Europe

this edition researched and updated by
David Abram, Nicky Agate, Robert Alcock, Rob Andrews,
Andrew Benson, Jules Brown, Belinda Dixon, Lucia Graves,
Matthew Hancock, Sharon Harris, Rob Humphreys,
Daniel Jacobs, Rachel Kaberry, Phil Lee, Norm Longley,
Lucy Mallows, Lone Mouritsen, Patrick O'Connell, Mike Parker,
Catherine Phillips, James Proctor, Donald Reid, Paul Smith,
Daphne Thambaki, Carl Thompson, Jeroen Van Marle,
Geoff Wallis and Richard Watkins

ROUGH
GUIDES

www.roughguides.com

iii

Introduction to

Europe

The collapse of the division between eastern and western Europe at the end of the 1980s, and the ever closer ties among the fifteen countries of the European Union, have contributed to a feeling that Europe is increasingly becoming a single entity. In part, this is a superficial analysis, but although true European unity still remains a distant dream, developments such as the introduction of the euro, the creation of the frontier-free Schengen Group and the opening of the Channel Tunnel have done much to bring it closer. The expected 2004 expansion of the EU (see box on p.vii) will no doubt contribute to the process.

Conventionally, the **geographical boundaries** of Europe are the Ural Mountains in the east, the Atlantic Coast in the north and west, and the Mediterranean in the south. However, within these rough parameters Europe is massively diverse. The environment changes radically within very short distances, with bleak mountain ranges never far from broad, fertile plains, and deep, ancient forests close to scattered lake systems or river gorges. Politically and ethnically, too, it is an extraordinary patchwork: Slavic peoples are scattered through central Europe from Poland in the north to Serbia and Bulgaria in the south; the Finnish and Estonian languages bear no resemblance to the tongues of their Baltic and Scandinavian neighbours, but more to that of Hungary, over 1000km south; meanwhile Romansch, akin to ancient Latin, is spoken in the valleys of southeastern Switzerland, while the Basques of the western Pyrenees have a language unrelated to any others known. These differences have become more political of late with the rise of nationalism that coincided with the fall of Communism, and borders are even now being redrawn, not always peacefully, and usually along lines of language, race or religion.

This book is a little eccentric in its **definition of Europe**. We have excluded countries such as Albania, Belarus, Moldova and Ukraine, which are too far off the beaten track to be on most people's European "grand tour", while of the war-torn and strife-riven republics that have been carved out of the former Yugoslavia, only Slovenia and Croatia have been included as easily accessible and currently safe to visit. On the other hand, we cover countries such as Morocco and Turkey that are not strictly part of Europe, in the main because they are easy to reach on a European tour and are included by the InterRail pass. We also have chapters on Russia, Estonia, Latvia and Lithuania, though these countries are *not* covered by the InterRail pass.

Where to go

Where you head for obviously depends on your tastes and the kind of vacation you want: you can sample mountain air and winter sports in the Alps of France, Austria or Switzerland, lie on a beach in the swanky resorts of the south of France or Italy, or view architecture and works of art in the great cities of London, Paris, Florence and Amsterdam. Suffice to say, the lifting of restrictions on travel

Working in Europe

There are plenty of ways of supplementing your travel budget in Europe. Bar- and restaurant-work is fine, so long as you speak the local language, but grape-picking is the perennial favourite with travellers. Help is needed from August to October – and in far more countries than you may at first think, from Germany in the north, by way of eastern European countries such as Hungary, to the more familiar vineyards of France, Italy and Spain.

in eastern Europe, with only a handful of countries still requiring visas and nothing like the bureaucratic regulations there were before, means that the Continent really is there for the travelling – something manifest in the increasingly good-value rail passes (see pp.20–29) that cover most of the countries in this book. Although you may want to make a long hop or two by air, rail is *the* way to see the Continent, highlighting the diversity of the place when you travel in a few hours from the cool temperatures of northern Europe to the rich and sultry climes of the Mediterranean. In fact, with the richness and diversity of its culture, climate, landscapes and peoples, there is no more exciting place to travel.

The European Union

The original European Economic Community (EEC), formed by the Treaty of Rome in 1957, had six members: France, Germany, Italy, Belgium, the Netherlands and Luxembourg. By the time the Maastricht Treaty came into force in 1993, changing the organization's name to the **European Union** (EU), the original six had been joined by Denmark, Ireland and the UK (1973), Greece (1981), Portugal and Spain (1986), with Austria, Finland and Sweden joining in 1995, making a total of fifteen member states. Norway voted in a 1972 referendum to stay out, but in 2004, ten new members are expected to join: eight east European countries (the Czech Republic, Estonia, Latvia, Lithuania, Hungary, Poland, Slovakia and Slovenia), plus the Mediterranean island states of Cyprus and Malta, bringing the number of members to twenty-five.

Whether this Union, headed by a Council of Ministers and a directly elected European Parliament, should move towards becoming a fully fledged United States of Europe, or confine itself to being just a trading block, is a matter of some controversy. The original six members – though less so Italy under Berlusconi's far-right administration – tend to favour further political union leading to a federal Europe. Britain and Denmark are the countries most consistently opposed to moves in that direction.

When to go

Europe's **climate** is as variable as everything else about the Continent. In **northwestern Europe** – Benelux, Denmark, southwestern Norway, most of France and parts of Germany, as well as the British Isles – the climate is basically a cool temperate one, with the chance of rain all year round and no great extremes of either cold or hot weather. There is no bad time to travel in most of this part of Europe, although the winter months (Nov–March) can be damp and miserable – especially in the upland regions – and obviously the summer period (May–Sept) sees the most reliable and driest weather.

In **eastern Europe** – to the right of a north–south line drawn roughly through the heart of Germany and extending down as far as the western edge of Bulgaria (taking in eastern Germany, Poland, central Russia, the Baltic states, southern Sweden, the Czech and Slovak republics, Austria, Switzerland, Hungary and Romania) – the climatic conditions are more extreme, with freezing winters and sometimes sweltering summers. Here the transitional spring and autumn seasons are the most pleasant time to travel; deep midwinter, especially, can be very unpleasant, although it doesn't have the dampness associated with the northwestern European climate.

Southern Europe, principally the countries that border the Mediterranean and associated seas – southern France, Italy, Spain, Portugal, Greece

Festivals

Wherever you find yourself in Europe, you'll not be far away from some annual event or other. From Venice's extravagant **Carnival** (Feb) to Munich's boozy **Oktoberfest** (Sept–Oct), by way of the **Pamplona Bull Run** (July) and the **Edinburgh Arts Festival** (Aug), you can be sure of coinciding your trip with at least one of Europe's big events. Should you do so, however, be sure to book your accommodation in advance – as this can fill up months in advance for the bigger events.

and western Turkey – has the most hospitable climate in Europe, with a general pattern of warm, dry summers and mild winters. Travel is possible at any time of year here, although the peak summer months can be very hot and very busy and the deep winter ones can see some rain.

There are, too, marked regional variations within these three broad groupings. As they're such large countries, inland Spain and France can, for example, see a **continental** type of weather as extreme as any in central Europe, and the Alpine areas of Italy, Austria and Switzerland – and other **mountain areas** such as the Pyrenees, Apennines and parts of the Balkans – have a climate mainly influenced by altitude, which means short summers and long winters that always see snow. There are also, of course, the northern regions of Russia and Scandinavia, which have an **Arctic climate** – again, bitterly cold, though with some surprisingly warm weather during the short summer when much of the region is warmed by the Gulf Stream. Winter sees the sun barely rise at all in these areas, while high summer can mean almost constant daylight.

There are obviously **other considerations** when deciding when to go. If you're planning to visit fairly touristed areas, especially beach resorts in the Mediterranean, avoid July and August, when the weather can be too hot and the resorts at their most congested. Bear in mind, also, that in a number of countries in Europe everyone takes their vacation at the same time (this is certainly true in France, Spain and Italy, where everyone goes away in August). Find out the holiday month beforehand for the countries where you intend to travel, since you can expect the crush to be especially bad in the resorts; meanwhile, in the cities the only other people around will be fellow tourists, which can be miserable. In northern Scandinavia the climatic extremes are such that you'll find opening times severely restricted, and even road and rail lines closed, outside the May to September period, making travel futile if not impossible. In mountainous areas, things stay open for the winter sports season (Dec–April), though outside the main resorts you'll again find many things closed. On the other hand, mid-April to mid-June can be a quiet period in many mountain resorts, when you may have much of the place to yourself.

Average daily maximum temperatures in °C/°F

	Jan	Feb	Mar	Apr	May	June	July	Aug	Sept	Oct	Nov	Dec
Amsterdam	4/40	5/42	9/49	13/56	18/64	21/70	22/72	22/71	19/67	14/57	9/48	6/42
Ankara	4/40	6/42	11/51	17/63	23/73	26/78	30/86	31/87	26/78	21/69	14/57	6/43
Athens	13/55	14/57	16/60	20/68	25/77	30/86	33/92	33/92	29/84	24/75	19/66	15/58
Berlin	2/35	3/37	8/46	13/56	19/66	22/72	24/75	23/74	20/68	13/56	7/45	3/38
Brussels	4/40	7/42	10/51	14/58	18/65	22/72	23/73	22/72	21/69	15/60	9/48	6/42
Bratislava	-1/30	0/30	5/41	10/50	13/58	12/54	20/68	19/67	16/61	10/50	4/40	0/32
Bucharest	1/34	4/40	10/50	18/64	23/74	27/81	30/86	30/85	25/78	18/65	10/49	4/40
Budapest	1/34	4/40	10/50	17/62	22/71	26/78	28/82	27/81	23/74	16/61	8/47	4/40
Copenhagen	2/36	2/36	5/41	10/51	16/61	19/67	22/71	21/70	18/64	12/54	7/45	4/40
Dublin	8/46	8/47	10/50	13/55	15/60	18/65	20/67	19/67	17/63	14/57	10/51	8/47
Helsinki	-3/26	-4/25	0/32	6/44	14/56	19/66	22/71	20/68	15/59	8/47	3/37	-1/31
İstanbul	8/46	9/47	11/51	16/60	21/69	25/77	28/82	28/82	24/76	20/68	15/59	11/51
Lisbon	14/57	15/59	17/63	20/67	21/71	25/77	27/81	28/82	26/79	22/72	17/63	15/58
London	6/43	7/44	10/50	13/56	17/62	20/69	22/71	22/71	19/65	14/58	10/50	7/45
Luxembourg	3/37	4/40	10/49	14/57	18/65	21/70	23/73	22/71	19/66	13/56	7/44	4/40
Madrid	9/47	11/52	15/59	18/65	21/70	27/80	31/87	30/85	25/77	19/65	13/55	9/48
Moscow	-9/15	-6/22	0/32	10/50	19/66	21/70	23/73	22/72	16/61	9/48	2/35	-5/24
Oslo	-2/28	-1/30	4/40	10/50	16/61	20/68	22/72	21/70	16/60	9/48	3/38	0/32
Paris	6/43	7/44	12/54	16/60	20/68	23/73	25/76	24/75	21/70	16/60	10/50	7/44
Prague	0/31	1/34	7/44	12/54	18/64	21/70	23/73	22/72	18/65	12/53	5/42	1/34
Rabat	17/63	18/65	20/68	22/71	23/73	26/78	28/82	30/83	27/81	25/77	21/70	18/65
Riga	-4/25	-3/27	2/35	10/50	16/61	21/69	22/71	21/70	17/63	11/52	4/40	-2/29
Rome	11/52	13/55	15/59	19/66	23/74	28/82	30/87	30/86	26/79	22/71	16/61	13/55
Sofia	2/35	4/40	10/50	16/60	21/69	24/76	27/81	26/79	22/70	17/63	9/48	4/40
Stockholm	-1/30	-1/30	3/37	8/47	14/58	19/67	22/71	20/68	15/60	9/49	5/40	2/35
Tallinn	-4/25	-4/25	0/32	7/45	14/57	19/66	20/68	19/66	15/59	10/50	3/38	-1/30
Vienna	1/34	3/38	8/47	15/58	19/67	23/73	25/76	24/75	20/68	14/56	7/45	3/37
Vilnius	-5/25	-3/26	1/34	12/54	18/65	21/71	23/74	22/71	17/62	11/52	4/40	-3/26
Warsaw	0/32	0/32	6/42	12/53	20/67	23/73	24/75	23/73	19/66	13/55	6/42	2/35
Zürich	2/36	5/41	10/51	15/59	19/67	23/73	25/76	24/75	20/69	14/57	7/45	3/39

30

things not to miss

It's not possible to see everything that Europe has to offer in one trip – and we don't suggest you try. What follows is a selective and subjective taste of the continent's highlights: outstanding natural features, spectacular cities, festivals, history and beautiful architecture. They're arranged in five colour-coded categories to help you find the very best things to see, do and experience. All entries have a page reference to take you straight into the guide, where you can find out more.

01 Carnevale, Venice Page **611** • Don a costume, get a mask and join the crowds congregating in the squares for this pre-Lent festival.

02 Ronda, Spain Page **972** • Perhaps the most spectacularly sited of Andalucía's Pueblos Blancos.

03 The Edinburgh Festival Page **192** • Europe's biggest arts festival.

04 Ljublijana, Slovenia Page **929** • Stunning architecture, a hilltop castle and leafy riverside cafés.

05 Oktoberfest, Germany Page **453** • An orgy of beer drinking, spiced up by fairground rides that are so hairy they're banned in the US.

06 Cappadocia, Turkey Page **1123** • Water and wind have created a land of fantastic forms from the soft tufa rock, including forests of cones, table mountains and canyon-like valleys.

07 **Belgian chocolates** Page **98** • Many would say that Belgium's chocolates are the finest in Europe.

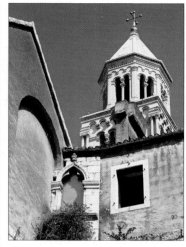

08 **Diocletian's Palace, Split** Page **239** • Extraordinary 1700-year-old palace housing shops, restaurants and bars.

09 **Avignon, Provence** Page **400** • The great city of the popes and for centuries one of the major artistic centres of France.

10 **Sighişoara** Page 870 • Beautiful, quiet medieval town in the heart of Transylvania.

11 **Tate Modern, London** Page **139** • London's new modern-art gallery, spectacularly housed in a former power station.

12 **Amsterdam's canals** Page 743 • The Venice of the north? Maybe not, but definitely an experience in their own right.

13 **The Kremlin, Russia** Page **887** • Evocative complex of political, architectural and artistic associations.

14 **Kaffee und Kuchen** Page **77** • Have a Viennese coffee and a fabulously gooey cake in one of Central Europe's great coffee houses.

15 **Island hopping, Greece** Page **513–529** • Old-town charm, deserted beaches or full-on party-town atmosphere – whatever you're looking for, you'll find a Greek island that suits you.

16 **Nyhavn, Copenhagen** Page **283** • Canalside bars and cafés in this district are *the* place to be seen in summer.

17 Temple Expiatiori de la Sagrada Família, Barcelona

Page **1002** ● Without doubt Antoni Gaudí's most famous creation, with eight towers each rising to over 100m.

ACTIVITIES | CONSUME | EVENTS | NATURE | SIGHTS |

18 Viking history, Norway
Page **776** • A fascinating insight into this misunderstood race – made most accessible at the Viking Ships Museum, Oslo.

19 Nevsky Monastery Page
899 • This Russian Orthodox complex is a heady blend of incense and icons.

20 Atlas Mountains, Morocco Page 711 • Get away from it all on a hiking trip into these world-famous mountains. Any tourist office can give you details of organized trips.

21 **Food, France** Page **343** • French food is amongst the finest in the world and the range of cheeses alone gives an idea of the quality on offer.

22 **The Parthenon, Athens** Page **496** • The heart of The Acropolis, one of Greece's oldest settlements.

23 Sevilla April Feria, Spain
Page **965** • A full week of flamenco, parades and bullfights in a frenziedly enthusiastic atmosphere.

24 Trekking in Lapland, Finland
Page **337** • Trek across the tundra of Lapland, where, if you're lucky, you might even see reindeer grazing.

25 Prague
Page **255** • One of Europe's most beautiful cities; an unmissable stop on any trip.

26 **Cloth Hall, Kraków** Page **810** • Buy wonderful handcrafted gifts in characterful surroundings at the heart of one of Europe's most beautiful squares.

27 **Király Baths, Budapest** Page **542** • Relax in the steamy healing waters to enjoy this typically Hungarian experience.

28 Guinness, Ireland Page **557** • All over Europe you'll find Irish theme-bars offering selling draft Guinness, but none can compare to the stuff served back home.

29 Northern Lights, Sweden Page **1038** • One of the natural wonders of the world.

30 Tatra mountains, Poland/Slovakia Page **814/917** • Fantastic hiking opportunities in these towering peaks that form the border between Slovakia and Poland.

Contents

Using the Rough Guide

We've tried to make this Rough Guide a good read and easy to use. The book is divided into five main sections, and you should be able to find whatever you want in one of them.

Colour section

The front colour section offers a quick survey of Europe. The **introduction** aims to give you a feel for the place, with suggestions on where to go and when. Next, our authors round up their favourite aspects of Europe in the **things not to miss** section – whether it's great food, amazing sights or a spectacular festival. Right after this comes a contents list.

Basics

The Basics section covers all the **pre-departure** nitty-gritty to help you plan your trip. This is where to find out about getting to Europe by air, sea and land, the various rail passes and routes that cover the continent, what paperwork you'll need, what to do about money and insurance, how to find accommodation, opportunities for working – in fact just about every piece of **general practical information** you might need.

Guide

This is the heart of the Rough Guide, divided into user-friendly chapters, each of which covers a specific country. Every chapter starts with a list of **highlights** and an **introduction** that helps you to decide where to go,

depending on your time and budget. The introduction prefaces the mini **basics** section, covering country-specific practicalities like public transport and food and drink. Chapters then move on to **detailed coverage** of your destination. We start most **town accounts** with information on arrival and accommodation, followed by a tour of the sights, and finally reviews of places to eat and drink, and details of nightlife. Longer accounts also have a directory of practical **listings**. Each chapter concludes with details of **public transport** routes for the country.

Language

Here you'll find lists of all the essential **words and phrases** you might need on your trip, arranged by language.

Index + small print

Apart from a **full index**, which includes maps as well as places, this section covers publishing information, credits and acknowledgements, and also has our contact details in case you want to send in updates and corrections to the book – or suggestions as to how we might improve it.

Map and chapter list

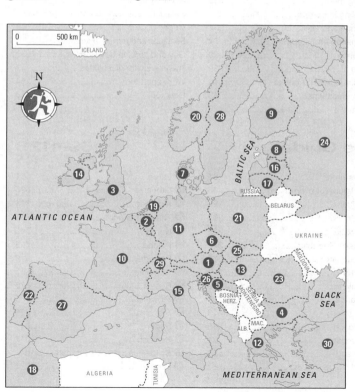

Contents

Language

1129–1140

Index and small print

1141–1153

CONTENTS

Map symbols

maps are listed in the full index using coloured text

------	National boundary	⊠	Post office
—■—	Railway	ⓘ	Information office
═══	Road	Ⓒ	Telephone
═══	Pedestrianized street	@	Internet access
- - - -	Path	★	Bus stop
▥▥▥	Steps	Ⓜ	Metro station
— —	Ferry route	Ⓢ	S-Bahn
——	Waterway	Ⓤ	U-Bahn
▪▪▪▪	Wall	Ⓣ	Tram stop
⋏	Mountains	⊖	London Underground Station
▲	Peak	▣	Parking
☼	Hill	⊠	Gate
↯	Viewpoint	▪	Building
ⵣ	Fountain	⊣	Church
◆	Point of interest	⬭	Stadium
ᐃ	Monastery	▨	Park
♦	Museum	⌐+	Christian cemetery
✡	Synagogue	⌐Y	Muslim cemetery
☪	Mosque	⌐⌐	Jewish cemetery
⊞	Hospital	▒	Beach

Basics

Basics

Getting there

Airfares always depend on the season, with the highest being roughly mid-June to early September and over the Christmas period, with cheaper deals available for the rest of the year, particularly during the winter months (Nov–March), when fewer people are travelling. Note also that flying on weekends can add $20–60/£15–50 to the round-trip fare; price ranges quoted below assume mid-week travel.

Barring special offers, the cheapest of the airlines' published fares is usually an **Apex** ticket, although this will carry certain restrictions: you have to book – and pay – at least twenty-one days before departure, spend at least seven days abroad (maximum stay three months), and you tend to get penalized if you change your schedule. There are also winter **Super Apex** tickets, sometimes known as "Eurosavers" – slightly cheaper than an ordinary Apex, but limiting your stay to between seven and twenty-one days. Some airlines also issue **Special Apex** tickets to people younger than 24, often extending the maximum stay to a year. Many airlines offer youth or student fares to **under 25s**; a passport or driving licence is sufficient proof of age, though these tickets are subject to availability and can have eccentric booking conditions. It's worth remembering that most cheap return fares will only give a percentage refund if you need to cancel or alter your journey, so make sure you check the restrictions carefully before buying a ticket.

You can often cut costs by going through a **specialist flight agent** – either a consolidator, who buys up blocks of tickets from the airlines and sells them at a discount, or a **discount agent**, who in addition to dealing with discounted flights may also offer special student and youth fares and a range of other travel-related services such as travel insurance, rail passes and tours. Some agents specialize in **charter flights**, which may be cheaper than anything available on a scheduled flight, but again departure dates are fixed and withdrawal penalties are high. Be advised however that the pool of travel companies is swimming with sharks – exercise caution, especially when dealing with small firms that are not well-established, and

never deal with a company that demands cash up front or refuses to accept credit cards.

If Europe is only one stop on a longer journey, and especially if you are based in Australia or New Zealand, you might want to consider buying a **Round-the-World (RTW) ticket**. Some travel agents can sell you an "off-the-shelf" RTW ticket that will have you touching down in about half a dozen cities (London, Paris, Amsterdam, Rome, Athens and Moscow are on many off-the-shelf itineraries); others will have to assemble one for you, which can be tailored to your needs but is apt to be more expensive. Figure on US$1700/Aus$2800 for a RTW ticket including one or two European stopovers.

Booking flights online

Many airlines and discount travel websites offer you the opportunity to book your tickets online, cutting out the costs of agents and middlemen. Good deals can often be found through discount or auction sites, as well as through the airlines' own websites.

Useful websites

ⓦ**www.airfares.co.uk** Easy-to-use flight search and booking from Britain and Ireland only.

ⓦ**www.cheapflights.com** Bookings from Britain and Ireland only. Flight deals, travel agents, plus links to other travel sites.

ⓦ**www.cheaptickets.com** Discount flight specialists.

ⓦ**www.etn.nl/discount.htm** International hub for on-line consolidators, discount agents and bucket shops, maintained by the non-profit European Travel Network.

ⓦ**www.expedia.com** Discount airfares, all-airline search engine and daily deals.

@ **www.flyaow.com** Online air travel info and reservations site.

@ **www.geocities.com/Thavery2000** Has an extensive list of airline toll-free numbers.

@ **www.hotwire.com** Bookings from the US only. Last-minute savings of up to forty percent on regular published fares. Travellers must be at least 18 and there are no refunds, transfers or changes allowed. Log-in required.

@ **www.lastminute.com** Bookings from the UK only. Offers good last-minute deals.

@ **www.priceline.com** Name-your-own-price website that has deals at around forty percent below standard fares. You cannot specify flight times (although you do specify dates) and the tickets are non-refundable, non-transferable and non-changeable.

@ **www.skyauction.com** Bookings from the US only. Auctions tickets and travel packages using a "second bid" scheme. The best strategy is to bid the maximum you're willing to pay, since if you win you'll pay just enough to beat the runner-up regardless of your maximum bid.

@ **www.smilinjack.com/airlines.htm** Lists an up-to-date compilation of airline website addresses.

@ **www.travelocity.com** Destination guides, hot web fares and best deals for accommodation as well as fares. Provides access to the travel agent system SABRE, the most comprehensive central reservations system in the US.

@ **www.travelshop.com.au** Australian website offering discounted flights and insurance.

@ **travel.yahoo.com** Incorporates a lot of Rough Guide material in its coverage of destination countries and cities across the world, with information about places to eat, sleep, etc.

From the US and Canada

The air space between North America and Europe is one of the most heavily travelled in the world. It is served by literally dozens of airlines, both US carriers and the national airlines of almost every European country, and there is consequently a huge range of seats at a huge range of prices. It all depends on when and from where you're travelling, and, of course, where you want to go. There are, however, a number of "gateway" cities into which you'll find a greater – and cheaper – choice of flights.

You'll often find the cheapest fare by leaving from the airline's "hub" – New York, Atlanta, Dallas, Chicago, Los Angeles, San Francisco, Seattle, Vancouver, Toronto and Montreal are the main ones; hub cities also tend to have nonstop flights, with no changes at all. You do, however, need to be flexible: London, Paris, and Amsterdam are usually the cheapest "gateway cities" in Europe, simply because they are served by more flights; Milan, Rome and Frankfurt run a close second in some cases. Flying mid-week rather than at the weekend is also a few dollars cheaper.

Flights from eastern and central US

There are lots of options from most of the **eastern hub cities**, though the best deals are generally out of New York and Chicago to London. Official Apex round-trip fares bought one to two weeks in advance from New York to London with the major carriers, such as Virgin Atlantic (the best in terms of service), British Airways or American, are around $330–390 in low season, $650–730 in high season, plus taxes. You should, how-ever, be able to find discounted fares, with-out the need to book three months in advance, for around $300/$550, especially if you're a student or under-26. From Chicago, official Apex fares to London are $495/$830 depending on the season, with more flexible discounted tickets at around $375/$605. To give an idea of other alternatives, discount-ed tickets from New York can be found for $350/600 to Paris ($410/740 from Chicago), $320/700 to Frankfurt ($400/780 from Chicago), $360/680 to Madrid ($400/750 from Chicago), and $450/870 to Athens ($500/980 from Chicago). There may also be Special Limited promotional offers which appear from time to time, especially in the off-peak seasons; Virgin Atlantic, for exam-ple, usually have New York–London fares in late winter for $99 each way, no advance purchase necessary.

Flights from the US west coast

From the **west coast** it's much the same story. The big airlines fly at least three times a week (sometimes daily) from Los Angeles, San Francisco and Seattle to the main European cities. The major carriers have plenty of flights, with round-trip ninety-day-advance Apex fares from LA starting at

$555/880 to London depending on season. Again, you can avoid the three-month advance booking and length of stay restrictions and still find a comparatively inexpensive fare by going to a discount agent or youth travel specialist, where you can find tickets for $400/650 (depending on the time of year) for a round trip to London, $420/800 to Paris, $450/860 to Frankfurt, $460/830 to Madrid, and $570/1050 to Athens.

Flights from Canada

Most of the big airlines fly to the major European hubs from **Montreal** and **Toronto** at least once daily (three times a week for the smaller airlines). From Toronto, London is your cheapest option, with the lowest round-trip fares, direct with the airline, costing around CDN$620/975 (depending on the time of year). From Montreal to Paris you can expect to pay CDN$1000/1250. Once again, a discount/student specialist such as Travel CUTS should be able to find a fare that's more flexible and, possibly, cheaper; current examples of discounted fares include CDN$810/1000 from Toronto to London and CDN$950/1100 from Montreal to Paris.

Flights from **Vancouver** have become more convenient since the expansion of the airport, with daily flights to London and other European cities now on offer. Round-trip fares to London can be had for around CDN$1040/1350, depending on the season.

Airlines in North America

Aer Lingus ☎1-800/223-6537, 🌐www.aerlingus.ie
Aero California ☎1-800/237-6225
Aeroflot US ☎1-888/340-6400, Canada ☎416/642 1653, 🌐www.aeroflot.com
Air Canada ☎1-888/247-2262, 🌐www.aircanada.ca
Air France US ☎1-800/237-2747, Canada ☎1-800/667-2747, 🌐www.airfrance.com
Alitalia US ☎1-800/223-5730, Canada ☎1-800/361-8336, 🌐www.alitalia.com
American Airlines ☎1-800/433-7300, 🌐www.aa.com
Austrian Airlines ☎1-800/843-0002, 🌐www.aua.com
Balkan Bulgarian Airlines ☎1-800/852-0944, 🌐www.balkanair.com
British Airways ☎1-800/247-9297, 🌐www.ba.com

British Midland ☎1-800/788-0555, 🌐www.flybmi.com
Continental Airlines ☎1-800/231-0856, 🌐www.continental.com
Swiss Air Lines ☎1-800/221-4750, 🌐www.swissairlines.com
Czech Airlines US ☎1-877/359-6629 or 212/765-6022, Canada ☎416/363-3174, 🌐www.czechairlines.com
Delta Air Lines ☎1-800/241-4141, 🌐www.delta.com
Finnair ☎1-800/950-5000, 🌐www.finnair.com
Iberia ☎1-800/772-4642, 🌐www.iberia.com
KLM/Northwest ☎1-800/447-4747, 🌐www.klm.com
LOT Polish Airlines US ☎1-800/223-0593, Canada ☎1-800/668-5928, 🌐www.lot.com
Lufthansa US ☎1-800/645-3880, Canada ☎1-800/563-5954, 🌐www.lufthansa-usa.com
Malev Hungarian Airlines ☎1-800/223-6884 or 212/757-6446, 🌐www.hungarianairlines.com
Martinair Holland ☎1-800/627-8462, 🌐www.martinairusa.com
Olympic Airways ☎1-800/223-1226 or 718/896-7393, 🌐www.olympic-airways.gr
Royal Air Maroc ☎1-800/344-6726 or 212/750-6071, 🌐www.royalairmaroc.com
SAS (Scandinavian Airlines) ☎1-800/221-2350, 🌐www.scandinavian.net
TAP Air Portugal ☎1-800/221-7370, 🌐www.tap-airportugal.pt
Tarom Romanian Air ☎212/560-0840, 🌐tarom.digiro.net/index_en.html
Turkish Airlines ☎1-800/874-8875, 🌐www.thy.com
United Airlines ☎1-800/538-2929, 🌐www.ual.com
Virgin Atlantic Airways ☎1-800/862-8621, 🌐www.virgin-atlantic.com
US Airways ☎1-800/622-1015, 🌐www.usairways.com

Discount travel companies in North America

Air Brokers International ☎1-800/883-3273 or 415/397-1383, 🌐www.airbrokers.com. Consolidator and specialist in RTW tickets.
Council Travel ☎1-800/226-8624, 🌐www.counciltravel.com. Nationwide organization that mostly, but by no means exclusively, specializes in student/budget travel. Flights from the US only.
Educational Travel Center ☎1-800/747-5551 or 608/256-5551, 🌐www.edtrav.com. Student/youth discount agent.
High Adventure Travel ☎1-800/350-0612 or 415/912-5600, 🌐www.airtreks.com. Round-the-world

tickets. The website features an interactive database that lets you build and price your own RTW itinerary.

New Frontiers/Nouvelles ☎1-800/677-0720 or 212/986-6006, ⊛www.newfrontiers.com. Discount-travel firm.

Skylink US ☎1-800/247-6659 or 212/573-8980, Canada ☎1-800/759-5465, ⊛www.skylinkus.com. Consolidator.

STA Travel ☎1-800/777-0112 or 1-800/781-4040, ⊛www.sta-travel.com. Independent travel specialist; can also provide student IDs, travel insurance and rail passes.

Student Flights ☎1-800/255-8000 or 480/951-1177, ⊛www.isecard.com. Student/youth fares, student IDs.

TFI Tours International ☎1-800/745-8000 or 212/736-1140, ⊛www.lowestairprice.com. Consolidator.

Travac ☎1-800/872-8800, ⊛www.thetravelsite.com. Consolidator and charter broker.

Travelers Advantage ☎1-877/259-2691, ⊛www.travelersadvantage.com. Discount travel club; annual membership fee required ($1 for three months' trial).

Travel Avenue ☎1-800/333-3335, ⊛www.travelavenue.com. Full-service travel agent that offers discounts in the form of rebates.

Travel Cuts Canada ☎1-800/667-2887, US ☎1-866/246-9762, ⊛www.travelcuts.com. Canadian-based student-travel organization.

Whole Earth Travel ☎1-800/326 2009 or 212/864 2000, ⊛www.airhitch.org. Stand-by seat broker: for a set price, they guarantee to get you on a flight as close to your preferred destination as possible, within a week. Western Europe only.

Worldtek Travel ☎1-800/243-1723, ⊛www.worldtek.com. Discount travel agency.

From Britain and Ireland

For destinations in northwestern Europe, train, long-distance bus and crossing the Channel by ferry tend to be best value for money, but the further you go the cheaper air travel becomes, and it's normally cheaper to fly than take the train to most parts of southern Europe, although special deals on rail passes can bring prices down considerably.

By plane

As ever, the best way to find the cheapest **flight** is to shop around: air travel in Europe is still highly regulated, which means that the prices quoted by the airlines can usually be undercut considerably, even on Apex fares,

by going to an agent. During the summer you can reach most of the countries of southern Europe – Portugal, Spain, Italy, Greece – on **charter flights**, block-booked by package holiday firms and usually having a few seats left over which they sell off cheap through selected **agents**, sometimes known as "bucket shops". Though they are inevitably rather restricted, with fixed return dates, a maximum validity of a month, and no chance of cancelling or changing your ticket once you've bought it, they can be very cheap – so much so in some cases that it's actually worth just using the outward portion if the return date doesn't suit. There are also flight agents who specialize in low-cost, discounted flights (charter and scheduled), some of them – like STA Travel in Britain, usitNOW in Ireland – concentrating on deals for youths and students, though they can be a good source of bargains for everyone. In addition, there are agents specializing in offers to a specific country or group of countries on both charters and regular scheduled departures.

Flights from Britain

London is predictably Britain's main hub for air travel, offering the highest frequency of flights and widest choice of destinations, but **Manchester** has flights to most parts of Europe, and there are also regular flights to the Continent from Birmingham, Bristol, Cardiff, Glasgow, Edinburgh, Leeds/ Bradford and Newcastle. Failing that, you can get a BA or British Midland flight from most UK airports (but not from Birmingham) to London, and take an onward flight from there, or fly to Paris with Air France, or Amsterdam with KLM, and change there.

For discounted flights, in London, check the ads in the *Evening Standard*, *Time Out* or free magazines such as *TNT*; elsewhere, look in local listings magazines or the travel sections of the Sunday broadsheets. To give a rough idea of prices booked through agents on scheduled flights in high season, reckon on paying, not including departure taxes, £60–100 to Paris, Brussels or Amsterdam; £100–200 to Scandinavia; £90–250 to the major cities of Spain or Italy; £150–280 to Athens, £140–300 to Istanbul; £100–175 to the major cities of eastern Europe. Many agents also do "open jaw" tickets, flying you into one city and out from another, not necessarily even in the same country. **One-way tickets** are normally very poor value, but some of the new "no-nonsense" airlines such as Ryanair, Go and EasyJet charge single fares each way and are often much cheaper than other airlines for return fares too. Excellent deals can also be found on Ceefax, Teletext and the internet (see p.9).

Flights from Ireland

There are direct flights **from Dublin** to most major cities in mainland Europe, and connections from those or from London to practically any airport you want to fly to. There are also one or two direct flights to the Continent **from Shannon and Cork**. You may save a little money travelling by land, sea or even air to London and buying your flight there, but the small amount you'd save hardly makes it worthwhile, and if you're going to London by surface routes, you may as well go the whole hog and carry on that way into Europe.

From Belfast, there are direct flights with EasyJet to Amsterdam and BA to Paris. For other destinations, you'll have to change at one of those, or at London (served by EasyJet, British Midland and BA) or Manchester (served by BA).

Airlines in Britain and Ireland

Adria UK ☎020/7734 4630, ⊛www.adria.si
Aer Arann Ireland ☎1890/462726 or 01/814 1058, ⊛www.aerarann.ie
Aer Lingus UK ☎0845/973 7747, Ireland ☎01/886 8888, ⊛www.aerlingus.ie
Aeroflot UK ☎020/7355 2233, Ireland ☎01/844 6166, ⊛www.aeroflot.com
Air France UK ☎0845/0845 111, Ireland ☎01/605 0383, ⊛www.airfrance.co.uk
Alitalia UK ☎0870/5448 259, Ireland ☎01/677 5171, ⊛www.alitalia.it
Austrian Airlines UK ☎0845/601 0948, ⊛www.aua.com
Balkan Airlines UK ☎020/7637 7637, ⊛www.balkan.com
Britannia Airways UK ☎01582/424155, ⊛www.britanniaairways.com
British Airways UK ☎0845/77 333 77, Ireland ☎1800/626 747, ⊛www.ba.com
British European UK ☎0870/567 6676, ⊛www.british-european.com

British Midland UK ☎0870/607 0555, Ireland ☎01/407 3036, ⊛www.flybmi.com
Buzz UK ☎0870/240 7070, ⊛www.buzzaway.com
Croatian Airlines UK ☎020/8563 0022, ⊛www.croatiaairlines.hr
Swiss Air Lines UK ☎0845/601 0956, Ireland ☎01890/200515, ⊛www.swissairlines.com
CSA Czech Airlines UK ☎020/7255 1898, Ireland ☎01/814 4626, ⊛www.csa.cz/en
EasyJet UK ☎0870/600 0000, ⊛www.easyjet.com
Estonian Airlines UK ☎020/7333 0196, ⊛www.estonian-air.ee
Ethiopian Airlines UK ☎020/8987 7000, ⊛www.flyethiopian.com
Finnair UK ☎020/7408 1222, Ireland ☎01/844 6565, ⊛www.finnair.com
Go UK ☎0870/607 6543, ⊛www.go-fly.com
Iberia Airlines UK ☎0845/601 2854, Ireland ☎01/407 3017, ⊛www.iberiaairlines.co.uk
KLM UK ☎08705/074074, ⊛www.klmuk.com
Lauda Air UK ☎020/7630 5924, ⊛www.laudaair.co.uk
Lithuanian Airlines ☎01293/579900, ⊛www.lal.lt
LOT Polish Airlines UK ☎020/7580 5037, ⊛www.lot.com
Lufthansa UK ☎0845/7737 747, Ireland ☎01/844 5544, ⊛www.lufthansa.com
Malev Hungarian Airlines UK ☎020/7439 0577, ⊛www.malev.hu
Olympic Airways UK ☎0870/606 0460, ⊛www.olympic-airways.co.uk
Royal Air Maroc UK ☎020/7439 4361, ⊛www.royalairmaroc.com
Ryanair UK ☎0870/156 9569, Ireland ☎01/609 7800, ⊛www.ryanair.com
Sabena UK ☎0845/601 0933, Ireland ☎1800/200512, ⊛www.sabena.com
SAS Scandinavian Airlines UK ☎0845/607 2772, Ireland ☎01/844 5440, ⊛www.scandinavian.net
TAP Air Portugal UK ☎020/7630 0900, Ireland ☎01/679 8844, ⊛www.tap-airportugal.pt
Tarom Romanian Airlines UK ☎020/7224 3693, ⊛http://tarom.digirow.net
Turkish Airlines UK ☎020/7766 9300, ⊛www.turkishairlines.com
Virgin Express UK ☎020/7744 0004, ⊛www.virgin-express.com

Travel agents in Britain and Ireland

Aran Travel International Ireland ☎091/562595, ⊛homepages.iol.ie/~arantvl/aranmain.htm. Good-value flights.
Bridge the World UK ☎020/7911 0900, ⊛www.bridgetheworld.com. Specializing in RTW tickets, with good deals aimed at the backpacker market.

CIE Tours International Ireland ☎01/703 1888, ⓦwww.cietours.ie. General flight and tour agent.

Go Holidays Ireland ☎01/874 4126, ⓦwww.goholidays.ie. Package tour specialists.

Joe Walsh Tours Dublin ☎01/872 2555 or 676 3053, Cork ☎021/427 7959, ⓦwww .joewalshtours.ie. General budget fares agent.

Lee Travel Ireland ☎021/277111, ⓦwww.leetravel.ie. Flights and holidays worldwide.

McCarthy's Travel Ireland ☎021/427 0127, ⓦwww.mccarthystravel.ie. General flight agent.

North South Travel UK ☎01245/608291, ⓦwww .northsouthtravel.co.uk. Friendly, competitive travel agency, offering discounted fares worldwide – profits are used to support projects in the developing world, especially the promotion of sustainable tourism.

STA Travel UK ☎0870/160 6070, ⓦwww .statravel.co.uk. Worldwide specialists in low-cost flights and tours for students and under-26s, though other customers are welcome.

Top Deck UK ☎020/7370 4555, ⓦwww .topdecktravel.co.uk. Long-established agent dealing in discount flights.

Trailfinders UK ☎020/7628 7628, ⓦwww.trailfinders.com, Ireland ☎01/677 7888, ⓦwww.trailfinders.ie. One of the best-informed and most efficient agents for independent travellers; produce a very useful quarterly magazine worth checking for RTW routes.

Travel CUTS UK ☎020/7255 2082, ⓦwww .travelcuts.co.uk. British branch of Canada's main youth and student travel specialist.

usit NOW Republic of Ireland ☎01/602 1600, Northern Ireland ☎028/9032 7111, ⓦwww.usitnow .ie. Ireland's main student and youth travel specialists.

By train

There are now direct **trains** for foot passengers from London to Paris (14 daily, 3hr) and Brussels (7 daily, 3hr 15min) operated by Eurostar through the Channel Tunnel. Tickets for under-26s start at £50 one-way, £79 return. For over-26s, the cheapest ticket is a weekend day return, which costs less than a single fare at £70. Through-ticket combinations for Eurostar, plus onward connections from Brussels and Paris, can be booked through Trainseurope, International Rail and European Rail.

Other rail journeys from Britain involve some kind of **sea crossing**, by ferry or, sometimes, catamaran. Current return fares from London (which include the crossing) are £58 to Paris, £65 to Brussels, £79 to Amsterdam, and £170 to Berlin. They can be bought at Charing Cross and some other stations, or from International Rail or Trainseurope. For some destinations, there are cheaper APEX fares (£50 to Amsterdam, £146 to Berlin, for example) requiring advance booking and subject to greater restrictions. Five-day return tickets to Paris and Brussels are also available, priced £49. Otherwise, international tickets are valid for two months and allow for stopovers on the way, providing you stick to the prescribed route (there may be a choice, with different fares applicable). One-way fares are generally around two-thirds the price of a return fare. If you're **under 26** you're entitled to all sorts of special deals, not least youth fares, which offer cut-price rail fares to European destinations. Also issued by International Rail and Trainseurope, these tickets are also valid for two months with stopovers permitted en route. Examples of under-26 return ticket prices are: £48 to Paris, £43 to Brussels, £64 to Amsterdam and £151 to Berlin.

Whatever your age and whether you cross the Channel by ferry or through the tunnel, **through tickets** to European destinations beyond France and Germany are becoming harder to find, largely because most intercity routes in Europe are now covered by superfast, deluxe services with "special" (high, in other words) fares which cannot be paid as part of a through ticket. You could, for example, buy a ticket from London to Rome for £167 return, but you wouldn't be able to use it on any through train from Paris to Italy, so you'd have to travel by local services, changing along the way. Trainseurope and International Railways are the best people to contact for through tickets.

From Ireland, direct rail tickets to Europe via Britain generally include both boat connections, and are available from Iarnród Éireann's Continental Rail Desk in the Republic, or Northern Ireland Railways in the North, with discounted **under-26 tickets** available from these, or from UsitNOW.

During the summer, especially if you're travelling at night or a long distance, it's best to make reservations on most legs of your journey, and on some trains (most French TGV services for example) it is compulsory.

At night, couchettes in six-berth compartments cost around £6–15 per person, sleeper cars cost around £20–60, depending on the train, and may be two-, three- or four-bed.

For **rail passes** and other types of discounted rail travel, see "Travelling in Europe", p.20.

Rail contacts in Britain and Ireland

European Rail UK ☏020/7387 0444, ⊛www.europeanrail.com
Eurostar UK ☏0870/160 6600, ⊛www.eurostar.com
Eurotunnel UK ☏0870/535 3535, ⊛www.eurotunnel.com
Iarnród Éireann (Continental Rail Desk) Ireland ☏01/836 6222, ⊛www.irishrail.ie
International Rail UK ☏01962/773646, ⊛www.international-rail.com
Northern Ireland Railways Northern Ireland ☏028/9089 9411, ⊛www.nirailways.co.uk
Rail Europe UK ☏0870/584 8848, ⊛www.raileurope.co.uk. SNCF French Railways.
Trainseurope UK ☏01354/660222, ⊛www.trainseurope.co.uk

By bus

A long-distance **bus**, although much less comfortable than the train, is at least a little cheaper. The main operator based in Britain is Eurolines, who have a network of routes spanning the Continent – north as far as Scandinavia, east to Poland and the Baltic states, and south to Spain, Portugal and Morocco. Prices can be up to a third less than the equivalent train fare, and there are marginally cheaper fares on most services for those under 26, which undercut BIJ rail rates for the same journey. Current Eurolines fares from London's Victoria Coach Station to Paris, Brussels or Amsterdam start at £32 one-way, £49 return (£35/54 without a youth reduction). Berlin is £47/76 (£53/84); Nice £56/86 (£62/95); Madrid £76/116 (£90/137); and Stockholm £87/139 (£95/152). For many destinations, there is a cheaper **APEX** fare for return journeys booked at least a week in advance (£69 to Berlin, Nice or Madrid, for example). Slightly higher fares apply at Easter, in July and August and from mid-December to the beginning of January. Add-on fares of £6.50–13.50 one-way,

£10–20 return are available for connecting services from other British cities. The German-based firm Gullivers offer an alternative service to Amsterdam, Brussels, Berlin, Hamburg and Hanover, via the Channel Tunnel, and Anglia International serve all of those, plus Prague, Kosice (Slovakia), Copenhagen, Oslo, Gothenburg (Sweden) and Moscow. Eurolines also have **Minipass** tickets from London to two or more European cities and back, valid for ninety days: London–Paris–Brussels–London costs £55, London–Amsterdam–Paris–London is £68, and London–Amsterdam–Brussels–Paris–London or London–Cologne–Paris–London each cost £69. Alternatively, you might consider Eurolines's thirty- and sixty-day passes, or one of the various passes offered by Busabout for their services around the Continent (see "Travelling in Europe", p.30), with a "London Link" to take you across the channel.

Bus contacts in Britain and Ireland

Anglia-Lines UK ☏0870/608 8806, ⊛www.anglia-lines.co.uk
Busabout UK ☏020/7950 1661, ⊛www.busabout.com
Eurolines UK ☏0870/514 3219, Ireland ☏01/836 6111, ⊛www.eurolines.co.uk. Tickets can also be purchased from any Eurolines or National Express agent (☏0870/580 8080, ⊛www.nationalexpress.co.uk or ⊛www.gobycoach.com).
Gullivers UK ☏0800/4855 4837, ⊛www.gullivers.de
Ulsterbus Northern Ireland ☏028/9033 7003, ⊛www.ulsterbus.co.uk

By ferry

There are numerous **ferry services** between Ireland and Britain, and between the British Isles and Europe. Which service you use will depend on where exactly you are coming from and which part of Europe you are aiming for. Ferries from the southeast of Ireland and the south coast of England connect with northern France and Spain; those from Kent in the southeast of England reach Normandy in northern France and Belgium; those from the east coast and northeast of England cross the North Sea to Holland, Germany and Scandinavia.

Sea crossings from Britain and Ireland

From Britain

ROUTE	COMPANY	FREQUENCY	CROSSING TIME	FOOT PASSENGER (min full adult o/w fare)
BRITAIN – EUROPE				
Dover–Calais	SeaFrance	15 daily	1hr 30min	£17
Dover–Calais	P&O Stena	20–35 daily	1hr 15min	£26
Dover–Calais (catamaran)	Hoverspeed	8–13 daily	1hr	£24
Dover–Dunkirk	Norfolk Line	4–7 daily	2hr	not allowed
Dover–Ostend (catamaran)	Hoverspeed	2 daily 22 Mar– 6 Jan	2hr	£24
Dover–Zeebrugge	P&O Stena	3–4 daily	4hr	not allowed
Harwich–Cuxhaven	DFDS Seaways	3–4 weekly	16hr 45min	£29–54
Harwich–Esbjerg	DFDS Seaways	3–4 weekly	19hr 15min	£49–89
Harwich–Hook of Holland	Stena	2 daily	6hr 30min–7hr 15min	£26
Harwich–Hook of Holland (fast ferry)	Stena	1–2 daily	3hr 40min	£26
Hull–Rotterdam	P&O North Sea Ferries	1 daily	10hr	£48–67
Hull–Zeebrugge	P&O North Sea Ferries	1 daily	12hr 30min	£48–67
Lerwick[1]–Bergen	Smyril Line	1 weekly May–Sept	12hr 30min	£48–68
Newcastle–Amsterdam	DFDS Seaways	daily	15hr	£39–64
Newcastle–Haugesund, Stavanger, Bergen	Fjord Line	2–3 weekly (exc mid-Jan)	17hr 30min–30hr 30min	£50–120
Newcastle–Kristiansand, Gothenburg	DFDS Seaways	2 weekly	17hr 15min–25hr 30min	£64–134
Newhaven–Dieppe	Hoverspeed	1–2 daily	4hr	£26
Newhaven–Dieppe (fast ferry)	Hoverspeed	1–3 daily Mar–Oct	2hr	£28
Newhaven–Dieppe	Transmanche Ferries	2–4 daily	4hr	£26
Plymouth–Roscoff[2]	Brittany Ferries	1–12 weekly	6hr–7hr 30min	£35–72
Plymouth–Santander	Brittany Ferries	2 weekly March–Nov	24hr	£61–107
Poole–Cherbourg	Brittany Ferries	1–2 daily[3]	4hr 15min–5hr 45min	£32–61
Poole–Cherbourg (catamaran)	Brittany Ferries/Condor	1 daily mid-May–Sept	2hr 10min	£38–64
Poole–St Malo[4]	Condor	1 daily May–Sept	4hr 35min	£29–30
Portsmouth–Bilbao	P&O Portsmouth	1–2 weekly except mid-Jan	35hr	£24–56
Portsmouth–Caen	Brittany Ferries	2–3 daily	6hr–6hr 45min	£21–67
Portsmouth–Cherbourg	P&O Portsmouth	1–22 weekly	5hr–7hr	£24–56
Portsmouth–Cherbourg	Condor	1 weekly July–Sept	5hr	not allowed
Portsmouth–Cherbourg	P&O Portsmouth	2–3 daily Apr–Sept	2hr 45min	£27–48
Portsmouth–Cherbourg (catamaran)	P&O Portsmouth	2–3 daily	5hr 30min–7hr 30min	£24–40
Portsmouth–Le Havre	P&O Portsmouth	2–3 daily	5hr 30min–7hr 30min	£24–40
Portsmouth–St Malo	Brittany Ferries	7–8 weekly	9hr–10hr 30min	£38–74
Weymouth–St Malo[5]	Condor	7 weekly March–Sept	5hr 30min	£29–30

[1] connecting service from Aberdeen • [2] a few winter sailings serve St Malo instead, taking 8hr • [3] except Jan and mid-Feb to mid-March • [4] via Jersey or Guernsey • [5] changing vessel at Guernsey

From Ireland

ROUTE	COMPANY	FREQUENCY	CROSSING TIME	FOOT PASSENGER (min full adult o/w fare including hidden supps)
IRELAND–BRITAIN				
Belfast–Heysham (catamaran)	Seacat	1–2 daily Mar–Sept	4hr	£22–29
Belfast–Liverpool	NorseMerchant Ferries	1–2 daily	8hr 30min	£25–40
Belfast–Stranraer	Stena	2 daily	3hr 15min	£14–19
Belfast–Stranraer (fast ferry)	Stena	4–5 daily	1hr 45min	£14–24
Belfast–Troon (catamaran)	Seacat	2–3 daily	2hr 30min	£11–20
Larne–Cairnryan	P&O Irish Sea	4–9 daily	2hr 15min	£19–27
Larne–Cairnryan (fast ferry)	P&O Irish Sea	5 daily March–Sept	1hr	£23–27
Larne–Fleetwood	P&O Irish Sea	2–3 daily	8hr	not allowed
Larne–Troon	P&O Irish Sea	6 weekly	4hr	not allowed
Dublin–Holyhead	Irish Ferries	2 daily	3hr 15min	€25–31
Dublin–Holyhead (fast ferry)	Irish Ferries	3–4 daily	1hr 50min	€33–39
Dublin–Holyhead	Stena	2 daily	3hr	€29–37
Dublin–Liverpool	NorseMerchant Ferries	1–2 daily	7hr 30min	€25–45
Dublin–Liverpool (catamaran)	P&O Irish Sea	11–12 weekly	7hr 30min	not allowed
Dublin–Mostyn	P&O Irish Sea	1–2 daily	6hr–7hr 30min	€29–39
Dun Laoghaire–Holyhead (fast ferry)	Seacat	3–4 daily	1hr 40min	€28–36
Rosslare–Fishguard	Stena	1–2 daily	3hr 30min	€22
Rosslare–Fishguard (catamaran)	Stena	2–4 daily Apr–Sept	1hr 50min	€28–38
Rosslare–Pembroke	Irish Ferries	2 daily	3hr 45min	€25–31
Cork–Swansea	Swansea–Cork Ferries	3–6 weekly	10hr	€30–43
IRELAND–EUROPE				
Cork–Roscoff	Brittany Ferries	1 weekly April–Sept	14hr	€50–169
Dublin–Cherbourg	P&O Irish Sea	1 weekly June–Aug	18hr	not allowed
Rosslare–Cherbourg	Irish Ferries	2–4 weekly	19hr 30min	€60–120
Rosslare–Cherbourg	P&O Irish Sea	3 weekly	18hr	not allowed
Rosslare–Roscoff	Irish Ferries	1–3 weekly April–Sept	17hr	€60–120

Fares on sailings from the Republic are quoted in euros, from Northern Ireland in sterling.

Ferry operators in Britain

Brittany Ferries ☏0870/536 0360,
☷www.brittanyferries.com. Portsmouth to Caen
and St Malo; Poole to Cherbourg; Plymouth to
Roscoff and Santander.

Condor Ferries ☏0845/245 2000,
☷www.condorferries.co.uk. Poole to St Malo via
Jersey or Guernsey; Weymouth to St Malo via
Guernsey; Portsmouth to Cherbourg.

DFDS Seaways ☏0870/533 3000,
☷www.dfdsseaways.co.uk. Harwich to Esbjerg and
Cuxhaven; Newcastle to Amsterdam (Ijmuiden),
Gothenburg and Kristiansand.

Fjord Line ☏0191/296 1313, ☷www.fjordline.co
.uk. Newcastle to Stavanger, Haugesund and Bergen.

Hoverspeed ☏0870/240 8282,
☷www.hoverspeed.com. Dover to Calais and
Ostend; Newhaven to Dieppe.

Norfolk Line ☏0870/870 1020,
☷www.norfolkline.com. Dover to Dunkirk.

P&O Portsmouth ☏0870/242 4999,
☷www.poportsmouth.com. Portsmouth to Bilbao,
Cherbourg and Le Havre.

P&O North Sea Ferries ☏0870/129 6002,
☷www.ponsf.com. Hull to Zeebrugge and
Rotterdam.

P&O Stena ☏0870/600 0600, ☷www.posl.com.
Dover to Calais and Zeebrugge.

SeaFrance ☏0870/571 1711, ☷www.seafrance
.com. Dover to Calais.

Smyril Line ☏01224/572615, ☷www.smyril-line
.fo. Lerwick to Bergen, with connecting P&O Scottish
service from Aberdeen.

Stena Line ☏0870/570 7070, ☷www.stenaline
.co.uk. Harwich to Hook of Holland.

Transmanche Ferries ☏0800/917 1201, ☷www
.transmancheferries.com. Newhaven to Dieppe.

Ferry operators in Ireland

Brittany Ferries Republic ☏021/277 705,
Northern Ireland ☏0870/901 2400; ☷www
.brittanyferries.ie. Cork to Roscoff (March–Oct only).

Irish Ferries Republic ☏01/661 0511, UK
☏0800/018 2211; ☷www.irishferries.com. Dublin
to Holyhead; Rosslare to Pembroke, Cherbourg and
Roscoff.

NorseMerchant Ferries Republic ☏1890/313131,
UK ☏0870/600 4321; ☷www.norsemerchant.com.
Belfast and Dublin to Liverpool.

P&O Irish Sea Republic ☏1800/406049, UK
☏0870/242 4777; ☷www.poirishsea.com. Larne
to Cairnryan, Fleetwood and Troon; Dublin to Liverpool
and Mostyn; Dublin and Rosslare to Cherbourg.

Sea Cat UK ☏0870/552 3523, Republic
☏1800/551743; ☷www.steam-packet.com.

Belfast to Heysham, Troon and Isle of Man; Dublin to
Liverpool and Isle of Man.

Stena Line Republic ☏01/204 7777, Northern
Ireland ☏028/9074 7747, rest of UK ☏0870/570
7070; ☷www.stenaline.co.uk. Rosslare to
Fishguard; Dun Laoghaire and Dublin to Holyhead;
Belfast to Stranraer.

Swansea–Cork Ferries Republic ☏021/427
1166, UK ☏01792/456116; ☷www.swansea-
cork.ie. Cork to Swansea.

From Australia and New Zealand

There are flights from Melbourne, Sydney,
Adelaide, Brisbane and Perth to most
European capitals, and there really is not a
great deal of difference in the fares to the
busiest destinations – a scheduled return
airfare from Sydney to London, Paris, Rome,
Madrid, Athens or Frankfurt should be available through travel agents for around
A\$1500 in low season. A one-way ticket will
cost slightly more than half that, while a
return flight from Auckland to Europe will
cost approximately NZ\$2000 in low season.
Asian airlines often work out cheapest, and
may throw in a stopover, while there are
often bargain deals to be had from
Melbourne to Athens on Olympic Airways –
ring around first.

For RTW deals and other **low-price tickets**, the most reliable operator is STA, who
also supply packages with companies such
as Contiki and Busabout and can issue rail
passes. STA can also advise on visa regulations for Australian and New Zealand citizens – and for a fee will do all the paperwork
for you.

Airlines in Australia and New Zealand

Aer Lingus Australia ☏02/9244 2123, New
Zealand ☏09/308 3351, ☷www.aerlingus.ie
Aeroflot Australia ☏02/9262 2233,
☷www.aeroflot.com
Air France Australia ☏1300/361400 or 02/9244
2100, ☷www.airfrance.com
Air New Zealand Australia ☏13 24 76, New
Zealand ☏0800/737 000, ☷www.airnz.com
Alitalia Australia ☏1300/0361 400,
☷www.alitalia.com
British Airways Australia ☏02/8904 8800, New
Zealand ☏09/356 8690, ☷www.ba.com

Cathay Pacific Australia ☎13 17 47, New Zealand ☎09/379 0861 or 0508/800 454, ⓦwww.cathaypacific.com

Swiss Air Lines Australia ☎1800/221339, New Zealand ☎09/358 3216, ⓦwww.swissairlines.com

Czech Airlines Australia ☎02/9247 7706, ⓦwww.csa.cz/en

Egypt Air Australia ☎02/9267 6979, ⓦwww.egyptair.com.eg

Finnair Australia ☎02/9244 2299, New Zealand ☎09/308 3365, ⓦwww.finnair.com

Garuda Australia ☎02/9334 9970, New Zealand ☎09/366 1862, ⓦwww.garuda-indonesia.com

Gulf Air Australia ☎02/9244 2199, New Zealand ☎09/308 3366, ⓦwww.gulfairco.com

Japan Airlines Australia ☎02/9272 1111, New Zealand ☎09/379 9906, ⓦwww.japanair.com

KLM Australia ☎1300/303 747, New Zealand ☎09/309 1782, ⓦwww.klm.com

Lauda Air Australia ☎02/9251 6155, New Zealand ☎09/308 3368, ⓦwww.laudaair.com

LOT Polish Airlines Australia ☎02/9244 2466, New Zealand ☎09/308 3369, ⓦwww.lot.com

Lufthansa Australia ☎1300/655 727 or 02/9367 3887, New Zealand ☎09/303 1529 or 008/945 220, ⓦwww.lufthansa.com

Malaysia Airlines Australia ☎13 26 27, New Zealand ☎0800/657 472, ⓦwww.mas.com.my

Olympic Airways Australia ☎1800/221 663 or 02/9251 1040, ⓦwww.olympic-airways.com

Qantas Australia ☎13 13 13, New Zealand ☎09/357 8900, ⓦwww.qantas.com.au

Royal Jordanian Airlines Australia ☎02/9244 2701, ⓦwww.rja.com.jo

Scandinavian Airlines (SAS) Australia ☎02/9299 9800, ⓦwww.scandinavian.net

Singapore Airlines Australia ☎13 10 11, New Zealand ☎09/303 2129 or 0800/808 909, ⓦwww.singaporeair.com

Tap Air Portugal Australia ☎02/9244 2344, New Zealand ☎09/308 3373, ⓦwww.tap-airportugal.pt

Tarom Romanian Airlines Australia ☎02/9262 1144, ⓦhttp://tarom.digiro.net

Thai Airways Australia ☎1300/651 960, New Zealand ☎09/377 3886, ⓦwww.thaiair.com

Turkish Airlines Australia ☎02/9299 8400, ⓦwww.turkishairlines.com

Virgin Atlantic Airways Australia ☎02/9244 2747, New Zealand ☎09/308 3377, ⓦwww.virgin-atlantic.com

Travel agents in Australia and New Zealand

Anywhere Travel Australia ☎02/9663 0411 or 018/401 014, ⓔanywhere@ozemail.com.au

Budget Travel New Zealand ☎09/366 0061 or 0800/808 040, ⓦwww.budgettravel.co.nz

Destinations Unlimited New Zealand ☎09/373 4033

Flight Centres Australia ☎02/9235 3522 or 13/1600, New Zealand ☎09/358 4310, ⓦwww.flightcentre.com.au

Northern Gateway Australia ☎08/8941 1394, ⓦwww.northerngateway.com.au

STA Travel Australia ☎1300/360 960, ⓦwww.statravel.com.au, New Zealand ☎0508/782 872, ⓦwww.statravel.co.nz

Student Uni Travel (SUT) Australia ☎02/9232 8444, ⓦww.sut.com.au, New Zealand ☎09/379 4224, ⓦwww.sut.co.nz

Thomas Cook Australia ☎13/1771 or 1800/801 002, ⓦwww.thomascook.com.au, New Zealand ☎09/379 3920, ⓦwww.thomascook.co.nz

Travel.com, Australia ☎02/9249 5444 or 1300/130482, ⓦwww.travel.com.au, New Zealand ☎09/359 3860, ⓦwww.travel.co.nz

Trailfinders Australia ☎02/9247 7666

Travelling in Europe

It's easy enough to travel in Europe, and a number of special deals and passes can make it fairly economical too. Air links are extensive, but also expensive, give or take the odd charter deal in season. In any case, you really appreciate the diversity of Europe best at ground level, by way of its enormous and generally efficient web of rail, road and ferry connections.

By train

Though to some extent it depends on where you intend to spend most of your time, **train** is the best way to make a tour of Europe. The rail network in most countries is comprehensive and the Continent boasts some of the most scenic rail journeys you could make anywhere in the world. Train travel is relatively cheap, too, even in the richer parts of northwest Europe, where – apart from Britain (whose rail system is in a state of virtual collapse following privatization) – trains are heavily subsidized, and prices are brought down further by the multiplicity of passes and discount cards available, both Europe-wide (**InterRail** for those based in Europe or the British Isles, **Eurail** for anyone based elsewhere) and on an individual country basis. We've covered the various passes here, as well as the most important international routes and most useful addresses; supplementary details, including frequencies and journey times of domestic services, are given throughout the guide in each country's "Travel details" section.

If you intend to do a lot of rail travel, the *Thomas Cook European Timetable* is an essential investment, detailing the main lines throughout Europe, as well as ferry connections, and is updated monthly. Thomas Cook also publish a rail map of Europe, which may be a good supplement to our own train map on pp.22–23.

Finally, whenever you board an international train in Europe, check the route of the car you are in, since trains frequently split, with different carriages going to different destinations.

Europe-wide rail passes

For young Europeans, probably the most popular of all the ways of travelling around the Continent is the **InterRail pass**, a ticket for unlimited travel on rail lines the length and breadth of Europe. InterRail passes are available from main stations and international rail agents in all countries covered by the scheme. For **contacts in Britain and Ireland**, see p.15. A zoning system applies for the European countries valid under the pass, as follows:

Zone A Britain and Ireland
Zone B Sweden, Norway and Finland
Zone C Denmark, Germany, Switzerland and Austria
Zone D Poland, the Czech Republic, Slovakia, Hungary and Croatia
Zone E France, Belgium, the Netherlands and Luxembourg
Zone F Spain, Portugal and Morocco
Zone G Italy, Slovenia, Greece and Turkey
Zone H Bulgaria, Romania, Yugoslavia and the Republic of Macedonia

The zones you want to travel in determine the price, which starts at £119 for those under 26 (over 26, £169) for a one-zone card valid for twelve days, £139/209 for twenty-two days; cards for more than one zone are valid for a month and cost £189/265 for two zones, £209/299 for three zones and £249/355 for all the zones. To qualify, you need to have been resident in one of the participating countries for six months or more; you also need a valid passport. For further details and price updates, see RailEurope's InterRail website at ⓦ www.inter-rail.co.uk.

Increasingly with InterRail passes, you need to pay **supplements** on most European express trains, all of them on some routes, and certainly all the most convenient ones (28 of the 29 daily trains between Paris and Brussels carry a supplement, for example, and the remaining service takes more than three times as long to cover the distance). Even where there is in theory no supplement, there is often a compulsory reservation fee, which may cost you double if you only find out about it once you're on the train.

Non-European residents aren't eligible for InterRail passes, though many agents don't in fact check residential qualifications. Better still, a **Eurail pass**, which should be bought outside Europe (but can be obtained from RailEurope in London by non-residents who were unable to get it at home), gives unlimited travel in seventeen countries – Austria, Belgium, Denmark, Finland, France, Germany, Greece, Hungary, Ireland, Italy, Luxembourg, the Netherlands, Norway, Portugal, Spain, Sweden and Switzerland – fewer than InterRail, but valid for more express trains, thus saving money on supplements. The **Eurail Youthpass** (for under-26s) costs US$401 for fifteen days, US$518 for twenty-one days, US$644 for one month, US$910 for two months, and US$1120 for three months; if you're 26 or over you'll have to buy a first-class pass, available for fifteen days (US$572), twenty one days (US$740), one month (US$918), two months (US$1298) and three months (US$1606). If there are between two and five of you travelling together, the **Eurail Saverpass** (first class only) can knock about fifteen percent off the cost of the standard Eurail offerings. You stand a better chance of getting your money's worth out of a **Eurail Flexipass**, which is good for a certain number of travel days in a two-month period. This, too, comes in under-26 and first-class versions: ten days costs US$473 for under-26s, US$674 for first-class travel; and fifteen days, US$622/888. There's also a **Saver Flexipass** for two to five people travelling together. A scaled-down version of the Flexipass, the **Europass** allows travel in France, Germany, Italy, Spain and Switzerland for US$253/360 for five days in two months, rising to US$497/710 for fifteen days, with prices in between for six, eight or ten days; there is also the option of adding adjacent "associate" countries. Eurail passes are available from the agents listed on pp.15 & 29, though note that this pass was superseded by the Eurail Selectpass within a few months of this book going to press.

National rail passes

Some European countries provide a **national rail pass**, which can be good value if you're doing a lot of travelling within one country, or a EuroDomino (also called a Freedom Pass), which you buy before you leave. Main second-class options are listed below (there are first-class versions of most EuroDominos, Railpasses and Flexipasses, plus first-class passes for Bulgaria, Hungary, Portugal, Romania and the Balkans). In general passes quoted in pounds or dollars need to be bought before you leave home, either from the office of the national rail company or national tourist office, or, in North America, from RailEurope, the general sales agent for most European railroads; they can be ordered online at ⓦ www.raileurope.com /us. There is no pass as such for the Baltics (Estonia, Latvia and Lithuania) or Russia.

Austria The VORTEILSCard rail pass gives a year's half-price travel throughout Austria for €93.75. A EuroDomino pass costs from £54 (£70 for over-26s) for three days up to £81/107 for eight days. An Austrian Railpass gives three days' free travel in a fifteen-day period for $107, plus up to five additional days at $15 each. Also covered by Eastern Europe passes.

Belgium A Belgian Tourrail gives five days' unlimited travel within a one-month period for €58, and the Go Pass allows under-26s ten single journeys of any length in six months for €39 (the over-26 version, Rail Pass, costs €58), but on weekdays it is only valid for five days. A EuroDomino pass costs from £27 (£36 for over-26s) for three days up to £41/59 for eight days. Also covered by Benelux passes.

Benelux A Benelux Tourrail card gives five days' travel in a month on the Netherlands, Belgium and Luxembourg railways for $104 ($155 for over-26s, $233 for two people travelling together).

Britain The BritRail pass, available from British Rail agents outside Britain, qualifies you for unlimited rail travel throughout England, Wales and Scotland for four days at $149 ($185 for over-26s), eight days at $215 ($265), fifteen at $279 ($399), twenty-two at $355 ($499), or a month at $419 ($599). It also gives a discount of around twelve percent on Eurostar Channel Tunnel services, and can be bought as a package with the discounted cross-Channel ticket. Alternatively, the BritRail Flexipass gives unlimited travel on any four days in two months for $185 ($235 for over-26s), eight for $239 ($339); or

INTERNATIONAL RAIL ROUTES

N

Trondheim

Bergen

OSLO

Stavanger

Glasgow

Edinburgh

Gothenburg

Frederikshaven

Århus

Belfast

DUBLIN

COPENHAGEN

Hamburg

AMSTERDAM

The Hague

Hannover

BERLIN

LONDON

Ostend

Calais

Cologne

BRUSSELS

Lille

Frankfurt

PARIS

Nürnberg

LUXEMBOURG

Regensburg

Munich

Nantes

Tours

Basel

Zürich

Salzburg

Geneva

BERN

LJUBLJANA

A Coruña

Bordeaux

Lyon

Milan

Santander

Bayonne

Venice

Oporto

Bilbao

Pau

Genoa

Toulouse

Florence

Marseille

Zaragoza

Nice

MADRID

LISBON

Barcelona

Sevilla

ROME

Valencia

Málaga

Naples

Tangier

Fes

Palermo

Casablanca

Marrakesh

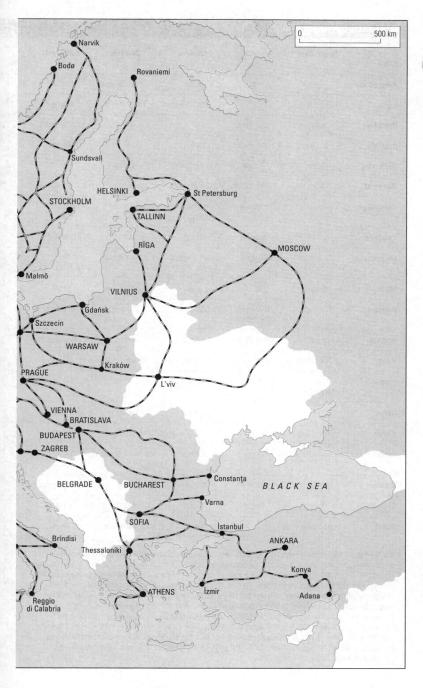

TO / FROM	Amsterdam	Berlin	Bratislava	Brussels	Bucharest
Amsterdam	–	3 (6hr)	Berlin	22 (2hr 55min)	Vienna
Berlin	3 (6hr 15min)	–	1 (9hr 50min)	1 (8hr 45min)	Prague
Bratislava	Berlin	1 (9hr 45min)	–	Vienna	1 (16hr 15min)
Brussels	22 (3h)	1 (8hr 45min)	Vienna	–	Vienna
Bucharest	Vienna	Prague	1 (17hr 55min)	Vienna	–
Budapest	Vienna	2 (12hr 10min)	8 (2hr 25min) [4]	Vienna	6 (13hr 40min)
Copenhagen	Duisburg [1]	Hamburg	Hamburg & Prague	Hamburg	Budapest & Munich
Ljubljana	Munich	Munich	Vienna	Munich	Budapest
Luxembourg	Brussels	Cologne	Zurich & Vienna	22 (2hr 40min)	Zurich & Budapest
Milan	Basel	Munich	Vienna	2 (11hr 55min)	Vienna
Moscow	Hanover [b]	3–7 weekly (27hr 15min) [b]	1 (35hr 5min) [b]	Cologne [b]	1 (45hr 5min) [u]
Munich	1 (10hr 50min)	7 (6hr 40min)	Vienna	1 (11hr)	Budapest
Paris	7 (4hr 50min)	1 (11hr 35min)	Vienna	25 (1hr 25min)	Vienna
Prague	3 weekly (14hr 40min)	5 (5hr 15min)	7 (4hr 30min)	Cologne [5]	1 (23hr)
Rome	Munich	Munich	Vienna	Milan	Vienna
Vienna	1 (14hr 25min)	2 (9hr 50min)	10 (1hr 10min) [4]	1 (14hr 25min)	1 (18hr)
Vilnius	Warsaw & Berlin [3]	Warsaw [3]	Warsaw [3]	Warsaw & Cologne [3]	Warsaw [3]
Warsaw	Berlin	4 (5hr 50min)	2 (8hr 20min)	Cologne	1 (27hr 40min)
Zagreb	Munich	Munich	Vienna	Munich	Budapest
Zurich	1 (8hr 50min)	1 (11hr 40min)	Vienna	2 (7hr 45min)	Vienna

This chart shows the number of direct daily trains between European capitals and the fastest scheduled time by ordinary services where practical (those with a supplement will be faster, and may be your only choice). Where there is no direct service, a suggested interchange point is given instead, but note that you may have to pick up your connecting service from a different terminal, and that you may have to wait several hours for your connection: you could take it as an opportunity to wander round town, with your bags at the left luggage deposit in the meantime, or to freshen up – many major stations have washing facilities. Depending on the time of day, or day of the week, you may be able to get to your destination more quickly or conveniently with one or two extra changes of train. Note too that most trains to Russia and the Baltic states pass through Belarus or Ukraine, and that you may therefore need a transit visa to use them (see p.32). Direct services to Athens, Istanbul and Sofia pass through Belgrade and sometimes Skopje, so you may wish to check on the current political situation in Yugoslavia, the republic of Macedonia and the neighbouring countries before deciding to use them.

Budapest	Copenhagen	Ljubljana	Luxembourg	Milan
Vienna	Duisburg[1]	Munich	Brussels	Basel
2 (2hr 15min)	Hamburg	Munich	Cologne	Munich
8 (2hr 25min)[4]	Prague & Hamburg	Vienna	Vienna & Zurich	Vienna
Vienna	Hamburg	Munich	22 (2hr 35min)	2 (12hr)
7 (13hr)	Munich & Budapest	Budapest	Budapest & Zurich	Vienna
–	Munich	3 (8hr 30min)	Zurich	Venice
Cologne	–	Munich	Cologne	Munich
3 (8hr 40min)	Munich	–	Zurich	Venice
Zurich	Cologne	Zurich	–	2 (8hr 55min)
Venice	Stuttgart	Venice	2 (8hr 50min)	–
1 (39hr 10min)[u]	Hanover & Hamburg[b]	Zagreb[6u]	Cologne[b]	Vienna[7b]
2 (7hr 50min)	1 (14hr 30min)	3 (6hr 20min)	Strasbourg	3 (7hr 20min)
Munich	Hamburg	Munich	6 (3hr 35min)	3 (6hr 50min)
5 (7hrs)	Hamburg	Munich	Frankfurt & Cologne	Munich
Trieste	Munich	Trieste	Milan	26 (4hr 30min)
7 (2hr 35min)[4]	Munich	2 (6hr 15min)	Zurich	1 (11hr 45min)
Warsaw[3]	Warsaw, Berlin & Hamburg[3]	Warsaw & Vienna[3]	Warsaw & Cologne[3]	Warsaw & Vienna[3]
2 (10hr 50min)	Berlin & Hamburg	Vienna	Cologne	Vienna
4 (5hr 5min)	Munich	6 (2hr 20min)	Zurich	Venice
1 (13hr)	Stuttgart	1 (11hr)	2 (5hr)	9 (3hr 40min)

[1] On days when there is no direct train between Copenhagen and Duisburg, change at Osnabrück and Hamburg instead.
[2] On days when there is no direct train, change at Dresden.
[3] The Warsaw–Vilnius train should not be routed via Belarus, but check before travelling. On days when there is no direct connection, change (also) at Şeştokai
[4] There is also a hydrofoil service in summer.
[5] On days when there is no direct service between Cologne and Prague, change also at Frankfurt.
[6] On days when there is no direct service between Zagreb and Moscow, change (also) at Budapest.
[7] On days when there is no direct service between Vienna and Moscow, change (also) at Warsaw.
[b] via Belarus – transit visa needed.
[u] via Ukraine – transit visa needed.

International train routes

TO FROM	Moscow	Munich	Paris	Prague	Rome
Amsterdam	Hanover[b]	1 (11hr)	7 (4hr 45min)	3 weekly (14hr 15min)[2]	Munich
Berlin	3–7 weekly (28hr)[b]	7 (6hr 45min)	1 (11hr 30min)	5 (5hr 10min)	Munich
Bratislava	1 (33hr)[b]	Vienna	Vienna	7 (4hr 15min)	Vienna
Brussels	Cologne[b]	1 (11hr 20min)	25 (1hr 25min)	Cologne[5]	Milan
Bucharest	1 (46hr)[u]	Budapest	Vienna	1 (23hr 45min)	Vienna
Budapest	1 (39hr 50min)[u]	2 (7hr 45min)	Munich	5 (6hr 45min)	Trieste
Copenhagen	Hamburg & Hanover[b]	1 (14hr 40min)	Hamburg	Hamburg	Munich
Ljubljana	Zagreb[6u]	3 (6hr 25min)	Munich	Munich	Trieste
Luxembourg	Cologne[b]	Strasbourg	6 (3hr 35min)	Cologne & Frankfurt	Milan
Milan	Vienna[7b]	3 (7hr 20min)	3 (6hr 50min)	Munich	26 (4hr 30min)
Moscow	–	Prague[b]	Cologne[b]	1 (35hr 25min)[b]	Vienna[7b]
Munich	Prague[b]	–	4 (8hr 35min)	1 (9hr)	2 (10hr 30min)
Paris	Cologne[b]	4 (8hr 30min)	–	Frankfurt	1 (14hr 50min)
Prague	1 (33hr 40min)	1 (8hr 20min)	Frankfurt	–	Munich
Rome	Vienna[7b]	2 (10hr 35min)	1 (14hr 20min)	Munich	–
Vienna	4–7 weekly (33hr 30min)[7b]	4 (4hr 50min)	2 (13hr 35min)	4 (4hr 25min)	1 (13hr 35min)
Vilnius	2–3 (14h 55minr)[b]	Warsaw & Prague[3]	Warsaw & Cologne[3]	Warsaw[3]	Vienna & Warsaw[3]
Warsaw	3–4 (17hr 50min)[b]	Prague	Cologne	3 (9hr 40min)	Vienna
Zagreb	3 weekly (48hr 40min)[6u]	3 (8hr 40min)	Munich	Munich	Trieste
Zurich	Prague[b]	4 (4hr 15min)	3 (6hr)	Munich	1 (11hr 30min)

This chart shows the number of direct daily trains between European capitals and the fastest scheduled time by ordinary services where practical (those with a supplement will be faster, and may be your only choice). Where there is no direct service, a suggested interchange point is given instead, but note that you may have to pick up your connecting service from a different terminal, and that you may have to wait several hours for your connection: you could take it as an opportunity to wander round town, with your bags at the left luggage deposit in the meantime, or to freshen up – many major stations have washing facilities. Depending on the time of day, or day of the week, you may be able to get to your destination more quickly or conveniently with one or two extra changes of train. Note too that most trains to Russia and the Baltic states pass through Belarus or Ukraine, and that you may therefore need a transit visa to use them (see p.32). Direct services to Athens, Istanbul and Sofia pass through Belgrade and sometimes Skopje, so you may wish to check on the current political situation in Yugoslavia, the republic of Macedonia and the neighbouring countries before deciding to use them.

Vienna	Vilnius	Warsaw	Zagreb	Zurich
1 (14hr 30min)	Berlin & Warsaw [3]	Berlin	Munich	1 (9hr)
2 (9hr 50min)	Warsaw [3]	4 (5hr 50min)	Munich	1 (11hr 55min)
4 (1hr 10min) [4]	Warsaw [3]	2 (8hr 15min)	Vienna	Vienna
1 (14hr 45min)	Cologne & Warsaw [3]	Cologne	Munich	2 (7hr 45min)
1 (17hr 50min)	Warsaw [3]	1 (28hr)	Budapest	Vienna
7 (2hr 40min) [4]	Warsaw [3]	2 (10hr 45min)	4 (5hr)	1 (12hr 45min)
Munich	Hamburg, Berlin & Warsaw [3]	Hamburg & Berlin	Munich	Stuttgart
2 (6hr 15min)	Vienna & Warsaw [3]	Vienna	6 (2hr 20min)	1 (11hr 55min)
Zurich	Cologne & Warsaw [3]	Cologne	Zurich	2 (5hr)
1 (12hr 30min)	Vienna & Warsaw [3]	Vienna	Venice	9 (3hr 40min)
4–7 weekly (34hr 40min) [7b]	2–3 (14hr 45min) [b]	2–3 (19hr 45min) [b]	3 weekly (51hr) [6u]	Prague [b]
4 (4hr 55min)	Prague & Warsaw [3]	Prague	3 (8hr 35min)	4 (4hr 15min)
2 (13hr 30min)	Cologne & Warsaw [3]	Cologne	Munich	3 (6hr)
4 (4hr 35min)	Warsaw [3]	3 (9hr 30min)	Munich	Munich
1 (13hr 40min)	Vienna & Warsaw [3]	Vienna	Trieste	1 (12hr 20min)
–	Warsaw [3]	2 (8hr 10min)	2 (6hr 35min)	3 (9hr 10min)
Warsaw [3]	–	every 2 days (9hr 55min) [3]	Warsaw & Vienna [3]	Warsaw & Vienna [3]
2 (8hr 15min)	every 2 days (10hr 15min)	–	Vienna	Vienna
2 (6hr 30min)	Vienna & Warsaw [3]	Vienna	–	1 (14hr 25min)
3 (9hr 30min)	Vienna & Warsaw [3]	Vienna	1 (13hr 30min)	–

[1] On days when there is no direct train between Copenhagen and Duisburg, change at Osnabrück and Hamburg instead.
[2] On days when there is no direct train, change at Dresden.
[3] The Warsaw–Vilnius train should not be routed via Belarus, but check before travelling. On days when there is no direct connection, change (also) at Şeştokai
[4] There is also a hydrofoil service in summer.
[5] On days when there is no direct service between Cologne and Prague, change also at Frankfurt.
[6] On days when there is no direct service between Zagreb and Moscow, change (also) at Budapest.
[7] On days when there is no direct service between Vienna and Moscow, change (also) at Warsaw.
[b] via Belarus – transit visa needed.
[u] via Ukraine – transit visa needed.

fifteen for $359 ($515). Other passes include the Freedom of Scotland Pass, giving four days' travel in Scotland in an eight-day period at $134, eight days in fifteen at $168, twelve days in twenty at $219, and the Freedom of Wales pass, which gives unlimited bus travel in Wales for eight days with unlimited rail travel on any four of them for $85, or unlimited bus travel for fifteen days with unlimited rail travel on any eight of them for $159. With a BritRail pass plus Ireland, you get five days' travel in a month throughout Britain and Ireland (plus a round trip on Stena Line Irish Sea ferries) for $399, or ten days for $569. Available in Britain, the Young Person's Railcard costs £18 and gives a 33 percent reduction to full-time students and under-26s for a year.

Bulgaria A EuroDomino pass costs from £22 (£27 for over-26s) for three days up to £41/54 for eight days.

Croatia A EuroDomino pass costs from £34 (the same for over-26s) for three days up to £52/57 for eight days.

Czech Republic A EuroDomino pass costs from £22 (£29 for over-26s) for three days up to £49/58 for eight days. A Czech Flexipass gives three days' free travel in a fifteen-day period for $48, plus up to five additional days at $6 each. Also covered by Eastern Europe passes.

Denmark A EuroDomino pass costs from £41 (£53 for over-26s) for three days up to £78/101 for eight days. For ScanRail passes see Scandinavia.

Eastern Europe A European East Pass gives five days' free travel in a month in Austria, the Czech Republic, Hungary, Poland and Slovakia for $154, plus up to five additional days at $18 each.

Finland Finnrail passes are valid for unlimited rail travel on three, five or ten days in a month and cost $108, $144 and $194 respectively. A EuroDomino pass costs from £56 (£74 for over-26s) for three days up to £103/139 for eight days. For ScanRail passes see Scandinavia.

France A EuroDomino pass costs from £84 (£115 for over-26s) for three days up to £155/204 for eight days. The France Railpass costs $210 for any four days' travel in a month, with up to six additional rail days at $30 each ($171 plus $25 per additional day each for two to five people travelling together). For under-26s, the France Youthpass gives four days' travel in a month for $148, with up to six additional days at $18 each. A France'n'Italy Pass gives four days' free travel in two months throughout France and Italy for $199 (over-26s $239), with up to six additional days at $21 ($25) each.

Germany The German Rail BahnCard gives a year of unlimited half-price travel on all trains in Germany and costs €140 (under-23s, students and spouses

of holders €70). A EuroDomino pass costs from £89 (£118 for over-26s) for three days up to £125/176 for eight days. A German Rail Pass costs $142 ($180 for over-26s, $270 for two travelling together) for any four days' travel in a month, rising to $216 ($316, $474) for ten (with prices in between for five to nine days).

Greece A EuroDomino pass costs from £32 (£41 for over-26s) for three days up to £55/73 for eight days.

Hungary A EuroDomino pass costs from £25 (£32 for over-26s) for three days up to £54/71 for eight days. Also covered by Eastern Europe passes.

Ireland Irish Rail's Rover ticket buys unlimited rail travel in the Republic and the North on any five days out of fifteen for €107, with an Irish Explorer Rail Ticket (the same deal in the Republic only) at €87. Use the Emerald Card on rail and bus in the Republic and the North at €147 for eight days in fifteen and €255 for fifteen days in thirty, or the Irish Explorer Rail and Bus Ticket for eight days in fifteen in the Republic only at €128. A EuroDomino pass costs from £39 sterling (£43 for over-26s) for three days up to £76/81 for eight days and is valid only in the Republic. See Britain for details of the BritRail Pass plus Ireland (not available in Britain or Ireland).

Italy A two-month Chilometrico ticket is valid for 3000km of travel, or twenty journeys if shorter, for up to five people within two months for €116.72 each, a lot more expensive if bought abroad. A EuroDomino pass costs from £70 (£94 for over-26s) for three days up to £107/139 for eight days. The Italy Railcard gives unlimited rail travel for eight days at $159, fifteen at $249, twenty-one at $289, or thirty at $348. A Flexi RailCard gives four days in a month for $159 (over-26s $191), eight days for $223 ($268), or twelve days for $286 ($343). A France'n'Italy Pass gives four days' free travel in two months throughout France and Italy for $199 (over-26s $239), with up to six additional days at $21 ($25) each.

Luxembourg One-day rail passes are €4.40 each, €17.60 for a book of 5. A EuroDomino pass costs from £10 (£14 for over-26s) for three days up to £15/18 for eight days. A Luxembourg Card covering buses too costs €9 for one day, €16 for any two days in two weeks, and €22 for any three days in two weeks, with free entry to numerous sights as well. See also Benelux.

Morocco A EuroDomino pass costs from £22 (£24 for over-26s) for three days up to £46/52 for eight days.

Netherlands A Dagskaart (Day Travel Card) gives a day's unlimited travel for €35.60. A Zomertoer (Summer Tour) ticket giving free travel on any three days in ten during July and August costs €45 for one person, €59 for two travelling together,

€54/72.50 for one covering bus services too. A HollandRail Pass gives three days' free travel in a month at $52 for one person, $78 for two travelling together (over-26s $65/98), or five days for $79/119 ($98/147). A EuroDomino pass costs from £25 (£34 for over-26s) for three days up to £62/81 for eight days. See also Benelux.

Norway A Norway Railpass gives three days' free travel in a month for $146, four days for $182, or five days for $202. A EuroDomino pass costs from £86 (£115 for over-26s) for three days up to £157/204 for eight days. For ScanRail passes see Scandinavia.

Poland Polrail passes cost £48 (£73 for over-26s) for eight days travel, £58/82 for fifteen, £64/92 for twenty-one, and £81/116 for a month. A EuroDomino pass costs from £30 (£36 for over-26s) for three days up to £59/73 for eight days. Also covered by Eastern Europe passes.

Portugal A Bilhete Turistico pass, which costs €100 for a week's rail travel, €170 for two weeks, and €250 for three, is really only worthwhile for first-class travel, which it allows. A EuroDomino pass costs from £27 (£41 for over-26s) for three days up to £54/68 for eight days.

Romania A EuroDomino pass costs from £25 (£34 for over-26s) for three days up to £54/81 for eight days.

Scandinavia The ScanRail pass is valid on the rail networks of Denmark, Norway, Sweden and Finland and costs $161 ($214 for over-26s) for five days' travel in two months, $216 ($288) for ten days in two months, and $249 ($332) for twenty-one days unlimited.

Slovakia A EuroDomino pass costs from £20 (£26 for over-26s) for three days up to £34/46 for eight days. Also covered by Eastern Europe passes.

Slovenia A EuroDomino pass costs from £25 (£34 for over-26s) for three days up to £39/52 for eight days.

Spain A EuroDomino pass costs from £55 (£73 for over-26s) for three days up to £129/168 for eight days. The Spain Flexipass gives three days' free travel in a two-month period for $155, plus $30 each for up to seven additional days.

Sweden EuroDomino passes for Sweden cost from £84 (£105 for over-26s) for three days up to £130/164 for eight days. The Sweden Railpass gives three days' free travel in a month for $158, four days for $175, five for $195. ScanRail passes are also valid (see Scandinavia).

Switzerland The Swiss Pass, valid for unlimited travel on rail, bus and ferry routes, costs $120 for four days ($160 for over-26s, $136 each for two or more people travelling together), $169 ($225/192)

for eight days, $203 ($270/230) for fifteen, $237 ($315/268) for twenty-two, and $263 ($350/298) for a month. Alternatives are the Swiss Flexipass (giving three to eight days in a month at $156–282, or $132–240 each for two or more travelling together), the Swiss Half-Fare Card (fifty percent discount on rail travel for a month for £42), and the Swiss Card (free travel between border or airport and your main resort plus fifty percent discount on other tickets for a month at $110). A EuroDomino pass costs from £51 (£68 for over-26s) for three days up to £79/105 for eight days.

Turkey A EuroDomino pass costs from £14 (£18 for over-26s) for three days up to £28/37 for eight days.

Rail contacts

For rail contacts in Britain and Ireland, see p.15.

In North America

BritRail Travel US ☎1-888/BRITRAIL or 212/490-6688, Canada, ☎1-800/361-RAIL, ⌨www.raileurope.com. British and European passes.
CIE Tours International ☎1-800/243-8687, ⌨www.cietours.com. Irish passes.
CIT Rail US ☎1-800/223-7987 or 212/730-2400, Canada ☎1-800/361-7799, ⌨www.fs-on-line.com. Eurail, Europass, German and Italian passes.
DER Travel ☎1-888/337-7350, ⌨www.dertravel.com/rail. European and many individual country passes.
European Rail Services Canada ☎1-800/205-5800 or 416/695-1211, ⌨www.europeanrailservices.com. European and many individual country passes.
Europrail International Canada ☎1-888/667-9734, ⌨www.europrail.net. European and many individual country passes.
Online Travel ☎1-800/660-5300, ⌨www.eurorail.com. European and many individual country passes.
Orbis Polish Travel Bureau ☎1-800/TO-POLAND, ⌨www.orbis-usa.com. Passes for Poland.
Rail Europe US ☎1-800/438-7245, Canada ☎1-800/361-7245, ⌨www.raileurope.com/us. Official Eurail agent in North America; sells the widest range of regional and individual country passes.
ScanTours ☎1-800/223 7226 or 310/636 4656, ⌨www.scantours.com. Eurail, Scandinavian and other European country passes.

In Australia and New Zealand

Rail Plus Australia ☎1300/555 003 or 03/9642 8644, @info@railplus.com.au, New Zealand ☎09/303 2484. Sells Eurail, Europass and Britrail passes.

Bentours Australia ☎02/9241 1353. Scandinavian rail and bus passes.
CIT World Travel Australia ☎02/9267 1255 or 03/9650 5510, ⊛www.cittravel.com.au. Eurail, Europass and Italian rail passes.
Trailfinders Australia ☎02/9247 7666, ⊛www.trailfinder.com.au. All Europe passes.

By bus

On the whole, you'll find yourself using buses only for the odd local trip, since long-distance journeys between major European cities are generally slow and uncomfortable and not particularly cheap, especially if you have a rail pass. If you have a limited itinerary, however, a **bus pass** or **circular bus ticket** can undercut a rail pass, especially for over-26s. The **Eurolines** pass is valid for unlimited travel between 31 cities in Europe and the British Isles (though, with certain exceptions, it is not supposed to be used for journeys that do not cross international frontiers). It costs £99 (£117 for over-26s) for fifteen days in low season and £130/155 in high season; for one month it's £136/167 and £186/229 and for two months it's £167/211 and £205/267. Alternatively, **Busabout** run services for their own pass holders every two to four days in summer, taking in the major cities of nine European countries, with add-on connections to two more, plus a link to London and through tickets from elsewhere in Britain and Ireland. Two-week Busabout passes are £159 for youth or student card-holders, £179 for oth-ers, rising to £219/249 for twenty-one days, £289/392 for a month, £439/489 for two months, £529/589 for three and £629/699 for the whole season (April–Oct). There are also Flexipasses for any six, ten or fifteen days in two months (£149/169, £229/259 and £329/369 respectively), twenty days in three months (£429/479), and twenty-five days in four months (£499/549), with additional days at £25/30. There are "early bird" discounts on two- to four-week Busabout passes and six- to fifteen-day Flexipasses if first used before mid-May. Busabout passes are available at travel agents in Britain, North America, Australia and New Zealand (enquiries at: UK ☎020/7950 1661, US ☎1-800/664 4046, Canada ☎416/322 8468, Australia ☎1300/301 776, New Zealand ☎09/309 5973; ⊛www.busabout.com).

By ferry

Travelling by **ferry** is often the most practical way to get from one part of Europe to another, the obvious routes being from the mainland to the Mediterranean islands, as well as moving between the countries bordering the Baltic and Adriatic Seas. There are countless routes across the whole of Europe serving a huge range of destinations, too numerous to outline here, so where possible we've given the details of ferries to other countries within individual *Guide* accounts. For further details of schedules and operators, see the *Thomas Cook European Timetable*, or see ⊛www .ex.ac.uk/~mspunter/ifg.

Red tape and visas

Since the lifting of many immigration restrictions for European Union members in January 1993, border-crossing for most EU nationals has become a much less formal procedure, with holders of most passports just having to wave their documents at border officials. Border controls between some countries, Scandinavian states in particular, are virtually nonexistent, and fifteen countries (Austria, Belgium, Denmark, Finland, France, Germany, Greece, Iceland, Italy, Luxembourg, the Netherlands, Norway, Portugal, Spain and Sweden), known as the Schengen Group, now have joint visas, valid for travel in all and, in theory, with no immigration controls between them – though this may mean more ID checks within those countries.

Citizens of the UK (but not other British passport holders), Ireland, Australia, New Zealand, Canada and the US do not need a **visa** to enter most European countries (current exceptions are listed in the next paragraph), and can usually stay for one to three months, depending on nationality; for some countries, passports must be valid at least six months beyond the end of stay. Always check on visa requirements before travelling, as they can and do change (this especially applies to Canadian, Australian and New Zealand citizens intending to visit eastern European countries), though EU countries should never require visas from British or Irish citizens.

Everyone needs a **visa** to visit Russia. **American**, **British** and **Irish citizens** need them for Turkey (available at the border). **Canadians** need them for the Czech Republic, Estonia, Latvia, Poland and Turkey (last one available at the border). **Australians** require visas to visit the Czech Republic, Hungary, Latvia, Poland, Romania and Turkey (last two available at the border); **New Zealanders** need them for Latvia, Poland and Romania (last one available at the border). Note that the three Baltic states (Estonia, Latvia and Lithuania) all allow entry to Canadians and certain other nationalities who have a valid visa for any one of them. You will also need transit visas if crossing the Ukraine or Belarus (when travelling for example from Poland, Slovakia, Hungary or Romania to Moscow).

Finally, don't leave it too late to get a passport before leaving home, since by post this can take four weeks or longer in the summer and is rather irksome to do in person.

Customs

Customs and duty-free restrictions vary throughout Europe, but are standard for travellers arriving in the EU at one litre of spirits, plus two litres of table wine, plus 200 cigarettes (or 250g tobacco, or fifty cigars). Since the inauguration of the Single Market, there is no longer any duty-free allowance for travel within the EU, but travellers between EU countries can effectively carry as much in the way of duty-paid goods as they want (so long as they are for personal use). Remember that carrying contraband such as controlled drugs, firearms or pornography is illegal, not to mention foolhardy in the extreme. If you are carrying prescribed drugs of any kind, it might be a good idea to have a copy of the prescription to flash at suspicious customs officers. If in doubt consult the relevant embassy.

Passport offices

Australia 12 Talbot St, Forrest, Canberra, ACT 2603 ☏02/6295 1376 (others in Newcastle, Melbourne, Brisbane, Adelaide, Perth, Hobart and Darwin). Applications can be made at most post offices. Information on line at ⊛ www.passports.gov.au.
Canada Applications by mail: Dept of Foreign Affairs and International Trade, Ottawa, ON K1A 0G3 ☏1-800/567-6868. Walk-in offices in major cities nationwide. Information on line at ⊛ www.dfait-maeci.gc.ca/passport.
Ireland Setanta Centre, Molesworth St, Dublin 2 ☏1890/426888; 1a South Mall, Cork

☎1890/426900. Information on line at ⌨www.irlgov
.ie/iveagh/services/passports/passportfacilities.htm.
New Zealand Level 4, 450 Queen St, PO Box
3291, Auckland ☎0800/225050 (others in
Christchurch, Manukau and Wellington).
Information on line at ⌨www.passports.govt.nz.
UK 80 Eccleston Square, London SW1V 1PN
☎0870/521 0410 (others in Belfast, Durham,
Glasgow, Liverpool, Newport and Peterborough).
Applications can be made at any post office.
Information on line at ⌨www.passport.gov.uk.
US 1111 19th St NW, Washington, DC 20524
☎202/647 0518 (others in Boston, Chicago,
Honolulu, Houston, Los Angeles, Miami, New
Orleans, New York, Norwalk (Connecticut),
Philadelphia, San Francisco and Seattle).
Information and application forms available online
at ⌨travel.state.gov/passport_services.html.

European embassies

AUSTRIA US 3524 International Court, NW,
Washington, DC 20008–3022 ☎202/895 6700;
Canada 445 Wilbrod St, Ottowa, ON K1N 6M7
☎613/789 1444; **UK** 18 Belgrave Mews West,
London SW1X 8HU ☎020/7235 3731; **Ireland** 15
Ailesbury Ct, 93 Ailesbury Rd, Dublin 4 ☎01/269
4577; **Australia** PO Box 375, Manuka, Canberra,
ACT 2603 ☎02/6295 1533; **New Zealand** 57
Willis St, Wellington ☎04/499 6393.

BELGIUM US 3330 Garfield St, NW, Washington,
DC 20008 ☎202/333 6900; **Canada** 80 Elgin St,
4th floor, Ottawa, ON K1P 1B7 ☎613/236 7267;
UK 103–105 Eaton Sq, London SW1W 9AB
☎020/7470 3700; **Ireland** 2 Shrewsbury Rd,
Dublin 4 ☎01/269 2082; **Australia** 19 Arkana St,
Yarralumla, Canberra, ACT 2600 ☎02/6273 2501;
New Zealand 12th floor, Axon House, 1–3
Willeston St, PO Box 3379, Wellington ☎04/917
0237.

BRITAIN US 3100 Massachusetts Ave, NW,
Washington, DC 20008 ☎202/588 6500; **Canada**
80 Elgin St, Ottawa, ON K1P 5K7 ☎613/237 1530;
Ireland 29 Merrion Rd, Dublin 4 ☎01/205 3700;
Australia Commonwealth Ave, Canberra, ACT
2600 ☎02/6270 6666; **New Zealand** 44 Hill St,
PO Box 1812, Wellington ☎04/472 6049.

BULGARIA US 1621 22nd St, NW, Washington, DC
20008 ☎202/387 7969; **Canada** 325 Stewart St,
Ottawa, ON K1N 6K5 ☎613/789 3215; **UK**
186–188 Queens Gate, London SW7 5HL
☎020/7584 9400; **Ireland** 22 Burlington Rd,
Dublin 4 ☎01/660 3293; **Australia** 4 Carlotta St,
Double Bay, NSW 2028 ☎02/9327 7581.

CROATIA US 2343 Massachusetts Ave, NW,
Washington, DC 20008 ☎202/588 5899; **Canada**

229 Chapel St, Ottawa, ON K1N 7Y6 ☎613/562
7820; **UK** 21 Conway St, London W1P 5HL
☎020/7387 2022; **Australia** 14 Jindalee Cres,
O'Malley, Canberra, ACT 2606 ☎02/6286 6988;
New Zealand 131 Lincoln Rd, Henderson,
Auckland ☎09/836 5581.

CZECH REPUBLIC US 3900 Spring of Freedom
St, NW, Washington, DC 20008 ☎202/274 9100;
Canada 251 Cooper St, Ottawa, ON K2P 0G2
☎613/562 3875; **UK** 26 Kensington Palace Gdns,
London W8 4QY ☎020/7243 1115; **Ireland** 57
Northumberland Rd, Ballsbridge, Dublin 4
☎01/668 1135; **Australia** 38 Culgoa Circuit,
O'Malley, Canberra, ACT 2606 ☎02/6290 1386.

DENMARK US 3200 Whitehaven St, NW,
Washington, DC 20008–3683 ☎202/234 4300;
Canada 47 Clarence St, Suite 450, Ottawa, ON
K1N 9K1 ☎613/562 1811; **UK** 55 Sloane St,
London SW1X 9SR ☎020/7333 0200; **Ireland**
121–122 St Stephen's Green, Dublin 2 ☎01/475
6404; **Australia** 15 Hunter St, Yarralumla,
Canberra, ACT 2600 ☎02/6273 2195; **New
Zealand** Level 7, 45 Johnston St, PO Box 10874,
Wellington ☎04/471 0520.

ESTONIA US 2131 Massachusetts Ave, NW,
Washington, DC 20008 ☎202/588 0101; **Canada**
958 Broadview Ave, Toronto, ON M4K 2R6
☎416/461 0764; **UK** 16 Hyde Park Gate, London
SW7 5DG ☎020/7589 3428; **Ireland** 24 Merlyn
Park, Dublin 4 ☎01/269 1552; **Australia** 86
Louisa Rd, Birchgrove, Sydney, NSW 2041
☎02/9810 7468.

FINLAND US 3301 Massachusetts Ave, NW,
Washington, DC 20008 ☎202/298 5800; **Canada**
55 Metcalfe St, Suite 850, Ottawa, ON K1P 6L5
☎613/236 2389; **UK** 38 Chesham Pl, London
SW1W 8HW ☎020/7838 6200; **Ireland** Russell
House, Stokes Pl, St Stephen's Green, Dublin 2
☎01/478 1344; **Australia** 10 Darwin Ave,
Yarralumla, Canberra, ACT 2600 ☎02/6273 3800;
New Zealand 44–52 The Terrace, 6th floor, PO
Box 2402, Wellington ☎04/499 4599.

FRANCE US 4101 Reservoir Rd, NW, Washington,
DC 20007 ☎202/944 6000; **Canada** 42 Sussex
Drive, Ottawa, ON K1M 2C9 ☎613/789 1795; **UK**
58 Knightsbridge, London SW1X 7JT ☎020/7201
1000; **Ireland** 36 Ailesbury Rd, Ballsbridge, Dublin 4
☎01/260 1666; **Australia** 6 Perth Ave, Yarralumla,
Canberra, ACT 2600 ☎02/6216 0100; **New Zealand**
Rural Bank House, 34–42 Manners St, 12th floor,
PO Box 11343, Wellington ☎04/384 2555.

GERMANY US 4645 Reservoir Rd, NW,
Washington, DC 20007–1998 ☎202/298 4000;
Canada 1 Waverley St, 14th floor, Ottawa, ON K2P
0T8 ☎613/232 1101; **UK** 23 Belgrave Square,

London SW1X 8PZ ☎020/7824 1300; **Ireland** 31 Trimleston Ave, Booterstown, Blackrock, Co Dublin ☎01/269 3011; **Australia** 119 Empire Circuit, Yarralumla, Canberra, ACT 2600 ☎02/6270 1911; **New Zealand** 90–92 Hobson St, PO Box 1687, Thorndon, Wellington ☎04/473 6063.

GREECE US 2221 Massachusetts Ave, NW, Washington, DC 20008 ☎202/939 5800; **Canada** 76–80 MacLaren St, Ottawa, ON K2P 0K6 ☎613/238 6271; **UK** 1a Holland Park, London W11 3TP ☎020/7229 3850; **Ireland** 1 Upper Pembroke St, Dublin 2 ☎01/676 7254; **Australia** 9 Turrana St, Yarralumla, Canberra, ACT 2600 ☎02/6273 3011; **New Zealand** 10th floor, 5–7 Willeston St, PO Box 24066, Wellington ☎04/473 7775.

HUNGARY US 3910 Shoemaker St, NW, Washington, DC 20008 ☎202/362 6730; **Canada** 299 Waverley St, Ottawa, ON K2P 0V9 ☎613/230 2717; **UK** 35 Eaton Pl, London SW1X 8BY ☎020/7235 5218; **Ireland** 2 Fitzwilliam Pl, Dublin 2 ☎01/661 2902; **Australia** 17 Beale Cres, Deakin, Canberra, ACT 2600 ☎02/6282 3226; **New Zealand** 7/1a Picton St, Ponsonby, Auckland ☎09/376 3609.

IRELAND US 2234 Massachusetts Ave, NW, Washington, DC 20008 ☎202/462 3939; **Canada** 130 Albert St, Suite 1105, Ottawa, ON K1P 5G4 ☎613/233 6281; **UK** 17 Grosvenor Pl, London SW1X 7HR ☎020/7235 2171; **Australia** 20 Arkana St, Yarralumla, Canberra, ACT 2600 ☎02/6273 3022.

ITALY US 1601 Fuller St, NW, Washington, DC 20009 ☎202/328 5500; **Canada** 275 Slater St, 21st floor, Ottawa, ON K1P 5H9 ☎613/232 2401; **UK** 14 Three Kings Yard, Davies St, London W1K 4EH ☎020/7312 2200; **Ireland** 63–65 Northumberland Rd, Dublin 4 ☎01/660 1744; **Australia** 12 Grey St, Deakin, Canberra, ACT 2600 ☎02/6273 3333; **New Zealand** 34–38 Grant Rd, Thorndon, PO Box 463, Wellington ☎04/473 5339.

LATVIA US 4325 17th St, NW, Washington, DC 20011 ☎202/726 8213; **Canada** 280 Albert St, Suite 300, Ottawa, ON K1P 5G8 ☎613/238 6014; **UK** 45 Nottingham Pl, London W1U 5LY ☎020/7312 0040; **Australia** 32 Parnell St, Strathfield, Sydney, NSW ☎02/9745 5981.

LITHUANIA US 2622 16th St, NW, Washington, DC 20009 ☎202/234 5860; **Canada** 130 Albert St, Suite 204, Ottawa, ON K1P 5G4 ☎613/567 5458; **UK** 84 Gloucester Pl, London W1U 6AU ☎020/7486 6401.

LUXEMBOURG US 2200 Massachusetts Ave, NW, Washington, DC 20008 ☎202/265 4171; **UK** 27 Wilton Crescent, London SW1X 8SD ☎020/7235 6961.

MOROCCO US 1601 21st St, NW, Washington, DC 20009 ☎202/462 7979; **Canada** 38 Range Rd, Ottawa, ON K1N 8J4 ☎613/236 7391; **UK** 49 Queen's Gate Gdns, London SW7 5NE ☎020/7581 5001; **Ireland** 53 Raglan Rd, Ballsbridge, Dublin 4 ☎01/660 9449.

NETHERLANDS US 4200 Linnean Ave, NW, Washington, DC 20008 ☎202/244 5300; **Canada** 350 Albert St, Suite 2020, Ottawa, ON K1R 1A4 ☎613/237 5030; **UK** 38 Hyde Park Gate, London SW7 5DP ☎020/7590 3200; **Ireland** 160 Merrion Rd, Dublin 4 ☎01/269 3444; **Australia** 120 Empire Circuit, Yarralumla, Canberra, ACT 2600 ☎02/6273 3111; **New Zealand** Investment Centre, 10th Floor, Ballance St/Featherstone St, PO Box 840, Wellington ☎04/471 6390.

NORWAY US 2720 34th St, NW, Washington, DC 20008–2714 ☎202/333 6000; **Canada** 90 Sparks St, Suite 532, Ottawa, ON K1P 5B4 ☎613/238 6571; **UK** 25 Belgrave Sq, London SW1X 8QD ☎020/7591 5500; **Ireland** 34 Molesworth St, Dublin 2 ☎01/662 1800; **Australia** 17 Hunter St, Yarralumla, Canberra, ACT 2600 ☎02/6273 3444; **New Zealand** 61 Molesworth St, Wellington ☎04/471 2503.

POLAND US 2640 16th St, NW, Washington, DC 20009 ☎202/234 3800; **Canada** 443 Daly Ave, Ottawa, ON K1N 6H3 ☎613/789 0468; **UK** 47 Portland Pl, London W1B 1JH ☎020/7580 4324; **Ireland** 5 Ailesbury Rd, Dublin 4 ☎01/283 0855; **Australia** 7 Turrana St, Yarralumla, Canberra, ACT 2600 ☎02/6273 1208; **New Zealand** 17 Upland Rd, PO Box 10211, Kelburn, Wellington ☎04/475 9453.

PORTUGAL US 2125 Kalorama Rd, NW, Washington, DC 20008 ☎202/328 8610; **Canada** 645 Island Park Drive, Ottawa, ON K1Y 0B8 ☎613/729 0883; **UK** 11 Belgrave Sq, London SW1X 8PP ☎020/7235 5331; **Ireland** Knocksinna House, Foxrock, Dublin 18 ☎01/289 4416; **Australia** 23 Culgoa Circuit, O'Malley, Canberra, ACT 2606 ☎02/6290 1733.

ROMANIA US 1607 23rd St, NW, Washington, DC 20008 ☎202/232 3694; **Canada** 655 Rideau St, Ottawa, ON K1N 6A3 ☎613/789 3709; **UK** Arundel House, 4 Palace Green, London W8 4QD ☎020/7937 9666; **Ireland** 47 Ailesbury Rd, Dublin 4 ☎01/269 2852; **Australia** 4 Dalman Cres, O'Malley, Canberra, ACT 2606 ☎02/6286 2343.

RUSSIA US 2650 Wisconsin Ave, NW, Washington, DC 20007 ☎202/298 5700; **Canada** 285 Charlotte St, Ottawa ON K1N 8L5 ☎613/235 4341; visa section 52 Range Rd, Ottawa, ON K1N 8J5 ☎613/236 7220; **UK** 13 Kensington Palace Gdns,

London W8 4QX ☎020/7229 3628; **Ireland** 186 Orwell Rd, Rathgar, Dublin 14 ☎01/492 2048; **Australia** 78 Canberra Ave, Griffith, Canberra, ACT 2603 ☎02/6295 9033; **New Zealand** 57 Messines Rd, Karori, Wellington ☎04/476 6113.

SLOVAKIA US 2201 Wisconsin Ave, Suite 250, NW, Washington, DC 20007 ☎202/965 5160; **Canada** 50 Rideau Terr, Ottawa, ON K1M 2A1 ☎613/749 4442; **UK** 25 Kensington Palace Gdns, London W8 4QY ☎020/7313 6470; **Ireland** 20 Clyde Rd, Ballsbridge, Dublin 4 ☎01/660 0012; **Australia** 47 Culgoa Circuit, O'Malley, Canberra, ACT 2606 ☎02/6290 1516.

SLOVENIA US 1525 New Hampshire Ave, NW, Washington, DC 20036–1203 ☎202/667 5363; **Canada** 150 Metcalfe St, Suite 2101, Ottawa, ON K2P 1P1 ☎613/565 5781; **UK** 10 Little College St, London SW1P 3SH ☎020/7222 5400; **Australia** Level 6, Advance Bank Centre, 60 Marcus Clark St, Canberra, ACT 2601 ☎02/6243 4830.

SPAIN US 2375 Pennsylvania Ave, NW, Washington, DC 20037 ☎202/452 0100; **Canada** 74 Stanley Ave, Ottawa, ON K1M 1P4 ☎613/747 2252; **UK** 39 Chesham Pl, London SW1X 8SB ☎020/7235 5555, visa section 20 Draycott Place, London SW3 2RZ ☎0906/550 8970 – premium-rate charge; **Ireland** 17a Merlyn Park, Dublin 4 ☎01/269 1640; **Australia** 15 Arkana St, Yarralumla, Canberra, ACT 2600 ☎02/6273 3555.

SWEDEN US 1501 M St, NW, Washington, DC 20005–1702 ☎202/467 2600; **Canada** Mercury Ct, 377 Dalhousie St, Ottawa, ON K1N 9N8 ☎613/241 8553; **UK** 11 Montagu Place, London W1H 2AL ☎020/7917 6400; **Ireland** Sun Alliance House, 13–17 Dawson St, Dublin 2 ☎01/671 5822; **Australia** 5 Turrana St, Yarralumla, Canberra, ACT 2600 ☎02/6270 2700; **New Zealand** 13th floor, Vogel Bldg, Aitken St, Thorndon, PO Box 12538, Wellington ☎04/499 9895.

SWITZERLAND US 2900 Cathedral Ave, NW, Washington, DC 20008–3499 ☎202/745 7900; **Canada** 5 Marlborough Ave, Ottawa, ON K1N 8E6 ☎613/235 1837; **UK** 16–18 Montagu Place, London W1H 2BQ ☎020/7616 6000; **Ireland** 6 Ailesbury Rd, Ballsbridge, Dublin 4 ☎01/218 6382; **Australia** 7 Melbourne Ave, Forrest, Canberra, ACT 2603 ☎02/6273 3977; **New Zealand** Panama House, 22 Panama St, Wellington ☎04/472 1593.

TURKEY US 2525 Massachusetts Ave, NW, Washington, DC 20008 ☎202/612 6700; **Canada** 197 Wurtemburg St, Ottawa, ON K1N 8L9 ☎613/789 4044; **UK** 43 Belgrave Sq, London SW1X 8PA ☎020/7393 0202; **Ireland** 11 Clyde Rd, Ballsbridge, Dublin 4 ☎01/668 5240; **Australia** 60 Mugga Way, Red Hill, Canberra, ACT 2603 ☎02/6295 0227; **New Zealand** 15–17 Murphy St, Level 8, PO Box 12248, Wellington ☎04/472 1292.

Information and maps

Before you leave, it's worth contacting the tourist offices of the countries you're intending to visit, since most produce copious free leaflets, maps and brochures, some of which can be quite useful, both for planning your trip and when you're travelling. This is especially true for parts of central and eastern Europe, where up-to-date maps in particular are often harder to find in the country than in their tourist offices abroad. Also, note that Estonia, Latvia, Lithuania and Russia do not have official tourist offices, so it may help to contact their embassies for more information. For the rest of Europe, go easy, though: much of the information these places pump out can be picked up just as easily on your travels, and it can weigh a tonne.

Once you're travelling in Europe, you'll find on-the-spot information easy enough to pick up. Most countries have a well-equipped and widespread network of tourist offices that answer queries, dole out a range of (sometimes free) maps and brochures, and can often book accommodation, or at least advise you on the best-value places if you're stuck. Tourist offices are, as you might expect, better organized in northern Europe

– Scandinavia, the Netherlands, France – with branches in all but the smallest village, and mounds of information; in Greece, Turkey and eastern Europe you'll find fewer tourist offices and they'll be less helpful on the whole, sometimes offering no more than a couple of dog-eared brochures and a photocopied map. We've given further details, including a broad idea of opening hours, in "Practicalities" for each country.

Tourist information websites and offices abroad

If there is no office listed below for your home country, apply to your embassy.

AUSTRIA ⊛www.austria-tourism.at; **US** 500 5th Ave, Suite 800, New York, NY 10110 ☎212/944 6885; **Canada** 2 Bloor St W, Suite 400, Toronto, ON M4W 3E2 ☎416/967 3381; **UK** 14 Cork St, London W1S 3NS ☎020/7629 0461; **Ireland** Merrion Centre, Nutley Lane, PO Box 2506, Ballsbridge, Dublin 4 ☎01/283 0488; **Australia** 36 Carrington St, 1st Floor, Sydney, NSW 2000 ☎02/9299 3621.

BELGIUM ⊛www.visitbelgium.com; **US** 789 3rd Ave, Suite 1501, New York, NY 10017–7076 ☎212/758 8130; **Canada** PO Box 760, Succursale NDG, Montreal, PQ H4A 3S2 ☎514/457 2888; **UK** (for Brussels and Wallonia) 17 Marsh Wall, London E14 9FJ ☎020/7531 0390, (for Flanders) 31 Pepper St, E14 9RW ☎020/7867 0311.

BRITAIN ⊛www.visitbritain.com; **US** 551 5th Ave, 7th Floor, New York, NY 10176–0799 ☎1-800/GO 2 BRITAIN, or 625 North Michigan Ave, Suite 1001, Chicago IL 60611-1977 ☎312/787 0464, or 10880 Wilshire Bvd, Suite 570, Los Angeles, CA 90024 ☎310/470 2782; **Canada** 5915 Airport Rd, Suite 120, Mississauga, ON L4V 1T1 ☎1-888/VISIT UK; **Ireland** 18–19 College Green, Dublin 2 ☎01/670 8000; **Australia** Level 16, Gateway, 1 Macquaire Pl, Sydney, NSW 2000 ☎02/9377 4400; **New Zealand** Fay Richwhite Bldg, 151 Queen St, Auckland 1 ☎09/303 1446.

BULGARIA US c/o Balkantourist, 181 E 86th St, New York, NY 10028 ☎212/722 1110. Be warned: it is very difficult to get through by phone.

CROATIA ⊛www.croatia.hr; **US** 350 5th Ave, Suite 4003, New York, NY 10118 ☎212/279 8672; **UK** 2 The Lanchesters, 162–164 Fulham Palace Rd, London W6 9ER ☎020/8563 7979.

CZECH REPUBLIC ⊛www.visitczech.cz; **US** 1109 Madison Ave, New York, NY 10028 ☎212/288

0830; **Canada** c/o CSA, 401 Bay St, Suite 1510, Toronto, ON M5H 2Y4 ☎416/363 9928; **UK** 95 Great Portland St, London W1W 7NY ☎020/7291 9925.

DENMARK ⊛www.dt.dk; **US** 655 3rd Ave, New York, NY 10017–5617 ☎212/885 9700; **UK** 55 Sloane St, London SW1X 9SY ☎020/9262 5832; **Australia** c/o Finnesse Communications, Level 4, York St, Sydney, NSW 2000 ☎02/9290 1980.

ESTONIA ⊛www.tourism.ee

FINLAND ⊛www.mek.fi; **US** PO BOX 4649, Grand Central Station, New York, NY 10163–4649; **UK** PO Box 33213, London W6 8JX ☎020/7365 2512; **Ireland** contact by phone only ☎01/407 3362.

FRANCE ⊛www.franceguide.com; **US** 444 Madison Ave, 16th floor, New York, NY 10022 ☎410/286 8310, or 676 N Michigan Ave, Suite 3360, Chicago, IL 60611 ☎312/751 7800, or 9454 Wilshire Bvd, Suite 715, Beverly Hills, Los Angeles, CA 90212-2967 ☎310/271 6665; **Canada** 1981 av McGill College, Suite 490, Montreal, PQ H3A 2W9 ☎514/876 9880; **UK** 178 Piccadilly, London W1V 0AL ☎0906/824 4123; **Ireland** 10 Suffolk St, Dublin 2 ☎01/679 8066; **Australia** 25 Bligh St, Level 22, Sydney, NSW 2000 ☎02/9231 5244.

GERMANY ⊛www.germany-tourism.de; **US** 122 E 42nd St, 52nd Floor, New York, NY 10168–0072 ☎212/661 7200; **Canada** PO Box 65162, Toronto, ON M4K 3Z2 ☎1-877/315 6237; **UK** PO Box 2695, London W1A 3TN ☎020/7317 0908; **Australia** c/o German-Australian Chamber of Industry and Commerce, PO Box A980, South Sydney, NSW 1235 ☎02/9267 8148.

GREECE ⊛www.gnto.gr; **US** Olympic Tower, 645 5th Ave, New York, NY 10022 ☎212/421 5777; **Canada** 91 Pollard St, 2nd floor, 1300 Bay St, Toronto, ON M5R 1G4 ☎416/968 2220 or 1170 pl Frère André, 3rd Floor, Montreal, PQ H3B 3C6, ☎514/871 1535; **UK** 4 Conduit St, London W1R ODJ ☎020/7734 5997; **Australia** 51 Pitt St, Sydney, NSW 2000 ☎02/9241 1663.

HUNGARY ⊛www.hungarytourism.hu; **US** 150 E 58th St, 33rd Floor, New York, NY 10155–3398 ☎212/355 0240; **UK** 46 Eaton Place, London SW1X 8AL ☎020/7823 1055.

IRELAND ⊛www.ireland.travel.ie; **US** 345 Park Ave, 17th Floor, New York, NY 10154 ☎1-800/223 6470; **Canada** 2 Bloor St W, Suite 1501, Toronto, ON M4W 3E2 ☎1-800/223 6470; **UK** Ireland Desk, BTA, 1 Lower Regent St, London SW1Y 4NR ☎0800/039 7000; **Australia** 5th Level, 36 Carrington St, Sydney, NSW 2000 ☎02/9299 6177; **New Zealand** 18 Shortland St, 6th floor, Private Bag 92136, Auckland 1 ☎09/379 8720.

ITALY ✆www.enit.it; **US** 630 5th Ave, Suite 1565, New York, NY 10111 ☎212/245 4822, or 500 N Michigan Ave, Suite 2240, Chicago, IL 60611 ☎312/644 0996, or 12400, Wilshire Bvd, Suite 550, Los Angeles, CA 90025 ☎310/820 1898; **Canada** 175 Bloor St E, Suite 907, South Tower, Toronto, ON M4W 3R8 ☎416/925 4882; **UK** 1 Princes St, London W1R 2AY ☎020/7408 1254; **Australia** 44 Market St, Level 26, Sydney, NSW 2000 ☎02/9262 1666.

LUXEMBOURG ✆www.luxembourg.co.uk; **US** 17 Beekman Pl, New York, NY 10022 ☎212/935 8888; **UK** 122–124 Regent St, London W1B 5SA ☎020/7434 2800.

MOROCCO ✆www.tourism-in-morocco.com; **US** 20 E 46th St, Suite 1201, New York, NY 10017 ☎212/557 2520, or PO Box 2263, Lake Buena Vista, FL 32830 ☎407/827 5337; **Canada** 1800 av McGill College, Suite 2425, Montreal, PQ H3A 2J6 ☎514/842 8111–2; **UK** 205 Regent St, London W1R 7DE ☎020/7437 0073; **Australia** 11 West St, North Sydney, NSW 2060 ☎02/9922 4999.

NETHERLANDS ✆www.holland.com; **US** 355 Lexington Ave, 19th floor, New York, NY 10017 ☎1-888/GO HOLLAND; **Canada** 25 Adelaide St E, Suite 710, Toronto, ON M5C 1Y2 ☎416/363 1577; **UK** PO Box 30783, London WC2B 6DH ☎020/7539 7950.

NORWAY ✆www.visitnorway.com; **US** 655 3rd Ave, Suite 1810, New York, NY 10017 ☎212/885 9700; **UK** 5th floor, Charles House, 5 Lower Regent St, London SW1Y 4LR ☎020/7839 2650.

POLAND ✆www.polandtour.org; **US** 275 Madison Ave, Suite 1711, New York, NY 10016 ☎212/338 9412; **UK** 310–312 Regent St, 1st floor, London W1R 5AJ ☎020/7580 8811.

PORTUGAL ✆www.portugal-insite.pt; **US** 590 5th Ave, New York, 4th floor, NY 10036–4785 ☎212/719 3985; **Canada** 60 Bloor St W, Suite 1005, Toronto, ON M4W 3B8 ☎416/921 7376; **UK** 22–25a Sackville St, 4th Floor, London W1X 1DE ☎0906/364 0610 – premium rates charged for calls; **Ireland** 54 Dawson St, Dublin 2 ☎01/670 9133.

ROMANIA ✆www.romaniatourism.com; **US** 14 E 38th St, 12th floor, New York, NY 10016 ☎212/545 8484; **UK** 22 New Cavendish St, London W1G 8TT ☎020/7224 3692.

RUSSIA ✆www.russia-travel.com; **US** 130 W 42nd St, Suite 412, New York, NY 10036 ☎1-877/221 7120.

SLOVENIA ✆www.slovenia-tourism.si; **US** 345 E 12th St, New York, NY 10003 ☎212/358 9686; **UK** 49 Conduit St, London W1R 9FB ☎020/7287 7133.

SPAIN ✆www.tourspain.es; **US** 666 5th Ave, New York, NY 10103 ☎212/265 8822, or 845 N Michigan Ave, Suite 915E, Chicago IL 60611 ☎312/642 7188, or 8383 Wilshire Bvd, Suite 960, Beverley Hills, CA 90211 ☎323/658 7188; **Canada** 2 Bloor St W, 34th floor, Toronto, ON M4W 3E2 ☎416/961 3131; **UK** 22–23 Manchester Sq, London W1U 3PX ☎020/7486 8077.

SWEDEN ✆www.visit-sweden.com; **US** PO Box 4649, Grand Central Stn, New York, NY 10163–4649 ☎212/885 9764; **UK** 5 Upper Montagu St, London W1H 2AG ☎020/7724 5872. Worldwide toll-free number: ☎+800/3080 3080.

SWITZERLAND ✆www.myswitzerland.com; **US** 608 5th Ave, New York, NY 10020 ☎011-800/1002 0030; **UK** Swiss Centre, 10 Wardour St, London W1D 6QF ☎00-800/1002 0030; Worldwide toll-free number: ☎+800/1002 0030.

TURKEY ✆www.turizm.gov.tr; **US** 821 UN Plaza, New York, NY 10017 ☎212/687 2194–5, or 1717 Massachusetts Ave, Suite 306, Washington, DC 20036 ☎202/612 6800–1; **Canada** 360 Albert St, Suite 801, Ottawa, ON K1R 7X7, ☎613/230 8654; **UK** 170–173 Piccadilly, 1st Floor, London W1V 9DD ☎020/7629 7771; **Australia** Unit 17, Level 3, 428 George St, Sydney, NSW 2000 ☎02/9223 3055.

Maps

Whether you're doing a grand tour or confining yourself to one or two countries you will need a decent **map**. Though you can often buy these on the spot, you may want to get them in advance to plan your trip – if you know what you want, then contact Stanfords in London (perhaps the world's best map shop) or Rand McNally in the US; both sell maps by mail order.

We've recommended the best maps of individual countries throughout the book. In general, though, the best series are Bartholomew/RV, Kümmerley & Frey and Hallwag; and, in North America, those published by Rand McNally. For plans of over fifty European cities, the Falk series of detailed, indexed maps are excellent, and easy to use. Geo-Center's 1:1,250,000 double-sided Europe map is one of the best covering the entire Continent, clear, with a large scale, showing roads, railways and relief. Other good road maps covering the whole of Europe include Lascelles's (1:3,750,000), Hallwag's (1:3,600,000), Freytag and Berndt's (1:3,500,000), and

Philip's (1:3,500,000), all of which show the road networks pretty well, though they omit most of Turkey and Morocco; of the four, only Hallwag's shows railways, and not very clearly. Michelin's (1:3,000,000) is cheaper but less clear. Kümmerley and Frey's (1:5,000,000) covers Turkey and Morocco but omits road numbers. Among other 1:5,000,000 maps, Collins's and Penguin's both show the main road and rail routes pretty clearly. For extensive motoring, it is better to get a large-page road atlas such as Michelin's Tourist and Motoring Atlas. If you intend to travel mainly by rail, on the other hand, it might be worth getting the Thomas Cook Rail Map of Europe.

Map outlets

In the US and Canada

Adventurous Traveler Bookstore 102 Lake St, Burlington, VT 05401 ☎1-800/282-3963, ⊛www.adventuroustraveler.com.

Book Passage 51 Tamal Vista Blvd, Corte Madera, CA 94925 ☎1-800/999-7909, ⊛www .bookpassage.com.

Distant Lands 56 S Raymond Ave, Pasadena, CA 91105 ☎1-800/310-3220, ⊛www.distantlands.com.

Elliot Bay Book Company 101 S Main St, Seattle, WA 98104 ☎1-800/962-5311, ⊛www.elliotbaybook.com.

Forsyth Travel Library 226 Westchester Ave, White Plains, NY 10604 ☎1-800/367-7984, ⊛www.forsyth.com.

Globe Corner Bookstore 28 Church St, Cambridge, MA 02138 ☎1-800/358-6013, ⊛www.globercorner.com.

GORP Books & Maps ☎1-877/440-4677, ⊛www.gorp.com/gorp/books/main.htm.

Map Link 30 S La Patera Lane, Unit 5, Santa Barbara, CA 93117 ☎805/692-6777, ⊛www.maplink.com.

Rand McNally ☎1-800/333-0136, ⊛www .randmcnally.com. Around thirty stores across the US; dial ext 2111 or check the website for the nearest location.

Travel Books and Language Center 4437 Wisconsin Ave NW, Washington, DC 20016 ☎1-800/ 220-2665, ⊛www.bookweb.org/bookstore/travelbks.

The Travel Bug Bookstore 2667 W Broadway,

Vancouver, BC V6K 2G2 ☎604/737-1122, ⊛www.swifty.com/tbug.

World of Maps 1235 Wellington St, Ottawa, ON K1Y 3A3 ☎1-800/214-8524, ⊛www.worldofmaps .com.

In the UK and Ireland

Blackwell's Map and Travel Shop 50 Broad St, Oxford OX1 3BQ ☎01865/793550, ⊛http://maps .blackwell.co.uk/index.html.

Easons Bookshop 40 O'Connell St, Dublin 1 ☎01/873 3811, ⊛www.eason.ie.

Heffers Map and Travel 20 Trinity St, Cambridge CB2 1TJ ☎01223/568 568, ⊛www.heffers.co.uk.

Hodges Figgis Bookshop 56–58 Dawson St, Dublin 2 ☎01/677 4754, ⊛www.hodgesfiggis.com.

John Smith & Son 100 Cathedral St, Glasgow G4 0RD ☎0141/552 3377, ⊛www.johnsmith.co.uk.

James Thin Booksellers 53–59 South Bridge Edinburgh EH1 1YS ☎0131/622 8222, ⊛www .jthin.co.uk.

The Map Shop 30a Belvoir St, Leicester LE1 6QH ☎0116/247 1400, ⊛www.mapshopleicester.co.uk.

National Map Centre 22–24 Caxton St, London SW1H 0QU ☎020/7222 2466, ⊛www.mapsnmc .co.uk.

Newcastle Map Centre 55 Grey St, Newcastle-upon-Tyne, NE1 6EF ☎0191/261 5622.

Stanfords 12–14 Long Acre, WC2E 9LP ☎020/7836 1321, ⊛www.stanfords.co.uk, ©sales@stanfords.co.uk. Maps available by mail, phone order, or email. Other branches within British Airways offices at 156 Regent St, London W1R 5TA ☎020/7434 4744 and 29 Corn St, Bristol BS1 1HT ☎0117/929 9966.

The Travel Bookshop 13–15 Blenheim Crescent, W11 2EE ☎020/7229 5260, ⊛www.thetravelbookshop.co.uk.

In Australia and New Zealand

The Map Shop 6–10 Peel St, Adelaide, SA 5000 ☎08/8231 2033, ⊛www.mapshop.net.au.

Mapland 372 Little Bourke St, Melbourne, Victoria 3000, ☎03/9670 4383, ⊛www.mapland.com.au.

MapWorld 173 Gloucester St, Christchurch, New Zealand ☎0800/627 967 or 03/374 5399, ⊛www.mapworld.co.nz.

Perth Map Centre 1/884 Hay St, Perth, WA 6000, ☎08/9322 5733, ⊛www.perthmap.com.au.

Specialty Maps 46 Albert St, Auckland 1001 ☎09/307 2217, ⊛www.ubdonline.co.nz/maps.

Insurance

Wherever you're travelling from, it's a very good idea to have some kind of **travel insurance**. Before paying for a new policy, however, it's worth checking whether you are already covered: some all-risks home insurance policies may cover your possessions when overseas, and many private medical schemes include cover when abroad. In Canada, provincial health plans usually provide partial cover for medical mishaps overseas, while holders of official student/teacher/youth cards in Canada and the US are entitled to meagre accident coverage and hospital in-patient benefits. Students will often find that their student health coverage extends during the vacations and for one term beyond the date of last enrolment.

After exhausting the possibilities above, you might want to contact a specialist travel insurance company, or consider the travel insurance deal we offer (see box below). A typical **travel insurance policy** usually provides cover for the loss of baggage, tickets and – up to a certain limit – cash or cheques, as well as cancellation or curtailment of your journey. Most of them exclude so-called **dangerous sports** unless an extra premium is paid: in Europe this can mean anything from scuba-diving to mountaineering, skiing and even bungee-jumping. Many policies can be chopped and changed to exclude coverage you don't need – for example, sickness and accident benefits can often be excluded or included at will. If you do take **medical coverage**, ascertain whether benefits will be paid as treatment proceeds or only after you return home, and whether there is a 24-hour medical emergency number. When securing baggage cover, make sure that the per-article limit – typically under £500 – will cover your most valuable possession. If you need to make a claim, you should keep receipts for medicines and medical treatment, and in the event you have anything stolen, you must obtain an official statement from the police.

Despite EU health care privileges, **British and Irish** residents would do well to take out an insurance policy before travelling to

Rough Guides travel insurance

Rough Guides offers its own travel insurance, customized for our readers by a leading UK broker and backed by a Lloyds underwriter. It's available for anyone, of any nationality and any age, travelling anywhere in the world.

There are two main Rough Guide insurance plans: **Essential**, for basic, no-frills cover; and **Premier**, with more generous and extensive benefits. Alternatively, you can take out **annual multi-trip insurance**, which covers you for any number of trips throughout the year (with a maximum of sixty days for any one trip). A European policy covers all the places in this book (including Morocco, Turkey, Russia west of the Urals, and, if bought elsewhere, the UK). Unlike many policies, the Rough Guides schemes are calculated by the day, so if you're travelling for 27 days rather than a month, that's all you pay for. If you intend to be away for the whole year, the Adventurer policy will cover you for 365 days. Each plan can be supplemented with a "Hazardous Activities Premium" if you plan to indulge in sports considered dangerous, such as skiing, scuba-diving or trekking.

For a policy quote, call the Rough Guide Insurance Line on US freefone ☏1-866/220 5588, UK freefone ☏0800/015 0906 or, if you're calling from elsewhere, ☏+44 1243/621046. Alternatively, get a quote or buy online at ⒲www.roughguides.com/insurance.

cover against theft, loss and illness or injury. Travel agents and tour operators are likely to require some sort of insurance when you book a package holiday, though according to UK law they can't make you buy their own (other than a £1 premium for "schedule airline failure"). If you have a good all-risks home insurance policy it may cover your possessions against loss or theft even when overseas. Many private medical schemes such as BUPA and PPP also offer coverage plans for abroad, including baggage loss, cancellation or curtailment and cash replacement as well as sickness or accident.

Health

There aren't many particular health problems you'll encounter travelling in Europe. You don't need to have any inoculations for any of the countries covered in this book, although for Morocco and Turkey typhoid jabs are advised, and for some parts of Turkey, even malaria pills are a good idea for much of the year. When travelling, remember to be up-to-date with your polio and tetanus boosters.

EU citizens resident in the UK or Ireland are covered by reciprocal health agreements for free or reduced-cost emergency treatment in many of the countries in this book (main exceptions are the Baltic states, Switzerland, Slovenia, Morocco and Turkey). To claim this, you will often need only your passport, but you may also be asked for your NHS card or proof of residence. In EU countries and Norway, far from it being simpler, you'll also need **form E111**, available from post offices, DSS offices and travel agents, which you must get before you leave. Without an E111 you won't be turned away from hospitals but you will almost certainly have to pay for any treatment or medicines. Also, in practice, some countries' doctors and hospitals charge anyway and it's up to you to claim reimbursement when you return home. Make sure you are insured for potential medical expenses, and keep copies of receipts and prescriptions.

Tap water in most countries is drinkable, though you may prefer bottled mineral water, either for the taste (mains supply in some places can be very hard or heavily chlorinated), or to be on the safe side, though you only need to avoid tap water altogether in southern Morocco and parts of Turkey. Diarrhoea and sickness from tap water or food are reasonably likely in the south, if only in a mild form. The best thing to do is carry anti-diarrhoea tablets with you at all times. One of the biggest problems you may face if travelling in southern Europe is the sun: don't spend too much time in direct sunlight if you're not used to it, and certainly not without any kind of sun block cream; just half an hour on your first day's sunbathing is probably the limit – more than this can leave you beetroot-red and nauseated. **Mosquitoes**, too, are a problem Europewide, especially in the south and places where there's a lot of water around – the Netherlands, for example, harbours particularly virulent species. It's hard to know what to do about them: most people develop an immunity to bites after a few days' exposure; until then an antihistamine cream such as Phenergan can ease the itching. As for repellents, citronella oil is excellent, though not long-lasting. Finally, **AIDS** is as much of a problem in Europe as it is in the rest of the world, and it hardly needs saying that unprotected casual sex is highly inadvisable.

For minor health problems it's easiest to go to the local **pharmacy**. You'll find these pretty much everywhere and we've detailed out-of-hours ones in the text. In more serious cases contact your nearest consulate, who will have a list of English-speaking doctors, as will the local tourist office, and in the larger cities we've listed the most convenient casualty departments (emergency rooms).

Costs, money and banks

It's hard to generalize about what you're likely to spend travelling around Europe. Some countries – Norway, Switzerland and the UK – are among the priciest places to be in the world, while in others you can live like a lord on next to nothing – Turkey, for example. The collapse of the eastern European economy means that many of the countries there appear very inexpensive if you're coming from the west. However, the absorption of a number of the previously inexpensive countries of southern Europe into the EU means their costs are becoming much more in tune with the European mainstream.

Accommodation will be the largest single cost, and can really determine where you decide to travel. For example, it's hard to find a double hotel room anywhere in Scandinavia – perhaps the most expensive part of the Continent – for much under £40/$65 a night, whereas in most parts of southern Europe, and even in France, you might be paying under half that on average. Everywhere, though, even in Scandinavia, there is some form of bottom-line accommodation available, and there's always a hostel on hand. In general, reckon on a minimum budget of around £10/$15 a night per person in most parts of Europe.

Food and drink costs also vary wildly, although again in most parts of Europe you can assume that a restaurant meal will cost on average £5–10/$8–15 a head, with prices at the top end of the scale in Scandinavia, at the bottom end in eastern and southern Europe. **Transport** costs are something you can pin down more exactly if you have a rail pass. Nowhere, though, are transport costs a major burden, except perhaps in Britain where public transport is less heavily subsidized than elsewhere. Local city transport, too, is usually good, clean and efficient, and is normally fairly cheap, even in the pricier countries of northern Europe. It's hard to pinpoint an average daily budget for touring the Continent, but a bottom-line survival figure – camping, self-catering, hitching, etc – might be around £15/$25 a day per person; building in an investment for a rail pass, staying in hostels and eating out occa-

The euro

On 1 January 1999, eleven EU countries – Austria, Belgium, Finland, France, Germany, Ireland, Italy, Luxembourg, the Netherlands, Portugal and Spain, subsequently joined by Greece – fixed their exchange rates to a new currency, **the euro (€)**, which is now the single currency for all of them. The remaining three EU countries (the UK, Denmark and Sweden) are expected to join the euro zone eventually, though their politicians may have a hard time convincing voters that it is a good idea. The British government has promised a referendum before joining; Denmark had one and voted against; but attitudes in those countries are expected to change as the euro becomes established.

Euro coins come in **denominations** of 1, 2, 5, 10, 20 and 50 cents and 1 and 2 euros. One side of the coin states the denomination, and is the same everywhere, while the other side has a different design in each issuing country. Notes come in denominations of 5, 10, 20, 50, 100, 200 and 500 euros, and each has the same design in all countries, though the first letter of the serial number tells you where the note was issued (L for Finland, M for Portugal, N for Austria, P for the Netherlands, R for Luxembourg, S for Italy, T for Ireland, U for France, V for Spain, X for Germany, Y for Greece and Z for Belgium, with J, K and W reserved for the UK, Sweden and Denmark). All the notes and coins are legal tender throughout the euro zone, regardless of their country of issue.

Prices and exchange rates

In the *Guide* we've quoted **prices** in local currency wherever possible, except in those countries where the weakness of the currency and the inflation rate combine to make this a meaningless exercise. In these cases – parts of eastern Europe and Turkey – we've used either US dollars, pounds sterling or Deutschmarks, depending on which hard currency is most commonly used within that country.

The current **exchange rates** are given in each country's own practicalities section, but bear in mind that in the case of certain less stable currencies, the approximate rates quoted may fluctuate considerably. The latest market rates (bank rates will not be as good) can be found on Oanda's universal currency converter at ⓦ www.oanda.com/converter/classic.

For **accommodation** prices, we've used a standard coding system throughout the *Guide*: see p.46 for details.

---

sionally would bring this up to perhaps £20/$30 a day; while staying in private rooms or hotels and eating out once a day would mean a personal daily budget of at least £25/$40. Obviously in the more expensive countries of northern Europe you might be spending more than this, but on a wide tour this would be balanced out by spending less in southern and eastern Europe, where everything is much cheaper.

When you are travelling also makes a difference. Accommodation rates tend to go up across the board in July and August, when everyone is on vacation – although paradoxically there are good deals in Scandinavia during these months. Also bear in mind that in capital cities and major resorts in the peak season everything will be a grade more expensive than anywhere else, especially if you're there when something special is going on, for example in Munich during the Beer Festival, Pamplona for the running of the bulls or Siena during the Palio. These are, in any case, times when you will be lucky to find a room at all without having booked.

As for ways of **cutting costs**, there are plenty. It makes sense, obviously, to spend less on transport by investing in some kind of rail pass. Always try to plan in advance. Although it's good to be flexible, buying one-off rail tickets can add a huge amount to your travel budget. The most obvious way to save on accommodation is to use hostels; you can also save by planning to make some of your longer trips at night, when the cost of a couchette may undercut the cost of a night's accommodation. It's best not to be too spartan when it comes to food costs,

but doing a certain amount of self-catering, especially at lunchtime when it's just as easy (and probably nicer) to have a picnic lunch rather than eat in a restaurant or café, will save money.

Youth and student discounts

If you're a student, an **ISIC card** is well worth investing in. It can get you reduced (usually fifty percent, sometimes free) entry to museums and other sights – costs which can eat their way into your budget alarmingly if you're doing a lot of sightseeing – as well as qualifying you for other discounts in certain cities; it can also save you money on some transport costs, notably ferries, and especially if you are over 26. For Americans there's also a health benefit, providing up to $3000 in emergency medical coverage and $100 a day for sixty days in hospital, plus a 24-hour hotline to call in the event of a medical, legal or financial emergency. The card costs $22 in the US, $16 in Canada, £6 in the UK, €12.70 in Ireland, $16.50 in Australia and $21 in New Zealand. If you are not a student but under 26, get an **International Youth Travel Card**, which costs US$22/£7 and can in some countries give much the same sort of reductions. Teachers qualify for the International **Teacher Identity Card**, offering similar discounts. All these cards are available from youth travel specialists such as Council Travel, STA and Travel CUTS. Basically, it's worth flashing one or the other at every opportunity to see what you can get.

Cash and travellers' cheques

A safe way to carry your money is in **travellers' cheques**, in either dollars, euros or pounds sterling. These are available for a small commission from any bank. Strictly speaking, you should order them in advance but this isn't always necessary in larger branches, or if you get them direct from offices of the issuing companies. The usual fee for travellers' cheque sales is one or two percent, though this may be waived if you buy the cheques through a bank where you have an account. It pays to get a selection of denominations. Make sure to keep the purchase agreement and a record of cheque serial numbers safe and separate from the cheques themselves. In the event that cheques are lost or stolen, the issuing company will expect you to report the loss forthwith to their local office; most companies claim to replace lost or stolen cheques within 24 hours. The most commonly accepted travellers' cheques are American Express, Visa and Thomas Cook/Mastercard. Most cheques issued by banks will be one of these three brands. You'll usually pay commission again when you cash each cheque; this varies from country to country but is normally another one percent or so, or a flat rate, in which case it makes sense to cash as many as possible at once, though in some countries it's a flat rate per cheque. Keep a record of the cheques as you cash them, as you can get the value of all uncashed cheques refunded immediately if you lose them.

In many countries **banks** are the only places where you can legally change money, and they often offer the best exchange rates and lowest commission. Local banking hours are given in the text. Outside these times there are normally bureaux de change, often at train stations and airports, though rates and/or commissions may well be less favourable (always check the rate of commission first – it is sometimes as high as ten percent), and even automatic money-changing machines. Try to avoid changing money or cheques in hotels, where the exchange rates are generally very poor.

Credit and debit cards

You'll find that most hotels, shops and restaurants in Europe accept the major **credit cards**, although they're less useful in eastern Europe, where you shouldn't depend on being able to use one. Credit cards can also come in handy as a backup source of funds, and can even save on exchange-rate commissions; just be sure someone back home is taking care of the bills if you're away for more than a month. Your card will also enable you to get **cash advances** from certain ATMs, mostly in western Europe. Note, however, that there will be a transaction fee (a set figure or a percentage of the total withdrawn, whichever is the higher; usually around 1.5 percent), and there will be a maximum amount you can draw at one time – check your limit with your card issuer. There may also be a minimum amount you can withdraw, which varies from one country to the next, but it's usually at least the equivalent of £50–100/ $80–150 in local currency.

A compromise between travellers' cheques and plastic is Visa TravelMoney, a disposable pre-paid debit card with a PIN that works in all ATMs which take Visa cards. You load up your account with funds before leaving home, and when they run out, you simply throw the card away. You can buy up to nine cards to access the same funds – useful for couples or families travelling together – and it's a good idea to buy at least one extra as a back-up in case of loss or theft. There is also a 24-hour toll-free customer assistance number (available at ℡+1-410/581-9994 (US) and ⊛http://usa .visa.com/personal/secure_with_visa/lost_your _card.html#numbs). The card is available in most countries from branches of Thomas Cook and Citicorp. For more information, check the Visa TravelMoney website at ⊛http://usa.visa.com/personal/cards/visa _travel_money.html.

Wiring money

Having **money wired** from home is never cheap, and should be considered as a last resort. Funds can be sent to most countries via MoneyGram and Western Union. Both companies' fees depend on the amount being transferred, but as an example, wiring £700/$1000 will cost around £40/$60. The funds should be available for collection (usually in local currency) from the company's local agent within minutes of being sent; you can do this in person at the company's nearest office (in the UK all post offices are agents for MoneyGram), or over the phone using your credit card with Western Union. It's also possible, and slightly cheaper, to have money wired from a bank in your home country to one in Europe, but this is much slower (two working days is the norm, but a couple of weeks is not unheard of) and less reliable; if you go down this route, the person wiring the funds will need to know the routing number of the destination bank. A compromise option is Thomas Cook's Telegraphic Transfer service, which costs £15 plus one percent of the amount to be sent (minimum charge £25), and takes one to two days to arrive.

If you have no money in your account, and there is no one you can persuade to send you any, then the options are inevitably limited. You can either find some casual, cash-in-hand work (see p.54), sell blood (not possible in all European countries), or, as a last resort, throw yourself on the mercy of your nearest consulate. They won't be very sympathetic or even helpful, but they may cash a cheque drawn on a home bank and supported by a cheque card. They might, if there's nothing else for it, repatriate you, though bear in mind your passport will be confiscated as soon as you set foot in your home country and you'll have to pay back all costs incurred (at top-whack rates). They never lend money.

Money-wiring companies

Moneygram US and Canada ☎1-800/926 9400, UK ☎0800/6663 9472, Republic of Ireland ☎1850/205800, Australia ☎1800/230 100, New Zealand ☎09/379 8243 or 0800/262 263, international toll-free number ☎+800/8971 8971, ⊛www.moneygram.com

Thomas Cook US ☎1-800/287 7362, Canada ☎1-888/823-4732, Britain ☎01733/318922, Northern Ireland ☎028/9055 0030, Republic of Ireland ☎01/677 1307, ⊛www.us.thomascook.com

Western Union US and Canada ☎1-800/325 6000, UK ☎0800/833833, Republic of Ireland ☎1800/395395, Australia ☎1800/649565, New Zealand ☎09/270 0050, ⊛www.westernunion.com

Communications

Communications throughout northwestern Europe are generally excellent: public phones are readily available and normally work, and the postal system is reasonably efficient and easy to use. In southern Europe, services are sometimes less impressive, notably in Italy and Spain where the post is still not overly reliable, though it has improved a lot in recent years; and in eastern Europe the infrastructure is still very poor and services consequently unpredictable.

Mail

For buying stamps and, sometimes, making telephone calls, we've listed the **central post offices** in major cities and given an idea of opening hours. Bear in mind, though, that throughout much of Europe you can avoid the queues in post offices by buying stamps from newsagents and the like. If you know in advance where you're going to be and when, it is possible to receive mail through the **poste restante** (general delivery) system, whereby letters addressed "poste restante" and sent to the main post office in any town or city will be kept – for at least two weeks and usually for a month – under your name for collection at the relevant counter. When collecting mail, make sure you take your passport for identification, and bear in mind that there's a possibility of letters being misfiled by someone unfamiliar with your language; if there is nothing under your surname it may have been filed under your first name.

Telephones

It is often possible, especially in western Europe, to make **international calls** from a public call box; this can often be more trouble than it's worth from a coin phone due to the constant need to feed in change, although most countries now have phone cards, making the whole process much easier. Otherwise, you can go to a **post office**, or a **special telephone bureau**, where you can make a call from a private booth and pay afterwards. Most countries have these in one form or another, and the local tourist office will point you in the right direction. Wherever possible, avoid using the telephone in your **hotel room** – it costs the earth.

To **dial any country** in this book from Britain, Ireland or New Zealand, dial ☏00, then the country code, then the city/area code, if there is one, less the initial zero (except in Italy, Russia and the Baltics, where it must be dialled; from the US and most of Canada, the international access code is ☏011, from Australia it's ☏0011 – otherwise the procedure is the same. To call home from most European countries, dial ☏00,

then the country code, then the city code (less the initial zero if there is one), then the subscriber number. The exception is Russia, where you dial ☏8, wait for a continuous dialling tone and then dial ☏10 followed by the country code, etc; in Estonia, it's ☏8-00 – you need only wait for a new tone after the 8 on old phones. For **collect calls**, Home Country Direct services are available in most of the places covered in this book. In Britain and some other countries, international calling cards available from newsagents enable you to call North America, Australia and New Zealand very cheaply. Most North American, British, Irish and Australasian phone companies either allow you to call home from abroad on a **credit card**, or billed to your home number (call your company's customer service line before you leave to find out their toll-free access codes from the countries you will be visiting), or else will issue an **international calling card** which can be used worldwide, and for which you will be billed on your return. If you want a calling card and do not already have one, leave yourself a few weeks to arrange it before leaving.

Mobile phones from North America are unlikely to work in Europe – for details of which phones will work outside the US and Canada, contact your provider. Mobiles from the British Isles, Australia and New Zealand can be used in most parts of Europe, and a lot of countries – certainly in western Europe – have nearly universal coverage, but for all bar the very top-of-the-range packages, you'll have to inform your provider before

International dialling codes

Andorra ☏376	Gibraltar ☏350	Norway ☏47
Australia ☏61	Greece ☏30	Poland ☏48
Austria ☏43	Hungary ☏36	Portugal ☏351
Belgium ☏32	Ireland ☏353	Romania ☏40
Bulgaria ☏359	Italy ☏39	Russia ☏7
Canada ☏1	Latvia ☏371	Slovakia ☏421
Croatia ☏385	Liechtenstein ☏423	Slovenia ☏386
Czech Republic ☏420	Lithuania ☏370	Spain ☏34
Denmark ☏45	Luxembourg ☏352	Sweden ☏46
Estonia ☏372	Monaco ☏377	Switzerland ☏41
Finland ☏358	Morocco ☏212	Turkey ☏90
France ☏33	Netherlands ☏31	UK ☏44
Germany ☏49	New Zealand ☏64	US ☏1

leaving home to get international access switched on. Also note that it will not always be possible to charge up or replace your **pre-paid cards**, so again check beforehand and if necessary remember to bring enough credit with you. A standard two-pin socket is used on the Continent so you may need an **adaptor** for charging up.

Internet and email

Europe still lags some way behind the US in terms of **internet** access, and surfing the web is usually more expensive due to the high rates charged for local phone calls. Nonetheless, things are improving all the time: more and more internet cafés are opening up, and it is becoming increasingly easy to access the web and send and receive **email**. That being the case, a good way to keep in touch is to open up an account with one of the free **internet email sites** that can be accessed from anywhere, for example YahooMail (⊛www.yahoo.com) and Hotmail (⊛www.hotmail.com), so that you can receive emails while on the road.

The media

British **newspapers and magazines** are fairly widely available in Europe, sometimes on the day of publication (in Belgium and the Netherlands, for example), more often the day after. They do, however, cost around three times as much as they do at home. Exceptions are the *Guardian* and *Financial Times*, which print special European editions that are cheaper and available on the day of issue. You can also find the terminally dull and self-righteous *International Herald Tribune* just about everywhere, as well as the uninspiring *USA Today*; if you're lucky you may come across the odd *New York Times* or *Washington Post*, but don't count on it outside the major centres. What you will find are *Time*, *Newsweek* and *The Economist* pretty much everywhere, as well as a host of British and American glossies.

It's cheaper to get your news by tuning a **radio** into the BBC World Service (still considered to have the most reliable news of all the media), Radio Canada, the Voice of America, or one of the many local news broadcasts in English. In northern France, the Netherlands and Belgium you can pick up BBC domestic services as well. BBC World Service frequencies include: 6195kHz, 9410kHz, 12,095kHz and 15,485kHz on shortwave, or in western Europe 648kHz MW, and in southeastern Europe 1323kHz MW (programme details at ⊛www.bbc.co.uk /worldservice). Radio Canada can be picked up at 8–10pm GMT on 5850kHz (details at ⊛www.rcinet.ca). The Voice of America can be found during the day on 1197kHz, at night on 6105kHz or 15,205kHz, among other frequencies – further details and full schedules on their website on ⊛www.voa.gov.

With the advent of cable and satellite channels, **television** has become more of a pan-European medium than radio. Sky TV, Superchannel, CNN, Eurosport and the European version of MTV are all popular across the Continent and normally available in the pricier hotels. In many parts of Europe there is, in any case, a reasonably wide choice (by British, if not by American, standards) of terrestrial channels, since a border is never far away and you can often pick up at least one other country's TV stations. This is at its most extreme in Belgium and the southern Netherlands, where as well as all the satellite and cable channels you can pick up Dutch and Belgian TV, French TV, BBC1 and BBC2, all the German stations, and even the state Italian channel.

Accommodation

Although it is obviously one of the more crucial costs to consider when planning your trip, accommodation needn't be a stumbling block to a budget-conscious tour of Europe. Indeed, even in Europe's pricier reaches the hostel system means there is always an affordable place to stay, and if you're prepared to camp you can get by on very little while staying at some excellently equipped sites. The one thing you should bear in mind is that in the more popular cities and resorts – Florence, Venice, Amsterdam, Prague, Barcelona, the Algarve – things can get chock-a-block during the peak summer months, and even if you've got plenty of money to throw around you should book in advance.

Hostels

The cheapest way for young people to travel around Europe is by using the extensive network of hostels that covers the Continent. Some of these are **private** places, but by far the majority are **official hostels**, members of Hostelling International (**HI**), which incorporates the national youth hostel associations of each country in the world. Youth hostelling isn't the hearty, up-at-the-crack-of-dawn and early-to-bed business it once was; indeed, hostels have been keen to shed this image of late and now appeal to a wider public, and in many countries they simply represent the best-value overnight accommodation available. Most are clean, well-run places, always offering dormitory accommodation, some – especially in Scandinavia and other parts of northern Europe – offering a range of private single and double rooms, or rooms with four to six beds. Many hostels also either have self-catering facilities or provide low-cost meals, and the larger ones have a range of other facilities – a swimming pool, games room, common room, etc. There is no age limit (except in Bavaria), but where there is limited space, priority is given to those under 26.

Strictly speaking, to use an HI hostel you have to be a member, although if there is room you can stay at most hostels by simply paying extra – and you can often join the HI on the spot. If you do intend to do a lot of hostelling, however, it is certainly worth joining, which you can do by becoming a member of your home country's hostelling association. Annual **membership** costs are low everywhere. We've detailed the hostelling situation in each country in the text, as well as giving the name and address of the relevant national hostelling organization if you want further information. The *HI Guide to Europe*, available from bookstores and national hostelling associations, is a good investment at £8/$13.95, detailing every official hostel in Europe (but not Morocco, which is covered by the *HI Guide to Africa, the Americas, Asia and the Pacific*).

Accommodation price codes

Throughout this guide, accommodation is coded on a scale of ❶ to ❾, the code indicating the lowest price per person per night you could expect to pay in each establishment in high season. With hostels this is the nightly rate per person; with hotels, the price is arrived at by dividing the cost of the cheapest double room by two. The prices indicated by the codes are as follows:

❶ under £5/$7 (€8)
❷ £5–10/$7–14 (€8–16)
❸ £10–15/$14–21 (€16–24)
❹ £15–20/$21–28 (€24–33)
❺ £20–25/$28–35 (€33–41)
❻ £25–30/$35–43 (€41–49)
❼ £30–35/$43–50 (€49–57)
❽ £35–40/$50–57 (€57–65)
❾ £40/$57 (€65) and over

Youth hostel associations

Australia Australia Youth Hostels Association, 422 Kent St, Sydney ☎02/9261 1111, ⊛www.yha.com.au. Annual membership A$52, renewal A$32; life membership A$320.

Canada Hostelling International/Canadian Hostelling Association, Room 400, 205 Catherine St, Ottawa, ON K2P 1C3 ☎1-800/663 5777 or 613/237 7884, ⊛www.hostellingintl.ca. Sells membership valid from 16 to 28 months, depending on when you buy it; 28 months costs $35, life membership $175 (both plus tax).

England and Wales Youth Hostel Association (YHA), Trevelyan House, 8 St Stephen's Hill, St Albans, Herts AL1 2DY ☎0870/870 8808, ⊛www.yha.org.uk. Annual membership £13, life membership £190.

Ireland An Óige, 61 Mountjoy St, Dublin 7 ☎01/8430 4555, ⊛www.irelandyha.org. Annual membership €15, life membership €75.

New Zealand New Zealand Youth Hostels Association, 173 Gloucester St, Christchurch ☎03/379 9970, ⊛www.yha.co.nz. Annual membership NZ$40, renewal NZ$30; life membership NZ$300.

Northern Ireland Hostelling International Northern Ireland, 22–32 Donegall Rd, Belfast BT12 5JN ☎028/9032 4733, ⊛www.hini.org.uk. Annual membership £10, life membership £75.

Scottish Youth Hostel Association 7 Glebe Crescent, Stirling, FK8 2JA ☎0870/155 3255, ⊛www.syha.org.uk. Annual membership £6.

US Hostelling International-American Youth Hostels (HI-AYH), 733 15th St NW, Suite 840, PO Box 37613, Washington, DC 20005 ☎202/783-6161, ⊛www.hiayh.org. Annual membership $25, life membership $250.

Hotels and pensions

If you've got a bit more money to spend, you may want to upgrade from hostel accommodation to something a little more comfortable and private. With **hotels** you can really spend as much or as little as you like. Most hotels in Europe are graded on some kind of star system. One- and two-star category hotels are plain and simple on the whole, usually family-run, with a number of rooms without private facilities; sometimes breakfast won't be included. In three-star hotels all the rooms will have private facilities, prices will normally include breakfast and there may well be a phone or TV in the room; while four- and five-star places will certainly have

all these, perhaps on a plusher, roomier basis, perhaps also including access to other facilities – sauna, swimming pool, etc. In the really top-level places breakfast, oddly enough, isn't always included. When it is, in the Netherlands, Britain or Germany, it's fairly sumptuous; in France it wouldn't amount to much anyway and it's no hardship to grab a croissant and coffee in the nearest café.

Obviously **prices** vary greatly, but you're rarely going to be paying less than £10/$15 for a double room even in southern Europe, while in the Netherlands the average price is around £25/$40, and in Scandinavia somewhat higher than that. In some countries **pensions** or **B&Bs** (variously known as guesthouses, *pensão*, *gasthausen* or numerous other names) – smaller, simpler affairs, usually with just a few rooms, that are sometimes part of a larger family house – are a cheaper alternative. In some countries these advertise with a sign in the window; in others they can be booked through the tourist office, which may demand a small fee. There are various other kinds of accommodation – apartments, farmhouses, cottages, *paradores* (in Spain), *gîtes* (in France), etc – but most are geared to longer-term stays and we have only detailed them where relevant.

For information on the accommodation pricing codes we've used throughout the text, see the box opposite.

Camping

The cheapest form of accommodation is, of course, the **campsite**, either pitching your own tent or parking your caravan or camper van. Most sites make a charge per person, plus a charge per plot and another per vehicle. Obviously you'll pay less if you're travelling on foot – maybe just a couple of pounds per night between two people – but parking a car or camper van doesn't add a lot to the cost. Bear in mind also, especially in countries like France where camping is very popular, that facilities can be excellent – though the better the facilities, the pricier the site. If you're on foot you should add in the cost and inconvenience of getting to the site, since most are on the outskirts of towns, sometimes further. Some sites have **cabins**, which you can stay in for a little extra, although these are usually fairly basic affairs, only really worth considering in regions like Scandinavia where budget options are thin on the ground. In Britain, the AA issue a *Caravan and Camping Europe* guide (£9.99), which provides a **list of campsites** in eleven west European countries. Alternatively, **tourist offices** can recommend well-equipped and conveniently located sites.

If you're planning to do a lot of camping, an **international camping carnet** is a good investment. The carnet gives discounts at member sites, serves as useful identification, and is obligatory on some sites in Portugal and some Scandinavian countries. Many campsites will take it instead of making you surrender your passport during your stay, and it covers you for third-party insurance when camping. However, the carnet is not recognized in Sweden, where you may have to join their own carnet scheme. In the **US and Canada**, the carnet is available from Family Campers and RVers (FCRV), 4804 Transit Rd, Building 2, Depew, NY 14043 (☎1-800/245-9755, ⊛www.fcrv.org. FCRV annual membership costs $25, and the carnet an additional $10. In the **UK and Ireland**, the carnet costs £4.50, and is available to members of the Camping and Caravanning Club, Greenfields House, Westwood Way, Coventry, CV4 8JH (☎024/7669 4995, ⊛www.campingandcaravanningclub.co.uk), and Carefree Travel Service (☎024/7642 2024), the foreign touring arm of the same company, which provides the carnet free if you take out insurance with them.

As for **camping rough**, it's a fine idea if you can get away with it – though perhaps an entire trip of rough camping is in reality too gruelling to be truly enjoyable. In some countries it's easy – indeed in parts of Scandinavia it is a legal right, and in Greece and other southern European countries you can usually find a bit of beach to pitch down on – but in others it's almost a non-starter and can get you into trouble with the law.

Sexual harassment, crime and personal safety

Travelling around Europe should be relatively trouble-free, but, as in any part of the world, there is always the chance of petty theft. However, conditions do vary greatly from, say, Scandinavia, where you're unlikely to encounter much trouble of any kind, to the crime-ridden inner-city areas of metropolises such as London and Paris, and poorer countries such as Morocco, Turkey and southern Italy, where tourists are an obvious target.

In order to minimize the risks, you should take some basic **precautions**. First and perhaps most important, you should try not to look too much like a tourist: appearing lost, even if you are, is to be avoided if you can; neither is it a good idea, especially in southern Europe, to walk around draped with cameras or expensive jewellery – the professional bag-snatchers who tour train stations can have your watch or camera off in seconds. If you're waiting for a train, keep your eyes (and hands if necessary) on your bags at all times; if you want to sleep, put every- thing valuable under your head as a pillow. You should be cautious when choosing a train compartment and avoid any situation that makes you feel uncomfortable. If staying in a hostel, take your valuables out with you unless there's a very secure store for them on the premises; some people even make photocopies of their more crucial documentation and leave them at home; a copy of your address book, certainly, can be a good idea.

If the worst happens and you do have something stolen, inform the **police** immediately (we've included details of the main city police stations in the text); get a statement from them detailing exactly what has been lost, which you'll need for your insurance claim back home. Generally you'll find the police sympathetic enough, sometimes able to speak English, though unwilling to do much more than make out a report for you.

As for **offences** you might commit, it's hardly necessary to state that **drugs** such as cocaine, heroin, LSD and ecstasy are illegal all over Europe, and although use of cannabis is widespread in most countries, and legally tolerated in some (famously in the Netherlands, for example), you are never allowed to possess more than a small amount for personal use, and unlicensed sale remains illegal. Penalties for possession of hard drugs and psychedelics can be severe; in certain countries, such as Turkey, even possession of cannabis can result in a hefty prison sentence, and your consulate is unlikely to plead any kind of case for you. Other, more minor, misdemeanours you should be wary of committing include **sleeping rough**, which is more tolerated in some parts of Europe than others and should be undertaken everywhere with a certain amount of circumspection, and **topless sunbathing**, which is now fairly common throughout southern Europe but still often frowned upon, especially in parts of Greece, Turkey and Italy. As always, be sensitive, and err on the side of caution. It's also worth remembering that, in theory, it is illegal to be on the streets without an official **ID card or passport** throughout most of mainland Europe (except the Netherlands and Scandinavia). Finally, although it's much less of an issue than it once was, avoid photography around sensitive military sites or installations – you may be arrested as a spy.

One of the major irritants for women travelling through Europe is **sexual harassment**, which in Italy, Greece, Turkey, Spain and Morocco especially can be almost constant for women travelling alone or with another woman, and can put certain areas completely out of bounds. Southern European coastal areas, especially, can be a real problem, where women tourists are often regarded as being on the lookout for sex. By far the most common kind of harassment you'll come across simply consists of street whistles and cat-calls; occasionally it's more sinister and very occasionally it can be dangerous. Indifference is often the best policy, avoiding eye contact with men and at the same time appearing as confident and purposeful as possible. If this doesn't make you feel any more comfortable, shouting a few choice phrases in the local language is a good idea; don't, however, shout in English, which often seems to encourage them. You may also come across gropers on crowded buses and trains, in which case you should complain as loudly as possible in any language – the ensuing scene should be enough to deter your assailant. The best way of avoiding more dangerous situations is to simply be as suspicious as possible: don't ever get yourself into a situation where you're alone with a man you don't know.

Festivals and annual events

There is always some annual event or other happening in Europe, and some of the bigger shindigs can be reason enough for visiting a place, some are even worth planning your entire trip around. Be warned, though, that if you're intending to visit a place during its annual festival you need to plan well in advance, since accommodation can be booked up months beforehand, especially for the larger, more internationally known events.

Religious and traditional festivals

Many of the festivals and annual events you'll come across were – and in many cases still are – **religion-inspired affairs**, centring on a local miracle or saint's day. **Easter**, certainly, is celebrated throughout Europe, with most verve and ceremony in Catholic and Orthodox Europe, where Easter Sunday or Monday is usually marked with some sort of procession; it's especially enthusiastically celebrated in Greece, where it is more important than Christmas, though be aware that the Orthodox Church's Easter can in fact fall a week or two either side of the Western festival. Earlier in the year, traditionally at the beginning of **Lent** in February, **Carnival** (or Mardi Gras) is celebrated, most conspicuously (and perhaps most stagily) in Venice, which explodes in a riot of posing and colour to become one of Italy's major tourist draws at this time of year. There are smaller, perhaps more authentic carnivals in **Viareggio**, also in Italy, and in Germany, Belgium and the Netherlands, most notably in **Cologne**, **Maastricht** and tiny Binche in the Ardennes, where you can view some 1500 costumed *Gilles* or dancers in the streets. Also in Belgium, in mid-Lent, catch if you can the procession of white-clad *Blanc Moussis* through the streets of **Stavelot** in the Ardennes – one of Europe's oddest sights. Other religious festivals you might base a trip around include: the *Festa di San Gennaro* three times a year in **Naples**, when the dried blood of the city's patron saint is supposed to liquefy to prevent disaster befalling the place – it rarely fails; the Ommegang procession through the heart of **Brussels** city centre to commemo-rate a medieval miracle; the Heilig Bloed procession in **Bruges**, when a much-venerated relic of Christ's blood is carried shoulder-high through the town; and, in Italy, the annual procession across **Venice**'s Grand Canal to the church of the Madonna della Salute to recall the deliverance of the city from a seventeenth-century plague. In Morocco and Turkey, where the predominant religion is Islam, and in the Muslim areas of Bulgaria, **Ramadan**, commemorating the revelation of the Koran to Muhammad, is observed. The most important Muslim festival, it lasts a month, during which time Muslims fast from sunrise until sunset – although otherwise, as far as is possible, life carries on as normal.

There are, of course, other, equally long-established events that have a less obvious foundation. One of the best-known is the April *Feria* in **Seville**, a week's worth of flamenco music and dancing, parades and bullfights, in a frenziedly enthusiastic atmosphere. Also in Spain, for a week in early July, the San Fermín festival in **Pamplona** is if anything even more famous, its centrepiece – the running of the bulls along with local macho men, through the streets of the city – drawing tourists from all over the world, though there is much more to the festival than that. Also in July, at the beginning of the month (and again in mid-August), the Palio in **Siena** is perhaps the most spectacular annual event in Italy, a bareback horse race between representatives of the different quarters of the city around the main square, its origins dating back to medieval times. It's a brutal affair, with few rules and a great sense of deeply felt rivalry, and, although there are other Palio events in Italy, it's like no other horse race you'll ever see. At least as big a deal as the Palio and San Fermín is the **Munich** *Oktoberfest*, a huge beer festival and fair that goes on throughout the last two weeks in September. Unlike most events of its size in Europe it's less than two hundred years old, but it attracts vast numbers of people to consume gluttonous quantities of beer and food. **London**'s *Notting Hill Carnival*, held at the end of August, is also a recent phenomenon, a predominantly Black and Caribbean celebration that's become the world's second biggest street carnival after Rio. Other, smaller events include the great **Venice** *Regata Storica*, each September, a trial of skill for the city's gondoliers, and the gorgeous annual displays and processions of flowers in the **Dutch bulbfield towns** in April and May.

Arts festivals

Festivals celebrating all or one specific aspect of the **arts** are held all over Europe throughout the year, though particularly in summer, when the weather is better suited to outdoor events. Of general international arts festivals, the **Edinburgh Arts Festival** held every August is perhaps the best known and most enjoyable, not to mention one of the most innovative, with a mass of top-notch and fringe events in every medium, from rock to cabaret to modern experimental music, dance and drama. For three weeks every year the whole city is given over to the festival and it's a wonderful time to be around if you don't mind the crowds and have booked somewhere to stay in advance. There is another major general arts festival in **Spoleto**, the *Festival dei Due Mondi*, held over two months each summer, which is Italy's leading international arts festival, though on a somewhat smaller scale than Edinburgh, while the midsummer **Avignon**

festival in southern France is slanted towards drama but hosts plenty of other events besides and is again a great time to be in town. Smaller general arts festivals, though still attracting a variety of international names, include the **Holland Festival**, held in Amsterdam in June; the **Flanders Festival**, an umbrella title for all sorts of dramatic and musical events held mainly in the medieval buildings of Bruges and Ghent in July and August; and the **Dubrovnik Summer Festival**, with a host of musical events and theatre performances against the backdrop of the town's beautiful Renaissance centre.

As regards more specialist gatherings, the **Montreux Jazz Festival** in July and the **North Sea Jazz Festival** in The Hague in mid-July are the Continent's premier jazz jamborees, while the same month sees the beginning of the **Salzburg Music Festival**, perhaps the foremost – if also the most conservative – serious music festival in Europe, though **London's Prom season** (July–Sept) maintains very high standards at egalitarian prices. **Florence's Maggio Musicale** is also worth catching, a festival of opera and classical music that runs from late April until early July. Less highbrow musical forms – rock, folk, etc – are celebrated, most conspicuously at the huge **Glastonbury festival** in Britain; at the **Pink Pop Festival**, held every June in Geleen near Maastricht in the Netherlands; and the **Roskilde Festival** in Denmark. Look out also for the **WOMAD** get-togethers, a number of which are usually held each year at a variety of sites all over Europe, celebrating World, folk and roots music, and the excellent and still relatively small **Cambridge Folk Festival** in late July. For **films**, there is, of course, **Cannes**, though this is more of an industry affair than anything else, and the **Venice** and **Berlin** film festivals, which are more geared to the general public.

Gay and lesbian travellers

Gay men and lesbians will find most of Europe a tolerant part of the world in which to travel, the west rather more so than the east. Most countries have at least in part legalized homosexual relationships, and the only part of Europe covered in this guide where homosexual acts are still against the law is Romania. Laws still in the main apply to male homosexuality; lesbianism, it would seem, doesn't officially exist, so it is in theory legal everywhere. The homosexual age of consent is, however, usually different from the heterosexual one – on average 18 years of age as opposed to 15 or 16. In general, the Netherlands and Scandinavia (except Finland) are the most tolerant parts of the Continent, with anti-discrimination legislation and official recognition of lesbian and gay partnerships. Reactionary laws against "outraging public decency" or "promotion" of homosexuality exist in Russia, Turkey, England, Wales and Northern Ireland (but not Scotland).

Most cities of any size, at least in northern Europe, have a few bars or cafés frequented by **gay men**, and it's not hard to make contact with other gay people. In the major northern capitals, certainly, the gay scene is usually fairly sophisticated, with any number of bars, bookshops, clubs and gay organizations and switchboards, though things are usually firmly slanted towards gay men. The gay capital of Europe is perhaps Amsterdam, but there is plenty of interest for gay men in London, Paris, Copenhagen, and, to a lesser extent, Madrid and Barcelona. In southern Europe, things are less developed: the main cities may have the odd gay bar, but it may not advertise itself as such, and outside of the capitals there won't be many obvious places to meet at all. **Lesbians** can likewise usually find somewhere to meet with other gay women in northern Europe, albeit on a much smaller scale than gay men, while elsewhere, in southern and eastern Europe, word-of-mouth is about the only course open. We've detailed the best of the gay scenes of the major cities in the text; for further information, contact the organizations listed below.

Contacts for gay and lesbian travellers

Damron Company PO Box 422458, San Francisco, CA 94142 ☎1-800/462-6654 or 415/255-0404, ⓦwww.damron.com. Publishes a men's and a women's guide, and an accommodation guide

and gay road atlas, all mainly on North America but covering major European cities too.
Ferrari Publications PO Box 37887, Phoenix, AZ 85069 ☎1-800/962-2912 or 602/863-2408, ⓦwww.ferrariguides.com. Publishes *Ferrari Gay Travel A to Z*, a worldwide gay and lesbian guide; *Inn Places*, a worldwide accommodation guide; the guides *Men's Travel in Your Pocket* and *Women's Travel in Your Pocket*.
International Gay & Lesbian Travel Association 4331 N Federal Hwy, Suite 304, Ft Lauderdale, FL 33308 ☎1-800/448-8550, ⓦwww.iglta.org. Trade group that can provide a list of gay- and lesbian-owned or -friendly travel agents, accommodation and other travel businesses.
Madison Travel 118 Western Rd, Hove, East Sussex NN3 1DB ☎01273/202532, ⓦwww.madisontravel.co.uk. Established travel agents specializing in packages to gay- and lesbian-friendly mainstream destinations, and also to gay/lesbian destinations.
Parkside Travel 70 Glen Osmond Rd, Parkside, SA 5063 ☎08/8274 1222 or 1800/888501, ⓔhwtravel@senet.com.au. Gay travel agent associated with local branch of Hervey World Travel; all aspects of gay and lesbian travel worldwide.
Silke's Travel 263 Oxford St, Darlinghurst, NSW 2010 ☎02/9380 6244 or 1800/807860, ⓦwww.silkes.com.au. Long-established gay and lesbian specialist, with the emphasis on women's travel.
Tearaway Travel 52 Porter St, Prahan, Vic 3181 ☎03/9510 6344, ⓔtearaway@bigpond.com. Gay-specific business dealing with international and domestic travel.
Spartacus Gay Guide Bruno Gmünder Verlag, PO Box 610104, 10921 Berlin ☎49-30/6100 1120; at

Bookazine Co, 75 Hook Rd, Bayonne, NJ 07002
☎1-800/548 3855; at Turnaround, Unit 3, Olympia
Trading Estate, Coburg Rd, London N22 6TZ
☎020/8829 3000; at Bulldog Books, PO Box 300,
Beaconsfield, NSW 2014 ☎02/9699 3507.
International gay guide with information on meeting
and cruising spots for gay men, but nothing much for
lesbians.
🖳 www.gaytravel.co.uk UK-based online gay and
lesbian travel agent, offering good deals on all types
of holiday. Also lists gay- and lesbian-friendly hotels
around the world.

Gay and Lesbian Travel 🖳 www.galta.com.au.
Australian-based directory and links for gay and
lesbian travel worldwide.
Gay Travel 🖳 www.gaytravel.com. Site for trip
planning, bookings, and general information about
international travel.
Pinkstay 🖳 www.pinkstay.com. Austalian-based
organization with information on everything from visa
information to finding accommodation and work
around the world.

 # Travellers with disabilities

It's easier for disabled people to get around in northern Europe than in the south
and east, which is not surprising given the fact that this part of the Continent is
more developed in every other way. Wheelchair access to public buildings is,
however, far from easy in many countries, as is wheelchair accessibility to public transport – indeed, the only big-city underground systems that are accessible
are those in Berlin, Amsterdam, Stockholm and Helsinki, with the rest lagging far
behind; buses, too, are in general out of bounds to wheelchair users, although
airport facilities are improving, as are those on the cross-Channel ferries. As for
rail services, these vary greatly: France, for example, has very good facilities for
disabled passengers, as have Belgium, Denmark and Austria, but many other
countries make little, if any, provision. Things in general are improving however,
particularly within the EU, where new accessibility regulations are gradually coming into force.

Your particular disability may govern
whether you decide to see Europe on a
package tour or **independently**. There are
any number of specialist tour-operators,
mostly catering for physically disabled travellers, and the number of non-specialist
operators who cater for disabled clients is
increasing.

Pressure on space means that it is impossible for us to detail wheelchair-access
arrangements for everywhere we list in the
Guide; neither can we detail the best and
worst of the operators. For more **information on disabled travel abroad** you should
get in touch with the organizations listed
below. As well as their publications, look out
for *Access London* and *Access Paris,* with
information specific to those cities, published by Access Project in the UK.

Contacts for travellers with disabilities

In the US and Canada

Access-Able 🖳 www.access-able.com. Online
resource for travellers with disabilities.
Directions Unlimited 123 Green Lane, Bedford
Hills, NY 10507 ☎1-800/533-5343 or 914/241-
1700. Tour operator specializing in custom tours for
people with disabilities.
Mobility International US 451 Broadway,
Eugene, OR 97401, voice and TDD ☎541/343-
1284, 🖳 www.miusa.org. Information and referral
services, access guides, tours and exchange
programmes. Annual membership $35 (includes
quarterly newsletter).
**Society for the Advancement of Travelers
with Handicaps (SATH)** 347 5th Ave, New York,
NY 10016 ☎212/447-7284, 🖳 www.sath.org. Non-

profit educational organization that passes queries on to its members as appropriate; allow plenty of time for a response.

Travel Information Service ☏ 215/456-9600. Telephone-only information and referral service.

Twin Peaks Press Box 129, Vancouver, WA 98661 ☏ 360/694-2462 or 1-800/637-2256, 🖤 www.twinpeak.virtualave.net. Publisher of the *Directory of Travel Agencies for the Disabled* ($19.95), listing more than 370 agencies worldwide; *Travel for the Disabled* ($19.95); the *Directory of Accessible Van Rentals* ($12.95) and *Wheelchair Vagabond* ($19.95), loaded with personal tips.

Wheels Up! ☏ 1-888/389-4335, 🖤 www.wheelsup .com. Provides discounted airfare, tour and cruise prices for disabled travellers, also publishes a free monthly newsletter and has a comprehensive website.

In the UK and Ireland

Access Travel 6 The Hillock, Astley, Lancashire M29 7GW ☏ 01942/888844, 🖤 www.access-travel .co.uk. Small tour-operator that can arrange flights, transfer and accommodation in France, Spain, Portugal and parts of Greece.

Disability Action Group 2 Annadale Ave, Belfast BT7 3JH, ☏ 028/9049 1011. Provides information about access for disabled travellers abroad.

Holiday Care 2nd floor, Imperial Building, Victoria Rd, Horley, Surrey RH6 7PZ ☏ 01293/774535, Minicom ☏ 01293/776943, 🖤 www.holidaycare .org.uk. Provides free lists of accessible accommodation abroad. Information on financial help for holidays available.

Irish Wheelchair Association Blackheath Drive, Clontarf, Dublin 3 ☏ 01/833 8241, ✉ iwa@iol.ie. Useful information provided about travelling abroad with a wheelchair.

Tripscope Alexandra House, Albany Rd, Brentford, Middlesex TW8 0NE ☏ 08457/585641, 🖤 www.justmobility.co.uk/tripscope. This registered charity provides a national telephone information service offering free transport and travel advice for people with a mobility problem.

In Australia and New Zealand

ACROD (Australian Council for Rehabilitation of the Disabled) PO Box 60, Curtin ACT 2605 ☏ 02/6282 4333; 24 Cabarita Rd, Cabarita NSW 2137 ☏ 02/9743 2699. Provides lists of travel agencies and tour operators for people with disabilities.

Disabled Persons Assembly 4/173–175 Victoria St, Wellington ☏ 04/801 9100. Resource centre with lists of travel agencies and tour operators for people with disabilities.

Work and study

The opportunities for working or studying your way around Europe are almost unlimited, especially for citizens of EU nations, who benefit from the easing of restrictions on the movement of labour. You can either fix something up before you leave home and build your trip around that, or simply look out for casual labour on your travels, treating it as a way of topping up your vacation cash. Certainly the best way of discovering a country properly is to work there, learning the language if you can and discovering something about the culture. Study opportunities are also a good way of absorbing yourself in the local culture, but they invariably need to be fixed up in advance; check the newspapers for ads or contact one of the main organizations (listed on p.56) direct.

There are any number of jobs you can pick up on the road to supplement your spending money while you're travelling. It's normally not hard to find **bar or restaurant work**, especially in large resort areas during the summer, and your chances will be greater if you can speak the local language – although being able to speak English may be your greatest asset in the more touristy areas; you may be asked for documentation, in which case you're better off in an EU member-state, but it's unlikely. Don't be afraid to march straight in and ask, or check the noticeboards in local bars, hostels or colleges, or the local newspapers, particularly the English-language ones. Cleaning jobs, nannying and **au pair** work are also common, if not spectacularly well paid, often just providing room and board plus pocket money. Some of them can be fixed up on the spot, while others need to be organized before you leave home. If you're staying in a place for a while, you can always place an ad or a notice yourself offering your services. The other big casual earner is farmwork, particularly **grape-picking**, which is an option from August to October, when the vines are being harvested. The best country for this is France, but there's sometimes work in Germany too. Once again, you're unlikely to be asked for any kind of documentation. Also in France, along the Côte d'Azur, and in other yacht-havens in Greece and parts of southern Spain, there is sometimes **crewing** work available, though you'll obviously need some sailing experience. If this isn't up your street but you want something active to last the whole summer, try tour operators, who are often on the lookout for **travel couriers**, though this is something better arranged from home. If you're really serious, get in touch with the companies that run bus tours for young people around Europe, who are often keen to take on new blood.

Rather better paid, and equally widespread, if only during the September to June period, is **teaching English as a foreign language** (TEFL), which is something you normally (though not exclusively) need to fix up from home. People are desperate to learn English all over Europe, but it is becoming harder to find English-teaching jobs without some kind of TEFL qualification. If you do organize work on the spot you may have to leave the country while your employers apply for a work permit. You'll normally be paid a liveable local salary, sometimes with somewhere to live thrown in as well, and you can often supplement your income with much more lucrative private lessons. The TEFL teaching season is reversed in Britain and to a lesser extent Ireland, with plenty of work available during the summer in London and on the English south coast

(but again, some kind of TEFL qualification is pretty well indispensable).

If you want to know more about working in Europe, get hold of one of several handy **publications**. In Britain, *Overseas Jobs Express* (☎01273/699611, ⊛www .overseasjobs.com) is a fortnightly publication with a range of job vacancies, available by subscription only. The publishers Vacation Work (☎01865/241978, ⊛www.vacationwork .co.uk) produce the useful *Work your Way around the World* by Sue Griffiths and *Summer Jobs Abroad* by David Woodworth and Ian Collier, which has details of places you could try before leaving home; for more on TEFL possibilities, check out Sue Griffiths, *Teaching English Abroad*. Kuperard publish Mark Hempshell's *Working Holidays Abroad – A Practical Guide*, which also has some good leads for short-term work. Travel magazines such as *Wanderlust* (every two months; £2.80) have a job section that often advertises opportunities with tour companies.

Studying abroad invariably means learning a language, doing an intensive course that lasts between two weeks and three months and staying with a local family. There are plenty of places you can do this, and you should reckon on paying around £200/$300 a week including room and board. If you know a language well, you could also apply to do a short course in another subject at a local university; scan the classified sections of the newspapers back home, and keep an eye out when you're on the spot. The website ⊛www.studyabroad.com has useful listings and links to study and work programmes worldwide. The EU runs a programme called **Erasmus** (part of a wider project called Socrates) in which university students from Britain and Ireland can obtain mobility grants to study in one of 26 European countries (including the other EU countries, plus Bulgaria, the Czech Republic, Estonia, Hungary, Latvia, Lithuania, Norway, Poland, Romania, Slovakia and Slovenia) for three months to a full academic year if their university participates in the programme. Anyone interested should check with their university's international relations office, or on the Erasmus/Socrates website at ⊛europa.eu.int/comm/education/socrates/erasmus/home.html.

Study and work contacts

AFS Intercultural Programs US, 198 Madison Ave, 8th Floor, New York, NY 10016 ☏1-800/AFS INFO or 212/299 9000; Canada, 1290, rue St-Denis, Suite 600, Montreal, PQ H2X 3J7, ☏1-800/361 7248 or 514/288 3282; UK, Leeming House, Vicar Lane, Leeds LS2 7JF, ☏0113/242 6136; Australia, Level 5, 418A Elizabeth St, Surry Hills, NSW 2010, ☏1300/131716; New Zealand, PO Box 5562, Level 3, 125 Featherston St, Wellington, ☏0800/600300 or 04/494 6020; ✆www.afs.org. Worldwide, UN-recognized organization running summer experiential programmes to foster international understanding.

American Institute for Foreign Study US, River Plaza, 9 W Broad St, Stamford, CT 06902–3788, ☏1-800/727 2437, ✆www.aifs.com. Language study and cultural immersion for the summer or school year in Austria, Britain, the Czech Republic, France, Ireland, Italy, the Netherlands, Poland, Russia and Spain.

ASSE International US, 228 North Coast Highway, Laguna Beach, CA 92651, ☏1-800/333 3802; Canada, 7 Rue de la Commune Ouest, Suite 204, Montreal, PQ H2Y 2C5, ☏1-800/361 3214; UK, PO Box 20, Harwich, Essex CO12 4DQ, ☏01255/506347; Australia, c/o Southern Cross Cultural Exchange, Locked Bag 1200, Mt Eliza, Vic 3930, ☏03/9775 4711; New Zealand, PO Box 35697, 1311 Browns Way, Auckland; ✆www.asse .com. International student exchanges to Scandinavia, Germany, Switzerland, the Netherlands, France, Spain, Italy, Estonia, the Czech Republic, Slovakia, Poland, Portugal and the UK; also offers summer language programmes in most of those.

Association for International Practical Training US, 10400 Little Patuxent Pkwy, Suite 250, Columbia, MD 21044–3510, ☏410/997 2200, ✆www.aipt.org. Summer internships in various European countries for students who have completed at least two years of college in science, agriculture, engineering or architecture.

Australians Studying Abroad Australia, 1/970 High St, Armadale, Vic 3143, ☏1800/645 755 or 03/9509 1955, ✆www.asatravinfo.com.au. Study tours focusing on art and culture.

British Council Central Bureau for Educational Visits and Exchanges UK, 10 Spring Gdns, London SW1A 2BN, ☏020/7930 8466, ✆www.britishcouncil.org/cbeve. Enables teachers to find out about development programmes abroad, or gap year students to take part in foreign language assistant programmes in France and Germany. Also recruits qualified EFL teachers for schools in Europe and elsewhere.

Council on International Educational Exchange (CIEE) US, 205 E 42nd St, New York, NY 10017 ☏1-800/2COUNCIL, ✆www.ciee.org /study; UK, 52 Poland St, London W1F 7AB, ☏020/7478 2000; Australia, Level 8, University Centre, 210 Clarence St, Sydney, NSW 2000, ☏02/9373 2730, ✆www.councilexchanges.org.au. An international organization worth contacting for advice on studying, working and volunteering in Europe. They run summer-semester and one-year study programmes, and volunteer projects, in Belgium, the Czech Republic, France, Hungary, the Netherlands, Poland, Russia, Spain, Turkey and the UK.

Experiment in International Living ☏1-800/345-2929, ✆www.usexperiment.org. Summer programme for high-school students in France, Ireland, Italy, Poland, Spain, Switzerland, Turkey and the UK.

School for International Training US, Kipling Rd, PO Box 676, Brattleboro, VT 05302, ☏1-800/336-1616 or 802/257 7751, ✆www.sit.edu /studyabroad. Accredited college semesters abroad, comprising language and cultural studies, homestay and other academic work in Croatia, the Czech Republic, France, Germany, Ireland, Morocco, the Netherlands, Russia, Spain and Switzerland.

Directory

Bargaining The only places where you need really do any bargaining when shopping are in Turkey – in the bazaars and carpet shops – and in the souks of Morocco. Everywhere else, even in the less developed parts of southern Italy and Greece, people would think it odd if you tried to haggle.

Contraceptives Condoms are available everywhere, and are normally reliable international brands such as Durex, at least in northwestern Europe; the condoms in eastern European countries, Morocco and Turkey are of uncertain quality, however – so it's best to stock up in advance. The pill is available everywhere, too, though often only on prescription; again, bring a sufficient supply.

Electric current The supply in Europe is 220v (240v in the British Isles), which means that anything on North American voltage normally needs a transformer. However, one or two countries (notably Spain and Morocco) still have a few places

Conversion charts

Clothing and shoe sizes

Dresses

Continental	42	44	46	48	50	52
American	8	10	12	14	16	18
British	10	12	14	16	18	20

Men's suits

Continental	46	48	50	52	54	56
American	36	38	40	42	44	46
British	36	38	40	42	44	46

Men's shirts

Continental	36	38	41	43	45
American	14	15	16	17	18
British	14	15	16	17	18

Women's shoes

Continental	36	37	38	39	40	41
American	5	5	6	7	8	$8^1/_2$
British	3	4	5	5	$6^1/_2$	7

Men's shoes

Continental	41	42	43	44	45	46
American	8	$8^1/_2$	$9^1/_2$	$10^1/_2$	$11^1/_2$	12
British		7	$7^1/_2$	$8^1/_2$	$9^1/_2$	$10^1/_2$

Metric conversions

1 centimetre = approx 0.394 inches; 1 inch = approx 2.5cm; 1 foot = approx 30cm.

1 metre = approx 1.094 yards or 39 inches; 1 yard = approx 0.914m.

1 hectare = approx 2.47 acres; 1 acre = approx 0.405 ha.

1 kilometre = approx 0.621 miles; 1 mile = approx 1.609km; 5 miles = approx 8km.

1 kilo = approx 2.2lb; 1lb = approx 454g/0.454kg; 1oz = approx 28.3g.

1 litre = approx 2.11 US pints; 1 US pint = approx 0.473 litres; 1 US quart = approx 0.946 litres.

1 litre = approx 0.264 US gallons; 1 US gallon = approx 3.785 litres.

1 litre = approx 1.76 UK pints; 1 UK pint = approx 0.568 litres; 1 UK gallon = approx 4.54litres.

1 US pint = approx 0.834 UK pint; 1 UK pint = approx 1.2 US pints; 6 US pints = approx 5 UK pints.

Temperature

To convert Celsius to Fahrenheit, multiply by nine, divide by five and add 32.

To convert Fahrenheit to Celsius, take away 32, multiply by five and divide by nine.

Celsius	0	10	20	30	40
Fahrenheit	32	50	68	86	104

on 110v or 120v, so check before plugging in. Continental, Moroccan and Turkish sockets take two round pins, British and Irish ones take three square pins. A travel plug which adapts to all these systems is useful to carry.

Left luggage Almost every train station of any size has facilities for left luggage, either lockers or a desk that's open long hours every day. We've given details in the major capital accounts.

Tampons In western and southern Europe you can buy tampons in all chemists and supermarkets, although in parts of eastern Europe they can still be hard to come by. If you're travelling in the east for any length of time, it's best to bring your own supply.

Time The places covered in this book are in four time zones. Britain, Ireland, Portugal and Morocco are in principle on GMT (or UTC), which is five hours ahead of Eastern Standard Time, eight hours ahead of Pacific Standard Time, eight hours behind West Australia, ten hours behind eastern Australia, and twelve hours behind New Zealand. Most of the Continent is an hour ahead of that, with Finland, Estonia, Latvia, Lithuania, Romania, Bulgaria, Greece and

Turkey two hours ahead, and Moscow and St Petersburg on GMT+3. All of these countries except Estonia, Lithuania and Morocco have daylight saving time in summer. Thankfully, they usually manage to all change over at the same time nowadays, but this change, along with daylight saving in North America, Australia and New Zealand, can mean a further hour or two's difference.

Tipping Although it varies from one country to the next, tipping is not really the serious business it is in North America, but in many countries it is customary to leave at least something in most restaurants and cafés, if only rounding the bill up to the next major denomination. Even in swankier establishments, a ten percent tip is sufficient, and you shouldn't feel obliged to tip at all if the service has been bad, certainly not if service has been included in the bill. In smarter hotels you should tip hall porters, etc. Cab drivers expect a tip in Britain and Ireland, but not necessarily on the Continent. The opposite is true of bartenders (but if you want to tip a bartender in Britain or Ireland, buy them a drink).

Guide

Austria

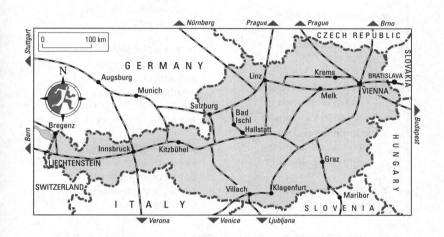

Austria highlights

✳ **Zentralfriedhof**
Fascinating enormous cemetery in the heart of Vienna; the final resting place of Strauss and Beethoven. See p.76

✳ **Schönbrunn Palace**
Extremely opulent Viennese palace. See p.76

✳ **Vienna's Coffee Houses**
An unmissable part of any trip to the city: get your *Kaffee und Kuchen*, sit back and watch the world go by. See p.77

✳ **Melk's Benedictine Monastery** Exquisite religious excess. See p.79

✳ **Höhensalzburg** The largest, completely preserved fortress in central Europe giving panoramic views across Salzburg city. See p.85

✳ **The Sound of Music Tour** Cheesy, but fun and almost compulsory whether you like the movie or not! The Hills Are Alive... See p.86

✳ **Hallstatt** UNESCO World Heritage Site in the the Salzkammergut, this is picture-postcard Austria. See p.88

Introduction and basics

For centuries the heart of the Habsburg Empire, which played a pivotal role in the political and cultural destiny of Europe, Austria underwent decades of change and uncertainty in the twentieth century. The interwar state, shorn of its empire and racked by economic problems and political strife, fell prey to the promises of Nazi Germany. After World War II, denazification was pretty desultory, since most Austrians preferred to forget their wartime role. Postwar economic stability encouraged an emphasis on social policy as the guiding principle of national life, and the growth of a low-key patriotism. With the end of the Cold War, the country returned to the heart of Europe, finally joining the EU in 1995.

From time to time, however, Austria's reactionary past has come back to haunt it, most notably in 1986 during the **Waldheim affair**, when the president's wartime record was called into question. Then, in February 2000, the right-wing People's Party (ÖVP) formed a coalition with the far-right **Freedom Party** (FPÖ). The EU immediately froze bilateral relations with Austria, but the protest eventually petered out. The ÖVP/FPÖ coalition may turn out to be a short-term exercise in political pragmatism rather than the start of a new dark age, but the persistence of xenophobic attitudes and their exploitation by the populist right continue to be a source of concern.

Politics aside, Austria is primarily known for two contrasting attractions – the fading imperial glories of Vienna, and the variety of its Alpine hinterland. **Vienna** is the gateway to much of central Europe and a good place to soak up the culture of *Mitteleuropa* before heading towards the Magyar and Slav lands over which the city once held sway. Less renowned provincial capitals such as **Graz** and **Linz** provide a similar level of culture and vitality. The most dramatic of Austria's Alpine scenery is west of here, in and around the **Tyrol**, whose capital, **Innsbruck**, provides the best base for exploration.

Salzburg, between Innsbruck and Vienna, represents urban Austria at its most picturesque, an intoxicating Baroque city within easy striking distance of the mountains and lakes of the **Salzkammergut**.

Information and maps

Tourist offices are plentiful and come under an assortment of names (usually *Information, Tourismusverband, Verkehrsamt, Fremdenverkehrs-verein* or other variants). All are helpful and well organized, often hand out free maps and almost always book accommodation, sometimes for a small fee, a deposit, or both. They are open all day, every day, in the larger cities during the summer; outside this period, and in smaller towns and remote areas, times may be restricted to a few hours on weekday mornings and afternoons.

There are plenty of good general **maps** of Austria; one of the best is the 1:500,000 Freytag & Berndt. The 1:200,000 Generalkarte series of regional maps are useful for lengthier touring, as are the more detailed 1:50,000 Freytag & Berndt Wanderkarten and rival Kompass Wanderkarten, both covering all the Alpine districts and many rural eastern areas as well.

Austria on the net

ⓦ**www.anto.com** Austrian Tourist Board website
ⓦ**wwww.austriatoday.at** Website version of the monthly English-language newspaper
ⓦ **www.info.wien.at** Vienna's Tourist Board site
ⓦ **www.austrosearch.at** Search engine for all things Austrian
ⓦ **www.tiscover.com** Detailed information in English and German on all regions of the country

Money and banks

Austria is one of twelve European Union countries who have switched over to the **euro** (€).

Banking hours tend to be Mon–Fri 8am–12.30pm & 1.30–3pm; in Vienna they're Mon–Wed & Fri 8am–3pm, Thurs 8am–5.30pm (smaller Viennese branches take an hour for lunch). Post offices charge slightly less commission on **exchange** than do banks, and in larger cities they are open longer hours.

Communications

Most **post offices** are open Mon–Fri 8am–noon & 2–6pm; in larger cities they do without the lunch break and also open Sat 8–10am; some are open 24hr. **Stamps** can also be bought at tobacconists (*Tabak-Trafik*).

The smallest coin accepted in **public phones** is 20¢; a couple should suffice for a local call; insert 50¢ and upwards if calling long distance, or buy a **phone card** (*Telefonkarte*; €3.60 or €6.90), available from tobacconists. You can make **international calls** from all public phones, but it's easier to do so from larger post offices, which have booths. The operator number for domestic calls is ☎1611, for international it's ☎1616.

Internet access is largely limited to the big cities. Expect to pay around €5/hr.

Getting around

Austria's public transport system is fast, efficient and comprehensive, with trains covering the country, supplemented in remoter regions by buses.

Trains and buses

Austrian Federal Railways (Österreichische Bundesbahnen or ÖBB; @www.oebb.at) run a punctual, clean and comfortable network, which includes most towns of any size. **Trains** marked EC or EN (EuroCity and EuroNight international expresses), ICE or IC (Austrian InterCity expresses) are the fastest. Those designated D (*Schnellzug*) or E (*Eilzug*) are next, stopping at most intermediate points, while the *Regionalzug* (R) is the slowest service, stopping at all stations. **Fares** are calculated according to distance, with the first 100km costing €14; 200km costing €23; 500km, about €43.60. In terms of **passes** a Eurorail (see p.20) is the only real option. The national timetable (*Kursbuch*), detailing the whole network, costs €7.50; leaflets covering major routes are free.

Austria's **Bahn-** and **Postbus** system fills the gaps in the network, serving the remoter villages and otherwise inaccessible Alpine valleys. Where there is a choice, you will find trains easier and quicker, and bus fares are only slightly cheaper at around €9.50 per 100km. As a general rule, *Bahnbus* services, operated by ÖBB, depart from outside train stations; the *Postbus* tends to stop outside the post office. Daily and weekly regional **travelcards** (*Netzkarte*), covering both trains and buses, are available in many regions, but prices and areas of coverage vary widely from place to place.

Cycling

Austria is bicycle-friendly, with **cycle lanes** in all major towns. All except the smallest train stations rent out bikes for €13 per day (€8.70 with a valid rail ticket). You can return them to any station for an extra fee of €6.50/€3.30.

Accommodation

Outside popular tourist spots such as Vienna and Salzburg, accommodation need not be too expensive, and, although it can be a scramble in July and August, finding a room doesn't present too many problems. Most tourist offices book accommodation with little fuss, usually for a fee (€2–3) and/or a deposit.

Hotels, pensions and private rooms

A high standard of cleanliness and comfort can usually be taken for granted in Austrian **hotels**, although in resorts and larger towns prices can be high. Outside of Vienna, expect to pay a minimum of €35 for a double with bathroom, slightly less for rooms with shared facilities. Good-value **B&B** is usually available in the many small family-run hotels known as *Gasthöfe* and *Gasthaüser*, with prices starting at €35 for a double. In the larger towns and cities a **pension** or **Frühstückspension** in large apartment blocks will offer similar prices. Most (though not all) tourist offices also have a stock of **private rooms**, although in well-travelled rural areas where the locals depend a great deal on tourism, roadside signs offering *Zimmer Frei* are fairly ubiquitous anyway. Prices for a double room are usually €30–45.

Hostels and student accommodation

HI Hostels (*Jugendherberge* or *Jugend-gästehaus*) are fairly widespread, with around 100 in all. Each is run by one of two organizations: the Österreichischer Jugendherbergsverband (ÖJHV; ☎01/533 5353, ⊛www.oejhv.or.at) or the Österreichischer Jugendherbergswerk (ÖJHW; ☎01/533 1833, ⊛www.oejhw.or.at). Standards vary from the basic, hearty rural variety to the well-appointed (but crowded) places in larger cities. **Rates** are €10–18, normally including a nominal breakfast. Sheet sleeping bags are obligatory, although the cost of renting one is often included in the charge. Many hostels also serve lunch and dinner for an additional €3.50–5.50.

Camping

Austria's high standards of accommodation are reflected in the country's **campsites**, the vast majority of which have laundry facilities, shops and snack bars, as well as the standard necessities. Most are open May–Sept, although in the winter-sports resorts of western Austria many never close. Prices vary enormously depending on the facilities available and the season. In general, you can expect to pay €4–6 per person, €3–9 per pitch.

Food and drink

Eating out in Austria is marginally cheaper than self-catering, but both will take a large chunk out of your daily expenses. By contrast, **drinking** is remarkably affordable, especially wine, and the country's bars and cafés are among its real joys.

Food

For ready-made snacks, try a bakery (*Bäckerei*) or confectioner's (*Konditorei*), which sell sweet pastries and cakes, as well as sandwiches. **Fast food** centres on the *Würstelstand*, which sells hot dogs, *Bratwurst* (grilled sausage), *Käsekrainer* (spicy sausage with cheese), *Bosna* (spicy, thin Balkan sausage) and *Currywurst*, usually chopped up and served with a *Semmel* or bread roll, along with a dollop of *Senf* (mustard) and *Dose* (can) of beer. *Schnell-Imbiss* or *Bufet* places serve similar fare, augmented by hamburgers and simple grills.

It's difficult to make hard distinctions between places to eat and places to drink – most places offer **snacks and meals** of some kind. Similarly, it's possible just to have a drink in most restaurants. Food served up in town-centre *Kaffeehäuser* or cafés and bars can actually be great value, with light meals and snacks starting at about €5; all restaurant and café menus have filling central European standbys such as spicy *Serbische Bohnensuppe* (Serbian bean soup) and *Gulaschsuppe* (goulash soup) for less than €4. Main dishes (*Hauptspeisen*) are dominated by *Schnitzel* (tenderized veal) often accompanied by potatoes and a vegetable or salad: *Wienerschnitzel* is fried in breadcrumbs, *Pariser* in batter, *Natur* served on its own or with a creamy sauce. In general you can expect to pay €6.50–9.50 for a standard main course, though set lunchtime menus (*Mittagsmenü*) always offer a wide range of cheaper dishes. Desserts (*Mehlspeisen*) include sweets and pastries: various types of Torte (including the famous rich chocolate *Sachertorte*); strudel, cheesecake; and *Palatschinken* (pancake, with various nut or jam fillings) are all common.

Drink

For urban Austrians, daytime drinking traditionally centres on the *Kaffeehaus*, relaxed places furnished with a stock of the day's newspapers and serving alcoholic and soft drinks, snacks and cakes, alongside a wide range of different coffees: a *Schwarzer* is small and black, a *Brauner* comes with a little milk, while a *Melange* is half-coffee and half-milk; a *Kurzer* is a small espresso; an

Einspönner a glass of black coffee topped with *Schlag*, the ubiquitous whipped cream that is offered with most pastries and cakes. A cup of coffee in one of these places is pricey at around €2.50–3 and numerous stand-up **coffee bars** are a much cheaper alternative at €1.50 a cup.

Also commonplace is the **Café-Konditorei**, or **Kaffee-Konditorei** where a vast, tempting array of traditional freshly baked Austrian cakes and pastries are usually on offer. *Apfelstrudel* is apple and raisins wrapped in pastry and topped with icing sugar. *Mohnstrudel* resembles *Apfelstrudel*, but has a poppyseed and raisin filling. *Topfenstrudel* has a sweet curd cheese filling while *Linzertorte* is a jam tart with almond pastry.

Night-time drinking centres on a growing number of youthful **bars** and cafés, although more traditional *Bierstuben* and *Weinstuben* are still thick on the ground, especially in rural areas. Austrian **beers**, while of a high standard, don't come in the infinite variety found in Germany. Most places serve the local brew on tap, either by the *Krügerl* (half/litre, €2.90–3), *Seidel* (third/litre, €1.80) or *Pfiff* (fifth/litre, €0.80–1.30), while also keeping a few international speciality beers in bottles. Wine, drunk by the *Viertel* (25cl mug) or the *Achterl* (12.5cl glass), is often cheaper than other alcoholic drinks and is widely consumed. The *Weinkeller* is the place to go for this or, in the vine-producing areas, a *Heuriger* or *Buschenshenk* – a traditional tavern, customarily serving cold food as well. In autumn a lot of places serve *Sturm*, a misty, part-fermented concoction made from newly harvested grapes.

Opening hours and holidays

Traditionally, **opening hours** for shops are Mon–Fri 9am–noon & 2–6pm, with late opening on Thurs till 7.30/8pm & Sat 8am–noon; on the first Sat of the month they open 8am–5pm. It's increasingly common for shops to open all day every Sat and some shops in the larger towns and cities also stay open at lunchtimes. The only shops you're likely to find open outside these hours – and on Sun and on public holidays – are the small general stores at the main train stations and airports. Note that many **cafés** and **restaurants** also have a weekly *Ruhetag* (closing day).

All shops and banks will be closed, and most museums will at least have reduced hours, on the following **public holidays**: Jan 1; Jan 6; Easter Mon; May 1; Ascension Day; Whit Mon; Corpus Christi; Aug 15; Oct 26; Nov 1; Dec 8; Dec 25 & 26.

Emergencies

Austria is an extremely law-abiding country and it is a reasonably safe place to travel. This doesn't prevent the tabloids from complaining about the increase in urban **crime**, which the political right attributes to East Europeans. Austrian **police** are armed, and are not renowned for their friendliness, especially towards other races. There are few places where female travellers will feel ill at ease, except for some outer districts of Vienna and Graz.

As for **health**, city hospital casualty departments will treat you and ask questions later. For prescriptions, **pharmacies** or *Apotheke* tend to follow normal shopping hours. A rota system covers night-time and weekend opening; each pharmacy has details of this posted up in the window.

Emergency Numbers
Police ☏133
Ambulance ☏144
Fire ☏122.

Vienna

Most people visit **VIENNA** with a vivid image in their minds: a romantic place full of Habsburg nostalgia and musical resonances. Visually it's unlikely to disappoint: an eclectic feast of architectural styles, from High Baroque through monumental imperial projects from the late nineteenth century to Modernist experiments and enlightened municipal planning. However, the capital often seems aloof from the rest of the country; Alpine Austrians look on it as an alien eastern metropolis with an impenetrable dialect, staffed by an army of fund-draining bureaucrats.

The first settlement of any substance here, Roman Vindobona, was never much more than a garrison town, and it was only with the rise of the Babenberg dynasty in the tenth century that Vienna became an important centre. In 1278 the city fell to Rudolf of Habsburg, but had to compete for centuries with Prague, Linz and Graz as the imperial residence on account of its vulnerability to attack from the Turks, who first laid siege to it in 1529. It was only with the removal of the Turkish threat in 1683 that the court based itself here permanently. The great aristocratic families, grown fat on the profits of the Turkish wars, flooded in to build palaces and summer residences in a frenzy of construction that gave Vienna its Baroque character.

Imperial Vienna was never a wholly German city; as the capital of a cosmopolitan empire, it attracted great minds from all over central Europe. By the end of the Habsburg era it had become a breeding ground for the ideological movements of the age: nationalism, socialism, Zionism and anti-Semitism all flourished here. This turbulence was reflected in the cultural sphere, and the ghosts of Freud, Klimt, Schiele, Mahler and Schönberg are nowadays bigger tourist draws than old standbys such as the Lipizzaner horses and the Vienna Boys' Choir. There is more to Vienna than *fin-de-siècle* decadence, however; a strong, home-grown, youthful culture, together with influences from former Eastern Bloc neighbours, has once more placed the city at the heart of European cultural life.

Arrival and information

Trains from the west and from Hungary terminate at the Westbahnhof, five U-Bahn stops from the city centre; services from eastern Europe, Italy and the Balkans arrive at the Südbahnhof, south of the city centre (Südtiroler Platz U-Bahnor tram #D); services from Lower Austria and the odd train from Prague arrive at Franz-Josefs-Bahnhof, north of the centre (tram #D); while the airport is served by Wien-Nord in the northeast (U-Bahn Praterstern). Long-distance **buses** arrive at Marxergasse on the corner of Invalidenstrasse, east of the city centre (U-Bahn Wien-Mitte/Landstrasse); while **DDSG boat services** (ⓦwww.ddsg-blue-danube.at) from further up the Danube, or from Bratislava or Budapest, disembark at the Schiffahrtszentrum by the Reichsbrücke, some way northeast of the city centre – the nearest station (U-Bahn Vorgartenstrasse) is five minutes' walk away, one block west of Mexicoplatz. The **airport**, Flughafen Wien-Schwechat (ⓦwww.viennaairport.com) lies around 20km southeast of the city. It's connected to the centre by S-Bahn line S7; trains (every 30min; journey time 30min; €2.80 single, €1.40 with a travel pass) run to Wien-Nord, from where you can make a connection to the more central Wien-Mitte. Buses (every 20min; journey time 20min; €5.80 single) run to the City Air Terminal (adjacent to Wien-Mitte). There are also hourly buses to the Südbahnhof and Westbahnhof (see below).

All points of arrival have **tourist kiosks** which can help with accommodation. The main central **tourist office**, which can also arrange accommodation, is behind the opera house on Albertinaplatz (daily 9am–7pm; ☎24 555, ⓦwww.info.wien.at). There's an **information centre** for young people, *Jugendinfo*, at Babenbergerstrasse 1 (Mon–Sat noon–7pm; ☎1799, ⓦwww.jugendinfowien.at), on the corner of the Ringstrasse.

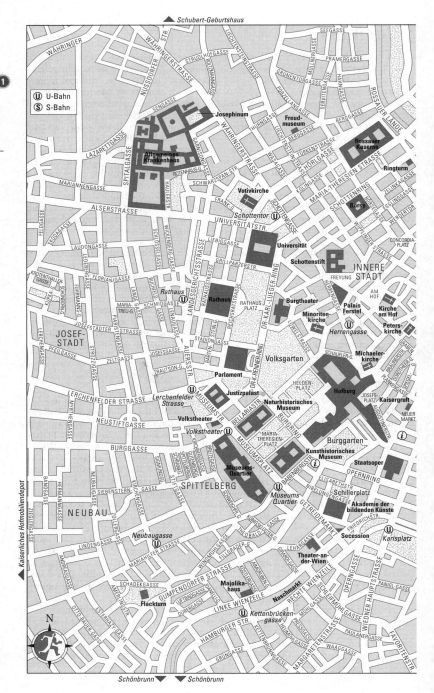

▲ *Schubert-Geburtshaus*

Ⓤ U-Bahn
Ⓢ S-Bahn

WÄHRINGER STR.

Schubert-Geburtshaus

WÄHRINGERSTRASSE

SEEGASSE

STRUDLHOFGASSE

LIECHTENSTEINSTR.

BOLTZMANNGASSE

MÜLLNERGASSE

PRAMERGASSE

NUSSDORFER STRASSE

SENGASSE

SPITALGASSE

LAZARETTGASSE

GARNISONGASSE

HAUFGASSE

ROTENHAUS-G.

SCHWARZSPAN-STR.

THURNGASSE

BERGGASSE

SERVITENGASSE

GRÜNENTORGASSE

PORZELLANGASSE

GRUNENTORGASSE

ROSSAUER LÄNDE

BERGGASSE

ZELINKAGASSE

Josephinum

Freud-
museum

Rossauer
Kaserne

Ringturm

Allgemeines
Krankenhaus

MARIANNENGASSE

ALSERSTRASSE

WICKENBURG-GASSE

WÄHRINGERSTRASSE

VAAGASSE

HÖRLGASSE

TÜRKENSTRASSE

KOLINGASSE

MARIA-THERESIEN STRASSE

SCHOTTENRING

Votivkirche

Schottentor Ⓤ

Börse

FELDGASSE

SKODAGASSE

LAUDONGASSE

FLORIANIGASSE

LEDERERGASSE

KROTENTHALLER
GASSE

SCHÖNBORNG.

FUHRMANNS-G.

SCHLÖSSELGASSE

LANGE GASSE

BUCHFELDG.

LIEBIGGASSE

UNIVERSITÄTSTR.

FRANK-G.

Schottentor Ⓤ

Universität

Schottenstift

INNERE
STADT

FREYUNG

CONCORDIA-
PLATZ

WIPPLINGER STRASSE

WERDERTOR

JOSEFS-
STADT

JOSEFSTÄDTER STRASSE

PFEILGASSE

PARISERGASSE

STROZZIGASSE

ZELTGASSE

JOSEFSGASSE

TRAUTSON-G.

MARIA-
TREU-G.

SCHMIDGASSE

LENAUGASSE

Rathaus

Rathaus

RATHAUS
PLATZ

LANDESGERICHTSSTRASSE

REICHSRATSSTRASSE

GRILLPARZERSTR.

DR.-KARL-LUEGER-RING

Burgtheater

Minoriten-
kirche

Palais
Ferstel

Kirche
am Hof

AM
HOF

Peters-
kirche

Herrengasse

Michaeler-
kirche

HERRENGASSE

SCHAUFLER-G.

GRABEN

KOHLMARKT

PLANKENG.

DOROTHEERG.

SPIEGELG.

STALLBURGG.

SEILERG.

LERCHENFELDER STRASSE

MYRTHENGASSE

NEUSTIFTGASSE

BURGGASSE

LERCHENGASSE

STADIONGASSE

BARTENSTEIN-G.

AUERSPERGSTR.

DR.-RENNER-RING

JOSEFSGASSE

Volksgarten

Parlament

Justizpalast

HELDEN-
PLATZ

Naturhistorisches
Museum

BURGRING

Hofburg

JOSEFS-
PLATZ

Kaisergruft

NEUER
MARKT

AUGUSTINERSTR.

Volkstheater

Volkstheater Ⓤ

MUSEUMSTR.

BELLARIASTR.

MARIA-
THERESIEN-
PLATZ

MUSEUMSPLATZ

BABENBERGERSTR.

Museums-
Quartier

Kunsthistorisches
Museum

Burggarten

Staatsoper

OPERNRING

NEUBAU

SPITTELBERG

SIGMUNDSGASSE

STIFTGASSE

SCHOTTENFELDG.

KIRCHENGASSE

NEUBAUGASSE

Ⓤ Museums-
Quartier

GETREIDEMARKT

NIBELUNGENGASSE

Schillerplatz

Akademie der
bildenden Künste

ELISABETHSTR.

HERMANNGASSE

ZIEGLERGASSE

BANDGASSE

SIEBENSTERN-
GASSE

ZOLLERGASSE

LINDENGASSE

MARIAHILFER STRASSE

Neubaugasse Ⓤ

WIDMMANNGASSE

FILLGRADER-G.

THEOBALDG.

Secession

Karlsplatz Ⓤ

FRIEDRICHSTR.

KANDLG.

ANDREASGASSE

SCHWEIGHOFERG.

Theater-an-
der-Wien

AMERLINGSTR.

SCHADEKGASSE

DÜRERGASSE

STRASSE

GUMPENDORFER STRASSE

MARIAHILFER STRASSE

LINKE WIENZEILE

Majolika-
haus

Naschmarkt

RECHTE WIENZEILE

SCHLEIFMÜHLGASSE

MARGARETENSTRASSE

WIEDNER HAUPTSTRASSE

FAVORITENSTRASSE

▲ *Kaiserliches Hofmobiliendepot*

Flackturm

OTTO-BAUER-GASSE

ESTERHÁZYGASSE

GFRORNERGASSE

LUFTBADGASSE

JONELG.

KÖSTLERGASSE

Kettenbrücken-
gasse Ⓤ

HAMBURGER STR.

KETTENBRÜCKENGASSE

MÜHLGASSE

PRESSGASSE

WAAGGASSE

PANIGL-GASSE

PAULANERGASSE

N

68

▼ *Schönbrunn* ▼ *Schönbrunn*

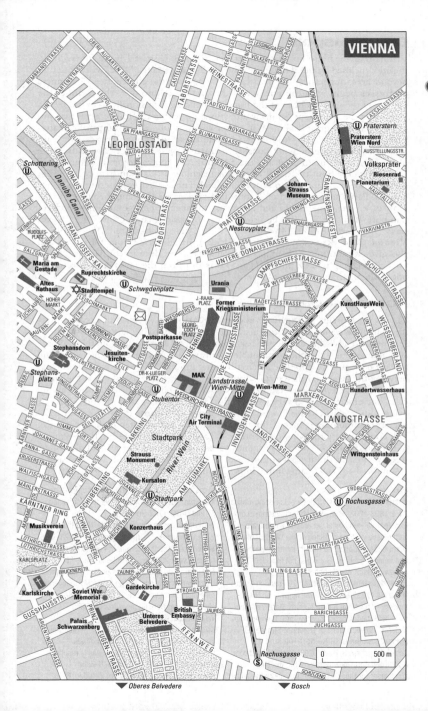

VIENNA

LEOPOLDSTADT

Praterstern

Praterstern
Wien Nord

AUSTELLUNGSSTR.

Volksprater

Riesenrad
Planetarium

Schottering

Danube Canal

Johann-
Strauss
Museum

Nestroyplatz

Maria am
Gestade

Ruprechtskirche

Altes
Rathaus

Stadttempel

Schwedenplatz

Urania

KunstHausWein

J-RAAB-
PLATZ

Former
Kriegsministerium

Postsparkasse

GEORG-
COCH-
PLATZ

Stephansdom

Jesuiten-
kirche

DR-K-LUEGER
PLATZ

MAK

Stephans-
platz

Stubentor

Landstrasse/
Wien-Mitte

Wien-Mitte

Hundertwasserhaus

LANDSTRASSE

City
Air Terminal

Stadtpark

Strauss
Monument

Kursalon

River Wein

Wittgensteinhaus

Stadtpark

Rochusgasse

Konzerthaus

Musikverein

Karlskirche

Soviet War
Memorial

Gardekirche

British
Embassy

Palais
Schwarzenberg

Unteres
Belvedere

Rochusgasse

0   500 m

▼ Oberes Belvedere   ▼ Bosch

City transport

Vienna is divided into numbered **districts** (*Bezirke*). District 1 is the Innere Stadt, the area enclosed by the Ringstrasse; districts 2–9 are arranged clockwise around it; beyond here, districts 10–23 are a fair way out from the city centre. All Viennese **addresses** begin with the number of the district, followed by the name of the street, and then the number of the house or building, occasionally followed by the number of the apartment. So many attractions are within the Innere Stadt that you can do and see a great deal on foot. Otherwise, you'll be reliant on **public transport**, which runs 5am–midnight (outside these times night buses run from Schwedenplatz). The network consists of **trams** (*Strassenbahn* or *Bim*), **buses**, the ultra-clean **U-Bahn** (metro) and the **S-Bahn** (fast commuter trains). You should buy your ticket from the ticket booths or machines at U-Bahn stations and from tobacconists, and punch it on board buses and trams or before entering the U- or S-Bahn. **Fares** are calculated on a zonal basis: tickets for the central zone (covering most of Vienna) cost €1.30 and allow any number of changes, on any mode of transport. If you're going to be using public transport a fair bit, invest in a **travel pass** (*Netzkarte*; €4.30/24hr, €10.90/72hr); the much-touted *Wien-Karte* or **Vienna Card** (ⓦwww.wienkarte.at; €15.25) includes a 72-hour travel pass and also gives various minor discounts at local attractions. Be warned that the penalty for fare-dodging is €40, plus the fare. **Taxis** run from the ranks around town; to book, call ☎31330, 40100 or 60160.

Accommodation

There's no shortage of expensive **accommodation** in Vienna, but extreme pressure on the cheaper end of the market means that booking ahead is essential in summer and advisable during the rest of the year. It's hard to find anything affordable and central – the cheapest double rooms within easy reach of the centre will set you back at least €50. The likeliest hunting grounds are in the western districts between the Ring and the Gürtel (districts 5–9); places here are often on the upper floors of characterful nineteenth-century apartment buildings. Vienna's **hostels** are clean and efficient and so very popular; the HI ones all have daytime lock-outs.

The tourist offices have a limited number of **private rooms** (☎24 555; from €22/person; minimum three nights), but these go quickly and are often in distant suburbs. You could also try the Mitwohnzentrale, 8, Laudongasse 7 (Mon–Fri 10am–2pm & 3–6pm; ☎01/402 60 61), which tends to have cheaper properties and also offers weekly rates; or the nearby youth travel specialists ÖKISTA, at 9 Türkenstrasse 8 (Mon–Wed & Fri 9.30am–4pm, Thurs 9.30am–5.30pm; ☎01/401 48).

Hostels

Hostel Ruthensteiner 15 Robert-Hamerling-Gasse 24 ☎1893 4202, ⓦwww.hostelruthensteiner.com. Excellent VIP-run hostel set around a courtyard, within easy walking distance of the Westbahnhof. Dorm beds, doubles and triples. Internet, kitchen, and laundry facilities. Breakfast not included. No curfew. U-Bahn Westbahnhof. ❷

Jugendgästehaus Brigittenau 20 Friedrich-Engels-Platz 24 ☎332 8294, ⓦwww.oejhv.or.at. Huge, modern HI hostel in a dour suburb. Dorms and en-suite bunk-bed doubles. Curfew 1am. Tram #N from U-Bahn Schwedenplatz or Dresdner Strasse. ❷

Jugendgästehaus Hütteldorf-Hacking 13 Schlossberggasse 8 ☎877 0263, ℮jgh@wigast.com. A 220-bed dorm-only hostel, out in the sticks, convenient for those who wish to explore the wilds of the Lainzer Tiergarten and Schönbrunn. Curfew 11.45pm, but night key available for a small fee. S- and U-Bahn Hütteldorf. ❷

Jugendherberge Myrthengasse/Neustiftgasse 7 Myrthengasse 7 & Neustiftgasse 85 ☎523 6316, ⓦwww.oejhv.or.at. Most central of the official hostels, with 200-plus dorm beds divided between two addresses, round the corner from each other. Book well in advance and go to the Myrthengasse reception on arrival. Curfew 1am. Bus #48A or short walk up Neustiftgasse from U-Bahn Volkstheater. ❷

Kolpingfamilie Wien-Miedling 12 Bendlgasse 10–12 ☎813 5478, ⓦwww.kolpinghaus-wien12.at. Large, modern hostel easily reached from the city centre. No curfew. U-Bahn Niederhofstrasse. Breakfast not included. ❷

Turmherberge Don Bosco 3 Lechnerstrasse 12
☎713 1494. In a church tower in the back end of
Landstrasse. Curfew 11.45pm. Closed Dec–Feb. U-
Bahn Kardinal-Nagl-Platz. ❶
Wombat's 15 Grangasse 6 ☎897 2336,
ⓦwww.wombats.at. Plain dorm beds and bunk-
bed doubles and a party atmosphere at this laid-
back hostel, within easy walking distance of U-
Bahn Westbahnhof. Internet access and laundry
facilities. No curfew. ❷

Hotels and pensions
Pension Dr Geissler 1 Postgasse 14 ☎533 28
03, ⓔhotelpension.dr.geissler@aon.at. Modern
central pension; rooms with shared facilities are
among the cheapest in the Innere Stadt. U-Bahn
Schwedenplatz. ❹
Pension Kraml 6 Brauergasse 5 ☎587 8588,
ⓦwww.pensionkraml.at. Smart, clean, modern,
friendly, reliable and cheap pension off
Mariahilferstrasse. U-Bahn
Zieglergasse/Neubaugasse. ❸
Hotel Kugel 7 Siebensterngasse 43 ☎523 3355,
ⓦwww.hotelkugel.at. Clost to Spittelberg's
numerous restaurants and bars. Plain but clean
rooms; continental breakfast. U-Bahn
Neubaugasse. ❸

Pension Lindenhof 7 Lindengasse 4 ☎523 04
98, ⓔpensionlindenhof@yahoo.com. Appealing
rooms with creaky parquet flooring in a lugubrious
building off Mariahilferstrasse. U-Bahn
Neubaugasse. ❹
Hotel Post 1 Fleischmarkt 24 ☎515 83-0,
ⓦwww.hotel-post-wien.at. A civilized, very large
central hotel with big old rooms and modern
furnishings. U-Bahn Schwedenplatz. ❹
Pension Wild 8 Lange Gasse 10 ☎406 5174,
ⓦwww.pension-wild.com. Laid-back pension, a
short walk from the Ring, popular with
backpackers and gay travellers. Booking essential.
U-Bahn Lerchenfelder Strasse. ❹

Campsites
Camping Rodaun 23, An der Au 2 ☎888 4154.
By a stream in the very southwestern outskirts,
near the Wienerwald. Tram #60 from U-Bahn
Hietzing to its terminus, then 5-min walk. Closed
mid-Nov to mid-April.
Wien West 14, Hüttelbergstrasse 80 ☎914 2314,
ⓦwww.wiencamping.at. In the plush, far-western
suburbs of Vienna, close to the Wienerwald, with
four-bed bungalows to rent (April–Oct; €29). Bus
#151 from U-Bahn Hütteldorf, or a 15min walk
from tram #49 terminus. Closed Feb.

The City

For all its grandiosity, Vienna is surprisingly compact: the historical centre or **Innere
Stadt**, bound to the northeast by the Danube canal and surrounded on all other
sides by the majestic sweep of the **Ringstrasse**, is just 1km wide at its broadest
point. From the Ringstrasse, the main arteries of communication radiate outwards
before reaching another ring road, the **Gürtel** (literally "belt"), further west. Most
of the important sights are concentrated in the central district and along the Ring,
but there are important outlying sights such as the imperial palace at **Schönbrunn**
and the funfair and parklands of the **Prater**. Judicious use of public transport
enables you to travel from one side of the city to the other in less than thirty minutes, so you should be able see a great deal in a couple of days.

Stephansplatz

The obvious place to begin a tour of the city is **Stephansplatz**, the lively pedestrianized central square dominated by the hoary Gothic bulk of the **Stephansdom**
(Mon–Sat 9am–noon & 1–5pm, Sun 12.30–5pm). The first thing that strikes you as
you enter the gloomy, high-vaulted interior is that, despite the tourists,
Stephansdom is still very much a place of worship. The highlight in the nave is the
early sixteenth-century carved stone pulpit with portraits of the four fathers of the
Christian church, and a self-portrait by the sculptor who peers from a window
below the pulpit stairs. The area beyond the transepts is roped off, so to get a good
look at the Wiener Neustädter Altar, a masterpiece of late Gothic art, and, to its
right, the tomb of the Holy Roman Emperor Friedrich III, you must sign up for a
guided tour (English tours: April–Oct daily 3.45pm; €2.90).

Other features of interest include the **catacombs** (Mon–Sat 10–11.30am &
1.30–4.30pm, Sun 1.30–4.30pm; every 30min; €2.90), where, among other
macabre remains, the entrails of illustrious Habsburgs are housed in bronze caskets;

the north or Eagle Tower, which can be ascended by lift (daily: April–Oct 9am–6/6.30pm; Nov–March 8.30am–5pm; €2.90) for a look at the *Pummerin* (Great Bell); and the spire, 137m high and nicknamed *Steffl* ("Little Stephen"; daily 9am–5.30pm; €2.20), which is reached via a blind scramble up internal stairways and has better views than the north tower. Finally, the seventeenth-century Archbishop's Palace, on the north side of the cathedal at Stephansplatz 6, contains the **Dom-** and **Diözesanmuseum** (Tues–Sat 10am–5pm; €5.10), in which the church silver is outshone by a collection of fifteenth-century devotional paintings.

East of Stephansplatz

The warren of alleyways to the north and east of the cathedral preserve something of the medieval character of the city, although the architecture reflects centuries of continuous rebuilding. The medieval house on Raubensteingasse 8 where **Mozart** died while at work on his **Requiem** has long since disappeared, but is commemorated by a small memorial on the ground floor of the Steffl department store that now occupies the site. The only one of the composer's residences to survive is the so-called **Figarohaus**, immediately east of the cathedral at Domgasse 5 (Tues–Sun 9am–6pm; €1.80), though there's little to see inside. A much more intriguing find is the **Treasury of the Order of Teutonic Knights**, around the corner at Singerstrasse 7 (May–Oct Mon, Thurs & Sun 10am–noon, Wed 3–5pm, Fri & Sat 10am–noon & 3–5pm; Nov–April closed Fri am & all Sun; €3.60), where you can view ceremonial regalia and domestic trinkets assembled by seven centuries of Grand Masters.

To the north of Stephansdom, one of the prettiest little squares in Vienna, **Judenplatz**, is now dominated by a bleak concrete **Holocaust Memorial**, designed by British sculptor Rachel Whiteread and unveiled in 2000. Judenplatz stands on the site of the city's medieval Jewish ghetto and you can view the foundations of an old synagogue at the excellent **Museum Judenplatz** at no. 8 (Mon–Thurs & Sun 10am–6pm, Fri 10am–2pm; closed Sat; €3.05), which has an interactive multimedia exhibition on Jewish life in the ghetto.

Further east, the seventeenth-century **Jesuitenkirche** on Dr.-Ignaz-Seipel-Platz is by far the most awesome High Baroque church in Vienna. Inside, the most striking features are the red and green barley-sugar spiral columns, the exquisitely carved pews and the clever trompe l'oeil dome. Beyond it, on Georg-Coch-Platz is the early Modernist **Postsparkasse** (Mon–Wed & Fri 8am–3pm, Thurs 8am–5.30pm; free), completed in 1912 by Otto Wagner.

Nearby, on the far side of Stubenring, is Vienna's most enjoyable museum, known simply as the **MAK** (Tues 10am–midnight, Wed–Sun 10am–6pm; €6.50; ⓦwww.mak.at). The highlights of its superlative, eclectic collection, dating from the Romanesque period to the twentieth century, are Klimt's *Stoclet Frieze* and the unrivalled collection of Wiener Werkstätte products. But what really sets it apart is its provocative early 1990s makeover, which gave some of Austria's leading designers free rein to create a unique series of rooms, each one individually designed.

Kärntnerstrasse, Graben and Kohlmarkt

From Stephansplatz, **Kärntnerstrasse** leads off southwest, a continuous pedestrianized ribbon lined with street entertainers and elegant shops that ends at the city's illustrious **Staatsoper** (ⓦwww.wiener-staatsoper.at), opened in 1869 as the first phase of the development of the Ringstrasse. You can visit the opera house (€4.40), but a more unusual tribute to the city's musical genius can be found down Annagasse at the new **Haus der Musik** (daily 10am–10pm; ⓦwww.haus-der-musik-wien.at; €8), a hugely enjoyable, state-of-the-art exhibition on the nature of sound, filled with high-tech installations.

Halfway along Kärntnerstrasse and one block to the west lies **Neuer Markt**, centred on the writhing figures of the Donnerbrunnen, a copy of an eighteenth-century fountain in which animated nudes symbolize four of the rivers feeding into the

Danube. At the southwest exit of the square, the Kapuzinerkirche houses the **Kaisergruft** (daily 9.30am–4pm; €2.90), where Habsburg family members were interred from 1633. Maria Theresia reputedly came here on the eighteenth of every month to commune with the remains of her late husband Franz Stephan, and was eventually placed beside him in a riotously ornamented sarcophagus of stunning proportions – a stark contrast to the humble, unadorned coffin of her enlightened successor, Josef II.

The prime shopping streets of **Graben** and **Kohlmarkt**, which lead northwest off Stephansplatz, retain an air of exclusivity that Kärntnerstrasse has lost. Just off Graben, at Dorotheergasse 11, is the city's intriguing Jüdisches Museum (daily except Sat 10am–6pm, Thurs till 9pm; €5.10; ⓦwww.jmw.at). The emphasis of the museum's excellent exhibitions on the first floor is on contemporary Jewish life, while on the second floor, visitors are confronted with a series of free-standing glass panels imprinted with holograms, ghostly images of the city's once vast Jewish population.

At the far end of Kohlmarkt is Michaelerplatz, site of the **Looshaus**. Built as a department store in 1911 by pioneering Modernist Adolf Loos, it marked a total break with the Jugendstil confections of Otto Wagner. Its initial unpopularity was largely due to the fact that it was constructed directly opposite the statue-laden nineteenth-century Michaelertor, entrance to the Habsburgs' city residence, the Hofburg.

The Hofburg

The **Hofburg** (ⓦwww.hofburg.at) is a real hotch-potch of a place, with no natural centre, no symmetry and no obvious main entrance. Apart from being the seat of the Austrian president, it now contains a range of museums with imperial connections, beginning with the rather dull parade of **Kaiserappartements** (daily 9am–4.30pm; €5.80) on the north side of the main courtyard. To the southeast is the brightly painted entrance to the Schweizerhof, a smaller courtyard where you'll find the much more impressive **Schatzkammer** (daily except Tues 10am–6pm; €7.30), which holds some of the finest medieval craftsmanship and jewellery in Europe, including the imperial regalia and relics of the Holy Roman Empire as well as the Habsburgs' own crown jewels. Steps beside the Schatzkammer lead up to the **Burgkapelle** (Jan–June & mid-Sept to Dec Mon–Thurs 11am–3pm, Fri 11am–1pm; €1.10), primarily known as the venue for Mass with the **Vienna Boys' Choir** (mid-Sept to June Sun 9.15am; ⓦwww.wsk.at), for which you can obtain free, standing-room only tickets from 8.30am.

Another monument to the Habsburgs' hoarding instincts is the ornate Baroque **Prunksaal** (mid-May to Oct Mon–Wed, Fri & Sat 10am–4pm, Thurs 10am–7pm, Sun 10am–1pm; Nov to mid-May Mon–Sat 10am–2pm; closed Sept; €4.40; ⓦwww.onb.ac.at), overlooking Josefsplatz and worth a glimpse for its frescoes, globes and gold-bound volumes. On the other side of Josefsplatz, a door leads to the imperial stables, home to the performing white horses of the **Spanish Riding School** (performances March–June & Sept–Dec times vary; training sessions same months Tues–Sat 10am–noon; performances €14.50 standing, €22–165 sitting; training sessions €7.30; ⓦwww.spanische-reitschule.com). Tickets for performances are hard to come by, but training sessions are also open to the public and tickets for this are sold at the Josefsplatz entrance box office; the queue is at its worst early on, but by 11am it's usually easy enough to get in.

South of Josefsplatz, down Augustinerstrasse, lies the **Albertina** (ⓦwww.albertina.at), home to one of the largest collections of **graphic arts** in the world, with works by the likes of Raphael, Rembrandt, Dürer, Leonardo, Michelangelo, Rubens, Bosch, Picasso, Klimt, Schiele and Kokoschka. The Albertina has newly expanded exhibition halls, an international study centre, a winter garden, and a restaurant on the terrace, and whatever the exhibition, it's worth a look.

To the west of the Hofburg is Heldenplatz, an enormous open space partially enclosed by the great curve of the palace's **Neue Burg**, a bombastic neo-

Renaissance edifice completed in 1913. Steps lead up to a series of **museums** (daily except Tues 10am–6pm; €7.50), all of which are covered by one ticket. The exhibits include musical instruments, arms and armour, and finds of Austrian archeologists from Ephesus in Asia Minor. A separate entrance leads to the **Museum für Volkerkünde** (daily except Tues 10am–4/6pm; €7.27), which features the collections of Captain Cook, Aztec treasures and other ethnographical exhibits.

The Kunsthistorisches and the MuseumsQuartier

Across the Ring from Heldenplatz, Maria-Theresien-Platz is framed by two pompous neo-Renaissance museums designed to accommodate the vast imperial collections. On the right is the **Naturhistorisches Museum** (daily except Tues 9am–6pm, Wed till 9pm; €2.20; ⊕www.nhm.at), which has changed little since it was opened by Franz-Josef over a hundred years ago. Basically a depository for rocks and stuffed fauna, it also boasts Celtic grave finds from the Salzkammergut village of Hallstatt, plus a copy of the *Venus of Willendorf*, a small stone figure carved by Paleolithic inhabitants of the Danube valley 25,000 years ago.

On the left is one of the richest museums in the world, the **Kunsthistorisches Museum** (Tues–Sun 10am–6pm; €9; ⊕www.khm.at). Its ground floor is largely given over to decorative arts and the ancient world, with impressive Egyptian, Greek and Roman collections, while the fine arts section (also open Thurs till 9pm) upstairs boasts Gothic-infused canvases of Danubian painters such as Altdorfer and the two Cranachs, as well as pieces by Rubens, Caravaggio, Velázquez and Rembrandt. However, it's the unparalleled collection of Pieter Bruegel the Elder that attracts most visitors, pictures such as *The Meeting of Lent and Carnival* and the famous winter scenery of the *Return of the Hunters* portraying the seasons and peasant festivities of the sixteenth-century Netherlands (then Habsburg dominions).

Stand between the two big museums, with your back to the Hofburg, and you will find yourself confronted with Vienna's **MuseumsQuartier** (⊕www.mqw.at). Housed in the former imperial stables, it hopes to do for Vienna what the Tate Modern has done for London. It is the new home to the city's chief permanent collection of Modern Art and to the Leopold Museum (Mon &Wed–Sun 10am–7pm, Fri till 9pm; €9; ⊕www.leopoldmuseum.org), the world's biggest collection of works by Egon Schiele.

Rathausplatz and around

By now you will have crossed the **Ringstrasse**, built to fill the gap created when the last of the city's fortifications were demolished in 1857 and subsequently lined with monumental civic buildings – "Ringstrasse Historicism" became a byword for the bombastic taste of the late Habsburg bourgeoisie. The broad sweep of the Ring wasn't just a symbol of imperial and municipal prestige: it was designed to facilitate the mobility of cannons in the event of any rebellious incursions from the proletarian districts beyond.

Rathausplatz, to the northwest of the Hofburg, is the Ringstrasse's showpiece square, framed by no fewer than four monumental public buildings – the Rathaus, the Burgtheater, Parliament and the University – all completed in the 1880s. The most imposing building of the four is the cathedralesque **Rathaus**, parts of which are accessible only as part of a guided tour (Mon, Wed & Fri 1pm; free). Directly opposite the Rathaus stands the **Burgtheater**, flanked by two grandiose staircases decorated with frescoes by, among others, Gustav Klimt (guided tours only Tues, Thurs & Fri 9am & 3pm, Sat 3pm, Sun 11am & 3pm; €3.60; ⊕www .burgtheater.at). The **Parlament** is an imposing pastiche of Greco-Roman styles fronted by a monumental statue of Pallas Athene (guided tours only mid-Sept to June Mon–Thurs 11am & 3pm, Fri 11am, 1pm, 2pm & 3pm; July to mid-Sept Mon–Fri 9am, 10am & 11am & 1pm, 2pm & 3pm; free; ⊕www.parlament.gv.at).

Not far north of Rathausplatz is the former home of Sigmund Freud, who moved to the second floor of Berggasse 19, six blocks north of the Ring, in 1891 and stayed there until June 4, 1938, when he and his family fled to London. His apartment, now the **Freud Museum** (daily: July–Sept 9am–6pm; Oct–June 9am–5pm; €5; ⓦwww.freud-museum.at; tram #D to Schlickgasse), is a place of pilgrimage, even though Freud took almost all his possessions with him into exile. His hat, coat and walking stick are still here, however, and there's home-movie footage from the 1930s, but the only room with any original decor is the waiting room.

Karlsplatz

Karlsplatz should be one of Vienna's showpiece squares. Instead, the western half is little more than a vast traffic interchange, with pedestrians relegated to a set of seedy subways that give access to the U-Bahn and stretch north as far as the Staatsoper. Immediately above the subway are Otto Wagner's elegant Jugendstil **Station Karlsplatz** pavilions, now used as a café (daily 10am–7pm) and exhibition space (April–Oct Tues–Sun 1–4.30pm; €1.80). Rising majestically above everything around it, the **Karlskirche** (Mon–Sat 9–11.30am & 1–5pm, Sun 1–5pm; €2.90), designed by Fischer von Erlach, is, without doubt, the city's finest Baroque church. A huge Italianate dome with a Neoclassical portico, flanked by two giant pillars modelled on Trajan's Column, it's an eclectic and rather self-conscious mixture of styles, built to impress. The Modernist **Historisches Museum der Stadt Wien** (Tues–Sun 9am–6pm; €3.63) next door includes three floors of medieval sculpture and painting, arms and armour recalling the city's struggles against the Turks, a reconstruction of Adolf Loos's ascetic living quarters, several works by Klimt and Schiele, and a model of the city as it was before the Ring was built.

Over on the west side of Karlsplatz stands the **Secession** building, completed in 1898 as the headquarters of Vienna's Art Nouveau movement. Led by Gustav Klimt, this younger generation rebelled against academic historicism in favour of something more modern, although the Jugendstil they initiated was in many ways equally nostalgic. The building itself is a case in point, though the "gilded cabbage" that crowns it is in a league of its own. One of Klimt's most characteristic works, the **Beethoven Frieze**, created for an exhibition of 1902, remains on permanent display in the basement, while the rest of the building is used for contemporary exhibitions (Tues–Sun 10am–6pm, Thurs till 8pm; €5.50; ⓦwww.secession.at). Immediately behind the Secession, on Schillerplatz, is the **Akademie der bildenden Künste** (Tues–Sun 10am–4pm; €3.63; ⓦwww.akbild.ac.at), which has an often overlooked collection, strong on Flemish works, including Bosch's triptych, *The Last Judgement*.

South of the Ring

Immediately south of the Ring, beyond the Soviet war memorial and fountain on Schwarzenbergplatz (one stop on tram #71 or walk up Rennweg), lies the **Belvedere**, the finest palace complex in the whole of Vienna, at least from the outside. Two magnificent Baroque mansions, designed by Lukas von Hildebrandt for Prince Eugene of Savoy, face each other across a sloping formal garden, commanding a superb view over central Vienna. Today, the loftier of the two palaces, the **Oberes Belvedere** (Tues–Sun 10am–6pm; €7.50; ⓦwww.belvedere.at), houses one of the most popular art galleries in Vienna, with an unrivalled collection of paintings by Gustav Klimt, plus a few choice works by Egon Schiele and Oskar Kokoschka. The same ticket lets you into the **Unteres Belvedere**, which preserves more of its original, lavish decor than the Oberes Belvedere, and for that reason it's worth exploring the **Barock-Museum** (same hours and ticket) now installed in its rooms.

Beyond the Belvedere, the area around the Südbahnhof has a distinctly Balkan feel, with scattered ethnic bars and restaurants providing a meeting place for emigrants from the former Yugoslavia and Turkey. Heading southeast from the Südbahnhof through the Schweizer Garten brings you to the city's former **Arsenal**, a huge complex of barracks and munitions factories that also houses the **Heeresgeschichtliches Museum** (daily except Fri 9am–5pm; €5.10; ⓦwww

.bmlv.gv.at/hgm), built in 1856 to glorify the imperial army. Among the exhibits is the Gräf & Stift open-top car in which Archduke Ferdinand and his wife Sophie Chotek were assassinated in Sarajevo in June 1914; his bloodstained uniform lies nearby.

Ten minutes' walk from here (or tram #71 from Schwarzenbergplatz) is the **St Marxer Friedhof**, on Leberstrasse (daily 7am–dusk), Vienna's principal cemetery from 1784 to 1874. Planted with a rather lovely selection of trees, the cemetery today gives little indication of the bleak and forbidding place it must have been when, on a rainy night in December 1791, **Mozart** was given a pauper's burial in an unmarked mass grave with no one present but the grave-diggers. A memorial marking the area in which the composer was interred – a broken column accompanied by a cherub – was first raised in 1859. The original, however, now stands in Vienna's greatest necropolis, the **Zentralfriedhof** on Simmeringer Hauptstrasse, penultimate stop on the #71 tram line (daily: March–Oct 7am–6/7pm; Nov–Feb 8am–5pm), in which graves of eminent Viennese are grouped by profession. The musicians, principally Mozart, Beethoven, Schubert, Brahms and the Strauss family, lie a short way beyond Gate 2, to the left of the central avenue.

East of the Ring

One of Vienna's most popular tourist attractions, the brightly coloured kitsch **Hundertwasserhaus** (tram #N to Hetzgasse from Schwedenplatz U-Bahn), lies in the unassuming residential area of Landstrasse, east of the Ring. Following his philosophy that "the straight line is godless", the Austrian artist Friedensreich Hundertwasser (1928–2000) transformed some dour council housing on the corner of Löwengasse and Kegelgasse into a higgledy-piggledy ensemble that caught the popular imagination. Understandably, the residents were none too happy when hordes of pilgrims began ringing on their doorbells, asking to be shown round; Hundertwasser obliged with a shopping arcade opposite, called **Kalke Village**, the most disconcerting aspect of which is his penchant for uneven floors. There's another of Hundertwasser's Gaudí-esque conversions, **KunstHausWien** (daily 10am–7pm; €8, Mon €4; ®www.kunsthauswien.com), three blocks north up Untere Weissgerberstrasse, featuring a gallery devoted to Hundertwasser's own paintings and inventions, and temporary exhibitions by other headline-grabbing contemporary artists.

On the other side of the Danube canal, which runs east of the centre, is **Leopoldstadt**, home to a thriving Jewish community until the Nazi Holocaust. The district's main attraction is the **Prater** (U-Bahn Praterstern), a large expanse of parkland that stretches for miles between the Danube canal and the river itself. Formerly the royal hunting grounds, the public were allowed access to the Prater by Josef II, who often walked here himself, quixotically ordering passing members of the public not to salute him. The funfair at the northern end is renowned for the **Riesenrad** (daily: March, April & Oct 10am–10pm; May–Sept 9am–midnight; Nov to early Jan 10am–6pm; €7.50), the giant Ferris wheel featured in Carol Reed's film *The Third Man*. You can take U1 east from Praterstern to the **Donauinsel**, an island in the middle of the Danube crisscrossed with cycle paths and the city's most popular bathing area throughout the summer.

Schönbrunn

The biggest attraction in the west of the city is the imperial summer palace of **Schönbrunn**, reachable by U4 to Schönbrunn or Hietzing. This was originally a royal hunting lodge until Leopold I commissioned Fischer von Erlach to draw up plans for a palace on the model of residences like Versailles. The plans proved too expensive, however, and what was eventually completed during the reign of Maria Theresia, was, for all its size and elegance, far more modest. To visit the palace rooms or **Prunkräume** (daily: 8.30am–4.30/5pm; ☎01/8111 3239; ®www.schoenbrunn .at), there's a choice of two tours: the "Imperial Tour" (€7.50), which takes in 22 state rooms, and the "Grand Tour" (€9.80), which includes all 40 rooms. There's little point in opting for the shorter tour, since it misses out the best rooms – such as the Millions Room, a rosewood-panelled room covered from floor to ceiling with wildly irregular Rococo cartouches, each holding a Persian miniature watercolour. Both tours include English-language hand-held audioguides; there are guided tours – also in English – of the "Grand Tour" (€14).

There are coaches and carriages to see in the **Wagenburg** (April–Oct daily 9am–6pm; Nov–March Tues–Sun 10am–4pm; €4.36) in the right wing, but it's better to concentrate on strolling through the **Schlosspark** (daily 6am–dusk; free), with its frolicking fountain statuary, its maze (daily: April–Oct 9am–4.30/7pm) and Gloriette, a hilltop colonnaded monument, now a café (daily 9am–dusk), from which you can enjoy splendid views back towards the city. The park also holds Vienna's Tiergarten or **Zoo** (daily 9am–dusk; €6.90) and **Palmenhaus** (daily: May–Sept 9.30am–6pm; Oct–April 9.30am–5pm; €3.30), a glasshouse full of tropical ferns.

Eating and drinking

Vienna has a huge variety of places to **eat and drink** as well as a wide range of cuisines, from Balkan to South American. Vienna is, of course, also home of the *Kaffeehaus*, and has by far the largest selection in the country. In summer a visit to a wine tavern (*Heuriger*), to sample their produce along with traditional fare, is also extremely popular; you'll find *Heurigen* in Vienna's outlying districts such as Grinzing (tram #38) or Stammersdorf (tram #31). For **snacks**, head for a *Wurstelstand* or one of the lunchtime stand-up snack bars selling bite-size open-topped sandwiches (*Brötchen*) in the city centre. The **Naschmarkt** itself – the city's main fruit and veg market off Karlsplatz – is a great place to assemble a picnic or grab a tasty take-away and is also home to numerous cheap cafés attached to the various stalls. Another budget option is the student **Mensas**, which serve subsidized three-course lunches; ask for details from the tourist office. You don't have to be a student, and some, like the Technical University *Mensa* on Resselgasse, behind Karlsplatz, are even open during the holidays.

Cafés

Aera 1 Gonzagagasse 11. Relaxing café upstairs serving tasty food; live bands in dimly lit cellar downstairs. Open till 2am. U-Bahn Schwedenplatz.

Alt Wien 1 Bäckerstrasse 9. Dark, smoky *Kaffeehaus*. Good food, if you can find a table. Open till 2am. U-Bahn Stephansplatz.

Berg 9 Berggasse 8. Trendy modern café, with good food and relaxed, mostly gay, clientele. Open till 1am. U-Bahn Schottentor.

Central 1 Herrengasse 14. Traditional meeting place of Vienna's intelligentsia, and Trotsky's favourite café, this is probably the most ornate of Vienna's cafés. Closes 8pm. U-Bahn Herrengasse.

Demel 1 Kohlmarkt 14. Vienna's most prestigious and priciest café/patisserie. U-Bahn Herrengasse.

Diglas 1 Fleischmarkt 16. Homely café offering a mellow respite from the outside world. Pastries and a wide selection of teas. Piano music every Wed 5–8pm. U-Bahn Stephansplatz.

Drechsler 6 Linke Wienzeile 22. Opens at 4am for the stallholders of the Naschmarkt. A good place for breakfast after the bars and clubs have closed. Closed Sun. U-Bahn Kettenbrückengasse.

Europa 7 Zollergasse 8. Lively, spacious café that attracts a trendy crowd; food is a tasty mixture of Viennese and Italian. Open till 5am. U-Bahn Neubaugasse.

Hawelka 1 Dorotheegasse 6. Famed for its smoky, Bohemian atmosphere, this is a popular drinking venue. Open till 2am. Closed Tues. U-Bahn Stephansplatz.

Landtmann 1 Dr-Karl-Lueger-Ring 4. One of the poshest of the *Kaffeehäuser* – and a favourite with Freud – with a high quota of politicians and Burgtheater actors. U-Bahn Herrengasse/Schottentor.

Palmenhaus 1 Burggarten. Stylish modern café set amidst the palms of the greenhouse in the Burggarten behind the Hofburg. Open till 2am. U-Bahn Karlsplatz.

Prückel 1 Stubenring 24. Great original 1950s decor; opposite the MAK. U-Bahn Stubentor.

Savoy 6 Linke Wienzeile 36. Wonderfully scruffy, but ornate *fin-de-siècle* decor, packed with boho bargain-hunters during Sat flea market. Closed Sun. U-Bahn Kettenbrückengasse.

Sperl 6 Gumpendorferstrasse 11. The *fin-de-siècle*

interior is one of the finest set pieces of the Vienna coffee-house scene. July & Aug closed Sun. U-Bahn Karlsplatz/Babenbergerstrasse.

Stein 9 Währingerstrasse 6 ❻ www,café-stein.com. Big, trendy, designer café, with funky music, online facilities and decent food. Open till 1am. U-Bahn Schottentor.

Restaurants

Beim Czaak 1 Postgasse 15. Cosy and smart with traditional food and lovely dark green wood panelling and low-lighting. Closed Sun. U-Bahn Schwedenplatz.

Figlmüller 1 Wollzeile 5. Very popular; this is the place in the city centre to eat Wienerschnitzel. U-Bahn Stephansplatz.

Fischer Bräu 19 Billrothstrasse 17. Civilized micro-brewery near the Gürtel, serving lots of tasty food. Open till 1am. U-Bahn Nussdorferstrasse.

Hunger-Künstler 6 Gumpendorferstrasse 48. Candlelit restaurant serving Vorarlberg specialities and plenty of veggie options. Open till 2am. U-Bahn Kettenbrückengasse.

Margherita 1 Wallnerstrasse 4. Smart, bustling Neapolitan pizza and pasta joint in the inner court of the Palais Esterházy. Closed Sun. U-Bahn Herrengasse.

Osteria Venexiana 3 Rennweg 11/corner of Marokkanergasse. Delicious Venetian menu in this small, attractive restaurant, just round the corner from the Unteres Belvedere. Tram #71.

Schnitzelwirt 7 Neubaugasse 52. Another great place to eat Wienerschnitzel – and cheaper than *Figlmüller*. Closed Sun. Tram #49.

Schweizerhaus 2 Strasse des 1 Mai 116. Czech-owned restaurant in the Prater; known for its draught beer and grilled pigs' trotters (Steltzen). Closed Nov–Feb. U-Bahn Praterstern.

Siebenstern Bräu 7 Siebensterngasse 19. Popular modern *Bierkeller* that brews its own beer and serves solid Viennese food. U-Bahn Volkstheater/Neubaugasse.

Wrenkh 1 Bauernmarkt 10. Fashionable vegetarian restaurant just north of Stephansplatz. Closed Sun.

Nightlife

Vienna's late-night **bars** are concentrated in three main areas: the central Bermuda Triangle of Rabensteig, Seitenstetten-gasse, Ruprechtsplatz where you're bound to find somewhere that appeals; the Naschmarkt, where late-night licences abound, and the Spittelberg, between Burggasse and Siebensterngasse. At **clubs**, you may have to pay an entrance fee, though it's rarely more than €7.50; for the latest information, visit ❻ www.club.at. The local **listings magazine**, *Falter* (❻ www.falter.at), has comprehensive details of the week's cultural programme and is pretty easy to decipher, even if you have scant German. The tourist office also publishes the free monthly *Programm*.

You can catch high-class international **opera** and **ballet** at the Staatsoper, 1, Opernring 2 (❻ www.wiener-staatsoper.at), and opera and operetta at the Volksoper, 9, Währingerstrasse 78 (❻ www.volksoper.at). There's a huge number of **classical music** venues, of which the principal ones are the Musikverein, 1, Karlsplatz 6 (❻ www.musikverein-wien.at), home of the Vienna Philharmonic, and the Konzerthaus, 3, Lothringerstrasse 20 (❻ www.konzerthaus.at). Bookings can be made for all these venues at Bundestheaterkassen, 1, Hanuschgasse 3 (☏ 01/51444 2960; ❻ www.oebthv.gv.at), though you can usually get cheap standing-room tickets by queuing up an hour before a performance.

Musikcafés, live venues and clubs

American Bar 1 Kärntnerstrasse 59. Small, dark late-night bar with a rich interior designed by Adolf Loos. Open till 2am. U-Bahn Stephansplatz.

B72 8 Stadtbahnbögen 72, Hernalser Gürtel. Dark, designer club underneath the U-Bahn arches – features a mixture of DJs and live indie bands. Open till 4am. U-Bahn Alserstrasse.

Blue Box 7 Richtergasse 8. *Musikcafé* with resident DJs and a good snack menu. Open till 2am or later. U-Bahn Neubaugasse.

Chelsea 8 U-Bahnbögen 29–31, Lerchenfelder Gürtel. Favourite venue with up-and-coming Brit guitar bands; situated underneath the U-Bahn. U-Bahn Thaliastrasse.

Flex Donaukanal ❻ www.flex.at. A popular club that also has live bands, as well as the odd art installation. Open till 4am. U-Bahn Schottenring.

Porgy & Bess 1 Riemergasse 11 ❻ www.porgy.or.at. A converted porn cinema provides the new home for Vienna's top jazz venue, attracting acts from all over the world. U-Bahn Stubentor.

Rhiz 8 Stadtbahnbögen 37–38, Lerchenfelder Gürtel; ⓦwww.rhiz.org. Bar/café/club, with several DJs spinning everything from dance to trance. Open until 4am. U-Bahn Lerchenfelder Strasse.
Rosa-Lila-Villa 6 Linke Wienzeile 102. Gay and lesbian centre housing a café/restaurant with a nice leafy courtyard. A good place to pick up information about events. Open till 2am. U-Bahn Pilgramgasse.
Shultz 7 Siebensterngasse. Large, trendy bar with outdoor seating and good cocktails.
U4 12 Schönbrunnerstrasse 222 ⓦwww.u4club.com.

Dark, cavernous disco, mostly break beats and house, with frequent gigs; a Mecca of the alternative crowd. Gay and lesbian night on Thurs. Open till 4am. U-Bahn Meidling-Hauptstrasse.
Volksgarten 1 Burgring 1 ⓦwww.volksgarten.at. Situated in the park of the same name, Vienna's longest-running club. A firm favourite with the dance crowd. Open till 5am. U-Bahn Volkstheater.
w.u.k. 9 Währingerstrasse 59 ⓦwww.wuk.at. Old school now an arts venue run by a sprinkling of anarchists and others. Café, live music and much more. Open till 2am. Tram #40, #41 or #42.

Listings

Bike rental Viennabikes in the central district (☎0676 757 0715; ⓦwww.viennabike.at): Bright pink and blue bicycles available free from any one of 235 stands in the city – €2 deposit slots into the bicycle and is returned after use rather like a supermarket trolley. Otherwise, try Pedal Power 2 Austellungstrasse 3 (☎729 7234; ⓦwww .pedalpower.at; €27/day).
Embassies Australia, 4 Mattiellistrasse 2–4 ☎512 85 80; Canada, 1 Laurenzerberg 2 ☎531 38 30; Ireland, 3 Hilton Centre, Landstrasse Hauptstrasse 2 ☎715 42 46; UK, 3 Jauresgasse 12 ☎71 61 30;

US, 9 Boltzmanngasse 16 ☎313 39.
Exchange Outside banking hours, try the offices at the Westbahnhof (daily 7am–10pm) or the Südbahnhof (daily 6.30am–9pm).
Hospital Allgemeines Krankenhaus, 9, Währinger Gürtel 18–20; U-Bahn Michelbeuern-AKH.
Internet Bignet at 1 Mariahilferstrasse 27, 1 Kartnerstrasse 61, and 1 Hoher Markt 8; Surfland.c@fe at 1 Krugerstrasse 10.
Laundry 8 Josefstädter Strasse 59 (Mon–Fri 7.30am–7.30pm; tram #J).
Post office 1 Fleischmarkt 19.

The Danube Valley

Heading west from Vienna, there are two alternative routes for onward travel: to Salzburg, around three hours away, and then on to Munich or Innsbruck; or a more leisurely route following the Danube through the **Wachau**, a tortuously winding stretch of water where vine-bearing, ruin-encrusted hills roll down to the river from the north. This is an Austria decidedly different from either cosmopolitan Vienna or the Alpine southwest, and accommodation here is generally cheaper than in either place. At the eastern entrance to the region, within easy reach of Vienna by train, is the historic town of Krems, with its older, medieval suburb of Stein; further on lies **Melk**, with its superb Benedictine monastery overlooking the river. Transport to Salzburg from Melk is pretty straightforward, although the industrialized, but culturally vibrant, northern city of **Linz** has enough of interest to make a further stopoff worthwhile. Melk is reached on the main line from Vienna's Westbahnhof.

The most stylish way to travel is by boat. The **DDSG boat service** (ⓦwww.ddsg-blue-danube.at) operates at weekends between Vienna, Linz and Passau during the summer and year-round services between Krems and Melk, the most scenic stretch. The journey takes about three hours upstream, two in the opposite direction, and costs about €18 each way; making your way along the river by shorter hops will work out more expensive, although Eurail holders can travel free and those with an InterRail get a fifty percent reduction.

Melk

For real High Baroque excess, head for the Benedictine monastery at **MELK** – a pilgrimage centre associated with the Irish missionary St Coloman – designed by local architect Jakob Prandtauer in the first half of the eighteenth century. The monumental coffee-cake monastery, perched on a bluff over the river, dominates the town. Highlights of the interior (mid-April to mid-Nov daily 9am–6pm; mid-Nov to mid-April guided tours only 11am & 2pm; €6, plus €1.70 for guided tour; ☎02752/52312 232, ⊛www.stiftmelk.at) are the exquisite library, with a cherub-infested ceiling by Troger, and the monastery church, with similarly impressive work by Rottmayr.

Melk's **river station** is about ten minutes' walk north of town. The **train station** is at the head of Bahnhofstrasse, which leads directly into the old town. The **tourist office**, Babenbergstrasse 1 (April–June, Sept & Oct Mon–Fri 9am–noon & 2–5/6pm, Sat 10am–2pm; July & Aug Mon–Sat 9am–7pm & Sun 10am–2pm; ☎02752/52307, ⊛www.tiscover.com/melk), has a substantial stock of **private rooms**, though most are out of the centre. The **HI hostel** is ten minutes' walk from the tourist office, at Abt Karl Strasse 42 (☎02752/52681, ©oejh-wien-noe @telecom.at; closed Nov–Feb; ❷). A similar distance in the opposite direction is the town's **campsite**, *Melker Camping* (☎02752/53291, ©faehrhaus-jensch@melker .net; closed Dec–Feb), by the river station.

Linz

Away from its heavy industrial suburbs, the Upper Austrian capital of **LINZ** is a pleasant Baroque city straddling the Danube. It's greatest claim to fame is as the childhood home of Adolf Hitler, something about which the local tourist board is understandably coy.

A tour of the city should perhaps start at the rectangular expanse of the **Hauptplatz** or main square, with its tall, pastel-coloured facades, and central Trinity Column, crowned by a gilded sunburst. The pea-green **Alter Dom** (daily 7am–7pm) to the southeast of the square is an unusually stern piece of seventeenth-century architecture. In the **Pfarrkirche** round the corner to the north, a gargantuan marble slab contains Emperor Friedrich III's heart (the rest of him is in Vienna's Stephansdom). To the west of Hauptplatz lies a pedestrianized quarter rich in Baroque houses leading up to the fifteenth-century **Schloss**, Tummelplatz 10 (Tues–Fri 9am–6pm, Sat & Sun 10am–5pm; €4), two blocks west of Hauptplatz, the former residence of Emperor Friedrich III, who made Linz the imperial capital for four years from 1489. Inside, there's little to see save for a good view across the Danube. The castle's museum is particularly strong on medieval weaponry, musical instruments and folk art – it also contains a large but uneven art collection with a smattering of works by Klimt, Schiele and Kokoschka plus a wonderful room of exquisite *fin-de-siècle* glassware and accessories.

The suburb of Urfahr, on the north bank of the river, hosts Linz's latest attraction, the **Ars Electronica Center**, Hauptstrasse 2 (Wed–Sun 10am–6pm; €6.18; ⊛www.aec.at), a museum dedicated to new technology, immediately on your right after you've crossed the bridge. Even if you're barely computer-literate, this place is fun, and though most of the instructions are in German, the helpful staff speak English. You can play around with various pieces of state-of-the-art computer equipment, but the highlight is a visit to the "CAVE", a virtual reality room with 3D projections on the walls and floor – you need to get here early to book a ticket for this (no extra charge).

Also in Urfahr, on the first floor of the supremely unattractive Lentia 2000 shopping centre on Blütenstrasse, is the **Neue Galerie** (mid-June to mid-Oct Mon–Fri 10am–6pm, Thur till 10pm, Sat 10am–1pm; €5; ⊛www.neuegalerie.linz.at), which has a small, permanent collection of modern art, including a few works by Klimt, Kokoschka, Schiele and their lesser-known contemporaries. The only other reason to visit Urfahr is to take a ride on the **Pöstlingbergbahn**, a narrow-gauge railway which climbs to the eighteenth-century pilgrimage church of Pöstlingberg – a good vantage point for sweeping views of the valley; trains leave from a twee station at the end of the #3 tram line (daily 5.40am–8.20pm; every 20min; €3.20).

Practicalities

Linz's **train station** is 2km south of the centre, on the far side of the city's main artery, Landstrasse; tram #3 runs to the central Hauptplatz. There's a **tourist office** in the Altes Rathaus on Hauptplatz (Mon–Fri 8am–6/7pm, Sat & Sun 9/10am–6/7pm; ☏0732/7070 1777). Affordable **accommodation** is thin on the ground, the only feasible options in the centre are the *Wilder Mann*, ten minutes' walk from the station at Goethestrasse 14 (☏0732/65 60 78, ✆wilder-mann @aon.at; ❸), whose rooms come with en-suite showers but shared hallway WCs; the similarly equipped *Goldenes Dachl*, Hafnerstrasse 27 (☏0732/77 58 97; ❸), one block south of the neo-Gothic city cathedral; and the *Goldener Anker*, just off the main square at Hofgasse 5 (☏0732/77 10 88, ✆goldeneranker@nusurf.at; ❹), which has some en-suite rooms. There are two **hostels**, both with self-contained double rooms: *Jugendgastehaus Linz* at Stanglhofweg 3 (☏0732/66 44 34, ✆jgh@oejhv.or.at; closed mid-Dec to mid-Jan; ❸; take bus #17 from the train station); and *Landesjugendherberge Lentia* at Blütenstrasse 23 (☏0732/73 70 78, ✆ljh-linz.post@ooe.gv.at; ❷) in the Lentia 2000 shopping centre across the river in Urfahr. The best **campsite** is on the Pleschinger See (☏0732/24 78 70, ✆kolmer@ione.at; closed Oct–April), 3km northeast of the centre on the Danube; take bus #33 or #33a from Reindlstrasse in Urfahr.

There are plenty of **bars and restaurants** around the Hauptplatz and in the largely pedestrianized streets immediately to the west. *Mangolds*, Hauptplatz 6, is a self-service vegetarian café with cheap but tasty food and a great salad bar; while *Klosterhof*, Landstrasse 30, serves solid Austrian food in the labyrinthine rooms of a former monastery – it also boasts the city's largest beer garden. *Gelbes Krokodil* (closed Sat & Sun lunch), Dametzstrasse 30, is a superb, stylish café inside the city's Moviemento arts cinema, with an excellent selection of Med-influenced food and good wine. *Traxlmayr*, Promenade 16, southwest of Hauptplatz, a traditional coffee house and local institution, is a good place to treat yourself to a slice of *Linzer Torte*, the local chocolate cake, washed down with excellent coffee. *Alte Welt*, Hauptplatz 4 (closed Sun), is a trendy **wine bar** that features regular live jazz, folk- and world-music bands; alternatively try one of the *Weinkellers* along the river front in Urfahr, all good places to sample the white wines of the Mühlviertel, the vine-covered hills north of the city. Otherwise, most charicterful of the downtown drinking dives is *Café Ex-Blatt*, Waltherstrasse 15, a popular studenty pub decked out with nostalgic posters and adverts. *Posthof*, 2km east of the centre at Posthofgasse 43 (🖥www.posthof.at; bus #21 from the train station), organizes regular gigs and **club nights**; while *Cembranikeller*, 500m northwest of the station at Kellergasse 4, organizes regular rave parties – look out for posters advertising both. There's free **internet access** at Ars Electronica (see p.80) but you have to buy a ticket to the museum first. Otherwise, try Bignet, Promenade 3.

Southeast Austria

Austria's **southeastern** corner, despite the subalpine terrain of the central province of Styria and the sun-baked plains of the Burgenland, is bypassed by most visitors. The area contains a wealth of diffuse attractions, though these demand leisurely exploration, and the obvious focus of concentrated interest is the Styrian provincial capital of **Graz**.

Graz

Austria's second largest city, **GRAZ** owes its importance to the defence of central Europe against the Turks. From the fifteenth century, it was constantly under arms, rendering it far more secure than Vienna. This led to a modest seventeenth-century flowering of the arts; the Baroque style appeared first in Graz. During the last years of the empire, the city's mild climate made it a popular retirement choice for ageing officers

1

and civil servants, and its reputation as a conservative town swarming with pensioners has proved almost impossible to shake off. Nowadays, however, it is a rich and culturally varied city, with a varied nightlife, thanks in part to its large student population.

Graz is compact and easy to explore, most sights being within striking distance of **Hauptplatz**, a broad market square centred on a statue of the Habsburg Archduke Johann, a popular nineteenth-century benefactor. Herrengasse leads off to the south towards the **Landhaus**, a sixteenth-century town hall with Italianate arcading in the courtyard. Next door **Zeughaus**, Herrengasse 16 (Tues–Sun 9/10am–3/5pm; €4.40), is an armoury whose galleries bristle with weaponry used to keep the Turks at bay. The main attraction west of Herrengasse is the **Landesmuseum Joanneum** (✇www.museum-joanneum.at), founded by Archduke Johann, a vast collection housed in different locations; entrance to the natural history section (Tues–Sun 9am–4pm; €4.40) is at Raubergasse 10, while the more interesting **Alte Galerie** (Tues–Sun 10am–5pm; €4.40) at Neutorgasse 45 houses a collection rich in Gothic devotional paintings. A fifteenth-century altarpiece by the illustrious Tyrolean painter Michael Pacher depicts the martyrdom of Thomas à Becket, and, among other Flemish paintings, there's a grippingly macabre *Triumph of Death* by Brueghel.

On the other side of Herrengasse, Stempfergasse leads into a neighbourhood of narrow alleyways that dog-leg their way up the hill towards the **Mausoleum of Ferdinand II** (May–Oct Mon–Sat 11am–noon & 2–3pm; Nov & Dec 11am only; closed till April for renovation; €0.70). It's a fine example of the early Baroque style, begun in 1614 when its intended incumbent was a healthy 36-year-old. Next door is the **Domkirche**, immediately north of which is the **Burg**, an erstwhile imperial residence now given over to local government offices; peer through the archway at the end of the first courtyard to view the unique double spiral of a fifteenth-century Gothic staircase. From here Hofgasse descends to the bustling shopping street of **Sporgasse**, where the Saurau palace at no. 25 features a Turkish figure throwing himself from a small window.

A short way north of Hauptplatz, down Sackstrasse, the **Neue Galerie** (Tues–Sun 10am–6pm; €4.40), housed in the seventeenth-century Herberstein Palace, displays nineteenth- and twentieth-century works including a sprinkling of Klimts and Schieles. From Schlossbergplatz a balustraded stone staircase zigzags up to the **Schlossberg**, a wooded hill overlooking the town; reached by either the Schlossberg lift (daily 8am–9pm; €1.50) or Schlossbergbahn funicular, a little further along Sackstrasse (9am–10pm; every 15min; €2.20). The Schloss from which its name derives was destroyed by Napoleon in 1809; only two prominent features survive – the sixteenth-century **Uhrturm** or clock tower, whose steep overhanging roof figures prominently in the town's tourist literature, and the more distant **Glockenturm** or bell tower of the same period. Paths descend south from the Schlossberg to the elegant sweep of the **Stadtpark**, a leafy barrier between the city and the residential suburbs beyond.

Some 4km west of the town centre, at the end of tram line #1, are the luxurious state rooms of **Schloss Eggenburg**, Eggenberger Allee 90 (May–Oct daily 9am–5pm; €5.81), built in 1625 for Hans Ulrich of Eggenburg, Ferdinand II's First Minister. Tickets include a guided tour of the state rooms as well as the Schloss's museums. The archeological collection is strong on prehistory, its most valued exhibit being the Strettweg chariot – a remarkable wheeled platform dating from the eighth century BC, peopled by small, weapon-wielding figures.

Practicalities

Graz's **train station** is on the western edge of town, a fifteen-minute walk or short tram ride (#1, #3 #6 or #7) from the central Hauptplatz. There's a **tourist office** at the station (Mon–Sat 9am–6pm, Sun 10am–6pm; ✆0316/80750) and a bigger one 200m from Hauptplatz at Herrengasse 16 (same hours and number), which can book private rooms, although these are almost all a lengthy bus ride from the centre. **Internet** access is available at *Sit 'n' Surf*, Hans-Sachs-Gasse 10.

Conveniently located **accommodation** can by found at *Hotel Alter Telegraph*, Grabenstrasse 12 (℡0316/686 558, ✉altertelegraph@aon.at; ➍), and *Pension Rückert*, Rückertgasse 4 (℡316/32 30 31; closed June; ➍), in a leafy suburb 2km east of the centre; take tram #1 from the train station to Teggethofplatz. The town's **HI youth hostel** is four blocks south of the station at Idlhofgasse 74 (℡0316/71 48 76; dorms ➌) and offers simple dorms and comfy en-suite doubles; it's justifiably popular so book in advance. *Camping Central* is the only **campsite**, south of the centre at Martinhof-strasse 3 (℡0676/378 5102, ⓦwww.tiscover.at/campingcentral; bus #32 from Jakominiplatz).

Graz is foremost among Austria's provincial cities in preserving the culture of the **Kaffeehaus**. *Hofcafé Edegger Tax*, Hofgasse 8, is the refuge of the city's more sedate citizens; the modern *Operncafé*, Opernring 22, attracts a youthful crowd and is equally popular in the evening; whilst *Café Promenade*, Erzherzog-Johann-Allee, is an attractive pavilion in the Stadtpark. For something more substantial than munching a *Wurst* on Hauptplatz or visiting the fishy *Nordsee* outlet on Herrenstrasse, try *Gambrinuskeller*, Farbergasse 6–8 (closed Sun), which has a wide choice of reasonably priced **food**, including kebabs, stuffed peppers and other Balkan dishes; or *Glockenspielkeller*, Mehlplatz 3, with more standard Austrian fare and pleasant outdoor seating. *Pizzeria Catharina*, Sporgasse 32, has a wide range of inexpensive pizzas, and *Zu den 3 goldenen Kugeln*, east of the centre in the University district, on the corner of Goethestrasse and Heinrichstrasse, doles out dirt-cheap Schnitzel-and-chips fare. Many of the best places to **drink** are in the alleys around the Hauptplatz – *MI*, Färberplatz, is a swish designer bar, while the lively *Flann O'Brien's*, Paradiesgasse, is the best of the Irish pubs. It's also worth venturing out to the cafés and bars which cluster in the streets around the university, east of the Stadtpark: *Café Harrach*, Harrachgasse 26, is good, and *Bier Baron*, Heinrichstrasse 56, is a student favourite, serving inexpensive food. *Park House*, a pavilion in the Stadtpark, is a late bar with resident DJs. Other **clubbing venues** include the Kulturhauskeller, a studenty dive at Elisabethstrasse 31 (ⓦwww.kulturhauskeller.com); and *Arcadium*, Griesgasse 25 (ⓦwww.arcadium.at), which organizes themed nights with guest DJs. Graz also has a summer classical **music festival**, with various concerts held all over the city from late June to late July (information on ℡0316/825 000; ⓦwww.styriarte.com).

Salzburg and the Salzkammergut

Salzburg, straddling the border with Germany, is Austria's most heavily touristed city after Vienna – a magnet for those seeking the best of the country's Baroque heritage and a taste of subalpine scenery. The most accessible and popular of these mountain areas is the **Salzkammergut**, a region of glacier-carved lakes and craggy peaks a couple of hours east by bus or train.

Salzburg

Thomas Bernhard, writer and acerbic critic of the postwar state, spent his formative years in **SALZBURG**, later referring to his home town as "a fatal illness", whose Catholicism, conservatism and sheer snobbery drove its citizens to a miserable end. Yet for many visitors Salzburg represents the quintessential Austria, offering the best of the country's Baroque architecture, subalpine air, and a musical heritage largely provided by the city's most famous son, Wolfgang Amadeus Mozart, whose bright-eyed visage peers from every box of the city's ubiquitous chocolate delicacy, the *Mozartkügel*. The city, once home to the renowned singing Von-Trapp family immortalized in the movie *The Sound of Music*, wastes no time in cashing in on the connection via a variety of tours and shows.

The City

Salzburg's compact centre straddles the River Salzach: the ensemble of archiepiscopal buildings on the west bank form a tight-knit network of alleys and squares, overlooked by the brooding presence of the medieval Hohensalzburg castle. From here it's a short hop over the river to a narrow ribbon of essential sights on the east bank.

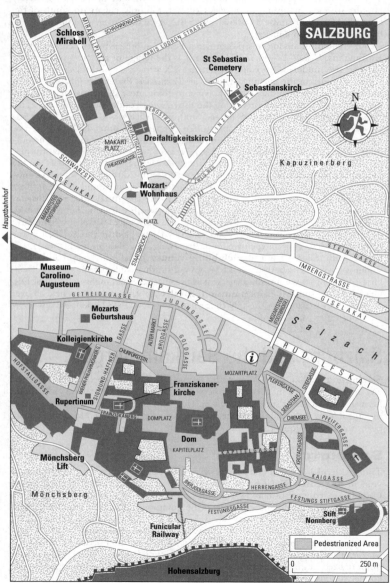

The west bank

From the **Staatsbrücke**, the main bridge across the River Salzach, tourists are funneled along the west bank's Judengasse and up into **Mozartplatz**, home to a statue of the composer and overlooked by the **Glockenspiel**, a seventeenth-century musical clock whose chimes attract crowds at 7am, 11am and 6pm. The complex of Baroque buildings on the right exudes the ecclesiastical and temporal power wielded by Salzburg's archbishops, whose erstwhile living quarters – the **Residenz** – dominate the west side of the adjacent **Residenzplatz**. You can make a self-guided audio-tour of the lavish state rooms (daily 10am–5pm; €6.60); one floor above, the **Residenzgalerie** (daily 10am–5pm; Oct–March closed Wed; ⊕www.salzburg.gv.at /residenzgalerie; €4.70) offers a fine display of archiepiscopal acquisitions, including works by Rembrandt and Caravaggio, and a fairly comprehensive collection of Flemish works. From here arches lead through to **Domplatz**, dominated by the pale marble facade of the **Dom** – an impressively cavernous Renaissance structure put up by Archbishop Wolf Dietrich in 1628, and decorated with dazzling ceiling frescoes. The cathedral **museum** (mid-May to mid-Oct Mon–Sat 10am–5pm, Sun 1–6pm; €4.40; ⊕www.dommuseum.salzbergkirchen.net) holds a collection of artworks and curiosities assembled by seventeenth-century Archbishop Guidobaldo Thun.

At the opposite end of the Domplatz an archway leads through to the Gothic **Franziskanerkirche**, a thirteenth-century reconstruction of an eighth-century edifice that houses a fine Baroque altar by Fischer von Erlach around an earlier, Gothic Madonna and Child sculpted by the Tyrolean master Michael Pacher. The altar is enclosed by an arc of nine chapels, adorned in a frenzy of stucco ornamentation. Look out also for the twelfth-century marble lion that guards the stairway to the pulpit. Around the corner is the **Rupertinum**, Wiener-Philharmonikergasse 9 (mid-July to Sept Mon & Thurs–Sun 10am–5pm, Wed until 9pm; Oct to mid-July open Tues, closed Mon; ⊕www.rupertinum.at; €7.27), a picture gallery devoted to twentieth-century work, particularly Kirchner and other German well-knowns, which hosts touring exhibitions; it also has a secluded café. Art exhibitions often grace the cavernous interior of Fischer von Erlach's graceless **Kollegienkirche** or University Church, on the adjacent Universitätsplatz. Around the back of the church, Hofstallgasse is dominated by the modern **Festspielhaus**, a principal venue for the Salzburg festival. Northeast of here, the **Museum Carolino-Augusteum**, Museumplatz 1 (Tues–Sun 9/10am–5/6pm; ⊕www.smca.at; €3.20), contains Roman finds from the town centre, including reconstructed mosaics retrieved from beneath Mozartplatz, more Gothic religious art, and a room devoted to moralistic works by the late-nineteenth-century local painter Hans Makart. On the far side of the square, the **Haus der Natur** (daily 9am–5pm; ⊕www.hausdernatur.at; €4.50) crams in five floors of science and natural history, with exhibits ranging from live piranha fish to space rockets. From here Getreidegasse leads east back towards the centre, lined with opulent boutiques, painted facades and wrought-iron shop signs. At no. 9 is **Mozart's Geburtshaus** (daily 9am–5.30/6.30pm; ⊕www.mozarteum.at; €5.50, or €9 combined ticket with Mozart's Wohnhaus). Born here in 1756, the musical prodigy lived here till the age of 17. Now a rather overcrowded place of pilgrimage, it harbours some fascinating period instruments, including a baby-sized violin used by the composer as a child.

You can get up to the **Höhensalzburg** (daily 9am–5/6pm; €3.55; ⊕www.salzburg-burgen.at), which commands excellent views across town from Mönchberg; you can get there by funicular (daily 9am–10pm; every 10min; €6.35) from Kapitelplatz behind the cathedral, although the journey on foot isn't as hard or as time-consuming as it looks. Begun around 1070 to provide the city's then powerful archbishops with a refuge from belligerent German princes, the fortress was gradually transformed into a more salubrious courtly seat. State rooms can be visited with a CD audio guide, although a roam around the ramparts and passageways of the castle is enough to gain a feel for the place. Paths lead east from the fortress to another piece of pre-Baroque Salzburg, the **Stift Nonnberg**, whose church is a largely fifteenth-century Gothic rebuilding of an earlier Romanesque structure.

The east bank

Streets on the eastern bank of the river radiate out from **Platzl**, a small square at the foot of the **Kapuzinerberg**, named after a Capuchin monastery at the summit. It can be scaled in five minutes: the climb is rewarded with excellent views of Salzburg's domes and spires. Linzergasse heads east from Platz towards the **Sebastianskirche** and its fascinating graveyard, last resting place of the Renaissance humanist and alchemist Paracelsus and home to the mausoleum of Wolf Dietrich, tiled with an almost Islamic delicacy. Two blocks northwest of Platzl, on Makartplatz, is **Mozart's Wohnhaus**, the family home from 1773 to 1787 (daily 9am–5.30/7pm; ❽www.mozarteum.at; €5.50, or €9 combined ticket with Mozart's Geburtshaus), containing an engrossing multimedia history of the composer and his times. Fischer von Erlach's **Dreifaltigkeitskirche** or Church of the Holy Trinity stands nearby, notable for the elegant curve of its exterior and murky frescoes by Rottmayr inside. Dreifaltigkeitsgasse brings you to the **Schloss Mirabell**, on the site of a previous palace built by Wolf Dietrich for his mistress Salome, with whom the energetic prelate was rumoured to have sired a dozen children. Completely rebuilt by Lukas von Hildebrandt in the early eighteenth century, and further reconstructed after a fire in the nineteenth, it now houses local government buildings and a prestigious concert hall. Its most outstanding features are the cherub-lined staircase by Baroque master George Raphael Donner and the ornate gardens, the rose-filled high ground of the adjoining Kurgarten which offers a much-photographed view back across the city towards the Höhensalzburg.

Practicalities

Salzburg's **airport** is 5km west of town on the Innsbrucker Bundesstrasse and is linked to the city's train station by bus #77. It's 1km into town from the train station, but there are regular buses (#2, #5, #6, #51 & #55) to Ferdinand-Hanusch-Platz or Rudolfskai on the fringes of the Old Town; a 24-hr pass (*Tageskarte*) costs €2.90. There's a **tourist kiosk** at the train station (platform 2a; daily 8.30/9am–8/9pm), and a larger **tourist office** at Mozartplatz 5 (daily 9am–6/8pm; ☎0662/889 8733,; ❽www.salzburginfo.at). Both offices have accommodation details and book rooms; they also sell the Salzburg card (€18/24hr, €23.40/48hr), which gives you unlimited use of public transport and free entry to many of the sights. Panorama Tours, St Andrakirche/Mirabellplatz (☎0662/874 029, ❽www.panoramatours.com) run a number of **tours**, including what they bill as *The Original Sound of Music Tour.*

The **Salzburg Festival** (last week July & all Aug; ☎0662/840 310, ❽www.salzburgfestival.at) has been running since 1920 and is one of Europe's premier festivals of classical music, opera and theatre. Tickets are hard to come by: write to Salzburger Festspiele, Postfach 140, A-5020 Salzburg, for programme and booking details. Some standing places for the outdoor performances are available on a stand-by basis; check with the box office on Hofstallgasse (☎0662/844 5579). Numerous other classical music concerts – many of them Mozart-related – take place in Salzburg all year round. The Salzburg Ticket Service (❽www.salzburgticket.com), inside the tourist office on Mozartplatz, is the best place for information.

Of the **hostels**, most conveniently placed are the *YO-HO International Youth Hotel Obermair*, Paracelsusstrasse 9 (☎0662/87 96 49, ❽www.yoho.at; ❷), a lively place nicely poised between the train station and main sights; and the HI-affiliated *Haunspergstrasse* hostel, three blocks west of the train station at Haunspergstrasse 27 (☎0662/87 50 30, ❽www.hostel-ehh.at, ❷, midnight curfew; July & Aug). As for **hotels**, rooms fill quickly in summer and can be pricey. The *Schwarzes Rössl*, Priesterhausgasse 6 (☎0662/87 44 26; ❽www.academia-hotels.at ❸; July–Sept), is a marvellous, creaky old building in a good location; *Bergland*, Rupertgasse 15 (☎0662/87 23 18, ❽www.berglandhotel.at; ❺), is a friendly place on the right bank, 1km northeast of the centre – handy for both sightseeing and the train station. *Goldene Krone*, also on the left bank at Linzergasse 48 (☎0662/87 23 00; ❺), is an old-fashioned pension-style place with small but comfortable ensuites. *Camping Nord -Sam, Samstrasse* 22a, is the most convenient **campsite**, bus #29 from Mirabellplatz (℡0662/64 04 94, ✆www.camping-nord-sam.com; mid-May to mid-Sept).

There are plenty of outlets around the Old Town offering sandwiches and **snacks**; *Fischkrieg,* Ferdinand-Hanusch-Platz, is a renowned riverside snackbar serving up everything from fishburgers to grilled squid. Salzburg is full of elegant **cafés**; the most renowned are *Tomasselli,* Alte Markt 9, and *Bazar,* Schwarzstrasse 3, on the east bank with a nice terrace overlooking the Salzach. For more substantial eating, *Resch & Lieblich,* next to the Festspielhaus at Toscaninihof 1, offers good-value Austrian cuisine in dining rooms carved out of the cliff of the Hohensalzburg hill. *Gablerbräu,* Linzergasse 9, serves good Austrian grub and has several vegetarian options, as does *Stieglkeller,* Festungsgasse 10 (May–Sept only), which provides pleasant outdoor seating on the way up to the Burg – it's also a good place for drinking beer on warm evenings. *Sternbrau* is a massive beer garden and restaurant complex occupying two courtyards between Griesgasse and Getriedegasse. *Zur Glocke,* Schanzlgasse 2, is a smaller establishment just east of the old town with homely Austrian cooking; as has *Gasthof Alter Fuchs,* Linzergasse 47–49. There are numerous raucous night-time **drinking** venues along Rudolfskai on the left bank – *O'Malley's* and *Shamrock* are two of the best – and Giselakai opposite on the right bank. *Zwettlers Gastwirtschaft,* just off Mozartplatz at Kaigasse 3, is a relaxing pub with good food and blues music. Further afield, *Augustiner Bräu,* Augustinerstrasse 4–6, is a vast open-air courtyard fifteen minutes northeast of the centre serving huge mugs of locally brewed beer; while *Shakespeare,* Hubert-Sattler-Gasse 12, is a jazzy east-bank café/restaurant which often has themed DJ nights in the back room. **Club events** also take place in *Arge Nonntal,* also a venue for theatre and live gigs, 15 minutes' southwest of the Old Town at Mühlbacherhofweg 5.

Listings

Consulates UK Alter Markt 4 ℡0662/848133; US Alter Markt 1/3 ℡0662/848776.

Exchange Outside banking hours, try: the exchange counter at the main train station (daily 7/7.30am–8.30/9pm); Salzburger Sparkasse at the airport (daily 8am–4pm); or the exchange counter on Alte Markt (Mon–Fri 8.30am–4.30pm, Sat 9.30am–1pm; Nov–June Mon–Fri only).

Hospital Müllner Hauptstrasse 48 ℡0662/4482.

Internet access Bignet, Judengasse 5–7; Piterfun, opposite the train station at Ferdinand-Porsche-Strasse 7.

Left luggage Lockers at the main station.

Pharmacy Elisabethstrasse 1 (℡0662/871 484).

Post office Residenzplatz 9.

The Salzkammergut

The peaks of the **Salzkammergut** may not be as lofty as those further south, but the glacier-carved troughs that separate them make for some spectacular scenery. Most of the towns and villages here are modest places, quiet for much of the year until the annual summer influx of visitors. The area has plentiful private rooms and *Gasthöfe.* The natural transport and commercial hub of the region is the nineteenth-century spa town of **Bad Ischl**, 60km east of Salzburg, close by two of the most scenic Salzkammergut lakes – the **Wolfgangersee** and **Hallstättersee**. You can reach Bad Ischl by train by way of a branch line off the main Salzburg–Vienna route from Attnang-Puchheim – or from Stainach-Irdning on the Graz–Salzburg route to the south. From Salzburg, a bus is the most direct route.

St Wolfgang

Hourly buses from Salzburg to Bad Ischl run east along the southern shores of the Wolfgangersee, though they bypass the lake's main attraction, the village of **ST WOLFGANG**, on the opposite shore. Get off the bus at the village of Strobl, at the lake's eastern end, and pick up a connecting bus to the village from there. Popular with package-tourists, St Wolfgang can be crowded in summer, but you should make a point of stopping off, if only to visit the **Pfarrkirche**, just above the lake shore, which contains a high altar by Michael Pacher. An extravagantly pinnacled structure measuring some 12m high, the altar was probably built with the help of the artist's brother Friedrich and was completed sometime between 1471 and 1481 in Pacher's home town of Bruneck before being carted over the Alps to St Wolfgang. Brightly gilded, sculpted scenes of the *Coronation of the Virgin* form the altar's centrepiece, while the outer panels of the altar wings depict scenes from the Life of St Wolfgang. From Ash Wednesday to the day before Palm Sunday the wings are opened further to allow a glimpse of the eight richly coloured paintings from the Life of Christ. Ascents of the local peak, the **Schafberg**, by mountain railway (May–Oct; €19 return; InterRail/Eurail concessions), are possible from a station on the western edge of town.

There are two **tourist offices**: the chief one is at the eastern entrance to the tunnel (Mon–Fri 9am–8pm, Sat 9am–noon & 2–8pm, Sun 2–8pm; ☎06138/2239, ⬤www .salzkammergut.at/wolfgangsee), the other at the western end of the tunnel in the Michael-Pacher-Haus (Mon–Fri 9am–noon & 2–5pm); both can arrange **accommodation**.

Bad Ischl

The elegant town houses, fountains and gardens of **BAD ISCHL** have an air of bourgeois repose. The soothing properties of the waters here prompted the penultimate Habsburg emperor, Franz Josef, to summer here in the **Kaiservilla** (April Sat & Sun 9–11.45am & 1–5.15pm; May to mid-Oct daily same times; €9.50; park only €3), across the River Ischl from the centre. Beyond the villa (which is crammed with victims of the emperor's hunting expeditions) stretches a park containing the **Marmorschlössel** (April–Oct daily 9.30am–5pm; €1.50), an exquisite neo-Gothic garden retreat built for the Empress Elizabeth; it now houses a small museum of photography.

Both the **bus** and **train stations** are on the eastern fringe of the town centre, a few steps away from the **tourist office**, at Bahnhofstrasse 6 (Mon–Fri 9am–7pm, Sat 9am–3pm, Sun 10am–1pm; ☎06132/27757, ⬤www.badischl.at), who will direct you to the town's numerous **private rooms**. There's a modern, functional **HI hostel** near the swimming pool at Am Rechensteg 5 (☎06132/26577, ✉jgh.badischl@oejhv.or.at; ❸); and a clean and comfy **pension**, *Eglmoos*, at Eglmoosgasse 14 (☎06132/23154; ❸). **Internet** access is at the main post office, not far from the tourist office.

Hallstatt

The real jewel of the Salzkammergut is the UNESCO World Heritage Site of **HALLSTATT**, occupying a dramatic position 20km south of Bad Ischl on the western shores of Hallstättersee, jutting out into the lake at the base of a precipitous cliff. Before the building of the road along the western side of the lake, local transport was provided by a sharp-prowed boat known as a *Fuhr*, propelled by a single paddle at the stern, rather like a punt; a few still ply the lake, emerging from the characteristic wooden boathouses that line the shore.

Hallstatt gave its name to a distinct period of Iron Age culture after Celtic remains were discovered in the salt mines above the town. Many of the finds which made the town famous date back to the ninth century BC, and can now be seen in the **World Heritage Hallstatt Museum** (April–Oct daily 9am–6/7pm; Nov–March Tues–Sun 10am–4pm; €6; ⬤www.museum-hallstatt.at); they include wooden mining implements, pit props and hide rucksacks used by Iron Age miners, alongside more ornamental objects such as jewellery and ornate dagger handles. It is also full of the natural historical and anthropological collections of Friedrich Morton, the archeologist who worked on the sites in the 1930s. Tableaux on the history of salt mining illustrate working conditions through the centuries.

Hallstatt's **Pfarrkirche**, uphill from the water's edge, has a south portal adorned with Calvary scenes painted around 1500. Inside, the most interesting of the winged altars is the late-Gothic one on the right, with its heavily gilded statuettes of the Madonna and Child flanked by St Catherine (the patron of woodcutters, on the left) and St Barbara (the patron of miners); high relief scenes from the lives of Mary and Christ are depicted on the wings. In the graveyard outside stands a small stone structure known as the **Beinhaus** (daily 10am–6pm; €1), traditionally the repository for the skulls of villagers, with their bones neatly stacked below like fire-wood. The skulls, some of them quite recent, are inscribed with the names of the deceased and dates of their death, and are often decorated with finely painted floral patterns. Steep paths behind the graveyard lead up to a highland valley, the Salzachtal, where the **salt mines** that provided the area's prosperity can be viewed only on a guided tour (daily: May to Oct 9.30am–3/4.30pm; €14). You can also take the **funicular** (€7.50 return) up here from the nearby suburb of Lahn.

Hallstatt's **train station** is on the opposite side of the lake to the town, a local ferry meeting all incoming trains. However, after 6pm trains don't stop here and instead continue on to the village of Obertraun, 5km away along the shores of the lake. Hallstatt's **tourist office** is centrally located at Postfach 7 (July & Aug Mon–Fri 9am–6pm, Sat 10am–2pm, Sun 10am–2pm; Sept–June Mon–Fri 9am–noon & 1–5pm; ☎06134/8208, ⊛www.hallstatt.net) and can arrange **accommodation** in private rooms or guest houses. *Gasthaus zur Mühle*, set back from the landing stage at Kirchenweg 36 (☎06134/8318; ❷), has dorm beds, as well as some doubles. *Bräugasthof*, Seestrasse 120, is a very pleasant **place to eat** with a lakeside terrace and a competitively priced range of fresh fish.

Western Austria

West of Salzburg towards the mountain province of the **Tirol**, the grandiose scenery of Austria's Alpine heartland begins to unfold in earnest. Most of the trains from Vienna and Salzburg travel through a corner of Bavaria before joining the Inn valley and climbing back into Austria to the Tirolean capital, **Innsbruck**. A less direct but more scenic route (and one you will be more likely to follow if coming from Graz and the southeast) cuts between the Kitzbühler Alpen and the majestic **Hoher Tauern** (site of Austria's highest peak, the Grossglockner), before joining the River Inn at Wörgl. Settlements such as the exclusive resort-town of **Kitzbühel** provide potential stopoffs on the way, although it's Innsbruck that offers the most convenient mix of urban sights and Alpine splendour. Further west towards Switzerland, **Bregenz**, on the shores of Lake Constance, makes for a tranquil stop before pressing on.

Innsbruck

Located high in the Alps, with ski resorts within easy reach, **INNSBRUCK** is as rich in history as any other Austrian city: Maximilian I based the imperial court here in the 1490s, suddenly placing this provincial Alpine town at the heart of European politics and culture. It remained an imperial residence for a century and a half, so it's perhaps not surprising that its incorporation into Bavaria (a move precipitated by the Napoleonic carve-up of Europe) produced an insurrectionary movement under the local hero after whom so many streets and squares are named – Andreas Hofer.

Most of what you will want to see in Innsbruck is confined to the central precincts of the **Altstadt**, a small area bounded by the river and the Graben, following the course of the moat, which used to surround the medieval town. Leading up to this, Innsbruck's main artery is **Maria-Theresien-Strasse**, famed for the view north towards the great rock wall of the Nordkette, the mountain that dominates the city. At its southern end, three blocks west of the train station down Salurnerstrasse, the triumphal arch, **Triumphpforte**, was built in advance of celebrations marking the marriage of Maria Theresia's son Leopold in 1756. Halfway along, the **Annasäule**, a column supporting a statue of the Virgin, but named after St Anne, who appears at the base, was erected to commemorate the retreat of the Bavarians, who had been menacing the Tirol, on St Anne's day (July 26), 1703.

North of here, Herzog-Friedrich-Strasse leads into the centre, opening out into a plaza lined with arcaded medieval buildings. Commanding attention at the plaza's southern end is the **Goldenes Dachl**, or golden roof (though the tiles which give the roof its name are actually copper), built in the 1490s to cover an oriel window from which the court of Kaiser Maximilian could observe the square below. Inside is the **Maximilianeum** (May–Oct: daily 10am–6pm; Nov–April Tues–Sun 10am–12.30pm & 2–5pm; @www.tiroler-landesmuseum.at; €3.63), a flashy and insubstantial museum of Maximilian's life and times, although it does include an entertaining video-style documentary about the man in English. An alley to the right leads down to Domplatz and the **Domkirche St Jakob**, home to a valuable *Madonna and Child* by German master Lucas Cranach the Elder, although it is buried in the fussy Baroque detail of the altar. The adjacent **Hofburg**, entered from Rennweg, at the end of Hofgasse around the corner, has late-medieval roots but was remodelled in the eighteenth century, its Rococo state apartments crammed with imperial portraits and opulent furniture (daily 10am–5pm; €5.45; @www.tirol.com/hofburg-ibk).

At the head of the Rennweg is the **Hofkirche**, an outwardly unassuming building which nevertheless contains the most impressive of Innsbruck's imperial monuments, the **Cenotaph of Emperor Maximilian** (Mon–Sat 9/10am–5/5.30pm; €2.20; combined ticket with Tiroler Volkskunstmuseum €4.35). This extraordinary project was originally envisaged as a series of 40 larger-than-life statues, 100 statuettes and 32 busts of Roman emperors, representing both the real and the spiritual ancestors of Maximilian, but in the end only 32 of the statuettes and 20 of the busts were completed. The resulting ensemble is still impressive, though the effect is dulled slightly by the knowledge that the emperor is actually buried at the other end of Austria in Wiener Neustadt. Upstairs is the Silberkapelle or silver chapel, named after the silver Madonna that adorns the far wall. The chapel was built by sixteenth-century Archduke Ferdinand II (one of Maximilian's grandsons) in honour of his beloved first wife Philippine Welser – whose grave, and relief, lies against one wall.

Entrance to the Hofkirche is through the same door as the **Tiroler Volkskunstmuseum** (Mon–Sat 9am–5pm, Sun 9am–noon; @www.volkunstmuseum .cnt.at; €4.35; price includes entrance to the Hofkirche), which features wonderful recreations of traditional wood-panelled Tirolean peasant interiors and models of Tirolean village architecture. The **Tiroler Landesmuseum Ferdinandeum**, a short walk south at Museumstrasse 15 (May–Sept: daily 10am–5pm; Oct–April Tues–Sat 10am–noon & 2–5pm, Sun 9am–noon; €4.38; @www.tiroler-landesmuseum.at), contains one of the best collections of Gothic paintings in the country. Most originate from the churches of the South Tirol (now Alto-Adige in Italy), although some are by the "Pustertal painters" based around Bruneck (now Brunico in Italy) in the East Tirol, pre-eminent among whom were Michael and Friedrich Pacher, who imported Italian Renaissance techniques into German painting and sculpture.

Also worth a visit is **Schloss Ambras** (April–Oct daily 10am–5pm; Nov–March closed Tues; €7.50; @www.khm.at/ambras), 2km southeast of the centre and accessible by tram #6. It was the home of the above-mentioned **Archduke Ferdinand** of Tirol and still houses his cabinet of curiosities, a wondrously wide-ranging collection of artworks and objects from around the globe.

The quickest route to higher altitudes is the **Hungerburgbahn** (daily 8/8.30am–5/6pm; €4.02 return), which leaves from a station at the end of Rennweg (end of tram lines #1 and #6), calling at an intermediate station for the **Alpenzoo** (daily 9am–5/6pm; €5.10; @www.alpenzoo.at) before reaching the

Hungerburg plateau itself, a good base for hikes. A three-stage sequence of cable cars continues from here to just below the summit of the **Nordkette**, where you can enjoy stupendous views of the high alps to the south.

Practicalities

The **tourist kiosk** in the forecourt of Innsbruck's **train station** (daily: June–Sept 8am–10pm, Oct–May 9am–9pm) offers a speedy room-booking service for a small fee and a refundable deposit. The main **tourist office** is at Burggraben 3 (daily 9am–6pm, Sun 9am–6pm; ☎0512/583 766, ⊛www.innsbruck-tourismus.com). Both offices sell the "Innsbruck Card" (€19/24hr; €24/48hr), which allows free travel in the centre and entry to all the sights.

Best of the **hostels** is the HI-affiliated *Jugendherberge Innsbruck*, 4km east of the centre at Reichenauerstrasse 147 (☎0512/346179, ⊛www.youth-hostel-innsbruck .at; ❸), which has both dorm rooms and en-suite doubles – bus O from Museumstrasse trundles past. Other options include: *Paula*, Weiherburggasse 15 (☎0512/29 22 62; ⊛www.pensionpaula.at; ❹), a friendly **pension** with fine views across the city from a hillside spot north of the Inn; the *Gasthof Innrain*, Innrain 38 (☎0512/58 89 81; ⊛www.gasthof-innrain.com; ❹), a small *Gasthof* on the south bank of the river; and *Hotel-Pension Binder*, Dr-Glatz-Strasse 20 (☎0512/33 43 6, ⊛www .info.hotelbinder.at; ❹), clean and friendly, in a suburban street twenty minutes south of the centre. The only **campsite** is *Innsbruck Kranebitten*, Kranebitnner Allee 214, 5km west of the city centre (☎0512/28 41 80, ⓔcampinnsbruck@hotmail.com; closed Nov–March); take bus #LK from Boznerplatz, a block west of the station.

The streets around the Goldenes Dachl are a good source of **places to eat**, packed with old coaching inns transformed into restaurants; one of the more atmospheric is the *Ottoburg* at Herzog-Friedrich-Strasse 1, with solid Austrian fare and at least one **vegetarian** main dish. Other central options include: *Stiftskeller*, Stiftgasse 1, offering a good choice of fresh fish; and *La Cucina*, Museumstrasse 26, with a wide range of reasonably priced pizza and pasta. *Philippine*, ten minutes south of the centre at Müllerstrasse 9, is an eccentrically decorated restaurant with plenty of vegetarian dishes. There are plenty of convivial **drinking venues** in Innsbruck's old town, many of which also do decent food: *Café Central*, Gilmstrasse 5, is a venerable old coffeehouse serving up excellent pastries and cakes as well as decent breakfasts; while *Elferhaus*, on Herzog-Friedrich-Strasse, is a perennially popular beer bar that also does decent pub grub. *Prometheus*, Hofgasse 2, has an intimate student bar upstairs and a disco in the cellar; while *Weli*, under the railway arches just east of the centre at Viaduktbogen 26, is an informal café/bar with good food. *Innkeller*, on the other side of the river at Innstrasse 1, is another popular late-night haunt. *Treibhaus*, Angerzellgasse 8, is the place to look for live jazz, folk and alternative theatre.

Listings

Consulates UK, Kaiserjaeger Strasse 2 ☎0512/58 83 20.
Exchange Outside banking hours, try the tourist office, Burggraben 3.
Hospital Universitätklinik, Anichstrasse 35 ☎0512/50 40.

Internet access Café-bar Piccolo, Maria-Theresien-Strasse 16; and internet Café, Brunecker Strasse 12, opposite the train station. Also, at the tourist office.
Post office Maximilianstrasse 2.

Bregenz

Stretched along the southern shores of Lake Constance, **BREGENZ** is an obvious staging post on journeys into neighbouring Bavaria, Liechtenstein and Switzerland. The Vorarlbergers who live here speak a dialect close to Swiss German, and have always considered themselves separate from the rest of Austria. In November 1918 they declared independence and requested union with Switzerland, but this was denied by the Great Powers.

At first sight Bregenz is curiously disjointed, the tranquil lakeside parks cut off from town by the main road and rail links along the shore of Lake Constance. Most points of interest are located in the old town, up the hill from the lake, around **St Martinsturm**, an early seventeenth-century tower crowned by a bulbous wooden dome. The small **Militarmuseum** inside (May–Sept Tues–Sun 9am–6pm; €1) contains arms and armour, and views down towards the lake. Up the street from here is the seventeenth-century **town hall**, an immense half-timbered construction with a steeply inclined roof. Down in the modern town nearest the lake on Kornmarkt, the **Kunsthaus Bregenz** (Tues–Sun 10am–6pm, Thurs till 9pm; €3.50; ⍟www.kunsthaus-bregenz.at) is a coolly modernist green cube that hosts high-profile modern art exhibitions. The **Vorarlberger Landesmuseum**, Kornmarkt 1 (Tues–Sun 9am–noon & 2–5pm; €1.50; ⍟www.vlm.at), has some outstanding paintings by sixteenth-century artists like Wolf Huber and Jörg Frosch and a selection of portraits and Classical scenes by Angelika Kauffmann, the Vorarlberg painter who achieved success in late eighteenth-century London. Beyond here, leafy **parklands** line the lake, at the western end of which stands the **Festspielhaus**, a modern concert hall built to accommodate the operatic and orchestral concerts of the Bregenz Festival (usually last week in July to mid-Aug; ☏%05574/4076, ⍟www.festspiele.com). The most popular excursion from Bregenz, however, is by cable car from a station at the eastern end of town to the **Pfänder** (daily 9am–7pm; €9.50; ⍟www.pfaenderbahn.at), a wooded hill commanding an excellent panorama of the lake. An alternative route is via the Pfänderweg, a worthwhile hour-and-a-half walk that takes you to the top through the wooded hillside.

Practicalities

The **tourist office**, Bahnhofstrasse 14 (July–Sept Mon–Sat 9am–7pm; Oct–June Mon–Fri 9am–6pm, Sat 9am–noon; ☏05574/49590), can book **rooms**. *Gästehaus Tannenbach*, im Gehren 1 (t%05574/44174; closed Oct–April; ❹), is the friendliest of the smaller pensions, in a quiet street east of the centre; *Pension Sonne*, Kaiserstrasse 8 (☏05574/642572, ⍟www.bregenz.at/sonne; ❹), is the best of the budget hotels in the central. The HI **hostel** west of the train station at Mehrerauerstrasse 5 (☏05574/42867, ⍟www.jgh.at; ❷) offers dorms as well as swanky doubles; while *Seecamping*, Bodengasse 7, is a large **campsite** by the lake, 2km west of town. *Günz*, Anton-Schneider-Strasse 38, is one of the cheapest sources of traditional Austrian **food** in town; *Zum Goldener Hirschen*, Kirchstrasse 8, is a more atmospheric, pub-like venue with slightly more expensive eats. Best of the central **bars** are *1 Akt*, Kornmarktstrasse 24, and the stylish but cosy *Flexibel*, Rathausgasse 27. *S'logo*, at Kirchstrasse 47 is an **internet** café.

Travel details

Trains

Vienna to: Bregenz (8 daily; 10hr); Graz (every 2hr; 2hr 40min); Innsbruck (every 2hr; 5hr 20min); Linz (1–2 daily; 2hr); Krems (hourly; 1hr 15min); Melk (every 1–2hr; 1hr); Salzburg (every 1–2hr; 3hr 20min).
Bad Ischl to: St Wolfgang (hourly; 40min).
Graz to: Innsbruck (7 daily; 6hr); Linz (every 2hr; 3hr 30min); Salzburg (8 daily; 4hr 30min).
Innsbruck to: Bregenz (10 daily; 3hr).

Salzburg to: Innsbruck (8 daily; 2hr 30min); Linz (hourly; 1hr 20min).

Buses

Bad Ischl to: Hallstatt (5–7 daily; 40min); Salzburg (hourly; 1hr 40min); St Wolfgang (hourly; 45min).
Krems to: Melk (3–4 daily; 1hr).
Linz to: St Florian (Mon–Fri every 2hr; 35min).
Salzburg to: Bad Ischl (hourly; 1hr 30min).

Belgium and Luxembourg

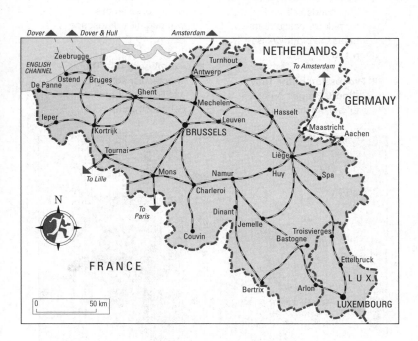

Belgium and Luxembourg highlights

✳ Grand-Place, Brussels
Wonderfully preserved, with beautiful guildhouses, in the heart of the city. See p.103

✳ Het Gravensteen, Ghent
This handsome and formidable castle dominates the old town. See p.113

✳ Procession of the Holy Blood, Bruges A colourful but solemn religious procession each Ascension Day. See p.118

✳ Canoeing in the Ardennes Great opportunities, mostly along the River Lesse, in this wooded, hilly landscape. See p.119

✳ Luxembourg City The spectacular setting alone justifies a visit to this tiny capital city. See p.121

Introduction and basics

A **federal country**, with three official languages and an intense regional rivalry, Belgium has a cultural diversity that belies its rather dull reputation. Its population of around ten million is divided between Flemish-speakers (about sixty percent) and French-speaking Walloons (forty percent), with a few pockets of German-speakers in the east. Prosperity has shifted back and forth between the two leading communities over the centuries, and relations have long been acrimonious. The constitution was redrawn in 1980 on a federal basis, with three separate entities: the Flemish North, Walloon South, and Brussels, which is officially bilingual (although its population is eighty percent French-speaking).

The north and south of **Belgium** are visually very different. Marking the meeting of the two, **Brussels**, the capital, is a culturally varied city at the heart of the European Union. The **north**, made up of the provinces of West and East Flanders, Antwerp, Limburg and much of Brabant, is mainly flat, with a landscape and architecture not unlike Holland. **Antwerp** is the second city, a bustling old port with doses of high art, redolent of its sixteenth-century golden age. Further west lie the great historic cities, **Bruges** and **Ghent**, with a stunning concentration of Flemish art and architecture. By contrast, Belgium's most scenically rewarding region, the **Ardennes**, an area of deep, wooded valleys, high elevations and dark caverns, sprawls across the south of the country with the attractive town of **Namur** the obvious gateway.

The Ardennes reach across the border into the northern part of the **Grand Duchy of Luxembourg**, a verdant landscape of rushing rivers and high hills topped with crumbling castles. The best base for rural expeditions is **Luxembourg City**, a pleasant town with a splendid rugged setting. The city has a population of around 80,000, which makes it one of the continent's smallest capitals.

Information and maps

In both Belgium and Luxembourg there are **tourist offices** in all but the smallest of villages. They usually provide free local maps, and in the larger towns offer a free accommodation-booking service too (see p.9). The best general **map** is the clear and easy-to-use Baedeker & AA Belgium and Luxembourg (1:250,000) map.

Money and banks

Belgium and Luxembourg are two of the twelve European Union countries who have switched over to the (€). **Banks** are the best places to change money and are generally open Mon–Fri 9am–4/4.30pm in both countries, though some have a one-hour lunch break between noon and 2pm. **ATMs** are commonplace in all the cities and larger towns.

Communications

Post offices are open Mon–Fri 9am–noon & 1.30/2–4/5pm. Some open Saturday mornings, too. Many public **phones** only take

---

Belgium and Luxembourg on the net

ⓦ **www.artsite.be** Details of Belgium's best-known art galleries and museums.
ⓦ **www.belgique-tourisme.net** Information on Brussels and southern Belgium.
ⓦ **www.luxembourg.co.uk** Official site of the Luxembourg Ministry of Tourism.
ⓦ **www.visitflanders.com** Information on Brussels and the Flanders region.

phonecards, which are available from newsagents and post offices. There are no area codes in either country. The international operator numbers are ☎ 1324 in Belgium, ☎ 0010 in Luxembourg. **Mobile phone** coverage is good and visitors can pick up a signal in all but the remotest spots. **Internet** access is increasingly widespread with at least one or two internet cafés in all the larger cities, though you will be struggling out in the countryside; libraries are often a good bet where all else fails.

Getting around

Travelling around Belgium is rarely a problem. Distances are short, and an efficient, reasonably priced train service links all the major centres. Luxembourg, on the other hand, can be problematic: the train network is not extensive and bus timetables demand careful study.

Trains and buses

Operated by SNCB, **Belgium's rail system** is comprehensive and efficient, and fares are comparatively low. InterRail and Eurail passes are valid throughout the network, as are a number of other regional passes – see p.21 for further details. SNCB also publish information on their various offers and services in their comprehensive **timetable book**, which has an English-language section and is available at major train stations. As so much of Belgium is covered by the rail network, **buses** are only really used for travelling short distances, or in parts of the Ardennes where rail lines are thin on the ground.

Luxembourg's railways are run by CFL. There's one main north–south route down the middle of the country with Luxembourg City as the hub and a handful of branch lines fanning out from the capital, but most of the country can only be reached by **bus**. Fares are comparable with those in Belgium, and there are a number of passes available, giving unlimited train and bus travel (see p.30).

Cycling

The modest distances and flat terrain make **cycling in Belgium** a fairly effortless way of getting around. Cycling in most big cities and on the majority of trunk roads, however, can be precarious, but once you've reached the countryside, there are dozens of clearly signposted routes to follow. You can take your own bike on a train (€4.50/journey), or rent one from one of around thirty train stations during the summer (around €8.80/day); note that some train excursion tickets include the cost of **bike rental**. For a list of train stations offering bike rental, get a copy of Belgian Railways' Train & Vélo leaflet.

In **Luxembourg** you can rent bikes for around €10 a day, and take your own bike on trains for €1.50 per journey. The Luxembourg Tourist Office has leaflets showing cycle routes and also sells cycling guides.

Accommodation

Inevitably, **hotel accommodation** is one of the major expenses you will incur on a trip to Belgium or Luxembourg – indeed, if you're after a degree of comfort, it's going to be the costliest item by far. There are, however, budget alternatives, principally the no-frills end of the hotel market, **private rooms** arranged via the local tourist office and **hostels**.

Hotels and private rooms

In both countries prices range from around €40–50 for a double room in the cheapest one-star **hotel** to €100 in big city hotels – much more if you go for somewhere luxurious. Breakfast is normally (but not always) included in the room rate. During the summer you'd be well advised to book ahead. Hotel **reservations** can be made for free through most tourist offices on the day itself – the deposit they require is subtracted from your final hotel bill.

Private rooms can be booked through local tourist offices too. Expect to pay €25–35 a night for a double, but be aware that they are often inconveniently situated on the outskirts of cities and towns. An exception is in Bruges, where rooms can be booked direct and many are in the city centre.

Hostels and student rooms

Belgium has more than thirty **HI hostels**, run by two separate organizations: In Flanders, Vlaamse Jeugdherbergcentrale, Van Stralenstraat 40, B-2060 Antwerp ☎032 32 72 18, ⓦwww.vjh.be, in Wallonia, Les Auberges de Jeunesse de Wallonie, rue de la Sablonnière 28, B-1000 Brussels ☎022 19 56 76, ⓦwww.laj.be. Most charge a flat rate per person of around €12 for members, otherwise €15, breakfast included; many also offer meals for €5.00–7.50. During the summer you should book ahead wherever possible.

Some of the larger cities – Bruges, Antwerp and Brussels, for example – have a number of **privately run hostels**. These normally charge about €12.50 for a dorm bed and are often just as comfortable as their HI counterparts. You'll also find some universities offering **student rooms** for rent during the summer vacation, Ghent being a good example. Rooms are basic but rates are reasonable – reckon on about €15 per person per night.

There are fourteen **HI hostels in Luxembourg**, all of which are members of the Centrale des Auberges de Jeunesse Luxembourgeoises (CAJL), place de la Gare 24, Galerie Kons, L-1616 Luxembourg ☎26 29 35 00, ⓦwww.youthhostels.lu. Rates for HI members are €14–16 per person (non-members can expect to pay a further €3–5). Breakfast is always included; lunch or dinner is an extra €5–8.

Camping

Camping is a popular pastime in both Belgium and Luxembourg, but many sites are located with the motorist in mind. There are around five hundred sites **in Belgium**, most of them well-equipped and listed in the Belgian Tourist Office's Camping leaflet, broadly classified on a one- to five-star basis. The vast majority are one-star establishments, for which two adults plus tent can expect to pay €10–15 per night; surprisingly most four-star sites rarely cost much more – add about €3.50 – though the occasional five-star campsite is more like a recreation park and here the price can reach around €45.

Luxembourg has a little over one hundred campsites, all detailed in the free booklet available from the national tourist board. They are classified into three broad bands. The majority are in Category 1, the best-equipped and most expensive classification. Prices vary considerably, even within each category, but are usually €1.50–€3.50 per person, plus €3–5 for a site.

In both countries, it can be a good idea to **reserve ahead** during peak season; phone numbers are listed in the free camping booklets, and in Luxembourg the national tourist board will gladly make a campsite reservation on your behalf (☎42 82 82 10).

Food and drink

Belgian cuisine is held in high regard, second only to French; the country also offers a wide range of ethnic food. Luxembourg's food is less varied and more Germanic – but you can still eat out extremely well. As for drink, **beer** is one of the real delights of Belgium, and Luxembourg produces some very drinkable white **wines** along its side of the River Moselle.

Food

Southern Belgian cuisine is not unlike traditional French, retaining its neighbour's fondness for rich sauces and ingredients. In **Flanders** the food is more akin to that of Holland, with many interesting traditional dishes. Pork, beef, game, fish and seafood, especially mussels, are staple items, often cooked with butter, cream and herbs, or sometimes beer. Soups, too, are common: hearty affairs, especially in the south and the **Ardennes**, a region also renowned for its smoked ham and pâté.

In both countries, many **bars** offer inexpensive meals, at least at lunchtimes, and a host of **cafés** serve basic dishes – omelettes, steak or mussels with chips (virtually the Belgian national dish). The distinction between the two is, however, becoming increasingly blurred with **café/bars** often the most fashionable place to be, especially in the city. Most places have a dish of the day for €10–12. **Restaurants** are almost always more expensive, but the food they offer is almost always excellent. A main course will rarely cost under €9.50, with €15 being a more usual price.

Belgium is also renowned for its **chocolate**. The big Belgian chocolatiers, Godiva and Leonidas, have shops in all the main towns and cities, and their pralines and truffles are almost worth the trip alone. Of the two, Leonidas is the cheaper; reckon on spending €15 or so for 500g of their chocolates.

Drink

Drinking **beer in Belgium** is a real treat. The most common brands are Stella Artois, Jupiler and Maes, but this merely scrapes the surface. There are several hundred **speciality beers**, usually served by the bottle but occasionally on draught, from dark stouts to fruit beers, wheat beers and brown ales – something to suit any palate and enough to swamp the hardiest liver. The most famous are probably the strong ales brewed by the country's five Trappist monasteries, the most widely available being Chimay. **Luxembourg** doesn't really compete, but it's three most popular brews – Diekirch, Mousel and Bofferding – are pleasant enough lagers. Bar prices don't vary greatly: in both countries you'll pay around €1.50 for a glass of beer and from €3.50 for a bottle.

French **wines** are the most commonly available, although Luxembourg is a wine producer, and its white and sparkling wines, produced along the north bank of the Moselle, are very drinkable: in the shops they go for around €6–9 a bottle of sparkling stuff, €6 for ordinary white wine. In restaurants they'll cost two or three times as much.

There's no national Belgian **spirit**, but all the usual brands are widely available. You will also find Dutch-style **jenever** in most bars in the north. In Luxembourg spirits are cheaper than elsewhere in northern Europe. You'll also come across home-produced **eau de vie**, distilled from various fruits and around fifty percent alcohol by volume.

Opening hours and holidays

In both countries, the weekend fades painlessly into the week with some shops staying closed till late on Monday morning, even in major cities. Nonetheless, normal **shopping hours** are Mon–Sat 9/10am–6/7pm; most supermarkets stay open till 8/9pm on Fri and many smaller places shut early on Sat. In the big cities, a smattering of convenience stores (*magasins de nuit/avondwinkels*) stay open either all night or until around 1/2am daily, and some souvenir shops open late or on Sun too. At the other extreme, some shops close for a half-day (Wed or Thurs am), though this tradition has died out in all but the smaller towns and villages.

Shops, banks and many museums are closed on the following **public holidays**: Jan 1; Easter Mon; May 1; Ascension Day (40 days after Easter); Whit Mon; Assumption (mid-Aug); Nov 1; Nov 11 (Belgium only); & Dec 25. In addition, the Luxembourg national day is June 23, Belgium's is July 21.

Emergencies

Belgium and Luxembourg are relatively free of street crime and you shouldn't have much cause to come into contact with the **police**. As far as **personal safety** goes, it's fairly safe to walk anywhere in the centres of the larger cities at any time of day, though the rougher neighbourhoods of all the big cities – primarily Brussels and Antwerp – are still best avoided, especially after dark. If you are unlucky enough to have something stolen, report it immediately to the nearest police station and get a report number, or better

Emergency Numbers

Belgium
Ambulance & Fire ☏100; Police ☏ 101.

Luxembourg
Ambulance & Fire ☏112; Police ☏113.

still a copy of the statement itself, for your insurance claim when you get home.

With regard to **medical emergencies**, if you're reliant on free treatment within the EU health scheme, try to remember to make this clear to the ambulance staff, and, if you're whisked off to hospital, to the medic you subsequently encounter. If you are British, it's a good idea to hand over a photocopy of your E111 on arrival at hospital to ensure your non-private status is clearly understood. In terms of describing symptoms, you can anticipate that someone will speak English in Flemish Belgium and in Brussels and Luxembourg, though in parts of Wallonia you'll be struggling unless you have some rudimentary grasp of French.

Outside normal working hours, all **pharmacies** are expected to display a list of open alternatives on their windows. Weekend rotas are also listed in local newspapers.

Brussels

Wherever else you go in Belgium, it's likely that at some point you'll wind up in **BRUSSELS**. The city is the major gateway for flights into the country; it's on the main road routes heading inland from the Channel ports via the Flemish art towns; Eurostar trains arrive here direct from London via the Channel Tunnel; and, in addition, it's a convenient stopover on the train between France and the Netherlands.

Brussels takes its name from Broekzele, or "village of the marsh", which grew up in the sixth century on the trade route between Cologne and the towns of Bruges and Ghent. Under the Habsburgs, the town flourished, eventually becoming capital of the Spanish Netherlands. In the nineteenth century it became the capital of the newly independent Belgium, and was kitted out with all the attributes of a modern European capital. Since World War II, the city's appointment as headquarters of both NATO and the EU has instigated many major development projects, not least a metro system.

It's true that Brussels has a reputation as a dull centre of commerce and bureaucracy, but this is thoroughly unfair. Brussels has architecture and museums to rank with the best of Europe, a well-preserved medieval centre and an energetic nightlife. It's also very much an international city with European civil servants and business folk, plus immigrants from Africa, Turkey and the Mediterranean, making up a quarter of the population.

Arrival and information

Brussels has three main **train stations** – Bruxelles-Nord, Bruxelles-Centrale and Bruxelles-Midi, each a few minutes apart; almost all **domestic** trains stop at all three. The majority of **international** services only stop at Bruxelles-Midi, including Eurostar trains and Thalys express trains from Amsterdam, Paris, Cologne and Aachen.

Bruxelles-Centrale is, as its name suggests, the most central of the city's three main stations, a five-minute walk from the Grand-Place; **Bruxelles-Nord** lies in the business area just north of the main ring road; and **Bruxelles-Midi** is south of the city centre. To transfer from one of the three main stations to another, simply jump on the next available mainline train. Eurolines **buses** arrive at the Gare du Nord complex. The **airport** is in Zaventem – 13km northeast of the city centre – and from here there are three trains an hour to the city's three main train stations (30min; €2.40).

There are two **tourist offices** in the city centre. The main one is the **BI-TC**, on the Grand-Place (May–Sept daily 9am–6pm; March, April & Oct–Dec closes 2pm on Sun; Jan & Feb closed all Sun; ☎025 13 89 40, ⊛www.tib.be). They have oodles of information on the city. The **Belgian tourist information centre**, nearby at rue du Marché aux Herbes 63 (Mon–Fri 9am–6/7pm, Sat & Sun 9am–1pm & 2–6/7pm; Nov–April closed Sun pm; ☎025 04 03 90), has information on the rest of Belgium.

Language

In Brussels, the **languages** of the French- and Flemish-speaking communities have parity. This means that every instance of the written word, from road signs to the yellow pages, has by law to appear in both languages. Visitors soon adjust, but on arrival this can be confusing, especially in the names of the city's three main train stations: Bruxelles-Nord (in Flemish it's Brussel-Noord), Bruxelles-Centrale (Brussel-Centraal), and, bewilderingly, Bruxelles-Midi (Brussel-Zuid). Note that for simplicity we've used the French version of street names, sights, etc in this account.

City transport

The easiest way to get around central Brussels is to **walk**, but to reach some of the more widely dispersed attractions you'll need to use **public transport**. Operated by STIB (☎025 15 20 00, ⓦwww.stib.be), the system runs on a mixture of bus, tram, premetro (underground tram) and metro lines and covers the city comprehensively. A single flat-fare **ticket** costs €1.40, a strip of five €6, and a strip of ten

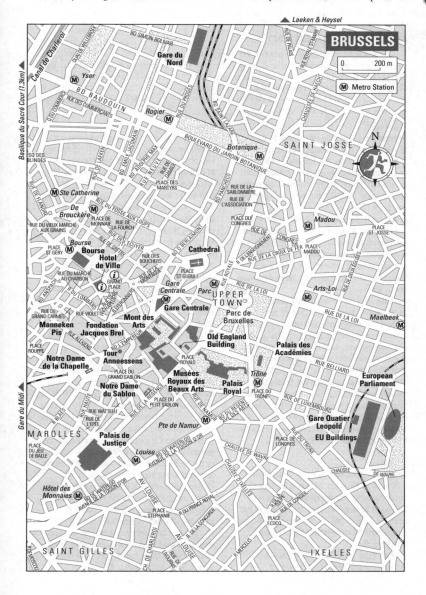

▲ Laeken & Heysel

BRUSSELS

0   200 m

Ⓜ Metro Station

€9 – all available from tram and bus drivers, metro kiosks and ticket machines, STIB information offices in the Port de Namur, Midi and Rogier stations, and some newsagents. A **day-pass**, allowing unlimited travel on public transport for 24hr, costs €3.60. Spot fines for fare-dodging are heavy. Services run from 6am until midnight; route maps are available free from the tourist office and from STIB information kiosks. **Taxis** can be picked up from ranks around the city – notably on Bourse and place De Brouckère. To book, phone Taxis Verts (☏023 49 49 49) or Taxis Orange (☏023 49 43 43).

Accommodation

Brussels has no shortage of **places to stay**, but given the number of visitors, finding a room can be hard, particularly in summer, and it's best to book ahead at least for your first night. Staying in a hotel on or around the narrow lanes near the Grand-Place is an attractive and central option. The tourist office and Bed & Brussels, rue Kindermans 5, 1050 Brussels (☏026 46 07 37, ⓦwww.BnB-brussels.be), provide reservation services.

Hostels

Bruegel rue du Saint Esprit 2 ☏025 11 04 36, ⓦwww.vjh.be. This HI hostel, housed in a smart and modern building, has 135 beds. It's fairly central and a basic breakfast is included. Dorms sleep six to twelve, double and quadruple rooms also available. Curfew 1am. Métro Gare Centrale. Dorms ❷

CHAB rue Traversière 8 ☏022 17 01 58, ⓦwww.ping.be/chab. A rambling, spacious hostel with a good reputation, though it can seem chaotic. Sinks in all rooms, but shared showers and toilets. No curfew. Breakfast included. Sheet rental €3.50. One-, two- and four-bed rooms. Métro Botanique. Dorms ❷

Jacques Brel rue de la Sablonnière 30 ☏022 18 01 87, ⓦwww.planet.be/aubjeun. HI hostel – modern and comfortable, and with a hotel-like atmosphere. Showers in every room; bar, restaurant and meeting room. Beds in two- to twelve-bedded dorms. Métro Madou or Botanique. Dorms ❷

New Sleep Well rue du Damier 23 ☏022 18 50 50, ⓦwww.sleepwell.be. Bright and breezy hostel in a recently refurbished building, a five-minute walk from place Rogier. Hotel-style facilities including a bar; good disabled access. Sheet rental €3.50. Advance booking essential. One-, two-, three- and four-bed rooms. Métro Rogier. Dorms ❷

Hotels

Les Bluets rue Berckmans 124, Saint Gilles ☏025 34 39 83, ⓔbluets@swing.be. Charming, family-run hotel with ten en-suite rooms in a handsome terrace house one block south of the petit ring. Immaculate *fin de siècle* decor. Advance reservations recommended. Métro Hôtel des Monnaies. ❹

George V rue 't Kint 23 ☏025 13 50 93, ⓦwww.george5.com. A ramshackle old hotel in an atmospheric if somewhat down-at-heel neighbourhood of big, balconied tenement blocks. Rooms are plain and modern, but with clean and well-appointed en suites. Prémétro Bourse. ❹

Mirabeau place Fontainas 18 ☏025 11 19 72, ⓔhotel.mirabeau@skynet.be. Welcoming hotel with thirty neat, modern en-suite rooms. Occupies a good-looking, early twentieth-century, seven-storey block and overlooks a busy square bordering bld Anspach. Prémétro Anneessens. ❹

Résidence Rembrandt rue de la Concorde 42, Ixelles ☏025 12 71 39, ⓔrembrandt@brutele.be. Popular, pleasant pension-style hotel. Thirteen clean and comfortable rooms – six en suite – and kitsch bygones in the foyer. Located on a dispiriting street off avenue Louise, near place Stéphanie. Trams #93 and #94 run along ave Louise. ❹

Sabina rue du Nord 78 ☏022 18 26 37, ⓦwww.hotelsabina.com. Twenty-four, workaday, en-suite rooms in a late nineteenth-century terrace town house. Located in an appealing residential area that was once a favourite haunt of the city's Victorian bourgeoisie. Métro Madou. ❹

Saint-Michel Grand-Place 15 ☏025 11 09 56, ⓔhotelsaintmichel@hotmail.com. One of the city's most distinctive hotels and the only one that looks out over the Grand-Place. It occupies an old guildhouse on the east side of the square, but the grandness of the facade isn't universally matched by the rooms inside – which range from the basic and small at the back of the building to more elegant period rooms at the front. If you're a light sleeper, revellers on the Grand-Place may well disturb your slumbers. Prémétro Bourse. ❹

La Tasse d'Argent rue du Congrès 48 ☏022 18 83 75. A popular, family-run hotel with just eight modest, modern rooms in a good-looking, *fin de siècle* mansion about five minutes' walk north of the cathedral. Métro Madou. ❹

The City

Central Brussels is bordered by a rough pentagon of boulevards – the **petit ring** – which follows the course of the medieval city walls. It is divided between the Upper and Lower Towns, the neighbourhoods generally becoming more bourgeois the higher you go. The greater part of the centre is occupied by the **Lower Town**, of which the Grand-Place – perhaps the best-preserved city square in Europe – is the focus. South of here, the busy centre fades into the old working-class streets of the Marolles district and Gare du Midi, now a relatively depressed, predominantly immigrant area; north, the shopping street of rue Neuve leads up to place Rogier and the office blocks that surround the Gare du Nord. The **Upper Town** is quite different in feel from the rest of the centre, with statuesque buildings lining wide, classical boulevards and squares. **Beyond the ring** several places are worth a visit, particularly the Musée Victor Horta.

The Lower Town

The obvious place to begin any tour of the **Lower Town** is the **Grand-Place**, the commercial hub of the city since the Middle Ages. With its stupendous tower, the **Hôtel de Ville** (tours in English: April–Sept Tues & Wed 3.15pm, Sun 12.15pm; Oct–March Tues only 3.15pm; €2.50) dominates the square, and inside you can view various official rooms; most dazzling is the sixteenth-century council chamber, decorated with gilt moulding, faded tapestries and an oak floor inlaid with ebony. But the real glory of the Grand-Place lies in the **guildhouses**, built in the early eighteenth century, their slender facades swirling with exuberant carving and sculpture. At the end of the row, on the west side of the square at no. 1, the **Roi d'Espagne** was once the headquarters of the guild of bakers and is named after its bust of Charles II, the last of the Spanish Habsburgs; Moorish and Native American prisoners flank Charles, symbolizing his mastery of a vast empire. At no. 4 is the **Maison de Sac**, the headquarters of the carpenters and coopers; the upper storeys were appropriately designed by a cabinet-maker, and feature pilasters and caryatids resembling the ornate legs of Baroque furniture. Next door, the **Maison de la Louve** boasts an elegant pilastered facade fronting the former home of the archers' guild, studded with pious representations of concepts such as Peace and Discord. Adjoining it, at no. 6, the **Maison du Cornet** was the headquarters of the boatsmen's guild, a fanciful creation of 1697 whose top storey resembles the stern of a ship. The adjacent **Maison du Renard** was the house of the haberdashers' guild; on the ground floor animated cherubs in bas-relief play at haberdashery, while a scrawny, gilded fox – after which the house is named – squats above the door.

Most of the northern side of the square is taken up by the sturdy neo-Gothic **Maison du Roi**, a reconstruction of a sixteenth-century building that now houses the **Musée de la Ville de Bruxelles** (Tues–Fri 10am–5pm, Sat & Sun 10am–1pm; €2.50). Here you'll find an eclectic mix of locally manufactured tapestries, ceramics, pewterware and porcelain.

Rue de l'Etuve leads south from the Grand-Place down to the **Manneken Pis**, a diminutive statue of a little boy pissing that's supposed to embody the "irreverent spirit" of the city and is today one of Brussels' biggest tourist draws. Jerome Duquesnoy cast the original statue in the 1600s, but it was stolen several times and the current one is a copy. From here it's another short hop to place de la Vieille-Halle aux Blés and the **Fondation internationale Jacques Brel** (Tues–Sat 11am–6pm; €5), a small but inventive museum celebrating the life and times of the Belgian singer Jacques Brel (1933-78). Brel became famous in the 1960s as a singer of mournful *chansons*. Suitably quirky, the museum begins with a false lift that actually doesn't move at all – despite the sounds – and beyond you can hear Brel pouring out his feelings on a mock-up stage and in a replica bar with juke box. From here, it's a short walk south to boulevard de l'Empereur, a busy carriageway that disfigures this part of the centre. Across the boulevard, you'll spy the crumbling brickwork of **La Tour Anneessens**, a chunky remnant of the medieval city wall, while to the south gleams the recently restored **Notre Dame de la Chapelle** (June–Sept Mon–Sat 9am–5pm & Sun 11.30am–4.30pm; Oct–May daily 12.30–4.30pm; free), a sprawling Gothic structure founded in 1134 that is the city's oldest church,. Running south from the church, rue Haute and parallel rue Blaes form the spine of the **Quartier Marolles** – an earthy neighbourhood of cheap restaurants, shops and bars that grew up in the seventeenth century as a centre for artisans working on the nearby mansions of Sablon. Today, gentrification is creeping in, but it's got some way to go, and **place du Jeu de Balle**, the heart of Marolles, is still the scene of the city's best **flea market** (daily from 7am), at its busiest on Sundays.

The Upper Town

The steep slope that marks the start of the **Upper Town** rises just a couple of minutes' walk from the Grand-Place at the east end of rue d'Arenberg. Here you'll find the city's **Cathedral** (daily 8am–6pm; free), a splendid Brabantine-Gothic building begun in 1220 and sporting a striking twin-towered, whitestone facade. Inside, the triple-aisled nave is an airy affair supported by plain, heavy-duty columns and displaying a massive oak pulpit featuring Adam and Eve. Look out also for the gorgeous sixteenth-century **stained glass** windows in the transepts and above the main doors.

Five minutes' walk south of the cathedral, the so-called **Mont des Arts** also occupies the slopes of the Upper Town, its collection of severe geometric buildings given over to a variety of government- and arts-related activities. In the middle, a wide stairway climbs up towards **place Royale** and **rue Royale**, the dead-straight backbone of the Upper Town. On the left here is the **Old England Building**, one of the finest examples of Art Nouveau in the city. It is now home to the **Musée des Instruments de Musique**, rue Montagne de la Cour 2 (Tues–Fri 9.30am–5pm, Thurs until 8pm, Sat & Sun 10am–5pm; €4), which contains around 1500 instruments and a string of interactive displays. Around the corner, the **Palais Royal** (late July to Sept Tues–Sun 10.30am–4.30pm; free) is something of a disappointment, a sombre conversion of some eighteenth-century town houses that serve as the official residence of the Belgian royals.

Just off place Royale, at the start of rue de la Régence, the **Musées Royaux des Beaux Arts** (Tues–Sun 10am–5pm; €5 for both museums) comprise two museums: the Musée d'Art Moderne and the Musée d'Art Ancien. Together they make up Belgium's most satisfying all-round collection of fine art, with marvellous collections of work by the likes of Pieter Bruegel the Elder, Rubens and the surrealists Paul Delvaux and René Magritte. The permanent collection is vast, but a system of colour-coded zones makes it easy to negotiate your way around. In the **Musée d'Art Ancien**, the **blue zone** takes in paintings of the fifteenth and sixteenth centuries, including works by Lucas Cranach, Quentin Matsys, Rogier van der Weyden and Pieter Bruegel the Elder's haunting *The Fall of Icarus*. The **brown zone** concentrates on work of the seventeenth and eighteenth centuries, notably some glorious canvases by Rubens and his contemporaries Jacob Jordaens and Anthony van Dyck. Moving on into the **Musée d'Art Moderne**, the **yellow zone** begins with the Social Realism of Charles de Groux and Constantin Meunier and continues with a collection of Neoclassical paintings, most notably by Jacques-Louis David, whose famous *Death of Marat* is displayed here. Then come the Symbolists, including several works by Fernand Khnopff, and a separate section devoted to the disconcerting canvases of James Ensor. The **green zone** boasts an extremely varied collection of modern art and sculpture, laid out on six subterranean levels. There are fine examples of Fauvism, Cubism, Futurism, Expressionism, and, above all, Surrealism, with the oddly erotic works of Paul Delvaux and a small show of paintings by Magritte.

From the Beaux Arts it's a short stroll south to the **place du Petit Sablon**, decorated with 48 statues representing the medieval guilds, and a fountain surmounted by the Counts Egmont and Hoorn, beheaded on the Grand-Place for their opposition to Spanish tyranny in the 1500s. On the opposite side of rue de la Régence stands the fifteenth-century church of **Notre Dame du Sablon**, built after a statue of Mary with powers of healing was brought by boat from Antwerp, an event still celebrated each July by the Ommegang procession. Behind the church, the sloping wedge of **place du Grand Sablon** is the centre of one of the city's wealthiest districts and scene of a lively weekend antiques market.

Nearby, at the southern end of rue de la Régence, is the immense – and immensely ugly - **Palais de Justice**. Built in 1883, it is actually larger than St Peter's in Rome.

Outside the petit ring: the parks and outer boroughs

Brussels by no means ends with the petit ring. To the east of the ring road, the **Quartier Leopold** has been colonized by the huge concrete and glass high-rises of the EU, notably the winged **Berlaymont** building beside Métro Schuman. The latest addition to the sprawling EU complex is the lavish **European Union Parliament building** (free guided tours: Mon–Thurs 10am & 5pm, Fri 10am, Sat 10am, 11.30am & 2.30pm; mid-Oct to mid-April Mon–Fri only; none in Aug), an imposing structure topped off by a spectacular curved glass roof. It's a couple of minutes' walk from place du Luxembourg, behind the Gare Quartier Leopold train station.

Just south of the petit ring is **St Gilles**, a gritty multiracial borough that stretches from the refinement of avenue Louise in the east to the solidly immigrant quarters around the Gare du Midi. The main reason to trek out here is the **Musée Victor Horta**, the former home of the Belgian Art Nouveau architect at rue Américaine 25 (Tues–Sun 2–5.30pm; €5); take tram #91 or #92 from place Louise. The exterior is modest, but inside are all the architect's trademarks: crisp, bright rooms spiralling around a superbly worked staircase, stained glass, sculpture and ornate furniture and panelling.

Some 3km north of the ring road, **Laeken** is the royal suburb of Brussels. Its large public **park** is best known for the **Atomium** (daily 9/10am–5.30/7.30pm; €5.45), a model of a molecule expanded 165 billion times, which was built for the 1958 World Fair. Poking its very distinctive head into the sky, the structure has become something of a symbol of the city, but its interior can only muster up an unremarkable exhibition on the construction of – and the concepts behind – itself.

Eating and drinking

Brussels has an international reputation for the quality of its cuisine, and even at the dowdiest snack bar you'll find that the food is well-prepared and generously seasoned – and then there are the city's **restaurants**, many of which equal any in Paris. Traditional Bruxellois dishes are canny amalgamations of Walloon and Flemish ingredients and cooking styles. In addition, the city is among Europe's best for sampling a wide range of different cuisines – from the Turkish restaurants of St Josse to Spanish, Vietnamese and Japanese. You can also eat magnificent fish and seafood, especially around the fashionable district of Ste Catherine.

Eating out is rarely cheap, but **prices** are usually justified by the quality. It's also hard to distinguish between the less expensive restaurants and the city's **cafés**, some of which provide the tastiest food in town. In addition, many **bars** serve food, some including traditional Brussels cuisine. For **fast food**, there are plenty of stands and kebab places around the Grand-Place.

For **drinking**, the enormous variety of bars and cafés is one of the city's real joys – sumptuous Art Nouveau cafés, speciality-beer bars with literally hundreds of different varieties of ale, and, of course, more modern hangouts. Many of the centrally located bars are much frequented by tourists and expats, but outside the centre, and even tucked away off the Grand-Place, there are places that remain refreshingly local. Bars stay open late – most until 2 or 3am, some until dawn.

Restaurants and cafés

On and around the Grand-Place

Le Cirio rue de la Bourse 18. One of Brussels'
oldest bars, sumptuously decorated in *fin de siècle*
style, though now somewhat frayed round the
edges. Once frequented, they say, by Jacques Brel.

Le Falstaff rue Henri Maus 17–23. Art Nouveau
café next to the Bourse, attracting a mixed bag of
tourists, gays, Eurocrats and bourgeois Bruxellois.
Full of atmosphere, and so crowded in the evenings
that you're unlikely to find a seat. Inexpensive beer
and sandwiches, plus pastries to swoon for.

't Kelderke Grand-Place 15 ☎025 13 73 44.
Busy cellar restaurant specializing in traditional
Bruxellois dishes. Serves an excellent *lapin à la
gueuze* (rabbit cooked in gueuze) and a superb
carbonnades flamandes à la bière (beef in beer).

Totem rue de la Grande Île 42. Tucked away
down a sidestreet off boulevard Anspach, this
friendly, fashionable restaurant is a hit with
veggies, who come here for the organic soups,
fresh salads and a delicious selection of cakes
and pastries. Has a good choice of organic wines
and serves meat dishes too. Closed Mon; no
credit cards.

On and around place Ste Catherine

Bij den Boer quai aux Briques 60 ☎025 12 61
22. There's nothing pretentious here in this good
old neighbourhood café/bar with its tiled floor and
bygones on the wall. A great place for a drink or a
meal, though the service can be slow. The seafood
is delicious and reasonably priced. Closed Sun.

Iberica rue de Flandre 8 ☎025 11 79 36.
Agreeable Spanish restaurant offering all the
classics. Tapas around €6. Closed Wed.

Kasbah rue Antoine Dansaert 20. Popular with a
youthful crowd, this Moroccan eatery is famous
for serving enormous portions of couscous and
other North African specialities. Vibrant and
fashionable.

La Marée rue du Flandre 99 ☎025 11 00 40.
Outstanding, pocket-sized restaurant, and not to
be confused with its namesake on rue au Beurre.
The speciality is seafood, always fresh and always
prepared in a simple, direct manner. Frugal decor
that somehow manages to feel quite cosy. Closed
Sun eve & Mon.

La Papaye Verte rue Antoine Dansaert 53. First-
rate Vietnamese food at bargain basement prices.

Good range of vegetarian options. Smart,
authentically Vietnamese interior.

Le Pré Salé rue de Flandre 16 ☎025 13 43 23.
Friendly, old-fashioned neighbourhood restaurant
providing a nice alternative to the swankier eateries
of the district. Very Bruxellois. Great mussels, fish
and other Belgian specialities. Closed Mon.

Bars

On and around the Grand-Place

À la Bécasse, rue de Tabora 11. This old-
fashioned bar has long wooden benches, ancient
blue and white tiles on the walls and serves beer
in earthenware jugs.

Au Bon Vieux Temps rue du Marché aux Herbes
12. Cosy old place tucked down an alley. Has tile-
inlaid tables and a handsome seventeenth-century
chimney piece. Popular with British servicemen
just after the end of World War II, the bar still has
comforting old-fashioned signs advertising
Mackenzies' Port and Bass pale ale. A great place
for a quiet drink.

La Fleur en Papier Doré rue des Alexiens 53.
Cluttered, cosy locals' bar whose walls are
covered with doodles and poems. Was once one of
the chosen drinking places of René Magritte.

Le Greenwich rue des Chartreux 7. Brussels'
traditional chess café with a lovely old wood-
panelled and mirrored interior. Laid-back
atmosphere.

À l'Imaige de Nostre-Dame rue du Marché aux
Herbes 6. A welcoming, quirky little bar situated at
the end of a long, narrow alley. Decorated like an
old Dutch kitchen. Good range of speciality beers.

À la Mort Subite rue Montagne aux Herbes
Potagères 7. Twenties bar just northeast of the
square that loaned its name to a widely available
bottled beer. A long, narrow room with nicotine-
stained walls and mirrors, a dissolute-arty clientèle
and an animated atmosphere. Snacks served.

Au Soleil rue Marché au Charbon 86. Popular bar
with a wide choice of beers, crowded nightly till
late with a young, trendy crowd.

Toone Impasse Schuddeveld 6, off Petite rue des
Bouchers. Bar belonging to the Toone puppet
theatre. Two small rooms with old posters on
rough plaster walls, a reasonably priced beer list, a
modest selection of snacks, and a soundtrack of
classical and jazz, make it one of the centre's
more congenial watering-holes.

Nightlife

Although it's not as lively a scene as in some European capitals, Brussels is a reasonably good place to catch **live bands**. **Club** culture has also made some headway in

the city and, although it's hardly cutting edge stuff, there are several good venues in the centre. As a general rule, clubs **open** Thursday to Saturday from 11pm to 5/6am and entry **prices** are low – rarely more than €10 and many of the smaller clubs have no cover at all, though you should tip the bouncer (€2 or so) on the way out.

For **listings** of concerts and events, check the *What's On* section of the weekly *Bulletin*, the city's English-language magazine. **Tickets** for most things are available from Fnac in the City 2 complex, rue Neuve (☎022 09 22 11).

Live music venues

AB bld Anspach 110 ☎02548 2424. One of the capital's premier rock venues. Has a reputation for showcasing prime local bands. Prémétro Bourse. Closed in July & Aug.

Le Cercle rue Ste Anne 20 ☎025 14 03 53. Small, unremarkable venue, but the live music is a real attraction – everything from jazz and Latino to *chanson* three or four times a week. Just off place du Grand Sablon.

Forest National ave du Globe 36 ☎090 00 09 91. The main arena for big-name international acts. Tram #18.

Magazin 4 rue du Magasin 4 ☎022 23 34 74. In an old warehouse off bld d'Anvers, this is a favourite venue for up-and-coming local indie bands. Open only when there's a gig – call for details. Métro Yser.

Sounds rue de la Tulipe 28, Ixelles ☎025 12 92 50. Atmospheric jazz café off place Ferdinand Cocq in Ixelles. Has showcased local and internationally acclaimed jazz acts for over twenty years. Live music most nights, but the biggies usually appear on Sat. Closed Sun.

VK rue de l'Ecole 76 ☎024 14 29 7. Regularly features top-class hip-hop, ragga, rock and indie acts and occasionally puts on the odd punk band

too – it's probably the best cutting-edge "alternative" venue in the capital. Just to the west of Métro Comte de Flandre – an area with a bad reputation: take a taxi.

Clubs

Le Bazaar rue des Capucins 63. Split-level club with a competent restaurant upstairs and a dance-floor below, offering funk, soul, rock and indie. In the Marolles, off rue Haute – and below the Palais de Justice. Closed Sun.

The Fuse rue Blaes 208. Large, young, and vibrant techno, jungle and house club in the Marolles district. Big-name, international DJs a regular feature. Chill-out rooms and visuals. Métro Porte de Hal. Sat only.

Le Pacha rue de l'Écuyer 41. Much vaunted Ibiza import. Spectacular stuff, with all the fury and action you might expect. Fri is funk, '60s and '70s rock, soul and house, Sat is house music, Sun is gay night. Closed Mon–Thurs.

Who's Who Land rue du Poinçon 17. A short walk east of Prémétro Annessens, this is one of the capital's runaway success stories. A trendy house club, it's always packed with legions of revellers. Classic techno and house anthems are blasted out until the wee hours. Sat only.

Listings

Embassies Australia, rue Guimard 6–8 ☎022 86 05 00; Canada, ave de Tervuren 2 ☎027 41 06 11; Ireland, rue Froissart 89 ☎022 30 53 37; New Zealand, bld du Régent 47–48 ☎025 12 10 40; UK, rue d'Arlon 85 ☎022 87 62 11; US, bld du Régent 27 ☎025 08 21 11.

Exchange Crédit Général Automatic Exchange at Grand-Place 7 (24hr).

Internet easyEverything, place De Brouckère 9.

Laundry Wash Club, place St Géry 25.

Left luggage At the train stations.

Pharmacy Multipharma, rue du Marché aux Poulets 37.

Post office First floor, Centre Monnaie, pl de la Monnaie.

Northern Belgium

The region north of Brussels is Flemish-speaking and possesses a distinctive and vibrant cultural identity. It's dull countryside on the whole, but a string of fine historic cities more than compensates. **Antwerp**, a large old port with many reminders of its sixteenth-century golden age, is due north of Brussels. To the west, in Flanders, lie two fascinating cities – **Ghent** and **Bruges** – both became prosperous during the Middle Ages on the cloth trade and their ancient centres are now graced by a wonderful medley of early Flemish art and architecture. All three cities have great bars and fine restaurants.

There are two major **ports** along this stretch of coast: Zeebrugge with ferries from Hull and Dover, and Ostend with catamaran services from Dover. In **OSTEND**, ferries dock right by the **train station**; in **ZEEBRUGGE** they dock out on a mole 2km from the train station, so check with the ferry company to make sure they provide onward bus connections. There's a seasonal **tourist office** inside Ostend train station (July & Aug daily 9am–1pm & 4–7.30pm), but nothing handy for ferry passengers in Zeebrugge.

Antwerp

Belgium's second city, **ANTWERP**, fans out from the east bank of the Scheldt about 50km north of Brussels. Many people prefer it to the capital and indeed it does have a denser concentration of things to see, not least some fine churches and distinguished museums – reminders of its auspicious past as centre of a wide trading empire. In recent years, the city has effectively become the capital of Flemish Belgium, a lively cultural centre with a spirited nightlife. On the surface it's not a wealthy city, but its diamond industry (centred on Centraal Station) is the world's largest. There is also the enormous legacy of Rubens, some of whose finest works adorn Antwerp's galleries and churches.

Arrival, information and accommodation

Antwerp has two mainline train stations, Antwerp Berchem and **Centraal Station**; the latter, 2km east of the main square, Grote Markt, is the one you want for the city centre. **Trams** #2 and #15 run from the Diamant prémétro (underground tram) station beside Centraal Station to the centre. **Transport information** is available from Diamant station (Mon–Fri 8am–12.30pm & 1.30–4pm); they also sell **tickets** – a standard single fare on any part of the system costs €1, a ten-strip *Rittenkaart* €7.50 and a 24-hour pass (*dagpas*) €2.90. One-way tickets can also be bought direct from the driver and all tickets can be bought at prémétro stations and at selected shops and newsstands. The **tourist office** is at Grote Markt 15 (Mon–Sat 9am–6pm, Sun 9am–5pm; ☎032 32 01 03, ⊛www.visitantwerpen.be) and **internet access** is available at *easyEverything*, Century Center, De Keyserlei 58–60.

Antwerp has the range of hotels you'd expect of Belgium's second city, plus a number of good hostels. Consequently, finding **accommodation** is rarely difficult, although there are surprisingly few places in the centre. Many mid-priced and budget places are clustered in the scruffy area around Centraal Station, where you should exercise caution at night, particularly if travelling alone. The tourist office has a comprehensive list of places and will make **bookings** on your behalf.

Hostels

Antwerp Youth Hostel Eric Sasselaan 2 ☎032 38 02 73, ⊛www.vjh.be. HI hostel close to the ring road, 5km south of the centre. Around 130 beds in four-, six- and eight-bedded rooms. Canteen, self-catering facilities and a laundry room. Tram #2 from Centraal Station. ❷

New International Youth Hotel Provinciestraat 256 ☎032 30 05 22, ⊛www.niyh.be. Dorm beds, doubles and some en suite, just ten minutes' walk from Centraal Station. To get here head south down Pelikaanstraat, turn left along Plantin en Moretuslei, and take the third right. ❸

Scoutel Jeugdverblifcentrum Stoomstraat 3 ☎032 26 46 06, ⊛www.vvksm.be. Spick and span hostel-cum-hotel offering frugal but perfectly adequate doubles and triples with breakfast. It's about five minutes' walk from Centraal Station. No curfew (guests have their own keys), but reception closes 6pm. Reservations are advised. Discounts for the under-26s. ❸

Hotels

Cammerpoorte Nationalestraat 38 ☎032 31 97 36. Budget, two-star hotel with forty plain modern rooms. Close to the Grote Markt. ❺

ANTWERP

Ⓜ Tram/Metro Stations

N

◄ International Zeemanshuis

◄ Campsite & Antwerpen Youth Hostel

▼ Museum voor Schone Kunsten

Schelde

0   200 m

Nationaal Scheepvaartmuseum

Vleeshuis

St Pauluskerk

Stadhuis

ⓘ

GROTE MARKT

Plantin-Moretus Museum

Cathedral

OLV

Groen-plaats

Beurs

Ⓜ

St Jacobskerk

Mayer van den Bergh Museum

Rubenshuis

Wapper

Opera Ⓜ

Centraal Station

Ⓜ

Diamant

PELIKAANSTRAAT

FRANKLIN ROOSEVELT PLAATS

MEIR

FRANKRIJKLEI

DAMBRUGGERSTRAAT

VAN SCHOONHOVENSTRAAT

KONINGIN ASTRIDPLEIN

HOLLANDSTR

ROTTERDAMSTR

OLIFANTSTR

ITALIELIE

ROODESTRAAT

PAARDENMARKT

VEKESTRAAT

VENUSSTRAAT

PRINSSTRAAT

KEIZERSTRAAT

BLINDESTR

MUTSAERTSTR

ST PAULSSTRAAT

MINDERBROEDERSRUI

HOFSTR

OUDE BEURS

KAASRUI

MELKMARKT

EIERMARKT

SCHOENMARKT

REYNDERSSTRAAT

HOOGSTR

VLAMINCKVELD

KAMMENSTRAAT

NATIONALE STRAAT

STEENHOUWERSVEST

PLANTINKAAI

KLOOSTERSTRAAT

ST-ANDRIES PLAATS

PREKERSSTRAAT

MINSTRAAT

DRIJVER

LANGE NIEUWE STRAAT

MEISTRAAT

OUDE VAARTPLAATS

LEOPOLDSTRAAT

LOMBARDENVEST

K. GASTHUISSTRAAT

WIESSTR

HUIDEVETTERSTR

ST KATELIJNEVEST

VINGERLINGSTRAAT

LANG HERENTALSESTR

QUELLINSTRAAT

RUBENSLEI

LEYS STR

GEMEENTESTRAAT

VAN ARTEVELDESTR

VAN STRALENSTR

KONINGSSTRAAT

STATIESTR

VESTINGSTRAAT

APPELMANSSTRAAT

ANNEESSENSSTR

DE KEYSERLEI

ARENBERGSTR

THEATER-PLEIN

GRAAN-MARKT

KOMEDIE PLEIN

JODENSTR

MEIR

EIKENSTRAAT

ST JACOBS MARKT

KIPDORP

WOLSTRAAT

PRINSESSTRAAT

KLAPDORP

VEKESTRAAT

ZIRKSTR

L GASTHUISSTRAAT

BREDESTR

BEGIJNSTR

VLEMINCKVELD

VRIJDAG MARKT

VLIERSTR

GROTE PIETER POTSTR

VLAMINCKVELD

PLOEGSTR   KIEVSTR

VAN WESEBEKESTRAAT

VAN WESEBEKESTRAAT

GROENPLAATS

HANDSCHOENMARKT

KORNMARKT

OUDE KORNMARKT

PELGRIMSTRAAT

SINT JANSVLIET

VRIJDAG MARKT

SCHUTTERSHOFSTRAAT

VESTINGSTR

OSYSTRAAT

GRAMAYESTRAAT

VAN EHRBORNSTRAAT

Eden Lange Herentalsestraat 25 ☏ 032 33 06 08.
Chain hotel in the diamond district. The modern
rooms are perfectly adequate but quite plain – and
stand by for attack in the mosquito season.
Breakfasts are very good. ❺

Ibis Antwerpen Centrum Meistraat 39 ☏ 032 31
88 30. Chain hotel with routine modern rooms
hidden behind a ghastly concrete exterior; all is
compensated for by a decent location, close to the
Rubenshuis. ❺

Internationaal Zeemanshuis Falconrui 21 ☏ 032
27 54 33, ⊛ www.zeemanshuis.be. Spartan but
perfectly acceptable en-suite doubles ten minutes'
walk north of the Grote Markt. ❹

Tourist Hotel Pelikaanstraat 20 ☏ 032 32 58 70.
Straightforward, modern rooms near Centraal
Station – OK for a night or two, though
Pelikaanstraat can be noisy. ❸

The City

The centre of Antwerp is the spacious **Grote Markt**, at the heart of which stands
the **Brabo fountain**, a haphazard pile of rocks surmounted by a bronze of Silvius
Brabo, the city's first hero, depicted flinging the hand of the giant Antigonus – who
terrorized passing ships – into the Scheldt. The north side of Grote Markt is lined
with daintily restored sixteenth-century **guildhouses**, though they are overshadowed by the **Stadhuis** (tours Mon–Wed & Fri 11am, 2pm & 3pm, Sat 2pm &
3pm; €1), completed in 1566, and one of the most important buildings of the
Northern Renaissance. Among rooms you can visit are the Leys Room, named
after Baron Hendrik Leys, who painted the frescoes in the 1860s, and the Wedding
Room, which has a chimney piece decorated with two caryatids carved by the
architect Cornelius Floris.

Southeast of Grote Markt, the **Onze Lieve Vrouwe Cathedral** (Mon–Fri
10am–5pm, Sat 10am–3pm, Sun 1–4pm; €2.50) is one of the finest Gothic churches in Belgium, mostly the work of Jan and Pieter Appelmans in the middle of the
fifteenth century. Inside, the seven-aisled nave is breathtaking, if only because of its
sense of space, an impression that's reinforced by the bright, light stonework
revealed by a recent refurbishment. Four early paintings by **Rubens** are displayed
here, the most beautiful of which is the *Descent from the Cross*, a triptych painted
after the artist's return from Italy.

It takes about five minutes to walk southwest from the cathedral to the **Plantin-
Moretus Museum**, on Vrijdagmarkt (Tues–Sun 10am–5pm; €4), which occupies
the grand old mansion of Rubens' father-in-law, the printer Christopher Plantin.
One of Antwerp's most interesting museums, it provides a marvellous insight into
how Plantin and his family conducted their business.

From here it's a brief stroll to the riverfront and the **Nationaal
Scheepvaartmuseum** (Tues–Sun 10am–5pm; €4) – the maritime museum in the
Steen, the remaining gatehouse of what was once an impressive medieval fortress, at
the end of Suikerrui. Inside, the cramped rooms feature exhibits on inland navigation, shipbuilding and waterfront life, while the open-air section has a long line of
tugs and barges under a rickety corrugated roof. Crossing Jordaenskaai, it's a short
walk east to the impressively gabled **Vleeshuis** (Tues–Sun 10am–5pm; €2.50), built
for the guild of butchers in 1503 and now used to display a substantial but incoherent collection of applied arts – everything from antique musical instruments to
medieval woodcarvings.

Just north of here, along Vleeshouwersstraat, **St Pauluskerk** (May–Sept daily
2–5pm) is a dignified late Gothic church built for the Dominicans in the early sixteenth century. Inside, the airy and elegant nave is decorated by a series of paintings
depicting the Fifteen Mysteries of the Rosary, including Rubens' exquisite *Scourging
at the Pillar* of 1617.

Ten minutes' walk east from the OLV Cathedral is the **Rubenshuis**, Wapper 9
(Tues–Sun 10am–5pm; €5), the former home and studio of Rubens, now restored
as a (very popular) museum. Unfortunately, there are only one or two of his less
distinguished paintings here, but the restoration of the rooms is convincing. Rubens
died in 1640 and was buried in **St Jacobskerk**, just to the north at Lange

Nieuwstraat 73 (April–Oct Mon–Sat 2–5pm; €1.80). The artist and his immediate family are buried in the chapel behind the high altar, where, in one of his last works, *Our Lady Surrounded by Saints*, he appears himself as St George, his two wives as Martha and Mary, and his father as St Jerome.

About ten minutes' walk southwest of Rubenshuis, the **Mayer van den Bergh Museum**, at Lange Gasthuisstraat 19 (Tues–Sun 10am–5pm; €4), contains delightful examples of the applied arts, from tapestries to ceramics, silverware, illuminated manuscripts and furniture, in a crowded reconstruction of a sixteenth-century town house. There are also some excellent paintings, including works by Quentin Matsys and Jan Mostaert, but the museum's most celebrated work is **Bruegel**'s *Dulle Griet* or "Mad Meg", a misogynistic allegory in which a woman, loaded down with possessions, stalks the gates of Hell.

About twenty minutes' walk further south, the **Museum voor Schone Kunsten** (Tues–Sun 10am–5pm; €4) has one of the country's better fine art collections. Its early Flemish section features paintings by Jan van Eyck, Memling, Rogier van der Weyden and Quentin Matsys. **Rubens** has two large rooms to himself, in which one very large canvas stands out: the *Adoration of the Magi*, a beautifully human work apparently completed in a fortnight. The museum also displays a comprehensive collection of modern Belgian art with Paul Delvaux and James Ensor being particularly well-represented.

Eating and drinking

Antwerp is an enjoyable and inexpensive place to **eat**, full of informal café/restaurants that excel at combining traditional Flemish, Mediterranean and French cuisines – several of the best are clustered on Suikerrui and Grote Pieter Potstraat near the Grote Markt, and there's another concentration in the vicinity of Hendrik Conscienceplein. For **fast food**, try the kebab and falafel places on Oude Koornmarkt. Antwerp is also a fine place to **drink**, the narrow lanes of its centre dotted with small and atmospheric bars.

Cafés and restaurants
Het Dagelijks Brood Steenhouwersvest 48. An enjoyable and distinctively artsy café serving wholesome soups and light meals.
Facade Hendrik Conscienceplein 18. A laid-back, funky café with good music and inexpensive vegetarian, meat and fish dishes.
De Matelote Haarstraat 9 ☎032 31 32 07. Modish, pastel-painted fish restaurant off Grote Pieter Potstraat, near the Grote Markt. Closed Sun.
Pizzeria Antonio Grote Markt 6. Tasty and swiftly served pasta and pizza at reasonable prices.
De Stoemppot Vlasmarkt 12. *Stoemp* is a traditional Flemish dish consisting of puréed meat and vegetables – and this is the best place in town to eat it. Closed Wed.

Bars
Café de Muze Melkmarkt 15. With its bare brick walls and retro film posters, this laid-back and central café-bar is a popular spot. Occasional live music – mainly jazz and blues.
Den Engel Grote Markt 3. Traditional, very Flemish bar bang in the centre of town.
Het Elfde Gebod Torfbrug 10. On one of the tiny squares fronting the north side of the cathedral, this bar is something of a tourist trap, but it's still worth visiting for the kitsch religious statues which cram the interior; avoid the food.
Kulminator Vleminckveld 32–34. This long-established, laid-back bar lays claim to a stock of 500 beers.
De Vagant Reyndersstraat 21. Specialist gin bar serving an extravagant range of Belgian and Dutch jenevers in spruce, modern surroundings.
De Volle Maan Oude Koornmarkt 7. Lively, likeable and offbeat bar close to the Grote Markt.

Ghent

The largest town in western Europe during the thirteenth and fourteenth centuries, **GHENT** was at the heart of the medieval Flemish cloth trade. By 1350, the city boasted a population of 50,000, of whom no less than 5000 were directly involved in the industry. However, the cloth trade began to decline in the early sixteenth century and Ghent decayed – until better times finally returned in the nineteenth century when the city was industrialized. It is now the third largest city in Belgium.

The best place to start exploring is at the mainly Gothic **St Baaf's Cathedral**, squeezed into the corner of St Baafsplein, bang in the centre of town (daily: 8.30am–5/6pm). Inside, a small chapel (Mon–Sat 9.30/10.30am–4/5pm, Sun 1/2–5pm; €2.50) holds Ghent's greatest treasure, the altarpiece of the *Adoration of the Mystic Lamb*, a wonderful early fifteenth-century work by Jan van Eyck. The inside panels reveal God the Father, the Virgin and John the Baptist on the upper level, while down below the Lamb of God is depicted in a sort of earthly paradise, approached by saints, popes, patriarchs and godly knights.

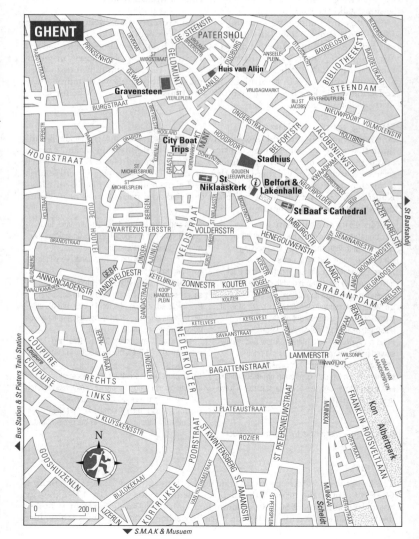

▼ S.M.A.K & Musuem

Just west of St Baaf's, the fifteenth-century **Lakenhalle** now holds the tourist office and little else; its first-floor entrance leads to the adjoining **Belfry** (mid-March to mid-Nov 10am–1 & 2–6pm; €3), a much-amended edifice from the fourteenth century. A glass-sided lift climbs up to the roof for excellent views over the city centre. A few strides away to the north is the **Stadhuis** (tours: May–Oct Mon–Thurs; check tourist office for latest times; €3), whose long facade was erected in two phases: the earlier, fancier carving is to the north, but the money ran out and so the rest of the building was completed in a much plainer style.

A short walk west of the Stadhuis, **Graslei** forms the eastern side of the old city harbour and is home to a splendid series of gabled guildhouses dating from medieval times. From here, it's another short haul to the sinister-looking **Het Gravensteen** (daily 9am–5/6pm; €6.20), the Castle of the Counts of Flanders, where a self-guided tour leads through a labyrinth of cold, stark rooms and chambers. Nearby, just to the east, are the narrow cobbled lanes and alleys of the **Patershol**, a pocket-sized district that was formerly home to the city's weavers, but is now Ghent's main restaurant quarter. Here you'll find the **Huis van Alijn**, Kraanlei 65 (Tues–Sun 11am–5pm; €2.50), a folk museum sited in a series of restored almshouses and boasting a delightful chain of period rooms depicting local life and work in the eighteenth and nineteenth centuries.

Strolling south from the centre along Ghent's main shopping street, Veldstraat, it takes about twenty minutes to reach the **Museum voor Schone Kunsten** at Nicolaas de Liemaeckereplein 3 (Tues–Sun 10am–6pm; €2.50). The museum displays a first-rate sample of Flemish paintings, including two exquisite works by Hieronymus Bosch, along with work by the likes of Pieter Bruegel the Younger, Jordaens and Van Dyck. Opposite, the old casino has been turned into **SMAK** (Tues–Sun 10am–6pm; ⓦwww.smak.be; €5), a museum of contemporary art that is well-known for its adventurous programme of temporary exhibitions.

Practicalities

Of Ghent's two **train stations**, the most useful is **St Pieters**, 2km south of the centre and connected to it by **trams** #1, #10, #11, #12 and #13. The **tourist office** is in the crypt of the Lakenhalle, right in the centre on the Botermarkt (daily: April–Oct 9.30am–6.30pm; Nov–March 9.30am–4.30pm; ☏09226 5232, ⓦwww.gent.be). The best way of seeing the sights is on **foot**, but Ghent is a large city and you may find you have to use a **tram** or **bus** at some point. Standard single fares cost €1, a ten-journey *Rittenkaart* €7.50 and a day pass €2.90. Single tickets can be bought direct from the driver; passes are sold at shops and kiosks all over town. The handiest place to access the **internet** is the *Coffee Lounge*, across from the tourist office at Botermarkt 6.

Ghent has around twenty **hotels**, ranging from the delightful to the mundanely modern, as well as a bright, cheerful and centrally located **hostel**. As for **eating out**, Ghent's numerous **cafés** and **restaurants** offer the very best of Flemish and French cuisines, with a sprinkling of Italian, Chinese and Arab places. The fancier restaurants are concentrated in and around the Patershol, while less expensive spots, including a rash of fast food joints, cluster on the Korenmarkt. Ghent has lots of great **bars** too.

Hostels and student rooms

Ghent Youth Hostel Jeugdherberg De Draecke, St Widostraat 11 ☏092 33 70 50, ⒠youthhostel.gent @skynet.be. Excellent, well-equipped hostel in the city centre, five minutes' walk north of the Korenmarkt. Over a hundred beds, in two-, three-, four-, five- and six-bed rooms. Facilities include lockers, currency exchange, bike rental and a bar. Breakfast included, and lunch and dinner offered. Advance reservations advised. Dorm beds ❷, rooms from ❸

Universitaire Homes ☏092 64 71 2. Offers student rooms at several sites across the south of town. Mid-July to late Sept only. ❷

Private rooms

Brooderie Jan Breydelstraat 8 ☏092 25 06 23. The Brooderie is an appealing café (see below) handily located near the Korenmarkt and its owners rent out three neat and trim little rooms above it. Breakfast is excellent. ❹

Hotels

Boatel Voorhuitkaai 29A ☎092 67 10 30, ⓦwww .theboatel.com. Certainly the most distinctive of the city's hotels – as its name implies, it's a converted boat, and an imaginatively and immaculately refurbished canal barge to be precise. The seven bedrooms are decked out in crisp, modern style and breakfasts, taken on the poop deck, are first rate. Moored in one of the outer canals, a fifteen-minute walk east from the centre. ❻

Flandria Centrum Barrestraat 3 ☎092 23 06 26, ⓦwww.flandria-centrum.be. Somewhat dishevelled hotel in the narrow sidestreets off the Reep, five minutes' walk northeast of the cathedral. After the youth hostel, these are the least expensive rooms in the centre. All sixteen (modest) rooms are en suite. ❹

Poortackere Monasterium Oude Houtlei 58 ☎092 69 22 10 ⓦwww.poortackere.com. This unusual hotel-cum-guesthouse occupies a rambling former monastery dating from the nineteenth century. Guests have a choice between en suites in the hotel section and the more authentic monastic-cell experience in the guest house, either en suite or shared facilities. Located five minutes' walk west of Veldstraat. ❹

Cafés and restaurants

Avalon Geldmunt 32. Vegetarian restaurant offering a wide range of well-prepared food served in several rooms and on the terrace in summer. Mon–Sat noon–2pm.

Brooderie Jan Breydelstraat 8. Pleasant and informal café with a health-food slant. Wholesome breakfasts, lunches, sandwiches and salads. Centrally located, near the castle. B&B above the café too (see p.113). Closed Mon.

Malatesta Korenmarkt 35. Informal, fashionable café/restaurant; modern decor and good pizza and pasta dishes at very affordable prices. Closed Tues.

Pakhuis Schuurkenstraat 4. A lively bistro-brasserie Occupies an old warehouse down a narrow alley near St Michielsbrug with acres of glass and metal. Offers an extensive menu – Flemish and French and beyond. Good for just a drink too. Closed Sun.

Bars and clubs

Bardot Oude Beestenmarkt 8. This new hip venue is one of the top places in town. Regular DJs offer house, techno and plenty of the newest sounds. Wed–Sat 8pm–5am.

't Dreupelkot Groentenmarkt 10. Cosy bar specializing in jenever, of which it stocks more than 100 brands. Down a little alley, next door to the famous *Het Waterhuis* (see below).

Pink Flamingos Onderstraat 55. Weird, wonderful and the height of kitsch – film stars, religion, Barbie-dolls; if it's cheesy it's somewhere in the decor. Great place for an aperitif or one of their large selection of cocktails.

De Tap en de Tepel Gewad 7. Charming, candlelit bar with an open fire and a clutter of antique furnishings. Wine is the main deal here, served with a good selection of cheeses. Wed–Sat from noon.

Het Waterhuis aan de Bierkant Groentenmarkt 9. More than 100 types of beer are available in this engaging, canal-side bar near the castle. Popular with tourists and locals alike.

Bruges

"Somewhere within the dingy casing lay the ancient city, like a notorious jewel, too stared at, talked of, trafficked over." So wrote Graham Greene of **BRUGES**. It's true that Bruges' reputation as one of the most perfectly preserved medieval cities in Europe has made it the most popular tourist destination in Belgium, packed with visitors throughout the summer. Inevitably, the crowds tend to overwhelm the city's charms, but you would be mad to come to Flanders and miss the place – its intimate, winding streets, woven around a pattern of narrow canals and lined with ancient buildings, live up to even the most inflated hype.

Bruges boomed throughout the Middle Ages, sharing effective control of the **cloth trade** with its two great rivals, Ghent and Ieper, its weavers turning English wool into items of clothing that were exported all over the world. It was an immensely profitable business and at its height the town was one of the richest in Europe. By the end of the fifteenth century, though, Bruges was in decline, partly because of a recession in the cloth trade, but principally because the Zwin river – the city's vital link to the North Sea – was silting up. By the 1530s its sea trade had collapsed completely, and Bruges simply withered away. Frozen in time, Bruges escaped damage in both world wars to emerge the perfect tourist attraction.

Arrival, information and accommodation

Bruges **train station** adjoins the **bus station** about 2km southwest of the town centre. Local **buses** leaving from outside the train station for the the main square or Markt. Inside the train station, there's a **tourist office** (Mon–Sat 10am–6pm; ☎050 44 86 86), which concentrates on hotel reservations. The main **tourist office** is right in the centre of town at Burg 11 (Mon–Fri 9.30am–5/6.30pm, Sat & Sun 9.30/10am–noon/1pm & 2–5.30/6.30pm; ☎050 44 86 86, ⊛www.brugge.be); it, too, offers an accommodation-booking service.

Bruges has over one hundred hotels, dozens of private rooms and several youth hostels, but still can't accommodate all its visitors at the height of the season. If you're arriving in July or August, be sure to **book ahead** or, at a pinch, make sure you get here in the morning. Given the crush, many visitors use the **accommodation service** provided by the tourist office – it's free, efficient and can save you a lot of hassle.

Hostels

Bauhaus International Youth Hotel Langestraat 135 ☎050 34 10 93, ⊛www.bauhaus.be. Laid-back hostel with dorms sleeping up to eight and a mish-mash of doubles and triples. There's bike rental, currency exchange and coin-operated lockers. Situated fifteen minutes' walk east of the Burg, next to the *Bauhaus Hotel* (see below). ❶
Charlie Rockets Hoogstraat 19 ☎050 33 06 60, ⊛www.charlierockets.com. New kid on the block, this place steals a march on its rivals by dint of being so much closer to the Markt. Has eleven rooms on two floors above a busy American-style bar. Breakfast €2 extra. Dorms ❶
Passage Dweersstraat 26 ☎050 34 02 32. The best hostel in Bruges. Accommodates fifty people in ten comfortable dorms, each with shared bathrooms. About ten minutes' walk west of the Markt. The *Passage Hôtel* next door is also a bargain (see below). Dorms ❶

Private rooms

Salvators Korte Vulderstraat 7 ☎050 33 19 21, ⊛www.hotelsalvators.be. This smart place offers three rooms, two en suite, in an attractive, well-maintained, three-storey brick house. Central location. ❸
Mr Van Nevel Carmersstraat 13 ☎050 34 68 60, ✉robert.vannevel@advalvas.be. Two unassuming

guest rooms with shared bathroom near the Spiegelrei canal. No credit cards. ❸

Hotels

Bauhaus Hotel Langestraat 133 ☎050 34 10 93, ⊛www.bauhaus.be. Twenty rooms with shared facilities, plus one en suite. Don't expect too much in the way of creature comforts, but the atmosphere is usually agreeable and the clientele friendly. ❸
Cordoeanier Cordoeaniersstraat 18 ☎050 33 90 51, ⊛www.cordoeanier.be. Medium-sized, family-run hotel handily located in the narrow side streets a couple of minutes north of the Burg. Mosquitoes can be a problem here, but the small rooms are clean and pleasant. ❹
Jacobs Baliestraat 1 ☎050 33 98 31, ⊛www.hoteljacobs.be. Pleasant hotel in a creatively modernized old brick building complete with a precipitous crowstep gable. Occupies a quiet location in one of the more attractive parts of the centre, a ten-minute walk to the northeast of the Markt. ❹
Passage Hotel Dweersstraat 28 ☎050 34 02 32. Ten simple but well-maintained rooms – four en suite - ten minutes' stroll west of the Markt. It's a very popular spot, so advance booking is essential. Also has a busy bar that's a favourite with backpackers. ❷

The City

The older sections of Bruges fan out from two central squares, Markt and Burg. **Markt**, edged on three sides by nineteenth-century gabled buildings, is the larger of the two, an impressive open space, on the south side of which the mighty **Belfry** (Tues–Sun 9.30am–5pm; €5) was built in the thirteenth century when the town

Museum pass

A **musuem pass**, available from any of the participating museums, covers six of Bruges' central museums: the Stadhuis, Renaissancezaal 't Brugse Vrije, Arentshuis, Gruuthuse, St Jans Hospitaal and Groeninge. It costs €15.

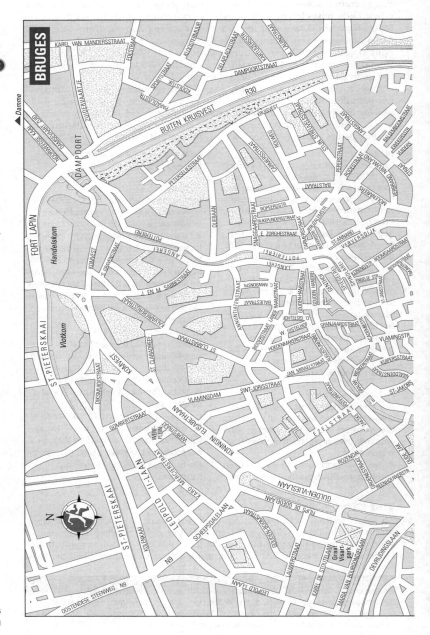

BRUGES

▲ Damme

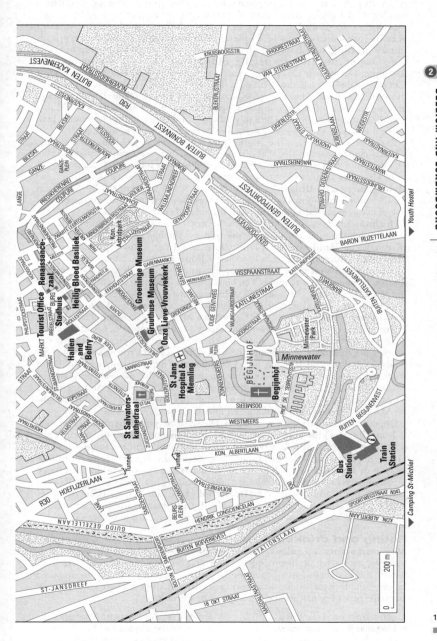

▶ Youth Hostel

▶ Camping St-Michiel

117

was at its richest and most extravagant. It is attached to the rectangular **Hallen**, a much-restored edifice dating from the thirteenth century, its style and structure modelled on the cloth hall at Ieper. Entry to the Belfry is via the Hallen. Inside, a very narrow staircase leads up to the roof. From the Markt, Breidelstraat leads through to **Burg**, whose southern half is fringed by the city's finest group of buildings. One of the best is the **Heilig Bloed Basiliek** (daily 9.30am–noon & 2–4/6pm; Oct–March closed Wed pm; free), named after a phial of the blood of Christ brought back here from Jerusalem by the Crusaders – one of the holiest relics in medieval Christendom. It divides into a shadowy **Lower Chapel**, built to house another relic, that of St Basil; and an **Upper Chapel** where the phial is stored in a grandiose silver tabernacle. The Holy Blood is still venerated on Ascension Day, when it is carried through the town in a colourful but solemn procession.

To the left of the basilica, the **Stadhuis** has a beautiful, turreted sandstone facade, a much-copied exterior that dates from 1376. Inside, the magnificent Gothic Hall of 1400 (Tues–Sun 9.30am–5pm; €2.50) is well worth a look for its ornate decoration. The price of admission covers entry to the former alderman's mansion, the **Renaissancezaal 't Brugse Vrije** (Tues–Sun 9.30am–12.30pm & 1.30–5pm), also on the square; it has just one exhibit: an enormous sixteenth-century marble and oak chimney piece carved in honour of the ruling Habsburgs.

Heading south from the Burg, through the archway next to the Stadhuis, it's a brief walk to both the eighteenth-century Vismarkt and the huddle of picturesque houses that make up **Huidenvettersplein**. Close by, **Dijver** follows the canal to the **Groeninge Museum** at no. 12 (Tues–Sun 9.30am–5pm), which reopens this spring following refurbishment. It houses a superb sample of Flemish paintings from the fourteenth to twentieth centuries. The best section is the early Flemish work, including several canvases by Jan van Eyck, who lived and worked in Bruges from 1430 until his death eleven years later. There's also work by Hieronymus Bosch and Gerard David. Further along, at no. 17, the **Gruuthuse Museum** (Tues–Sun 9.30am–5pm; €5 or museum pass), sited in a rambling fifteenth-century mansion, has a varied collection of fine and applied art, including intricately carved altar pieces and many different types of antique furniture. Beyond, the **Onze Lieve Vrouwekerk** (Tues–Sat 9.30am–12.30pm & 1.30–5pm, Sun 1.30–5pm) is a massive shambles of different dates and styles, among whose treasures is a delicate marble *Madonna and Child* by Michelangelo, an influential early work brought from Tuscany by a Flemish merchant. The chancel (€2.50) is home to the mausoleums of Charles the Bold and his daughter Mary of Burgundy; both striking examples of Renaissance carving.

Opposite the church, the large medieval ward of **St Jans Hospitaal** (Tues–Sun 9.30am–5pm; €7) has been turned into a lavish museum celebrating the city's history in general and St John's hospital in particular. In addition, the old hospital chapel displays a small but exquisite collection of paintings by **Hans Memling**. Born near Frankfurt in 1433, Memling spent most of his working life in Bruges, producing serene but warmly coloured and stunningly beautiful paintings. From St Jans, it's a quick stroll down to the **Begijnhof** (daily 9am–6pm), a circle of whitewashed houses around a tidy green. Nearby, the extraordinarily picturesque **Minnewater** was once used as a town harbour, and still has a dinky lock gate.

Eating and drinking

Most **restaurants** and **cafés** are geared up for tourists. Consequently, standards are variable, with a whole slew of places churning out some pretty mediocre stuff. There are, of course, lots of exceptions – including the places we recommend below – and these are well worth seeking out. Bruges also has a very good range of **bars**, the pick of which sell a wide range of Belgian beers.

Cafés and restaurants
Het Dagelijks Brood Philipstockstraat 21. Excellent bread shop which doubles as a

wholefood café. Mouth-watering homemade soup and bread makes a meal in itself for just €7, or you can chomp away on a range of snacks and cakes. Handy location, just off the Burg. Closed Tues.

Gran Kaffee de Passage Dweersstraat 26. This lively café is extremely popular with backpackers, many of whom have bunked down in the nearby *Passage Hostel* (see above). Serves up a good and filling line in Flemish food with many dishes cooked in beer. Mussels are featured, too, along with vegetarian options.

Lokkedize Korte Vuldersstraat 33. Sympathetic bar/café, all subdued lighting, fresh flowers and jazz music, serving up a good line in Mediterranean food. Closed Sun & Mon.

De Vlaamsche Pot Helmstraat 3–5. Informal and friendly, this restaurant, with its cosy furnishings and fittings, is justifiably popular. The menu is confined to a few traditional Flemish dishes, each competently prepared; excellent value.

Bars

Het Brugs Beertje Kemelstraat 5. Small and friendly speciality beer bar that claims a stock of 300 beers. Five minutes' walk southwest of the Markt, off Steenstraat. Closed Wed.

Cohiba Zilverstraat 38. Idiosyncratic bar popular with a fashionable, thirty-something crew. Closed Sun & Mon.

Het Dreupelhuisje Kemelstraat 9. Tiny and eminently agreeable, laid-back bar specializing in jenevers and advocaats, of which it has an outstanding range. Closed Tues.

Oud Vlissinghe Blekerstraat 2. With its wood panelling, antique paintings and long wooden tables, this is one of the oldest and most distinctive bars in Bruges. Relaxed and easy-going atmosphere with the emphasis on quiet conversation. Five minutes' walk from Jan van Eyckplein. Closed Mon & Tues.

De Republiek Sint-Jacobsstraat 38. Arguably one of the most fashionable and certainly one of the most popular café/bars in town with an arty, sometimes alternative crew. Filling snacks, including vegetarian and pastas.

De Vuurmolen Kraanplein 5. Not far from the Markt, this crowded bar is a lively spot with a reasonably wide range of beers and some of the best DJs in town– techno through house and beyond.

Southern Belgium

South of Brussels lies French-speaking Belgium, where a belt of heavy industry interrupts the rolling farmland that precedes the high wooded hills of the **Ardennes**. The latter spreads over three provinces – Namur in the west, Luxembourg in the south and Liège in the east – and is a great place for hiking and canoeing. The best gateway town for the Ardennes is the lively provincial centre of **Namur**, an hour from Brussels by train.

Namur

NAMUR is a pleasant and appealing town straddling the confluence of the rivers Sambre and Meuse, with the narrow streets of its antique centre dotted with elegant, eighteenth-century mansions, its nightlife lent vigour by the university. Occupying an important strategic location, it has been fought over time and again. The main result of all this military activity has been the construction of the massive, rambling **Citadel** (early April & June–Sept daily 11am–6pm; late April & May Sat & Sun only 11am–6pm; €6), which rolls along the top of the steep bluff overlooking the south bank of the Sambre. Originally constructed in medieval times, the citadel has been remodelled on several occasions and its assorted redoubts, underground passages, artillery emplacements and barracks span several centuries – and can take a couple of days to explore, though you can speed things up by taking the miniature train round the stronghold.

Cutting through the old town centre is **rue de l'Ange** and its continuation **rue de Fer**, which together comprise the main shopping street. A few metres east of here, the **Trésor du Prieuré d'Oignies**, rue Julie Billiart 17 (Tues–Sat 10am–noon & 2–5pm, Sun 2–5pm; €1.25), is Namur's best – and smallest – museum. Located in a nunnery, it holds a spellbinding collection of reliquaries and devotional pieces created by local craftsman Hugo d'Oignies in the first half of the thirteenth century; the nuns give the guided tour in English.

Practicalities

Namur's **train** and **bus station** is on the northern edge of the city centre on place de la Station. Close by is the **tourist office** on square Léopold, itself at the north end of rue de Fer (daily 9.30am–6pm; ☏081 24 64 49, ⊛www.ville.namur.be); here, you can get advice on cycling, walking and canoeing in the Ardennes. There's also a seasonal **tourist information chalet** (April–Sept daily 9.30am–6pm), ten minutes' walk away, over the Sambre bridge near the south end of rue de l'Ange.

Namur hardly goes overboard when it comes to **accommodation**, but there are a couple of budget options – including a **hostel** - and the tourist office has a small supply of **private rooms** (❹). There is an excellent selection of **restaurants** in town and a good supply of lively **bars**, many of them clustered in the quaint, pedestrianized squares just west of rue de l'Ange – on and around place Marché-aux-Légumes and neighbouring place Chanoine Descamps.

Accommodation

Auberge de Jeunesse avenue Félicien Rops 8 ☏081 22 36 88, ⓔnamur@laj.be. This 100-bed hostel occupies a big old house on the southern edge of town on the banks of the Meuse past the casino. There's no lock-out and the hostel has a kitchen, laundry and self-service restaurant. It's 3km from the train station; buses #3 or #4 run here from the centre. ❷

Beauregard avenue Baron de Moreau 1 ☏081 23 00 28, ⊛www.diamond.hotels.com. Part of Namur's casino complex, this hotel has attractive, large and modern rooms, some with a river-view and balcony. It's a ten-minute walk south of the centre, on the banks of the Meuse below the citadel. An excellent breakfast is included in the price. ❻

Grand Hôtel de Flandre pl de la Station 14 ☏081 23 18 68. Competent if slightly dog-eared hotel directly opposite the station. ❹

Opera Parisien rue Emile Cuvelier 16 ☏081 22 63 79. Adequate if uninspiring hotel in a routine modern building close to the town centre on the corner of rue Emile Cuvelier and rue Pépin. ❸

Restaurants

La Bonne Fourchette rue Notre Dame 112. Pint-sized, informal and family-run restaurant down below the citadel on the way to the casino. A little off the beaten track, so the prices are very reasonable and the food is delicious. Closed Wed.

La Fondue rue St Jean 19. Medium-sized restaurant serving excellent fondues and steaks. Just off place Marché-aux-Légumes.

Le Moulin à Poivre rue Bas de la Place 23. Cosy little restaurant offering tasty French food from premises just off place d'Armes.

Bars

Le Chapitre rue du Séminaire 4. Unassuming, sedate little bar with an extensive beer list. Behind the cathedral.

Henry's Bar pl St Aubain 3. Right by the cathedral, this is a big loud brasserie in the best tradition.

Le Monde à L'Envers rue Lelièvre 28. Lively, fashionable bar just up from the cathedral. A favourite spot for university students.

Piano Bar pl Marché-aux-Légumes. One of Namur's most popular bars. Live jazz Fri & Sat from 10pm.

Luxembourg

Some 100km southeast of Namur, across the border from the Belgian province of Luxembourg, the **Grand Duchy of Luxembourg** is one of Europe's smallest sovereign states, a tiny principality with a population of around 420,000. Many travellers tend to write it off as a dull and expensive financial centre, but this is a mistake. The northern part of the principality boasts charming scenery in the green forested hills of the Ardennes and is within easy reach – by road, rail and bus – of **Luxembourg City**, the country's eminently agreeable and dramatically sited capital. Home to around a fifth of the population, Luxembourg City is the country's only genuinely urban environment, and well worth one or two nights' stay. After exploring the city, you may want to see something of the rest of the **Grand Duchy** and the place to head for is the village of **Vianden** with its clifftop castle.

As regards **language**, every native speaks the indigenous language, Letzebuergesch – a dialect of German that sounds a bit like Dutch – but most also speak French and German and many speak English too.

Luxembourg City

LUXEMBOURG CITY is one of the most spectacularly situated capitals in Europe, the deep canyons of its two rivers, the Alzette and Pétrusse, lending it an almost perfect strategic location. It's a tiny place by capital-city standards and broadly divides into three distinct sections. The **old town**, on the northern side of the Pétrusse valley, is not noticeably ancient, but its tight grid of streets, home to most of the city's sights, makes for a pleasant, lively area by day. On the opposite side of the Pétrusse, connected by two bridges, is the **modern city** – less attractive and of interest only for its train station and cheap hotels. The **valleys** themselves, far below and most easily accessible by lift from place St-Esprit, are a curious mixture of houses, allotments and parkland, banking steeply up to the massive bastions that secure the old centre.

The **Old Town** focuses on two squares, the more important of which is **place d'Armes**, fringed with cafés and restaurants. To the north lie the city's principal shops, mainly along **Grande Rue**, while on the southern side a small alley cuts through to the larger **place Guillaume**, the venue of Luxembourg's main general market (Wed & Fri am) and flanked by the bland buildings of the city authorities.

Not far away, a group of patrician mansions on Marché aux Poissons holds the city's largest museum, the **Musée National d'Histoire et d'Art** (Tues–Sun 10am–5pm; €4), where there's an enjoyable sample of fifteenth- and sixteenth-century Dutch and Flemish paintings. East of the museum lie the **Casements du Bock** (daily March–Oct 10am–5pm; €1.70), underground fortifications built by the Spaniards in the eighteenth century. The city occupies an ideal defensive position and its defences were reinforced time and again – hence the massive bastions and subterranean artillery galleries of today. These particular casements are the most diverting to visit – though several others are also open throughout the summer – and afterwards you can follow the dramatic **chemin de la Corniche**, which tracks along the side of the cliff with great views of the slate-roofed houses of **Grund** down below. It leads to the gigantic **Citadelle du St-Esprit**, whose top has been levelled off and turned in part into a leafy park.

Practicalities

The **train station**, fifteen minutes' walk south of the city centre proper, is the hub of all **city bus** lines and close to many of the city's cheapest (but dreariest) hotels. There is a branch of the national **tourist office** inside the station (June–Sept Mon–Sat 9am–7pm, Sun 9am–12.30pm & 2–6pm; Oct–May daily 9.15am–12.30pm & 1.45–6pm; ☎42 82 82 20). It sells the **Luxembourg Card**, which entitles you to unlimited use of public transport throughout the Grand Duchy and admission to selected museums and attractions; a one-day card costs €8.70, the two- and three-day cards €14.90 and €21.10 respectively. The busier city **tourist office**, in the centre on place d'Armes (April–Sept Mon–Sat 9am–7pm, Sun 10am–6pm; Oct–March Mon–Sat 9am–6pm; ☎22 28 09), offers much the same facilities, but, as its name suggests, deals only with the city. There is a reasonable urban **bus** system (€1.10/journey), but Luxembourg City is small enough to make **walking** the best way of getting around.

Most of the city's **hotels** are clustered near the train station, which is the least interesting part of town. You're much better off staying in the Old Town and won't necessarily pay much more to do so, though you are limited to just a handful of places. Budget accommodation is available at the **hostel** below the Bock fortress.

As for **cafés** and **restaurants**, the city's Old Town is crowded with inexpensive places. French cuisine is popular here, but traditional Luxembourgish dishes are found on many menus too, mostly meaty affairs such as neck of pork with broad beans (*judd mat gaardebounen*) or black sausage (*blutwurst*). Keep an eye out also for *Gromperenkichelchen* (potato cakes usually served with apple sauce) – and, in winter, stalls and cafés selling *Glühwein* (mulled wine). As for **nightlife**, there's a lively bar

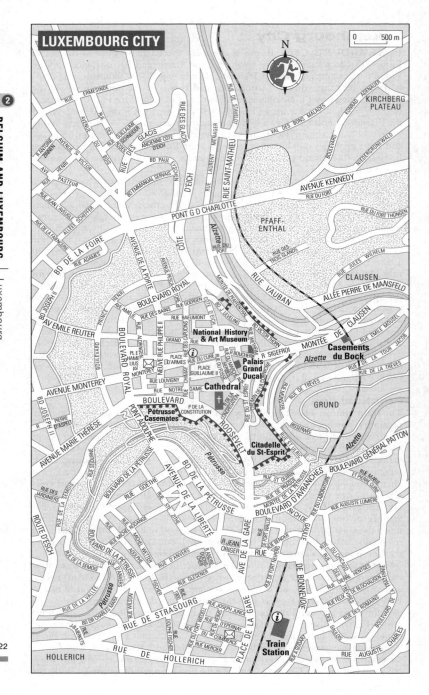

LUXEMBOURG CITY

0   500 m

N

KIRCHBERG PLATEAU

RUE ERMESINDE

RUE DES GLACIS

RUE DE STAVELOT

VAL DES BONS MALADES

KONRAD ADENAUER

BOULEVARD NIEDERGRUNEWALD

R ANTOINE ZINNEN

AVENUE S VICTOR

RUE DU BOIS

ANCIENNE CÔTE D'EICH

RUE MENAGER

RUE LAURENT MENAGER

AVENUE KENNEDY

RUE DU FORT THÜNGEN

AVE HENRI

RUE PASTEUR

BD PAUL EYSCHEN

RUE SAINT-MATHIEU

RUE DU FORT

RUE JEAN LAFAGE-LE SCHEFER

ALLEE MARCONI

BD EMMANUEL SERVAIS

PFAFF-ENTHAL

AVE DE LA FAIENCERIE

PONT G D CHARLOTTE

RUE DU PORT

RUE DES TROIS GLANDS

RUE JULES WILHELM

BD DE LA FOIRE

RUE ADAMES

AVENUE DE LA PORTE

CÔTE D'EICH

Alzette

RUE VAUBAN

CLAUSEN

ALLÉE PIERRE DE MANSFELD

BD JOSEPH II

AV EMILE REUTER

AVENUE PESCATORE

BOULEVARD ROYAL

RUE GOERGEN

RUE BAEUMONT

MONTÉE DE CLAUSEN

RUE EMILE MOUSEL

PRINCE HENRI

AVE AMELIE

RUE DES BAINS

CÔTE D'EICH

BD F.D. KLEVELING

National History & Art Museum

R SIGEFROI

Casements du Bock

RUE DE LA TOUR JACOB

BOULEVARD ROYAL

RUE ALDRINGEN

GRAND RUE NEUVE RUE PHILIPPE II

RUE CHIMAY

RUE DU CURÉ

RUE DES CAPUCINS

BOUCHERIE

RUE NOTGER THORN

Palais Grand Ducal

MONTÉE DE CLAUSEN

RUE DE TRÈVES

PL DE LA HAMELIUS

AV MONTEREY

PLACE D'ARMES

i

PLACE GUILLAUME II

RUE DU FOSSÉ

RUE DE L'EAU

RUE DE TRÈVES

AVENUE MONTEREY

RUE LOUVIGNY

RUE NOTRE DAME

Cathedral

RUE DE L'ESPRIT

GRUND

BD JOSEPH II

BOULEVARD

P DE LA CONSTITUTION

RUE DE CONGRÉGATION

RUE SOSTHÈNE WEIS

Alzette

RUE PIERRE D'ASPELT

Pétrusse Casemates

PONT ADOLPHE

ROOSEVELT

BISSERWEE

BOULEVARD GÉNÉRAL PATTON

AVENUE MARIE THÉRÈSE

RUE SÉCURANE

Pétrusse

RUE ST ULRIC

Citadelle du St-Esprit

RUE MARIE ET PIERRE CURIE

RUE DES JARDINIERS

BD DE LA PÉTRUSSE

BD DE LA PÉTRUSSE

RUE GOETHE

RUE ST JEAN

AVENUE DE LA PÉTRUSSE

RUE ST QUIRIN

RUE DE PRAGUE

MONTÉE DE LA PÉTRUSSE

BOULEVARD D'AVRANCHES

AV CH DE GAULLE

RUE DU LABORATOIRE

RUE AUGUSTE LUMIERE

ROUTE D'ESCH

RUE DE LA SEMOIS

RUE MICHEL RODANGE

RUE MICHEL WELTER

AVENUE DE LA LIBERTÉ

RUE D'ANVERS

RUE GLESENER

RUE JEAN ORIGER

AVE DE LA GARE

RUE DE FORT WALLIS

RUE DE FORT NEIPPERG

RUE DU CHICAGO

RUE DU CORT

RUE DES HENTGES

RUE DE BONNEVOIE

RUE DE LA VALLÉE

BD DR CHARLES MARX

RUE D'ANVERS

RUE 1900

RUE FISCHER

RUE JOSEPH JUNCK

RUE D'EPERNAY

RUE DE FORT WEDELL

RUE DU FORT ELISABETH

RUE FÉLIX DE BLOCHAUSEN

RUE DES ROMAINS

BOULEVARD DE LA FRATERNITÉ

J B MERCELS

RUE DE STRASBOURG

RUE JOSEPH FISCHER

RUE MERCIER

RUE DU COMMERCE

PLACE DE LA GARE

i

Train Station

RUE A GODART

RUE AUGUSTE CHARLES

HOLLERICH

RUE DE HOLLERICH

and club scene, with bars in the Old Town and Grund, and clubs mostly west of the train station in Hollerich. Opening hours are fairly elastic, but bars usually stay open till around 1am, clubs till 3am.

Hostel

Luxembourg youth hostel rue du Fort Olisy 2 ☏22 68 89, ✉luxembourg@youthhostels.lu. This barracks-like HI hostel is 3km northeast of the station on the edge of the centre in the Alzette valley; take bus #9. It has a laundry and cooking facilities and breakfast is Included.Dorms ❶

Hotels

Empire place de la Gare 34 ☏48 52 52. Straightforward modern hotel with 35 en-suite rooms opposite the station. Hardly sets the pulse racing, but is perfectly adequate. ❺
Francais place d'Armes 14 ☏47 45 34. This attractive place has smart and spotless rooms furnished in a crisp modern style. Great location, too, on the Old Town's main square. ❼
Schintgen rue Notre Dame 6 ☏22 28 44, ✉schintgen@pt.lu. Bang in the middle of the Old Town, this simple, unassuming hotel is short on accessories, but it is reasonably priced. ❺

Cafés and restaurants

Brasserie Chimay rue Chimay 15. Small, pleasantly old-fashioned café/restaurant off place d'Armes.

Traditional, straightforward dishes at inexpensive prices.
Francais place d'Armes 14. The pavement café of the *Hotel Francais* offers tasty salads and a wide-ranging menu including several Luxembourgish favourites. Excellent value daily specials.
Giorgio's Pizzeria rue du Nord 11. A sociable and eminently fashionable place tucked away off côte d'Eich in the Old Town. Closed Sun.
Maison des Brasseurs Grande Rue 48. On a modern shopping street just to the north of place d'Armes, this long-established and smartly decorated restaurant sells delicious Luxembourgish dishes. Sauerkraut is the house speciality. Closed Sun.

Nightlife

Chiggeri rue du Nord 15. Groovy bar in the Old Town that has a great atmosphere, funky decor and a mixed straight and gay clientele.
Conquest rue du Palais de Justice 7. Gay club in the Old Town. House music. Closed Sun.
Sodaz Café Bar rue de la Boucherie 16. Small and crowded bar featuring cocktails plus soul and rock.

Listings

Bike rental rue Bisserwé 8, Grund (☏47 96 23 83; €10/day, discounts for under-26s; advance booking advised).
Embassies Ireland, rte d'Arlon 28 ☏45 06 10; UK, bld Roosevelt 14 ☏22 98 64; US, bld E. Servais 22 ☏46 01 23.
Internet Chiggeri, rue du Nord 15.

Laundry Quick-Wash, rue de Strasbourg 31 (☏48 78 33).
Left luggage At the train station.
Pharmacies Goedert, pl d'Armes 5; Mortier, ave de la Gare 11.
Post office place E. Hamilius (Mon–Sat 7am–7pm).

Travel details

Trains

Antwerp to: Bruges (hourly; 1hr 20min); Brussels (every 30min; 40min); Ghent (every 30min; 50min); Ostend (hourly; 1hr 40min).
Bruges to: Antwerp (hourly; 1hr 20min); Brussels (every 30min; 1hr); Ostend (every 20min; 15min); Zeebrugge (hourly; 15min).
Brussels to: Antwerp (every 30min; 40min); Bruges (every 30min; 1hr); Ghent (every 30min; 40min); Luxembourg City (every 2hr; 2hr 30min); Namur (hourly; 50min); Ostend (hourly; 1hr 20min).
Ghent Antwerp (every 30min; 50min); Bruges

(every 20min; 25min); Brussels (every 30min; 40min); Ostend (every 30min; 50min).
Luxembourg City to: Brussels (hourly; 2hr 30min); Namur (hourly; 1hr 40min).
Namur to: Brussels (hourly; 50min); Luxembourg City (hourly; 1hr 40min).
Ostend to: Antwerp (hourly; 1hr 40min); Bruges (every 20min; 15min); Brussels (hourly; 1hr 20min); Ghent (every 30min; 50min).

Ferries

For Channel crossings, see pp.16–17.

Britain

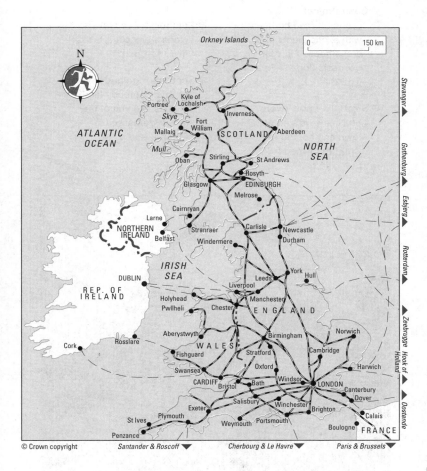

Orkney Islands

0   150 km

N

ATLANTIC
OCEAN

Portree
Kyle of
Lochalsh
Skye
Mallaig
Fort
William
Inverness
SCOTLAND
Aberdeen

Mull
Oban
Stirling
St Andrews
NORTH
SEA

Rosyth
Glasgow
EDINBURGH

Melrose

Cairnryan

Larne
NORTHERN
IRELAND
Belfast
Stranraer
Carlisle
Newcastle
Durham

Windermere

IRISH
SEA
DUBLIN
Leeds
York
Hull

Liverpool

REP. OF
IRELAND
Holyhead
Pwllheli
Chester
Manchester

E N G L A N D

Aberystwyth
Birmingham
Norwich

Cork
Rosslare
W A L E S
Stratford
Cambridge

Fishguard
Oxford
Harwich

Swansea
Windsor

CARDIFF
Bristol
Bath
LONDON
Canterbury
Dover

Salisbury
Winchester
Brighton

St Ives
Plymouth
Exeter
Calais

Weymouth
Portsmouth
Boulogne
FRANCE

Penzance

Stavanger

Gothenburg

Esbjerg

Rotterdam

Zeebrugge Hook of
Holland

Oostende

© Crown copyright   Santander & Roscoff ▼   Cherbourg & Le Havre ▼   Paris & Brussels ▼

Britain highlights

✳ **Tate Modern** London's new modern-art gallery, spectacularly housed in a former power station. See p.139

✳ **Eden Project** Disused clay pit turned hothouse, with exotic plants and crops housed in vast geodesic domes. See p.157

✳ **Stratford-upon-Avon** Shakespeare's home town and host to the world-renowned RSC. See p.162

✳ **Snowdonia** Dramatic Welsh range offers hiking and climbing opportunities, including an ascent of the country's highest mountain. See p.183

✳ **Edinburgh Festival** The world's biggest arts festival. See p.191

✳ **Scottish Highlands** Dramatic, moody landscapes in some of the last wildernesses in Europe. See p.198

Introduction and basics

The single most important thing to remember when travelling round Britain* is that you're visiting not one country, but three: England, Wales and Scotland. That means contending with three capital cities (London, Cardiff and Edinburgh) and three sets of national identity – not to mention the myriad accent shifts as you move between them.

England remains the dominant and most urbanized member of the British partnership, but crossing the border into predominantly rural **Wales** brings you into an unmistakably Celtic land, while in **Scotland** (a nation whose absorption into the state was rather more recent) the presence of a profoundly non-English worldview is striking.

For cultural sightseeing as for nightlife, **London** is a ceaselessly entertaining city, and is the one place that features on everyone's itinerary. Within the heavily built-up southeast, **Brighton** and **Canterbury** offer contrasting diversions – the former an appealing seaside resort, the latter one of Britain's finest medieval cities. The southwest of England, with the rugged moorlands of **Devon** and the rocky coastline of **Cornwall**, is an altogether wilder region, albeit one that pulls in droves of visitors in the height of summer. The chief attractions of central England are the university cities of **Oxford** and **Cambridge**, and Shakespeare's home town, **Stratford-upon-Avon**. Further north, the former industrial cities of **Manchester**, **Liverpool** and **Newcastle** are lively places, and **York** has splendid historical treasures, but the landscape is again the real magnet, especially the uplands of the **Lake District**. For true wilderness, however, you're better off heading to the **Welsh** mountains or **Scottish Highlands**. The finest of Scotland's lochs, glens and peaks, and the magnificent scenery of the west coast islands, can be reached easily from the contrasting cities of **Glasgow** and **Edinburgh** – the latter perhaps the most attractive urban landscape in Britain.

Information and maps

Tourist offices (usually called Tourist Information Centres) exist in virtually every British town. They're usually open Mon–Sat 9am–5.30/6pm, some also open Sun in summer. All offer a basic range of information on accommodation, local public transport and maps. In many cases this is free, but a growing number make a small charge for an accommodation list or a town guide. National Parks (such as the Lake District, Exmoor and Dartmoor) also have their own Information Centres, which are better for guidance on local walks and outdoor pursuits.

The most comprehensive series of **maps** is produced by the Ordnance Survey (⊛ www.ordsvy.gov.uk). Their 1:50,000 Landranger series covers the whole country, while the more detailed 1:25,000 Explorer series is invaluable for serious walking. The

---

Britain on the net

⊛ **www.visitbritain.com** Tourist board site with links to regional sites

⊛ **www.pti.org.uk** Information on public transport

⊛ **www.seaview.co.uk** Covers ferry routes and links

⊛ **www.backpackers.co.uk** General information and tips for travellers

⊛ **www.knowhere.co.uk** Irreverent local knowledge

---

*Note that "Britain" is a geographical term, referring to the largest of the British Isles. "United Kingdom" is a political term, referring to a state comprising England, Scotland, Wales and Northern Ireland. Northern Ireland, part of the political union of the United Kingdom, is covered with the rest of the island of Ireland on p.580.

Outdoor Leisure series (also 1:25,000) is devoted to Britain's National Parks and Areas of Outstanding National Beauty.

Money and banks

Britain is one of the few EU countries *not* to have embraced the euro. The **pound** (£) sterling remains the national currency and is divided into 100 pence; there are coins of 1p, 2p, 5p, 10p, 20p, 50p, £1 and £2; and notes of £5, £10, £20 and £50. Banknotes issued by Scottish banks (among them a £1 note) can be used throughout Britain; in reality, however, many businesses outside Scotland are unwilling to accept them.

Normal **banking hours** are Mon–Fri 9.30am–4.30pm. Some branches open on Sat, but times can vary. Most banks have **ATMs** that accept a wide range of debit and credit cards.

Communications

Post offices are usually open Mon–Fri 9am–5.30pm, Sat 9am–12.30/1pm, though some town-centre offices may have extended hours. **Stamps** can be bought at post office counters, vending machines outside post offices and at many newsagents and shops.

Most public **phones** are operated by BT, though you'll also see other companies' phone boxes in a variety of designs, especially in London. Most BT phones take all coins from 10p upwards (minimum charge 20p), as well as **phonecards**, available from post offices and most newsagents in denominations of £3, £5, £10 and £20. An increasing number accept credit cards too. Newsagents can sell you good-value cards from other phone companies for making **international** calls. **Domestic** calls are cheapest from 6pm to 8am and at weekends; ☎0845 numbers are charged at local rate; ☎0870 at long-distance rate; ☎07 and ☎09 are very expensive. For the operator (domestic/international) call ☎100/☎155; for directory enquiries ☎192/☎153.

Internet cafés are common in the major cities, and you'll also find access at some hostels, main train stations, and in London,

some public phones. Prices vary, but £1 should be enough for you to reply to your email.

Getting around

Public transport in Britain has been shaken up by large-scale privatization in recent years, but promised price-cuts have failed to materialize, leaving costs still among the highest in Europe. However, despite what you may have heard about the state of the network, most places are still accessible by **train** and/or **coach** (as long distance **buses** are known).

Trains

Following privatization, standard **fares** have become extremely expensive and the system notoriously less reliable. **Eurail** passes aren't valid in Britain but **InterRail** gives a thirty-percent discount; for details of other passes valid across the network, see p.20.

Cheap deals for train travel do exist, but the bafflingly complicated pricing system makes them hard to find. Generally speaking, avoid rush hours, especially Fri eve, and book your ticket as far in advance as you can to get the best deals – **saver**, **supersaver** or **superapex** tickets are generally the best deals on intercity routes. Always ask the person selling you your ticket to specify the cheapest options open to you; if you don't, there's a good chance you'll end up paying the so-called "**standard fare**", which is often twice the price of other tickets on the same route and provides no more frills than the cheap deals.

If travelling on routes between London and other major cities, and especially at weekends, during public holidays or around Christmas you should **book a seat**. Reservations are usually free if made at the same time as ticket purchase, although on some routes you'll have to pay an extra £1.

For details of all train services, call ☎0845/748 4950, or check ⊛www.rail.co.uk or ⊛www.thetrainline.com.

Coaches and buses

The long-distance **coach** services run by **National Express** (☎0870/580 8080, www.gobycoach.com) duplicate many intercity rail routes, very often at half the price or less. The frequency of service is often comparable to rail, and in some instances the difference in journey time is minimal. Coaches are comfortable, and some have drinks and sandwiches available on board. If you're a student or under 26 you can buy a **Coachcard** (£8), which gives a quarter off standard fares. The **Tourist Trail Pass**, only available within Britain, offers unlimited travel for two days in three (£49, £39 with a Coachcard), or five (£85/£69), eight (£135/£99) or fifteen (£190/£145) days in thirty. These are valid on National Express through-routes to Scotland, but not on services within Scotland itself. These are provided by the sister company Scottish Citylink (℡0870/550 5050, www.citylink. co.uk), which has its own Explorer Pass for three (£33), five (£55) or ten days (£85) within ten; it also lets you travel free on Inverness–Aberdeen trains and half-price on some island ferries.

Local bus services are run by a bewildering array of companies, some private, some not. As a rule, the further away from urban areas you get, the less frequent and more expensive bus services become, but there are very few rural areas which aren't served by at least the occasional minibus.

Accommodation

Budget **accommodation** isn't hard to come by in Britain. Many tourist offices will book local rooms for you, but you should expect to pay a ten percent deposit for this service. Most also operate a "Book a Bed Ahead" service for accommodation in other towns, which usually costs around £3.

Hotels and B&Bs

Hotels in Britain are generally of a high quality but are also expensive – in tourist cities it's hard to find a double for less than £50 a night. Fortunately, there's a wide range of budget accommodation in the form of **guest houses** and **B&Bs** – often a comfortable room in a family home, followed by a substantial breakfast, from around £15 a head (a bit more in the affluent south, and a lot more

in London). Many B&Bs have only a few rooms so advance booking is advisable.

Hostels and camping

Britain has an extensive network of **HI hostels**; all of those listed in the *Guide* can be contacted by email via their respective **websites** (see p.47). In Scotland, a bed for the night can cost as little as £4, except in the cities, where you can pay more than twice that. In England and Wales the charge for under-18s is nearer £10 (considerably higher in London); over-18s pay around fifty percent more. Catering varies with the size of the hostel, from a set meal at a set time in the smaller ones to a cafeteria system in the bigger ones. **Privately run hostels** are generally of a comparable standard and can be several pounds cheaper than their HI counterparts.

There are more than 750 official **campsites** in Britain, charging from £8 per tent per night. In the countryside farmers will let you camp in a field if you ask, sometimes charging a couple of pounds for the privilege. Camping rough is illegal in designated parkland and nature reserves.

Food and drink

British **food** has long had a poor reputation, but things have been changing in recent years and it's now possible to eat well and cheaply, thanks chiefly to the inspiration of Britain's various ethnic communities. Social life, however, has always focused more on **drinking** than eating, and a pub is often the best introduction to the life of a town.

Food

In many B&Bs you'll be offered an "**English breakfast**" – basically sausage, bacon and fried eggs – although most places will give you the option of cereal, toast and fruit as well. Every major town will have its upmarket restaurant specializing in classic meat-based British food, but for most visitors the quintessential British meal is **fish and chips**, a dish that can vary from the succulently fresh to the indigestibly greasy. However, the once ubiquitous fish-and-chip shop ("chippy") is now outnumbered on Britain's high streets by pizza, kebab and burger joints. Less threatened is the so-called **"greasy spoon"**, generally a down-at-heel diner where the average menu will include bacon sandwiches and high-cholesterol variations on sausages, fried eggs, bacon and chips.

Many **pubs** also serve food, usually at lunchtime only; menus consist of meat-and-vegetable dishes such as steak-and-kidney pie, shepherd's pie (minced lamb topped with potato), chops or steaks, accompanied by boiled potatoes and plain veg, but the range and quality is improving and some so-called **gastro-pubs** can offer menus to rival any restaurant. There's also an increasing number of **vegetarian** restaurants, especially in the larger towns, but most places – including the pub menus – will make some attempt to cater for vegetarians.

For sit-down dining, though, the innumerable outlets for **non-British cuisine** offer the best-value meals. In every town of any size you'll find Chinese, Indian (the "curry house" has become a national institution to rival the chippy) and Italian eateries, and more – from Caribbean to Thai – with London and the industrial cities of the north holding the widest choice and the finest quality.

Drink

Drinking traditionally takes place in the **pub**, where a standard range of draught **beers** – sold by the pint or half-pint – generates most of the business here, although imported bottled beers are also popular. Beers fall into two distinct groups: cold, blond, fizzy lager and the very different darker ale, or bitter, which is flat, served at room temperature and varies in taste from brewer to brewer. Many pubs also serve tea and coffee, and all have soft drinks. In England, pubs are generally open Mon–Sat 11am–11pm, Sun noon–10.30pm (though some close daily 3–5.30pm); hours are often longer in Scotland, while Sun closing is common in Wales. In bigger towns there's an increasing number of **wine bars**, European-style cafés and brasseries, which also serve food.

In Scotland, the national drink is of course **whisky**, a spirit of far greater subtlety than bland mass-marketed blended whiskies might lead you to believe. The best are the single malts, produced by often very small

distilleries from local spring water. Most English and Welsh pubs sell only two or three whiskies (invariably blends); you'll generally find the best malt selections in pubs in Scotland.

Opening hours and holidays

General **shop hours** are Mon–Sat 9am–5.30/6pm, although an increasing number of places in big town are also open Sun (usually 10am–4pm) and till 7/8pm at least once a week. In Scotland you'll find more places open on Sun than in England, and in Wales far fewer. Many small towns still have an "early closing day" when shops close at 1pm (often Wed or Thurs).

In England and Wales, **public holidays** ("bank holidays") are: Jan 1; Good Fri; Easter Mon; first Mon in May; last Mon in May; last Mon in Aug; Christmas Day and Boxing Day (Dec 25 & 26). In Scotland: Jan 1, Jan 2 & Dec 25 are the only fixed public holidays – otherwise towns are left to pick their own holidays.

Museums and monuments

Many of Britain's national **museums** are free, but stately homes and monuments are often administered by the state-run **English Heritage** (**EH** in opening times through the *Guide*; ⊛www.english-heritage.org.uk) and **Historic Scotland** (**SH**; ⊛www.historic-scotland.gov.uk); while in Wales **CADW** (**CADW**; ⊛www.cadw.wales.gov.uk) owns several dramatic ruins. The trio run a joint membership scheme – if you join one, admission to sites run by the other two is half-price – good value if you intend to visit more than half-a-dozen, since entry fees can be high. Annual fees to join EH/HS/Cadw are £31/£26/£22. You can join EH/Cadw for £18/15 if you're under 21, or HS for £20 if you're a full-time student. The privately run **National Trust** (**NT**; ⊛www.nationaltrust.org .uk) and **National Trust for Scotland** (**NTS**; ⊛www.nts.org.uk) also run a large number of gardens and stately homes nationwide; annual membership of NT/NTS costs £30/£27 (£15/£12 for under-25s), and each pass is recognized by the other, as well as by EH, HS and CADW. All these let you join online or at any of their properties.

The **Great British Heritage Pass**, which covers entry to sites administered by all the organizations above and many others too, is worth considering; it's available from the British Travel Centre and Tourist Information Centres (seven days £35; fifteen days £46; one month £60), as well as worldwide agents. All but the biggest churches and cathedrals are free, although most charge for access to towers, museums, cloisters and the like, and nearly all request donations.

Emergencies

Although the traditional image of the friendly British bobby has become tarnished by recent exposés of racism and corruption, **police** remain approachable and helpful. Tourists aren't a particular target for criminals except perhaps in the crowds of central London, where you should be on your guard against pickpockets. Britain's bigger conurbations all contain inner-city areas where you may feel uneasy after dark, but these are usually away from tourist sights.

Pharmacists can dispense only a limited range of drugs without a doctor's prescription. Most are open standard shop hours, though in large towns some may stay open as late as 10pm. Local newspapers carry lists of **late-opening** pharmacies. Opening times of doctors' surgeries vary greatly; in any case, you can always turn up at the accident and emergency (A&E) department of a local **hospital** for complaints that require immediate attention.

Emergency Numbers

Police, Fire & Ambulance ☎999.

London

With a population of well over seven million, **LONDON** is by far Europe's biggest city, spreading over an area of more than 1500sq km from its core on the River Thames. This is where the country's news and money are made, and if Londoners' sense of superiority causes some resentment in the regions, it's undeniable that the city has a unique aura of excitement and success. However, all this comes at a price; with high accommodation and transport costs, this is one of the most expensive city's in the world.

London is a thrilling place to visit. Thanks to the frenzy of lottery and millennium-funding of the last few years, virutally all of London's world-class museums and galleries have been reinvented, from the British Museum to the Tate Modern, and the vast majority are free of charge. London also boasts the world's largest observation wheel and the first new bridge to cross the Thames for over a hundred years. Of course, the traditional sights – from Big Ben to the Tower of London – continue to draw in millions of tourists every year. Yet there's also much enjoyment to be had from the city's Georgian squares, riverside walks and its sizeable, very central parks: Hyde Park, Green Park and St James's – not to mention Hampstead Heath, Greenwich and Kew on the periphery.

The **Romans** founded the town of Londinium on the north bank of the Thames soon after invading Britain in 43 AD, but the city's expansion didn't really begin until the eleventh century, when the last successful invader of Britain, **William of Normandy**, became in 1066 the first king of England to be crowned in Westminster Abbey. Subsequent monarchs left their imprint, but many of the city's finest structures were destroyed in a few days in 1666, when the **Great Fire of London** razed over 13,000 houses and nearly ninety churches. Christopher Wren was commissioned to replace much of the lost architecture, and rose to the challenge by designing such masterpieces as St Paul's Cathedral. Unfortunately, only a portion of the post-Fire splendours has survived, due partly to the bombing raids of the **Blitz** in World War II and partly to some equally disfiguring postwar development. However, the special atmosphere comes less from the look of the streets than from the life on its streets. This has been a multicultural city since at least the seventeenth century, when it was a haven for Huguenot (French Protestant) refugees. Today, London is by far Europe's most **multicultural city**, continuing to absorb immigrant communities from all over the world.

Arrival

Flying into London, you'll arrive at one of the capital's three **international airports**: Heathrow, Gatwick or Stansted – all of which are less than an hour from the city centre. From **Heathrow**, twelve miles west of the city, the Piccadilly Line **underground** runs to central London in about an hour (£3.60), or there's the Heathrow Express **rail** link to Paddington Station (every 15min; 15min; £12). There's also **National Express** service to Victoria Coach Station (every 30min; 45min; £7) or **Airbus #2** which goes to several destinations throughout the city terminating at Euston (every 30min; 1hr 30min; £8). After midnight, **night bus #N9** runs to Trafalgar Square (every 30min; 55min; £1). **Gatwick**, thirty miles to the south, is connected by several **train** companies: the Gatwick Express speeds to Victoria Station (every 15–30min; 35min; £11), although South Central trains on the same route are cheaper (every 15–30min; 40min; £8.20); Thameslink trains run to Blackfriars and King's Cross (Mon–Sat every 15–30min; 45min; £9.80). **Stansted**, 34 miles to the northeast, is served by Stansted Express **trains** to Liverpool St Station (every 15–30min; 45min; £13). **Airbus #6** runs to Victoria Coach Station (every 30min; 1hr 30min; £8).

Eurostar **trains** from Paris or Brussels through the Channel Tunnel terminate at Waterloo International. Trains from the English Channel ports arrive at Victoria,

Liverpool St or Charing Cross, while those from elsewhere in Britain come into one of London's numerous mainline termini (see p.9), all of which have tube stations. **Buses** from around Britain and continental Europe arrive at Victoria Coach Station, 500m walk south of Victoria Station.

Note that London is divided up by area **postcodes**, used by everyone to locate addresses. It's an arcane system that's difficult for first-time visitors to pick up, but here are a few central districts: W1 is the West End of Soho, Mayfair and Marylebone; Bloomsbury is WC1; Covent Garden is WC2.

Information

London Tourist Board (LTB, ⓦ www.londontown.com) has a desk in the tube station for Heathrow Terminals 1, 2 and 3 (daily 8am–6pm), but the main central office is near Piccadilly in the **British Visitor Centre**, 1 Regent St (Mon–Fri 9/9.30am–6.30pm, Sat & Sun 9/10am–4/5pm). There are also offices at Waterloo International (daily 8.30am–10.30pm), Liverpool St tube station (daily 8am–6/7pm), and in Victoria Station (Mon–Sat 8/9am–7/9pm, Sun 8am–6.15pm). None of these offices accept telephone queries but LTB's well-designed website is crammed with useful material. The **British Tourist Authority** has an enquiry line (ⓣ 020/8846 9000, ⓦ ww.visitbritain.com).

City transport

The **London Transport information office** at Piccadilly Circus tube station (daily 9am–6pm; ⓦ www.londontransport.co.uk) will provide free transport maps, with other desks at Euston, Heathrow Terminals 1, 2 & 3, King's Cross, Liverpool St and Victoria. There's also a 24-hour phone line for information on all bus, tube and boat services (ⓣ 020/7222 1234).

The quickest way to get around London is by **Underground**, or **Tube**, as it's known to all Londoners (daily 5.30/7.30am–midnight). Tickets are bought from machines or ticket counters in all station entrance halls, or from many newsagents. A one-way journey in central Zone 1 costs £1.60, or you can buy a Carnet of ten tickets for £11.50. Better value is a **Travelcard**, valid for buses and suburban trains and the tube. A Day Travelcard (Mon–Fri after 9.30am, Sat & Sun all day) costs £4.10 for Zones 1–2, enough to cover virtually everything you'll want to see; £5 for all six zones, which includes Heathrow. If you're travelling before 9.30am (Mon–Fri), you need an **LT card** instead, valid all day on buses and tubes only, and costing £5.30 for Zones 1–2. A bargain weekend Travelcard costs £6.10 for Zones 1–2. Weekly Travelcards cost £16.20 for Zone 1, or £19.30 for Zones 1–2; to buy Weekly Travelcards you need ID and a passport-sized photo. **Visitor Travelcards**, which come packaged with discount vouchers for city attractions, are only available outside the UK (see website).

Without a travelcard, any bus journey in the central zone costs £1; normally you pay the driver on entering, although older buses with an open rear platform are staffed by a fare-collecting conductor. A lot of bus stops are **request stops**, so if you don't hold your arm out the bus will drive past. After midnight, **night buses** (prefixed with the letter "N") take over, with services radiating out from Trafalgar Square (every 20min–1hr). All fares are £1, and Travelcards are valid.

River-boat services on the Thames are fairly limited. Westminster Pier, beside Westminster Bridge, Embankment Pier and Waterloo Pier near the London Eye are the main central embarkation points. Among the many routeings are boats east to the Tower of London (every 40min; 30min; £5.20) and Greenwich (50min; £6.30), and west to Kew (3 daily; 1hr 30min; £9) and Hampton Court (3 daily; 3hr 30min; £12). Return fares are much better value than singles and Travelcards give you a 33 percent discount.

If you're in a group of three or more, London's metered **black cabs** (taxis) can be an economical way of riding across the centre; from Euston to Victoria should cost

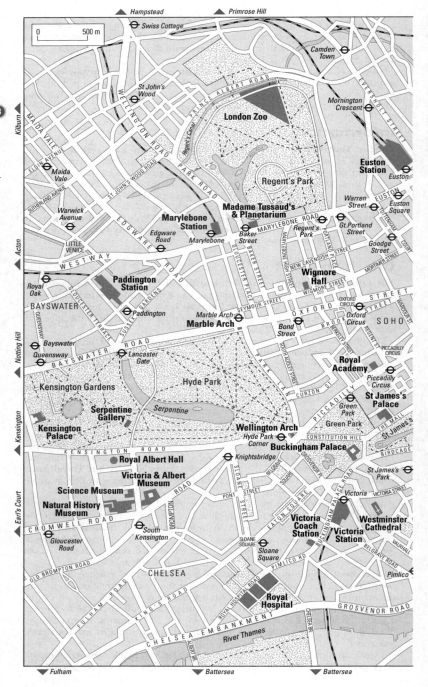

▲ Hampstead   ▲ Primrose Hill

⊖ Swiss Cottage

Camden
Town ⊖

Kilburn ◄

St John's
Wood

London Zoo

Mornington
Crescent ⊖

EVERSHOLT STREET

Maida
Vale ⊖

Elgin Avenue

Sutherland Avenue

Warwick
Avenue ⊖

MAIDA VALE

PRINCE ALBERT ROAD

Regent's Canal

Regent's Park

Euston
Station
⊖ Euston

Acton ◄

LITTLE
VENICE

WELLINGTON ROAD

ST JOHN'S WOOD ROAD

PARK ROAD

EDGWARE ROAD

Edgware
Road ⊖

Marylebone
Station

Marylebone ⊖

Madame Tussaud's
& Planetarium

Baker
Street ⊖

MARYLEBONE ROAD

Regent's
Park ⊖

Warren
Street ⊖

EUSTON

Euston
Square ⊖

Gt.Portland
Street ⊖

Goodge
Street ⊖

NEW CAVENDISH STREET

MORTIMER STREET

TOTTENHAM COURT

Bayswater ◄

Royal
Oak ⊖

BAYSWATER

QUEENSWAY

GLOUCESTER TERRACE

WESTWAY

Paddington
Station

⊖ Paddington

GLOUCESTER PLACE

BAKER STREET

MARYLEBONE HIGH STREET

PORTLAND PLACE

Wigmore
Hall

WIGMORE STREET

OXFORD

OXFORD
CIRCUS ⊖

Oxford
Circus ⊖

STREET

WARDOUR ST

SOHO

Notting Hill ◄

Bayswater ⊖

Queensway ⊖

BAYSWATER ROAD

SUSSEX GARDENS

Lancaster
Gate ⊖

Kensington Gardens

Marble Arch ⊖

Marble Arch

Hyde Park

SEYMOUR STREET

Bond
Street ⊖

SOUTH AUDLEY STREET

PARK LANE

BROOK STREET

BERKELEY STREET

REGENT'S STREET

PICCADILLY
CIRCUS ⊖

Piccadilly
Circus

Royal
Academy

Kensington ◄

Kensington
Palace

Serpentine
Gallery

Serpentine

Wellington Arch

Hyde Park
Corner ⊖

CURZON ST

PICCADILLY

CONSTITUTION HILL

Green
Park ⊖

Green Park

St James's
Palace

St James's ⊖

THE MALL

BIRDCAGE

Earl's Court ◄

KENSINGTON ROAD

Royal Albert Hall ●

Victoria & Albert
Museum

Science Museum

Natural History
Museum

CROMWELL ROAD

Gloucester
Road ⊖

OLD BROMPTON ROAD

⊖ South
Kensington

BROMPTON ROAD

Knightsbridge ⊖

SLOANE STREET

PONT STREET

BELGRAVE SQUARE

EATON SQUARE

SLOANE
SQUARE

Sloane
Square ⊖

CHELSEA

KING'S ROAD

FULHAM ROAD

ROYAL HOSPITAL ROAD

Buckingham Palace

BUCKINGHAM PALACE ROAD

GROSVENOR PL

St James's
Park ⊖

Victoria ⊖ VICTORIA STREET

Victoria
Coach
Station

Victoria
Station ⊖

Westminster
Cathedral

BELGRAVE ROAD

VAUXHALL

Pimlico ⊖

PIMLICO RD

Royal
Hospital

GROSVENOR ROAD

CHELSEA EMBANKMENT

ALBERT BR

CHELSEA BR

River Thames

▼ Fulham   ▼ Battersea   ▼ Battersea

0 ———— 500 m

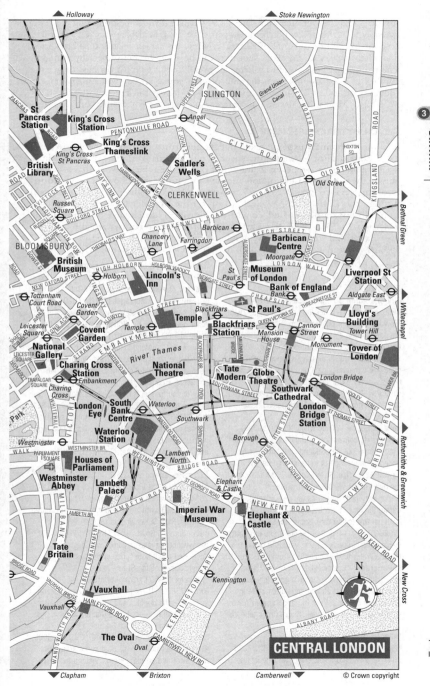

ISLINGTON

Grand Union Canal

NEW NORTH ROAD

ROAD

PANCRAS ROAD

St Pancras Station

King's Cross Station

⊖ Angel

PENTONVILLE ROAD

CITY ROAD

HOXTON SQ

KINGSLAND

King's Cross St Pancras

King's Cross Thameslink

ST JOHN ST

GOSWELL ROAD

FARRINGDON ROAD

ROSEBERY AVENUE

Sadler's Wells

OLD STREET

⊖ Old Street

GRAY'S INN ROAD

British Library

EUSTON ROAD

▶ Bethnal Green

Russell Square

GUILFORD STREET

CLERKENWELL

CLERKENWELL ROAD

OLD STREET

GOWER ST

TAVISTOCK PLACE

SOUTHAMPTON ROW

THEOBALD'S WAY

⊖ Chancery Lane

⊖ Barbican

BEECH STREET

Barbican Centre

BLOOMSBURY

THEOBALD'S ROAD

Farringdon ⊖

Moorgate

LONDON WALL

MOORGATE

▶ Whitechapel

British Museum

HIGH HOLBORN

HOLBORN VIADUCT

ALDERSGATE STREET

Museum of London

Liverpool St Station ⊖

⊖ Holborn

Lincoln's Inn

NEWGATE STREET

St Paul's ⊖

Bank of England

GOWER S

NEW OXFORD STREET

KINGSWAY

Tottenham Court Road ⊖

CHEAPSIDE

Bank ⊖

THREADNEEDLE ST

⊖ Aldgate East

CHARING CROSS ROAD

Covent Garden ⊖

DRURY LANE

ALDWYCH

FLEET STREET

Blackfriars

✠ **St Paul's**

QUEEN VICTORIA ST

Lloyd's Building

Temple

Blackfriars Station

⊖ Cannon Street

Tower Hill ⊖

LONG ACRE

Covent Garden

Temple ⊖

BLACKFRIARS BR.

Mansion House ⊖

Monument ⊖

Tower of London

Leicester Square ⊖

ST MARTIN'S LANE

EMBANKMENT

SOUTHWARK BRIDGE

Cannon Street

LEICESTER SQUARE

National Gallery

River Thames

HAYMARKET

TRAFALGAR SQUARE

Charing Cross Station

National Theatre

Tate Modern

Globe Theatre

London Bridge ⊖

TOWER BR

Park

Charing Cross

Embankment ⊖

Southwark Cathedral

TOOLEY STREET

▶ Rotherhithe & Greenwich

WHITEHALL

London Eye

South Bank Centre

Waterloo

SOUTHWARK STREET

Southwark ⊖

ST THOMAS STREET

London Bridge Station

VICTORIA

Waterloo Station

WATERLOO ROAD

Borough ⊖

LONG LANE

BRIDGE ROAD

Westminster ⊖

WESTMINSTER BR.

Lambeth North ⊖

BOROUGH ROAD

BOROUGH HIGH STREET

GREAT DOVER STREET

WALK

PARLIAMENT SQUARE

WESTMINSTER

Houses of Parliament

Westminster Abbey

Lambeth Palace

LAMBETH BR.

ST GEORGE'S ROAD

Elephant & Castle ⊖

TOWER

NEW KENT ROAD

LAMBETH ROAD

Imperial War Museum

Elephant & Castle

BRIDGE ROAD

OLD KENT ROAD

MILLBANK

Tate Britain

ALBERT EMBANKMENT

KENNINGTON ROAD

KENNINGTON PARK ROAD

WALWORTH ROAD

▶ New Cross

BRIDGE ROAD

VAUXHALL BRIDGE

Vauxhall

HARLEYFORD ROAD

Vauxhall ⊖

Kennington ⊖

ALBANY ROAD

WANDSWORTH ROAD

The Oval

Oval ⊖

CAMBERWELL NEW RD

KENNINGTON ROAD

N

🏃

CENTRAL LONDON

135

around £10. However, after 8pm, fares go sky high and you're best off using the Tube. A yellow light over the windscreen tells you if the cab is available – just wave to hail it. To book in advance, call ☎020/7272 0272. **Minicabs** are less reliable than black cabs, since their drivers are untrained, but they can be a lot cheaper (especially at night). There are hundreds of minicab firms all over London – you'd do best to get the number of a local outfit from the pub or club you're at. For women drivers, call Ladycabs on ☎020/7254 3501; for gay/lesbian drivers call Freedom Cars ☎020/ 7734 1313. Most minicabs are not metered, so check the fare before you get going.

Accommodation

London is extremely expensive, and budget **accommodation** in the centre tends to be poor quality. However, the sheer size of the place means you'll have little trouble finding a room, even in midsummer, and the tube network makes staying outside the centre a feasible option. All the LTB offices listed above operate a **room booking service**, which costs £5, or you can book by phone with a credit card through the LTB (☎020/7932 2020) or via the internet (ⓦwww.londontown .com). To book a **hostel bed**, contact the individual hostels, or for HI hostels, the YHA (☎020/7373 3400, ⓦwww.yha.org.uk). **Student rooms** are also available over Easter and from July to September: contact Imperial College (☎020/7594 9507, ⓦwww.ad.ic.ac.uk) or the LSE (☎020/7955 7370, ⓦwww.lse.ac.uk).

Hostels

HI hostels
City of London 36 Carter Lane, EC4 ☎020/7236 4965. In the City – a desolate area at night – with crowded dorms or private rooms. St Paul's or Blackfriars tube. ❺
Earl's Court 38 Bolton Gardens, SW5 ☎020/7373 7083. Comfortable and fairly capacious, with good-value meals. Earl's Court tube. ❺
Hampstead Heath 4 Wellgarth Rd, NW1 ☎020/8458 9054. One of the biggest and best-appointed, near the wilds of Hampstead Heath. Golders Green tube. ❺
Holland House Holland Walk, W8 ☎020/7937 0748. Fairly convenient for the centre, with a nice location overlooking parkland, and large dorms. Holland Park or High St Kensington tube. ❺
Oxford St 14 Noel St, W1 ☎020/7734 1618. In the heart of the West End, but with only 75 beds, it fills up very fast. Discounts for weekly stays. Oxford Circus or Tottenham Court Rd tube. ❺
Rotherhithe Island Yard, Salter Rd, SE16 ☎020/7232 2114. Rather far out to the east, but a viable option in peak season, with 320 beds. Canada Water tube or bus #381 from Waterloo. ❺
St Pancras 79 Euston Rd, NW1 ☎020/7388 9998. Sparkling new hostel in a good location opposite St Pancras station and within walking distance of both the West End and Camden Town, with small dorms and twins. King's Cross tube. ❺

Other hostels
Leinster Inn 7–12 Leinster Sq, W2 ☎020/7229 9641, ⓦwww.astorhotels.com. The biggest and

liveliest of the Astor hostels, close to Notting Hill, with a variety of rooms from singles to dorms. Under 30s only. Queensway or Notting Hill Gate tube. ❹
Museum Inn 27 Montague St, W1 ☎020/7580 5360, ⓦwww.astorhotels.com. The quietest of the Astor hostels, near the British Museum, with the usual friendly young crowd. Russell Sq tube. ❹
Generator Compton Place, W1 ☎020/7388 7666, ⓦwww.the-generator.co.uk. Neon-lit post-industrial decor, and a youthful clientele. No sharing with strangers, so prices get cheaper the more you have in your posse. Russell Sq or Euston tube. ❹
St Christopher's Village 121 Borough High St, SE1 ☎020/7407 1856, ⓦwww.st-christophers.co.uk. Upbeat and cheerful hostel in a series of buildings near London Bridge, with a café and late bar onsite and cosmopolitan clientele. London Bridge tube. ❹

Hotels and B&Bs
Abbey House 11 Vicarage Gate, W8 ☎020/7727 2594, ⓦwww.abbeyhousekensington.com. Victorian B&B, with large, bright rooms with shared facilities. High St Kensington tube. ❽
Cavendish 75 Gower St, WC1 ☎020/7636 9079, ⓦwww.hotelcavendish.com. Clean, tastefully decorated guest house, one of the best in Bloomsbury. Goodge St tube. ❺
Crescent 49–50 Cartwright Gardens, WC1 ☎020/7387 1515, ⓦwww.crescenthoteloflondon .com. En-suite doubles and a few bargain singles in a beautiful Regency house that are a cut above the rest. Euston or Russell Sq tube. ❽
Dover 42–44 Belgrave Rd, SW1 ☎020/7821 9085, ⓦwww.dover-hotel.co.uk. Best in the area, with nice decor and en-suite rooms. Victoria tube. ❼

Garden Court 30–31 Kensington Gardens Sq, W2 ☎ 020/7229 2553, ⊛ www.gardencourthotel.co.uk. Presentable, family-run hotel near Portobello Market. Bayswater tube. ❻

Philbeach 30–31 Philbeach Gardens, SW5 ☎ 020/7373 1244, ⊛ www.philbeachhotel.freeserve.co.uk. London's busiest gay hotel, with a popular restaurant attached. Earl's Court tube. ❻

Ridgemount 65–67 Gower St, WC1 ☎ 020/7636 1141, ⊛ www.ridgemounthotel.co.uk. Old-fashioned family-run Bloomsbury hotel with a garden and a laundry service. Goodge St tube. ❻

Rushmore Hotel 11 Trebovir Rd, SW5 ☎ 020/7370 3839, ⊛ www.rushmore.activehotels.com. A cut above the average in this often dreary Earl's Court area. Earl's Court tube. ❽

Oxford House 92–94 Cambridge St, SW1 ☎ 020/7834 6467. Very friendly B&B with pristine rooms and shared facilities; booking essential. Victoria tube. ❻

Strand Continental Hotel 143 Strand, WC2 ☎ 020/7836 4880. Tiny Indian-run hotel offering very basic rooms with shared facilties; an unbeatable central London bargain. Covent Garden or Temple tube. ❺

Woodville House and **Morgan House** 107 & 120 Ebury St ☎ 020/7730 1048, ⊛ www.woodvillehouse .co.uk. Jointly run above-average B&Bs, some en-suite rooms. Patio gardens and great breakfasts. Victoria tube. ❼

Campsites

Abbey Wood Federation Rd, SE2 ☎ 020/8311 7708. Enormous, well-equipped Caravan Club site east of Greenwich. Maximum two weeks' stay in summer. Train from Charing Cross to Abbey Wood.

Crystal Palace Crystal Palace Parade ☎ 020/8778 7155. Caravan Club site, maximum two weeks' stay in summer. Train from Victoria or London Bridge to Crystal Palace.

The City

The majority of sights are north of the **River Thames**, but there's no single focus of interest. One of the few areas that's manageable on foot is the area around Whitehall, with **Trafalgar Square** at one end and Parliament Square at the other, with **Buckingham Palace** to the west. The busiest, most popular area for visitors and Londoners alike is the **West End**, centred on Leicester Square and Piccadilly Circus, and home to the majority of the city's theatres and cinemas.

The financial district lies a mile or so to the east, and is known, confusingly, as the **City of London**, at once the most ancient and most modern part of London. Over on the other side of the river, the **South Bank** has become a prime tourist destination thanks to, among others, the London Eye, the Tate Modern and Shakespeare's Globe. Further afield, **Greenwich** makes for a great day out, as do the Royal Botanic Gardens at **Kew**, and the outlying royal palaces of **Hampton Court** and **Windsor Castle**.

Trafalgar Square and the National Gallery

Despite being little more than a glorified traffic island, **Trafalgar Square** is still one of London's grandest architectural set-pieces. The square's focal point is **Nelson's Column**, featuring the one-eyed admiral who died whilst defeating the French at the 1805 Battle of Trafalgar. Four lions (and innumerable pigeons) guard the column's base, and two adjacent fountains are a magnet for overheating sightseers during the summer.

Extending across the north side of the square is the bulk of the **National Gallery** (daily 10am–6pm, Wed till 9pm; free; ⊛ www.nationalgallery.org.uk), one of the world's great art collections. A quick tally of the National's Italian masterpieces includes works by Piero della Francesca, Raphael, Botticelli, Michelangelo, Leonardo da Vinci, Caravaggio, Titian and Veronese. From Spain there are dazzling pieces by Velázquez (including the *Rokeby Venus*), El Greco and Goya. From the Low Countries there's Memlinck, van Eyck (the *Arnolfini Marriage*), Rubens, and some of Rembrandt's most searching portraits. The collection also includes several very famous Impressionist and Post-Impressionist works by the likes of Seurat, Cézanne, Van Gogh and Monet. If you want to take the art chronologically, you should start in the Sainsbury Wing, a mildly postmodern annexe on the west side.

Round the side of the National Gallery, in St Martin's Place, is the **National**

Portrait Gallery (daily 10am–6pm, Thur & Fri till 9pm; free; ⊛www.npg.org.uk), which houses portraits of the great and good from Hans Holbein's larger-than-life drawing of Henry VIII, to photographs of the latest pop stars and footballers.

The Mall and Buckingham Palace

The tree-lined sweep of **The Mall** runs from Trafalgar Square, through the imposing Admiralty Arch, and on to **Buckingham Palace** (Aug & Sept daily 9.30am–4.15pm; £11.50; ⊛www.royal.gov.uk). Popularly known as "Buck House", the palace has served as the monarch's permanent residence only since the accession of Queen Victoria in 1837. The building's exterior, last remodelled in 1913, is as bland as could be; inside, it's all suitably lavish, but only worth a visit to view the van Dycks and Rembrandts on the walls. There's more high-class art on display in the newly revamped **Queen's Gallery** (daily 10am–4.30pm; £6.50), on the south side of the palace.

When Buckingham Palace is closed, most folk simply mill about outside the gates, with the largest crowds assembling for the **Changing of the Guard** (May–Aug daily 11.30am; Sept–April alternate days; no ceremony if it rains). However, you're better off heading for the **Horse Guards** building on Whitehall (see below), where a more elaborate equestrian ceremony takes place (Mon–Sat 11am, Sun 10am). Wherever you watch the Changing of the Guard, you can relax afterwards in nearby **St James's Park**, immaculately laid out south of the Mall, its lake providing an inner-city reserve for wildfowl and a recreation area for the employees of Whitehall.

Whitehall

Heading south from Trafalgar Square is the broad sweep of **Whitehall**, lined with government buildings and civil service offices. The original Whitehall was a palace built for King Henry VIII and subsequently extended, but virtually the only bit to survive a fire in 1698 is the supremely elegant **Banqueting House** (Mon–Sat 10am–5pm; £3.90; ⊛www.hrp.org.uk), begun by Inigo Jones in the Palladian style in 1619 and decorated with vast ceiling paintings by Rubens, glorifying the Stuart dynasty. They were commissioned by James' son Charles I – who on January 30, 1649, stepped onto the executioner's scaffold from one of the building's front windows.

Further down this west side of Whitehall is London's most famous address, **10 Downing St**, residence of the Prime Minister since 1732. During World War II, the Cabinet was forced to vacate Downing St in favour of a bunker in nearby King Charles St. The **Cabinet War Rooms** (daily 9.30/10am–6pm; £5; ⊛www .iwm.org.uk) – left more or less as they were in 1945 – provide a glimpse of the claustrophobic suites from which Winston Churchill directed wartime operations.

The Houses of Parliament and Westminster Abbey

Clearly visible at the south end of Whitehall is one of London's best-known buildings, the Palace of Westminster, better known as the **Houses of Parliament**. The city's finest Gothic Revival building and symbol of a nation once confident of its place at the centre of the world, it's distinguished above all by the ornate, gilded clock tower popularly known as **Big Ben**, after the thirteen-ton bell that it houses. The original royal palace, built by Edward the Confessor in the eleventh century, burnt down in 1834. The only relic of the medieval palace to survive is the magnificent Westminster Hall, which can be glimpsed en route to the **public galleries** (Mon–Thurs from 4.30pm, Fri from 10am), from which you can watch parliament's proceedings. To avoid the queues, turn up after 6pm, when most tourists have disappeared. It's also possible to go on a **guided tour** (Aug & Sept Mon–Sat; £7) of the building (excluding Big Ben).

The Houses of Parliament dwarf their much older neighbour, **Westminster Abbey** (Mon–Fri 9.30am–4.45pm, Wed also 6–8pm, Sat 9.30am–2.45pm; £6;

tory of England: it has been the venue for all but two coronations since the time of
William the Conqueror, and the site of more or less every royal burial for five hundred years until George II. Many of the nation's most celebrated citizens are honoured here, too, and the interior is crowded with monuments, reliefs and statuary.
Entry is currently via the north door, and the highlights include the **Lady Chapel**,
with its wonderful fan vaulting, the much venerated Shrine of Edward the
Confessor, which you can now only peek into, and **Poets' Corner**, where the likes
of Chaucer, Tennyson, T.S. Eliot and many others are buried, and still more, like
Shakespeare, are honoured. On your way out, don't miss the Great Cloister, which
gives access to the **Chapter House** (daily 10am–4/5.30pm; £2.50, or £1 with
abbey ticket), with its thirteenth-century paving stones, the **Pyx Chamber** (daily
10.30am–4pm), formerly the royal treasury, and the Norman **Undercroft
Museum** (daily 10.30am–4pm), in which several generations of royal death-masks
are displayed.

Tate Britain

From Parliament Square the unprepossessing Millbank runs south to the **Tate
Britain** (daily 10am–5.50pm; free; @www.tate.org.uk; Pimlico tube). Displaying
British art from 1500 onwards, plus a whole wing devoted to Turner, it also showcases contemporary British artists. The galleries are rehung more or less annually,
but always include a fair selection of works by Hogarth, Constable, Gainsborough,
Reynolds, Blake, Spencer, Bacon, Hockney and others. The gallery also runs contemporary art's prestigious, and often controversial, Turner prize. Every autumn, the
finalists' work is displayed for a month or two prior to the prize-giving.

Covent Garden and the British Museum

Northeast of Trafalgar Square lies the attractive area of **Covent Garden**, centred
on the Piazza, London's oldest planned square, laid out in the 1630s, and now centred on the nineteenth-century market hall that housed London's principal fruit
and vegetable market until the 1970s. The structure now shelters a gaggle of tasteful
shops and arty stalls. On the western side, by Jones's classical St Paul's Church, is a
semi-institutionalized venue for buskers and more ambitious street performers. In
the Piazza's southeast corner is the **London Transport Museum** (daily
10am–6pm, Fri from 11am; £5.95; @www.ltmuseum.co.uk), a fun scamper
through the history – and possible future – of public transport in the city.

From here it's a short walk northwards up fashionable Neal St and across New
Oxford St into the district of Bloomsbury, home to the **British Museum** on Great
Russell St (daily 10am–5.30pm, Thurs & Fri till 8.30pm; free; @www.british-muse-
um.ac.uk). One of the great museums of the world, and Britain's most popular
tourist attraction (after Blackpool). The building itself is the grandest of London's
Greek Revival edifices, and is now even more amazing, thanks to Norman Foster's
glass-and-steel covered Great Court, at the centre of which stands the **Round
Reading Room**, where Karl Marx penned *Das Kapital*.

With over four million exhibits, the BM is far too big to be seen in one go – so
head for the two or three displays that interest you most. The museum's Roman
and Greek antiquities are second to none, but the exhibits that steal the headlines
are the **Elgin Marbles**, taken from the Parthenon in Athens by Lord Elgin in 1801
and still the cause of discord between the British and Greek governments. Upstairs,
there's a vast Egyptian mummy collection, the 2000-year-old Lindow Man, preserved in a Cheshire bog after his sacrificial death, and the famous twelfth-century
Lewis Chessmen, carved from walrus ivory. Two of the most remarkable treasure
troves on this floor were found in East Anglia: Saxon pieces from Sutton Hoo, and
the Roman silverwork known as the Mildenhall Treasure.

The City of London

Once the fortified heart of the capital, the **City of London**, also known as the Square Mile, is now its financial district. Few people actually live here, making it a desolate place after nightfall and at the weekend. Postwar redevelopment and the 1666 Fire of London destroyed most of the old City, but the area's finest structure, **St Paul's Cathedral** (Mon–Sat 8.30am–4pm; £5; St Paul's tube), was designed by Christopher Wren. The most distinctive feature of this Baroque edifice is the dome, second in size only to St Peter's in Rome, and still a dominating presence on the London skyline. The interior of the church is filled with dull imperialist funerary monuments, for the most part, but a staircase in the south transept leads up to a series of galleries in the dome. The internal **Whispering Gallery** is the first, so called because of its acoustic properties – words whispered to the wall on one side are distinctly audible on the other. The broad exterior Stone Gallery and the uppermost Golden Gallery both offer good panoramas over London. The **crypt** is the resting place of Wren himself, along with Turner, Reynolds and other artists, but the most imposing sarcophagi are the twin black monstrosities occupied by the Duke of Wellington and Lord Nelson.

The eastern extent of the City is marked by the **Tower of London** (daily 9/10am–4/6pm; £11; ⊛www.hrp.org.uk), on the river a mile southeast of St Paul's. Despite all the hype and heritage claptrap, it remains one of London's most remarkable buildings, site of some of the goriest events in the nation's history, and somewhere all visitors should explore. For a start, the Tower is the most perfectly preserved (albeit heavily restored) medieval fortress in the country, begun by William the Conqueror, and pretty much completed by the end of the thirteenth century. Before you set off exploring, take one of the free tours given by the "Beefeaters", ex-servicemen in Tudor costume. The central White Tower holds part of the **Royal Armouries** collection (the rest resides in Leeds), and, on the second floor, the Norman Chapel of St John, London's oldest church. Close by is Tower Green, where the likes of Lady Jane Grey, Anne Boleyn and Catherine Howard were beheaded. The Waterloo Barracks house the **Crown Jewels**, among which are the three largest cut diamonds in the world. On the south side of the complex, the **Bloody Tower** is where the murder of the "Princes in the Tower", Edward V and his brother, is thought to have taken place. Below lies **Traitor's Gate**, through which prisoners arrived after having been ferried down the Thames from the courts of justice at Westminster.

River views from here are dominated by the twin towers of **Tower Bridge**, completed in 1894 and now one of London's most famous landmarks. The raising of the bascules to allow tall ships through remains an impressive sight. Sadly, though, you can only the visit the walkways linking the summits of the towers by joining a guided tour dubbed the "Tower Bridge Experience" (daily 9.30am–6pm; £4.50; ⊛www.towerbridge. org.uk).

The South Bank

The **South Bank** of the Thames is home to London's most prominent new landmark, the **London Eye** (daily 10am–8pm; £9.50; ⊛www.ba-londoneye.com), a 135m-tall observation wheel that revolves slowly and silently over the Thames. A full-circle "flight" in one its pods takes thirty minutes and lifts you high above the city. From the Eye, a riverside footpath heads east past the **South Bank Centre** (⊛www.sbc.org.uk), London's concrete "culture bunker", for a mile or so before reaching Bankside, the old entertainment district of Tudor and Stuart London.

Contemporary Bankside is dominated by the austere power station, which has been magically transformed into the **Tate Modern** (daily 10am–6pm, Fri & Sat till 10pm; free; ⊛www.tate.org.uk). The collection is arranged thematically, and minor rehangs take place every six months or so, but you're pretty much guaranteed to see works by Monet, Bonnard, Matisse, Picasso, Dalí, Mondrian, Warhol, Beuys and Rothko. Directly outside Tate Modern is Norman Foster's **Millennium**

Bridge, London's famous bouncing bridge, which wobbled so worryingly when it first opened in 2000 that it was closed for repairs for almost two years. It's open again now and will take you effortlessly over to St Paul's Cathedral (see above).

Seriously dwarfed by the Tate Modern is the equally spectacular **Shakespeare's Globe Theatre** (⊛www.shakespeares-globe.org), a reconstruction of the polygonal playhouse where most of the Bard's later works were first performed. The Globe's pricey but stylish **exhibition** (daily 10am–5pm; £7.50) is well worth a visit, and includes a guided tour of the theatre, except in the afternooons during the summer – at this time, however, you'd be better off watching a show.

One other national institution on the south bank worth seeking out is the **Imperial War Museum**, on Lambeth Rd, half a mile south of Waterloo station (daily 10am–6pm; free; ⊛www.iwm.org.uk; Lambeth North tube). This is by far the best military museum in the country, its treatment of the subject wide-ranging and fairly sober. The museum also contains the nation's only permanent **Holocaust Exhibition**, which pulls few punches and has made a valiant attempt to avoid depicting the victims of the Holocaust as nameless masses by focusing on individual cases, interspersing the archive footage with eyewitness accounts from survivors.

Hyde Park and west to Notting Hill

The best way to approach **Hyde Park**, London's largest central green space, is from the southeastern corner known as Hyde Park Corner. Here, in the middle of the traffic interchange, stands the **Wellington Arch** (Wed–Sun 10am–4/5/6pm; £2.50), erected in 1828 to commemorate Wellington's victories in the Napoleonic Wars. The arch now houses a small exhibition on London's outdoor memorials. Wellington himself used to live at **Apsley House** (Tues–Sun 11am–5pm; £4.50), overlooking the arch, and now home to the Wellington Museum, which holds works by Velázquez, Goya, Rubens and Canova.

In the middle of Hyde Park is the **Serpentine** lake, with a popular lido towards its centre; the nearby **Serpentine Gallery** (daily 10am–6pm; free; ⊛www.serpentine gallery.org) hosts excellent contemporary art exhibitions. Nearby stands the **Albert Memorial**, an over-decorated Gothic canopy covering a gilded statue of Queen Victoria's much-mourned consort, who died in 1861. To the west the park merges into Kensington Gardens, leading to **Kensington Palace** (daily 10am–6pm; £8.80; ⊛www.hrp.org.uk), a modestly proportioned Jacobean brick mansion that was Princess Diana's London residence following her separation from Prince Charles. The highlights of the sparsely furnished state apartments are the *trompe l'oeil* ceiling paintings by William Kent, and the oil paintings in the King's Gallery.

South Kensington museums

London's richest concentration of free museums lies to the south of Hyde Park. In terms of sheer variety and scale, the **Victoria and Albert Museum** (daily 10am–5.45pm; Wed also 6.30-9.30pm; free; ⊛www.vam.ac.uk), on Cromwell Rd, is the greatest museum of applied arts in the world. The most celebrated of the V&A's numerous exhibits are the **Raphael Cartoons**, seven vast biblical paintings that served as templates for a set of tapestries destined for the Sistine Chapel. Other highlights include the largest collection of Indian art outside India, the new British Galleries, plaster casts of European art's greatest sculptures, twentieth-century *objets d'art*, more Constable paintings than the Tate and a decent collection of Rodin sculptures.

Established as a technological counterpart to the V&A, the **Science Museum** on Exhibition Rd (daily 10am–6pm; free; ⊛www.nmsi.ac.uk) is undeniably impressive. First off, visit the Making of the Modern World, a display of inventions such as *Puffing Billy*, the world's oldest surviving steam train, and a Ford Model T, the world's first mass-produced car. From here, the darkened, ultra-purple **Wellcome Wing** beckons you on, its ground floor dominated by the floating, sloping under-belly of the museum's IMAX cinema (£6.95). The four floors of the Wellcome

Wing are filled with high-tech hands-on gadgetry, which makes some of the galleries in the rest of the museum look decidedly dated.

The nearby **Natural History Museum**, back on Cromwell Rd (Mon–Sat 10am–5.50pm, Sun 11am–5.50pm; ®www.nhm.ac.uk), is London's most handsome museum. Most folk come here with the kids to see the Dinosaur gallery, and wince at the Creepy-Crawlies. Even more stunning, however, are the new Earth Galleries, a visually exciting romp through the earth's evolution. The most popular sections are the slightly tasteless Kobe earthquake simulator, and the spectacular display of gems and crystals in the Earth's Treasury.

North London: Regent's Park to Hampstead

As with almost all of London's royal parks, Londoners have Henry VIII to thank for **Regent's Park**, which he confiscated from the Church for yet more hunting grounds. Flanked by some of the city's most elegant residential buildings, the park is best known for **London Zoo** (daily 10am–4/5.30pm; £11; ®www.londonzoo.co.uk), one of the world's oldest and most varied collections of animals, which hides in the northeastern corner.

A short stroll from the southwestern corner of the park, on busy Marylebone Rd, is one of London's most enduring tourist traps, **Madame Tussaud's** (daily 9.30/10am–5.30pm; £14.95; ®www.madame-tussauds.com), which has been pulling in the crowds since the good lady arrived in 1802 with the sculpted heads of guillotined aristocrats. The entrance fee might be extortionate, the likenesses risible, but you can still rely on finding some of London's biggest queues here. Tickets to Madame Tussaud's include entry into the neighbouring **London Planetarium** (Mon–Fri 10/11.30am–5pm; shows every 30min; Planetarium only £2.45), which features a standard romp through the basics of astronomy accompanied by high-tech visuals and cosmic astro-babble.

Just five minutes' walk from the north side of the park lies bustling **Camden Town**, host to a vast **weekend market** that sprawls around the canal, spilling over several locations either side of the main street. Camden gets so crowded that the tube station is deemed exit-only on Sunday afternoons. Further north still is the affluent suburb of **Hampstead**, which gives access to Hampstead Heath, one of the few genuinely wild areas left within reach of central London. One major attraction east of Hampstead is **Highgate Cemetery**, ranged on both sides of Swains Lane (Highgate or Archway tube). Highgate's most famous corpse is **Karl Marx**, who lies in the East Cemetery (daily 10am–4/5pm; £1); more intriguing and atmospheric is the overgrown West Cemetery (guided tours only: phone ®020/83401834 to check), with its spooky Egyptian Avenue and terraced catacombs.

Greenwich

Some nine miles east of central London, **Greenwich** (pronounced "gren-itch") is one of London's most beguiling spots. At its heart is the architectural set-piece of the former Royal Naval College overlooking the Thames; nearby are two prime tourist sights: the Royal Observatory and the National Maritime Museum. Transport links are good: boats run regularly from Westminster Pier, trains run from Charing Cross, and the Docklands Light Railway scoots east from the Bank or Tower Gateway in the City via the redeveloped Docklands, south to the **Cutty Sark**, which stands in a dry dock next to Greenwich pier (daily 10am–5pm; £3.50; ®www.cuttysark.org.uk). This majestic vessel was one of the last of the clippers, sail-powered cargo ships built for speed and used on long-distance routes to bring wool, tea and other produce to London from the far-flung corners of the Empire.

Hugging the riverfront to the east is Wren's beautifully symmetrical Baroque ensemble of the **Old Royal Naval College** (Mon–Sat 10am–5pm, Sun 12.30–5pm; £3, free after 3.30pm & all Sun; ®www.greenwichfoundation.org.uk). Across the road the **National Maritime Museum** (daily 10am–6pm; free;

@www.nmm.ac.uk) exhibits model ships, charts and globes, and has been wonder-fully rejuvenated with some inventive new galleries under an enormous glazed roof. Inigo Jones's adjacent **Queen's House**, Britain's first Neoclassical building, also forms part of the museum. From here Greenwich Park stretches up the hill, crowned by the Wren-inspired **Royal Observatory** (daily 10am–6pm; free), home of Greenwich Mean Time and Zero Longitude. As well as housing numerous timepieces, telescopes and navigational equipment, the museum also has a fascinating exhibition on the search for longitude and displays four of the marine clocks designed by John Harrison.

Clearly visible from the vantage point of Greenwich Park is the **Millennium Dome**, designed by Richard Rogers for the one-year only millennium extravaganza.

Out west: Kew to Windsor

Boats ply westwards from Westminster Pier, upstream to **Kew** where you'll find the **Royal Botanic Gardens** (daily 9.30am–dusk; £5; Kew Gardens tube; @www.kew.org), established in 1759, and now home to over 50,000 species grown in the plantations and glasshouses of a beautiful 300-acre site.

Further upstream, thirteen miles southwest of the centre and also served by river-boat, is the finest of England's royal mansions, **Hampton Court Palace** (daily 9.30/10.15am–4.30/6pm; £10.80; train from Waterloo; @www.hrp.org.uk). Built in 1516 by the upwardly mobile Cardinal Wolsey, it was purloined enlarged and improved by Henry VIII, and later rebuilt by William III who hired Wren to remodel the buildings. The palace is laid out into six thematic walking tours, with costumed guided tours available at no extra charge. If your energy is lacking, the most rewarding sections are Henry VIII's State Apartments, which feature the glorious double hammerbeamed Great Hall, the King's Apartments, and the Tudor Kitchens. There's plenty more to see in the grounds: the Great Vine, the Lower Orangery, which houses Mantegna's *The Triumphs of Caesar*, and, of course, the famous **Maze**, laid out in 1714, lies just north of the palace.

WINDSOR, 21 miles west of central London, is dominated by **Windsor Castle** (daily 9.45am–4.15/5.15pm; £11.50; train from Waterloo; @www.royal.gov.uk). The castle began its days as a wooden fortress built by William the Conqueror, with numerous later monarchs having had a hand in its evolution. It's an undeniably awesome sight, but the small selection of rooms open to the public are relatively unexciting; the only exception is the Perpendicular Gothic glory of St George's Chapel, resting place of numerous monarchs.

Eating and drinking

London is a great place in which to **eat out**. You can sample more or less any kind of cuisine here, and wherever you come from, you should find something new and quite possibly unique. The only drawback is that eating out can also be very expensive. For those on a budget, however, there are still plenty of options: London has some of the best Cantonese restaurants in Europe, top Indian and Bangladeshi food, and numerous French, Greek, Italian, Japanese, Spanish and Thai restaurants.

London's great period of pub building took place in the Victorian era, to which many **pubs** still pay homage; genuine Victorian interiors are increasingly difficult to find, as are genuinely individual pubs – chain pubs are as ubiquitous in London as elsewhere in the country. As for modern **bars**, there are countless numbers of them, with more opening and closing as each year goes by, and an eternally young, hip clientele seemingly oblivious to the sky high prices.

Snacks and quick meals

Café in the Crypt St Martin-in-the-Fields church, Trafalgar Sq. The self-service buffet food is nothing special, but there are regular veggie dishes and the handy location makes this an ideal refuelling spot. Charing Cross tube.

Centrale 16 Moor St, W1. Tiny, friendly Italian café that serves up huge plates of steaming, garlicky pasta, as well as omelettes, chicken and chops for around £5. Leicester Square tube.

Food For Thought 31 Neal St, WC2. Very small vegetarian restaurant – the inexpensive food is delicious, but don't expect to linger. Covent Garden tube.

Gaby's 30 Charing Cross Rd, WC2. Busy café serving a wide range of home-cooked veggie and Middle Eastern specialities. Hard to beat for value, choice and location. Leicester Sq tube.

India Club 143 Strand, WC2. Faded period charm about this long-established, inexpensive Anglo-Indian eatery, sandwiched between floors of the Strand Continental Hotel. Covent Garden or Temple tube.

Lee Ho Fook 4 Macclesfield St, cnr Dansey Place, Chinatown, W1. No English sign. An authentic Chinese barbecue house, tiny, bright and fast-paced. Leicester Sq tube.

Mô 25 Heddon St, W1. The ultimate Arabic pastiche, and a successful one at that. This tearoom, just off Regent St, serves delicious snacks and is a great place to hang out. Piccadilly Circus tube.

Pollo 20 Old Compton St, Soho W1. The best-value Italian food in town. Always packed, though the queues move quickly. Leicester Sq tube.

Saucebarorganicdiner 214 Camden High St, NW1. Organic fast food – burgers, wraps and sandwiches – with a juice and cocktail bar attached. Camden Town tube.

Stockpot 18 Old Compton St, W1. Chain of cafés serving filling bistro-style stews and such like at rock-bottom prices. Soho Leicester Sq tube. Branches all across town.

Wagamama 4 Streatham St, Bloomsbury WC1. Austere, minimalist canteen-style place where the diners share long benches and slurp huge bowls of noodle soup and stir-fry plates. Expect to queue and don't expect to linger. Tottenham Court Rd tube. Branches all across town.

Restaurants

Abu Ali 136–138 George St, W1. Spartan place serving honest Lebanese fare that's terrific value for money. Marble Arch tube.

Alounak 44 Westbourne Grove, W2. This place turns out really good, really cheap Iranian grub, washed down with black tea. Queensway or Bayswater tube.

Aroma II 118 Shaftesbury Avenue, W1. Bright, modernist Chinese restaurant with an exhaustive menu ranging from noodles to braised sea slug. Leicester Sq tube.

Belgo Centraal 50 Earlham St, WC2. Hugely popular Belgian restaurant serving heaps of mussels and other hearty fare, as well as beer, of

course. The lunchtime deals are hard to beat. Covent Garden tube.

Café Pacifico 5 Langley St, WC2. Rated as the best Mexican in central London, though that isn't saying much. Fairly quiet during the day, unbelievably noisy in the evening. Good bar. Covent Garden tube.

China City White Bear Yard, 25s Lisle St, WC2. Large restaurant with *dim sum* that's up there with the best, and service that is Chinatown brusque. Leicester Sq tube.

Kettner's 29 Romilly St, W1. Grand old place with high ceilings and a pianist, that's actually part of the Pizza Express chain and consequently cheaper than it looks. Leicester Sq tube. Pizza Express has branches all over the city.

Mandalay 444 Edgware Rd, W2. Small, non-smoking restaurant that serves pure, freshly cooked, unexpurgated Burmese cuisine. Closed Sun. Edgware Rd tube.

Tokyo Diner 2 Newport Place, WC2. Minimalist decor, and inexpensive sushi and sumo fast food on the edge of Chinatown. Leicester Square tube.

Pubs and bars

Albert 52 Victoria St, SW1. Handily situated pub serving good food, including hearty breakfasts in the upstairs restaurant. St James's Park tube.

Anchor Bankside 34 Park St, SE1. Old Bankside inn, with tables overlooking the river – handy for the Tate Modern. London Bridge, Southwark or Blackfriars tube.

Blackfriar 174 Queen Victoria St, City. Art Nouveau landmark, handy for the City sights. Closed Sat & Sun. Blackfriars tube.

Bunch of Grapes 207 Brompton Rd, SW3. Popular High Victorian pub that is the perfect place for a post-V&A pint, pie and chips. South Kensington tube.

Cutty Sark Ballast Quay off Lassell St, Greenwich. Ancient riverside pub with a nautical theme, outside tables and fine views of Docklands and the Dome. Cutty Sark DLR, then walk downstream.

Dog & Duck 18 Bateman St, Soho. Tiny pub that retains much of its old character and a loyal clientele. Leicester Sq tube.

Flask 14 Flask Walk, NW3. Convivial local, close to the station and serving good food and real ale. Hampstead tube.

George Inn 77 Borough High St. Half a magnificent seventeenth-century coaching inn, now owned by the National Trust. Borough or London Bridge tube.

Lamb 94 Lamb's Conduit St, Bloomsbury. Pleasant pub with a well-preserved Victorian interior. Russell Sq tube.

Lamb & Flag 33 Rose St, WC2. Busy, atmospheric pub tucked away down an alley between Garrick and Floral streets. Covent Garden tube.

Museum Tavern 49 Great Russell St, WC1. Large old pub, right opposite the main entrance to the British Museum, once Marx's favourite. Tottenham Court Rd tube.

Paviour's Arms Page St, SW1. Untouched Art Deco pub, close to Tate Britain with cheap Thai food. Pimlico tube.

Salisbury 90 St Martin's Lane, WC2. One of the most beautifully preserved Victorian pubs in the centre. Leicester Sq tube.

The Social 5 Little Portland St, W1. Bacchanalian, industrial club/bar, with great DJs playing everything from rock to rap, a truly hedonistic-cum-alcoholic crowd. Oxford Circus tube. Closed Sun.

Two Floors 3 Kingly St, W1. Relaxed, modernist Soho bar attracting a mixed straight/gay crowd, with pumping music. Closed Sun. Oxford Circus or Piccadilly Circus tube.

Nightlife

On any night of the week London offers a bewildering range of things to do after dark, ranging from top-flight opera and theatre to clubs. The **listings magazine** *Time Out* (every Tues), is essential if you want to get the most out of this city, giving full details of prices and access, plus previews and reviews. If you're looking for **dance music**, then welcome to Europe's party capital, with everything from hip-hop to house, techno to trance, samba to soca. The **gay and lesbian** scenes in London are also livelier than almost anywhere else in Europe, with a vast range of venues from quiet pubs to cruisy bars and frenetic clubs. London's **theatre** scene is dominated by big musicals, but there's plenty of other stuff on offer, too. Cut-price stand-by tickets can sometimes be had on the day; otherwise head for the large booth in Leicester Square selling **half-price theatre tickets** (Mon–Sat 10am–7pm, Sun noon–3pm) for that day's performances at all West End theatres (note that they specialize in the top end of the price range). An even better bargain are the standing tickets for £3 for the **Proms** (July–Sept) the annual classical music festival held at the Royal Albert Hall, or the free classical concerts that take place during weekday lunchtimes in the City's churches.

Live music venues

12-Bar Club 23 Denmark Place. A combination of live blues and contemporary country seven nights a week. Tottenham Court Rd tube.

100 Club 100 Oxford St, W1. The 100 Club is an unpretentious and inexpensive jazz venue – in a very central location. Tottenham Court Rd tube.

Astoria 157 Charing Cross Rd, WC2. One of London's best-used venues – a large balconied theatre that has live bands and clubs. Tottenham Court Rd tube.

Borderline Orange Yard, Manette St, W1. Intimate venue with diverse musical policy, and a good place to catch new bands. Also has club nights. Tottenham Court Rd tube.

Forum 9–17 Highgate Rd, NW5. Perhaps the capital's best medium-sized venue – large enough to attract established bands, but also a prime spot for newer talent. Kentish Town tube.

Jazz Café 5 Parkway, NW1. Futuristic, white-walled venue with an adventurous booking policy exploring Latin, rap, funk, hip-hop and musical fusions. Camden Town tube.

Ronnie Scott's 47 Frith St, W1. The most famous jazz club in London, small, smoky and rather precious, but featuring top-line names. Leicester Sq tube.

Subterania 12 Acklam Rd, W10. One of the original live music/club crossover venues in an arch under a bridge. The crowd is as trendy as the music, which is often dance-oriented. Ladbroke Grove tube.

ULU Manning Hall, Malet St, WC1. The University of London Union (yoo-loo), with an exceptionally cheap bar and loud bands. Goodge St or Russell Sq tube.

Underworld 174 Camden High St, NW1. This labyrinthine venue is good for new bands and has sporadic club nights. Camden Town tube.

Clubs and discos

Bagley's Studios King's Cross Freight Depot, off York Way, N1. Vast warehouse-style venue. with a different DJ in each of the three rooms, and a chill-out bar complete with sofas. King's Cross tube.

Bar Rumba 36 Shaftesbury Ave, W1. Small West End venue with a programme of Latin, jazz-based and funk dance. Piccadilly Circus tube.

Camden Palace 1a Camden High St, NW1. Most often home to Balearic beats; great lights, great sound, heaving crowds. Mornington Crescent tube.

The End 16a West Central St, WC1. A club designed by clubbers for clubbers – large spacious with chrome minimalist decor. Tottenham Court Rd tube.

Fabric 77a Charterhouse St, EC1. If you're seriously into dance music then there really isn't a better weekend venue in London. Get there early. Farringdon tube.

Home 1 Leicester Sq, WC2. Multifloored superclub with some of the best resident DJs in Britain and one of the finest sound systems around. Leicester Sq tube.

Ministry of Sound 103 Gaunt St, SE1. Vast, state-of-the-art club with an exceptional sound system. Corporate clubbing, but it still draws the top talent. Elephant & Castle tube.

The Scala 278 Pentonvlle Rd, N1. One of London's best clubs, holding unusual and multi-faceted nights that take in film, live bands and music from hip hop to deep house. King's Cross tube.

Velvet Room 143 Charing Cross Rd, WC2. Very cool, velvet-dripping interior; house, techno and drum 'n' bass tunes. Tottenham Court Rd tube.

Gay and lesbian nightlife

Black Cap 171 Camden High St, NW1. Drag and cabaret acts of wildly varying quality almost every night; upstairs bar is quieter, and opens onto a lush and lovely summer roof garden. Camden Town tube.

Brief Encounter 41–43 St Martin's Lane, WC2. A popular pre-*Heaven* or post-opera hangout; the front bar is light, the back bar dark, and both are busy. Leicester Square tube.

Candy Bar 4 Carlisle St, W1. Britain's first seven-day all-girl bar offers a retro-style cocktail bar-cum-pool room upstairs; a noisy, beery ground level cruising bar. Tottenham Court Rd tube.

First Out 52 St Giles High St, WC2. The West End's original gay café/bar, and still permanently packed, serving good veggie food at reasonable prices. *Girl Friday* is a busy women-only Fri night pre-club session. Tottenham Court Rd tube.

Freedom 60 Wardour St, Soho, W1. Hip, busy café/bar attracting a mixed gay/straight crowd. Leicester Sq tube.

G.A.Y. at *The Astoria*, 157 Charing Cross Rd, WC2. Huge, unpretentious and fun-loving dance nights for a young crowd on Fri & Sat. Tottenham Court Rd tube.

Heaven under the Arches Villiers St, WC2. Britain's most popular gay club, this legendary, 2000-capacity club continues to reign supreme. Charing Cross tube.

Liquid Lounge 275 Pentonville Rd, N1. Happy-go-lucky weekend dance-bar popular with a young, indie-minded crowd. DJs and reliably cheap beer. Kings Cross tube.

Vespa Lounge Under Centrepoint House, St. Giles High St, WC1. London's newest girl bar sets up

shop at weekends, and it gets busy. Pool table, video screen, and a mostly young crowd. Tottenham Court Rd tube.

Theatre, cinema and the arts

Barbican Centre Silk St, EC2. London home of Royal Shakespeare Company, and venue for a wide range of concerts from classical to world music. Barbican or Moorgate tube.

BFI London Imax Centre South Bank, SE1. Remarkable state-of-the-art glazed drum in the middle of a roundabout showing the usual IMAX fodder. Waterloo tube.

Donmar Warehouse Earlham St, WC2. Spiritual home of Sam Mendes, and the best bet for a central off-West End show. Covent Garden tube.

English National Opera Coliseum, St Martin's Lane, WC2. More radical and democratic than the ROH, with opera (in English) and ballet. Leicester Sq tube.

ICA Nash House, The Mall, SW1. Theatre, dance, films and art at London's enduringly avant-garde HQ. Charing Cross tube.

National Film Theatre South Bank, SE1. London's only really serious arts cinema, with six different films shown each day on two screens. Waterloo tube.

National Theatre South Bank Centre, South Bank, SE1. The NT has three separate theatres, and consistently good productions – some sell out months in advance, but discounted dayseats available from 10am. Waterloo tube.

Open Air Theatre Regent's Park, Inner Circle, NW1. If the weather's good, there's nothing quite like a dose of al fresco Shakespeare, or a musical, play or concert. Regent's Park tube.

Prince Charles 2–7 Leicester Place, WC2. The bargain basement of London's cinemas, with a programme of new movies, classics and cult favourites. Leicester Square tube.

Royal Opera House Bow St, WC2. Newly refurbished, but still as expensive as ever – 44 discounted day seats available. Covent Garden tube.

Sadler's Wells Rosebery Avenue, EC1. London's biggest dance venue puts on a mixed bag of contemporary dance, kids' shows and ballet. Angel tube.

Shakespeare's Globe New Globe Walk, SE1. Replica open-air Elizabethan theatre that puts on shows from mid-May to mid-Sept, with standing tickets for £5. London Bridge, Blackfriars or Southwark tube.

Wigmore Hall 36 Wigmore St, W1. Intimate and elegant classical recital venue, just off Oxford St, that remains many Londoners' favourite. Bond St or Oxford Circus tube.

Listings

Embassies Australia, Australia House, Strand, WC2 ☎020/7379 4334; Canada, MacDonald House, 1 Grosvenor Square, W1 ☎020/7258 6600; Ireland, 17 Grosvenor Place, SW1 ☎020/7235 2171; New Zealand, New Zealand House, 80 Haymarket, SW1 ☎020/7930 8422; South Africa, South Africa House, Trafalgar Square, WC2 ☎020/7451 7299; US, 24 Grosvenor Square, W1 ☎020/7499 9000.

Exchange Shopping areas such as Oxford St and Covent Garden are littered with private exchange offices, and there are 24hr booths at the biggest central tube stations, but their rates are always worse than the banks. You'll find branches of all major banks around Oxford St, Regent St and Piccadilly.

Hospital St Mary's Hospital, Praed St, W2, Paddington tube ☎020/7886 6666; University College Hospital, Grafton Way, WC1, Euston Square tube; ☎020/7387 9300.

Internet access easyEverything: 9 Tottenham Court Rd (Tottenham Court Rd tube), 358 Oxford St (Bond St tube), 7 The Strand (Charing Cross tube) and across the city.

Left luggage At all airport terminals and major train stations.

Lost property On a bus or tube, call ☎020/7486 2496; on a train ☎020/7401 7861; in a black taxi ☎020/7833 0996.

Pharmacies Bliss, 5 Marble Arch, W1 (daily 9am–midnight).

Police 10 Vine St, W1 ☎020/7437 1212.

Post office 24–28 William IV St, WC2 4DL (Leicester Sq or Charing Cross tube).

Southeast England

Nestling in self-satisfied prosperity, **southeast England** is the richest part of the country, due to its agricultural wealth and proximity to the capital. Swift, frequent rail and coach services make it ideal for day-trips from London. Medieval ecclesiastical power-bases such as **Canterbury** and **Winchester** offer an introduction to the nation's history; while on the coast is the upbeat, hedonistic resort of **Brighton**, London's playground by the sea.

DOVER is the main port of entry along this stretch of coast, and the country's busiest. An uninspiring place in itself, Dover's famous **White Cliffs** are best enjoyed from a boat several miles out, although you can amble around on the grassy summit. **Ferries** (Calais and Zeebrugge) use the Eastern Docks, while **Hoverspeed** (Calais and Ostend) uses the Hoverport, south of the centre. The main **train station**, for services to Canterbury and London (last one 10.30pm), is Dover Priory, ten minutes' walk west of the centre and served by free shuttle buses from both docks. **Coaches** to London (last one 8.30pm) pick up from both docks and the town-centre **bus station** on Pencester Rd. The **tourist office** is on Townwall St (daily 8/9am–6/7.30pm; ☎01304/205108, ❷www.whitecliffscountry.org.uk).

Canterbury

CANTERBURY, one of England's oldest centres of Christianity, was home to the country's most famous martyr, Archbishop Thomas à Becket, who fell victim to Church–State rivalry in 1170. It became one of northern Europe's great pilgrimage sites, as Chaucer's *Canterbury Tales* attest, until Henry VIII had the martyr's shrine demolished in 1538. The cathedral remains the focal point of a compact centre, which is enclosed on three sides by medieval walls. Today, as well as hosting a sizeable student population, it's thronged with visitors, but remains relatively unspoilt.

Built in stages from 1070 onwards, the vast **Cathedral** (Mon–Sat 9am–7pm, Sun 12.30–2.30pm & 4.30–5.30pm; £3.50, free on Sun; ❷www.canterbury-cathedral.org) derives its distinctive presence from the perpendicular thrust of the late Gothic towers, dominated by the central, sixteenth-century Bell Harry tower. Notable features of the high vaulted interior are the tombs of Henry IV and his wife, and a gilded effigy of the Black Prince, both in the Trinity Chapel behind the main altar. The site of Becket's murder is marked by a modern shrine in the northwest transept, with a crude sculpture of the supposed weapons suspended above. Steps descend from here to the Romanesque arches of the **crypt**, one of the few remaining visible relics of the Norman cathedral.

East of the cathedral, across the ring road, are the evocative ruins of **St Augustine's Abbey** (daily 10am–4/6pm; £2.60; EH), on the site of a church founded by St Augustine, who began the conversion of the English in 597. Most of the town's other sights are located on or near High St. The **Eastbridge Hospital** (Mon–Sat 10am–4.45pm; £1), opposite the library, was founded in the twelfth century to provide poor pilgrims with shelter, and a thirteenth-century wall painting of Christ is still faintly visible in the upstairs refectory. The **West Gate**, at the far end of St Peter's St (a continuation of High St), is the city's last remaining medieval gate, housing a small museum (Mon–Sat 11am–12.30pm & 1.30–3.30pm; £1; ⓦ www.canterbury-museums.co.uk) featuring weaponry used by the medieval city guard. The best exposition of local history is provided by the interactive **Heritage Museum**, on Stour St (Mon–Sat 10.30am–5pm, Sun 1.30–5pm; Nov–May closed Sun; £1.90; ⓦ www.canterbury-museums.co.uk).

Practicalities

Canterbury has two **train stations**, Canterbury East for services from London Victoria and Dover Priory, and Canterbury West for services from London Charing Cross – the stations are ten minutes south and northwest of the centre respectively. The **bus station** is on St George's Lane, just below the High St. The **tourist office** is just off the High St at 34 St Margaret's St (daily 9.30am–5/6pm; Oct–April closed Sun; ☎ 01227/766567, ⓦ www.canterbury.co.uk); it will book a room for you for a small fee, a service which is often necessary in the summer months.

Accommodation

Hostels

YHA 54 New Dover Rd ☎ 01227/462911, ⓦ www.yha .org.uk. HI hostel a mile southeast of the centre. ❸
KiPPS hostel 40 Nunnery Fields ☎ 01227/786121, ⓦ www.kipps-hostel.com. A short walk south of the centre. ❸

Guest houses

Ann's House 63 London Rd ☎ 01227/768767.

Traditional Victorian villa offering comfortable rooms, most en suite. ❺
St Stephen's Guest House 100 St Stephen's Rd ☎ 01227/767644. Ten minutes' walk north along the river Stour, this place has excellent value en suites. ❺
Wincheap Guest House 94 Wincheap ☎ 01227/ 762309. Good-value Victorian B&B near East station. ❹

Eating and drinking

Bell & Crown 10 Palace St. A friendly medieval pub with excellent home-cooked food.
Billabong 5 St Margaret's St. Along with the *Hobgoblin* (see below), this is a popular student haunt.
Café des Amis du Mexique 95 St Dunstan's St. Serves popular Mexican fare.

Chaopraya River 2 Dover St. Serves tasty, affordable Thai food.
Hobgoblin 40 St Peter's St. Another spot popular with a young, studenty crowd.
Miller's Arms on Mill Lane. A picturesque riverside pub with its own restaurant.
Tapas en Las Trece 13 Palace St. Tasty tapas for around £5 a dish. Occasional live music too.

Brighton

BRIGHTON has been a prime target for day-tripping Londoners since the Prince Regent, later George IV, started holidaying here in the 1770s with his mistress and thus began a trend for the "dirty weekend". This is one of Britain's most entertaining seaside resorts, and has recently emerged from tawdry seediness to embrace a new, fashionable hedonism which is turning the heads of London's style gurus. The wide range of nightlife owes much to the large student population, and there's a colourful music and arts **festival** (ⓦ www.brighton-festival.org.uk), which runs for three weeks in May.

From Brighton's **train station** on Queen's Rd it's a ten-minute stroll straight
down to the **seafront**, a four-mile-long pebble beach bordered by a balustered
promenade. (Coaches arrive at the Pool Valley **bus station**, very near the front.) The
wonderfully tacky **Palace Pier** is an obligatory call, basically a half-mile amusement
arcade lined with booths selling fish and chips, candyfloss and assorted tat. Near here
the antiquated locomotives of **Volk's Railway** (April to mid-Sept daily 11am–5pm;
£1.60 return), the first electric train in the country, run eastward towards the Marina
and the nudist beach. On the western seafront you can see – but not enter – the
brooding **West Pier**, damaged in World War II and then severed from the mainland
following a hurricane in 1987 and restored to its former glory in 2002.

A block back from the seafront are **The Lanes**, a shopping area of narrow alleys
preserving the layout, but little of the ambience, of the fishing port that Brighton
once was. Inland from here, overlooking the traffic heavy Old Steine, is the distinctive
Royal Pavilion (daily 10am–5/6pm; £4.50; ⊛ www.royalpavilion.brighton.co.uk),
a wedding-cake confection of pagodas, minarets and domes built in 1817 as a pleasure palace for the Prince Regent. Just around the corner on Church St is
Brighton's **Museum and Art Gallery** (Mon, Tues & Thurs–Sat 10am–5pm, Sun
2–5pm; free), with nondescript paintings tempered by interesting displays of Art
Nouveau and Art Deco furniture and Dalí's surreal sofa based on Mae West's lips; it
also hosts regular temporary exhibitions. North of Church St is the arty, bohemian
quarter of **North Laine**, with plenty of second-hand clothes-, record- and junk-
shops interspersed with stylish boutiques and coffee houses.

Practicalities
Brighton has a fast and frequent **train** service from London (Victoria, King's Cross
and London Bridge) and Gatwick Airport. The **tourist office** is at 10
Bartholomew Sq in The Lanes (daily 9/10am–4/6pm; ☎01273/292599, ⊛ www
.brighton.co.uk).

Cafés and **restaurants** abound, with a particularly good selection around North
Laine. Many also offer student discounts. For drinking, the **pubs** around The Lanes
are the place to head for, too. Brighton has a frenetic **nightlife** scene, livelier than
just about anywhere outside London. We've listed a few of the most highly related
places below, but for full listings, pick up a copy of *Insight* (£1) from newsagents or
the free magazines *The Latest* and *Source*, available from the tourist office, popular
bars and clubs. Brighton also has a lively **gay scene**; we've listed a few of the more
popular places below, but for full details check out ⊛ www.gay.brighton.co.uk.

Accommodation
Hostels
Baggies Backpackers 33 Oriental Place
☎01273/733740, ⊛ www.cisweb.co.uk/baggies.
Just beyond the West Pier and more spacious than
the *Brighton Backpackers*. ❸
Brighton Backpackers 75 Middle St ☎01273/
777717, ⊛ www.brightonbackpackers.com. Just off
the seafront and a much livelier option than the HI
place; has a quieter annexe around the corner. ❸
YHA Patcham Place ☎01629/556196, ⊛ www

.yha.org.uk. HI hostel four miles north of Brighton
on the A23 London Rd; take bus #5a. ❸

Guest houses
Four Seasons 3 Upper Rock Gdns ☎01273/673574,
ⓔ joehalfpenny@compuserve.com. Cosy place
with good veggie options for breakfast. ❺
Sea Spray 25 New Steine ☎01273/680332,
ⓔ seaspray@brighton.co.uk. Good-value place, all
rooms have showers. ❺

Eating, drinking and nightlife
Cafés and restaurants
Bombay Aloo 39 Ship St. In The Lanes; check out
the £5 eat-all-you-can buffet.
Food for Friends 17 Prince Albert St. A classy
budget wholefood veggie eatery.

Grinder 10 Kensington Gardens. Trip-hoppy place
on The Lanes with a balcony upstairs.
Havana 33 Duke St. An urbane bistro-bar in a
faux-colonial setting.

Pubs

The Aquarium 6 Steine St. A popular, central gay pub.

Dr Brighton's 16 Kings Rd. Another popular gay haunt, this one on the seafront.

Hector's House Grand Parade. A favourite student hangout.

Prince Albert 48 Trafalgar St. A pre-club venue near the station.

Clubs and live music venues

Concorde 2 Madeira Shelter. Live music venue; also has comedy night on Tues and club nights at w/ends.

Escape 10 Marine Parade. Brighton's trendiest club, specializing in funk and techno.

Honey Club 214 Kings Rd Arches. Garage, House and hip-hop.

Revenge 32 Old Steine. Predominantly gay venue. Mon night is cabaret.

Winchester

WINCHESTER's rural tranquillity betrays little of its former role as the political and ecclesiastical power base of southern England. A town of Roman foundation fifty miles southwest of London, Winchester rose to prominence in the ninth century as King Alfred the Great's capital, and remained influential well into the Middle Ages. The shrine of St Swithin, Alfred's tutor and Bishop of Winchester, made the town an important destination for pilgrims, and the flow of European merchants to the annual St Giles' fair replenished the civic coffers.

Alfred's statue stands at the eastern end of the Broadway, the town's main thoroughfare, which becomes High St as it progresses west towards the train station. To the south of here is the **Cathedral** (daily 7.30am–6.30pm; £3.50 donation requested; ®www.winchester-cathedral.org.uk); much of its exterior is twelfth century, although some earlier masonry is visible, in particular the Norman stonework of the south transept. Above the high altar are mortuary chests holding the remains of the pre-Conquest kings of England. The Angel chapel contains sixteenth-century wall paintings of the miracles of the Virgin Mary, although a modern protective replica now covers the originals. Jane Austen is buried on the south side of the nave; the inscription on the floor slab remembers her merely as the daughter of a local clergyman, ignoring her renown as a novelist.

Immediately outside are traces of the original Saxon cathedral, built by Cenwalh, king of Wessex, in the mid-seventh century. The true grandeur of this structure is shown by a model in the **City Museum** (Mon–Sat 10am–5pm; Oct–March closed Mon; free) on the western side of the cathedral close; other exhibits include mosaics and pottery from Roman Winchester. Further west along High St is the thirteenth-century **Great Hall** (daily 10am–4/5pm; free), a banqueting chamber used by successive kings of England and renowned for what is alleged to be King Arthur's Round Table – but the piece, which now hangs from the wall, is probably fourteenth-century (and so about 500 years too young). It seems to have been repainted with portraits and the names of King Arthur's knights for the visit of Emperor Charles V, who was entertained here by Henry VIII in 1522.

South of the Cathedral is the fourteenth-century Pilgrims Hall, from where a signposted route leads through a medieval quarter to **Winchester College**, the oldest of Britain's public schools. It's then a half-hour stroll across the Water Meadow to the almshouse of **St Cross** (Mon–Sat 9.30am–3.30/5pm; £2), founded in 1136, whose church contains a triptych by the Flemish painter Mabuse. Continuing a medieval tradition, needy wayfarers may still apply for the "dole" here – a tiny portion of bread and beer.

Practicalities

Winchester's **train station** is about a mile northwest of the cathedral on Stockbridge Rd. The **bus terminal** is on Broadway, just opposite the Guildhall, in which the **tourist office** is situated (Mon–Sat 10am–5/6pm, Sun 11am–2pm; Oct–May closed Sun; ☎01962/840500, ®www.winchester.gov.uk). Winchester's affluence is reflected in both the style and prices of its **B&Bs**, most of which cluster in the streets between St Cross and Christchurch roads, south of town. *The Farrells*, 5 Ranelagh Rd (℡01962/869555; ❺), is a cosy option, or try the slightly cheaper *Sullivans*, 29 Stockbridge Rd, beside the train station (℡01962/862027; ❹). There's also a lovely **hostel** in the *City Mill*, 1 Water Lane, just east of Alfred's statue (℡01962/853723; closed Oct–Feb; ❷). For **food**, the fine old *Wykeham Arms*, 75 Kingsgate St, offers imaginative meals served in a labyrinthine interior, while *Noah's*, Jewry St, provides good-value, cosmopolitan dishes.

England's West Country

England's "West Country" has never been a precise geographical term, and there will always be a certain amount of argument as to where it actually starts. But as a broad generalization, the cosmopolitan feel of the southeast begins to fade into a slower, rural pace of life from **Salisbury** onwards, becoming more pronounced the further west you travel. In Neolithic times a rich and powerful culture evolved here, as shown by monuments such as **Stonehenge** and **Avebury**, and the isolated moorland sites of inland **Cornwall**. Urban attractions of western England include **Bristol** and the well-preserved Regency spa town of **Bath**; those in search of rural peace and quiet should head for the compelling bleakness of **Dartmoor**. The southwestern extremities of Britain include some of the most beautiful stretches of coastline, its rugged, rocky shores battered by the Atlantic, although the excellent sandy beaches make it one of the country's busiest corners over the summer. All of the region's major centres can be reached fairly easily by train or coach from London. Local bus services cover most areas, although in the rural depths of Dartmoor they can be very sparse indeed. Consult the tourist office website ✆www.westcountrynow.com.

Salisbury and around

SALISBURY's central feature is the elegant spire of its **Cathedral** (daily 7.15am–6.15/8.15pm; £3.50 donation requested; ✆www.salisburycathedral.org.uk), the tallest in the country, rising over 400ft above the lawns of the cathedral close. With the exception of the spire, the cathedral was almost entirely completed in the thirteenth century, and is one of the few great English churches that is not a hotch-potch of different styles. Prominent among the features of the interior are the fourteenth-century clock just inside the north porch, one of the oldest working timepieces in the country, and an exceptional Tudor memorial to the Earl of Hertford, Lady Jane Grey's brother-in-law, in the Lady Chapel at the eastern end of the church. An octagonal **chapterhouse**, approached via the extensive **cloisters** (Mon–Sat 9.30am–5.30/7.45pm, Sun noon–5.30pm; free), holds a collection of precious manuscripts, among which is one of the four original copies of the Magna Carta.

Most of Salisbury's remaining sights are grouped in a sequence of historic houses around The Close, the old walled inner town around the cathedral. The **Salisbury and South Wiltshire Museum**, opposite the main portal of the cathedral on West Walk (Mon–Sat 10am–5pm; July & Aug also Sun 2–5pm; £3.50), is a good place to bone up on the Neolithic history of Wessex before heading out to Stonehenge and Avebury. The **Mompesson House** on The Close's North Walk (April–Oct Mon–Wed, Sat & Sun noon–5.30pm; £3.90) is a fine eighteenth-century house complete with Georgian furniture and fittings. For the postcard view of the cathedral immortalized by John Constable, wander across the meadows and over the River Avon to **HARNHAM**, where you can have lunch or a drink at the *Old Mill* pub.

A ten-minute hop on any Andover- or Amesbury-bound bus takes you to the ruins of **Old Sarum** (daily 9/10am–4/6pm; £2), abandoned in the fourteenth century when the bishopric moved to Salisbury. Traces of the medieval town are visible in the outlines of its Norman cathedral and castle mound, but the ditch-encircled site is far older, populated in Iron Age, Roman and Saxon times.

Practicalities

It's a short walk southeast from Salisbury's **train station** (services from London Waterloo) across the River Avon into town. **Buses** from nearby Winchester and elsewhere terminate behind Endless St, a block south of which is the **tourist office**, just off Market Square (daily 9.30/10.30am–4.30/6pm; closed Sun in winter; ☎01722/334956, ⊛www.visitsalisbury.com).

Accommodation

Hostels

HI hostel Milford Hill House, Milford Hill ☎01722/327572. Excellent hostel five minutes east of the city centre, it also allows camping. ❸
Matt & Tiggy's Salt Lane ☎01722/327443. Small, privately run hostel near the bus station. ❸

Hotels and guest houses

Clovelly 17 Mill Rd ☎01722/322055, ⊛www .clovellyhotel.co.uk. Good-value hotel, close to the train station. No smoking. ❼
Glen Lyn 6 Bellamy Lane ☎01722/327880, ⊛www.glenlynbandbatsalisbury.co.uk. Elegant Victorian guest house ten minutes' walk from the centre. ❹
Town House 1 Bridge St ☎01722/415386. Bland but clean en-suite rooms over this centrally located pub. ❹

Eating and drinking

Bishop's Mill Bridge St. Popular pub offering outdoor seating and bar meals.
Haunch of Venison Minster St. Atmospheric pub serving good food.

Michael Snell's Tea Rooms St Thomas's Square. Traditional tea rooms, serving snacks and delicious buns. Closed Sun.
Moloko 5 Bridge St. Cool café and cocktail bar, serving croissants, panini and salads.

Stonehenge

The uplands northwest of Salisbury were a thriving centre of Neolithic civilization, the greatest legacy of which is **Stonehenge** (daily 9/9.30am–4/7pm; £4.40). It is served by buses from Salisbury. You can also take a tour – ask at the bus station for details – or get an Explorer (£5.50) or Wiltshire Rover (£6) pass, which are valid all day and include travel to Avebury and Bath.

The monument's age is being constantly revised as research progresses, but it's known that it was built in several distinct stages and adapted to the needs of successive cultures. The first Stonehenge probably consisted of a circular ditch dug in around 3000 BC. This was followed by the construction within the ditch of two concentric circles of forty bluestones, thought to have originated in the Preseli area of Wales. During the next half-century, the outer circle and inner horseshoe were put in place, made up of local Wiltshire sarsen stones up to 21ft in height topped by horizontal slabs. The way in which the sun's rays penetrate the central enclosure at dawn on midsummer's day has led to speculation about Stonehenge's role as either an astronomical observatory or a place of sun worship, but knowledge of the cultures responsible for building it is too scanty to reach any firm conclusions. The stones themselves are controversially fenced off to prevent the erosion caused by thousands of visitors, but it makes the visit a slightly disappointing experience. The only way to enter the circle itself is to take a **guided tour** (apply on ☎01980/626267 or at ⊛www.english-heritage.org.uk; £10).

Avebury

Salisbury also serves as a base for visiting the equally important – and much more atmospheric – Neolithic site at **AVEBURY**. Buses #5 and #6 run here daily from Salisbury.

The Avebury monoliths were probably erected soon after 2500 BC, and the main circle – with a diameter of some 400m – easily beats Stonehenge in terms of scale, even if it is not as impressive for its architectural sophistication. The atmosphere here is far more relaxed, however, and you can contemplate the grassy site armed with a pint or two from the *Red Lion* village pub, set right beside the main stone circle. Avebury's **Alexander Keiller Museum** (daily 10am–4/6pm; Nov–March closed Sun; £4) has displays on the monoliths as well as other ancient sites in the vicinity, while the **Barn Gallery** (same times, same ticket) favours a more interactive approach. Both places are worth visiting before or after exploring the cluster of archeological sites to the south of Avebury, best approached along the (signposted) **West Kennet Avenue**, two lines of standing stones thought to have been a processional way. Originally this ran two miles south to the so-called **Sanctuary**, possibly a gathering place of religious significance from around 3000 BC, of which little remains today. More compelling is the enormous conical mound of **Silbury Hill** just west of here, Europe's largest neolithic construction, dating from around 2600 BC. Signposted up a track on the other side of the A4, **West Kennet Long Barrow** is an impressive stone passage grave in use for over 1500 years from about 3700 BC.

From the Sanctuary at Overton Hill, hikers can loop northeast on a section of the **Ridgeway**, a 4000-year-old prehistoric highway which may once have run the breadth of Britain; it can still be walked or cycled as far as Tring, in the Chilterns. Get details from Avebury's **tourist office** on Green St (daily 10/10.30am–4.30/5.30pm; closed Sun in winter; ☎01672/539425).

Bath

BATH is an ancient Roman spa revived in the eighteenth-century for the tastes of the wealthy upper classes. Extensive reconstruction put into effect by neoclassicist architects John Wood and his son, John Wood the Younger, gives the town its distinctive appearance, with terraces of weathered sandstone fringed by spindly black railings. The hot spring that gave the city its name was dedicated to Sulis, the Celtic goddess of the waters, and provided the centrepiece of an extensive **bath complex** in the Roman era; the baths are now restored and can be visited (daily 9.30am–5.30pm; July–Aug till 10pm; ◍www.romanbaths.co.uk; £8). The pools, pipes and underfloor heating are remarkable demonstrations of the ingenuity of Roman engineering. The **Pump Room** (free), built above the Roman site in the eighteenth century, is the place to sample the waters while listening to genteel tunes from the resident chamber ensemble; and from late 2002 you'll be able to bathe or receive any number of health treatments in the modern **Bath Millennium Spa** (daily 7am–10pm) a few blocks away. The neighbouring **Abbey** (daily 9am–4.30/6pm; £2 donation requested) is renowned for the lofty fifteenth-century vault of its choir and the dense carpet of gravestones and memorials that cover the floor. The Abbey's **Heritage Vaults** (Mon–Sat 10am–4pm; £2) house Saxon and Norman sculpture and a reconstruction of the original building.

The best of Bath's eighteenth-century architecture is on the high ground to the north of the town centre, where the well-proportioned urban planning of the Woods is best showcased by the elegant Circus and the adjacent **Royal Crescent**. The house at 1 Royal Crescent is now a museum (Tues–Sun 10.30am–4/5pm; closed Jan to mid-Feb; £4), showing how the Crescent's houses would have looked in the Regency period. The social calendar of Bath's elite centred on John Wood the Younger's **Assembly Rooms** (daily 10am–5pm; free), just east of the Circus; recently renovated, it includes the interesting **Museum of Costume** in the basement (daily: 10am–5pm; ◍www.museumofcostume.co.uk; £5; combined ticket with bath complex £10.50).

The triple arches of Pulteney Bridge lead northeast from the town centre across the River Avon and up Great Pulteney St to the **Holburne Art Museum** (Tues–Sat 10am–5pm, Sun 2.30–5.30pm; closed mid-Dec to mid-Feb; ◍www.bath.ac.uk/holburne; £3.50), which contains silver, porcelain and furniture from the Regency period, as well as some fine art, including works by Gainsborough. Just south of the town centre **Herschel House**, 19 New King St

(March–Oct daily 2–5pm; Nov–Feb Sat & Sun only same times; £3.50; Ⓦwww.bath-preservation-trust.org.uk), showcases another eighteenth-century interior, this one housing the home-made telescope with which astronomer William Herschel first spotted Uranus in 1781.

Practicalities

The **train** and **bus stations** are both on Manvers St, five minutes south of the centre. The **tourist office** is just off the Abbey churchyard (Mon–Sat 9.30am–5/6pm, Sun 10am–4pm; ☎01225/477101, Ⓦwww.visitbath.co.uk).

The main tourist thoroughfares and neighbouring backstreets provide more **tea-rooms** than you can handle. We've listed some of the best, along with the best **restaurants** and **pubs**, below. Bath also hosts the eclectic *International Music Festival* (Ⓦwww.bathmusicfest.org.uk) in May and June. For **internet** access and coffee try the *Green Park Brasserie* at Old Green Park Station, off James St (☎01225/338565; £3/hr).

Accommodation

Hostels

Backpackers' Hostel 13 Pierrepoint St ☎01225/446787, Ⓦwww.hostels.co.uk. Relaxed and centrally located, just five minutes' walk north of the train and bus stations. ❸

YHA Bathwick Hill ☎01225/465674. A mile and a half east of town; take bus #18. ❸

Guest houses

Henry 6 Henry St ☎01225/424052. Near the Abbey, with more rooms than most, but still books up quickly. No en suites. ❺

Holly Villa 14 Pulteney Gardens ☎01225/310331, Ⓔhollyvilla.bb@ukgateway.net. Friendly place close to the Kennet and Avon canal, with six rooms, all en suite, and a nice garden. No smoking. No credit cards. ❹

Eating and drinking

Cafés and restaurants

Café Retro 18 York St. Popular café and bistro with an inventive international menu.

Demuth's 2 North Parade Passage off Abbey Green. Stylish vegetarian restaurant.

Walrus and Carpenter Barton St. Friendly place behind the theatre, serving steaks and burgers as well as veggie dishes.

Pubs

The Bell Walcot St. Grungy pub with garden and live music Mon and Wed eve, plus Sun lunch.

Pig & Fiddle Saracen St. Real ales, outside terraces, table football and food. Very popular.

The Porter 15 George St. Cheap meals at lunchtime and a pre-club crowd in the evenings.

Bristol

Situated on a succession of lumpy hills twelve miles beyond Bath and just inland from the mouth of the Avon, the city of **BRISTOL** grew rich on transatlantic trade – slaving, in particular – in the early part of the nineteenth century. It doesn't have quite the status now that it did then, but the city remains a wealthy, commercial centre, home to computer and aviation industries, a major university and a thriving cultural scene.

The city centre – in so much as there is one – is an elongated traffic interchange, **The Centre**, well away from the stations. Its southern end gives onto the **Floating Harbour**, an area of waterways that formed the commercial hub of the old town and now the location of numerous bars and restaurants as well as two of Bristol's best contemporary arts venues, housed in converted warehouses on either side of the water: the **Arnolfini** (exhibitions Mon–Sat 10am–7pm, Thurs till 9pm, Sun noon–7pm; free; Ⓦwww.arnolfini.demon.co.uk) and the **Watershed Arts Centre** (Ⓦwww.watershed.co.uk); both have pleasant, reasonably priced cafés which serve food and stay open late. Behind the Watershed lies the "at-Bristol" complex (Ⓦwww.at-bristol.org.uk), where two interactive centres – **Explore** (daily 10am–6pm; £7.50), a hands-on technology park, and **Wildwalk** (same times;

£6.50), a hi-tech wildlife museum – are overshadowed by a giant **IMAX cinema** (screenings Mon–Wed 10am–4.45pm, Thurs & Fri 10am–8.30pm, Sat & Sun 12.30–8.30pm; £6.50); a ticket for all three costs £16.50. From the Arnolfini, on Prince's Wharf, a swing bridge leads to the quayside **Bristol Industrial Museum** (Mon–Wed, Sat & Sun 10am–5pm; Nov–March Sat & Sun only; free), with cars and ship models. Just east of here rises the **Church of St Mary Redcliffe** (daily 8am–5/8pm), a glorious Gothic confection begun in the thirteenth century. To the west of the Industrial Museum, ten minutes' walk or a brief ride on the harbour ferry brings you to the **Maritime Heritage Centre** (daily 10am–4.30/5.30pm; £6.25), celebrating Bristol's shipbuilding past and providing access to Brunel's **SS Great Britain** (🖰www.ss-great-britain.com), the first propeller-driven iron ship, launched from this dock in 1843, and to a replica of the **Matthew**, which carried John Cabot to America in 1497.

Uphill from The Centre, past College Green – flanked by the city's **Cathedral** (not a patch on St Mary's) – you can follow Park St to the university's Wills Memorial Building, a Victorian neo-Gothic monster endowed by the local tobacco dynasty. The street opposite leads to **Brandon Hill**, topped by a splendid folly, **Cabot Tower** (daily 8am–dusk; free), from where there are views over much of the city, with the old docks spread out below you to the south, the suburb of Clifton and its suspension bridge to the west.

The rest of your time is best spent wandering around **CLIFTON**, whose airy terraces are reminiscent of the Georgian splendours of nearby Bath. It's a somewhat genteel quarter, but full of enticing pubs and with a spectacular focus in the **Clifton Suspension Bridge** (🖰www.clifton-suspension-bridge.org.uk), the creation of the indefatigable engineer and railway builder Isambard Kingdom Brunel, spanning the limestone abyss of the Avon Gorge. On a height above the bridge, the diminutive **Observatory** (daily 11am/noon–4/5pm; closed when cloudy; £1), holds a Victorian camera obscura which encompasses views of the gorge and bridge, and provides access to a steep tunnel ending at Giant's Cave, a ledge on the side of the gorge (same times; £1).

Practicalities

Bristol's Temple Meads **train station** is a five-minute bus ride southeast of the centre, or a fifteen-minute walk. The **bus station** is close to the Broadmead shopping centre on Marlborough St. There's a **tourist office** in the at-Bristol complex on Harbourside (daily 10am–6pm; ☎0117/926 0767; 🖰www.visitbristol.co.uk).

There are two **hostels** in town and plenty of **private rooms** available, mostly in the pleasant suburby of Clifton. For **food and drink**, the stretch between Clifton and the city centre offers a vast choice of ethnic eats and late bars. For nightlife **listings** galore check out the magazine *Venue* (🖰www.venue.co.uk) available from most bars and clubs. Arnolfini and Watershed both have arts **cinemas**, and there's a renowned **theatre** company at the Old Vic on King St. Bristol's vibrant **music** scene has produced a host of influential names (Tricky, Massive Attack, Portishead). Top **clubs** are listed below. OnCoffee.net, 11 Christmas Steps (☎0117/9251100; £3/hr), is a friendly **internet** café.

Accommodation

Hostels

YHA 14 Narrow Quay ☎0117/922 1659. Splendidly situated HI hostel in an old wharfside building next to the Arnolfini. ❸

Bristol Backpackers 17 St Stephen's St ☎0117/925 7900, 🖰www.bristolbackpackers.co.uk. Friendly place in the heart of the pub district. ❸

Hotels and guest houses

Oakfield Hotel 52 Oakfield Rd ☎0117/973 5556. A mile from the centre in Clifton; the public rooms are gloomy but the rooms are fine. No en suites. NO credit cards. ❹

St Michael's Guest House 145 St Michael's Hill ☎0177/907 7820. Simple rooms over one of Cotham's most popular cafés. No en suites. ❹

Eating, drinking and nightlife

Eating and drinking

Mud Dock Café The Grove. In the harbourside area, this funky restaurant/bar also has regular DJs most nights.

Riverstation The Grove. A good-value deli/bar with a classier restaurant upstairs.

Tantric Jazz Café 39 St Nicholas St. Serves up middle-eastern cuisine, live music and a bohemian atmosphere.

Nightlife

Academy Frogmore St. Live bands and international Djs. Open Thurs–Sat.

Thekla The Grove. Great riverboat venue staging regular club nights Thurs–Sat.

Winn's 23–25 West St, Old Market ⓦwww.winnsclub.com. Cheerful, central gay club. Thurs is student night, Sun is themed-party night.

Wells and Glastonbury

A small town dwarfed by its extraordinary cathedral, **WELLS** is served by shoals of buses from nearby Bath and Bristol, all arriving at Princes Rd bus station, five minutes from the centre. Follow Cuthbert St eastwards from here to the picturesque inn-lined Market Place, and the **tourist office** in the Town Hall (daily 9.30/10am–4/5.30pm; ☏01749/672552). From here a gateway leads through to The Close, bringing you face to face with an intoxicating array of Gothic statuary, mostly from the 1230s and 1240s. Inside the majestic **Cathedral** (7am–6/7pm; ⓦwww.wellscathedral.org.uk; donation £4.50), the great interlacing "scissor-arches" at the crossing were devised to support the unstable tower; in the north transept a fourteenth-century clock strikes the quarter-hours. South of the cathedral, a drawbridge leads across a moat to the **Bishop's Palace** (Easter–Oct Tues–Fri 10.30am–5pm, Sun 1–5pm; Aug daily 10.30am–6pm; £3.50), where opulently furnished rooms are watched over by portraits of former bishops. On the other side of the cathedral are the **town museum** (Easter–Oct daily 10am–5.30/8pm; Nov–Easter Mon & Wed–Sun 11am–4pm; £2.50) and the **Vicar's Close**, a row of fourteenth-century terraced houses. The tourist office has a list of B&Bs, but the nearest **hostel** (☏01934/742494; ❸) is six miles northwest in the village of **CHEDDAR**, reached on bus #126 or #826. The dramatic **Cheddar Gorge**, formed by the collapse of a cave system, is walkable from here.

Buses #163, #376 and #977 head southeast from Wells to **GLASTONBURY**, a small rural town whose associations with the Holy Grail and King Arthur have made it a magnet for those with a taste for the mystical – the **Tor**, a natural mound overlooking the town, is identified with the Isle of Avalon. Joseph of Arimathea, a relation of the Virgin Mary, is also said to have owned land nearby, and to have brought Mary and Jesus here; William Blake's poem *Jerusalem* replays the legend: "And did those feet in ancient time / Walk upon England's mountains green?" Glastonbury itself is not much more than a High St, the lower end of which, around the Market Cross, is overrun by New Age book- and crystal-shops. The impressive ruins of the **Abbey** are approached around the corner from Magdalene St (daily 9.30/10am–4.30/6pm; £3.50; ⓦwww.glastonburyabbey.com); this was the oldest Christian establishment in continuous use in England until Henry VIII ordered its near-destruction. The choir is alleged to hold the tomb of King Arthur and Guinevere. A mile to the east is the Tor, at the base of which stands the natural spring known as **Chalice Well** (daily 10am/noon–4/6pm; ⓦwww.chalicewell.org.uk; £2.20). The ferrous waters that flow from the hillside here were popularly thought to have gained their colour from the blood of Christ, supposedly flowing from the Holy Grail, buried here by Joseph of Arimathea. On top of the Tor stands the remains of a fourteenth-century church; the views from here are spectacular and it is a popular place from which to see the sunrise on the summer solstice.

By nightfall Glastonbury reverts to sleepy rural stillness – except over the summer solstice and during the **Glastonbury Festival**, which is held on a nearby farm over a weekend in mid-June and draws around 80,000 people to its binge of music, drugs and events. The **tourist office**, housed in the Tribunal on High St, sells tickets (daily 10am–4/5.30pm; ☎01458/832954, ⊛www.glastonburytic.co.uk). If you'd like to stay, note that there's a friendly crowd at the *Glastonbury Backpackers* **hostel** on Market Place (☎01458/833353, ⊛www.backpackers-online.com/glastonbury; ❷). The *Isle of Avalon* **campsite** is a short walk up Northload St from the centre (☎01458/833618). For **food and drink**, the *Backpackers* has cheap, filling meals and a lively bar with events; you'll also find well-priced veggie food at *Rainbow's End* on the High St.

Exeter

The county town of Devon, **EXETER** is the first stop for travellers to England's westernmost counties of Devon and Cornwall, and makes a feasible base for visiting a clutch of attractions within an easy bus-ride, including Dartmoor (see below). The city itself, once an inland port which flourished on the medieval wool trade, has plenty to occupy a day or two's exploration. The most distinctive feature of the skyline, **St Peter's Cathedral** (daily 8am–5/7.30pm; £3 donation requested; ⊛www.exeter-cathedral.org.uk), is a stately monument made conspicuous by the two great Norman towers flanking the nave. The facade's ornate Gothic screen, made up of three tiers of sculpted (and very weathered) figures – including various medieval kings – was begun around 1360, part of a rebuilding programme which left only the Norman towers from the original construction. Inside, you can admire the longest unbroken Gothic ceiling in the world, intricately rib-vaulted, and the thirteenth-century Lady Chapel and Chapter House. Elsewhere in town, the **Royal Albert Memorial Museum** on Queen St (Mon–Sat 10am–5pm; free) is worth a visit for its imaginative review of the city's various building styles, and the old **Quayside** area, on the banks of the River Exe, is the place to head for cafés, pubs and clubs.

Exeter has two **train stations**, Exeter Central and St David's, the latter a little way out from the centre of town. **Buses** stop at the station on Paris St, right across from the **tourist office** (July & Aug Mon–Sat 9am–5pm, Sun 10am–4pm; rest of year Mon–Fri 9am–5pm, Sat 9am–1pm & 2–5pm; ☎01392/265700, ⊛www.thisisexeter .co.uk). *Globe Backpackers*, 71 Holloway St (☎01392/215521, ⊛www.globebackpackers .freeserve.co.uk; ❸), is a clean and central independent **hostel**; the **HI hostel** lies two miles south of the city centre on Countess Wear Rd (☎01392/873329; ❸). *Herbie's*, 15 North St (closed all Sun & Mon eve), is a good wholefood **restaurant**, and there are cheap eats at the Quayside. Two of the best **clubs** are in the centre: the *Cavern Club*, in Gandy St and the *Timepiece*, Little Castle St. Finally, Saddles & Paddles **rents bikes** and **canoes** (☎01392/424241, ⊛www.saddlepaddle.co.uk), good for exploring the Exeter Canal, which runs for five miles from the Quayside area to Topsham and beyond.

Dartmoor

Dartmoor (⊛www.dartmoor-npa.gov.uk) is one of England's most beautiful wilderness areas, an expanse of wild uplands in the heart of Devon, some 75 miles southwest of Bristol. It's home to an indigenous breed of wild pony and dotted with **tors**, characteristic wind-eroded pillars of granite. The main focus for visitors in the middle of the park is **POSTBRIDGE**, reached by local bus from the nearest city, Plymouth. Famous for its medieval bridge over the East Dart river, this is a good starting point for walks in the woodlands surrounding Bellever Tor to the south. Postbridge's **tourist office**, on the main road through the village (daily 10am–4/5pm; ☎01822/880272), can supply information on the national park. The nearest **hostel** is at Bellever, one mile south (☎01822/880227; closed Nov–March; ❸).

The most untamed parts of the moor, around its highest points of High Willhays and Yes Tor, are above the market town of **OKEHAMPTON** – served by regular buses from Plymouth and Exeter. Despite the stark beauty of the terrain, this part of the moor is used by the Ministry of Defence as a firing range: details of times when it's safe to walk the moor are available from the **tourist office** on Fore St (Easter–May & Oct Mon–Sat 10am–4.30pm; June–Sept daily 10am–5pm; Nov–Easter Mon, Fri & Sat 10am–4.30pm; ☎01837/53020). Okehampton has a couple of attractions in its own right. The **Museum of Dartmoor Life** next to the tourist office (June–Sept daily 10am–5pm; Oct–Feb Mon–Fri 10am–4pm; March–May Mon–Sat 10am–4/5pm; £2) offers interesting anthropological insights, including a look at life in one of the Dartmoor longhouses, the stone and turf huts in which the moorland natives used to live. Surrounded by woods one mile southwest of town is the now crumbling Norman keep of **Okehampton Castle** (April–Oct daily 10am–5/6pm; £2.50). There's an **HI hostel** in a converted goods shed at the station (☎01837/53916; closed Dec & Jan; ❸).

The Eden Project

In the heart of Cornwall, England's most southwesterly county, is one of the newest and highest-profile attractions in the country; the **Eden Project** (daily 10am–4.30/6pm; £9.80; ⊛www.edenproject.com) lies four miles northeast of St Austell (bus #T9 from St Austell train station or #T10 in summer from Newquay). Occupying a 160-foot-deep disused clay pit, the centre showcases the diversity of the planet's plant-life in an imaginative, sometimes wacky, but refreshingly ungimmicky style. At centre stage of the stunningly landscaped site are two vast geodesic "biomes", or conservatories: one holding groves of olive and citrus trees, cacti and other plants more usually found in the warm, temperate zones of the Mediterranean, southern Africa and southwestern USA; the larger of the two recreates a tropical zone, with teak and mahogany trees, and has a waterfall and river gushing through it. Equally impressive are the external grounds, where plantations of bamboo, tea, hops, hemp and tobacco are interspersed with brilliant swathes of flowers. The whole "living theatre" presents a constantly changing spectacle, and should ideally be visited in different seasons. Allow at least half a day for a full exploration, but arrive early to avoid congestion. There are timed "story-telling" sessions, a lawn-carpeted arena where Celtic and other music is played, and good food on hand.

Penzance and around

The busy port of **PENZANCE** forms the natural gateway to the westernmost extremity of Cornwall – and, indeed, England – the Penwith Peninsula, and all the major sights of the region can be reached on day-trips from here. From the **train station**, at the northern end of town, Market Jew St threads its way through the town centre, culminating in the Neoclassical facade of Market House, fronted by a statue of local-born chemist and inventor Humphry Davy. West of here, a series of parks and gardens punctuate the quiet residential streets overlooking the promenade. The **Penlee House Gallery and Museum**, off Morrab Rd (Mon–Sat 10/10.30am–4.30/5pm; £2, free on Sat), features works by members of the Newlyn school, late nineteenth-century painters of local seascapes.

The view east across the bay is dominated by **St Michael's Mount**, site of a fortified medieval monastery perched on an offshore pinnacle of rock. At low tide, the Mount is joined by a cobbled causeway to the mainland village of Marazion (regular buses from Penzance); at high tide, a boat can ferry you over (£1). You can amble around part of the Mount's shoreline, but most of the rock lies within the grounds of the **castle**, now a stately home belonging to Lord St Levan (April–Oct Mon–Fri 10.30am–5.30pm, plus most weekends; Nov–March in good weather only; £4.60).

The other obvious excursion is to **Land's End**, the cliffy extremity of the Penwith Peninsula, accessible on frequent buses from Penzance. Despite the hold it exerts over the popular imagination, the site itself may fail to live up to expectations – especially now that a small theme park has been built here – and it's worthwhile using the coastal path to explore some of the less frequented spots of the peninsula. One and a half miles south of Land's End you'll find rugged beauty at **Mill Bay**, while there are acres of beaches the same distance north at **Whitesand Bay**, and more spectacular headlands around **Cape Cornwall**, four miles north of Land's End.

Practicalities

Penzance's **train** and **bus stations** are at the northeastern end of town, a step away from Market Jew St. The **tourist office** (May–Sept Mon–Sat 9am–5/6pm, Sun 10am–1pm; Oct–April Mon–Fri 9am–5pm, Sat 10am–1pm; ℡01736/362207, ✆www.go-cornwall.com) is by the bus station. **B&Bs** congregate at the western end of town around Morrab Rd. The **HI hostel**, Castle Horneck, Alverton (℡01736/362666; ❸), is a short walk along the Land's End road, or there's *Penzance Backpackers*, Alexandra Rd (℡01736/363836, ✆www.pzbackpack.ndirect.co.uk; ❷). Near Whitesand Bay and Land's End, the excellent *Land's End Backpackers' Hostel* is at Whitesands Lodge (℡01736/871776, ✆www.whitesandslodge.co.uk; ❸). *Co-Co's Tapas Bar*, Chapel St, has **snacks** and cakes as well as coffee and beer; *Dandelions*, on Causeway, is a veggie café. Town-centre **pubs** include the *Star* on Market Jew St, or the more touristy *Admiral Benbow* on Chapel St, a seventeenth-century house with maritime fittings. Look out for live music and other performances at the *Acorn Theatre*, Parade St.

St Ives and the north Cornwall coast

Across the peninsula from Penzance on Cornwall's north coast, the fishing village of **ST IVES** is the quintessential Cornish resort, featuring a maze of narrow streets lined with whitewashed cottages, sandy beaches and lush subtropical flora. The village's erstwhile tranquillity attracted several major artists throughout the twentieth century – Ben Nicholson, Barbara Hepworth and Naum Gabo among them. You can see examples of the work of these and others of the various St Ives schools at the **Tate Gallery**, overlooking Porthmeor Beach (daily 10am–4.30/5.30pm; Nov–Feb closed Mon; £4.10; ✆www.tate.org.uk/stives). A combined ticket (£6.95) admits you to the **Barbara Hepworth Museum** on Barnoon Hill (same hours), which preserves the studio of the modernist sculptor. Her photos of Cornwall quoits and landscapes provide clues to the inspiration behind her sleek monoliths, many splendid examples of which are displayed in the garden. Of the town's three beaches, the north-facing Porthmeor occasionally has good surf, and boards can be rented at the beach.

The **train station** is at Porthminster Beach, just north of the **bus station** on Station Hill. The **tourist office** in the Guildhall, St An Pol (Easter–Sept Mon–Sat 9am–5.30/6pm, Sun 10am–1/4pm; Oct–Easter Mon–Fri 9am–5pm, Sat 10am–1pm; ℡01736/796297, ✆www.go-cornwall.com), is a couple of minutes from both stations. Nearby is the *St Ives Backpackers* **hostel**, in a restored Wesleyan chapel on The Stennack (℡01736/799444, ✆www.backpackers.co.uk/st-ives; ❸).

Newquay, Padstow and Tintagel

Buffeted by Atlantic currents, Cornwall's cliffy **north coast** has a harsh grandeur, and is the area of the West Country most favoured by the surfing set. King of the surf resorts is **NEWQUAY**, whose somewhat tacky centre is surrounded by seven miles of golden sands, including **Fistral Beach**, the venue for surfing championships. However, unless you're dedicated to sand and surf, or drawn by the clubbing scene – Newquay's hectic nightlife is legendary – you could skip Newquay in favour of less packed resorts along this coast. Ten miles north, **PADSTOW** makes a more appealing base for some first-class beaches nearby, such as **Constantine Bay**, four miles west, and **Polzeath**, on the eastern side of the Camel estuary. Primarily a fishing port, Padstow is renowned for its fish restaurants, not least those belonging to celebrity chef **Rick Stein**. He has three eateries in town: the pricey *Seafood Restaurant* (℡01841/532700), which is one of the country's top eateries, and consequently booked up weeks in advance; the more moderately priced *St Petroc's Bistro*, 4 New St (℡01841/532700; closed Mon); and the casual *Rick Stein's Café*, 10 Middle St (closed Sun), which serves lunchtime snacks and moderately priced meals in the evening.

Across the Camel estuary, twelve miles northwest of Padstow, the village of **TINTAGEL** trades on its associations with King Arthur. Even if you're bored by all the money-spinning hocus-pocus surrounding the legend, **Tintagel Castle** (daily 10am–4/7pm; £3), supposedly the birthplace of the Once and Future King, merits a visit, its black and tattered ruins straddling an outcrop above the sea. Dating from the Norman era, there is little to connect the stronghold with the real-life Arthur, though traces of an early Christian community have been found here. It's an evocative spot, with splendidly craggy coastline to either side, the coast path running along the cliff-top.

Practicalities

There are **tourist offices** at Newquay, Marcus Hill (May–Sept Mon–Sat 9.30am–4.30/5.30pm, Sun 9.30am–12.30pm; ℡01637/854020, www.newquay.co.uk), and Padstow, on the harbourside (April–Oct daily 9.30am–5pm; Nov–March closed weekends; ℡01841/533449, www.padstow.uk.com). Newquay has numerous campsites and **hostels**, including *Newquay International Backpackers*, 69 Tower Rd (℡01637/879366, www.backpackers.co.uk/newquay; ❸), and *Matt's Surf Lodge*, 110 Mount Wise (℡01637/874651, www.matts-surf-lodge.co.uk; ❸). Two **HI hostels** in the region enjoy superb locations: just off the beach at Constantine Bay, near Padstow (℡01841/520322; ❸), and about a mile south of Tintagel at Dunderhole Point (℡01840/770334).

Central England

Central England was the powerhouse of the Industrial Revolution, and although large portions of the Midlands are greener than most people realize, it is still predominantly a region of gritty manufacturing towns. Birmingham, at the hub of the industrial sprawl, may boast one of the best concert halls and orchestras in the country, but it is still unlikely to feature on a quickstop national tour. It is the university town of **Oxford** and **Stratford-upon-Avon**, the birthplace of William Shakespeare, to the south and west, that are the main draw here; and, in the far east of the region, the other university town of **Cambridge**.

Oxford

Think of **OXFORD** and inevitably you think of its university, revered as one of the world's great academic institutions, inhabiting honey-coloured stone buildings set around ivy-clad quadrangles. Much of this is accurate enough, but although the university dominates central Oxford, the wider city has an entirely different character, its economy built on the car plants of Cowley.

The **university** has long operated a collegiate system in which students and tutors live, work and take their meals together in the same complex of buildings – usually a couple of quadrangles ("quads") with a chapel, library and dining hall – and taken together the colleges form a dense maze of historic buildings in the heart of the city. Access may be restricted during term-time, and many colleges close to visitors entirely in May and June, when exams are approaching.

The City

The main point of reference is **Carfax**, a central crossroads overlooked by the chunky **Carfax Tower** (daily 10am–3.30/5.30pm; £1.20), the first of many opportunities to enjoy a panorama of Oxford's "dreaming spires". From here, head south

OXFORD

Hostel ▲

Punts

River Cherwell

St Catherine's College

Magdalen Grove

Magdalen College

MAGDALEN BRIDGE

Botanical Gardens

River Cherwell

LONGWALL STREET

HIGH STREET

ROSE LANE

CITY WALL

New College

Christ Church Meadow

River Thames (Isis) ▶

QUEEN'S LANE

JOWETT WALK

Queen's College

MANSFIELD ROAD

All Soul's College

Merton College

DEAD MAN'S WALK

SAVILE ROAD

HOLYWELL STREET

Holywell Music Room

NEW COLLEGE LANE

Oriel College

University College

MERTON STREET

Corpus Christi College

Wadham College

Sheldonian Theatre

Bodleian Library

CATTE STREET

ORIEL SQUARE

Cathedral

PARKS ROAD

New Bodleian Library

Radcliffe Camera

University Church

BRASENOSE LANE

BEAR LANE

ALFRED STREET

BROAD STREET

TURL STREET

Christ Church College

BLUE BOAR STREET

St John's College

Trinity College

Balliol College

Exeter College

SHIP STREET

MARKET STREET

ST ALDATES

QUEEN STREET

CARFAX

The Oxford Story

ST GILES

CORNMARKET

Covered Market

Carfax Tower

St Museum of Oxford

MOMA

PEMBROKE STREET

BREWER STREET

ROSE PLACE

MAGDALEN STREET

ST MICHAEL'S STREET

Oxford Union

ST EBBE'S STREET

Playhouse Theatre

BEAUMONT STREET

NEW INN HALL STREET

Nuffield College

NEW ROAD

CASTLE STREET

PUSEY LANE

Ashmolean Museum

GEORGE STREET

GLOUCESTER STREET

ST JOHN'S STREET

Market

Gloucester Green Coach Station

WORCESTER STREET

HYTHE BRIDGE STREET

PARK END STREET

PARADISE STREET

Ruskin College

Worcester College

Oxford Canal

HOLLYBUSH ROW

N

▲ A34, (M40) Birmingham

Train Station ▲

100 m

0

© Crown copyright

down St Aldates to the biggest of Oxford's colleges, **Christ Church** (daily 9.30/11.30am–5.30pm; £4; ☎01865/276492). The main entrance passes underneath the dome of Tom Tower, built in 1681 by Christopher Wren, before opening onto the vast expanse of Tom Quad, mostly dating from the college's foundation in the sixteenth century. It is an indication of the prestige and wealth of the college that the city's late Norman **Cathedral** also serves as the college chapel. The complex also holds the college's **Picture Gallery**, with a strong collection of Italian Renaissance paintings.

South of the college, **Christ Church Meadow** offers gentle walks – either east to the River Cherwell or south to the Thames, perversely referred to hereabouts as the Isis. Alternatively, wander northeast to the cluster of especially beguiling colleges that hugs the High St. Just to the south of here, **Merton** (Mon–Fri 2–4pm, Sat & Sun 10am–4pm; free; ☎01865/276310) is perhaps the prettiest college, founded in the thirteenth century and complete with the beautiful Mob Quad. At the rear of Merton College, Dead Man's Walk heads east to join Rose Lane, which emerges at the eastern end of the High St beside the **Botanical Gardens** (daily 9am– 4.30/5.30pm; £2) and the River Cherwell, where you can rent punts in summer. Opposite is the fifteenth-century bell tower of **Magdalen College** (pronounced "maudlin"; daily noon/2–6pm; £2; ☎01865/276000); the Cloister Quad of the same period is the most striking of its courtyards.

Many of the university's most important and imposing buildings lie just to the north of the High St. The most dramatic is the Italianate **Radcliffe Camera**. Built in the 1730s by James Gibbs, it is now used as a reading room for the **Bodleian Library**, whose main building is immediately to the north in the Old Schools Quad. Most of the library is closed to the general public, but you can see part of the immense collection of ancient manuscripts on a guided tour of **Duke Humfrey's library** (March–Oct Mon–Fri 10.30am, 11.30am, 2pm & 3pm, Sat & Sun 10.30am & 11.30am; £3.50). The adjacent **Sheldonian Theatre** (Mon–Sat 10am–12.30pm & 2–3.30/4.30pm; £1.50), a copy of the Theatre of Marcellus in Rome, was designed by Christopher Wren and is now a venue for concerts and university functions. West from the Sheldonian is the **Ashmolean Museum** (Tues–Sat 10am–5pm, Sun noon/2–5pm; June–Aug Thurs till 7pm; free), which occupies a mammoth building on the corner of Beaumont St and St Giles. The building is enormous and so is the collection. Highlights include the Egyptian rooms with their well-preserved mummies and sarcophagi; the Islamic Art room, which holds superb Islamic ceramics; and the Chinese Art rooms.

Practicalities

From Oxford's **train station**, it's a ten-minute walk to the centre. Long distance and many county-wide buses terminate at the central Gloucester Green **bus station**, which is by the **tourist office** (Mon–Sat 9.30am–5pm, Sun 10am–3.30pm; Oct– March closed Sun; ☎01865/726871, ⊛www.visitoxford.org). You'll find **internet** access at Internet Exchange, Costa Coffee, 8 George St. Bike Zone at 6 Lincoln House, Market St (☎01865/728877), is the best place for **bike rental**. For **listings** of upcoming gigs and concerts, consult *This Month in Oxford*, available free at the tourist office.

Accommodation

Hostels

New Oxford Youth Hostel 2A Botley Rd ☎01865/ 727275, ⊛www.yha.org.uk. Next door to the train station, this popular HI hostel has 184 beds divided up into two-, four- and six-bedded rooms. Inexpensive meals available plus self-catering. Advance booking recommended. No curfew. **4**

Oxford Backpackers Hostel 9A Hythe Bridge St ☎01865/721761, ⊜oxford@hostels.co.uk. Independent hostel, with ten bunkrooms holding a maximum of ten people each. Fully equipped kitchen, laundry, bar and internet facilities. Handy location, between the train station and the centre. Advance booking recommended. No curfew. **3**

Guest houses
Becket Guest House 5 Becket St ☎01865/724675. Modest but well-run bay-windowed guest house in a plain terrace close to the train station. Most rooms are en suite. ⑤

Isis Guest House 45–53 Iffley Rd ☎01865/248894. Large college house, just across Magdalen Bridge. Good value, but spartan. Open July–Sept only. ④

St Michael's Guest House 26 St Michael's St ☎01865/242101. Often full, this friendly, well-kept B&B, in a cosy three-storey terrace house, has unsurprising furnishings and fittings, but a charming, central location. ⑤

Eating, drinking and nightlife
Snacks and cafés
Beat Café Little Clarendon St. Hippified café with fancy decor and stained glass windows selling a good line in inexpensive sandwiches, salads and smoothies.

George and Davies Little Clarendon St. Ice-cream parlour that stays open well after the pubs and cinemas.

Nosebag 6 St Michael's St. A civilized but unassuming place, with floral decor and classical background music. The food attracts queues at lunchtime; not so in the evening, when it is a good place for a quick but wholesome meal. Good selection of veggie food.

Restaurants
Bangkok House 42a Hythe Bridge St ☎01865/200705. Best Oriental restaurant in town, with superb Thai food and excellent service. The mixed starter and the coconut-milk curries are particularly good. Closed Sun & Mon lunch.

Pizza Express 8 Golden Cross, Cornmarket ☎01865/790442. In an imaginatively renovated Tudor building, this reliable chain offers the best-value pizzas in central Oxford. Expect a long wait at weekends.

Pubs and bars
Eagle & Child 49 St Giles. This pub was once the haunt of J.R.R. Tolkien, C.S. Lewis and other literary types, and still attracts a comparatively genteel mix of professionals and academics.

Lamb & Flag St Giles. Generations of university students have hung out in this old pub, which comes complete with low-beamed ceilings and a series of cramped but cosy rooms. Good range of ales.

White Horse 52 Broad St. A tiny, old pub with snug rooms, pictures of old university sports teams on the walls and Real Ales. It was used as a set for the *Inspector Morse* series.

Live music and clubs
The Coven Oxpens Rd ☎01865/242770. Formerly a gay disco, but now gone more or less straight. Tacky grottoes for tête-a-têtes, but generally a good atmosphere and decent music with techno/acid/hard house featuring prominently. Closed Sun & Mon.

Old Fire Station (aka **OFS**) 40 George St ☎01865/794494. Multi-purpose venue with musicals and theatre, plus regular DJ club nights (Fri & Sat).

Zodiac 190 Cowley Rd ☎01865/420042. Oxford's most respected indie and dance venue, with live bands throughout the week. Closed Sun.

Stratford-upon-Avon

STRATFORD-UPON-AVON makes the most of its association with William Shakespeare, who was born here on April 23, 1564. There are five restored properties recalling the Bard, three in the town itself and two on the outskirts. If you've time to visit them all, it's worth considering a combined ticket (£8.50/three town properties, £12/five), available at the tourist office (see below); otherwise save your

The Royal Shakespeare Company (RSC)

The **RSC** (☻www.rsc.org.uk) works on a repertory system, which means you could stay in Stratford for a few days and see four or five different **plays**. Tickets start at around £5 for standing room and a restricted view, rising to £40 for the best seats in the house. However, very popular shows get booked up months in advance. There are three theatres – The Other Place, the Swan and the Royal Shakespeare – and one central **box office** (Mon–Sat from 9am; ☎01789/403403).

money and go and watch the excellent Royal Shakespeare Company at one of its three theatres.

Top of everyone's Bardic itinerary is the **Birthplace Museum** (daily 9/10am–4/5pm; £6), comprising an ugly modern visitor centre attached to the heavily restored half-timbered building on Henley St where the great man was born. The visitor centre pokes into every corner of Shakespeare's life and times, making the most of what little hard evidence there is. A short walk away is **Nash's House**, Chapel St (daily 9.30/10am–4/5pm; £3.50), once the property of Thomas Nash, first husband of Shakespeare's granddaughter, Elizabeth Hall. The ground floor is kitted out with a pleasant assortment of period furnishings and upstairs has more of the same, plus a competent potted biography of Shakespeare. Chapel St continues south as Church St. At the end, turn left along Old Town St for Stratford's most impressive medieval house, **Hall's Croft** (daily 9.30/10am–4/5pm; £3.50). The former home of Shakespeare's elder daughter, Susanna, and her doctor husband, John Hall, the immaculately maintained Croft, with its creaking wooden floors, beamed ceilings and fine kitchen range, holds a fascinating display on Elizabethan medicine. Beyond, Old Town St steers right to reach the handsome **Holy Trinity Church** (Mon–Sat 8.30/9am–4/6pm, Sun 2–5pm; free), whose mellow, honey-coloured stonework is enhanced by its riverside setting. Shakespeare lies buried here in the **chancel** (£1), his remains overseen by a sedate and studious memorial plaque and effigy added just seven years after his death.

Situated about a mile west of the town centre in Shottery is **Anne Hathaway's Cottage** (daily 9/9.30am–4/5pm; £4.50), whose dinky wooden beams and thatching were home to Anne before she married Shakespeare. There's also **Mary Arden's House**, three miles northwest of the town centre in Wilmcote (same times; £5.50), which was the home of Shakespeare's mother and is now a well-furnished example of an Elizabethan farmhouse.

Practicalities

Stratford's **train station** is on the northwestern edge of town, ten minutes' walk from the centre. Now the end of the line, it receives hourly shuttles from Birmingham and frequent trains from Warwick (for London Paddington or London Marylebone). Local **bus services** arrive and depart from Bridge St in the centre; long-distance buses pull into the Riverside station on the east side of town, off Bridgeway. The **tourist office** (Mon–Sat 9am–5/6pm, Sun 11am–4/5pm; ☎01789/293127, ⊛www.shakespeare-country.co.uk) is located a couple of minutes' walk from the bus station by the bridge at the junction of Bridgeway and Bridgefoot. They operate an efficient **accommodation booking hotline** (Mon–Fri 9.30am–4.30pm; ☎01789/415061; £3).

Accommodation

Hostel
Stratford-upon-Avon Youth Hostel Hemmingford House, Alveston ☎01789/297093,⊛www.yha.org .uk. HI hostel occupying a rambling Georgian mansion on the edge of the pretty village of Alveston, two miles east of the town centre on the B4086. Has dormitories and family rooms, some en suite. Laundry, internet access and self-catering. Evening meals too. Regular buses from Stratford's Riverside bus station. ❷

Guest houses
Chadwyns Guest House 6 Broad Walk ☎01789/ 269077, ⊛www.chadwyns.freeserve.co.uk. Just off Evesham Place, this well-maintained, most agreeable guest house occupies pleasant Victorian premises and offers seven en-suite rooms. Great breakfasts with vegetarian options. ❺
Parkfield Guest House 3 Broad Walk ☎01789/293313, ⊜parkfiel@btinternet.com. Very pleasant B&B in a rambling Victorian house down a residential street off Evesham Place. Most of the rooms are en suite. Less than ten minutes' walk from the centre. ❺
Woodstock Guest House 30 Grove Rd ☎01789/ 299881, ⊜woodstockhouse@compuserve.com. A smart B&B ten minutes' walk from the centre, by the start of the path to Anne Hathaway's Cottage. It has five extremely comfortable bedrooms, all en suite. No credit cards. ❺

Campsite
Stratford Racecourse Camp Site Luddington Rd
☎01789/267949. Well-equipped camping and
caravan site one mile southwest of the town
centre. Regular buses into town (not Sun). Closed
Oct–March. Tent pitches from £4.

Eating and drinking
Restaurants and cafés
Kingfisher Fish Bar 13 Ely St. The best fish-and-chip shop in town. A five-minute walk from the
theatres. Takeaway only. Closed Sun.
Lamb's Café Bistro 12 Sheep St ☎01789/
292554. Smart restaurant serving a mouth-watering
range of stylish English and continental dishes. A
good option for pasta lovers.
The Opposition 13 Sheep St ☎01789/269980.
Top-quality, imaginative international cuisine in a
busy but amiable atmosphere. The dishes of the day,
chalked up on a board inside, are excellent value.

Pubs
Dirty Duck 53 Waterside. The archetypal actors'
pub, stuffed to the gunwales every night with a
vocal entourage of RSC employees and hangers-on. Essential viewing.
The Garrick Inn 25 High St. Arguably the town's
most photogenic and best-preserved old ale
house: exposed beams, real ales and good food.
Windmill Inn Church St. Popular pub of cosy little
rooms with low-beamed ceilings. A good range of
beers too.

Cambridge

Tradition has it that the University of **CAMBRIDGE** was founded by refugees
from Oxford, who fled the town after one of their number was lynched by hostile
townsfolk in the 1220s. There's been rivalry between the two institutions ever since,
but what distinguishes Cambridge is "**the Backs**" – the green swathe of land straddling the River Cam, which overlooks the backs of the old colleges, and provides
the town's most enduring image of grand academic architecture.

A logical place to begin a tour is **King's College**, whose much celebrated **King's
College Chapel** (term time Mon–Fri 9.30am–3.30pm, Sat 9.30am–3.15pm, Sun
1.15–2.15pm; rest of year Mon–Sat 9.30am–4.30pm, Sun 10am–5pm; £3.50) is an
extraordinarily beautiful building. King's flanks **King's Parade**, originally the
medieval High St, at the northern end of which is the **Senate House**, the scene of
graduation ceremonies on the last Saturday in June, when champagne corks fly
around the rabbit-fur collars and black gowns.

Nearby Trinity St holds the main entrance to **Gonville and Caius College**,
known simply as Caius (pronounced "keys"), whose two adjoining courts boast
three fancy gates representing a different stage on the path to academic enlightenment. On the south side, the "Gate of Honour" leads into Senate House Passage,
which itself heads west to **Clare College** (daily 10am–5pm; £2). One of seven
colleges founded by women, Clare's plain period-piece courtyard leads to one of
the most picturesque of all the bridges over the Cam, **Clare Bridge**. Beyond lies
the Fellows' Garden, one of the loveliest college gardens open to the public (times
as college).

Just to the north of Caius, **Trinity College** (daily 10am–5pm; £1) is the largest
of the Cambridge colleges and to ram home the point it also has the largest courtyard. A statue of Henry VIII, who founded the college in 1546, sits in majesty over
Trinity's **Great Gate**, his sceptre replaced with a chair leg by a student wit. Beyond
lies the vast asymmetrical expanse of **Great Court**, which displays a fine range of
Tudor buildings, the oldest of which is the fifteenth-century clock tower – the
annual race against its midnight chimes is now common currency thanks to the
film *Chariots of Fire*. To get through to **Nevile's Court** – where Newton first calculated the speed of sound – you must pass through "the screens", a passage separating the Hall from the kitchens, a common feature of Oxbridge colleges. The west
end of Nevile's Court is enclosed by the university's most famous building after
King's College Chapel, the **Wren Library** (term time Mon–Fri noon–2pm, Sat
10.30am–12.30pm; rest of year Mon–Fri only; free).

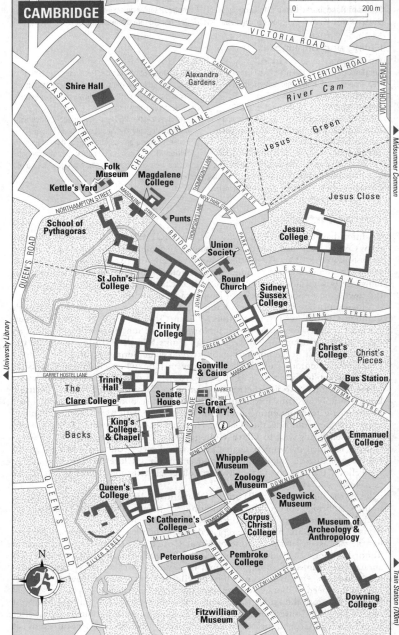

CAMBRIDGE

0   200 m

VICTORIA ROAD

CASTLE STREET

HERTFORD STREET

ALPHA ROAD

CARLYLE ROAD

Alexandra
Gardens

CHESTERTON ROAD

VICTORIA AVENUE

► Midsummer Common

River Cam

CHESTERTON LANE

Jesus   Green

Shire Hall

THOMPSON'S LANE

PARK PARADE

Jesus Close

Folk
Museum

Magdalene
College

NEW PARK STREET

Kettle's Yard

NORTHAMPTON STREET

MAGDALENE STREET

Punts

BRIDGE STREET

THOMPSON'S LANE

Jesus
College

School of
Pythagoras

Union
Society

PARK STREET

JESUS   LANE

QUEEN'S ROAD

◄ University Library

St John's
College

ST JOHN'S ST

Round
Church

Sidney
Sussex
College

KING   STREET

Trinity
College

GREEN STREET

SIDNEY STREET

HOBSON STREET

Christ's
College

Christ's
Pieces

Gonville
& Caius

MARKET ST

DRUMMER STREET

Bus Station

GARRET HOSTEL LANE

Trinity
Hall

MARKET
HILL

PETTY CURY

ST ANDREW'S STREET

The

Clare College

Senate
House

Great
St Mary's

ℹ

Emmanuel
College

Backs

King's
College
& Chapel

KING'S PARADE

BENE'T STREET

Whipple
Museum

DOWNING STREET

Zoology
Museum

Sedgwick
Museum

Queen's
College

St Catherine's
College

PEMBROKE ST

Corpus
Christi
College

Museum of
Archeology &
Anthropology

TENNIS COURT ROAD

FITZWILLIAM ST

► Train Station (700m)

QUEEN'S ROAD

SILVER STREET

MILL LANE

Peterhouse

Pembroke
College

TRUMPINGTON STREET

Downing
College

N

Fitzwilliam
Museum

© Crown copyright

Doubling back along King's Parade, it takes about five minutes to reach **Queens' College** (daily 10am–4.30pm; £1.20), accessed through the gate on Queen's Lane, just off Silver St. Here, the **Old Court** and the **Cloister Court** are twin fairy-tale Tudor courtyards, with the first of the two the perfect illustration of the original collegiate ideal with kitchens, library, chapel, hall and rooms all set around a tiny green. Equally eye-catching is the wooden **Mathematical Bridge** over the Cam, a copy of the mid-eighteenth-century original which, it was claimed, would stay in place even if the nuts and bolts were removed. Back outside Queens', it's a short hop to the River Cam, where you can go for a **punting** – the quintessential Cambridge activity. **Punt rental** is available at the bridge (roughly £12/hour).

From Queens', it's another short stroll to the **Fitzwilliam Museum** (Tues–Sat 10am–5pm, Sun 2.15–5pm; £3 donation suggested). Of all the museums in Cambridge, this is the best with the Lower Galleries containing a wealth of classical antiquities, while the Upper Galleries concentrate on painting and sculpture both from Europe and Britain. The post-1945 gallery is packed with a fascinating selection including pieces by the likes of Lucian Freud, David Hockney and Henry Moore.

Practicalities

Cambridge **train station** is a mile or so southeast of the city centre, off Hills Rd. It's an easy but tedious twenty-minute walk into the centre, or take shuttle bus #3. The **bus station** is centrally located on Drummer St, right by Christ's Pieces. The **tourist office** is also central, on Wheeler St, off King's Parade (Mon–Fri 10am–5.30/6pm, Sat 10am–5pm, Sun 11am–4pm; Nov–March closed Sun; ☎01223/322640; ⊛www.tourismcambridge.com). They operate a useful **accommodation booking service**. For the latest information, get Adhoc's *What's On?*, a free, monthly **listings** magazine, available at the tourist office and larger bookshops. There are several **bike rental** outlets, including Geoff's Bike Hire, near the train station at 65 Devonshire Rd (☎01223/365629; £7/day).

Accommodation

Hostels
Cambridge YHA 97 Tenison Rd ☎01223/354601, ⊛www.yha.org.uk. This well-equipped HI hostel has laundry and self-catering facilities, a cycle store, a games room and a small courtyard garden. It's close to the train station – off Station Rd. ❸
YMCA Queen Anne House, Gonville Place ☎01223/356998. Central location on the south side of Parker's Piece. Singles and doubles, with breakfast included. Very busy during summer; book well in advance. ❹

Guest houses and B&Bs
Benson House 24 Huntingdon Rd ☎01223/311594. Pleasant, well-kept guest house in a demure brick house, just north of Magdalene Bridge near New Hall College. Five rooms, three en suite. ❺
Netley Lodge 112 Chesterton Rd ☎01223/363845. Cosy B&B in a Victorian town house a long but manageable walk from the centre. Three attractively furnished bedrooms, two en suite. No credit cards. ❺.
Sleeperz Hotel Station Rd ☎01223/304050, ⊛www.sleeperz.com. This popular hotel is in an imaginatively converted granary warehouse, right outside the train station. Most of the rooms are bunk-style affairs done out in the manner of a ship's cabin, and there are a few doubles too. All are en suite, with shower and TV. ❺

Eating, drinking and nightlife

Restaurants and cafés
Clowns 54 King St. Italian-style cappuccino and cakes, sandwiches and snacks, plus newspapers to browse.
Efes 80 King St ☎01223/350491. Intimate Turkish restaurant, with chargrilled meats prepared under your nose and a decent *meze* selection.

Eraina Taverna 2 Free School Lane ☎01223/368786. Packed Greek taverna that satisfies the hungry hordes with huge platefuls of stews and grills, as well as pizzas, curries and a whole host of other menu madness.
Rainbow Vegetarian Bistro 9a King's Parade ☎01223/321551. Vegetarian restaurant with main

courses – ranging from couscous to lasagne and Indonesian *gado-gado* – all under £7. Good-value breakfasts and organic wines served with meals. Closed Sun.

Pubs, bars and clubs
Champion of the Thames 68 King St. Gratifyingly old-fashioned central pub with decent beer and a student/academic clientele.

Eagle Bene't St. An ancient inn with a cobbled courtyard where Crick and Watson sought inspiration in the 1950s, at the time of their discovery of DNA. It's been tarted up since and gets horribly crowded, but is still worth a pint of anyone's time.
Junction Clifton Rd ☏01223/511511. Rock, Indie, jazz, reggae or soul gigs, plus occasional comedy acts and dance groups at this popular arts and entertainments venue.

Northern England

The main draw of **northern England** is the **Lake District**, a scenic region just thirty miles across, taking in stone-built villages, sixteen major lakes and the steeply pitched faces of England's highest mountains. However, to restrict yourself purely to the outdoors would be to do a disservice to cities such as **Manchester** and **Liverpool** on the northwest coast, and **Newcastle** on the northeast, whose centres are alive with the ostentatious civic architecture of nineteenth-century capitalism and twenty-first century renewal. An entirely different angle on northern history is provided by the great medieval ecclesiastical centres of **Durham** and **York**, where famous cathedrals provide a focus for extensive medieval remains.

Manchester

Few cities in the world have embraced social change so heartily as **MANCHES-TER**. From engine of the Industrial Revolution to test-bed of contemporary urban design, the city has no realistic provincial rival in England. After a massive IRA bomb destroyed much of the centre in 1996, rebuilding has transformed the city, and with a huge student population, a lively Gay Village, and a venerable history of churning out talent for the twin glories of British culture – music and football – Manchester today hosts one of the country's most vibrant social and cultural scenes.

From the main Piccadilly train station, it's a few minutes' walk northwest to **Piccadilly Gardens** (hub of the local tram and bus network). North of the gardens is what's been dubbed the **Northern Quarter**, an edgy old wholesale district full of boutiques, music stores, bars and cafés. West of the gardens, **St Ann's Square** took the brunt of the 1996 bomb but has now been thoroughly transformed into a pedestrianized shopping area. The square is home to the **Royal Exchange** building, which houses the famous Royal Exchange Theatre, while New Cathedral St runs through the landscaped expanse of **Exchange Square** to the demure fifteenth-century **Cathedral**. South down Deansgate brings you to the Victorian Gothic **John Rylands Library** at no. 150 (Mon–Fri 10am–5.30pm, Sat 10am–1pm; free), which exhibits a changing selection of rare items, from Egyptian papyri to early examples of European printing. Keep on down Deansgate and turn right into Liverpool Rd for a celebration of the triumphs of industrialization at the superb **Museum of Science and Industry** (daily 10am–5pm; free; admission charge for special exhibitions; ⍟www.msim.org.uk), where exhibits include working steam engines, textile machinery, a hands-on science centre and a glimpse of the Manchester sewer system. Fifteen minutes' walk east, on Albert Square, stands the city's finest Victorian Gothic building, its **Town Hall** (Mon–Fri 9am–5pm; free), whose Great Hall features paintings depicting decisive moments from Manchester's past. There's more terrific art a block to the east at the newly expanded **City Art Gallery** on Mosley St (daily 10am–5pm; free; ⍟www.cityartgalleries.org.uk), including the country's finest public collection of works by the Pre-Raphaelite Brotherhood.

Metrolink trams run from Piccadilly Gardens to **Salford Quays**, scene of a massive urban renewal scheme in the old dock area. Centrepiece is the spectacular waterfront **Lowry Centre** (daily from 9.30am; free; @ www.thelowry.com), where – as well as theatre and gallery space (Mon–Sun 11am–5/8pm; free) – there's always room devoted to the work of the artist after whom the centre is named, L.S. Lowry, best-known for his "matchstick men" scenes. To reach the centre, take the tram to Broadway, or you can walk down the docks from the Salford Quays stop. A footbridge runs across the docks to the new **Imperial War Museum North** (@ www.iwm.org.uk/north), housed in a strikingly designed broken-globe complex. It's as resonant in its way as the other great building that looms in the near distance, **Old Trafford**, home of **Manchester United Football Club**, whose museum is sited in the North Stand (daily 9.30am–5pm; museum and tour £8.50, museum only £5.50; advance booking essential, ☎ 0161/877 8631, @ www.manutd.com).

Practicalities

Most **trains** arrive at Piccadilly station, on the city's east side. **Coaches** stop at Chorlton St, just west of Piccadilly. The **airport** is ten miles south, with a direct 24-hour train service to Piccadilly. The **Manchester Visitor Centre** is in the town hall extension on Lloyd St, at St Peter's Square (Mon–Sat 10am–5.30pm, Sun 11am–4pm; ☎ 0161/234 3157, @ www.manchester.gov.uk/visitorcentre), with branches in both airport terminals. There's 24-hour **internet** access at easyEverything, 18 Exchange St, St Ann's Square. **Youth hostel and backpacker beds** are easy to come by, while the Visitor Centre can help with university accommodation (summer only) and budget B&B (though most of these are well out of the city centre).

For cheap **eating**, head a couple of blocks east of the visitor centre to **Chinatown**, where noodle-and-rice cafés mingle with flash Cantonese restaurants. Alternatively, the scores of restaurants along Wilmslow Rd in Rusholme (buses #40–49), otherwise known as "Curry Mile", feature some of Britain's best (and cheapest) Asian cooking. The trendiest places to **drink** are in the Castlefield area around Liverpool Rd; along Deansgate Locks (Whitworth St West); in the Northern Quarter around Oldham St; and the Gay Village on the Rochdale Canal. Don't miss a pint in one of Manchester's classic Victorian city-centre **pubs** either.

For details of the city's **nightlife**, pick up a copy of the fortnightly *City Life*. For **live music** catch up-and-coming bands at *The Roadhouse*, Newton St; bigger acts play the *Academy* and the *Students' Union* on Oxford Rd. **Bridgewater Hall** on Lower Mosley St (☎ 0161/907 9000, @ www.bridgewater-hall.co.uk) is home of the world-famous Hallé Orchestra (founded 1857), while the **Cornerhouse**, 70 Oxford St (☎ 0161/200 1500, @ www.cornerhouse.org), is the city's centre for contemporary arts, with a cinema, exhibitions, café and bar.

Accommodation

Manchester Backpackers' Hostel 64 Cromwell Rd, Stretford ☎ 0161/865 9296. Two miles out of the centre, with laundry facilities, kitchen, TV lounge and pool table. Dorms and twins/doubles available. Metrolink to Stretford. ❷
Manchester YHA Potato Wharf, Castlefield ☎ 0161/839 9960, @ www.yha.org.uk. Opposite the Science and Industry Museum. Well-designed HI hostel (all rooms have private bathroom), which comes with all mod cons; breakfast included. ❹
The Ox 71 Liverpool Rd ☎ 0161/839 7740, @ www.theox.co.uk. Nine rooms above a classy pub opposite the Science and Industry Museum. The food is good; breakfast is extra (£2–6). ❺
Woodies 19 Blossom St, Ancoats ☎ 0161/228

3456. Independent backpackers', handy for the Northern Quarter. Around fifty beds in dorms, singles and doubles, plus internet access, free tea and coffee, laundry and left-luggage facilities. ❷

Cafés and restaurants

Café Pop 34–36 Oldham St. Retro Northern Quarter café full of 70s' kitsch, with veggie fry-ups, hefty sandwiches, omelettes and the like. Closed Sun.
Dimitri's 1 Campfield Arcade, Deansgate. Pick and mix from the Greek/Spanish/Italian menu, or grab an arcade table and sip a drink.
Eighth Day 107–111 Oxford Rd. Manchester's oldest organic-vegetarian café – shop, takeaway and juice bar upstairs, café/restaurant downstairs.
Wong Chu 63 Faulkner St. The best of the budget

Chinatown eateries, this no-frills joint serves up enormous portions of Cantonese staples.

Shere Khan 52 Wilmslow Rd, Rusholme. Popular Indian brasserie, serving marvellous kebabs, and great *karahi* and *biryani* dishes.

Bars, pubs and clubs

Dry Bar 28–30 Oldham St. The first of the designer café/bars on the scene, and catalyst for much of what has gone in the Northern Quarter.

Dukes '92 Castle St, Castlefield. Former stableblock for goods horses on the Duke of Bridgewater's canal, now a pub serving a great-value range of pâtés and cheeses.

Metz 3 Brazil St. Enjoyable warehouse bar and restaurant in the Gay Village with summer deck.

Mr Thomas' Chop House 52 Cross St. Victorian pub with a Dickensian feel to its nooks and crannies.

Mumbo 35a King St. The city's first tea-bar, with sipping and eating on three floors.

Paradise Factory 112–116 Princess St. One of the hottest clubs on the scene, with regular gay and lesbian nights.

Sankey's Soap Beehive Mill, Jersey St, Ancoats. Many people's favourite Fri/Sat night out, brought to you by the Tribal Gathering crew.

Liverpool

Once Britain's main transatlantic port and the empire's second city, **LIVERPOOL** spent too many of the twentieth-century postwar years struggling against adversity. Things are looking up at last, as economic and social regeneration brightens the centre and the old docks on the River Mersey. Acerbic wit and loyalty to one of the city's two great football teams are the linchpins of Liverpudlian "Scouse" culture, along with an underlying pride in the local musical heritage – fair enough from the city that produced The Beatles.

Immediately opposite the main **Lime St station**, **St George's Hall** exemplifies the municipal classicism that spread throughout industrial Britain early in the nineteenth century. Just north of the hall, on William Brown St, is the renowned **Walker Art Gallery** (Mon–Sat 10am–5pm, Sun noon–5pm; free), providing a representative jaunt through British art history, with Turner, Gainsborough, Joseph Wright of Derby and Stubbs all well represented. Nearby, the **Liverpool Museum** (same hours; free) comprises five floors of varied exhibits featuring anthropology, stuffed beasts, Amazonian rain forests and a planetarium.

From here it's a fifteen-minute walk west to the **Pier Head** and Liverpool's waterfront, from where it's worth taking a "Ferry 'cross the Mersey" (*a la* Gerry and the Pacemakers) to Birkenhead for the views back towards the city (£1.10 each way). A short stroll to the south is the **Albert Dock**, showpiece of the renovated docks area, whose main focus is the **Tate Gallery** (Tues–Sun 10am–6pm; free; ⊛www.tate.org.uk), showing off exhibits on four floors; there's a great café here, too. Occupying the other side of the dock is the **Maritime Museum** (Mon–Sat 10am–5pm, Sun noon–5pm; free), housing – amongst other highlights – an exhibition detailing the shocking conditions forced upon African slaves in the eighteenth and nineteenth centuries, as well as Liverpool's key role in the slave trade. The Albert Dock is also home to **The Beatles Story** (daily 10am–5/6pm; £7.95), a multimedia attempt to capture the essence of the Fab Four's rise from Hamburg rags to Abbey Rd riches. Continuing the theme, the area back in the city centre around **Mathew St** has been designated the "**Cavern Quarter**", its buildings (including a re-built version of the original *Cavern Club*, where The Beatles played in the Sixties), pubs and shops providing an excuse to wallow in nostalgia. You can take a "Magical Mystery Tour" of other sites associated with the band, such as Penny Lane and Strawberry Fields, on board a double-decker bus (daily tours; book through Cavern City Tours, ☏0151/236 9091 or Mersey Tourism, ☏0151/709 3285; £10.95, or £15 with The Beatles Story) – and join in with moptops galore at the **International Beatles Festival** on the last weekend of August.

To the east and south of Lime St are the city's two eye-catching twentieth-century cathedrals. The Roman Catholic **Metropolitan Cathedral of Christ the King** (daily 8am–6pm; free), ten minutes' walk up Mount Pleasant, is a vast inverted funnel of a building. Hope St, opposite, runs to the Anglican **Liverpool Cathedral** (same times; £2 donation), the largest in the country. Designed by Sir Giles Gilbert Scott in 1903, this neo-Gothic mass of pale-red stone wasn't completed until 1978.

Practicalities

Trains arrive at Lime St station, on the eastern edge of the city centre; **coaches** stop on Norton St, northeast of the station. The **airport** is eight miles southeast (take bus #80/180, or the pricier express bus #500 into the centre). **Ferry** arrivals – from the Isle of Man, Dublin and Belfast – dock at the terminals just north of Pier Head, close to Albert Dock. Tourist information is available from two handy offices: one centrally located in **Queen Square** (Mon–Sat 9am–5.30pm, Sun 10.30am–4.30pm), the other at **Albert Dock** at the Atlantic Pavilion (daily 10am–5.30pm); both share the same enquiries number and website (☏0906/680 6886, ⊛www.visitliverpool.com). There's **internet access** at Planet Electra, 36 London Rd (daily 10am–6pm). Budget **accommodation** is available at a variety of places, including a terrific youth hostel a short walk from Albert Dock and, from July to early September, in self-catering **student halls** at John Moores University (☏0151/709 3197) and the University of Liverpool (☏0151/794 6440).

There's a wide range of inexpensive ethnic **food** found around Mount Pleasant and Hardman and Bold streets, while cafés within both cathedrals offer good-value lunches. Berry and Nelson streets form the heart of Liverpool's **Chinatown**, where you'll find more reasonable choices. Liverpool's **pubs and bars** stay open later than most, and Fleet St, Slater St, Wood St and Concert Square (off Bold St) are where all the action is. The *Picket*, 24 Hardman St, and the *Lomax and L2*, 11–13 Hotham St, are the best **live music venues** for local bands, while the *Royal Court Theatre*, Roe St, gets the pick of the touring bands. The **Bluecoat Arts Centre** on School Lane (☏0151/709 5297, ⊛www.bluecoatartscentre.com) is always worth a look for drama, dance, poetry, comedy, music and art. Liverpool also has some excellent **music festivals**, particularly the Summer Pops (July) and the Party at the Pier (Aug) for big-name pop and rock. The evening paper, the *Liverpool Echo*, has **listings** of what's on.

Accommodation

Aachen 89–91 Mount Pleasant ☏0151/709 3477, ⊛www.aachenhotel.co.uk. The most popular budget hotel, with value-for-money rooms and big "eat-as-much-as-you-like" breakfasts. ➎

Embassie Youth Hostel 1 Falkner Square ☏0151/707 1089. Twenty minutes' walk from Lime St station (bus #80), west of the Anglican cathedral; showers, tea, toast and coffee included in the price. ➋

Liverpool Youth Hostel Wapping ☏0151/709 8888, ⊛www.yha.org.uk. One of the best HI hostels, just south of Albert Dock. Smart two-, three-, four- or six-bed rooms, all with private bathroom. Price includes breakfast. ➍

Cafés and restaurants

Bluecoat Café Bar Bluecoat Chambers, School Lane. Good-value, mostly veggie, food – salad bar, baked potatoes and dips – served throughout the day. Closed Sun.

Far East 27–35 Berry St. One of the longest-serving and most reliable of Liverpool's Cantonese eating houses, with authentic *dim sum* (noon–6pm).

Green Fish Café 11 Upper Newington St. Cool vegetarian café off Renshaw St.

Life Café 1a Bold St. The eighteenth-century Lyceum Library makes a grand backdrop for this late-opening café/bar.

Number Seven Café 7 Falkner St. Laid-back restaurant with a daily changing blackboard menu of contemporary flavours – good for a splurge.

Tabac 126 Bold St. Contemporary café/bar, serving a wide-ranging menu.

Pubs, bars and clubs

The Baltic Fleet 33a Wapping. Restored pub with a great period feel.

The Cavern Club 10 Mathew St. The self-styled "most famous club in the world" puts on live bands Thurs–Sun.

Cream Wolstenholme Square, off Hanover St. Liverpool's best club, featuring big DJ names.

The Philharmonic 36 Hope St. A traditional watering-hole boasting mosaic floors, tiling, gilded wrought-iron gates and marble decor in the gents.

The Lake District

The site of England's highest peaks and its biggest concentration of lakes, the gla-cier-carved **Lake District** is the nation's most popular walking and hiking area. The weather changes quickly here, but the sudden shifts of light on the bracken and moorland grasses, and on the slate of the local buildings, are part of the area's appeal. For a twice-daily updated **weather forecast** of the region phone ☏017687/75757. The most direct way of reaching the Lake District is via the west coast main line **train** route from London Euston towards Glasgow, disembarking at Lancaster, from where bus #555 runs through the Lake District, calling at Windermere, Ambleside, Grasmere and Keswick. Alternatively, you could get off at Oxenholme, north of Lancaster, connecting with a branch line service to Windermere; and there are also direct services from Manchester to Windermere. A National Express **coach** service runs daily from London Victoria to the Lake District, while local Stagecoach **buses** go everywhere in the region – an **Explorer Ticket** (£6.50/day, £15/four days) is valid on the entire network and can be bought on the bus. Cumbria Traveline (daily 7am–8pm; ☏0870/608 2608, ⊛www.traveline.org.uk) can advise about local bus, train, coach and ferry services.

Windermere, Bowness, Ambleside and around

Largest and southernmost of the lakes, **Windermere** is also one of the most crowded in summer. The town of **WINDERMERE** itself (where the train stops) is set a mile or so back from the lake and, other than the short climb up to the view-point of **Orrest Head**, offers little to do. Instead, stroll down (or catch the #599 bus from outside the station) to the prettier sister town of **BOWNESS** on the lakeshore. Windermere's **tourist office** is just outside the train station (daily 9am–6/7.30pm; ☏015394/46499), steps from the cosy *Backpackers Hostel* in the Old Bakery (☏015394/46374, ⊛www.lakedistrictbackpackers.co.uk; ③) at the top of High St. A top B&B choice nearby is *Brendan Chase*, 1–3 College Rd (☏015394/45638; ④). The nearest HI hostel is *High Cross* at Bridge Lane (☏015394/43543, ⊛www@yha.org.uk; ③) at **Troutbeck**, two miles northwest of Windermere; they have a shuttle-bus, which meets trains at Windermere. Accommodation in Bowness tends to be more expensive; but don't miss a drink in *The Hole in't Wall* pub, behind the church, the town's oldest hostelry.

Ferries on the lake are operated by Windermere Lake Cruises (☏015394/31188, ⊛www.windermere-lakecruises.co.uk), which runs boats to Lakeside at the southern tip (£6.20 return) or to Waterhead (for Ambleside) at the northern end (£6 return). A 24-hour **Freedom-of-the-Lake ticket** costs £10.50. There are also boat services to the excellent National Park Visitor Centre at **Brockhole** (April–Oct daily 10am–5pm; ☏015394/46601, ⊛www.lake-district.gov.uk), also reached on the #555 or #599 buses from Windermere.

From Waterhead, it's a mile north to **AMBLESIDE** – or take bus #555 from Windermere and Bowness. Stroll along Rydal Rd to the **Ambleside Museum** (daily 10am–5pm; £2.50) for the lowdown on lakeland writers and artists, and make time too for a more unusual gallery, **The Homes of Football**, 100 Lake Rd (daily 10am–5pm; free), a permanent archive of over 60,000 images of the country's stadiums and fans. The **tourist office** is in the Central Buildings by the Market Cross (daily 9am–5.30pm; ☏015394/32582). One of the Lake District's best-sited **HI hostels** fronts the lake at Waterhead (☏015394/32304, ⊛www@yha.org.uk; ③), while B&Bs line central Ambleside streets like Church St and Compston Rd. Cheapest rates are at *Linda's B&B and Bunkhouse* at *Shirland*, Compston Rd (☏015394/32999; ③). *Zeffirelli's*, on Compston Rd, specializes in inexpensive vege-tarian **food**, either in the daytime *Garden Café* or upstairs in the pizza-and-pasta restaurant.

The nearest **campsite** to Ambleside is *Low Wray National Trust Campsite* (☏015394/32810; closed Nov–Easter) three miles south – hourly bus #505/506 passes within a mile. In addition, the #516 **bus** from Ambleside runs four miles west to the hamlet of **Elterwater**, centred on a tiny green and boasting another HI hostel, *Elterwater Langdale* (℡015394/37245, ⓦwww@yha.org.uk; ❸), as well as the fantastic *Britannia Inn* (℡015394/37210, ⓦwww.britinn.co.uk; ❼), an old lakeland pub with tasty food. The hikes around here, and three miles further up the valley in **Langdale**, are famously good.

Hawkshead and Coniston

Ferries shuttle from Bowness piers across Windermere to Sawrey, from where it's a steep two-mile walk (or minibus ride) to the hamlet of **NEAR SAWREY** and Beatrix Potter's beloved house, **Hill Top** (April–Oct Mon–Wed, Sat & Sun 11am–5pm; £4). It's another two miles to the whitewashed cottages of **HAWK-SHEAD** (also served by bus #505/506 from Ambleside), which is refreshingly peaceful after the hurly-burly of Windermere. There are some marvellous village pubs (the *King's Arms* is the best) and **Hawkshead Grammar School**, where Wordsworth was a pupil (Easter–Oct Mon–Sat 10am–12.30pm & 1.30–5pm, Sun 1–5pm; £2). The **tourist office** at the main car park (Easter–Oct daily 9.30am–6pm; Nov–Easter Fri–Sun 10am–3.30pm; ℡015394/36525) handles a range of B&Bs and farmhouse stays, but the family-oriented **HI hostel**, *Esthwaite Lodge* (℡015394/36293, ⓦwww@yha.org.uk; ❸), a mile south of town, is worth investigating. There's espresso and cake in the *Minstrel's Gallery* **café** on the main square.

Walking through **Grizedale Forest** from Hawkshead and descending towards the graceful **Coniston Water** is a good way of reaching **CONISTON** village, a cluster of houses nestling beneath the craggy Old Man of Coniston (which you can climb in 2hr). Bus #505/506 comes this way too. There's an **HI hostel** just north of the village at Holly How (℡015394/41323, ⓦwww.yha.org.uk; ❸), and another more peaceful one above Coniston on the slopes of Old Man, at Coppermines House (℡015394/41261; ❸). The nearest **campsite** is the *Coniston Hall Campsite*, Haws Bank (℡015394/41223; booking essential), a mile south of town by the lake. The vegetarian *Beech Tree Guesthouse*, on Yewdale Rd (℡015394/41717; ❺), is pick of the B&Bs; best **pub** is the *Sun Hotel*, an old inn 200m uphill from the bridge in the centre. The *Village Pantry* bakery on Yewdale Rd has **internet access**. The most popular walk from Coniston is to **Tarn Hows**, two miles northeast, a serene lake with several vantage points across the hills.

The wooden **Coniston Launch** (℡015394/36216, ⓦwww.lakefell.co.uk) operates a year-round lake service on two routes, north and south (£3.60 & £5.80 return). This, along with the **Steam Yacht Gondola** (£4.80 return), is the best means of reaching the elegant lakeside villa, **Brantwood** (mid-March to mid-Nov daily 11am–5.30pm; rest of year Wed–Sun 11am–4.30pm; £7.50, house only £4.50, gardens only £2; ⓦwww.brantwood.org.uk). Once inhabited by the art historian John Ruskin, whose work provided the theoretical substance for that of the Pre-Raphaelites, the house is full of Ruskin's own drawings and sketches, as well as items relating to the painters he inspired; there's a good café too.

Rydal and Grasmere

The trusty #555 bus connects Windermere and Ambleside with the heart of Wordsworth country. **RYDAL**, three miles northwest of Ambleside, was where Wordsworth made his home from 1813 until his death in 1850; his house, **Rydal Mount** (daily 9.30/10am–4/5pm; Nov–Feb closed Tues; £4), is famous largely for the gardens laid out by Wordsworth himself. Paths on either side of Rydal Water cover the two miles to **GRASMERE**, site of Wordsworth's more famous abode, **Dove Cottage** (daily 9.30am–5.30pm; closed mid-Jan to mid-Feb; £5; ⓦwww.wordsworth.org.uk). The adjoining museum has portraits and manuscripts relating to Wordsworth, Coleridge – who regularly hiked over from Keswick to visit him here – and De Quincey, author of *Confessions of an English Opium-Eater* and biographer of the Lake poets, who took over Dove Cottage after Wordsworth's move to Rydal. Wordsworth and his sister Dorothy lie in simple graves in the churchyard of St Oswald's, in the village. Grasmere's **tourist office** is on Redbank Rd, by the main car park (daily 9.30/10am–3.30/5pm; ☎015394/35245). The *Dove Cottage Tea Rooms and Restaurant* is the nicest spot for **tearoom** favourites (at night, prices shoot up for fashionable dinners). The **HI hostel** choices are *Butterlip How*, 150 yards north of the green on Easedale Rd, and simpler *Thorney How*, under a mile further along the unlit road (both ☎015394/35316, ⊛www@yha.org.uk; ❸). There's also the excellent *Grasmere Independent Hostel* at Broadrayne Farm (☎015394/35055, ⊛www.grasmere-accommodation.co.uk; ❸), just north of town on the A591, near the *Travellers' Rest* **pub** (which serves bar meals).

Keswick and Derwent Water

Principal centre for the northern lakes, **KESWICK** (pronounced "kez-ick") lies on the northern fringes of **Derwent Water**, one of the few stretches of water in the area which can be walked all the way around – although the **Keswick Launch** (Easter–Nov daily; Dec–Easter Sat & Sun; £5 round-trip, 80p per stage) runs right around the lake too. The easiest hike is up **Latrigg Fell** to the north (2–3hr), giving splendid views; the trek up **Skiddaw** (5hr) is more demanding, but the easiest of the many true mountain hikes around and about. Keswick itself was an important wool and leather centre until around 1500, when these trades were supplanted by the discovery of local graphite. **The Cumberland Pencil Museum**, at Greta Bridge, on Main St (daily 9.30am–4pm; £2.50; ⊛www.pencils.co.uk), tells the whole story entertainingly. Otherwise, the best thing to do is to hike a mile and a half eastwards to **Castlerigg Stone Circle**, a Neolithic monument commanding a spectacular view, or take the #77/77A bus ride down into **Borrowdale**, south of town, perhaps the most beautiful valley in England.

Buses use the terminal behind Lakes Foodstore, off Main St. Keswick's **tourist office** is in the Moot Hall, Market Sq (daily 9.30am–5.30/7pm; ☎017687/72645, ⊛www.keswick.org), and there's **internet access** at U-Compute, above the post office at 48 Main St. The local **HI hostel** is on Station Rd by the river (☎017687/72484; ⊛www@yha.org.uk; ❸); there's another on the eastern shores of Derwentwater, two miles south, in Barrow House (☎017687/77246, ⊛www@yha.org.uk; ❸); bus #77/77A and the Keswick Launch come this way. **B&Bs** cluster along Bank and Stanger streets, near the post office, and around Southey, Blencathra and Eskin streets. *Bridgedale Guesthouse*, 101 Main St (☎017687/73914; ❸), is the best value, just around the corner from the bus station. Local **campsites** – by the lake and up near Castlerigg Stone Circle – are always busy; check on space with the tourist office. Keswick's most agreeable **café** is the *Lakeland Pedlar*, Henderson's Yard, off Main St, serving breakfasts and veggie food, and there are fine **pub** meals and good beer at the *George Hotel*, St John St, and the *Four In Hand* on Lake Rd.

York

It's the spectacular Gothic Minster, alleyways and ancient stone walls that draw tourists to **YORK**, but the city's character-forming experiences go back a lot further than that. It became the principal northern headquarters of the Romans and, when Emperor Severus decided to split the administration of Britain in two, he made it one of the capitals. The city's position as the north's spiritual capital dates from 627, when Edwin of Northumbria adopted Christianity. Northumbrian power crumbled in the face of a Danish invasion that swept through York in 866, destroying one of the finest libraries in western Europe in the process. By 876 one of the Danish leaders, Halfdan, had settled here with half the Viking army, beginning a century of Scandinavian rule.

Best introduction to York is a stroll along the **city walls** (daily till dusk), a three-

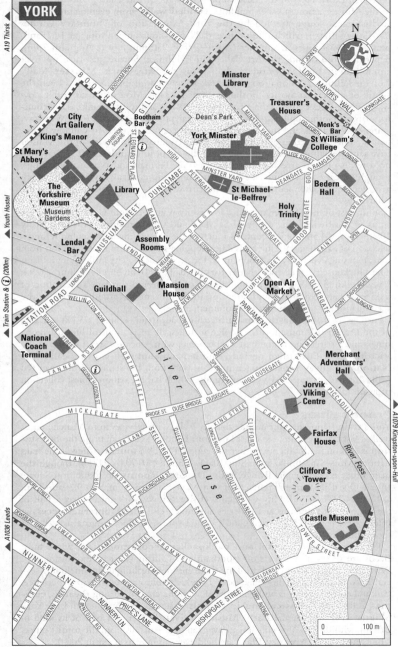

YORK

- A19 Thirsk
- Youth Hostel
- Train Station & ⓘ (200m)
- A1036 Leeds
- A1079 Kingston-upon-Hull

Minster Library
PORTLAND STREET
TERRACE
BOOTHAM
BOOTHAM ROW
GILLYGATE
MARYGATE
City Art Gallery
King's Manor
Bootham Bar
EXHIBITION SQUARE
ST LEONARD'S PLACE
Dean's Park
MINSTER YARD
Treasurer's House
LORD MAYOR'S WALK
ST JOHN'S ST
MONKGATE
Monk's Bar
OGLEFORTH
St William's College
ALDWARK
St Mary's Abbey
The Yorkshire Museum
Museum Gardens
York Minster
HIGH PETERGATE
DEANGATE
COLLEGE STREET
St Michael-le-Belfrey
Bedern Hall
BEDERN
GOODRAMGATE
Holy Trinity
SAINT ANDREWGATE
SPEN LN
Library
MUSEUM STREET
DUNCOMBE PLACE
BLAKE ST
STONEGATE
LOW PETERGATE
GRAPE LANE
SWINEGATE
KING'S SQ
GOODRAMGATE
COLLIERGATE
Lendal Bar
LENDAL
LENDAL BRIDGE
Assembly Rooms
ST HELEN'S SQUARE
LITTLE STONEGATE
DAVYGATE
CHURCH STREET
Open Air Market
SHAMBLES
SAINT SAVIOURGATE
SAINT HUNGATE
Guildhall
Mansion House
NEW STREET
CONEY STREET
PARLIAMENT ST
FOSSGATE
STATION ROAD
WELLINGTON ROW
ROUGIER STREET
National Coach Terminal
TANNER ROW
GEORGE HUDSON ST
NORTH STREET
MARKET STREET
SPURRIERGATE
HIGH OUSEGATE
PAVEMENT
COPPERGATE
PICCADILLY
Merchant Adventurers' Hall
Jorvik Viking Centre
River Foss
MICKLEGATE
BRIDGE ST
OUSE BRIDGE
OUSEGATE
KING STREET
CASTLEGATE
Fairfax House
TRINITY LANE
FETTER LANE
SKELDERGATE
QUEEN'S STAITH
KING'S STAITH
CLIFFORD STREET
Clifford's Tower
PRIORY STREET
BISHOPHILL JUNIOR
BISHOPHILL SENIOR
BUCKINGHAM ST
SOUTH ESPLANADE
SKELDERGATE
Castle Museum
DEWSBURY TERRACE
LOWER PRIORY STREET
FAIRFAX STREET
HAMPDEN STREET
VICTOR STREET
CROMWELL ROAD
TOWER STREET
SKELDERGATE BRIDGE
TERRY AVENUE
NUNNERY LANE
DALE STREET
SWANN STREET
VICTOR ST
NUNNERY LN
BENEDICT RD
KYME STREET
NEWTON TERRACE
PRICE'S LANE
GATE HILL TERRACE
BISHOPGATE STREET
River Ouse

N

0 — 100 m

175

© Crown copyright

mile circuit that takes in the various medieval Bars, or gates, and grants fine views of the Minster, amongst other buildings. **Guided walks**, from evening ghost walks to historical tours, are led by the York Association of Voluntary Guides (℡01904/640780), which offers a free, daily, two-hour guided tour (at 10.15am), plus additional tours in summer (April–Oct at 2.15pm; July & Aug also 7pm), departing from outside the Art Gallery in Exhibition Square; just turn up. Ever since Edwin built a wooden chapel on the site, **York Minster** (daily 7am–6/8.30pm; £3 donation requested; ☯www.yorkminster.org) has been the centre of spiritual authority for the north of England. Most of what's visible now was built in stages between the 1220s and the 1470s, and today it ranks as the country's largest Gothic building. Inside, the apocalyptic scenes of the **East Window**, completed in 1405, and the abstract thirteenth-century *Five Sisters* window represent the finest collection of stained glass in the country. Various parts of the Minster have separate admission charges, including the **crypt and undercroft** (£3), which hold remnants and artefacts from the previous Roman and Norman buildings, though best use of a limited budget is to climb the **central tower** (£3), which gives views over the medieval pattern of narrow streets to the south, known as the **Shambles**.

Southwest of the Minster, just outside the city walls, Museum Gardens lead to the ruins of the Benedictine abbey of St Mary and the **Yorkshire Museum** (daily 10am–5pm; £4.50), which contains much of the abbey's medieval sculpture, and a selection of Saxon and Viking finds. The shopping streets spread south and east from here, focusing eventually on Coppergate, former site of the city's Viking settlement. The blockbuster experience that is **Jorvik** (daily 9/10am–4.30/5.30pm; £6.95; ☯www.vikingjorvik.com) provides a taste of the period through a recreation of Viking streets, complete with appropriate smells and recorded sounds, to the accompaniment of an informative commentary.

Further south, the **Castle Museum** (daily 9.30/10am–4/5pm; £5.75) was one of the first British museums to indulge in full-scale recreations of life in bygone times, and it's still one of the best of the genre, with evocative street scenes of the Victorian and Edwardian periods. Another museum well worth a call is the **National Railway Museum**, ten minutes' walk from the station on Leeman Rd (daily 10am–6pm; free; ☯www.nrm.org.uk), which has the nation's finest collection of steam locomotives.

Practicalities

York's **train** station lies just outside the city walls, with services from Manchester, as well as fast trains on the east coast line from London and Edinburgh; the **bus station** is at Rougier St, slightly nearer the centre. There's a **tourist office** at the train station (Mon–Sat 9am–5/8pm, Sun 10am–4/5pm; ℡01904/621756), though the main office is over Lendal Bridge, in the **De Grey Rooms**, on Exhibition Square (April–Oct daily 9am–6/7pm; rest of year Mon–Sat 9am–5pm, Sun 9.30am–3pm; ℡01904/621756). York City Council **website**, ☯www.york.gov.uk, has details of the major sites, museums and galleries and much else. There's **internet access** at Internet Exchange, 13 Stonegate, and Coffee Express, 60 Goodramgate, as well as at the youth hostels.

There's some good **hostel and backpacker accommodation**, while most B&Bs are in the side-streets off Bootham and Clifton (west of Exhibition Sq). When it comes to eating and drinking there are some real highlights, including several historic **pubs** and the remarkable *Betty's*, the ultimate **tea-shop** experience. Cultural entertainment is wide and varied, with the city supporting **theatres**, **cinemas** and regular **classical music recitals**, often in its churches and the York Minster itself. The annual **Early Music Festival** (July), is the best of its kind in Britain, with dozens of events spread over ten days – details from the tourist office. The famous **York Mystery Plays** are held every four years (next in 2004).

Accommodation

Arnot House 17 Grosvenor Terrace, Bootham ☎01904/641966, ⊛www.arnothouseyork.co.uk. Classy Victorian family house preserving many of its original features. Four no-smoking en-suite rooms. ❻

City Guest House 68 Monkgate ☎01904/622483, ⊛www.cityguesthouse.co.uk. Central, non-smoking, family-run guest house with budget rates, not far from the Minster. ❺

York Backpackers Hostel Micklegate House, 88–90 Micklegate ☎01904/627720, ⊛www.yorkbackpackers.mcmail.com. Dorm space, doubles and family rooms in a rather grand building, former home of the High Sheriff of Yorkshire. There's a self-catering kitchen, laundry, TV and games room, and licensed bar. ❸

York International Youth Hostel Water End, Clifton ☎01904/653147, ⊛www@yha.org.uk. HI hostel in large mansion, twenty minutes' walk along Bootham from the tourist office. Four-bedded dorms and some private rooms (book in advance), a café and large garden. ❹

York Youth Hotel 11–13 Bishophill Senior, off Micklegate ☎01904/625904, ⊛www.yorkyouthhotel.com. Dorms, singles and twin rooms; breakfast extra. Also a kitchen, laundry, games room and TV lounge. ❸

Cafés and restaurants

Betty's 6–8 St Helen's Square. If there are tea shops in heaven they'll be like *Betty's*, a York institution with a permanent queue for seats, despite the (relatively) high prices.

Blake Head Vegetarian Café 104 Micklegate. Bookstore/café with patio for freshly baked cakes, pâtés, quiche, brunch, salads and soups – a favoured student hangout.

The Patio 13 Swinegate Court East, off Grape Lane. Plenty of choice in this informal café/restaurant, from overly stuffed baguettes and wraps to a plate of bangers and mash. Closed Sun & Mon eve.

Pizza Express River House, 17 Museum St. Grand old riverside club rooms with sought-after balcony, the venue for this chain's usual menu of good-quality pizzas.

The Rubicon 5–7 Little Stonegate. Contemporary style and vegetarian world flavours, so there's nut roast and veggie lasagne but also masala dhal and burritos on offer.

Spurriergate Centre St Michael's Church, Spurriergate. Quiche, salads and baked potatoes served in the impressive interior of twelfth-century St Michael's. Closed Sun.

Pubs

Black Swan Peasholme Green. York's oldest (sixteenth-century) pub with some superb stone flagging and wood panelling. Home of the city's folk club.

Judge's Lodging Cellar Bar 9 Lendal. Cosy drinking hole with good beer, in the eighteenth-century cellars of a smart hotel.

King's Arms King's Staithe. Close to the Ouse Bridge, this has a fine riverside setting with outdoor tables.

The Three-Legged Mare 15 High Petergate. York Brewery's cosy outlet for its own quality beer and definitely a pub for grown-ups – no juke box, no video games and no kids.

Durham

Seen from the train, **DURHAM** presents a magnificent sight, with cathedral and castle perched atop a bluff enclosed by a loop of the River Wear, and linked to the suburbs by a series of sturdy bridges. Nowadays a quiet provincial town with a strong student presence, Durham was once one of northern England's power bases: the Bishops of Durham were virtual royal agents in the north for much of the medieval era, responsible for defending a crucial border province frequently menaced by the Scots.

The town initially owed its reputation to the possession of the remains of St Cuthbert, an early prior of Lindisfarne, which were evacuated to Durham in the ninth century because of Viking raids. Since then, his shrine has dominated the eastern end of the spectacular **Cathedral** (daily 9.30am–6/8pm; £3 donation). The cathedral itself is the finest example of Norman architecture in England, with the nave, completed in 1128, the first to use pointed arches, raising the interior dimensions to dizzying heights. Medieval frescoes depicting St Cuthbert are just visible in the Galilee Chapel, which also contains the tomb of the Venerable Bede, England's first historian. The original coffin of St Cuthbert and other antiquities can be seen in the **Treasures of St Cuthbert** exhibition in the undercroft

(Mon–Sat 10am–4.30pm, Sun 2–4.30pm; £2), while the **tower** gives the usual breathtaking views (Mon–Sat 9.30/10am–3/4pm; £2). On the opposite side of Palace Green is the Norman **Castle** (Easter–Sept daily 10am–12.30pm & 2–4pm; Oct–Easter Mon, Wed, Sat & Sun 2–4pm; £3; ⊛www.durhamcastle.com), and both cathedral and castle are surrounded by North and South Bailey, a continuous street that curves around the hillside, lined with eighteenth- and nineteenth-century buildings. A half-hour stroll follows a pathway on the wooded river bank below, all the way around the cathedral's peninsula, passing a succession of elegant bridges.

Practicalities

The **train station** is ten minutes' walk from the centre, via either of two bridges over the Wear. The **bus station** is just to the south on North Rd. **Minibuses** link the cathedral with the bus station. The **tourist office** is in the Gala Theatre, at Millennium Place (Mon–Sat 9.30am–5.30pm, Sun 10am–4pm; July & Aug Mon–Sat till 8pm ☎0191/384 3720, ⊛www.durham.gov.uk). **B&Bs** are concentrated on Gilesgate, northeast of Market Place, and around Crossgate, south of the bus station. Good bets include *Green Grove*, 99 Gilesgate (☎0191/384 4361; ❹), and *Castle View Guest House*, 4 Crossgate (☎0191/386 8852, ⊛www.castle-view.net; ❻). There's no hostel, so the **cheapest beds** in town are at the university – either dorms or rooms (☎0191/374 3863; outside term times; ❹). The nearest **campsite**, *Grange*, is three miles northeast of the city towards Sunderland on Meadow Lane, Carrville (☎0191/384 4778); take bus #220/222.

For good value **food**, *Vennel's Café*, Saddler's Yard, serves snacks in a lovely little hidden courtyard off Saddler St, while the *Almshouse* on Palace Green, near the cathedral, conjures up meals for around £5 (till 8pm in summer). For **drinking**, try the *Market Tavern* on the marketplace for a traditional pub, or the lively *Hogshead*, 58 Saddler St. *Cathedrals*, in the old police station on Court Lane, has something for everyone – rooftop restaurant, bistro, microbrewery and coffee house. The **Gala Theatre** at Millennium Place is focus of the latest in the arts and drama.

Newcastle upon Tyne

Once a tough, industrial city with a proud shipbuilding heritage, **NEWCASTLE** has retained its undeniable raw vigour, which has served it well during the decimation of local industry. These days, it is streets ahead of its rivals in the northeast, and has a slew of good galleries and music venues. It also serves as a good base for explorations of **Hadrian's Wall**, a Roman-era barricade that stretches from coast to coast.

Arriving by train, your first view is of the River Tyne and its redeveloped quaysides, along with the five bridges that join Newcastle to Gateshead. The single steel arch of the **Tyne Bridge**, built in 1929, and the high-tech "winking" **Millennium Bridge**, completed in 2001, are world-renowned trademarks. Newcastle's centre owes a lot of its character to John Dobson, who remodelled the city along Neoclassical lines in the early nineteenth century. His most imposing legacy is the sweep of **Grey St**, leading north from the cathedral – just east of the station – to the lofty Grecian column of Grey's Monument, the city's central landmark. Newcastle's status as a border stronghold is remembered in the **castle**, with its Norman keep (daily 9.30am–4.30/5.30pm; Oct–March closed Mon; £1.50). The city's main art collection is housed in the **Laing Art Gallery** on New Bridge St, east of the monument (Mon–Sat 10am–5pm, Sun 2–5pm; free), but, like most local attractions, it has been dwarfed by the opening of the **Baltic Centre for Contemporary Art** (⊛www.balticmill.com), on the southern banks of the Tyne opposite Quayside. The converted former Baltic Flour Mill is second only in scale to London's Tate Modern and, as well as galleries, it accommodates artists' studios, workshops, performance space and cinema, plus a bar and two restaurants. The Baltic will be joined by the similarly ambitious **Music Centre Gateshead** (due to open in summer 2003), a billowing steel, aluminium and glass structure that will be home to the Northern Sinfonia.

Practicalities

Newcastle's **train station** is five minutes' walk south of the centre; the **coach station**, on Gallowgate, is a couple of minutes west. The **ferry port** (for crossings from Amsterdam and Scandinavia) is in North Shields, seven miles east, with connecting buses running to the centre, and the **airport** is six miles north, linked by metro. There are **tourist offices** in Central Station (June–Sept Mon–Fri 10am–8pm, Sat 9am–5pm, Sun 10am–4pm; Oct–May Mon–Sat 10am–5pm; ☎0191/277 8000, 🌐www.newcastle.gov.uk) and at 132 Grainger St (June–Sept Mon–Sat 9.30am–5.30pm, Thurs till 7.30pm, Sun 10am–4pm; rest of year closed Sun; same number). **Internet** access is available at *Internet Exchange*, 26–30 Market St.

The **HI hostel** is at 107 Jesmond Rd (☎0191/281 2570, 🌐www.yha.org.uk; ❸). Jesmond – a mile north of the centre – is also the main location for **B&Bs**, which are clustered around Osborne Rd; try the *George* at no. 88 (☎0191/281 4442; ❺), or the *Westland* round the corner at 27 Osborne Ave (☎0191/281 0412; ❺). The University of Northumbria (☎0191/227 4024; July–Sept only; ❸) offers bargain B&B in its halls of residence.

Local institutions for cheap **eats** are the *Side Café Bistro*, 1–3 The Side, and *Pani's*, 61 High Bridge St, off Grey St. City-centre **pubs** and bars are clustered around Bigg Market, a block east of Grey St, although there are trendier (and pricier) options down on the quayside. Be sure to check out the *Crown Posada*, 31 The Side, and *The Cooperage*, 32 The Close, both of them cosy drinking dens, or close by on Quayside, the sleek and stylish *Pitcher & Piano* has fine views of the river. The city's foremost **dance club** venue is the *Foundation*, 57 Melbourne St; also look out for **live bands** performing at the university Students' Union on Haymarket.

Hadrian's Wall

The turf and stone **Hadrian's Wall** (🌐www.hadrians-wall.org), separating Roman England from barbarian Scotland, was punctuated by "mile castles", strong points spaced at one-mile intervals, and by sixteen more substantially garrisoned forts. A day-trip from Newcastle will suffice to see a little of the wall, and regular trains and hourly buses (#685) between Newcastle and Carlisle pass by many of the sites. The best base, however, is the market town of **HEXHAM**, 45 minutes west of Newcastle by train or bus. It has a **tourist office**, in the main town car park (daily 9/10am–5/6pm; Nov–Easter closed Sun; ☎01434/65220, 🌐www.tynedale.gov.uk) and plenty of accommodation including a basic **HI hostel** in Acomb (☎01434/602864; ❷), two miles from Hexham, and several reasonably priced B&Bs. Other budget accommodation along the Wall is available at the *Once Brewed* HI hostel (☎01434/344360, 📧oncebrewed@yha.org.uk; ❸) and the *Hadrian Lodge* backpackers at Haydon Bridge (☎01434/688688, 🌐www.hadrianlodge.co.uk; ❷), both near some of the finest preserved sections of Hadrian's Wall and the excavated fort of **Vindolanda**. A **bus service** (late-May to late-Sept; #AD122; day rover ticket £5.50) links Hexham with Carlisle via all the main sites along Hadrian's Wall; on Sundays it links through to Newcastle.

Wales

The relationship between England and **Wales** (Cymru in Welsh) has never been entirely easy. Impatient with constant demarcation disputes, the eighth-century Mercian king Offa constructed a dyke to separate the two countries; today, a long-distance footpath follows its route from near Chepstow in the south to Prestatyn in the north, still marking the border to this day. During Edward I's reign the last of the Welsh native princes, Llywelyn ap Gruffudd, was killed, and Wales passed uneasily under English rule. Trouble flared again with the rebellion of Owain Glyndûr in the fifteenth century, but the Welsh prince Henry Tudor's defeat of Richard III at the Battle of Bosworth crowned him King Henry VII of England and paved the way for the 1536 Act of Union, which joined the English and Welsh in restless but perpetual partnership. The arrival of the 1999 National Assembly for Wales, the first all-Wales tier of government for nearly six hundred years, may well indicate that power is dribbling back.

Contact with England has watered down indigenous Welsh culture: bricked-up, decaying chapels stand as reminders of the days when Sunday services and chapel choirs were central to community life. The **Eisteddfod festivals** of Welsh music, poetry and dance still take place throughout the country in summer – the *Royal National Eisteddfod* (⊛ www.eisteddfod.org.uk), a very Welsh affair that breaks out in a different location every August, and the *Llangollen International Musical Eisteddfod* (⊛ www.international-eisteddfod.co.uk), held on the first full week in July, being the best-known examples. The Welsh language is undergoing a revival and you'll see it on bilingual road signs all over the country, although you're most likely to hear it spoken in the North, West and Mid-Wales. Some Welsh place-names have never been anglicized, but where alternative names do exist, we've given them in the text.

Much of the country, particularly the **Brecon Beacons** in the south and **Snowdonia** in the north, is relentlessly mountainous and offers wonderful walking and climbing terrain. **Pembrokeshire** to the west boasts a spectacular rugged coastline, dotted with offshore island nature reserves. The biggest towns, including the capital **Cardiff** in the south, **Aberystwyth** in the west, and **Caernarfon** in the north, all cling to the coastal lowlands, but even then the mountains are no more than a bus-ride away. **Holyhead**, on the island of **Anglesey**, is the main British port for ferry sailings to the Irish capital, Dublin.

Cardiff

The Welsh capital **CARDIFF** (Caerdydd) is rapidly picking itself up after the collapse of the coal-mining industry, and in the last couple of years has gained added status as the home of the Welsh Assembly, wielding powers newly devolved from London. The city's narrow Victorian arcades are interspersed with new shopping centres and wide pedestrian precincts. Long-distance coaches, and buses from the airport, arrive at the **bus terminal**, right beside Cardiff Central **train station**, south of the city centre off Penarth Rd (local trains use Queen St station instead, east of the centre). There's a **tourist office** on Wood St (Mon–Sat 9am–5/6pm, Tues opens 10am, Sun 10am–2pm; ☎029/2022 7281, ✉ enquiries@cardifftic.co.uk).

The geographical and historical heart of the city is **Cardiff Castle** (tours daily 9.30am–4.30/6pm; £5.25, winter tours £3.15, grounds only £2.60). Standing on a Roman site developed by the Normans, the castle was embellished by William Burges in the 1860s, and each room is now a wonderful example of Victorian "medieval" decoration; best of all are the Chaucer Room, the Banqueting Hall, the Arab Room and the Fairy-tale Nursery. Five minutes' walk northeast, the **National Museum and Gallery** in Cathays Park (Tues–Sun 10am–5pm; free; ⊛ www.nmgw.ac.uk/nmgc) houses a fine collection of Impressionist paintings, and natural history and archeological exhibits. A half-hour walk south of the centre is the **Cardiff Bay** area, also reached by bus #8 from Central Station, or a train from Queen St. Once known as Tiger Bay, the long-derelict area (birthplace of singer Shirley Bassey) has seen massive redevelopment since the opening of the Welsh Assembly in 1999; now you'll find waterfront walks, glittering new architecture and an old Norwegian seamen's chapel, converted into a cosy café.

Attractions near Cardiff include the **Museum of Welsh Life** at St Fagans, four miles west of the centre on bus #32. This 100-acre open-air museum is packed with reconstructed rural and industrial heritage buildings from all over Wales (daily 10am–5/6pm; free; ⊛ www.nmgw.ac.uk/mwl); every May Day, a huge fair is held here. Fans of William Burges' elaborate interiors shouldn't miss the fairy-tale **Castell Coch** at Tongwynlais, five miles north of town on bus #136 (April–Oct daily 9.30am–5/6pm; Nov–March Mon–Sat 9.30am–4pm, Sun 11am–4pm; £2.50). Built on the site of a thirteenth-century castle and perched dramatically on a steep, forested hillside, Burges' lavish Victorian showpiece was commissioned by the third Lord Bute as a country retreat, complete with turrets and a fully-operational portcullis and drawbridge.

Cardiff's **HI hostel** is a couple of miles north of the centre at 2 Wedal Rd (℡029/2046 2303, ☜www.yha.org.uk; ❸), or you could try the excellent *Cardiff International Backpacker*, just west of the centre across the River Taff at 98 Neville St (℡029/2034 5577; ❸). **B&Bs** include *Acorn Lodge*, 182 Cathedral Rd, Pontcanna (℡029/2022 1373; ❹), fifteen minutes' walk west of the centre; the best budget hotel is the trendy **Big Sleep Hotel**, Bute Terrace (℡029/2063 6363, ☜www.the-bigsleephotel.com; ❻), opposite the Cardiff International Arena.

To **eat** laver bread and other Welsh delicacies, head for *Celtic Cauldron* in the shopping arcade opposite the castle. *Cibo*, 83 Pontcanna St, is a small Italian trattoria serving sandwiches and more substantial fare, while the café in the Norwegian church by Cardiff Bay is great for salads and snacks. Ale-lovers can sample the local bitter surrounded by rugby memorabilia in the *Old Arcade* pub, Church St. **Internet** access is available from *Cardiff Cybercafé*, 9 Duke St.

South Wales

The region's most spectacular historic monument is accessible from the old market town of **CHEPSTOW** (Cas-Gwent), itself ringed on three sides by thirteenth-century walls and on the fourth by the River Wye. Within the town, the Wye bridge gives stunning views of cliff-faces soaring above the river and of the first stone **castle** in Britain, built by the Normans in 1067, a year after William the Conqueror's victory at Hastings (April–Oct daily 9.30am–5/6pm; Nov–March Mon–Sat 9.30am–4pm, Sun 11am–4pm; £3). Opposite the castle is Gwy House, an eighteenth-century town house that now features the unassuming **Chepstow Museum** (Mon–Sat 11am–1pm & 2–5pm, Sun 2–5pm; £1). However, nothing within the town can match the six-mile stroll north along the Wye to the impossibly romantic ruins of **Tintern Abbey**, built by the Cistercians in 1131, rebuilt 150 years later and now in a state of majestic disrepair (same hours as Chepstow castle; £2.50). The nave walls rise to such a height that, from a distance, you might think the magnificent Gothic church still stood intact beneath the overhang of the wooded cliff – only when you get close do you find the roof is long gone. If you don't fancy walking, catch bus #69 (every 2hr), which runs from Chepstow to Tintern and on to Monmouth, eight miles north. You can top up for the return journey in the fourteenth-century *Moon and Sixpence* **pub** – almost a mile north of the Abbey by the river – which does excellent food. For information on Chepstow and the popular **Offa's Dyke Path** contact the **tourist office** on Bridge St (daily 9.30/10am–4/6pm; ℡01291/623772). The *Coach and Horses Inn* on Welsh St offers **B&B** (℡01291/622626; ❺), or you could head one mile east across the Wye to the characterful *Upper Sedbury House* (℡01291/627173; ❹). St Pier Caravan & **Camping**, at Port Skewett (℡01291/425114) is the only cheap option in the area. Take the Caldicot and Newport bus four miles west.

Newport and around

First stop in Wales for mainline trains from Bristol and London is **NEWPORT** (Casnewydd), also served by buses and local trains from Chepstow. An unexciting town, Newport nevertheless does have its claim to fame: the legendary *TJ's* pub music venue, 14 Clarence Place (just over the river from the station), was where Kurt Cobain proposed to Courtney Love. Three miles northeast, and almost contiguous, is **CAERLEON**, a small, traffic-bedevilled town that preserves the extensive remains of its important Roman forebear, Isca. The state-of-the-art **Legionary Museum**, High St (Mon–Sat 10am–4.30/6pm, Sun 2–4.30/6pm; free;

@www.nmgw.ac.uk/rlm), contains finds from all the adjacent sites. The museum stands opposite the road leading to the less dramatic remains of the barracks and grassed-over amphitheatre (free). Beside the museum is the **tourist office** (Mon–Sat 9.30am–5pm; ☎01633/842962), while further down the High St are the **Fortress Baths**, built on the site of a 75 AD bath-house (same hours as museum; £2). Caerleon is more amenable to stay in than Newport, and has three good **B&Bs**, including *Pendragon*, 18 Cross St (☎01633/430871; ❺).

Bus #23 from Newport runs fourteen miles north to **BLAENAFON**, a town recently awarded the status of UNESCO World Heritage Site for its place in the Industrial Revolution. It is home to both a vast ironworks museum and, housed in a defunct coal-mine a mile west of town, the **Big Pit Mining Museum** (March–Nov daily 9.30am–5pm; free), which gives a revealing glimpse of working life in the South Wales valleys. The mine closed in 1980, and former miners are now employed as guides. The full tour involves descending 294ft in a miners' cage to inspect coalfaces, underground roadways and haulage engines that are almost 200 years old.

The Brecon Beacons

The **Brecon Beacons National Park** occupies a swathe of rocky uplands stretching from the English border to the remote moorlands above Swansea – perfect walking territory. The Beacons themselves, a pair of hills 2900ft high accessed from Brecon town, share the limelight with the **Black Mountains** north of Crickhowell. Bus #21 (every 2hr, not Sun) runs from Newport to Brecon, passing through Abergavenny and Crickhowell, but trains from Newport veer off into England after Abergavenny.

The market town of **ABERGAVENNY** (Y Fenni) sits in a fold between seven green hills at the eastern edge of the park, about fifteen miles north of Newport. Before setting out for the mountains, pick up maps from the combined **tourist office** and **national park information office** (daily 9.30/10am–4.30/6pm; ☎01873/857588) at Swan Meadow beside the bus station – and check what sort of weather you can expect, as sudden mists are common. The most accessible walking areas are the **Sugar Loaf** (1955ft), four miles northwest, and **Holy Mountain** (Skirrid Fawr; 1595ft), three miles north. The *Black Sheep* **hostel** opposite the train station offers dorm beds (☎01873/859125; ❸). Plenty of **B&Bs** line Monmouth Rd on the five-minute walk between the train station and the town centre; *Maes Glas* on Raglan Terrace is best (☎01873/854494; ❹). For good value **eating** try the *Greyhound Vaults* on Market St or for excellent Chinese but terrible service head for the *Peking Chef* on Cross St.

CRICKHOWELL (Crughywel), a friendly village with a fine seventeenth-century bridge five miles west of Abergavenny, is a more picturesque point to begin your explorations. A six-mile hike into the Black Mountains from Crickhowell takes you through remote and occasionally bleak countryside to tiny **Partrishow Church**; inside, you'll find a rare carved fifteenth-century rood screen complete with dragon, and an ancient mural of the grim reaper. Beaufort St in Crickhowell holds both the **tourist office** (April–Oct daily 9am–1pm & 2–5pm; ☎01873/812105), and *Greenhill Villas* **B&B** (☎01873/811177; ❹).

The largest central Brecon Beacons rise just south of **BRECON** (Aberhonddu), a lively little town eight miles west of Crickhowell that springs to life in mid-August for the huge international Brecon Jazz Festival. For details of the numerous trekking routes into the Beacons and an extensive programme of guided walks, call in at the park's **information office**, which shares premises with the **tourist office** in the Cattle Market car park beside Safeway (daily 9/10am–5/6pm; ☎01874/622485, @www.brecon.co.uk). **B&Bs** abound, including *Tirbach*, 13 Alexandra Rd (☎01874 /624551; ❹); both *Pickwick House*, St John's Rd (☎01874/624322; ❹), and *Beacons*, in a rambling town house at 16 Bridge St (☎01874/623339, @www.beacons.brecon .co.uk; ❹), also cook excellent evening meals. The *Ty'n-y-Caeau* **hostel** is two miles east of Brecon at Groessford (☎01874/665270; ❷), a mile off the Abergavenny bus route, while the *Held Bunkhouse* hostel is in Cantref (☎01874/624646; ❸), a mile southwest of town.

Pembroke and the southwest

PEMBROKE (Penfro), birthplace of Henry VII, is a sleepy town at the southwestern extremity of the country, lying at the heart of the Pembrokeshire Coast National Park and easily accessible by train from Cardiff. Centrepiece is the magnificent water-surrounded **Castle** (daily 9.30/10am–4/6pm; £3), whose circular keep, dating from 1200, offers fine views of the countryside. The castle overshadows the high street where shops are shoehorned into an assortment of Tudor and Georgian buildings, one of them housing the **Museum of the Home**, an eclectic mix of exhibits ranging from toys and games to fashion accessories (May–Sept Mon–Thurs 11am–5pm; £1.50). The Visitor Centre on Commons Rd includes the tourist office (daily 10am–5.30pm; ☎01646/622388). *Beech House* is the best-value **B&B** in town, 78 Main St (☎01646/683740; ❸). The nearest **HI hostel** is six miles east at Manorbier (☎01834/871803; ❸), accessible by train. Regular **ferries** to Rosslare in Ireland (4hr) leave from Pembroke Dock, two miles north of the town.

The **Pembrokeshire Coast National Park** sweeps all the way around the edge of the southwestern peninsula of Wales, and the coastal path includes some of the country's most stunning and remote scenery, offering sheer cliff-faces, panoramic sea views and excellent seabird-watching. Tricky though it may be without a car, it's worth getting to **St Govan's Head** – directly south of Pembroke near Bosherston – where a thousand-year-old chapel clings, barely credibly, to the rock face.

From Pembroke, bus #359 runs north to Haverfordwest where you can catch bus #411 sixteen miles west to **ST DAVID'S** (Tyddewi), one of the most enchanting spots in Britain, where a breathtakingly beautiful **Cathedral**, delicately tinted purple, green and yellow by a combination of lichen and geology, hides in a dip below the High St. Constructed between 1180 and 1522, but heavily restored in the nineteenth century, it hosts a prestigious classical music festival each May. Across a thin trickle of river thousands of jackdaws congregate around the extensive remains of the magnificent fourteenth-century **Bishop's Palace** (Easter–Oct daily 9.30am–5/6pm; Nov–Easter Mon–Sat 9.30am–4pm, Sun noon–2pm; £2), which adds to the beauty of the setting. There's a **hostel** at Llaethdy, two miles west of town (☎01437/720345; ❸), and bus 411 takes you to the **HI hostel** off the St David's Rd, near the attractive little village of Solva (☎01437/721940; ❸). For central **B&Bs**: try *Pen Albro*, 18 Goat St (☎01437/721865; ❹), or *Y Glennydd*, 51 Nun St (☎01437/720576; ❹). The **tourist office** is at the top of the High St (Easter–Oct daily 9.30am–5.30pm; Nov–Easter Mon–Sat 10am–4pm; ☎01437/720392, ✆www.stdavids.co.uk).

Seventeen miles further north on bus #411 – and at the end of the main train line from Cardiff and London – is **FISHGUARD** (Abergwaun), an attractive fishing port that's another embarkation point for Rosslare, with ferries and catamarans departing daily from alongside the train station. *Hamilton Backpackers Lodge*, a **hostel** near the tourist office at 21 Hamilton St (☎01348/874797; dorms ❷), and *Glanmoy Lodge*, ten minutes from the port on Tref-Wrgi Rd (☎01348/874333; ❺), are used to people arriving late or departing early.

Mid-Wales

Mid-Wales, an area of wild mountain roads, hidden valleys and genteel ex-spa towns, is the least visited part of the country, perhaps because access is a little trickier than elsewhere. Nevertheless, it's worth making the effort, because it's here that you'll discover the traditional rural Wales, in quiet towns where the pub conversation takes place in Welsh rather than English. But this is also Wales at its most "alternative" – look out for healthfood shops and trendy bookshops, their owners often escapees from England's industrial Midlands' sprawl.

Trains run into mid–Wales from Shrewsbury, accessible on the main line north from Cardiff. Three miles inside Wales is **WELSHPOOL** (Y Trallwng), a market town full of the distinctive black-and-white half-timbered houses typical of the *Marches*, the Welsh–English borders. It's worth a stop simply to visit the thirteenth-century **Powis Castle**, a gorgeous red limestone building that's been continuously inhabited for five hundred years (April–Oct Wed–Sun 1–5pm; July & Aug also Tues; £7.50). The castle houses Wales' best collection of furniture, tapestries and pictures, as well as the Clive of India collection of Indian treasures. Capability Brown designed the lovely terraced **gardens** (same days 11am–6pm; free with castle ticket, or £5 separately). The **tourist office** is on Church St (daily 10am–5/6pm; ☎01938/552043). One of the many **B&Bs** is *Montgomery House* on Salop Rd (☎01938/552693; ❸).

Trains terminate at **ABERYSTWYTH**, a lively, thoroughly Welsh seaside resort of neat Victorian terraces and a thriving student culture. The train station is ten minutes' east of the seafront, but if you walk north up Terrace Rd, you'll come to the **tourist office** (daily 10am–5/6pm; ☎01970/612125); upstairs, the **Ceredigion Museum** (free) contains coracles once used by local fishermen as well as a reconstructed cottage interior. The flavour of the town is best appreciated on the seafront, where one of Edward I's castles bestrides a windy headland to the south. There's also a Victorian camera obscura further north, which can be reached via a clanking cliff train (Easter–Oct daily 10am–6pm; £2 return). For a more extended rail trip, you could take the very popular **Vale of Rheidol** narrow-gauge steam train to **Devil's Bridge**, a canyon where three bridges of assorted ages and in assorted conditions span a dramatic waterfall (April–Oct; 3hr return trip, 1hr to Devil's Bridge; £12).

The seafront is lined with genteel **guest houses**, all much of a muchness; try *Yr Hafod*, 1 Marine Terrace (☎01970/617579; ❹). Out of term-time, contact University College about B&B in **student halls** (☎01970/621960; ❹). *The Treehouse*, on Eastgate, is a great daytime vegetarian cafe. Check out the university's Arts Centre on Penglais Hill for films, plays, exhibitions and other events.

North of Aberystwyth the train passes through a succession of seaside resorts, some small and discreet, others large and upfront, before reaching **HARLECH**, where one of the best of Edward I's great castles, later Owen Glyndûr's residence, towers above everything else on a rocky crag overlooking the sea (April–Oct daily 9.30am–4/6pm; Nov–March Mon–Sat 9.30am–4pm, Sun 11am–4pm; £3); the ramparts offer panoramic views over the mountains of Snowdonia on one side and Tremadog Bay on the other. The town itself huddles apologetically behind the castle with little to say for itself, but if you want **to stay**, try the *Aris Guesthouse*, 4 Pen-y-Bryn (☎01766/780409; ❻), or the *Plas Newydd* hostel, three miles south by bus #38 or train in Llanbedr (☎01341/241287; ❸). The **tourist office** is on the High St in town (Easter–Oct daily 10am–6pm; ☎01766/780658).

Midway between Aberystwyth and Harlech is down-at-heel **Barmouth**, from where you can catch bus #94 inland to **DOLGELLAU**, a base for exploring **Cadair Idris** (2930ft). The mountain looms over the southern side of town, its summit accessible via a tough six-mile, five-hour trek along the Pony Path starting three miles south of Dolgellau at Ty Nant – just one of the many walks in the area. The **tourist office** is on central Eldon Sq, right by the bus stop (Easter–Oct daily 10am–5/6pm; Nov–Easter closed Tues & Wed; ☎01341/422888). There's a decent independent **hostel** in the shape of *Plas Isa* on Lion St (☎01341/440666; ❸) or you could make for *Kings* **hostel** at Penmaenpool, four miles west, off the #28 bus route (☎01341/422392; ❷).

North Wales

Snowdonia National Park is the glory of **North Wales**, with some of the most dramatic mountain scenery Britain has to offer – jagged peaks, towering waterfalls and glacial lakes decorating every roadside. Not surprisingly, walkers congregate here in large numbers, and the villages around the area's highest peak, Snowdon (3650ft), see steady tourist traffic even in the bleakest months of the year. Whatever season you're here, make sure you're equipped with suitable shoes, warm clothing, and food and drink to see you through any unexpected hitches.

There are two main routes into North Wales. From Porthmadog, a few miles north of Harlech, **buses** skirt the base of Snowdon west to Caernarfon and Llanberis, and east to Blaenau Ffestiniog; while mainline **trains** from Crewe and Chester hug the north coast through Conwy and Bangor to Holyhead, with a branch line heading south to Betws-y-Coed and Blaenau Ffestiniog.

Blaenau Ffestiniog and Betws-y-Coed

A private train (call for times; ☎01766/512340, ⍵www.festrail.co.uk) twists and loops inland from Porthmadog up to the slate-quarrying town of **BLAENAU FFESTINIOG**, a fourteen-mile journey through a corner of the Snowdonia National Park. On a grey day, Blaenau Ffestiniog can look particularly desolate, but it's worth a call for the **Llechwedd Slate Caverns** a mile north, reached by bus. A train takes visitors into the side of the mountain, past an underground lake and spectacular caverns to the very bottom of the mine, on Britain's steepest train incline (daily 10am–4.15/5.15pm; £11. single tour £7.25; ⍵www.llechwedd.co.uk). Should the brooding scenery have cast its spell over you, **B&B** can be had at *Afallon*, Manod Rd (☎01766/830468; ❹).

Most people push on to **BETWS-Y-COED**, ten miles northeast by ordinary train. A popular base for Snowdonia National Park – though no serious walks start here – the town has one of the prettiest settings in Wales but is overrun with visitors in summer, many coming here just to see the **Swallow Falls** in the wooded Llugwy Valley, two miles west of town. If you want to stay to appreciate the wood-and-water setting after the day-trippers have moved on, try the **B&B** above the *Riverside Restaurant*, Holyhead Rd (☎01690/710650; ❹), though keen walkers would be better catered for at the **hostel** at Capel Curig, six miles west by bus #19 (☎01690/720225; ❸). In Betws-y-Coed the *Royal Oak Hotel* and *Pont-y-Pair*, both on Holyhead Rd, do reasonable bar meals and are the liveliest places for a drink. Beside the station sits the **tourist office** (daily 9/10am–4/6pm; ☎01690/710426, ⍵www.betws-y-coed.co.uk). From Betws-y-Coed there are trains and buses to Llandudno Junction, on the main Chester–Holyhead line.

Conwy and Caernarfon

A couple of miles west of Llandudno Junction is **CONWY**, where Edward I's magnificent **Castle** (April–Oct daily 9.30am–5/6pm; Nov–March Mon–Sat 9.30am–4pm, Sun 11am–4pm; £3.60) and the town walls have been listed by UNESCO as a World Heritage Site. Inside you'll also find the **tourist office** (same times; ☎01492/592248). The ramparts offer fine views of Thomas Telford's recently restored 1826 **suspension bridge** (April–Oct Tues–Sun 10am–5pm; July & Aug also Mon; £1) over the River Conwy. For **B&B** try the popular *Gwynedd Guesthouse*, 10 Upper Gate St (☎01492/596537; ❸), or the *Pen-y-Bryn*, 28 High St (☎01492/596445; ❹). Otherwise, there's the *Larkhill* **HI hostel**, Sychnant Pass Rd, just west of the centre (☎01492/593571; ❸).

West of Conwy, trains pass through Bangor on the way to Holyhead. To get to **CAERNARFON** – the springboard for trips into Snowdonia from the north – you'll need bus #5, #5A or #5B from the bus station off Bangor High St. **Caernarfon Castle** (daily: April–Oct 9.30am–5/6pm; Nov–March 9.30/11am–4pm; £4.20), built in 1283 and arguably the most splendid castle in Britain, completely dominates the town. Little of the interior has survived, however, and the three-acre space is largely grassed over; it is here that the Princes of Wales are invested.

Buses to Penllyn St stop on Castle Sq, close to the **tourist office** on Castle St (daily 10am–6pm; Nov–Easter closed Wed; ☎01286/672232). In town, the cheapest place **to stay** is *Totters*, an excellent backpacker hostel at 2 High St (☎01286/672963; ❷); *Isfryn Guesthouse*, 11 Church St (☎01286/675628; ❸) is another good bet.

Llanberis and Snowdon

Regular buses run the seven miles northeast from Caernarfon to **LLANBERIS**, a lakeside village bursting to grow into a town in the shadow of **Snowdon**, at 3560ft the highest mountain in England and Wales. With the biggest concentration of guest houses, hostels and restaurants in Snowdonia, Llanberis offers the perfect base for even the most tentative mountain exploration. The longest but easiest ascent of the mountain is the Llanberis Path, a signposted five-mile hike (3hr) that is manageable by anyone reasonably fit, although the final stretch up to the Yr Wyddfa summit involves a bit of a scramble. Alternatively, you can cop out and take the generally steam-hauled **Snowdon Mountain Railway** (daily mid-March to October; £16.90), which operates from Llanberis to the summit café, pub and post office, weather permitting (note that in adverse conditions trains may terminate at Clogwyn, three-quarters of the way up the mountain). Return tickets permit half an hour's viewing from the summit. The slate quarries that seared Llanberis's surroundings now lie idle, with the **Welsh Slate Museum** (daily 9.30/10am–4.30/5.30pm; free; ⑩www.nmgw.ac.uk/wsm) remaining as a memorial to the workers' tough lives. Nearby, the Dinorwig Pumped Storage Hydro Station is carved out of the mountain and can be visited on underground tours starting at the **Electric Mountain Museum** (daily 9.30/10.30am–4.30/5.30pm; Feb–Easter Thurs–Sun only; Jan closed; £5), whose displays take a Disney approach to the complexities of Welsh history.

Buses stop near the **tourist office**, 41a High St (daily 10am–4/6pm; Nov–March closed Mon & Tues; ☏01286/870765). Walkers have a good choice of **accommodation**. There are several different **HI hostels**, all served by Gwynedd bus #11 from Llanberis, and each at the base of a footpath up Snowdon: *Llanberis*, Llwyn Celyn (☏01286/870280; ❷); *Snowdon Ranger*, Rhyd Ddu (☏01286/650391; ❷); *Bryn Gwynant*, Nantgwynant (☏01766/890251; ❷); and *Pen-y-Pass*, Nantgwynant (☏01286/870428; ❷). Llanberis's High St is lined with small **hotels**: try *The Heights* at no. 74 (☏01286/871179; ❺), which also has eight-bed dorms (❷), or *Dolafon*, another pleasant B&B (☏01286/870933; ❺). The enduringly popular *Pete's Eats*, 40 High St, satisfies walkers' appetites.

Anglesey

The Menai Bridge was built by Thomas Telford in 1826 to connect North Wales with the island of **Anglesey** (Ynys Môn) across the Menai Straits, and it's one of the two chief sights on the little island, even though it's been superseded by a newer rival alongside. The other draw is the last of Edward I's masterpieces, **Beaumaris Castle** (April–Oct daily 9.30am–5/6pm; Nov–March Mon–Sat 9.30am–4pm, Sun 11am–4pm; £2.50), reached by bus #53, #57 or #58 from Bangor. The giant castle was built in 1295 to guard the straits and has a fairy-tale moat enclosing its twelve sturdy towers. Nonetheless, most tourist traffic in this direction speeds past to **HOLYHEAD** (Caergybi), the busiest Welsh **ferry-port**, with several daily ferry and catamaran sailings leaving for Dublin (see p.17). **B&Bs** galore are within a few minutes' walk of the combined bus, train and ferry terminal, including *Glan Ifor*, 8 Walthew Ave (☏01407/764238; ❸) and many more on the same street. The **tourist office** is on Penrhos Beach Rd (daily 10am–4.30/5.30pm; ☏01407/762622, ⑩www.holyhead.com).

Scotland

Scotland is a model example of how a small nation can retain its identity within the confines of a larger one. Unlike the Welsh, the Scots successfully repulsed the expansionist designs of England, and when the "old enemies" first formed a union in 1603, it was because King James VI of Scotland inherited the English throne, though the parliaments were not united for another hundred years. Even then, Scotland retained many of its own institutions, notably distinctive legal and educational systems, and in 1997 the Scots voted to re-establish a parliament; elections were held in May 1999, and by 2000 it was taking a full and active role in day-by-day affairs.

Most of the population clusters in the narrow central belt between the two principal cities: stately **Edinburgh**, the national capital, with its magnificent architecture and imperious natural setting, and earthy **Glasgow**, a powerhouse of the Industrial Revolution and still a hard-working, hard-playing place. The third city, **Aberdeen**, set in one of the rare strips of lowland in the north, has grown fabulously wealthy on the proceeds of offshore oil, its pristine granite buildings and abundant parks and gardens looking smarter than ever. Yet it's the **Highlands**, severely depopulated but comprising over two-thirds of the total area, which for most people is the enduring image of Scotland. The dramatic landscapes are enhanced by the volatile climate, producing an extraordinary variety of moods and colours. Here you'll find some of the last wildernesses in Europe, though even the highest mountain, **Ben Nevis**, is an uncomplicated ascent for the average walker and much of the scenery – such as the famous **Loch Lomond** and **Loch Ness** – can be enjoyed without too much effort.

Edinburgh

EDINBURGH, showcase capital of Scotland, is a historic, cosmopolitan and cultured city. Its stone-built houses, historic buildings and fairy-tale castle, perched on the rocky crag of an extinct volcano, make it visually stunning and it is little surprise that this city is the most popular draw for tourists in Scotland. The 430,000 population swells massively in high season, peaking in mid-August during the **Festival**, when an estimated one million visitors come to town for the biggest arts event in Europe. Yet despite this annual invasion, this dynamic European capital with the boost in confidence the recent arrival of the Scottish parliament has provided is still emphatically Scottish in character and atmosphere.

The centre has two distinct parts. The castle rock is the core of the medieval city, where nobles and servants lived side by side for centuries within tight defensive walls. Edinburgh earned the nickname "Auld Reekie" for the smog and smell generated by the cramped inhabitants of this **Old Town**, where the streets flowed with sewage tipped out of tenement windows and disease was rife. The riddle of medieval streets and alleyways remained a rundown slum well into the last century. The **New Town** was begun in the late 1700s on farmland lying to the north of the castle rock. Edinburgh's wealthier residents speculated profitably on tracts of this land and engaged the services of eminent architects in their development. The result is an outstanding example of Georgian town planning, still largely intact.

Arrival, information and accommodation

Edinburgh **airport** is seven miles west of the centre; there are bus connections around the clock to the city. **Trains** pull into Waverley Station, bang in the centre; the New Town and Princes St lie to the north, the Old Town and the castle to the south. The **bus** terminal is on St Andrew Square, just north of Princes St. The best way to **get around** the city centre is on foot. There's also a good local bus service; day passes (£2.20, £1.50 off-peak) are available on board. The main **tourist office** is at 3 Princes St, above the station on the top level of Princes Mall (July & Aug Mon–Sat 9am–8pm, Sun 10am–8pm; rest of year Mon–Sat 9am–5/7pm, Sun 10am–4/7pm; ☎0131/473 3800, ⊛www.edinburgh.org).

The tourist office has full listings of **accommodation**, and will book rooms for a £3 fee. Central hotels and hostels book up quickly in peak season, but **B&B** is easier to come by, with prices starting from £15 per person. In addition, you can get **student rooms** over the summer; try Napier University (☎0131/455 4331; ➍) or Pollock Hall, Edinburgh University (☎0131/651 2007; ➐). **Campsites** are on the

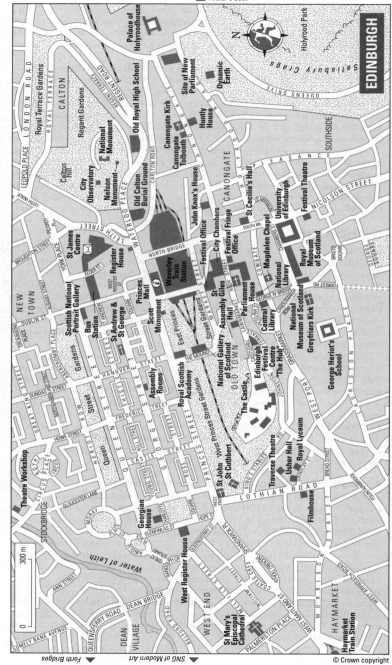

▲ Arthur's Seat

EDINBURGH

Holyrood Park

QUEENS DRIVE

Salisbury Crags

N

Palace of Holyroodhouse

LONDON ROAD

Royal Terrace Gardens
ROYAL TERRACE

REGENT TERRACE

Regent Gardens

CALTON

Old Royal High School

Site of New Parliament

Dynamic Earth

SOUTHSIDE

PLEASANCE

Canongate Kirk

Huntly House

Canongate Tolbooth

National Monument

LEOPOLD PLACE

Calton Hill

City Observatory

Nelson Monument

Old Calton Burial Ground

CARLTON ROAD

CANONGATE

John Knox's House

St Cecilia's Hall

University of Edinburgh

Festival Theatre

NICOLSON STREET

BRISTO SQUARE

GEORGE SQUARE

LEITH WALK

PICARDY PL

Theatre Workshop

LEITH STREET

WATERLOO PLACE

York PLACE

BROUGHTON STREET

St James Centre

Register House

NEW TOWN

DUBLIN ST

ALBANY STREET

Scottish National Portrait Gallery

Bus Station

St Andrew & St George

St Andrew Square

Gardens

WEST REGISTER STREET

ELDER ST

Princes Mall

Scott Monument

Waverley Train Station

NORTH BRIDGE

Festival Office

City Chambers

Festival Fringe Office

SOUTH BR.

Magdalen Chapel

National Library

Royal Museum of Scotland

CHAMBERS ST

East Princes Street Gardens

St Giles

Assembly Hall

Parliament House

HIGH STREET

COWGATE

GEORGE IV BRIDGE

Central Library

National Museum of Scotland

Greyfriars Kirk

George Heriot's School

LAURISTON PLACE

FORREST RD

DRUMMOND PLACE

GREAT KING STREET

NORTHUMBERLAND ST

ABERCROMBY PLACE

HERIOT ROW

DUNDAS STREET

HOWE STREET

Street

HANOVER STREET

THISTLE STREET

Assembly Rooms

Royal Scottish Academy

Queen

FREDERICK STREET

Street

West Princes Street Gardens

National Gallery of Scotland

Edinburgh Festival Centre

The Hub

The Castle

CASTLE STREET

QUEEN STREET

GEORGE STREET

ROSE STREET

PRINCES STREET

LAWNMARKET

GRASSMARKET

JOHNSTON TERRACE

West Port

WEST PORT

YOUNG STREET

HILL STREET

STOCKBRIDGE

CIRCUS PLACE

ROYAL CIRCUS

GLOUCESTER LANE

MORAY PLACE

Georgian House

CHARLOTTE SQUARE

HOPE ST

GLENFINLAS ST

West Register House

West End

St John

St Cuthbert

Traverse Theatre

Royal Lyceum

Usher Hall

Filmhouse

LOTHIAN ROAD

GRINDLAY ST

BREAD STREET

KING'S STABLES RD

SPITTAL ST

Water of Leith

AINSLIE PLACE

GREAT STUART ST

ANN STREET

DEAN BRIDGE

BELFORD ROAD

DEAN VILLAGE

QUEENSFERRY ROAD

COMELY BANK AVENUE

St Mary's Episcopal Cathedral

WEST END

PALMERSTON PLACE

MELVILLE STREET

COATES CRES

WILLIAM STREET

ATHOLL CRESCENT

MORRISON STREET

HAYMARKET

Haymarket Train Station

WEST APPROACH ROAD

300 m

0

▼ Forth Bridges

▲ SNG of Modern Art

© Crown copyright

fringes of the city. If you want to stay **during the Festival** (mid–Aug to early Sept), you'll need to book months in advance.

Hostels

Argyle 14 Argyle Place, Marchmont ☎0131/667 9991, ⊛www.argyle-backpackers.com. Quieter hostel, with small dorms and a dozen double/twin rooms. Pleasant location in studenty Marchmont. ❸

Brodies 12 High St, Old Town ☎0131/556 6770, ⊛www.brodieshostels.co.uk. Tucked down a typical Old Town close, it's cosier than many others, but with limited communal areas. ❸

Bruntsfield 7 Bruntsfield Crescent, Bruntsfield ☎0131/447 2994, ⊛www.syha.org.uk. Large HI hostel a mile south of Princes Street. ❸

Castle Rock 15 Johnston Terrace, Old Town ☎0131/225 9666, ⊛www.scotlands-top-hostels .com. Busy 200-bed hostel tucked below the castle ramparts. ❸

Edinburgh Backpackers 65 Cockburn St, Old Town ☎0131/220 1717, ⊛www.hoppo.com. Big hostel with a great central location in a side street off the Royal Mile. ❸

Eglinton Hostel 18 Eglinton Crescent, Haymarket ☎0131/337 1120, ⊛www.syha.org.uk. More expensive but more central of the two HI hostels, in a characterful town house west of the centre. ❸

High Street Hostel 8 Blackfriars St, Old Town ☎0131/557 3984, ⊛www.scotlands-top-hostels .com. Large but lively and well known hostel in a sixteenth-century building just off the Royal Mile. ❸

St Christopher's Inns 9–13 Market St, Old Town ☎0131/226 1446, ⊛www.st-christophers.co.uk. Edinburgh's first mega-hostel; 110 beds (all bunks) with smaller rooms as well as dorms. ❹

Royal Mile Backpackers 105 High St, Old Town ☎0131/557 6120, ⊛www.scotlands-top-hostels .com. Small hostel popular with longer-term residents; shares facilities with the nearby *High Street Hostel*. ❸

Hotels and B&Bs

Ardenlee Guest House 9 Eyre Place ☎0131/556 2838. Welcoming, non-smoking guest house near the Royal Botanic Garden, with spacious rooms. ❼

Six Mary's Place Raeburn Place ☎0131/332 8965, ⊛www.sixmarysplace.co.uk. Collectively run "alternative" guest house; has a no-smoking policy and offers excellent home-cooked vegetarian meals. ❽

Stuart House 12 E Claremont St ☎0131/557 9030, ⊛www.stuartguesthouse.co.uk. Cosy, bright Georgian house in the Broughton area. No smoking. ❽

Bar Java 48–50 Constitution St, Leith ☎0131/553 2020. Simple but brightly designed rooms above one of Leith's funkiest bars. Food and drink available till late in the bar itself. ❻

Cluaran House 47 Leamington Terrace, Viewforth ☎0131/221 0047, ⊛www.cluaran-house-edinburgh.co.uk. Pleasant B&B in a nicely decorated, non-smoking house near Brunstfield serving wholefood breakfasts. ❽

The Greenhouse 14 Hartington Gardens, Viewforth ☎0131/622 7634, ⊛www.greenhouse-edinburgh .com. A fully vegetarian/vegan guest house, where a relaxed atmosphere prevails. ❼

International Guest House 37 Mayfield Gardens, Mayfield ☎0131/667 2511, ⊛www.accommodation -edinburgh.com. One of the best Southside guest houses, with comfortable well equipped rooms. ❼

Teviotdale House Hotel 53 Grange Loan, Grange ☎0131/667 4376, ⓔteviotdale.house@btinternet .com. Peaceful non-smoking hotel, offering luxurious standards at reasonable prices. Particularly good (and huge) home-cooked Scottish breakfasts. ❼

Campsites

Davidson's Mains Caravan Site Marine Drive, Silverknowes ☎0131/312 6874. Pleasantly located close to the shore in the northwestern suburbs, 30min from the centre on bus #28.

Mortonhall Caravan Park 38 Mortonhall Gate, Frogston Rd ☎0131/664 1533. A good site, five miles south of the centre, near the Braid Hills; take bus #11(marked Captain's Rd) or #31 from the centre of town. Closed Nov–Feb.

The Old Town

The cobbled **Royal Mile** – composed of Castlehill, Lawnmarket, High St and Canongate – is the central thoroughfare of the **Old Town**, running down a prominent ridge to the Palace of Holyroodhouse (see below) from the **Castle** (daily 9.30am–5/6pm; £7.50). The castle is thought to have evolved from an Iron Age fort, the sheer volcanic rock on which it stands providing formidable defence on three sides. Within its precincts are St Margaret's Chapel, probably the oldest building in the city, the Great Hall with its magnificent hammerbeam roof, the ancient crown jewels of Scotland and the even older Stone of Destiny – coronation stone of the kings of Scotland that was returned north of the border in 1996 after a 700-

year stay in London. There's a large military museum here, too, and the castle esplanade provides a dramatic setting for the world-famous Military Tattoo, an unashamed display of martial pomp staged during the Festival. Year round, at 1pm (not Sun) a cannon shot is fired from the castle.

Descending Castlehill from the Esplanade you'll pass the **Scotch Whisky Heritage Centre** (daily 9.30am/10am–5.30/6.30pm; £6.50), which offers an informative and entertaining introduction to Scotland's national beverage. A little further down in an imposing black Gothic church building is **The Hub** (daily 8am–late; free), permanent home of the Edinburgh International Festival, where you'll find a pleasant café/bistro, a bookshop and various quirky art installations. A little further down, leading off the far side of Lawnmarket, Lady Stair's Close is home to the **Writers' Museum** (Mon–Sat 10am–5pm; during Festival also Sun 2–5pm; free), dedicated to Sir Walter Scott, Robert Burns and Robert Louis Stevenson.

At the southern end of Lawnmarket, George IV Bridge leads south from the Royal Mile to Chambers St; here the **National Museum of Scotland** (Mon–Sat 10am–5pm, Tues till 8pm, Sun noon–5pm; free; ⊛www.nms.ac.uk), housed in a striking modern sandstone building, contains many Scottish artefacts, ranging from Celtic treasures to twentieth-century icons. Immediately next door is the **Royal Museum** (same times), a soaring Victorian pile housing a rich collection of colonial acquisitions. The area south of here is dominated by **Edinburgh University**, Scotland's largest with over 15,000 students.

Back on the Royal Mile, High St starts at Parliament Square, dominated by the **High Kirk of St Giles** (daily 9am–5/7pm), whose beautiful crown-shaped spire is an Edinburgh landmark. Inside, the Thistle Chapel (1911) is an amazing display of mock-Gothic woodcarving. Outside, near the west door, the heart-shaped cobble pattern set in the cobbles is the Heart of Midlothian – traditionally, passers-by spit on it for luck. On the south side of Parliament Square are the neoclassical law courts, incorporating the seventeenth-century **Parliament House**, under whose spectacular hammerbeam roof the Scottish parliament met until the 1707 Union.

The final section of the Royal Mile, Canongate, starts just beyond medieval **John Knox's House** (July & Aug Mon–Sat 10am–5pm, Sun noon–5pm; rest of year closed Sun), which juts out into the street. Reputedly the home of the city's famously fierce Calvinist cleric, its bare interiors give a good idea of the labyrinthine layout of Old Town houses. The final section of Canongate is dominated by the new Scottish **Parliament**, a costly and controversial but undoubtedly striking piece of contemporary architecture which is set to open in 2003. South of this, the most interesting of various modern buildings is the futuristic tented structure of **Our Dynamic Earth** (April–Oct daily 10am–6pm; Nov–March Wed–Sat 10am–5pm; £7.95), a trendy exhibition on the earth and the environment using hi-tech audio-visual-tactile displays.

In complete contrast to the modern vision of the Parliament is the **Palace of Holyroodhouse** (daily 9.30am–4.30/6pm; £6.50), the Royal Family's official Scottish residence, which principally dates from the seventeenth century. The public are admitted to the sumptuous state rooms and historic apartments unless the royals are in residence or when there are garden parties. The palace looks out over Holyrood Park, 650 acres of wilderness in the heart of the city, where fine walks lead across parkland up to the arc of the **Salisbury Crags** and **Arthur's Seat** beyond; a fairly stiff climb is rewarded by magnificent views over the city and out to the Firth of Forth.

The New Town

The clear divide between the Old and **New Town** is the wide grassy valley of Princes St Gardens, along the north side of which runs **Princes St**, the main shopping area, with chain stores crammed in cheek-by-jowl. Amongst the gardens halfway along Princes St, the Mound leads to the **National Gallery of Scotland** (Mon–Sat 10am–5pm, Sun noon–5pm; free), an Athenian-style sandstone building. One of the best small collections of pre-twentieth century art in Europe, it includes works by major European artists, including Botticelli, Raphael, Titian, Rembrandt, Vermeer, Degas, Gauguin and Van Gogh. The Scottish collection is relatively limit-ed, though it's worth looking out for the charming *Reverend Robert Walker Skating* by Henry Raeburn – a postcard favourite. The National Gallery is currently under-going a major upgrade, during which sections of its exterior will be hidden by scaf-folding until at least 2005; the gallery remains open throughout.

East of the National Gallery the spire of the **Scott Monument** (daily 9am–4/8pm; £2.50) stands out, decorated with figures from Sir Walter's novels and now oddly piebald following restoration work. You can climb the tightly winding internal spiral staircase to get some inspiring – if heady – views of the city below and hills beyond. Nearby George St, which runs parallel to Princes St, is fast becoming the domain of designer-label shops; but suave Charlotte Sq, at its western end, remains the most elegant square in the New Town. The **National Trust for Scotland** has its HQ at no. 27 – you can go inside to view a small art collection or enjoy a refined cup of tea in the Georgian dining room, while on the opposite side of the square at no. 7 the **Georgian House** (March–Oct Mon–Sat 10am–5pm, Sun 2–5pm; £5) is a pristinely restored period piece. North of George St is the broad avenue of Queen St, at whose eastern end stands the **Scottish National Portrait Gallery** (Mon–Sat 10am–5pm, Sun noon–5pm; free). The remarkable red sandstone building is modelled on the Doge's Palace in Venice; inside the collection of portraits offers an engaging procession through Scottish history with famous Scots such as Bonnie Prince Charlie and Mary, Queen of Scots on display alongside contemporary heroes such as Sean Connery and Alex Ferguson.

In the northwest corner of the New Town lies **Stockbridge**, a smart residential suburb with bohemian pretensions – especially noticeable around the huddle of old mill buildings known as Dean Village. From here Belford Rd leads up to the **Scottish National Gallery of Modern Art** and the **Dean Gallery** extension opposite (both Mon–Sat 10am–5pm, Sun noon–5pm; free); the two offer an acces-sible introduction to all the notable movements of twentieth century art, displaying work by the likes of Matisse, Picasso, Giacometti and Mondrian, as well as modern Scottish artists such as the Colourists and industrial sculptor Sir Eduardo Paolozzi.

Another luscious retreat from the city is offered by the **Royal Botanic Garden** (daily 9.30am–dusk; free) on the north side of Stockbridge, entered from either Arboretum Place or Inverleith Row; it's served by buses #14, #17, #23 or #27 from the city centre. Covering seventy acres, the gardens support a vast array of rare plants from around the world in their landscaped grounds and magnificent hothouses.

Eating, drinking and nightlife

Edinburgh is well served with **restaurants**, but – as with accommodation – there's a lot of pressure on space. Edinburgh's **cafés** are among the most enjoyable spots in the city – serving coffee, food and often alcohol too, and sometimes doubling as exhibition and performance spaces during the Festival. The city's many **bars** are among the most congenial in the country, with live music a frequent bonus.

Edinburgh has a lively **nightlife**, and venues change name and location with such speed that the only way to keep up with what's going on is to get hold of *The List*, a comprehensive **listings** magazine published fortnightly. The best **theatre** is the *Traverse*, 10 Cambridge St, and there's an excellent art-house **cinema**, *The Filmhouse*, nearby at 88 Lothian Road. **Gay nightlife** is centred on the top of Leith Walk, notably at *CC Bloom's* and *Planet Out*, next to the Playhouse on Greenside Place.

Cafés and restaurants

Blue Moon 36 Broughton St. Coffee, snacks and filling meals at this friendly lesbian/gay café; all welcome.

Café Mediterraneo 73 Broughton St ☎0131/557 6900. Deli with a small dining space serving good quality Italian food at great prices.

Elephant House 21 George IV Bridge. Popular café near the university with a cavernous back room.

Favorit Teviot Pl and 30–32 Leven St, Bruntsfield. Modern café/diner open till 3am.

Kalpna 2 St Patrick Sq ☏0131/667 9890. Prize-winning vegetarian Indian; lunchtime buffet £5. Closed Sun.

Henderson's 94 Hanover St. Self-service restaurant with a lively atmosphere, good-value vegetarian food and occasional live music.

Lost Sock Diner 11 East London St, Broughton. Burgers, wraps and blackboard specials at low prices in this quirky laundrette-cum-diner.

Mamma's American Pizza Company 30 Grassmarket. Good pizzas and a lively atmosphere that often spills out onto the Grassmarket cobbles.

Niji 25a Thistle St ☏0131/220 5254. Excellent noodle and Sushi bar. Closed Sun.

Mussel Inn 61–65 Rose St ☏0131/225 5979. Owned by two Scottish shellfish farmers, you can feast on a kilo of mussels and a basket of chips for under £10.

Le Sept 7 Old Fishmarket Close ☏0131/225 5428. Long established French brasserie serving filling savoury crepes and good fish dishes.

Susie's Diner 51 West Nicolson St ☏0131/667 8729. Popular student veggie/vegan café.

Pubs and bars

City Café 19 Blair St. A stylish yet inviting café/bar that is popular with the pre-club crowd.

Garibaldi's 97a Hanover St. A basement Mexican bar serving authentic dishes and cocktails alongside a dancefloor.

Human Be-In 2–8 West Crosscauseway. Super-trendy student bar serving excellent food.

Last Drop Tavern 74 Grassmarket. A late-closing studenty pub.

Malt Shovel 11 Cockburn St. Good beer, plenty of local colour and a wide choice of single malt whiskies; live jazz some evenings.

The Outhouse 12a Broughton St Lane. Pre-club bar and beer garden.

Live music venues and clubs

Ego 14 Picardy Pl. Popular club playing house and trance to a mixed crowd.

La Belle Angèle 11 Hasties Close. Latin, soul, hip-hop and jazz at this club.

Cavendish West Tollcross. Popular club with long-running reggae/ragga and R&B night on Sat.

Liquid Room 9c Victoria St. Live music venue, showcasing indie and local R&B bands.

Royal Oak Infirmary St. Venue for Scottish folk music.

Venue 15 Calton Rd. Music venue hosting up-and-coming indie bands.

Whistlebinkies 4–6 South Bridge. Rock venue.

The Edinburgh Festival

The city's essential cultural event is the **Edinburgh Festival** (🌐www.edinburghfestivals .co.uk), by far the world's largest arts jamboree, which was founded in 1947 and now attracts thousands of artists from August to early September. The event is, in fact, several different festivals taking place at around the same time: the *Edinburgh International Festival* traditionally presents highbrow fare; but it's the frenetic **Fringe** that gives Edinburgh its unique buzz during August, with all sorts of unlikely venues turned into performance spaces for a bewildering array of artists. In addition, there's a *Film Festival* focusing on the latest movies, a *Jazz Festival*, and a *Book Festival*. **Tickets** are available at the venues and from the International Festival Office, The Hub, Castlehill (☏0131/473 2000), or the Fringe Office, 180 High St (☏0131/226 5257).

Listings

Bike rental Biketrax, 11 Lochrin Place ☏0131/228 6333; Edinburgh Cycle Hire, 29 Blackfriars St ☏0131/556 5560.

Banks and exchange Several big branches on and around Andrew, Hanover and George squares.

Consulates Australia, 69 George St ☏0131/624 3333; Canada, 30 Lothian Rd ☏0131/220 4333; USA, 3 Regent Terrace ☏0131/556 8315.

Hospitals Royal Infirmary, Lauriston Place ☏0131/ 536 1000.

Internet access easyEverything, 58 Rose St; Tourist Information Centre, Princes Mall.

Laundry Capital Launderette, 208 Dalkeith Rd, Newington; Tarvit Launderette, 7–9 Tarvit St, Tollcross.

Left luggage Lockers at Waverley Station and St Andrew Sq bus station.

Pharmacy Boots, 48 Shandwick Place.

Police Fettes Ave ☏0131/311 3131.

Post office St James' Shopping Centre, off Leith St.

Glasgow

GLASGOW is the largest city in Scotland, home to 750,000 people. It once thrived on the tobacco trade with the American colonies, on cotton production and, most famously, on the shipbuilding on the River Clyde. The civic architecture of Victorian Glasgow was as grand as any in Britain, and the West End suburbs were regarded as among the best designed in the country. Since this heyday, however, it has not enjoyed the best of reputations. The Gorbals area became notorious as one of the worst slums in Europe, and the city's association with violence and heavy drinking stuck to it like a curse. However, like many British cities, rejuvenated Glasgow has undergone another change of image, symbolized by its selection as the European City of Culture in 1990 and City of Architecture and Design in 1999, titles which recognize that the city has broken the industrial shackles of the past and evolved into a city of stature and confidence.

The City

Glasgow's centre lies on the north bank of the Clyde, around the grandiose **George Square**, a little way east of Central Station. Just south of the square, down Queen St, is the **Gallery of Modern Art** (Mon–Thurs & Sat 10am–5pm, Fri & Sun 11am–5pm; free). Formerly a "temple of commerce" built by one of the eighteenth-century tobacco lords, it now houses an exciting collection of contemporary Scots art, notably works by Peter Howson and John Bellany. A short way west on Mitchell Lane, just off Buchanan St, **The Lighthouse** (Mon–Sat 10.30am–5.30pm, Thurs till 7pm, Sun noon–5pm; 32.50) was the first commission of Glasgow's famous architect Charles Rennie Mackintosh, whose distinctively streamlined Art Nouveau designs appear in shops all over the city; inside is an exhibition devoted to the man.

Down by the river, southeast of George Sq, is Glasgow Green, site of the **People's Palace** (Mon–Thurs & Sat 10am–5pm, Fri & Sun 11am–5pm; free), opened in 1898 as a cultural centre for the area. It now records the social history of the city, giving most of its space to memorabilia of Victorian Glasgow. Northeast of George Sq is the **Cathedral** on Castle St (Mon–Sat 9.30am–4/6pm, Sun 2–4/5pm). Built in 1136, destroyed in 1192 and rebuilt soon after, it's the only Scottish mainland cathedral to have escaped the hands of the country's sixteenth-century religious reformers, whose hatred of anything that smacked of idolatry wrecked many of Scotland's ancient churches. Just as interesting as the cathedral is the adjacent **Necropolis**, a hilltop cemetery for the magnates who made Glasgow rich; there are great views across the city from here.

North and west of George Square, just off Glasgow's most famous thoroughfare, **Sauchiehall Street**, is the **Glasgow School of Art**, 167 Renfrew St, a remarkable building designed by Mackintosh that is a fusion of Scottish manor house solidity and modernist refinement. The interior, making maximum use of natural light, was also furnished and fitted entirely by the architect, and can be seen on a guided tour (Mon–Fri 11am & 2pm, Sat 10.30am & 11.30am; £5; ☎0141/353 4526). A short distance north is the **Tenement House**, 145 Buccleuch St (March–Oct daily 2–5pm; £3.20); with box beds and gas lamps it's an intriguing if sanitized vision of working-class life. About fifteen minutes' walk west, past the salubrious crescents of the West End, **Kelvingrove Park** is home to the **Glasgow Art Gallery and Museum** (Mon–Thurs & Sat 10am–5pm, Fri & Sun 11am–5pm; free), a stunning red sandstone building housing a first-rate collection of art and artefacts. Its particular strengths are pictures from Italy, the Low Countries and nineteenth-century France, and there are notable pieces from Rembrandt, Degas, Millet, Van Gogh and Monet, as well as an impressive body of Scottish painting.

About four miles south of the centre, in **Pollok Country Park** (bus #45, #47, #48 or #57 from Union St, or train to Pollokshaws West), is the astonishing **Burrell Collection**, housed in a custom-built gallery (Mon–Thurs & Sat 10am–5pm, Fri & Sun 11am–5pm; free). Sir William Burrell began collecting at the age of 15 and kept going until his death at 96, buying an average of two pieces a week. Works by Memling, Cézanne, Degas, Bellini and Géricault feature among the paintings, while in adjoining galleries there are pieces from ancient Rome and Greece, medieval European arts and crafts, and a massive selection of Chinese artefacts, with outstanding ceramics, jades and bronzes. Somewhat overshadowed, the nearby **Pollok House** (daily 10am–5pm; £4, free in winter) is a lovely eighteenth-century mansion containing paintings by El Greco, Goya and Murillo, and works by William Blake.

Practicalities

Glasgow airport (☎0141/887 1111) is eight miles west of the city, with regular buses shuttling to Buchanan St **bus station**; **Prestwick airport** (☎01292/ 479822), thirty miles south, is connected to the city centre by train. Glasgow has two main **train stations**, Central, which serves all points south, and Queen St, for Edinburgh and the north. It's an easy city to explore on foot – you can walk from the centre to Kelvingrove Park in about forty minutes. Should you tire of the pavements, the **Underground** is cheap and easy, operating on a circular chain of fifteen stations with a flat fare of 90p (day-pass £1.60). The **Strathclyde Travel Centre**, above St Enoch underground station (Mon–Sat 8.30am–5.30pm), has information on all public transport, as well as discount passes. The helpful **tourist office** is on the south side of George Sq, near the top of Queen St (Mon–Sat 9am–6/8pm, Sun 10am–6pm; Oct–April closed Sun; ☎0141/204 4400, ⊛www.seeglasgow.com); there's a smaller office at the airport (Mon–Sat 7.30am–5pm; ☎0141/848 4440).

Accommodation

During summer, the universities of Glasgow (☎0141/330 5385) and Strathclyde (☎0141/553 4148) also let out rooms (❸).

Hostels and B&Bs

Alamo 46 Gray St ☎0141/339 2395, ⊛www .alamoguesthouse.com. Attractive B&B near Kelvingrove. ❹

Euro Hostel 318 Clyde St ☎0141/222 2828; ⊛www.euro-hostels.com. Very central, 360-bed hostel. ❹

Glasgow SYHA 7 Park Terrace ☎0141/332 3004. ⊛www.syha.org.uk. Attractive location, near Kelvingrove Park. ❸

Scott 417 Woodside Rd ☎0141/339 3750. Another good B&B, close to Kelvingrove underground. ❹

Campsites

Craigendmuir Park Campsie View ☎0141/779 4159. Four miles northeast of the centre; take a train to Stepps, from where it's a fifteen-minute walk.

Eating, drinking and nightlife

There are plenty of inexpensive **eating** options in the city centre and a huge number of **pubs** in which to down a pint. As for **nightlife**, the fortnightly magazine *The List* is the best source of club listings, but pick of the crop are *The Arches*, on Midland St, and *The Tunnel*, 84 Mitchell St. You can often find innovative, challenging theatre at the Citizens' or Tramway theatres, both on the south side of the river, while the **Centre for Contemporary Arts** (or CCA), 346 Sauchiehall St, has a reputation for a programme of controversial performances and exhibitions. The wonderful Glasgow Film Theatre, Rose St, shows art films and old favourites.

Cafés and restaurants

Ashoka Ashton Lane. Excellent-value Indian restaurant.

Corinthian 191 Ingram Rd, Ultra-ornate tea rooms, worth a visit for the decor alone.

Grassroots Café 97 St George's Rd. Innovative organic food in bright and airy surroundings.

Grosvenor Café 31 Ashton Lane. Just off Byres Rd in the West End, this is one of the best places

in town for inexpensive snacks.

Insomnia 38 Woodlands Rd. Bargain prices at this 24-hr café, packed with a post-club crowd in the wee hours.

University Café Byres Rd. A period piece where you can fill up on basic but filling fare.

Willow Tea Rooms 217 Sauchiehall St. Mackintosh-designed place, good for a light meal.

Pubs and live music venues

Bar 10 10 Mitchell St. A good example of a traditional Glasgow style bar.
Bargo Albion St. A trendy pre-club DJ-bar in fashionable Merchant city.
Del Monica's 68 Virginia St. The liveliest gay bar in town.

The Horseshoe Bar 17 Drury St. Has the longest bar in the UK and plenty of atmosphere.
King Tut's Wah Wah Hut 272a Vincent St. Famous as the place where Oasis were discovered, and still hosts excellent gigs.
Scotia 112 Stockwell St. Has live folk music.

Listings

Bike rental Dales, 150 Dobbies Loan ☎0141/332 2705; West End Cycles, 16 Chancellor St ☎0141/357 1344.
Hospitals Royal Infirmary, 84 Castle St ☎0141/211 4000.
Internet access easyEverything, 57–61 St Vincent St; Internet Exchange, 136 Sauchiehall St.

Laundry Harvey's, 161 Great Western Rd; Laundromat, 39 Bank St; Majestic Launderette, 1110 Argyle St.
Pharmacy Boots, Buchanan Galleries.
Police Pitt St ☎0141/532 2000.
Post office 47 St Vincent St.

Melrose and around

If you've only time to visit one town in the Scottish Borders, the upland region that lies between England and Scotland, then **MELROSE**, 37 miles south of Edinburgh, is the obvious choice. Tucked in between the River Tweed and the gorse-backed Eildon Hills, tiny Melrose is the most beguiling of towns, its narrow streets trimmed by a harmonious ensemble of styles, from pretty little cottages and tweedy shops to high-standing Georgian and Victorian facades. Its chief draw is its ruined **Abbey** (April–Sept daily 9.30am–6.30pm; Oct–March Mon–Sat 9.30am–4.30pm, Sun 2–4.30pm; £3.30), the finest of the Border abbeys. It's best seen on a bright morning, with the sun streaming through the tracery of the exquisite east and south windows and illuminating the richly sculpted capitals and cornices of the nave.

The Scots Baronial house of **Abbotsford** (June–Sept daily 9.30am–5pm; mid-March to May & Oct Mon–Sat 9.30am–5pm, Sun 2–5pm; £4), three miles west of Melrose, was designed to satisfy the Romantic inclinations of **Sir Walter Scott**, who lived here from 1812 until his death twenty years later. Despite all the exterior pomp, the interior is surprisingly small and poky, with just six rooms open for viewing, starting with the wood-panelled study where Scott banged out the Waverley novels at a furious rate to try and pay off his debts. Even more aesthetically pleasing is Scott's burial place, **Dryburgh Abbey** (times as for Melrose Abbey; £2.80), five miles southeast of Melrose. The romantic setting is second to none, though the abbey ruins are much less substantial than at Melrose. Virtually nothing survives of the nave, but the transepts have fared better and now serve as a burial ground for Scott, and Field Marshal Haig, the World War I commander responsible for needless slaughter of millions.

Buses to Melrose stop in Market Sq, from where it's a short walk north to the abbey ruins and the **tourist office**, opposite (March–Oct Mon–Sat 9.30/10am–5/6.30pm; ☎01896/822555). The **HI hostel** is in an old Victorian villa overlooking the abbey (☎01896/822521; ❷). There's a plentiful supply of **B&Bs**, most notable of which is *Braidwood*, on Buccleuch St (☎01896/822488; ❺). The old coaching inns in the village offer quality **meals**: *Burt's* does good bar meals, as does *The Ship*.

St Andrews

Well-groomed **ST ANDREWS**, on the coast, 56 miles northeast of Edinburgh, has the air of a place of importance. Retaining memories of its days as medieval Scotland's metropolis, it is the country's oldest university town, the Scottish answer to Oxford or Cambridge with a snob-appeal to match. The upper-class English accents that you hear everywhere in term time certainly haven't diminished now that the university is playing host to Prince William's undergraduate years.

St Andrews has an exalted place in Scottish sporting history too. Entering the town from the Edinburgh road, you pass no fewer than four golf links, the last of which is the **Old Course**, the most famous and – in the opinion of Jack Nicklaus – the best in the world. At the southern end of the Old Course, down towards the waterfront, is the award-winning **British Golf Museum** (April–Oct daily 9.30am–5.30pm; Nov–March Mon & Thurs–Sun 11am–3pm; £3.75); if you want to step onto the famous fairways, head to the **Himalayas** putting green, located right by the first hole and only 80p per round. Immediately south of the Old Course begins North St, one of St Andrews' two main arteries. Much of it is taken up by university buildings, with the tower of **St Salvator's College** rising proudly above all else. Together with the adjoining chapel, this dates from 1450 and is the earliest surviving part of the university. Further east, you can reach the ruined **Castle** on North Castle St (April–Sept daily 9.30am–6.30pm; Oct–March Mon–Sat 9.30am–4.30pm, Sun 2–4.30pm; £2, or combined ticket with cathedral £4). Commanding a prominent headland, it began as a fortress, but was partly transformed by the local archbishops into a Renaissance palace, of which little more than the facade survives. A short distance further along the coast is the equally ruined Gothic **Cathedral** (same times), the mother church of medieval Scotland and the largest and grandest ever built in the country. Even though little more than the cemetery survives, the intact east wall and the exposed foundations give an idea of the vast scale of what has been lost. With the entrance ticket (prices as castle) you can get a token to ascend the austere Romanesque **St Rule's Tower** – part of the priory that the cathedral replaced – for superb views over the sea and town.

Practicalities

You can reach St Andrews by **bus** on a day-trip from Edinburgh or Stirling. There are no direct trains, though frequent buses connect with the train station five miles away in Leuchars (where the parish church incorporates the most beautiful and intact piece of Norman architecture in Scotland). St Andrews' **tourist office**, 70 Market St (Mon–Sat 9.30am–7pm, Sun 10am–5pm; shorter hours in winter; ☎01334/472021, ⊛www.standrews.com), will book **rooms** for a ten percent deposit – worth paying in the summer and during big golf tournaments, when **accommodation** is in short supply. The only **hostel** in the area is *St Andrews Tourist Hostel* on St Mary's Pl (☎01334/479911; ❸). *Doune House*, 5 Murray Place (☎01334/475195; ⊛www.dounehouse.co.uk; ❼), and *Craigmore*, 3 Murray Park (☎01334/472142; ❼), are two options of the many on those streets. For **eating**, student favourites are *The Inn on North Street*, 127 North St, and the Mexican *La Pasada* on St Mary's Place; for a touch of tongue-in-cheek Scottish kitsch and decent food try *Saltire Scottish Restaurant*, 11 Crails Lane. Most **pubs** are concentrated on Market St and South St; best of the bunch are *Central*, 1 Market St, *Ma Belle's*, 40 The Scores, both popular student joints, while *Broons Bistro and Bar* beside the New Picture House cinema on North St is a trendier spot with live music sessions.

Stirling

Occupying a key strategic position between the Highlands and Lowlands at the easiest crossing of the River Forth, **STIRLING** has played a major role throughout Scottish history. With its castle and steep, cobbled streets, it can appear like a smaller version of Edinburgh. Imperiously set on a rocky crag, the atmospheric and explorable **Castle** (daily 9.30am–5/6.30pm; £6.50, includes Argyll's Lodging) combined the functions of a fortress with those of a royal palace. Highlights within the complex are the **Royal Palace**, dating from the late Renaissance, and the earlier **Great Hall**, where recent restoration, including a complete rebuilding of the vast hammerbeam roof, has revealed the original form and scale.

The oldest part of Stirling is grouped around the streets leading up to the castle. Just downhill, on Castle Wynd, stands a richly decorated facade, all that remains of

Mar's Wark, one of two imposing Renaissance town houses. The other, **Argyll's Lodging**, is intact, with some rooms furnished in period style (same times and ticket as castle). Beyond stands the Gothic **Church of the Holy Rude** (May–Sept Mon–Fri 10am–5pm), which boasts a fine timber roof. Here the infant James VI – later James I of the United Kingdom – was crowned King of Scotland in 1567. From here, Broad St slopes down to the lower town, passing the **Tolbooth**, the city's newly restored arts and cultural centre. Stirling is famous as the scene of Sir William Wallace's battlefield victory over the English in 1297, a crucial episode in the Wars of Independence (as portrayed in the film *Braveheart*). The Scottish hero was commemorated in Victorian times by the **Wallace Monument** (daily 10am–4/6pm; £3.95), about a mile further north near the university. Though the refurbished building seems ugly close up, compensation comes in the stupendous views – finer even than those from the castle.

The train and bus stations are both five minutes' walk from the **tourist office**, 41 Dumbarton Rd, in the lower part of town (July & Aug Mon–Sat 9am–7.30pm, Sun 9.30am–6.30pm; rest of year Mon–Sat 9/10am–5/6pm; ☎01786/475019, ⓦwww.scottish.heartlands.org). The **HI hostel**, St John St, is a little characterless but occupies a great setting at the top of town in a converted church (☎01786/473442; ❸), while *Willy Wallace Independent Hostel*, 77 Murray Place, is a lively, welcoming backpacker **hostel** (☎01786/446773; ❸). Of the many guest houses, *No. 10*, 10 Gladstone Place, is especially friendly (☎01786/472681; ⓦwww.cameron-10.co.uk; ❺). The picturesque *Witches' Craig* **campsite** is three miles east of town on bus #62, off the St Andrews road (☎01786/474947; closed Nov–March). Try the lively *Barton Bar and Bistro*, Barton St, or the slightly more upmarket *Yill & Kail* at 39 Broad St for decent **meals** and relaxed drinking.

Loch Lomond

Loch Lomond – the largest stretch of fresh water in Britain – is the epitome of Scottish scenic splendour, thanks in large part to the ballad that fondly recalls its "bonnie, bonnie banks". The easiest way to get to the loch is to take one of the frequent trains from Glasgow Queen St Station to **BALLOCH** at its southwestern tip, from where you can take a cruise around the 33 islands nearby. The **western shore** is very developed, with the upgraded A82 zipping along its banks. The only place to find any peace and quiet now is on the **eastern shore**, large sections of which are only accessible via the footpath which forms part of the West Highland Way. The easiest access to the graceful peak of **Ben Lomond** (3192ft) is from Rowardennan, from which it's a straightforward three-hour hike to the summit; you can reach Rowardennan by ferry from Inverbeg on the western shore.

Opposite Balloch train station there's a **tourist office** (daily: April–Oct 9.30/10am–5/6.30pm; ☎01389/753533); they'll find you a **B&B** – of which there's a plentiful supply – without charge. A couple of miles northwest of Balloch is Scotland's most beautiful **HI hostel**, complete with resident ghost (☎01389/850226; ❷); and there's another alluringly sited HI hostel at Rowardennan (☎01360/870259; ❷). There are **campsites** in all the villages.

Mull and Iona

The **Isle of Mull** is the most accessible of all the Hebridean islands off the west coast of Scotland: just forty minutes by ferry from Oban, which is linked by train to Glasgow. The chief appeal of the island of **Mull** is its remarkably undulating coastline – three hundred miles of it in total. Despite its proximity to the mainland, the slower pace of life is clearly apparent: most roads are single lane, with only a handful of buses linking the main settlements. **CRAIGNURE**, the ferry terminal for boats from Oban (4–6 daily; 40min; £3.65 single), is otherwise little more than a smattering of cottages. It does, however, have the island's main **tourist office** (daily 8.30/10am–5/7pm; ☎01680/812377), a decent pub, bike rental and a campsite.

Two castles lie immediately southeast of Craignure. The first, **Torosay Castle** (Easter to mid-Oct daily 10.30am–5.30pm; £4.50), is a full-blown Scots Baronial creation, set in a magnificent garden (open dawn to dusk) complete with eighteenth-century statues. The mile-and-a-half between Craignure and the castle is covered by the diminutive, narrow-gauge **Mull Rail** (Easter to mid-Oct; £3.50 return). A further two miles' walk along the bay is **Duart Castle** (May to mid-Oct daily 10.30am–6pm; £3.80); stronghold of the MacLean clan from the thirteenth century, it was restored earlier last century – you can peek in the dungeons and ascend to the rooftops.

Mull's "capital", **TOBERMORY**, 22 miles northwest of Craignure, is easily the most attractive fishing port on the west coast of Scotland, its clusters of brightly coloured houses and boats sheltering in a bay backed by a steep bluff. For a list of the local **B&Bs** head for the **tourist office** (April–Oct daily 9/10am–5/6pm; ℡01688/302182), in the Cal-Mac ticket office at the northern end of the harbour. The island's **HI hostel** (℡01688/302481; ❷; closed Nov–Feb) is on Main St, near *Fàilte*, one of the best of the many guest houses (℡01688/302495; ❺; closed Nov–March). Also on Main St is the *Mishnish Hotel* **pub**, popular for the live folk music at the weekends and during the festival.

At the opposite end of Mull, 35 miles west of Craignure, is the **Isle of Iona**. Just three miles long and not much more than a mile wide, Iona has been a place of pilgrimage for several centuries. For it was to this flat Hebridean island that St Columba fled from Ireland in 563 and established a monastery that was responsible for the conversion of more or less all of pagan Scotland. No buildings remain from Columba's time: the present **Abbey** (daily 9.30am–4.30/6.30pm; £2.80), which dominates all views of the island, dates from a re-establishment of monasticism here by the Benedictines in around 1200; it was extensively rebuilt in the fifteenth and sixteenth centuries, and restored wholesale last century. Iona's oldest building, **St Oran's Chapel**, lies south of the abbey, and boasts an eleventh-century door. It stands at the centre of the sacred burial ground, Reilig Odhrain, which is said to contain the graves of sixty kings of Norway, Ireland, France and Scotland, including the two immortalized by Shakespeare – Duncan and Macbeth. In front stand three delicately carved **crosses** from the eighth and ninth centuries, among the masterpieces of European sculpture of the Dark Ages.

Reached in a few minutes by regular ferry from Fionnphort, Iona is a very popular day-trip from Oban in summer. To appreciate its special atmosphere and to have time to see the whole island, it's best to stay the night here. Camping is not permitted on Iona, but there is a **hostel** (℡01681/700642; ❷), a mile or so from the ferry, past the abbey; for **B&B**, try *Sithean House* (℡01681/700331; ❹), a mile from the ferry on the west side of the island; the better of the two **hotels** is the *Argyll* (℡01681/700334; ❺).

A basaltic mass rising direct from the sea, the **Isle of Staffa** is the northern end of Ireland's Giant's Causeway, and is the most romantic and dramatic of Scotland's plethora of uninhabited islands. On one side, its perpendicular rockface has been cut into caverns of cathedral-like dimensions, notably **Fingal's Cave**, whose haunting noises inspired Mendelssohn's *Hebrides Overture*. To get to Staffa, jump aboard the Iolaire (℡01681/700358; £12.50), which sails out of Fionnphort and Iona.

Skye

Jutting out from the mainland, the bare and bony promontories of the **Isle of Skye** fringe a deeply indented coastline. The most popular destination on the island is the **Cuillin ridge**, whose jagged peaks dominate the island during clear weather; equally dramatic in their own way are the rock formations of the Trotternish peninsula in the north. The easiest way to reach Skye is either to catch a **ferry** from the train terminus of Mallaig, or by **bus** (via the controversial Skye Bridge) from the train terminus of Kyle of Lochalsh.

Either way, you'll end up in the southeast corner of the island, where there's a concentration of hostels. From Mallaig, you disembark in **ARMADALE**, where there's an **HI hostel** (☎01471/844260; ❷; closed Oct–mid March) along the shore from the harbour. From Kyle of Lochalsh, you arrive in **KYLEAKIN**, which has an **HI hostel** a few minutes' walk from the dock (☎01599/534585; ❷) with the laid-back *Skye Backpackers* nearby (☎01599/534510; ❷). Both the above places are preferable to **BROADFORD**, a charmless village further inland, which does, how-ever, have a small **tourist office** (April–Oct Mon–Sat 9.30am–5/5.30pm; June–Sept also Sun 10am–2pm; ☎01471/822361).

The best approach to the **Cuillin**, whose sharp snowcapped peaks rise mirage-like from the flatness of the surrounding terrain, is via **ELGOL**, fourteen miles southwest of Broadford at the end of the most dramatic road in Skye. From here there are **boat trips** to Loch Coruisk on the *Bella Jane* (☎0800/731 3089), after which you can walk the eight miles up gentle Glen Sligachan to the welcoming *Sligachan Hotel* (☎01478/650204; ❼) and adjacent **campsite** (closed Nov–March). Serious hikers head for **GLENBRITTLE**, ten miles southwest of Sligachan and north of the Cuillin, where there's an **HI hostel** (☎01478/640278; ❷; closed Oct–Feb) and a **campsite** not far away by the sandy beach (☎01478/640404; closed Nov–March).

The only real town on Skye is the "capital", **PORTREE**, an attractive fishing port in the north of the island. Here you'll find the island's main **tourist office** just off Bridge St (Mon–Sat 9am–5.30/8pm; April–Oct also Sun 10am–4pm; ☎01478/612133). The town has several **hostels**, the smartest of which is the *Portree Independent Hostel* (☎01478/613737; ❷), housed in the Old Post Office on the Green. Of the dozens of **B&Bs**, try *Conusg* (☎01478612426; ❹; closed Oct–Easter), in a quiet spot by the *Cuillin Hills Hotel*. **Food** in Portree can be pricey, but the fish and chips down by the harbour are excellent.

From Portress, head north up the east coast of the **Trotternish** peninsula. Some nine miles from Portree, at the edge of the Storr ridge, is a distinctive 165-foot obelisk known as the **Old Man of Storr**, while a further ten miles north, rising above Staffin Bay, are the **Quiraing** – a spectacular forest of mighty pinnacles and savage rock formations, including the Needle, the Prison and the Table, where the locals used to play shinty. The straggling village of **UIG**, on the west coast, has fer-ries to the islands of the Outer Hebrides, including Harris and North Uist, as well as an **HI hostel** (☎01470/542211; ❷; closed Nov–March), high up above the har-bour, a mile or so from the ferry terminal.

Inverness

Capital of the Highlands, **INVERNESS** is 160 miles north of Edinburgh, the train line between the two traversing the gentle countryside of Perthshire before skirting the stark Cairngorm mountains. Approaching from Skye in the west, there's the magnificent eighty-mile train journey from Kyle of Lochalsh. Inverness **airport** (☎01667/464000) is seven miles east of town.

Inverness has a fine setting astride the River Ness at the head of the Beauly Firth, but despite having been a place of importance for a millennium – it was probably the capital of the Pictish kingdom and the site of Macbeth's castle – there's nothing remarkable to see, nor any particularly strong sense of character. The chief attrac-tions of historical interest lie some six miles east of town, reached by regular buses. **Culloden Moor** was the scene in 1746 of the last pitched battle on British soil, when the troops of "Butcher" Cumberland crushed Bonnie Prince Charlie's Jacobite army in just forty minutes. This ended forever Stuart ambitions of main-taining the monarchy, and marked the beginning of the break-up of the clan system which had ruled Highland society for centuries. A **visitor centre** (daily 9/10am–4/6pm; closed Jan; £4) has displays describing the action. About a mile south of the battlefield are the **Clava Cairns**, a late-Neolithic burial site compris-ing three impressive stone cairns. Six miles further east is **Cawdor Castle**

(May–Oct daily 10am–5.30pm; £5.90), immortalized by Shakespeare in *Macbeth*, set in lovely gardens and parkland. The original fourteenth-century keep has grown towers, turrets and battlements over the years, and approached over its drawbridge it's real fairy-tale stuff.

As well as the only big choice of shops, restaurants and nightlife in the Highlands, you'll find **B&Bs** by the score in Inverness. These tend to fill up in summer, and the **tourist office** on Castle Wynd (June–Aug Mon–Fri 9am–5/8pm, Sat & Sun 9.30am–5pm; rest of year Mon–Fri 9am–5pm, Sat 10am–4pm; ℡01463/234353, ⓦwww.host.co.uk) charges £3 to find a room. The modern **HI hostel** is on Victoria Drive, off Milburn Rd (℡01463/231771; ❸); there are plenty of independent hostels, including the non-smoking *Bazpackers*, at the top of Castle St (℡01463/717663; ❷). Also try the *Eastgate Backpackers*, 98 Eastgate (℡01463/718756; ❸), which has a wide range of facilities including internet access, bike rental and laundry. There are **campsites** at Culloden (closed Nov–Feb), on the road to Loch Ness, and within Inverness at Bught Park, west of the river. Inverness and around is best explored by bike: contact *Barney's*, 35 Castle St (℡01463/232249).

Loch Ness

Loch Ness forms part of the natural fault line known as the Great Glen, which slices across the Highlands between Inverness and Fort William. In the early 1800s, Thomas Telford linked the glen's lochs by means of the **Caledonian Canal**, enabling ships to pass between the North Sea and the Atlantic without having to navigate Scotland's treacherous northern coast. Today, pleasure-craft galore now ply the route, with **cruises** from Inverness (summer only; book at tourist office) providing the most straightforward way of seeing the terrain. Most visitors are eager to catch a glimpse the elusive Loch Ness Monster. Tales of **"Nessie"** date back at least as far as the seventh century, when the monster came out second best in an altercation with St Columba. However, the possibility that a mysterious prehistoric creature might be living in the loch only attracted worldwide attention in the 1930s, when sightings were reported during the construction of the road along its western shore. Numerous appearances have been reported since, but even the most hi-tech surveys of the loch have failed to come up with conclusive evidence. To find out the whole story, take a bus to **DRUMNADROCHIT**, fourteen miles southwest of Inverness, where the most informative displays are at the **Loch Ness 2000 Exhibition** (daily: July & Aug 9am–8pm; shorter hours at other times; £5.95). Most photographs allegedly showing the monster have been taken a couple of miles further south, around the ruined **Castle Urquhart** (daily 9.30am–4.30/8.30pm; £3.80), one of Scotland's most beautifully sited fortresses.

Aberdeen

Set on the eastern coast some 120 miles north of Edinburgh, **ABERDEEN** is the third city of Scotland. Solid and hard-wearing like the distinctive silver-grey granite used for so many of its buildings, it has been nicknamed the "Silver City", although its wealth is built on black gold – North Sea oil.

Until a hundred years ago, Aberdeen was two separate towns a couple of miles apart, based around the mouths of the rivers Dee and Don. While Old Aberdeen slumbered in academic and ecclesiastical tranquillity, the newer town became a major port and commercial centre, and was subject to grandiose planning schemes. The most ambitious of these, in the early nineteenth century, included the layout of spacious **Union St**, a block north of the bus and train stations, which runs for more than a mile east–west across the centre. Despite the grand buildings, Union St today is fairly tawdry, with uninspiring shops and the continual drone of traffic. Best of the sights is down Shiprow, near the eastern end of Union St, where Provost Ross's House is a sixteenth-century mansion now containing the award-winning **Maritime Museum** (Mon–Sat 10am–5pm, Sun noon–3pm; free), which describes

Aberdeen's relationship with the sea through imaginative displays, films and models, including a thirty-foot oil rig. A further short walk downhill is the bustling **harbour** area, seen at its best in the early morning, before the daily fish market winds down at 8am. Across Union St from Shiprow is Broad St, dominated by **Marischal College**, the younger half of Aberdeen University. Its facade, a century-old historicist extravaganza, is probably the most spectacular piece of granite architecture in existence. Nestling in stranded isolation behind the hideous municipal offices opposite is the oldest surviving residential building in the city, **Provost Skene's House** (Mon–Sat 10am–5pm, Sun 1–4pm; free). Highlight of the interior is the sixteenth-century Painted Gallery, whose wooden ceiling is covered with depictions of religious scenes. Past this, on Schoolhill, the city's **Art Gallery** (Mon–Sat 10am–5pm, Sun 1–4pm; free) has an excellent collection, including a clutch of Impressionist paintings and some strong modern British art. Less than a mile east of Union St is the best **beach** to be found in any British city, a great two-mile sweep of clean sand, very popular in summer.

Twenty minutes north of the centre by bus #20, **Old Aberdeen** preserves the atmosphere of a cloistered academic community. Dominating High St is **King's College**, the university's older half. The chapel (Mon–Fri 9am–5pm), founded just a few years after the college at the end of the fifteenth century, boasts an outstanding crown spire; inside is a remarkably complete set of flamboyant late medieval furnishings. Over St Machar Drive lies the **Chanonry**, formerly a walled precinct and still with many fine houses, and, at the end, the former cathedral, **St Machar's** (daily 9am–5pm), Aberdeen's first great granite construction. Its early fifteenth-century facade is a highly original, fortress-like design; equally impressive is the huge sixteenth-century heraldic ceiling covering the nave, which bears the coats of arms of the royal houses of Europe and the bishops and nobles of Scotland. A walk of about a mile through Seaton Park leads to Bridgend of Balgownie, a cluster of restored houses, beyond which is the **Brig o' Balgownie**, a graceful, single-arched, fourteenth-century bridge.

Practicalities

Aberdeen **airport** is seven miles northwest of the city; both **bus** and **train** stations are on Guild St, 200m south of Union St. The **tourist office** (July & Aug Mon–Sat 9.30am–7pm, Sun 10am–4pm; Oct–May Mon–Fri 9.30am–5pm, Sat 10am–2/4pm; ☎01224/88828) is in Provost Ross' House, Shiproy St. It can help with finding B&B; the **HI hostel** is at 8 Queen's Rd (☎01224/646988; ❸); take buses #14, #15, #23 and #27. One of Aberdeen's perennially popular spots for **eating** is the *Ashvale*, 46 Great Western Rd, long rated as one of Britain's best fish-and-chip shops. Cheap meals can also be found at *Café 52*, on The Green near Union St, and at the café at the *Lemon Tree Arts Centre*, 5 West North St. For **drinking**, the *Prince of Wales* on St Nicholas Lane is Aberdeen's most colourful real ale pub. In Old Aberdeen, the *St Machar Bar*, 97 High St, is a popular student hangout.

Travel details

Trains

London to: Aberdeen (6 daily; 7hr 30min); Aberystwyth (change at Birmingham; 14 daily; 5hr); Bath (every 15min; 1hr 20min); Brighton (every 15min; 50mins); Bristol (every 30min; 1hr 45mins); Cambridge (every 15min; 45min); Canterbury (every 30min; 1hr 20min–2hr 10min); Cardiff (hourly; 2hr–2hr 20min); Dover (every 30min; 1hr 45min); Durham (hourly; 2hr 45min); Edinburgh (every 30min; 4hr–4hr 30min); Glasgow (15 daily; 5hr 30min); Liverpool (hourly; 2hr 50min); Manchester (20 daily; 2hr 40min); Newcastle (every 30min; 2hr 50min); Newport (every 30min; 1hr 45min); Oxford (every 20–30min; 1hr); Penzance (8 daily; 5hr 30min–6hr); Stratford-upon-Avon (5 daily; 2hr 15min); Winchester (every 15min; 1hr); York (every 30min; 2hr 15min).

Bristol to: Bath (24 daily; 15min); Cardiff (every 30min; 50min–1hr); Manchester (5 daily; 3hr 30min); Oxford (11 daily; 1hr 20min); Salisbury (hourly; 1hr 10min); York (6 daily; 4hr).
Edinburgh to: Aberdeen (hourly; 2hr 30min); Durham (hourly; 2hr); Glasgow (every 15min; 1hr); Inverness (6 daily; 3hr 30min); Newcastle (every 30min; 1hr 30min); Leuchars for St Andrews (hourly; 1hr 20min); Stirling (every hour; 1hr); York (hourly; 2hr 30min).
Glasgow to: Aberdeen (hourly; 2hr 20min); Inverness (some change at Perth; 8 daily; 4hr); Preston for Liverpool and Manchester (13 daily; 1hr 30min); Newcastle (every 2hr; 2hr 30min); Stirling (every 30min; 30min).
Inverness to: Aberdeen (10 daily; 2hr 15min); Kyle of Lochalsh for Skye (Mon–Sat 3 daily, Sun 1 daily; 2hr 30min); Stirling (some change at Perth; 9 daily; 2hr 30min).
Liverpool to: Cardiff (some change at Crewe; 13 daily; 4hr); Manchester (every 20min; 1hr); Preston for Glasgow and Edinburgh (hourly; 1hr); York (hourly; 2hr 20min).
Manchester to: Newcastle (12 daily; 2hr 50min); York (every 30min; 1hr 40min); Preston for Glasgow (every 20min; 1hr); Windermere (5 daily; 2hr 10min).

Buses

London to: Aberdeen (2 daily; 12hr); Aberystwyth (1 daily; 6hr 45min); Bangor (for Holyhead; 1 daily; 8hr 30min); Bath (13 daily; 2hr 20min); Brighton (hourly; 2hr); Bristol (hourly; 2hr 50min); Cambridge (hourly; 1hr 50min); Canterbury (hourly; 1hr 50min); Cardiff (6 daily; 3hr 10min); Dover (hourly; 2hr 15min–2hr 45min); Durham (5 daily; 5hr 30min); Edinburgh (4 daily; 8hr 30min–9hr 10min); Glasgow (5 daily; 7hr 45min–8hr 50 min); Inverness (2 daily; 12hr 20min–13hr 10min);

Liverpool (5 daily; 4hr 45min); Manchester (7 daily; 4hr 35min); Newcastle (5 daily; 6hr); Newport (6 daily; 2hr 45min); Oxford (every 12min; 1hr 30min–2hr); Penzance (5 daily; 7hr 45min–9hr 15min); Salisbury (2–3 daily; 2hr 45min); Stirling (2 daily; 9hr); Stratford (3 daily; 2hr 45min–3hr 15min); Winchester (9 daily; 2hr); York (3 daily; 4hr 30min).
Bristol to: Bath (every 30min; 50min); Cardiff (hourly; 1hr 10min); Manchester (2 daily; 6hr); Oxford (4 daily; 2hr 30min); Salisbury (1 daily; 3hr); Wells (1 daily; 1hr 20min).
Edinburgh to: Aberdeen (change at Perth or Dundee; hourly; 3hr 20min); Durham (1 daily; 4hr 30min); Glasgow (every 20min; 1hr 10min); Inverness (hourly; 4hr); Kyle of Lochalsh for Skye (1 daily 2hr 15min); Manchester (3 daily; 5hr 30min); Melrose (every 30min; 2hr 15min); Newcastle (3 daily; 3hr); St Andrews (every 30min; 2hr–3hr); Stirling (every 30min; 1hr 50min).
Glasgow to: Aberdeen (hourly; 3hr 30min); Inverness (every 15mins; 4hr 5min); Liverpool (2 daily; 4hr 40min–5hr 15min); Manchester (3 daily; 5hr 30min); Newcastle (every 2hr; 2hr 30min); St Andrews (12 daily; 2hr 20min); Stirling (every 30min; 30min).
Inverness to: Aberdeen (10 daily; 2hr 15min); Stirling (2 daily; 3hr 20min).
Liverpool to: Cardiff (4 daily; 5hr 40min–6hr 40min); Manchester (hourly; 50min); Newcastle (3 daily; 4hr 30min–7hr 30min); Oxford (4 daily; 5hr 30min); Stratford (1 daily; 4hr 35min); Windermere (2 daily; 4hr 30min–5hr 45min); York (2 daily; 3hr 40min–5hr).
Manchester to: Durham (3 daily; 4hr 15min–4hr 45min); Glasgow (2 daily; 4hr 30min–5hr); Leeds (14 daily; 2hr); Newcastle (5 daily; 4hr 50min); Windermere (2 daily; 2hr 45min–4hr); York (3 daily; 3hr 20min).

Bulgaria

Bulgaria highlights

✳ Aleksandâr Nevski Cathedral, Sofia One of the most awe-inspiring buildings in the Balkans. **See p.212**

✳ Rila Monastery Bulgaria's largest and most beautiful monastery, in the mountains south of Sofia. **See p215**

✳ Plovdiv's Old Quarter A wealth of brightly painted National Revival houses, art galleries and Roman remains. **See p.217**

✳ Koprivshtitsa This picturesque village boasts Bulgaria's finest ensemble of National Revival architecture. **See p.219**

✳ Varna Archeological Museum Bulgaria's finest collection of Neolithic and Roman antiquities. **See p.221**

✳ Nesebâr The Black Sea Coast's top resort, boasting several fine medieval churches. **See p.222**

Introduction and basics

If Westerners have an image of **Bulgaria**, it tends to be coloured by the murky intrigues of Balkan politics, with tales of poisoned umbrellas and plots to kill the pope. The nation has come a long way, though, since it threw off the 500-year-old yoke of the Ottoman Empire in the 1870s, and is now struggling to cope with the aftermath of Communist misrule. The Socialists retained power through the early 1990s and moves towards free-market reforms were slow, to say the least. The election of a right-of-centre government in April 1997 brought some measure of stability, while in 2001, the former King, Simeon II, was democratically elected as prime minister; his party has pledged to fight institutional corruption, speed up the privatization process and prepare the country for membership of both the EU and NATO. In the meantime, low wages and high unemployment remain ever-present features of life here; the growing number of beggars on the city streets bear testimony to the economic malaise. Recent war in neighbouring Serbia and unrest in Macedonia have also taken their toll.

Independent travel here is not common, but there are relatively few restrictions, the costs are low, and for the committed there is much to take in. The main attractions are the mountainous scenery and the web of towns and villages with a crafts tradition, where you'll find the wonderfully romantic architecture of the National Revival era. Foremost among these are **Koprivshtitsa** in the Sredna Gora range, **Bansko** in the Pirin mountains and **Plovdiv**, the second largest city. The monasteries can be stunning, too – the finest, **Rila**, is on every tourist's itinerary. For city life, the bustling, if rather faded capital, **Sofia**, and the cosmopolitan coastal resort of **Varna** are the places to aim for.

Information and maps

There is no publicly funded **tourist office** in Bulgaria. Most main towns have agencies, working on commission, who will book accommodation and transport for you, but are off little use for other information. While hotel and travel agency staff in Sofia and the larger towns generally speak some English, knowledge of foreign languages elsewhere in the country is patchy; younger people are more likely to know a few words of English, but German is the preferred second language in the coastal resorts. Wherever you go, street signs, public signs and menus will almost invariably be written in **Cyrillic**.

The best **maps** of Bulgaria and of Sofia are those produced by Datamap, and these are widely available.

Money and banks

The local currency is the **lev** (Lv), which is divided into 100 stotinki (st). Notes come in denominations of 1, 2, 5, 10, 20 and 50 leva, and there are coins of 1, 2, 5, 10, 20 and 50 stotinki. Since it was revalued in 1999, the lev has been stable, although hotels, travel agencies and the like nearly always quote prices in US dollars, and this form has been followed in the text. Nonetheless, you can pay in the local currency, and, occasionally,

---

Bulgaria on the web

ⓦ **www.bulgaria.com** Comprehensive and practical travel information
ⓦ **www.hotelsbulgaria.com** Online hotel-booking facility
ⓦ **www.online.bg** News site
ⓦ **www.travel-bulgaria.com** Practical information on news and politics, as well as travel

in euros, worked out at the current daily exchange rate. Museums and galleries, though, always charge in leva, and foreigners are required to pay substantially more for entry than Bulgarians. Producing a student ID card may get you a discount.

Banks are open Mon–Fri 9am–4pm, while ATMs are a familiar sight in most big towns. Exchange bureaux, offering variable rates, are widespread. Be careful, though, as some may try and give you a lower rate for older banknotes, or may refuse to change them altogether. Also watch out for black market moneychangers who approach unwary foreigners with offers of better rates – if they sound too good to be true, they are. Many smaller banks and offices won't accept **travellers' cheques**, and while Visa and Mastercard are gaining greater acceptance, **credit cards** are generally accepted only at the more expensive shops and hotels.

Be sure to keep a ready supply of coins and 1 lev notes for small purchases, as shops are often unable to change larger denomination notes.

Communications

Post offices (*Poshta*) are open Mon–Sat 8.30am–7.30pm. The main office will have a poste restante, but postal officers tend to return mail to sender if not claimed immediately.

Coin-operated **public phones** rarely work, and it's far better to use one that takes cards. **Phonecards** (*fonkarta*) are available from post offices and some street kiosks and shops. International calls can be made from any public phone. The operator number for domestic calls is ☎121, for international calls ☎0123.

Internet cafés are beginning to appear in the larger towns and cities, but access is still scanty in smaller towns, and connection times can be slow. Costs are variable, but you will rarely pay more than 1.50Lv per hour.

Body language

Bulgarians shake their heads when they mean "yes" and nod when they mean "no". Sometimes they reverse these gestures if they know they're speaking to foreigners,

thereby complicating the issue further. Emphatic use of the words *da* (yes) and *ne* (no) should be enough to avoid misunderstandings.

Getting around

Public transport in Bulgaria is inexpensive, but vehicles and carriages are old and not always very clean. Bear in mind that bus and train journeys are notoriously slow – a product of mountainous terrain and badly maintained routes. Travelling by bus is usually the quickest way of getting between major towns and cities, and there's an ever-growing number of privately run bus companies which ply these routes; these are generally quicker still, and more comfortable, though you'll pay slightly more.

Trains

Bulgarian State Railways (BDZh) can get you to most towns; trains are punctual, if slow, and fares low; it is always worth paying the extra third or so to travel first class (*purva klassa*) – if nothing else, you will have more room. Express services (*Ekspresen*) are restricted to trunk routes, but on all except the humblest branch lines you'll find so-called Rapid (*bârz vlak*) trains. Where possible, use these rather than the snail-like *pât-nicheski* services. Long-distance/overnight trains have reasonably priced couchettes (*kushet*) and/or sleepers (*spalen vagon*). For these, on all expresses and many rapids, you need seat **reservations** (*zapazeni mesta*) as well as **tickets** (*bileti*). To ensure a seat in a non-smoking carriage (*myasto nepooshachi*), you will have to specify this when booking. In large towns, it's usually easier to obtain tickets and reservations from **railway booking offices** (*byuro za bileti*) or **transport service bureaux** (*kompleksni transportni uslugi*) rather than at the station, and wise to book a day in advance. Tickets can only be bought on the day of travel at the station. Advance bookings are required for **international tickets** and are bought through the Rila Agency; branches can be found in all major cities. Most stations have **left-luggage offices** (*garderob*). Both InterRail and Eurail passes are valid in Bulgaria.

Buses

Most places are accessible by **bus** (*avtobus*), though in more remote areas there may only be one or two (unreliable) services a day. Generally, you can buy a ticket at least an hour in advance when travelling between towns, but on some routes they're only sold when the bus arrives. On rural routes, tickets are often sold by the driver rather than at the terminal.

Accommodation

Although foreigners are required to pay five to ten times the rate charged to Bulgarians, **accommodation** in Bulgaria is still very cheap by Western standards. Prices are normally quoted in US dollars, and though you *can* pay in local currency, it may cost you slightly more.

Hotels and private rooms

Most one- and two-star **hotels** (for the most part uninspiring high-rise blocks) rent doubles from around £10/$16 per person, a little more in Sofia and Plovdiv. Cosier family-run hotels are common on the coast and in village resorts such as Koprivshtitsa and Bansko.

Private rooms (*chastni kvartiri*) are available in most large towns, and are usually administered by accommodation agencies, although in the smaller resorts you can usually find a room by asking around – expect to pay around £10–15/$16–24 for a double, more in Sofia and Plovdiv. Single travellers usually get a small reduction on the price of a double. The quality varies enormously, and it's rarely possible to inspect the place first, but as a rule, private rooms in big cities will be in large residential blocks, while those in village resorts can often be in atmospheric, traditional houses.

Hostels and campsites

Hostels (*Turisticheska spalnya*) are thin on the ground, although those that exist (in Sofia or Plovdiv, for example) are well run and accustomed to foreigners.

Some towns of interest have a **campsite** (*Kamping*) on the outskirts, although these are few and far between, and can be unkempt affairs with bad connections to the town centre. The majority have two-person chalets (£5–10/$8–16 per night). **Camping rough** is illegal and punishable with a fine.

Food and drink

Fresh fruit and vegetables have long formed the basis of Bulgarian cuisine, a tradition rarely reflected in restaurants, where menus have become pretty standardized and uninspiring. Grilled meats are the backbone of most restaurant meals, although you'll sometimes find more traditional roasted or stewed dishes.

Food

Sit-down meals are eaten in either a **restorant** (restaurant) or a **mehana** (taverna). There's little difference between the two, save for the fact that a *mehana* is likely to offer folksy decor and a wider range of traditional Bulgarian dishes. Wherever you go, you're unlikely to spend more than 15Lv for a main course, salad and drink.

Foremost among **snacks** are *kebapcheta*, (grilled sausages), or variations such as *shishche* (shish kebab) or *kiofteta* (meatballs). Another favourite is the *banitsa*, a flaky-pastry envelope with a filling – usually cheese; it's sold by street vendors in the morning and evening, to people going to and from work. Elsewhere, *sandvichi* (sandwiches) and *pitsi* (pizzas) dominate the fast-food repertoire. Pork (*svinsko*), veal (*teleshko*), chicken (*pile*) and offal, in various forms, all make a strong appearance on restaurant menus, usually accompanied by potatoes (*kartofi*) and a couple of vegetables, as well as bread.

The most characteristic **traditional Bulgarian dishes** are those baked and served in earthenware pots. The best-known dish is *gyuvech* (which literally means "earthenware dish"), a rich stew comprising peppers, aubergines and beans, to which is added either meat or meat stock. *Kavarma*, a spicy meat stew (either pork or chicken), is prepared in a similar fashion. Fish dishes (*riba*) are most common on the coast.

Vegetarian meals (*yastia bez meso*) are

hard to obtain, although *gyuveche* (a variety of *gyuvech* featuring baked vegetables) and *kachkaval pane* (cheese fried in bread-crumbs) are worth trying, as is *tarator*, a traditional cold summer soup, made with cucumber and yoghurt.

Bulgarians consider their **yoghurt** (*kiselo mlyako*) the world's finest, and hardly miss a day without consuming a glass.

Drink

The quality of Bulgarian **wines** is constantly improving, and the industry now exports worldwide. Among the best reds are the heavy, mellow Melnik, and rich, dark Mavrud. Dimyat is a good, dry white wine, though if you prefer the sweeter variety, try Karlovski Misket (Muscatel) or Tramminer.

Cheap native **spirits** are highly potent, and should be drunk diluted with water in the case of *mastika* (like ouzo in Greece) or downed in one, Balkan-style, in the case of *rakiya* – brandy made from either plums (*slivova*) or grapes (*grozdova*). Bulgarian **beer** is as good as any, and brands such as Kamenitza, Zagorka and Astika are much preferable to pricey imported alternatives.

Coffee (*kafe*) usually comes *espresso* style, though at smarter outlets you will also encounter forms of *kapuchino*. **Tea** (*chai*) is nearly always herbal – ask for *cheren chai* (literally "black tea") if you want the real stuff, normally served with lemon.

Opening hours and public holidays

Big-city **shops and supermarkets** are generally open Mon–Sat 8.30am–6pm or later. In rural areas and small towns, an unofficial siesta may prevail between noon and 3pm. Many shops, offices, banks and museums are closed on the following **public holidays**: Jan 1; March 3; Easter Sun; Easter Mon; May 1; May 24; Sep 6; Dec 25 & 26. Additional public holidays may occasionally be called by the government.

Emergencies

Petty theft is a danger on the coast, and the Bulgarian **police** can be slow in filling out insurance reports unless you're insistent. **Consulates** may be helpful in some respects, but they never lend cash to nationals who've run out or been robbed. Foreign tourists are still a novelty in much of the country, and **women** travelling alone can expect to encounter stares, comments and sometimes worse from macho types, and discos on the coast are pretty much seen as cattle-markets. A firm rebuff should be enough to cope with most situations.

If you need a **doctor** (*lekar*) or dentist (*zâbolekar*), go to the nearest *Poliklinika* (health centre), whose staff might well speak English or German. Emergency treatment is free of charge although you must pay for **medicines** – larger towns will have at least one 24-hour pharmacy.

> ### Emergency Numbers
>
> Police ☏166; Ambulance ☏150; Fire ☏160

Sofia

One of Europe's least known and least glamorous capital cities, **SOFIA**, with its dilapidated old buildings and crumbling roads, can appear an uninspiring place to first-time visitors. However, much has been done in recent years to revitalize the heart of the city, and once you've settled in and begun to explore, you'll find it a surprisingly laid-back place, especially on fine spring days, when its lush public gardens and pavement cafés buzz with life. Urban pursuits can be combined with the outdoor possibilities offered by verdant **Mount Vitosha**, just 12km to the south.

The city was founded by a Thracian tribe some 3000 years ago, and various **Roman ruins** attest to its zenith as the regional Imperial capital of **Serdica** in the fourth century. The Bulgars didn't arrive on the scene until the ninth century, and with the notable exception of the thirteenth-century Boyana Church, their cultural monuments largely disappeared during the Turkish occupation (1381–1878), of which the sole visible legacy is a couple of stately **mosques**. The finest architecture postdates Bulgaria's liberation from the Turks: handsome public buildings and parks, and the magnificent **Aleksandâr Nevski Cathedral**.

Arrival and information

Trains arrive at **Central Station** (*Tsentralna Gara*), a dingy concrete hangar harbouring a couple of exchange bureaux and snack bars, but little else to welcome the visitor. Five minutes' ride along bul Knyaginya Mariya Luiza (tram #1 or #7 or minibus #2) is Sveta Nedelya Square, within walking distance of several hotels and the main accommodation bureaux (see below). Most national **buses** arrive in the various bus parks situated around the *Hotel Princess*, just opposite the train station, although some Bansko services and Blagoevgrad buses (for connections to Rila monastery) use the Ovcha Kupel terminal, 5km southwest of the centre along bul Tsar Boris III (tram #5 from behind the Law Courts). International buses (daily connections with Istanbul, Thessaloniki, Athens and Skopje) arrive either near the *Hotel Princess* or at a small terminal at Damian Gruev 38, ten minutes walk west of the centre. The best way to get into town from **Sofia Airport** is to catch a minibus (#30), which runs every ten to fifteen minutes until around 10pm, and operates like a shared taxi. It will take you to the city centre for 1Lv. Bus #84, running every ten to twenty minutes, takes a more tortuous route and drops you, rather inconveniently, outside Borisova Gradina, at the eastern edge of the city centre; the last bus leaves the airport at around 11.30pm. Taxis might well try to charge you an exorbitant $20, or even more, so be sure to negotiate a reasonable price first ($10).

The nearest you'll get to a **tourist office** is the friendly Odysseia-In, at bul Stamboliiski 20, entrance on ul Lavele (Mon–Fri 9am–6.30pm; ☎02/989-0538, ®www.newtravel.com). The weekly English-language *Sofia Echo*, sold at some newsstands (most reliably the one in Tzum), is a good source for local news and **listings**. Also handy is the *Sofia City Guide*, a glossy monthly publication containing general information, available from some hotel reception desks.

City transport

The **public transport** network – consisting of buses (*avtobus*), trolleybuses (*troleibus*), a one-line metro system, and trams (*tramvai*) – runs between 5am and midnight and is cheap and efficient. There's a **flat fare** of around 40st on all urban routes; tickets (*bileti*) are sold from street kiosks, and, occasionally, on board, and must be punched as you enter the vehicle (inspections are frequent and there are spot fines for fare-dodgers). Kiosks at the main tram stops sell one-day tickets (*karta za edin den*; 2Lv) and five-day tickets (*karta za pet dena*; 9Lv). Metro tickets must be bought from the station; a "combination ticket" (*kombiniran bilet*) costs 50st and is valid for one metro and one bus or tram journey. **Taxis** should charge about 1Lv/km until nightfall, after which rates double. Make sure the driver has his clock

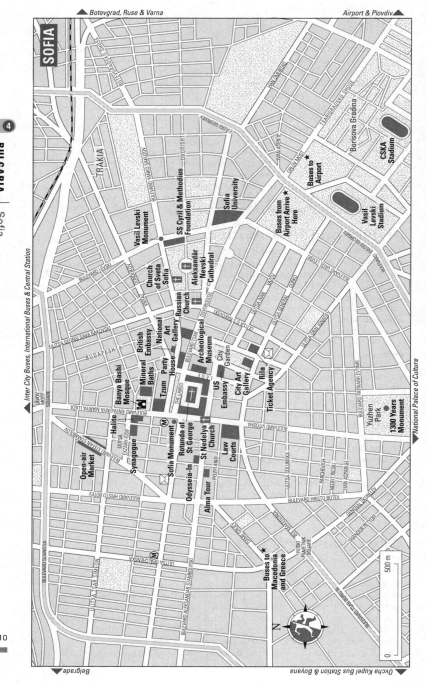

SOFIA

▲ Botevgrad, Ruse & Varna

Airport & Plovdiv ▲

◀ Inter City Buses, International Buses & Central Station

◀ Belgrade

Ovcha Kupel Bus Station & Boyana ▼

National Palace of Culture ▶

TRAKIA

BUDAPESHTA

Open-air Market

Synagogue

Halite

Sofia Monument

Odysseia-In

Alma Tour

Banya Bashi Mosque

Mineral Baths

Tzum

National Art Gallery

British Embassy

Party House

Vasil Levski Monument

Church of Sveta Sofia

Russian Church

Aleksandar Nevski Cathedral

SS Cyril & Methodius Foundation

Sofia University

Buses to Airport

Buses from Airport Arrive Here

Vasil Levski Stadium

CSKA Stadium

Borisova Gradina

Archeological Museum

City Garden

US Embassy

City Art Gallery

Rila Ticket Agency

Rotunda of St George

St Nedelya Church

Law Courts

Yuzhen Park

1300 Years Monument

Buses to Macedonia and Greece

N

0   500 m

210

running, though. Additionally, there's a fleet of private **minibuses** (*marshrutka*), acting like shared taxis and covering around forty different routes across the city for a flat fare of 1Lv. Destinations and routes are displayed on the front of the vehicles – in Cyrillic – and passengers flag them down like normal taxis.

Accommodation

As you might expect, accommodation in the capital tends to be slightly dearer than elsewhere, but there are a number of small, reasonably priced **hotels** in the centre, as well as a few good **hostels**. All fill up quickly, though, especially in summer, and advance bookings are advisable. **Private rooms**, of varying standards, can be booked by agencies such as Alma Tour, at bul Stamboliiski 27b (Mon–Fri 9am–5pm, Sat 9am–4pm; ☎02/987-7233; ❸). Odysseia-In (see p.209) can book rooms in the smaller private hotels both here and throughout the country.

Hostels

Art Hostel Angel Kânchev 21a ☎02/987-0545, ✆www.art-hostel.com. Sofia's trendiest hostel, with two six-bed dorms, hosting monthly art exhibitions, live music and dance and drama performances. Guests have access to a kitchen and tea room, while breakfast and dinner can be provided for a small extra charge. Internet and laundry facilities are also on hand. ❷

Hostel Sofia Pozitano 16 ☎02/989-8582, ✉hostelsofia@usa.net. Despite the grubby external appearance, this very central two-dorm, thirteen-bed hostel, just west of Sveta Nedelya Square, is a clean and well-run establishment, with shared kitchen, bathroom and cable TV. Breakfast included. ❷

Yellow Hostel Ami Bue 50 ☎02/546383, ✉petroff@consultant.com. New hostel, a ten-minute walk south west of the city centre, with two small dorms and extra alfresco sleeping space on the roof terrace in summer. Also provides TV, internet and laundry facilities. ❷

Hotels

Baldzhieva ul Tsar Asen 23 ☎02/981-1257. Small hotel, in a smart town house one block west of bul Vitosha. Rooms are clean and cosy, all with phone, fridge, TV and WC. ❺

Enny Pop Bogomil 46 ☎02/983-1649. Basic but reasonable little hotel – one of the cheapest in central Sofia – just off bul Knyaginya Mariya Luiza, and not far from the train station. Shared facilities. ❷

Ganesha Al von Humboldt 26 ☎02/971-9228. Neat rooms with en-suite shower and satellite TV, in a converted apartment block. Midway between the city centre and the airport. Bus #213 or #313 from the train station, bus #84 or minibus #30 from the airport to the *Hotel Pliska* stop. ❸

Lyulin ul Serdica 8 ☎02/940-2147. Well-located, if somewhat characterless hotel, offering small en-suite rooms in an anonymous apartment block, right behind Tzum. ❹.

Maya Trapezitsa 4 ☎02/894-611. Large, homely rooms, some with great views over Sveta Nedelya Square, in an apartment block just off the Largo. Shared bathrooms. ❹

Niky Neofit Rilski 16 ☎02/511-915. Tiny but comfortable pine-panelled rooms in a small, modern hotel with its own restaurant, in a sidestreet off bul Vitosha. Shared bathrooms. ❸

Tsar Asen ul Tsar Asen 68 ☎02/547-801. Small and basic family-run pension on the same street as the much more expensive *Baldzhieva*. A bargain for this central spot. ❷

The City

At the heart of Sofia is **ploshtad Sveta Nedelya**, a pedestrianized square dominated by the **Sveta Nedelya** church, built after the liberation as the successor to a number of churches that have stood here since medieval times. Running south of the square is **Bulevard Vitosha**, Sofia's main shopping street, which leads to **Yuzhen Park**, where you'll also find the cavernous **National Palace of Culture** (NDK), the city's principal concert and exhibition centre. Heading north from pl. Sveta Nedelya, you'll come to the **Largo**, an elongated plaza flanked on three sides by severe monumental buildings, the most arresting of which is the towering monolith of the former **Party House**, originally the home of the Communist hierarchy, and now serving as government offices.

An underpass gives access from ploshtad Sveta Nedelya to a sunken shop-lined plaza, with the tiny **Church of Sveta Petka Samardzhiiska** (daily 8am–7pm;

5Lv) at its centre. Dating back to the twelfth century, the church contains fragmentary and much-restored frescoes, while national hero Vasil Levski is rumoured to be buried beneath the crypt. The plaza extends westwards to the Serdica metro station, watched over by the **Sofia Monument**, representing the eponymous Goddess of Wisdom – the city's new symbol. On the northern side of the Largo is the Council of Ministers (Bulgaria's cabinet) and Sofia's upmarket shopping mall, **Tzum**.

Just beyond, on **Bulevard Knyaginya Mariya Luiza**, you'll find the **Banya Bashi Mosque**, built in 1576 by Hadzhi Mimar Sonah, who also designed the great mosque at Edirne in Turkey. Behind stand Sofia's **mineral baths**, housed in a yellow and red-striped *fin-de-siècle* building, which, although partially restored in recent years, still remains largely derelict. Locals gather daily to bottle the hot, sulphurous water, which gushes into the long stone troughs outside. Right opposite the mosque is the **Halite**, an elegant building dating from the early 1900s, housing the city's central food hall, with three floors of shops and restaurants.

On the southern flank of the Largo, the *Sheraton Hotel*'s sombre wings run round a courtyard containing Sofia's oldest church, the fourth-century **Rotunda of St George**. It houses frescoes from the eighth century onwards, although most eyes are drawn to the fourteenth-century Christ Pantokrator, surrounded by a frieze of 22 prophets, in the dome. Alongside is the **Presidency**, guarded by soldiers in colourful nineteenth-century garb (Changing of the Guard hourly). Immediately to the east, a fifteenth-century mosque now holds the **Archeological Museum** (Tues–Sun 10.30am–4.30pm; 3Lv), whose prize exhibit is the magnificent gold cauldron and cups of the Thracian Vâlchitrân treasure. Also on show is a collection of Thracian armour, medieval church wall paintings and numerous Roman tombstones.

A little further along is **ploshtad Aleksandâr Battenberg**, named after the German aristocrat chosen to be the newly independent country's first monarch in 1878. The square, surfaced with attractive yellow bricks, was once the scene of Communist rallies and, until its demolition in 1999, was dominated by the mausoleum of Georgi Dimitrov, first leader of the People's Republic of Bulgaria. On the northern side of the square is the dilapidated former **Royal Palace**, though the dreary National Art Gallery and Ethnographic Museum housed here today are of little note; instead, try the **City Art Gallery** (Tues–Sat 10am–6pm, Sun 11am–5pm; free) in the City Garden, immediately to the south, which stages monthly exhibitions of contemporary Bulgarian art.

Follow the yellow brick **Bulevard Tsar Osvoboditel** east, and you'll see the **Russian Church**, a stunning golden-domed confection, with an emerald spire and an exuberant mosaic-tiled exterior, concealing a dark, candle-scented interior. Just beyond is a particularly busy road junction; turn left, up ul Rakovski, where a glint of gold betrays the proximity of the **Aleksandâr Nevski Cathedral**, one of the finest pieces of architecture in the Balkans. Financed by public subscription and built between 1882 and 1924 to honour the 200,000 Russian casualties of the 1877–78 War of Liberation, it's a magnificent structure, bulging with domes and semi-domes and glittering with gold leaf. Within the gloomy interior, a beardless Christ sits enthroned above the altar, and numerous scenes from his life, painted in a humanistic style, adorn the walls. Many other frescoes have peeled and darkened considerably over the years, and the whole building is currently undergoing major restoration. The **crypt**, entered from outside (Mon & Wed–Sun 10am–6pm; 3Lv), contains a superb collection of **icons** from all over the country. Pride of place goes to a fifteenth century double-sided icon from Sozopol, carrying an image of the Virgin on one side and the Crucifixion on the other.

On the northeastern edge of the cathedral square, an imposing gallery houses the **SS Cyril and Methodius Foundation** (Tues–Sun 11am–6.30pm; 2Lv), an international art collection which devotes a lot of space to Indian wood-carvings and second-division French artists, though there are a few sketches by the likes of Millet and Renoir, and a couple of Rodin busts. Heading west across the square, you'll pass two recumbent lions flanking the Tomb of the Unknown Soldier, set beside the wall of the plain, brown-brick **Church of Sveta Sofia**. Originally raised during the sixth-century, it has been much restored since.

The best route from here is to cut down past the **Parliament** building onto pl Narodno Sâbranie, watched over by an equestrian statue of the Russian Tsar, Alexander II, known as the "Liberator" (*Osvoboditel*). From here, it's a brief stroll along bul Tsar Osvoboditel, past **Sofia University**, to **Borisova Gradina**, named after Bulgaria's interwar monarch, Boris III. The largest in Sofia, the park has a rich variety of flowers and trees, outdoor bars, two football stadiums and two huge Communist monuments, still impressive despite the graffiti and rubbish scattered around them.

Mount Vitosha

A wooded granite mass 20km long and 16km wide, **Mount Vitosha** is where Sofians come for picnics and skiing – and the ascent of its highest peak, the 2290m **Cherni Vrâh**, has become a traditional test of stamina. Getting here on public transport is straightforward, although there are fewer buses on weekdays than at weekends.

One approach is to take tram #5 from behind the Law Courts to Ovcha Kupel bus station, then change to bus #61, which climbs through the forests towards **ZLATNI MOSTOVE**, a beauty spot on the western shoulder of Mount Vitosha beside the so-called **Stone River**. Beneath the large boulders running down the mountainside is a rivulet, which once attracted gold-panners. Trails lead up beside the rivulet towards the mountain's upper reaches: Cherni Vrâh is about two to three hours' walk from here.

Another route is on tram #9 or #12 from Graf Ignatiev to the Hladilnika terminus on bul Cherni Vrâh, and then bus #66 to the resort centre of **ALEKO**. Aleko can also be reached by taking bus #64 or #93 from Hladilnika to the suburb of **Dragalevtsi**, where there's a **chairlift** (*lifta*; daily in winter season; rest of year w/ends only); or taking bus #122 from Hladilnika to **Simeonovo**, starting point for the Aleko-bound **gondola** (winter daily; rest of year w/ends only). Aleko is a thriving winter sports centre, with pistes to suit all and a couple of ski schools that also rent out gear; outside the ski season, there are plenty of walking trails to explore (Cherni Vrâh is an easy forty-metre walk from here). The resort is well-served with snack bars and restaurants throughout the year.

Eating, drinking and entertainment

Eating and drinking in Sofia can be remarkably cheap, with new **restaurants** and **bars** opening all the time. Numerous fast-food outlets serve up the usual range of burgers, sandwiches and kebabs, while restaurants offering reasonable, though rather standardized, menus of grilled meats, salads and chips are on the increase in the city centre. In addition, there are now plenty of pricier restaurants, offering a range of international cuisine, from Brazilian to Serbian, but don't expect total authenticity.

The cheapest places to grab a beer or a coffee are the many cafés and kiosks around bul Vitosha or in the city's public gardens, while for night-time entertainment, there's an ever-growing number of **clubs**, most playing a mix of pop and the ubiquitous local "folk pop"(*chalga*). Jazz and Latino music are also popular.

Restaurants

Baalbek Vasil Levski 4. Highly regarded Lebanese establishment, with sit-down restaurant upstairs and fast-food counter (offering kebabs, shawarma and falafel) on the ground floor.

Chen Rakovski 86. Popular Chinese restaurant with authentic food, just opposite the opera house.

The Friends corner of Graf Ignatiev and Rakovski.

Smart self-service restaurant offering a range of Bulgarian specialities. Also has a bar and takeout kebab counter.

Goody's Sveta Nedelya 3. Bright and breezy fast-food place, serving up burgers, sandwiches and salads, with large outdoor seating area.

Happy Bar and Grill Sveta Nedelya 4. Very popular, home-grown fast-food chain, with friendly,

English-speaking waitresses. Tasty though fairly standardized range of dishes, mostly of the salad, grilled meat and chips variety.

Perfect In the sunken plaza beneath Tzum. Bright, modern place, offering reasonably priced Bulgarian and international dishes, including grills, fish, salads and pizzas.

Pizza Troll Vitosha 27. A little cramped and smoky, but it's still one of the better pizza and pasta restaurants in the centre, with vaguely Art Nouveau decor. There's another branch on Graf Ignatiev.

Ramayana Hristo Belchev 32. Pretty authentic Indian restaurant one block east of bul Vitosha, with a range of vegetarian options.

Trops-kâshta Graf Ignatiev 12. Good value buffet-style restaurant offering tasty – if invariably luke-warm – Bulgarian standards. There's another branch in the basement of the Hali, bul Knyaginya Mariya Luiza.

Cafés, bars and discos

Biblioteka Vasil Levski 88. Busy rock and pop-oriented disco, featuring high-profile bands and a karaoke bar, beneath the National Library building. Cover charge.

Club Lavazza Vitosha 13. Very smart place for coffee and cakes, which also offers light meals, and an excellent value English breakfast.

Caramba Tsar Osvoboditel 4. Sofia's premier Latino club, featuring different Latin rhythms nightly.

Chervilo Tsar Osvoboditel 8. Bar and disco with a different style of music every night, and a resident DJ.

Miss Kapriz Angel Kânchev 2. Bright and airy café/bar serving pizzas, coffee and cakes.

Pri Kmeta Parizhka 3. Roomy basement beer hall, serving good food, and with a nightly disco offering a mix of Bulgarian and Latino music.

Quo Vadis Moskovska, near the Levski Monument. Late night beer and dance hall with live music ranging from local folk acts to tango. Open till 4am.

Schveik Vitosha 1A. Basement beer hall just off Vitosha, serving meaty snacks. Live band nightly.

Sturgaloto Rakovski 124. Busy bar and disco, featuring popular local bands on weekends and new talent on week nights. Also serves light snacks.

Swingin' Hall Dragan Tsankov 8. Modern suburban bar serving imported drinks at Western prices. Live music (usually pop/rock or jazz) on two stages. Open well after midnight. Cover charge.

Listings

Embassies and consulates Australia, ul Trakia 37 ☎ 02/946-1334; Canada, Asen Zlatarov 11 ☎ 02/943-3704; UK, Moskovska 9 ☎ 02/933-9222; US, ul Sâborna 1 ☎ 02/937-5100.

Gay Sofia Bulgarian Gay Organization, bul Vasil Levski 3 (☎ 02/987-6872, ⓦ www.bgogemini.org); Spartacus, a gay club, can be found in the underpass below the university (Wed–Sun 11pm–5am).

Internet access Ultima Internet Centre, Lavele 16 (daily 9am–11.30pm); Infocafe, Graf Ignatiev 32 (daily 9am–10.30pm); Cyberzone, Rakovski 149 (daily 9am–10.30pm).

Hospital Pirogov hospital, bul Totleben 21 ☎ 02/51531.

Pharmacies pl Sveta Nedelya 5.

Post office ul General Gurko (daily 7am–9pm).

Southern Bulgaria

Trains heading from Bulgaria to Greece follow the Struma Valley south from Sofia, skirting some of the country's most grandiose mountains on the way. Formerly noted for their bandits and hermits, the Rila and Pirin Mountains contain Bulgaria's highest peaks, swathed in forests and dotted with alpine lakes. If time is short, the place to head for is the most revered of Bulgarian monasteries, **Rila**, lying some 30km east of the main southbound route. **Bansko**, on the eastern side of the Pirin range, is a small detour from the main north–south route, and boasts a wealth of traditional architecture. As well as being one of the country's newest **skiing** resorts, Bansko also makes a good base for **hiking**.

Another much-travelled route heads southeast from Sofia towards Istanbul, through the Plain of Thrace, a fertile region that was the heartland of the ancient Thracians, whose origins date back to the third millennium BC. The main road and rail lines now linking Istanbul and Sofia essentially follow the course of the Roman Serdica–Constantinople road, past towns ruled by the Ottomans for so long that foreigners used to call this "European Turkey". Of these, the most important is **Plovdiv**, Bulgaria's second city, whose old quarter is a wonderful melange of National Revival mansions and classical remains. Some 30km south of Plovdiv is **Bachkovo Monastery**, containing Bulgaria's most vivid frescoes.

Rila Monastery

Home to the best-known of Bulgaria's monasteries, famed for its architecture and mountainous setting, and declared a world heritage monument by UNESCO, **RILA** receives a steady stream of visitors, many of them day-trippers from Sofia (tours from around $30/day). There's also a twice-daily bus service (summer-only), which leaves from Sofia's Ovcha Kupel terminal. Otherwise, public transport is so meagre that you'll have to stay the night: catch a bus or train from Sofia to Blagoevgrad in the Struma Valley, where you can catch local buses to Rila village, 27km short of Rila Monastery. Here, you can change to one of three daily buses to the monastery itself.

The single road to the **Rila Monastery** runs above the foaming River Rilska, fed by springs from the surrounding pine-clad mountains. Even today there's a palpable sense of isolation, and it's easy to see why **Ivan Rilski** chose this valley to escape the savagery of feudal life and the laxity of the established monasteries at the end of the ninth century. The current foundation, 4km from Ivan's original hermitage, was plundered during the eighteenth century and repairs had hardly begun when the whole structure burned down in 1833. Its resurrection was presented as a religious and patriotic duty: public donations poured in throughout the nineteenth century, and the east wing was built as recently as 1961 to display the treasury.

Ringed by mighty walls, the monastery has the outward appearance of a fortress, but this impression is negated by the beauty of the interior, which even the crowds can't mar. Graceful arches above the flagstoned courtyard support tiers of monastic cells, and stairways ascend to wooden balconies. Bold red stripes and black-and-white check patterns enliven the facade, contrasting with the sombre mountains behind and creating a harmony between the cloisters and the **church**. Richly coloured frescoes shelter beneath the church porch and cover much of its interior. The iconostasis is particularly splendid, almost 10m wide and covered by a mass of intricate carvings and gold leaf.

Beside the church is **Hrelyo's Tower**, the sole remaining building from the fourteenth century. Cauldrons, which were once used to prepare food for pilgrims, occupy the soot-encrusted kitchen on the ground floor of the north wing, while on the floors above you can inspect the spartan refectory and panelled guest rooms. Beneath the east wing is the **treasury** (daily 8am–5pm; 2Lv), where, amongst other things, you can view a miniature cross, carved with more than 1500 tiny human figures by the monk Raphael during the 1790s.

Practicalities

It's possible to **stay** in the monastery cells, if you don't mind the lack of hot water and the curfew (summer 8pm; winter 5pm; ➋). Otherwise, try the cheaper *Turisticheska spalnya* (➊) just outside the monastery's eastern gate, the *Hotel Tsarev Vrah* (☎07054/2280; ➍), about 200m further on, or the older *Hotel Rilets* (☎07054/2106; ➌), 2km further east. Near the *Rilets* the primitive *Bor* **campsite** occupies an attractive riverside site. The more comfortable *Camping Zodiac* (☎07054/2291), another 200m east, rents out four-person chalets (➋).

For **snacks**, delicious bread can be obtained at the bakery (which is run by monks), just outside the monastery's east gate. For more substantial meals, the **restaurants** at the hotels *Tsarev Vrah* and *Rilets* are preferable to the outlets near the monastery gates, which sometimes overcharge stray foreigners. **Nightlife** is limited to the bar of the *Rilets*, where there's sometimes a disco.

Bansko and around

Lying some 40km east of the main Struma valley route, **BANSKO** is the main centre for walking and skiing on the eastern slopes of the Pirin mountains. It's a traditional agricultural centre and a growing tourist resort, boasting a wealth of stone-built nineteenth-century farmhouses and a number of small hotels. Though connected to Sofia and other towns by bus (see p.224), Bansko can also be reached by a narrow-gauge railway, which leaves the main Sofia–Plovdiv line at **Septemvri** and forges its way across the highlands. It's one of the most scenic trips in the Balkans, but also one of the slowest, taking five hours to cover just over 100km.

Bansko centres on the modern pedestrianized pl Nikola Vaptsarov, where the **Nikola Vaptsarov Museum** (Mon–Fri 8am–6pm, Sat & Sun 8am–noon & 2–6pm; 2Lv) contains a display relating to the local-born poet and socialist martyr, as well as housing a crafts exhibition where you can purchase distinctive local rugs. Immediately north of here, pl Vâzrazhdane is watched over by the solid stone tower of the **Church of Sveta Troitsa**, whose interior contains exquisite nineteenth-century frescoes and icons. On the opposite side of the square, the **Rilski Convent** contains an **Icon Museum** (Mon–Fri 9am–noon & 2–5pm; 2Lv) devoted to the achievements of Bansko's nineteenth-century icon painters.

The easiest way of getting into the **Pirin mountains** from Bansko is to head west – on foot or by taxi – via a steep fourteen kilometre uphill climb to the Vihren hut; dorm **accommodation** is available here (❷). This is the main trailhead for hikes towards the 2914m summit of **Mt Vihren** (Bulgaria's second-highest peak), or gentler rambles around the meadows and lakes nearby.

Practicalities

There are eight buses a day to Bansko from Sofia, although if you're approaching the area from Rila, it's far easier to head for Blagoevgrad in the Struma valley and change buses there. Bansko's **bus and train stations** are on the northern fringes of town, ten minutes' walk from the central pl Vaptsarov, where you'll find the main **tourist office** (irregular hours, ☎07443/5048). More reliable is the **Pirin Tourist Forum**, Stefan Milenkov 3, Blagoevgrad (Mon–Fri 8.30am–6.30pm; ☎073/81458, ⓦwww.pirin-tourism.bg), which is the best source of information on hiking and accommodation in the region. Best of the family-run **hotels** are: the friendly *Yatse*, in a quiet area ten minutes' walk from the centre at Gotse Delchev 21 (☎07443/ 3538; ❸); *Dzhangal*, close by at Gotse Delchev 24 (☎07443/2661; ❸), featuring a garden, barbecue and sauna; and *Bâlgariya*, fifteen minutes south of the centre at Hristo Matov 2 (☎07443/3006; ❷), with a sauna and solarium on site. For **eating**, there are over forty mehanas offering traditional specialities: *Sirleshtova Kâshta*, *Molerova Mehana* and *Dyado Pene*, all around the main square, are among the most atmospheric.

Plovdiv

Bulgaria's second largest city, **PLOVDIV**, is, in many ways, a more modern and urbane place than Sofia, which locals tend to regard as a provincial backwater. The old town embodies Plovdiv's long history – Thracian fortifications subsumed by Macedonian masonry, overlaid with Roman and Byzantine walls, and by great timber-framed mansions erected during the Bulgarian renaissance, symbolically looking down upon the derelict Ottoman mosques and artisans' dwellings of the lower town. But Plovdiv isn't just another museum town: the city's arts festivals and trade fairs are the biggest in the country, and its restaurants and bars are equal to those of the capital.

Arrival and accommodation

The **train station** is on the southern fringe of the centre, on bul Hristo Botev, and the two **bus stations** are nearby: Rodopi, serving the mountain resorts to the south, is just on the other side of the tracks; while Yug, serving the southeast, is one block east. Private **rooms** (❷) can be booked through Esperansa, Ivan Vazov 14 (daily 11am–5pm; ☎032/260653). Basic **hostel** accommodation is available in the atmospheric *Turisticheski Dom* (☎032/633211; ❷) in the old town at ul Slaveikov 5. **Hotel** prices in Plovdiv tend to be relatively high; two of the cheapest options are the ageing, high-rise *Leipzig*, bul Ruski 70 (☎032/632250; ❸), and the much smaller *Trakia*, just north of the railway station at ul Ivan Vazov 84 (☎032/624101; ❸). Both have their own restaurants. Cheaper – and more comfortable – hotels can be found in the town of **Asenovgrad**, 20km to the south and served by half-hourly buses from the Yug bus station; try *Nic*, a pleasant, modernized town house not far from the centre at ul Zahari Stoianov 6 (☎0331/22777; ❷). The *Gorski Kat* **campsite** (☎032/551360) is located some 4km west of Plovdiv, and can be reached by bus #222 from outside the train station.

The City

Plovdiv centres on the large **ploshtad Tsentralen**, dominated by the monolithic *Hotel Trimontium Princess*. Heading north from here, the pedestrianized bul Knyaz Aleksandâr Battenberg, lined with shops, cafés and bars, leads onto the attractive **ploshtad Dzhumaya**, where stallholders gather to sell a range of touristy knick-knacks, including paintings, jewellery and icons. The ruins of a **Roman Stadium**, visible in a pit beneath the square, are just a fragment of the arena where up to 30,000 spectators watched gladiatorial spectacles. Among the variously styled buildings here, the **Dzhumaya Mosque** (daily), with its diamond-patterned minaret and lead-sheathed domes, steals the show; it's believed that the mosque, sadly now looking a little dilapidated, dates back to the reign of Sultan Murad II (1359–85). From the square, ul Raiko Daskalov continues north to meet bul 6 Septemvri; turning westwards you'll find ploshtad Sâedinenie and two small museums. The **Historical Museum** (Mon–Sat 9am–noon & 1–6pm; 2Lv) holds the usual, patriotic exhibitions, while next door, the **Archeological Museum** (Mon–Fri 9am–12.30pm & 1–5.30pm; 2Lv) has a rather more interesting display of Thracian and Roman artefacts, including a curious plaque depicting a three-headed Thracian Rider.

With its cobbled streets and colourful mansions covering one of Plovdiv's three hills, the **Old Quarter** is a painter's dream and a cartographer's nightmare. As good a route as any is to start from pl Dzhumaya and head east up ul Sâborna. Blackened **fortress walls** dating from Byzantine times can be seen around Sâborna and other streets, sometimes incorporated into the dozens of timber-framed **National Revival** houses that are Plovdiv's speciality. Outside and within, the walls are frequently decorated with niches, floral motifs or false columns, painted in the style known as *alafranga*. Turn right, up steps beside the **Church of Sveta Bogoroditsa**, and continue, along twisting cobbled lanes, to the **Roman Theatre** (daily 9am–5pm; 3Lv), the best preserved in the country, and still an impressive venue for regular concerts and plays. Back on Sâborna, the **State Gallery of Fine Arts** (Mon–Sat 9am–12.30pm & 1–5.30pm; 2Lv) holds an extensive collection of nineteenth- and twentieth-century Bulgarian paintings, including some fine portraits by Stanislav Dospevski. Further along, the **Church of SS Constantine and Elena** contains a fine gilt iconostasis, partly decorated by the prolific nineteenth-century artist Zahari Zograf, whose work also appears in the adjacent **Museum of Icons** (Mon–Sat 9am–12.30pm & 1–5.30pm; 2Lv). A little further uphill is the richly decorated **Kuyumdzhioglu House**, now home to the **Ethnographic Museum** (Tues–Thurs, Sat & Sun 9am–noon & 2–5pm; 3Lv). Folk costumes and crafts are on display on the ground floor, while upstairs, the elegantly furnished rooms reflect the former owner's taste for Viennese and French Baroque. Heading west from the Hisar Gate, a road leads downhill to ul Artin Gidikov, where, at no. 4, the **Hindlian House** (daily 9am–noon/5.15pm; 3Lv), former home of an Armenian merchant, harbours some of Plovdiv's most evocative nineteenth-century interiors.

Eating and drinking

Plovdiv's best **restaurants** are in the old town, many occupying elegant old houses, and serving good, traditional Bulgarian food. The *Apoloniya*, ul Vasil Kânchev 1, *Ulpia*, at ul 4 Yanuari 17, and the excellent *Philipopol*, Konstantin Stoilov 56b, all specialize in authentic Bulgarian fare. In the new town, bul Battenberg is awash with cheaper fast-food outlets, though better quality can be found away from the main drag; *The Red Dragon*, on the corner of bul Ruski and ul Filip Makedonski, is a good Chinese restaurant, serving generous portions, while *Malâk Bunardzhik*, ul Volga 1, at the foot of the Hill of the Liberators, is a very smart but surprisingly cheap restaurant serving excellent Bulgarian cuisine.

Drinking takes place in the pavement cafés of bul Battenberg. *Dreams*, at bul Battenberg 42, is a popular spot for coffee, cocktails and cakes, while *Dzhumayata*, built into the side of the Dzhumaya mosque, serves authentic Turkish coffee and sweets, such as baklava. The *Caligula Club*, bul Battenberg 30, is a good central spot for an alfresco beer, with a late night disco. *Morris*, north of the river at bul Maritsa 122, is a trendy nightclub with regular live music. For **internet** access, try Royal, ul Naiden Gerov 6 (just off bul Battenberg) or Fantasy, bul Battenberg 31.

Bachkovo Monastery

The most attractive destination to the south of Plovdiv is **Bachkovo Monastery** (daily dawn–dusk; free), around 30km away and an easy day-trip from the city (hourly buses from Rodopi station to Smolyan or Zlatograd). Founded in 1038 by two Georgians in the service of the Byzantine Empire, this is Bulgaria's second largest monastery and, like Rila, has been declared a UNESCO World Heritage Site.

A great iron-studded door admits visitors to the cobble-stoned courtyard, surrounded by wooden galleries and adorned with colourful frescoes. Along one wall is a pictorial narrative of the monastery's history, showing Bachkovo roughly as it appears today, and watched over by the Madonna and Child. Beneath the vaulted porch of Bachkovo's principal church, **Sveta Bogoroditsa**, are frescoes depicting the horrors in store for sinners; the entrance itself is more optimistic, overseen as it is by the Holy Trinity. Floral motifs in a naive style decorate the beams of the interior, where you can view a fourteenth-century Georgian icon of the Virgin, though legend claims it to be the original handiwork of St Luke.

The church of **St Nicholas**, originally founded during the nineteenth century, features a fine *Last Judgement* covering the porch exterior, which includes a portrait of the artist, Zahari Zograf. Finally, not far from the main gate is the recently restored **Ossuary**, which dates from the eleventh century and contains a number of early medieval frescoes, but sadly, it's rarely open to visitors.

You can normally **stay** in the monastery (☎03327-277; ❶), although at the time of writing, the guest quarters were closed for major repairs; phone ahead to check availability. There are three **restaurants** just outside – *Vodopada*, with its mini waterfall, is the best.

Travelling on from Plovdiv

There's a nightly **train** to Istanbul, which leaves Plovdiv at 10.05pm; Turkish visas can be bought for £10 (British citizens), US$45 (US and Canadian citizens), or US$20 (Australian and New Zealand citizens) at the Kapikule frontier – have the exact sum ready in cash, as they don't always have change and won't let you in without it. Other nationals should contact the Turkish consulate, at ul Filip Makedonski 10 (☎032/632309), for current visa prices. Several agencies at the Yug bus station sell tickets for **international buses**; *Hebros Bus* (daily 7.30am-7pm, ☎032/626916) is an agent for Eurolines, and books seats on buses to Greece, Turkey and Western Europe.

Northern Bulgaria

Routes from Sofia to the Black Sea coast take you through the mountainous terrain of central and northern Bulgaria – a gruelling eight- or nine-hour ride that's worth interrupting to savour something of the country's heartland. For over a thousand years, Stara Planina – known to foreigners as the **Balkan range** – has been the cradle of the Bulgarian nation. It was here that the Khans established the First Kingdom. Here, too, after a period of Byzantine control, that the Boyars proclaimed the Second Kingdom and created a magnificent capital at **Veliko Târnovo**. Closer by, the **Sredna Gora** (Central Range) was inhabited as early as the fifth millennium BC, but for Bulgarians this forested region is best known as the Land of the April Rising, the nineteenth-century rebellion for which the picturesque town of **Koprivshtitsa** will always be remembered.

Although they lie some way off the main rail lines from Sofia, neither Veliko Târnovo nor Koprivshtitsa is difficult to reach. The former lies just south of Gorna Oryahovitsa, a major rail junction midway between Varna and Sofia, from where you can pick up a local train or bus; the latter is served by a stop on the Sofia–Burgas line, whose four daily trains in each direction are met by local buses to ferry you the 12km to the village itself.

Koprivshtitsa

Seen from a distance, **KOPRIVSHTITSA** looks almost too lovely to be real, its half-timbered houses lying in a valley amid wooded hills. It would be an oasis of rural calm if not for the tourists drawn by the superb architecture and Bulgarians paying homage to a landmark in their nation's history. From the Bridge of the First Shot to the Place of the Scimitar Charge, there's hardly a part of Koprivshtitsa that isn't named for an episode or participant in the **April Rising of 1876**. As neighbouring towns were burned by the Bashibazouks – the irregular troops recruited by the Turks to put the rebels in their place – refugees flooded into Koprivshtitsa, spreading panic. The rebels eventually took to the hills while local traders bribed the Bashibazouks to spare the village – and so Koprivshtitsa survived unscathed, to be admired by subsequent generations as a symbol of heroism.

Buses arrive at a small station south of the main square, from where a street running off to the west leads to the **Oslekov House** (Mon 9.30am–noon & Tues–Sun 9.30am–5.30pm; 2Lv), where pillars of cedar wood support a facade decorated with scenes of Italian cities. Its Summer Guest Room is particularly impressive, with a vast wooden ceiling carved with geometric motifs. Further along, the street joins ul Debelyanov, which straddles a hill between two bridges and boasts some more lovely buildings. Near the Surlya Bridge is the birthplace of the poet **Dimcho Debelyanov** (Tues–Sun 9.30am–5.30pm; 2Lv), who is buried in the grounds of the hilltop **Church of the Holy Virgin**, just to the south. Built in 1817 and partly sunk into the ground to comply with Ottoman restrictions, the church contains icons by nineteenth-century artist Zahari Zograf. A gate at the rear of the churchyard leads to the birthplace of **Todor Kableshkov** (same times and price as the Debelyanov House), leader of the local rebels. Kableshkov's house now displays the insurgents' silk banner embroidered with the Bulgarian Lion and "Liberty or Death!" and weapons used in the Uprising.

Continuing south, cross the **Bridge of the First Shot**, which spans the Byala Reka stream, and head up ul Nikola Belodezhdov, and you'll come to the **Lyutov House** (same times and price as the Debelyanov House), once home to a wealthy yoghurt merchant and today housing some of Koprivshtitsa's most sumptuous interiors, and especially noted for its colourful murals depicting palaces, temples and world cities.

On the opposite side of the River Topolnitsa at the southern end of the village, steps lead up to the birthplace of another major figure in the uprising, **Georgi**

Benkovski (daily, except Tuesday, 9.30am-5.30pm; 2Lv). A tailor by profession, he made the insurgents' banner and uniforms and commanded a rebel band on Mount Eledzhik, which fought its way north until it was wiped out near Teteven. Returning towards the main square along the eastern bank of the river you'll find the birth-place of **Lyuben Karavelov** (same times and price as the Benkovski House), who published émigré newspapers from exile in Bucharest, advocating armed struggle against the Ottomans. His printing press and other oddments are on display.

A **tourist office** (irregular hours; ☎07184/2191,✉ koprivshitza@hotmail.com) on the main square books private **rooms** in charming village houses (❷). The near-by **museum centre** (daily 10am–6pm; ☎07184/2180) is also a good source of information; in addition, it sells combined tickets (5Lv) covering entry to all six museum houses and you can hire an English-speaking guide for an hour long tour (10Lv). The *Byaloto Konche* (☎07184/2250; ❷), across the road from the Oslekov House, has delightful rooms in the National Revival style, while *Zdravets*, near the Lyutov House at ul Nikola Belovezhdov (☎07184/2286; ❷), has neat modern rooms in an attractive wooden house with a large garden. For **eating and drink-ing**, the best places to sample traditional food are the *Dyado Liben Inn*, in a fine nineteenth-century mansion opposite the main square, and *Lomeva Kashta*, a folk-style restaurant just north of the square.

Veliko Târnovo

With its dramatic medieval fortifications and huddles of antique houses teetering over the lovely River Yantra, **VELIKO TÂRNOVO** holds a uniquely important place in the minds of Bulgarians. When the National Assembly met here to draft Bulgaria's first constitution in 1879, it did so in the former capital of the Second Kingdom (1185–1396), whose civilization was snuffed out by the Turks. It was here, too, that the communists chose to proclaim the People's Republic in 1944.

Modern Târnovo centres on **ploshtad Mayka Bâlgariya**: from here bul Nezavisimost (which becomes ul Stefan Stambolov after a few hundred metres) heads northeast into the network of narrow streets, which curve above the River Yantra and mark out the old town, with its photogenic houses. Alleyways climb from Stefan Stambolov to the peaceful old **Varosh Quarter**, where you'll find a couple of nineteenth-century churches.

Continuing along Stefan Stambolov, you'll notice steps leading off downhill to **ul General Gurko**; don't miss the **Sarafina House** at no. 88 (Mon–Fri 8am–noon & 1–5pm; 4Lv), whose elegant restored interior is notable for the splendid octagonal vestibule and a panelled rosette ceiling. Rejoining Stefan Stambolov and continuing downhill, you'll find the blue-and-white building where the first Bulgarian parlia-ment assembled in 1879. It's now home to the **Museum of the National Revival and the Constituent Assembly** (Mon & Wed–Sun 8am–noon & 1–6pm; 4Lv), where you can see a reconstruction of the original assembly hall, and a collection of icons.

From here, Ivan Vazov leads directly to the medieval fortress, **Tsarevets** (daily 8am–7pm; 4Lv). The boyars Petâr and Asen led a successful rebellion against Byzantium from this citadel in 1185, and Tsarevets remained the centre of Bulgarian power until 1393, when, after a three-month siege, it fell to the Turks. The partially restored fortress is entered via the **Asenova Gate** halfway along the western ramparts. To the right, paths lead round to **Baldwin's Tower**, where Baldwin of Flanders, the so-called Latin Emperor of Byzantium, was incarcerated by Tsar Kaloyan. Above lie the ruins of the royal palace and a reconstruction of the thirteenth-century **Church of the Blessed Saviour**.

All **trains** between Sofia and Varna stop at Gorna Oryahovitsa, from where local trains (6 daily) cover the remaining 12km to Veliko Târnovo **train station**, which stands 2km south of the city centre – buses #4 and #13 run to pl Mayka Bâlgariya. The *Comfort* **hotel**, in the Varosh quarter at ul Paneyot Tipografov 5 (☎062/28728;

❸), is a basic, family-run pension, with splendid views of the Tsarevets. Nearby, at ul Yanaki Donchev 22, is the *Deyan* (☎062/30532; ❸), a small, simple place with shared bathrooms. The *Bolyarski Stan* **camping site** can be found on the western outskirts of the town, and is served by bus #110. The best **restaurants** are the traditional *Mehanas* just off Stefan Stambolov – follow signs pointing down the steps to find *Mehana Belite Brezi*. Nearby, the *Mehana Mecha Dupka* serves authentic Bulgarian fare in a cellar below ul Rakovski, with nightly music and dancing. For **drinking**, there are numerous cafés and bars around town; *Yasna*, on pl Slaveykov, is a good spot for coffee or cocktails. **Internet** access is available at Prolink, ul Dondukov 17.

The coast

The Black Sea resorts have been popular holiday haunts for more than a century, though it wasn't until the 1960s that the coastline was developed for mass tourism, with Communist party officials from across the former Eastern Bloc descending on the beaches each year for a spot of socialist fun in the sun. Since then, the **resorts** have mushroomed, growing increasingly sophisticated as the prototype mega-complexes have been followed by holiday villages. With fine weather practically guaranteed, the selling of the coast has been a success in economic terms, but with the exception of ancient **Sozopol** and touristy **Nesebâr**, there's little to please the eye. Of the coast's two cities – **Varna** and Burgas – the former is by far preferable as a base for getting to the less-developed spots.

Varna

VARNA'S origins date back almost five millennia, but it wasn't until seafaring Greeks founded a colony here in 585 BC that the town became a port. The modern city is a port for both commercial freighters and the navy, as well as being a popular tourist resort in its own right. It's a cosmopolitan place and a nice one to stroll through: Baroque, nineteenth century and contemporary architecture pleasantly blended with shady promenades and a handsome seaside garden.

Social life revolves around **ploshtad Nezavisimost**, where the opera house and theatre provide a backdrop for a gathering of restaurants and cafés. The square is the starting point of Varna's evening promenade, which flows eastward from here along bul Knyaz Boris I and towards bul Slivnitsa and the seaside gardens. Beyond the opera house, Varna's main lateral boulevard cuts through pl Mitropolit Simeon to the domed **Cathedral of the Assumption**. Constructed in 1886 along the lines of St Petersburg's cathedral, it contains a splendid iconostasis and bishop's throne, with armrests carved in the form of magnificent winged panthers.

The **Archeology Museum** on the corner of Mariya Luiza and Slivnitsa (Tues–Sat 10am–5pm; 2Lv) houses one of Bulgaria's finest collections of antiquities. Most impressive are the skeletons and gold jewellery, some dating back almost 6000 years, recovered from a Neolithic necropolis on the outskirts of town. Upstairs the array of Greek and Roman artefacts includes an extensive display of funerary sculpture, and there's also a gallery of icons.

South of the centre, on ul Han Krum, are the extensive remains of the third-century **Roman baths** (Mon–Fri 9am–5pm & Sat 10am–5pm; 3Lv), which played such a central role in the social life of the city. It's still possible to discern the various bathing areas and the once huge exercise hall. Ten minutes west of here on ul Panagyurishte is the **Ethnographic Museum** (Tues–Sun 10am–5pm; 2Lv), where you can see displays illustrating traditional local crafts, folk costumes and reconstructions of nineteenth century interiors. At the southern edge of the Sea Gardens, the **Navy Museum** (daily 10am–5pm; 2Lv) houses a musty collection of naval relics, with some rusting armaments, including a helicopter, in the gardens.

Meanwhile, the boat responsible for the Bulgarian Navy's only victory - the *Drazki* - is embedded on the waterfront outside; it sank the Turkish cruiser *Hamidie* off Cape Kaliakra in 1912.

Practicalities

Each of the main points of arrival has good bus connections with the centre. The **bus terminal** (bus #1, #22 or #41) is a ten minute journey northwest of the centre on bul Vladislav Varnenchik; Varna **airport** is about a 50 minute ride (#409) in the same direction; the **train station** is ten minutes' walk south of the centre along ul Tsar Simeon.

Private rooms in central Varna (❷) can be obtained from the Isak accommodation bureau, inside the train station (daily 7am–10.30pm), or from CM92 George, across the road at Tsar Simeon 36b (daily 7am–7pm; ☎052/630776), which is also a good source for maps and general information. Best of the cheap **hotels** are the slightly decrepit *Voennomorski Klub*, opposite the cathedral at bul Varnenchik 2 (☎052/238312; ❷), and the rather more modern *Trite Delfina*, near the train station at ul Gabrovo 27 (☎052/600911; ❸). Closer to the beach, at ul Slivnitsa 33, is the high-rise *Cherno More* (☎052/232110; ❸), reasonably priced, though past its prime.

Varna has no shortage of **eating and drinking** venues: for authentic Bulgarian standards, try *Arkitekt*, a traditionally furnished wooden town house with a pleasant courtyard garden at ul Musala 10; while for pizzas and other light meals, *The Red Fox Pub* at M Koloni 4, is a good bet; as you might expect, given the name, it also has an English-style bar. There are plenty of other **bars** to choose from along bul Knyaz Boris I, while in summer, the **beach**, reached by steps from the seaside gardens, is lined with open-air bars and fish restaurants, such as *Tonga* and *Zhatra*, and a seemingly unending strip of **nightclubs**. Outside high season, though, it's pretty dismal. For **internet access**, try Doom, ul 27 July 13 (daily 9am–11pm), or Cyber X, Knyaz Boris I 53 (daily 9.30am–10pm).

The southern coast

The south coast's prime urban centre and transport hub, **BURGAS** can be reached by train from Sofia and Plovdiv, or by bus from Varna, and provides easy access to the museum town of Nesebâr to the north or Sozopol to the south. Burgas's train and bus stations are both located at the southern edge of town, near the port. Bypassed by most tourists, the pedestrianized city centre, lined with smart boutiques, bars and cafés, is pleasant enough, though its best feature is the Sea Gardens, overlooking the beach at the eastern end of town. More attractive and better cared for than Varna's, they are laid out with pristine flowerbeds, statues and a wide variety of plant life. If you need to stay, contact Dimant, ul Tsar Simeon 15 (daily 8am–8pm; ☎056/840779), which can book **private rooms** (❶). The city's few **hotels** are pricey; most central is the towering *Bulgaria* (☎056/842820; ❹) just north of the train station at ul Alexandrovska 21.

Nesebâr

Founded by Greek colonists from Megara, **NESEBÂR** – 35km northeast of Burgas and served by buses every 45 minutes – grew into a thriving port during the Byzantine era, and ownership alternated between Bulgaria and Byzantium until the Ottomans captured it in 1453. The town remained an important centre of Greek culture and the seat of a bishop under Turkish rule, which left Nesebâr's **Byzantine churches** reasonably intact. Nowadays the town depends on them for its tourist appeal, demonstrated by the often overwhelming stream of summer visitors crossing the man-made isthmus that connects the old town with the mainland. Outside the hectic summer season, the place seems eerily deserted, with little open other than a few sleepy cafés.

Buses arrive at the harbour at the western end of town, above which stands the

Archeological Museum (summer only: Mon–Fri 9am–7pm, Sat & Sun 9am–1.30pm & 2–7pm; 3Lv). There's an array of Greek tombstones and medieval icons on display, though one of the more intriguing artefacts is a small Hellenistic statue showing a triple image of Hecate, goddess of witches. Immediately beyond the museum is **Christ Pantokrator**, the first of Nesebâr's churches. Dating from the fourteenth-century, its ceramic inlays and red brick motifs are characteristic of late Byzantine architecture, and it features an unusual frieze of swastikas – an ancient symbol of the sun and continual change. It's currently in use as an art shop. Downhill on ul Mitropolitska is the eleventh century church of **St John the Baptist** (now an art gallery), only one of whose frescoes – a seventeenth century depiction St Marina – still survives.

Overhung by half-timbered houses, ul Aheloi branches off from ul Mitropolitska towards the **Church of Sveti Spas** (summer only: Mon–Fri 10am–1.30pm & 2–5.30pm, Sat & Sun 10am–1.30pm; 2Lv), outwardly unremarkable but filled with seventeenth-century frescoes. Diagonally opposite are the now ruined **Church of the Archangels Michael and Gabriel**, and the **Church of Sveta Paraskeva**, patterned with green ceramic inlays. A few steps to the east lies the ruined **Old Metropolitan Church**, dominating a plaza filled with pavement cafés, street traders and hawkers. The church itself dates back to the sixth century, and it was here that bishops officiated during the city's heyday. South of the town's main street, down ul Ribarska, lies the **New Metropolitan Church** (*Sveti Stefan*; daily 9am–1pm & 2–6pm; 2Lv), whose interior fresco of the Forty Martyrs, on the west wall, gives pride of place to the patron who financed the church's enlargement during the fifteenth century. Downhill from here is the ruined **Church of St John Aliturgetos**, standing in splendid isolation beside the shore and representing the zenith of Byzantine architecture in Bulgaria. Its exterior employs limestone, red bricks, crosses, mussel shells and ceramic plaques for decoration.

Accommodation can be hard to come by during the busy summer season, and advance bookings are advisable. **Private rooms** (**2**), many in fine old houses, can be booked through Stoyanovi-94, signposted down an alley off ul Mesembriya (irregular hours, ☎0554/45880). The *Hotel Rai*, at ul Sadala 7 (☎0554/46094; **3**), is a small and comfortable family-run place on the northern side of the peninsula, while the nearby, unnamed, pension at ul Kraybrezhna 20 (☎0554/42329; **2**) is one of the cheapest places in town. There are plenty of places to **eat**, although most restaurants are aimed at the passing tourist crowd, serving predictably mediocre food. Two of the better restaurants are the *Kapetanska Sreshta*, overlooking the harbour, and the sea-facing *Neptun*, towards the far end of town. Snacks are available from summertime kiosks along the waterfront.

Sozopol

SOZOPOL, the oldest settlement on the coast, was founded in the seventh century BC by Greek colonists from Miletus, who called the town Apollonia and prospered by trading textiles and wine for honey and corn. Today it's a busy fishing port and holiday resort, especially popular with East European tourists. The **Archeological Museum** (Mon–Fri 9am–5pm, Sat & Sun 10am–2pm; 2Lv), hidden behind the library, holds an extensive collection of amphorae and barnacle-encrusted stone anchors, dredged from the surrounding waters, as well as a display of exquisitely decorated Greek vases. There's little else in the way of specific sights, though Sozopol's charm owes much to its old wooden houses. With space at a premium, their upper storeys project so far out that houses on opposite sides of the narrow, cobbled streets almost meet.

The hourly **buses** from Burgas arrive at the southern edge of the old town. **Accommodation** can be even harder to find during summer than in Nesebâr; some places may insist on minimum stays of up to a week. The Lotos bureau at ul Musala 7 (irregular hours, ☎05514/2282) can arrange rooms (**2**). **Hotels** can all be found in the new part of town; *Alfa-Beta*, ul Republikanska 9 (☎05514/3614; ❸), is a small pension with a pleasant breakfast garden, while uphill from here at ul Vihren 28 is the modern *Orion* (☎05514/3193; ❸), whose en-suite rooms have TV and balconies. The *Poseidon*, ul Apoloniya 7, and the *Vyatarna Melnitsa*, ul Morski Skali 27, are a couple of good, if touristy **restaurants**.

Travel details

Trains

Sofia to: Blagoevgrad (5 daily; 2hr 30min–3hr 30min); Burgas (4 daily; 6–8hr); Gorna Oryahovitsa (6 daily; 4hr 30min); Koprivshtitsa (6 daily; 1hr 40min–2hr 20min); Plovdiv (12 daily; 2hr–3hr 30min); Varna (5 daily; 8–9hr).
Gorna Oryahovitsa to: Veliko Târnovo (6 daily; 20-30min).
Plovdiv to: Burgas (4 daily; 5hr); Sofia (13 daily; 2hr–3hr 30min); Varna (3 daily; 5 hr).

Buses

Sofia to: Bansko (8 daily; 3hr); Burgas (8 daily; 7hr); Koprivshtitsa (1 daily; 2hr); Plovdiv (hourly; 2hr); Rila monastery (2 daily in summer; 3hr); Varna (5 daily; 7hr); Veliko Târnovo (8 daily; 4hr).
Blagoevgrad to: Bansko (8 daily; 1hr); Rila village (4 daily; 40min).
Burgas to: Nesebâr (every 45min; 50min); Sozopol (hourly; 40min); Varna (4 daily; 3hr).
Gorna Oryahovitsa to: Veliko Târnovo (every 30min; 30min).
Plovdiv to: Asenovgrad (every 30min; 30min); Bachkovo (hourly; 40min); Sofia (hourly; 2hr).
Rila village to: Rila monastery (3 daily; 30min).

5

Croatia

Croatia highlights

✳ **Amphitheatre, Pula** This magnificent arena is the sixth largest in the world. **See p.236**

✳ **Windsurfing, Bol** The Adriatic's most attractive beaches also provide the best windsurfing opportunities. **See p.241**

✳ **Diocletian's Palace, Split** This extraordinary 1,700 year old palace houses shops, restaurants and bars, as well as some fascinating remains. **See p.239**

✳ **Vis Island** One of the coast's lushest and most peaceful islands. **See p.243**

✳ **City Walls, Dubrovnik** Sensational views of the Old Town and the Adriatic from the 25m high city walls. **See p.246**

✳ **Dubrovnik Summer Festival** Classical concerts and theatre at Croatia's most prestigious festival. **See p.248**

Introduction and basics

Croatia (Hrvatska) has come a long way since the summer of 1991, when foreign tourists fled from a region standing on the verge of war. Now that stability has returned, visitors are steadily coming back to a country which boasts one of the most outstanding stretches of coastline that Europe has to offer. Croatia was an independent kingdom in the tenth century, but fell under the rule of Hungary in the eleventh and was subsequently absorbed by the Austro-Hungarian Empire before becoming part of the new state of Yugoslavia in 1918. Croatian aspirations were frustrated by a Yugoslav state which was initially dominated by Serbs, and then (after 1945) ruled by Communists. Croatia's declaration of independence on June 25, 1991 was fiercely contested by a Serb-dominated Yugoslav army eager to preserve their control over areas in which groups of ethnic Serbs lived. The period of war – and fragile, UN-supervised ceasefire that followed – was finally brought to a close by Croatian offensives during the summer of 1995.

Croatia's capital, **Zagreb**, is a typical central-European metropolis, combining elegant nineteenth-century architecture with plenty of cultural diversions and a vibrant café scene. At the northern end of the Adriatic coast, the peninsula of **Istria** contains many of the country's most developed resorts, with old Venetian towns such as **Poreč** and **Rovinj** rubbing shoulders with the raffish port of **Pula**. Further south lies **Dalmatia**, a dramatic, mountain-fringed stretch of coastline studded with islands. Dalmatia's main town is **Split**, an ancient Roman settlement and modern port which provides a jumping-off point to the enchanting islands of **Brač**, **Hvar**, **Vis** and **Korčula**, on which you'll find lively fishing villages and the best of the beaches. South of Split lies the medieval walled city of **Dubrovnik**, site of an important festival in the summer and a magical place to be whatever the season.

Information and maps

Most towns of any size have a **tourist office** (*turistički ured*) run by the local authority, which will happily give out brochures and local maps; English is widely spoken in these places. Few offices book private rooms, but they will at least direct you to an agency that does. Freytag & Berndt produce a good 1:600,000 **map** of Croatia, Slovenia and Bosnia-Hercegovina, as well as 1:100,000 regional maps of Istria and the Dalmatian coast.

Money and banks

The local currency is the **kuna** (kn), which is divided into 100 lipa. Coins come in denominations of 1, 2, 5, 10, 20 and 50 lipa, and 1, 2, and 5 kuna; and there are notes of 5, 10, 20, 50, 100, 200, 500 and 1000 kuna. Accommodation and ferry prices are often quoted in euros, but you still pay in kuna.

Croatia on the net

ⓦ **www.croatia.hr** Croatia's tourist board site
ⓦ **www.zagreb-touristinfo.hr** Zagreb's main website
ⓦ **www.istra.com** One of the better regional sites
ⓦ **www.dalmacija.net** Comprehensive coverage of the Dalmatian islands and online accommodation booking service
ⓦ **www.dubrovnik.online.com** Excellent city site, including message board

Banks (*banka*) are open Mon–Fri 7.30am–7/8pm (sometimes with a break for lunch), Sat 7.30am–1pm. Money can also be changed in post offices, travel agencies and exchange bureaux (*mjenjačnica*), which have more flexible hours. **Credit cards** are accepted in a large number of hotels and restaurants, and you can use them to get cash from ATMs and the bigger banks.

Communications

Post offices (*pošta* or HPT) are open Mon–Fri 7/8am–8pm, Sat 8am–1pm. In big towns and resorts, some are open daily and until 10pm. Stamps (*marke*) can also be bought at newsstands.

Public phones use magnetic cards (*telekarta*), which come in denominations of 13kn, 24kn, 38kn and 67kn; you can buy these from post offices or newspaper kiosks. When making long-distance and international calls, it's usually easier to go to the post office, where you're assigned a cabin and given the bill afterwards.

Internet access is readily available in the capital and most towns and cities; expect to pay around 20kn per hour.

Getting around

Trains are of limited value in a country with such a small rail network, although they do connect Zagreb with the coastal towns of Rijeka and Split. Elsewhere, Croatia is well served by an extensive and reliable **bus network.** **Ferries** offer a leisurely way of getting up and down the coast, and provide the only transport to Croatia's many Adriatic islands.

Trains and buses

Croatian railways (Hrvatske željeznice; ⊛www.hznet.hr) run a smooth and efficient service. **Trains** (*vlak*, plural *vlakovi*) are divided into *putnički* (slow ones which stop at every halt) and *IC* (intercity trains which are faster and more expensive). There's an overnight service from Zagreb to Split, for which places in couchettes (*kušet*) and sleeping cars (*spalnica*) are best booked in

advance. Timetables (*vozni red*) are usually displayed on boards in stations – *odlazak* means departure, *dolazak* arrival.

Croatia's **bus network** is run by a confusing array of small local companies, but services are well integrated and bus stations tend to be well-organized affairs with clearly listed departure times and efficient booking facilities. If you're at a big city bus station, tickets (*karta*) must be obtained from ticket windows before boarding the bus. Elsewhere, they can be bought from the driver. You'll be charged around 5kn for items of baggage to be stored in the hold.

Ferries

Jadrolinija (⊛www.jadrolinija.hr) operate **ferry services** down the coast on the Rijeka–Zadar–Split–Korčula–Dubrovnik route at least once a day in both directions between June and August, and two or three times weekly for the rest of the year. Rijeka to Dubrovnik is a 22-hour journey, involving one night on the boat. In addition, ferries link Split with the islands of Brač, Hvar, Vis and Korčula. Ferries are also a good way of moving on from Croatia, with connections to Italy (Split and Zadar to Ancona, Pula and Brioni to Trieste and Dubrovnik to Bari) and Greece (Dubrovnik to Igoumenitsa).

Prices (often quoted in dollars or euros, but payable in kuna) are reasonable for short trips: Split to Hvar costs around $4. For longer journeys, prices vary greatly according to the level of comfort you require. The cheapest Rijeka–Dubrovnik fare, in high season, is $29), while you'll pay double that for a couchette-style bunk bed, and three times more for a bed in a well-appointed cabin (breakfast included); bicycles travel free of charge. Book in advance for longer journeys wherever possible; addresses and phone numbers are provided in the text where relevant.

Accommodation

Private rooms have long been the mainstay of Croatian tourism, especially on the coast, and represent an inexpensive way of finding a bed for the night. There are well-appointed campsites all along the Adriatic coast, although Croatian **hotels** tend to be bland and overpriced.

Hotels and private rooms

Croatian **hotels** are generally modern multi-storey affairs providing modern comforts but little atmosphere. Although the international five-star grading system is being introduced, most Croatian hotels are still classified by letter: generally speaking, C-class (one-star) hotels have rooms with shared WC and bathroom; B-class (two- to three-star) have rooms with en-suite facilities; A-class (four-star) is business class; and L-class (five-star) are in the international luxury bracket. A double room in a C-class establishment will cost around £30/$45, although these tend to be in very short supply, and in most places you'll be dependent on B-class hotels, where you should expect to pay £40/$60 a double.

Private rooms (*privatne sobe*) are available just about everywhere in Croatia. Bookings are made through the local tourist office or private travel agencies. Agencies are usually open daily 8am–8/9pm in summer, although they may take a long break on Sunday afternoons. Prices are around £8/$12 per person for a simple double sharing a WC and bathroom, £10/$14 for a double with en-suite facilities; stays of less than three nights are often subject to a surcharge of thirty percent or over. Places fill up quickly in July and August, when it's a good idea to arrive early or book ahead. Single travellers will sometimes find it difficult to get a room at all at this time, unless they're prepared to pay the price of a double; at other times, you could expect to get a thirty percent discount on the room rate. It is very likely that you will be offered rooms by elderly ladies waiting outside train, bus and ferry stations, particularly in Southern Dalmatia. Whilst they can be alarmingly persistent, don't be afraid to take a room offered in this manner, but be sure to establish the location of the room and agree a price before setting off – and if anything makes you feel uncomfortable about the situation, don't go. If taking a room this way expect to pay around twenty percent less than you would with an agency.

However you find a room, you can usually examine it before committing to paying for it.

Hostels and campsites

HI hostels are thin on the ground, although those that exist – mostly in the big cities – are generally clean and well run. You can get details, and make reservations, from Hrvatski Ferijalni i Hostelski Savez, Dežmanova 9, Zagreb (℡01/48-47-474, ✉hfhs-cms@zg.hinet.hr). In addition, **student rooms** are often let out cheap to travellers during the summer vacation (usually mid-July to Aug). For both, expect to pay £8–10/$12–$14 for a bed.

Campsites (most open May–Sept) abound on the Adriatic coast, and tend to be large-scale, well-appointed affairs with plentiful facilities, restaurants and shops.. Two people travelling with a tent can expect to pay roughly £8/$12 each.

Food and drink

There's a varied and distinctive range of cuisine on offer in Croatia, largely because the country straddles two culinary cultures: the fish-and-seafood-dominated cuisine of the Mediterranean, and the hearty meat-oriented fare of central Europe.

Food

Basic **self-catering** and picnic ingredients such as cheese (*sir*), vegetables (*povrće*) and fruit (*voće*) can be bought at a supermarket (*samoposluga*) or open-air market (*tržnica*). Bread (*kruh*) is bought from either a supermarket or a *pekara* (bakery). For breakfasts and fast food, look out for street stalls or snack-food outlets selling *burek*, a flaky pastry filled with cheese; or grilled meats such as *ćevapčići* (rissoles of minced beef, pork or lamb), and *pljeskavica* (a hamburger-like mixture of the same meats).

For a more relaxed, sit-down meal, a **restaurant** menu (*jelovnik*) will usually include Croatian speciality starters such as *pršut* (home-cured ham) and *paški sir* (piquant hard cheese), as well as a range of soups (*juha*). Typical main courses include *punjene paprike* (peppers stuffed with rice and meat), *gulaš* (goulasch) or some kind of *odrezak* (fillet of meat, often pan-fried), usually either *svinjski* (pork) or *teleški* (veal). *Mješano meso* is a mixed grill. Lamb, often roasted, is *jagnjetina*. Traditional dishes from the area around Zagreb include *purica z mlincima* (turkey with pasta noodles) and *štrukli* (ravioli-like blobs of pasta dough with a cheese filling). One typically Dalmatian dish is *pašticada* (beef and bacon cooked in vinegar and wine). On the coast, you'll be regaled with every kind of seafood. *Riba* (fish) can come either *na žaru* (grilled) or *u pečnici* (baked). *Brodet* is a hot peppery fish stew. Otherwise, the main menu items to look out for on the coast are *lignje* (squid), *škampi* (unpeeled prawns eaten with the fingers), *rakovica* (crab), *oštrige* (oysters), *kalamari* (squid), *školjke* (mussels) and *jastog* (lobster); *crni rižoto* is risotto with squid. No Croatian town is without at least one pizzeria, often the cheapest place to eat and the easiest, if not the most imaginative, source of a **vegetarian** meal.

Typical **desserts** include *palačinke* (pancakes), *voćna salata* (fruit salad) and *sladoled* (ice cream).

Drink

Daytime drinking takes place in a *kavana* (café) or a *slastičarnica* (patisserie). **Coffee** (*kava*) is usually served black unless specified otherwise – ask for *mlijeko* (milk) or *šlag* (cream). Tea (*čaj*) is widely available, but is drunk without milk.

Night-time drinking takes place in a growing number of small *kafići* or café/bars. Croatian **beer** (*pivo*) is of the light lager variety; Karlovačko and Ožujsko are two good local brands to look out for. The local wine (*vino*) is consistently good and reasonably cheap. In Dalmatia there are some pleasant whites, crisp dry wines such as Kastelet, Grk

and Pošip, as well as reds such as the dark heady Dingač and Babić. In Istria, Semion is a bone-dry white, and Teran a light fresh red. Local spirits include *loza*, a clear grape-based spirit; *travarica*, herbal brandy; *vinjak*, locally produced cognac, and *Maraskino*, a cherry liqueur from Dalmatia.

Opening hours and holidays

Most **shops** open Mon–Fri 8am–8pm, Sat 8am–1pm, although many supermarkets, outdoor markets and the like are open daily 7am–7pm. **Museum and gallery** times vary from place to place, although most are closed Mon.

All shops and banks will be closed on the following **public holidays**: Jan 1; Jan 6; Easter Mon; May 1; May 30; June 22; Aug 5; Aug 15; Nov 1; & Dec 25 & 26.

Emergencies

The crime rate in Croatia is low by European standards. Croatian **police** (*policija*) are generally helpful when dealing with holiday-makers, although they can be slow when filling out reports. Police often make routine checks on identity cards and other documents; always carry your **passport**.

Hospital treatment is free to EU citizens. **Pharmacies** (*ljekarna*) tend to follow normal shopping hours, and a rota system covers night-time and weekend opening; details are posted in the window of each pharmacy.

Emergency Numbers

Police ☏92; Ambulance ☏94; Fire ☏93

Zagreb

Capital of an independent state since 1991, **ZAGREB** has served as the cultural and political focus of Croatia since the Middle Ages. The city grew out of two medieval communities, **Kaptol**, to the east, and **Gradec**, to the west, each sited on a hill and divided by a river long since dried up but nowadays marked by a street known as Tkalčićeva. Zagreb grew rapidly in the nineteenth century, and the majority of its buildings are relatively well-preserved, grand, peach-coloured monuments to the self-esteem of the Austro-Hungarian Empire. Nowadays, with a population topping one million, Zagreb is the boisterous capital of a newly self-confident nation. A handful of good museums and a vibrant nightlife ensure that a few days here will be well spent.

Arrival, information and city transport

Zagreb's central **train station** is on Tomislavov Trg, on the southern edge of the city centre, a ten-minute walk from Trg bana Jelačića, the main square. The main **bus station** is a fifteen-minute walk east of the train station, at the junction of Branimirova and Držićeva – trams #2, #3 and #6 run between the two stations, with #6 continuing to the main square. Zagreb **airport** is 10km southeast of the city; Croatia Airlines buses run to the main bus station (6am–8pm, every 30min; 25kn).

There are two **tourist offices** in central Zagreb; the main one is at Trg bana Jelačića 11 (Mon–Fri 8.30am–8pm, Sat 9am–5pm, Sun 10am–2pm; ☎01/48-14-051, ⊛www.zagreb-touristinfo.hr), the other is at Trg N. Zrinskog 14 (Mon, Wed & Fri 9am–5pm, Tues & Thurs 9am–6pm; ☎01/49-21-645). Both sell the **Zagreb Card** (72hr, 60kn), which gives unlimited city transport and good discounts in museums and restaurants. The superb *Zagreb In Your Pocket* (20kn), available from the tourist offices, hotels and shops, is by far the best source of information on the city.

Zagreb has an efficient and comprehensive **tram** network and, to a lesser extent, bus network, though much of the city centre can easily be seen on foot. For both buses and trams in the centre, there's a flat fare per journey of 7kn; **tickets** (*karte*) are sold from cigarette and newspaper kiosks. Day tickets (*dnevne karte*) cost 16kn. Validate your ticket by punching it in the machines on board the trams. The train station and Trg bana Jelačića are the two main hubs of the city transport system.

Accommodation

Zagreb has very little in the way of budget **accommodation**. **Private rooms** (❸) can be arranged through the Evistas agency at Šenoina 28, midway between the train and bus stations (Mon–Fri 9am–8pm, Sat 9am–5pm; ☎01/48-39-546, ⊛evistas@zg.tel.hr).

In additionto the hostels listed below, some **student rooms** are available (mid-July to late Sept only; ❹). The two main locations are at Cvjetno naselje, Odranska 8 (☎01/61-91-245; tram #14 or #17 from Trg bana Jelačića), and Stjepan Radić, Jarunska 2 (☎01/36-34-255; tram #17 from Trg bana Jelačića). The nearest **campsite** (☎01/65-30-444) is 10km southwest of town at the *Plitvice Motel* beside the main Zagreb–Ljubljana motorway – there's no public transport.

Hostels

HI hostel Petrinjska 77 ☎01/48-41-261. Convenient location, just five minutes' walk from the railway station, compensates (just) for the grubby, noisy interior. Dorms ❷

Ravnice hostel Ravnice 1 38b ☎23-32-325, ⊛vpesjak@lnet.hr. Fabulous and welcoming new hostel east of the centre. Tram #7 or #12 to Dubrava, then ten minutes' walk south along Ravnice. Dorms ❷

Hotels

Astoria Petrinjska 71 ☎01/48-41-222, ⊛hotel-astoria@zg.tel.hr. Slightly careworn though clean en suites; all rooms have TV, too. Convenient for the train and bus stations. ❶

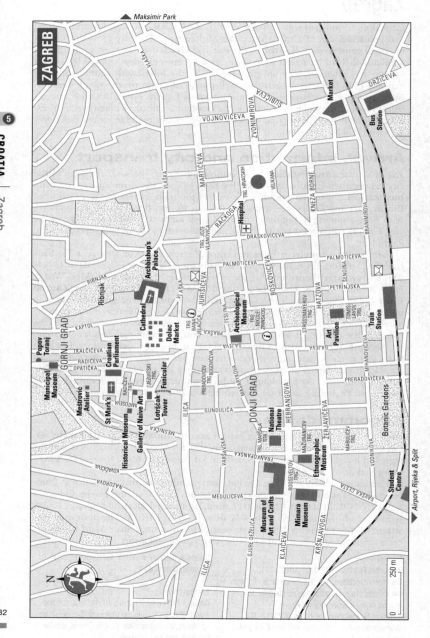

▲ Maksimir Park

ZAGREB

VLAŠKA

SUBIĆEVA
ZVONIMIROVA
VOJNOVIĆEVA
MARTIĆEVA
Market
DRŽIĆEVA
Bus
Station

VLAŠKA

RAČKOGA
TRG HRVATSKIH VELIKANA
Hospital
TRG JOŽE VLAHOVIĆA
DRAŠKOVIĆEVA
KNEZA BORNE
BRANIMIROVA

Archbishop's
Palace

RIBNJAK
Ribnjak
KAPTOL

Cathedral
VLAŠKA
JURIŠIĆEVA
PALMOTIĆEVA
BOŠKOVIĆEVA
PALMOTIĆEVA

Dolac
Market
TRG BANA JELAČIĆA
TESLINA
PRAŠKA
TRG NIKOLE ZRINSKOG
Archeological
Museum
STROSSMAYEROV TRG
HATZOVA
PETRINJSKA
SENOINA

Popov
Toranj
GORNJI GRAD
TKALČIĆEVA
RADIĆEVA
OPATIČKA

Croatian
Parliament
ĆIRILOMETODSKA
RADIĆEV TRG
JEZUITSKI TRG
GAJEVA

Municipal
Museum
Meštrović
Atelier
St Mark's
Historical Museum
Gallery of Naive Art
MATOŠEVA

Lotršćak
Tower
Funicular
ILICA
MESNIČKA

DONJI GRAD
PRERADOVIĆEV TRG
MASARYKOVA
GUNDULIĆA
GAJEVA
TOMIŠLAVOV TRG
Art
Pavilion
Train
Station
MIHANOVIĆEVA
PRERADOVIĆEVA

KOVAČIĆEVA
NAZOROVA
VARŠAVSKA
National
Theatre
TRG MARŠALA TITA
FRANKOPANSKA
HEBRANGOVA
ŽERJAVIĆEVA
Botanic Gardens
VODNIKOVA
SAVSKA CESTA

MEDULIĆEVA
Museum of
Art and Crafts
ROOSEVELTOV TRG
MAŽURANIĆEV TRG
Ethnographic
Museum
MARULIĆEV TRG
Student
Centre
▼ Airport, Rijeka & Split

GJURE DEŽELIĆA
Mimara
Museum
KLAIĆEVA
KRŠNJAVOGA
ILICA

N

0   250 m

Dora Trnjanska 11f ☎01/46-55-088, ☜www
.zeljeznicko-ugostiteljstvo.hr. This simple but cheery
place, ten-minutes' walk south of the train station
(via the subway), has clean, wood-furnished
rooms. Breakfast not included. ❸
Ilica Ilica 102 ☎01/37-77-522, ☜www.hotel-
ilica.hr. Modern, smart and friendly B&B with en-
suite rooms 1.5km west of the main square.
Popular, so book in advance. ❹

Jadran Vlaška 50 ☎01/45-53-777. Cheapest of
the central hotels, with en-suite rooms. Just east
of the city centre and fifteen minutes' walk from
the train station at the top end of Draskovićeva. ❹
Slíško Supilova 13 %01/61-84-777,
☜www.slisko.hr. Clean, comfortable and
welcoming hotel 300m east of the main bus
station. ❹

The City

Modern Zagreb falls neatly into three parts. **Donji Grad** or "Lower Town", which
extends north from the train station to **Trg bana Jelačića**, the main square, is the
bustling centre of the modern city. Uphill from here, to the northeast and the
northwest, are the older quarters of **Kaptol** (the "Cathedral Chapter") and **Gradec**
(the "Upper Town"), both peaceful districts of ancient mansions, quiet squares and
leafy parks.

Donji Grad

Tomislavov Trg, opposite the train station, is the first in a series of three shady,
green squares which form the backbone of the lower town. Its main attraction is
the **Art Pavilion** (Mon–Sat 11am–7pm, Sun 10am–1pm; 20kn; free Mon; ☜www
.umjetnicki-paviljon), built in 1898 and now hosting art exhibitions in its gilded
stucco and mock-marble interior. There's little to divert you in the second of the
squares, but beyond, in the last of the three – **Trg Nikole Zrinjskog** – lies the
Archeological Museum (Tues–Fri 10am–5pm, Sat & Sun 10am–1pm; 20kn;
☜www.arheoloski.hr); the museum has pieces from prehistoric times to the Middle
Ages, including pottery fragments from the fourth century BC Vučedol culture,
ancient Roman and Greek artefacts and Egyptian antiquities.

Walk up from here and you're on **Trg bana Jelačića**, flanked by cafés, hotels and
department stores, and hectic with the whizz of trams and hurrying pedestrians.
The statue in the centre is of the nineteenth-century governor of Croatia, Josip
Jelačić. Running west from the square, below Gradec hill, is **Ilica**, the city's main
shopping street. A little way along it and off to the right, you can take a **funicular**
(daily 6.30am–9pm, every 10min; 2.5kn) up to Strossmayerovo Šetaliste; alternatively, cut down via **Preradovićev Trg**, a small lively square where there's a flower
market, to **Trg maršala Tita**. This is a grandiose open space, centred on the late
nineteenth-century **National Theatre**, a solid ochre-coloured pile behind a piece
by Ivan Meštrović, the strangely erotic *Well of Life*. Across the square, the **Museum
of Arts and Crafts** (Tues–Fri 10am–6pm, Sat & Sun 10am–1pm; 20kn; ☜www
.muo.hr) boasts an impressive display of furniture, ceramics, clothes and textiles
from the Renaissance to the present day. On the southern side of the square, on Trg
Ivana Mažuranića, the **Ethnographic Museum** (Tues–Thurs 10am–6pm, Fri–Sun
10am–1pm; 15kn) has a collection of costumes from every corner of the country, as
well as an engaging heap of artefacts brought back from the South Pacific, Asia and
Africa.

A couple of minutes west, on Rooseveltov Trg, lies Zagreb's most prestigious art
collection, the **Mimara Museum** (Tues–Sat 10am–5pm, Sun 10am–2pm; 20kn;
☜www.mimara.hr), housing the art and archeological collection of Ante Topić
Mimara, a native of Zagreb who spent much of his life in Austria. Ground-floor
exhibits include ancient glass from Egypt, Greece, Syria and the Roman Empire,
oriental carpets from the seventeenth to ninenteenth centuries, and Chinese art
from the Shang through to the Song dynasty. Upstairs, there's a collection of
European paintings.

Kaptol and Gradec

Behind Trg bana Jelačiča, the filigree spires of Zagreb's **Cathedral** mark the edge of the district (and street) known as **Kaptol**, ringed by the ivy-cloaked turrets of the eighteenth-century **Archbishop's Palace** – a "sumptuous Kremlin" fancied the archeologist Arthur Evans before its decimation by an earthquake in 1880. After the disaster, the cathedral was rebuilt in neo-Gothic style, a high, bare structure inside, with very little left from the years before the earthquake. Behind the altar lies a shrine to Archbishop Stepinac, head of the Croat church in the 1940s, imprisoned by the Communists after World War II, and beatified by the Pope in 1998.

Immediately west of Kaptol, **Gradec** is the most ancient and atmospheric part of Zagreb, a leafy, tranquil backwater of tiny streets, small squares and Baroque palaces, whose mottled brown roofs peek out from the hill to the west. From Trg bana Jelačiča, make your way to the **Dolac** market, which occupies several tiers immediately beyond the square; this is the city's main food-market, a feast of fruit, vegetables, meat and fish held every morning. From the far side of Dolac market, **Tkalčićeva** spears north, following the course of the river which once formed the boundary between Kaptol and Gradec. Entry to Gradec proper from here is by way of **Krvavi Most**, which connects the street with Radićeva. On the far side of Radićeva, the **Kamenita Vrata** is a gloomy tunnel with a small shrine that formed part of Gradec's original fortifications. Close by, the fourteenth-century **Kula Lotršćak** (Tues–Fri noon–8pm, Sat & Sun 10am–7pm; 10kn) marks the top station of the funicular (see above). There are fantastic views from here over the rest of the city and the plains beyond. North of the tower, the **Gallery of Naive Art**, Ćirilometodska 3 (Tues–Fri 10am–6pm, Sat & Sun 10am–1pm; 10kn; ⓦwww.hmnu.org), is an impressive collection of work by the naive, peasant artists of rural Croatia. At the northern end of Ćirilometodska, **Markov Trg** marks the centre of Gradec – fringed by government offices, the square's focus is the squat **Church of St Mark**, a much renovated place whose tiled roof displays the coats-of-arms of the constituent parts of Croatia.

Just north of Markov Trg, at Mletačka 8, is the **Meštrović Atelier** (Tues–Fri 9am–2pm, Sat 10am–6pm; 10kn), an exhibition dedicated to Croatia's most famous twentieth-century artist – in the sculptor's former home and studio. On display are sketches, photographs, memorabilia from exhibitions worldwide, and small-scale studies of his more familiar public creations. Left off Markov Trg, the **Historical Museum of Croatia**, at Matoševa 9 (Mon–Fri 10am–5pm, Sat & Sun 10am–1pm; 10kn; ⓦwww.hismus.hr), is the venue for prestigious temporary exhibitions. The **Municipal Museum**, at Opatička 20 (Tues–Fri 10am–6pm, Sat & Sun 10am–1pm; 20kn), close to the thirteenth-century **Popov Toranj**, is perhaps more appealing, telling the tale of Zagreb's development from medieval times to the early twentieth century with the help of paintings and lumber from the city's wealthier households, and the original seventeenth-century statues that once adorned the portals of the city's cathedral.

Eating and drinking

Whilst not outstanding, Zagreb's **restaurant** scene is becoming more varied, and there's no shortage of budget places to eat. There's a wide range of Croatian cuisine, including several superb seafood restaurants, and any number of pizzerias. Expect to pay 50–70kn for a decent meal in any of the places listed below. For **snack food**, head to the area around Dolac market. There's a 24-hour bakery, *Pekarna Dora*, between the train station and the centre at Strossmayerov Trg 8 and **picnic supplies** can be purchased from Dolac or the Veterinaria supermarket (daily 7am–midnight) in the subterranean shopping centre in front of the train station.

Zagreb has a wealth of **cafés and bars** offering outdoor seating in the pedestrian area around Gajeva and Bogovićeva – particularly along Tkalčićeva, just north of Trg bana Jelačiča.

Restaurants

Boban Gajeva 9. Popular and central pasta place in the vaulted basement of the stylish café of the same name.

Cantinetta Teslina 14. Good-quality Croatian and Italian food just south of the main square. Chic, but not too expensive. Closed Sun.

Club Havana Perkovčeva 2. This brilliant Cuban restaurant, located under the *Press Club*, has high-class food, sophisticated decor and attentive waiting staff, making It the most engaging place In town to eat. Closed Sun.

Kaptolska Klet Kaptol 5. Ordinary-looking restaurant serving a decent selection of above-average, and not too pricey, grilled meats; the fabulous courtyard seating affords terrific views of the cathedral spires.

Lenuci Zrinjevac 15. Large, subtly decorated Mexican restaurant and cocktail bar.

Lopud Kaptol 10. Well-respected seafood restaurant, offering fresh fish flown in each morning from Dubrovnik. Closed Sun.

Nokturno Skalinska 4. In a side street just off Tkalčićeva, offering serviceable pizzas, varied lasagnes, and good salads.

Pivnica Medvedgrad Savska 56. Located 1.5km southwest of the centre, this huge beer hall serves up large, cheap portions of grilled meats; the beer, brewed on the premises, is excellent, too.

Rubelj Frankopanska 2 & Dolac market. Cheapest central place for simple but tasty grilled-meat standards.

Stari Fijaker Mesnička 6. A dimly lit, intimate restaurant serving local cuisine.

Cafés and bars

Bulldog Bogovićeva 6. A typically elegant Zagreb bar and pavement café, this is one of the most popular meeting places in the town centre.

Dobar Zvuk Gajeva 18. Popular café-bar with cheap drinks and a moderately bohemian clientele.

Kaptol Kaptol 4. Small, sticky and a lot of fun, this pub has an energy rarely found In other Zagreb establishments.

Kolding Berislavićeva 8. Civilized cellar bar with turn-of-the-century furnishings. Good place for an intimate drink.

Melin Košarska 19. This energetic pub is a terrific alternative to the posier establishments nearby.

Tolkien's Katarinin Trg. Funky, *Lord of the Rings* inspired place on a quiet square In Gradec.

Zrin Berislavićeva 3. Mellow, charming and extremely tasteful café, conducive to contemplative drinking.

Nightlife

Zagreb offers a rich and varied diet of high culture, with the **National Theatre**, Trg maršala Tita 15 (ticket office Mon–Fri 10am–1pm & 5–7.30pm, Sat 10am–1pm & 1hr 30min before each performance, Sun 30min before each performance; ℡01/48-28-532), providing the focus for serious, Croatian-language **drama**, as well as **opera** and **ballet**. The city's main **orchestral-music** venue is the **Lisinski Concert Hall** south of the train station at Trg Stjepana Radića 4 (ticket office Mon–Fri 9am–8pm, Sat 9am–2pm; ℡01/61-21-166). Intimate **chamber-music** concerts take place at the **Croatian Musical Institute**, Gundulićeva 6 (℡01/48-30-822). The free monthly pamphlet *Events and Performances*, available from the Zagreb tourist office, contains **listings** in English of all forthcoming events.

Zagreb nightlife centres on a clutch of established, and reasonably varied, **discos** and **clubs** – many presenting the best opportunities for catching live rock and jazz; the best are listed below.

Discos and clubs

Aquarius Aleja Mira bb. At the eastern end of Lake Jarun, 4km southwest of the centre, the place specializes in techno and drum 'n' bass. Occasional host to live bands. Tues–Sat 9pm–6am.

BP Club Teslina 7. Established jazz club and relaxed late-night drinking haunt. Daily 5pm–1am.

Gjuro II Medveščak 2. Relaxed cellar club with varied programme of dance and alternative rock, with regular live music. Wed–Sun 9pm–2am.

Močvara Tvornica Jedinstvo building, Trnjanski nasip. Unpretentious cultural centre in an old factory on the banks of the River Sava. Live gigs (usually alternative rock), film shows and club nights – something happening every night. Take any bus heading for Novi Zagreb and alight just before the bridge – the club is on your right. Mon–Fri 8pm–4am, Sat & Sun 10am–4am.

Saloon Tuškanac 1a. Legendary meeting place in a leafy corner of town, 500m west of the centre. Music is an enjoyable mish-mash of commercial disco. Tues–Sat 10pm–4am.

Tvornica Šubićeva 1. Former ballroom just north of the bus station, now hosting live rock, club nights and theatre. Daily 10pm–4am.

Listings

Istria

A large peninsula jutting into the northern Adriatic, **Istria** is Croatian tourism at its most developed. Many of the towns here were tourist resorts in the nineteenth century, and in recent years their proximity to northern Europe has ensured an annual influx of sun-seekers from Germany, Austria and the Netherlands. Yet the growth of modern hotel complexes, sprawling campsites and (mainly concrete) beaches has done little to detract from the essential charm of the region. This stretch of the coast was under Venetian rule for 400 years and there's still a fair-sized Italian community, with Italian very much the second language. Istria's largest centre is the port city of **Pula**, which, with its Roman amphitheatre and other relics of Roman occupation, is a rewarding place to spend a couple of days. On the western side of the peninsula, resort towns such as **Poreč** and **Rovinj**, with their cobbled piazzas and shuttered houses, are almost overwhelmingly pretty.

Pula

Once the chief port of the Austro-Hungarian Empire, **PULA** is an engaging combination of working port, naval base and brash riviera town. The Romans put the city squarely on the map when they arrived in 177 BC, transforming it into an important commercial centre. The most obvious relic of their rule is the first century BC **Amphitheatre** (daily: June–Sept 8am–9pm; Oct–May 9am–5pm; 16kn) just north of the centre, a great grey elliptical skein of connecting arches, silhouetted against the skyline from wherever you stand in the city. It's the sixth largest in the world, and once had space for over 23,000 spectators. The outer shell is fairly complete, as is one of the towers, up which a slightly hair-raising climb gives a good sense of the enormity of the structure and a view of Pula's industrious harbour. The cavernous rooms underneath, which would have been used for keeping wild animals and Christians before they met their death, are now given over to piles of crusty amphorae and reconstructed olive presses.

South of the amphitheatre, central Pula circles a pyramidal hill, scaled by secluded streets and topped with a star-shaped Venetian fortress. On the eastern side of the hill, Istarska – which later becomes Giardini – leads down to the first-century BC **Triumphal Arch of the Sergians**, through which ul Sergijevaca, a lively pedestrianized thoroughfare, leads in turn to a square known as **Forum** – site of the ancient Roman forum and now the centre of Pula's old quarter. On the far side of here, the slim form of the **Temple of Augustus** was built between 2 BC and 14 AD to celebrate the cult of the emperor; its imposing Corinthian columns, still intact, make it one of the best examples of a Roman temple outside Italy.

Heading north from Forum along Kandlerova leads to Pula's **Cathedral** (check with tourist office for opening times), a broad, simple and very spacious structure that is another mixture of periods and styles: a fifteenth-century renovation of a Romanesque basilica built on the foundations of a Roman temple. From the cathedral, you can follow streets up to the top of the hill, the site of the original Roman Capitol and now the home of a mossy seventeenth-century **fortress**, built by the Venetians and housing a pretty inessential local museum. You're better off following tracks to the far side of the fortress where there are the remains of a small **Roman Theatre** and the **Archeological Museum** (May–Sept Mon–Sat 9am–8pm, Sun 10am–3pm; Oct–April Mon–Fri 9am–3pm; 12kn), which has pillars and toga-clad statues mingling haphazardly with ceramics, jewellery and trinkets from all over Istria, some dating back to prehistoric times.

Practicalities

Pula's **train station** is a ten-minute walk north of the centre, at the far end of Kolodvorska; the **bus station** is along Istarska, just south of the amphitheatre. The **tourist office** is in the Forum (June–Sept daily 9am–10pm; Oct–May Mon–Sat 9am–8pm; ☎052/219-197, ⊛www.gradpula.com). **Private rooms** (**❷**) can be booked through Arenatours, Splitska Ulica 1 (☎052/218-696, ⊜arenaturist @pu.tel.hr), or Atlas, Ulica Starih Statuta 1 (☎052/214-172). There's a **HI hostel** at Valsaline bay, 4km south of the centre (☎052/391-124, ⊜hfhs-pula@pu.hinet.hr; **❷**); take bus #2 or #7 from Giardini to Vila Idola and then bear right towards the bay. Cheapest of the **hotels** is the Veli Jože, 1km south of the centre at Bečka 7 (☎052/551-182; **❸**); more central, but more expensive, is the *Omir*, slightly uphill from Giardini at Sergia Dobrića 6 (☎052/213-944; **❹**). The nearest **campsite** is Stoja, on a rocky wooded peninsula 3km southeast of town (☎052/387-144); take bus #1 from Giardini.

The vast **market** on Narodni Trg will yield all the provisions you'll need. Most **eating out** options are around the arena, Forum and Kandlerova: *Delfin*, opposite the cathedral at Kandlerova 17, offers inexpensive fish dishes; *Jupiter*, below the fortress at Castropola 38, is easily the best of the pizzerias; and *Pompei*, just off Sergijevaca at Clarissova 1, does good pasta dishes and salads. Best of the **drinking** haunts are *Ulix*, an elegant bar next to the triumphal arch; *Bounty Pub*, an animated place with plenty of outdoor seating two blocks east of the arch at Veronska 8; and *Voodoo*, in the basement at Marulićeva 1, which has live music at weekends. During the summer, the liveliest party venues are in Verudela, 3km south of town. There's **internet access** at *Enigma*, Kandlerova 19, and *Oigi*, on Glavinićev, by the Triumphal Arch.

Rovinj

ROVINJ, lies 40km north of Pula, its harbour a likeable mix of fishing boats and swanky yachts, its quaysides a blend of sunshaded café-tables and the thick orange of fishermen's nets. From the main square, **Trg maršala Tita**, the Baroque **Vrata svetog Križa** leads up to Grisia Ulica, lined with galleries selling local art. It climbs steeply through the heart of the old town to **St Euphemia's Church** (daily 10am–noon & 4–7pm), dominating Rovinj from the top of its peninsula. This eighteenth-century church, Baroque in style, has the sixth-century sarcophagus of the saint inside; you can climb its 58-metre-high tower (same times; 10kn). Back on maršala Tita, the **Town Museum** (May–Sept Mon–Sat 9am–12.30pm & 6–9pm; Oct–April Tues–Sat 10am–1.30pm; 10kn) has the usual collection of archeological oddments, antique furniture and Croatian art. North of here is **Trg Valdibora**, home to a small fruit and vegetable market.

Paths on the south side of Rovinj's busy harbour lead south towards **Zlatni rt**, a densely forested cape, crisscrossed by tracks and fringed by rocky **beaches**. Other spots for bathing can be found on the two islands just offshore from Rovinj – **Sveta Katerina**, the nearer of the two, and **Crveni otok**, just outside Rovinj's bay; both are linked by boats from the harbour (every 30min).

Rovinj's **bus station** is five minutes' walk southeast of its centre, just off Trg na lokvi, at the junction of Carrera and Carducci. The **tourist office** is located at

Obula Pina Budicin 12 (June–Sept daily 8am–9pm; rest of year Mon–Sat 8am–3pm; ☎052/811-566, ⊛www.istra.com/rovinj). **Private rooms** (❷) can be obtained from Natale, Carducci 3 (☎052/813-365, ⊛www.natale.hr), and Onio, Aldo Rismondo 19 (☎052/811-155); both are near the bus station. The only reasonably priced **hotel** in town is the *Rovinj*, Svetoga Križa 59 (☎052/840-758, ⓔhotel-rovinj@pu.hinet.hr; ❺). The nearest **campsite** is the *Polari* (☎052/801-501), 3km south and reached by regular bus. The harbourfront area is teeming with places to **eat and drink**. Away from here, *da Sergio*, at Grisia 11, is the best place for pizza; while *Konoba Veli Jože*, at Svetog Križa 1, has top-notch seafood.

Poreč

POREČ, 30km north of Rovinj, is Istria's largest and busiest resort. Another peninsula town with an ordered mesh of streets dating from its days as a Roman encampment, Poreč's star historic turn is the **Basilica of Euphrasius** just off Eufrazijeva (daily 7.30am–7pm; free), a sixth-century Byzantine structure harbouring mosaics claimed by some to be comparable with those at Ravenna. The basilica is at the heart of a religious complex, established by Bishop Euphrasius in 543; entry is through the **Atrium**, an arcaded courtyard that was heavily restored in the nineteenth century, but still has ancient bits of masonry incorporated in its walls. Beyond lies the **Bishop's Palace** (daily 10am–3pm; 10kn), a seventeenth-century building harbouring a display of mosaic fragments that once adorned the basilica floor. To the left of here is the octagonal **Baptistry**. The **basilica** itself is a rather bare structure, save for the wall mosaics above the altar which are studded with semi-precious gems, encrusted with mother-of-pearl and emblazoned with Euphrasius's personal monogram. The central part of the composition shows the Madonna and Child, flanked by a worldly Euphrasius holding a model of his church.

Due east of the basilica is ul Dekumanska, which follows the line of the ancient Roman main street and opens out into a square busy with buskers and tourists. The **Poreč Museum** in the Baroque Sinčić Palace at ul Dekumanska 9 (daily 9am–noon & 4–7pm; 10kn) displays Greek and Roman finds from the area. South of here, towards the end of the peninsula, is the distinctive thirteenth-century **Romanesque House**, with an unusual projecting wooden balcony; it's now a venue for art shows. Further on is **Trg Marafor**, with its remains of Roman temples to Mars and Neptune.

As an alternative to the crowded **beaches** of the old town, take a boat from the jetty next to the Marina (7am–midnight, every 30min; 15kn) to the nearby island of **Sveti Nikola**, or walk south beyond the marina where pathways head along a rocky coastline shaded by gnarled pines.

Practicalities

Poreč's **bus station** is just outside the town centre, behind the marina. From here, it's a five-minute walk to the **tourist office** at Zagrebačka 11 (May–Sept daily 8am–10pm; Oct–April daily 8am–3pm & 4.30–7.30pm; ☎052/451-458, ⊛www.istra.com/porec). For **private rooms** (❷), contact Atlas, at Eufrazijeva 63 (☎052/432-273). The friendly and central *Hotel Poreč*, just behind the bus station on Rade Končara 1 (☎052/451-811, ⊛www.hotelporec.com; ❺), has neat, comfortable rooms. The closest **campsites** are at the Zelena Laguna complex, a few kilometres south – *Zelena Laguna* (☎052/ 410-541) and, further south, *Bijela Uvala* (☎052/410-551) – reachable by hourly bus from the bus station.

There is a large **supermarket** next to the bus station. As for **restaurants**, there's a good sprinkling of places in the old town: *Sarajevo Grill*, just off Dekumanska on Matije Vlačica, has an array of meat dishes; while *Istra*, on the corner of Obala maršala Tita and Bože Milanovića, is one of the best places to eat fish. The area around Trg Svobode is the place for **cafés** and **bars**, many with outdoor seating. There's **internet access** at *Cybermac*, M. Graholica 1.

Moving on from Istria: Rijeka

Travelling on from Istria towards Zagreb or Dalmatia, most routes lead through the brusque port city of **RIJEKA**, hardly worth a stopoff in its own right but an important transport hub for onward travel: regular buses run from here to Zagreb, Split and Dubrovnik, and it's the starting point for the Jadrolinija coastal ferry, which calls in at Split and Dubrovnik on its way south. Rijeka's train and bus stations are about 400m apart; the former at the western end of Trpimirova, the latter at the eastern end of the same street on Trg Žabica. The **Jadrolinija ferry office** (daily 7am–6/8pm; ☎051/211-444) is along the waterfront from the bus station at Riva 16.

Dalmatia

Stretching from Zadar in the north to the Montenegrin border in the south, **Dalmatia** possesses one of Europe's most dramatic shorelines, the sheer wall of Croatia's mountain ranges sweeping down to the sea from stark, grey heights, scattering islands in their path. For centuries, the region was ruled by Venice, spawning towns, churches and an architecture that wouldn't look out of place on the other side of the water. All along, well-preserved medieval towns sit on tiny islands or just above the sea on slim peninsulas, beneath a grizzled karst landscape that drops precipitously into some of the clearest – and cleanest – water in the Mediterranean. The main attractions are in the south: the provincial capital **Split** is served by buses and trains from Zagreb and provides onward bus connections with the walled city of **Dubrovnik**. Ferry connections to the best of the islands – **Brač**, **Hvar**, **Vis** and **Korčula** – are also from Split.

Split

By far the largest city in the region, and its major transit hub, **SPLIT** is one of the most enticing spots on the Dalmatian coast; a hectic city, full of shouting stall-owners and travellers on the move. At the heart of all this, hemmed in by the sprawling estates and a modern harbour, lies a crumbling old town built within the precincts of **Diocletian's Palace**, one of the most outstanding classical remains in Europe. Built as a retirement home by Dalmatian-born Roman Emperor Diocletian in AD 305, it has been modified over the centuries, but has remained the core of Split.

The best place to start a tour of the palace area is on the seaward side, through the **Bronze Gate**, a functional gateway giving access to the sea that once came right up to the palace itself. Inside, you find yourself in a vaulted hall, from which imposing steps lead through the now domeless vestibule to the **Peristyle**. Once the central courtyard of the palace complex, these days the Peristyle serves as the main town square, crowded with cafés and surrounded by remnants of the stately arches that once framed the square. At the southern end, steps lead up to the **vestibule**, a round, formerly domed building that is the only part of the **imperial apartments** to be left anything like intact. You can get some idea of the grandeur of the old apartments by visiting the **subterranean halls** (daily: July & Aug 8am–8pm; Sept–June 8am–noon & 4–7pm; 6kn) beneath the houses which now stand on the site; the entrance is to the left of the Bronze Gate.

On the east side of the Peristyle stands one of two black granite Egyptian sphinxes, dating from around 15 BC, that flanked the entrance to Diocletian's mausoleum; the octagonal building, surrounded by an arcade of Corinthian columns, has since been converted into Split's **Cathedral** (Mon–Sat 7am–noon & 4–7pm). On the right of the entrance is the **campanile** (same hours; 5kn), a Romanesque structure much restored in the late nineteenth century – from the top, the views across the city are splendid. As for the cathedral itself, the walnut and oak main **doorway** is one of its most impressive features – carved with an inspired comic strip showing scenes from the life of Christ, it is the work of local artist Andrija Buvina and dates from 1214. Inside is an odd hotchpotch of styles, the dome ringed by two series of decorative Corinthian columns and a frieze that contains portraits of Diocletian and his wife. The **pulpit** is a beautifully proportioned example of Romanesque art, sitting on capitals tangled with snakes, strange beasts and foliage. But the church's finest feature is on the Altar of St Anastasius – a cruelly realistic *Flagellation of Christ*, completed by local artist Juraj Dalmatinac in 1448.

North of the cathedral and reached by following Dioklecijanova is the grandest and best preserved of the palace gates, the **Golden Gate**. Just outside there's another piece by Meštrović, a gigantic statue of the fourth-century Bishop **Grgur Ninski**.

Fifteen minutes' walk northwest of here, the **Archeological Museum** at Zrinsko Frankopanska 25 (June–Sept Tues–Fri 9am–1pm & 5–8pm, Sat & Sun 9am–noon; Oct–May Tues–Fri 9am–2pm, Sat & Sun 10am–1pm; 10kn) contains comprehensive displays of Illyrian, Greek, medieval and Roman artefacts. Outside, the arcaded courtyard is crammed with a wonderful array of Greek, Roman and early Christian gravestones, sarcophagi and decorative sculpture.

If you want some peace and quiet, head for the woods of the **Marjan peninsula** west of the old town. It's accessible from Obala hrvatskog narodnog preporoda via Sperun and then Senjska, which cuts up through the slopes of the **Varoš** district. Most of Marjan's visitors stick to the road around the edge of the promontory with its scattering of tiny rocky **beaches**; the Bene beach, on the far northern side, is especially popular. From the road, tracks lead up into the heart of the Marjan Park, which is thickly wooded with pines, rising to its peak at 175m. The main historical attractions of Marjan are on the lower, southern edge, along Šetalište Ivana Meštrovića. Highlight of these lies some fifteen minutes west of the centre (bus #12 from the seafront). The **Meštrović Gallery**, Ivana Meštrovića 46 (Tues–Sat 10am–4/6pm, Sun 10am–2/3pm; 15kn, includes entrance to Kaštelet), is another Croatian shrine, housed in the ostentatious neoclassical building that was built – and lived in – by Croatia's most famous twentieth-century artist, the sculptor Ivan Meštrović (1883–1962). This fabulous collection consists largely of boldly fashioned bodies curled into elegant poses. Meštrović's former workshop, **Kaštelet** (same times and ticket), is 300m up the same road, and contains a chapel decorated with one of Meštrović's most important set-piece works: a series of wood-carved reliefs showing scenes from the Stations of the Cross.

Practicalities

The main **bus and train stations** are next to each other on Obala Kneza Domagoja, five minutes walk round the harbour from the centre; the **ferry terminal** for both domestic and international ferries – and the Jadrolinija booking office – is a few hundred metres south of here. Split **airport** is 16km west of town; Croatia Airlines buses connect with scheduled flights and run to the waterfront Riva (25kn); alternatively the #37 Split–Trogir bus runs from the main road outside the airport to the suburban bus station (13kn).

Split's **tourist office** is in the Peristyle of the Palace (June–Sept Mon–Sat 9am–9pm, Sun 9am–1pm; Oct–May Mon–Fri 9am–7.30pm, Sat 9am–1pm; ☏021/355-088, ⊚www.visitsplit.com). **Private rooms** (❷) can be booked through Turist Biro, on the waterfront at Obala narodnog preporoda 12 (☏021/342-142). Cheapest of the **hotels** are the *Slavija* at Buvinova 3 in the old town (☏021/347-053; ❸), which has basic rooms, some with shower; and the slightly more comfortable *Bellevue* on the western fringes of the old town at bana Jelačića 2 (☏021/585-701; ❹).

The daily **market** at the eastern edge of the old town is the place to shop for fruit, veg and local cheeses. There are few **restaurants** in the old town, although *Sarajevo*, Domaldova 6, has a good range of Croatian meat and fish dishes. Further afield, *Galija* at Matošića 2 on the western fringes of the old town, is the best of the pizzerias; while *Konoba kod Jože* at Sredmanuška 4, ten minutes northeast of the old town, is an atmospheric place specializing in seafood. *Konoba Varo*, up behind the *Bellevue Hotel* at ban Mladenova 7, is another traditional Dalmatian restaurant.

For **cafés**, the busy waterfront Riva is a good spot, as is the old town, whose many small squares yield clusters of options: on Mihovilova širina, *Song* and *Shook* are fairly upbeat places, whilst just around the corner, at Dosud 10, is the *Getto Club*, a welcome alternative to the posier establishments round about. For quieter, more reflective options, head to Majstora Jurja and, in particular, *Teak Caffe*. Other places worth trying are *Planet Jazz*, a bohemian hangout on Grgura Ninskog, and the similar *Jazz III* on Vukičovićeva. The beach at Bačvice, a few minutes' walk south past the railway station, is a popular party place in summer. For **internet access** head to Internet, Games & Books, 200m north of the train station on Obala kneza domagoja, or *Issa*, at Dobrić 12 in the old town.

Brač

The third largest island on the Adriatic coast, **BRAČ** is famous for its milk-white marble, which has been used in places as diverse as Berlin's Reichstag, the high altar of Liverpool's Metropolitan Cathedral, the White House in Washington – and, of course, Diocletian's Palace. In addition to the marble, a great many islanders were once dependent on the grape harvest, though the phylloxera (vine lice) epidemics of the late nineteenth century and early twentieth century forced many of them to emigrate. Even today, as you cross Brač's interior, the signs of this depopulation are all around in the tumbledown walls and overgrown fields.

The easiest way to reach Brač is by **ferry** from Split to **Supetar**, an engagingly laid-back fishing port on the north side of the island, from where it's a straightforward bus journey to **Bol**, a major windsurfing centre on the island's south coast and site of one of the Adriatic's most beautiful beaches.

Supetar

Though the largest town on the island, **SUPETAR** is a rather sleepy village onto which package tourism has been painlessly grafted. There's little of specific interest, save for several attractive shingle **beaches** which stretch west from the harbour, and the **Petrinović Mausoleum**, a neo-Byzantine confection on a wooded promontory 1km west of town, built by sculptor Toma Rosandić to honour a local businessman.

Supetar's **tourist office** beside the ferry dock at Porat 1 (June–Sept daily 8am–10pm; Oct–May Mon–Fri 10am–4pm; ☎021/630-551, ⊛www.supetar.hr) has information on the whole island. **Private rooms** (❷) are available from Supetar Travel (☎021/631-374), behind the bus station, and Atlas (☎021/631-105) on the harbourfront. The *Palute*, 1.5km west of the harbour at Put pašike 16 (☎021/631-541; ❸), is a friendly **pension**, whilst the *Britanida*, 200m east of the ferry dock at Hrvatskih velikana 26 (☎021/631-038; ❹), is the best **hotel** option. There are two **campsites** just east of the ferry dock. Best of the places to **eat** on the harbourfront is *Palute* at Porat 4, which serves good grilled fish. *Vinotoka*, just inland from the harbour at Dobova 6, has a wide range of traditional Croatian food and an extensive choice of local wines. The clear waters around Supetar are perfect for **scuba diving**; the Dive Center Kaktus in the *Kaktus Hotel* complex (☎021/630-421; closed Nov–March) rents out gear and arranges scuba and snorkelling courses (from 200kn), as well as renting out mountain bikes (11kn/day).

Bol

Stranded on the far side of the Vidova Gora mountains, there's no denying the beauty of **BOL**'s setting, or the charm of its old stone houses. However, the main attraction of the village is its beach, **Zlatni rat**, which lies to the west of the centre along the wooded shoreline. The sandy cape juts into the sea like an extended finger, changing shape from season to season as the wind plays across it. Unsurprisingly, it does get very crowded during summer. While you're here, look in at the late-fif-teenth-century **Dominican Monastery** (daily 10am–noon & 5–9pm; 10kn). Dramatically perched on a bluff just east of central Bol, the monastery museum holds a *Madonna with Child* by Tintoretto in its small collection.

Buses from Supetar stop just west of Bol's harbour, at the far end of which stands the **tourist office** (June–Aug daily 8am–10pm; Sept–May Mon–Fri 8.30am–3pm; ☎021/635-638, ⊛www.bol.hr). **Private rooms** (❷) can be booked through Boltours, 100m west of the bus stop at Vladimira Nazora 18 (☎021/635-693, ⊛www.boltours.com), and there are several **campsites** in the new part of town uphill from the centre. For **eating**, there are numerous places along the waterfront, although *Gust*, above the harbour at F. Radića 14, has the widest range of tradition-al food. Big Blue (☎021/306-222, ⊛www.big-blue-sport.hr), with offices next to the tourist office and in front of the *Hotel Borak*, is the best of several **windsurfing** centres; as well as board rental (60kn/hr) and a range of courses for beginners, they also rent out sea kayaks (25kn/hr) and **mountain bikes** (110kn/day).

Hvar

One of the most hyped of all the Croatian islands, **HVAR** is undeniably beautiful – a slim, green slice of land punctured by jagged inlets and cloaked with hills of spongy lavender. Tourist development hasn't been too crass, and the island's main centre, **Hvar Town**, retains much of its old Venetian charm. **Ferries** from Split arrive at Stari Grad, 4km further east, from where buses run into Hvar Town (every 30min); the Dubrovnik–Rijeka coastal ferry stops at Hvar Town itself.

The best view of **HVAR TOWN** is from the sea, the tiny town hugging the bay, grainy-white and brown with green splashes of palms and pines bursting from every crack and cranny. At the centre, the main square is flanked to the south by the arcaded bulk of the Venetian arsenal, the upper storey of which was added in 1612 to house a **theatre** (daily: summer 10am–noon & 8–11pm; winter 10am–noon; 10kn), the oldest in Croatia and one of the first in Europe. The theatre has since been converted to a cinema, but its painted Baroque interior has survived pretty much intact. At the eastern end of the square is Hvar's **Cathedral** (usually open mornings), a sixteenth-century construction with an eighteenth-century facade that's a characteristic mixture of Gothic and Renaissance styles. Inside is rou-tine enough, but the **Bishop's Treasury** (daily: summer 9am–noon & 5–7pm; winter 10am–noon; 10kn) is worth the entry fee for its small but fine selection of chalices and reliquaries.

The rest of the old town stretches back from the piazza in an elegant confusion of twisting lanes and alleys. Up above, the **Fortress** (daily: May–Sept daily 8am–dusk; 10kn) is a good example of sixteenth-century military architecture. The views over Hvar and the islands beyond are well worth the trek to the top. From the fort you can pick out the fifteenth-century **Franciscan Monastery** (summer Mon–Fri 10am–noon & 5–7pm; winter 10am–noon; 10kn), to the left of the harbour. The monastery has a small collection of paintings, mostly obscure Venetian; next door, the monastic **church** is pleasingly simple, with beautifully carved choir stalls.

The **beaches** nearest to town are rocky and crowded, and it's best to make your way towards the **Pakleni otoci**, just to the west. Easily reached by water taxi from the harbour (about 15kn each way), the Pakleni are a chain of eleven wooded islands, three of which cater for tourists with simple bars and restaurants: Jerolim island is the nearest; next is Marinkovac; then Sv Klement, the largest of the islands. Bear in mind that camping is forbidden throughout Pakleni.

Practicalities

Hvar Town's **tourist office** (June–Sept daily 8am–2pm & 4–10pm; Oct–May Mon–Fri 8am–1pm; ☎021/741-059, ⊛www.dalmacija.net/hvar) is on the water-front below the theatre. For **private rooms** (❷), head for the Mengola agency, also on the harbour (☎021/742-099, ⊚www.mengola.hr), or Pelegrin, by the ferry dock (☎021/742-250, ⊚pelegrin@Inet.hr). The **hotels** *Dalmacija*, on the eastern side of the harbour (☎021/741-120; ➎), and the *Delfin*, over on the western side (☎021/741-168; ➎), are as reasonable as you'll get here. The Milna **campsite** (☎021/745-027) is 2km southeast of town on Milna Bay.

There are dozens of **restaurants** in Hvar Town, none of which is too expensive. *Kod Kapetana*, next to the *Delfin hotel*, dishes up splendid seafood, with terrific terrace views to boot; while *Hanibal*, on the main square, has a slightly pricier, but wider ranging menu. *Macondo*, signposted in a backstreet uphill from the harbour, is a good place for meat and fish. For **drinking**, there are several cafés and bars around the harbour: *Sidro*, *Atelier* and *Carpe Diem* are three of the best.

Vis

Compact, humpy, and at first glance a little forbidding, **VIS** is situated further off-shore than any other of Croatia's inhabited Adriatic islands. Closed to foreigners for military reasons until 1989, the island has never been overrun by tourists, and even now depends much more heavily on independent tourism than its package-oriented neighbours. Croatia's bohemian youth seem to have fallen in love with the place over the last decade, drawn by its wild mountainous scenery, two good-looking towns, **Vis Town** and **Komiža**, and a brace of fine wines, including the white Vugava and the red Viški plavac.

Ferries and, in summer, **hydrofoils** from Split arrive at Vis Town, from where **buses** depart for Komiža on the western side of the island.

Vis Town

VIS TOWN is attractively sited, a sedate arc of grey-brown houses on a deeply indented bay, above which looms a steep escarpment covered with the remains of abandoned agricultural terraces. The most attractive parts of town are east of the ferry landing in the suburb of **Kut**, a largely sixteenth-century tangle of narrow cobbled streets overlooked by the summer houses built by nobles from Hvar. The stone balconies and staircases give the place an aristocratic air, but there are no specific buildings to visit. Heading west around the bay soon brings you to a small peninsula, from which the campanile of the **Franciscan monastery of St Hieronymous** rises gracefully alongside a huddle of cypresses. The town's small pebbly **beach** is just beyond.

The **tourist office** (May–Sept Mon–Sat 8am–1pm & 4–8pm, Sun 8am–1pm; Oct–April Mon–Fri 9am–1pm; ☎021/717-017, ⊚www.tz-vis.hr) is just to the right of the ferry dock. **Private rooms** (➋) can be booked through Ionios, Obala Sv Jurja 37 (☎021/711-532, ⊚ionios@st.hinet.hr). Best of the **hotels** are the stately turn-of-the-century *Tamaris*, on the waterfront at Obala Sv Jurja 20 (☎021/711-350; ➍), and the smaller, pension-like *Paula*, at Petra Hektorovića 2 (☎021/711-362, ⊚paula-hotel@st.tel.hr; ➌) in Kut. **Restaurants** worth checking out include *Paula* and *Val*, both in Kut, and *Dionis*, just east of the *Tamaris* in Vis Town.

Komiža

KOMIŽA, 10km from Vis Town, is the island's main fishing port – a compact town with a palm-fringed seafront on one side and a ring of mountains on the other. Dominating the southern end of the harbour is the **Kaštel**, a stubby sixteenth-century fortress which now holds a **Fishing Museum** (daily: July & Aug 9am–noon & 6–10pm; June & Sept 9–10am & 7–10pm; 15kn).

Rearing up above Komiža to the southeast is **Mount Hum**, at 587m Vis's highest point. To climb it you can either scramble up a series of tracks which ascend steeply from behind the Benedictine monastery, 1km south of town, or follow the road as it works its way round the southern side of the island, and turn left to the hamlet of Žena Glava (about 10km in all). There's a wonderful view of the Adriatic from the top, with the pale grey stripe of the Italian coastline far away to the west, and the mountains of the Croatian mainland to the east.

Buses from Vis Town terminate about 100m behind the harbour, from where it's a short walk southwards to the **tourist office** (July & Aug daily 8am–10pm; rest of year Mon–Fri 8am–1pm; ☎021/713-455), on the Riva just beyond the Kaštel. The town's **hotel**, the *Biševo* (☎021/713-095; ❺), is at the northern end of the bay, and there are **private rooms** (❷) available through Darlić & Darlić, on the harbourfront (☎021/713 760, ⓦwww.darlic-travel.hr), and Srebrnatours at Ribarska 4 (☎021/713 668, ⓔsandra.vitaljic@st.tel.hr). There are a couple of pizzerias on the harbour, and one very good seafood **restaurant**, *Bako*, just off Ribarska. For **drinking**, head for the tiny main square, Škor, which is ringed by lively cafébars.

Korčula

Like so many islands along this coast, **KORČULA** was first settled by the Greeks, who gave it the name Korkyra Melaina or "Black Corfu" for its dark and densely wooded appearance. Even now, it's one of the greenest of the Adriatic islands, and one of the most popular. The island's main settlement is **Korčula Town**, and the rest of the island, although beautifully wild, lacks any real centres. The main coastal **ferry** docks at Korčula Town harbour. In addition, local ferries travel daily between Split and Vela Luka at the western end of Korčula island, from where there's a connecting bus service to Korčula Town. There's also a **bus service** from Dubrovnik, which crosses the narrow stretch of water dividing the island from the mainland by ferry from Orebić.

KORČULA TOWN sits on a beetle-shaped hump of land, a medieval walled city ribbed with a series of narrow streets that branch off the spine of the main street like the veins of a leaf. The Venetians first arrived here in the eleventh century, and stayed, on and off, for nearly eight centuries. Their influence is particularly evident in Korčula's old town, which huddles around the **Cathedral of St Mark**, squeezed into a space between the buildings that roughly passes for a main square. The cathedral facade is decorated with a gorgeous fluted rose window and a bizarre cornice frilled with strange gargoyles. The interior, reached through a door framed by statues of Adam and Eve, is one of the loveliest in the region – a curious mixture of styles, ranging from the Gothic forms of the nave to the Renaissance northern aisle, tacked on in the sixteenth century. The best of the church's treasures have been removed to the **Bishop's Treasury** (daily: May–June, Sept & Oct 10am–1pm; July & Aug also 4–8pm; 8kn), a couple of doors down. This small collection of fine and sacral art is one of the best in the country, with an exquisite set of paintings, including a striking *Portrait of a Man* by Carpaccio and a Leonardo da Vinci sketch of a soldier wearing a costume bearing a striking resemblance to that of the Moreška dancers (see below). Opposite the treasury, a former Venetian palace holds the **Town Museum** (daily: May–Oct 9am–1pm; July & August till 9pm; 10kn), whose more modest display contains a plaster cast of a fourth-century BC Greek tablet from Lumbarda – the earliest evidence of civilization on Korčula.

Close by the main square, down a turning to the right, is another remnant from Venetian times, the so-called **House of Marco Polo** (summer daily 10am–1pm & 5–7pm; 10kn). Korčula claims to be the birthplace of Marco Polo, although it seems unlikely that he had any connection with this seventeenth-century house, which these days is little more than an empty shell with some terrible twentieth-century prints.

Your best bet for **beaches** is to head off by **water taxi** from the old harbour to one of the **Skoji** islands just offshore. The largest and nearest of these is **Badija**, where there are some secluded rocky beaches, a couple of snack bars and a naturist section. There's also a sandy beach just beyond the village of **Lumbarda**, 8km south of Korčula (reached by hourly bus in the summer).

Practicalities

Korčula's **bus station** is 400m southeast of the old town. Work your way round to the northwestern side of the peninsula to find the **tourist office** (June–Sept Mon–Sat 8am–9pm, Sun 8am–3pm; Oct–May Mon–Sat 8am–3pm; ☎021/715-701; ⓦwww.korcula.net). **Private rooms** (❷) are handled by Marko Polo (☎020/715-400, ⓔmarko-polo-tours@du.tel.hr), whose office is between the bus station and the entrance to the old town. Cheapest of the **hotels** is the *Badija*, accessible by taxi boat from the harbour (☎020/711-115; ❸), a spartan but idyllically situated place in a former Franciscan monastery on Badija. The *Park* is a package-tour-oriented place in a bay southeast of the centre (☎020/726-004; ❺). The nearest **campsite** is *Autocamp Kalac* (☎020/726-336), about 3km southeast of town and reached by hourly buses for Lumbarda.

Not surprisingly, most **restaurants** in the old town tend to be expensive. One exception is the excellent *Adio Mare*, near Marco Polo's House and justifiably popular; arrive early to get a table. Another good choice is *Gradski Podrum*, just inside the main gate of the old town. A cheaper and more functional alternative is *Planjak* at Plokata 21. Wherever you eat, do try some of the excellent **local wines**: the delicious dry white Grk from Lumbarda, Posip from Smokvica, or the headache-inducing red Dingač from Postup on Peljesac.

Performances of Korčula's famous **folk dance**, the **Moreška**, take place outside the main gate to the old town in summer every Thursday evening (tickets from Marko Polo; 50kn). This frantic, sword-based dance is the story of a conflict between the Christians (in red) and the Moors (in black): the heroine, Bula, is kidnapped by the evil foreign king and his army, and her betrothed tries to win her back in a ritualized sword fight which takes place within a shifting circle of dancers.

Dubrovnik

DUBROVNIK, the jewel in the crown of Croatian tourism, is a beautifully preserved medieval fortified city. First settled by Roman refugees in the early seventh century, and given the name Ragusa, the town soon exploited its favourable position on the Adriatic with a maritime and commercial genius unmatched anywhere else in Europe. By the mid-fourteenth century, having shaken off the yoke of first the Byzantines and then the Venetians, it had become a successful and self-contained city state, its merchants trading far and wide. Dubrovnik fended off the attentions of the Ottoman Empire and continued to prosper until 1667, when an earthquake devastated the city, killing around 5000 people. Though the city-state survived, it fell into decline and, in 1808, was formally dissolved by Napoleon. An eight-month siege by Yugoslav forces in the early 1990s caused much destruction, but the city swiftly recovered and is now firmly back on the tourist map.

Arrival, information and accommodation

Both **ferry and bus terminals** are located in the port suburb of Gruž, 3km west of town. The main western entrance to the old town, the Pile Gate, is a thirty-minute slog along ul Ante Starčevića and you'd be better off catching a bus – #1a and #3 from the ferry terminal, #1a, #3 or #6 from behind the bus station. Tickets for local buses are bought from the driver (exact change only; 10kn) or from newspaper kiosks (7kn). Dubrovnik's **airport** is 20km south of the city, close to the resort town of Cavtat; Croatia Airways buses meet arrivals and run to the station (30kn).

The **tourist office** is located just up from Pile Gate at Ante Starčevića 7 (June–Sept daily 9am–8pm; Oct–May Mon–Sat 9am–7pm, Sun 9am–3pm; ☎020/427-591; ⓦwww.dubrovnik.laus.hr). **Private rooms** (❷) can be booked through Gulliver, opposite the ferry terminal at Obala Stjepana Radića 32 (☎020/313-300, ⓦwww.gulliver.hr); and Atlas, downhill from the Pile Gate at Svetog Djurdja 1 (☎020/442-574, ⓔatlas-pile@atlas.tel.hr), and just off Luža square in the old town at Lučarica 1 (☎020/442-591). There are four comfortable rooms

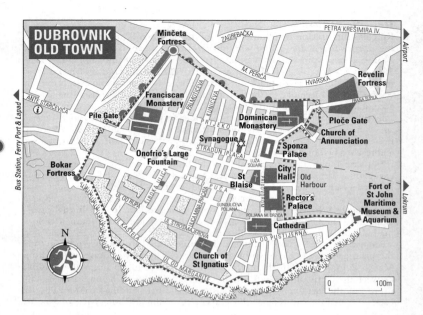

at *Dubrovnik B&B*, opposite the Ploce Gate, at Frank Supila 1 (☎020/201-5591, ⓦwww.dubrovnikbedandbreakfast.com; book in advance; ❹). There's a basic, well-run **HI hostel** at bana Jelačića 15/17 (☎020/423-241, ⓔhfhs.du@du.hinet.hr; ❷) – head up Ante Starčevića from the bus station and turn uphill to the right after five minutes. Affordable **hotels** are in short supply: the hostel-like *Hotel Gruž*, opposite the ferry terminal at Pionirska 4 (%020/418-977; ❸); the *Petka*, also opposite the terminal at Obala Stjepan Radića 38 (020/418-008; ❺); and the *Lero*, 1.5km west of Pile Gate at Iva Vojnovića 14 (☎020/332-122, ⓔhotel-lero@du.tel.hr; ❺), are the best options. The free, monthly *Dubrovnik Riviera*, available from hotels and the tourist office, is a great **pocket guide** listing bus and ferry timetables as well as forthcoming events.

The City

The **Pile Gate**, main entrance to the old town, is a fifteenth-century construction complete with a statue of St Blaise, the city's protector, set in a niche above the arch. The best way to get your bearings is by making a tour of the fabulous **city walls** (daily: summer 9am–9pm; winter 9am–4pm; 15kn), 25m high and with all its towers intact. Of the various towers and bastions that punctuate the walls, the 1455 **Minčeta fortress**, which marks the northeastern side, is by far the most imposing.

Within the walls, Dubrovnik is a sea of roofs faded into a pastel patchwork, punctured now and then by a sculpted dome or tower. At ground level, just inside the Pile Gate, **Onofrio's Large Fountain**, built in 1444, is a domed affair at which visitors to this hygiene-conscious city had to wash themselves before they were allowed any further. Across the street is the fourteenth-century **Franciscan Monastery** complex (free access); its treasury (daily 9am–4/5pm; 5kn) holds some fine Gothic reliquaries and manuscripts tracing the development of musical scoring, together with relics from the apothecary's shop, dating from 1317 and claiming to be the oldest in Europe.

From outside the monastery church, **Stradun** (also known as Placa), the city's main street, runs dead straight across the old town, its limestone surface polished to a slippery shine by the tramping of thousands of feet. Its far end broadens into the pigeon-choked **Luža Square**, the centre of the medieval town and even today hub of much of its activity. On the left, the **Sponza Palace** was once the customs house and mint, with a facade that's an elegant weld of florid Venetian Gothic and more sedate Renaissance forms; its majestic courtyard is given over to contemporary art exhibitions. Across the square, the Baroque-style **Church of St Blaise**, built in 1714 to replace an earlier church, serves as a graceful counterpoint to the palace. Outside the church stands the carved figure of an armoured knight, known as **Orlando's Column** and once the focal point of the city-state. On the eastern side of the square a Gothic arch leads through to an alley which winds past the **Dominican monastery**. Here, an arcaded courtyard filled with palms and orange trees leads to a small **museum** (daily 9am–5/6pm; 10kn), with outstanding examples of local sixteenth-century religious art.

Back on Luža, a street leads round the back of St Balaise towards the fifteenth-century **Rector's Palace**, the seat of the Ragusan government, in which the incumbent Rector sat out his month's term of office. Today it's given over to the **City Museum** (summer daily 9am–6pm; winter Mon–Sat 9am–2pm; 10kn), though for the most part it's a rather paltry collection, with mediocre sixteenth-century paintings and dull furniture.

Immediately south of the palace, Dubrovnik's seventeenth-century **Cathedral** is a rather plain building, although there's an impressive Titian polyptych of *The Assumption* inside. The **Treasury** (daily: summer 9am–8pm; winter 9am–noon & 3–7pm; 5kn) boasts a twelfth-century reliquary containg the skull of St Blaise; an exquisite piece in the shape of a Byzantine crown, the reliquary is stuck with portraits of saints and frosted with delicate gold and enamel filigree work.

From the cathedral, it's a short walk through to the small harbour, dominated by the monolithic hulk of the **Fort of St John**, which now houses a downstairs **aquarium** (daily: summer 9am–9pm; winter 9am–1pm; 15kn); upstairs is the **maritime museum** (summer daily 9am–6pm; winter Tues–Sun 9am–2pm; 10kn), which traces the history of Ragusan sea power through a display of naval artefacts and model boats.

Walking back east from here, you skirt one of the city's oldest quarters, **Pustijerna**, much of which predates the seventeenth-century earthquake. On the far side, the **Church of St Ignatius**, Dubrovnik's largest, is a Jesuit confection, modelled, like most Jesuit places of worship, on the enormous church of Gesù in Rome. The steps that lead down from here also had a Roman model – the Spanish Steps – and they sweep down to **Gunduliceva Poljana**, the square behind the cathedral which is the site of the city's morning fruit and vegetable market.

The noisy and crowded main city **beach** is a short walk east of the old town; a better bet is to head for the less crowded, and somewhat cleaner, beach on the Lapad peninsula, 5km to the west, or to catch one of the **boats** from the old city jetty (April–Oct 9am–6pm, every 30min, journey time 10min; 30kn return) to the wooded island of **Lokrum**. Crisscrossed by shady paths overhung by pines, Lokrum has some extensive rocky beaches running along the eastern end of the island, and there's a nudist section (FKK) at the far eastern tip.

Eating and drinking

For self-catering, there are morning fruit-and-vegetable **markets** (not Sun) on Gundulićeva Poljana. For **snacks**, try the sandwich bars lining the alleys running uphill from Stradun, the best of which is *Buffet Škola* on Antuninska. There's no shortage of **restaurants** in the old town, though many on Prijeko, the street running parallel to Stradun to the north, make too much of a hard sell, which is generally offputting: head instead for *Kamenica*, at Gundulićeva poljana 8, a simple place serving up cheap portions of *girice* (tiny deep-fried fish) and *kamenice* (oysters); or *Baracuda*, a tiny pizzeria on Božidarevičeva; alternatively, there's *Konoba Posat*, uz Posat 1, a large garden terrace just outside the Pile Gate which is good for grilled meats; and the tiny, but enjoyable Mexican restaurant, *Tres Miyos*, just north of the old town at Hvarska 6.

The pavement cafés at the eastern end of Stradun are popular spots for daytime and evening drinking, but for something with a bit more character, head for the smaller **cafébars** in the backstreets: *Hard Jazz Café Troubadur*, on Bunićeva Poljana, has live jazz most nights; *Otok*, Pobijana 8, is an alternative cultural centre whose cafébar attracts bohemian types; and *Pivnica Karaka*, at Izme Đ Polača 5, will satisfy those seeking a more beery evening. Outside the centre, ulica bana Jelačića, just above the bus station, is lined with bars buzzing until late on summer evenings. For clubbing, *Latino Club Fuego*, outside the Pile Gate, and *Esperanza*, near the bus station at Put Republike 30, are mainstream places. Live music and themed disco nights take place at the Karantena, a cultural centre just beyond Pile Gate on Frana Supila.

Dubrovnik's prestigious **Summer Festival** (July 10 to Aug 25; ☏020/412-288, ⓦwww.dubrovnik-festival.hr) is a good, if crowded, time to be around, with classical concerts and theatre performances in most of the city's courtyards, squares and bastions. Book tickets well in advance.

Listings

Consulates UK, Petilovrijenci 2 ☏311-466.
Exchange Dubrovačka Banka, Stradun (Mon–Fri 7.30am–1pm & 2–8pm, Sat 7.30am–1pm); Gospodarsko-Kreditna Banka, Pile Gate (daily 8am–8pm).
Hospital Roka Mišetiča bb ☏431-777.
Internet access Dubrovnik Internet Centar, Brsalje 1 (daily 10am–10pm; 20kn/hr); DuNet

Club, Put Republike 7 (Mon–Fri 8am–10pm; Sat 10am–10pm; 15kn/hr).
Left luggage At the bus station (daily 6am–9.00pm).
Pharmacy Obala S. Radiča 44.
Post office Put Republike 28 (Mon–Fri 8am–8pm, Sat 8am–7pm, Sun 8am–noon); A. Starčevića 2 (Mon–Fri 8am–3pm).

Travel details

Trains

Zagreb to: Pula (2 daily; 6hr 40min); Rijeka (6 daily; 4hr); Split (2 daily; 8hr–9hr).
Pula to: Zagreb (2 daily; 6hr 40min).

Buses

Zagreb to: Dubrovnik (6 daily; 11hr); Poreč (8 daily; 5hr); Pula (12 daily; 6hr); Rijeka (hourly; 4hr); Rovinj (5 daily; 9hr); Split (hourly; 7-9hr).
Dubrovnik to: Korčula (1 daily; 3hr 30min); Rijeka (6 daily); Split (15 daily; 4hr 30min); Zagreb (8 daily; 11hr).
Hvar Town to: Starigrad (7 daily; 35min).
Poreč to: Rijeka (5 daily; 2hr 30min); Pula (9 daily; 2hr); Zagreb (7 daily; 7hr).
Pula to: Dubrovnik (1 daily; 14hr); Poreč (8 daily; 2hr); Rijeka (hourly; 2hr 30min); Rovinj (12 daily; 1hr); Split (3 daily; 10hr); Zagreb (12 daily; 6hr).
Rijeka to: Dubrovnik (4 daily; 13hr); Pula (hourly; 2hr 30min); Split (4 daily; 8hr); Zagreb (hourly; 4hr).
Rovinj to: Poreč (8 daily; 45min); Pula (12 daily; 1hr); Rijeka (8 daily; 5hr).

Split to: Dubrovnik (hourly; 4hr 30min); Pula (3 daily; 10hr); Rijeka (12 daily; 8hr); Zagreb (hourly; 7-9hr).
Supetar to: Bol (5 daily; 1hr).

Ferries

Services from Dubrovnik and Rijeka run daily in summer and twice weekly at other times.

Brač to: Split (7 daily; 1hr).
Dubrovnik to: Korčula (4hr); Hvar (Stari Grad; 7hr); Split (9hr);
Rijeka (21hr).
Hvar to: Korčula (2 weekly; 45min); Split (1 weekly; 2hr; Stari Grad: 3–4 daily; 2hr); Vis (1 weekly; 1hr 15min).
Korčula to: Hvar (2 weekly; 45min); Split (1-2 daily; 3hr).
Rijeka to: Split (12hr); Hvar (Stari Grad; 14hr); Korčula (18hr); Dubrovnik (20hr).
Split to: Brač (7 daily; 1hr); Dubrovnik (1 daily; 9hr); Hvar (1 daily; 2hr; Stari Grad: 3–4 daily; 2hr); Korčula (1–2 daily; 3hr); Rijeka (1 daily; 12hr); Vis (1–2 daily; 2hr 30min).
Vis to: Hvar (1 weekly; 1hr 15min); Split (1–2 daily; 2hr 30min).

Czech Republic

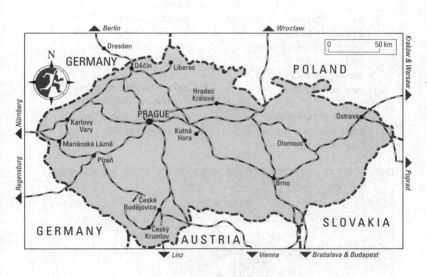

Czech Republic highlights

✳ **Prague Castle** Home to the cathedral, royal palace and numerous art galleries, with great views across the city. **See p.259**

✳ **Josefov, Prague** The former Jewish Quarter is home to six synagogues and an evocative medieval Jewish cemetery. **See p.261**

✳ **Obecní dům, Prague** The city's finest Art Nouveau building, housing two restaurants, a café, bar, art gallery and concert hall. **See p.262**

✳ **A Budvar at the Masné krámy, České Budějovice** Converted medieval butchers' stalls selling the original Czech version of Budweiser. **See p.265**

✳ **Český Krumlov** A gem of a medieval town, tucked into a bend of the River Vltava. **See p.265**

Introduction and basics

Czechoslovakia's "Velvet Revolution" in November 1989 was probably the most unequivocably positive of eastern Europe's anti-Communist upheavals, as the Czechs and Slovaks shrugged off 41 years of Communist rule without a shot being fired. But the euphoria and unity of those first few months evaporated more quickly than anyone could have imagined. Just three years on, the country split into two separate states: the Czech Republic and Slovakia. The Czechs – always the most urbane, agnostic and liberal of the Slav nations – have fared well, although they are now having to contend with rising crime and an increasing cost of living.

Almost untouched by the wars of the twentieth century, the capital, **Prague**, is justifiably one of the most popular destinations in Europe. An incredibly beautiful city with a wealth of architecture, from Gothic cathedrals and Baroque palaces to Art Nouveau cafés and Cubist villas, it's also a lively meeting place for young people from all over Europe. The rolling countryside of **Bohemia** is swathed in forests and studded with well-preserved medieval towns and castles, especially in the south around **České Budějovice**. In the west, you'll find the old watering-holes of the European aristocracy, the spa towns of **Karlovy Vary** and **Mariánské Lázně**. The country's eastern province, **Moravia**, is every bit as beautiful, only less touristed. **Olomouc** is the most attractive town here, but **Brno**, the regional capital, has its own peculiar pleasures.

Information and maps

Most cities and towns have their own **tourist offices** (*informační centrum*), where you should find an English-speaker who can attempt to answer any questions. A comprehensive range of **maps** is available. You can buy them, often very cheaply, from bookshops, petrol stations and some hotels – ask for a *plán města* (town plan) or *mapa okolí* (regional map). For hiking, Shocart produce a 1:50,000 *turistická mapa* series detailing the country's complex network of marked footpaths, as well as a 1:75,000 *cykloturistické* series, and a 1:100,000 series.

Money and banks

The local **currency** is the Czech crown, or *koruna česká* (Kč), which is divided into one hundred hellers or *haléř* (h). Coins come in 10h, 20h, 50h, 1Kč, 2Kč, 5Kč, 10Kč, 20Kč and 50Kč; notes as 20Kč, 50Kč, 100Kč, 200Kč, 500Kč, 1000Kč and 2000Kč (less frequently 5000Kč). The crown is fully convertible, though you may still find problems getting hold of any in foreign banks.

Banks are the best places to change money; they're open Mon–Fri 8am–5pm, though some close early on Fri. Assistants are generally more helpful and likely to speak English at branches of foreign banks, although charges can be a bit higher. **Travellers' cheques** are the traditional way to carry funds, but they are no longer the cheapest nor the most convenient. Credit

---

Czech Republic on the net

ⓦ **www.czech.cz** Basic information on the whole country

ⓦ **www. pis.cz** Prague's tourist office site

ⓦ **www.praguepost.com** Online version of the capital's own English-language paper

ⓦ **www.radio.cz/english** Updated news and weather

ⓦ **www.ticketpro.cz**, ⓦ **www.ticketstream.cz**, ⓦ **www.ticketsbti.cz** Three good sites for finding out what's on in Prague and booking tickets online

and debit cards, which you can use to make withdrawals from **ATMs**, are more useful, though it's a good idea to keep some hard currency in cash for emergencies.

Communications

Most **post offices** (*pošta*) are open Mon–Fri 8am–5pm, Sat 8am–noon. Look for the right sign to avoid queuing unnecessarily: *známky* (stamps), *dopisy* (letters) or *balky* (parcels). You can also buy **stamps** from tobacconists and kiosks, though often only for domestic mail; current rates are 9Kč for postcards within Europe and 12Kč to the rest of the world.

The majority of **public phones** only take phone cards (*telefonní karty*), currently available in 50, 100 and 150 units from post offices, tobacconists and some shops. You can make local and international calls from all card phones, all of which have instructions in English.

There's usually at least one **internet café** in every Czech city and major town; charges are around free to 100Kč/hr.

Phone changes

In September 2002, all Czech regional prefixes became an integral part of **telephone numbers**. Thus in Prague, the first digit of all phone numbers is now **2** and it is necessary to dial this even when calling from within the city. All new Czech phone numbers should therefore now have **nine digits**.

Getting around

The most pleasant way of travelling around the Czech Republic is by **train** (*vlak*) – it's scenic, safe and inexpensive, although fares are gradually creeping up. If you're in a hurry, however, **buses** (*autobusy*) are nearly always quicker and more frequent.

Trains

The Czech Republic has one of the most comprehensive rail networks in Europe.

Czech Railways (České dráhy or ČD, ⓦ www.cdrail.cz) run two main types of **trains**: *rychlík* (R) or *spěšný* (Sp) trains are the faster ones which stop only at major towns, while *osobní* trains stop at just about every station, averaging as little as 30kph. Fast trains are further divided into SuperCity (SC), which are first class only, EuroCity (EC) or InterCity (IC), for which you need to pay a supplement, and Expres (Ex), for which you don't. **Tickets** (*jízdenky*) for domestic journeys can be bought at the station (*nádraží*) before or on the day of departure. Fares are still cheap – a second-class single from Prague to Brno costs around £8/$12 – but they're rising. ČD runs reasonably priced **sleepers** to and from a number of cities in neighbouring countries. You must, however, book as far in advance as possible and in any case no later than six hours before departure. **InterRail** passes are valid; **Eurail** passes are not.

Buses

Regional **buses** – mostly run by the state bus company, Česká státní automobilová doprava (ČSAD) – travel to most destinations, with private companies such as ČEBUS providing an alternative on popular intercity routes. Bus stations are usually next to the train station, and if there's no separate terminal you'll have to buy your ticket from the driver. It's essential to book your ticket at least a day in advance if you're travelling at the weekend, on a public holiday or early in the morning on one of the main routes. Useful **websites** for times and information include ⓦ www .vlak-bus.cz and ⓦ www.jizdnirady.cz.

Accommodation

Accommodation remains the most expensive aspect of travelling in the Czech Republic. There is no organized hostel system, as such, though some places are now affiliated with Hostelling International. Private rooms are available all over the country, and more often than not the local tourist office will help to book a room. To book accommodation **online** try ⓦ www.avetravel.cz or ⓦ www.marys.cz.

Hotels and private rooms

Hotels are still occasionally priced up for foreigners and are in any case fairly expensive, especially in Prague. Most old state hotels have been refurbished by their new owners, and many new hotels and pensions have opened, particularly in the more heavily touristed areas. In the newer places, continental or buffet-style breakfast is normally included. Ignore the star system as it is no guarantee of quality, service or atmosphere. With ongoing privatization, refurbishment and renovation work, make it a rule to check hotel prices before you book.

Private rooms are available in Prague, Brno and several other towns on the tourist trail, and are a good bet, though not as widespread as they used to be. Elsewhere, just keep your eyes peeled for signs saying *Zimmer Frei*. Prices start at around 300Kč per person per night, but expect to pay more in Prague.

Hostels and campsites

Prague now has a number of **hostels**, which offer varying degrees of discomfort. The student travel organization CKM can arrange cheap **student accommodation** in the big university towns during July and August and usually charge 200Kč per person for dorm beds. The KMC (Club of Young Travellers), at Karolíny Světlé 30 in Prague (☎222 220 347, ✆www.kmc.cz), is an umbrella organization for youth hostels throughout the republic who can help organize accommodation for you.

Campsites, known as *autokemp*, are plentiful all over the Republic; the facilities are often basic and the ones known as *tábořiště* are even more rudimentary. Most have simple **chalets** (*chaty* or *bungolovy*) for anything upwards of 500Kč for two people. Very few sites remain open all year, and most don't open until May, closing sometime in September. Even though prices are sometimes inflated for foreigners, camping charges remain minimal.

Food and drink

The good news is that you can eat and drink very cheaply in the Czech Republic. The bad news is that forty years of culinary isolation and centralization under the Communists introduced few innovations to **Czech cuisine**, with its predilection for pork, gravy, dumplings and pickled cabbage – still, washed down with divine **Czech beer**, anything tastes good.

Food

Despite the recent arrival of cereals into Czech homes, the whole concept of **breakfast** (*snídaně*) as such is alien to the Czechs, though in hotels and pensions you'll probably get the standard coffee, roll and cheese or salami. Popular street **snacks** include *bramborák*, a potato pancake with flecks of bacon, *párek*, a frankfurter dipped in mustard or ketchup and shoved in a white roll, and *smažený sýr*– a slab of melted cheese fried in breadcrumbs and served in a roll (*v housce*) with tartar sauce.

More and more Czech cafés have proper espresso machines serving half-decent **coffee** (*káva*); elsewhere, the Czechs drink Turkish-style or *turecká*, with grains at the bottom of the cup. The **cake shop** (*cukrárna*) is an important part of the country's social life, particularly on Sundays when it's often the only place that's open, although the cakes aren't up to Austrian standards.

In and around Prague, eating out is inexpensive; **restaurants** (*restaurace*) always display their menus and prices outside. They serve hot meals from about 11am until 11pm (10pm outside Prague). Most **pubs** (*pivnice*) also serve a menu of basic hot dishes, as do **wine cellars** (*vinárna*) – often the most stylish places around.

Most lunchtime menus start with **soup** (*polévka*), one of the country's culinary strong points. **Main courses** are overwhelmingly based on pork (*vepřový*) or beef (*hovězí*), but one treat is carp (*kapr*), traditional at Christmas and cheaply and widely offered just about everywhere, along with trout (*pstruh*). Goose (*husa*), duck (*kachna*) and wild boar (*kanci maso*) dishes are also generally delicious. Main courses are served with different varieties of **dumpling** (*knedlíky*) or **vegetables**, most commonly potatoes (*brambory*) and sauerkraut (*zelí*). With the exception of *palačinky* (pancakes) filled with chocolate or fruit, cream, delicious fruit dumplings (*ovocné knedlíky*) and ice cream, **desserts**, where they exist at all, can be pretty uninspiring.

Drink

Even the most simple *bufet* (self-service cafeteria) in the Czech Lands almost invariably has draught beer (*pivo*). The **pub** (*pivnice*), most of which close around 11pm, is still a predominantly male affair, with heavy drinking the norm; **wine bars** (*vinárna*) and restaurants are generally far more upmarket and **cocktail bars** have now opened up in most main towns.

The Czech Republic tops the world league table of **beer** consumption, even beating the Germans – hardly surprising since its beer ranks among the best in the world. The most natural starting point for any beer tour is the Bohemian city of **Plzeň** (Pilsen), whose local lager is the original Pils. The other big brewing town is **České Budějovice** (Budweis), home to Budvar, a mild beer by Bohemian standards but still leagues ahead of the American Budweiser. The burgeoning in-house breweries offer some great brews, as do the hundreds of small breweries dotted around the country.

The republic also produces a modest selection of medium-quality **wines**; the largest wine-producing region is southern Moravia. The home-production of firewater is a national pastime, resulting in some almost terminally strong concoctions, most famously a plum brandy called *slivovice*. The most well-known Czech **spirit** is Becherovka, a medicinal herbal tipple from Karlovy Vary, known as a *beton* when ordered with ice and tonic.

Opening hours and holidays

Shops are open Mon–Fri 9am–5pm, with some, and most supermarkets, staying open till 6pm or later. Smaller shops close for lunch between noon and 2pm, while others stay open late on Thurs. In larger towns, some shops stay open all day at weekends, and the **corner shop** (*večerka*) stays open daily till 11pm.

Public holidays include Jan 1; Easter Mon; May 1; May 8 (VE Day 1945); July 5 (Introduction of Christianity into the Czech Lands by SS Cyril and Methodius); July 6 (Anniversary of the Martyrdom of Jan Hus); Sept 28 (Czech state day); Oct 28 (Anniversary of the Foundation of the Republic); Nov 17 (The Battle for Freedom and Democracy Day); Dec 24, 25 & 26.

Emergencies

In the last decade, public confidence in the **police** (*policie*) has declined as the crime level has risen. For tourists, theft from cars is the biggest worry, although pickpockets are as rife as in any European capital in the centre of Prague, particularly in the Old Town Square, on the #22 tram, in the metro and in the main railway stations. Although everyone is obliged to carry some form of ID and you should theoretically carry your **passport** with you at all times, you're highly unlikely to get stopped unless you're driving a car bearing foreign plates or if you are non-white, so you may choose to leave your ID in the hotel safe.

Minor ailments can be easily dealt with at a **pharmacy** (*lékárna*), but language is likely to be a problem outside the capital. If it's a repeat prescription you want, take any empty bottles or remaining pills along with you. If the pharmacist can't help, they'll be able to direct you to a **hospital** (*nemocnice*). If you do have to pay for any medication, keep the receipts for claiming on your insurance once you're home.

Emergency numbers

Police ☏150; Ambulance ☏155; Fire ☏158.

Prague

Prague (Praha) is one of the least "eastern" European cities you could imagine. Architecturally it is a revelation: few other cities anywhere in Europe look so good – and no other European capital can present six hundred years of architecture so completely untouched by natural disaster or war.

Prague rose to prominence in the ninth century under Prince Bořivoj, its first Christian ruler and founder of the Přemyslid dynasty. His grandson, Prince Václav, became the **Good "King" Wenceslas** of the Christmas carol and the country's patron saint. The city prospered from its position on the central European trade routes, but it was after the dynasty died out in 1306 that Prague enjoyed its **golden age**. In just thirty years Holy Roman Emperor Charles IV transformed it into one of the most important cities in fourteenth-century Europe, founding an entire new town, Nové Město, to accommodate the influx of students. Following the execution of the reformist preacher Jan Hus in 1415, the country became engulfed in **religious wars**, and trouble broke out again between the Protestant nobles and the Catholic Habsburgs in 1618. The full force of the Counter-Reformation was brought to bear on the city's people, though the spurt of Baroque rebuilding that went with it gave Prague its most striking architectural aspect.

After two centuries as little more than a provincial town in the Habsburg Empire, Prague was dragged out of the doldrums by the **Industrial Revolution** and the **národní obrození**, the Czech national revival that led to the foundation of the **First Republic** in 1918. Shortly after World War II, which it survived substantially unscathed, Prague disappeared completely behind the Iron Curtain. The city briefly re-emerged onto the world stage during the **Prague Spring** in 1968, but the decisive break came in November 1989, when a peaceful student demonstration, brutally broken up by the police, triggered off the **Velvet Revolution**, which eventually toppled the Communist government. The popular unity of that period is now history, but there is still a great sense of new-found potential in the capital, which has been transformed by restorations over the last decade.

Arrival and information

Prague's **airport**, Ruzyně, is 10km northwest of the city. The cheapest way of getting into town is by taking local bus #119 (every 15–20min) the 20-minute ride to Dejvická metro station. Alternatively, there's the ČEDAZ **express minibus** (every 30min), which stops first at Dejvická metro station, and ends up at náměstí Republiky (90Kč). The express minibuses will also take you straight to your hotel for around 360Kč per drop-off – a bargain if there's a few of you. Avoid so-called "fixed price" taxis. Arriving by **train** from the west, you're most likely to end up at Praha hlavní nádraží. It's only a short walk to Wenceslas Square from here (though inadvisable at night), and there's also a metro station inside the station. International expresses, passing through Prague, often stop only at Praha-Holešovice, north of the city centre (metro Nádraží Holešovice). Some trains from Moravia and Slovakia wind up at the central Masarykovo nádraží (metro Náměstí Republiky); and trains from the south at Praha-Smíchov (metro Smíchovské nádraží). There are lockers

---

Entry to sights of interest

If you want to see the interior of a building, nine times out of ten you'll be forced to go on a **guided tour** that will last at least 45 minutes. Ask for an *anglický* text, an often unintentionally hilarious English résumé.

Entrance tickets to most sights of interest throughout the Czech Republic rarely cost more than 50–100Kč, so prices are only quoted in this chapter where the entrance fee is prohibitive; the last tour usually leaves an hour before the advertised closing time.

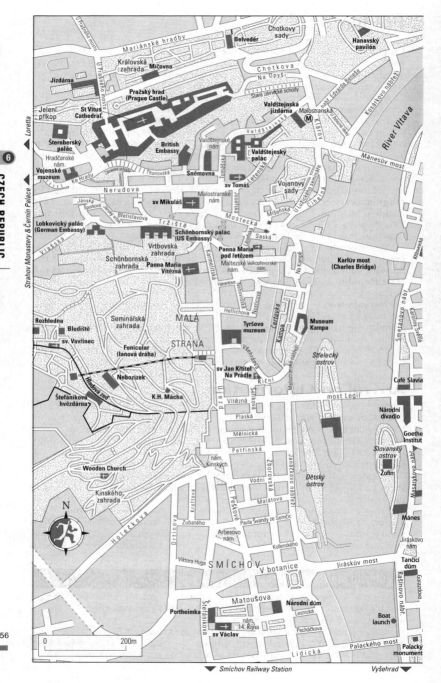

Strahov Monastery & Černín Palace ◀ Loretta

Mariánské hradby

Belvedér

Chotkovy sady

Hanavský pavilón

Královská zahrada Míčovna

Jízdárna

Chotkova

Na Opyši

U Prašného mostu

Pražský hrad
(Prague Castle)

Staré zámecké schody

Valdštejnská jízdárna

Malostranská Ⓜ Klárov

nábř. Edvarda Beneše

Kosárkovo nábřeží

River Vltava

Jelení příkop

St Vítus Cathedral

Mánesův most

Šternberský palác

Hradčanské nám.

British Embassy

Valdštejnské nám.

Valdštejnská

Valdštejnský palác

Vojanovy sady

U Lužického semináře

Cihelná

Vojenské muzeum

Ke Hradu

zámecké schody

Thunovská

Sněmovna

Tomášská

Letenská

sv Tomáš

Nerudova

Jánská Šporkova

Břetislavova

sv Mikuláš

Malostranské nám.

Mostecká

Míšeňská

Na Kampě

Karlův most
(Charles Bridge)

Kizovnická

Lobkovický palác
(German Embassy)

Vlašská

Tržiště

Schönbornský palác
(US Embassy)

Karmelitská

Lázeňská

Saská

Vrtbovská zahrada

Panna Maria pod řetězem

Maltézské nám. Velkopřevorské nám.

Schönbornská zahrada

Panna Maria Vítězná

Harantova

Nebovidská

Nosticova

Smetanovo nábř.

Karolíny Světlé

Rozhledna

Bludiště

Seminářská zahrada

MALÁ

Hellichova

Všehrdova

Lázeňská

Tyršovo muzeum

Museum Kampa

Střelecký ostrov

sv. Vavřinec

Funicular
(lanová dráha)

STRANA

Maltézské nábř.

Kampa

Café Slavia

Nebozízek

sv Jan Křtitel Na Prádle

Říční

most Legií

Národní divadlo

Hladová zeď

K.H. Mácha

Úpze

Vítězná

Seříkova

Goethe Institut

Štefánikova hvězdárna

Plaská

Mělnická

Slovanský ostrov

Žofín

Wooden Church

Petřínská

nám. Kinských

Zborovská

Janáčkovo nábřeží

Dětský ostrov

Masarykovo nábř.

Mánes

Kinského zahrada

N

Vodní

Malátova

Jiráskovo nám.

Holečkova

Plzeňská

Ditinova

Kroftova

El. Peškové

Zubatého

Pavla Švandy ze Semčic

Arbesovo nám.

Kořenského

Jiráskův most

Tančící dům

Gorazdova

Viktora Huga

SMÍCHOV

V botanice

Rašínovo nábř.

Portheimka

Matoušova

Lesnická

Národní dům

Boat launch

Štefánikova

nám. 14. Října

Pecháčkova

Palackého most

Palacký monument

sv Václav

Lidická

0   200m

▼ Smíchov Railway Station   Vyšehrad ▼

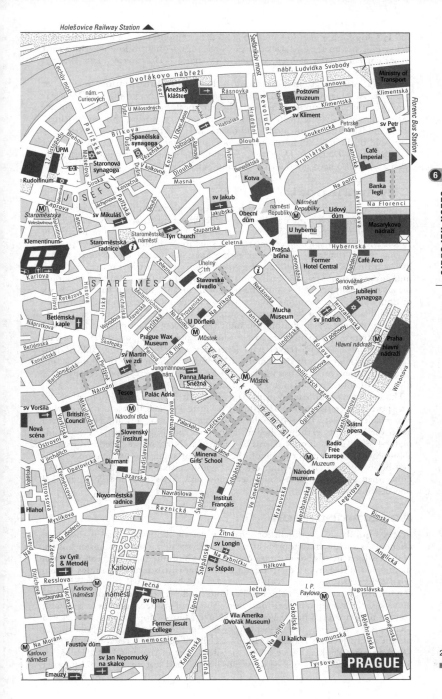

Čechův most
Dvořákovo nábřeží
nábř. Ludvíka Svobody
Ministry of Transport
nám. Curieových
Kozí
Anežský klášter
Rásnovka
Lannova
Klimentská
17 listopadu
Pařížská
Bílkova
Dušní
U Milosrdných
Anežská
Haštalská
Revoluční
Nová mlýn
Poštovní muzeum
Klimentská
sv Kliment
Petrské nám.
sv Petr
Florenc Bus Station ▶
ÚPM
Masełská
Elišky Krásnohorské
Bílkova
Dušní
Haštalská
Řásnovka
Vězeňská
Kozí
Soukenická
Rudolfinum
Valentinská
Pařížská
Vězeňská
V kolkovně
Dlouhá
Rybná
Benediktská
Truhlářská
Café Imperial
JOSEFOV
Kaprova
Staronová synagoga
Jachymova
Masná
Na poříčí
Banka Legii
Staroměstská
Veleslavínova
Žatecká
Dušní
Kostečná
sv Mikuláš
sv Jakub
Jakubská
náměstí Republiky
Náměstí Republiky
Lidový dům
Na Florenci
Masarykovo nádraží
Klementinum
Staroměstská radnice
Staroměstské náměstí
Týn Church
Štupartská
Celetná
Obecní dům
U hybernů
Hybernská
Havlíčkova
Karlova
STARÉ MĚSTO
Zelená
Uhelný trh
Stavovské divadlo
Prašná brána
Former Hotel Central
Café Arco
Karlova
Liliová
Retězová
Husova
Jilská
Michalská
Melantrichova
Havelská
Na příkopě
Nekázanka
Senovážná
Senovážné nám.
Jubilejní synagoga
Betlémská kaple
Náprstkova
Betlémská
Konviktská
Jalská
Vejvodova
Rytířská
Provaznická
Panská
Mucha Museum
sv Jindřich
Jeruzalémská
Bartolomějská
Skořepka
Perštýn
28 října
U Dörflerů
Můstek
Indřišská
Růžová
U půjčovny
Hlavní nádraží
Praha hlavní nádraží
sv Martin ve zdi
Prague Wax Museum
Václavské
Jungmannovo nám.
Panna Maria Sněžná
Můstek
Politických vězňů
Olivova
Wilsonova
sv Voršila
British Council
Voršilská
Mikulandská
Národní
Tesco
Palác Adria
náměstí
Vodičkova
Štěpánská
Opletalova
Washingtonova
Nová scéna
Ostrovní
Spálená
Národní třída
Slovenský institut
Jungmannova
Palackého
Ve Smečkách
Krakovská
Muzeum
Radio Free Europe
Státní opera
V jirchářích
Diamant
Vladislavova
Minerva Girls' School
V jámě
Mezibranská
Legerova
Voršilská
Klementova
Černá
Lazarská
Navrátilova
Školská
Štěpánská
Národní muzeum
Hlahol
Myslíkova
Novoměstská radnice
Řeznická
Institut Français
Žitná
Anglická
Na Zderaze
Na zbořenci
Na Rybníčku
sv Longin
Štěpánská
Na Štěpán
sv Štěpán
Hálkova
Římská
Ječná
I. P. Pavlova
Jugoslávská
sv Cyril & Metoděj
Karlovo
Resslova
Karlovo náměstí
náměstí
sv Ignác
Ječná
Lipová
Sokolská
Na bojišti
Bělehradská
Londýnská
Dittrichova
Jenštejnská
Václavská
Former Jesuit College
Vila Amerika (Dvořák Museum)
Rumunská
Na Moráni
Karlovo náměstí
Faustův dům
U nemocnice
Kateřinská
Viničná
Ke Karlovu
U kalicha
Emauzy
sv Jan Nepomucký na skalce
Tyršova

PRAGUE

and **left-luggage** offices (open 24hr) at all these stations. The main **bus station** is Praha-Florenc, on the eastern edge of Nové Město (metro Florenc). **Busabout buses** currently arrive at Arena Hostel, U výstaviště 1, Holešovice (metro Nádraží Holešovice).

The best place to go for information is the **Prague Information Service**, or PIS (Pražská informační služba), whose main branch is at Na příkopě 20 (Mon–Fri 9am–6/7pm, Sat & Sun 9am–3/5pm). The staff speak English, but their helpfulness varies enormously; they can usually answer most enquiries, and can organize accommodation, sell maps, guides and theatre tickets. As for listings, it's worth getting hold of the free English-language monthly *Culture in Prague/Česká kultura* or the fortnightly *Do města/ Downtown*. The English-language newspaper *Prague Post* (every Wed), also has a good selective listings section.

City transport

Prague's city centre is reasonably small and best explored on foot, but to cross the city quickly, or reach some of the more widely dispersed attractions, you'll need to use the public transport system (*dopravní podnik* or *DP*). There are two main types of **ticket**: the 12Kč *přestupní jízdenka*, which is valid for an hour (1hr 30min off-peak), during which time you may change metro lines, trams and buses as often as you like, and the 8Kč *nepřestupní jízdenka*, which allows you to travel for up to fifteen minutes on a single tram or bus, or up to four stops on the metro (not including the one you start at). Tickets must be bought in advance from a tobacconist, kiosk or from one of the extraordinarily complicated ticket machines inside all metro stations and at some tram stops; basically, you want to hit the "8" or "12" button, followed by the *výdej/enter* button. You must validate your ticket on board or at the metro entrance. If you're going to be using the public transport system a lot, it's worth getting hold of a **travel pass** (*časová jízdenka*; 1000Kč/24hr, 200Kč/72hr, 250Kč/week); write your name and date of birth on the reverse of the ticket and validate it when you first use it. Plain-clothes inspectors (*revizoří*) check tickets – it's a fine of 400Kč on the spot if it's not valid.

The fast Soviet-built **metro** (daily 5am–midnight) is the most useful form of city transport. The **trams** (every 10–20min) navigate Prague's hills and cobbles with remarkable dexterity. Tram #22, whose runs includes Vinohrady and Hradčany, is a good way to sightsee, though beware of pickpockets. Night trams #51–58 (midnight–4.30am; every 40min) all pass by Lazarská in Nové Město. The horror stories about Prague **taxi** drivers ripping off tourists are too numerous to mention, so your best bet is to flag a taxi down or call the English-speaking AAA (☎233 113 311), rather than go to the mafia-controlled ranks on Václavské náměstí, Národní and outside Obecní dům.

Accommodation

Prague's **hotels** are exorbitant for what you get and booking ahead is absolutely essential. As a result, most tourists on a budget now stay in private rooms or hostels, both of which are easy to organize on arrival. At both the main international train stations and at the airport, there are numerous **accommodation agencies** dealing with private rooms (from ❷): the largest and best is AVE (☎257 555 176, ⓦ www.avetravel.cz), which also has 350 hotels and pensions on its books. Prague's university, the Karolinum, rents out over a thousand **student rooms** in summer; contact the booking office at Voršilská 1, Nové Město (Mon–Fri only; ☎224 913 692; beds available June to mid-Sept; from ❶). Another organization specializing in summer-only dorms is Traveller's Hostels, a chain of centrally located **hostels** (from ❷); their main booking office is also the site of one of the hostels at Dlouhá 33, Staré Město (☎224 826 662, ⓦ www.travellers.cz) and features a bar and internet access.

Hostels

Clown and Bard Bořivojova 102, Žižkov ☎222 716 453, Ⓦwww.crownandbard.com. Clean hostel with laid-back atmosphere and loads of staged events. Laundry facilities. No curfew. Doubles as well as dorms. Tram #5, #9 or #26 to Lipanská from metro Hlavní nádraží. **❷**

Klub Haitat Na Zderaze 10, Nové Město ☎224 921 706, Ⓔhostel@iol.cz. The best of Prague's hostels, offering a discount to HI members, located a short walk from Karlovo náměstí. Rates include breakfast. Book ahead. Metro Karlovo náměsti. **❷**

Hostel Týn Týnská 19, Staré Město ☎222 734 590, Ⓦwww.hostel.cz. The most centrally located hostel. Six-bed dorms and simple doubles. Metro Náměstí Republiky. Dorms **❷**

Sokol Újezd 40, Malá Strana ☎257 007 397. Shambolic student hostel in sports centre in a great location; the entrance is on Všehrdova. Tram #12 or #22 from metro Malostranská. **❶**

Traveller's Hostel Dlouhá 33, Staré Město ☎224 826 662, Ⓦwww.travellers.cz. Centrally located; booking office above the *Roxy* nightclub. Metro Náměstí Republiky. **❷**

Hotels and pensions

Avalon-Tara Havelská 15 ☎224 228 083, Ⓔavalon-tara@volny.cz. Perfect location right over the market on Havelská, with seven very small, plainly furnished but clean rooms. Metro Můstek. **❹**

Betlem Club Betlemské náměstí 9, Staré Město ☎222 221 574, Ⓦwww.betlemclub.cz. Cheerful pension just west of Národní. Metro Národní třída. **❺**

Cloister Inn/Pension Unitas Bartolomějská 9, Staré Město ☎224 211 020, Ⓦwww.cloister-inn.com. Hotel-cum-hostel in a centrally located former nunnery; rooms range from the clean and bright to claustrophobic converted secret-police prison cells (where Havel was once detained). Metro Národní třída. **❸**

Dum U velké boty Vlašská 30, Malá Strana ☎257 311 107. The most delightful, tastefully decorated pension, run by a very welcoming couple. Metro Malostranská. **❼**

Expres Skořepka 5, Staré Město ☎224 211 801, Ⓦwww.hotel-expres.wz.cz. Simple, central hotel with friendly staff, breakfast included. Metro Národní třída. **❹**

Imperial Na Poříčí 15, Nové Město ☎222 316 012, Ⓦwww.hotelimperial.cz. Friendly, atmospheric and spotless rooms with shared facilities in an Art Nouveau hotel on the edge of the old town, with a great café below. **❺**

U krále Jiřího Liliová 10, Staré Město ☎224 248 797, Ⓦwww.kinggeorge.cz. Eight slightly kitsch rooms above a set of bars, deep in the heart of the old town. Metro Staroměstská. **❻**

U medvídků Na Perštýně 7 ☎224 211 916 Ⓦwww.umedvidku.cz. Plainly furnished rooms above famous Prague pub and something of an Old Town bargain; booking ahead essential. Metro Národní třída. **❺**

The City

The **River Vltava** divides the capital into two unequal halves: the steeply inclined left bank, which accommodates the castle district of Hradčany and Malá Strana, and the more gentle, sprawling right bank, which includes Staré Město, Josefov and Nové Město. **Hradčany**, on the hill, contains the most obvious sights – the castle, the cathedral and the old royal palace. Below Hradčany, **Malá Strana** (Little Quarter), with its narrow eighteenth-century streets, is the city's ministerial and diplomatic quarter, though its Baroque gardens are there for all to enjoy. Over the river, on the right bank, **Staré Město** (Old Town) is a web of alleys and passage-ways centred on the city's most beautiful square, Staroměstské náměsti. Enclosed within the boundaries of Staré Město is **Josefov**, the old Jewish quarter, now down to a handful of synagogues and a cemetery. **Nové Město** (New Town), the focus of the modern city, covers the largest area, laid out in long wide boulevards – most famously Wenceslas Square – stretching south and east of the old town.

Hradčany

Hradčany is wholly dominated by the city's omnipresent landmark, **Prague Castle**, or Pražský hrad (Ⓦwww.hrad.cz), the vast hilltop complex that looks out over the city centre from the west bank of the River Vltava. Viewed from the Charles Bridge (Karlův most), Prague Castle stands aloof from the rest of the city, protected by a rather austere palatial facade that's breached only by the great mass of **St Vitus Cathedral** (Mon–Sat 9am–4/5pm, Sun noon–4/5pm). Building started under Charles IV, who summoned the precocious 23-year-old German mason **Peter Parler** to work on the church. But only the choir and the south transept were finished when Charles died in 1399, and the whole structure wasn't completed until 1929. The eastern section recalls the building's authentic Gothic roots and the south door, or **Golden Gate** (Zlatá brána), is also pure Parler in style.

The Cathedral is the country's largest church, and, once inside, it's difficult not to be impressed by its sheer height. The grand chapel of **sv Václav**, by the south door, is easily the main attraction. Built by Parler, its rich decoration resembles the inside of a jewel casket: the gilded walls are inlaid with over 1300 semiprecious stones, set around ethereal fourteenth-century Biblical frescoes, while above, the tragedy of Wenceslas unfolds in later paintings. A door in the south wall leads to the coronation chamber, which houses the Bohemian crown jewels, including the gold crown of St Wenceslas. At the centre of the choir, within a fine Renaissance grill, cherubs lark about on the sixteenth-century marble **Imperial Mausoleum**, commissioned by Rudolf II for his grandfather, Ferdinand I, and father, Maximilian II.

If you want to see the choir or the ambulatory, you'll need to buy a **ticket** (220Kč), valid for three days, which also gives you entry into a handful of other sights in the castle, including the **Old Royal Palace** (Starý královský palác), just across the courtyard from the south door of the cathedral, and home to the princes and kings of Bohemia from the eleventh to the seventeenth centuries. It's a sandwich of royal apartments built by successive generations – these days you enter at the third and top floor, built at the end of the fifteenth century. The massive Vladislav Hall (Vladislavský sál) is where the early Bohemian kings were elected, and where every president since Masaryk has been sworn into office – including Václav Havel on December 29, 1989.

Don't be fooled by the uninspiring red facade of the **Basilica of sv Jiří** (Basilica of St George) – this is Prague's most beautiful Romanesque monument (and a popular venue for events), its inside meticulously restored to re-create the crumble-coloured basilica which replaced the original tenth-century church in 1173. Next door, the **Convent of sv Jiří** (Jiřský klášter), founded in 973, now houses the National Gallery's **Rudolfine and Baroque art collection** (Tues–Sun 10am–6pm; ⑩www.ngprague.cz), mostly of specialist interest only, though including a brief taste of the overtly sensual and erotic Mannerist paintings from the reign of Rudolf II (1576–1612). Round the corner from the convent is the **Golden Lane** (Zlatá ulička), a blind and crowded alley of miniature sixteenth-century cottages in dolly-mixture colours. A plaque at no. 22 commemorates Franz Kafka's brief sojourn here during World War I.

North of the castle walls, across the Powder Bridge (Prasný most), is the entrance to the **Královská zahrada** (April–Oct daily 10am–6pm), founded by Ferdinand I and still the best-kept gardens in the country, with functioning fountains and immaculately cropped lawns. At the end of the gardens is Prague's most celebrated Renaissance legacy, the **Belvedér** (Tues–Sun 10am–6pm), a delicately arcaded summer house, now an art gallery.

Hradčanské náměstí fans out from the castle's main gates, surrounded by the oversized palaces of the old nobility. A passage down the side of the Archbishop's Palace leads to the early eighteenth-century **Šternberg Palace** (Tues–Sun 10am–6pm; ⑩www.ngprague.cz), housing the National Gallery's relatively modest **Old European art collection** (ie non-Czech), which primarily consists of works from the fifteenth to eighteenth centuries, the most significant of which is the *Festival of the Rosary* by Dürer.

Malá Strana

More than anywhere else, **Malá Strana** conforms to the image of Prague as the quintessential Baroque city. Its focus is the sloping, cobbled **Malostranské náměstí**, a busy square split in two by the former Jesuit seminary and church of **sv**

Mikuláš (daily 9am–4pm; tower till 6pm; Nov–March tower Sat & Sun only), possibly the most magnificent Baroque building in the city. Nothing of the plain west facade prepares you for the overwhelming High Baroque interior – the fresco in the nave alone covers over 1500sq m, and portrays some of the more fanciful feats of St Nicholas.

Follow Tomášská north from the square and you'll enter Vladštejnská, flanked on one side by the gargantuan Valdštejn Palace, and on the other by the **Ledeburská zahrada** (April–Oct daily 10am–6pm). These terraced gardens, which connect higher up with the Zahrada na valech beneath the Castle, are one of the chief joys of Malá Strana. This is where the royal vineyards used to be, and the gardens command superb views over Prague.

South of the main square, a continuation of Karmelitská brings you to the funicular railway up **Petřín** hill (daily 9.15am–8.45pm, every 10–15min), a better green space than most in Prague, and a good place for a picnic and views from Petřín tower (April–Oct daily 10am–7pm; Nov–March Sat & Sun 10am–5pm).

Staré Město

Staré Město, founded in the early thirteenth century, is where most of the capital's shops, restaurants and pubs are located. It is linked to Malá Strana by the city's most familiar monument, the **Charles Bridge** (Karlův most), begun in 1357. The statues that line it – brilliant pieces of Jesuit propaganda added during the Counter-Reformation – have made it renowned throughout Europe and choked throughout the year. Cross to Staré Město and head down the narrow, crowded **Karlova**, which winds past the massive **Klementinum** (Mon–Fri 2–8pm, Sat & Sun 10am–8pm; Nov–March Sat & Sun only; 100Kč), the former Jesuit College, completed just before the order were turfed out of the country in 1773. It now serves as the national library and state technical library, though you can visit the spectacular Baroque library and the astronomical tower on a short guided tour.

At the end of the street lies **Staroměstské náměstí**, the most spectacular square in Prague and the city's main marketplace from the eleventh century. At its centre is the dramatic Art Nouveau **Jan Hus Monument**, featuring the great fifteenth-century religious reformer. The best-known sight on the square, however, is the **Astronomical Clock** (chimes hourly 8am–8pm), which features a mechanical performance by Christ, the Apostles and a few extras. The clock is an integral part of **Staroměstská radnice**, the town hall, inside which you can view a few chambers (Mon 11am–5pm, Tues–Sun 9am–6pm), climb the tower and get a close-up view of the aforementioned mechanical figures. Staré Město's most impressive Gothic structure is the mighty **Týn Church**, whose towers rise above the two arcaded houses which otherwise obscure its facade. Behind, at the end of Týnská, lies the **Ungelt**, a stunning fortified courtyard where customs used to be collected; it houses the Renaissance Granovský palace plus some very upmarket shops and cafés.

Josefov

Within Staré Město lies **Josefov**, the Jewish quarter of the city until the end of the nineteenth century, when this ghetto area was demolished in order to create a beautiful bourgeois district on Parisian lines. The writer **Franz Kafka** spent most of his life in and around Josefov, and the destruction of the Jewish quarter, which continued throughout his childhood, had a profound effect on his psyche; a small exhibition (Tues–Sat 10am–6pm) on the site of his birthplace tells the story of his life.

The "sights" of Josefov are covered by one ticket, available from any of the quarter's box offices (daily except Sat & Jewish holidays 9am–4.30/6pm; 280Kč, plus another 200Kč for the Old-New Synagogue). The best place to begin is the **Pinkas Synagogue** on Široká, which contains a chilling memorial to the 77,297

Czechoslovak Jews who were killed during the Holocaust – the names of all the victims cover the walls, while children's drawings from the Theresienstadt (Terezín) camp are displayed in the women's gallery. From here, you enter the **Old Jewish Cemetery** (Starý Židovský hřbitov), established in the fifteenth century and in use until 1787, by which time there were some 100,000 graves here piled on top of one another. Get there before the crowds, and the jumble of 12,000 Gothic, Renaissance and Baroque tombstones are a poignant reminder of the ghetto, its inhabitants subjected to overcrowding even in death.

Halfway down **Pařížská**, Prague's most glamorous shopping street, is the steep brick gable of the **Old-New Synagogue**, completed in the fourteenth century and still the religious centre of Prague's Jewish community. Originally it was known simply as the New Synagogue, but after several fires gutted the ghetto it became the oldest synagogue building in the quarter – hence its name.

Opposite the synagogue is the **Židovská radnice**, the old Jewish town hall founded in the sixteenth century and later turned into a creamy-pink Baroque house crowned by a wooden clocktower. In addition to the four main clocks, there's one on the north gable, which (like the Hebrew script) goes "backwards". The nearby Baroque **Klaus Synagogue** on U Starého hřbitová and the neo-Gothic **Maisel Synagogue** on Maiselova display some beautiful religious objects and portray the history of the Jews in the Czech lands until the eighteenth century, while the highly ornate neo-Byzantine **Spanish Synagogue**, at Věženská 1, on the other side of Pařížská, contains an exhibition on the more recent history of the city's Jewish community from 1781.

Nové Město

Nové Město, now a sprawling late nineteenth-century bourgeois quarter, was actually founded in 1348 by Charles IV. The borderline between Staré and Nové Město is made up by the continuous boulevards of **Národní** and **Na příkopě**, a boomerang curve that follows the course of the old moat. The former was the unlikely setting for the November 17 demonstration that sparked off the Velvet Revolution.

At the river end of Národní is the gold-crested **National Theatre**, a proud symbol of the Czech nation. Refused money by the Austrian state, Czechs of all classes dug deep into their pockets to raise funds for the venture themselves. Halfway along Na příkopě you can visit the **Mucha Museum**, at Panská 7 (daily 10am–6pm; 120Kč; Ⓦwww.mucha.cz), dedicated to the country's best-known artist, Alfons Mucha.

At the far end of Na příkopě, on náměstí Republiky, stands the **Obecní dům**, where you can see more of Mucha's work. Begun in 1903, it was decorated inside and out with the help of almost every artist connected with the Czech Secession. The easiest way of soaking up the dramatic interior, covered with Art Nouveau mosaics and pendulous chandeliers, is to have a reasonably pricey but delicious meal in the French restaurant to the right or a coffee in the equally dazzling café to the left. Alternatively, you can go on a guided tour of the interior; tickets are available from the new information centre (daily 10am–6pm; 150Kč; Ⓦwww.obecni-dum.cz).

Cross the boulevard at its central point and you're into the pivot of modern Prague and the political focus of the events of November 1989 – the wide, gently sloping **Wenceslas Square** (**Václavské náměstí**). The square's history of protest goes back to the Prague Spring of 1968: towards the top end, there's a small memorial to the victims of Communism, the most famous of whom, the 21-year-old student Jan Palach, set himself alight on this very spot in January 1969 in protest against the Soviet occupation. A six-lane freeway effectively cuts off the square from the **National Museum** (daily 9/10am–5/6pm), one of the great symbols of the nineteenth-century Czech national revival, with its monumental glass cupola, sculptural decoration and frescoes from Czech history. However, unless you're a geologist or a zoologist you're likely to remain unmoved by the exhibits.

Trade Fair Palace: Museum of Modern Art

One reason to hop on a tram is to visit the city's modern-art museum, housed in a vast functionalist 1920s building known as the **Trade Fair Palace** (Tues–Sun 10am–6pm; 180Kč; ®www.ngprague.cz), on Dukelských hrdinu 47 (tram #5 from náměstí Republiky). The museum's *raison d'être* is its unrivalled permanent collection of nineteenth- and twentieth-century Czech art, but it also houses the National Gallery's modest collection of nineteenth- and twentieth-century European art, including works by Klimt, Schiele, Picasso and the French Impressionists, as well as temporary exhibitions of contemporary Czech and foreign art.

Eating

Angel Café Opatovická 3, Nové Město. Sleek, light, minimalist decor and seriously delicious designer cooking available at this resolutely expat café/restaurant. Closed Mon–Wed & Sun eve.

Bar Bar Všehrdova 17, Malá Strana. Arty crêperie with big, cheap salads and sweet and savoury pancakes.

Dynamo Pštrossova 29, Nové Město. Eye-catching retro 1960s designer decor, competent fish, chicken, steak and pasta dishes make this place a popular, trendy little spot.

Jarmark Vodičkova 30, Nové Město. Popular, inexpensive self-service steak and salad buffet in the Lucerna pasáž, where the chef prepares your food in front of you; a few veggie dishes on offer, too.

Lotos Platnéřská 13, Staré Město. Veggie wholefood versions of Czech cuisine – this is your chance to have a meat-free pork and dumplings. No smoking but there is alcohol.

Ostroff Střelecký ostrov, Nové Město. Very popular basement Italian restaurant and summer terrace on the first island you come to on the most Legií.

Pizzeria Kmotra V jirchářích 12, Nové Město. Hugely popular basement pizza place in the backstreets behind Národní.

Radost FX Café Bělehradská 120, Vinohrady. Outstanding veggie food attracts ultra-fashionable crowd; open till very late, brunch at weekends.

U sádlů Klimentská 2. Deliberately over-the-top themed medieval banqueting hall serving inexpensive hearty fare and lashings of frothing ale.

Drinking

The choice of Prague **cafés** is pretty varied – from Art Nouveau relics and swish espresso bars (both of which are called *kavárna* and are licensed), to simple sugar and caffeine joints (*cukrárna*). For no-nonsense boozing you need to head for a **pub** (*pivnice*), which invariably serves excellent beer by the half-litre, but many of which close around 11pm. For late-night drinking, head for one of the clubs or all-night bars.

Café Slavia Národní 1, Nové Město. Famous café, opposite the National Theatre.

Café Imperial Na poříčí 15, Nové Město. An endearingly shabby yet grand Habsburg-era *Kaffeehaus* which has retained its original, tiled decor.

Café Louvre Národní 20. With high ceiling, mirrors, daily papers and a billiard hall, this first-floor café is a resurrected Habsburg-era *Kaffeehaus*.

Dahab Dlouhá 33, Staré Město. The mother of all Prague teahouses, a vast Bedouin tent of a place serving tasty Middle Eastern snacks, couscous and hookahs to a background of funky world music.

Globe Pštrossova 6, Nové Město. Large, buzzing café, at the back of the English-language bookstore of the same name, that's a serious expat hangout, but enjoyable nevertheless.

Jo's Bar Malostranské náměstí 7, Malá Strana. A narrow bar in Malá Strana that is the original expat/backpacker hangout. Tex-Mex food served all day, bottled beer only and a heaving crowd guaranteed most evenings. Downstairs is *Jo's Garáž* disco.

Obecní dům náměstí Republiky 5, Nové Město. Glorious Art Nouveau decor, impeccable service, good cake trolley and even a few internet terminals.

Pivovarský dům Lipova 15, Nové Město. In-house brewery offering everything from wheat- to banana-beer – along with excellent Czech pub grub and good service.

Velryba Opatovická 24, Nové Město. Smoky and studenty café, with cheap Czech food and an art gallery in the basement.

Nightlife

As far as live music is concerned, the classical scene still has the edge in Prague. Some better **jazz clubs**, **discos** and **nightclubs** have sprouted up. Predictably enough, with a playwright as president, **theatre** in Prague is thriving; without knowing the language, however, your scope is limited, though there's a tradition of innovative mime, puppetry and "black light" theatre in the city. **Tickets** are cheap and available from any Ticketpro outlet (there's one in the PIS office) as well as from the venues themselves. As for particular areas, in the summer Hradčany hosts many open-air concerts and plays.

Classical concerts take place throughout the year in concert halls and churches, the biggest event being the Prague Spring **international music festival** (ⓦwww.festival.cz), which traditionally begins on May 12, the day of Smetana's death, with a performance of *Má vlast*, and finishes on June 2 with a rendition of Beethoven's Ninth. Watch out for concerts in the churches and palaces, as well as in the main venues (listed below).

Finally, Prague does not have a large, nor very upfront **gay and lesbian scene**, but there are a few bars and clubs worth checking out: *Friends*, Náprstkova 1, Staré Město, is a friendly, laid-back mixed gay/lesbian cellar bar in the centre of the old town, while *Gejzee…r*, Vinohradská 40 (closed Mon & Sun), is Prague's largest and most popular gay club with dance floor, DJs and the inevitable darkroom.

Classical music and opera

Smetanova síň Obecní dům, náměstí Republiky 5, Nové Město. Fantastically ornate and recently renovated Art Nouveau concert hall which is home to the excellent Prague Symphony Orchestra.
Rudolfinum Alsovo nábřeží 12, Staré Město ⓦwww.rudolfinum.cz. Stunning Neo-Renaissance concert hall and home to the Czech Philharmonic.
Státní opera Praha Wilsonova 4, Nové Město ⓦwww.opera.cz. The former German opera house and the city's second-choice venue for opera and ballet.
Stavovské divadlo Ovocný trh 1, Staré Město ⓦwww.narodni-divadlo.cz. Prague's main opera house, which witnessed the première of Mozart's Don Giovanni.

Clubs and live venues

AghaRTA Jazz Centrum Krakovská 5, Nové Město ⓦwww.agharta.cz. Prague's best jazz club with a good mix of top-name foreigners and locals.

Karlovy lázně Novotného lavka 1, Staré Město ⓦwww.karlovylazne.c. Mega, high-tech club by the Charles Bridge; techno on the top floor, progressively more retro as you descend to the internet café on the ground floor.
Lucerna Music Bar Vodičkova 36, Nové Město ⓦwww.musicbar.cz. Central, small dance space, live music, occasionally jazz.
Palác Akropolis Kubelíkova 27, Žižkov ⓦwww.palacakropolis.cz. Decent live arts/world music venue in the backstreets of Žižkov, renowned for Romany and other ethnic music festivals. Tram #5, #9 or #26.
Radost FX Bělehradská 120, Vinohrady ⓦwww.radostfx.cz. Still the slickest (and longest-running) all-round dance club venue in Prague, with a great veggie café attached.
Roxy Dlouhá 33, Staré Město ⓦwww.roxy.cz. The Roxy is a great little venue: a laid-back rambling old theatre with an interesting programme of events from arty films and exhibitions to live acts and DJ nights.

Listings

Embassies Australia, Klimentská 10, Nové Město ☏251 018 350; Canada, Mickiewiczova 6, Hradčany ☏272 101 800; New Zealand, Dykova 19, Vinohrady ☏222 514 672; Ireland, Tržiště 15, Malá Strana ☏257 530 061; UK, Thunovská 14, Malá Strana ☏257 402 111; US, Tržiště 15, Malá ☏257 530 663.
Exchange There's a 24-hour exchange service at the airport but banks and ATMs are your best bet.
Internet access Terminal Bar, Soukenická 6, Nové Město. Prague's trendiest internet café is also a

great place to chill out, especially in the downstairs retro bar.
Laundry Laundry Kings, Dejvická 16, Dejvice (Mon–Fri 6am–10pm, Sat & Sun 8am–10pm).
Pharmacy Palackého 5, Nové Město ☏224 946 982 (open 24hr).
Post office Jindřišská 14, Nové Město (daily 7am–8pm); 24-hour service for parcels, telegrams and telephones at Hybernská 15 by Masarykovo nádraží.

Bohemia

Prague is the natural centre and capital of Bohemia; the rest divides easily into four geographical districts. South Bohemia, bordered by the Šumava Mountains, is the least spoilt; its largest town by far is the brewing centre of **České Budějovice**, and its chief attraction, aside from the thickly forested hills, is a series of well-preserved medieval towns, whose undisputed gem is **Český Krumlov**. Neighbouring West Bohemia has a similar mix of rolling woods and hills, despite the industrial nature of its capital **Plzeň**, home of Pilsen beer and the Škoda empire. Beyond here, as you approach the German border, Bohemia's famous spa region unfolds, with magnificent resorts such as **Mariánské Lázně** and **Karlovy Vary** enjoying sparkling reputations. North Bohemia has real problems: devastated by industrialization, many parts are virtually uninhabitable. East Bohemia has suffered indirectly from the polluting industries of its neighbour, but remains relatively blight-free. There's some great walking and climbing country here, but the only essential stop on a quick tour is the silver-mining centre of **Kutná Hora**.

České Budějovice

Since its foundation in 1265, **ČESKÉ BUDĚJOVICE** – just two hours by train from Prague – has been a self-assured place, convinced of its own importance. Its wealth, based on medieval silver mines and its position on the salt route from Linz to Prague, was wiped out in the seventeenth century by war and fire, but the Habsburgs lavishly reconstructed most of České Budějovice in the eighteenth century. Its real renown, however, is for its local brew Budvar, better known abroad under its original German name, Budweiser.

České Budějovice has a compact old town that's only a five-minute walk from the **train** and **bus stations**, both situated to the east of the city centre, along the pedestrianized Lannova třída. The medieval grid plan leads inevitably to the magnificent central **náměstí Přemysla Otakara II**, one of Europe's largest market squares. Its buildings are elegant enough, but it's the arcades and the octagonal **Samson's Fountain** – once the only tap in town – that make the greatest impression. The 72-metre status symbol, the **Black Tower** (Černá věž), one of the few survivors of the 1641 fire, leans gently to one side of the square; its roof gallery (April–Oct Tues–Sun 10am–6pm; July & Aug also Mon 10am–6pm) provides superb views. The **Budvar brewery** is off the road to Prague, on Karolíny Světlé (bus #2), and has a newly refurbished *pivnice* inside the nasty titanium-blue headquarters; (☏387 705 341, ⊛www.budweiser.cz for information on guided tours).

České Budějovice's popularity with neighbouring Austrians and Germans means that **hotels** tend to be expensive. The best-value options are *Penzion Klika* (☏387 318 360, ⊛www.klika-penzion.cz; ❸), Zátkovo nábřeží 17, on the western edge of the old town; or *Hotel Malý pivovar*, Karla IV 8–10 (☏386 360 471, ⊛www.budvar.cz; ❻). There's a friendly **tourist office** at no. 2 on the main square (June–Sept Mon–Fri 8.30am–6pm, Sat 8.30am–5pm, Sun 10am–4pm; Oct–May Mon–Fri 9am–5pm, Sat 9am–3pm; ☏386 801 413), too, where you can book accommodation. From July to September rooms are available in **student halls**, located at Studentská 15 (☏387 774 201; ❶). There's also a good **campsite**, *Dlouhá louka* at Stromovká 8 (☏387 210 601; bus #16 from station). The most famous **pub** in town is *Masné krámy* at Krajinská 29, which serves huge quantities of Budvar all day. The Budvar-run *Malý pivovar* is also widely recommended for great pub **food** and beer, as is the *Hotel Zvon* on the main square – head for the pub section, rather than the more expensive restaurant.

Český Krumlov

Squeezed into a tight S-bend of the River Vltava, **ČESKÝ KRUMLOV** is undoubtedly one of the most picturesque towns in the country, having hardly changed in the last three hundred years. This, however, is no secret, and the crowds are getting increasingly thick throughout the summer.

The **train station** is twenty minutes' walk north of the old town, up a precipitous set of steps, while the **bus station** is just outside the old town. The twisting River Vltava divides the town into two: the circular staré město on the right bank and the Latrán quarter on the hillier left. For centuries, the focal point has been the **Castle** (April–Oct Tues–Sun 9am–noon & 1–4/6pm; 140Kč English-language tour) in the Latrán quarter, as good a place as any to begin a roam. There's a choice of two hour-long guided tours: one concentrating on feudal opulence, the other peaking at the castle's eighteenth-century Rococo ballroom. Another covered walkway puts you high above the town in the unexpectedly expansive **terraced gardens**.

The houses leaning in on Latrán lead to a wooden ramp-like bridge which connects with the staré město. Head straight up the soft incline of Radniční to the main square, where a long, white Renaissance entablature connects two-and-a-half Gothic houses to create the **town hall**. On the other side, the high lancet windows of the church of **St Vitus** rise above the ramshackle rooftops. Continuing east off the square, down Horní, the beautiful sixteenth-century Jesuit college now provides space for the *Hotel Růže*. Opposite, the local **museum** (Tues–Fri 9am–4pm, Sat & Sun 1–4pm) includes a reconstructed seventeenth-century shop interior among its exhibits. The **Egon Schiele Art Centrum** (daily 10am–6pm; 120Kč), on Široká, has a whole series of galleries and exhibition halls housed in a fifteenth-century former brewery in the staré město devoted to the Austrian painter Egon Schiele, who lived here briefly in 1911.

There's a helpful **tourist office** (daily 9am–5pm; ☎380 711 650, ⓦwww .ckrumlov.cz) at nám. Svornosti in the staré město, which can organize accommodation for you. *Hotel Růže*, Horní 24 (☎380 772 100, ⓦwww.hotelruze.cz; ➒), is the town's most beautiful and grand old **hotel**; the friendly **pub/pension**, *Na louži*, Kájovská 66 (☎380 711 280, ⓦwww.nalouzi.cz; ➌), is a good bet. The central HI *Travellers Hostel* at Soukenická 43 (☎380 711 345; ➋) has bike rental, a barbecue and other amenities. An even cheaper option is the **hostel** *Krumlov House* (☎380 711 935; ➊); to get there follow Horní out of the old town and turn right towards Rooseveltova 68. There's also a primitive **campsite** (☎380 728 670; closed Oct–May), 2km south on road 160 to Nové Spolí. As far as **eating** goes, there's a wide choice: *Papa's Living Restaurant*, Latrán 13, offers funky Mexican, Italian and veggie dishes, while the fish restaurant *Rybařská bašta*, off Široká, is good value. **Drinking** is best done at the *Eggenberg*, the brewery tap, on the eastern edge of the Latrán quarter, or at the aforementioned *Na louži* which also serves Eggenberg.

Plzeň

PLZEŇ (Pilsen) is Bohemia's second city, with a population of 170,000. Despite its industrial character, there are compensations – eclectic architecture (including the recently restored Great Synagogue) and an unending supply of (probably) the best **beer** in the world. Plzeň's **train stations** are works of art in themselves: your likeliest point of arrival is the Hlavní nádraží, just a little east of the city centre. The **bus terminal** is on the west side of town. From both stations, the city centre is only a short walk away.

The main square, **náměstí Republiky**, presents a full range of architectural styles, starting with the exalted heights of the Gothic cathedral of **sv Bartoloměj**, its green spire (daily 10am–6pm) reaching up almost 103m. Over the way rises the sgraffitoed Renaissance **Old Town Hall**, self-importantly one storey higher than the rest of the square. Here and there other old buildings survive, but the vast majority of Plzeň's buildings hail from the city's heyday during the industrial expansion around the turn of the century.

But the reason most people come to Plzeň is to sample its famous 12° Plzeňský Prazdroj, or **Pilsner Urquell** (its Germanized export name). Beer has been brewed in the town since it was founded in 1295, but it wasn't until 1842 that the famous Bürgerliches Brauhaus was built, after a near-riot by the townsfolk over the declining quality of their brew. For a **guided tour** of the **brewery** (75Kč; ⓦwww.pilsner-urquell.cz), you can either book in advance or simply show up and join one of the roughly hourly tours (in English). You could, of course, just settle for a half-litre of the stuff at the vast *Na spílce* pub (daily from 11am), beyond the brewery's triumphal arch.

Finding a vacancy in one of Plzeň's **hotels** presents few problems, though rooms don't come cheap. The best-value rooms in town are the three at *Pension Bárová*, Solní 8 (☎377 236 652; ❸), just off the main square; or there are even better ones at the grandiose *Continental*, Zbrojnická 8 (☎377 235 292, ⓦwww.hotelcontinental.cz; ❹). **Private rooms** and other accommodation are available at the **tourist office** (daily 10am–3.30/5pm; ☎377 032 750, ⓦwww.plzen-city.cz), at nám. Republiky 41. Alternatively, you can stay at the **hostel** at Bolevecká 30 (❶; tram #4 north along Karlovarská). Bus #20 from the train station will drop you at the *Bílá hora* **campsite** (closed Oct–March), on 28 října (☎377 562 225) in the northern suburb of the same name.

All the hotels have **restaurants** attached but for cheap meals you might as well combine your **eating** with your **drinking**. Apart from *Na stílce*, you can get cheap grub at the wood-panelled *U Salzmannů* at Pražská 8. Gambrinus, Plzeň's other main beer, is best at *Žumbera* at Bezručova 14.

Mariánské Lázně

Once one of the most fashionable European spas – and a regular haunt of King Edward VII, who also came for the golf – **MARIÁNSKÉ LÁZNĚ** is far less exclusive today. The riotous, *fin-de-siècle* architecture is gradually being restored and the spa now surveys busloads of elderly Germans getting the full works. Buses and trains stop 3km from the spa, from where trolleybus #5 runs up Hlavní třída to the centre. Sumptuous, regal buildings, most dating from the second half of the nineteenth century, rise up from the pine-clad surroundings – an appropriate backdrop for the genteel classical music festivals hosted annually here.

The focal point of the spa is the **Kolonáda**. This beautiful wrought-iron colonnade gently curves like a whale-ribbed railway station, the atmosphere relentlessly genteel and sober, although the view has been marred by a functionless concrete splat left by Communist developers. Access to the colonnade's life-giving faucets is restricted (daily 6am–noon & 4–6pm), though the spa's first and foremost **spring**, Křížový pramen, is accessible round the clock. Mariánské Lázně's altitude lends an almost subalpine freshness to the air, and **walking** is as important to "the cure" as the various specialized treatments. At the end of the Kolonáda, by the "singing fountain", there's a map showing the marked walks in the area.

Rooms are getting increasingly pricey, but try the *Zlatý zámek*, Klíčová 4 (☎354 623 924; ❷), which is exceptional value for its central locale. The *Kossuth/Suvuorov*, Ruská 77 (☎354 622 861, ⓦwww.orea.cz; ❸), parallel to the main street, is pretty basic, but the *fin-de-siècle Polonia*, Hlavní třída 50 (☎354 622 451, ⓦwww.orea.cz; ❹) has rooms overlooking the spa gardens. Accommodation is also available from the **tourist office** at Hlavní 47 (Mon–Fri 9am–6pm, Sat & Sun 9am–5pm; ☎354 622 474, ⓦwww.marienbad.cz), which has its own **internet café** (daily 9am–6pm; 2Kč/min), plus seven private rooms (❷) without bath or shower, which are the cheapest in town. The *Classic* **restaurant**, just down from the *Excelsior* at Hlavní třída 50, is especially recommended for vegetarians; the neighbouring *Café Polonia* is probably Mariánské Lázně's most opulent surviving **café** offering stucco decoration as rich as its cakes.

Karlovy Vary

KARLOVY VARY, undisputed king of the Bohemian spas, is one of the most cosmopolitan Czech towns. Its international clientele – largely Russians – annually doubles the local population, which is further supplemented by thousands of able-bodied tourists in summer, the greatest number of whom are German.

There are two **train stations**, one by the bus station and one by the River Ohře. Don't get off from the Prague bus at the **bus station** on Varšavská; along with almost everyone else, hop off at Tržnice, one stop before, which is far more central. Half a kilometre south, the pedestrianized **spa quarter** stretches along the winding Teplá Valley. Unfortunately, many visitors' first impressions are marred by the inex-cusable concrete scab of **Thermal** sanatorium, for whose sake a large slice of the old town bit the dust. However, its open-air spring-water **swimming pool** is superb and offers unbeatable views. As the valley narrows, the river disappears under a wide terrace in front of the graceful **Mlýnská kolonáda**, each of whose four springs is more scalding than the last.

Most powerful of the town's twelve springs is the **Vřídlo**, which belches out over 2500 gallons every hour. The smooth marble floor of the modern **Vřídelní kolonáda** (the old fountain was melted down for armaments by the Nazis) allows patients to shuffle up and down contentedly, while inside the glass rotunda the geyser shoots hot water forty feet upwards. Clouds of steam obscure a view of Dientzenhofer's Baroque masterpiece, the **church of sv Maria Magdalána**, pitched nearby on a precipitous site. South of the Sprudel is Karlovy Vary's most famous shopping street, the **Stará louka**. Its shops are beginning once more to exude the snobbery of former days – there's even a branch of Versace at the far end of the street. At Stará louka 30 is the **Grand Hotel Pupp**. Founded in 1701 as the greatest hotel in the world, it still has a certain snooty grandeur.

It's best to start looking for **accommodation** early in the day – Karlovy Vary is a very fashionable spa town so nothing comes dirt cheap. *W Privat*, an office on náměstí Republiky (Mon–Fri 8.30am–5pm, Sat & Sun 9am–1pm), can organize **private rooms**. Moderately priced **hotels** include the *U tří mouřenínů*, Stará louka 2 (☎353 235 054, ⓦwww.abaka.com/czech/kucera; ❹), which occupies a prime central location; for something significantly cheaper, you'll have to head out of town beyond the railway station to the comfortable pension *Clara*, Na kopečku 23 (☎353 449 983; ❷). Karlovy Vary's most central **campsite** is at *Motel Gejzír* (☎353 225 101; closed Nov–March), on Slovenská; take bus #7 from the bus station. For **eating**, head for the *Zámecký vrch*, an intimate restaurant up at no. 14 on the street of the same name, the Moravian wine cellar at *Promenáda*, Tržiště 31, or *Embassy*, Nová louka 21. The *Elefant Café* on Stará louka is the nearest Karlovy Vary comes to an elegant Habsburg-style **café**.

Kutná Hora

KUTNÁ HORA, 60km east of the capital, was once one of the most important towns in this neck of the Habsburg Empire. In 1308 Václav II founded the royal mint here, and the town's sudden wealth allowed it to underwrite the construction of one of the most magnificent churches in central Europe, plus a number of other prestigious monuments. By the late Middle Ages its population was equal to that of London, its shantytown suburbs straggling across what are now green fields. When the silver mines dried up at the end of the sixteenth century, Kutná Hora's impor-tance came to an abrupt end.

The easiest way to get here from Prague is by bus, as the main train station is sev-eral kilometres from the centre, whereas the buses stop just across the ring road. The small houses that line the town's medieval lanes give little idea of its former glories, and the same goes for **Palackého náměstí**, nominally the main square though it's no showpiece. A narrow alleyway on the south side of the square leads to the leafy Havlíčkovo náměstí, off which is the **Italian Court**, where Florentine workers produced Prague's silver *Groschen*, a coin used throughout central Europe until the nineteenth century. Better still, head for the **Mining Museum** (April–Oct Tues–Sun 9am–5/6pm), the other side of sv Jakub, the town's oldest church. Here, you can visit some of the medieval mines that were discovered beneath an old fort in the 1960s.

The Jesuits arrived too late to exploit the town's silver stocks, but with their own funds they built a **Jesuit College** on the ridge to the southwest of town. With its gallery of saints and holy men, it was a crude attempt to eclipse the astounding achievement of the neighbouring Gothic **Cathedral of sv Barbora** (Tues–Sun: May–Sept 9am–5.30pm; Oct–April 9am–11.30am & 1/2–3.30pm). Not to be out-done by the St Vitus Cathedral in Prague, the miners of Kutná Hora financed the construction of a great cathedral of their own, dedicated to Barbara, the patron saint of miners and gunners. The foundations were probably laid by Peter Parler in the 1380s, but work was interrupted by the Hussite wars, and the church remained unfinished until the late 1800s. From the outside it's an incredible sight, bristling with pinnacles, finials and flying buttresses supporting a roof of three tent-like tow-ers and unequal needle-sharp spires. Inside, light streams through the plain glass, illuminating a vaulted nave whose ribs form branches and petals stamped with coats of arms belonging to Václav II and the miners' guilds.

While you're in Kutná Hora, don't miss the weird subterranean *kostnice* or **ossuary** (daily: April–Sept 8am–6pm; Oct–March 9am–noon & 1–4/5pm), over-flowing with 40,000 complete sets of bones, moulded into sculptures and decora-tions by František Rint in the nineteenth century. To get there, take bus #1 or #4 to the giant tobacco factory; you'll find the ossuary behind a Baroque church.

The **tourist office** at Palackeho náměstí 377 (Mon–Fri 9am–5/6.30pm; April–Oct also Sat & Sun 9am–5pm; ☎327 512 378, ⓦwww.kutnahora.cz) can book you **private rooms**. *U rytířů*, on Rejskovo náměstí (☎327 512 256; ❷), is a simple inexpensive pension, while *Hotel Anna*, Vladislavova (☎327 516 315; ❸), is a bit more upmarket. The nearest **campsite** is the unlikely sounding *Santa Barbara* on Česká (☎327 512 051; closed Nov–March), 800m from the cathedral, with hot showers and a restaurant.

Moravia

Wedged between Bohemia and Slovakia, **Moravia** is the smallest of the three provinces that once made up Czechoslovakia, but possibly the prettiest, friendliest and most bucolic. Although the North Moravian corridor is heavily industrialized and has suffered from increasingly high unemployment over the past decade, much of the region is rural and the folk roots, traditions and religion here are strongly felt. The Moravian capital, **Brno**, a once-grand nineteenth-century city, is within easy striking distance of Moravia's spectacular **karst region**. In the northern half of the province, the Baroque riches of the Moravian prince-bishopric have left their mark on the old capital, **Olomouc**, now a thriving university town and one of the region's main attractions.

Brno

As the second largest city in the Czech Republic, with a couple of really good museums and galleries plus a handful of other sights and a fair bit of nightlife, **BRNO** is worth a day of anyone's time. The city was a late developer, the first cloth factory being founded in 1766, but by the end of the nineteenth century this was easily the largest city in Moravia. Between the wars Brno enjoyed a cultural boom, heralded by the 1928 Exhibition of Contemporary Culture, which provided an impetus for much of the city's modernist architecture. After the war, Brno's

German-speakers (one quarter of the population) were sent packing on foot to Vienna. Capital fled with the capitalists and centralized state funds were diverted to Prague and Bratislava, pushing Brno firmly into third (now second) place.

A steady stream of people plough up and down **Masarykova**, the main shopping route. Don't let that stop you from looking up at the five-storey mansions, some laden with a fantastic mantle of decoration. Follow the flow north and you'll end up at **náměstí Svobody** – far short of magnificent but nonetheless the place where most of Brno comes to shop. To the left halfway up Masarykova is **Zelný trh**, a low-key vegetable market on a sloping cobbled square, with a huge fountain by Fischer von Erlach in its centre. At the top of the square, the plain mass of the Dietrichstein Palace contains the **Moravian Museum** (Tues–Sat 9am–5pm), a worthy collection of ancient and medieval artefacts. Much more interesting, if only for its macabre value, is the **Capuchin Crypt** (Tues–Sat 9am–noon & 2–4.30pm, Sun 11–11.45am & 2–4.30pm) to the far south of the square, a gruesome collection of dead monks and top nobs mummified in the crypt of the Capuchin church.

Clearly visible from Zelný trh is the **Old Town Hall** (daily 7am–8pm). Anton Pilgram's Gothic doorway is its best feature, the thistly pinnacle above the statue of Justice symbolically twisted – Pilgram's revenge on the town aldermen who short-changed him for his work. Inside, the courtyards and passageways are jam-packed with tour groups, most of them here to see the so-called Brno dragon (actually a stuffed crocodile) and the Brno Wheel, made in 1636 by a cartwright from nearby Lednice. If you're still hazy on the geography of the town, the tower is worth a climb for the panorama across the red-tiled rooftops.

Southwest of the square, the Petrov hill – on which the **Cathedral of SS Peter and Paul** stands – is one of the best places to escape to from the choked streets below. The cathedral's needle-sharp Gothic spires dominate the skyline for miles around, but close up, the crude nineteenth-century rebuilding has made it a lukewarm affair.

On the western edge of the city centre, the **UPM** on Husova (Tues–Sun 10am–6pm) contains one of the country's best collections of modern applied art, displaying everything from avant-garde photomontages to swirling Art Nouveau vases; it also has excellent temporary shows. At the **Pražák Palace** (Tues–Sun 10am–6pm), a little further down the road, there's a very good cross-section of twentieth-century Czech art on permanent display. Skulking in the woods above the gallery is the barely visible **Špilberk Castle** (Tues–Sun 9am–5/6pm), one of the worst prisons in the Habsburg Empire, and later the Brno Gestapo jail; the dungeons (*kasematy*) are now open to the public, while the local city museum occupies the upper floors.

Practicalities

Brno's main **train and bus station** sit closely together, on the edge of the city centre; the train station has lockers and a 24-hour left-luggage office. Most of Brno's sights are within easy walking distance of the train station, although **trams** will take you almost anywhere in the city within minutes. You need to buy either a 7Kč ticket for ten minutes' travel or a 12Kč ticket, valid for forty minutes and allowing changes between trams or buses. Tickets must be bought beforehand from kiosks, hotel lobbies or yellow ticket machines, and validated on board.

The main **tourist office** is in the Old Town Hall at Radnická 8 (Mon–Fri 8am–6pm, Sat & Sun 9am–5pm; ☎542 320 758, ⓦwww.brno.cz); it can help with **accommodation** – Brno hosts many trade fairs, so it's wise to book ahead. One of the cheapest **hotels** is the budget *Amphone*, třída. kpt. Jaroše 29 (☎545 428 310; ❹), a short walk from the old town. *Pegas*, Jakubská 4 (☎542 210 104; ❻), just off Česká, is more central and above a microbrewery. Best of Brno's **campsites** is the *Radka* site (☎546 215 821; closed Sept–May; tram #1, #3 or #11), 10km northwest of the city on the shores of the Brno dam, at Brneňska prehrada-kninia.

The **eating and drinking** scene has improved enormously in the last decade.

The most popular café around is the Italian-run *Adria*, on Masarykova 31, which serves great ice cream and pizzas, but if you want to sit outside and sup beer Czech-style, try *Špaliček*, at the top of Zelný trh, which has tables outside in summer and lashings of the local Starobrno beer, or the replica functionalist café, *Zemanova kavárna*, near the Janáček Theatre. The microbrewery, *Pegas*, on Jakubská, is deservedly popular, or you could swing by *Elektra*, a cellar pub with decent food on Běhounská, or *Taj*, a decent first-floor Indian restaurant opposite. **Internet cafés** include *Internetová kavárna mladých* at Josefská 15 and *@Internet café* at Lidická 17.

Moravian karst region

Well worth a visit is the limestone **karst region** just over 25km northeast of Brno. The best way to get there by public transport is to catch an early morning train from Brno out to Blansko-Macocha station, and walk 200m southwards to the bus station. From here, buses depart for Skalní Mlýn, location of the main ticket office and information centre for the caves. The **Punkevní cave** (daily 8.20am–2/3.50pm) is the cave to head for – it's the biggest and best and includes an underground boat trip. To reach the cave, walk or catch the Eko-Train; there are also bikes for rent. Alternatively, it's a very nice walk (5km) through the woods from Blansko; follow the green waymarkers.

Olomouc

Occupying the crucial Morava crossing-point on the road to Kraków, **OLOMOUC** (pronounced "Olla-moats") was the capital of Moravia from the Middle Ages to the mid-seventeenth century and the seat of the bishopric for even longer. All this attracted the destructive attention of Swedish troops in the Thirty Years War, though the wealth of the Church and its strategic trading position kept the place going. And with a well-preserved old town, sloping cobbled squares and a plethora of Baroque fountains, not to mention a healthy quota of university students and a few interesting festivals, Olomouc has a great deal going for it.

The **staré město** is a strange contorted shape, squeezed in the middle by an arm of the Morava. The train station is 1.5km east, so on arrival take any tram heading west up Masarykova and get off after three or four stops; the bus station is even further out, and connected to the centre by tram #4. In the western half of the old town, all roads lead to the city's two central cobbled main squares, which are hinged to one another at right angles. At the centre of the upper square, the irregular **Horní náměstí**, stands the amalgamation of buildings that collectively make up the **town hall**. From its creamy rendering the occasional late Gothic or Renaissance gesture emerges – notably the handsome lanterned tower soaring to its conclusion of baubles and pinnacles. On the north side, next to the arcade of shops, is an astronomical clock, which was destroyed in the war. The remake chimes all right, but the hourly mechanical show is disappointing.

Big enough to be a chapel, the **Holy Trinity Column** to the west of the town hall is the country's largest plague column; many such monuments were erected as thanksgiving for deliverance from the forces of Protestantism, but few are left standing. Set into the west facade of the square is the **Moravian Theatre**, where Mahler arrived as the newly appointed *Kapellmeister* in 1883; the local press took an instant dislike to him, and he lasted just three months. **Fountains** grace each of Olomouc's six ancient market squares. Horní náměstí boasts two: Hercules, looking unusually athletic for his years, and a vigorous depiction of Julius Caesar bucking on a steed that coughs water from its mouth.

Two of the city's best-looking backstreets, Školní and Michalská, lead southeast from Horní náměstí, up to the **church of sv Michal**, plain on the outside but inside clad in a masterly excess of Baroque. Firmly wedged between the two sections of the old town is the obligatory **Jesuit church of Panna Maria Sněžná**, deemed particularly necessary in a city where Protestantism had spread like wildfire in the sixteenth century. Jutting out into the road, it signals the gateway to the less hectic part of town. The great mass of the former Jesuit College, now the **Palacký University**, dominates the first square, náměstí Republiky, opposite which is the dull town museum and, next door, the vastly superior **Museum of Art** (Tues–Sun 10am–6pm); the top floor houses a fascinating selection of twentieth-century works by local-born artists and features a viewing tower.

Three blocks east of náměstí Republiky, the **Cathedral**, or Dóm, of sv Václav comes into view. Though it started life as a Romanesque basilica, the current structure is mostly nineteenth-century neo-Gothic. However, the walls and pillars of the nave are prettily painted in Romanesque style, and the crypt (Wed–Sun 9/11am–4/5pm) has a wonderful display of gory reliquaries and priestly sartorial wealth.

Practicalities

The **tourist office** in the town hall, at Horní nám. 1(Mon–Fri 8.30am–5pm; ☎585 513 392, ⓦwww.olomoucko.cz), will book **private rooms** for you. Cheap rooms are hard to come by in Olomouc – the cheapest **hotel** in town is the *Sigma* (☎585 232 076; ❷), opposite the train station at Jeremenkova 36; a better bet is *Na hradbách*, Hrnčířská 14 (☎585 233 243; ⓔaquaveri@iol.cz; ❷), a small, inexpensive, four-bed **pension** hidden away in one of the city's prettiest, quietest backstreets. For real budget accommodation head down Ztracená to the student travel agency CKM (Mon–Fri 9am–5pm) at Denisova 4. Note that rooms can be even harder to come by in May when the Spring **Music Festival** follows the **Flower Festival**.

For **restaurants**, the *U červeného volka* on Dolní náměstí is a cheap place with a wide range of veggie dishes, but *Caesar Pizzeria* in the cobbled vaults under the town hall is by far the most popular joint in town. A good range of cakes can be found in the *Maruška cukrárna* at 28 října or the *Café Mahler*, at Horní náměstí 11. In the evenings, head for a backstreet **pub** like the reasonably priced *U bakaláre*, on Žerotinovo náměstí. The *U-Klub*, at the Studentcentrum at the far end of Křížovského, has occasional DJs and bands.

Travel details

Trains

Prague to: Brno (hourly; 3hr–3hr 30min); České Budějovice (8–9 daily; 2hr 15min–3hr); Karlovy Vary (3 daily; 3hr 20min–4hr); Mariánské Lázně (every 2hr; 2hr); Olomouc (every 1–2hr; 3hr–3hr 30min); Plzeň (hourly; 1hr 40min–2hr 15min).
Brno to: Olomouc (hourly; 1hr 30min–2hr 30min).
České Budějovice to: Brno (4–5 daily; 4hr 20min); Český Krumlov (9 daily; 1hr); Plzeň (hourly; 1hr 50min–3hr 15min).

Mariánské Lázně to: Karlovy Vary (6–7 daily; 1hr 40min); Plzeň (every 2hr; 1hr–1hr 15min).
Plzeň to: Brno (3 daily; 6hr 45min).

Buses

Prague to: Brno (hourly; 2hr); České Budějovice (up to 20 daily; 2hr 20min–3hr 45min); Český Krumlov (up to 14 daily; 3hr–5hr); Karlovy Vary (hourly; 2hr 30min); Kutná Hora (32 daily; 55min–1hr 40min); Olomouc (2 daily; 4hr).

Denmark

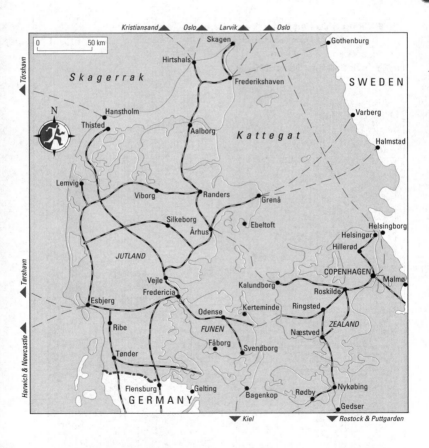

Denmark highlights

* **Ny Carlsberg Glyptotek, Copenhagen** The city's finest gallery, with the biggest collection of Etruscan art outside Italy. **See p.284**

* **Viking Ship Museum, Roskilde** Five excellent specimens of Viking shipbuilding. **See p.290**

* **Fireworks at Tivoli** A perfect end to an evening in Copenhagen. **See p.284**

Introduction and basics

Between Scandinavia proper and mainland Europe, **Denmark** is a difficult country to pin down. In many ways it shares the characteristics of both regions: it's an EU member, and has prices and drinking laws that are broadly in line with those in the rest of Europe. But Denmark's social policies and its style of government are distinctly Scandinavian: social benefits and the standard of living are high, and its politics are very much that of consensus.

Denmark is the easiest Scandinavian country in which to travel, but its **landscape** is the least dramatic: very green and flat, largely farmland interrupted by innumerable pretty villages. Apart from a scattering of small islands, three main landmasses make up the country – the islands of Zealand and Funen and the peninsula of Jutland, which extends northwards from Germany.

Most visitors make for **Zealand** (Sjælland), and, more specifically, **Copenhagen**, the country's one large city and an exciting focal point, with a beautiful old centre, a good array of museums and a boisterous nightlife. Zealand's smaller neighbour, **Funen** (Fyn), has only one real urban draw, **Odense**; otherwise, it's a sedate place, renowned for cute villages and sandy beaches. **Jutland** (Jylland) has a truly individual flavour: as well as Denmark's most varied scenery, ranging from soft green hills to desolate heathlands, it is home to **Århus** and **Aalborg**, two of the liveliest cities outside the capital.

Information and maps

All towns and some villages will have a **tourist office**, who can sometimes help with accommodation and change money. They're **open** daily, with long hours, in the most popular places, but have much reduced hours from October to March. All airports and many train stations also offer a hotel booking service.

The best general **map** of Denmark is the one by *Hallwag*. The **HI Association map** is also very informative; available free of charge at ⓦwww.danhostel.dk.

Money and banks

Danish currency is the **krone** (plural kroner). It's made up of 100 øre, and comes in notes of 50kr, 100kr, 200kr, 500kr, 1000kr, and coins of 25øre, 50øre, 1kr, 2kr, 5kr, 10kr, 20kr.

Banking hours are Mon–Fri 10am–4pm, Thurs till 6pm; and banks are generally the best places to **exchange cash** and travellers' cheques; there's a uniform commission of 25kr per transaction. Forex bureaux charge only 20kr per transaction, but they are few and far between. Most airports and ferry terminals have late-opening exchange facilities, and automatic cash machines are everywhere.

Communications

Post offices are open Mon–Fri 9.30/ 10am–5/5.30pm, Sat 9.30/10am–noon/1pm, with reduced hours in smaller communities. You can also buy stamps from most newsagents.

Denmark on the net

ⓦ**www.visitdenmark.dk** Official Danish Tourist Board site
ⓦ**www.useit.dk** For budget travellers; focuses mainly on Copenhagen
ⓦ**www.aok.dk** Covering most of Zealand
ⓦ**www.visitcopenhagen.dk** Official Copenhagen tourist site
ⓦ**www.rejseplanen.dk** Public transport journey planner

Public phones come in two forms. Coin-operated ones are white and require a minimum of 2 x 1kr for a local call (the machines irritatingly swallow one of the coins if the number is engaged), and 5kr for international calls; **phonecards** for the blue phones comes in denominations of 30kr, 50kr and 100kr and work out a little cheaper. The operator number for domestic calls is ☎118, for international call it's ☎113 (both 7kr/min); almost all operators speaking English.

Internet access is free at most libraries and some tourist offices. Internet cafés can be found in most towns.

Getting around

Denmark has a swift and easy to use **public transport** system. Trains, buses and ferries are punctual and efficient, and the timetables are well integrated.

Trains and buses

Trains are the best way to get about. Danish State Railways (Danske Statsbaner or DSB; ⓦwww.dsb.dk) — run an exhaustive and reliable network. Train types range from the large inter-city expresses (*Lyntog*) to smaller local trains (*regionaltog*). **InterRail** and **Eurail** passes are valid on all DSB trains, as is the ScanRail pass (see p.29).

There are few places that trains do not serve, and all of these can easily be reached by **buses**, which often supplement the train timetable – some operated privately, some by DSB itself – and on these **railcards** are valid.

DSB's **timetable** or *Køreplan* (free) details all train, bus and ferry services, including the S-train system in Copenhagen and all private services; smaller timetables detailing specific routes are available free at tourist offices and station booking counters.

Ferries

Ferries link all the Danish islands. Where applicable, train and bus fares include the cost of crossings (although you can also pay at the terminal and walk on). Routes and prices are covered on the very useful HI map (see above).

Cycling

Cycling is the best way to appreciate Denmark's flat landscape, which is criss-crossed by **cycle routes** (maps and information at ⓦwww.dcf.dk). Most country roads have sparse vehicle traffic and all large towns have cycle tracks. Bikes can be rented at youth hostels, tourist offices and some train stations, as well as from bike shops (from 50kr/day, 200–250kr/week; 200–500kr deposit). All trains and most long-distance buses accept bikes, but you'll have to pay according to the zonal system used to calculate passenger tickets – 50kr to take your bike from Copenhagen to Århus by train with 20kr on top if you want to reserve a space in advance; 70kr by bus.

Accommodation

While less costly than the rest of Scandinavia, **accommodation** is still a major expense in Denmark. Hotels, however, are by no means off-limits if you are prepared to seek out the better offers, and both the youth hostels and campsites are uniformly of a high standard.

Hotels and private rooms

Most Danish **hotel** rooms are en suite and have phone and TV; expect to pay around 700kr for a double, although most large towns have hotels offering rooms without bathrooms for as little as 500kr for a double. One advantage of staying in a hotel is the inclusive all-you-can-eat breakfast – so large you won't need to buy lunch. It's a good idea to book in advance, especially in peak season, which you can do through tourist-office websites. Tourist offices can also supply details of **private rooms**, which will cost 400–500kr a double. Alternatively, **farm-stays** (*Bondegårdsferie*) are becoming increasingly popular in Denmark; information and catalogues from ⓦwww.bondegaards-ferie.dk.

Hostels and sleep-ins

Hostels are by far the cheapest option. Every town has one and they have a high degree of comfort, most offering a choice of

private rooms, often with en-suite toilets
and showers, as well as dorm accommodation; nearly all have cooking facilities. Rates
are around 100kr per person for a dorm
bed; non-HI members pay an extra 30kr a
night. If you're doing a lot of hostelling, it's
worth contacting Danhostel Danmarks
Vandrerhjem (☎33.31.36.12, ⑩www.
danhostel.dk) for their free hostel guide.

Cheaper still are **sleep-ins**, predominantly
found in major towns and often open only in
summer (May–Aug). You need your own
sleeping bag, sometimes only one night's
stay is permitted and there is sometimes an
age restriction. The local tourist office will
have the latest details, as these sleep-ins do
tend to come and go quickly.

Campsites and cabins

If you don't already have an International
Camping Card (see p.48), you'll need to get
hold of a **Camping Card Scandinavia**
(80kr), which is available at official campsites
and is valid on all sites in Scandinavia until
the year's end. A Transit Pass (20kr) can be
used for a single overnight stay.

All **sites are open** at least from June to
August, many from April to September, while
a few stay open all year. There's a rigid **grading system**: one-star sites have drinking
water and toilets; two-stars have, in addition,
showers, laundry and a food shop within
1km; three-stars, by far the majority, have all
the above plus a TV-room, shop, cafeteria,
etc. Prices vary only slightly, three-stars
charging 52–62kr per person, others a few
kroner less. **Camping rough** without permission is illegal, and an on-the-spot fine
may be imposed.

Many campsites also have **cabin accommodation**, usually with cooking facilities, for
2000kr–4000kr per week for a six-berth
place, although they are often fully booked in
summer. Tourist offices will give you a free
leaflet listing all sites.

Food and drink

There are plenty of ways to **eat** affordably
and healthily in Denmark, and with plenty of
variety, too. Much the same applies to **drink**:
the only Scandinavian country free of social

drinking taboos, Denmark is an imbiber's
delight – both for its choice of tipples and
the number of places they can be sampled.

Food

Traditional Danish **food** centres on meat and
fish, served with potatoes and another, usually boiled, vegetable. **Breakfast** (*morgen-
mad*) can be the tastiest Danish meal, and
almost all hotels and hostels offer a sumptuous breakfast: a table laden with cereals,
bread, cheese, boiled eggs, fruit juice, milk,
coffee and tea, for around 40kr. Breakfast
elsewhere is less substantial, although
brunch, served from 11am until mid-afternoon, is a filling option for late starters, consisting of variations on American, English,
French and Australian breakfasts for 40–90kr.

For daytime **snacks**, you can buy *smørrebrød* – open sandwiches heaped with meat,
fish or cheese, and assorted trimmings – for
9–25kr from special shops, at least one of
which will be open until 10pm. There are
also **fast-food stands** (*pølsevogn*) in all
main streets and at train stations, serving
various hot sausages (*pølser*) and hot dogs,
toasted sandwiches (*parisertoast*) and chips
(*pommes frites*). Cafés sell **Danish pastries**
(*wienerbrød*), tastier and much less sweet
than the imitations sold elsewhere, along
with the tea and coffee, and you can usually
get a generous sandwich or filling portion of
salad (usually served with fresh bread) for
around 50kr.

You can also find an excellent-value set
lunch (*frokost*) at restaurants and bodegas
(bars that sells no-frills food). *Tilbud* is the
"special", *dagens ret* the "dish of the day",
and you can expect to pay around 40kr for
these, 80–100kr for a three-course set
lunch. Open **buffets**, where you can help
yourself to as much as you like, will set you
back 60–80kr. American burger franchises
are commonplace, as are pizzerias.
Shawarmas and China Boxes are also easy
to find in most larger towns and both cost
around 25kr. You can also get a filling but
ordinary self-service meat, fish or omelette
lunch in a supermarket cafeteria for 50–90kr.

Dinner (*aftensmad*) is, predictably, the
most expensive meal of the day as the same
Danish restaurants that are promising for
lunch turn into expense-account affairs at

night, although many still will have good-value buffets. Many **youth hostels** serve filling evening meals for 50–65kr. For 70–90kr you can get a meal in a Chinese or Middle Eastern restaurant. Sadly, If you plan to save money by **self-catering**, head for Netto or Fakta supermarkets, where the food and drink are cheap and of excellent quality.

Drink

Although you can buy booze much more cheaply from supermarkets, the most sociable places to **drink** are pubs and cafés, where the emphasis is on beer. There are also bars and bodegas, in which, as a very general rule, the mood tends to favour wines and spirits and the customers are a bit older. The cheapest **beer** is bottled, the so-called gold beer (*Guldøl* or *Elefantøl*; 20–30kr/bottle) is the strongest. Draught beer (*Fadøl*) is more expensive (15–30kr/250ml, 30–45kr/500ml) and a touch weaker than the bottled stuff, but tastes fresher and is increasingly popular. The most common brands are Carlsberg and Tuborg; Lys Pilsner is a very low alcohol lager, more like a soft drink. Most international **wines** (from 25kr) and **spirits** (15–35kr) are widely available. You should also investigate the many varieties of the schnapps-like **Akvavit**, which Danes consume as eagerly as beer; a tasty relative is the hot and strong **Gammel Dansk Bitter Dram** – Akvavit-based but made with bitters and drunk occasionally at breakfast time.

Opening hours and holidays

Standard **shop hours** are Mon–Fri 9.30/10am–5.30/7pm, Sat 9/9.30am–2/5pm. All shops and banks are closed, and public transport and many museums run to Sun schedules on the following **public holidays**: Jan 1; Maundy Thurs to Easter Mon; Prayer Day (4th Fri after Easter); Ascension (40th day after Easter); Whit Sun & Mon; Constitution Day (June 5); Dec 24 (pm only); Dec 25 & Dec 26. On **International Workers' Day**, May 1, many offices and shops close at noon.

Emergencies

You're unlikely to have little direct contact with Danish **police**, as street crime and hassle are minimal in Denmark – but if you do, you'll find them helpful and almost certainly able to speak English. For prescriptions, doctors' consultations and dental work – but not hospital visits – you have to pay on the spot, but to get a full refund, take your receipt, E111 and passport to the local health office.

Emergency numbers
All emergencies ☏112

Copenhagen and around

COPENHAGEN, as any Dane will tell you, is no introduction to Denmark; indeed, a greater contrast with the sleepy provincialism of the rest of the country would be hard to find. Despite that, the city completely dominates Denmark: it is the seat of all the nation's institutions – politics, finance and the arts. It is also easily Scandinavia's most affordable capital, and one of Europe's most user-friendly cities: welcoming and compact, with a centre largely given over to pedestrians. There are first-rate galleries to visit and a worthy batch of smaller museums. In summer, there's also a lively range of street entertainment, while at night there's a plethora of cosy bars and an intimate club and live-music network that can hardly be bettered.

There was no more than a tiny fishing settlement here until the twelfth century, when Bishop Absalon oversaw the building of a castle on the site of the present Christiansborg. The settlement's prosperity grew after Erik of Pomerania granted special privileges and imposed the Sound Toll on vessels passing through the Øresund, then under Danish control, thus giving the expanding city tidy profits and enabling a self-confident trading centre to flourish. Following the demise of the Hanseatic ports, the city became the Baltic's principal harbour, earning the name København ("merchant's port"), and in 1443 it was made the Danish capital. A century later, Christian IV began the building programme that was the basis of the modern city: Rosenborg Slot, Børsen, Rundetårn and the districts of Nyboder and Christianshavn date from this time. In 1669, Frederik III graced the city with its first royal palace, Amalienborg.

Arrival and information

Kastrup Airport is 8km from the centre and connected to it by train (6 hourly 5am–midnight; 1 hourly at other times; journey time 13min; 21kr). All **trains** pull into Central Station, near Vesterbrogade; **long-distance buses** from elsewhere in Denmark stop either here or a short bus or S-train ride from the centre. **Ferries** and catamarans dock close to Nyhavn, a few minutes' walk from the centre.

The **tourist office** is across the road from the train station at Bernstorffsgade 1 (May–Aug Mon–Sat 9am–8pm, Sun 10am–6pm; rest of year Mon–Fri 9am–4.30pm, Sat 9am–1.30pm; ⓣ70.22.24.42, ⓦwww.visitcopenhagen.dk), who can arrange your accommodation for a 60kr fee. Far better for youth and budget-oriented information, however, is **Use-It**, centrally located in the Huset complex at Rådhusstræde 13 (mid-June to mid-Sept daily 9am–7pm; rest of year Mon–Wed 11am–4pm, Thurs till 6pm, Fri till 2pm; ⓣ33.73.06.20, ⓦwww.useit.dk). It provides a wide range of help for travellers, including poste restante and free email, luggage storage facilities and the very useful free magazine, *Playtime*.

Consider, also, buying the **Copenhagen Card** (215kr/24hr, 375kr/48hr, 495kr/72hr), which is valid for the entire public transport network (including much of eastern Zealand) and gives entry to most museums in the area. It's available at tourist offices, hotels, travel agents and the train station.

City transport

An integrated network of **buses** and electric **S-trains** (S-tog) covers Copenhagen and the surrounding areas from 5.30am to 12.30am; outside these hours a night bus (*Natbus*) network operates. Route maps can be picked up free of charge from stations. InterRail or Eurail cards are valid on the S-trains, otherwise the best option is a Copenhagen Card (see above); the **24-timer ticket** (85kr), which covers the same area, but doesn't include admission to museums; or the **Klippekort** (90kr/two-zone, 120kr/three-zone), which consists of ten stamps, each giving unlimited transfers for one hour within the designated zones (make sure you stamp your ticket when boarding the bus or in machines on station platforms to validate it). For a single journey, get a **Billet** (14kr), which is also valid for one hour, and unlimited transfers, within two zones. *Billets* can be bought on board buses or at train stations, *Klippekort* and *24-timers* at stations and HT Kortsalg kiosks. A passenger without a valid ticket faces an instant fine of 500kr.

Finally, under the **City Bike scheme** (summer only; ⑩www.citybike.dk), you can borrow bikes from racks across the city for a deposit of 20kr, which is returned when the bike is locked back into any other city rack after use. You'll be fined if

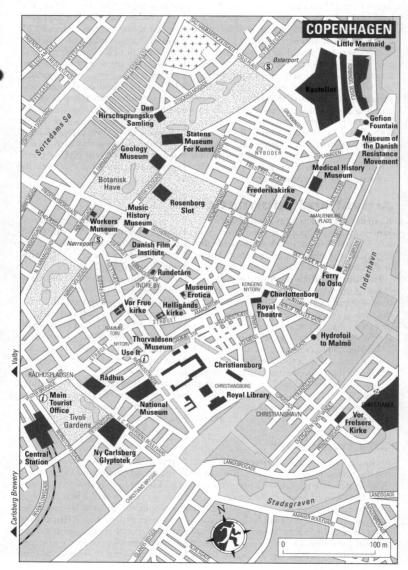

you use the bikes outside the city limits (the old rampart lakes mark the border) and you'll need to get yourself some lights if you want to cycle at night as you'll be fined if you're caught without any.

Accommodation

Accommodation is not easy to come by in Copenhagen, especially if you arrive late, or during July and August, when it's essential to book in advance. Most of the cheaper **hotels** are just outside the centre, around Istedgade, a slightly seedy area on the far side of the train station, and there's a good range of mid-priced hotels around Nyhavn, on the opposite side of the Indre By. Check with the tourist office early in the day and they may find you a double room for as little as 450kr; **private rooms** (❸), most of which are in the inner suburbs, will be an S-train ride away from the centre. Copenhagen has a great, though less central, selection of **hostels**, and space is only likely to be a problem in the peak summer months, when you should call ahead or turn up as early as possible to be sure of a place (*Use It* keeps a daily list of availability). Breakfast is not included in the prices given, unless otherwise stated.

Hostels and sleep-ins

Bellahøj Vandrehjem Herbergsvejen 8, Brønshøj ☎38.28.97.15, ⓦwww.danhostel.dk/bellahoej. HI hostel with large dorms, but more cosy than its rivals, and just fifteen minutes from the city centre on buses #2 and #11, nightbus #82N. No curfew. Closed mid-Jan to March. ❷

City Public Hostel Absalonsgade 8, Vesterbro ☎32.31.20.70, ⓦwww.city-public-hostel.dk. Noisy sixty-bed dorm on the lower floor, less crowded conditions on other levels. Just ten minutes' walk from the train station. Buses #6 and #28 stop close by. No curfew. Breakfast 20k. Closed Sept–April. ❸

Copenhagen Hostel Vejlands allé 200, Amager ☎32.52.29.08, ⓦwww.danhostel.dk/copenhagen. HI hostel with frugal two- and five-bed rooms. Bus #46, or E or A line S-train to Sjælør then bus #100S towards Svanemøllen; in all a 30–40min journey. Or a good twenty minutes' walk from the airport. No curfew. Closed Dec to mid-Jan. ❷

Hotel Jørgensens Rømersgade 11 ☎33.13.81.86, ⓦwww.hoteljoergensen.dk. A stone's throw from Nørreport station on Israels Plads. Mostly dorms of six, nine and twelve beds, with a few basic doubles. Popular with gay travellers. Age limit 35. Breakfast 120kr. Dorms ❸

Ishøj Strand Hostel, Ishøj Strandvej 13, Ishøj ☎43.53.50.15, ⓦwww.danhostel.dk/ishoj. A great five-star HI hostel, next to Køge beach park and the Arken modern art gallery. Thirty minutes from the centre on A or E line S-trains. ❷

Sleep In, Blegdamsvej 132, Østerbro ☎35.26.50.59, ⓦwww.sleep-in.dk. North of the city centre, next to Fælledparken and within walking distance of lively Sankt Hans Torv. Basic but adequate four- and six-bed dorms. Bus #1, #6 or #14, nightbus #85N or #95N. July & Aug only. ❷

Sleep-In-Fact Valdemarsgade 14 ☎33.79.67.79, ⓦwww.sleep-in-fact.dk. In the heart of Vesterbro, this is a sports centre out of season. Fifteen minutes' walk from the Central Station or bus #6. Closed mid-Aug to mid-June. Small and basic breakfast included. ❸

Sleep In Green Ravnsborggade 18, Nørrebro ☎35.37.77.77, ⓦwww.sleep-in-green.dk. Close to Sankt Hans Torv's café- and bar-life, this place has 68 dorm beds. Bus #5 or #16, nightbus #81N or 84N. Organic breakfast 30kr. Closed mid-Oct to May. ❷

Sleep in Heaven Struensegade 7, Nørrebro ☎35.35.46.48, ⓦwww.sleepinheaven.com. Two vast halls, the largest with 76 beds divided into four- and eight-bed compartments. Pleasant atmosphere, with youthful staff and occasional free gigs. Ten minutes from the centre by bus #8, #12 or #13, nightbus #92N. No curfew. ❸

YWCA Interpoint Valdemarsgade 15, Vesterbro ☎33.31.15.74). Four-, six- and ten-bed rooms. Fifteen minutes' walk from Central Station or bus #3, #6 or #16. Closed mid-Aug to Mid-June. ❷

Hotels

Absalon Hotel Helgolandsgade 15–19 ☎33.24.22.11 ⓦwww.absalon-hotel.dk. Very large family-run hotel, near Central Station. Most rooms en suite, but some (cheaper ones) aren't. Breakfast included. ❻

Bertrams Hotel Vesterbrogade 107a ☎33.25.04.05. Relaxed and cosy, modelled on Agatha Christie's *Bertrams* in London, a quiet haven in lively Vesterbro. Large rooms, some end suite. Bus #6 or #28. Breakfast buffet included. ❼

Hotel Cab Inn Scandinavia Vodroffsvej 55, Frederiksberg ☎35.36.11.11, ⓦwww.cab-inn.dk. Inspired by the Oslo ferry, 200 small en-suite cabins. Breakfast 50kr. ❻

Saga Hotel Colbjørnsensgade 18–20 ☎ 33.24.49.44, ⓦ www.sagahotel.dk. Cheap, central hotel, a stone's throw from Central Station (head out the back exit). On the edge of the red light district. Shared bathrooms. Breakfast included. ➏

Campsites

Absalon Korsdalsvej 132, Rødovre ☎ 36.41.06.00, ⓦ www.dcu.dk. Reasonable site 9km southwest of the city. S-train line B to Brøndbyøster, then fifteen minutes' walk or bus #550S, nightbus #93N. Open all year.

Bellahøj Camping Hvidkildevej 66 ☎ 38.10.11.50. Near the hostel of the same name. Central but grim, with long queues for the showers. Bus #11 or S-train F or M to Fuglebakken, nightbus #82N. Open June–Aug.

Charlottenlund Strandpark Strandvejen 144, Charlottenlund ☎ 39.62.36.88, ⓦ www.campingcopenhagen.dk. Beautifully situated at Charlottenlund Beach. Bus #6 or nightbus #85N. Open mid-May to mid-Sept.

FDM Camping Tangloppen, Ishøj Havn, Ishøj ☎ 43.54.07.67, ⓦ www.fdm.dk. Near the Ishøj hostel, 14km from the centre, but a fantastic location near both a beach and a plethora of watersports facilities. S-train A or E, then a ten-minute walk. Open May to mid-Sept.

The City

Indre By forms the city's inner core, an intricate maze of streets, squares and alleys. The main way in is from the buzzing open space of Rådhuspladsen, where you'll find the **Rådhus** (tours: Mon–Fri 3pm, Sat 10 &11am; 30kr), which has an elegant *fin-de-siècle* hall and a **bell tower** (separate tours: June–Sept Mon–Fri 10am, noon & 2pm, Sat noon; Oct–May Mon–Sat noon; 20kr)that gives wonderful views over the city. **Jens Olsen's World Clock** (10kr), in a room close to the entrance, took 27 years to perfect; it contains a 570,000-year calendar, plotting solar and lunar eclipses and various planetary orbits, as well as telling the local time – all with astounding accuracy.

Strøget and around

Beyond Rådhuspladsen, **Strøget**, a lively, pedestrianized street, leads into the heart of the city. The liveliest part is around Gammeltorv and Nytorv, squares on either side of Strøget, where there's a morning fruit and vegetable market, and jewellery and bric-a-brac stalls. A few minutes further on is the **Helligånds Kirke** (daily noon–4pm), founded in the fourteenth century and largely rebuilt from 1728 onwards, it is one of the oldest churches in the city. Strøget ends at **Kongens Nytorv**, the city's largest square, with an equestrian statue of its creator, Christian V, in the centre and a couple of grandly ageing structures around two of its shallow angles, most notably the **Danish Royal Theatre** and **Charlottenborg** – finished in 1683, at the same time as the square itself, for a son of Frederik III. Since 1754 it has been the home of the **Royal Academy of Art** (daily 10am–5pm, Wed till 7pm; 20kr; ⓦ www.charlottenborg-art.dk), which hosts decidedly eclectic art exhibitions in its spacious rooms.

There's more to see among the tangle of buildings and streets **west of Strøget**, not least the old university area, sometimes called the Latin Quarter, where the **Vor Frue Kirke** (Mon–Sat 8.30am–5pm, Sun noon–3pm), Copenhagen's cathedral, dates from 1829. The figure of Christ behind the altar and the solemn statues of the Apostles, crafted by Bertel Thorvaldsen and his pupils, merit a quick call. Northeast, the **Rundetårn** (June–Aug Mon–Sat 10am–5/8pm, Sun noon–5/8pm; 20kr), whose summit is reached by a spiral ramp, was built by Christian IV as an observatory. Close by, the **Music History Museum**, just off Kultorvet at Åbenrå 30 (May–Sept Mon & Wed–Sun 1–3.50pm; Oct–April also closed Thurs; 30kr), holds an impressive collection of musical instruments and sound-making devices, spanning the globe and the last thousand years. Over Nørre Voldgade, the **Workers Museum** at Rømersgade 22 (July–Oct daily 10am–4pm; rest of the year closed Mon; 50kr) is an engrossing guide to working-class life in Copenhagen from 1930 to 1959, using reconstructions and authentic period materials.

Nørrebro, northwest of the train station, has shed its crime-related reputation and is now a lively, young area that houses an ever increasing number of trendy fashion shops and buzzes right through the night.

North of Indre By

Gothersgade, the road marking the northern perimeter of Indre By, is home to the **Cinematek** (Tues–Fri 9.30am–10pm, Sat & Sun 12.30–10pm; free, movies 50kr; ⓦwww.cinemateket.dk), housing a three screen art-house cinema, a *videotek* section with free film showings, and a museum and library with exhibits on the city's early film industry. There's a profound change of mood once you cross Gothersgade: the congenial alleys of the old city give way to long, broad streets and proud, aristocratic structures. Running from Kongens Nytorv, a slender canal divides the two sides of **Nyhavn**, picturesquely lined by eighteenth-century houses – now bars and cafés, which are *the* place to be seen enjoying a beer in summer. Just north, the cobbled **Amalienborg Plads** centres on a statue of Frederik V flanked by four identical Rococo palaces. Two serve as royal residences, and there's a changing of the guard at noon, if the monarch is at home. Between the square and the harbour are the lavish gardens of Amaliehaven; in the opposite direction is the great marble dome of **Frederikskirke**, also known as "Marmorkirken" or marble church (Mon–Thurs 10am–5pm, Wed till 6pm, Fri–Sun noon–5pm), which was modelled on St Peter's in Rome. Begun in 1749, it remained unfinished until a century and a half later because of the enormous costs involved. Further along Bredgade, a German armoured car commandeered by Danes to bring news of the Nazi surrender marks the entrance to the **Museum of the Danish Resistance Movement** (Tues–Sat 10/11am–3/4pm, Sun 10/11am–4/5pm; 30kr, free on Wed).

The road behind the museum crosses into the grounds of the **Kastellet** (daily 6am–sunset; free), a fortress built by Christian IV and expanded by his successors through the seventeenth century. It's now occupied by the Danish army and closed to the public, but on a nearby corner the **Little Mermaid** has, since its unveiling in 1913, been one of the city's major tourist attractions; a bronze statue of a Hans Christian Andersen character, it was sculpted by Edvard Erichsen and paid for by the founder of the Carlsberg brewery. A short walk to the south, the spectacular **Gefion Fountain** shows the goddess Gefion with her four sons, whom she's turned into oxen having been promised, in return, as much land as she can plough in a single night.

West of here lies **Nyboder**, a curious area of narrow streets lined with rows of compact yellow dwellings, originally built by Christian IV to encourage his sailors to live in the city. The oldest (and cutest) houses can be found along Skt. Pauls Gade. Across Sølvgade from Nyboder is the main entrance to **Rosenborg Slot** (May–Oct daily 10/11am–3/5pm; Nov–April Tues–Sun 11am–2pm; 60kr). This Dutch-Renaissance-style palace served as the main residence of Christian IV and, until the end of the nineteenth century, of the monarchs who succeeded him. The main building displays the rooms and furnishings used by the regal occupants, although the highlight is the downstairs treasury, which displays the crown jewels and rich accessories worn by Christian IV. Adjacent to Rosenborg Slot is **Kongens Have**, the city's oldest public park and a popular place for picnics, while on the west side is the **Botanical Garden** (daily 8.30am–4/6pm; winter closed Mon; free).

The neighbouring **Statens Museum for Kunst** (daily 10am–5pm, Wed till 8pm; 50kr, free on Wed; ⓦwww.smk.dk) holds a mammoth collection of art, from minor Picassos and major pieces by Matisse and Braque, Cranach, El Greco, Titian, Rubens, Poussin and Claude Lorrain – although it's the grotesque pieces by Emil Nolde that steal the show. The new section houses mostly contemporary Danish art. The Skagen artists (see p.299), known for their interesting use of light, are amongst a nearby collection of twentieth-century Danish art across the park, at **Den Hirschsprungske Samling** on Stockholmsgade (daily 11am–4pm, Wed till 9pm; 25kr, free on Wed; ⓦwww.hirschsprung.dk).

Christiansborg

Christiansborg sits on the island of Slotsholmen, tenuously connected to Indre By by several short bridges. It was here, in the twelfth century, that Bishop Absalon built the castle that instigated the city. The drab royal palace completed in 1916 that now occupies the site is primarily given over to government offices and the state parliament or **Folketinget** (guided tours July–Sept daily at 2pm; rest of year Sun only; free). Close to the bus stop on Christiansborg Slotsplads is the doorway to the **Ruins under Christiansborg** (May–Sept daily 9.30am–3.30pm; Oct–April closed Mon, Wed & Fri; 20kr), where a staircase leads down to the remains of Absalon's original building; it's surprisingly absorbing, the mood enhanced by the semi-darkness and lack of external noise. **The Royal Reception Rooms** (guided tours May–Sept daily at 11am, 1pm & 3pm; Oct–April Tues, Thurs & Sat at 11am & 3pm, Sun at 3pm; 40kr), in the palace's north wing and used by the royal family to entertain important visitors, are worth a peek.

On the far side of Slotsholmen, the **Thorvaldsens Museum** (Tues–Sun 10am–5pm; 20kr, Wed free) is the home of an enormous collection of work and memorabilia (and the body) of Denmark's most famous sculptor, who lived from 1770 to 1844. There's another major collection a short walk away over the Slotsholmen moat, in the **National Museum** (same times; 40kr, Wed free; ⊛www.natmus.dk), which has excellent displays on Denmark's prehistory and Viking days – jewellery, sacrificial gifts, and even bodies, all remarkably well preserved by Danish peat bogs.

Christianshavn and Christiania

From Christiansborg, a bridge crosses to **Christianshavn**, built by Christian IV as an autonomous new town in the early sixteenth century as housing for shipbuilding workers. It was given features more common to Dutch ports of the time, even down to small canals, and in parts is more redolent of Amsterdam than Copenhagen. Reaching skywards on the far side of Torvegade is the blue-and-gold spire of **Vor Frelsers Kirke** (daily 11/12am–3.30/4.30pm; tower April–Oct only; free, tower 20kr), whose helter-skelter outside staircase was added to the otherwise plain church in the mid-eighteenth century, making it one of the city's most recognizable features.

A few streets from Vor Frelsers Kirke, **Christiania** is a former barracks area that was colonized by hippies after declaring itself a **"free city"** in 1971. A pseudo-Statue of Liberty greets visitors as they pass under the little arched entrance and head for the open hash market, known as *Puscherstreet*, where smoking is tolerated by the government. Bob Marley and John Lennon blare out from the bars and the area is awash with psychedelic painting. Residents ask visitors not to camp or point cameras directly at them. There are two-hour guided tours of the area (daily noon–3pm on the hour; 30kr; ☏32.57.96.70 ⊛www.christiania.org); individuals can just turn up, but if possible book at least one day in advance.

Along Vesterbrogade

Hectic **Vesterbrogade** begins on the far side of Rådhuspladsen, and its first attraction is perhaps Copenhagen's most famous, the **Tivoli Gardens** (mid-April to Sept daily 11am–11pm/1am 50kr), whose opening each year marks the beginning of summer. Throughout the season, the gardens feature fairground rides, fireworks, fountains, and a variety of nightly entertainment in the central arena. It's rather overrated and expensive, but you can still have an enjoyable evening wandering among the revellers of all ages. On the other side of Tietgensgade, the **Ny Carlsberg Glyptotek** (Tues–Sun 10am–4pm; 30kr, Wed & Sun free; ⊛www. glyptoteket.dk) is Copenhagen's finest gallery, with an array of Greek, Roman and Egyptian art and artefacts, as well as what is considered the biggest and best collection of Etruscan art outside Italy. There are also excellent examples of modern

European art, including a collection of Degas casts, Manet's *Absinthe Drinker* and works by Man Ray, Chagall and Picasso.

Directly behind the station begins **Vesterbro** proper, the city's fomer red light district currently undergoing a bit of a gentrification process as home of Copenhagen's wealthier students and young families. In the narrow streets between Vesterbrogade and Istedgade, a few pornography shops remain as evidence of the area's former role. At Vesterbrogade 59, the **City Museum** (Mon & Wed–Sun 10am/1pm–4pm; 20kr, Fri free) contains reconstructed ramshackle house fronts and tradesmen's signs from early Copenhagen, a large room recording the form Christian IV gave the city, and a collection of memorabilia concerning the nineteenth-century Danish philosopher Søren Kierkegaard. Further along Vesterbrogade, down Pile Allé and along Gamle Carlsberg Vej (buses #6 and #18), the exhibition at **Carlsberg Brewery Visitors Center** (Tues–Sun 10am–4pm; free) is well worth seeing, if only for the free booze provided at the end.

Eating and drinking

There's a wide choice of **eating** options in the city centre; the areas around Kultorvet and along Studiestræde are loaded with great places to eat. Farther afield, Nørrebro across Peblinge Søen draws the trendy set, and Vesterbrogade turns up a number of lower-key places, better the further you venture. An almost unchartable network of **cafés** and bars serving drinks and snacks covers Copenhagen. The best are in or close to Indre By, and it's no hardship to sample several on the same night, though bear in mind that on Fridays and Saturdays you'll probably need to queue.

If you're **self-catering**, there are numerous *smørrebrød* outlets – Domhusets Smørrebrød, Kattesundet 18, and Centrum Smørrebrød, Vesterbrogade 6C, are two of the most central – and there's a Netto at Nørre Voldgade 94, Fiolstræde 9, Landemærket 11 and Store Kongensgade 47, Fakta is on Nørrebrogade 14–16 and on Borgergade 27.

Brunches, Snacks and fast food

Amokka Dag Hammerskjölds Allé 38–40. A coffee temple near Østerport station serving more varieties of coffee than you can imagine. Also sells sandwiches, etc. Outdoor seating in summer.

Bang & Jensen Istedgade 130. Popular café at the quieter end of Istedgade, serving a renowned brunch until 4pm and sandwiches all day.

Café Europa Amagertorv 1. Its coffee is said to be the best in town, and it also sells fabulous cakes, sandwiches and light meals. Outdoor seating on Strøget.

Café Sommersko Kronprinsensgade 6. A popular café, whose filling Sunday brunch (veggie options available) is particularly recommended.

Den Sorte Gryde, Istedgade 108. Legendary huge burgers, but also good traditional Danish fare.

Front Page Sortedams Dosseringen 21. Overlooking one of the city's finest lakes, this is a perfect spot for a quiet coffee or beer and light snacks.

Husets Café Rådhusstræde 13. Sandwich spot located in the Huset complex, which doubles as a jazz venue in the evenings. Closed Sun.

La Galette Larsbjørnstræde 9. Authentic Breton pancakes made with organic buckwheat and an array of fillings – from smoked salmon to

chocolate and chestnut mousse.

Morgenstedet Langgade in Christiania. Tasty and mostly organic vegan and vegetarian salads, snacks and meals at very affordable prices. No smoking, No alcohol. Closed Tues.

Pussy Galore's Flying Circus Sankt Hans Torv 30. Trendy brunch spot with outdoor seating on the square. Brunch served till 4pm. Also popular in the evening, when beer and wine take priority.

The Taco Shop Nørre Farimagsgade 57. The best taco spot in town. Take out only.

Restaurants

Ankara Vesterbrogade 35. Popular Turkish restaurant with an all-you-can-eat lunchtime buffet for 49kr, 69kr in the eve.

Atlas Bar Larsbjørnstræde 18. Eco-restaurant/café serving tasty Asian and South American dishes. The portions are enormous, with main courses from 100kr. Closed Sun.

Circus Rosenvængets Allé 7. A trendy butcher-cum-hairdresser-cum-restaurant with French-inspired dishes. Keep an eye out for the 1900 murials, depicting a cow's journey from the field to the butchers' shop.

Den Grønne Kælder Pilestræde 48. A simple tiled-floor vegetarian eatery. Closed Sun.

Delicatessen Vesterbrogade 120. Cosy basement restaurant serving outstanding international dishes, tapas from 20kr a plate. Take out available.

Hackenbusch Vesterbrogade 124. Colourful café/bar with an inventive blackboard menu.

Nyhavns Færgekro Nyhavn 5. Slightly pricey, but the lunchtime fish-laden buffet (89kr) cannot be surpassed. Outdoor seating in summer.

RizRaz Kompagnistræde 20. Excellent value Mediterranean food; lunchtime buffet 49kr, 59kr in the eve.

Shezan Viktoriagarde 22. The first Pakistani restaurant in Copenhagen and still going strong. Main courses from 50kr, with plenty of vegetarian dishes.

Spiseloppen Christiania. It's won culinary accolades, and hiked up its prices, but the *Spiseloppen* is still great and the portions generous. Meals from 140kr. Closed Mon.

Thai Esan Lille Istedgade 7. Bargain Thai food in a very popular restaurant.

Bars

Bibendum Nansengade 24. The city's hottest new winebar also serves tapas.

Café Ludvigsen Sundevedsgade 2. Vesterbro's most popular pool bar, complete with jukebox and inexpensive beer. Crammed at weekends.

Charlie's Bar Pilestræde 33. Award-winning Real Ale pub.

Café Louise Nørrebrogade 5. Open through to 4am daily, 9am at weekends,this once traditional bar has become a legendary last stop after a big night out. You have to ring a door bell to get in.

Dan Turell Store Regnegade 3. Something of an institution with the artier student crowd, this place is packed at weekends, when it's open till 4am.

Drop Inn Kompagnistræde 34. Easy going and unpretentious place near Huset with live blues or rock almost every night. Cheap beer and late opening hours.

Hviids Vinstue Kongens Nytorv 19. Old-fashioned bar with crowded rooms patrolled by uniformed waiters. Outdoor seating in summer.

Kulkafeen Teglgårdsstræde 5. Cosy café that gets going in the evening and has live music on Sat.

Krasnapolsky Vestergade 10. Danish avant-garde art on the wall reflects the trend-setting reputation of this ultramodern watering hole. DJs Thurs, Fri & Sat. Tasty food too.

Krut's karport Øster Farrimagsgade 12. Small and slightly run down but nonetheless very popular and one of the few bars selling absinthe.

The Moose Sværtegade 5. Tiny-looking bar that stretches back into a spacious room with pool tables. "Happy hour" 9pm till 2am.

Peder Hvitfeldt P. Hvitfeldtsstræde 15. Immensely popular spit-and-sawdust place. Come early if you want a seat.

Sebastopol Sankt Hans Torv 2. Trendy spot on the Sankt Hans Torv square that catches the last rays of sun and therefore gathers large crowds in summer. Good brunches too.

Supergejl Nørrebrogade 184. New popular café/bar, especially among the younger crowd. Funky DJ Fri & Sat.

Universitetscaféen Fiolstræde 2. A prime location, long hours (until 5am), outdoor seating in summer and live blues or rock every Thurs.

Nightlife

The city is a pretty good place for **live music**. Major international names visit regularly, and there are always plenty of minor gigs in cafés and bars, often free during the week. For **listings** of what's on, pick up the free *Nat & Dag* or *Gaffa*, from cafés and music shops. Clubs and discos are busy from midnight and 5am, with fairly easy-going dress codes; drinks are seldom hiked-up and admission is fairly cheap (from 40kr).

Live music, clubs and discos

Barcelona Fælledvej 21. This swanky hangout is very much the place to be seen. Fri & Sat it's *Bar'Cuda* and becomes a sweaty cavern of funk and soul till 5am. Free.

Copenhagen JazzHouse Niels Hemmingsensgade 10 ⊛ www.jazzhouse. Laid-back jazz venue, followed by a jazz, funk or mainstream disco.

Barfly & Britannia, Løvstræde 4. A new multi-storey temple of entertainment. The bottom half

plays music from the 70s and 80s, the top two floors techno and mainstream pop. Pool tables and pinball machines too. Open Wed–Sat till 5/6am.

Distotek In Nørregade 1. Cavernous disco playing mainstream hits.. Entrance fee (from 50kr) includes free drinks all night. Thurs till 6am, Fri & Sat till 10am.

Femøren and **Tiøren**, Amager. Two open-air rock venues hosting local and international bands from June to Aug on the beach at Amager. Bus #12 or #13.

JazzHuset Vognporten Rådhusstræde 13. In the same building as Use-It, with regular live bands. Mon–Thurs Be bop, Fri & Sat jazz.

Klaptræet, Kultorvet 11. A café/bar during the week, at weekends it hosts DJs with a dancefloor out back. Open till 5am.

Loppen Bådsmandsstræde 43, Christiania. Regular rock, jazz and performance artists. Discos follow live music events Fri & Sat. Open till 5am.

Mojo Løngangstræde 21 ⓦ www.mojo.dk. Renowned jazz and blues evenings – live music every night. Happy hour 8–10pm.

Park Café Østerbrogade 79 ⓦ www.parkcafe.dk. Popular café/music venue. Thurs–Sat, it's home to *Kitty Club*, with mainstream disco upstairs, live music downstairs.

Pumpehuset Studiestræde 52 ⓦ www.pumpwhuset .dk. Venue for mainstream rock, hip-hop and funk from around the world.

Rust Guldbergsgade 8, Nørrebro ⓦ www.rust.dk. Huge complex hosting rock bands on a main stage, and three dancefloors playing everything from Break Beat to Latin jazz. Closed Mon.

Sabor Latino Vester Voldgade 85. Popular Latin dance venue. Free Salsa lessons Thurs–Sat 10–11pm.

Stengade 30 Stengade 18 ⓦ www.stengade30.dk. Mixed bag of live music and dance events, and a popular hardcore metal venue. Techno Thurs. Closed Mon.

Stereo Bar Linnésgade 16A. Once-trendy bar that's mellowed with age, with a dancefloor in the basement playing mostly House. Open till 3am.

Vega Enghavevej 40 ⓦ www.vega.dk. A large multi-levelled centre with DJs at Lille Vega and concerts at Store Vega. Plays House, Techno and Disco. Over 20s only.

Gay Copenhagen

Copenhagen has a lively **gay scene**. For all **information**, contact the National Organization for Gay Men and Women at Teglgårdstræde 13 (☎33.13.19.48, ⓦwww.lbl.dk), or get hold of a copy of *Pan* magazine. As for gay **bars**, the *Cosy Bar*, Studiestræde 24, is frequented by gay men of all ages, while *Sebastian*, Hyskenstræde 10, draws a predominantly young trendy crowd. *Pan Club*, Knabrostræde 3, part of the largest gay centre in the country, has a great disco (Thurs is *Carma Club* for women only). *Masken*, Studiestræde 33, has a great bar and disco, often featuring drag shows. Of primarily lesbian places *Kvindehuset*, Gothersgade 37 (☎33.14.28.04), has a café and disco, *XXBar*, every third Friday of the month as well as other regular events. *Jeppes Club*, Allégade 25, is a lesbian meeting place open the first and last Friday of the month (9pm–3am).

Listings

Bike rental Københavns Cykelbørs, Gothersgade 157; Københavns Cykler, Reventlowsgade 11; Østerport Cykler, Oslo Plads 9.

Embassies Australia, Dampfærgevej 26 ☎70.26 .36.76; Canada, Kristen Bernikowsgade 1 ☎33.48 .32.00; Ireland, Østbanegade 21 ☎35.42.32.33; Netherlands, Toldbodgade 33 ☎33.70.72.00; New Zealand, use UK; UK, Kastelsvej 40 ☎35.44.52.00; US, Dag Hammerskjölds Allé 24 ☎35.55.31.44.

Exchange Arbejdernes Landsbank, Vestrebrogade 5 (24hr); Den Danske Bank at the Airport (daily 6am–10pm); Forex at the Central Station (daily 8am–9pm). Kontanten ATMs everywhere.

Hospital Rigshospitalet, Blegdamsvej 9 ☎35.45.35.45.

Internet cafés Free at Usit, Rådhusstræde 13, and the Royal Library, Søren Kirkegaard Plads 1. Otherwise, Boomtown, Axeltorv 1–3; Faraos Cigarer, Skindergade 27; MåneBase Alpha, Elmegade 20, Nørrebro; Nethulen, Istedgade 114, Vesterbro.

Left luggage Free for a day at Usit, Rådhusstræde 13. Otherwise, lockers at Central Station.

Pharmacies Steno Apotek, Vesterbrogade 6; Sønderbro Apotek, Amagerbrogade 158. Both 24hr.

Police ☎33.25.14.48

Post office Main office: Tietgensgade 37; also at Central Station.

Short trips from Copenhagen

If the weather's good, take a trip to the Amager **beaches** on bus #12 or #13 along Øresundsvej. On the other side of the airport from the beaches lies **DRAGØR**, an atmospheric cobbled fishing village which has good local history collections in the

Dragør Museum (May–Sept Tues–Sun noon–4pm; 20kr), by the harbour, and the **Amager Museum** (same times and price), just off the Copenhagen road at the western edge of the village. From the city, take buses #30, #36 or #350S. Alternatively, if you're in the mood for an amusement park but can't afford Tivoli, venture out to **BAKKEN** (end March to Aug daily noon/2pm–midnight; free; 198kr daypass), close to the Klampenborg stop at the end of lines C and F on the S-train. This has been an amusement park since the sixteenth century, and besides swings and rollercoasters it offers pleasant woods of oak and beech, which were once royal hunting grounds.

The most noteworthy attractions are a little further out. Fifteen minutes' walk from Rungsted Kyst train station, the **Karen Blixen Museum** (May–Sept Tues–Sun 10am–5pm; Oct–April Wed–Sun 11am/1pm–4pm; 35kr) is housed in the former home of Isak Dinesen, author of out *Out of Africa*. In **HUMLEBÆK**, 10km further north and a short walk from its train station, you'll find **Louisiana**, an excellent modern art gallery, at Gammel Strandvej 13 (daily 10am–5pm, Wed till 10pm; 68kr); its setting alone is worth the journey, harmoniously combining art, architecture and the natural landscape.

The rest of Zealand

As home to the capital, **Zealand** is Denmark's most important and most visited region, and, with a swift metropolitan transport network covering almost half of the island, you can always make it back to the capital in time for an evening drink. North of Copenhagen, **Helsingør**, the departure point for ferries to Sweden, is the site of the Kronborg Slot – though Frederiksborg Slot, at nearby **Hillerød**, is, if anything, more impressive. West of Copenhagen, and on the main route to Funen, is **Roskilde**, its extravagant cathedral the resting place for Danish monarchs, and with a gorgeous location on the Roskilde fjord – from where five Viking boats were salvaged and are now restored and displayed in a specially built museum.

Three **ferry** lines make the twenty-minute crossing from Helsingør to Helsingborg in **Sweden**. Scandlines is the main one (every 20–30min; 16kr), leaving from the main terminal by the train station. Otherwise, there's Sundbusserne (6.30am–7.30pm every 20min; 19kr), and HH Ferries (8kr), the latter docking a good walk from central Helsingborg. **Rail passes** are valid on all three and the Copenhagen Card gives a fifty percent discount.

Hillerød

Last stop on lines A and E of the S-train, **HILLERØD** has a castle to rival the Kronborg Slot (see Helsingør, below): **Frederiksborg Slot** (daily 10/11am–3/5pm; 50kr) lies decorously across three small islands on an artificial lake. The Frederiksborg ferry does a half hour trip on the castle lake in summer (20kr). Buses #701, #702 and #703 run from the train station to the castle, but it's only a twenty-minute signposted walk.

The castle was rebuilt at the turn of the seventeenth century in Dutch Renaissance style and the unusual design – prolific use of towers and spires, pointed Gothic arches and flowery window ornamentation – still dominates. There's an illustrated guide to the interior(40kr), but most rooms have detailed descriptions in English pasted up on the walls. Two rooms deserve special mention: the exquisite chapel, where monarchs were anointed between 1671 and 1840, and the Great Hall above, bare but for the staggering wall- and ceiling-decorations: tapestries, wall-reliefs, portraits and a glistening black marble fireplace.

The **tourist office** at Slangerupgade 2 (Mon–Fri 10am–5/6pm, Sat 10am–1/3pm; ☎48.24.26.26, ⓦwww.hillerodturist.dk;) offers **private rooms** (❷), for a 25kr booking fee. Few of the **hotels** can match the prices in Copenhagen, but you could try *Hotel Hillerød*, Milnersvej 41 (☎48.24.08.00, ❾www.hotelhillerod.dk; ❽). Less expensive are beds at the *Nordiske Lejerskole og Kursuscenter*, Lejerskolevej 4 (☎48.26.19.86, ❾www.nordlejr.dk; ❸). The **campsite** is on Blytækkervej 18, by the agricultural showground, 1km from the centre (☎48.26.48.54, ❾www.hillerodcamping .dk); it has cabins, too (Easter to mid-Sept). The *Spisestedet Leonora*, in one of the castle's gatehouses, serves fantastic *smørrebrød* (from 35kr a piece); while *Engelhardt's Cafe*, at Slotsarkaderne 112, serves good-value sandwiches and light **snacks**.

Helsingør

First impressions of **HELSINGØR** are none too enticing, but away from the hustle of its terminals it is a quiet and likeable town. Its position on the four-kilometre strip of water linking the North Sea and the Baltic brought the town prosperity when, in 1429, the Sound Toll was imposed on passing vessels. Today, it's once again an important waterway, with ferries across it to Helsingborg, accounting for most of Helsingør's through-traffic.

The town's great tourist draw is **Kronborg Slot** (May–Sept daily 10.30am–5pm; rest of year Tues–Sun 11am–3/4pm; 40kr, 60kr joint ticket with the Maritime Museum; Copenhagen Card not valid), principally because of its literary associations as Elsinore Castle, whose ramparts Shakespeare's Prince Hamlet supposedly strode. The playwright never actually visited Helsingør, and the tenth-century character Amleth on whom his hero was based long predates the castle, but there's nevertheless a thriving Hamlet souvenir business. The present castle dates from the sixteenth century and though various bits have been destroyed and rebuilt since, it remains a grand affair, enhanced immeasurably by its setting; the interior, particularly the royal chapel, is spectacularly ornate. The castle also houses the national **Maritime Museum** (30kr, 60kr joint ticket with the castle itself), an uninteresting collection of model ships and nautical knick-knacks.

Away from Kronborg and the harbour area, Helsingør has a well-preserved medieval quarter. **Stengade** is the main pedestrianized street, linked by a number of narrow alleyways to Axeltorv, the town's small market square and a good spot for a beer. Near the corner of Stengade and Skt. Annagade, the newly renovated spired **Skt. Olai's Kirke** (Mon–Fri 10am–2/4pm) is now Helsingør's cathedral. Just beyond is the **Karmeliterklostret**, the best-preserved medieval monastic complex in Scandinavia (Mon–Fri 10am–2/3pm; 20kr). Its former hospital contains the **Town Museum** (daily noon–4pm; 10kr), which prided itself on brain operations – the unnerving tools of which are still here, together with diagrams of the corrective procedures used.

Practicalities

Trains from Copenhagen arrive at the noisy station attached to the **ferry terminal**. The **tourist office**, on Havnepladsen 3 (Mon–Fri 9am–4/5/6pm, Sat 10am–1/3pm; ☎49.21.13.33, ❾www.helsingorturist.dk), will book **private rooms** (❸) for a 50kr booking fee. The closest thing to a cheap **hotel** is *Hotel Skandia*, Bramstræde 1 (☎49.21.09.02, ❾www.hotel-skandia.dk; ❺). More affordably, there is a **youth hostel** (☎49.21.16.40, ❾www.helsingorhostel.dk; ❷) on the beach, twenty minutes' walk north along Ndr. Strandvej (the coastal road), or take bus #340 from the station. The **campsite** (☎49.28.12.12, ❾www.helsingorcamping.dk) at Strandaleen 2 is closer to town and also by a beach, between the main road and the sea; take the private train – Hornbæk banen (Copenhagen Card valid, rail passes not) – to Marienlyst or bus #340. For **food**, *Rådmands Davids Hus*, Strandgade 70, is a prime lunchtime spot for its daily specials; *Møllers Conditori*, Stengade 39, Denmark's oldest bakery, has sizeable sandwiches and Danish pastries to follow; or try the varied delights of *Færgegården*, Stengade 81, three ethnic restaurants in one place – Chinese, Mexican and Greek – all with good value buffets starting at 50kr.

Roskilde

ROSKILDE, half an hour by train from the capital, was the base of the Danish church in the twelfth century and as a consequence became the nation's capital. Its importance waned after the Reformation, and it came to function mainly as a market town for the neighbouring rural communities – which it still is, as well as being dormitory town for Copenhagen. Its ancient centre is one of Denmark's most appealing – well worth a look on your way west.

Showpiece is the fabulous **Roskilde Domkirke** (Mon–Sat 9/10am–3.45/4.45pm, Sun 12.30–3.45/4.45pm; 15kr), founded in 1170 and largely completed by the fourteenth century, although bits have been added since. Four royal chapels house a claustrophobic collection of regal remains: twenty kings and seventeen queens. The most richly endowed chapel is that of Christian IV, a previously austere resting place jazzed up in the early nineteenth century with bronze statues, frescoes and vast paintings of scenes from his reign. A roofed passageway, the **Arch of Absalon**, runs from the Cathedral into the **Roskilde Palace**, housing the **Palace Collections** (mid-May to mid-Sept daily 11am–4pm; rest of the year Sat & Sun 2–4pm; 25kr): paintings, furniture and other artefacts belonging to the wealthiest Roskilde families of the eighteenth and nineteenth centuries. In the same building is the **Museum of Contemporary Art** (Tues–Fri 11am–5pm, Sat & Sun noon–4pm; 20kr, Wed free), hosting temporary exhibitions and including a charming sculpture garden.

The town's history is recorded in the **Roskilde Museum** at Skt. Ols Gade 18 (daily 11am–4pm; 25kr), with strong sections on medieval pottery and toys, although time is better spent at the absorbing **Viking Ship Museum** (daily 9/10am–4/5pm; 60kr; ⊕www.vikingeskibsmuseet.dk), in Strandengen on the banks of the fjord. Inside, five excellent specimens of Viking shipbuilding are proudly displayed: a deepsea trader, a merchant ship, a warship, a ferry and a longship, each one retrieved from the fjord where they had been sunk to block invading forces. There's also the Museum Island, where you can watch new Viking ships being built.

The **tourist office** (Mon–Fri 9am–4/5/6pm, Sat 10am–1/2pm; ⊕46.35.27.00, ⊕www.visitroskilde.dk) is at Gullandsstræde 15, a short walk from the main square. There's a **campsite** (⊕46.75.79.96, ⊕www.roskildecamping.dk; April to mid-Sept) on the wooded edge of the fjord 4km away – an appealing setting, which makes it very crowded at peak times; take bus #603 from the centre towards Veddelev. The wonderful new **youth hostel** on Vindeboder 7 is nextdoor to the Viking Ship Museum on the harbour (⊕46.35.21.84, ⊕www.danhostel.dk/roskilde; ❷); take bus #605 towards Boserup. Both will be booked solid during the **Roskilde Festival** (⊕www.roskilde-festival.dk), one of the largest open-air rock events in Europe, attracting around ninety thousand people annually. The festival takes place late June/early July and there's a special free camping ground beside the festival site, to which shuttle buses run from the train station every ten minutes. For **lunch**, head to *Bogart Café* on Algade; for a beer try the informal *Café Grunk* on Store Gråbrødrestræde.

Funen

Known as the Garden of Denmark, partly for the lawn-like neatness of its fields, partly for the fruit and vegetables grown in them, **Funen** is the smaller of the two main Danish islands. The pastoral outlook of the place and the coastline draw many visitors, but its attractions are low-profile cultural sights, such as the collections of the "Funen painters" and the birthplaces of writer Hans Christian Andersen and composer Carl Nielsen. **Odense**, Denmark's third city, is the island's main urban attraction. Close to this, the former fishing town of **Kerteminde** has a faded charm, and is near the *Ladby Boat*, an important Viking relic.

Odense

ODENSE is proud to be the birthplace of Denmark's best-loved writer, Hans Christian Andersen, as well as the childhood home of composer Carl Nielsen. Named after Odin, chief of the pagan gods, this is one of the oldest settlements in the country. Much of the pleasantly sleepy city is pedestrianized and there's a good cycle network, too. There's a range of good museums to visit and the **nightlife** is surprisingly lively, with a focus on live music and jazz.

The Town

The city's major attraction is the **Hans Christian Andersen Museum** at Hans Jensen Stræde 37–45 (mid-June to Aug daily 9am–7pm; rest of the year Tues–Sun 10am–4pm; ⊛www.odmus.dk; 35kr), in the house where the writer was born in 1805. The son of a hard-up cobbler, Andersen was only really accepted in his own country towards the end of his life, which was perhaps why he travelled widely and often, leaving Odense at the first opportunity. The museum is stuffed with intriguing items, including school reports, manuscripts and paraphernalia from his travels. One room has been recreated as his Copenhagen study and a separate gallery has an audio collection of the writer's best-known tales and a slide-show of his life.

The area around the museum, all half-timbered houses and clean, car-free cobbled streets, nonetheless lacks character; indeed, if Andersen were around he'd hardly recognize the neighbourhood, which is now one of Odense's most expensive. For far more realistic local history, head to **Bymuseet Møntergården**, a few streets away at Overgade 48–50 (Tues–Sun 10am–4pm; 15kr), where there's an engrossing assemblage of artefacts dating from the city's earliest settlements to the Nazi occupation. There's more about Andersen at Munkemøllestræde 3–5, between Skt. Knud Kirkestræde and Horsetorvet, in the tiny **Hans Christian Andersen's Childhood Home** (daily 10/11am–3/4pm; 10kr), where Andersen lived from 1807 to 1819. More interesting, though, is the nearby **Skt. Knud's Kirke** (Mon–Sat 9/10am–4/5pm, Sun noon–3pm; free), whose crypt holds the remains of King Knud II and his brother Benedikt, both slain in 1086 by Jutish farmers angry at the taxes Knud imposed on them – Knud was canonized soon after. The cathedral is the only example of pure Gothic church architecture in the country; its finely detailed sixteenth-century wooden altarpiece is one of the greatest works of the Lübeck master, Claus Berg.

The **Funen Art Gallery** at Jernbanegade 13 (Tues–Sun 10am–4pm; ⊛www.odmus.dk; 30kr), just a few minutes' walk from Skt. Knud's, gives a good indication of the region's importance to the Danish art world during the late nineteenth century; a number of Funen-based painters abandoned portraiture for impressionistic landscapes and studies recording the lives of the peasantry and this collection contains some stirring works by Vilhelm Hammershøi, P.S. Krøyer, Michael and Anne Ancher, and H.A. Brendekilde's enormously emotive *Udslidt*. A short walk east, at Claus Bergs Gade 11, is the **Carl Nielsen Museum** (Jan–Aug Thurs–Sun noon–4pm; rest of the year Thurs & Fri 4–8pm, Sun noon–4pm; 25kr). Born in a village just outside Odense, Nielsen is best remembered in Denmark for his popular songs, though it was his operas, choral pieces and symphonies that established him as a major international composer. The exhibits, detailing Nielsen's life and achievements, are enlivened by the accomplished sculptures of his wife, Anne Marie, and you can listen to some of his work on headphones.

West of the centre and well worth a visit is the **Brandts Klædefabrik**, on Brandts Passage just off Vestergade, a large former textile factory now given over to a number of cultural endeavours: an art school, a cinema, a music library, several cafés and restaurants, and four museums (July & Aug daily 10am–5pm; rest of year Tues–Sun 10am–5pm; 50kr combined ticket; ⊛www.brandts.dk). In the large halls that once housed the huge machinery are the **Brandts Art Gallery** (30kr), which displays work of high-flying new talent in art and design, and the **Museum of**

Photographic Art (25kr), featuring the cream of modern (and some not so modern) art photography. On the third floor the **Danish Museum of Printing** (25kr), with its bulky machines and devices, chronicles the development of printing, book binding and illustrating from the Middle Ages to the present. Further down Brandts Passage, upstairs at no. 27, the **Time Collection** (25kr) gives a fascinating insight into the development of fashion and interior design since the turn of the last century.

South of the centre at Sejerskovvej 20 is **Funen Village** (April–Oct Tues–Sun 9.30/10am–5/7pm; mid-June to mid-Aug also Mon; Nov–March Sun 11am–3pm; 55kr), a reconstructed nineteenth-century village made up of buildings from all over Funen. In summer, some of the old trades are revived in the former workshops and crafthouses, and free shows are staged at the open-air theatre. Bus #21, #22 and #42 run to the village from the city centre (get off at the sign Den Fynske Landsby).

Practicalities

The **train station** is a ten-minute walk from the city centre. All long-distance **buses** terminate here, too, and it's also where you'll find the **tourist office** (mid-June to Aug Mon–Fri 9.30am–7pm, Sat & Sun 10am–4/5pm; rest of year Mon–Fri 9.30am–4.30pm, Sat 10am–1pm; ☎66.12.75.20, ⊛www.odenseturist.dk) on the Vestergade side of the Rådhus – follow the signs. The tourist office sells the useful **Adventure Pass** (100kr/24hr, 140kr/48hr), which gives a discount on most museums and unlimited travel on all local buses.

The only cheap **hotels** are *Det Lille Hotel*, Dronningensgade 5 (☎66.12.28.21; ❺), and *Ydes*, Hans Tausens Gade 11 (☎66.12.11.31, ⊛www.ydes.dk; ❹). There are two **hostels**: one by the train station at Østre Stationsvej 31 (☎66.11.04.25, ⊛www.cityhostel.dk; ❷); and the quieter one at Kragsbjergvej 121 (☎66.13.04.25, ⊛www.odense-danhostel.dk; ❷; closed Dec to mid-Feb) – take bus #61 south to Tornbjerg or Fraugde and get out along Munkebjergvej at the junction with Vissenbjergvej. The closest **campsite** (☎66.11.47.02) is at Odensevej 102, near the Funen Village, and has cabins as well as tent space; take buses #21, #22, #23 or #24 from the Rådhus or station to Højby. There's free **internet** access in the large local library in the train station; otherwise, try No Limit Cyber Café, Albani Torv 5, or Net Café 5000, Vindegade 43.

There are plenty of **restaurants** and **snack bars** in the city centre. *Den Gyldne ovn* on Fisketorvet is a reliable spot for freshly made sandwiches, while the best pizzeria is *Pizzeria Ristorante Italiano*, Vesterbro 9. You might also try the Mexican dishes at *Tortilla Flat*, Frederiksgade 38, or the inexpensive café in the Badstuen cultural centre, Østre Stationsvej 26. For a **drink**, try *Carlsen's Kvarter*, an inexpensive pub on Læssøgade that sometimes hosts Danish folk music, or the fashionable *Café Biografen* in Brandts Passage. As for **nightlife**, Jazzhus Dexter, Vindegade 65 (⊛www.dexter.dk), is the place to head for jazz, while the Badstuen cultural centre (⊛www.badstuen.dk) and Rytmeposten, across the road at Østre Stationsvej 35 (⊛www.rytmeposten.dk), host raucous live bands. Cabarbaret, Vintapperstræde 39, is host to a hosttest **club scene** at weekends.

Kerteminde and around

A thirty-minute bus ride (#890) northeast from Odense takes you to **KERTE-MINDE**, a sailing and holiday centre that has a prettily preserved nucleus of shops and houses around its fifteenth-century Skt. Laurentius Kirke. Across the road from the bus station on Magrethes Plads 1, **Fjord & Bæltcentret** (mid-Feb to mid-Aug daily 10am–4/6pm; 70kr; ⊛www.gounderwater.com) is a state-of-the-art aquarium with a fifty-metre long underwater tunnel from where you can see seals and porpoises in their natural sea environment. On Strandgade, the **Town Museum – Farvergården** (Tues–Sun 10am–4pm; 15kr) has five reconstructed craft workshops and a collection of local fishing equipment. Kerteminde was home to the late-nine-teenth-century ornithological painter Johannes Larsen, and a fairly lengthy stroll around the marina and along Møllebakken brings you to the **Johannes Larsen Museum** (June–Aug daily 10am–5pm; rest of year Tues–Sun 10/11am–4pm; 50kr; ⓦwww.kert-mus.dk) – the painter's house, kept as it was when he lived there, with knick-knacks, canvases and, in the dining room, his astonishing wall-paintings.

Ladby Boat

About 6km from Kerteminde, along the banks of the fjord at Vikingvej 123, is the **Ladby Boat** (March–Oct Tues–Sun 10am–4/5pm; June–Aug also Mon; Nov–Feb Wed–Sun 11am–3pm; 25kr; ⓦwww.kert-mus.dk), a vessel dredged up from the fjord and found to be the burial place of a Viking chieftain. The craft, along with the weapons, hunting dogs and horses that accompanied the deceased on his jour-ney to Valhalla, are now kept in a small purpose-built museum. Infrequent bus #482 stops 1.5km away at Ladby, from where there are the signs to the museum; but it's also a pleasant and easy walk or cycle ride, from Kerteminde.

Jutland

Long ago, the Jutes, the people of **Jutland**, were a separate tribe from the more warlike Danes who occupied the eastern islands. In pagan times, the peninsula had its own rulers and much power, and it was here that the ninth-century monarch Harald Bluetooth began the process that turned the two tribes into a unified Christian nation. By the Viking era, however, the battling Danes had spread west, absorbing the Jutes, and real power gradually shifted towards Zealand, where it has largely stayed ever since. Unhurried lifestyles and rural calm are thus the overriding impression of Jutland for most visitors; indeed, its distance from Copenhagen makes it the most distinct and interesting area in the country. In the south, Schleswig is a territory long battled over by Denmark and Germany, though beyond the immacu-lately restored **Ribe** town, it holds little of abiding interest. **Århus**, halfway up the eastern coast, is Jutland's main urban centre and Denmark's second city. Further inland, the landscape is the country's most dramatic – stark heather-clad moors, dense forests and swooping gorges. Ancient **Viborg** is the best base for this, from where you can head north to vibrant **Aalborg**, on the southern bank of the Limfjord, which cuts deep into Jutland this far north – across which the landscape reaches a crescendo of storm-lashed savagery around **Skagen**, on the very tip of the peninsula.

There are two international **ferry ports** in the region, Esbjerg, north of Ribe, with services to Britain, and Frederikshavn, in the far north of the region, with connections to Sweden and Norway. **ESBJERG**'s passenger harbour is twenty minutes' walk from the centre and **trains** to and from Copenhagen connect direct-ly with ferries at the harbour. The main train station is at the end of Skolegade, where, at no. 33, you'll find the **tourist office** (Mon–Fri 9/10am–5pm, Sat 9.30/ 10am–1/3.30pm; ☏75.12.55.99, ⓦwww.esb-jerg-tourist.dk). **FREDERIKSHAVN**'s ferry terminal is near Havnepladsen, not far from the centre. All buses and most trains terminate at the central **train station**, a short walk from the town centre; some continue to the ferry terminal itself. The **tourist office** is close by at Skandiatorv 1 (Mon–Sat 9am–4/7pm, Sun 11am–2/7pm; ☏98.42.32.66, ⓦwww .frederikshavn-tourist.dk).

Ribe

Exquisitely preserved **RIBE** was once a major stopover point for pilgrims on their way to Rome, as well as a significant port, until thwarted by the Reformation and the silting-up of the harbour. Since then, not much appears to have changed. The surrounding marshlands, which have prevented the development of any large-scale industry, and a long-standing preservation programmes have enabled Ribe to keep it medieval appearance and size, making it a delight to wander around.

From the train station, Dagmarsgade leads to Torvet and the towering **Domkirke** (daily 10am/noon–4/5.30pm), begun around 1150. Only the "Cat's Head Door" on the south side remains from the original construction, and the church's interior is not as spectacular as its long history might suggest, though you can normally climb the red-brick tower and peer out over the town. Behind the cathedral, the **Weis' Stue** is a tiny inn built around 1600, from which the nightwatchman of Ribe makes his rounds – a throwback to the days when Danish towns were patrolled by guards looking for unattended candles, though these days he stops at points of interest to explain the town's history to tourists (May to mid-Sept 10pm; June–Aug also 8pm; free). The **Viking Museum** (April–Sept daily 10am–4/6pm; July & Aug Wed till 9pm; Nov–March closed Mon; 50kr; ⓦwwwribesvikinger.dk), nearby on Odins Plads, has an informative display on Ribe's past. If you haven't had enough of Vikings, you can watch their daily life being re-enacted at the **Ribe Vikingecenter** (May–Sept Mon–Fri 11am–4/4.30pm; July & Aug daily; 50kr; ⓦwwwribesvikingecenter.dk), 2km south of the town centre at Lustrupvej.

The **tourist office** (Mon–Fri 9.30am–4/5pm, Sat 10am–1/5pm; ☎75.42.15.00, ⓦwww.ribetourist.dk) is behind the cathedral, opposite the Weis' Stue; it has a full list of **private homes** with rooms to rent (❸). There's also a **youth hostel** (☎75.42.06.20, ⓦwww.danhostel.dk/ribe; ❷; closed Dec & Jan), on the opposite side of the river from Skibbroen: cross the river bridge and turn left into Skt. Peders Gade. Failing that, try *Weis' Stue* (☎75.42.07.00; ❺), opposite the atmospheric but expensive *Hotel Dagmar* (☎75.42.00.33, ⓦwww.hoteldagmar.dk; ❽), the oldest hotel in Denmark. The nearest **campsite**, which also has cabins, is 1.5km from Ribe, along Farupvej (☎75.41.07.77; bus #715 on weekdays; closed Nov to Easter). For **food**, try *Restaurant Backhaus*, Grydergade 12, with good value portions of steaks or burgers. *Kolvig Café and Restaurant*, next to Skibroen, offers filling salads and sandwiches at reasonable prices with relaxed riverside seating. There's excellent coffee in *Valdemar Sejr* next to the art gallery on Sct. Nicolaj Gade, which is also a good spot for **drinks** and **music** in the evening. *Stenbohus*, on Stenbogade, attracts artists, students and musicians and has live blues, folk or rock bands at least once a week.

Århus

At the geographical heart of the country and often regarded as Denmark's cultural capital, **ÅRHUS** typifies all that's good about Danish cities: it's small enough to get to know in a few hours, yet big and lively enough to fill both days and nights. Despite Viking-era origins, the city's present-day prosperity is due to its long, sheltered bay, on which the first harbour was constructed during the fifteenth century, and the more recent advent of railways, which made Århus a nationally important trade and transport centre.

Arrival, information and accommodation

Trains, **buses** and **ferries** all stop on the southern edge of the city centre. Frequent buses from the **airport** run to the train station (45min; 55kr). The **tourist office** is a short walk from the stations, in Park Allé (Mon–Fri 9.30am–4.30/6pm, Sat 10am–1/5pm; mid-June to mid-Sept also Sun 9.30am–1pm; ☎89.40.67.00, ⓦwww.visitaarhus.com), on the first floor of the city's Rådhus, and can arrange private rooms (❷) for a 25kr booking fee.

Buses form the city's **public transport system**, which is divided into four zones: one and two cover the centre; three and four reach into the country; a basic ticket costs 14kr from machines on board and is valid for any number of journeys for two hours from the time stamped on it. And while it's easy to get around on

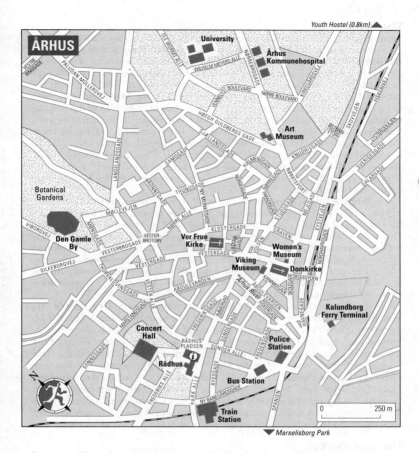

ÅRHUS

University
Århus
Kommunehospital

Art
Museum

Botanical
Gardens

Den Gamle
By

Vor Frue
Kirke

Women's
Museum

Viking
Museum

Domkirke

Kalundborg
Ferry Terminal

Concert
Hall

Rådhus

Police
Station

Bus Station

Train
Station

0   250 m

Marselisborg Park

foot – you'll need buses only to get to the beaches or woods on the outskirts – it might be worth considering the **Århus Pass** (88kr/24hr, 110kr/48hr, 155kr/week), which, along with unlimited bus travel, covers entrance to most museums and sightseeing tours (book these at the tourist office first).

There's a **youth hostel** 4km from the centre at Marienlundsvej 10 (℡86.16.72 .98, ⓦwww.hostel-aarhus.dk; ❷; bus #1, #6, #8, #9, #16, #56 or #58), in the middle of Risskov wood and close to Den Permanente beach, to which locals flock in summer. The *Århus City Sleep-In*, Havnegade 20 (℡86.19.20.55, ⓦwww.citysleep-in.dk; ❷), is more central and has an impressive range of facilities for travellers. There are just three reasonably priced central **hotels**: *Hotel Guldsmeden* at Guldsmedegade 40 (℡86.13.45.56; ⓦwww.hotelguldsmeden.dk; ❺), *Hotel Cab Inn Århus*, Kannikegade 14 (℡86.75.70.00, ⓦwww.cab-inn.dk; ❻), and the new *Sportshotellet*, Stadion Allé 70 (℡86.14.30.00, ⓦwww.aarhusindraetspark.dk; ❺) There's also a good B&B: *Get In*, Jens Baggesensvej 43 (℡86.10.86.14, ⓦwww.get-in .dk; ❹). Of a number of **campsites**, the two most useful are *Blommehaven* (ⓦwww.blommehaven.dk; closed early Sept to March; bus #6 or #19), overlooking the bay 3km south of the city centre, and *Århus Nord* 8km north (ⓦwww.dk-camping .dk/aarhusnord; bus #117 or #118 from the bus station); both have cabins.

The City

Søndergade is the city's main street, a pedestrianized strip that leads down into Bispetorvet and the old centre, the streets of which form a web around the **Domkirke** (Mon–Sat 10am–3/4pm), a massive Gothic church, most of which dates from the fifteenth century. The area around it makes for a leisurely stroll, with browsable shops and enticing cafés. On Clements Torv, across the road from the cathedral in the basement under Nordea, the **Viking Museum** (Mon–Fri 10am–4pm, Thurs till 6pm; free) displays finds that include sections of the original ramparts and some craftsmen's tools. West along Vestergade, the thirteenth-century **Vor Frue Kirke** (Mon–Fri 10am–2pm, Sat 10am–noon) is the site of three churches, most notable of which is the atmospheric eleventh-century crypt church, discovered beneath. Look in at the main church, for Claus Berg's altarpiece, and, through the cloister remaining from the pre-Reformation monastery (now an old folks' home), for the medieval frescoes in the third church, depicting local workers rather than biblical scenes.

The **Århus Rådhus**, home to the tourist office, is a controversial 1940s building and one of the modern city's major sights. You're free to walk in and look for yourself, but it's best to take a guided tour (mid-June to Aug Mon–Fri at 11am; 10kr). Above the entrance hangs Hagedorn Olsen's huge mural, *A Human Society*, symbolically depicting the city emerging from World War II. Perhaps most interesting are the walls of the small civic room; Albert Naur, who designed them during the Nazi occupation, concealed various Allied insignia in their intricate floral patterns. Finally, a lift (noon & 2pm; 5kr, included in the tour) climbs to the bell tower for a view over the city and across the bay.

It's a short walk from here to the city's best-known attraction, **Den Gamle By**, on Viborgvej (daily: June–Aug 9am–6pm; rest of year 10/11am–3/5pm; 70kr; ⓦwww.dengamleby.dk), an open-air museum of traditional Danish life, with seventy-odd half-timbered town houses taken from across the country. Many of the craftsmen's buildings are used for their original purpose, the overall aim of the place being to give an impression of an old Danish market town, something it does very effectively. Fans of Danish art may well prefer to visit the **Århus Art Museum** (Tues–Sun 10am–5pm, Wed till 8pm; 40kr ⓦwww.aarhuskunstmuseum.dk) in Vennelystparken, a little way north, with works from the late eighteenth century to the modern day, including the radiant canvases of Asger Jorn and Richard Mortensen, and Bjørn Nørgaard's sculptured version of Christian IV's tomb.

The outskirts

On Sundays Århus resembles a ghost town, most locals spending the day in the parks or beaches on the city's outskirts. The closest **beaches** are north of the city at Riis Skov, easily reached with buses #6 or #16. Otherwise, the Marselisborg Skov is the city's largest park, home to the **Marselisborg Slot**, summer residence of the Danish royals, the landscaped grounds of which can be visited when the monarch isn't staying. Further east, paths run down to rarely crowded pebbly beaches, and, near the junction of Ørneredevej and Thorsmøllevej, to the Dyrehaven or Deer Park. A few kilometres further on, the **Moesgård Prehistoric Museum** (daily 10am–4/5pm; Oct–March closed Mon; 35kr; ⓦwww.moesmus.dk), reached direct on bus #6, details Danish civilizations from the Stone Age onwards with copious finds and easy-to-follow illustrations. Its most notable exhibit is the "Grauballe Man", a body dated 80 BC discovered in a peat bog west of town and thus amazingly well preserved. From the museum, a "prehistoric trail" runs 3km to the sea, past a scattering of reassembled dwellings, monuments and burial places.

Eating, drinking and nightlife

Many of the old-town **cafés** and **restaurants** offer lunchtime specials for around 55kr; try theatrical *Pind's Café* at Skolegade 11, which often looks shut but does excellent *smørrebrød*. *Athena*, on the first floor on Storetorv, is also good value, as are the highly rated **vegetarian** meals at *Restaurant Gyngen*, Mejlgade 53, and *Hokus Pokus*, Mejlgade 28. Åboulevarden, along the northern bank of the river, has a string of trendy eating and drinking venues; here, try *Cross Café* for their generous brunch platters. For superb Danish pastry, head to *Emmerys*, Guldsmedegade 24–26, the city's oldest patisserie; the bakery is organic and the cakes to die for. For **self-catering**, there's a late-opening supermarket (8am–midnight) at the train station.

Århus and Aalborg, further north, are the only places in Denmark with a **nightlife** to match that of Copenhagen. The city has particularly good **bars**, many situated in the streets close to the cathedral, including the movie-themed *Casablanca* at Rosensgade 12, the pricey *Carlton* nearby at no. 23, *Den Smagløse* at Klostertorv 7, and *Englen* on Studsgade (which also does good food). Around the corner, *Masken* on Store Torv is also worth a try, with impressive masks from around the globe decorating the walls. The cream of Danish and international rock acts can be found at *Voxhall*, Vester Allé 15, and *Train*, Toldbogade 6; *Fatter Eskil*, Skolegade 25, and *Kulturgyngen*, Fronthuset, Mejlgade 53, have more run-of-the-mill blues bands. *Plasma*, Klostergade 34, currently hosts the hottest **club scene**, while the leading **jazz** venue is the smoky, atmospheric *Bent J*, at Nèrre Allé 66.

Listings

Bike rental Cykelværkstedet Morten Mengel, Mejlgade 41.
Hospitals Århus Kommunehospital, on Nørrebrogade.
Internet Gate 58, Vestergade 58; Net House

Computercafé, Nørre Allé 66A.
Pharmacy Løve Apoteket, Store Torv 5 (24hr).
Police Århus Politistation, Ridderstræde 1
☏87.31.14.48.
Post office On Banegårdpladsen, by the station.

Viborg

For a long time the junction of the major roads across Jutland, **VIBORG** was once one of the most important communities in the country. From Knud in 1027 to Christian V in 1655, all Danish kings were crowned here, and until the early nineteenth century the town was the seat of a provincial assembly. As the national administrative axis shifted towards Zealand, however, Viborg's importance waned, and although it still has the high court of West Denmark, it's now primarily a market town for the local farming community.

The twin towers of the **Domkirke** (Mon–Sat 10/11am–3/4pm, Sun noon–3/4pm) are the most visible feature of the compact town centre, and the most compelling reminder of Viborg's former glories. The interior is dominated by the brilliant frescoes of Joakim Skovgaard, whose work can also be seen in the **Skovgaard Museum** (daily 1.30–5pm; May–Sept also 10am–12.30pm; May–Sept 10kr, otherwise free), inside the former Rådhus across Gammel Torv. For a broader perspective of Viborg's past, keep an hour spare for exploring the **Viborgs Stiftsmuseum** on the northern side of Hjultorvet between Vestergade and Skt. Mathias Gade (mid-June to Aug daily 11am–5pm; rest of year Mon–Fri 2–5pm, Sat & Sun 11am–5pm; 20kr), which has everything from prehistoric artefacts to clothes, furniture and household appliances.

The **tourist office** on Nytorv (Mon–Fri 9am–4/5pm, Sat 9.30am–12.30/3pm; ☏86.61.16.66, ✆www.viborg.dk) can advise on **accommodation**. In town, *Palads Hotel*, 5 Sct. Mathias Gade (☏86.62.37.00, ✆www.hotelpalads.dk; ❾), often has reduced rates. The more affordable **youth hostel** (☏86.67.17.81, ✆www.danhostel.dk/viborg; ❷) and **campsite** (with cabins) are both 2km across the lake from the town centre, along Vinkelvej (bus #707). Best places for **food** are the historic *Brygger Bauers Grotter*, Sct. Mathias Gade 61, with Danish lunch platters from 60kr and a more expensive dinner menu. For a lighter snack, coffee or salad try *Café Morville*, Hjultorvet 2, next to the Stiftsmuseum.

Aalborg

The main city of north Jutland and the fourth largest in Denmark, **AALBORG** hugs the southern bank of the Limfjord and boasts a nightlife and music scene to rival Copenhagen's. The most obvious place to spend a night or two before venturing into the wilder countryside beyond, Aalborg is the main transport terminus for the region, and boasts a well-preserved centre dating from its seventeenth-century trading heyday. The era is perhaps best exemplified by the Jens Bangs Stenhus opposite the tourist office, a grandiose five-storey affair in the Dutch Renaissance style, which has functioned as a pharmacy since it was built. The commercial roots of the city are further evidenced by the collection of portraits of the town's merchants that hang inside the **Budolfi Domkirke** (Mon–Fri 9am–3/4pm, Sat 9am–noon/2pm), behind. The cathedral is a small but elegant specimen of the Gothic style, built on the site of an eleventh-century wooden church, from which a few tombs remain, embedded in the walls close to the altar. Outside, across the square, the **Aalborg Historical Museum** at Algade 48 (Tues–Sun 10am–5pm, 20kr; ⑩www.aahm.dk) has fairly routine displays, apart from an impressive glasswork collection. Behind here, just off Gammel Torv, the fifteenth-century **Monastery of the Holy Ghost** is now the home of 25 senior citizens, but guided tours can be arranged through the tourist office, taking in the monks' refectory, kept largely unchanged since the last monk left, and the small Friar's room, the only part of the monastery in which nuns (from the adjoining nunnery) were permitted. Most interesting, however, are the frescoes that cover the entire ceiling of the chapel.

On the other side of Østerågade, the sixteenth-century **Aalborghus Slot** is worth a visit for its **dungeon** (May–Oct Mon–Fri 8am–3pm; free) and the underground passages (till 9pm). Fifteen minutes' walk out of the centre on Kong Christians Allé, the **North Jutland Art Museum** (Tues–Sun 10am–5pm, 30kr; ⑩www.nordjyllandskunstmusem.dk; buses #5, #8, #10 or #11) is one of the country's best modern art collections, featuring works by Max Ernst, Andy Warhol, Le Corbusier and Claes Oldenburg, alongside many Danish contributions. On the hill behind the museum is the **Aalborg Tower** (daily 10/11am–5/7pm; 20kr), from which there's a grand view over the city and the Limfjord. The **Aalborg Maritime Museum** (daily 10am–4/6pm; 60kr; ⑩www.aalborgmarinemuseum.dk), 2km west of the centre at Vestrefjordvej 81 (buses #2 and #8), recalls the city's shipbuilding days – centrepiece is the *Springeren*, a 54-metre-long submarine.

Practicalities

The **tourist office** is centrally placed at Østerågade 8 (Mon–Fri 9am–4.30/5.30pm, Sat 10am–1/4pm; ☎98.12.60.22, ⑩www.visitaalborg.com). The cheapest **hotels** are the basic *Aalborg Sømandshjem*, Østerbro 27 (☎98.12.19.00, ⑩www.hotel-aalborg.com; ❻), *Prinsen Hotel*, Prinsensgade 14–16 (☎98.13.37.33, ⑩www.prinsen-hotel.dk; ❻), and the slightly cosier *Hotellet Krogen*, Skibstedsvej 4 (☎98.12.17.05, ⑩www.krogen.dk; ❻). There's a large **youth hostel**, *Fjordparken* (☎98.11.60.44, ⑩www.danhostelnord.dk/aalborg; reservations necessary; ❷), 3km west of the town on the Limfjord bank beside the marina – take bus #8 from the centre to the end of its route. There's a **campsite** nearby, too: *Strandparken* (☎89.12.76.29, ⑩www.strandparken.dk; closed mid-Sept to mid-April). For a little more adventure, catch the half-hourly **ferry** (☎98.11.78.23; 6.30am–11.15pm; 12kr) from near the campsite to Egholm, an island in Limfjord with free camping under open-sided shelters. For **food and drink**, head for Jomfru Ane Gade, a small street close to the harbour between Bispensgade and Borgergade, on which a number of restaurants/bars advertise daily specials: try *Fyrtøjet* at no.7, or *Dirch's Regensen* at no.16. Aalborg Kongres & Kultur Center at Europa Pads 4 (☎99.35.55.65, ⑩www.akkc.dk) is the city's new **theatre** and **concert venue**. For smaller gigs head for *Skråen*, Standvejen 18 (☎98.12.21.89, ⑩www.skraaen.dk).

Skagen

About 100km north of Aalborg, **SKAGEN** perches at the very top of Jutland amid a breathtaking landscape of heather-topped sand dunes. It can be reached by private bus or train (Eurail not valid, Scanrail and InterRail fifty percent reduction on both) roughly once an hour. The bus is the best choice if you're planning to stay at the Skagen youth hostel, as it stops right outside.

Sunlight seems to gain extra brightness as it bounces off the two seas which collide off Skagen's coast, something which attracted the **Skagen artists** in the late nineteenth century. They arrived in the small fishing community during 1873 and 1874 and often met in the bar of *Brøndum's Hotel*, off Brøndumsvej, the grounds of which now house the **Skagen Museum** (April & Oct Tues–Sun 11am–4pm; May–Sept daily 10am–5/6pm; Nov–March Wed–Fri 1–4pm, Sat & Sun 11am–3pm; 50kr). Many of the canvases depict local scenes, using the town's strong natural light to capture subtleties of colour. Nearby, at Markvej 2–4, **Michael and Anna Anchers' Hus** (April–Oct daily 10/11am–3/6pm; Nov–March Sat & Sun 11am–3pm; 40kr), home to one of the group's leading lights and his wife, herself a skilful painter, evokes the atmosphere of the time through an assortment of used tubes of paint, piles of canvases, paintings, sketches, books and ornaments.

The artists made Skagen fashionable, and the town continues to be a popular holiday destination. But it still bears many marks of its tough past as a fishing community, the history of which is excellently documented in **Skagens By og Egnsmuseum** on P.K. Nielsensvej 8–10, a fifteen-minute walk south of the centre along Skt. Laurentii Vej (May–Sept Mon–Fri 10am–4/5pm, Sat & Sun 11am–4pm; July daily till 6pm; rest of year Mon–Fri only 10/11am–3/4pm; 30kr). Amid the dunes south of town, a further twenty minutes' walk along Skt. Laurentii Vej, Damstedvej and Gammel Kirkesti, is **Den Tilsandede Kirke** (June–Aug 11am–5pm; 10kr). This fourteenth-century church was swallowed by sandstorms during the eighteenth century. Part of the tower is open to the public, while the floor and cemetery lie beneath the sands. The impressive new **Skagen Odde Naturcenter** (daily 10am–4/10pm; 65kr) is designed by Jørn Utzon, architect of the Sydney Opera House, and centred on the themes of sand, water, wind and light. The forces of nature can be further appreciated at Grenen, 4km north of Skagen (hourly bus #79 in summer), along Skt. Laurentii Vej, Fyrvej and the beach, where two seas – the Kattegat and Skagerrak – meet with a powerful clashing of waves. You can get to the tip by a tractor-drawn bus (April–Oct; 15kr return) aptly named the *Sandormen* (lugworm) – although it's an enjoyable walk as the scenery is beautiful.

Practicalities

The combined **bus and train station** is on Skt. Laurentii Vej, and plays host to the **tourist office** (mid-June to early-Aug Mon–Sat 9am–7pm, Sun 10am–4pm; rest of year Mon–Fri 9am–3/5pm, Sat & Sun 10am–1/2pm; ☎98.44.13.77, ⓦwww.skagen-tourist.dk). *Brøndum's Hotel*, Anchervej 3 (☎98.44.15.55, ⓦwww.broendumshotel.dk; ❽), is by far the most atmospheric spot to stay – book well ahead in summer. A little cheaper are *Skagen Sømandshjem*, Østre Strandvej 2 (☎98.44.25.88; ❻), which also serves up bargain meals; *Den Gamle Skibssmedie*, Vestre Standvej 28 (☎98.44.67.16; ❺); and *Clausens Hotel*, Skt. Laurentii Vej 35 (☎98.45.01.66, ⓦwww.clausenshotel.dk; ❼). There are two **youth hostels**: one at Rolighedsvej 2 (☎98.44.22.00, ⓦwww.danhostelnord.dk/skagen; no dorms; ❷), the other at Højensvej 32 in Gammel Skagen (☎98.44.13.56, ⓦwww.skaw.dk/hostel; ❹; closed mid-Oct to Easter), 3km west of Skagen; take bus #79. Of a number of **campsites**, the most accessible are *Grenen* (☎98.44.25.46, ⓦwww.grenencamping .dk; closed early Sept to May), to the north along Fyrvej, which has cabins, and *Poul Eeg's* (☎98.44.14.70; closed Sept to mid-May), on Batterivej, left off Oddenvej just before the town centre.

Travel details

Trains

Copenhagen to: Aalborg (hourly; 4hr 40min, last train at 8pm); Århus (36 daily; 2hr 45min to 3hr 10min); Helsingør (every 20min; 50min); Odense (58 daily; 1hr 30min); Roskilde (8 an hour; 22min).
Århus to: Aalborg (32 daily; 1hr 25min); Viiborg (hourly; 1hr 10min).
Helsingør to: Hillerød (2 hourly; 30min).
Odense to: Århus (38 daily; 1hr 30min).
Roskilde to: Odense (43 daily, 1hr 10min).

Buses

Copenhagen to: Aalborg (3 daily; 4hr 45min); Århus (7 daily; 3hr to 3hr 30min, depending ferry crossing).
Odense to: Kerteminde (5 an hour; 40min).

Ferry

Kalundborg to: Århus (3–8 daily; 2hr 30min).

Estonia

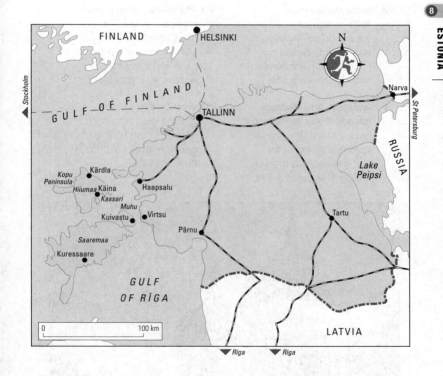

Estonia highlights

* **Tallinn's Old Town** Within medieval turreted walls, this ancient corner of the city is beautifully preserved. See p.309

* **Nevsky Cathedral, Tallinn** High on Toompea, this Russian orthodox cathedral is a heady blend of incense and icons. See p.310

* **Saaremaa and Hiiumaa islands** If you like wilderness and walking, these islands are perfect for that get-away-from-it-all feeling. See pp.313–314

* **Kuressaare Castle, Saaremaa Island** The best-preserved medieval castle in the region. See p.314

* **Café Wilde, Tartu** A calm, relaxed tea house in the heart of Estonia. Huge pots of tea, newspapers, cake and internet access. See p.315

* **Pärnu Beach** Enjoy a bracing dip in the Baltic or take a mud bath in one of many local spas. See p.316

Introduction and basics

It's a tribute to the resilience of the **Estonians** that in the decade or so since the Declaration of Independence in August 1991 they've transformed their country from a dour outpost of the former Soviet Union into a viable nation with the most stable economy in the Baltic region. This is even more impressive in the light of the fact that Estonians have ruled their own country for barely thirty years out of the past eight hundred. A Finno-Ugric people related to the Finns, the Estonians have had the misfortune to be surrounded by powerful, warlike neighbours. First conquered by the Danes at the start of the thirteenth century, then German crusading knights, then Swedes and Russians snatched its brief independence at the end of World War I. This brief freedom was extinguished by the Soviets in 1940 and Estonia disappeared from view again only to emerge from the Soviet shadow in 1991.

Estonia's capital, **Tallinn**, is an atmospheric city with a magnificent medieval centre and lively nightlife. Two other major cities, **Tartu**, a historic university town, and **Pärnu**, a major seaside resort, are worth a day or so each. Estonia's small population means that the countryside – around forty percent of which is covered by forest and much of the rest by lakes – is generally empty and unspoiled. To get a feel for it at its best, head for the Baltic islands of **Saaremaa** and **Hiiumaa**. **Kuressaare**, capital of the former, is home to one of the finest castles in the Baltics.

Information and maps

The Estonian national tourist association operates **tourist offices** in all the places covered in this chapter, which can be useful for booking B&Bs and hotel rooms.

The useful Kümmerly & Frey 1:1,000,000 **map** of the Baltic States covers Estonia and includes a rudimentary street plan of central Tallinn. The best detailed street map of Tallinn is the *Falk Plan*, which includes enlarged Inner and Old Town sections and also covers public transport routes.

The following terms or their abbreviations are commonly encountered in Estonian **addresses**: *mantee* (mnt.), meaning road; *puistee* (pst.), avenue; *tänav* (tn.), street. Normally, when giving an address or naming a street in Estonia the term *tänav* is not actually used – the street's name alone is enough.

Money and banks

The local currency is the **kroon**, normally abbreviated to EEK (Eesti kroon – Estonian Crown), and is divided into 100 sents. Notes come in 1, 2, 5, 10, 25, 50, 100 and 500EEK denominations and coins in 0.05, 0.10, 0.20, 0.50, 1 and 5 EEK denominations. The kroon is now pegged to the euro (€1 = 15.65EEK), meaning that the current exchange rate is 25EEK to £1 and 17EEK to $1.

Bank (*pank*) opening hours are Mon–Fri 9am–4pm, many staying open in larger towns till 6pm and most also opening Sat 9am–2/4pm. As well as exchanging cash,

---

Estonia on the net

ⓦwww.visitestonia.com Tourist board site
ⓦwww.ee Search engine and good starting point
ⓦwww.estica.org General information from the Estonian Institute
ⓦwww.weekend.ee Entertainment listings
ⓦwww.baltictimes.com Weekly English-language newspaper

major banks will also cash **travellers' cheques** and give you an advance on your credit card for a commission of around three percent. ATMs taking all the usual international cards are now widely available. **Credit cards** can be used in some of the more expensive hotels, restaurants and stores, but outside the capital cash is the most commonly accepted method of payment.

Communications

Post offices (*postkontor*) open Mon–Fri 9am–7pm & Sat 9am–3pm. You can buy stamps here and at some shops, hotels and kiosks.

Most **public phones** now operate on magnetic cards (available in denominations of 30, 50 and 100EEK), for both local and long-distance calls. You'll find **internet cafés** in Tallinn and Tartu, but they're still rare elsewhere. Expect to pay from 50EEK/hr.

Getting around

Places covered in this chapter are all easily reached by **bus**. The **rail network** has been cut back so drastically in recent years that you're unlikely to use those parts of it that still survive, save perhaps for international services.

Both train and bus information is available from station timetable boards – the Estonian for departure is *väljub*, and arrival is *saabub*.

Train

Ticket windows at **train stations** are marked *linnalähedane*l for suburban lines; *piletite müük* for national services; and *rahvusvaheline* for international lines. Tickets for the last need to be bought 45min in advance. Long-distance services are divided either *reisirong* (passenger) or *kiir* (fast). Both are slow, but the latter, usually requiring a reservation, stop only at every second village.

Bus

Bus tickets can be bought either from the **bus** station ticket office or direct from the driver. It's best to buy long-distance tickets

in advance if you're travelling at the height of summer or at weekends, especially to the islands. Opt for an express (*ekspress*) bus if possible to avoid frequent stops. Normally **luggage** is taken on board – if you have a large bag you may have to pay a nominal fee to have it stowed in the luggage compartment. Buses are also the best method for travelling to the other Baltic countries with services linking Tallinn, Vilnius and Rīga.

Accommodation

Though cheaper than in Western Europe, **accommodation** in Estonia will still take a large chunk out of most budgets. It is possible to keep costs down by staying in private rooms, and most towns have one or two decent budget hotels.

Private rooms and hotels

Booking a **private room** is often the cheapest option, usually costing 200–400EEK per person. This can be arranged through local tourist offices or private agencies. You should be able to find plain but clean **hotel** rooms for 300–500EEK per person, often in converted student hostels or apartment buildings, and better value for money than the purpose-built Soviet-era places. There's a growing number of small **guest houses** and mid-range pension-type establishments in the more popular destinations; expect to pay between 200–350EEK per night. Prices for mid-range places usually include breakfast, and many places accept credit cards. In all but the very cheapest hotels there will usually be at least one English-speaking member of staff.

Hostels and campsites

Estonia has a network of **hostels**, often just student dorms converted for the summer. Contact the Estonian Youth Hostel Association in Tallinn (☎372/6461 455, ☻www.baltichostels.net) for the latest details. Hostel beds, where available, cost 100–200EEK per person. An ex-Soviet phenomenon is the cabin **campsite** (*kämping*), usually offering accommodation in three- to four-bed cabins (shared facilities) for 180–260EEK per person; many of them will also let you pitch a tent, which works out slightly cheaper than sleeping under a roof.

Food and drink

Elderly expats aside, not too many people come to Estonia for the food. The national cuisine consists mainly of pig by-products teamed with potatoes and other vegetable-patch produce. You're likely to encounter indigenous recipes in Estonian restaurants where, in true post-Soviet style, stodgy meat and two veg dishes dominate most menus.

Food

Soup (*supp*), dark bread (*leib*), sour cream (*hapukoor*) and herring (*heeringas*) figure prominently in the Estonian diet, a culinary legacy of the country's largely peasant past, and if you like your food without frills you can eat very well here. A typical **national dish** is *verevorst* and *mulgikapsad* (blood sausage and sauerkraut), and you're also likely to encounter various kinds of smoked fish, particularly eel (*angerjas*), perch (*ahven*) and pike (*haug*).

You'd have to be invited into a local home to enjoy Estonian food at its best, unfortunately, as the average **restaurant** (*restoran*) tends to serve up hearty international meat dishes, the most common of which is *karbonaad* – pork chop (sometimes fried in batter) – with potatoes and seasonal vegetables. You might occasionally encounter game, and several ethnic restaurants break the culinary monotony in Tallinn. **Vegetarianism** is not a widely understood concept here.

When eating out you're best off heading for bars and cafés, many of which serve snack dishes and even full meals, and where the bill is likely to be less than in a restaurant. By and large you should be able to have a decent meal (two courses and a drink) for less than 130EEK and you'd have to really push the boat out for the bill to come to more than 200EEK.

If you really want to keep costs down then try one of the various **fast-food** options. Some places going under the name of café (*kohvik*) are essentially canteen-style restaurants where you can pick up main courses and dishes-of-the-day for as little as 30EEK, as well as basic soups, salads and sweets. There's also a growing number of pizzerias, many of which offer a range of pasta dishes. For self-catering, **food shopping** poses no major problems with staples, such as bread, cheese, smoked meat and tinned fish, all available in supermarkets, and fresh fruit and vegetables available in markets.

Drink

Estonians are enthusiastic drinkers with **beer** (*õlu*) being the most popular tipple. The principal local brands are *Saku* and *A. Le Coq*, both of which are rather tame lager-style brews, although both companies also produce stronger, dark beers – the strongest are found on the islands (*Saaremaa õlu* is the best known). In bars a lot of people favour **vodka** (*viin*) with mixers which, thanks to generous measures, is a more cost-effective route to oblivion. **Local alcoholic specialities** include *hõõgvein* (mulled wine) and *Vana Tallinn*, a pungent dark liqueur which some suicidal souls mix with vodka.

An ever-increasing range of pubs and bars – most of which imitate Irish or American models – are beginning to take over the Estonian drinking scene, especially in Tallinn. If you're not boozing, head for a *kohvik* (café), where alcohol is still served, but getting drunk is not a priority. **Coffee** (*kohv*) is usually of the filter variety, and **tea** (*tee*) is served without milk.

Opening hours and holidays

Most **shops** open Mon–Fri 9/10am–6/7pm & Sat 10am–2/3pm. Some food shops stay open till 10pm or later and are also open Sun. **Public holidays**, when most shops and all banks are closed, are: Jan 1; Feb 24 (Independence Day); March 14 (Language Day); Good Fri; Easter Mon; May 1; Whitsun; June 23 (Victory Day); June 24 (St John's Day); Aug 20 (Restoration of Independence); Dec 25 & 26.

Emergencies

Estonians claim that their country is a hotbed of crime and that visitors run a routine risk of being robbed and murdered, particularly in Tallinn. The truth is that while theft and street crime are probably on the rise, they're still at lower levels than in most other European cities, and if you keep your wits about you and avoid staggering around the backstreets drunk after dark you should come to no harm. The Estonian **police**

(*politsei*) are mostly very young and some may speak a little English, but don't bank on it. As far as **health** goes, though emergency health care is free in Estonia, the country's hospitals are under-equipped and if you fall seriously ill it's best to head for home if possible. No immunizations are required for Estonia.

Emergency numbers

Police ☏110; Ambulance ☏112; Fire ☏112.

Tallinn

The port city of **TALLINN**, Estonia's compact, human-scale capital, has been shaped by nearly a millennium of outside influence. Its name, derived from the Estonian name for "Danish Fort" (*taani linnus*), is a reminder of the fact that the city was founded by the Danes at the beginning of the thirteenth century, and since that time political control has nearly always been in the hands of foreigners – Germans, Swedes and Russians. The Germans have undoubtedly had the most lasting influence on the city; Tallinn was one of the leading cities of the Hanseatic League, the German-dominated association of Baltic trading cities, and for centuries it was known to the outside world by its German name, Reval. Even when Estonia was ruled by the kings of Sweden and the tsars of Russia, the city's public life was controlled by the German nobility, and its commerce run by German merchants. Today reminders of foreign rule abound in the streets of Tallinn, where each of the city's one-time rulers have left their mark.

Arrival, information and city transport

Tallinn's international **train station** is at Toompuiestee 35, just northwest of the Old Town, while the city's **bus terminal** is at Lastekodu 46, 2km southeast of the centre – trams #2 and #4 run from nearby Tartu mnt. to the main square Viru väljak. Arriving by **sea**, the passenger port is just northeast of the centre at Sadama 25. The **airport** is 3km southeast of the city centre and linked to Viru väljak by bus #2 (every 30min; 15EEK). Tallinn's **tourist office**, Raekoja Plats 10 (May–Sept Mon–Fri 9am–8pm, Sat & Sun 10am–6pm; Oct–April Mon–Fri 9am–5pm, Sat 10am–4pm; ℡0/645 7777, ✆tourism.tallinn.ee), sells various maps and city guides and has limited information about other destinations in Estonia. You can also buy a **Tallinn Card** here (24hr 205EEK; 48hr 275EEK; 72hr 325EEK) which gives unlimited use of public transport, discounts and savings at museums and other sights. For advice about what's on in the city check out the widely available free paper *Tallinn This Week*, the *City Paper*, or the informative *Tallinn In Your Pocket* city guide.

Though most of Tallinn's sights can be covered on foot, the city has an extensive **tram**, **bus** and **trolleybus** network should you need to travel further afield. Services are frequent and cheap, with tickets (*talongid*) common to all three systems available from kiosks near stops for 10EEK or from the driver for 15EEK. Tickets should be validated using the on-board punches. **Taxis** are reasonably cheap (around 10EEK/km, slightly more after 10pm) though as a foreigner you may occasionally find your meter running faster than it should. Most companies have a minimum charge of 25EEK, but a taxi from one point in the city centre to another should never exceed 50EEK.

Accommodation

There's a shortage of cheap and mid-range hotels in central Tallinn, making **private rooms** the best value for money if you want to be close to the heart of things. Bed & Breakfast Rasastra, a few steps north of Viru väljak at Mere 4 (daily 9.30am–6pm; ℡0/6616 291, ✉rasastra@online.ee), offers rooms (**❷**) in family homes throughout the Baltics and private apartments for longer stays.

Hostels

Merevaik Sõpruse 182 ✆0/655 3767. Faded but clean singles, doubles and triples in a red-brick block 3km southwest of the Old Town. Trolleybus #2 or #3 from Vabaduse väljak to the Linnu stop. Ten percent discount for HI and ISIC cardholders. **❷**

Vana Tom VSike-Karja 1 ℡0/631 3252. In the Old Town, this place has clean dorms doubles.

Discounts for HI, Peace Corps members and those who bring their own sleeping bag. Dorms **❷**

Guest house and B&Bs

Dorell Karu 39 ℡0/626 1200, ✆www.hot.ee/dorell. A ten-minute walk from the Old Town, this place offers shared facilities or fairly basic en-suite rooms. Entrance via a passage on Narva mnt. **❷**

Eeslitall Dunkri 4/6 ☎0/631 3755, ⓦwww.eeslitall
.ee. Small, simple but central pension. ❸
Kelluka Kelluka tee 11 ☎0/623 8811, ⓦwww
.kelluka.ee. Quiet guest house on the edge of
town. Facilities include a sauna and pool. Bus #5
from the centre to the Helmiku stop. ❹
Kristiine Luha 16 ☎0/646 4600,

ⓦwww.kristiine.ee. Quiet, friendly place on two
floors of a grey office block, around 15min from
the centre. Rooms are plain but en suite and have
TV. Bus #5, #18, #36 from Vabaduse väljak or tram
#3, #4 from PSrnu mnt. to the Luha stop. ❸
Old House Bed & Breakfast Uus 22 ☎0/641
1464, ⓦwww.oldhouse.ee. Small and friendly five-

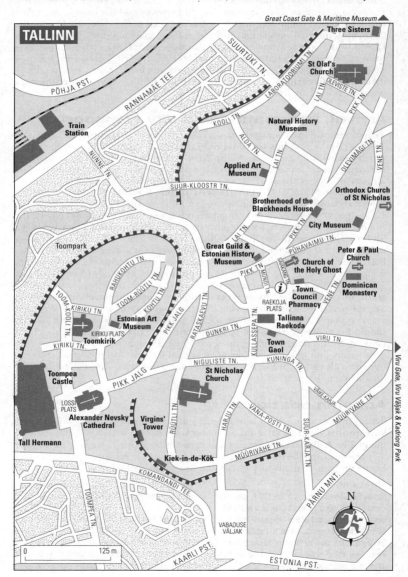

TALLINN

Great Coast Gate & Maritime Museum ▲

Three Sisters

St Olaf's Church

SUURTÜKI TN.
PÕHJA PST.
RANNAMÄE TEE
LABORATOORIUMI TN.
OLEVISTE TN.
PIKK TN.
LAI TN.

Train Station

KOOLI TN.
ALDA TN.
LAI TN.

Natural History Museum

NUNNE TN.
OLEVIMÄGI TN.
VENE TN.

SUUR-KLOOSTR TN.
Applied Art Museum

Orthodox Church of St Nicholas

Brotherhood of the Blackheads House

City Museum

PIKK TN.

Toompark

Great Guild & Estonian History Museum

PÜHAVAIMU TN.
Peter & Paul Church

RAHUKOHTU TN.
TOOM-RÜÜTLI TN.
KOHTU TN.
PIKK TN.
SAIAKANG TN.
MÜNDI TN.
Church of the Holy Ghost

Dominican Monastery

Estonian Art Museum
KIRIKU TN.
TOOM-KOOLI TN.
KIRIKU PLATS
Toomkirik
KIRIKU TN.
PIKK JALG
RATASKAEVU TN.
DUNKRI TN.
KULLASSEPA TN.
RAEKOJA PLATS
ℹ️
Town Council Pharmacy
Tallinna Raekoda

Town Gaol

VIRU TN.

NIGULISTE TN.
KUNINGA TN.

Toompea Castle
PIKK JALG
St Nicholas Church

VANA-POSTI TN.
HARJU TN.
SUUR-KARJA TN.
MÜÜRIVAHE TN.

LOSSI PLATS
Alexander Nevsky Cathedral
Virgins' Tower
RÜÜTLI TN.
VÄIKE-KARJA

Tall Hermann

Kiek-in-de-Kök
MÜÜRIVAHE TN.

KOMANDANDI TEE

TOOMPEA TN.

PARNU MNT.

N

VABADUSE VÄLJAK

0   125 m

KAARLI PST.
ESTONIA PST.

Viru Gate, Viru Väljak & Kadriorg Park ▶

room guest house in the Old Town; all rooms with shared facilities. ❸
PÄÄSU Sõpruse 182 ☎0/654 2013, ⓔpaasu@mail.ee. Unpretentious place occupying the same building as the *Merevaik* hostel (see above). Rooms have dated furnishings, but all are clean and with TV. Shared facilities. ❷

TKTK Üliopilashotell Nomme tee 47 ☎0/655 2679. Hotel attached to a student hostel some 3km southwest of the centre, offering plain, cheap rooms. One bathroom for every two rooms. No breakfast. Bus #17 or #17a from Vabaduse väljak to Koolimaja, or trolleybus #4 from the train station to Tedre. ❷

The City

The heart of Tallinn and location of most of its sights is the **Old Town**, once enclosed by the city's medieval walls. At its centre is the **Raekoja plats**, the medieval marketplace, above which looms **Toompea**, the hilltop stronghold of the German Knights who controlled the city during the Middle Ages. Outside the city centre, **Kadriorg Park**, a peaceful wooded area to the east with a cluster of historic buildings and a view of the sea, and the **Open Air Museum**, to the west, are both worth a visit.

Around Raekoja plats

Raekoja plats, the cobbled and gently sloping market square at the heart of the Old Town, is as old as the city itself. On its southern side stands an imposing reminder of the Hanseatic past: the fifteenth-century **Town Hall** (Tallinna Raekoda), which boasts an elegant arcade of gothic arches at ground level, and a delicate, slender steeple at its northern end. Near the summit of the slender steeple, Vana Toomas, a sixteenth-century weather vane depicting a medieval mercenary, has become Tallinn's city emblem.

Of the other old buildings that line the square, the most venerable is the **Town Council Pharmacy** in the northeastern corner, whose dull grey facade dates from the seventeenth century, though the building is known to have existed in 1422 and may be much older. If this leaves you underwhelmed, head for the former Town Gaol behind the town hall at Raekoja 4/6, which now houses the **Town Prison Museum of Photography** (April–Oct Mon & Thurs–Sun 11am–5pm; Nov–March Thurs–Tues 10.30am–6pm 10EEK), an entertaining little photographic collection with views of Tallinn from the days when it was still known as Reval, and portraits of Estonians in traditional costume (English captions).

Close to Raekoja plats are a couple of churches that neatly underline the social divisions of medieval Tallinn. The fourteenth-century **Church of the Holy Ghost** (daily 10am–2pm), tucked away on Pühavaimu and reached via a small passage called Saiakang tSnav next to the Raeapteek, is the city's most appealing church, a small Gothic building with stuccoed limestone walls, stepped gables and a tall, verdigris-coated spire. Originally the Town Hall chapel, it later became the place where the native Estonian population worshipped, and in 1535 priests here compiled an Estonian-language Lutheran catechism, an important affirmation of identity at a time when most Estonians had been reduced to serf status. The ornate clock set in the wall above the entrance dates from 1680 and is the oldest in Tallinn.

Contrasting sharply is the late Gothic **St Nicholas Church**, sitting on raised open ground just southwest of Raekoja plats. These days the church serves as a **museum and concert hall** (Wed–Sun 10am–5pm; 35EEK); guided tours of the Silver Chamber can be arranged in advance. Organ music every Sat & Sun at 4pm; usually 100EEK.

Toompea

After Raekoja plats the most obvious place to head is **Toompea**, the hill where the Danes built their fortress after conquering what is now Tallinn in 1219. According to legend, Toompea is also the grave of Kalev, the mythical ancestor of the Estonians. The most atmospheric approach is through the sturdy gate tower – built

by the Teutonic Knights to contain the Old Town's inhabitants in times of unrest –
at the foot of Pikk jalg. This is the cobbled continuation of Pikk, the Old Town's
main street, and climbs up to Lossi plats, dominated by the incongruous-looking
Alexander Nevsky Cathedral (daily 8am–7pm). This gaudy, onion-domed concoction, complete with souvenir shop, was built at the end of the nineteenth century for the city's Orthodox population; it is an enduring reminder of the two centuries Tallinn spent under tsarist rule.

At the head of Lossi plats is **Toompea Castle**, on the site of the original Danish
fortification. Today's castle is the descendant of a stone fortress built by the Knights
of the Sword, the Germanic crusaders who kicked out the Danes in 1227 and controlled the city until 1238 (when the Danes returned). The castle has been altered
by every conqueror who raised their flag above it since then; these days it wears a
shocking-pink Baroque facade, the result of an eighteenth-century rebuild for
Catherine the Great. The northern and western walls are the most original part of
the castle, and include three defensive towers, the most impressive of which is the
fifty-metre **Tall Hermann** at the southwestern corner, dating from 1371.

Toompea Castle is now home to the Riigikogu, Estonia's parliament, and is therefore out of bounds to the public, but nearby a couple of towers that formed part of
the Old Town fortifications are accessible. A narrow archway in the medieval walls
just south of the Alexander Nevsky Cathedral leads to the ironically named
Virgins' Tower, which was once a prison for prostitutes and is now home to a
café/bar. A little south of here on Komandandi tee is the imposing **Kiek-in-de-
Kök tower** dating from 1475; it now contains a **museum** (May–Sept Tues–Sun
10am–5pm; Oct–April Wed–Sun 10am–5pm; 15EEK) devoted to the history of
Tallinn fortifications, with all exhibits labelled in English.

From Lossi plats, Toom Kooli leads north to the **Toomkirik** (Tues–Sun
9am–5pm), the city's understated Lutheran cathedral, originally a wooden church
built here by the Danes soon after their arrival in Tallinn. A stone's throw from the
Toomkirik, in a peppermint green neo-Renaissance palace, is the **Estonian Art
Museum**, Kiriku plats 1 (Wed–Sun 11am–6pm; 10EEK), housed here temporarily,
pending the construction of a new building in Kadriorg park. This small museum
displays a range of works that includes everything from nineteenth-century studies
of Tallinn and portraits of peasants in traditional costume to twentieth-century
paintings heavily influenced by European artistic trends like Expressionism.

Elsewhere in the Old Town

The remainder of the Old Town contains the commercial streets of medieval Tallinn,
lined by merchants' residences and warehouses. Pikk tänav, running northeast from
Pikk jalg gate and linking Toompea with the port area, has some of the city's most
important secular buildings from the Hanseatic period, kicking off with the **Great
Guild** at Pikk 17. Completed in 1430 this was the city's main guild, meeting place
of the German merchants who controlled the city's wealth. Its gloomy Gothic facade
now fronts the **Estonian History Museum** (11am–6pm; closed Wed; 10EEK)
where a predictable array of weaponry, domestic objects and jewellery offers an
uninspiring history of Estonia from the Stone Age to the eighteenth century.

If the appearance of their headquarters is anything to go by, the guild who occupied the **Brotherhood of the Blackheads House**, Pikk 26, were a more exuberant bunch than the merchants of the Great Guild. The Renaissance facade of
this building, inset with an elaborate stone portal and richly decorated door, cuts a
bit of dash amid the stolidity of Pikk. The Brotherhood moved here in 1531 and
remained until the guild was abolished by the Soviets in 1940. It now houses a concert hall and is worth a peep inside, for free if there's no concert playing at the time.

Continuing along Pikk brings you to the **St Olaf's Church**, first mentioned in
1267 and named in honour of King Olaf II of Norway, who was canonized for battling against pagans in Scandinavia. Were it not for its size, this slab-towered Gothic
structure would not be particularly eye-catching, and extensive renovation between

1829 and 1840 has left it with an unexceptional nineteenth-century interior. The church is chiefly famous for the height of its spire which reaches today 124m. According to local legend the citizens of Tallinn wanted the church to have the highest spire in the world to attract passing ships and bring trade to the city. Whether Tallinn's prosperity during the Middle Ages had anything to do with the church spire is not known, but between 1625 and 1820 the church burned down eight times as a result of lightning striking the tower.

Bearing witness to the city's medieval wealth are the Old Town's merchants' houses. The best examples are the **Three Sisters**, a gabled group at Pikk 71. Supremely functional with loading hatches and winch-arms set into their facades, these would have served as combined dwelling places, warehouses and offices, and are among the city's best-preserved Hanseatic buildings. At its far end Pikk is straddled by the **Great Coast Gate**, a sixteenth-century city gate flanked by two towers. The larger of these, the aptly named Fat Margaret Tower, has walls four-metres thick and now houses the **Estonian Maritime Museum** (Wed–Sun 10am–6pm; 25EEK; some English captions), a surprisingly diverting collection of model boats and nautical ephemera.

West of Lai is one of the longest-surviving sections of Tallinn's medieval city wall, complete with nine towers – to reach it, head down Suur-Kloostri. The walls that surrounded the Old Town were largely constructed during the fourteenth century, but they were added to and enhanced over succeeding centuries until improvements in artillery rendered them obsolete during the eighteenth century. Today, 2km of city wall still survives, along with eighteen towers.

The suburbs

Kadriorg Park, a large, heavily wooded park 2km east of the Old Town, is closely associated with the Russian Tsar Peter the Great, who first visited Tallinn in 1711, the year after the Russian conquest. The main entrance to the park is at the junction of Weizenbergi tänav and J. Poska (tram #1 or #3 from Viru väljak). Weizenbergi cuts through the park, running straight past **Kadriorg Palace**, a Baroque residence designed by the Italian architect Niccolò Michetti, which Peter had built for his wife Catherine. These days the palace is the official home of the **Museum of Foreign Art** (May–Sept Tues–Sun 10am–5pm; Oct–April Wed–Sun 10am–5pm; 35EEK), with a highly recommended selection of European art through the centuries. The smaller palace behind it is now home to Estonia's president. While waiting for the palace to be completed, Peter lived in a small cottage in the park grounds, at the junction of Weizenbergi and Mäekalda. Today this houses the **Peter the Great House Museum** (mid-May to Sept Wed–Sun 10.30am–6pm, 10EEK) with furniture from the time Peter lived there, along with a few objects from the palace.

The path down Mäekalda from Peter's cottage leads, after around fifteen minutes, to Narva mnt. On the other side of this busy road is the **Lauluväljak**, a vast amphitheatre that's the venue for Estonia's Song Festivals. These gatherings, featuring massed choirs thousands strong, have been an important form of national expression since the first all-Estonia Song Festival was held in Tartu in 1869, and are held every two years. The present structure, which can accommodate 15,000 singers (with room for a further 30,000 or so on the platform in front of the stage), went up in 1960. The grounds were filled to capacity for the September 1988 festival – a significant public expression of longing for independence from Soviet rule, which gave rise to the epithet "Singing Revolution".

A tree-lined avenue runs downhill from the amphitheatre to Pirita tee, which runs along the seashore. Turn right here and continue north for 750m to reach **Maarjamäe Palace**, a neo-Gothic residence built for a Russian count in the 1870s, which looks out over Tallinn Bay at Pirita tee. The building now houses a branch of the **History Museum** (March–Oct Wed–Sun 11am–6pm; Nov–Feb Wed–Sun 10am–5pm 10EEK), covering the mid-nineteenth century onwards, and is far more interesting and imaginative than its city-centre counterpart. Most exhibits have English captions, but the earlier sections are in Estonian and Russian only.

At the other end of Tallinn, on the western outskirts of the town, is the **Open-Air Museum** (daily: May–Aug 10am–8pm; Sept & Oct 10am–6pm; Nov–April 10am–4pm; 25EEK), a collection of eighteenth- and nineteenth-century village buildings gathered here from around the country and illustrating how Estonian farms developed. Visitors can also view a wooden church and a windmill, though for many the biggest attraction is the Kolu Kõrts café which serves up traditional bean soup and beer. The museum site slopes down to the sea and is known by the Italian name Rocca al Mare, christened by a merchant who built himself a mansion here in the late nineteenth century. To get to the museum, take bus #21 from the train station or trolleybus #6 from Vabaduse väljak.

Eating, drinking and nightlife

Meat and potatoes figure heavily on most **restaurant** menus in Tallinn, with alternatives available in a handful of ethnic places. Vegetarians are not well catered for, though a few places make a token effort. Many **cafés** and **bars** also offer snacks and full meals, and are usually a cheaper option; many feature live music or dancing. Most of Tallinn's **clubs** cater for a mainstream crowd. More underground, cutting-edge dance music events change location frequently and are advertised by flyposters, or try asking around in the city's hipper bars. Expect to pay 50–150EEK admission.

Cafés and snacks

Apollo Bookstore café Viru 23. Above the book shop there's a comfortable little café with strong coffee, organic tea and wicked chocolate cake. Three swift internet terminals.

Coffe Vanaturu Kael 8. Good place for a breakfast pastry or a pasta-based lunch, just off the main square.

Balti Sepik Süda 1. Café with its own bakery and eight computer terminals provided by Internetti.

Maiasmokk Pikk 16. Tallinn's most venerable café – founded in 1864 – with a beautiful wood-panelled interior. Queue up for your coffee and pastry, then, like the regulars, take your used dishes back when you're done.

Mocha Vene 1. Quiet café with good coffee, pastries and salads.

Stockmann Department Store Liivalaia 53, 5th floor. Self-service restaurant with excellent sandwiches and salads; also has internet access.

Tristan ja Isolde Raekoja plats 1. Dark, atmospheric café in the town hall with a full range of drinks and tasty salads and cakes.

Restaurants

Buon Giorno Müürivahe 17. Good place for soups, pasta dishes and cheap specials.

Café Anglais Raekoja plats 14. Excellent coffee and hot chocolate, and sumptuous range of salads and sweets. More expensive than average, but worth the price for fresh vegetables.

Eeslitall Restoran Dunkri 4/6. Probably Tallinn's most famous restaurant, with a formal dining room

on the ground floor and a more relaxed cellar downstairs. Bar features live jazz at weekends.

Elevant Vene 5. Chic Indian restaurant with affordable range of dishes, including plenty of vegetarian choices.

Golden Dragon Pikk 37. Highly recommended Chinese place with a large variety of fish and vegetarian options.

Kuldse Notsu Kõrts Dunkri 8. Serves Estonian country dishes accompanied by folk music in the evenings.

Pizza Americana Müürivahe 2. Excellent deep-pan pizzas and a range of inexpensive pasta dishes.

Pudru ja Pasta Pikk 35. Cellar bar/restaurant with small but imaginative range of inexpensive pasta and meat-and-potato standards.

Bars

Diesel Boots Lai 25. "Genuine American Bar" packed with ephemera that draws a local crowd.

Guitar Safari Muurivahe 22. Popular venue for live cover-bands and dancing.

Hell Hunt Pikk 39. The most congenial and perhaps most authentic of Tallinn's Irish bars. A basement and outside seating to the rear. Imaginative pub food.

Molly Malone's Möndi 2. Large pub just off Raekoja plats – a blend of ex-pat haunt, tourist pub and local yuppy meeting-place. Frequent live music by cover bands and pub-grub menu.

Nimega Baar Suur-Karja 13. Bar and disco opened by a Scottish football fan. DJs and live music at weekends.

Nimeta Baar, Suur-Karja 4/6. Sister venture of the *Nimega Baar*, offering curry and kebabs. International soccer matches screened live.

VS PSrnu mnt. 28. Hip new addition to the bar scene featuring industrial decor, late-night DJs (in the basement) and great food.

X-Baar Sauna 1. Relaxed gay bar with bright pink decor.

Live music and discos

Café Amigo in the Viru Hotel, Viru väljak 4. Heaving but likeable place playing mainstream dance music for locals and tourists into the early hours. Frequent appearances by Estonian bands.

Hollywood Club Vana-Posti 8. Popular Old Town dance club specializing in commercial techno. Trendy and busy. No trainers. Wed–Fri only.

Spirit Mere pst. 6E. Ultra-cool designer bar with alternative dance music and occasional gay nights. Café open daily, club nights Wed–Sat. Admission charge.

Terrarium Sadama 6. Filling up rapidly with the dance crowd. Visiting international DJs and beautiful young things in this minimalist club by the port. Closed Sun–Tues.

Von Krahli Bar Rataskaevu 10/12. Hip hangout that's always packed with a bohemian crowd. Frequent live music and dancing.

Listings

Embassies UK, Wismari 6 ☎0/667 4700; US, Kentmanni 20 ☎0/668 8100.

Exchange Outside banking hours, try the Monex exchange offices in the ferry dock, or the Kaubamaja or Stockmann department stores (all daily 9am–8pm).

Hospital Ravi 18 ☎0/602 7000; 24hr information ☎0/620 7015, ⓦwww.keskhaigla.ee.

Internet access Central Post Office, 2nd floor Narva mnt 1; @5, Gonsiori 2.

Laundry Vendlus, Pärnu 48 (Mon–Sat 8am–8pm, Sun 8am–5pm).

Left luggage At the bus and train stations.

Pharmacies Tonismae Apteek, Tõnismägi 5; Tallinna Linna Apteek, Pä Apteek, Pärnu mnt. 10.

Police Pärnu mnt. 11 ☎0/6123 523.

Post office Narva mnt. 1, opposite the *Viru Hotel*.

The rest of Estonia

The islands of **Saaremaa** and **Hiiumaa**, off the west coast of Estonia, are both easily reached from Tallinn and immensely popular as holiday-home destinations. Saaremaa, the largest of Estonia's 1500 islands, is also the most developed. Hiiumaa is roughly half the size of its neighbour and remains remarkably unspoilt, its forests and coastline ripe for exploration. On the mainland, **Tartu**, the former Hansa city of Dorpat and some 190km southeast of Tallinn, is regarded by many Estonians as the spiritual capital of Estonia, thanks to its role in the nineteenth-century National Awakening. These days it's a laid-back university town with a population of 100,000 and a small and easily walkable Old Town. **Pärnu**, Estonia's fifth largest city, lies to the west of west of Tartu. There are a handful of sights in its Old Town, but the city's main claim to fame is as the country's main resort, its sandy beach drawing thousands of visitors every summer – especially in July, for its jazz festival.

Saaremaa

Cloaked with pine trees and juniper bushes, and littered with glacial boulders, the island of **SAAREMAA** is a tranquil place. It was the last part of Estonia to come under foreign control (when the Knights of the Sword captured it in 1227) and the locals have always maintained a strong-minded indifference to the influence of foreign occupiers – a fact that has led many to claim that the island is one of the most authentically Estonian parts of the country. To get here, take a ferry from Virtsu on the mainland to Kuivastu on nearby Muhu island, which is linked to Saaremaa by a causeway.

Approaching **KURESSAARE**, Saaremaa's main town, don't be put off by the ugly Soviet-era industrial zone that surrounds it – the centre remains much as it was before World War II and is home to one of the finest castles in the Baltic region. From the bus station on Pihtla turn left onto Tallinna in order to reach **Kesk väljak**, the main square. Here you'll find Kuressaare's second oldest building (after the castle), the yellow-painted **Town Hall**, dating from 1670, its door guarded by stone lions; facing it is the **Weigh House**, another yellow building with a stepped gable.

From the square, Lossi runs south past a monument to the dead of the 1918–20 War of Independence, past the eighteenth-century **Nikolai kirik**, a white Orthodox church with green onion domes, and on to the magnificent **Kuressaare Castle**, a vast fortress built from locally quarried dolomite. Set on an artificial island surrounded by a moat, the castle was founded during the 1260s as a stronghold for the bishop of Ösel-Wiek who controlled western Estonia from his base at Haapsalu on the mainland. What you see today dates largely from the fourteenth century and is a formidable structure, protected by huge seventeenth-century ramparts. The labyrinthine keep houses the **Saaremaa Regional Museum** (Wed–Sun 11am–7pm; 30EEK), an interesting but confusingly laid-out collection covering the history and culture of the island from prehistoric times to date. The various sections are summarized in English. It's also possible to view the spartan living quarters of the bishops on the ground floor and climb the watchtowers. **Tall Hermann**, the eastern (and thinner) corner tower, is linked to the rest of the keep only by a wooden drawbridge.

The **tourist office** is in the town hall (June–Aug daily 9am–7pm; rest of year Mon–Fri 9am–5pm; ☎45/33120), and will book **private rooms** across the island for around 150EEK per person. About the cheapest **place to stay** in town is the *Guesthouse Mardi*, Vallimaa 5a (☎45/24633; ❷), which is part hotel, part hostel; the hostel beds, available from May to August, are in double and triple rooms, with bathrooms shared between two rooms. The *Arabella Guesthouse*, Tomi 12 (☎45/55885; ❸), is also more of an upmarket hostel with around fifty double rooms, each with its own shower and toilet. On the outskirts of town at Piibelehe 4, *Piibelehe Holiday Home* (☎45/36206; ❷) has two guest rooms with shared bathroom/toilet; traditional Saaremaa breakfasts are included. Alternatively, try the *Ovelia Majutus* at Suve 8 (☎45/55732; ❷), another family-run B&B.

For **food**, the *Classic* kohvik, Lossi 9, has an excellent selection of pasta, salads, omelettes and pancakes, or pour your own coffee and select from a tempting array of pastries at the *Vannalinna Kohvipood* café at Kauba 10. Be sure to sample *Saaremaa*, the locally brewed beer, which packs more of a punch than watery *Saku*. To sample it in situ, head for *Veski*, Pärnu 19, a pub in an old windmill, which also dishes up basic food (pork and potato variations). *Budweiser Pub*, Kauba 6, has Czech and German beers on tap, a pool table and pub grub, Estonian-style. **Internet** access is available in the dark and gloomy *Piljardisaal* Billiard Hall, at Raekoja 1.

Hiiumaa and Kassari

Most of **HIIUMAA** island is forested – elk, wild boar and lynx are among the local fauna – with swathes of peat moor and swamp at its heart. The sandy, rocky soil is of little agricultural use and supports a permanent population of just 12,000, but, like Saaremaa, Hiiumaa is a very popular holiday destination. Mainland ferries arrive at Heltermaa from Rohuküla, on the mainland near Haapsalu. A ferry service also runs to Sõru, on Hiiumaa's southern tip, in summer from Triigi on Saaremaa, but is not met by buses.

Hiiumaa's capital is **KÄRDLA**, an uneventful little town that serves as the island's main transport hub. Its centre is just south of the bus station at **Kesk väljak**. The **tourist office**, nearby at Kesk väljak 1 (Mon–Fri 9am–5pm; ☎46/22233, ⓦwww.hiiumaa.ee), can arrange **accommodation**. Alternatively, try *Sõnajala Hotel*, at the western end of town on Leigri väljak (☎46/31220), which has simple rooms and shared facilities (❷), or *Nuutri*, a small hostel just east of the main square at Nuutri 4 (☎46/98715; ❷). The *Eesti Posti Puhkekeskus* hostel, Posti 13 (☎46/91871;

❷), has twenty places plus a campsite, sauna and grill. You can pick up **food** from shops and cafés on the main square; try the café/bar *Arteesia* on the main square, or *Priiankru* at Sadama 4.

Regular buses head 20km south from Kärdla to the village of **KÄINA**, a useful jumping-off point for Hiiumaa's small neighbour, **KASSARI**. Kassari contains some of the most unspoilt juniper-covered heathland in the region and is small enough to be covered on foot if you make a day of it. If you want to **stay** overnight, try the well-appointed hotel *Liilia* at Hiiu mnt. 22 in Käina (☏46/36146; ❹), which has a good **restaurant**.

Tartu

The major city of south-central Estonia, and less than three hours away from Tallinn by bus, **TARTU**'s main sights lie between **Cathedral Hill**, right in the centre of Tartu, and the River Emajõgi. The train station is about 500m southwest of the city centre at Vaksali 6, and the bus station is just east of the centre at Turu 2.

Tartu's focal point is its cobbled **Town Hall Square**, lined by prim Neoclassical buildings, the most eye-catching of which is the **Town Hall**, a toy-town edifice at the head of the square, painted lilac and purple and topped by a spire. The neoclassical architectural theme continues in the yellow and white stucco facade of the main **Tartu University** building at Ülikooli 18, a couple of hundred metres north of the square.

A hundred metres or so beyond the university is the red-brick shell of the Gothic **St John's Church**, founded in 1330, bombed out in 1944 and now undergoing extensive restoration. The building is inaccessible, but from the street you can admire the unusual terracotta sculptures in niches that surround the main entrance. From behind the Town Hall, Lossi climbs **Cathedral Hill**, now a pleasant park with a few historic buildings dotted among its trees. On the way up, the street passes beneath **Inglisild**, a brightly painted wooden bridge dating from the nineteenth century. At the top of the hill you'll find the remains of the red-brick **Cathedral**, built by the Knights of the Sword in the thirteenth century. Tacked onto the end of the cathedral is a new building housing the **University History Museum** (Wed–Sun 11am–5pm; 20EEK), with three floors of ancient-looking text books, scientific instruments, and the sabres and flags brandished by nineteenth-century student fraternities.

Within a few minutes' walk of Cathedral Hill is the **Estonian National Museum**, J. Kuperjanovi 9 (Wed–Sun 11am–6pm; 20EEK). Devoted to peasant life and the development of agriculture in Estonia, it includes some imaginatively recreated farmhouse interiors and a detailed display of folk costume from all over the country; there's good English labelling, too.

Practicalities

Tartu's **tourist office** is at Raekoja plats 14 (Mon–Fri 10am–6pm, Sat 10am–3pm; ☏7/432 141, ⊛www.tartu.ee). There are a number of small **guest houses** (❷) in the suburbs offering accommodation, although few of the hosts speak English and you're best off making reservations through the tourist office. *Carolina*, a comfy B&B, lies 4km north of the centre at Kreuzwaldi 15 (☏7/422 070; ❸); to get there, take bus #6 from the station to the Teemeistri stop. A more central option, *B&B Herne*, at Herne 59 (☏7/441 959; ❸), has a sauna, tent places and internet facilities. The *Oru Villa*, Oru 1 (☏7/422 894, ⊛oruvilla.ee; ❸), a 1920s Jugendstil villa, provides rooms with atmosphere and a sense of history.

For fast **food** try the *Pronto Pizzeria* or *Zum Zum*, the latter serving soups, sandwiches and meat-and-potato main course. For a **drink**, the superb *Wilde*, Vallikraavi 4, offers tea, coffee, alcohol and atmosphere. Alternatively, head to *Zavood*, a bohemian dive just north of the centre at Lai 30. *Atlantis*, on the opposite bank of the river from the centre at Narva mnt 2, is a large and lively mainstream **disco**;

and the basement bar at *Tsink Plekk Pang* has themed DJ nights at weekends. **Club** nights also take place at *Varjend 2000*, a graffiti-covered bunker 500m south of the centre on Pargi; and at *Pattaya*, Turu 21, a. hot new club, southeast of the bus station. There's an **internet café**, *Virtuaal* (daily 11am–midnight; 30EEK/hr), at Pikk 40, on the opposite side of the Emajõgi from the centre.

Pärnu

The main town on Estonia's southwestern coast, **PÄRNU** comes into its own in summer, when the faded beach resort fills with visitors intent on making the most of the brief good weather. The sandy beaches are popular with young families, but the festivals cater to an alternative, cultural crowd and the mud baths of the many sanatorium spas are a must. The historic sights are mostly clustered in its **Old Town**. The bus station is on Pikk at the northeastern edge of the Old Town (information & ticket office at Ringi 3, round the corner), and the **train station** is about 5km east of the centre at Riia mnt. 116.

Rüütli, lined with two-storey wooden houses, is the Old Town's main thoroughfare, cutting east–west through the centre. Near the junction with Aia is the **Pärnu Museum**, Rüütli 53 (Wed–Sun 10am–6pm, 30EEK), devoted to local history, and housing some of Estonia's oldest archeological finds as well as examples of local traditional costume. The oldest building in town is the **Red Tower**, a fifteenth-century remnant of the medieval city walls on Hommiku, running north from Rüütli a few blocks west of the museum. Despite its name the tower is white – only the roof and window frames are red – and it now houses an antiques shop.

Pühavaimu, a few blocks to the west, has a pair of respectable-looking seventeenth-century houses near the junction with Malms, one in lemon yellow, the other in washed-out green with a large gabled vestibule. Moving west from Pühavaimu along Uus leads to the **Catherine Church**, a green-domed and multispired Orthodox church dating from 1760 and named after the Russian empress Catherine the Great. The interior is abundantly furnished with icons but is open for services only.

From here, Vee runs down to **Kuninga**, the Old Town's other major street, at the western end of which is the seventeenth-century **Tallinn Gate**, an elegant relic of the Swedish occupation set into the remains of the city ramparts and now home to a bar. Kuninga heads east to the Lutheran **Elizabeth Church** (Mon–Fri 10am–2pm) dating from 1747, with a maroon and ochre Baroque exterior and plain, wood-panelled interior. From here, Nikolai leads south to Esplanaadi, where the **Chaplin Centre** (daily 9am–9pm; 15EEK) occupies the former Communist party HQ at no. 10. Taken over by local artists in the post-independence years, it holds regular shows, film festivals and a collection of contemporary Estonian paintings and other works donated by international artists, including Yoko Ono. South of here Nikolai joins Supeluse, which runs down to the city's **resort area**, passing beneath the trees of the Rannapark, a shady park separating the town from the beach. At the southern end of Supeluse are the grand, colonnaded neoclassical **Pärnu Mud-Baths**, built in 1926, and painted in the familiar ochre. Nearby is Pärnu's sandy, white beach, packed at weekends and on public holidays.

Practicalities

The **tourist office** is at Rüütli 16 (June–Aug Mon–Sat 9am–6pm, Sun 10am–3pm; rest of year Mon–Fri 9am–5pm; ☎44/73000, ⊛www.parnu.ee). **Private rooms** (❶) are available from Tanni Vakoma, a block east of the bus station at Hommiku 5 (☎44/31070). The best **hotels** lie between the town centre and the beach: try the *Vesiroos*, Esplanaadi 42a (☎44/30940; ❸), which has a few en suites and the only outdoor swimming-pool in town. Alternatively, try the **hostel** *Lõuna*, at Lõuna 2 (☎44/30943; ❷), which is well-situated and can provide breakfast; or the *Niidu*, 3km out of town at Niidu 3 (☎44/38058; ❷), which offers kitchen facilities.

Linnakamping Green, 3km east of the centre at Suur-Jõe 50b (closed Oct–April), has cabins as well as tent pitches.

For **food**, try *Kohvik Georg*, Rüütli 43, an inexpensive self-service restaurant open until 7.30pm; *Steffani*, Nikolai 24, which has a big choice of pizza and pasta dishes; or *Mõnus Margarita*, Akadeemia 5 – a lively Tex-Mex joint with reasonable prices. The best of the **drinking** venues also do good food – try *Väike Klaus*, a pub-style venue at Supeluse 3 with a meaty Estonian menu. *Sunset Club*, Ranna pst 3, on the Baltic shore, hosts beach-side music events. For **internet** access, head to the Chaplin Centre (see above; 30EEK/hr).

Travel details

Trains

Tallinn to: Pärnu (2 daily; 3hr); Tartu (3 daily; 3hr 20min).

Buses

Tallinn to: Haapsalu (7 daily; 2hr); Kaina (1 daily; 5hr); Kärdla (3 daily; 5hr); Kuressaare (6 daily; 4hr 30min); Pärnu (12 daily; 2hr); Tartu (every 30min; 2hr 30min).

Kuressaare to: Tallinn (6 daily; 4hr 30min).
Pärnu to: Tallinn (12 daily; 2hr).
Tartu to: Tallinn (every 30min; 2hr 30min).

Ferries

Rohuküla to: Heltermaa for Hiiumaa (12 daily; 2hr).
Triigi to: Sõru for Hiiummaa (summer only; 5 daily; 1hr 30min).
Virtsu to: Kuivastu for Saaremaa (12–20 daily; 30min).

Finland

Finland highlights

* **Tuomiokirkko, Helsinki**
  The Lutheran cathedral is the capital's most evocative sight. See p.331

* **Aura river, Turku** Stroll along the tree-lined banks, through the heart of Finland's former capital. See p.332

* **Lenin museum, Tampere**
  A fascinating opportunity to delve into the long and mutually respectful relationship between Lenin and Finland. See p.333

* **Olavinlinna castle, Savonlinna.** The best preserved medieval castle in Finland, it once marked the frontier between Sweden and Russia. See p.334

* **Crossing the Arctic Circle, Rovaniemi.** The trip everybody wants to make. See p.336

* **Pielpajärvi wilderness church, Inari.** Trek across the tundra of Lapland to reach this former Sami outpost. See p.337

Introduction and basics

Scandinavia's most culturally isolated and least understood country, **Finland** has been independent only since 1917, having been ruled for hundreds of years by first the Swedes and then the Tsarist Russians. Much of its history involves a struggle for recognition and survival, and so modern-day Finns have a well-developed sense of their own culture, manifest in the widely popular Golden Age paintings of Gallen-Kallela and others, the music of Sibelius, the National Romantic style of architecture, and the deeply ingrained values of rural life.

Finland is mostly flat and punctuated by huge forests and lakes, but has wide regional variations. The south contains the least dramatic scenery, but the capital, **Helsinki**, more than compensates, with its brilliant architecture and superb collections of national history and art. Stretching from the Russian border in the east to the industrial city of Tampere, the vast waters of the **Lake Region** provide a natural means of transport for the timber industry – indeed, water here is a more common sight than land. Towns lie on narrow ridges between lakes, giving even major manufacturing centres green and easily accessible surrounds. North of here, Finland ranges from the flat western coast of **Ostrobothnia** to the thickly forested heartland of **Kainuu** and gradually rising fells of **Lapland**, Finland's most alluring terrain and home to the Sami, the semi-nomadic reindeer herders found all over northern Scandinavia.

Information and maps

Most towns have some sort of **tourist office**, which sometimes book accommodation. In summer they generally open daily 9am–7pm in more popular centres; in winter, opening hours are much reduced and some don't open at all. The best general **map** of Finland is the *freytag & berndt* one; there is also an excellent map in the *Finland: Budget Accommodation* booklet, available from tourist offices.

Money and banks

Finland is one of twelve European Union countries who have switched over to the **euro** (€).

Banks are open Mon–Fri 9.15am–4.15pm. Some banks have exchange desks at transport terminals, and ATMs are widely available. You can also change money at hotels, but the rates are generally poor.

Communications

Communications in Finland are dependable and quick. **Post offices** are generally open 9am–5pm, with later hours in Helsinki. **Public phones** are ubiquitous. You'll need a phone card (*puhelukortti*; €5–15), available at post offices and tourist offices, to make use of them. Some phones also accept major credit cards. **International calls** are cheapest between 10pm and 8am. Operator numbers are ☏118 for domestic calls and ☏92020 for international calls.

Finland on the net

ⓦ**www.finland-tourism.com** The Finnish tourist board site
ⓦ**www.finland.org** General facts about Finland
ⓦ**www.sauna.fi** The Finnish Sauna Society
ⓦ**www.srm.inet.org** Finnish Youth Hostels Association

Free **internet access** is readily available, even in the most out-of-the-way places. The first place to look is the local library, though you may need to book a few hours in advance. Tourist offices often have online access too.

Getting around

You'll have few headaches getting around Finland. For the most part **trains** and **buses** integrate well, and you'll only need to plan with care when travelling through the remoter areas of the far north and east.

Trains and buses

Trains are operated by Finnish State Railways (**VR**). Large, comfortable Express and InterCity trains, plus a growing number of super-smooth tilting Pendolino trains, serve the principal cities several times a day. Elsewhere, especially on east–west hauls through sparsely populated regions, trains are often tiny or replaced by buses on which rail passes are still valid. **InterRail** and **ScanRail** passes (see p.29) are valid on all trains. The best and most understandable **timetable** is the *Rail Pocket Guide* published by VR and available from all train stations and tourist offices.

Buses – privately run, but with a common ticket system – cover the whole country, but are most useful in the north. Tickets can be purchased at bus stations and most travel agents; only ordinary one-way tickets can be bought on board. The **timetable** (*Pikavuoroaikataulut*), available at all main bus stations, lists all bus routes.

Flying

With a range of discounts aimed particularly at under-26s, domestic flights with Finnair (ⓦwww.finnair.com) can be comparatively cheap as well as time-saving. However, the only time you'll find flying a truly economic option is if you are planning to visit Lapland and the far north of the country. The company also offer a variety of off-peak summer reductions which can be checked at travel agents or tourist offices once you're in the country.

Accommodation

Hotels are expensive in Finland, but special offers during the summer months mean that you will be able to sleep well on a budget in high season, but may have difficulty finding anything affordable out of season; the reverse of the norm. **Bookings** can be made through Hotel Booking Centre (ⓣ09/22881400), inside the City Tourist Office in Helsinki. The free *Finland: Budget Accommodation* booklet, available from any tourist office, contains a comprehensive list of hostels and campsites; it also has an excellent map of the country.

Hotels

Most **hotels** come with TV, phone and private bathrooms, and large eat-as-much-as-you-can buffet breakfasts. Taking advantage of discount schemes and summer reductions, such as the Finncheque, can cut prices to around €35 per person for double rooms. **Finncheque** must be arranged through the Finnish Tourist Board or a specialist travel agent before arriving in Finland; it entitles the holder to an unlimited number of vouchers, for use between mid-May and Sept, each voucher entitling the holder to a hotel room in participating chains; there's often a surcharge (€13.50) in more expensive hotels, but in other places lunch is thrown in. The **Scanhotel** chain offers a similar system, which works out to about €75 for a double room, including breakfast, but once again look out for surcharges. In many towns you'll also find **tourist hotels** (*matkustajakoti*), offering less frills than standard hotels and charging €35–50 per person, although they are often full during summer. **Summer hotels** (*kesähotelli*; June–Aug only) are another option, offering decent accommodation in student blocks for €25–45 per person, normally with breakfast thrown in.

Hostels

The cheapest option, and always spotlessly clean, are the **HI hostels** (*retkeilymaja*; ⓦwww.srm.inet.org). There are around 100 throughout the country and each city has at least one. It's always advisable to book ahead, especially between June and August.

Note that many hostels close altogether from mid-August till June. Hostels range from the basic dormitory type to those with two-bedded rooms and a bathroom between three. Bedlinen, if not included, costs an extra €3.50–5; Finnish health regulations prohibit the use of sleeping bags in hostels. HI cards, while not obligatory, reduce an overnight stay by €2.50.

Campsites and camping cottages

Official **campsites** (*leirintäalue*) are plentiful. Most open May or June until August or September, although some stay open longer and a few all year. Sites are star rated, and many three-star sites also have **camping cottages** often with TV, sauna and kitchen. The cost for two people sharing a tent is €5–15, depending on site facilities; cabins cost €100–500 per week. It's advisable to book cabins as far ahead as possible in July and August. You'll need either an International Camping Card or a National Camping Card; the latter (€3.40), available at all sites, is valid for a year.

Food and drink

Restaurants can be pricey, but you can keep a rein on the expense by taking advantage of special lunchtime deals and self-catering. Though tempered by many regulations, **alcohol** is more widely available and considerably less expensive than in the rest of Scandinavia.

Food

Though it may at first seem a stodgy, unsophisticated cuisine, **Finnish food** is an interesting mix of Western and Eastern influences, with Scandinavian-style fish specialities and exotic meats such as reindeer and elk alongside dishes that bear a Russian stamp – pastries, and casseroles strong on cabbage and pork. **Breakfasts** (*aamiainen*) are a sumptuous affair: a buffet of herring, eggs, cereals, cheese, salami and bread. Later in the day you can lunch on the economical **snacks** sold in market halls (*kauppahalli*) or in the adjoining cafés. Most train

stations and some bus stations and supermarkets also have cafeterias offering a selection of snacks and light meals, and the Grilli and Nakkikioski street stands turn out burgers and hot dogs for €2.50–3.50. Otherwise, campus **mensas** are the cheapest places to get a hot dish (€2–4). Theoretically, you have to be a student, but you are unlikely to be asked for ID. In regular restaurants or *ravintola*, **lunch** (*lounas*) deals offer good value, with many places offering a lunchtime buffet table (*voileipäpöytä* or *seisova pöytä*) stacked with a choice of traditional goodies for a set price of €8.50–13. Pizzerias are another good bet, serving lunch specials for €6–9.

For **evening meals** in smaller towns there will no doubt be a cheap pizzeria or *ravintola*, serving up standard plates of meat and two veg. In Helsinki and the big towns there are usually a good range of options, including Chinese and Thai. Prices run from €6 for a cheap pizza to €50 for a substantial meal plus drinks in a smart restaurant.

Drink

Whilst the attitude to **drinking** can seem austere, Finland has a truly staggering problem with alcoholism and in some of the smaller towns bars can be quite depressing places. In Helsinki and the bigger towns, however, the drinking culture is more sophisticated and you'll be able to find numerous appealing places to have a jar or two.

Beer (*olut*) falls into three categories: "light beer" (I-Olut), like a soft drink; "medium strength beer" (*Keskiolut*, III-Olut), perceptibly alcoholic, sold in shops and cafés; and "strong beer" (A-Olut or IV-Olut), on a par with the stronger European beers, and only available at fully licensed restaurants, clubs and ALKO shops. Strong beers, such as Lapin Kulta and Koff, cost about €1.35 per 300ml bottle. Imported beers go for €1.50–2 per bottle. As for **spirits**, Finlandia vodka is €27 per litre and Koskenkorva, a rougher vodka, €25 per litre.

Most restaurants are fully licensed, and many are frequented more for drinking than eating. **Bars** are usually open till midnight or 1am and service stops half an hour before closing. You have to be 18 to buy beer and wine, 20 to buy spirits. Expect to queue to get into popular bars, as there's no standing allowed, so you'll only be let in if there's a seat free. Remember to tip the doorman (*portsari*; €1), if there is one, on leaving; if there isn't, then there'll almost certainly be an obligatory cloakroom fee (also €1).

The main – and cheapest – outlet for alcohol of any kind is the ubiquitous government-run **ALKO** shops: Mon–Thurs 10am–5pm, Fri 10am–6pm; Oct–April also Sat 9am–2pm.

Opening hours and holidays

Shops open Mon–Fri 9am–6pm, Sat 9am–4pm. Along with banks, they close on **public holidays**, when most public transport and museums run to a Sun schedule: Jan 1; Jan 6 (Epiphany); Good Fri & Easter Mon; May 1; Midsummer's Eve & Day; All Saints' Day; Dec 6; Dec 24, 25 & 26.

Emergencies

You probably won't have much cause to come into contact with the Finnish **police**, though if you do they are likely to speak English. As for **health problems**, if you're insured, you'll save time by seeing a doctor at a private health centre (*Lääkäriasema*) rather than queuing at a national health centre (*Terveyskeskus*). Medicines must be paid for at a **pharmacy** (*apteekki*), generally open daily 9am–6pm; outside these times, a telephone number for emergency help is displayed on every pharmacy's front door.

Emergency numbers

All emergencies ☏112.

Helsinki

The southern coast of Finland is the most populated, industrialized and richest part of the country, with the densest concentration, not surprisingly, around the capital, **HELSINKI**. A city of half a million people, Helsinki is quite different from the other Scandinavian capitals, closer both in mood and looks to the major cities of eastern Europe. For a century an outpost of the Russian Empire, its very shape and form is derived from its powerful neighbour. Yet through the twentieth century it has become a showcase of independent Finland, much of its impressive architecture drawing inspiration from the dawning of Finnish nationalism and the rise of the republic. The streets have a youthful buzz, the short summer bringing crowds along the boulevards and at outdoor cafés and restaurants. At night the pace picks up, with a great selection of pubs and clubs and free rock concerts in the numerous parks.

Arrival, information and city transport

All points of arrival are close to the city centre: the **ferry** terminals are less than 1km from the centre; the **train station** is in the heart of the city; the **long-distance bus station** is a short way up Simonkatu; and the **airport**, Vantaa, is 20km to the north, connected by buses to the Finnair terminal at the central train station (every 15–30min; €4.90).

The **City Tourist Office** at Pohjoisesplanadi 19 (Mon–Fri 9am–6/8pm, Sat & Sun 9am–4/6pm; ☏09/169 3757, ✆www.hel.fi/tourism), stocks the useful, free listings magazines *Helsinki This Week*, *City* and *Helsinki Happens*. If you're staying a while, consider purchasing a **Helsinki Card** (€24/24hr €38/72hr), giving unlimited travel on public transport and free entry to more than forty museums. For information on the rest of the country, use the **Finnish Tourist Board** across the road at Eteläesplanadi 4 (Mon–Fri 9am–5pm; May–Sept also Sat & Sun 11am–3pm; ☏09/4176 9300, ✆www.mek.fi).

Most sights are within easy walking distance of each other. However, quick hops across the centre are easily done on the efficient **public transport** system (trams, buses and a small metro). One-way tickets can be bought on board (€2) or from the bus station, tourist office or kiosks around the centre (€1.40), while a **tourist ticket** (€4.20/one day, €8.40/three day, €12.60/five day) permits unlimited use of the whole network for the period covered. **Tram** #3T, which follows a figure-of-eight route around the centre, has probably the most useful route.

Accommodation

There's plenty of **accommodation** in Helsinki, the bulk of it mid-range **hotels**. However, there are a number of cheaper, if less luxurious, **tourist hotels**, providing basic accommodation in private rooms without bathrooms, and a few **hostels**, though space can be tight in summer. You can book hotel rooms and hostel beds at the **Hotel Booking Centre** at the train station for a fee of €5 in person or for free by email or phone (June–Aug Mon–Sat 9am–7pm, Sun 10am–6pm; rest of year Mon–Fri 9am–5pm; ☏09/2288 1400, ✉hotel@helsinkiexpert.fi).

Hostels and tourist hotels

Hostel Academica Hietaniemenkatu 14 ☏09/1311 4334. On the fringes of the city centre with dorms and double rooms. HI and student card discounts. June to Aug only. ❸

Erottajanpuisto Uudenmaankatu 9 ☏09/642169. Conveniently positioned for the buses, with singles to quadruples. ❹

Eurohostel Linnankatu 9 ☏09/622 0470. The biggest hostel in Finland, close to the ferry terminals and with a free sauna. ❸

Omapohja Itäinen Teatterikuja 3 ☏09/666 211. Dorms and smaller rooms, some en suite. ❹

Stadion Hostel in the Olympic Stadium ☏09/477 8480. Out of the centre by 2km and often crowded, but cheap and open all year. Trams #3T, #7A, #7B and #10 to stadium, then follow the signs. ❸

Summer Hotel Satakunta Lapinrinne 1 ☏09/6958 5231. Centrally located, doubles as an HI hostel. June–Aug only. ❸

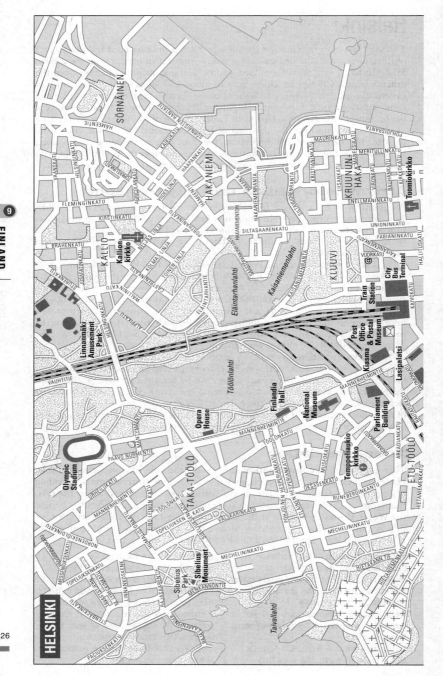

HELSINKI

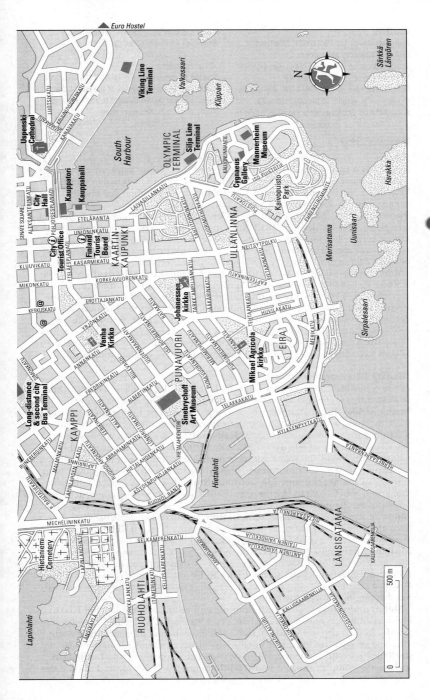

Hotels

Anna Annankatu 1 ℡09/616621. Small and central, with a cosy atmosphere. ❻

Arthur Vuorikatu 19b ℡09/173441. Good-quality hotel, with some en-suite rooms. ❹

Finn Kalevankatu 3b ℡09/6844 360. A peaceful, modern place, virtually in the city centre. ❹

Kongressikoti Snellmaninkatu 15a ℡09/1356839.

Clean and cosy place close to Senate square. Discounts for longer stays. ❹

Campsites

Rastila Karavaanikatu 4 ℡09/321 6551. Located 13km east of the city centre, at the end of the metro line and served by night buses #90N and #93N till 1.30am. Also has cabins.

The City

Following a devastating fire and the city's appointment as Finland's capital in 1812, Helsinki was totally rebuilt in a style befitting its new status: a grid of wide streets and Neoclassical brick buildings modelled on the then Russian capital, St Petersburg. From **Senate Square** to **Esplanadi** the grandeur has endured. The square itself is dominated by the exquisite form of the recently renovated **Tuomiokirkko** (Mon–Sat 9am–6pm, Sun noon–6pm), designed by Engel and completed after his death in 1852. After the elegance of the exterior, the spartan Lutheran interior comes as a disappointment; better is the gloomily atmospheric **crypt** (same times as cathedral; entrance on Kirkkokatu), now often used for exhibitions. Walking east, the square at the end of Aleksanterinkatu is overlooked by the onion domes of the Russian Orthodox **Uspenski Cathedral** (Mon–Sat 9.30am–4pm, Sun noon–3pm, Oct–April closed Mon; tram #3). Inside, a rich display of icons glitters while incense mingles with the sound of Slavonic choirs. Beyond is Katajanokka, a wedge of land extending between the harbours, where a dockland development programme is converting the old warehouses into pricey new restaurants and apartments. Just a block south of Senate Square, the new **City Museum** at Sofiankatu 4 (Mon–Fri 9am–5pm, Sat & Sun 11am–5pm; €3) offers a hi-tech record of Helsinki life in an impressive permanent exhibition called "Time".

Along Mannerheimintie

Across a mishmash of tramlines from the harbour is Esplanadi, a wide tree-lined boulevard that is Helsinki at its most charming. South of here, on Annankatu, is the **Vanha kirkko**, Engel's humble wooden structure, the first Lutheran church to be built in Helsinki after it became the capital. A few blocks from the end of Kasarminkatu is the large and rocky **Kaivopuisto** park, where nobility from St Petersburg came to sample the waters at its 1830s spa house. However, it's beyond the northern end of Bulevardi that most of the city's attractions can be found. On the corner of Aleksanterinkatu and Mannerheimintie is the Constructivist brick exterior of the **Stockmann Department Store**. Europe's largest, it sells everything from bubble gum to Persian rugs. Further along Mannerheimintie, steps head down to the **Tunneli** shopping complex, which leads to one of the city's most enjoyable structures, **Helsinki train station**, a solid yet graceful building dating from 1914. Beside the station is the imposing granite **National Theatre**, home of Finnish drama since 1872. Directly opposite the bus station is the **Atheneum Art Museum**, Kaivokatu 2 (Tues–Fri 9am–6/8pm, Sat & Sun 11am–5pm; €7.50). Its stirring selection of late-nineteenth-century works – including Akseli Gallén-Kallela and Albert Edelfelt's scenes from the Finnish epic, the *Kalevala*, and Juho Rissanen's moody studies of peasant life – recalls a time when the spirit of nationalism was surging through the country.

Mannerheimintie spears north from the city centre, past the striking **Kiasma**, Helsinki's museum of contemporary art (Tues 9am–5pm, Wed–Sun 10am–8.30pm; €5.50). Its gleaming steel-clad exterior and high-tech interior make it well worth a visit, and its collection includes installations in which sound, moving images and smell add a sensory dimension to the experience. Opposite is the **Lasipalatsi**, a multimedia complex situated in a recently renovated 1930s classic Functionalist building, inside which are trendy shops and cafés and the excellent **Cable Book Library** (Mon–Thurs 10am–10pm, Sat & Sun noon–6pm), offering free internet access. Further along on the left, the **Parliament Building** (guided tours Sat 11am & noon, Sun noon & 1pm; July & Aug also Mon–Fri 2pm; free), with its pompous columns and choking air of solemnity, was completed in 1931. North of here is the **National Museum** (Tues–Sun 11am–6/8pm; €4), its design drawing on the country's medieval churches and granite castles. The exhibits, from prehistory to the present, are exhaustive; it's best to concentrate on a few specific sections, such as the marvellously restored seventeenth-century manor house interior and the ethnographic displays from the nation's varied regions.

Directly opposite the National Museum, **Finlandia Hall** (guided tours by appointment; ☎09/402 4246; free) was designed in the 1970s by the country's premier architect, Alvar Aalto. Inside, Aalto's characteristic asymmetry and wave pattern (his surname means "wave") are everywhere, from the walls and ceilings through to the lamps and vases. A little further up Mannerheimintie, the **Olympic Stadium** is clearly visible; originally intended for the 1940 Olympics, it hosted the second postwar games in 1952. Its **tower** (Mon–Fri 9am–8pm, Sat & Sun 9am–6pm; €2) gives an unsurpassed view over the city and a chunk of the southern coast. Back towards the city centre, the **Hietaniemi Cemetery** houses the graves of some of the big names of Finnish history – Mannerheim, Engel and Alvar Aalto, whose witty little tombstone, with its chopped Neoclassical column, stands beside the main entrance. East of here, at Lutherinkatu 3, is the late-1960s **Temppeliaukio kirkko** (Mon–Fri 10am–8pm, Sat till 6pm, Sun noon–1.45pm & 3.15–5.45pm; closed Tues 1–2pm and during services; tram #3B). Blasted from a single lump of granite beneath a domed copper roof, it's a thrill to be inside.

Suomenlinna

Built by the Swedes in 1748 to protect Helsinki from seaborne attack, the fortress of **Suomenlinna** stands on five interconnected islands and is the biggest sea fortress in the world. It's reachable by ferry (every 30min) from the harbour: you can either visit independently, or take one of the hour-long summer **guided walking tours**, beginning close to the ferry stage and conducted in English (June–Aug daily 10.30am, 1pm & 3pm; €5). Suomenlinna has a few museums, none particularly riveting. The best of the lot is **Suomenlinna Museum** (March–Oct Sat & Sun 10/11am–56/pm; €5) which contains a permanent exhibition on the island, but it is the views from the island back across the water towards the capital that are truly superb.

Eating and drinking

Many places offer good-value **lunchtime** deals, and there are plenty of affordable ethnic **restaurants** and fastfood *grillis* for the evenings. At the end of Eteläesplanadi the old market hall, **Kauppahalli** (Mon–Fri 8am–7pm, Sat 8am–4pm), is good for snacks and reindeer kebabs. Helsinki has several **student mensas**, two of which are centrally located at Aleksanterinkatu 5 and Yliopistonkatu 3; both are open during term time, and one or the other will be open through summer.

Drinking can be enjoyed in the city's many pub-like restaurants; on Fridays and Saturdays it's best to arrive as early as possible to get a seat. Most places also serve food, although the grub is seldom at its best in the evening. There are ALKO shops at Fabianinkatu 9–11 and Kaivokatu 10.

Restaurants and cafés

Café Ekberg Bulevardi 9. Nineteenth-century fixtures and a *fin-de-siècle* atmosphere, with starched waitresses bringing expensive sandwiches and pastries to marble tables.
Café Fazer Kluuvikatu 3. Owned by Finland's biggest chocolate company, with justly celebrated pastries.

Kasakka Meritullinkatu 13. Great atmosphere and food in this old-style Russian restaurant.
Lappi Annankatu 22. Great Lapland food in a restaurant done out in tacky log cabin style. Lunchtime specials are good value, but prices escalate in the evenings.

Lasipalatsi Mannerheimintie 22–24. Decent modern Finnish food served in a classic Functionalist style building with great views of Kiasma and the street life below.

Mamma Rosa Runeberginkatu 55. A classic pizzeria also serving fish steaks and pasta.

Namaskar Mannerheimintie 100. Popular evening buffet and plenty of vegetarian options.

Saslik Neitystpolku 12. Pricey but delicious authentic Russian grub.

Strindberg Pohjoisesplanadi 33. The upstairs restaurant serves contemporary Scandinavian cuisine, while the street level café is one of *the* places in town to see and be seen.

Bars

Ateljee Bar on the roof of *Hotel Torni*, Yrjönkatu 26. The best views of Helsinki in a stylish atmosphere.

Bar Nº9 Uudenmaankatu 9. A popular hangout for professionals at lunchtime and bohos in the evening, it has a beer list and menu as cosmopolitan as its staff. Food is reasonably cheap and filling and there is always a vegetarian option.

Bulevardia Bulevardi 34. Art Deco fittings and reasonably priced lunchtime specials.

Elite Eteläinen Hesperiankatu 22. Once the haunt of the city's artists, many of whom settled their bill with the paintings that line the walls. Especially good in summer, when you can drink on the terrace.

St Urho's Pub Museokatu 10. One of the most popular student pubs. Guitars, a piano, etc available for jam sessions.

Vanha Mannerheimintie 3. Self-service and comparatively cheap café/bar. Arrive early for a seat on the balcony overlooking the streets below. The cellar is given over to a smoky beerhall, whilst other parts of the building serve as an indie/rock concert venue.

Nightlife

Helsinki has a vibrant night scene, with several venues putting on a steady diet of **live music** and free gigs almost every summer Sunday in Kaivopuisto park. There is also a wide range of **clubs and discos**, which charge a small admission fee (around €5). For details of **what's on**, read the entertainments page of *Helsingin Sanomat*, or the free fortnightly paper, *City*, found in record shops, bookshops, department stores and tourist offices. **Tickets** can be booked at Tiketti, Yrjönkatu 29c (Mon–Fri 9am–5pm; ☎0600/11 616 premium rate call).

Botta Museokatu 10. Vibrant dance music of various hues most nights.

Kerma Erottaja 7. One of the grooviest places in town. Seventies-style decor and funky Latin rhythms abound. Open till 4am at w/ends.

KY-Exit Pohjoinen Rautatiekatu 21. Sometimes has international bands; more often lively disco nights.

Saunabar Eerikinkatu 27. With a sauna attached and a legendary Sun night DJ spot, this is one the most idiosyncratic places in town.

Soda Uudenmaankatu 16–20. Losing its edge a little, but still a good night out. Dance music downstairs; bar and guest DJs upstairs.

Storyville Museokatu 8. Popular venue for nightly live jazz. Good food, too.

Gay Helsinki

Always the slowest of the Scandinavian countries to reform sexuality laws, Finland finally decriminalized homosexuality in 1971 and introduced partnership laws in 2001. In recent years, however, the gay scene in Helsinki has flourished and today there's an impressive number of exclusively gay and gay-friendly establishments. For the latest details, pick up a copy of the monthly *Z* **magazine** – in Finnish only but with a useful listings section – widely available in larger newsagents, or drop into SETA, Hietalahdenkatu 2b 16, the state-supported gay organization (☎09/6123233, ⓦwww.seta.fi).

Con Hombres Eerikinkatu 14. The most popular bar in Helsinki and one of the oldest in the country. If it's quiet elsewhere, the chances are there'll be people here. Very cruisy at weekends.

DTM (Don't Tell Mamma) Annankatu 32 ⓦwww.dtm.fi. The capital's legendary night club and *the* place to go, with occasional drag shows and house music most nights.

Hercules Lönnrotinkatu 4b. Not quite as trendy as *DTM*, but still attracting a mixed crowd, this club plays varied music, including some of Finland's best offerings.

Lost and Found & Hideaway Annankatu 6. Two bars on two floors, with a small dancefloor downstairs. Very popular at weekends with a mixed crowd.

Mann's Street Mannerheimintie 12 (upstairs). If you're looking for karaoke, Finnish music and older gay men, you'll find generous helpings here.

Room Erottajankatu. Next to *Lost and Found* and one of Helsinki's better neighbourhood bars; attracts the young and beautiful.

Listings

Embassies Canada, Pohjoisesplanadi 25b ☎09/171 141; Ireland, Erottajankatu 7A ☎09/646 006; UK, Itäinen Puistotie 17 ☎09/2286 5100; US, Itäinen Puistotie 14a ☎09/171 931. Australia, contact Stockholm embassy (see p.1029).
Exchange Other than the banks, try at the airport (6.30am–11pm) or the train station (daily 8am–9pm).
Hospital Marian Hospital, Lapinlahdenkatu 16 ☎09/4711.
Internet Café Aalto, 2nd floor Akateeminen

Kirjakauppa, Keskuskatu 1; Wave Bar cafe, Vuorikatu 16; Netcup, Aleksanterinkatu 52; mbar in the Lasipalatsi, Mannerheimintie 22–24.
Laundry Punavuorenkatu 3.
Left luggage Long-distance bus station and at train station.
Pharmacies Yliopiston Apteekki, Mannerheimintie 96 (24hr).
Police Pieni Roobertinkatu 1–3 ☎1891.
Post office Elielaukio 2F.

Around Helsinki: Porvoo

Fifty kilometres east of Helsinki, **PORVOO** is one of the oldest towns on the south coast and one of Finland's most charming. Its narrow cobbled streets, lined by small wooden buildings, give a sense of the Finnish life which predated the capital's bold squares and neoclassical geometry.

Close to the station, the **Johan Ludwig Runeberg House**, Aleksanterinkatu 3 (Mon–Sat 10am–4pm, Sun 11am–5pm; Sept–April closed Mon & Tues; €4), is where the famed Finnish poet lived from 1852 while a teacher at the town school; despite writing in Swedish, one of his poems provided the lyrics for the Finnish national anthem. The old town is built around the hill on the other side of Mannerheimkatu, crowned by the fifteenth-century **Tuomiokirkko** (May–Sept Mon–Fri 10am–6pm, Sat 10am–2pm, Sun 2–5pm; Oct–April Tues–Sat 10am–2pm, Sun 2–4pm), where Alexander I proclaimed Finland a Russian Grand Duchy and convened the first Finnish Diet. This, and other aspects of the town's past, can be explored in the **Porvoo Museum** (daily 11am/noon–4pm; Sept–April closed Mon & Tues; €5) at the foot of the hill in the main square; the collection of furnishings, musical instruments and oddities mostly date from the days of Russian rule.

Buses run daily from Helsinki to Porvoo (€25 one way), arriving opposite the **tourist office**, which is at Rihkamakatu 4 (Mon–Fri 9.30am–4.30/6pm, Sat & Sun 10am–2/4pm; Sept to mid-June closed Sun; ☎019/520 2316, ⓦwww.porvoo.fi). There's a **hostel** at Linnankoskenkatu 1–3 (☎019/523 0012; ❶), and a **campsite** (☎019/581 967; June to mid-Aug), 1.5km from the town centre. The cheapest place **to eat** is *Rosso* at Piispankatu 21.

The southwest

The area immediately west of Helsinki is probably the blandest section of the country – endless forests interrupted only by modest-sized patches of water and virtually identical villages and small towns. The far southwestern corner, however, is more interesting, with islands and inlets around a jagged shoreline and some of the country's distinctive Finnish-Swedish coastal communities. The country's former capital, **Turku**, is historically and visually one of Finland's most enticing cities.

Turku

TURKU was once the national capital, but lost its status in 1812 and most of its buildings in a ferocious fire in 1827. These days it's a small and sociable city, bristling with history and culture and with a sparkling nightlife, thanks to the students from its two universities.

To get to grips with Turku and its pivotal place in Finnish history, cut through the centre to the river. This tree-framed space was, before the great fire of 1827, the bustling heart of the community, and is overlooked by Turku's **Tuomiokirkko** (daily 9am–8pm except during services), erected in the thirteenth century and still the centre of the Finnish Church. Despite repeated fires, a number of features survive, notably the ornate seventeenth-century tomb of Torsten Stålhandske, commander of the Finnish cavalry during the Thirty Years War. On top of a small hill near the cathedral, you'll see the wooden dome of the **Engel Observatory**, which currently houses the **Turku Art Museum** (Tues–Thurs 11am–6pm, Fri–Sun 10am–4pm; €5.50–7, according to the exhibition). The museum contains one of the better collections of Finnish art, with works by all the great names of the country's golden age plus a commendable stock of moderns. Retrace your steps to the riverbank to find Turku's newest and most splendid museum, the combined **Aboa Vetus and Ars Nova** (daily 11am–7pm; mid-Sept to April closed Mon; €7). Digging the foundations of the modern art gallery revealed a warren of medieval lanes, now on view beneath the glass floor of the building. The gallery itself comprises 350 striking works plus temporary exhibitions, and there's a great café too.

Just north of the cathedral is the sleek low form of the **Sibelius Museum** (Tues–Sun 11am–4pm, Wed also 6–8pm; €3), which – although Sibelius had no direct connection with Turku – displays family photo albums and manuscripts, the great man's hat, walking stick and even his final half-smoked cigar. A short walk away, on the southern bank of the river at Itäinen Rantakatu 38, the **Wäinö Aaltonen Museum** (Tues–Sun 11am–7pm; from €4, depending on exhibition) is devoted to the best-known modern Finnish sculptor, who grew up close to Turku and studied at the local art school – his imaginative and sensitive work turns up in every major Finnish town. Crossing back over Aurajoki and down Linnankatu and then towards the mouth of the river will bring you to **Turku Castle** (daily 10am–3/6pm; mid-Sept to mid-April closed Mon; €5). The featureless exterior conceals a maze of cobbled courtyards, corridors and staircases, with a bewildering array of intriguing finds and displays. The castle probably went up around 1280; the seat of government for centuries, its gradual expansion accounts for the patchwork architecture.

Practicalities

The river Aura splits the city, its tree-lined banks forming a natural promenade as well as a useful landmark. On the northern side of the river is Turku's central grid, where you'll find the **tourist office** at Aurakatu 4 (Mon–Fri 8.30am–6pm, Sat & Sun 9am–4pm; ☎02/262 7444). Both the **train** and **bus station** are within easy walking distance of the river, just north of the centre; for the Stockholm ferry, stay on the train for the terminal, 2km west, or catch bus #1 on Linnankatu. There's an **InterRail Centre** at Eerikinkatu 7 (mid-July to mid-Aug), right by the river, where you can shower, leave luggage, rent bicycles and eat cheaply.

There are some good deals to be had at Turku's mid-range **hotels**, especially if you make an early reservation and pick a weekend. Try *Hotel Julia*, Eerikinkatu 4 (☎02/336 311; ❹), or for a real slice of luxury and character try *Park Hotel*, Rauhankatu 1 (☎02/273 2555; ❻). Alvar Aalto fans should stay at *Quality Hotel Ateljee* (☎02/336 111; ❺), Humalistonkatu 7, housed in a building designed by Finland's most famous architect; ask for room no. 422 or 534. The excellent **hostel**, *Hostel Turku*, is by the river at Linnankatu 39 (☎02/262 7680; ❸); take bus #1 or #30. The nearest **campsite** (☎050/559 0139; June to mid-Aug; bus #8) is on the island of Ruissalo, which has two sandy beaches and overlooks Turku harbour. There's free **internet** access at the central library, Linnankatu 2.

For excellent **food** at sensible prices, it's worth trekking out to *Turun Hotelli Ravintola Oppilaitos* in the Data Centre, close to Turku hospital (take the train one stop to Kupittaa); run by the catering college, the food and service are excellent. In the centre, *Gadolinia*, a **student mensa**, part of Åbo Akademi on Porthaninkatu, offers the cheapest food; or there's *Pizzeria Dennis*, Linnankatu 17, for affordably priced pizza. Near the tourist office **Market Square** (*Kauppatori*) sells fresh produce, and in summer is full of open-air cafés; nearby, the effervescent market hall or **Kauppahalli** (Mon–Fri 8am–5pm, Sat 8am–2pm) offers a slightly more upmarket choice of delis and other eateries. Top-notch food can be had at *Herman*, Läntinen Rantakatu 37, in a bright, airy storehouse dating from 1849, with excellent lunches (€7). Floating restaurants change each summer, but look out for *Papa Joe* and *Svarte Rudolph*. The most popular **drinking** venue is *Uusi Apteekki*, Kaskenkatu 1, which, true to its name, is an old pharmacy complete with ancient fittings.

The Lake Region

About a third of Finland is consumed by the **Lake Region**, a huge area of bays, inlets and islands, interspersed with dense forests. Despite holding much of Finland's industry, it's a tranquil, verdant region, and even **Tampere**, the major industrial city, enjoys a peaceful lakeside setting. The eastern part of the region is the most atmospheric, slender ridges furred with conifers linking the few sizeable landmasses. While the regional centre, **Savonlinna**, stretches delectably across several islands and boasts a superb medieval castle.

Tampere

TAMPERE, a leafy place of parks and lakes, is Finland's biggest manufacturing centre and Scandinavia's largest inland city. Its rapid growth began just over a century ago, when the Scotsman James Finlayson opened a textile factory, drawing labour from rural areas where traditional crafts were in decline. Metalwork and shoe factories soon followed, their owners paternally promoting a vigorous local arts scene for the workforce. Free outdoor concerts, lavish theatrical productions and one of the best modern art collections in Finland maintain such traditions to this day.

Almost everything of consequence is within the central section, a thin strip of land bordered on two sides by lakes Näsijärvi and Pyhäjärvi. The main streets run off either side of Hämeenkatu, which leads directly from the train station across Hämeensilta. Left off Hämeenkatu, up slender Hämeenpuisto, the **Lenin Museum** (Mon–Fri 9am–6pm, Sat & Sun 11am–4pm; €4) remembers the time when Lenin lived in Finland and attended the Tampere conferences, held in what is now the museum. Nearby, at Puutarhakatu 34, the **Art Museum of Tampere** (Tues–Sun 10am–6pm; €4) holds temporary exhibitions, but if you're looking for Finnish art you might be better off visiting the **Hiekka Art Gallery**, a few minutes' walk away at Pirkankatu 6 (Tues–Thurs 3–6pm, Sun noon–3pm; €4), which has sketches by Gallen-Kallela and Helene Schjerfbeck. Better still is the tremendous **Sara Hildén Art Museum** (daily 11am–6pm; €4), built on the shores of Näsijärvi, a quirky collection of Finnish and foreign modern works; take bus #16 from the centre.

Practicalities

The city's **tourist office** is by the river, 500m from the **train station** at Verkatehtaankatu 2 (Mon–Fri 8.30am–5/8pm; June–Aug also Sat & Sun 11am–3pm; ☎03/3146 6800, ❽www.tampere.fi), and a similar distance along Hatanpään from the **bus station**. Along with all the usual services, the tourist office also offers free **internet access**. Central, moderately priced **hotels** include the *Victoria*, Itsenäisyydenkatu 1 (☎03/242 5111; ❺), and *Sokos Hotel Villa*, Sumeliuksenkatu 14 (☎03/262 6267; ❺). There are various **hostels**, the best being the *Uimahallin maja*, an HI hostel centrally located at Pirkankatu 10–12 (☎03/222 9460; ❸), and the *NNKY* opposite the cathedral at Tuomiokirkonkatu 12a

(☎03/2524020; June–Aug; ❸). The nearest **campsite** is *Härmälä*, 5km south (☎03/2651355; mid-May to late Aug; bus #1), which also has cabins.

The cheapest places to eat are the **student mensas** at the university at the end of Yliopistonkatu; the usual pizza joints such as *Paprika* on the second floor of the *Hostel Uimahallion Maja*, Pirkankatu 10–12; and, for relaxed posing, *Café Strindberg*, opposite the train station. For a local speciality, try *mustamakkara*, a type of black sausage, at the Laukontori open-air **market** by the rapids. For **drinking**, the busiest and trendiest place is *Café Europa* at Aleksanterinkatu, which, despite its name, is more bar than café. Also worth a look is *Plevna*, a German-style beer hall in Finlayson's converted factory on Kuninkaankatu, which is especially busy at weekends; for live music, head for *Tullikamari*, a **nightclub** in an old customs house on Itsenäsyydenkatu behind the train station.

Savonlinna and around

SAVONLINNA is one of the most relaxed towns in Finland, a woodworking centre that also makes a decent living from tourism and its renowned **opera festival** (ⓦwww.operafestival.fi) in July. It's packed throughout summer, so book well ahead if you're visiting at this time. Out of peak season, its streets and beaches are uncluttered, and the town's easy-going mood makes it a pleasant place to linger.

The best locations for soaking up the atmosphere are the **harbour** and **market square** at the end of Olavinkatu, where you can cast an eye over the grand **Seurahuone Hotel**, with its Art Nouveau fripperies. Follow the harbour around Linnankatu, or better still around the sandy edge of Pihlajavesi, which brings you to atmospheric and surprisingly well-preserved **Olavinlinna Castle** (guided tours daily 10am–3/5pm; €5), perched on a small island. Founded in 1475, the castle witnessed a series of bloody conflicts until the Russians claimed possession of it in 1743 and relegated it to the status of town jail. Nearby is the **Savonlinna Regional Museum** (July to mid-Aug daily 11am–5/8pm; rest of the year closed Mon; €3), which occupies an old granary and displays an intriguing account of the evolution of local life, with rock paintings and ancient amber carved with human figures.

Practicalities

There are two **train stations**; be sure to get off at Savonlinna-Kauppatori, just across the main bridge from the **tourist office**, Puistokatu 1 (June & Aug daily 8am–6pm, till 10pm during festival; rest of year, Mon–Fri 9am–4pm; ☎015/517 510, ⓦwww.travel.fi/fin/Savonlinna). The **bus station** is off the main island, but within easy walking distance of the town centre. **Bikes** can be rented at several places on Olavinkatu, including at Koponen, no. 42 (☎015/533977). For information and tickets for the **festival** visit the opera office, Olavinkatu 27 (☎015/476 7515, ⓦwww.operafestival.fi).

The most central **accommodation** is at the *Perehotelli Hospits*, Linnankatu 20 (☎015/515661; ❺). There is a **hostel**, *Malakias*, Pihlajavedenkatu 6 (☎015/533 283; July to early Aug only; ❸), 2km west of the centre along Tulliportinkatu and then Savontie, and a summer hotel, the *Vuorilinna*, on Kasinonsaari (☎015/739 5494; ❺), five minutes over the bridge from the marketplace. The nearest **campsite** is 7km from the centre at Vuohimäki (☎015/537 353; June–Aug; bus #4). Good, cheap **food** is available at the pizza joints along Olavinkatu and Tulliportinkatu. *Majakka*, Satamakatu 11, offers good Finnish nosh at lunchtime, though the most adventurous place to try is *Paviljonki*, Rajalatiendenkatu 4, where Finland's top trainee chefs serve their latest creations.

Around Savonlinna

Savonlinna boasts beautiful scenery all around, and the place to sample it is **Punkaharju Ridge**, a narrow strip of land between the Puruvesi and Pihlajavesi lakes, 28km from town. Locals say it has the healthiest air in the world, super-oxygenated by abundant conifers. With the water never more than a few metres away on either side, this is the Lake Region at its most breathtakingly beautiful. The ridge is traversable by road and rail, both running into the town of Punkaharju and passing the incredible **Retretti Arts Centre** (June–Aug daily 10am–5pm/6pm; €15), set in caves gouged into three-billion-year-old rock and with a large sculpture park outside in which fibreglass figures by Olavi Lanu are entwined with natural forms. Trains and buses make the short journey between Savonlinna and Retretti.

Northern Finland

The northern regions of Ostrobothnia and Lapland take up a vast portion of Finland – one third of the country lies north of the Arctic Circle. It is sparsely populated and predominantly rural, with small communities often separated by long distances. The coast of **Ostrobothnia** is affluent due to the adjacent flat and fertile farmland; busy and expanding **Oulu** is the region's major city as well as a centre of high-tech expertise, though it maintains a pleasing small-town atmosphere. Further north, **Lapland** is a remote and wild territory whose wide open spaces are home to several thousand Sami, who have lived in harmony with this harsh environment for millennia. Here, though the long winters are eerily dark, summer days are long and bright with the Midnight Sun. Moving around is fairly easy as there is an extensive bus service and regular flights from Helsinki. Make sure you try Lappish cuisine, too – fresh cloudberries, smoked reindeer and wild salmon are highlights. **Rovaniemi** is the rather bland gateway to the Arctic North; from here a road leads on towards **Sodankylä** and **Inari**, both convenient bases, and on to Norway.

Oulu

OULU with its renowned university is a leading light in Finland's burgeoning computing and microchip industries. During the last century it was the centre of the world's tar industry and the city's affluence and vibrant cultural scene date from that time, though the old buildings clustered around the river bank are now somewhat overshadowed by the faceless office blocks of the past twenty years. In the centre of town on Kirkkokatu, the **City Hall** retains some of the grandeur of the late nineteenth century, when it was a luxury hotel, and you can peek in at the wall paintings and enclosed gardens. Further along Kirkkokatu, the copper-domed and stuccoed **Tuomiokirkko** (daily 11am/noon–1/8pm), seems anachronistic amid the bulky blocks of modern Oulu. Across the small canal just to the north, the **North Ostrobothnia Museum** (Mon–Thurs 8am–4pm, Sat & Sun 11am–5pm; €1.70) has a large regional collection with a good Sami section.

The connected **train and bus stations** are linked to the city centre by several parallel streets feeding to the *kauppatori* and *kauppahalli* (**markets**) by the water beyond. The **tourist office** is at Torikatu 10 (Mon–Fri 9am–4/6pm; mid-June to mid-Aug also Sat 10am–3pm; ℡08/5584 1330, ⓦwww.oulutourism.fi). Low-cost **accommodation** in the centre is available at the *Hotel Turisti*, opposite the train station at Rautatienkatu 9 (℡08/375233; ❺), which provides hostel-type accommodation during summer, when it takes the overspill from the official **hostel** at Kajaanintie 36 (℡08/880 3311; ❸; June–Aug), a fifteen-minute walk from the train station. There's a **campsite** (℡08/5586 1351) with cabins on Hietasaari Island, 4km from town; take bus #5 from outside the tourist office. Oulu boasts some charming **cafés** including *Sokeri Jussi* in an old salt warehouse on Pikisaari just over the bridge from the mainland, while *Katri Antell* on Rotuaari (Mon–Fri 8.30am–5pm, Sat 9am–2.30pm) is justly famed for its luscious, but expensive, cakes. Cheapest **meals** are at the pizzerias – *Fantasia* serves the best and also has a selection of Finnish dishes; *Oskarin* Kellari, opposite the train station, also serves a stuff-your-face lunch buffet for about €7.50. For **nightlife** try the eclectic *Panimo*, Kappurienkatu 13, a pub that is generally stuffed with Oulu's young and trendy.

Rovaniemi

Easily reached by rail, **ROVANIEMI** is touted as the capital of Lapland, though its administrative buildings and busy shopping streets are a far cry from the surrounding rural hinterland. The elegant wooden houses of old Rovaniemi were razed by departing Germans at the close of World War II, and the town was completely rebuilt during the late 1940s.

Aside from eating reindeer in the local restaurants, the best way to prepare yourself for what lies further north is to visit the 172m long glass tunnel of **Arktikum**, Pohjoisranta 4 (mid-June–Aug daily 10am–6pm; Sept–April closed Mon; €10; ᴡww.arktikum.fi), symbolically pointing north across the Ounasjoki river. Subterranean galleries along one side house the **Provincial Museum of Lapland** with genuine Sami crafts and costumes alongside the imitations sold in souvenir shops to emphasize the romanticization of their culture. Across the corridor is the **Arctic Centre**, which gives a thorough treatment of all things circumpolar. For a couple of weeks either side of midsummer, the **Midnight Sun** is visible from Rovaniemi, the best vantage points being either the striking bridge over the Ounaskoski or atop the forested and mosquito-infested hill, Ounasvaara, across the bridge.

The remaining sight is on the south side of town near the **bus** and **train stations**, where pristine Aalto-designed civic buildings line Hallituskatu. The city **library** (Mon–Thurs 11am–8pm, Fri 11am–5pm, Sat 11am–4pm) has a **Lapland Department** with a staggering hoard of books in many languages covering every Sami-related subject. Most other things of interest are outside town, not least the **Arctic Circle**, 8km north and connected by the hourly bus #8 from the railway station. On the circle is the **Santa Claus Village** (daily 9/10am–5/7pm; free), a large log cabin where you can meet Father Christmas all year round and leave your name for a Christmas card from Santa himself.

Practicalities

The main **tourist office** is at Rovakatu 21 (Mon–Fri 8am–46/pm; June–Aug also Sat & Sun 10am–4pm; ☎016/346270, ᴡww.rovaniemi.fi). The **hostel**, *Tervashonka* at Hallituskatu 16 (☎016/344644; ❸), is always crowded in summer – try to book in advance. Otherwise you can fall back on the **guest houses**, the best of which are within five minutes' walk of the train station: *Matka Borealis* is nearest at Asemieskatu 1 (☎016/3420130; ❹), whilst *Matka Outa*, Ukkoherrantie 16 (☎016/312474; ❹), is towards the town centre. The only other budget accommodation is the **campsite** (☎016/345 304; June–Aug) on the far bank of Ounaskoski, facing town, a thirty-minute walk from the station. For filling **food** at very reasonable prices try *Café Kisälli*, Korkalonkatu 35 (Mon–Fri 8.30am–5pm), or *Martina*, Koskikatu 11, for good value pizzas and pasta dishes.

Sodankylä

A two-hour bus ride north of Rovaniemi, **SODANKYLÄ** is worth a short stop-off on the road north to Inari. The **bus station** is at the northern end of the main street, Jäämerentie, where you will also find the **tourist office** at no. 7 (Mon–Fri 9am–5pm; July also Sat & Sun 9am–2pm; ☎016/618168). Next door is the **Andreas Alariesto Art Gallery** (Mon–Fri 10am–5pm, Sat 10am–4/5pm, Sun noon–6pm; €5), which has an engaging collection of Alariesto's early-twentieth century bold, colourful paintings, depicting the life, struggles and myths of the Sami. Just behind, towards the Kitinen River, is Lapland's **oldest surviving church**, dating from 1689, its plain roof of rough-hewn timbers crowding in on the narrowest of naves.

A good time to come to Sodankylä is in mid-June for Lapland's biggest annual cultural event, the **Midnight Sun Film Festival** (☎016/614 52, ᴡww.msfilm-festival.fi), but you will need to book **accommodation** well ahead. At other times there should be no problem in finding somewhere to stay. The *Kolme Veljestä* guest house, north of the bus station, at Ivalontie 1 (☎016/611216, ✉majatalo.kolmevel-jesta@pp.inet.fi; ❷), has comfortable rooms with breakfast, and use of the kitchen and sauna, included in the room rate. There's a **campsite** (☎016/612181; June to mid-Aug) just across the river, which also has cabins. Places to **eat** can be found along Jäämerentie with good pizzas at no. 25, *Pizza-Pirkko,* and good value Lapland dishes at the *Revontuli* at no. 9.

Inari

Roughly 220km north of Sodankylä, **INARI** lies along the fringes of Inarijärvi, one of Finland's largest lakes, and makes a rather attractive base from which to further explore this part of Lapland. The **bus** stops outside the **tourist office** (Mon–Fri 9/10am–4/7pm; June–Sept also Sat & Sun 10am–3pm; ☎016/661666, ✉inari.info@seo.inet.fi), on the main street, Inarintie, before continuing to Karasjok in Norway and the North Cape (latter June to late Aug only). Staff here have information on guided snow scooter trips in winter and fishing trips around the lake in summer. Close by is the excellent "Siida", the **Sami Museum** (daily 9/10am–5/8pm; Oct–May closed Mon; €7), one of the best museums in Lapland. An excellent outdoor section gives you an idea of how the Sami survived in Arctic conditions in their tepees, or *kota*, while the indoor section has a well-laid-out exhibition on all aspects of life in the Arctic.

Towards the northern end of the village, summer boat tours (€12) depart from under the bridge to the ancient Sami holy site on the island of **Ukonkivi**; a plaque marks an ancient site of worship rumoured to have been a place of sacrifice. If walking's your thing then check out the pretty **Pielpajärvi Wilderness Church**, a two-hour well-signposted 7km hike from the village. There was a church on this site as far back as 1646, and the present one dates from 1754.

Accommodation should not be too problematic, though Inari does get very busy during the summer. The *Inarin Kultahovi* (☎016/671221; ✉inarin.kulta-hovi@co.inet.fi; ❼) at Saarikoskentie 2 is a basic hotel with a decent **restaurant**. The *Uruniemi* **campsite** (☎016/671331, ✉pentti.kangasniemi@uruniemi.inet.fi; Oct–April advanced booking obligatory) is about 3km south of the village in a lovely location right by the lake.

Travel details

Trains

Helsinki to: Jyväskylä (12 daily; 3hr 30min); Oulu (8 daily; 7hr); Rovaniemi (5 daily; 9hr 45min); Tampere (hourly; 2hr); Turku (12 daily; 2hr).
Oulu to: Rovaniemi (5 daily; 3hr).
Rovaniemi to: Helsinki (5 daily, 9hr 45min); Oulu (5 daily; 3hr).
Savonlinna to: Parikkala for Helsinki (2 daily; 50min).
Tampere to: Helsinki (hourly; 2hr); Oulu (7 daily; 5hr); Savonlinna (2 daily; 5hr); Turku (8 daily; 2hr).
Turku to: Tampere (8 daily; 2hr).

Flights

Helsinki to: Ivalo for Inari (2–3 daily; 1hr 40min); Oulu (10–15 daily; 1hr) Rovaniemi (5–7daily; 1hr 20min).

Buses

Helsinki to: Porvoo (15 daily; 1hr).
Rovaniemi to: Sodankylä (5 daily; 1hr 45min); Inari (4 daily; 5hr 30min); North Cape (1 daily June to late Aug 10hr 30min).
Sodankylä to: Inari (4 daily; 3hr 30min).
Inari to: North Cape (1 daily June to late Aug; 5hr 30min); Rovaniemi (4 daily; 5hr 30min).

Ferries

Helsinki to: Stockholm (2 daily; 17 hr); Tallinn (15–25 daily; 1hr 40 min–4 hr); Rostock (3 weekly June to early Sept; 24hr).
Turku to: Stockholm (4 daily 10hr–11hr).

France

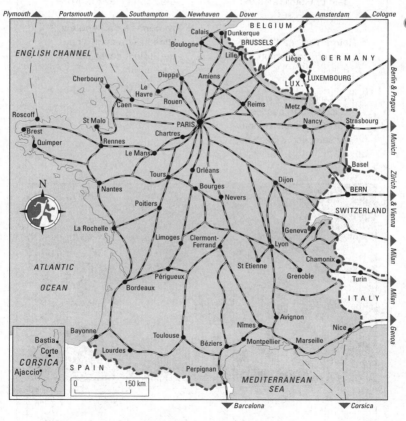

France highlights

* **The Louvre, Paris** Vast place, home to some of the most important artworks in the world. See p.352

* **Chartres Cathedral** A gem of Gothic architecture. See p.362

* **Reims** The heart of the Champagne region. See p.364

* **The Loire Valley** Not only studded with castles, but also a great region for sampling wine. See p.371

* **Carcassonne** A fairy-tale medieval city. See p.385

* **Palais des Papes, Avignon** Perhaps the most impressive medieval monument in the country. See p.401

* **Promenade des Anglais, Nice** Take a stroll along the Riviera coastline. See p.407

Introduction and basics

Straddling the continent between the Iberian peninsula and the nations of central Europe, **France** is a core country on any European tour. It would be hard to exhaust its diversity in a lifetime of visits. Each area looks different, feels different, has its own style of architecture and food and often its own *patois* or dialect. There is an astonishing variety of things to see, from the Gothic cathedrals of the north, through the boulevards and museums of Paris, to the Roman monuments of the south and the beaches of the Mediterranean and Atlantic coasts.

Travelling in France is easy. Budget restaurants and hotels proliferate; the rail and road networks are efficient; and the tourist information service is highly organized. As for where to go, it's hard to know where to begin. If you arrive from the north, you may pass through the Channel ports – Calais or Boulogne – or those of **Normandy**, to **Paris**, one of Europe's most elegant and compelling capitals. To the west lie the rocky coasts of **Brittany** and, further south, the châteaux of the **Loire**, although most people push on south to the limestone hills of **Provence**, the canyons of the **Pyrenees** on the Spanish border, or the glorious coastline of the **Côte d'Azur** towards Italy. There are good reasons, however, for taking things more slowly, not least the Germanic towns of **Alsace** in the east, the gorgeous hills and valleys of the **Lot** and the **Dordogne**, and, more adventurously, the high and rugged French heartland of the **Massif Central**.

Information and maps

You'll find a Syndicat d'Initiative (SI) or Office du Tourisme in practically every town and in many villages, giving local **information**, listings of things to see, free maps and, occasionally, bike rental. Some can book accommodation anywhere in France. In larger cities and tourist resorts these will be open every day during the high season, often without a break, although times are greatly cut back in most places in the winter months.

The best **map** of France is the Michelin no. 989 (1:1,000,000). For more regional detail, the Michelin yellow series (scale 1:200,000) is better. If you're planning to walk or cycle, check out the IGN green (1:100,000 and 1:50,000) and blue (1:25,000) maps.

Money and banks

France is one of twelve European Union countries which have switched over to the **euro** (€).

The best place to change money is a bank: standard **banking hours** are Mon–Fri 9am–noon & 2–4.30pm, some are also open on Saturdays. Rates of exchange and commissions vary greatly, but the Banque Nationale de Paris often gives the best rate for the least commission. The **exchange** counters – at the train stations of all big cities and usually one or two in the town centre as well – have longer opening hours, though normally offer a much worse deal. You can also change money at post offices and some tourist offices, and draw cash direct from **ATMs**, which are ubiquitous.

France on the net

ⓦ **www.tourisme.fr** French Tourist Board
ⓦ **www.franceguide.com** Excellent resource, with links to many tourist offices
ⓦ **www.discoverfrance.net** Useful tourist information, with links to other sites
ⓦ **www.viafrance.com** Information on festivals, expos, events and concerts
ⓦ **www.monum.fr** Information on major historical monuments

Communications

Post offices *(la Poste)* are generally open Mon–Fri 9am–7pm, Sat 8am–noon. You can also buy **stamps** *(timbres)* from *tabacs*.

International **phone calls** can be made from any box *(cabine)*. They take **phonecards** *(télécartes)*, available from post offices, *tabacs* and train station ticket counters. For calls within France – local or long distance – dial all ten digits of the number. The **operator** number is ☎12. To call Monaco from France, prefix the eight-digit number with ☎00377.

All towns have cybercafés offering **internet access** for around €4/hr. Post offices also offer access: to use their terminals you need a prepaid card costing €7.60 for the first hour. Street-side kiosks in major cities are operated by France Telecom *télécartes*.

Getting around

With the most extensive **rail network** in western Europe, run by the SNCF (⊛ www.sncf.com), France is a country best travelled by train. The only areas not well served are the mountains, where rail routes are replaced by SNCF **buses**. Private bus services tend to be uncoordinated.

Trains and buses

SNCF **trains** are generally clean, fast and frequent. **Fares** are reasonable, with a 300km journey costing around €30 and a 600km journey roughly €53 off-peak in second class. InterRail and Eurail **passes** are valid throughout the network, as is the Eurodomino (see p.21); though the numerous and ultrafast **TGV**s *(Trains à Grande Vitesse)* require compulsory reservation (€1.50–3) plus a supplement at peak times. The slowest trains are those marked *Autorail* in the timetable, stopping at all stations. All tickets (not passes) must be stamped in the orange machines in station foyers. Rail journeys may be broken any time, anywhere, for up to 24hr. On night trains, a **couchette** will cost an extra €14.

Regional **rail maps** and **timetables** are on sale at *tabacs*, and leaflet timetables are available free at every train station *(gare*

SNCF). All but the smallest stations have an information desk and most have *consignes automatiques* – coin-operated left-luggage lockers. Many also rent bicycles (see below).

The designation *Autocar* at the top of a timetable column means it's an **SNCF bus service**, on which rail tickets and passes are valid. Apart from these, the only time you'll need to take a **bus** is in cities; indeed the most frustrating thing about buses is that they rarely serve regions outside the SNCF network – which is precisely where you need them.

Cycling

Keen **cyclists** are much admired in France. Traffic keeps at a respectful distance (except in the big cities) and restaurants and hotels go out of their way to find a safe place for your bike. Bikes go free on some SNCF trains, though on others you have to pay €30 to send it to your destination – for details, consult the free leaflet *Train et Vélo*, available from most stations. Some SNCF stations also **rent bikes** for around €7.50 per day plus a €150 or €200 deposit (or a credit card number). You can return the bike to any other specified station.

Accommodation

For most of the year it's possible to turn up in any French town and find **accommodation**. Booking a couple of nights in advance can, however, be reassuring, and is essential from mid-July to mid-Aug, when the French take their holidays. The first weekend of August is the busiest time of all, though campsites still normally have room for tents.

Hotels

All French **hotels** are officially graded, and prices are relatively uniform. Ungraded and single-star hotels cost €15–30/double, two-stars €23–45; breakfast is sometimes extra, but you will nearly always do better at a café. Note that It is illegal for hotels to insist on your taking meals, but they sometimes do, and in busy resorts you may not find a room unless you agree. In country areas you will come across **chambres d'hôte** – B&B in a house or on a farm. These vary in standard and are rarely cheap, usually costing the equivalent of a two-star hotel.

Full lists of accommodation for each province are available from any French Government Tourist Office or from local SIs. In peak season it is worth getting hold of these, together with a handbook for the **Logis de France** – independent hotels, promoted for their consistently good food and reasonably priced rooms, and recognizable by their green and yellow logo.

Hostels and foyers

France boasts a wide network of official **hostels** (*auberges de jeunesse*), and most are of a high standard. However, at €6–14 for a dorm bed (more in Paris), they are sometimes no less expensive for a couple than the cheapest hotel room – particularly if you take into account fares to their sometimes remote locations. There are two youth hostel associations: the Fédération Unie des Auberges de Jeunesse, 27 rue Pajol, 75018 Paris (℡01.44.89.87.27, ✆www.fuaj.org), and the Ligue Française pour les Auberges de Jeunesse, 67 rue Vergniaud, 75013 Paris (℡01.44.16.78.78). **HI membership** covers both, though only those of the former are detailed in the HI handbook.

A few large towns provide a more luxurious standard of hostel accommodation in **Foyers des Jeunes Travailleurs/-euses**, residential hostels for young workers and students, charging around €11 for a room. Most also have a good canteen. In rural areas, **gîtes d'étape** – often run by the local village or municipality and less formal than the hostels – provide bunk beds and simple kitchen facilities. Tourist offices can provide listings and sell guides to *gîtes* and *chambres d'hôte*.

Campsites

Practically every village and town in the country has at least one **campsite**: thousands of French people choose to spend their holidays under canvas. The cheapest – starting at €4 per person per night – is usually the *Camping Municipal*, normally clean, well-equipped and in a prime location. On the coast especially, there are superior campsites where prices are similar to a hotel room for what can be extensive facilities.

Inland, camping on somebody's farm is a cheaper alternative, but never **camp rough** without permission: farmers have been known to shoot first and ask questions later. Lists of sites are available from tourist offices and at ✆www.campingfrance.com.

Food and drink

French **food and drink** is as good a reason as any for a visit to France. Cooking has art status, the top chefs are stars, and dining out is a national pastime, whether it's at the local brasserie or a famed house of *haute cuisine*. Eating out in France isn't particularly cheap, but as long as you avoid tourist hot spots, you should be able to get decent *plats du jour* with wine for around €15 or so.

Food

Generally the best place to eat **breakfast** is in a bar or café. Most serve *baguettes* (French bread) and have a basket of croissants on the counter to which you can help yourself; the waiter will keep an eye on how much you've eaten and bill you accordingly. **Coffee** is invariably espresso and strong. *Un café* or *un express* is black; *un crème* is with milk; *un grand café* is a large cup. In the morning, ask for *café au lait* – espresso in a large cup or bowl with plenty of hot milk. **Tea** (*thé*) is less popular, though most cafés and restaurants will have it on their menus. Hot chocolate (*chocolat chaud*) can also be had in any café. Every bar or café displays a full price list for drinks at the bar (*au comptoir*), sitting inside (*la salle*), or outside (*la terrasse*) – each progressively more expensive.

Cafés are often the best option for a light **lunch** as well, serving omelettes, sandwiches (generally half-baguettes filled with cheese or meat), and *croque-monsieur* and *-madame* (variations on the grilled cheese sandwich). On street stalls you'll also find *frites* (chips/french fries), *crêpes*, *galettes* (wholewheat pancakes) and *gaufres* (waffles). For **takeaway**, there's nothing to beat the ready-made dishes – salads and fully prepared main courses – from a *charcuterie* (delicatessen), which are also available at supermarket *charcuterie* counters. Buy by weight, or ask for *une tranche* (a slice), *une* *barquette* (a carton) or *une part* (a portion).

You can also eat lunch at a **brasserie** – like a restaurant, but open all day and geared to quicker meals; **restaurants** tend to stick to the traditional meal times of noon–2pm & 7–9.30/10.30pm. In major cities, town centre brasseries often serve until 11pm or midnight. Prices at both are posted outside. Normally there is a choice between one or more *menus fixes* as well as *à la carte*; the latter is more expensive, but often the only option available after 9pm. Look out, at lunchtime and in the evening, for the **plat du jour** (daily special), which for €10–15 in a cheap restaurant will often be the most interesting and best-value thing on the menu. *Service compris* means the service is included; if not, you need to add fifteen percent. Wine (*vin*) or a drink *(boisson)* may be included in a *menu fixe*, but when ordering your own wine ask for *un quart*, *un demi-litre* or *une carafe* (a litre). You'll normally be given the house wine unless you specify otherwise.

Drink

Where you can eat you can usually **drink**, and vice versa. Drinking is done most often at a **café** and at a leisurely pace, whether taken as an *apéritif* before eating, a *digestif* after eating, or as a meal's accompaniment. **Wine** *(vin)* is drunk at just about every meal or social occasion. *Vin de table* or *vin ordinaire* (table wine) is generally drinkable and always cheap, and in wine-producing areas can be very good indeed. Wines marked *AOC (Appellation d'Origine Contrôlée)* are another matter. They can be excellent value at the lower end of the scale – favourable domestic taxes keep prices down to €1.50 or so a bottle – but serious wines command serious prices. In a café, a glass of wine is simply *un rouge* or *un blanc*. If you select an *AOC* wine you may have the choice of a round glass (*un ballon*) or a smaller glass *(un verre)*.

Most of the **beers** you'll find comprise the familiar Belgian and German names, plus home-grown brands. Beer on tap *(à la pression)* is France's cheapest alcoholic drink, alongside wine – just ask for *une pression*. Stronger alcohol is drunk by some people from 5am as a pre-work fortifier, right through the day: **cognac** or **armagnac** brandies, dozens of *eaux-de-vie* (spirits distilled from fruit) and **liqueurs**. Measures are generous, but don't come cheap. **Pastis** is a refreshing and inexpensive aniseed-flavoured liquor (popular brands are Pernod and Ricard), drunk diluted with water and ice *(glaçons)*.

Commonly available **soft drinks** include fresh orange/lemon juice *(orange pressée/ citron pressé)*, while bottled **spring water** *(eau minérale)* – either sparkling *(gazeuse)* or still *(eau plate)* – is everywhere, but you can ask for tap water *(l'eau du robinet)*, which is free.

Opening hours and holidays

The basic **working hours** in France are 8am–noon & 2–7pm. Sunday and Monday are the standard **closing days**, though you'll always find at least one *boulangerie* (bakery) open. **Museums** open at around 10am and close 5/6pm, with reduced hours outside the mid-May to mid-Sept season, sometimes even outside July and Aug; they also tend to close on Mon or Tues, usually the latter.

All shops, museums and offices are closed on the following **national holidays**: Jan 1; Easter Sun & Mon; May 1; May 8; Ascension Day; Whit Sun & Mon; July 14; Aug 15; Nov 1; Nov 11; Dec 25.

Emergencies

There are two main types of French police – the **Police Nationale** and the **Gendarmerie Nationale** – which are, for all practical purposes, indistinguishable; you can report a theft, or other incident, to either. You can be stopped at anytime and asked to produce ID, so always carry your passport.

Under the French social security system every **hospital** visit, doctor's consultation and prescribed medicine is charged, though in an emergency not upfront. Although all employed French people are entitled to a refund of 70–75 percent of their medical expenses, this can still leave a hefty shortfall,

10

especially after a stay in hospital. In **emergencies** you will always be admitted to the local hospital *(hôpital)*, whether under your own power or by ambulance. To find a **doctor**, stop at any *pharmacie* and ask for an address. Consultation fees for a visit should be €15–23 and in any case you'll be given a *Feuille de Soins* (Statement of Treatment) for your insurance claims. Prescriptions should be taken to a *pharmacie*, which is also equipped – and obliged – to give first aid (for a fee). For minor illnesses **pharmacists** will dispense free advice and a wide range of medication.

Emergency numbers

Police ☎17; Ambulance ☎15; Fire ☎18.

Paris

PARIS is the paragon of style – perhaps the most captivating city in Europe. Yet it is also a deeply traditional, village-like and, in parts, dilapidated metropolis. Famous names and events are instilled with a glamour that elevates the city and its people to a legendary realm, and it is still keen to preserve its status as an artistic, intellectual and literary pacesetter.

From a shaky start, the kings of France gradually extended their control from Paris over their feudal rivals, centralizing administrative, legal, financial and political power as they did so. The supremely autocratic Louis XIV made the city into a glorious symbol of the pre-eminence of the state, a tradition his successors have been happy to follow. Napoleon I added to the Louvre and built the Arc de Triomphe, the Madeleine and the Arc du Carrousel, while Napoleon III had Baron Haussmann redraw the city centre. The habit of breaking architectural moulds has continued with the Pompidou Centre's luridly coloured tubing, the landmark steel-and-glass Louvre Pyramide, the enormous hollow cube of the Grande Arche de la Défense and the new L-shaped glass towers of the Bibliothèque Nationale.

The most tangible pleasures of Paris are to be found in its **street life** and along the lively banks of the river Seine. Few cities can compete with the cafés, bars and restaurants – trendy and traditional, local and cosmopolitan, humble and pretentious – that line every street and boulevard. And the city's compactness makes it possible to experience the individual feel of the different *quartiers*. You can move easily, even on foot, from the calm, almost small-town atmosphere of **Montmartre** and the Latin Quarter to the busy commercial centres of the **Bourse** and **Opéra** or the aristocratic mansions of the **Marais**. An imposing backdrop is provided by the monumental architecture of the **Arc de Triomphe**, the **Louvre**, the **Eiffel Tower**, the **Hôtel de Ville**, the bridges and the institutions of the state. As for entertainment, Paris is a world **cinema** capital, while the best Parisian **music** encompasses jazz, avant-garde, salsa and, currently, Europe's most vibrant African music scene.

Paris is divided into twenty postal districts, known as **arrondissements**, which are used by everyone to locate addresses. The first, or *premier* (abbreviated as 1er), is centred on the Louvre, with the rest (abbreviated as 2e, 3e, 4e) spiralling outwards in a clockwise direction: the inner hub of the city, where most of the major sights and museums are located, is covered by the first six *arrondissements*.

Arrival and information

Paris has two main **airports**: Roissy-Charles de Gaulle and Orly. **Charles de Gaulle**, or CDG for short, is 23km northeast and connected to the Gare du Nord by Roissyrail, a combination of free shuttle bus and the RER train line B (every 8min 5am–midnight; 35min; €7.60). There's also the Roissybus, which departs from both terminals and terminates at métro Opéra (every 15min 6am–11pm; 45min; €8), or two Air France bus lines, which depart from both terminals to métro Charles-de-Gaulle-Étoile and Porte Maillot (every 12min 5.45am–11pm; €10), or to Gare Montparnasse and Gare de Lyon (every 30min 7am–9pm; €11.50). **Orly**, 14km south of Paris, has two bus–rail links: Orly-Rail to the Gare d'Austerlitz and other Left Bank stops (every 20min 5.50am–10.50pm; €5.15); and Orlyval, a fast train shuttle link to RER line B station Antony then connection to the métro stations Denfert-Rochereau, St-Michel and Châtelet (every 10min 6.30/7am–10.30/11pm; €8.65). Air France buses go to the Gare des Invalides via Montparnasse (every 12min 6am–11.30pm; 30min; €7.50), Orlybus goes to métro Denfert-Rochereau (every 15min 6am–11.30pm; 30min; €5.50) and Jetbus (every 15min; 6.20am–10.30pm, 15min; €4.80) goes to the métro station Villejuif-Louis Aragon at the end of line 7. A door-to-door **shuttle** from either airport costs €15–23 (T01.43.90.91.91, Wwww.parishuttle.com).

Paris has six mainline **train** stations, all of which are served by the métro. You can buy national and international train tickets at any mainline station. Eurostar trains from London, as well as trains from northern France, Belgium, Holland, northern Germany and Scandinavia, arrive at the **Gare du Nord**; Eurostar have their own booking offices and departure lounge on a raised tier at one side of the station. The **Gare de l'Est** serves eastern France, Luxembourg, southern Germany, northern Switzerland, Austria and eastern Europe; **Gare St-Lazare** serves the Normandy coast; **Gare de Lyon** serves the south, the Alps, western Switzerland, Italy and Greece; **Gare Montparnasse** serves Chartres, Brittany and the Atlantic coast; **Gare d'Austerlitz** serves the Loire Valley, the southwest and Spain. All long-distance **buses** except Gulliver's and Hoverspeed use the main *gare routière* at **Bagnolet** in eastern Paris (métro Gallieni, last stop on line #3); Gulliver's coaches arrive at the corner of rue Maubeuge and blvd de La Chapelle near the Gare du Nord; Hoverspeed coaches arrive at 165 av de Clichy, 17e (métro Porte de Clichy or Brochant).

The main **tourist office** is at 127 av des Champs-Élysées, métro Georges V (daily 9am–8pm; Nov–Easter Sun 11am–7pm; ☎08.36.68.31.12, ⓦwww.paris-touristoffice .com). They have maps and leaflets, and can book last-minute accommodation for a fee of €1.20–8.30, depending on the category of hotel. There's an annexe of the tourist office at the Gare de Lyon (Mon–Sat 8am–8pm) and a seasonal office by the Eiffel Tower (May–Sept daily 11am–6.40pm).

City transport

Central Paris is relatively small, with a public transport system that is cheap, fast and meticulously signposted. The **métro** (abbreviated as M°) is the simplest way of getting around: stations are widespread, and the lines are colour-coded and numbered – with directions at stations signposted with the names of the end-station. The métro operates from 5.30am to 12.30am, after which **night buses** *(Noctambus)* run on eighteen routes from place du Châtelet near the Hôtel de Ville (every 30min–1hr 1am to 5.30am). Nightbus stops are marked with a black and yellow owl. The regular bus network runs from 6.30am until around 8.30pm.

Free route **maps** are available at métro stations, bus terminals and tourist offices. Flat-fare **tickets** (€1.30) are valid on buses, the métro and, within the city limits (zones 1–2), the RER express rail lines (the RER extends out into the suburbs; zones 3–5); tickets can be bought individually or, for slightly less, in **carnets** of ten (€9.30). Be sure to keep your ticket until the end of the journey; you'll be fined on the spot if you can't produce one. If you plan on using the network extensively, then consider buying a one-day *Mobilis* pass (€5/zones 1–2, €11.70/zones 1–5). Also available is the *Paris Visites* (€8.35/one day, €18.25/three days, €26.65/five days; zones 1–3), valid for the funicular, Montmartrobus and Noctambus, RER and short-distance mainline trains, with certain museum and monument reductions thrown in; however, the discounts are rather measly and don't include most of the major sights.

Accommodation

Compared to other European capitals, Paris is a relatively cheap place to spend the night – a double room in a decent and centrally located **hotel** can be found for as little as €27 – although you should always book in advance. There are also numerous **hostels**, runs by three organizations: the official French Youth Hostel Association (FUAJ), which is open to HI members only; the Maison Internationale de la Jeunesse et des Étudiants (MIJE); and the Union des Centres de Rencontre Internationaux de France (UCRIF).

Hostels

Aloha 1 rue Borromé, 15e ☎01.42.73.03.03, ⓦwww.aloha.fr. A popular, young and noisy independent with its own bar serving cheap beer. M° Volontaires. ❸

Auberge Internationale des Jeunes 10 rue Trousseau, 11e ☎01.47.00.62.00, ⓦwww.aijparis .com. Despite the official-sounding name, this is a laid-back (but very noisy) independent in a great location 5min from the Bastille. M° Ledru-Rollin. ❷

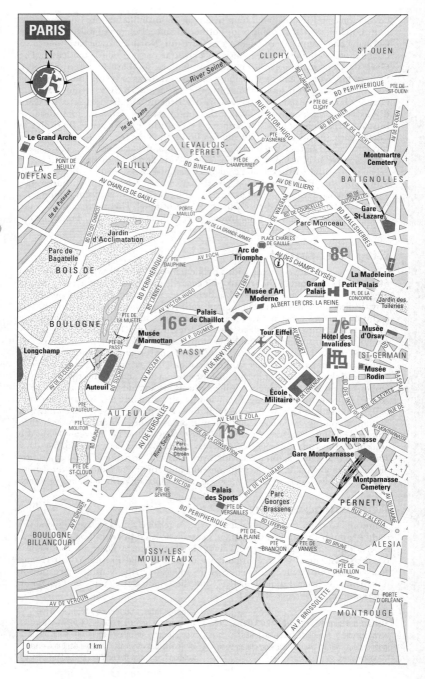

PARIS

N

CLICHY ST-OUEN

River Seine

Le Grand Arche

LA DÉFENSE

PONT DE NEUILLY

NEUILLY

LEVALLOIS-PERRET

BATIGNOLLES

Montmartre Cemetery

Jardin d'Acclimatation

Parc de Bagatelle

BOIS DE

BOULOGNE

17e

PORTE MAILLOT

Arc de Triomphe

Parc Monceau

Gare St-Lazare

8e

La Madeleine

Longchamp

Musée Marmottan

16e

Palais de Chaillot

Musée d'Art Moderne

Grand Palais

Petit Palais

PL DE LA CONCORDE

Jardin des Tuileries

Auteuil

Tour Eiffel

Hôtel des Invalides

7e

Musée d'Orsay

ST-GERMAIN

AUTEUIL

PASSY

École Militaire

Musée Rodin

15e

Tour Montparnasse

Gare Montparnasse

Palais des Sports

Parc Georges Brassens

Montparnasse Cemetery

PERNETY

ALESIA

BOULOGNE BILLANCOURT

ISSY-LES-MOULINEAUX

MONTROUGE

PORTE D'ORLÉANS

0   1 km

10

FRANCE

348

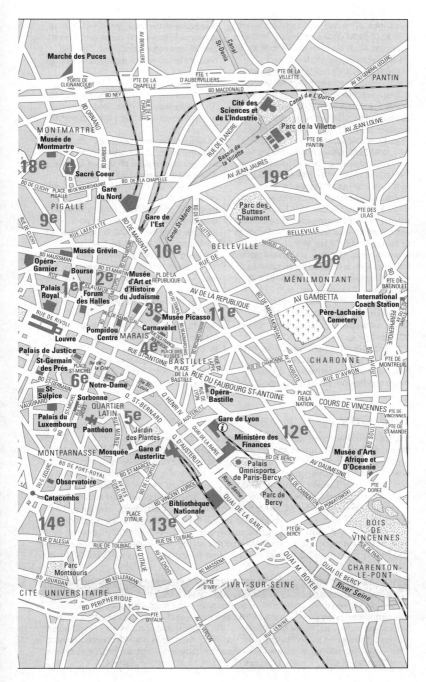

Marché des Puces

PANTIN

Canal St-Denis

Canal de L'Ourcq

PTE DE LA VILLETTE

AV DU GENERAL-LECLERC

PORTE DE CLIGNANCOURT

PTE DE LA CHAPELLE

PTE D'AUBERVILLIERS

BD MACDONALD

BD NEY

Cité des Sciences et de L'Industrie

Parc de la Villette

PTE DE PANTIN

AV JEAN LOLIVE

MONTMARTRE

Musée de Montmartre

18e

Sacré Coeur

BD ORNANO

RUE DE LA CHAPELLE

RUE DE FLANDRE

Bassin de la Villette

AV JEAN JAURÈS

19e

BD BARBES

BD DE CLICHY

PIGALLE

PLACE PIGALLE

BD DE ROCHECHOUART

BD DE LA CHAPELLE

Gare du Nord

Parc des Buttes-Chaumont

PTE DES LILAS

9e

PIGALLE

RUE LAFAYETTE

Gare de l'Est

BD DE MAGENTA

Canal St-Martin

BD DE LA VILLETTE

BELLEVILLE

BELLEVILLE

MANUEL JOSÉ QUINO

RUE DE CLICHY

Musée Grévin

BD HAUSSMAN

Opéra Garnier

Bourse

2e

BD ST-MARTIN

Musée d'Art et d'Histoire du Judaïsme

PL DE LA RÉPUBLIQUE

10e

RUE DE

20e

MÉNILMONTANT

PTE DE BAGNOLET

RUE

1er

Palais Royal

REAUMUR

Forum des Halles

RUE DE RAMBUTEAU

3e

Musée Picasso

AV DE LA REPUBLIQUE

BD DE MENILMONTANT

AV GAMBETTA

International Coach Station

RUE DE RIVOLI

Pompidou Centre

Louvre

MARAIS

Carnavelet

4e

PLACE DES VOSGES

11e

Père-Lachaise Cemetery

BD DAVOUT

PTE DE BAGNOLET

Palais de Justice

St-Germain des Prés

Île de la Cité

PLACE ST-MICHEL

RUE ST-ANTOINE

Île St-Louis

BASTILLE

PLACE DE LA BASTILLE

RUE DU FAUBOURG ST-ANTOINE

RUE DE CHARONNE

CHARONNE

PTE DE MONTREUIL

BD ST-GERMAIN

St-Sulpice

6e

Notre-Dame

Q. ST-BERNARD

Q. HENRI IV

RUE DE LYON

Opéra-Bastille

PLACE DE LA NATION

COURS DE VINCENNES

PTE DE VINCENNES

VAUGIRARD

Sorbonne

QUARTIER LATIN

5e

Q. D'AUSTERLITZ

Gare de Lyon

PTE DE ST-MANDE

Palais du Luxembourg

Panthéon

Jardin des Plantes

Ministère des Finances

12e

BD

MONTPARNASSE

Mosquée

Gare d'Austerlitz

QUAI DE LA RAPEE

BD DE BERCY

AV DAUMESNIL

Musée d'Arts Afrique et D'Oceanie

BD DE PORT-ROYAL

BD ST-MARCEL

RIVER SEINE

Palais Omnisports de Paris-Bercy

PTE DOREE

Observatoire

BD VINCENT AURIOL

QUAI DE LA GARE

Parc de Bercy

BD PONIATOWSKI

Catacombs

PLACE D'ITALIE

Bibliothèque Nationale

BOIS DE VINCENNES

14e

13e

PTE DE BERCY

RUE D'ALESIA

RUE DE TOLBIAC

RUE DE TOLBIAC

AV D'ITALIE

QUAI M. BOYER

QUAI DE BERCY

CHARENTON-LE-PONT

Parc Montsouris

BD JOURDAN

BD KELLERMAN

BD MASSENA

IVRY-SUR-SEINE

River Seine

RUE DE PARIS

CITÉ UNIVERSITAIRE

BD PERIPHERIQUE

PTE D'IVRY

PTE D'ITALIE

RUE LENINE

BVJ Centre 20 rue Jean-Jacques-Rousseau, 1er
☎01.53.00.90.90, ⓦwww.ucrif.asso.fr; M° Louvre
Rivoli); and 44 rue des Bernadins, 5e (☎01.43.29
.34.80, ⓦwww.ucrif.asso.fr; M° Maubert-
Mutualité). Central, efficient UCRIF hostels with
little to distinguish each from the other. Both ③
D'Artagnan 80 rue Vitruve, 20e ☎01.40.32.34.56,
ⓦwww.fuaj.org. Enormous FUAJ hostel with good
facilities, but it's a fair way out on the eastern
fringes of the city. M° Porte de Bagnolet. ③
Jules Ferry 8 bd Jules-Ferry, 11e
☎01.43.57.55.60, ⓦwww.fuaj.org. The smaller
and more central of the two FUAJ hostels – in the
lively area at the foot of the Belleville hill. Get there
early – it fills up fast. M° République. ③
Le Fauconnier 11 rue du Fauconnier, 4e ☎01.42
.74.23.45, ⓦwww.mije.com. MIJE place in a
superbly renovated seventeenth-century mansion
with a courtyard. Breakfast included. M° St-Paul. ③
Le Fourcy 6 rue de Fourcy, 4e ☎01.42.74.23.45,
ⓦwww.mije.com. MIJE place in a beautiful mansion
with small, four- to eight-bed dorms. Breakfast
included and restaurant on site. M° St-Paul. ③
Maubuisson 12 rue des Barres, 4e ☎01.42.74
.23.45, ⓦwww.mije.com. MIJE hostel in a
magnificent medieval building in a quiet street.
Singles and doubles available. Breakfast included.
M° Pont-Marie. ③
3 Canards (Three Ducks) 6 place Étienne-Pernet,
15e ☎01.48.42.04.05, ⓦwww.3ducks.fr.
Independent with bar, beer and use of kitchen.
Book ahead May–Oct. M° Félix Faure. ③

Woodstock 48 rue Rodier, 9e ☎01.48.78.87.76,
ⓦwww.woodstock.fr. This independent is in the
heart of Montmartre. Friendly staff, cheap bar,
courtyard and a lively atmosphere. M° Anvers. ③

Hotels
Burq Bonséjour 11 rue Burq, 18e ☎01.42.54.22
.53. Friendly place with clean, good-value rooms
on a quiet street in the centre of Montmartre. M°
Abbesses. ②
Le Central 6 rue Descartes, 5e ☎01.46.33.57.93.
Clean and decent accommodation on top of the
Montagne Ste-Geneviève. M° Maubert-Mutualité. ③
Grand Hôtel du Loiret 8 rue des Mauvais-
Garçons, 4e ☎01.48.87.77.00. Simple place but
good value. M° Hotel-de-Ville. ④
Henri IV 25 place Dauphine, 1er ☎01.43.54.44.53.
Well-known cheapie in the beautiful place
Dauphine on the Île de la Cité. Breakfast included.
Booking essential. M° Pont-Neuf. ②
Marignan 13 rue du Sommerard, 5e ☎01.43.54
.63.81. One of the best backpacker bargains in
town, with free laundry and self-catering facilities
provided. You'll need to book a month ahead in
summer. M° Maubert-Mutualité. ③
du Palais 2 quai de la Mégisserie, 1er
☎01.42.36.98.25. Cheap and ideally located, on
the riverbank, with some good views over Paris.
M° Bastille. ③
Tiquetonne 6 rue Tiquetonne, 2e ☎01.42.36.94.58.
Good-value place in a small, attractive street.
Closed Aug. M° Étienne-Marcel. ③

The City

Paris is split into two halves by the Seine. On the north of the river, the **Right
Bank** *(rive droite)* is home to the grand boulevards and most monumental buildings, many dating from Haussmann's nineteenth-century redevelopment, and is
where you'll probably spend most time, during the day at least. The top museums
are here – the Louvre and Beaubourg, to name just two – as well as the city's
widest range of shops around rue de Rivoli and Les Halles; and there are also
peaceful quarters like the Marais for idle strolling. The **Left Bank** *(rive gauche)* has a
noticeably different feel, its very name conjuring Bohemian, dissident, intellectual
connotations, and something of this atmosphere survives in the city's best range of
bars and restaurants, and its most wanderable streets: the areas around St-Germain
and St-Michel are full of nooks and crannies to explore. Parts of Paris, of course,

---

Museum pass

If you plan to see more than a few museums during your stay, it's a good idea to invest
in a **museum pass** (€15/one day, €30/three days, €45/five days), available at all participating museums, some tourist offices, the larger métro stations and FNAC ticket
offices (there's one in Les Halles). Note that many **museums** offer discounted entry to
the under-25s and have reduced fees for all on Sundays – and are often free on the
first Sunday of every month. Most are closed on Mondays or Tuesdays.

don't sit easily in either category. **Montmartre**, rising up to the north of the centre, has managed to retain a village-like, almost rural atmosphere despite the daily influx of tourists, with its colourful mix of locals and artists. The dilapidated quarters of **eastern Paris**, undisturbed by tourism, offer a rich, ethnically diverse slice of Parisian streetlife; in direct contrast, the ground-breaking science museum in the recently renovated **Parc de la Villette** celebrates technological wonder.

The Arc de Triomphe, Champs-Élysées and place de la Concorde

Voie Triomphale (Triumphal Way) stretches in a straight line from the Louvre to the corporate skyscrapers at La Défense, 9km northwest, and has some of the city's most famous landmarks. The best view is from the top of the **Arc de Triomphe**, Napoleon's homage to the armies of France and himself (daily 10am–10.30/11pm; €7, €4.50 for under-25s; métro Charles-de-Gaulle-Étoile), at the centre of **place Charles-de-Gaulle** – which is still better known as place de l'Étoile – where traffic swarms from the twelve avenues leading into it. From here, Paris's most famous street, the **Champs-Élysées**, sweeps gracefully southeast to the equally traffic-bound **place de la Concorde**, whose centrepiece, an obelisk from the temple of Luxor, was given to the city by the viceroy of Egypt in 1829. The symmetry continues beyond the square in the formal layout of the **Jardin des Tuileries** (daily 8/9am–7/8pm; métro Concorde), which stretches down to the Louvre. Towards the river, the **Orangerie** (currently undergoing renovation; due for completion 2004) displays Monet's largest water-lily paintings, as well as Cézanne's southern landscapes and portraits by van Dongen, Utrillo and Modigliani.

The Louvre

On the east side of the Jardin des Tuileries is the home of the *Mona Lisa*, the **Louvre** (Mon & Wed–Sun 9am–6/9.45pm; €7.50, €5 after 3pm and all day Sun; métro Palais Royal-Musée du Louvre/Louvre-Rivoli; ⑩www.louvre.com). The building was first opened to the public in 1793, during the Revolution, and within a decade Napoleon had made it the largest art collection on earth with the takings from his empire. It's a vast collection that would take months to see in detail.

I.M. Pei's stunning **glass pyramid** is the main entrance, with an alternative entrance at the Portes des Lions. Recent building work has allowed the excavation of what remains of the **medieval Louvre** under the Cour Carrée – Philippe-Auguste's twelfth-century fortress and Charles V's fourteenth-century palace conversion. The foundations and archeological findings are on show along with a permanent exhibition on the history of the Louvre on the *entresol* floor in the Sully wing. **Oriental Antiquities** – including the recently presented Islamic Art collection – covers the Sumerian, Babylonian, Assyrian and Phoenician civilizations, plus the art of ancient Persia. **Egyptian Antiquities** comprise jewellery, domestic objects, sandals, sarcophagi and dozens of examples of the delicate naturalism of Egyptian decorative technique, and statues like the pink granite *Mastaba Sphinx*. **Greek and Roman Antiquities**, divided between the Denon and Sully wings, include the *Winged Victory of Samothrace* and the famous *Venus de Milo*. The **Objets d'Art** collection is heavily weighted on the side of imperial opulence, but also includes a great deal of impressive tapestry as well as smaller, less public items, such as the carved Parisian ivories of the thirteenth century and the Limoges enamels. **Sculpture** covers the entire development of the art in France from Romanesque to Rodin, all in the new Richelieu wing, plus Italian and northern European sculpture in Denon, including Michelangelo's *Slaves*, designed for the tomb of Pope Julius II.

The largest section by far, however, is **Painting**: French from the year dot to mid-nineteenth century, along with Italian, Dutch, German, Flemish and Spanish. The *Mona Lisa* (in Denon) is the painting most people head for, and it is normally swamped with onlookers; hardly anyone pays the slightest attention to the other Leonardos nearby, such as the *Virgin of the Rocks*. There is a good selection of other

Italian paintings, including works by Giotto, Botticelli, Titian, Tintoretto and Mantegna (a *Crucifixion*), one of Uccello's *Battle of San Romano* series and, most strikingly, Paolo Veronese's huge *Marriage at Cana*, painted in 1563. Among the Flemish and Dutch paintings in the Richelieu Wing are Quentin Matsys' moralistic *Moneychanger and his Wife*, Memling's *Mystic Marriage of St Catherine*, Rembrandt's masterful *Supper at Emmaus*, and several works by Rubens. The works of Caravaggio are also richly represented, and the two exquisite Vermeers in the last part of the Richelieu are certainly worth the wait. There are French paintings of all periods, notably works by Poussin and later canvases by the great nineteenth-century artists David, Ingres and Delacroix. Géricault's harrowing *Raft of Medusa* made his name as an artist.

The Opéra, Les Halles and the Pompidou Centre

A short walk north of the Louvre is the **Opéra-Garnier**, on place de l'Opéra. A preposterously ornate building, it was designed by Charles Garnier and built in 1875 as the venue for opera in Paris, but since the completion of the Opéra-Bastille in 1989 it has been used chiefly for ballet. You can see the splendid interior (daily 10am–5pm; €4.88; métro Opéra), including the auditorium, where the domed ceiling is the work of Chagall; there's also a small museum. A short walk northeast brings you to the **Musée Grévin**, 10 blvd Montmartre (daily 10am–7pm; €15; métro Richelieu-Drouot; ⊛www.musee-grevin.com), a Paris institution since 1882 that displays around 500 wax statues of celebrities and historical figures. South of here is the area around the former **Les Halles** (a covered market), which was redeveloped in the 1970s amid widespread opposition and is now promoted as the heart of trendy Paris. In truth, the multi-layered shopping precinct at its core, the **Forum des Halles**, is a tacky affair, and it can be unsafe, too, especially at night – hence the high-profile police presence. During the day the main flow of feet is from here a little way east to the **Pompidou Centre** (métro Rambuteau; ⊛www.centrepompidou.fr). This seminal design by Renzo Piano and Richard Rogers was the first public structure to manifest the hi-tech notion of displaying its services on the outside, the tubing colour-coded according to function, leaving maximum space for the interior. Inside, the **Multimedia Library** (11am/noon–10pm, closed Tues) remains hugely popular, as does the ever-growing collection of the **Musée National d'Art Moderne** (11am–9pm, closed Tues; €5.49, €3.51 for under-25s), with pieces from the late Impressionists to the present day.

The Marais, the Bastille and Île St-Louis

Just east of Beaubourg, the **Marais** is a formerly fashionable aristocratic district that until some 35 years ago was one of the city's poorer quarters. Regentrification has since turned the renovated mansions into museums, offices and chic apartments flanked by designer clothes shops. A little way down the main drag, rue des Francs-Bourgeois, one of the grandest Marais mansions houses the **Musée Carnavalet** (entrance around the corner at 23 rue de Sévigné; Tues–Sun 10am–5.40pm; €6, €4.50 for under-25s; métro St-Paul), which presents the history of Paris from the reign of François I to the early twentieth century, with models, maps and plans, reconstructions of interiors and mementoes of the 1789 Revolution. Slightly further north, at 71 rue du Temple, the **Musée d'Art et d'Histoire du Judaïsme** (Mon–Fri 11am–6pm, Sun 10am–6pm; €6.10, €3.81 for under 26s; métro Rambuteau) has a fascinating display of Jewish artefacts and historical documents as well as some fine modern paintings by the likes of Chagall and Soutine. A short walk east, another mansion, the proud seventeenth-century Hôtel Juigné Salé at 5 rue de Thorigny, is home to the **Musée Picasso** (9.30am–5.30/6pm, closed Tues; €5.50, €4 on Sun and for under-25s; métro St-Paul). It is an overwhelming collection, much of which was the artist's personal property, and comprises the largest number of his works anywhere.

At the far end of rue des Francs-Bourgeois, off to the right, **place des Vosges** (originally known as Place Royale) is a masterpiece of aristocratic urban planning, a vast square of stone and brick symmetry built for Henri IV and Louis XIII. At no. 6, the **Maison Victor Hugo** (Tues–Sun 10am–5.40pm; €5.50; métro Bastille) is the former home of the writer of *Les Misérables*; not surprisingly, a whole room is devoted to posters of the various stage productions of the musical based on the book.

A short walk southeast, heading for the landmark column with the gilded "Spirit of Liberty", is **place de la Bastille**, the site of the Bastille that was famously stormed in 1789. The column was erected not to commemorate the surrender of the prison, which was subsequently demolished, but the July Revolution of 1830 – although it is the 1789 Bastille Day that France celebrates every July 14. The Bicentennial in 1989 was marked by the inauguration of the **Opéra-Bastille**, on the far side of the square, a bloated building that caused great controversy when it went up – a "hippopotamus in a bathtub", one critic called it.

Just south from here, across Henri IV bridge, the **Île St-Louis** is one of the centre's swankier quarters, with no monuments or museums, just high houses on single-lane streets. It's a peaceful and atmospheric route through to the Île de la Cité, either strolling down the centre along the shop-filled rue Île-St-Louis – a real weekend promenade with pedestrians taking over the street, many intent on queuing for an ice-cream at the famous *Berthillon* – or along the tree-lined *quais* down by the Seine. It is particularly atmospheric at night as the lights from the *Bateaux Mouches* cast shadows of the trees over the buildings, whose lit-up windows offer a glimpse of their elegant interiors.

Île de la Cité

Île de la Cité is where Paris began. It is the original site of the Roman garrison and later of the palace of the Merovingian kings and the counts of Paris, who in 987 became kings of France. Nowadays the main lure is the astounding **Cathédrale de Notre-Dame** (daily 8am–6.45/7.45pm; métro Cité), begun in 1163 under the auspices of Bishop de Sully and completed around 1345. In the nineteenth century, Viollet-le-Duc carried out extensive renovation work, remaking most of the statuary and adding the steeple and baleful-looking gargoyles, which you can see close up if you brave the 387-step ascent of the **towers** (daily 9.30/10am–6/10pm; €5.50). The sculpture of the west front portals is amazingly detailed, dating mainly from the twelfth and thirteenth centuries, while, inside, the immediately striking feature is the dramatic contrast between the darkness of the nave and the light falling on the first great clustered pillars of the choir. All this light is admitted by the end walls of the transepts, nearly two-thirds glass, including two magnificent rose windows in imperial purple that were added in 1267. In front of the cathedral, the **crypte archéologique** (Tues–Sun 10am–5.40pm; €3.30) holds the remains of the original cathedral, as well as of streets and houses of the Cité back as far as the Roman era.

At the western end of the island, the dull mass of the **Palais de Justice** swallowed up the palace that was home to the French kings until the bloody revolt of 1358 frightened them into the greater security of the Louvre. The only part of the older complex that remains in its entirety is Louis IX's **Ste-Chapelle** at 4 blvd du Palais (daily 9.30am–6pm; €5.50, €8 joint ticket with the Conciergerie; métro Cité). This was built to house a collection of holy relics and one of the finest achievements of French Gothic style, lent a fragility by its height and huge expanses of glorious stained glass, most of which is original. You should also visit the **Conciergerie**, Paris's oldest prison, whose entrance is around the corner facing the river on quai de l'Horloge (same times and prices). This was where Marie-Antoinette and, in their turn, the leading figures of the Revolution were incarcerated before execution. Its chief interest is the enormous late-Gothic Salle des Gens d'Armes, canteen and recreation room of the royal household staff, as well as Marie-Antoinette's cell and various macabre mementoes of the guillotine's victims. Outside the Conciergerie is Paris's first public clock, the **Tour de l'Horloge**, built in 1370.

The Eiffel Tower, Les Invalides and the Musée d'Orsay

A short walk south of place de l'Étoile is the **Musée d'Art Moderne de la Ville de Paris** in the Palais de Tokyo, 11 av du Président-Wilson (Tues–Sun 10am–5.30/6.45pm; €4.57; métro Iéna). This displays examples of the schools and trends of twentieth-century art, as well as sculpture and painting by contemporary artists. Among the most spectacular works on show are Robert and Sonia Delaunay's huge whirling wheels and cogs of rainbow colour, the leaping figures of Matisse's *La Danse* and Dufy's enormous mural, *La Fée Électricité* (done for the electricity board), illustrating the story of electricity from Aristotle to the modern power station in 250 colourful panels. The western wing of the Palais de Tokyo houses Paris's new **Site de Création Contemporaine** (Tues–Sun noon–midnight; €5; métro Iéna), a highly designed space given over to contemporary art exhibitions. A short walk down the river, at **Trocadéro**, the terrace of the Palais de Chaillot gives splendid vistas across the river to the **Eiffel Tower**. Though no conventional beauty, the tower is nonetheless an amazing structure, at 300m the tallest building in the world when it was completed by Gustave Eiffel in 1889. Reactions to it were violent, but it stole the show at the 1889 Exposition, for which it had been constructed. A **lift** will takes you straight to the top (daily 9/9.30am–11pm/midnight; €9.90; métro Bir Hakeim/RER Champ de Mars; ☻www.tour-eiffel .fr); if you're fit enough, you can save money by walking up as far as the second level (704 stairs; €3), from where you can join the lift for the final leg (€3). Daytime queues for the final stage can be massive, and the effort is only really worth it on an absolutely clear day. At night the queues are much shorter and the views often more impressive.

To the east, the **Esplanade des Invalides** strikes south from the river to the wide facade of the **Hôtel des Invalides**, built as a home for invalided soldiers on the orders of Louis XIV and topped by a distinctive gilded dome which is a real Paris landmark. One of its two churches was intended as a mausoleum for the king but now contains the mortal **remains of Napoleon** (daily 10am–6pm; €6) in a gallery decorated with friezes and captioned with quotations of awesome conceit from the great man. Immediately east, the **Musée Rodin** at no. 77, on the corner of rue de Varenne, is in the beautiful eighteenth-century mansion that the sculptor leased from the State in return for the gift of all his work on his death (Tues–Sun 9.30am–4.45/5.45pm; €5, €3 for under-25s; métro Varenne; ☻www.musee-rodin.fr).

A little way northeast along the river, on the quai d'Orsay, the **Musée d'Orsay** (Tues–Sun 9/10am–6pm, Thurs till 9.45pm; €7, €5 on Sun and for under-25s; RER Musée d'Orsay/métro Solférino; ☻www.musee-orsay.fr), converted from a disused train station in the mid-1980s, houses an outstanding collection of painting and sculpture from the pre-modern period (1848–1914). On the ground floor are works by the likes of Ingres, Delacroix, Degas, Daumier, Corot and Millet; on the top floor are landscapes and outdoor scenes by Renoir, Sisley, Pissarro and Monet. Cézanne is also wonderfully represented, as are Van Gogh, Gauguin, Seurat and Toulouse-Lautrec. The middle floor is dominated by sculpture, with some amazing works by Rodin, and several rooms of Art Nouveau and Jugendstil pieces.

The Latin Quarter, St-Germain and Montparnasse

The warren of medieval lanes around the boulevards St-Michel and St-Germain is known as the **Quartier Latin** because of the university that was here right up to 1789. The pivotal point of the area is **place St-Michel**, where the tree-lined **boulevard St-Michel** begins, its cafés and shops jammed with people – mainly young and, in summer, largely foreign. **Rue de la Huchette**, gathering-place of beatniks and bums in the 1950s, is now a bit of a tacky tourist trap, as is the adjoining rue Xavier-Privas. Close to the St-Michel/St-Germain junction, the walls of the third-century Roman baths are visible in the garden of the **Hôtel de Cluny** on place Paul-Poinlevé. This sixteenth-century mansion, built by the abbots of the powerful Cluny monastery as their Paris pied-à-terre, now houses the **Musée**

National du Moyen Age – Thermes de Cluny (Mon & Wed–Sun 9.15am–5.45pm; €5.50, €4 on Sun and for under-25s; métro Cluny-La Sorbonne), a treasure-house of medieval art that includes some wonderful, finely detailed tapestries. The real masterpiece is *La Dame à la Licorne* – six highly symbolic medieval scenes, probably made in Brussels in the late fifteenth century.

Immediately south of here, the **Montagne Ste-Geneviève** slopes up to the domed **Panthéon**, Louis XIV's thankyou to Geneviève, patron saint of Paris, for curing him of illness, which was transformed during the Revolution into a mausoleum for the great: its incumbents include Voltaire, Rousseau, Zola and Hugo (daily 9.30/10am–6.15/6.30pm; €7, €4.50 for under-25s; métro Cardinal Lemoine/RER Luxembourg). Down rue Soufflot from here, across blvd St-Michel, you might prefer to while away a few hours in the elegant surrounds of the **Jardin du Luxembourg** (daily 8/9am–7/8pm; métro Luxembourg), laid out by Marie de Médici, Henri IV's widow, to remind her of the Palazzo Pitti and Giardino di Bóboli of her native Florence. They are the chief recreation ground of the Left Bank, with tennis courts, a *boules* pitch, toy yachts to rent on the pond and, in the southeast corner, a miniature orchard of elaborately espaliered pear trees.

Beyond the Luxembourg gardens, the northern half of the 6e *arrondissement* is one of the most attractive parts of the city, full of bookshops, art galleries, antique shops, cafés and restaurants. It is also, perhaps, its most culturally historic: Picasso painted *Guernica* in rue des Grands-Augustins; in rue Visconti, Delacroix painted and Balzac's printing business went bust; and in parallel rue des Beaux-Arts, Oscar Wilde died and the crazy poet Gérard de Nerval went walking with a lobster on a blue ribbon. **Place St-Germain-des-Prés**, the hub of the *quartier*, is the site of the *Deux Magots* café, renowned for the number of politico-literary backsides that have shined its seats. On the other side of the Luxembourg gardens, **Montparnasse** also trades on its association with the colourful characters of the interwar years, many of whom were habitués of the cafés *Select*, *Coupole*, *Dôme* and *Rotonde* on blvd du Montparnasse. Close by, the colossal 59-storey skyscraper **Tour Montparnasse**, av du Maine, has become one of the city's principal landmarks since its construction in 1973; it can be climbed for less than the Eiffel Tower, but it is more than 100m shorter (daily 9.30am–10.30/11.30pm; €7.60; métro Montparnasse-Bienvenue). A short walk down blvd Edgar-Quinet, the **Montparnasse cemetery** (daily 9/9.30am–5.30/6pm; free; métro Raspail) has plenty of illustrious names, from Baudelaire to Sartre and André Citroën to Serge Gainsbourg.

Montmartre and eastern Paris

Montmartre lies in the middle of the largely working-class 18e *arrondissement*, a mixture of depressing slums towards the Gare du Nord and Gare de l'Est, and respectable, almost countrified pockets around its main focus on the hill, the **Butte Montmartre**. You can get up here by **funicular** from place Suzanne-Valadon or, for a quieter and prettier approach – though not for the unfit – climb stairs via place des Abbesses. The **place du Tertre** is the heart of touristic Montmartre, photogenic but totally bogus, jammed with day-trippers, overpriced restaurants and "artists" doing quick portraits while you wait. Crowning the Butte is the nineteenth-century **Sacré-Cœur** (daily 6am–10.30pm; free; métro Anvers/Abbesses), along with the Eiffel Tower one of the classics of the Paris skyline, although the best thing about it is the **view** from the top (dome and crypt daily 10am–5.45pm; €2.50).

North of place du Tertre, the house that holds the **Musée de Montmartre** at 12 rue Cortot (Tues–Sun 11am–6pm; €3.81; métro Lamarck-Caulaincourt) was rented at various times by Renoir, Dufy, Suzanne Valadon and her alcoholic son Utrillo, but its exhibits are disappointing. Close by, off rue Lepic, the **Moulin de la Galette** is the only survivor of Montmartre's forty-odd windmills, which were immortalized by Renoir. Down the hill from here the artistic associations continue in the **Moulin Rouge** on blvd de Clichy, although these days it's a mere shadow of its former self. This stretch – known as **Pigalle** – has always been a sleazy neighbourhood, the centre of the boulevard occupied by sideshows, the pavements dotted with transvestite prostitutes. At the western end, a little way up rue Caulaincourt, the **Montmartre cemetery** (daily 9/9.30am–5.30/6pm; métro Place de Clichy) holds the graves of Zola, Stendhal, Berlioz, Degas, Offenbach and François Truffaut among others.

East of Montmartre, the **Bassin de la Villette** and the **canals** at the northeastern gate of the city were for generations the centre of a densely populated working-class district but have recently become the subject of yet another big Paris redevelopment, whose major extravagance is the **Cité des Sciences et de l'Industrie** (Tues–Sun 10am–6/7pm; €7.50; métro Porte de la Villette; ❻www.cite-sciences.fr) in the **Parc de la Villette**, built into the concrete hulk of the abandoned abattoirs on the north side of the canal de l'Ourcq. Three times the size of the Pompidou Centre, this is the most astounding monument to be added to the capital in the last two decades, and is worth visiting for the interior alone – all glass and stainless steel, cantilevered platforms and suspended walkways, the different levels linked by lifts and escalators around a huge central space. Its permanent exhibition, Explora, on the top two floors, is the science museum to end all science museums, covering everything from microbes and maths to outer space.

South of La Villette, Paris' **eastern** districts – Belleville and Ménilmontant – are among the poorest of the city and not on most visitors' itineraries. However, the **Père-Lachaise cemetery**, on blvd de Ménilmontant, draws a fair number of tourists (daily 7.30/9am–5.30/6pm; métro Père-Lachaise), most of them heading for Jim Morrison's small, guarded grave in the east of the cemetery and Oscar Wilde's more extravagant tomb. There are countless famous others buried here – Edith Piaf, Modigliani, Abélard and Héloïse, Sarah Bernhardt, Ingres and Corot, Delacroix and Balzac, to name only a few.

The Beaux Quartiers, Bois de Boulogne and La Défense

South and west of the Arc de Triomphe lie the so-called **Beaux Quartiers**, the 16e and 17e *arrondissements*, in turns aristocratic and rich, bourgeois and staid districts, mainly residential, which hold little of interest save the wonderful **Musée Marmottan**, 2 rue Louis-Boilly (Tues–Sun 10am–6pm; €6.50; métro La Muette), whose Monet paintings were bequeathed by the artist's son. Among them is the canvas entitled *Impression, Soleil Levant*, an 1872 rendering of a misty sunrise over Le Havre, whose title unwittingly gave the Impressionist movement its name. Beyond the museum, the **Bois de Boulogne**, running down the west side of the 16e, is the city's largest open space, supposedly modelled on London's Hyde Park.

La Défense has been elevated to one of the top places of pilgrimage for visitors to Paris by the breathtaking **Grande Arche** (métro Grande-Arche-de-la-Défense), a 112m high hollow cube clad in white marble. Suspended within its hollow are open lift shafts and a "cloud canopy". You can ride up to the top (daily 10am–7pm; €7), but the views – right down the Voie Triomphale 6km to the Arc de Triomphe – are no more impressive than those gained from the series of steps which lead up to the Arch. Between here and the river is the business complex of La Défense, a perfect monument to capitalism that lacks any formal pattern to its dizzying arrangement of towers. Bizarre artworks transform the nightmare into comic entertainment, with Joan Miró's giant wobbly creatures and Alexander Calder's red iron interspersed between a coloured plastic waterfall and concrete flower-beds.

Eating

Eating out in Paris need not be an enormous extravagance. There are numerous fixed-price menus from €12, providing simple but well-cooked French fare, and a wide range of ethnic restaurants – North and West African, Chinese, Japanese, Vietnamese, Greek and lots more, though they are not necessarily any cheaper. Being vegetarian in Paris is not always easy, but there are a handful of vegetarian restaurants; Indian, Jewish and Italian restaurants are also a good bet for non-meat dishes. Anyone in possession of an ISIC card is eligible to apply for tickets for the **university restaurants** run by CROUS, 39 av Georges–Bernanos, 5e (☎01.40.55 .55.55); CROUS can provide a list of addresses, but you must buy your tickets from the restaurants themselves.

Snacks, sandwiches, cakes and ice cream

Berthillon 31 rue St-Louis-en-l'Île, 4e. Long queues for superb ice creams and sorbets. Closed Mon & Tues. M° Pont Marie.

Le Loir dans la Théière 3 rue des Rosiers, 4e. Peaceful retreat with laid-back, quirky atmosphere, leather armchairs, big tables and naive paintings on the walls. Sun brunch, superb midday *tartes* and omelettes, fruit teas and cakes served all day. M° St-Paul.

Mosquée de Paris 39 rue Geoffroy St Hilaire, 5e. Tea and cakes in this oasis of calm, popular with women. The boisterous restaurant next door serves some of Paris's best couscous. M° Jussieu.

A Priori Thé 35 Galerie-Vivienne, 2e. Classy *salon de thé* in a charming nineteenth-century gallery. More substantial dishes available, too. M° Pyramides/Sentier.

La Samaritaine 19 rue de la Monnaie, 1er. Wonderful views over the Pont Neuf, la Monnaie and the Conciergerie from the inexpensive self-service rooftop café of this Art Deco department store. M° Pont Neuf.

La Tartine 24 rue de Rivoli, 4e. A good selection of affordable wines, plus excellent cheese and snacks. Closed Tues & all Aug. M° St-Paul.

Restaurants and brasseries

Bistro de la Sorbonne 4 rue Toullier, 5e. Large portions of traditional French and North African dishes in a noisy, friendly ambience. Closed Sun. M° Place Monge.

Chardenoux 1 rue Jules-Vallès, 11e. An authentic oldie that still serves solid meaty fare at moderate prices. M° Charonne.

Chartier 7 rue du Faubourg-Montmartre, 9e. Good cheap food in an original and splendid turn-of-the-century soup kitchen. Expect to queue. M° Le Peletier.

Chez Paul 13 rue de Charonne, 11e. Lopsided corner building housing a small, popular restaurant serving traditional and affordable food. M° Bastille.

Le Commerce 51 rue du Commerce, 15e. Long-established place serving nourishing, inexpensive food. M° Commerce.

Flo 7 cours des Petites-Écuries, 10e. Handsome old-time brasserie, where you eat elbow-to-elbow at long tables. Excellent food and thoroughly enjoyable atmosphere. M° Château d'Eau.

La Fresque 100 rue Rambuteau, 1er. Good-value traditional French food served in an ex snail-merchant's hall. M° Les Halles.

Goldenberg 7 rue des Rosiers, 4e. Paris's best-known Jewish restaurant, Its borscht, blinis, strudels and other central European dishes are a real treat. M° St-Paul.

Higuma 32 rue Ste-Anne, 1er. Authentic Japanese noodle bar serving cheap, filling dishes and set menus. M° Pyramides.

Le Muniche 7 rue St-Benoît, 6e. Appealing old-style eatery with an oyster bar, mirrors and theatre posters, serving classic French brasserie fare. Can get crowded. M° St-Germain-des-Prés.

Perraudin 157 rue St-Jacques, 5e. Well-known traditional bistro with good-value lunchtime menus. Prices double in the evenings. M° Cluny La Sorbonne.

Le Petit Prince 12 rue Lanneau, 5e. Good food in a restaurant full of charm in one of the Latin Quarter's oldest lanes. M° Cardinal Lemoine.

Le Petit St-Benoît 4 rue St-Benoît, 6e. A simple, genuine and very appealing local. Solid traditional fare. M° Mabillon.

La Petite Légume 36 rue des Boulangers, 5e. Tiny homely vegetarian café with a mezzanine level and an organic, macrobiotic approach; though they do serve a bit of fish. Downstairs it feels like you're in someone's kitchen. Closed Sun. M° Jussieu.

Port de Pidjiguiti 28 rue Etex, 18e. Pleasant atmosphere and excellent food in this place run by a village in the West African state of Guinea-Bissau, whose inhabitants take turns in staffing the restaurant; all profits go to the village. M° Guy Môcquet.

Le Temps des Cerises 18–20 rue de la Butte-aux-Cailles, 13e. A well-established workers' co-op with elbow-to-elbow seating. M° Corvisart.

Thoumieux 79 rue St-Dominique, 7e. Large and popular place in this rather smart district serving standard French fare. M° Invalides.

Drinking

Most squares and boulevards have **cafés** spreading out onto the pavements and, although these are usually the priciest places to drink, it can be worth shelling out for a coffee for the chance to observe the streetlife. The Left Bank has some of the city's best-known and longest-established cafés, while the presence of the university means there are plenty of places to drink around place de la Sorbonne and rue Soufflot. The Bastille is now livelier than ever as the Opéra and rocketing property values bring headlong development, as is Les Halles – though the latter's trade is principally among out-of-towners up for the bright lights. The Marais offers small crowded watering holes and many gay bars; there are plenty of bars in Montmartre; while Ménilmontant and Belleville are popular but less obvious drinking haunts. You'll also find **wine bars**, the best of which are long-established places serving food as well as decent wine by the glass. There are plenty of establishments more geared to **beer**, most inspired by Belgian or British watering holes.

Bar de la Fontaine 1 rue de Charonne, 11e. Perfect corner spot for watching a slice of life from the pavement tables. An easygoing place where the clientele ranges from old characters in berets to a casual but hip twenty-something crowd, with a soundtrack of funk and soul. Open until 1 or 2am. M° Bastille.

Le Dépanneur 27 rue Fontaine, 9e. Popular all-night bar on a busy corner just down from place Blanche and the Moulin Rouge. M° Blanche.

Les Deux Magots 170 blvd St-Germain, 6e. Former haunt of Sartre and numerous famous others from the postwar years. Touristy now, with a terrace often besieged by buskers. Open till 2am; closed one week in Jan. M° St-Germain-des-Prés.

Café de l'Industrie corner of rue Sedaine and rue St-Sabin, 11e. Rugs on the floor around solid old wooden tables, paintings and miscellaneous

objects on the walls, and a young, unpretentious crowd. M° Bastille.

Café de la Mairie 8 place St-Sulpice, 6e. Famous yet unpretentious café that holds an enviable position overlooking the enormous St Sulpice church. M° St-Sulpice.

Le Rubis 10 rue du Marché-St-Honoré, 1er. One of the oldest wine bars in Paris, with a reputation for having some of the best wines, plus excellent snacks and *plats du jour*. M° Tuileries.

Le Sélect 99 blvd du Montparnasse, 6e. The least spoilt of the swanky Montparnasse cafés, still thriving since its 1920s heyday. M° Vavin.

Web Bar 32 rue de Picardie, 3e. This internet café is very Marais-chic, a multimedia centre that has films and videos on its menu, as well as offering low-tech storytelling and chess. Mon–Fri 8.30am–2am, Sat & Sun noon–2am. M° Temple.

Nightlife

Nightlife is as lively and diverse here as you would expect. The city's reputation for **live music** is impeccable; Paris is a centre of world music second-to-none in Europe, and there is excellent live jazz in numerous St-Germain and Les Halles clubs. The tradition of *chansons* – epitomized by Edith Piaf and developed to its greatest heights by Leo Ferré, Georges Brassens and Jacques Brel – endures, too, and there's an almost limitless choice of classical music and opera. Should you be after a place to dance, **clubs** come and go as rapidly as in any other large city, but there are one or two long-established places that won't let you down; most clubs open around 11pm, some stay open until sunrise. For **what's on** listings, there are two weekly guides, *Pariscope* (@ www.pariscope.fr; €0.40) and *L'Officiel des Spectacles* (€0.35), which both come out on Wednesdays; the former is easier to use and has a small *Time Out* section in English. The best places to get **tickets** are FNAC, Forum des Halles, 1–5 rue Pierre-Lescot, level 3 (métro Les Halles), and the Virgin Megastore, 56–60 av des Champs-Élysées (métro Franklin Roosevelt).

Live music venues

Le Bataclan 50 blvd Voltaire, 11e ☎01.43.14.35.35. One of the best larger rock venues. M° Oberkampf.

La Cigale 120 blvd de Rochechouart, 18e. Old-

fashioned theatre with an eclectic programme of rock. Long a fixture on the Pigalle scene. M° Anvers.

Divan du Monde 75 rue des Martyrs, 18e. Youthful venue in a café whose regulars once included Toulouse-Lautrec. An eclectic programme with a focus on world music. M° Pigalle.

La Guinguette Pirate quai de la Gare, 13e. Beautiful Chinese barge, moored alongside the quay in front of the Bibliothèque Nationale, hosting funk, reggae, rock and folk concerts. M° Bibliothèque.

New Morning 7–9 rue des Petites-Écuries, 10e. Famed jazz venue where blues, Latin and world music now also hold sway. M° Château d'Eau.

Petit Journal St-Michel 71 bd St-Michel, 5e. A small, smoky bar, long frequented by Left Bank student types, with good, mainly French, traditional and mainstream jazz. Music from 10pm. M° Luxembourg.

Satellit' Café 44 rue de la Folie-Méricourt, 11e. Multicultural acoustic evenings, anything from swing to folk, Brazilian to Balkan. M° République.

Clubs and discos

Les Bains 7 rue du Bourg-l'Abbé, 3e. A former Turkish bath-house, this is currently one of the hippest clubs in Paris playing house and garage with hip-hop on Wed. If you can get past the door policy, the spectacle of punters plunging into the pool by the dance floor awaits. M° Etienne Marcel.

Balajo 9 rue de Lappe, 11e. Old-style music hall or *bal musette* with extravagant 1930s decor and music ranging from mazurkas and tangos to slurpy *chansons*. Closed Mon & Aug. M° Bastille.

La Java 105 rue du Faubourg-du-Temple, 11e. Live Latin bands Thurs–Sat followed by DJs playing similar sounds. Older, energetic and friendly crowd. M° Goncourt.

La Locomotive 90 blvd de Clichy, 18e. Enormous hi-tech nightclub next to the legendary *Moulin Rouge* with two crowded dance floors and a very young crowd. M° Place de Clichy.

Rex Club 5 blvd Poissonnière, 2e. A happening club with strictly electronic music – house, drum'n'bass, etc. M° Bonne Nouvelle.

Classical music, opera and ballet

Salle des Concerts 221 av Jean-Jaurès, 19e ☎01.44.84.44.84. Adjustable concert hall with seating for 800–1200 listeners. The programme covers ancient music, contemporary works, jazz, *chansons* and world music. M° Porte-de-Pantin.

Salle Pleyel 252 rue du Faubourg-St-Honoré, 8e ☎01.45.61.53.00. The Orchestre de Paris performs here most frequently along with visiting international orchestras. M° Ternes.

Théâtre des Champs-Élysées 15 av Montaigne, 8e ☎01.49.52.50.50. Home to the Orchestre National de France, but also hosts international superstar conductors, ballet troups and operas. M° Alma-Marceau.

Théâtre Musical de Paris (Châtelet) 1 place du Châtelet, 1er ☎01.40.28.28.40, ⓦwww.chatelettheatre.com. As well as operas, the programme includes visiting ballets, concerts and solo recitals. M° Châtelet.

Opéra-Bastille 120 rue de Lyon, 12e ☎08.36.69.78.68, ⓦwww.opera-de-paris.fr. Paris's ultra-modern opera house is now the main place to see opera. Tickets cost €10 to €105, with the cheapest seats only available to personal callers; unfilled seats are sold at a discount to students five minutes before the curtain goes up. M° Bastille.

Opéra-Garnier place de l'Opéra, 9e ☎08.36.69.78.68, ⓦwww.opera-de-paris.fr. The original opera house now stages smaller operas and ballet productions. M° Opéra.

Films

There are over 350 **films** showing in Paris in any one week. Tickets cost around €7.50, €5.30 for students. Almost all of the huge selection of foreign films will be shown at some cinemas in their original language – *v.o.* in the listings (as opposed to *v.f.*, which means it's dubbed into French). Committed film freaks should head to the small *cinémathèques*, which show a choice of over fifty movies a week; tickets are only €4.75. The Forum des Images in the Forum des Halles, 2 Grande Galerie, Porte Eustache (métro Les Halles), is an excellent-value venue for the bizarre or obscure on celluloid; its repertoires are always based around a theme.

Gay and lesbian Paris

Paris has a well-established **gay scene** concentrated in the Halles, Marais and Bastille areas, and there are numerous gay organizations. For **information** visit the main gay and lesbian bookshop, Les Mots à la Bouche, 6 rue Ste-Croix-de-la-Bretonnerie, 4e (☎01.42.78.88.30, ⓦwww.motalabouche.com; métro Hôtel de

Ville); or the handy Centre Gai et Lesbien, 3 rue Keller, 11e (☎01.43.57.21.47, ⊛www.cglparis.org; métro Bastille), which has its own café. The CGL also produces a free guide map to gay Paris and a monthly publication, *Le 3 Keller*.

Banana Café 13 rue de la Ferronnerie, 1er. Popular, expensive and very fashionable. Try and catch the cabaret and go-go dancing. M° Châtelet/Les Halles.

Bar Hôtel Central 33 rue Vieille-du-Temple, 4e. The oldest gay local in the Marais. Small, friendly and always crowded. M° Hôtel de Ville.

Le Piano Zinc 49 rue des Blancs-Manteaux, 4e. A happy riot of songs, music-hall acts and dance, from 10pm onwards. One of the few venues patronized by both lesbians and gay men. Closed Mon. M° St-Paul.

Le Queen 102 av des Champs-Élysées, 8e. Very trendy mainstream gay club, with a strict door policy. It's also one of the hippest spots in town for heterosexuals – if they can get in. Mainly house music with big-name guest DJs. M° Georges V.

Le Quetzal 10 rue de la Verrerie, 4e. A trendy gay bar crammed with a well-toned and stylish clientele, with space for dancing. M° Hôtel de Ville.

Les Scandaleuses 8 rue des Écouffes, 4e. Trendy women-only bar in the Marais. Lively atmosphere guaranteed. M° St-Paul.

Listings

Bike rental Paris Vélo, 4 rue du Fer-à-Moulin, 5e ☎01.43.37.59.22 (M° Censier Daubenton); Paris à Vélo C'est Sympa, 37 blvd Bourdon, 4e ☎01.48.87.60.01 (M° Bastille).

Embassies Australia, 4 rue Jean-Rey, 15e ☎01.40.59.33.00 (M° Bir Hakeim); Canada, 35 av Montaigne, 8e ☎01.44.43.29.00 (M° Franklin Roosevelt); Ireland, 4 rue Rude, 16e ☎01.44.17 .67.00 (M° léna); New Zealand, 7 rue Léonard-de-Vinci, 16e ☎01.45.01.43.43 (M° Victor Hugo); UK, 35 rue Faubourg-St-Honoré, 8e ☎01.44.51.31.00 (M° St-Phillippe du Roule); US, 2 rue St Florentin, 1er ☎01.43.12.22.22 (M° Concorde).

Exchange Crédit Commercial de France, 103 av des Champs-Élysées, 8e (M° Georges V); also counters at main train stations.

Hospital 24hr medical help from SOS-Médecins ☎01.47.07.77.77.

Internet Cyber Cube, 5 rue Mignon, 6e (M° Odéon), 12 rue Daval, 11e (M° Bastille), and 3 rue Molière, 1er (M° Pyramides); Cyber Café Latino, 13 rue de l'École Polytechnique, 5e (M° Maubert-Mutualité); easyEverything, 37 blvd de Sébastopol, 1er (M° Châtelet/Les-Halles), 6 rue de la Harpe (M° St-Michel), and 15 rue de Rome (M° St-Lazare).

Left luggage Lockers at all train stations and *consignes* for bigger items.

Pharmacies Dérhy, 84 av des Champs-Élysées, 8e (M° Georges V).

Police 7 blvd du Palais, 4e ☎01.53.71.53.71 (M° Châtelet).

Post office 52 rue du Louvre, 1er (M° Louvre).

Around Paris

Around 32km east of Paris is **Disneyland Paris** (daily 9am–8pm; €36; RER A to Marne-la-Vallée; ⊛www.disneylandparis.com), a 5000-acre slice of the US grafted onto a bleak tract of the Bassin Parisien. For all the jokes about "Disneybland", the theatricality and professionalism of the place elevate it head and shoulders above any other theme park in Europe.

American pleasure parks aside, the most popular day-trip from Paris is undoubtedly to **Versailles**, but the most rewarding, the cathedral at **Chartres**.

Versailles

The **Palace of Versailles** (Tues–Sun 9am–5.30/6.30pm; €7.50, €5.30 after 3.30pm; ⊛www.chateauversailles.com) is one of the three most visited monuments in France. The palace, 16km west of Paris, is the apotheosis of French regal indulgence, its decor a grotesque homage to two of the greatest of all self-propagandists, Louis XIV (the "Sun King") and Napoleon. It's more impressive for its size than anything else, which, by any standards, is incredible. The most amazing room is perhaps the **Hall of Mirrors**, although the mirrors are not the originals; this is, more importantly, the room in which the Treaty of Versailles was signed, so bringing World War I to an end. You can also visit the state apartments of the king and queen, and the **royal chapel**, a grand structure that ranks among France's finest

Baroque creations. Outside, the **park** is something of a relief, and you could wander for hours through its vast extent. It is inevitably a very ordered affair, but the scenery becomes less formal the further you go from the palace, especially around the **Grand** and **Petit Trianons** (Tues–Sun noon–5.30/6.30pm; €5 for both). Beyond is **Le Hameau**, an area of thatched cottages, a mill and a dairy set around a lake where Marie Antoinette played at being a shepherdess.

The easiest way to get to Versailles is the half-hourly RER line C5 from Gare d'Austerlitz to Versailles-Rive Gauche (30min; €4.75 return).

Chartres

About 35km southwest of Versailles, an hour by train from Paris-Montparnasse, **CHARTRES** is a small and relatively undistinguished town. However, its **Cathédrale Notre-Dame** (daily 8am–7.15/8pm; ⦿ www.diocesechartres.com) is one of the finest examples of Gothic architecture in Europe. Its size and hilltop position are awe-inspiring, and there are more than enough visible wonders to enthral: the geometry of the building, unique in being almost unaltered since its consecration; the Renaissance choir screen and the hosts of sculpted figures above each transept door; and the shining symmetries of the stained glass, 130 windows in all, virtually all of which are original, dating from the twelfth and thirteenth centuries – the light coming through the rose windows is one of the wonders of Chartres. There's also a treasury and crypt, and you can climb the north **tower** (€4).

Though the cathedral is the main reason for coming here, Chartres town is not entirely without appeal, with a small old quarter and a picturesque district of bridges and old houses down by the river Eure. The **Musée des Beaux-Arts** in the former episcopal palace just north of the cathedral (Mon & Wed–Sat 10am–noon & 2–5/6pm, Sun 2–5/6pm; €2.40) has some beautiful tapestries, a room full of Vlaminck paintings, and Zurbarán's *St Lucy*, as well as good temporary exhibitions. The **tourist office** is in front of the cathedral, at place de la Cathédrale (Mon–Sat 9/10am–6/7pm, Sun 9.30/10am–1pm & 2.30–4.30/5.30pm; ☎02.37.18.26.26, ⦿ www.ville-chartres.fr), and can help with accommodation. Rue du Cygne is the place to look for **restaurants**.

The north

Northern France includes some of the most industrial and densely populated parts of the country. However, it is possible that you'll both arrive and leave France via this region, and there are curiosities within easy reach of the Channel ports – of which only **Boulogne** is worth a visit in its own right. Further south, the *maisons* and vineyards of the **Champagne** region are the main draw, for which the best base is **Reims**, which also has a fine cathedral.

The **main port** of entry is **CALAIS**, France's busiest passenger port with the shortest and most frequent connections to Dover, England. There's a **free bus service** during the day from the ferry dock alongside Calais-Maritime train station to place d'Armes and on to the central Calais-Ville **train station** in Calais-Sud. The **tourist office** is at 12 blvd Clemenceau (Mon–Sat 9am–7pm, Sun 10am–1pm; ☎03.21.96.26.40, ⦿ www.ot-calais.fr) and has an accommodation service, for which there is a small charge.

Boulogne

BOULOGNE is the one northern Channel port that might tempt you to stay. Its **Ville Basse**, centring on **place Dalton**, is home to some of the best *charcuteries* and *pâtisseries* in the north, as well as an impressive array of fish restaurants. Rising above, the **Ville Haute** is one of the gems of the northeast coast, flanked by grassy ramparts that give impressive views over the town and port. Inside the walls, the

Basilique Notre-Dame is something of an oddity, raised by the town's vicar in the nineteenth century without any architectural knowledge or advice. Its **crypt** (Tues–Sun 2–5pm; €2) has frescoed remains of the previous Romanesque building and relics of a Roman temple to Diana, while the main part of the church has a curious statue of the Virgin and Child on a boat-chariot, drawn here on its own wheels from Lourdes. Also worth a visit is **Nausicaa**, blvd St-Beuve (daily 9.30am–6.30/8pm; €9), claimed to be the largest marine complex in Europe.

The **tourist office** (Mon–Sat 9am–12.30pm & 1.30–6.30pm, Sun 10.15am–1pm; ☎03.21.10.88.10, ⊛www.tourisme-boulognesurmer.com), over the bridge as you leave the ferry terminal, can advise on availability of rooms, which in summer fill early. Your best bet is the friendly **hostel** in front of the train station, 56 place Rouget de Lisle (☎03.21.99.15.30, ⊜boulogne-sur-mer@fuaj.org; ❷). Most of the budget **hotels** are around the port area: try *Alexandra*, 93 rue Thiers (☎03.21.30.52.22; ❷), or *Hôtel les Arts*, 102 blvd Gambetta (☎03.21.31.53.31; ❸). For **eating**, there are dozens of possibilities around place Dalton and the cathedral, but you need to be selective. The brasserie *Chez Jules*, 8 place Dalton, is always a good bet and serves food all day. Opposite the cathedral on rue de Lille, *Estaminet du Château* offers inexpensive menus in a pleasant setting. Near place Dalton is the *Hamiot* restaurant, a decent alternative, while *La Houblonnière*, 8 rue Monsigny, has a vast international selection of brews to wash down its plats du jour.

Lille

By far the largest city in the far north of France, **LILLE** is the very symbol of French industry and working-class politics, but suffers from some of the country's worst poverty and racial conflict, and a crime rate rivalled only by Paris and Marseille. There is regionalism – the Lillois sprinkle their speech with a French-Flemish patois and, to an extent, assert a Flemish identity – but there is also classic French affluence here: the city has a lovely old quarter, along with some vibrant and prosperous commercial areas, and it's a place that takes its culture and its restaurants very seriously. Though not a prime destination, it is a stop for Eurostar trains between London and Paris, and is worth at least a night.

At the heart of the old quarter is the **Grand Place**. Also known as place du Général de Gaulle, who was born here in 1890, it's a busy square dominated by the old exchange building, the lavishly ornate **Ancienne Bourse**. A few minutes' walk north is the **Hospice Comtesse**, rue de la Monnaie, which is perhaps Lille's main sight. This former hospital now contains a selection of Dutch, Flemish and French paintings on loan from the Palais des Beaux-Arts in its old ward, the **Salle des Malades** (Mon 2–6pm, Wed–Fri 10am–12.30pm & 2–6pm, Sat & Sun 10am–6pm; €2.30). South of the old quarter lies the modern place Rihour, beyond which the stylish rue de Béthune leads into café-lined **place Béthune**, and on to blvd de la Liberté and the city's **Palais des Beaux-Arts** on place de la République (Mon 2–6pm, Wed–Sun noon–6pm, Fri till 8pm; €7).

The **train station** is only a few minutes' walk from the old town. The **tourist office** is in the old Palais Rihour on place Rihour (Mon–Sat 9.30am–6.30pm, Sun 10am–noon & 2–5pm; ☎03.21.21.94.21, ⊛www.lille.cci.fr). The *Hôtel Flandres Angleterre*, at 13 place de la Gare (☎03.20.06.04.12; ❹), is a reasonable and pleasant place to stay; you could also try the *Hôtel de France* at 10 rue de Béthune (☎03.20.57.14.78; ❸), which is right in the centre. The **hostel is** near the Hôtel de Ville at 12 rue Malpart (☎03.20.57.13.57; ⊜lille@fuaj.org; ❷). The nearest **campsite** is *Les Ramiers*, 10km north of the centre in Bondues (☎03.20.23.13.42; bus #35/36). The main area for **restaurants** is around place Rihour and place Béthune. For mussels – a local speciality – the brasseries around the station are as good as any in town, and *La Galetière*, 4 place Louise-de-Bettignies, is a pleasant crêperie. For **drinking**, monied local students hang around *Café 'Imaginaire* on place Louise-de-Bettignies.

Reims

Laid flat by World War I artillery, **REIMS** is not the most inspiring of cities, although there are two good reasons for visiting: it's the best centre (along with Épernay) for the Champagne region, and it's home to one of the country's most impressive Gothic cathedrals, once scene of the coronations of French monarchs. The battered west front of the **Cathédrale** is still a rare delight, with an array of restored and remarkably expressive statuary – although many of the originals have been removed to the former bishop's palace (see below). Inside, the stained glass includes stunning designs by Marc Chagall in the east chapel and glorifications of the champagne-making process in the south transept. Next door to the cathedral, the **Palais du Tau** (July & Aug daily 9.30am–6.30pm; rest of year Tues–Sun 9.30/10am–noon/12.30pm & 2–6pm; €5.30), in the bishop's palace, is worth a visit to see some of the dislodged west-front figures: there are grinning angels, friendly looking gargoyles and a superb Eve. The building also preserves the paraphernalia of Charles X's coronation in 1824. Most of the early kings were buried in Reims's oldest building, sited 1km east of the cathedral – the eleventh-century **Basilique St-Rémi** (daily 8/9am–dusk/7pm). Part of a former Benedictine abbey, it's an immensely spacious building that preserves its Romanesque choir and ambulatory chapels. You can also visit the adjacent monastic buildings, with more displays of stone sculpture and tapestries.

If you're in Reims for the **champagne**, head to place des Droits-de-l'Homme and place St-Niçaise, around which are most of the Reims *maisons*; most charge a small fee for their tours. If you're limiting yourself to one, the **Maison Veuve Clicquot**, 1 place des Droits-de-l'Homme (by appointment only; free; ℡03.26.89.53.90, ⊛www.veuve-clicquot.com), is one of the least pompous. There's also **Pommery**, at 5 place du Général-Gouraud (April–Oct daily 10am–4pm; Nov–March by appointment only; €7.50; ℡03.26.61.62.56, ⊛www.pommery .com), and **Taittinger**, 9 place St-Niçaise (Mon–Fri 9.30–noon & 2–4.30pm, Sat & Sun 9–11am & 2–5pm; Dec–Feb closed Sat & Sun; €5.50; ⊛www.taittinger.com).

Reims **train station** is on the northwest edge of the town centre, on Square Colbert. It's a five-minute walk to the **tourist office**, which is at 2 rue Guillaume de Machault (Mon–Sat 9am–6/7pm, Sun 10/11am–5/6pm; ℡03.26.77.45.25, ⊛www.tourisme.fr/reims). Among central **hotels**, the *Thillois*, 17 rue de Thillois (℡03.26.40.65.65; ❷), and the *Alsace*, 6 rue Général Sarrail (℡03.26.47.44.08; ❷), are the most affordable, and there's a *Centre International* with **dorm beds** south of the centre at Parc Léo Lagrange (℡03.26.40.52.60, ⊛www.cis-reims.com; ❷), twenty minutes' walk from the station. For **food**, place Drouet d'Erlon is lined with cafés and restaurants: try *A Casa Mia* at no. 84 or the more upmarket *l'Apostrophe* at no. 59. There's **internet** access at Clique et Croque, 27 rue de Vesle.

Normandy

To the French, the essence of **Normandy** is its produce: this is the land of butter and cream, famous cheeses and seafood, cider and calvados. Yet parts of Normandy are among the most economically depressed of the whole country. The Normans themselves have a reputation for being insular and conservative, with a hatred of Parisians with weekend homes in the region. Along the coast, there are occasional surprises, notably the picturesque harbour at **Honfleur**. Inland, it's hard to pin down specific highlights; the pleasures lie in the feel of particular landscapes – lush meadows and orchards, half-timbered houses, and the food and drink for which the region is famous. Of urban centres, **Rouen**, the Norman capital, is by far the most compelling.

The **main ports** of entry along this stretch of coast are Le Havre, Cherbourg and Dieppe. **LE HAVRE** is France's second largest port after Marseille and takes up half the Seine estuary, extending far further than the town itself. The **tourist office** (Mon–Sat 9am–6.30/7pm, Sun 10am–12.30/1pm; June–Sept also Sun 2.30–6pm; ✆02.32.74.04.04, ✇www.lehavretourisme.com) is on the seafront at 186 blvd Clemenceau. Bus #1 or #3 makes the 2km journey from the **train station**, which is on cours de la République. **CHERBOURG** is situated at the top end of the Cotentin Peninsula. Its **tourist office** (Mon–Sat 9am–12.30pm & 2–6pm; ✆02.33.93.52.02, ✇www.ot-cherbourg-cotentin.fr) is near the ferry terminal at 2 quai Alexandre and the **train station** is on av François-Millet – a ten-minute walk from the ferry terminal behind the inner dock. **DIEPPE** is smaller and much more enjoyable, with a good market and a castle. Its **tourist office** is beside the ferry terminal on Pont Ango (Mon–Sat 9am–noon/1pm & 2–6/8pm; summer also Sun 10am–1pm & 3–6pm; ✆02.32.14.40.60, ✇www.mairie-dieppe.fr); its **train station** is about 800m southwest of the ferry terminal.

Honfleur

HONFLEUR is the best-preserved of the Normandy ports and a near-perfect seaside town. The ancient port still functions and although only pleasure craft now make use of the moorings in the harbour basin, fishing boats tie up alongside the pier close by, and there are usually freshly caught fish for sale either directly from the boats or from stands on the pier. It's all highly picturesque, and not so different from the town that had such appeal to artists in the late nineteenth century.

It's this artistic past – and a present-day concentration of galleries and painters – which dominates Honfleur. The town owes most to Eugène Boudin, forerunner of Impressionism, who was born and worked in the town, trained the 15-year-old Monet, and was joined here for various periods by Pissarro, Renoir and Cézanne. There's a good selection of his work in the **Musée Eugène Boudin**, west of the port on place Erik-Satie (March to Sept Mon & Wed–Sun 10am–noon & 2–6pm; Oct–Dec Mon & Wed–Fri 2.30–5pm, Sat & Sun 10am–noon & 2.30–5pm; closed Jan & Feb; €5) – quite appealing here in context, particularly the crayon seascapes, along with an impressive set of works by Dufy and Monet. The composer, musician, artist and author Erik Satie was born in Honfleur, and the rooms of his childhood home have been innovatively converted into an exhibition of his life and works. **Les Maisons Satie**, 76 blvd Charles V (Mon & Wed–Sun 10/10.30am–6/7pm; €5), is no conventional museum, however. Visitors are conducted through a series of innovative "stage sets" by the man himself – or rather his words and music – by way of an infra-red controlled headset. Expect flying giant pears and indoor rainshowers, rather than dusty artefacts – all very entertaining and insightful, like a walk through the mind of the artist.

Honfleur is on the direct **bus** route between Caen and Le Havre (4 buses daily); the town's nearest **train station** is at Deauville, connected by bus #20 (takes 20min). The **tourist office** is on place Arthur Boudin (July & Aug daily 9.30am–7pm; rest of year Mon–Sat 9.30am–12.30pm & 2–6.30pm, Sun 10am–5pm; ✆02.31.89.23.30, ✇www.ot-honfleur.fr). None of Honfleur's **hotels** are very affordable – the *Cascades*, 17 place Thiers (✆02.31.89.05.83; ❸), is the best bet, or there's a **campsite**, *Du Phare*, at the west end of blvd Charles V on place Jean de Vienne (✆02.31.89.10.26; closed Oct–March). The most reasonable **restaurants** and **bars** are on rue Haute, on the way up to the Boudin museum: try *Au P'tit Mareyeur* at no. 4. At the harbour itself, it's hard to beat *Le Vieux Honfleur*, 13 quai St Étienne.

Bayeux

BAYEUX's perfectly preserved medieval ensemble, magnificent cathedral and world-famous tapestry depicting the 1066 invasion of England by William the Conqueror make it one of the high points of Normandy. However, it receives an influx of summer tourists that can make its charms pall somewhat.

The **Bayeux Tapestry** is housed in the **Centre Guillaume le Conquérant**, clearly signposted on rue de Nesmond (daily 9am–6/7pm; Nov–March closed 12.30–2pm; €6.40). Visits begin with a projection of slides on swathes of canvas, before moving on to an almost full-length reproduction of the original, complete with photographic extracts and detailed commentary. Upstairs in the theatre there's a film (in alternate French and English versions) on the general context and craft of the piece, and beyond this the tapestry itself, a 70m strip of linen embroidered over nine centuries ago with coloured wools. It records scenes from the Norman Conquest, as well as incidental details of domestic and daily life, which run along the bottom as a counterpoint. The tapestry was commissioned for the consecration of the nearby **Cathédrale Notre-Dame** in 1077 – and, despite some eighteenth-century vandalism, the Romanesque plan of the church is still intact. The **crypt**, entirely unaltered, is a beauty, its columns graced with frescoes of angels playing trumpets and bagpipes. Also well worth a visit while in Bayeux is the **Memorial Museum to the Battle of Normandy** on blvd Fabian Ware (daily 9.30/10am–6/6.30pm; Oct–April closed 12.30–2pm; €5.40). The numerous original documents, life-size models, equipment and videos dramatically capture the most decisive chapter in the battle to re-establish peace in Europe during the war.

Bayeux's **train station** is on the southern side of town, on blvd Sadi Carnot. The **tourist office**, at Pont St Jean (Mon–Sat 9am–7pm, Sun 9am–12.30pm & 2–6.30pm; Oct–June closed Mon–Sat 12.30–2pm & all Sun; ☎02.31.51.28.28, ⍟www.bayeux-tourism.com), might be able to help you find reasonable **accommodation**. Most affordable of the **hotels** are the *Mogador*, 20 rue Alain Chartier (☎02.31.92.24.58; ❸), and *la Gare*, 26 place de la Gare (☎02.31.92.10.70; ❷). The *Family Home* at 39 rue du Général de Dais (☎02.31.92.15.22; ❶), north of the cathedral, functions as a friendly and decent **hostel**, and serves good food too. The nearest **campsite** is on blvd d'Eindhoven, a fifteen-minute walk from the centre (☎02.31.92.08.93). Most of the **restaurants** are on the pedestrianized rue St-Jean – *La Rapière* at no. 53 is the most popular, *La Table du Terroir* at no. 42 serves good solid French cuisine.

Mont St-Michel

The island of **Mont St-Michel**, site of a marvellous **Gothic abbey** (tours daily 9.30am–7pm; €7), on the far western edge of Normandy, is a big draw. The abbey church, long known as the Merveille, is visible from all around the bay, and it becomes more awe-inspiring the closer you get. The granite structure was sculpted to match the contours of the hill, and though space was always limited, the building has grown through the centuries in ever more ingenious uses of geometry; but the current dour state of the stone walls is a far cry from the way the monastery would have looked in medieval times, brightly painted and festooned with tapestries.

To stay on the island, head up the one twisting street to the *du Guesclin* (☎02.33.60.14.10; ❹), with excellent rooms and a reasonable **restaurant**. There's a **campsite** (☎02.33.60.09.33; closed Nov–Jan) near the causeway to the island. The nearest **train station** is at Pontorson, 6km south, from where you can rent a bike or take the expensive bus to the Mont.

Rouen

ROUEN is another city that was flattened during World War II, although a flood of money was spent on restoring it. The result is an attractive, if in parts fake, medieval centre complete with half-timbered houses, cobbled streets and impressive churches. A prominent point in the centre, between place du Vieux-Marché and the cathedral, is the **Gros Horloge**, a colourful one-handed clock which spans the street named after it. You can climb up the **belfry** and see the surrounding towers and spires arraying themselves in startling density. Just off here is the **Cathédrale de Notre-Dame** (Mon 2–6pm, Tues–Sun 8am–6/7pm), a Gothic masterpiece built in the twelfth and thirteenth centuries, although various vertical extensions have since been added. The west facade, intricately sculpted like the rest of the exterior, was Monet's subject for his series of celebrated studies of changing light.

The church of **St-Ouen**, in a park a short walk northeast, is larger than the cathedral and has far less decoration, so that the Gothic proportions have a more instant impact. Close by, the church of St-Maclou is more flamboyant, although perhaps the real interest is in its adjacent **Aître St-Maclou**, once a cemetery for plague victims, which still has its original macabre decorations. Also worth a visit is the **Musée Flaubert et d'Histoire de la Médicine** in the Hôpital Hôtel-Dieu on the corner of rue de Lecat and rue du Contrat-Social (Tues 10am–6pm, Wed–Sat 10am–noon & 2–6pm; €1.80), dedicated to Rouen's most famous novelist, Gustave Flaubert, whose father was chief surgeon at the medical school here.

The main **train station**, Rouen Rive-Droite, is a ten-minute walk or one metro stop from the centre. The bus station is just off the southern end of the main rue Jeanne d'Arc. The **tourist office** is opposite the cathedral at 25 place de la Cathédrale (Mon–Sat 9am–6/7pm, Sun 9.30am–12.30pm & 2–6pm; Oct–April closed Sun pm; ℡02.32.08.32.40, ✆www.mairie-rouen.fr). Choice of the **hotels** are: the *Sphinx*, 130 rue Beauvoisine (℡02.35.71.35.86; ❷); *des Carmes*, 33 pl des Carmes (℡02.35.71.92.31; ❸); and *Le Palais*, 12 rue du Tambour (℡02.35.71.41.40; ❷). The town's **campsite** is 5km northwest on rue Jules-Ferry in Déville-lès-Rouen (℡02.35.74.07.59; bus #2 from Théâtre des Arts). Rouen has a reputation for good **food**, and its most famous dish, duckling (*caneton*), can be enjoyed quite affordably at *Pascaline*, 5 rue de la Poterne. For good basic meals, the south side of place du Vieux-Marché and the north side of St-Maclou church are both lined with good-quality restaurants. You can access the **internet** at Cybernetics, 59 pl du Vieux-Marché, and Place Net, 37 rue de la République.

Giverny

GIVERNY is famous for **Monet's house and gardens**, complete with water-lily pond (April–Oct Tues–Sun 10am–6pm; €5.50, €4 for gardens only; ✆www.fondation-monet.com). Monet lived here from 1883 until his death in 1926 and the gardens that he laid out were considered by many of his friends to be his masterpiece; the best months to visit are May and June, when the rhododendrons flower around the lily pond and the wisteria over the Japanese bridge, but it is overwhelmingly beautiful at any time of year. There aren't any paintings on show, however; the house is filled with Monet's collection of Japanese prints.

The easiest way to get to Giverny is to take a train to nearby **VERNON**, then either rent a bike or take the *Gisor* bus from the station (not Mon). There's a **hostel** in Vernon, at 28 av de l'Île-de-France (℡02.32.51.66.48; ❶), and the *Auberge La Musardière*, 123 rue Claude Monet in Giverny itself (℡02.32.21.03.18; ❸).

Brittany

For generations the people of **Brittany** risked their lives fishing and trading on the violent seas or struggling with the arid soil of the interior, and their resilience is tinged with Celtic culture: mystical, musical, sometimes morbid, sometimes vital and inspired. Unified with France in 1532, the Bretons have seen their language steadily eradicated, and the interior severely depopulated. Today, the people still tend to treat France as a separate country, even if few of them actively support Breton nationalism. The recent economic resurgence, helped partly by summer tourism, has largely been due to local initiatives; at the same time, a Celtic artistic identity has been revived at festivals of traditional Breton music, poetry and dance.

For most visitors to Brittany, the **coast** is the dominant feature. After the Côte d'Azur, this is the most popular summer resort area in France, and the attractions are obvious – white sand beaches, towering cliffs and offshore islands. Whether you approach across the Channel by ferry, or along the coast from Normandy, the River Rance, guarded by **St-Malo** on its estuary and **Dinan** 20km upstream, makes a spectacular introduction to Brittany. To the **west** stretches a varied coastline culminating in one of the most seductive of the islands, the **Île de Bréhat**. Brittany's **southern coast** takes in Europe's most famous prehistoric site, the alignments of **Carnac**, and although the beaches are not as spectacular as Finistère's, the water is warmer. Of the cities, **Vannes** has one of the liveliest medieval town centres.

Brittany's **main port** is **ROSCOFF**, on the northwestern tip of Brittany. Follow the signs from the **ferry terminal** to the town centre; the **train station** is 100m south of the town on rue Ropartz Morvan. The **tourist office** is at 46 rue Gambetta (July & Aug Mon–Sat 9am–12.30pm & 1.30–7pm, Sun 10am–12.30pm; rest of year Mon–Sat 9am–noon & 2–6pm; ☎02.98.61.12.13, ⊛www.sb-roscoff.fr/Roscoff).

St-Malo

ST-MALO, walled and built with the same grey granite as Mont St-Michel, presents its best face to the River Rance and the sea. Once within the old ramparts, it can seem a little grim and squat, and overrun by summer tourists; but away from the thoroughfares of the tiny **citadel**, with its high seventeenth-century houses, random exploration is fun and you can surface to the light on the ramparts or head through them to the nearby beaches. The **town museum**, in the castle to the right as you enter Porte St-Vincent (daily 10am–noon & 2–6pm; winter closed Mon; €4.40), glorifies, on several exhausting floors, St-Malo's sources of wealth and fame – colonialism, slave-trading and privateering among them.

Buses drop you at the main city gate, the **Porte St-Vincent**, while **trains** stop on the other side of the docks, a ten-minute walk away. The **tourist office** is on the corner of Esplanade St-Vincent and av Louis Martin beside the Bassin Duguay-Trouin (July & Aug Mon–Sat 8.30am–8pm, Sun 10am–7pm; April–June & Sept Mon–Sat 9am–12.30pm & 1.30–6/7pm, Sun 10am–noon & 2.30–6pm; rest of year closed Sun; ☎02.99.56.64.48, ⊛www.ville-saint-malo.fr). It's always more difficult to find **accommodation** in the old city, despite the extraordinary number of hotels, but rooms at *La Rotonde*, 1 place Châteaubriand (☎02.99.40.47.97; ❸), and *Le Louvre*, 2 rue des Marins (☎02.99.40.86.62; ❸), are worth trying. Otherwise, there's an array near the station. In the suburb of **Paramé**, 2km northeast of the train station, is an often-crowded hostel at 37 av R.P. Umbricht (☎02.99.40.29.80; ❷; bus #2). There's a municipal **campsite**, *Cité d'Aleth*, on allée Gaston Buy (☎02.99.81.60.91), near some shops and the beach. Most of the citadel's **restaurants** are pricey tourist traps, so you're better off at the *crêperies* and *mouleries* such as *Le P'tit Crêpier*, 6 rue Sainte-Barbe, and *Le Brick*, 5 rue Jacques-Cartier. **Internet** access is available at Cyber Com at 75 blvd des Talards.

Dinan

A short distance along the river Rance lies **DINAN**, in contrast one of the most enyoyable towns in Brittany. Its **citadel** has been preserved almost intact within a three-kilometre circuit of walls, inside which lies a warren of beautiful late-medieval houses. It's almost too good to be true and time is easily spent rambling from crêperie to café, admiring the houses on the way. Unfortunately, there's only one small stretch of the **ramparts** that you can walk along – from the gardens behind St-Sauveur to just short of the Tour Sillon – but you get a good general overview from the **Tour de l'Horloge** (April & May daily 2–6pm; June–Sept daily 10am–6.30pm; €2.50). Another good view can be had from the **Château Duchesse Anne** (June–Sept daily 10am–6.30pm; rest of year closed noon–2pm & Tues; €3.90). An inevitable target of any Dinan wanderings is the church of **St-Sauveur**, a real mix of styles, with a Romanesque porch and eighteenth-century steeple.

Dinan's **train station** is a ten-minute walk away from place Duclos. The **tourist office** (daily 9am–7.30pm; winter closed 12.30–2pm & Sun; ☎02.96.87.69.76, ⓦwww.dinan-tourisme.com) is opposite the Tour de l'Horloge. The less pricey **hotels** are near the station: *De l'Océan*, 9 pl du 11-Novembre (☎02.96.39.21.51; ❷), is as good as any. Within the walls there's *La Duchesse Anne* at 10 place Duguesclin (☎02.96.39.09.43; ❸). Dinan's **hostel** (☎02.96.39.10.83, ⓦdinan@fuaj.org; ❶) is attractively set in the Moulin de Méen near the port at Taden, about 3km away, while the closest **campsite** is at 103 rue Châteaubriand (☎02.96.39.11.96; closed Oct–May), which runs parallel to the western ramparts. Of the wide choice of **eating places**, one of the best bets is *Crêperie Pizzéria d'Armor*, 15 place des Cordeliers. For **internet** access, try @rospace on rue de la Chaux (closed Sun & Mon).

Quimper and around

QUIMPER, capital of the ancient diocese and kingdom of Cornouaille, is the oldest Breton city, founded according to legend by St Corentin, who came here across the channel to the place they named Little Britain some time between the fourth and seventh centuries. It's a laidback place, with old granite buildings, two rivers and the rising woods of Mont Frugy overlooking the centre of town.

The town focuses on the enormous Gothic **Cathédrale St-Corentin**. The **Musée des Beaux-Arts** is next to the Hôtel de Ville at 40 place St-Corentin (July & Aug daily 10am–7pm; rest of year closed noon–2pm & Tues; €3.85), and has an amazing collection of drawings by Cocteau, Max Jacob and Gustave Doré (shown in rotation) and nineteenth- and twentieth-century paintings of the famed Pont-Aven school. To see pottery made on an industrial scale, and an exhibition of the changing styles since the first Quimper *ateliers* of the late seventeenth century, head for rue Jean-Baptiste Bosquet, where you'll find the **Faïenceries de Quimper** (guided visits only; ☎08.00.62.65.10; €3) and the **Musée de la Faïence** (April–Oct Mon–Sat 10am–6pm; €4).

The adjacent **train** and **bus stations** are a short walk east along the river from the town centre. The **tourist office** is on the south bank at 7 rue de la Déesse, place de la Résistance (July & Aug Mon–Sat 9am–7pm, Sun 10am–1pm & 3–6pm; June & Sept closed Sun pm; rest of year closed all Sun & Mon–Sat 12.30–1.30pm; ☎02.98.53.04.05, ⓦwww.bretagne-4villes.com). Budget **hotels** include the *Hôtel de la Gare*, near the station at 17 av de la Gare (☎02.98.90.00.81; ❹), and *le Derby*, at no. 13 (☎02.98.52.06.91; ❷). The **hostel** (☎02.98.64.97.97; ❶) and **campsite** (☎02.98.55.61.09) are downstream on av des Oiseaux in the Bois du Séminaire – take bus #1 from place de la Résistance. For **food**, a good bet is the *Crêperie au Vieux Quimper*, 20 rue Verdelet, a typically Breton dining experience. Note that rooms book up fast for the last full week of July, when the town hosts the **Festival de Cornouaille**, a jamboree of Breton music, costume and dance.

Boats down the Odet to the coast leave from the end of quai de l'Odet, opposite the Faïenceries, a winding journey to the upmarket resort of **BÉNODET**, where there's a long sheltered beach; for times and prices call ☎02.98.57.00.58. **Hotels** are comparatively expensive, but there are several large **campsites**. There are more **beaches** along the coast between Penmarch and Loctudy and beyond, about an hour by bus from Quimper. Another possibility is a trip to the **Pointe du Raz**, the Land's End of France, a series of plummeting fissures, filling and draining with deafening force, above which you can walk on precarious paths.

Carnac and around

About 10km along the coast from the functional port of Lorient, **CARNAC** is home to one of the most important prehistoric sites in Europe, a congregation of some two thousand or so **menhirs** stretching for more than 4km to the north of the village, long predating the Pyramids or Stonehenge. The stones may have been part of an observatory for the motions of the moon, but no one really knows. Though many have been pillaged, the megaliths remain an amazing site. The main alignments, fenced from the public, are viewed from a raised platform at one end of the plain. There's plenty of information on them at the **Musée de la Préhistoire**, 10 place de la Chapelle, near rue du Tumulus in Carnac-Ville (May–Sept Mon–Fri 10am–6.30pm, Sat & Sun 10am–noon & 2–6.30pm; rest of year Mon & Wed–Sun 10am–noon & 2–5pm; ⊛www.museedecarnac.com; €4.65).

Carnac itself, made up of Carnac-Ville and the newer seaside resort of Carnac-Plage, is extremely popular. **Buses** arrive at the main **tourist office** at 74 av des Druides in Carnac-Plage (July & Aug Mon–Sat 9am–7pm, Sun 3–7pm; rest of year Mon–Sat 9am–noon & 2–6pm; ☏02.97.52.13.52, ⊛www.ot-carnac.fr). The office has an annexe on place de l'Eglise (April–Oct only). Among the town's **hotels**, the *Ratelier*, 4 chemin du Douet (☏02.97.52.05.04; ❸), is a good deal, as is the central *Chez Nous*, 5 pl de la Chapelle (☏02.97.52.07.28; ❸). The best of the many **beaches** is the smallest, the **Men Dû**, just off the road towards La Trinité. For **camping**, by the sea, head for *Men Dû* (☏02.97.52.04.23; ⊛www.camping-du-mendu.com); the best site, though, is *La Grande Métairie* (☏02.97.52.24.01), opposite the stones.

South of Carnac, the **Presqu'île de Quiberon** is well worth a visit. The town of **QUIBERON** itself is a lively port, and provides a jumping-off point for boats out to the nearby islands or simply a base for the peninsula. The ocean-facing shore, known as the **Côte Sauvage**, is a wild and unswimmable stretch, but the sheltered eastern side has safe and calm sandy beaches, and offers plenty of **campsites**. In Quiberon, **Port Maria**, the fishing harbour, is the most active part of town and has the best concentration of **hotels**, though they're often full in high season – try *Le Neptune* at 4 quai de Houat (☏02.97.50.09.62; ❸), or *Au Bon Accueil*, 6 quai de Houat (☏02.97.50.07.92; ❸), which also has a very good fish restaurant. The **hostel**, *Les Filets Bleus*, 45 rue du Roch-Priol (☏02.97.50.15.54; ❷; closed Oct–March), is set back from the sea about 1km southeast of the train station. A vast array of fish **restaurants** line the seafront, and **cafés** by the long bathing beach are also enjoyable. The **train station**, with services in July and August only, is a couple of minutes north of the centre on place de la Gare. The **tourist office** is at 14 rue de Verdun (July & Aug Mon–Sat 9am–12.30pm & 2–6.30pm, Sun 9am–12.30pm & 3–6pm; rest of year closed Sun; ☏02.97.50.07.84, ⊛www.quiberon.com).

Vannes and the Golfe de Morbihan

VANNES is one of the most historic towns in Brittany – it was here that the Breton assembly ratified the Act of Union with France in 1532. Its old centre is a chaotic web of streets crammed around the cathedral and enclosed by ramparts and gardens. Opposite the cathedral is **La Cohue**, the building where the Act of Union was ratified. Nowadays it houses the **Musée de Vannes** (daily 1.30–6pm; €4), with the local Beaux-Arts museum on its top floor, and a gallery downstairs for temporary exhibitions.

Vannes' harbour is a channelled inlet of the ragged-edged **Golfe de Morbihan**, which lets in the tides through a narrow gap. By popular tradition, the **islands** scattered around this enclosure used to number the days of the year, though for centuries the waters have been rising and there are now fewer than one for each week. Of these, thirty are privately owned, while two – the Île aux Moines and Île d'Arz – have small communities and regular ferry services, and end up being crowded in summer. You can take a **boat tour** around the rest, a compelling trip through a baffling muddle of channels, megalithic ruins, stone circles and solitary menhirs; contact Navix (☏02.97.46.60.00) or Isle (☏02.97.46.18.19) for details.

It's fifteen minutes' walk south from the **train station** to the centre at place de la République. The **tourist office** is at 1 rue Thiers (July & Aug Mon–Sat 9am–6pm, Sun 9.30am–1pm & 2–6pm; rest of year Mon–Sat 9.30am–12.30pm & 2–6pm;

☏02.97.47.24.34, ⓦwww.pays-de-vannes.com/tourisme). Vannes has the best choice of **hotels** anywhere around the Golfe de Morbihan: two good ones are *Le Bretagne*, 36 rue du Mené, in the old town (☏02.97.47.20.21; ❷), and *Le Marina* overlooking the port at 4 place Gambetta (☏02.97.47.22.81; ❷). For **food**, the *St-Ex*, on place Valencia, serves decent crêpes and has a pleasant terrace.

Nantes

Though **NANTES**, the former capital, is these days not officially a part of Brittany, it remains to its inhabitants an integral part of the province. Crucial to its self-image is the **Château des Ducs**, subjected to a certain amount of damage over the centuries, but still preserving the form in which it was built by two of the last rulers of independent Brittany, François II and his daughter Duchess Anne, who was born here in 1477. The most significant act in the castle's history was the signing of the Edict of Nantes by Henri IV in 1598, which ended the Wars of Religion and granted Protestantism a certain degree of tolerance. You can walk into the courtyard and up onto the low ramparts for free, and visit temporary exhibitions in the Harnachement building, but the rest of the castle is undergoing a huge renovation in order to become the Museum of the History of Nantes and its Region, due for completion by 2008. In 1800 the castle's arsenal exploded, shattering the stained glass of the **Cathédrale de St-Pierre et St-Paul**, 200m away, just one of many disasters that have befallen the church. Its soaring heights are home to the tomb of François II and his wife, Margaret. Back past the château, the **Île Feydeau**, once an island, was the birthplace of **Jules Verne**; the museum dedicated to him is at 3 rue de l'Hermitage (Mon & Wed–Sat 10am–noon & 2–5pm, Sun 2–5pm; €1.50).

The **train station** is a short way east of the castle. For **accommodation**, try the *Cœur du Loire*, 3 rue Anatole-le-Braz (☏02.40.74.35.61; ❷), *Hôtel de l'Océan*, 11 rue du Maréchal-de-Lattre-de-Tassigny (☏02.40.69.73.51; ❷), or *Fourcroy*, 11 rue Fourcroy (☏02.40.44.68.00; ❷). The city's **hostel** is at 2 place de la Manu, and is a ten-minute walk east of the train station along the tram tracks, or by tram #1 to Beaujoire (☏02.40.29.29.20; ❷). The **tourist office** is on place du Commerce (May–Sept Mon–Sat 10am–7pm, Sun 10am–1pm & 1.30–6pm; rest of year closed Sun; ☏02.40.20.60.00, ⓦwww.nantes-tourisme.com) in an appealing, largely pedestrian area that is a good source of **restaurants**. **Internet** access is at Cyber Salon on Place Viarme, and Cyber City at 14 rue de Strasbourg.

The Loire

The sheer density of **châteaux** can be daunting when choosing where to go in the **Loire**, but if you pick your castles selectively – the best are those at **Chenonceaux** and **Loches** – this can be one of the most enjoyable of all French regions. The most salient features of the Loire itself are whirlpools, vicious currents and a propensity to flood. No one swims in or boats on the Loire, nor are any goods carried along it – it's just there, the longest river in France. The stretch above Saumur is the loveliest on the lower reaches, the land to the south planted with vines and sunflowers. Other than the châteaux, the region has few sights; of the towns, **Tours** is good for museums, while **Saumur** is perfect for indolence.

Saumur and around

SAUMUR is a peaceful and pretty town, and a good place to base yourself, with Angers and Chinon within easy reach and the vineyards of St-Hilaire-St-Florent, which produce Saumur's famous sparkling wines, just 4km south on the road to Angers. It has a **château** (June–Sept daily 9.30am–6pm; rest of year Mon & Wed–Sun 9.30am–noon & 2–5.30pm; €6), where you can visit dungeons and a watchtower, and be guided around two museums – the **Musée des Arts Décoratifs** and the **Musée du Cheval**.

The **train station** is on the north bank of the river; from here cross over the bridge to the island, then over another bridge to the main part of the town on the south bank. Saumur's main street, rue d'Orléans, cuts back through the south-bank sector; the **tourist office** is at the foot of the second bridge, on place de la Bilange (May–Sept Mon–Sat 9.15am–6/7pm, Sun 10.30am–12.30pm & 2.30–5.30pm; Oct–April closed 12.30–2pm & Sun pm; ☎02.41.40.20.60, ⊛www.saumur-tourisme.com). The best **hotel** is *Le Cristal*, 10 place de la République (☎02.41.51.09.54; ❸), with river views from most rooms; alternatively there's the *Central*, at 23 rue Daillé (☎02.41.51.05.78; ❸). On the Île d'Offard, connected by bridges to both banks of the town, there's a good **hostel** at the eastern end of rue de Verden (☎02.41.40.30.00; ❷), and a **campsite** next door. The best area for **eating** is around place St-Pierre: *Auberge St-Pierre*, at no. 6, has a fairly cheap menu, or try *Les Forges de St-Pierre*. The *Le Cristal* hotel offers **internet** access.

The **Abbaye de Fontévraud** (daily: June–Sept 9am–6.30pm; rest of year 9.30am–12.30pm & 2–5/6pm; €5.50), 13km southeast of Saumur on bus #16, was founded in 1099 as both a nunnery and a monastery with an abbess in charge – a radical move, even if the post was filled solely by queens and princesses. The premises had to be immense to house and separate not only nuns and monks but also the sick and the repentant prostitutes. A prison from the Revolution until 1963, its most famous inmate was the writer Jean Genet, but its chief significance is as the burial ground of the Plantagenet kings. Four tombstone effigies remain, of Henry II, Eleanor of Aquitaine, Richard the Lionheart and Isabelle of Angoulême (King John's wife).

Chinon

The first of the big Loire **châteaux** is at **CHINON** (daily: April–Sept 9.15am–6.15pm; Nov–Feb 9.30am–noon & 2.15–5pm; €4.42). This was one of the few places in which Charles VII could stay while Henry V of England held Paris and the title to the French throne. Charles' situation changed with the arrival here in 1429 of Joan of Arc, who persuaded him to give her an army. All that remains of the scene of this encounter, the Grande Salle, is a wall and first-floor fireplace. More interesting is the **Tour Coudray**, to the west, covered with intricate thirteenth-century graffiti carved by imprisoned and doomed Templar knights. Below the castle, the town is a tacky and rather sterile place, with very few **hotels** and everything closed up long before midnight. The two least expensive places to stay are the *Point du Jour*, 102 quai Jeanne-d'Arc (☎02.47.93.07.20; ❷), and the *Jeanne d'Arc*, 11 rue Voltaire (☎02.47.93.02.85; ❸). The **campsite** (☎02.47.93.08.35) is across the river at Île-Auger. The **tourist office** is on place Hofheim (May–Sept daily 9am–7pm; Oct–April Mon–Sat 10am–noon & 2–6pm; ☎02.47.93.17.85, ⊛www.chinon.com). The most reasonable **restaurant** is *Les Années 30*, 78 rue Voltaire. L'Astrol@b, 28 rue Rabelais (closed Sun & Mon) offers **internet** access.

Tours and around

A little way upriver, **TOURS**, set on the Loire and a good base for seeing châteaux and enjoying the surrounding vineyards, has a delightful old town and a handful of decent museums. The main street is rue Nationale, a short walk down which is the **Musée du Compagnonnage** (daily 9am–noon/12.30pm & 2–6pm; Oct–May closed Tues; €4), which documents the origins and militant activity of the guilds that built the châteaux. Next door is the **Musée des Vins** (Mon & Wed–Sun 9am–noon & 2–6pm; €2.50), which provides a comprehensive study of the history, mythology and production of the wondrous liquid. Over beside the **Cathédrale St-Gatien**, with its crumbling, Gothic frontage, the city's third museum, the

Musée des Beaux-Arts on place François Sicard (9am–12.45pm & 2–6pm, closed Tues; €4.60), has some beauties in its rambling collection – *Christ in the Garden of Olives* and the *Resurrection* by Mantegna, and Frans Hals' portrait of Descartes. The museum's top treasure, however, Rembrandt's *Flight into Egypt*, is difficult to see through the security glass. In the opposite direction, west of rue Nationale, Tours' **Old Town** crowds around place St-Pierre-le-Puellier, whose medieval half-timbered houses and bulging stairway towers are the city's showpieces.

The **tourist office** is in front of the train station at 78–82 rue Bernard-Palissy (Mon–Sat 8.30am–7pm, Sun 10am–12.30pm & 2.30–5pm; winter closed 12.30–1.30pm & Sun pm; ☎02.47.70.37.37, ✆www.tourism-touraine.com). There are plenty of reasonably priced **hotels**: the *Regina*, 2 rue Pimbert (☎02.47.05.25.36; ❷), and *Mon Hôtel*, 40 rue de la Préfecture (☎02.47.05.67.53; ❷) are two of the cheapest, as is the *Central Hôtel*, 21 rue Berthelot (☎02.47.05.46.44; ❷), which has good rooms in an excellent location in the old town. At the time of writing the official **hostel** was closed and awaiting relocation; an alternative for the under-25s is *Le Foyer*, 16 rue Bernard-Palissy (☎02.47.60.51.51; ❷). The nearest **campsite**, *Les Acacias* (☎02.47.44.08.16), is east of town, on the south bank of the Loire. Rue du Grand-Marché and rue de la Rôtisserie, on the periphery of old Tours, and rue Colbert, which runs down to the cathedral, are the most promising streets for **restaurants**. Try *Le Petit Patrimoine* at 58 rue Colbert for good French food, or *Comme Autre Fouée* at 11 rue de la Monnaie for good-value local specialities. Annexe Informatique, at 8 rue Gambetta, offers **internet** access.

Villandry, Chenonceaux and Loches

The most popular attraction close to Tours is the **château** of **VILLANDRY**, about 13km west, where there are some extraordinary Renaissance **gardens** set out on several terraces with marvellous views over the river (daily 9am–5/6.30pm; gardens till 5.30/7.30pm; €7.50, €5 gardens only). The château holds Spanish paintings and a Moorish ceiling from Toledo. There's no public transport, but if you rent a bike it's a wonderful ride along the banks of the Cher.

Perhaps the finest of all the region's **châteaux**, however, is that straddling the river at **CHENONCEAUX** (daily 9am–4.30/7pm; €7.60), about 15km from Villandry and accessible by train from Tours or Blois. The building went up in the 1520s and was the home of Diane de Poitiers, the lover of Henry II. There's plenty to see – floors of tapestries, paintings and furniture, not least Zurbarán's penetrating depiction of Archimedes in the Salle François I.

The **château** at **LOCHES**, an hour by train southeast of Tours, is visually the most impressive of the Loire fortresses, with ramparts and a huddle of houses below still partly enclosed by the outer wall of the medieval town (daily 9am–5/7pm; Oct–March closed noon–2pm; €3.70). You can climb to the top of the keep, poke around in the dungeons and torture chamber and visit the royal lodgings, where Charles VII and his three successors had their residence.

Orléans

Due south of Paris, poor **ORLÉANS** feels compelled to recuperate the glory it enjoyed when Joan of Arc delivered the city from the English in 1429. Unsurprisingly, it is Joan of Arc who is the main draw here today. The north transept of the wonderful **Cathédrale Ste-Croix** (daily 9am–4/6.16pm; winter closed noon–2pm) holds her pedestal, supported by two golden leopards (representing the English) on an altar carved with the battle scene; the late nineteenth-century stained-glass windows in the nave tell the story of her life, with caricatures of the loutish Anglo-Saxons and snooty French nobles; and there's more on her at the **Maison de Jeanne d'Arc** on place Général-de-Gaulle (May–Oct Tues–Sun 10am–12.15pm & 1.30–6pm; Nov–April Tues–Sun 1.30–6pm; €3). If you've had your fill of Joan of Arc, head for the modern art collection in the basement of the

Musée des Beaux-Arts, opposite the Hôtel de Ville (Tues–Sun 11am–6pm, Wed till 8pm; €3), with works by Picasso, Miró, Dufy, Renoir and Monet.

The **train station** and **tourist office** (Mon–Sat 9/10am–1pm & 2–6.30pm; ☎02.38.24.05.05, ✆www.ville-orleans.fr) are on opposite sides of rue Albert I, north of the town centre, connected by rue de la République to the central place du Martroi. There's an annexe to the tourist office near the cathedral at 6 rue Jeanne d'Arc (Mon 2–6pm; Tues–Sun 10am–6pm). There are cheap **hotels** near the station, including the pleasant *Hôtel de Paris*, 29 rue Faubourg-Bannier (☎02.38.53.39.58; ❸), and in the centre, you could try the *Charles Sanglier*, 8 rue Charles Sanglier (☎02.38.53.38.50; ❸). The **hostel** is at 14 rue Faubourg-Madeleine to the west of town, accessible on bus #4 from the train station (☎02.38.62.45.75; ❶; closed Dec & Jan). Bus #6 goes to the **campsite** at St-Jean-de-la-Ruelle, 2km out on the Blois road, rue de la Roche (☎02.38.88.39.39; July & Aug only). Rue de Bourgogne, parallel to the river, has a good choice of snack bars and **restaurants** of which *La Petite Marmite*, at no. 178, serving traditional French food, is one of the best. Another good bet for decent French cuisine is *La Chancellerie*, at 27 place Martroi. You can access the **internet** at Odysseus, 32 rue du Colombier.

Poitou-Charente and the Atlantic coast

The summer light, the warmth, the fields of sunflowers and the siesta-silent air of the farmhouses of **Poitou-Charente** give the first exciting promise of the south. The coast has great charm in places – it remains distinctly Atlantic, with dunes, pine forests and misty mud flats, and lacks much of the glitz and glamour of the Côte d'Azur. The principal port, **La Rochelle**, is one of the prettiest and most distinctive towns in France, and the island of **Ré**, out of season at least, is lovely, with kilometres of sandy beaches. **Poitiers** is a likely entry point to the region, a pleasant enough town with an attractive old centre. South of here, the valley of the Charente river, slow and green, epitomizes blue-overalled, peasant France, accessible on boat trips from **Cognac**, itself famous for the eponymous brandy.

Poitiers

POITIERS is a country town with a charm that comes from a long and sometimes influential history as seat of the dukes of Aquitaine, discernible in the winding lines of the streets and the breadth of architectural fashions of its buildings. The tree-lined **place Leclerc**, and **place de Gaulle** just a few streets north, are the two poles of communal life, flanked by cafés and bustling market stalls. Between is a web of streets, with rue Gambetta cutting north past the **Palais de Justice** (June–Sept daily 9am–6pm; rest of year closed Sat & Sun; free), whose nineteenth-century facade hides the twelfth-century great hall of the dukes of Aquitaine. This magnificent room is where Jean, Duc de Berry, held his sumptuous court in the late fourteenth century, seated on the intricately carved dais at the far end of the room. In one corner, stairs give access to the **Maubergeon Tower**, the old castle keep. The stairs lead out onto the roof with a memorable view over the town.

Across from the Palais is one of the most idiosyncratic churches in France, **Notre-Dame-la-Grande** (daily 8am–7pm), whose west front is loaded with enthralling sculpture, typical of the Poitou brand of Romanesque. The interior, crudely overlaid with nineteenth-century frescoes, is not nearly as interesting. There is another unusual church a little way east, literally in the middle of rue Jean-Jaurès as you head towards the River Clain. This is the mid-fourth-century **Baptistère St-Jean** (April–Oct Mon & Wed–Sun 10.30am–12.30pm & 3–6pm; Nov–March same days 2.30–4.30pm; €0.60), reputedly the oldest Christian building in France and until the seventeenth century the only place in town to conduct a proper baptism; the font was the octagonal pool sunk into the floor. There are also some ancient and faded **frescoes** on the walls, including the Emperor Constantine on horseback.

Poitiers **train station** is at the foot of the hill that forms the kernel of the town, from where it's a ten-minute walk up to the centre. Cheap **hotels** nearby include the *Hotel Bistrot du Gare* at 131 Blvd du Grand Cerf (☎05.49.58.56.30; ❷), and the *Petite Villette*, 14 blvd de l'Abbé de Frémont (☎05.49.41.41.33; ❷); in the town centre there's the attractive *Hôtel du Plat d'Étain*, 7–9 rue du Plat d'Étain (☎05.49.41.04.80; ❸). The **hostel** is at allée Roger Tagault (☎05.49.30.09.70; ❷; bus #3) and there's a municipal **campsite** on rue du Porteau, 2km north of the town (☎05.49.41.44.88; closed Oct–March; bus #7). The **tourist office** is at 45 Place Charles de Gaulle (Mon–Sat 9.30/10am–6/7.30pm, Sun 10am–6pm; Oct–May closed Sun; ☎05.49.52.35.35, ⊛www.mairie-poitiers.fr). As for **eating**, *Le St-Hubert*, 13 rue Cloche Perse, does regional food at reasonable prices, and *Le Cappuccino*, on rue de l'Université, is one of several good Italians. Le Maillon, 20–22 rue de la Chaîne, offers **internet** access (closed Sat & Sun).

La Rochelle

LA ROCHELLE is the most attractive seaside town in France, with a beautiful seventeenth- and eighteenth-century centre and waterfront and a lively, bustling air. The town has a long history. Eleanor of Aquitaine gave it a charter in 1199, and it rapidly became a port of major importance, trading in salt and wine, the principal terminus for trade with the French colonies in the West Indies and Canada. Indeed, many of the settlers, especially in Canada, came from this part of France.

From the visitor's point of view, most attractions lie in the area behind the waterfront, between the harbour and place de Verdun. The heavy Gothic gateway of the **Porte de la Grosse Horloge** straddles the entrance to the old town, dominating the pleasure-boat-filled inner harbour, overlooked by two towers. Through the Grosse Horloge, the main shopping street, **rue du Palais**, is lined by eighteenth-century houses and arcaded shop fronts. To the west, especially in rue de l'Escale, are the discreet residences of the eighteenth-century shipowners and chandlers, while to the east, rue du Temple leads to the **Hôtel de Ville**, begun in the reign of Henri IV, whose initials, intertwined with those of Marie de Médici, are carved on the ground-floor gallery. It's a beautiful specimen of frenchified Italian taste, adorned with niches and statues and coffered ceilings. There's more of this rich world in the **Musée du Nouveau Monde**, 10 rue Fleuriau (Mon & Wed–Sat 10.30am–12.30pm & 1.30–6pm, Sun 3–6pm; €3.50), which occupies the former residence of the Fleuriau family, who, like many of their fellow Rochelais, made fortunes from slaving and West Indian sugar, spices and coffee. The new, hugely enjoyable **aquarium** (daily 9/10am–8/11pm; €10), by the marina, is also well worth a look, with impressive collections of indigenous and tropical species, albeit in a rather Disneyesque setting.

Practicalities

From the **train station**, it's ten minutes down av de Gaulle to the town centre. The **tourist office** is by the harbour on place de la Petite Sirène, Quai de Gabut (May–Sept Mon–Sat 9am–6/8pm, Sun 10/11am–5pm; rest of year closed noon–2pm & Sun; ⊛www.ville-larochelle.fr). Finding **accommodation** can be a problem in season. There's a **hostel** in av des Minimes to the west (☎05.46.44.43.11; ❷; bus #10 from place de Verdun or the train station) and two **campsites** – the *Soleil* by the hostel (☎05.46.44.42.53; closed Oct–April) and the *Port Neuf*, on the northwestern side of town on blvd A. Rondeau (☎05.46.43.81.20; bus #6 from Grosse Horloge). Of the handful of budget **hotels**, the best cetnral bets are the *Bordeaux,* 45 rue St-Nicolas (☎05.46.41.31.22; ❸), which is atmospheric but a bit noisy, and the friendly *Henri-IV*, 31 rue des

Gentilshommes (℡05.46.41.25.79; ❸). For **food**, try the area around rue du Port and rue St-Sauveur just off the waterfront, and rue St-Nicolas. *À Côté de Chez Fred*, 34 rue St-Nicolas, serves fresh fish in a homely atmosphere, and *Café de la Poste*, place de l'Hôtel de Ville, also has decent menus. For **internet** access, there's *Café Expo*, 18 rue des Dames, which also serves good pasta; and, on the other side of town AAT Web Conception, av Amérigo Vespucci.

For **beaches**, you're best off crossing over to the **Île de Ré**, a long narrow island immediately west of La Rochelle (buses from place de Verdun or pricey boat trips from the Vieux Port), which is surrounded by sandy strands. Out of season it has a slow, misty charm, with life in its little ports revolving around the cultivation of oysters and mussels, although in the summer you'll find it packed.

Cognac

COGNAC is a sunny, prosperous, little town, best-known for its brandy distilleries, which reveal themselves through the heady scent that pervades the air. The **tourist office**, close by the central place François I, 16 rue du 14-Juillet (Mon–Sat 9am–7pm, Sun 10.30am–4pm; winter closed 12.30–2pm & Sun; ℡05.45.82.06.71, ⓦwww.tourism-cognac.com), has information on visiting the various cognac *chais*, most of which are at the end of Grand-Rue, which winds through the old quarter of town. Perhaps the best for a visit are those of Hennessy (daily: March–Dec 10am–5/6pm; Jan & Feb by appointment; €4.60; ℡05.45.35.72.68, ⓦwww.hennessy-cognac.com), a seventh-generation family firm of Irish origin, where tours begin with a film explaining what's what in the world of cognac. Hennessy alone keeps 180,000 barrels in stock; all are regularly checked and various blends made from barrel to barrel. Only the best is kept, a choice which depends on the taste buds of the maître du chais. At Hennessy the job has been in the same family for six generations; the present heir apparent has already been under his father's tutelage for nineteen years and is still said to not yet be fully qualified.

From the **train station**, take rue Mousnier, then rue Bayard, which leads you up rue du 14-Juillet to place François I. There are a couple of **cafés** and a reasonable **brasserie** on the square or try the excellent *La Boîte-à-Sel*, 68 av Victor-Hugo. The cheapest **rooms** are at *Le Cheval Blanc*, 6–8 place Bayard (℡05.45.82.09.55; ❸); while the *Hotel d'Orléans* at 25 rue d'Angoulême (℡05.45.82.01.26; ❸) is slightly more upmarket. Upstream from the bridge, the oak woods of the Parc François I stretch along the riverbank to the town **campsite** (℡05.42.32.13.32).

Aquitaine, the Dordogne and the Lot

Steamy, moist and green, the southwest of France can feel like a lower-latitude England. In the **Dordogne** heartlands, the country is certainly beautiful, but the more famous spots, especially in the Dordogne valley, have become oppressively crowded in season. **Bordeaux**, with its international airport, is the main entry point to the region, and makes an especially stimulating base for those interested in wine. East of Bordeaux, the **Périgord Blanc** is named for the light, white colour of its rock outcrops – undulating, fertile, wooded country, rising in the north and east to the edge of the Massif Central. The regional capital is **Périgueux**, which, because of its central position and relative ease of access, makes the best base for the whole region, especially for the cave paintings at **Les Eyzies** and around. The **Périgord Noir** is the stretch of territory from Bergerac to Brive. It's this area that people tend to think of when you say Dordogne – most of the picture-book villages are here and it is here that the cuisine is at its richest and the prices at their highest. To the south lies the drier, poorer and more sparsely populated region through which the **Lot** river flows, an ideal area to hike, bike and camp.

Bordeaux

Famous the world over for the **wines** of the surrounding countryside, **BORDEAUX** is a big, bustling city, though outside its grand eighteenth-century centre, it's not a particularly attractive place, and there are surprisingly few major sights of interest. Nevertheless, it is a vibrant city with a large student population, and it makes a great base for exploring the area. Wine *aficionados*, of course, won't be disappointed; the biennial **Fête de Vin**, a four day celebration of local viticulture and gastronomy held in June, is one of the biggest of its kind, and it's a great time to be in town. You'll need your own transport to explore the surrounding countryside, though it's the wines, rather than the landscape, that are the draw. More interesting are the vast pine-covered expanses of **Les Landes** to the south, and the wild Atlantic **beaches**.

The centre of the city is the café-lined **place Gambetta**, a once majestic square conceived in the time of Louis XV. Its house fronts, arcaded at street level, are decorated with rows of carved masks and surround a beautifully tended garden. In one corner, the eighteenth-century arch of the **Porte Dijeaux** spans the street. East, cours de l'Intendance, full of chic shops, leads to the impeccably classical **Grand Théâtre** on place de la Comédie, built in 1780 and faced with an immense colonnaded portico topped by Muses and Graces. From here, smart streets radiate out. Sanded and tree-lined **allée de Tourny** leads to a statue of Tourny, the eighteenth-century administrator who was prime mover of the city's golden age. Cours du 30-juillet leads into the vast gravelled expanse of **Esplanade des Quinconces**, said to be Europe's largest municipal square, with an enormous memorial to the Girondins, the influential local deputies to the Revolutionary Assembly of 1789, purged by Robespierre as counter-revolutionaries.

Rue Ste-Catherine, the city's main pedestrianized shopping street, leads down from place de la Comédie towards the best of the city's museums, the **Musée d'Aquitaine** at 20 cours Pasteur (Tues–Sun 11am–6pm; €4), an excellent though poorly labelled collection, illustrating the history of the region from prehistoric times through to the 1800s. A couple of blocks east stands the cathedral of **St-André**, with its slender, towering twin spires. The surrounding square is attractive, with its enticing pavement cafés and, at its western end, the classical **Hôtel de Ville**. Just around the corner on cours d'Albret, the **Musée des Beaux-Arts** (Mon & Wed–Sun 11am–6pm; €4) has a small but commendable collection, including works by Rubens, Matisse and Renoir. Look out, too, for Pierre Lacour's wonderfully evocative Bordeaux dockside scene, *Quai des Chartrons*, painted in 1804. Just north of the cathedral, on the corner of rue des Trois Conils and rue Vital Carles, is the **Centre Jean Moulin** (Mon–Fri 11am–6pm, Sat & Sun 2–6pm; free), dedicated to the wartime resistance leader, and holding displays chronicling the fight against Nazi occupation and the horrors of the concentration camps.

Practicalities

Bordeaux **airport**, 12km west of the city, is connected by regular shuttle **buses** (daily 6am–10.45pm; 30–45min; €5.80) to place Gambetta and the train station. **Trains** arrive at **gare St-Jean**, linked to the town centre by bus #1, #7 or #8. There's a small annexe at the station, but the main **tourist office** is in the centre of town at 12 cours du 30-Juillet, just north of place de la Comédie (Mon–Sat 9am–7/8pm, Sun 9/10am–4.30/7pm; ☎05.56.00.66.00, ⓦwww.bordeaux-tourisme.com). For **accommodation**, you could try the *Hôtelière la Terrasse*, 20 rue St-Vincent de Paul (☎05.56.33.46.46, ⓦwww.hotellaterrasse.fr; ❷); or for a bit more comfort, there are several reasonably priced places in the centre, such as *Bristol* at 4 rue Bouffard (☎05.56.81.85.01; ❸), and the *Acanthe* at 12 rue St-Rémi (☎05.56.81.66.58; ❸). The large **hostel** is near the station, at 22 cours Barbey (☎05.56.33.00.70; ❷; 11pm curfew). Note that, though the city centre is walkable, you'll need to use the **bus network** to cover longer distances; tickets (€1.15), valid for one journey only, are available on board, but it's cheaper to buy packs of ten from a *tabac*.

There are a lot of inexpensive **restaurants** in the station quarter, and along the left bank of the river near the station. In the centre of town, wholesome meals and terrace drinks are available at the very popular *Café des Arts* on the corner of rue St-Catherine and cours Victor-Hugo. For typical French cooking try *Croc-Loup*, 45 rue du Loup, or *Le Bistro d'Édouard*, 16 place du Parlement. Rue St-Rémi has a good range of international restaurants, including *Peperoni*, serving up pasta and pizzas at no. 57. The city is home to a good selection of lively **bars**, including the *Frog & Rosbif*, a themed "British" pub at 23 rue Ausone, and the Cuban style *Calle Ocho* at 24 rue des Pilliers-de-Tutelle. There's **internet access** at Cyberstation, 23 cours Pasteur.

Bordeaux's vineyards

Along with Burgundy and Champagne, the **wines** of Bordeaux form the Holy Trinity of French viticulture. The reds in particular – known as **claret** to the English – have graced the tables of the discerning for many a century. The countryside that produces them stretches north, east and south of the city, and is the largest quality wine district in the world. North along the west bank of the brown, island-spotted Gironde estuary are **Médoc** and **Haut-Médoc**, whose wines have a full-bodied, smoky taste and a reputation for improving with age. Across the Gironde – via seven ferries a day from Lamarque to Vauban-fortified Blaye – the green slopes of the *côtes* of **Bourg** and **Blaye** are home to heavier reds, less pricey than anything on the opposite side of the river. South of the city is the domain of the great whites, the super-dry **Graves** and the sweet dessert wines of **Sauternes**, which get their flavour from grapes left to rot on the vine. East, on the other side of the River Garonne, are the **Premières Côtes de Bordeaux**, which form the first slopes of the **Entre-Deux-Mers** – by far the prettiest countryside in the Bordeaux wine region – whose wines are good but not so fine as the Médocs and Graves, and less fine than the superlative reds of **Pomerol**, **Fronsac** and **St-Émilion**, just to the north of the River Dordogne.

The Bordeaux tourist office has information detailing all the châteaux that allow **visits and wine-tasting**, as does the Maison du Vin de Bordeaux, opposite at 3 cours du 30-Juillet (Mon–Thurs 8.30am–6pm, Fri 8.30am–5.30pm; May–Oct also Sat 9am–4.30pm; ☏05.56.00.22.88). Getting to any of these places without your own transport is hard work, and the easiest option is to join one of the interesting and informative wine **tours** organized by Bordeaux's tourist office (May–Oct daily at 1.30pm; Nov–April Wed & Sat only; €26, including tasting), which are well worth the money. Alternatively, you could take advantage of the tourist office's *Bordeaux Découverte* package (from €74): two nights accommodation, guided tours of Bordeaux and a wine château, including tasting, a free pass for the city's museums, and a bottle of wine.

Périgueux

PÉRIGUEUX, a busy and prosperous market town, makes a good base for seeing the best of the Dordogne's prehistoric caves. The centre of town focuses on **place Bugeaud**, a ten-minute walk from the train station. Ahead, down rue Taillefer, the **Cathédrale de St-Front** – its square, pineapple-capped belfry surging above the roofs of the surrounding medieval houses – is one of the most distinctive Romanesque churches in France, modelled on the Holy Apostles in what was then Constantinople. Outside, place de la Clautre gives on to Périgueux's renovated **old quarter**, with a number of fine Renaissance houses, particularly along rue Limogeanne. The **Musée du Périgord**, at the end of rue St-Front on the cours de Tourny (Mon & Wed–Fri 10/11am–5/6pm, Sat & Sun 1–6pm; €3.50), has some beautiful Gallo-Roman mosaics from local sites. There are some exquisite Limoges enamels near the exit; look out especially for the portraits of the twelve Caesars.

The **tourist office** is at 26 place Francheville (Mon–Sat 9am–6/7pm; June–Sept also Sun 10am–6pm; ☎05.53.53.10.63, ⓦ www.ville-perigueux.fr), next to the Tour Mataguerre, the last remnant of the town's medieval defences. There are some good inexpensive **hotels** in the centre of town: try the riverside *Les Barris*, 2 rue Pierre Magne (☎05.53.53.04.05; ❸), which has a great view of the cathedral. Opposite the train station, at 14 rue Denis-Papin, is the more modern *Comfort Hôtel Régina* (☎05.53.08.40.44; ❸). Alternatively, there is a **campsite** on the river, *de Barnabé* (☎05.53.53.41.45). Surprisingly, Périgueux isn't greatly blessed with good **restaurants**, but *Hercule Poirot*, 2 rue de la Nation, and the rather cheaper *L'Amandier*, 12 rue Eguillerie, are good places to try some of the local specialities.

The Vézère valley caves

Half-an-hour or so by train from Périgueux is a luxuriant cliff-cut region riddled with **caves** and subterranean streams. Human skeletons were first unearthed here in 1868, and an incredible wealth of archeological evidence of the life of late Stone Age people has since been found. The paintings that adorn the caves – perhaps to aid fertility or hunting rituals – are remarkable not only for their age, but also for their exquisite colouring and the skill with which they are drawn.

LES EYZIES is the centre of the region, a rambling, unattractive village given over to tourism. **Trains** run daily to Les Eyzies from Périgueux, and the Périgueux tourist office issues a sheet detailing how to get there and back in a day. Worth a glance before or after visiting the caves is the **Musée National de la Préhistoire** (Mon & Wed–Sun 9.30am–noon & 2–5/7pm; €3.40), which exhibits prehistoric artefacts and art objects including copies of one of the most beautiful pieces of Stone Age art – two clay bison from the Tuc d'Audoubert cave in the Pyrenees. Just outside Les Eyzies, off the road to Sarlat, the tunnel-like **Grotte de Font de Gaume** (9/10am–noon & 2–5/6pm, closed Wed; €5.50, Sun half-price) contains dozens of polychrome paintings. Most miraculous of all is a frieze of five bison discovered in 1966 during cleaning operations, the colour remarkably preserved by a protective layer of calcite. Only twenty people are allowed in at any one time and tickets sell out fast; to be sure of a place, get there at least an hour before opening. The Les Eyzies **tourist office** on place de la Mairie (July & Aug daily 9am–8pm; June & Sept Mon–Sat 9am–7pm, Sun 10am–noon & 2–6pm; rest of year Mon–Sat 9am–noon & 2–6pm; ☎05.53.06.97.05, ⓦwww.leseyzies.com) has information on private rooms in the area and rents out **bikes**.

Abri du Cap-Blanc (April–Oct daily 9.30/10am–noon & 2–6/7pm; €5.20) is a steep but manageable 7km bike ride from Les Eyzies. Not a cave but a rock shelter, its sculpted frieze of horses and bison, dating from 12,000 BC, is polished and set off against a pockmarked background in extraordinary high relief. Of the ten surviving prehistoric sculptures in France, this is the best. The road up takes you past the **Grotte des Combarelles** (9/10am–noon & 2–5/6pm, closed Wed; €5.50, Sun half-price), whose engravings of humans, reindeer and mammoths dating from the Magdalanian period are also worth a visit.

Up the valley of the Vézère river northeast of Les Eyzies, **MONTIGNAC** is more attractive than Les Eyzies, but of prime interest for the cave paintings at nearby **Lascaux** – or, rather, for a tantalizing replica, Lascaux II (April–Sept daily 9/9.30am–6.30/8pm; Oct & Nov daily 10am–12.30pm & 2–6pm; Dec Tues–Sun 10am–noon & 2–5.30pm; €7.80); the original has been closed since 1963 due to deterioration caused by the breath and body heat of visitors. Executed 17,000 years ago, the paintings are said to be the finest prehistoric works in existence. There are five or six identifiable styles, and subjects include the bison, mammoth and horse, plus the biggest-known prehistoric drawing in existence, a 5.5-metre bull with astonishingly expressive head and face. Tickets are available from the **tourist office**, on place Bertran de Born (July–Sept daily 9am–7pm; rest of year closed noon–2pm & Sun; ☎05.53.51.82.60, ⓦwww.bienvenue-montignac.com); visits last forty minutes, and the commentary is in French, with English translations if requested.

Montignac is short on even moderately priced **accommodation**, though the *Hôtel de la Grotte*, 63 rue du 4-Septembre (☎05.53.51.80.48; ❷), is a rare exception. There is also a **campsite** a short walk away on the riverbank (☎05.53.51.83.95; closed Nov–March).

Bergerac and the Dordogne valley

Lying on the banks of the Dordogne southeast of Périgueux, **BERGERAC** is the main market centre for the surrounding maize, vine and tobacco farms. Devastated in the Wars of Religion, when most of its Protestant population fled overseas, it is essentially a modern town, yet it is still attractive. What's left of the old quarter has a lot of charm, with numerous late-medieval houses. In rue de l'Ancien-Pont, the seventeenth-century Maison Peyrarède houses a **tobacco museum** (Mon–Sat 10am–noon & 2–5/6pm, Sun 2.30–6.30pm; €3), detailing the history of the weed, with collections of pipes and tools of the trade. Bergerac is the mainstay of the French tobacco-growing industry, somewhat in the doldrums today since the traditional *brune* (brown cigarette tobacco) is gradually being superseded by the *blonde*, which is oven-cured and therefore a lot less labour-intensive to make.

The **train station** is on av du 108e Régiment d'Infantrie, a short walk north of the town centre. The **tourist office** is at 97 rue Neuve d'Argenson (July & Aug daily 9.30am–7pm; rest of year Mon–Sat 9.30am–1pm & 2–7pm; ☎05.53.57.03.11, ⓦwww.bergerac-tourisme.com). For **accommodation**, try *Le Colombier de Cyrano et Roxane*, 17 place de la Myrpe (☎05.53.57.96.70; ❸), a lovely small hotel in a renovated sixteenth century house, or for a bit more luxury, the *Hôtel de Bordeaux*, 38 place Gambetta (☎05.53.57.12.83; ❹), a three-star place with a swimming pool and pleasant garden. There's also a **campsite**, *La Pelouse* (☎05.53.57.06.67), ten minutes' walk north of the centre, by the river.

The Pyrenees

Basque-speaking and wet in the west, snowy and patois-speaking in the middle, dry and Catalan in the east, **the Pyrenees** are physically beautiful, culturally varied and a great deal less developed than the Alps. The whole range is marvellous walking country, especially the central region around the **Parc National des Pyrénées**, with its 3000-metre peaks, streams, forests, flowers and wildlife. If you're a serious hiker, it's possible to walk all the way across from Atlantic to Mediterranean between June and September, following the GR10 or the more difficult *Haute Randonnée Pyrénéenne* – although bear in mind that these are big mountains, and to cover any of the main walks you'll need hiking boots and, despite the southerly latitude, warm and windproof clothing. As for more conventional tourist attractions, the **Basque coast** is lovely but very popular, suffering from seaside sprawl and a massive surfeit of campsites: **St-Jean-de-Luz** is by far the prettiest of the resorts; **Bayonne** is the most attractive town, with an excellent Basque museum and art gallery; and **Biarritz** has the best surf. The foothill towns, on the whole, are dull, though **Pau** is worth a day or two, while **Lourdes** is a monster of kitsch that has to be seen to be believed.

Biarritz

BIARRITZ is a nineteenth-century resort once patronized by the French Emperor, Napoléon III – who built a seaside palace for his wife here – and an impressive list of European aristocracy and royalty, including Britain's Edward VII; today it still has an air of quiet gentility out of season, while its crashing waves make it Europe's premier summer surfing venue, with a prestigious competition held each July.

The town's beaches – particularly the central **Grande Plage**, watched over by the Art Deco **Casino** – are the main attraction, while there are also a few small museums to provide diversion on a rainy day. The **Musée de la Mer**, on the Esplanade du Rocher de la Vierge (daily: June–Sept 9.30am–7pm; July & Aug till midnight; rest of the year Tues–Sun 9.30am–12.30pm & 2–6pm; €7.20) has an interesting collection from the Bay of Biscay in its aquarium, and a roof-top seal pool. Sweet-toothed visitors may prefer a look round the small **Musée du Chocolat**, 14 av Beaurivage (daily 10am–noon & 2.30–6/7pm; €5), with its gallery of remarkably intricate sculptures, all made out of chocolate. It also boasts an unrivalled display of vintage chocolate moulds and machinery. **Asiatica**, meanwhile, at 1 rue Guy Petit (Mon–Fri 10.30am–7pm, Sat–Sun 2–8pm; €7), holds one of Europe's most important collections of oriental art, dating from prehistoric times to the modern day.

Biarritz **train station** is 3km southeast of the centre at the end of av Kennedy. Buses #2 and #9 run to place d'Ixelles, where you'll find the **tourist office** (daily: July & Aug 8am–8pm; rest of year 9/10am–5/6pm; ☎05.59.22.37.00, ⌨www.biarritz .tm.fr). There's plenty of reasonably priced **accommodation** in town: try the charming *Maïtagaria*, 34 av Carnot (☎05.59.24.26.65; ❸), an elegant nineteenth century house in a central, though quiet, residential area, or the small *Hostellerie Victoria*, 12 av Reine Victoria (☎05.59.24.08.21; ❸), towards the northern edge of town. There's a **hostel** at 8 rue Chiquito de Cambo (☎05.59.41.76.00; ❷), 2km southwest of the centre. For **food**, *Bistrot des Halles*, 1 rue du Centre, serves generously portioned, tasty fish dishes; for grills and *frites* head to *Le Surfing*, behind Plage de la Côte des Basques, which is festooned with antique boards. With Spain just a stone's throw away, tapas bars are much in evidence, including *El Callejon*, 5 rue Monhaut, which hosts regular flamenco dancing. Just south of town on the Plage d'Ilbarritz is the hip *Blue Cargo*, which serves fish and salads on the terrace; its tent-bar gets packed after midnight. **Internet** access is available at the tourist office.

Bayonne

BAYONNE is a virtual continuation of Biarritz, although standing 6km back from the Atlantic, it has been protected from any major exploitation by tourism. This is fortunate, for with its half-timbered houses, their shutters painted in the Basque tones of green and red, it is a distinctive and enjoyable town. It is situated at the junction of the Nive and Adour rivers, with the centre grouped closely around the banks of the Nive. **Place de la Liberté** is the main town square, close to the confluence of the two rivers and full of cafés and *pâtisseries*; alongside the Hôtel de Ville on the square is a stop for bus #1 bound for Biarritz and the beaches. On the opposite side of the river, on the Quai des Corsaires – in the area known as "Petit Bayonne" – is the excellent **Musée Basque** (daily: May–Oct 10am–6.30pm; Nov–April 10am–1.30pm & 2–6pm; €5.30), which gives a comprehensive overview of modern Basque culture. The city's second museum, the **Musée Bonnat** on nearby rue Jacques Lafitte (Mon & Wed–Sun 10am–12.30pm & 2–6pm; €3), is an unexpected treasury of art, with works by, among others, Michelangelo, Raphael, Rubens and Degas. Across the Nive, the **Cathédrale Ste-Marie** (Mon–Sat 7.30am–noon & 3–7pm, Sun 3.30–6.30pm; free) looks its best from a distance, its twin towers and steeple rising with airy grace above the houses.

Bayonne's **train station** is in the quarter of St-Esprit on the opposite bank of the Adour from the centre, ten minutes' walk along the Pont St-Esprit. The **tourist office** is a short way west of the Hôtel de Ville, on place des Basques (Mon–Sat 9/10am–6/7pm; July & Aug also Sun 10am–1pm; ☎05.59.46.01.46, ⌨www.bay-onne-tourisme.com). Budget **accommodation** is available at the basic *Hôtel des Basques* at 4 rue des Lisses (☎05.59.59.08.02; ❷). A more comfortable choice is the *Monbar*, at 24 rue Pannecau, Petit Bayonne (☎05.59.59.26.80; ❸). The closest **campsite** is the well-equipped *La Chêneraie* (☎05.59.55.01.31; closed Oct–March), in the St-Frédéric quarter on the north bank of the Adour. The best area for **cafés and restaurants** in Bayonne is Petit Bayonne –*Le P'tit Chalut*, 24 Quai Galuperie, offers decent seafood and tapas, while the *Auberge du Cheval Blanc*, 68 rue Bourgneuf, has a Michelin star, but is still good value. For **live music** and a pint of Guinness, head to *Katie Daly's* on pl de la Liberté. **Internet** access is available at Cyber Net Café, 9 pl de la République.

St-Jean-de-Luz

ST-JEAN-DE-LUZ is by far the most attractive resort on the Basque coast. Although it gets crowded and its main seafront is undistinguished, it boasts a long curve of beautiful fine sand. It is also a thriving fishing port, and the old houses around the harbour, both in St-Jean and across the water in Ciboure (effectively the same town) are very picturesque. At the heart of town is **place Louis XIV**, with its cafés, bandstand and plane trees. The seventeenth-century **Maison Louis XIV** (Mon–Sat June–Sept 10.30am–noon & 2.30–5.30/6.30pm; €4.60) on the harbour side of the square, was where Louis XIV stayed at the time of his marriage to Maria Theresa in 1660, and the suitably stately building houses a fine array of period furnishings. A short distance up rue Gambetta, on the town side of the square, is the large church of **St-Jean-Baptiste**, where Louis and Maria Theresa were married.

The **train station** is on place de Verdun, close to the **tourist office** on place du Maréchal-Foch (Mon–Sat 9am–12.30pm & 2–7/8pm; July & Aug also Sun 10.30am–1pm & 3–7pm; ☎05.59.26.03.16; ⊛www.saint-jean-de-luz.com). There are several **hotels** near the train station: *Le Verdun*, 13 av de Verdun (☎05.59.26.02.55; ❹), is comfortable and has a restaurant attached; alternatively try *Hôtel de Paris* at 1 blvd du Commandant Passicot (☎05.59.85.20.20; ❸). There are plenty of **campsites** in the vicinity, all grouped together a few kilometres northeast of the town; try the *Chibau Berria* (☎05.59.26.11.94), left off the N10.

Pau and the mountains

Once capital of the viscounty of Béarn, **PAU** has had a turbulent history, suffering atrocities from both sides in the sixteenth century Wars of Religion, while maintaining its independence from the French crown until being annexed by Louis XIII in 1620; even today many of the Béarnais speak *Occitan* rather than French. Pau is an attractive and prosperous university town, occupying a grand natural site on a steep scarp overlooking the Gave de Pau, and from its **boulevard des Pyrénées**, the promenade running along the rim of the scarp, there are superb **views** of the higher peaks. Not surprisingly, Pau has become the most popular starting point for the Parc National des Pyrénées, and it's well-equipped for the purpose. Foremost among Pau's own attractions is the **Château**, at the western end of blvd des Pyrénées, now home to a museum (daily 9.30am–12.15pm & 1.30-5.30pm; €3.80) with sumptuous period furniture, mainly eighteenth and nineteenth century.

Pau is probably the best large base for launching into the highest parts of the Pyrenees, since the **Parc National des Pyrénées Occidentales** lies to the south of the town. It's possible to hitch-hike up to the spectacular main passes of **Col d'Aubisque** and **Col du Tourmalet**, though you may well find that you get left on the top by drivers coming up for the view and going back down the same way. The tourist office in Pau supplies walking information and will recommend local organizations that run **guided hikes**. More specialist knowledge can be gleaned from the Club Alpin Français, 5 rue René Fournets in Pau (☎05.59.27.71.81).

Practicalities

From the **train station** down by the river, a free funicular shuttles you up to blvd des Pyrénées. The **bus station** is off place Clemenceau, on rue Gachet. The **tourist office** is at the end of place Royale (Mon–Sat 9am–6/6.30pm, Sun 9am–1pm;

☎05.59.27.27.08, ⊛www.ville-pau.fr). There's a **hostel** at 30 rue Michel-Houneau
(☎05.59.30.45.77; ❷). For **hotels**, try the quiet and hospitable *d'Albret*, 11 rue
Jeanne d'Albret (☎05.59.27.81.58; ❷), or *Le Matisse*, 17 rue Mathieu-Lalanne
(☎05.59.27.73.80; ❷). The municipal **campsite** is on blvd du Cami-Salié
(☎05.59.02.30.49; closed Oct–May), off av Sallenave, 5km north of town.
Restaurants are numerous, too, especially towards the château: *La Brochetterie*, 16
rue Henri IV, has reasonably priced menus and a pleasant family atmosphere; *O'
Gascon*, 13 rue de Château, is equally good, offering local specialities.

Lourdes

LOURDES, about 30km southeast of Pau, has just one function. Around five million Catholic **pilgrims** arrive here each year, and the town is totally given over to
catering for them. Before 1858, Lourdes was hardly more than a village, but in that
year Bernadette Soubirous, the 14-year-old daughter of a poor miller, had the first
of eighteen visions of the Virgin Mary in a spot called the Grotte de Massabielle, by
the Gave de Pau. Since then Lourdes has grown a great deal, and it is now one of
the region's biggest attractions, many of its visitors hoping for a miraculous cure.

Practically every shop is given over to the sale of religious kitsch – Bernadette
can be found in every shape and size adorning barometers, key rings, bottles and
candles. The architecture of the **Cité Religieuse** has grown up around the Gave de
Pau and is scarcely any better. The **grotto** is a moisture-blackened overhang by the
riverside with a statue of the Virgin in waxwork white and baby blue. Suspended in
front is a row of rusting crutches, *ex votos* offered by the hopeful. Up above is the
first church built here, dating from 1871, and below this a massive subterranean
basilica, reputedly able to hold twenty thousand people at one time.

The **train station** is on the northeastern edge of town. The **tourist office**,
which can help with accommodation, is on place Peyramale; turn right outside the
station and then left down Chaussée Maransin (Mon–Sat 9am–noon & 2–6/7pm;
Easter–Oct also Sun 11am–6pm; ☎05.62.42.77.40, ⊛www.lourdes-france.com).
There's an abundance of inexpensive **hotels** on av de la Gare, and more en route to
the Grotte and around the castle. **Hostel** accommodation can be had on the western edge of town, ten minutes' walk from the centre, at the *Centre Pax Christi*, route
de la Forêt (☎05.62.94.00.66; ❶; closed Nov–March). There are several **campsites**
– the nearest is *La Poste*, 26 rue de Langelle (☎05.62.94.40.35; closed Nov–March),
east off the Chaussée Maransin and near the post office. If everything is full, consider staying in **TARBES**, twenty minutes from Lourdes by train, which has a **hostel**
at 88 av Alsace-Lorraine (☎05.62.38.91.20; ❶), and cheap **hotels** near its station.

Languedoc and Roussillon

Languedoc is more an idea than a geographical entity. The modern region covers
only a fraction of the lands which stretched south from Bordeaux and Lyon into
Spain and northwest Italy where once *Occitan* or the *langue d'oc* was spoken.
Although things are changing, the sense of being Occitanian remains strong, a
regional identity that dates back to the Middle Ages, when its castles and fortified
villages were the final refuges of the Cathars, a heretical religious sect. The old
Roman town of **Nîmes** is one entry point; beyond, **Montpellier** is a good base,
though otherwise the coast is not generally noteworthy, the beaches for the most
part bleak strands, windswept and cut off from their hinterland by marshy lakes.
They have the bonus of relatively unpolluted and uncrowded water, but even this is
under threat from development. **Béziers** is an enjoyable urban diversion, as is
Toulouse, the elegant cultural capital.

South of Languedoc, **Roussillon**, or French Catalonia, maintains much of its
Catalan identity, though by contrast with the Basques there is little support nowa-

days for political independence or reunification with Spanish Catalunya, of which it was a part until the seventeenth century. Its countryside is its best feature, its hills and valleys providing some fine walking. The coast is again something of a disappointment, although the region's main town, **Perpignan**, is an attractive place.

Nîmes

NÎMES is inescapably linked to two things: Rome – whose influence is manifest in some of the most extensive Roman remains in Europe – and denim, a word corrupted from *de Nîmes*. Denim was first manufactured as *serge* in the city's textile mills and exported by a certain Mr Levi-Strauss to the USA to clothe miners.

The old centre of Nîmes spreads northwards from place des Arènes, site of the magnificent first-century **Arena** (daily 9am–noon & 2–5/6.30pm; €4.30), one of the best-preserved Roman arenas in the world, which can still hold the 20,000 spectators for whom it was designed. Four centuries after it was built, and with the Roman Empire crumbling away, the arena was turned into a fortress by invading Visigoths. Eventually, it became a slum, home to some two thousand people until the early 1800s. Today it has recovered something of its former role: in summer it hosts bullfights, opera and an international jazz festival. Northeast along Boulevard Victor Hugo is the **Maison Carrée** (daily 9am–noon & 2.30pm–6/7pm; free), a compact temple built in 5 AD and celebrated for its harmony of proportion.

The **Cathedral** on place aux Herbes was mutilated in the Wars of Religion and significantly altered in the nineteenth century. Next to the cathedral in the Bishop's Palace, the **Musée du Vieux Nîmes** (daily 11am–6pm; €4.30) has interesting displays of Renaissance furnishings and decor, while the **Musée Archéologique** (Tues–Sun 11am–6pm; €4.30) on blvd Amiral-Courbet, holds a sizeable collection of Roman inscriptions. Further out, across rue de la Libération, the **Musée des Beaux-Arts** on rue Cité Foulc (Tues–Sun 11am–6pm; €4.30) prides itself on a huge Gallo-Roman mosaic showing the *Marriage of Admetus*, as well as its fine collection of French and Italian paintings. You can buy a **museum pass** (€9.15) from the Arena, which gives access to all sites for three days.

Nîmes **train station** is at the end of av Feuchères. The main **tourist office** is at 6 rue Auguste, by the Maison Carrée (Mon–Sat 8/9am–7/8pm, Sun 10am–6pm; ☎04.66.58.38.00, ⓦ www.ot-nimes.fr). To stay in the heart of things, try the excellent value *Hôtel du Temple*, 1 rue de l'Amphithéâtre (☎04.66.67.28.51; ❷), or nearby *Cat*, 22 blvd Amiral-Courbet (☎04.66.67.22.85; ❷). There's a **hostel** 2km northwest of town on Chemin de la Cigale (☎04.66.23.25.04; ❶), which also has tent space. The main **campsite** is the *Domaine de la Bastide* on route de Générac (☎04.66.38.09.21), 5km south of the centre. For superb regional **food** at reasonable prices, try *Le Jardin d'Hadrien*, 111 rue Enclos-Rey. Place du Marché and place aux Herbes are home to several good cafés and brasseries, while blvd Victor Hugo has plenty of lively spots for a drink. Netgames offers **internet** access just behind the temple, at place de la Maison Carrée.

Montpellier

MONTPELLIER is a vibrant, youthful city, renowned for its ancient university, once attended by such luminaries as Petrarch and Rabelais. Ruled over by the Kings of Mallorca for almost a hundred and fifty years during the Middle Ages, it's a cosmopolitan place, which today is the regional capital of Languedoc-Roussillon. At the town's hub is **place de la Comédie**, a grand oval square paved with cream-coloured marble and surrounded by cafés. The **Opéra**, an ornate nineteenth-century theatre, presides over one end, while the other end leads onto the pleasant park of the **Champs du Mars**. Nearby is the **Musée Fabre** (Tues–Sun 9.30am–5/5.30pm; €3.80), which has a vast collection of largely French paintings, including works by Delacroix and David. Behind the Opéra lie the tangled, hilly lanes of Montpellier's **old quarter**, full of seventeenth- and eighteenth-century mansions and small museums. One of the more interesting, at 7 rue Jacques-Coeur, is the **Musée Languedocien** (Mon–Sat 2–5pm; €5), which houses an eclectic display of ceramics, furniture and tapestries. Further along, on place Pétrarque, are another two local history museums: the **Musée du Vieux Montpellier** (Tues–Sat 9am–noon & 1.30–5pm; free) concentrates on civic history, while the slightly more rewarding **Musée Fougau** (Wed & Thurs 3–6.30pm; free) holds a collection of traditional folk costumes. At the end of rue Foch, on the western edge of town, are the formal gardens of the **Place du Peyrou**. The **Jardin des Plantes**, just north of here, with its alleys of exotic trees, is France's oldest botanical garden, founded by Henri IV in 1593 (Mon–Sat 8.30/10am–noon & 2-5/6pm).

The **train station** is next to the **bus station** on the southern edge of town, a short walk down rue Maguelone. The main **tourist office** is in the passage du Tourisme, at the top end of place de la Comédie (Mon–Fri 9am–6.30/7.30pm, Sat 10am–6pm, Sun 10am–1pm & 2–5pm; ☎04.67.60.60.60, ✆www.ot-montpellier.fr); there's also a desk in the station during July and August. There are numerous **hotels** between the station and place de la Comédie: the basic *Majestic*, 4 rue du Cheval-Blanc (☎04.67.66.26.85; ❷), and *des Étuves*, 24 rue des Étuves (☎04.67.60.78.19; ❷), are both worth a try. The **hostel** is on rue des Écoles-Laïques (☎04.67.60.32.22; ❷), and there's a municipal **campsite** (☎04.67.15.11.61) just south of town on the D21 (bus #28). Of the large number of **restaurants** in town, try *La Diligence*, 2 pl Pétrarque, or *Chez Marceau*, 7 pl de la Chapelle Neuve, for traditional French cuisine. *Tripti Kulai*, 20 rue Jacques-Coeur, is a good vegetarian restaurant. For **internet** access, make for Cybersurf, 22 pl du Millénaire.

Béziers

Though no longer the rich city it was in its nineteenth-century heyday, **BÉZIERS** is the capital of the Languedoc **wine** country and consequently popular with visitors keen on wine-tasting. The first view of the old town as you come in from the west is spectacular. From the Pont-Neuf across the River Orb, you look upstream at the sturdy golden arches of the **Pont-Vieux**, with the fortress-like **Cathedral** crowning the steep-banked hill behind. The thirteenth century building is of little interest in itself, but from the top of the cathedral's tower there's a superb view out across the vine-dominated surrounding landscape, while the **cloister** gives access to a terraced garden overlooking the river. The narrow medieval streets of the old quarter make for a pleasant stroll, with their mixture of sunny southern elegance and dilapidation, and reminders of the town's turbulent history are never far away. Centre of Béziers' life are the lively **allées Paul-Riquet**, a broad, leafy esplanade laid out in the nineteenth century and lined with cafés and restaurants; the *allées* run from an elaborate theatre in the north to the English-style park of the **Plateau des Poètes**, designed by the creators of the Bois de Boulogne in Paris.

Arriving at Béziers **train station**, the best way into town is through the Plateau des Poètes. The **tourist office** is at 29 av St-Saëns (July & Aug daily 9am–7pm; rest of year Mon–Sat 9am–noon & 2/3–6/6.30pm; ☎04.67.76.47.00, ✆www.ville-beziers .fr). For **hotels**, try the attractive *Hôtel des Poètes*, 80 allées Paul-Riquet (☎04.67.76.38.66; ❸), the central *Angleterre*, 22 place Jean-Jaurès (☎04.67.28.48.42; ❸), or the *Hôtel du Théâtre*, 13 rue Coquille (☎04.67.49.13.43; ❹). For **eating**, there are several places on allées Paul-Riquet, or try *Le Cep d'Or* at 7 rue Viennet, which specializes in seafood.

Carcassonne

CARCASSONNE, on the main Toulouse–Montpellier train link, is one of the most dramatic (if also most commercialized) towns in Languedoc. It owes its division into two separate "towns", the **Cité** and **Ville Basse**, to the Cathar wars of the Middle Ages. Following Simon de Montfort's capture of the town in 1209, its people tried to restore their traditional ruling family, the Trencavels, in 1240. In reprisal

King Louis IX expelled them, only permitting their return on condition they built on the low ground by the River Aude.

The main attraction is the **Cité**, a double-walled and turreted **fortress-town** crowning the hill above the Aude like a scene from a medieval fairy-tale. Viollet-le-Duc rescued it from ruin in 1844, and his rather romantic restoration has been furiously debated ever since. Inevitably, it's become a real tourist trap, with its narrow lanes lined with innumerable souvenir shops and regularly crammed with hordes of day-trippers. There is no charge for admission to the main part of the city, or the grassy *lices* (moat) between the walls. However, to see the inner fortress of the **Château Comtal**, with its small **museum** of medieval sculpture, and to walk along the walls, you have to join a guided tour (daily 9.30am–5/7.30pm; €5.50). In addition to wandering the narrow streets, don't miss the beautiful church of **St-Nazaire** at the end of rue St-Louis (Mon–Sat 9–11.45am & 1.45–5/7pm, Sun 9–10.45am & 2–5/7pm), a serene combination of Romanesque nave with carved capitals, and Gothic transepts and choir. Especially attractive are the two colourful Rose windows, dating from the thirteenth and fourteenth centuries.

The **tourist office** is at 15 blvd Camille-Pelletan, at the end of place Gambetta in the Ville Basse (9am–12.30pm & 1.30–6pm, closed Sun pm; ☎04.68.10.24.30, ⓦwww.tourisme.fr/carcassonne), with an annexe in the Tours Narbonnaises in the Cité (daily 9am–6/7pm). **Accommodation** in the Cité is pricey, apart from the 120 bed **hostel** on rue du Vicomte Trencavel (☎04.68.25.23.16; ⓔcarcassonne@fuaj.org; ❷; closed mid-Dec end Jan), and you're better off at a **hotel** in the Ville Basse such as the basic but reasonable *Relais du Square*, 51 rue du Pont Vieux (☎04.68.72.31.72; ❷). The nearest **campsite**, *Camping de la Cité*, is off route de St-Hilaire (☎04.68.25 .11.17) just west of the Cité. There's an abundance of reasonably priced **restaurants** in the Cité, with several touristy, but very good, brasseries located on place Marcou – try *Le Trouvère* at no. 1, where you can also taste the locally brewed *Trencavel*.

Toulouse

TOULOUSE, with its historic, pink-coloured buildings, is one of the most vibrant provincial cities in France, a result of a policy to make it the centre of hi-tech industry. Always an aviation centre – St-Exupéry and Mermoz flew out from here on their pioneering flights over Africa in the 1920s – Toulouse is now home to Aérospatiale, the driving force behind Concorde, Airbus and the Ariane space rocket. Added zest comes from its large student population, second only to that of Paris.

The centre of the city is a rough hexagon clamped around a bend in the wide, brown Garonne. The **Musée des Augustins**, 21 rue de Metz (Mon & Wed–Sun 10am–6pm, Wed till 9pm; €2.20), incorporates the two cloisters of an Augustinian priory and houses collections of outstanding Romanesque and Gothic sculpture, much of it saved from the now-vanished churches of Toulouse's golden age. Outside the museum, the main shopping street, **rue Alsace-Lorraine**, runs north. West of here are the cobbled streets of the **old city**, lined with the ornate *hôtels* of the merchants who grew rich on the woad trade, the city's economy base until the sixteenth century. The predominant building material is the flat Toulousain brick, whose cheerful rosy colour gives the city its nickname of *ville rose*. Best known of these palaces is the **Hôtel Assézat**, towards the river end of rue de Metz, which houses the marvellous private art collection of the **Fondation Bemberg** (Tues–Sun 10am–12.30pm & 1.30–6pm, Thurs till 9pm; €4.60), which includes excellent works by Bonnard. Modern art is on display at **Les Abattoirs**, a vaulted nineteenth-century building on the west bank of the Garonne at 76 allées Charles de Fitte (Tues–Sun noon–8pm; ⓦwww.lesabattoirs.org; €6.10). One highlight is an enormous theatre backdrop painted by Picasso, entitled *La dépouille de Minotaure en costume d'Arlequin*.

The **place du Capitole** is the site of Toulouse's huge classical town hall and is today a great meeting-place, with numerous cafés and a weekday market. Rue du Taur leads northwards to **place St-Sernin** and the largest Romanesque church in

France, the **basilica de St-Sernin**. Begun in 1080 to accommodate the passing hordes of pilgrims, it is one of the loveliest examples of its kind. Inside, the Holy Bodies Circuit (€2) is lined with a succession of richly housed relics and adorned with exceptional eleventh-century marble bas-reliefs. Steps lead down to a crypt, housing more saintly remains and a treasury. Opposite the church is the **Musée St-Raymond** (daily 10am-6/7pm; €2.20), with exhibits charting the history of the Roman town of *Tolosa*, as Toulouse was then known, including mosaics, sculptures and some magnificent Celtic gold torques. West of place du Capitole, on rue Lakanal, the church of **Les Jacobins** is another unmissable ecclesiastical building, started in 1230 by the Dominicans. It's a huge fortress-like rectangle of unadorned brick, with an interior divided by a central row of slender pillars from whose capitals spring a colourful splay of vaulting ribs. Beneath the altar lie the bones of the philosopher St Thomas Aquinas, while on the north side is a calming cloister (€2.30) and a hall which hosts regular temporary art exhibitions.

Practicalities

Trains and buses arrive at the **gare Matabiau**, twenty minutes' walk from the centre down allées Jean-Jaurès or a five-minute métro ride. The **tourist office** is just behind place du Capitole, in a restored medieval tower on pl Charles de Gaulle (Mon–Sat 9am–12.30pm & 2–6/7pm, Sun 10am–12.30pm & 2–5/6.15pm; ☎05.61.11.02.22, ⊛ www.ot-toulouse.fr). Best of the city's central budget **hotels** are the *Castellane*, 17 rue Castellane (☎05.61.62.18.82; ❸), the *Royal*, 6 rue Labéda (☎05.61.12.41.41; ❸), *des Ambassadeurs*, 68 rue Bayard (☎05.61.62.65.84; ❷), and *St-Severin*, next door at 69 (☎05.61.62.71.39; ❷). The closest **campsite** is on the chemin du Pont de Rupé, just north of the city (☎05.61.70.07.35); take bus #59 from place Jeanne-d'Arc. There are plenty of very good **restaurants** in town. *Flunch*, a self-service buffet-style place at 28 allées Jean-Jaurès, offers excellent value, while for higher quality regional cuisine, try *La Cave au Cassoulet*, 54 rue Peyrolières, or *La Gourmandine*, 15 pl Victor-Hugo. The food market on this square also houses several good, small lunchtime restaurants, while if you're just looking for a snack, *Pain Soleil*, 23 rue du Taur, does good hot pasties. **Bars** are similarly plentiful: *Le Chat d'Oc* at 7 rue de Metz has a wide range of beers. Cyber Média-Net, 19 rue des Lois, offers **internet** access.

Albi

Though not itself an important centre of Catharism, **ALBI** gave its name to both the heresy and the crusade to suppress it (Albigensian). Today it is a small industrial town an hour's train ride northeast of Toulouse, with two sights of interest. The first, the **Cathédrale Ste-Cécile** (daily 9am–noon & 2–6.30/7pm), is visible the moment you arrive at the train station, dwarfing the town. The brutal, fortress-like exterior expresses the power and authority the church had over the townspeople. The vast hall-like nave is richly decorated with colourful Italian paintings. Opposite the east end of the cathedral, rue Mariès leads into the shopping streets of the **old town**, but the most interesting sight is next door in the powerful red-brick Palais de la Berbie, which houses the **Musée Toulouse-Lautrec** (9/10am–noon & 2–5/6pm, closed Tues; €4.50). There's a huge collection of the local lad's paintings, drawings, lithographs and posters, from the earliest work to his very last.

The **tourist office** is on the corner of Palais de la Berbie and place Ste-Cécile (Mon–Sat 9am–12.30pm & 2–6/7.30pm, Sun 10am–12.30pm & 2.30–5/6.30pm; ☎05.63.49.48.80, ⊛www.mairie-albi.fr). There's a basic *Auberge de Jeunesse* **hostel** at 13 rue de la République (☎05.63.54.53.65; ❶), with very low-priced dorm beds; inexpensive **hotels** include the *Terminus*, by the station at 33 av Maréchal Joffre (☎05.63.47.09.76; ❸), and the more central *St-Clair*, 8 rue St-Clair (☎05.63.54.25.66; ❸). The nearest **campsite** is the *Camping de Caussels*, about 2km east on the D999 (☎05.63.60.37.06; closed Nov–March). For local **cuisine**, try *Le Lautrec*, 13 rue Toulouse-Lautrec, or *Lou Sicret*, 1 rue Timbal.

Perpignan

This far south, climate and geography alone would ensure a palpable Spanish influence, but **PERPIGNAN** is in fact of Spanish origin, being as it is the home of refugees from the Civil War and their descendants. The southern influence is further augmented by a sizeable North African community, including both Arabs and white French settlers repatriated after Algerian independence in 1962. While there are few memorable monuments, this is a pleasant city with a lively street life. Its heyday was the thirteenth and fourteenth centuries, when the kings of Mallorca held their court here, and it wasn't until 1659 that it finally became part of the French state.

The centre of Perpignan is marked by the palm trees and smart cafés of **place Arago**. From here rue Alsace-Lorraine and rue de la Loge lead past the massive iron gates of the classical Hôtel de Ville to the tiny **place de la Loge**, the focus of the renovated old core, dominated by the **Loge de Mer**, a late fourteenth-century Gothic building designed to hold the city's stock exchange and a maritime court. North up rue Louis-Blanc is one of the city's few remaining fortifications, the crenellated fourteenth-century gate of **Le Castillet**, now home to the **Casa Païral**, a fascinating **museum** of Roussillon's Catalan folk culture (Mon & Wed–Sun 9/9.30am–6/7pm; €3.80). In the gloomy nave of the fourteenth-century **Cathédrale St-Jean**, down rue St-Jean and across place Gambetta, are some elaborate Catalan altarpieces, while a side-chapel to the south, somewhat incongruously, houses a Rhenish altarpiece dating from around 1400. Through place des Esplanades, crowning the hill which dominates the southern part of the old town, is the **Palais des Rois de Majorque** (daily 9/10am–5/6pm; €3). Vauban's walls surround it now, but the two-storey palace and its great arcaded courtyard date from the late thirteenth century. The Spanish–Moorish influence lends sophistication and finesse to the architecture and detailing, particularly the beautiful marble porch to the lower of the two chapels.

To get to the centre from the **train station**, follow av Général-de-Gaulle to place de la Catalogne, and then continue along blvd Clemenceau as far as Le Castillet. The **tourist office** is a short stroll from here, in the Palais des Congrès at the end of blvd Wilson (Mon–Sat 9am–6/7pm, Sun 9/10am–noon & 2–5/6pm; ☏04.68.66.30.30, ⊛www.perpignantourisme.com). The **bus station** is by Pont Arago, on av Général-Leclerc. The best place for **accommodation** is around the station: try the basic but comfortable *Avenir*, 11 rue de l'Avenir (☏04.68.34.20.30; ❷). The **hostel** (☏04.68.34.63.32; ❶) is about 1km from the station in Parc de la Pépinière by the river. The **campsite**, *Le Catalan*, is on route de Bompas (☏04.68.63.16.92), north of town. The station is also a good area for inexpensive **food** - for traditional Catalan fare, try *Le Perroquet*, 1 av Général-de-Gaulle.

The Massif Central

Thickly forested, and sliced by numerous rivers and lakes, the **Massif Central**, occupying a huge swathe of the middle of France, is geologically the oldest part of the country, and culturally one of the most firmly rooted in the past. Industry and tourism have made few inroads here, and the people remain rural and taciturn, with an enduring sense of regional identity. The heart of the region is the **Auvergne**, a wild, inaccessible landscape dotted with extinct volcanic peaks known as *puys*, much of it now incorporated into the **Parc Naturel Régional des Volcans d'Auvergne**, France's largest regional park. To the southeast are the gentler wooded hills of the **Cévennes** that form part of the **Parc National des Cévennes**. Only a handful of towns have gained a foothold in this rugged terrain. **Le Puy**, spiked with jagged pinnacles of lava and with a majestic cathedral, is the most compelling, but there is appeal, too, in the provincial capital, **Clermont-Ferrand**.

Clermont-Ferrand and around

CLERMONT-FERRAND is an incongruous capital for rustic Auvergne – a live-ly, youthful city with a major university and a manufacturing base (it's the HQ of the Michelin organization). Although hardly resplendent with cultural treats, it has a well-preserved historic centre and is an ideal base for this side of the Massif and the nearby spectacle of **Puy de Dôme** and the Parc des Volcans.

Clermont and neighbouring Montferrand were united in 1631 to form a single city, but you're likely to spend most of your time in the former, since what is left of Vieux Montferrand stands out on a limb to the east. Clermont's most immediate feature is its *ville-noire* aspect – so-called for the local black volcanic rock used in the construction of many of its buildings. On the edge of old Clermont, the huge and soulless **place de Jaude** is the hub of the city and its main shopping area. In the centre stands a rousing statue of the Gallic chieftain Vercingétorix, who in 53 BC led his people to their only – and indecisive – victory over Julius Caesar just south of the town. North from place de Jaude, **place St-Pierre** is the site of Clermont's principal market, with a morning food **market**, at its liveliest on Saturdays. The nearby **Musée du Ranquet**, in a sixteenth-century building at 34 rue des Gras (Tues–Sun 10am-6pm; €2), is one of the city's best museums, with displays on local history back to Roman times.

The streets gather up to the dark and soaring **Cathédrale Notre-Dame**, whose strong volcanic stone made it possible to build vaults and pillars of unheard-of slen-derness and height; off the nave, the **Tour de la Bayette** (summer Mon–Sat 2–6pm, Sun 3–6pm; €1.50) gives extensive views across the city. A short step northeast of the cathedral, on place Delille, stands Clermont's other great church, the **Basilique Notre-Dame du Port**, a beautiful building, pure Auvergnat Romanesque, that is on the UNESCO World Heritage list.

Practicalities

The **train station** is on av de l'URSS, east of the centre, and is connected by fre-quent buses with place de Jaude. The **tourist office** is on place de la Victoire (Mon–Fri 9am–6/7pm, Sat 10am–1pm & 2–6pm, Sun 9.30/10am–12.30pm & 2–6pm; ☎04.73.98.65.00, ⊛www.clermont-fd.com), with lots of information on **hiking** and **mountain-biking** in the area. Clermont's **hostel** is at 55 av de l'URSS (☎04.73.92.26.39; ❷; closed Nov–March), two minutes' walk right of the station. There's a cluster of **hotels** outside the station, of which the *Grand Hôtel du Midi*, 39 av de l'URSS (☎04.73.92.44.98; ❸), is one of the least expensive; nearer the centre is the *Foch*, 22 rue Maréchal-Foch (☎04.73.93.48.40; ❸). The nearest **campsite**, *L'Oclède*, is at Royat to the west (☎04.73.35.97.05; closed Nov–March; bus #41). For **food**, the very popular *Crêperie 1513*, 3 rue des Chaussetiers, has a fine setting in a medieval mansion opposite the cathedral, while *Le Café Pascal* and *Le Bar d'O*, both nearby on pl de la Victoire, offer excellent value *plats du jour*. The **Internet Café** is at 34 rue Ballainvilliers.

Le Puy

LE PUY sprawls across a broad basin in the mountains in a muddle of red roofs barbed with poles of volcanic rock; both landscape and architecture are totally the-atrical. In medieval times it was the assembly point for pilgrims heading for Santiago de Compostela in Spain, and amid the cobbled streets of the old town are some of the most richly endowed churches in the land. The surrounding countryside is an added attraction. And the town still produces its famous green *Le Puy* lentils.

The **old town**, reached by climbing the sequence of steep streets and steps that terrace the town's *puy* foundation, is dominated by the **Cathedral** – almost Byzantine in style, striped with alternate layers of light and dark stone and capped with a line of small cupolas. The Black Virgin inside is a copy of a revered original burned during the Revolution, and is still paraded through the town every August

15. Other, lesser treasures are displayed at the back of the church in the sacristy, beyond which is the entrance to the beautiful twelfth-century **cloister** (daily 9.30am–noon/12.30pm & 2–4.30/6.30pm; €4). At the highest point in the town is the giant crimson statue of the **Virgin and Child**, fashioned from the metal of guns captured in the Crimean War; you can pay €3 to climb to the top for some stunning views. The nearby church of **St-Michel** (daily 9/10am–noon & 2–5/7pm; €2), sitting on the peak of an even steeper *puy*, the Rocher d'Aiguilhe, is an eleventh-century construction that seems to grow out of the rock itself. It's a tough ascent, but one you should definitely make: St-Michel is a quirky little building decorated with mosaics, arabesques and trefoil arches, its bizarre shape following that of the available flat ground. Back down below, Le Puy's old lanes form an uncluttered and wonderful maze, while in the new part of town, beyond the squat Tour Pannessac, **place de Breuil** and **place Michelet** form the social hub, where you'll find spacious public gardens and the **Musée Crozatier** (May–Sept daily 10am–noon & 2–4/6pm; Oct–April closed Tues; €3), with exhibits illustrating the local lace industry.

Buses and trains arrive at place du Maréchal-Leclerc, a ten-minute walk from place de Breuil and the **tourist office** (Easter–Oct daily 8.30am–noon & 1.30–6.15/7.30pm; Oct–Easter Sun 10am–noon; ☎04.71.09.38.41, ◉www.ot-lep-uyenvelay.fr), and within easy striking distance of some reasonably priced **hotels**, including the *Régional*, 36 blvd Maréchal-Fayolle (☎04.71.09.37.74; ❸). There's a **hostel** at the Centre Pierre-Cardinal, 9 rue Jules-Vallès (☎04.71.05.52.40; ❶), and a **campsite**, *Bouthézard*, half-an-hour's walk from the station along chemin de Roderie (☎04.71.09.55.09; bus #6). For inexpensive regional **food**, try *L'Âme des Poètes* or *Comme à la Maison*, both on rue Séguret.

Burgundy

Peaceful, rural **Burgundy** is one of the most prosperous regions of modern France and was for a long time independent from the French state. In the fifteenth century its dukes ruled an empire that embraced much of northeastern France, Belgium and the Netherlands, with revenues equalled only by Venice. Everywhere there is startling evidence of this former wealth and power, both secular and religious. **Dijon**, the capital, is a slick and prosperous town with plenty of remnants of old Burgundy; to the north, **Sens** is a worthy stop-off, as is the great abbey of **Vézelay**. South, there are the famous **vineyards**, whose produce has been a major moneymaker since Louis XIV's doctor prescribed the stuff for the royal dyspepsia. **Beaune** is a good centre for sampling the best of the wine. And be sure to try local specialities such as *escargots à la bourguignonne*, *bœuf bourguignon* and *coq au vin*.

Vézelay

The abbey church of **La Madeleine** (daily 7am–8pm) at **VÉZELAY**, one of the seminal buildings of the Romanesque period, was saved from collapse by Viollet-le-Duc in 1840. The church was home, it was thought, to the bones of Mary Magdalene, and so was a major pilgrimage site and assembly point for pilgrims heading for Santiago de Compostela in Spain; today it is a UNESCO World Heritage site. Just inside, the colossal narthex was added around 1150 to accommodate the pilgrims, and is striking for the superb sculpture on its central doorway; on the outer arch there are small-scale medallions of the zodiac signs and labours of the months. The long body of the church is vaulted by arches of alternating black and white stone, edged with fretted mouldings, and the supporting pillars are crowned with finely cut capitals depicting scenes from the Bible, classical mythology, allegories and morality stories, in complete contrast to the clean, soaring lines of the early Gothic choir beyond.

There's a small **tourist office** on the right in rue St-Pierre as you go up towards the abbey (daily 10am–1pm & 2–6pm; Nov–May closed Thurs; ☎03.86.33.23.69, ✉vezelay.otsi@ipoint.fr). Of several reasonable **hotels**, try *Hôtel de la Poste et du Lion* on place Champ-du-Foire (☎03.86.33.21.23; ❸); there's an HI **hostel** 1km along route de l'Étang (☎03.86.33.24.18; Dec–March by reservation only; ❶).

Dijon

DIJON grew out of its strategic position on the merchant route from Britain up the Seine and across the Alps to the Adriatic. But it was as capital of the dukes of Burgundy from 1000 until the late 1400s that it knew its finest hour. The dukes used their tremendous wealth and power to make Dijon one of Europe's greatest centres of art, learning and science. Though it lost some of this status with incorporation into the French kingdom in 1477, it has remained one of the pre-eminent provincial cities, especially since the industrial boom of the mid-nineteenth century.

You sense Dijon's former glory more in the lavish houses of its burghers than in the former seat of the dukes, the **Palais des Ducs**, an undistinguished building from the outside and one that has had many alterations, especially in the sixteenth and seventeenth centuries when it became the Parliament of Burgundy. In fact, the only outward reminders of the dukes' building are the fifteenth-century **Tour Philippe le Bon** (daily 9am–noon & 1.45–5.30pm; €2.30), from whose terrace on the clearest of days you can supposedly see Mont Blanc, and the fourteenth-century **Tour de Bar**, which now houses Dijon's **Musée des Beaux-Arts** (Mon & Wed–Sun 9.30/10am–5/6pm; €3.40, free on Sun), with a collection of paintings representing many different schools and periods from Titian and Rubens to Monet and Manet, as well as religious artefacts, ivories and tapestries.

The palace looks onto **place de la Libération**, a gracious semicircular space designed in the late seventeenth century and bordered by houses of honey-coloured stone. Behind it is the tiny, enclosed **place des Ducs** and a maze of lanes flanked by beautiful old houses, best of which are those on **rue des Forges**. Parallel to rue des Forges, **rue de la Chouette** passes the north side of the impressive thirteenth-century Gothic church of **Notre-Dame**, whose north wall holds a small sculpted owl (*chouette*), which people touch for luck and which gives the street its name. At the end of the street is the attractive **place François-Rude**, a favourite summer hangout, crowded with café tables. Just to the south, the **Musée Archéologique**, 5 rue Docteur-Maret (9am–6pm, closed Tues; Oct–May also closed 12.30–1.30pm; €2.20, free on Sun), has interesting Gallo-Roman funerary bas-reliefs depicting the perennial Gallic preoccupation with food and wine, and a collection of *ex votos* from the source of the Seine, among them the little bronze of the goddess Sequana (Seine), upright in her bird-prowed boat. Being the mustard capital of France, Dijon, of course, has a museum dedicated to the stuff: the diverting **Musée de la Moutarde Amora** on Quai Nicolas Rohin (tours only: mid-June to mid-Sept Mon–Sat 3pm; rest of year Wed & Sat only; €3); tickets should be bought from the tourist office.

Practicalities

The **train station** is at the end of av Maréchal-Foch, beside the bus station and five minutes from place Darcy, site of the main **tourist office** (May to mid-Oct daily 9am–8pm; rest of year Mon–Sat 10am–6pm, Sun 10am–noon & 2–6pm; ☎03.80.44.11.44, ❂www.ot-dijon.fr). Another tourist office is at 34 rue des Forges (May to mid-Oct Mon–Sat 9.30am–1pm & 2–6pm; rest of year Mon–Fri 9am–noon & 2–6pm). The official **hostel** is 4km from the centre at 1 blvd Champollion (☎03.80.72.95.20; ❷) – take bus #5 from place Grangier. As for **hotels**, try the noisy but welcoming *Monge* at 20 rue Monge (☎03.80.30.55.41; ❷), or, at no. 64, the *Hostellerie Sauvage* (☎03.80.41.31.21; ❸). The nearest **campsite** is by the lake off blvd Chanoine Kir (☎03.80.43.54.72; closed Nov–March; bus #12).

There's no problem finding a good **restaurant** in this centre of *haute cuisine*, though locating affordable places is harder. A good bet is bustling rue Berbisey, which has plenty of cafés and restaurants. With a student card, you can eat in the very cheap university restaurant at 3 rue Docteur-Maret in the centre of town, while the *Coum' Chez Eux*, 68 rue J.J. Rousseau, is just a little more upmarket. For a **drink**, try *La Marina* and *Flannery's Pub* – lively bars near the cathedral – or *Le Café des Grand Ducs*, 96 rue de la Liberté. Multirezo, in the bus station, offers **internet** access.

The Burgundy vineyards

Burgundy's best **wines** come from a narrow strip of hillside – the **Côte d'Or**, which runs southwest from Dijon to Santenay. It is divided into two regions – **Côte de Nuits** and **Côte de Beaune**. With few exceptions, the reds of the Côte de Nuits are considered the better of the two: they are richer, age better and, consequently, cost more. Côte de Beaune is known particularly for its whites, such as Meursault, Montrachet and Puligny. The countryside hereabouts is attractive: the steep scarp of the *côte*, wooded along the top, is cut by deep little valleys called *combes*, where local rock climbers hone their skills. The villages, strung along the N74 through the town of Beaune and beyond, are sleepy and exceedingly prosperous, full of houses inhabited by well-heeled *vignerons*. There are numerous *caves* at which to sample produce before you buy – note that the former is meant to be a prelude to the latter. If you are buying, be aware that the *Hautes Côtes* (both Nuits and Beaune), from the top of the slope, are lower in price – and cachet.

Beaune

BEAUNE, the principal town of the Côte d'Or, has many charms, but is totally devoted to tourism. Chief attraction is the fifteenth-century hospital, the **Hôtel-Dieu** on the corner of place de la Halle (daily 9am–5.30/6.30pm; rest of year closed 11.30–2am; €5.10), whose vast stone-flagged hall has an impressive painted timber roof and until quite recently continued to serve its original purpose. It is here that the Hospices de Beaune's wines are auctioned during the annual *Trois Glorieuses*, the prices paid setting the pattern for the season. The private residence of the dukes of Burgundy on rue d'Enfer now contains the **Musée du Vin** (daily 9.30am–6pm; Dec–March closed Tues; €5.10), with giant winepresses and an interesting collection of tools of the trade. At the other end of rue d'Enfer, the church of **Notre-Dame** (Mon–Sat 9.30am–12.30pm & 2–7pm, Sun 2–7pm) has five tapestries from the fifteenth century depicting the Life of the Virgin, commissioned by the Rolin family.

From the **train station**, the town centre is 500m up av du 8-Septembre, across the boulevard, and left onto rue des Tonneliers. **Buses** leave from outside the walls at the end of rue Maufoux. The **tourist office** is opposite the Hôtel-Dieu on rue de l'Hôtel-Dieu (Mon–Sat 9.30am–6/8pm, Sun 9.30/10am–1pm & 2–5/6pm; ℡03.80.26.21.30, ⊛www.ot-beaune.fr) and has information on wine tours. **Accommodation** is pricey: it's cheaper to make Dijon or Chalon your base, but should you need to stay here, try *Hôtel Foch* (℡03.80.24.05.65; ❷), just to the west of town at 24 blvd Foch, or the *Foyer des Jeunes Travailleurs* opposite the hospital on av Guigone-de-Salins (℡03.80.24.88.00; ❷). There's a **campsite**, *Les Cent Vignes* (℡03.80.22.03.91), 1km out on rue Auguste Dubois off rue du Faubourg-St-Nicolas. **Eating** can also be expensive. The best places for budget meals are rue Monge, place Carnot and rue de Lorraine. *Le Carnot* at 18 rue Carnot is a good cafeteria, and menus at the *La Cave à Crêpes*, 21 blvd St-Jacques, start at €7.50. The massive number of **wine** sellers trying to lure you in to sample their wares can leave you feeling overwhelmed, tipsy or both, but one or two of the centrally located vendors are well worth a visit: try the *Caves des Cordeliers* on 6 rue de l'Hôtel-Dieu (daily: June–Sept 9.30am–7pm; rest of year 9.30–11.45am & 2–5.45pm; €3.80, including tasting).

Alsace and Lorraine

France's eastern borderlands were a battleground for centuries. Disputed since the Middle Ages, in the twentieth century they became the scene of some of the worst fighting of two world wars. The democratically minded burghers of **Alsace**, the more beautiful of the two provinces, created a plethora of well-heeled semi-autonomous towns for themselves centuries before their eighteenth-century incorporation into the French state: neat, well-ordered places full of Germanic fripperies adorning the houses – but the Alsatian people remain fiercely and proudly French, despite the German dialect spoken by many. The mélange of cultures is at its most vivid and picturesque in the string of little wine towns that punctuate the *Route du Vin* along the eastern margin of the wet and woody **Vosges** mountains, and in the great cathedral city of **Strasbourg**. By comparison, the province of **Lorraine**, though it has suffered much the same vicissitudes, is rather wan, the elegant eighteenth-century provincial capital of **Nancy** being the main exception.

Nancy

NANCY, capital of Lorraine, is lighter and more southern in feel than its close neighbour and provincial capital Metz, with a relatively untouched eighteenth-century core that was the work of the last of the independent dukes of Lorraine, Stanislas Leczinski, dethroned King of Poland and father-in-law of Louis XV. During the twenty-odd years of his office in the mid-eighteenth century he ordered some of the most successful urban redevelopment of the period in all France.

The centre of this is **place Stanislas**, a supremely elegant, partially enclosed square at the far end of rue Stanislas, whose south side is taken up by the **Hôtel de Ville**, its roof line topped by florid urns and lozenge-shaped lanterns dangling from the beaks of gilded cockerels. On the west side of the square, the excellent **Musée des Beaux-Arts** (Mon & Wed–Sun 10am–6pm; €4.57, €6.10 joint ticket with Musée de l'École) boasts work by Bonnard, Dufy, Modigliani and Matisse. A little north, at 64 Grande-Rue, is the **Musée Lorrain** (May–Sept Mon & Wed–Sun 10am–12.30pm & 2–6pm; €3.10), devoted to Lorraine's history and with a room of etchings by the seventeenth-century artist, Jacques Callot, whose concern with social issues presaged much nineteenth- and twentieth-century art. It's only a twenty-minute walk to the **Musée de l'École de Nancy**, 36–38 rue Sergent-Blandan (Wed–Sun 10.30am–6pm; €4.57, €6.10 joint ticket with Musée des Beaux-Arts). It holds a collection of Art Nouveau furniture and furnishings, arranged as if in a private house – evidence of Nancy's prominence in the movement, a branch of which was founded here by Emile Gallé, a local manufacturer of glass and ceramics.

The **train station** is at the end of rue Stanislas, a five-minute walk from place Stanislas, where you'll find the **tourist office** (Mon–Sat 9am–6/7pm, Sun 10am–1/5pm; ☎03.83.35.22.41, ⓦwww.ot-nancy.fr). For cheap **hotels**, there's the *Poincaré*, 81 rue Raymond-Poincaré, west of the train station (☎03.83.40.25.99; ❷), and the trendy new *4A*, 32 Ave du XXe Corps (☎03.83.37.99.66, ⓦwww.voyages4a.com; ❷). There's a **hostel** out at the Centre d'Accueil, Château de Rémicourt, Villers-lès-Nancy (☎03.83.27.73.67; ❶); bus #4, #16 or #26 to St-Fiacre. *Camping de Brabois* (☎03.83.27.18.28, ⓔcampeoles.brabois@wanadoo.fr) is the nearest **campsite**. For reasonably priced **food**, Grande-Rue and rue des Ponts offer the best choice. Try *Chez Bagot*, at 45 Grande-Rue. The ornate café *L'Excelsior*, across place Thiers from the train station, is a beautiful place for a coffee and a hearty meal. For **internet** access, head to *e-café*, 11 rue des Quatre-Églises.

Strasbourg

The prosperous and attractive capital of Alsace, **STRASBOURG** is big enough to have a metropolitan air, but with a cheerful cosiness that prevents if from being

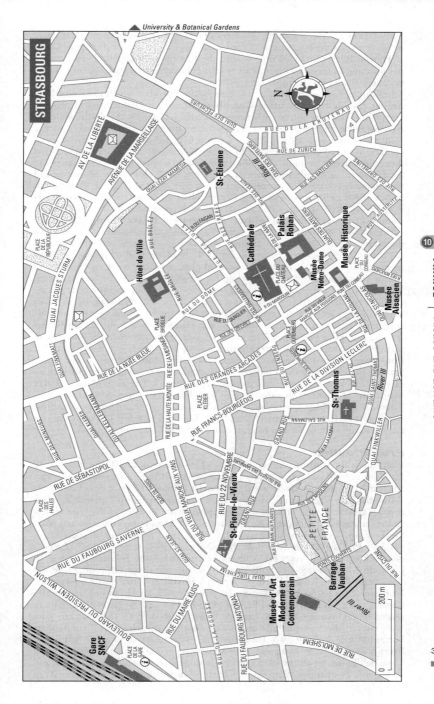

STRASBOURG

University & Botanical Gardens

N

AV DE LA LIBERTÉ

AVENUE DE LA MARSEILLAISE

QUAI DES PÊCHEURS

RUE DE LA KRUTENAU

RUE DE ZURICH

QUAI DES BATELIERS

RUE DES BATELIERS

RUE DES ORPHELINS

QUAI LEZAY MARNÉSIA

QUAI DES BATELIERS

St-Étienne

QUAI AU HERON

Palais
Rohan

Cathédrale

RUE D'AUSTERLITZ

Musée Historique

Musée
Notre-Dame

PLACE DU
CORBEAU

RUE BRÛLÉE

RUE DU FAISAN

RUE DES FRÈRES

Hôtel de Ville

RUE DU MARQUIN

Musée
Alsacien

QUAI JACQUES STURM

PLACE
DE LA RÉPUBLIQUE

RUE BRÛLÉE

RUE DU DÔME

PLACE DU CHÂTEAU

PONT DU CORBEAU

RUE DES COUPLES

QUAI SAINT-NICOLAS

PLACE
BROGLIE

RUE DU SANGLIER

RUE DES ORFÈVRES

RUE DU VIEUX MARCHÉ AUX POISSONS

QUAI DE LA BRUCHE

RUE DES GRANDES ARCADES

PLACE
GUTENBERG

RUE DE LA DIVISION LECLERC

RUE DE LA NUÉE BLEUE

RUE DE LA MÉSANGE

RUE DE LA HAUTE MONTÉE

PLACE
KLEBER

RUE GUTENBERG

St-Thomas

RUE SAINT-THOMAS

River III

QUAI KELLERMANN

RUE FRANCS-BOURGEOIS

GRAND RUE

RUE SALZMANN

ALLÉE LA MARSEILLAISE

RUE DES MINEURS

QUAI FINKWILLER

RUE DE SÉBASTOPOL

RUE DU 22 NOVEMBRE

QUAI DU VIEUX MARCHÉ AUX VINS

RUE DES DENTELLES

RUE DES MOULINS

PLACE
DES
HALLES

St-Pierre-le-Vieux

PETITE
FRANCE

RUE DU FAUBOURG SAVERNE

QUAI SAINT-JEAN

QUAI TURCKHEIM

RUE DU BAIN AUX PLANTES

PONTS COUVERTS

RUE DU DÔME

GRAND RUE

RUE DE LA COURSE

RUE DU MAIRE KUSS

Musée d' Art
Moderne et
Contemporain

Barrage
Vauban

River III

RUE DE MOLSHEIM

BOULEVARD DU PRÉSIDENT WILSON

RUE DU FAUBOURG NATIONAL

Gare
SNCF

PLACE
DE LA
GARE

200 m

0

393

overwhelming. It has one of the loveliest cathedrals in France, an ancient but active university and is the current seat of the Council of Europe and the European Court of Human Rights, and part-time base of the European Parliament. Even if you're not planning to spend much time in eastern France, Strasbourg is a genuine highlight and well worth a detour.

Strasbourg focuses on two main squares, the busy but much defaced **place Kléber**, and, to the south, **place Gutenberg**, named after the pioneer of printing type, who lived here in the early fifteenth century. Close by, the **Cathédrale de Notre-Dame** (daily 8.30/9am–4.30/7pm) soars from a square of crooked-roofed medieval houses, with a spire of such delicate, flaky lightness it seems the work of confectioners rather than masons. In the south transept the slender triple-tiered thirteenth-century column, the **Pilier des Anges**, is decorated with some of the most graceful and expressive statuary of its age. Look also at the enormous and tremendously complicated **astrological clock** (visits 12.15–12.30pm; €0.80), built by Schwilgué of Strasbourg in 1842; visitors roll up in droves to witness its crowning performance – striking the hour of noon with unerring accuracy at 12.30pm.

South of the cathedral the **Musée de l'Oeuvre Notre-Dame**, 2 place du Château (Mon & Wed–Sun 10am–6pm; €3), houses the original sculptures from the cathedral exterior, damaged in the Revolution and replaced today by convincing copies. There's also the eleventh-century *Wissembourg Christ*, perhaps the oldest representation of a human figure in stained glass, from the previous cathedral, as well as the original parchment drawings for the statuary for the present cathedral. Just north of the old centre, across the river, **place de la République** is surrounded by vast neo-Gothic edifices erected during the Prussian occupation (1870–1918), a few hundred metres beyond which are the imposing pieces of contemporary architecture that are home to the European Court of Human Rights and the European Parliament. The opposite edge of the city centre is much more picturesque. Around **quai Turckheim**, four square towers guard the so-called **Ponts Couverts** over a series of canals. This beautiful area, known as the Petite France, has winding streets bordered by sixteenth- and seventeenth-century houses with carved woodwork and decked with flowers. The new **Musée d'Art Moderne et Contemporain**, 1 place Jean-Hans-Arp (Tues–Sun 11am–7pm, Thurs till 10pm; €4.50), stands on the west bank of the river and houses an impressive collection featuring Monet, Klimt, Ernst, Klee and Jean Arp. Just upstream you can see a dam built by Vauban to protect the city from waterborne assault.

Practicalities

From the **train station** take rue du Maire-Kuss and cross the Rhine into rue du 22-Novembre and continue to place Kléber, from where rue des Grandes-Arcades heads south to place Gutenberg and the **tourist office** at 17 place de la Cathédrale (Mon–Sat 9am–7pm, Sun 9am–6pm; ⓦwww.strasbourg.com). The tourist office also has annexes in the underground shopping centre in front of the train station and at the Pont de l'Europe, at the German border. **Hotels** are expensive and often booked up: excellent value are the *Hôtel de l'Ill*, 8 rue des Bateliers (☎03.88.36.20.01; ❷). and *Hôtel du Rhin*, 7–8 place de la Gare (☎03.88.32.35.00, ⓦwww.hotel-du-rhin.com; ❷). A little more upmarket, the *Hôtel des Arts* is at 10 place du Marché-aux-Cochons-de-Lait, in the old town (☎03.88.37.98.37, ⓦwww.hotel-arts.fr; ❸). There's a modern **hostel** at 9 rue de l'Auberge-de-Jeunesse (☎03.88.30.26.46; ❶; closed Jan; bus #2), an HI hostel on rue des Cavaliers, close to the Pont de l'Europe (☎03.88.45.54.20; ❶; bus #21), and more central hostel beds at *CIARUS*, 7 rue de Finkmatt (☎03.88.15.27.88; ❶; 1am curfew); rates at the latter include meals. The nearest **campsite** is at 2 rue Robert Forrer (☎03.88.30.25.46). For **food**, the *FEC* student canteen on place St-Étienne has rock-bottom prices and good meals. Otherwise, eating out can be pricey. *Flam's*, 1 rue de l'Epine, serves the local speciality, *tarte flambée*, a pizza-like onion tart; and *La Victoire*, 24 quai des Pêcheurs, is a lively studenty place. The city abounds in

wine bars and **beer halls**: *L'Académie de la Bière*, 17 rue Adolphe Seyboth, is its most serious beer palace; *La Salamandre*, 3 rue Paul-Janet, is a good place for live music, and is open until 1am or later. **Internet** access is available at *Midi Minuit*, 5 place du Corbeau.

The Alps

Rousseau wrote in his *Confessions*, "I need torrents, rocks, pine trees, dark forests, mountains, rugged paths to go up and down, precipices at my elbow to give me a good fright." And these are, in essence, the principal joys of the French **Alps**. Along the mountains' western edge, **Grenoble** and **Annecy** are the gateways to the highest parts, although you really need to spend several days here to create time for anything more strenuous than viewing the peaks from your hotel window. There are four **national or regional parks** – Vanoise, Écrins, Queyras (the least busy) and Vercors (the gentlest) – each of which is ideal walking country, as is the professionals' **Grande Traversée des Alpes**, which crosses all the major massifs from Lake Geneva to Nice. But on a quick tour you're best off grabbing a taster at **Chamonix**, principal base for accessing **Mont Blanc** on the French–Italian border, or simply doing day walks from the main centres. All **routes** are clearly marked and equipped with refuge huts and *gîtes d'étape*. The CIMES office in Grenoble can provide detailed information on GR paths, and local tourist offices often produce detailed maps of walks in their areas. Bear in mind that anywhere above 2000m will be free of snow only from early July until mid-September.

Grenoble

The economic and intellectual capital of the French Alps, **GRENOBLE** is a thriving city, beautifully situated on the Drac and Isère rivers. The old centre, south of the Isère, focuses on place Grenette and place Notre Dame, both popular with local students lounging in the many outdoor cafés. The city celebrates local boy Stendhal, author of *The Black and the Red*, in the **Musée Stendhal**, 1 rue Hector Berlioz (Tues–Sat 9/10am–noon & 2–6pm; free). The **Musée de Grenoble** on place de Lavalette (Mon–Sun 11am–7pm, Wed closes 10pm; €3.80) boasts an excellent collection of nineteenth and twentieth century paintings; it also has some good temporary exhibitions. For an insight into the region, visit the **Musée Dauphinois** (Mon & Wed–Sun 10am–6/7pm; €3), which occupies the former convent of Ste-Marie-d'en-Haut, on rue Maurice-Gignoux. The French Resistance were particularly active in the Vercors Massif near Grenoble during World War II, and are commemorated – along with victims of the Holocaust – in the **Musée de la Résistance et de la Déportation**, 14 rue Hébert (Mon & Wed–Sun 9/10am–6pm; €3). Finally, the one thing you shouldn't miss is the trip by **téléférique** from the riverside quai Stéphane Jay up to **Fort de la Bastille** on the steep slopes above the north bank of the Isère (9.45/11am-7.30pm/midnight; €5.30 one-way). It's a hair-raising ride to an otherwise uninteresting fort, but the view over the surrounding mountains and valleys, and down onto the town, is stunning.

The **train station** and **bus station** are on the western edge of the centre, at the end of av Félix-Viallet. The **tourist office** is at 14 rue de la République, near place Grenette (daily 9am–7pm; ☎04.76.03.37.53, ⊛www.grenoble-isere-tourisme.com). The CIMES desk in the same office will provide detailed information on hiking and climbing. There are numerous **hotels** near the station, among them the *Alizé* at 1 place de la Gare (☎04.76.43.12.91; ➋). The *Bellevue* (☎04.76.46.69.34; ➌), on the corner of quai Stéphane-Jay and rue Belgrade, has simple rooms with river views. There's a **hostel** 4km to the south of town in Échirolles (☎04.76.09.33.52, ⓔ grenoble-echirolles@fuaj.org; ➋; bus #1). There's a **campsite** 4km to the west, in Seyssins (☎04.76.96.45.73). For reasonably priced local **food** there's a wide selection of cafés and brasseries between place St-André and place Notre-Dame; try *Le Valgo* at 2 rue St Hughes. For **internet** access go to Le New Age Cyber Café, 16 place Notre-Dame.

Annecy

ANNECY is undeniably pretty, perched at the edge of a turquoise lake with views of Alpine peaks. The town inevitably gets busy with tourists, although it also serves as a transit point for hikers. The most interesting part of the city is a warren of seventeenth-century lanes and passages cut through by branches of the Canal du Thiou, which drains the Lac d'Annecy into the River Fier. Opposite the **Hôtel de Ville**, in the main square, is the fifteenth-century church of **St-Maurice**, originally built for a Dominican convent, with attractive Flamboyant windows and walls leaning outwards to an alarming degree. South of here, across the canal bridge, is the grand old **Palais de l'Île** and **rue Ste-Claire**, the main street of the old town, with arcaded shops and houses. From rue de l'Île the narrow Rampe du Château leads up to the **Musée du Château** (April–Sept daily 10am–6pm; rest of year closed Mon & Tues; €4.60), the former home of the counts of Genevois, which now houses Bronze Age and Roman archeological finds, Savoyard popular art, furniture, and, on the top floor, an excellent display illustrating the geology of the Alps.

The **train** and **bus** station complex is five minutes' walk northwest of the centre. The **tourist office** is on rue Jean Jaurès (Mon–Sat 9am–12.30pm & 1.45–6.30pm; July & Aug also Sun same times; ☎04.50.45.00.33, ⊛www.lac-annecy.com), and has a 1:50,000 map of the Annecy area with walking trails marked. The **hostel**, 4 route du Semnoz (☎04.50.45.33.19; ❷), and hotels fill up fast, so it's advisable to book. For rooms close to the centre, try the *Hôtel des Pâquiers*, 3 rue de Pâquier (☎04.50 .51.09.67; ❸); further out, the *Belvédère*, 7 chemin de Belvédère (☎04.50.45.04.90; ❷; closed Oct–April), has great views over the lake. The **campsite** is off blvd de la Corniche, just south of town (☎04.50.45.48.30). A clutch of **restaurants** can be found around the château: *Restaurant des Arts*, 4 passage de l'Île, occupies an especially pleasant position. Also good are the *Auberge de Savoie*, 1 place St-François, a pricey fish restaurant; and *Taverne de Maître Kanter*, 2 quai Perrière. There are round-the-lake **boat trips** from Compagnie des Bateaux, 2 place aux Bois, by the mouth of the Thiou canal (☎04.50.51.08.40; from €9.30). **Bikes** can be rented at Little Big Shop on rue Carnot.

Chamonix and Mont Blanc

At 4807m, **Mont Blanc** is both Europe's highest mountain and the Alps' biggest draw, but by walking you can soon get away from the worst of the crowds. The two approach routes come together at Le Fayet, where the **tramway du Mont-Blanc** begins its haul to the **Nid d'Aigle** (1hr 15min), a vantage point on the northwest slope. There's more exciting access 30km further on, at the resort of **CHA-MONIX**, via the expensive **téléférique** (€30 return) to the **Aiguille du Midi** (3842m), a terrifying granite pinnacle on which the *téléférique* station and a restaurant are precariously balanced. The view of Mont Blanc from here is incredible. At your feet is the snowy plateau of the **Col du Midi**, with the glaciers of the Vallée Blanche and Géant crawling off left at their millennial pace. To the right, a steep snowfield leads to the "easy" ridge route to the summit with its cap of ice. You must, however, go before 9am, because the summit usually clouds over towards midday and the crowds become intolerable. Be sure also to take warm clothes: even on a summer's day it can be well below zero at the top.

Finding **accommodation** in the area can be a big problem. There are some budget **hotels**, but you will need to book in advance; try *La Boule de Neige*, 362 rue Vallot (☎04.50.53.04.48; ❸). You might have more luck at the comfortable and welcoming **hostel** just west of Chamonix at 127 Montée Jacques-Balmat in Les Pèlerins en Haut (☎04.50.53.14.52, ⊜ chamonix@fuaj.org; ❷); take a bus to

Pèlerins-École, from where the hostel is signposted. Otherwise, ask at the Chamonix **tourist office**, near the church at 45 place du Triangle de l'Amitié (daily 8.30am–12.30pm & 2–7/7.30pm; ☎04.50.53.00.24, ⊛www.chamonix.com). **Campsites** are numerous; most convenient are *Les Molliases* (☎04.50.53.16.81) on the left of the main road, going west from Chamonix towards the Mont Blanc tunnel entrance, and *Les Arolles* (☎04.50.53.14.30), on the opposite side of the road, fifteen minutes' walk from the station.

Rhône Valley and Provence

Of all the regions of France, **Provence** is the most irresistible, with attractions that range from the high mountains of the southern Alps to the wild plains of the Camargue. Yet, apart from the coast, large areas remain remarkably unscathed by development. Its complete integration into France dates only from the nineteenth century and, although the Provençal language is rarely heard, the accent is distinctive even to a foreign ear. The main problem is choosing where to go. The **Rhône valley**, north–south route of ancient armies, medieval traders and modern rail and road, is nowadays fairly industrialized, and other than the big city delights of **Lyon** – not strictly in Provence but the main gateway for the region – there's not much to detain you before the Roman city of **Orange** and the old papal stronghold of **Avignon**, the latter with a wonderful summer festival. Deeper into Provence, on the edge of the flamingo-filled lagoons of the **Camargue**, **Arles** is another ancient Roman settlement, retaining a superb amphitheatre.

Lyon

LYON, the third-largest city in France, became a UNESCO World Heritage site in 1998, one of only five urban sites in the world thus honoured. Its charms are manifold, not least its gastronomy: there are more restaurants per square metre here than anywhere else on earth. It also has a beautifully preserved old quarter and an elegant town centre of grand boulevards and public squares. With a population of more than two million, including over 100,000 university students, there is a vibrant nightlife and cultural scene, boasting one of the few national operas outside Paris and a major summer-long **festival**, *Les Nuits de Fourvière*, celebrating theatre, cinema, music and dance.

Arrival, information and accommodation

Lyon-St-Exupéry **airport** is off the Grenoble autoroute, 45 minutes from the centre by bus (daily 5am–9pm, every 20min; €8.20). The TGV train station, **Gare de la Part-Dieu**, is on blvd Marius Vivier-Merle, in the heart of the commercial district on the east bank of the Rhône, and connected to the centre by a regular métro service. Other **trains** arrive at the **Gare de Perrache**, on what was once the tip of the peninsula. **Buses** arrive at one of several bus stations dotted around town. The **tourist office** is on the southeast corner of place Bellecour (daily 9/10am–6/7pm; ☎04.72.77.69.69, ⊛www.lyon-france.com), where you can pick up maps for the city métro, tram and bus system, and book guided tours of Lyon. Tickets for **city transport** cost a flat €1.20, or you can buy a **carnet** of ten for €10.40; the tourist office's **liberté ticket** gives unlimited travel on trams, buses and métro for a day (€3.80). The Lyon **City Card**, also available at the tourist office, covers entry to all museums, monuments, tours and transport (€15/1 day, €25/2 days, €30/3 days). Under 18s can take advantage of the half price "Junior" version. *Le Petit Bulletin* is a free, and very useful, weekly listings newspaper, available from shops and restaurants all around town. For **accommodation** close to the centre, try the comfortable *Elysée*, 92 rue Edouard Herriot (☎04.78.42.03.15; ❸). Nearer the Gare de Perrache is the clean and homely *Vaubecour*, at 28 rue Vaubecour

(℡04.78.37.44.91; **②**). The modern *Athéna Part-Dieu*, at 45 blvd Marius Vivier Merle (℡04.72.68.88.44; **④**), right beside the TGV station, is a very handy option, and consequently often booked up. Vieux Lyon has a **hostel** at 41–45 montée du Chemin Neuf (℡04.78.15.05.50; **②**), with great city views. The closest **campsite** is the Porte de Lyon at Dardilly (℡04.78.35.64.55), a ten-minute ride by bus #89 from the bus station in Gare de Vaise, north of the city.

The City

Directly in front of Gare de Perrache is the green square of **place Carnot** which leads to the pedestrian rue Victor Hugo, in turn opening out onto the vast **place Bellecour**, where even the statue of Louis XIV on horseback looks small. On rue

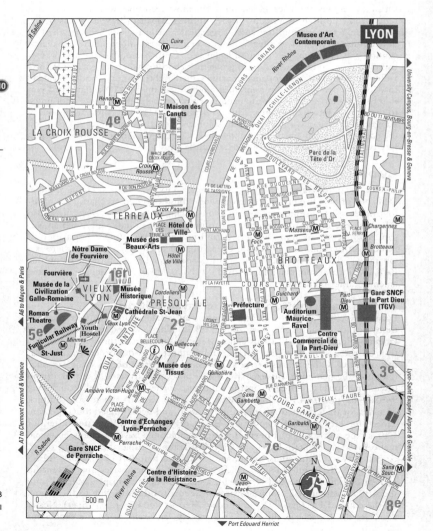

de la Charité, which runs parallel to rue Victor Hugo on the Rhône side, is the **Musée des Tissus** (Tues–Sun 10am–5.30pm; €4.60; métro Bellecour), a surprisingly interesting collection of fabrics, clothes and tapestries dating from ancient Egypt to the present. From here, push straight on up the busy rue de la République, past place Bellecour. Turning left leads to quai St-Antoine, lined in the mornings with a colourful food market; a Sunday book market lies just upriver. Heading back to the centre of Presqu'île is **Place des Terreaux**, the centrepiece of which is an imposing nineteenth-century fountain sculpted by Bartholdi, more famously responsible for New York's Statue of Liberty. The square also features the splendidly ornate **Hôtel de Ville**, as well as the **Musée des Beaux-Arts** (Mon & Wed–Sun 10.30am–6pm; €3.80; métro Hôtel de Ville). This absorbing collection includes ancient Egyptian, Greek and Roman artefacts as well as works by Rubens, Renoir and Picasso.

North of Place des Terreaux, the old silk weavers' district of **La Croix-Rousse** is still a working-class area, but today only twenty or so people work on the computerized looms that are kept in business by the restoration and maintenance of the palaces and châteaux. You can watch the traditional looms in action at **La Maison des Canuts** at 10 rue d'Ivry, one block north of place de la Croix-Rousse (Mon–Sat 8.30/9am–noon & 2–6.30pm; €2; @www.maisondescanuts.com; métro Croix Rousse). From here, cut through the narrow streets of the district to the river and cross to **Vieux Lyon**. The tangled streets on the left bank of the Saône form an attractive muddle of cobbled lanes and Renaissance facades, riddled with the famous *traboules*, or covered alleyways running between streets. Originally used to transport silk safely through town, they later served as escape routes and hideouts for the Resistance during WWII. The **Musée Historique de Lyon** on place du Petit-Collège (Mon & Wed–Sun 10.45am–6pm; €3.80; métro Vieux Lyon) has a good collection of Nevers ceramics, although the **Musée de la Marionnette** (same hours and ticket) on an upper floor of the same fifteenth-century mansion is more engaging, containing the eighteenth-century Lyonnais creations *Guignol* and *Madelon* (the French Punch and Judy), which you can see in action at **Théâtre Guignol**, 2 rue Louis Carrand (Wed & Sat 3pm & 4.30pm, Sun 3pm; @04.78.28.92.57).

Rue St-Jean ends at the **Cathédrale St-Jean**, built between the twelfth and fifteenth centuries, and though damaged during WWII, its thirteenth-century stained glass above the altar and in the rose windows of the transepts is in perfect condition, as is the magnificent fourteenth century clock. Just beyond the cathedral, at métro Vieux Lyon on av Adolphe-Max, is a **funicular station**, from which you can ascend to the two **Roman theatres** on rue de l'Antiquaille (daily 7am–7/9pm; free), and the excellent **Musée de la Civilisation Gallo-Romaine** at 17 rue Cléberg (Tues–Sun 10am–6pm; €3). The drab concrete building houses a wealth of artefacts from the ancient Roman city of Lugdunum, as Lyon was then known, including some superb mosaics, and the lower half of the famed "Claudian Table", a large bronze plaque recording a speech made by the locally born Emperor, Claudius. From here, it's a short walk to the late nineteenth-century **Basilique de Notre-Dame**, a gaudy showcase of multicoloured marble and mosaic. The belvedere behind the church affords an impressive view of Lyon and its curving rivers.

Reminders of the war are never far away in France and this is particularly true of Lyon where the **Centre d'Histoire de la Résistance et de la Déportation** at 14 av Berthelot (Wed–Sun 9am–5.30pm; €3.80) tells of the immense courage and ingenuity of the French resistance, and also serves as a poignant memorial to the city's Jews who were deported to concentration camps.

Eating, drinking and nightlife

Lyon is the self-proclaimed gastronomic capital of France, and not without reason. It has hundreds of **restaurants** offering delicious, if somewhat heavy, Lyonnais fare. Vegetarians will be disappointed, however, as its specialities focus on meat and offal, most famously in its *quenelles* (soufflé-like dumplings) and *andouillletes* (hefty tripe sausages). Lyon is crammed with touristy restaurants claiming to be *bouchons*, typical Lyon wine bars serving food. For the real thing, try *Chabert et Fils*, 11 rue des Marronniers, serving excellent local fare in evocative, *fin-de-siècle* surroundings; or, straight opposite at no. 8, *Le Bouchon des Carnivores*, which offers a beef-heavy menu, and walls covered with paintings, photos and models of bulls. Other options include the *Café des Fédérations*, 10 rue du Major Martin (closed Sat, Sun & Aug), and *Café 203*, by the Opera House at 9 rue du Garet, which is popular with Lyon's trendy set and offers excellent-value menus. *Le Confort Imperial*, meanwhile, at 10 rue Confort, serves very good Chinese food. If you just want a light meal or a **drink**, try the *Bar Americain-Café Anglais*, 24 rue de la République. There are two **internet** cafés worth trying: *Connectik*, 19 quai St Antoine, which has a bar; and *Raconte-moi La Terre*, 38 rue Thomassin (closed Sun), with a bookshop specializing in travel literature. Lyon also boasts a few **gay bars**: head for *La Ruche* at 22 rue Gentil, with 1930s' decor; or *Le Village* at 8 rue St-Georges (women only).

Orange

Around 100km south of Lyon, **ORANGE** is the first major stop in Provence proper, a pleasant town originally built by Julius Caesar for his troops as a reward for the successful conquest of Gaul. Aside from a **triumphal arch** on the north edge of town, adorned with friezes celebrating the campaign, the main feature from this period is the **Roman theatre** (daily 9am–noon & 1.30–5/6.30pm; €5 joint ticket with the municipal museum), the best-preserved example in existence. The finest view of the theatre is from the St-Eutrope hill, into which it is built, past the remains of the forum. At the top of the hill are the ruins of the short-lived seventeenth-century **castle** of the princes of Orange; Louis XIV had it destroyed and annexed the principality to France – a small price to pay for William of Orange, ruler of the Netherlands and, later, also king of England.

The **train station** is about 1.5km east of the centre, at the end of av Frédéric-Mistral; the nearest bus stop is at the bottom of rue Jean-Reboul, first left out of the station. Bus #2 takes you to the ancient theatre and – at the next stop – the **tourist office** at 5 cours Aristide-Briand (Mon–Sat 10am–1pm & 2–5/6pm; April–Sept also Sun 10am–6pm ☏04.90.34.77.88, ⊛www.provence-orange.com); there's an annexe at place des Frères Mounet, close to the theatre (same times). Of the **hotels**, the *Arcotel*, 8 place aux Herbes (☏04.90.34.09.23; ❸), is central, appealing and good value. Orange's **campsite**, *Le Jonquier* (☏04.90.34.49.48; closed Nov–March), is northwest on rue Alexis-Carrel. For **food**, *La Fringale* on rue de Tourre has affordable *plats du jour*, and *Le Yaca*, 24 place Silvian, has a generous choice of dishes in an old vaulted hall. If it's full, try *La Roselière* at 4 rue du Renoyer, or *Le Parvis*, 3 cours des Pourtoules.

Avignon

AVIGNON, great city of the popes and for centuries one of the major artistic centres of France, is today one of the country's major tourist attractions and always crowded in summer. It is an immaculately preserved medieval town, and it's worth putting up with the inevitable queues and the camcorder-wielding crowds to enjoy its unique stock of monuments, churches and museums. During the drama **festival** in July, it's the only place to be.

Central Avignon is enclosed by medieval **walls**, built by one of the nine popes who based themselves here in the fourteenth century, away from the anarchic feuding and rival popes of Rome. Centre of town is **place de l'Horloge**, lined with cafés and market stalls on summer evenings, just beyond which is the enormous **Palais des Papes** (daily 9.30am–5.45/8pm; ⊛www.palais-des-papes.com, €9.50, €11 joint ticket with Pont d'Avignon). The denuded interior gives little indication of the richness of the papal court, although the building is impressive for sheer size alone. The nearby **Musée du Petit Palais** (Mon & Wed–Sun 9.30/10am–1pm &

2-5.30/6pm; €6) houses a collection of religious art from the thirteenth to sixteenth centuries, while more modern works are on show at the **Musée Calvet**, 65 rue Joseph Verner (Mon & Wed–Sun 10am–1pm & 2–6pm; €6) and in the **Collection Lambert**, 5 rue Violette (Tues–Sun 11am–7pm; €5.5). Jutting out halfway across the river is the famous **Pont d'Avignon** (same times as Palais des Papes; €3.50). The struggle to keep the bridge in good repair against the ravages of the Rhône was finally abandoned in 1660, three-and-a-half centuries after it was built, and today just 4 of the original 22 arches survive. The free **Discovery Passport**, valid for fifteen days and available from the tourist office, gives reductions of between twenty and fifty percent on entrance fees to all monuments and museums.

Practicalities

Avignon's **train station** is by the porte de la République on blvd St-Roch, on the southern edge of the centre. There's a separate TGV station in the Quartier de Courtine, to the west, and reached by regular shuttle bus from the stop just inside the main gate. The **tourist office** is a short walk from the main station at 41 cours Jean-Jaurès (April–Oct Mon–Sat 9am–5/8pm, Sun 9/10am–5pm; Nov–March closed Sun pm; ☎04.32.74.32.74, ⊛www.ot-avignon.fr), and there's another office open daily at the Pont d'Avignon. Even outside festival time, finding **accommodation** can be a problem. One of the cheaper options is the *Monclar*, 13 av Monclar (☎04.90.86.20.14; ②), an attractive eighteenth century house just round the corner from the train station. Other reasonable choices include *Le Parc*, 18 rue Agricol Perdiguier (☎04.90.82.71.55; ③), and the *Innova*, 100 rue Joseph-Vernet (☎04.90.82.54.10; ③). There's a **hostel**, the *Auberge Bagatelle* (☎04.90.86.30.39; ②), across the river on Île de la Barthelasse, which also has a **campsite**; take bus #10 or #11 to the bridge, from where you can cross to the island.

    Eating on a budget is easy. The touristy brasseries on place de l'Horloge all do well-priced meals and are pleasant places to sit outside – try *Les Domaines*. Alternatively, try *Vert Citron*. *Maison Nani*, 29 rue Théodore Aubanel, a lively place, also popular with locals, which does good *plats du jour*. Place de l'Horloge also has plenty of places to sip an early evening **drink**. **Internet** is available at Cyberdrome, 68 rue Guillaume, and the tourist office.

The festival

Avignon's **festival**, held every July, is a great time to be in town. Theatre dominates, but opera, classical music, film and street theatre are also featured. Much of it takes place in the Palais des Papes and other interesting locations, while the streets are given over to the fringe. Around 200,000 spectators come here for the show, so doing any normal sightseeing becomes virtually impossible. The festival headquarters, open from May to July, is at l'Espace St-Louis, 20 rue du Portail Boquier (☎04.90.14.14.60, ⊛www.festival-avignon.com); as well as providing the main festival programme and information, it shows videos and a collection of festival memorabilia dating back to the event's inception in 1947.

Arles

Around 25km south of Avignon, **ARLES** was one of the most important settlements of Gaul, providing grain for most of the western Roman empire, as well as being a crucial port and shipbuilding centre – indeed, in the fourth century it became the capital of Gaul, Britain and Spain. Today, Arles is a picturesque town with a laid-back Mediterranean atmosphere and well-preserved vestiges of its illustrious past – not least a marvellous Roman amphitheatre. Arles' most famous inhabitant, **Vincent van Gogh**, spent a fruitful, if turbulent, year here, producing some of his most famous works, including *Starry Night* and *Evening Café*, yet not one of his paintings remains in the town.

Boulevard des Lices is the main street, along with rue Jean-Jaurès and its continuation, rue Hôtel-de-Ville. The most obvious place to start exploring is the central place de la République, between rue Jean-Jaurès and rue Hôtel-de-Ville, highlight of which is the Cathédrale St-Trophime, whose doorway is one of the most famous bits of twelfth-century Provençal carving, depicting a *Last Judgement* trumpeted by angels playing with the enthusiasm of jazz musicians. The cloister (daily 9/10am–4/6.30pm; €3.5), with its mix of Romanesque and Gothic architecture, is also worth a look. Immediately east of the cathedral is the Théâtre-Antique (daily Nov–April 9/10–11.30am & 2–4.30/6.30pm; €3) although the nearby Arènes (daily Nov–April 9/10am–4.30/6.30pm; €4) is the town's most impressive Roman structure. Built in the first century AD, it originally seated 20,000, and is still used for bullfights.

For a better insight into Roman Arles, head for the **Musée de l'Arles Antique** (daily 9/10am–5/7pm; €5.35), west of the town centre on the spit of land between the Rhône and the Canal du Rhône, where fabulous mosaics, sarcophagi and sculpture illuminate Arles' early history. Housed in a splendid medieval building once used by the Knights of the Order of Malta, the **Musée Réattu** (daily 9/10am–11.30am/12.30pm & 2–4/6.30pm; €4) hosts a fine collection of modern art, including sketches and sculptures by Picasso. Opposite are the remains of the fourth century **Roman baths**.

Practicalities

The **train station** is a few blocks north of the Arènes, close to the Porte de la Cavalerie. The **tourist office** is opposite rue Jean-Jaurès on blvd des Lices (April–Sept daily 9am–7pm; Oct–March Mon–Sat 9am–6pm, Sun 10am–2.30pm; ℡04.90.18.41.20, ⓦ www.arles.org), and provides a hotel booking service. For central **accommodation**, try the *Mirador* at 3 rue Voltaire (℡04.90.96.28.05; ❷), or *De l'Amphithéâtre* at 5 rue Diderot (℡04.90.96.10.30; ⓦwww.hotelamphitheatre.fr; ❸), a wonderfully renovated seventeenth century mansion with small, neat rooms. There's a **hostel** at 20 av Maréchal-Foch (℡04.90.96.18.25; ❷; closed Jan), a five-minute walk from the tourist office. Of the five **campsites** within easy reach of the city, the most pleasant is *La Bienheureuse* (℡04.90.98.48.06), 7km out on N453 at Raphèle-les-Arles and with a restaurant and regular bus connections; closer to town is *Camping City*, 67 route de la Crau (℡04.90.93.08.86; ⓦwww.camping-city.com). To sample traditional Provençal **cuisine**, try *La Gueule du Loup*, 39 rue des Arènes, or *Lou Peyrou*, 18 blvd Georges Clémenceau. **Internet** is available at Connexion, 10 rue du 4 septembre (closed Sun).

The Camargue

The flat, marshy delta area immediately south of Arles – the **Camargue** – is a unique area that is used as a breeding-ground for the bulls used in *corridas* around here, along with the horses that their herdsmen ride. The true wildlife of the area is made up of flamingos, marsh- and seabirds, and a rich flora of reeds, wild flowers and juniper trees. The only town is **SAINTES-MARIES-DE-LA-MER**, best known for the annual **Gypsy Festival** held each May, and which is linked by a regular **bus** service to Arles. It's a pleasant, though touristy, place, with some fine sandy beaches, while if you're interested in bird-watching or touring the lagoons, your first port of call should be the **tourist office** on 5 av Van Gogh (daily 9am–6/7pm; ℡04.90.97.82.55; ⓦwww.saintes-maries.camargue.fr), which has information on a number of organized cycle, horse and boat tours of the Camargue. There are also several places to rent your own bicycles and horses, if you prefer to explore alone. Reasonably priced **hotels** include *Le Bleu Marine*, 15 av du Docteur Cambon (℡04.90.97.77.00; ❸), and, slightly further from the sea, at 14 rue Camille-Pelletan, *Le Mirage* (℡04.90.97.80.43; ❸), which also has a restaurant serving Camarguais specialities. The imaginative **Musée Carmarguais**, halfway between Gimeaux and Albaron on the D570, documents the traditions and livelihoods of the Camarguais people and the region's main products, rice and salt (April–Sept daily 9.15/10.15am–4.45/6.45pm; Oct–March closed Tues; €4.60).

Marseille and the Côte d'Azur

The **Côte d'Azur**, synonymous with wealth and luxury, is one of the most built-up and expensive stretches of coast anywhere in the world. While its reputation as a pricey playground for the chic and the international super-rich is still very much intact, that doesn't mean that holidaying here is necessarily more expensive than elsewhere in France, providing you avoid the more obvious tourist traps. The coast's eastern reaches are its most spectacular, the mountains breaking their fall just a few metres before levelling off to the shore. **St-Tropez** is an expensive high spot, though only **Nice** has real substance – a major city with the second busiest airport in the country. At the opposite end of the coast, the vast, cosmopolitan sprawl of **Marseille** is quite different, with its big-city buzz and unique, down-to-earth charm. July and August are, of course, the busiest months of the year, when accommodation can be hard to come by; and May can be equally hectic, with both **Monaco**'s Grand Prix and **Cannes**' Film Festival, pulling in the crowds.

Marseille

France's most populous city after Paris, **MARSEILLE** has been a major centre of international maritime trade ever since it was founded by Greek colonists, some 2500 years ago. Like the capital, the city has suffered plagues, religious bigotry, republican and royalist terror and had its own Commune and Bastille-storming. It was the presence of so many revolutionaries from this city marching to Paris in 1792 that gave the name *Marseillaise* to the national anthem. Though this down-to-earth, working city has little of the glamour of its ritzy Riviera neighbours, it is nevertheless a vibrant and exciting place, with a cosmopolitan population including large numbers of Italians and North Africans. In addition, it's a world-class diving and sailing centre, and, surprisingly, it's also France's second fashion capital.

The old harbour, or **Vieux Port**, is a good place to indulge in the sedentary pleasures of observing the city's streetlife. Two fortresses guard the entrance to the harbour, a little way south of which is the **Basilique St-Victor** (daily 8am–7.15pm), the city's oldest church. It looks and feels like a fortress – the walls of the choir are almost 3m thick – and you can visit the crypt and catacombs (daily 8.30am–6.30pm; €2). On the northern side of the harbour is the former old town of Marseille, known as **Le Panier**, a densely populated area that was dynamited by the Nazis, who deported around 20,000 people from here. Nowadays it's a largely working class quarter, although it's becoming a fashionable area for the young and bohemian. After the war, archeologists reaped the benefits of the destruction by finding remains of the Roman docks equipped with vast storage jars for foodstuffs, now housed in the small **Musée des Docks Romains on place Vivaux** (Tues–Sun10/11am–5/6pm; €2). The quarter's main attraction, though, is **La Vieille Charité**, a Baroque seventeenth century church and hospice complex, on rue de la Charité, which is now home to a couple of museums, including the **Musée d'Archéologie Méditerranéenne** (Tues–Sun 10/11am–5/6pm; €2). Of most interest is the excellent Egyptian collection, with its array of mummified animals, while there are also galleries devoted to Greek, Etruscan and Phoenician antiquities.

Leading north from the Vieux Port is **La Canebière**, Marseille's main street. Just off the lower end, on busy cours Belsunce, the **Centre Bourse** is a giant mall, oddly, also home to an excellent museum of finds from Roman Marseille, the **Musée d'Histoire de Marseille** (Mon–Sat noon–7pm; €3), which includes the well-preserved remains of a third-century Roman merchant vessel, and a small fishing boat, dating back to the sixth century BC. There's also a garden, where you can explore the scanty remains of the Roman docks, now some way from the modern seafront. At the far eastern end of La Canebière, the **Palais Longchamp** (bus #81) was the grandiose conclusion of an aqueduct bringing water from the outlying hills to the city. Water is still pumped into the middle of the central colonnade of the building, whose left wing houses the **Musée des Beaux-Arts** (Tues–Sun 10/11am–5/6pm; €2), which holds a fair collection of French and Italian paintings, with works by Tiepolo, Millet, Corot and Marseille's own Pierre Puget on show. South of La Canebière are Marseille's main shopping streets, rue Paradis, rue St-Ferréol and rue de Rome, and the **Musée Cantini**, 19 rue Grignan (Tues–Sun 10/11am–5/6pm; €3), a collection of twentieth-century art with pieces by Dufy, Léger and Picasso.

A twenty-minute boat ride offshore is the **Château d'If**, the notorious island fortress that figured in Dumas' great adventure story, *The Count of Monte Cristo*. In reality, no one ever escaped, and most prisoners, incarcerated for political or religious reasons, ended their days here. The relatively comfortable cells on the upper floor, with their large fireplaces and windows, held the more distinguished internees, such as the Count of Mirabeau, while the less fortunate were herded into the gloomy dungeons downstairs. Hourly boats leave for the island from the Quai des Belges (€8 return, plus €4 admission to the château).

Practicalities

Marseille's main train station, **gare St-Charles**, is on the northern edge of the 1er *arrondissement*, round the corner from the **bus station** on place Victor-Hugo. The best way of getting around is to walk, although if you need to cover longer distances fast the **public transport** system – bus, tram and métro – is efficient enough, and tickets cost €1.40 from métro stations and on buses. The **tourist office** is at 4 La Canebière, down by the harbour (Mon–Sat 9am–7/7.30pm, Sun 10am–5/6pm; ☎04.91.13.89.00, ⊚www.marseille-tourisme.com), and offers a free **accommodation** booking service. Among the budget **hotels**, *La Maison du petit Canard*, 2 impasse St-Françoise (☎04.91.91.40.31; ❸), is a small, friendly place in the middle of the Panier district; *Alizé*, 35 Quai des Belges (☎04.91.33.66.97; ❸), is basic, but in a good central position; while the *Béarn*, 63 rue Sylvabelle (☎04.91.37.75.83; ❷), is a few blocks east of the harbour. For a bit more luxury, try *La Résidence du Vieux Port* at 18 Quai du Port (☎04.91.91.91.22; ❻). There's only one **hostel**, the *Bois Luzy*, allée des Primevères, 12e (☎04.91.49.06.18; ❷; 11.30pm curfew), housed in an old château; take bus #8 from La Canebière.

Marseille's speciality is *bouillabaisse*, a delicious fish stew served in most **restaurants** around the Vieux Port; the finest place to try it is *Le Miramar*, 12 quai du Port (☎04.91.91.10.40), a local institution with high prices that books up fast. The best low-priced meals can be found on trendy cours d'Estienne d'Orves, which is laid out with numerous **brasseries**: *Le plat Provençal* at no. 28 does very good *plats du jour*. *Les Arcenaulx*, at 25 cours Estienne d'Orves, serves light meals, and has a wonderful tea room, surrounded by shelves of books.

For **nightlife**, the clubs around cours d'Estienne-d'Orves and cours Julien are the places to head for, though prices tend to be high. *Café Julien*, 39 cours Julien, is a popular **bar** with live music at weekends. *L'Énigme*, 22 rue Beauveau, is a camp **gay club**. **Internet** access is available at *Infocafé*, 1 Quai de Rive-Neuve.

St-Tropez and around

The heart of **ST-TROPEZ** is surprisingly village-like, gathered around a port founded by the ancient Greeks and made up of a web of cobbled alleys and butter-coloured houses. Rustic it is not, however: the place was transformed in 1956 after the arrival of Roger Vadim, who filmed **Brigitte Bardot** in *Et Dieu Créa La Femme (And God Created Woman)*.

The road into St-Tropez splits in two as it enters the village, with the **bus station** between them; a short distance beyond on place Georges Grammont is the **Musée de l'Annonciade** (Wed–Sun 10am–noon & 3–6/7pm; €4.60) – a reason in itself for coming here, with works by Matisse, Signac and Derain. Beyond the museum, the **Vieux Port** is the centre of the town, a regular promenade for orange-tanned yacht owners and an international crowd of wealthy style-slaves. Up from here, at the end of quai Jean-Jaurès, rue de la Mairie passes the **Town Hall**, with a street to the left leading down to the rocky Baie de la Glaye, and, along rue de la Ponche, the fishing port with a tiny **beach**. Both these spots are miraculously free from commercialization. Beyond the fishing port, roads lead up to the sixteenth-century **Citadelle**, which has a drab maritime museum but marvellous views from the ramparts, or along to Les Graniers and further **beaches** on Baie des Canoubiers – accessible by a coastal path and by frequent **bus** service.

St-Tropez has no train service. **Buses** arrive at the **gare routière** on av Général-de-Gaulle, a short walk from quai Jean-Jaurès, where you'll find the **tourist office** (daily 9.30am–1pm & 3–7/8.30pm; ☎04.94.97.45.21, ⊛www.nova.fr/saint-tropez). **Hotels** are pricey and regularly full in summer, with few staying open for the winter. *Lou Cagnard*, 18 av Paul Roussel (☎04.94.97.04.24; ❺), is one option, or you could also try *La Méditerranée*, place Croix Fer (☎04.94.97.00.44; ❹), though you'll need to book well in advance. There's a better choice of accommodation in **ST-RAPHAËL**, north of St-Tropez; *Beau Séjour* (☎04.94.95.03.75; ❸) on promenade René-Coty is one of the cheapest hotels here. **Camping** poses similar problems: the two closest sites to St-Tropez are on the plage du Pampelonne and cost a fortune. Better is *Les Tournels* on route de Camarat near Ramatuelle (☎04.94.55.90.90). There are plenty **restaurants** on rue Clemenceau and place des Lices, but don't expect any bargains: try *La Patate* or *Café des Arts*.

Cannes

Fishing village turned millionaires' playground, **CANNES** is chiefly known for the **International Film Festival**, held in May, during which time the place is overrun by the denizens of Movieland, their hangers-on, and a small army of paparazzi. The seafront promenade, **La Croisette**, and the **Vieux Port** form the focus of Cannes life, while the old town, **Le Suquet**, on the steep hill overlooking the bay from the west, with its quaint winding streets and eleventh century castle, is a pleasant place to wander. Meanwhile, the attractive **îles de Lérins**, composed of touristy **Ste Marguerite** and the quieter **St Honorat**, home to a Cistercian monastery, are just a fifteen-minute ferry ride from the Vieux Port (€8).

The **train station** is on rue Jean-Jaurès, a short walk north of the centre along rue des Serbes. Finding accommodation can be a problem during high season, and all but impossible during the Film Festival, when prices are bumped up considerably. There are several budget **hotels** around the train station: try the *Bourgogne*, 11 rue du 24-Août (☎04.93.38.36.73; ❷), or nearby *Little Palace*, at no. 18 (☎04.92.98.18.18; ❸). Another option, a little closer to the seafront, is the cosy *Albe*, 31 rue Bivouac Napoléon (☎04.97.06.21.21; ❸). The nearest **campsite** is *Parc Bellevue*, 67 av Maurice Chevalier (☎04.93.47.28.97; bus #2 or #9). There's a **tourist office** at the train station (daily 9am–noon & 2–6pm), with the main office in the Palais des Festivals on the waterfront (daily 9am–7pm; ☎04.93.39.24.53, ⊛ www.cannes-on-line.com). Le Suquet is full of **restaurants**, which get cheaper as you reach the top. *Au Bec Fin*, 12 rue du 24-août, has superb traditional cooking and good *plats du jour*; *Le Sevrina*, 3 rue Félix Faure, serves pizza, pasta and fondue; and *Le Bouchon d'Objectif*, 10 rue de Constantine, is an excellent, reasonably priced bistro. Cannes abounds with **nightclubs**, though prices, as you might expect, are high; try *Deep Purple* (closed Mon), 17 rue des Frères Pradignac. **Internet** access is available at *Station-Cyber*, 32 rue Jean-Jaurès.

Nice

NICE, capital of the French Riviera and fifth-largest city in the country, grew into a major tourist resort in the nineteenth century, when large numbers of foreign visitors – many of them British – were drawn here by the health-giving properties of the mild Mediterranean climate. The most obvious legacy of these early holiday-makers is the famous **promenade des Anglais** stretching along the pebble beach, laid out by nineteenth-century English residents to facilitate their afternoon stroll by the sea, while Russian aristocrats erected an **Orthodox Cathedral** at the end of av Nicolas II, not far from the train station. These days, it's a busy, bustling city with an incredible amount of traffic, but it's still a lovely place, with a beautiful location and attractive historical centre. The city also makes the best base for visiting the Riviera coast, which stretches for 30km, east to the Italian border and west to Cannes. The **Carnival of Nice** (Feb/early March) packs out the town, with parades and music culminating at Mardi Gras, a city-wide party that takes up every street.

The **old town** nestles around the hill of Nice's former château, a rambling collection of narrow alleys lined with tall, rust-and-ochre houses, sadly scarred by a bewildering amount of graffiti, and centring on place Rossetti and the Baroque **Cathédrale Ste-Réparate**. Nearby is the entrance to the **parc du Château** (there's an elevator and stairway by the Tour Bellanda, at the eastern end of the Quai des États-Unis), decked out in a mock-Grecian style harking back to the original Greek settlement of Nikea. The point of climbing the stairs, apart from enjoying the perfumed greenery, is the view stretching west over the bay. Nearby, on Promenade des Arts, is the **Musée d'Art Moderne et d'Art Contemporain** (10am–6pm, closed Tues; €3.80), with a collection of Pop Art and neo-Realist work, including pieces by Andy Warhol and Roy Lichtenstein. The **Musée des Beaux-Arts** (Tues–Sun 10am–noon & 2–6pm; €3.80), meanwhile, is on the other side of town at 33 av des Baumettes, with a superb collection of works dating from the fifteenth to the twentieth century.

Up above the city centre, **Cimiez**, a posh suburb reached by bus #15 from av Thiers, was the social centre of the town's elite some seventeen centuries ago, when the city was capital of the Roman province of Alpes-Maritimae. Excavations of the Roman baths are housed, along with accompanying archeological finds, in the **Musée d'Archéologie**, 160 av des Arènes (Tues–Sun 10am–noon/1pm & 2–5/6pm; €3.80). Overlooking the baths is the wonderful **Musée Matisse** (10am–5/6pm, closed Tues; €3.80): Nice was the artist's home for much of his life, and the collection covers every period and includes models for the chapel in Vence, a complete set of the books that he illustrated, and *Fleurs et Fruits*, a large decorative piece created for a Californian villa by Matisse in 1953. Amongst the paintings are the 1919 *Tempête à Nice* and *Fenêtre à Tahiti*, painted in 1936.

Practicalities

Nice **airport**, the busiest in France after Paris, is 6km southwest of the city and connected to its train station by bus #23 (daily 6am–9pm; 30min; €1.30) and centre by shuttle bus (every 15min; €4). The main **train station**, Nice-Ville, is ten minutes' walk northwest from the centre, at the top of av Jean-Médecin. There's a **tourist office** next to the station on av Thiers (Mon–Sat 8am–7/8pm; May–Sept also Sun 9am–6pm) and an annexe at the airport (daily 8am–10pm), but the main office is at 5 promenade des Anglais (Mon–Sat 8/9am–6/8pm; May–Sept also Sun 9am–6pm; ☏04.92.14.48.00, ⊕www.nicetourism.com). For **city transport**, single bus tickets (€1) can be bought on board, while *carnets* of ten (€8.50) are available from kiosks and *tabacs*, who also sell the one-, five- and seven-day bus pass (€3.80, €13, €17), as do Sunbus, 10 av Félix-Faure.

There are lots of cheap, though not terribly attractive, **hotels** around the train station, including *Les Orangers*, 10bis av Durante (☏04.93.87.51.41; ❸; closed Nov). There's a better choice in the centre of town, such as the friendly *Carlyna,* 2 rue

Sacha Guitry (☎04.93.80.77.21; ❹), and the *Cronstadt*, 3 rue Cronstadt (☎04.93.82.00.30; ❹). The **hostel** is 4km out of town on route Forestière du Mont Alban (☎04.93.89.23.64; ❷); take bus #14 from place Masséna. The tourist office has a list of **campsites** in the area.

The old town stays up late and is full of **restaurants**. Marché aux Fleurs (not to be missed in the mornings for its colourful market) is lined with restaurants, their tables spilling outdoors, but they tend to be quite pricey. *Pasta Basta*, 18 rue de la Préfecture, offers very good value *plats du jour*; while *Chez René Socca*, 2 rue Miralhéti, serves Niçois specialities at busy outdoor tables, including great *socca*, a pancake made from chickpea flour. *Passez à Table*, 30 rue Pertinax, serves vegetarian meals and organic produce. *Wayne's* **bar** on rue de la Préfecture has live music and is popular with backpackers. For the best ice-cream in town, head for *Fenocchio* on place Rossetti, where you can sample such novelties as lavender, tomato and thyme. *La Florentine*, on the corner of rue de France and rue Meyerbeer, in the new part of town, is a great place for authentic Italian coffee and pastries. For **internet** access, try Cyber Point at 10 av Félix Faure.

Monaco

The tiny independent principality of **MONACO**, with its tight concentration of gleaming modern banks and offices, rears up over the rocky Riviera coast like a Mediterranean Hong Kong. Identified worldwide with gambling and motor-racing, this overcrowded tax-haven is also one of the greatest sites for property speculation anywhere. Finding out about the workings of the regime is not easy, but it is clear that there is no opposition to the ruling family, the Grimaldis, who have held power here for more than seven centuries. The present Prince, Rainier III – who famously married American actress, Grace Kelly – has been on the throne since 1949. A copy of every French law is sent to Monaco, reworded, and put to the Prince: if he likes it, it is passed; if not, it's not. There is a parliament of limited function elected by Monagesque nationals – who comprise about sixteen percent of the population – but there's no opposition to the Prince's rule.

The three-kilometre-long state consists of the old town of **Monaco-Ville** around the palace on a high promontory; the new suburb and marina of **Fontvieille** in its western shadow; **La Condamine** behind the harbour on the other side of the rock; **Larvotto**, to the east with its artificial beaches of imported sand; and, in the middle, **MONTE CARLO**. There are relatively few conventional sights, only the toy-town palace (Changing of the Guard daily at noon) and assorted museums in the old town, the most interesting – and expensive – of which is the **Musée Océanographique**, overlooking the sea on av St-Martin (daily 9/10am–6/7pm; €11). The upper floors house displays reflecting the maritime interests of the museum's founder, Prince Albert I, including models of his ships and the stuffed and skeletal remains of his prize catches, including a gigantic fin whale. Most visitors, though, head straight for the superb **aquarium** in the basement, where, amongst other things, you can see a full-sized, living coral reef, transplanted from the Red Sea into a 40,000 litre tank, and inhabited by a rich array of colourful fish. Also unmissable is the famous **Casino** (daily noon–dawn), with its riotously Rococo American Room and European Gaming Rooms; admission (€10) is for over 21s only – and you'll be refused entry if you don't look enough like a gambler.

Monaco's labyrinthine **train station** is on av Prince-Pierre in La Condamine, a short walk from the **bus station** on place d'Armes. Bus #4, direction Larvotto, takes you from the train station to the Casino-Tourism stop, near the **tourist office** at 2a blvd des Moulins (Mon–Sat 9am–7pm, Sun 10am–noon; ☎92.16.61.66, ⊛www.monaco-tourisme.com). Monaco's one good public service is the clean, efficient and free **lift system** for steep north–south journeys. **Accommodation** is often in short supply, especially when the Grand Prix is in town. La Condamine is your best bet: try *Cosmopolite*, 4 rue de la Turbie

(☎93.30.16.95; ❷), or its neighbour, *Hôtel de France* (☎93.30.24.64; ❸). If you're under 26 or a student under 31, and arrive early enough, you might get a **dorm bed** at the *Centre de Jeunesse Princesse Stéphanie,* near the station at 24 av Prince-Pierre (☎93.50.83.20; ❷). La Condamine and the old town are the places to look for **restaurants**, but you'll be hard pressed to find anything affordable – though *Costa Monaco*, 178 blvd Princesse Charlotte, Monte Carlo, does serve surprisingly cheap light meals and sandwiches.

Corsica

Despite nearly two-and-a-half centuries of French rule, the island of **CORSICA** has more in common culturally with Italy than with its governing country, as testified by a profusion of Italianate churches and a language that's closely related to the Tuscan dialect. A history of repeated invasion has strengthened the cultural identity of an island whose reputation for violence and xenophobia has overshadowed the more hospitable nature of its inhabitants. The island, over one third of which is Regional Park, comprises an amazing diversity of landscapes: its magnificent rocky coastline is interspersed with outstanding beaches, while the inland mountains offer numerous opportunities for hiking. The extensive forests and sparkling rivers provide the locals with a rich supply of game and fresh fish: regional specialities include wild boar, blackbird pâté, cured hams and sausages.

Two French *départements* divide Corsica, each with its own capital: Napoleon's birthplace, **Ajaccio**, is on the southwest coast, while **Bastia** faces Italy in the north. The old capital of **Corte** is one of many fortress towns that characterize the interior. Of the coastal resorts, **Calvi** draws tourists with its massive citadelle and long sandy beach; while **Bonifacio**, huddled on the southernmost point facing Sardinia, is superbly located, with a tightly packed grid of Genoan houses perched atop limestone cliffs buffeted by the clearest water in the Mediterranean. Trains connect Ajaccio, Bastia, Corte and Calvi; for Bonifacio you're reliant on **buses**.

Ajaccio

Set in a magnificent bay, **AJACCIO** combines all the ingredients of the archetypal Mediterranean resort with its palm trees, spacious squares, yachts and street cafés. **Napoleon**, who was born here in 1769, gave the town fame, but did little else for the place except to make it the island capital for the brief period of his empire; and while you can visit his family house, now a museum, there's not a great deal else to see. It is, however, a pleasant place to spend some time, particularly around the ancient streets surrounding the fifteenth-century Genoese citadelle.

Cours Napoléon is the main thoroughfare, running parallel to the sea and culminating in place Général-de-Gaulle, which in turn leads onto **place Foch**, a shady, palm-lined square bordered by cafés and restaurants and open to the sea. The most rewarding attractions are the **Musée Fesch** (Mon 1–5.15/6.30pm, Tues–Sun

---

Ferries to Corsica

For full details, go to ⓦwww.corsicaferries.com, ⓦwww.corsica-marittima.com, ⓦwww.mobylines.it or ⓦwww.sncm.fr.

Genoa (Italy) to: Bastia (June–Sept 2–4 weekly; 6–11hr).
Livorno (Italy) to: Bastia (April–Oct 1–6 daily; 4–7hr).
Marseille to: Ajaccio (3–7 weekly; 4hr 30min–11hr); Bastia (1–3 weekly; 10hr).

Nice to: Ajaccio (1–6 weekly; 12hr); Bastia (3–24 weekly; 6–7hr); Calvi (2–5 weekly; 2hr 45min).
Toulon to: Ajaccio (April–Sept 1–3 weekly; 10hr); Bastia (April–Oct 1–3 weekly; 8hr 30min).

9.15am–12.15pm & 2.15–5.15/6.30pm; €5.40), halfway down rue Cardinal-Fesch, and home to an important collection of Italian paintings from the fifteenth and sixteenth centuries – the legacy of Napoléon's step-uncle Cardinal Joseph Fesch – and the **Chapelle Impériale** (€1.50 extra), where the Bonaparte family vaults have been gathered.

As for **beaches**, head for the one that is twenty minutes' walk southwest down the promenade. Better still, jump on one of the hourly buses that run from the *terminal routier* to the beaches beyond Porticcio, on the far southern side of the gulf.

Practicalities

The **airport**, Campo dell'Oro, is 8km southeast and connected to the town by hourly bus #8. The **ferry port** and **bus station** occupy the same building in the town centre, but the **train station** is a ten-minute walk north along the seafront. The **tourist office** (summer Mon–Sat 9am–8.30pm, Sun 9am–1pm; winter Mon–Fri 8am–6pm, Sat 8am–noon & 2–5pm; ☎04.95.51.53.03, ⊛www.tourisme .fr/ajaccio) occupies the ground floor of the Hôtel de Ville in place Foch, directly opposite the market square.

Budget **accommodation** is thin on the ground and books up fast. Try *Le Dauphin*, just north of the ferry port/bus station on blvd Sampiero (☎04.95.21.12.94; ❸); *Hôtel Du Palais*, just off cours Napoleon at 5 avenue Bévérini-Vico (☎04.95.22.73.68; ❹); or *Marengo*, twenty minutes' walk from the centre at 2 rue Marengo (☎04.95.21.43.66; ❸). The most convenient **campsite** is *Le Barbicaja*, 5km west (☎04.95.52.01.17; closed Nov–March); take bus #5 from place de Gaulle.

For location, the **restaurants** along the quai de la Citadelle are hard to beat, though the seafood served up tends to be mediocre; stick to pizza and a *pichet* of house red and you'll not go far wrong. Alternatively, head for the restaurants lining the rue des Halles, the alley behind the covered market: *Les Halles* is an old favourite, as is *L'Aquarium*, two doors down. **Bars and cafés** take up much pavement space, with cocktail bars and *glaciers* lining the seafront behind the beach. *Safari*, by the beach at 18 blvd Lantivy, is popular, while the innovative *Café de la Flore*, opposite Palais Fesch, hosts live jazz. La Marge, 4 rue Emanuelle-Arène, offers **internet** access, as does U Borgu, 52 rue Fesch.

Bastia

BASTIA is a charismatic harbour town, its crumbling buildings set against a backdrop of bare hills. Now a thriving commercial port, it was the island capital under the Genoese and has remained a working town with few concessions to tourism. It has much to recommend it: the dilapidated Vieux Port, a sprinkling of Baroque churches, the imposing citadel, or bastion, from which the town gets its name, and the vast place St-Nicolas, lined with trees and cafés open to the sea.

The most appealing area is the **Vieux Port**, the site of the original fishing village around which the town grew, nowadays a tranquil backwater. Dominating the harbour are the twin towers of **Église St-Jean-Baptiste**, the largest but not the most interesting church in Bastia, which shoulders the place du Marché, where a lively **market** takes place each morning. The narrow streets nearby, a flaking conglomeration of tenement blocks in attractive decay, are known as **Terra Vecchia**. Close by, in rue Napoléon, are two Baroque churches whose dull facades belie their interiors. Halfway up the street stands the little **Oratoire de l'Immaculée Conception**, dating from 1611, a Genoese showplace used for state occasions such as the inauguration of the Anglo-Corsican parliament in the 1760s.

Bastia's **airport**, Poretta, is 16km south of town off RN197. Shuttle **buses** to the centre (€7.60) stop opposite the **train station**, located above place St-Nicolas; other buses stop at the top of boulevard Paoli or outside the train station. **Ferries** use the Nouveau Port, five minutes' walk from the centre. The **tourist office** in place St-Nicolas (8am–6/7pm; Oct–May closed Sun) is only worth dropping into for bus timetables. **Accommodation** can be hard to find, especially at the height of the season. Pick of the budget bunch is the *Central*, 3 rue Miot (☎04.95.31.71.12; ❸), just off the place St-Nicolas; alternatively, there's the *Riviera*, 1 rue du Nouveau Port (☎04.95.31.07.16; ❹), and the *Univers*, 3 av du Maréchal-Sébastiani (☎04.95.31.03.38; ❺). Top **campsite** is *Camping Casanova* (☎04.95.33.28.90; closed Nov–Feb), 4km north at Miomo; take the Erbalunga bus from opposite the tourist office. The Vieux Port and nearby market place are crammed with **restaurants**. For lunch, *La Table du Marché* (☎04.95.31.64.25), on the east side of place du Marché, has the best deal. In the evening, head for the outdoor **cafés** on the harbourside or the quirky *Chez Jo La Braise* (☎04.95.31.36.97).

Corte

Set against a spectacular backdrop of craggy mountains, **CORTE**, the island's only interior town, is regarded as the spiritual capital of Corsica, as this is where Pascal Paoli had his seat of government during the brief period of independence in the eighteenth century. Paoli founded a university here which was reopened in the early 1980s, and its student population add a much needed bit of life. For outdoor enthusiasts, this is also an ideal base for trekking into the island's watershed, with two superb gorges stretching west into the heart of the mountains.

The main street, **cours Paoli**, runs the length of town, culminating in place Paoli, a pleasant market square lined with cafés. A cobbled ramp leads from there up to the Ville Haute, where you can still see the bullet marks made by Genoese soldiers during the War of Independence in tiny **place Gaffori**. The statue is of General Gaffori, one of Paoli's right-hand men, who led the independent army in 1756. Continuing north you'll soon come to the gates of the **Citadelle**. Enclosed behind its well preserved ramparts is the **Museu di a Corsica** (Tues–Sun 10am–6/8pm; June–Sept also Mon; Nov & Dec closed Sun; €5.5), hosting a collection of old farming implements that's far less compelling than the recently erected building itself. Best views of the citadelle, the town and its valley are from the **Belvédère**, a platform opposite the tower which you don't have to pay to reach.

Corte's **train station** is 1km east of town at the foot of the hill near the university. **Buses** stop at the south end of cours Paoli. The **tourist office** is within the citadelle (Mon–Fri 9am–1pm & 2–6/8pm; ☎04.95.46.26.70, ⊛www.corte-tourism.com), with a summer-only annexe at the train station. **Accommodation** is plentiful and cheap by comparison with the rest of the island. Head for the *Hôtel HR*, near the train station on allée du 9 Septembre (☎04.95.45.11.11; ❷), a charmless, but cheap, converted police station; the more characterful *de la Poste*, 2 place Padoue (☎04.95.46.01.37; ❸); or the smart, friendly and efficient *du Nord et de L'Europe*, halfway along cours Paoli (☎04.95.46.00.68; ❷). Of the five **campsites**, much the nicest is the *Ferme Equestre l'Albadu* (☎04.95.46.24.55), fifteen minutes' walk away – follow the main road south down the hill from place Paoli and take the second right after crossing the second river bridge – with superb views. For **restaurants**, of the many around place Gaffori, the *Paglia Orba* on av Xavier Luciani is your best bet, with plenty of vegetarian options; for a more inspiring location try *U Museu*, huddled beneath the citadelle's walls and serving a superb goat's cheese salad and tasty wild boar stew.

Calvi

Seen from the water, the great citadelle of **CALVI** resembles a floating island, sharply defined by a hazy backdrop of snowcapped mountains. Home to the Paratroop Regiment of the Foreign Legion, this is the island's third port and draws thousands of tourists for its 6km of sandy beach. It's a light-hearted holiday town, its marina packed with boats, many of them the huge yachts of international glitterati. It became a Genoese stronghold in 1268, when its inhabitants were granted special privileges for being loyal citizens; their motto *Civitas Calvis Semper Fidelis* is inscribed above the gate into the citadelle, or **Haute Ville**, a labyrinth of cobbled lanes and stairways rising from **place Christophe Colomb**, the square linking the two parts of town. The name of the *place* derives from the local belief that the discoverer of the New World was born here, in a now ruined house on the edge of the citadelle. The assertion is hotly disputed by historians, but this hasn't stopped locals from claiming Columbus as one of their own. You'll come across his image in many of the shops, restaurants and hotels scattered around the **Basse Ville**, which backs onto the marina. To reach the **beach**, keep walking past the boats.

The **airport** is 8km southeast, with only **taxis** (€12–15) to get you into town. **Trains** stop behind the marina, and close by is the stop for **buses** from Bastia. The **ferry port** is below the citadelle, at the far end of the quai Lantivy. The **tourist office** is on quai Landry (daily 9am–5/7pm; winter closed noon–2pm & all Sun; ☎04.95.65.16.67, ◍www.calvitravel.com), with a summer annexe at the citadelle gate. The cheapest and most convenient **accommodation** is at *BVJ Corsotel* (☎04.95.65.14.16; ❷ closed Nov–April), in a grand building overlooking the marina, where rates include breakfast and an evening meal; alternatively, there's the *Hôtel de Centre* (☎04.95.65.02.01; ❷), hidden away in the Basse Ville at 12 rue Alsace-Lorraine. The long pine forest behind the sands shelter a string of large **campsites**, among which *la Pinède* (☎04.95.65.17.00), 2km out of town, is one of the smartest; you can reach it on the hourly trains from Calvi station. **Restaurants** cram the streets of the Basse Ville; of the options along quai Landry, the *Pizzeria Cappuccino* is suprisingly affordable; further into the old quarter, *U San Carlu*, place St-Charles, serves excellent seafood at reasonable prices; lively but touristy *La Santa Maria*, 14 rue Clemenceau, turns out some unusual Corsican specialities such as *stifatu,* a tasty blend of stuffed meats; while the famous piano bar and restaurant *Chez Tao* is worth a visit for its impressive views of the bay.

Bonifacio

The port of **BONIFACIO** is superbly isolated on a narrow peninsula of dazzling white limestone at Corsica's southernmost point, only minutes by boat from Sardinia (see p.673). For five hundred years Bonifacio was a virtually independent republic, and a sense of detachment from the rest of Corsica persists, with many Bonifaciens still speaking their own dialect. It has become a chic holiday spot and sailing centre, and can be unbearably overcrowded in midsummer.

The **Haute Ville** is connected to the marina by a steep flight of steps at the west end of the quay. Within the massive fortifications of the citadelle, it's an alluring maze of dusty streets, its houses displaying pointed arches and closed arcades unique to Bonifacio. From the edge of the ramparts there's a glorious view across the straits to Sardinia. In rue de Palais de Garde, in front of the drawbridge at the top of the steps, is **Église Ste-Marie-Majeure**, its facade hidden by the loggia from where Genoese officers dispensed justice in the thirteenth century. Also in the Haute Ville is the **Cimetière Marin**, a walled cemetery at the far end of the promontory filled with elaborate mausoleums. Down in the marina, a **boat excursion** (€11.50) round the base of the cliffs is well worth it for a fantastic view of the town and also to the **sea-caves**, grottoes where the rock glitters with rainbow colours and the turquoise sea is deeply translucent. The closest **beach** is **plage de la Catena**, 1km west of the port, a ten-minute walk on the Ajaccio road then left down a track just before the *Araguina* campsite. Some outstanding beaches lie to the north of Bonifacio, most notably **Golfe de Santa Manza**, 5km north along the road to Porto Vecchio, and **plage de la Rondinara**, 5km further.

Ferries from Santa Teresa on Sardinia dock at the far end of the quay; **buses** from Ajaccio stop in the car park by the marina. The **tourist office** is on Place de l'Europe (9am–noon & 2–6/8pm; Nov–April closed Sat pm & all Sun; ☎04.95.73.11.88, ◍www.bonifacio.com). Most affordable **hotel** is *Étrangers*, av

Sylver Bohn (☎04.95.73.01.09; ❸). **Campsites** include *L'Araguina*, 500m past the marina on the Ajaccio road (☎04.95.73.02.96), and *Campo di Leccia* (☎04.95.73.03.09), opposite the U Farniente building. For **food**, head for *Le Rustic*, 16 rue Fred Scamaroni, and *Café de la Poste*, at no. 6, both very popular with the locals. For **internet** access, head to Boni Boom on quai Comparetti.

Travel details

Trains

Paris to: Bordeaux (hourly; 3hr); Boulogne (7 daily; 3hr); Calais (6 daily; 3hr 10min); Clermont-Ferrand (8 daily; 4hr); Dieppe (hourly; 2hr 20min); Dijon (hourly; 1hr 40min); Le Havre (10 daily; 2hr); Lille (hourly; 1hr); Lyon (hourly; 2hr); Marseille (13 daily; 4hr); Montpellier (14 daily; 4hr 30min); Nancy (14 daily; 2hr 30min); Nice (9 daily; 6hr 30min); Nîmes (14 daily; 4hr); Poitiers (hourly; 1hr 30min); Reims (11 daily; 1hr 40min); Rouen (hourly; 1hr); Strasbourg (13 daily; 4hr); Toulouse (10 daily; 5hr 30min); Tours (hourly; 1hr).
Ajaccio to: Bastia (4 daily; 3hr 30min); Calvi (2 daily; 3hr 30min); Corte (4 daily; 2hr).
Bastia to: Ajaccio (4 daily; 3hr 30min); Calvi (2 daily; 3hr 30min); Corte (4 daily; 2hr).
Bergerac to: Sarlat (3 daily; 1hr 30min).
Bordeaux to: Bayonne-Biarritz (10 daily; 1hr 10min); Bergerac (4 daily; 1hr 20min); Marseille (8 daily; 6–7hr); Nice (8 daily; 9–10hr); Périgueux (13 daily; 1hr 20min); Toulouse (16 daily; 2hr).
Calvi to: Ajaccio (2 daily; 3hr 30min); Bastia (2 daily; 3hr 30min); Corte (2 daily; 2hr 30min).
Clermont-Ferrand to: Marseille (7 daily; 6hr); Nîmes (3 daily; 4hr 50min); Toulouse (4 daily; 6hr).
Corte to: Ajaccio (4 daily; 2hr); Bastia (4 daily; 2hr); Calvi (2 daily; 2hr 30min).
Dijon to: Beaune (11 daily; 25min); Lyon (20 daily; 1hr 45min).
Le Puy to: Lyon (10 daily; 2hr 30min).
Lyon to: Avignon (19 daily; 2hr 30min); Grenoble (hourly; 1hr 45min); Marseille (11 daily; 3hr 30min); Orange (7 daily; 2hr).

Nancy to: Strasbourg (11 daily; 1hr 20min).
Nice to: Marseille (13 daily; 2hr 30min); St-Raphaël (hourly; 1hr 30min).
Nîmes to: Arles (10 daily; 20min); Avignon (hourly; 30min); Clermont-Ferrand (3 daily; 4hr 50min); Marseille (10 daily; 1hr 30min); Montpellier (hourly; 30min); Perpignan (hourly; 2hr 10min; change at Narbonne).
Périgueux to: Les Eyzies (5 daily; 30min).
Poitiers to: Bordeaux (14 daily; 1hr 50min); La Rochelle (8 daily; 1hr 30min).
Rennes to: Nantes (7 daily; 2hr); Quimper (7 daily; 2hr 30min); St-Malo (9 daily; 1hr 15min).
Sens to: Dijon (6 daily; 2hr).
Toulouse to: Albi (hourly; 1hr); Bayonne-Biarritz (3 daily; 4hr); Bordeaux (9 daily; 2hr); Clermont-Ferrand (2 daily; 7hr); Lourdes (12 daily; 2hr 20min); Lyon (5 daily; 5–6hr); Marseille (10 daily; 4hr 30min); Pau (6 daily; 2hr 30min).
Tours to: Azay-le-Rideau (8 daily; 30min); Chinon (8 daily; 1hr); Lyon (5 daily; 5hr).

Buses

Ajaccio to: Bastia (2 daily; 3hr); Bonifacio (2 daily; 3hr); Corte (2 daily; 3hr).
Corte to: Ajaccio (2 daily; 2hr); Bastia (2 daily; 2hr).

Ferries

For Channel crossings, see p.15; for Corsica crossings, see p.409.

Germany

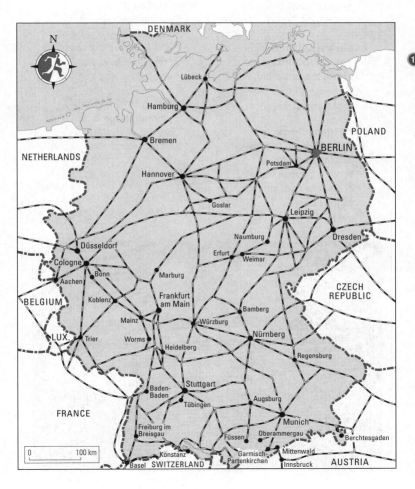

Germany highlights

❋ **Speicherstadt, Hamburg**
A free port since 1189,
Hamburg's warehouse
district remains the
largest complex of its
kind in the world and is a
magical place to stroll
around. See p.419

❋ **Cologne's Dom** Once the
tallest structures in the
world, this is Gothic
grandeur on a massive
scale. See p.429

❋ **The Rhine Gorge** A
cruise through this spec-
tacular 80km valley
takes in peaceful towns,
ancient castles and the
alluring Lorelei. See
p.435

❋ **Zugspitze, Bavarian Alps**
See into four countries
from the summit of
Germany's loftiest moun-
tain. See p.455

❋ **Reichstag, Berlin**
Dramatic history and
cool modernity combine
impressively at the seat
of the German parlia-
ment. See p.469

❋ **Zwinger, Dresden** This
Baroque palace is now
home to several excel-
lent museums. See
p.480

Introduction and basics

The stereotype of **Germany** as the great monolith of western Europe has always been a long way from the truth. Regional characteristics are a strong feature of German life, and there are many hangovers from the days when the country was a patchwork of independent states. To travel from the ancient ports of the north, across the open fields of the German plain, down through the Ruhr conurbation, and on to the forests, mountains and cosmopolitan cities of the south is to experience a variety as great as any continental country can offer.

Several of Germany's cities have the air of national capitals. **Cologne**, though enmeshed in one of Europe's most intensively industrialized regions, is rich in monuments. Bavaria's capital, **Munich**, is another star attraction, with great museums and galleries. **Berlin**, the nucleus of the turmoil of reunification, has an atmosphere at times electrifying, while **Nürnberg** retains more than a trace of its bygone glory. **Hamburg**, burned to the ground by a firestorm in 1943, is now a pleasant city with nightlife comparable to Berlin's. **Frankfurt**, the economic dynamo of postwar reconstruction, looks on itself as the "real" capital of the country, while **Stuttgart** and **Düsseldorf**, with their corporate skyscrapers and consumerist buzz, contest the title of champion of German economic success. In the east, as well as Berlin, there's the Baroque splendour of **Dresden**.

Engaging as they are, these cities suffered considerable damage in World War II and have been subjected to some heavy-handed redevelopment, so in many respects it's the smaller towns of Germany that offer the richer experience. There's nowhere as well-loved as the university city of **Heidelberg**, while **Trier, Bamberg, Regensburg, Rothenburg** and **Marburg** in the west and **Potsdam** and **Meissen** in the east are all attractive places that reward exploration.

Among the scenic highlights are the **Bavarian Alps** (on Munich's doorstep), the **Bodensee** (Lake Constance), the **Black Forest** and the valley of the **Rhine**, whose majestic sweep has spawned a rich fund of legends and folklore.

Information and maps

You'll find a **tourist office** (*Fremdenverkehrsamt*) in virtually every town in Germany. These are almost universally friendly and very efficient, providing large amounts of often useful literature and maps. The major cities share the same phone number for information: simply dial the local code followed by 1 94 33. The best general **maps** are those by RV or Kümmerly and Frey, whose 1:500,000 map is the most detailed single sheet of the country available. Specialist maps marking **cycling routes** or **alpine hikes** can be bought in the relevant regions.

Money and banks

Germany is one of twelve European Union countries who have switched over to the **euro** (€).

11

GERMANY | Basics

Germany on the net

- Ⓦ **www.germany-tourism.de** Official German tourist site
- Ⓦ **www.falk-germany.de** City maps
- Ⓦ **www.dhm.de** Information on the country's museums
- Ⓦ **www.galerie.de** Information on the country's galleries and artists
- Ⓦ **www.eventguide.rm.net** Information on events
- Ⓦ **www.openair.de** Information on festivals

Exchange facilities can be found in most banks and in post offices and commercial exchange shops called *Wechselstuben*. The Deutsches Reisebank has branches in the train stations of most main cities, which are generally open daily, often until 10/11pm. Basic **banking hours** are Mon–Fri 9am–noon & 1.30–3.30pm, with late opening on Thurs till 6pm. **Credit cards** are used relatively infrequently, though they are becoming more popular.

Communications

Post offices are open Mon–Fri 8am–6pm & Sat 8am–noon. **Poste restante** services are available at the main post offices in any given town: collect mail from the counter marked *Postlagernde Sendungen*. Mail is usually only held for a couple of weeks.

You can **phone abroad** from all pay phones except those marked "National"; telephone cards (€5) are widely used. The **operator number** is ☏03. **Internet access** is easy to find in larger towns and cities; although the cybercafé has limited popularity, many department stores (notably the Karstadt chain) offer the facility. Expect to pay around €3–4/hr.

Getting around

While it may not be cheap, getting around Germany is quick and easy. Barely an inch of the country is untouched by a reliable **public transport** system, and it's a simple matter to jump from **train** to **bus** on the integrated network.

Trains

By far the best form of public transport in **Germany** is the **train**, operated by the national company Deutsche Bahn. **Fares** are €0.14/km second class, exclusive of supplements, and a return costs the same as two one-way tickets. The most luxurious service is the 280kph **InterCityExpress (ICE)**, otherwise the fastest and most comfortable trains are the **InterCity (IC)** and **EuroCity (EC)**. **InterRegio (IR)** trains offer a swift service along less heavily used routes.

Around major cities, the **S-Bahn** is a commuter network on which InterRail and Eurail cards are valid, as they are on all other services.

InterRail or **Eurail** passes are both valid throughout the network. Supplements apply on both for sleepers, and on fast trains for InterRail pass holders. The colossal national **timetable** (*Kursbuch*) can be bought from stations for €12.75, though it's too bulky to be easily portable.

Buses

If you must forsake the trains for **buses**, you'll find no decline in efficiency. Many are run by regional co-operatives in association with DB, although there are a few privately operated routes on which rail passes cannot be used. You're most likely to need buses in remote rural areas, or along designated "scenic routes" where scheduled services are more luxurious than on standard routes and buses pause at major points of interest.

Cycling

Cyclists are well catered for in Germany: many smaller roads have marked cycle paths, and bike-only lanes are a common sight in cities and towns. Between April and October, the best place to **rent a bike** is from a railway station participating in the **Fahrrad am Bahnhof** scheme (around €6/day). You can return it to any other participating station and holders of the various rail passes get a fifty percent discount.

Accommodation

Be it high-rise city hotels or half-timbered guest houses in the country, **accommodation** of all types is easy to find in Germany, and it can often be good value.

Hotels

An immensely complicated grading system applies to German **hotels**, but they're all more or less the same: clean, comfortable and functional. Just take care not to turn up in a large town or city during a trade fair, or *Messe* – hotels often double their rates and still get booked solid. In country areas, prices start at about €17.50 for a single, €30 for a double; in cities, expect to pay an extra €5–10 extra for something similar. Hotels in eastern Germany are overwhelmingly geared to the business market, but the situation is much better for the budget traveller in holiday areas.

Pensions, guest houses and private rooms

To escape the formality of a hotel, look for one of the plentiful **pensions**, which may be rooms above a bar or restaurant or simply space in a private house. In urban areas these cost roughly the same as hotels – they're usually a little cheaper in the countryside. An increasingly prevalent budget option is **B&B** accommodation in a private house (look for signs saying *Fremdenzimmer* or *Zimmer frei*). Prices vary but start at around €15 for a single, €25 for a double. Particularly plentiful along the main touring routes are **country inns** or **guesthouses** (*Gasthöfe* or *Gasthäuser*), charging upwards of €25 a night for a double (more in popular areas).

The best budget option in the east is a room in a **private house**, of which thousands have now become available. Prices vary widely and may cost as much as €25 per person in the cities. Nearly all **tourist offices** will book you a room for a fee and there are also a number of private agencies that may give a better deal.

Hostels

In Germany, you're never far away from an **HI hostel** (*Jugendherberge*), but at any time of the year (especially summer weekends) they're liable to be block-booked by school groups, so book as far in advance as possible. Hostels divide into categories according to location and facilities. The most basic cost around €10; the most luxurious – which go under the youth guest house (*Jugendgästehaus*) designation – charge upwards of €20. Except in youth guest houses, HI members over 27 pay around €2 more per night; non-members, if admitted at all, will be charged an extra €2 per night. Note that in **Bavaria** those over-27 cannot use hostels at all, unless they're accompanying children. The German YHA is DJH, Bismarkstr. 8, 32756 Detmold (☎00 49-52 31/7 40 10, ⊛www.djh.de); you can email any of the HI hostels through the website.

Campsites

Big, well-managed **campsites** are a feature all over Germany. Even the most basic have toilets, washing facilities and a shop, while the grandest are virtually open-air hotels with swimming pools and supermarkets. Prices are based on facilities and location, comprising a fee per person and per tent (each €2.50–5), plus extra fees for vehicles. Many sites are full from June to September, so arrive early in the afternoon. Most close for winter, but those in popular skiing areas remain open all year.

Food and drink

German food is both good value and high quality, but it helps if you share the national penchant for solid, fatty fare accompanied by compensating fresh vegetables.

Food

The vast majority of German hotels and guest houses include **breakfast** in the price of the room. Typically, you'll be offered a small platter of cold meats and cheeses, with a selection of breads, marmalades, jams and honey, and sometimes muesli.

Elegant **cafés** are a popular institution in Germany, serving a choice of coffee and cream cakes, pastries or hand-made chocolates. More substantial food is available from **butcher's shops**; you can generally choose from a variety of freshly roasted meats to make up a hot sandwich. The easiest option for a snack is to head for the ubiquitous **Imbiss** stands and shops, serving a range of sausages, plus meatballs, hamburgers and chips; the better ones have soups, schnitzels, chops, spit-roasted chickens and salads too.

All **restaurants** display their menus and prices by the door. Hot meals are usually served throughout the day. Most of the *Gaststätte*, *Gasthaus*, *Gasthof*, *Brauhaus* or *Wirtschaft* establishments belong to a brewery and function as a meeting point, drinking haven and cheap restaurant. Their cuisine resembles hearty German home cooking, and portions are usually generous. Main courses are overwhelmingly based on pork, served with a variety of sauces. Sausages feature regularly, and can be surprisingly tasty, with distinct regional varieties. **Vegetarians** will find east Germany extremely difficult – menus are almost exclusively for carnivores. However, student towns and popular stopover points are slowly becoming more veggie-friendly, and visitors to Germany in spring can't fail to notice the curious annual obsession with asparagus.

Germany's multicultural society is mirrored in its wide variety of **ethnic** eateries. Italian restaurants are generally the most reliable, but there are also plenty offering Balkan, Greek, Turkish and Chinese cooking. In the largest cities, a host of other cuisines can be found as well.

Drink

For serious **beer** drinkers, Germany is paradise; around forty percent of the world's breweries are to be found here, with some eight hundred in Bavaria alone. A beer tour of Germany should really begin in **Munich**. The city's beer gardens and beer halls are the most famous drinking dens in the country, offering a wide variety of premier products, from dark lagers through tart *Weizens* to powerful *Bocks*. **Cologne** holds the world record for the number of city breweries, all of which produce the jealously guarded *Kölsch*. **Düsseldorf** has its own distinctive brew, the dark *Alt*, but wherever you go you can be fairly sure of getting a locally brewed beer.

Most people's knowledge of German **wine** starts and ends with Liebfraumilch, a medium-sweet wine. Sadly, its success has obscured the quality of other German wines, especially those made from the Riesling grape. The vast majority of German wine is white, since the northern climate doesn't ripen red grapes reliably. If, after a week or so, you're pining for a glass of red, try a *Spätburgunder*.

Apart from beer and wine, there's nothing very distinctive about German drink, save for **Apfelwein**, a variant of cider. The most popular **spirits** are the fiery *Korn* and after-dinner liqueurs, which are mostly fruit-based.

Opening hours and public holidays

Most **shops** in Germany open at 8.30am and, by law, close weekdays at 8pm, Sat at 4pm and all Sun (except for bakers, who may open for a couple of hours between 11am and 3pm). Smaller shops also cllose noon–2pm. Exceptions are pharmacies and shops in and around train stations, which stay open late and at weekends. **Museums** and **historic monuments** are, with few exceptions (mainly in Bavaria), closed on Mon. Most museums offer half-price entry for students with valid ID.

Public holidays are: Jan 1; Jan 6 (regional); Good Fri; Easter Mon; May 1; Ascension Day; Whit Monday; Corpus Christi (regional); Aug 15 (regional); Oct 3; Nov 1 (regional); Dec 25 & 26.

Emergencies

The German **police** (*Polizei*) are not renowned for their friendliness, but they usually treat foreigners with courtesy. Reporting **thefts** at local police stations is straightforward, but inevitably there'll be a great deal of bureaucracy to wade through. The level of theft in the former GDR has increased dramatically with unemployment, but, provided you take the normal precautions, there's no real risk. All **drugs** are illegal in Germany, and anyone caught with them will face either prison or deportation: consulates will not be sympathetic towards those held on drug charges.

German **doctors** generally speak English, but to be certain, ask your consulate for a list of English-speaking doctors in the major cities. **Pharmacies** (*Apotheken*) can deal with many minor complaints and again will often speak English. In the west you'll find international *Apotheken* in most large towns, who will be able to fill a prescription in any European language. All pharmacies display a rota of 24-hour *Apotheken*.

Emergency numbers

Police ☎110; Ambulance & Fire ☎112

Northern Germany

Hamburg, Germany's second city, is infamous for the sleaze of the Reeperbahn, but it has plenty more sparkling nightlife to offer and a centre with enjoyably contrasting neighbourhoods. In this generally unprepossessing region, another maritime city, **Lübeck**, has the strongest pull, with a similar appeal to the mercantile towns of the Low Countries. To the north, Schleswig-Holstein's mix of dyke-protected marsh, peat bog and farmland holds few rewarding sights, but to the south lies the diverse region of Lower Saxony. **Hannover**, its capital, is worth a visit for its museums and gardens. The province's smaller towns present a fascinating contrast – the mining town of **Goslar**, in particular, is unlike any other in the world. Near the centre of Lower Saxony is **Bremen**, the region's largest city and, like Hamburg, a Land in its own right.

Hamburg

Stylish media centre and second largest port in Europe, **HAMBURG** has a certain coolness and sense of openness. Its skyline is dominated by the pale green of its copper spires and domes, but a few houses and the churches are all that's left from before the last century. The Great Fire of 1842 was a main cause of this loss, followed by demolition to make way for the warehouse area, and bombing during World War II. Much of the subsequent rebuilding might not be especially beautiful, but it has preserved the city's human scale. Two-thirds of Hamburg is occupied by parks, lakes or tree-lined canals, giving a rural feel to this major industrial centres.

Arrival, information and accommodation

An Airport Express connects the **airport** to the **train station** in the eastern end of the city centre, close to Adnauerallee (every 15min; 25min; €4.35). **Ferries** from Britain dock at Fischerhafen on Grosse Elbstrasse, from where buses run to Altona Station, west of town. Ferries from elsewhere dock at St Pauli Landungsbrücken. The **tourist office** in the station (daily 7am–11pm; ☎0 40/30 05 13 00, ✉info@hamburg-tourismus.de) has a full room-finding service. Pick up the **Hamburg Card** (€6.80/day, €14/three days) here, too, which gives free or reduced admission to most of the city's museums as well as use of public transport.

Close to Sternschanze station (north of St Pauli; U-Bahn #3, S-Bahn #21 or #31) are two **hostels**: *Backpacker Hostel Instant Sleep*, Max-Brauer-Allee 277 (☎0 40/43 18 23 10, ⊛www.instantsleep.de; ❷), and *Schanzenstern*, Bartelsstr. 12 (☎0 40/4 39 84 41, ⊛www.schanzenstern.de; ❸). **Hotels** are not cheap, though there's plenty of choice, particularly near the train station: try *Annenhof*, Lange Reihe 23 (☎0 40/24 34 26; ❸), which is clean and homely; or small but stylish *Sarah Petersen* at no. 50 (☎0 40/24 98 26, ⊛www.galerie-hotel-sarah-petersen.de; ❹). **B&B** is available through *bed&breakfast*, Müggenkampstrasse 59 (☎0 40/491 56 66; ❸).

The City

Hamburg has no obvious centre, but the best place to begin an exploration is the oldest and liveliest area, the **harbour**, dominated by the clock tower and green dome of the **St Pauli Landungsbrücken**. To the east is the late-nineteenth-century **Speicherstadt**, whose tall, ornate warehouses are still very much in use: you'll see bundles of Oriental carpets being hoisted, and smell spices and coffee wafting on the breeze. The Speicherstadt is within the **Freihafen** (customs-free zone), into which you can walk unrestricted. It's a magical place to stroll around and crisscross the bridges – Hamburg has more than Venice or Amsterdam.

Just to the north is the nightlife centre of **St Pauli**, whose main artery is the notorious **Reeperbahn** – an ugly and unassuming street by day, ugly but sizzling with neon at night. The main road along the waterfront on St Pauli's edge is the **Hafenstrasse**, which runs west to the suburb of **Altona**, formerly a separate city

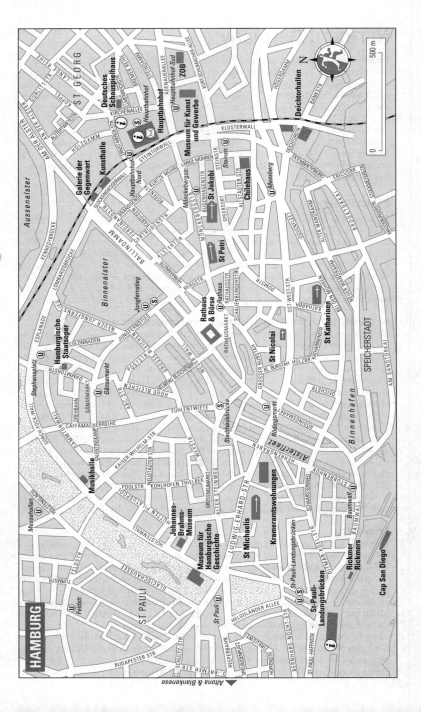

ruled by the Holstein dukes. Its reputation for racial tolerance is one of the reasons it grew, and it still has a large Portuguese population – and good, very cheap Portuguese restaurants. On the waterfront here, one of the city's main weekly events takes place: the **Fischmarkt**. Come very early on Sunday and you'll find yourself in an amazing hubbub – if you want to buy bananas by the crate or a two-metre-tall potted palm, this is the place to do it; the market by no means sells only fish. Everything is in full swing by 6am; by 10am trading has ceased; by 11am it's over.

Hamburg's commercial and shopping district centres on **Binnenalster** lake and the neo-Renaissance **Rathaus** – a magnificently pompous demonstration of the city's power and wealth in the nineteenth century. Southeast of here, at the junction of Burchardstrasse and Pumpen, is Hamburg's most original building, the **Chilehaus**, designed by the Expressionist architect Fritz Höger and rising like the prow of a huge ocean liner. From the Rathausmarkt, continue up **Poststrasse** to the heart of Hamburg's exclusive shopping area, which puts London's Bond Street in the shade.

Just north of the train station is the **Kunsthalle**, the city's one unmissable art collection (Tues–Sun 10am–6pm, Thurs till 9pm; €7.50; ✆www.hamburger-kunsthalle.de). There are three altarpieces by Master Bertram, the first German painter identifiable by name, and a Dutch and Flemish section where two Rembrandts take centre stage, but it is the nineteenth-century German section that is the museum's main strength. Next door to the Kunsthalle is the **Galerie der Gegenwart** (same times and ticket), where contemporary art is represented.

Eating and drinking

Some of the best **places to eat** are northwest of the city centre, in the Univiertel or the Schanzenviertel around Schulterblatt and Schanzenstrasse (two minutes' walk south of Sternschanze station). For **snacks**, the stalls in front of the Rathaus are pricey but delicious, while most café-bars have food as well as drinks and sometimes music. Good choices include *Frank & Frei*, Schanzenstr. 93, and *Oma's Alte Apotheke*, directly opposite at no. 85. Also worth trying is *Erika's Eck*, Sternstr. 98 (1am–2pm), which serves one of the best breakfasts in the city. For **traditional German cuisine** and fish dishes, the best-known addresses in the city centre include *Alt Hamburger Aalspeicher*, Deichstr. 43, and *Nikolaikeller*, Cremon 36, whilst *Sagres*, at Vorsetzen 42, is one of many good and inexpensive Portuguese restaurants in the vicinity of the harbour. If an inexpensive fill-up is a priority, it's worth seeking out *Einstein*, Bahrenfelder Chaussee 45. Best of the cheapies around the main station area is *Yildiz Kebab Haus*, Lange Reihe 43, which manages to be spacious and snug at the same time, and where the huge dishes cost around €5.

Nightlife

Hamburg's **nightlife** is among the best the country has to offer – for up-to-the-minute **listings**, pick up a copy of *Szene* or *Prinz* magazine. St Pauli is the city's main venue for live music, with big-name bands mostly playing at weekends. Entry is around €10.

Betty Ford Klinik Grosse Freiheit 6. The finest in house music, according to those in the know. Fri & Sat only.

Bunker Feldstrasse 66, Heiligengeistfeld. Swanky venue featuring a VIP lounge, two dance floors and four bars, one of them a sushi bar. Fri & Sat only.

Grosse Freiheit Grosse Freiheit 36. A tourist attraction in itself, Hamburg's leading live venue books major acts most weekends.

Gum Hamburger Berg 12–13. The name stands for Global Underground Music; an unusual club housed in a former brothel. Fri & Sat only.

Grünspan Grosse Freiheit 58. A paradise for those who like their rock uncompromisingly heavy. Closed Sun, Mon & Tues.

Kaiserkeller Grosse Freiheit club basement. Massive subterranean club with themed alternative music nights.

Logo Grindelallee 5. Hosts mainly English and American underground bands.

Gay Hamburg

The best way to find out what's on in the lively **gay scene** is through the magazine *Du und Ich* and the free sheet *Gay Express*.

Absolut Hans-Albers-Platz 15. Mixed gay/straight crowd attracted by the excellent DJs and welcoming atmosphere. Sat only. Entry €10.

Fabrik Barnerstrasse 36 ℮ info@fabrik.de. Various gay and lesbian parties take place at one of Altona's most popular party venues.

Frauenkneip Stresemannstrasse 60. The city's leading address for women only. Closed Tues & Sun.

Male Pulverteich 17. Intimate club featuring a cruising area, café and cocktail bar. Wed, Fri & Sat.

Listings

Bike rental From the tourist office in the train station.

Consulates UK, Harvestehuder Weg 8a ℡ 0 40/4 48 03 20; Ireland, Feldbrunnenstr. 43 ℡ 0 40/44 18 62 13; US, Alsterufer 28 ℡ 0 40/41 17 10.

Hospital Krankenhaus Bethesda, Glindersweg. 80 ℡ 0 40/72 55 44 12.

Internet access Internet café Fun Club,

Fischersallee 78; at discount telecom shop, Int. Telecom, Kirchenallee 9; also at Hauptbahnhof-Süd station.

Left luggage At the train station.

Pharmacy Apotheke an der Bergstrasse, Bergstr. 26.

Post office At the Kirchenallee exit from the train station.

Lübeck

LÜBECK's Altstadt was made a UNESCO heritage site in 1987, the first northern European city to be so honoured. Set on an egg-shaped island surrounded by the water defences of the Trave and the city moat, it is a five-minute walk from the city's train station, past the twin-towered **Holstentor**, the city's emblem. Built in 1477, the tower leans horrifyingly, but that shouldn't put you off calling in at its small **Historical Museum** (Tues–Sun 10am–4/5pm; April–Sept also Mon; €2.60), a useful introduction to the city and Hanseatic history. On the waterfront to the right of the Holstentor is a row of lovely gabled buildings – the **Salzspeicher**.

Straight ahead over the bridge and up Holstenstrasse, the first church on the right is the Gothic **Petrikirche**, one of many buildings to suffer during the Allied bombing of March 1942. An elevator goes to the top of its spire (March–Dec daily 10am–4/6pm; €2) for great views over the town. Back across Holstenstrasse is the Markt and the imposing **Rathaus** (tours Mon–Fri at 11am, noon & 3pm; €2), displaying the city's characteristic brickwork. Opposite is the **Konditorei-café Niederegger**, renowned for its vast marzipan display; its old-style first-floor café is surprisingly affordable. Behind the north wing of the town hall is the **Marienkirche**, Germany's oldest brick-built Gothic church. Severely damaged in 1942, the restored interior now makes a light and lofty backdrop for the church's treasures: a magnificent 1518 carved altar, a life-size figure of John the Evangelist dating from 1505, a beautiful Gothic gilded tabernacle and some fourteenth-century murals.

The imposing **Katharinenkirche**, on the corner of Königsstrasse and Glockengiesserstrasse, boasts three sculptures on its west facade by Ernst Barlach; he was commissioned to make a series of nine in the early 1930s, but had completed only these when his work was banned by the Nazis. Just north of Glockengiesserstrasse, sharing an entrance in Breite Strasse, are the **Behnhaus** and the **Drägerhaus**, two patricians' houses now converted into a museum (Tues–Sun 10am–4/5pm; April–Sept also Mon; €2.60, free first Fri of the month). The former has a good collection of paintings, including works by Kirchner and Munch, while the latter's impressive interior contains nineteenth-century furniture and porcelain.

The nearby **Jakobikirche**, a sailors' church built in the thirteenth and fourteenth centuries, has Gothic wall paintings on its square pillars. On the other side of the Breite Strasse is a Renaissance house that used to belong to the sailors' guild, the **Haus der Schiffergesellschaft**. A tavern since 1535, it is decked out with all sorts of seagoing paraphernalia, and features on the programme of every tour group. East of here is the thirteenth-century **Heiligen-Geist-Hospital** (Tues–Sun 10am–4/5pm; free), one of the best-preserved hospices from this period.

At the opposite end of the Altstadt are the **St-Annen-Museum** and the **Dom**. The museum (Tues–Sun 10am–4/5pm; April–Sept also Mon; €2.60, free first Fri of the month) has a first-rate collection of domestic, civic and church art and history from the thirteenth to the eighteenth century, including a magnificent *Passion* triptych by Memling. The large brick-built Dom, founded in 1173, contains an enormous triumphal cross by Bernt Notke.

Practicalities

The **train station**, just west of the Altstadt, houses a **tourist office** (Mon–Fri 10am–6pm, Sat 10am–2pm; ☎04 51/7 02 02 78, ⊛www.lübecker-verkehrsverein.de); there's another at Breite Str. 62 (Mon–Fri 9.30am–6/7pm, Sat 10am–3pm, Sun 10am–2pm; ⊛www.luebeck-tourismus.de). For getting around, pick up a **Lübeck Card** (€5/day, €10/three days), which can be used on public transport and for reduced entrance fees for museums and harbour-trips. The cheapest **hotel** is Stadt Lübeck, Am Bahnhof 21 (☎04 51/83 8 83; ❺). The best **hostel** is *Rucksackhotel Backpackers* in the Werkhof complex at Kanalstr. 70 (☎04 51/70 68 92; ❷); the HI place is at Gertrudenkirchhof 4 (☎04 51/3 34 33, ⊛jghluebeck@djh-nordmark.de; ❷); its more luxurious counterpart is at Mengstr. 33 (☎04 51/7 02 03 99; ❷) in the historic centre. Lübeck has a good choice of **cafés** and eating places. The *Ratskeller*, Markt 13, offers traditional German cuisine, while *Schmidt's*, Dr-Julius-Leber-Str. 60–62, has a highly eclectic menu and *Tipasa*, Schlumacherstr. 12–14, has cheap bistro-type dishes, highly popular with students. *Café Affenbrot*, part of the aforementioned Werkhof, has tasty veggie food and cakes. The Engelsgrube is the best street for bars.

From Lübeck **ferries** cross to Helsinki, Finland, with Farhre Helsinki (3 weekly; ☎04 51/5 89 90) and Fin-Lines (3 weekly; ☎04 51/1 50 74 43).

Bremen

BREMEN was declared an autonomous Land in 1949, and since then it's had a reputation for being the most politically radical part of the country, electing the first Green MPs in 1979. The main area of historical interest is the **Altstadt**, on the Weser's northeast bank, reached by walking straight ahead from the train station. At the top of Sögestrasse, Bremen's main shopping street, is the **Liebfrauenkirche**, a Gothic hall church engulfed by a flower market.

The **Marktplatz** ahead of the church is relatively small but attractive, and dominated by the **Rathaus**, one of the most splendid buildings in northern Germany. You can visit the main reception rooms as part of a tour (Mon–Sat 11am, noon, 3pm & 4pm, Sun 11am & noon; €4), which are awash with gilded wallpaper and ornate carving. To the left of the Rathaus is a vast **statue of Roland**, erected in 1404 as a symbol of Bremen's independence from its archbishop; he now stares at the modern Parliament building, one of the ugliest edifices to disgrace a German town.

On a small rise beyond the Rathaus stands the **Dom**, its brooding interior ranging from Romanesque to late Gothic. In the crypt are some fine works of art, notably an eleventh-century Christ and a magnificent thirteenth-century font. Off the southeast corner is the **Bleikeller** (€1.20); a macabre attraction is provided by the corpses that were discovered here when the room was opened up, perfectly preserved in the air-free environment.

Böttcherstrasse, off the south side of Marktplatz, was transformed in the 1920s by the Bremen coffee magnate Ludwig Roselius into a Gothic-cum-Art Nouveau fantasy. Craft workshops are tucked in among the bronze reliefs, the arches and the turrets, and there's a musical clock depicting the history of transatlantic crossings. The only old house in the street is the **Roselius-Haus**, now a museum of art and furniture (Tues–Sun 11am–6pm; €4); the best works are paintings by the Cranachs and an alabaster statue of St Barbara by Riemenschneider. Adjacent is the **Paula-Modersohn-Becker-Haus** (same times and ticket), containing a number of paintings by the artist, who lived in nearby Worpswede.

Tucked away between the Dom and the river is a small, extraordinarily well-preserved area of medieval fishing houses known as the **Schnoorviertel**. Just east of the Schnoorviertel at Am Wall 207, the **Kunsthalle** (Wed–Sun 10am–5pm, Tues till 9pm; €5; ⓦwww.kunsthalle-bremen.de) houses a superb array of nineteenth- and early twentieth-century paintings, including some forty works by Modersohn-Becker.

Practicalities

The **train station** is just north of the city centre; immediately outside is the **tourist office** (Mon–Fri 9.30am–6.30/8pm, Sat & Sun 9.30am–4pm; ☎01805/10 10 30, ⓦwww.bremen-tourism.de). Bremen's **HI hostel** is in the western part of the old town at Kalkstr. 6 (☎04 21/17 13 69; ❷) and has an unparalleled view over the River Weser. **To stay**, try the central *Heinisch*, Wachmannstr. 26 (☎04 21/34 29 25; ❹), with spotless en-suite rooms; *Weltevreden*, Am Dobben 62 (☎04 21/780 15; ❹), with fourteen rooms in varying styles, between the city centre and the Ostertorviertel; or *Weser*, Hastedter Osterdeich 205 (☎04 21/44 35 29; ❸).

Bremen has a number of good **café/bars** and is also known for its fish specialities (particularly eel), best sampled in the gemütlich old restaurants of the Altstadt and Schnoorviertel. Try also *café Engel*, Ostertorsteinweg 31, which offers inexpensive daily specials. The city is also home of **Beck's**, one of Germany's most heavily exported beers, but the products of Haake-Beck are the ones to go for in the city itself; try them at the *Kleiner Ratskeller*, Hinter dem Schütting 11.

Hannover

HANNOVER has a closer relationship with Britain than any other German city, a consequence of the 1701 Act of Settlement, which resulted in Georg Ludwig of Hannover becoming King George I of the United Kingdom in 1714. As well as a monarch, Britain gained a great composer: anticipating the accession, the court director of music, Georg Friedrich Händel, had established himself in London by the time his employer arrived, and went on to write his finest works there. Hannover's showpiece is not a great cathedral, palace or town hall, but a series of gardens, which are among the most impressive in Europe. Add this to a number of first-class museums and there's plenty here to keep you occupied for a couple of days.

The City centre

Hannover has had to reconstruct itself after almost total demolition by World War II bombing, and the from the train station isn't prepossessing, with a bland pedestrian precinct stretching ahead. Underneath runs the Passarelle, a sort of subterranean bazaar-cum-piazza that at night is a little disconcerting.

Standing at Hannover's most popular rendezvous, the **café Kröpcke**, the most imposing building in view is the Neoclassical Opernhaus, perhaps the finest of the city's public buildings. A short distance southwest, a few streets of rebuilt half-timbered buildings convey some impression of the medieval town; most notable is the high-gabled fifteenth-century **Altes Rathaus**, its elaborate brickwork enlivened with colourful glazed tiles. Alongside is the fourteenth-century **Marktkirche**, whose bulky tower has long been the emblem of the city; inside, there's some miraculously preserved stained glass in the east windows. Close by, at Pferdestr. 6, the **Historisches Museum** (Wed–Sun 10am–4/6pm, Tues till 8pm; €3, free Fri) incorporates the sole remnant of the city walls. The displays include some state coaches, a section illustrating the changing face of Hannover, and several reconstructed interiors from farmhouses in the province.

Southwards, across the Friedrichswall, is the **Neues Rathaus**, a Baroque-cum-neo-Gothic extravaganza whose dome gives the best views of the city (April–Oct daily 9.30/10am–6pm; €2). Next door, the **Kestner-Museum** (Tues–Sun 11am–6pm, Wed till 8pm; €1.50 or €2.60 combined ticket with Rathaus, free Fri; Ⓦwww.kestner-museum.de) is a compact and eclectic decorative arts museum. Round the back of the Rathaus on Willy-Brandt-Allee is the **Niedersächsisches Landesmuseum** (Tues–Sun 10am–5pm, Thurs till 7pm; €3; Ⓦwww.nlmh.de), housing an excellent collection of paintings from the Middle Ages to the early twentieth century. On the first floor, the archeology department's showpieces are the bodies of prehistoric men preserved in the peat bogs of Lower Saxony, along with the contents of several graves and an array of Bronze Age jewellery.

A bit further down the road, the **Sprengel-Museum** (Tues–Sun 10am–6/8pm; €3.50; Ⓦwww.sprengel-museum.de) is one of the most exciting modern art galleries in Germany. Much of the display space is given over to changing exhibitions of photography, graphics and experimental art-forms, but there's also a first-rate permanent display of twentieth-century painting and sculpture. Focal point is a huge range of work by Hannover's own Kurt Schwitters.

Herrenhausen

The royal gardens of **Herrenhausen**, summer residence of the Hannover court, can be reached by U-Bahn #4 or #5 from the Kröpcke, but it's better to pick up the free tourist office plan of the complex and walk through it. Proceeding north from town along Nienburgerstrasse, you reach the least remarkable of the gardens – the **Welfengarten** – first; it lies to the right, dominated by the huge neo-Gothic Welfenpalais, now occupied by the university.

To the left, the dead straight Herrenhäuser Allee cuts through the **Georgengarten**, an English-style landscaped garden with an artificial lake. This garden was created as a foil to the magnificent formal **Grosser Garten** (daily 8am–4.30/8pm; €3, free in winter), the city's pride and joy. If possible, time your visit to coincide with the playing of the fountains (April–Sept daily 11am–noon & 2/3–5pm) or when the illuminations are switched on (May–Aug Wed–Sun at 9pm; €3). Just inside the entrance gate is one of the most striking features, the Hedge Theatre, a permanent amphitheatre whose hedges double as scenery and changing rooms. In the adjoining **Georgengarten** is the **Wilhelm Busch Museum** (Tues–Sun 10am–5/6pm; €4.50; Ⓦwww.wilhelm-busch-museum.de), which features a collection of works by the eponymous father of the comic-strip cartoon.

Across Herrenhäuser Strasse to the north of the Grosser Garten is the **Berggarten** (same times and ticket), set up to shelter rare and exotic plants. Some compensation for the loss of the palace in the last war is provided by a number of courtly buildings to the west along Herrenhäuser Strasse. One of these, the **Fürstenhaus**, is a sort of museum of the House of Hannover (Tues–Sun 10am–5/6pm; €3.30).

Practicalities

The **train station** is in the centre of town; behind is the bus station. The **tourist office** is to the right of the train station in the post office building at Ernst-August-Platz 2 (Mon–Fri 9am–6pm, Sat 9am–2pm; ☎05 11/16 84 97 00, Ⓦwww.hannover-tourism.de). Pick up a Hannover Card here (€8/day, €12/three days), covering public transport and entrance to the main museums and sights.

There's an **HI hostel** at Ferdinand-Wilhelm-Fricke-Weg 1 (☎05 11/1 31 76 74, Ⓔjh-hannover@djh-hannover.de; ❷); take U-Bahn #3 or #7 to Fischerhof, from where it's a five-minute walk to the left over the bridge, then right. For €6.50 the tourist office will book you into a **hotel**. As a centre of the trade fair industry, Hannover charges fancy prices – normally the lowest rates in the centre are at *Flora*, Heinrichstr. 36 (☎05 11/38 39 10; ❹), and *Gildehof*, Joachimstr. 6 (☎05 11/36 36 80; ❹); or you could try the pricier *Reverey*, Aegidiendamm 8 (☎05 11/88 37 11; ❻).

For **snacks** head for the Markthalle, where German, Italian, Spanish and Turkish stallholders sell wonderful examples of their cooking. Alternatively, try the shops around Goetheplatz. Good **cafés** include the aforementioned *Kröpcke*, whilst bars serving food include *café Safran*, Königsworther Str. 39, *Weinloch*, Burgstr. 33, and *Hannen-Fass* on Knochenhauerstr. 36. The best-known live music venue is the renowned Jazz Club on Am Lindener Berge 38. **Internet access** is at Cyberbar, Grosse Packhofstr. 39–45, or Das Netz, Humboldtstr. 1.

Goslar

The stereotype of a mining town immediately conjures up images of grim terraced houses and louring machinery. **GOSLAR**, superbly located at the northern edge of the gentle wooded Harz mountains, could not be more different. For one thing, the mining here was always of a very superior nature – silver was discovered in the nearby Rammelsberg in the tenth century, and the town soon became the "treasure chest of the Holy Roman Empire". The presence of a POW hospital during World War II spared it from bombing, and Goslar can claim to have more old houses than any other town in Germany, ensuring its place as a UNESCO World Heritage site.

Although it hosts an attractive market every Tuesday and Friday morning, the central **Marktplatz** is best seen empty to fully appreciate its gorgeous visual variety, with its elegantly Gothic **Rathaus** (daily 11am–4pm; €2) and roofs of bright red tiles and contrasting grey slate. The Huldigungssaal in the Rathaus contains a dazzling array of medieval wall and ceiling paintings, with the most valuable items hidden in altar niches and closets behind the panelling.

Just behind the Rathaus is the **Marktkirche**, facing the sixteenth-century **Brusttuch**, with its top storey crammed with satirical carvings. Goslar's half-timbered beauty begins in earnest in the streets behind the church – the Frankenberg Quarter – the oldest houses lying in the Bergstrasse and Schreiberstrasse areas. An especially fine Baroque specimen is the **Siemenshaus** at their junction. Turning right into Bergstrasse, wind your way up to the roughly hewn **Frankenberger Kirche**, situated in tranquil solitude on the boundaries of the Altstadt. Some faint thirteenth-century frescoes compete in vain for attention against a Baroque pulpit.

Down Peterstrasse, past a variety of attractive buildings, lies the remarkable **Kaiserpfalz**. Built at the beginning of the eleventh century, the Kaiserpfalz continued to flourish until a fire gutted it in 1289 – it was rescued from disrepair by the future Kaiser Wilhelm I in 1868. Much of the interior (daily 10am–4/5pm; €4.50) is occupied by the vast Reichssaal, decorated with romantic depictions of the emperors. Below the Kaiserpfalz, a large car park fills the former site of the **Dom**, pulled down in 1822 due to lack of funds for restoration. Only the entrance hall with its facade of thirteenth-century statues survived. Down the Abzucht stream to the right is the **Goslarer Museum** (April–Oct Tues–Sun 10am–4/5pm; €3), which contains the bronze Krodo altar from the Dom and a section on mining.

A ten-minute walk northwest of Marktplatz brings you to the **Mönchehaus Museum** (Tues–Sat 10am–5pm, Sun 10am–1pm; €3). A black-and-white half-timbered building over 450 years old, it's the curious home to Goslar's modern art collection. East of here, the **Jakobikirche** contains a moving Pietà by the great but elusive sixteenth-century sculptor, Hans Witten. Finally, the silver mine in the Rammelsberg hill on the southern edge of town – the spot where silver was first discovered in this vicinity – has been opened to the public as a **mining museum** (daily 9am–6pm; €8.50; ⊛www.rammelsburg.de).

Practicalities

The **tourist office** is at Marktplatz 7 (Mon–Fri 9.15am–5/6pm, Sat 9.30am–2/4pm, Sun 9.30am–2pm; Nov–April closed Sun; ☎0 53 21/7 80 60, ⊛www.goslarinfo.de). A few minutes' walk from the **train station** at the northern end of town is the excellent *Gästehaus Elisabeth Müller*, Schieferweg 6 (☎0 53 21/2 30 98; ❸). The attractively quaint **HI hostel**, Rammelsberger Str. 25 (☎0 53 21/2 22 40, ⊛jh-goslar@djh-hannover.de; ❷), is ten minutes' walk from the centre. Of the

hotels, the eighteenth-century *Zur Börse*, Bergstr. 53 (☎0 53 21/3 45 10; ❹), is one of the prettiest. For **restaurants**, try *Köpi am Markt*, Worthstr. 10, which does salads and steaks; *Worthmühle*, Worthstr. 4, good for provincial cooking; and *Kaiserkelle*, Marktstr. 25, a hospitable *Kneipe*.

Central Germany

Central Germany is the most populous region of the country and home to the zone of heaviest industrialization – the **Ruhrgebiet**. Within this conurbation, **Cologne** is the outstanding city, managing to preserve many of the splendours of its long centuries as a free state. Neighbouring **Bonn** is another historic city, renowned for being the birthplace of Beethoven long before becoming a seat of ministerial power, a position it still holds to a degree. The other city of top-class historical interest is **Aachen**, the original capital of the Holy Roman Empire. Swish, cosmopolitan Düsseldorf is the capital of present-day North Rhine-Westphalia (Nordrhein-Westfalen), but of little interest to the casual tourist.

The adjoining province of Rhineland-Palatinate (Rheinland-Pfalz) is the land of the national epic, of the alluring Lorelei, of robber barons and of the traders who used the river routes to make the country rich. Nowadays pleasure cruisers run through the **Rhine gorge**, past a wonderful landscape of rocks, vines, white-painted towns and ruined castles. Industry exists only in isolated pockets, and **Mainz**, the state capital, only just ranks among the forty largest cities in Germany. Its monuments, though, merit more than a passing glance, while **Trier** preserves the finest buildings of classical antiquity this side of the Alps.

In the province of Hesse (Hessen), dynamic **Frankfurt** dominates, with its banking and communications industries providing the region's real economic base. Of the historical centres here, the old university town of **Marburg** is of particular interest.

Cologne

COLOGNE (Köln), with a population of just over a million, is the colossus of the Rhine–Ruhr sprawl and its huge Gothic Dom is the country's most visited monument. Try and coincide your visit with the annual **Carnival** in the early spring or the **Christmas market**, both of which attract visitors from all over Europe. The city also ranks high as a **beer** centre, with some two dozen breweries, all of which produce the distinctive **Kölsch**.

Founded by the Romans in 33 BC, Cologne owed much of its development to ecclesiastical affairs. A bishopric was established in the fourth century, and saints Severin, Gereon and Ursula were all martyred here. In the twelfth century Cologne acquired the relics of the Three Magi from Milan, thus increasing its standing as one of the greatest centres of pilgrimage in northern Europe. Situated on the intersection of the Rhine and several major trade routes, medieval Cologne became immensely rich – and the largest city in Germany. Later decline was partially reversed in the eighteenth century with the exploitation of an Italian recipe for distilling flower blossoms into almost pure alcohol. Originally created as an aphrodisiac, it was marketed here as a toilet water, achieving worldwide fame as **eau de Cologne**.

Arrival, information and accommodation

The **train station** is immediately below the Dom; directly behind is the **bus station**. Coming from the **airport**, bus #170 runs from both terminals (every 15min; journey time 20min) to the train station. The **tourist office**, at Unter Fettenhennen 19, in front of the Dom (Mon–Sat 8am–9/10.30pm, Sun 9am–7/10.30pm; ☎02 21/22 13 04 00, ⊛www.koelntourismus.de), publishes a monthly guide to what's on, *Köln-Monatsvorschau* (€1.20). Cologne's **public transport** network is a mixture of buses and trams, the latter becoming the U-Bahn around the centre. Fares are high, so it's best to get a pass (€5.15/day, €12.95/three days) or the **Welcome Card** (€9/day, €19/three days), which also covers entrance to some sights.

Accommodation is mainly geared to trade fairs, but it is plentifully scattered all over the city. For a hotel room, the best advice is to pay the €3 the tourist office charges to find you a place (same-day only); they often offer special discounts. Cologne also has a good range of **hostel** accommodation.

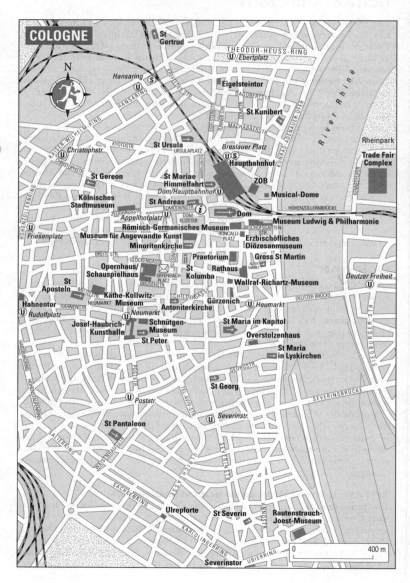

Hostels

Köln Deutz City Hostel Siegesstr. 5a ☎ 02 21/81 47 11. Newly renovated HI-hostel close to Deutz station, directly across the Rhine from the Altstadt. ❸

Köln Riehl City Hostel An der Schanz 14 ☎ 02 21/76 70 81. Another HI hostel tucked away in the quiet northern suburb of Riehl; take U-Bahn #15 or #16 to Boltensternstrasse. ❸

Station Backpacker's Hostel Marzellenstr. 44–48 ☎ 02 21/9 12 53 01, ✆ station@hostel-cologne.de. Comfortable and privately run, this hostel is also the most central. ❷

Station Hostel and Bar Rheingasse 34-36 ☎ 02 21/23 02 47. Another branch of *Station Backpacker's*, ten minutes' walk from the station. ❸

Hotels and pensions

Das Kleine Stapelhäuschen, Fischmarkt 1–3 ☎ 02 21/2 57 78 62, ✆ stapelhaeuschen @compuserve.com. Welcoming and characterful hotel/restaurant in the heart of the Altstadt, overlooking the Rhein. ❹

Im Kupferkessel Probsteigasse 6 ☎ 02 21/13 53 38. Good-value rooms, complete with mini-bars, in a location just far enough from the centre to be peaceful. ❺

Jansen Richard-Wagner-Str. 18 ☎ 02 21/25 18 75. Six-room pension; all rooms have TV. ❹

Rossner Jakordenstr. 19 ☎ 02 21/12 27 03. Homely and clean, and looking exactly as it must in the 1950s, this is the pick of the cluster of hotels behind the station. ❸

The Dom

One of the largest Gothic buildings ever constructed, Cologne's **Dom** is built on a scale that reflects its power – the archbishop was one of the seven Electors of the Holy Roman Empire, and the Dom remains the seat of the Primate of Germany. Impetus for its creation came with the arrival of the alleged relics of the Magi; when it came to commissioning a church of appropriate grandeur, it was decided to adopt the new Gothic style rather than the late Romanesque style still in vogue at the time.

The **chancel** was completed in 1322, but then the extravagant ambition of the plans began to take its toll. In 1560 the project was abandoned, to be resumed only in the nineteenth century. What you see today is an act of homage from one age to another. The **spires** were the tallest structures in the world, but were soon dwarfed by the Eiffel Tower and are no longer even the highest in Cologne. All the same, it's a climb up of 509 steps to the top of the south tower for a panorama over the city and the Rhine (daily 9am–4/6pm; €2, €5 combined ticket with Schatzkammer).

From the west door your eye is immediately drawn down the length of the building to the **high altar**, with the spectacular golden shrine to the Magi, made in 1181. It's one of three masterpieces to be found here; the others are in the chapels at the entrance to the ambulatory. On the north side is the ninth-century **Gero crucifix**, the most important monumental sculpture of its period, while the corresponding chapel to the south has the greatest achievement of the fifteenth-century Cologne school of painters, the *Adoration of the Magi* by Stefan Lochner.

The new **Domschatzkammer** (daily 10am–6pm; €4) in the cellars, entered from the north side of the building, contains a stunning array of treasury items, the original sculptures from the medieval south portal and items excavated from Merovingian royal graves. Also worth a visit, the **Diocesan Museum**, just outside on Roncalliplatz (11am–6pm, closed Thurs; free; ⊛ www.kolumba.de), contains another beautiful Lochner, *Madonna of the Violets*.

The rest of the city

In a modern building right next to the Dom, the **Museum Ludwig** (Tues–Sun 10/11am–6/8pm; €5.50; ⊛ www.museenkoeln.de) is one of Germany's premier collections of modern art. Among German works there are superb portraits by Dix and sculptures by Barlach. Picasso and Andy Warhol also feature. Part of the building is given over to the Agfa-Foto-Historama, which shows old photographic equipment and a selection of prints from the vast holdings of the local company.

The neighbouring **Römisch–Germanisches Museum** (Tues–Sun 10am–5pm; €4; ⊛ www.museenkoeln.de) is one of Germany's most important archeological museums. Its collection of Roman glass is reckoned to be the world's finest, but of more general appeal is the dazzling array of jewellery on the first floor, mostly dating from the Dark Ages. Its star exhibit is the Dionysus Mosaic, the finest work of its kind in northern Europe; created for a patrician villa in about 200 AD, it covers some 70sqm.

For nearly 600 years, **Gross St Martin**'s tower, surrounded by four turrets, was the dominant feature of the Cologne skyline; the rest of the church seems rather truncated for such a splendid adornment, although the interior has a pleasing simplicity. From the Alter Markt just beyond, you can see the irregular octagonal tower of the **Rathaus**, a real fricassee of styles, the highlight being the graceful Renaissance loggia. Just in front of the entrance to the Rathaus, a steel and glass pyramid stands over the **Mikwe** (Mon–Thurs 8am–4.45pm, Fri 8am–noon, Sat 10am–4pm, Sun 11am–1pm; free). This is the only remnant of the Jewish ghetto, which was razed soon after the expulsion order of 1424.

Proceeding south, you soon come to the strikingly angular **Wallraf-Richartz-Museum** (Tues–Sun 10/11am–6/8pm; €5.50; @www.museenkoeln.de), whose holdings are centred on the fifteenth-century Cologne school. The gems of the display are the two large triptychs by the Master of St Bartholomew, from the school's final flowering at the beginning of the sixteenth century. There are also pieces by Dürer, Lucas Cranach and Rembrandt. The museum is joined onto the burned-out church of **Alt St Alban**, left in this state as a war memorial.

Continuing in a southerly direction, go down Rheingasse to see the step-gabled **Overstolzenhaus**, the finest mansion in the city. A stroll southwest from here takes you to **St Pantaleon**, the oldest church in the city. North up Poststrasse and Peterstrasse is **St Peter**, a Gothic church with gleaming stained-glass windows. Rubens, whose childhood was spent in Cologne, painted its altarpiece.

Next door, the church of **St Cäcilien** now houses the **Schnütgen-Museum** (Tues–Sun 10/11am–5pm; €3; @www.museenkoeln.de), a collection of all kinds of Rhineland religious art except paintings. There are some wonderful ivories, but the most famous piece is a painted bust of a woman, carved by one of the Parler family and thought to be the portrait of a relative. Across the road and down Antongasse is the tiny Gothic **Antoniterkirche**, housing one of the most famous twentieth-century sculptures, Barlach's *Memorial Angel*.

Following Tunisstr. northwards until it meets Gereonstr. brings you to **St Gereon**, a church without parallel in European architecture. Its kernel is an oval fourth-century chapel, which, after various additions, became the basis of a four-storey decagon in the early thirteenth century. From here you can return towards the Dom, passing the stately **St Andreas**, worth a look for its frescoes and the Maccabees shrine, a notable piece of early sixteenth-century craftsmanship. If you then strike north you'll come to **St Ursula**, with its prominent sturdy tower. From here the **Eigelsteintor**, an impressive survival of the medieval fortifications, is reached via the street of the same name. Dagobertstrasse then leads east to **St Kunibert**, the final fling of the Romanesque in the early thirteenth century, completed just as work began on the Dom. It's also the last church to be restored after war damage, with the nave and massive facade not yet joined up.

Eating, drinking and entertainment

Cologne crams over three thousand pubs, bars and cafés into a relatively small area. Their ubiquitous feature is the city's unique beer, **Kölsch**. Light and aromatically bitter, it's served in a tall, thin glass (*Stange*), which holds only a fifth of a litre – hence its rather effete image among other German beer drinkers. Best places to try it are the **Brauhäuser**, brewery-owned beer halls, which, although staffed by horribly matey waiters called *Köbes*, are definitely worth sampling, not least because they serve some of the cheapest and tastiest food in the city.

Cologne's **nightspots** are concentrated in several distinct quarters. Most obvious of these is the area around Gross St Martin in the Altstadt, which catches the tourists and businessmen, yet manages to create a distinctive atmosphere in places.

Beer halls

Alt-Köln Trankgasse 7–9. Notable for both the intricate clock mechanism on the outside and the no-nonsense slabs of salmon steak served inside.
Brauhaus Sion Unter Taschenmacher 5. Frequented mainly by locals, despite its proximity to the Dom; the menu concentrates on variations of *Wurst* and knuckles of pork leg.
Früh am Dom Am Hof 12–14. Located opposite the Dom, this Brauhaus is heavily touristed and serves excellent food. Opens for breakfast 8–11am.
Päffgen Friesenstr. 64–68. Less touristy than the places near the Dom, and brews *Kölsch* on the premises.
Zur Malzmühle Heumarkt 6. Traditional Hausbrauerei, which brews its own malty *Malzmühlenkölsch*.

Bars

Chlodwig-Eck Annostr. 1. Popular Südstadt meeting place, with live sport TV and Mediterranean-flavoured food.

Filmdose Zülpicher Str. 39. Fun pub that's packed with students enjoying a post-lecture *Kölsch*; it has a tiny cabaret stage and also shows films in English.
Gilberts Pinte Engelbertstr. 1. Laid-back student bar with plenty of atmosphere.
Opera Alteburger Str. 1. Brightly coloured, youth-oriented place with daily specialities on the menu.
Papa Joe's Em Streckstrumpf Buttermarkt 37. Cosier, smaller, somewhat overpriced version of the *Klimperkasten* (see below) – and Germany's oldest jazz bar.
Papa Joe's Klimperkasten Alter Markt 50. Deservedly popular Altstadt bar with twenties decor and live trad jazz.
Peppermint Hohenstauffenring 23. Popular late-night joint that springs into action around midnight. Happy hour 5–7pm.
Schmelztiegel Luxemburger Str. 34. Located in a former pharmacy, the relaxed "melting pot" now offers eleven varieties of *Kölsch* to combat most ailments.

Carnival

Though the **Carnival** actually begins as early as November 11, the real business begins with Weiberfastnacht on the Thursday prior to the seventh Sunday before Easter. A ceremony at 10am in the Alter Markt leads to the official inauguration of the festival, with the mayor handing over the keys of the city to Prinz Carnival, who assumes command for the duration. At 3pm there's the first of the great processions and in the evening the series of costume balls begins – with singing and dancing in the streets and taverns as an alternative. On the Saturday morning there's the Funkenbiwak, featuring the Rote und Blaue Funken, men who, dressed up in eighteenth-century military outfits, disobey every order. On Sunday the Schul- und Veedleszög, largely featuring children, forms a prelude to the more spectacular Rosenmontagzug (Rose Monday Parade). After this, the festival runs down, but there are numerous smaller parades in the suburbs on Shrove Tuesday, while the restaurants offer special fish menus on Ash Wednesday. The grandstand seats along the route are expensive for the Rose Monday Parade but good value on the Sunday; don't forget it's free, and certainly more fun, simply to mingle with the crowds.

Listings

Bike rental Rent-a-Bike, Sedanstr. 27 ☎02 21/72 36 27.
Hospital Alexianer Krankenhaus, Kölner Str. 64 ☎02 21/9 17 00.
Internet Voice Store Callshop, Bahnhofsvorplatz 1; Future Point, Richmodstr. 13.
Laundry Waschsalon, Pantaleonsmühlengasse 42, in the Altstadt.

Left luggage At the train station.
Pharmacy An der Rennbahn Apotheke. Branches through Cologne, including the station and at Neumarkt 2.
Post office Breite Str. 6–26; sub-branch at the station.

Bonn

BONN, Cologne's neighbour, served as West Germany's capital from 1949 until the unification of 1990, when Berlin was restored to its former status. Bonn has managed to preserve an important administrative role, however, remaining the seat of seven ministries and a host of other governmental bodies. It is also an historic town in its own right, chiefly renowned as the birthplace of Beethoven.

The small **Altstadt** is now a pedestrianized shopping area centred on two spacious squares. The square to the east is named after the huge Romanesque **Münster**, whose central octagonal tower with its soaring spire is the city's most prominent landmark. The pink Rococo **Rathaus** adds a touch of colour to the other square, the Markt, which still hosts a market each weekday. A couple of minutes' walk north of here, at Bonngasse 20, is the **Beethoven–Haus** (daily 10am–4/6pm; €8), one of the few old buildings in the centre to have escaped wartime devastation. Beethoven served his musical apprenticeship at the Electoral court, but left the city for good at the age of 22, though this hasn't deterred Bonn from building up the best collection of memorabilia of its favourite son. The Altstadt's second dominant building is the Baroque **Schloss**, an enormously long construction that was formerly the seat of the Archbishop-Electors of Cologne and is now used by the university.

Bonn's **government quarter**, a mile south of the city centre, was saddled with a temporary status. As a result, nothing was custom-built, but rather government offices utilized existing buildings, such as the **Villa Hammerschmidt** and the **Palais Schaumburg** – pompous nineteenth-century buildings now used as plush conference venues. The **Museumsmeile**, planned as a cultural accompaniment to the government quarter, is home to the **Kunstmuseum** (Tues–Sun 10am–6pm, Wed till 9pm; €6), the municipal gallery of modern art, which is especially strong in its representation of the Expressionists, and the **Kunst- und Ausstellungshalle der Bundesrepublik Deutschland** (Tues–Sun 10am–7/9pm; ⓦwww.bundeskunsthalle.de), a monumental postmodern arts centre for temporary exhibitions.

Practicalities

The **train station** lies in the middle of the city; close by is the **bus station**, whose local services, along with the **trams** (which become the U-Bahn in the city centre), form part of a system integrated with that of Cologne. As the attractions are well spaced out, it's advisable to buy a public transport pass (€5.15/day, €12.25/three days) or the one-day **BonnCard** (€12.25), which covers public transport plus entrance to the museums. You can get them from the **tourist office**, Windeckstr. 9 (Mon–Sat 9am–4/6.30pm, Sun 10am–2pm; ☎02 28/77 50 00, ⓦwww.bonn.de).

The **hostel** is at Haager Weg 42 (☎02 28/28 99 70, ✉jh-bonn@djh-rheinland .de; ❸) in the suburb of Venusberg, served by bus #621. Central **Hotels** include the *Savoy*, Berliner Freiheit 17 (☎02 28/72 59 70; ❻), the hospitable *Deutsches Haus*, Kasernenstr. 19-21 (☎02 28/63 37 77; ❹), and the pastel-shaded *Mozart*, Mozartstr. 1 (☎02 28/65 90 71, ⓦwww.hotel-mozart-bonn.de; ❹).

For **places to eat** try: *Cassius Garten*, Maximilianstr. 28d, which offers a mouthwatering choice of vegetarian food; *Don Quijote*, Oxfordstr. 18, the most affordable of a surprising number of Spanish restaurants; *Grand' Italia*, Bischofsplatz 1, the best of many Italian places; *Em Höttche*, Markt 4, a good traditional *Gaststätte* next to the Rathaus; or *Im Bären*, Acherstr. 1–3, an excellent brewery-owned place. Many of the best **bars** are in the Altstadt. *Brauhaus Bönnsch*, Sterntorbrücke 4, produces a distinctive blond ale and does good-value meals, while *Zebulon*, Stockenstr. 19, is a big favourite with arts students, particularly for breakfast.

Aachen

Now a frontier post – it borders both Belgium and the Netherlands – **AACHEN** once played a far grander role. Around the late eighth century the city became the hub of the great empire of Charlemagne, a choice made partly for strategic reasons but also because of the presence of hot springs – exercising in these waters was one of the emperor's favourite pastimes.

The centre is ten minutes from the train station – down Bahnhofstrasse then left into Theaterstrasse. Although the surviving architectural legacy of Charlemagne is small, Aachen retains its crowning jewel, the former **Palace chapel**. Now the heart of the **Dom**, the original octagon had to be enlarged by adding the Gothic chancel to accommodate the number of pilgrims that poured in. Some original furnishings – including the great bronze doors – survive, but these are overshadowed by the additions of Charlemagne's successors. Adorning the main altar is the **Pala d'Oro**, an eleventh-century altar front embossed with scenes of the Passion. At the end of the chancel, the gilded **shrine of Charlemagne**, finished in 1215 after fifty years' work, contains the remains of the emperor. In the gallery is the imperial throne, which was long thought to have been made for the coronation of Otto I, thus initiating the tradition of emperors being crowned at Aachen. Recent tests, however, have all but conclusively proved that it actually dates back to the time of Charlemagne. To see the throne you have to join a tour (daily; €2.50).

Charlemagne's palace once extended across the Katschhof, now lined with ugly modern buildings, to the site of the fourteenth-century **Rathaus**, which incorporates two of the palace's towers. Fronting the **Markt**, which boasts the finest of the medieval houses left in the city, its facade is lined with the figures of 50 Holy Roman Emperors, 31 of whom were crowned in Aachen. The glory of the interior (daily 10am–1pm & 2–5pm; €1.50) is the much-restored Kaisersaal, repository of the **crown jewels** – in reproduction. The originals have been in Vienna since the early nineteenth century, when they were commandeered by the Habsburgs.

Practicalities

The **tourist office** occupies the Atrium Elisenbrunnen on Friedrich-Wilhelm-Platz (Mon–Fri 9am–6pm, Sat 9am–2pm; ☎02 41/180 29 60, ✆www.aachen-tourist.de). The **HI hostel** is southwest of the centre, at Maria-Theresia-Allee 260 (☎02 41/71 10 10, ✉jh-aachen@djh-rheinland.de; ❷); take bus #2 as far as Brüsseler Ring or Ronheide. The cheaper **hotels** can be found near the train station; try: *Dura*, Lagerhausstr. 5 (☎02 41/40 31 35; ❸); *Hesse am Marschiertor*, Friedlandstr. 20 (☎02 41/47 05 40; ❹); or *Marx*, Hubertusstr 33–35 (☎02 41/3 75 41, ✆www.hotel-marx.de; ❹). A spiced gingerbread called **Printen** is the main local speciality, and the place to eat it is the old coffee house *Leo van den Daele* at Büchel 18. The most celebrated **bar/restaurant** is *Postwagen*, Markt 40, built onto the end of the Rathaus, with a cheerful Baroque exterior and wonderful cramped rooms inside. The student quarter centres on Pontstrasse, where *Tangente* and *Atlantis* – which share a terrace at no.141 – are popular haunts and *Labyrinth* at no. 156 is a large pub serving Greek-style food. *Café Kittel*, at no. 37, is a relaxed café/bar with garden.

Mainz

At the confluence of the Rhine and Main, **MAINZ** developed in the eighth century, when St Boniface made it the main centre of the Church north of the Alps. Later, the local archbishop came to be one of the most powerful princes in the Holy Roman Empire, and further prestige came through **Johannes Gutenberg**, who revolutionized the art of printing here. Since the Napoleonic period it has never managed to recover its former status, and its strategic location inevitably made it a prime target of World War II bombers. Nonetheless, it's an agreeable mixture of old and new, and makes a good place to stay if you're flying in or out of Frankfurt, as the airport lies on the S-Bahn line linking the two cities.

Rearing high above the centre of Mainz is the **Dom**, crowded in by eighteenth-century houses, though most of what can be seen dates from the twelfth century. Choirs at both ends of the building indicate its status as an imperial cathedral, with one area for the emperor and one for the clergy; the solemn and spacious interior contains the sculptured tombs of archbishops from the thirteenth to nineteenth century. The **Diocesan Museum** (Tues–Sun 10am–5pm; free), off the cloisters, contains fragments from the demolished rood screen carved by the mason known as the Master of Naumburg from his work in the eastern German city of that name.

On Tuesday, Friday and Saturday mornings the spacious **Markt**, with its riotously colourful fountain, is packed with market stalls and is unmissable. Dominating the adjoining Liebfrauenplatz, the resplendent pink Haus zum Römischen Kaiser houses the offices of the **Gutenberg Museum** (Tues–Sat 9am–5pm, Sun 11am–3pm; €3; ℗www.gutenberg.de) – the actual displays are in a modern extension behind. It's a fitting tribute to one of the greatest inventors of all time, whose pioneering development of movable type led to the mass-scale production of books. In 1978, the museum acquired the last Gutenberg **Bible** still in private hands – made in the 1450s, it's one of only forty-odd surviving examples.

Across Schöfferstrasse from the Dom, Ludwigstrasse runs to Schillerplatz and Schillerstrasse, both lined with Renaissance and Baroque palaces. Up the hill by Gaustrasse is the Gothic **St Stephan** (daily 10am–noon & 2–5pm), whose priest persuaded Marc Chagall to make a series of stained-glass windows. Symbolizing the reconciliation between France and Germany, Christian and Jew, the nine windows were finished in November 1984, a few months before Chagall's death. Down Grosse Bleiche – which runs from the end of Schillerstrasse to the river – are the old imperial stables, now home of the **Landesmuseum Mainz** (Tues–Sun 10am–5pm, Tues till 8pm; €3, free Sat). The outstanding archeology department includes a hall of Roman sculptural remains, dominated by the Jupitersäule, the most important Roman triumphal column in Germany.

Further along is the Schloss, the enormous former palace of the Archbishop-Electors, a superbly swaggering Renaissance building. The interior was completely rebuilt after the war, and now contains the **Römisch-Germanisches Museum** (Tues–Sun 10am–6pm; free), a confusing mix of original antiquities and copies.

Practicalities

The **train station** is northwest of the city centre, while the **tourist office** (Mon–Fri 9am–6pm, Sat 10am–3pm; ℗0 61 31/28 62 10, ℗www.info-mainz.de) is in the Brückenturm am Rathaus at the corner of Rheinstrasse. Near the station are some of the least expensive **hotels**, such as *Terminus*, Alicenstr. 4 (℗0 61 31/22 98 76, ℗hotel-terminus@debitel.net; ❹), which has 28 en-suite rooms. *Stadt Coblenz*, Rheinstr. 49 (℗0 61 31/22 76 02; ❹), is more conveniently located near the Dom, though the front rooms suffer from excessive street noise. Alternatively, there's the **HI hostel** (℗0 61 31/8 53 32, ℗jh-mainz@djh-info.de; ❷), in the wooded heights of Am Fort Weisenau and reached by buses #61 and #62.

Mainz boasts more vineyards than any other German city, and you don't need to stray far from the Dom if you fancy a **wine** crawl. Some *Weinstuben* are open in the evenings only, such as the oldest, *Alt Deutsche Weinstube*, Liebfrauenplatz 7, which offers cheap daily dishes. Even better **food** is available at *Weinhaus Schreiner*, Rheinstr. 38. Though Mainz is a wine rather than a beer city, it has an excellent home-brew **pub**, *Eisgrub-Bräu*, Weissliliengasse 4, which serves inexpensive buffet lunches. The hottest **nightspots** include *KUZ*, Dagobertstr. 20b, and *Jazzid*, in the Malakoff-Center, Rheinstr. 4.

The Rhine gorge

North of Mainz, the Rhine bends westwards and continues its stately but undramatic journey – then suddenly, at Bingen, the river widens and swings north into the spectacular 80km **Rhine gorge**. This waterway may have become one of Europe's major tourist magnets, but the pleasure steamers are still outnumbered by commercial barges – a reminder of the river's crucial role in the German economy.

In summer, inexpensive accommodation is scarce and heavily booked. Spring and autumn are the best times to visit. Rail and road lines lie on each side of the river and, although there are no bridges between Bingen and Koblenz, there are fairly frequent ferries, enabling you to hop from one side of the river to the other. However, it's undeniably most fun by boat. **River cruises** depart from Mainz, where there's also a K-D Line office (☎0 61 31/23 28 00, ⊛www.k-d.com). Fares aren't cheap – from Mainz to St Goar costs €26.40 one way and €30.80 return – though Eurail is valid and other rail passes attract a discount on certain routes.

Arguably the most famous point along the Rhine is the **Lorelei**, a much-photographed rocky projection where, legend has it, a blonde woman would lure passing mariners to their doom with her siren song. The rock itself can also be spotted from trains heading north from Koblenz, since the track runs right along the banks of the Rhine as it passes through the gorge. At **BACHARACH**, 10km downstream from Bingen, the chunky castle of **Burg Stahleck** now houses the local **hostel** (☎0 67 43/12 66, ⊛jh-bacharach@djh-info.de; ❷), while moderately priced hotels are clustered in Blücherstrasse, Langstrasse and Oberstrasse. Bacharach itself dates back to Roman times, and sections of the original town wall remain. The local **campsite** is at Strandbadweg. From **KAUB**, a few kilometres on, you get a great view of the **Pfalz**, a white-walled toll fortress standing on an island that has become a famous Rhineland symbol (Tues–Sun 9am–1pm & 2–5/6pm; €3.60 including ferry). This stronghold enabled the lords of **Burg Gutenfels** to extract a toll from passing ships well into the nineteenth century. Burg Gutenfels as you see it today is a late-nineteenth-century rebuild of the original thirteenth-century castle. There are **camping** facilities at *Am Bacharach* on Blücherstrasse.

Koblenz

KOBLENZ stands where the Rhine and Mosel meet. The centre is at its best in the area around the confluence at **Deutsches Eck**, close to which stands the fine Romanesque church of **St Kastor**. However, the most commanding sights are across the Rhine in **Ehrenbreitstein**, where the Baroque **Residenz** of the Electors of Trier is overshadowed by the **Festung**. One of the largest fortresses in the world, it is now home to the **Landesmuseum Koblenz** (mid-March to Nov daily 9am–5pm; €2) and one of the best **hostels** in Germany (☎02 61/97 28 70; ❷; bus #8, #9 or #10).

Koblenz's main **tourist office** (Mon–Fri 9am–6/8pm, Sat & Sun 10am–4/6/8pm; ☎02 61/30 38 80, ⊛www.koblenz.de) is opposite the **train and bus stations**, which are a little to the southwest of the centre. **Hotel** rooms are reasonably priced: try *Sessellift*, Obertal 22 (☎02 61/7 52 56; ❸); or *Jan van Werth*, Van-Werth-Str. 9 (☎02 61/3 65 00; ❸). The **campsite**, *Schartwiesenweg*, is at Lützel (☎02 61/80 24 89; closed mid-Oct to March), directly opposite Deutsches Eck; a ferry crosses the Mosel here in summer, while another crosses the Rhine further south.

Trier

The oldest city in Germany, **TRIER** was once the capital of the Western Roman Empire, and a residence of the Emperor Constantine. Nowadays, it has the less exalted role of regional centre for the upper Mosel valley, its relaxed air a world away from the status it formerly held. Despite a turbulent history, an amazing amount of the city's past has been preserved, in particular the most impressive group of Roman monuments north of the Alps.

The centre of modern Trier corresponds roughly to the Roman city and can easily be covered on foot. From the train station, it's a few minutes' walk down Theodor-Heuss-Allee to the **Porta Nigra**, northern gateway to Roman Trier. Nearby, housed in a former monastery, is the **Städtisches Museum** (Tues–Sun 9am–3/5pm; April–Oct also Mon; €2.60), which contains some notable medieval sculptures plus a good ancient history section featuring Egyptian and Roman artefacts. From here, Simeonstrasse runs down to the **Hauptmarkt**, a busy pedestrian shopping area, with stalls selling fruit and flowers. The finest of the Hauptmarkt's medieval monuments is the thirteenth-century **Dreikönigshaus**, once a secure home in uncertain times for a rich merchant family. At the southern end of the Hauptmarkt a Baroque portal leads to the Gothic **St Gangolf**, built by the burghers of Trier in an attempt to aggravate the archbishops, whose political power they resented.

Up Sternstr. from the Hauptmarkt is the magnificent Romanesque **Dom** on the site of a huge original dating from 325 AD and built for Constantine. The present building dates from 1030, and the facade has not changed significantly since then. Inside, the relative austerity is enlivened by devotional and decorative features added through the centuries. The **Schatzkammer** (Mon–Sat 10/11am–4/5pm, Sun 1.30–4/5pm; €1.50) has many examples of the work of local goldsmiths, notably a tenth-century portable altar. From the cloisters there's a good view of the ensemble and the adjacent **Liebfrauenkirche**, one of Germany's first Gothic churches. Facing the north side of the Dom on Windstrasse is the **Bischöfliches Museum** (Mon–Sat 9am–1pm & 2–5pm, Sun 1–5pm; €2) with a fourth-century ceiling painting from the palace which preceded the Dom and some important sculptures, including most of the original statues from the facade of the Liebfrauenkirche.

From here, Liebfrauenstrasse goes past the ritzy Palais Kesselstadt to the **Konstantinbasilika**. Built as Constantine's throne hall, its dimensions are awe-inspiring: 30m high and 75m long, it is completely self-supporting. It became a church for the local Protestant community in the nineteenth century, a role it still fills. Next door, the **Rokoko-Palais der Kurfürsten** was built in 1756 for an archbishop who felt that the adjoining old Schloss wasn't good enough for him. Its pink facade overlooks the Palastgarten, setting for the **Rheinisches Landesmuseum** (9.30/10.30am–5pm; Nov–April closed Mon; €5.50). Easily the best of Trier's museums, its collection brings to life the sophistication and complexity of Roman civilization; prize exhibit is the Neumagener Weinschiff, a Roman sculpture of a wine ship.

A few minutes further south, the **Kaiserthermen** was once one of the largest bath complexes in the Roman world. The extensive underground heating system has survived, and you can walk around the service channels and passages. From the Kaiserthermen the route to the **Amphitheatre** is well signposted. The oldest of Trier's surviving Roman buildings, it was built around 100 AD and had a capacity of 20,000. Head back towards the town centre down Olewiger Strasse and then Südallee and you'll come to the **Barbarathermen**, Trier's second set of Roman baths. Built in the second century, they are now little more than piles of rock and vaguely defined foundations. Midway between the baths and the Hauptmarkt, at Brückenstr. 10, the **Karl-Marx-Haus** (Mon 1/2–5pm, Tues–Sun 10am–1pm & 2–5/6pm; €2) explains the life and work of Trier's most influential son in detail that verges on the excruciating.

Practicalities

Trier's **tourist office** is at An der Porta Nigra (Mon–Sat 9am–5/6pm, Sun 10am–1/3pm; ☎97 80 80, ⊛www.trier.de). It sells the **Trier-Card** (€9), which covers entrance to the museums and various other discounts over three consecutive days. Cheapest **internet** access is at the *Telecafe*, Theodor-Heuss-Allee 21, just outside the train station. There's a large **HI hostel** at An der Jugendherberge 4 (☎06 51/14 66 20, ⊛jh-trier@djh-info.de; ➋) on the banks of the Mosel. *Kolpinghaus Warsburger Hof*, Dietrichstr. 42 (☎06 51/97 52 50; ➋), is the best-value **hotel**; it has dorm beds as well as individual rooms, and is ideally situated in the Altstadt. Otherwise, the most central hotel is the recently revamped *Zur Glocke*, Glockenstr. 12 (☎06 51/7 31 09; ➌). There's a **campsite**, *Trier City* (☎0651/86921; closed Dec & Jan), on the western bank of the Mosel at Luxemburger Str. 81. There are plenty of places where you can get good and inexpensive **food**: the best bet is *Astarix*, Karl-Marx-Str. 11, a big, relaxed student bar; or try *Zum Domstein*, Hauptmarkt 5, whose eclectic menu includes Roman-style dishes, regional creations and some good vegetarian options. Among the many possibilities for tasting the local wines is the late-opening **bar** of the prestigious Reichsgraf von Kesselstatt estates, at Liebfrauenstr. 10. The bright and breezy *InFlagranti*, Viehmarkt 14, is a student favourite, while *Palais* on Stockplatz is a trendy **bar–cum–disco**.

Frankfurt

Straddling the Main just before it meets the Rhine, **FRANKFURT** is a city with two faces. The cut-throat financial capital of Germany, with its fulcrum in the Westend district, it's also a civilized place that spends more per year on the arts than any other city in Europe. In fact, Frankfurt is a thriving recreational centre for the whole of Hesse, with a good selection of theatres and galleries, and an even better range of museums. Over half of the city, including almost all of the centre, was destroyed during the war and the rebuilders opted for innovation rather than restoration. The result is a skyline that smacks more of Chicago than of Germany.

Arrival, information and accommodation

Frankfurt **airport** is a major point of entry into Germany, and there are regular rail links between it and most German cities, with a regular service (every 10min) to the main **train station**. The airport is also linked to the train station by two S-Bahn lines, run by the regional transport company (RMV), which is also responsible for bus, tram and U-Bahn services. Ticket prices vary according to the time of travel, making it better to invest in the one-day ticket (€4.35) or, better still, the **Frankfurt Card** (€7.50/day, €11/two days), which is available from tourist offices and allows travel throughout the city, plus reduced entry charges to most museums (though many are free on Wed). From the train station it's a fifteen-minute walk to the centre, or take U-Bahn line #4 or #5, or tram #11. There are two main **tourist offices**: in the train station (Mon–Fri 8am–9pm, Sat & Sun 9am–6pm; ☎0 69/21 23 88 00, ✉www.frankfurt-tourismus.de), and at Römerberg 27 (10am–4/5.30pm; same number). Free **listings magazines**, *Fritz* and *Strandgut*, are available at both.

Accommodation is pricey, thanks to the expense-account clientele. Most reasonably priced options are in the sleazy environs of the train station, close to the Kaiserstrasse red-light district. The pick of the inexpensive hotels are listed below.

Hostel
HI hostel Deutschherrnufer 12 ☎0 69/6 10 01 50. The best budget option in town, with 470 places in dorms of up to twelve beds each. In Sachsenhausen and reached by bus #46 from the train station. ❷

Hotels
Atlas Zimmerweg 1 ☎0 69/72 39 46. Friendly place with bright, airy rooms within walking distance of the station but away from the sleazy side of things. Recommended. ❹
Backer Mendelssohnstr. 92 ☎0 69/74 79 92. Pleasant enough place close to the university,

although use of the showers will cost you €2 a time. U-Bahn line #6 or #7 to Westend. ❸
Glockshuber Mainzer Landstr. 120 ☎74 26 28. Pleasant budget hotel just north of the train station, away from the sleazier streets. ❹
Gölz Beethovenstr. 44 ☎0 69/74 67 35, ✉hotelgoelz@aol.com. Small, traditionally furnished hotel located on a quiet, tree-lined avenue in the Westend district. ❺
Royal Wallstr. 17 ☎0 69/62 30 26, ✉www .royal-primus-hotels.de. Functional but good-value hotel in the heart of Sachsenhausen, close to some of the well-known apple wine taverns. ❺

The City

The city centre is defined by the old city walls, now transformed into a semi-circular stretch of public gardens. **Römerberg** is the historical and, roughly speaking, geographical centre of the city. Charlemagne built his fort on this low hill to protect the ford that gave Frankfurt its name – Frankonovurd (Ford of the Franks). Römerberg was still the heart of the city, and an essentially medieval quarter, at the start of World War II, but it was flattened in two air raids in March 1944.

The most significant survivor was the thirteenth-century St Bartholomäus or **Dom**, and even that emerged with only its main walls intact. Before the construction of the skyscrapers it was the tallest building in the city, as befitted the venue for the election and coronation of the Holy Roman Emperors. To the right of the choir is the restored **Wahlkapelle**, where the seven Electors used to make their final choice of emperor.

To the north, in Domstrasse, the **Museum für Moderne Kunst** (Tues–Sun 10am–8pm; €5; ⓦwww.mmk-frankfurt.de) features some of the major names in postwar American and German art. At the opposite end of the Römerberg is the building that gave the area its name – the **Römer**, formerly the Rathaus. Its distinctive facade, with its triple-stepped gables, fronts the Römerplatz market square, on whose southern side stands the former court chapel, the **Nikolaikirche**. The interior is refreshingly restrained; though the church was given a Gothic face-lift, the lines of the original Romanesque structure are visible on the inside. The **Saalhof**, an amalgamation of imperial buildings now housing the Historisches Museum, is nearby on Mainkai, overlooking the river. Its twelfth-century chapel is all that remains of the palace complex, which grew up in the Middle Ages. The **museum** (Tues–Sun 10am–5pm, Wed till 8pm; €4) contains a good local-history collection, with an eye-opening section on the devastation caused by the bombing.

A short distance to the west, on Untermainkai, is the **Karmeliterkloster**, where Jörg Ratgeb's 80-metre-long al secco cycle of the life of Jesus occupies the cloister. The southern part of the complex houses the **Museum für Vor- and Frühgeschichte** (Tues–Sun 10am–5pm, Wed till 8pm; €4), a collection devoted to early and prehistory. Just north of here, at Grosser Hirschgraben 23, is the **Goethehaus und Goethe-Museum** (daily 9/10am–4/6pm; €5; ⓦwww.goethe-haus-frankfurt.de), the house where Goethe was born and raised. It has been made to look as much as possible like it did when Goethe lived here, and there are even a few objects that somehow survived the war.

A couple of minutes away on the Liebfrauenberg is the fifteenth-century **Liebfrauenkirche** – its unusual altar, a huge alabaster and gilt affair, sits well in the dusky pink interior. A little to the northwest of the **Hauptwache** (originally a guard house) is the **Börse**, Frankfurt's stock exchange. Entry to the viewing area, to watch the deals being struck, must be arranged at least one month in advance (☎069/2 10 10). Appropriately, two of the most expensive shopping streets in the city are just around the corner. **Goethestrasse** is Frankfurt's Bond Street, all expensive jewellers and designer clothes shops, while **Grosse Bockenheimer Strasse** is home to upmarket delicatessens and smarter restaurants. This area is characterized by gleaming skyscrapers, one of which admits the public to its 86th-floor outside viewing platform; the **Main Tower** (10am–7/9pm; €4.50) is the place to come for an unrivalled vista of Frankfurt, doubly impressive by night.

East of here, the garden of **Peterskirche** is notable for its unusual and moving memorial to victims of AIDS in Frankfurt; designed by Thomas Fecht, *Verletzte Liebe* ("Wounded Love") is a wall studded with nails, one for each fatality; there are currently over eight hundred nails.

Sachsenhausen

For a laid-back evening out, head for **Sachsenhausen**, the city-within-a-city on the south bank of the Main. The network of streets around Affentorplatz are home to the famous **apple wine** (*Ebbelwei*) houses. There's entertainment of a different sort to be had on **Schaumainkai**, which runs between the Eiserner Steg and the Friedensbrücke; if you're here on a Saturday, the **fleamarket** is worth a browse. Schaumainkai's biggest draw is the **Städel** located at no. 63 (Tues–Sun 10am–5pm, Wed till 8pm; €6; ⓦwww.staedelmuseum.de), one of the most comprehensive art galleries in Europe. All the big names in German art are represented, including Dürer, both Holbeins, Cranach and Altdorfer. The **Museum für Angewandte Kunst**, at no. 15 (Tues–Sun 10am–8pm; €5; ⓦwww.mak.frankfurt.de), has a huge collection of applied art, divided into four sections: European, featuring a unique collection of furniture models, glassware and ceramics; Islamic, with some fine carpets; Far Eastern, with lots of jade and lacquer work plus a liberal sprinkling of porcelain and sculptures; and finally a section devoted to books and writing. The **Deutsches Filmmuseum**, no. 41 (Tues–Sun 10am–5pm, Wed till 8pm, Sat from 2pm; €2.50; ⓦwww.deutsches-filmmuseum.de), is Germany's biggest and best film museum, and has its own cinema. The **Deutsches Architekturmuseum**, no. 43 (Tues–Sun 10am–5pm, Wed till 8pm; €4, free Wed; ⓦwww.dam-online.de), is installed in an avant-garde conversion of a nineteenth-century villa; the highpoint is the "house within a house" which dominates the museum like an oversized dolls' house.

Eating, drinking and nightlife

Not surprisingly, Frankfurt has a wealth of gastronomic possibilities, from the ultra-trendy joints found in the Westend to the cheapo Italian restaurants of Bockenheim, the working-class/boho/student quarter. Whether it's vegan breakfast or Japanese afternoon tea you're after, you'll be able to find it somewhere in the city – though you might have to travel some distance to get it. Frankfurt's nightlife is pretty eclectic, too. Perhaps its best-known locale is Kleine Bockenheimer Strasse, aka Jazzgasse, the centre of Frankfurt's jazz scene.

Apple wine taverns

Adolf Wagner Schweizer Str. 71. One of the best of the taverns, with a lively clientele of all ages and a cosy garden terrace. Roomy, but frequently packed out.

Atschel Wallstr. 7. This offers a more extensive menu than many of its counterparts, and has bargain set lunches. Closed Mon.

Zum Eichkatzerl Dreieichstr. 29. An excellent traditional tavern with a large courtyard; particularly popular on account of its low-priced food. Closed Mon.

Zum Gemalten Haus Schweizer Str. 67. A bit kitsch with its oil-painted facade and stained-glass windows, yet quite intimate and lively, with long rows of tables outside. Closed Mon & Tues.

Bars, cafés and café/bars

café Laumer Bockenheimer Landstr. 67. One of Frankfurt's oldest cafés, halfway up the Westend's main thoroughfare. The all-day breakfasts are a true indulgence.

Club Voltaire Kleine Hochstr. 5. Tasty, good food with a Spanish bias, and a fairly eclectic clientele including left-wing political activists, artists and gays. Frequent events include musical improvization evenings and political debates. From 6pm.

Dichtung und Wahrheit Am Salzhaus 1. Named after one of Goethe's works, this literary venue is littered with books and newspapers, and attracts a healthy mix of people.

Harvey's Bornheimer Landstr. 64. Slick, high-ceilinged colonnaded bar in an appealing end-of-terrace building, which in the evening hosts a mainly gay and lesbian crowd.

Restaurants

Bistro Rosa Grüneburgweg 25. The walls hung with pictures of pigs lend an element of kitsch, but the very select menu is excellent. Closed Mon.

Cantina Mescal Schweizer Str. 77. Trendy if predictable Mexican food, Latin music, bizarre cocktails and service with a smile.

Iwase Vibeler Str. 31. Reasonably priced Japanese, with seating at the counter or the few tables. Closed Mon.

Knoblauch, Staufenstr. 39. Friendly, intimate little place where the seasonal dishes come liberally laced with garlic.

Nibelungenschänke Nibelungenallee 55. Typical Greek food at very reasonable prices. Attracts a young crowd and is usually open till 1am. U-Bahn line #5.

Stars und Starlet Friedrich-Ebert-Anlage 49. In the basement of the Messeturm, this American-style restaurant has wonderful fantasy decor and excellent-value set lunches.

Tse Yang Kaiserstr. 67. One of several good Chinese restaurants near the train station, leaning heavily on Cantonese cuisine.

Music and discos

Batschkapp Maybachstr. 24, ⓦwww.batschkapp.de. Grimy, sweaty and fantastic venue for top-rank indie bands.

Brotfabri Bachmannstr. 2–4. One of the most innovative venues in the city, featuring live and disco music from all over the world, with salsa, African and Asian sounds particularly popular. Also has a café and a Spanish restaurant.

Jazzkeller Kleine Bockenheimer Str. 18a. This atmospheric cellar is Frankfurt's premier jazz venue. Closed Sun.

U60311 Rossmarkt Unterführung. Hardcore techno club that is always packed to the rafters; be prepared to queue.

Listings

Bike rental Per Pedale, Leipziger Str. 4 ☎0 69/70 76 91 10.
Consulates UK, Bockenheimer Landstr. 42 ☎0 69/1 70 00 20; US, Siesmayerstr. 21 ☎0 69/7 53 50.
Exchange Travellers cheques and cash exchange at Römerberg 28.
Hospital Bürgerhospital, Nibelungenallee 37–41 ☎069/1 50 00.

Internet CyberRyder, Töngesgasse 31; Telecafe, Mainzer Landstr. 99.
Laundry Wash World, Moselstr. 17.
Left luggage At the train station.
Pharmacy At the train station.
Post office Goetheplatz 2–4; sub-branch on ground floor of Karstadt department store, Zeil.

Marburg

About 80km north of Frankfurt, the university town of **MARBURG**, the cradle of Hesse and its original capital, clusters on the slopes of the Lahn valley in a maze of narrow streets and medieval buildings, crowned by an impressive castle. It has a relaxed and lively atmosphere, and has been touched by war less than almost any other city in the country.

The most important building is the **Elisabethkirche** (daily 9/10am–4/6pm; chancel €2), the first Gothic church in Germany. It was erected to house the remains of St Elisabeth, who died here in 1231. Inside, the church is a museum of German religious art, statues and frescoes; Elisabeth's thirteenth-century shrine is in the sacristy. Nearby, the Steinweg, a stepped street hemmed in by half-timbered buildings, leads to the **Marktplatz**, centre of the **Altstadt** and focal point of nightlife. From the Marktplatz make your way up Rittergasse to the thirteenth-century **Marienkirche**, just past which a flight of steps rises to the **Schloss** (Tues–Sun 10/11am–5/6pm; €2.60). Begun by Sophie, the daughter of St Elisabeth, the bulk of what can be seen today dates from the fifteenth and sixteenth centuries.

Marburg's **train station** is on the right bank of the Lahn at the northern end of town. The **tourist office** is at Am Pilgrimstein 26 (Mon–Fri 9am–6pm; Sat 10am–4pm; ☎0 64 21/9 91 20, ⊛www.marburg.de). The **HI hostel** has a pleasant riverside setting at Jahnstr. 1 (☎0 64 21/2 34 61, ✉marburg@djh-hessen.de; ❸), a little to the south of the Altstadt. Most central **hotels** are a little pricey – *Gästehaus Müller*, Deutschhausstr. 29 (☎0 64 21/6 56 59; ❹), is perhaps the best value. **Camping** facilities are over the river at Trojedamm 47 (☎0 64 21/2 13 31). For **eating and drinking**, two enduring student favourites are *café Barfuss*, Barfüsserstr. 33, and *Hinkelstein*, Markt 18. *Alter Ritter*, Steinweg 44, is a classy restaurant offering good-value set lunches.

Southern Germany

Baden-Württemberg is the most prosperous part of the country. The motor car was invented here in the late nineteenth century, and the region has stayed at the forefront of world technology ever since, with the region's largest city, **Stuttgart**, still home of Mercedes and Porsche. Germany's most famous university city, **Heidelberg**, is here, and the spa resort of **Baden-Baden** remains wonderfully evocative of its nineteenth-century heyday as the playground of Europe's aristocracy. The scenery of the province is wonderful too: its western and southern boundaries are defined by the Rhine and its bulge into Germany's largest lake, the **Bodensee** (Lake Constance); within the curve of the river lies the **Black Forest**, source of another of the continent's principal waterways, the Danube.

Bavaria is the home of all the German clichés: beer-swilling Lederhosen-clad men, sausage dogs, sauerkraut and Wurst. But that's only a small part of the picture, and almost entirely restricted to the Alpine region south of the magnificent state capital **Munich**. In the state's western region, around its pristine capital **Augsburg**, the food is less pork and sausages and more pasta and sauces, and the landscape gentle farming country ideal for camping and cycling holidays. To the north lies **Nürnberg**, centre of a region of vineyards and nature parks, while eastern Bavaria – apart from its capital **Regensburg** – is relatively poor; life in its highland forests revolves around logging and workshop industries such as glass production.

One practical note: **travellers over 27** are barred from using Bavarian youth hostels, but reasonable alternatives can usually be found, and you'll only be handicapped if you're on the tightest of budgets.

Heidelberg

Home to Germany's oldest university, **HEIDELBERG** is majestically set on the banks of the swift-flowing Neckar between ranges of wooded hills. Since the days of the Grand Tour it has seduced travellers like no other German city. Centrepiece is the **Schloss**, a compendium of magnificent buildings, somehow increased in stature by their ruined condition. Founded at the start of the thirteenth century, its expansion gathered momentum in the middle of the sixteenth century, when the Electors converted to Protestantism, and began the construction of the most splendid Renaissance buildings in Germany. Friedrich V's ham-fisted attempt to establish a Protestant, anti-Habsburg majority in the Electoral college led to the Thirty Years War, which devastated the country. However, it was French designs on the region in 1689 that led to the destruction of Heidelberg and its Schloss; after this, the Electorship passed to a Catholic branch of the family who, unable to establish a rapport with the locals, abandoned Heidelberg.

The Schloss can be reached from the Kornmarkt by **funicular** (€3 return), which continues to the Königstuhl viewpoint; you can walk up via the Burgweg. At the southeastern corner is the most romantic of the ruins, now generally known as the **Gesprengter Turm**; a collapsed section lies intact in the moat, leaving a clear view into the interior. In the **Schlosshof** (8am–5.30pm; €2; free access outside these hours), what really catches your eye is the group of Renaissance palaces on the north and east sides. The triple loggia of the earlier **Saalbau** forms a link to the swaggering **Friedrichsbau**, which supports a pantheon of the House of Wittelsbach, beginning with Charlemagne, the alleged founder of the dynasty. The statues now on view are copies; the originals can be seen inside, along with a number of restored rooms that have been decked out in period style.

The finest surviving buildings in the **Altstadt** are grouped on **Marktplatz**, in the middle of which is the sandstone **Heiliggeistkirche**, whose domed tower is one of the city's most prominent landmarks. Note the tiny shopping booths between its buttresses, a feature ever since the church was built. Inside, it's light, airy and uncluttered, but was not always so, as the church was built to house the mausoleum of the Palatinate Electors; only one tomb remains. Facing the church is the only mansion to survive the seventeenth-century devastations, the **Haus zum Ritter**, so called for the statue of St George on the pediment. The most striking Baroque building in Heidelberg is the **Alte Brücke**, reached from the Marktplatz down Steingasse; dating from the 1780s, it was blown up in the last war, but has been painstakingly rebuilt. The **Palais Rischer** on Untere Strasse was the most famous venue for one of the university's more risible traditions, the *Mensur*, or fencing match. Every vital organ was padded, but wounds were frequent and prized as badges of courage; for optimum prestige, salt was rubbed into them, leaving scars that would remain for life.

One side of **Universitätsplatz**, the heart of the old town, is occupied by the **Alte Universität** (April–Oct Mon–Sat 10am–4pm; Nov–March Tues–Fri 10am–4pm; €2.50), which dates back to the first quarter of the eighteenth century, though its *Aula* or graduation hall is a grand example of nineteenth-century Romanticism. The rest of the square is occupied by the **Neue Universität**, backed by American money and erected in 1931. The oddest of Heidelberg's traditions was that its students used not to be subject to civil jurisdiction: offenders were dealt

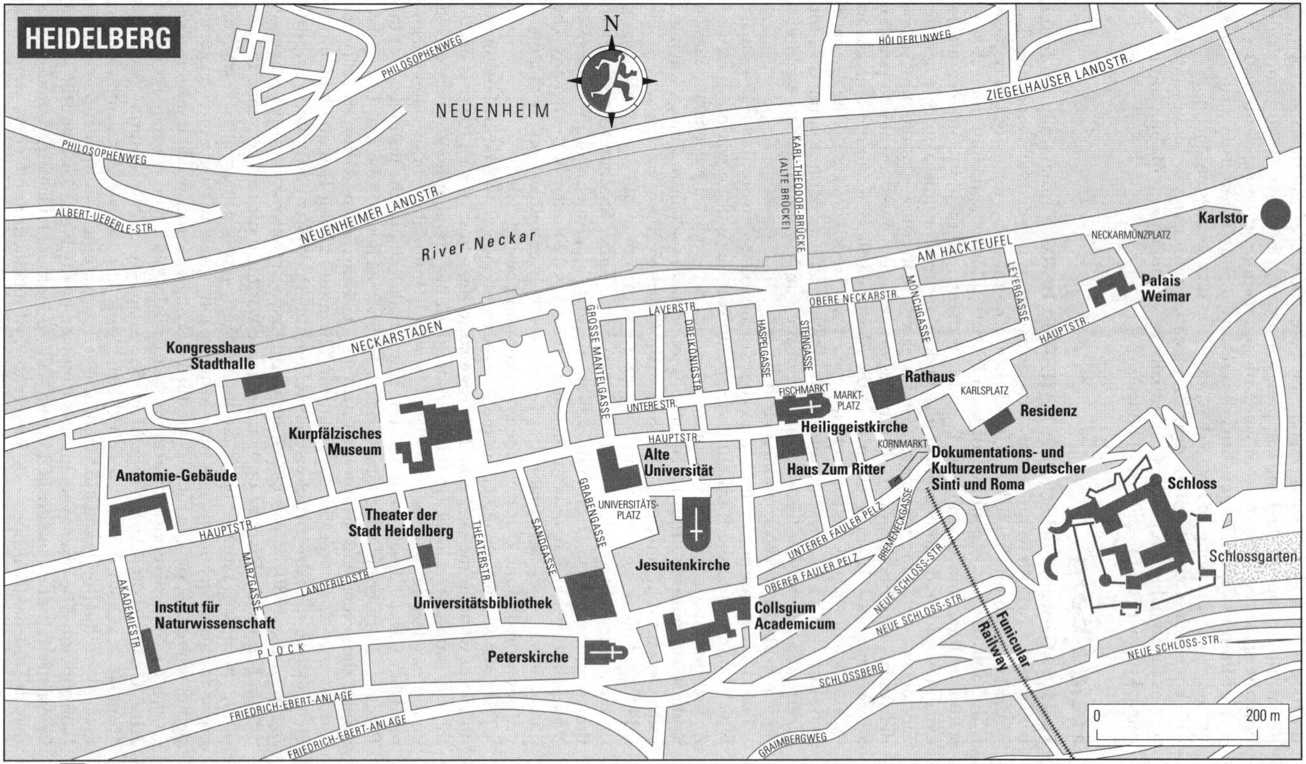

HEIDELBERG
N
NEUENHEIM
PHILOSOPHENWEG
HÖLDERLINWEG
ZIEGELHAUSER LANDSTR.
ALBERT-UEBERLE-STR.
NEUENHEIMER LANDSTR.
River Neckar
KARL-THEODOR-BRÜCKE
(ALTE BRÜCKE)
Karlstor
NECKARMÜNZPLATZ
AM HACKTEUFEL
Palais Weimar
LEYERGASSE
HAUPTSTR.
MÖNCHGASSE
OBERE NECKARSTR.
STEINGASSE
HASPELGASSE
DREIKÖNIGSTR.
LAVERSTR.
GROSSE MANTELGASSE
NECKARSTADEN
Kongresshaus Stadthalle
Rathaus
KARLSPLATZ
Residenz
FISCHMARKT
MARKT-PLATZ
UNTERE STR.
Heiliggeistkirche
KORNMARKT
Dokumentations- und Kulturzentrum Deutscher Sinti und Roma
Schloss
Schlossgarten
Kurpfälzisches Museum
Alte Universität
Haus Zum Ritter
Anatomie-Gebäude
UNIVERSITÄTS-PLATZ
GRABENGASSE
Theater der Stadt Heidelberg
THEATERSTR.
SANDGASSE
Jesuitenkirche
UNTERER FAULER PELZ
BREMENECKGASSE
OBERER FAULER PELZ
NEUE SCHLOSS-STR.
Funicular Railway
AKADEMIESTR.
MARZGASSE
LANDFRIEDSTR.
Institut für Naturwissenschaft
Universitätsbibliothek
Collsgium Academicum
PLÖCK
Peterskirche
SCHLOSSBERG
FRIEDRICH-EBERT-ANLAGE
GRAIMBERGWEG
0
200 m

Hauptbahnhof, Post Office & Tourist Office

with by the university authorities, and could serve their punishment at leisure. Now a protected monument, the **Students' Prison** (same times and ticket as Alte Universität) is on Augustinergasse; used from 1712 to 1914, the spartan cells are covered with graffiti.

Practicalities

First impressions of Heidelberg are a let down: the **train and bus station** are in an anonymous quarter fifteen minutes' walk west of the centre, with the dreary Kurfürsten-Anlage leading towards town. The **tourist office** is on the square outside (Mon–Sat 9am–6/7pm, Sun 10am–6pm; ☎06221/14220, ✆www.cvb-heidelberg.de).

The **hostel** is on the north bank of the Neckar, about 4km from the centre, at Tiergartenstr. 5 (☎0 62 21/41 20 66, ✆jh-heidelberg@t-online.de; ➋); take bus #11. There are a large number of **hotels**, but they are often booked solid: the chart outside the tourist office details any vacancies. The only real budget options are *Jeske*, in the heart of the city at Mittelbadgasse 2 (☎0 62 21/2 37 33; ➍); *Elite*, Bunsenstr. 15 (☎0 62 21/2 57 34; ➎); *Schmitt*, Blumenstr. 54 (☎0 62 21/2 72 96; ➎); and *Astoria*, over the river at Rahmengasse 30 (☎0 62 21/40 29 29; ➍).

The **student taverns** are a must: known for their basic dishes at reasonable prices, they are still regularly patronized, even if tourists make up most of the clientele these days. At the eastern end of Hauptstrasse are the two most famous: *Zum Sepp'l* at no. 213, popular for its Wiener Schnitzel; and *Roter Ochsen* at no. 217, which serves excellent home-made goulash. Slightly less touristy is the oldest **tavern**, *Schnookeloch*, at Haspelgasse 8. Among other traditional **restaurants**, try *Essighaus*, Plöck 97, or *Goldener Hecht*, Steingasse 2. Most **drinking** spots are along Untere Strasse; best of the bunch is characterful *Destille*. Elsewhere, the *Weisser Schwan Biermuseum* at Hauptstr. 143 has 101 varieties of **beer**, while *Vetter*, Steingasse 9, has its own small house brewery. The mid-nineteenth-century *Knösel*, Haspelgasse 20, is the oldest of Heidelberg's **cafés**; its speciality is Heidelberger Studentenkuss, a dark chocolate filled with praline and nougat. For something more like a **bistro** set-up, call in at the crowded *café Journal*, Hauptstr. 162. There's an **internet café** on Universitätsplatz, although student ID is required.

Stuttgart

STUTTGART is home to such German success stories as Bosch, Porsche and Daimler-Benz – all in the vanguard of the German economic miracle, and together having established the city at the forefront of European industry. Yet Stuttgart was slow to develop. Founded around 950 as a stud farm (Stutengarten), it became a town only in the fourteenth century, and lay in the shadow of its more venerable neighbours up to the early nineteenth century. Though not the comeliest of cities, it has a range of superb museums, and a varied cultural scene and nightlife.

From the train station, Königstrasse passes the dull modern Dom and enters Schlossplatz, on the south of which is the **Altes Schloss**, home to the **Württembergisches Landesmuseum** (Wed–Sun 10am–5pm, Tues closes 1pm; €2.60). Highlight of this richly varied museum is the Kunstkammer of the House of Württemberg, displayed in one of the corner towers: the first floor has small bronze sculptures of mainly Italian origin, while the second is laid out in the manner of a Renaissance curio cabinet. Upstairs, in the main part of the building, is a large collection of Swabian devotional sculptures and an archeology section that includes excavations from Troy, Roman antiquities, the grave of a Celtic prince and Frankish jewellery. The top floor has musical instruments and a wonderful array of clocks.

To the north of Schlossplatz, facing the straggling complex of the Staatstheater across Konrad-Adenauer-Strasse, is the **Staatsgalerie** (Tues–Sun 10am–6pm, Thurs till 9pm; first Sat in month till midnight; €4.60). The most startling work in the entire gallery is the huge, violently expressive *Herrenberg Altar* by Jörg Ratgeb, whose reputation rests almost entirely on this work. The equally idiosyncratic Hans Baldung is also represented, as are Cranach, Memling and Rembrandt.

On the other side of Schlossplatz, the **Altes Schloss** overlooks **Schillerplatz**, Stuttgart's sole example of an old-world square. Presiding in the middle is a pensive statue of Schiller himself, erected the year after his death by the Danish sculptor Bertel Thorwaldsen. At the back of Schillerplatz is the **Stiftskirche**, the choir of which is lined with one of the most important pieces of German Renaissance sculpture, an ancestral gallery of the counts and dukes of Württemberg.

The car museums

Set up in 1986 to celebrate the centenary of the invention of the motor car by Gottlieb Daimler and Carl Benz, the **Mercedes-Benz Museum** (Tues–Sun 9am–5pm; free) is an absolute must. Even entering here is an experience – you take S-Bahn #1 to Gottlieb-Daimler-Stadion, or bus #56 to the works entrance, from where you're whisked in a sealed minibus to the museum doors. The earliest vehicle on display is the Daimler Reitwagen of 1885, the first ever motorbike, which was capable of 12kph. Daimler's first Mercedes dates from 1902. Other exhibits include fire engines, motorboats, aeroplanes and buses; but it's the luxury cars and the machines specially designed for world record attempts that steal the show.

The **Porsche Museum**, Porschestrasse 42, is right beside the Neuwirtshaus station on S-Bahn line #6 (daily 9am–4/5pm; free). Ferdinand Porsche made his name when Hitler commissioned him to create the original Volkswagen, precursor of the Beetle, the ultimate mass-market car. For his own enterprise, Porsche concentrated on the opposite end of the economic spectrum. The vehicles on show illustrate all the company's cars from the 356 Roadster of 1948 to current models.

Practicalities

The **train station** is in the centre of town; immediately behind it is the **bus station**. S-Bahn #2 and #3 provide a link to the **airport** every twenty minutes. There's a **tourist office** in front of the train station at Königstr. 1a (Mon–Fri 9.30am–8.30pm, Sat & Sun 9.30/10.30am–6pm; ☏07 11/2 22 82 40, ⓦwww.stuttgart-tourist.de). The integrated public transport network comprises buses, trams, the U-Bahn and main-line and S-Bahn trains; a 24-hour ticket costs €4.70. Alternatively, there's the StuttCard Plus (€14), valid for three days and covering all public transport, admission to most museums and a range of reductions and numerous freebies, including drinks and food; the basic StuttCard (€8.50) gives the same benefits with the exception of public transport.

The **HI hostel** is fifteen minutes' walk east of the train station at Haussmannstr. 27 (☏07 11/24 15 83, ⓔjh-stuttgart@t-online.de; ❷); there's also a privately run one, the *Jugendgästehaus Stuttgart*, at Richard-Wagner-Str. 2–4a (☏07 11/24 11 32; ❸). Average **hotel** rates are high, but you could try *Eckel*, Vorsteigstr. 10 (☏0711/29 09 95; ❹); *Museum-Stube*, Hospitalstr. 9 (☏07 11/29 68 10; ❹); or *Alte Mira*, Büchsenstr. 24 (☏07 11/2 22 95 02; ❹).

Though fancy **restaurants** abound, there are a few places offering traditional Swabian dishes at low cost – for good-quality food and drink try the numerous **Weinstuben**. *Zur Kiste*, Kanalstr. 2, is the best-known of these, but the widest choice of wines is at *Weinhaus Stetter*, Rosenstr. 32. For a **beer hall** setup try *Ketterer*, Marienstr. 3b. For **nightlife** details, pick up the tourist office's *Lift Stuttgart* and *Prinz Stuttgart*, both available from newsagents for €1. *Schlesinger International*, Schloss Str. 28, is a popular hangout; the former punk haunt of *Exil*, Filderstr. 61, now belongs to arty types, with jazz and blues in a laid-back atmosphere. Jazz also features at *Laboratorium*, Wagenburgerstr. 147, popular with the Green Party contingent. In an old rail tunnel, *Röhre*, Neckarstr. 34, platforms live bands, playing everything from jazz to punk, and is also a disco patronized by fashion-conscious locals. *Café Stella*, Haupstuatter Str. 57, is a trendy **café/bar**.

Consulates UK Breite Str. 2 ☎07 11/1626 90; US, Urbanstr. 7 ☎07 11/21 02 21.
Exchange Landesbank Baden-Württemberg, Königstr. 3–5; Reisebank, entrance of the train station.
Hospital Marienhospital, Böheimstr. 37 ☎07 11/6 48 90.

Internet Café California, Schellingstr. 7; Karstadt, Königstr. 1.
Laundry Lavomagic, Katharinenstr. 21c.
Left luggage At the train station.
Pharmacy Apotheke im Hauptbahnhof, Arnulf-Klett-Platz 2; Europa Apotheke, Königstr. 10b.
Post office Königsbau on Schillerplatz.

Tübingen

TÜBINGEN is sited above the willow-lined banks of the Neckar, some 55km upstream from Stuttgart. Over half the population of 70,000 is in some way connected with the university, and the current size of the town is due entirely to the twentieth-century boom in higher education.

The old town is a visual treat, a mixture of brightly painted half-timbered and gabled houses grouped into twisting and plunging alleys. Two large squares provide a setting for communal activities. The first, **Holzmarkt**, is dominated by the **Stiftskirche St Georg** (daily 9am–4/5pm), a gaunt, late-Gothic church with a fine interior. In the chancel (Easter–Oct Fri–Sun 11.30am–5pm; €1) an outstanding series of stained-glass windows casts reflections on the pantheon of the House of Württemberg, the thirteen tombs showing the development of Swabian sculpture in the Gothic and Renaissance periods.

Overlooking the banks of the Neckar on Bursagasse, the street immediately below, is the **Hölderlinturm** (Tues–Fri 10am–noon & 3–5pm, Sat & Sun 2–5pm; €1.50). Originally part of the medieval fortifications, it's named after Friedrich Hölderlin, who lived here in the care of a carpenter's family, hopelessly but harmlessly insane, from 1807 until his death 36 years later. There's a collection of memorabilia of the poet, now regarded as one of the greatest Germany ever produced.

The **Markt**, heart of old Tübingen, is a short walk uphill from here. It preserves many of its Renaissance mansions, along with a fountain dedicated to Neptune, around which markets are held on Mondays, Wednesdays and Fridays. Burgsteige, one of the oldest and handsomest streets in town, climbs steeply from the corner of the Markt to **Schloss Hohentübingen**, Renaissance successor to the original eleventh-century castle. One wing is now given over to the **Schausammlungen der Universität** (Mon–Fri 9am–5pm; in holidays by request; free), one of the largest university museums in the world, with archeology, history and ethnology displays. The northwestern part of town, immediately below the Schloss, has some of the city's oldest and most spectacular half-timbered buildings, such as the old municipal **Kornhaus** on the alley of the same name, and the **Fruchtschranne**, formerly the storehouse for the yields of the ducal orchards, on Bachgasse.

Practicalities

The **train and bus stations** are side by side, just five minutes' walk from the old town. At the edge of Eberhardsbrücke is the **tourist office** (Mon–Fri 9am–7pm, Sat 9am–5pm; May–Oct also Sun 2–5pm; ☎0 70 71/9 13 60, ✆www.tuebingen-info.de). **Hotels** aren't plentiful and tend to be expensive; the best bet is *Am Schloss*, Burgsteige 18 (☎0 70 71/9 29 40; ❺), or try the **hostel** on the banks of the Neckar, a short walk from the station at Gartenstr. 22/2 (☎0 70 71/2 30 02, ✉jh-tuebingen@t-online.de; ❷); the tourist office also has a list of private rooms. To reach the **campsite**, also with a riverside setting at Rappenberghalde, turn left on leaving the train station, and cross at Alleenbrücke. The best **restaurant** in the centre is *Forelle*, a wine bar at Kronenstr. 8. Giant pancakes are the speciality of the *Ratskeller*, Haaggasse 4, while *Marktschenke*, Markt 11, is a lively student bar.

11

GERMANY | Southern Germany

The Black Forest region

Stretching 170km north to south, and up to 60km east to west, the **Black Forest** is the largest German forest and the most beautiful. As late as the 1920s, much of this area was an eerie wilderness, a refuge for boars and bandits. Nowadays most of the villages have been opened up as spa and health resorts, brimming with shops selling tacky souvenirs, while the old trails have become gravel paths smoothed down for easier walking. Yet by no means all the modernizations are drawbacks. Railway fans, for example, will find several of the most spectacular lines in Europe here. It should be noted, though, that the trains tend to stick to the valleys and that bus services are much reduced outside the tourist season.

Most of the Black Forest is associated with the Margravate of Baden, whose old capital, **Baden–Baden**, is at the northern fringe of the forest, in a fertile orchard and vine-growing area. The only city actually surrounded by the forest is **Freiburg im Breisgau**, one of the most enticing in the country.

Baden-Baden

The therapeutic value of **BADEN-BADEN**'s hot springs was discovered by the Romans, but the town's rise to international fame only came about as a result of Napoleon's creation of the buffer state of Baden in 1806. The Grand Dukes promoted their ancestors' old seat as a modern resort, and began embellishing it with handsome buildings such as the **Kurhaus** and its integral casino. The easiest way to see these is to take a guided tour (daily 9.30/10am–noon; €3; ⓔinfo@kurhaus-baden-baden.de); highlight is the **Winter Garden**, with its glass cupola, Chinese vases and solid gold roulette table. A day ticket, with no obligation to participate, is €2.60.

South of the Kurhaus runs Baden-Baden's most famous thoroughfare, the **Lichtentaler Allee**, landscaped with exotic trees and shrubs and flanked by buildings such as the Parisian-style theatre and the **Kunsthalle**, which often hosts major exhibitions of twentieth-century art. Immediately north of the Kurhaus is the **Trinkhalle**, whose arcades shelter vast frescoes illustrating legends of the town and the nearby countryside.

Little remains today of the old town, almost completely destroyed in a single day in 1689, the result of a fire started by French troops. However, halfway up the Florintinerberg is the **Marktplatz**, and the **Stiftskirche**, a Gothic hall church containing one of the masterpieces of European sculpture, an enormous sandstone *Crucifixion* by Nicolaus Gerhaert von Leyden. Hidden under the Stiftskirche are the remains of the Roman Imperial Baths; the more modest **Römerbad** (Easter–Oct daily 10am–noon & 1.30–4pm; €1.30), just east on Römerplatz, was probably for soldiers. Above the ruins is the **Friedrichsbad** (Mon–Sat 9am–10pm, Sun noon–8pm), begun in 1869 and grand as a Renaissance palace. Speciality of the house is a three-hour "Roman-Irish Bath", which will set you back €21 (€29 for soap-brush massage); a glass of thermal water will set you back just €0.05.

Practicalities

Baden-Baden is on the fast Karlsruhe–Freiburg line, but the **train station** is 4km northwest of the centre in the suburb of Oos; take bus #201, #205 or #216 into the centre. The **tourist office** is in the Trinkhalle on Kaiserallee (daily 10am–6.30pm; ☎0 72 21/27 52 00, ⓦwww.baden-baden.de). A few **rooms** are available in private houses (**②**). Baden-Baden's **hostel** is between the train station and the centre at Hardbergstr. 34 (☎0 72 21/5 22 23, ⓔjh-baden-baden@t-online.de; **②**); take bus #201, #205 or #216 to Grosse-Dollen-Strasse, from where the way is signposted. The main group of cheap **hotels** is in Oos: try *Goldener Stern*, Ooser Hauptstr. 16 (☎0 72 21/6 15 09; **❸**), or *Adler*, Ooser Hauptstr. 1 (☎0 72 21/6 18 58; **❹**). Among places to **eat and drink**, *Münchener Löwenbräu*, Gernsbacher Str. 9, is a good choice; complete with beer garden, it's like a little corner of Bavaria, and serves excellent meals. For a trendy atmosphere, try *Leo's*,

Luisenstr. 10, while for solid, reasonably priced German food, there's *Rathaustglöckel*, Steinstr. 7.

Freiburg im Breisgau

FREIBURG IM BREISGAU basks in a laid-back atmosphere that seems completely un-German. A university town since 1457, its youthful presence is maintained all year round with the help of a varied programme of festivals.

The dark red sandstone **Münster** was originally built as a parish church, the costs being met entirely by the local citizens. Begun in about 1200, it has a masterly Gothic nave, resplendent with flying buttresses, gargoyles and statues – the magnificent sculptures of the west porch are the most important German works of their time. To get a decent look at Baldung's *Coronation of the Virgin* altarpiece, take a guided tour of the ambulatory chapels (Mon–Fri 11am & 2pm; €2), which contain some wonderful pieces – including a retable by the two Holbeins, and a silver crucifix from the first Münster. From the **tower** (March–Nov Mon–Sat 10am–5pm, Sun 1–5pm; €1.50) there's a fine panorama of the city and forest.

A peculiarity of Freiburg is the system of rivulets known as the **Bächle**, which run in deep gulleys all over the city. Formerly used for watering animals, and as a fire-fighting provision, they have their purpose even today, helping to keep the city cool. Following the main channel of the Bächle southwards, you come to the **Schwaben Tor**, one of two surviving towers of the medieval fortifications. On Oberlinden, just in front, is **Zum Roten Bären**, which is generally considered to be Germany's oldest inn. Just to the west is Salzstrasse, where the **Augustinermuseum** (Tues–Sun 10am–5pm; €2, free first Sun of month) houses works of art from the Münster and a few top-class pictures, including the most important paintings by the mysterious draughtsman known as Master of the Housebook. South of here, on Marienstrasse, the **Museum of Modern Art** (same times; free) has a good cross-section of twentieth-century German painting. From here, follow Fischerau, the old fishermen's street, and you come to the other thirteenth-century tower, the **Martinstor**, in the middle of Freiburg's central axis, Kaiser-Josef-Strasse.

On the west side of the Münster, the **Neues Rathaus**, **Altes Rathaus** and the plain Franciscan friary church of **St Martin** stand around a shady chestnut-lined square. In the alley behind St Martin is the cheerful Gothic facade of the **Haus zum Wallfisch**, for two years the home of the great humanist Erasmus, who was forced to flee from Basel by the religious struggles there. A few minutes to the west, in the Columbipark opposite the tourist office, is the **Museum of Pre- and Early History** (same times; voluntary donation), which has important archeological collections relating to the Black Forest region.

Practicalities

The **train station**, with the bus station on its southern side, is about ten minutes' walk west from the city centre. Following Eisenbahnstrasse, you come to the **tourist office** at Rotteckring 14 (Mon–Fri 9.30am–6/8pm, Sat 9.30am–2/5pm, Sun 10am–noon; ☎07 61/3 88 18 80, ⊛www.freiburg.de). For €1.60, they will find you a room; after closing time, there's an electronic noticeboard equipped with a phone, which lists vacancies. **Internet** is available at the Kaufhof department store on Kaiser-Joseph-Str (€3/hr). Among **hotels** with a central location, the cheapest is *Schemmer*, Eschholzstr. 63 (☎07 61/20 74 90, ✉angelavr@t-online.de; ❸). The 443-bed **HI hostel** is at Karthäuserstr. 151 (☎07 61/6 76 56, ✉jh-freiburg@t-online.de; ❷), at the extreme eastern end of the city, reached by tram #1 to Hasemannstrasse. Nearby, slightly nearer town, is the *Hirzberg* **campsite**; *Mösle-Park* (closed Nov to mid-March) is on the opposite side of the river.

For **restaurants**, try: *Oberkirchs Weinstuben*, Münsterplatz 22, a top-notch but not expensive wine cellar serving Baden specialities; *Zur Traube* just behind at Schusterstr. 17, which is equally good; *Kleiner Meyerhof*, Rathausgasse 27, for hearty

South German cooking; or *Grosser Meyerhof*, Grünwälderstr. 3, which has a large garden terrace. One of the trendiest places to be seen is *Uni-café*, Niemensstr. 7, which serves a wide selection of **coffees** and has good **snacks**. Freiburg now ranks as one of the leading German cities for jazz, thanks to the *Jazzhaus* at Schnewlinstr. 1, which has **concerts** every evening.

Konstanz and the Bodensee

In the far south of the province, **KONSTANZ** lies at the tip of a tongue of land sticking out into the **Bodensee** (Lake Constance), which is really a swelling in the River Rhine. The town itself is split by the water: the **Altstadt** is a German enclave on the Swiss side of the lake. It's a cosy little place, with a convivial atmosphere in summer, when street cafés invite long pauses and the water is a bustle of sails.

The most prominent church is the **Münster**, set on the highest point of the Altstadt. It was here in 1417 that the papal court tried the reformer Johannes Hus for heresy – the spot on which he stood during his trial is marked in the central aisle. Konstanz's major museum is the **Rosgartenmuseum** on the street of the same name (closed until late summer 2003; check with tourist office for latest details), which has a fine collection of local archeological finds, plus art and craft exhibits from the Middle Ages.

The **tourist office** is located alongside the **train station** at Bahnhofplatz 13 (Mon–Fri 9.30am–12.30pm & 2–6pm; April–Oct also Sat 9am–4pm & Sun 10am–1pm; ☎0 75 31/13 30 30, ⓦwww.konstanz.de); they can book accommodation for you in private rooms (❷). The **hostel** is at Zur Allmannshöhe 18 (☎0 75 31/3 22 60, ⓔjh-konstanz@t-online.de; ❷); take bus #4 from the train station to Jugendherberge, or #1 to Post Allmannsdorf. If you'd prefer a **hotel**, however, try *Gretel* at Zollenstr. 6–8 (☎0 75 31/2 32 83; ❸), or *Graf Zeppelin*, Am St. Stephansplatz 15 (☎0 75 31/2 37 80, ⓔbashkin@t-online-de; ❹). Information on **cruises** and **ferries** is available from the Bodensee-Verkehrsdienst at Hafenstr. 6 (☎0 7531/28 13 98). Ferries regularly leave Konstanz for destinations all over the lake: perhaps the most interesting longer trip is to the Rheinfall in Switzerland (€17.90), along one of the Rhine's most scenic stretches to Europe's largest waterfall.

Munich

Founded in 1158, **MUNICH** has been the capital of Bavaria since 1503, and as far as the locals are concerned it may as well be the centre of the universe. Münchener pride themselves on their special status; even people who have made Munich their home for most of their lives are still called *Zugereiste* (newcomers). Next to Berlin, Munich is Germany's most popular city, with everything you'd expect in a cosmopolitan capital. Yet it's small enough to be digestible in one visit, and it's got the added bonus of a great setting, with the mountains and Alpine lakes just an hour's drive away. The best time of year to come here is from June to early October, when the beer gardens, street cafés and bars are in full swing.

Arrival, information and city transport

Munich's **airport**, Franz Josef Strauss Flughafen, is connected to the **train station** by S-Bahn #1 or #8. There are **tourist offices** at Bahnhofplatz 2 (daily 10am–6pm; ☎0 89/23 39 65 00; ⓦwww.muenchen-tourist.de) and in the Rathaus on Marienplatz (Mon–Sat 10am–8pm, Sun 10am–4pm). They will book rooms, and provide brochures about the city and what's on. The bus station is a stone's throw from the train station. The *Insel* booth on Hauptwache also provides transport information and sells advance tickets.

Day tickets for all **public transport** in the central city area cost €4.50 (€9 for whole system). The Munich Welcome Card (€6.50/day, €15.50/three days) covers all public transport and entitles the bearer to big discounts on 38 different attractions. Tickets can be bought from the automatic machines in all U-Bahn stations, at some bus and tram stops, and inside trams. If you're making several journeys across the city, it's far more economical to invest in a strip card (€9/ten), and stamp two strips for every zone crossed – the zones are shown on maps at stations and tram and bus stops. For journeys of up to two S- or U-Bahn stops, or up to four bus or tram stops, only one strip needs to be cancelled. Tickets must be stamped before any journey – those without a validated ticket face an on-the-spot fine of €30.

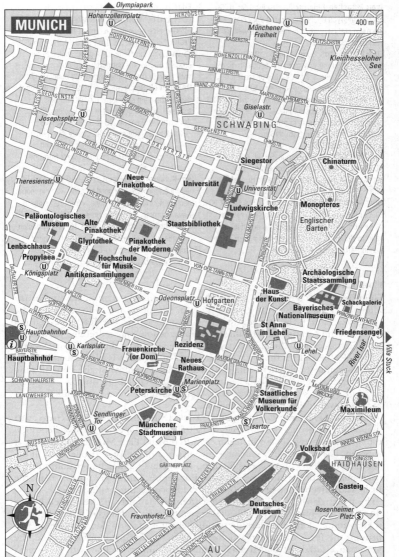

▼ Tierpark Hellabrunn (3km) & Bavaria Filmstadt (5km)

Accommodation

Cheap **accommodation** can be hard to find, especially during the high season in the summer, though prices are fairly constant throughout the year. If you're going to be in town during the Oktoberfest, it's essential to book your room well in advance. Details of the pick of the hotels, hostels and campsites are given below. Many pensions offer rooms with three to six beds, a good alternative to the hostels.

Hostels

4you München Hirtenstr. 18 ⊕0 89/5 52 16 60, ⊛www.the4you.de. Friendly outfit very close to the main station, with some singles as well as standard dorms. ❷.

Burg Schwaneck Burgweg 4–6 ⊕0 89/7 93 06 43. HI hostel some way from the centre in an old castle on the river. S-Bahn #7 to Pullach, then follow signs to the Jugendherberge. ❸

DJH Jugendgästehaus Miesingstr. 4 ⊕0 89/7 23 65 60, ⊛JGHMuenchen@djh-bayern.de. Smaller, more upmarket HI hostel in attractive grounds. U-Bahn to Harras, then tram #16 to Boschetsriederstr. ❸

DJH München Wendl-Dietrich-Str. 20 ⊕0 89/13 11 56, ⊛JHMuenchen@djh-bayern.de. The largest, most central and most basic HI hostel, with 535 beds. U-Bahn to Rotkreuzplatz. ❸

Haus International Elisabethstr. 87 ⊕0 89/12 00 60. Centrally located in Schwabing, 186 rooms range from five beds to singles. No age limit. U-Bahn to Hohenzollernplatz, then bus #33 or tram #12 to Barbarastrasse. ❸

Hotels and pensions

Eder Zweigstr. 8 ⊕0 89/55 46 60. Cosy hotel in a quiet road between the train station and Marienplatz, offering nice appointed rooms at the price. ❹

Frank Schellingstr. 24 ⊕0 89/28 14 51, ⊛www.pension-frank.de. A good choice in the student quarter for both price and atmosphere, with homely rooms in a creaky old building. ❹

Haberstock Schillerstr. 4 ⊕0 89/55 78 55. Right beside the train station with basic, no frills facilities, but it's good value nonetheless. ❹

Jedermann Bayerstr. 95 ⊕0 89/54 32 40, ⊛www.hotel-jedermann.de. Classy, family-run hotel located well away from any noise and seediness, but just five minutes' walk from the train station. ❹

Am Kaiserplatz Kaiserplatz 12 ⊕0 89/34 91 90. Very friendly place in a good location with big rooms, each done in a different style – from red satin to Bavarian rustic. Six-bed rooms can be arranged. ❸

Steinberg Ohmstr. 9 ⊕0 89/33 10 11, ⊛pension .steinberg@t-online.de. Friendly and in a good location near Giselastr. U-Bahn station. Some rooms have bathtubs. ❹

The City

The central **Marienplatz** is always thronged, with street musicians and artists entertaining the crowds. At 11am and noon, the square fills with tourists as the tuneless carillon in the Rathaus tower jingles into action. The **Rathaus** itself is a late nineteenth-century neo-Gothic monstrosity whose only redeeming features are the café in its cool and breezy courtyard and the view from the **tower** (by elevator; €1.50). To the right is the plain Gothic tower of the Altes Rathaus, rebuilt in the fifteenth-century style after being destroyed in the war. Close by, the **Peterskirche** looks out across the busy Viktualienmarkt; the oldest church in Munich, it's notable for its grisly relics of St Munditia, patron saint of single women, and for the view from its **tower** (daily 9/10am–6/7pm; €2).

Almost next to the Viktualienmarkt is the **Münchener Stadtmuseum** (Tues–Sun 10am–6pm; €2.50; ⊛www.stadtmuseum-online.de), the excellent local history museum, which also incorporates a Photo and Film Museum and a Puppet Museum. The last is highly recommended: it's one of the largest collections in the world, and includes puppets ranging from Indian and Chinese paper dolls to large mechanical European creations. Southwest of here, at Sendlinger Str. 62, stands the small **Asamkirche**, one of the most splendid Rococo churches in Bavaria.

The pedestrian Kaufingerstrasse, west from Marienplatz, is overlooked by the **Dom**. The red-brick Gothic cathedral is seen to its best advantage from a distance, its twin onion-domed **towers** (by elevator April–Oct Mon–Sat 10am–5pm; €3) forming the focus of the city's skyline. A little further up Kaufingerstrasse, the Renaissance facade of **St Michael** stands unassumingly in line with the street's other buildings. In the **crypt** (Mon–Fri 10am–1pm & 2–4.30pm, Sat 10am–3pm;

€2) you'll find the coffins of the Wittelsbach dynasty – a candle is always burning at the foot of mad castle-builder Ludwig II's.

North of Marienplatz is the posh end of the city centre. From fashionable **Maximilianstrasse**, the little Kosttor road leads straight to the **Hofbräuhaus**, Munich's largest and most famous drinking hall. Nearby, with its Baroque facade standing proud on the Odeonsplatz, is one of the city's most regal churches, the **Theatinerkirche**, whose golden-yellow towers and green copper dome add a splash of colour to the roofscape.

The palace of the Wittelsbachs, the **Residenz** (daily 9am–4/6pm; €4) stands across the square from the Theatinerkirche. One of Europe's finest Renaissance buildings, it was so badly damaged in the last war that it had to be almost totally rebuilt. To see the whole thing you have to go on two consecutive visits, as parts of the immense complex are shut in the morning and others in the afternoon. On the morning tour you see the Antiquarium, the oldest part of the palace; in the afternoon, the two very contrasting chapels and the Baroque Golden Hall. A separate ticket is necessary to see the fabulous treasures of the **Schatzkammer** (same hours; €4, €7 combined ticket); star piece is the dazzling stone-encrusted statuette of St George, made around 1590.

Munich's most overwhelming museum – the **Deutsches Museum** (daily 9am–5pm; €6; ⌽www.deutsches-museum.de) – occupies the mid-stream island of Isarinsel. Covering every conceivable aspect of technical endeavour, from the first flint tools to the research labs of modern industry, this is the most compendious collection of its type in Germany. Another gargantuan collection lies further north – the **Bayerisches Nationalmuseum**, Prinzregentenstr. 3 (Tues–Sun 10am–5pm, Thurs till 8pm; €3, free Sun; ⌽www.bayerisches-nationalmuseum. de), houses a rambling collection of decorative arts. Close by, at Prinzregentenstr. 1, the Nazi-era **Haus der Kunst** (daily 10am–10pm; variable entrance charges) hosts temporary exhibitions. But it is the **Alte Pinakothek**, Barerstr. 27 (Tues–Sun 10am–5pm, Thurs till 10pm; €5, free Sun; ⌽www.pinakotheken-muenchen.de), that is the main draw: one of the largest galleries in Europe, it houses the world's finest assembly of German art. Among the collection are pieces by Dürer, Cranach the Elder and Albrecht Altdorfer; but centrepiece is the collection of works by Rubens, with 62 paintings displaying the scope of the artist's prodigious output.

Just off Königsplatz at Luisenstr. 30 is the **Lenbachhaus** (Tues–Sun 10am–6pm; €6), the nineteenth-century villa that belonged to the Bavarian painter Franz von Lenbach. It's a pleasant setting for some of German art's most interesting modern painters, the highlights coming with the group known as Der Blaue Reiter, whose members included Kandinsky, Klee, Marc and Macke. Recent exhibitions have also featured contemporary German art.

Nymphenburg

Schloss Nymphenburg (daily 9am–4/6pm; €3.50, €7.50 combined ticket with pavilions and Marstall), the summer residence of the Wittelsbachs, is reached by tram #17 from the train station. Its kernel is a small Italianate palace begun in 1664 for the Electress Adelaide, who dedicated it to the goddess Flora and her nymphs – hence the name. The Marstall, or stables, contain notable collections of historic coaches and porcelain, but more enticing than the palace itself are the wonderful park and its four distinct pavilions. Three were designed by Joseph Effner: the **Magdalenenklause**, built to resemble a ruined hermitage; the **Pagodenburg**, used for the most exclusive parties thrown by the court; and the **Badenburg**, which, like the **Pagodenburg**, reflects an interest in the art of China. For all their charm, Effner's pavilions are overshadowed by the stunning **Amalienburg**, the hunting lodge built behind the south wing of the Schloss by his successor as court architect, François Cuvilliés. This supreme expression of the Rococo style marries a cunning design – which makes the little building seem like a full-scale palace – with the most extravagant decoration imaginable.

Dachau

DACHAU, now reverted to a picturesque town on the northern edge of Munich, was the site of Germany's first **concentration camp** (Tues–Sun 9am–5pm; free). The motto that greeted arrivals at the gates has taken its chilling place in the history of Third Reich brutality: Arbeit Macht Frei, "Work Brings Freedom". Original buildings still standing include this gateway, the administration block, the deeply unsettling Bunker cell-block, two crematoria and the gas chambers, which were never used. However, a replica hut gives an idea of the conditions under which prisoners were forced to live, and the permanent exhibition of photographs speaks volumes. Turn up at 11.30am or 3.30pm and you can also view the short, deeply disturbing, documentary *KZ-Dachau* in English. There are also weekend tours in English at 12.30pm. Get there by taking bus #724 or #726 from Dachau S-Bahn station.

Eating and drinking

It's easy to eat well on a budget here. **Mensas** are the cheapest places; you're supposed to have a valid student card to eat here, but no one seems to check. The most central one is at Leopoldstr. 15 (closed Sat & Sun), and there are two more in the main building at Schellingstrasse and at the Technical University, Arcisstr. 17. The *Gaststätten* offer filling soups, salads and sandwich-type dishes, too. Not surprisingly, **drinking** is central to Munich social life and apart from the *Gaststätten* and beer gardens, it also has a lively café/bar culture, which carries on well into the early hours. The place to head is Haidhausen, across the river to the southeast of the centre. Though tamer than Berlin's Kreuzberg and Prenzlauer Berg, it has a good mix of bars, cafés and restaurants, a good alternative to glitzy Schwabing.

Cafés, café/bars and wine bars

Alter Simpl Türkenstr. 57. Famous literary café/bar that spawned the satirical magazine *Simplicissimus*, now a favoured student haunt.

café Kreutzkamm Maffeistr. 4. Airy and elegant, and one of the best (and most expensive) *Kaffee und Kuchen* establishments.

Pfälzer Weinprobierstuben Residenzstr. 1. Despite the chandeliers, this is an unpretentious place serving excellent wines from the Palatinate.

Weintrödler Brienner Str. 10. Late-night wine bar (closes 6am) with welcoming dark-wood booths; the last boozer to close.

Restaurants

Adria Leopoldstr. 19. Popular late-night Italian, right next to Giselastr. U-Bahn, with good food at reasonable prices.

Bella Italia Herzog-Wilhelm-Str. 8. One of a small chain of inexpensive Italian restaurants.

Bernard & Bernard Innere Wiener Str. 32. Newly renovated but still a great place for crepes, in Haidhausen.

Donisl Weinstr. 1. A fine old Munich *Gaststätte* with an ornate gallery, dating back to the early eighteenth century.

Haxnbauer Münzstr. 6. Specializes in the delicious roasted pork knuckles that are such a high point of German cuisine; the lamb version is no less tasty.

Prinz Myshkin Hackenstr, 2. Best vegetarian place in the centre, specializing in oven-baked Italian specialities.

Thai-China Bahnhofplatz 1 (entrance on Schützenstr.). Unbeatable value for Indian food too; also does take out.

Schelling Salon Schellingstr. 54. Good for their large cheap breakfasts and also for playing pool.

Beer gardens and beer halls

Augustinerbräu Neuhauser Str. 27. One of several beer halls on this central street, with an unusually long menu and wonderfully evocative *fin-de-siècle* decor.

Augustinerkeller Arnulfstr. 52, near the Hackerbrücke S-Bahn stop. A shady island of green, hidden in one of Munich's grottier quarters.

Aumeister Sondermeierstr. 1. At the northern end of the Englischer Garten; a good place for daytime breaks.

Hofbräuhaus Platzl 9. The most famous, though nowadays, at least during the tourist season, it's by far the least authentic of any on this list.

Hofbräukeller Innere Wiener Str. 19. Nestling under ancient chestnut trees; very popular in the evenings.

Weisses Bräuhaus Im Tal 10. Famous for the favourite Munich snack of *Weisswurt*, a white sausage which should traditionally only be eaten before noon.

Music, nightlife and festivals

Munich has a great deal to offer musically, from classical concerts to rock. Best sources for **information** on what's happening are the *Münchener Stadtzeitung* or *In München*, both available at any kiosk, or the monthly *Monatsprogram* from the tourist office or the English-language *Munich Found*. For **jazz concerts** – a major feature of Munich nightlife – check the monthly *Münchener Jazz-Zeitung*. Munich has three first-rate symphony orchestras – the Münchener Philharmoniker, the Bayrisches Rundfunk Sinfonie Orchester and the Staatsorchester – as well as eleven major theatres and numerous fringe theatres. Advance tickets for plays and concerts can be bought at the relevant box offices or commercial ticket shops such as the one located in the Marienplatz U-Bahn station. Opera tickets can be bought at Max-Joseph-Platz 2, or from the box office in the Nationaltheater one hour before performances begin. As for **clubs**, a trendy new area is Kunstpark Ost (S- or U-Bahn to Ostbahnhof), a mini-city of clubs housed in a network of old factory buildings that attracts upwards of 30,000 ravers on any given weekend.

Clubs and live music venues

Crash Ainmillerstr. 10. Stage for heavy rock, although the odd 80s night is not unknown.

Kaffee Giesing Bergstr. 5. Venue for small bands and solo artists.

Muffathalle Zellstr. 4. On evenings when bands aren't performing live, expect regular dance nights and even philosophical readings.

Nachtwerk Landsberger Str. 185. Draws a young crowd on Fri and Sat, and stages occasional up-and-coming acts.

Olympiapark Free rock concerts by the lake in summer; they usually get going around 2pm at weekends.

Schwabinger Podium Wagnerstr. 1. Chiefly for aficionados of Dixieland.

Sugar Shack Herzogspitalstr. 6. Mainstream disco.

Unterfahrt Einsteinstr. 42. Showcase for avant-garde jazz, with many big names gracing the stage.

Classical music, opera and theatre

Cuvilliéstheater in the Residenz. Premier venue for drama, plus the occasional chamber music recital.

Deutsches Theater Schwanthalerstr. 13. A changing programme of home-grown talent and international musical spectaculars.

Gasteig Rosenheimer Str. 5. One of the two main venues for classical concerts.

Herkulessaal in the Residenz. The other big classical concert hall.

Staatsoper or **Nationaltheater** Max-Josef-Platz 1. Munich's answer to Covent Garden, with grand opera and ballet.

Residenztheater Max-Josef-Platz 1. Traditional dramatic fare.

Staatstheater Am Gärtnerplatz Am Gärtnerplatz. Mixed programme of operetta, musicals and popular operas.

The Oktoberfest and other events

The **Oktoberfest**, held on the Theresienwiese fairground from the penultimate Saturday in September for the next sixteen days, is an orgy of beer drinking, spiced up by fairground rides that are so hairy they're banned in the US. The fair is so big that the grounds are divided along four main avenues, creating a boisterous city of its own, heaving from morning till night. **Fasching**, Munich's carnival, is an excuse for fancy-dress balls and general shenanigans from mid-January until the beginning of Lent. More sedate is **Auer Dult**, a traditional market that takes place on the Mariahilfplatz during the last weeks of April, July and October each year; there are stalls selling food, craftware and antiques, and there's also a fairground.

Listings

Bike rental From the train station, opposite platform 31.

Consulates UK, Bürkleinstr 10 ☏0 89/21 10 90; Canada, Tal 29 ☏0 89/2 19 95 70; Ireland, Denningerstr. 15 ☏0 89/20 80 59 90; US, Königinstr. 5 ☏0 89/2 88 80.

Exchange The bank at the train station is open daily 6am–11pm.

Gay Munich Despite Bavaria's deep conservatism, Munich has an active and visible gay scene. *Our Munich* is a gay listings mag and there's a shop of the same name at Müllerstr. 36–38. Cafés that cater predominantly for lesbians are *Inge's Karotte*, Baaderstr. 13, *Frauencafé im Kofra*, Baldestr. 8, and *Mädchenpower-café*, Baldestr. 16. The following male gay bars are well known: *Colibri*,

Utzschneiderstr. 8, *Juice*, Buttermelcherstr. 2a, and *Klimperkasten*, Maistr. 28.
Hospital Technische Universität München, Ismaninger Str. 22 ☎0 89/4 14 00.
Internet easyEverything, directly in front of the train station.

Laundry Amalienstr. 61; Ismaninger Str. 45.
Pharmacy Bahnhof-Apotheke, Bahnhofplatz 2; Internationale Ludwigs-Apotheke, Neuhauser Str. 11.
Post office Bahnhofplatz 1.

The Bavarian Alps

It's among the picture-book scenery of the **Alps** that you'll find the Bavarian folklore and customs that are the subject of so many tourist brochures, and the region also encompasses some of the most famous places in the province, such as the Olympic ski resort of **Garmisch-Partenkirchen**, and the fantasy castle of **Neuschwanstein**, just one of the lunatic palaces built for King Ludwig II of Bavaria. The western reaches are generally cheaper and less touristy, partly because they're not so easily accessible to Munich's weekend crowds. Many make the trip out to **Oberammergau**, though, a traditional Alpine village projected into the spotlight of worldwide fame on account of its Passion Play. In contrast, much of the eastern region of **Berchtesgaden** is heavily geared to the tourist trade, but if you go outside the high season of July and August, you should have a good chance of avoiding the crowds and not straining your finances.

Hohenschwangau and Neuschwanstein

Lying between the Forggensee reservoir and the Ammer mountains, around 100km by rail from Munich, **FÜSSEN** and the adjacent town of **SCHWANGAU** are the bases for visiting Bavaria's two most popular castles. **Schloss Hohenschwangau** (daily 9am–4/6pm; €7), originally built in the twelfth century but heavily restored in the nineteenth, was where Ludwig spent his youth. A mark of his individualism is left in the bedroom, where he had the ceiling painted with stars that were spotlit in the evenings. **Schloss Neuschwanstein** (same times; €7), the ultimate storybook castle, was built by Ludwig a little higher up the mountain. The architectural hotchpotch includes Byzantine throne hall and an artificial grotto. Left incomplete at Ludwig's death, it's a monument to a very sad and lonely man.

The nearest **hostel** is in Füssen, at Mariahilferstr. 5 (☎0 83 62/77 54; ❷). An inexpensive guest house near the castles is *Pension Weiher*, Hofwiesenweg 11 (☎0 83 62/8 11 61; ❹). The **tourist office** at Kaiser-Maximilian-Platz 1 (Mon–Fri 8.30am–6pm, Sat 9am–1pm; ☎0 83 62/9 38 50, ⓦwww.fuessen.de) in Füssen can book accommodation. Füssen is also the end of the much-publicized **Romantic Road** from Würzburg via Augsburg, served by special **tour buses** in season.

Oberammergau and Schloss Linderhof

From Murnau, midway between Munich and Garmisch-Partenkirchen, a branch line runs to **OBERAMMERGAU**, world famous for its **Passion Play**, first performed in 1633 as thanks for being spared by a plague epidemic. The show takes place every ten years (next in 2010) between May and October, with a cast of local villagers. Many of Oberammergau's houses have traditional outside frescoes of religious or Alpine scenes, which you can see as either quaint or kitsch – that goes for the wood carvings in the local souvenir shops, too.

From here it's a short bus ride to **Schloss Linderhof** (daily 10am–4/6pm; €6, €4.50 in winter), one of the architectural fantasies conjured for Ludwig. Though built as a discreet private residence, it has a reception room with intricate gold-painted carvings, stucco ornamentation, and a throne canopy draped in ermine curtains. The real attraction is the delightful **park**: Italianate terraces, cascades and manicured flowerbeds give way to an English garden design that gradually blends into the forests of the mountain beyond. A number of romantic little buildings are dotted around the park, the most remarkable of which is the Venus Grotto. Based on the set for Wagner's opera *Tannhäuser* (Ludwig was the composer's principal patron), it has an illuminated lake supporting a huge floating golden conch in which the king would sometimes take rides.

Garmisch-Partenkirchen and Mittenwald

GARMISCH-PARTENKIRCHEN is the most famous town in the German Alps, partly because it's at the foot of the highest mountain – the **Zugspitze** (2966m) – and partly because it hosted the Winter Olympics in 1936. It has excellent facilities for skiing, skating and other winter sports, as well as abundant accommodation, a full list of which can be obtained from the **tourist office** at Richard-Strauss-Platz 2 (Mon–Sat 8am–6pm, Sun 10am–noon; ☎0 88 21/18 00, ⊛www.garmisch-partenkirchen.de). The ascent of Zugspitze by **rack–railway** and cable car (both €42, €33 in winter) is the most memorable local excursion.

MITTENWALD, which remains a community rather than a resort, is just 15km down the road and the main rail line from Munich. The Karwendl mountain towering above Mittenwald is a highly popular climbing destination, and the view from the top is one of the most exhilarating and dramatic in Germany; a **cable car** goes there (€18 return). The **tourist office**, at Dammkarstr. 3 (Mon–Fri 8am–noon & 1–5pm; July & Aug also Sat 10am–noon; ☎0 88 23/3 39 81, ⊛www.mittenwald .de), will reserve rooms and provide free maps of the area. There are plenty of good **guest houses** in the village, such as *Franziska*, Innsbrucker Str. 24 (☎0 88 23/9 20 30; ❺), and *Bergfrühling*, Dammkarstr. 12 (☎0 88 23/80 89; ❹). The nearest **campsite** is 3km north, on the road to Garmisch.

Berchtesgaden

Almost entirely surrounded by mountains at Bavaria's southeastern extremity, the area around **BERCHTESGADEN** has a magical atmosphere, especially in the mornings, when mists rise from the lakes and swirl around lush valleys and rocky mountainsides. The town is easily reached by rail from Munich and from Salzburg in Austria, which is just 23km to the north.

The town is famous for its **salt mine** (May to mid-Oct daily 9am–5pm; mid-Oct to April Mon–Sat 12.30–3.30pm; €12), where a small train will take you deep into the mountainside; you have to don protective clothing and descend on wooden slides. The region's other star attraction is **Königssee**, Germany's highest lake, which bends around the foot of the spiky Watzmann 5km south of the town and can be reached by regular buses. There are **cruises** on the Königssee all year round (to St. Bartholoma €10.50; €13.50 return). You can also take a cable car up the Jenner, immediately above the lake (€18 return). There are some great mountain trails to take you out of the crowds – maps of suggested walking routes can be bought at the **tourist office** opposite the train station (Mon–Fri 8am–5/6pm, Sat 8/9am–noon/5pm; late June to mid-Oct also Sun 9am–3pm; ☎0 86 52/96 70, ⊛www.berchtesgaden.de).

The area is still associated with **Adolf Hitler**, who rented a house in the nearby village of **Obersalzberg**, which he later enlarged into the **Berghof**, a stately retreat where he could meet foreign dignitaries. It was blown up by the Allies, and the ruins are now overgrown. High above the village on the Kehlstein, the Kehlsteinhaus, Hitler's "**Eagle's Nest**", survives as a restaurant, and can be reached by special bus from Obersalzberg (May to mid-Oct; €12 return).

Berchtesgaden has plenty of reasonable guest house **accommodation**. Options include *Haus am Hang*, Göllsteinbichl 3 (☎0 86 52/43 5 90; ❷), *Hansererhäusl*, Hansererweg 8 (☎0 86 52/25 23; ❷), *Gästehaus Alpina*, Ramsauer Str. 6 (☎0 86 52/25 17; ❸), and *Haus Achental*, Ramsauer Str. 4 (☎0 86 52/45 49; ❸). The tourist office can help with booking rooms and will direct you to any of the five campsites in the valley.

Augsburg

Innovations, both religious and secular, have found fertile ground in **AUGSBURG**, 70km from Munich. Luther's reforms found their earliest support here, and in 1514 the city built the world's first housing estate for the poor, the Fuggerei – an institution still in use today. The citizens of Augsburg have gone to great lengths to restore the city's appearance to that of its medieval heyday, yet this isn't just a museum piece. There's lively cultural action ranging from Mozart festivals to jazz and cabaret, and the university provides a thriving alternative scene to keep the place on its toes.

Heart of the city is the spacious cobbled **Rathausplatz**, which turns into a massive open-air café during the summer and into a glittering market at Christmas. At the baseline of this great semicircle stands the massive **Rathaus**; inside, the spick-and-span **Goldener Saal** (daily 10am–6pm; €1.50), with its gold-leaf pillars and marble floor, recalls the period when the Fugger banking dynasty made Augsburg one of the financial centres of Europe.

To the south, **Maximilianstrasse** is lined by merchants' palaces and punctuated by fountains. Beyond the Mercury fountain, the **Fuggerhäuser** stand proudly to the right; built in 1515 by Jacob Fugger "the Rich", they still belong to his loaded descendants, but you can walk through the main door to see the luxurious arcaded courtyard. Opposite the Hercules fountain is the **Schaezler Palais** (Tues–Sun 10am–5pm; €3), through the courtyard of which is the Dominican nunnery of St Catherine and the **State Gallery**. At the far end of Maximilianstrasse, Lutheran **St Ulrich** is dwarfed by the Catholic basilica of **St Ulrich-und-Afra**, resting place of the city's joint patron saints.

At the other end of the town's axis, the **Dom** stands in the grounds of the former Episcopal palace, now the seat of the regional government. Founded by St Ulrich in the tenth century, it has the oldest stained-glass windows still in position. There are also a number of altarpieces by Hans Holbein the Elder. The famous Romanesque bronze doors are now on view in the **Diocesan Museum St Afra** (Tues–Sat 10am–5pm, Sun 2–5pm, first Fri of the month till 9pm; €2.50) in the cloisters.

For a charge of one "Our Father", one "Hail Mary" and one Creed daily, plus €90 per annum, good Catholic paupers can retire to the **Fuggerei** at the age of 55. With an entrance in the Jacoberstrasse, it's a town within a town, and compared with modern housing estates is a real idyll, the cloister-like atmosphere disturbed only by the odd ringing doorbell. **Number 13** (March–Dec daily 9am–6pm; €1) in the Mittlere Gasse is one of only two houses from the original foundation; today it's full of furnishings from the sixteenth to the eighteenth century.

On the other side of town, in Annastrasse, stands **St Anna**, where the **Fuggerkapelle** marks the belated German debut of the full-blooded Italian Renaissance style, a spin-off of the family's extensive business interests in Italy. It was in St Anna that the final confrontation between the papal court and Luther took place in 1518. Luther found refuge with the Carmelites of St Anna when he was summoned to see the pope's legate, and today his room and several others in the old monastery have been turned into the **Lutherstiege** (Tues–Sun 10am–12.30pm & 3–5pm; free), a museum of the reformer's life and times.

Practicalities

The **tourist office** (Mon–Fri 9am–6pm, Sat 10am–1pm; ☏08 21/50 20 70, ✆www.augsburg.de) is a couple of minutes from the **train station** at Bahnhofstr. 7: there's also a branch on Rathausplatz (Mon–Fri 9am–6pm, Sat 10am–4pm; May–Oct also Sun 10am–4pm). Good **pensions** are to be found in the suburb of Lechhausen, 1.5km from the city centre and connected by three bus routes and tram #1: *Bayerische Löwe*, Linke Brandstr. 2 (☏08 21/70 28 70; ❸), *Linderhof*, Aspernstr. 38 (☏08 21/71 30 16; ❸), and *Märkl*, Schillerstr. 20 (☏08 21/79 14 99; ❸). The **hostel** is three minutes' walk from the Dom, at Beim Pfaffenkeller 3 (☏08

21/3 39 09; ❷). The cheapest places for **snacks** are the market and meat halls off Annastrasse, where you'll find several good *Imbiss* stands. Moving upmarket, excellent Swabian **meals** are served at the *Fuggerei-Stube*, Jakobergstr. 26. For **drinking**, *Kreslesmühle*, Barfüsserstr. 4, is a popular café/bar and arts centre; Striese, Kirchgasse 1, is also a theatre and music venue.

Regensburg

The undisturbed medieval panorama of central **REGENSBURG** and its stunning location on the banks of the Danube make it a great place to spend a couple of days. The best view of the medieval skyline is from the twelfth-century **Steinerne Brücke**, which was the only safe and fortified crossing along the entire length of the Danube at the time it was built, and thus had tremendous value for the city as a trading centre. On the left, just past the medieval salt depot, the **Historische Wurstküche** (daily 8am–7pm) originally functioned as the bridge workers' kitchen. It's been run by the same family for generations and serves little else but delicious Regensburg sausages.

A short way south the Gothic **Dom** comes into full view. Begun around 1250, it replaced a Romanesque church of which the **Eselsturm** is the only remaining part above ground. Highlights include the late thirteenth-century statues of the Annunciation and the fourteenth-century stained-glass windows in the south transept. In the cloisters – accessible only on tours (May–Oct Mon–Sat 10am, 11am & 2pm, Sun noon & 2pm; Nov–April Mon–Sat 11am, Sun noon; €2.50) – the **Allerheiligenkapelle** still has many Romanesque frescoes. Concerts and services are a musical treat here, as the **Domspatzen** is one of the finest choirs in the country.

The best of the city's merchant and patrician houses are to be seen on the **Haidplatz**. The largest building on the square is the **Haus zum Goldenen Kreuz**, where Emperor Charles V used to meet a local girl called Barbara Blomberg: their son, John of Austria, was born here in 1547 and died Governor of the Netherlands in 1578. The nearby **Thon-Dittmer Palais** is one of the main cultural venues, concerts and plays being held in its courtyard in summer. A few minutes' walk away, the Neupfarrplatz is the centre of Regensburg's commercial life; the **Neupfarrkirche** occupies the site of the old synagogue, wrecked during the 1519 expulsion.

After the Dom, the town's most important Gothic structure is the **Altes Rathaus** on Kohlenmarkt. To appreciate its grand scale, you need to take a tour of the **Reichstagsmuseum** (tours May–Sept Mon–Sat 3pm; €2.50). On nearby Keplerstrasse, the **Kepler-Gedächtnishaus** (Tues–Sun 10am–noon & 2–4pm; Nov–March closed Sun pm; €2) is dedicated to the great astronomer Johann Kepler, who died in Regensburg. Another museum worth looking at is the **Historical Museum on Dachauplatz** (Tues–Sun 10am–4pm; €2) – especially the section on Albrecht Altdorfer, one of Germany's greatest artists, and a leading local politician.

Schloss Thurn und Taxis (tours April–Oct Mon–Fri 11am, 2pm, 3pm & 4pm, Sat & Sun also 10am; Nov–March Sat & Sun only 10am, 11am, 2pm & 3pm; €8), home of the Prince of Thurn und Taxis, is situated in the city's southern quarter, in the converted monastic buildings of the abbey of St Emmeram. The former cloisters represent some of the finest Gothic architecture to be found in Germany, while the nineteenth-century state rooms contain some wonderful Brussels tapestries recording the family's illustrious history. In the neoclassical Marstall are two museums: the **Marstallmuseum** (April–Oct Mon–Fri 11am–5pm, Sat & Sun 10am–5pm; €4.50 combined ticket with Thurn und Taxis Museum), which holds travelling and ceremonial coaches and winter sleighs, and the **Thurn und Taxis Museum** (April–Oct Mon–Fri 11am–5pm, Sat & Sun 10am–5pm; Nov–March Sat & Sun only; ticket as for Marstallmuseum), which has displays of decorative art.

Practicalities

Maximilianstrasse leads straight from the train station to the centre. The **tourist office** is in the Altes Rathaus (Mon–Fri 8.30am–6pm, Sat 9am–4pm, Sun 9.30am–2.30/4pm; ☎09 41/5 07 44 10, ⊛www.regensburg.de). The **hostel**, Wöhrdstr. 60 (☎09 41/5 74 02; ❸), is about five minutes' walk from the heart of things, on an island in the Danube, and offers a choice of half or full board. Cheapest **hotel** in the town centre is *Am Peterstor*, Fröhliche-Türken-Str. 12 (☎09 41/5 45 45; ❸). Directly opposite there's another good deal at no. 11, although the rooms at *Zum Fröhliche Türken* (☎09 41/5 36 51; ❹) are beginning to show their age. Just the other side of the Steinerne Brücke, *Spitalgarten*, St Katharinen-Platz 1 (☎09 41/8 47 74; ❹), is conveniently sited next to the best beer garden. The **campsite** is about twenty minutes' walk from the centre, next to the Danube at Weinweg 40.

There are plenty of **places to eat**. Two *Gaststätten* with traditional and moderately priced Bavarian fare are *Alte Münz*, Fischmarkt 8, and *Kneitinger*, Arnulfsplatz 3. For more of a bar-type atmosphere, usually with good music, try *Rote Löwe*, Rote Löwengasse 10, *Amopola*, Am Römling 1, or *Jalapenos*, Schottenstr. 4, a Latin-laced local with a well-stocked bar. Netzblick, Am Römling 9, is an **internet café** (daily 6pm–1am). Popular student hangouts are *Schwedenkugel*, Haaggasse 15, and *Goldene Ente*, Badstr. 32. For a traditional **beer garden**, take bus #6 or #10 south to *Kneitinger-Keller*, at Galgenbergstr. 18 near the university, or for a great location on one of the Danube islands, try the *Spitalgarten* on St Katharinen-Platz.

Nürnberg

Founded in the eleventh century, **NÜRNBERG** rapidly rose to become the unofficial capital of Germany, its position at the intersection of major trading routes leading to economic prosperity and political power. The arts flourished too, though the most brilliant period was not to come until the late fifteenth century, when the roll call of citizens was led by Albrecht Dürer. Like many other wealthy European cities, Nürnberg went into gradual economic and social decline once the sea routes to the Americas and Far East had been established; moreover, adoption of the Reformation cost the city the patronage of the Catholic emperors. It made a comeback in the nineteenth century, when it became the focus for the Pan-German movement, and the Germanisches Nationalmuseum – the most important collection of the country's arts and crafts – was founded at this time.

The Altstadt has some great **nightlife**. In the summer, particularly, it is alive with street theatre and music, and open-air concerts liven up the parks and stadiums.

Arrival, information and accommodation

The main **tourist office** (Mon–Sat 9am–7pm; ☎09 11/2 33 61 32, ⊛www.nuernberg.de) is at Königstr. 93 in front of the train station, at the entrance to the Altstadt. There's another office at Hauptmarkt 18, within the Altstadt (May–Sept Mon–Sat 9am–6pm, Sun 10am–4pm; Oct–April closed Sun; ☎09 11/2 33 61 35). The Nürnberg KulTour Ticket (€14.50) covers two days' travel on the public transport network plus entrance to over thirty museums and sights. **Internet** access is available at the Maximum shopping complex, where Färberstr. meets Frauengasse.

The official **HI hostel** has a wonderful location within the Kaiserburg, overlooking the Altstadt (☎091 1/2 30 93 60; ❸). The popular *Lettem Sleep* hostel at Frauentormauer 42 (☎09 11/9 92 81 28; ❷) offers free tea, coffee and internet access, and there's another privately run **youth hotel** to the north of the city at Rathsbergstr. 300 (☎09 11/5 21 60 92; ❸); despite the name, no age restrictions apply. Try to avoid arriving on a Sunday, since many **pensions** are closed for the day. The cheapest reasonably central options include: *Vater Jahn*, Jahnstr. 13 (☎09 11/44 45 07; ❸), *Melanchthon*, Melanchthonplatz 1 (☎09 11/41 26 26; ❹), and the twelve-room *Altstadt*, Hintere Ledergasse 4 (☎09 11/22 61 02; ❹). Closer to the castle at Schildgasse 14–16, *Burghotel Stammhaus* (☎09 11/20 30 40) has chintzy rooms with large balconies, and there's even a mini swimming pool in the cellar.

The City

On January 2, 1945, a storm of bombs reduced ninety percent of Nürnberg's centre to ash and rubble, but you'd never guess it from the meticulous postwar rebuilding. Covering about 4sq km, the reconstructed medieval core is surrounded by its ancient city walls and neatly spliced by the River Pegnitz. To walk from one end to the other takes about twenty minutes, but much of the centre, especially the area around the castle – known as the **Burgviertel** – is on a steep hill. It's not all medieval pictures, either. Significant areas of modern architecture and open spaces are nearby, ensuring a refreshing mix of old and new.

One of the highest points of the city is occupied by the **Kaiserburg** (daily 9/10am–4/6pm; €5), whose earliest surviving part is the eastern **Fünfeckturm**, dating from the eleventh century. A century later, Frederick Barbarossa extended the castle to the west: his **Sinwellturm**, built directly on the rock, can be ascended for the best of all the views. Another survivor of this period is the **Kaiserkapelle**, whose upper level was reserved for the use of the emperor, with the courtiers confined to the lower tier. At the extreme east end of the complex is the **Luginslandturm**, erected by the city council in the fourteenth century. At the end of the fifteenth century, the Luginslandturm was joined to the Fünfeckturm by the vast Kaiserstallung – originally a cereal warehouse and later a stable, it's now home to the HI hostel.

The area around the **Tiergärtner Tor** next to the Kaiserburg is one of the most attractive parts of the old town centre, a meeting point for summertime street vendors, artists and musicians. Virtually next door, the **Dürer Haus** (Tues–Sun 10am–5pm, Thurs till 8pm; €4) is where the painter, engraver, scientist, writer, traveller and politician lived from 1509 to 1528, and is one of the very few original houses still standing. Don't come here looking for original Dürer paintings, though: there are only copies, plus works by artists paying homage to the man. Dürer is buried in the St Johannisfriedhof, a few minutes' walk away, along Johannisstrasse.

Nürnberg's oldest and most important church, the twin-towered **Sebalduskirche**, is just down the road from the Fembohaus. Founded in the thirteenth century and altered a century later, it contains an astonishing array of works of art. Particularly striking are the bronze shrine of St Sebald and some pieces by Veit Stoss, Nürnberg's most famous sculptor: an expressive *Crucifixion* on the pillar behind the shrine and three stone reliefs in the chancel.

The **Hauptmarkt**, commercial heart of the city and the main venue for weekly markets (and the famous Christmas market), is a couple of minutes' walk away. Its east side is bounded by the **Frauenkirche**, on whose facade a clockwork mechanism known as the *Männleinlaufen* tinkles away at noon. Also on the Hauptmarkt is a replica of the famous **Schöner Brunnen**, looking like a lost church spire; the original parts are on display in the Germanisches Nationalmuseum.

South of the Hauptmarkt, the Museumsbrücke crosses the river, giving a good view of the **Fleischbrücke** to the right, and the **Heilig–Geist–Spital** – one of the largest hospitals built in the Middle Ages – on the left. Passing the oldest house in the city, the thirteenth-century **Nassauer Haus**, you shortly come to the **Lorenzkirche**, built about fifty years after the Sebalduskirche, its counterpart on the other side of the water. The nave has a resplendent rose window, while the chancel is lit by gleaming stained glass. The graceful late fifteenth-century tabernacle, some 20m high, was carved by Adam Kraft, who depicted himself as a pensive figure crouching at the base. Equally spectacular is the larger-than-life *Annunciation* by Veit Stoss, suspended above the high altar.

The **Germanisches Nationalmuseum** occupies a fourteenth-century monastery on Kornmarkt (Tues–Sun 10am–5pm, Wed till 9pm; €4). On the ground floor the displays follow a roughly chronological layout, beginning with

Bronze Age items and moving onto medieval sculptures and carvings, outstanding among which are *The Seven Stations of the Cross* by Adam Kraft and works by Tilman Riemenschneider and Veit Stoss. German painting at its Renaissance peak dominates the first floor, with pieces by Dürer, Altdorfer, Baldung and Cranach. The following rooms focus on the diversity of Nürnberg's achievements during the Renaissance. The strong tradition of gold- and silver-smithing is shown to best effect in the superb model of a three-masted ship, while the city's leading role in the fast-developing science of geography is exemplified by the first globe of the earth, made by Martin Behaim in 1491 – just before the discovery of America.

For a complete contrast, head back east to the **Neues Museum** (Tues–Fri 10am–8pm, Sat & Sun 10am–6pm; €3.50) on Klarissenplatz, which is rapidly gaining a reputation as one of Germany's most important design museums. The collection provides an impressive panorama of artistic developments since the 1960s.

The Zeppelin and Mars fields

In virtually everyone's mind, "Nuremberg" conjures up thoughts of **Nazi rallies** and **war-crime trials**. As the city council is eager to point out, the Nazis' choice of Nürnberg had less to do with local support of Nazi ideology, and more to do with what the medieval city represented in German history. The rallies were held on the **Zeppelin and Mars fields** in the suburb of Luitpoldhain (tram #9 from the centre). A permanent exhibition documenting the history of the rally grounds and the ruthless misuse of power under National Socialism is now housed in Albert Speer's Congress Hall. **Fascination and Terror** (Tues–Fri 10am–8pm, Sat & Sun 10am–6pm; €5; tram #4 to Dutzendteich) is a multimedia information centre occupying the northernmost wing of this gargantuan but unfinished structure. The "**Nürnberg Laws**" of 1935 deprived Jews of their citizenship and forbade relations between Jews and Gentiles. It was through these laws that the Nazis justified their extermination of six million Jews, 10,000 of whom came from Nürnberg. Only ten remained here after the war. It was highly significant that the war criminals of the Nazi regime were tried in the city that saw their proudest demonstrations of power.

Eating, drinking and nightlife

Nürnberg is the liveliest Bavarian city after Munich, with a wealth of Studentenkneipen and café/bars catering for the students. The cheapest **meals** in town are to be found in the university **Mensa**, in the northeastern corner of the Altstadt. Otherwise there are plenty of *Imbiss*-type snack-joints in the pedestrian zone between St Lorenz and the Ehekarussel. In the Altstadt, good places to eat include *Bratwurst-Häusle*, Rathausplatz 1, the most celebrated of the city's sausage restaurants, and the excellent and reasonable *Nassauer Keller*, Karolinerstr. 2, installed in an atmospheric thirteenth-century cellar. In *Spitalgasse*, Heilig-Geist-Spital serves hearty fare in the setting of a medieval hospital building. At Bergstr. 19 is *Schwarzer Bauer*, the **pub** of the Altstadthof's celebrated house brewery. Another place that brews its own beer is the 450-seat *Barfüsser*, which occupies the cavernous cellars of the Mauthalle at Hallplatz 2. For a combination of beer haven and music bar, make for *Starclub*, Maxtorgraben 33. Ruhestörung, Tetzelgasse 21, is one of the most fashionable **café/bars**. The tiny, excellent café/bar *Meisengeige*, Am Laufer Schlagturm 3, caters for a mixed crowd, and its small cinema shows an offbeat selection of films. The trendiest **nightclub** in Nürnberg is Mach 1, Kaiserstr. 1–9, with four different bars and some good lighting effects (closed Mon & Tues). To find out what else is going on, get either the *Monatsmagazin* from the tourist office, or the *Plärrer* magazine from any kiosk.

Rothenburg ob der Tauber

The tourist itinerary known as the **Romantic Road** winds its way along the length of western Bavaria and runs through the most visited medieval town in

Germany: **ROTHENBURG OB DER TAUBER**, 50km west of Nürnberg. It is connected by a branch railway with Steinach, on the Augsburg–Würzburg line; to reach Nürnberg, you need to change here and again at Ansbach. There are also scores of bus tours along the chain of half-timbered villages that comprise the Romantic Road.

It takes about an hour to walk around the fourteenth-century walls of Rothenburg, the ultimate museum piece. The promontory on the western side of town is the site of the **Burgtor** watchtower – the oldest of all the 24 towers – and the **Blasiuskapelle**, with murals from the fourteenth century. The nearby Herrngasse leads up to the town centre, and is the widest street in Rothenburg, once home to the local nobs.

The sloping **Marktplatz** is dominated by the arcaded front of the Renaissance Rathaus, which supplanted the Gothic building that stands behind it. The sixty-metre tower of the **Gotisches Rathaus** (April–Oct daily 9.30am–12.30pm & 1.30–5pm; Dec noon–3pm; €1) is the highest point in Rothenburg and provides the best view of the town and surrounding countryside. The other main attractions on the Marktplatz are the figures on each side of the three clocks of the **Ratsherrntrinkstube**, which seven times daily re-enact an episode that allegedly occurred during the Thirty Years War. The fearsome Johann Tilly agreed that Rothenburg should be spared if one of the councillors could drain in one draught a tankard holding over three litres of wine. A former burgomaster duly sank the contents of the so-called Meistertrunk, then needed three days to sleep off the effects. On the opposite side of the Marktplatz is Rothenburg's largest building, the Gothic **St Jakob-Kirche** (April–Oct daily 9am–5.30pm; Nov, Jan & March daily 10am–noon & 2–4pm; Dec daily 10am–5pm; €1.50), rising above the sea of red roofs like a great ship; the entrance fee is worth paying purely to see Tilman Riemenschneider's exquisite limewood *Holy Blood Altar*. Of the local museums, the most fascinating is the **Kriminalmuseum** at Burggasse 3 (daily: April–Oct 9.30am–6pm; Nov–March 1/2–4pm; €3.20), which contains collections of medieval torture instruments and related objects such as the beer barrels that drunks were forced to walk around in.

There are many cheap **pensions** and **inns** in Rothenburg; worth trying are the charming old-fashioned *Pöschel*, Wenggasse 22 (⊕0 98 61/34 30, ©pension .poeschel@t-online.de; ❸), the hugely welcoming *Raidel*, in a Medieval house on the same street at no. 3 (⊕0 98 61/31 15, ⊛www.romanticroad.com/raidel; ❸), and the quiet *Hofmann*, Stollengasse 29 (⊕0 98 61/33 71; ❸). The two **hostels** – *Rossmühle* and its annexe *Spitalhof* (⊕0 98 61/45 10; both ❷) – are in beautifully restored houses off the bottom of the Spitalgasse, and room rates drop the longer you stay. Private **rooms** are the next cheapest option (❷): details are available at the highly efficient **tourist office** on Marktplatz (Mon–Fri 9am–12pm & 1–5/6pm, Sat 10am–1/3pm; ⊕0 98 61/4 04 92, ⊛www.rothenburg.de). Interesting **local specialities** include the Schneeball (snowball), a complex confectionery creation, best washed down with a mug of Mauerblümchentee (wallflower tea).

Würzburg

Terminus of the Romantic Road, **WÜRZBURG** straddles the River Main some 60km north of Rothenburg, and can be reached either by bus from there or by train from Nürnberg, Augsburg or Munich. During the night of March 16, 1945, it got the same treatment from Allied bombers that Nürnberg had received two months earlier. Würzburg has been less successful in rebuilding itself, but a number of outstanding sights and the town's location among a landscape of vineyards easily justify a visit.

Bracketed by the river and the Residenz, the old town is focused on the **Marktplatz**, where a daily food market ensures a lively bustle. Just off the square, the **Haus zum Falken** is the city's prize example of a Rococo townhouse, perfectly restored to the very last stucco curl. Overlooking the Markt is the Gothic **Marienkapelle**, which has an intriguing *Annunciation* above the northern portal: a band leads from God to Mary's ear, a baby sliding towards her along its folds.

Halfway down the Kürschnerhof, leading off the Marktplatz, the **Neumünster's** dusky pink facade stands out among the postwar houses. The church was built over the graves of saints Kilian, Kolonat and Totnan, Irish missionaries martyred in 689 for trying to Christianize the region. The Kiliani festival, at the beginning of July, is the region's most important religious event, drawing thousands of pilgrims to the crypt where the saints are buried. The **Dom**, again consecrated to St Kilian, is virtually next door; it was burned out in 1945, so only the exterior is true to the original Romanesque.

The **Residenz** (mid-April to mid-Oct Mon–Sun 9am–6pm, Thurs till 8pm; rest of year daily 10am–4pm; €8) was intended to show that the Würzburg bishops could hold their own among such great European courts as Versailles. Construction was left largely in the hands of Balthasar Neumann, whose famed staircase is covered by the largest fresco in the world. An allegory extolling the fame of the prince-bishops in the most immodest way imaginable, it was painted by the greatest decorator of the age, Giambattista Tiepolo. The tour of the palace goes through the plain stuccoed Weisser Saal, before plunging into the opulence of the Kaisersaal; once reserved for the use of the emperor, it now provides a glamorous setting for the June Mozart Festival. The marble, the gold-leaf stucco and the sparkling chandeliers produce an effect of dazzling magnificence, but finest of all are more frescoes by Tiepolo. Tucked discreetly into the southwest corner of the palace in order not to spoil the symmetry, the Hofkirche is a brilliant early example of Neumann's illusionism – the interior, based on a series of ovals, appears much larger than it really is. Both side altars are by Tiepolo.

On the other side of the Dom, the twelfth-century **Alte Mainbrücke** – the oldest bridge over the Main – leads towards the Festung Marienberg; if you don't fancy the climb to the castle, take bus #9 from the bridge. This was home to the ruling bishops from the thirteenth century until 1750, when they shifted to the Residenz. The devastations of foreign armies – the Swedes, the Prussians, the Allies in the last war – have been so great that although much of the original structure has been restored, the interiors are largely missing. The medieval core contains the round Marienkirche, one of Germany's oldest churches, as well as the Brunnenhaus, whose 105-metre well was chiselled through the rock in around 1200. Surrounding this are a number of other buildings, including the Renaissance **Fürstenbau** (Tues–Sun 9/10am–4.30/6pm; €3). The **Mainfränkisches Museum** (Tues–Sun 10am–4/5pm; €3, €4 combined ticket with Fürstenbau) in the former arsenal contains sculptures by Riemenschneider and examples of all genres of art across the ages, as well as an interesting display on Franconian wine.

During work on the Residenz, Neumann also took time to build the **Käppele**, a pilgrimage church imperiously perched on the heights to the south of the Marienberg. Apart from the opportunity to see the interior, lavishly covered with frescoes and stucco, it's worth visiting for the view from the terrace – the finest in Würzburg.

Practicalities

The **train station** is at the northern end of the city centre, while the **tourist office** is in the Haus zum Falken (Mon–Fri 10am–6pm, Sat 10am–2pm; April–Oct also Sun 10am–2pm; ☎09 31/37 23 35, ⊛www.wuerzburg.de). There are two reasonably priced **pensions** between the station and the centre: *Siegel*, Reisgrubengasse 7 (☎09 31/5 29 41; ❹), and *Spehnkuch*, Röntgenring 7 (☎09 31/5 47 52; ❹). The 254-bed **hostel**, Burkarderstr. 44 (☎09 31/4 25 90 or 4 25 95; ❸; tram #3 or #5), is situated below the Marienberg. The nearest **campsite** is about 4km south in Heidingsfeld (bus #16 from Barbarossaplatz).

Best places for Franconian **food** are *Bürgerspital*, Theaterstr. 19, and *Juliusspital*,

Juliuspromenade 19. *Zur Stadt Mainz*, Semmelstr. 39, though excellent, is the tourist spot in town, printing its menus in five languages as well as Braille. For student **bars** go to Sanderstrasse in the south of town − *Till Eulenspiegel*, at no. 1a, is particularly good; while at no. 5 there's an **internet café**, *H@ackm@c*.

Bamberg

The citizens of **BAMBERG**, 60km north of Nürnberg and 95km east of Würzburg, knock back more beer per head than anywhere else in the country: ten breweries produce thirty different kinds of ale, most notably the distinctive smoky **Rauchbier**. Bamberg's isolation has preserved it from the ravages of war, and today it is one of the most beautiful small towns in the world, where most European styles from the Romanesque onwards have left a mark.

Heart of the lower town is the **Maxplatz**, dominated by Balthasar Neumann's **Neues Rathaus**. A daily market is held here and on the adjoining Grüner Markt, which stands in the shadow of the huge Jesuit church of St Martin. On an islet anchoring the Obere Brücke to the Untere Brücke is the picturesque **Altes Rathaus**. Except for the half-timbered section overhanging the rapids, the original Gothic building was transformed into the Rococo style. The famous **Klein–Venedig** (Little Venice) of medieval fishermen's houses is best seen from the Untere Brücke.

Uphill, the spacious, sloping **Domplatz** is lined with a superb variety of buildings. The **Kaiserdom** was consecrated in 1012, but the present structure of golden sandstone is the result of a slow rebuilding that continued throughout the thirteenth century. The astonishing array of sculpture was initially executed in orthodox Romanesque style, best seen in the Fürstenportal on the north side of the nave, where figures of the Apostles are carved below a *Last Judgement*. The most famous sculpture is inside − the enigmatic **Bamberg Rider**, one of the first equestrian statues to be made since classical antiquity. Focus of the nave is the white limestone tomb of the canonized imperial couple Heinrich II and Kunigunde; Tilman Riemenschneider laboured away for fourteen years on this sarcophagus, whose reliefs depict scenes taken from the life and times of the couple.

Opposite the cathedral, the Ratstube is a Renaissance gem, now containing the **Historical Museum** (May–Oct Tues–Sun 9am–5pm; €2.10), which covers local history from the Stone Age to the twentieth century, as well as Bamberg's rich art history. Adjoining it is the **Reiche Tor**, where Heinrich and Kunigunde appear once more, leading into the huge courtyard of the Alte Hofhaltung, the former Episcopal palace. Across the street is the building that supplanted it, the huge Baroque **Neue Residenz** (tours daily: 9am–4/6pm; free). Inside is the Staatsgalerie Bamberg, with medieval and Baroque paintings by German masters.

From the rose garden behind the Neue Residenz is a view of Michaelsburg, crowned by a huge **Abtei**. Much of the Romanesque shell of the church remains, but the interior is an awesome hotchpotch: lavish Rococo furnishings, tombs of Bamberg bishops and a ceiling depicting over 600 medicinal herbs. The cellars house the **Fränkisches Brauereimuseum** (April–Oct Wed–Sun 1–5pm; €2) − even if you're not interested in beer, it's worth coming for the wonderful panorama over the city.

Another place for a great view is the path up to the **Altenburg**, a ruined castle at the end of the very steep Altenburger Strasse. En route, up Untere Kaulberg and past Karmelitenplatz, you'll find the **Karmelitenkloster**. The church is again Baroque, but the Romanesque cloister (daily 8.30–11.30am & 2.30–5.30pm; free), the largest in Germany, has been preserved.

Practicalities

The **train station** is fifteen minutes' walk northeast of the centre. The **tourist office** (Mon–Fri 9am–3pm; May–Sept & Dec also Sun 10am–2pm; ☎09 51/87 11 61, ⊛www.tourismus.bamberg.de) is at Geyerswörthstr. 3. Among several inexpensive **hotels** are *Bamberger Weissbierhaus*, Obere Königstr 38 (℡09 51/2 55 03; ❸), and *Zum Alten Goldenen Anker*, Untere Sandstr. 73 (℡09 51/6 65 05; ❹). The **hostel** is 2km south of the centre at Oberer Leinritt 70 (℡09 51/5 60 02; ❷), reached by buses #1, #7, #11 from the train station to ZOB Promenade, then bus #18 to Regnitzufer. The local **campsite** (℡09 51/5 63 20) is another 2km downriver – also reached by bus #18.

Two **restaurants** worth trying are *Schlenkerla*, Dominikanerstr. 6, which is famous for its Rauchbier, and *Kaiserdom-Stuben*, Urbanstr. 18, which is good for vegetarian dishes. Three of the best **cafés** are *Am Dom*, Ringleinsgasse 2, *Michaelsberg*, Michaelsberg 10e, and the summer *Rosengarten* in the Neue Residenz. Good places to try the local **beers** are four beer cellar-cum-gardens: *Spezial*, on Obere Stephansberg 47; *Greiffenklau*, Laurenziplatz 20; *Keesmann*, Wunderburg 5; and *Mahr's-Bräu*, Oberer Stephansberg 36.

Berlin

BERLIN is something of a weather-vane of modern European history, yet its rise to national prominence was a long and slow process. For five centuries, its fortunes were tied to those of the hugely ambitious Hohenzollern dynasty, serving as capital of their ever-expanding state, which was successively known as Brandenburg, then Brandenburg-Prussia, and finally as the Kingdom of Prussia. As Prussia played the vanguard role in the belated achievement of national unity in 1871, Berlin duly became Imperial Germany's capital. It maintained that role in the Weimar Republic after World War I, and during the Nazis' Third Reich. Following defeat in World War II, however, the city was partitioned by the victorious Allies, and as a result served as the frontline of the Cold War. In 1961, its division into two hostile sectors was given a very visible expression by the construction of the notorious Berlin Wall.

After the Wall fell in 1989, Berlin's status as capital of Germany (which it had never officially lost, despite the relocation of the West German government to Bonn) was confirmed. However, although Berlin narrowly won the bitter fight to become the main governmental seat, Bonn has been left with an important second-ary role. This is a calculated measure designed to ensure that Berlin – with its deeply tainted historical record – does not become too powerful or dominant within Germany. Thus the vast rebuilding and re-development that the city is cur-rently undergoing is something of a delicate balance. There is a clear need to increase the population (which had fallen by more than a million from its prewar level), and to create a city that is a worthy capital of Europe's most powerful nation, yet at the same time to ensure that it does not become a direct German counter-part of London or Paris.

The speed of change in the past few years has been astounding. Much of the new Berlin is already in place: parliament sits in the renovated Reichstag; Potsdamer Platz, formerly a field in the Wall's death strip, is now a bustling entertainment quar-ter; and some of the city's world-class museum collections have been put back together again. However, the transformation of the city will go on for another decade at least, ensuring that it will continue to be an exciting place to visit.

Arrival, information and city transport

Most flights to Berlin arrive at Tegel **airport**, from where frequent #X9 express or local #109 buses (€2.10) run to Zoo Station (Bahnhof Zoologischer Garten), cen-tral point for the western side of the city. The JetExpressBus TXL provides connec-tion to Unter den Linden and the east, though tickets are more expensive (€5). Most international coaches stop at the bus station near the Funkturm, linked to the centre by #149 buses or U-Bahn from Kaiserdamm.

Berlin's **tourist office** is in the Europa Center at Budapester Str. 45 (Mon–Sat 8.30am–8.30pm, Sun 10am–6.30pm; ☎0 30/25 00 25, ⊛www.berlin-tourism.de), with additional offices at the Brandenburg Gate (daily 9.30am–6pm) and the Fernsehturm on Alexanderplatz (daily 10am–6pm). Smaller "Info Points" can be found at Tegel Airport and the KaDeWe department store, Tauentzienstr. 21–24. Berlin has two **listings magazines**, *Zitty* (⊛www.zitty.de; €2.30) and *Tip* (⊛www.tip-berlin.de; €2.50), published on alternate weeks.

The **U-Bahn** underground system is efficient and extensive; trains run from 4am to approximately 12.30am, an hour later on Friday and Saturday. The **S-Bahn**, whose stops are further apart, travels to the outer suburbs (such as Wannsee) and out of the city boundaries (to Potsdam, for instance). The city **bus network** – and the **tram system** in eastern Berlin – covers most of the gaps left by the U-Bahn: night buses run at intervals of around twenty minutes, although the routes often differ from daytime ones; agents in the U-Bahn stations can usually provide a map. **Tickets** can be bought from machines at U-Bahn station entrances, on trams, or from bus drivers; good for any mode of transport, they cost €2.10, allow you to travel in two of the three tariff zones, and are valid for two hours after stamping. Longer trips, from central Berlin to Potsdam for example, cost €2.40. An Einzelfahrschein Kurzstreckentarif, or short-trip ticket, costs €1.20 and allows you to travel up to three train or six bus stops. A day ticket is €6.10 for two tariff zones, €6.30 for all three. You can also buy a weekly ticket for €22 (2 zones) or €28 (3 zones). There are on-the-spot fines of €30 for those without a valid ticket or pass.

Accommodation

Accommodation in high season can be very hard to find, and if booking your own place in the western part it's best to call at least a couple of weeks in advance. If you turn up with nothing arranged, head for the tourist office in the Europa Center as it offers a free hotel-**booking service**; most of the accommodation listed can be booked on their website. For longer stays, contact one of the **Mitwohnzentrale** organizations, which will find you a room, usually for a minimum of seven nights. Try the Home Company at Joachimstaler Str. 17 (Mon–Fri 9am–6pm, Sat 11am–2pm; ☎0 30/1 94 45, ⊛www.homecompany.de), an easy walk from Zoo Station.

Hostels

Bax Pax Skalitzer Str. 104 ☎0 30/69 51 83 22. Laid-back with clean, bright-as-a-button rooms, this backpacker outfit offers cooking facilities and a rare chance to sleep in a VW Beetle. Görlitzer Bahnhof U-Bahn. ❷

The Circus Rosa-Luxemburg-Str. 39–41 & Weinbergsweg 1a both ☎0 30/28 39 14 33, ⊛www.circus-berlin.de. Clean, welcoming and traveller-oriented bases, with internet access, breakfast service near the action in the east. No curfew. Rosa Luxemburg Platz U-Bahn & Rosenthaler Platz U-Bahn. ❷

Jugendherberge JGH Berlin Kluckstr. 3 ☎0 30/2 61 10 98, ⊛www.jugendherberge.de. Slightly clinical HI-option in a quiet location between the two city centres. Dorms must be booked two weeks ahead. No curfew. Bus #129 to "Gedenkstätte Deutscher Widerstand". ❷

Jugendgästehaus am Zoo Hardenbergstr. 9a ☎0 30/3 12 94 10. Rough and ready but extremely popular hostel; excellent location in the western side of the city. No curfew. Zoologischer Garten U- and S-Bahn or Ernst-Reuter-Platz U-Bahn. ❸

Mitte's Backpacker Hostel Chausseestr. 102 ☎0 30/28 39 09 65, ⊛www.backpacker.de. Zinnowitzer Str. In a renovated factory building on the city's east side, this welcoming hangout features themed rooms including the "honeymoon suite". No curfew. U-Bahn line #6. ❷

Hotels

Acksel Haus Belforter Str. 21 ☎0 30/44 33 76 33. Small, effortlessly stylish hotel in the midst of the lively Prenzlauer Berg scene. ❹

Altberlin am Potsdamer Platz Potsdamer Str. 67 ☎0 30/26 06 70. Large pension just a few minutes' walk from the Tiergarten museums, recently refurbished with turn-of-the-century trappings. ❽

Artemisia Brandenburgischestr. 18 ☎0 30/8 73 89 05, ⊛www.artemisia-berlin.com. One of the city's women-only hotels, with airy pastel-coloured rooms throughout and a pleasant roof terrace. ❻

Artist Hotelpension Die Loge Friedrichstr. 115
☎ 0 30/2 80 75 13. Seven well-equipped rooms
with an earthy, arty charm. ④
Bogota Schlüterstr. 45 ☎ 0 30/8 81 50 01,
⊛ www.hotelbogota.de. Traditional style, including
a dozen four-bed rooms, in a stuffy but
comfortable 1911 building. ⑤

Bregenz Bregenzer Str. 5 ☎ 0 30/8 81 43 07,
⊛ www.hotelbregenz-berlin.de. Very quiet and
cosy family-run set-up only a five minute walk
from the Ku'damm. Children are welcome. ④
Charlot Giesebrechtr. 17 ☎ 0 30/3 27 96 60.
Neatly restored but impersonal mid-range hotel
near Adenauerplatz. Good value for money. ④

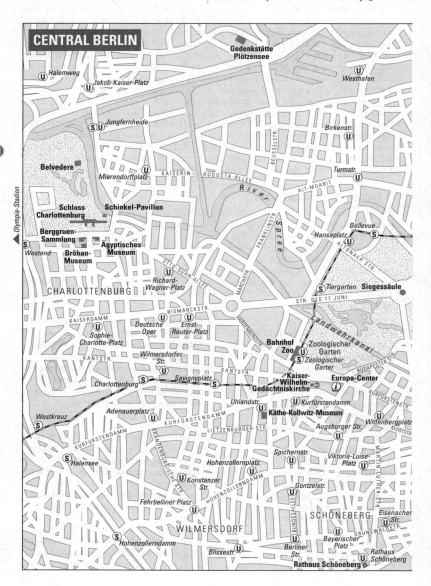

Hansablick Flotowstr. 6 ☏ 0 30/3 90 48 00. Well-appointed hotel in a quiet location, on the far side of the Tiergarten, yet close to the city's western hub. **⑦**

Merkur Torstr. 156 ☏ 0 30/2 82 82 97. Comfortable rooms, including one with five beds, within easy walking distance of city-centre

attractions and local nightlife. Most rooms have showers. **④**

Unter den Linden Unter den Linden 14 ☏ 030/23 81 10, ⓦ www.hotel-unter-den-linden.de. Vintage East German hotel, now renovated throughout, located at the historic intersection of Unter den Linden and Friedrichstrasse. **⑥**

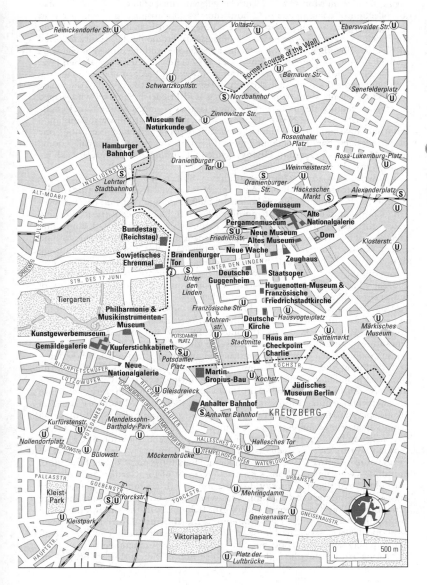

Eastern Berlin

The most atmospheric approach to eastern Berlin starts at the **Brandenburg Gate** and leads up **Unter den Linden**, a stately broad boulevard that is rapidly reassuming its prewar role as one of Berlin's most important thoroughfares. A recent addition to the avenue, located just to the east of Friedrichstrasse, is the **Deutsche Guggenheim Berlin**, Unter den Linden 13–15 (daily 11am–8pm, Thurs till 10pm; €3, free on Mon; ⊛www.deutsche-guggenheim-berlin.de), which, as well as its collection of contemporary art, hosts three to four major exhibitions per year. Lining the wide promenade beyond are a host of historic buildings restored from the rubble of the war, starting with the Neoclassical Humboldt University, followed by the Alte Bibliothek, the flawless Deutsche Staatsoper and the domed St Hedwig's Cathedral, built for the city's Catholics in 1747. The cathedral faces **Bebelplatz**, the site of the infamous Nazi bookburning of May 10, 1933; an unusual memorial – an underground room visible through a glass panel set in the centre of the square – marks the event. More than anyone, it was Karl Friedrich Schinkel who shaped nineteenth-century Berlin. One of his most famous creations can be found opposite the Staatsoper: the **Neue Wache**, a former royal guardhouse resembling a Roman temple and now a memorial to victims of war and tyranny. Next door, one of Berlin's finest Baroque buildings, the old Prussian Zeughaus or Arsenal, is home to the **Museum of German History** (closed till autumn 2003; temporary exhibitions on historical themes in the Kronprinzenpalais across the road).

Following Charlottenstrasse south from Unter den Linden leads to the **Gendarmenmarkt**, much of whose appeal is derived from the **Französische Kirche** on the northern side of the square. Built as a church for Berlin's influential Huguenot community at the beginning of the eighteenth century, it also now houses the **Hugenottenmuseum** (daily 11am/noon–5pm; €1.60), documenting their way of life. At the southern end of the square, the **Deutsche Kirche** was built around the same time for the city's Reformed community. It houses an engrossing though wordy historical exhibition, "Questions of German History" (Tues–Sun 10am–6pm; free). Schinkel's Neoclassical Schauspielhaus sits between the two churches. Friedrichstrasse, a high-class shopping district with an eclectic mix of modernist architecture, lies a block west of here.

At the eastern end of Unter den Linden lies the **Schlossplatz**, former site of the imperial palace, now home to the abandoned parliament building of the former GDR, the Palast der Republik. It stands at the midpoint of a city-centre island whose northwestern part, **Museumsinsel**, is the location of some of the best of Berlin's museums. An extensive reconstruction programme, however, has closed several of them: the Neues Museum will remain dark until 2008 and the Bodemuseum until 2004. The **Alte Nationalgalerie** (Tues–Sun 10am–6pm, Thurs till 10pm; €6, free first Sun of month; ⊛www.smpk.de) houses the city's collection of nineteenth-century European art. Currently, the **Altes Museum** (Tues–Sun 10am–6pm; €6, free first Sun on month; ticket gives same-day admission to all Berlin's state-owned museums; ⊛www.smpk.de), arguably Schinkel's most impressive surviving building, displays part of the city's excellent collection of Greek and Roman antiquities as well as all kinds of temporary exhibitions. The **Pergamonmuseum** (Tues–Sun 10am–6pm, Thurs till 10pm; €6, free first Sun of month; ⊛www.smpk.de) houses the treasure trove of the German archeologists who plundered the ancient world in the nineteenth century, and includes two must-sees: the spectacular Pergamon Altar, which dates from 160 BC, and the huge Processional Way from sixth-century BC Babylon. On the other side of the Pergamon, adjacent to the Altes Museum, is the **Berliner Dom**, built between 1894 and 1905 to serve the House of Hohenzollern as a family church; its vault houses ninety sarcophagi containing the remains of various members of the line.

To reach **Alexanderplatz**, the commercial hub of eastern Berlin, head along

Karl-Liebknecht-Strasse past the Neptunbrunnen fountain and the thirteenth-century Marienkirche, Berlin's oldest parish church. Like every other building in the vicinity, the church is overshadowed by the gigantic **Fernsehturm** or TV tower (daily 9am–midnight/1am; €6; ⊛www.berlinerfernsehturm.de), whose observation platform offers unbeatable views of the whole city from a height of 203m. Southwest of here lies the **Nikolaiviertel**, a modern development that attempts to recreate the winding streets and small houses of this part of prewar Berlin, which was razed overnight on June 16, 1944. At the centre of it all is the **Nikolaikirche** (Tues–Sun 10am–6pm; €1.50, free Wed), a rebuilt thirteenth-century structure that is Berlin's oldest parish church. Not far away on Mühlendamm is the rebuilt Rococo **Ephraim-Palais** (same times and ticket), housing a collection of Berlin art from the reign of Frederick the Great to 1945.

Western Berlin

Zoo Station is at the centre of the city's western side: a short walk south and you're at the eastern end of the Kurfürstendamm or **Ku'damm**, a 3.5-kilometre strip of ritzy shops, cinemas, bars and cafés. The great landmark here is the **Kaiser-Wilhelm-Gedächtniskirche**, destroyed by British bombing in November 1943, and left as a reminder of the horrors of war. There's little to do on the Ku'damm other than spend money, and there's only one cultural attraction nearby, the **Käthe-Kollwitz-Museum** at Fasanenstr. 24 (Mon & Wed–Sun 11am–6pm; €5; ⊛www.kaethe-kollwitz.de), devoted to the drawings and prints of the left-wing and pacifist artist Käthe Kollwitz.

The **Zoologischer Garten** itself (daily 9am–5.15/6pm; €8; ⊛www.zoo-berlin .de) forms the beginning of the Tiergarten, a restful expanse of woodland and a good place to wander along the banks of the Landwehrkanal. At the centre of Strasse des 17 Juni, the broad avenue that cuts through the Tiergarten, rises the **Siegessäule** (daily 9.30am–5.30/7pm; €1.20), a victory column celebrating Prussia's military successes; its summit offers a good view of the surrounding area, but you'll have to climb 585 steps to get there. Strasse des 17 Juni comes to an end at the **Brandenburg Gate**, built as a city gate-cum-triumphal arch in 1791. A little way north stands the **Reichstag**, the nineteenth-century home of the German parliament – it was remodelled by Norman Foster for the resumption of its historic role in April 1999. Foster's glass cupola has become a landmark, and a trip to the top (daily 8am–10pm; free) affords a stunning view of the city. Immediately behind the Reichstag, it's now only just possible to make out the course of the **Berlin Wall**, which divided the city for 28 years until November 9, 1989.

The heart of prewar Berlin used to be to the south of the Brandenburg Gate, its core formed by **Potsdamer Platz**. A huge commercial project here, involving various eateries, theatres and a shopping mall, attempts to recreate the area's former liveliness but apart from the impressive tent-like Sony Center on the northern side, there is little that's original. Just to the east, near the corner of Wilhelmstrasse and An der Kolonnade, lies the site of **Hitler's bunker**, where the Führer spent his last days, issuing meaningless orders as the Battle of Berlin raged above.

West of Potsdamer Platz lies the Kulturforum, a series of museums centred on the unmissable **Gemäldegalerie**, Matthäikirchplatz 8 (Tues–Sun 10am–6pm, Thurs till 10pm; €6, free first Sun of month; ⊛www.smpk.de). In it the world-class collection of old masters, covering all the main European schools, ranges from the Middle Ages to the late eighteenth century. Highlights of the German section include Cranach's tongue-in-cheek *The Fountain of Youth* and Holbein's *The Danzig Merchant Georg Gisze*. The interconnected building to the north houses the **Kunstgewerbemuseum** (Tues–Sun 10/11am–6pm; €3 if visited separately, free first Sun of month; ⊛www.smpk.de), a sparkling collection of European arts and crafts from Byzantium to Bauhaus. Opposite are the Philharmonie, the home of the

Berlin Philharmonic, and the **Musikinstrumenten-Museum** (Tues–Sun 9/10am–5pm; €3, free first Sun of month), a collection of weird and wonderful musical instruments. At Potsdamer Str. 50, a couple of minutes' walk to the south, is the **Neue Nationalgalerie** (Tues–Sun 10/11am–6pm, Thurs till 10pm; €6, free first Sun of month; ⊛www.smpk.de), which has a good collection of twentieth century German paintings, best of which are the Berlin portraits and cityscapes by George Grosz and Otto Dix.

Southeast of here, the **Martin-Gropius-Bau** at Niederkirchner Str. 7 (10am–8/10pm, closed Tues; admission varies; ⊛www.gropiusbau.de) is now a venue for prestigious temporary art exhibitions. Next door an open-air exhibition, **The Topography of Terror** (daily 10am–6/8pm; free; ⊛www.topographie.de), occupies the former site of Gestapo and SS headquarters and documents their history. From here it's a ten-minute walk down Wilhelmstrasse and Kochstrasse to the site of the notorious Checkpoint Charlie; evidence of the trauma the Wall caused is still on hand in the **Haus am Checkpoint Charlie** at Friedrichstr. 43-45 (daily 9am–10pm; €7; ⊛www.mauer-museum.com), which tells the history of the Wall and the stories of those who tried to break through.

The checkpoint area marks the northern limit of **Kreuzberg**, famed for its large immigrant community, its self-styled "alternative" inhabitants and nightlife. Daniel Libeskind's striking new **Jewish Museum Berlin** (daily 10am–8/10pm; €5; ⊛www.jmberlin.de) documents the culture, achievements, and tragic history of Berlin's Jewish community. Southwest is the slightly more upscale Schöneberg district, where the most famous attraction is the **Rathaus Schöneberg** on Martin-Luther-Strasse, where, in 1963, John F. Kennedy made his celebrated "Ich bin ein Berliner" speech.

Way over to the northwest of the Tiergarten stretches the district of **Charlottenburg**, its most significant target being the sumptuously restored **Schloss Charlottenburg** (Tues–Sun 10/11am–6pm; €7). Commissioned by the future Queen Sophie Charlotte in 1695, it was added to throughout the eighteenth and early nineteenth centuries. The entry price includes a tour of the main state apartments, self-guided visits to the private chambers (where the Prussian crown jewels can be seen), the Knobelsdorff-Flügel with its wonderful array of paintings by Watteau and other eighteenth-century French artists, and the Belvedere and Mausoleum in the park. Just to the south, at Schloss-Str. 70, is the **Ägyptisches Museum** (Tues–Sun 10am–6pm; €6, free first Sun of month; ⊛www.smpk.de), a fabulous collection of Egyptian antiquities; the famous bust of Nefertiti can be seen on the first floor. Also worth visiting is the **Berggruen Collection: Picasso and His Era** (Tues–Sun 10/11am–6pm; €6, free first Sun of month; ⊛www.smpk.de) directly opposite, which houses some seventy paintings of the Spanish artist.

The southwestern suburb of Dahlem, reached by U-Bahn line #1 to Dahlem-Dorf, is home to the **Dahlem Museums** (Tues–Sun 10/11am–6pm; €3, free first Sun of month; ⊛www.smpk.de). Since the Gemäldegalerie moved to the Tiergarten, the Dahlem complex is no longer the must-see it once was, but it still impresses. Check out the rich and imaginatively laid out Museum of Ethnology, featuring treasures from Asia, the Pacific and South Sea Islands. The collections of the Museums for East Asian and Indian Art (the latter featuring a spectacular group of Buddhist cave paintings from the Silk Road) are also worth a visit.

West of Charlottenburg, U-Bahn line #2 runs to the Olympia Stadion station; a signposted walk (15min) brings you to the vast **Olympic Stadium** itself (Wed & Sun 10am–6pm; €2.50), one of the few Nazi buildings left intact in the city.

For a break from the city pressure, you could take a trip to the **Grunewald** forest and beaches on the **Havel** lakes. To get to the beach, take S-Bahn #1 or #7 to Nikolassee station, from where it's a ten-minute walk to **Strandbad Wannsee** (April–Sept daily 8/10am–7/8pm; €4), a one-kilometre strip of pale sand that's the largest inland beach in Europe.

Eating, drinking and nightlife

The range and quality of **restaurants** in Berlin is unmatched in any other German city, and there's a wealth of **bars**, from Bavarian-style beer halls to sleek cocktail lounges. Cheapest way of warding off hunger is to use the **Imbiss** snack stands, or one of the **Mensas**, officially for German students but usually open to anyone who looks the part. Eating out in a restaurant won't break the bank, though, with prices for a main course usually between €6 and €16.

The **nightlife** in Berlin is worthy of any European capital. In Eastern Berlin there's a fast-developing scene: around Oranienburger Strasse, Rosenthaler Strasse, and Gipsstrasse in the Mitte neighbourhood are dozens of new bars and clubs that attract a young professional crowd as well as tourists, while further north, the streets around Käthe-Kollwitz–Platz and the Wasserturm in Prenzlauer Berg are a bit more "alternative" (to get there take the U-Bahn from Alexanderplatz to either Eberswalder Strasse or Schönhauser Allee). Western Berlin has four focal points for drinking: Savignyplatz is for conspicuous good-timers; Kreuzberg drinkers include political activists and punks; the area around Nollendorfplatz (northwestern Schönberg) and Winterfeldtplatz is the territory of sped-out all-nighters and the pushing-on-forty crew; central Schöneberg bars are on the whole more mixed and more relaxed. Unless you're into drunken businessmen, avoid the Ku'damm and the rip-off joints around the Europa Center. Berlin is very much a city that wakes up when others are going to sleep – don't bother turning up before midnight for the all-night clubs in Kreuzberg and Schöneberg. For more sedate nightlife there are a number of theatres and one of Europe's great orchestras. To find out what's on, buy one of the listings magazines *Tip*, *Zitty* or *Prinz*, get the Berlin *Programm* leaflet, or look for the flyposters about town.

Snacks

Al Rai Grosse Hamburger Str. 20/21, Mitte. Spacious, informal place where you can linger long over your tea and Arab specialities such as couscous and felafels.

Brooklyn Oranienstr. 176, Kreuzberg. Wonderful, inexpensive American-style hero sandwiches, cheesecake and brownies.

Soup Kultur Kurfürstendamm 224. A closet-sized place that offers a budget-priced selection of ten often exotic and always delicious soups. Close Sun.

Restaurants

Astor Oranienburger Str. 84. A snug and casual restaurant serving great fish and chips, home-made soups and large American breakfasts.

Athener Grill Meinekestr. 22. More moderately priced than it's appearance suggests, this Greek restaurant serves hearty fare in a quiet spot off the Ku'damm.

Café Aroma Hochkirchstr. 8 ☏ 0 30/7 82 58 21. Well above average, inexpensive Italian. One of the best places to eat in east Schöneberg; it's advisable to book after 8pm.

Carib Motzstr. 30. Classical Caribbean cuisine including curried goat, friendly service, lethal rum cocktails.

Dachgarten On top of the Reichstag, Platz der Republik ☏ 0 30/22 62 99 33. Fanciful German and continental nouvelle cuisine, not cheap, but in an unbeatable location. Booking recommended.

Don Sushi Propststr. 1. Tucked away in a corner of the Nikolaiviertel, this is the place to sample outlandish sushi creations.

Gugelhof Kollwitzstr. 59. Stylish and popular Alsatian restaurant in the trendy Kollwitzplatz neighbourhood; the set meals are the best value.

Kellerrestaurant im Brecht-Haus Chausseestr. 125 ☏ 0 30/28 28 43. A cellar restaurant in the basement of Brecht's old house and decorated with Brecht memorabilia. Viennese specialities supposedly dreamt up by Brecht's wife, Helen Weigel, make this a very popular place. Worth booking.

Merhaba Hasenheide 39. Highly rated Turkish restaurant that's usually packed with locals. A selection of the starters here can be more interesting than a main course.

Nam-Chi Schönhauser Allee 187. Shiny, modern place serving authentic spicy Thai dishes.

Pasternak Knaackstr. 24. Intimate Russian restaurant in the thick of the bustling scene in Prenzlauer Berg; also open for breakfast.

Publique Yorckstr. 62 ☏ 030/786 9469. Friendly café-cum-restaurant serving everything from Argentinian rump steak to chili con carne till 2am.

Restaurant am Wasserturm Knaackstr. 22. Occupying the same building as Pasternak, favourite old Eastern European Jewish dishes and surprises from Jewish cuisine.

Restauration 1900 Husemannstr. 1. An institution even before reunification. Excellent if unsurprising German food.

Tuk-Tuk Grossgörschenstr. 2 ⓣ030/781 1588. Amiable Indonesian near Kleistpark U-Bahn, with an extensive vegetarian selection. Enquire about the heat of your dish before ordering.

Bars and cafés

808 Bar & Lounge Oranienburger Str. 42/43. Large, somewhat plain cocktail lounge with upscale appointments and customers.

Anderes Ufer Hauptstr. 157. Cramped yet casual gay café that's something of an institution in the city.

Bar am Lützowplatz Lützowplatz 7. The longest bar in the city. A dangerously great place.

Begine Potsdamer Str. 139. Stylishly decorated women-only bar/bistro/gallery with limited choice of inexpensive food.

Café Adler Friedrichstr. 206. Classically furnished, smoky café next to the site of the Checkpoint Charlie border crossing. Moderately priced breakfasts and meals.

Café Einstein Kurfürstenstr. 58. Housed in a seemingly ancient mansion, this is about as close as you'll get to the ambience of the prewar Berlin *Kaffeehaus*, with international newspapers and breakfast served daily till 2pm.

Obst & Gemüse Oranienburger Str. 48. Snug, old-style bar that's a mainstay of the area's active nightlife; packed after 10pm.

The Pips Auguststr. 84. Very popular bar and dance club of bright colours and designer furnishings; different cocktail offers every day.

Schwarzes Café Kantstr. 148. Kantstrasse's best hangout for the young and chic, with a relaxed atmosphere, good music and Kölsch on tap. Open Mon till 3am, Tues from noon and Wed–Sun round the clock.

Silberstein Oranienburger Str. 27. One of eastern Berlin's trendiest bars, thanks to over-the-top designer furniture and fashion-conscious clientele.

VEB OZ Auguststr. 92. Hopelessly tacky but fun bar that attracts a crowd of punks and their admirers. Often loud but usually amiable nevertheless.

Zum Nussbaum Am Nussbaum 3. In the heart of the Nikolaiviertel and overshadowed by the Nikolaikirche, this is a convincing 1980s replica of a prewar *Kneipe*.

Discos, clubs and rock venues

90 Grad Dennewitzstr. 37. Practically an institution, this long-lived, predominantly gay club still maintains its cutting edge, although gaining entry is never a formality.

ColumbiaFritz Columbiadamm 9–11 ⓣ0 30/6 98 12 80. Renovated 1950s movie theatre with a very modern light show. Now hosts moderately good rock groups.

Duncker Dunckerstr. 64 ⓣ0 30/4 45 95 09. Indie gigs and frequent club evenings attract a party-hard local crowd. Small but atmospheric venue with deep sofas inside and open-air gigs in the back yard in summer.

Junction Bar Gneisenaustr. 18 ⓣ0 30/6 94 66 02. A fixture on the local jazz circuit, with nightly concerts and DJs at the weekends.

Matrix Warschauer Platz 18. Famous disco that aims to satisfy all tastes across three dance floors. House, soul, rock and more.

Privat Club Pücklerstr. 34. Highly intimate basement club with an eclectic and often unpredictable mix of sounds and cartoons flickering across the walls.

SO 36 Oranienstr. 190. Dark and punky cult club with a mainly gay and lesbian following. Spontaneous outbreaks of belly-dancing are not unknown.

Sophienclub Sophienstr. 6. Equal numbers of loyal locals and curious tourists let their hair down at this large basement club with a new 70s-style facelift.

Classical music

Deutsche Oper Bismarckstr. 35 ⓣ0 30/3 41 02 49. Good Classical concerts, plus opera and ballet in a large, modern venue.

Komische Oper Behrenstr. 55–57 ⓣ0 30/47 99 74 00. The house orchestra performs classical and contemporary music, and some very good opera productions are staged here.

Konzerthaus Berlin Schauspielhaus am Gendarmenmarkt, Gendarmenmarkt 2 ⓣ0 30/2 03 09 21 01. Home to the Berlin Sinfonie Orchester and host to visiting orchestras.

Philharmonie Herbert-von-Karajan-Str. 1 ⓣ0 30/25 48 80. Custom-built home of the world's most celebrated orchestra, the Berlin Philharmonic. In 2002 musical director Sir Simon Rattle takes over from Claudio Abbado.

Staatsoper Unter den Linden 7 ⓣ0 30/20 35 45 55. Excellent operatic productions in one of central Berlin's most beautiful buildings.

Theatre

Berliner Ensemble Bertolt-Brecht-Platz 1 ⓣ0 30/2 82 31 60. The official Brecht theatre.

Maxim Gorki Theater Am Festungsgraben 2 ⓣ0 30/20 22 11 15. Consistently good productions of modern works.

Schaubühne am Lehniner Platz Kurfürstendamm 153 ⓣ0 30/89 00 23. State-of-the-art theatre for

performances of the classics and some experimental pieces.
Varieté Chamäleon Rosenthaler Str. 40–41, Mitte ☎0 30/2 82 71 18. Cabaret and variety theatre in the beautiful early twentieth-century Hackescher Höfe complex.

Listings

Bicycle rental Fahradstation, Friedrichstrasse station ☎0 30/20 45 45 00; Pedal Power, Grossbeerenstr. 53 ☎0 30/78 99 19 39. From €10/day, €35/week; deposit, insurance payment and passport required.
Embassies and consulates Australia, Friedrichstr. 200 ☎0 30/8 80 08 80; Canada, Friedrichstr. 95 ☎0 30/20 31 20; Ireland, Friedrichstr. 200 ☎0 30/22 07 20; New Zealand, Friedrichstr. 60 ☎0 30/20 62 10; UK, Wilhelmstr. 70/71 ☎0 30/20 45 70; US, Neustädtische Kirchstr. 4–5 ☎0 30/2 38 51 74.
Exchange ReiseBank, at the main entrance to the Zoo Station (daily 7.30am–10pm) and in the Friedrichstrasse station (daily 7.30am–7.30pm).

Hospitals Charité University Clinic, Schumannstr. 20/21 ☎0 30/2 80 20; Prenzlauer Berg Hospital, Fröbelstr. 15 ☎0 30/4 24 20; Spandau Hospital, Neue Bergstr. 6 ☎0 30/3 38 70.
Internet easyEverything, corner of Kurfürstendamm and Meinekestr; Surf and Sushi, Oranienburgerstr. 17.
Laundry Rosenthaler Str. 71; Hermannstr. 74–75.
Left luggage At major stations, such as Zoo and Friedrichstrasse.
Pharmacies Europa-Apotheke, Europa Center, Tauentzienstr. 9.
Police Platz der Luftbrücke 6 ☎0 30/69 95.
Post office Joachimsthaler Str. 7.

Eastern Germany

By the time the former German Democratic Republic was fully incorporated into the Federal Republic of Germany, just one year after the peaceful revolution of autumn 1989 (the so-called Wende), most vestiges of the old political system had been swept away. Yet there is still a long way to go before the two parts of the country achieve parity, and the cities of eastern Germany remain in the process of social and economic change. While for visitors this transformation can be fascinating, for many citizens of the former GDR it is problematic.

Berlin stands apart from the rest of the east, but its sense of excitement finds an echo in the two other main cities – **Leipzig**, which provided the vanguard of the revolution, and **Dresden**, the beautiful Saxon capital so ruthlessly destroyed in 1945. Equally enticing are some of the smaller places, which retain more of the appearance and atmosphere of prewar Germany than anywhere in the west, notably **Erfurt**, capital of the ancient province of Thuringia, nearby **Weimar**, the small cathedral towns of **Naumburg** and **Meissen**, and the old Prussian royal seat of **Potsdam**. Although much of eastern Germany is monotonous – its heartland was once a vast swamp – it is by no means the drab industrial landscape you might imagine.

Potsdam

The favourite residence of Frederick the Great, **POTSDAM** is an easy and excellent day-trip from Berlin. From Alexanderplatz, Friedrichstrasse or Zoologischer Garten S-Bahn line #7 will take you directly to Potsdam's main station. This lies on the opposite side of the Havel from the historic centre, whose skyline is dominated by the huge dome of the Nikolaikirche, one of Schinkel's most admired designs, albeit one that was built posthumously.

Stretching for 2km west of the centre is **Park Sanssouci** (daily 9am–dusk; free; joint ticket covering entry to the Schloss, Bildergalerie, Neue Kammern, Orangerie and Neues Palais €15; ☻www.spsg.de), the fabled retreat of the Prussian kings. These days it's too often overrun by visitors – to avoid the crowds, visit on a weekday, Frederick the Great worked closely with his court architect Georg Wenzeslaus von Knobelsdorff on designing **Schloss Sanssouci** (tours Tues–Sun 9am–4/5pm; €8), which was to be a place where the king could escape Berlin and his wife Elizabeth Christine, neither of which he cared for. Begun in 1744, it's a surprisingly modest one-storey Baroque affair, topped by a copper dome and ornamental statues looking out over vine terraces. Frederick loved the Schloss so much that he intended to be buried here, and had a tomb excavated for himself in front of the eastern wing; in 1991 his body was finally moved here. Inside is a frenzy of Rococo, spread through the twelve rooms where Frederick lived and entertained his guests. The most eye-catching chambers are the opulent **Marble Hall** and the **Concert Room**, where the flute-playing king had eminent musicians play his own works on concert evenings.

West of the palace, overlooking the ornamental Holländischer Garten, is the **Bildergalerie** (mid-May to mid-Oct Tues–Sun 10am–5pm; €2), a restrained Baroque creation that contains paintings by Rubens, Van Dyck and Caravaggio. On the opposite side of the Schloss, steps lead down to the **Neue Kammern** (mid-May to mid-Oct Tues–Sun 10am–5pm; €3), the architectural twin of the Bildergalerie, originally used as an orangery and later as a guest house. Immediately to the west of the Neue Kammern is the prim Sizilianischer Garten, crammed with coniferous trees and subtropical plants, complementing the Nordische Garten just to the north.

From the west of the Sizilianischer Garten, Maulbeerallee cuts through the park and ascends to the **Orangerie** (mid-May to mid-Oct Tues–Sun 10am–5pm; €3), an Italianate Renaissance-style structure with belvedere towers. A series of terraces with curved retaining walls sporting water spouts in the shape of lions' heads leads to the sandy-coloured building, whose slightly down-at-heel appearance lends it added character.

To the west through the trees rises the **Neues Palais** (9am–4/5pm, closed Fri; €5), another massive Rococo extravaganza from Frederick's time. The main entrance is on the western facade, approached via gates flanked by stone sentry boxes. The interior is predictably opulent, though a couple of highlights stand out: the vast and startling Grottensaal on the ground floor decorated entirely with shells and semi-precious stones to form images of lizards and dragons, and the equally huge Marmorsaal, with its beautiful floor of patterned marble slabs. The southern wing (which these days houses a small café) contains Frederick's apartments and the theatre where the king enjoyed Italian opera and French plays.

Leipzig

LEIPZIG has always been among the most dynamic of German cities. Its trade fairs have a tradition dating back to the Middle Ages and remained important during the Communist years, so that there was never the degree of isolation from outside influences experienced by so many cities behind the Iron Curtain.

Most points of interest are conveniently placed within the old centre. Following Nikolaistrasse due south from the train station brings you to the **Nikolaikirche**, one of the two main civic churches and a rallying point during the Wende. Although a sombre medieval structure outside, inside the church is a real eye-grabber, its coffered vault supported by fluted columns whose capitals sprout like palm trees. A couple of blocks to the west is the Markt, whose eastern side is entirely occupied by the **Altes Rathaus** (Tues–Sun 10am–6pm; €2.50, free first Sun in month), built in the grandest German Renaissance style with elaborate gables, an asymmetrical tower and the longest inscription to be found on any building in the world. The ground floor retains its traditional function as a covered walkway with shops; the upper storeys now house the local-history museum. On the north side of the square is another handsome public building from Renaissance times, the old weighing house or **Alte Waage**. To the rear of the Altes Rathaus, approached by a graceful double flight of steps, is the **Alte Handelsbörse**, a Baroque gem that was formerly the trade exchange headquarters. The nearby Handelshof at Grimmaische Str. 1–7 is the temporary home of the **Museum der Bildenden Künste** (Tues & Thurs–Sun 10am–6pm, Wed 1–9.30pm; €2.50), a distinguished collection of old masters, including Cranach, Hals and Rubens. This is due to move into its new custom-built premises on Sachsenplatz in late 2003.

Following Barfussgässchen off the western side of the Markt brings you to Kleine Fleischergasse and the cheerful Baroque **Zum Coffe Baum**. One of the German pioneers of the coffee craze that followed the Turkish invasion of central Europe in the late seventeenth century, it gained further fame courtesy of Robert Schumann, who came here regularly. On its second floor is the **Museum Coffe Baum** (daily 11am–7pm; free), which illustrates the history of European coffee culture. Klostergasse leads southwards to the Thomaskirche, the senior of the two big civic churches, and the place where Johann Sebastian Bach served for the last 27 years of his life. Predominantly Gothic, the church has been altered down the centuries, notably by the addition of the galleries in line with the Protestant emphasis on preaching. The most remarkable feature is its musical tradition: the **Thomanerchor**, which Bach once directed, can usually be heard on Fridays (6pm), Saturdays (3pm) and during the Sunday service (9.30am). Directly across from the church is the **Bach–Museum** (daily 10am–5pm; €3; ⓦwww.bach-leipzig.de), with an extensive show of mementos of the great composer. Close by, at Dittrichring 24, is another historically important museum, the Round Corner or **Runde Ecke** (daily 10am–6pm; free), which commemorates victims who suffered at the hands of the Stasi, East Germany's secret police.

The southeastern part of the Altstadt is the academic quarter. On Schillerstrasse, east of the Neues Rathaus, the **Egyptian Museum** (Tues–Sat 1–5pm, Sun 10am–1pm; €2) contains nineteenth-century finds by archeologists from Leipzig University. Beyond is a fragment of the old fortifications, the **Moritzbastei**, beside which stands the **Gewandhaus**, the ultramodern home of the oldest orchestra in the world, and still one of the best.

Practicalities

The enormous **train station** is at the northeastern end of the Ring, which encircles the old part of the city. The **tourist office**, directly opposite at Richard-Wagner Str. 1 (Mon–Fri 9am–7pm, Sat 9am–4pm, Sun 9am–2pm; ☏03 41/7 10 42 60, ⓦwww.leipzig.de), can book private rooms (❸) and sells the Leipzig Card (€5.90/day, €11.50/three days), which covers public transport costs plus entrance fees to the main museums and sights.

Other **accommodation** options include the privately owned *Hostel Sleepy Lion*, just west of the centre at Käthe Kollwitz-Str. 3 (☏03 41/9 93 94 80, ⓦwww.hostel-leipzig.de; ❷); the HI hostel at Volksgartenstr. 24 (☏03 41/24 57 00, ✉jhleipzig@djh-sachsen.de; ❷; tram #1 to Löbauer Strasse); and the campsite, *Auensee*, at Gustav-Esche-Str. 5 (☏03 41/4 65 16 00; tram #10). Most hotels and pensions are prohibitively priced: exceptions include *Weisses Ross*, Ross-Str. 20 (☏03 41/9 60 59 51; ❹), and the two pensions, *Am Nordplatz*, Nordstr. 58 (☏03 41/9 60 31 43; ❺), a short walk west of the train station, and *Christin*, south of the centre at Kochstr. 4 (☏03 41/2 32 93 66; ❹).

Leipzig offers mainly traditional German taverns with the occasional ethnic restaurant, giving a good choice when it comes to **eating**. Many of the best spots are conveniently close to the Markt. *Zum Coffe Baum*, Kleine Fleischergasse 4, is unmissable, whether for *Kaffee und Kuchen* or a full meal. Tucked underneath the Mädler-Passage, one of the covered shopping malls off Grimmaischer Strasse at the southeastern end of the Markt, is *Auerbachs Keller*, an historic and quite formal restaurant that was the setting for a scene in Goethe's *Faust*. Good choices for a hearty, reasonably priced German meal are the rambling old *Thüringer Hof*, Burgstr. 19, and *Apels Garten*, Kolonnadenstr. 2, which uses recipes from a 300-year-old cookbook. *Varadero*, Barfussgässchen 8, is a popular Cuban restaurant – a hangover of the political allegiances of the recent past – specializing in grills and cocktails. *Spizz*, Markt 9, is a live music bar with regular jazz features. The city is also famous for its satirical **cabaret**: if your German's up to it, try Pfeffermühle in the same building as the Bach-Museum, or SanftWut in the Mädler-Passage.

Naumburg

The old cathedral city of **NAUMBURG** is situated on the fast rail line between Leipzig and Weimar, and reachable from both in well under an hour. Rather neglected in recent decades, it is well on the way to reclaiming its former status as one of Germany's most distinctive towns. The historic centre, set on heights overlooking the Saale valley, is dominated by the **Dom**, which shows medieval German architecture and sculpture at their peak. Though it was built as the seat of the local prince-bishop, with choirs at both ends of the building to emphasize its status as an imperial cathedral, it has been no more than a Protestant parish church since the Reformation. The thirteenth-century builders began by erecting the eastern choir, complete with its almost Oriental towers, in a florid Romanesque style. However, by the time the west choir was finished – minus one of the towers, which was finally built to the original plans a century ago – Gothic had taken over completely. Pride of the **interior** (April–Sept Mon–Sat 9am–6pm, Sun noon–6pm; reduced hours out of season; €4) are the sculptures by the so-called **Master of Naumburg**. His rood screen, illustrating the Passion, imbues the figures with a humanity and a realism previously absent from religious art, and the twelve life-size statues of the Dom's founders in the west choir are each given a distinctive characterization. Particularly outstanding are the couple Ekkehardt and Uta, who have come to symbolize the Germans' romantic view of their chivalric medieval past.

From the Dom, Steinweg and then Herrenstrasse – each with its fair share of fine houses – lead eastwards to the central **Markt**. The square is dominated by the Renaissance **Rathaus**, whose huge curved gables served as a model for other mansions in the city. Rising to the south is the curiously elongated **Stadtkirche St Wenzel**, which was the burghers' answer to the prince-bishop's Dom. In the Baroque period, this late Gothic church was given an interior face-lift, including the provision of a magnificent organ; look out also for two paintings by Cranach.

More fine mansions are to be seen on Jakobstrasse, which leads eastwards from the Markt. Also well worth a visit is the **Marientor**, at the edge of the inner ring road directly to the north of the Markt. This double gateway, one of the best-preserved in the country, is the only significant reminder these days of the fifteenth-century fortifications.

Naumburg's **train station** is northwest of the historic centre. The **tourist office** at Markt 6 (Mon–Fri 9am–6pm, Sat 9am–2/4pm, Sun 10am–1pm; Nov–March closed Sun; ☎0 34 45/20 16 14, ⊛www.naumburg-tourismus.de) can book private rooms (❷). Alternatively, there's a HI **hostel** way to the south of the centre at Am Tennisplatz 9 (☎0 34 45/70 34 22, ⊜jh-naumburg@djh-sachsen-anhalt.de; ❷). **Hotels** include *Zum Alten Krug*, Lindenring 44 (☎0 34 45/20 04 06; ❹). Among **restaurants**, the *Ratskeller* in the Rathaus and *Café Kaffeklatsch*, Herrenstr. 9, are recommended.

Weimar

Despite its modest size, **WEIMAR** has played a role in the development of German culture that is unmatched: Goethe, Schiller, Herder and Nietzsche all made it their home, as did the Cranachs and Bach, and the architects and designers of the Bauhaus school. Its part in the politics of Germany is scarcely less significant: Weimar was chosen as the seat of government of the democratic republic established after World War I, a regime whose failure ended with the Nazi accession. One of the most notorious concentration camps was to be built here, and its preservation is a shocking reminder of Germany's double-edged contribution to the history of modern Europe. It served as European City of Culture in 1999, and for the years prior to this was subject to a frantic programme of restoration that has once again established its immaculate appearance.

The Town

Weimar preserves the appearance and atmosphere of its heyday as the capital of the Duchy of Saxe-Weimar, whose population never rose much above 100,000. The seat of power was the **Schloss** (Tues–Sun 10am–4.30/6pm; €4; ⚉www.kunst-sammlungen-weimar.de), set by the River Ilm at the eastern edge of the town centre, a Neoclassical complex of a size more appropriate for ruling a mighty empire. On the ground floor is a collection of old masters, including pieces by both Cranachs, and Dürer's portraits of the Nürnberg patrician couple, Hans and Elspeth Tucher. Upstairs are some fine original interiors and German paintings from the Enlightenment era.

Just west of the Schloss on Herderplatz stands the **Stadtkirche St Peter und Paul** (daily 10/11am–noon & 2–3/4pm), usually known as the Herderkirche in honour of the poet who was its pastor for three decades. Inside are several impressive tombs plus a large triptych by the Cranachs. South of Herderplatz is the spacious **Markt**, lined by an unusually disparate jumble of buildings, of which the most eye-catching is the green and white gabled **Stadthaus** on the eastern side, opposite the neo-Gothic **Rathaus**. Schillerstrasse snakes away from the southwest corner of the Markt to the **Schillerhaus** (9am–4/6pm, closed Tues; €3), the home of the poet, dramatist and historian for the last three years of his life. Beyond lies Theaterplatz, in the centre of which is a large monument to Goethe and Schiller. The **Nationaltheater** on the west side of the square was founded and directed by Goethe, though the present building, for all its stern Neoclassical appearance, is a modern pastiche. Opposite is the **Wittumspalais** (Tues–Sun 9/10am–4/6pm; €3), a Baroque palace containing some of the finest interiors of Weimar plus mementos of the Enlightenment philosopher-poet, Christoph-Martin Wieland.

Last of the literary museums is **Goethewohnhaus und Nationalmuseum** (Tues–Sun 9am–4/6pm; €5), on Frauenplan south of the Markt, where Goethe lived for some fifty years until his death in 1832. In the adjoining museum his achievement is chronicled with typically Teutonic detail. From the Goethewohnhaus, Marienstrasse continues to the **Liszthaus** (Tues–Sun 9am–1pm & 2–4/6pm; €2), home of the Hungarian composer and virtuoso pianist for the last seventeen years of his life, when he was director of Weimar's orchestra and opera. A few minutes' walk west down Geschwister-Scholl-Strasse is the **Hochschule für Architektur und Bauwesen**, where Walter Gropius established the original Bauhaus in 1919. Further to the west is the **Alter Friedhof** or Old Cemetery, site of the Neoclassical mausoleum of Goethe and Schiller (9am–1pm & 2–4/6pm, closed Tues; €1.50).

The **Park an der Ilm** stretches from the Schloss to the southern edge of town on both sides of the river. Almost due east of the Liszthaus, on the opposite bank, is **Goethes Gartenhaus** (9/10am–4/6pm, closed Tues; €2.50), where the writer stayed when he first came to Weimar in 1776 as a ducal administrator. Further south and back on the west bank is the ducal summer house, known as the **Römisches Haus** (9/10am–4/6pm, closed Mon; €2). At the south edge of town, in the suburb of Oberweimar, there's the full-blown summer palace of **Schloss Belvedere** (10am–4.30/6pm, closed Mon; €3; ⚉www.kunstsammlungen-weimar.de), whose light and airy Rococo forms a refreshing contrast to the Neoclassical solemnity of so much of the town. The **orangery** (closed for renovation at time of writing; check with tourist office for latest details) contains a collection of historic coaches, while the surroundings were transformed under Goethe's supervision into a jardin anglais.

Finally, the **Konzentrationslager Buchenwald** (Tues–Sun 8.45/9.45am–5/6pm; free) is situated to the north of Weimar on the Ettersberg heights, and can be reached by bus (hourly from just south of the train station). Over 240,000 prisoners were incarcerated in this concentration camp, with 65,000 dying here, among them the interwar leader of the German Communist Party, Ernst Thälmann. This gave the place a special significance for the GDR authorities, now tarnished by the emergence of evidence that the Russians used it after the war for their own political opponents.

Practicalities

Weimar's **train station**, on the main line between Leipzig and Erfurt, is a twenty-minute walk north of the main sights. One of the **tourist offices** (daily 10am–8pm) is to be found there; another, much larger one, is in the Stadthaus at Markt 10 (Mon–Fri 9.30/10am–6pm, Sat & Sun 9.30/10am–2/4pm; ☎0 36 43/2 40 00, ⊚www.weimar.de). Both can arrange **accommodation** in private rooms (❷). There are neat and tidy HI **hostels** at Humboldtstr. 17 (☎0 36 43/85 07 92; ❷), Carl-August-Allee 13 (☎0 36 43/85 04 90; ❷) and, 5km south of the centre, at Zum Wilden Graben 12 (☎0 36 43/85 07 50; ❷). Reasonably priced **pensions** include *Am Berkaer Bahnhof*, Peter-Cornelius-Str. 7 (☎0 36 43/20 20 10; ❹), and the tastefully furnished *Savina II*, Meyerstr. 60 (☎0 36 43/8 66 90; ❸). The *Residenz-Café* on Grüner Markt is recommended for coffee and cakes, and you shouldn't leave Weimar without sampling a Thuringian bratwurst, reputedly the most flavoursome variety in Germany. For a more substantial meal, try the places on the Markt, such as the inevitable *Ratskeller* or the atmospheric and surprisingly affordable *Elephantenkeller* under the Hotel Elephant.

Erfurt

Of all Germany's major cities, it's **ERFURT**, twenty minutes from Weimar by train, that is most redolent of prewar Germany. Although it lost a couple of important monuments in bombing raids, it was otherwise little damaged in World War II, while its streets of grandiose *fin-de-siècle* shops were saved by the Communist authorities from the developers who would have demolished them had the city been on the other side of the Iron Curtain.

The vast open space of the Domplatz is the heart of the city centre. Imperiously set on the hill above, and reached via a monumental stairway, the **Dom** perches on a mighty fortress-like crypt. It's entered by a magnificent fourteenth-century porch, which bears statues of the Apostles on one side, the Wise and Foolish Virgins on the other. Inside, the richly carved stalls and gleaming windows in the choir stand out, and the nave is jam-packed with works of art, the most notable being the so-called Wolfram, a Romanesque candelabrum in the shape of a man, and a spectacular font. Alongside the Dom is the **Severikirche**, a pure early Gothic hall church containing the tomb of the saint after whom it's named, a fourteenth-century masterpiece by an anonymous sculptor whose work adorns several of the city's churches.

From Domplatz, Marktstrasse leads east to Fischmarkt, lined by handsome Renaissance mansions and the nineteenth-century **Rathaus**. Just beyond is the **Krämerbrücke**: walking along, you have the illusion of entering a narrow medieval alley but it is actually a bridge lined with shops and galleries. On the west bank, to the north of the Krämerbrücke, is the imposing Gothic facade of the **University**; the rest of the building was a casualty of World War II. However, its outstanding collection of old manuscripts survived, as did the academic church, the **Michaeliskirche**, which has a fine late Gothic chapel.

Across the river is the **Augustinerkloster** (tours Mon–Sat 10am–noon & 2–4/5pm, Sun 11am; Nov–March closed Mon; €3.10; ⊚www.augustinerkloster .de), one of many monasteries in Erfurt, the profusion of which earned the town its nickname of "little Rome". This one is best known – it was here that Luther served as a novice, then a monk, between 1505 and 1511. A visit to his cell forms part of the tour, which also includes the cloister and the typically austere church, which is enlivened by a fine stained-glass window depicting the life of St Augustine.

Of the other monastic churches, pride of place goes to the **Predigerkirche** just south of Fischmarkt. Built by the Dominicans, it's extremely plain on the outside, but the interior is a masterpiece of spatial harmony in the purest Gothic style, and has preserved its layout and furnishings intact. Bombing wrecked the nave of the Franciscan **Barfüsserkirche**, over the river to the south, but the choir has been restored to house a small museum of religious art (April–Oct Tues–Sun 10am–1pm & 2–6pm; €1). This is a branch of the **Angermuseum** (Tues–Sun 10am–6pm; €1.50), in a Baroque mansion at the intersection of two of the main shopping streets, Bahnhofstrasse and Anger. Highlight here is the display of medieval artefacts, including more sculptures by the master who carved the tomb in the Severikirche. A fine collection of German painting from the Renaissance to modern times is also featured.

Erfurt's **train station** is situated at the southeastern corner of the city centre. The **tourist office** (Mon–Fri 10am–6/7pm, Sat & Sun 10am–4pm; ☎03 61/6 64 00, ⓦwww.erfurt-tourist-info.de) at Fischmarkt 27 can book **rooms** in private houses and small pensions (❸). There are two HI hostels south of the centre: one at Hochheimerstr. 12 (☎03 61/5 62 67 05, ⓔjh-erfurt@djh-thueringen.de; ❷; tram #5 to the Steigerstrasse terminus) and a smaller, pricier one at Klingenstr. 4 (same contact details; ❸). Reasonably priced hotels include *Daberstedt*, Buddestr. 2 (☎03 61/3 73 34 61; ❸), and *Haus zum Pfauen*, Marbacher Gasse 12–13 (☎03 61/2 11 11 00; ❸). The latter has a **restaurant** and brews its own beer according to a six-teenth-century recipe.

Dresden

Generally regarded as Germany's most beautiful and culturally significant city, **DRESDEN** survived World War II largely unscathed until the night of February 13, 1945. Then, in a matter of hours, it was reduced to ruins in the most savage sat-uration bombing ever mounted prior to Vietnam – according to official figures at least 35,000 civilians died (though the total was probably considerably higher), as the city was packed with people fleeing the advancing Red Army. With this back-ground, it's all the more remarkable that Dresden is the one city in the former GDR that has slotted easily into the economic framework of the reunited Germany, and the post-Communist authorities are now brilliantly restoring the his-toric buildings. Today Dresden is a dynamic gateway between the East and West.

Arrival, information and accommodation

Dresden has two main **train stations** – the Hauptbahnhof, south of the Altstadt, and the Neustadt, at the northwestern corner of the Neustadt district across the Elbe and only slightly further away from the main sights. One of the **tourist offices** (Mon–Fri 9am–7pm, Sat 9am–4pm; ☎03 51/49 19 20, ⓦwww.dresden-tourist.de) is in a pavilion at Prager Str. 10, a short walk from the Hauptbahnhof; the other is in the heart of the Altstadt, in the Schinkelwache on Theaterplatz (Mon–Fri 10am–6pm, Sat & Sun 10am–4pm). Both sell the Dresden Card (€16/two days), which covers public transport, entry to twelve museums and sundry discounts. Otherwise, there's the 24-hour transport ticket (€4) and a sepa-rate day ticket for the museums (€6.10).

The tourist offices can book private **rooms** and **pensions** (❸). There are two privately owned **hostels** in Neustadt, well placed for nightlife in the Hechtviertel artists' ghetto: the supremely relaxed and homely *Mondpalast*, Katharinenstr. 11–13 (☎03 51/8 04 60 61, ⓦwww.mondpalast.de; ❷), and the brand-new *Die Boofe*, Hechtstr. 10 (☎03 51/8 01 33 61, ⓦwww.boofe.com; ❷; tram #8 from the Hauptbahnhof to Bischofsweg), which has its own sauna. The much larger HI hos-tel is just to the southwest of the Altstadt sights at Maternistr. 22 (☎03 51/49 26 20; ❸). Another hostel offering excellent rooms at the price is the *City-Herberge*, just to the east of the Altstadt at Lingnerallee 3 (☎03 51/4 85 99 00; ❸). Among the budg-et **hotels** are *Am Birkenhain*, Barbarastr. 76 (☎03 51/8 51 40; ❹), which lies close to the Pieschen S-Bahn station. Unless you're travelling alone, the three gargantuan Ibis hotels on Prager Str. are good value; try *Königstein* (☎03 51/4 85 64 42, ⓦwww.ibishotel.com; ❺). The *Mockritz* **campsite** is at Boderitzer Str. 30 (☎03 51/4 71 52 50; bus #76 from the Hauptbahnhof).

The City

If you arrive at the Hauptbahnhof, you see the worst of modern Dresden first: the **Prager Strasse**, a vast Stalinist pedestrian precinct with the standard cocktail of high-rise luxury hotels, public offices, boxlike flats and a few fountains and statues thrown in for relief. At the far end, beyond the inner ring road, is the **Altmarkt**, which was much extended after its wartime destruction; the only building of note that remains is the **Kreuzkirche**, a church which mixes a Baroque body with a Neoclassical tower. On Saturdays at 6pm, and at the 9.30am Sunday service, you can usually hear the **Kreuzchor**, one of the world's leading church choirs. Behind stands the **Rathaus**, built in the early twentieth century in a lumbering Historicist style.

North of here, the **Albertinum** (10am–6pm, closed Thurs; €3.60; ⓦwww.staatl-kunstsammlungen-dresden.de) houses the Gemäldegalerie Neue Meister, whose highlights include one of the greatest of Romantic paintings, Friedrich's *Cross in the Mountains*. Works by most of the French Impressionists and their German contemporaries precede a section devoted to the Expressionists of the Brücke group, which was founded in Dresden. For the time being, the Albertinum is also home to the major part of the **Grünes Gewölbe** or Green Vault, a dazzling array of treasury items including the Baroque fancies created by the Saxon Electors' own jeweller, Johann Melchior Dinglinger.

West of the Albertinum is the **Neumarkt**, formerly dominated by the round, domed Frauenkirche. Only a fragment of wall was left standing after the war, and the Communists decided to leave it in this condition as a memorial. After fierce controversy, the decision was taken in 1991 to rebuild it completely, and you can now savour the slightly odd experience of watching a Baroque church rise from a modern building site.

The colossal **Residenzschloss** (Tues–Sun 10am–6pm; €2.60; ⓦwww.staatl-kunstsammlungen-dresden.de) of the Electors of Saxony was also wrecked in the war, and the rebuilding programme now under way is a massive task, though the projected completion date of 2006 – the city's 800th anniversary – now looks achievable. Sooner or later, the miraculously preserved **Mirror Rooms** (currently closed) will re-house the entire Grünes Gewölbe collection; in the meantime, an exhibition on the history of the building in the Georgenbau includes reconstructed display cabinets in which some of the older items are displayed. The main tower, the **Hausmannsturm**, can be ascended (April–Oct only; included in entrance ticket) for a view over the complex and the city. At the end of nearby Augustusstrasse is the Baroque **Hofkirche** (or Dom). The existence of this Catholic church in a staunchly Protestant province is explained by the fact that the Saxon rulers converted in order to gain the Polish throne. In the gleaming white interior is an ornate pulpit by the great sculptor of Dresden Baroque, **Balthasar Permoser**. The plush **Staatsoper** (tours at times posted; €5) opposite was built by the leading architect of nineteenth-century Dresden, Gottfried Semper, and saw the first performances of Wagner's *The Flying Dutchman* and *Tannhäuser*, and Richard Strauss's *Der Rosenkavalier*.

The Zwinger

Baroque Dresden's great glory was the palace known as the **Zwinger**, which faces the Residenzschloss. Less severely damaged in the war, it was quickly restored, and is currently undergoing further repairs. It's a daringly original building: a vast open space with fountains surrounded by a single-storey gallery linking two-storey pavilions, and entered by grandiose gateways. The effect is further enhanced by superbly expressive decoration by Permoser.

The Zwinger contains several museums. Beautifully displayed in the southeastern pavilion, entered from Sophienstrasse, is the **Porzellansammlung** (ⓦwww.staatl-kunstsammlungen-dresden.de); products from the famous Meissen factory are extensively featured. A small natural history display, the **Tierkundemuseum** (Wed–Mon 9am–5pm; €1), is housed in the southern gallery. The southwestern pavilion is known as the **Mathematisch-Physikalischer Salon** (10am–6pm, closed Thurs; €1.50), and offers a fascinating array of globes, clocks and scientific instruments. In the northeastern part of the nineteenth-century extension by Semper is the **Rüstkammer** (Tues–Sun 10am–6pm; €1.60; ⓦwww.staatl-kunst-sammlungen-dresden.de), housing an armoury, including the sword of Elector Frederick the Valiant, and the coronation robes of Augustus the Strong.

The extension also contains the **Gemäldegalerie Alte Meister** (Tues–Sun 10am–6pm; €3.60; ⓦwww.staatl-kunstsammlungen-dresden.de). The Saxon Electors' collection of old masters ranks among the dozen best in the world, and includes some of the most familiar Italian Renaissance paintings: Raphael's *Sistine Madonna*, Titian's *Christ and the Pharisees* and Veronese's *Marriage at Cana*. The German section includes Dürer's *Dresden Altarpiece*, Holbein's *Le Sieur de Morette* and Cranach's *Duke Henry the Pious*. Van Eyck's *Madonna and Child* triptych, executed with miniaturist precision, kicks off a distinguished Low Countries section in which Rubens and Rembrandt are extensively featured.

The Neustadt and Schloss Pillnitz

Across the Elbe, the Neustadt was a planned Baroque town and its layout is still obvious, even if few of the original buildings survive. In the centre of the Markt rises the **Goldener Reiter**, a gilded equestrian statue of the Elector Augustus the Strong. The Neustadt's central axis, Hauptstrasse, preserves several Baroque houses by Pöppelmann, along with the same architect's Dreikönigskirche, only recently restored following war damage. In the park overlooking the Elbe is the most esoteric creation of Dresden Baroque, the **Japanisches Palais**, which now contains archeological and ethnographic museums (Tues–Sun 10am–6pm; various entry fees). You don't have to pay to see the courtyard, a fantasy inspired by the eighteenth-century infatuation with the Orient.

Schloss Pillnitz, which lies 10km up the Elbe at the extreme edge of the city boundary, is another Pöppelmann creation, completed in 1830 and inspired by the mystique of the East; it's also the only part of the city's Baroque heritage to escape war damage altogether. There are actually two summer palaces here: the **Wasserpalais** (May–Oct 9.30am–5.30pm, closed Tues; €1.60; ⓦwww.staatl-kunst-sammlungen-dresden.de), directly above the river, contains a museum of applied arts; the **Bergpalais** (May–Oct Tues–Sun 9.30am–5pm; €1.60), across the courtyard, is an almost exact replica, whose apartments are themselves the main exhibits. Pillnitz can be reached directly by taking tram #1 or #2 from Postplatz to Comeniusplatz and changing there to bus #83.

Eating, drinking and nightlife

There's a wide choice of **restaurants** in Dresden. Options in the Altstadt include the *Ratskeller*, Dr-Kulz-Ring 19, which serves hearty local dishes; *Szeged*, Wilsdruffer Str. 4, offering both Hungarian and German cuisine; and the three establishments in the Italienisches Dörfchen, Theaterplatz 3. In Neustadt, *Am Thor*, Hauptstr. 35, is a worthy survivor from GDR days; *Kügelgenhaus*, Hauptstr. 13, is an atmospheric restaurant-cum-beer cellar in a fine Baroque building; *El Perro Borracho* is a highly regarded Spanish eatery in the intriguing Kunsthof alleyway off Alaunstrasse; and *Pfund's*, Bautzner Str. 79, is a café/restaurant attached to a wonderful dairy shop with immaculately restored Jugendstil decor. Far less formal is the *Schlemmerland* complex on Pragerstr., where you'll find plenty of cheap and cheerful fast-food outlets under one roof. At night, the liveliest areas are the outer fringes of the Neustadt, and the Univiertel to the south of the Hauptbahnhof. Trendy **bars** in the former include *Raskolnikov*, Böhmische Str. 34, and *Planwirtschaft*, Louisenstr. 20; in the latter, *Café B. liebig*, Liebigstr. 24, and *Müllers Café*, Bergstr. 78, are two enduring favourites. *Scheune*, Alaunstr. 36–40, is a Neustadt arts centre with a café, beer garden, live music and theatre and gay and lesbian nights, while *Mona Lisa* on the corner of Louisenstr. and Kamenzerstr. is an achingly hip haunt for locals.

Meissen

The porcelain-producing town of **MEISSEN** is one of the most photogenic cities in Germany. Unlike Dresden, it survived World War II almost unscathed. Walking towards the centre from the train station, you see the commandingly sited castle almost immediately. The present building, the **Albrechtsburg** (daily 10am–5/6pm; closed Jan; €3.50; ❦www.albrechtsburg-meissen.de), is a late fifteenth-century combination of military fortress and residential palace. Cocooned within the castle precinct is the **Dom** (daily 9/10am–4/6pm; €2). For the most part it's a pure Gothic structure, but the distinctive openwork spires that dominate Meissen's skyline were added only in the first decade of the twentieth century. Inside, look out for the superb brass tomb plates of the Saxon dukes; the rood screen with its colourful altarpiece by Cranach; and the statues of the founders in the choir, made in the great Naumburg workshop.

Between the castle hill and the Elbe lies the atmospheric **Altstadt**, a series of twisting and meandering streets. Centrepiece is the **Markt**, dominated by the Renaissance **Rathaus**. On its own small square to the side is the Flamboyant Gothic **Frauenkirche**, whose carillon, fashioned from local porcelain, can be heard six times daily. The church's tower (May–Oct daily 10am–12pm & 1–4pm; €1) commands a superb view of the city. On the terrace just above is the celebrated **Gasthaus Vinzenz Richter**, a half-timbered tavern that preserves an eighteenth-century winepress. The wines served here are said to be the best in eastern Germany.

The **Staatliche Porzellan-Manufaktur Meissen** (tours daily 9am–5/6pm; €3), about 1.5km south of the Markt, is most easily reached by going down Fleischer Gasse, then continuing straight down Neugasse; it's also close to the S-Bahn terminus, Meissen-Triebischtal. Alternatively, there's a city bus from the station (hourly 10am–5pm). This is the latest factory to manufacture Dresden china, whose invention came about when Augustus the Strong imprisoned the alchemist Johann Friedrich Böttger, ordering him to produce some gold. Instead, he invented the first true European porcelain, according to a formula that remains secret. In addition to seeing the works, you can also view the **museum** (same hours; €4.50), which displays many of the factories' finest achievements, most notably some gloriously over-the-top Rococo fripperies made by the most talented artist ever employed here, Joachim Kaendler.

The **tourist office** at Markt 3 (Mon–Fri 9/10am–6pm, Sat & Sun 10am–3/4pm; Jan closed weekends; ☎0 35 21/4 19 40, ❦www.meissen.de) books private **rooms** (❸). There are also a couple of reasonably priced pensions with a central location: *Burkhardt*, Neugasse 29 (☎0 35 21/45 81 98; ❸) and *Im Kleinen Haus*, Leinewebergasse 3 (☎0 35 21/45 30 18). The youth hostel is at Wilsdruffer Str. 28 (☎0 35 21/45 30 65; ❷). For **eating and drinking**, the one unmissable place is the aforementioned *Vinzenz Richter*; other possibilities include *Domkeller*, Domplatz 9, and *Bahrmanns Brauereikeller*, Webergetailsasse 2.

Travel details

Trains

Berlin to: Dresden (every 2hr; 2hr 15min); Frankfurt (hourly; 4hr); Hamburg (hourly; 2hr 30min); Hannover (hourly; 2hr); Leipzig (hourly; 2hr); Munich (every 30min; 7–8hr); Weimar (every 2hr; 3hr).

Cologne to: Aachen (every 30min; 1hr); Düsseldorf (frequent; 25min); Frankfurt (hourly; 2hr 15min); Heidelberg (hourly; 2hr 30min); Mainz (every 20min; 1hr 45min); Stuttgart (hourly; 3hr 25min).

Dresden to: Meissen (every 30min; 50min).

Frankfurt to: Baden-Baden (hourly; 1hr 30min); Berlin (hourly; 4–6hr); Cologne (hourly; 2hr 15min); Hamburg (hourly; 3hr 45min); Hannover (hourly; 2hr 20min); Heidelberg (every 30min; 1hr); Munich (hourly; 4hr); Nürnberg (hourly; 2hr); Würzburg (twice hourly; 1hr).

Hamburg to: Bremen (hourly; 1hr); Hannover (every 30min; 1hr 25min); Lübeck (every 30min; 40min).

Hannover to: Goslar (hourly; 1hr 20min); Heidelberg (every 2hr; 4hr 40min).

Koblenz to: Trier (hourly; 1hr 30min).

Leipzig to: Dresden (hourly; 1hr 40min); Meissen (hourly; 2–3hr); Naumburg (hourly; 35min); Weimar (hourly; 1hr 25min).

Mainz to: Koblenz (frequent; 50min); Worms (every 30min; 40min).

Munich to: Augsburg (every 20min; 30min); Nürnberg (every 30min; 1hr 30min–2hr 30min); Regensburg (hourly; 1hr 30min); Würzburg (every 30min; 2hr 20min).

Nürnberg to: Bamberg (every 30min; 45min); Munich (hourly; 1hr 30min); Regensburg (hourly; 1hr).

Stuttgart to: Freiburg (hourly; 2hr); Heidelberg (every 30min; 1hr); Konstanz (hourly; 2hr 40min).

Greece

Greece highlights

✳ **The Acropolis, Athens** One of the archetypal images of Western culture. See p.496

✳ **Monemvasiá** The old Byzantine town and fortress rise spectacularly from this island-like rock. See p.502

✳ **Olympia** Atmospheric ancient site where the Olympic Games were born. See p.504

✳ **Delphi** Centre of the world, according to the ancient Greeks, and site of the famous oracle. See p.505

✳ **Metéora** Awe-inspiring Byzantine monasteries perched atop extraordinary rock formations. See p.507

✳ **Santoríni (Thíra)** Volcanic island with the most spectacular sunset over the caldera cliff. See p.516

✳ **Knossós, Crete** This 3500-year old palace is the largest and most impressive Minoan site. See p.525

✳ **Samariá Gorge, Crete** This is the longest gorge in Europe, and one of the most beautiful. See p.528

Introduction and basics

With 166 inhabited islands and a landscape that ranges from Mediterranean to Balkan, **Greece** has enough appeal to fill months of travel. The historic sites span four millennia of civilization, encompassing the renowned – such as Mycenae, Olympia, Delphi and the Parthenon in **Athens** – and the obscure, where a visit can still seem like a personal discovery. The **beaches** are distributed along a convoluted coastline equal in length to that of France, and they range from islands where the boat calls once or twice a week to hip, cosmopolitan resorts.

Modern Greece is the sum of an extraordinary diversity of **influences**. Romans, Arabs, Franks, Venetians, Slavs, Albanians, Turks, Italians, to say nothing of the great Byzantine Empire, have all been here and gone since the time of Alexander the Great. All have left their mark: the Byzantines in countless churches and monasteries, and in ghost towns such as **Mystra**; the Venetians in impregnable fortifications such as **Monemvasiá** in the Peloponnese; the Franks in crag-top castles, again in the Peloponnese but also in the east Aegean. Most obvious, perhaps, is the heritage of four hundred years of Ottoman Turkish rule which exercised an inestimable influence on music, cuisine and the way of life.

From even before the fall of Byzantium, the Greek country people – peasants, fishermen, shepherds – created one of the most vigorous and truly **popular cultures** in Europe, which endured until quite recently in the songs and dances, costumes, embroidery, furniture and the white houses of popular image. Since the 1970s most of this has disappeared under the impact of Western consumer values, and is now, at best, relegated to museums, but the architectural and musical heritage in particular have undergone a recent renaissance.

Information and maps

The **National Tourist Organization of Greece (EOT)** publishes an impressive array of free regional pamphlets and maps. There are EOT offices in many of the larger towns and resorts; in other places, try **municipal tourist offices**. The **tourist police**, a branch of the local police, can usually provide you with lists of rooms to let, and will assist if you have a serious complaint about a hotel or restaurant.

The most reliable **maps** of Greece are published in Athens: Road Editions (ⓦwww.road.gr) has the best maps for mountainous regions and islands, while Emvelia Editions (ⓦwww.emvelia.gr) maps include useful town plans.

Money and banks

Greece is one of twelve European Union countries who have switched over to the **euro** (€).

Banks are normally open Mon–Thurs 8am–2pm, Fri 8am–1.30pm. They usually charge a flat fee (€2–3) to exchange money, the National Bank usually being the cheapest; travel agencies and designated money-

Greece on the net

- ⓦ**www.gnto.gr** National tourist board
- ⓦ**www.athensnews.gr** Useful and literate English-language daily
- ⓦ**www.greekislands.gr** Online reservations for travel in the Cyclades and Crete
- ⓦ**www.all-hotels.gr** Comprehensive listings of accommodation facilities
- ⓦ**www.greekferries.gr** Information on ferry and hydrofoil schedules

exchange booths may give a poorer rate, but often levy a sliding two-percent commission, which makes them a better deal than the banks for changing small amounts. There are plenty of **ATMs** that accept foreign cards, especially in resort areas; only Alpha Bank machines accept Amex.

Communications

Post offices are generally open Mon–Fri 7.30am–2pm; in big towns and major tourist centres, hours may extend into the evening and even weekends. **Stamps** can also be bought at kiosks. **Poste restante** is reasonably efficient. American Express holds mail for customers only at its offices in Athens, Thessaloníki, Iráklio, Rhodes and Corfu.

Public phones are almost always card-operated. You can buy phone cards from newsagents and kiosks. It is possible to make collect (reverse-charge) or charge-card calls from these phones, but you need credit on a Greek phone-card to begin. The **operator number** is ☏151 for domestic calls, ☏161 for international. **Internet access** is good; all big towns have several places, and there is usually at least one place on the more visited islands. Prices are around €4.50–6/hr.

Getting around

Though there are a few trains, it is buses that form the basic means of **public transport** on the mainland. And, of course, ferries and hyrdofoils link the mainland to the islands.

Buses

Bus services on the major routes – both on the mainland and islands – are highly efficient, with the national network run by a syndicate of bus companies known as the **KTEL**. However, even in medium-sized towns there can be several widely spaced termini for services in different directions, so make sure you have the right station for your departure. Ticketing is computerized for the major intercity lines, with assigned seating,

so such buses often get fully booked. On smaller rural routes, tickets are generally dispensed on the spot, with some standing allowed. On the islands, buses usually run between the port and main town for ferry arrivals and departures.

Trains

The **rail network**, run by **OSE**, is limited to the mainland, and trains are slower than the equivalent buses – except on the growing number of showcase IC (intercity) lines, which cost more. However, most trains are cheaper than buses, and some of the routes are highlights in their own right. If you're starting a journey at the initial station of a run you can reserve a seat at no extra cost; at most intermediate points, it's first-come, first-served. **Eurail** and **InterRail** are valid, though passholders must make reservations like other passengers.

Ferries and hydrofoils

Schedules for **ferries** and **hydrofoils** are notoriously erratic. The most reliable, up-to-date information is available from the local **port police** (*limenarhío*), at Pireás and on all larger islands. Regular ferry tickets are, in general, best bought on the day of departure, unless you need to reserve a cabin – although from March 23 to 25, over Easter weekend and during August it's best to book several days in advance. The cheapest ticket is **deck class**. **Hydrofoils** and **high-speed catamarans** are roughly twice as fast and twice as expensive as ordinary ferries. In season, **kaïkia** (caiques) sail between adjacent islands, and to a few of the more obscure ones. The only firm information you'll get about them is on the quayside.

Accommodation

Greece has a vast amount of tourist **accommodation**, and most of the year you can rely on turning up pretty much anywhere and finding a room. Only around Easter and in July and August are you likely to experience problems; at these times, it's worth heading off the standard tourist routes, and/or arriving at each new place early in the day.

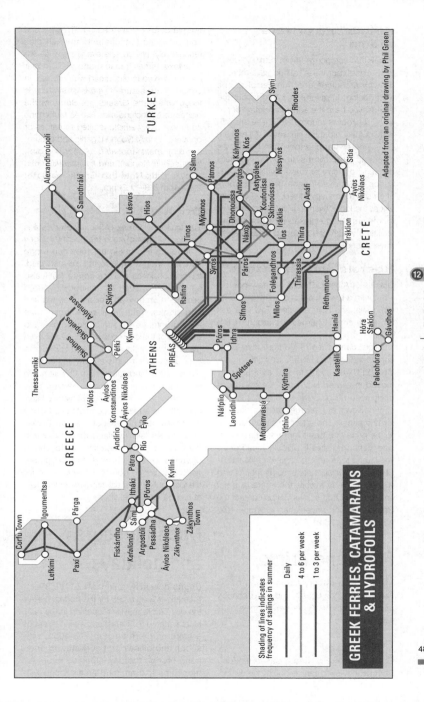

GREEK FERRIES, CATAMARANS & HYDROFOILS

Shading of lines indicates frequency of sailings in summer

Daily

4 to 6 per week

1 to 3 per week

Adapted from an original drawing by Phil Green

GREECE | Basics

12

Hotels and private rooms

Hotels are categorized from "Luxury" down to "E-class", but these ratings have more to do with amenities and number of rooms than pricing. In resorts and throughout the islands, you have the additional option of privately let **rooms** (*dhomátia*). These are officially divided into three classes (A–C) and are often somewhat cheaper than hotels. As often as not, rooms find you: owners descend on ferry or bus arrivals to fill any space they have. In smaller places you'll often see rooms advertised, or you can just ask at the local taverna or café. Increasingly, rooms are being eclipsed by **self-catering** facilities, which can be good value; ask at travel agencies.

Hostels and campsites

Outside of Athens, Greece has few **hostels** – but with a few exceptions, they tend to be run-down, and non- affiliated. Few ever ask for an HI card. Charges are around €8 a night.

Official **campsites** range from fairly basic compounds on the islands to highly organized EOT-run complexes, all generally **closed in winter** (Nov–April). Casual places rarely cost much above €3 a night per person; however, at the larger sites it's possible for two people and a tent to almost add up to the price of a basic room. Camping outside authorized sites is officially forbidden. If you intend to do this, be aware of local sensibilities, especially near seaside resorts and villages. Once in a while the regulations get enforced. For further information contact the Greek Camping Association, Sólonos 102, Athens (☎010 36 21 560).

Food and drink

There's no snobbery about eating out in Greece; everyone does it, and it's reasonably priced – around €13 per person for a meal with house wine.

Food

Greeks generally don't eat breakfast. **Snacks**, however, can be one of the distinc-

tive pleasures of Greek eating. *Tyrópites* and *spanakópites* (cheese and spinach pies respectively) are on sale everywhere, as are *Souvlákia* (small kebabs) and *yíros* (doner kebab), served in *píta* bread with garnish. In choosing a **restaurant**, the best strategy is to go where the Greeks go. Some of the dishes to try include *moussakás* (aubergine and meat pie), *yemistá* (stuffed tomatoes or peppers), *tzatzíki* (yoghurt, garlic and cucumber dip), *melitzanosaláta* (aubergine dip), *khtapódhi* (octopus), and *kalamarákia* (fried baby-squid). Note that Greeks eat **late**: 2.30–4pm & 9–11.30pm.

Drink

The traditional Greek coffee shop or **café** is the central pivot of life in the country villages – although like tavernas, they can range from the sophisticated to the old-fashioned. Its main business is Greek **coffee**, but it also serves spirits such as aniseed-flavoured **oúzo** and brandy, as well as beer, tea and soft drinks. Take your pre-dinner *oúzo* around 6pm, as the sun begins to sink and the heat of the day cools: you'll be served a glass of water alongside, to be tipped into your *oúzo* until it turns a milky white. **Bars** are a 1990s innovation, now ubiquitous in the largest towns and holiday resorts. They are often housed in buildings of historic interest, with the added enticements of a techno soundtrack and ultra-trendy clientele. Drinks, at about €5, are invariably more expensive than at a café. Tavernas offer a better choice of **wines**. Boutari, Tsantali and Calliga are good, low-priced bottles. Otherwise, go for the local bulk wines: ask for *hýma* or *varelísio*, at around €4.50 per litre.

Opening hours and holidays

Shops generally open from 8.30/9.30am, then take a long break for the hottest part of the day before maybe reopening in the mid-to late afternoon. Tourist areas tend to adopt a more northern timetable, though, with shops and offices probably staying open right through the day. Opening hours for **museums** and **ancient sites** change with exasperating frequency. Smaller sites generally close for a long siesta (even where they're not supposed to), as do **monasteries**. Many state-owned museums and sites are free for students from EU countries (a valid card is required, but not necessarily an ISIC). Non-EU students, and all over-65s, generally pay half-price.

There's a vast range of **public holidays** and festivals. The most important, when almost everything will be closed, are: Jan 1; Jan 6; first Mon of Lent; March 25; May 1; Easter Sun; Whit Mon; Aug 15; Oct 28; Dec 24–27.

Emergencies

The most common causes of a run-in with the **police** are nude bathing or sunbathing, breaking into archeological sites after-hours, and camping outside an authorized site.

Topless bathing may now be legal on virtually all Greek beaches but, especially in smaller places, you should be aware of local sensitivities before stripping off.

For minor medical complaints go to the local **pharmacy**. If you regularly use any drug you should bring along a copy of the prescription together with the generic name of the drug. For serious medical attention you'll find moderately priced English-speaking doctors in all the bigger towns or resorts; consult the tourist police for some names. Emergency treatment is free in state **hospitals**, though you'll only get the most basic level of nursing care. Even with an E111 form, you may have to pay up front for medications.

Emergency numbers

Police ☎110; Ambulance ☎166; Fire ☎199.

Athens and around

ATHENS has been inhabited continuously for over 7000 years. Its acropolis, protected by a ring of mountains and commanding views of all approaches from the sea, was a natural choice for prehistoric settlement. Its development into a city-state and artistic centre reached its zenith in the fifth century BC with a flourish of art, architecture, literature and philosophy that pervaded Western culture forever after. Since World War II, the city's population has risen from 700,000 to four million – and is now home to more than a third of the country's population. The speed of this process is reflected in the city's chaotic mix of retro and contemporary: cutting-edge clothes shops and designer bars stand by the remnants of the Ottoman bazaar, and crumbling Neoclassical mansions are dwarfed by brutalist 1960s apartment blocks.

The ancient sites are only the most obvious of Athens' attractions. There are attractive cafés, landscaped stair-streets, and markets; startling views from the hills of Lykavitós and Filopáppou; and, around the foot of the Acropolis, scattered monuments of the Byzantine, medieval and nineteenth-century town. Outside the city, the **Temple of Poseidon** at Sounion is the most popular trip, and rightly so, with its dramatic clifftop position.

The port of **PIREÁS**, effectively an extension of Athens, is the main terminus for the island and for international and inter-island **ferries**. It connects to Athens by the metro: Pireás is the last stop heading southwest from Monastiráki. The other port, **RAFÍNA**, is on the east coast of the Attic peninsula and a useful departure point for many of the Cyladic and north Aegean islands. There's a regular bus service connecting it with central Athens.

Arrival and information

From Eleftherios Venizelos **airport**, take the E94 express **bus** (every 15–30min 6am–midnight) from outside arrivals to the metro stop Ethnikí Ámyna and then continue into the centre. Alternatively, take the E95 express bus all the way to central Sýndagma Square (every 25–35min), or the E96 express bus to Pireás port (every 20–40min). Tickets for each cost €2.93 and are valid on all Athens public transport for a day. Beware that in dense traffic it can take up to two hours to cover the 25km to the city centre.

International **trains** arrive at the Stathmós Laríssis in the northwest of the city centre, connected by metro to Sýndagma. The virtually adjacent Stathmós Peloponníssou handles traffic to and from the Peloponnese. **Buses** from northern Greece and the Peloponnese arrive at Kifissoú 100, ten minutes from the centre by bus #051. Buses from central Greece (not Delphi) arrive closer to the centre at Liossíon 260, north of the train stations (bus #024 to Sýndagma). Most international buses drop off at the train station or Kifissoú 100; a few will drop you right in the city centre. Arriving by **boat** at Pireás, the simplest access to the centre is by metro to Sýndagma or Omónia stations.

The city's main EOT **tourist office** is at Amerikís 2, near Sýndagma Square (Mon–Fri 9am–4pm; ☏010 33 10 565).

City transport

All **public transport** operates daily from around 5.30am to midnight. Athens' bus and trolley network is extensive but very crowded at peak times. Line #1 of the **metro** runs from Pireás to Kifissiá, with stops at Monastiráki, Thissío and Omónia; Line #2 runs from Dháfni to Sepólia via Sýndagma and a station at the foot of the Acropolis; Line #3 heads east from Sýndagma to Ethnikí Ámyna. Tickets are available at all stations from automatic coin-op dispensers or staffed windows. A one-day travel card (€2.90), which can be bought from metro stations, gives you the run of all buses and all metro lines. Tickets for **buses** must be bought in advance from kiosks. **Taxis** can be surprisingly difficult to hail, but are very inexpensive: fares around the city centre should rarely come to more than €3. Taxi drivers will often pick up a whole string of passengers along the way, each passenger paying the full fare for their journey – so if you're picked up by an already occupied taxi, memorize the meter reading; you'll pay from then on, including a €1.50 minimum.

Accommodation

Accommodation can be packed to the gills in midsummer – August especially – but for most of the year there is a good range. You can reserve at the tourist office for hotels of C-class and above.

Hostels

Aphrodite Einárdhou 12, cnr Mihaïl Vódha 65 ☎010 88 10 589, ✉e hostel-aphrodite@ ath.forthnet.gr. Between the main train station and Platía Viktorías, this friendly hostel has a bar/restaurant and internet access. All rooms have a/c. Dorms ❶

Festos Youth and Student Guesthouse Filellínon 18 ☎010 32 32 455, ✉consolas@netplan.gr. Centrally placed, if often overcrowded and noisy hostel on the edge of Pláka. Dorms ❶

Hostel #5 Dhamaréos 75, Pangráti ☎010 75 19 530. Friendly place in an appealing neighbourhood with cooking and laundry facilities, and no curfew. A bit remote: trolley #2/#11 stops round the corner. ❶

International Youth Hostel Victor Hugo 16 ☎010 52 34 170. Athens' cheapest option, an official HI hostel with a cheerful atmosphere, well-kept facilities and helpful staff, though the location isn't wonderful. Bus #1/#12 to Karaïskáki Square nearby. ❶

Hotels

Acropolis House Kódrou 6–8 ☎010 32 22 344. Clean, well-sited pension on a pedestrian street. Most rooms are en suite and some have a/c. ❹

Adonis Kódrou 3 ☎010324 9737. C-class hotel with plain, en-suite rooms and a stunning view of the Acropolis from the rooftop bar. Breakfast included. ❺

Exarhion Themistokléous 55, Exárhia ☎010 38 01 256. Sixties high-rise that's superbly placed (and priced) for the studenty nightlife. TV and a/c in all rooms. ❸

Orion Emm. Benáki 105, corner Anexartisías, Exárhia ☎010 38 28 441. Quiet, well-run budget hotel across from the Lófos Stréfi park – a steep final walk to get there, yet close to many attractions. Rooftop kitchen and common area with an amazing view. ❸

Student and Travellers' Inn Kydhathinéon 16 ☎010 32 44 808, ✉student-inn@ath.forthnet.gr. Excellent location for this popular, clean and well-run former hostel. Singles, doubles and triples, with shared bathrooms, as well as luggage storage and internet. ❸

Tempi Eólou 29 ☎010 32 13 175. Upgraded hotel, with very helpful staff; well sited on a pedestrian street in the bazaar. Doubles and triples, some with private bathroom. ❸

Campsites

Nea Kifissia Potamoú 60 Néa Kifissiá ☎010 620 56 46. In a leafy suburb, this year-round place has its own swimming pool. Metro to Kifissiá then bus #528 behind the station.

Várkiza Camping at Km27 on the Athens–Sounion road ☎010 897 36 14. Large year-round site by the beach, 20km south of the centre. Bus #Ø (July & Aug) from Odhós Panepistimíou or #A3 from Amalías Avenue to Glyfáda then #115 to Várkiza.

The City

Pláka is the best place to begin exploring the city. One of the few parts of Athens with charm and architectural merit, its narrow winding streets and stairs are lined with nineteenth-century Neoclassical houses. An attractive approach is to follow **Odhós Kydhathinéon**, a pedestrian walkway starting on Odhós Filellínon, south of Sýndagma. It continues through café-crowded Platía Filomoússou Eterías to **Odhós Adhrianoú**, which runs nearly the whole east–west length of Pláka from Hadrian's Arch to the Thissíon.

The downhill, northerly section of Adhrianoú is largely commercial as far as the Roman Forum. But a few steps south from Kydhathinéon, there's a quiet and

CENTRAL ATHENS

Párnitha, Lamía & the North ◀

Pl. Attikís ◀

Ambelókipi, Kifissiá & Marathon ▲

LOCAL BUSES
- **A** Rafína and Soúnion
- **B** Glyfádha, Voúla and the beaches
- **C** Soúnion extra stop and # 40 stop
- **D** # 051 terminal
- **E** # E95 airport bus
- **Ⓜ** Metro Station

Panathenaïkós Stadium

Yennádhion Library

Evangelismós Hospital

Evangelismós Ⓜ

Lykavitós Theatre

Áyios Yeóryios

Funicular

Cycladic Art

LYKAVITOS

EXARHIA

Lófos Strefí

National Archeological Museum

Pedhíon Áreos

YIS

Akadhimía

Panepistímiou Ⓜ

OSE

National Library

Polytekhnío

Main Post Office

Ⓔ

Red Cross

OTE

Omónia Ⓜ

OTE

Pl. Viktorías Ⓜ

Ⓐ

Central

Laríssis Train Station Ⓜ

Pelopónnissou Train Station

Kifissoú 100 Bus Station ▲

Liossíon 260 Bus Station ▲

Liossíon 100 Bus Station, Kórinthos & the Peloponnese ▼

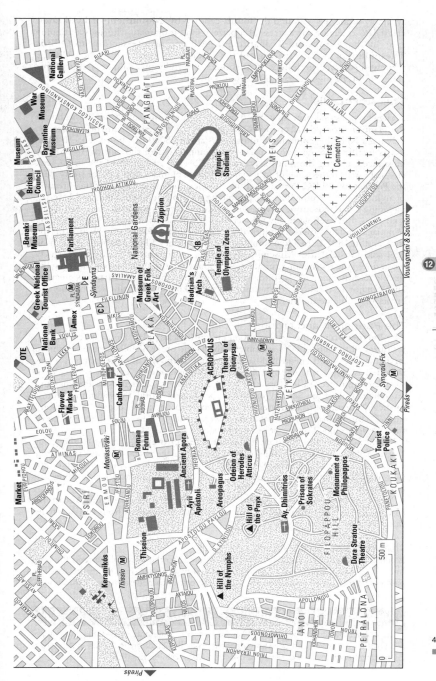

GREECE

12

495

attractive sitting space around the fourth-century-BC **Monument of Lysikrates**, erected to celebrate the success of a prize-winning dramatic chorus. Continuing straight ahead from the Kydhathinéon–Adhriánou intersection up **Odhós Thespídhos**, you reach the edge of the Acropolis precinct. Up to the right, the whitewashed Cycladic houses of Anafiótika cheerfully proclaim an architect-free zone amidst the highest crags of the Acropolis rock.

The Acropolis

A rugged limestone plateau, watered by springs and rising an abrupt 100m out of the plain of Attica, the **Acropolis** was one of the earliest settlements in Greece, drawing a Neolithic community to its slopes around 5000 BC. In Mycenaean times it was fortified around a royal palace and temples where the cult of Athena was introduced. During the ninth century BC, it became the heart of the first Greek city-state, and in the wake of Athenian military supremacy and a peace treaty with the Persians in 449 BC, Pericles had the complex reconstructed under the direction of architect and sculptor Pheidias, producing most of the monuments visible today, including the **Parthenon**. Having survived more or less intact for over two thousand years, the Acropolis finally fell victim to the demands of war. In 1687 besieging Venetians ignited a Turkish gunpowder magazine in the Parthenon, blasting off the roof, and in 1801 Lord Elgin removed the frieze (the "Elgin Marbles"), which he later sold to the British Museum. Meanwhile, generations of visitors have slowly worn down the Parthenon's surfaces; and, more recently, smog has been turning the marble to dust. Since 1981, visitors have been barred from the Parthenon's precinct, and a major restoration programme is proceeding sporadically; scaffolding and cranes may obscure the view.

The Parthenon and around

The **Parthenon** was the first great building in Pericles's plan. Designed by Iktinos, it utilizes all the refinements available to the Doric order of architecture to achieve an extraordinary and unequalled harmony. Built on the site of earlier temples, it was intended as a new sanctuary for Athena and a house for her cult image, a colossal wooden statue decked in ivory and gold plate that was designed by Pheidias and considered one of the Seven Wonders of the Ancient World; the sculpture was lost in ancient times, but its characteristics are known through later copies. "Parthenon" means "virgins' chamber" and initially referred only to a room at the west end of the temple occupied by the priestesses of Athena.

To the north of the Parthenon stands the **Erechtheion**, the last of the great works of Pericles. Here, in symbolic reconciliation, Athena and the city's old patron Poseidon-Erechtheus were both worshipped. On the south side, in the Porch of the Caryatids, the Ionic line is transformed into six maidens (caryatids) holding the entablature on their heads.

Placed discreetly on a level below that of the main monuments, the **Acropolis Museum** contains nearly all of the portable objects removed from the Acropolis since 1834.

The west and south slopes

Rock-hewn stairs immediately below the entrance to the Acropolis ascend the low hill of the **Areopagus**, site of the court of criminal justice. Following the road or path over the flank of the Acropolis, you come out onto pedestrianized Dhionysíou

Access to the ancient sites

The **entry ticket** to the Acropolis (€12, €6 to non-EU students, free to EU students) is valid for two days and allows free access to all the other ancient sites in Athens. **Opening hours** for all are: Mon 11am–4/7pm, Tues–Sun 8am–4/7pm.

Areopayítou, by the Odeion of Herodes Atticus (see below). Turning right, a network of paths leads up **Filopáppou Hill**, its summit capped by a grandiose monument to a Roman senator and consul, Filopappos. Just north of the main path, which follows a line of truncated ancient walls, is the church of **Áyios Dhimítrios**, with Byzantine frescoes. Above the church, further to the north, rises the **Hill of the Pnyx**, a meeting place in classical times for the democratic assembly.

The second-century Roman **Odeion of Herodes Atticus**, restored for performances of music and classical drama during the summer festival (the only time it's open), dominates the south slope of the Acropolis hill. The main interest hereabouts lies in the earlier Greek sites to the east, pre-eminent among which is the **Theatre of Dionysos**, beside the main site entrance on Dhionysíou Areopayítou. One of the most evocative locations in the city, it was here that the masterpieces of Aeschylus, Sophocles, Euripides and Aristophanes were first performed. The ruins are impressive; the theatre, rebuilt in the fourth century BC, could hold some 17,000 spectators.

The Agora and Roman Forum

Northwest of the Acropolis, the **Agora** was the nexus of ancient Athenian city life, where the various claims of administration, commerce, market and public assembly competed for space. The site is a confused jumble of ruins, dating from various stages of building between the sixth century BC and the fifth century AD. For some idea of what you are surveying, the place to head for is the **museum**, housed in the rebuilt Stoa of Attalos. In the far corner of the agora precinct sits the nearly intact but distinctly clunky Doric **Temple of Hephaistos**, otherwise known as the **Thissíon** from the exploits of Theseus depicted on its friezes.

The **Roman Forum**, or Roman agora, was built as an extension of the Hellenistic agora by Julius Caesar and Augustus. The best-preserved and easily the most intriguing of the ruins, though, is the graceful, octagonal structure known as the **Tower of the Winds**. It was designed in the first century BC by a Syrian astronomer, and served as a compass, sundial, weather vane and water clock powered by a stream from one of the Acropolis springs. Each face of the tower is adorned with a relief of a figure floating through the air, personifying the eight winds.

Sýndagma Square, the National Gardens and Lykavitós

All roads lead to Platía Syndágmatos – **Sýndagma Square** – with its busy metro station. Geared to tourism, with a main post office, banks, luxury hotels, American Express, airline and travel offices grouped around, it has convenience but not much else to recommend it. Behind the parliament buildings on the square, the **National Gardens** provide the most refreshing spot in the city, a luxuriant tangle of trees, shrubs and creepers, whose shade, duck ponds, cafés and sparkling irrigation channels bring relief from the heat and pollution of summer. At the southern end of the park stands **Hadrian's Arch**, erected by the Roman emperor to mark the edge of the classical city and the beginning of his own. Directly behind are the sixteen surviving columns of the 104 that originally comprised the **Temple of Olympian Zeus** – the largest in Greece, dedicated by Hadrian in 131 AD.

At the northeastern corner of the National Gardens is the fascinating and much-overlooked **Benáki Museum**, Koumbári 1 (Mon–Sat 9am–5pm, Thurs till midnight, Sun 9am–3pm; €6, free on Thurs), with a collection that features Mycenaean jewellery, Greek costumes, memorabilia of the Greek War of Independence and historical documents, engravings and paintings.

Taking the second left off Vassilísis Sofías after the Benáki Museum will bring you to the **Museum of Cycladic and Ancient Greek Art**, Neofítou Dhouká 4 (Mon–Fri 10am–4pm, Sat 10am–3pm; €3), which in the quality of its display methods is streets ahead of anything else in Athens.

North, past the posh shopping district of Kolonáki, a **funicular** at the corner of Dhorás Dhistría and Ploutárhou (daily 8.45/10.30am–12.20am; €1.50) begins its ascent to the summit of **Lykavitós**. The principal path up the hill begins here, too, rambling up through the woods. On top, the chapel of Áyios Yeóryios provides the main focus. There's a café on the adjacent terrace and another, more pleasant one, halfway down; both have views spectacular enough to excuse the high prices.

Eating, drinking and entertainment

If it's character you're after, Pláka's hills and stepped lanes can still provide a pleasant evening's setting for a meal, despite the touts and tourist hype. But for good-value, good-quality fare, it's best to head for neighbourhoods such as Psyrrí and Exárhia. Quintessentially Greek **ouzerí** and **mezedhopolía** sell *mezédhes* (hors d'oeuvres) along with the drinks, which can be a substantial meal on their own. Bars, cinemas, exhibitions and nightlife venues change fast and often, so it's useful to have a copy of the English-language daily *Athens News* (⊛ www.athensnews.gr), which has **listings** for clubs, galleries, concerts and films.

The summer **Athens Festival** (early June to late Sept) encompasses classical Greek theatre, established and contemporary dance, classical music, big-name jazz, traditional Greek music and a smattering of rock shows. Most performances take place at the Herodes Atticus theatre, which is memorable in itself on a warm summer's evening. There are also special bus excursions to the great ancient theatre at Epidaurus. The main **festival box office** is at Stadhíou 4 (March–Sept Mon–Fri 8.30am–4pm, Sat 9am–2.30pm; ☎010 32 21 459, ⊛ www.greekfestival.gr).

Restaurants

Barba Yannis Emmanouíl Benáki 94. Vast menu of inexpensive home-style food. Food is best at lunch, but it's open till 1.30am.

Iy Ipiros Platía Ayíou Filíppou, Monastiráki. Long-established lunchtime taverna at the heart of the flea market; good value and great for people-watching.

Rozalia Valtetsíou 58, Exárhia. The best all-round taverna near the triangular plaza. Garden open in summer.

Iy Taverna tou Psyrri Eskhýlou 12, Psyrrí. The only straightforward taverna in a zone dominated by *ouzerí*, this excels at grilled/fried seafood, vegetable starters and wine from basement barrels. Arrive early or queue for a table.

O Thanasis Mitropóleos 69, Monastiráki. Reckoned the best *souvláki* and kebab in this district. Always packed with locals at lunchtime, worth the wait. Take out or eat in.

Ouzerí and mezedhopolía

To Athinaïkon Themistokléous 2, cnr Panepistimíou. Long-established *ouzerí* with marble tables and old posters, popular with local office workers at lunch, and strongest on fresh seafood. Closed Sun.

Kafenio Dhioskouri Dhioskoúron, Pláka. Popular bar/café, where seafood snacks are served at tables with an unbeatable view of the ancient agora.

Filistron Apostólou Pávlou 23, Thissío. Excellent all-round *ouzerí*; best in the evening when the roof terrace allows unimpeded views of the Acropolis.

Listings

Embassies and consulates Australia, Tsóha 24 ☎010 64 50 404; Canada, I Yennadhíou 4 ☎010 72 73 400; Ireland, Vassiléos Konstandínou 7 ☎010 72 32 771; New Zealand, Xenías 24☎010 77 10 112; UK, Ploutárhou 1, Kolonáki ☎010 72 36 211; US, Vassilísis Sofías av 91 ☎010 72 12 951.

Hospital Call ☎171 for the address of the nearest hospital, and take a taxi. KAT, way out in Maroússi (with its own metro stop), is the designated Greater Athens emergency ward.

Internet Downtown Internet, Platía Omonía 10; Museum Internet Café, Patission 46; Sofokleous.com Internet Café, Stadhíou 5.

Laundry Angélou Yerónda 10, off Platía Filomoússou Eterías, Pláka; and at Dhidhótou 46, Exárhia.

Pharmacies Bakakos, Platía Omonía. Outside hours, check the rota on any pharmacy window of call ☎107.

Post office Eólou 100, just off Omónia; on Sýndagma.

Around Athens: The Temple of Poseidon at Sounion

The 70km of coast south of Athens – dubbed the **Apollo Coast** – has some good but highly developed beaches. At weekends the sands fill fast, as do the innumerable bars, restaurants and discos. If this is what you're after, then resorts such as Glyfádha and Vouliagméni are functional enough. But for most visitors, the coast's attraction is at the end of the road. **Cape Sounion** is one of the most imposing spots in Greece, and on its tip stands the fifth-century BC **Temple of Poseidon** (daily 10am–sunset; €3), built in the time of Pericles as part of a sanctuary to the sea god. In summer there is faint hope of solitude unless you slip into the site before the tours arrive, but the temple is as evocative a ruin as Greece can offer. Doric in style, it preserves sixteen of its thirty-four columns, and the view from the temple is stunning. Below the promontory are several coves, the most sheltered of which is a five-minute walk east from the car park and site entrance. The main Soúnio **beach** is more crowded, but has a group of tavernas at the far end, which, considering the location, are reasonably priced. There's a single **campsite** about 5km short of the cape, the *Bacchus* (☎0292 39 572).

Buses to Soúnion leave every thirty minutes from the KTEL terminal on Mavromatéon at the southwest corner of the Pédhion Áreos park in central Athens. They alternate between coastal and inland services, the latter slightly longer and more expensive (the coastal route takes around 2hr).

The Peloponnese

The appeal of the **Peloponnese** is hard to overstate. This southern peninsula, technically an island since the cutting of the Corinth Canal, seems to have the best of almost everything Greek. Its ancient sites include the Homeric palace of Agamemnon at **Mycenae**, the Greek theatre at **Epidaurus** and the sanctuary of **Olympia**, host of the Olympic Games for a millennium. The medieval remains are scarcely less rich, with the fabulous castle at **Acrocorinth**; the strange tower-houses and churches of the **Máni**; and the extraordinary Byzantine towns of **Mystra** and **Monemvasiá**. The Peloponnesian **beaches**, especially along the west coast, are among the finest and least developed in the country.

The usual approach from Athens is via modern Corinth; frequent buses and trains run this way. A more attractive method is by hydrofoil, via the islands of the Argo-Saronic; the route runs from Pireás south to Monemvasiá. **PÁTRA** is the **major port** in the Peloponnese. The **EOT office** (☎0610 620 353) and the **tourist police** (☎0610 451 833) are at the entrance to the Italy ferry building. The main **bus station** (☎0610 273 936) is midway along the waterside; there's another on the harbour road.

Ancient Corinth

Whoever possessed **CORINTH** – the ancient city that displaced Athens as capital of the Greek province in Roman times – had control of trade between northern

Greece and the Peloponnese, and a link between the Ionian and Aegean seas. It's not surprising, then, that the city's history is characterized by invasions and power struggles. The Romans finally razed it in 146 BC. The site lay in ruins for a century before being refounded, on a majestic scale, by Julius Caesar in 44 BC. Again in ruins, the remains of the city occupy a rambling site below the acropolis hill of **Acrocorinth**, itself littered with medieval remains. To explore both you really need a full day, or better still, to stay close by. The modern village of **ARHÉA KÓRINTHOS** spreads back around the main archeological zone, where you'll find good **accommodation** at *Hotel Shadow* (℡07410 31 481; ❸); there's also a scattering of **rooms** to rent in the backstreets.

The **main excavated site** (daily 8am–5/7pm; €3.50) is dominated by the remains of the Roman city. You enter from the south side, which leads straight into the **Roman agora**. The real focus, however, is a survival from the classical Greek era: the fifth-century BC **Temple of Apollo**, whose seven austere Doric columns stand slightly above the level of the forum. Towering 575m above the lower town, **Acrocorinth** (summer daily 8am–7pm; winter Tues–Sun 8.30am–3pm; free) is an amazing mass of rock still largely encircled by 2km of wall. During the Middle Ages this ancient acropolis of Corinth became one of Greece's most powerful fortresses. It's a 4km climb up (about 1hr), but well worth it. Amid the sixty-acre site, you wander through a jumble of semi-ruined chapels, mosques, houses and battlements, erected in turn by Greeks, Romans, Byzantines, Crusaders, Venetians and Ottomans.

There are frequent **bus** and **train services** from Athens and Pátra to **modern Corinth**, from where you can catch a local bus to the main site.

Mykínes (Mycenae)

The modern village of **MYKÍNES** lies 2km southwest of the ancient site of **MYCENAE**, tucked into a fold of the hills just east of the highway from Kórinthos to Árgos. Agamemnon's citadel, "well-built **Mycenae**, rich in gold", as Homer wrote, was uncovered in 1874 by the German archeologist Heinrich Schliemann, whose work was impelled by his belief that there was a factual basis to Homer's epics; the brilliantly crafted gold and sophisticated architecture that he found bore out the accuracy of Homer's epithets. The buildings unearthed by Schliemann show signs of having been occupied from around 1950 BC to 1100 BC, when the town, though still prosperous, was abandoned. No coherent explanation has been found for this event, but war among rival kingdoms was probably a major factor.

You enter the **Citadel of Mycenae** (daily 8am–5/7pm; €4.50) through the mighty **Lion Gate**. Inside the walls to the right is **Grave Circle A**, the cemetery which Schliemann believed to contain the bodies of Agamemnon and his followers, murdered on their triumphant return from Troy. In fact the burials date from about three centuries before the Trojan war, but they were certainly royal, and the finds (now in Athens' National Archeological Museum) are among the richest yet unearthed. Schliemann took the extensive **South House**, beyond the grave circle, to be the Palace of Agamemnon. But a much grander building, which must have been the **Royal Palace**, was later discovered on the summit of the acropolis. Rebuilt in the thirteenth century BC, probably at the same time as the Lion Gate, like all Mycenaean palaces it is centred on a **Great Court**. The small rooms to the north are believed to have been royal apartments and in one of them the remains of a red stuccoed bath have led to its fanciful identification as the spot of Agamemnon's murder.

Only the ruling elite were permitted to live within the citadel itself; outside its walls lay the main part of the town. The extensive remains of **merchants' houses** have been uncovered near to the road, beside a second grave circle. A few minutes walk down the road from the main site is the astonishing **Treasury of Atreus**, a royal burial vault entered through a majestic fifteen-metre corridor. Set above the chamber doorway is a lintel formed by two immense slabs of stone, one of which – a staggering 9m long – is estimated to weigh 118 tonnes.

There's a **train station** at Fíkhti, 2km west of Mykínes; most of the KTEL buses will drop you off here as well. There are numerous bus trips here from Athens, making this a popular day-trip destination. **To stay**, try the *Rooms Dassis* (☎07510 76 123; ❸), *Hotel Belle Hélène*, up the hill towards the site (☎07510 76 225; ❸), or one of the two fairly central **campsites**, *Mycenae* (☎07510 76 121) and *Atreus* (☎07510 76 221). The village has plenty of **restaurants**, all geared to the lunchtime bus-tour trade.

Náfplio

NÁFPLIO – a lively, beautifully sited town with a fading elegance, inherited from when it was briefly the first capital of modern Greece – makes an attractive base for exploring the Argolídha area and resting up by the sea. The main fort, the **Palamídhi** (daily 8.30am–3pm; €2.50), is most directly approached by 899 stone-hewn steps up from Polyzoïdhou street, by the side of a Venetian bastion. Within the walls are three self-contained castles, all built by the Venetians in the 1710s. The **Íts Kalé** ("Inner Citadel" in Turkish), to the west, occupies the ancient acropolis, whose walls were adapted by successive medieval occupants. The third fort, the photogenic **Boúrtzi**, occupies the islet offshore from the harbour and allowed the Venetians to close the shallow shipping channel with a chain. In the town itself, **Platía Syndágmatos**, the main square, is the focus of most interest and a great place to relax drinking coffee.

Buses arrive on Odhós Syngroú, just south of the interlocking squares Platía Trión Navárhon and Platía Kapodhístrias, themselves just west of the **train station**. There are also summertime **hydrofoil** connections to the Argo-Saronic islands, and to Pireás and Monemvasiá. The EOT **tourist office** is at 25-Martíou 2 (daily 9am–1pm & 4–8pm; ☎07520 24 444). **Hotels** are generally overpriced, the most reasonable being *Hotel Economou* fifteen minutes' walk from the centre at Argonaftón 22, between the roads to Árgos and Toló (☎07520 23 955; ❷). Private **rooms**, most of which cluster on the slope south of the main square, can be a better deal. For **eating**, try *Kakanarakis*, Vassilísis Ólgas 18, or *Omorfi Taverna* at no. 16.

Epídhavros (Epidaurus)

From the sixth century BC to Roman times, **EPÍDHAVROS**, 30km east of Náfplio, was a major spa and religious centre; its **Sanctuary of Asclepius** was the most famous of all shrines dedicated to the god of healing. The magnificently preserved 14,000-seat theatre (daily 8.30am–5/9pm; €4.50), built in the fourth century BC, merged so well into the landscape that it was rediscovered only last century. Constructed with mathematical precision, it has near-perfect acoustics: from the highest of the 54 tiers of seats you can hear coins dropped in the orchestra. Close by is a small **museum** (Mon noon–5/7pm, Tues–Sun 8am–5/7pm; same ticket as theatre) containing various statuary and frieze fragments. The sanctuary itself encompasses hospitals, dwellings for the priest-physicians, and hotels and amusements for the fashionable visitors.

Most people take in Epídhavros as a day-trip from Náfplio, but a memorable experience is to catch an evening classical theatre **performance** (summer only Fri & Sat; ⊛www.greekfestival.gr). You can **camp** near the car park or stay in **LYGOURIÓ**, 5km north, at *Hotel Alkyon* (☎07530 22 002; ❸). There is also a campsite on the beach at **Néa Epídhavros**, *Diamantis* (☎07130 31 181). The nearest **restaurant** to the campsite is *Oasis* on the Lygourió road, but *Leonides* in the village proper is better.

Mystra

A glorious, airy place, hugging a steep flank of Taïyettos, **MYSTRA** is an astonishingly complete Byzantine city that once sheltered a population of some 40,000. The castle on its summit was built in 1249 by Guillaume II de Villehardouin, fourth

Frankish Prince of the Morea (as the Peloponnese was then known), and together with the fortresses of Monemvasiá and the Máni it guarded his territory. In 1262 the Byzantines drove out the Franks and established the Despotate of Mystra. This isolated triangle of land in the southeastern Peloponnese enjoyed considerable autonomy from Constantinople, flowering as a brilliant cultural centre in the fourteenth and early fifteenth centuries and only falling to the Ottomans in 1460, seven years after the Byzantine capital was conquered.

The site of the **Byzantine city** (daily 8am–2/8pm; €3.50) has two entrances on the road up from Néos Mystrás: it makes sense to take the bus to the top entrance, then explore a leisurely downhill route. Following this course, the first identifiable building that you come to is the fourteenth century church of **Ayía Sofía**. The chapel's finest feature is its floor, made from polychrome marble. The **Kástro**, reached by a path that climbs directly from the upper gate, maintains the Frankish design of its thirteenth-century construction, though modified by successive occupants.

Heading down from Ayía Sofía, there is a choice of routes. The right fork winds past the ruins of a Byzantine mansion, while the left fork is more interesting, passing the massively fortified **Náfplio Gate** and the vast, multi-storeyed complex of the **Despots' Palace**. At the **Monemvasiá Gate**, linking the upper and lower towns, turn right for the **Pandánassa convent**. The church, whose name means "Queen of the World", is the finest that survives in the town, a perfectly proportioned blend of Byzantine and Gothic. Further down on this side of the lower town make sure you see the diminutive **Perívleptos monastery**, whose single-domed church, partly carved out of the rock, contains Mystra's most complete cycle of frescoes, almost all of which date from the fourteenth century. The **Mitrópolis**, or cathedral, immediately beyond the gateway, ranks as the oldest of Mystra's churches, built from 1270 onward. A marble slab set in its floor is carved with the symbol of the Paleologos dynasty, the double-headed eagle of Byzantium, commemorating the spot where Constantine XI Paleologos, the last emperor, was crowned in 1449.

Practicalities

The modern village, **NÉOS MYSTRÁS**, is a small roadside community whose half-dozen tavernas are crowded with tour buses by day and revert to a low-key life at night. **Accommodation** is limited: there's the *Hotel Byzantion* (⊕07310 83 309, Ⓔmedotels@otenet.gr; ➍) and *Khristina Vahaviolou* (⊕07310 20 047; ➌). Nearby **SPÁRTI** (ancient Sparta, though there's little left to see) is a good alternative base, with the friendly *Cecil*, Paleológou 125, near the top of Paleológou (⊕07310 24 980; ➋), and *Apollon*, Thermopýlon 84 (⊕07310 22 491; ➌). One **campsite**, 2.5km from Spárti, is *Mystras* (⊕07410 22 724); closer to Mystra itself is *Castle View* (⊕07310 83 303). There are a number of reasonable **restaurants** in Spárti, including *Averof*, Paleológou 77, and *Diethnes*, Paleológou 105. Spárti's bus station is at the far eastern end of Lykoúrgou, but buses for Mystrá depart from the corner of Lykoúrgou and Leonídhou, on the west side of the central square.

Monemvasiá

Set impregnably on a great eruption of rock connected to the mainland by a kilometre-long causeway, the Byzantine seaport of **MONEMVASIÁ** is a place of grand, haunted atmosphere. At the start of the thirteenth century it was the Byzantines' sole possession in the Morea, eventually being taken by the Franks in 1249 after three years of siege. Regained by the Byzantines as part of the ransom for the captured Guillaume de Villehardouin, it served as the chief commercial port of the Despotate of the Morea. At its peak in the Byzantine era, Monemvasiá had a population of almost 60,000.

You can get there by road or, more enjoyably, by sea. There are more or less daily

hydrofoils in season, linking it with Pireás and the Argo-Saronic islands, dropping off midway along the causeway. **Buses** connect with Spárti and Athens three times daily, and with Yíthio twice daily in season only, arriving in the village of **YÉFIRA** on the mainland, where most **accommodation** is located. There are several reasonable hotels near the causeway – try the *Monemvassia* (☎07320 61 381; ❸) – plus numerous pensions and rooms. The nearest **campsite**, *Kapsis Paradise*, is 3.5km south of Yéfira near a reasonable beach. Rooms on the rock are much more expensive, but worth the splurge: try the long-established *Malvasia* (☎07320 61 323; ❺). The best **taverna** is *Matoula*; and *Marianthi* for a variety of delicious pies.

The **Lower Town** once sheltered forty churches and over 800 homes, an incredible mass of building threaded by an intricate network of alleys. A single main street harbours most of the restored houses, plus cafés, tavernas and a scattering of shops. The foremost monument is the **Mitrópolis**, the cathedral built by Emperor Andronikos II Komnenos in 1293, and the largest medieval church in southern Greece. Across the square, the tenth-century domed church of **Áyios Pétros** was transformed by the Ottomans into a mosque and is now a small **museum** of local finds (unpredictable opening hours). Towards the sea is a third church, the **Khrysafítissa**, with its bell hanging from an old acacia tree in the courtyard. It was restored and adapted by the Venetians in the eighteenth century, when for twenty-odd years they took the Peloponnese from the Ottomans. The climb to the **Upper Town** is highly worthwhile, not least for the solitude. Its fortifications, like those of the lower town, are substantially intact; within, the site is a ruin, though infinitely larger than you could imagine from below.

Yíthio and the Máni peninsula

YÍTHIO, Sparta's ancient port, is the gateway to the dramatic Máni peninsula and one of the south's most attractive seaside towns. Its somewhat low-key harbour, with occasional ferries, has a graceful nineteenth-century waterside. Out to sea, tethered by a long narrow causeway, is the islet of **Marathoníssi** (ancient Kranae), where Paris and Helen of Troy spent their first night after her abduction from Sparta. **Buses** drop you close to the centre of town, and finding **accommodation** should be a matter of a stroll along the waterfront Vassiléos Pávlou, where there is, amongst others, the *Kondogiannis* pension, at no. 19 (☎07330 22 518; ❸). There are several summer **campsites** (*Meltemi* and *Yíthio Bay* are good choices) along the huge Mavrovoúni beach, which begins 3km south of town off the Areópoli road. For **eating**, try the *Iy Nautila* or *Korali* ouzeris at the head of the port.

The southernmost peninsula of Greece, the **Máni peninsula**, stretches from Yíthio in the east and Kalamáta in the west down to Cape Ténaro, mythical entrance to the underworld. It is a wild and arid landscape with an idiosyncratic culture and history: nowhere in Greece does a region seem so close to its medieval past. The quickest way into it is to take a bus from Yíthio to **AREÓPOLI**, gateway to the so-called Inner Máni. There are **rooms** at a number of tower-houses, including *Pyrgos Tsimova* (☎07330 51 301; ❹), or there's the *Hotel Kouris* on the main square (☎07330 51 340; ❹). There are regular buses from here north to Stoúpa, Kardhamýli and Kalamáta (a change in Ítylo is usually involved).

The real attractions lie to the north of Areópoli, along the eighty-kilometre road to Kalamáta, which has views as dramatic and beautiful as any in Greece. There are numerous paths along the mountain ridge for hiking and a series of small **beaches**, beginning at **ÁYIOS NIKÓLAOS**, which has fish tavernas and rooms such as the *Skafidakia* (☎07210 77 698; ❷), and extending more or less through to Kardhamýli. **STOÚPA**, which has possibly the best sands, is now geared very much to tourism, with several small hotels – friendliest and most reasonable of which is *Lefktron* (☎07210 77 322; ❸) – a **campsite** five minutes' walk from Kalógria beach, a supermarket and tavernas. **KARDHAMÝLI**, 8km north, remains a beautiful place despite its commercialization and busy road, with a long pebble beach and a restored tower-house quarter. *Lela's* (☏07210 73 541; ❸) has some good rooms, while *Anniska's* mini apartments (☏07210 73 600; ❹) are right on the beach.

If you get as far as **Kalamáta** – the largest city in the area – then ancient **Pýlos**, the impressive medieval fortresses of **Methóni** and **Koróni** and the superb beach at **Finikoúnda** are all close enough to be taken in as day trips.

Olympia

The historic resonance of **OLYMPIA**, which for over a millennium hosted the Panhellenic Games, is rivalled only by Delphi or Mycenae. Its site, too, ranks with this company, for although the ruins are confusing, the setting is as perfect as could be imagined: a luxuriant valley of wild olive and plane trees beside the twin rivers of Alfiós and Kladhéos, overlooked by the pine-covered hill of Krónos. The contests at Olympia probably began around the eleventh century BC, slowly developing over the next two centuries from a local festival to a major quadrennial celebration attended by states from throughout the Greek world. From the very beginning, the main Olympic events were athletic, but the great gathering of people expanded the games' importance: nobles and ambassadors negotiated treaties here, while merchants chased contacts and sculptors and poets sought commissions. The games eventually fell victim to the Christian Emperor Theodosius's crackdown on pagan festivities in 391–2 AD, and his successor ordered the destruction of the temples, a process completed by invasion, earthquakes and, lastly, by the River Alfiós changing its course to cover the sanctuary site. There it remained, covered by seven metres of silt and sand, until the 1870s.

The entrance to the **ancient site** (daily 8.30am–3/7pm; €3.50, or €6 joint ticket with museum) leads along the west side of the sacred precinct wall past a group of public and official buildings, including a structure adapted as a Byzantine church. This was originally the studio of Pheidias, the fifth-century BC sculptor responsible for the great cult statue in the focus of the precinct, the great Doric **Temple of Zeus**. Built between 470 and 456 BC, it was as large as the Parthenon and its decoration rivalled the finest in Athens. The great gold and ivory cult statue by Pheidias was displayed in the *cella*, and here, too, the Olympian flame was kept alight from the time of the games until the following spring – a tradition continued at an altar for the modern games. The smaller **Temple of Hera**, behind, was the first built here; prior to its completion in the seventh century BC, the sanctuary had only open-air altars, dedicated to Zeus and a variety of other cult gods. Rebuilt in the Doric style in the sixth century BC, it's the most complete structure on the site. Finally, though, what makes sense of Olympia is the 200-metre track of the **Stadium** itself. The start and finish lines are still there, as are the judges' thrones in the middle and seating banked to each side. The tiers accommodated up to 30,000 spectators, with a smaller number on the southern slope overlooking the **Hippodrome** where chariot races were held. Finally, in the **archeological museum** (Mon 11am/noon–5/7pm, Tues–Sun 8/8.30am–5/7pm; €3.50), the centrepiece is the statuary from the Temple of Zeus, displayed in the vast main hall. Most famous of the individual sculptures is the **Hermes of Praxiteles**, dating from the fourth century BC; one of the best-preserved of all Classical sculptures, it retains traces of its original paint.

Most people arrive at Olympia **via Pýrgos**, which has frequent buses to the site, plus numerous connections to Pátra and a couple daily to Kalamáta. The modern town of **OLYMBÍA** has grown up merely to serve the excavations and tourist trade. The **tourist office** is on the south side of Praxitélous Kondhýli (Mon–Sat 9am–3pm; ☏06240 23 100). Among **hotels**, the least expensive is *Hercules*, by the church (☏06240 22 696; ❷). There is also a **hostel** at Praxitélous Kondhýli 18 (☏06240 22 580; ❶). The closest **campsite**, *Diana*, just off the main road, has a pool and good facilities. For **eating**, most of the tavernas offer standard tourist meals at mildly inflated prices; honourable exceptions include *O Kladhios*, a beautiful and authentic grill near the river.

Central and northern Greece

Central Greece has an indeterminate character, consisting mostly of vast agricultural plains dotted with rather drab market and industrial towns. The highlights all lie at the fringes: **Delphi** above all, and further northeast the forested slopes of **Mount Pílion** with its magnificent villages and alluring beaches or northwest at the unworldly rock-monasteries of the **Metéora**. Access to these monasteries is through **Kalambáka**, from where the **Katára pass** over the Píndhos Mountains brings you into **Epirus**, the region with the strongest identity in mainland Greece. En route lies **Métsovo**, perhaps the easiest location for a taste of mountain life, though increasingly commercialized. Nearby **Ioánnina**, once the stronghold of the notorious Ali Pasha, remains a town of some character, and serves as the main transport hub for trips into the relatively unspoilt villages of the **Zagóri**, the **Vikos gorge** and the archeological site of **Dodona**.

The northern provinces of **Macedonia** and **Thrace** have only been part of the Greek state since 1913 and 1923 respectively. As such, the region stands slightly apart from the rest of the nation – an impression reinforced for visitors by scenery and climate that are essentially Balkan. The only areas to draw more than a scattering of summer visitors are **Mount Olympus** and **Halkidhikí**, the latter providing the beach-playground for the Macedonian capital of **Thessaloníki** and also sheltering the "Monks' Republic" of **Mount Áthos**.

IGOUMENÍTSA is Greece's third **passenger port** after Pireás and Pátra, with almost hourly ferries to Corfu, and several daily to Italy. The **tourist office** is next to the customs house on the under-used central quay (daily 7am–2pm; ☎06650 22 227). Note that if you wish to **travel on** to Bulgaria, Romania or Turkey, there are frequent bus and train services from Thessaloníki, although you have to get your visas in Athens.

Delphi

Access to the extraordinary site of **DELPHI**, 150km northwest of Athens, is straightforward: a half-dozen buses run there from the capital daily, and services are as frequent from **Livádhia**, the nearest rail terminus. With its site raised on the slopes of a high mountain terrace and dwarfed by the ominous crags of Parnassós, it's easy to see why the ancients believed Delphi to be the centre of the earth. But what confirmed this status was the discovery of a chasm that exuded strange vapours and reduced all comers to frenzied, incoherent and obviously prophetic mutterings. For over a thousand years a steady stream of pilgrims worked their way up the dangerous mountain paths to seek divine direction, until the oracle eventually expired with the demise of paganism in the fourth century AD.

You enter the **Sacred Precinct of Apollo** (daily 7.30am–5/7pm;; €3.50 or €5.90 joint ticket with museum) by way of a small agora, enclosed by ruins of Roman porticoes and shops for the sale of votive offerings. The paved **Sacred Way** begins after a few stairs, zigzagging uphill between the foundations of memorials and treasuries, to the **Temple of Apollo**. Of the main body of the temple only the foundations stood when it was uncovered by in the 1890s; they have, however, re-erected six Doric columns, giving a vertical line to the ruins and providing some idea of its former dominance over the sanctuary. In the innermost part of the temple was a dark cell where the priestess would officiate; no sign of cave or chasm has been found, but it is likely that it was closed by earthquakes. The theatre and stadium used for the main events of the Pythian games are on terraces above the temple. The **theatre**, built in the fourth century BC, was closely connected with Dionysos, god of the arts and wine, who reigned in Delphi over the winter months when Apollo was absent and the oracle was silent. A steep path leads up through cool pine groves to the stadium, which was banked with stone seats only in Roman times. The **museum** (Mon–Fri 7.30/8.30am–3/6.45pm, Sat & Sun 8.30am–2.45pm;

€3.50) contains a collection of archaic sculpture matched only by finds on the Acropolis in Athens. Its most famous exhibit is *The Charioteer*, one of the few surviving bronzes of the fifth century BC.

Following the road east of the sanctuary towards Aráhova, you reach a sharp bend. To the left, marked by niches for votive offerings and the remains of an archaic fountain house, the celebrated **Castalian spring** still flows from a cleft in the cliffs. Visitors to Delphi were obliged to purify themselves in its waters, usually by washing their hair, though murderers had to take the full plunge. Across and below the road from the spring is the **Marmaria** or Sanctuary of Athena Pronoia (daily 8am–5/7pm; free), the "Guardian of the Temple". The precinct's most conspicuous building is the **Tholos**, a fourth-century BC rotunda whose purpose is a mystery. Outside the precinct on the northwest side, above the Marmaria, is a **gymnasium**, also built in the fourth century BC but later enlarged by the Romans.

Practicalities

The modern village of **DHELFÍ** has a quick turnaround of visitors, so finding a place to stay should present few problems. There are upwards of twenty **hotels** and pensions, plus a few rooms to let, though there is no low season: in winter, skiers throng the place. Best value of the budget hotels is the E-class *Odysseus* at Iséa 1, corner Fillelínon (✆02650 82 235; ❸), and the *Sun View*, Apóllonos 84 (✆02650 82 349; ❸). The nearest official **campsite** is *Apollon* (✆02650 82 750), less than 1km west towards Ámfissa, with an acceptable **restaurant**. Other eating options aren't brilliant; try *Taverna Vakchos* or *Omfalos*, both on Apollonos street. The helpful **tourist office** (Mon–Fri 8am–2.30pm; ✆02650 82 900), with up-to-date transport schedules, is in the town hall.

The Pílion peninsula

There is something decidedly un-Mediterranean about the **Pílion peninsula**, with its lush fruit orchards and dense broadleaf forests. Water gurgles from crevices beside every road, and summers are a good deal cooler than in the rest of central Greece. Pílion villages are idiosyncratic too, sprawling affairs with sumptuous mansions and barn-like churches lining their cobbled streets. Add to the scenery and architecture a dozen or so excellent beaches, and easy access from Athens and Thessaloníki, and it's no wonder that this is a well-loved corner of Greece: avoid July, August, Easter and Christmas unless you wish to camp out.

The most visited part of the peninsula lies just north and east of the industrial city of **Vólos**. The bus station catering for the twenty-plus Pílion villages is at Grigoríou Lambráki, a short walk south of the train station. If your time is limited, the best single targets are the recognized showcases of Makrinítsa and Vyzítsa. **MAKRINÍTSA** has become a bit commercialized, with fairly overpriced lodging in a bevy of restored mansions, though frequent connections to Vólos make day-trips easy. Remoter **VYZÍTSA** has equally good connections, with better possibilities of staying cheaply – try *Rooms Aphrodite* (✆04230 86 484; ❷), west of the square – and eating cheaply – try *Taverna O Yiorgaras* on the road east. The less homogeneous village of **MILIÉS**, 3km east, also has some accommodation and the wonderful *Korbas* bakery, by the bus stop.

The largest village on the Pílion – almost a small town – is **ZAGORÁ**, destination of fairly regular buses across the peninsula's summit ridge. Unlike its seashore neighbours, Zagorá has a life independent of tourism, and is more appealing than first impressions suggest. You're also more likely to find a room here in season, for example at *Room Yiannis Halkias* (✆04260 22 159; ❸), than down at **HOREFTÓ**, 8km below, where you might try the hotel *Erato* (✆04260 22 445; ❸). There's also a good **campsite** at the south end of the main beach here; another cove beckons north of the resort.

Just before Zagorá, a junction funnels traffic southeast to **TSANGARÁDHA**, also the terminus of two daily buses from Miliés. Though nearly as large as Zagorá, it may not seem so, divided as it is into four distinct quarters along several kilometres of road. Reasonable accommodation is difficult to come by, though you might enquire at *Villa ton Rodhon* (☎04260 49 340; ❹) in Ayía Paraskeví. Eating out is generally uninviting; most people do so at **MOÚRESSI**, 3km northwest, where two adjacent tavernas dish out Pílion specialities at fairly moderate prices. **KISSÓS**, still further towards Zagorá, is another possibility for staying and dining, with its excellent, inexpensive *Xenonas Kissos* (☎04260 31 214; ❸).

Most visitors, however, stay at one of several nearby beaches, the best on this shore of the peninsula. **ÁYIOS IOÁNNIS**, 6km below Kissós, is an overblown resort with plenty of accommodation – you can try *Hotel Evripidis* (☎04260 31 338; ❸). If it's too busy for your tastes, head south along the sand, past the crowded campsite, to **Papá Neró beach** or further still to postcard-perfect **DAMOÚHARI**, with its tiny ruined castle and fishing anchorage. The area's most scenic beach is reached by following a winding 7km road from the south end of Tsangarádha to **Mylopótamos**; unfortunately it gets very crowded in high season. For more solitude, you can engage in the hour-and-a-half walk from Damoúhari or Tsangarádha to beautiful **Fakistra beach**; beware that there are no facilities on this beach.

Kalambáka and the Metéora

There are few more exciting places to arrive at than **KALAMBÁKA**. The shabby town itself you hardly notice, for your eye is immediately drawn upwards to the weird grey cylinders of rock overhead. These are the outlying monoliths of the extraordinary valley of **the Metéora**. To the right you can make out the monastery of Ayíou Stefánou, firmly entrenched on a massive pedestal; beyond stretches a chaos of spikes, cones and stubbier, rounded cliffs, beaten into bizarre shapes by the action of the sea that covered the Plain of Thessaly around fifty million years ago. The earliest religious communities in the valley emerged during the late tenth century, when hermits made their homes in the caves that score many of the rocks. In 1336 they were joined by two monks from Mount Áthos, one of whom established the first monastery here. Today, put firmly on the map by films such as the James Bond *For Your Eyes Only*, the four most accessible monasteries are essentially museums. Only two, Ayías Triádhos and Ayíou Stefánou, continue to function with a primarily religious purpose.

From Kastráki the road loops between huge outcrops of rock, passing below the chapel-hermitage of **Doúpiani** before reaching a track to the left, which winds up a low rock to the fourteenth-century **Ayíou Nikoláou** (9am–3.30pm, closed Fri). A small, recently restored monastery, this has some superb sixteenth-century frescoes in its main chapel. Next to it on a needle-thin shaft is **Ayía Moní**, ruined and empty since an earthquake in 1858. Between Ayíou Nikoláou and Ayía Moní a clear path leads up a ravine between assorted monoliths; soon, at a fork, you've the option of bearing left for Megálou Meteórou or right to Varlaám, the two also linked by a higher access road. **Varlaám** (9am–2pm & 3.15–5pm, closed Thurs) ranks as one of the oldest and most beautiful monasteries in the valley. It also retains its old ascent tower; until 1923 the only way of reaching the monasteries was by being hauled up in a net drawn by rope and windlass, or by the equally perilous retractable ladders. Today, however, you can reach the monastery safely, if breathlessly, via the 195 steps cut into the side of the rock. From Varlaám the path system takes you northwest to **Megálou Meteórou** (10am–5pm, closed Thurs). This is the grandest of the monasteries and also the highest, built 415m above the surrounding ground. Next you follow the main access road east, ignoring the turning back down for Kastráki, until you reach the signed access path for the tiny, compact convent of **Roussánou** (daily 9am–5pm), approached in the final moment across a dizzying bridge from an adjacent rock. This has perhaps the most extraordinary site of all the monasteries, its walls built right on the edge of a sharp blade of rock. It's less than half-an-hour from Roussánou to the fourteenth-century **Ayías Triádhos**

(9am–12.30pm & 3–5pm, closed Thurs), approached up 130 steps carved into a tunnel in the rock. Although Ayías Triádhos teeters above a deep ravine and its little garden ends in a precipitous drop, there is a 3km, well-marked cobbled trail at the bottom of the monastery's steps back to Kalambáka, which saves a long trudge back around the circuit. **Ayíou Stefánou** (9am–2pm & 3.30–6pm, closed Mon), the last and easternmost of the monasteries, is a further fifteen minutes' walk from Ayías Triádhos; bombed in World War II, it's the one to omit if you've run out of time.

Each monastery levies an **admission charge** of €1.50 and operates a strict **dress code**: skirts for women, long trousers for men and covered arms for both sexes.

Practicalities

Visiting the Metéora demands a full day, which means staying at least one night in Kalambáka or at the village of Kastráki, right in the shadow of the rocks. **KALAMBÁKA** is characterless but pleasant enough, with plentiful **accommodation**. Good budget choices in the quieter, upper portion of town towards Kastráki include *Hotel Meteora*, Ploutárhou 13 (℡04320 22 367; ❸), and *Koka Roka Rooms*, Kanári 21 (℡04320 24 554; ℡e kokaroka@yahoo.com; ❸). **KASTRÁKI** is twenty minutes' walk out of Kalambáka; there are regular buses in season. Along the way you pass the busy *Vrahos*, the first of two **campsites**, offering rock-climbing lessons (℡04320 22 293); the other, *Boufidhis/The Cave* (℡04320 24 802), is smaller but quieter, grassier and incomparably set under the pinnacles of the monasteries. Kastráki also has hundreds of rooms to rent, mostly better value than in Kalambáka (though avoid the main road); good examples include *Ziogas Rooms* (℡04320 24 037; ❸) and the more basic ones at *The Cave* campsite (❷). The best-value **eating** is at the tiny *Ziogas* grill (eve only).

The Katára pass

West of Kalambáka, the **Katára pass** cuts across the central range of the Píndhos to link Thessaly and Epirus. The route is one of the most spectacular in the country, and is covered by two buses daily between **Tríkala** and **Ioánnina**.

MÉTSOVO spreads just west of the Katára pass, a high mountain town built on two sides of a ravine and encircled by a mighty range of peaks. It is a startling site: from below the main road the eighteenth- and nineteenth-century stone houses, with their wooden balconies and modern tile roofs, wind down the ravine to the main platía, where a few old men still loiter after Sunday Mass, magnificent in full traditional dress. The town **museum** occupies the Arhondikó Tosítsa (tours 9am–1.30pm & 4–6pm, closed Thurs; €1.50), a mansion restored to the full glory of its eighteenth-century past, with panelled rooms, rugs and a fine collection of crafts and costumes. For **eating**, the restaurant of *Hotel Athinai* is excellent for casserole dishes. Métsovo has quite a range of **accommodation** and apart from around July 26, date of the main local **festival**, and during the ski season, you'll have little difficulty getting a room. You can try the *Filoxenia* (℡06560 41 021; ❸), below the platía with ravine views from some rooms.

Ioánnina and around

Descending from Métsovo, you approach **IOÁNNINA** through more spectacular folds of the Píndhos Mountains. The fortifications of the old town, once the capital of the Albanian Muslim chieftain Ali Pasha, are punctuated by towers and minarets. From this base Ali, "the Lion of Ioannina", carved out of the Ottoman Empire a kingdom encompassing much of western Greece, an act of rebellion that foreshadowed wider defiance in the Greeks' own War of Independence. Disappointingly, most of the city is modern and undistinguished. However, the fortifications of Ali's citadel, the **Kástro**, survive more or less intact, and this is an obvious point to stroll towards. Apart from the Kástro, the most enjoyable quarter is the old **bazaar** area, outside the citadel's main gate. If you're planning a visit to Dodona, check out the

Archeological Museum (Tues–Sun 8.30am–3pm; €1.50), just off Dhimokratías square, which has a fascinating collection of lead tablets inscribed with questions to the Dodona oracle.

The island of **Nissí** is served by water-buses (every 30min) from the quay northwest of the Froúrio. Its village, founded during the sixteenth century, is flanked by several beautiful, diminutive monasteries. You can stay on the island at the spotless rooms kept by the Dellas family (☎06510 84 494; ❷). In the city itself, the best budget lodging is in the area between the bazaar and the central plazas; try *Esperia*, Kaplání 3 (☎06510 24 111; ❸). The pleasant, mosquito-free, lakeshore *Limnopoula* **campsite** (☎06510 25 265) is 2km out of town on the Pérama/airport road. Besides the **tavernas** at Nissí, more standard fare can be found immediately opposite the citadel gate, where the two rival grills *To Kourmanio* and *To Manteio* vie for your custom. The main **bus** station is at Zozimádhon 4, serving most points north and west; a smaller terminal at Bizaníou 19 connects Dodona and villages south and east. The **tourist office** at Dhódhonis 39, south of the centre, can provide information on the whole Epirus region.

Dodona

At remote and mountainous **DODONA**, 22km southwest of Ioánnina, lie the ruins of the **Oracle of Zeus**, dominated by a vast amphitheatre. This is the oldest oracle in Greece: worship of Zeus through his sacred oak tree at Dodona seems to have begun around 1900 BC. Entering the **ancient site** (daily 8am–5/7pm; €1.50) you are immediately confronted by the massive western wall of the theatre. Able to seat 17,000, it is one of the largest on the Greek mainland, built during the time of Pyrrhus (297–272 BC). Nowadays in summer, plays are sporadically but atmospherically performed: ask at the tourist office in Ioánnina. Beside the theatre are the foundations of a *bouleuterion* (council house), beyond which lie the complex ruins of the **Sanctuary of Zeus**, site of the ancient oracle.

Transport to Dodona is sparse, with at most two badly timed **buses** a day from Ioánnina (Mon, Wed & Fri only). A return trip by **taxi** from Ioánnina with an hour at the site costs around €18. There are, however, some lovely spots to **camp**, and a friendly if basic **taverna** in the neighbouring modern village of **DHODHÓNI**, which also has rooms run by Stefanos Nastos (☎06510 71 106; ❷).

Zagóri and the Víkos Gorge

Few parts of Greece are more surprising, or beguiling, than **Zagóri**, the infertile region to the north of Ioánnina. It is the last place you might expect to find some of the Greece's most imposing architecture, yet the *Zagorohória*, as the 46 villages of Zagóri are called, are full of grand stone mansions, enclosed by semi-fortified walls and with deep-eaved gateways opening on to immaculately cobbled streets.

In the northwest corner of the region, the awesome trench of the **Víkos Gorge** – its walls nearly 1000m high in places – separates the villages of western and central Zagóri. A hike through or around Víkos is the highlight of any visit to the area, the usual starting point being the handsome village of **MONODHÉNDHRI**. There are twice-daily buses from Ioánnina (Mon, Wed & Fri only); The only real budget option here is *Katerina's Pension* (☎06530 71 300; ❷). Much the clearest **path into the gorge**, marked as the long-distance O3, starts beside Áyios Athanásios church; the route is fairly straightforward, and it takes under five hours to reach the point where the gorge begins to open out. From here the best option is to follow the O3 path to **MEGÁLO PÁPINGO**, two hours further on. A hillside village of fifty or so houses along a tributary of the Voïdhomátis river, it offers abundant if pricey accommodation; most reasonable is *Pension Koulis* (☎06530 41 138; ❸). Around half the size of its neighbour, **MIKRÓ PÁPINGO** just uphill has one main inn, *Xenon O Dhias* (☎06530 41 257; ❸). Bus services to Ioánnina are erratic (in theory four weekly in summer). The alternative is to trail-walk west two and a half hours to the village of **Káto Klidhoniá**, where there are regular buses along the Kónitsa–Ioánnina highway. If you are looking for more adventure, there is an extreme sports centre at *Taxiarches Hotel* by the entrance of Arísti village, Western Zagóri (℡06530 41 888, ✉taxiarches@hol.gr).

Thessaloníki

Second city of Greece and administrative centre for Macedonia and Thrace, **THES-SALONÍKI** has a very different feel from Athens – more Balkan-European and modern. During the Byzantine era, it was the second city after Constantinople, reaching a cultural "Golden Age" until the Ottoman conquest in 1430. As recently as the 1920s, the city's population was as mixed as any in the Balkans: besides the Ottomans, who had been in occupation for close on five centuries, there were Slavs, Albanians and the largest European **Jewish** community of the period – 80,000 at its peak. Today, however, there is little to keep you – aside from a visit to the excellent archeological museum; but this is the place to arrange permits for Mt Áthos and make onward connections to the Halkidhikí beaches, or to Bulgaria or Turkey.

The **Archeological Museum** (Mon 10.30am/12.30–5/7pm, Tues–Sun 8.30am–3/7pm; €4.50) is a couple of minutes from the White Tower, the last surviving bastion of the city's medieval walls. The museum contains many of the finds from the tombs of Philip II of Macedon and others at the ancient Macedonian capital of Aegae (modern Veryína). They include startling amounts of gold and silver – masks, crowns, necklaces, earrings, bracelets – all of extraordinary craftsmanship, although the exhibits are now slightly depleted following the transfer of many items back to a purpose-built underground gallery at Veryína itself.

Practicalities

The **train station** on the west side of town is a short walk from the central grid of streets and the waterfront. **Buses** arrive at one of five KTEL terminals nearby. From the **airport**, 16km out at Mikrá, bus #78 runs hourly to the train station (6am–11pm). The EOT **tourist office** is at Platía Aristotélous 8 (Mon–Fri 7.30am–3pm, Sat 8.30am–6pm, Sun 10am–5pm; ℡0310 271 888).

Outside the fair-and-festival season (Sept–Nov), hotel vacancies are reasonably easy to find, though not, as a rule, very attractive or good value. Modest **hotels** are clustered along the noisy beginning of busy Egnatía, including the *Atlantis*, at no. 14 (℡031/540 131; ❸), and *Nea Mitropolis*, just north of Egnatía at Syngroú 22 (℡0310 525 540; ❸). The closest **campsites** are at the beach resorts of Ayía Triádha (24km away) and Órmos Epanomís (33km); the latter is better, served by bus #69 from Platía Dhikastiríon. To **eat**, *Platia Athonos* on Dhragoúmi, an alley off Platía Athonos, is one of the more dependable of several *ouzerís* in this area; and *Kamares*, Ayíou Yeoryíou 11, just behind the Rotunda, is another option. **Bars** and **clubs** tend to be concentrated in the rehabilitated warehouse area southeast of Platía Eleftherías known as Ladhádhika; *Zythos*, Platía Katoúni 5, is one of the best bars, with dozens of well-kept foreign beers. The main indoor **music** venue is the multi-disciplinary complex *Mylos*, out in an old flour mill at Andhréou Yeoryíou 56, where you can also find bars, a summer cinema and exhibition galleries.

Listings

Consulates Australia, Kifisías 46, Kalamriá ℡0310 482 322; Canada, Tsimiskí 17 ℡0310 256 350; UK, Venizélou 8 ℡0310 278 006; US Níkis 59 ℡0310 241 905. If you need a visa for onward travel, get it in Athens.

Exchange 24hr automatic machine at Platía Aristotélous 8.

Hospital Yenikó Kedrikó, Ethnikís Amýnis 41

℡0310 211 211.

Internet The Link, Goúnari 50; Planet, Svólou 55.

Laundry Bianca, Antoniádhou 3; Freskádha, Filíppou 105.

Mount Áthos permits Take your passport to the Grafío Proskynitón Ayíou Órous (Mount Áthos Pilgrims' Office), Konstandínou Karamanlí 14, first floor (Mon–Fri 9am–2pm, Sat 10am–noon); they will issue an entry permit for a specified day. Call ☎0310 861 611 (English-speaking) for instructions on faxing your details.

Pharmacy Zofráfou, Tsimiskí 75 ☎0310 244 184.
Post office Aristotélous 26.

Mount Olympus

Highest, most magical and most dramatic of all Greek mountains, **Mount Olympus** – the mythical seat of the gods – rears straight up nearly 3000m from the shores of the Thermaíkos gulf, south of Thessaloníki. Dense forests cover its lower slopes and its wild flowers are gorgeous. If you're equipped with decent boots and warm clothing, no special expertise is necessary to get to the top between mid-June and October, though it's a long hard pull, and at any time of year Olympus must be treated with respect: its weather is notoriously fickle and it regularly claims lives.

The best base is the village of **LITÓHORO** on the eastern side. The station for trains from Thessaloníki is 9km from the village, with rare connecting buses; or you can get a bus direct from Thessaloníki. Cheapest **accommodation** is the plain *Hotel Markesia*, Dhionýsou 5 (☎03520 81 831; ❷), just down from main street 28-Oktovríou. Best **eats** are at *Dhamaskinia*, uphill on Vassiléos Konstandínou, or *Psistaria Zeus*, at the start of the road up the mountain.

You'd do well to buy a proper **map** of the range in Athens or Thessaloníki (#31 Road Editions 1:50,000 is adequate). Four to five hours' walking along the well-marked, scenic E4 long-distance path up the Mavrólongos canyon brings you to **Priónia**, also the end of the much longer road and with the last reliable water source. From Priónia there's a sharper three-hour climb along a trail to the *Spilios Agapitos* **refuge** (☎03520 81 800; ❶; closed mid-Oct to mid–May). It's best to stay overnight here, as you need to make an early start for the three-hour ascent to **Mýtikas**, the highest peak (2917m); the summit frequently clouds up towards mid-day. The path continues behind the refuge, reaching a signposted fork above the tree line in about an hour; straight on, then right, takes you to Mýtikas via the ridge known as Kakí Skála, while the abrupt right reaches the *Yiosos Apostolidhis* **hut** in one hour (☎03520 82 300; ❶; mid-Sept to July), from where there's an enjoyable loop down to the **Gortsiá** trailhead and from there back down into the Mavrólongos canyon, via the ancient monastery of Ayíou Dhionysíou.

Halkidhikí and Mount Áthos

The squid-shaped peninsula of **Halkidhikí** begins at a perforated edge of lakes east of Thessaloníki and extends into three prongs of land – Kassándhra, Sithonía and Áthos – trailing like tentacles into the Aegean Sea. **Kassándhra** and **Sithonía** are Thessaloníki's beach-playground, hosting some of the fastest-growing holiday resorts in Greece. Both are connected to Thessaloníki by bus, but neither peninsula is easy to travel around on public transport. You really have to pick a place and stay there, perhaps renting a scooter for local excursions. Áfytos is by far the most attractive place on Kassándhra, while Sithonía is marginally less packaged, with low-key resorts at Kalamítsi, Pórto Koufó and Toróni.

Mount Áthos, the easternmost peninsula, is in all ways separate: a "Holy Mountain" whose monastic population, semi-autonomous from the Greek state, excludes all women – even as visitors. For men who wish to experience Athonite life, all that's required is a visit to the pilgrims' office in Thessaloníki (see p.510) to arrange the necessary admission paperwork. You need to be over the age 18, and demonstrate a religious or scholarly interest in Áthos, to be given an entry pass allowing up to four days' stay on the holy mountain, moving to a different monastery each night. A visit is highly recommended, though you can't hope to see more than a fraction of the twenty main monasteries in the time allotted. Choose between the "museum monasteries" of Meyístis Lávras, Vatopedhíou, Ivíron or Dhionysíou with their wealth of treasures and art, or the more modestly endowed cloisters where the brothers will make more time for you, such as Osíou Grigoríou, Pandokrátoros and the Serbian foundation of Hilandharíou.

Both Ierissós and Ouranópoli, villages at the top of the peninsula and the usual gateways to Áthos, are served by several daily buses from Thessaloníki. **IERISSÓS** has many rooms to let and the friendly if slightly noisy *Hotel Marcos* (☎03770 22 518; ❷); in summer boats sail daily at 8.30am (not Tues or Wed) to the monasteries of Áthos's northeast shore. It's often best to continue to the busy resort of **OURANÓPOLI**, the last settlement before you reach the monastic domains. **Accommodation** is plentiful, with numerous rooms and a few budget hotels, such as *Diana* (☎03770 71 052; ❷). It's from here that the most reliable ferries depart for the southwest shore of monastic Áthos, daily at 9.45am. Allow time to queue up at the Grafío Proskynitón (Pilgrims' Bureau) to exchange your reservation from the Thessaloníki office for a full-fledged **pass** (€24, €12 for students) allowing you to stay overnight at any of the major monasteries.

From the usual entry port of **DHÁFNI** on the southwest coast, there are more possibilities of moving about by boat and bus, but walking between the religious communities on a dwindling trail network is an integral part of the Athonite experience, so you should be reasonably fit and self-sufficient in dry snack food, as the two meals offered each day tend to be spartan. Most monks pay scant attention to foreigners, so you get more of an idea of the magnificent scenery and engaging architecture than of the religious life, though it's hard to avoid tangling with the disorienting daily schedule, dictated by the hours of sun and darkness. Also, some monasteries have become so visited that you must book a bed by phone in advance; the Pilgrims' Bureau provides a list of contact numbers.

The southern Aegean islands

The **Argo-Saronic** islands are the nearest archipelago to Athens and one of the busiest: more than any other group, these islands are at their best outside peak season. To the east, the **Cyclades** is the most satisfying Greek archipelago for island-hopping. The majority of these islands are arid and rocky, with brilliant-white, cubist architecture. The impact of tourism is haphazard, and though some English is spoken in most places, a slight detour could have you groping for your Greek phrasebook. **Íos**, the original hippie island, is still a backpackers' paradise, while **Mýkonos** – with its teeming old town, nude beaches and highly sophisticated clubs and bars (many of them gay) – is by far the most visited of the group. After these, **Páros**, **Sífnos**, **Náxos** and **Thíra** are currently most popular, their beaches and main towns drastically overcrowded in July and August. The one major ancient site worth making time for is **Delos**, the commercial and religious centre of the classical Greek world. Almost all of the Cyclades are served by boats from Pireás, but there are also ferries from Rafína.

Further east still, the **Dodecanese** lie so close to the Turkish coast that some are almost within hailing distance of the shore. The islands were only included in the modern Greek state in 1948 after centuries of occupation by Crusaders, Ottomans and Italians. Medieval **Rhodes** is the most famous, but almost every Dodecanese has its classical remains, its Crusaders' castle, its traditional villages and grandiose Art Deco public buildings. The main islands are connected almost daily with each other, and none is hard to reach. Rhodes is the main transport hub, with services to Turkey, Cyprus and Israel, as well as connections with Crete, the northeastern Aegean islands, the Cyclades and the mainland (Thessaloníki and Pireás).

Ídhra

The port and town of **ÍDHRA**, with its tiers of stone mansions and tiled white houses climbing up from a perfect horseshoe harbour, forms a beautiful spectacle.

Unfortunately, from Easter to September it's packed to the gills, and the seafront becomes one uninterrupted outdoor café (there are no private cars on Ídhra). Dozens of mansions were built here, mostly during the eighteenth century, on the accumulated wealth of a merchant fleet which traded as far afield as America. There's no lack of expensive cafés and **restaurants** on the waterfront, but better value is to be had inland, for example at *Xiri Elia* and the much-loved *Yeitoniko* (alias *Manolis & Christina's*). **Hotels** and pensions are overpriced; reasonable-value places include *Erofili* (℡02980 54 049; ❷) and *Hotel Amarillis* (℡02980 53 611; ❹).

As far as beaches are concerned, on the opposite side of the harbour a coastal path leads to a pebbly but popular stretch, just before **KAMÍNI**, where there are a pair of reasonable pensions and a good year-round taverna, *Christina*. Thirty minutes' walk beyond Kamíni (or a boat ride from the port) will bring you to **VLYHÓS**, a small hamlet with pricier rooms and three tavernas. **Camping** is tolerated here, and the swimming between the pebble shore and an islet is good.

Sífnos

Although **Sífnos** often gets crowded, its modest size means that wherever you stay, you can reach the rest of the island by the excellent bus service to all points or on foot over a network of old stone pathways. **KAMÁRES**, the port, is tucked at the base of high bare cliffs in the west. **Accommodation** can be expensive – the budget option are the rooms above the Katsoulakis Tourist Agency (℡02840 32 362; ❸) close to the quay. There are other places behind the beach, including a mediocre **campsite**, and the reasonable *Hotel Stavros* (℡02840 31 641; ❸), just past the church. The best **meals** are at the quayside *Meropi*.

A steep twenty-minute bus ride takes you up to **APOLLONÍA**, a rambling collage of flagstones, belfries and flowered courtyards. The island bank, post office and tourist police are all here, but rooms, though plentiful, are even more likely to be full than at Kamáres. Outside of high season, there will be vacancies along the road to Fáros; quieter, and pricier, digs are along the stair-street north of the main square, or you can apply to the travel agency Aegean Thesaurus (℡02840 31 151). As an alternative base, head for **KÁSTRO**, a forty-minute trail walk or regular bus ride below Apollonía on the east coast; built on a rocky outcrop with an almost sheer drop to the sea on three sides, this medieval capital of the island retains much of its character. There are many rooms at the lower end of the village, such as *Marianna* (℡02840 33 681; ❷).

At the southern end of the island, 12km from Apollonía by frequent bus, lies the busy beach resort of **PLATÝS YIALÓS**. It has a poor campsite and numerous rooms to let, as well as tavernas, bakeries and supermarkets. For something more original, ask the driver to drop you off at the bus stop for **Chrissopigí** (from where it's a ten-minute walk down a path), where the beach is less crowded, there is an excellent taverna and a postcard-perfect monastery. Heading northeast to **FÁROS**, you will find a mediocre sandy beach, plenty of rooms and good, cheap tavernas. Perhaps the finest walk is through the hills to **VATHÝ**, around three hours from Apollonía's Katavatí "suburb". A fishing and ex-pottery village on a stunning funnel-shaped bay, Vathý is the most attractive base on the island: there are **rooms** to let, the cheapest being *Manolis* (℡02840 71 111; ❷) which is also a **taverna**, as is *To Tsikali,* behind the tiny monastery. An alternative route here is by regular bus from Apollonía.

Mýkonos

Mýkonos has become the most popular and expensive of the Cyclades, visited by nearly a million tourists a year. But if you don't mind the crowds the upscale capital is one of the most beautiful of all island towns. Dazzlingly white, it's the archetypal island-postcard image, with sugar-cube buildings stacked around a cluster of seafront fishermen's dwellings.

The **airport** is about 3km out of Mýkonos Town (also known as Hóra), a short taxi ride away. **Ferries** and cruise ships dock at the northern jetty, where you'll be met by a horde of owners hustling hotels and rooms; you'd do better to proceed to the helpful Mýkonos **accommodation centre** in town (☎02890 23 160) – be aware that a private room is likely to be cheaper than staying in a hotel on the nearby beaches. As for **hotels** in town, out of season you might consider *Philippi* at Kaloyéra 25 (☎02890 22 294; ❹). Otherwise there are very lively official **camp-sites** at Paradise (☎02890 22 852, ℮paradise@paradise.myk.forthnet.gr) and Paránga (☎02890 24 578) beaches. The harbour curves around past the dull, central beach, behind which is the **bus station** for Áyios Stéfanos. Continue along the seafront to the southern jetty for the **tourist police** (☎02890 22 482) and kaïkia to Delos. A second **bus terminus**, for beaches to the south of town, is right at the other end of Hóra, beyond the windmills.

Around Kaloyéra is a promising area for **food**. Cheaper eats are at *Nikos*, behind the town hall, and *Yiavroútas* on Mitropóleos. **Drinking** haunts are over in the south of the town (known as "Little Venice"); try *Kástro's* or *Caprice* for an early-evening cocktail, moving on later to *Montparnasse*, which is fairly swanky. The **nightlife** in town is every bit as good – and expensive – as it's cracked up to be. Among the most durable nightspots are *Remezzo*, with sunset views, and *Pierro's*, once the main draw for the island's substantial gay contingent, but now mixed. Just off K. Yiorgoúli, the *Skandinavian Bar-Disco* is a cheap, nonstop party bar, while *Cavo Paradiso* near Paradise camping is the after-hours club for party animals.

Mýkonos beaches

The closest decent beach is **ÁYIOS STÉFANOS** (4km north), connected by a very regular bus service. Better to make for **PLATÝS YIALÓS**, 4km south, though you won't be alone there. A kaïki service from Mýkonos town connects almost all the beaches east of Platýs Yialós: gorgeous, pale-sand **PARÁNGA** beach, popular with campers; **PARADISE**, well sheltered by its headland, predominantly nudist, with two tavernas; and **SUPER PARADISE**, which has a friendly atmosphere and another taverna. Probably the island's best beach is **ELIÁ**: it's a broad sandy stretch with a verdant backdrop, split in two by a rocky area. It boasts a few restaurants, including the excellent *Mattheos*, and a waterslide park (10am–midnight; €12; free daily bus from Hóra).

Delos

The remains of ancient **DELOS** (Tues–Sun 8.30am–3pm; €4.40), though skeletal and swarming now with lizards and tourists, give some idea of the past grandeur of this sacred isle a few sea-miles west of Mýkonos. The kaïki trip gives you three hours on the island – barely enough time to take in the main attractions, but it's no longer possible to stay the night.

Delos' ancient claim to fame is as the place where Leto gave birth to the divine twins Artemis and Apollo; one of the first things you see on arrival is the **Sanctuary of Apollo**, while three Temples of Apollo stand in a row along the Sacred Way. To the east towards the museum you pass the **Sanctuary of Dionysos** with its marble phalluses' on tall pillars. To the north is the **Sacred Lake** where Leto gave birth: guarding it is a group of lions, masterfully executed in the seventh century BC. Set out in the other direction from the agora and you enter the residential area, known as the **Theatre Quarter**. There are some nice mosaics to be seen: one in the **House of the Trident**, better ones in the **House of the Masks**, including a vigorous portrayal of Dionysos riding on a panther's back. The **Theatre** itself, though much ravaged, offers some fine views.

Páros and Andíparos

With a little of everything – old villages, monasteries, fishing harbour and a labyrinthine capital – **Páros** is a good point to begin your island wanderings, with boat connections to virtually the entire Aegean, though things have become nearly as expensive and commercialized here as on Mýkonos. All ferries dock at **PARIKÍA**, the main town, with its ranks of white houses punctuated by the occasional Venetian-style building and church domes. Just outside the central clutter, the town also has one of the most interesting churches in the Aegean – the **Ekatondapylianí**, or "Church of One Hundred Gates". The original construction was overseen in the sixth century by Isidore of Miletus but the work was carried out by his pupil Ignatius. The **Archeological Museum** (Tues–Sun 8am–3pm; €1.50) is just behind the church; its prize exhibit is a portion of the Parian Chronicle, a social and cultural history of Greece up to 264 BC, engraved in marble.

You'll be met off the ferry by locals offering rooms; avoid offers of properties to the north as they're invariably a long walk away, though there is a crowded **campsite**, the *Koula*, at the northern end of the town beach. The better *Parasporos* campsite is 2km south of town (☎02840 21 100). Among pensions and hotels not blockbooked by tour operators, try the *Pension Festos* (☎02840 21 635; ②) and the smart *Hotel Argonauta*, close to the National Bank (☎02840 21 440, ✉hotel@argonauta.gr; ④). For **food**, *Trata* to the left of the cemetery of the ancient city is good for fish. The most popular cocktail bars extend along the seafront, tucked into a series of open squares.

The second village of Páros, **NÁOUSSA** (reached by regular buses leaving from the stop 100m or so to the left off where ferries dock), was until the early 1990s an unspoilt town, but a rash of new concrete hotels has all but swamped its character. Despite this development, there are some pleasant beaches nearby, while rooms are marginally cheaper than in Parikía – track them down with the help of the tourist office just over the bridge, west from the harbour. There are two **campsites**, out of town towards **Kolymbíthres** and **Sánta María** beaches, both better than the mosquito-plagued one in Parikía, and various **tavernas**, all of which are pretty good, specializing in fresh fish and seafood: start with *Barbarossas* or *Vengera*.

There are boats from Parikía to the island of **ANDÍPAROS** (hourly in high season; 40min), making it a convenient day trip. There is plenty of **accommodation**, including a campsite. The best beaches are at Psaralíki, Glýfa, Ághios Yeóryios and Kalógeros; kaïkia make daily trips around the island, stopping at them all.

Náxos

Náxos is the largest and most fertile of the Cyclades. The Venetian occupation left towers and fortified mansions scattered throughout the island, while medieval Cretan refugees bestowed a singular character upon the eastern settlements. A long causeway protecting the harbour connects **NÁXOS TOWN** with the islet of Palátia, where the huge stone portal of an unfinished **Temple of Apollo** still stands. Most of the town's life goes on down by the port or in the streets just behind it; stepped lanes behind lead up past crumbling balconies and through low arches to the fortified **kástro**, from where the Venetians ruled over the Cyclades. In the same area you will find the **Archeological Museum** (Tues–Sun 8.30am–2.30pm; €3), with an important early sculpture collection and a Hellenistic mosaic on the roof terrace.

Tourism has reached such a level that an annexe of purpose-built **accommodation** extends south of the town centre, since rooms downtown are of a uniformly poor standard and overpriced. The helpful private **tourist office** near the jetty (summer daily 9am–11pm; ☎02850 25 201) can book rooms around the island. In-town **hotels** are better on the cooler north slope of the *kástro*: best budget options are the Dionyssos youth hostel (☎02850 22 331; ②) and the hotel *Panorama* on Amfitrítis (☎02850 24 404; ④). Along the quayside, cafés and **restaurants** are abundant, if a bit expensive; *Iy Kali Kardhia* is worth a visit. There's an **internet** café on the town square.

The island's best **beaches** are regularly served by buses in season. **ÁYIOS YEÓRYIOS**, a lengthy sandy bay south of the hotel quarter, lies within walking distance. There are several tavernas here and four mosquito-prone campsites; further south at **ÁYIOS PROKÓPIOS** beach you will find the good *Apollon* campsite, or you could follow the tracks a little further – an hour-plus walk from town – to **AYÍA ÁNNA**, a small port where there are plenty of rooms to let and a few modest tavernas. Beyond the headland stretches less-developed **PLÁKA** beach, a 5km long vegetation-fringed expanse of white sand which comfortably holds the summer crowds of nudists and campers from the two friendly campsites.

Náxos also serves as a convenient entry point to the **East Cyclades**, a chain of six small islands still unaffected by mass tourism. In high season local boat *Express Skopelitis* leaves Náxos town at 3pm calling at Koufonnísi, Skhinoússa, Irakliá and Donoússa, where you will find basic accommodation and good beaches (free camping may be tolerated; check with the locals first). The end point of this journey is the island of **AMORGÓS**, with dramatic mountain scenery and crystal-blue seas. It is best to stay at the port of **EGIÁLI**, where you will find a friendly campsite and plenty of rooms to let. Make sure that you visit the postcard-pretty village of **HÓRA**, and the spectacular **monastery of Hozoviótissa**, dramatically situated on a cliff high above the sea.

Íos

No other island attracts the same vast crowds as **Íos**, yet the island hasn't been commercialized in quite the same way as, say, Mýkonos, since many visitors are young and impecunious, though the island is being driven steadily more upmarket. You might be tempted to grab a room in **YIALÓS** as you arrive, though it's the most expensive place on the island to stay. A refurbished **campsite** is to the west of the harbour, although there are also two other remoter sites. Yialós beach, five minutes' walk from the harbour, is fringed by hotels and lodgings, but loud music seems to be accepted on the beach and obligatory in the tavernas. Most of the cheaper rooms are in **HÓRA**, a twenty-minute walk (or a short bus ride) up the mountain behind the port, with dorms as well as the usual rooms and hotels. Every evening the streets throb to music from competing **clubs** (mostly free, though drinks tend to be expensive). The *Ios Club* is an antidote to standard techno-pop and a good place to watch the sunset.

The most popular stop on the island's bus routes is **MYLOPÓTAS**, site of a magnificent beach and a mini-resort. By day, bodies cover every inch of the bus-stop end of the sand: for a bit more space head the other way, where there are dunes behind the beach. There are two **campsites**, *Purple Pig* (✆02860 91 302) and *Far Out* (✆02860 91 468), which also has bungalows. For **rooms**, try *Drakos Pension* (✆02860 91 281; ❹) to the right of the bus stop, also with a well-respected taverna. From Yialós, daily day-trip boats depart at around 10am to **MANGANÁRI** on the south coast, the beach to go to for serious all-over tans. There's a better atmosphere, though, at **ÁYIOS THEODHÓTIS**, up on the northeast coast, served by daily buses from Yialós.

Santoríni (Thíra)

As the ferry manoeuvres into **Santoríni**, gaunt, sheer cliffs loom hundreds of feet above. Nothing grows to soften the view, and the only colours are the reddish-brown, black and grey pumice striations of the cliff face. As early as 3000 BC Santoríni developed as an outpost of Minoan civilization until, around 1450 BC, the volcano-island erupted; island and settlements were both destroyed and, it is thought, the great Minoan civilizations on Crete went with them.

Some small ferries and excursion boats dock at **SKÁLA FIRÁ**, but most vessels use the somewhat grim port of **ÓRMOS ATHINIÓS**. Half-rebuilt after a devastating earthquake in 1956, the island capital **FIRÁ** lurches dementedly at the cliff's edge. Besieged by day-trippers from cruise-ships, it's become incredibly tacky of late, the most grossly commercialized spot on what can seem a grossly commercialized island. There is no shortage of **rooms**, as well as three **hostels**; the official HI one is at the northern part of town (☎02860 22 387; ❶). The **campsite** is well-signposted 500m east of the bus terminal. Firá is not a place to linger, but it is worth having a look at the **Archeological Museum** (Tues–Sun 8am–2.30pm; €3) near the cable car to the north of town, and at the **Museum of Prehistoric Thíra** (Tues-Sun 8.30am-3pm; free), between the cathedral and the bus station. **Bus services** are plentiful enough between the town and beaches. **Internet** access is at *Lava*, on the main street close to Firá Square.

Near the northwest tip of the island is one of the most dramatic towns of the Cyclades, **ÍA**, a curious mix of pristine white reconstruction and tumbledown ruins clinging to the cliff face. It's also much the calmest place on Santoríni, and with the presence of a post office, travel agencies and an excellent **youth hostel** (☎02860 71 465; ❷), there's no reason to feel stuck in Firá.

Beaches on Santoríni are bizarre: long black stretches of volcanic sand which get blisteringly hot in the afternoon sun. There's little to choose between **KAMÁRI** and **PERÍSSA**, the two main resorts: both have long beaches and a mass of restaurants, rooms and apartments; neither is for those seeking solitude. Períssa gets more backpackers, has the better campsite and a well-run hostel, *Anna* (☎02860 82 182; ❷). Camping rough is forbidden. Kamári and Períssa are separated by the **Mésa Vounó** headland, on which stood classical (post-eruption) **THÍRA** (Tues–Sun 9am–3pm; free); most of the ruins are difficult to place, but the views are awesome. Evidence of the Minoan colony was found at **AKROTÍRI** (summer Tues–Sat 8.30am–3pm; €15), a town buried under banks of volcanic ash at the southwest tip of the island, and reached by bus from Firá or Períssa. Tunnels through the ash uncovered structures two and three storeys high; lavish frescoes adorned the walls and Cretan pottery was found stored in a chamber. Make sure you have a swim at the quite spectacular **Kókkini Ámmos beach**, a short walk from the site.

Rhodes

It's no surprise that **Rhodes** is among the most visited of Greek islands. Not only is its east coast lined with sandy beaches, but the core of the capital is a beautiful and remarkably preserved medieval city. **RHODES TOWN** divides into two unequal parts: the compact old walled city, and the new town which sprawls around it in three directions. First thing to meet the eye, and dominating the northeast sector of the city's fortifications, is the **Palace of the Grand Masters** (Mon 2.30–9pm; Tues–Fri 8.30am–9pm; €6). There are two excellent **museums** on the ground floor: one devoted to medieval Rhodes, the other to ancient Rhodes. The heavily restored **Street of the Knights** (Odhós Ippotón) leads due east from the front of the palace. The "Inns" lining it housed the Knights of St John for two centuries, and at the bottom of the slope the Knights' Hospital has been restored as the **Archeological Museum** (Tues–Sun 8.30am–3pm; €2.40), where the star exhibits are two statues of Aphrodite. Across the way is the recently restored **Byzantine Museum** (same hours; €1.50), housed in the knights' chapel and highlighting the island's icons and frescoes. Leaving the Palace and heading south, it's hard to miss the most conspicuous Ottoman monument in Rhodes, the candy-striped, recently restored **Süleymaniye Mosque**.

Affordable **accommodation** abounds in the old town and is contained almost entirely in the quad bounded by Odhós Omírou, Sokrátous, Perikléos and Ippodhámou. Quiet, good-value places include *Apollo Rooms*, Omírou 28C (☎02410 63 894; ❷); *Pension Pink Elephant* on Timahídhas, off Irodhótou (☎02410 22 469; ❸), and the modernized, en-suite *Hotel Spot*, Perikleous 21 (☎02410 34 737; ❸). There's a **hostel** at Eryíou 12, just off Ayíou Fanouríou (☎02410 30 491; ❶). **Eating** cheaply can be more of a problem; try the little alleys and backstreets well south of Sokrátous. Here you'll find *Anthony's* on the corner of Pythagóra and Omírou, for fresh *souvláki* in characterful surroundings (eve only). Better value can be had just outside the walls, for instance at *To Steno*, Ayíon Anaryíron 29, 400m southwest of the Ayíou Athanasíou gate. The **post office**, most **banks** (there are just two in the old town), the EOT **tourist office** (Mon–Fri 7.40am–3pm; ☎02410 23 255) and the **police** are all in the new town, mostly northwest of the Italian-built New Market. **Buses** for the rest of the island leave from two terminals within sight of the market. Most central **internet** café is *Rock Style* at Dhimokratías 7, just southwest of the old town.

Around the island

Heading down the east coast from Rhodes Town, the giant promontory of **Tsambíka**, 26km south, is the first place to seriously consider stopping – there's an excellent eponymous beach just south of the headland, reached by a 1.5km slip road. The best overnight base on this stretch of coast is probably **HARÁKI**, a tiny port with rooms and tavernas overlooked by a ruinous castle. **LÍNDHOS**, Rhodes' number-two tourist attraction, erupts 12km south of Haráki. Like Rhodes Town itself, its charm is undermined by commercialism and crowds, and there are relatively few self-catering houses that aren't block-booked through package companies – find vacancies through Pallas Travel (☎02440 31 494). On the hill above the town, the scaffolding-swathed **Temple of Athena** stands inside the inevitable knights' castle (summer Mon 12.30–7pm, Tues–Fri 8am–7pm; €6). Líndhos' beaches are crowded and overrated, but you'll find better ones heading south past Lárdhos, the start of 15km of intermittent coarse-sand beach up to and beyond the growing resort of **Yennádhi**. Inland near here, the Byzantine frescoes in the village church of **Asklipió** are the best on Rhodes.

Kós

Kós is the largest and most popular island in the Dodecanese after Rhodes, and there are superficial similarities between the two. Like its competitor, the harbour here is also guarded by a castle of the Knights of St John, the streets are lined with grandiose Italian public buildings, and minarets and palm trees punctuate extensive Greek and Roman remains. Except for Kós Town and Mastihári, there aren't many non-package travellers: in high season you'll be lucky to find any sort of room at all, except perhaps at the far west end of the island.

Mostly modern **KÓS TOWN**, levelled by a 1933 earthquake, spreads out from the harbour. The helpful municipal **tourist office** (July & Aug daily 7am–9pm; spring & autumn Mon–Fri 9am–8pm, Sat 8am–3pm; winter Mon–Fri 8am–3pm; ☎02420 29 200), 500m south of the ferry dock on the shore road, offers maps and ferry schedules. Long-distance **buses** arrive 500m west of the tourist office. Among budget **accommodation**, try the clean and friendly *Pension Alexis*, Irodhótou 9 (☎02420 28 798; ❷; closed Dec–Feb), and *Hotel Afendoulis*, 600m south at Evripýlou 1 (☎02420 25 321; ❸; closed Dec–March). The official **campsite** (☎02420 23 275) is thirty minutes' walk along the scrappy beach to the southeast of town; there are also frequent buses. Avoid the waterfront **restaurants** in favour of such inland outfits as *Australia-Sydney* on Vassiléos Pávlou. **Internet** access is at *Café del Mare*, Megálou Alexándhrou 4a.

Apart from the **castle** (Tues–Sun 8am–2.30pm; €2.40), the town's main attraction is its wealth of Hellenistic and Roman remains, the largest single section of which is the ancient **agora**, reached from the castle or the main square next to the **Archeological Museum** (same hours; €2.40). Next to the castle, scaffolding props up the branches of the so-called Hippocrates plane tree, which does have a fair claim as one of the oldest trees in Europe. Hippocrates is also honoured by the **Asklepion** (Tues–Sun 8am–pm; €2.40), a temple to Asclepius and renowned centre of Hippocratic teaching, 45 minutes on foot (or a short bus ride) from town. The road to the Asklepion passes through the bi-ethnic village of **PLATÁNI**, where the island's ethnic Turkish minority run the *Arap* and *Sherif* tavernas (summer only), serving excellent, affordable food.

For beaches you'll need to ride the long-distance buses, or else find your own transport. Around 12km west of Kós town, **TINGÁKI** is easily accessible and thus oversubscribed. **MASTIHÁRI**, 30km from Kos town, has a decent beach and non-package-tour rooms, as well as regular ferries to Kálymnos. Continuing west, buses run as far as **KÉFALOS**, which squats on a bluff looking back down the length of Kós. Well before Kéfalos are **Áyios Stéfanos**, where the exquisite remains of a mosaic-floored fifth-century basilica overlook tiny Kastrí islet, and **KAMÁRI**, the resort just below Kéfalos. Beaches begin at Kamári and extend east past Ayios Stéfanos for 7km, virtually without interruption; "Paradise" has the most facilities, but "Magic" (officially Polémi) and Langhádes are calmer and more scenic.

Pátmos

It was in a cave on **Pátmos** that St John the Divine wrote the Book of Revelation, and the monastery which commemorates him, founded here in 1088, dominates the island both physically and politically. While the monks no longer run Pátmos as they did for more than six centuries, their influence has stopped most of the island going the way of Rhodes or Kós. **SKÁLA**, the port and main town, is the chief exception, crowded on summer days with day-trippers from Kós and Rhodes or cruise-ship shoppers. **Accommodation** touts meet all ferries and hydrofoils, and their offerings tend to be a long walk inland – not necessarily a bad thing, as the waterfront is noisy. Hotels to book in advance include *Blue Bay* (⊕02470 31 165; ❹; closed Nov–April), just east of town, also with the town's main **internet** café; or *Diethnes* well inland (⊕02470 31 357; ❸; closed Nov–March). Among **restaurants**, try the seafood *ouzerí To Hiliomodhi*. The next bay north of the main harbour shelters **MÉLOÏ BEACH**, with a well-run campsite and excellent taverna, *Stefanos*. For swimming, the next beach, **AGRIOLIVÁDHI**, is usually less crowded.

The **Monastery of St John** (daily 8am–1pm) shelters behind massive defences in the hilltop capital of **HÓRA**. There is a bus up, but the thirty-minute walk by a beautiful old cobbled path puts you in a more appropriate frame of mind. Just over halfway is the **Monastery of the Apocalypse**, built around the cave where St John heard the voice of God issuing from a cleft in the rock. This is merely a fore-taste, however, of the main monastery, behind whose fortifications have been pre-served a fantastic array of religious treasures dating back to medieval times (museum €3.50). Hóra itself is a beautiful little town whose antiquated alleys shelter over forty churches and monasteries, plus dozens of shipowners' mansions dating from the island's heyday in the seventeenth and eighteenth centuries. If you're deter-mined to stay here – and there is a total of only about fifty beds – it's best to make morning enquiries at the recommended taverna *Vangelis*, on the inner square. From Hóra a good road runs above the forgettable package resort of Gríkou to the isth-mus of **Stavrós**, from where a thirty-minute trail leads to the excellent beach, with one seasonal taverna, at **PSILÍ ÁMMOS** (summer kaïki from Skála). There are more good beaches in the north of the island, particularly **LIVÁDHI YERÁNOU**, shaded by tamarisk groves and with a decent taverna, and **LÁMBI** with volcanic pebbles and another quality taverna.

The northern Aegean islands

The seven scattered islands of the **northeastern Aegean** form a rather arbitrary archipelago. Local tour operators do a thriving business shuttling passengers for absurdly high tariffs between the easternmost islands and the Turkish coast. **Sámos** is the most visited, and has – until a week-long forest fire devastated a fifth of the island in July 2000 – perhaps the most verdant and beautiful. **Híos** is culturally interesting, while **Lésvos** is more of an acquired taste, though once you get a feel for the island you may find it hard to leave. The **Sporades**, in the northwestern

Aegean, are a very easy group to island-hop and well connected with Athens by bus and ferry via Áyios Konstandínos or Kými (for Skýros only), and with Vólos.

Sámos

Sámos was the wealthiest island in the Aegean during the seventh century BC, but fell on hard times thereafter; today its economy is heavily dependent on package tourism. Except for express boats, all **ferries** to and from Pireás and the Cyclades call at both Karlóvassi in the west and Vathý in the east; additionally there are services to the Dodecanese out of Pythagório in the south. **VATHÝ**, the capital, lines the steep-sided shore of its namesake bay and is of minimal interest except for its hill quarter of tottering, tile-roofed houses, Áno Vathý, and an excellent **archeological museum** (Tues–Sun 8.30am–2.30pm; €2.40) which has a wealth of peculiar votive offerings and a huge, five-metre statue of an idealized youth. The **tourist office** is at 25-Martíou 4 (summer Mon–Fri 9am–2pm; ☎02730 28 530). **Accommodation** without tour-group allotment includes the welcoming *Pension Avli*, housed in a former convent at Áreos 2 (☎02730 22 939; ❷), and the basic *Pension Ionia*, Manóli Kalomíri 5 (☎02730 28 782; ❷). For **food**, head inland to *Ta Kotopoula* at Plátanos junction, or the pricier but good-value *Ouzeri Apanemia*, at the south end of the front.

West of Vathý, the busy resort of **KOKKÁRI** is enchantingly set between twin headlands at the base of still partly forested mountains. Nearby beaches are pebbly and exposed, prompting its role as a major windsurfers' resort. Some 13km west is untouristed **ÁYIOS KONSTANDÍNOS**, with three modest pensions, including *Atlantis* (☎02730 94 329; ❷). Less than an hour's walk west from functional Karlóvassi, **POTÁMI** is a popular beach ringed by forest and weird rock formations; for more solitude you can continue another hour or so on foot to the two bays of **Mikró Seitáni** (pebbles) and **Megálo Seitáni** (sand). But for an amenitied beach resort in the west of the island, you'll need to shift south to **VOTSALÁKIA**, almost 2km of sand and pebbles lined with accommodation. *Emmanuel Dhespotakis* (☎02730 31 258; ❸) has a few non-packaged **rooms** at the west end of the developed strip; *Loukoulos* is the most unique and interesting **taverna**.

Híos

Increasing numbers of foreigners are discovering **Híos** beyond its port city and single resort strip – fascinating villages, an important Byzantine monument and a healthy complement of beaches. **HÍOS TOWN** is always full of life, with a shambling old bazaar district, some excellent authentic tavernas, and a regular evening promenade along the waterfront. There's relatively cheap **accommodation** along and just behind the waterfront; the helpful **tourist office**, Kanári 18 (daily 7am–3/10pm; winter closed Sat & Sun; ☎02710 44 389), has comprehensive lists. The best-value and quietest include *Rooms Alex*, Mihaïl Livanoú 29 (☎02710 26 054; ❷), and *Hios Rooms*, Kokáli 1 (☎02710 20 198; ❷). For **eating out** try *Ouzeri Theodhosiou*, where the big ferries dock, or *O Hotzas*, well inland at Yeoryíou Kondhýli 3. Green long-distance **buses** run from the terminal south of the central park to most of the villages, though services to the north are sparse. The closest decent beach is **KARFÁS** (7km; frequent blue bus), a long if narrow sweep of sand, unfortunately overwhelmed by package tours; the best independent **accommodation** is *Markos' Place* (☎02710 31 990; ❸; closed Dec–March), in a disused monastery.

The monastery of **Néa Moní** (daily 8am–1pm & 4–8pm; free), founded by Byzantine emperor Constantine IX in 1042, is the most beautiful and important medieval building on the Greek islands. There are special KTEL bus excursions (Mon, Wed & Fr at 10am; €2). Once a community of 600 monks, the monastery was pillaged during Ottoman atrocities in 1822 and most of its inmates put to the sword. While here, make sure you plan a visit to the deserted medieval village of **ANÁVATOS**, about 9km to the northwest of Néa Moní, set on a dramatic 300-metre-high rock formation.

The hillsides of **southern Híos** are home to the mastic bush, whose resin – for centuries the base of paints and cosmetics – was the source of local wealth before petrochemicals came along. **PYRGÍ**, 24km from the port, is one of the liveliest and most colourful of the "mastic villages", its houses elaborately embossed with geometric patterns cut into the plaster and then outlined with paint. Pyrgí has a handful of rooms and some good beaches nearby, the closest being Emborió, 5km from Pyrgí and served by occasional buses in summer; eating is, however, better at the equally impressive **MESTÁ**, 11km west, with two good tavernas on its square.

Lésvos

Lésvos, birthplace of Sappho, the ancient world's foremost woman poet, may not at first strike the visitor as particularly beautiful, but the rocky volcanic landscape of pine and olive groves grows on you. Despite the inroads of tourism, this is still by and large a working island, with few large hotels outside the capital, Mytilíni, and the resorts of Skála Kallonís and Mólyvos.

MÓLYVOS, on the northwestern coast, is easily the most attractive spot on Lésvos. Tiers of sturdy, red-tiled houses mount the slopes between the picturesque harbour and the Genoese castle. There are plenty of rooms to let and a campsite east of town. The **tourist office** is by the bus stop (summer daily 8am–3pm & 6.30–8.30pm; ☎02530 71 347). The main lower road, past the tourist office, heads towards the picturesque harbour, where *The Captain's Table* is the best-value taverna. The best beach is at **SKÁLA ERESSOÚ** in the far southwest. There are a few rooms to let here. Tavernas with wooden terraces line the beach – try *Adonis* or *Blue Sardine*.

The Sporades

The three northern **Sporades** – package-tourist haven Skiáthos, Alónissos and **Skópelos**, the pick of the trio – have good beaches, transparent waters and thick pine forests. **Skýros**, the fourth island, is slightly isolated from the others, less scenic, but with perhaps the most character; for a relatively uncommercialized island within a day's travel of Athens it is hard to beat.

Skópelos

More rugged and better cultivated than neighbouring Skiáthos, **Skópelos** is also very much more attractive. **SKÓPELOS TOWN** slopes down one corner of a huge, almost circular bay. There are dozens of rooms to let – take up one of the offers when you land or call the Roomowners Association (☎04240 24 576) for vacancies. The most reliable waterfront **tavernas** are *To Aktaion* and *Spyros*. Make sure you try the famous local fried cheese pie (*skopelítiki tirópita*). Within the town, spread below the oddly whitewashed ruins of a Venetian *kástro*, are an enormous number of churches – 123 reputedly, though some are small enough to be mistaken for houses. **Buses** run along the island's one asphalt road to Loutráki about seven times daily, stopping at the turn-offs to all the main beaches and villages. **STÁFYLOS** beach, 4km out of town, is the closest, but it's small, rocky and increasingly crowded; the overflow, much of it nudist, flees to **VELANIÓ**, just east. Much more promising, if you're after isolation and are content to walk, is **AGNÓNDAS** (with tavernas and rooms), a fifteen-minute walk or short kaïki ride from the sand beach at Limnonári. The large resort of **Pánormos** has become overdeveloped, but slightly further on, **MILIÁ** offers a tremendous 1.5km sweep of tiny pebbles beneath a bank of pines.

Skýros

Skýros was until recently a very traditional and idiosyncratic island. The older men still wear the vaguely Cretan costume of cap, vest, baggy trousers, leggings and clogs, while the women favour yellow scarves and long embroidered skirts. Skýros also has some particularly lively **festivals** – notably the Apokriatiká (pre-Lenten) carnival's "Goat Dance", performed by masked revellers in the village streets. A **bus** connects Linariá – a functional little port with a few tourist facilities – to **SKÝROS TOWN**, perched on a high rock rising precipitously from the coast. Traces of classical walls can still be made out among the ruins of the Venetian *kástro*; within the walls is the crumbling, tenth-century monastery of **Áyios Yeóryios**. There are several hotels and plenty of rooms to let in private houses; you'll be met with offers as you descend from the bus. Skyros Travel (☏02220 91 123) on the main street can help with accommodation. Eating out, you'll find most tavernas overpriced and mediocre, *Khristina's* and *Maryetis* being exceptions. The campsite is down the hill at the fishing village of **MAGAZIÁ**, with rooms and tavernas fronting the best beach on the island. The most rewarding walk is a four-hour traverse of the island by rough jeep track to **ATSÍTSA** on the west coast.

The Ionian islands

The six **Ionian islands** are, both geographically and culturally, a mixture of Greece and Italy. Floating on the haze of the Adriatic, their green silhouettes come as a shock to those more used to the stark outlines of the Aegean. The islands were the Homeric realm of Odysseus and here alone of all modern Greek territory the Ottomans never held sway. After the fall of Byzantium, possession passed to the Venetians, and the islands became a keystone in that city-state's maritime empire from 1386 until its collapse in 1797. Tourism has hit **Corfu** in a big way – so much so that it's one of the few islands known to locals and foreigners by completely different names. None of the other islands has endured anything like Corfu's scale of development, although the process seems well advanced on parts of **Zákynthos**. For a less sullied experience, head for the trio of **Kefalloniá**, **Itháki** and **Lefkádha**.

Corfu (Kérkyra)

Corfu's natural appeal remains an intense experience, if sometimes a beleaguered one, for it has more package hotels and holiday villas than any other Greek island. The commercialism is apparent the moment you step ashore at the ferry dock, or cover the 2km from the airport (local buses #2 an d#3 leave from 500m north of the terminal gates). **KÉRKYRA TOWN**, the capital, has a lot more going for it than first exposure to the summer crowds might indicate. The cafés on the Esplanade and in the arcaded Listón have a civilized air, and the **Palace of SS Michael and George** at the north end of the Spianádha is worth visiting for its Asiatic museum (Tues–Sun 8.30am–3pm; €2.50) and Municipal Art Gallery (daily 9am–9pm; €1.50). The **Byzantine Museum** (Tues–Sun 9am–3pm; €1.50) and the cathedral are both interesting, as is the **Archeological Museum**, Vraíla 3 (Tues–Sun 8.30am–3pm; €2.40), where the small but intriguing collection features a 2500-year-old Medusa pediment. The island's patron saint, Spirýdhon, is entombed in a silver-covered coffin in his own church on Vouthrótou, and four times a year, to the accompaniment of much celebration and feasting, the relics are paraded through the streets. Some 5km south of town lies the picturesque island of **Vlahérna**, which is capped by a small monastery and joined to the plush mainland suburb of Kanóni by a short causeway.

There are several agencies along Vassíleos Konstandínou that can arrange your accommodation; the **tourist office** on the corner of Vouleftón and Mantazárou (Mon–Fri 8am–2pm; ☏06610 37 520) also has lists of **rooms**. Otherwise, try the least expensive old-town **hotel**, *Europa*, Yitsiáli 10, near the new port (☏06610 39 304; ❸). The nearest **campsite** is *Dionysos Camping Village* (☏06610 91 417) at Dhassiá, 8km north. For **eating out**, try *Aleko's Beach*, at the jetty below the Palace of St Michael and St George.

Around the island

The coast north of the port has been remorselessly developed as far as Pyrgí, and much of it is best written off. The best spot is **PEROULÁDHES**, a genuine, somewhat run-down village with a spectacular beach of brick-red sand below wind-eroded cliffs. On the west coast, **PALEOKASTRÍTSA** has gone the way of all package locations, though its coves are on a beautiful stretch of coast. Expensive villas and hotels are present in abundance, plus a few campsites, which are, however, some distance from the town. If you just want a **room**, search uphill in the villages of Lákones and Makrádhes, 5km away. The tiny village of **VÁTOS**, just inland from west-coast Érmones, is the one place within easy reach of Kérkyra Town that has an easy, relaxed feel to it and reasonable rooms and tavernas. Campers pitch tents down towards **Myrtiótissa Beach**, though they sometimes get encouraged to use the official site, *Vatos Camping*, near the village. Nearby **PÉLEKAS** is rather busy, but it's a good alternative base, with simple tavernas, a hostel and rooms. Further south, **ÁYIOS GÓRDHIS** beach is more remote but that hasn't spared it from the crowds who come to admire the cliff-girt setting or patronize the *Pink Palace* (☎06610 53 103; ❷), a holiday village/resort right on the sand.

Beyond Messongí stretches the flat, sandy southern tip of Corfu. **ÁYIOS YEÓRYIOS**, on the southwest coast, consists of a developed area just before its beautiful beach, which extends north alongside the peaceful Korissíon lagoon. **KÁVOS**, near the cape itself, rates with its many **clubs** and **discos** as the nightlife capital of the island; for daytime solitude and swimming, you can walk to beaches beyond the nearby hamlets of Sparterá and Dhragotiná.

Kefalloniá

Kefalloniá is the largest, and at first glance least glamorous, of the Ionian islands; the 1953 earthquake that rocked the archipelago was especially devastating here, with almost every town and village levelled. Couple that with the islanders' legendary eccentricity, and with poor infrastructure, it's no wonder tourism didn't take off until the late 1980s. Already popular with the Italians, the island has, more recently, been attracting large numbers of British tourists, in no small part thanks to the success of Louis de Bernières' novel, *Captain Corelli's Mandolin*, which was set here. There's plenty of interest: beaches to compare with the best on Corfu or Zákynthos, good local wine, and the partly forested mass of Mount Énos (1632m). The island's size, skeletal bus service and shortage of summer accommodation make renting a motorbike or car a must for extensive exploration.

Ferries mostly dock at **SÁMI** on the east coast; few people linger here, though there is an excellent campsite, *Karavomilos Beach* (☎06740 22 480). **AYÍA EVFIMÍA**, 10km north, makes a far more attractive base, with the small but smart *Moustakis* hotel (☎06740 61 030; ❹) and *Dendrinos*, arguably the best taverna on Kefalloniá. Between the two towns, 3km from Sámi, the **Melissáni cave** (daily 8am–sunset; €4.70), a partly submerged Capri-type "blue grotto", is well worth a stop. Southeast from Sámi you find the resorts of **PÓROS**, with ferries to Kyllíni on the Peloponnese. You may have to continue around the cape, past excellent beaches, to find accommodation in the coastal village of Lourdháta. Just inland, detour to the Venetian **castle of Áyios Yeóryios** (Tues–Sat 8am–8pm, Sun 8am–2pm; €1.50).

ARGOSTÓLI, with occasional ferries to Kyllíni and Zákynthos, is the bustling, inevitably concrete island capital. The waterfront **tourist office** (Mon–Fri 7.30am–2.30pm & 5pm–10pm, Sat 9am–1pm; ☎06710 22 248) keeps comprehensive lists of **accommodation**; you're best off with private rooms as hotels are expensive. The newly refurbished **Archeological Museum** (Tues–Sun 8.30am–3pm; €1.50) is second only to Corfu's in the archipelago. Heading north, you find the beach of **MÝRTOS**, considered the best one on the island, although lacking in facilities; the closest place to **stay** is the almost bus-less **ÁSSOS**, a fishing port perched on a narrow isthmus linking it to a castellated headland. At the end of the line, **FISKÁRDHO**, with its eighteenth-century houses, is the most expensive place on the island; the main reason to come would be for the daily **ferry** to Lefkádha island, and sometimes to Itháki.

Itháki

Despite its proximity to Kefalloniá, there's still very little tourist development to spoil **Itháki**, Odysseus's capital. There are no sandy beaches, but the island is good walking country, with a handful of small fishing villages and various coves to swim from. **Ferries** from Pátra and Kefalloniá (and, in peak season, from Corfu) land at the main port and the village-sized capital of **VATHÝ**, at the back of a deep bay within a bay. **Rooms** are fairly easy to come by; they tend, however, to be inconspicuous, and are best sought by nosing around the backstreets south of the ferry dock. There's ample choice for **food**, with seven or eight tavernas, the seafront *To Kohyli* being the best of a remarkably similar bunch.

In season the usual small boats shuttle tourists from the harbour to a series of tiny coves along the peninsula northeast of Vathý. The pebble-and-sand **beaches** between Cape Skhinós and Sarakíniko Bay are excellent. Two daily **buses** run north along the main road out of Vathý to **STAVRÓS**, a fair-sized village with a couple of tavernas and some rooms. There's an Homeric site nearby that may be the location for Odysseus's castle. **FRÍKES**, a thirty-minute walk downhill beyond Stavrós, is smaller but has a handful of tavernas, rooms and a pebbly strip of beach. This is where the seasonal **ferries** dock, to and from Lefkádha and Fiskárdho on northern Kefalloniá; the port is linked to Vathý by the same bus as Stavrós.

Zákynthos

Zákynthos was hit hardest by the 1953 earthquake, and the island's grand old capital was completely destroyed. Although some of its beautiful Venetian churches have been restored, it's a town of limited appeal and the attraction for travellers lies more in the thick vineyards, orchards and olive groves of the interior, and some excellent beaches. Under two hours from Kyllíni on the mainland, Zákynthos now gets close to half a million visitors a year. Most tourists, though, are conveniently housed in one place, Laganás, on the south coast; if you avoid July and August, and steer clear of Laganás and the developing villages of Argási and Tsiliví, there is still a peaceful Zákynthos to be found. The most tangible hints of the former glory of **ZÁKYNTHOS TOWN** are in **Platía Solomoú**, the grand and spacious main square. At its waterside corner stands the beautiful fifteenth-century sandstone church of **Áyios Nikólaos**, whose paintings and icons are displayed in the imposing **Zákynthos Museum** (Tues–Sun 8am–2.30pm; €2.35) by the town hall. The large church of **Áyios Dhionýsios** was one of the few buildings left standing after the earthquake, and murals still cover the interior. If you've a couple of hours to fill, walk up the cobbled path to the town's massive **Venetian fortress** (daily 8am–2/7.30pm; €1.50) for great views across the town and sea. The **tourist police** on waterfront Lombárdhou have information about **accommodation** and **bus** services. The Roomowners Association (☎06950 49 498) also has vacancies all over the island. Good-value hotels include *Egli* at the corner of Loútzi and Lombárdhou (☎06950 28 317; ❸). **Eating places** are thin on the ground; *Taverna Arekia* is excellent and has authentic live music, but it's a twenty-minute walk north along the east road. To get to the **beaches**, buses depart from the station on Filitá (one block back from the seafront), but since the island is fairly flat, apart from the north and west, this is an ideal place to rent a **bike** – available from Moto-Saki, opposite the phone office. In the summer a number of boats depart from the quay for day-trips around the island, visiting the Blue Caves, Shipwreck Bay and Cape Kerí caves.

Crete

With its flourishing agricultural economy, **CRETE** is one of the few islands that could probably support itself without tourists. Nevertheless, tourism is heavily promoted. The northeast coast in particular is overdeveloped and, though there are parts of the south and west coasts that have not been spoiled, they are getting harder and harder to find. By contrast, the high mountains of the interior are barely touched.

Crete is distinguished as the home of the **Minoan** civilization, Europe's earliest, which made the island the centre of a maritime trading empire as early as 2000 BC and produced artworks unsurpassed in the ancient world. Control of the island passed from Greeks to Romans to Saracens, through the Byzantine Empire to Venice, and finally to Turkey for more than two centuries. Almost wherever you go, you'll find some reminder of the island's history. The first priority is to get away from the capital **Iráklio** as quickly as possible, having first paid a visit to its superb archeological museum and the Minoan palace at nearby **Knossos**. There's another great Minoan site at **Mália** on the north coast, while to the south are Roman ruins at **Gortys**. For many people, unexpected highlights turn out to be Crete's **Venetian forts** (dominant at **Réthymno**) and its **Byzantine churches**. To get away from it all, head west towards **Haniá** and the smaller, less well-connected places along the south and west coasts; it is in this area that the mighty **White Mountains** rise, while below them yawns the famous **Samariá Gorge**, a magnet for trekkers.

Iráklio and around

The best way to approach **IRÁKLIO** is by sea; that way you see the city as it should be seen, with Mount Ioúktas rising behind and the Psilorítis range to the west. As you get closer, it's the city walls which first stand out, still dominating and fully encircling the oldest part of town, and finally you sail in past the great fort defending the harbour entrance. Unfortunately, big ships no longer dock in the old port but at great modern concrete wharves alongside – which neatly sums up Iráklio itself: many of the old parts have been restored, but they're of no relevance to the dust and noise which characterize much of the city today. The only realy sight of interest is the **Archeological Museum**, just off the north side of the main square, Platía Eleftherías (Mon noon–7pm, Tues–Sun 8am–7pm; €6). It hosts a fabulous if bewilderingly large collection that includes almost every important prehistoric and Minoan find on Crete (go early or late in the day to avoid tour groups).

Directly opposite the museum is the EOT **tourist office** (Mon–Fri 8.30am–5pm; ☎0810 228 225). Finding a **room** is usually not a problem, except in August. There is a friendly and comfortable non-HI hostel at Výronos 5 (☎0810 286 281; ❶). The nearest **campsite**, *Creta Camping* at Káto Goúves (☎08970 41 400), lies 16km east; Hersónissos-bound buses will drop you there. Of the **places to eat**, try *Geroplatanos*, with a tranquil terrace in the small pedestrianized square fronting the church of Áyios Titos, just off Fountain Square. On the same square there is a stylish **bar**, *Pagopoleion*, which has been imaginatively converted from an old ice factory. **Internet** access is at Gallery Games, Korái 14, and Netc@fé, Odós 1878, 4. **Buses** for all points east along the coastal highway and to the east and southeast of the island leave from the station near the ferry dock on the south (or town) side of the coast road; services west leave from the terminal opposite.

Knossós

The largest of the Minoan palaces, **KNOSSÓS** reached its cultural peak over 3500 years ago, though a town of some importance persisted here until well into the Roman era. It lies on a low, largely artificial hill some 5km southeast of Iráklio amid hillsides rich in lesser remains spanning twenty-five centuries. As soon as you enter the **Palace of Knossós** (daily 8am–5/7pm; €4.50) through the West Court, the ancient ceremonial entrance, it is clear how the legends of the Labyrinth of the Minotaur grew up around it. Even with a detailed plan, it's almost impossible to find your way around the site systematically. Evidence of a luxurious lifestyle is plainest in the **Queen's Suite**, off the grand **Hall of the Colonnades** at the bottom of the stunningly impressive **Grand Staircase**. Going up the Grand Staircase to the floor above the Queen's domain, you come to a set of rooms in a sterner vein, generally regarded as the **King's quarters**. The staircase opens into a grandiose reception chamber known as the **Hall of the Royal Guard**, its walls decorated in repeated shield patterns. Continuing to the top of the staircase you emerge onto the broad **Central Court**, which would once have been enclosed by the walls of the buildings all around. On the far side, in the northwestern corner of the courtyard, is the entrance to one of Knossós' most atmospheric survivals, the **Throne Room**, in all probability the seat of a priestess rather than a ruler.

Gortys, Phaestos and Mátala

About 1km west of Áyii Dhéka, where the bus drops you off, **GORTYS** (daily 8am–7pm; €4) is the ruined capital of the Roman province of Cyrenaica, which included not only Crete but also much of North Africa. Cutting across the fields to the south of the fenced site will give you some idea of the scale of this city at its zenith (approximately the third century AD); here, an enormous variety of other remains are strewn across your route, including an impressive **theatre**, a huge administrative complex and three temples. At the main entrance to the **fenced site**, alongside and to the north of the road, is the ruinous but still impressive basilica of **Áyios Títos**, the saint who converted Crete and was also its first bishop. Beyond this is the **Odeion**, which houses the most important discovery on the site, the Law Code – an inscription measuring about 10m by 3m.

Some 17km west of Gortys along the main highway lies the **Palace of Phaestos** (daily 8am–7pm; €4), another of the island's key Minoan sites. Unlike Knossós, the palace was not substantially reconstructed and requires a little more imagination. But the location is stunning, a hillside position giving a commanding view over the Messará plain. The palace was constructed in the seventeenth century BC on the ruins of a previous palace, destroyed by a terrific earthquake. Merely following your nose will enable you to find the Theatral Area with an imposing staircase, royal apartments, storerooms with huge ceramic *pithoi* for storing oil, wine and grain, and a magnificent Central Court, the focus of all Minoan palaces.

MÁTALA is the best-known beach hereabouts, widely promoted because of the famous **caves** cut into the cliffs above its beautiful beach. These ancient tombs used to be almost permanently inhabited by a sizeable hippie community; nowadays the town is full of package tourists and tries hard to present a respectable image. The cliffs were long ago cleared out and nowadays comprise a fenced-off **archeological site** (April–Sept daily 10am–4pm; €1.50). Should the crowds get too much, make the twenty-minute clamber over the rocks to another excellent stretch of sand, known locally as "Red Beach".

Mália and Áyios Nikólaos

With. its crowded sandy beach, the resort of **MÁLIA**, 31km east of Iráklio, lives for the party-holiday spirit:. The raucous side of town lies along the snaking, 1km long beach road, replete with supermarkets, souvenir shops, video bars and nightclubs which erupt into a pulsating cacophony from around midnight. *Zoo* is one of the top choices along here; others (mostly British-owned) include *Cloud* and *Cosmos*. **Eating** is of the pie-and-chips variety, but if you head into the **old town**, on the inland side of the main road, you'll find welcoming tavernas around Platía Ayíou Dhimitríou and rooms at *Esperia* (☏08970 31 086; ❸). Some 3km east are the atmospheric ruins of the **Palace of Mália** (Tues–Sun 8.30am–3pm; €2.50), much less visited than Knossós or Phaestos, but with a virtually intact ground plan.

About the same distance again east, **ÁYIOS NIKÓLAOS** is set around a supposedly bottomless salt lake, now connected to the sea to form an inner harbour.
Both lake and port are surrounded by restaurants and bars, all of which charge well
above normal, and the town itself is permanently crammed with tourists, many of
whom are distinctly surprised to find themselves in a place with no decent beach. If
you're after clubs, crowds and souvenirs, though, this is the place for you. Finding a
cheap **room**, however, is virtually impossible in season; try the backpackerish *Green
House*, Modhátsou 15 (℡08410 22 025; **❷**). The helpful **tourist office** (April–Oct
daily 8am–9.30pm; ℡08410 22 357), by the bridge dividing the lake and harbour,
has accommodation lists. **Internet** access is at Café Peripou, 28-Oktovríou 25.

Following the coast road 8km north you find **ELOÚNDA**, a resort on a more
acceptable scale. It's a spectacular bus ride with a series of impeccable views over a
gulf dotted with islands and moored supertankers. From Eloúnda, kaïkia run to the
fortress-rock of **SPINALÓNGA**. As a bastion of the Venetian defence, this tiny
islet withstood the Turkish invaders for 45 years after the rest of Crete had fallen; in
more recent decades it served as a leper colony.

Sitía and Váï beach

The port and main town of the relatively unexploited eastern edge of Crete,
SITÍA offers a plethora of waterside restaurants, a long sandy beach and a lazy
lifestyle little affected by the thousands of visitors in peak season. You pass the
friendly **hostel** (℡08430 22 693; **❶**) as you come into Sitía from Áyios Nikólaos
on the main road. The **tourist office** is on the seafront (Mon–Fri 9am–2.30pm &
5-8.30pm; ℡08430 23 300). For **food**, there are inexpensive options in the streets
behind the waterfront, such as *Mixos*, Kornárou 117, while *Itanos Cafe* at the start of
the Beach Road does good *mezédhes*.

The superb **Váï beach** has become somewhat commercialized in recent years,
with charges for parking and shower use. The beach itself is famous above all for its
palm trees, creating an illusion of a Caribbean island. Now a fenced (and guarded)
natural park, you will not be allowed to sleep on the main beach, but you should be
able to get some peace at some of the smaller beaches north and south (watch your
belongings – this seems to be the one place on Crete with crime on any scale).

Réthymno

The old town of **RÉTHYMNO** remains one of the most beautiful of Crete's major
cities. A wide sandy beach and palm-lined promenade border a labyrinthine tangle
of Venetian and Turkish houses. Medieval minarets lend an exotic air to the skyline,
while dominating everything from the west is the superbly preserved outline of the
fortress built by the Venetians after a series of pirate raids had devastated the town.

When you get off the bus, walk east, with the fortress to your left, to reach the
beach and the centre; the seafront **tourist office** (April–Sept Mon–Fri 8am–7pm;
℡08310 56 350) can provide a town map. To explore, follow Arkadhíou, the street
which curves around to the north immediately inland from the beach, and then
continue towards the **fortress** (Tues–Sun 8am–7pm; €2.40). There are plenty of
rooms, although you may struggle to find something if you turn up on spec in
August; try *Olga's Pension*, Soulíou 57, slightly west of the central Rimóndi
Fountain (℡08310 54 896; **❷**). The **hostel**, Tombázi 45 (℡08310 22 848; **❶**), is a
passable alternative, or there's a **campsite**, *Camping Elizabeth* (℡08310 28 694),
about 4km east along the beach and served by frequent buses from the main bus
station. There's an unbroken line of **tavernas**, cafés and cocktail bars right around
the waterside and into the area around the old port, but the sea view comes at a
price. You'll find an assortment of better-value places around the seventeenth-century Venetian **Rimóndi Fountain**: tucked into an alley behind here is *Kyria María*,
a cosy taverna serving economical fare. **Bars** and **nightlife** concentrate in the same
general area, particularly towards the western end of the town beach.

Haniá

HANIÁ is the spiritual capital of Crete; for many it is also the island's most attractive city – especially in spring, when the Lefká Óri's snowcapped peaks seem to hover above the roofs. Although it is for the most part modern, the small outer harbour is surrounded by a jumble of Venetian streets that survived the wartime bombardments. The **bus station** is on Odhós Kydhonías, within easy walking distance of the centre: turn right, then left down the side of Platía 1866 and you'll emerge at a major road junction opposite the top of Halídhon, the main street of the old quarter. **Boats** dock about 10km away at the port of Soúdha: there are frequent city buses which will drop you by the market on the fringes of the old town.

The **port area** is the oldest and the most interesting part of town. The little hill that rises behind the landmark domes of the quayside **Mosque of the Janissaries** is called **Kastélli**, site of the earliest habitation and core of the Venetian and Turkish towns. Beneath the hill, on the inner harbour, the arches of sixteenth-century Venetian arsenals survive alongside remains of the outer walls. Behind the harbour lie the less picturesque but more lively sections of the old city. Around the ordinary cathedral up Halídhon street there are some of the more animated shopping areas, particularly leather-dominated **Odhós Skrídhlof**. In the direction of the Spiántza quarter are ancient alleys with tumbledown Venetian stonework and overhanging wooden balconies that appear little touched by modern tourism.

Haniá's **beaches** all lie to the west: the packed **city beach** is a ten-minute walk beyond the Maritime Museum, but for good sand you're better off taking the local bus from the east side of Platía 1866 along the coast road to Kalamáki. In between you'll find emptier stretches if you're prepared to walk from Haniá.

Practicalities

The **tourist office** is in the new town at Kriári 40, just off Platía 1866 (Mon–Fri 8am–2.30pm; ☎08210 92 624). There are plenty of **rooms** on offer, but in season you may face a long search. *Pension Fidias*, Kalinikoú Sarpáki 8, behind the cathedral (☎08210 52 494; ❷), is exceptionally friendly and comfortable, and run along hostel lines (dorms ❶). Popular *Pension Lena*, Theotokopoúlou 60 (☎08210 86 860; ❷), near the Maritime Museum, is a wonderfully restored house. The **campsite**, *Camping Hania* (☎08210 31 138), lies on the coast 4km west, served by city bus from Platía 1866. Both the inner and outer harbours are circled by **cafés**, **tavernas** and **bars**, although most are overpriced. You can stock up on food at the bustling and colourful **market**, three blocks east from the northern end of Platía 1866, which is housed inside a nineteenth-century steel-framed copy of the market at Marseille. There's a series of **bars** around the twin harbours, particularly along Odhós Sarpidhóna off the inner harbour. Along the inner harbour quayside *Prime Vision Ariadne* is a popular dance **club**, and the nearby *Four Seasons* bar has a popular terrace. Haniá is also a good place to catch local Cretan lýra **music**, especially at *Café Kriti*, Kallérgon 22, one block inland from the harbour. **Internet** access is at Café Vranas, next to Vranas Studios.

The Samariá Gorge

It's easy to visit the beautiful **Gorge of Samariá** – Europe's longest – as a day-trip from Haniá. You should catch the early bus (6.15am) to avoid the full heat of the day while walking through the gorge, though be warned that you will not be alone: there are often as many as four coachloads setting off before dawn for the dramatic climb into the White Mountains. The **gorge** (May–Oct; €3.60; ☎08210 67 179) begins at a stepped path descending steeply from the southern lip of the Omalós Plain through almost alpine scenery of pines, wild flowers and un-Cretan greenery. At an average pace with regular stops, the 18km walk down takes five to six hours; solid shoes are vital. There's plenty of water from springs and streams (except in Sept & Oct), but nothing to eat. Small churches and viewpoints dot the route, and about halfway down you pass the abandoned village of Samariá, now home to a wardens' station, with picnic facilities and (filthy) toilets. Further down, the path levels out and the walls close in to the narrowest point – the spectacular *Sidherespórtes* or **Iron Gates**, a mere 3m wide and rising sheer for over 300m.

When you finally get down to the sea, the village of **AYÍA ROÚMELI** is all but abandoned until you reach the beach, a mirage of iced drinks and a cluster of expensive tavernas with equally pricey rooms to let. If you aim to get back to Haniá, buy your **boat** ticket immediately, especially if you want an afternoon on the beach: the last boat tends to sell out first. Boats run west towards the pleasant resorts of Soúyia and Paleohóra, good beach on which to wait for a bus to Haniá; but most of your fellow gorge walkers will be taking boats east to the less desirable Hóra Sfakíon, where up to fifty daily buses run to Haniá and other places around the island.

Travel details

Buses

Athens to: Corfu (4 daily; 11hr); Corinth (hourly; 1hr 30min); Delphi (6 daily; 3hr); Ioánnina (8 daily; 7hr 30min); Kefalloniá (3 daily; 7hr); Kými, for Skýros ferries (6 daily; 3hr 30min); Mycenae (hourly; 2hr); Náfplio (hourly; 2hr 30min); Olympia (4 daily; 5hr 30min); Pátra (every 30min; 3hr); Kalamáta (12 daily; 4hr 30min); Lárissa (Mt Olympus; 6 daily; 4h 30min); Rafína (every 30min; 1hr 30min); Sounion (every 30min; 2hr); Spárti (10 daily; 4hr 30min); Thessaloníki (10 daily; 7hr 30min); Vólos (10 daily; 5hr 20min); Zákynthos (5 daily; 6hr).

Corinth to: Ancient Corinth (hourly; 20min); Árgos (hourly; 1hr); Kalamáta (10 daily; 3hr–4hr); Mycenae-Fíkhti (hourly; 30min); Náfplio (hourly; 1hr 30min); Spárti (8 daily; 3hr–4hr).

Ioánnina to: Igoumenítsa (9 daily; 2hr); Métsovo (2–3 daily, 1hr 30min); Dodona (3 weekly; 40min); Tríkala (2 daily; 4hr).

Kalamáta to: Areópoli (4 daily; 1hr 30min); Kóroni (8 daily; 1hr 30min); Methóni via Pýlos (5 daily; 1hr 30min); Pátra (2 daily; 4hr); Pýlos (8 daily; 1hr).

Lárissa (Mt Olympus) to: Kalambáka (hourly; 2hr); Litóhoro junction (hourly; 1hr 45min).

Náfplio to: Epidaurus (5 daily; 45min); Mycenae (3 daily; 30min).

Pýrgos to: Kalamáta (2 daily; 2hr); Olympia (hourly; 45min); Pátra (10–11 daily; 2hr).

Thessaloníki to: Ierissós (5–7 daily; 3hr 30min); Ioánnina (5 daily except Tues; 7hr); Kalambáka (7 daily; 4hr 30min); Litóhoro (7 daily; 1hr 30min); Ouranoúpoli (5–7 daily; 3hr 45min); Vólos (4 daily; 4hr).

Vólos to: Áyios Ioánnis (2 daily; 2hr 30min); Kalambáka (4 daily; 3hr); Lárissa (Mt Olympus; hourly; 1hr 15min); Makrinítsa (10 daily; 50min); Miliés (6 daily; 1hr); Tsangarádha (2 daily; 2hr); Vyzítsa (6 daily; 1hr 10min); Zagorá (4 daily; 2hr).

Trains

Athens to: Corinth (12 daily; 1hr 30min–2hr); Kalamáta (3 daily; 7hr); Kalambáka via Paleofársala (4 daily; 5–6hr 30min); Mycenae (5 daily; 2hr 45min); Náfplio (2 daily; 3hr–3hr 30min); Pátra (8 daily; 3hr 30min); Thessaloníki (9 daily, including 1 sleeper; 6–8hr); Vólos (6 daily; 4hr–6hr 30min).

Pátra to: Corinth (8 daily; 1hr 30min); Kalamáta (1 daily; 5hr); Pýrgos (7 daily; 2hr).

Thessaloníki to: Litóhoro (6 daily; 1hr 40min); Vólos (2 daily; 2hr).

Vólos to: Athens (2 daily; 5hr); Kalambáka (2 daily; 2hr 45min); Lárissa (Mt Olympus; 11 daily; 1hr).

Ferries and hydrofoils

Áyios Konstandínos to: Skópelos (2–4 daily; 1hr 45min–3hr 30min).

Híos to: Lésvos (6–10 weekly; 4hr); Sámos (2–5 weekly; 2hr–5hr).

Íos to: Náxos (3 daily; 3hr); Páros (2 daily; 5hr); Thíra (1–2 daily; 2hr).

Iráklio to: Pireás (3 daily; 12hr) also fast ferry (1 daily; 6hr); Páros & Cyclades (1 daily; 7hr); Rhodes (2–3 weekly; 11hr).

Kefalloniá to: Zákynthos (summer 2 daily; 1hr 30min); Itháki (summer 1 daily; 1hr).

Kós to: Pátmos (2–4 daily; 2hr 30min–5hr); Rhodes (2–4 daily; 2–4hr).

Kyllíni to: Kefalloniá (2 daily; 1hr 45min); Zákynthos (7 daily; 3 in winter; 1hr 30min).

Kými to: Skýros (1–2 daily; 2hr 30min).

Lésvos to: Híos (5–9 weekly; 4hr); Thessaloníki (2 weekly; 14hr).

Náxos to: Íos (3 daily; 3hr); Iráklio (3 weekly; 6hr); Páros (3 daily; 1hr); Thíra (3 daily; 4hr).

Pátra to: Corfu (3–5 daily; 8–10hr); Itháki (2 daily; 4hr); Kefaloniá (2 daily; 2hr 30min).

Pireás to: Crete (2–4 daily; 12hr); Híos (6–7 weekly; 10hr); Íos (3–6 daily; 10hr); Kós (13 weekly; 12hr); Lésvos (6–7 weekly; 14hr); Mýkonos (2 daily; 5hr); Náxos (4 daily; 8hr); Páros (4 daily; 7hr); Pátmos (2 daily; 11hr); Rhodes (19 weekly; 18–23hr); Sámos (daily; 6–14hr); Sífnos (2 daily; 3-5hr); Thíra (2–5 daily; 10–12hr).

Rafína to: Mýkonos, Páros, Náxos, Íos, Thíra (all 1–2 daily; 3–7hr).

Rhodes to: Crete (Sitía/Áyios Nikólaos; 2–3 weekly; 13hr); Kós (2 daily; 4hr); Pátmos (2 daily; 8h).

Sámos to: Kós (4–9 weekly; 3hr 45min); Pátmos (2 weekly; 1hr 30min–3hr); Rhodes (1 weekly; 9hr).

Thessaloníki to: Híos (1–2 weekly; 15hr); Iráklio (2–5 weekly; 21hr); Lésvos (1–2 weekly; 15hr); Skýros (2–4 weekly; 3–7hr); Skópelos (summer daily; 3hr).

Thíra to: Íos (3 daily; 2hr); Iráklio (5 weekly; 5hr); Mýkonos (1 daily; 7hr); Náxos (3 daily; 4hr); Páros (3 daily; 5hr).

Vólos to: Skópelos (2–4 daily; 2hr 30min–5hr).

Hungary

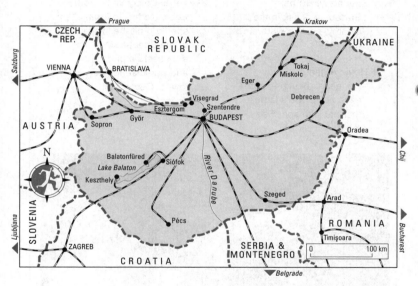

Hungary highlights

* **Communist Statue Park, Budapest** Graveyard for statues of old dictators, an ironic open-air museum. See p.542

* **Széchenyi Baths, Budapest** Relax in the steamy, healing waters. See p.543

* **Hévíz** A genuine Hungarian health experience at Europe's largest thermal-lake spa. See p.549

* **Pécs** Terrace cafés, brightly-coloured buildings and laid-back attitude; a young, fun destination. See p.550

* **Széoasszony Vally, near Eger**. No trip to Eger should omit the "Valley of the Beautiful Woman", a horseshoe of cellars and paradise for wine lovers. See p.551

Introduction and basics

Visitors who refer to **Hungary** as a Balkan country risk getting a lecture on how this small, landlocked nation of 10 million people differs from "all those Slavs": locals are strongly conscious of themselves as **Magyar** – a race that transplanted itself from Central Asia into the heart of Europe over a thousand years ago.

The magnificent capital, **Budapest** (split into historic Buda and vibrant Pest), with its coffee houses, Turkish baths and fad for Habsburg bric-a-brac, has a strong whiff of Mitteleuropa – that ambient culture that welcomed Beethoven in Budapest and Hungarian-born Liszt in Vienna, and continues with a new wave of writers, film directors, artists and other media figures. But there is also an eager modern feel to the place, with international fashions snapped up and adapted to local tastes. Outside the capital, there is much to divert the traveller. **Lake Balaton**, in the west, with its string of brash resorts, styles itself as the "Nation's Playground", while other highlights of the region include historic **Sopron**, within spitting distance of Vienna, and Turkish-flavoured **Pécs**. The forested **Northern Uplands** in the far northeast towards Ukraine envelop the famous wine centre of **Eger**.

Information and maps

You'll find branches of **Tourinform**, the Hungarian National Tourist Office in the capital and in larger towns across the country; branches are open Mon–Fri 9am–5/8pm; summer also open Sat & Sun. They do not book accommodation, but do have information on where rooms and beds are available, including the small booklet *Hungarian Hotel Guide*, and *Camping*. There are also **local tourist offices** in larger towns (Savariatourist, Balatontourist, etc, according

to the region), where you can **book rooms**; opening hours are Mon–Fri 9am–4/6pm; summer also Sat 8am–1pm.

It's cheapest to buy your **maps** in Hungary: the best is Cartographia's full-country fold-out sheet (1:450,000; 550Ft).

Money and banks

The local currency is the **forint** (Ft), which comes in notes of 200, 500, 1000, 2000, 5000, 10,000 and 20,000Ft, and in coins of 1, 2, 5, 10, 20, 50 and 100Ft (the 50Ft coin is easily confused with the 10Ft coin). The best rates of exchange are offered by regional tourist offices and the banks. Changing money at large hotels or at the growing number of exchange offices leaves you substantially worse off. Avoid the black market.

Standard **banking hours** are Mon–Thurs 8am–4pm, Fri 8am–3pm. Budapest also has a large number of **ATMs**, and more are appearing in larger towns across the country, though you should not rely on finding one. You can use a **credit card** to pay in many hotels, restaurants and tourist shops, but outside the main tourist centres they're of little use.

Communications

Larger **post offices** (*posta*) are usually open Mon–Fri 8am–6pm, Sat 8am–1pm. Smaller branches close at 3pm and don't always open on Saturdays. **Poste restante** mail

Hungary on the net

ⓦ**www.tourinform.hu** National tourist office
ⓦ**www.travelport.hu** Excellent general site
ⓦ**www.budapestsun.com** Entertainment listings
ⓦ**www.elvira.hu** Train timetables and information

should be addressed "Poste restante, Posta", followed by the name of the town.

You can make local calls from **public phones**, where 20Ft is the minimum charge (40Ft if you're calling a mobile phone), or, better, from **cardphones** – they're increasingly common, and you have less chance of losing your money; cards come in 50 and 120 units and can be bought from post offices and newsstands. To make **national calls**, dial ⊕06, wait for the buzzing tone, then dial the area code and number. You can make **international calls** from most public phones: dial ⊕00, wait for the buzzing tone, then carry on dialling the country code as usual.

Internet access is widely available (usually 500–700Ft/hr), particularly in Budapest; most larger towns will also have at least one internet café.

Getting around

Although it doesn't break any speed records, **public transport** reaches most parts of Hungary, and fares are very low. The only problem is getting information, for staff rarely speak anything but Hungarian, although German is spoken around Lake Balaton.

Trains

The centralization of the MÁV **rail network** means that many cross-country journeys are easier if you travel via Budapest. Intercity **trains** are the fastest way of getting to the major towns, though seat reservations, made at any MÁV office, are compulsory and cost an extra 400Ft; *személyvonat* trains, which stop at every hamlet en route, do not incur the additional reservation fee. Most international, intercity and some express trains have buffets, but it is best to take food and drink with you if you're embarking on a long trip. You can buy tickets *(jegy)* for domestic services at the station *(pályaudvar* or *vasútállomás)* on the day of departure, but it's best to buy tickets for international trains *(nemzetközi gyorsvonat)* at least 36hr in advance. You're permitted to break your journey once. When buying your ticket, specify whether you want a one-way

ticket *(egy útra)*, or a return *(retur* or *oda-vissza)*. **InterRail** and **Eurail** passes are both valid.

Buses

Volán runs the bulk of Hungary's **buses**, which are often the quickest way to travel between the smaller towns. Schedules are clearly displayed in bus terminals; arrive early to confirm the departure bay and get a seat. For **long-distance services** from Budapest and the major towns, you can buy tickets with a seat booking up to thirty minutes before departure; after that, you get them from the driver (and risk standing). In rural areas, tickets are only available on board and there may be only one bus a day.

Accommodation

There's plenty of **accommodation** available, but costs have risen dramatically in recent years. More upmarket places tend to quote prices in euros (they'll usually accept US dollars or pounds sterling too); private rooms and hostels charge in forints. The cheapest places tend to fill up during high season, so it's wise to make bookings if you're heading somewhere that has limited accommodation.

Hostels and dormitories

Hostels go under various names: in provincial towns they're called *turistaszálló*, but in the highland areas they go by the name of *turistaház*. Local tourist offices can provide details and make bookings. They can also guide you to **student dormitories**, which are usually even cheaper: rooms are rented out in July and August, and are often available at weekends year-round.

Private rooms

Private rooms *(fizetővendégszoba)* – B&B-style in a private home – are an inexpensive way of staying near town centres, and are often quite appealing. Such accommodation can be arranged through local tourist offices for a small fee or by dealing direct with the owner (there'll be a sign outside saying either *szoba kiadó* or *Zimmer Frei)*. Doubles range from 2000Ft in provincial towns to around 4000Ft in Budapest and around the Balaton; singles usually pay the full double rate, though there may be a small reduction. Rooms in a town's *belváros* (inner sector) are likely to be much better than those in outlying zones.

In some towns and resorts it's possible to rent whole **apartments**, while regional tourist offices can arrange home accommodation in villages through the village tourism *(falusi turizmus)* network, the central office of which is in Budapest at VII, Király utca 93 ☎1/352-1433, ✉ebudapest3@tourinform.hu.

Hotels

Of the **hotels** *(szálló* or *szálloda)*, three-star places have become most common; luxury four- and five-star establishments are still mainly confined to Budapest and major resorts, while humble one- and two-star joints are getting rarer. Outside Budapest and Lake Balaton (where prices are thirty percent higher), a three-star hotel will charge from around 11000Ft (€45) for a double room with bath, TV, etc; solo travellers often have to pay this too, since singles are rare. A similar rating system is used for **inns** *(fogadó)* and **pensions** *(panzió)*, which charge a little less than hotels, though prices in the middle range often turn out very similar.

Bungalows and campsites

Throughout Hungary, campsites and bungalows come together in complexes. **Bungalows** *(faház)* proliferate around resorts and on the larger campsites; prices depend on their amenities and size. The first-class bungalows – with well-equipped kitchens, hot water and a sitting room or terrace – are excellent, and will cost a few thousand forints, while the most primitive at least have clean bedding and don't leak. **Campsites** (usually signposted *Kemping*) likewise range from de luxe to third class. The more elaborate places include a restaurant and shops but tend to be overcrowded; second- or third-class sites often have a more pleasant ambience. In high season, expect to pay anything up to 2500Ft, more around Lake Balaton.

Food and drink

For foreigners, the archetypal **Hungarian dish** is goulash – historically a soup made of potatoes and whatever meat was available, which was later flavoured with paprika. Today, meat is still a central part of the Hungarian diet.

Food

Hungarians like a calorific **breakfast** *(reggeli)* that includes cheese, eggs or salami, plus bread and jam. **Coffee houses** *(kávéház)* are coming back into fashion, reclaiming their places at the heart of Budapest's cultural life. You'll find many serving breakfast and everywhere you can count on a coffee with milk *(tejeskávé)* or whipped cream *(tejszínhabbal)*. Asking for a cappuccino is acceptable even in smaller towns, although most Hungarians take their coffee short and strong *(eszpresszó)*.

A whole range of places sell **snacks**, including bakeries and delicatessens *(csemege)*, which display a tempting spread of salads, open sandwiches, pickles and cold meats. Numerous **patisseries** *(cukrászda)* pander to the Magyar fondness for sweet things. Pancakes *(palacsinta)* with fillings are very popular, as are strudels *(rétes)* and a staggering array of cakes and other sticky items. On the streets you can buy, in summer, corn-on-the-cob *(kukorica)* and in winter, roasted chestnuts *(gesztenye)*; while stalls selling fried fish *(sült hal)* are common in towns near rivers or lakes. In covered and open–air markets you'll also find various inexpensive diners.

Hungarians have a variety of words implying fine distinctions among **restaurants**. In theory an *étterem* is a proper restaurant, while a *vendéglő* approximates to the Western notion of a bistro; however, these distinctions are very thin now. The old word for a roadside inn, *csárda*, is often used today by folksy, touristy restaurants. Traditionally, the main meal of the day is **lunch**, when some places offer set menus *(napi menű)*, a basic meal at moderate prices. Keep an eye on prices: gone are the days when even the top restaurants were cheap; but there are still plenty of places where you can eat well and sink a few beers for under 1000Ft. Always check your bill carefully as foreigners are a common target for being ripped off.

Starters *(előételek)* range from soup *(leves)* to the popular *Hortobágyi palacsinta* (pancakes stuffed with mince and doused in a creamy paprika sauce) and the more extravagant *libamáj* (goose liver), though nobody will mind if you just have a **main course** *(főételek)*. Hungarians like most things fried in breadcrumbs, such as *rántott csirkecomb* (chicken drumstick), but they also have a taste for *marhapörkölt* (beef stew). In traditional places the only choice for **vegetarians** will be breaded and fried cheese, mushrooms or cauliflower *(rántott sajt/gomba/karfiol)*, though prospects are better in the scores of international restaurants sprouting up around the capital. In the countryside, pork and lard still rules.

Drink

Hungary's mild climate and diversity of soils is perfect for **wine** *(bor)*, which is perennially cheap, whether you buy it by the bottle *(üveg)* or the glass *(pohár)*. Wine bars *(borozó)* are ubiquitous, while true grape devotees make pilgrimages to the wine cellars *(borpince)* around Pécs and Eger. **Spirits** are inexpensive, if you stick to native brands; the best-known types of brandy *(pálinka)* are distilled from apricots *(barack)* and plums *(szilva)*, the latter often available in private homes in a mouth-scorching home-distilled version. **Beer** *(sör)* of the lager type *(világos)* predominates, although you can also find **brown ale** *(barna)*: these come in draught form *(csapolt sör)* or in bottles *(üveges sör)*. Local brands to look out for are Pécsi Szalon sör and Soproni Ászok.

Opening hours and holidays

Shops are generally open Mon–Fri 10am–6pm, Sat 10am–1pm. Most things closed down for the following **public holidays**: Jan 1; March 15; Easter Mon; May 1; Whit Mon; Aug 20; Oct 23; Dec 25 & 26.

Emergencies

The **police** *(rendörség)* are badly paid and under-trained, which doesn't make for good policing. However, most foreign tourists are treated with respect – unless they're suspected of black-marketeering, drug smuggling or driving under the influence of alcohol. Be sure to always carry your passport or a photocopy at least. Most police officers have at least a smattering of German, but rarely any other foreign language. Should you be arrested or need legal advice, ask to contact your embassy or consulate.

All towns and some villages have a **pharmacy** *(gyógyszertár or patika)*, with staff – often German-speaking – authorized to issue a wide range of drugs. (However, if you need specific medication, you should bring a supply with you.) Opening hours are generally Mon–Fri 9am–6pm, Sat 9am–noon or 1pm; signs in the window give the location or telephone number of all-night pharmacies *(ügyeletes gógyszertár)*.

Tourist offices can direct you to local **medical centres** or **doctors' surgeries** *(orvosi rendelő)*; these will probably be in private *(magán)* practice, so be sure to carry health insurance.

Budapest

The importance of **BUDAPEST** to Hungary is difficult to overestimate. Around two million people – one-fifth of the population – live in the city, and everything converges here: wealth, political power, cultural life and transport. Surveying the city from Castle Hill, it's obvious why Budapest was dubbed the "Pearl of the Danube". It's grand buildings and sweeping bridges look magnificent, especially when floodlit or illuminated by the barrage of fireworks launched from **Gellért Hill** on St Stephen's Day.

Castle Hill (Várhegy) is the most prominent feature of the **Buda** district, a plateau one mile long laden with old mansions and a huge palace, commanding the **Watertown**. Buda and its twin, **Pest**, have a surfeit of other fine sights, including museums and galleries, restaurants, bars and a wide variety of entertainments, accessible by efficient, inexpensive public transport. A host of new nightclubs show that the city is making up for its dreary postwar past, though it is still true to say that many people get up early and then slope off at around 10pm, interrupting work with breaks in patisseries and *eszpresszó* bars. Ease yourself into Budapest life by wallowing away an afternoon in one of the city's **thermal baths** (*gyógyfürdő*). A basic ticket covers three hours in the pools, sauna and steamrooms (*gőzfürdő*), while supplementary tickets are available for such delights as the mud baths (*iszapfürdő*) and massages (*masszázs*).

Arrival, information

Most points of arrival are fifteen to thirty minutes from the centre. There are three main **train stations**, all of which are directly connected by **metro** with the central **Deák tér** metro station in the Belváros, the city centre district of Pest: Keleti station handles most international trains, including those from Vienna (Südbahnhof), Belgrade, Bucharest, Zagreb and Bratislava, as well as domestic arrivals from Sopron and Eger; Nyugati station handles trains from Prague and Bratislava, some from Bucharest, and domestic ones from the Danube Bend; and Déli station has one train a day from Vienna (Westbahnhof), the odd train from Zagreb, and domestic services from Pécs and Lake Balaton. From Ferihegy **airport**, there's a half-hourly shuttle bus (800Ft from Terminals 2A and 2B) which stops in front of the *Kempinski Hotel* on Erzsébet tér, by Deák tér metro station, as well as an Airport Minibus, which will take you to wherever you're staying (1800Ft; book it in the terminal building). The airport taxi-drivers are notorious sharks. The central **bus station** is also at Erzsébet tér, serving international destinations and routes to Transdanubia. Also in Pest, Népstadion bus station (red metro) serves areas east of the Danube; and Árpád híd bus station (blue metro) serves the Danube Bend. **Hydrofoils** from Vienna dock alongside the Belváros embankment.

The best source of practical information is the friendly **Tourinform** (daily 8am–8pm; ☎1/438-8080, ⊛www.tourinform.hu), just around the corner from Deák tér metro at Sütő utca 2, behind the big yellow Lutheran church; other branches are on Liszt Ferenc tér, at Nyugati train station, and in the Castle District on Szentháromság tér. Other useful offices include the **Vista Tourist Center**, Paulay Ede utca 7 (Mon–Fri 9am–8pm, Sat & Sun 10am–6pm; ☎1/267-8603, ⊛www.vista.hu), the **IBUSZ tourist office**, Ferenciek tere 10 (Mon–Fri 8.15am–5pm; ☎1/485-2700, ⊛www.ibusz.hu), and **Budapest Tourist**, in the subway in front of Nyugati train station (Mon–Fri 9am–4pm; ☎1/342-6521). The weekly *Budapest Sun* has **listings** of what's on, as does *Where Budapest*, a free monthly events guide available in many hotel foyers.

A **Budapest Card** (two days 3700Ft, three days 4500Ft), available at tourist offices, hotels and major metro station ticket offices, gives unlimited travel on public transport, free admission to a long list of museums, reductions on the airport minibus (buying single tickets with the card gets you a bigger reduction than buy-

ARPAD BRIDGE

Kiscelli Museum

Pálvölgyi Stalactite Cave

Roman
Amphitheatre

Árpad híd
Bus Station

SZEPVÖLGYI UT

Szemlöhegy Cave

Szépvölgyi út
HÉV Station

Palatinus
Baths

XIII

DRÁVA UTCA

II

RÓZSADOMB

Margit
Island

Hajós Baths

VICTOR HUGO UTCA

Lehel Tér
Market

Lukács Baths

VI

Gül Baba Tomb

MÁRCZIBÁNYI
TÉR

MARGIT BRIDGE

SZILÁGYI ERZSÉBET FASOR

Király
Baths

SZ. ISTVÁN KRT

Nyugati
Train Station

Moszkva tér

Parliament

Oktogon

HÉV Terminal and
Batthyány tér Metro

KOSSUTH
TÉR

BATHORY UTCA

Opera
House

Music
Academy

XII

Mátyás
Church

SZABADSÁG
TÉR

St Stephen's
Basilica

Déli Train Station
and Metro

Szentháromság
tér

CASTLE
HILL

BUDA

PEST

V

ROOSEVELT
TÉR

Clark
Ádám
tér

CHAIN BRIDGE

JÓZSEF ATTILA U

Funicular

Buda Palace

Vörösmarty
tér

Deák tér

ℹ

Synagogue

KÁROLY KÖRÚT

Astoria

RÁKÓCZI

ATTILA ÚT

Ferenciek tere

XI

Rác Baths

Rudas Baths

International
Landing
Stage

Main
Market
Hall

IX

Citadella

GELLÉRT HILL

Economics
University

Gellért Baths

Farkasréti Cemetery

13

HUNGARY

538

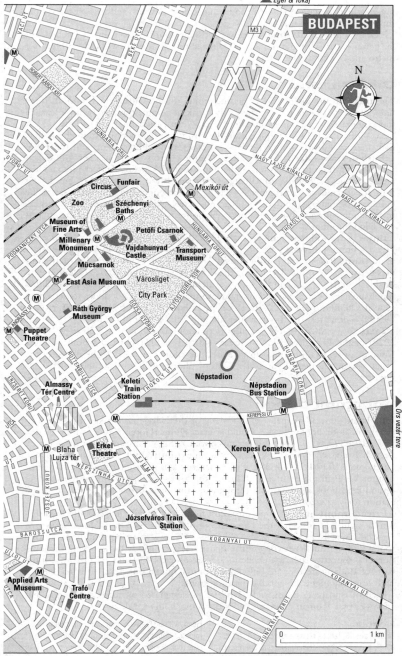

Eger & Tokaj

BUDAPEST

M3

XV

N

XIV

NAGY LAJOS KIRÁLY UT

NAGY LAJOS KIRÁLY UT

Mexikói út Ⓜ

Funfair

Circus

Zoo

Széchenyi Baths Ⓜ

Museum of Fine Arts

Millenary Monument Ⓜ

Petőfi Csarnok

Vajdahunyad Castle

Transport Museum

Műcsarnok

East Asia Museum Ⓜ

Városliget City Park

Ⓜ

Ráth György Museum

Puppet Theatre Ⓜ

Ⓜ

Népstadion

Keleti Train Station

Népstadion Bus Station

Almassy Tér Centre

VII

Ⓜ

KEREPESI UT

Ⓜ

Blaha Lujza tér Ⓜ

Erkel Theatre

Kerepesi Cemetery

VIII

Józsefváros Train Station

KOBANYAI UT

Applied Arts Museum Ⓜ

Trafó Centre

KOBANYAI UT

13

HUNGARY

Őrs vezér tere

0   1 km

539

Népliget Bus Station & Ferihegy Airport

ing a return), certain sightseeing tours and cultural events, and discounts in some shops, restaurants and thermal baths.

Pick up a proper **city map** as soon as possible; tourist offices supply freebies, but far better is the wirebound 1:25,000 Budapest Atlas, from newsstands in Deák tér metro and bookshops (1500Ft).

City transport

The **metro** is the easiest way of getting around (daily 4.30am–11.15pm). Its three lines intersect at Deák tér, and there's little risk of going astray once you've learned to recognize the signs: *bejsrat* (entrance), *kijsrat* (exit), *vonal* (line) and *felé* (towards). A basic 106Ft ticket (130Ft if bought on the bus) is valid for a journey along one line, and is also valid for a single journey on buses, trolleybuses, trams and the **HÉV suburban train** as far as the city limits. On the metro you can also get 75Ft tickets for journeys of up to three stops, and combination tickets for transferring to another metro line. Rather than queueing at a metro station, it's quicker to buy tickets from street stands or newsagents. Tickets have to be punched in the machines at the entrances of metro stations, or on board buses, trolleybuses and trams: inspectors are increasingly common, often waiting at the bottom of the escalators to check tickets and hand out fines.

Buses (*busz*) with red numbers make limited stops, while those with the red suffix "E" run nonstop between termini; all run every ten minutes or so during the day – as do **trams** (*villamos*) and **trolleybuses** (*trolibusz*) – and every thirty to sixty minutes between 11pm and dawn along those routes with a night service (denoted with the black suffix "É"). When the metro or trams are not running on a line, you'll find supplementary buses (*pótlóbusz*) operating in their place. It's a good idea to get a **pass** (one day 850Ft, three day 1700Ft), or buy a book of tickets (ten 1000Ft, twenty 1950Ft) – don't tear them out, as they are only valid if kept in the book.

Taxis are inexpensive, but are also a common rip-off. Go for Főtaxi (☎1/222-2222) or the English-speaking Citytaxi (☎1/211-1111), both of whom charge a basic fee of up to 200Ft plus up to 200Ft per kilometre; they can be hailed in the street, but are cheapest if you order them by phone, giving the number you're calling from.

Accommodation

Hotels are generally expensive, and many of the better places expect payment in euros. For hotel bookings, you should contact HungarHotels, Petőfi Ssndor utca 16 (☎1/318-3393, ⊛www.danubiusgroup.com); IBUSZ,V,Vörösmarty tér 6, facing the British Embassy (☎1/317-0532, ⊛www.ibusz.hu); American Express, V, Deák Ferenc utca 10 (☎1/235-4330), which charges a $20 service fee; or the Vista Visitor Center,VI, Paulay Ede utca 7 (☎1/267-8603, ⊛www.vista.hu). Another budget option is to book a **hostel** bed through the Tourist Information Centre in Keleti Station (☎1/413-2062).

Private rooms in downtown areas cost from 4000Ft (8000Ft–12000Ft high season) a night and are often the cheapest option. Tribus Non-stop Hotel Service,V, Apsczai Csere Jsnos utca 1 (24hr; ☎1/266-8042, ⊛www.tribus.hu), book private rooms and apartments. A copy of the *Budapest Atlas* is handy for checking the location of prospective sites: preferable locales are districts V,VI and VII in Pest, and the parts of Buda nearest Castle Hill. **Apartments**, rented out from 8000Ft (12000Ft high season) a night, are good-value for groups.

Each of Budapest's 23 districts (*kerületek*) is designated on maps, street signs and addresses by a Roman numeral; "V" is Belváros, "I" the Castle district.

Hostels

Back Pack XI, Takscs Menyhért utca 33 ☎1/385-8946, ✉backpackguest@hotmail.com. Charming, clean, with a shaded garden, and only twenty minutes from the centre. Lots of city information, plus rock climbing and cave trips. Tram #49 or bus

#7 to Tétényi Òt stop in Buda. Dorms **❶**
Citadella I, Citadella sétány ☎1/466-5794,
🖦www.hotels.hu/hotelcitadella. Breathtaking
views of the city; get there early to get a bunk, but
note that the neighbouring nightclub sets the
whole place shaking at weekends. Dorms **❶**
Disksport Szálló XIII, Dózsa György út 152 ☎1/340
-8585, 🖦www.travellers-hostels.com. Singles,
doubles and dorms in a clean but run-down hostel
near the centre, with internet access. **❷**
Landler XI, Bartók Béla út 17 ☎1/463-3622,
🖦www.hotels.hu/hostellandler. An older hostel
with high ceilings near the Gellért Baths, housed in
the Baross Gábor Kollégium. June to Sept only.
Tram #47 or #49 from Deák tér. **❷**
Museum Guest House VIII, Mikszáth Kálmán tér
4, 1st floor ☎1/318-9508,
✉museumgh@freemail.c3.hu. In a street behind
the National Museum, handy for central bars and
cafés. Three clean dorms, each with seven or eight
mattresses on the floor. Free internet in the eve. **❶**
Strawberry Youth Hostel IX, Kinizsi utca 2–6

☎1/217-3033, 🖦www.strawberryhostel.com. The
newer of two hostels of the same name, with basic
furniture in rooms with two, three or four beds.
June to Sept only. Blue metro line to Kálvin tér. **❷**

Hotels and pensions

ELTE Peregrinus Vendégház V, Szerb utca 3 ☎1/
266-4911. Located in a quiet backstreet in central
Pest, this friendly, elegant place is attached to the
university; 25 rooms, available year round. **❺**
Jager-Trio Panzió XI, Ördögorom út 20 ☎1/246-
4558, ✉jagertrio@axelero.hu. Small pension on
the edge of the city in the Buda hills, close to the
end of the bus #8 route. **❸**
Medosz VI, Jókai tér 6 ☎1/374-3000.
Comfortable lodging in an ugly but well located
building near the Oktogon. **❹**
San Marcó Panzió III, San Marcó utca 6 ☎1/388-
9997, ✉saiban@elender.hu. Small, friendly
pension in northern Buda, five rooms, three with
private bathrooms. Famous for its hearty
breakfasts. **❹**

The City

The **River Danube** (Duna) determines basic orientation, with **Pest** sprawled
across the eastern plain and **Buda** reclining on the hilly west bank. Castle Hill is the
historic focal point of Buda, home of the Royal Palace and for many years the government. Across the water, Pest has always been the commercial focus, with its hub
around the old city centre or Belváros. Construction of the first permanent bridge
between the two in 1849 led to rapid expansion, then unification in 1873.

Buda

Seen from the embankments, **Buda** looks irresistibly romantic with its palatial
buildings, archaic spires and outsize statues rising from rugged hills. Its centre,
Castle Hill, is easily reached from the city centre via the **Chain Bridge**, opened
in 1849 and the first permanent bridge between Buda and Pest. From the busy
square on its western side, Clark Ádám tér, you can ride up Castle Hill by the nineteenth-century funicular or **Sikló** (daily 7.30am–10pm; 400Ft up, 300Ft down).
Alternativly,take the red metro to Moszkva tér and the *Várbusz* from there.

By midday, **Szentháromság tér**, the square at the heart of the district, is
crammed with tourists, buskers, handicraft vendors and other entrepreneurs, a multilingual spectacle played out against the backdrop of the wildly asymmetrical
Mátyás Church (Mon–Fri 9am–5pm, Sat 9am–1pm, Sun 1–5pm; 300Ft, 600Ft
with audio guide). The church is a riotous nineteenth-century re-creation of the
medieval spirit, grafted onto those portions of the thirteenth-century structure that
survived 150 years of Ottoman rule – when the church was turned into a mosque
– and the siege of 1686, which brought the Ottoman occupation to an end. An
equestrian statue of **King Stephen** stands just outside the church, commemorating
the ruler who forced Catholicism onto his subjects, thus aligning Hungary with the
culture of Western Europe. The **Fishermen's Bastion** or Halászbástya (open 24hr;
mid-March to end Oct 8.30am–11pm 300Ft; otherwise free) is a white rampart
with cloisters and seven turrets, framing the view of Parliament across the river.

Medieval architectural features have survived along **Országház utca**, at the
northern end of which the quasi-Gothic **Mary Magdalene Tower** still dominates
Kapisztrán tér, albeit gutted and transformed into an art gallery. To the south of

HUNGARY | Budapest

Szentháromság tér the street widens as it approaches the **Buda Palace**. The fortifications and dwellings built by Béla III after the thirteenth-century Mongol invasion were replaced by ever more luxurious palaces; the most recent reconstruction dates from after the devastation wrought in World War II. The northern Wing houses the **Museum of Contemporary Art (Ludwig Collection)** (Tues–Sun 10am–6pm; 400Ft), which has pieces by the likes of Picasso, Hockney and Lichtenstein as well as by younger Hungarian artists such as Attila Szűcs. The **National Gallery** (Tues–Sun 10am–4/6pm; 500Ft), occupying the central wings B, C and D, contains Hungarian art since the Middle Ages. Gothic stone-carvings, altars and painted panels fill the ground floor, while nineteenth-century painting, including major Hungarian artists such as Csontváry, Rippl-Rónai and Munkácsy, dominates upstairs. On the far side of the Lion Courtyard, the **Budapest History Museum** in Wing E (Wed–Mon 10am–4/6pm; 600Ft) gives the history of the territory that makes up the city, from prehistoric finds on display on the top floor down to the marbled and flagstoned halls of the Renaissance palace deep underground.

Watertown (Víziváros), a wedge-shaped tangle of narrow streets between Castle Hill and the river to the north of the Chain Bridge, was once the poor quarter housing fishermen, craftsmen and their families. Today it's a reclusive neighbourhood of old mansions meeting at odd angles on the hillside, reached by alleys which mostly consist of steps rising from the main street, Fő utca. North along Fő utca stand the **Király baths** (men only Mon, Wed & Fri 9am–9pm; women only Tues & Thurs 6.30am–7pm, Sat 6.30am–1pm; 700Ft), distinguishable by four copper cupolas.

South of Watertown rises **Gellért Hill** (Gellérthegy), crowned by the **Liberation Monument**, one of the few Soviet monuments to survive the fall of the Iron Curtain, and the **Citadella**, a low fortress built by the Habsburgs to cow the population after the 1848–49 revolution. Nowadays the fort contains nothing more sinister than a few exhibits, a tourist hostel, a new terrace bar and an overpriced restaurant. Descending the southern slopes of the hill through the playgrounds of Jubileumi Park, you'll come to the **Gellért baths**, at the side of *Hotel Gellért*. The best-publicized of the city's baths, they were built in 1913, and the grandeur of the entrance hall is continued in the main pool (Mon–Fri 6am–7pm, Sat & Sun 6am–5/7pm; 1800Ft). You can get cheaper tickets just for the stunning thermal baths (which close earlier at weekends; separate baths for men and women), but it's worth paying to enjoy the beauty of the whole complex. Further north, by the Erzsébet Bridge, are the men-only **Rudas baths** (Mon–Fri 6am–7pm, Sat & Sun 6am–1pm; 650Ft, 900Ft for steam bath), Budapest's most atmospheric Turkish baths, whose interior has hardly changed since it was constructed in 1556.

Budapest's ironically nostalgic **Communist Statue Park** (*Szoborpark*, daily 10am–sunset, 300Ft) also lies on this side of the river and is well worth a detour. Featuring monumental statues of Marx, Engels and Lenin, it is, however, stuck out in district XXII. To get there, take tram #19 or #49 along Bartók Béla út from the Hotel Gellért to the terminus in Buda's district XI; from here take a yellow bus from bay 2 to Diósd-Érd (a total journey time of 50min).

Pest

Pest, busier and more vital than Buda, is the place where things are decided, made and sold. Much of the architecture and general layout dates from the late nineteenth century, when boulevards, public buildings and apartment houses were built on a scale appropriate to the Habsburg Empire's second city and the capital of Hungary, which celebrated its 1000th anniversary in 1896. The **Belváros** revels in its cosmopolitanism, with shops selling the latest fashions and French perfumes, posters proclaiming the arrival of Hollywood films and international rock groups, and streets noisy with the sound of foreign cars and languages. The main square, **Vörösmarty tér**, busy with portraitists, conjurers, violinists and other performers, is dominated by crowded café terraces. The most venerable institution here is the **Gerbeaud** patisserie, the favourite of Budapest's high society since the late nineteenth century, and now packed with tourists. The city's most chic shopping street, **Váci utca**, runs south from the square, parallel to the river and thronged with people. Passing the Pesti Theatre, where 12-year-old Liszt made his concert debut, the crowds flow down to **Ferenciek tere**, overlooking which is a slab of gilt-and-gingerbread architecture, the **Párizsi udvar**, home to an ice-cream parlour and IBUSZ office, but chiefly known for its "Parisian arcade", adorned with arabesques and stained glass. Váci utca continues south to the **Main Market Hall**, with its fancy ironwork, porcelain tiles and stalls festooned with strings of paprika and garlic.

Peering over the rooftops to the north of Vörösmarty tér is the dome of **St Stephen's Basilica**, from the top of which there's a good view over the city (dome: April–Oct daily 10am–5/7pm; 500Ft). On his name day, August 20, St Stephen's mummified hand and other holy relics are paraded round the building; the rest of the year, the hand is on show in a side chapel. Just north of the Basilica, dominating the banks of the Danube, is the large dome of the **Parliament**, a stupendous nineteenth-century creation befitting a small country with old longings for grandeur. In 1999 the ambitious young prime minister Viktor Orbán displayed his nationalist leanings by transferring the old **Coronation Regalia** from the National Museum to the Parliament. Reputedly the very crown, orb and sceptre used by King Stephen, the regalia is now thought to be a combination of two crowns used by Stephen's successors; nevertheless it's still seen as a symbol of Hungarian statehood. There are daily **tours** of the building – in English – if parliamentary business allows (10am & 2pm; 1700Ft; tickets from Gate X, half way along the east front).

To the east of the Basilica, **Andrássy ut** runs dead straight for 2.5km, a parade of grand buildings laden with gold leaf, dryads and colonnades, including the magnificent Opera House at no. 22. Its shops and sidewalk cafés retain some of the style that made the avenue so fashionable in the 1890s. The boulevard culminates at **Hősök tere**, built to mark the 1000th anniversary of the Magyar conquest. Its centrepiece is the **Millennary Monument**, portraying Prince Árpád and his chieftains grouped around a 36m-high column topped by the Archangel Gabriel, and half-encircled by a colonnade displaying statues of Hungary's most illustrious leaders, from King Stephen to Kossuth. Also on the square, the **Museum of Fine Arts** (Tues–Sun 10am–5.30pm; 700Ft) contains Egyptian funerary relics, Greek and Roman ceramics, and paintings and drawings by European masters from the thirteenth to twentieth centuries – including Dürer, El Greco, Velázquez and Bronzino. Behind the museum lies **Budapest Zoo** (daily 9am–4/7pm; 1500Ft), worth a visit for the architecture alone – the Palm House, the Elephant House and the Aviary in particular. Opposite the zoo, the yellow neo-Baroque walls of the **Széchenyi baths** (daily 6am–6pm; 1800Ft) contain one of Europe's largest spa complexes. Watch locals play chess on floating boards while wallowing in the steam.

Back towards the centre of the Belváros, on the corner of Wesselényi and Dohány utca, stands the dramatic main **Synagogue**, whose Byzantine-Moorish architecture has been undergoing much-needed restoration; the interior is now complete and utterly magnificent. In the **National Jewish Museum** next door (Mon–Thurs 10am–3pm, Fri 10am–2pm, Sun 10am–2pm; 600Ft), exhibits dating back to the Middle Ages are opposed by a harrowing Holocaust exhibition, which casts a chill over the third section, portraying Jewish cultural life today. In the streets behind the synagogue lies Pest's main **Jewish quarter**. In recent years the small Jewish community that survived the Holocaust has become much more visible in the city, although even here, where the community is strongest, it keeps a low profile. Along Dob utca there is the *Fröhlich* kosher coffee shop at no. 22, a wigmaker at no. 31, and at no. 35, by the entrance to the orthodox community buildings, a kosher butcher's (Mon–Thurs 8am–3.30pm, Fri 8–11am), while further along in Klauzál tér you can buy excellent kosher *slivovitz* in the cellar of no. 16 (Thurs 2.30–4.30pm, Fri 11.30am–2pm).

Eating and drinking

Magyar cooking has been overtaken in Budapest's **restaurants** by scores of places devoted to international cuisine. Prices by Western standards are very reasonable, and your budget should stretch to at least one binge in a top-flight place. The following categories – *cukrsszdas* (patisseries) for sweet pastries and coffee, restaurants (for eating), and bars and beer halls (for drinking) – are to an extent arbitrary, since all restaurants serve alcohol and all bars serve some food, while *eszpresszós* (cafés) feature both, plus coffee and pastries.

Patisseries

Angelika I, Batthyány tér 7. The former convent has been modernized by the *Café Miro* crew (see below), with techno soundtrack, a lively terrace and elderly locals hanging in there.

Central V, Károlyi Mihály utca 9. Large old coffee house recently restored to its former glory, with a broad menu ranging from cheap to very expensive.

Eckermann VI, Andrássy út 24. Big coffees and internet access (from 2pm) in this popular café next to the Goethe Institute. Closed Sun.

Fröhlich VII, Dob utca 22. A kosher patisserie five minutes' walk from the Dohány utca synagogue, presided over by the Fröhlich family. Specialities include *flódni* (an apple, walnut and poppy-seed cake). Closed Sat & Jewish holidays.

Gerbeaud V, Vörösmarty tér 7. A popular and very grand place in central Pest. A coffee and a torte will set you back around 900Ft; the same rich pastries are cheaper in *Kis Gerbeaud* around the corner. Gets unbearably full in summer.

Múzeum Cukrsszda VIII, Múzeum kör út 10. Friendly hangout by the National Museum. Fresh pastries arrive at dawn.

Müvész VI, Andrássy út 29. Another grand old coffee house, less touristy and cheaper than *Gerbeaud*.

Ruszwurm's I, Szentháromság utca 7. Excellent cakes, served production-line fashion to those taking a break from sightseeing on Castle Hill, who crowd its diminutive interior.

Fast food, self-service and snack bars

Duran Sandwich Bar V, Október 6 utca 15. A sandwich and coffee bar – still, oddly enough, a rare combination in Budapest. Closed Sun.

Falafel Faloda VI, Paulay Ede utca 53. Best of the city's falafel joints. Closed Sat & Sun.

Museum of Contemporary Art I, Wing A, Buda Royal Palace. Excellent café on the museum's upper floor, with fast service and very tasty Hungarian food. Best value on Castle Hill – but you'll have to pay admission to the museum first! Closed Mon.

Marie Kristensen Sandwich Bar IX, Ráday utca 7. The Danish flavour is hard to spot; this is just a decent regular sandwich bar behind Kálvin tér. Closed Sun.

Self-service canteen V, Szende Pál utca 3. Very cheap lunches with the local office workers behind Vörösmarty tér. Nothing translated, so just point to what you want. Closed Sat & Sun.

Tower Restaurant 10th floor, Central European University, V, Nádor utca 9. Excellent inexpensive café, run by the same people as the Ludwig Museum café and open to all. Closed Sat & Sun.

Restaurants

Abszint VI, Andrássy út 34. Reasonably priced Provencale cuisine in a young, fun setting. Budding visionary poets can taste a Bulgarian version of absinthe.

Al-Amir VII, Király utca 17. Syrian restaurant serving excellent salads and hummus, making it a haven for vegetarians in a city of carnivores. No alcohol served. Cash only.

Café Kör V, Sas utca 17 ☎1/311-0053. Popular place near the Basilica with excellent food and fine wines. Menu supplemented by specials written up on the wall. Booking essential. Closed Sun.

Gandhi V, Vigyázó Ferenc utca 4. An oasis of spiritual calm in the city serving a range of international vegetarian dishes.

Gundel XIV, Állatkerti út 2 ☎1/468-4040. Prides itself as the flagship of Hungarian cuisine and has prices that are high by Western standards. On Sunday, though, you can eat your fill for 3900Ft at their bargain brunch. Booking essential. Closed Sun eve.

Kádár étkezde VII, Klauzsl tér 9. Jewish home cooking in the old quarter. Friendly, very efficient staff serve lunches of boiled beef in fruit sauces. Closed Sun.

Márkus Vendéglő II, Lövőház utca 17. Welcoming, inexpensive Hungarian restaurant near Moszkva tér. Daily 11am–1am.

Náncsi Néni II, Ördögsrok út 80 ☎1/397-2742. Large, popular garden restaurant in the leafy suburb of Hűvösvölgy, ten minutes' walk from the terminus of bus #56. Booking advisable.

Papageno V, Semmelweis utca 10. Small, friendly new establishment with top chefs specializing in French and Italian cuisine. Closed Sun.

Bars, wine bars and beer halls

Bambi I, Bem tér. Wonderful old bar from the socialist era serving breakfast, snack lunches, dry-looking cakes and alcohol.

Buena Vista VI, Liszt Ferenc tér 5. Popular new bar near the Music Academy on a square where cafés all spill out under the trees. Good restaurant upstairs, plus their own beer in the cellar bar.

Café Miro I, Úri utca 30. A trendy bar in the Castle district which often has live music.

Castro IX, Ráday utca 35. A lively new place on Ráday utca, a street popular with students and lined with cafés and bars. Internet access too.

Darshan Udvar VIII, Krúdy Gyula utca 7. The largest bar in a growing complex of bars, cafés and shops. Set at the back of the courtyard, with oriental/hippie decorations, good food, world music and leisurely service.

Gusto's II, Frankel Leó ut 12. Tiny bar near Buda side of Margit Bridge, serving the best tiramisù in town. Closed Sun.

Eklektika V, Semmelweis utca 21. Arty, gay-friendly bar with 1960s furniture, art exhibitions, a pasta/salad menu and women-only evenings on the second Sat of the month.

Old Man's Music Pub VII, Akácfa utca 13. Large, popular joint in the centre of Pest, live local acts and good food.

Zöld Pardon XI, by the Buda end of Petőfi Bridge, a large outdoor bar with live music sprawling across the grass near the university quarter, popular with students. March–Oct only.

Entertainment and nightlife

Star events in the capital's cultural year are the **Budapest Spring Festival** (two weeks in March or April) and the **Autumn Music Weeks** (late Sept to late Oct), both of which attract the cream of Hungary's artists and top international acts. There's also scores of classical and popular concerts during the summer. On **St Stephen's Day** (Aug 20) the area around the Royal Palace becomes one big folk and crafts fair, and in the evening the population lines the embankments to watch the fireworks.

You'll have to check the posters and listings publications for information on **rock concerts**. The four main venues for **alternative concerts**, **folk music** and **modern dance** events are the Petőfi Csarnok in the Vsrosliget (☎1/363-3730, ☏www.petoficsarnok.hu); the Almássy tér Cultural Centre at VII, Almássy tér 6 (☎1/342-0387, ☏www.almassy.hu); the Trafó at IX, Liliom utca 41 (☎1/456-2040, ☏www.trafo.hu); a revamped transformer station in Pest; and the Fonó at XI, Sztregova utca 3 (☎1/206-5300, ☏www.fono.hu), in Buda. **Tickets** for most events can be had through the Filharmonia Ticket office, Mérleg utca 10 (☎1/318-0281); Ticket Express for classical music, VI, Andrássy út 18 (☎1/312-0000); Music Mix at V, Vsci utca 33 (☎1/266-7736); and Publika for rock and jazz at VII, Károly körút 9 (☎1/322-2010).

New **clubs and discos** are opening all the time, and the rave and floating party scene is growing constantly: check flyers and posters around town, or look in the "Könnyű" section of *Pesti Est*, the free listings magazine in cinema foyers. There's also a variety of cheap **student clubs**, the liveliest being Közgáz behind the Economics University at Fővsm tér 8 (☎1/215-4359).

Nightclubs

Angyal VII, Szövetség utca 33. Budapest's premier gay club: looks like an airport lounge but has an interesting crowd. Sat is men only. Thurs–Sun.

Capella V, Belgrád rakpart 23. Drag queens, jungle music and lots of tat: just the place for a night on the town.

Cha Cha Cha IX, Kálvin tér subway. Despite its strange location, this place attracts a big crowd spilling out into the concourse and has DJs at weekends. Closed Sun.

Romkert I, Döbrentei tér 9. Outside bar attracting a wealthy young crowd, that's one of the few places you can dance outside until the early hours. Good bar food; worth booking a table if you're eating. March–Oct only.

Süss Fel Nap V, Honvéd utca 40. Heaving, lively place attracting a young crowd.

Trocadero Café V, Szent István körút 15. Excellent Latin music and dancing just up from Nyugáti Station. Closed Sun & Mon.

Listings

Embassies and consulates Australia, XII, Királyhágó tér 8–9 ☎1/457-9777; Canada, XII, Budakeszi út 32 ☎1/392-3360; Ireland, V, Szabadság tér 7, 7th floor, Bank Center ☎1/302-9600; New Zealand, VI, Teréz körút 38, 4th floor ☎1/428-2208; UK, V, Harmincad utca 6 ☎1/266-2888; US, V, Szabadság tér 12 ☎1/475-4400.

Exchange Gönc Szövetkezeti Takarékpénztsr at V, Rákóczi út 5; Magyar Külkereskedelmi Bank at Türr István utca at the top of Vsci utca, Pest; Tribus tourist office V, Apsczai Csere Jsnos utca 1.

Hospital V, Hold utca 19, behind the US embassy ☎1/311-6816; II, Ganz utca 13–15 ☎1/202-1370.

Internet Eckermann Café, VI, Andrássy út 24, near the Opera House (closed Sun); Enternet at V, Deák Ferenc utca 15, corner of Vörösmarty tér; Libri Könyvpalota, VII, Rákóczi út 12 (closed Sun); Vista Visitor Center, VI, Paulay Ede utca 7.

Pharmacy Alkotás utca 2, opposite Déli station; Teréz körút 41, near Oktogon.

Post office V, Petőfi utca 13.

Around Budapest: Szentendre

To escape Budapest's humid summers, many people flock north of the city to the **Danube Bend**, one of the grandest stretches of the river. The historic town of **SZENTENDRE** on the west bank is the most popular day-trip from the capital (40min by HÉV train from Batthyány tér; 1hr 30min by boat from Vigadótér pier), a friendly maze of houses painted in autumn colours, secret gardens, and alleys leading to hilltop churches – the perfect spot for an artists' colony, which is what it became in the 1920s, when artists moved out from the city to make the most of the superb natural light. Szentendre's original character was largely shaped by Serbs seeking refuge from the Ottomans. Their townhouses – now converted into galleries, shops and cafés – form a set piece around **Fő tér**, now a stage for musicians and mime-artists.

On the north side of the square is **Blagovestenska Church** (Tues–Sun 10am–5pm; winter open for worship only; 100Ft) – whose iconostasis, painted by Mikhail Zivkovic (1776–1824), suggests the richness of the Serbs' artistry and faith. Just around the corner at Vastagh György utca 1 stands the wonderful **Margit Kovács Museum** (daily 10am–5/6pm; closed Mon in winter; 450Ft), displaying the lifetime work of Hungary's best-known ceramicist, born in 1902. Above Fő tér there's a fine view over Szentendre's steeply banked rooftops and gardens from the hilltop **Templom tér**, where frequent craft fairs help finance the restoration of the Catholic parish church there. Opposite the church, paintings whose fierce brush strokes and sketching were a challenge to the canons of classicism during the 1890s hang in the **Béla Czóbel Museum** (April–Sept Wed–Sun 10am–6pm; 300Ft), beyond which the spire of the **Serbian Orthodox Cathedral** pokes above a walled garden; tourists are generally not admitted, but you can see the cathedral iconostasis and treasury in the adjacent **museum** (March–Dec Tues–Sun 10am–4/6pm; Jan & Feb Fri–Sun only; 200Ft). An hourly bus runs from the HÉV terminal out along Szabadságforrás út to Szentendre's fascinating **Village Museum** (April–Nov daily 9am–5/7pm; 600Ft; ⓦwww.skanzen.hu), which has reconstructed villages from five regions of Hungary (more are planned). During the summer, on alternate weekends, there are demonstrations of traditional craft techniques, including pottery, baking and basket-making.

For **information**, both on the town and the Danube Bend, head to the branch of Tourinform at Dumtsa Jenő utca 22 (Mon–Fri 9am–4.30pm, Sat & Sun 10am–2pm; ☎26/317-965, ✉szentendre@tourinform.hu). For **accommodation**, the best budget options are the *Aradi Panzió*, Aradi utca 4 (☎26/314-274; ❷), near the HÉV station; and *Ilona Panzió*, Rákóczi F. utca 11 (☎26/313-599; ❷), in a pleasant location in the centre of town. IBUSZ, Bogdsnyi utca 11 (Mon–Fri 10am–4/6pm; summer also Sat & Sun 10am–1pm; ☎26/310-181) can arrange **private rooms**. A lot of people end up camping rough on Szentendre Island or at the **official campsite** on Pap Island (☎26/310-697; closed Oct–April) – accessible by ferry or bus respectively. Most **restaurants** are concentrated in and around Fő tér;

the *Aranysárkány*, Alkotmány utca 1/a, and *Rab Ráby*, Kucsera Ferenc utca 1, are two popular choices, and *Palapa*, Dumtsa J 14/a, is an excellent Mexican bar/restaurant. **Café terraces** line up along the Danube – *Szerb Kisvendéglő*, Dunakorzó 4, provides meaty Balkan snacks, too.

Western Hungary

The major tourist attraction to the west of the capital is **Lake Balaton**, over-romantically labelled the "Hungarian sea". Despite the fact that rising prices are pushing out natives in favour of Austrians and Germans, this is still very much the nation's playground, with vacation resorts lining both shores. On the northern bank, development has been limited to some extent by reedbanks and cooler, deeper water, giving tourism a different slant – the spa town of **Balatonfüred** is the main draw here. Historic **Tihany** offers fine sightseeing, while anyone whose social life doesn't take off in **Keszthely** can go soak themselves in the thermal lake at **Hévíz**.

More than other regions in Hungary, the western region of **Transdanubia** is a patchwork land, an ethnic and social hybrid. Its valleys and hills, forests and mud flats have been a melting pot since Roman times: settled by Magyars, Serbs, Slovaks and Germans; torn asunder and occupied by Ottomans and Habsburgs; transformed from a state of near-feudalism into brutal collectives; and now operating under modern capitalism. All the main towns display evidence of this evolution, especially **Sopron**, with its well-preserved medieval centre, and **Pécs**, which boasts an Ottoman mosque and minaret.

Balatonfüred

The Romans were the first to imbibe the curative waters of **BALATONFÜRED**, and nowadays some 30,000 people come every year for treatment in its sanatoriums. A busy harbour and skyscraper hotels dominate approaches to the town, but the centre has a sedate, convalescent atmosphere, typified by the embankment promenade, Rabindranath Tagore sétány, named after the Bengali poet who came here in 1926. Above the tree-lined promenade lies **Gyógy tér**, where you can drink the Kossuth spring's carbonic water at a pagoda-like structure.

The **bus and train stations** are next door to each other on Castricum tér, midway between the old town and the lake. **Ferries** from Tihany dock at the pier at the western end of the promenade. For **information** on the town and region, head to the Tourinform office by the Balatonarács train station – the stop before Balatonfüred – at Petőfi utca 68 off the main Tihany road (Mon–Fri 9am–5/7pm; summer also Sat 9am–1pm; ☎87/580-480, ✉balatonfured@tourinform.hu), or the Balatontourist office at the *Füred* campsite (May–Aug 6/7am–7/10pm; ☎87/580-241). Of the **accommodation** available, best bets are: the *Korona Panzió*, Vörösmarty utca 4 (☎87/343-278, ⌨www.hotels.hu/korona_panzio; ➌), a decent pension; lakeside *Tagore*, Deák Ferenc utca 56 (☎87/343-173; closed Nov–April; ➌); *Blaha Lujza*, Blaha Lujza utca 4 (☎87/581-210, ⌨www.hotelblaha.hu; ➌), with an elegant restaurant in actress Lujza Blaha's former summer villa; and *Fortuna*, Honvéd utca 3 (☎87/343-037; closed Oct–April; ➌). Alternatively, you can arrange **private rooms** through Balatontourist, or IBUSZ in the Arany Csillag store, Zsigmond utca 2 (☎87/482-248). There are **dorms** at Széchenyi Ferenc Kollégium in Iskola utca, though those in the old town can be a long way from the water. The big lakeside *Füred* **campsite**, Szechenyi utca 24 (☎87/580-241), is west of town, beyond the *Füred* and *Marina* hotels. **Restaurants** and **snack bars** line up along Tagore sétány, there's a clutch of over-priced tourist traps on Vitorlás tér near the Mahart ferry pier, better to head east to the friendly *Borcsa Restaurant* in front of the *Tagore* hotel, or walk uphill to the *Hotel Park Restaurant*, Jókai Mór utca 24, with an open-air grill and substantial three-course menu for under 1000Ft.

Tihany

The historic centre of **TIHANY**, self-proclaimed "Pearl of the Balaton", sits above the harbour where the **ferries** from Balatonfüred dock; you'll find it by following the winding steps up between a screen of trees, and you'll know you've arrived by the mass of tourist boutiques and stalls crowding the streets. Tihany's **Benedictine Abbey**, 2km north of the docks, on top of the hill, was established in 1055 at the request of Andrew I, whose body now lies in the crypt. A few paces north from the abbey brings you to the **Open-Air Folk Museum**, a collection of old cottages giving a feel of life in the village in the early twentieth century (May–Sept Tues–Sun 10am–6pm; 200Ft). Around Petőfi and Csokonai streets, houses are built of grey basalt tufa, with windows and doors outlined in white, and porticoed terraces. Even without a map it's easy to stumble upon the **Inner Lake** (Belső-tó), whose sunlit surface is visible from the abbey. From its southern bank, a path runs through vineyards, orchards and lavender fields past the Aranyház geyser cones and down to Tihanyi-rév.

Since trains bypass the peninsula, your alternative method of arrival – other than the ferry – is by **bus** from Balatonfüred. There's a **Tourinform** office up by the abbey at Kossuth utca 20 (℡87/448-804, ✉tihany@tourinform.hu). Hotel prices, like everything else in Tihany, are exorbitant by Hungarian standards. The neighbouring **campsite** or **private rooms** are the only affordable options: book at Balatontourist, Kossuth utca 12 (April–Oct Mon–Sat 8am–6.30pm, Sun 8am–1pm; Nov–March Mon–Fri 8am–4.30pm, Sat 8am–1pm; ℡87/448-519), or Tihany Tourist, Kossuth utca 11 (April–Oct daily 9am–4/8pm; ℡87/448-481, ✉tihany.tourist@axelero.hu). The *Oazis* **restaurant**, Major utca 47, has good food and friendly staff.

Keszthely and around

Absorbing thousands of visitors gracefully, **KESZTHELY**, Balaton's best hangout, has some good bars and restaurants, a thermal lake at nearby Hévíz, and a university to give it some life of its own. Keszthely's waterfront has two bays (one for swimming, the other for ferries) formed by man-made piers, a slew of parkland backed by plush hotels and miniature golf courses, and dozens of fast-food joints and bars. In the evenings, action shifts from the water to the centre, where the bars and restaurants work at full steam.

Walking up from the train station along Martírok útja, you'll pass the **Balaton Museum** at the junction with Kossuth Lajos utca (Tues–Sat 9am–5pm; 300Ft), with exhibits on the region's history and wildlife. From Fő tér onwards, with its much-remodelled Gothic church, Kossuth utca is given over to cafés, vendors, buskers and strollers and leads up towards the **Festetics Palace**, founded in 1745 by Count GyörgyFestetics (July & Aug daily 9am–6pm; rest of year Tues–Sun 10am–5pm; 1500Ft), which attracted the leading lights of Magyar literature from the nineteenth century onwards. The building's highlights are its gilt, mirrored ballroom and the Helikon Library, a masterpiece of joinery and carving. It stages regular summer concerts.

The **dock** and the **train station** are roughly ten minutes' walk south of the centre along Erzsébet királyné útja. The train station is five minutes' walk southwest of the cluster of lakeside hotels along Kazinczy utca, where some intercity buses also terminate. Most **buses**, however, drop off on Fő tér, halfway along Kossuth utca, the main drag. There's a **Tourinform** office at Kossuth utca 28 (June to mid-Sept Mon–Fri 9am–8pm, Sat & Sun 9am–6pm; rest of year Mon–Fri 9am–5pm, Sat 10am–1pm; ℡83/314-144). For budget **accommodation**, private rooms are your best bet and are available from KeszthelyTourist, Kossuth utca 25 (Oct–April Mon–Sat 8am–5pm, May–Sept daily 9am–8/9pm; ℡83/312-031, ✇www.keszthelytourist.hu). For information on rooms in college **dorms** (July & Aug daily; rest of year weekends only), ask at either tourist office. There are two **campsites** just south of the train station and the big, expensive *CastrumCamping* 1500m along the shore in the opposite direction (☎83/312-120). For food, the friendly *Oázis* **restaurant**, down Szalasztó utca from the palace at Rákóczi tér 3 (Mon–Fri 11am–4pm), has an excellent salad and vegetarian self-service bar, while the *Eldorado Étterem*, Kossuth utca 14, by the Festetics Palace gates has a good range of fish dishes. Local student hangouts are the trio of bars opposite the post office on Kossuth Lajos utca, whilst the smart *Pelzo Café*, next to the Gothic parish church on Fő tér, is ideal for a coffee stop. There's **internet** access at *Stones Café*, on the corner of Bem utca and Kisfaludy utca.

Hévíz

Half-hourly buses from Keszthely train station run to **HÉVÍZ**, a spa based around Europe's largest thermal lake, **Hévízi Gyógy-tó**. The wooden terraces surrounding the **Tófürdő** (daily 8.30am/9am–4/5pm; 3hr 550Ft, all day 1100Ft) have a vaguely *fin-de-siècle* appearance, but the ambience is contemporary, with people sipping beer while bobbing on the murky, egg-scented lake in rented inner-tubes. Otherwise, Hévíz seems to consist of rest homes and costly hotels, with a late-night **bar** and **casino** in the *Hotel Thermál*. An inexpensive place to **stay** is *Pannon*, Széchenyi utca 23 (☎83/340-482, ✉pannonhotels@axelero.hu; ❷), near the centre of town, or you could try the slightly smarter *Piroska Panzió*, Kossuth utca 10 (☎83/342-698; ❷). Hévíz Tourist, Rákóczi utca 2 (Mon–Fri 8.30am–4.30pm, Sat 9am–1pm; ☎83/341-348, ✉heviztour@axelero.hu), is an **accommodation**-booking agency.

Sopron and around

SOPRON – the nearest big Hungarian town to Vienna, and is consequently a popular destination for Austrian residents – has 240 listed buildings, which allow it to claim to be "the most historic town in Hungary". The horseshoe-shaped Belváros (old town) is north of Széchenyi tér and the main train station. At the southern end, **Orsolya tér** features Renaissance edifices dripping with loggias and carved protrusions, and a Gothic church. Heading north towards the main square, **Új utca** (New Street – one of the town's oldest thoroughfares) is a gentle curve of arched dwellings painted in red, yellow and pink, with chunky cobblestones and pavements. At no. 22 stands one of the **synagogues** that flourished when the street was known as Zsidó utca (Jewish Street); Sopron's Jewish community survived the expulsion of 1526 only to be all-but-annihilated during World War II. The main source of interest is up ahead on Fő tér, a parade of Gothic and Baroque architecture partly overshadowed by the **Goat Church** – so called, so legend has it, because its construction was financed by a goatherd whose flock unearthed a cache of loot. The Renaissance **Storno House**, once visited by King Mátyás and Count Széchenyi, now exhibits Roman, Celtic and Avar relics, plus mementoes of Liszt. North of the square rises Sopron's symbol, the **Firewatch Tower** (April–Oct Tues–Sat 10am–6pm; 300Ft), founded upon the stones of a fortress originally laid out by the Romans. From the top there's a stunning view of the town's narrow streets and weathered rooftops. The "Gate of Loyalty" at the base of the tower commemorates the townfolk's decision, when offered the choice of Austrian citizenship in 1921, to remain Magyar subjects. Walk through it and you'll emerge onto Előkapu, a short street where the houses are laid out in a saw-toothed pattern.

Practicalities

The **train station** is on Mátyás Király utca, 500m south of Széchenyi tér and the old town; Sopron is linked to Vienna by a fast intercity service, though it's not on the main Budapest–Vienna route. The **bus station** is to the northwest of the old town, five minutes' walk along Lackner Kristóf utca from Ógabona tér. There's a **Tourinform** at Előkapu 11 (June–Oct Mon–Fri 9am–5pm, Sat 9am–noon; Nov–May Mon–Fri 9am–4pm; ☎99/338-892, ✉sopron@tourinform.hu). **Private rooms** and student accommodation can be arranged through Lokomotiv Tourist,

Várkerület 90 (Mon–Fri 8.30am–4.30pm, Sat 8am–noon; ☎99/311-111, ⓔloktur@gysev.hu)´, and Ciklámen Tourist, Ógabona tér 8 (Mon–Fri 8am–4pm, Sat 8am–1pm; ☎99/312-040). For **accommodation**, try *Bástya Panzió*, Patak utca 40 (☎99/325-325; ❷), or *Jégverem Panzió*, Jégverem utca 1 (☎99/312-004; ❷), good-value pensions just across the Ikva Stream to the northeast of town. The *Lövér* **campsite** is 4km south of town – take bus #12 from Deák tér; you'll need to book in advance through Ciklsmen Tourist. There are some terrific places **to eat**, including *Várkerület Söröző*, Várkerület 83, serving Hungarian dishes, and *Rókalyukhoz*, opposite, with an extensive and eclectic international menu. Up on Fövényverem utca, *Ameli* at no. 15 serves superb fish dishes (closed Mon), or try *Fekete Bárány* opposite. *Café Dakar*, Vsrkerület 86, is the place to go for cakes and coffees. To sample the local **wines**, head for the *Cezár* cellar, Hátsókapu utca 2, or *Gyógygödör Borozó*, Fő tér 4; both are open daily until 10pm.

The Esterhszy Palace

Some 27km east of Sopron (hourly buses) lies a monument to one of the country's most famous dynasties: the **Esterhszy Palace** at Fertőd (Tues–Sun 10am–6pm; 1000Ft). Originally minor nobility, the Esterhszy family began its rise thanks to Miklós Esterhszy I (1583–1645), who married two rich widows, sided with the Habsburgs, and got himself elevated to count. The palace itself was begun by his grandson, Miklós the Ostentatious, who inherited 600,000 acres and a dukedom in 1762. With its 126 rooms, fronted by a vast horseshoe courtyard where Hussars once pranced to the music of Haydn – Esterhszy's resident maestro for many years – the palace was intended to rival Versailles. Recently renovated, highlights include a **candle-lit guided tour** (every Sat eve; 1500Ft). Climb the tower (200Ft) for a view of the manicured gardens. You can **stay** in the palace – though the accommodation is all Socialist Realist: rooms with two, three, four or more beds and shared showers are available in the east wing (booking essential; ☎99/537-649; ❶).

Pécs

The town of **PÉCS** is one of Transdanubia's largest and most attractive towns; indeed, it lays claim to being the finest town in the country, with its tiled rooftops climbing the vine-laden slopes of the Mecsek range. Besides some fine museums, the fifth-oldest university in Europe (founded in 1367) and a great market, Pécs contains Hungary's best examples of **Islamic architecture**, a legacy of the long Ottoman occupation. Heading up Bajcsy-Zsilinszky út from the bus terminal, or by bus #30 from the train station towards the centre, you'll pass Kossuth tér and Pécs's **synagogue** (closed for renovation). The beautiful nineteenth-century interior is a haunting place, with Romantic frescoes swirling around a space emptied by the murder of almost 4000 Jews – ten times the number that live in Pécs today. During the Ottoman occupation (1543–1686), a similar fate befell the Christian population, whose principal church was converted into the **Mosque of Gazi Kasim Pasha** (mid-April to mid-Oct Mon–Sat 10am–noon/4pm, Sun 11.30am–2/4pm; donations) to the north on Széchenyi tér. In a twist of history, the mosque has changed sides again and operates as the City Centre Catholic Parish Church. Also on the square is a gallery of contemporary work by local artists and an **Archeological Museum** (Tues–Sun 10am–2pm; 150Ft) displaying items testifying to a Roman presence between the first and fifth centuries. From here you can follow either Káptalan or Janus Pannonius utca towards the **Cathedral**. Though its architects have incorporated a crypt and side-chapels from eleventh- to fourteenth-century churches, the cathedral is predominantly nineteenth-century neo-Romanesque..

Practicalities

Both train and bus stations are roughly twenty minutes' walk from the centre: the **train station** is south of the centre on Indoház tér, the **bus station** northeast of here on Zsolyom utca. There's a branch of **Tourinform** at Széchenyi tér 9

(June–Sept Mon–Fri 8am–7pm, Sat & Sun 9am–6pm; rest of year Mon–Fri 8am–4pm; ☎72/213-315, ✉baranya-m@tourinform.hu).

Most of the central **hotels** are expensive – the best-value option is *Főnix Hotel* just off Széchenyi tér, Hunyádi út 2 (☎72/311-680; ❷). Convenient for the station is the good-value *Vig Apst Hotel*, Msrtirok utca 14 (☎72/313-340; ❷). The renovated and extended *Hotel Laterum*, 3km west of the centre at Hajnóczy utca 37 (☎72/252-113; ❷), has a restaurant, beer hall, gym and laundry amongst its many facilities, while *Familia Privst Camping*, 3km east at Gyöngyösi utca 6 (☎72/327-034, ❶), has a more homely atmosphere. For inexpensive, central accommodation, book a **private room** or **student hostel bed** through Mecsek Tours, Széchenyi tér 1 (☎72/513-370, ✉utir@mecsektours.hu) or IBUSZ, Apsca utca 1 (☎72/212-157). *Mandulss* **campsite**, Ángyán János utca 2 (☎72/515-655; closed mid-Oct to mid-April; bus #34; ❷), is just 2km north of the centre, but up a steep, winding hill.

When it comes to **eating**, *Aranykacsa*, Teréz utca 4, is excellent, while wholesome Hungarian food is the order of the day at the magnificently decorated *Dóm Étterem*, Király utca 3. Similarly top-notch Hungarian cuisine is served at the classy *Fortuna Étterem*, Ferencesek utca 32. The very classy *Morik* café, on Jokai tér, is the place for coffee, and Király utca abounds with pizzerias and cafés. In summer, the **beer garden** of *Rózsakert* on Janus Pannonius utca is very pleasant; **bars** are more numerous in the western part of the Belváros, south of the centre. Pécs has its own brewery in Rókusalja utca, and the local beer is served up in the *Kiskorsó* pub. **Internet** access is available in the café next to the *Fortuna* restaurant.

Finally, **Pécs Fair**, held on the morning of the first Sunday – and the Friday and Saturday immediately before – of each month, sees some hard bargaining and hard drinking, and there are smaller markets on the same site every Sunday. Bus #50 carries local shoppers from outside the Konzum store in Rákóczi utca to the brand new Pécs Plaza mall opposite the fair; get a ticket from a newsstand or the train station before boarding. Pécs is also an excellent starting-point for heading to the nearby wine region of Villány to the south – ask at Tourinform for further information.

Eastern Hungary

The hilly and forested northern region of **eastern Hungary** will not feature prominently in any hurried tour of the country, but nobody should overlook the famous wine-producing town of **EGER**, where the Valley of the Beautiful Woman attracts wine-lovers from all over Europe. Its colourful architecture suffused by sunshine, Eger seems a fitting place of origin for Egri Bikavér, the famous red wine marketed abroad as "Bull's Blood", which brings hordes of visitors to the town. Despite occasional problems with accommodation, it's a fine place to hangout and wander around, not to mention all the opportunities for drinking. The Neoclassical Cathedral, designed by József Hild and constructed between 1831 and 1836, is five minutes' walk southwest from Dobó István tér, the main square. The florid **Lyceum** directly opposite the cathedral is worth visiting for its library (April–Sept Tues–Sun 9.30am–3pm; Oct–March Sat & Sun 9.30am–1.30pm; 300Ft), whose beautiful floor and fittings are made of polished oak. While in the building, check out the **observatory**, at the top of the tower in the east wing (same hours and ticket), where a nineteenth-century *camera obscura* projects a view of the entire town. Close by, facing Széchenyi utca, stands the **Archbishop's Palace**, a U-shaped Baroque pile with fancy wrought-iron gates; in its right wing you'll find the treasury and a history of the bishopric of Eger (April–Oct Tues–Sat 9am–5pm; Nov–March Mon–Fri 8am–4pm; 120Ft).

Heading back towards the centre along Bajcsy-Zsilinsky utca you'll come out on the pleasant **Dobó István tér**. Cross the bridge and head to the left to find Eger's most photographed structure, a slender fourteen-sided **minaret** (April–Oct

9am–5pm; 100Ft), looking rather lonely without its mosque, which was demolished during a nineteenth-century building boom. Alternatively, head uphill from the square to the gates of the **Castle** (daily 8/9am–5/8pm, limited access Mon; 500Ft, Mon400Ft). From the bastion overlooking the main gate, a path leads up to the ticket office and the fifteenth-century **Bishop's Palace**. Here, tapestries, ceramics, Turkish handicrafts and weaponry fill the museum upstairs, while downstairs are temporary exhibits and a Hall of Heroes, where a life-size marble István Dobó lies amid a bodyguard of heroes of the 1552 siege in which 2000 soldiers and Eger's women repulsed a Turkish force six times their number.

Just west of town, in the Szépasszony Valley, local **vineyards** produce four types of wine – Muskotály (Muscatel), Bikavér (Bull's Blood), Leányka (medium-dry white with a hint of herbs) and Medoc Noir (rich, dark and sweet red) – and it's possible to sample all of them in the cellars there. Finding the right cellar is a matter of luck and taste, but you could try Auntie Anci's Olaszrizling at no. 28 or the Medoc Noir in Sándor Arvai's at no. 31. Cellars tend to close by 8pm. Take a **taxi** (around 800Ft; ☎36/411-222) or attempt the twenty-minute walk back uphill to town.

Practicalities

Trains from Budapest-Keleti arrive at the station on Állomástér; to reach the centre, walk up the road to Deák Ferenc út, catch bus #10 or #12, and get off when you see the cupola of the cathedral. There's a **Tourinform/Eger Tourist** office at Bajcsy-Zsilinszky utca 9 (mid-June to Aug Mon–Fri 9am–6pm, Sat & Sun 9am–1pm; rest of year Mon–Fri 9am–5pm, Sat 9am–1pm; ☎36/510-270, ✆www.egertourist.hu). For **student hostels** and **private rooms** contact IBUSZ, Széchenyi utca 9 (☎36/311-451, ✉eger@iroda.ibusz.hu), or Express, Széchenyi utca 28 (☎36/427-757). Alternatively, along from the castle, there's the *Tourist Motel*, Mekcsey utca 2 (☎36/429-014; ❶); the *Hotel Minaret*, Harangöntő utca 5 (☎36/410-020, ✉hotelminaret@matavnet.hu; ❷); or the classier *Senator Ház Hotel*, Dobó István tér 11 (☎36/320-466, ✆www.hotels.hu/senatorhaz; ❹). There are two **campsites**: *Autós Caraván Camping* to the north, Rskóczi út 79 (☎36/410-558; closed mid-Oct to mid-April; bus #10/#11), and *Tulipsn* in the Szepasszony Valley (☎36/410-580). Two of the best **restaurants** are *Efendi*, Kossuth utca 19, and *Fehér szarvas Vadásztanya*, Klapka utca 8.

Travel details

Trains

Budapest to: Balatonfüred (every 1–2hr; 2hr 15min); Pécs (10 daily; 2hr 30min–3hr); Sopron (8 daily; 2hr 50min); Szentendre (every 15–30min; 45min); Eger (6 daily; 1hr 30min–2hr 30min).

Buses

Budapest to: Balatonfüred (2 daily); Eger (hourly); Esztergom (every 30min–1hr); Hévíz (2 daily); Keszthely (2 daily); Sopron (4 daily); Szeged (5 daily); Szentendre (every 30min–1hr); Visegrád (hourly).
Badacsony to: Keszthely (hourly).
Balatonfüred to: Tihany (hourly).
Esztergom to: Visegrád (hourly).
Keszthely to: Hévíz (every 30min).
Szentendre to: Esztergom & Visegrád (hourly).
Visegrád to: Esztergom (hourly).

Ferries

Usually operating April–Oct/Nov, weather permitting
Budapest to: Esztergom (1–2 daily; 5hr 20min); Szentendre (1–3 daily; 1hr 40min); Visegrád (2–4 daily; 3hr 20min).
Esztergom to: Budapest (1–2 daily; 4hr); Szentendre (2 daily; 3hr).

Hydrofoils

Usually operating April–Oct/Nov, weather permitting
Budapest to: Esztergom (2 at weekends; 1hr 20min); Vienna (1–2 daily; 6hr 20min); Visegrád (1 at weekends; 50min).

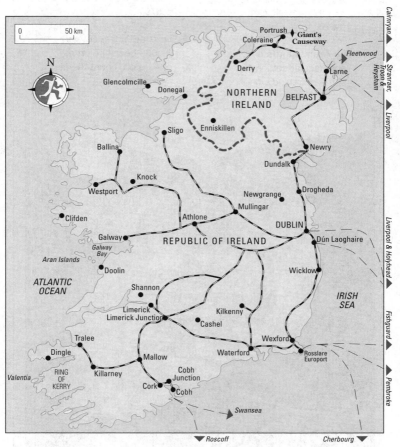

Ireland

Ireland highlights

Introduction and basics

Ireland's attractions are its landscape and people – both in the **Republic** and **Northern Ireland**. Few visitors are disappointed by the stock Irish images: the rain-hazed loughs and wild coastlines, the talent for conversation and wealth of traditional music. While Ireland's urban centres have undergone transformations based on high-tech industry, the rural landscape remains relatively unchanged.

Especially in the Irish-speaking Gaeltacht areas, there's a strong and enduring **oral tradition**. The speech of the country, moulded by the rhythms of the ancient tongue, inspired such literary greats as Yeats, Joyce, Beckett and Heaney. **Traditional music**, too, is thriving, and you can find sessions in many pubs.

The **west coast** draws most visitors; its coastline and offshore islands – especially **Aran** – combine vertiginous cliffs, boulder-strewn wastes and violent mountains. In Northern Ireland the principal draw is the bizarre basalt formation of the **Giant's Causeway**. The **interior** is less spectacular, but the southern pastures and low wooded hills, and the wide peat bogs of the midlands, are the classic landscapes of Ireland. Of the **inland waterways**, the most alluring is the island-studded **Lough Erne**, easily reached from Enniskillen.

If time is limited, one of the best options is to combine a visit to **Dublin** with the mountains and monastic ruins of County Wicklow. Dublin is an extraordinary mix of youthfulness and tradition, of rejuvenated Georgian squares and vibrant pubs. **Belfast**, victim of a perennial bad press, vies with Dublin in the vitality of its nightlife, while the cities of **Cork** and **Galway** in particular sparkle with newfound energy.

No introduction can cope with the complexities of Ireland's **politics**, which permeate every aspect of daily life, most visibly in the North. However, regardless of partisan politics, Irish hospitality is as warm as the brochures say, on both sides of the border.

Information and maps

Tourist information in the Republic is handled by **Bord Fáilte**, in the North by the **Northern Ireland Tourist Board**. There are branches in many towns and these can help in finding accommodation.

The best **maps** are the Michelin 1:400,000 (#405) and the AA 1:350,000. The four Ordnance Survey 1:250,000 regional Holiday Maps are useful, but their 1:50,000 Discovery series is generally the best option for walkers.

Money and banks

The currencies of the Republic and Northern Ireland are respectively the **euro** (€) and the **pound sterling** (£). Standard **bank hours** are Mon–Fri 10am–4pm (Republic) and Mon–Fri 9.30am–4.30pm (Northern Ireland). In less populated areas banks may close for lunch and, in some cases, may only open on certain days of the week, so it's wise to change money in the large towns.

There are **ATMs** throughout Ireland – though not in all villages – and most accept a variety of cards.

14

IRELAND | Basics

Ireland on the net

@**www.ireland.travel.ie** Irish Tourist Board
@**www.discovernorthernireland.com** Northern Ireland Tourist Board
@**www.ireland.com** Irish Times site with up-to-date info on Dublin
@**www.local.ie** Region-by-region breakdown
@**www.heritageireland.ie** Official site for monuments and cultural institutions

Communications

Main **post offices** are open Mon–Fri 9am–5.30pm, Sat 9am–1pm. Stamps are sometimes available in newsagents. You can make domestic and international calls from **pay phones** and **card phones** throughout Ireland (it's worth carrying a phonecard, since coin-operated phones are rare in rural areas). International calls are best made at weekends or after 6pm on weekdays when rates are lower. For the **operator** call ✆10 (domestic) or ✆114 (international) in the Republic; ✆100/✆155 in Northern Ireland. All phone numbers in **Northern Ireland** comprise the UK area code ✆028 plus an eight-digit local number; but calls from the Republic to the North use the code prefix ✆048 instead, followed by the eight-digit number.

Internet access is widely available. Most cities have cybercafés, and smaller places may have Internet booths in post offices, hostels, supermarkets and even a few pubs. Rates are around €6 or £4/hr.

Getting around

Public transport is generally reliable, though sometimes slow and often infrequent in rural areas (with many having no Sunday service).

Trains

In the Republic, Irish Rail (Iarnród Éireann) operates **trains** to most major towns and cities. Few routes run north–south across the country, so, although you can get to the west easily by train, you can't use the railways to explore the west coast. The Dublin–Belfast line is the only **cross-border service**.

Train travel is not cheap, so look for off-peak fares: the system is complicated, and it's always worth asking about any special deals. In the **Republic**, the **InterRail** pass entitles visitors to unlimited free travel, while Irish citizens travel half-price; in **Northern Ireland**, all visitors (including Irish citizens) again travel free, and UK citizens get a 75-percent discount.

For train **timetables**, check ⊛www.irishrail.ie (Republic), or ⊛www.translink.co.uk (North).

Buses

Routeings can be complex and slow on the Republic's national bus service – **Bus Éireann**. Fares are generally far lower than for trains, especially midweek. If you are going to be using buses a lot, pick up a free **timetable** from any major bus station; remote villages may only have a couple of buses a week, so knowing when they run is essential. **Private buses** operate on major routes and are often cheaper than the national service.

In the North, **Ulsterbus** runs regular and reliable services, particularly to towns not served by the rail network, with Citybus operating within Belfast.

Cycling

Cycling can be an enjoyable way to see Ireland. It's relatively cheap to **rent a bike** in most towns in the Republic, and at a limited number of places in the North. Raleigh is the biggest national operator (about €13/day, €60/week; €50 deposit; for nearest outlet call ✆01/626 1333). However, local dealers (including some hostels) are often less expensive. In the North, tourist offices have lists of local operators; rates are around £10 per day. In the Republic it costs an extra €8 to carry a bike on a bus, and €3–8 on a train in the Republic, though not all buses or trains can carry bikes; check in advance. In the North, it's an additional 25 percent to the price of each journey.

Accommodation

Though **camping** is the cheapest option, it can be hampered by tricky terrain and the constant possibility of rain. Next up in price, **hostels** vary greatly, but offer the essential basics, and can be very good indeed. Above these come **B&Bs**, guest houses and **hotels**, usually registered with and graded by the tourist boards.

B&Bs and hotels

B&Bs vary enormously, but most are welcoming, warm and clean. Expect to pay from around €24/£16 per person; en-suite facilities are usually a little more and most **hotels** are generally pricier. For an extra €3/£2, you can book through tourist offices or by phoning the international toll-free line ☎800/668 668 66 in the Republic, or ☎0800/783 5740 in the North. Booking ahead is always advisable during high season.

Hostels

Hostels run by both **An Óige** (the Irish Youth Hostel Association) and **HINI** (Hostelling International Northern Ireland) are affiliated to Hostelling International. Some may close during the daytime and have evening curfews. HI membership is required at all these hostels, and overnight fees start at €10 in the Republic, €14 in Dublin; and £8–12 in the North.

Independent hostels are often more interesting places to stay. Very often cosy and informal, they don't have curfews, though some cram people in to the point of discomfort. Hostels usually belong to either **Independent Holiday Hostels** (☎01/836 4700, ✆www.hostels-ireland.com) which has a book-ahead system during high season, or the **Independent Hostels Ireland** network (☎073/30130, ✆www.holiday-hound.com/ihi). There are a very small number of dangerous and disreputable hostels around, so it's a good idea to check the Rough Guide or ask around locally before booking in at a non-approved hostel. In the Republic, expect to pay €10–15 for a dorm bed (more in Galway, Cork and Dublin), €14–20 per person for private rooms where available; in the North, it's £8–12/£14–18.

Camping

Camping usually costs around €8 a night in the Republic, £6 in the North. In out-of-the-way places nobody minds where you pitch. Farmers in heavily touristed areas may ask for a small contribution to use their land, but other than this you can expect to camp for free in areas where there's no official site. Note, though, that in the Republic you can't camp in the state forests – but the North's forest parks contain some of its best campsites. Some **hostels** also let you camp on their land for around €8/£5.

Food and drink

Ireland now has a wide choice of sophisticated cuisine in most towns and resorts. In smaller, rural places, the food you'll find as a traveller will tend to be simple and hearty, and often excellent.

Food

Irish **food** is meat-orientated. Many B&Bs provide a hearty "traditional" **Irish breakfast** of sausages, bacon and eggs, although many now offer vegetarian alternatives. **Pub lunch** staples are usually meat or fish and two veg; sometimes with a few veggie options. Vegetarian restaurants or cafés are sparse outside major cities and some of the more tourist-influenced areas. Most towns have **fast-food** outlets, but old-fashioned fish-and-chips are a better bet, especially on the coast. For the occasional binge, there are some very good **seafood** restaurants, particularly along the southwest and west coast, serving fresh catch-of-the-day. Most towns have daytime **cafés** serving a selection of hot dishes, salads, soups, sandwiches and cakes.

Drink

Especially in rural areas, the **pub** is the social heart of the community and here you'll most often find the proverbial **craic** ("crack"), a particular blend of Irish fun involving good company, witty conversation and laughter, frequently against a backdrop of music. Many pubs have late licences on certain nights until 1am.

The classic Irish drink is **Guinness**, best in Dublin, home of the brewery, while the Cork stouts, Beamish and Murphy's, have their devotees. If you want a pint of English-style keg **bitter**, try Smithwicks, while **lager** brands include Carlsberg, Harp and Budweiser. The price of a pint starts at around €3.20, rising to €4 in Dublin. Irish **whiskeys** may seem expensive, but the measures are large: try Paddy, Jameson's, Powers or Bushmills.

Opening hours and holidays

Business and shop **opening hours** across Ireland are roughly Mon–Sat 9am–6pm, with some late openings (usually Thurs or Fri), half-days and Sunday opening. Away from the bigger towns, hours are much more flexible, with later closing times. The bigger **museums** and attractions will normally be open regular shop hours, while smaller places may open only in the afternoon. Many sites away from the main tourist trails are open only during the summer months.

Public holidays are: in the **Republic**, Jan 1; St Patrick's Day (March 17); Good Fri, Easter Mon; May 5; June 2; Aug 4; Oct 27; Dec 25 & 26. In the **North**, Jan 1; St Patrick's Day (March 17); Easter Mon; May 5 & 26; July 12; Aug 25; Dec 25 & 26.

Emergencies

The **police** in the Republic are known as the **Gardaí** (pronounced "gar-dee") or "guards", while in Northern Ireland, the **PSNI** (Police Service of Northern Ireland) deals with all general civic policing. The North is subject to UK law and is heavily policed, with several "emergency measures" permanently in effect. Despite security relaxations you may occasionally find yourself being quizzed about your details. Be co-operative and polite and you should have no difficulties.

Hospitals and medical facilities are of a high standard; you'll rarely be far from a hospital, and both Northern Ireland and the Republic are within the E111 scheme. Even the most remote rural areas will have a local doctor on 24-hour call. Most **pharmacies** are open standard shop hours, though in large towns some may stay open as late as 10pm; they can dispense only a limited range of drugs without a doctor's prescription.

Emergency Numbers

☏ 999 for all emergencies.

Dublin and around

Set on the banks of the River Liffey, **DUBLIN** is splendidly monumental, but also a youthful city with a lively nightlife. Ireland's vibrant economy has brought extensive urban regeneration, but there's still much deprivation here. It's this collision of the old and the new, the slick and the shabby, that makes Dublin the exciting, aggravating, energetic place it is.

Dublin really began as the Viking trading post Dubh Linn (Dark Pool), which soon amalgamated with the Celtic settlement of **Baile Átha Cliath** (Town of the Hurdle Ford) – still the Irish name for the city. Most early buildings were wooden, so only the two cathedrals, part of the castle and several churches date from before the seventeenth century. The city's fabric is essentially **Georgian**, when the Anglo-Irish gentry began to invest their income in new townhouses. After the 1801 Act of Union Dublin entered a long economic decline, but remained the focus of much of the agitation that eventually led to independence. The 1829 Emancipation Act secured a limited role for Catholics in the administration of the city, and Dublin was later the birthplace of the Gaelic League which helped catalyse an Irish national consciousness by nurturing the native language and culture. The long struggle for independence came to a head during the **Easter Rising** of 1916, a rebellion commemorated by a host of monuments in Dublin.

Arrival and information

Trains arrive at either **Heuston Station** on the South Side of the city, or **Connolly Station** on the North Side. All **Buses** arrive at **Busáras**, the central bus station off Beresford Place, just behind the Customs House. From the **airport**, six miles north, the official airlink bus #747 or #748 runs to Busáras (every 10min; €4.50; 25min), and the privately run Aircoach serves the main shopping areas and hotels (every 15min; €5). **Boats** dock at either **Dún Laoghaire**, six miles south, connected to the centre by the **DART** (Dublin Area Rapid Transport; 20min), or at the closer **Dublin Port** (bus #53); through-coaches from Britain usually drop you at Busáras.

Dublin's main **tourist office** is on Suffolk St, off College Green (Mon–Sat 9am–5.30/6.30pm; July & Aug also Sun 10.30am–3pm; ⊕www.visitdublin.com). There are other branches at 14 Upper O'Connell St, the Dún Laoghaire ferry terminal and the airport. Their accommodation service (⊕1800/668 668) costs €3 per booking. The **USITNow** office on Aston Quay, near O'Connell Bridge on the South Side (Mon–Fri 9.30am–6.30pm, Thurs till 8pm, Sat 9.30am–5pm; ⊕01/677 8117; ⊕www.usitnow.ie), also books B&Bs during the summer, and has its own hostel and a travel agency offering student discounts. For what's-on **listings**, see the free *Event Guide* or *In Dublin* (€2.48), or, for music events, *Hot Press* (€3.17).

City transport

Dublin has an extensive **bus** network – but without a pass, you'll need lots of change, as all buses are exact-fare-only. The maximum fare is €1.65, a one-day bus pass is €4.50, though a pack of five one-day passes costs only €14, or there are bus and rail passes (including DART) for one day/three days (€6/€13.30). Students pay €13.30 for a seven-day bus pass. Free bus timetables are available from Dublin Bus, 59 Upper O'Connell St. The **DART** links Howth to the north of the city with Bray to the south (maximum fare €2.95). **Nitelink** buses cost €4–6, depending on your destination.

Accommodation

Although Dublin has lots of **accommodation** in all price ranges, anywhere central is liable to be full at weekends, around St Patrick's Day (March 17), during Easter week and in high summer, so it's always wise to **book ahead**. **Hotels** are generally

CENTRAL DUBLIN

N

500 m
0

Connolly Station
Bus Station
Custom House
Pearse Station
National Gallery
Merrion Square
Leinster House
National Library
National Museum
Mansion House
Trinity College
St. Stephens Green
Royal College of Surgeons
Civic Museum
Bank of Ireland
USITnow
Abbey Theatre
James Joyce Statue
Dublin Bus ★
O'Connell Street
GPO
James Joyce Centre
Dublin Writers' Museum
Rotunda Hospital
Hugh Lane Gallery
Kings Inns
City Hall
Dublin Castle
Christ Church Cathedral
St Patrick's Cathedral
Four Courts
Dvblinia
St Michan's
Old Jameson Distillery
Collins Barracks
Guinness Brewery
Guinness Storehouse
Heuston Station

River Liffey

▲ Phoenix Park   ▲ Irish Museum of Modern Art   ▲ Kilmainham Gaol

expensive, and often no more comfortable than good **guesthouses**, but out-of-season reductions can be considerable; the tourist office in Suffolk St has a list of recommended accommodation. Most of the better **B&Bs** are in the suburbs, but this isn't such a problem, given the good public transport. All hotels, guest houses and B&Bs listed have en-suite facilities. The **hostel** booking service, *Irelandfound,* is at 10 Lower Abbey St (daily 9am–9pm; ☎01/856 1211; €2 booking fee). All hostels listed provide free breakfast, unless stated.

Hostels

Abbey Court 29 Bachelors Walk ☎01/878 0700, ✉info@abbey-court.com. Close to O'Connell Bridge, with all rooms en suite. Dorms ❹

Abraham House 82 Lower Gardiner St ☎01/855 0600; ✉stay@abraham-house.ie. Large, well-run complex with en-suite and shared facilities. Kitchen and laundry. Dorms ❺

Avalon House 55 Aungier St ☎01/475 0001, ✉info@avalon-house.com. Impressive Victorian building near St Stephen's Green. Cramped dorms and twin or four-bedded rooms, sharing unisex bathrooms. Friendly and noisy, with a good café. Dorms ❸

Barnacles Temple Bar House 19 Temple Lane ☎01/671 6277, ⊛www.barnacles.ie. Modern place in the heart of Temple Bar. All rooms en suite. Dorms ❸

Brewery Hostel 22-23 Thomas St ☎01/473 8600, ✉brewery@indigo.ie. Housed in a fine converted library near the Guinness Brewery and often has space when other hostels are full. Breakfast not provided. Dorms ❸

Globetrotters Tourist Hotel 46 Lower Gardiner St ☎01/873 5893, ✉gtrotter@indigo.ie. Upmarket hostel where security-locked dorms and individual bed lights make for a peaceful night's sleep. Dorms ❸

Isaacs Hostel 26 Frenchman's Lane ☎01/855 6215, ✉hostel@isaacs.ie. Housed in an eighteenth century wine warehouse – no breakfast, but a good café on site. Dorms ❸

Kinlay House Christchurch 2–12 Lord Edward St ☎01/679 6644, ✉kinlay.dublin@usitworld.com. Bright and cheerful USITNow hostel near Christ Church Cathedral. Doubles, quadruples and six-bed dorms with en-suite facilities. Café, laundry facilities and kitchen. Dorms ❸

Litton Lane Hostel 2–4 Litton Lane ☎01/872 8389, ✉litton@indigo.ie. Situated off Bachelor's Walk on the North Side, in a converted warehouse that was once a major recording studio. The showers are excellent and there are no problems with security. Dorms ❸ ,

Mount Eccles Court 42 North Great George's St ☎01/873 0826, ✉info@eccleshostel.com. A splendid converted house in a fine North Side Georgian street. Great kitchen and helpful staff. Dorms ❸

Guest houses, B&Bs and hotels

Clifden Guesthouse 32 Gardiner Place ☎01/874 6364, ✉bnb@indigo.ie. Friendly guest house in a slightly run-down street close to the city centre and Busáras. ❾

The Gate Hotel 80–82 Parnell St ☎01/872 2500. One of the North Side's best budget options with twenty en-suite rooms and car parking. ❺

Harding Hotel Copper Alley, Fishamble St ☎01/679 6500, ⊛www.iol.ie/usitacom. Extremely popular, well-furnished budget hotel in a prime Christchurch location. Breakfast extra. ❽

Kilronan Guesthouse 70 Adelaide Rd ☎01/475 5266, ✉info@dublinn.com. Handily placed, very comfortable Georgian house just south of St Stephen's Green. ❾

Marian Guesthouse 21 Upper Gardiner St ☎01/874 4129. Friendly, good-value guesthouse close to the city centre. ❺

St Jude's Guesthouse 17 Pembroke Park ☎01/668 0928. Comfortable accommodation in a quiet Ballsbridge location. ❻

Campsites

Comac Valley Caravan and Camping Park Corkegh Regional Park, off the Naas Rd, Clondalkin ☎01/464 0644. Pleasant site with views of the Dublin Mountains. Bus #68 or #69.

Shankill Caravan and Camping Park ☎01/282 0011. Close to the DART stop at Shankill – or take bus #45 or #84 from the city centre.

The City

A healthy rivalry exists between Dublin's North and South sides. The fashionable **South Side** can lay claim to the city's trendy bars, restaurants and shops, especially in the cobbled alleys of buzzing **Temple Bar** leading down to the river, and most of its historic monuments, centred on **Trinity College**, **Grafton St** and **St Stephen's**

Green. But the **North Side**, with its long-standing working-class neighbourhoods and inner-city communities, vaunts itself as the real heart of the city. Across the bridges from Temple Bar are the shopping districts around **O'Connell St**, where you'll find a taste of the old Dublin, particularly along **Moore St** where traders ply their wares in melodic tones. You'll also find here a fair amount of graceful – if slightly shabby – residential streets and squares, with plenty of interest in the museums and cultural centres around **Parnell Square**. In the North Side in particular, you should be wary of straying off the main streets after dark.

The South side

The Vikings sited their assembly and burial ground near what is now **College Green**, where **Trinity College** is the most famous landmark. Founded in 1592, it played a major role in the development of a Protestant Anglo-Irish tradition: right up to 1966, Catholics had to obtain a special dispensation to study here, though nowadays roughly seventy percent of the students are Catholic. The stern grey- and mellow red-brick buildings are ranged around cobbled quadrangles in a grander version of the quads at Oxford and Cambridge. **The Old Library** (Mon–Sat 9.30am–5pm, Sun noon–4.30pm; €6) owns numerous Irish manuscripts. Pride of place goes to the ninth-century **Book of Kells**, which totals 680 pages but was rebound in the 1950s into four volumes, of which two are on show at any one time, one open at a completely illuminated page, the other at a text page, itself adorned with patterns and fantastic animals intertwined with the capitals. The **Book of Durrow** is equally interesting: it is the first of the great Irish illuminated manuscripts, dating from between 650 and 680, and has, unusually, a whole page given over to abstract ornament. In summer there are guided tours of Trinity, and an audiovisual presentation of Dublin's history, the **Dublin Experience**, in the arts block (late May to early Oct daily 10am–5pm; €4.20).

Facing Trinity across the busy interchange, the imposing **Bank of Ireland** was built in 1729, originally as the parliament of independent Ireland. After the Act of Union in 1801, the building was sold to the bank, which still adheres to tradition by having a guard in a top hat and tailcoat, and a coal fire in the lobby. You can visit the former House of Lords (tours Tues 10.30am, 11.30am & 1.45pm) and the grand Cash Hall for free during working hours.

Just south of here, the streets around pedestrianized **Grafton St** frame Dublin's quality shopping area – chic, sophisticated and expensive. After spotting the statue of Molly Malone (nicknamed "the tart with the cart"), drop into **Bewley's** coffee house, whose dark wood and marble-tabled interior is a great place to sit and watch people; there's even a small **museum** tracing the history of this Dublin institution.

Continuing south you'll arrive at the northwest corner of **St Stephen's Green**, whose pleasant gardens with ponds and a lake are the focus of Georgian city planning. Running off beside the swanky *Shelbourne Hotel*, Kildare St harbours the imposing Leinster House, built in 1745 as the Duke of Leinster's townhouse, and now the seat of the Irish parliament, the **Dáil** (open out of session; booking essential; ☎01/618 3333). Alongside are the rotundas of the **National Library** and the **National Museum** (Tues–Sat 10am–5pm, Sun 2–5pm; free), the repository of the treasures of ancient Ireland. Much of its prehistoric gold was found in peat-bogs, as were a sacrificed human and the Lurgan Longboat. The Treasury and the Viking exhibition display such masterpieces as the Ardagh Chalice and Tara Brooch, St Patrick's Bell and the Cross of Cong. The brooch is perhaps the greatest piece of Irish metalwork and is decorated both on the front and the back, where the intricate filigree could be seen only by the wearer.

Around the block, the other side of Leinster House overlooks **Merrion Square**, the finest Georgian plaza in Dublin. No. 1 was once the home of Oscar Wilde, and a flamboyant statue in the green opposite shows the writer draped insouciantly over a rock; on Sundays, the square's railings are used by artists flogging their wares. Here, the **National Gallery** (Mon–Sat 9.30am–5.30pm, Thurs until 8.30pm, Sun noon–5pm; free; @www.nationalgallery.ie) owns a fair spread of European old masters and French Impressionists, but the real draw is the trove of Irish paintings, ranging from formal portraits and landscape paintings of the Anglo-Irish era to the modernist creations of Mainie Jellett, Evie Hone and Roderic O'Conor. Best of all is the new permanent exhibition devoted to the work of Ireland's best-known painter, Jack B. Yeats, tracing his development from Dublin illustrator to expressionist interpreter of Connemara sea- and landscapes.

Temple bar and west to Kilmainham

Dame St, the main thoroughfare leading west from College Green, marks the southern edge of the redeveloped **Temple Bar** quarter, whose fashionable restaurants, pubs, boutiques and arts centres make this one of the liveliest parts of town.

Uphill, tucked away behind City Hall, **Dublin Castle** (Mon–Fri 10am–5pm, Sat & Sun 2–5pm; €4) was founded by the Normans, and symbolized British power over Ireland for 700 years. Though parts date back to 1207, it was largely rebuilt in the eighteenth century. Tours of the State Apartments reveal much about the tastes and foibles of the viceroys and while you can see the lovely Chapel Royal, the real highlights are the excavations of Norman and Viking fortifications in the Lower Yard. The Clock Tower building now houses the **Chester Beatty Library** (Mon–Fri 10am–5pm, Sat 11am–5pm, Sun 1–5pm; Oct–April closed Mon; free; @www.cbl.ie), a sumptuous and massive collection of books, manuscripts, objects and paintings amassed by Sir Arthur Chester Beatty on his travels around Europe, the Middle and Far East. Over the brow of Dublin Hill, **Christ Church Cathedral** (daily 9.45/10am–5pm; €3 donation; @www.cccdub.ie) is a resonant monument built in 1190 by the Norman baron, Richard de Clare, "Strongbow". The north wall of the nave has leaned eighteen inches outwards since the roof collapsed in 1562. The crypt now houses a small museum (€3) of the Cathedral's treasures. The former Synod Hall, connected to Christ Church by an overhead bridge, contains **Dvblinia** (daily 10/11am–4/5pm; €5.75; @www.dublinia.ie), an array of presentations, models and tableaux depicting Dublin's medieval past and Viking and Norman artefacts excavated at nearby Wood Quay.

Five minutes' walk south from Christ Church is Dublin's other great Norman edifice, **St Patrick's Cathedral** (daily 9am–5/6pm; Nov–Feb Sun closes 3pm; €3.50; @www.stpatrickscathedral.ie). Founded in 1191, the cathedral is replete with relics of Jonathan Swift, its dean from 1713 to 1747. To the right of the entrance are memorials to both him and Esther Johnson, the "Stella" with whom he had a passionate though apparently platonic relationship, while the north pulpit contains Swift's writing table, chair, portrait and death mask. Handel's *Messiah* received its first performance here in 1742.

A mile west of Christ Church, the **Guinness Brewery** covers 64 acres on either side of James's St. Founded in 1759, Guinness has the distinction of being the world's largest single beer-exporting company, dispatching some 300 million pints a year. Set in the centre of the brewery, the **Guinness Storehouse** (daily 9.30am–5pm; €12; @www.guinness.com) presents a comprehensive exhibition detailing the history of this famous stout, visits ending with reputedly the best pint of Guinness in Dublin, in the panoramic *Gravity* bar with superb views over the city.

Regular buses (#78A, #79 and #90) ply the road out to Heuston Station and the **Royal Hospital Kilmainham**, Ireland's first Neoclassical building, dating from 1680, which now houses the **Irish Museum of Modern Art** (Tues–Sat 10am–5.30pm, Sun noon–5.30pm; free; @www.modernart.ie), with excellent permanent and visiting exhibitions. If you exit via the west wing and head towards the gateway at the end of the avenue, you'll emerge near **Kilmainham Gaol** (April–Sept daily 9/10am–4/4.45pm; €4.40; @www.heritageireland.ie), where the British incarcerated patriots such as Charles Stewart Parnell, Pádraig Pearse and James Connolly (the last two were executed here). A superb museum on both crime and political history sets the tone for guided tours of the gaol.

The North Side

Crossing O'Connell Bridge from College Green, the view of the Georgian Custom House downstream is marred by a railway viaduct, and many of the handsome buildings on **O'Connell St**, the main avenue on the North Side, have – with the exception of the General Post Office – been spoiled by tacky facades. A rejuvenation programme is currently underway to restore some of the boulevard's former glory and reduce the number of traffic lanes. Halfway down O'Connell St looms the **General Post Office**, the insurgents' headquarters in the 1916 Easter Rising; only the facade survived the fighting, and its pillars are still scarred by bullets. Across the road on the corner of Essex St North is a **statue of James Joyce**. At the same junction, on the site of what was the city's most famous landmark, Nelson's Pillar (it was destroyed in an explosion in 1966), it's planned to erect an illuminated stainless-steel spike – the **Monument of Light** – representing the city's hopes for the new millennium.

At the northern end of O'Connell St lies Parnell Square, one of the first of Dublin's Georgian squares. Its plain red-brick houses are broken by the grey stone **Hugh Lane Municipal Art Gallery** (Tues–Sat 9.30am–5/6pm, Sun 11am–5pm; free; ⊛www.hughlane.ie), originally the townhouse of the Earl of Charlemont and the focus of fashionable Dublin before the city centre moved south of the river. The gallery exhibits work by nineteenth- and twentieth-century Irish and international masters, and features a reconstruction of Francis Bacon's working studio (€7.60) following a bequest from the artist's estate. Nearby at nos. 18–19, the **Dublin Writers Museum** (Mon–Sat 10am–5/6pm, Sun noon–5pm; €5.50) whisks you through Irish literary history from early Christian writings up to Samuel Beckett and Brendan Behan. Especially worth visiting is the well-stocked bookshop and the summertime Zen garden. Two blocks east of Parnell Square, at 35 North Great George's St, the **James Joyce Centre** (Mon–Sat 9.30am–5pm, Sun 12.30–5pm; €4.50; ⊛www.jamesjoyce.ie) runs intriguing walking tours of the novelist's haunts (☏01/878 8547).

Half-a-mile to the west, on Church St, you'll find **St Michan's Church** (March–Oct Mon–Fri 10am–12.30pm & 2–4.30pm, Sat 10am–12.45pm; rest of year Mon–Fri 12.30–3.30pm, Sat 10am–12.45pm; €3), the oldest on the North Side, founded in 1095. The crypt is famous for its "mummified" bodies, preserved by the constant temperature and dry air pervaded by methane gas. The oldest – thought to have been a Crusader – dates back 700 years. At the bottom of Church St, on the bank of the Liffey, stands the **Four Courts**. Like the Custom House down river, it's a grand eighteenth-century edifice by James Gandon that has been restored after serious damage during the Civil War, which followed the 1921 treaty.

One block west on Bow St is the **Old Jameson Distillery** (daily 9.30am–6pm; €6.50); tours cover the history and method of distilling what the Irish called *uisce beatha* ("water of life", anglicized to whiskey) – which differs from Scotch whisky by being thrice-distilled and lacking a peaty undertone – and end with a tasting session involving five different types of whiskey, Scotch and bourbon. Outside, lifts ferry you up to the top of the old distillery **chimney** (Mon–Sat 10am–5.30pm, Sun 11am–5.30pm; €6), where an observation platform provides panoramic views of the city.

On the first Sunday of each month (9am–4pm; best at midday), the nearby cobbled **Smithfield** is the site of horse sales attended by Travellers who race their ponies bareback through the streets. Further west is the **Collins Barracks** (Tues–Sat 10am–5pm, Sun 2–5pm; free), an annexe of the National Museum housing its decorative arts collection and occasional special exhibitions. Finally, there's **Phoenix Park**, one of the largest urban parks in the world (bus #10 from O'Connell St or bus #37 from Lower Abbey St); originally priory land, it's now home to the Presidential Lodge, and attractions such as **Dublin Zoo** (Mon–Sat 9.30am–5/6pm, Sun 10.30am–5/6pm; €9.80; ⊛www.dublinzoo.ie). The visitor centre (daily 9.30/10am–4.30/6pm; €2.50; ⊛www.heritageireland.ie) has an exhibition on the park's history and wildlife and tickets include a tour of the adjacent **Ashtown Castle**, a seventeenth century tower house.

Eating, drinking and entertainment

Thanks to a recent gastronomic revolution in Dublin, most kinds of **food** are now widely available, especially in the eateries of Temple Bar. Note that many **cafés** and **restaurants** serve lunch at much lower prices than they'll charge in the evening (when it's wise to reserve a table); while Dublin's 800 **pubs** offer anything from soup and sandwiches to a full carvery at lunchtime. The **music** scene – much of which is based in the pubs – is volatile, so it's always best to check on the latest action by reading the *Event Guide* or *Hot Press*. Nightclubs along Leeson St (known as "The Strip"), at the southeastern corner of St Stephen's Green, are mostly pretty dire; the trendier clubs closer to Dame St are a better bet. Dublin's **theatres** are among the best in Europe.

Restaurants and cafés

Alpha Café 37 Wicklow St. A well-kept secret just off Grafton St with old-fashioned homely menu at great prices. Closed Sun.

Bewley's 78 Grafton St; 11–12 Westmoreland St; 40 Mary St. An essential food experience in Dublin, serving everything from a sticky bun to a full meal. Check out the lunchtime theatre programme in Grafton St, with combined lunch and show ticket for €10.50. Open from 7.30am; closes Grafton St 11.30pm; Westmoreland St 7.30pm; Mary St 6pm.

Cornucopia 21 Wicklow St. A wholefood shop with one of the city's few vegetarian cafés.

Elephant and Castle 18 Temple Bar ☏01/679 3121. Busy diner-cum-brasserie with burgers and Cajun-Creole dishes; classy without being posey.

Fresh Powerscourt Townhouse Centre, off Grafton St. Delicious vegetarian food, at tables overlooking the atrium. Closed Sun.

Govinda's 4 Aungier St. Huge helpings of dhal and rice and tasty vegetarian curries plus daily veggie specials, served by a very friendly team.

Irish Film Centre 6 Eustace St, Temple Bar ☏01/677 8788. Delicious, inventive food in elegantly minimal surroundings. Watch a film or just soak up the atmosphere.

Leo Burdock's 2 Werburgh St. Dublin's best fish-and-chips – takeaway only. Closed Sun.

Mao Café and Bar 2–3 Chatham Row ☏01/670 4899. Communist-chic themed restaurant serving reasonably priced rice- and noodle-based dishes with excellent service.

Pizza Stop 6 Chatham Lane ℅01/679 6712. Tasty all-day Italian menu of pizza and pasta favourites, an economical option for evening dining.

Probe Café South Great George's St Market Arcade. Excellent, reasonably priced café offering everything from Irish stew to fajitas. Reductions for students. Closed Sun.

Steps of Rome 1 Chatham Court. Limited seating area, though has great slabs of highly original pizza available to take away also. Good vegetarian options.

The Winding Stair 40 Lower Ormond Quay. Quaint bookshop downstairs, wholefood café and coffee shop on two upper floors with great-value hearty lunches.

Pubs

Davy Byrne's 21 Duke St. An object of pilgrimage for *Ulysses* fans, since Leopold Bloom stopped by here for a snack. Despite the pastel-toned refit, it's still a good pub, and serves oysters at lunchtime.

The Duke Duke St. The starting point for "Dublin's Literary Pub Crawl" (€10).

The Globe South Great George's St. Trendy hangout with loud music. Backs onto *RiRa*, an intimate but very lively club.

Kehoe's South Anne St. Wonderful snugs for privacy to sip your pint.

The Long Hall South Great George's St. Victorian pub encrusted with mirrors and antique clocks.

McDaid's 3 Harry St. Excellent Guinness in Brendan Behan's former local.

Mulligan's 8 Poolbeg St. Shabby and smoky, but always packed in the evenings; many claim that it serves the best Guinness in Dublin.

Neary's 1 Chatham St. Plenty of bevelled glass and shiny wood, plus Liberty-print curtains to show some style appropriate for its theatrical clientele.

Ryan's Parkgate St, across the river from Heuston Station. Another pub famous for its wood-lined snugs.

Stag's Head Dame Court, Dame St, almost opposite the Central Bank. Wonderfully intimate pub, all mahogany, stained glass and mirrors. Good lunches, too.

Music pubs, clubs and venues

The Brazen Head 20 Lower Bridge St. The oldest pub in Dublin, with traditional music nightly from 9.30pm.

The Cobblestone 77 North King St, Smithfield. Popular old-fashioned bar with nightly traditional music downstairs and more formal gigs upstairs.

Eamonn Doran's 3A Crown Alley. Long-standing music venue with everything from indie bands to regular club nights.

Fireworks Tara St. Converted fire station on three floors, where trendy Dubliners queue up to pose.
International Bar 23 Wicklow St. Large, smoke-filled saloon with gigs and comedy club upstairs – mostly rock bands, but also solo acts on Tues.
Oliver St John Gogarty's 57/58 Fleet St. Lively tourist pub with Irish music upstairs, the starting point for "Dublin's Musical Pub Crawl" (€9). The adjoining *Left Bank Bar* often has live jazz and blues.
The Olympia 74 Dame St. Hosts regular top-name gigs in an intimate theatre setting.
Red Box and **POD** 35 Harcourt St. Two hugely popular clubs, housed in an old railway station, offering a variety of different regular nights and events.
Temple Bar Music Centre Curved St. Everything from traditional acts to salsa, with live recording of all gigs.
Tivoli Theatre 135–138 Francis St. The latest "in" venue – reckoned to have the best sound system in Dublin.
Vicar St Thomas St. Arguably Dublin's best music venue with an innovative, wide-ranging programme of singers and bands.

Whelans 25 Wexford St. Very lively pub with nightly gigs and frequent bar extensions.

Theatres

Abbey Theatre Lower Abbey St ☏01/878 7222, ⊛www.abbeytheatre.ie. Founded in 1904 by W.B. Yeats and Lady Gregory, the *Abbey*'s golden era was when writers like Yeats, J.M. Synge and later Sean O'Casey were its house playwrights. It's still known for its productions of older Irish plays, but does encourage younger writers. The building also houses the *Peacock Theatre*, which stages more experimental shows.
Gaiety Theatre South King St ☏01/677 1717, ⊛www.iom.com/gaietytheatre. Dublin's oldest theatre stages a mix of musical comedy, revues and occasional opera, plus popular dance clubs Fri and Sat.
Gate Theatre Cavendish Row, Parnell Square ☏01/874 4045, ⊛www.gate-theatre.ie. Another of Dublin's literary institutions, staging classic and modern Irish theatre.
Project 39 Essex St East, Temple Bar ☏01/679 6622. Temple Bar's long-standing project continues to mount experimental and politically sensitive theatre.

Listings

Bike rental Cycle Ways, 185 Parnell St, opposite Ilac shopping centre ☏01/873 4748.
Embassies Australia, Fitzwilton House, Wilton Terrace ☏01/676 1517; Canada, 64–65 St Stephen's Green ☏01/478 1988; UK, 31–33 Merrion Rd ☏01/205 3700; US, 42 Elgin Rd, Ballsbridge ☏01/668 8777.
Exchange Thomas Cook, 118 Grafton St; General Post Office; most city-centre banks.
Hospital South Side: St James's, St James St ☏01/410 3000; North Side: Mater Misericordae Hospital, Eccles St ☏01/803 2000.

Internet Planet Cyber Café, St Andrew's St, near Suffolk St tourist office.
Laundry All American Launderette, Wicklow Court, South Great George's St.
Left luggage Busáras, Heuston and Connolly stations.
Pharmacy O'Connell's, 55 O'Connell St.
Police Harcourt Terrace ☏01/666 9500.
Post office O'Connell St.

Around Dublin

County Wicklow, easily accessible to the south of Dublin, has some of Ireland's most spectacular mountain scenery and the impressive monastic monuments of **Glendalough**. To the north of the city is the Brú na Bóinne complex of prehistoric remains, the most important and spectacular of which is **Newgrange**.

Glendalough

The early Celtic monastery of **GLENDALOUGH**, eighteen miles south of Dublin, is one of the most important monastic sites in Ireland, with a tangible quality of peace and spirituality that's only marginally disturbed by coach parties. Transport is easy: the St Kevin's Bus Service (☏01/281 8119; €15 return) runs at 11.30am from outside the Royal College of Surgeons on St Stephen's Green, returning at 4.15pm. The huge **visitors' centre** (daily 9.30am–5/6pm; €2.50;

@www.heritageireland.com) features an excellent exhibition and video show; entrance includes a guided tour of the site. The **Monastery** was founded by St Kevin in the sixth century, and became famous throughout Europe for its learning. The **Cathedral**, which dates from the early ninth century, has an impressive ornamental east window; the saint's burial spot is marked by the massive granite **St Kevin's Cross**, carved around 1150. The **round tower**, whose door is ten feet above the ground, was probably used as a refuge in times of trouble. Glendalough's most famous building is the solid barrel-vaulted stone oratory of **St Kevin's Church**; although it may well date from Saint Kevin's time, the round-tower belfry is eleventh-century, and the structure has clearly been altered many times. There are more monastic antiquities among the cliffs around the **Upper Lake**: the site of St Kevin's original church, the **Temple-na-Skellig**, is on a platform approached by a flight of stone steps, accessible only by boat, and **St Kevin's Bed**, a rocky ledge high up the cliff, is said to be where the holy man used to sleep in an attempt to escape the unwelcome advances of a young girl. Best accommodation in the area is the outstanding An Óige **hostel**, about half-a-mile up the valley (⊕0404/45342, ⊜glendaloughyh@ireland.com; ❸).

Newgrange

The main N1 Belfast road and the railway pass through **Drogheda**, from where it's a short bus hop to the great **NEWGRANGE** tumulus (daily 9/9.30am–5/7pm; €5; @www.heritageireland.com); enter by the Brú na Bóinne visitor centre, and, since it's very popular, you may have a long wait. Raised around 5000 years ago and completely restored, the mound of earth and loose stone covers the chambers of a remarkable passage grave. The outer ring of **standing stones**, of which only twelve uprights now remain, was unique among passage grave tombs. Perhaps the most important feature is the unique **roof-box** several feet in from the tunnel mouth. This contains a slit through which, at the **winter solstice**, the light of the rising sun fills the chamber with a sudden blaze of orange light. The entry passage, about three feet wide, leads into the **central chamber**, where the stones are carved with intricate decoration.

Southern Ireland

The southeast is often Ireland's sunniest and driest corner, and the region's medieval and Anglo-Norman history is richly concentrated in **Kilkenny**, a bustling, quaint inland town, while to the west, at the heart of County Tipperary is the **Rock of Cashel**, a spectacular natural formation topped with Christian buildings from virtually every period. In the southwest, **Cork** is both relaxed and spirited, the perfect place to ease yourself into the exhilarations of the west coast.

Rosslare and Wexford

Ferries from Wales (Fishguard and Pembroke) and France (Cherbourg and Roscoff) arrive at **Rosslare Harbour/Europort**, on the southeastern tip of Ireland. Trains depart daily from the pier for Wexford, Waterford and Dublin, and there's also a daily bus service to Dublin and the west. There's a **tourist desk** in the terminal open for incoming sailings (May–Sept, except early mornings; ⊕053/33622); otherwise, try the Kilrane tourist office, just over a mile from the dock along the N25 (May–Sept daily 11am–8pm; Oct–April Tues–Sun 2–8pm; ⊕053/33232). There's an An Óige **hostel** a short walk from the ferry in Goulding St (⊕053/33399, ⊜rosslareyh@oceanfreenet; ❷), though *Kirwan House Hostel*, 13 miles away in **WEXFORD**, 3 Mary St (⊕053/21208, ⊜kirwanhostel@eircom.net; ❷), is a more appealing place to spend your first night in Ireland.

Kilkenny

KILKENNY is Ireland's finest medieval city, its castle set above the broad sweep of the River Nore and its narrow streets laced with carefully maintained buildings. In 1641, the city became virtually the capital of Ireland, with the founding of a parliament known as the Confederation of Kilkenny. The power of this short-lived attempt to unite the resistance to English persecution of Catholicism had greatly diminished by the time Cromwell's wreckers arrived in 1650. Kilkenny never recovered its prosperity, but enough remains to attest to its former importance.

The **bus and train stations** are just north of the city, at the top of John St. Following this road over the river and climbing Rose Inn St brings you to the **tourist office** (Mon–Sat 9am–5/7pm, May–Sept also Sun 11am–1pm & 2–5pm; ☎056/51500), housed in the sixteenth-century **Shee Alms House**. At the top of Rose Inn St to the left is the broad **Parade**, which leads up to the castle. To the right, the High St passes the eighteenth-century **Tholsel**, once the centre of the city's financial dealings and now now the town hall. Beyond is **Parliament St**, the main thoroughfare, where the **Rothe House** (Mon–Sat 10.30am/1–5/6pm, Sun 3–5pm; €3) provides a unique example of an Irish Tudor merchant's home, comprising three separate houses linked by cobbled courtyards. The highlight of this end of town is the thirteenth-century **St Canice's Cathedral** (Mon–Sat 9/10am–1pm & 2–4/6pm, Sun 2–4/6pm; donations). Rich in carvings, it has a fine array of sixteenth-century monuments, many in black Kilkenny limestone (which looks remarkably like marble). The **round tower** next to the church (weather permitting; €1.50) is all that remains of the monastic settlement reputedly founded by St Canice in the sixth century; there are superb views from the top.

It's the imposing **Castle**, though, which defines Kilkenny (tours daily: April–Sept 9.30/10.30am–5/7pm; rest of year 10.30–11am/12.45pm & 2–5pm; €4.40; ✺www.heritageireland.com). Seat of the Butler family, the castle was founded in the twelfth century and radically altered by the nineteenth century. Within the castle the library, drawing room, bedrooms and Long Gallery of family portraits are open for viewing, as well as the **Butler Gallery**, housing an exhibition of modern art. The castle's kitchen is a tearoom in summer.

Practicalities

Kilkenny is well served by **B&Bs**, although in the summer the city can get crowded and during festival weeks in June and August you'll need to book in advance. *Bregagh* on Dean St (☎056/22315; ❺) is very central; also within walking distance of the centre is *Celtic House*, 18 Michael St (☎056/62249; ❺). *Banville's*, 49 Walkin St (☎056/70182, ✉mbanville@eircom.net; ❺), is also good. There's an An Óige **hostel**, *Foulksrath Castle*, at Jenkinstown (☎056/67674; ❷), eight miles north along the N77; Buggy's buses run to the hostel three times a day from the Parade near the castle. The friendly *Kilkenny Tourist Hostel*, 35 Parliament St (☎056/63541, ✉kilkennyhostel@eircom.net; ❷), is a more central option. There's **camping** at *Tree Grove* (☎056/70302), a mile outside the city, or further south near Bennettsbridge at *Nore Valley Park* (☎056/27229).

An influx of artists and craftspeople to the area in pursuit of the good life has boosted the town's restaurants and pubs. Among popular **eating** places are *Café Sol* on William St, great for lazy breakfasts, *Fl'éva* on High St, and *Pierre's* on Parliament St for authentic French food. The **café** in the Kilkenny Design Centre, opposite the castle, serves excellent home-cooked lunches; alternatively *The Gourmet Store* on High St has tasty sandwiches for a takeaway lunch. There are several good spots for **bar food**: *Kyteler's Inn*, St Kieran St, serves food in medieval surroundings, while *Lenehan's* on Barrack St has traditional Irish cooking popular with the locals. You won't be hard pushed to find **music**: try *Cleere's* on Parliament St or *Ryan's* on Friary St. *Tynan's* on the Bridge is worth a visit for its cosy Victorian interior. The weekly *Kilkenny People* has information about what's on. The town is renowned for its "The Cat Laughs" comedy **festival** in June (✆www.thecatlaughs.com), and the Kilkenny Arts Festival in August (✆www.kilkennyarts.ie).

The Rock of Cashel

Approached from the north or west, the **Rock of Cashel** (daily 9am–4/7.30pm; €4.40; ✆www.heritageireland.com) appears as a mirage of crenellations rising bolt upright from the vast encircling plain. The rock, less than a quarter of a mile wide, is one of Ireland's most extraordinary architectural sites and is also the place where St Patrick is supposed to have used a shamrock to explain the doctrine of the Trinity.

CASHEL, a ten-minute walk east of the Rock, is easily reached by bus from Dublin. Approaching from here, the first thing you'll encounter on the Rock is the fifteenth-century **Hall of the Vicars**, whose vaulted undercroft today contains the original **St Patrick's Cross**. Tradition has it that the cross's huge plinth was the coronation stone of the High Kings of Munster. **Cormac's Chapel**, built in the 1130s, is the earliest and most beautiful of Ireland's Romanesque churches; both north and south doors feature intricate carving, while inside, the alleged sarcophagus of King Cormac has an exquisite design of interlacing serpents and ribbon decoration. The graceful limestone **Cathedral**, begun a century after Cormac's chapel, is Anglo-Norman in conception, with its Gothic arches and lancet windows; a door in the south transept gives access to the tower, and in the north transept some panels from sixteenth-century altar-tombs survive, one with an intricately carved retinue of saints. The tapering **Round Tower** is the earliest building on the Rock, perhaps dating from the tenth century, though the officially accepted date is early twelfth century. From the grounds of the Rock you can look down at the thirteenth-century Hore Abbey on the plain below.

Cashel's **tourist office** (Mon–Sat 9am–6pm; June & July also Sun 11am–5pm; ✆062/61333) is in the market house on Main St alongside the **Cashel of the Kings Heritage Centre** (9.30am–5.30/8pm; Sept–March closed Sat & Sun; free), where a small exhibition covers the history of the town. The **Bolton Library** (April–Oct daily 10am–5.30pm; €2), on John St, off Main St, houses a fine collection of early manuscripts and rare maps. Cashel has two excellent **hostels**, both a short walk from the Rock: *O'Brien's Holiday Lodge*, off the Dundrun Rd (✆062/61003; ❷; also with camping), and *Cashel Holiday Hostel*, 6 John St (✆062/62330; ❷). For **B&B**, try *Abbey House*, 1 Dominic St (✆062/61104, ✉teachnamainstreet@eircom.net; ❺), or *Maryville*, Bank Place (✆062/61098, ✉maryville@iol.ie; ❺).

Cork

Everywhere in **CORK** there's evidence of the city's history as a great mercantile centre, with grey stone quaysides, old warehouses, and elegant, quirky bridges spanning the River Lee to each side of the island core – but the city's lively, cosmopolitan atmosphere and large student population, combined with a vibrant social and cultural scene, are equally powerful draws. **St Finbarre** founded an abbey here in the seventh century, but the Vikings wrecked it in 820 before building a new settlement on one of the islands in the marshes, and eventually integrating with the native Celts. Massive stone walls built by invading Normans in the twelfth century were destroyed by Williamite forces at the **Siege of Cork** in 1690, after which waterborne trade brought increasing prosperity, as witnessed by the city's fine eighteenth-century bow-fronted houses and ostentatious nineteenth-century churches.

The graceful arc of **St Patrick's St** – which with **Grand Parade** forms the commercial heart of the centre – is crammed with major chain stores and modest traditional businesses. Just off St Patrick's St on Princes St, the sumptuous **English Market** offers the chance to sample the local delicacies tripe and drisheen (the lining of a sheep's stomach served with peppered blood-sausage). On the far side of St

Patrick's St, chic Paul St is a gateway to the bijou environs of French Church St and Carey's Lane. The downstream end of the island, where many of the quays are still in use, gives the clearest sense of the old port city. In the west the island is predominantly residential, though Fitzgerald Park is the home of the **Cork Public Museum** (Mon–Sat 11am–1pm & 2.15–5/6pm, Sun 3–5pm; free), which focuses on Republican history with side exhibits on the city trades and guilds, silver and glassware and local natural history.

North of the River Lee is **Shandon**, a reminder of Cork's eighteenth-century status as the most important port in Europe for dairy products. The most striking survival is the **Cork Butter Exchange**, stout nineteenth-century Neoclassical buildings recently given over to craft workshops. The old butter market itself, now renovated to house the Firkin Crane Theatre, sits in a cobbled square. To the rear is the pleasant Georgian church of **St Anne Shandon** (Mon–Sat 9am–6pm; €5 @www.shandonsteeple.com), easily recognizable from all over the city by its weather vane – an eleven-foot salmon. The church tower (€4.40) gives excellent views and an opportunity to ring the famous bells: a good stock of sheet tunes is provided. West of here in Sunday's Well is the nineteenth-century **Cork City Gaol** (daily 9.30/10am–4/5pm; €5), with an excellent taped tour focusing on social history. From here, you can walk back to the town centre via the Shaky Bridge and Fitzgerald Park.

Practicalities

The **bus station** is at Parnell Place alongside Merchant's Quay, while the **train station** is about one mile out of the city centre on Lower Glanmire Rd. **Ferries** from Swansea and Roscoff arrive at Ringaskiddy, some ten miles out, from where there's a bus into the centre. The **tourist office** is on Grand Parade (Mon–Sat 9.30am–4.30/7pm; July & Aug also Sun 10am–1pm; ☎021/425 5100, @www.cork-kerry.travel.ie).

For **B&B**, try *Number Forty Eight*, 48 Lower Glanmire Rd (☎021/450 5790; ❺); *Westbourne House*, Western Rd (☎021/427 6153; ❹); or the many along Western Rd, near the university, and Lower Glanmire Rd, near the train station. For **hostels** try *Sheila's*, 4 Belgrave Place, Wellington Rd (☎021/450 5562, @info@sheilashostel.ie; ❷); *Kelly's Hostel*, 25 Summerhill South (☎021/472 2124; ❷); or the refurbished An Óige place, at 1–2 Redclyffe along Western Rd (☎021/454 3289, @corkyh@gofree.indigo.ie; ❷), fifteen-minutes' walk from the centre and just over a mile from the train station; take bus #8 to University College Cork). **Internet** access is at *webworkhouse*, 8a Winthrop St.

For **food**, *The Quay Co-op*, 24 Sullivan's Quay, and *Café Paradiso*, on Lancaster Quay, are excellent vegetarian restaurants serving local produce; trendy *Pi* on Washington St is good for a reasonably priced pizza lunch; *Yumi Yucki* in the Triskel Arts Centre, Tobin St, is another fashionable lunch option for sushi and seafood; *Farm Gate* upstairs in the English Market has great home-cooked breakfasts and lunches. There's plenty of **traditional Irish music**: the best spots are the *Corner Bar* on Coburg St; *An Spailpín Fánach*, South Main St; *Gable's*, Douglas St; and *The Lobby*, Union Quay (which has rock and indie too).

Cork's best **club** is *The Savoy* on Patrick St, with DJs and live music; *The Bodega* on Coal Quay is a popular late café-bar with regular jazz sessions; and there's an international **jazz festival** in late October. For **theatre**, the *Granary Theatre* on the Mardyke (☎021/490 4275) has a year-round cutting-edge fringe programme, while *Triskel Arts Centre* in Tobin St (☎021/427 2022) is a lively spot with a cinema, exhibitions, readings and concerts. *Crawford Art Gallery* in Academy St is worth a visit for its permanent and visiting collections and excellent café. The *Kino Cinema* on Washington St screens independent films and is part-host for the excellent **film festival** in October (@www.corkfilmfest.org). For **listings** of what's on get the free *Whazon?* or the *Evening Echo*.

The west coast

If you've come to Ireland for mountainous scenery, sea and remoteness, you'll find them all in County Kerry. By far the most visited area is the town of **Killarney** and a scenic route around the perimeter of the Iveragh Peninsula known as the **Ring of Kerry**. Despite the region's popularity, it's easy to lose all contact with modern civilization, whether you head for the mountains or the sea. The **Dingle Peninsula**, to the north, is on a smaller scale, but equally magical and peppered with ancient remains. **Galway** is an exceptionally enjoyable, free-spirited sort of place, and a gathering point for young travellers. West of the city lies **Connemara**, a magnificently wild coastal terrain of wind, rock and water, with the nearby, elementally beautiful **Aran Islands**, in the mouth of Galway Bay. Up the coast the landscape softens around the historic town of **Westport**, while further north, **Sligo** has plenty of associations with the poet Yeats and a lively, bustling feel. In the far northwest **County Donegal**'s scenery is especially rich with a spectacular two-hundred-mile folded coastline whose highlight is **Slieve League** with its awesome sea cliffs, the highest in Europe.

There are plenty of international **flights** directly into the region, to Shannon airport near Limerick or the smaller Knock airport near Westport.

Killarney and around

Although **KILLARNEY** has been commercialized to saturation point and has little of architectural interest, its location amid some of the best lakes, mountains and woodland in Ireland more than compensates. The town is essentially one main street and a couple of side roads, full of souvenir shops, cafés, pubs, restaurants and B&Bs. Pony traps and jaunting cars line up while their owners talk visitors into taking trips through the surrounding country. It's all done with bags of charm, true to Killarney's long tradition of profitably hosting the visiting masses since its establishment as a resort in the mid-eighteenth century. Around the town, three spectacular lakes – Lough Leane, Muckross Lake and the Upper Lake – form an appetizer for MacGillycuddy's Reeks, the highest mountains in Ireland. **Cycling** is a great way of seeing the terrain, and makes good sense because local transport is sparse (David Sheehan at Market Cross and O'Sullivan's in Main St both offer **bike rental**).

The entrance gates to the **Knockreer Estate**, part of the Killarney National Park, are just over the road from Killarney's cathedral. A short walk through the grounds takes you to the banks of **Lough Leane**, where tall wooded hills plunge into the water, with the peaks rising behind to the highest, **Carrauntoohill** (3414ft). The main path through the estate leads to the restored fifteenth-century tower of **Ross Castle** (April–Sept daily 9am–5/6.30pm; Oct Tues–Sat 10am–5pm; €3.80; gardens free), the last place in the area to succumb to Cromwell's forces in 1652.

A mile or so south of Killarney is the **Muckross Estate**; aim first for **Muckross Abbey**, for both the ruin itself and its calm, contemplative location. Founded by the Franciscans in the mid-fifteenth century, it was suppressed by Henry VIII; the friars returned, but were finally driven out by Cromwell in 1652. Back at the main road, signposts direct you to **Muckross House** (daily 9am–5.30/7pm; €5 or €7.50 joint ticket with farm), a solid nineteenth-century neo-Elizabethan mansion with wonderful gardens and also a traditional working farm. The estate gives access to well-trodden paths along the shores of the Muckross Lake where you can see one of Killarney's celebrated beauty spots, the **Meeting of the Waters**. Actually a parting, it has a profusion of indigenous and flowering subtropical plants on the left of the Old Weir Bridge. Close by is the massive shoulder of Torc Mountain, shrugging off **Torc Waterfall**. The Upper Lake is beautiful, too, but still firmly on the tourist trail, with the main road running along one side up to Ladies' View, from where the view is truly amazing.

West of Killarney is the **Gap of Dunloe**, a natural defile formed by glacial over-flow that cuts the mountains in two. Rather than joining the continual stream of expensive jaunting cars, you'd do better to walk the four miles in the late afternoon, when the cars have gone home and the light is at its most magical. **Kate Kearney's Cottage**, a hamlet located six miles from Killarney at the foot of the track leading up to the Gap, is the last place for food and water before **Lord Brandon's Cottage**, a summer tearoom (Easter–Nov), seven miles away on the other side of the valley. The track winds its way up the desolate valley between high rock cliffs and water-falls, past a chain of icy loughs and tarns, to the top, where you find yourself in what feels like one of the remotest places in the world: the **Black Valley**. Named after its entire population perished during the famine (1845–49), it's now inhabited by a mere handful of families, and was the very last valley in Ireland to get electricity. There's a wonderfully isolated An Óige **hostel** here too (☎064/34712; ❷; closed Dec–Feb). From here, the quickest way to Killarney is to carry on down to Lord Brandon's Cottage and take the boat back across the Upper Lake.

Practicalities

B&Bs abound in Killarney, though in high season it's worth booking ahead through the **tourist office**, on Beech Rd off New St (Mon–Sat 9/10am–5.30/6pm; June–Sept also Sun; ☎064/31633, ⊛www.cork-kerry.travel.ie). The An Óige **hostel** (☎064/31240, ⊜anoige@killarney.iol.ie; ❷) is three miles west of town along the Killorglin road at Aghadoe, but there are several alternatives in Killarney itself: *Killarney Railway Hostel* is opposite the station (☎064/35299, ⊜railwayhostel@eir-com.net; ❷); *The Súgan Hostel* is minutes away on Lewis Rd (☎064/33104; ❷); bustling *Neptune's Town Hostel* is in the middle of town on New St (☎064/35255, ⊜neptune@eircom.net; ❷); and *Park Hostel* is up the hill off Cork Rd, opposite the petrol station (☎064/32119; ❷). There's a **campsite** at the *Fossa Holiday Hostel*, just past the Aghadoe hostel (☎064/31497, ⊜fossaholidays@eircom.net; ❷; closed Oct–March). Places to **eat and drink** are thick on the ground: one of the best is *Bricín*, on High St, along with *The Caragh* on New St; or try *Sceilig* on High St, all serving hearty food. *Café Internet* on New St (Mon–Sat 9.30am–10pm, Sun noon–9pm; ☎064/36711) provides **internet** access. Evening **entertainment** is everywhere as you walk the streets; pick up *The Kerryman* for listings.

The Ring of Kerry

Most tourists view the spectacular scenery of the 110-mile **Ring of Kerry**, west of Killarney, without ever leaving their coach or car. So, anyone straying from the road or waiting until the buses stop running in the afternoon will experience the slow twilights of the Atlantic seaboard in perfect seclusion. **Cycling** the Ring takes three days, and a bike will let you get onto the largely deserted mountain roads. Buses from Killarney go right around the Ring in summer (May–Sept 2 daily); for the rest of the year they travel along the northern coast as far as Caherciveen.

Valentia Island and around

Heading anticlockwise on the main N70 around the Ring of Kerry, at **Kells Bay** the road veers inland towards **CAHERCIVEEN**, a long, narrow street of a town and also the main shopping centre for the western part of the peninsula. It has an independent **hostel**, *Sive*, 15 East End (☎066/947 2717, ⊜sivehostel@oceanfree.net; ❷), with camping facilities. Beyond here, lanes lead out to **VALENTIA ISLAND**, Europe's most westerly harbour, its position on the Gulf Stream giving it a mild, balmy climate. Access to the island is easiest by **ferry** from Reenard Point (two-and-a-half miles from Caherciveen) to **Knightstown**. Its main street has a few shops, a post office offering free maps of the island, and a couple of bars. The much-touted **Grotto** – Valentia's highest point – is a gaping slate cavern with a crude statue of the Virgin perched two hundred feet up amid dripping icy water. More exciting is the spectacular cliff scenery to the northwest. You should book ahead for **accommodation** during the summer season. The Knightstown An Óige **hostel** (☎066/947 6154; ②; closed Oct–May) has space for forty, though facilities are spartan. The *Royal Pier Bar* runs an independent hostel in the village (☎066/947 6144, ✉royalpier-val@ireland.com; ②), or for **B&B** try *Spring Acre* (☎066/947 6141; ④).

The stretch of coast south of Valentia is wild and almost deserted, apart from a scattering of farms and fishing villages. Sweet-smelling, tussocky grass dotted with wild flowers is raked by Atlantic winds, ending in abrupt cliffs or sandy beaches. The An Óige **hostel** (☎066/947 9229; ②; closed Oct–March) in **BALLINSKEL-LIGS** is pretty basic but sells supplies. Monks from the Skellig Islands retreated to Ballinskelligs Abbey in the thirteenth century; today, the village is a focus of the Kerry *Gaeltacht* (Irish-speaking area), busy in summer with schoolchildren and students learning Irish. **WATERVILLE** may be touristy, but it does have a certain grace. Formerly a popular resort, it has an air of consequence that contrasts with the wild Atlantic views and is the best base on the Ring for exploring the coast and the mountainous country inland. For **B&B** try *Klondyke House*, New Line Rd (☎066/947 4119, ✇homepage.eircom.net/~klondykehouse; ⑤), or *Ashling House*, Main St (☎066/947 4247; ⑤; closed Nov–Feb); and there's the independent hostel, *Bru na Domoda* at Maistir Gaoithe (☎066/947 4782, ✉maistirgaoithe@tinet.ie; ②; closed Nov to mid-May).

The Dingle Peninsula

The **Dingle Peninsula** is a place of intense, shifting beauty. Spectacular mountains, long sandy beaches and the splinter-slatted mass of rocks that defines the extraordinary coast at Slea Head all conspire to ensure that, remote though it is, the peninsula is firmly on the tourist trail. Here is one of the greatest concentrations of Celtic ruins in Ireland, and the now uninhabited Blasket Islands once generated a wealth of Irish literature.

Served by several daily buses from Killarney, **DINGLE** makes the best base for exploring the peninsula. Now little more than a few streets by the side of **Dingle Bay**, Dingle was Kerry's leading port in medieval times, later becoming a centre for smuggling. There's no shortage of **accommodation**, and the **tourist office** in Strand St (daily 9.30am–1pm & 2.15–5.15/6pm; ☎066/915 1188) will book places. Although many of Dingle's **B&Bs** are fairly expensive, the central *Connor's*, Dykegate St (☎066/915 1598; ④), is comfortable and reasonably-priced. *Boland's* on Goat St (☎066/915 1426, ✇homepage.eircom.net/~bolanddingle; ⑤) is another reliable option. For **hostels**, try the *Grapevine*, Dykegate St (☎066/915 1434; ②); *Ballintaggart House*, one mile before Dingle Town (☎066/915 1454, ✉info@dingleaccommodation.com; ②; closed Nov to mid-March); or the beautifully situated *Seacrest Hostel* (☎066/915 1390, ✉seacrest@indigo.ie; ②), near Lispole. Dingle's top **restaurants** serve excellent seafood, landed just a few hundred yards away. Try *Doyle's* or the *Half Door* on John St for a good, if pricey, meal. *Greaney's*, on the corner of Dykegate and Strand streets, offers good cheap lunches and dinners; *Nithe le n-ithe* deli on Main St does tasty gourmet sandwiches. **Internet** access is at *Dingle Internet Café* on Main St. The best **pubs** for traditional music are *An Droichead Beag* on Main St (nightly) and *O'Flaherty's* on Bridge St (Fri & Sat).

West of Dingle town

Cycling is the best way to explore the peninsula; there are bikes available at Foxy John's on Main St and Paddy's on Dykegate St. Public transport in the west of the peninsula amounts to a **bus** from Dingle to Dunquin (July & Aug daily; rest of year Mon & Thurs).

The Irish-speaking area west of Dingle is rich with relics of the ancient Gaelic and early Christian cultures and the main concentration of monuments lies between Ventry and Slea Head. First off there's the spectacular **Dun Beag** (daily 9am–6/8pm; €2), about four miles out from Ventry. A promontory fort, its defences include four earthen rings, with an underground escape route by the main entrance. West of here, the hillside above the road is studded with stone beehive huts, cave dwellings, souterrains, forts, churches, standing stones and crosses – over 500 of them in all. The beehive huts were being built and used for storage until the late nineteenth century, but among ancient buildings like the **Fahan group** you're looking over a landscape that's remained essentially unchanged for centuries.

At **Slea Head** the view encompasses the desolate, splintered masses of the **Blasket Islands**, uninhabited since 1953, though there are some summer residents. In the summer, boats bound for **Great Blasket** depart from the pier just south of Dunquin (daily weather permitting; €18 return; ⊛www.kerryweb.ie/destination-kerry/blasket/blasket.html). Great Blasket's delights are simple ones: tramping the footpaths that crisscross the island, sitting on the beaches watching the seals and dolphins, or savouring the amazing sunsets. There is accommodation at the *Great Blasket Hostel* on the island (☎087/852232, ⊜info@greatblasketisland.com; ❸; closed Nov–March); you can camp for free and there's a café serving good, cheap vegetarian meals. At **DUNQUIN**, there's an An Óige **hostel** (☎066/915 6121, ❷), and **B&B** in *Kruger's* pub (☎066/915 6127; ❹).

A couple of miles north around the headland from Dunquin stands **BALLY-FERRITER**, with the *Black Cat* **hostel** (☎066/915 6286; ❷). From here, the little northward lanes lead to the 500-foot cliffs at Sybil Head or to Smerwick Harbour and **Dún an Óir** (Golden Fort). The single most impressive early Christian monument on the peninsula is the **Gallarus oratory** (April–Oct daily 9am–8pm; €2.50) three miles further east, built sometime between the ninth and twelfth centuries of unmortared stone and still watertight. It's the best-preserved example of around twenty such oratories in Ireland, and represents a transition between the round beehive huts and the later rectangular churches, an example of which is to be found a mile to the north at **KILMALKEDAR**, with a nave dating from the mid-twelfth century and a corbelled stone roof.

Galway and around

The city of **GALWAY** continues to justify its reputation as the party capital of Ireland. University College Galway guarantees a high number of young people in term-time, but the energy is most evident during Galway's **festivals**, especially the Arts Festival in the last two weeks in July (⊛www.galwayartsfestival.ie). For locals, however, the most important event is the **Galway Races**, usually held in the last week of July. You'll have to pre-book accommodation during these weeks.

Galway began as a crossing point on the River Corrib, and developed as a strong Anglo-Norman colony. Granted city status in 1484 by Richard III, it developed a flourishing trade with the Continent, especially Spain. When Cromwellian forces arrived in 1652, however, the city was besieged for ninety days and went into a decline from which it has only recently recovered. The prosperity of maritime Galway was expressed in the distinctive townhouses of the merchant class, remnants of which are littered around the city, even though recent development has destroyed some of the city's character. The **Browne doorway** in Eyre Square is one such monument, a bay window and doorway with the coats of arms of the Browne and Lynch families, dated 1627. Just about the finest medieval townhouse in Ireland is fifteenth century **Lynch's Castle** in Shop St – along with Quay St, the social hub of Galway. Now housing the Allied Irish Bank, it has a stone facade decorated with carved panels, gargoyles and a lion devouring another animal.

There are two churches of interest: the **Collegiate Church of St Nicholas** and the **Cathedral of Our Lady Assumed into Heaven and St Nicholas**. The former, founded in 1320, is the largest medieval church in Ireland. The Cathedral, in hideous contrast, sits on the banks of the river like a huge toad, its copper dome seeping green slime down the formica-bright limestone walls. Down by the river Corrib stands the **Spanish Arch**: more evocative in name than in reality, it's a sixteenth-century structure that was used to protect galleons unloading wine and rum. Cross the bridge over the river into the **Claddagh** district, the old fishing village that once stood outside the city walls and gave the world the Claddagh ring as a symbol of love and fidelity. Past the Claddagh the river widens out into **Galway Bay**; for a pleasant sea walk follow the road until it reaches **Salthill**, the city's seaside resort. There are several beaches along the prom, though for the best you'll have to leave the city behind and head two miles past Salthill to **Silverstrand** on the Barna road. Once past Barna and into Connemara the beaches become quieter and more idyllic.

Practicalities

The **bus and train stations** are off Eyre Square, on the northern edge of the city centre. The **tourist office** (Mon–Fri 9am–5.45pm, Sat 9am–12.45pm; July & Aug daily 9am–7.45pm; ☎091/537700, ⊛www.westireland.travel.ie) is a short stroll away on Forster St, and has an accommodation service. The best budget **accommodation** includes *Kinlay House Galway*, Merchant's Rd (☎091/565244, ⊛kingal@usit.ie; ❸), and *Barnacles Quay Street House*, 10 Quay St (☎091/568644, ⊛www.barnacles.ie; ❷). For **B&B** head for *Ardawn House*, 31 College Rd (☎091/568833; ❻), or *Crookhaven*, 96 Father Griffin Rd (☎091/589019; ❺). There are **campsites** at *Ballyloughnane Caravan Park* on Dublin Rd (closed Oct–April), and several in Salthill, the most pleasant being *Hunter's* at Silver Strand, four miles west on the coast road (closed Oct–Easter). The Celtic e-centre by Kinlay House on Merchant's Rd offers discounted international calls and **internet** access.

The bars are the lungs of this city, and even the most abstemious travellers are going to find themselves sucked in. Good-value **pub food** is served around midday at *The Quays*, Quay St, *Busker Browne's*, Cross St, and *McSwiggan's* in Eyre St; for a more adventurous menu with a Latin influence, head for *BarCuba* on Eyre Square. In Quay St, *McDonagh's Seafood Bar* is a must for seafood at any time of day, while on Cross St, *The Latin Quarter* is a popular spot for brunch and lunch. *Food for Thought* on Abbeygate St is a veggie café and excellent noodle dishes can be enjoyed at *Da Tang Noodle House*, Middle St.

The Quay St area of the city leading down to the river is known as the "left bank" due to the proliferation of popular pubs, restaurants and cafés. *The Quays* bar is one of the city's best-loved, along with the nearby *Front Door* on Cross St. Among the best places to hear **traditional music** are *Taaffes* on Shop St, the old fashioned *Tigh Neachtain* on Cross St and *The Crane* bar across the river on William St West. For nightly live music, *Róisín Dubh* in Dominick St attracts leading Irish and international names. Galway also has its fair share of **clubs**: *ClubCuba*, Eyre Square, is a huge draw while other popular venues include *GPO*, Eglinton St, and *Le Metro* in the Radisson Hotel, Lough Atalia Rd. For **listings**, see the weekly *Galway Advertiser*.

The Aran Islands

The **Aran Islands** – Inishmore, Inishmaan and Inisheer – lying thirty miles out across the mouth of Galway Bay, are spectacular settings for a wealth of early remains and some of the finest archeological sites in Europe. The isolation of the Irish-speaking islands prolonged the continuation of a unique, ancient culture into the early twentieth century. There are daily **ferries** to Inishmore year-round, but less frequently to the other islands, departing from Galway city, Rossaveal (20 miles west by bus) and Doolin in County Clare – the cost of a return trip ranges from €13 to €25, depending on the season, with some student reductions and good-value accommodation packages. Book through Island Ferries at Galway tourist office (☎091/568903); O'Brien Shipping, New Docks, Galway city (☎091/567676); or Doolin Ferry Company (☎065/707 4455). You can also **fly** with Aer Árann (☎091/593034, ⊛www.aerarann.ie); book at Galway tourist office.

Although **INISHMORE** is the most tourist-orientated of the Aran Islands, its wealth of dramatic ancient sites overrides such considerations. It's a long strip of an island, a great tilted plateau of limestone with a scattering of villages along the sheltered northerly coast. The land slants up to the southern edge, where tremendous cliffs rip along the entire shoreline. As far as the eye can see is a tremendous patterning of stone, some of it the bare pavements of grey rock split in bold diagonal grooves, gridded by dry-stone walls. The ferry docks at **Kilronan**, where the cheapest place to stay is the *Kilronan Hostel* (℡099/61255; ②), though the island's tranquillity is best enjoyed at the relaxing *Mainistir House Hostel* (℡099/61318, ✉mainistirhouse@eircom.net; ②), twenty minutes' walk from the pier. **B&Bs** can be booked through the Kilronan **tourist office** (daily 10am–4/6.45pm; ℡099/61263), or when you buy your ferry ticket. Seafood is the island's great speciality, with most of the popular restaurants located in Kilronan: *Dún Aonghasa* has a varied and reasonably priced menu; *Joe Watty's* bar serves good soups and stews; the *Aran Fisherman* has an extensive seafood menu; and *Café Pota Stoir*, based in the Heritage Centre, does delicious homemade soups and cakes. For **bike rental**, there's Aran Bicycle Hire beside the pier, or Mullin & Burke by the *Aran Islands Hostel*. Alternatively, take the minibus up through the island's villages and walk back from any point. Most of Inishmore's sights are to the northwest of Kilronan; the first hamlet in this direction is Mainistir, from where it's a short signposted walk to the twelfth-century church of **Teampall Chiaráin**, the most interesting of the ecclesiastical sites on Inishmore. Three miles or so down the main road is Kilmurvey, a fifteen-minute walk from the most spectacular of Aran's prehistoric sites, **Dún Aengus**. This massive ring fort, lodged on the edge of three hundred foot sea cliffs, has an inner citadel of precise blocks of grey stone, their symmetry echoing the almost geometric regularity of the land's limestone pavementing. Nearby **Dún Eoghanachta** is a huge drum of a stone fort, set in a lonely field with the Connemara mountains as a backdrop. It's accessible by tiny lanes from Dún Aengus with a detailed map; otherwise retrace your steps to Kilmurvey and follow the road west for just over a mile. At the **seven churches**, just east of Eoghannacht, there are ancient slabs commemorating seven Romans who died here, testifying to the far-reaching influence of Aran's monasteries. The site is, in fact, that of two churches and several domestic buildings, dating from the eighth to the thirteenth centuries, and includes St Brendan's grave, adorned by an early cross with interlaced patterns.

From Inishmore, it's an easy hop by boat to the other two islands; all the ferry companies run daily services. In comparison with Inishmore, **INISHMAAN** is lush, its stone walls forming a maze that chequers off tiny fields of grass and clover. The island's main sight is **Dún Chonchubhair**: built some time between the first and seventh centuries, its massive oval wall is almost intact and commands great views. Inishmaan's indifference to tourism means that amenities for visitors are minimal; if you arrive on spec ask at the pub for information (℡099/73003) – it's a warm and friendly place which also serves snacks in summer. For **B&B** try *Ard Álainn* (℡099/73027; ④; closed Oct–March); or *An Dun* (℡099/73047; ⑤).

INISHEER, at just under two miles across, is the smallest of the Aran Islands. Tourism has a key role here; Inisheer doesn't have the archeological wealth of Inishmore, nor the wild solitude of Inishmaan. A great plug of rock dominates the island, its rough, pale-grey stone dripping with greenery, topped by the fifteenth-century **O'Brien's Castle**, standing inside an ancient ring fort. Set around it are low fields, a small community of pubs and houses, and windswept sand dunes. The **tourist office** hut by the pier (June–Sept daily 10am–7pm) will give you a map and a list of **B&Bs**; try *Uí Chongaile's*, Lioseinee, West Village (℡099/75025; ④). There's also a **hostel**, *Brú Radharc na Mara* (℡099/75024, ✉maire.searraigh@ocean-free.net; ②) and a **campsite** near the pier. Meals are available all day at *Radharc na Mara* (closed Oct–May). For **music**, head for *Tigh Ned's* bar.

Stay in Touch & Save!

Visit **www.roughguides.ekit.com**
or call toll-free *1-800-707-0031 in the US*

Contact Me
www.roughguides.ekit.com

NAME

To leave me a FREE voicemail: Dial 1-800-706-1333

Press [*] [2] & enter my eKit account #

And leave me a message!

Or send me an email:

Powered by

Contact Me
www.roughguides.ekit.com

NAME

To leave me a FREE voicemail: Dial 1-800-706-1333

Press [*] [2] & enter my eKit account #

And leave me a message!

Or send me an email:

Powered by

Carry this card with you!

To a make a call:

1. Dial the access number for the country you are in, from any touchtone phone

2. Enter your eKit account #

   & Press [#] followed by your PIN

   & Press [#]

3. Press [2], then dial the country code, area code and phone number

   Follow instructions for additional options.

Powered by

ROUGH GUIDES

Doolin and The Cliffs of Moher

One of the liveliest, if touristic places on the west coast, is the Clare village of **DOOLIN**, accessible by **Bus Éireann** from Galway. It's set near a treacherous sandy beach and famed for a steady supply of **traditional music** in its three bars all summer. There's plenty of **accommodation** including *Paddy's Doolin Hostel* (☎065/707 4006, ✉doolinhostel@eircom.net; ❷; closed Dec & Jan); *Rainbow Hostel* (☎065/707 4415, ✉rainbowhostel@eircom.net; ❷); *Flanagan's Village Hostel* (☎065/707 4564; ❷); and *Aille River Hostel* (☎065/707 4260, ✉ailleriver@esat-clear.ie; ❷) which offers **camping** as well. There's also a summer campsite by the pier. All of Doolin's pubs serve excellent **food**; the *Lazy Lobster* by the pier and *Doolin Café* are two of the best restaurants. By the pier, from which a ferry runs to the **Aran Islands**, bold shelves of limestone pavement step into the sea. The **Cliffs of Moher**, four miles south of Doolin, are the area's most famous tourist spot, their great bands of shale and sandstone rising 660 feet above the waves.

Connemara

The great asset of **CLIFDEN** – capital of the beautiful region of Connemara – is its position, perched above the boulder-strewn estuary of the Owenglin River, with the circling jumble of the Twelve Bens providing a magnificent backdrop. Clifden tries hard to cultivate Galway's cosmopolitan atmosphere, and it attracts a fair number of young Dubliners, too, revving up the life of this rural town. The **tourist office** on Galway Rd (Mon–Sat 9/10am–5/6pm; also July & Aug Sun 10am–5pm; ☎095/21163, ✆www.irelandwest.travel.ie) has lists of the plentiful **B&Bs** around Clifden, though these can be very busy in July and August. In town, try the good value *Ben View House*, Bridge St (☎095/21256, ✆www.connemara.net/benviewhouse; ❺), or the renovated *Clifden House*, further down the same street (☎095/21187, ✆www.clifdon.com; ❺). Clifden has a couple of **hostels**, best of which is the excellent *Clifden Town Hostel*, Market St (☎095/21076, ✉seancth@eircom.net; ❷). Two of the nicest **bars** for drink and music are *Mannion's* and *E.J. King's* on Market St, both of which also serve **food**. *Mitchell's* has a varied, reasonably priced menu, while for evening meals at €15 and upwards, try *Derryclare Seafood Restaurant*. Clifden is a good base for getting out into the Connemara countryside, and to do this you really need your own transport; there are plenty of places for **bike rental**, including John Mannion on Bridge St.

Westport

Set on the shores of Clew Bay at the end of a rail line from Dublin, **WESTPORT** is one of the west's liveliest spots. Planned by the eighteenth-century architect James Wyatt, its formal layout comes as quite a surprise in the midst of the west. The craggy **Croagh Patrick** makes an imposing background to the town, standing at 2510 feet above the bay; the climb is a strenuous one, but your reward is spectacular views. St Patrick reputedly prayed on the mountain for forty days for the conversion of the Irish to Christianity, and on the last Sunday of July many tackle the pilgrimage to the summit barefoot. Another attraction is **Westport House** (summer Mon–Fri 11.30am–5.30pm, Sat & Sun 1.30–5.30pm; €12; ✆www.westporthouse.ie), a mile or so out of town towards the bay. The beautifully designed house dates from 1730 and is privately owned: the present family are direct descendants of legendary pirate Grace O'Malley of Clew Bay. Inside the house is a *Holy Family* by Rubens and an upstairs room with intricate Chinese wallpaper dating from 1780.

Buses drop off on Mill St in the centre; the **train** station is on Altamount St (☎098/25253), ten minutes north of the centre. Westport's **hostels** include the enormous *Club Atlantic* on Altamount St (☎098/26644; ❷; closed Nov–Feb) and, a little further out of town, *The Granary* on Quay Rd (☎098/25903; ❷; closed

Nov–March). There are plenty of **B&Bs** – check for availability at the **tourist office** on James St (Mon–Sat 9am–6pm; July & Aug also Sun; ☎098/25711). *O'Malley's* on Bridge St is a popular **eating** choice while the Mediterranean-style *Sol Rio* on Bridge St is a good lunch option. For more formal Italian food, *La Bella Vita* on High St is excellent. The restaurant at *Quay Cottage*, the entrance to Westport House, serves enormous salmon salads and plenty of vegetarian food; the nearby complex of refurbished waterside buildings brims with people, pubs and more expensive restaurants. The best **music** pubs are on Bridge St – *The West* is hugely popular and *Matt Molloy's Bar*, owned by the eponymous Chieftains' flute player, occasionally features visiting celebrities and is a hive of activity during Westport's **Arts Festival** at the end of September.

Sligo and around

SLIGO is, after Derry, the biggest town in the northwest of Ireland and a focal point for the area. During the Famine its population fell by a third, but recovery began at the end of the nineteenth century and the upswing has continued to the present.

The legacy of **W.B. Yeats** – perhaps Ireland's best-loved poet – is still strongly felt in the town: the **Yeats Memorial Building** on Hyde Bridge (Mon–Sat 10am–4.30pm; €2.50) features a photographic exhibition and film on his life, and houses a branch of the **tourist office**, the main branch of which is on Temple St (June–Aug daily 9am–8pm; rest of year Mon–Fri 9am–5/6pm; ☎071/61201, ⓦwww.northwestireland.travel.ie). En route to see the poet's Nobel Prize for Literature and other memorabilia in the **Sligo County Museum** on Stephen St (June–Sept Mon–Sat 10am–noon & 2–5pm; rest of year 2–5pm only; free), admire his flamboyant bronze image outside the Ulster Bank. Further along the street, the **Model Arts Centre** on The Mall (Tues–Sat 10am–5.30pm; free) is home to a collection of paintings and drawings by the poet's brother Jack B. Yeats. His later works like *The Graveyard Wall* and *The Sea and the Lighthouse* are especially evocative of the area's life and atmosphere. The gallery also houses a good representation of modern Irish art and stages visiting exhibitions. Heading back towards the town centre, take a left onto Bridge St and cross the Garavogue to reach the thirteenth-century **Dominican Friary** on Abbey St. The modern visitor centre (April–Oct daily 10am–6pm; €1.90, guided tours on request) provides an informative introduction to many of its existing features, including the last remaining sculptured high altar in the country and an impressive cloistered arcade.

Buses and **trains** arrive at the station on Lord Edward St, five minutes west of the centre. For **bike rental**, try Gary's Cycles on Lower Quay St (☎071/45418). One of the most central **B&Bs** is *Renaté House*, 9 Upper John St (☎071/62014; ⑤); or try *St Anne's* (☎071/43188; ⑥) or *Pearse Lodge* (☎071/61090; ⑥), two good options on Pearse Rd. **Hostels** include the central and popular *White House* on Markievicz Rd (☎071/45160; ❷), sometimes overcrowded in the summer; the *Yeats County Hostel*, Lord Edward St (☎071/46876; ❷), well-run and near the train station; or the very comfortable *Harbour House*, Finisklin Rd (☎071/71547, ⓔharbourhouse@eircom.net; ❷), a desolate mile-long walk from the centre which women may feel uncomfortable undertaking alone. There are **campsites** five miles from town at Rosses Point to the north (bus #473) and Strandhill to the west (bus #472); both have fine beaches and Strandhill, while unsafe for swimming, draws in plenty of surfers. Most pubs in Sligo serve decent **bar lunches**: *Hargadon's* on O'Connell St has fine old traditional snugs; the *Garavogue* on Stephen St has a river terrace and serves excellent international food and bar snacks all day. For top pizza head for *Bistro Bianconni* restaurant on O'Connell St; *The Loft* on Lord Edward St has an extensive menu of world cuisine. Sligo does well for **pubs**: tiny *Shoot the Crows* on Castle St is popular with the arty set, and *Fiddler's Creek* along the river on Rockwood Parade is always lively. Best for **traditional music** are *Sheela na Gig* on

Bridge St, owned by local trad stars Dervish, with nightly summer sessions; *Earley's* bar across the road also has regular sessions. A pre-club hangout is *The Belfry*, with adjoining nightclub *Toff's* on Kennedy Parade, the town's favourite night-spot. Check the weekly *Sligo Champion* for listings.

Donegal Town

Regular buses connect Sligo to **DONEGAL TOWN**, a bustling place focused around its old marketplace, the Diamond. Donegal is a fine base from which to explore the stunning coastal countryside and inland hills and loughs, though just about the only thing to see in the town itself is the well-preserved shell of **O'Donnell's Castle** on Tírchonaill St by the Diamond (Easter–Oct daily 10am–6pm; €3.80), a fine example of Jacobean architecture. On the left bank of the River Eske stand the few ruined remains of **Donegal Friary**, while on the opposite bank a woodland path known as Bank Walk offers wonderful views of **Donegal Bay** and towards the **Blue Stack Mountains**, which rise at the northern end of Lough Eske.

There are dozens of **B&Bs** in town, and to avoid a lot of walking it's simplest to call at the **tourist office** on the Quay (Easter–Sept Mon–Sat 9am–5/8pm July & Aug also Sun; ☎073/21148, ⊛www.ireland-northwest.travel.ie). There are two **hostels** off the Killybegs road just outside town: the nearest is *Donegal Town Independent Hostel* (☎073/22805, ✉lincunn8@eircom.net; ❷), with camping facilities, while An Óige *Ball Hill Hostel* is about three miles out on the north side of Donegal Bay (☎073/21174; ❷; closed Oct–Easter). **Eating** places are plentiful. You'll find excellent burgers and pizza at the *Harbour*, opposite the tourist office, and a substantial cheap meal at the *Atlantic Café* on Main St. Many **pubs** serve lunches and are good evening watering holes. The *Olde Castle Bar*, next to the castle, is fine for a quiet daytime drink; *McGroarty's* on the Diamond has a good bar menu and a weekly traditional session; while *The Scotsman* on Bridge St has regular open traditional sessions. The *Abbey Hotel* on the Diamond hosts a popular **disco** on Saturday and Sunday nights. For **bike rental** head for the Bike Shop on Waterloo St.

Slieve League and Glencolmcille

To the west of Donegal Town lies one of the most stupendous landscapes in Ireland – the stark and beautiful **Teelin Bay** and the majestic Slieve League cliffs. An ideal base for exploring the region is one of the best independent **hostels** in the country, the *Derrylahan Independent Hostel* (☎073/38079, ✉derrylahan@eircom.net; ❷), on the seaside road between **KILCAR** and **CARRICK**; it also has a **campsite**.

There are two routes up to the ridge of **Slieve League**: a back route following the signpost to Baile Mór just before Teelin, and the road route from Teelin to Bunglass, a thousand sheer feet above the sea. The former path, only a few feet wide in places and dangerous in windy weather, has you looking up continually at the ridge known as One Man's Path, on which walkers seem the size of pins, while the frontal approach swings you up to one of the most thrilling cliff scenes in the world, the **Amharc Mór**. On a good day you can see a third of Ireland from the summit.

One Man's Path across the summit leads via Malinbeg and Malinmore to **GLEN-COLMCILLE** – the Glen of St Columbcille, the name by which Columba was known after his conversion. A place of pilgrimage since the seventh century, following Columba's stay in the valley, every June 9 at midnight the locals commence a three-hour barefoot itinerary of the cross-inscribed slabs that stud the valley basin, finishing up with Mass at 3am in the small church. If you want to attempt *Turas Cholmcille* ("Columba's Journey") yourself, get a map of the route from the **Folk Village Museum** (Easter–Sept daily noon/11am–6pm; €2.75). The museum itself is a cluster of replica, period-furnished thatched cottages, including a National School and a Shebeen house. A path up to the left from here leads to the wonderfully positioned *Dooey Hostel* (☎073/30130, ⊛www.holidayhound.com/dooeyhostel; ➋). The best **food** in Glencolmcille is at *An Cistin*, part of the Foras Cultúir Uladh complex, or there's the *Lace House Restaurant* on the main street above the **tourist office** (June–Aug daily 10am–6pm; ☎073/30116). **B&Bs** include *Brackendale* (☎073/30038; ➎) and *Corner House* (☎073/30021; ➎; closed Oct–March), both near *Biddy's Bar* in the village centre.

Northern Ireland

Both the pace of political change and the uncertainty of its future continue to characterise **Northern Ireland**. In May 1998, after thirty years of "The Troubles", its people overwhelmingly voted in support of a political settlement and, it was hoped, an end to political and sectarian violence. Although an assembly was elected and an executive formed in November 1999, deep mistrust and suspicion continue to exist on both sides, with issues such as the decommissioning of IRA weaponry and inter-community tensions still rife in parts of Belfast. Despite the political instability the north remains a pretty safe place for tourists. **Belfast** and **Derry** – two lively and attractive cities – have no obvious security presence beyond the occasional hovering army helicopter. The northern coastline – especially the weird geometry of the **Giant's Causeway** – is as spectacular as anything in Ireland. Over to the southwest is the great **Lough Erne**, a huge lake complex dotted with islands and surrounded by richly beautiful countryside, and **Enniskillen**, a town resonant with history.

Belfast

A quarter of Northern Ireland's population lives in the capital, **BELFAST**. While the legacy of "The Troubles" is clearly visible in the landscape of areas like West Belfast – the peace walls, derelict buildings and political murals – security measures have been considerably eased and the place buzzes with a tangible sense of optimism engendered by the peace process and economic rejuvenation.

Belfast began life as a cluster of forts guarding a ford across the River Farset, which nowadays runs beneath High St. However, its history doesn't really begin until 1604, when Sir Arthur Chichester was "planted" in the area by James I. By the eighteenth century the cloth trade and shipbuilding had expanded tremendously, and the population increased ten-fold in a century. It was then noted for its liberalism, but in the nineteenth century the sectarian divide became wider and increasingly violent. Although Partition and the creation of Northern Ireland with Belfast as its capital inevitably boosted the city's status, the Troubles exacerbated the industrial decline which hit much of the British Isles during the 1980s. However, a massive programme of regeneration commenced in the 1990s at the first signs of peace, fuelled by the billions of pounds pumped in from Britain, the European Union and the International Fund for Ireland in the hope of ensuing political stability. While a stable democracy has yet to be achieved and the city still bears physical and psychological scars from years of violence, it seems to become livelier each year.

Arrival, information and accommodation

Flights arrive at **Belfast International Airport**, nineteen miles west of town (buses every 30min to Europa bus station; £5), or **Belfast City Airport**, three miles northeast (bus #21 to city centre; £2). **Ferries** dock at Donegall Quay (15min walk to centre, £3 taxi-ride); a little further north at Corry Rd (taxi £4); further north again on West Bank Rd (taxi £5); or 20 miles north at Larne (bus or train into centre). Most **trains** call at Great Victoria St Station in the centre, though those from Dublin terminate at Central Station on East Bridge St. **Buses** from

Derry, the Republic, the airports and ferry docks arrive at Europa bus station beside Great Victoria St train station; buses from the north coast use Laganside Buscentre in Queen's Square. A regular Centrelink bus connects all bus and train stations. The excellent **Citybus** company covers nearly everywhere you'll want to go; it's worth buying a multi-journey ticket (£3.40) for four daily journeys, available from newsagents and the Citybus kiosk in Donegall Square West, which can also provide a free bus map. **Ulsterbus** serves the outlying areas; and there are special weekend **late-night buses** from Donegall Square West (Fri & Sat 1–2am; £3). Full details for all buses and trains are available at ☻ www.translink.co.uk.

The **Belfast Welcome Centre** is at 47 Donegall Place (Mon–Fri 9am–5.30/7pm; Sat 9am–5.30pm; June–Sept also Sun noon–5pm; ☎ 028/9024 6609, ☻ www.gotobelfast.com), with information and an accommodation booking service as well as left-luggage facilities and an internet café. **Bord Fáilte**, for information about the Republic, is at 52 Castle St (Mon–Fri 9am–5pm; June–Sept also Sat 9am–12.30pm; ☎ 028/9032 7888).

Many of Belfast's numerous **B&Bs** are on the south side of the city in the university area, and there are several budget options.

Hostels

The Ark 18 University St ☎ 028/9032 9626, ☻ www.arkhostel.com. Friendly, comfortable hostel close to the university. ❷

Arnie's Backpackers 63 Fitzwilliam St ☎ 028/9024 2867. Cheerful and relaxed independent hostel, also near the university. ❷

Belfast International Youth Hostel 22–32 Donegall Rd ☎ 028/9031 5435, ☻ www.hini.org.uk. Large, well-equipped but characterless new hostel in the city centre. ❷

Linen House Hostel 18 Kent St ☎ 028/9058 6400, ☻ www.belfasthostel.com. Large, but welcoming, centrally located hostel. ❷

Hotels and B&Bs

Botanic Lodge 87 Botanic Ave ☎ 028/9032 7682. Popular, family-run B&B; 16 rooms, but only two en suite. ❺

Eglantine Guest House 21 Eglantine Ave ☎ 028/9066 7585. Eight cosy B&B rooms in a Victorian house. ❺

The Kitchen Bar 16–18 Victoria Sq ☎ 028/9032 4091. Comfortable accommodation above one of the city's best pubs. ❻

Liserin 17 Eglantine Ave ☎ 028/9066 0769. Well-run six-room B&B in the university area. ❺

The City

Belfast **City Hall**, presiding over central **Donegall Square**, is an austere building (tours June–Sept Mon–Fri 10.30am, 11.30am & 2.30pm, Sat 2.30pm; rest of year Mon–Sat 2.30pm; free), its civic purpose almost subservient to its role in propagating the ethics of Presbyterian power. At the northwest corner of the square stands **The Linen Hall Library** (Mon–Fri 9.30am–5.30pm, Sat 9.30am–4pm; ☻ www.linenhall.com), where the Political Collection houses over 80,000 publications dealing with every aspect of Northern Ireland's political life since 1966. The streets leading north off Donegall Square North take you into the main shopping area. Towards the river, either side of Ann St, you're in the narrow alleyways known as **The Entries**, where you'll find some great old saloon bars. At the end of High St the clock tower is a good position from which to view the world's second- and third-largest cranes, Goliath and Samson, across the river in the Harland & Wolff shipyard where the **Titanic** was built. North of the clock tower is a series of grand edifices which grew out of a similar civic vanity to that invested in the City Hall. The restored **Customs House**, a Corinthian-style building, is the first you'll see, but the most monolithic is the Protestant **St Anne's Cathedral** at the junction of Donegall and Talbot streets, a neo-Romanesque basilica started in 1899. Across the river from the Customs House is the face of a new Belfast, the ambitious **Odyssey** development (☻ www.theodyssey.co.uk) housing a sports stadium, cinema complex, science exhibition centre, shopping malls and Ireland's first *Hard Rock Café*. Further along the waterside is the impressive Waterfront Hall concert venue (☻ www.waterfront.co.uk).

IRELAND | Northern Ireland

The university area inhabits part of the stretch of **South Belfast** known as "The Golden Mile", starting at the **Grand Opera House** on Great Victoria St, an area littered with eating places, pubs and bars, B&Bs and guest houses. Among the attractions is the **Crown Liquor Saloon**, one of the greatest of the old Victorian gin palaces. Further south on University Rd lies the university quarter, of which **Queen's University** is the architectural centrepiece, flanked by the most satisfying Georgian terrace in Belfast, University Square. Just south of the university are the verdant **Botanic Gardens** whose Palm House (Mon–Fri 10am–4/5pm, Sat & Sun 2–4/5pm; free) was the first of its kind in the world. Also in the Botanic Gardens is the **Ulster Museum** (Mon–Fri 10am–5pm, Sat 1–5pm, Sun 2–5pm; free, except for some major exhibitions; bus #69/#70/#71; ⓦwww.ulstermuseum.org.uk), with its collection of Irish art, history and natural sciences, and treasures salvaged from the Spanish Armada ships which foundered off the Giant's Causeway in 1588.

Eating, drinking and entertainment

Many of the best places to **eat** and the liveliest **pubs** can be found around Great Victoria St and in the university area, and Belfast's best entertainment is **music** in the pubs. Good sources of information are *The Big List*, available free in pubs and record shops, and the *Belfast Evening Telegraph*.

Restaurants and cafés

Archana 53 Dublin Rd ☎028/9032 3713. Indian Balti house with *Little India*, a fine Indian vegetarian restaurant, downstairs.

Bewley's Donegall Arcade. Branch of the famous Dublin coffee house serving good-value breakfasts, lunches and snacks.

Café Conor 11a Stranmillis Rd. Stylish café beside the Botanic Gardens with hot food specials and breakfasts.

Chez Delbart (aka **Frogities**) 10 Bradbury Place ☎028/9023 8020. French food at good prices, though you often have to queue.

Delaney's 19 Lombard St. Economical, wholesome food from a restaurant handily placed in the main shopping area. Mon–Sat 9am–5pm, Thurs until 9pm.

La Salsa 23 University Rd ☎028/9024 4588. One of Ireland's few Mexican restaurants and decorated accordingly.

Láziz 99 Botanic Ave ☎028/9023 4888. Splendid Moroccan restaurant serving beautifully presented and extremely tasty specialities.

Maggie May's 45 Botanic Ave ☎028/9032 2662. Huge, economically priced portions with lots of veggie choices.

Sun Kee 38 Donegall Pass ☎028/021 2016. No-frills decor, but superbly adventurous Chinese food, popular with the local Chinese community.

Villa Italia 39 University Rd ☎028/9032 8356. Queues outside are the best indicator of this reasonably priced Italian restaurant's popularity.

Pubs and music

The Apartment Donegall Sq West. Trendy city centre hangout featuring two bars on three floors.

Bar Twelve Lower Crescent. Fashionable spot in the university area, popular with young clubbers.

The Basement Donegall Sq East. Basement bar with a stylish interior, cosmopolitan atmosphere and regular DJs at weekends.

Crown Liquor Saloon 46 Great Victoria St. The city's most famous pub, decked out like a spa bath, with a good range of Ulster food and Strangford oysters in season.

The Empire 42 Botanic Ave. Music hall and cellar bar in converted church with regular music and popular comedy club (Tues).

The John Hewitt Donegall St. Owned by Belfast Unemployed Resource Centre, this popular bar has some of Belfast's best traditional sessions (Tues, Wed & Sun evenings plus Sat 5pm).

Kelly's Cellars 30 Bank St. One of the city's oldest and finest traditional bars.

The Kitchen Bar 16 Victoria Sq. Fine old bar, tucked away behind Ann St – great value lunches and traditional sessions (Fri & Sun).

Madden's Smithfield. Unpretentious and atmospheric pub, with regular traditional sessions (Fri & Sat).

The Morning Star 17 Pottinger's Entry. Old-fashioned bar serving great food in the restaurant upstairs, with a very cheap lunchtime buffet downstairs.

Morrison's Spirit Grocer's 21 Bedford St. Retro bar with interesting lunchtime food.

The Rotterdam 54 Pilot St. Names big and small play in this docklands venue. First-class sounds.

Listings

Exchange Thomas Cook, 11 Donegall Place; and at the banks.

Hospitals Belfast City Hospital, Lisburn Rd ☎028/9032 9241; Royal Victoria, Grosvenor Rd ☎028/9024 0503.

Internet Broncos Web, 122 Great Victoria St; Revelations, 27 Shaftesbury Sq.

Left luggage Belfast Welcome Centre, 47 Donegall Place.

Police North Queen St ☎028/9065 0222.

Post office Castle Place.

The Giant's Causeway and around

Since 1693, when the Royal Geographical Society publicized it as one of the great wonders of the natural world, the **Giant's Causeway**, 65 miles north of Belfast on the coast, has been a major tourist attraction. Consisting of an estimated 37,000 polygonal basalt columns, it's the result of a massive subterranean explosion some sixty million years ago which spewed out a huge mass of molten basalt onto the surface and, as it cooled, solidified into what are, essentially, massive polygonal crystals. Public transport is well-organized in summer. **Trains** from Belfast go to **COLERAINE**, and some go on to **PORTRUSH**; from either, you can catch the "**open-topper**" bus (July & Aug 4 daily) to the Causeway, or from Portrush there's bus #172. The scenic Antrim Coaster coach (Goldline Express #252) runs from Belfast Laganside Buscentre direct to the Causeway (June–Sept twice daily). The Causeway's **visitor centre** (daily 10am–5/7pm; ☎028/2073 1855; free; car parking £3) has information and a small exhibition. Taking the path down the cliffs from the visitor centre (or the shuttle bus; every 15min; £1 return) brings you to the most spectacular of the blocks where many people linger, but if you push on, you'll be rewarded with relative solitude and views of some of the more impressive formations high in the cliffs. One of these, **Chimney Point**, has an appearance so bizarre that it persuaded the ships of the Spanish Armada to open fire on it, believing that they were attacking Dunluce Castle, a few miles further west. An alternative two-mile circuit follows the spectacular clifftop path from the visitor centre, with views across to Scotland, to a flight of 162 steps leading down the cliff to a set of 40ft basalt columns known as the **Organ Pipes**, from where paths lead round to the shuttle-bus stop alongside the Causeway proper.

Derry

DERRY lies at the foot of Lough Foyle, less than three miles from the border with the Republic. The city presents a beguiling picture, its two hillsides terraced with pastel-shaded houses punctuated by stone spires, and, being two-thirds Catholic, has a very different atmosphere from Belfast. However, until recently Derry's Catholic majority was denied its civil rights by gerrymandering, which ensured that the Protestant minority maintained control of all important local institutions. The situation came to a head after the Protestant Apprentice Boys' March in August 1969, when the police attempted to storm the Catholic estates of the Bogside. In the ensuing tension, British troops were widely deployed for the first time in Northern Ireland. On January 31, 1972, the crisis deepened when British paratroopers opened fire on civilians, killing thirteen unarmed demonstrators in what became known as **Bloody Sunday**. Derry is now greatly changed: tensions eased considerably here long before Belfast, thanks in part to a determinedly even-handed local council, although defiant murals remain and marching is still a contentious issue. The city centre has undergone much regeneration too, while Derry has gained a justifiable reputation for innovation in the arts.

The City

You can walk the entire mile-long circuit of Derry's **city walls** – some of the best-preserved defences left standing in Europe. Reinforced by bulwarks, bastions and a parapeted earth rampart, the walls encircle the original medieval street pattern with four gateways – Shipquay, Butcher, Bishop and Ferryquay – surviving from the first construction, in slightly revised form.

You're more than likely to make your approach from the **Guildhall Square**, once the old quay. Most of the city's cannon are lined up here, between Shipquay and Magazine gates, their noses peering out above the ramparts. A reconstruction of the medieval **O'Doherty Tower** (Tues–Sat 10am–5pm; July & Aug also Sun 2–5pm; £4.20) houses a splendid display outlining the turbulent historic development of the city. Turning left at **Shipquay Gate**, the promenade doglegs at Water Bastion where the River Foyle once lapped the walls at high tide. Continue on to Newgate Bastion and **Ferryquay Gate**, where you can look out across the river to the Waterside area, once primarily Protestant, now almost half Catholic – further evidence of the lessening of the city's political tensions. Between Ferryquay and Bishop's Gate the major sight is the Protestant **St Columb's Cathedral** (Mon–Sat 9am–1pm & 2–4/5pm; £1 donation), just within the south section of the walls; it overlooks the Fountain, the Protestant enclave immediately outside the same stretch of walls, and offers one of the best views of the city. The cathedral was built in 1633, the first post-Reformation cathedral to be constructed in the British Isles. In 1688/89 Derry played a key part in the Williamite victory over the Catholic King James II by holding out against a fifteen-week siege that cost the lives of one-quarter of the city's population. The cathedral was used as a battery during the siege, and in the entrance porch you'll find the cannonball shot into the grounds by the besieging army with proposals for the city's surrender.

Back on the walls, you'll pass the white sandstone **courthouse** next to Bishop's Gate and you'll see, downhill to the left, the only remaining tower of the old Derry jail. At the **Double Bastion** sits the Roaring Meg cannon, used during the siege, while down in the valley below are the streets of the Bogside. These were once the undisputed preserve of the IRA, and **Free Derry Corner** marks the site of the original barricades erected against the British army at the height of the Troubles. Nearby are the Bloody Sunday and Hunger Strikers' memorials, while several large murals commemorate victims of the fighting. Further along the city wall is the **Royal Bastion** lookout point, former site of the Rev. George Walker statue which was blown up in 1973. It is in Walker's and their predecessors' memory that the Protestant Apprentice Boys march round the walls every August 12.

Practicalities

Trains from Belfast arrive on the east bank of the Foyle; the city centre is a short walk away across Craigavon Bridge. **Buses** arrive at Foyle St beside Guildhall Square. City of Derry **airport** is seven miles northeast, connected to the centre by bus. The **tourist office** is at 44 Foyle St (July–Sept daily 9/10am–5/7pm; rest of year Mon–Fri 9am–5pm; ☎028/7126 7284) and contains branches of both Bord Fáilte and the Northern Ireland Tourist Board. **Hostel** accommodation includes the 150-bed *Derry International Hostel* in the city centre at 4–6 Magazine St (☎028/7137 2273, @derrycitytours.aol.com; ❷), and *Steve's Backpackers* at 4 Asylum Rd, half-a-mile down Strand Rd (☎028/7137 7989; ❷). For **B&Bs** try the excellent-value *The Saddler's House*, 36 Great James St (☎028/7126 9691, @www.the-saddlershouse.com; ❻), or *Clarence House*, 15 Northland Rd (☎028/7126 5342; ❺). Places for **eating out** include *The Leprechaun*, 23 Strand Rd, for delicious home-baking and hot meals, and *The Gallery* on Shipquay St, offering tasty and reasonably priced meals; *Badger's Bar*, 16 Orchard St, is another good option. **Internet** access is available at *Bean-There.Com*, 20 The Diamond (closed Sun in winter). The **pubs** are the best bet for entertainment. Students congregate at *Café Roc* where Rock and Strand roads meet; upstairs *Earth Niteclub* is hugely popular. *Sandino's* on Water St attracts an arty crowd; *Metro* at the bottom of Shipquay St, *Mullan's* on three floors at Little James St, and the central *Strand Bar*, Waterloo St just outside the northern walls, is the best bet for **traditional music** venues, including the *Dungloe Bar, The Rocking Chair* and *Peadar O'Donnell's*. Pick up the free monthly **listings** magazine, *The Beat*, at bars and cafés.

Enniskillen

ENNISKILLEN sits on a lake island, a narrow ribbon of water passing each side of the town between the Lower and Upper **Lough Erne**. The water loops its way around the core of the town, its glassy surface lending Enniskillen a sense of calm and reflecting the mini-turrets of **Enniskillen Castle**. Rebuilt by William Cole, to whom the British gave Enniskillen in 1609, the castle houses the **Watergate History and Heritage Centre** and the **Regimental Museum of the Royal Inniskilling Fusiliers** in the keep (July & Aug Mon 2–5pm, Tues–Fri 10am–5pm, Sat & Sun 2–5pm; May & Sept closed Sun; rest of year closed Sat & Sun; £2), a proud, polished display of the uniforms, flags and paraphernalia of the town's historic regiments. A mile along the Belfast road stands **Castle Coole** (July & Aug daily noon–6pm; June Mon & Wed–Sun same times; March–May & Sept Sat & Sun only; grounds daily 10am–4/8pm; £3.50). A perfect Palladian building of Portland stone, with an interior of fine plasterwork and superb furnishings, it sits in a beautiful landscaped garden.

Opposite the **bus station** on Wellington Rd is the **tourist office** (Mon–Fri 9am–5.30/7pm; Easter–Sept also Sat & Sun 10/11am–5/6pm; ☎028/6632 3110, ⊛www.fermanaghlakelands.com). A new HINI **hostel**, *The Bridges*, is on Belmore St by the war memorial (☎028/6634 0110, ⊛www.hini.org.uk; ❸). **B&Bs** are across the town's western bridges, along the A46 Derrygonnelly road and along the Sligo road. For **eating out**, try *Franco's* in Queen Elizabeth Rd, or the Indian *Kamal Mahal* in Water St, off High St. Several **bars** along High St and its continuation, Townhall St, provide pub food, particularly *The Vintage* and *Pat's Bar*. You'll find occasional **traditional sessions** at the *Blakes of the Hollow* on Townhall St. *The Vintage* has regular live music and DJs.

Lough Erne

The earliest people to settle in this region lived on and around the two lakes of **Lough Erne** which features many *crannogs* (Celtic artificial islands). The maze of waterways protected the settlers from invaders and created an enduring cultural isolation. Stone carvings suggests that Christianity was accepted far more slowly here than elsewhere: several pagan idols have been found on Christian sites, and the early Christian remains on the islands reveal the influence of pagan culture.

The easiest place to visit is **Devenish Island**, two miles northwest of Enniskillen. A monastic settlement was founded here by St Molaise in the sixth century and it remained an important religious centre up until the Plantations. It's a delightful setting and the considerable ruins span the entire medieval period. There are regular **ferries** (Easter–Sept) from Trory Point, four miles north of Enniskillen on the A32 road (£2.50; check times with tourist office). Ferries (April–Sept; £3) also leave from the marina at **Castle Archdale** forest park, on the eastern shore, near Lisnarick to **White Island**, whose ruined abbey bears early Christian carvings that look eerily pagan. The most disconcerting is the lewd female figure known as a Sheila-na-Gig, with bulging cheeks, a big grin, open legs and arms pointing to her genitals.

Travel details

Trains

Details given below refer to weekday services; extra services may run on Mondays and Fridays, fewer on Sundays.

Dublin to: Belfast (8 daily; 2hr 5min); Cork (9 daily; 2hr 40min–3hr 20min); Galway (5 daily; 2hr 45min); Killarney (6 daily; 3hr 40min); Limerick (11 daily; 2hr 20min–3hr); Rosslare (3 daily; 3hr 10min); Sligo (3 daily; 3hr 15min); Westport (3 daily; 3hr 50min).

Belfast to: Derry (7 daily; 2hr 40min); Dublin (8 daily; 2hr 5min); Larne Harbour (15 daily; 55min).

Coleraine to: Portrush, for Giant's Causeway (7 daily; 15min).

Cork to: Dublin (9 daily; 2hr 40min–3hr 20min); Killarney (5 daily; 2hr).

Derry to: Belfast (7 daily; 2hr 40min); Coleraine (7 daily; 40min).

Galway to: Dublin (5 daily; 2hr 45min).

Killarney to: Cork (5 daily; 2hr); Dublin (4 daily; 3hr 40min).

Sligo to: Dublin (3 daily; 3hr 15min).

Westport to: Dublin (3 daily; 3hr 50min).

Buses

Details below cover Bus Éireann or Ulsterbus services on summer weekdays; extra services may run on Fridays, fewer in winter and on Sundays.

Dublin to: Belfast (7 daily; 3hr); Cork (6 daily; 4hr 30min); Derry (6 daily; 4hr 30min); Donegal (5 daily; 4hr 30min); Enniskillen (5 daily; 3hr 40min); Galway (13 daily; 3hr 30min); Killarney (5 daily; 6hr); Sligo (4 daily; 4hr); Westport (3 daily; 5hr).

Belfast to: Derry (19 daily; 1hr 40min); Dublin (7 daily; 3hr); Enniskillen (10 daily; 2hr 40min); Galway (3 daily; 7hr); Sligo (3 daily; 4hr).

Cork to: Dublin (6 daily; 4hr 30min); Killarney (7 daily; 2hr 30min).

Derry to: Donegal (5 daily; 1hr 30min); Dublin (5 daily; 4hr 15min); Enniskillen (7 daily; 1hr 30min); Sligo (7 daily; 2hr 45min).

Donegal to: Derry (4 daily; 1hr 30min); Dublin (5 daily; 4hr 30min); Glencolmcille (3 daily; 1hr 25min); Sligo (5 daily; 1hr).

Enniskillen to: Belfast (8 daily; 2hr 35min); Derry (7 daily; 1hr 30min); Dublin (5 daily; 3hr 40min).

Galway to: Clifden (2–5 daily; 1hr 45min–2hr 20min); Cork (5 daily, 4hr); Doolin (2 daily; 2hr); Dublin (13 daily; 3hr 30min); Killarney (6 daily; 4hr 35min).

Killarney to: Dingle (5 daily; 2hr); Waterville via Caherciveen (2–3 daily; 2hr); Dublin (5 daily; 6hr).

Sligo to: Belfast (3 daily; 4hr); Derry (7 daily; 2hr 45min); Enniskillen (3 daily; 1hr 25min); Galway (5 daily; 2hr 45min).

Italy

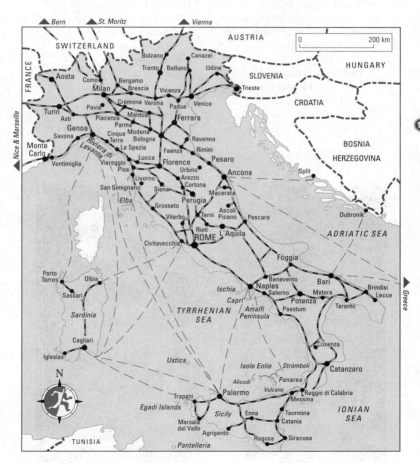

Italy highlights

* **Via Garibaldi, Genoa**
Lined with frescoed
Renaissance palaces of
awe-inspiring opulence.
See p.602

* **Grand Canal, Venice**
Catch an ordinary water-
bus – at night, for maxi-
mum effect. See p.605

* **The Palio, Siena** The
event of the year in this
wonderfully preserved
medieval town centre.
See p.634

* **Palatine Hill, Rome**
Huge, wonderfully tran-
quil, archeological gar-
den in the heart of the
city. See p.650

* **Pompei** Buried by ashes
from Vesuvius in 79AD,
the vast excavations of
this Roman town are
hauntingly evocative.
See p.663

* **Valle Dei Templi,
Agrigento, Sicily** Some
say these Greek temples
are better than any in
Greece. See p.673

Introduction and basics

Of all the countries in Europe, **Italy** is perhaps the hardest to classify. It is a modern, industrialized nation; it is the harbinger of style, its designers leading the way with each season's fashions. But it is also a Mediterranean country, with all that that implies. Agricultural land covers much of the country, a lot of it, especially in the south, still owned under almost feudal conditions. In towns and villages all over the country, life stops during the middle of the day for a siesta. It remains strongly family-oriented, with an emphasis on the traditions and rituals of the Catholic Church, and it is not unusual to find people living with their parents until their early 30s.

If there is a single national characteristic, it's to embrace life to the full, manifest in the hundreds of local **festivals** taking place on any given day and the importance placed on good food. It is also a very sociable society and Italians spend a lot of time in public places, whether during the collective evening stroll or *passeggiata,* or out in the piazza of a summer evening. There is also, of course, the country's enormous cultural legacy: Tuscany alone has more classified historical monuments than any country in the world and every region retains its own relics of an artistic tradition generally acknowledged to be the world's richest.

Italy wasn't unified until 1861, a fact that's borne out by the regional nature of the place today. The country breaks down into nineteen distinct *regione*, but the sharpest division is between north and south. The north is one of the most advanced industrial societies in the world; the south is by contrast one of the most economically depressed areas in Europe.

In the northwest, the regions of Piemonte and Lombardy – and the two main centres of **Turin** and **Milan** – epitomize the wealthy north. Liguria, the small coastal province to the south, has long been known as the "Italian Riviera" and is accordingly crowded with sun-seeking holiday-makers for much of the summer season. But it's a beautiful stretch of coast, and its capital, **Genoa**, is a bustling port with a long seafaring tradition. The interest of the northeastern regions of the Veneto and Friuli-Venezia Giulia is of course **Venice** itself, a unique city, and every bit as beautiful as its reputation would suggest – though this means you won't be alone in appreciating it. If the crowds are too much, there's also the arc of historic towns outside the city – **Verona**, **Padua** and **Vicenza**. To the south, the region of Emilia-Romagna has been at the heart of Italy's postwar industrial boom. Its coast is popular among Italians, especially **Rimini**, Italy's brashest seaside resort; and there are also the ancient centres of **Ravenna**, **Parma** and **Bologna**, the capital – one of Italy's liveliest but least appreciated cities.

Central Italy perhaps represents the most commonly perceived image of the country, and **Tuscany**, with its classic rolling countryside and the art-packed towns of **Florence**, **Pisa** and **Siena**, is one of its most visited regions. Neighbouring **Umbria** is similar in all but its relative emptiness, though it gets fuller every year, as visitors flock into towns such as Perugia, Spoleto and Assisi – and unspoilt Urbino in adjacent Marche. Lazio, to the south, is a poor and desolate region whose focal point is **Rome**, Italy's capital,

Italy on the net

- ⓦ**www.enit.it** Official Tourist Board site
- ⓦ**www.virgilio.it** Italian search engine with good travel and tourism links
- ⓦ**www.paginegialle.it** Italian Yellow Pages
- ⓦ**www.beniculturali.it** Listings of national monuments and information on festivals, etc

the one city in the country with allegiance neither to the north nor south.

Beyond Rome, **Naples**, capital of Campania, a petulant, unforgettable city, is the spiritual heart of the Italian south, and is close to some of Italy's finest ancient sites in **Pompeii** and **Herculaneum**, not to mention its most spectacular stretch of coast around **Amalfi**. Puglia, the "heel" of Italy, has underrated pleasures – the souk-like quality of its capital, **Bari**, and more notably **Lecce**, a baroque gem of a city. As for **Sicily**, the island is a law unto itself, a wide mix of attractions ranging from some of the finest preserved Hellenic treasures in Europe, to the drama of Mount Etna and one of the country's fanciest beach resorts in **Taormina**. Sardinia, too, feels far removed from the mainland, especially in its relatively undiscovered interior, though you may be content with its fine beaches.

Information and maps

Most Italian towns, major train stations and airports have a **tourist office** – *ufficio di turismo*. Very small or out-of-the-way villages may have a tiny office known as a Pro Loco. Most tourist offices will give out **maps** of their local area for free, but if you want an indexed town plan, get Studio FMB's or Falk's, both of which covers the country's towns and cities. The clearest and best-value large-scale road map of Italy is the Michelin 1:1,000,000. Michelin also produce 1:400,000 maps of the north and south, as well as Sicily and Sardinia.

Money and banks

Italy is one of twelve European Union countries which have changed over to a single currency, the **euro** (€).

Banking hours are Mon–Fri 8.30am– 1.30pm & 3.30–7.30pm. There are ATMs pretty much everywhere, and this is generally the cheapest way of getting local currency. If you need to change cash or travellers' cheques, then the **exchange bureaux** are a better choice than the banks. Otherwise, the larger hotels will change money and travellers' cheques – in larger towns and cities the rate is invariably better at the train station exchange bureau.

Communications

Post office opening hours are Mon–Fri 8am–6.30pm, with branches in larger towns and cities opening on Saturdays too. Stamps can also be bought at *tabacchi* – ask for *posta prioritaria* if you want letters to arrive home before you do. Public **telephones** are run by several companies, but all are card-operated; get a phone card (*scheda telefonica*), available from *tabacchi* and newsstands for €2.50, €5 and €7.50. Bars will often have a phone you can use, and there are offices at the larger train stations where you can make a metered call from a kiosk. For all land-line calls – local, long-distance and international – dial all digits, including the 0 and the area code. Note however, that **mobile phone** numbers no longer have the prefix 0 and you need to omit the 0 even when dialling any old numbers. For **directory enquiries**, call ☎176 (intenational) or ☎412 then dial 3 (domestic).

Italy is improving rapidly when it comes to **internet access**. You'll find at least one place in most towns. Hourly rates vary from €1 in the south to €5 in big cities.

Getting around

Trains make for the easiest way of travelling around – the system is cheap and fairly efficient and far preferable to the fragmented and grindingly slow **bus network**.

Trains

Apart from a few private lines, Italian **trains** are operated by Italian State Railways (Ferrovie dello Stato or FS). For most journeys you'll have a choice between Eurostar/Intercity – for which you have to pay a supplement of thirty percent (and reserve for Eurostar) – and ordinary trains. Of these ordinary trains, some, such as the Regionale, can be extremely slow – check before boarding. Fares are calculated by the kilometre.

InterRail and **Eurail** passes are valid on the whole FS network – though, as mentioned above, you'll have to pay a supplement on the fast trains – and there are specific Italian passes available (see p.28).

Buses

Almost everywhere is connected by some kind of **bus** service, but schedules can be sketchy, and are drastically reduced – sometimes nonexistent – at weekends. It's worth knowing that in rural areas timetables are often designed with the working or school day in mind, making for some frighteningly early starts and occasionally no buses at all during school holidays. Tickets are generally bought at *tabacchi* or the bus terminal rather than on board.

Accommodation

Accommodation is fairly reliable: hotels are star-rated and required to post their prices clearly in each room. Most tourist offices have details of hotel rates in their town or region, and you can usually expect them to be broadly accurate. In the major cities and resorts, booking ahead is often a good idea, particularly during the summer months.

One peculiar Italian institution is the confusingly named *albergo diurno* or day hotel, an establishment providing bathrooms, showers, hairdressers and the like – but no accommodation. You'll find them at train stations and they're usually open daily 6am–midnight.

Hotels and B&Bs

Hotels in Italy come with a confusing variety of names. *Locanda* are historically the most basic option, although the word is sometimes used to denote something quite fancy these days; *pensione* too can be little different from the regular *alberghi* or hotels. Prices do vary greatly between the poor south and the wealthy north, and between cities and the country, but on average, you can expect to pay about €35 for a double without private bathroom in a one-star hotel, and a

minimum of about €75 for a double in a three-star. In very busy places you might have to stay a minimum of three nights, and many proprietors will add the price of breakfast to your bill whether you want it or not; try to resist this – you can eat more cheaply in a bar. Whatever happens, establish the full price of your room before you accept it. It is advisable to book ahead in high season and during holidays; many of the hotels listed are small and fill up quickly.

There is a growing number of **B&Bs** in Italy, which are sometimes in spectacular locations. Many cost as much as a hotel, but it is worth asking the tourist office for a list, if for no other reason than to experience Italian family life first-hand.

Hostels

There are around sixty **hostels** in Italy, charging €12–26 for a dorm bed for HI members; for two people travelling together, they don't represent a massive saving on the cheapest double hotel room. You'll need to book ahead in the summer months. A full list of hostels is available from the Associazione Italiana Alberghi per la Gioventù, Via Cavour 44, 00184 Roma (☎06.487.1152, ⊛www .hostels-aig.org).

Student accommodation

In some cities it's also possible to stay in **student accommodation** during the summer; accommodation is generally in individual rooms and can work out cheaper than a hotel. Again, you'll need to book in advance. It is also worth trying religious foundations: convents and monasteries often have cheap rooms, the only disadvantage being a curfew.

Campsites

Camping is not as popular in Italy as it is in some other European countries, but there are plenty of sites, and most of them are well equipped. The snag is that they're expensive, and, once you've added the cost of a tent, don't always work out a great deal cheaper than staying in a hostel. Prices are around €3–5 per person daily, plus €3.50–8.50 for a caravan or tent, and around €3 for a vehicle. If you're camping extensively, check out ⊛www.camping.it for a full list of sites.

Food and drink

There are few places in the world where you can eat and drink as well as you can in Italy. The food is seasonal, healthy and simple, and there are distinct regional cuisines that are worth exploring. The peasant traditions persist and it is not surprising to find a wine made by the restaurant's proprietor on the list, or that the *fava* (broad beans) come from his cousin's garden. Enjoy, and don't be afraid to ask how something is made or what the *piatti tipici* or local dishes are. Food is one of the Italians' great pleasures and everyone wants to talk about it.

Food

Italians invented fast food, and you will quickly have to master the art of eating and drinking standing up: there is often no seating and some bars charge more if you sit down. Most Italians start their day in a bar, their **breakfast** consisting of a cappuccino and a *cornetto* – a croissant which is particularly good *con crema*. At **lunchtime**, bars sell *tramezzini*, sandwiches on white bread that can be toasted, and *panini*. Another stopgap is *arancini*, fried meat or cheese-filled rice balls, substantial enough for a light lunch. Markets are also a good source of cheap food. Among other delicacies you should try fresh figs (*fichi*), ripe green tomatoes (*pomodori verdi*) and strawberry-flavoured grapes (*uva di fragola).*

Italian **ice cream** (*gelato*) is justifiably famous: a cone (*un cono*) is an indispensable accessory to the evening *passeggiata*. Most bars have a fairly good selection, but for the best choice go to a *gelateria*.

For **sit-down food**, the cheapest thing you can eat is **pizza** – usually thin and flat, and, if you're lucky, cooked in the traditional way in wood-fired ovens. There are stand-up counters selling slices (*pizza al taglio*) and folded over pizza (*calzone*) as well as fully fledged restaurants. Full meals are generally served in a **trattoria** or a **ristorante**, which often do a fixed price *menu turistico* – although cheap this is not always very good. Traditionally, a trattoria is the cheaper of the two, offering home-style cooking. In either, pasta dishes go for around €4–6, and although pasta is considered to be a starter

there's usually not a problem just having this; the main fish or meat courses will normally be €5–8. Bear in mind that almost everywhere you'll pay about €1.50 per person extra for bread (*pane),* which is brought to your table automatically. Fish is generally either served whole or by weight. Vegetables or salads – *contorni* – are ordered separately: potatoes will invariably be fried, salads either green (*verde*) or mixed (*mista*). Afterwards you get a choice of fresh fruit (*frutta*) and desserts (*dolci*) – which can usually be avoided in favour of an ice cream at a gelateria afterwards. Note that as well as the **cover charge** (*coperto*), service (*servizio*) will often be added, generally about ten percent. If service isn't included you should tip about the same amount, though trattorias outside the large cities won't necessarily expect this.

Drink

Although many Italian children are brought up on wine, there's not the same emphasis on dedicated drinking as there is in Britain or the US. **Bars** are less social centres than functional places for a quick coffee or beer. You pay first at the cash desk (*la cassa*), present your receipt (*scontrino*) and give your order. In the south of the country it's customary to leave a small tip on the counter, though no one will object if you don't. Bear in mind that sitting down sometimes costs twice as much, especially if you sit outside. **Coffee** is always excellent, small and black (*espresso,* or just *caffé*), with a dash of milk (*macchiato*) or cream (*con panna*) or white and frothy (*cappuccino*); try also a *granita* – cold coffee with crushed ice, usually topped with cream. **Tea** (*te*) comes with lemon (*con limone*) unless you ask for milk (*con latte*); there are usually several types, and vanilla flavoured tea (*alla vaniglia*) is worth trying; it's also served cold (*te freddo*). As for **soft drinks**, a *spremuta* is a fresh fruit juice; there's also crushed-ice fruit *granitas*, and the usual range of fizzy drinks and concentrated juices. In winter, try a hot punch – *punch alla livornese*, an alcoholic coffee drink found in Tuscany, is one of the best.

Beer (*birra*) usually comes in one-third or two-third litre bottles. Most common and cheapest are the Italian brands, Peroni and

Dreher, both of which are very drinkable; in most bars you have a choice of this or draught beer (*alla spina*). All the usual **spirits** are on sale and known mostly by their generic names; a generous shot costs from about €1.50. There's also **grappa**, made from the leftovers of the wine-making process and something of an acquired taste. You'll also find **fortified wines** and a daunting selection of liqueurs; Amaro is a bitter after-dinner drink, Amaretto much sweeter with a strong taste of marzipan, Sambuca a sticky-sweet aniseed concoction, Limoncello a lemon-flavoured digestif. **Wine** is invariably drunk with meals, and is still very cheap. Try the local stuff: ask for *vino sfuso* or simply *un mezzo* (a half litre), or *un quarto* (a quarter), sometimes served straight from the barrel, particularly down south. Bottled wine is pricier but still good value; expect to pay around €6.50 a bottle in a restaurant.

Opening hours and holidays

Most **shops and businesses** open Mon–Sat 8/9am–1pm & 4–7/8pm, though in the north, offices work to a 9am–5pm day. Everything, except bars and restaurants, closes on Sunday, though you might find fish shops in some coastal towns and *pasticcerias* or cake shops open until lunchtime. Closing days for restaurants and bars are given in the text wherever possible. Most **churches** keep similar hours to the shops, unless otherwise stated.

Museums traditionally open Tues–Sat 9am–2pm, Sun 9am–1pm, and are closed on Mondays; but many now have greatly extended hours. Most archeological sites open daily from 9am until late – usually one hour before sunset.

Everything closes for the following **national holidays**: Jan 1; Jan 6; Easter Mon; April 25; May 1; Aug 15; Nov 1; Dec 8; Dec 25 & 26.

Emergencies

Despite what you hear about the mafia, most of the crime you're likely to come across in Italy is of the small-time variety, prevalent in the major cities and the south of the country, where gangs of *scippatori* operate, snatching handbags, wallets, jewellery, etc. You can minimize the risk of this by being discreet, not flashing anything of value, keeping a firm hand on your camera and bag, and never leaving anything valuable in your car. If it comes to the worst, you'll have some dealings with the **police**. In Italy these come in many forms: the *Polizia Urbana/Vigili Urbani* are mainly concerned with directing the traffic and punishing parking offences; the *Polizia Stradale* patrol highways; the *Carabinieri*, with their military-style uniforms and white shoulder belts, deal with general crime, public order and drug control; but it's the *Polizia Statale* to whom thefts should generally be reported.

Italian **pharmacies** (*farmacia*) are well qualified to give you advice on minor ailments, and to dispense prescriptions, and there's generally one open all night in the bigger towns and cities. They work on a rota system; you'll find the address of the nearest open one on any pharmacy door. If you are more seriously ill, call an ambulance or go to the *Pronto Soccorso* (casualty) section of the nearest **hospital**.

Emergency numbers

Police ☏112; Ambulance ☏113; Fire ☏115.

The northwest

The **northwest** of Italy is many people's first experience of the country, and in many ways represents its least "Italian" aspect, at least in the regions of **Piemonte** and **Val d'Aosta**, where French is still spoken by some as a first language. **Turin**, on the main rail and road route from France to Milan, is the obvious first stop, the first capital of Italy after the Unification in 1860 and a grand city with many reminders of its past as seat of the Savoy dukes, later the Italian royals. To the east, **Lombardy** was long viewed by northerners as the heart of Italy – emperors from Charlemagne to Napoleon came here to be crowned – and northern European business magnates continue to take its capital, Milan, more seriously than Rome. The region's landscape has paid the price for economic success: industry chokes the peripheries of towns and spreads its tentacles into the northern lakes and mountain valleys. Nonetheless, Lombardy has its attractions. **Milan** is a natural gateway to the region, an upbeat city with plenty to see, and **Mantua** – which flourished during the Middle Ages and Renaissance – retains its historical character. The region of **Liguria** to the south has perhaps the country's most spectacular stretch of coastline. Chief town of the province is the sprawling port of **Genoa**, west of which is one long ribbon of hotels. Southeast, towards Tuscany, is more rugged, the mix of mountains and fishing villages "discovered" by the Romantics in the late eighteenth century preparing the way for the first package tourists in the early twentieth century. Now the whole area explodes into a ruck every July and August, with people coming to resorts like **Portofino** strictly for pose value – although stretches like the **Cinque Terre** are still well worth discovering.

Turin

"Do you know Turin?" wrote Nietzsche, "It is a city after my own heart…a princely residence of the seventeenth century, which has only one taste giving commands to everything, the court and its nobility. Aristocratic calm is preserved in everything: there are no nasty suburbs." Although **TURIN**'s traffic-choked streets are no longer calm, and its suburbs, built by Fiat, a vast company that virtually owns the city, are as nasty as any in Italy, the city still boasts gracious Baroque avenues, opulent palaces, sumptuous churches and splendid collections of Egyptian antiquities and northern European paintings.

The grid plan of the city's Baroque centre makes finding your way around easy. **Via Roma** is the central spine, a grand affair lined with designer shops and ritzy cafés and punctuated by the city's most elegant piazzas, most notably **Piazza San Carlo**. Around the corner, the **Museo Egizio** (Tues–Sun 8.30am–7.30pm; €6.50) holds a superb collection of Egyptian antiquities, gathered together in the late eighteenth century under the aegis of Carlo Emanuele III. There are gorgeously decorated mummy cases, an intriguing assortment of everyday objects and, the undoubted highlight, the Tomb of Kha, the burial chamber of a 1400 BC architect, and his wife, Merit, discovered in 1906 at Deir-el-Medina. Above the museum, the **Galleria Sabauda** (Tues–Sun 8.30am–7.30pm; €4) was built around the Savoys' private collection and is still firmly stamped with their taste – a miscellany of Italian paintings, supplemented by a fine Dutch and Flemish collection, including works by Memling, Brueghel, David Teniers Jnr and Van Dyck.

Around the corner, the fifteenth-century **Duomo** houses the **Turin Shroud**, which is usually kept under wraps and only on display to the public during holy years but a copy is on display by the altar. This piece of cloth, imprinted with the image of a man's body, had long been claimed as the shroud in which Christ was wrapped after his crucifixion. However, in 1989 carbon-dating tests showed it to be a fake, made between 1260 and 1390. Beyond the Duomo, the elegant **Piazza della Repubblica** was designed by the eighteenth century architect Juvarra. To the back of the square is the **Palazzo Reale** which has a peaceful garden to its rear

(Tues–Sun 9am–7pm; free). Next to the fountains in the square is **Palazzo Madama**, whose baroque exterior conceals its origins as a Roman fortress.

The porticoes of Via Po lead down to the river, past the **Mole Antonelliana**, Via Montebello 20, which houses Turin's new **Museo Nazionale del Cinema** (Tues–Sun 9am–8pm, Sat till 11pm; €5.20, €6.80 with lift to top of the Mole). Turin was the birthplace of Italian cinema in the 1910s and 1920s, and the museum houses a magnificent collection including a huge series of magic lanterns. Via Po ends in the vast arcaded **Piazza Vittorio Veneto**. Along the river from here, **Parco del Valentino** is one of Italy's largest parks, home to the **Borgo e Rocca Medioevale** (Tues–Sun 9am–7pm; €3), a fake medieval village and castle, built with the same materials and techniques as the originals, for the General Italian exhibition of 1884. Further south still, the **Museo dell'Automobile** at Corso Unità d'Italia 40 (Tues–Sun 10am–6.30pm, Thurs till 10pm, Sun till 8.30pm; €5; bus #34 from Piazza Marconi) traces the development of the motor car, with one of the first Fiats, a bulky 1899 model, the gleaming Isotta Fraschini driven by Gloria Swanson in *Sunset Boulevard*, and, the pride of the collection, the 1907 Itala which won the Peking to Paris race in the same year.

Practicalities

Turin's main **train station**, Porta Nuova, is on Corso Vittorio Emanuele, at the foot of Via Roma, convenient for the city centre and hotels. There are two **tourist offices** – the main one is at Piazza Castello 161 (Mon–Sat 9.30am–7pm, Sun 9.30am–3pm; ☎011.535.181, ⊛www.turismotorino.org) and a smaller one at the train station (same hours). The **Torino Card** (€14/two days) gives free transport on buses, entrance to all museums and discounts on some theatre and concert tickets.

Accommodation

Many of Turin's budget **hotels** are in the sleazy quarter off Via Nizza, convenient enough but not an advisable choice, particularly for women travelling alone. Somewhat safer, but more expensive, are the streets opposite Porta Nuova, close to Piazza Carlo Felice. There are also a number of fairly reasonably priced hotels west of Piazza Castello.

Hostel

Ostello Torino Via Alby 1 ☎011.660.2939. Friendly HI place with small rooms, internet access, and all just thirty minutes' walk from Porta Nuova; take bus #52. ❷

Hotels

Canelli Via San Dalmazzo 7 ☎011.537.166. Close to the pedestrian area of Via Garibaldi is the cheapest option and very central. ❷

Hotel Mobledor Via Accademia Albertina 1 ☎011.812.5805. A small friendly one-star hotel in an excellent location. ❸

Paradiso Via Berthollet 3 ☎011.669.8678. Extremely clean one-star hotel with friendly proprietors. ❷

Campsite

Villa Rey Strada Val San Martino Superiore, 27. On the far side of the river south of the hostel; take bus #61 from Porta Nuova, and then bus #56.

Eating, drinking and nightlife

There are snack bars on Via Nizza, some tempting delicatessens on Via Lagrange and a superb *rosticceria* on Corso Vittorio Emanuele. For local fare, reasonably priced **restaurants** include the *Vecchio Piemonte*, Corso Vinzaglio 21, and *Cucco*, Corso Casale 89. Make sure you look in on one of the city's *fin-de-siècle* **cafés**, most of which have an atmosphere that more than compensates for the steep prices. In *Baratti* and *Milano*, Piazza Castello 29, genteel Torinese sip tea in a rarefied ambience of mirrors, chandeliers and carved wood. The glitzy *Caffè San Carlo*, Piazza San Carlo 156, is reputedly a favoured haunt of politicians and industrialists, while *Fiorio*, Via Po 8, was once the haunt of Cavour, and is now visited mostly for its ice cream. **Internet access** is available at Internet Train, Via Carlo Alberto 18. Later on in the **evening**, Via Carlo Alberto and Via San Quintino are the areas to check out. Of specific **bars**, *Bar Elena* in Piazza Vittorio is popular, or for **live music**, try *Doctor Sax*, Murazzi di Lungo Po Cadorna 4 (Afro, jazz and rock), or *Doks Dora* on Lungo Dora.

Milan

The dynamo behind the country's economic miracle, **MILAN** is a city like no other. It's foggy in winter, muggy in summer, and is a fast-paced business city in which consumerism and the work ethic rule. But it's a historic city, with enough churches and museums to keep you busy for a week – much of the city a testament to the prestige-building of the Visconti dynasty and their successors, the Sforzas, who ruled here in Renaissance times – and the contemporary aspects of the place represent the leading edge of Italy's fashion and design industry, not to mention a nightlife scene that is the country's most varied.

Arrival, information and accommodation

Most international **trains** pull in at the monumental Stazione Centrale, northeast of the centre on Piazza Duca d'Aosta, on metro lines #2 and #3 (MM2 or MM3). **Buses** arrive at and depart from Piazza Castello, in front of the Castello Sforzesco. Of Milan's two **airports**, Linate is the closer, 7km from the city centre, connected with the airport bus terminal at Stazione Centrale (every 20min 5.40am–10pm; journey time 20min; €2.50). There are also ordinary city buses (#73; €1) until around midnight from Linate to Piazza San Babila. The other airport, **Malpensa**, is 50km away towards Lago Maggiore. It's connected by train with Cadorna station (every 30min; €4.50) and by bus with Stazione Centrale until 10.30pm (€5.50).

The main **tourist offices** are at the Stazione Centrale (Mon–Sat 9am–1.30pm, 3–6pm; ☎02.8645.4033) and Via Marconi 1, off Piazza Duomo (Mon–Fri 8.45am–1pm, 2–6pm Sat & Sun 9am–1pm & 2/3–6/7pm; same number). Both have the free **listings** guide, *Milan is Milan*. **Public transport** in Milan is an efficient network of trams, buses and metro that runs from 6am to midnight, when night buses take over until 1am. Tickets (valid 1hr 15min; €1), can be used for one journey only on the metro; alternatively buy a *blochetto* of ten tickets (€9.20), or a 24-hour ticket (€3), from the Centrale or Duomo metro stations.

Milan is more a business than a tourist city, and its **accommodation** is geared to the expense-account traveller. However, there are plenty of one star hotels, mostly concentrated in the area around Stazione Centrale, and along Viale Vittorio Veneto and Corso Buenos Aires.

Hostels

ACISJF Corso Garibaldi 121 ☎02.290.00164. Run by nuns and open to women under 25 only. Accommodation is in four-bedded rooms. MM Moscova. ❸

Piero Rotta Via Salmoiraghi 2 ☎02.392.67095. Out in the northwest suburbs near the San Siro stadium, this HI place is cheap but not especially welcoming. MM QT8. ❷

Hotels

Arno Via Lazzaretto 17 ☎02.670.5509. Modest one-star place near the station. Gets packed from March to July. ❸

Casa Mia Viale V. Veneto 30 ☎02.657.5249. The best option near the station. ❺

Pensione Eva Via Lazzaretto 17 ☎02.670.6093. Similar to *Arno*. ❸

San Tomaso at Viale Tunisia 6 ☎02.295.14747, ⓦ www.italiaabc.it/hotelsantomaso. Popular hotel in the commercial centre. Rooms have TV, phone and there's internet access too. ❹

Siena on Via P. Castaldi 17 (entrance on Via Lazzaretto) ☎02.295.16108. Small and clean. ❹

Speronari Via Speronari 4 ☎02.864.61125. Friendly and very central, close to the cathedral. ❺

Hotel Trieste Via M.Polo 13 ☎02.65.54405, ⓦ www.htrieste.it. Two-star hotel in tranquil area of town, near the centre. ❹

Campsite

Autodromo Via Santa Maria Alle Sleve ☎0.39.387.771. In Monza, 20km from the centre, in the park near the Formula One circuit; take a bus from Stazione Centrale. Closed Oct–March.

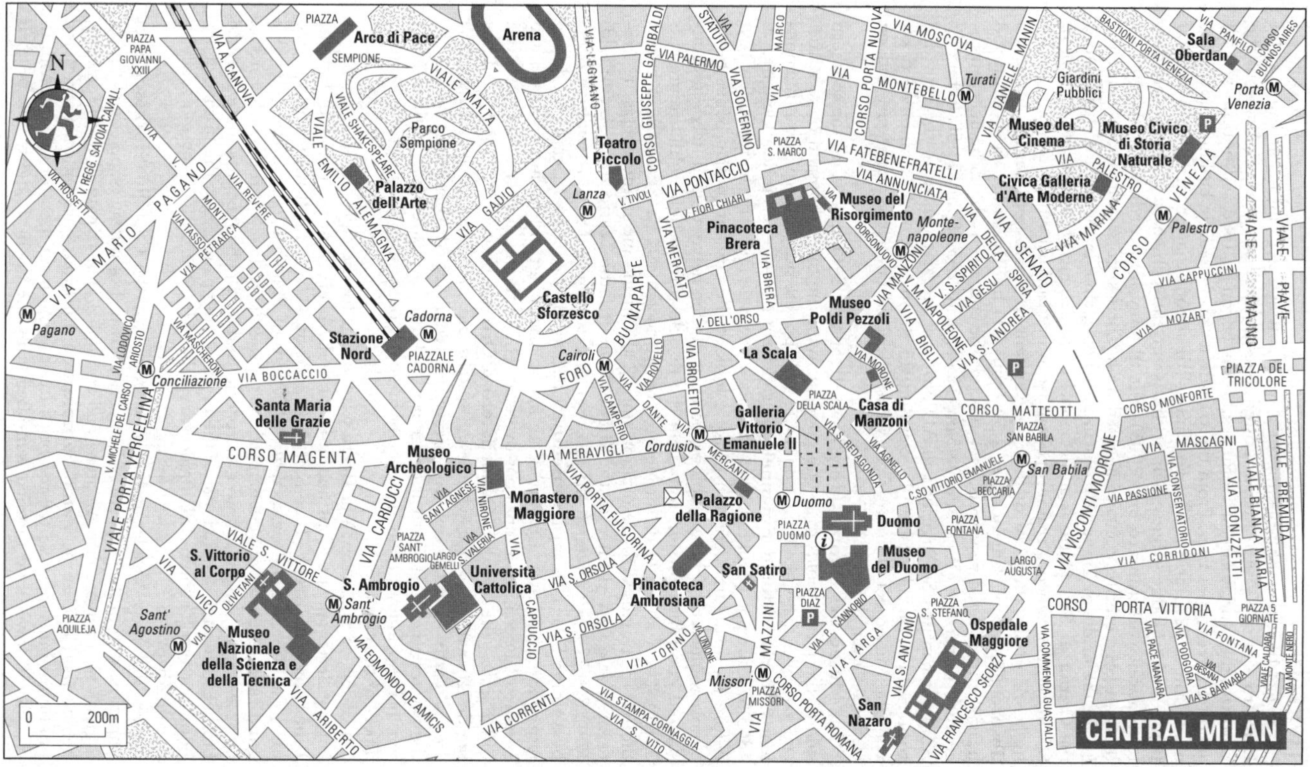
CENTRAL MILAN
0 200m
N
Arco di Pace
Arena
Parco Sempione
Palazzo dell'Arte
Castello Sforzesco
Stazione Nord
Cadorna
Piazzale Cadorna
Teatro Piccolo
Lanza
Pinacoteca Brera
Museo del Risorgimento
Monte-napoleone
Museo Poldi Pezzoli
La Scala
Casa di Manzoni
Galleria Vittorio Emanuele II
Cairoli
Cordusio
Duomo
Piazza Duomo
Museo del Duomo
Palazzo della Ragione
San Satiro
Pinacoteca Ambrosiana
Missori
San Nazaro
Ospedale Maggiore
San Babila
Museo Archeologico
Monastero Maggiore
Università Cattolica
S. Ambrogio
Sant' Ambrogio
S. Vittorio al Corpo
Museo Nazionale della Scienza e della Tecnica
Sant' Agostino
Santa Maria delle Grazie
Conciliazione
Pagano
Turati
Palestro
Porta Venezia
Sala Oberdan
Giardini Pubblici
Museo del Cinema
Museo Civico di Storia Naturale
Civica Galleria d'Arte Moderne
Corso Magenta
Corso Matteotti
Corso Porta Vittoria
Corso Porta Romana
Corso Venezia
Via Manzoni
Via Montenapoleone
Via della Spiga
Via Brera
Via Dante
Via Torino
Via Mazzini
Viale Piave
Viale Majno
Via Moscova
Via Senato
Corso Porta Nuova
Corso Giuseppe Garibaldi
Via Boccaccio
Via Carducci
Viale Porta Vercellina
Via Mario Pagano
Via Visconti Modrone
Via Francesco Sforza
Via Larga
Via Meravigli
Via Porta Fulcorina
Foro Buonaparte
Corso Monforte
Viale Bianca Maria
Via Donizzetti
Piazza del Tricolore
Piazza 5 Giornate
Via Edmondo de Amicis
Viale Premuda
Via Correnti

The City

Historic Milan lies at the centre of a web of streets zeroing in on **Piazza del Duomo**, the city's main hub, a mostly pedestrianized square that's home to the **Duomo**, the world's largest Gothic cathedral, begun in 1386 and not finished till almost five centuries later. From the outside it's an incredible building, notable as much for its decoration as its size and with a front that's a strange mixture of Baroque and Gothic – but much of this is currently obscured thanks to ongoing restoration work (due to end 2005). The gloomy interior holds, among other things, a large crucifix containing a nail from Christ's cross, crafted to become the bit for the bridle of Emperor Constantine's horse; close by, beneath the presbytery, the **Cripta di San Carlo** is an octagonal crypt designed to house the remains of St Charles Borromeo, a zealous sixteenth-century cardinal who was canonized for his work among the poor of the city. Adjacent to Borromeo's resting place, the **Tesoro** (Tues–Sun 9am–noon & 2.30–6pm; €1) has Byzantine ivory-work and heavily embroidered vestments; back towards the entrance is the cathedral's fourth-century **Baptistry** (Tues–Sun 9.45am–12.45pm & 2–5.45pm; €1.50) where St Ambrose baptised St Augustine in AD 387. You can also get up to the cathedral **roof** (9am–4.15/5.45pm; €5 by elevator, €3.50 on foot, or €7 combined ticket with the Museo del Duomo), from where there are fine views of the city and, on clear days, even the Alps.

The **Museo del Duomo** (daily 10am–1.15pm & 3–6pm; €6), on the southern side of the piazza, holds casts of a good many of the three thousand or so statues and gargoyles that spike the Duomo. On the opposite side of the piazza is the opulent **Galleria Vittorio Emanuele**, a cruciform glass-domed gallery designed in 1865 by Giuseppe Mengoni, who was killed when he fell from the roof a few days before the inaugural ceremony. Take a look at the circular mosaic beneath the cupola composed of the symbols of the cities of then newly unified Italy – it's considered good luck to spin round on the testicles of the bull (which represents Turin). The Galleria leads through to the world-famous **La Scala** opera house, though this is closed for restoration until 2004. In the meantime operas are performed at a new theatre in the Bicocca suburb, the Teatro degli Arcimboldi (℡02.860.775, ℠www.teatroallascala.org). La Scala opened in 1778 with an opera by Antonio Salieri. Its small **museum**, at Palazzo Busca, Corso Magenta 71, during restoration, contains composers' death masks, plaster casts of conductors' hands and a statue of Puccini in a capacious overcoat. The shopping quarter to the northeast of La Scala – the so-called **Quadrilatero d'Oro** – is home to the shops of all the big designer names, along with design studios and contemporary art galleries. The area is worth a stroll, if only to observe the better-heeled Milanese searching out the perfect objet d'art for their designer pads. Indeed, to leave Milan without looking in the windows of its designer boutiques would be to miss out on a crucial aspect of the city.

A couple of blocks east, **Via Brera** sets the tone for the city's arty quarter with its fancy galleries and art shops, and, at its far end, Milan's most prestigious gallery, the **Pinacoteca di Brera** (Tues–Sun 8.30am–7pm; €4.14), filled with works looted from the churches and aristocratic collections of French-occupied Italy. There's a good representation of Venetian painters – works by Paolo Veronese, Tintoretto, Gentile Bellini and his follower, Carpaccio, and a *Pietà* by Gentile's more talented brother, Giovanni, deemed one of the most moving paintings in the history of art. Look out also for Piero della Francesca's chilly *Madonna*, perhaps the most famous painting here.

West of the Via Accademia down Via Pontaccio, the **Castello Sforzesco** rises imperiously from the mayhem of Foro Buonaparte, laid out by Napoleon as part of a grand plan for the city. An arena and triumphal arch remain from the scheme, behind the castle in the **Parco Sempione**, a notorious hangout for junkies and prostitutes, but otherwise the red-brick castle is the main focus of interest, with its crenellated towers and fortified walls. Begun by the Viscontis and rebuilt by their successors, the Sforzas, whose court was one of the most powerful and cultured of the Renaissance, the castle houses, along with a number of run-of-the-mill collections, the **Museo d'Arte Antica** and **Pinacoteca** (both Tues–Sun 9am–5.30pm; free) – the former including Michelangelo's *Rondanini Pietà*, the latter a cycle of monochrome frescoes illustrating the Griselda story from Boccaccio's *Decameron* and paintings by Vincenzo Foppa, the leading Milanese artist before Leonardo da Vinci.

South of the castle, the church of **Santa Maria delle Grazie** is the main attraction. An originally Gothic pile, partially rebuilt by Bramante (who added the massive dome), it is famous for its fresco of the **Last Supper** by Leonardo da Vinci, which covers one wall of the refectory. Advance booking is essential (call ☎02.498.7588; viewing Tues–Sun 8.15am–6.45pm; €6.50, plus €1 booking fee).

Eating, drinking and nightlife

Food in workaholic Milan, at lunchtime at least, is more of a necessity than a pleasure, with the city centre dominated by *paninoteche* and fast-food outlets. *Luini*, Via S. Radegonda 16, just east of the Duomo, is justifiably popular for delicious *panzerotti*; *Crota Piemunteisa*, Piazza Beccaria 10, has a vast array of chunky sandwiches for around €2.60, and a few tables; or try *Il Fornaio* on the opposite side of the piazza, for pizzas. For **sit-down meals**, *Il Cantinone*, Via Agnello 19, is a famous old trattoria and bar, with home-made pasta and some choice wines; *La Bruschetta*, Piazza Beccaria 12, is one of the best city-centre pizzerias, though you'll have to wait for a table. *Grand Italia*, Via Palermo 5, is cheaper and just as good. The *Cozzeria*, via Muratori Lodovico 7, serves mussels by the kilo and does a delicious lemon and peperoncino sorbet; at no. 10 on the same street *Giulio pane e ojo* (☎02.535.6189) is a trendy and inexpensive trattoria; while *Circolo del Liberty*, at via Savona 20, is an eccentric, intimate restaurant run by a talkative Neapolitan. Further out, there's *Da Abele*, Via della Temperanza 5 (MM Pasteur), a long-established, cosy and very popular haunt that specializes in risotto. In the Città Studi, *Lo Smeraldo*, Via Baracchini 9, serves thirty types of pizza.

Milan's **nightlife** centres on two areas – the streets around the Brera gallery and the Navigli and Ticinese quarters. Popular bars include *Caffe Roma*, Via Ancona 4; the refined *Old Fashion*, Viale Alemagna 6, which has an outdoor disco in summer; and *La Banque*, Via Porrone 6, a trendy bar and night-spot that used to be a bank. *Bar Magenta*, Via Carducci 13, is a liberty-style bar, timelessly posey and usually packed. *Scimmie*, Via Ascanio Sforza 49, is another popular stage, small and buzzy and mainly hosting jazz; while *Tunnel*, Via Sammartini, right by Stazione Centrale, puts on alternative rock. Among many clubs, *Loolapaloosa*, Corso Corno 15, is a popular student hangout; *Rolling Stone*, Corso XXII Marzo, plays a wide range of music and is an enormous place that sometime hosts big-name rock bands. *Hollywood*, Corso Como 15, is a long-established club with an airport theme. And among **gay clubs**, the *One Way Club* via F.Cavalotti 204, is a popular spot (Fri & Sat; entrance with Arci Gay membership).

There's also, of course, **La Scala**, temporarily at the Teatro Arcimboldi, one of the world's most prestigious opera houses, whose season runs from December to July. Although seats are expensive and can sell out months in advance, there is often a reasonable chance of picking up a seat in the gods an hour or so before a performance.

Listings

Consulates Australia, Via Borgogna 2 ☎02.77.70421; Canada, Via V. Pisani 19 ☎02.67.581; UK, Via San Paolo 7 ☎02.723.001; US, Via Principe Amedeo 2/10 ☎02.290.351.
Exchange The office in Stazione Centrale is your best bet.
Hospital Fatebenefratelli hospital, Corso Porta Nuova 23 ☎02.63.631; Ospedale Maggiore

Policlinico, Via Francesco Sforza 35 ☎02.55.031.
Internet access Internet Corner, Centro Telecom, Galleria Vittorio Emanuele.
Laundry Lavanderia, Via Vigevano 20, near Porta Genova.
Pharmacy Stazione Centrale.
Police Via Montebello ☎02.62.261.
Post office Via Cordusio 4, off Piazza Cordusio.

Mantua

Aldous Huxley called it the most romantic city in the world, and with an Arabian nights skyline rising above its three encircling lakes, **MANTUA** is undeniably evocative. It was the birthplace of Vergil, the scene of Verdi's *Rigoletto*, and its history is one of equally operatic plots, most of them perpetrated by the Gonzagas, who ruled the town for three centuries and left two splendid palaces – the Palazzo Ducale, with Mantegna's stunning fresco of the Gonzaga court, and Palazzo Tè, whose frescoes have entertained generations of visitors with their combination of steamy erotica and illusionistic fantasy.

Historic Mantua centres on four interlinking squares. **Piazza Mantegna** is dominated by the facade of Alberti's **Sant'Andrea**, an unfinished basilica commissioned by Lodovico II Gonzaga, who felt that the existing medieval church was neither impressive enough to represent the splendour of his state, nor large enough to hold the droves of people who flocked here to see the holy relic of Christ's blood that had been found on the site. Inside, an octagonal balustrade stands above the crypt where the holy relic is kept in two vases, copies of originals designed by Cellini and stolen by the Austrians in 1846. There are also wall-paintings designed by Mantegna and executed by his students, one of whom was Correggio; Mantegna himself is buried in the church, in one of the north aisle chapels, his tomb topped with a bust that's said to be a self-portrait. Opposite Sant'Andrea and sunk below the present level of the busy **Piazza dell'Erbe**, Mantua's oldest church, the eleventh-century **Rotonda**, narrowly escaped destruction under Lodovico's city-improvement plans, and still contains traces of twelfth- and thirteenth-century frescoes.

The dark underpassage beneath the red-brick **Broletto**, the medieval town hall, leads into **Piazza Broletto**, beyond which the sombre **Piazza Sordello** is flanked by the Baroque facade of the **Duomo**, which conceals a rich interior designed by Giulio Romano, and the **Palazzo Ducale** (Tues–Sun 8.45am–7.15pm; €6.50), an enormous complex that was once the largest palace in Europe, with a population of over a thousand. When it was sacked by the Habsburgs in 1630, eighty carriages were needed to carry the two thousand works of art contained in its five hundred rooms. Only a few of these are open to visitors, and to see them you have to take a guided tour. In the Salone del Fiume there's a trompe l'oeil garden complete with painted creepers and two fountains; the Sala degli Specchi, further on, has a notice outside signed by Monteverdi, who worked as court musician to Vincenzo I and gave frequent concerts of new works. Vincenzo also employed Rubens, whose *Adoration of the Magi* in the Salone degli Arcieri shows the Gonzaga family of 1604. However, the palace's real treasure is in the Castello di San Giorgio beyond, where you can see Mantegna's frescoes of the Gonzaga family, splendidly restored in the so-called Camera degli Sposi.

Mantua's other main sight, the **Palazzo Tè**, on the opposite side of town (Mon 1–6pm, Tues–Sun 9am–6pm; €8), was designed for Federico Gonzaga and his mistress, Isabella Boschetta, by Giulio Romano, and a tour of it is like a voyage around Giulio's imagination, a sumptuous world where very little is what it seems. In the Sala dei Cavalli, horses stand before an illusionistic background in which simulated marble, fake pilasters and mock reliefs reveal distant landscapes. The function of the Salotta di Psiche, further on, is undocumented, but the sultry frescoes, and its proximity to Federico's bedroom, might give a few clues. The ceiling paintings tell the story of Cupid and Psyche with some dizzying *sotto in su* (from the bottom up) works by Giulio. On the walls, too, are racy pieces, covered with orgiastic wedding-feast scenes, watched over by the giant Polyphemus, perched above the fireplace, while, beyond, the extraordinary Sala dei Giganti shows the destruction of the giants by the gods, with cracking pillars, toppling brickwork and screaming giants appearing to crash down into the room.

Practicalities

The city centre is a ten-minute walk from the **train station** down Via Solferino. The **tourist office** (Mon–Sat 8.30am–12.30pm & 3–6pm, Sun 9am–noon; ☎0376.328.253, ✆www.comune.mantova.it) is around the corner from Sant'Andrea. Budget **accommodation** is almost non-existent in Mantua. Of the less expensive hotels, you could try the *ABC*, Piazza Don Leoni 25 (☎0376 .323347; ❺), or the *Bianchi Stazione*, next door (☎0376.326.465; ❺), both opposite the station, or the *Broletto* (☎0376.223.678; ❼), a good value three-star at Via Accademia 1. Otherwise, you'll have to stay outside the town – the *Marago* 3km away in Virgiliana has cheap doubles (☎0376.370.313, ✆www.ristorante.marago.com; ❸; take bus #25). For inexpensive **food**, the cheapest place is the *Il Punto* self-service at Via Solferino 36, near the train station. Failing that, try the *Bella Napoli*, Piazza Cavalotti 14, which serves good pizza, or the atmospheric *Leoncino Rosso*, Via Giustiziati 33, off Piazza Broletto. For tasty pasta try *Osteria dei Canossa*, Vicolo Albergo 3.

Genoa

GENOA is is a marvellously eclectic city, centring on the port that had made it one of the five Italian maritime republics by the thirteenth century. Later, during the Unification era, the city was a base for radical thought. Mazzini, one of the main protagonists in Italy's unification, was born here, and in 1860 Garibaldi set sail for Sicily with his "Thousand" from the city's harbour. After forty years of economic decline the city started reinvesting in the 1990s. State funding to celebrate the 500th anniversary of Columbus's 1492 voyage paid for the renovation of some of the city's frescoed late-Renaissance palaces and the old port area, with Genoa's most famous son of modern times, Renzo Piano, taking a leading role. The tidying-up hasn't sanitized the old town, a set of winding alleys that form the core of the city, between the stations and the waterfront, and which are still dark and slightly threatening.

Arrival, information and accommodation

Trains from Ventimiglia and points west arrive at Stazione Principe in Piazza Acquaverde, just above the port; trains from La Spezia, Rome and points south arrive at Stazione Brignole, Piazza Verdi, on the other side of the city centre; trains from Milan and Turin usually stop at both, but if you have to travel between the two, take bus #18 or #37. **Ferries** arrive at the Stazione Marittima, ten minutes' walk downhill from Stazione Principe. **Getting around** is best done on foot; if you do need to take a bus, get a ticket from a *tabacchi* or newspaper stand. There is a **tourist office** at Stazione Principe (Mon–Sat 9.30am–1pm & 1.30–6pm; ☎010.246.2633, ✆www.apt.genova.it), and another at Porto Antico, Palazzina S. Maria (Mon–Sat 9am–1pm & 2–6pm, Sun 9am–noon; ☎010.248.711, ✆www.comune.genova.it). Both have *Passport*, a free **listings** guide. If you plan to visit several museums and other tourist attractions, it may be worth your while getting a **Museum Card** (from the train station and tourist office; €10.30/three days, €15.50/one week).

There are plenty of one-star **hotels** in the city centre, but many are grim and depressing. Good areas to try are the roads bordering the old town, and Piazza Colombo and Via XX Settembre, near Stazione Brignole.

Hostel
Genova Via Costanzi 120 ☎010.242.2457. Friendly, clean and well-run HI place with great views down over the port north of the centre; take bus #40 from Stazione Brignole. ❷

Hotels
Cairoli Via Cairoli 14/4 ☎010.246.1454,
✆www.venere.it search Cairoli. A very pleasant two-star, handy for the old town and Stazione Principe. ❺
Carletto Via Colombo 16/4 ☎010.588.412, ✆www.paginegialle.it/h-carletto. Central and quiet, a good fallback option if the *Soana* is full. ❸
Nettuno Via Mercantini 16 ☎010.362.8106. On the seaview walkway on Corso Italia. ❸

Soana Via XX Settembre 23/8/a ☎010.562.814,
🖳www.hotelsoana.it. Friendly two-star place ten
minutes' walk from Stazione Brignole. ❹

Campsites

Villa Doria Via Al Campeggio Villa Doria 15, Pegli
☎010.696.9600, 🖳www.camping.it/liguria/
villadoria. Set in parkland, 8km from Genoa, with
its own café, shop and solarium. Take a train to
Pegli and then #93 bus.

The City

Genoa spreads outwards from its **old town** around the port in a confusion of tiny
alleyways and old palaces; its people speak an impenetrable dialect – a mixture of
Neapolitan, Calabrese and Portuguese. From 1384 to 1515, except for brief periods
of foreign domination, the doges ruled the city from the ornate stuccoed **Palazzo
Ducale** in Piazza Matteotti (Tues–Sun 9am–9pm; prices vary; 🖳www.palazzodu-
cale.genova.it), across from which the dour **Gesù** church, designed by Pellegrino
Tibaldi at the end of the sixteenth century, contains Guido Reni's *Assumption* and
two paintings by Rubens. Close by, the Gothic **Cattedrale di San Lorenzo** is
home to the Renaissance chapel of St John the Baptist, whose remains once rested
in the thirteenth-century sarcophagus. After a particularly bad storm, priests carried
his casket through the city to placate the sea, and a commemorative procession
takes place each June 24 to honour him. His reliquary is in the treasury (tours
Mon–Sat 9am–noon & 3–6pm; €5.16; book on ☎010.247.1831), along with a polished quartz plate on which, legend says, Salome received his severed head. Also on
display is a glass dish given to Solomon by the Queen of Sheba, and used at the
Last Supper. East from the adjacent Piazza Ferrari, **Via XX Settembre**, Genoa's
commercial nucleus, has big chain stores and pavement cafés in the arcades.

South across **Via San Bernardo**, another busy street, the mosaic spire of the
church of **Sant'Agostino** marks the adjacent **Museo dell'Architettura e
Scultura Ligure** (Tues–Sat 9am–7pm, Sun 9am–12.30pm; €3.10), built around
the cloister of a thirteenth-century monastery, with a collection of Roman and
Romanesque fragments from other churches, as well as wood carvings and ancient
maps of Genoa. Down on the waterfront, ruined by a hideous concrete over-pass,
the sea once came up to the vaulted arcades of **Piazza Caricamento**, a hive of
activity, fringed by cafés and market stalls. Customs inspectors, and subsequently the
city's elected governors, set up in the **Palazzo San Giorgio** on the edge of the
square, some rooms of which are open to the public (Sat 10am–6pm; free). Beyond,
the waterfront has been the subject of a massive restoration project, manifest most
obviously in the huge **Aquarium** (Mon–Fri 9.30am–6.30pm, Sat & Sun
9.30am–8pm; Oct–March closed Mon; €11.60; 🖳www.acquariodigenova.it).
Behind Piazza Caricamento is a thriving commercial zone centred on **Piazza
Banchi**, formerly the heart of the medieval city, off which the long Via San Luca
leads to the **Galleria Nazionale di Palazzo Spinola** (Tues–Sat 9am–7pm, Sun
2–7pm; €4), with work by the Sicilian master Antonello da Messina and an
Adoration of the Magi by Joos van Cleve.

North of here, **Via Garibaldi** is lined with frescoed and stuccoed Renaissance
palaces; two are now museums and if you peek into courtyards and buildings you
will catch a glimpse of the rest. The **Palazzo Bianco** (Tues–Sat 9am–1pm, Wed &
Sat till 7pm, Sun 10am–6pm; €5 joint ticket with Palazzo Rosso) holds paintings
by Genoese artists and others, including Van Dyck and Rubens, and a good general
gathering of Flemish art. The **Palazzo Rosso** across the road (same hours and ticket as Palazzo Bianco) has works by Titian, Caravaggio and Dürer, but it's the decor
that really impresses: fantastic chandeliers, mirrors, an excess of gilding, and frescoed
ceilings. Behind, Genoa heads up the hill like the steps of an amphitheatre, a part of
town best seen by way of the **funicular** (bus tickets valid) from Piazza del Portello
up to Sant'Anna. The view from the top is much hyped, but the trip is more
absorbing than anything you'll see when you arrive.

Eating, drinking, nightlife and beaches

For cheap **lunches, snacks** and **picnic** ingredients, try the Via de Pre near the station and the covered Mercato Orientale, halfway down Via XX Settembre in the old cloisters of an Augustinian monastery, or *Gran Ristoro* on Sottoripa, which does good panini. A popular fish **restaurant** is the hectic *Da Vittorio*, opposite Piazza Caricamento on Sottoripa; it can be difficult to get a table. *Sâ Pesta*, Via Giustiniani 16, is a well-known source of good local cooking, including farinata, a thin chickpea-based pancake, but it closes early. The no-nonsense and endearingly chaotic *Trattoria da Maria*, Via Testadoro 14/b, just off Via XXV Aprile, also serves up simple Ligurian cooking at rock-bottom prices. The *Ostaja do Castello*, Salita Sanda Maria di Castello 32, on the other side of the Old Town, is a similar family-run trattoria. Late night, young people congregate on the **bars** around Piazza delle Erbe, and popular discos include *Estoril*, on Corso Italia 7d, and the *Matilda Caffe* on Via D'Annunzio 19. The *Louisiana Jazz Club*, Via S Sebastiano 36R, *Cezanne* on Via Cecchi 7r, and *Mako*, Corso Italia 28r, all have live music.

As for **beaches**, you need to travel some way before you really feel free of Genoa's sprawl, and it's probably best to accept that sunbathing isn't part of the Genoese experience. If you fancy a swim, though, the small district of **Nervi**, on the eastern side of the city, is probably the most attractive easily reached spot – take bus #15 from Piazza Caricamento.

The Riviera di Levante

The stretch of coast east from Genoa, the **Riviera di Levante**, is not the place to come for a relaxing beach holiday. The ports that once survived on navigation, fishing and coral diving have now experienced thirty years of tourism; the coastline is still wild and beautiful in parts, but the sense of remoteness has gone. **PORTOFINO**, at the extremity of the Monte Portofino headland, manages to be both attractive and offputting at the same time, a wealthy resort but a beautiful one. It's well worth making the two-and-a-half-hour walk to San Fruttuoso's beach and thirteenth-century Abbey (June–Sept Mon–Fri 10am–6pm, Sat & Sun 10am–3.45pm; Oct–May closed Mon; €6; ☎0185.772.703). Boats run there, too, for those who would rather sooner not walk. On the corniche road 3km out of Portofino, the sparkling cove at **PARAGGI** is a good place for a swim, with a couple of bars set back from the beach, and you can take a bus to Ruta, from where you can either slog on foot to the summit of Monte Portofino or catch another bus to Portofino Vetta, from where it's twenty minutes' walk to the top. On very clear days the views are fantastic.

SANTA MARGHERITA LIGURE is a small, thoroughly attractive resort, with palm trees along its front and a minuscule pebble beach and concrete jetties to swim from. If you'd like **to stay**, try *Albergo Annabella*, Via Costasecca 10, just off Piazza Mazzini (☎0185.286.531; **⑤**), or *Albergo Fasce*, a little further up the road at Via L. Bozzo 3 (☎0185.286.435; **⑤**), which has a dozen bikes that guests can use free of charge. For **food**, try *Trattoria Biacin*, just off the seafront square at Via Algeria 9, or the long-established *Da Pezzi*, around the corner at Via Cavour 21, a canteen-like locals' hangout serving pasta and grills, and takeaway snacks for lunch. The **tourist office** is on Via XXV Aprile (Mon–Sun 9am–12.30pm & 3–5.30pm; ☎018.287.485, ⑩www.apttigullio.liguria.it).

RAPALLO crowds around the first bay along in the gulf, a highly developed though still attractive resort that used to be patronized by a number of writers: Max Beerbohm lived in Rapallo, attracting a vast coterie, and Ezra Pound wrote the first thirty of his Cantos here between 1925 and 1930. There are decent **places to stay** in the centre of town, most notably the *Pensione Bandoni*, Via Marsala 24/3 (☎0185.50.423; **❸**); alternatively, try the *Fernanda*, along the front at Via Milite Ignoto 9 (☎0185.50.244; **⑤**), cosy enough, but more expensive for less pleasant rooms. There are a couple of campsites, *Rapallo* at Via San Lazzaro 4 (☎0185.262.018) and the *Miraflores* at Via Savagna 10 (☎0185.263.000). Perhaps the least expensive and most authentic place to **eat** is *Bansin* at Via Venezia 49, in the heart of the old town; while *Da Mario*, Piazza Garibaldi 23, is a good, moderately priced fish restaurant.

   LEVANTO, further east still, is one of the most pleasant resorts in this area, with a long stretch of sandy beach, plentiful accommodation and food options, and a decent campsite, the *Aquadolce*, in the centre of town. It's a good base from which to explore the **CINQUE TERRE**, five small villages perched on tiny cliff-bound inlets to the west. Levanto's **tourist office** is in Piazza Cavour (☎0187.808.125, ⓦwwwaptcinqueterre.sp.it). For **accommodation**, try *Pensione Garden*, right by the sea at Corso Italia 8 (☎0187.808.173; ❸); if that's full, or you have a little more money, try the slightly cosier atmosphere of the *Europa*, up the street at Via Dante 41 (☎0187.808.126; ❺; June–Sept half board obligatory). For **food** and late-night **drinks**, the *Caffè Roma*, on the square round the corner from the *Pensione Garden*, has a small, reasonably priced restaurant out the back.

The northeast

The **northeast** of the country has the most appealing – and versatile – regions. The appeal of **Venice** hardly needs stating: it's one of Europe's truly unique urban landscapes, and is an unmissable part of any European tour. The region around Venice – the **Veneto** – is a prosperous one, where virtually every acre still bears the imprint of Venetian rule. **Padua** and **Verona** are the main attractions, with their masterpieces by Giotto, Donatello and Mantegna, and a profusion of great buildings from Roman times to the Renaissance. Much of the countryside is dull and flat, only perking up to the north with the high peaks of the Dolomite range. East, on the former Yugoslav border, **Trieste** is capital of the partly Slav region of **Friuli-Venezia Giulia**, a Habsburg city only united with Italy after World War II. South, between Lombardy and Tuscany, stretching from the Adriatic coast almost to the shores of the Mediterranean, **Emilia–Romagna** is the heartland of northern Italy, a patchwork of ducal territories formerly ruled by a handful of families, whose castles and fortresses remain in well-preserved medieval towns. Carving a straight route through the heart of the region, from Milan to Rimini on the coast, the Via Emilia is a central and obvious reference point, a Roman military road constructed in 187 BC that was part of the medieval pilgrim's route to Rome and the way east for crusaders to Ravenna and Venice. **Bologna**, the region's capital, is one of Italy's largest cities, but despite having one of the most beautifully preserved centres in the country, it's relatively neglected by tourists. North of Bologna is **Ferrara**, a Renaissance town run for hundreds of years by the Este family, and these days Italy's premier bicycle city. Nearby is **Parma**, a wealthy provincial town that is worth visiting for its paintings by Parmigianino and Correggio. The coast is less interesting, and the water polluted, but, just south of the Po delta, **Ravenna** boasts probably the finest set of Byzantine mosaics in the world.

Venice

The first-time visitor to **VENICE** arrives with a heavy burden of expectations, most of which are well-founded. It is an extraordinarily beautiful city and the major sights, such as the basilica and piazza of San Marco, are all they are cracked up to be. The downside is that Venice is deluged with tourists, the annual influx exceeding the city's population two-hundredfold; and it is expensive.

   The city first rose to prominence when traders stole the body of St Mark from Alexandria in 828, to signal their independence from Byzantium. Venice later exploited the trading networks and markets of Byzantium and the East, aided by the Crusades, and by the twelfth century had achieved unprecedented prosperity. The Sacking of Constantinople in 1204 left much of the Roman Empire under the city's sway. Following the defeat of Genoa in 1380, Venice became the unrivalled trading power of the region, and by the middle of the fifteenth century was in possession of a mainland empire that was to survive several centuries. Decline had set in by the eighteenth century, however, and Venice became known as a playground for the rich. By the nineteenth century it was a well-established destination on the Grand Tour and today some twenty million visitors come here annually. Without them, Venice would barely exist at all.

Arrival, information and city transport

Flights arrive at the city's **Marco Polo** airport, on the edge of the lagoon, linked to the city centre by ACTV bus #5 (€1) or ATVO bus (€2), or the more expensive waterbus (from €10). All road traffic comes into the city at **Piazzale Roma**, at the head of the Canal Grande, from where waterbus services run to the San Marco area, stopping off at Santa Lucia **train station**, the next stop along the Canal Grande. The main **tourist office** is at San Marco 71/f, a couple of minutes' walk east of the square (daily 9.40am–3.20pm; ☎041.5298.711, ⓦwww.turismovenezia.it; www.comune.venezia.it). There are also desks in the Casinò da Caffè by the San Marco waterbus stop, at the train station, and at the airport. Pick up the free English-language **listings magazines**, *Leo* and *Un Ospite di Venezia* (ⓦwww.aguestinvenice.com), from any of them; you can also buy the **Museum Pass** (€15.50), which gives entry to the main museums (but not the Accademia or Guggenheim), and the **Chorus Pass** (€8), which gives entry to fourteen churches, including the Madonna dell'Orto.

In most cases the speediest way of **getting around** Venice is on foot – you can cross the whole city in an hour. It is sometimes faster, and more fun, to take a waterbus (*vaporetto*). **Tickets** are available from most landing stages and all shops displaying the ACTV sign. Flat-rate fares are €3.10 for any one continuous journey, though most one-stop journeys cost just €1.50. Tickets bought on board are subject to a surcharge, and the spot-fine for not having a valid ticket is €15.50, so it's a good idea to buy a block of ten (*un blochetto*) or a tourist ticket (€9.30/one day, €18.08/three day, €30.99/one week). Timetables are posted at each stop and the tourist office's city map has a route plan. In addition, the **traghetti** that cross the Canal Grande (€0.40/trip) are a cheap way of getting a ride on a gondola. Otherwise, the **gondola** is an adjunct of the tourist industry: to hire one costs from €62 for fifty minutes, plus €31 for each additional twenty-five minutes – be sure to confirm the charge beforehand.

Accommodation

Accommodation is the major expense in Venice, although there are inexpensive options, not least a number of **hostels**, most owned by religious foundations. You should always book ahead. However, if you do turn up without somewhere to stay, then try one of the following **booking offices**: at the train station (daily 8am–9pm), on the Tronchetto (daily 9am–8pm), at Piazzale Roma (daily 9am–9pm), at Marco Polo airport (daily 9am/noon–7pm), and at the autostrada's Venice exit (8am–8pm).

Hostels

Domus Cavanis Rio Terrà Foscarini, Dorsoduro 896 ☎041.522.2826. Catholic-run place, with separate rooms for men and women. ❸

Domus Civica Calle Campazzo, San Polo 3082 ☎041.721.103. A student house in winter, open to women travellers only from June to Sept. Curfew 11.30pm. ❸

Foresteria Valdese Santa Maria Formosa, Castello 5170 ☎041.528.6797. Three large dorms, and a few rooms for two to four people. Difficult to find – go from Campo Santa Maria Formosa along Calle Lunga,

and it's at the foot of the bridge at the far end. ❸

Ostello Venezia Fondamenta delle Zitelle, Giudecca 86 ☎041.523.8211. The official HI hostel, in a superb location looking at San Marco from the island of Giudecca. Curfew 11pm. Waterbus #82 from the station. ❷

Hotels

Antico Capon Campo S. Margherita, Dorsoduro 3004/B ☎041.528.5292. Situated on one of the city's most atmospheric squares, in the heart of the student district. ❻

Bernardi Semenzato Calle dell'Oca, Cannaregio 4366 ☎041.522.7257. Two-star place with welcoming and helpful English-speaking owners. **④**
Ca' Fóscari Calle della Frescada, Dorsoduro 3887B ☎041.710.401. Quiet, well decorated and relaxed place, tucked away in a tiny alley near San Tomà. **⑤**
Caneva Ramo della Fava, Castello 5515

☎041.522.8118. Overlooking the Rio della Fava on the approach to the busy Campo San Bartolomeo, yet very peaceful. **⑥**
Casa Gerotto Calderan Campo S. Geremia 283, Cannaregio ☎041.715.361. Welcoming place not far from the train station. Dorm beds also available. **⑤**, dorms **③**

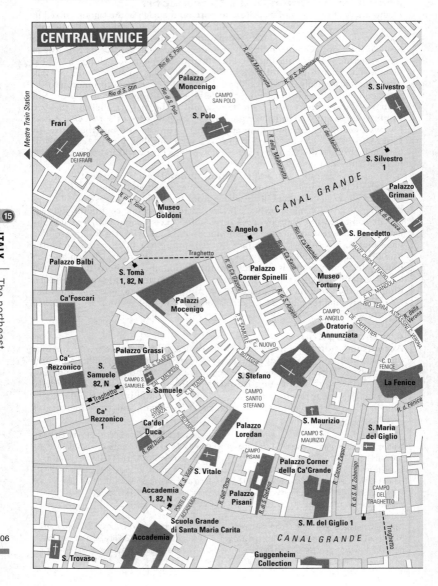

ITALY | The northeast

Casa Petrarca Calle delle Colonne, San Marco 4394 ☏041.520.0430. Friendly place with just six rooms. The cheapest near the Piazza. ⑥

Zecchini Lista di Spagna 130, Cannaregio ☏041.716.321. Three star run by Antica Casa Carettoni. ④

The City

The 118 islands of central Venice are divided into six districts known as *sestieri*. The *sestiere* of **San Marco** is home to the majority of the essential sights, and is accordingly the most expensive and most crowded district of the city. On the east it's bor-

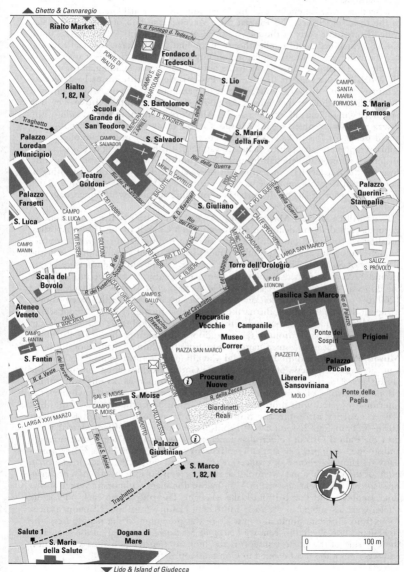

▲ Ghetto & Cannaregio

▼ Lido & Island of Giudecca

dered by **Castello**, on the north by **Cannaregio**. On the other side of the Canal Grande, the largest of the *sestieri* is **Dorsoduro**, which stretches from the fashionable quarter at the southern tip of the canal to the docks in the west. **Santa Croce**, named after a now demolished church, roughly follows the curve of the Canal Grande from Piazzale Roma to a point just short of the Rialto, where it joins the smartest and commercially most active of the districts on this bank – **San Polo**.

San Marco

The section of Venice enclosed by the lower loop of the Canal Grande is the Venice of the travel brochures. The **Piazza San Marco** is the hub of most activity, signalled from most parts of the city by the **Campanile** (daily 9.30am–4.15/6pm; €4.10), which began life as a lighthouse in the ninth century, but is in fact a reconstruction: the original tower collapsed on July 14, 1902. It is the tallest structure in the city, and from the top you can make out virtually every building, but not a single canal. Away to the left stretches the **Procuratie Vecchie**, an early-sixteenth-century structure that was converted into a palace by Napoleon, who connected the building with the other side of the piazza – the **Procuratie Nuove** – by way of a new wing. Generally known as the **Ala Napoleonica**, this short side of the Piazza is partly occupied by the **Museo Correr** (daily 9am–5/7pm; €9.50 combined ticket for Piazza San Marco museums), whose vast historical collection – coins, weapons, regalia, prints, mediocre paintings – is heavy-going unless you have an intense interest in Venetian history. The **Quadreria** on the second floor is no rival for the Accademia's collection, but does set out the evolution of painting in Venice from the thirteenth century to around 1500, and contains some gems, including a print of Jacopo de'Barbari's astonishing aerial view of Venice, engraved in 1500.

The **Basilica di San Marco** (daily 9.45am–5pm; €1.50) is the most exotic of Europe's cathedrals, modelled on Constantinople's Church of the Twelve Apostles, finished in 1094 and embellished over the succeeding centuries with trophies brought back from abroad – proof of Venice's secular might and thus of the spiritual power of St Mark. The Romanesque carvings of the central door were begun around 1225 and finished in the early fourteenth century, while the mosaic above the doorway on the far left – *The Arrival of the Body of St Mark* – was made around 1260 (the only early mosaic left on the main facade) and includes the oldest-known image of the basilica. Inside, the narthex holds more mosaics, Old Testament scenes on the domes and arches, together with *The Madonna with Apostles and Evangelists* in the niches of the bay in front of the main door – dating from the 1060s, the oldest mosaics in San Marco. A steep staircase goes from the church's main door up to the **Museo Marciano** and the **Loggia dei Cavalli** (daily 9.45am–5pm; €1.50), where you can enjoy fine views of the city and the Gothic carvings along the apex of the facade, as well as the horses in question, replicas of Roman works thieved from the Hippodrome of Constantinople (the genuine articles are inside). Downstairs, the interior is covered with more mosaics, most dating from the middle of the thirteenth century, although the **Sanctuary**, off the south transept (Mon–Sat 10am–5.30pm, Sun 2–4pm; €1.50), holds the most precious of San Marco's treasures, the **Pala d'Oro** or golden altar panel, commissioned in 976 in Constantinople and studded with precious stones. The **Treasury**, nearby (same times; €2), is a similarly dazzling warehouse of chalices, reliquaries and candelabra. Back in the main body of the church, don't overlook the **rood screen**'s marble figures of *The Virgin, St Mark and the Apostles*, carved in 1394 by the dominant sculptors in Venice at that time, Jacobello and Pietro Paolo Dalle Masegne. The **pulpits** on each side of the screen were assembled in the early fourteenth century from miscellaneous panels, some from Constantinople; the new doge was presented to the people from the right-hand one. The tenth-century *Icon of the Madonna of Nicopeia* (in the chapel on the east side of the north transept) is the most revered religious image in Venice, and was one of the most revered in Constantinople.

The adjacent **Palazzo Ducale** (daily 9am–5/7pm; €9.50 combined ticket for Piazza San Marco museums) was principally the residence of the doge. Like San Marco, it has been rebuilt many times since its foundation in the first years of the ninth century, but the earliest parts of the current structure date from 1340. Parts of it can be marched through fairly briskly, its walls covered with acres of wearisome canvas, although you should linger in the **Anticollegio**, one of the palace's finest rooms and home to four pictures by Tintoretto and Veronese's characteristically benign *Rape of Europa*. The cycle of paintings on the ceiling of the adjoining Sala del Collegio is also by Veronese, and he features strongly again in the most stupendous room in the building – the Sala del Maggior Consiglio, where his ceiling panel of the Apotheosis of Venice is suspended over the dais from which the doge oversaw the sessions of the city assembly. The backdrop is the immense *Paradiso* painted at the end of his life by Tintoretto, with the aid of his son, Domenico. From here you descend quickly to the underbelly of the Venetian state, crossing the **Ponte dei Sospiri** (Bridge of Sighs) to the prisons, and then back over the water to the Pozzi, the cells for the most hardened malefactors.

Dorsoduro

Some of the finest architecture in Venice is to be found in **Dorsoduro**, but few visitors wander off the strip that runs between the main sights of the area, the first of which, the **Galleria dell'Accademia** (Mon 8.15am–2pm, Tues–Sun till 7.15pm; €6.50), has one of the finest collections of European art, following the history of Venetian painting from the fourteenth to the eighteenth centuries. The gallery is laid out in roughly chronological order and includes paintings by Paolo Veneziano, Carpaccio, Mantegna, Giovanni Bellini, and one of the most mysterious of Italian paintings, Giorgione's *Tempest*. Tintoretto weighs in with three typically energetic pieces illustrating the legend of St Mark, and an entire wall is filled by Paolo Veronese's *Christ in the House of Levi* – called *The Last Supper* until the authorities objected to its lack of reverence. Finally, in room 24 there's Titian's *Presentation of the Virgin*, painted for the place where it hangs.

Five minutes' walk from the Accademia is the unfinished Palazzo Venier dei Leoni, home of the **Guggenheim Collection** (10am–6pm. closed Tues; €8), and of Peggy Guggenheim for thirty years until her death in 1979. Her private collection is an eclectic mix of pieces from her favourite modernist movements and artists, including works by Brancusi, De Chirico, Max Ernst and Malevich. Continuing along the line of the Canal Grande, you'll come to the church of Santa Maria della Salute; better known simply as the **Salute**, it was built to fulfil a Senate decree of 1630 that a new church be dedicated to Mary if the city were delivered from plague. Every November 21 there's a procession from San Marco to the church, over a specially constructed pontoon bridge, to give thanks for the city's good health, still a major event on the Venetian calendar. In 1656, a hoard of Titian paintings were moved here and are now housed in the sacristy (€2), along with the *Marriage at Cana* by Tintoretto, featuring portraits of a number of the artist's friends.

San Polo

On the northeastern edge of **San Polo** is the former trading district of **Rialto**. It still hosts the Rialto market on the far side of the Rialto Bridge, a lively affair and one of the few places in the city where it's possible to hear nothing but Italian spoken. The main reason people visit San Polo, however, is to see the mountainous brick church of the **Santa Maria Gloriosa dei Frari** west of here (Mon–Sat 9am–6pm, Sun 1–6pm; €2), whose collection of artworks includes a rare couple of paintings by Titian – most notably his *Assumption*, painted in 1518, a swirling piece of compositional bravura for which there was no precedent in Venetian art. Titian is buried in the church, the spot marked by a bombastic nineteenth-century monument; opposite, the equally pompous mausoleum of Canova was erected by pupils of the sculptor, following a design he had made for the tomb of Titian.

At the rear of the Frari is the **Scuola Grande di San Rocco** (daily 9am–4/5.30pm; €5.16), home to a cycle of more than fifty major paintings by Tintoretto – including, in the main hall, three large ceiling panels featuring Old Testament references to the alleviation of physical suffering (coded declarations of the Scuola's charitable activities), while around the walls are New Testament themes.

Cannaregio

In the northernmost section of Venice, **Cannaregio**, you can go from the bustle of the **train station** to some of the quietest and prettiest parts of the city in a matter of minutes. The district has the dubious distinction of containing the world's first **Ghetto**: in 1516, all the city's Jews were ordered to move to the island of the Ghetto Nuovo, an enclave which was sealed at night by Christian curfew guards. Even now it looks quite different from the rest of Venice, many of its buildings relatively high-rise due to the restrictions on the growth of the area. A couple of the oldest synagogues – the **Scola Levantina**, founded in 1538, and the **Scola Spagnola**, founded twenty years later – are still in use and can be viewed on an informative guided tour that leaves on the half-hour, organized by the **Jewish Museum** in Campo Ghetto Nuovo (Mon–Fri & Sun 10am–5.30/7pm; tours till 4.30pm; €3, tours €8). The district also contains one of the most beautiful palazzi in Venice, the **Ca D'Oro** or Golden House (Mon 8.15am–2pm, Tues–Sun till 7.15pm; €3), the facade of which once glowed with gold leaf; and what is arguably the finest Gothic church in Venice, the **Madonna dell'Orto** (€2), which contains Tintoretto's tomb and two of his paintings.

Castello

Castello is home among other things to the **Miracoli** church (€2), built in the 1480s to house a painting of the Madonna that was believed to have performed a number of miracles, such as reviving a man who had spent half an hour lying at the bottom of the Giudecca canal. East of here, the **Campo San Zanipolo** is the most impressive open space in Venice after Piazza San Marco, dominated by the huge brick church of **San Zanipolo**, founded by the Dominicans in 1246 and finally consecrated in 1430. The church is best known for the tombs and monuments around the walls, the memorials of some 25 doges, most impressive of which is the tomb of Doge Michele Morosini on the right of the chancel. The other essential sight in this area is to the east of San Marco – the **Scuola di San Giorgio degli Schiavoni** (Tues–Sat 9.30am–12.30pm & 3.30–6.30pm, Sun 9.30am–12.30pm; €3), set up by Venice's Slav population in 1451. The building dates from the early sixteenth century, and its interior looks much as it would have then, with a superb cycle painted by Vittore Carpaccio between 1502 and 1509 on the ground floor.

Venice's other islands

Immediately south of the Palazzo Ducale, Palladio's church of **San Giorgio Maggiore** stands on the island of the same name and has two pictures by Tintoretto in the chancel – *The Fall of Manna* and *The Last Supper*, perhaps the most famous of all his images, painted as a pair in the last years of the artist's life. On the left of the choir a corridor leads to the **Campanile** (€3), rebuilt in 1791 after the collapse of its predecessor and one of the two best vantage points in the city.

The long island of **La Giudecca**, to the west, was where the wealthiest aristocrats of early Renaissance Venice built their villas, and in places you can still see traces of their gardens, although the present-day suburb is a strange mixture of decrepitude and vitality. The main reason to come is the Franciscan church of the **Redentore** (€2), designed by Palladio in 1577 in thanks for Venice's deliverance from a plague that killed a third of the population. Sadly, the church is in a bad state of repair, and a rope prevents visitors going beyond the nave, but you can see its best paintings in the sacristy, as well as a curious gallery of eighteenth-century wax heads of illustrious Franciscans.

Sheltering Venice from the open sea, the thin strand of the **Lido** used to be the focus of the annual hullaballoo of Venice's "Marriage to the Sea", when the doge went out to the Porto di Lido to drop a gold ring into the brine and then disembarked for mass at San Nicolò al Lido. Later it became the smartest bathing resort in Italy, and although it's no longer as chic as it was when Thomas Mann set *Death in Venice* here, there's less room on its beaches now than ever before; indeed, unless you're staying at one of the flashy hotels on the seafront, or are prepared to pay a ludicrous fee to rent a beach hut, you won't even be allowed to get on the Lido sand. There are public beaches at the northern and southern ends of the island – though the water is, as you would expect, filthy.

Of the major islands lying to the north of Venice, **Murano** is chiefly famed as the home of Venice's glass-blowing industry. Its main *fondamente* are crowded with shops selling the mostly revolting products of the **furnaces**, but the process of manufacture is more interesting. There are numerous furnaces to visit, all free of charge. There's also the **Museo de Vetro** in the Palazzo Giustinian (10am–5pm, closed Wed; €4), which displays Roman pieces and the earliest surviving examples of Murano glass from the fifteenth century. The nearby island of **Burano**, on the other hand, is still largely a fishing community, although there is also a thriving trade in **lace-making** here, and the main street is crammed with shops selling Burano- and Venetian-point lace. The skills are taught at the Scuola dei Merletti in Piazza Baldessare Galuppi, which also houses a small museum, **Museo del Merletto** (10am–5pm, closed Mon; €4), with work dating back as far as the sixteenth century.

Eating and drinking

Bars, cafés and pasticcerie

Bar Paolin Campo Santo Stefano, San Marco. Thought by many to be the makers of the best ice cream in Venice; the outside tables also have one of the finest settings in the city. Closed Fri.

Caffe Florian St Mark's Square. World famous cafe, where American writer Ernest Hemingway invented the eponymous and lethal Gin-Martini cocktail.

Cantinone gia Schiavi Fondamenta Maravegie, Dorsoduro. Great wine shop and bar opposite San Trovaso church. Closed Sun.

Do Mori Calle Do Mori, San Polo. Narrow, standing-only bar, catering for the Rialto traders and locals – the best of a number of bars in the area, it serves delicious snacks. Closed Wed pm & all Sun.

Enoteca Al Volto Calle Cavalli (near Campo S. Luca), San Marco. Stocks 1300 wines from Italy and elsewhere, some cheap, many not; good snacks, too. Closed Sun.

Gelateria Nico Záttere ai Gesuati, Dorsoduro. High spot of a wander in the area, celebrated for an artery-clogging creation called a *gianduiotto* – a block of praline ice cream in whipped cream. Closed Thurs.

Marchini Ponte San Maurizio, San Marco. The most delicious and expensive of Venetian pasticcerie.

Restaurants

Al Cugnai Piscina del Forner, Dorsoduro. Good-value trattoria close to the Accademia. Get there by 8pm or be prepared to queue. Closed Mon.

Alle Oche Calle del Tintor (south side of Campo S. Giacomo dell'Orio), San Polo. Eighty-odd varieties of inexpensive pizza.

Antico Mola Fondamenta degli Ormesini, Cannaregio. Originally a family-run, local place, but becoming trendier by the year. Still good food and good value. Closed Wed.

Paradiso Perduto Fondamenta della Misericordia, Cannaregio. Fronted by a popular bar, with a lively relaxed atmosphere and occasional live music. Closed Wed.

Rosticceria San Bartolomeo Calle della Bissa, San Marco. Glorified snack bar serving good-value meals.

Trattoria Altanella Calle dell'Erbe, Giudecca. Succulent fish dishes, and a terrace overlooking the island's central canal. Good for a treat. Closed Mon & Tues.

Trattoria Pizzeria Casa Mia Calle dell'Oca, Cannaregio. Very popular trattoria-pizzeria close to St Apostoli Chuch. Closed Tues.

The Carnevale

Perhaps the city's most famous annual event is the **Carnevale**, which occupies the ten days leading up to Lent, finishing on Shrove Tuesday with a masked ball for the glitterati and dancing in the Piazza for the plebs. It was revived in the late 1970s, and after three years gained support from the city authorities, who now organize various pageants and performances. It's also a time to see and be seen: people don costumes and in the evening congregate in the squares. Masks are on sale throughout the year in Venice, but new mask- and costume-shops suddenly appear during Carnevale, and Campo San Maurizio sprouts a marquee with mask-making demonstrations.

Listings

Consulates UK, Palazzo Querini, Accademia, Dorsoduro 1051 ☎041.522.7207. The nearest US consulate is in Milan; travellers from Canada, Australia, New Zealand and Ireland should contact the embassy in Rome.
Complaints The dedicated tourist complaint line is ☎800.355.920.
Exchange American Express, Salizzada San Moisè, San Marco.
Hospital Ospedale Civili Riunti di Venezia, Campo Santi Giovanni e Paolo ☎041.523.0000.

Internet Net House, Campo Santo Stefano 2967–2958.
Laundry Ai Tre Ponti, Santa Croce 274; Salizzada del Pistor, Cannaregio 4553, near Santi Apostoli.
Left luggage At the train station.
Pharmacies Farmacia Baldiserotto, Via Garibaldi 1778; or consult *Un Ospite di Venezia* or ⓦwww.turismovenezia.it for full list.
Police Via Nicoldi 24, Marghera ☎041.271.5511.
Post office Fondaco dei Tedeschi, by the Rialto Bridge.

Padua

Extensively rebuilt after damage caused by bombing during World War II, and hemmed in by the sprawl which accompanied its development as the Veneto's most important economic centre, **PADUA** is not the most alluring city in northern Italy; however, it is one of the most ancient, and plentiful evidence remains of its lineage. A former Roman settlement, the city was a place of pilgrimage following the death of St Anthony here, and it later became an artistic and intellectual centre: Donatello and Mantegna both worked here, and in the seventeenth century Galileo researched at the university, where the medical faculty was one of the most ambitious in Europe.

Just outside the city centre, through a gap in the Renaissance walls off Corso Garibaldi, the Giotto frescoes in the **Cappella degli Scrovegni** (daily 9am–6/7pm; by appointment only; book at least 72hr in advance on ☎20.100.20; €11 for joint ticket with Musei Civici) are the reason for coming to Padua. Commissioned in 1303 by Enrico Scrovegni in atonement for his father's usury, the chapel's walls are covered with illustrations of the life of Mary, Jesus and the story of the Passion – a cycle, arranged in three tiers and painted against a backdrop of saturated blue, that is one of the high points in the development of European art in its innovative attention to the inner nature of its subjects. Beneath the main pictures are shown the vices and virtues in human (usually female) form, while on the wall above the door is the *Last Judgement*. Directly above the door is a portrait of Scrovegni presenting the chapel; his tomb is at the far end, behind the altar, with its statues by Giovanni Pisano. The adjacent **Musei Civici** (Tues–Sun 9am–5pm; €9) contains an assembly of fourteenth- to nineteenth-century art from the Veneto and further afield, the high point being a *Crucifixion* by Giotto that was once in the Scrovegni chapel, a superbly presented archeological museum and one of the world's largest collections of coins and medals. Nearby, the church of the **Eremitani**, built at the turn of the fourteenth century, but almost completely wrecked by bombing in 1944, has been fastidiously rebuilt, although the frescoes by Mantegna that used to be here were almost totally lost, and can now be assessed only from a few fuzzy photographs and some fragments on the right of the high altar.

South of here, on the other side of the centre, the main sight of the Piazza del Santo is Donatello's **Monument to Gattamelata** of 1453, the earliest large bronze sculpture of the Renaissance. On one side of the square, the basilica of San Antonio or **Il Santo** (daily 6.30am–7/7.45pm) was built to house the body of St Anthony, and its Cappella del Santo has a sequence of panels showing scenes from his life, carved between 1505 and 1577, and **Cappella del Tesoro** (8am–noon & 2.30–7pm), which houses the tongue and chin of St Anthony in a head-shaped reliquary.

From the basilica, Via Umberto leads back towards the **University**, established in 1221, and older than any other in Italy except Bologna. The main block is the **Palazzo del Bò**, where Galileo taught physics from 1592 to 1610, declaiming from a lectern that is still on show, though the major sight is the sixteenth-century anatomy theatre (tours March–Oct Mon, Wed & Fri 3pm, 4pm & 5pm, Tues, Thurs & Sat 9am, 10am & 11am; €2.50). The area west of here, around the **Piazza della Frutta** and **Piazza delle Erbe**, is effectively the hub of the city. Separating the two squares is the extraordinary **Palazzo della Ragione** (Tues–Sun 9am–6/7pm; €6), which, at the time of its construction in the early 1200s, sported frescoes by Giotto and his assistants. These were destroyed by fire in 1420 and most of the extant frescoes (1425–1440) are by Nicola Miretto. Close by, Padua's **Duomo** is an unlovely church whose design was cribbed from drawings by Michelangelo, though the adjacent Romanesque **Baptistry** is one of the unproclaimed delights of Padua, lined with some fourteenth-century frescoes by Giusto de'Menabuoi – a cycle which makes a fascinating comparison with Giotto's in the Cappella degli Scrovegni.

Practicalities

The **train station** is at the far end of Corso del Popolo, a few minutes' walk north of the city walls. There's a **tourist office** at the station (Mon–Sat 9am–6pm, Sun 9am–noon), but the main office is in Galleria Pedrocchi, just off Via 8 Febbraio (Mon–Sat 9am–12.30pm & 3–7pm; ☎049.876.7927, ⓦwww.apt.padova.it). Of many affordable **hotels**, *Verdi*, Via Dondi dell'Orologio 7 (☎049.875.5774; ❸), is particularly friendly. Another good budget option is *Junior*, Via L. Faggin 2 (☎049.611.756; ❸), just behind the station. The **HI hostel** is at Via A. Aleardi 30 (☎049.875.2219; ❷; curfew 11pm), and has internet access; take bus #3, #8, or #18 from the station. The nearest **campsite** is 15km away at Via Roma 123 in Montegrotto Terme, served by frequent trains (15min). As for **food**, the *rosticceria* in Via Daniele Manin offers a wide variety of snacks, while *Pane e Foccaccia* on Via del Santo has excellent pizza slices. For a more relaxed session at only slightly greater expense, try the excellent Osteria *l'Anfora*, Via dei Soncin 13; two good cheap restaurants are *Da Giovanni* at Via Maroncelli and *Pago Pago* at Via Galilei 59. On Piazza Cavour, *Pe Pen* (closed Sun) has a wonderful range of pizzas, with seats on the square in summer. The *Dotto*, Via Randaccio 23, is a superb mid-range restaurant.

Verona

The easy-going city of **VERONA** is the largest city of the Veneto, and, with its wealth of Roman sites and streets of pink-hued medieval buildings, one of its most interesting. First settled by the Romans, it later became an independent city-state, reaching its zenith in the thirteenth century under the Scaligeri family. Ruthless in the exercise of power, the Scaligeri were at the same time energetic patrons of the arts, and many of Verona's finest buildings date from the century of their rule. With their fall, the Viscontis of Milan assumed control of the city, which was later absorbed into the Venetian empire.

The city centre clusters in a deep bend in the River Adige, the main sight of its southern reaches the central hub of **Piazza Brà** and its mighty Roman **Arena** (Tues–Sun: July & Aug 9am–3pm; rest of year 8am–7pm; €3.10, first Sun of month €1.40; ⓦwww.arena.it). Dating from the first century AD, and originally with seating for some 20,000, this is the third-largest surviving Roman amphitheatre, and offers a tremendous panorama from the topmost of the 44 marble tiers. Nowadays it is used as an **opera** venue for big summer productions such as Aida. North, **Via Mazzini**, a narrow traffic-free street lined with expensive shops, leads to a group of squares, most noteworthy of which is the **Piazza dei Signori**, flanked by the medieval **Palazzo degli Scaligeri** – the residence of the Scaligeri. At right angles to this is the fifteenth-century **Loggia del Consiglio**, the former assembly hall of the city council and Verona's outstanding early Renaissance building, while, close by, the twelfth-century **Torre dei Lamberti** (Tues–Sun 9am–6pm; €2.07 by elevator, €1.55 on foot) gives dizzying views of the city. Beyond the square, in front of the Romanesque church of Santa Maria Antica, the **Arche Scaligere** are the elaborate Gothic funerary monuments of Verona's first family, in a wrought-iron palisade decorated with ladder motifs, the emblem of the Scaligeri. Mastino I ("Mastiff"), founder of the dynasty, is buried in the simple tomb against the wall of the church; Mastino II is to the left of the entrance, opposite the most florid of the tombs, that of **Cansignorio** ("Top Dog"); while over the side entrance of the church is an equestrian statue of **Cangrande I** ("Big Dog") – a copy of the original now in Verona's Castelvecchio. Towards the river from here is the church of **Sant'Anastasia** (Tues–Sat 9/10am–6/4pm, Sun 1–5/6pm; €2, €5 combined ticket for all Verona churches), a mainly Gothic church, completed in the late fifteenth century, with Pisanello's delicately coloured fresco of *St George and the Princess* in the sacristy. Verona's **Duomo** (Tues–Sat 10am–5.30pm, Sun 1.30–5.30pm; €1.03) lies just around the river's bend, a mixture of Romanesque and Gothic styles that houses an *Assumption* by Titian in an architectural frame by Sansovino, who also designed the choir.

In the opposite direction, off Piazza delle Erbe at Via Cappello 23, is the **Casa di Giulietta**, a well-preserved fourteenth-century structure, though there's no connection between this house and the historical character to whom Shakespeare's Juliet is distantly related (Tues–Sun 9am–7pm; €3.10). South of here, on the junction of Via Diaz and Corso Porta Borsari, the **Porta dei Borsari** is a fine Roman monument, with an inscription that dates it to 265 AD, though it's almost certainly older than that. Some way down Corso Cavour from here, the Arco dei Gavi is a first-century Roman triumphal arch, beyond which the **Castelvecchio** (Tues–Sun 8am–7pm; €3.10, free on first Sun of the month) houses a collection of paintings, jewellery and weapons, as well as the equestrian figure of Cangrande I.

A kilometre or so northwest of here, the **Basilica di San Zeno Maggiore** (€2) is one of the most significant Romanesque churches in northern Italy, put up in the first half of the twelfth century. Its rose window, representing the Wheel of Fortune, dates from then, as does the magnificent portal, whose lintels bear sculptures representing the months, while the door has bronze panels depicting scenes from the Bible and the miracles of San Zeno. The simple interior is covered with frescoes, but the most compulsive image is the altar's luminous *Madonna and saints* by Mantegna.

Practicalities

The **train station** is twenty minutes outside the city centre, connected with Piazza Brà by a #11, #12, #13 or #14 bus. There's a **tourist office** at the train station (Mon–Sat 8/9am–6/7.30pm, Sun 9am–noon; winter closed Sun; ☎045.800.0861, ⓦwww.tourism.verona.it) and at the Cortile del Tribunale, close to the Arche Scaligere (Tues–Sun 10am–7pm). Of **hotels**, the *Al Castello*, Corso Cavour 43 (☎045.800.4403; ❻), has recently refurbished rooms, *Catullo*, Via Catullo 1 (☎045.800.2786; ❸), is in a central position just off Via Mazzini. Verona's **HI hostel** is at Via Fontana del Ferro 15 (☎045.590.360; ❷), on the north side of the river behind the Teatro Romano (bus #73 or #90), close to which there's a pleasant summer campsite. There's also the *Casa della Giovane*, Via Pigna 7 (☎045.596.880; ❷), in the old centre, for women only.

Among **eating** options, *Alla Costa*, Via della Costa 2, serves good pizzas, as does *Pizzeria Arena*, Vicolo Tre Marchetti 1; *Pero d'Oro*, Via Ponte Pignolo 25, serves inexpensive but genuine Veronese dishes. For evening **drinks**, the ultra-friendly, but pricey, *Bottega del Vino* in Vicolo Scudo di Francia, just off the north end of Via Mazzini, is an old bar with a selection of wines from all over Italy. For a less touristy ambience, try *Al Carro Armato*, Vicolo Gatto 2a, or *Osteria Al Duomo*, Via Duomo 7a.

Trieste

Backed by a white limestone plateau and facing the blue Adriatic, **TRIESTE** is in a potentially idyllic setting – get close up, however, and you see that a lot of the place is run-down, and the water uninviting, which is why most visitors pass straight through. The city itself is a strange place, its massive Neoclassical architecture dating from the time when it was the Habsburg Empire's southern port. It has long been a city of political extremes. Yugoslavia and the Allies fought over it until 1954, when the city and a connecting strip of coast were secured for Italy. The neo-Fascist MSI party has always done well here, and there's even a local anti-Slav party, Lista per Trieste. The city was also home to the writers James Joyce and Italo Svevo.

The social centre of Trieste is the huge **Piazza dell'Unità d'Italia**, opening onto the harbour and flanked by the vast bulks of the **Palazzo del Comune** and **Palazzo di Governo**. The focal point of the city's history is the hill of San Giusto, with its castle and cathedral, accessible on bus #24. The **Castello** (Tues–Sun 9am–sunset; €1.55 with museum) is a fifteenth-century Venetian fortress, built near the site of the Roman forum, whose ramparts are worth a walk and whose museum (Tues–Sun 9am–1pm) houses a collection of antique weaponry. The **Cattedrale di San Giusto** (daily 8am–noon & 3.30–7.30pm) is a typically Triestine synthesis of styles, with a predominantly Romanesque facade including five Roman columns and a Gothic rose window. Inside, between Byzantine pillars, there are fine thirteenth-century frescoes of St Justus, a Christian martyr killed during the persecutions of Diocletian. More disturbingly, on the southern side of the city, the **Risiera di San Sabba** at Rattodella Pileria 43 (Tues–Sun 9am–1pm; April & May till 7pm; free), on the #10 bus route, was one of Italy's two concentration camps. A permanent exhibition serves as a reminder of Fascist crimes in the region.

Practicalities

The central **train station** is on Piazza Libertà, on the northern edge of the city centre. There's a tourist information desk here, but the main **tourist office** is at Piazza Unita D'Italia 4b (Mon–Sat 9am–7pm, Sun 10am–1pm & 4–7pm; ☎040.347.8312, ⊛www.triestetourism.it). There are many reasonable **hotels**, nicest of which are the *Centro*, Via Roma 13 (☎040.371.116; ❸), the *Blaue Krone*, Via XXX Ottobre 12 (☎040.631.882; ❸), and the *Istria*, Via Timeus 5 (☎040 371343; ❹). The **HI hostel** is 8km out of the city at Viale Miramare 331 (☎040.224.102; ❷) – take bus #6 from the tourist office, then bus #36. The nearest **campsite** is in nearby Obelisco, on the #4 bus route.

For **snacks** and light meals, *Pepi Sciavo* in Via Cassa di Risparmio is a favourite student lunch-stop, with excellent sausages and sauerkraut. Another student hangout is *Notorious* in Via del Bosco – sandwiches and salads on the ground floor and a good cheap trattoria on the first floor. Decent pizzas can be had at *Il Barattolo* in Piazza Sant'Antonio Nuovo. For more substantial food, try the excellent *Da Giovanni*, at Via Lazzaro 14, or the popular *Galleria Fabris* at Piazza Dalmazia 4 which serves cheap pizzas and fish. The city's favourite **café** is the *Caffè San Marco*, which has occupied its premises on Via G. Battisti for some eighty years. The *Caffè Tommaseo* on Piazza Tommaseo was a rendezvous for Italian nationalists in the last century and although refurbished still makes a pleasant, if pricey refuge in the summer heat. The *Caffè Walter* at Via San Niccolo 31 has *fin-de-siècle* decor and free nibbles in the afternoon, while among the bars, *Public House* at Via San Lazzaro 9, and *Osteria de Libero*, Via Risorta 8, are both atmospheric places.

Bologna

The capital of Emilia-Romagna, **BOLOGNA** is the oldest University town in Europe and teems with students and bookshops. Up until the last elections, when it fell to the right, "Red Bologna" had been the Italian Communist Party's stronghold and spiritual home since World War II. It also boasts some of the richest food in

Italy. The city centre is still startlingly medieval in plan, and has enough curiosities to warrant several days' exploration. Bologna, though, is really enjoyable just for itself, with a busy cultural life and a café and bar scene that is one of the most convivial in northern Italy.

Arrival, information and accommodation

Bologna's **airport** is northwest of the centre, linked to the train station on Piazza delle Medaglie d'Oro, at the end of Via dell'Indipendenza, by Airbus (€3.60). There are **tourist information** booths at the airport (Mon–Sat 8am–8pm, Sun 9am–3pm) and at the train station (Mon–Sat 9am–7pm, Sun 8.30am–2.30pm), and a main office at Piazza Maggiore 6 (Mon–Sat 8.30am–7pm, Sun 8.30am–2.30pm); for telephone enquiries, there's a call centre with a hotel-booking facility (☎051.24.6541, ⊛www.comune.bologna.it).

In terms of **places to stay**, Bologna is not geared up for tourists, least of all for those travelling on a tight budget, and the trade fairs during high season make booking ahead imperative. The least expensive place to stay is the official **HI hostel**, *Due Torri*, 6km outside the centre of town at Via Viadagola 5 (☎051.501.810; ❷; curfew midnight); take bus #93 from Via Irnerio. Among the few affordable **hotels** are the centrally positioned *Garisenda*, Via Rizzoli 9, Galleria del Leone 1 (☎051.224.369; ❹), *Minerva*, Via De Monari 3 (☎051.239.652; ❸), and the *Panorama*, Via Livraghi 1 (☎051.221.802; ❸). More expensive is the *Accademia*, nicely situated at Via Belli Arti 6 (☎051.232.318; ❹). For **camping**, the *Camping Hotel and Residence*, Via Romita 12/4a (☎051.325.016, ⊛www.hotelcamping.com), near the exhibition centre, has a swimming pool.

The City

Bologna's city centre is quite compact, and the buzzing **Piazza Maggiore** is the obvious place to make for first. On its western side, the **Palazzo Comunale** has two galleries: the **Museo Morandi** and the **Collezioni Comunali D'Arte** (Tues–Sun 10am–6pm; €4), while on the square's south side, the church of **San Petronio** is the city's largest, intended originally to have been larger than St Peter's in Rome, and one of the finest Gothic brick buildings in Italy. You can see the beginnings of the planned side aisle on the left of the building and there are models of what the church was supposed to look like in the **museum** (10am–12.30pm, closed Tues); otherwise the most intriguing features are a beautiful carving of *Madonna and Child* by Jacopo della Quercia, above the central portal, and an astronomical clock – a long brass meridian line set at an angle across the floor, with a hole left in the roof for the sun to shine through on the right spot. The adjacent **Piazza Nettuno** has an extravagant statue of Neptune that was fashioned by Giambologna in 1566.

Across Via dell'Archiginnasio from here, and down the street, Bologna's university – the **Archiginnasio** – was founded at more or less the same time as the Piazza Maggiore was laid out, predating the rest of Europe's universities, though it didn't get a special building until 1565. The most interesting part is the recently renovated **Teatro Anatomico** (Mon–Sat 9am–1pm; free), the original medical faculty dissection theatre, whose tiers of seats surround an extraordinary professor's chair, covered with a canopy supported by figures known as *gli spellati* – the skinned ones. South, down Via Garibaldi, Piazza San Domenico, with its strange canopied tombs holding the bones of medieval law scholars, is the site of the church of **San Domenico**, built in 1251 to house the relics of St Dominic. The bones rest in the *Arca di San Domenico*, a fifteenth-century work that was principally the creation of Nicola Pisano. He and his pupils were responsible for the reliefs illustrating the saint's life; the statues on top were the work of Pisano himself; Nicola dell'Arca was responsible for the canopy; and the angel and figures of saints Proculus and Petronius were the work of a very young Michelangelo.

North of here, the eastern section of Bologna's centro storico preserves many of the older university departments, housed for the most part in large seventeenth-and eighteenth-century palaces. At Piazza di Porta Ravegnana, the **Torre degli Asinelli** (daily 9am–5/6pm; €2.60) and perilously leaning **Torre Garisenda** are together known as the *Due Torri*, the only survivors of literally hundreds of towers that were scattered across the city during the Middle Ages. From here, Via San Stefano leads down past a complex of four – originally seven – churches, collectively known as **Santo Stefano**. The striking polygonal church of San Sepolcro, reached through the church of Crocifisso, is about the most interesting: the basin in its courtyard is by tradition the one used by Pilate to wash his hands after he condemned Christ to death, while, inside, the bones of St Petronius provide a pleasingly kitsch focus, held in a tomb modelled on the Church of the Holy Sepulchre in Jerusalem. A doorway leads from here through to San Vitale e Agricola, Bologna's oldest church, built from discarded Roman fragments in the fifth century; while the fourth church, the Trinitá, lies across the courtyard.

Eating, drinking and nightlife

For **picnics**, try Mercato delle Erbe, Via Ugo Bassi 2, biggest and liveliest of the city's markets, or the small but inviting market on Via Draperie. For **snacks**, *Altero*, at Via Indipendenza 33 or Via Ugo Bassi 10, is best for pizza by the slice; *La Torinese*, under the vaults of Palazzo del Podestà in Piazza Maggiore, does daily quiches and stuffed vegetables. Of **restaurants** *Centro*, Via Indipendenza 45, and *Bassotto*, Via Ugo Bassi 8 (lunchtimes only), serve quality fast food in comfortable surroundings. *Nino's*, Via Volturno 9 (off Via dell'Indipendenza), serves inexpensive pizza and pasta; and the self-service *Lazzarini*, Via Clavature 1 (Mon–Sat 7am–8pm), is cheap but more stylish than most. For a **drink**, there are plenty of good bars on Via Pratello and in the student quarter, and plenty of late-opening *osterie* all over town that have been the mainstay of Bolognese **nightlife** for a few hundred years. *Matusel*, at Via Bertolini 2, close to the university, is a lively and noisy example, with reasonably priced full meals; *Osteria Senzanome*, Via Senzanome 42, serves good meals and has a wide choice of beers and wines; and *Marieina*, at Via San Felice 137, close to the city gate, is old and dark, with good wine and snacks. For events, the excellent English-language **listings** magazine *Talkabout* (Ⓦwww.talkabout.it) has details of what's on.

Ferrara

Ferrara is one of the first planned Renaissance towns in Europe, and it is Italy's bicycle city, with more bikes per head than any other town. It also has the longest stretch of intact city walls in Italy (9.5km). A republic, it was controlled by the noble Este family for over 500 years. The Este were active patrons of the arts, including artists such as Pisanello and Titian, and the poet Ariosto. Their most impressive legacy, however, is the sixteenth century redesign commissioned from the architect and town planner Biagio Rossetti – who built the straight new roads of Corso Biagio Rossetti and Corso Ercole I d'Este – as well as the famous Palazzo dei Diamanti. After the Este family line failed, the town fell into a sharp decline, and by the eighteenth century it was a ghost town. The town – these days known for its annual **palio**, a horse race held in May (Ⓦwww.paliodiferrara.it) – was once renowned for its fragrant gardens, from the orange grove within the castle (still there), to the trees and fountains along the defensive town walls (long gone).

Starting in Ferrara's main square, the magisterial **Castello d'Estense** (9.30am–5pm, closed Mon; €4.10; €1 supplement to visit Torre dei Leoni) rises from a toy-town moat. In 1385 Duke Niccolo II knocked down the homes and workshops of the old Borgo to build this fortress to protect the Este family from the people. Inside the dungeons the barely legible testimonies of prisoners can just be seen, scratched on the walls or written on the ceiling in candle smoke. In 1425 the prison briefly held the ill-fated lovers Ugo and Parisina, the son and 20-year old wife of Marquis Niccolo III, who were later beheaded.

A short walk down the Corso Ercole I d'Este, the flower of Biagio Rossetti's work in Ferrara is the **Palazzo dei Diamanti**, at the crossroads of his two streets, the Corso Biagio Rossetti and Corso Ercole I d'Este. The stone building is ridged with pyramid-shaped blocks. Inside it is frescoed and contains four museums; of the permanent collections, the **Pinacoteca Nazionale** (Tues–Sun 9am–1/2pm, Thurs till 7pm; €4) is of the most interest, with works by Serafino da Modena, Garofalo, Dosso Dossi and Bastianino.

On the other side of the Castello is the thirteenth century **Duomo** (daily 7.30am–noon & 3.30–6.30pm). A mixture of Romanesque and Gothic styles, it has a magnificent facade with a carved portal portraying the Last Judgement, in part the work of Wiligelmus. East of here is the **Museo Ebraico** (tours Mon–Thurs & Sun 10am, 11am, noon; €4), which remembers the Jewish community that lived here until World War II – the main synagogue was destroyed by Italian Fascists in 1944. Further east is the **Palazzo Schifanoia**, Via Scandiana 23 (Tues–Sun 9am–6pm; €4.20), another renaissance palace built by the Estense, with marvellous frescoes, including a three-tiered cycle in the Salone dei Mesi, and a painted and stuccoed ceiling in the Sala dei Virtu by Domenico di Paris.

Practicalities

It's a ten-minute walk along Viale Cavour from the **train station** to the centre of Ferrara. There's a tourist information office just inside the station (daily 9am–1pm & 2–6pm), but the main **tourist office** is in the *castello* courtyard (same hours; ☏0532.209.370); there's a **bicycle rental** point next door (closed Sun; €7/day). A **Card Musei** (€12.40), available from the tourist office, gives access to most museums. Ferrara's **HI hostel** *Ostello Estense*, Corso Biagio Rossetti 24 (☏0532.204.227; ➋), is housed in an historic building with frescoed ceilings near Palazzo dei Diamanti. Among **hotels and B&Bs** try Casa degli Artisti, Via Vittoria 66 (☏0532.761.038; ➋), the *Daniela*, via Arginone 198, a twenty-minute walk west of the station (☏0532.773.104; ➍), or San Paolo, Via Baluardi 9 (☏0532.762.040; ➎). The closest **campsite**, *Estense*, is at Via Gramicia 5 (☏0532.752.396; closed Oct–April); take bus #1 from the station to Piazzale San Giovanni, and it is ten minutes' walk from there.

Ferrara is well-known for its cross-shaped bread; there are two **bakeries** on Via Garibaldi or try the historic *Forno Perdonati*, via San Romano 108, which also does good pizza. For **ice-cream**, the popular place is *Leon D'Oro*, opposite the Duomo, which does a mean almond ice. The town's historic **café**, famed for its coffee, cake and aperitifs, is *Europa*, Corso della Giovecca 51. For **meals**, try *Trattoria Volano* on via Volano, dating from the seventeenth century; *Hostaria Savonarola*, off Piazza Savonarola; *l'Osteria*, Via de Romei 51; or *L'Oca Giuliva*, Via Boccacanale di Santo Stefano – an *enoteca* that does good food. There are two atmospheric **bars** serving wine in Via Adelardi by the Duomo - *Due Gobbi* and *Al Brindisi*, much frequented by students. There's also *Enoteca*, Via Contrari 52, a very trendy bar with buzzing music and outside tables.

Parma

PARMA is about as comfortable a town as you could wish for. The measured pace of its streets, the abundance of its restaurants and the general air of provincial affluence are almost cloyingly pleasant. There is plenty to see, not least the works of two key late Renaissance artists – Correggio and Parmigianino.

Piazza Garibaldi is the fulcrum of Parma; its packed-out cafés and surrounding alleyways are home to much of the town's nightlife. The mustard-coloured **Palazzo del Governatore** flanks the square, behind which the Renaissance church of the **Madonna della Steccata** stands, apparently using Bramante's original plan for St Peter's as a model. Inside there are frescoes by a number of sixteenth-century painters, notably Parmigianino, who spent the last ten years of his life on this work, and was eventually sacked for breach of contract by the disgruntled church authorities. Five minutes' walk away, the beautiful Romanesque **Duomo**, dating from the eleventh century, holds earlier work by Parmigianino in its south transept, painted when the artist was a pupil of Correggio – one of whose most famous works, a 1534 fresco of the *Assumption*, can be seen in the central cupola. There's more by Correggio in the cupola of **San Giovanni Evangelista** behind the Duomo. You should also visit the Duomo's octagonal **Baptistry** (€2.58), considered to be Benedetto Antelami's finest work, built in 1196. Antelami sculpted the frieze that surrounds the building, and was also responsible for the reliefs inside, including a series of fourteen statues representing the months and seasons. Take the spiral staircase to the top for a closer view of the frescoes on the ceiling, by an unknown thirteenth-century artist. More Correggio frescoes can be seen in the **Camera di San Paolo** (Tues–Sun 8.30am–2pm; €2.10) of the former Benedictine convent off Via Melloni, a few minutes north.

East of the cathedral square, the **Museo Glauco-Lombardi** at Via Garibaldi 15 (Tues–Sat 10am–3pm, Sun 9am–1pm; €4) recalls later times, with a display of memorabilia relating to Marie-Louise of Austria, who reigned here after the defeat of her husband Napoleon at Waterloo. Just across Piazza Marconi from here, it's hard to miss Parma's biggest monument, the **Palazzo della Pilotta**, begun for Alessandro Farnese in the sixteenth century and rebuilt after World War II bombing to house a number of Parma's museums, notably the city's main art gallery, the **Galleria Nazionale** (Tues–Sun 9am–1.30pm; €6, includes admission to Teatro Farnese). The hi-tech display includes more work by Correggio and Parmigianino, and the remarkable *Apostles at the Sepulchre* and *Funeral of the Virgin* by Carracci – massive canvases suspended each side of a gantry at the top of the building. The **Teatro Farnese**, which you pass through to get to the gallery, was almost entirely destroyed in 1944 and has been virtually rebuilt. Up a floor, the **Museo Archeologico Nazionale** (Mon–Sun 8.30am–7.30pm; €2) is less enticing but still worth a glance, with finds from the Etruscan city of Velleia and the prehistoric lake villages around Parma.

Practicalities

Parma's **train station** is fifteen minutes' walk from the central Piazza Garibaldi, or a short ride on bus #7, #8, #9 or #10. The main **tourist office** is on Strada Melloni (Mon–Sat 9am–7pm, Sun 9am–1pm; ☎0521.218.889, ⓦwww.turismo .comune.parma.it/turismo). Finding a **place to stay** can be tricky. There's an official **HI hostel** with **campsite** at Parco Cittadella 5 (☎0521.961.434; ❷; closed Oct–March; curfew 11pm); take bus #9 or, after 8pm, #E. Among **hotels** near the station, the *Leon d'Oro* at Viale A. Fratti 4 (☎0521.773.182; ❸) has a **restaurant** attached. Good eateries include the central *Lazzaro*, Via XX Marzo 14 (☎0521 .208.944; ❹), a small *locanda*. Pizzeria Ristorante *L'Artista*, Via Bruno Longhi 3/a, does good pizzas and has friendly English-speaking owners. At **night**, a young clientele drinks at *Bottiglia Azzura*, Borgo Felino 63; another good *enoteca* is *Ombre Rosse*, vicolo Giandemaria 4; both also do food. There's an annual Verdi **festival** in May; the Teatro Regio on Via Garibaldi (☎0521.218.678) is renowned for its **opera**.

Ravenna

When **RAVENNA** became capital of the Western Roman Empire 1500 years ago, it was more by quirk of fate than design. The Emperor Honorius, alarmed by armies invading from the north, moved his court from Rome to this obscure town on the Romagna coast because it was easy to defend, surrounded by marshland, and situated close to the port of Classis – the biggest Roman naval base on the Adriatic. Honorius' anxiety proved well founded – Rome was sacked by the Goths in 410 – but Ravenna's days of glory were brief, and it, too, fell in 473. Yet the Ostrogoth king Theodoric continued to beautify the city, and it wasn't long before it was taken by the Byzantines, who were responsible for Ravenna's most glorious era – the city's mosaics are generally acknowledged to be one of the crowning achievements of Byzantine art.

The best of the mosaics are in the basilica of **San Vitale**, ten minutes northwest of the centre, a fairly typical Byzantine church, begun in 525 AD under Theodoric and finished in 548 under Justinian, which formed the basis for the great church of Aya Sofia in Constantinople fifteen years later. The mosaics are in the apse, arranged in a rigid hierarchy, with Old Testament scenes across the semicircular lunettes of the choir, Christ, the Apostles and sons of San Vitale on the arch, and, on the semidome of the apse, a beardless Christ presenting a model of the church to San Vitale and Bishop Ecclesius. On the side walls of the apse are portraits of the Emperor Justinian and his wife Theodora, Justinian's foot resting on that of his general, Belisarius, who reclaimed the city from the Goths, while Theodora looks on, her expression giving some hint of the cruelty for which she was apparently notorious.

Across from the basilica is the tiny **Mausoleo di Galla Placidia**, named after the half-sister of Honorius, who later became regent of the Western Empire and was responsible for much of the grandeur of Ravenna's early days, though it's unlikely that the building ever held her bones. Inside, the mosaics glow with a deep blue lustre, most in an earlier style than San Vitale's, full of Roman and naturalistic motifs. Stars around a golden cross spread across the vaulted ceiling, while at each end are representations of St Lawrence, with the gridiron on which he was martyred, and the Good Shepherd, with one of his flock. Adjacent to San Vitale, housed in the former cloisters of the church, the **National Museum of Antiquities** (Tues–Sun 8.30am–7pm; €4.10) contains items from this and later periods, most notably a sixth-century statue of Hercules capturing a stag, and the so-called "Veil of Classis", decorated with portraits of Veronese bishops of the eighth and ninth centuries.

There are more fine mosaics east of here, on the busy Via di Roma, in the basilica of **Sant'Apollinare Nuovo**, another sixth-century building by Theodoric. The mosaics run the length of the nave and depict ceremonial processions of martyrs bearing gifts for an enthroned Christ and Virgin through an avenue of date palms. Some of the scenery is specific to Ravenna: you can make out what used to be the harbour at nearby Classe against the city behind, out of which rises Theodoric's palace. Five minutes' walk up Via di Roma, the **Arian Baptistry**, also known as the Basilica dello Spirito Santo, has a fine mosaic ceiling showing the twelve Apostles and the baptism of Christ. Via Diaz leads from here down to Piazza del Popolo, the centre of Ravenna, a couple of minutes away from which, on Piazza Duomo, the **Museo Arcivescovile** has mosaic fragments from around the city and the sixth-century Oratorio Sant'Andrea, adorned with birds above a Christ dressed in the uniform of a Roman centurion. The **Neonian Baptistry** next door is a conversion from a Roman bath house. The original floor level has sunk into the marshy ground, and you can see the remains of the previous building 3m below.

Ravenna was also the final resting place of the exiled poet **Dante Alighieri**; he wrote the final part of the Divine Comedy, *Paradise*, here and you can visit his tomb on Via Alighieri (free).

Practicalities

Ravenna has a compact city centre, and it's only a short walk from the **train station** on Piazza Farini, along Viale Farini and Via A. Diaz, to the central Piazza del

Ravenna's sights

There is a **combined ticket** (€6) covering most of Ravenna's sights, including San Vitale, the Mausoleo di Galla Placida, Sant'Apollinare Nuovo, the Arian Baptistry, the Neonian Baptistry and the Museo Arcivescovile (when it reopens). Available from any of the participating museums, it is valid for one visit to each for a year. **Opening times** for all are daily 9am–7pm.

Popolo. The **tourist office** is at Via Salara 8/12 (daily 8.30am–4/7pm; ☎544.35.404, ⓦwww.turismo.ravenna.it). There are very few one-star **hotels**, including the *Al Giaciglio*, Via Rocca Brancaleone 42 (☎0544.39.403; ❸), which has a decent restaurant. There's an **HI hostel**, the *Ostello Dante*, at Via Aurelio Nicolodi 12 (☎0544.421.164; ❷), ten minutes' walk out of town or bus #1 from outside the station. A more central alternative is the *Residenza Galletti Abbiosi*, Via di Roma 140 (☎0544.215.127; ❸), which is run by monks, has some frescoed rooms and no curfew. Ravenna's best places to **eat** are between the Duomo and Piazza San Francesco. *Ca' De Ven*, at Via C. Ricci 24, has a large selection of Emilia-Romagnan wine and decent food. Back towards the square, on Via Mentana, *Da Renato*, and its sister restaurant next door, *Guidarello*, on Via R. Gessi, both do traditional local food. *Ristorante Scai*, Piazza Baracca 20, close to San Vitale, specializes in roast meat and game; it also serves pizzas in the evening. There are **mensas** at S. Apollinaire Nuovo and Via G. Oberdan 8.

Central Italy

The Italian heartland of **Tuscany** represents the archetypal image of the country – its walled towns and rolling, vineyard-covered hills the classic backdrops of Renaissance art. **Florence** is the first port of call in this region, from the Uffizi gallery's masterpieces to the great fresco cycles in the churches and the wealth of Florentine sculpture in the city's museums. **Siena** is one of the great medieval cities of Europe, it's also the scene of Tuscany's one unmissable festival – the **Palio** – which sees bareback horse riders careering around the cobbled central square. The other major cities, **Pisa** and **Lucca**, both have medieval splendours – Pisa its Leaning Tower and cathedral ensemble, Lucca a string of Romanesque churches – and there are, of course, the smaller hill towns, of which **San Gimignano**, the "city of the towers", is the best known. The provincial capital of the upper Arno region, **Arezzo**, an hour's train ride from Florence, is also worth a stop, if only for its marvellous series of paintings by Piero della Francesca, while to the east lies **Umbria**, a beautiful region of rolling hills, woods and valleys – not unlike Tuscany but as yet less discovered. Most visitors head for the capital, **Perugia**, for **Assisi** – with its extraordinary frescoes by Giotto in the Basilica di San Francesco – or **Orvieto**, where the Duomo is one of the greatest Gothic buildings in the country, though lesser-known places like **Gubbio**, ranked as the most perfect medieval centre in Italy, and **Spoleto**, for many the outstanding Umbrian town, are worth taking in, too. Further east still, the **Marche** repeats much the same sort of pleasures, the town of **Urbino** in the north of the region, with its superb Renaissance ducal palace, providing a deserved highlight.

ANCONA is the mid-Adriatic's **largest port**. A bland, modern place, rebuilt after the war, it has little to distract you in itself, but is useful for connections to Greece and Croatia. Regular buses run along the seafront from the train station to the port. The main **tourist office** is at Via Thaon de Revel 4 (Mon–Fri 9am–1pm & 3–6pm, Sat 9am–1pm & 3–6pm, Sun 9am–1pm; ☎071.358.991, ⓦwww.marcheturismo.it).

Florence

Ever since the nineteenth-century revival of interest in the art of the Renaissance, **FLORENCE** has been a shrine to the cult of the beautiful. It is a city of incomparable indoor pleasures, its chapels, galleries and museums an inexhaustible treasure, embodying the complex, exhilarating and often elusive spirit of the Renaissance more fully than any other place in the country. The city became the centre of artistic patronage in Italy under the Medici family, who made their fortune in banking and ruled Florence as an independent state for three centuries, most auspiciously

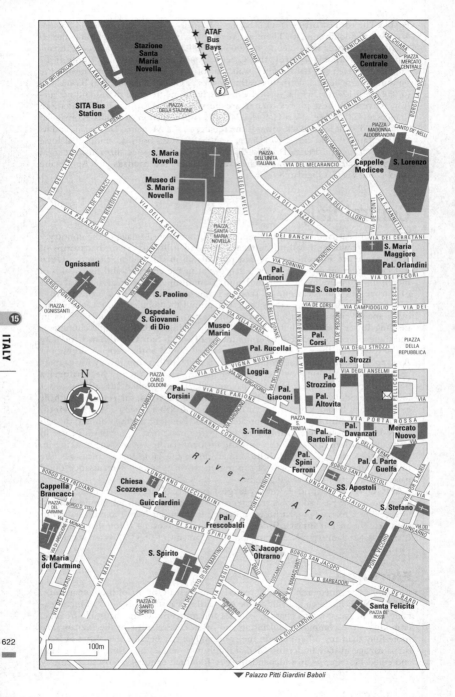

▼ Palazzo Pitti Giardini Baboli

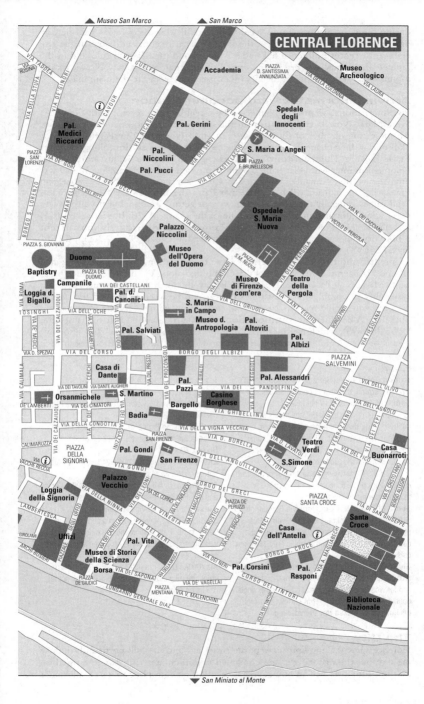

CENTRAL FLORENCE

Accademia

Museo Archeologico

Pal. Medici Riccardi

Pal. Gerini

Spedale degli Innocenti

PIAZZA D. SANTISSIMA ANNUNZIATA

Pal. Niccolini

Pal. Pucci

S. Maria d. Angeli

PIAZZA F. BRUNELLESCHI

PIAZZA SAN LORENZO

Ospedale S. Maria Nuova

Palazzo Niccolini

PIAZZA S. GIOVANNI

Duomo

Baptistry

Museo dell'Opera del Duomo

PIAZZA DEL DUOMO

PIAZZA SM NUOVA

Teatro della Pergola

Campanile

Loggia d. Bigallo

Pal. d. Canonici

Museo di Firenze com'era

S. Maria in Campo

Pal. Salviati

Museo d. Antropologia

Pal. Altoviti

Pal. Albizi

PIAZZA SALVEMINI

Casa di Dante

Pal. Pazzi

Pal. Alessandri

Orsanmichele

S. Martino

Casino Borghese

Badia

Bargello

Pal. Gondi

San Firenze

Teatro Verdi

S.Simone

PIAZZA DELLA SIGNORIA

Casa Buonarroti

Palazzo Vecchio

Loggia della Signoria

PIAZZA DE' PERUZZI

PIAZZA SANTA CROCE

Santa Croce

Uffizi

Casa dell'Antella

Pal. Vita

Museo di Storia della Scienza

Borsa

Pal. Corsini

Pal. Rasponi

PIAZZA DE'GIUDICI

PIAZZA MENTANA

LUNGARNO GENERALE DIAZ

Biblioteca Nazionale

15

ITALY

623

during the years of Lorenzo de' Medici, tagged "Il Magnifico", who held fiercely onto Florentine independence in the face of papal resentment. Later, in the late eighteenth century, Florence fell under Austrian and then French rule, and in the nineteenth century was briefly the capital of the kingdom of Italy. Nowadays the monuments and paintings of the city's Renaissance heyday are the main draw.

Arrival, information and accommodation

Pisa international **airport** is connected by a regular train service with Florence's Santa Maria Novella **train station** in the city centre; the journey takes an hour. An increasing number of flights now come into Florence's tiny Perètola airport, 5km out of the city and connected by bus to the main **bus station**, alongside Santa Maria Novella. The main **tourist offices** are at Via Cavour 7r, just north of the Duomo (summer Mon–Sat 9am–6.30pm, Sun 9am–1pm; ☏055.290.832, ⊛www .firenze.turismo.toscana.it), at Borgo San Croce 29r, near Piazza Santa Croce, and Piazza della Stazione. All have free maps and the useful *City Guide* booklet. **Walking** is generally the most efficient way of getting around, but if you want to cover a long distance in a hurry, take one of the orange ATAF **buses**; tickets (€1) are valid for one hour and can be bought from tabacchi. Alternatively, you can **rent a bike** from Florence by Bike at Via San Zanobi 120R (daily 9am–7.30pm; €2.50/ hr, €12/day).

Florence's most affordable **hotels** are close to the station, in particular along and around Via Faenza and the parallel Via Fiume, and along Via della Scala and Piazza Santa Maria Novella; you could also try Via Cavour, north of the Duomo. However, availability is a problem at most times of year, and between Easter and the start of October you should really book in advance. If you need help, try the Informazioni Turistiche Alberghiere **accommodation office** at the station (daily 8.45am–8pm; ☏055.282.893), which can make last-minute reservations for a fee. They also have details of the emergency **camping area** provided by the city authorities in high season.

Hostels

Istituto Gould Via dei Serragli 49 ☏055.212.576. Over in Oltrarno. It's wise to book in advance. **❸**

Ostello Villa Camerata Viale Righi 2 ☏055.601.451. The official HI hostel lies in a beautiful park, thirty minutes out of town on bus #17 from the train station. Doors open at 1pm; phone ahead. **❷**

Santa Monaca Via Santa Monaca 6 ☏055.268.338, ⊛www.ostello.it. In Oltrarno; 1am curfew. Very popular hostel in a converted fifteenth-century convent. **❷**

Suore Oblate dell'Assunzione Via Borgo Pinti 15 ☏055.248.0582. Not far from the Duomo, this place is run by missionaries. Use of kitchen and common room. Singles and doubles only. Midnight curfew. **❹**

Suore Oblate dello Spirito Santo Via Nazionale 8 ☏055.239.8202. A few steps from the station, and for women only. Very clean and pleasant; single, double and triple rooms; 11pm curfew; two-night minimum stay. Closed Nov to mid-June. **❸**

Hotels

Azzi/Locanda degli Artisti Via Faenza 56 ☏055.213.806. Probably the most pleasant of six reasonably priced *pensioni* on the upper floors of this building. **❹**

Brunetta Borgo Pinti 5 ☏055.247.8134. Friendly place in the historic centre, just east of the Duomo. **❺**

Elite Via della Scala 12 ☏055.215.395. Two-star hotel near Santa Maria Novella. **❹**

Firenze Piazza dei Donati 4 ☏055.214203. Clean and comfortable en-suite rooms. No credit cards. **❺**

Kursaal e Ausonia Via Nazionale 24 ☏055.496.547, ⊛www.kursonia.com. Halfway between the train station and the market, this welcoming place has some en suites and internet access. **❺**

Maxim Via Dei Calzaiuoli 11 ☏055.217.474. A small, friendly one-star hotel near Duomo, some rooms en suite. **❺**

The City

Florence sprawls along both sides of the Arno and into the hills north and south of the city, but the major sights are contained within an area that can be crossed on foot in a little over half an hour. Perhaps the most obvious place to start exploring is the **Piazza della Signoria**, fringed on one side by the graceful late-fourteenth-century **Loggia della Signoria** and dotted with statuary, most famously a copy of Michelangelo's *David*. The square is dominated by the colossal **Palazzo Vecchio**, Florence's fortress-like town hall (Mon–Sun 9am–7/11pm, Thurs closes 2pm; €5.70), begun in the last year of the thirteenth century as the home of the *Signoria*, the highest tier of the city's republican government. The Medici were only in residence here for nine years, but left their mark – notably Cosimo I's relentless eulogies to his family in the state rooms. The huge Salone dei Cinquecento, built at the end of the fifteenth century, is full of heroic murals by Vasari, though it is redeemed by the presence of Michelangelo's *Victory*, facing the entrance door, originally sculpted for Pope Julius II's tomb but donated to the Medici by the artist's nephew. The bizarre Studiolo di Francesco I was also created by Vasari, and decorated by several of Florence's prominent Mannerist artists as a retreat for the introverted son of Cosimo.

Immediately south of the piazza, the **Galleria degli Uffizi** (Tues–Sun 8.30am–6.50pm; summer Sat till 10pm; advisable to book ☎055.294.883; €6.50) is the greatest picture gallery in Italy, with a collection of masterpieces that is impossible to take in on a single visit. There are works from the early Renaissance, including three altarpieces of the *Madonna Enthroned* by Cimabue, Duccio and Giotto; Uccello's *Battle of San Romano* – demonstrating the artist's obsessional interest in perspectival effects – which once hung in Lorenzo il Magnifico's bed chamber; and plentiful works by Filippo Lippi, his *Madonna and Child with Two Angels* one of the best-known Renaissance images of the Madonna. Close by, there's a fine *Madonna* by Botticelli, who in the next room is represented by some of his most famous works, notably *Primavera* and the *Birth of Venus*; look also at the huge *Portinari Altarpiece* by Botticelli's Flemish contemporary Hugo van der Goes, a work whose naturalism greatly influenced the artists of Florence. The Uffizi doesn't own a finished painting that's entirely by Leonardo da Vinci, but there's a celebrated *Annunciation* that's mainly by him and the angel in profile that he painted in Verrocchio's *Baptism*. Room 18, the octagonal Tribuna, houses the most important of the Medici sculptures, first among which is the *Medici Venus*, along with some chillingly precise portraits by Bronzino and Vasari's portrait of Lorenzo il Magnifico, painted long after the death of its subject. Michelangelo's *Doni Tondo* is his only completed easel painting, its contorted gestures and virulent colours studied and imitated by the Mannerist painters of the sixteenth century. Separating the two Mannerist groups are a number of compositions by Raphael and Titian, while later rooms include some large works by Rubens, Van Dyck, Caravaggio and Rembrandt.

To get a comprehensive idea of the Renaissance achievement in Florence, you need to visit the **Museo Nazionale del Bargello**, just north in Via del Proconsolo (Tues–Sat 8.15am–1.50pm; €4). The first part of the collection focuses on Michelangelo. Beyond, the more flamboyant art of Cellini and Giambologna is exhibited, including Giambologna's best-known creation, the nimble figure of *Mercury*. Out in the courtyard, at the top of its external staircase, the first-floor loggia has been turned into an aviary for Giambologna's bronze birds, imported from the Medici villa at Castello, while a nearby room displays work by Donatello. His sexually ambiguous bronze *David*, the first freestanding nude figure since classical times, was cast in the early 1430s. Upstairs, the Sala dei Bronzetti has Italy's best assembly of small Renaissance bronzes, with plentiful evidence of Giambologna's virtuosity, and a further room holds Renaissance portrait busts.

Parallel to Via del Proconsolo on the opposite side of Piazza della Signoria is **Via dei Calzaiuoli**, one of the city's more animated streets and home to the church of **Orsanmichele** (closed first and last Mon of the month), whose exterior is decorated by a number of early Renaissance sculptures, including a *John the Baptist* by Ghiberti, the first life-size bronze statue of the Renaissance. The streets west of the Signoria retain a medieval character. About 500m northwest, off Via della Scala, the partly Gothic church of **Santa Maria Novella** (Mon–Thurs 9.30am–5pm, Fri–Sun 1–5pm; €2.58) is home to Masaccio's extraordinary fresco of *The Trinity*, one of the earliest works in which perspective and classical proportion were rigorously employed. The church's **cloisters** are richly decorated with frescoes by Uccello and his workshop.

The Duomo and around

North of the Signoria, the **Duomo** (Mon–Sat 8.30am–7.30pm) was built between the late thirteenth and mid-fifteenth centuries to an ambitious design, originally the brainchild of Arnolfo di Cambio and realized finally by Filippo Brunelleschi, who completed the majestic dome – the largest in existence until this century. The fourth largest church in the world, its ambience is more that of a great assembly hall than of a devotional building, its most conspicuous pieces of decoration two memorials to *condottieri* – Uccello's monument to Sir John Hawkwood, painted in 1436, and Castagno's monument to Niccolò da Tolentino, created twenty years later – and seven stained-glass roundels designed by Uccello, Ghiberti, Castagno and Donatello, best inspected from a gallery that forms part of the route to the top of the dome (€6). The views at the very top are as stupendous as you would expect.

Next door to the Duomo, the **Campanile** (daily 8.30am–7.30pm; €6) was begun in 1334 by Giotto and continued after his death by Andrea Pisano and Francesco Talenti. The only part of the tower built exactly as Giotto designed it is the lower storey, studded with two rows of remarkable bas-reliefs, the lower one illustrating the *Creation of Man and the Arts and Industries* carved by Pisano. The figures of *Prophets and Sibyls* in the second-storey niches are by Donatello and others. Opposite, the **Baptistry** (Mon–Sat noon–6.30pm; Sun 8.30am–2pm; €3), generally thought to date from the sixth or seventh century, is the oldest building in the city. Its most famous embellishments, the gilded bronze doors, were cast in the early fifteenth century by Lorenzo Ghiberti, and were described by Michelangelo as "so beautiful they are worthy to be the gates of Paradise". They're a primer of early Renaissance art, innovatively using perspective, gesture and sophisticated grouping of subjects to convey the human drama of each scene. Ghiberti included a self-portrait in the frame of the left-hand door – his is the fourth head from the top of the right-hand band. Inside, the Baptistry is equally stunning, with a thirteenth-century mosaic floor and ceiling and the tomb of Pope John XXIII, draped by a superb marble canopy, the work of Donatello and his pupil Michelozzo.

Since the early fifteenth century the maintenance of the Duomo has been supervised from the building at Piazza del Duomo 9, nowadays housing the **Museo dell'Opera del Duomo** (Mon–Sat 9am–7.30pm, Sun 9am–2pm; €6), the repository of the most precious and fragile works of art from the buildings around, including Brunelleschi's death mask; models of the dome and a variety of tools and machines devised by the architect; Michelangelo's anguished late *Pietà*; Pisano's bas-reliefs and Donatello's figures for the campanile; and four of Ghiberti's door panels from the Baptistry.

North of the Duomo

The church of **San Lorenzo**, north of the Baptistry, has good claim to be the oldest church in Florence, and for the best part of three hundred years was the city's cathedral. Rebuilt by Brunelleschi in the mid-fifteenth century, the interior is a fine example of early Renaissance church design. Inside are two bronze pulpits by Donatello, while further pieces by him adorn Brunelleschi's neighbouring Sagrestia Vecchia – principally the two pairs of bronze doors, the large reliefs of *SS Cosmas and Damian* and *SS Lawrence and Stephen*. At the top of the left aisle and through the cloisters, the **Biblioteca Medicea-Laurenziana** (Mon–Sat 9am–1pm; free) was designed by Michelangelo in 1524; its most startling feature is the vestibule, a room almost filled by a flight of steps resembling a solidified lava flow. Michelangelo's most celebrated contribution to the San Lorenzo buildings, however, is the Sagrestia Nuova, part of the **Cappelle Medicee** (Tues–Sun 8.15am–5pm; €6), which contains the fabulous Medici tombs, carved between 1524 and 1533. To the left is the tomb of Lorenzo, duke of Urbino, the grandson of Lorenzo il Magnifico, bearing figures of *Dawn and Dusk* to sum up his contemplative nature. Opposite is the tomb of Lorenzo il Magnifico's youngest son, Giuliano, his supposedly more active character symbolized by *Day and Night*.

Just east of here, the **Galleria dell'Accademia** (Tues–Sun 8.15am–6.50pm; summer Sat till 10pm; €6.50) was Europe's first school of drawing. Its collection of paintings is impressive, but most people come to view the sculpture of Michelangelo, specifically his **David**. Finished in 1504, when Michelangelo was just 29, and carved from a gigantic block of marble, it's an incomparable show of technical bravura. The gallery also houses his remarkable unfinished *Slaves*.

The Santa Croce district

Down by the river, the church of **Santa Croce** (Mon–Sat 9.30am–noon & 3–5.30pm, Sun 3–5.30pm), was begun in 1294, possibly by the architect of the Duomo, Arnolfo di Cambio, and is full of tombstones and commemorative monuments, including Vasari's monument to Michelangelo, and, on the opposite side of the church, the tomb of Galileo, built in 1737 when it was finally agreed to give the great scientist a Christian burial. Most visitors, however, come to see the frescoes by Giotto in the Cappella Peruzzi and the Cappella Bardi (on the right of the chancel), which shows scenes from the lives of St John the Baptist and St John the Evangelist. The **Museo dell'Opera di Santa Croce**, off the first cloister (10am–5pm, closed Wed; €4.13), houses a miscellany of works of art, the best of which are Cimabue's flood-damaged *Crucifixion* and Donatello's enormous gilded *St Louis of Toulouse*. Also visit Brunelleschi's **Cappella dei Pazzi**, at the end of the first cloister, designed in the 1430s and completed in the 1470s, several years after the architect's death, with decorations by Luca della Robbia.

Oltrarno and San Miniato

The thirteenth-century **Ponte Vecchio**, loaded with jewellers' shops, which overhang the water, leads from the city centre across the river to the district of **Oltrarno**, dominated by the massive bulk of the **Palazzo Pitti**. Nowadays the fifteenth-century palace and its sumptuous garden – the Giardino di Bóboli – contain six separate museums. The **Galleria Palatina** (Tues–Sun 8.15am–6.50pm; summer Sat till 10pm; €8.50) has superb displays of the art of Raphael and Titian, including a number of Titian's most trenchant portraits. Much of the rest of the first floor comprises the **Appartamenti Monumentali** (included in the Galleria Palatina ticket), the Pitti's state rooms, while on the floor above, the **Galleria d'Arte Moderna** (Tues–Sat 8.15am–2pm; €5) is a chronological survey of primarily Tuscan art from the mid-eighteenth century to 1945. The Pitti's enormous formal garden, the **Giardino di Bóboli** (Tues–Sun 8.15am–4.30/7.30pm; €2), is full of Mannerist embellishments, including the Grotta del Buontalenti; among its fake stalactites are shepherds and sheep and replicas of Michelangelo's *Slaves*, replacing the originals that were here until 1908. In the eastern corner of the gardens is **Forte di Belvedere** (same times; free), a star-shaped fortress built in 1590, which can only be entered through Porta San Giorgio at the top of the hill.

About 500m northwest of the Palazzo Pitti, the church of **Santa Maria del Carmine** is visited for the frescoes of Filippino Lippi in its Cappella Brancacci (Mon & Wed–Sat 10am–5pm, Sun 1–5pm; €3.10) by Masaccio – recently, and controversially, restored. In the opposite direction, the multicoloured facade of **San Miniato al Monte** (daily 8am–12.30pm & 2.30–7.30pm) lures troops of visitors up the hill. The interior is like no other in the city, and its general form has changed little since the mid-eleventh century. In the lower part of the church, don't overlook the intricately patterned panels of the pavement, from 1207, and the tabernacle between the choir stairs, designed in 1448 by Michelozzo.

Eating and drinking

The best place to find **picnic food** and **snacks** is the **Mercato Centrale**, just east of the train station, which also has bars charging prices lower than elsewhere in the city. There are also plenty of city-centre **bars**, along Via de' Panzani, Via de' Cerretani, Via Por Santa Maria and Via Guicciardini, whose snacky food offers ample compensation for their lack of character. Otherwise, try a **vinaio**, a wine cellar/snack bar that serves *crostini* and other snacks. The *vinaio I Fratellini* at Via Cimatori 38 is a perfect example, as is *Lo Skipper* at Via Alfani 70, in the university area. For classier snacks, try the *panini* and pasta at *Fiaschetteria Balducci*, Via de' Neri 17, or the similar fare at *Fiaschetteria da Il Latini*, Via del Palchetti 6r, behind Palazzo Rucellai. Another Florentine speciality is the **friggitoria**, serving polenta, potatoes and apple croquettes – try the one at Via Sant'Antonino 50, which also sells pizza, or *Antico Noé* at Volta di San Piero 6, which does burgers and salads and has a restaurant next door. For ice cream, leader of the pack is *Vivoli*, near Santa Croce at Via Isola delle Stinche 7r (closed Mon).

Restaurants

Benvenuto Via Mosca 16/5, off Via de' Neri. Looks more like a delicatessen than a trattoria from the street; the *gnocchi* and *arista* are delicious.

Dante Piazza Nazario Sauro 10r. Friendly pizzeria with a dozen types of spaghetti on the menu too.

Da Mario Via Rosina 2r. Popular with students and market workers – be prepared to queue and share a table. Closed evenings.

Palle d'Oro Via Sant'Antonio 45r. Station area eatery that's halfway between a *rosticceria* and a trattoria. Also does sandwiches to take away.

Trattoria Borgo Antico Piazza Santo Spirito 6r. Busy trattoria on a quiet Oltrarno square, with excellent seafood, home-made pasta and tables outside in summer.

Trattoria Casalinga Via Michelozzi 9r. Oltrarno restaurant, off Via Maggio, that offers just about the best low-cost authentic Tuscan dishes in town. Always crowded.

Za-Za Piazza del Mercato Centrale 26r. A few tables on ground level, but a bigger canteen below.

Nightlife and festivals

For late **at night**, *Dolce Vita*, on Piazza del Carmine, is a trendy hangout that also stages small-scale art exhibitions. *Porfirio Rubirosa*, Viale Strozzi 38r, is where the *bella gente* drop in before heading for a late dinner or disco. In the Santa Croce district, *Rex*, Via Fiesolana 25r, has good music, a varied clientele, and serves snacks and cocktails, while in Oltrarno, *Zoe* on Via dei Renail 13/R is a posey but atmospheric cocktail bar. *Tenax*, on Via Pratese 47, is the city's biggest disco and one of its leading venues for new and established bands. *Yab Yum*, Via de' Sassetti 5r, is a city-centre disco playing the best of new dance music; and *Space Electronic*, Via Palazzuolo 37, is the favourite disco of young foreigners, open nightly. For information on what's on, call in at Box Office, Via Alamanni 39 (☎055.210.804), or consult the listings magazines *Firenze Spettacolo* and *Informa Città*.

As for **festivals**, in May music lovers may want to catch the *Maggio Musicale* festival (⊛www.maggiofiorentino.com), and the *Festa di San Giovanni* on 24th June, Florence's saint's day, sees a massive fireworks display.

Listings

Consulates UK, Lungarno Corsini 2 ☎055.284.133; US, Lungarno Vespucci 38 ☎055.239.8276.

Exchange Esercizio Promozione Turismo, Via Condotta 42.

Hospital Santa Maria Nuova, Piazza Santa Maria Nuova 1 ☎055.27.581. English-speaking doctors on 24-hour call at the Tourist Medical Service, Via Lorenzo il Magnifico 59 ☎055.475.411.

Internet access Internet Train, Via Guelfa 24a, Via dell'Oriuolo 40r, Borgo San Jacopo 30r.

Laundry Onda Blu, Via degli Alfani 24r; Wash & Dry, Via della Scala 52–54r.

Pharmacies All-night pharmacy at the train station; Molteni, Via dei Calzaiuoli 7r; All' Insegna del Moro, Piazza San Giovanni 20r.

Police Via Zara 2 ☎055.49.771.

Post office Via Pellicceria 3.

Fiesole

A long-established Florentine retreat from the summer heat and crowds, **FIESOLE** spreads over a cluster of hilltops some 8km northeast of Florence. The #7 ATAF bus runs there from Florence's train station to Piazza Mino (every 15min; journey time 20min). The **tourist office** is on Piazza Mino 37 (daily 8.30am–7.30pm; ☎055.597.8372). Fiesole's main square is home to the **Duomo**, in which the Cappella Salutati, right of the choir, contains two fine pieces carved by Mino da Fiesole in the mid-fifteenth century. From here, Via San Francesco leads up to a terrace which gives a remarkable panorama of Florence, just above which the church of **Sant'Alessandro**, founded in the sixth century on the site of Etruscan and Roman temples, has a beautiful basilical interior with onion marble columns. Around the back of the Duomo, in Via Marini, is the entrance to the **Teatro Romano** and **Museo Archeologico** (daily 9.30am–7pm; €6.20). Built in the first century BC, the 3000-seat theatre is still used for performances during the *Estate Fiesolana* festival. Most of the museum exhibits were discovered in this area, and encompass pieces from the Bronze Age to the Roman occupation. The narrow Via Vecchia Fiesolana leads from just west of the main square to the hamlet of **SAN DOMENICO**, 1500m southwest. Fra Angelico was once prior of the Dominican monastery here, and the church retains a *Madonna and Angels* by him; the chapterhouse also has a Fra Angelico fresco of *The Crucifixion*. Five minutes' walk northwest from San Domenico brings you to the **Badia Fiesolana**, formerly Fiesole's cathedral and altered by Cosimo il Vecchio in the 1460s, who left the magnificent Romanesque facade intact while transforming the interior into a superb Renaissance building.

San Gimignano

SAN GIMIGNANO – "delle Belle Torri" – is one of the best-known towns in Tuscany. Its image as a "Medieval Manhattan", with its skyline of towers, has caught the tourist imagination. From May to October, it is very busy, and to really get a feel for the place you should come out of season. If you can't, aim to spend the night here – in the evenings the town takes on a very different pace and atmosphere. It's also worth knowing that there's a **combined ticket** (€7.50) for all the town's civic **museums**, available at any of the participating sites.

Founded around the eighth century, San Gimignano was a force to be reckoned with in the Middle Ages, with a population of fifteen thousand (twice the present number). Nowadays it's not much more than a village: you could walk across it in fifteen minutes, and around the walls in an hour. The main entrance gate, facing the bus terminal on the south side of town, is **Porta San Giovanni**, from where Via San Giovanni leads to the town's interlocking main squares, **Piazza della Cisterna** and Piazza del Duomo. You enter the Piazza della Cisterna through another majestic gateway, the **Arco dei Becci**, part of the original fortifications before the town expanded in the twelfth century. The more austere **Piazza Duomo**, off to the left, is flanked by the **Collegiata** church, frescoed with Old and New Testament scenes. Best, though, is the superb **fresco cycle** by Ghirlandaio in the Cappella di Santa Fina, depicting the trials of a local saint (Mon–Sat 9.30am–5/7.30pm, Sun 1–5pm; €3.50). There's more work by Ghirlandaio to the left of the cathedral – a fresco of the Annunciation on the courtyard loggia – while the **Palazzo del Popolo**, next door (daily 9.30am–7pm; €5), gives you the chance to climb the **Torre Grossa** (€4.10), the town's highest surviving tower and the only one you can ascend. The same building is home to a number of rooms given over to the **Museo Civico**, the first of which, frescoed with hunting scenes, is known as the Sala di Dante and houses Lippo Memmi's *Maestà*, modelled on that of Simone Martini in Siena. North from Piazza Duomo, **Via San Matteo** is one of the grandest and best preserved of the city streets, with quiet alleyways running down to the walls. At the

Museo Criminale Medioevale (daily 10am–5.30/7pm; €8; not covered by combined ticket) at Via del Castello 1, you get a no-holds-barred exploration of the medieval torturer's mind.

Practicalities

Accommodation lists are available from the **tourist office** on Piazza del Duomo (daily 9am–1pm & 2/3–6/7pm; ☎0577.940.008, ⊛www.sangimignano.com), but from May to September you'll save a lot of frustration by using the Associazione Extralberghiere at Piazza della Cisterna 6 (daily 9.30am–7.30pm; ☎0577.943.111), which can arrange **private rooms** without commission; or at the pro loco Association, Piazza del Duomo 1 (daily 9am–7pm; ☎0577.940.809), which offers a similar service for hotel accommodation for those who turn up in person. San Gimignano's **hotels** are expensive; one of the cheapest is the three-star *Da Graziano* at Via Matteotti 39/a (☎0577.940.101, ⊛www.hoteldagraziano.it; ❹). For **camping**, the nearest site is *Il Boschetto*, 3km downhill at Santa Lucia (☎0577.940.352). One of the most popular **restaurants**, and a fraction cheaper than most, is *Le Vecchie Mura* at Via Piandornella 15, off Via San Giovanni. The *Trattoria Chiribiri* in Piazza della Madonna 1 serves a good selection of pasta dishes. For **snacks**, tasty pizza is served by the slice at Via San Giovanni 38.

Arezzo

About 50km southeast of Florence, **AREZZO** was one of the most important settlements of the Etruscan federation and a prosperous independent republic in the Middle Ages, later falling under the sway of Florence. During the Renaissance, Petrarch, Pietro Aretino and Vasari brought lasting prestige to the city, yet it was an outsider – Piero della Francesca – who gave Arezzo its permanent Renaissance monument, the glorious frescoed choir in the Basilica of **San Francesco** (Mon–Sat 9am–5.30pm, Sun 1–5.30pm; advance booking necessary; ☎0575.352 .727, ⊛www.pierodellafrancesca.it; €5.03). Located to the left of Corso Italia, which leads from the **lower town** to the more interesting **older quarter** at the top of the hill, the church was built in the early fourteenth century. A century later Piero della Francesca was commissioned to paint the choir with a cycle depicting *The Legend of the True Cross*, one of the most radiant creations of the period.

Further up the Corso, the twelfth-century **Pieve di Santa Maria** is one of the finest Romanesque structures in Tuscany, with some wonderful early-thirteenth-century carvings of the months over the portal. The fourteenth-century campanile, known locally as "the tower of the hundred holes", has become the emblem of the town. On the other side of the church, the dramatically sloping Piazza Grande is bordered by the tiered facade of the **Palazzetto della Fraternità dei Laci**, with a Gothic ground floor and fifteenth-century upper storeys, and Vasari's **loggia**, occupied by shops that in some instances still have their original stone counters. At the highest point of the town, the large unfussy **Duomo**, begun in the late thirteenth century, has stained-glass windows from around 1520, terracottas by the della Robbia family, and a tiny fresco of the *Magdalene* by Piero della Francesca. A short distance in the opposite direction from the Duomo, the church of **San Domenico** has a dolorous *Crucifix* by Cimabue. Signs point the way to the nearby **Casa di Giorgio Vasari** at Via XX Settembre 55 (Mon & Wed–Sat 9am–7.30pm, Sun 9am–12.30pm; free), designed by the celebrated biographer-architect-painter for himself and coated with his own lurid frescoes.

Practicalities

The **train station** is a short walk from the centre along Via Monaco. The **tourist office** is outside the station at Piazza della Repubblica 28 (summer Mon–Sat 9.30am–1.30pm & 3.30–6.30pm, Sun 9.30am–1pm; ☎0575.377.678, ⊛www.turismo.toscana.it). **Rooms** are hard to come by on the first weekend of every month (because of the massive antiques fair), and at the end of August and beginning of September. The most convenient, affordable **hotel** is *La Toscana*, Via M. Perennio 56 (☎0575.21.692; ❸), on the main road coming in from the west. Alternatively, try the centrally located *Astoria*, Via Guido Monaco 54 (☎0575.24.361; ❹), or the *Cecco*, at Corso Italia 215 (☎0575.20.986; ⊛www.hotelcecco.com; ❹). The nearest **hostel**, *Ostello Villa Severi*, is some way out of town at Via Redi 13 (☎0575.299.047; ❷); take bus #4 from the train station. For **restaurants**, *Da Guido*, Via Madonna del Prato 85, is a basic local trattoria, and for more pricey but high-quality Tuscan cuisine, try *La Buca di San Francesco*, by San Francesco church.

Siena

During the Middle Ages **SIENA** was one of the major cities of Europe. Virtually the size of Paris, it controlled most of southern Tuscany and its flourishing wool industry dominated the trade routes from France to Rome. The city developed a highly sophisticated civic life, with its own written constitution and a quasi-democratic government. Nowadays it's the perfect antidote to Florence. Self-contained and still rural in parts behind its medieval walls, its great attraction is its own cityscape – a majestic Gothic whole that could be enjoyed without venturing into a single museum. To get the most from it you'll need to stay, especially if you want to see its spectacular horse race, the **Palio** – though you'll definitely need to book during this time (July & Aug).

The City

The centre of Siena is almost entirely medieval in plan and appearance, and has been effectively pedestrianized since the 1960s. At its heart, the **Campo**, with its amphitheatre curve, is an almost organic piece of city planning, and still the focus of city life. The **Palazzo Comunale** (daily 10am–5.30/7pm; €9.50 combined ticket) with its 107m tall bell-tower, the **Torre del Mangia** (€5.50), occupies virtually the entire south side, and although it's still in use as Siena's town hall, its principal rooms have been converted into a **museum** (€6.50) of former public rooms, frescoed with themes integral to the secular life of the medieval city. Best of these are the Sala del Mappamondo, on the wall of which is the fabulous *Maestà* of Simone Martini, an acknowledged masterpiece of Sienese art, painted in 1315 and touched up (the site was damp) six years later, and the former Sale dei Nove, the "Room of the Nine", decorated with Lorenzetti's *Allegories of Good and Bad Government*, commissioned in 1377 to remind the councillors of their duties. At the top end of the Campo, the fifteenth-century **Loggia di Mercanzia**, built as a dealing room for merchants, marks the intersection of the city centre's principal streets. From here Via Banchi di Sotto leads up to the **Palazzo Piccolomini**, housing the **state archive** (closed for restoration at time of writing), which displays the painted covers of the *Tavolette di Biccherna*, the city accounts.

From the Campo, **Via di Città** cuts across the oldest quarter of the city, fronted by some of Siena's finest private palazzi. At the end of the street, Via San Pietro leads to the **Pinacoteca Nazionale** (summer Mon 8.30am–1.30pm, Tues–Sat 8.15am–7.15pm, Sun 8am–1pm; €4), a roll call of Sienese Gothic painting housed in a fourteenth-century palace. In the opposite direction Via di Capitano leads up to the **Duomo**, completed to virtually its present size around 1215; plans to enlarge the church withered with Siena's medieval prosperity, and the vast skeleton of an unfinished extension still stands at the north end of the cathedral square. The Duomo is in any case a delight, its style an amazing conglomeration of Romanesque and Gothic, delineated by bands of black and white marble on its facade. This theme is continued in the sgraffito marble pavement, which begins with geometric patterns outside the church and takes off into a startling sequence of 56 panels within, completed between 1349 and 1547; virtually every artist who worked in the city tried his hand on a design. The rest of the interior is equally

Chianti

Osservanza

Train Station & Campsite

Florence

N

VIA CHIANTIGIANA
VIALE PIETRO TOSELLI
VIA SIMONE MARTINI
RAVACCIANO
VIA DUCCIO DI BONINSEGNA
VIA B. PERUZZI
VIALE LIPPO MEMMI
VIA SIMONE MARTINI
VIA DOMENICO BECCAFUMI
Fonte d'Ovile
Oratorio di San Bernardino
San Francesco
VIALE SARDEGNA
VIA GIUSEPPE MAZZINI
Porta Ovile
VIA DEL COMUNE
Santa Maria di Provenzano
San Cristoforo
VIA DEL ROSSI
San Donato
Barriera San Lorenzo
VIA GARIBALDO
VIA PIAN D'OVILE
TERZO DI CAMOLLIA
VIA DI VALLEROZZI
VIA DEL PIAN
VIA DELL'OVILE
Palazzo Salimbeni
BANCHI
VIA DEL
VIA DELL'
VIA DELLE
VIA N. BIXIO
VIA CAMPANSI
VIA DEL PIGNATTELLO
VIA DON GIOVANNI MINZONI
Fonte Nuova
VIA DELLA STUFA SECCA
PIAZZA DEL SALE
Sant'Andrea
VIA DEI MONTANINI
PIAZZA SALIMBENI
VIA S. CATERINA
V. DI S.PIETRO
VIA DI CAMOLLIA
PIAZZA GRAMSCI
PIAZZA MATTEOTTI
VIA DEI TERMINI
VIA DI CAMOLLIA
Porta Camollia
VIA DI BIAGIO DI MONTLUC
VALE A. DIAZ
VIALE RINALDO FRANCI
VIALE TOZZI
PIAZZA S. DOMENICO
VIA RICASOLI
VIA B. PAVE
VIALE VITTORIO EMANUELE II
Fontegiusta
La Lizza
VIALE CESARE MACCARI
Stadio Comunale
Fortezza
VIALE DEI MILLE
VIALE V. VENETO
VIA V. VENETO
VIALE XXV APRILE

▲ Arezzo

► Buonconvento

SIENA

Porta Pispini

San Raimondo

VIA ROMA
VIA ENEA SILVIO PICCOLOMINI

Santa Maria
dei Servi

Palazzo
Bianchi

Porta
Romana

Santo
Spirito

San Giovannanino
della Staffa

San Giorgio

TERZO DI SAN MARTINO

San Martino

Palazzo
Piccolomini

Logge del Papa

VIA PORTA GIUSTIZIA

Porta Tufi

► Autostrada

Palazzo Bandini

San Vigilio

Loggia d.
Mercanzia

IL CAMPO

Palazzo
Pubblico

San Giuseppe

Sant'Agostino

Parcheggio
Il Campo **P**

Santa
Caterina

Fonte-
branda

Museo
dell'Opera
del Duomo

Pinacoteca
Nazionale

San Pietro

Orto
Botanico

San Domenica

Porta
Fontebranda

San Sebastiano

Duomo

Ospedale di
Santa Maria
della Scala

TERZO DI CITTÀ

San Niccolò
e Lucia

Palazzo
Pollini

Porta
Laterina

Santa Maria
del Carmine

Parcheggio
Il Duomo **P**

Porta S. Marco

► Autostrada

0   200m

ITALY

633

15

arresting: among its greatest treasures are Nicola Pisano's font with its high-relief details of the *Life of Jesus* and *Last Judgement*, and a bronze Donatello statue of St John the Baptist in the north transept. Midway along the nave, the **Libreria Piccolomini** (daily 9/10am–1pm & 2–5/7.30pm; €1.50), signalled by Pinturicchio's brilliantly coloured fresco of the *Coronation of Pius II*, has further frescoes by Pinturicchio and his pupils (including Raphael).

Behind the cathedral, the **Baptistry** (daily 9/10am–1pm & 2–5/7.30pm; €2.50) houses a Renaissance font with panels illustrating John the Baptist's life by della Quercia and Donatello. Visit also the **Museo dell'Opera Metropolitana** (daily 9am–1.30/7.30pm; €5.50), which occupies part of the cathedral's planned extension and houses Pisano's original statues from the facade. Upstairs is a fine array of panels and the cathedral's original altarpiece, a haunting Byzantine icon known as the *Madonna dagli Occhi Grossi* ("Madonna of the Big Eyes"). The painting that repays a visit most, however, is the cathedral's second altarpiece, Duccio's *Maestà*, completed in 1311 and generally thought to be the climax of the Sienese style.

Practicalities

Buses stop along Viale Curtatone, by the Basilica of San Domenico; the **train station** is less convenient, 2km northeast, connected with Piazza Matteotti, at the top end of Via Curtatone, by shuttle bus. **Accommodation** is less of a struggle than in Florence, though it still pays to phone ahead. If you haven't, make your way either to the Cooperativa Hotels Promotion booth opposite San Domenico on Via Curtatone (Mon–Sat 9am–7/8pm; ☎0577.288.084, ☻www.hotelsiena.com), which can book rooms; or to the **tourist office** at Piazza del Campo 56 (daily 10am–1pm & 3–8pm; ☎0577.280.551, ☻www.siena.turismo.toscana.it), which provides an accommodation list. Otherwise, try *Tre Donzelle*, Via Donzelle 5 (☎0577.280.358; ❸), which has good clean rooms; the small, smart *Piccolo Hotel Etruria* at no. 3 (☎0577.280.358; ❹), right in the heart of town; *La Perla*, Via delle Terme 25 (☎0577.47.144; ❹), a regular pensione in a very central location, just two blocks north of the Campo; or the *Bernini* at Via della Sapienza 15 (☎0577.289.047, ☻www.albergobernini.com; ❹), which has stunning views to the Duomo. The **HI hostel** is at Via Fiorentina 89 (closed for restoration at time of writing; ☎0577.522.12; ❷), 2km northwest of the centre; take bus #10 or #15 from Piazza Gramsci or, if you're coming from Florence, ask the bus driver to let you off at "Lo Stellino". The nearest **campsite** is the well-maintained *Campeggio Siena Colleverde*, Strada di Scacciapensieri 47, 2km north (☎0577.280.044; closed mid-Nov to mid-March; bus #3 from Piazza Gramsci).

Restaurants cost a bit over the odds in Siena, especially if you want to eat out in the Campo. For a **snack**, there's pizza by weight at Via delle Terme 10, and an extravagantly stocked deli, the *Pizzicheria Morbidi*, at Via Banchi di Sotto 27. The cheapest **sit-down** alternative is the *Mensa Universitaria*, Via Sant'Agata 1 (closed Sun & all Aug); there's another mensa at Via Bandini 47. *Gallo Nero*, Via del Porrione 65–67 and the unpretentious café *Carla e Franca*, Via di Pantaneto 138, which serves pizza and pasta. Up a notch in price, the *Osteria Le Logge*, in an old *farmacia* in Via del Porrione 33, is a popular trattoria, while out towards San Lorenzo at Corso San Antonio 4, *Osteria Chiacchieria* is a rustic and welcoming option. For **ice cream**, try *Nannini Gelateria*, at the Piazza Matteotti end of Banchi di Sopra, or *La Costarella* just off the Campo near the corner of Via di Città and Via dei Pellegrini.

The Palio

The Siena **Palio** is the most spectacular festival event in Italy, a bareback horse race around the Campo contested twice a year (July 2 & Aug 16) between the ancient wards – or *contrade* – of the city. Each of the seventeen contrade has its own church, social centre and museum, and a heraldic animal motif, displayed in a modern fountain-sculpture in its individual piazza. Each *contrada* has a traditional rival, and ensuring it loses is as important as winning. Although there's a big build-up, the race itself lasts little more than a minute. Most spectators crowd into the centre of the Campo; for the best view, you need to have found a position on the inner rail by 2pm and to keep it for the next six hours.

Pisa

There's no escaping the Leaning Tower in **PISA**. The medieval bell tower is one of the world's most familiar images and yet its beauty still comes as a surprise. It is set in chessboard formation alongside the Duomo and Baptistry on the manicured grass of the **Campo dei Miracoli** (daily 8/9am–5/7.30pm; admission to all four museums, but excluding the tower, €10) where most buildings belong to the city's "Golden Age" – the twelfth and thirteenth centuries, when Pisa was one of the great Mediterranean powers. Perhaps the strangest thing about the **Leaning Tower** (€15), begun in 1173, is that it has always tilted; subsidence disrupted the foundations when it had reached just three of its eight storeys. For the next 180 years a succession of architects were brought in to try to correct the tilt, until 1350 when the angle was accepted and the tower completed. Eight centuries on, it was thought to be nearing its limit: the overhang is over 5m, and the tower, supported by steel wires, was closed to the public in the 1990s – though following the recent success of attempts to stop the tilt increasing, the tower was reopened to the public again in 2001. The **Duomo** (€2) was begun a century earlier, its facade – with its delicate balance of black and white marble, and tiers of arcades – setting the model for Pisa's highly distinctive brand of Romanesque. The interior continues the use of black and white marble, and with its long arcades of columns has an almost Oriental aspect. Most of the artworks are Renaissance or later, a notable exception being Cimabue's mosaic of *Christ in Majesty* in the apse. Its acknowledged highlight is the astonishingly detailed Gothic pulpit by Giovanni Pisano.

The third building of the Miracoli ensemble, the circular **Baptistry**, is a slightly bizarre mix of Romanesque and Gothic, embellished with statuary (now displayed in the museo) by Giovanni Pisano and his father Nicola, as well as another pulpit, sculpted by Nicola in 1260 – his first major commission. Along the north side of the Campo is the **Camposanto**, a cloistered cemetery built towards the end of the thirteenth century. Most of the cloister's frescoes were destroyed by Allied bombing in World War II, but two masterpieces survived relatively unscathed – a fourteenth-century *Triumph of Death* and *Last Judgement* in the Cappella Ammanati, a ruthless catalogue of horrors painted around the time of the Black Death. At the southeast corner of the Campo, a vast array of pieces from the Duomo and Baptistry are displayed in the **Museo dell'Opera del Duomo**, a huge collection that includes statuary by each of the Pisano family.

Away from the Campo dei Miracoli, Pisa takes on a very different character, as tourists give way to students at the still-thriving university. It's nonetheless a quiet place, eerily so at night, set around a series of erratic squares and arcaded streets, and with clusters of Romanesque churches and, along the banks of the Arno, a number of fine palazzi. The **Piazza dei Cavalieri** is an obvious first stop, a large square that was the centre of medieval Pisa, before being remodelled by Vasari as the headquarters of the Knights of St Stephen, whose palace, the curving **Palazzo dei Cavalieri**, topped with busts of the Medici, faces the order's church of **San Stefano**. A short walk east along the river, the **Museo Nazionale di San Matteo** (Tues–Sat 9am–7.30pm, Sun 9am–1.30pm; €4), housed in a twelfth-century convent, displays fourteenth-century paintings, antique armour and wooden shields used in the annual *Gioco del Ponte* pageant.

Practicalities

Pisa's **train station** is south of the centre on Piazza della Stazione, a ten-minute walk from the Campo dei Miracoli; or catch bus #3. From the **airport**, take the

ITALY | Central Italy

hourly Florence train for the five-minute journey. There are two **tourist offices**: one to the left of the station as you leave (Mon–Fri 8.30am–5.30/7pm, Sat & Sun 9am–5pm; ☎050.422.91, ◉www.pisa.turismo.toscana.it) and another in the north-east corner of the Campo dei Miracoli (Mon–Sat 8.30am–5.30/7pm, Sun 10.30am–4.30pm; ☎050.560.464). You can buy a **Biglietto Unico** (€12.91/eight days) for all musuems except the Leaning Tower. The most attractive budget **hotels** are grouped around the Campo dei Miracoli, and the best of the lot is the elegant old *Albergo Gronchi* in Piazza Arcivescovado (☎050.561.823; ❷). Others include the *Locanda Galileo*, Via Santa Maria (☎050.40.621; ❸), and *Pensione Helvetia*, Via G. Boschi 31, off Piazza Arcivescovado (☎050.553.084; ❸). You could also try the *La Torre*, Via C. Battisti 17 (☎050.252.20; ❹). A good women-only alternative, five minutes' walk from the station (first right), is the *Casa della Giovane*, Via Corridoni 31 (☎050.43.061; ❸). The nearest **hostel** is at Via Pietrasantina 15 (☎050.890.622; ❷); take bus #3 from the station or Campo dei Miracoli. The city **campsite**, *Campeggio Torre Pendente*, is 1km west of the Campo dei Miracoli at Viale delle Cascine 86 (☎050.561.704; closed Nov–March) – a large, well-maintained site, with a restaurant and shop.

There are some good-value **places to eat** a few blocks south of the tower, around the market on Piazza delle Vettovaglie. One of the best is *Vineria di Piazza*, Piazza delle Vettovaglie 13, which does good soups; try also the slightly dearer trat-toria *La Mescita*, Via Cavalca 2, on the corner of the piazza. Over to the west, *Pizzeria da Cassio*, Piazza Cavallotti 14, is a good *tavola calda*, and the university building on Via Martiri, off Piazza Cavalieri, has a **mensa** (closed mid-July to mid-Sept). Pisa is known for its **Gioco del Ponte**, held on the last Sunday in June, when teams from the north and south banks of the city stage a series of "battles", including pushing a seven-tonne carriage over the Ponte di Mezzo. But the town's most magical event is the **Luminara** on June 16, when buildings along the river are festooned with candles to celebrate San Ranieri, the city's patron saint.

Lucca

LUCCA is as graceful a provincial capital as they come, set inside a thick swathe of Renaissance walls, and with a quiet, almost entirely medieval street plan. Palazzi and the odd tower dot the streets, at intervals overlooked by a brilliantly decorated Romanesque facade.

The most enjoyable way to get your bearings is to follow the path around the top of the **Walls** – nearly 4km in extent and built with genuine defensive capability in the early sixteenth century, before being transformed to their present, garden aspect by the Bourbon ruler, Marie Louise. In the centre of town, just east of the main Piazza Napoleone on Piazza San Martino, the **Duomo of San Martino** (daily 7am–5/7pm) was in part sculpted by Nicola Pisano. The great hall-like interior includes paintings by Tintoretto, Ghirlandaio and Filippino Lippi. The most famous item, however, Jacopo della Quercia's **Tomb of Ilaria del Carretto** (Mon–Sat 9.30am–4.45/6.45pm, Sun 9–10am & 1/3–5pm; €2), has been restored so vigor-ously that one expert declared it had been ruined – prompting a libel action from the restorer. Lucca's finest sculptor was Matteo Civitali, whose *Tempietto* in the north aisle was sculpted to house the city's most famous relic, the *Volto Santo* – said to be the "true effigy of Christ" and the focus for international pilgrimage.

Northwest of the Duomo across Via Fililungo, the facade of **San Michele in Foro** church (daily 7.30am–8pm) is a triumph of eccentricity, each of its loggia columns different, some twisted, others sculpted or candy-striped. Giacomo Puccini was born almost opposite at Via di Poggio 30, and his home, the **Casa di Puccini** (Tues–Sun 10am–1pm & 3–6pm; €3), is now a school of music with a small muse-um, featuring the Steinway piano on which he composed *Turandot*, along with original scores and photographs from premieres. At the end of the street in Via Galli Tassi is the seventeenth-century **Palazzo Mansi**, which houses a **Pinacoteca**

Nazionale (Tues–Sat 9am–7pm, Sun 9am–2pm; €4), an indifferent collection, but the Rococo palace itself is the real attraction – particularly the spectacularly gilded bridal suite.

Be sure to visit the remarkable **Piazza Anfiteatro**, a circuit of medieval buildings whose foundations are the arches of the Roman amphitheatre. Just southeast, and perhaps the strangest sight in Lucca, is the **Casa-Torre Guinigi** (daily 9/10am–5.30/8pm; €3.10), the fifteenth-century home of Lucca's leading family, with a battlemented tower surmounted by holm oaks whose roots have grown into the room below. Much of it is being restored, but from Via San Andrea you can climb it for one of the best views over the city. Across the narrow canal on Via della Quarquonia, the fifteenth-century **Villa Guinigi** is now the home to Lucca's major museum of art and sculpture, the **Museo Nazionale Guinigi** (Tues–Sat 9am–7pm; Sun 9am–2pm; €6.50), with a good deal of lively Romanesque sculpture from the city and some work by the cathedral's maestro, Matteo Civitali.

Practicalities

The **train station** is just south of the city walls, an easy walk or short bus ride from the centre. One of the most pleasant ways of exploring Lucca is to **rent a bike** (€10.50/day); the **tourist office** on the north side of Piazza Verdi (daily: summer 9am–7pm; winter 9.30am–5.30pm; ☎0583.442.944, ⊛www.luccatourist .it) has details. Finding **accommodation** is a problem at almost any time of year, but of the hotels, the *Melecchi* at Via Romana 37 (☎0583.950.234; ❹), *Stipino* at Via Romana 95 (☎0583.495.077; ❺), and *Diana* at Via del Molinetto 11 (☎0583.492.202; ❹) are all worth a try. After these the best bet is the *Moderno*, Via Civitali 38 (☎0583.558.40; ❹). The **HI hostel**, *San Frediano*, is at Via della Cavallerizza 12 (☎0583.469.957; ❷), next to the church of San Frediano in the centre of town. For **food**, try the *Trattoria da Guido*, Via C. Battisti 28; *Trattoria da Leo*, Via Tegrimi 1; *Trattoria da Giulio*, Via delle Conce 47; or *Ristorante all'Olivo*, Piazza S. Quirico 1. For excellent pizza, with good **beer**, try the *Gli Orti di Via Elisa*, Via Elisa 17.

Perugia

The provincial capital, **PERUGIA** is the most obvious base to kick off a tour of Umbria. It's an oddly mixed town, with a medieval centre and not a little industry: Buitoni, the pasta people, are based here, and it's also where Italy's best chocolate, Perugini, is made.

Perugia hinges on a single street, **Corso Vannucci**, a broad pedestrian thoroughfare constantly buzzing with action. At the far end, the austere **Piazza Quattro Novembre** is backed by the plain-faced **Duomo San Lorenzo** (daily 8am–noon & 4pm–sunset), recently reopened after damage caused by an earthquake in 1983, although the interior – home to the so-called Virgin's "wedding ring", an unwieldy piece of agate that changes colour according to the character of the person wearing it – isn't especially interesting. The Perugians keep the ring locked up in fifteen boxes fitted into one another like Russian dolls, each opened with a key held by a different person; it's brought out for public viewing every July 30. The centrepiece of the piazza is the **Fontana Maggiore**, sculpted by the father-and-son team Nicola and Giovanni Pisano and describing episodes from the Old Testament, classical myth, Aesop's fables and the twelve months of the year. Opposite rises the gaunt mass of the **Palazzo dei Priori**, worth a glance inside for its frescoed **Sala dei Notari** (Tues–Sun 9am–1pm & 3–7pm; free). A few doors down at Corso Vannucci 25 is the **Collegio di Cambio** (Jan, March–Oct & Dec Mon–Sat 9am–12.30pm & 2.30–5.30pm, Sun 9am–12.30pm; Nov & Feb Tues–Sat 8am–2pm, Sun 9am–12.30pm; €2.60), the town's medieval money-exchange, frescoed by Perugino. The palace also houses the **Galleria Nazionale di Umbria** (Mon–Sat 8.30am–7.30pm, Sun 9am–1pm; closed first Mon of each month;

€6.50), one of central Italy's best galleries – a twelve-room romp through the history of Umbrian painting, with works by Perugino and Pinturrichio along with one or two stunning Tuscan masterpieces.

The best streets to wander around to get a feel of the old city are either side of the Duomo. **Via dei Priori** is the most characteristic, leading down to Agostino di Duccio's colourful **Oratorio di San Bernardino**, whose richly embellished facade is by far the best piece of sculpture in the city. From here you can wander through the northern part of the centre, along Via A. Pascoli, to the **Arco di Augusto**, whose lowest section is now one of the few remaining monuments of Etruscan Perugia. On the other side of town, along **Corso Cavour**, is the large church of **San Domenico**, one of whose chapels holds a superb carved arch by Agostino di Duccio, and, to the right of the altar, the tomb of Pope Benedict XI. In the church's cloisters, the **Museo Archeologico Nazionale dell'Umbria** (Mon 2.30–7.30pm, Tues–Sun 8.30am–7.30pm; €2) has one of the most extensive Etruscan collections around.

Practicalities

Trains arrive well away from the centre of Perugia on Piazza V. Veneto; buses #6, #7, #9, #11, #13d, #13s or #15 make the fifteen-minute journey from here to Piazza Italia or Piazza Matteotti. The **tourist office** is on Piazza IV Novembre 3 (Mon–Sat 8.30am–1.30pm & 3.30–6.30pm, Sun 9am–1pm; ☎075.573.6458, ⓦwww.umbria2000.it). There are two **HI hostels**: *Spagnoli*, near the station on Via Cortonese 4 (☎075.501.1366; ❷), and *Torri Baldelli Mombelli* at Via Manicomi (☎075.591.3991; bus #8 or #16 from Perugia). As for **hotels**, try *Rosalba*, at Via del Circo 7 (☎075.572.0626; ❹); *Etruria*, just off the Corso at Via della Luna 21 (☎075.572.3730; ❸); or *Anna*, centrally placed at Via dei Priori 48 (☎075.573.6304; ❸). On the **food** front, *Osteria del Gambero*, Via Baldeschi 17 (closed Mon), has healthy Umbrian specialities, and *La Botte*, Via Volte della Pace 33 (closed Sun), is a decent pizzeria. On Via dei Priori 7, *Papaya* is a good bar with plenty of seating and decent *panini*. The reasonably priced *Dal mì Cocco*, Corso Garibaldi 12, with a student clientele, offers traditional cuisine (closed Mon). For **entertainment**, try *Bliz Caffe* at Corso Vannucci 99, which does cocktails, *Bratislava* at Via Fiorenzuola 12, near Corso Cavour, which has live music on selected nights, and *Caffe Morlacchi*, Piazza Morlacchi 6–8, which has live jazz. There's **internet access** at Internet Point, Via Ulisse Rocchi 4.

Gubbio

GUBBIO is the most thoroughly medieval of Umbrian towns, an immediately likeable place that holds onto its charm despite an ever-increasing influx of tourists. The first high peaks of the Apennines rising behind give the place the feel of a mountain outpost – something it's always been, in fact. The best (and most scenic) approach is by frequent bus from Perugia, or by train from Foligno to Fossato di Vico, 19km away but with an hourly connecting bus.

Centre-stage on the windswept Piazza della Signoria is the immense fourteenth-century **Palazzo dei Consoli** (daily 10am–1pm & 2/3–5/6pm), whose crenellated outline and campanile command your attention for miles around. Council officials and leading citizens met to discuss business here in the cavernous Salone dell'Arengo, from which the word "harangue" is derived. The building holds the **Museo Civico** (Tues–Sun same times; €3.62), unremarkable except for the famous Eugubine Tablets, Umbria's most important archeological find and the only extant record of the ancient Umbrian language. Admission to the museum also gets you into the five-roomed **Pinacoteca** upstairs, worth a look for works by the Gubbian School. On the hillside above the town, the **Basilica of Sant'Ubaldo** is the place Gubbians drive to on Sunday mornings, a pleasant spot with a handy bar and great views, connected with the town's Porta Romana by a slightly scary funicular

(€4.65 return). There's not much to see in the basilica itself, except the body of the town's patron saint, Ubaldo, who's missing three fingers, hacked off by his manservant as a religious keepsake. You can't miss the big wooden pillars, though, featured in Gubbio's annual *Corsa dei Ceri* (May 15), a race to the basilica from the town that's second only to Siena's Palio in terms of its exuberance.

You shouldn't have any problem finding somewhere **to stay** in Gubbio, though the place does get busy. The **tourist office**, Piazza Oderisi 6 (Mon–Sat 8.30am–1.30pm & 3–6pm, Sun 9am–12.30pm; ☎075.922.0693, ⑩www.comune .gubbio.pg.it), may be able to help; or try the *Locanda del Duca*, Via Piccardi 3 (☎075.927.7753; ❸), or *Grotta dell'Angelo*, Via Gioia 47 (☎075.927.1747; ❸), which both have excellent restaurants. There are two **campsites** for Gubbio, both in Loc. Ortoguidone – four-star *Villa Ortoguidone County Club* (☎075.927.2037) and three-star *Città di Gùbbio* (both ☎075.927.2037, ⑩www.agriturgubbio.com; closed Oct–March). There's a good selection of places **to eat**: if you want to be outdoors, try the *Trattoria di San Martino*, Via dei Consoli 8 (closed Tues); alternatively, try the classier *Taverna del Lupo*, Via Ansidei 21 (closed Mon).

Assisi

Thanks to St Francis, Italy's premier saint and founder of the Franciscan order, **ASSISI** is Umbria's best-known town, and suffers as a result, crammed with people for ten months of the year. But it has a medieval hill-town charm and quietens down in the evening. An earthquake in September 1997 caused extensive damage to parts of the town, most notably to the Basilica di San Francesco, but restoration is now complete and the basilica is, mercifully, almost back to its original splendour.

The **Basilica di San Francesco** at the end of Via San Francisci (daily 6.30am–7.30pm; ⑩www.sanfrancescoassisi.org) is justly famed as Umbria's single greatest glory, and one of the most overwhelming collections of art outside a gallery anywhere in the world. Begun in 1228, two years after the saint's death, it was financed by donations that flooded in from all over the world. The sombre **Lower Church** is the earlier of the two churches that make up the basilica, its complicated floor plan and claustrophobic vaults intended to create a mood of meditative introspection. Francis lies under the floor in a crypt only brought to light in 1818. Frescoes cover almost every available space, and span a century of continuous artistic development, from the anonymous early works above the altar, through Cimabue's over-restored *Madonna, Child and Angels with St Francis* in the right transept to work by the Sienese School painters, Simone Martini and Pietro Lorenzetti. The **Upper Church**, built to a light and airy Gothic plan, is richly decorated, too, with dazzling frescoes on the life of St Francis, some of which at least are considered to be the work of Giotto. The **treasury** contains a rich collection of paintings, reliquaries and religious clutter.

There's not a great deal to see in Assisi's small centre. A nondescript **Museo Civico** in the crypt of the now defunct church of San Nicolo on central Piazza del Comune (daily 10am–1pm & 2/3–5/7pm; €2.10) includes Etruscan fragments and the so-called **Tempio di Minerva**, six columns and a pediment from a Roman temple of the first century. A short trek up the steep Via di San Rufino from here, the thirteenth-century **Duomo** has the font used to baptize St Francis and St Clare, and close by is the **Basilica di Santa Chiara**, burial place of St Francis's devoted early companion. Consecrated in 1265, the church is a virtual facsimile of the basilica up the road, and is home to the macabre blackened body of Clare herself and a Byzantine crucifix famous for having bowed to Francis and commanded him to embark on his sacred mission.

Practicalities

Assisi's **train station** is 5km south of town, connected to it by half-hourly buses. The **tourist office**, Piazza del Comune 12 (Mon–Sat 9am–1pm & 3–6pm, Sun

9am–1pm; ☎075.812.450, ⓦwww.umbria2000.it), has details of private rooms. Otherwise, the functional *Italia*, off the central Piazza del Comune at Vicolo della Fortezza 2 (☎075.812.625; ❸; closed Dec–Feb), is about the cheapest place **to stay**; *La Rocca*, Via Porta Perlici 27 (☎075.812.284; ❸), is also a fair bet, as is the *Anfiteatro Romano*, close by at Via Anfiteatro Romano 4 (☎075.813.025; ❸). There are also pilgrim **hostels** (*Case Religiose di Ospitalità*) all over town: the *Suore del Giglio*, Via San Francesco 13 (☎075.812.267; ❸), is the best as far as location goes. There's a big **campsite** and **hostel** at Fontemaggio (☎075.813.636; ❸), 3km out on the road to the monastery of Eremo delle Carceri – take bus #20 or #34l; and the official **HI hostel**, *Ostello della Pace*, at Via di Valecchie (☎075.816.767; ❸), but be warned – it may make you stay half-board. For **food**, try the reasonably priced pizzeria, *Il Pozzo Romano*, on Via Sant'Agnese near Santa Chiara (closed Thurs); *Pallotta*, Via San Rufino 4 (closed Tues); or *I Monaci*, Via A Fortini 10, off Via Fontebella on the Scaletti del Metastasio (closed Wed). Otherwise, the *La Rocca* hotel (see above) has a good no-frills restaurant. To use the **internet**, try Bar del Corso, Via Corso Mazzini.

Spoleto

SPOLETO is Umbria's most compelling town, remarkable for its extremely pretty position and several of Italy's most ancient Romanesque churches. The lower town, where you arrive, was badly damaged by World War II bombing, and doesn't hold much of interest, so it's best to take a bus straight to the upper town. There's no single, central piazza, but the place to head for is **Piazza Libertà**, site of a much-restored first-century **Roman Theatre**, visible at all times, but also visitable more closely in conjunction with the **Museo Archeologico** (Mon–Sat 9am–7pm, Sun 9am–1pm; €2). The adjoining **Piazza della Fontana** has more Roman remains, best of which is the **Arco di Druso**, built to honour the minor campaign victories of Drusus, son of Tiberius. The homely **Piazza del Mercato**, beyond, is a fine opportunity to take in some streetlife, and from there it's a short walk to the **Duomo**, whose facade of restrained elegance is one of the most memorable in the region. Inside, various Baroque embellishments are eclipsed by the superlative apse frescoes of the fifteenth-century Florentine artist Fra Lippo Lippi, dominated by his final masterpiece, a *Coronation of the Virgin*. He died shortly after their completion (amid rumours that he was poisoned for seducing the daughter of a local noble family) and was interred here in a tomb designed by his son, Filippino. You should also take the short walk out to the **Ponte delle Torri**, a picture-postcard favourite, and an astonishing piece of medieval engineering, best seen as part of a circular walk around the base of the **Rocca** – everyone's idea of a cartoon castle, with towers, crenellations and sheer walls; it served until recently as a high-security prison, home to Pope John Paul II's would-be assassin and leading members of the Red Brigades.

Practicalities

Spoleto's **train station** is 1km north of the town centre. The **tourist office** is on central Piazza della Libertà (daily 9/10am–1pm & 4–7pm; ☎0743.238.920, ⓦwww.umbria2000.it). If you're planning on **staying** in town, try the central and reasonably priced *Pensione dell'Angelo*, Via Arco del Druso 25 (☎0743.222.385; ❹). If that's full, then the only other vaguely affordable place in the upper town is the *Pensione Aurora*, off Piazza Libertà at Via dell'Apollinare 3 (☎0743.220.315; ❹). The lower town is very much a second choice, but there are more likely to be rooms available. The **hostel**, *Villa Redenta*, is at Via di villa Redenta 1 (☎0743.22.49.36; ❷). The closest **campsite** is the tiny but very pleasant *Camping Monteluco*, behind San Pietro (☎0743.220.358; closed Oct–March). For **food**, the best basic trattoria is *Trattoria del Festival*, Via Brignone 8 (closed Fri); *Il Panciolle*, Via del Duomo 3–4 (closed Wed), is also a popular choice and has a terrace. *Pecchiarda*, in Vicolo S.

Giovanni off Via delle Postierno in the lower town, has a pleasant enclosed garden (closed Thurs), but if you want something really special, go to *Pentagramma*, off Piazza Libertà at Via T. Martani 4 (closed Mon).

In June and July Spoleto plays host to the country's leading international arts festival, the **Festival dei Due Mondi**. The jet-set audiences – and ticket prices to match – can be off-putting, but there's also an Edinburgh-type fringe with lots of film, jazz, buskers and so on. Tickets and information are available from the festival office at Via del Duomo 8 (April–July & Sept–Dec Mon–Fri 9.30am–1.30pm & 2.30–7pm; June & July also Sat & Sun same times; ☎0743.45.028, ❀www .spoletofestival.it).

Orvieto

Out on a limb from the rest of Umbria, **ORVIETO** is flooded with tourists in summer, most of whom are drawn by its **Duomo**, one of the greatest Gothic buildings in Italy, built, according to tradition, to celebrate the so-called Miracle of Bolsena (1263), in which a doubting priest celebrating Mass in a church on the nearby Lago di Bolsena noticed real blood dripping from the Host onto the altar-cloth. The stained linen was whisked off to Pope Urban IV, who was in Orvieto to escape the heat and political hassle of Rome, and the building was constructed over the ensuing three centuries, in a surprisingly unified example of the Romanesque-Gothic style. The star turn is the facade, a riot of columns, spires, bas-reliefs, sculptures and dazzling colour, just about held together by four enormous fluted columns, the work of the master mason Lorenzo Maitini and his pupils, describing episodes from the Old and New Testaments in staggering detail. Inside, the church is surprisingly plain by comparison, mainly distinguished by the **Cappella di San Brizo** (Mon–Sat 10am–12.45pm & 2.30–6/7.15pm, Sun 2.30–5.45/6.45pm; €3; tickets from the tourist office), which holds Luca Signorelli's fresco of the *Last Judgement*, a realistic yet grotesque work, full of beautifully observed muscular figures that greatly influenced Michelangelo's celebrated cycle in the Vatican's Sistine Chapel. Signorelli, suitably clad in black, includes himself with Fra Angelico in the lower left-hand corner of *The Sermon of the Antichrist*, both calmly looking on as someone is garrotted at their feet. The twin Cappella del Corporale contains the sacred *corporale* (altar cloth) itself, locked away in a massive, jewel-encrusted casket (an accurate facsimile of the facade).

Next to the Duomo, the **Museo dell'Opera del Duomo** (closed for restoration at time of writing) has paintings by Martini, several important thirteen-century sculptures by Arnolfo di Cambio and Andrea Pisano, and a lovely font filled with Escher-like carved fishes. Opposite, the **Museo Greco** (daily 10.30am–1pm & 2/3–5.30/6.30pm; €2.50) features a fairly predictable collection of vases and assorted fragments excavated from local tombs. Moving north up Via del Duomo, you come to **Corso Cavour**, the town's pedestrianized main drag, at the far end of which, across Piazza Cahen, is **Il Pozzo di San Patrizio** (daily 10am–6/7pm; €3.50), the novelty act of the town, a huge cylindrical well, commissioned in 1527 by Pope Clement VII to guarantee the town's water supply during an expected siege by the imperial army. It's a dank but striking piece of engineering, named after its alleged similarity to the Irish cave where St Patrick died in 493, supposedly aged 133.

Practicalities

Bus #1 makes a regular trip from the distant **train station** to Piazza XXIX Marzo, a short way north of the Duomo. A more charming alternative is the funicular up to Piazza Cahen, from where minibuses wind through the twisting streets to Piazza del Duomo. The **tourist office** is at Piazza del Duomo 24 (Mon–Fri 8.15am–2pm & 4–7pm, Sat & Sun 10am–6pm; ☎0763.341.772, ❀www.comune.orvieto.tr.it). Of **hotels**, try the pleasant *Posta*, Via Luca Signorelli 18 (☎0763.341.909; ❹). Orvieto has several religious foundations which rent out rooms including the Istituto SS Salvatore, Via del Popolo 1 (☎0463.342.910; ❸), and the Villa Mercede at Via Soliana 2 (☎0763.341.766; ❸). The central **hostel**, *Porziuncola*, is very small and located at Loc. Cappuccini 8 (☎0763.341.387; ❶). The nearest **campsite** is the *Orvieto*, 10km away on Lago di Corbara (take the bus to Baschi/Civitella). There's a group of cheap **restaurants** at the bottom of Corso Cavour, though the best-value eating is close to the Duomo, at Via Maitani 15, a canteen affair run by a co-operative, offering a choice between a restaurant and self-service trattoria (closed Sun). *La Grotta*, Via Signorelli 5, off Via del Duomo (closed Mon), is a standard, friendly trattoria, and the *Antico Bucchero*, Via de' Cartari 4, is a popular restaurant with reasonable prices (closed Wed). The *Bottega del Buon Vino*, Via della Cave 26, is a wine **bar** that's good for staples and has a few outside tables. **Internet** access is at Caffé Montanucci, Corso Cavour 23.

Urbino

For the second half of the fifteenth century, **URBINO** was one of the most prestigious courts in Europe, ruled by the remarkable Federico da Montefeltro, who employed a number of the greatest artists and architects of the time to build and decorate his palace in the town. At one time it was reckoned the most beautiful in all Italy, and it does seem from contemporary accounts that fifteenth-century Urbino was an extraordinarily civilized place, a measured and urbane society in which life was lived without indulgence.

In the centre of Urbino, the **Palazzo Ducale** is a fitting monument to Federico, home now to the **Galleria Nazionale delle Marche** (Mon 8.30am–2pm, Tues–Sun 8.30am–7.15pm; €4), although it's the building itself that makes the biggest impression. Among the paintings in the Appartamento del Duca are Piero della Francesca's strange *Flagellation*, and the *Ideal City*, a famous perspective painting of a symmetrical and deserted cityscape long attributed to Piero but now thought to be by one of his followers. There's also Paolo Uccello's last work, the six-panelled *Profanation of the Host*, and, in the same room, a portrait of Federico da Montefeltro by the Spanish artist Pedro Berruguete. The most interesting and best preserved of the palazzo's rooms is Federico's Studiolo, a triumph of illusory perspective created by intarsia. Shelves appear to protrude from the walls, cupboard doors seem to swing open to reveal lines of books, a letter lies in an apparently half-open drawer. Even more remarkable are the delicately hued landscapes of Urbino as it might appear from one of the surrounding hills, and the life-like squirrel perching next to a bowl of fruit.

Urbino is a lively university town, and its bustling streets – a pleasant jumble of Renaissance and medieval houses – can be a welcome antidote to the rarefied atmosphere of the Palazzo Ducale. You can wind down in one of the many bars and trattorias, or take a picnic up to the gardens within the **Fortezza Albornoz**, from where you'll get great views of the town and the countryside, out to **San Bernardino**, a fine Renaissance church 2km away that is the resting place of the Montefeltros.

Urbino is notoriously difficult to reach – the best approach is by **bus** from Pésaro, about 30km away on the coast (last one leaves at around 8pm). Buses stop in Borgo Mercatale, at the foot of the Palazzo Ducale, which is reached either by lift or by Francesco di Giorgio Martini's spiral staircase. For **accommodation**, the cheapest options are **private rooms**, most of which are on Via Budassi – lists available from the **tourist office** on Piazza Rinascimento (Mon–Sat 9am–1pm & 3–6pm, Sun 9am–1pm; ☎0722.2613, ❻www.comune.urbino.ps.it); you can also check the **internet** here for free. The most convenient **hotels** are the newly refurbished *Italia*, Corso Garibaldi 32 (☎0722.2701; ❹), and the *San Giovanni*, Via Barocci 13 (☎0722.2827; ❷; closed July). The best deals for **food** are at the university mensa on Piazza San Filippo, or the *Self-Service Franco* on Via del Poggio (both closed Sun). If your budget's not too tight, try *Il Girarrosto*, off Via Raffaello at Piazza San

Francesco 3, which serves good traditional food (lunch daily; dinner Thurs–Sun), and *L'Angolo Divino* on Via Sant'Andrea 14 is a fine *osteria*.

Rome

Of all Italy's historic cities, it's **ROME** that exerts the most compelling fascination. There's arguably more to see here than in any other city in the world, with the relics of more than two thousand years of continuous occupation. For the traveller, it is the sheer weight of history in the city that is most evident, its various eras crowding in on each other to an almost breathtaking degree. There are the classical features – the Colosseum, the Forum and spectacular Palatine Hill – and relics from the early Christian period in ancient basilicas; while the fountains and churches of the Baroque period go a long way to determining the look of the city centre. But these are just part of the picture, which is an almost continuous one right up to the present day, taking in Romanesque churches, Renaissance palazzi, Rococo fountains and the ponderous buildings of post-Unification, often all found within a few paces of each other.

Rome is not an easy place to absorb on one visit, and you need to approach things slowly. On foot it's easy to lose a sense of direction in the twisting old streets, and in any case you're so likely to see something interesting that detours and stopoffs are inevitable.

Arrival, information and city transport

The main **train station** is Termini, meeting-point of the metro lines and city bus routes. Rome has two **airports**: Leonardo da Vinci, better known as **Fiumicino**, handles all scheduled flights; Ciampino is for charter services only. Two train services link Fiumicino to Rome: one to Termini (every 30min; €8.80), the other goes to Trastevere, Ostiense and Tiburtina stations (every 20min; €4.70). A taxi will cost at least €40. From Ciampino, take a Cotral bus to Anagnina on metro line A, from where it's a twenty-minute ride to Termini on the metro. Information is available from the **Tourist Call Centre** (daily 9am–7pm; ☎06.3600.4399), which has up-to-the-minute information in five languages; the **tourist information** booth at Fiumicino airport (Mon–Sat 8am–7pm; ☎06.65954471); and the **main tourist office** at Via Parigi 5 (Mon–Sat 9am–7pm; ☎06.4889.9200). There are also information kiosks dotted around the city (daily 9am–6pm.)

The best way to get around Rome is to **walk**. That said, its **public transport** is both reliable and cheap. A day pass (BIG; €3.10) can be bought from any newspaper stall or tabaccaio, or the ATAC booth on Piazza dei Cinquecento, where they also sell decent transport maps. The buses and the metro stop around 11.30pm (Sat 12.30pm), after which a network of **night buses** takes over, serving most parts of the city until about 5.30am. **Taxis** are costly; hail one in the street, or try the ranks at Termini, Piazza Venezia, Piazza San Silvestro; alternatively call ☎06.3570, 06.5551 or 06.6645 to book one. The meter should start at €2.33.

Accommodation

In summer Rome is as crowded as you might expect, so be sure to book as far in advance as possible. If you can't, make straight for the tourist office to save your legs. Many of the city's cheaper hotels are handily located close to Termini station.

Hostels

Hostel Alessandro Via Vicenza 42 ☎06.446.1958, ⊛www.hostelalessandro.com. Friendly, international staff, full use of kitchen. No curfew. ❸

Colors Via Boezio 31 ☎06.687.4030, ⊛www .colorshotel.com. In Prati, near St Peter's. Clean, friendly, good value, use of kitchen. Dorms ❸

Fawlty Towers Via Magenta 39 ☎06.445.4802, ⊛www.fawltytowers.org. Near the station,

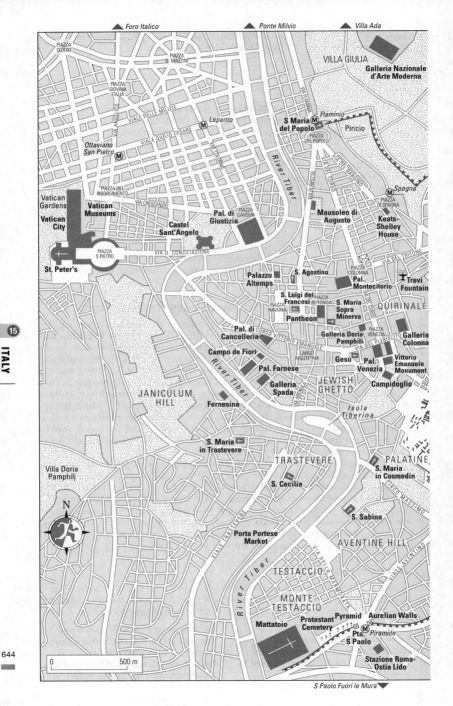

PIAZZA
CLODIO

PIAZZA
G. MAZZINI

VILLA GIULIA

Galleria Nazionale
d'Arte Moderna

PIAZZA
GIOVINA
ITALIA

VIALE DELLE MILIZIE

VIA FLAMINIA

Lepanto

Ⓜ Flaminio

S Maria Ⓜ
del Popolo

Pincio

VIALE GIULIO CESARE

VIA DEL CORSO

Ottaviano
San Pietro Ⓜ

PIAZZA
DEL POPOLO

VIA COLONNA

River Tiber

VIA DEL BABUINO

PIAZZA DEL
RISORGIMENTO

Ⓜ Spagna

VIA CRESCENZIO

Vatican
Gardens

Vatican
Museums

Pal. di
Giustizia

PIAZZA
CAVOUR

VIA DI RIPETTA

PIAZZA
DI SPAGNA

Castel
Sant'Angelo

Mausoleo di
Augusto

Keats-
Shelley
House

Vatican
City

PIAZZA
S PIETRO

VIA D. CONCILIAZIONE

VIA DEL TRITONE

St. Peter's

Palazzo
Altemps

S. Agostino

PIAZZA
COLONNA

Pal.
Montecitorio

† Trevi
Fountain

S. Luigi dei
Francesi

PIAZZA
ROTONDA

S. Maria
Sopra
Minerva

QUIRINALE

PIAZZA
NAVONA

Pantheon

Pal. di
Cancelleria

CORSO VITTORIO EMANUELE

Galleria Doria
Pamphili

PIAZZA
DEL PLEBISCITO

Galleria
Colonna

Campo de Fiori

LARGO
ARGENTINA

Gesù

VIA DEL PLEBISCITO

Pal.
Venezia

Vittorio
Emanuele
Monument

Pal. Farnese

River Tiber

VIA ARENULA

JEWISH
GHETTO

Campidoglio

Galleria
Spada

Isola
Tiberina

JANICULUM
HILL

Fernesina

S. Maria
in Trastevere

TRASTEVERE

PALATINE

S. Maria
in Cosmedin

CIRCO MASSIMO

S. Cecilia

Villa Doria
Pamphilj

N

S. Sabina

VIALE TRASTEVERE

Porta Portese
Market

AVENTINE HILL

VIA DELLA MARMORATA

VIALE AVENTINO

River Tiber

TESTACCIO

MONTE
TESTACCIO

Pyramid

Aurelian Walls

Mattatoio

Protestant
Cemetery

Ⓜ Piramide

Pta.
S Paolo

Stazione Roma-
Ostia Lido

0   500 m

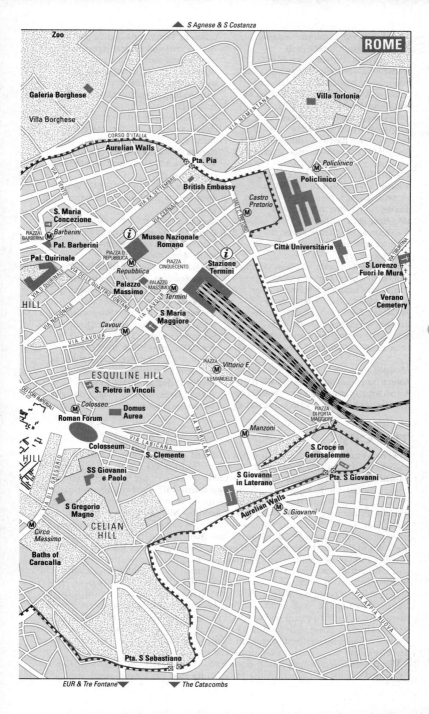

Zoo

Galeria Borghese

Villa Borghese

Villa Torlonia

CORSO D'ITALIA

Aurelian Walls

Pta. Pia

British Embassy

Policlinico

Policlinico

Castro
Pretorio

S. Maria
Concezione

Barberini

Pal. Barberini

Pal. Quirinale

Museo Nazionale
Romano

Repubblica

Città Universitària

Stazione
Termini

S Lorenzo
Fuori le Mura

HILL

Palazzo
Massimo

PIAZZA
CINQUECENTO

PALAZZO
MASSIMO

Termini

Verano
Cemetery

S Maria
Maggiore

Cavour

ESQUILINE HILL

PIAZZA
Vittorio E.
V. EMANUELE II

S. Pietro in Vincoli

Colosseo

Roman Forum

Domus
Aurea

PIAZZA
DI PORTA
MAGGIORE

Colosseum

Manzoni

S. Clemente

S Croce in
Gerusalemme

SS Giovanni
e Paolo

S Giovanni
in Laterano

Pta. S Giovanni

S Gregorio
Magno

HILL

CELIAN
HILL

Aurelian Walls

S. Giovanni

Circo
Massimo

Baths of
Caracalla

Pta. S Sebastiano

EUR & Tre Fontane

The Catacombs

efficient, clean, with all amenities, including internet, kitchen use, satellite TV. ❸

Hotel Ottaviano Via Ottaviano 6 ⊕06.3973.7253, ⓦwww.pensioneottaviano.com. Excellently situated, friendly private hotel/hostel, just outside the Vatican walls. Take Metro line A to Ottaviano. ❸

Hotel Sandy Via Cavour 136 ⊕06.488.4585, ⓦwww.sandyhostel.com. Good value, central young people's hotel/hostel. Metro Cavour. ❸

Ostello del Foro Italico Viale delle Olimpiadi 61 ⊕06.324.2571, ⓦwww.hostelbooking.com. Rome's vast HI hostel. Metro line A to Ottaviano, then bus #32. Breakfast included. Midnight curfew. ❷

Marello Via Urbana 50 ⊕06.482.5361. Run by the oblates of St Joseph, this place has singles and doubles, many en suite. Very central. ❸

M&J Place Hostel Via Solferino 9 ⊕06.446.2802, ⓦwww.mejplacehostel.com. Just out of the station and to the right; facilities include kitchen and internet access. ❸

Protezione della Giovane Via Urbana 158 ⊕06 .488.148. This convent for the "protection of young women" is for under 28s only. Friendly, central and cheap. Curfew 10.30am. No breakfast. ❷

YWCA Via C. Balbo 4 ⊕06.488.3917. For all travellers, and more conveniently situated than the HI hostel; ten minutes' walk from Termini. Breakfast included (not Sun). Curfew midnight. ❹

Hotels

Abruzzi Piazza della Rotonda 69 ⊕06.679.2021, ⓦwww.hoteldegliabruzzi.com. Bang in front of the Pantheon, and as such you pay for the location. ❺

Campo de' Fiori Via del Biscione 6 ⊕06.6880 .6865, ⓦwww.hotelcampodefiori.com. Friendly, clean, colourful place, beautiful views over the medieval quarter from its roof terrace. ❻

Della Lunetta Piazza del Paradiso 68 ⊕06.686.1080. An unspectacular hotel in a great location. ❺

Katty Via Palestro 35 ⊕06.490.079. One of the cheaper, more pleasant options east of the station. ❹

Marsala Via Marsala 36 ⊕06.444.1262, ⓔhotelmarsala@iol.it. Pleasant, clean hotel close to the station. ❺

Monaco Via Flavia 84 ⊕06.474.4335. Very welcoming and clean; between the station and Via Veneto. ❺

Navona Via dei Sediari 8 ⊕06.686.4203, ⓦwww.hotelnavona.com. Perfectly placed *pensione* run by a friendly Italian–Australian couple. Metro Colosseo. ❻

Perugia Via del Colosseo 7 ⊕06.679.7200, ⓔhtlperugia@lol.lt. On a peaceful but central street. Breakfast included. Metro Colosseo. ❺

Prati Via Crescenzio 89 ⊕06.687.5357, ⓦwww.hotelprati-roma.com. Two-star hotel on the Vatican side of the river with a nice, family-run feel. Metro Ottaviano. ❺

Rosetta Via Cavour 295 ⊕06.4782.3069, ⓔhotel_rosetta@iol.it. Nice location close to the Colosseum. Metro Colosseo. ❺

Sole Via del Biscione 76 ⊕06.6880.6873, ⓦwww.solealbiscione.lt. Near Piazza del Campo dei Fiori, one of the nicest city-centre locations. ❺

The City

Piazza Venezia is a good central place to start your wanderings, flanked by the **Palazzo di Venezia** and overlooked by the hideous **Vittorio Emanuele Monument** or Altar of the Nation, erected at the turn of the twentieth century to commemorate Unification. Behind, the **Capitoline Hill**, formerly the spiritual and political centre of the Roman Empire, is home to one of Rome's most elegant squares, **Piazza del Campidoglio**, designed by Michelangelo in the 1550s for Pope Paul III, and flanked by the two branches of one of the city's most important museums of antique art – the **Capitoline Museums** (Tues–Sun 8.30am–8pm; €6.20). On the left, the **Palazzo Nuovo** concentrates some of the best of the city's Roman and Greek sculpture and Renaissance painting – numerous works by Reni and Tintoretto, a vast picture by Guercino that used to hang in St Peter's, some nice small-scale work by Annibale Carracci, an early work by Ludovico Carracci, *Head of a Boy*, and Caravaggio's *St John the Baptist*. Behind the square, a road skirts the Forum down to the small church of **San Giuseppe dei Falegnami**, built above the prison where St Peter is said to have been held – you can see the bars to which he was chained, along with the spring the saint is said to have created in which to baptize other prisoners, and, at the top of the staircase, an imprint claimed to be of St Peter's head as he was tumbled down the stairs.

Via del Plebiscito forges west from Piazza Venezia past the church of **Gesù**, a high, wide Baroque church of the Jesuit order that has served as the model for

Jesuit churches everywhere. It's notable for its size (the left transept is surmounted by the largest single piece of lapis lazuli in existence) and the richness of its interior, especially the paintings of Baciccio in the dome and the ceiling's ingenious trompe l'oeil, which oozes out of its frame in a tangle of writhing bodies, flowing drapery and stucco angels. Crossing over, streets wind down to **Piazza di Campo dei Fiori**, home to a morning market and surrounded by restaurants and bars. South of the Campo, at the end of Via dei Balestrari, the **Galleria Spada** (Tues–Sun 8.30am–7pm; €5) is decorated in the manner of a Roman noble family and displays a small collection of paintings, best of which are a couple of portraits by Reni. To the left off the courtyard is a crafty trompe l'oeil tunnel by Borromini, whose trick perspective makes it appear four times its actual length. Across Via Arenula, through and beyond the Jewish Ghetto, the broad open space of **Piazza della Bocca di Verità** is home to two of the city's better-preserved Roman temples, the **Temple of Fortuna Virilis** and the circular **Temple of Hercules Victor**, both of which date from the end of the second century BC, though the church of **Santa Maria in Cosmedin**, on the far side of the square, is more interesting, a typically Roman medieval basilica with a huge marble altar and surround and a colourful and ingenious Cosmati mosaic floor – one of the city's finest. Outside in the portico, the **Bocca di Verità** gives the square its name, an ancient Roman drain cover in the shape of an enormous face that tradition says will swallow the hand of anyone who doesn't tell the truth.

The Centro Storico

You need to walk a little way northwest from the Capitoline Hill to find the real city centre of Rome, the **Centro Storico**, circled by a bend in the Tiber, above Corso Vittorio Emanuele. The old Campus Martius of Roman times, it later became the heart of the Renaissance city, and is now an unruly knot of narrow streets holding some of the best of Rome's classical and Baroque heritage, as well as its street- and nightlife.

The boundary of the historic centre to the east, **Via del Corso**, is Rome's main shopping street and cuts straight through the heart of the city centre. Walking north from Piazza Venezia, the first building on the left is the **Galleria Doria Pamphili** (10am–5pm; closed Thurs & last half of Aug; €7.30), one of many galleries housed in palaces belonging to Roman patrician families. Its collection includes Rome's best cache of Dutch and Flemish paintings, canvases by Caravaggio and Velázquez's painting of Pope Innocent X. The second left after the palace leads into Piazza Sant'Ignazio, an odd little square dominated by the church of **Sant'Ignazio**, which has a marvellous ceiling by Pozzo showing the entry of St Ignatius into paradise, employing sledgehammer trompe l'oeil effects, notably in the mock cupola painted into the dome of the crossing. Stand on the disc in the centre of the nave for the full effect.

Follow Via di Seminario from here and you're standing in front of the **Pantheon** (daily 8.30/9am–6.30pm; free) on Piazza della Rotonda, the most complete ancient Roman structure in the city, finished around 125 AD. Inside, the diameter of the dome and height of the building are precisely equal, and the hole in the dome's centre is a full 9m across; there are no visible arches or vaults to hold the whole thing up; instead, they're sunk into the concrete of the walls of the building. It would have been richly decorated, the coffered ceiling was covered in solid bronze until the seventeenth century, and the niches were filled with statues of the gods.

There's more artistic splendour on view behind the Pantheon, in the church of **Santa Maria sopra Minerva**, one of the city's art-treasure churches, crammed with the tombs and gifts of wealthy Roman families. Of these, the Carafa chapel, in the south transept, is the best known, holding Filippino Lippi's fresco of *The Assumption*, below which one painting shows a hopeful Oliviero Carafa being presented to the Virgin Mary by Thomas Aquinas; another depicts Aquinas confounding the heretics in the sight of two beautiful young boys – the future Medici popes

Leo X and Clement VII. You should look, too, at the figure of *Christ Bearing the Cross*, on the left-hand side of the main altar, a serene work painted for the church by Michelangelo in 1521.

In the opposite direction from the Pantheon, **Piazza Navona** is the most appealing square in Rome, an almost entirely enclosed space fringed with cafés and restaurants that follows the lines of the Emperor Domitian's chariot arena. Pope Innocent X built most of the grandiose palaces that surround it in the seventeenth century and commissioned Borromini to design the church of **Sant'Agnese** on the west side. The church, typically squeezed into the tightest of spaces by Borromini, supposedly stands on the spot where St Agnes, exposed naked to the public in the stadium, miraculously grew hair to cover herself. The **Fontana dei Quattro Fiumi** opposite, one of three that punctuate the square, is by Borromini's arch-rival, Bernini; each figure represents one of the four great rivers of the world – the Nile, Danube, Ganges and Plate – though only the horse, symbolizing the Danube, was actually carved by Bernini himself. It is astonishing to think that Mussolini once planned to plough a boulevard straight through the piazza.

Just out of the north end, you'll find **Palazzo Altemps** (Tues–Sun 9am–7pm; €5), functioning as part of the Museo Nazionale Romano and featuring the unmissable ancient statuary collected by the Ludovisi family. The highlight is the original fifth-century-BC Greek throne, embellished with a delicate relief of the birth of Aphrodite. East of Altemps, the Renaissance façade of the church of **Sant'Agostino** is not much to look at but the church's handful of art treasures might draw you in – among them Raphael's vibrant *Isaiah*, on the third pillar on the left, Sansovino's craggy *St Anne, Virgin and Child*, and, in the first chapel on the left, a *Madonna and Pilgrims* by Caravaggio, which is badly lit, so come prepared with coins for the light box. There's more work by Caravaggio down Via della Scrofa, in the French national church of **San Luigi dei Francesi**, in the last chapel on the left: early works, describing the life and martyrdom of St Matthew, best of which is the *Calling of St Matthew* on the left wall – Matthew is the dissolute-looking youth on the far left, illuminated by a shaft of sunlight. A little way up Via della Ripetta from here, the **Ara Pacis Augustae** (closed for restoration) was built in 13 BC to celebrate Augustus' victory over Spain and Gaul. It supports a fragmented frieze showing Augustus himself, his wife Livia, Tiberius, Agrippa, and various children clutching the togas of the elders, the last of whom is said to be the young Claudius.

At the far end of Via di Ripetta the **Piazza del Popolo** provides an impressive entrance to the city, all symmetry and grand vistas, although its real attraction is the church of **Santa Maria del Popolo**, which holds some of the best Renaissance art of any Roman church, including frescoes by Pinturicchio in the south aisle and two fine tombs by Andrea Sansovino. Two pictures by Caravaggio get most attention – the *Conversion of St Paul* and the *Crucifixion of St Peter*.

Villa Borghese

At the northern edge of the city centre, the **Villa Borghese** (Metro Flaminio or Spagna), now beautifully restored, is made up of the grounds of the seventeenth-century palace of Cardinal Scipione Borghese – a vast and peaceful area of woods, lakes and grass. The main attraction is the **Galleria Borghese** (Tues–Sun 9am–7pm; €8.03; book on ☏06.328.0010), which has an assortment of works collected by Scipione Borghese, notably sculptures by Bernini and a small, but fine collection of paintings: *Aeneas and Anchises, Rape of Proserpine, Apollo and Daphne* and *David*.

The Villa Borghese's two other major museums are on the other side of the park, along the Viale delle Belle Arti. Of these, **Museo Nazionale di Villa Giulia** (Tues–Sun 8.30am–7.30pm; €4) is the world's primary collection of Etruscan treasures. Best among the sculpture is the group of *Apollo and Hercules*, from the site of Veio, north of Rome, and the remarkable *Sarcophagus of a Married Couple* from Cerveteri. Other highlights include the *Cistae* recovered from tombs around

Praeneste – drum-like objects, engraved and adorned with figures, that were supposed to hold all the things needed for the care of the body after death – and marvellously intricate pieces of gold jewellery, delicately worked into tiny animals.

The **Galleria Nazionale d'Arte Moderna** (Tues–Sun 8.30am–7.20pm; €6.50) houses an undistinguished collection of nineteenth- and twentieth-century Italian art including works by Modigliani, Di Chirico, Boccion and other Futurists, along with the odd Cézanne, Mondrian and Klimt.

East of Via del Corso

The area immediately southeast of Piazza del Popolo is travellers' Rome, historically the artistic quarter of the city, with a distinctly cosmopolitan air. At the centre of the district, **Piazza di Spagna** is a long, thin square centring on the distinctive boat-shaped **Barcaccia** fountain, the last work of Bernini's father. Opposite, the **Keats–Shelley Memorial House** (Mon–Sat 9/11am–1pm & 3–6pm; €3), where John Keats died in 1821, now serves as an archive of English-language literary and historical works and a museum of literary mementoes. Beside the house, the **Spanish Steps** – a venue for international posing – sweep up to the **Trinità dei Monti**, a largely sixteenth-century church that holds a couple of works by Daniel da Volterra, notably a soft flowing fresco of *The Assumption* in the third chapel on the right, which includes a portrait of his teacher Michelangelo. His *Deposition*, across the nave, is also worth a glance; it was painted from a series of drawings by Michelangelo.

From the church, follow Via Sistina to **Piazza Barberini**, a busy traffic junction, in the centre of which is Bernini's **Fontana del Tritone**. **Via Veneto** bends north from here, its pricey bars and restaurants once the haunt of Rome's Beautiful People but now home of high-class tack and overpriced sleaze. A little way up, the Capuchin **Church of the Immaculate Conception** is worth visiting for its cemetery (9am–noon & 3–6pm, closed Thurs; donation requested); the bones of four thousand monks line the walls of a series of chapels in rococo patterns or as fully clothed skeletons, their faces peering out of their cowls in expressions of agony.

Back across **Piazza Barberini**, the Palazzo Barberini is home to the **Galleria d'Arte Antica** (Tues–Sun 9am–7pm; closed winter; €5; book on ☏06 328101), which displays a rich patchwork of mainly Italian art from the early Renaissance to late Baroque period. In addition to canvases by Tintoretto, Titian and El Greco, highlights include Filippo Lippi's warmly maternal *Madonna and Child*, painted in 1437, and Raphael's beguiling *Fornarina*. But perhaps the most impressive feature of the gallery is the building itself, the epitome of Baroque grandeur worked on at different times by the most favoured architects of the day: Bernini, Borromini and Maderno. The Salone is guaranteed to impress, its ceiling frescoed by Pietro da Cortona in one of the best examples of exuberant Baroque trompe l'oeil work, a manic rendering of *The Triumph of Divine Providence*.

East down Via del Tritone from Piazza Barberini, hidden among a tight web of narrow, apparently aimless streets, is one of Rome's more surprising sights, easy to stumble upon by accident – the **Fontane di Trevi**, a huge Baroque gush of water over statues and rocks built onto the back of a Renaissance palace. Originally commissioned from Bernini by Pope Urban VIII, it wasn't begun until Niccolo Salvi took up the project in 1723. The Trevi fountain is now best known for Anita Ekberg's frolics in Fellini's film *La Dolce Vita*. Unless you enjoy crowds, go very early or in the middle of the night.

Five minutes from the gallery, **Via Nazionale**, one of Rome's main shopping streets, lined with boutiques, leads up to **Piazza della Repubblica**, a stern but rather tawdry semicircle of buildings that occupies part of the site of Diocletian's Baths, the scanty remains of which lie across the square in the church of **Santa Maria degli Angeli**. Michelangelo is also said to have had a hand in modifying another part of the baths, the courtyard that makes up part of the **Museo Nazionale Romano** behind the church (closed for restoration). The museum's collection of Greek and Roman antiquities is second only to the Vatican's and is now partly housed in the **Palazzo Altemps**, **Palazzo Braschi** and the **Palazzo Massimo** across the square at Piazza dei Cinquecento 68 (Tues–Sun 9am–7.45pm; €6), a recently restored building featuring a series of Roman busts, mosaics and fresco fragments. The top floor gallery contains stunning, sylvan frescoes from a country villa that belonged to the emperor Augustus's wife Livia, and some of the best examples of mosaics from Roman villas around the world. Close by on Via XX Settembre, the church of **Santa Maria della Vittoria** was built by Carlo Maderno and its interior is one of the most elaborate examples of Baroque decoration in Rome, its ceiling and walls pitted with carving, and statues crammed into remote corners like an overstuffed attic. The church's best-known feature is Bernini's melodramatic carving of the *Ecstasy of St Theresa*, the centrepiece of the sepulchral chapel of Cardinal Cornaro.

Southeast of Piazza Venezia

From Piazza Venezia **Via dei Fori Imperiali** cuts south, a soulless boulevard whose main pedestrians are tourists rooting about among the ancient sites. Just off Piazza Venezia, **Trajan's Column** was erected to celebrate the emperor's colonization of Dacia (modern day Romania) and its reliefs iillustrate the highlights of the Dacian campaign. Across the road is the **Roman Forum, Palatine Hill and Colosseum** (Tues–Sun 9am–6pm/1hr before sunset; forum free, rest €8), in ancient times the centre of what was a very large city. Following the downfall of the city to various barbarian invaders, the area was left in ruin, its relics quarried for construction in other parts of Rome during medieval and Renaissance times.

Running through the core of the Forum, the **Via Sacra** was the best-known street of ancient Rome. At the bottom of the Capitoline Hill, the **Arch of Septimus Severus** was built in the early third century AD to commemorate the emperor's 10th anniversary in power, and the grassy, wide-open scatter of paving and beached columns in front of it was the place where most of the life of the city took place. Nearby, the **Curia** is one of the few complete structures here, a huge building that was begun in 80 BC, restored by Julius Caesar soon after and rebuilt by Diocletian in the third century AD. The Senate met here during the Republican period, and augurs would come to announce the wishes of the gods. On the opposite side is the **House of the Vestal Virgins**, where lived the six women charged with the responsibility of keeping the sacred flame of Vesta alight: four floors of rooms around a central courtyard, with the round **Temple of Vesta** at the near end. On the far side of the site, the **Basilica of Constantine and Maxentius** is probably the Forum's most impressive remains. It's said that Michelangelo studied the hexagonal coffered arches here when grappling with the dome of St Peter's. From the basilica, the Via Sacra climbs to the **Arch of Titus** on a low arm of the Palatine Hill – its reliefs showing the spoils of the sacking of Jerusalem being carried off by eager Romans. Just to the north is the Forum Museum (Antiquarium Forense) – a small collection of Iron Age burial urns and pre-Roman artefacts.

Turning right at the Arch of Titus takes you up to the **Palatine Hill**, now a stunningly beautiful archeological garden. In the days of the Republic, the Palatine was the most desirable address in Rome (from it is derived our word "palace"), and the big names continued to colonize it during the imperial era, trying to outdo each other with ever larger and more magnificent dwellings. The gargantuan **Domus Augustana** spreads to the far brink of the hill. You can look down from here onto its vast central courtyard and maze-like fountain, and wander through a handful of its bare rooms. From close by, steps lead down to the **Cryptoporticus**, a passage built by Nero to link the Palatine with his palace on the far side of the Colosseum, and decorated along part of its length with well-preserved Roman stuccowork. A left turn leads to the **House of Livia**, originally believed to have been the residence of the wife of Augustus, whose courtyard and rooms are decorated with scanty frescoes. Turn right down the passage and up some steps and you're in the

Farnese Gardens, among the first botanical gardens in Europe, laid out by Alessandro Farnese in the mid-sixteenth century and now a tidily planted refuge from the exposed heat of the ruins. The terrace here looks back over the Forum, while the terrace at the opposite end looks down on the real centre of Rome's ancient beginning – an Iron Age hut, known as the **House of Romulus**, the best preserved part of a ninth-century village, and the so-called **Lupercal**, beyond, which tradition says was the cave where Romulus and Remus were suckled by the she-wolf.

Immediately outside the Forum, the fourth-century **Arch of Constantine** marks the end of the Via Sacra. Across from here, the **Colosseum** is Rome's most awe-inspiring ancient monument, begun by the Emperor Vespasian around 72 AD and finished by his son Titus about eight years later – an event celebrated by 100 days of games. The Romans flocked here for gladiatorial contests and cruel spectacles that pitted man against animal, animal against animal – scenes recently dramatized in the film *Gladiator*. They even had mock sea battles – the arena could be flooded in minutes. After the games were outlawed in the fifth century, the Colosseum was pillaged for building material, and is now little more than a shell. The structure of the place is still easy to see, however, and has served as a model for stadia around the world ever since.

Close by is Nero's **Domus Aurea** (daily 9am–8pm, €5; booking recommended, ☏06.3996.7700). The entrance is opposite the Colosseum, off Via Labicana, a short walk up some steps on the Oppian Hill. The whole complex was built by Nero as his private house and helped to make him even more unpopular than before. The palace covered a full square mile, and its extravagant halls were decorated in the most lavish style: masterful frescoes and carved stucco painted in rich colours, and covered in gold leaf. Little remains. Filled with rubble 35 years after Nero's death, and stripped of its marbles, when the site was first rediscovered hundreds of years later, it was thought to be some sort of mystical cave or grotto.

It's a short walk from here down Via San Giovanni in Laterano to the church of **San Clemente**, a light, twelfth-century basilica that encapsulates the continuity of history in the city. It's a conglomeration of three places of worship. The ground-floor church is a superb example of a medieval basilica, with some fine mosaics in the apse. Downstairs (€3), there's the nave of an earlier church, dated back to 392 AD. At the eastern end and down another level are the remains of a Roman apartment building – a labyrinthine set of rooms including a Mithraic temple of the late second century standing next to a first-century imperial block.

The same street leads to the basilica of **San Giovanni in Laterano**, Rome's cathedral and the seat of the pope until the Unification of Italy. There has been a church on this site since the fourth century, the first established by Constantine. The present building, reworked by Borromini in the mid-seventeenth century, evokes Rome's staggering wealth of history. The doors were taken from the Curia of the Roman Forum. Inside, the first pillar on the left of the right-hand aisle shows a fragment of Giotto's fresco of Boniface VIII, proclaiming the first Holy Year in 1300, while further on, a more recent monument commemorates Sylvester I, bishop of Rome during much of Constantine's reign, and incorporates part of his original tomb, said to sweat and rattle its bones when a pope is about to die. Behind the papal altar are the reliquaries for the heads of SS Peter and Paul, though the relics themselves were stolen in the early 1800s. Outside, the cloisters (€3) are one of the most pleasing parts of the complex, decorated with early thirteenth-century Cosmati work. Next door, the **Baptistry** is the oldest surviving in the Christian world, an octagonal structure built by Constantine, rebuilt during the fifth century, and now carefully restored after a 1993 car bomb damaged the stonework and some of the frescoes. On the other side of the church the **Scala Santa** is claimed to be the staircase from Pontius Pilate's house down which Christ walked after his trial. The 28 steps are protected by boards, and the only way you're allowed to climb them is on your knees – which pilgrims do regularly.

On the far side of the road from the Colosseum, the main feature of interest on the Esquiline Hill is the church of **San Pietro in Vincoli**, one of Rome's most delightfully plain churches, built to house an important relic: the chains of St Peter from his imprisonment in Jerusalem, along with those that bound him when a prisoner in Rome. These can still be seen in the glass case on the altar, but most people come for Michelangelo's unfinished Tomb of Pope Julius II in the southern aisle. The figure of Moses, pictured as descended from Sinai to find the Israelites worshipping the golden calf, and flanked by the gentle figures of Leah and Rachel, is one of the artist's most arresting works. Steps lead down from San Pietro to **Via Cavour**, a busy central thoroughfare that carves a route up to Termini past the basilica of **Santa Maria Maggiore**, one of the city's four great basilicas, with a broad nave fringed on both sides with strikingly well-kept mosaics, most of which date from the church's construction and tell of incidents from the Old Testament. The Sistine chapel, on the right, holds the elaborate tomb of Sixtus V, while the equally fancy Pauline chapel opposite has a venerated twelfth-century *Madonna* topped with a panel showing the legendary tracing of the church's plan after a miraculous August snowfall.

South of the centre

On the southern side of the Palatine Hill is the **Circo Massimo**, a long green expanse that was ancient Rome's chariot racing track. The arena once held a crowd of 200,000, but now a litter of stones at the Viale Aventino end is all that remains. Across the far side of Piazza di Porta Capena, the **Baths of Caracalla** (Mon 9am–1pm, Tues–Sun 9am–1hr before sunset; €5) are better preserved, and give a much better sense of the scale of Roman architecture. It's a short walk from behind the baths down Via Gitto to the Protestant Cemetery (Tues–Sun, 9am–5pm; donations expected), accessible direct on metro line B (Piramide stop), the burial place of Keats and Shelley – a small, tranquil enclave, crouched behind the mossy pyramidal tomb of Caius Cestius.

San Paolo fuori le Mura, 2km south, is one of the four patriarchal basilicas of Rome, occupying the supposed site of St Paul's tomb. Of the four, it has fared least well over the years, and the church you see is largely a nineteenth-century reconstruction after a devastating fire. It is a huge, impressive building, and home to a handful of ancient features: in the south transept, the Paschal Candlestick is a remarkable piece of Romanesque carving, supported by half-human beasts and rising through entwined tendrils and strangely human limbs and bodies to scenes from Christ's life; the bronze aisle doors date from 1070, and the Cosmati cloister, just behind here, is probably Rome's finest, its spiralling, mosaic-encrusted columns enclosing a peaceful rose garden.

Further south still, on the edge of the city, the **Via Appia** was the most important of all the Roman trade routes. Its sides are lined with the underground burial cemeteries or **Catacombs** of the first Christians. There are five complexes in all, dating from the first to the fourth centuries, almost entirely emptied of bodies now but still decorated with the primitive signs and frescoes that were the hallmark of the then-burgeoning Christian movement. You can get to the main grouping on bus #218 from the Colosseum (Via San Gregorio in Laterano), but the only ones of any significance are the catacombs of **San Callisto** (8.30am–noon & 2.30–5pm; closed Wed & all Feb; €5), burial place of all the third-century popes, whose tombs are preserved in the papal crypt, and the site of some well-preserved seventh- and eighth-century frescoes; and those of **San Sebastiano** 500m further on (9am–noon & 2.30–5pm; closed Sun & mid-Nov to mid-Dec; €5) under a basilica that was originally built by Constantine. Tours take in paintings of doves and fish, a contemporary carved oil lamp and inscriptions dating the tombs themselves – although the most striking features are three pagan tombs discovered when archeologists were burrowing beneath the floor of the basilica upstairs. Nearby graffiti records the fact that this was indeed, albeit temporarily, where the Apostles Peter and Paul rested.

Trastevere

Across the Tiber from the centre of town, **Trastevere** is a small, tightly knit neighbourhood that was once the artisan quarter of the city and has since become gentrified. It is now home to much of its most vibrant and youthful nightlife – and some of Rome's best restaurants. The best time to come is on Sunday morning, when the **Porta Portese** flea market stretches down Via Portuense to Trastevere station in a congested medley of junk, antiques and clothing. Afterwards, stroll north up Via Anicia to the church of **Santa Cecilia in Trastevere**, built over the site of the second-century home of the patron saint of music. Locked in the hot chamber of her own baths for several days, she sang her way through the ordeal until her head was hacked half off with an axe. At the back of the church you can see excavations of the baths, though hints at restoration have robbed these of any atmosphere. If you get the chance, have a peek at the Singing Gallery's beautifully coloured and tender **frescoes** by Piero Cavallini (c.1293; Tues–Thurs 10am–noon, Sun 11.30am–12.15pm; donation expected).

Santa Cecilia is situated in the quieter part of Trastevere, on the southern side of Viale Trastevere, the wide boulevard which cuts through the centre of the district. There's more life on the other side centred on **Piazza Santa Maria in Trastevere**, named after the church of **Santa Maria in Trastevere** – held to be the first official church in Rome, built on a site where a fountain of oil is said to have sprung on the day of Christ's birth and sporting some of the city's most impressive mosaics, also by Cavallini. North towards the Tiber, the **Villa Farnesina** is known for its Renaissance murals, including a Raphael-designed painting of *Cupid and Psyche*, completed in 1517 by the artist's assistants. Raphael did, however, manage to finish the *Galatea* next door. The other paintings in the room are by Sebastiano del Piombo and the architect of the building, Peruzzi, who also decorated the upstairs Salone delle Prospettive, which shows trompe l'oeil galleries with views of contemporary Rome – one of the earliest examples of the technique.

Castel Sant'Angelo, St Peter's and the Vatican Museums

Across the Tiber from Rome's old centre, the **Castel Sant'Angelo** (Tues–Sun 9am–8/10pm; €6.20; Metro Lepanto) was the burial place of the Emperor Hadrian. In the sixteenth century, the pope converted the building for use as a fortress and built a passageway to link it with the Vatican as a refuge in times of siege. Inside, rooms hold swords, armour, guns and the like, while below, dungeons and storerooms are testament to the castle's grisly past as the city's most notorious Renaissance prison. Upstairs, the official papal apartments, accessible from the terrace, are extravagantly decorated with lewd frescoes amid paintings by Poussin, Jordaens and others.

Via della Conciliazione, which Mussolini ploughed through the old *borgo* to seal a pact with the pope, leads to the **Vatican City** (Metro Cipro), a tiny territory surrounded by high walls on its far side and on the near side opening its doors to the rest of the city and its pilgrims in the form of Bernini's **Piazza San Pietro**. The basilica of St Peter's (daily 7am–6/7pm; free) is the replacement of a basilica built during the time of Constantine, to a plan initially conceived at the turn of the fifteenth century by Bramante and finished off, heavily modified, over a century later by Carlo Maderno, making it something of a bridge between the Renaissance and Baroque eras. The inside is full of features from the Baroque period, although the first thing you see, on the right, is Michelangelo's *Pietà*, completed when he was just 24 and, following an attack in 1972, displayed behind glass. To the right is the Holy Door, opened by the pope for 2000, which he had declared a holy year; in all other years it remains bricked up. On the right-hand side of the nave, the bronze statue of St Peter was cast in the thirteenth century by Arnolfo di Cambio and has its right foot polished smooth by the attentions of pilgrims. Bronze was also the material used in Bernini's massive 28m high baldachino, the centrepiece of the sculptor's embellishment of the interior. Bernini's feverish sculpting decorates the apse, too, his *cattedra* enclosing the supposed chair of St Peter in a curvy marble and stucco throne. An entrance off the aisle leads to the **treasury** (daily 9am–5/6pm; €4.20), while back at the central crossing, steps lead down to the **Vatican Grottoes** (daily 7/8am–5/6pm), where a number of popes are buried in grandiose tombs – in the main, those not distinguished enough to be buried up above. Under the portico, to the right of the main doors, you can ascend to the **roof and dome** (by lift €4.20) – from where the views over the city are glorious.

A five-minute walk out of the northern side of the piazza takes you up to the only part of the Vatican Palace you can visit independently, the **Vatican Museums** (Mon–Sat 8.45am–4.45pm, last Sun of month 8.45am–1.45pm; €10, free Sun) – quite simply the largest, richest museum complex in the world, stuffed with booty from every period of the city's history. There's no point in trying to see everything on one visit; you'd do far better to select what you want to see and aim to return another time if you can. It's worth also taking account of the official, colour-coded routes that are constructed for varying amounts of time and interest and can take anything from 45 minutes to the best part of a day.

Start off at the **Raphael Stanze**, at the opposite end of the building to the entrance, a set of rooms decorated for Pope Julius II by Raphael among others. Of the two most interesting rooms, the **Stanza Eliodoro** is home to the *Expulsion of Heliodorus from the Temple*, an allusion to the military success of Julius II, depicted on the left in portrait. Not to be outdone, Leo X, Julius's successor, in the *Meeting of Attila and St Leo* opposite, ordered Raphael to substitute his head for that of Julius II, turning the painting into an allegory of the Battle of Ravenna at which he was present; thus he appears twice, as pope and as the equally portly Medici cardinal just behind. In the same room, the *Mass at Bolsena* shows Julius again on the right, pictured in attendance at a famous thirteenth-century miracle in Orvieto (see p.641). The next room, the **Stanza della Segnatura** or pope's study, was decorated between 1512 and 1514, and its *School of Athens*, on the near wall as you come in, is perhaps Raphael's most renowned work, a representation of the "Triumph of Scientific Truth" in which all the great minds from antiquity are present.

Steps lead down from the Raphael Stanze to the **Sistine Chapel**, built for Pope Sixtus IV in 1481, which serves as the pope's private chapel and hosts the conclaves of cardinals for the election of each new pontiff. The **paintings** down each side wall are contemporary with the building, depictions of scenes from the lives of Moses and Christ by Perugino, Botticelli and Ghirlandaio among others. But it's the **ceiling frescoes** of Ghirlandaio's pupil, Michelangelo, depicting the *Creation*, that everyone comes to see, executed almost single-handed over a period of about four years, again for Pope Julius II. Whether the ceiling has been improved by the controversial recent restoration is a moot point, but the virtuosity of the work remains stunning. The *Last Judgement*, on the west wall of the chapel, was painted by Michelangelo over twenty years later, and is quite possibly the most inspired large-scale painting you'll ever see. The nudity caused controversy from the start, and the pope's zealous successor, Pius IV, would have had the painting removed had not Michelangelo's pupil, Daniele da Volterra, carefully added coverings – some of which have been left by the restorers – to the more obvious nudes, earning himself the nickname of the "breeches-maker".

Having seen the Raphael rooms and the Sistine Chapel, you've barely scratched the surface of the Vatican. At the opposite end of the Vatican Palace are grouped most of the other museums. In the main body of the palace, the small **Museo Pio-Clementino** holds some of the best of the Vatican's classical statuary, including the serene *Apollo Belvedere*, a Roman copy of a fourth-century BC original, and the second-century BC *Laocoön*, which depicts the treacherous priest of Apollo being crushed with his sons by serpents. Near the Pio-Clementino museum, the **Museo Chiaramonti** and **Braccio Nuovo** hold more classical sculpture, the Museo Egizio has lots of mummies, and the **Museo Gregoriano Etrusco** offers sculpture, funerary art and applied art from the sites of southern Etruria. In a separate building, the **Pinacoteca** has works from the Early to High Renaissance: pieces by Crivelli, Lippi and Giotto; the rich backdrops and elegantly clad figures of the Umbrian painters Perugino and Pinturrichio; Raphael's unfinished *Transfiguration*, which hung above the artist as he lay in state; Leonardo's *St Jerome*; and Caravaggio's *Descent from the Cross* – a warts 'n' all canvas that is imitated successfully by Reni's *Crucifixion of St Peter* in the same room.

Eating and drinking

You can **eat** cheaply and well in Rome. Restaurants cluster near Campo dei Fiori and Piazza Navona, but Trastevere is Rome's traditional restaurant ghetto and the home of some fine and reasonably priced eateries.

Snacks, cakes and ice cream

Al Settimo Gelo via Vodice 21. On the corner with via Oslavia and worth the hike for their *cioccolato al peperoncino*, or their heavenly cardamom-flavoured ice. Metro Lepanto.

Ciampini Piazza San Lorenzo in Lucina. Expensive, but it's so popular, and the ice cream here is so good, that they don't even need to put it out on display.

Il Delfino Corso V. Emanuele 67. Central and very busy cafeteria with a huge choice of snacks and full meals. Good for a fast fill-up.

Il Forno del Ghetto Via del Portico d'Ottavia 1. Unmarked Jewish bakery with marvellous ricotta and dried fruit-filled cakes. Closed Sat.

Il Gelato di San Crispino Via della Panetteria 42. Close to the Trevi fountain and considered Rome's best. Closed Tues.

Giolitti Via Offici Uffici del Vicaro 40. An Italian institution that once had a reputation for the country's top ice cream. Overrated, crowded, but has a choice of seventy flavours. Closed Mon.

Pascucci Via di Torre Argentina 20. Just the thing after hours of sightseeing – a Roman *frullato*, the local version of a milkshake.

Sciam Via del Pellegrino 56. A Middle Eastern-style tea room, done up in truly lavish style, offering exotic teas and treats.

Tre Scalini Piazza Navona. Renowned for its absolutely remarkable *tartufo*. Closed Wed.

Restaurants

Al Leoncino Via del Leoncino 28. Inexpensive city-centre pizzeria.

Ai Marmi Viale Trastevere 53–59 ☎06.580.0919. Rome's most traditional pizzeria, with regional extras such as deep-fried stuffed olives and batter-fried cod. Closed Wed.

Da Baffetto Via Governo Vecchio 114. An old-fashioned pizzeria, swamped by tourists, but still good value. Expect to queue. Eve only.

Filetti di Baccala Largo dei Librari 88. Paper-covered Formica tables, cheap wine and beer, and

fried fish dishes. Eve only. Closed Sun & all Aug.

Grappola d'Oro Piazza della Cancelleria 80 ☎06.689.7080. Curiously untouched place with genuine Roman cuisine and a timeless trattoria feel. Closed Sun.

Da Giggetto Via del Portico d'Ottavia 21a ☎06.686.1105. Much pricier than most, but worth it for the Romano–Jewish cooking. Closed Mon.

L'Insalata Ricca Largo di Chiavari 85 ☎06.6880.3656. Relaxed place, with interesting salads and hearty pastas.

Osteria Dell' Angelo Via Bettolo 24 ☎06.372.9470. A short walk from St Peter's and off the tourist trail. Good, basic Italian cooking, excellent value set menu in the evening. Book, or get there by 8pm for a seat.

Pizzeria Da Poeta Vicolo del Bologna 45. One of the best pizzerias in Rome. Closed Mon.

Silvio Via Urbana 67–69 ☎06.48.6531. Classic Italian cooking at this unpretentious restaurant. Closed Mon. Near Metro Cavour.

Tram Tram Via dei Reti 44–46. San Lorenzo district's top student favourite, featuring regional Pugliese cooking. Closed Mon.

Da Vittorio Via San Cosimato 14a. Neapolitan pizza in the heart of Trastevere. Closed Mon.

Bars and birrerias

Bar della Pace Via della Pace 5. Just off Piazza Navona, this is the summer bar to be seen in, with outside tables full of Rome's self-consciously beautiful people.

Enoteca Cavour Via Cavour 313. At the Forum end of Via Cavour, a handy retreat with an easy-going studenty feel, lots of wine and bottled beers and (slightly overpriced) snacks.

Il Fico Piazza del Fico. Late at night the piazza thrums with the bars' young Roman clientele; escape inside for a cocktail-bar atmosphere.

Jonathan's Angels Via della Fossa 18, next door to *Il Fico*. This colourful bar presents an explosion of kitsch decor.

La Locandiera Via di Sora, 12. Tiny, atmospheric

vineria serving good *bruschetta* and *ciambelle*, and has a roaring fire in winter.

Ombre Rosse Piazza Sant'Egidio 12. Trastevere's liveliest venue, offering a huge menu of drinks and good light snacks, plus newspapers in several languages.

La Scala Piazza della Scala. The most popular Trastevere *birreria* – big, bustling and crowded.

Vineria Campo dei Fiori 15. Fashionable *vineria* that spills out into the square during the summer.

Nightlife

Roman **nightlife** still retains some of the smart ethos satirized in Fellini's *Dolce Vita*. **Discos and clubs** cover the range: there are vast glittering palaces with stunning lights and sound systems, places that are not much more than upmarket bars with music, and other, more down-to-earth places to dance, playing a more interesting selection of music to a younger crowd (entrance from €5), with the *centri sociali* (see below) offering an innovative alternative to the mainstream scene, usually on a "pay what you can" basis. Rome's **rock scene** is a fairly limp affair, and the city is much more in its element with **jazz**, with lots of venues and a wide choice of styles performed by a healthy array of local talent. Most clubs close during July and August, or move to locations on the coast, but *Estate Romana* organizes many outdoor locations all over Rome for concerts, discos, bars and cinemas. Many top international groups participate. You may have to pay a membership fee on top of the admission price. Drinks, though, are generally no more expensive than you'd pay in the average bar.

The city's best source of **listings** is the magazine *Roma C'è* issued on Friday with a section in English, or the *TrovaRoma* supplement published with the Thursday edition of *La Repubblica*.

Centri sociali

In the suburbs of Rome, **centri sociali** have opened in abandoned public buildings, mostly by students, who offer a cheap, alternative programme of concerts, films and parties. The students are politically active, and work with newly arrived immigrants, the events they organize are among the more interesting that take place in Rome. We recommend a couple here, but for full listings see *Roma C'è* and *Il Manifesto*.

Forte Prenestino Via F. del Pino. Situated in an abandoned nineteenth-century fortress. Offers two big arenas for concerts and a beehive of smaller spaces used for exhibitions, cinema, a disco and a bar.

Villaggio Globale Ex-Mattatoio In the old slaughterhouse in Testaccio, partly run by the Senegalese community in Rome, which organizes concerts, parties and exhibitions, helped by a grant from local authorities.

Discos and clubs

L'Alibi Via Monte Testaccio 44. Predominantly but not exclusively male venue that's one of Rome's best gay clubs. Downstairs cellar disco and upstairs open-air bar.

Black Out Club Via Saturnia 18. Popular disco playing a mix of house, punk and grunge.

Gilda Via Mario de' Fiori 97. Slick, stylish club, the focus for the city's minor (and would-be) celebs.

Goa Via Libetta 13. An ethnic feel to accentuate the house, techno and trance high-energy dance atmosphere.

Siva Via del Cardello 13a. Seventies and eighties disco just off Via Cavour.

Live music: rock, jazz and Latin

Alexanderplatz Via Ostia 9 ☎06.3974.2171. Rome's foremost jazz club/restaurant. Reservations recommended.

Alpheus Via del Commercio 36–38. A four-roomed venue with concerts, a disco, theatrical performances and a bar.

Berimbau Via dei Fienaroli 30/b. Live Latin-American music and Brazilian drinks.

Big Mama Vicolo San Francesco a Ripa 18. Trastevere-based jazz/blues club of long standing. Closed July–Sept.

Blue Knight Via delle Fornaci 8–10. Bar and

gelateria on the ground floor; downstairs there's live music Thurs–Sat.

Caffè Latino Via di Monte Testaccio 96. Multi-event club in the newly hip area near the Protestant cemetery. Best at weekends when it's crowded and more atmospheric.

Charity Café Via Panisperna 68. Tiny club with live jazz music and great ambience.

Circolo degli Artisti Via Casilina Vecchia 42. Huge bar and disco with more alternative live music. Cheap and fun.

Fonclea Via Crescenzio 82a. Long running jazz/salsa outfit, with live music most nights. Metro Ottaviano.

Classical music, opera and film

For **classical music**, the city's churches host a wide range of choral, chamber and organ recitals, many of them free. International names appear at Rome's new Auditorium (✆800.90.70.80). The Accademia di Santa Cecilia (✆06.6880.1044) stages concerts by its own or visiting orchestras at Via della Conciliazione 4 and, in summer, in the gardens of the Villa Giulia. Rome's **opera** scene concentrates on the Teatro dell'Opera, on the Via Firenze, Piazza B. Gigli in winter (box office Mon–Sat 9am–5pm; ✆06.481.601) and at various outdoor venues in summer. Purists should be prepared for a carnival atmosphere and plenty of unscheduled intervals. Rome's two **English-language cinemas** are the Pasquino, Piazza Sant'Egidio 10 on Vicolo del Piede in Trastevere (✆06.580.3622), and the Quirinetta at Via Minghetti 4 (✆06.679.0012). Other cinemas occasionally showing English-language films are the Nuovo Sacher, Largo Ascianghi 1 (✆06.581.8116), and Alcazar, Via Cardinal Merry del Val 14 (✆06.588.0099).

Festivals

Much of Rome's nightlife moves outdoors during the summer, all part of the *Estate Romana* programme; festivals offer live music, movies, markets and munchies and may be a more appealing option than the clubs on a hot summer evening.

La Festa di Noantri Viale Trastevere and around. Medieval Trastevere's traditional summer festival in honour of the Virgin, with street stalls selling all sorts of snacks and trinkets, and a grand finale of fireworks. The main event is the Virgin's effigy being hauled joyously from the church of Santa Agata to that of San Crisogono, and back again. Last two weeks of July.

La Festa dell'Unità Venues change annually; check *Roma C'è* for details. Throughout the summer, this cheery hotchpotch of music, film, eateries, games and other attractions – much of it free – is the re-founded Communist Party's way of reminding people of what fun the Left can be.

Fiesta Capannelle Via Appia Nuova 1245. Based at Rome's racecourse in the southeast of the city, this festival has a Latin American flavour. Metro A to Subagosto, then bus #354 to Ippodromo Capannelle. Mid-June to Aug.

Testaccio Village Viale del Campo Boario. Just behind the old Testaccio slaughterhouse, this nightly festival draws a young crowd for the bars and stalls, live bands (rock, Latin and jazz) and DJs. Metro B to Piramide, night bus #40N back. June–Sept.

Tevere Expo Tiber Embankment, main entrance by Castel Sant'Angelo. Atmospheric annual handicrafts fair along the river; nighttime stalls, bars and live entertainment. Mid-June to July.

Listings

Embassies Australia, Via Alessandria 215 ✆06.852.721; Canada, Via G.b. de Rossi 27 ✆06.445.981; New Zealand, Via Zara 28 ✆06.441.7171; UK, Via XX Settembre 80 ✆06.422.00001; US, Via V. Veneto 121 ✆06.46.741.

Exchange Two offices at Termini station operate out of banking hours; also Cambio Rosati, Via Nazionale 186 ✆06.488.5498.

Hospital ✆06.884.0113 for 24-hour assistance.

Most central hospital: Santo Spirito, Lungotevere in Sassia 1 ✆06.68.351; International Medical Centre ✆06.488.2371.

Internet access easyInternet Café, Piazza Barberini; TreviNet Pl@ce, Via in Arcione 103.

Left luggage At Termini station.

Pharmacies PIRAM, Via Nazionale 228; at Stazione Termini. Rota posted on pharmacy doors.

Police Questura, Via S. Vitale ✆06.4686.

Post office Piazza San Silvestro 18–20.

Tivoli

Just 40km from Rome, **TIVOLI** has always been a retreat from the city. In classical days it was a retirement town for wealthy Romans; later, during Renaissance times, it again became the playground of the moneyed classes.

Most people head first for the **Villa d'Este** (Tues–Sun 8.30am–7.30pm/1hr before sunset; €6.50), the country villa of Cardinal Ippolito d'Este, across the main square of Largo Garibaldi. It's the gardens rather than the villa itself that they come to see, peeling away down the hill in a succession of terraces – probably the most contrived gardens in Italy, interrupted at decent intervals by one playful fountain after another, unfortunately not all in working order. The town's other attraction, the **Villa Gregoriana** (closed for restoration at the time of writing), is a park with waterfalls created when Pope Gregory XVI diverted the flow of the river here in 1831 to ease periodic flooding of the town. The lush, overgrown vegetation descends into a gorge over 60m deep. There are two main waterfalls – the *Grande Cascata* on the far side, and a small Bernini-designed one at the neck of the gorge. The path winds down to the bottom of the canyon, where you can get right up close to the pounding water, the dark shapes of the rock glowering overhead.

At the bottom of the hill, fifteen minutes' walk off the main Rome road (CAT bus #4 from Largo Garibaldi), the **Villa Adriana** (daily 8.30am–6.30pm; €6.50) casts the inventions of the Tivoli popes and cardinals into the shade. This was probably the largest and most sumptuous villa in the Roman Empire, the retirement home of the Emperor Hadrian for a short while between 135 AD and his death three years later, and it is now one of the most soothing spots around Rome. Hadrian was a great traveller and a keen architect, and parts of the villa were inspired by buildings he had seen around the world. Highlights include the Canopus, on the far side of the site and – perhaps the most photographed part of the site – the **Teatro Marittimo**, with its island in the middle of a circular pond, to which it's thought Hadrian retired at siesta time.

Buses run here daily from Rome's Rebibbia Ponte Mammolo station, and dropping off at Tivoli's main Largo Garibaldi. Opposite here is the **tourist office** (Mon & Sat 9am–2pm, Tues–Fri 8am–2pm & 3–6pm; ☎0774.334.522).

Ostia Antica

Another popular side trip from Rome is to **OSTIA ANTICA**. There are, in fact, two Ostias, both reachable by regular train from Rome's Piramide station: one, Lido di Ostia, is an over-visited seaside resort that is well worth avoiding; the other, the stop before the Lido, is for the excavations of the port of Ostia Antica. On a par with anything you'll see in Rome itself, the site (Tues–Sun 8.30am–7pm/1hr before sunset; €4) is grouped around the town's commercial centre, otherwise known as the **Piazzale di Corporazione** with the remains of shops and trading offices still fringing it, the mosaics in front of which denote their trade. Flanking one side of the square, the **Theatre** has been much restored but is nonetheless impressive, enlarged in the second century to hold up to four thousand people. On the left of the square, the **House of Apulius** preserves mosaic floors and, beyond, a dark aisled mithraeum with more mosaics illustrating the cult. Behind here, the **Casa di Diana** is probably the best-preserved private house in Ostia, with a dark set of rooms around a central courtyard, and again with a mithraeum at the back. You can climb up to its roof for a fine view of the rest of the site, afterwards crossing the road to the **Thermopolium** – an ancient Roman café, complete with seats, counter, display shelves and even wall paintings of parts of the menu. North of the Casa di Diana, the **Museum** (Tues–Sat 9am–4.30pm, Sun 9am–1pm; same ticket) holds a variety of articles from the site, including frescoes, and some fine sarcophagi and statuary. Left from here, the **Forum** centres on the Capitol building, reached by a wide flight of steps.

The south

The Italian south or *mezzogiorno* is quite a different experience from the north; indeed, few countries are more tangibly divided into two distinct, often antagonistic, regions. While the north is rich, the south is among the poorest areas in Europe, with a rate of unemployment around twice that of the north. The dialect down here is different, too, sounding almost Arabic sometimes. Indeed the south's "capital", Naples, is often compared to Cairo. For most people, **Naples**, officially the regional capital of **Campania** and only a couple of hours south of Rome, is the obvious focus, an utterly compelling city. The **Bay of Naples** is dense in interest, with the ancient sites of Pompeii and Herculaneum just half an hour outside – probably Italy's best-preserved and most revealing Roman remains – and the island of Capri, swarmed over by tourists these days but so beautiful that a day there is by no means time squandered. South of Naples, the **Amalfi Coast** is probably Europe's most dramatic stretch of coastline, harbouring some enticing – if crowded – beach resorts. **Puglia** – the long strip of land that makes up the "heel" of Italy – was for centuries a strategic province, invaded and colonized by just about every major power of the day. Apart from the Baroque wonders of **Lecce**, **Puglia** is really a province you pass through on the way elsewhere, not least to Bari and Brindisi with their ferry connections to Croatia and Greece (see below). **Basilicata** and **Calabria** are also to some extent transit regions, although in many ways they represent the quintessence of the *mezzogiorno* – culturally impoverished, underdeveloped and – owing to emigration – sparsely populated.

Ferries between **BARI** and Greece and Croatia dock at Maríttima station, next to the old city. From here, it is a short **bus ride** or 45-minute walk to the **tourist office** – Piazza Aldo Moro (Mon–Fri 8am–2pm, Tues & Thurs till 5.30pm; ☎080.524.2361, ⑩www.pugliaturismo.com/aptbari) – and the nearby **train station**. **BRÍNDISI** is about 100km southeast of Bari and has useful connections to Greece. Ferries dock at Maríttima station on Via del Mare, from where it's a few minutes' walk to the bottom of Corso Garibaldi, and another twenty minutes to the **train station** in Piazza Crispi. Lots of **buses** run down Corso Umberto and Corso Garibaldi. There's a **tourist office** on Viale Regina Margherita 43 (summer daily Mon–Fri 8.30am–2pm & 3–7pm; winter Sat only 8.30am–1pm; ☎0831.523.072, ⑩www.pugliaturismo.com/aptbrindisi).

Naples

Wherever else you travel south of Rome, the chances are that you'll wind up in **NAPLES**. It's the kind of city people visit with preconceptions, and it rarely disappoints: it is filthy, large and overbearing; it is crime-infested; and it is most definitely like nowhere else in Italy – something the inhabitants will be keener than anyone to tell you. One thing, though, is certain: a couple of days here and you're likely to be as staunch a defender of the place as its most devoted inhabitants. Few cities on earth excite such fierce loyalties.

Arrival, information and city transport

Naples' **Capodochino Airport** is northwest of the centre at Viale Umberto Maddalena, connected with Piazza Garibaldi by buses #14 and #15 (every 15min; journey time 30min). There's also a blue official airport bus (6am–midnight every 30min), which will take you straight to the port, Piazza Municipio and Piazza Garibaldi. **Trains** arrive at Napoli Centrale on Piazza Garibaldi, the main hub of all transport services. There is a tourist office at the train station (Mon–Sat 9am–8pm, Sun 9am–1.30pm), and a branch at the airport (daily 9am–7pm), but the **main office** is at Piazza Gesù Nuovo dei Martiri 58 (Mon–Sat 9am–8pm, Sun 9am–2.30pm; ☎081.551.2701, ⑩www.inaples.it). All have copies of the free **listings** booklet *Qui Napoli*, handy for ferry and bus times.

The only way to really get around Naples and stay sane is to walk. However, this is a large, sprawling city, so you'll need to use some form of public transport sooner or later. City **buses** are much the best option; buy tickets in advance from tobacconists or the booth on Piazza Garibaldi. There is also the **metropolitana**, a small underground network worth trying if only for the contemporary art on display, and **funiculars** scaling the hill of the Vómero from stations at piazzas Montesanto, Amedeo and Augusto. For **trips around the bay** in either direction, there are three rail systems, the most useful of which is the **Circumvesuviana**, which runs from its station on Corso Garibaldi around the Bay of Naples as far as Sorrento in about an hour. If you are around for more than a day, invest in the **Artecard**, which gives sixty hours of transport and entrance to six museums (€13).

Accommodation

A good many of the city's cheaper **hotels** are situated around Piazza Garibaldi, within spitting distance of the train station and not badly placed for the rest of town. A word of warning: don't go with any of the touts in the station.

Hostel

Hostel Pensione Mancini Via Mancini 33 ☏081.553.6731, ⌨ www.hostelpensionemancini .com. Small, welcoming place right across the piazza from the station. Dorms, singles and doubles. Breakfast included. ❸

Ostello Mergellina Salita della Grotta 23 ☏081.761.2346. HI site in an attractive location with an amazing view – very popular. Breakfast included. Metro to the Mergellina (not the train station), or bus #152 from Piazza Garibaldi. ❷

Hotels

Bella Capri Via Melisurgo 4 ☏081.552.9494, ⌨ www.bellacapri.it. On the main port, on the top floor of a modern block, with great views of Mt Vesuvius and Capri. ❹

Casanova Corso Garibaldi 333 ☏081.268.287, ✉ hcasanova@tin.it. Close to Piazza Garibaldi, with its own roof garden. ❸

Hotel Eden Corso Novara 9 ☏081.285.690, ✉ hotel_eden_napoli@libero.it. Sizeable and friendly, on right as you leave the station. ❸

Hotel Ginevra Via Genova 116 ☏081.554.1757, ⌨ www.hotelginevra.it. Family-run one-star, friendly and helpful. ❸

Hotel Garibaldi Via Mancini 11 ☏081.563.0656. Two-star place with good facilities, two minutes from the station. ❸

Soggiorno Imperia Piazza Luigi Miraglia 386 ☏081.459.347. Homely, clean hotel, offering kitchen and laundry facilities right in the *centro storico*. Breakfast included. ❸

Campsite

Vulcano Solfatara Via Solfatara 161, Pozzuoli ☏081.526.7413. Well-equipped site, with swimming pool and restaurant; also offers internet access. Bus #152 from Piazza Garibaldi, or metro to Pozzuoli then ten-minute walk uphill. Closed Nov–March.

The City

Naples is a large city, with a centre that has many different focuses. The area between the vast and busy Piazza Garibaldi, where you will arrive, and Via Toledo, the main street a mile or so west, makes up the old part of the city – the **centro storico**. Buildings rise high on either side of the narrow, crowded streets; there's little light, not even much sense of the rest of the city outside – certainly not of the proximity of the sea. The two main drags here are Via dei Tribunali and Via San Biagio dei Librai, both a maelstrom of hurrying pedestrians, revving cars and buzzing scooters. **Via dei Tribunali** cuts through to **Via Duomo**, where you'll find the tucked-away **Duomo**, a Gothic building from the early thirteenth century dedicated to San Gennaro, the patron saint of the city. San Gennaro was martyred in 305 AD. Two phials of his blood miraculously liquefy three times a year – on the first Saturday in May (when a procession leads from the church of Santa Chiara to the cathedral) and on September 19 and December 16. If the blood refuses to liquefy – which luckily is rare – disaster is supposed to befall the city. The first chapel on the right as you walk into the cathedral holds the precious phials and Gennaro's skull in a silver bust-reliquary from 1305. Downstairs, the **Crypt of San Gennaro**

(Mon–Sat, 9.30am–1pm & 4.30–7pm, Sun 9am–noon; €3) is one of the finest examples of Renaissance art in Naples, founded by Cardinal Carafa and holding the tombs of both San Gennaro and Pope Innocent IV.

Across Via Duomo, Via dei Tribunali continues on into the heart of the old city: the **Spaccanapoli**, the city's busiest and architecturally richest quarter. Cut down to its other main axis, **Via San Biagio dei Librai**, which leads west to **Piazza San Domenico Maggiore**, marked by the **Guglia di San Domenico** – built in 1737, it is one of many whimsical Baroque obelisks that pop up all over the city. The **church** of the same name flanks the north side of the square, an originally Gothic building from 1289, one of whose chapels holds a miraculous painting of the *Crucifixion* which is said to have spoken to St Thomas Aquinas during his time at the adjacent monastery. North, Via de Sanctis leads off right to one of the city's odder monuments, the **Cappella Sansevero** (Mon & Wed–Sat 10am–5/7pm, Sun 10am–1.30pm; €5), the tomb-chapel of the di Sangro family, decorated by the sculptor Giuseppe Sammartino in the mid-eighteenth century with some remarkable carving including a starkly realistic dead *Christ*. The chapel downstairs, commissioned by alchemist Prince Raimondo, contains the gruesome results of some of his experiments: two bodies under glass, their capillaries and organs preserved by a mysterious liquid developed by the prince.

Continuing west, the **Gesù Nuovo** church is most notable for its lava-stone facade. Originally part of a fifteenth-century palace that stood here, prickled with pyramids that give it an impregnable, prison-like air. Facing the Gesù church, the church of **Santa Chiara** is quite different, a Provençal-Gothic structure built in 1328 and rebuilt after World War II with an austerity that's pleasing after the excesses opposite. The attached **cloister** (Mon–Sat 9.30am–1pm & 2.30–5.30pm, Sun 9.30–11am; €4), lushly planted and covered with colourful majolica tiles depicting bucolic scenes of life outside, is one of the gems of the city.

Piazza del Municipio is a busy traffic junction that stretches down to the waterfront, dominated by the brooding hulk of the **Castel Nuovo**. Built in 1282 by the Angevins and later the royal residence of the Aragon monarchs, it now contains the **Museo Civico** (Mon–Sat 9am–7pm; €5.16), which holds periodic exhibitions in a series of elaborate Gothic rooms. The entrance of the Castel incorporates a triumphal arch built in 1454 to commemorate the taking of the city by Alfonso I, the first Aragon ruler. Just beyond the castle, on the left, the **Teatro San Carlo** (closed for restoration at time of writing) is still the largest opera house in Italy, and one of the most distinguished in the world. Beyond, at the bottom of the main shopping street of Via Toledo, the dignified **Palazzo Reale** (9am–8pm, closed Wed; €4) was built in 1602 to accommodate a visit by Philip III of Spain. Upstairs, the palace's first-floor rooms are decorated with gilded furniture, trompe l'oeil ceilings, overbearing tapestries and lots of undistinguished seventeenth- and eighteenth-century paintings.

Via Toledo leads north from Piazza Trieste e Trento to the **Museo Archeologico Nazionale** (Wed–Mon 9am–7.30pm; €6.50) – Naples' most essential sight, home to the Farnese collection of antiquities from Lazio and Campania, and the best of the finds from the nearby Roman sites of Pompeii and Herculaneum. The ground floor concentrates on sculpture, including the *Farnese Bull* and *Farnese Hercules* from the Baths of Caracalla in Rome. The mezzanine floor at the back houses the museum's collection of mosaics, remarkably preserved works giving a superb insight into ordinary Roman customs, beliefs and humour. Upstairs, the wall paintings from the villas of Pompeii and Herculaneum are the museum's other major draw, rich in colour and invention. There are also everyday items from the Campanian cities – glass, silver, ceramics, charred pieces of rope, even foodstuffs – together with a model layout of Pompeii in cork. The other side of the first floor has sculptures in bronze from the **Villa dei Papiri** in Herculaneum, including a superb *Hermes at Rest*, a languid *Resting Satyr* and a convincingly woozy *Drunken Silenus*.

At the top of the hill is the city's other major museum, the **Palazzo Reale di Capodimonte** (Tues–Sun 8.30am–7.30pm; €7.50; bus #24 from Piazza Dante), the former residence of the Bourbon King Charles III, built in 1738 and now housing the **Museo Nazionale di Capodimonte**. This has a superb collection of Renaissance paintings, including a couple of Brueghels, *The Misanthrope* and *The Blind*, canvases by Perugino and Pinturicchio, an elegant *Madonna and Child with Angels* by Botticelli and Lippi's soft, sensitive *Annunciation*.

Vómero, the district topping the hill immediately above the old city, can be reached on the Montesanto funicular. Go up to the star-shaped fortress of **Castel Sant'Elmo** (Tues–Sun 9am–7pm; €1.50), occupying Naples' highest point. Built in the fourteenth century, it now hosts exhibitions and concerts, and boasts the very best views of Naples.

Eating, drinking and nightlife

Naples is the home of **pizza**. If you're just after a **snack**, you can pick something up from the city's **street markets** – the Forcella quarter market on the far side of Piazza Garibaldi or the fish market at Porta Nolana, off to the left. There are also plenty of snack places around Piazza Garibaldi. **Restaurants** are best in the historic centre: *L'Antica Pizzeria "da Michele"*, Via Cesare Sersale 1–3, on the corner of Via Colletta (closed Sun), is the cheapest in town and possibly the most authentic; alternatively, try *La Trianon da Ciro* at Parco Margherita 27. Pushing on into the depths of the old centre, *Pizzeria Sorbillo*, Via Pie di Grotta (closed Sun), is a tiny, old-fashioned treat. *Bellini*, at Via Santa Maria di Constantinopoli 80 (closed Sun eve), one of the city's longest-established restaurants, is a good place for a splurge. On the other side of Via Toledo, *Brandi*, Salita Sant'Anna di Palazzo 1–2, off Via Chiaia (closed Mon), is possibly Naples' most famous pizzeria – very friendly, and serving pasta too. *Da Tonino*, Via Santa Teresa e Chiara 47, is an excellent historic trattoria, and cheap. Near the port itself, *Da Antonio*, Via de Pretis 143 (closed Sat), is an unpretentious place serving great regional specialities at moderate prices, while along the seafront closer to the City Park, *Zi Carmela*, Via Nicolò Tommaseo 11–12 (closed Mon), has special pizzas and inventive seafood pastas.

As for **nightlife**, the beautiful Piazza Bellini is a trendy drinking spot, where tables spill out from the surrounding bars. Of these *Intra Moenia*, at number 70, offers snacks and salads as well as internet access.

Listings

Consulates UK, Via dei Mille 40 ☎081.423.8911; US, Piazza della Repubblica ☎081.583.8111.

Exchange Outside banking hours at Stazione Centrale (daily 7am–9pm).

Hospital Ospedale Nuovo Pellegrini via FM Briganti 255 ☎081.254.5291.

Internet access By Tightrope, Piazza Bellini 74; Multimedia Napoli, Via Sapienza 43.

Laundry Bolle Blu, Corso Novara 62 (close Sun).

Pharmacy At Stazione Centrale (24hr).

Police Via Medina 75 ☎081.794.1111.

Post office Piazza Matteotti, off Via Toledo.

The Bay of Naples

For the Romans, the **Bay of Naples** was the land of plenty, a blessed region with a mild climate, gorgeous scenery and hence a favourite vacation and retirement area for the city's nobility. Later, when Naples became the final stop on the Grand Tour, the relics of its heady Roman period only added to the charm. However, these days it's hard to tell where Naples ends and the countryside begins, the city sprawling around the Bay in an industrial and residential mess that is quite at odds with the region's popular image. It's only when you reach **Sorrento** in the east, or the islands that dot the Bay, that you really feel free of it all. Of the islands, **Capri** is the best place to visit if you're here for a short time. There's also, of course, the ever-brooding presence of **Vesuvius**, and the incomparable Roman sites of **Herculaneum** and **Pompeii**.

Herculaneum and Vesuvius

The first point of any interest travelling east is the town of **ERCOLANO**, the modern offshoot of the ancient site of **Herculaneum**, which was destroyed by the eruption of Vesuvius on August 2, 79 AD. It's worth stopping here for two reasons: to see the excavations of the site and to climb to the summit of **Vesuvius** – to which buses run from outside the train station. If you're planning to both visit Herculaneum and scale Vesuvius in one day, though, be sure to see Vesuvius first, and set off reasonably early – buses stop running up the mountain at lunchtime, leaving you the afternoon free to wander around the site.

Situated at the seaward end of Ercolano's main street, **Herculaneum** (daily 8.30am–7.30pm, last entry 6.30pm; €10, €18 including Pompeii) was a residential town in Roman times, much smaller than Pompeii, and as such it's a more manageable site – less architecturally impressive, but better preserved and more easily taken in on a single visit. Because it wasn't a commercial town, there is no central open space or forum, just streets of villas and shops, cut as usual by two very straight main streets. The **House of the Mosaic Atrium** at the bottom end of the main street, Cardo IV, retains its mosaic-laid courtyard, corrugated by the force of the tufa, behind which the **House of the Deer** contains corridors decorated with richly coloured still lifes and a bawdy statue of a drunken Hercules seemingly about to piss all over the visitors. There's also a large **Thermae** or bath complex with a domed *frigidarium* decorated with frescoes of fish and a *caldarium* containing a plunge bath at one end and a scallop-shell apse complete with washbasin and water pipes. The women's bath complex has a mosaiced floor of Triton and sea creatures. Opposite, the **House of Neptune and Amphitrite**, holding a sparklingly preserved wall mosaic of the god and goddess, and frescoes of flowers and vegetables, served in lieu of a garden. Under the house is a wine shop, stocked with amphorae in wooden racks, left as they lay when disaster struck. Close by in the **Casa del Bel Cortile** are some skeletons poignantly lying in the same attitude as they were in 79 AD. Further down on the opposite side of the road in the **House of the Wooden Partition**, there's a room with the marital bed still intact, and in the house nearby a perfectly preserved coiled rope.

Since its first eruption in 79 AD, when it buried the towns and inhabitants of Pompeii and Herculaneum, **Vesuvius** has dominated the lives of those who live on the Bay of Naples. It's still an active volcano, the only one on mainland Europe, and there have been hundreds of eruptions over the years, but only two of real significance: one in December 1631 that engulfed many nearby towns and killed 3000 people; and the last, in March 1944, which caused widespread devastation, though no one was actually killed. The people who live here still fear the reawakening of Vesuvius, and with good reason – scientists calculate it should erupt every thirty years or so, and it hasn't since 1944.

There are two ways to make the **ascent**. Trasporti Vesuviani run bus services from Ercolano train station to a car park and huddle of souvenir shops and cafés close to the crater; don't listen to the taxi drivers at the station who will try and persuade you there is no bus. The walk up to the crater from the car park where the bus stops takes about half an hour, across barren gravel on marked-out paths. At the top (admission €6), the crater is a deep, wide, jagged ashtray of red rock emitting the odd plume of smoke, though since the last eruption effectively sealed up the main crevice, this is much less evident than it once was. You can walk most of the way around, but take it easy – the fences are old and rickety.

Pompeii

The other Roman town destroyed by Vesuvius, **Pompeii** (daily 8.30am–5/7.30pm; €10; ☎081.857.5347, ⊛www.pompeiisites.org) was one of Campania's most important commercial centres. Out of a total population of 20,000, it's thought that only 2000 actually perished, asphyxiated by the toxic fumes of the volcanic debris, their homes buried in several metres of volcanic ash and pumice. In effect, the eruption froze Pompeii in time, and the excavations here have probably yielded more information about the life of Roman citizens during the imperial era than any other site. The full horror of their way of death is apparent in plaster casts made from the shapes their bodies left in the volcanic ash. Note, however, that most of the best mosaics and murals have found their way to the Archeological Museum in Naples.

The site covers a wide area, and seeing it properly takes half a day at least. Entering the site from the Pompeii-Villa dei Misteri side, the **Forum** is the first real feature of significance, a slim open space surrounded by the ruins of what would have been some of the town's most important official buildings. North from here, the **House of the Tragic Poet** is named after its mosaics of a theatrical production and a poet inside, though the "Cave Canem" (Beware of the Dog) mosaic by the main entrance is more eye-catching. Close by, the residents of the **House of the Faun** must have been a friendlier lot, its "Ave" (Welcome) mosaic outside beckoning you in to view the atrium and the copy of a tiny bronze dancing faun that gives the villa its name. On the street behind, the **House of the Vettii** is one of the most delightful houses in Pompeii, a merchant villa ranged around a lovely central peristyle that gives the best possible impression of the domestic environment of the city's upper middle classes. The first room on the right off the peristyle holds the best of Pompeii's murals viewable in situ: the one on the left shows the young Hercules struggling with serpents, while, through the villa's kitchen, a small room that's normally kept locked has erotic works showing various techniques of lovemaking, together with a potent-looking statue of Priapus from which women were supposed to drink to ensure fertility.

On the other side of the site, the **Grand Theatre** is very well preserved and still used for performances, as is the **Little Theatre** on its far left side. Walk up to the **Amphitheatre**, one of Italy's most intact and also its oldest, dating from 80 BC. Next door, the **Palestra** is a vast parade ground that was used by Pompeii's youth for sport and exercise. One last place you shouldn't miss is the **Villa dei Misteri**, outside the main site, a short walk from the Porta Ercolano and accessible on the same ticket. This is probably the best preserved of all Pompeii's palatial houses, and it derives its name from a series of excellently preserved paintings in one of its larger chambers: depictions of the initiation rites of a young woman into the Dionysiac Mysteries, an orgiastic cult transplanted to Italy from Greece in the Republican era and at times partially outlawed for its excesses.

To **reach Pompeii from Naples**, take the Circumvesuviana to Pompeii-Villa dei Misteri (direction Sorrento); this leaves you right outside the western entrance to the site. The Circumvesuviana also runs to Pompeii-Santuario, outside the site's eastern entrance (direction Sarno), or you can take the main-line train (direction Salerno) to the main Pompeii FS station, on the south side of the modern town. It makes most sense to see the site from Naples, but there is an **HI hostel**, *Casa del Pellegrino*, at Via Duca D'Aosta 4 (☎081.850.8644; ❷), 200m from Circumvesuviana Metro, and a large and well-equipped **campsite**, *Zeus*, right outside the Pompeii-Villa dei Misteri station. The **tourist office** is on Piazza Esedra (Mon–Sat 8.30am–7pm; ☎081 850 7255) – turn right outside Pompeii-Villa dei Misteri station.

Sorrento

Topping the rocky cliffs close to the end of its peninsula, **SORRENTO** is unashamedly a resort, its inspired location and mild climate having drawn foreigners from all over Europe for close on two hundred years. Nowadays it caters mostly to the package-tour industry, but is none the worse for it – a bright, lively place that retains its southern Italian roots. Cheap restaurants aren't hard to find; neither is reasonably priced accommodation; and there's no better place outside Naples itself from which to explore the rugged Amalfi shore and the islands of the Bay.

Sorrento's centre is **Piazza Tasso**, five minutes from the train station along the busy Corso Italia, the streets around which are pedestrianized for the lively evening *passeggiata*. Strange as it may seem, Sorrento isn't particularly well provided with beaches: most people make do with the rocks and a tiny, crowded strip of sand at **Marina Grande** – fifteen minutes' walk or a short bus ride from Piazza Tasso – or simply use the wooden jetties. If you don't fancy this, try the beaches further along, such as the tiny **Regina Giovanna** at Punta del Capo, again connected by bus from Piazza Tasso, where the ruins of the Roman Villa Pollio Felix make a unique place to bathe.

There's a **tourist office** in the large yellow Circolo dei Foresteri building at Via de Maio 35, just off Piazza Sant'Antonino (Mon–Sat 8.30am–7pm; ☎081.807.4033, ⓦww.sorrentotourism.com), which can help with accommodation. There's a **hostel** close to the station at Via degli Aranci 160 (☎081.807.2925; ❷); walk out of the station, turn left on the main road and it's a little way down on your left. Among a number of centrally placed **hotels**, try the *City*, Corso Italia 221 (☎081.877.2210; ❹), and the *Astoria* on Via Santa Maria delle Grazie 24 (☎081.807.4030; ❹, including breakfast). The cheapest and closest **campsite** is *Nube d'Argento* (closed Nov–March), ten minutes' walk from Piazza Tasso in the direction of Marina Grande at Via del Capo 12. For **eating**, the *Ristorante Sant'Antonino*, off Piazza Antonino, is good value. For late-night boozing and **nightlife**, there are the town's English-style pubs: try the *English Inn*, or *Chaplin's*, almost opposite, on Corso Italia.

Capri

Sheering out of the sea off the far end of the Sorrentine peninsula, the island of **CAPRI** has long been the most sought-after part of the Bay of Naples. During Roman times the emperor Tiberius retreated here to indulge in legendary debauchery until his death in 37 AD. Later, the discovery of the Blue Grotto and the island's remarkable natural landscape coincided with the rise of tourism; the island has attracted a steady flow of artists and writers and, more recently, inquisitive tourists, ever since. Inevitably, Capri is a crowded and expensive place, and in July and August it's sensible to give it a miss. But it would be hard to find a place with more inspiring views, and it's easy enough to visit on a day-trip. There are regular **ferries** to Capri from Naples' Molo Beverello, at the bottom of Piazza Municipio, and regular **hydrofoils** from the Mergellina jetty a couple of miles north of here – and also from Sorrento. For more information, consult the daily newspaper, *Il Mattino*.

Ferries and hydrofoils dock at **MARINA GRANDE**, the waterside extension of Capri town, which perches on the hill above, connected by funicular. There's not much to actually see, but it's very pretty, its winding, hilly alleyways converging on the dinky main square of **Piazza Umberto**. The **Certosa San Giacomo** (Tues–Sat 9am–2pm, Sun 9am–1pm; free) on the far side of the town is a run-down old monastery with a handful of paintings, and the Giardini Augustos next door give tremendous views of the coast below and the towering jagged cliffs above. From here you can wind down to **MARINA PICCOLA**, a huddle of houses and restaurants around a few patches of pebble beach – pleasantly uncrowded out of season, though in season it's heaving. You can also reach the ruins of Tiberius' villa, the **Villa Jovis**, from Capri town (daily 9am–1hr before sunset; €2), a steep thirty-minute trek east. The site is among Capri's most exhilarating, with incredible vistas of the Bay, although there's not much left of the villa.

The island's other main settlement, **ANACAPRI**, is less picturesque than Capri town, its tacky main square flanked by souvenir shops, boutiques and touristy restaurants. But during the season, a chair-lift operates from here up **Monte Solaro**, at 596m the island's highest point, and you can also get to the island's most famous attraction, the **Blue Grotto**, from here – a good 45-minute trek down Via Lo Pozzo or reachable by bus from the main square; at €8.10 it's a bit of a rip-off, with boatmen whisking visitors through the grotto in five minutes flat, but in the late afternoons, after the tourists have gone, you can swim into the cave for nothing – change at the bar next to the entrance. Time is better spent at Axel Munthe's **Villa San Michele** (daily 9am–6pm; €5), a light, airy house that was home to the

Swedish writer for a number of years, and is filled with his furniture and knick-knacks, as well as Roman artefacts.

The main **tourist office** is on Piazza Umberto in Capri town (Mon–Sat 9am–8.30pm, Sun 9am–1pm & 3.30–6.45pm; ☎081.837.0686), with another useful branch on Via G. Orlandi in Anacapri (same times; ☎081.837.1524). If you're on a tight budget, you'd be advised not to **stay overnight**. However, if you need or want to, try *Stella Maris*, Via Roma 27 (☎081.837.0452; ❻), or the family-run *Villa Eva* in Anacapri, Via La Fabbrica 8 (☎081.837.1549; ❻), a garden paradise with pool, breakfast included. Even if you don't stay, **eating** is an expense, and you might prefer to fix a **picnic**: in Capri town there is a supermarket and bakery a little way down Via Botteghe off Piazza Umberto, and well-stocked food stores at Via Roma 13 and 30. For inexpensive sit-down food, *Di Giorgio* in Via Roma (closed Tues) is your best bet. For seafood, try rather pricey *Da Gemma* in Via Madre Serafina 6 (closed Mon out of season), just off the south side of the piazza, up the steps, past the church and bearing right through the tunnel.

The Amalfi Coast

Occupying the southern side of Sorrento's peninsula, the **Amalfi Coast** lays claim to being Europe's most beautiful stretch of coast, its corniche road winding around the towering cliffs. It's an incredible ride.

AMALFI is the largest town and an established seaside resort since Edwardian times, when the British upper classes spent their winters here. An independent republic in Byzantine times, Amalfi was one of the great naval powers with a population of some seventy thousand. Vanquished by the Normans in 1131, it was devastated by an earthquake in 1343. A few remnants of Amalfi's past glories survive, and the town has a crumbly attractiveness that makes it fun to wander through. The **Duomo**, at the top of a steep flight of steps, dominates the main piazza, its decorated, almost gaudy facade topped by a glazed tiled cupola that's typical of the region. Inside, it's a mixture of Saracen and Romanesque styles, though now heavily restored, with a major relic in the body of St Andrew buried in its crypt. The most appealing part of the building is the cloister (daily 9am–9pm; €2.50) – oddly Arabic in feel, with its whitewashed arches and palms. Close by, the **Museo Civico** (same hours & ticket) displays the original *Tavoliere Amalfitane* – the book of maritime laws which governed the republic, and the rest of the Mediterranean, until 1570. Beyond these, the focus is along the busy seafront, where there's an acceptably crowded **beach**.

The **tourist office** is at Corso delle Repubbliche Marinare 27–29 (Mon–Fri 8.30am–1.30pm & 3–5.15pm, Sat 8.30am–noon; ☎089.871.107, ☻www.amalfi coast.it), next door to the post office. The cheapest **hotels** are the *Proto*, off Via Genova down Salita dei Curiali 4 (☎089.871.003; ❺), and the *Lidomare*, just off the main square at Via Piccolomini 9 (☎089.871.332, ☻www.lidomare.it; ❻); both include breakfast in their room rates. The popular **hostel-cum-hotel** *A' Scalinatella*, is out of town at Piazza Umberto I 5–6, Atrani (☎089.871.492, ☻www.hostelscalinatella.com; ❸), with a free beach close by. For **eating**, try *La Taverna del Duca*, Piazza Spirito Santo 26 (closed Thurs); *Trattoria da Gemma* (closed Wed), opposite; or *Il Mulino* further up the hill on Via delle Cartiere.

The best views of the coast can be had inland from Amalfi, in **RAVELLO**. This was also an independent republic for a while, and for a time an outpost of the Amalfi city-state; now it's not much more than a large village, but its unrivalled location, spread across the top of one of the coast's mountains, makes it more than worth the thirty-minute bus ride up from Amalfi. Buses drop off on the main **Piazza Vescovado**, outside the **Duomo**: an eleventh-century church dedicated to St Pantaleone, a fourth-century saint whose blood – kept in a chapel on the left-hand side – is supposed to liquefy like that of Naples' San Gennaro, twice a year on May 19 and August 27. Ten minutes away, the gardens of the **Villa Cimbrone** (daily 9am–sunset; €4.10), laid out by a Yorkshire aristocrat earlier this century, spread across the furthest tip of Ravello's ridge. Most of the villa itself is not open to visitors, though it's worth peeking into the crumbly, flower-hung cloister as you go in, and the open crypt down the steps from here. Best bit of the gardens is the belvedere at the far end of the main path, giving marvellous views over the sea below. **Tourist information** is available at Piazza Duomo 10 (Mon–Fri 9am–1pm & 3–5pm; ☎089.857.096, ❀www.ravelloarts.org).

Lecce

Puglia, the long strip of land that makes up the "heel" of Italy, has little to detain you, save for the town of **LECCE** – the so-called "Baroque Florence" of the south. Walking its alleys, there's still a sense of jaw-dropping excitement at discovering its Baroque buildings, with forests of vines, flowers and statues enveloping the stonework. Carved from a soft sandstone, the buildings are one of the high-points in Italian architecture, and very different from the heavy Baroque of Rome. Built for wealthy families, churchmen and merchants during the fifteenth to seventeenth centuries, when Lecce was at the height of its power, these buildings are some of the most beautiful examples of the style – some of the most impressive were designed by Giuseppe Zimbale, known as Lo Zingarello.

The heart of Lecce is the **Piazza Sant'Oronzo**, centred on a statue of the saint by Zingarello. In the middle is the tiny (deconsecrated) church of San Marco, a reminder of the economic importance of the Venetian community in Lecce. To one side of the square is the **Anfiteatro Romano**, which would have held 20,000 people and dates from the second century AD, but was only rediscovered in the nineteenth century. It is a short distance from the **Castello** (undergoing restoration at the time of writing) built by Charles V and the only major part of the sixteenth century fortifications left.

Walk north from here up to **Santa Croce** (daily 8am–noon & 5–7pm), the most famous of the Lecce churches – and the best thing about it has to be Zingarello's facade, where delicate engravings and a riot of putti and grotesques soften the Baroque outline of the building. Inside, the excess continues with a riot of stars, flowers and foliage covering everything from the top of columns to chapel altar-pieces. Next door, the yellow stone **Palazzo del Governo**, a former Celestine monastery, is another Zingarello building.

West of here is the **Porta Napoli**, a triumphal arch put up in honour of Charles V. The obelisk was added in 1822 to celebrate the visit of Bourbon king Ferdinand I. From here it is a short walk to the **Monastero** – now part of Lecce University, where Baroque detail has been added to the inside courtyard. Round the corner, a walk though a narrow remembrance garden to the town cemetery takes you to the Norman church of **SS Nicolo E Cataldo** (open for occasional morning services only) whose front has been decorated in the Baroque style.

Back down Via Palmieri on the **Piazza del Duomo**, a harmonious square surrounded by Baroque palazzi, is the **Duomo** (daily 8am–noon & 5–7pm), another of Zingarello's works, and an explosion of Baroque detail – although its main entrance, on the Piazza Vescovile, is much more restrained.

Practicalities

The main **tourist office** is at Corso Vittorio Emanuele 24, near the Cathedral (Mon–Fri 9am–1pm & 4–7pm, Sat 9am–1pm; ☎0832.248.092, ❀www.pugliaturismo.it/lecce). Budget **accommodation** is limited. The cheapest hotel is the two-star *Cappello*, in Via Montegrappa near the station (☎0832.308.881; ❸); alternatively, there are private rooms to rent – try Andreina Goffredo, viale Marche 15 (☎0832.231.724; ❸). Lecce's nearest **campsite** is *Torre Rinalda* at Litoranea Salentina 152 (☎0832.382.161; closed Oct–May; bus from Piazza Sant'Oronzo.

You'll find good **snacks** at *Bar della Cotognata Leccese*, in Via Marconi 51, and excellent coffee and brioches at *Avio* on the corner of Via Trinchese/Via 25 Luglio. For **full meals** try the cheap student haunt *Osteria da Angiulino*, hidden along Via Principe di Savoia 24; the classier *Alle Due Corti*, via Leonardo Prato 42, which has an interesting local menu; or the old-fashioned *Trattoria Casareccia*, via Costadura 9, which is a bit of a local institution. In the **evening**, a good place to have an aperitif is *Tito Schipa* on piazza Sant'Oronzo – expensive, but they give you so many nibbles you may be able to give supper a miss. For live **music**, try *Cagliostro* on Via Cairoli 25, which has cool decor, jazz and cocktails, and is a fine place to spot some of the beautiful people; just round the corner is the quieter *Caffè Letterario*, Via G Paladini. Otherwise, try one of the many bars in the area around Via Vittorio Emanuele where the evening *passaggiata* takes place. **Internet access** is available at Chatwin Netcafé, Via Isabella Catriota 8.

Sicily

Coming from the Italian mainland, **SICILY** feels socially and culturally separate from Europe. Occupying a strategically vital position, this largest island in the Mediterranean has a history and outlook that has less in common with its modern parent than of its erstwhile rulers – from the Greeks who first settled the east coast in the eighth century BC, through a dazzling array of Romans, Arabs, Normans, French and Spanish, to the Bourbons, seen off by Garibaldi in 1860. Substantial relics of these ages remain – temples, theatres and churches are scattered across the island. And there are other, more immediate hints of Sicily's unique past – a hybrid Sicilian language is still widely spoken in the countryside and the food is noticeably spicier, and its sweets (candied fruits and marzipan), have a middle-eastern flavour.

Inevitably perhaps, most points of interest are on the coast: the interior of the island is mountainous, sparsely populated and relatively inaccessible. The capital, **Palermo**, is a memorable first stop, a bustling city with an unrivalled display of Norman art and architecture and Baroque churches. The most obvious other trips are to the chic resort of **Taormina** – although if you are looking for fewer crowds and cleaner water you'd be advised to go to the west or south coasts. Near Taormina you can skirt around the foothills and even up to the craters of **Mount Etna**, and to the ancient Greek centre of **Siracusa**, with its wonderful architecture and ancient remains. To the south, the greatest draw is the grouping of temples at **Agrigento**, the biggest concentration of the island's Greek remnants.

To **get to Sicily**, you can simply take a **train** from the mainland – they travel across the Straits of Messina on the **ferries** from Villa San Giovanni and continue on the other side.

Palermo and around

In its own wide bay underneath the limestone bulk of Monte Pellegrino, **PALERMO** is stupendously sited. Originally a Phoenician, then a Carthaginian colony, this remarkable city was long considered a prize worth capturing, and under Saracen and Norman rule in the ninth to twelfth centuries it became the greatest city in Europe, famed for the wealth of its court and peerless as a centre of learning. Nowadays it's a brash but exciting city, a fascinating place to be as much for strolling and consuming as for specific attractions. But Palermo's monuments, its unique series of Baroque and Arabo-Norman churches, the unparalleled mosaic work and excellent museums are also the equal of anything on the mainland.

The heart of the old city is the **Quattro Canti**, erected in 1611; just around the corner is Piazza Pretoria, home to the **Chiesa di S Caterina**, whose spectacular Baroque interiors can be seen only at Easter; and the **Palazzo della Aquila**, seat of the local government, whose opulent interiors are open daily (not Sun). In the next street, the church of **La Martorana** (Mon–Sat 8am–1pm & 3.30–5.30pm, Sun

8.30am–1pm) is one of the finest survivors of the medieval city; its slim twelfth-century campanile and series of spectacular mosaics are well worth a visit.

In the district of Albergheria, a warren of tiny streets southwest of the centre, you'll find the deconsecrated church of **San Giovanni degli Eremiti** (Mon–Fri 8.30am–noon & 2.30–6pm; €4.50), built in 1148 and the most obviously Arabic of the city's Norman relics, with five ochre domes topping a small church that was built upon the remains of an earlier mosque. A path leads up through citrus trees to the church, behind which lie its celebrated late-thirteenth-century cloisters. From here it's a few paces north to the **Palazzo dei Normanni** (Mon, Fri & Sat 9am–noon unless parliament is sitting), whose entrance is on Piazza Indipendenza; it was originally built by the Saracens and was enlarged considerably by the Normans, under whom it housed the most magnificent of medieval European courts. Sadly, there are only a few mosaics left from those times, and most of the interior is now taken up by the Sicilian parliament, reinstated in 1947. The Palazzo also houses the beautiful **Cappella Palatina** (Mon–Fri 9–11.45am & 3–4.45pm, Sat 9–11.45am, Sun 9–10am & noon–1pm), the private royal chapel of Roger II, built between 1132 and 1143 and almost entirely covered in twelfth-century mosaics.

On the far side of Corso V. Emanuele from here, the **Cattedrale** (Mon–Sat 7am–7pm, Sun 8am–1.30pm & 4–7pm) is a more substantial Norman relic, an odd building mainly because of the eighteenth-century alterations which added the dome and spoiled the fine lines of the tawny stone. Still, the triple-apsed eastern end and the lovely matching towers are all original; the interior is cold and Neoclassical, the only items of interest the fine portal and wooden doors and the royal tombs, containing the remains of some of Sicily's most famous monarchs.

Across Via Roma, the **Museo Archeologico Regionale** (daily 9am–1pm, Tues, Wed & Fri also 3–6.15pm; €4.13) is a magnificent collection of artefacts, mainly from the island's Greek and Roman sites. Two cloisters hold anchors and other retrieved hardware from the sea off the Sicilian coast, and there are rich stone carvings from the temple site of Selinunte. In the opposite direction from Santa Zita lies the depressed area around the old harbour, La Cala, and, across Corso V. Emanuele on Via Alloro, Sicily's **Galleria Regionale** (Mon–Sat 9am–2pm, Tues & Thurs also 3–8.30pm, Sun 9am–12.30pm; €4.13), a stunning medieval art collection that includes a magnificent fifteenth-century fresco of the *Triumph of Death*, work by the fifteenth-century sculptor Francesco Laurana and paintings by Antonello da Messina. The third of Palermo's showpiece museums, the **Museo Etnografico Pitrè** (9am–8pm, closed Fri; €4.13) lies on the edge of La Favorita, a large park 3km from Piazza Castelnuovo (bus #106 or #806 from Piazza Sturzo, behind the Politeama, or from Viale della Libertà). This is the key exhibition of Sicilian folklore and culture on the island, with a wealth of carts painted with bright scenes from the story of the Paladins, a reconstructed puppet theatre and dozens of expressive puppets, plus a whole series of intricately worked terracotta figures, dolls and games.

Practicalities

Trains all pull in at the southern end of Via Roma, from where buses #101 and #102 run to the centre. **Ferry and hydrofoil** services dock, just off Via Francesco Crispi, from where it's a ten-minute walk up Via E. Amari to Piazza Castelnuovo. There are **tourist offices** inside the train station (Mon–Fri 8am–2pm & 3–6pm) and at Piazza Castelnuovo 34 (same hours; ☏091.583.847). For **internet** access try Accademia Internet, Via Cala 64 (☏091.611.8483) or Internet Shop, Via Napoli 32/34.

Most of the budget hotel **accommodation** is on and around the southern ends of Via Maqueda and Via Roma, near the train station: the *Olimpia*, just before Corso Vittorio Emanuele (☏091.616.1276; ❷), has rooms overlooking Piazza Cassa di Risparmio; or try *Vittoria*, Via Maqueda 8 (☏091.616.2437; ❷); or the atmospheric

Orientale at no. 26 (☎091.616.5727; ❸). If you're **camping**, take bus #101 to the stadium then #616 or #628 out to Sferracavallo, 13km northwest of the city, where the beaches are good and there are two sites: the *Campeggio Internazionale Trinacria* on Via Barcarello (☎091.530.590), with two-bedded **cabins**, and the cheaper *degli Ulivi* (☎091.533.021), on Via Pegaso.

For authentic Sicilian **fast food**, the old-style *Antica Focacceria*, Via A. Paternostro 58, off Corso Vittorio Emanuele, is the place to go. Alternatively, try the busy *Pizzeria Italia* at Via Orologio 54, off Via Maqueda. For **full-blown meals**, the city's best bargain is *Trattoria-Pizzeria Enzo*, Via Maurolico 17/19, close to the station, while the *Trattoria Primavera* on Piazza Bologni has an excellent-value set meal. On warm evenings a young crowd spills out onto the street from the *Bottiglieria del Mássimo*, a **wine bar** with pavement seating at Via Spinuzza 59, near the Teatro Mássimo and at the various bars and cafés behind the church of Sant'Ignazio All'Olivella. There's a major theatrical and puppetry tradition in Palermo – recognized by UNESCO in 2001 – and there are five **puppet theatres**; one of the best is *Cuticchio*, Via Bara all'Olivella 95. Look out, too, for *Lapis Palermo*, a fortnightly **listings** guide.

Monreale

Sicily's most extraordinary medieval mosaics are to be seen in the Norman cathedral at **MONREALE**, a small hill town 8km southwest of Palermo and accessible on bus #389 from Piazza dell'Indipendenza, a twenty-minute journey. The **Duomo** mosaics (daily 8am–6pm) represent the apex of Sicilian-Norman art, and were almost certainly executed by Greek and Byzantine craftsmen, revealing a unitary plan and inspiration: your eyes are drawn to the all-embracing figure of Christ in the central apse – an awesome and pivotal mosaic, the head and shoulders alone almost 20m high. Underneath sit an enthroned Virgin and Child, attendant angels and ranks of saints, each individually and subtly coloured and identified by name. No less remarkable are the nave mosaics, an animated series starting with the Creation to the right of the altar and running around the entire church. Ask at the desk by the entrance to climb the **tower** (€1.55) in the southwest corner of the cathedral – an unusual and precarious vantage point. The **cloisters** (Mon–Sat 9am–7pm, Sun 9am–1pm; €4.13), part of the original Benedictine monastery, form an elegant arcaded quadrangle, with some 216 twin columns that are a riot of detail and imagination.

Taormina and around

On Sicily's eastern coast, and dominating two grand sweeping bays, **TAORMINA** is the island's best-known resort. The outstanding remains of its classical theatre, with Mount Etna as an unparalleled backdrop, arrested passing travellers when Taormina was no more than a medieval hill village, and these days it's virtually impossible to find anywhere to stay between June and August. Despite this, Taormina retains all of its romantic small-town charm, the main traffic-free street, Corso V. Emanuele, lined with fifteenth- to nineteenth-century palazzi interspersed with small, intimate piazzas. The **Teatro Greco** (daily 9am–1hr before sunset; €4.50), however – signposted from just about everywhere – is the only real sight, founded by Greeks in the third century BC, though most of what's left is a Roman rebuilding from the first century AD, when the stage and lower seats were cut back to provide room and a deep trench dug in the orchestra to accommodate the animals and fighters used in gladiatorial contests. These days it has a summer season of Greek plays (in Italian).

The **train station** is way below town, from where it's a steep thirty-minute walk up or a short bus ride to the centre. There is a **tourist office** at the station (Mon–Sat 8.30am–1.30pm & 4–7pm) but the main office is in Palazzo Corvaja, Piazza Santa Caterina (same hours; ☎0942.23.243, ⊛www.taormina-ol.it). There are good **accommodation** possibilities along Via Bagnoli Croce – try *Il Leone* at no. 124–126 (☎0942.23.878; ❸); alternatively, there's the tiny but cheap *Diana* at Via di Giovanni 6, nearby (☎0942.23.898; ❸). There is also an **HI Hostel**, *Ulisse*,

Vico San Francesco de Paola 9, (☎0942.231.93; ❷), which offers good home-cooked evening meals; its rival, *Taormina's Odyssey* at Trav A on Via G.Martino (☎0942.245.33; ❷), has largely mixed rooms. **Eating** in Taormina is relatively pricey compared to the rest of Sicily – if money is tight, try the good **rosticceria** just up from Porta Messina, on the corner of Via Timeo and Via Patrizio. Among the less expensive **trattorias** are *La Botte*, Piazza Santa Domenica 4, and *Il Baccanale* in Piazza Filea, which has outdoor tables and similar prices – both close to Via Bagnoli Croce – or try *Trattoria Siciliana*, a quieter place outside Porta Catania at Salita Ospedale 9.

The closest beach to town is at **MAZZARÓ**, with its much-photographed islet. It's about a thirty-minute descent on foot, but the preferable option is to use the cable car (every 15 min; €2) from Via Pirandello. The beach-bars and restaurants at **SPISONE**, 1km or so further north, are also reachable by path from Taormina, this time from below the cemetery in town. From Spisone, the coast opens out and the beach gets wider. Some 5km north of Taormina, **LETOJANNI** is a little resort in its own right, with a few fishing boats on a sandy beach, two campsites and regular buses and trains back to Taormina. Roomier and better for swimming are the sands south of Taormina at **GIARDINI-NAXOS**, which is an excellent alternative source of accommodation and food. Prices tend to be a good bit cheaper than in Taormina and in high season it's worth trying here first. The **tourist office** at Taormina's station and Immobiliare Naxos, Via V. Emanuele 58, in Giardini-Naxos (☎0942.51.184) can help find you **accommodation**. For **eating**, good pizzas and fresh fish can be had at *Fratelli Marano*, Via Naxos 181. *Da Angelina*, on Via Euboea by the pier, serves well-priced pizzas and home-made pasta and has great views. Also good is *La Conchiglia*, Via Naxos 221, specializing in Sicilian meat dishes.

Mount Etna

Mount Etna's massive bulk looms over much of the coastal route south of Taormina, and, if you don't have the time to reach the summit, rail services provide some alternative volcanic thrills in a ride around the base of the volcano from **GIARRE-RIPOSTO**, thirty minutes by train or bus from Taormina; InterRail passes are not valid, and if you make the entire trip to Catania (€5.16 one way), allow four hours. As for the **ascent**, this is a spectacular trip worth every effort to make – though without your own transport that effort can be considerable. At 3323m, Etna is a fairly substantial mountain; the fact that it's also one of the world's biggest volcanoes (and still active) only adds to the draw. Some of the eruptions have been disastrous: in 1669 Catania was wrecked; this century the Circumetnea rail line has been repeatedly ruptured by lava flows, and, in 1979, nine people were killed on the edge of the main crater. In 1997, 1998 and 2001 the eruptions were high, but not life-theatening; and you'll not be in any danger, provided you heed the warnings as you get closer to the top. There are several approaches. On **public transport**, you'll need to come via **NICOLOSI**, an hour from Catania by frequent bus, one of which (8am from Catania train station) continues on up to a huddle of souvenir shops and restaurants; arriving on this bus, you'll have enough time to make it to the top and back for the return bus to Catania (4.45pm). From here you have two options: you can take a **cable car** up to about 2500m (€20 return), from where a guide can take you by jeep to the Torre del Filósofo (April–Oct; €38 return, including cable car); or you can walk, following the rough minibus track (3–4hr each way). However you go, take warm clothes, good shoes and glasses to keep the flying grit out of your eyes. The highest you're allowed to get is 2900m, and though there's only a rope across the ground to prevent you from climbing further, it would be foolish to do so.

Siracusa

Further down Sicily's eastern seaboard, **SIRACUSA** (ancient Syracuse) was first colonized by Greeks in 733 BC and grew to become their main power base in Sicily. Today the city boasts some of the best Greek archeological remains anywhere, and also has a strong Baroque character in its old town, squeezed onto the island of Ortygia, by the harbour. **Ortygia** makes a good place to start exploring the city. At the centre of the island, the most obvious attraction is the **Duomo**, set in an elongated piazza studded with Baroque architecture, and itself incorporating twelve fluted columns belonging to the temple that originally stood here. Round the corner, the severe thirteenth-century Palazzo Bellomo houses the **Museo Regionale d'Arte Medioevale e Moderna** (Tues–Sun 9am–1.30pm, Wed also 3am–6pm; €2.50), an outstanding collection of medieval art. North of the train station, the city is mainly new and commercial, though there are also the best of Siracusa's archeological sights here: it is a short walk, or take #15 bus from Ortygia's Largo XXV Luglio as far as Viale Teocrito, from where you should walk east for the **Museo Archeologico** (Tues–Sun 9am–1pm & 3.30–7.30/6.30pm; €4.50), which holds a wealth of material from the early Greek colonies. Round the corner, the ruined church of **San Giovanni Evangelista** has interesting catacombs (Mon–Wed, Fri & Sat 9am–1pm, 3.30–5pm; €3.50); an earthquake in 1693 destroyed the church, which was never rebuilt.

Siracusa's extensive **Parco Archeologico** (daily 9am–2hr before sunset; €4.50) is a twenty-minute walk west of the Museo Archeologico (or bus #15 from Largo XXV Luglio). Here, the **Ara di Ierone II**, an enormous altar of the third century BC, is the first thing you see, but the main highlight of the park is the **Teatro Greco**, cut out of the rock and looking down towards the sea. It's much bigger than the one at Taormina, capable of holding around 15,000 people (though is less impressive, scenically), and also has a summer season of Greek plays. At the top is a tiny waterfall in the Ninfeo cave, the outlet from a 30km long aqueduct dug out by hand in the fifth century BC, and surrounding it are the remains of looted Byzantine tombs.

Nearby, the **Latomia del Paradiso**, a leafy quarry, is best known for its unusually shaped cavern that Dionysius is supposed to have used as a prison, the **Orecchio di Dionigi** – a high, S-shaped cave 65m long: Caravaggio, a visitor in 1586, coined the name after the shape of the entrance, but the acoustic properties are such that it's not impossible to imagine Dionysius eavesdropping on his prisoners from a vantage point above. The other large cave down here – though you can't go into it – is known as the **Ropemaker's cave**, because its damp conditions made it ideal for the craft.

Going back up the entrance path, on the left-hand side is the entrance to the last section of the park, the neglected-looking **Roman amphitheatre**. This has a central rectangular-shaped construction, which was probably used for water fights, and just below the small church at the top of the path down to the Parco Archeologico is the Roman water storage tank that would have supplied water for this; the tank was converted into a church in the sixth century.

Practicalities

Siracusa's **train station** is on the mainland, a twenty-minute walk from Ortygia. AST **buses** arrive either in Piazza della Poste, just over the bridge on Ortygia, or else in Piazzale Marconi, in the modern town; SAIS buses stop in Via Trieste, close by Piazza della Poste. There's a privately run tourist point, *Syrako*, in Ortygia at Via Ruggero Settimo 19 (Mon–Sat 9am–1pm & 3–7pm; ☏0931.241.33); the **main tourist office** is in the new town at Via San Sebastiano 43 opposite the church of San Giovanni Evangelista (Mon–Sat 8.30am–1.30pm & 3.30–6.15pm, Sun 9am–1pm; ☏0931.481.200, ⊛www.apt-siracusa.it).

Accommodation choices aren't spectacular and in high season you'll need to book in advance. Try the *Aretusa* at Via Francesco Crispi 75 (☏0931.24.211; ❸), or the *Centrale*, Corso Umberto 141 (☏0931.60.528; ❷), just off Piazzale Marconi. The nearest **campsite**, *Agriturist Rinaura* (☏0931.721.224), is 5km away – take bus #21,

#22 or #23 from Corso Umberto or Piazza delle Poste. The nearest **HI Hostel** – *Il Castello*, Via Fratellli Bandiera (℗0931.571.534) – is 30km away in the lovely Baroque town of Noto; take a train from Siracusa.

As for **restaurants**, *La Siciliana*, Via Savoia 17, has a wide range of pizzas, and the *Trattoria Archimede*, Via Gemmellaro 8, frequented by locals, is inexpensive and good for fish. *Spaghetteria do Scogghiu*, Via Scina 11, has a huge selection of cheap pasta and is popular at night. And *Da Antonio*, Via Gimillaro 34, is a trattoria with good home cooking. Good **bars** and cafés are easy to come by; one of the best, the *Bar Del Ponte*, at the end of the Ponte Nuovo on Ortygia, serves good breakfasts.

Agrigento

Halfway along Sicily's southern littoral, **AGRIGENTO** is primarily of interest for the substantial remains of Pindar's "most beautiful city of mortals", strung out along a ridge facing the sea a few kilometres below town. The series of Doric temples here, mostly dating from the fifth century BC, are the most evocative of Sicilian remains. They are also the focus of a constant procession of tour buses, so budget accommodation should be booked in advance.

A road winds down from the modern city to the **Valle dei Templi**, buses #1, #2 and #3 dropping you at a car park between the two separate zones of **archeological remains** (daily 8.30am–5/7pm; €4.50, or €6 with the museum). The eastern zone is home to the scattered remains of the oldest of the temples, the **Tempio di Ercole**, probably begun in the last decades of the sixth century BC, and the better-preserved **Tempio della Concordia**, dated to around 430 BC, with fine views of the city and sea, and preserved that well because it was turned into a church in the Byzantine era. There's also the **Tempio di Giunone**, an engaging half-ruin standing at the very edge of the ridge. The western zone, back along the path and beyond the car park, is less impressive but it's fun to wander around the vast tangle of stone and fallen masonry from a variety of temples – get a little off the path and you'll easily lose the other tourists. Most notable is the mammoth construction that was the **Tempio di Giove**, or Temple of Olympian Zeus, the largest Doric temple ever known, though never completed, left in ruins by the Carthaginians and further damaged by earthquakes. The small piece that is standing is a nineteenth century reconstruction. Around the site there are also some early Christian and Byzantine tombs. Via dei Templi leads back to the town from the car park via the excellent **Museo Nazionale Archeologico** (daily 9am–1.30pm, Wed–Sat also 2–6.30pm; €4.50, or €6 with the archeological site) – an extraordinarily rich collection devoted to finds from the city and the surrounding area.

Trains arrive at the edge of the old town, outside which – on Piazza Marconi – buses leave for the temples. The **tourist office** is nearby at Via Cesare Battisti 15 (Mon–Fri 8am–1pm & 3pm–dusk; ℗0922.204.54), at the eastern end of Via Atenea. There's also an information box at the Valle dei Templi site. Among **hotels** worth trying are the *Amici*, in via Acrone next to the station (℗0922.402.831; **❸**); *Concordia*, at Piazza San Francesco 11 (℗0922.596.266; **❸**); and the *Bella Napoli*, Piazza Lena 6 (℗0922.20.435; **❹**). You can camp 5km away at the coastal resort of San Leone; take bus #2 or #2/ from outside the train station. You can **eat** cheaply and well at *Trattoria Atenea*, Via Ficani 12, an alley above Via Atenea, or at *La Forchetta*, next door to the *Concordia* hotel.

Sardinia

A little under 200km from the Italian mainland, slightly more than that from the North African coast of Tunisia, **Sardinia** is way off most tourist itineraries. Relatively free of large cities or heavy industry, the island boasts some of the country's cleanest, least crowded beaches, and, though not known for its cultural riches, holds some fascinating vestiges of the various civilizations that have passed through. In addition to Roman and Carthaginian ruins, Genoan fortresses and a string of lovely Pisan churches, there are striking remnants of Sardinia's only significant native culture, known as the nuraghic civilization after the 7000 stone constructions that litter the landscape.

On the whole, Sardinia's smaller centres are the most attractive, but the capital, **Cágliari** – for many the arrival point – shouldn't be written off. With good facilities for eating and sleeping, it makes a useful base for exploring the southern third of the island. The other main ferry port and airport is **Olbia** in the north, little more than a transit town for visitors to the nearby Costa Smeralda, though budget travellers are unlikely to want to spend time in this uncomfortable mix of opulence and suburbia.

In the northwest of the island, **Sássari** and **Alghero** manifest the deepest imprint of the long Spanish presence in Sardinia, with the latter having developed into the chief package resort. Inland, **Nuoro** has impressive literary credentials and a good ethnographic museum. As Sardinia's biggest interior town, it also makes a useful stopover for visiting some of the more remote mountain areas, where you can find what remains of the island's traditional culture, best embodied in the numerous village **festivals**.

The island boasts a good network of **public transport** – bus and train – that will get you to all but the remoter areas. Note, however, that Interail/Eurail passes are not valid for the smaller (private) rail lines.

Getting to Sardinia

There are frequent daily **flights** from the Italian mainland to the island's three airports, at Cágliari, Olbia and Fertília (for Alghero and Sássari). Cheaper but slower are the overnight **ferries** to Cágliari, Arbatax (halfway up the island's eastern coast), Olbia, Golfo degli Aranci (near Olbia) and Porto Torres (on Sardinia's northwestern corner) from mainland Italy (Civitavécchia, Genoa, Livorno, Naples) – as well as from Sicily, Tunis, Corsica and France. In high summer, **fast ferries** connect Genoa, Civitavécchia and Fiumicino to the island, though fares are higher than on the regular ferries, and seats quickly get booked up.

Cágliari

Rising up from its port and crowned by an old citadel squeezed within a protective ring of Pisan fortifications, **CÁGLIARI** has been Sardinia's capital at least since Roman times and is still the island's biggest town. Nonetheless, its centre is easily explored on foot, and offers sophistication and charm in its tangle of narrow lanes.

Almost all the wandering you will want to do in Cágliari is encompassed within the old quarter. The most evocative entry to this is from the monumental **Bastione San Remy** on Piazza Costituzione. It's worth the haul up the grandiose flight of steps inside for the views over the port and the lagoons beyond – especially at sunset.

From the bastion, you can wander off in any direction to enter the intricate maze of Cágliari's citadel, traditionally the seat of the administration, aristocracy and highest ecclesiastical offices. It has been little altered since the Middle Ages, though the tidy Romanesque facade on the **Cattedrale** (daily 8am–1pm & 4–8pm) in Piazza Palazzo is in fact a fake, added in the twentieth century in the old Pisan style. The main structure dates originally from the thirteenth century but has gone through what D.H. Lawrence called "the mincing machine of the ages, and oozed out Baroque and sausagey." Inside, a couple of massive stone pulpits flank the main doors: they were crafted as a single piece around 1160 to grace Pisa's cathedral, but were later presented to Cágliari along with the same sculptor's set of lions, now adorning the outside of the building.

At the opposite end of Piazza Palazzo a road leads into the smaller Piazza dell'Arsenale, site of the **Museo Archeologico Nazionale** (Tues–Sun 9am–7pm;

€4), a must for anyone interested in Sardinia's past. The island's most important Phoenician, Carthaginian and Roman finds are gathered here, but everything pales beside the museum's greatest pieces, from Sardinia's **nuraghic** culture. Of these, the most eye-catching is a series of bronze statuettes, ranging from about 15cm to 45cm in height, spindly and highly stylized, but packed with invention and quirky humour. Off the piazza stands the **Torre San Pancrazio**, from which it's only a short walk to Via dell'Università and the **Torre dell'Elefante**, named after the small carving of an elephant on one side; the towers were erected by Pisa after it had wrested the city from the Genoans in 1305 and formed the main bulwarks of the city's defences. Both have a half-finished look about them, with the side facing the old town completely open, but they've been fitted with steps, which you can climb for stupendous views over the city and coast (April–Sept Tues–Sun 9am–1pm & 3.30–5.30/5pm; free). Nearby, Viale Buon Cammino leads to the **Anfiteatro Romano** (Tues–Sun: April–Oct 9am–1pm & 3–7pm; Nov–March 9am–4pm; free). Cut out of solid rock in the second century AD, the amphitheatre could hold the entire city's population of twenty thousand.

Practicalities

Cágliari's **port** lies in the heart of the town, opposite Via Roma. The **airport** sits beside the Stagno di Cágliari, the city's largest lagoon, fifteen minutes' bus ride west of town. There are **tourist offices** at the port, and opposite the **train and bus stations** on Piazza Matteotti, but the main office covering the whole of Sardinia is at Via Mameli 97 (all daily 8.30am–1pm & 3–6pm; ☎070.669.255).

Cágliari has a good selection of budget **hotels**, but book ahead in high season. Best choice is *Pensione Vittoria* at Via Roma 75 (☎070.657.970; ❹); if this is full, nearby Via Sardegna has several basic choices, including *Palmas* at no. 14 (☎070.651.679; ❷) and *La Perla* at no. 18 (☎070.669.446; ❸). Away from the seafront, try the central *La Terrazza* at Via S. Margherita 21 (☎070.668.652; ❹). The nearest **campsite** is at Quartu Sant'Elena, a 45-minute bus ride east along the coast, where the *Pini e Mare* (☎070.803.103; July & Aug; ❹) also has bungalows.

Most of Cágliari's **restaurants** are clustered around Via Sardegna. *Da Serafino*, at Via Sardegna 109, is extremely good value and popular with the locals. *Da Lillicu* at Via Sardegna 78 is plain but authentic, offering Sardinian specialities and delicious fish. Seafood-lovers will do well at the *Stella Marina di Montecristo*, at the end of Via Sardegna, where it meets Via Regina Margherita. In the centre try the trattoria *Crackers*, Corso Vittorio Emanuele 195, for a fusion of Sardinian and Piemontese cooking. Away from the port area, try *Il Gatto*, just off Piazza del Cármine at Viale Trieste 15, for seafood or meat dishes. For a **snack** and a beer, drop in on *Il Merlo Parlante* in Via Portascalas, an alley off Corso Vittorio Emanuele, where you can find drink, music and *panini* (open eve only). Down by the port, the bars on Via Roma make good breakfast stops, while there are several decent pizza and sandwich places in the alleys running off it.

Su Nuraxi

If you have no time to see any other of Sardinia's ancient stone *nuraghi*, make a point of visiting **Su Nuraxi**, the biggest and most famous of them and a good taste of the primitive grandeur of the island's only indigenous civilization. The snag is access: the site lies 1km outside the village of **BARÚMINI**, 50km north of Cágliari, to which there are only two daily buses, which stop here en route to Désulo and Samugheo.

At Barúmini, turn left at the main crossroads and walk the last leg to Su Nuraxi (daily 9am–4/7pm; €4.20). Its dialect name means simply "the *nuragh*" and not only is it the biggest *nuraghic* complex on the island, but it's also thought to be the oldest, dating probably from around 1500 BC. Comprising a bulky fortress surrounded by the remains of a village, Su Nuraxi was a palace complex at the very least – possibly a capital city. The central tower once reached 21m (now shrunk to less than 15m), and its outer defences and inner chambers are connected by passageways and stairs. The whole complex is thought to have been covered with earth by Sards and Carthaginians at the time of the Roman conquest, which may account for its excellent state of preservation.

Nuoro and around

Superbly sited beneath the soaring peak of Monte Ortobene opposite the stark heights of Sopramonte, **NUORO** is an insular little town. No place on the island, however, can match its extraordinary literary fame. The best-known Sard poet, **Sebastiano Satta** (1867–1914), was Nuorese, as was the author **Grazia Deledda** (1871–1936), who won the Nobel Prize for Literature in 1927.

Nuoro's **old quarter** is the most compelling part of town, spread around the pedestrianized hub of **Corso Garibaldi**, along which the *passeggiata* takes place. Otherwise the main attraction is the impressive **Museo Etnografico** (daily 9am–1pm & 3–7/8pm; €2.58) on Via Mereu, a ten-minute walk from the Corso on the other side of Piazza Vittorio Emanuele, which contains Sardinia's most comprehensive range of local costumes, jewellery, masks, carpets and other handicrafts.

As many as three thousand of the costumes are aired at Nuoro's biggest annual **festival**, the **Festa del Redentore**, usually taking place on the penultimate Sunday of August and involving participants from all over the island, but especially the villages of the Barbágia. The religious festivities are held on August 29, when a procession from town weaves up to the 955m summit of **Monte Ortobene**, 8km away, where a bronze **statue** of the Redeemer stands, poised in an attitude of swirling motion with stunning views of the gorge separating Nuoro from the Sopramonte.

Practicalities

Nuoro's **train station** is a twenty-minute walk from the centre of town along Via Lamármora. Buses stop outside here and at Via Brigata Sássari (parallel to Via Lamármora). Nuoro's **tourist office** is on Piazza Italia (May–Sept daily 9am–1pm & 4–7pm; Oct–April Mon–Fri 10.30am–1pm, Tues & Wed also 4–6pm; ☎0784.30.083, ⌨www.nuoro.com) and is useful for a street-map. The few **hotels** are mostly antiquated and often full. Right opposite the station on Via Lamarmora, the *Grazia Deledda* (☎0784.31.257; ❻) is grand, otherwise try the *Grillo*, a modern and characterless place, but centrally located at Via Monsignor Melas 14 (☎0784.38.668; ❺). Nuoro's **restaurants** are equally hard to track down, but they offer good-quality fare at reasonable prices, for example the excellent *Tascusi* at Via Aspromonte 13, near the top end of the the Corso, where local dishes are served in simple white rooms decorated with Sard art. You'll find a more boisterous atmosphere at *Ciusa*, a plain pizzeria-restaurant popular with locals at Viale Ciusa 53, on the western end of town. Also worth trying is *Il Rifugio*, Vicolo del Pozzo 4, an excellent trattoria-pizzeria.

Sássari and around

While Cágliari was Pisa's base of operations during the Middle Ages, **SÁSSARI**, an inland town in northwestern Sardinia, was the Genoan capital, ruled by the Doria family, whose power reached throughout the Mediterranean. Under the Aragonese it became an important centre of Spanish hegemony, and the Spanish stamp is still strong.

The **old quarter**, a network of alleys and piazzas bisected by the main Corso Vittorio Emanuele, is a good area for aimless wandering, but take a look at the **Duomo**, whose florid facade is Sardinia's most imposing example of Baroque architecture, added to a simpler Aragonese-Gothic base from the fifteenth and sixteenth centuries. The only other item worth searching out is the late Renaissance **Fonte Rosello**, at the bottom of a flight of steps accessible from Corso Trinità, in the northern part of the old town. The fountain is elaborately carved with dolphins and four statues representing the seasons, the work of Genoese stonemasons.

Connected by a series of squares to the old quarter, the **newer town** is centred on the grandiose Piazza Italia. Leading off the piazza is Via Roma, site of the **Museo Sanna** (Tues–Sun 9am–7/8pm; €4.10), Sardinia's second archeological museum; it's a good substitute if you've missed the main one at Cágliari, and like the Cágliari museum its most interesting exhibits are *nuraghic* sculptures.

Roughly 15km inland from Sássari, on the main road to Olbia, rises the tall bell tower of **Santa Trinità di Saccárgia**, its conspicuous zebra-striped facade marking its Pisan origins. Built in 1116, the church owes its remote location to a divine visitation, informing the wife of the *giudice* of Logudoro that she was pregnant. It has survived remarkably well, with lovely Gothic capitals at the top of the entrance porch.

Practicalities

The **train station** is at the bottom of the old town's Corso Vittorio Emanuele. All **buses** arrive at the semicircular Emiciclo Garibaldi, south of the tourist office. PANI buses run from Via Bellini 5, just off Via Roma. Sássari's **tourist office** is at Viale Umberto 72 (Mon–Thurs 9am–1pm & 4–6pm, Fri 9am–1pm; ☎079.231.777, ◍www.regione.sardegna.it/azstss.), a couple of blocks up from the museum. **Staying** in Sássari can be a real problem. Try the *Giusy* (☎079.233.327; ❸), conveniently near the station on Piazza Sant'Antonio, or the conference hotel *Frank Hotel* (☎079.276.456; ❹). Among a range of **restaurants** in town try *Da Bruno*, a cheap pizzeria with tables outside on Piazza Matteotti, or *Fainé Sassu*, off Piazza Castello at Via Usai 17 (closed Sun & June–Sept), which specializes in *fainé*, a sort of pancake made of chickpea flour, either plain or cooked with onions, sausage or anchovies. For a full meal, try *Il Posto*, a friendly trattoria in the new town at Via Enrico Costa 16, or Da Gesuino, at Via Torres 15.

Alghero

Some 36km southwest of Sássari, **ALGHERO** owes its predominantly Catalan flavour to a wholesale Hispanicization that followed the overthrow of the Genoese Doria family by Pedro IV of Aragon in 1354. The traces are still strong in the old town today, with its flamboyant churches, wrought-iron balconies and narrow cobbled streets named in both Italian and Catalan.

A walk around the old town should include the seven defensive **towers** that dominate Alghero's centre and surrounding walls. From the **Giardino Púbblico**, the **Porta Terra** is the first of the massive bulwarks: known as the Jewish Tower, it was erected at the expense of the prosperous Jewish community before their expulsion in 1492. Beyond is a puzzle of lanes, at the heart of which the pedestrianized Via Carlo Alberto, Via Principe Umberto and Via Roma have most of the bars and shops. At the bottom of Via Umberto stands Alghero's sixteenth-century **Cattedrale**. Its neoclassical entrance is round the other side on Via Manno; inside, the lofty nave's alternating pillars and columns rise to an impressive octagonal dome. In fact, most of Alghero's finest architecture dates from the same period, and is built in a similar Catalan–Gothic style. Two of the best examples are a short walk away: the **Palazzo d'Albis** on Piazza Cívica and the elegantly austere Jewish palace **Palau Reial** in Via Sant'Erasmo.

The best of the excursions you can take from the port is to **Neptune's Grotto** (hourly during summer; €10, not including entry to the grotto). The ride takes you west along the coast past the long bay of Porto Conte as far as the point of **Capo Caccia**, where the spectacular sheer cliffs are riddled by deep marine caves. The most impressive is the **Grotta di Nettuno** (daily 9/10am–2/7pm; €8), a long snaking passage delving far into the rock, into which tours are led, single-file, past dramatically lit and fantastical stalagmites and stalactites. A cheaper alternative to the boat tour is to take the bus to Capo Caccia.

Practicalities

Trains arrive some way out of the centre and are connected to the port by shuttle bus. **Buses** arrive in Via Catalogna, on the Giardino Públbico. Alghero's **tourist office** is on the corner of the Giardino Públbico (Easter–June Mon–Sat 8am–1pm & 5–8pm, Sun 9am–1pm; July–Sept daily 8am–8pm; Oct–Easter Mon–Sat 8am–2pm; ℡079.979.054, ✆www.infoalghero.it). The best-value **hotel** in town is the *San Francesco* (℡079.980.330; ❺), in the heart of the old town at Via Machin 2, just behind San Francesco church; each of its clean, quiet rooms has a bathroom. There's a cheaper alternative in the newer part of town: the *Normandie*, on Via Enrico Mattei, between Via Kennedy and Via Giovanni XXIII (℡079.975.302; ❸), with shared bathrooms. *La Mariposa* **campsite** (℡079.950.360; April to mid-Oct), 2km north of town, has direct access to the beach; while the **hostel**, *Giuliani* (℡079.930.353; ❷), is 6km along the coast at Fert'lia, reachable by local bus.

Alghero's **restaurants** are renowned for seafood, inventively prepared and well presented – spring and winter are the best seasons. *La Lépanto* on Via Carlo Alberto, off Piazza Sulis, is excellent, as is *Da Pietro*, at Via Machin 20, with cheaper prices though less atmosphere. The *Machiavello* at Via Cavour 7 has a stunning view, and *Trattoria Maristella* at Via Fratelli Kennedy 9 is a popular joint. If for **snacks**, the fast-food joints by the port aren't bad.

Travel details

Trains

Bari to: Bríndisi (hourly; 1hr 30min).

Bologna to: Ferrara (10 daily; 30min); Florence (7 daily; 1hr 30min); Milan (11 daily; 2hr–2hr 35min); Ravenna (15 daily; 1hr 25min); Rimini (hourly; 1hr 20min).

Cágliari to: Macomer (6 daily; 2–3hr); Olbia (4 daily; 4hr 30min); Oristano (hourly; 1hr–1hr 30 min); Sássari (3 daily; 3hr 40min).

Ferrara to: Rimini (2 daily; 2hr 15min).

Florence to: Arezzo (hourly; 1hr); Bologna (every 30min hourly; 1hr–1hr 30min); Genoa (hourly 6 daily; 3hr 10min–4hr 30min); Lucca (hourly; 1hr 5min–1hr 50min); Milan (18 daily; 2hr 50min–4hr 50min); Naples (9 daily; 4hr); Perugia (11 daily; 2hr 10min); Pisa (every 30min; 55min); Rome (hourly; 2hr 15min–3hr 30min); Venice (hourly; 3hr 25min–4hr 10min); Verona (14 daily; 2hr 40min–3hr 40min).

Genoa to: Bologna (3 daily; 3hr); Milan (hourly; 2hr); Naples (4 daily; 8hr); Pisa (every 2hr; 2hr 30min); Rome (every 2hr; 6hr).

Milan to: Bergamo (5 daily; 50min); Bologna (hourly; 2hr–2hr 35min); Brescia (every 15min; 45min–1hr 10min); Como (12 daily; 30min); Rome (10 daily; 4hr); Venice (hourly; 3hr).

Naples to: Bríndisi (1 daily; 6hr 30min); Palermo (4 daily; 9hr 30min).

Padua to: Bologna (34 daily; 1hr 25min); Milan (25 daily; 2hr 30min); Verona (hourly; 50min).

Palermo to: Agrigento (11 daily; 2hr); Catania (5 daily; 3hr 10min).

Parma to: Brescia (8 daily; 1hr 45min).

Perugia to: Assisi (hourly; 20min); Florence (11 daily; 2hr 10min); Rome (14 daily; 2hr 5min–4hr).

Pisa to: Florence (hourly; 1hr); Livorno (every 30min; 15min); Lucca (hourly; 30min).

Rome to: Ancona (8 daily; 3hr 15min–6hr); Bologna (12 daily; 3hr 20min); Florence (hourly 10 daily; 2hr–3hr 30min); Milan (12 daily hourly; 3hr–5hr 40min); Naples (hourly; 2hr 30min).

Sássari to: Alghero (11 daily; 35min); Cágliari (3 daily; 3hr 40min); Macomer (4 daily; 1hr 35min); Olbia (4 daily; 2hr); Oristano (4 daily; 2hr 35min).

Turin to: Genoa (15 daily; 1hr 45min); Milan (hourly; 1hr 45min).

Venice to: Bologna (hourly; 2hr); Florence (hourly; 3hr 15min); Milan (hourly; 3hr); Padua (hourly; 30min); Trieste (hourly; 2hr 10min); Verona (hourly; 1hr 30min).

Verona to: Milan (hourly; 1hr 30min); Padua (hourly; 55min); Rome (6 daily; 6hr); Venice (hourly; 1hr 30min).

Buses

Cágliari to: Macomer (5 daily; 2hr 30min); Nuoro (4 daily; 3hr 30min); Oristano (5 daily; 1hr 30min); Sássari (7 daily; 3hr 15min–4hr).

Sássari to: Alghero (hourly; 1hr); Bosa (1–4 daily; 2hr 15min); Cágliari (7 daily; 3hr 15min–3hr 45min); Olbia (2 daily; 1hr 45min); Stintino (2–6 daily; 1hr 15min).

Ferries

Cágliari to: Civitavécchia (1 daily; 14hr); Genoa (1 weekly in summer; 21hr); Naples (1 weekly; 16hr); Palermo (1 weekly; 13hr 30min); Trápani (1 weekly; 11hr); Tunis (1 weekly; 35hr 30min).

Genoa to: Bastia (1 weekly; 9hr); Cágliari (2 weekly in summer; 20 hr); Olbia (at least 7 weekly in summer; 13 hr); Palermo (6 weekly; 20 hr); Porto Torres (7 weekly; 12 hr).

Naples to: Capri (6 daily; 1hr 15min); Palermo (daily; 11hr); Sorrento (4 daily; 1hr 15min); Aeolian Islands (3–6 per week; 8 hrs overnight to Strómboli).

Olbia to: Civitavécchia (1daily; 8hr); Genoa (3–7 weekly in summer; 6hr); Livorno (1 daily; 10hr).

Porto Torres to: Genoa (June–Sept 1–2 daily; 12hr); Toulon, France (May–Sept 1 weekly; 9hr; Oct–Apr 1 weekly; 16hr).

Reggio di Calabria to: Messina (15–25 daily; 45min).

Santa Teresa di Gallura to: Bonifacio (2–12 daily; 50min).

Sorrento to: Capri (4 daily; 50min).

Villa San Giovanni to: Messina (every 15min; 45min).

Hydrofoils

Naples to: Capri (17 daily; 40min); Sorrento (7 daily; 40min); Aeolian Islands (2–4 per day; 4 hrs to Strombóli).

Olbia to: Civitavécchia (6–7 weekly; 4–6 hr).

Palermo to: Naples (daily; 4hr).

Reggio di Calabria to: Messina (12 daily; 20min); Naples (summer 1 daily; 6hr).

Sorrento to: Capri (12 daily; 20min).

Latvia

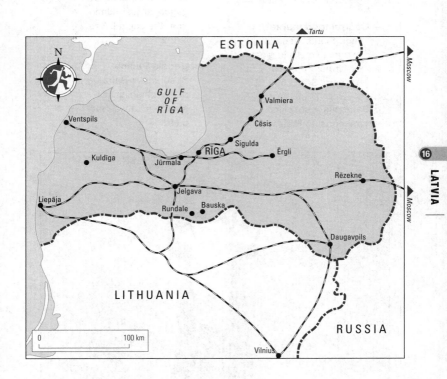

Latvia highlights

* **Milda, the freedom monument** An elegant, stylized female figure holds aloft three stars; Latvia's symbol of independence. See p.689

* **Central food market, Rīga** Sights, sounds and pungent smells in gigantic former Zeppelin hangars. See p.690

* **Salaspils** A shocking memorial to Rīga's Jewish population. See p.692

* **Jūrmala coastline** Fresh air, sand dunes, pine forests and faded elegance, all just 40min from the capital. See p.692

* **Rundāle Palace** Spectacular Baroque palace, highlight of southern Latvia. See p.693

Introduction and basics

The history of Latvia, like that of its neighbour Estonia, is largely one of foreign occupation. The indigenous Balts were overwhelmed at the start of the thirteenth century by German crusading knights, who massacred and enslaved them in the name of Christianity. The Germans continued to dominate both land and trade even after political control passed to the Polish-Lithuanian Commonwealth, then Sweden and finally Russia. During the second half of the nineteenth century the Latvians began to reassert their identity, achieving independence following the 1918–20 war in which they beat off both the Soviets and the Germans. This hard-won independence was extinguished by Soviet annexation in 1940. As conditions in the Soviet Union relaxed during the late 1980s demands for increased autonomy turned into calls for independence, and on August 21, 1991, as the attempted coup against Gorbachev disintegrated in Moscow, Latvia declared its independence for the second time.

These days Latvia is engaged in turning over the economy to private ownership and struggling to reverse Soviet-era stagnation and neglect. Environmental damage aside, the most enduring **legacy** of Soviet occupation is a Russian minority population of thirty percent.

The most obvious destination in Latvia is **Rīga**, a city whose architectural treasures have largely survived five decades of isolation. Places within easy reach of the capital include the palace of **Rundāle**, the resort area of **Jūrmala**, and the gently scenic **Gauja Valley** with the attractive small towns of Sigulda and Cēsis. Latvia also has hundreds of miles of unspoilt **coast** as well as endless **forests** inland.

Information and maps

Tourist information centres run by the Latvian tourist board (ⓦwww.latviatravel.com) are beginning to appear in major centres. The Kümmerly & Frey 1:1,000,000 **map** of the Baltic States includes Latvia, and has a basic street plan of Rīga. If you're travelling extensively in Latvia it's worth investing in the 1:300,000 Euromap map. Jāņa Sēta, Elizabetes 83–85, Rīga, is well-stocked with guides, and publishes its own maps of the region. The Falk Plan of Rīga includes enlarged sections and public transport routes. *Rīga in your Pocket* is an excellent English-language **listings** guide to the capital, with features on attractions elsewhere in the country.

Money and banks

Latvia's unit of currency is the **lat** (plural lati), normally abbreviated to Ls, which is divided into 100 santimi. Coins come in 0.01, 0.02, 0.05, 0.10, 0.20, 0.50, 1 and 2Ls and notes in 5, 10, 20, 50, 100 and 500Ls. At the time of writing £1 was worth 0.9Ls and $1 was worth 0.6Ls.

Bank (*banka*) opening times vary, but in Rīga there should be some open 10am–5pm or later. Outside the capital many close at

---

Latvia on the net

ⓦ **www.virtualriga.com** Information on travel, entertainment and accommodation
ⓦ **www.latviansonline.com** News and features in English
ⓦ **www.tvnet.lv/en/** Welcome to Latvia site with useful links
ⓦ **www.eunet.lv/Riga/** Site for the free *Riga This Week* listings magazine
ⓦ **www.latviatourism.lv** State tourism portal
ⓦ **www.latviatourism.com** Private tour office with many useful links

1pm and all are closed on Saturday and Sunday. Most major banks like the Hansa Banka, Rīgas Komercbanka and Unibank will cash **travellers' cheques** (Thomas Cook and American Express preferred) and some give advances on major credit cards.

In Rīga some major hotels will also cash travellers' cheques and accept credit cards. **Exchanging cash** presents few problems, even outside banking hours, as Rīga is full of currency exchange offices (*valūtas apmaiņa*), often little more than kiosks in unlikely locations like food shops. There are also **cash machines** (ATMs) throughout the country. **Credit cards** are only useful in Rīga's more expensive restaurants and stores, and in some petrol stations.

Communications

Post offices (*pasts*) generally open Mon–Fri 8am–7pm. For **telephone** calls there are modern digital call boxes operated using magnetic cards which come in 2, 5 and 10Ls denominations and can be bought at the post office and most stores. Latvia is in the process of switching from analogue to digital but the whole telephone system, while good, is confusing and area codes are in flux. When in Latvia, for all calls to analogue phones (those with six-digit numbers) you should dial 2 before the six-digit number. If you're calling a digital phone (those with seven-digit numbers) from an analogue phone, dial 1 and wait for a tone before dialling the number. The Rīga city code (2) should be used if you're calling the capital from elsewhere in the country, but is omitted when you're calling from abroad. To make a direct **international** call from digital phones, dial 00 followed by the country code, area code and number. Analogue users must dial 8, wait for the tone, then dial the country code, area code and number.

Rīga is well served by an increasing number of **Internet** cafés, although they are yet to appear in any of the regional centres. Prices are around 1L/hr.

Getting around

The destinations covered in this chapter are all easily reached by bus and/or rail. Buses are generally slightly quicker, but more expensive, than trains.

Trains and buses

Train tickets should be bought in advance – stations have separate windows for long-distance (*starpilsetu*) and suburban (*pirpilsetu*) trains. Long-distance services are divided into "passenger" (*pasažieru vilciens*) and "fast" (*ātrs*) – both painfully slow but the latter, usually requiring a reservation, won't stop at every second village. Train **information** is available from station timetable boards – the Latvian for departure is *atiet*, and arrival is *pienāk*.

It's best to buy long-distance **bus** tickets in advance. Opt for an express (*ekspresis*) bus if possible to avoid frequent stops. Normally luggage is taken on board – if you have a particularly large bag you may have to pay extra to stow it in the luggage compartment. Buses are also useful for travelling to other Baltic countries, with services linking Rīga with Tallinn and Vilnius.

Accommodation

Outside of Rīga and Jūrmala accommodation possibilities are fairly limited and even in tourist areas towns will often only have a couple of hotels and perhaps a campsite to their name.

Hotels and private rooms

Rīga has **hotels** at both the opulent and fleapit ends of the scale, but not much in between. Away from the capital, even in tourist areas like Jūrmala and the Gauja Valley, your only choice is likely to be either cheap Soviet-era dives with no facilities or overpriced Soviet-era places with leaky en-suite plumbing and a broken TV in your room. In Rīga, a number of private room agencies now offer value for money accommodation.

Hostels, student halls and camping

Hostel accommodation exists in Rīga and it's also possible to find rooms in student halls of residence during college vacations – although non-Latvian speakers are often greeted by bemused staff who don't understand English. Such options don't really exist elsewhere in the country, where the only choice open for budget travellers is to head for a campsite (*kempings*), with basic cabins and shared toilets and washing facilities, and usually space for tents.

Food and drink

Latvian **cooking** is based around meat, fish, potatoes and dairy products, with vegetables of the kind people can grow on their own plots. For **drinking**, Rīga has some excellent bars, and though some are expensive, you shouldn't have trouble finding somewhere affordable.

Food

Popular **starters** include cabbage soup (*svaigu kāpostu zupa*) – often almost a meal in itself – and sprats with onions (*šprotes ar sīpoliem*). Most **main courses** are meat- or fish-based – if you want to try something indigenous go for *cūkas galerts* (pork in aspic) or *rasols* (potato salad with herring, beetroot and apple). Popular fish dishes include herring (*siļķe*) and fried, smoked or salted eel (*zutis*). **Desserts** are normally based around forest berries – try *debess manna* (creamed wheat, cranberries and vanilla sauce).

Eating out in Latvia, particularly in Rīga, is often expensive; two people can easily run up a bill of 20Ls. Keep costs down by dining in fast-food places serving indigenous snacks such as *pīrāgi* (blobs of dough with various stuffings) or *pelmeņi* (East-European ravioli). In Rīga you'll also find a few ethnic restaurants offering vegetarian options. Eating in cafés and bars is another cheap option, and self-catering should be no problem as food shops are well stocked with picnic staples.

Drink

The main alcoholic drink in Latvia is **beer** (*alus*). A lot of places serve imported beer but the local brews are fine, and usually cheaper – the most common brand is Aldaris. Worth trying once (and probably only once) is Rīgas Melnais Balzāms, or Rīga black balsam, a kind of bitter made from a secret recipe combining various roots and herbs.

Outside the capital there isn't a great choice of watering-holes, but most places will have at least one bar, café or restaurant. If you want to sample local drinking culture head for a **beer bar**, almost exclusively male hangouts dedicated to serious imbibing, while for something more civilized, try a café. **Coffee** (*kafija*) and **tea** (*tēja*) are usually served black – if you want milk (*piens*) and/or sugar (*cukurs*) you'll have to ask.

Opening hours and holidays

Shops usually open Mon–Fri 8/10am–6/8pm, though some close for an hour at lunchtime. A few food shops open until 10pm and also open Sunday. Most shops and all banks close on the following **public holidays**: Jan 1; Good Fri; Easter Day; May 1; Second Sun in May (Mothers' Day); June 23; June 24 (St John's Day); Nov 18 (National Day); Dec 25, 26 & 31.

Emergencies

Latvia has a major organized crime problem, but activities are unlikely to affect the average visitor. **Theft** is the biggest hazard, and if you're staying in a cheap hotel it's best not to leave valuables in your room. Muggings and casual violence are not unknown in Rīga, but you can minimize the risks by avoiding the backstreets after dark. Latvian **police** (*policija*) are unlikely to speak much, if any, English.

No **immunizations** are necessary for Latvia and emergency medical care is free, though if you fall ill head for home if possible as the country's medical facilities are run-down.

Emergency Numbers

Police ☎02; Ambulance ☎03; Fire ☎01.

RĪGA

RĪGA is the undisputed Baltic metropolis, a major port and industrial centre of nearly a million people. The city was founded by Albert von Buxhoeveden, a German canon who arrived in 1201 with twenty shiploads of crusaders to convert the Latvian tribes to Christianity. The main Hanseatic outpost in the region, Rīga was run by German nobles and merchants even when wider political control passed to other powers, starting with the Polish-Lithuanian Commonwealth in the late sixteenth century. After a subsequent period of Swedish rule Rīga became part of the Russian Empire in 1710 and during the second half of the nineteenth century it developed into a major manufacturing centre. Badly damaged during World War I, the city made a comeback during the first Latvian independence and remained a major centre after the country was swallowed up by the Soviet Union in 1940. Under the Soviets, the influx of Russian immigrants reduced the Latvians to a minority in their own capital – thirty percent of the city's population is now Russian, with a further sixteen percent made up of other non-Latvian nationalities. These days Rīga has a boom-town feel with a small but conspicuous section of the population making big bucks from the get-rich-quick opportunities thrown up by the switch to full-blown market economics.

Arrival, information and city transport

Rīga's main **train station** (Centrālā Stacija) and **bus station** (Autoosta) are just south of Old Rīga and within easy walking distance of the centre. The sea passenger terminal (Jūras pasažieru stacija) is to the north of the centre. **Trams** #5, #7 or #9 run from the stop in front of the terminal on Ausekļa iela into the centre of town (two stops). Rīga airport (Lidosta Rīga) is at Skulte, 8km southwest of the centre; bus #22 (0.20Ls) runs approximately every thirty minutes from the airport to the train station between 6am and 10.30pm; a taxi will cost around 7Ls.

There are **tourist offices** at the airport (daily 9am–9pm; ☎720 7800) and on the Old Town's main square, Rātslaukums (daily 10am–7pm; ☎704 4377, ✉tourinfo@rcc.lv), both of which have leaflets and hotel lists. They also sell the **Rīga Card** (8Ls for 24hr, 12Ls for 48hr, 16Ls for 72hr) which gives unlimited use of public transport and discounts, but it's worth doing a few sums to see whether it will save you any money on your planned itinerary. The excellent English-language guides *Rīga in Your Pocket* (1.20Ls; ✇www.inyourpocket.com) and the free *Rīga This Week* are both available everywhere. Old Rīga is easily walkable, and you can also cover the New Town on foot. Outlying attractions are reached by bus, tram or trolleybus. Flat-fare single-journey **tickets** cost 0.20Ls, bought from the conductor. **Taxis** should cost 0.30Ls per kilometre during the day and 0.40Ls between 10pm and 6am, but watch out for rip-offs or non-functioning meters. Rīga Taxi (☎800 1010) is usually reliable.

Accommodation

Rīga has no shortage of expensive hotels and there are a number of very basic budget places too. What's lacking are comfortable, reasonably priced mid-range options. If you're looking for something in this bracket you may want to consider bed and breakfast accommodation in a private apartment. Patricia Ltd, Elizabetes 22–6 (Mon–Fri 9.15am–6pm, Sat & Sun 10.15am–1pm; ☎728 4868, ✉tourism@parks.lv), has private rooms from 15Ls a night (though they only accept payment in dollars and require a key deposit in dollars too) per person, mostly within walking distance of the centre. The Latvian Youth Hostel Association at Aldaru 8 (☎722 7207, ✇hostels.kolumbs.lv) can suggest hostels in different locations or check out the website ✇www.hostellinglatvia.com for ideas. *Rīga Technical University* **student hostel**, in the centre at Kaļķu 1 (☎708 9395), has double and

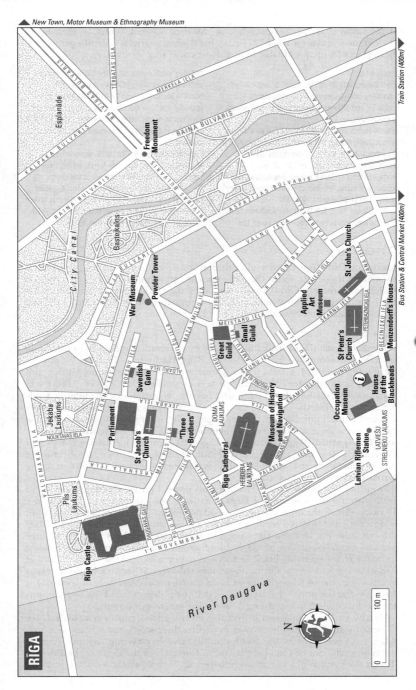

RĪGA

Train Station (400m) ▶

Bus Station & Central Market (400m) ▶

Esplanāde

Freedom Monument

City Canal

Bastejkalns

Powder Tower

War Museum

St John's Church

Applied Art Museum

Great Guild

Small Guild

St Peter's Church

Menzendorff's House

Swedish Gate

Parliament

St Jacob's Church

"Three Brothers"

Riga Cathedral

Museum of History and Navigation

Occupation Museum

House of the Blackheads

Jēkaba Laukums

Latvian Riflemen Statue

Pils Laukums

Riga Castle

River Daugava

N

RĪGA

16

LATVIA | Rīga

687

100 m
0

triple rooms at 3Ls per person; while the *Studentu Kopmītne* hostel, on the edge of the old town at Basteja 10 (☎721 6221), has doubles or triples from 6Ls per person. Both places fill up quickly due to their location, so ring in advance.

Hotels

ECB Barona iela 37 ☎729 8535. British-owned company offering eleven renovated rooms, with cable TV and shower, Internet access and airport pick-up service. ❸

Eliass Hamburgas 14 ☎751 8117. A welcoming atmospheric hostel, ten minutes from the centre in an attractive pre-war neighbourhood. ❷

Homestay Stokholmas 1 ☎755 3016, ✉diga@latnet.lv. Three rooms; one double, one single, one suite, in a friendly family home. Take tram 11 to Vizbijas prospekts. ❸

Laine Skolas 11 ☎728 9823, ✉info@laine.lv. A friendly and comfortable mid-range hotel, ten minutes' walk northeast of the old town. Rooms with shared facilities (❸) or en suites (❺).

Saulīte Merķeļa 12 ☎722 4546. Basic place opposite the train station, acceptable for a short stay. Some renovated rooms have en-suite WC and showers, but are more expensive than standard doubles. ❷

Tia Valdemāra 63 ☎733 3918, ⊛www.tia.lv. Modern hotel with sparsely-furnished but neat en suites, a 15-min walk northeast of the centre. ❸

Valdemārs Valdemāra 23 ☎733 4462. En-suite rooms in this Art Nouveau building have dull brown colour schemes but are spacious and clean. A 10-min walk northeast of the centre. ❸

The City

Vecrīga or **Old Rīga**, centred on Cathedral Square and neatly cut in two from east to west by Kaļķu iela, forms the city's nucleus and is home to most of its historic buildings. To the east Old Rīga is bordered by Bastejkalns Park, beyond which lies the New Town, the nineteenth- and early twentieth-century extension of the city which contains some remarkable Jugendstil architecture.

Old Rīga

Cathedral Square (Doma laukums) is edged by government offices and a sprinkling of cafés, and dominated by the red-brick **Rīga Cathedral** (Tues–Fri 1–5pm, Sat 10am–2pm; 0.50Ls), a towering agglomeration of Romanesque, Gothic and Baroque architecture. The cathedral was established in 1211 by Albert von Buxhoeveden, the founder of Rīga, who became its first bishop. The interior is relatively unadorned, the most eye-catching features being a florid pulpit from 1641 and a magnificent nineteenth-century organ with 6768 pipes. The east wing of the cathedral was once a monastery but now houses the **Rīga Museum of History and Navigation** (Rīgas vestures un kuģniecības muzejs), Palasta 4 (May–Sept Wed–Sun 10am–5pm, Oct–April Wed–Sun 11am–5pm; 1.20Ls), a collection of nautical ephemera and archeological finds. The ticket also gives admission to the **Cross Gallery** of the Cathedral.

From the Cathedral Square Pils iela runs down to leafy **Castle Square** (Pils laukums) and the nondescript **Rīga Castle** (Rīgas pils), built in 1515 by the Livonian Order (the organization of crusading knights who conquered the region), and recently restored as a residence for the Latvian president. Heading along Mazā Pils iela from Pils laukums takes you past the **Three Brothers** (Trīs brāli), three plain medieval houses, one of which dates from the fifteenth century and is thought to be the oldest surviving house in Latvia. A left turn into Jēkaba iela at the end of Mazā Pils iela leads to the thirteenth-century red-brick **St Jacob's Church** (Jēkaba baznīca), the seat of Rīga's Roman Catholic archbishop. Next door at Jēkaba 11 is Latvia's **Parliament** (Latvijas augstākā padome), housed in a pompous Renaissance-style building dating from the late nineteenth century.

Nearby on Torņa iela you'll find the seventeenth-century **Swedish Gate** (Zviedru vārti). This simple archway beneath a three-storey town house was built when Rīga was ruled by the Swedes, and is the sole surviving city gate. A more impressive relic can be found at the end of Torņa iela in the shape of the **Powder Tower** (Pulvertornis), a vast, fourteenth-century bastion whose red-brick walls are still embedded with cannonballs from various sieges. Today, it's home to the **Museum Of War** (Wed–Sun 10am–6pm; 0.50Ls; English-language leaflet 0.40Ls) with sections on the War of Liberation (1918–20), and on the volunteer Latvian Legion who served with the German Waffen SS during World War II.

Though it's not readily apparent, **Bastion Hill** – the park that slopes down to the city canal on the eastern edge of Old Rīga – is actually a vast earthworks built as part of the city's outer defences. It's also a reminder of Rīga's more recent history: on January 20, 1991 four people were killed here by sniper fire as Soviet OMON troops stormed the Latvian Ministry of the Interior on nearby Raiņa bulvāris during an attempted crackdown on Latvia's independence drive. Stones bearing the names of the victims mark where they fell near the Bastejas bulvaris entrance.

From the Swedish Gate Meistaru iela runs down to the **Great Guild Hall** (Lielā Ģilde) at Amatu 6, once the centre of commercial life in Hanseatic Rīga. Though it dates from the fourteenth century the building owes its present neo-Gothic appearance to a nineteenth-century facelift and now houses the Latvia State Philharmonic. South of Kaļķu iela on Skārņu iela is **St Peter's Church** (Pēterbaznīca; Tues–Sun 10am–6pm); a large red-brick structure with a graceful three-tiered spire, it's dedicated to the city's patron saint. A lift (same times; 1.60Ls) takes visitors to the church's gallery and observation platform, affording panoramic views over the city.

Before World War II the late-Gothic **House of the Blackheads** (Melngalvju nams, Tues–Sun 10am–5pm, 1Ls), headquarters of a guild of bachelor merchants and one of Rīga's most famous medieval buildings, stood to the west of St Peter's on what used to be the town hall square (Rātslaukums), which was destroyed in 1941, then totally rebuilt in celebration of Rīga's 800-year anniversary in 2001. These days the square, bereft of any other historic buildings, is known as **Latvian Riflemen's Square** (Latviešu Strēlnieku Laukums) in honour of the Latvian soldiers who fought with the Imperial Russian army during World War I, and then with the Bolsheviks, as the Latvian Red Riflemen, during the Russian Civil War. They are commemorated by a red marble statue depicting three stern figures clad in greatcoats and caps near the bridge at the western end of the square. Also on the square is the **Occupation Museum** of Latvia (Latvijas okupācijas muzejs; ⊛www.occupationmuseum.lv; May–Sept daily 11am–5pm, Oct–April Tues–Sun 11am–5pm; donations), formerly the Latvian Riflemen's Museum, but now devoted to Latvia's occupation by the Bolsheviks, Nazis and Soviets. Well presented and with some English-language texts, the display is an ideal introduction to Latvian contemporary history. Nearby at Grēcinieku 18 is **Menzendorff's House** (Mencendorfa nams; Wed–Sun 10am–5pm; 0.75Ls), an impeccably restored late-seventeenth-century merchant's house.

The New Town

The boulevards of the **New Town**, rolling east from Old Rīga, bear witness to a period of rapid urban expansion that began in 1857, when the city's medieval walls were demolished, and lasted right up until World War I. As Rīga grew into a major industrial centre and country-dwellers flocked to the city, four- and five-storey apartment buildings – many of them decorated with extravagant Jugendstil motifs – were erected to house the expanding middle class.

As you head east out along Kaļķu, which widens out and becomes Brīvības bulvāris, the defiantly modernist **Freedom Monument** (Brīvības piemineklis) dominates the view. This stylized female figure, placed here in 1935 and known as "Milda", holds aloft three stars symbolizing the three regions of Latvia. Incredibly, the monument survived the Soviet era, and nowadays two soldiers stand guard here in symbolic protection of Latvia's independence.

Running north from Brīvības bulvāris to the east of the Freedom Monument is the formal **Esplanade Park** with the **Cathedral of Christ's Nativity** (Kristus dzimsanas katedrāle) just inside its grounds. This late nineteenth-century mock-

Byzantine creation was recently returned to the city's Orthodox community after serving as a planetarium during the Soviet period. At the far end of the park is the **State Museum of Latvian Art** (Valsts mākslas muzejs), Valdemāra iela 10 (Wed–Mon 11am–5pm, Thurs 11am–7pm; 1.70Ls), housed in a grandiose Neoclassical building. Among the numerous nineteenth- and twentieth-century Latvian works inside, the odd street scenes and portraits of Jānis Tīdemanis (1897–1964) make the most lasting impression. Beyond the park it's worth continuing along Brīvības bulvāris as far as the **Alexander Nevsky Church** (Aleksandra Nevska Baznīca) at no. 56, an attractive little Orthodox church from the 1820s, partly concealed by trees on the southern side of the street.

Jugendstil architectural embellishments – florid stucco swirls surrounding doorways, stylized human faces incorporated into facades, and towers fancifully placed on top of buildings – can be seen on virtually every street of the New Town. One of the most famous examples is at **Elizabetes 10a and 10b**, an apartment building adorned with plaster flourishes and gargoyles, and topped by two vast impassive faces. It was designed by Mikhail Eisenstein, the architect father of film director Sergei; more of Eisenstein's creations can be seen a block north of here at Alberta iela 2, 2a, 4, 6, 8 and 13.

Elsewhere in central Rīga

A few hundred metres south of Old Rīga, near the bus and train stations, is the bustling **Central Market** (Centrālais tirgus), housed in a couple of hulking 1930s former Zeppelin hangars. As well as being a useful source of fruit and vegetables, the market is an interesting place to wander round – but keep an eye on your possessions. Five run-down blocks southeast of the market on Elijas iela, the white-painted **Jesus Church** (Jēzus Baznīca) is surrounded by a neighbourhood of decaying timber houses. Dating back to 1635, this is Rīga's oldest wooden church, though it's been rebuilt following fires a couple of times since then. The interior is unusual, with a circular central hall supported by wooden pillars. The church is overshadowed by the **Academy of Sciences** (Latvijas Zinātņu Akedemija) at Turgeņeva 19, a Soviet-era pile built in monumental "wedding-cake" style during the early 1960s and nicknamed "Stalin's Birthday Cake".

Rīga's **Ghetto**, the area originally inhabited by the city's Jews and to which the Nazis later restricted Rīga's Jewish inhabitants, was located about 1km southeast of the train station, in an area now bounded by Lāčplēša iela, Maskavas iela, Lauvas iela and Kalna iela. Most of its original inhabitants were murdered at Salaspils concentration camp, outside the city, between November 30 and December 8, 1941. The ghetto remained in operation, occupied by Jews from elsewhere in Europe until 1943, when it was liquidated on the orders of Himmler after the Warsaw Ghetto uprising. Rīga still has a several-thousand-strong Jewish community and their synagogue is at Peitavas 6–8 in the old town.

To the south of the former ghetto area, on **Rabbit Island** (Zaķu sala; bus #40 or #40A across the bridge), is Rīga's TV Tower. At 368m, it's one of the highest buildings in the world, and has a viewing platform and restaurant.

Eating, drinking and nightlife

If you're on a budget, many bars and cafés do **food** that is less expensive and often just as good as restaurant dishes. There are also plenty of inexpensive fast-food places. Many places have English-language menus. For **drinking**, most of the Old Town bars, particularly those around Cathedral Square, tend to be expensive and geared towards tourists and rich locals. A number of cheaper and more off-beat places can be found in the New Town. The majority of locals can't afford Rīga bar prices so they buy beer from kiosks and wander the streets.

Rīga has a reasonable number of **live music** venues, a few discos and some excellent clubs. **Gambling** is very big in the city.

Cafés and snacks

Café Opera Aspazijas 3. Even if you don't have time to catch a production, the marble and wood interior of the Opera House (✆www.opera.lv) coffee house is worth a visit. Daily 9am–6pm.

Coffee Nation Valdemāra 21. First of a predicted chain of Latvian espresso bars. Excellent cappuccino, cakes and pastries. Popular with film school students and intellectuals. Daily 8am–10pm.

Ķirbis Doma Laukums 1. Divine vegetarian food by the cathedral, with outdoor seating. Pick-and-mix from a wide range of dishes – plates are priced by weight. Mon–Fri 9am–11pm, Sat & Sun 10am–11pm.

Lido atpūtas centrs Krasta 76. Look out for the Lido chain of cafeteria–restaurants serving generous portions of Latvian meat-and-potato dishes. Cavernous cellar with two beer bars. Daily 10am–11pm.

Lido–Staburags Čaka 55. Another point-and-pile-your-plate-up for 2Ls. Traditional Latvian food served amidst old-fashioned oak rooms. Daily noon–1am.

Lido–Vērmanītis Elizabetes 65. All manner of tasty Baltic meat-and-potato dishes, plus salads and fruit bars on the ground floor, pizza and fast food in the cellar. Daily 8am–11pm.

Monte Kristo Ģertrūdes 27. Great coffee house serving pastries. Sun–Fri 9am–9pm, Sat noon–9pm.

Pelmeņi XL Kaļķu 7. Popular fast-food joint on the old town's main street offering Slavic ravioli – blobs of dough (*pelmeņi*) filled with meat or cheese. Mon–Sat 8am–9pm.

Pizza Lulū Ģertrūdes 27. Fashionable little pizzeria with reasonable prices. Open 24hrs.

Šefpavārs Vilhelms Šķūņu 6. Self-service, create your own pancake place near the Cathedral Square. Mon–Thurs 9am–10pm, Fri 9am–11pm, Sat 10am–11pm, Sun 10am–10pm.

Restaurants

Lidojošā Varde Elizabetes 31a. A New Town basement restaurant serving an eclectic international menu in Jugendstil-pastiche decor. Main courses from around 3Ls. Daily 10am–1am.

Mamma Mia Raiņa bulv 21. Bright and cheerful Italian restaurant with crisp pizzas and generous pasta and risottos. Daily 10am–midnight.

Pūt Vējiņ! Jauniela 18/22. Cheap burgers and pasta dishes on the ground floor, moderately-priced Latvian specialities in the restaurant *Blow Little Winds!* upstairs. Daily noon–midnight.

Rāma Barona 56. Hare-Krishna-run veggie place in the New Town with a tasty range of dirt-cheap Asian dishes. One of the few places in the city for vegans. Daily 9am–9pm.

Senā Rīga Aspazijas 22. Dine in rustic cabins while accordionists entertain you from on board a mocked-up pirate galleon, in a restaurant that forms part of the *Rīga Hotel*. The food is Latvian, portions are large and, if you choose carefully, the bill won't clean you out. Daily noon–midnight.

Slepenais Eksperiments Šķūņu 15 (entrance on Amatu). Salads and other dishes during the day and techno at night. Daily noon–4am; 1–2Ls.

Bars

Ala Audēju 11. Popular with young locals, with good, inexpensive cocktails. Open 1pm–2am.

Alus Sēta Tirgotu iela 6. Sample good, cheap Latvian ales accompanied by the national beer-snack – peas (*zirņi*) sprinkled with bacon bits. Outdoor seating in warm months. Daily 11am–1am.

A. Suns Elizabetes 83–85. Named after Dalí and Buñuel's collaboration *Un Chien Andalou*, this arty café/bar has an eclectic menu, with dishes from around 3Ls and some good vegetarian options. Mon–Wed 8am–1am, Thurs & Fri 8am–3am, Sat 11am–3am, Sun 11am–1am.

DECO Bars Dzirnavu 84. Snacks, great cocktails, music, dancing and excellent service. Sun–Thur 11am–1am, Fri & Sat 11am–5am.

Dickens Grēcinieku 11. Brit-pub with wide range of international beers, heaving with expats and locals every weekend. Top-notch pub grub in the restaurant section at the back. Daily 11am–1am.

M6 Mārstaļu 6. Loungey bar attracting laid-back arty-intellectual crowd at the back of the Old Town art gallery of the same name. Punk-goth-alternative misfits congregate in the cellar. Daily noon–11pm.

Možums Šķūņu 19. Guinness on tap and reasonable, albeit pricey, food. Sun noon–1am, Mon–Thurs 9am–1am, Fri 9am–3am, Sat noon–3am.

Paddy Whelan's Bar Grēcinieku 4. Big, lively Irish pub, popular with young locals and expats alike. Mon–Thurs 10am–midnight, Fri 10am–1am, Sat 11am–1am, Sun 11am–midnight.

Pulkvedim Neviens Neraksta Peldu 26/28. Hip bar with industrial-chic decor and alternative-leaning crowd. Serves meat and pasta during the day, becomes a club at night (when there's an admission charge). Frequent live bands. Sun–Thurs noon–2am, Fri & Sat noon–5am.

Live music and clubs

Četri Balti Krekli Vecpilsētas 12. Large upmarket cellar bar known for its Latvian-only music policy. Regular gigs by domestic rock-pop acts. Daily noon–5am.

Dizzi Music Club Mārstaļu 10 (entrance round the corner on Alksnāja). Chic modern jazz bar in the old town with frequent live music and upscale food. Wed–Sat 5pm–3am.

Karakums Lāčplēša 18. A popular café/bar with acoustic bands playing on the ground floor, and a dance floor upstairs with live bands or DJs providing the sounds. Daily 2pm–3am.

Metro Lāčplēša 5. Small and friendly cellar club 15min walk northeast of the centre, offering a much more cutting-edge menu of dance music than the bigger downtown clubs. Thurs–Sat 9am–6pm. 2Ls.

Pepsi Forums Kaļķu 24. Popular with Russian speakers, expats and beautiful young things. Bar, billiards and dancing. Daily 9pm–6am; 5Ls.

Purvs Matīsa 60. Stylish gay club whose name means "Swamp". Erotic performances, sometimes with audience participation. Wed–Sun 8pm–apm, 1–3Ls.

Saksofons Stabu 43. Small rock, jazz and blues venue with a bohemian clientele. The cocktails are cheap and potent. Daily 2pm–2am.

Slepenais Eksperiments Šķūņu 15, entrance at Amatu 4. Hip techno-oriented club in town with great interior decor, live bands and DJs. Fri midnight–5am, Sat 8pm–6am. 2Ls, 1Ls after 4am.

XXL Kalniņa 4. Gay club and restaurant attracting a mixed, dance-oriented crowd. Good food and wild decor. Open daily 4pm–6am, cover charge Tues–Sat 1-5Ls.

Listings

Bike rental Gandrs Kalnciema 28 ☎7614 775.

Embassies Canada, Doma laukums 4 ☎783 0141, ✉canembr@bkc.lv; UK, Alunāna 5 ☎733 8126, ✉british.embassy@apollo.lv; USA, Raiņa bulvaris 7 ☎721 0005.

Exchange Round-the-clock service at Marika, Basteja 14, Brīvības 30, Marijas 5, Merķeļa 10.

Hospital Ars, Skolas 5 ☎720 1001. Some English-speaking doctors.

Internet access Internet Kafejnīca, Elizabetes 75; Internet Klubs, Kalku 10, open 24hrs.

Laundry Miele, Elizabetes 85a. Open 24hr.

Left Luggage At the bus station (daily 6.30am–11pm). Lockers at the left-luggage office (Rokas Bagāīas) in the basement of the railway station (0.50–1Ls per day, 4.30am–midnight).

Pharmacies 24hr service at Rudens aptieka, Ģertrūdes 105 ☎724 4322.

Post office 24hr service on Brīvības bulvāris 19.

Day-trips from Rīga

For a taste of the rest of Latvia, a number of destinations within easy reach of Rīga make feasible **day-trips** from the capital.

The concentration camp at **SALASPILS**, 22km southeast of Rīga, is where most of Rīga's Jewish population perished during World War II. Around 100,000 people died here, including Jews from other countries who had been herded into the Rīga Ghetto after most of the indigenous Jewish population had been wiped out. Today the site is marked by monumental sculptures and a memorial, with the former locations of the barrack buildings outlined by white stones. To get there take a suburban train in the direction of Ogre and alight at Dārziņi station from where a clearly signposted path leads to the memorial, a walk of about fifteen minutes.

JŪRMALA or "Seashore" is the collective name for a string of small seaside resorts that line the Baltic coast for about 20km west of Rīga. Originally favoured by the tsarist nobility, it became the haunt of Latvian intellectuals between the wars. Today, its sandy beaches backed by dunes and pine woods seethe with people at weekends and on public holidays. Trains for Jūrmala leave the suburban terminus of Rīga's central station from platforms 3 and 4, with Majori, about 10km beyond Rīga city limits, the main stop. Here you'll find a number of restaurants and cafés along Jomas iela, the pedestrianized main street running east from the station square. Head north from here to Jūras iela, from where a few paths lead to the beach. The **tourist office** at Jomas 42 (June–Aug daily 9am–9pm, Sept–May daily 9am–7pm; ☎776 4276, ✆www.jurmalatour.lv) can arrange accommodation.

RUNDĀLE PALACE or Rundāles Pils (Wed–Sun: May–Oct 10am–6pm; Nov–April 10am–5pm; 1.50Ls), 77km south of Rīga, is one of the architectural wonders of Latvia. This 138-room Baroque palace, built in two phases during the 1730s and 1760s, was designed by Bartolomeo Rastrelli, the architect who created the Winter Palace in St Petersburg. It was privately owned until 1920 when it fell into disrepair, but meticulous restoration, begun in 1973, has largely returned it to its former glory. To get there take the bus to **Bauska** (®www.bauska.lv) and then a minibus for Rundāles Pils, from where it's a twenty-minute walk to the palace. Should you want to stay overnight, try the *Viesnīca Bauska*, Slimnīcas 7, Bauska (®39/23027; ❷) by the bus station.

Sigulda and Cēsis

SIGULDA, dotted with parks and clustered above the southern bank of the River Gauja, around 50km northeast of Rīga, is the **Gauja National Park**'s main centre and a good jumping-off point for exploring the rest of the Gauja Valley.

From the train station Raiņa iela runs north into town, passing the bus station on the way. After about 800m a right turn into Baznīca iela brings you to **Sigulda Church** (Siguldas Baznīca), built over seven hundred years ago, though much altered since. A left turn after the church leads, by way of **Sigulda New Castle** (Siguldas Jaunā Pils), a nineteenth-century manor house masquerading as a medieval castle, to the ruins of Sigulda Castle (Siguldas Pilsdrupas), a former stronghold of the Knights of the Sword. From here you can admire **Turaida Castle** (Turaidas Pils), perched on a bluff 3km away. To get there, catch one of the Turaida or Krimulda buses from Sigulda bus station, or walk there in about 45 minutes. Begin the walk by taking J. Poruka iela northwest from Sigulda church, and descending the wooden staircase at the end to the bridge across the Gauja river. On the far side of the bridge an asphalt path slopes down to the left, and runs past several sandstone caves before rejoining the main road just short of Turaida itself. Built on the site of an earlier stronghold by the bishop of Rīga in 1214, Turaida Castle was destroyed when lightning hit its gunpowder magazine in the eighteenth century. Extensively restored, these days it houses a local history **museum** (Tues–Sun 10am–5/6pm; 0.80Ls). Just before the castle is the eighteenth-century **Turaidas Church** (Turaidas Baznīcas), an appealing little wooden church with a Baroque tower that's one of the best-preserved examples of Latvian native architecture in the country. Sigulda is also the centre for a range of activities from horse-riding and bungee jumping to less energetic mini golf and bike hire (®www.sigulda.lv).

The well-preserved little town of **CĒSIS**, 35km northeast of Sigulda, is considered by many Latvians to have an atmosphere as close to that of prewar small-town Latvia as it's possible to get. One of the oldest towns in the country, it's the former seat of the master of the Livonian order and was also a member of the Hanseatic League. More recently Cēsis was the site of a crucial battle during the War of Independence, when a combined Latvian/Estonian force defeated the Iron Division of the German *Landeswehr* between June 19 and June 24, 1919.

From the **train** and **bus** stations walk down Raunas iela to Vienības Laukums, the town's main square. The attractive but run-down old town – a few narrow streets lined with flaking wooden buildings – lies to the south of here. On Rīgas iela just south of the square the remains of the old town gates have been excavated. Nearby, on Skolas iela, is the thirteenth-century **St John's Church** (Svēta Jāņa Baznīca), which contains the tombs of several masters of the Livonian order. East of the square are the remains of **Cēsis Castle** (Cēsu Pils) founded by the Knights of the Sword in 1209.

Travel details

Trains

Rīga to: Majori-Jūrmala (every 30 min; 40 min); Cēsis (9 daily; 1hr 30min); Moscow (2 daily; 17hr 30min); Sigulda (14 daily; 1hr); St Petersburg (1 daily; 14hr); Tallinn (1 daily; 7hr); Vilnius (1 daily; 6hr).

Buses

Rīga to: Bauska (30 daily; 1hr 30min); Cēsis (20 daily; 2hr); Kaunas (3 daily; 4hr 30min); Sigulda (every hour; 1hr); Tallinn (7 daily; 5hr 30min); Vilnius (5 daily; 6hr).
Sigulda to: Turaida (12 daily; 10min).

Lithuania

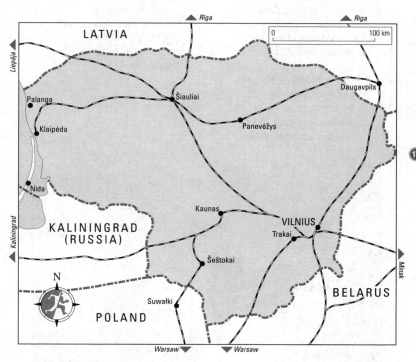

Lithuania highlights

* **St Anne's church, Vilnius** Napoleon wanted to take the little late Gothic masterpiece home to Paris. **See p.703**

* **Genocide museum** In the former KGB HQ, this museum is a shocking reminder of man's inhumanity. **See p.704**

* **Vilnius, Skonis ir Kvapas** Elegant tea house with gorgeous interiors and an impressive range of teas and coffees. **See p.705**

* **Trakai** A fairy-tale medieval castle sitting on its own little island amongst lush green countryside. **See p.706**

* **Couronian Spit** The wild, beautiful Couronian National Park was added to UNESCO's World Heritage List in 2000. **See p.709**

Introduction and basics

Unlike its Baltic neighbours, Lithuania once enjoyed a period of sustained independence. Having driven off the German Knights of the Sword in 1236 at Šiauliai, the Lithuanians emerged as a unified state under Grand Duke Gediminas (1316–41). The 1569 Union of Lublin established a combined Polish-Lithuanian state which reached its zenith under King Stefan Bathory, but the Great Northern War of 1700–21, in which Poland-Lithuania, Russia and Sweden battled for control of the Baltics, left the country devastated, and by the end of the eighteenth century most of Lithuania had fallen into Russian hands. Uprisings in 1830 and 1863 presaged a rise in nationalist feeling, and Russia's collapse in World War I enabled the Lithuanians to re-establish their independence. In July 1940, however, the country was effectively annexed by the USSR. German occupation from 1941 to 1944 wiped out Lithuania's Jewish population and wrecked the country, and things scarcely improved with the return of the Soviets. When Moscow eventually relaxed its hard line in the late 1980s, demands for greater autonomy led to the declaration of independence on March 11, 1990, way ahead of the other Baltic States. A prolonged stand-off came to a head on January 11, 1991 when Soviet forces killed fourteen people at Vilnius TV Tower, but as the anti-Gorbachev coup foundered in August 1991, the world recognized Lithuanian independence.

Travel in Lithuania presents no real hardships, and even in well-trodden destinations the volume of visitors is low, leaving you with the feeling that there's still much to discover here. Vilnius, with its Baroque old town, is the most architecturally beautiful of the Baltic capitals, while the second city, Kaunas, also has an attractive centre and a couple of unique museums, along with a handful of surprisingly good restaurants and bars. The port city of Klaipėda has a restored old town, and is a stopping-off point en route to the resorts of Neringa, a unique spit of sand dunes and forest that shields Lithuania from the Baltic.

Information and maps

Most of Lithuania's major towns now have **tourist offices** run by the state tourist board

(@www.tourism.lt), often offering accommodation listings and events calendars in English. Otherwise *Vilnius In Your Pocket* guide (available from bookshops, newsstands, tourist offices and some hotels; 8Lt) is the most indispensable source of practical information, with annual publications on Kaunas and Klaipėda also. If you're planning to travel extensively in Lithuania, the Euromap 1:300,000 **map** of the country is a useful investment. Regional maps and detailed street plans of Vilnius are available in bookshops and newspaper kiosks once you arrive. The Jāṇa Sēta plan of Vilnius comes as either a fold-out map or spiral-bound city atlas, and includes public transport.

Money and banks

Lithuania's unit of currency is the **litas** (usually abbreviated to Lt), which is divided into

Lithuania on the net

@**www.tourism.lt** National tourist board site with useful information
@**www.exploringvilnius.lt** Attractive city guide with photographs and listings
@**www.search.lt** Lithuanian search engine
@**www.lietuva.lt** General information about the country

100 *centai*. Coins come in denominations of 0.01, 0.02, 0.05, 0.10, 0.20, 0.50Lt and bank notes in 1, 2, 5, 10, 20, 50, 100 and 200Lt denominations. The litas is now pegged to the Euro (€1 = 3.45Lt), the current exchange rate is approximately 6Lt and 4Lt to $1. **Bank** (*bankas*) opening hours vary, though branches of the Vilniaus Bankas usually open Mon–Fri 8am–3/4pm. They generally give advances on Visa/Mastercard/AmEx cards and cash travellers' cheques (commission 2–3 percent). To exchange cash outside banking hours, find a currency exchange office (*valiutos keitykla*). Credit cards are most likely to be accepted in Vilnius.

Communications

In major towns, **post offices** (*paštas*) are open Mon–Fri 8am–6pm, Sat 8am–4pm; in smaller places hours are more restricted. Stamps are also available at some newspaper kiosks and tourist offices. Public **telephones** operate with cards (*telefono kortele*; 9Lt, 13Lt, 16Lt and 30Lt) from post offices and newspaper kiosks – the higher-denomination cards should suffice for a short-duration international call. To make a long-distance call, first dial 82 before dialling the area code and phone number. When calling Lithuania from abroad, the initial 82 is omitted. For international calls from Lithuania, dial 8, wait for the tone, followed by 10, then the country code, area code and phone number. There's a good choice of **Internet** cafés in Vilnius and a few in Kaunas.

Getting around

The destinations covered in this chapter are all easily reached by bus and/or train. Buses are generally slightly quicker and slightly more expensive than trains, though both are desperately slow.

Trains

Train tickets should be bought in advance – stations have separate windows for long-distance and suburban (priemiestinis or vieti-

nis) trains. Long-distance services are divided into "passenger" (keleivinis traukinys) and "fast" (greitas); the latter usually require a reservation. Train information is available from station timetable boards – the Lithuanian for departure is išvyksta, and arrival is atvyksta.

Buses

It's best to buy long-distance **bus** tickets in advance, and opt for an express (*ekspresas*) bus if possible, to avoid frequent stops. You can also pay for your ticket on board, although this doesn't guarantee you a seat. Normally luggage is taken on board, though large bags may have to go in the luggage compartment for a small charge. As well as being a viable means of getting around Lithuania, buses are also useful for travelling to other Baltic countries.

Accommodation

Accommodation in Lithuania is generally cheaper than in Western Europe. The best way to keep costs down is by staying in private rooms, as budget hotels tend to be pretty grim. If money isn't an issue, you'll have few problems finding a decent place to stay.

Private rooms and hotels

For budget travellers **private room** accommodation usually costs around 70–100Lt per person. The most ubiquitous and reliable agency is Litinterp, with offices in Vilnius, Klaipėda and Kaunas. Though fairly grim, if you don't mind spartan conditions you may be able to find rooms in Soviet-era budget hotels for as little as 40Lt for a double. Some cheap hotels can be dodgy – if things don't feel right (rooms show signs of past forced-entry, etc) don't stay. Smaller, mid-range places are starting to appear, charging upwards of 280Lt a double, and are usually preferable to similarly priced Soviet-era hotels which tend to be large and impersonal. In Vilnius and Kaunas you'll find innumerable international business-standard places charging 400Lt and upwards for a double.

Hostels and camping

Lithuania has a few **hostels** where you'll pay 24–32Lt per night. Space is limited and it's best to try and ring individual establishments in advance. An ex-Soviet phenomenon is the cabin **campsite** (*kempingas*), offering accommodation in three to four-bed cabins (usually primitive facilities are shared with other cabins) for around 20Lt per person. Many will also let you pitch a tent for slightly less. The downside is that they're often located a long way out of town. You can also camp wild in the countryside, subject to the approval of any landowner.

Food and drink

Lithuanian **cuisine**, based on traditional peasant dishes, is less bland than that of its Baltic neighbours, partly as a result of Polish influence. Typical **starters** include marinated mushrooms (*marinuoti grybai*), herring (*silkė*) and smoked sausage (*rukyta dešra*) along with cold beetroot soup (*šaltibarščiai*). Potatoes play a major role; one of the most commonly encountered dishes is *cepelinai*, or zeppelins – cylindrical potato dumplings stuffed with meat, mushrooms or cheese. Also popular are potato pancakes (*bulviniai blynai*), and cabbage leaves stuffed with minced meat (*balandėliai* or "*pigeons*"). **Desserts** include stewed fruit (*kompotas*), sweet fruit sauce (*kisielius*), and innumerable varieties of pancakes (*blynai*, *blyneliai* or *lietiniai* are synonyms for more or less the same thing).

Some **restaurants** serve indigenous cuisine, and even in a fairly upmarket place a meal shouldn't work out too expensive. Western fast food is making inroads, and Vilnius has a few ethnic places. Although **vegetarianism** has yet to establish itself, it's possible to find meat-free options on menus. Most cafés and bars do reasonably priced food.

Beer (*alus*) is the most popular alcoholic drink while the leading Lithuanian fire-waters are Starka, Trejos devynerios and Medziotoju – invigorating spirits flavoured with a variety of herbs.

Lively **bars** are sprouting up daily in Vilnius and Kaunas. Many ape American or Irish models, although there are also plenty of folksy Lithuanian places, while cafés (*kavine*) come in all shapes and sizes. **Coffee** (*kava*) and **tea** (*arbata*) are usually served black.

Opening hours and holidays

Opening hours for shops are 9/10am –6/7pm. Outside of Vilnius, some places take an hour off for lunch; most usually close on Sun (though some food shops stay open). Most shops and all banks will be closed on the following **public holidays**: Jan 1; Feb 16 (Old Independence Day); March 11 (New Independence Day); Easter Sun; Easter Mon; July 6 (Statehood Day); Nov 1; Dec 25 & 26.

Emergencies

Though many Lithuanians claim the streets are unsafe, you're unlikely to meet trouble if you're sensible. Nor is organized crime likely to affect the average visitor. Car theft and vandalism are the most common crimes.

The cash-starved Lithuanian police expect to be taken seriously – be polite if you have any dealings with them and you should have no problems. A few of the younger ones may speak a little English. Emergency health care is free in Lithuania but if you get seriously ill, head for home (or at least Western Europe).

Emergency Numbers

Police ☏02; Ambulance ☏03; Fire ☏01.

Vilnius

"Narrow cobblestone streets and an orgy of Baroque: almost like a Jesuit city some-where in the middle of Latin America", wrote the author Czesław Milosz of prewar **VILNIUS**. Soviet-era satellite suburbs aside, it's a description which still rings true today. Between the wars Vilnius, known as **Wilno**, belonged to Poland and was inhabited mainly by Poles and Jews, who played such a prominent role in the city's life that it was known as the "Northern Jerusalem". Though now firmly part of Lithuania, Vilnius is still a cosmopolitan place – around twenty percent of its popu-lation is Polish and another twenty percent is Russian – though with just 543,000 inhabitants it has an almost village-like atmosphere, making it an easy place to get to know.

Arrival, information and city transport

The main **train station** is at Geležinkelio 16, just south of the Old Town, and the main **bus station** is just across the road. There are exchange facilities at both, although you'll get a better rate at banks in the town centre. Trolleybus #2 takes you from the train station to the main Cathedral Square. Walking into the Old Town is feasible too. The **airport** is around 5km south of the city centre at Rodūnės kelias (☎2/306 666). From outside the main entrance bus #2 runs a cou-ple of times an hour to Lukiškių aikstė in the city centre, and takes approximately 25 minutes. Bus #1 will take you to the train and bus station area. **Tickets** for both buses cost 1Lt from the driver.

The **tourist offices** at Vilniaus 22 (Mon–Thurs 9am–6pm Fri 9am–5pm; ☎2/629 660, ✉turizm.info@vilnius.lt) and at Pilies 42 (Mon–Fri 10am–6pm; ☎2/626 470) offer maps, tours and information on hotels and museums, but your best bet is the excellent *Vilnius in Your Pocket* city guide (✆www.inyourpocket.com), costing 8Lt and available everywhere. Vilnius is well served by **public transport** with buses and trolleybuses covering most of the city. Tickets cost 0.80Lt from *kioskas* and 1Lt from the driver; validate your ticket by punching it in the machine on board. Alternatively, hail a minibus at any bus stop in the direction you're going, pay the driver 2Lt and you'll be dropped off at the stop you require. **Taxi** prices are usually reasonable and fares should cost no more than around 1–2Lt per kilometre. Telephoning for a taxi is one way of ensuring a fair rate; try Vilniaus Taxi (☎2/128 888).

Accommodation

Best value for money is offered by **private rooms**. *Litinterp*, Bernardinų 7/2 (Mon–Fri 8.30am–5.30pm, Sat 9am–3.30pm; ☎2/223 850, ✆www.litinterp.lt), is the longest-established agency, offering rooms in the Old Town – either with a host family or in *Litinterp's* own self-contained guesthouse – with singles from 70Lt and doubles from 120Lt. Similar deals are offered by the two Vilnius tourist offices, and the *Vilnius In Your Pocket* booth at the airport arrivals hall.

Hostels

Filaretai Filaretų 17 ☎2/154 627; bus #34 from the train station. HI-affiliated hostel, with kitchen, common room and washing machine. Fifteen minutes' walk east of the Old Town. ❶

JNN Hostel Ukmergės 25 ☎2/722 270, ✉centras@lvjc.elnet.lt. A slightly more upmarket place north of the river. Take bus #2 from the airport or trolleybus #5 from the train station to Žaliasis Tiltas followed by bus #2 or #46. ❷

Old Town Hostel Aušros Vartų 20–10 ☎2/625 357. HI-affiliated hostel near the train and bus stations; reservations essential. Cramped but comfortable. ❷

Teacher's University Hotel Vivulskio 36 ☎2/130 509. A choice of 68 rooms, 20-min walk west of the Old Town in a dull neighbourhood. Dorms ❶

Hotels

Apia Šv Ignoto 12 ☎2/123426, ✉apia@takas.lt. Friendly, five-room guesthouse in superb Old Town location. ❸

Rudninkų Vartai Rudninkų 15/46 ☎2/613916. Neat and tasteful, medium-sized place on the fringe of the Old Town, rooms arranged around a central courtyard. ⑥

Mikotel Pylimo 63 ☎2/609626, ✉mikotel@takas.lt. Small-size hotel a few steps away from the train and bus stations, with pristine modern en suites and quirky paintings in the hallways. ⑤

Šaulės Šaulės 15/23 ☎2/349 358, ✉saulesB&B@takas.lt. A fair distance out of town, but this family-run country lodge-style guest house has a lovely forest view. ③

VILNIUS

Hill of Three Crosses & St Peter & St Paul Church

KGB Museum & Parliament

ARSENALO GATVĖ
Lithuanian National Museum
Applied Art Museum
Gediminas Tower
Cathedral
Gedimino Kalnas
Clock Tower
KATEDROS AIKŠTĖ
Jewish Museum
Jewish Museum
SVENTARAGIO GATVĖ
BARBOROS RADVILAITĖS
Mickiewicz Museum
University
St Anne's Church & Benedictine Church
Presidential Palace
St John's Church
St Michael's Church
Mickiewicz Statue
Lithuanian Art Museum
Town Hall
St Casimir's Church
Artillery Bastion
Philharmonia
Holy Spirit Church
St Theresa's Church
Gates of Dawn

N
0   250 m

17

Bus Station ▼   ▼ Train Station

The City

At the centre of Vilnius, poised between the medieval and nineteenth-century parts of the city, is **Cathedral Square** (Katedros aikstė). To the south of here along Pilies gatvė and Didžioji gatvė is the **Old Town**, containing perhaps the most impressive concentration of Baroque architecture in northern Europe. West of the square in the New Town is **Gedimino prospektas**, a nineteenth-century boulevard and the focus of the city's commercial and administrative life. Wedged between the Old Town and the Gedimino prospektas areas, the traditionally **Jewish areas** of Vilnius were shorn of their populations in the 1941–1945 period, but retain some sights.

Cathedral Square and around

Cathedral Square is dominated by the Neoclassical **Cathedral** (daily 7am–7pm), its origins going back to the thirteenth century, when a wooden church is thought to have been built here on the site of a temple dedicated to Perkūnas, the god of thunder. The highlight of the airy, vaulted interior is the opulent **Chapel of St Kazimieras**, dedicated to the patron saint of Lithuania, whose remains lie in a silver casket in the chapel's main altar. Next to the cathedral on the square is the white **belfry**, once part of the fortifications of the vanished Lower Castle but now looking like a stranded Baroque lighthouse. Between the Cathedral and the belfry, locals can often be seen spinning round on a small coloured tile with the word *stebuklas* (miracle) written on it. This marks the spot from where, in 1989, two million people from the Baltic states formed a protest chain which stretched all the way to Tallinn in Estonia.

Rising behind the cathedral is the tree-clad **Gediminas Hill**, its summit crowned by the red-brick octagon of **Gediminas Tower**, one of the city's best-known landmarks. The first substantial fortification here was founded by Grand Duke Gediminas, the Lithuanian ruler who consolidated the country's independence. According to legend Gediminas dreamt of an iron wolf howling on a hill overlooking the River Vilnia and was told by a pagan priest to build a castle on the spot. The tower houses the **Vilnius Castle Museum** (Tues–Sun 11am–5/7pm; 4Lt, free on Wed in winter), showing the former extent of the Vilnius fortifications.

A hundred metres north of the cathedral in a former arsenal building is the **Lithuanian National Museum**, Arsenalo 1 (Wed–Sun 11am–5/6pm; 4Lt; free Wed in winter; ⓦwww.lnm.lt), covering the history of Lithuania from prehistoric times to 1940 but with mostly Lithuanian and Russian labelling. A little further north on Arsenalo, a separate department of the museum houses the Prehistoric Lithuania exhibition (same times; 4Lt). Nearby is the **Applied Art Museum**, Arsenalo 3 (Tues–Sun 11am–5/6pm; 8Lt, free Wed in winter), home to a glittering array of ecclesiastical treasures.

The Old Town

The **Old Town**, just south of Cathedral Square, is a network of narrow, often cobbled streets that forms the Baroque heart of Vilnius, with the pedestrianized **Pilies gatvė** cutting into it from the southeastern corner of the square. To the west of this street is **Vilnius University**, a jumble of buildings constructed between the sixteenth and eighteenth centuries around nine linked courtyards that extend west as far as Universiteto gatvė. Within its precincts is the beautiful, ornate **St John's Church** – access from Šv Jono gatvė. Founded during the fourteenth century, St John's was taken over by the Jesuits in 1561 and given to the university in 1737. Reconstruction after a fire in the same year has left it with its present Baroque facade, and a no-holds-barred Baroque altar inside. Climb the **bell tower**, separate from the main building, for excellent views of the city.

The **Presidential Palace**, just west of the university on **Daukanto aikstė**, was originally built during the sixteenth century as a merchant's residence and remodelled into its present Neoclassical form at the end of the eighteenth century, going on to serve as the residence of the Russian governor-general during the Tsarist period. Napoleon Bonaparte stayed here briefly during his ill-fated campaign against Russia in 1812. The emperor is said to have been so impressed by **St Anne's Church** (Tues–Sat 10am–3pm & 5.30–9pm, Sun 8am–1pm & 5–7pm) on Maironio gatvė, to the east of Pilies gatvė, that he wanted to take it back to Paris on the palm of his hand. Studded with skeletal, finger-like towers, and its facade overlaid with intricate brick traceries and fluting, this late-sixteenth-century structure is the finest Gothic building in Vilnius. Rising behind St Anne's is the Gothic facade of the much larger **Bernardine Church** from 1520. Its once fine Baroque interior suffered during its Soviet-era incarnation as home to the Vilnius Art Academy, and the building is now undergoing a much-needed renovation.

Just south of St Anne's and the Bernardine church is a **statue** commemorating the Polish Romantic poet Adam Mickiewicz (1798–1855), author of *Pan Tadeusz*, the Polish national epic. Nearby is the **A. Mickievičius Memorial Apartment** at Bernardinų 11 (Tues–Fri 10am–5pm, Sat & Sun 10am–2pm; 2Lt), whose rather paltry exhibits include a couple of chairs and a desk owned by Mickiewicz. **Bernardinų gatvė** is one of the Old Town's more appealing back streets, a narrow lane lined by seventeenth- and eighteenth-century houses.

Heading south Pilies becomes Main Street (Didžioji gatvė), with the restored Baroque palace at no. 4 housing the **Lithuanian Art Museum** (Tues–Sat noon–6pm, Sun noon–5pm; 5Lt; free on Wed in winter), a marvellous collection of sixteenth- to nineteenth-century paintings and sculptures from around the country. The colonnaded Neoclassical building standing at the end of **Town Hall Square** (Rotušės aikštė) has recently been restored to its original function as the town hall. The modern building behind it houses the **Contemporary Art Centre** (Tues–Sun 11am–6.30pm; 4Lt; free on Wed in winter), which hosts changing exhibitions of works by modern artists.

Just east of the square, **St Casimir's Church** (Mon–Fri 4–6.30pm, Sun 8am–2pm), dating from 1604 and the oldest Baroque church in the city, remains a striking building – its central cupola topped by an elaborate crown and cross symbolizing the royal ancestry of St Casimir, the son of King Casimir IV of Poland.

South of here, Didžioji becomes **Aušros Vartų gatvė**, a short distance along which a gateway on the left-hand side leads to the seventeenth-century **Church of the Holy Spirit**, Lithuania's main Orthodox church, a Baroque structure built on a low hill in the grounds of a monastery. In front of the large iconostasis, the bodies of three fourteenth-century martyred saints are displayed in a glass case, their faces swathed in cloth.

A little further along Aušros Vartų gatvė the seventeenth-century **St Theresa's Church** rises to the left of the street, another soaring testimony to the city's dominating architectural style. The end of the street is marked by the **Gates of Dawn**, the sole survivor of nine city gates that once studded the walls of Vilnius. A **Chapel** above the gate houses the city's most celebrated religious monument, the **White Madonna**, an image of the Virgin Mary said to have miraculous powers and revered by Polish Catholics.

East of Aušros Vartų gatvė on Boksto 20/18 is the **Artillery Bastion**, a seventeenth-century bastion that was once part of the city's outer fortification ring and which now houses a **museum** (Wed–Sun 10am–5pm; 2Lt, free on Wed in winter) of weapons and armour, though the setting is more interesting than the contents.

Jewish Vilnius

Before World War II Vilnius was one of the most important centres of Jewish life in eastern Europe. The Jews – first invited to settle in 1410 by Grand Duke Vytautas – made up around a third of the city's population, mainly concentrated in the eastern fringes of the Old Town around present-day Vokiečių gatvė, Žydų gatvė and Antokolskio gatvė. The **Great Synagogue** was located just off Žydų gatvė, on a site now occupied by a kindergarten.

Massacres of the Jewish population began soon after the Germans occupied Vilnius on June 24, 1941, and those who survived the initial killings found themselves herded into two **ghettos**. The smaller of these ghettos centred around Žydų, Antokolskio, Stiklių and Gaono streets and was liquidated in October 1941, while the larger occupied an area between Pylimo, Vokiečių, Lydos, Mikalojaus, Karmelitų and Arklių streets and was liquidated in September 1943. Most of the Jews of Vilnius perished in Paneriai forest on the southwestern edge of the city (see p.706).

Today, the Jewish population of Vilnius numbers only a few thousand. The city has one surviving **synagogue** at Pylimo 39 (Mon–Thurs 8–10am, Sun 7–9pm), out of the 96 that once existed. To find out about the history of Jewish Vilnius head for the **Lithuanian State Jewish Museum**, housed in various parts of the labyrinthine Jewish community offices at Pylimo 4 (Mon–Thurs 9am–5pm, Fri 9am–4pm; 2Lt, free on Wed in winter). The display includes items salvaged from the Great Synagogue and some of the exhibits are captioned in English. A second branch of the museum, the Catastrophe Exhibition, occupies a small green house nearby at Pamenkalnio 12 (Mon–Thurs 9am–5pm, Fri 9am–4pm; donations), and contains a harrowing display about the fate of Vilnius Jews during the war. The museum can also arrange "history of Jewish Vilnius" tours (☏2/620 730).

Nearby, the otherwise nondescript Kalinausko street is worth a visit to see the bronze head of rocker **Frank Zappa** perched on a column. Civil servant, Saulis Paukstys, founded the local Zappa fan club and commissioned the socialist realist sculptor Konstantinas Bogdanas, more accustomed to forging likenesses of Lenin, to create this unique tribute to Zappa.

Gedimino prospektas

Gedimino prospektas, named after the founder of the city, runs west from Cathedral Square, and was, in the past, named after St George, Mickiewicz, Stalin and Lenin, reflecting the succession of foreign powers that controlled the city. It was the main thoroughfare of nineteenth-century Vilnius, and remains the most important commercial street.

Lukiškių aikštė, around 600m west of Cathedral Square, is the former location of the city's Lenin statue, removed after the failed 1991 coup which precipitated the final break-up of the Soviet Union. The square has long played an infamous role in city history. After the 1863–64 uprising against the Russians, a number of rebels were publicly hanged here, while Gedimino 40, on the southern side of the square, was Lithuania's **KGB headquarters**. The building also served as Gestapo headquarters during the German occupation and more recently the Soviets incarcerated political prisoners in the basement. It's now the **Genocide Museum** (entrance at Aukų 2a; Tues–Sun 10am–4/6pm; 2Lt), with dank green cells and courtyard where prisoners were tortured and executed preserved in their pre-1991 state. The English-language cassette-tape commentary (8Lt) provides detailed background on the prison and its inmates.

At the far end of Gedimino prospektas stands Lithuania's graceless modern **Parliament Building**. Thousands gathered here on January 13, 1991, when Soviet troops threatened to occupy it following the killing of a dozen people at the TV Tower (see below). Facing the river some of the barricades built to defend the building have been preserved, complete with anti-Soviet graffiti; there's also a moving memorial commemorating those who died at the TV Tower and the seven border guards killed by Soviet special forces in July 1991. The 326-metre **TV Tower** (10am–9pm; 12Lt) itself is around 3km west of the centre in the Karoliniškės district – trolleybus #16 from the train station or #11 from Lukiškių aikštė; alight at the Televizijos bokštas stop on Sausio 13-Osios gatvė. At the tower's base, wooden crosses commemorate those killed here in the bloodiest event of the struggle for Baltic independence.

Eating, drinking and nightlife

There's a fast-growing range of **eateries** in Vilnius offering everything from Lithuanian to Lebanese cuisine – although the majority of places serve the standard meat-and-potatoes. There's little difference between eating and drinking venues: **bars** and **cafés** invariably serve snacks and meals and often represent better value for money than restaurants. Vilnius has a few **clubs** and **discos**, though you may have a better (and cheaper) time in some of the bars mentioned below. Cutting-edge DJ culture is limited to monthly rave parties organized by hip magazine *Ore*, but venues change: look out for posters or check the internet (®www.ore.lt) for details.

Cafés and snack bars

Afrika Pilies 28. Popular lunchtime stop-off on the Old Town's main street, offering a tasty range of salads, sandwiches and soups.

Bar Italia Gedimino 3a. Strong coffee and excellent sandwich and cake selection.

Greitai corner of Gedimino and Totorių. Classy cafeteria with cheap main courses (peruse the choice at the counter and point to what you want) and good-ish cakes.

Mano Kavinė Bokšto 7. Stylish place in the Old Town with chic, modernist decor, trendy young clientele, a wide range of snacks and speciality teas.

Pilies Menė Pilies 8. Flash modern café/bar with extensive pancake menu. Good place for a daytime coffee or night-time drink.

Presto Gedimino 32a. Bright modern coffee bar with an impressive range of brews, as well as salads and sumptuous cakes.

Skonis ir Kvapas Trakų 8. The most beautiful vaulted interior in town. Big pots of tea, excellent coffee, and an affordable range of hot meals.

Užupio Kavinė Užupio 2. Relaxed, mildly Bohemian place on the eastern fringes of the Old Town, with lime-tree-shaded outdoor terrace overlooking the Vilnia River.

Restaurants

Balti Drambliai Vilniaus 41. Vegetarian restaurant with friendly service, unusual non-smoking policy in the cellar and lively beer garden.

Čili Didžioji 5. Popular place for an inexpensive bite, with thin-crust and deep-pan pizzas. Six more branches, one at Gedimino 23.

Finjan Vokiečių 18. Middle-eastern place that looks like a fast-food café but charges restaurant prices. Good kebabs, shawarma and falafel and large portions.

Freskos Didžioji 31. Imaginative, well-presented modern European cuisine behind the Town Hall. Good value lunchtime salad buffet.

Lokys Stiklių 8/10. Reasonably priced Lithuanian cellar restaurant serving boar, elk and beaver meat alongside more traditional meat-and-potato favourites.

Po Saule Labdarių 8. French bistro with superb food at reasonable prices. Great place for a quick *tarte à l'oignon* or a more leisurely three-course meal.

Ritos Sléptuvė Goštauto 8. Excellent pizzas plus quiche, spaghetti and a few vegetarian options. Order local beer to keep your bill manageable. Good for breakfasts and dancing in the evening.

Savas Kampas Vokiečių 4. A cosy wood-furnished interior and extensive list of alcohol, with good pizzas too.

Žemaičių Smuklė Vokiečių 24. The top place for traditional Lithuanian cuisine. An excellent place to try *cepelinai* (potato dumplings stuffed with meat), or *žemaičių blynai* (potato pancakes). Warren of cellar rooms in winter, outdoor courtyard seating in summer.

Bars

Bix Etmonų 6. Great bar with industrial decor, karaoke nights and an enjoyable disco in the cellar – run by members of local rock band Bix. Food available.

Brodvėjaus Pubas Mėsinių 4. Popular drinking/dancing venue with live bands (Thurs–Sun) and DJs. Full menu of snacks and hot meals; lunchtime specials.

Prie Parlamento Gedimino 46. Big, popular café/bar with restaurant-standard food (excellent veggie options) and pub-style bar.

Prie Universiteto Dominikonų 9. British bar with dark interior and covered courtyard. Frequent live music, big-screen sport and extensive food menu.

Šuolaikinio Meno Centras In the Contemporary Art Centre at Vokiečių 2. Dark, minimalist café/bar which has long been a meeting place for arty types and nonconformists.

Clubs and discos

Gero Viskio Baras Pilies 34. Eternally popular Old-Town drinking joint both day and night. Aside from the main ground-floor bar there's a cocktail bar upstairs; cellar disco after 8pm.

Men's Factory Žygimantų 1, Gay bar and disco found at the north end of the Old Town, beside the river. Bar Wed–Thurs, disco Fri & Sat, closed Sun.

Ministerija Gedimino 46. In the cellar below Prie Parlamento, playing newish dance stuff as well as popular classics. Popular with ex-pats and beautiful young things.

Stiklių Tangomania Gedimino 31. Stylish place with smart clientele.

Ultra Imperiale Goštauto 12. Trendy place catering for a younger age group. Pop during the week and techno on Sat. Thurs–Sat only.

Listings

Embassies and Consulates Australia, Vilniaus 23 ☎2/123 369; Canada, Gedimino 64 ☎2/496 853; USA, Akmenų 6 ☎2/665 500; UK, Antakalnio 2 ☎2/122 070.
Exchange Gelezinkelio 6 (24hr).
Hospital Vilnius University Emergency Hospital, Šiltnamių 29 ☎2/169 140.

Internet access Bazė, Gedimino 50 (entrance round the corner on Rotundo); Collegium, Pilies 22; Netcafe, Antakalnio 36.
Pharmacies Gedimino Vaistinė, Gedimino 27.
Police Jogailos 3 ☎2/616 208.
Post office Gedimino prospektas 7.

Day-trips from the city

Beyond Vilnius, several places merit a day-trip. **PANERIAI**, the site where the Nazis and their Lithuanian accomplices murdered one hundred thousand people during World War II, lies within Vilnius city limits in a forest at the edge of a suburb, 10km southwest of the centre. Seventy thousand of those killed at Paneriai were Jews from Vilnius, who were systematically exterminated from the time the Germans arrived in June 1941 until they were driven out by the Soviet army in 1944. To get to Paneriai take a southwest-bound suburban train from Vilnius station and alight at Paneriai. From the station platform descend onto Agrastų gatvė, turn right and follow the road through the woods for about a kilometre. The entrance to the site is marked by the **Paneriai Memorial** – two stone slabs with Russian and Lithuanian inscriptions commemorating the murdered "Soviet citizens", flanking a central slab with an inscription in Hebrew commemorating "seventy thousand Jewish men, women and children". From the memorial a path leads to the **Paneriai Museum**, Agrastų 15 (9am–5pm, closed Tues; call to check ☎2/602 001; donations), with a small display detailing what happened here. Paths lead to the pits in the woods where the Nazis burnt the bodies of their victims and to another eight-metre pit where the bones of the dead were crushed.

TRAKAI, 25km west of Vilnius, is the former capital of the Grand Duchy of Lithuania. Founded during the fourteenth century and standing on a peninsula jutting out between two lakes, it's the site of two medieval castles. From the **train** and **bus stations** follow Vytauto gatvė to reach the main sights. After about 500m turn right down Kęstuaio gatvė to the remains of the **Peninsula Castle**, thought to have been built by Duke Kęstutis, son of Gediminas and father of Vytautas. Trakai is home to the **Karaites**, members of a Judaic sect whose ancestors were brought here from the Crimea by Grand Duke Vytautas to serve him as bodyguards, and whose distinctive wooden cottages line Karaimų gatvė, the northern continuation of Vytauto gatvė. Around two hundred inhabitants of Trakai are Karaites; Lithuania's smallest ethnic minority, they recognize only the laws of the Old Testament. Down the street at no. 30 is their wooden **Kenessa**, or prayer house, built in the early nineteenth century. A hundred metres or so beyond the Kenessa two wooden footbridges lead to the **Island Castle**, a cluster of red-brick towers built around 1400 on a small offshore island and one of Lithuania's most famous monuments. Built by Grand Duke Vytautas, under whom Lithuania reached the pinnacle of its power during the fifteenth century, it fell into ruin from the seventeenth century until a 1960s restoration returned it to its former glory. It now houses a **museum** (Tues–Sun 10am–5/7pm; 8Lt). The main **tower**, built around a galleried courtyard, is separated from the outer buildings by a moat – you cross a footbridge to enter. Within are exhibits covering the history of the castle, plus examples of medieval weaponry and wooden carvings.

The rest of Lithuania

Outside Vilnius, Lithuania is predominantly rural – a gently undulating, densely forested landscape scattered with lakes. However, it does boast at least one more major city in **Kaunas**, a genuine rival to Vilnius in terms of its historical importance to the Lithuanian nation. Further west, the main highlight of the coast is the holiday village of **Nida**, whose dramatic dunescapes and traditional timber architecture are reachable by ferry and bus from **Klaipėda**, the country's major port.

Kaunas

KAUNAS, 80km west of Vilnius and easily reached by bus or rail, is Lithuania's second city and seen by many Lithuanians as the true heart of their country. It served as provisional capital during the interwar period when Vilnius was part of Poland, and remains a major commercial and industrial centre. Nevertheless it's an attractive, easy-going city, with enough sights to merit at least a full day's visit.

The Old Town

The most interesting part of town is predictably the **Old Town**, or **Senamiestis**, centred around **Town Hall Square** (Rotušes aikštė), on a spur of land between the Neris and Nemunas rivers. The square is lined with fifteenth- and sixteenth-century merchants' houses in pastel stucco shades, but the overpowering feature is the magnificent **Town Hall**, its tiered Baroque facade rising to a graceful 53-metre tower. The other most eye-catching structure on the square is the seventeenth-century **Jesuit Church** on the southern side. Originally part of a larger college and monastery complex, the church was built in 1666. In 1825 the Russians handed it over to the Orthodox church, and later the Soviets turned it into a trade school, but the Baroque interior remains intact.

Northeast of the square, the red-brick tower of Kaunas' austere **Cathedral** can be seen at the start of Vilniaus gatvė. Dating back to the reign of Vytautas the Great, the cathedral was much added to in subsequent centuries. After the plain exterior, the lavish gilt and marble interior comes as a surprise. There are nine altars in total, though the large, statue-adorned Baroque high altar (1775) steals the limelight. Predating the cathedral by several centuries is **Kaunas Castle**, whose scant remains survive just northwest of the square. Little more than a restored tower and a couple of sections of wall are left, the rest washed away by the Neris, but in its day the fortification was a major obstacle to the Teutonic Knights.

South of the town square, the **Perkūnas House** at Aleksoto 6 is an elaborately gabled red-brick structure, thought to have been built as a Hansa office or possibly a Jesuit chapel, standing on the reputed site of a temple to Perkūnas, the pagan god of thunder. From here Aleksoto descends to the banks of the Nemunas and the glowering Vytautas Church, built by Vytautas the Great in around 1399.

The New Town

The main thoroughfare of Kaunas' **New Town** is **Freedom Avenue** (Laisvės alėja), a broad pedestrianized shopping street running east from the Old Town, which, bizarrely, was declared a no-smoking zone during the 1990s. At the junction with L. Sapiegos the street is enlivened by a bronze **statue of Vytautas the Great**, which faces the **City Garden** where, on May 14, 1972, the 19-year-old student Romas Kalanta immolated himself in protest against Soviet rule. Kalanta's death sparked anti-Soviet rioting, and he is commemorated by a memorial stone in the gardens.

Towards the eastern end of Freedom Avenue the silver-domed **Church of St Michael the Archangel** looms over Independence Square (Nepriklausomybes aikštė), while the striking modern building in the northeast corner is one of the best art galleries in the country, the **Mykolas Žilinskas Art Museum** (Tues–Sun

11am/noon–5/6pm; closed last Tues of every month; 3Lt), with a fine collection of Egyptian artefacts, Chinese porcelain and Lithuania's only Rubens.

Kaunas celebrates its role in sustaining Lithuanian national identity on **Unity Square** (Vienybės aikštė), at the junction of S. Daukanto and K. Donelaičio, a block north of Laisvės. Here a **monument** depicting liberty as a female figure faces an eternal flame flanked by traditional wooden crosses, with busts of prominent nine-teenth century Lithuanians between the two. Just north of the square, Kaunas has a unique art collection in the **A. Žmuidzinavičius Art Museum**, Putvinskio 64 (Tues–Sun 11am/noon–5/6pm; closed last Tues of every month; 5Lt). Better known as the **Devil's Museum**, this houses a vast collection of devil figures put together by the artist Antanas Žmuidzinavičius. Though most of the images are comic, there's also a sinister representation of Hitler and Stalin as devils dancing on a Lithuania composed of skulls. Heading east down Putvinskio brings you to the 1930s **funicular railway** (0.50Lt) which climbs up to the **Žaliakalnis** district to the north of the city centre, giving panoramic views. Near the upper terminal is the **Church of Christ's Resurrection**, a 1930s modernist edifice with a very tall white tower.

Before World War II Kaunas, like Vilnius, had a large **Jewish population**, but nearly all were killed during the war and little remains to remind of their presence, except the city's sole surviving **synagogue** at Ožeskienės 17 in the New Town and the ruins of two more at Zamenhofo 7 and 9. To find out about the fate of the Jews of Kaunas head out of town to the **Ninth Fort Museum**, Žemaičių plentas 73 (Wed–Sun 10am–5/6pm; 14Lt to see all three parts), housed in the tsarist-era fortress where the Jews were kept while awaiting execution. Take bus #23 or #35 from Šv. Gertrūdos just north of the Old Town.

Practicalities

There's a helpful **tourist office** just off Laisvės alėja at Mickievičiaus 36 (Mon–Fri 9am–6pm; April–Sept also Sat 9am–3pm; ☎37/323 436, ✉turizmas@takas.lt) doling out English-language leaflets and a free map. You can also pick up a copy of *Kaunas in Your Pocket* here (🌐www.inyourpocket.com; 4Lt). For **accommodation** the ever-reliable *Litinterp*, Kumelių 15–4 (☎37/228 718, 🌐www.litinterp.lt), can sort you out with a room in the centre for 60Lt single, 100Lt double. Central **hotels** include the unrenovated but tolerable *Monela*, Laisvės 35 (☎37/221 791; ❸); the gloomy but charmingly olde-worlde *Lietuva I*, Daukanto 21 (☎37/225 992, ✉metropol@takas.lt; ❸); and the hulking concrete *Takijoji Neris*, off Laisvės to the north at Donelaičio 27 (☎37/204 224, takneris@takas.lt; ❹).

To **eat** in style head for *Chez Eliza*, Vilniaus 30, with a French-influenced menu (main courses from 12Lt). For something more local try the *Bernelių Užeiga*, Valančiaus 9, where you can dine on meat and potatoes in an attractive rustic interior. *Pizza Jazz*, Laisvės alėja 68, does delicious thin-crust pizzas while *Dviese*, Vilniaus 8, is the place for deep-fried meat pies. **Cafés** and **bars** are often a good bet for eating too: *Avilys*, Vilniaus 9, is a chic establishment with a full range of meals and its own beer; *Elfų Šėlsmas*, Laisvės 93, offers drinking, dining and dancing in faux-rustic surroundings. The *Skliautai*, Rotušės aikštė 26, and the nearby *B.O.*, Muitinės 9, are the best places to hook up with a young, arty crowd. *Los Patrankos*, Savanorių 124, is the newest, biggest and friendliest of the techno-oriented **clubs**. *Mefistofelis*, Ignalinos 21, is a semi-official gay bar, but locals appear wary of new-comers. You can access the **Internet** at Dokeda, Mairono 13 (4Lt/hr), or Kavinė Internetas, Daukšos 12 (5–7Lt per hour).

Klaipėda and around

KLAIPĖDA, Lithuania's third largest city and most important port, lies on the Baltic coast, a long and tedious 275km by road or rail northwest of Vilnius. Though it has a handful of sights the city is of more interest as a staging post en route to **Neringa**, the Lithuanian name for the Couronian Spit which shields much of Lithuania's coast from the open Baltic.

Until 1919 a part of Germany known as **Memel**, Klaipėda is bisected by the River Danė. The main sights are in the **Old Town** on its southern bank, an area of half-timbered buildings and cobbled streets, at the heart of which is **Theatre Square** named after the ornate Neoclassical **Theatre** building on its northern side. In front of the theatre is **Anna's Fountain**, a replica of a famous prewar monument to the German poet Simon Dach (1605–1659), which depicts the heroine of his folksong *Ännchen von Tharau*. Southeast of the square, the **History Museum of Lithuania Minor**, Didžioji vandens 6 (Wed–Sun 11am–7pm; 3Lt), has local archeological finds, national costumes and ancient domestic implements.

In the **New Town**, on the northern side of the Danė, at Liepų 16, is Klaipėda's splendid red-brick Gothic-revival **Post Office**. Built between 1883 and 1893, it is a vivid reminder of imperial German civic pride, while a few doors along at Liepų 12, the **Clock Museum** (Tues–Sun noon–5.30pm; 4Lt) is stuffed with timepieces, including some magnificent seventeenth- and eighteenth-century examples.

Practicalities

Klaipėda's **tourist office** is just off Teatro aikštė at Tomo 2 (Mon–Fri 8.30am–5pm; summer also Sat 9am–2pm; ☎26/412186, ✉kltic@takas.lt). *Klaipėda in Your Pocket* (4Lt, from the tourist office or bookstores) is your best source of information about what's going on in town. Litinterp, Šimkaus 21/4 (Mon–Fri 8.30am–5.30pm; summer also Sat 10am–3pm; ☎26/311 490, ⌨www.litinterp.lt), has central **private rooms** (❷), and they can also help with rooms in Nida. *Klaipėda Travellers' Guesthouse*, Turgaus 3–4 (☎26/214 935, ✉oldtown@takas.lt; ❷), is a centrally located, friendly hostel. Reasonable mid-range **hotels** include the *Fortūna*, Poilsio 64 (☎26/348028; ❹), a small pension 4km south of the centre best booked in advance. Nearer the centre is the family-run pension *Prūsija*, Šimkaus 6 (☎26/412 081; ❹). There's an unofficial free **campsite** with no facilities at Giruliai, 8km north of Klaipėda next to the *Pajūris* sanatorium on Slaito (shuttle bus #8 from the centre).

Good places to **eat** in the Old Town are Galerija Pėda, Turgaus 10, whose tasty food looks as arty as the gallery it occupies; and *Būrų Užeiga*, Kepėjų 17, which serves up Lithuanian meat-and-potato favourites in homely surroundings. For **drinking**, *Kurpiai*, Kurpių 1, is a pub that also functions as the best jazz bar in the Baltics; while *Skandalas*, 10 minutes' northwest of the Old Town at Kanto 44, is an American-themed bar with a wide selection of food and drinks.

Neringa

NERINGA, or the Kuršių Nerija, is the Lithuanian section of the Couronian Spit, a 97-kilometre spit of land characterized by vast sand dunes and pine forests. Much of the spit can be seen as a day-trip from Klaipėda, although you need to stay a day or two to soak up the unique atmosphere. Ferries from the quayside towards the end of Žvejų gatvė in Klaipėda (sailings every 30min, 5am–3am; free) sail to **SMILTYNE** on the northern tip of the spit. From the landing stage, frequent minibuses (7.50Lt) run south towards the scenic, dune-dominated parts of the spit, terminating at Nida, 35km south.

NIDA is the most famous village on the spit – a small fishing community boasting several attractive streets of attractive wooden houses, although there's some lumpen Soviet resort architecture at its heart. To get a feel for the old fishing settlement head for **Naglių gatvė** and **Lotmisko gatvė** (5min south of the village centre bus stop). The roads are lined with single-storey blue- and brown-painted wooden houses, many with traditional thatched roofs. The **Etnografinė Žvejo Sodyba**, Naglių 4 (May–Sept Wed–Sun 11am–5pm; 3Lt), is a re-created nineteenth-century fisherman's cottage with simple wooden furnishings. From the end of Naglių a shore path runs to a flight of wooden steps leading up to the top of the **dunes** south of the village. From the summit you can gaze out across a Saharan sandscape to the Kaliningrad province, part of German East Prussia until 1945 but now belonging to the Russian Federation. At the northern end of the village is **Thomas Mann's**

House (May–Sept Tues–Sun 11am–5pm; 3Lt), the author's summer residence from 1930 to 1932. Nida's long, luxuriant beach stretches along the opposite, western side of the spit, a 20min walk through the forest from the village.

The **tourist office**, in the centre of the village at Taikos 4 (Mon–Fri 9am–1pm & 2–6pm; ☎259/52345), will find you a **private room** (❶). Litinterp back in Klaipėda can book rooms in advance, but for a slightly higher fee. Best of the numerous small **hotels** in town is the *Rasytė*, Lotmiskio 11 (☎259/52592; ❹), a wooden house in the heart of the old fishing settlement, although it's essential to book in advance. The larger and less atmospheric *Nidos Smiltė*, Skruzdynės 2 (☎259/52221; ❷), offers simple doubles with shared facilities and spartan cabins in the Nidos Pušynas holiday settlement nearby. For **food** head for *Seklyčia*, Lotmiškio 1 (daily 9am–midnight), which does simple dishes like *cepelinai* as well as more sophisticated meat and fish dishes. *Reidas*, just behind the bus station at Naglių 20, is a good place to try the delicious, locally smoked fish *ŗukyta žuvis*. It turns into a lively **bar** with rock music at night.

Travel details

Trains

Vilnius to: Kaunas (12 daily; 1hr 15min–2hr); Klaipėda (3 daily; 5hr); Rīga (2 daily; 9hr); Šeštokai (2 daily; 3hr 30min); Warsaw (1 daily; 11hr). The only way to get from Vilnius to Warsaw by train without passing through Belarus, for which you will need an expensive visa, is to travel indirectly via Šeštokai and Suwałœki.

Kaunas to: Klaipėda (3 daily; 3hr 30min); Rīga (1 daily; 7hr); Vilnius (12 daily; 1hr 15min–2hr).

Klaipėda to: Kaunas (3 daily; 3hr 30min); Vilnius (3 daily; 5hr).

Buses

Vilnius to: Kaunas (every 20–30min; 1hr 30min–2hr); Klaipėda (10–12 daily; 4hr); Rīga (5 daily; 6hr); Tallinn (2 daily; 11hr 40min); Warsaw (4 daily; 12hr).

Kaunas to: Klaipėda (10 daily; 3hr); Rīga (2 daily; 4hr 30min); Vilnius (every 20–30min; 1hr 30min–2hr).

Klaipėda to: Kaliningrad (2 daily; 3hr 50min); Kaunas (10 daily; 3hr); Nida (departures from Smiltynė; 8 daily; 50min); Vilnius (10–12 daily; 5hr).

Ferries

Kaunas to: Nida (hydrofoil service; June–Aug 1 daily; 4hr).

Morocco

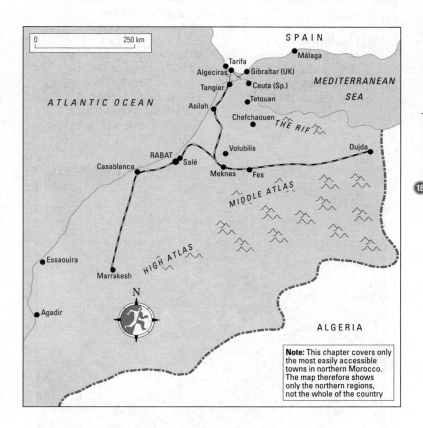

Note: This chapter covers only the most easily accessible towns in northern Morocco. The map therefore shows only the northern regions, not the whole of the country

Morocco highlights

* **Chefchaouen** Beautiful and very friendly little town in the Rif mountains, where the houses look like they're made of blue meringue. **See p.720**

* **Fes, Medina** An incredible labyrinth of alleys, sights and smells in the world's best-preserved medieval city. **See p.724**

* **Djemaa el Fna, Marrakesh** A spontaneous live circus in a large square in the middle of town, featuring everything from snake charmers to tooth pullers. **See p.729**

* **Essaouira** Arty and very laid-back beach resort where Jimi Hendrix once played impromptu concerts on the beach for his fellow hippies. **See p.734**

Introduction and basics

Just an hour's ferry ride from Spain, Morocco seems very far from Europe, with a deeply traditional Islamic culture. Throughout the country, despite its 44 years of French and Spanish colonial rule, a more distant past constantly makes its presence felt. Travel here is, if not always easy, an intense and rewarding experience.

Berbers, the indigenous population, make up over half of Morocco's population. Only around ten percent of Moroccans claim to be "pure" **Arabs**, though with a population shift to the industrialized cities, such distinctions are becoming less significant. More telling is the legacy of the **colonial** period: until independence in 1956, the country was divided into Spanish and French zones. The French, who ruled the larger and more heavily populated area, had the most lasting effect, building *Villes Nouvelles* (new towns) alongside the long-standing *Medinas* (old towns) in all the country's main cities, and created Casablanca in the image of Marseille. Today French is spoken alongside Arabic and the three Berber languages.

Most visitors' introduction to Morocco is **Tangier** in the north, still shaped by its heyday of "international" port status in the 1950s. To its south, in the Rif mountains, the town of **Chefchaouen** is a small-scale and enjoyably laid-back place, while inland lies the enthralling city of **Fes**, the greatest of the four imperial capitals (the others are Meknes, Rabat and Marrakesh), and unique in the Arab world for the chance to witness a city life that remains largely medieval. The sprawl of **Meknes**, with its ancient walls, and nearby Roman site of **Volubilis**, makes an easy day-trip from Fes, but justifies a day or two of exploration on its own.

The power axis of the nation lies on the coast in **Rabat** and **Casablanca**, respectively the seats of government and of industry and commerce. They've acquired their pre-eminence only in the last sixty years, so French and post-colonial influences are dominant: "Casa" looks more like Marseille than anything Moroccan, while the elegant, orderly capital, Rabat, houses some gems of Moroccan architecture. Further south, **Marrakesh** is an enduring fantasy that won't disappoint. The country's loveliest resort, **Essaouira**, a charming walled seaside town, lies within easy reach of Marrakesh and Casablanca.

Information, guides and maps

There's a **tourist office** (Délégation du Tourisme) run by the Office National Marocain du Tourisme (ONMT) in every major city. In addition, there's sometimes a locally funded Syndicat d'Initiative. They stock leaflets and maps, and can put you in touch with official guides.

In addition to the guides trained by the government, there are scores of young Moroccans offering their services. Some of these **"unofficial guides"** are genuine students, while others are out-and-out hustlers, though these have been clamped down on. If you do run across them, be polite but firm, and don't be intimidated. Note that it's illegal to harass tourists.

Good **maps** of Moroccan cities are hard to obtain locally or abroad. The most functional are those in the *Rough Guide to Morocco*.

MOROCCO | Basics

18

Morocco on the net

ⓦ**www.tourism-in-morocco.com** Tourist office info
ⓦ**www.geocities.com/TheTropics/4896/morocco.html** Information and links
ⓦ**www.lexicorient.com/morocco** Destinations
ⓦ**infoweb.magi.com/~morocco/morocco.html** History and culture
ⓦ**www.maroc.net** News and information

Money and banks

Morocco is inexpensive but poor, and **tips** can make a lot of difference. The unit of currency is the **dirham** (dh), divided into 100 centimes; in markets, prices may well be in centimes rather than dirhams. There are coins of 10, 20 and 50 centimes, and 1, 5 and 10 dirhams, and notes of 10, 20, 50, 100 and 200 dirhams. You can get dirhams in Algeciras and Gibraltar, and can usually change foreign notes on arrival at major sea- and airports. It can be difficult to change travellers' cheques until you reach a bank.

For **exchange** purposes, the most useful and efficient chain of banks is the **BMCE** (Banque Marocaine du Commerce Extérieur), which often has a separate *bureau de change* open longer hours and at weekends. **Travellers' cheques** incur a 10.70dh commission except at the state-run Bank al-Maghrib. Many banks give cash advances on **credit cards**, both of which can also be used in tourist hotels (but not cheap unclassified ones) and in the **ATMs** of all major banks.

Banking hours are: summer Mon–Fri 8am–2pm; winter Mon–Thurs 8.15–11.30am & 2.15–4.30pm, Fri 8.15–11.15am & 2.45–4.45pm. During Ramadan, banks open Mon–Fri 9am–2pm. In major resorts there's usually one bank with flexible hours and large hotels may also change money.

Communications

Post offices (PTT) open Mon–Thurs 8.30am–12.15pm & 2.30–6.30pm, Fri 8.30–11.30am & 3–6.30pm. Central post offices in large cities will be open longer hours, except in summer and Ramadan. In addition to the post offices, you can buy **stamps** at postcard shops and sometimes at tobacconists (look for three interlocking blue circles). Always post items at a PTT.

International **phone calls** are best made with a phonecard (from post offices and some tobacconists). Alternatively, there are privately run téléboutiques, open late, where you can sometimes also fax and make photocopies. Calls through hotels usually cost a lot more. Coin-operated pay phones accept 50c and 1dh coins; a short local call costs around 50c, and a few dirhams is enough for a long-distance one. Moroccan **phone numbers** have nine digits, all of which must be dialled.

Internet access is available pretty much everywhere, and at low rates: 10dh/hr is typical.

Getting around

Public transport by train, bus or collective grand taxi is, on the whole, good. Guidelines on **fares** are given in each section.

Trains

The **train** network is limited, but for travel between the major cities, trains are the best option. Major stations have free timetables, printed by ONCF (Ⓦwww.oncf.org.ma), the national train company. Second-class fares are comparable to what you'd pay for buses. In addition, there are couchettes (50dh extra) available in summer on trains from Tangier to Marrakesh (9hr 30min) and Fes (5hr 30min); these are worth the money for extra comfort and security.

Grands taxis and petits taxis

Collective **grands taxis** are usually big Peugeots or Mercedes, plying set routes for a set fare and are much quicker than buses, though the drivers can be reckless. Make clear you only want *une place* in a *collectif*, otherwise drivers may assume you want to charter the whole car.

Within towns **petits taxis** do short trips, carrying up to three people, with luggage on the roof. They queue in central locations and at stations and can be hailed on streets when they're empty. Payment – usually no more than 15dh – relates to distance travelled.

Buses

Buses are marginally cheaper than grands taxis, and cover longer distances, but are much slower. Buses run by CTM (the national company) are most reliable, with numbered seats and fixed schedules. An additional express service is run by Supratours, and is fast and comfortable. On small private-line buses, you generally have to pay a standard 5dh for your bags to go on the roof (this also covers unloading at your destination).

Accommodation

Accommodation is inexpensive, generally good value and usually pretty easy to find, except in the peak seasons (August, Christmas and Aïd el Kebir), and even then only in a handful of main cities and resorts. Cheap, unclassified **hotels** and *pensions* (charging about 100dh for a double) are mainly to be found in the Medinas, while hotels with stars tend to concentrate in the Villes Nouvelles.

At their best, **unclassified Medina hotels** are beautiful, traditional houses with white-washed rooms grouped around a central patio. The worst can be extremely dirty, and many have problems with water. Few have en-suite bathrooms, though *hammams* (public Turkish baths) are usually close at hand.

Classified hotels' star-ratings are fairly self-explanatory and prices are reasonable for all except five-star places. Except in Marrakesh, most hotels do not include **breakfast** in their room price.

HI **hostels** (*auberges de jeunesse*), often bright, breezy and friendly, offer an alternative to cheap hotels, but generally have strict rules requiring you to be in by 10pm and out by 10am daily. **Campsites** usually suffer the disadvantage of being well out of town. They tend to charge around 15dh per person plus the same again for your tent.

Food and drink

If your funds are limited, you'll probably be **eating** mainly in cheap local diners. Fancier restaurants, definitely worth an occasional splurge, are mostly to be found in the Ville Nouvelle, which is where you'll also find any bars.

Food

Moroccan **cooking** is good and filling. The main dish is usually a **tajine**, essentially a stew. Classic *tajines* include chicken with lemon and olives, and lamb with prunes and almonds. The most famous Moroccan dish – Berber rather than Arab in origin – is **couscous**, a huge bowl of steamed semolina piled with vegetables, mutton, chicken or fish.

Restaurant **starters** include *salade marocaine*, a finely chopped salad of tomato and cucumber, or soup, most often the spicy, bean-based *harira*, followed by couscous, *tajine*, kebab (*brochettes*), or something like a Western meat-and-two-veg main course. **Dessert** will probably be fruit, yoghurt or a pastry. Restaurants at all levels may offer a **set menu**, often a bargain at 60–100dh in even quite fancy places.

Vegetarians may have problems as the idea is not really understood, and meat stock may be added even to vegetable dishes. If you're fussy about such things, you will probably have to avoid main courses, and all soups bar the filling bean-and-olive-oil *baisara*.

If **invited** to a home, you'll probably find yourself using your hands rather than a knife and fork. Copy the locals and eat only with your right hand.

Drink

The national drink is **thé à la menthe** – green tea with a large bunch of mint and a massive amount of sugar. If you want them to hold back on the sugar, ask for it with *shweeya sukar* (a little) or *blé sukar* (none). Coffee (*café* or *qahwa* in Arabic) is best in French-style cafés. Many cafés and street stalls sell fresh-squeezed orange juice and, though water is generally safe to drink, **mineral water** is readily available.

As an Islamic nation, Morocco gives **alcohol** a low profile, and it's generally impossible to buy any in the Medinas. Moroccan **wines**, usually red, can be very good, while the best **beer** is Flag Speciale. **Bars** are totally male domains, except in tourist hotels – but even then they can be a bit rowdy.

Opening hours and holidays

Shops and stalls in the *souk* areas open roughly 9am–1pm & 3–6pm. Ville Nouvelle shops are also likely to close for lunch, and also once a week, usually Sunday.

Islamic **religious holidays** are calculated on the lunar calendar and change each year. In 2003 they fall as follows: Feb 11 (provisional), **Aïd el Kebir** (when Abraham offered to sacrifice his son for God); March 4, Muslim New Year; May 13, **Mouloud** (the birthday of Muhammad); roughly Oct 25 to Nov 23 **Ramadan** (when all Muslims fast from sunrise to sunset). Non-Muslims are not expected to observe Ramadan, but should be sensitive about not breaking the fast in public. The end of Ramadan is celebrated with **Aïd es Seghir** (aka Aïd el Fitr), a two-day holiday.

Secular holidays are considered less important, with most public services (except banks and offices) operating normally even during the two biggest ones – the Feast of the Throne (July 30), and Independence Day (Nov 18).

Emergencies

Street **robbery** is rare but not unknown, especially in Casablanca. **Hotels** are generally secure for depositing money; campsites considerably less so.

There are two main types of **police**. The grey-clad gendarmes with authority outside city limits, and the navy-clad sûreté in towns. There's sometimes a brigade of "tourist police" too.

Moroccan **pharmacists** are well trained and dispense a wide range of drugs. In most cities there is a night pharmacy, often at the town hall, and a rota of *pharmacies de garde* which stay open till late and at weekends. You can get a list of English-speaking **doctors** in major cities from consulates.

Steer clear of **hashish** and *kif* (marijuana) – it's illegal and buying it leaves you vulnerable to scams, and potentially large fines and prison sentences, though the police normally expect to be paid off.

Emergency Numbers

Police (Sûreté) ☎19
Gendarmes ☎177
Fire and Ambulance ☎15

Tangier

For the first half of the twentieth century **TANGIER** (*Tanja* in Arabic; *Tanger* in French) was an "International City" with its own laws and administration, plus an eclectic community of expats and refugees. With independence in 1956, this special status was removed and the expat colony dwindled. Today Tangier is a major port, halfway to becoming a mainstream tourist resort, but with hints of its decadent past.

Arrival and accommodation

Ferries dock at the terminal immediately below the Medina. The **CTM bus terminal** is at the port entrance, but the *gare routière* **bus station** used by private bus

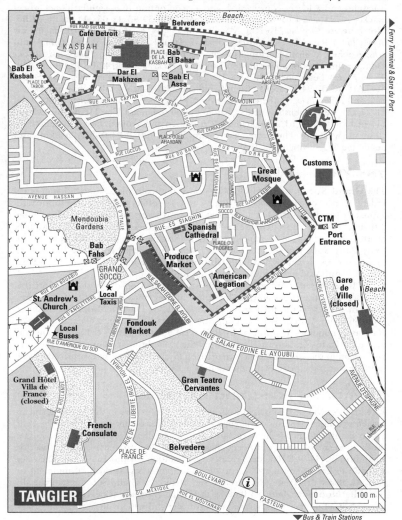

▼ Bus & Train Stations

companies and *grands taxis* is 1.5km inland on Av Youssef Ben Tachfine. All trains terminate at Tanger Morora (or Moghogha) station, 4km out on the Tetouan road (bus #13 from the port). Tangier's **airport** is 15km out of town, served by *grands taxis* to the *gare routière*. The **tourist office** is at 29 Bd Pasteur (Mon–Thurs 8.30am–noon & 2.30–6.30pm, Fri 8.30–11.30am & 3–6.30pm; July & Aug open lunch and weekends; ℡039 94 80 50), just down from Place de France.

There are dozens of **hotels** and **pensions**, but the city does get crowded in summer, when some places double their prices. In the **Medina**, *Mauretania*, 2 Rue des Almohades, aka Rue des Chrétiens (℡039 93 46 77; **❶**), has shared cold showers and toilets, but is clean. *Olid*, 12 Rue Mokhtar Ahardane, aka Rue des Postes (℡039 93 13 10; **❶**), has seen better days, but is good value for money, while *Palace*, 2 Rue Mokhtar Ahardane (℡039 93 61 28; **❶**), is more attractive with hot running water, balconies and a lovely courtyard. A good-value option in a slightly higher price bracket is *Mamora*, 19 Rue Mokhtar Ahardane (℡039 93 41 05; **❷**). In the **Ville Nouvelle** are *Magellan*, 16 Rue Magellan (℡039 37 23 19; **❶**), and *El Muniria* or *Tanger Inn*, 1 Rue Magellan (℡039 93 53 37; **❶**), the latter now a quiet, family-run *pension*, where William Burroughs wrote his most famous book, *The Naked Lunch*. On the main street opposite the tourist office is *Hôtel de Paris*, 42 Bd Pasteur (℡039 93 18 77; **❷**), best value in the area. Top choice on the seafront are *Miramar*, 168 Av des FAR (℡039 94 17 15; **❷**), friendly, old and a little shabby with a bar and restaurant; and *Marco Polo*, on the corner of Av d'Espagne and Rue El Antaki (℡039 94 11 24; **❷**), well established, with a bar and good restaurant. The **HI hostel**, 8 Rue El Antaki (℡039 94 61 27; **❶**; closed 10am–noon and 3–6pm), near the seafront, is clean and well run. The nearest **campsite**, *Tingis* (℡039 94 01 91), is 6km east, beside the Oued Moghogha lagoon.

The City

The **Grand Socco**, or Zoco Grande – once the main market square (and, since Independence, officially Place du 9 avril 1947) – offers the most straightforward approach to the **Medina**. The arch at the northwest corner opens onto Rue d'Italie, which becomes Rue de la Kasbah, the northern entrance to the Kasbah quarter. To the right, an opening onto Rue es Siaghin leads to the atmospheric but seedy **Petit Socco**, or Zoco Chico, the Medina's principal landmark. From here, though not easy to follow, **Rue des Almohades** (aka Rue des Chrétiens) and **Rue Ben Raisouli** lead to the lower gate of the Kasbah.

The **Kasbah** (citadel), walled off from the Medina on the highest rise of the coast, has been the palace and administrative quarter since Roman times. The main point of interest is the former Sultanate Palace, or **Dar el Makhzen** (Mon & Wed–Sun 9am–1pm & 3–6pm; 10dh), now converted into an excellent museum of crafts and antiquities. If you leave by Rue Riad Sultan and Bab el Kasbah, you pass under the **Café-Restaurant Detroit** (up the stairs through a doorway in the tunnel), set up in the 1960s by Beat writer Brion Gysin, and now an overpriced tourist spot but worth the price of a mint tea for the views.

Eating, drinking and nightlife

As with most Moroccan cities, the cheapest places to **eat** are in the **Medina**, and an authentic Tangier experience is people-watching over a mint tea at one of the Petit Socco **cafés**. Of the Medina's **restaurants**, the small and simple *Andaluz*, 7 Rue du Commerce, off the Petit Socco, has excellent, low-priced swordfish steak or fried shrimps. *Ahlen*, 8 Rue des Postes, serves traditional Moroccan dishes. The cafés around the Grand Socco are worth a look too; most stay open until midnight or later. Alcoholic drinks are not served in the Medina or Grand Socco restaurants. In the **Ville Nouvelle**, *Africa*, 83 Rue Salah Eddine el Ayoubi (aka Rue de la Plage), has a 50dh set menu and is licensed to serve beer and wine with meals, while *Hassi*

Baida next door offers a traditional Moroccan menu (without alcohol). *Agadir*, 21 Rue Prince Héretier Sidi Mohammed, uphill from Place de France, is small and friendly, serving French and Moroccan dishes, and *San Remo*, 15 Rue Ahmed Chaouki, specializes in Italian dishes and runs a takeaway pizzeria opposite. For Spanish seafood, including vast portions of fine paella, try the pricier *Romero*, 12 Rue Prince Moulay Abdallah, around the corner from the tourist office. On the **seafront**, many hotels have reliable European restaurants, including *Marco Polo* whose generous servings come at a fair price. As an alternative, try *L'Marsa*, 92 Av d'Espagne, with a roof terrace and offering excellent pasta and pizzas, with home-made ice cream too. Finally, back in town, the long-established *Rubis Grill*, at 3 Rue Ibn Rochd, off Rue Prince Moulay Abdallah, serves European dishes; the candlelit hacienda decor is a bit over the top but the food and service are exemplary.

For **drinking**, the *Tanger Inn*, the bar of the *Hôtel el Muniria* at 1 Rue Magellan (daily 9pm–1am), has been an institution since the days of the International Zone, decorated with photos of the Beat Generation authors who stayed at the hotel, but quiet midweek off-season. *Hôtel Miramar* on Av des FAR is a hard-drinking seafront spot. *Scott's* on Rue El Moutanabi, traditionally a gay disco, is worth a look for its decor, although nothing much happens here before midnight; take care leaving late at night – the best idea is to tip the doorman 5dh to order you a taxi. *Morocco Palace*, Av du Prince Moulay Abdallah, is a strange, sometimes slightly manic place with traditional Moroccan music and a belly-dancing floorshow.

Listings

American Express Voyages Schwartz, 54 Bd Pasteur ☏039 33 03 72.

Consulates UK, 41 Bd Mohammed V ☏039 94 15 57.

Exchange BMCE on Bd Pasteur is the most efficient with a bureau de change and ATM.

Internet Best place is Cybercafé Adam, 4 Rue Ibn Rochd (off Bd Pasteur); others include Euronet, 5 Rue Ahmed Chaouki (off Bd Pasteur).

Pharmacies There are several English-speaking pharmacies on Place de France and Bd Pasteur.

Post office Main PTT, 33 Bd Mohammed V.

Police Rue Ibn Toumert near the Prefecture; also 22 Rue Mountanabi.

Ceuta and Tetouan

A Spanish enclave which dates back to the sixteenth century, the port of **CEUTA** (*Sebta* in Arabic) is politically and culturally part of Spain. As the crossing here from Algeciras is quicker than to Tangier, this drab outpost has become a popular point of entry. Try to arrive early in the day so that you have plenty of time to move on. The Moroccan border is 3km south of town at **FNIDEQ**, reached by local bus from the seafront. Once across, the easiest transport is a shared *grand taxi* to Tetouan; buses are infrequent, though a couple of dirhams cheaper. There are cash-only exchange places at the frontier. If you get stuck here, *Pensión Charito*, c/Arrabal 5 (☏956 513 982; ❶), is cheap, as are others nearby. The **tourist office** at Muelle Cañonero Dato by the ferry dock (daily 9am–8pm; ☏956 506 275), or opposite the town hall (*ayuntamiento*) in Plaza de Africa (Mon–Fri 9am–8pm, Sat 9am–12.30pm; ☏956 501 410, ✆www.turiceuta.com), keeps a list of hotels.

Coming from Ceuta, you usually need to pick up onward transport at **TETOUAN**, a town with a walled Medina and a reputation for having the worst hustlers in Morocco, but a *grand taxi* from Fnideq will leave you close enough to the bus station to head straight out. There are regular **buses** to Meknes, Fes and destinations nationwide. For Tangier, Chefchaouen or Ceuta it's easiest to travel by **grand taxi**; those for Fnideq (Ceuta) leave from Boulevard de Mouquaouama, a stone's throw from the bus station, but those for Tangier and Chefchaouen leave from a stand some 2km west, up Boulevard de Mouquaouama to Place Moulay el

Mehdi, then west along Av Mohammed V to the end and ask someone. The ONCF office on Av 10 Mai, alongside Place Al Adala, sells **train** tickets that include a shuttle bus to the station at Tnine Sidi Lyamani. If you're stuck in Tetouan, cheap hotels near the bus station include the friendly *Principe*, 20 Av Youssef Ibn Tachfine (no phone; ❶), on the corner of Boulevard de Mouquaouama midway between the bus station and Place Moulay el Mehdi. Tetouan has a **tourist office**, a few metres east of Place Moulay el Mehdi at 30 Bd Mohammed V (Mon–Thurs 8.30am–noon & 2.30–6.30pm, Fri 8.30–11.30am & 3–6.30pm; ☎039 96 19 16).

Chefchaouen

Shut in by a fold of the Rif mountains, **CHEFCHAOUEN** (sometimes abbreviated to Chaouen or Xaouen) had, until the arrival of Spanish troops in 1920, been visited by just three Europeans. It's a town of extraordinary light and colour, its whitewash tinted with blue and edged by golden stone walls. *Pensions* are friendly and cheap and a few days here is one of the best introductions to Morocco.

Buses and **grands taxis** drop you outside the town walls; to reach the Medina, walk across the old marketplace to the tiny arched entrance, **Bab el Ain**. Through the gate a dominant but narrow lane winds up to the main square, the elongated **Place Outa el Hammam**. This is where most of the town's evening life takes place, while by day the town's focus is the **Kasbah**, a quiet ruin with shady gardens which occupies one side of the square. Beyond, the smaller **Place El Makhzen** is an elegant clearing with an old fountain and tourist pottery stalls.

Along and just off the main route through the Medina is a series of small **hotels**, the quietest of which is *Abie Khancha*, 75 Rue Lala el Hora (☎039 98 68 79; ❶), a converted house with an open courtyard and high terrace. Outside the Medina, nearer to transport, is the immaculate *Madrid*, Av Hassan II (☎039 98 74 96 or 97; ❷), and nearby is the cheap, good *Sevilla*, Av Allal Ben Abdallah (☎039 98 72 85; ❷). The **campsite** (☎039 98 69 79), up on the hill above town, by the modern *Hôtel Asma*, is inexpensive and can be crowded in summer. A very inexpensive but inconveniently located **HI hostel** adjoins the campsite (call via the campsite; ❶). A few of the **cafés** in the Place Outa el Hammam serve regular Moroccan meals; one of the best is the *Ali Baba*. Slightly pricier is *Tissemlal* (aka *Casa Hassan*), 22 Rue Targui, just up from Place Outa el Hammam, which serves delicious food in elegant surroundings. Outside the Medina, on Rue Moulay Ali Ben Rachid, are *Moulay Ali Ben Rachid* and *El Jasira*, popular with local residents.

Buses to Fes and Meknes are quite often full, so buy tickets a day in advance. Buses head to Tetouan at least eight times a day, or you can share a *grand taxi*. There are also buses to the Ceuta border.

Meknes and around

More than any other Moroccan town, **MEKNES** is associated with a single figure, the Sultan Moulay Ismail, in whose reign (1672–1727) the city went from provincial centre to spectacular capital with over fifty palaces and fifteen miles of exterior walls. A prosperous city today, its monuments reward a day's exploration.

Place El Hedim (the Square of Demolition and Renewal) originally formed the western corner of the Medina, but Moulay Ismail had the houses here demolished to provide a grand approach to his palace quarter. The **Dar Jamai** (daily except Tues, 9am–noon & 3–6pm; 10dh), at the back of the square, is one of the best examples of a nineteenth-century Moroccan palace, and the museum inside is one of the best in Morocco, with a fantastic display of Middle Atlas carpets.

The lane immediately to the left of the Dar Jamai takes you to the Medina's major market street: on your left is **Souk en Nejjarin**, the carpet souk; on your right, leading to the Great Mosque and Bou Inania Medersa, are the fancier goods offered in the **Souk es Sebbat**. The **Bou Inania Medersa** (daily 9am–noon & 3–6pm; 10dh), constructed around 1340–50, has an unusual ribbed dome over the entrance hall and from the roof you can look out to the tiled pyramids of the Great Mosque.

From Place el Hedim, the magnificent **Bab Mansour** leads into Place Lalla Aouda. Straight ahead bearing left, you come into another open square, on the right of which is the green-tiled dome of the **Koubba el Khayatine**, once a reception hall for ambassadors to the imperial court (daily 9am–noon & 3–6pm; 10dh). Below it, a stairway descends into a vast series of subterranean vaults, known as the **Prison of Christian Slaves**, though it was probably a storehouse or grana-ry. Ahead of the Koubba, within the wall and at right angles to it, are two modest gates. The one on the left opens onto a corridor of walls and, a few metres down, the entrance to **Moulay Ismail's Mausoleum** (daily 9am–noon & 3–6pm, closed Fri am; 10dh donation expected), where you can approach the sanctuary.

Past the mausoleum, a long-walled corridor leads to the **Heri as-Souani**, a series of storerooms and granaries once filled with provisions for siege or drought. From the roof garden café, you can gaze out across much of the Dar el Makhzen (Royal Palace) and the wonderfully still **Agdal Basin**, built as an irrigation reservoir and pleasure lake.

Practicalities

Meknes has two **train stations**, both in the Ville Nouvelle. All trains stop at both stations, but **Gare Amir Abdelkader** is more central than **Gare de Ville**. Private **buses** and most **grands taxis** arrive west of the Medina by Bab el Khemis; **CTM buses** arrive at their terminal on Av de Fès, near the Gare de Ville, and some *grands taxis* from Fes also drop you there. For bus connections from Meknes, and other matters, check at the helpful **tourist office**, 27 Place Administrative (Mon–Thurs 8.30am–noon & 2.30–6.30pm, Fri 8.30–11.30am & 3–6.30pm; ☎055 52 44 26).

Pick of the **Medina** hotels is *Maroc*, 7 Rue Rouamzine (☎055 53 00 75; ❶). The best budget choice in the **Ville Nouvelle** is friendly *Bordeaux*, 64 Av de la Gare (☎055 52 25 63; ❶), with a shaded garden, near the Gare de Ville and CTM bus station. *Touring*, 34 Av Allal Ben Abdallah (☎055 52 23 51; ❶), is the best of the one-star places, followed by *Majestic*, 19 Av Mohammed V (☎055 52 20 35; ❷), handy for the Gare El Amir Abdelkader. The **HI hostel**, Av Okba Ben Nafi (☎055 52 46 98; ❶), is an easy 1.5km walk northwest of the city centre. Arguably the best **campsite** in Morocco is *Aguedal* (☎055 55 53 96), south of the Imperial City, a twenty-minute walk from Place El Hedim, opposite the Heri as-Souani.

For straight Moroccan **food** the *Economique*, 123 Rue Dar Smen, opposite Bab Mansour, is a top Medina café/restaurant. Budget eats in the Ville Nouvelle include excellent, cheap fried fish at *Casse-Croute Driss*, 34 Rue Emir Abdelkader, and the *Lorraine* next door, which specializes in roast rabbit. Not so cheap but still reason-able are *Pizzeria Le Four* (pasta and pizzas) on Rue Atlas, near the *Hôtel Majestic*, and *La Coupole*, on the corner of Av Hassan II and Rue Ghana, serving Moroccan and European food (with a bar and nightclub). *Collier de la Colombe*, 67 Rue Driba, in an ornate mansion on the edge of the Medina. offers outstanding international cuisine and moderate prices. For a not too expensive splurge, the lovely *Riad*, in a section of original palace at 79 Ksar Chaacha in the Medina, serves well-prepared Moroccan dishes in beautifully restored rooms or outdoors beside a sunken garden. In the Ville Nouvelle, *Diafa* has great home cooking in what looks like a private house at 12 Rue Badr el Kobra (off Av Hassan II at its western end). There are plenty of **bars**, several in Ville Nouvelle hotels, including the swing-doors-and-saw-dust *Club de Nuit*, part of *Hôtel Excelsior* on Av des FAR.

Volubilis

Visible for miles, **VOLUBILIS** occupies the ledge of a long, high plateau and was the Roman Empire's most remote city. Direct Roman rule lasted little more than two centuries – the garrison withdrew in 285 AD to ease pressure elsewhere – but the city remained active well into the eighteenth century, when its marble was carried away for the building of Meknes. What you see today, well-excavated and maintained, are largely the ruins of second- and third-century AD buildings. The **entrance** (daily 9am–noon & 2.30–6pm; 20dh) is through a minor gate set into the city wall, built in 168 AD following a series of Berber insurrections. Just inside are the ticket office, a café/bar and a small **museum** of sculpture. The best of the finds made here –including a superb collection of bronzes – are in the Rabat museum. Volubilis has, however, retained the great majority of its **mosaics**, some thirty or so in a good state of preservation. **Getting there** from Meknes is easy enough – take a collective grand taxi for Moulay Idris and ask to be set down en route. The problem is getting back: if you're not prepared to hitch, you'll have to wait for a passing bus from Ouezzane, which could easily be a couple of hours. Alternatively, charter a *grand taxi* from Meknes – about 300dh for the round trip including waiting time.

Fes

The most ancient of the imperial capitals, **FES** stimulates the senses and seems to exist somewhere between the Middle Ages and the modern world. Some 200,000 of the city's half-million inhabitants live in the oldest part of the Medina, **Fes el Bali**, with a culture and atmosphere quite different from anywhere in mainland Europe.

Arrival, information and accommodation

The **train station** is in the Ville Nouvelle, fifteen minutes' walk from the hotels around Place Mohammed V. If you prefer to stay in the Medina, take a *petit taxi*, or walk down to Place de la Résistance (aka La Fiat) and pick up bus #9 to Dar Batha/Place de l'Istiqlal, near the western gate to Fes el Bali, Bab Boujeloud. The *gare routière* **bus station** is just outside the walls near Bab Boujeloud. The new terminal for CTM buses is off Rue Atlas, which links the far end of Av Mohammed V with Place d'Atlas. **Grands taxis** mostly operate from the *gare routière*; exceptions include those serving Meknes (from the train station). The **tourist office** is on Place de la Résistance (Mon–Fri 8.30am–noon & 2.30–6.30pm; ☎055 62 34 60), where you can find out about June's seven-day **Festival of World Sacred Music**; more details from the secretariat (☎055 74 05 35, ⓦwww.fezfestival.org).

There's a shortage of **hotel** space in all categories, so be prepared for higher-than-usual prices; booking ahead is advisable. For atmosphere and character, the **Medina** is the place to be, though you'll need an easy-going attitude towards size and cleanliness. The less engaging **Ville Nouvelle** has a wider choice of hotels.

Hostel
HI Hostel 18 Rue Abdeslam Seghrini ☎055 62 40 85. One of Morocco's best hostels – well-kept, friendly and spotlessly clean. ➋

Hotels in the Medina
Cascade Just inside Bab Boujeloud, Fes el Bali ☎055 63 84 42. An old building, with a useful public *hammam* (bath house) behind. Small rooms, but clean and friendly. ➋

Du Commerce Place des Alaouites, Fes el Djedid, facing the doors of the royal palace ☎055 62 22 31. Still owned by a Jewish family in what was the Jewish quarter; old, but comfortable and friendly, with a lively café at street level. ➋

Lamrani Talâa Seghira, Fes el Bali ☎055 63 44 11. Friendly with small but spotless rooms, mostly doubles, opposite a *hammam*. ➊

Pension Talaa 14 Talâa Seghira, Fes el Bali ☎055 63 33 59. A small place and slightly pricier than

FES EL BALI

▲ *Ouezzane & Chaouen* · *Taza & Oujda* ▲

Bab Ftouh

Bab Sidi Bujida

Andalusian Mosque

Medersa Es Sahrija

RUE KAID KHAMMAR

Oued Fes

ROUTE DU TOUR DE FES

Medersa El Oued

RUE SIDI YOUSSEF

Tanneries

Kairaouine Mosque

Seffarine Medersa

Local Buses & Petits Taxis

Medersa Misbahiya

Medersa Ech Cherratin

Mosque Er Rsif

Bab Jamaï

Mosque Bab Guissa

Bab El Guissa

Fondouk Guissa

Attarin Medersa

RUE SOUK EL ATTARIN

Zaouia Moulay Idriss II

Nejjarin Fondouk

Merenid Tombs

Cherabliyin Mosque

Fondouk

FES EL BALI

RUE CHERABLIYIN

RUE SIDI EL KHIYAT

Hammam

Fountain

▶ *Ville Nouvelle*

Borj Nord (Arms Museum)

Medersa Bou Inania

Clock

PLACE DE L'ISTIQLAL

AVE DE LA LIBERTÉ

ROUTE DU TOUR DE FES

AVENUE DES MEERNIDS

Bus Station & Grands Taxis

KASBAH EN NOUAR

Bab Boujeloud

Dar Batha

Lycée

Bab Mahrouk

PLACE BAGHDADI

Jardins de Boujeloud

ROUTE DU TOUR DE FES

ROUTE DES FRANÇAIS

0 · 300 m

18 **MOROCCO** | Fes

723

the other Medina cheapies, but also newer, cleaner and more comfortable. ❶

Hotels in the Ville Nouvelle
Amor 31 Rue Arabie Saoudite, formerly Rue du Pakistan ☎055 62 27 24. One block from Av Hassan II, behind the Bank al-Maghrib. Attractive tiled frontage, bar, restaurant and reasonable rooms. ❷
Grand Bd Abdallah Chefchaounei ☎055 93 20 26, ✉grandhotel@fesnet.net.ma. Old colonial hotel opposite the sunken park on Place Mohammed V. Refurbished, en-suite rooms, some very large. ❸
Mounia 60 Rue Asilah ☎055 65 07 71. Modern hotel with friendly management, plus restaurant and a popular bar (which can be noisy). ❸
Nouzha 7 Av Hassan Dkhissi ☎055 64 00 02 or 12. Splendidly decorated hotel in an out-of-centre district but only 20min walk from the centre.

Convenient for the CTM bus terminal. ❷
De la Paix 44 Av Hassan II ☎055 62 50 72, ✉hoteldelapaix@iam.net.ma. Tour-group hotel, recently refurbished, with a good seafood restaurant and a bar. ❸
Rex 32 Place Atlas ☎055 64 21 33. Built in 1910, this small, congenial hotel has been given a new lease of life by the nearby CTM terminal. ❶
Royal 36 Rue es Soudan ☎055 62 46 56. Handy for the train station. All rooms have a shower (some have toilets too), but they vary in quality; look before you book. ❶

Campsite
Camping International Route de Sefrou ☎055 61 80 61. Some 4km south of town, this site is pricey but has great facilities, including a pool in summer. Take bus #38 from Place de l'Atlas.

The City

The Medina is actually two cities: the newer section, **Fes el Djedid**, established in the thirteenth century, is mostly taken up by the Royal Palace. The older part, **Fes el Bali**, founded in the eighth century on the River Fes, was populated by refugees from Tunisia on one bank – the **Kairouine quarter** – and from Spain on the other bank – the **Andalusian quarter**. In practice, almost everything you will want to see is in the Kairouine quarter.

Getting lost is one of the great joys of the Medina, and a guide is not really necessary (you can always ask people for directions to Bab Boujeloud, Place Nejjarine or the Medersa el Attarin), but should you want to engage one, official guides wear a medallion to identify themselves, unofficial guides do not; both can be found at Bab Boujeloud. Never go shopping with either kind of guide however, as prices are liable to double. For a view over the whole city, take a hike up to the **Arms Museum** in the fort above the bus station (daily 8.30–11.30am; 10dh), from which the whole of Fes el Bali is laid out at your feet.

Talaa Kebira, the Medina's main artery, can be accessed by entering Bab Boujeloud, taking the first left and then turning right. About 100m down is the most brilliant of Fes's monuments, the **Medersa Bou Inania**, which comes close to perfection in every aspect of its construction, with beautiful carved wood, stucco and *zellij* tilework. Unfortunately it has been closed some years now for restoration, but will most definitely warrant a visit when it reopens.

Continuing down Talâa Kebira you reach the entrance to the **Souk el Attarin** (Souk of the Spice Vendors), the formal heart of the city. To the right, a street leads past the charming **Souk el Henna** – a tree-shaded square where traditional cosmetics are sold – to Place Nejjarin (Carpenters' Square). Here, next to the geometric tilework of the **Nejjarin Fountain**, is the imposing eighteenth-century **Nejjarin Fondouk**, now a woodwork museum (daily 10am–5.30pm, during Ramadan closes 4.30pm; 10dh), though the building is rather more interesting than its exhibits. Immediately to the right of the fountain, Talâa Seghira is an alternative route back to Bab Boujeloud, while the alley to the right of that is the aromatic **carpenters' souk**, ripe with the scent of sawn cedar, and top on the list of great Medina smells.

The street opposite the Nejjarin Fountain leads to the **Zaouia Moulay Idriss II**, one of the holiest buildings in the city. Buried here is the son and successor of Fes's founder, who continued his father's work. Only Muslims may enter to check out the *zellij* tilework, original wooden *minbar* (pulpit) and the tomb itself. Beyond it is the **Kissaria**, where fine fabrics are traded. Meanwhile, over to your left (on the other side of the Kissaria), Souk el Attarin comes to an end opposite the four-teenth-century **Attarin Medersa** (daily 9am–6pm; during Ramadan closes 4pm; 10dh), the finest of the city's medieval colleges after the Bou Inania.

To the right of the Medersa, a narrow street runs along the north side of the **Kairaouine Mosque**. Founded in 857 AD by a refugee from Kairouan in Tunisia, the Kairouine is one of the oldest universities in the world, and the fountainhead of Moroccan religious life. Its present dimensions, with sixteen aisles and room for 20,000 worshippers, are essentially the product of tenth- and twelfth-century reconstructions. Non-Muslims can look into the courtyard through the main door.

The street emerges in **Place Seffarine**, almost wilfully picturesque with its faience fountain, gnarled fig trees and metalworkers hammering away. On the west side of the square, the thirteenth-century **Seffarine Medersa** is still in use as a hostel for students at the Kairaouine (visitors may enter for a look at any reasonable hour without paying). If you're beginning to find the medieval prettiness of the central *souks* and *medersas* slightly unreal, then the area beyond the square should provide the antidote. The dyers' market – **Souk Sabbighin** – is directly south of the Seffarine Medersa, and is draped with fantastically coloured yarn and cloth dry-ing in the heat. Below, workers in grey toil over cauldrons of multicoloured dyes. Place er Rsif, nearby, has buses and taxis to the Ville Nouvelle.

The street to the left (north) of the Seffarine Medersa leads to the **tanneries**, constantly visited by tour groups with whom you could discreetly tag along if you get lost. Inside the tanneries (pay a tip to the *gardien*, usually 10dh, to enter), water deluges through holes that were once windows of houses, and hundreds of skins lie spread out on the rooftops, above vats of dye and the pigeon dung used to treat the leather, reminiscent of the pits of hell from Dante's *Inferno*. Straight on, the road eventually leads back round to the Attarin Medersa.

Eating and drinking

Cafés are plentiful in the Ville Nouvelle, with some of the most popular along Av Mohammed es Slaoui and Av Mohammed V. Fes el Bali has two main areas for **budget eating**: around Bab Boujeloud and along Rue Hormis (running from Souk el Attarin towards Bab Guissa), but for a cheap option, try the café/restau-rants near the municipal market in the Ville Nouvelle, on the left-hand side of Av Mohammed V as you walk from the post office.

For **bars**, you have to look a little harder. *Café Chope* on Av Mohammed V, south of Place Mohammed V, with its 1930s mock-classical interior, does good bar snacks, or try the hotel bars.

Bouanania Talâa Kebira, behind Bab Boujeloud. Rooftop or indoor eating, with *tajines* and other good food in large portions.

Chamonix 5 Rue Moukhtar Soussi, off Av Mohammed V. A reliable restaurant serving Moroccan and European dishes. Attracts a young crowd, and stays open late in summer.

La Cheminée 6 Av Lalla Asma (aka Rue Chenguit). Small and friendly licensed restaurant, moderate prices.

Chez Vittorio Pizzeria 21 Rue du Nador, opposite *Hôtel Central*. Pizza and pasta; reliable and good value, but not very exciting.

Fish Friture 138 Av Mohammed V, at the far end of a short passageway off the main street. Fish dishes are the mainstay (the paella's great), but there is much else on offer. Courteous and quick.

Des Jeunes (aka *Chez Hamid*), inside Bab Boujeloud. Cheap and basic – soups, kebabs, couscous and *pastilla* (poultry-filled pie – a Fes speciality).

Marrakesh 11 Rue Abes Tazi (between *Hôtel Mounia* and the old CTM terminal). Small, but good and inexpensive, with a limited menu of tasty food.

Zagora 5 Av Mohammed V in a small arcade, behind the Derby shoe shop. New and a little pretentious, but the food and service are well above average.

Listings

Exchange BMCE, Place Mohammed V, Place de l'Atlas and Place Florence (all with ATMs).

Internet Cyber Club, 70 Rue Bou Khessissat; Fes el Djedid, 2 Rue el Houria; and Place Mohammed V.

Pharmacies Night pharmacy in the *baladiya* (town hall) on Av Moulay Youssef (daily 9pm–8.30am). **Police** Commissariat Central is on Av Mohammed V behind the post office.

Post office Corner of avenues Mohammed V and Hassan II.

Rabat

Capital of the nation since 1912, **RABAT** is elegant, slightly self-conscious in its modern ways, and a little bit dull. However, its monuments punctuate the span of Moroccan history, and are among the country's most picturesque.

Arrival and accommodation

Rabat Ville **train station** is at the heart of the Ville Nouvelle, with most classified hotels situated only a few minutes' walk away (don't get off at the smaller Rabat Agdal train station, 2km from the centre). The main **bus terminal** is 5km west of the centre, served by local bus #30 and *petits taxis*. It's easier, if you're arriving by bus from the north, to get off in Salé across the river, and take a *grand taxi* from there into Rabat. **Grands taxis** for non-local destinations operate from outside the main bus station; those to Casa cost only a couple of dirhams more than the bus and leave more or less continuously. **Local bus services** radiate from the corner of Rue Nador and Bd Hassan II, where *petits taxis* and local *grands taxis* can be found.

Accommodation can fill up in midsummer and during festivals; it's best to phone ahead.

Hostel
HI Hostel 43 Rue Marrassa ☎037 72 57 69. Just outside the Medina walls north of Bd Hassan II. Closed 10am–noon. ❶

Hotels
Berlin 261 Av Mohammed V ☎037 72 34 35. Small hotel with hot showers. Centrally located above the Chinese restaurant *Hong Kong*. ❷
Central 2 Rue Al Basra ☎037 70 73 56. Central position near train station and alongside better-known *Hôtel Balima* on Av Mohammed V. A good budget choice and, with 34 rooms, likely to have space. ❶
Dorhmi 313 Av Mohammed V, Medina, just inside Bab Djedid ☎037 72 38 98. Above *Café Essalem* and Banque Populaire. Well furnished and maintained. ❶
Gaulois Corner of Rue Hims and Av Mohammed V ☎037 72 30 22. One of a cluster of budget hotels around the bottom end of Av Mohammed V. ❷
Majestic 121 Av Hassan II ☎037 72 29 97,

ℰ majestic@welcom.net.ma. Across the road from the Medina and still popular and good value after a complete make-over. ❷
D'Orsay 11 Av Moulay Youssef, on Place de la Gare ☎037 70 13 19. Convenient for train station and café/restaurants, this is a friendly, helpful and efficient hotel. ❷
Splendid 8 Rue Ghazza ☎037 72 32 83. Nice place whose best rooms overlook a courtyard. *Café-Restaurant Ghazza* opposite is good for breakfast and a snack any time. ❷
Terminus 384 Av Mohammed V ☎037 70 52 67. A good alternative to the *D'Orsay* round the corner. A large, featureless block, but the interior has been updated. ❸
Des Voyageurs 8 Souk Semarine, Medina, near Bab Djedid ☎037 72 37 20. Inexpensive, popular and often full. Clean, airy rooms but no showers. ❶

Campsites
Camping de la Plage (no phone). Across the river at Salé. Basic but well-managed.

The City

Rabat's compact **Medina** – the whole city until the French arrived in 1912 – is wedged on two sides by the sea and the river, on the others by the twelfth-century Almohad and fifteenth-century Andalusian walls. Laid out in a simple grid, its streets are very easy to navigate.

North lies the **Kasbah des Oudaïas**, a charming and evocative quarter whose principal gateway – **Bab el Kasbah** or Oudaïa Gate, built around 1195 – is one of the most ornate in the Moorish world. Its interior is now used for art exhibitions. Down the steps outside the gate, a lower, horseshoe arch leads directly to Moulay Ismail's palace, housing a **Museum of Moroccan Arts** (Mon & Wed–Sun 9.30am–noon & 3–5pm; 10dh), which features Berber and Arab jewellery and traditional costumes from most regions of Morocco. The adjoining **Andalusian Garden** – one of the most delightful spots in the city – was actually constructed by the French in the last century, though true to Arab Andalusian tradition, with deep, sunken beds of shrubs and flowering annuals.

The most ambitious of all Almohad buildings, the **Hassan Mosque** (daily 8.30am–6.30pm; free), with its vast minaret, dominates almost every view of the city. Designed by the Almohad ruler Yacoub el Mansour as the centrepiece of the new capital, the mosque seems to have been more or less abandoned at his death in 1199. The minaret, despite its apparent simplicity, is among the most complex of all Almohad structures: each facade is different, with a distinct combination of patterning, yet the whole intricacy of blind arcades and interlacing curves is based on just two formal designs. Facing the tower are the **Mosque and Mausoleum of Mohammed V**, begun on the sultan's death in 1961 and dedicated six years later. On the opposite side of the Ville Nouvelle from the mausoleum is the **Archeological Museum**, Rue Brihi (daily except Tue 9–11.30am & 2.30–6pm; 10dh), the most important in Morocco. Although small, it has an exceptional and beautiful collection of Roman-era bronzes, found mainly at Volubilis.

The most beautiful of Moroccan ruins, the royal burial ground called the **Chellah** (daily 8.30am–6pm; 10dh), is a startling sight as you emerge from the long avenues of the Ville Nouvelle, with its circuit of fourteenth-century walls, legacy of **Abou el Hassan** (1331–51), the greatest of Merenid rulers. Off to the left of the main gate are the partly excavated ruins of the Roman city that preceded the necropolis. A set of Islamic ruins are further down to the right, situated within a second inner sanctuary, approached along a broad path through half-wild gardens.

Eating and drinking

Rabat has a wide range of good **restaurants** serving both Moroccan and international dishes. As ever, the cheapest ones are to be found in the Medina. Just on the edge of the quarter, down Rue Mohammed V and along Rue Souika, there is a string of good everyday café/restaurants, with *Jeunesse*, 305 Av Mohammed V, and *Taghazoute,* round the corner at 7 Rue Sebbahi, among the better choices, the latter a good place for breakfast.

In the Ville Nouvelle, restaurants are grouped around the train station, Place de la Gare and Av Moulay Youssef. Try *Brasserie Française*, 3 Av Moulay Youssef, with an upstairs restaurant that is one of the best places to eat around the train station. *La Clef*, alongside *Hôtel d'Orsay* on Rue Hatim, serves good French and Moroccan dishes upstairs, and has a small bar downstairs. Worthwhile, but more expensive, choices include *Saïdoune*, in the mall at 467 Av Mohammed V, opposite *Hôtel Terminus*, a good Iraqi-run Lebanese restaurant. *Hong Kong*, 261 Av Mohammed V, does a tasty range of Chinese and Vietnamese dishes. *La Bamba* on Rue Tanta, behind *Hôtel Balima*, offers a choice of tourist, gastronomic and Moroccan set menus. For Italian specialities, go to *La Mamma* (with takeaway and home-delivery options), or the trendy *Equinox*, both also on Rue Tanta and with set and *à-la-carte* menus. Most of these serve beer and wine with meals.

Better suited for lunch is the alcohol-free *Café-Restaurant El Bahia*, set into the Andalusian wall on Bd Hassan II, with reasonably priced Moroccan dishes served in a pleasant courtyard, upstairs or on the street outside. If you're looking for a treat, try the more expensive *Restaurant de la Plage* on the beach below the Kasbah des Oudaïas (☏037 72 31 48), which specializes in fish.

Avenues Mohammed V and Allal Ben Abdallah have some good **cafés**, but **bars** are few and far between outside the main hotels. The one at the *Hôtel Balima* is as good a place as any. Late-night options include a string of disco-bars around Place de Melilla and on Rue Patrice Lumumba.

Listings

Embassies Australia represented by Canada; Canada, 13bis Rue Jaafar as Sadiq, Agdal ☏037 67 28 80; New Zealand represented by the UK; UK, 17 Bd Tour Hassan ☏037 72 09 05 or 06; USA, 2 Av de Marrakesh ☏037 76 22 65. Irish citizens covered by their embassy in Lisbon (see p.147), but may get help from the UK embassy.

Exchange Along Av Allal Ben Abdallah and Av Mohammed V. BMCE also has a *bureau de change* in Ville train station.
Internet Student Cyber, 83 Av Hassan II; Int Plus, second floor, 379 Av Mohammed V.
Police Av Tripoli, near the Cathedral. Police post at Bab Djedid.
Post office Halfway down Av Mohammed V.

Casablanca

Morocco's main city and economic capital, **CASABLANCA** is also North Africa's largest port, though its westernized image – with the almost total absence of women wearing head-coverings and its fancy beach clubs – masks what is still substantially a "first-generation" city with some of Morocco's most intense social problems. Film buffs will be disappointed to learn that Bogart's *Casablanca* wasn't shot here – the *Casablanca Café* commemorates it as a gimmick in the luxury *Hyatt Regency* hotel on Place des Nations-Unies, with T-shirts and baseball caps available.

The city's main monument, the **Grande Mosquée Hassan II** (tours daily except Fri 9am, 10am, 11am & 2pm; 100dh, students 50dh), opened in 1993, is the world's second largest mosque, with space for 100,000 worshippers, and a minaret that soars to a record 172m. Commissioned by the last king, who named it after himself, it cost an estimated £320m/US$500m, raised by not wholly voluntary public subscription. It's a twenty-minute walk northwest from the centre.

The French city centre and its formal colonial buildings already seem to belong to a different and distant age. Grouped around **Place Mohammed V**, and models for administrative architecture nationwide, they are built in a style called Mauresque, a French idealization of Moorish design, heavily influenced by Art Deco. The **Medina**, above the port and recently gentrified, is largely the product of the late nineteenth century, when Casa began its modest growth as a commercial centre.

Practicalities

Some trains stop only at the **Gare des Voyageurs** (2km southeast of the centre) rather than continuing to the far better-situated **Gare du Port**, between the town centre and the port. Bus #30 runs into town from the Voyageurs; otherwise, it's a twenty-minute walk or a *petit taxi* ride. The station for **CTM buses** is on Rue Léon l'Africain, behind *Hôtel Safir* on Av des FAR; other buses arrive at the *gare routière*, southeast of town on Route des Ouled Ziane. **Grands taxis** from Rabat arrive a block east of the CTM terminal, while those from points south come into a station south of town on the Route de Jadida in Beauséjour. The **tourist office** is inconveniently located south of the centre at 55 Rue Omar Slaoui (Mon–Fri 8.30am–noon & 2.30–6pm; ☏022 27 11 77); more convenient is the **Syndicat d'Initiative**, 98 Bd Mohammed V (Mon–Fri 8.30am–noon & 3–6.30pm, Sat 8.30am–noon & 3–5pm, Sun 9am–noon; ☏022 22 15 24).

Hotels are plentiful, though they run near capacity for much of the year. There are some unclassified hotels in the Medina, but the ones in the centre are better and no pricier: for example, *Mon Rêve*, 7 Rue Chaouia (☎022 31 14 39; ❶), is the best option in an area of cheap hotels, but often fills up, with *Colbert*, 38 Rue Chaouia (☎022 31 42 41; ❶), a good fall-back option. *Du Centre*, 1 Rue Sidi Belyout, corner of Av des FAR (☎022 44 61 80 or 81; ❷), is another golden oldie, with an antique lift and dicey wiring. *Terminus*, 184 Bd Ba Hamad (☎022 24 00 25; ❶), is handy for the Gare des Voyageurs, and for eating places nearby. *Foucauld*, 52 Rue Araibi Jilali (☎022 22 26 66; ❶), is great value, with en-suite rooms, and is near several good café/restaurants. Very central is *Plaza*, 18 Bd Houphouët Boigny (☎022 29 78 22; ❸), which has good facilities and front rooms offering views of the Grande Mosquée. The **HI hostel**, 6 Place Ahmed Bidaoui (☎022 22 05 51; ❶; closed 10am–noon), is a friendly, well-maintained place just inside the Medina and signposted from the nearby Gare du Port. The nearest **campsite**, *Oasis*, Av Jean Mermoz, Beauséjour (☎022 23 42 57), is 8km out on the P8 road to Azemmour and El Jadida (bus #31).

Casa has the reputation of being the best place to **eat** in Morocco, and if you can afford the fancier restaurant prices, this is certainly true. For those on a budget, some of the best possibilities lie in the smaller streets off Bd Mohammed V. *Rotisserie Centrale* is the best of the cheap grills on Rue Chaouia (aka Rue Colbert). Also very cheap is *Snack Bab Rkha* on Rue Bab Rkha, where it meets Rue Sidi Bou Smara and Bd Houphouët Boigny at the edge of the Medina. Of slightly pricier places offering reasonable set menus, *Le Buffet* at 99 Bd Mohammed V is good value and has cheap breakfasts too, and *L'Étoile Marocaine*, 107 Rue Allal Ben Abdallah, has an ambitious menu and a good atmosphere. Quite expensive by local standards is *Centre 2000*, by Casa Port station, with four good restaurants serving Spanish, French, Italian and Moroccan food. *Le Dauphin*, 115 Bd Houphouët Boigny, is a long-established and popular fish restaurant, worth queuing for, and the stylish *Petit Poucet*, 86 Bd Mohammed V, has a cheaper snack bar next door – one of the best places for some serious drinking.

Marrakesh

MARRAKESH (*Marrakech* in French) is a city of immense beauty, low, pink and tent-like before a great shaft of mountains. It's an immediately exciting place, especially around the vast space of its central square, the **Djemaa el Fna**, the stage for a long-established ritual in which shifting circles of onlookers gather around groups of acrobats, drummers, pipe musicians, dancers, storytellers and comedians. Unlike Fes, for so long its rival as the nation's capital but these days stagnating, Marrakesh's population is growing and it has a thriving industrial area; the city remains the most important market and administrative centre of southern Morocco.

Arrival, orientation and information

The **Djemaa el Fna** (referred to simply as "el Djemaa", or even "la Place") lies right at the heart of the Medina, and almost everything of interest is concentrated in the web of alleyways around it. Just to the west of the Djemaa, an unmistakable landmark is the minaret of the great **Koutoubia Mosque** (enchanting under floodlights at night), in the shadow of which begins **Avenue Mohammed V**, leading out of the Medina and up the length of the new city, **Gueliz**. It's a fairly long walk between Gueliz and the Medina, but there are plenty of taxis and the regular buses #1 and #16 between the two.

From the **train station**, alongside Gueliz, cross the street and take bus #3/#10 or a *petit taxi* (10–15dh) for Djemaa. The **bus terminal** is just outside the northwestern walls of the Medina by Bab Doukkala; from here it's a 20-minute walk to the Djemaa, or bus #6 (across the street from the main entrance), or a *petit taxi*

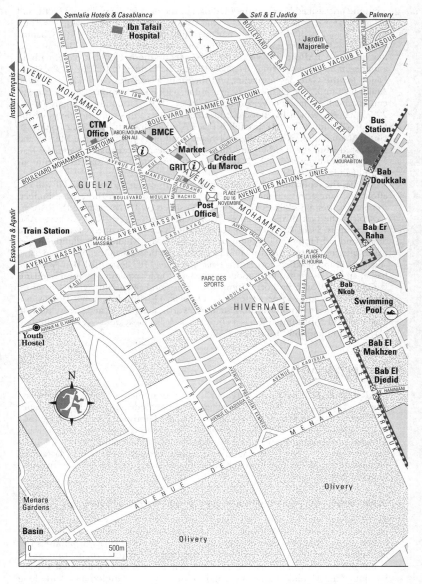

Ibn Tafail Hospital

Jardin Majorelle

BOULEVARD DE SAFI

AVENUE YACOUB EL MANSOUR

AVENUE MOHAMMED V

RUE IBN AICHA

BOULEVARD MOHAMMED ZERKTOUNI

BOULEVARD DE SAFI

AV. D'EL JADIDA

Bus Station

CTM Office

PLACE ABDELMOUMEN BEN ALI

BMCE

AVENUE DE FRANCE

BOULEVARD MOHAMMED ZERKTOUNI

AVENUE EL KATTABI

RUE DE LA LIBERTE

RUE SOURIYA

Market

Crédit du Maroc

PLACE MOURABITON

Bab Doukkala

i

RUE DE YOUGISLAVIE

RUE MAURITANIA

RUE EDDAHBI

GRIT *i*

MANSOUR EDDAHBI

G U E L I Z

AVENUE DES NATIONS-UNIES

AVENUE MOHAMMED V

Bab Er Raha

BOULEVARD MOULAY RACHID

RUE EL CADI AYAD

RUE EL BERAA

PLACE DU 16 NOVEMBRE

Post Office

PLACE DE LA LIBERTE, EL HOURIA

Train Station

PLACE EL MASSIRA

AVENUE HASSAN II

AVENUE HASSAN II

AVENUE YACOUB EL MARINI

Bab Nkob

RUE IBN KADI

AVENUE DU PRESIDENT KENNEDY

PARC DES SPORTS

AVENUE MOULAY EL HASSAN

Swimming Pool

H I V E R N A G E

AVENUE ECHOUHADA

BOULEVARD

Bab El Makhzen

AVENUE M. EL HANSALI

Youth Hostel

AVENUE DE FRANCE

AVENUE EL KADISSIA

Bab El Djedid

AV. HAMMAM

N

AVENUE EL KADISSIA

AVENUE DU PRESIDENT KENNEDY

AVENUE DE LA MENARA

YARMOUK

Menara Gardens

Basin

A V E N U E   D E   L A   M E N A R A

Olivery

Olivery

0 ——————— 500m

(8–10dh). CTM buses take you to their office in Gueliz. The **airport**, 5km south-west, is served by the erratic bus #11 (supposedly every half-hour to the Djemaa) – *petits* or *grands taxis* (40–50dh by day, 70–80dh at night) are a better option.

The tourist-friendly **GRIT** (*Groupement Régional d'Interêt Touristique*) is at 170 Av Mohammed V (July & Aug Mon–Fri 8.30am–3pm, Sat 8.30am–noon; rest of year

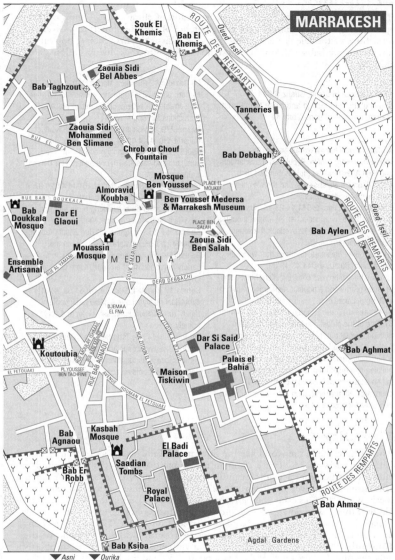

MARRAKESH

Souk El Khemis
Bab El Khemis
ROUTE DES REMPARTS
Oued Issil

Zaouia Sidi Bel Abbes
Bab Taghzout
RUE BAB TAGHZOUT
RUE ASSOUEL
RUE DE BAB KHEMIS
Tanneries

RUE EL GZA
Zaouia Sidi Mohammed Ben Slimane
Chrob ou Chouf Fountain
Bab Debbagh
PLACE EL MOUKEF

Mosque Ben Youssef
Almoravid Koubba
Ben Youssef Medersa & Marrakesh Museum
RUE BAB DOUKKALA

Bab Doukkala Mosque
Dar El Glaoui
PLACE BEN SALAH
Zaouia Sidi Ben Salah
Bab Aylen

Mouassin Mosque
M E D I N A
RUE AL YAMANI
SOUK SMARINE
ROUTE DES REMPARTS
Oued Issil

Ensemble Artisanal
DERB DEBBACHI

DJEMAA EL FNA

RUE RIAD ZITOUN EL KEDIM
RUE ZITOUN EL KEDIM
Dar Si Said Palace
Bab Aghmat

Koutoubia
RUE MOULAY ISMAIL
PL YOUSSEF BEN TACHFINE
EL FETOUAKI
AVENUE HOUMAN EL FETOUAKI
Palais el Bahia

Maison Tiskiwin

Bab Agnaou
Kasbah Mosque
El Badi Palace

Bab Er Robb
Saadian Tombs

Royal Palace
ROUTE DES REMPARTS
Bab Ahmar

Bab Ksiba
Agdal Gardens

▼Asni   ▼Ourika

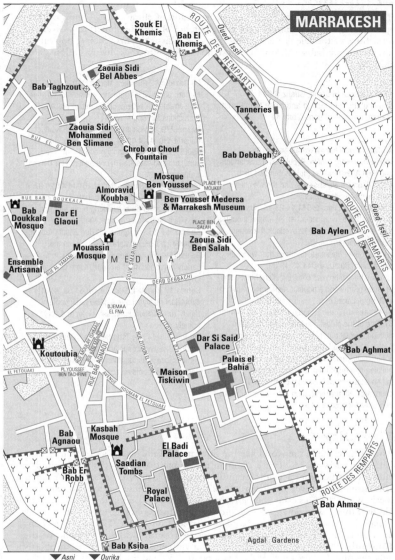

Mon–Fri 8.30am–noon & 2.30–6.30pm, Sat 8.30am–noon; ☏044 43 08 86).
There's not much at the **tourist office**, Place Abdelmoumen Ben Ali (July & Aug
Mon–Sat 8.30am–6.30pm; rest of year Mon–Sat 8.30/9–11.30am/noon &
2.30/3–6.30pm; during Ramadan Mon–Sat 9am–2.30pm; ☏044 43 61 79), or at
its branch office at Place Venus by the Koutoubia (same hours).

Accommodation

The **Medina**, as ever, has the main concentration of cheap places – most of them quite pleasant – and, unusually, has a fair number of classified hotels too. Given the attractions of the Djemaa el Fna and the *souks*, this is the first choice. Booking in advance is advisable. All our recommendations are in the Medina unless stated otherwise.

Hostels

HI Hostel Rue El Jahid, Geliz ☎044 44 77 13. Immaculate, refurbished and close to the train station, but closed 9am–2pm. **①**

Hotels

Ali Rue Moulay Ismail, ☎044 44 49 79, ✉hotelali@hotmail.com. Popular with overlanders and High Atlas trekkers (guides can be found here). Rooms have showers, and there's cheap dorm accommodation. **①**

CTM Djemaa el Fna, ☎044 44 23 25. Above the old bus station, with decent-sized rooms, though a little gloomy; rooms 28–32 overlook the square, as does the roof terrace. **①**

Farouk 66 Av Hassan II, on the corner with Rue Mauretania, Geliz, ☎044 43 19 89, ✉hotelfarouk@hotmail.com. Excellent hotel with en-suite rooms and a popular restaurant, within walking distance of the train station. **①**

De France 197 Rue Zitoun el Kedim ☎044 44 30 67. One of the oldest and best of the cheapies, nothing special but friendly with decent rooms. **①**

Gallia 30 Rue de la Recette, ☎044 44 59 13, ✉hotelgalliamarrakech@menara.net.ma. Pleasant building in a quiet road; airy and spotless rooms (all en suite and with air-con) off two tiled courtyards. Highly recommended – reserve by fax well ahead if possible. **③**

La Gazelle 12 Rue Bani Marine, ☎044 44 11 12. Modern place with bright airy rooms (not en suite), on a street with several cheap eating places. Reductions for long stays. **①**

Islane 279 Av Mohammed V, facing the Koutoubia minaret ☎044 44 00 81 or 83. Views of the Koutoubia and comfortable modern rooms (en suite, a/c and satellite TV) compensate for the traffic noise. **②**

Medina 1 Derb Sidi Bouloukat, ☎044 44 29 97. A real gem: low-priced, clean, friendly and good value, with an English-speaking proprietor and breakfast on the roof terrace. **①**

Sherazade 3 Derb Djama, off Rue Zitoun Kadem, ☎044 42 93 05, ✉sharazade@iam.net.ma. Beautifully restored merchant's house with a variety of rooms, most en suite, some with air-con. **②**

Souria 17 Rue de la Recette, ☎061 55 22 11, ✉hotelsouria@yahoo.fr. A deservedly popular family-run *pension*, spotlessly clean and very homely. **①**

Toulousain 44 Rue Tariq Ben Ziad, Geliz, ☎044 43 00 33, ⊛www.geocities.com/hotel_toulousain. Famous locally as the hotel used by the Peace Corps. Some rooms en suite. **①**

The City

There's nowhere in the world like the **Djemaa el Fna**: by day it's basically a market, with a few snake charmers and an occasional troupe of acrobats; in the late afternoon it becomes a whole carnival of musicians, storytellers and other entertainers; and in the evening dozens of stalls set up to dispense hot food to crowds of locals, while the musicians and performers continue. If you get tired of the spectacle, or if things slow down, you can move over to the rooftop terraces of the *Café de France* or the *Restaurant Argana* to gaze at it all from above. The absence of any architectural feature in the Djemaa serves to emphasize the drama of the **Koutoubia Minaret**. Nearly 70m high and visible for miles, it was begun shortly after the Almohad conquest of the city, around 1150, and displays many features that were to become widespread in Moroccan architecture – the wide band of ceramic inlay, the pyramid-shaped merlons, and the alternation of patterning on the facades.

The northern Medina

A lane opposite the *Café de France* on the Djemaa el Fna leads to a stuccowork arch that marks the beginning of the crowded **Souk Smarine**, an important thoroughfare traditionally dominated by textiles. Just before the red ochre arch at its end,

Souk Smarine narrows and you get a glimpse through the passageways to its right of the **Rahba Kedima**, a small and fairly ramshackle square whose most interesting features are its apothecary stalls. At the end of Rahba Kedima, a passageway to the left gives access to another, smaller square – a bustling, carpet-draped area known as la **Criée Berbère**, which is where slave auctions used to be held.

Cutting back to **Souk el Kebir**, which by now has taken over from the Smarine, you emerge at the **kissarias**, the covered markets at the heart of the *souks*. Kissarias traditionally sell more expensive products, which today means a predominance of Western designs and imports. Off to their right is **Souk des Bijoutiers**, a modest jewellers' lane, while at the north end is a convoluted web of alleys comprising the **Souk Cherratin**, essentially a leatherworkers' market.

If you bear left through this area and then turn right, you should arrive at the open space in front of the Ben Youssef Mosque. The originally fourteenth-century **Ben Youssef Medersa** (daily 9am–6pm; 20dh) – the annexe for students taking courses in the mosque – stands off a side street just to the east. It was almost completely rebuilt in the sixteenth century under the Saadians, with a strong Andalusian influence. Parts have exact parallels in the Alhambra Palace in Granada, and it seems likely that Muslim Spanish architects were employed in its construction. Next door, the **Marrakesh Museum** (daily 9am–6pm; 30dh) exhibits jewellery, art and sculpture, both old and new, in a beautifully restored nineteenth century palace. Almost facing it, just south of the Ben Youssef Mosque, the small **Almoravid Koubba** (daily 9am–6pm; 10dh) is easy to pass by, but it is the only building in the whole of Morocco from the eleventh century Almoravid dynasty still intact, and at the root of all Moroccan architecture. The motifs you've just seen in the *medersa* – the pine cones, palms and acanthus leaves – were all carved here first.

If you're keen to buy the best in the *souks*, you should study the more-or-less fixed prices of the range of crafts in the excellent **Ensemble Artesenal** (Mon–Sat 7.30am–7pm), just inside the ramparts on Av Mohammed V.

The southern Medina

South of Djemaa el Fna there are two places not to be missed: the Saadian Tombs and El Badi Palace, the ruined palace of Ahmed el Mansour. For the tombs, the simplest route from the Djemaa is to follow Rue Bab Agnaou outside the ramparts, then aim for the conspicuous minaret of the **Kasbah Mosque** – the minaret looks gaudy and modern but is in fact contemporary with the Koutoubia, and was restored to its original state in the 1960s. The narrow passageway to the tombs is well signposted from the right-hand corner of the mosque.

Sealed up by Moulay Ismail after he had destroyed the adjoining El Badi Palace, the sixteenth-century **Saadian Tombs** (daily 8.30–11.45am & 2.30–5.45pm; 10dh) lay half-ruined and half-forgotten for centuries but are now restored to their full glory. There are two main mausoleums in the enclosure. The finer is on the left as you come in, a beautiful group of three rooms built to house El Mansour's own tomb and completed within his lifetime. The tombs of over a hundred more Saadian princes and royal household members are scattered around the garden and courtyard, their gravestones likewise brilliantly tiled and often elaborately inscribed.

Though substantially in ruins, enough remains of Ahmed el Mansour's **El Badi Palace** (daily 8.30–11.45am & 2.30–5.45pm; 10dh) to suggest that its name – "The Incomparable" – was not entirely immodest. It took a later ruler, Moulay Ismail, over ten years of systematic work to strip the palace of everything movable or of value, and, even so, there's a lingering sense of luxury. What you see today is essentially the ceremonial part of the palace complex, planned for the reception of ambassadors. To the rear extends the central court, over 130m long and nearly as wide, and built on a substructure of vaults in order to allow the circulation of water through the pools and gardens. In the southwest corner of the complex is an ancient *minbar* (pulpit) from the Dwiria, or Koutoubia mosque; both mosque and *minbar* have been lovingly restored (admission is an extra 10dh).

Heading north from El Badi Palace, **Rue Zitoun el Djedid** leads back to the Djemaa, flanked by various nineteenth-century mansions. Many of these have been converted into carpet shops or tourist restaurants, but one of them has been kept as a museum, the **Palais El Bahia** (daily 8.30–11.45am & 2.30/3–5.45pm; 10dh; guided tour compulsory, with a tip of at least 10dh expected), former residence of a grand vizier. The palace is still used by the royal family (usually over the Western New Year) and there is no public admission at these times. The name of the building means "The Brilliance", but after the guided tour around the rambling palace courts and apartments you might feel this a somewhat tall claim. Also on this route is the **Dar Si Said** palace, which houses the **Museum of Moroccan Arts** (Mon, Wed, Thurs, Sat & Sun 9–11.45am & 2.30–5.45pm, Fri 9–11am & 3–5.45pm; 10dh). A further superb collection of Moroccan art and artefacts is housed in the **Maison Tiskiwin** (daily 10am–12.30pm & 3–5.30pm; 15dh), which lies between the El Bahia and Dar Si Said palaces at 8 Rue de la Bahia.

Eating and drinking

The most atmospheric place to eat is the Djemaa el Fna, where foodstalls set up around sunset and serve up everything from *harira* soup and couscous or tajine to stewed snails and sheep's heads, all eaten at trestle tables. For tea with a view, the terrace café of the *Hôtel CTM* overlooks the Djemaa el Fna, as do two relatively reasonable rooftop restaurants: *Argana* and *Hôtel Café de France*. As usual in Morocco, cheap restaurants tend to gather in the Medina, with posher places uptown in Gueliz, along with French-style cafés and virtually all the city's bars.

Hotel Ali Rue Moulay Ismail. The eat-all-you-like rooftop buffet here, served 7–11pm, is justifiably popular and great value at 60dh. There are also popular and great value lunchtime menus.

Chez Jack'line 63 Av Mohammed V, Gueliz. Italian, French and Moroccan dishes at moderate prices, with an 80dh set menu.

Hotel Farouk 66 Av Hassan II, Gueliz. The restaurant here offers an excellent-value set menu with soup, salad, couscous, tajine or brochettes,

followed by fruit, ice-cream or home-made yoghurt, for 50dh.

Café Snack Le Sindibad 216 Av Mohammed V, near the post office, Gueliz. Couscous, tajine or brochettes at 25–35dh a plate. Open 24hr.

Chez Bahia Riad Zitoun Kadim, 50m from Djemaa el Fna. Café/diner offering *pastilla*, tajine, breakfast and snacks at low prices.

El Bahja 66 Av Hassan II, Gueliz. The best of several decent choices in a street of cheap eateries.

Listings

Doctor Dr Abdelmajid Ben Tbib, 171 Av Mohammed V (☎044 43 10 30).

Exchange BMCE has branches with adjoining bureaux de change and ATMs in the Medina (Rue Moulay Ismail, facing Place de Foucauld) and Gueliz (114 Av Mohammed V).

Internet Super Cyber de la Place in an arcade off Rue Bani Marine by the *Hôtel Ichbilia*.

Pharmacies Place Djemaa el Fna at the top of Rue Bab Agnaou; Pharmacie de la Liberté, just off Place de la Liberté (or Houria).

Post office Place du 16 Novembre, midway along Av Mohammed V.

Essaouira

ESSAOUIRA, the nearest beach resort to Marrakesh, is a lovely eighteenth-century walled seaside town, with a vast expanse of largely empty beach. A favourite with the likes of Frank Zappa and Jimi Hendrix back in the 1960s, its tradition of hippie tourism has created a much more laid-back relationship between local residents and foreign visitors than you'll find in the rest of Morocco, and made Essaouira a centre for arts and crafts in addition to being the country's top surfing and windsurfing spot.

There are few formal "sights", but Essaouira is a great place just to walk around and the **ramparts** are the obvious place to start. Heading north along the lane at the end of Place Prince Moulay el Hassan, you can access the **Skala de la Ville**, the great sea bastion which runs along the northern cliffs. Along the top of it are a collection of European cannons, presented to Sultan Sidi Mohammed Ben Abdallah by ambitious nineteenth-century merchants, and at its end is the circular **North Bastion**, with panoramic views (closes at sunset). Along the Rue de Skala, built into the ramparts, are the **wood-carving workshops**, where artisans use thuja, a distinctive local hardwood. Marquetry and other woodwork, past and present, is displayed at the **Musée Sidi Mohammed Ben Abdallah** (daily except Tues 8.30am–7pm; Wed closed 12.30–2.30pm; 10dh), on Rue Derb Laâlouj, the road running down from the ramparts to Av de l'Istiqlal, along with carpets, costumes, jewellery and musical instruments, plus some interesting old photographs of Essaouira. The town's other **souks** spread around and to the south of two arcades, on either side of Rue Mohammed Zerktouni, and up towards the Mellah (former Jewish ghetto), in the northwest corner of the ramparts. Worth particular attention are the **Marché d'Épices** (spice market) and **Souk des Bijoutiers** (jewellers' market). Art studios and hippie-style clothing shops centre around Place Chefchaouni by the clocktower. By the harbour is another impressive sea bastion, the **Skala du Port**. The southern **beach** (the northern one is less attractive) extends for miles, past the Oued Ksob riverbed and the ruins of an old fort known as the **Bordj el Berod** – the inspiration for Jimi Hendrix's *Castles Made of Sand*.

Practicalities

Still largely contained within its ramparts, Essaouira is a simple place to get to grips with. At the northeast end of town is the **Bab Doukkala**; at the southwest is the town's pedestrianized main square, **Place Prince Moulay el Hassan**, and the fishing **harbour**. Between them run two main parallel streets: Av de l'Istiqlal/Av Mohammed Zerktouni and Rue Sidi Mohammed Ben Abdallah. The **tourist office** is on Av du Caire (Mon–Thurs 9–11.30am/noon & 3–6.30pm; ☎044 78 35 32).

Buses (both CTM and private lines) arrive at a new bus station, inconveniently sited on the outskirts of the town, about 500m (ten minutes' walk) northeast of Bab Doukkala. Especially at night, it's well worth taking a *petit taxi* (about 5dh) or horse-drawn calèche (about 10dh). **Grands taxis** also operate from the bus station, though they will drop arrivals at Bab Doukkala or Place Prince Moulay el Hassan. There is a *petit taxi* rank by the clocktower east of Place Prince Moulay el Hassan and calèches wait at Bab Doukkala.

Accommodation can be tight over Easter and in summer, when advance booking is recommended. Nonetheless, local residents may approach you with offers of rooms, and Jack's Kiosk, a newspaper shop on Place Prince Moulay el Hassan, displays ads for apartments. Of **hotels**, *Majestic*, opposite the museum, 40 Rue Laâlouj (☎044 47 49 09; ❶), has good, clean rooms, though a little cheerless; *Souiri*, 37 Rue El Attarine (☎044 47 53 39; ❶), is a popular and colourful hotel in the Medina, good value and centrally located, and the *Tafraout*, 7 Rue Marrakech (☎044 47 62 76; ❶), is clean and friendly with some en-suite rooms, but rather lacking in character. *Shahrazed*, 1 Rue Youssef el Fassi (☎044 47 29 77; ❷), is new, spacious and very comfortable, alongside the tourist office and opposite police headquarters; and *Sahara*, Av Okba Ibn Nafia (☎044 47 52 92; ❶), has big rooms around a central well, with en-suite hot showers. There's also a **campsite**, *Sidi Magdoul*, 1km south of town behind the lighthouse (☎044 47 21 96).

For an informal **meal**, you can do no better than eat at the line of grills down at the port, an Essaouira institution. A couple of snack bars on Av de l'Istiqlal offer the cheapest eats in town. Among the regular restaurants, try the budget *Essalam*, on Place Prince Moulay el Hassan, or the pricier *Petite Perle*, just off the clocktower square, with well-prepared dishes in a traditional setting. For a seafood splurge, you can't beat the two fish restaurants by the port, the long-established *Chez Sam's* and upmarket newcomer *Le Coquillage*, which is the first you come to.

Leaving for **Marrakesh**, there is a twice daily nonstop Supratours bus which leaves from Av Lalla Aicha, opposite Bab Marrakesh, at 6am and 4pm, arriving at Marrakesh train station; buy tickets from the kiosk here the day before. The best buses direct to **Casablanca** are the CTM Mumtaz Express (leaves Essaouira bus station daily at midnight, arrives 5am), or the cheaper 11.15am service; both are fast, comfortable and take you to the centre of Casa.

Travel details

Trains

Only direct trains listed here; for connections, consult ⊕ www.oncf.org.ma.
Casablanca Port to: Mohammed V airport (12–13 daily; 45min); Rabat (7–11 daily; 1hr).
Casablanca Voyageurs to: Fes (8 daily; 4hr 45min); Marrakesh (8 daily; 3hr 30min); Meknes (8 daily; 3hr 45min); Mohammed V airport (12–13 daily; 35min); Rabat (13 daily; 1hr); Tangier (3 daily; 5hr 40min).
Fes to: Casablanca Voyageurs (8 daily; 4hr 45min); Marrakesh (5 daily; 7hr 35min–10hr); Meknes (9 daily; 50min); Rabat (8 daily; 3hr 30min); Tangier (1 daily; 4hr 45min).
Marrakesh to: Casablanca Voyageurs (8 daily; 3hr 30min); Fes (5 daily; 7hr 35min–9hr 25min); Meknes (5 daily; 6hr 45min–8hr 30min); Rabat (8 daily; 4hr 20min); Tangier (1 daily; 9hr).
Meknes to: Casablanca Voyageurs (8 daily; 4hr); Marrakesh (5 daily; 6hr 45min–9hr 15min); Fes (9 daily; 50min); Rabat (8 daily; 2hr 20min); Tangier (1 daily; 4hr 10min).
Rabat to: Casablanca Voyageurs (13 daily; 1hr); Casablanca Port (7–11 daily; 1hr); Fes (8 daily; 3hr 45min); Marrakesh (8 daily; 4hr 15min); Meknes (8 daily; 2hr 45min); Tangier (3 daily; 4hr 40min).
Tangier Moghogha to: Casablanca Voyageurs (3 daily; 5hr 45min–6hr 15min); Fes (1 daily; 5hr 40min); Meknes (1 daily; 3hr 50min); Marrakesh (1 daily; 9hr 30min); Rabat (3 daily; 4hr 45min–5hr 15min).

Buses

Casablanca to: Essaouira (40 daily; 7hr); Fes (25 daily; 5hr 30min); Fnideq (for Ceuta) (15 daily; 7hr); Marrakesh (half-hourly; 4hr); Meknes (20 daily; 4hr 30min); Mohammed V airport (12 daily; 1hr); Rabat (frequent; 1hr 20min); Tetouan (23 daily; 6hr); Tangier (25 daily; 6hr 30min).
Chefchaouen to: Fes (8 daily; 5hr); Meknes (5 daily; 5hr 30min); Rabat (5 daily; 8hr 30min);

Tangier (8 daily; 3hr 30min); Tetouan (10 daily; 2hr).
Essaouira to: Casablanca (40 daily; 7hr); Rabat (9 daily; 8hr 30min); Marrakesh (14 daily; 3hr 30min).
Fes to: Casablanca (25 daily; 5hr 30min); Chefchaouen (8 daily; 5hr); Marrakesh (6 daily; 10hr); Meknes (frequent; 1hr); Rabat (30 daily; 4hr); Tangier (11 daily; 5hr 45min); Tetouan (7 daily; 5hr 20min).
Marrakesh to: Casablanca (half-hourly 4am–9pm; 4hr); Essaouira (9 daily; 3hr 30min); Fes (6 daily; 10hr); Meknes (5 daily; 9hr); Rabat (30 daily; 5hr 30min); Tangier (3 daily; 10hr).
Meknes to: Casablanca (20 daily; 4hr 30min); Chefchaouen (5 daily; 5hr 30min); Fes (frequent; 1hr); Marrakesh (5 daily; 9hr); Rabat (23 daily; 3hr); Tangier (14 daily; 8hr); Tetouan (7 daily; 6hr).
Rabat to: Casablanca (frequent; 1hr 20min); Essaouira (9 daily; 8hr 30min); Fes (30 daily; 4hr); Marrakesh (30 daily; 5hr 30min); Meknes (23 daily; 3hr); Salé (frequent; 15min); Tangier (25 daily; 5hr).
Tangier to: Casablanca (25 daily; 6hr 30min); Chefchaouen (8 daily; 3hr 30min); Fes (11 daily; 5hr 45min); Fnideq (for Ceuta) (10 daily; 1hr); Marrakesh (3 daily; 10hr); Meknes (14 daily; 8hr); Rabat (25 daily; 5hr); Tetouan (40 daily; 1hr 30min).
Tetouan to: Casablanca (23 daily; 6hr); Chefchaouen (10 daily; 2hr); Fnideq (for Ceuta) (40 daily; 1hr); Fes (7 daily; 5hr 20min); Meknes (7 daily; 6hr); Rabat (33 daily; 5hr); Tangier (40 daily; 1hr 30min).

Ferries and Hydrofoils

Ceuta to: Algeciras (20–36 daily; 35min–1hr 30min).
Tangier to: Algeciras (13–24 daily; 1hr 30min–2hr 30min); Tarifa (2 daily; 35min); Gibraltar (2 weekly; 1hr 15min).

The Netherlands

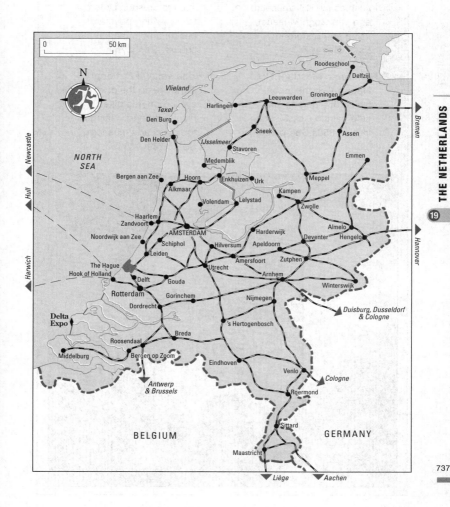

The Netherlands highlights

* **Amsterdam's canals**
  Cruise the canals and
  visit famous art venues
  such as the Rijksmuseum
  and Van Gogh Museum,
  using an Amsterdam
  Pass. **See p.743**

* **Panorama Mesdag, The
  Hague** Visit the astonishing 360 degree sea-
  side painting, by Mesdag
  in the 1880s.**See p.755**

* **Kobus Koch Café, Delft**
  Enjoy wonderful
  appeltart met slagboom
  in a picturesque Dutch
  town, writing postcards
  beside an old market
  square. **See p.757**

* **Hoge Veluwe National
  Park** Spend the day
  cycling on free bikes,
  picnicking and visiting a
  top class arts museum.
  See p.761

Introduction and basics

The Netherlands is a country partly reclaimed from the waters of the North Sea, and around half of it lies at or below sea level. Land reclamation has been the dominant motif of its history, with the result a country of unique images – flat, fertile landscapes punctuated by windmills and church spires; ornately gabled terraces flanking peaceful canals; and mile upon mile of grassy dunes, backing onto stretches of pristine sandy beach.

A leading colonial power, its mercantile fleets once challenged the best in the world for supremacy, and the country enjoyed a so-called "**Golden Age**" of prosperity in the seventeenth century. These days, the Netherlands is one of the most developed countries in the world, with the highest population density in Europe, its sixteen million or so inhabitants (most of whom speak English) concentrated into an area about the size of southern England.

Most people travel only to the uniquely atmospheric capital, **Amsterdam**: the rest of the country, despite its accessibility, is comparatively untouched by tourism. The west of the Netherlands is the most populated and historically interesting region, home to a group of towns known collectively as the **Randstad** (literally "rim town"). It's a good idea to forsake Amsterdam for a while and investigate places like Haarlem and Delft with their old canal-girded centres, or **The Hague** (Den Haag), stately home of the government with fine museums and easy beach access. Outside the Randstad, life moves more slowly. The remote province of Zeeland, in the southwest, is unlikely to feature on anyone's whistle-stop tour of the continent. In the north, **Groningen** is a busy cultural centre, lent verve by its large resident student population. To the south, the landscape undulates into heathy moorland, best experienced in the **Hoge Veluwe National Park**. Further south still lies the compelling city of **Maastricht**, squeezed between the German and Belgian borders.

Information and maps

"**VVV**" **tourist offices** are usually in town centres or by train stations, and have information in English, including maps and accommodation lists (a fee is payable); they will also book rooms, again for a small charge. The best general **map** is Kümmerley and Frey's; the Dutch motoring organization ANWB publishes an excellent series covering the whole country.

Money and banks

The Netherlands is one of twelve European Union countries which uses the **euro** (€). The current exchange rate is around €1.6 to £1 and €1 to US$1. **Banking hours** are Mon–Fri 9am–4/5pm; in larger cities some banks also open Thurs 7–9pm and occasionally on Saturday mornings. GWK **exchange offices**, usually at train stations, open late every day (24hr at Schiphol airport and Amsterdam Centraal Station); they change money and travellers' cheques, and give cash advances on all major credit cards. You can also change money at most VVV tourist offices, post offices and numerous *bureaux de change*, though the rates will be less favourable. **ATMs** dispense cash, though Visa card holders may have to search for a compatible machine. Always check that you can use a credit card; smaller

The Netherlands on the net

ⓦ**www.visitholland.com** National tourist board
ⓦ**www.ns.nl** Train information
ⓦ**www.bookings.nl** Online hotel bookings
ⓦ**www.museumjaarkaart.nl** Museum guide

places (including bed and breakfasts) may not accept them.

Communications

Dutch **post offices** open Mon–Fri 8.30am–5pm, Sat 8.30am–noon. All international post should go into the slot on red postboxes (often attached to a wall) marked "Overige". Public **phones** are widespread but almost all take phonecards or credit cards only; post offices and VVVs sell phonecards. Some train stations have a small number of coin-phones. The operator number is ☎0800/0410 (free); international directory enquiries is on ☎0900/8418 (premium rate). **Internet** access is easy in most parts of the country, with plenty of cafés as well as terminals at public libraries.

Getting around

Distances are short and urban **public transport** is efficient and cheap, running on an easy-to-understand ticketing system that covers the whole country.

Trains

The best way to get around is by train. The system, run by Nederlandse Spoorwegen (Dutch Railways), is one of Europe's finest: trains are fast, modern and frequent, fares relatively low, and the network of lines extremely comprehensive. There are various passes available to cut costs – ask at a station and have your passport ready. With any ticket, you're free to stop off en route and continue later that day.

Stations are well equipped and usually have a reasonably priced restaurant, left-luggage lockers (around €2 for 24hr), and a GWK change office. The NS **treintaxi** scheme (not valid in Amsterdam, Rotterdam or The Hague) means you pay €3 for a taxi to take you anywhere within the city limits from your destination train station, within a time span of 15min – very useful for smaller towns. Buy vouchers for *treintaxis* when you buy your train ticket.

Buses

For local transport **buses** are very efficient, and almost always run from ranks of bus stops next to the train station. **Ticketing** is simple. The whole country is divided into zones, and you need just one kind of ticket, a strippenkaart. The bus driver will cancel one strip on your *strippenkaart* for your journey plus one for each zone you travel through, and the tickets can be used by any number of people, cancelling the requisite number of strips each. You can buy 2-, 3- or 8-strip *strippenkaarts* from bus drivers, or the better-value 15-strip (€5.90) or 45-strip (€17) tickets in advance from train stations, tobacconists, local public transport offices and some VVVs.

Cycling

If you're not pushed for time, **cycling** is a lovely way to see the country. There's a nationwide system of well-signposted cycle paths, which often divert away from the main roads into the countryside; better bookshops sell cycling maps. You can rent bikes from all main train stations and also from outlets in almost any town and village. Never leave your bike unlocked, and don't leave it on the street overnight – most stations have a storage area.

Accommodation

Accommodation can be a little pricey, especially in places like Amsterdam and Haarlem, though a wide network of hostels and well-equipped campsites helps cut costs. Wherever you stay, book ahead during the summer and over holiday periods, especially Easter.

Hotels and private rooms

The cheapest one- or two-star double room, not en suite, starts at around €50. Three-star hotel rooms average out at around €80. Prices usually include a reasonable breakfast. You can reserve for free through the Netherlands Reservation Centre (🖱www.hotelres.nl), or at VVV offices (small charge).

THE NETHERLANDS | Basics

⑲

One way of cutting costs is to use private accommodation. Prices are usually quoted per person and are normally about €15. You can generally only book B&Bs through VVVs (who will sell you a list), although ✪www .bedandbreakfast.nl is useful.

Hostels and student rooms

There are about 35 HI **hostels** nationwide (✪www.njhc.org), charging €17–23 per person per night including breakfast (with a discount of €2.50 for HI members), more for single, double and family rooms. You can also often eat at hostels and some have kitchens where you can self-cater. Larger cities often have independent hostels with broadly similar prices, though standards are sometimes not as reliable. In a few cities, student accommodation is open during the holidays; ask at the local VVV.

Campsites and cabins

Camping is a serious option, with plenty of well equipped sites. Prices vary greatly, but you can generally expect to pay around €3 per person, plus €2–4 for a tent. Some sites also have cabins – book in advance – for up to four people, for around €34 a night.

Food and drink

The Netherlands is not renowned for its **food**, but there's an enormous variety of ethnic restaurants, especially Indonesian and Chinese, and, if you're selective, prices needn't break the bank. **Drinking**, too, is easily affordable: sampling the Dutch and Belgian beers in every region is one of the country's real pleasures.

Food

Dutch food tends to be plain, mainly steak, chicken or fish, along with soups and stews. **Breakfast** (ontbijt) is generally filling: rolls, cheese, ham, eggs, jam and honey, chocolate spread or peanut butter are the principal ingredients.

For the rest of the day, **fast-food** options include chips – frites or patat – sprinkled with salt, smothered with mayonnaise, curry,

satay or tomato sauce, and often complemented with kroketten (meat goulash coated in breadcrumbs and deep fried) or fricandel (a frankfurter-like sausage). Tastier, and good both as a snack and a full lunch, are **fish** specialities sold from street kiosks: salted raw herrings, smoked eel (gerookte paling), mackerel in a roll (broodje makreel), mussels and various kinds of deep-fried fish. A nationwide chain of fish restaurants, Noordzee, serves good-value fish-based sandwiches and light fish lunches. Another common snack is shoarma (kebab), sold in numerous Middle Eastern restaurants and takeaways, which generally also have the chickpea-based falafel, a good vegetarian stand-by.

The majority of **bars** serve at least sandwiches and rolls (boterham and broodjes – stokbrood if made with baguette); in winter, they serve erwtensoep, a thick pea soup with smoked sausage, and uitsmijters (literally "bouncers"), fried eggs on buttered bread, topped with ham or roast beef. **Restaurants** open in the evenings only, until around 11pm; if you're on a tight budget, stick to the dish of the day (dagschotels). Train station restaurants are a good standby, serving full meals for €7, and in university towns student restaurants serve meals for under €9. **Vegetarians** will have few problems: many places have at least one meat-free item, and you'll find veggie restaurants in most towns. Colonial history has led to hundreds of Surinamese and especially **Indonesian** restaurants; at the former try roti, flat bread with spicy curry; at the latter (which may also do Chinese food), go for a rijsttafel – rice or noodles served with a huge range of tasty side-dishes.

Drink

Most **drinking** is done either in a cosy brown café (bruine kroeg, named because of the colour of the tobacco-stained walls), or in more modern-looking bars, usually catering to a younger crowd. Most **bars** open till around 1am during the week, 2am at weekends. You may also come across proeflokalen or tasting houses, small, old-fashioned bars that close around 8pm. The most commonly consumed beverage is **beer**, usually served in small measures for about

19

€1 (ask for *een pils*); a bigger glass is *een vaasje*. The most common names are Heineken, Amstel, Oranjeboom and Grolsch, though there are other regional brews and you'll also come across plenty of Belgian brands. **Wine** is reasonably priced. The indigenous firewater is jenever or Dutch **gin**, served in small glasses and drunk straight; *oud* (old) is smooth, *jong* (young) packs more of a punch. **Coffee** is normally good and strong, while **tea** generally comes with lemon if anything. **Chocolate** is also popular, served hot or cold.

Opening hours and holidays

The Dutch weekend fades painlessly into the working week with many **shops** staying closed on Monday morning, even in major cities, although markets do open early. Otherwise, opening hours tend to be 9am–5.30/6pm, though certain shops stay open later on Thursday or Friday evenings, and city-centre supermarkets tend to close around 10pm. Night shops (*avondwinkels*) in major cities usually open 4pm–1/2am.

    Museum times are fairly uniform, generally Tues–Sat 10am–5pm, Sun 1–5pm. Shops and banks are closed, and museums adopt Sunday hours, on the following public holidays: Jan 1; Good Fri; Easter Sun & Mon; Queen's Day; May 5; May 13; Whitsun & Mon; Dec 5; Dec 25 & Dec 26.

Emergencies and drugs

It's generally **safe** to walk anywhere at any time of day, though be wary of pickpockets and badly lit or empty streets at night. You're unlikely to come into contact with the police force. As for **drugs**, people over the age of eighteen are legally allowed to buy five grammes of hashish or marijuana (less than one-fifth of one ounce) for personal use. Don't assume that the bar or café you're in permits dope-smoking; if in doubt, ask. Also bear in mind that the liberal attitude exists only in Amsterdam and the larger cities of the Randstad: elsewhere, public dope-smoking is frowned upon. All other narcotics – except fresh magic mushrooms – are illegal. Check out The Honest Cannabis Info Site (@www.thc.nl). **Pharmacies** (*apotheek*) are open Mon–Fri 8.30am–5.30pm. Outside these hours there'll be a note of the nearest open pharmacy on the door. Duty doctors at the Centrale Doktorsdienst (@0900/503 2042) offer general advice about medical symptoms; otherwise head for the casualty department of any hospital.

Emergency Numbers

Police, fire and ambulance @112.

Amsterdam

AMSTERDAM is a beguiling capital, a compact mix of the provincial and the cosmopolitan. It has a welcoming attitude towards visitors and a uniquely youthful orientation. For many, its world-class museums and galleries – notably the Rijksmuseum, with its collection of seventeenth-century Dutch paintings, and the Van Gogh Museum – are reason enough to visit.

Amsterdam was founded on a dam on the river Amstel in the thirteenth century. During the Reformation it rose in stature, taking trade away from Antwerp and becoming a haven for its religious refugees. Having shaken off the yoke of the Spanish, the city went from strength to strength in the seventeenth century, becoming the centre of a vast trading empire with colonies in Southeast Asia. Amsterdam accommodated its expansion with the cobweb of canals that gives the city its distinctive and elegant shape today. By the eighteenth century, Amsterdam was in gentle decline, re-emerging as a fashionable focus for the alternative movements of the 1960s. Despite a backlash in the 1980s, the city still takes a uniquely progressive approach to social issues and culture, with a buzz of open-air summer events, intimate clubs and bars, and relaxed attitude to soft drugs.

Arrival, information and city transport

Schiphol **airport** is connected by train with the main **Centraal Station** (every 15min; hourly at night), which is at the hub of all **bus** and **tram** routes and just five minutes' walk from central Dam Square. International buses arrive at Amstel Station, ten minutes south of Centraal Station by metro. For **information**, the main VVV is outside Centraal Station, Stationsplein 10 (daily 9am–5pm; ☏0900/400 4040, ⊛www.visitamsterdam.nl); there's another branch inside the station (Mon–Sat 8am–8pm, Sun 9am–5pm), a smaller kiosk on the Leidseplein corner of Leidsestraat (daily 9am–5pm, Thurs–Sat closes 7pm), and an office in the airport (daily 7am–10pm). Any of these can sell you an **Amsterdam Pass** (€26/day, €36/two days, €46/three days), which gives free or reduced entry to a selection of major attractions as well as free public transport and discounts at some restaurants. The VVV's monthly **listings** guide, *Day to Day* (€1), and *Infopocket Amsterdam* (€3) are both useful resources.

The excellent network of **trams**, **buses** and the small **metro** (all daily 6/7am–midnight) isn't expensive. The GVB public transport office in front of Centraal Station (Mon–Fri 7am–9pm, Sat & Sun 8am–9pm; winter closes 7pm; ☏0900/9292) has free route maps and an English guide to the ticketing system. As with the rest of the country, you use a *strippenkaart*. After midnight, **night buses** take over, running roughly hourly from Centraal Station to most parts of the city. **Taxis** are expensive, found in ranks on main city squares (Stationsplein, Dam Square, Leidseplein); to book one call ☏020/677 7777. **Bikes** can be rented from Centraal Station or from a number of firms around town (see p.752).

Accommodation

Hotels can be expensive, although the city's size means that you'll inevitably end up somewhere central. A viable alternative is to stay in one of the many **hostels** offering dorm beds and usually a few rooms. At peak periods throughout the year (April–September, but especially Easter) it's advisable to book ahead. The Amsterdam Reservation Centre (⊛www.amsterdamtourist.nl) can book accommodation for a €9 fee; it's especially useful for last-minute bookings. There are **campsites** at Vliegenbos (☏020/636 8855; closed Oct–March), a ten-minute bus ride away in Amsterdam North, and Gaasper Camping, Loosdrechtdreef 7 (☏020/696 7326, ⊛www.gaaspercamping-amsterdam.nl; closed Jan & Feb), way out in the southeast; take the metro to Gaasperplas.

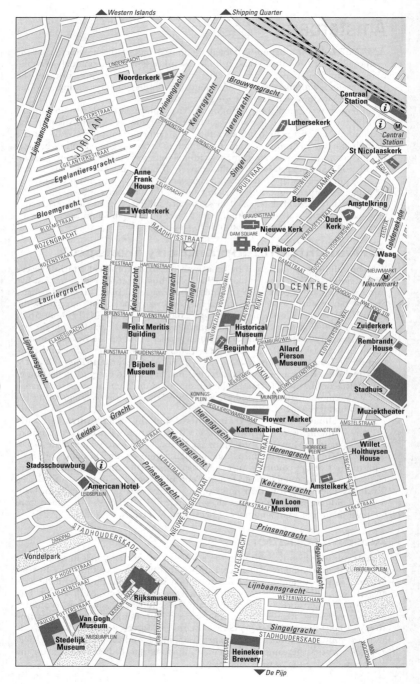

19

▲ Western Islands   ▲ Shipping Quarter

LINDENGRACHT

Noorderkerk

Brouwersgracht

Centraal
Station

ⓘ

ⓘ M

Central
Station

St Nicolaaskerk

WESTERSTRAAT

Lijnbaansgracht

JORDAAN

EGELANTIERSSTRAAT

Egelantiersgracht

Prinsengracht

Prinsenstraat

Keizersgracht

Herengracht

Herenstraat

Singel

Spuistraat

Luthersekerk

NIEUWENDIJK

DAMRAK

Beurs

Amstelkring

Anne
Frank
House

LELIEGRACHT

Bloemgracht

BLOEMSTRAAT

Westerkerk

RAADHUISSTRAAT

GRAVENSTRAAT

Nieuwe Kerk

DAM SQUARE

WARMOESSTRAAT

Oude
Kerk

Geldersekade

Gelderskade

ROZENSTRAAT

ROZENGRACHT

Lauriergracht

ELANDSGRACHT

✉

Royal Palace

Singel

Herengracht

Keizersgracht

Prinsengracht

REESTRAAT   HARTENSTRAAT

DAMSTRAAT

Waag

NIEUWMARKT

M

Nieuwmarkt

OLD CENTRE

OUDEZIJDS VOORBURGWAL

KALVERSTRAAT

ROKIN

BERENSTRAAT WOLVENSTRAAT

Felix Meritis
Building

Historical
Museum

Zuiderkerk

NIEUWEZIJDS VOORBURGWAL

Begijnhof

ⓘ

GRIMBURGWAL

Allard
Pierson
Museum

Rembrandt
House

OUDEHOOG STR.

NWE HOOG STR.

KLOVENIERSBURGWAL

Lijnbaansgracht

RUNSTRAAT   HUIDENSTRAAT

Bijbels
Museum

SPUI

HEILIGEWEG

ROKIN

NIEUWE DOELENSTRAAT

Stadhuis

Muziektheater

KONINGS-
PLEIN

MUNTPLEIN

Gracht

REGULIERSDWARSSTRAAT

Flower Market

AMSTELSTRAAT

Leidse

LEIDSESTRAAT

Herengracht

Kattenkabinet

REMBRANDTPLEIN

VIJZELSTRAAT

Herengracht

THORBECKE
PLEIN

Willet
Holthuysen
House

Stadsschouwburg ⓘ

KERKSTRAAT

Keizersgracht

Keizersgracht

Amstelkerk

UTRECHTSESTRAAT

American Hotel

LEIDSEPLEIN

Prinsengracht

NIEUWE SPIEGELSTRAAT

KERKSTRAAT

Van Loon
Museum

KERKSTRAAT

Vondelpark

ZANOPAD

STADHOUDERSKADE

P C HOOFTSTRAAT

Prinsengracht

Reguliersgracht

FREDERIKSPLEIN

JAN LUIJKENSTRAAT

PAULUS POTTERSTRAAT

VIJZELGRACHT

Lijnbaansgracht

WETERINGSCHANS

Rijksmuseum

MUSEUMSTRAAT

HOBBEMAKADE

Singelgracht

STADHOUDERSKADE

Van Gogh
Museum

Stedelijk
Museum

MUSEUMPLEIN

F BOLSTRAAT

Heineken
Brewery

▼ De Pijp

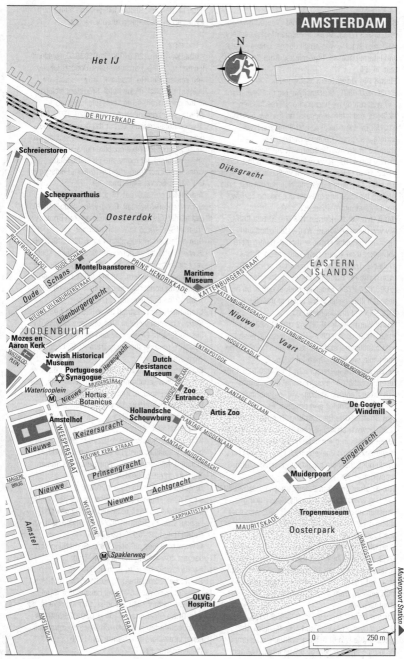

N

Het IJ

DE RUYTERKADE

TUNNEL

Schreierstoren

Dijksgracht

Scheepvaarthuis

Oosterdok

PRINS HENDRIKKADE

Montelbaanstoren

OUDE SCHANS

RECHTBOOMSSLOOT

Oude Schans

NIEUWE UILENBURGERSTRAAT

Uilenburgergracht

Maritime Museum

KATTENBURGERSTRAAT

KATTENBURGERGRACHT

EASTERN ISLANDS

Nieuwe

WITTENBURGERGRACHT

Vaart

OOSTENBURGERGRACHT

JODENBUURT

Mozes en Aaron Kerk

WATERLOO PLEIN

Jewish Historical Museum

Portuguese Synagogue

Houtgracht

ENTREPOTDOK

HOOGTEKADIJK

Waterlooplein

MUIDERSTRAAT

Nieuwe

Hortus Botanicus

Dutch Resistance Museum

PLANTAGE KERKLAAN

PLANTAGE DOKLAAN

Zoo Entrance

Artis Zoo

'De Gooyer' Windmill

Amstelhof

Hollandsche Schouwburg

PLANTAGE MIDDENLAAN

Keizersgracht

WEESPERSTRAAT

NIEUWE KERK STRAAT

PLANTAGE MUIDERGRACHT

Prinsengracht

Nieuwe

Singelgracht

MAGERE BRUG

Nieuwe

WEESPERPLEIN

Achtgracht

Muiderpoort

Amstel

Nieuwe

SARPHATISTRAAT

MAURITSKADE

Tropenmuseum

Oosterpark

LINNAEUSSTRAAT

M Spaklerweg

WIBAUTSTRAAT

AMSTELDIJK

OLVG Hospital

0   250 m

THE NETHERLANDS

19

Muiderpoort Station ▶

745

Hostels

Bob's Youth Hostel Nieuwezijds Voorburgwal 92 ☎020/623 0063. An old favourite of backpackers; lively and smoky, with small dorms, cheap meals and Internet access. Ten-minutes from Centraal Station. ②

Flying Pig Downtown Nieuwendijk 100 ☎020/420 6822, ⊛www.flyingpig.nl. Clean, large and well run by ex-backpackers. Free kitchen facilities and Internet access, no curfew, all-night bar. Not for faint-hearted anti-smokers. Five-minute walk from Centraal Station. ③

Flying Pig Palace Vondelpark Vossiusstraat 46 ☎020/400 4187, ⊛www.flyingpig.nl. Tram #1/#2/#5 to Leidseplein, then walk. On the edge of the city's big park; clean and well maintained. Free kitchen facilities and Internet access, no curfew, good tourist information. ③

Hans Brinker Kerkstraat 136 ☎020/622 0687, ⊛www.hans-brinker.nl. Well-established and raucously popular cheapie, though a little more upmarket than some. Café with cheap dishes available. Tram #1/#2/#5 to Prinsengracht. ③

International Budget Hostel Leidsegracht 76 ☎020/624 2784. Excellent budget option on a peaceful little canal in the heart of the city. Tram #1/#2/#5 to Prinsengracht. ③

Kabul Warmoesstraat 38–42 ☎020/623 7158/7059, ⊜ 620 0869. Huge, bustling hostel with multilingual staff, three minutes from station. Immaculately clean. Open 24 hours. ③

Keizersgracht Keizersgracht 15 ☎020/625 1364. Terrific location on a major canal five minutes' walk from Centraal Station, with a good mix of small dorms, singles and doubles. ③

The Shelter City Barndesteeg 21 ☎020/625 3230, ⊛www.shelter.nl. Non-evangelical Christian hostel smack in the middle of the red-light district: single-sex dorms, lockers, midnight curfew (1am weekends). Sizeable breakfast included. Metro Nieuwmarkt. ②

The Shelter Jordaan Bloemstraat 179 ☎020/624 4717, ⊛www.shelter.nl. Another easy-going Christian hostel in the Jordaan district, with very cheap beds. No smoking. Tram #13/#17 to Marnixstraat. ②

Stadsdoelen Kloveniersburgwal 97 ☎020/624 6832, ⊛www.njhc.org/stadsdoelen. The more accessible of the two HI hostels, with clean semi-private dorm rooms. HI members have priority in high season. Tram #4/#9/#16/#24/#25 to Muntplein. ③

Vondel Park Zandpad 5 ☎020/589 8996, ⊛www.njhc.org/vondelpark. For facilities, the better of the two HI hostels, with bar, restaurant, TV lounge and kitchen; also well located on the edge of the park. Secure lockers and a lift. Tram #1/#2/#5 to Leidseplein, then walk. ③

Hotels

Abba Overtoom 120 ☎020/618 3058. Conveniently located for the big art museums, Concertgebouw and Leidesplein. Rooms have showers and are quiet at the back of the hotel. Breakfast included in the price. Tram #5 to Leidseplein. ⑤

Arena 's-Gravesandestraat 51 ☎020/850 2400, ⊛www.hotelarena.nl. Out of the centre, but the best value in the city. On-site facilities include live music, tourist information, bike rental, a great bar and restaurant. All rooms are en suite. Metro Weesperplein or tram #6/#7/#10 from Leidseplein to Korte 's-Gravesandestraat. ③

Asterisk Den Texstraat 16 ☎020/626 2396, ⊛www.asteriskhotel.nl. Good-value budget hotel, just across the canal from the Heineken Brewery. Tram #16/#24/#25 to Weteringcircuit. ③

Bema Concertgebouwplein 19b ☎020/679 1396, ⊛www.hotel-bema.demon.nl. Small place, kept very clean by the English-speaking manager. The rooms are not modern, but are full of character. Handier for concerts and museums than nightlife. Tram #2/#5 to Museumplein. ④

Clemens Raadhuisstraat 39 ☎020/624 6089, ⊛www.clemenshotel.nl. One of many options on this hotel strip. Clean, neat and value for money. Ask for a room at the back. Tram #13/#17 to Westermarkt. ④

Euphemia Fokke Simonszstraat 1 ☎020/622 9045, ⊛www.euphemiahotel.com. A likeable, laid-back atmosphere: rooms are big and basic, with free showers and TVs. Very reasonable prices, which means it's usually full. Tram #16/#24/#25 to Weteringcircuit. ④

King Leidsekade 85–86 ☎020/624 9603. Clean but very small rooms in a small hotel. Breakfast included. Minimum three nights during summer. Tram #1/#2/#5 to Leidseplein. ④

Quentin Leidsekade 89 ☎020/626 2187. Friendly small hotel, often a stopover for bands performing at the Melkweg. Well regarded among gay and lesbian visitors. Tram #1/#2/#5 to Leidseplein. ④

Rokin Rokin 73 ☎020/626 7456, ⊛www.bookings.nl/hotels/rokin. Something of a bargain considering the location. Tram #4/#9/#16/#24/#25 to Dam or Spui. ⑤

St Nicolaas Spuistraat 1a ☎020/626 1384. Very pleasant, well-run little hotel housed in a former mattress factory (with a king-size lift to prove it). ⑥

Van Onna Bloemgracht 104 ☎020/626 5801. A quiet, comfortable, family-run place on a tranquil canal in the Jordaan. Tram #13/#17 to Westermarkt. ⑤

The City

Amsterdam is a small city, and, although the concentric canal system can be initially confusing, finding your bearings is straightforward. The medieval core boasts the best of the city's bustling streetlife and is home to shops, many bars and restaurants, fanning south from the nineteenth-century **Centraal Station**, one of Amsterdam's most resonant landmarks. From here, **Damrak** storms into the heart of the city, lined with overpriced restaurants and bobbing canal boats, and flanked on the left first by the stock exchange or **Beurs**, designed by the leading light of the Dutch modern movement, H.P. Berlage, and then by the enormous **De Bijenkorf** department store.

To the left off Damrak, the infamous **red-light district**, stretching across two canals – Oudezijds (abbreviated to O.Z.) Voorburgwal and O.Z. Achterburgwal – is one of the real sights of the city, thronged in high season with visitors keen to discover just how shocking it all is. The legalized prostitution on flagrant display here is world-renowned. The two canals, with their narrow connecting passages, are thronged with neon-lit "window brothels", where scantily clad women often stand or sit behind glass for up to 12 hours a day.

Behind the Beurs, off Warmoesstraat, the precincts of the **Oude Kerk** (Mon–Sat 11am–5pm, Sun 1–5pm; €3.60; ⊛www.oudekerk.nl) offer a reverential peace after the excesses of the red-light district; it's a bare, mostly fourteenth-century church with the memorial tablet of Rembrandt's first wife, Saskia van Uylenburg. Just beyond, **Zeedijk** leads to **Nieuwmarkt**, with the turreted **Waag** an original part of the city's fortifications. **Kloveniersburgwal**, heading south, was the outer of the three eastern canals of sixteenth-century Amsterdam and boasts, on the left, one of the city's most impressive canal houses, built for the Trip family in 1662. Further up on the right, the Oudemanhuispoort passage is filled with secondhand bookstalls.

At the southern end of Damrak, the **Dam** (or Dam Square), is the centre of the city, its War Memorial serving as a grim meeting place for tourists. On the western side, the **Royal Palace** (June–Oct daily 11am–5pm; Nov–May opening hours variable; €4.30; ⊛www.kon-paleisamsterdam.nl) was originally built as the city hall in the mid-seventeenth century. Vying for importance is the adjacent **Nieuwe Kerk** (open only during exhibitions; ⊛www.nieuwekerk.nl), a fifteenth-century structure rebuilt several times, and now used for exhibitions and state occasions.

South of Dam Square, **Rokin** follows the old course of the Amstel River, lined with grandiose nineteenth-century mansions. Running parallel, **Kalverstraat** is a monotonous strip of clothes shops, halfway down which, at no. 92, a gateway forms the entrance to the former orphanage that's now the **Amsterdam Historical Museum** (Mon–Fri 10am–5pm, Sat & Sun 1–5pm; €6.10; ⊛www.ahm.nl), where artefacts, paintings and documents survey the city's development from the thirteenth century. Just around the corner, off Sint Luciensteeg, the **Begijnhof** is a small court of seventeenth-century building where the poor and elderly celebrated Mass in a concealed Catholic Church. The plain English Reformed Church, taking up one side of the Begijnhof, has pulpit panels designed by the young Piet Mondriaan. Close by, the **Spui** (pronounced *spow*) is a lively corner of town whose mixture of bookshops and packed bars centres around a statue of a young boy known as *'t Lieverdje* (Little Darling). In the opposite direction, Kalverstraat comes to an end at **Muntplein** and the Munttoren – originally a mint and part of the city walls, topped with a spire by Hendrik de Keyser in 1620. Across the Singel canal is the fragrant daily **Flower Market**, while in the other direction Reguliersbreestraat turns left towards the loud restaurants of **Rembrandtplein**. To the south is Reguliersgracht, an appealing canal with seven distinctive steep bridges stretching in line from Thorbeckeplein.

The main canals and the Jordaan

Amsterdam's expansion in the seventeenth century was designed around three new canals, **Herengracht**, **Keizersgracht** and **Prinsengracht**, which formed a distinctive cobweb shape around the centre. Development was strictly controlled, resulting in the tall, very narrow residences with decorative gables you see today. The appeal lies in wandering along, taking in the calm of the tree-lined waterways, while looking into people's windows (Amsterdammers tend not to bother with curtains, a habit which lends the city an open and homely atmosphere). For shops, bars and restaurants, you're better off exploring the crossing-streets which connect the canals.

Herengracht remains the grandest, especially between Leidsestraat and Vijzelstraat, a stretch known as the "Golden Curve". To see the interior of one of the canal houses, head for the **Willet-Holthuysen House**, Herengracht 605 (daily 10/11am–5pm; €4.30; www.ahm.nl), splendidly decorated in Rococo style and containing a collection of glass and ceramics and a seventeenth-century kitchen.

On the corner of **Keizersgracht** and Leidsestraat, the designer department store Metz & Co has a top-floor café with one of the best views of the city. **Leidsestraat** itself is a long, slender shopping street across the main canals that broadens at its southern end into **Leidseplein**, focus of Amsterdam's nightlife, with a concentration of bars and restaurants. On the far corner, the Stadsschouwburg is the city's prime performance space after the Muziektheater, while behind, the fairy-castle *American Hotel* has a bar whose carefully co-ordinated furnishings are a fine example of Art Nouveau.

Immediately north of here, along **Prinsengracht**, is one of the city's loveliest neighbourhoods, focusing on the gracious tower of the **Westerkerk**, dating from 1631. Directly outside, a statue of Anne Frank, by the sculptor Marie Andriessen, signals the fact that the **Anne Frank House** (daily: April–Aug 9am–9pm; Sept–March 9am–7pm; closed Yom Kippur; €5.70; www.annefrank.nl), where the young diarist lived, is just a few steps away at Prinsengracht 263. Deservedly one of the most popular tourist attractions in town, arrive before 9am (or at the end of the day) and be prepared to queue. Anne, her family and friends went into hiding from the Nazis in July 1942, staying in the house for two years until they were betrayed and taken away to labour camps, an experience which only Anne's father survived. Anne Frank's diary was among the few things left behind, and was published in 1947, since when it has sold over thirteen million copies worldwide. The rooms the Franks lived in are left much as they were, even down to the movie-star pin-ups in Anne's bedroom and the marks on the wall recording the children's heights.

Across Prinsengracht to the west, the **Jordaan** is a beguiling area of narrow canals, narrower streets and architecturally varied houses. With some of the city's best bars and restaurants, alternative clothes shops and good outdoor markets, especially those on the square outside the Noorderkerk (a fabric market on Mondays and a popular farmers' market on Saturdays), it's a wonderful area to wander through. The hottest contemporary artists show work at the **Stedelijk Museum Bureau Amsterdam** gallery, Rozenstraat 59 (Tues–Sat 11am–5pm; www.smba.nl).

The Museum Quarter and south

Immediately south of Leidseplein begins the **Vondelpark**, the city's most enticing park, a regular forum for drama and other performance arts on summer weekends, when young Amsterdam flocks here to meet friends, laze by the lake and listen to music; in June, July and August there are free concerts every Sunday at 2pm. Southeast of the park is a residential district, with designer shops and delis along chic **P.C. Hooftstraat** and **Van Baerlestraat** and some of the city's major museums grouped around the grassy wedge of **Museumplein**.

The **Rijksmuseum**, Stadhouderskade 42 (daily 10am–5pm; €8.50; www.rijksmuseum.nl), has fine collections of medieval and Renaissance applied art, displays on Dutch history, a fine Asian collection and, most importantly, an array of seventeenth-century Dutch paintings that is among the best in the world. Most people head straight for one of the museum's great treasures, Rembrandt's *The Night Watch*, but there are many other examples of his work, along with portraits by Frans Hals, landscapes by Jan van Goyen and Jacob van Ruisdael, the riotous scenes of Jan Steen and the peaceful interiors of Vermeer and Pieter de Hooch.

Just south is the **Vincent Van Gogh Museum**, Paulus Potterstraat 7 (daily 10am–6pm; €8–€12; ❦www.vangoghmuseum.nl). Long queues can be a feature in high season so arrive early. The collection includes the early years in Holland, to the brighter works he painted after moving to Paris and then Arles, where he produced vivid canvases like *The Yellow House* and the *Sunflowers* series.

Just along the street at Paulus Potterstraat 13 is the modern-art **Stedelijk Museum** (daily 10/11am–5/6pm; €4.50; ❦www.stedelijk.nl). Much of its wide-ranging permanent collection is on display in July and August, and parts of it year-round. There's normally a good showing on the first floor, with drawings by Picasso, Matisse and their contemporaries, moving on to paintings by other major artists, including Van Gogh, Chagall, Kandinsky and Braque.

Further along Stadhouderskade from the Rijksmuseum, the **Heineken Brewery** runs tours (June to mid-Sept Mon–Fri 9.30am, 11am, 1pm & 2.30pm; July & Aug also Sat 11am, 1pm & 2.30pm; rest of year Mon–Fri 9.30am & 11am; €1; over-18s only), providing an overview of Heineken's history and the brewing process; afterwards you're given snacks and **free beer**. South of here is the neighbourhood known as **De Pijp** ("The Pipe") after its long, sombre canyons of brick tenements. This has always been one of the city's closest-knit communities, and one of its liveliest, with numerous inexpensive Surinamese and Turkish restaurants and a cheerful hub in the long slim thoroughfare of **Albert Cuypstraat**, whose **market** is the largest in the city.

East of the centre

East of Rembrandtplein across the Amstel, the large, squat **Muziektheater** and **Town Hall** flank **Waterlooplein**, home to the city's excellent flea market. Behind, Jodenbreestraat was once the main street of the Jodenhoek, the city's **Jewish quarter** (emptied by the Nazis in the 1940s), and is the site of the **Rembrandt House** at no.4 (Mon–Sat 10am–5pm, Sun 1–5pm; €6.80; ❦www.rembrandthuis.nl), which the painter bought at the height of his fame, living here for over twenty years. The interior was renovated in 1999 and displays a large number of the artist's engravings. Across the way, the excellent, award-winning **Jewish Historical Museum** (daily 11am–5pm; closed Yom Kippur; €3.60; ❦www.jhm.nl) is cleverly housed in a complex of Ashkenazi synagogues dating from the late seventeenth century and gives an imaginative introduction to Jewish life and beliefs.

Down Muiderstraat from here, the prim **Hortus Botanicus**, Plantage Middenlaan 2 (Mon–Fri 9am–4/5pm, Sat & Sun 11am–4/5pm; €3.40), is a pocket-sized botanical garden whose 8000 plant species make a wonderfully relaxed break; stop off for coffee and cakes in the orangery. Some 400m down Plantage Middenlaan stands the eye-catching Plancius Building, which houses the **Dutch Resistance Museum**, Plantage Kerklaan 2 (Tues–Fri 10am–5pm, Sat & Sun noon–5pm; €3.60). Here a variety of exhibits depict the ways in which the Dutch people opposed Nazi oppression. A short walk northwest, the **Maritime Museum** on Kattenburgerplein (Tues–Sun 10am–5pm; €6.60; ❦www.scheepvaartmuseum.nl), in a seventeenth-century arsenal, has maps, weapons and large models of sailing ships.

Eating and drinking

Amsterdam has an extensive supply of ethnic **restaurants**, especially Indonesian and Chinese, as well as *eetcafés* and bars which serve decent, well-priced food in an unpretentious setting. We've also listed a handful of places to get a snack, as well as the best of the city's so-called **coffeeshops**, where smoking dope is the primary pastime (ask to see "the menu"). You must be 18 or over to enter these, and don't expect alcohol to be served. Most open at 9am and close at 1am (2/3am at weekends). Check out the Smokers Guide (€3.50) or ❦www.smokersguide.com.

Cafés and snacks

Café Esprit Spui 10a. Swish modern café, with wonderful sandwiches and superb salads.

Da Antonio Singel 492. Enjoy tasty Dutch pancakes (pannekoek) while taking in the colourful sights of the Flower Market.

Gary's Muffins Prinsengracht 454, near Leidseplein; also Reguliersdwarsstraat 53. The best muffins and bagels in town, with big cups of coffee (and half-price refills).

Maoz Falafel Leidsestraat 85, near Leidsesplein; also Regulierbreestraat 45 and Muntplein 1. The best street-food in the city – falafel and as much salad as you can eat for €3.

The Pancake Bakery Prinsengracht 191. A large selection of pancakes.

Puccini Staalstraat 17–21, near Waterlooplein. Dreamy cakes, pastries and chocolates, all handmade.

Studio 2 Singel 504. Pleasantly situated, airy tearoom with a delicious selection of rolls and sandwiches.

Villa Zeezicht Torensteeg 3. Small place on the Singel canal, with excellent sandwiches and some of the best apple cake in the city.

Restaurants

Akbar Korte Leidsedwarsstraat 33, near Leidseplein. Fabulous South Indian food, with a fine choice across the board. Plenty for vegetarians.

De Blauwe Hollander Leidsekruisstraat 28, near Leidseplein. Good-value, generous portions of Dutch cuisine. Very popular; expect to share a table.

De Eetuin 2e Tuindwarsstraat 10, Jordaan. Hefty portions of Dutch food.

Hoi Tin Zeedijk 122, near Nieuwmarkt. One of the best places in the rather dodgy Chinatown, with an enormous menu (in English too) and some vegetarian dishes. Always busy.

Kam Yin Warmoesstraat 6. Excellent option for large portions of Chinese and Surinamese dishes.

Kilimanjaro Rapenburgerplein 6. Small, friendly place serving North African specialities. Closed Mon.

Keuken van 1870 Spuistraat 4. Former soup kitchen serving Dutch meat-and-potato staples.

De Rozenboom Rozenboomsteeg 6. Quaint little Dutch restaurant with good traditional food and a menu in English. Ideally situated, just off Spui.

Shiva Reguliersdwarsstraat 72. Outstanding Indian restaurant, with well-priced, expertly prepared food, including veggie.

De Vliegende Schotel Nieuwe Leliestraat 162, Jordaan. Best of the city's vegetarian restaurants, serving delicious food in large portions.

Bars

Café Vertigo Vondelpark 3. Attached to the Film Museum, a wonderful place to while away time with a spacious interior and a large terrace overlooking the park.

Last Waterhole Oudezijds Armsteeg 12. Red-light district refuge, with a lively, warm atmosphere and a fun-loving house band playing until dawn.

De Drie Fleschjes Gravenstraat 18, near Dam Square. Tasting house for spirits and liqueurs. No beer, and no seats either. Closes 8pm.

De Engelbewaarder Kloveniersburgwal 59. Former meeting place of Amsterdam's bookish types, with live jazz on Sunday afternoons.

't IJ Funenkade 7. Situated in the base of a windmill to the east of the centre, with exceptionally strong home-brewed beers. Wed–Sun 3–8pm.

De Jaren Nieuwe Doelenstraat 20–22, near Muntplein. Grand café overlooking the river – one of the best places to peruse the Sunday paper.

Koophandel Bloemgracht 49, Jordaan. Empty before midnight, this is the early-hours bar you dreamt about, in an old warehouse on one of Amsterdam's most picturesque canals. Open until at least 3am.

Lokaal 't Loosje Nieuwmarkt 32. Old-style "brown café" that's been here for 200 years.

Mulligans Amstel 100, near Rembrandtplein. Best Irish pub in the city, with superb traditional music.

Sound Garden Marnixstraat 164, Jordaan. Grunge bar, packed with people and noise, with a canalside terrace to retreat to.

De Tuin 2e Tuindwarsstraat 13. The Jordaan has some marvellously unpretentious bars, and this is one of the best. Agreeably unkempt.

De Twee Zwaantjes Prinsengracht 114. Tiny oddball Jordaan bar where locals sing along raucously to accordion music – you'll either love it or hate it.

Smoking coffeeshops

Dampkring (de) Handboogstraat 29. One of the best koffiehuises in town with nice decor and a refined menu. Favoured by tourists and locals, it can get busy.

Dolphin's Kerkstraat 39. Pleasant environment, with some decent music. Unusual as it serves alcohol. Good atmosphere, within easy reach of the Leidseplein.

El Guappo Nieuwe Nieuwstraat 31. Highly recommended, where staff from other coffeeshops unwind.

Global Chillage Kerkstraat 51. Celebrated slice of tie-dyed dope culture, with friendly staff.

Grasshopper Oudebrugsteeg 16 and other

outlets. One of the more welcoming large coffeeshops.

Greenhouse Effect Warmoesstraat 53. Better-than-average red-light district coffeeshop.

Paradox 1e Bloemdwarsstraat 2, Jordaan. Satisfies the munchies with outstanding natural food, including spectacular fresh-fruit concoctions. Closes 7pm.

Route 66 Warmoesstraat 77. A relaxing venue after a tour of the red light district. Has pool table

and snacks. The branch at Haringpakkerssteeg 8 has Internet facilities.

Siberië Brouwersgracht 11. Relaxed, long-standing place that's worth a visit whether you want to smoke or not. Has art exhibitions as well as an Internet facility.

The Bulldog Leidseplein 15 and a couple of other outlets. One of the oldest and biggest coffeehouses. It also can be the noisiest – not the place for a thoughtful smoke.

Nightlife

Amsterdam is a gathering spot for fringe performances, and buzzes with places offering a wide and inventive range of **entertainment**. Drinks prices are normally fifty percent or so more than what you pay in a bar, but entry prices are low and there's rarely any kind of door policy. Most places open around 10pm and close around 4am or slightly later. For more highbrow entertainment, the Concertgebouw assures Amsterdam a high ranking in the **classical music** stakes. The best source of information is the **Uitburo**, or **AUB**, in the Stadsschouwburg theatre on the corner of Marnixstraat and Leidseplein (daily 10am–6pm, Thurs until 9pm; ✆020/621 1211 or 0900/0191). Saturday's *Het Parool* newspaper has good **listings**.

Rock, jazz and world music venues

Akhnaton Nieuwzijds Kolk 25. A "Centre for World Culture", specializing in African and Latin American music and dance parties.

Alto Korte Leidsedwarsstraat 115, near Leidseplein. Legendary jazz café/bar, with free live music every night 9.30pm–3am. Big on atmosphere, not space. Bands are of a good standard too.

Arena 's-Gravesandestraat 51, near Oosterpark. Multimedia centre featuring live music every weekend, cultural events, a bar, coffeeshop and restaurant.

Bimhuis Oude Schans 73–77. Premier jazz venue. Big name concerts Thurs–Sat. Free workshop sessions Tues.

Casablanca Zeedijk 26. Live jazz every night.

Melkweg Lijnbaansgracht 234a, near Leidseplein. Amsterdam's most famous entertainment venue, with a young hip clientele. €7–17, plus €2.50 membership on the door. Closed Mon.

Paradiso Weteringschans 6–8, near Leidseplein. Set in a lovely old church, this well-known haunt of musos features both biggish names and up-and-coming bands.

Winston Kingdom Warmoesstraat 127. Small renovated venue with spoken word, jazz-poetry, R&B and punk/noise nights.

Clubs

Club Arena s'-Gravesandestraat 51. Large and spacious club, with a mixture of music from the 70s or 80s through to hip hop. Hotel guests (see listings) get a discount.

Club More Rozengracht 133, Amsterdam's finest dance club, with long queues.

Club Vision Olympisch Stadion 23. Relaxed club south of the city centre, playing noncommercial, futuristic house.

Dansen bij Jansen Handboogstraat 11, near Spui. Founded by students, and very popular; weekday discount with student ID.

Escape Rembrandtplein 11. Huge place packed at weekends, with several floors and top DJs. Wed–Sun only.

iT Amstelstraat 24, near Rembrandtplein. Large disco with popular and glamorous gay nights. Thurs & Sun are mixed gay/straight and attract a dressed-up, uninhibited crowd.

Mazzo Rozengracht 114, Jordaan. Perhaps the city's hippest and most laid-back club, with a choice of music to appeal to all tastes.

Multigroove Hemkade 48, in the nearby town of Zaandam. Famous for its illegal parties in the 1980s and 1990s, but now featuring the ultimate in hard house, techno and trance. No public transport.

Contemporary music, classical music and opera

Concertgebouw Concertgebouwplein 2–6 ☎020/
671 8345. One of the world's most dynamic
orchestras, playing in one of the finest halls, just
south of Museumplein.
Beurs van Berlage Damrak 213, city centre. The
splendid interior of the former stock exchange
hosts a wide selection of music from the Dutch
Philharmonic and Dutch Chamber Orchestras.

De IJsbreker Weesperzijde 23. Varied programme
of international modern, chamber and
experimental music €8–14. Also houses a
pleasant riverside café/bar. Tram #3/#6/#7/#10.
Muziektheater Amstel 3. Full opera programme.
Tickets sell quickly.
Stadsschouwburg Leidseplein 26. Somewhat
overshadowed by the Muziektheater, but still a
significant stage for opera and dance.

Film and theatre

Cinemas screen English-language movies, subtitled in Dutch, and rarely show for-
eign-language films without English subtitles. Amsterdam's cinemas excel in beautiful Art Deco interiors; watch alternative movies and big Hollywood offerings at the
lavish Tuschinski, Reguliersbreestraat 26, and check out the cult and classic flicks at
The Movies, Haarlemmerdijk 161, and Kriterion, Roeterstraat 12. The Film
Museum in Vondelpark shows all kinds of movies and has free open-air screenings
on summer weekends. For film listings get hold of a *Week Agenda* from any cinema.
The **theatre** company Toomler, Breitnerstraat 2, offers stand-up comedy in Dutch
and English, while Boom Chicago, Leidseplein 12, is a hugely popular rapid-fire
comedy troupe, performing nightly in English.

Gay Amsterdam

Amsterdam has one of the biggest and best-established **gay** scenes in Europe: attitudes are tolerant and facilities unequalled. The nationwide organization, COC,
Rozenstraat 14 (☎020/626 3087), can provide on-the-spot **information**, and has a
café and popular discos (men Fri, women Sat). For further advice contact the Gay
& Lesbian Switchboard (daily 10am–10pm; ☎020/623 6565, ⊛www.switch-
board.nl), the gay information point at Westermarkt (closed Oct–March) or look at
⊛www. gayamsterdam.com. For books, **Vrolijk**, Paleisstraat 135, bills itself as "the
largest gay and lesbian bookstore on the continent".

Gay Hotels

Golden Bear Kerkstraat 37 ☎020/ 624 4785.
Rooms are clean and spacious in this hotel located
not far from the busy Leidesplein, where trams #1
and #5 pass. ❺
ITC Hotel Prinsengracht 1051 ☎020/ 632 0230.
Friendly hotel in lovely old house, not far from
Rembrandtsplein and main gay areas. Tram #4 to
Prinsengracht. ❺
Liliane's Home Sarphatistraat 119. A women-only
hotel. ❺

Gay cafés and bars

Amstel Taveerne Amstel 54. Perhaps the best

established bar, at its most vivacious in summer
when the guys spill out onto the street.
April Reguliersdwarsstraat 37. Large and trendy,
with newspapers, coffee and cakes as well as
booze.
Camp Café Kerkstraat 45. Pleasant and clean
environment, with tasty dishes on offer.
Gaiety Amstel 14. Popular meeting place for gays,
with a predominantly young crowd.
Saarein Elandsstraat 119. Once the best-known
women-only/lesbian café, but now open to both
sexes.
De Steeg Halvemaansteeg 10. This is a tiny and
longtime favourite venue.

Listings

Bike tours Yellow Bike, Nieuwezijds Kolk 29
☎020 620 6940, ⊛www.yellowbike.nl
(€17/person).
Bike rental Cheapest from main train stations.
Also try: Bike City, Bloemgracht 70 ☎020/626
3721; Damstraat, just off Damstraat ☎020/625

5029; or MacBike, Mr Visserplein 2 ☎020/620
0985 and Marnixstraat 220 ☎020/626 6964. All
charge around €4.50 a day plus €100 deposit
with ID.
Embassies and consulates Note that most of
the following are in The Hague, not Amsterdam.

Australia, Carnegielaan 4, The Hague ☎070/310
8200; Canada, Sophialaan 7, The Hague
☎070/311 1600; Ireland, Dr Kuyperstraat 9, The
Hague ☎070/363 0993; New Zealand,
Carnegielaan 10, The Hague ☎070/346 9324; UK,
Koningslaan 44, Amsterdam ☎020/676 4343; US,
Museumplein 19, Amsterdam ☎020/664 5661.
Exchange GWK, Centraal Station and Leidseplein.
Change Express, Leidsestraat 105, Damrak 17 and

86, and Kalverstraat 150.
Hospital De Boelelaan 1117 ☎ 020/444 444.
Internet easyEverything, Reguliersbreestraat 22;
De Waag, Nieuwmarkt 4.
Laundry The Clean Brothers, Kerkstraat 56.
Left luggage Centraal Station.
Police Elandsgracht 117 ☎020/559 9111.
Post office Singel 250–256.

The Randstad towns

The string of towns known as the **Randstad**, or "rim town", situated amid a typically Dutch landscape of flat fields cut by canals, form the country's most populated
region and recall the seventeenth-century heyday of the provinces. Much of the
area is easily visited as day-trips from Amsterdam, but it's easy and more rewarding
to make a proper tour. **Haarlem** is definitely worth an overnight stop, while to the
south, the university centre of **Leiden** makes a pleasant detour before you reach
the refined tranquillity of **The Hague** and the busy urban centre of **Rotterdam**.
Nearby **Delft** and **Gouda** repay visits too, the former with one of the best-preserved centres in the region.

Haarlem

Just over fifteen minutes from Amsterdam by train, **HAARLEM** is an easily
absorbed city of around 150,000 people that sees itself as a cut above its neighbours
and makes a good alternative base for exploring North Holland, or even
Amsterdam itself.

The core of the city is **Grote Markt** and the adjoining Riviervischmarkt, flanked
by the gabled, originally fourteenth-century **Stadhuis** and the impressive bulk of
the **Grote Kerk of St Bavo** (Mon–Sat 10am–4pm; €1.30). Inside, the mighty
Christian Müller organ of 1738 is said to have been played by Handel and Mozart.
The town's main attraction is the **Frans Hals Museum**, Groot Heiligland 62
(Mon–Sat 11am–5pm, Sun noon–5pm; €4.50), a five-minute stroll from Grote
Markt in the Oudemannhuis almshouse. It houses a number of his lifelike seventeenth-century portraits, including the "Civic Guard" portraits which established
his reputation.

Back at the Grote Markt, take a look at the Frans Hals Museum's annexe, **De
Hallen** (Mon–Sat 11am–5pm, Sun noon–5pm; €3.40), an old meat-market building now filled with touring exhibitions and works by Haarlem-based Kees Verwey.

Practicalities

Haarlem **train station**, connected to Amsterdam and to Leiden by four trains an
hour, is on the north side of the city, about ten minutes' walk from the centre;
buses stop right outside.

The **VVV**, attached to the station (Mon–Fri 9.30am–5.30pm, Sat 10am–2pm;
☎0900/616 1600, ⊛www.vvvzk.nl), has maps and can book private rooms for a
small fee. Haarlem has a few reasonably priced and central **hotels**, including
Amadeus, Grote Markt 10 (☎023/ 532 4530; ❹), and *Carillon*, Grote Markt 27
(☎023/ 531 0591; ❺), both in the central square. *Charlie's*, Botermarkt 7 (❺), has
well appointed rooms, close to the centre, with breakfast at the café across the
square. *Die Raackse*, Raaks 1-3 (☎023/ 532 6629; ❺), has clean, en-suite rooms and
is close to the Grote Markt, as are *Joops Innercity Apartments*, Oude Groenmarkt 20
(☎023/ 532 2008; ❹). There's an **HI hostel** at Jan Gijzenpad 3 (☎023/537 3793;

❷; bus #2 from the station), and **campsites** among the dunes west of town, accessible on bus #81 from the station, including *Bloemendaal*, Zeeweg 72, in Bloemendaal-Aan-Zee (℡023/573 2178; closed Nov–March), and De Branding, Boulevard Barnaart 30, near Zandvoort (℡023/571 3035; closed Nov–March). Haarlem's own site, *De Liede*, is at Lieover 68 (℡023/533 2360; bus #2).

For **lunches**, *Café Mephisto*, Grote Markt 29, is open all day and serves Dutch food for €7–11, snacks for much less; try also *Café Brinkmann* on the same square. *Café de Karmeliet*, Spekstraat, is a lovely venue just beside the old church. *Café 1900*, Barteljorisstraat 10, is also a good place for lunch, serving drinks and snacks in a *fin-de-siècle* interior. In the evening, there's *Alfonso's* **restaurant**, Oude Groenmarkt 8, which does Tex-Mex meals for around €11; *Adagio*, Lange Veerstraat 17, which serves Italian meals for around €16; or the Indonesian *De Lachende Javaen* on Frankestraat, with *rijsttafels* from €18. *Ze Crack*, at the junction of Lange Veerstraat and Kleine Houtstraat, is a dim, smoky **bar** with good music and beer by the pint, or for a little traditional character, try the *proeflokaal* (a spirit-tasting room turned bar) *In den Uiver*, Riviervischmarkt 13.

Leiden and around

The charm of **LEIDEN** lies in the peace and prettiness of its gabled streets and canals, though the town's museums are varied and comprehensive enough to merit a visit in themselves. It's most appealing quarter is Rapenburg, a peaceful area of narrow pedestrian streets and canals that is home to the city's best-known attraction, the **Rijksmuseum Van Oudheden**, Rapenburg 28 (Tues–Fri 10am–5pm, Sat & Sun noon–5pm; €3.20), the country's principal archeological museum. Outside sits the first-century AD Temple of Teffeh while inside are more Egyptian artefacts, along with classical Greek and Roman sculpture and exhibits from prehistoric, Roman and medieval times. Across Rapenburg, a network of narrow streets converges on the **Pieterskerk** (daily 1.30–4pm; free). East of here, **Breestraat** marks the site of a vigorous **market** (Wed & Sat), which sprawls right over the sequence of bridges into Haarlemmerstraat, the town's major shopping street. Close by, the **Burcht** (daily 10/11am–11pm; free) is a shell of a fort, whose battlements you can clamber up for a view of Leiden. The nearby **Hooglandsekerk** (mid-May to mid-Sept Mon 1–3.30pm, Tues–Sat 11am–3.30/4pm; free) is a light, lofty church. Five minutes' walk away, Leiden's municipal museum, **Lakenhal**, Oude Singel 28–32 (Tues–Fri 10am–5pm, Sat & Sun noon–5pm; €3.60), has mixed rooms of furniture, tiles, glass and ceramics and a collection of paintings by Rembrandt and others. Around the corner on Molenwerf, the **Molenmuseum de Valk**, 2e Binnenvestgracht 1 (Tues–Sat 10am–5pm, Sun 1–5pm; €2.30), displays the history of windmills.

Practicalities

Leiden's **train** and **bus stations** are no more than ten minutes' walk from the centre. The **VVV**, a short walk from the stations at Stationsweg 2d (Mon–Fri 10am–6.30pm, Sat 10am–2pm; ℡0900/222 2333, ✆www.leiden.nl), can book private rooms (**❸**). The cheapest central **accommodation** is *The Rose*, Beestenmarkt 14 (℡071/514 6630; **❺**); fifteen minutes' walk out of the centre there's *Pension Witte Singel*, Singel 80 (℡071/512 4592; **❹**); and ten minutes from the stations, there's *Pension Schaefer*, Herensingel 1a (℡071/521 8104; **❸**). The closest **campsite** is *Koningshof* (℡071/402 6051), 6km north of Leiden (bus #40). For **lunch**, *M'n Broer*, by the Pieterskerk at Kloksteeg 7, has a reasonable Dutch menu, while *Barrera*, on Rapenburg, has good sandwiches. In the evening, *De Brasserie*, Lange Mare 38, has Dutch food; *Splinter* is a pleasant, reasonably priced vegetarian restaurant at Noordeinde 30; and the studenty *La Bota*, Herensteeg 11, by the Pieterskerk, has great-value food and beers. The Central Library, Nieuwstraat 4, has **Internet** access.

The bulbfields

Along with Haarlem to the north, Leiden and Delft are the best bases for seeing the Dutch **bulbfields** which flourish here in spring. The view from the train can be sufficient in itself as the line cuts directly through the main growing areas, the fields divided into stark geometric blocks of pure colour. Should you want to get closer, make a bee-line for **Lisse**, home to the **Keukenhof Gardens** (late-March to late-May daily 8am–7.30pm; €9; ⓦwww.keukenhof.nl), the largest flower gardens in the world. Some six million blooms are on show for their full flowering period, complemented by 5000 square metres of greenhouses. Special buses (#54) run daily to the Keukenhof from Leiden bus station twice an hour. You can also see the industry in action in **AALSMEER**, 23km north of Leiden, whose **flower auction**, held daily in a building the size of 125 football pitches (Mon–Fri 7.30–11am; €4.50; ⓦwww.vba.nl), trades roughly €1.5 billion of plants and flowers a year.

The Hague

With its urbane atmosphere, **THE HAGUE (Den Haag)** is different from any other Dutch city. Since the sixteenth century it's been the Netherlands' political capital though its older buildings are a rather subdued collection with little of Amsterdam's flamboyance. Diplomats and multinational businesses ensure that many of the city's hotels and restaurants are in the expense-account category, and the nightlife is similarly packaged. But, away from this, The Hague does have cheaper and livelier bars and restaurants, as well as some excellent museums.

Right in the centre, the **Binnenhof** is the home of the Dutch parliament with roots in the thirteenth century castle. The present complex is a rather mundane affair, the small **Hof Vijver** lake mirroring the symmetry of the facade; inside there's little to see except the **Ridderzaal**, a slender-turreted structure that can be viewed on regular guided tours from the information office at Binnenhof 8a (Mon–Sat 10am–3.45pm; €3.40). Immediately east, the **Royal Picture Gallery Mauritshuis**, Korte Vijverberg 8 (Tues–Sat 10am–5pm, Sun 11am–5pm; €6.80; ⓦwww.mauritshuis.nl), located in a magnificent seventeenth-century mansion, is of more interest, famous for its extensive range of Flemish and Dutch paintings including work by Vermeer, Rubens, Bruegel the Elder and Van Dyck. Down the street at Buitenhof 35, the **Prince William V Gallery** (Tues–Sun 11am–4pm; €1.40, free with Mauritshuis ticket) has paintings by Rembrandt, Jordaens and Paulus Potter in a reconstructed eighteenth-century gallery. About fifteen minutes' walk from the Mauritshuis at Zeestraat 65, **Panorama Mesdag** has an astonishing 360-degree painting of seaside scenes from the 1880s, said to be the world's largest, (Mon–Sat 10am–5pm; €4).

North, the **Gemeentemuseum**, Stadhouderslaan 41 (Tues–Sun 11am–5pm; €6.80; bus #4 from Centraal Station), contains superb collections of musical instruments and Islamic ceramics, and an array of modern art tracing the development of Dutch painting, with the world's largest collection of Mondriaan paintings. Halfway between The Hague and Scheveningen is one of the city's best-known attractions, the moderately diverting **Madurodam Miniature City** (daily 9am–6/8/10pm; €10; ⓦwww.madurodam.nl; tram #1/ #9), a scale model of a Dutch town.

Practicalities

The city has two **train stations** – "Den Haag HS" (short for Hollands Spoor) and, about 1km to the north, "Den Haag CS" (Centraal Station). Trains stop at one or the other and sometimes both; the latter is the more convenient, being next to the **VVV** (Mon–Sat 9am–5.30pm, July & Aug also Sun 10am–2pm; ☎0900/340 3505, ⓦwww.denhaag.com). **Accommodation** can be quite expensive. The VVV has a small stock of private rooms, or there's a cluster of seedy but reasonably priced hotels just outside Den Haag HS station: the cheapest is *Aristo*, Stationsweg 164–166 (☎070/389 0847; ❸), although you get a far better deal 4km north of the

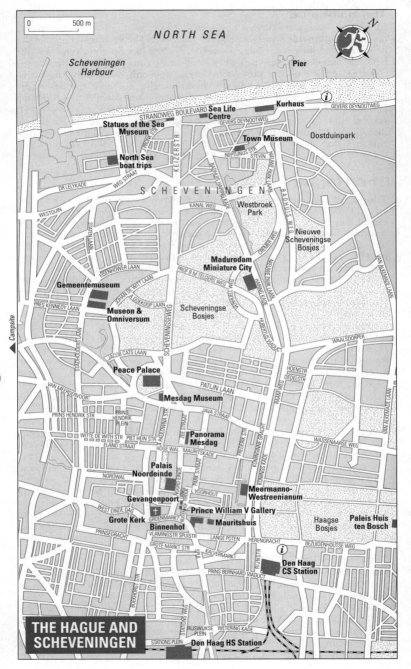

THE HAGUE AND SCHEVENINGEN

centre at the busy and developed beach resort of **Scheveningen**, where hotels are more plentiful and a little cheaper; it's a short ride on tram #1/#7/#9 from Den Haag CS, or tram #8/#11 from Den Haag HS. In Scheveningen, try *Bali*, Badhuisweg 1 (℡070/350 2434; ❺), or one of the group on the seafront road Zeekant that includes the comfortable *Aquarius*, Zeekant 107 (℡070/354 3543; ❻). There are three **hostels** in Scheveningen: *Scheveningen*, Gevers Deynootweg 2 (℡070/354 7003; ❸); *Marion*, Havenkade 3a (℡070/350 5050; ❸); and pleasant *HI City Hostel*, Scheepmakerstraat 27 (℡070/315 7878, ⓦwww.njhc/denhaag; ❸). The best **campsite** is *Kijkduinpark*, Machiel Vrijenhoeklaan 450 (℡070/448 2271), just behind the quiet beach at Kijkduin (bus #4 from CS or bus #26 from HS).

There are plenty of cheap places to **eat** around the town centre: *Greve*, Torenstraat 138, north of Grote Kerk, has snacks and full meals; *Pinelli*, Dagelikse Groenmarkt 31, serves pizzas; while Indonesian snacks are served at *Brasserie Surakarta*, Prinsestraat 13. There are several options on the streets around Denneweg and Frederikstraat, just north of Lange Voorhout, amongst them the popular vegetarian *De Dageraad*, Hooikade 4. *La Mano Maestra*, Noordelnde 138b, is a classy café, serving a wide range of coffees. In Scheveningen, the Haven harbour has some excellent places to eat fresh fish by the waterside: try the inexpensive *Bistro aan de Haven*, Lelykade 15, or the more upmarket *Ducdalf*, Lelykade 5. For **drinking**, aim for the studenty bar *Zwarte Ruiter* in the busy square south of The Hague's Grote Kerk. For **Internet** access try Internetcafé, Elandstraat 48 (℡070/363 6286).

Delft

DELFT, 2km inland from The Hague, has considerable charm, with its gabled red-roofed houses standing beside tree-lined canals. The pastel colours of the pavements, brickwork and bridges give the town a faded tranquillity – though one that can suffer beneath the tourist onslaught during summer. A good starting point is to follow the Historic Walk around the old town with a map from the VVV. The town is perhaps best known for **Delftware**, the delicate blue and white ceramics to which the town gave its name in the seventeenth century. **De Porceleyne Fles**, Rotterdamseweg 196, a factory producing Delftware, is open for visits (Mon–Sat 9am–5pm, April–Oct also Sun 9.30am–5pm; €2.30), and the **Huis Lambert van Meerten Museum**, Oude Delft 199 (Tues–Sat 10am–5pm, Sun 1–5pm; €2.30; ⓦwww.royaldelft.com), has a large collection of Delft and other tiles.

Markt is also a useful place to start exploring, with the **Oude Kerk** at one end and the Renaissance **Stadhuis** opposite. William the Silent is buried in this fine old church and you can climb the 370 steps of the tower for spectacular views of the countryside. South of here, **Wynhaven**, another old canal, leads to Hippolytusbuurt and the Gothic **Nieuwe Kerk** (same hours as Oude Kerk; €1.80), arguably the town's finest building, with an unhealthily leaning tower. The nearby **Prinsenhof,** William the Silent's base for his revolt against the Spanish and also where he was assassinated, has some decent collections of early Dutch art.

From the train station, aim for the big steeple you see on exit and it's a short walk into town to the **VVV** at Markt 83–85 (Mon–Fri 9am–5.30pm, Sat 9am–5pm; mid-April to Sept also Sun 10am–3pm; ℡015/212 6100, ⓦwww.vvvdelft.nl), which can find you the best **accommodation** deals in the centre. The town has some delightful family B&Bs: warmly recommended is *Oosteinde*, at Oosteinde 156 (℡015/213 4238; ❺), which is friendly and welcoming, with lovely rooms. At the cheaper end, try *Hotel Restaurant Radethuys*, Markt 38–40 (℡015/212 5115; ❸), or *Hotel Les Compagnons*, Markt 61–65 (℡015/215 8255; ❸). The campsite, *Delftse Hout*, is at Kortftlaan 5 (℡015/213 0040; bus #64 from station); of the two sites, the little one is best and cheapest. The least expensive **eating** is at a number of student mensas (term-time only) such as *De Koornbeurs* near the main square and *Jansbrug*, Kornmarkt 50–52; *Ladera* on Oosteinde also has good value food. *Kobus Koch* is a gem of a café/restaurant on the Beestenmarkt, 1; sampling the tasty *appeltart met* *slagboom* (apple pie with cream) is a must. *Willem Van Oranje*, centrally located on Markt, has pancakes, *uitsmijters* (ham or cheese with eggs), light meals for around €4.50 and three-course menus for €9. *Locus Publicus*, Brabantse Turfmarkt 67, is a popular local bar, serving a staggering array of beers as well as sandwiches. Further nightlife is provided by the nearby club *Speakers* which often features live music and a jazz bar, *The Piano Bar*. The library, Kruisstraat 71 (℡015/212 3450), has **internet** access.

Rotterdam

Just beyond Delft lies **ROTTERDAM**, at the heart of a maze of rivers and artificial waterways which form the outlet of the rivers Rhine (Rijn in Dutch) and Maas. An important port as far back as the fourteenth century, it was one of the major cities of the Dutch Republic, and is now the largest port in the world. The Luftwaffe bombed the town centre to pieces in 1940, and rebuilding has produced a modernistic assembly of concrete and glass. However, the city has its moments, not least in one of the best and most overlooked galleries in the country.

A nice feel for the city can be had by walking from the station (or taking #5 tram from just outside) down to the **Museumpark,** with its three museums. The **Boymans–Van Beuningen Museum**, Mathenesserlaan 18–20 (Tues–Sat 10am–5pm, Sun 11am–5pm; €6; ⓦwww.boijmans.rotterdam.nl), is an enormous museum, with a superb collection. The first floor contains work by Monet, Van Gogh, Picasso, Gauguin and Cézanne, while among the earlier canvases are several by Bosch, Bruegel the Elder and Rembrandt. A walk through the Museumpark brings you to the **Natuurmuseum** and the **Kunsthal** (both Tues–Sat 10am–5pm, Sun 11am–5pm; €6.50)**,** which houses contemporary art. Nearby the 185m-high **Spacetower** (daily: April–Sept 10am–5/10.30pm; €7) gives spectacular views.

Water taxis leave the Veerhaven and the Leuvehaven for the splendid *Hotel New York*, occupying the building where transatlantic cruise liners once docked. From here you can walk back to the centre over the futuristic bridge, the Erasmusbrug, an ideal spot for photos. Ten minutes' walk away is the **Maritime Museum** (Tues–Fri 10am–5pm, Sat & Sun 11am–5pm; €2.70) at the Leuvehaven. Close by is the seventeenth-century mansion at Korte Hoogstraat 31 that houses the **Schielandshuis Museum** (Tues–Fri 10am–5pm, Sat & Sun 11am–5pm; €2.70), with displays on the city's history. Another short walk away is the Oude Haven, where the curious **Kijkkubus** or cube houses can be seen. The picturesque **Delfshaven** is a good 45-minute walk southwest of Centraal Station – fifteen minutes by tram #6 or #9. Here, the **Dubbelde Palmboom Museum**, Voorhaven 12 (Tues–Fri 10am–5pm, Sat & Sun 11am–5pm; €2.70), displays the history of life in the Maas delta.

Practicalities

Rotterdam's large centre is bordered by its main rail terminal, **Centraal Station**, also the hub of a useful **tram** and **metro** system, though best avoided late at night. The main **VVV** office is a ten-minute walk away at Coolsingel 67 (Mon–Thurs 9.30am–6pm, Fri 9.30am–9pm, Sat 9.30am–5pm; April–Sept also Sun noon–5pm; ℡0900/403 4065, ⓦwww.vvv.rotterdam.nl), where you can pick up a comprehensive city brochure (€1.80). There are plenty of central, reasonably priced **hotels**. Southwest of the station is *Wilgenhof*, Heemraadssingel 92–94 (℡010/425 4892; ❺; tram #1/#7 or bus #38/#45). Immediately north of the station, *Bienvenue*, Spoorsingel 24 (℡010/466 9394; ❸), is excellent value. A five-minute walk from Wilhelminaplein metro, on the south bank of the Nieuwe Maas, is the *New York*, Koninginnenhoofd 1 (℡010/439 0500; ❸), with a great atmosphere and excellent restaurant. The **HI hostel**, *City Hostel Rotterdam*, is a 25-minute walk from the station, Rochussenstraat 107 (℡010/436 5763; ❷; tram #4). The nearest **campsite**, *Stadscamping* (℡010/415 3440), is north of the station at Kanaalweg 84 (bus #33).

The cheapest sit-down **meal** in town is at *Eetcafé Streetlife*, Jonker Franslaan 237; *De Eend*, Mauritsweg 29 (Mon–Fri 4.30–7.30pm), is also inexpensive. Oude and Nieuwe Binnenweg support a number of good *eetcafés*, including *Rotown*, Nieuwe Binnenweg 19. *De Consul*, Westersingel 28, serves a variety of dishes at reasonable prices, and vegetarians should head for *Eetcafé BlaBla*, Piet Heynstraat 35, in Delfshaven or the *Laughing Pig* in Kalingen. Rotterdam has a lively **nightlife** scene with *Grand Café Dudok*, off Beursplein on Meent, a good place to **drink**. For clubbing, the trendy *Now and Wow* at Sint Jobshaven plays house music, as does *Statts* on Westblaak. The *Waterfront* (Boompjeskade 10) plays a mixture including salsa, and *Jazzcafe Dizzy*, 's-Gravendijkwal 127, has regular live music.

From the **Leuvehaven** harbour, there are numerous **boat trips** through the harbour (year-round; 1hr 15min; €7.50), along the river delta (July & Aug; 2hr 15min; €12) and day-trips south to the Deltawerken (July & Aug; 7hr; €35; reserve in advance); contact Spido for details (☎010/275 9988, ⊛www.spido.nl).

Gouda

A pretty little place some 25km northeast of Rotterdam, **GOUDA** is almost everything you'd expect of a Dutch country town: a ring of quiet canals encircling ancient buildings and old quays. Its **Markt** is the largest in Holland, a reminder of the town's prominence as a centre of the medieval cloth trade, and later of the manufacture of cheeses and clay pipes. A touristy **cheese market** is held here every Thursday morning (10am–12.30pm) in June, July and August. Slap bang in the middle, the elegant Gothic **Stadhuis** dates from 1450; on the north side is the **Waag**, a tidy seventeenth-century building; the top two floors display cheesy matters (April–Oct Tues–Sun 1–5pm, Thurs 10am–5pm; €1.40). South, off the square, **St Janskerk** (April–Oct Mon–Sat 9am–5pm; Nov–March Mon–Sat 10am–4pm; €1.60) was built in the sixteenth century and is famous for its stained-glass windows.

Gouda's **train** and **bus stations** are north of the centre, ten minutes from the **VVV**, Markt 27 (Mon–Sat 9am–5pm; June–Aug also Sun noon–3pm; ☎0182/513666, ⊛www.vvv.groenehart.nl), which offers a limited supply of private rooms. The most reasonably priced **hotel** is *De Utrechtsche Dom*, fifteen minutes' walk from the train station at Geuzenstraat 6 (☎0182/528 833, ⊛www.rsnet.nl/hotel; ❸); otherwise, try *H't Trefpunt*, Westhaven 46 (☎0182/512879; ❹), or *De Keizerskroon*, Keizerstraat 11 (☎0182/528 096; ❺). For **food**, there are plenty of cafés catering to the swarms of summer day-trippers. You can eat cheaply at *'t Groot Stedelijk*, Markt 44, among other places; *'t Goudse Winkeltje*, Achter de Kerk 9a, has good pancakes; and you can get a decent Indonesian at *Warung Srikandi*, Lange Groenendaal 108. For a **drink**, find your way to the excellent *Eetcafé Vidocq*, Koster Gijzenstraat 8, or check out *Heeren Van Goude* on Zeugstraat.

Utrecht

"I groaned with the idea of living all winter in so shocking a place", wrote Boswell in 1763, and **UTRECHT**, surrounded by shopping centres and industrial developments, still promises little as you approach. But the centre, with its distinctive sunken canals – whose brick cellar warehouses have been converted into chic cafés and restaurants – is one of the country's most pleasant.

The focal point is the **Dom Tower**, built between 1321 and 1382, which at over 110m is the highest church tower in the country, soaring to a delicate octagonal lantern. A guided tour (Mon–Sat 10am–5pm, Sun noon–5pm; last entry 4pm; €3.40) takes you unnervingly close to the top, from where the gap between the tower and the Gothic **Dom Kerk** is most apparent. Only the eastern part of the cathedral remains today after the nave collapsed in 1674, but it's worth peering inside (Mon–Fri 10/11am–4/5pm, Sat 10am–3.30pm, Sun 2–4pm; free) and wandering through the Kloostergang, the fourteenth-century cloisters that link the cathedral to the chapterhouse. South of the church at Nieuwe Gracht 63, the national collection of ecclesiastical art, the **Catharijne Convent Museum** (Tues–Fri 10am–5pm, Sat & Sun 11am–5pm; €4.50; ⊛www.catharijneconvent.nl), has wonderful paintings, manuscripts and church ornaments from the ninth century on.

Train and **bus stations** both lead into the Hoog Catharijne shopping centre. The main **VVV** office is at Vredenburg 90 (Mon–Fri 9am–6pm, Sat 9am–5pm; ☎0900/414 1414, ⊛www.tref.nl/utrecht/vvv), a five-minute walk away. For **hotels**, try *Ouwi*, FC Donderstraat 12 (☎030/271 6303, ⊛www.bookings.nl; ❹), a fifteen-minute walk northeast of the centre; or *Parkhotel*, Tolsteegsingel 34 (☎030/251 6712; ❸), a similar distance southeast of the station. There's a nice **HI hostel**, *Ridderhofstad "Rhijnauwen"*, in an old country manor house 6km out at Rhijnauwenselaan 14, in Bunnik (☎030/656 1277; ❷; bus #40/#41 from the station). The pleasant *Strowis* hostel, Boothstraat 8 (☎030/238 0280, ⊛www.strowis.nl; ❹), is a more central option, a fifteen-minute walk from Centraal Station or a short ride on bus #3/#4/#8/#11 to the Janskerkhof stop, plus a two-minute walk. The well-equipped **campsite**, *De Berenkuil*, Ariënslaan 5 (☎030/271 3870), is served by bus #57. **Restaurants** are mainly situated along Oudegracht and the Lijnmarkt; the best is the moderately priced *Stadskasteel Oudaen* at no. 99, the oldest house in town, which serves beer from its own brewery downstairs. Also good is *Milky*, a vegetarian restaurant off the canal, Zakkerdragssteeg 22. A really cheap option is to go for a *dagschotel* at *Eetcafé De Baas*, Lijnmarkt 8, and there's the grand café *Stairway to Heaven*, Mariaplaats 11, with moderately priced meals and regular live music. The city's best **bars** cluster around the junction of Oude Gracht and the Lijnmarkt. The Central Library has **Internet** access.

Beyond the Randstad

Outside the Randstad towns, the Netherlands is relatively unknown territory to visitors. To the north, there's superb cycling and hiking to be had through scenic **dune reserves** and delightful villages, with easy access to pristine beaches. The island of **Texel** has the country's most complete beach experience, with plenty of birdlife. In the northeast, the main draw is **Groningen**, a lively, cosmopolitan town with a buzzing nightlife and a museum and art gallery. To the south, the countryside grows steadily more rolling as you head towards Germany. The **Hoge Veluwe National Park**, near Arnhem, boasts one of the country's best modern art museums and has cycle paths through a delightful landscape. Further south, in the provinces of North Brabant and Limburg, the landscape slowly fills out, rolling into a rougher countryside of farmland and forests and eventually into the hills around **Maastricht**, a city with a vibrant, pan-European air.

The island of Texel

The largest of the islands of the Waddenzee framing the north coast of the country – and the easiest to get to (2hr from Amsterdam) – **TEXEL** (*Tessel*) is a diverse and pretty island, and one of Europe's most important bird breeding-grounds. **Ferries** from Den Helder on the mainland depart every hour (around €4.50; coming from Amsterdam, ask for an all-in discounted "Waddenbiljet"). On the coast 3km southeast of Den Burg is **Oudeschild**, home to the **Beachcombers' Museum** (Juttersmuseum; Tues–Sat 10am–5pm; €3.60), a fascinating collection of marine junk from wrecks, while in the opposite direction is **De Koog**, with a good sandy beach and the **EcoMare** nature centre, Ruyslaan 92 (daily 9am–5pm; €5.70), highlight of which is a refuge for lost birds and seals (feeding at 11am & 3pm); they also organize excursions to the Wad, the banks of sand and mud to the east of the island, a gathering-place for seals.

Den Burg's **VVV** is at Emmalaan 66 (Mon–Fri 9am–6pm, Sat 9am–5pm; ☎0222/314741). The cheapest **hotel** is in Den Burg: *'t Koogerend*, Kogerstraat 94

(☎0222/313301; ❷), while there's a **hostel**, *Panorama*, at Schanseweg 7 (☎0222/315441; ❷). **Campers** are spoilt for choice: close to Den Burg is the small, well-run *De Koorn Aar*, Grensweg 388 (☎0222/312931; closed Nov–March); among the beachside dunes in De Koog is *Kogerstrand*, Badweg 33 (☎0222/317208; closed Nov–March); *Euroase Texel*, Bosrandweg 395 (☎0222/317290) also has bungalows on the beach; and there's *De Krim*, Roggeslootweg 6, in De Cocksdorp (☎0222/390111). The best **food** in Den Burg is *De Worsteltent*, Smitweg 6. In De Koog there are plenty of Mexican and Chinese restaurants, with *Het Pruttelhuus*, Dorpsstraat 170, a friendly local option, as well as *Café Sam-Sam* and *De Metro*, both on Dorpsstraat, for **drinking**.

Groningen

Heavily bombed in World War II, the northern city of **GRONINGEN** is an architectural jumble with few notable sights, but its large, prestigious university gives it a cosmopolitan feel quite unexpected in this rustic part of the country. The centre of town is the uninspired **Grote Markt**. At one corner is the **Martinikerk** (Easter–Nov Tues–Sat noon–5pm; €1.10); though the oldest parts of the church go back to 1180, most of it is mid-fifteenth-century Gothic. The vault paintings in the nave are beautifully restored. The city's biggest and best museum, the **Groninger Museum** (Tues–Sun 10am–5pm; €6.10; ☮www.groninger-museum.nl), is housed in spectacular pavilions across from the train station. The west pavilion is given over to travelling exhibitions but also houses the permanent art collection, including Rubens, Hague school paintings, and a number of late works by the Expressionists.

Practicalities

Groningen's **bus** and **train stations** are on the south side of town, fifteen minutes' walk from the **VVV** at Ged Kattendiep 6 (Mon–Fri 9am–5.30pm, Sat 10am–5pm; ☎0900/202 3050, ☮www.groningen.nl); they'll give you a short list of private rooms, though few are near the city centre. Otherwise, the cheapest **accommodation** is in the dorms of *Simplon Jongerenhotel*, north of the centre at Boterdiep 73 (☎050/313 5221, ☮www.xs4all.nl/~simplon; ❷). Three reasonably priced **hotels** are just south of the Grote Markt: *Friesland*, Kleine Pelsterstraat 4 (☎050/312 1307; ❸); *Garni Groningen*, Damsterdiep 94 (☎050/313 5435; ❹); and the likeable old *Weeva*, Gedempte Zuiderdiep 8 (☎050/312 9919; ❺), with a decent restaurant. Bus #4 from the train station runs via Peizerweg on a ten-minute ride to the **campsite** *Stadspark* (☎050/525 1624; closed mid-Oct to mid-March).

For Groningen's cheapest **food**, head for *Roezemoes*, Gedempte Zuiderdiep 15. Best of the rest are concentrated around Poelestraat: *Bistango*, at no. 14, is a decent Tex-Mex with veggie specialities; the pizzeria *Costa Smeralda* next door is slightly cheaper; *'t Pakhuis*, Peperstraat 8, has good Dutch snacks and a lively **bar** in an atmospheric building. On the south side of Grote Markt is a flank of outdoor **cafés**, best of which are the old-style brown café *Der Witz*, no. 47, and *Hooghoudt*, no. 42, which serves food until 4am at weekends. *De Smederij*, at Tuinstraat 2, is an *eetcafé* with a great atmosphere; in the opposite direction at Akerstraat 24, you'll find high-quality, moderately priced fish and vegetarian food in *Brussels Lof*.

Thanks to its large student population, Groningen has good **nightlife**. For **live music** try *Vera*, in the basement at Oosterstraat 44; or *Troubadour*, Peperstraat 19. *De Spieghel*, Peperstraat 11, has live jazz most nights. Good **clubs** include *Index*, Poelestraat 53, and *Palace*, Gelkingestraat 1, which occasionally hosts live bands. There's an **Internet** café at Turfsingel 94.

Hoge Veluwe National Park

Some 70km southeast of Amsterdam, and just north of of the town of Arnhem, is the huge and scenic **Hoge Veluwe National Park** (daily: April–Aug 8am–8/10pm; rest of year 9am–5.30/7pm; ☮www.hogeveluwe.nl; €5, or €10 combined ticket to the park and Kröller-Müller museum). Formerly the estate of wealthy local couple Anton and Helene Kröller-Müller, it has three entrances – one near the village of **Otterlo** on the northwest perimeter, another near **Hoenderloo** on the northeast edge, and a third to the south at **Rijzenburg**, near the village of Schaarsbergen.

The easiest way to get here is by **special bus** from Arnhem's train station (April–Oct Tues–Sun hourly; €4), which runs direct to the **Visitors' Centre** (daily 10am–5pm). The Centre is one of the five places from where you can pick up **white bicycles** which are available free to all visitors and which are by far the best way of exploring the park. Activities include walking **safaris** (€37, including lunch), rambles, birdwatching trips and photography courses. At the centre sits a terraced café/restaurant, *De Koperen Kop*. Also within the park is the **Museonder** (daily 10am–5pm), an underground natural history museum, and the **St Hubetus Hunting Lodge** (daily 10am–5pm), the former Art Deco home of the Kröller-Müllers, with free guided tours on offer. An unmissable sight is the **Kröller-Müller Museum** (Tues–Sun 10am–5pm; ⊛www.krollermuseum.nl; €10), a superb collection of fine art with paintings by Van Gogh, as well as Picasso, Seurat, Léger and Mondriaan. There's also a lovely **Sculptures Garden** (Tues–Sun 10am–4.30pm; same ticket as museum) behind the museum.

Trains run from Amsterdam to nearby **ARNHEM**, from where you can catch the special bus to the park. There's a VVV office nearby, at Willemsplein 8 (☎026/370 0226, ⊛www.vvvarnhem.nl), which can help you find **accommodation** in the area; note that there's an HI **hostel** at Diepenbrocklaan 27 (☎026/442 0114), just north of town towards the park (bus #3). To **stay in the park** itself, you can camp by the northeastern Hoenderloo entrance (☎055/378 2232; closed Dec–March).

Maastricht

Situated between Belgium and Germany, **MAASTRICHT** is one of the most delightful cities in the Netherlands. A cosmopolitan place, where three languages happily coexist, it's also one of the oldest towns in the country.

The busiest of Maastricht's many squares is **Markt**, at its most crowded during the Wednesday and Friday morning **market**. At the centre is the mid-seventeenth-century **Stadhuis** (Mon–Fri 8.30am–12.30pm & 2–5.30pm; free). Just west, **Vrijthof** is a grander open space flanked by a line of café terraces on one side and on the other by **St Servaaskerk** (daily 10am–5pm; €1.80), a tenth-century church. Next door is **St Janskerk** (Easter–Oct Mon–Sat 11am–4pm; free), with its high fifteenth-century Gothic **tower** (€1.10 donation). Maastricht's other main church, the **Onze Lieve Vrouwe Basiliek**, is a short walk south of Vrijthof, down Bredestraat, in a small shady square crammed with café tables.

On the other side of the square lies another of Maastricht's most appealing quarters, narrow streets winding out to the fast-flowing River Jeker and the **Helpoort** of 1229. Continuing south, the casemates in the **Waldeck Park** (guided tours: July & Aug daily 12.30pm & 2pm; rest of year Sun 2pm; €2.70) are further evidence of Maastricht's once impressive fortifications. Fifteen minutes' walk further south is the 110m hill of **St Pietersberg**. Of the ancient defensive tunnel systems under the hill, the **Zonneberg** is probably the better, situated on the far side of the hill at Casino Slavante (guided tours: July & Aug daily 2.15pm; €2.70). Just outside the city lies **Valkenburg,** which provides a base for walking the nearby hills and forests.

Practicalities

The centre of Maastricht is on the west bank of the river. You're likely to arrive, however, on the east bank, in the district known as Wijk, home to the **train** and **bus stations** and many of the city's hotels. The **airport** is north of the city at Beek, served by bus #61 to Markt and the train station (every 30min; takes 20min).

The **VVV** is in the centre at Kleine Straat 1, at the end of the main shopping street (Mon–Sat 9am–5/6pm, Sun 11am–3pm; Nov–April closed Sun; ☎043/325 2121, ⓦwww.visitmaastricht.nl); it has copies of *Uit In Maastricht* and a tourist guide with map and a list of private rooms. There are several good central **hotels**, including *La Cloche*, Bredestraat 41 (☎043/321 2407, ⓦwww.lacloche.com; ❺), and *Anno 1604*, Kattenstraat 11 (☎043/325 0165; ❸). Hotels conveniently located for the station and the city include the two-star *De Poshoorn*, Stationsstraat 47 (☎043/321 7334; ❺), and the one-star *Le Guide* at no. 17a (☎043/321 6176; ❹); the *Botel Maastricht* (☎043/321 9023; ❹) is moored on the river on Maasboulevard, not far from the Helpoort, and does an excellent breakfast. Low budget accommodation is also plentiful in Valkenburg. For **camping**, the large and well-equipped *De Dousberg* site (☎043/343 2171; closed Nov–March) is a ten-minute ride from the station on bus #11 (after 6.25pm, take bus #28 towards Pottenburg and ask the driver). The same bus also takes you to the **hostel** at Dousbergweg 4 (☎043/346 6777; ❷), which has access to open-air and indoor swimming pools.

Eating is never a problem in Maastricht. At the bottom end of the price scale, the street to head for is Koestraat where you'll find the excellent and cheap Indonesian *De Branding* at no. 5; the low-cost pizzeria *Alexandria* at no. 21; a good-value bakery around the corner; and the slightly upmarket *D'n Blind Genger*, no. 3, with a varied menu and nice atmosphere. Also nearby, down towards the river on Graanmarkt, *Caribbean Embassy* is an *eetcafé* with reasonably priced Caribbean specialities, and *Reitz*, Markt 75, is a Maastricht institution serving huge cones of thick Belgian-style *frites*. The **bars** on the east side of Vrijthof are packed in summer; *In den Ouden Vogelstruys*, on the corner of Platielstraat, is one of the nicest. Away from Vrijthof, *De Bóbbel*, on Wolfstraat just off Onze Lieve Vrouweplein, is a bareboards bar, lively in the early evening; *Falstaff*, on St Amorsplein, down Platielstraat from Vrijthof, is younger and noisier, with good music and a wide range of beers. For **live music** all year round try *D'n Awwe Stiene*, Kesselskade 43 (Wed, Fri & Sat 10pm–5am; €6–16). **Internet** access is at the *Centre Céramique*, five minutes from the station.

Travel details

Trains

Amsterdam to: Arnhem (for Hoge Veluwe National Park; every 30min; 1hr 10min); Groningen (every 30min; 2hr 20min); Haarlem (every 10min; 15min); The Hague (every 15min; 45min); Leiden (every 15min; 35min); Maastricht (hourly; 2hr 30min); Rotterdam (every 30min; 1hr 10min); Schiphol Airport (every 15min; 20min); Texel (via Den Helder; every 30min; 1hr 15min); Utrecht (every 30min; 30min).

Arnhem (for Hoge Veluwe National Park) to: Amsterdam (every 30min; 1hr 10min); Utrecht (every 10min; 35min).

Groningen to: Amsterdam (every 30min; 2hr 20min).

The Hague to: Delft (every 15min; 15min); Gouda (every 20min; 20min); Rotterdam (every 15min; 25min); Utrecht (every 20min; 40min).

Leiden to: Amsterdam (every 30min; 35min); The Hague (every 30min; 35min).

Maastricht to: Amsterdam (hourly; 2hr 30min).

Rotterdam to: Gouda (every 20min; 20min); Utrecht (every 20min; 45min).

Utrecht to: Arnhem (every 15min; 30min).

Norway

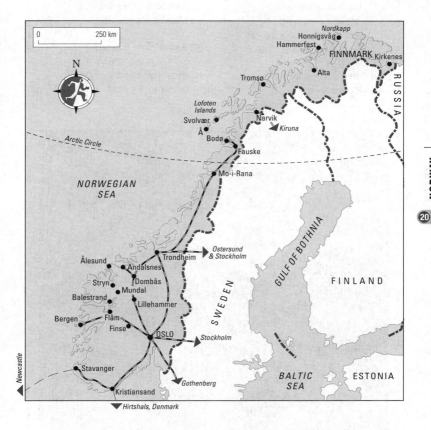

0   250 km

N

Nordkapp
Honnigsvåg
Hammerfest
FINNMARK Kirkenes

Tromsø

Alta

R U S S I A

Lofoten Islands
Svolvær
Å
Bodø

Narvik
Kiruna

Fauske

Arctic Circle

Mo-i-Rana

NORWEGIAN SEA

Ostersund & Stockholm

Ålesund
Trondheim
Andalsnes
Stryn Dombås
Balestrand Mundal
Bergen Flåm Lillehammer
Finse
OSLO *Stockholm*

S W E D E N

GULF OF BOTHNIA

FINLAND

Stavanger

Gothenberg

Newcastle

Kristiansand

Hirtshals, Denmark

BALTIC SEA   ESTONIA

NORWAY

20

Norway highlights

* **Viking Ships Museum, Oslo** A must on any tourist itinerary. See p.776

* **Vigeland Sculpture Park, Oslo** Scandinavia's finest – and most extraordinary – open-air sculpture. See p.776

* **Ferry across the Sognefjord** To Balestrand, for example, for the quintessential Norwegian experience. See p.783

* **The Jostedalsbreen glacier** Magnificent – hike to it or view it near Mundal See p.783

* **The Lofoten Islands** Some of the finest mountain scenery in the world. See p.788

Introduction and basics

In many ways **Norway** is still a land of unknowns. Comparatively quiet for a thousand years since the Vikings stamped their mark on Europe, the country nowadays often seems more than just geographically distant. Beyond Oslo and the famous fjords the rest of the country might as well be blank for all many visitors know – and, in a manner of speaking, large parts of it are. Vast stretches in the north and east are sparsely populated, and it is possible to travel for hours without seeing a soul.

Despite this isolation, Norway has had a pervasive influence. Traditionally its inhabitants were explorers, from the Vikings to more recent figures such as Amundsen, Nansen and Heyerdahl, while Norse language and traditions are common to many other isolated fishing communities, not least northwest Scotland and the Shetlands. At home, too, the Norwegian people have striven to escape the charge of national provincialism, touting the disproportionate number of acclaimed artists, writers and musicians (most notably Munch, Ibsen and Grieg) who have made their mark on the European scene. It's also a pleasing discovery that the great outdoors – great though it is – harbours some lively historical towns.

Beyond **Oslo**, one of the world's most prettily sited capitals, the major cities of interest are historic **Trondheim**, **Bergen**, on the edge of the fjords, and hilly, northern **Tromsø**. None is exactly super-charged, but they are likeable, imminently walkable cities, worth time for themselves as well as being good bases for exploring the startlingly handsome countryside. The perennial draw is, however, the **western fjords** – every bit as scenically stunning as they're cracked up to be. Dip into the region from Bergen or **Åndalsnes**, both accessible direct by train from Oslo, or take more time and appreciate the subtleties of the innumerable waterside towns and villages. Further north, the stunning **Lofoten Islands** are worth a trip for their calm atmosphere and sheer beauty. To the north of here, Norway grows increasingly barren, and the tourist trail focuses on the long journey to the North Cape, or **Nordkapp** – the northernmost accessible point of mainland Europe. The route leads through the province of **Finnmark**, a vast, eerily bleak wilderness where the Arctic tundra rolls as far as the eye can see, and one of the last strongholds of the Sami and their herds of reindeer.

Information and maps

Every town has a **tourist office**, usually with a stock of free maps, timetables and other bumph. Many book private rooms and hotel beds and some rent out bikes and change money. During the high season – late June to August – they normally open daily for long hours, while in the shoulder season they mostly adopt shop hours; many close down altogether in winter.

The best internationally available **map** of Norway is the *Hallwag International* 1:1,000,000, which comes complete with an index. If you're buying in Norway, the Statens Kartverk map is the best option; it also includes several city maps.

Norway on the net

ⓦ **www.visitnorway.no** Official Norwegian Tourist Board site

ⓦ **www.odin.dep.no/html/english** Norwegian government site with links to key information sources

ⓦ **www.museumnett.no** Comprehensive information on museums and current exhibitions

Money and banks

Norwegian currency is the **krone** (kr), which is divided into 100 **øre**. Coins in circulation are 50 øre, 1kr, 5kr, 10kr and 20kr; notes are for 50kr, 100kr, 200kr, 500kr and 1000kr. **Banking hours** are Mon–Fri 8.15am–3pm, till 5pm on Thurs; though many close half an hour earlier in summer. Most airports and some train stations have **exchange offices**, open evenings and weekends, and some tourist offices also change money, though at less favourable rates than the banks and post offices. Credit and debit cards are by far the easiest way of getting money: ATMs can be found in even the smaller towns.

Communications

Post office opening hours are usually Mon–Fri 8/8.30am–4pm, Sat 8/9am–1pm. **Stamps** are available from post offices, kiosks and most bookstores. Most **telephone boxes** take 1kr, 5kr, 10kr and 20kr coins, and there is a minimum 4kr charge. Coin-operated **phones** are gradually giving way to credit- and card-operated public telephones; cards come in denominations of 35kr (22 units), 98kr (65 units) and 210kr (150 units). The international access code is ☎00 47, and directory enquiries for Scandinavian countries is ☎1881, but note that these services are very expensive (10kr/min). To make an international collect call, dial ☎115. There are no area codes in Norway.

The Norwegians are into the **Internet** in a big way. Many hotels have Internet access, and most libraries offer free Internet access; you usually have to put your name on a list and then you'll get 30min online for free.

Getting around

Norway's **public transport system** is comprehensive and extraordinarily reliable. In the winter (especially in the north), services can be cut back severely, but no part of the country is isolated for long. A synopsis of all the main air, train, bus and ferry services is given in the free *NRI Guide to Transport and Accommodation* brochure, available in advance from the Norwegian Tourist Board; and there are detailed regional public transport timetables available at all local tourist offices.

Trains

Train services are operated by Norges Statsbaner (NSB) – Norwegian State Railways. There are four main routes. These link Oslo to Stockholm in the east, to Kristiansand and Stavanger in the southwest, to Bergen in the west and to Trondheim and on to Fauske and Bodø in the north. The nature of the country makes most of the routes engineering feats of some magnitude and worth a trip in their own right – the tiny Flåm line and sweeping Rauma run to Åndalsnes are exciting examples, and the journey from Oslo to Bergen is an impressive six-and-a-half-hour cross-country ride, taking in forests, waterfalls, mountains, bleak uplands and plunging valleys. **InterRail** and **Eurail** passes are valid, as is the **ScanRail** pass (see p.29). The ScanRail and InterRail passes and, to a lesser extent, the Eurail pass also provide large discounts on many major ferry crossings and long-distance bus journeys.

Buses

You'll need to use **buses** principally in the western fjords and the far north, though there is also a countrywide network of long-distance **express buses** connecting major towns. **Tickets** aren't especially expensive and are usually bought on board, although bus stations sell advance tickets too. Information on specific routes and timetables is available from local tourist offices or from **Nor-Way Bussekspress**, Karl Johans Gate 2, N–0154 Oslo 1 (☎23 00 24 40, ⊛www.nor-way.no).

Ferries

Travelling by **ferry** is one of the real pleasures of a trip to Norway. Rates are fixed nationally on a sliding scale. The tariff is reasonable, with a fifteen-minute ferry ride costing 15kr for foot passengers. Bus fares include the cost of any ferry journey made en route. Some of the busier routes have a control kiosk, where you pay on arrival, but for the most part a crew member comes round to collect fares either on the quayside or on board.

There's also the *Hurtigrute* (literally "rapid route"), a **coastal ferry** service, which shuttles up and down the Norwegian coast linking Bergen with Kirkenes and stopping off at over thirty ports on the way. **Tickets** for short jumps are quite expensive, certainly compared with the bus fares, and the full eleven-day return cruise (including a cabin and meals) goes for anywhere between 8000kr and 23,000kr. However, prices are reduced outside May to August, when under-26s can buy a special **coastal pass** (*kystpass*; 1750kr/three weeks). Get it on board on your first trip or at almost all travel agents at home or in Norway. Although it's a cruise ship you don't need to have a cabin: sleeping in the lounges or on deck is allowed – most have showers you can use on the lower corridors. Each ship has a 24-hour cafeteria and first-rate restaurants. Bikes travel free.

Accommodation

Inevitably, hotel **accommodation** is one of the major expenses you will incur on a trip to Norway – but there are budget alternatives, principally private rooms arranged via the tourist office, hostels and camping.

Hostels

For many budget travellers as well as hikers, climbers and skiers, **hostels** provide the accommodation mainstay – there are about ninety in all, spread right across the country and run by the Norwegian hostelling association, Norske Vandrerhjem, Dronningensgate 26, Oslo (☎23 13 93 00, ⊛www.vandr-erhjem.no). Prices vary greatly (100–180kr), although the more expensive ones nearly always include a first-rate breakfast. Most places also have a supply of doubles, often en suite, for 250–450kr per night. Non-members can use the hostels, but pay an extra 25kr a night. Between June and mid-September you should call ahead to check on space. Most hostels close 11am–4pm, and there's often an 11pm/midnight curfew.

Campsites and cabins

Camping is another way of keeping accommodation costs down. There are hundreds of official sites throughout the country and although many are situated with the motorist in mind, plenty of others are easily reached by public transport; the majority are of a high standard. Prices vary considerably, but on average expect to pay around 100kr per night for two people using a tent. The Norwegian Tourist Board details around four hundred campsites in their free *Camping* brochure.

Campsites also often have **cabins** (*hytter*), usually four-bedded affairs with kitchen facilities and sometimes a bathroom, for upwards of 300kr. **Camping rough**, as in Sweden, is a tradition enshrined in law. You can camp anywhere in open areas as long as you are at least 150m away from houses or cabins or otherwise have permission from the owner of the land.

Hotels, pensions and private rooms

Hotels are generally out of the reckoning for travellers on a budget – the cheapest double room will set you back around 700kr a night. Still, there are bargains to be found, particularly during summer, when most hotels have discounts of between twenty and forty percent. Remember also that the price of a hotel room almost always includes breakfast. **Guest houses** (*pensjonater*) in the more touristy towns are slightly cheaper at about 500kr a double; breakfast is usually extra. Tourist offices in larger towns can sometimes fix you up with a **private room** in someone's house for around 300–350kr a double, though there's a booking fee (15–25kr) on top and rooms are frequently out of the centre.

Food and drink

Norwegian food can be excellent: fish is plentiful, and carnivores can have a field day trying meats such as reindeer steak and elk. But it doesn't come cheap, and eating well on a tight budget may be a problem. The same can be said of **drinking**: buying from the supermarkets and Vinmonopolet (the state off-licences) is often the only way you'll afford a tipple: in a bar, beer costs 40kr/500ml.

Food

Breakfast (*frokost*) – a self-service affair of bread, cheese, eggs, preserves, cold meat and fish, washed down with unlimited tea and coffee – is usually excellent at hostels, and memorable in hotels. Almost everywhere breakfast is included in the price of a room; where it isn't, reckon on an extra 50–70kr. **Picnic food** is the best stand-by during the day, although there are a number of **fast-food** alternatives. The indigenous Norwegian variety, served up at street stalls (*gatekjøkken*), consists mainly of rather unappetising hot dogs (*varm pølse*), pizza slices and chicken and chips. A much better choice, and often no more expensive, is simply to get a *smørbrød*, a huge open sandwich heaped with a variety of garnishes. You'll see them in most **cafés** and **bakeries**. Good **coffee** is available everywhere and in cafeterias is usually half-price after the first cup. **Tea**, too, is ubiquitous, but usually served with lemon – if you want milk, ask for it.

The best deals for **sit-down food** are at lunchtime (*lunsj*), when self-service **kafeterias** offer a limited range of daily specials (*dagens rett*) – a fish or meat dish with vegetables or salad, often including a drink, sometimes bread, and occasionally coffee, too – that costs 70–90kr. Most department stores and large supermarkets have surprisingly good *kafeterias*; as do main railway stations, but these tend to be rather overpriced. In the larger towns you'll also find more original cafés called *kaffistovas*, which serve high-quality Norwegian food at quite reasonable prices. **Restaurants**, serving dinner (*middag*) and classic Norwegian food, are out of the range of most budgets – main courses average 200–220kr – but the seafood at the best of them is superb. Again, the best deals are at lunchtime, when some restaurants put out a *koldtbord* (the Norwegian *smörgåsbord*), where, for a fixed price (100–150kr), you can eat as much as you like for the three to four hours it's served. There are also a sizeable number of café/bars where a substantial main course and a couple of small beers will cost about 180kr.

Drink

Norwegian alcohol prices are among the highest in Europe. **Beer** is lager-like and comes in three strengths: class I is light, class II is what you get in supermarkets and is the most widely served in pubs, while class III is the strongest and only available at Vinmonopolet. If you are in Norway around Christmas, you should try some of the Christmas brews. Every year the different breweries are in fierce competition to win the coveted prizes organized by local and national newspapers. In the cities **bars** stay open until at least 1am and until 4am in many cases; in the smaller towns, they tend to close at around 11pm.

Wines and spirits can only be purchased from the state-controlled **Vinmonopolet**. **Spirits** are way over the top in price – though one local speciality worth trying at least once is *aquavit*, served ice-cold in little glasses and, at forty percent proof, real headache-inducing material. **Wines** are not cheap either – a good bottle costs from 85kr – but Vinmonopolet are known to be one of the best wine buyers in Europe, so you can, at least, be assured of the quality. There's generally at least one Vinmonopolet in each town, more in the cities; **opening hours** are usually Mon–Wed 10am–4/5pm, Thurs 10am–5/6pm, Fri 9am–4/6pm, Sat 9am–1/3pm.

Opening hours and holidays

Shop **opening hours** are usually Mon–Wed & Fri 9am–5pm, Thurs 9am–6/8pm, Sat 9am–1/3pm. Almost everything – including the supermarkets – is closed on Sunday. Newspaper kiosks (*Narvesen*) and takeaway food stalls are open every evening until 10 or 11pm. Most shops and businesses are closed on the following **public holidays**: Jan 1; Maundy Thurs; Good Fri; Easter Sun & Mon; May 1; Ascension Day (mid-May); May 17; Whit Sun & Mon; Dec 25 & 26.

20

Emergencies

Norway is in general a safe place to travel; the people are friendly and helpful, and petty crime is unusual. If you have to visit the **police** you'll usually find them amiable and normally able to speak English.

Most good hotels as well as pharmacies and tourist offices have lists of local doctors and dentists. Norway is not in the EU, but is a member of the EEA and thus operates reciprocal health agreements with all EU countries. This means that EU citizens get free **hospital treatment**, providing they're carrying an E111. Non-hospital treatment is not free, though EU citizens only pay part of the cost. These arrangements do not cover dental treatment or prescription charges. Prescriptions are taken to **pharmacies** (*apotek*) which – should they be closed – mostly carry a rota in the window advising of the nearest open pharmacy.

Emergency numbers

Police ☏112; Ambulance ☏113; Fire ☏110.

Oslo

Despite tourist-office endeavours, **OSLO** retains a low profile among European cities. Yet the city is definitely worth seeing. It has some of Europe's best museums, fields a street life that surprises most first-time visitors, and helps revive travellers weary of the austere northern wilderness.

Oslo is the oldest of the Scandinavian capital cities, founded around 1048 by Harald Hardråde. Several decimating fires and 600 years later, Oslo upped sticks and shifted west to its present site, abandoning its old name in favour of Christiania – after the seventeenth-century Danish king Christian IV responsible for the move. The new city prospered and by the time of the break with Denmark (and union with Sweden) in 1814, Christiania – indeed Norway as a whole – was clamouring for independence, something it finally achieved in 1905, though the city didn't revert to its original name for another twenty years. Today's city centre is largely the work of the late nineteenth and early twentieth centuries, an era reflected in the wide streets, dignified parks and gardens, solid buildings and long, consciously classical vistas. Its half a million inhabitants have room to spare in a city whose vast boundaries encompass huge areas of woods, sand and water, and much of the time you're as likely to be swimming or trail-walking as strolling the city centre.

Arrival and information

All **trains** arrive at Oslo Sentralstasjon, known as **Oslo S**, at the eastern end of the city centre. The central **bus terminal** is connected to Oslo S by a bridge on the northeast corner of the building; it handles most of the bus services within the city as well as those to and from the airport. Long-distance buses arrive and depart here too, but note that some services terminate on the south side of Oslo S at the bus stands beside Havnegata. **Ferries** arrive at either the Vippetangen quays, a fifteen-minute walk south of Oslo S, or at Hjortneskaia, some 3km west of the city centre; take bus #56 to the centre – an infrequent service, though it's mostly linked to ferry arrival times. Catamarans from Arendal, on the south coast, dock at the Palékaia, a five- to ten-minute walk south from Oslo S. Oslo's gleaming new **Gardermoen airport**, 45km north of the city, is linked to Oslo S by high-speed train and bus. The former is faster, the latter cheaper. There's also a second airport at Torp, 100km southwest of Oslo by the city of Sandefjord. Connecting buses take arrivals on to Oslo.

The main **tourist office** is on the harbourfront at Brynjulf Bulls plass 1 (April–Sept Mon–Sat 9am–5/7pm; Oct–March Mon–Fri 9am–4pm; ☎23 11 78 80, Ⓦ www.visitoslo.com). They stock the free monthly **listings** booklet *What's On*, and sell the useful **Oslo Card** (180kr/one day, 270kr/two days, 360kr/three days), which gives free admission to most of the museums, discounts in shops and restaurants and unlimited free travel on the transport system, including ferries.

City transport

The city's transport system is operated by AS Oslo Sporveier, whose **Trafikanten information office** is on Jernbanetorget, the pedestrianized square outside Oslo S (Mon–Fri 7am–8pm, Sat 8am–6pm www.trafikanten.no). They have a useful free transit map and a free timetable booklet, *Rutebok for Oslo*, which details every transport schedule in the city. Most **buses** stop running at around midnight, when **night buses** take over on certain routes. The **trams** are the preferred form of transportation for the people of Oslo. They run on eight lines, crossing the centre from east to west. The underground Tunnelbanen (**T-bane**) has eight lines, all of which converge to share a common slice of track that crosses the city centre from Majorstuen in the west to Tøyen in the east. Numerous **local ferries** cross the fjord to connect the city with its outlying districts and archipelagos. **Tickets** (flat-fare 22kr; travel pass 50kr/eight journeys, 135kr/seven days, 150kr/one month) are available from Trafikanten and are valid on trams, buses and the T-bane.

Accommodation

To appreciate the full flavour of the city, you're best off staying on or near the western reaches of Karl Johans gate, between the Stortinget and the Nationaltheatret. Many of the least expensive lodgings are, however, to be found in the vicinity of Oslo S. It is always well worth calling ahead to check on space, but you can cut the hassle by using the accommodation service provided by the tourist office, who also supply full accommodation lists and make reservations for a nominal fee. A good budget alternative to the hostels listed below is a **private room**, also booked by the tourist office; the supply rarely dries up, but note that there's often a minimum two–night stay.

Hostels

Ekeberg Vandrerhjem Kongsveien 82 ☏ 22 74 18 90, ⓔ oslo.ekeberg.hostel@vandrerhjem.no. Small, simple HI hostel occupying part of a school complex 4km southeast of Oslo S. Take tram #19 or the less frequent #18 from the centre and it is 100m from the Holtet tram stop. June to mid-Aug only. ❸

Oslo Haraldsheim Vandrerhjem Haraldsheimveien 4, Grefsen ☏ 22 22 29 65, ⓔ oslo.haraldsheim.hostel@vandrerhjem.no. The best of the three hostels, 4km northeast of the centre, with 71 rooms, mostly in four-bed dorms, the majority en-suite. Take tram #15 or #17 from Brugata to the Sinsenkrysset stop, from where it's a signposted ten-minute walk along a footpath. Advance booking necessary in summer. ❸

Oslo Vandrerhjem Holtekilen Michelets vei 55, 1320 Stabekk ☏ 67 51 80 40, ⓔ oslo.holtekilen.hostel@vandrerhjem.no. Located 10km west of the city centre, this place has a

dorm room (May–Sept only) and one- to four-bedded rooms. Kitchen, laundry facilities and restaurant. From Bussterminalen, take bus #151 to the Kveldsroveien bus stop; the hostel is 100m away on the right. ❸

Hotels

Bondeheimen Rosenkrantz gate 8 ☏ 23 21 41 00, ⓦ www.bondeheimen.com. One of Oslo's most delightful hotels, tastefully decorated with polished pine everywhere. It's a short walk north of Karl Johans gate – and the buffet breakfast, included in the price, is excellent. ❾

Perminalen Hotell Øvre Slottsgate 2 ☏ 23 09 30 81. Clean, basic and reasonably priced hotel/hostel close to the train station. ❹

Cochs Pensjonat Parkveien 25 ☏ 22 33 24 00, ⓦ www.cochs.no. Reasonable guest house with good deals on triples and quads with bathroom in the hall. Situated in the very nice area behind the palace. ❼

The city centre

Oslo's main street, **Karl Johans gate**, leads west up the slope from Oslo S train station. It begins unpromisingly with a clutter of tacky shops and hang-around junkies, but steps away at the corner of Dronningens gate is the curious **Basarhallene**, a circular building of two tiers, whose brick cloisters once housed the city's food market. The adjacent **Domkirke** (daily 10am–4pm) dates from the late seventeenth century, though its heavyweight tower was remodelled in 1850; plain and dour from the outside, the cathedral boasts an elegantly restored interior, its nave and transepts awash with maroon, green and gold paintwork. It's a brief stroll further up Karl Johans gate to the **Stortinget**, the parliament building, an imposing chunk of neo-Romanesque architecture that was completed in 1866. In front of the parliament, a narrow **park-piazza** flanks Karl Johans gate; in summer it teems with promenading city folk, while in winter people flock to its floodlit open-air skating rinks.

Lurking at the western end of the park is the Neoclassical **Nationaltheatret**, built in 1899 and fronted by a stodgy statue of playwright Henrik Ibsen. Beyond, up the hill, the **Royal Palace** is a monument to Norwegian openness; built between 1825 and 1848, when other monarchies were nervously counting their friends, it still stands without railings and walls, and the grounds – **Slottsparken** –

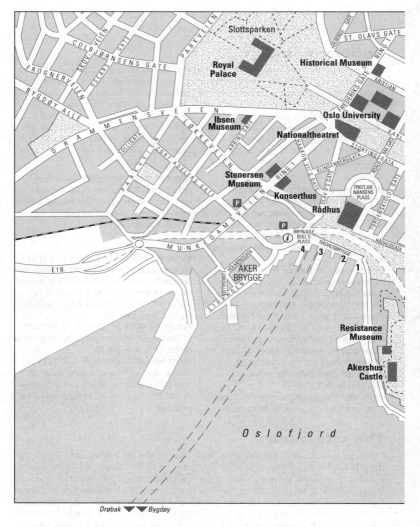

Drøbak ▼▼ Bygdøy

are open to the public. The daily changing of the guard (1.30pm) is a snappy affair, well worth a look. An equestrian statue of the king who built the palace, Karl XIV Johan, stands in front of the main facade.

Back on Karl Johans Gate, the nineteenth-century buildings of the **University** fit well in this monumental end of the city centre. Among them you will find Norway's largest and best collection of art at the **National Gallery**, Universitetsgata 13 (10am–4/6pm, Thurs till 8pm, closed Tues; free). Highlights include some wonderfully romantic, nineteenth-century landscapes by the likes of Johan Christian Dahl and Thomas Fearnley, and two rooms devoted to Edvard Munch, featuring the original version of the famous *Scream*. Heading south from the University buildings, you can't miss the monolithic brickwork of the **Rådhus** (daily 9am–4/5pm; free), the

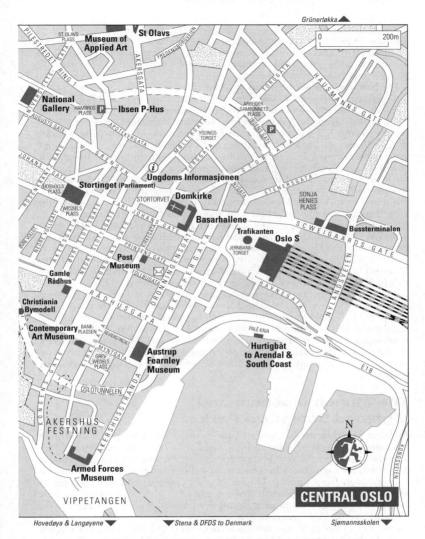

St Olavs

Museum of
Applied Art

St Olavs

National
Gallery HAMBROS
PLASS ■ Ibsen P-Hus

YOUNGS-
TORGET

ARBEIDER-
SAMFUNNETS
PLASS

ⓘ Ungdoms Informasjonen

Stortinget (Parliament)

STORTORVET Domkirke

SONJA
HENIES
PLASS

Basarhallene

Trafikanten

Oslo S Bussterminalen

JERNBANE-
TORGET

Post
Museum

Gamle
Rådhus

Christiania
Bymodell

Contemporary BANK-
Art Museum PLASSEN

Austrup
Fearnley
Museum

PALÉ KAIA

Hurtigbåt
to Arendal &
South Coast

AKERSHUS
FESTNING

Armed Forces
Museum

VIPPETANGEN

CENTRAL OSLO

N

Hovedøya & Langøyene ▼   ▼ Stena & DFDS to Denmark   Sjømannsskolen ▼

massive City Hall, opened in 1950 to celebrate the city's 900th anniversary. Few
people had a good word to say about the place when it was first built, but the
Rådhus has worn well, its twin towers a grandiose but somehow rather amiable
statement of civic pride. The interior – best seen on one of the frequent and free
guided tours – celebrates all things Norwegian; the main hall or Rådhushallen is
decorated with vast murals by several of the country's leading artists.

The Bygdøy peninsula

The most enjoyable way to reach the leafy **Bygdøy peninsula**, southwest of the
city centre, is by ferry #90, departing daily in summer (every 20min) from behind
the Rådhus. The two most popular attractions – the Viking Ships and the

Norwegian Folk museums – are within easy walking distance of the first stop, Dronningen pier; the other attractions are a stone's throw from Bygdøynes (the second stop). If you decide to walk between the two ferry stops, allow about fifteen minutes: the route is well signposted but dull. The alternative to the ferry is bus #30 (every 15min), which runs year-round.

The **Norwegian Folk Museum**, at Museumsveien 10 (daily 10/11am–3/6pm; 50/70kr), combines indoor collections of furniture, china and silverware with an open-air display of reassembled period farms, houses and other buildings. A few minutes' walk away, the **Viking Ships Museum** (daily 9/11am–4/6pm; 40kr) occupies a large hall specially constructed to house a trio of ninth-century Viking ships, with viewing platforms to enable you to see inside the hulls. The three oak vessels were retrieved from ritual burial mounds in southern Norway towards the end of the nineteenth century, each embalmed in a subsoil of clay, which accounts for their excellent state of preservation. The star exhibit is the **Oseberg ship**, thought to be the burial ship of a Viking chieftain's wife. Its ornately carved prow and stern rise high above the hull, where thirty oar-holes indicate the size of the crew. Treasure buried with the boat is on display at the back of the museum.

Down by Bygdøynes pier, the **Kon-Tiki Museum** (daily 9.30/10.30am–4/5.45pm; 35kr) displays the balsawood raft on which Thor Heyerdahl made his now legendary 1947 journey across the Pacific to prove that the first Polynesian settlers could have sailed from pre-Inca Peru. Over the road, in front of the **Fram Museum** (daily 9/11am–2.45/6.45pm; 30kr), is the *Gjøa*, the one-time sealing ship in which Roald Amundsen made the first complete sailing of the Northwest Passage in 1906. Another of Amundsen's ships, the polar vessel *Fram*, is displayed inside – this was the vessel that carried him to within striking distance of the South Pole in 1911. Complete with most of its original fittings, the interior gives a superb insight into the life and times of these early Arctic explorers. Next door, the **Norwegian Maritime Museum** (daily 10.30am–4/6pm; 30kr) is a sparkling new building that accommodates a fairly pedestrian collection of maritime artefacts. You'll probably be more taken with the café, a handy vantage point overlooking the bay.

The Munch Museum and Vigeland Sculpture Park

Also out of the centre but without question a major attraction, the **Munch Museum**, Tøyengata 53 (June to mid-Sept daily 10am–6pm; mid-Sept to May Tues–Fri 10am–4pm, Sat & Sun 11am–5pm; 60kr), is reachable by T-bane: get off at Tøyen and it's a signposted five-minute walk. Born in 1863, **Edvard Munch** is Norway's most famous painter. His lithographs and woodcuts, a dark catalogue of swirls and fog, are shown in one half of the gallery, and in the main gallery there are early paintings along with the great, signature works of the 1890s. The museum also owns no less than fifty versions of *The Scream*.

On the other side of the city and reachable on tram #12 and #15 from the centre (get off at Vigelandsparken), **Frogner Park** holds one of Oslo's most striking cultural targets in the **Vigeland Sculpture Park** (free access), which commemorates another modern Norwegian artist of world renown, **Gustav Vigeland**. The open-air sculptures, which Vigeland started in 1924 and was still working on when he died in 1943, are simply fantastic. A long series of life-size figures frowning, fighting and posing lead up to the central fountain, an enormous bowl representing the burden of life, supported by straining, sinewy bronze Goliaths while, underneath water tumbles out around clusters of playing and standing figures. The 20m obelisk up on the stepped embankment behind, and the grouped granite sculptures around it, comprise the summation of the work, a writhing mass that depicts the cycle of life as Vigeland saw it. The park comes to life in summer when the city's inhabitants come out to play and enjoy the green space.

The islands of the inner Oslofjord

The archipelago of low-lying, lightly forested **islands** in the **inner Oslofjord** is the city's summer playground. Although most of the islets are cluttered with summer homes, the least populated are favourite party venues for the city's preening youth. **Ferries** to the islands leave from the Vippetangen quay, at the foot of Akershusstranda – a twenty-minute walk, or a five-minute ride on bus #60, south from Jernbanetorget.

Conveniently, **Hovedøya** (ferry #92), the nearest island, is also the most interesting, its rolling hills incorporating both farmland and deciduous woods as well as the overgrown ruins of a twelfth-century Cistercian monastery. There are plenty of footpaths to wander, you can swim from the shingle beaches on the south shore, and there's a seasonal café opposite the monastery ruins. Camping is not permitted, however, as Hovedøya is a protected area – that's why there are no summer homes. The pick of the other islands is wooded **Langøyene** (ferry #94), the most southerly of the archipelago and the one with the best beaches. The H-shaped island has a **campsite**, *Langøyene Camping* (☎22 11 53 21; June to mid-Aug), and at night the ferries are full of people armed with sleeping bags and bottles, on their way to join swimming parties.

Eating

As befits a capital city, Oslo boasts scores of **eating places**, the sheer variety ensuring there's something to suit almost every budget. Those carefully counting the kroner will find it easy to buy bread, fruit, snacks and sandwiches from stalls, shops and kiosks across the city centre, while fast-food joints offering hamburgers and hot dogs (*pølser*) are legion. Far more interesting are the city's **cafés**. These run the gamut from homely family places to student haunts and ultra-fashionable hangouts, but nearly all of them serve inexpensive lunches and sometimes bargain evening meals too. It's worth noting that quite a few of the cafés detailed below could equally be slotted into our "Pubs and Bars" section as the distinction is often very blurred. Regular **restaurants** are more expensive and frequently rather formal, but even here it's possible to find some excellent deals, especially if you stick to pizza and pasta at one of the many Italian places.

Markets are always good for fruit and vegetables, and Oslo's principal open-air market is on Youngstorget (Mon–Sat 7am–2pm), a brief stroll north of the Domkirke along Torggata. In the eastern part of the city, around Trondheimsveien and the areas of Grünerløkka or Grønland, Turkish- and Pakistani-run shops offer reasonably priced vegetables, bread, olives and feta cheese. The city centre is dotted with **supermarkets** – Rimi, the biggest name, has an outlet in Grensen – and takeaway snacks are on sale from kiosks and **fast-food outlets** right across the city. Also, bakeries sell a reasonable range of sandwiches.

Cafés and restaurants

Arakataka Mariboes gate 7. Gourmet food, especially seafood, at extremely reasonable prices. On the east side of central Oslo.

Ett Glass Karl Johans gate 33, entrance round the corner on Rosenkrantz gate. Trendy, candlelit café/bar. Imaginative inexpensive menu focuses on Mediterranean-influenced light meals and lunches and provides some curious, often mouthwatering delights.

Den Gode Cafe Fredensborgveien. Reasonably priced snackfood and good coffee. At night the place turns into a relaxed bar for drinking and chatting; downstairs at weekends the *Bar Nede*

opens with a chilled atmosphere and cosy fireplace.

Kaffistova Rosenkrantz gate 8. Part of the Bondeheimen hotel, this spick-and-span self-service café serves tasty, traditional Norwegian cooking at very fair prices. There's usually a vegetarian option, too.

Krishna Cuisine Kirkeveien 59B. In the midle of busy Majorstukrysset, this is the city's best vegetarian option. Closed Sat & Sun.

Sult Thv Meyers gate 26. Serves innovative dishes using seasonal ingredients, at surprisingly low prices. The attached bar *Tørst* is one of Oslo's most popular spots.

Tullins cafe Tullins gate 2. Close to the National Gallery, this fashionable spot serves light meals, snacks and coffee in the daytime and turns into a café/bar at night. Reasonably priced.

Zoolounge Kristian August gate 7B. Stylish modern cafè/bar with nice snack/meal options, tasty coffee and posh drinks in the evening. Hip young crowd at nighttime DJ sessions.

Drinking

Downtown Oslo has a vibrant **bar** scene, a noisy, boisterous but generally good-tempered affair, at its most frenetic on summer weekends, when the city is crowded with visitors from all over Norway. The busiest mainstream bars are concentrated in the side streets near the Rådhus and down along the Aker Brygge, while other popular but less assertively heterosexual bars are clustered around Universitetsgata and on Rosenkrantz gate. Karl Johans gate also weighs in with a string of bars and in recent years nightlife has moved east – Grünerløkka is now *the* place to go and Grønland also has a couple of hotspots.

Bars and pubs

Bar Boca Thv Meyers gate 30. Tiny Fifties-retro bar, with the best dry Martinis in Norway. Get here early.

Dattera til Hagen Grønland 10. This trendy spot in the multicultural area of Grønland is a café during the day and a lively bar at night, sometimes with a DJ on the small first floor dance-floor.

Mono Pløens gate. Newly opened beer-haunt for students and the alternative crowd. Dark interior with old couches, velvet wallpaper and Sixties floor lamps. DJs play a good eclectic music selection.

Savoy Bar Universitetsgata 11. With its stained-glass windows and wood-panelled walls, this small, intimate bar is an agreeably low-key spot to nurse a beer. Part of the Savoy hotel.

Nightlife

Tracking down **live music** is straightforward enough – both international and local acts. **Jazz** fans are well served, with several first-rate nightspots dotted round the city centre. Oslo's busiest **nightclubs** are on and around Karl Johans gate, although lately some good places have opened in the areas of Grønland and Grünerløkka. Entry will set you back 50–100kr – though drinks prices are the same as anywhere else. Nothing gets going much before 11pm; closing times are generally 3–4am. For **entertainment listings** check *Natt & Dag*, a monthly Norwegian-language broadsheet available free from cafés, bars and shops.

Nightclubs, rock and jazz venues

BLÅ Brenneri veien 9c. Down by the river, this converted factory building holds one of the most exciting clubs in Oslo. Jazz concerts, literature readings and club nights with high-profile national and international DJs. Outdoor café/bar in summer.

Herr Nilsen C.J. Hambros plass 5. Great spot for live jazz and blues.

So What? Grensen 9. Indiemusic on the ground

floor, live acts and dance-floor in the blacker than black basement. Brings out the student club-hoppers.

Nye Enka Kirkegata. Popular pub on the ground floor, disco on the first. Attracts both gay and hetero party-goers.

Rockerfeller Music Hall Torggata 16. This former bathhouse is now one of Oslo's major concert venues, hosting well-known and up-and-coming bands – mostly rock or alternative.

Listings

Bike rental Glåmdal Cycle Hire, near the main tourist office ☎22 83 39 79 (265kr/day, 1000kr deposit).

Embassies Canada, Wergelandveien 7 ☎22 99 53 00; UK, Thomas Heftyes gate 8 ☎23 13 27 00; US, Drammensveien 18 ☎22 44 85 50. Australia and New Zealand use British embassy.

Exchange Outside normal banking hours, try the exchange office at Oslo S or the ATMs. Also 24hr

exchange at the airport.

Internet Akers Mik Internet café, Akersgaten 39. And at the libraries: most central Is at Drammensveien 42.

Laundry Mr Clean, Parkveien 6 at Welhavens gate.

Pharmacies Jernbanetorgets Apotek, Jernbanetorget 4b, by Oslo S (24hr).

Post offices Dronningens gate 15, corner of Prinsens gate.

Bergen and the Fjords

The **fjords** are the most familiar and alluring image of Norway: huge clefts in the landscape which occur along the west coast right up to the Russian border, though the most beguiling portion lies between Bergen and Ålesund. Wild, rugged and peaceful, this part of the country elicits inordinate amounts of purple prose from tourist office handouts, and for once it's rarely overstated. In the summer, the fjords are, it's true, patrolled by a steady flotilla of cruise ships, and the hills heave with hikers, but the crowds are rarely oppressive and what little development there has been is seldom intrusive.

Bergen, Norway's second largest city, is a handy springboard for the fjords, notably the **Flåm Valley** and its inspiring mountain railway, which trundles down to the Aurlandsfjord, a tiny arm of the mighty **Sognefjord**, Norway's longest and deepest. North of the Sognefjord, there is the smaller but less stimulating **Nordfjord**, though there's superb compensation in the **Jostedalsbreen** glacier, which nudges the fjord from the east. The tiny S-shaped **Geirangerfjord**, further north again, is magnificent too – narrow, sheer and rugged – while the northernmost **Romsdalsfjord** and its many branches and inlets reach pinnacles of isolation in the **Trollstigen** mountain highway.

By rail, you can only reach Bergen in the south and Åndalsnes in the north. For everything in between – including the Sognefjord, Nordfjord and the Jostedalsbreen glacier – **buses** and **ferries** together comprise a complicated but fully integrated system. It's a good idea to pick up full bus and ferry **timetables** from the local tourist office whenever you can. Catamarans and ferries are considered an extension of the train system, and holders of rail passes often qualify for fifty-percent discounts.

Bergen

Though known as one of the rainiest places in rainy Norway, **BERGEN** has a spectacular setting among seven hills and is one of the country's most enjoyable cities. There's plenty to see, from the fine surviving medieval buildings to a series of good museums. Bergen is also within easy reach of some of Norway's most spectacular scenic attractions, both around the city and further north. Founded in 1070, it was the largest and most important town in medieval Norway, a regular residence of the country's kings and queens, and later a Hanseatic port and religious centre, though precious little of that era survives today. Nowadays, the city centre divides into two distinct parts: the wharf area, **Bryggen**, adjacent to the Bergenhus fortress, once the working centre of the Hanseatic merchants and now the oldest part of Bergen; and the **modern centre**, which stretches inland from the head of the harbour and down along the Nordnes peninsula, taking in the best of Bergen's museums, cafés and bars.

The obvious place to start a visit is the **Torget**, an appealing harbourside plaza that's home to a colourful fish- and fresh-produce market. From here, it's a short stroll round to the **Bryggen**, where a string of distinctive wooden buildings line up along the wharf. These once housed the city's merchants and are now home to a string of shops, restaurants and bars. Although none of these structures was actually built by the Hanseatic Germans – most of the originals were destroyed by fire in 1702 – they carefully follow the original building line. Among them, the **Hanseatic Museum** (daily 9/11am–2/5pm; 40kr) is the best preserved, an early eighteenth-century merchant's dwelling kitted out in late-Hansa style. More than anything else, though, it's the gloomy warren-like layout of the place that impresses, as well as the all-pervading smell of fish. Good though this is, it's the **Bryggens Museum** (daily 10/11am–3/5pm; 30kr), just along the harbourfront, which is Bergen's showpiece. Here, a series of imaginative exhibitions attempts a complete reassembly of medieval life – from domestic implements, handicrafts and maritime

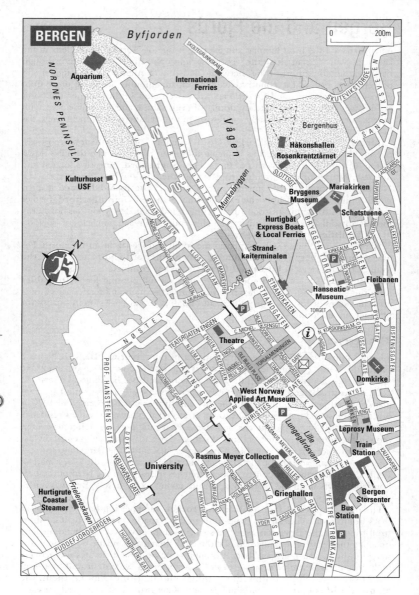

objects through to trading items – set in context by a set of twelfth-century foundations that were unearthed during the first archeological dig in the 1950s.

A few steps from the museum, **Øvregaten**, with its quaint clapboard houses, has long marked the boundary of the Bryggen. By walking along its length you'll soon reach the terminal of the **Fløibanen**, a dinky funicular railway (every 30min; 50kr return), which runs up to the top of 320m Mount Fløyen, from where there are panoramic views over the city.

About five minutes' walk from the funicular, in the modern centre, Bergen's four main **art museums** are on the south side of a pleasant, artificial lake. The pick of these is the **Rasmus Meyer Collection**, Rasmus Meyers Allé 3 (daily 11am–5pm; mid-Sept to mid-May closed Mon; 50kr), which holds an extensive collection of Norwegian painting, including many works by Edvard Munch.

Practicalities

Bergen is a busy international port and may well be your first stop in Norway. **International ferries** arrive at Skoltegrunnskaien, the quay just beyond Bergenhus fortress, on the east side of the harbour; **domestic ferries** line up on the opposite side of the harbour at the Strandkaiterminalen. The **train** and **bus stations** face Strømgaten, a five-minute walk east of the head of the harbour. The **airport**, 20km south of the city, is connected to the bus station by regular *flybussen* (every 20min; 60kr). The city is also a terminal port for the **coastal boat** (*Hurtigrute*), which leaves from the Frieleneskaien quay behind the university, about 1.5km south of the train station. The **tourist office** is a few metres from the head of the harbour at Vågsallmenning 1 (daily 8.30/9am–8/10pm; closes 4pm in winter; ☎55 55 20 00, ⊛www.visitbergen.com). It issues free copies of the *Bergen Guide*, an exhaustive consumer's guide to the city, and also sells the **Bergen Card** (165kr/day, 245kr/ two days), which allows travel on all the city's buses and free entrance to, or discounts on, most of the city's sights, including sightseeing trips. Flat-rate fare on public transport is otherwise 20kr per journey.

Accommodation

Budget accommodation is no great problem. As well as the places listed below, there are plenty of **private rooms** available; book through the tourist office.

Hostels

Bergen Vandrerhjem YMCA Nedre Korskirkealmenning 4 ☎55 60 60 55, ⊛ymca@online.no. Close to Torget, a five- to ten-minute walk from the train station. Has 200 dorm beds but fills quickly. Facilities include showers, kitchen and laundry. Closed mid-Sept to April. Dorms ❷

Intermission Kalfarveien 8 ☎55 30 04 00. Christian-run hostel close to the train station. Closed mid-Aug to mid-June. Dorms ❷

Montana Vandrerhjem Johan Blyttsveien 30, Landås ☎55 20 80 70, ⊛montvh@online.no. This large and comfortable hostel occupies lodge-like premises in the hills 6km east of the centre, with good views over the city. Dorms and doubles available. Bus #31 from Nygaten. Dorms ❹

Guesthouses and hotels

Crowded House Travel Lodge Håkonsgaten 27 ☎55 23 13 10, ⊛info@crowded-house.com. Lively, appealing place with bright and airy, if spartan, bedrooms. Self-catering facilities too. Halfway along traffic-clogged Håkonsgaten, five minutes' walk from the city centre. ❺

Hotel Rosenkrantz Rosenkrantzgaten 7 ☎55 30 14 00, ⊛rosenkrantz@rainbow-hotels.no. Efficient mid-range hotel in an old building just behind the Bryggen with very comfortable rooms and discounts in the summer. ❽

Skansen Pensjonat Vetrlidsallmenningen 29 ☎55 31 90 80, ⊛mail@skansen-pensjonat.no. Simple little place in a nineteenth-century stone house of elegant proportions just above – and up the steps from – the Fløibanen terminus. Has eight rooms, one en suite. ❸

Eating, drinking and nightlife

Bergen has a good supply of first-rate **restaurants**, concentrated in the Bryggen, with seafood a particular speciality. Less expensive – and more fashionable – are the city's café/restaurants, which often double up as lively **bars**, mostly found to the southwest of Ole Bulls plass, the main pedestrianized square just a couple of minutes' walk from the head of the harbour. **Cultural events** are fairly thick on the ground during the summer, with the largest annual shindig, the *Bergen International Festival*, and the *NATTJAZZ*, held for eleven days at the end of May.

Cafés, restaurants and bars

Bryggeloftet & Stuene Bryggen 11. Slightly staid and expensive restaurant, but it does serve the best and widest range of seafood in town.
Café Opera Engen 24. White wooden building near Ole Bulls plass, bustling with a fashionable crew drinking beer and good coffee. Tasty, filling snacks including some good veggie options. Crowded clublike venue in the evening.

Kafe Kippers Kulturhuset USF, Georgernes verft. Ultra groovy café/bar in an imaginatively recycled old herring factory, with delicious, inexpensive food and a prime seashore location; the terrace is the place to be on sunny summer days.
Naboen Restaurant Neumannsgate 20. Excellent, moderately priced meals at this easy-going restaurant, which features Swedish specialities. A student favourite.

Listings

Exchange Best bet is at the post office – competitive rates and longer opening hours than the banks.
Internet Library on Strømgaten (next to the train station).

Laundry Jarlens Vaskoteque, Lille Øvregate 17, near the funicular.
Pharmacy Apoteket Nordstjernen, at the Storsenter shopping mall.
Post office Olav Kyrres gate.

Around Bergen

There is more to Bergen than the city centre, not least a number of sights just outside the city limits, most notably Edvard Grieg's old lakeside home, **Troldhaugen**, which is – along with several other sights – easily reached on the special "**Attractions**" bus from outside the tourist office (June–Aug; 40kr). Further out, but still within day-tripping distance, are some of the fjords. If you're not journeying through the fjord region – the better option – you can get a taste by taking the train to Myrdal, at the head of the remarkable branch line down the valley to **Flåm** and the **Aurlandsfjord** – one of the most popular of all fjord trips. Pick up transport timetables from the tourist office or at the train station before you set out.

Troldhaugen

Troldhaugen (May–Sept daily 9am–6pm; rest of year Mon–Fri 10am–2pm; closed Dec & early Jan; 50kr) was Edvard Grieg's home for the last 22 years of his life. As well as the "Attractions" bus (see above), **buses** leaving from platforms #19, #20 and #21 run from Bergen's bus station – ask for the Hopsbroen stop and follow the signs for 1km. A visit begins at the **museum** where Grieg's life and times are exhaustively chronicled. The **house** itself is a pleasant and unassuming villa built in 1885, and still much as Grieg left it, with a jumble of photos, manuscripts and period furniture; the obligatory guided tour is quite entertaining. Grieg didn't, in fact, compose much at home, but preferred to walk round to a tiny **hut** he had built just along the shore. The hut survives beside a modern concert hall, the **Troldsalen**, where there are Grieg recitals from late June through to October: tickets for these, which include transport, are available from Bergen tourist office.

Flåm

If you're short on time but want to sample a slice of fjord scenery, make the train journey east from Bergen, through Voss, along the main rail line as far as barren Myrdal, from where specially built trains squeak down a branch line that plummets 900m into the **Flåm valley**. The track took four years to lay and is one of the steepest anywhere in the world. If time's not too tight, consider the "Norway in a nutshell" trip, which, as well as the magnificent train ride, includes a cruise on two of the narrowest "arms" of the Sognefjord from Flåm to Gudvangen and the spectacular bus ride from Gudvangen back to Voss and Bergen. The trip can be arranged from Oslo (1230kr; 16hr) and Bergen (630kr; 12hr) and tickets can be bought at any train station.

FLÅM village, the train's destination, lies alongside meadows and orchards on the Aurlandsfjord, a matchstick-thin branch of the Sognefjord. Hikers can get off the train at **Berekvam** station, the halfway point, and stroll down the winding country road from there. Flåm is a tiny village that can be packed with tourists on summer days, but out of season – or in the early evening during summer when the day-trippers have gone – it can be a wonderfully restful place. There are two good places **to stay**: the homely *Heimly Pensjonat* (☎57 63 23 00, ⓦwww.heimly.no; ❼), which provides simple but adequate lodgings in a modern block about 450m along the shore from the train station; and the excellent *Flåm Camping* (☎57 63 21 21, ⓔflaam.hostel@vandrerhjem.no; ❷; closed Oct–April), a combined **campsite** and **hostel** 200m from the train station. The **tourist office** is at the ferry dock (May & Sept Mon–Fri 10.30am–6.30pm; June–Aug daily 8.30am–8.30pm), by the train station, and has information on local hikes.

The Sognefjord and the Jostedalsbreen glacier

With the exception of Flåm, the southern shore of the **Sognefjord** remains sparse-ly populated and relatively inaccessible, whereas the north shore boasts a couple of appealing places. Top-of-the-list **BALESTRAND** is the prettiest base, a tourist destination since the mid-nineteenth century when it was discovered by European travellers in search of cool, clear air and mountain scenery. Buses (and express boats from Bergen and Flåm) arrive at the minuscule harbourfront, near which you'll find the **tourist office** (mid-June to mid-Sept Mon–Sat 7.30am–1pm & 3.30–5.30pm, Sun 8am–12.30pm & 4.30–5.30pm; ☎57 63 21 06, ⓦwww.alr.no). The comfort-able and very appealing *Kringsjå Hotel*, 100m from the tourist office, incorporates the local **hostel** (☎57 69 13 03; ⓔbalestrand.hostel@vandrerhjem.no; ❻, hostel ❹; late June to late Aug only). Another good choice is the relaxing *Midtnes Pensjonat* (☎57 69 11 33, ⓦwww.midtnes.no; ❻), about 300m from the dock behind the dinky little wooden church.

There's not too much to see in Balestrand itself, but several lovely places are with-in easy striking distance, particularly the delightful village of **MUNDAL**, on the Fjærlandsfjord. Mundal can be reached direct by ferry from Balestrand from June through to the middle of September and by bus throughout the rest of the year (change at Sogndal). Formerly one of the most isolated spots on the Sognefjord, **Fjærlandsfjord** is now connected to the road system, but Mundal retains its old-fashioned atmosphere and appearance, its handsome clapboard buildings occupying a wildly beautiful location. Mundal is also Norway's self-styled book town, and there are various **literature events** held here in the summer (ⓦwww.bokbyen.no or www.booktown.net). Mundal's **tourist office** is in the centre of the village (late May to early Sept daily 9.30am–5.30pm; ☎57 69 32 33). **Accommodation** is lim-ited. Choose from the splendid *Hotel Mundal* (☎57 69 31 01, ⓔmundal@fjordinfo.no; ❾; closed Oct–April), a quirky, old-fashioned sort of place, and the *Fjærland Fjordstue Hotell* (☎57 69 32 00, ⓔamenl@online.no; ❻), a well-tended family hotel with smart modern furnishings. A third option is *Bøyum Camping* (☎57 69 32 52) near the Bremuseum; they have huts (❸) as well as spaces for tents. Both hotels offer good, wholesome **food**.

Mundal's other advantage is its proximity to the southern edge of the **Jostedalsbreen glacier**, a vast ice plateau that dominates the whole of the inner Nordfjord region – Nordfjord being the next fjord system to the north. The glaci-er's 24 arms – or nodules – melt down into the nearby valleys, giving the local rivers and glacial lakes their distinctive blue-green colouring. In 1991, the glacier was placed within the **Jostedalsbreen Nasjonalpark** in order to co-ordinate its conservation. The main benefit of this for tourists has been to provide **guided gla-cier walks** (June–Sept; from around 230kr) on its various arms, ranging from two-hour excursions to all-day, fully equipped hikes. Equipment is provided, though you'll need good boots, warm clothes, gloves and hat, sunglasses and (usually) your own food and drink. One of the many places that takes bookings is the **Mundal tourist office**; glacier walks booked here mostly start at the Øygarden car park, about 7km from Mundal – transport from the village is included. If all this sounds too strenuous (and expensive), you can reach an arm of the glacier under your own steam – and without too much sweat – by strolling north from Mundal on Highway 5; about 6km north of the village, just before the tunnel, a signed side road leads the 200m to the **Bøyabreen** glacier arm; note, however, that you're not allowed to walk on it – gawpers only.

The Geirangerfjord

On the north side of the Jostedalsbreen glacier is the **Nordfjord**, but this fjord system does not have the scenic lustre of its more famous neighbours and you're much better off pressing on to the S-shaped **Geirangerfjord**, one of the region's smallest and most breathtaking fjords. A convoluted branch of the Storfjord, it cuts well inland, marked by impressive waterfalls and with a village at either end of its snake-like profile. You can reach the Geirangerfjord in dramatic style by bus from the north or south, but you'd do best to approach from the north if you can. From this direction, the journey begins in Åndalsnes (see below), from where Highway 63 wriggles over the mountains via the wonderful **Trollstigen Highway**, which climbs through some of the country's highest peaks before sweeping down to the Tafjord. From here, it's a quick ferry ride and dramatic journey along the Ørneveien, the Eagle's Highway, for a first view of the Geirangerfjord and the village that bears its name glinting in the distance. There is little as stunning anywhere in western Norway, and from mid-June to August it can all be seen on a twice-daily bus following this so-called "Golden Route".

GEIRANGER village enjoys a commanding position at one end of the fjord. However, it's hopelessly overdeveloped and your best bet, especially in high season, is to pass straight through, taking the ferry on to the hamlet of **HELLESYLT**, an hour's boat ride away through the double bend of the fjord. There's nothing much to the place, but by nightfall Hellesylt makes for a quiet and peaceful **overnight stay**. The ferry terminal is a few steps from the *Grand Hotel* (☎70 26 51 00; ⓦwww.grand-hotelhellesylt.no; ❼), a local landmark since its construction in 1871, though patchily renovated and enlarged – guests are put up in the modern annexe next door. The hotel's main competitor is the **hostel** (☎70 26 51 28; ❸; closed Sept–May), set on the hillside just above the village – just follow the signs. Alternatively, *Hellesylt Camping* (☎70 26 51 88) occupies the shadeless field beside the fjord about 400m from the quay. Usefully, Hellesylt is also on the main Bergen to Loen, Stryn and Ålesund bus route; **buses** stop near the jetty.

The Romdalsfjord and around

Travelling north from Oslo by train, the line forks at Dombås – the Dovre line continuing northwards over the fells to Trondheim (see opposite), the Rauma line beginning a thrilling, roller-coaster rattle west down through the mountains to the **Romsdalsfjord** (1hr 30min). Apart from the Sognefjord (see p.783), reached from Bergen, the Romsdalsfjord is the only other Norwegian fjord accessible by train, which explains the number of backpackers wandering its principal town of **ÅNDALSNES**, many people's first – sometimes only – contact with fjord country. Despite a wonderful setting between lofty peaks and looking-glass water, the town is unexciting, but it does make a convenient base for further explorations. Åndalsnes has an outstanding **hostel** (☎71 22 13 82; ⓔaandalsnes.hostel@vandrerhjem.no; ❸; closed mid-Sept to late May), which occupies a group of charming wooden buildings in a rural setting 2.5km along the E136 towards Ålesund. Another very good option is the riverside *Åndalsnes Camping og Motell* (☎71 22 16 29), with cabins (❹), rowboats and bikes for rent, a 25-minute walk from the train station – take the first left after the river on the road out to the hostel. The **tourist office** is at the train station (late June to Aug Mon–Sat 10am–7pm, Sun 1–7pm; rest of year Mon–Fri 9am–5pm; ☎71 22 16 22, ⓦwww.andalsnes.net), and has a free and comprehensive guide to local hikes as well as bus, boat and train timetables.

At the end of the E136, some 120km west of Åndalsnes, the fishing and ferry port of **ÅLESUND** is immediately – and obviously – different from any other Norwegian town. In 1904, a disastrous fire left 10,000 people homeless and the town centre destroyed. A hectic reconstruction programme saw almost the entire area rebuilt by 1907 in a style that borrowed heavily from the German Jugendstil movement. Kaiser Wilhelm II, who used to holiday hereabouts, gave assistance, and the architects ended up creating a strange but fetching hybrid of up-to-date foreign influences and folksy local elements, with dragons, faces, flowers and even a decorative pharaoh or two. The finest buildings are concentrated on the main street, **Kongensgate**, and around the slender, central harbour, the **Brosundet**.

Ålesund **bus station** is situated on the waterfront a few metres south of the Brosundet and across from the **tourist office** in the Rådhus (June–Aug Mon–Fri 8.30am–7pm, Sat 9am–5pm, Sun 11am–5pm; rest of year Mon–Fri 8.30am–4pm; ☎70 15 76 00, ✪www.visitalesund.com). The pick of the town's **hotels** are the *Comfort Home Hotel Bryggen*, an elegantly converted waterside warehouse at Apotekergata 1 (☎70 12 64 00; ✪www.bryggen-hotel.no; ❾), and the similar *Brosundet Gjestehus* along the street at no. 5 (☎70 12 10 00, ✪www.brosundet.no; ❽). There's also a small and central **hostel** at Parkgata 14, at the top of Rådstuggata (☎70 11 58 30, ✉aalesund.hostel@vandrerhjem.no; ❹; closed Oct–April). For **eating**, the *Sjøbua Fiskerestaurant*, Brunholmgata 1, is an expensive but first-rate seafood restaurant, which comes complete with its own lobster tank. A cheaper if much more mundane option is *Metz*, a café/restaurant overlooking the Brosundet; everyone flocks to its terrace in fine weather.

Northern Norway

The long, thin counties of **Trøndelag** and **Nordland** mark the transition from rural southern to blustery northern Norway. The main town of Trøndelag, appealing **Trondheim**, is easily accessible from Oslo by train, but north of here travelling becomes more of a slog as the distances between places grow ever greater. In **Nordland** things get wilder still, though save the scenery there's little of interest until you reach the steel town of **Mo-i-Rana**. Just north of here lies the **Arctic Circle**, beyond which the land becomes ever more spectacular, not least on the offshore chain of the **Lofoten Islands**, whose idyllic fishing villages (and cheap accommodation) richly merit a stop. Back on the mainland, **Narvik** is a modern port handling vast quantities of iron-ore amid some startling rocky surroundings. Further north still, the provinces of **Troms** and **Finnmark** are subtle in their appeal, but the travelling can be harder still, with **Tromsø**, a lively urban centre and university town, making the obvious stopping point. As for Finnmark, most visitors head straight for **Nordkapp**, from where the Midnight Sun is visible between early May and the end of July.

The **train** network reaches as far north as Fauske and Bodø, buses making the link to Narvik, from where a separate rail line runs to the border and then south through Sweden. Further north, access is either by the **coastal boat** (*Hurtigrute*) or bus. The boat takes just over two days to sail from Trondheim to Tromsø, two more to circumnavigate the huge fjords between Tromsø and Kirkenes, hard by the Russian border. Bus transport throughout the summer (and some of the winter) is efficient and regular, using the windswept E6 Arctic Highway as far as Kirkenes, with the E69 branching off to Nordkapp on the way.

Trondheim

TRONDHEIM, an atmospheric city with much of its eighteenth-century centre still intact, has been an important Norwegian power base for centuries, its success guaranteed by the excellence of its harbour and its position at the head of a wide and fertile valley. The early Norse parliament, or Ting, met here, and the city was once a major pilgrimage centre. The city centre sits on a small triangle of land, a pocket-sized area where the main sights – bar the marvellous cathedral – have an amiable low-key quality. Trondheim also possesses a clutch of good restaurants and a string of busy bars.

The City

The colossal **Nidaros Domkirke**, Scandinavia's largest medieval building, gloriously restored following the ravages of the Reformation and several fires, remains the focal point of the city centre (May to mid-Sept Mon–Fri 9am–3/6pm, Sat 9am–2pm, Sun 1–4pm; mid-Sept to April Mon–Fri noon–2.30pm, Sat 11.30am–2pm, Sun 1–3pm; 35kr). Taking Trondheim's former name (Nidaros means "mouth of the River Nid"), the cathedral is dedicated to King Olav, Norway's first Christian ruler, who was killed at the nearby battle of Stiklestad in 1030. After the battle, Olav's body was spirited away and buried here, his resting place marked by the erection of a chapel, which was altered and enlarged over the years to accommodate the growing bands of pilgrims, achieving cathedral status in 1152. Thereafter, it became the traditional burial place of Norwegian royalty and, since 1814, it has also been the place where Norwegian monarchs are crowned. The stonework of the early Gothic choir is especially fine, with the flying buttresses and pointed arches decorated with all manner of tiny heads and gargoyles. Inside, the gloomy half-light hides much of the lofty decorative work, but it is possible to examine the striking choir screen and font, both the work of the Norwegian sculptor Gustav Vigeland (1869–1943). If possible, visit in the early morning to avoid the tour-bus crowds.

Behind the Domkirke lies the heavily restored archbishop's palace, the **Erkebispegården**, a courtyard complex flanked by stone and brick wings of medieval provenance. The archbishops were kicked out during the Reformation and the palace was subsequently used as the city armoury. Some of the old weapons are now displayed in the west wing, which has been turned into the **Army and Resistance Museum** (March–Nov Sat & Sun 11am–4pm; June–Aug also Mon–Fri 9am–3pm; free). Its most interesting section, on the top floor, recalls the German occupation during World War II, dealing honestly with the sensitive issue of collaboration.

Near at hand is **Torvet**, the main city square, a spacious open area anchored by a statue of Olav Tryggvason, perched on a stone pillar like some medieval Nelson. The broad and pleasant avenues of Trondheim's centre radiate out from here; they date from the late seventeenth century, when they doubled as fire breaks. They were originally flanked by long rows of wooden buildings, now mostly replaced by uninspiring modern structures. One conspicuous survivor is the **Stiftsgården** (June to late Aug Mon–Sat 10am–3/5pm, Sun noon–5pm; guided tours hourly; 40kr), the yellow creation just north of Torvet on Munkegata. Built in 1774–1778 as the home of a provincial governor, it's now an official royal residence.

Practicalities

Trondheim is the first major northbound stop of the Bergen–Kirkenes **coastal boat**, which docks about 600m behind and to the north of Sentralstasjon, the combined **bus and train terminal**. Sentralstasjon is situated just over the bridge from the town centre, which occupies a small island at the mouth of the River Nid. The **tourist office** is bang in the middle of town on the main square, the Torvet (mid-May to Aug Mon–Fri 8.30am–6/10pm, Sat & Sun 10am–4/8pm; Sept to mid-May Mon–Fri 9am–4pm; ⓦwww.visit-trondheim.com). They can book **private rooms** (❸; 30kr fee). There's a large **HI hostel** at Weidemannsvei 41 (☎73 87 44 50, ⓔtrondheim.hostel@vandrerhjem.no; ❸; closed mid-Aug to mid-June), twenty minutes' hike east from the centre out over the Bakkebru bridge; bus #63 runs out in that direction from Sentralstasjon. More convenient alternatives include *Pensjonat Jarlen*, Kongensgate 40 (☎73 51 32 18; ❹), with frugal rooms at bargain prices, and the *Tulip Inn Rainbow Trondheim*, Kongensgate 15 (☎73 50 50 50, ✪www.rainbow-hotels.no;❼), a big and popular **hotel** offering well-maintained modern double rooms at reasonable rates. The city centre is best seen on foot, but if you're staying on the edge of town, take advantage of the brightly coloured **municipal bicycles** that are available from bike racks all over the centre; they are free, but you need 20kr to unlock them – as per a supermarket trolley.

For **eating**, the cafés and restaurants in the area of Bakklandet are a good choice. Try the *Dromedar*, Nedre Bakklandet 3, a fashionable café/bar offering tasty snacks and meals with a wholefood slant, or *Credo*, Ørjaveita 4, which has a very good ground-floor restaurant serving innovative seasonal food, and a bar above. The town has an active **nightlife**; the place to be is the Nedre Elvehavn area, where you'll find the very popular venue/bar/café *Blæst* in Dokkgata 8.

The Arctic Circle, Mo-i-Rana and Bodø

North of Trondheim, it's a long haul up the coast to the next major places of interest: Bodø, which is the main ferry port for the Lofoten Islands, and the gritty but likeable town of Narvik, respectively 730km and 908km away. You can cover most of the ground by train, a rattling good journey with the scenery becoming wilder and bleaker the further north you go. Departing Trondheim, it takes nine hours to reach Fauske, where the railway reaches its northern limit and turns west for the final 65km dash across to Bodø. On the way you cross the **Arctic Circle**, which, considering the amount of effort it takes to get there, is something of an anticlimax. The landscape, uninhabited for the most part, is, undeniably impressive – bare and bleak – but the gleaming **Arctic Circle Centre** (daily: May to early Sept 8/10am–6/10pm) disfigures the scene – a giant lampshade of a building plonked by the E6 highway and stuffed with every sort of tourist bauble imaginable: from "Polarsirkelen" certificates to specially stamped postcards. If you don't fancy making the long journey between Trondheim and Bodø in one hop, stop at **MO-I-RANA**, or simply "Mo", just south of the Arctic Circle. Formerly a grimy steel town, Mo has recently cleaned itself up and its leafy centre holds a pretty eighteenth-century church with a dinky onion dome. Mo has an excellent **hotel**, the *Meyergården* (☎75 13 40 00, ✪www.meyergarden.no; ❻), an extremely comfortable establishment on Ole Tobias Olsensgate, about 300m from the train station. For the adventurous, there are two great options for cave-walking here – one fairly straightforward tour to Grønligrotta and a more advanced trip into Setergrotta. Information on these tours is available from the **tourist office** (daily 9am–4pm, longer hours in summer; ☎75 13 92 00) in Ole Tobias Olsensgate.

Further north, **FAUSKE** is, along with Bodø, an important transport hub and one of the departure points of the Nord-Norgeekspressen bus service that complements the trains by carrying passengers as far as Nordkapp. These buses leave twice daily from beside Fauske train station, and tickets are purchased from the driver. There's a fifty-percent discount for InterRail and Scanrail pass holders on the first step of the route, to Narvik, a gorgeous five-hour run past fjords and snowy peaks. In Fauske, Storgata – also a part of the E6 – accommodates the handful of shops that pass for a town centre. Although it's a much better option to stay in Bodø (see below), there are a couple of useful **accommodation** options. At no. 82, you'll find the modern *Fauske Hotel* (☎75 60 20 00, ✉firmapost@fauskehotell.no; ❼), serving big breakfasts (from 7am; 60kr). Another option is the *Lundhøgda campsite* (☎75 64 39 66; closed Oct–April). In both cases, advance booking is advised.

An hour west of Fauske, **BODØ** is where the trains terminate. It's also a stop on the coastal-boat route and the main point of departure for the Lofoten Islands. The train station is midway between the dock for the coastal boat, about 700m to the northeast, and the Sentrumsterminalen, at Sjøgata 3, which is home to the bus station and the quays for both the southern Lofotens ferry (to Moskenes, Værøy and Røst) and the catamaran (*Hurtigbåt*) service to Stokmarknes, also on the Lofotens.

In the Sentrumsterminalen also is the **tourist office** (June–Aug Mon–Fri 9am–8pm, Sat 10am–8pm, Sun noon–8pm; rest of year Mon–Fri 9am–4pm, Thur till 6pm, Sat 10am–3pm; ☎75 54 80 00, ⓦwww.bodoe.com). If you're heading further north, note that the same half-price bus deal for rail pass holders travelling from Fauske to Narvik operates from Bodø to Narvik and points north too.

Bodø offers plenty of choice in **accommodation**. The tourist office has a small supply of **private rooms** both in the town and its environs (❸; 15–25kr booking fee). Alternatively, there's the no-frills **hostel** next door to the train station at Sjøgata 55 (☎75 52 11 22, ⓔbodo.hostel@vandrerhjem.no; ❸; closed Oct–April). Among several central hotels, the pick is the *Comfort Home Hotel Grand*, at Storgata 3 (☎75 54 61 00, ⓦwww.grand-bodo.no; ❼), whose handsome public rooms boast elegant Art Deco flourishes. For **eating**, easily the best bet is the Pizzakjeller'n, in the basement of the *Radisson SAS Hotel Bodø*, Storgata 2, where an enormous pizza for two will set you back around 170kr.

The Lofoten Islands

Stretched out in a skeletal curve across the Norwegian Sea, the **Lofoten Islands** are perfect for a simple, uncluttered few days. For somewhere so far north the weather is exceptionally mild, and there's plentiful **accommodation** (ⓦwww.lofotenholidays.com; from 400kr) in *rorbuer*, originally fishermen's shacks, but now usually well-equipped huts designed to accommodate from two to six people. In addition, the Lofotens have five hostels and plentiful campsites. The **coastal boat** calls at two ports, Stamsund and Svolvær, while the southern Lofoten ferry leaves Bodø for Moskenes, Værøy and Røst. There are also passenger express **boats**, which work out slightly cheaper than the coastal boat, linking both Bodø and Narvik with Svolvær. By **bus** the main long-distance services from the mainland to the Lofotens are from Bodø to Svolvær via Fauske and from Narvik to Svolvær.

The islands

The main town on **Austvågøy**, the largest and northernmost island of the group, is **SVOLVÆR**, a rather disappointing place, although it is a hub of island bus routes. Pick up island-wide information and bus schedules at the **tourist office**, located beside the main town square, by the harbour (mid-June to late Aug Mon–Fri 9am–7.30pm, Sat 10am–2pm, Sun 4–7pm; reduced hours rest of year). One of the most pleasant **places to stay** in Svolvær is *Sjøhuscamping* (☎76 07 03 36; ❹), by the seashore on Parkgata, five minutes' walk from the square, where the accommodation is in old boathouses and the price includes use of a well-equipped kitchen. Alternatively, the central *Hotel Aurora* (☎76 06 90 00; ❽) occupies a plain tower block and has perfectly adequate, en-suite rooms. Reachable by bus from Svolvær, **HENNINGSVÆR**, 23km to the southwest, is a much more beguiling village, its cramped and twisting lanes of brightly painted wooden houses lining a postcard-pretty harbour. It's well worth an **overnight stay**: try the centrally located *Den Siste Viking* (☎76 07 49 11, ⓔpostmaster@nordnorskklatreskole.no; ❸).

However, it's the next large island to the southwest, **Vestvågøy**, which captivates many travellers, due in no small part to the laid-back charm of **STAMSUND**, whose older buildings are strung along its rocky, fretted seashore. This is the first port of call for the **coastal boat** as it heads north from Bodø, and is much the best place to stay on the island. Getting there by **bus** from Austvågøy is reasonably easy, too, with several buses making the trip daily, though you do have to change at Leknes, 16km away to the west. In Stamsund, the first place to head for is the friendly **hostel** (☎76 08 93 34; ❶; closed late Oct to Dec), made up of several *rorbuer* perched over a pint-sized bay, about 1km down the road from the port and 200m from the Leknes bus stop. Fishing around here is first-class: the hostel rents out rowing boats and lines or you can go on an organized trip (150kr); afterwards, you can cook your catch on the hostel's wood-burning stoves. For touring the rest of Vestvågøy, the hostel rents out **bikes** (85kr/day).

By any standard the next two Lofoten islands, **Flakstadøya** and **Moskenesøya**, are extraordinarily beautiful. As the Lofotens taper towards their southerly conclusion, rearing peaks crimp a sea-shredded coastline studded with a string of fishing villages. Remarkably, the E10 travels along almost all of this dramatic shoreline, by way of tunnels and bridges, to **MOSKENES**, the **ferry port** midway between Bodø and the remote, southernmost bird islands of Værøy and Røst. Some 6km further on, the E10 ends at the tersely named **Å**, one of the Lofotens' most delightful villages, its huddle of old buildings rambling over a foreshore that's wedged in tight between the grey-green mountains and the surging sea. The same family owns the assortment of smart *rorbuer* (❸) that surround the dock, the adjacent **hostel** (❷), the bar and the only restaurant, where the seafood is very good; all **accommodation** can be reserved on ☎76 09 11 21; ✉aa.hostel@vandrerhjem.no. **Local bus** #101 runs along the length of the E10 from Leknes to Å once or twice daily from late June to late August, less frequently the rest of the year. Buses do not, however, tend to coincide with sailings to and from Moskenes. Consequently, if you're heading from the Moskenes ferry port to Å, you'll either have to walk – it's an easy 6km – or take a taxi (☎948 11 216, about 90kr).

Narvik

NARVIK was established less than a century ago as an ice-free port to handle the iron ore brought by train from northern Sweden, and the **iron ore docks** are still immediately conspicuous upon arrival, the rust-coloured machinery overwhelming the whole waterfront. Try and devote an hour or so to the **Krigsminne Museum** (mid-June to Aug Mon–Sat 10am–10pm, Sun 11am–5pm; March to mid-June & Sept daily 10am–4pm; 30kr), in the main square close to the docks. Run by the Red Cross, it documents the wartime German saturation bombing and bitter sea and air battles for control of the ore supplies, in which hundreds of foreign servicemen died alongside many locals.

The **train station** is at the north end of town and long-distance **buses** pull up outside. From here, it's a five- to ten-minute walk south along the main street to the main square, where the **tourist office** (mid-June to late Aug Mon–Fri 9am–7pm, Sat 10am–7pm, Sun noon–7pm; rest of year Mon–Fri 9/11am–4/5pm; ☎76 94 33 09) issues free maps and has a wide range of leaflets on the region's attractions. The best place **to stay** is the *Briedablikk Gjestehus*, Tore Hundsgate 41 (☎76 94 14 18, ⊛www.breidablikk.no; ❺), a well-tended guest house, a short, stiff walk from the tourist office at the top of Kinobakken.

On from Narvik

There's a choice of several routes on from Narvik. The **rail link**, cut through the mountains a century ago, runs east and then south into **Sweden**, reaching Kiruna in three and Stockholm in eighteen hours. It's a beautiful journey, but **bus** travellers, heading north on the *Nord-Norgeekspressen* to **Tromsø** and **Alta**, do no worse with a succession of switchback roads, lakeside forests, high peaks, gentle valleys and plunging, black-blue fjords. In summer, cut grass dries everywhere, stretched over wooden poles forming long lines on the hillsides like so much washing. Narvik is also connected to Svolvær, on the Lofotens, by bus and catamaran. Note that on all these buses and the catamaran InterRail and Scanrail pass holders get a fifty-per-cent discount.

Tromsø

TROMSØ was once known, rather preposterously, as the "Paris of the North", and the city still likes to think of itself as the capital of northern Norway, with two cathedrals, a clutch of reasonably interesting museums and an above-average (and affordable) nightlife, patronized by its high-profile student population. Certainly, as a base for this part of the country, it's hard to beat, set in magnificent landscape – dramatic mountains and craggy shoreline. In the centre of town, the **Domkirke** (Tues–Sat 10am–4pm, Sun 10am–2pm; free) reflects the town's nineteenth-century prosperity, the result of its barter trade with Russia. From the church, it's a short walk north along the harbourfront to the most diverting of the city's museums, the **Polar Museum** (daily 10/11am–3/7pm; 40kr), whose varied displays include skeletons retrieved from the permafrost of Svalbard and a detailed section on the polar explorer Roald Amundsen. On the other side of the water, over the spindly Tromsø Bridge, the white and ultramodern **Arctic Cathedral** (June to mid-Aug Mon–Sat 10am–8pm, Sun 1–8pm; mid-April to May & mid-Aug to Sept daily 3–6pm; 20kr) is spectacular, made up of eleven immense triangular concrete sections representing the eleven Apostles left after the betrayal.

Practicalities

The **coastal boat** docks in the centre of town at the foot of Kirkegata; **buses** arrive and leave from the adjacent car park. The **tourist office** is at Storgata 61, near the Domkirke (Mon–Fri 8.30am–4/6pm, Sat 10.30am–2/5pm; June to early Sept also 10.30am–2/5pm; ⓦwww.destinasjontromso.no). They have a small supply of **private rooms** (❸). The **hostel**, *Tromsø Vandrerhjem*, Åsgårdveien 9 (☎77 65 76 28, ⓔtromso.hostel@vandrerhjem.no; ❸; late June to mid-Aug only), is some 2km west of the quay; several city buses go near there – ask at the bus station. Alternatively, try one of two reasonable, if frugal **guest houses**: *Ami*, on the hillside directly west of the city centre at Skolegata 24 (☎77 68 22 08, ⓦwww.amihotel.no; ❹), or the *Nord*, nearby at Parkgata 4 (☎77 66 83 00, ⓦwww.hotellnord.no; ❹). The nearest **campsite**, *Tromsdalen Camping* (☎77 63 80 37), lies over the bridge on the mainland, about 1500m beyond the Arctic Cathedral. Tromsø has a varied selection of **restaurants**, **cafés** and **pubs**. For excellent coffee, pastries and light snacks try *Kaffebønna*, Strandtorvet 1. *Aunegården*, at Sjøgata 29, has everything from coffee and tasty cake to traditional Norwegian dishes. The *Sjømatrestauranten Arctandria* and the adjacent *Bifhuset*, Strandtorget 1, have excellent food, and there's a good, lively pub, *Skarven*. In the evening, *Blå Rock Café*, Strandgata 14, is a lively spot with a jukebox and a rock 'n' roll crowd.

Honningsvåg and Nordkapp

Connected to the mainland by an ambitious combination of tunnels and bridges, bleak and treeless Magerøya is Norway's most northerly island. The only settlement of any size here is **HONNINGSVÅG**, a crusty fishing village that makes a steady income from accommodating the hundreds of summertime tourists bent on visiting Nordkapp, just 34km away. Amongst several **hotels**, one of the more appealing is the *Rica Bryggen*, which occupies a plain but well-kept concrete high-rise down at the head of the harbour (☎78 47 28 88; ❾). Much cheaper is the **campsite/cabin** *Nordkapp* complex 8km away on the road to Nordkapp (☎78 47 33 77; ❸; closed late Sept to May). Long-distance buses arrive in the centre of Honningsvåg and there's a limited bus service on to Nordkapp (late June to mid-Aug 2 daily except Sat; 50min). When the buses aren't running, the only option is a taxi (800kr) – though note that the road is closed throughout the winter and often in spring too. Travellers with the **coastal boat**, which puts in at Honningsvåg, should note that there's a special coach on to Nordkapp and back within the two-and-a-half-hour stop. For **food** in Honningsvåg, there are a couple of takeaway kiosks along Storgata and a very good seafood restaurant at the *Best Western Honningsvåg Brygge Hotel*.

   NORDKAPP is only a cliff, 307m high, with an arguable claim to being the northernmost point of Europe. But there is something exhilarating about this bleak, wind-battered promontory. Originally a Sami sacrificial site, it was actually named by the English explorer Richard Chancellor in 1553, but it was not until the late nineteenth century that a visit by King Oscar II opened the tourist floodgates. These days the headland is occupied by **North Cape Hall** (daily: April to late May, Sept & early Oct noon/2–5pm; late May to early June till 1am; late May to late Aug 9am–midnight/2am; 175kr), an extremely flashy complex that contains souvenir shops, cafés, restaurants and huge windows from where you can survey the surging ocean below. The complex also has a **post office**, where you can get your letters specially stamped. Tourists gather here in numbers to watch the **Midnight Sun** (between early May and end of July).

Travel details

Trains

Åndalsnes to: Dombås (2 daily; 1hr 30min); Oslo (2 daily; 6hr 30min).

Dombås to: Trondheim (3–4 daily; 2hr 30min).

Myrdal to: Flåm (June–Sept 11–12 daily; Oct–May 4 daily; 50min).

Oslo to: Åndalsnes (2–3 daily; 6hr 30min); Bergen (4–5 daily; 6hr 30min); Trondheim (3–4 daily; 8hr 15min); Voss (4–5 daily; 5hr 40min).

Trondheim to: Bodø (2–3 daily; 10hr); Dombås (3–4 daily; 2hr 30min); Fauske (2–3 daily; 9hr 20min); Mo-i-Rana (2–3 daily; 7hr); Oslo (3–4 daily; 7hr); Stockholm (2 daily; 12hr).

Buses

Ålesund to: Bergen (1–2 daily; 10hr); Hellesylt (1–2 daily except Sat; 2hr 40min); Stryn (1–2 daily except Sat; 4hr); Trondheim (1–2 daily; 8hr 10min).

Alta to: Hammerfest (1–2 daily except Sat; 3hr); Honningsvåg (late June to mid-Aug 1–2 daily except Sat; 5hr); Kautokeino (1–2 daily except Sat; 2hr 30min); Tromsø (April to late Oct 1–2 daily; 7hr).

Åndalsnes to: Geiranger (mid-June to late Aug 2 daily; 3–4hr); Molde (3–7 daily; 1hr 30min); Ålesund (3–4 daily; 2hr 20min).

Balestrand to: Sogndal (2 daily; 1hr 10min).

Bergen to: Ålesund (1–2 daily; 10hr); Trondheim (1

daily; 14hr); Voss (4 daily; 1hr 45min).

Fauske to: Bodø (2–3 daily; 1hr 10min); Narvik (2 daily; 7hr).

Hammerfest to: Alta (1–2 daily except Sat; 3hr); Skaidi (1–2 daily except Sat; 1hr 15min).

Honningsvåg to: Nordkapp (late June to mid-Aug 2 daily except Sat; 50min).

Kautokeino to: Alta (1–2 daily except Sat; 2hr 30min).

Narvik to: Alta (1 daily; 14hr); Tromsø (1–2 daily; 4hr 40min).

Oslo to: Bergen (4–5 daily; 10hr).

Stryn to: Bergen (2 daily; 7hr); Oslo (1 daily; 8hr 30min).

Tromsø to: Alta (April to late Oct 1–2 daily; 7hr); Narvik (2 daily; 7hr); Nordkapp (late June to mid-Aug 1 daily except Sat; 14hr).

Trondheim to: Ålesund (2–3 daily; 8hr); Bergen (2 daily; 14hr); Kristiansund (2–3 daily; 5hr); Stryn (2 daily; 7hr 20min).

Voss to: Bergen (4 daily; 1hr 45min); Sogndal (2 daily; 3hr).

Catamaran ferries

Bergen to: Balestrand (1–2 daily; 4hr); Flåm (1–2 daily; 5hr 30min).

Bodø to: Svolvær (1 daily except Sat; 5hr 30min).

Narvik to: Svolvær (1 daily except Sat; 4hr).

Poland

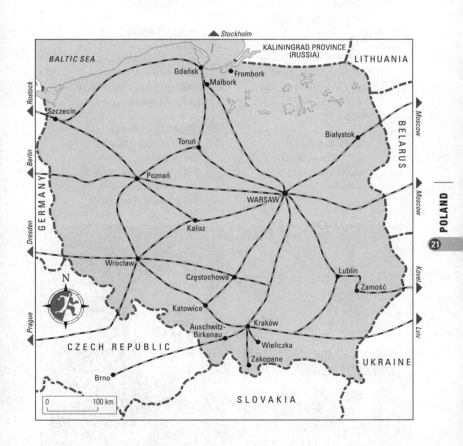

Poland highlights

✳ Old Town, Warsaw
Rebuilt from rubble after
World War II, this monu-
ment to Polish suffering
and recovery is also well
stocked with lively cafés
and restaurants. **See
p.801**

✳ The beach, Sopot A vast
stretch of white sand
near Poland's lively sum-
mertime capital, Sopot.
See p.806

✳ Cloth Hall, Kraków At the
heart of Europe's most
beautiful main squares.
See p.810

**✳ Auschwitz-Birkenau
camps** Fifty years on,
the Nazis' most infa-
mous death camps still
make a haunting impres-
sion. **See p.813**

✳ Tatra Mountains Hike
among the towering
peaks and crystal-clear
lakes and rest in the
charming mountain resort
of Zakopane. **See p.814**

✳ Old Town, Wrocław
Mostly overlooked by
the hordes heading for
Kraków, Wrocław has all
the beauty, but none of
the crowds. **See p.815**

Introduction and basics

Images of **Poland** flooded the world media throughout the 1980s. Strikes and riots at the Lenin Shipyards of Gdańsk were the harbingers of the disintegration of communism in Eastern Europe. The decade's end saw the establishment of a government led by the Solidarity trade union, followed by the victory of union leader Lech Wałęsa in Poland's first presidential election since the 1920s – though to many people's surprise, he lost the presidency in 1995 to "post-communist" Aleksander Kwasniewski, who remains in power with a right-wing parliament.

The pattern was familiar enough through the Eastern bloc, but the rebirth of democratic Poland was a uniquely Catholic revolution. The **Church** has always been the principal defender of the nation's identity, and its physical presence is inescapable in Baroque buildings, roadside shrines and images of the national icon, the Black Madonna. Encounters with the **people** are at the core of any experience of the country. On trains and buses, in the streets or the village bar, you'll never be stuck for opportunities for contact: Polish hospitality is legendary.

Unless you're driving to Poland, you're likely to begin your travels with one of the three major cities. Much of **Warsaw**, the capital, conforms to the stereotype of Eastern European greyness, but its historic centre, beautiful parks and vibrant nightlife are diverting enough. **Kraków**, the ancient royal capital, is the real crowd puller, rivalling the Central European elegance of Prague and Vienna. The Hanseatic city of **Gdańsk** offers a dynamic brew of politics and commerce, while nearby **Sopot** features golden beaches. German influences abound in the north and southwest of the country, in Gdańsk itself, in the austere castles and fortified settlements along the River Wisła (Vistula) and in the divided province of Silesia. Yet, to the north of Silesia, quintessentially Polish **Poznań** is revered as the cradle of the nation.

Poland has many regions of unspoilt natural beauty, none more popular than the alpine **Tatras**, the most exhilarating walking terrain in the country.

Information and maps

Most towns and cities have a **tourist office** (known as IT or *informacja turystyczna*); sometimes these are run by the local municipality and are rather good; sometimes, however, they're privately run travel agencies using the label to sell tours and tickets. In addition, two long-established tourist organizations which may be of help are **PTTK**, specializing in hiking tourism, and **Almatur**, a student travel bureau.

The best road **map** is Bartholomew's *Europmap: Poland* (1:800,000). Once you're in the country, you'll find EMPiK stores (on most high streets) are well stocked with regional and city maps. Most of these maps have tram and bus routes marked on them.

Money and banks

The Polish currency is the **złoty** (zł), which is divided into 100 groszy. Coins come in denominations of 1, 2, 5, 10, 20 and 50 groszy, and 1, 2 and 5 złoty; notes in

---

Poland on the net

- ⓦ **www.poland.pl** The official website with many links
- ⓦ **www.hotelsinpoland.com** Hotel booking site
- ⓦ **www.warsawvoice.pl** National and local news, events
- ⓦ **www.inyourpocket.com** City guides to Warsaw, Kraków, Gdańsk and Wrocław

denominations of 10, 20, 50, 100 and 200 złoty. There are about 4zł to the dollar and 6zł to the pound sterling.

The best way to get money is by using one of the many **ATMs**. Banks (usually open Mon–Fri 7.30am–5pm, Sat 7.30am–2pm) and exchange offices (kantors) offer similar **exchange rates**. Most kantors will not change travellers' cheques. Hotels offer poor exchange rates. Major **credit cards** are accepted by most hotels and restaurants, and you can arrange a cash advance on most cards; an increasing number of shops take plastic.

Communications

Post offices are identified by the name Urząd Pocztowy (Poczta for short). Theoretically, each city's head office has a **poste restante** facility: make sure that anyone addressing mail to you adds "No. 1" after the city's name. Head office opening hours are usually Mon–Sat 7/8am–8pm; branches close at 6pm or earlier.

For public **pay phones** you'll need to buy a phone card from a post office or newsagent kiosk. They come in denominations of 25, 50, 75 and 100 units (11.3zł, 20.4zł & 37.2zł) and can be used for international calls, though these are expensive.

You'll find at least one decent, central **internet café** in the larger towns; an hour online costs 4–10zł.

Getting around

Poland has comprehensive and cheap public transport services, though they can often be overcrowded and excruciatingly slow.

Trains

The reasonably efficient Polish State Railways (PKP) runs three main types of **trains**. Express services (*ekspresowy*), particularly the ones marked IC (intercity) or EC (Eurocity), are the ones to go for if you're travelling long distances, as they stop at the main cities only; seat reservations are compulsory and involve a small supplementary charge. So-called fast trains (*pośpieszny*)

have far more stops, and reservations are optional. The grubby normal services (*osobowy*) are best avoided: in rural areas they stop at every haystack.

Count on paying about £4/$5.5 for 100km of travel by train. It's sometimes worth paying the fifty percent extra to travel **first-class** or make a **reservation** (*miejscówka*), as sardine-like conditions are fairly common. Some long journeys are best done overnight; second-class sleepers are a bargain at around £7/$11 per person. For journeys of over 100km and for international trips you can **buy tickets** in advance at Orbis travel agencies (branches in all towns and cities). First- and second-class **PolRail passes** for the whole network are available in Poland for periods of eight (£100/$147 first-class, £67/$98 second-class), fifteen (£117/$171, £78/$114), 21 days (£134/$195, £89/$130) or a month (£167/$245, £112/$163). EuroDomino and InterRail passes are valid in Poland.

Buses

Intercity buses operated by **PKS**, the national bus company, may be cheaper than trains, but are slow and often overcrowded; there are few long-haul routes and no overnight journeys. In rural areas, notably the mountain regions, there's greater choice and convenience, and here the bus may be faster than the train. Main bus stations are usually alongside the train station. The private company **Polski Express** (☏022/620 03 26, ✆www.polskiexpress.pl) offers slightly pricier intercity journeys in rather more comfortable and faster buses – they're particularly useful if you're travelling on radial routes out from Warsaw, but are still much slower than trains. Many stations cannot allocate seats for services starting from another town – in such cases you have to buy a ticket from the driver. As with trains, Orbis offices are the best place to go if you want to book on an international route.

Accommodation

Accommodation will almost certainly account for most of your costs in Poland, though there are now plenty of cheap alternatives to the heavily touted international hotels. Look out for weekend reductions in big-city hotels. In addition, there are good deals to be had in several cities if you **book online**.

Hotels

Most Polish towns have at least one **budget hotel** offering spartan but habitable rooms with WC and shower located in the hallway, usually costing less than £8/$12 per person. Hotels in this category often include three- or four-person rooms, which work out very cheaply indeed if you're travelling as a group. Establishments offering additional comforts such as en-suite shower, TV and a decent breakfast need not cost a great deal more (reckon on £10–18/$14–25 per person), although standards in these **mid-range places** can be unpredictable: some rooms have wallpaper and fittings that haven't changed for decades, while others look like Scandinavian furniture showrooms. Hotels aiming at **international business standard** are often overpriced for what they are – especially in Warsaw.

Hostels

Poland has some two hundred **hostels** (*schroniska młodzieżowe*). Many are only open at the height of summer and are liable to be booked solid, while most of the year-round hostels still conform to the hair-shirt ideals of the movement's founders with lock-outs and curfews. Prices are rarely more than £4/$6 a head, though, and many hostels are located close to town centres. For a complete list, contact the Polish Youth Hostel Federation (PTSM), ul Chocimska 28, Warsaw (Mon–Fri 8am–3.30pm; ☎022/849 81 28, ⓦwww.ptsm.pl).

Alternatively you can ask the tourist offices about summer accommodation in **university hostels**; charges (including breakfast) are around £3/$4.50 for ISIC card-holding students and £5–7/$7.50–12 for others (no age limit), depending on whether they wish to share a room. They are often the best bet in summer, being as cheap as hostels without the restrictions, although they tend to be located in the suburbs. A generous number of **refuges** (clearly marked on hiking maps) enable you to make long-distance treks.

Private rooms

It's possible to get a **room in a private house** (*kwatery prywatne*) almost anywhere in the country. Those in the cities are often pretty shabby, although in mountain resorts they can be extremely comfortable. Several major cities have a **room-finding service**, usually known as the Biuro Zakwaterowania, and most tourist information offices will also help. Charges are around £8/$12 per person, £12/$18 in Warsaw. You'll be given a choice of location and category; it makes sense not to register for too many nights until you know you'll like the place. Many houses in rural holiday areas hang out signs saying *noclegi* (lodging) or *pokoje* (rooms). It's up to you to bargain: £3/$4.50 is the least you can expect to pay. Individuals with rooms to let may approach you at train stations – this can be the way to a bargain, but carries all the usual risks of an unofficial deal.

Camping

There are some four hundred **campsites** throughout the country; for a complete list see the *Campingi w Polsce* map, available from EMPiK and other bookshops. Apart from main holiday areas, they can be found in most cities: the ones on the outskirts are invariably linked by bus to the centre and often have the benefit of a peaceful location, all-day restaurant and swimming pool. Most open May–Sept only. Charges usually work out at less than £2/$3 a head, a bit more if you come by car. Many sites have chalets to rent which, though spartan, are good value at around £4/$6 per head. Camping rough, outside of the national parks, is fine so long as you're discreet.

Food and drink

Poles take their food seriously, providing meals of feast-like proportions for the most casual visitors. The cuisine is a complex mix of influences: Russian, German, Ukrainian, Lithuanian and Jewish traditions have all left their mark.

Food

Hotel **breakfasts** might include fried eggs with ham, mild frankfurters, a selection of cold meats and cheese, rolls and jam. If you need to find your own breakfast you could do worse than head for a **milk bar** (*bar mleczny*; usually open from early morning until 5/6pm), the traditional place for cheap and filling Polish snacks.

Traditional Polish **takeaway stands** usually sell *zapiekanki*, baguette-like pieces of bread topped with melted cheese, while some sell chips (*frytki*) with sausage (*kiełbasa*) or chicken (*kurczak*).

Many **restaurants** close late, but the older tradition of closing at 9 or 10pm persists in some places. First on the menu in most places are **soups**, varying from delicate dishes to concoctions that are virtually meals in themselves. Best known are *barszcz*, a spicy beetroot broth, and *żurek*, a soup made of fermented rye that tastes much better than it looks. The basis of most **main courses** is fried or grilled meat, such as *kotlet schabowy* (a pork cutlet). Two inexpensive specialities you'll find everywhere are *bigos* (cabbage stewed with meat) and *pierogi*, dumplings stuffed with meat and mushrooms, or with cottage cheese, onion and spices (*pierogi ruskie*). Pancakes (*naleśniki*) often come as a main course, stuffed with cottage cheese (*ze serem*). Fried potato pancakes (*placki ziemniaczane*) are particularly good, served in sour cream or spicy paprika sauce. The **cakes**, **pastries** and **other sweets** that can be found in cake shops (*cukiernia*) – even in small villages – are as good as any in Central Europe. *Sernik* (cheesecake) is a national favourite, as are *makowiec* (poppyseed cake), *drożdżówka* (a sponge cake, often topped with plums), and *babka piaskowa* (marble cake).

Drink

Poles' capacity for **alcohol** has never been in doubt, and drinking is a national pursuit. Poles can't compete with their Czech neighbours in the production and consumption of **beer** (*piwo*), but there are a number of fairly drinkable Polish brands. It's with **vodka** (*wódka*) that Poles really get into their stride. Ideally it is served neat, well chilled, in measures of 25 or 50 grams and knocked back in

one go. Best of the clear vodkas are *Żytnia* and *Wyborowa*. Of the **flavoured varieties**, first on most people's list is *żubrówka*, infused with bison grass.

Opening hours and holidays

Most **shops** open on weekdays from around 10am to 6pm, except food stores which may open as early as 6am and stay open well into the evening. Many shops close on Saturday afternoons and all day Sunday. RUCH kiosks, where you buy newspapers and municipal transport tickets, generally open at about 6am. Increasing numbers of street traders do business well into the evening, and you can find shops in major cities (particularly the EMPiK stores) offering late-night opening throughout the week. **Museums** and **historic monuments** almost invariably close one day per week, usually Monday. Entrance tends to cost very little, and is often free on one day of the week. **Public holidays** are: Jan 1; Easter Mon; May 1; May 3; Corpus Christi (May/June); Aug 15; Nov 1; Nov 11; Dec 25 & 26.

Emergencies

The biggest potential hassles are hotel room thefts, pickpocketing and car break-ins. Safely store your valuables when travelling by night train; on international trains it may be wise to book a couchette compartment with a lockable door. Polish **police** (*policja*) are courteous and helpful but may not speak English.

In a medical emergency most foreigners tend to rely on the pricey private medical centres run by **Medicover** (☎022/570 11 11, ⊛www.medicover.com).

Emergency numbers

Police ☎997, ambulance ☎999, fire ☎998.

Warsaw

First impressions of **WARSAW**, likely to be most visitors' first experience of Poland, are all too often negative. The years of communist rule did little for the city aesthetically, and there's sometimes a hollowness to the faithful reconstructions of earlier eras. The once tawdry state shopfronts have, however, given way to a host of colourful private initiatives.

Warsaw (*Warszawa*) became the capital of Poland in 1596, when **King Zygmunt III** moved his court here from Kraków. The city was badly damaged by the Swedes during the invasion of 1655 and then extensively reconstructed by the **Saxon kings** in the late seventeenth century. The **Partitions** abruptly terminated this golden age, as Warsaw was absorbed into Prussia in 1795. Napoleon's arrival in 1806 gave Varsovians brief hopes of liberation, but following the 1815 Congress of Vienna, the city was integrated into the Russian-controlled Congress **Kingdom of Poland**. It was only with the outbreak of World War I that Russian control began to crumble, and with the restoration of Polish independence in 1918, Warsaw reverted to its position as capital. Then, with the outbreak of World War II, came the progressive annihilation of the city. Hitler, infuriated by the 1943 Ghetto Uprising and the 1944 **Warsaw Uprising**, ordered the elimination of Warsaw; by the end of the war 850,000 Varsovians – two-thirds of the city's 1939 population – were dead or missing. The task of rebuilding took ten years of ceaseless labour.

Arrival and information

Okęcie international airport is 8km southwest of the Old Town: avoid the rip-off taxi drivers and take bus #175 (#611 at night) into town, which passes the main **train station**, Warszawa Centralna, in the modern centre, before arriving in the Old Town. There's a 24-hour left-luggage office at Warszawa Centralna, as well as lockers where you can store luggage for up to ten days. The main **bus station**, Centralny Dworzec PKS, is located right next to the Warszawa Zachodnia suburban train station, 3km west of Centralna station. To get into town from here catch any eastbound train or bus #127, #130, #517 or #E5. Intercity buses operated by Polski Express arrive at and depart from the bus stop on al Jana Pawła II, just outside the western entrance of Centralna train station.

The helpful IT office in the main hall of Centralna station (daily 8am–8pm; ☎022/524 11 41, ⊛www.warsawtour.pl) is the best source of general **information** and has excellent free city maps and brochures. There's another IT office on the corner of Plac Zamkowy at Krakowskie Przedmieście 89 (same times), as well as information booths at the airport arrivals hall and the main bus station.

For **what's on** listings in English consult either the monthly *Warsaw Insider* (⊛www.warsawinsider.com; 6zł) or the more detailed bi-monthly *Warsaw in Your Pocket* (⊛www.inyourpocket.com; 10zł). Both are available at information centres and at some hotels and bookstores.

City transport

Buses and **trams** are the main forms of transport and run until about 11pm; after that, night buses leave every thirty minutes from behind the Palace of Culture. There is also one **metro** line running through the centre of town (as far north as Ratusz station on Plac Bankowy).

Tickets for trams, buses and the metro are bought from green RUCH shacks or from automatic ticket machines and cost 2.4zł for a single trip, or 3.6zł for an hour. You need three tickets for night buses. You also need an extra ticket for bulky luggage. Punch your tickets in the machines on board – Warsaw's zealous inspectors are merciless. Day (7.2zł), three-day (12zł) and week (26zł) **passes** are also available from some kiosks.

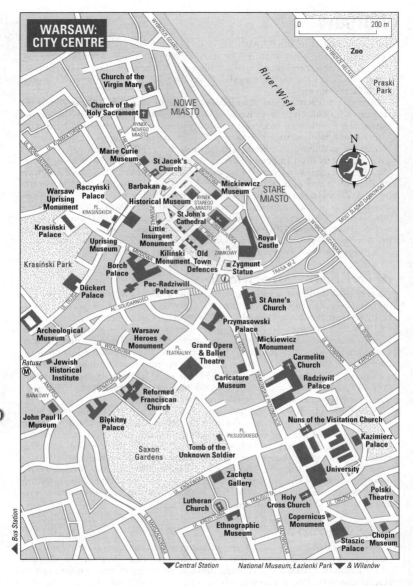

WARSAW: CITY CENTRE

Taxis cost about 1.8zł per kilometre. To avoid being ripped off take only taxis that have the price per kilometre, the name and the telephone number clearly marked. Don't get a taxi from outside the Centralna Station – go to the nearby ul Emilii Plater, or better still, book one; try Super Taxi (☎022/9622) or MPT (☎022/919).

Accommodation

Warsaw has a paltry collection of **hostels**, although during July and August the **student hostels** are another possibility, without those nasty lockouts and curfews – ask at the Centralna Station information centre. The best bet for help with hotel bookings are the Centralna station and Old Town IT offices (see above). Phoning ahead or booking is essential in summer.

Hostels

Agrykola ul Myśliwiecka 9 ☎022/622 91 10, ✉recepcja@hotelagrykola.pl. The city's best hostel, with clean modern rooms, friendly staff and no curfew. Near Łazienki park; take bus #151 from the station to the Rozbrat stop on the bridge. ❷

Przy Rynku ul Rynek Nowego Miasta 4 ☎022/831 50 33. The best of the summer hostels. ❷

Syrenka ul Karolkowa 53a ☎022/632 88 29. Take tram #12 or #24 from Centralna station six stops in the direction of Ochota (get off near the Wola department store). Lockout 5–10pm; curfew 11pm. ❷

Ul Smolna 30 ☎022/827 89 52. Barrack-like conditions but central location. A five-minute bus ride along al Jerozolimskie from the main station – any bus heading towards Nowy Świat will drop you at the corner of the street. Reception 4–9pm; curfew 11pm. ❷

Hotels

Harctour Niemcewicza 17 ☎022/659 00 11; ✉hharctur@beph.pl. Spartan but tolerable place 500m east of the main bus station. Some en suites. ❸

Ibis Centrum al Solidarności 165 ☎022/520 30 00; ✉h2894@accor-hotels.com. One of the few places offering good standards at genuinely mid-range prices. 2km west of the Old Town. ❺

Mazowiecki ul Mazowiecka 10 ☎022/827 23 65; ✉www.mazowiecki.com.pl. Renovated budget hotel, bang in the centre. Some en suites. ❹

Metalowcy ul Długa 29 ☎022/831 40 21. Slightly grubby basic rooms with shared bathrooms on the top floor of a building just west of the Old Town. ❷

Na Wodzie Wybrzeże Kościuszkowski ☎022/628 58 83. A central "boatel" with clean rooms, moored right next to Poniatowskiego bridge. Take any tram from Centralna station towards Praga and get off at the fourth stop, on the bridge. Closed Nov–April. ❷

Praski al Solidarności 61 ☎022/818 49 89. Clean, simple rooms, just across the river from the Old Town. The tram drops you right outside the hotel. ❹

Campsites

Camping Gromada ul Żwirki i Wigury 32 ☎022/825 43 91. Best and most popular of the Warsaw campsites, on the way to the airport – bus #188 or #175 will get you there. Cheap bungalows from 20zł.

Majawa Boh. Bitwy Warszawskiej 1920r. 15/17 ☎022/822 91 21. Good location just south of the bus station – take bus #154. Bungalows available for 70zł.

The City

Everything you'll want to see in Warsaw lies on the western bank of the **Wisła** (Vistula) river. It's here that you'll find the central business and shopping district, **Śródmieście**, grouped around Centralna station and the nearby Palace of Culture, with the more picturesque and tourist-friendly **Old Town** (Stare Miasto) just to the north.

The Old Town

The title "Old Town" – Stare Miasto – is in some respects a misnomer for the historic nucleus of Warsaw. After World War II this compact network of streets and alleyways lay in rubble, only to be painstakingly reconstructed in the decades afterwards. **Plac Zamkowy** (Castle Square), on the south side of the Old Town, is the obvious place to start a tour.

On the east side of the square is the former **Royal Castle** (☻www.zamek-krolewski.art.pl), once home to the royal family and seat of the Polish parliament, now the **Castle Museum** (Tues–Sat 10am–4pm, Sun 11am–4pm; 14zł). Though the structure is a replica, many of its furnishings are the originals, scooted into hiding during the first bombing raids. After passing the most lavish section of the castle, the **Royal Apartments of King Stanisław August**, you come to the magnificent **Canaletto Room**, with its views of Warsaw by Bernardo Bellotto, nephew of the famous Canaletto – whose name he appropriated to make his pictures sell better. Marvellous in their detail, these cityscapes provided important information for the architects rebuilding the city after the war.

On Świętojańska, north of the castle, stands **St John's Cathedral**, the oldest church in Warsaw. A few yards away, the Old Town Square is one of the most remarkable bits of postwar reconstruction anywhere in Europe. Flattened during the Warsaw Uprising, its three-storey merchants' houses have been rebuilt to their seventeenth- and eighteenth-century designs. The **Warsaw Historical Museum** (Tues & Thurs 11am–6pm, Wed & Fri 10am–3.30pm, Sat & Sun 10.30am–4pm; 5zł, free Sun) on the north side has an important section about the resistance to the Nazis. Don't miss the impressive English-language film about Warsaw's wartime destruction (Tues–Sat noon).

From the Rynek, ul Nowomiejska leads to the sixteenth-century **Barbakan**, which used to guard the Nowomiejska Gate, the northern entrance to the city. The fortress is part of the old town defences, which run all the way around from Plac Zamkowy to the northeastern edge of the district.

The New Town and the Ghetto

Cross the ramparts from the Barbakan and you're into the **New Town** (Nowe Miasto) district, which despite its name dates from the early fifteenth century, but was formally joined to Warsaw only at the end of the eighteenth. The heart of the district is the **Rynek Nowego Miasta**, once a commercial hub, now a soothing change from the bustle of the Old Town. Tucked into the eastern corner is the **Church of the Holy Sacrament**, commissioned by Queen Maria Sobieska in memory of her husband Jan's victory over the Turks at Vienna in 1683. West from the square, near the Warsaw Uprising monument, is the majestic **Krasiński Palace**, its facade bearing fine sculptures by Andreas Schlüter. To the south of the palace gardens stands the former Stock Exchange, now housing the extensive **John Paul II Collection** (Tues–Sat 10am–5pm; 5zł), featuring paintings from all periods between the Renaissance and the Impressionists.

West of here is the former **Ghetto** area. In 1939 there were an estimated 380,000 Jews living in and around Warsaw – one-third of the total population. By May 1945, the ghetto had been razed to the ground and around 300 Jews were left. The **Nożyk Synagogue** on ul Twarda is the only one of the Ghetto's three synagogues still standing. To the north of the Ghetto area, the **Ghetto Heroes Monument** was made from materials ordered by Hitler for a monument to the Reich's anticipated victory. You can get an idea of what most of Jewish Warsaw looked like in the miraculously untouched **ul Próżna**.

Śródmieście

The area stretching from the Old Town down towards Łazienki Park – **Śródmieście** – is the increasingly fast-paced heart of Warsaw, bisected by the Royal Way thoroughfare, which runs almost uninterrupted from Plac Zamkowy to the palace of Wilanów. **Krakowskie Przedmieście**, the first part of the Royal Way, is lined with historic buildings.

Even in a city not lacking in Baroque churches, the **Church of the Nuns of the Visitation** stands out, with its columned, statue-topped facade; it's also one of the very few buildings in central Warsaw to have come through World War II unscathed. Most of the rest of Krakowskie Przedmieście is taken up by **Warsaw University**. On the main campus courtyard stands the seventeenth-century **Kazimierz Palace**, once a royal summer residence, while across the street from the gates is the **Czapski Palace**, now home of the Academy of Fine Arts. Just south is the Baroque **Holy Cross Church**, wrecked in a two-week battle during the Warsaw Uprising; photographs of the distinctive figure of Christ left standing among the ruins became poignant emblems of Warsaw's suffering. On a pillar to the left side of the nave there's an urn containing Chopin's heart.

Biggest among Warsaw's palaces is the early-nineteenth-century **Staszic Palace**, now the headquarters of the Polish Academy of Sciences. South of here, the main street becomes **Nowy Świat** (New World), first settled in the mid-seventeenth century. Palaces of the aristocracy give way to shops and cafés as you move down this lively boulevard. West along al Jerozolimskie is the **National Museum** (Tues, Wed & Fri 10am–4pm, Thurs noon–5pm, Sat & Sun 10am–5pm; 13zł, free Sat), an impressive compendium of archeology and European paintings and sculptures – Caravaggio, Bellini, Brueghel and Rodin included. Further west lies the commercial heart of the city. Marszałkowska, the main north-south road cutting across Jerozolimskie, is lined with stores and boutiques. Towering over everything is the **Palace of Culture and Science**, a gift from Stalin that the Polish people could hardly refuse. Apart from a vast conference hall, the interior contains offices, theatres, nightclubs, cinemas, swimming pools and a casino. Locals joke that the platform on the thirtieth floor (daily 9am–6pm; 15zł) is the only viewpoint from which you can't see the palace.

Łazienki Park and Palace

South of the commercial district, on the east side of al Ujazdowskie, is the attractive and popular **Łazienki Park**. Once a hunting ground, the area was bought in the 1760s by King Stanisław August, who turned it into an English-style park and built the slender Neoclassical **Łazienki Palace** (Tues–Sun 9.30am–3pm; 11zł, Thurs free) across the park lake.

Oak-lined paths lead from the park entrance and the ponderous **Chopin Monument** to the palace. Most of the lavish furnishings, paintings and sculptures survived the war intact, having been hidden during the occupation. The stuccoed **ballroom** is lined with a tasteful collection of busts and sculptures. As the adjoining picture galleries demonstrate, Stanisław was a discerning art collector. Upstairs are the king's private apartments, most of them entirely reconstructed since the war. The park itself stays open till dusk.

Wilanów

The grandest of Warsaw's palaces, **Wilanów** (Mon & Wed–Sat 9.30am–2.30pm, Sun 9.30am–6pm; 15zł, free Thurs) makes an easy excursion from the city centre: take bus #180 south from anywhere along the main drag from the Old Town through Krakowskie Przedmieście and Nowy Świat to its terminus. King Jan Sobieski purchased the existing manor house and estate in 1677 and spent nearly twenty years turning it into the "Polish Versailles". Among the sixty-odd rooms you'll find styles ranging from the lavish early Baroque of the apartments of Jan Sobieski to the classical grace of the nineteenth-century Potocki rooms. The gate on the left side beyond the main entrance opens onto the stately **palace gardens** (9.30am till sunset; closed Tues; 2zł), while to the right before you enter is the **Poster Museum** (Tues–Fri 10am–4pm, Sat & Sun 10am–5pm; 4zł, free Wed), a mishmash of the inspired and the bizarre.

Eating and drinking

For basic snacks, **milk bars** and fast-food joints provide a good fill for under £3/$5. Though service is often bad and prices are higher than elsewhere in Poland, there are quite a few perfectly good **restaurants**. There's also an increasing number of decent **cafés and bars**.

Cafés and snack bars

Belle Epoque ul Freta 18. Sip tea amongst a wonderful collection of antiques – all for sale.
Coffeeheaven Nowy Świat 46. Sandwiches, cakes and good coffee.

Marak ul Świętokrzyska 18. Excellent, affordable and trendy new soup kitchen.
Mata Hari Nowy Świat 52. Tiny vegetarian

lunchroom with Asian specialities. Closed Sun.
Pod Barbakanem ul Mostowa 29. Milk bar with
prime location overlooking the Barbakan.
Uniwersytecki Krakowskie Przedmieście 20. Milk
bar frequented by students.

Restaurants

Kompania Piwna ul Podwale 25 ☎ 022/635 63
14. Rowdy cellar restaurant, with live traditional
music, huge portions of country-style food and
Czech beer.
Le Cedre al Solidarności 61 ☎ 022/670 11 66.
Excellent Lebanese cuisine.
Manufaktura ul Bednarska 28/30. Cheap and
central medieval-style pancake restaurant.
Pod Samsonem ul Freta 3/5. Good, cheap Jewish
food in simple surroundings.
Qchnia Artystyczna al Ujazdowskie 6. In
Ujazdowski Castle, with a wonderful view of
Łazienki Park from the terrace. Good vegetarian
selection.
Venezia ul Marzałkowska 10/16 ☎ 022/621 69
73. Excellent Italian food at reasonable prices.
Warsaw Tortilla Factory ul Wilcza 46 ☎ 022/621
86 22. A lively expat favourite with affordable Tex-
Mex food and great homemade lemonade.

Bars

Browar Soma ul Foksal 19. Busy central bar with
minimalist decor, a cool crowd, good home-
brewed beer (7zł) and DJs spinning alternative
dance discs at weekends.
Chimera ul Podwale 29. Wackily decorated,
relaxed cellar bar that attracts a fun-minded
crowd.
Kawiarnia Baumgart/Libera al Ujazdowskie 6.
Weird alternative bar inside Ujazdowski Castle.
Lolek ul Rokitnicka 20. Popular beer hall and
terrace in the middle of a park, with grilled food,
beer and live music. Metro: Pole Mokotowskie.
Między Nami ul Bracka 20. Relaxed gay-friendly
café/bar with good salads and an excellent
atmosphere.
Organza ul Sienkewicza 4. Large bar and
restaurant with good pastas and a lively crowd.
DJs work the basement club at weekends.
Szpilka pl Trzech Krzyży 18. Together with the
more glam *Szpulka* next door, this is where the
alternative set heads to be spotted. Decent food.
Utopia ul Jasna 1. Camp gay bar with comfy
couches and decent snacks.
Zakątek ul Chmielna 5/7. One of the cosiest bars
in town, with deep sofas and quiet music.

Nightlife and entertainment

English-language tips on nightlife venues can be found in the *Warsaw Insider* and
Warsaw In Your Pocket (see p.799). Warsaw **festivals** include the excellent Jazz
Jamboree in October, the *Festival of Contemporary Music* in September, and the five-
yearly *Chopin Piano Competition* – the next is in 2005.

Clubs, discos and live music

The **clubs** listed below all have something to recommend them in terms of decor,
choice of music or atmosphere.

Jazzgot pl Defilad 1. Grungy jazz club inside the
Palace of Culture (eastern entrance) with regular
gigs. Beware of bad beer though.
Paradise ul Wawelska 5. The main gay club in
Warsaw, southwest of the centre. Thurs–Sat only.
Piekarnia ul Młocinska 11. Has the latest
progressive dance music and prides itself on being
at the forefront of musical fashion. Thurs–Sat only.
Proxima ul Zwirki i Wigury 99a. Prime student
club offering unsophisticated diet of chart music.
Closed Sun.

Stodola ul Batorego 10. Student club with
different styles of music on different nights. Prime
venue for alternative rock gigs.
Tygmont ul Mazowiecka 6/8. Warsaw's top jazz
club, with regular gigs, good food and a smoke-
free environment.
Żuraw ul Żurawia 6/12. A good restaurant by day,
a throbbing club with Latino and salsa music on
weekend nights.

Listings

Embassies Australia, ul Nowogrodzka 11
☎ 022/521 34 44, ⊛ www.australia.pl/indexe.htm;
Canada, al Matejki 1/5 ⊛ 022/584 31 00,
⊛ www.canada.pl; Ireland, ul Humańska 10
☎ 022/849 66 55, ⊛ www.irlandia.pl; New Zealand,
ul Migdalowa 4 ☎ 022/645 14 07; UK, al Róż 1
☎ 022/628 10 01, ⊛ www.britishembassy.pl; US, al
Ujazdowskie 29 ☎ 022/628 30 41, ⊛ www.usinfo.pl.

Exchange ATMs are plentiful. Banks are the best option for travellers' cheques, while exchange offices will change cash without commission.
Internet access Casablanca, ul Krakowskie Przedmieście 4/6; EMPiK Megastore, Marszałkowska 116/122.
Laundry Alba, ul Chmielna 26 (closed Sun).

Medical services IMC Damian Hospital ☎022/847 33 13; CM Medical Centre ☎022/458 70 00.
Pharmacies Non-stop *apteka* on top floor of Centralna Station in main hall and at al Solidarności 149.
Post office Ul Świętokrzyska 31/33 (24hr).

Northern Poland

Even in a country accustomed to shifts in its borders, northern Poland presents an unusually tortuous historical puzzle. Successively the domain of a Germanic crusading order, of the Hansa merchants and of the Prussians, it's only in the last fifty years that the region has really become Polish. **Gdańsk**, **Sopot** and **Gdynia** – the **Tri-City**, as their conurbation is known – dominate the area from their coastal vantage point. The most enjoyable excursions from Gdańsk are to the medieval centres of **Malbork** and **Toruń**.

Gdańsk and around

Both the starting point of World War II and the birthplace of the Solidarity movement, Gdańsk has played more than a fleeting role on the world stage. Traces of its past can be seen in the steel skeletons of derelict shipyard cranes and the Hanseatic and Prussian-influenced architecture of the beautifully restored old town. After all the political and social upheavals of the last century the city is now busy reinventing itself as a popular student and tourist hub.

The **Główne Miasto** (Main Town) is the obvious starting point and is within easy walking distance of the train station. Entering it is like walking straight into a Hansa merchants' settlement, but its ancient appearance is deceptive: by May 1945 war had reduced the core of Gdańsk to ruins, leaving the city facing a laborious rebuilding programme. Huge stone gateways guard both entrances to **ul Długa**, the main thoroughfare. Start from the sixteenth-century gate at the top, **Brama Wyznna**, and you'll soon come across the huge tower of the **Town Hall**. Housing the **Historical Museum** (Mon–Sat 10am–4pm, Sun 11am–4pm; 5zł, Wed free), the lavish interior almost threatens to upstage the exhibits.

Past the Town Hall, the street opens onto the wide expanse of **Długi Targ**, where **Arthur's Court** (Dwór Artusa) stands out in a square filled with fine mansions. At the end of the street the archways of the **Brama Zielona** (Green Gate) open directly onto the waterfront. From the bridge over the Motława Canal you get a good view of the granaries on Spichlerze Island and along the old harbour quay. Halfway down is the largely original fifteenth-century **Gdańsk Crane**, the biggest in medieval Europe (Tues–Sun 10am–4pm; 4zł). A little further on is the **Central Maritime Museum** (Tues–Fri 10am–4pm; 12zł), with its exhibition of primitive boats and photographs illustrating the life of Polish writer Józef Korzeniowski, better known as Joseph Conrad.

All the streets back into the town from the waterfront are worth exploring, especially **Mariacka**, brimming with amber traders and cafés. Next up from the Brama Zielona is ul Chlebnicka, which ends at the gigantic **St Mary's Church**. Inside, the Chapel of 11,000 Virgins has a tortured Gothic crucifix, for which the artist apparently nailed his son-in-law to a cross as a model.

Dominating the waterside here is the seven-storey **Great Mill**, the biggest mill in medieval Europe. To the right of the crossway is the fourteenth-century **St Catherine's Church**, one of the nicest in the city and boasting a well-preserved and luminous interior. The most interesting part of the district is west along the canal from the mill, centred on the **Old Town Hall**, on the corner of ul Bielanska

POLAND | Northern Poland

㉑

and Korzenna. Looming large are the cranes of the famous **Gdańsk shipyards**, the crucible of the political strife of the 1980s. Outside the gates rears up the famous anchor-topped **monument** to the shipyard workers killed during the 1970s riots, while the nearby **Roads to Freedom** exhibition on ul Doki 1 (Tues–Sun 10am–4pm; 5zł) details the bloody struggle to topple communism.

The main attraction in the the southern part of old Gdańsk is the **National Art Museum** (Tues–Fri 9am–4pm, Sat & Sun 10am–4pm; 12zł; ⊛www.muzeum.narodowe.gda.pl), at Toruńska 1. There's enough local Gothic art and sculpture here to keep enthusiasts going all day.

Some 15km north of the city lies **SOPOT**, Poland's liveliest coastal centre, with a vast stretch of sandy beach. Once regarded as the "Monte Carlo of the Baltics", Sopot is Poland's fastest growing town and a magnet for young Polish party animals. Commuter trains run to and from Gdańsk and Sopot every ten minutes during the day. Sopot's main artery, Bohaterów Monte Cassino, packed with year-round bars and restaurants, runs east from the train station towards the seaside gardens and the pier, which affords excellent views of the coast.

Practicalities

Gdańsk's main **tourist office** is a couple of minutes northeast of the train station at ul Heweliusza 27 (Mon–Fri 9am–3/4pm; ☎058/301 43 55). Available from newsstands, the English-language city guide *Gdańsk in Your Pocket* is an invaluable source of hotel, restaurant and bar listings.

For **accommodation**, PTTK Gdańsk Tourist, in the mall opposite the train station at Podwale Grodzkie 8 (July & Aug daily 8am–8pm; rest of year Mon–Sat 8am–6pm Sun 8am–2pm; ☎058/301 26 34, ⊛www.gt.com.pl), offers private rooms (**❷**) in the town centre. The most central **hostel** is at ul Wałowa 21 (☎058/301 23 13; **❶**), a red-brick building with clean dorms ten minutes' walk from the main station. Of the cheaper **hotels**, try the central *Dom Harcerza*, ul Za Murami 2/10 (☎058/301 36 21), with dormitories (**❶**) and frugal doubles (**❷**), or the rather shabby *Zaułek*, ul Ogarna 107/108 (☎058/301 41 69; **❸**). Offering more comfort, *Dom Aktora* at ul Straganiarska 55/6 (☎058/301 59 01; **❺**) has snug en-suites with TV. Further out, a short bus ride from the centre, *Mac-Tur* on ul Beethovena 8 (☎058/306 29 90, ⊛www.mactur.gda.pl; **❸**) provides sparkling *pension* accommodation. In **Sopot**, *Pension Wanda*, 800m south of the pier at ul Poniatowskiego 7 (☎058/550 30 38; **❺**), offers comfy en-suites, while *Chemik*, 1km further south at Bitwy pod Plowcami 61 (☎058/551 12 09; **❸**), is a hideous concrete box which nevertheless harbours surprisingly good-value rooms. The most convenient **campsite** in Gdańsk is at ul Jelitkowska 23 (☎058/553 27 31; closed Oct–May), near the beach at Jelitkowo and a short walk from the terminus of trams #2, #6 or #8 from the train station.

For cheap **meals**, check out *Bar Neptun* at ul Długa 33/34, one of the city's classic milk bars (open till 6pm, closed Sun). The nearby *Bar Pod Rybą*, Długi Targ 35/38, something of a student institution, dishes up a variety of jacket potatoes. *Sphinx*, Długi Targ 31/32, serves up a reliable mix of middle-eastern food, while *Goldwasser Magic*, on the waterfront at ul Długie Pobrzeże 22, offers fresh snacks and light lunches at knockdown prices. The popular *Cocktail Bar Capri*, Długa 74, is the best place for coffee and cakes. For **drinking**, try *Kamiennica*, ul Mariacka 37/39, a wonderfully intimate bar, or the *Irish Pub*, ul Korzenna 33/35, frequented by an energetic crowd of young beer monsters, while *Gospoda Pod Wielkim Młynem*, Na Piaskach 1, is one of the most picturesque bars in town. Best of the **clubbing** venues is the sprawling *Parlement*, ul Św. Ducha 2.

In **Sopot**, *Bar Przystan*, al Wojska Polskiego 11, is one of the most famed fish restaurants in the city, while meat-eaters will appreciate the hearty helpings at *Harnaś*, ul Moniuszki 9. *Greenway*, ul Bohaterów Monte Cassino 67, serves excellent vegetarian cuisine. Sopot's **nightlife** centres around the main drag, ul

Bohaterów Monte Cassino. Film buffs might want to check out *Galeria Kińsky*, ul Kościuszki 10, a bar dedicated to local hero, actor Klaus Kinski. Further afield, *Sfinks*, in the middle of the park off Powstańców Warszawy, is known for its alternative crowd and unconventional music, while the nearby *Enzym*, ul Mamuszki 21, hosts a wide range of club nights.

Note that it's possible to catch a **ferry to Sweden** from the Tri-City. PolFerries, ul Przemysłowa 1 (☎058/343 18 87, ✆www.polferries.com.pl), runs a service from Gdańsk to Nynäshavn near Stockholm (June–Sept daily; Oct–May 3 weekly), while Stena Line, ul Kwiatkowskiego 60 (☎058/665 14 14, ✆www.stenaline.pl), sails daily from Gdynia to Karlskrona.

Malbork

Dating from the fourteenth-century, the castle of **MALBORK** is one of Poland's most spectacular fortresses. Built to serve as headquarters for the Teutonic Knights, it casts a threatening shadow over what is an otherwise sleepy town. The **train** and **bus stations** are sited next to each other about ten minutes' walk south of the castle; Malbork is on the main Warsaw line, so there are plenty of trains from Gdańsk (30–40min), as well as a regular bus service.

You approach the **fortress** (Tues–Sun: May–Sept 9am–7pm; Oct–April 9am–3pm, 19.50zł) through the old outer castle, a zone of utility buildings never rebuilt after the war. Passing over the moat and through the daunting main gate, you come to the **Middle Castle**. Spread out around an open courtyard, this part of the complex contains the Grand Master's palace, of which the **Main Refectory** is the highlight. From the Middle Castle a passage rises to the smaller courtyard of the **High Castle**, the oldest section of the fortress, harbouring the focus of the Knights' austere monasticism – the vast **Castle Church**.

Toruń

The biggest and most important of the Hanseatic trading centres along the Wisła, **TORUŃ** miraculously survived the recurrent wars afflicting the region, and the historic centre is a rich assembly of architectural styles. The principal stations are on opposite sides of the Old Town. Toruń Główny, the main **train station**, is 2km away south of the river; buses #22 and #27 (every 10min) run to pl Rapackiego, on the western edge of the Old Town. Exit the station beyond platform 4 and buy 1.6zł tickets from the kiosk beside the bus stop. From the **bus station** on ul Dabrowskiego it is a short walk south to the centre.

Highlight of the westerly Old Town area is the mansion-lined **Rynek**. Inside the austere fourteenth-century **Town Hall**, the **Town Museum** (Tues–Sun 10am–4pm, May–Sept until 6pm; 6zł) has a gorgeous collection of fourteenth-century stained glass, some fine sculptures and a good collection of artefacts from the fifty-odd local guilds. In the western corner of the Rynek stands the impressive medieval **Church of the Blessed Virgin Mary**.

South of the Rynek, at ul Kopernika 15/17, is the **Copernicus Museum** (Tues–Sun 10am–4/6pm; 5zł), installed in the high brick house where the great man was born and containing a collection of Copernicus artefacts and a sound-and-light show of fifteenth-century Toruń (2zł extra). The font in which Copernicus was baptized can be seen in the massive **St John's Cathedral** (Mon–Sat 9am–5.30pm May–Sept; 2zł) at the eastern end of ul Kopernica.

To the northeast lies the **New Town** district with a number of illustrious commercial residences grouped around the Rynek Nowomiejski. Ul Prosta leads north of the square to a park in which stands the former arsenal, now an **Ethnographic Museum** (10am–4/6pm daily; Oct–April closed Mon; 8zł), dealing with the customs and crafts of northern Poland, including an outdoor display of wooden buildings.

Practicalities

The **tourist office** at Rynek Staromejski 1, in the town hall (Mon & Sat 9am–4pm, Tues–Fri 9am–6pm; May–Sept also Sun 9am–1pm; ☎056/621 09 31, ⓦwww.it.torun.com.pl), hands out free maps and provides information about accommodation. For **hotels**, look no further than the excellent new *Hotelik w Centrum*, just east of the centre at ul Szumana 2 (☎056/652 22 46; ❶). All rooms have TV, there's a kitchen and internet access, and they can cook dinner for you for 10zł. If this is full, try the simple but clean *Dom Wycieczkowy PTTK*, north of the bus station at ul Szczecińska 16 (☎056/622 38 55; ❶), offering dorm beds and basic doubles. The two **hostels** are both about 3km from the centre – at ul Św. Józefa 22/24 to the northwest (☎056/659 61 84), and in an old fortress at ul Chobrego 86 to the northeast (☎056/655 82 36). The *Tramp* **campsite** at ul Kujawska 14 (☎056/654 71 87), a short walk west of the train station, also has bungalows sleeping four to six people.

Best of the cheap **places to eat** in town is the *Bar Mleczny*, on the corner of Rózana and Sw. Ducha, with a branch on ul Szcytna, offering filling soups and meaty snacks. Popular with students, *Manekin*, north of Rynek Nowomiejski at ul Wysoka 5, serves 53 varieties of excellent pancakes. Head for the vaulted rooms of *Staromiejska* at ul Szcytna 2–4 for cheap pasta dishes and pizzas, or to *U Sołtysa*, ul Mostowa 17, for Polish fare in folksy surroundings. Riverbank cafés provide numerous outdoor **drinking** opportunities. Otherwise, best of the regular bars is *Pod Aniołem*, a cellar under the town hall which sometimes hosts DJs and dancing. Other good choices are *Metropolis*, a lively restaurant, bar and club on ul Podmurna 28, and *Pod Krzywà Wiezą*, a tremendous bar in the Old Town battlements on ul Bankowa. Find the *Jeremi* **internet café** at Rynek Staromejski 33 (24hr).

Southern Poland

Southern Poland garners more visitors than any other region in the country, and its attractions are clear enough from just a glance at the map. The **Tatra Mountains**, which form the border with Slovakia, are Poland's grandest and most beautiful, snowcapped for much of the year and markedly alpine in feel. **Kraków** ranks with Prague and Vienna as one of the architectural gems of Central Europe, but its significance for Poles goes well beyond the aesthetic, for this was the country's ancient royal capital, and the Catholic Church has often looked to Kraków for guidance – Pope John Paul II was Archbishop of Kraków until his election in 1978. Equally important are Kraków's Jewish roots: until World War II, this was one of the great Jewish centres in Europe, a past whose fabric remains clear in the old Jewish area of Kazimierz, and whose culmination is starkly enshrined at the death camps of **Auschwitz–Birkenau**, west of the city.

Kraków

KRAKÓW was the only major city in the country to come through World War II essentially undamaged, and its assembly of monuments has now been listed by UNESCO as one of the world's most significant historic sites. Although swarming with visitors in summer, the city's Old Town retains an atmosphere of *fin-de-siècle* stateliness, and its streets are a cavalcade of churches and aristocratic palaces. A longtime university centre, Kraków has a tangible buzz of arty youthfulness, and boasts a wealth of nightlife opportunities to match.

Arrival and information

Kraków Główny, the central **train station**, and the main **bus station** just opposite, are five minutes' walk northeast of the city's historic centre. The city **tourist office**

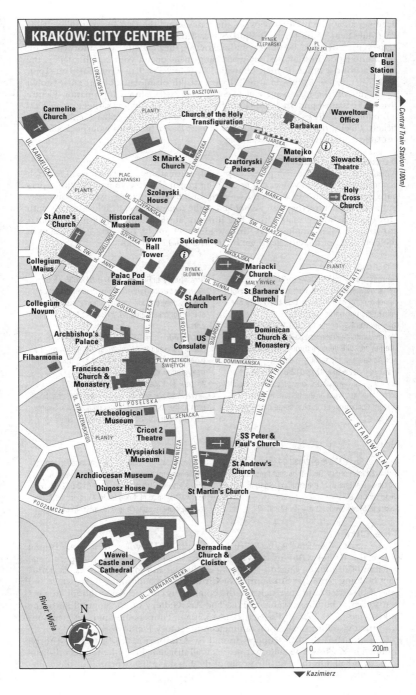

KRAKÓW: CITY CENTRE

RYNEK KLEPARSKI

PL MATEJKI

Central Bus Station

UL. PAWIA

UL. LOBZOWSKA

UL. BASZTOWA

PLANTY

Carmelite Church

Church of the Holy Transfiguration

Barbakan

Waweltour Office

UL. PIJARSKA

St Mark's Church

Czartoryski Palace

Matejko Museum

Słowacki Theatre

UL. KARMELICKA

PLAC SZCZEPAŃSKI

UL. SŁAWKOWSKA

SW. MARKA

Holy Cross Church

PLANTY

Szołayski House

UL. SZCZEPAŃSKA

UL. SW. JANA

UL. FLORIAŃSKA

SW. TOMASZA

SW. KRZYŻA

St Anne's Church

Historical Museum

UL. SZEWSKA

Town Hall Tower

Sukiennice

MIKOŁAJSKA

PLANTY

WESTERPLATTE

Collegium Maius

UL. SW. ANNY

UL. JAGIELLOŃSKA

RYNEK GŁÓWNY

Mariacki Church

MAŁY RYNEK

Pałac Pod Baranami

UL. SIENNA

St Barbara's Church

Collegium Novum

UL. WIŚLNA

GOŁĘBIA

St Adalbert's Church

UL. BRACKA

UL. GRODZKA

Archbishop's Palace

US Consulate

SIOLARSKA

Dominican Church & Monastery

Filharmonia

PL WYSZTKICH ŚWIĘTYCH

UL. DOMINIKAŃSKA

UL. SW. GERTRUDY

UL. STAROWIŚLNA

Franciscan Church & Monastery

UL. STRASZEWSKIEGO

UL. POSELSKA

Archeological Museum

UL. SENACKA

PLANTY

Cricot 2 Theatre

SS Peter & Paul's Church

Wyspiański Museum

UL. KANONICZA

UL. GRODZKA

St Andrew's Church

Archdiocesan Museum

Długosz House

St Martin's Church

PODZAMCZE

Wawel Castle and Cathedral

Bernadine Church & Cloister

UL. BERNARDYŃSKA

UL. STRADOMSKA

River Wisła

N

0   200m

Kazimierz

POLAND | Kraków

21

809

occupies a circular pavilion between the stations and the Old Town at ul Szpitalna 25 (May–Sept Mon–Fri 8am–8pm, Sat & Sun 9am–5pm; Oct–April Mon–Fri 8am–4pm; ☎012/432 00 60, ⊛www.krakow.pl); they can give you information on accommodation possibilities but won't ring them up on your behalf. Staff at the regional tourist office, Rynek Główny 1/3 (Mon–Fri 9am–6pm, Sat 9am–1pm; ☎012/421 77 06, ⊛www.mcit.pol), have a wealth of information on out-of-town sights. Just off the main square at ul Św. Jana 2, the Cultural Information Centre (Mon–Fri 10am–6pm, Sat 10am–4pm; ☎012/421 77 87, ⊛www.karnet.krakow2000 .pl) publishes **listings** of cultural events in a monthly booklet called *Karnet* and sells tickets. Finally, the bi-monthly *Kraków in Your Pocket* (wwww.inyourpocket.com), available from newsstands, is invaluable.

Accommodation

Kraków is one of Europe's prime city-break destinations – so you'll need to book accommodation in advance. If you can't, be prepared to try your luck with a **private room**, which run at around 40–50zł for a double, but may well be some way out from the centre; they can be booked at the tourist office, which also deals with **student hostels**, available from late June to late September. The most popular **campsite**, Krak Camping, ul Radzikowskiego 99 (☎012/637 21 22), is located in the northwest of the city; get there by trams #4, #12 and #44.

Hostels

Express Hostel ul Wrocławska 91 ☎012/633 88 62; ⊛www.express91.pl. Well-equipped student complex north of the centre. Bus #130 from the train station (towards *Azory*). ❶

Nawojka ul Reymonta 11 ☎012/633 58 77, ⊛www.bratniak.krakow.pl/nawojka. Student dorm offering en-suite doubles throughout the year, as well as cheaper rooms July–Sept. ❷

Piast ul Piastowska 47 ☎012/637 49 33, ⊛www.piast.bratniak.krakow.pl. Large university dormitory 3km west of the centre. Regular student accommodation plus some higher-grade rooms. ❷

Strawberry ul Racławicka 9 ☎012/636 15 00, ⊛www.strawberryhostel.com. 2km northwest of the city centre. Look for their shuttle bus from the station, or take trams #4, #12 or #14. July & Aug only. ❶

Ul Oleandry 4 ☎012/633 88 22. The main hostel, ten minutes' walk west of the centre, is a gloomy, grey place. Tram #15 or #18 from the train station. ❶

Żaczek al 3 Maja 5 ☎012/633 19 14, ⊛www.zakzek.com.pl. Well-placed students' hostel next to the main youth hostel (see above). Simple doubles with shared facilities and en suites. ❷

Hotels

Mistia ul Szlak 73a ☎012/633 29 26, ⊛www.mistia.org.pl. Decent budget hotel five minutes' walk north of the stations. Spartan but clean rooms. ❸

Saski ul Sławkowska 3 ☎012/421 42 22,

⊛www.hotelsaski.com.pl. Central location, great ambience and a wonderful antique lift. ❸

Trzy Kafki al Słowackiego 29 ☎012/632 94 18, ⊛www.trzykafki.pl. Good budget option, with clean rooms, laundry service and an internet café. ❷

The City

At the heart of Kraków is the **Stare Miasto**, the Old Town, with its great central square, the **Rynek Główny**. It was the largest square of medieval Europe: a huge expanse of flagstones, ringed by magnificent houses and towering spires. Its dominant building is the vast **Sukiennice** or **Cloth Hall**, rebuilt in the Renaissance and one of the most distinctive sights in the country. Its commercial traditions are perpetuated by a bustling covered market. The **Art Gallery** on the upper floor of the Sukiennice (Tues, Wed & Fri–Sun 10am–3.30pm, Thurs noon–6pm; 7zł, free Sun) is worth a visit for its collection of nineteenth-century Polish works.

To its south is the tiny copper-domed **St Adalbert's**, the first church to be founded in Kraków. The tall tower nearby is all that remains of the fourteenth-century town hall. On the east side is one of the finest Gothic structures in the country, the **Mariacki Church** (St Mary's; 11.30am–6pm, Sun 2–6pm; 4zł), the taller of its towers topped by an amazing ensemble of spires. Legend has it that during one of the Tatar raids, a guard watching from the tower saw the invaders approaching and took up his trumpet to raise the alarm; his warning was cut short by an arrow through the throat. Every hour on the hour a trumpeter plays the sombre *hejnał* melody, halting abruptly at the point the watchman was supposed to have been hit. Highlight of the church is the majestic high altar at the far east end. Carved between 1477 and 1489 by Veit Stoss, this huge limewood polyptych is one of the finest examples of late-Gothic art; at noon (Sundays and saints' days excluded) the altar is opened to reveal the inner panel of the Dormition of the Virgin, an amazing tableau of life-size figures.

North of the Rynek

Of the three streets leading north off the Rynek, **ul Floriańska** is the busiest and most striking, with fragments of medieval and Renaissance architecture among the shops. **Floriańska Gate**, at the end of the street, marks the edge of the Old Town proper. A square, robust fourteenth-century structure, it's part of a small section of fortifications saved when the old defensive walls were pulled down in the early nineteenth century. Beyond is the **Barbakan** (daily 10am–5pm; 4zł) a bulbous, spiky fort, added in 1498.

Back through Floriańska Gate, a right turn down the narrow ul Pijarska brings you to the **Czartoryski Palace**, housing Kraków's finest art collection (Tues & Thurs 9am–3.30pm, Wed & Fri 11am–6pm, Sat & Sun 10am–3.30pm; 7zł, free Sun). An intriguing highlight is the collection of Turkish trophies from the Battle of Vienna (1683). The picture galleries offer a rich display of art and sculpture ranging from thirteenth- to eighteenth-century works, the most famous being Rembrandt's brooding *Landscape Before a Storm* and Leonardo da Vinci's *Lady with an Ermine*.

The university district

West from the Rynek is the **university area**, whose heart is the Gothic Collegium Maius building, at ul Jagiellońska 15. Now the **University Museum**, the Collegium is open to guided tours only (Mon–Fri 11am–4.20pm, Sat 11am–1.20pm; 7zł; ☎012/422 05 49), for which you need to book places at least a day in advance. Inside, the ground-floor rooms retain the mathematical and geographical murals once used for teaching. In the treasury, the most valued possession is the Jagiellonian globe (1510), featuring the earliest-known map of America.

Wawel Hill

For over five hundred years, **Wawel Hill** was the seat of Poland's monarchy. The original **Cathedral** (May–Sept Mon–Sat 9am–3pm, Sun 12.15pm–3pm; 4zł) was built here around the time King Bolesław the Brave established the Kraków bishopric in 1020, but the present brick-and-sandstone basilica is essentially Gothic. All bar four of Poland's forty-five monarchs are buried in the cathedral, and their tombs and side chapels are like a directory of Central European architecture, art and sculpture of the last six centuries, not least the Gothic **Holy Cross Chapel**, the Baroque mausoleum of the seventeenth-century Wasa dynasty, followed by the high spot of the whole cathedral, the opulent **Zygmuntowska chapel**.

Arrive early or book ahead if you want to visit the museums in the **Wawel Castle**; the ticket office (open 9am–3pm, Sun 10am–3pm; ☎012/422 16 97) only sells a limited number of tickets each day. The magnificent **State Rooms** (Mon 9.30am–noon, Tues & Fri 9.30am–4pm, Wed, Thurs & Sat 9.30am–3pm, Sun 10am–3pm; 12zł, Mon free) are furnished with Renaissance paintings, furniture and tapestries. A tour of the **Royal Private Apartments** (same times, but closed Mon; 15zł) reveals the King's rooms as well as some eighteenth-century apartments. Although much of the contents had been sold by the time of the Partitions to pay off marriage dowries and debts of state, the **Royal Treasury and Armoury** (same times and pricing as the State Rooms) features some fine items such as the burial crown of Zygmunt August.

The **Lost Wawel** exhibition (same times as the State Rooms; 6zł, Mon free), beneath the old kitchens south of the cathedral, takes you past the excavated remains of the hill's most ancient buildings, including the foundations of the tenth-century **Rotunda of SS Felix and Adauctus**, the oldest church in Poland.

Return to ground level via the **Dragon's Den** (daily May–Oct 10am–5pm; 3zł), a spiral staircase leading to a cavern. Legend has it that Smok the dragon lived here, feeding on a steady diet of children, cattle and unsuccessful knights. A clever peasant boy, Krak, fed him a sheep stuffed with sulphur; to quench the burning Smok drank half the Wisła, causing him to explode.

Kazimierz

South from Wawel Hill lies the **Kazimierz** district, which in 1495 became the city's Jewish quarter. Kazimierz grew to become one of the main cultural centres of Polish Jewry, but in March 1941 the entire Jewish population of the city was crammed into a tiny ghetto over the river. After waves of deportations to the concentration camps, the ghetto was finally liquidated in March 1943, thus ending seven centuries of Jewish life in Kraków.

The tiny **Remu'h Synagogue** at ul Szeroka 40 (Mon–Fri 9am–4pm; 5zł) is one of two still functioning in the quarter. The tombstones of its cemetery were buried and therefore largely saved from Nazi ransacking. Fragments of tombstones have been collaged together to form an impressive wall just inside the entrance. The grandest of all the Kazimierz synagogues was the **Old Synagogue** on ul Szeroka, the oldest surviving Jewish religious building in Poland. Since the war it's been carefully restored and turned into a **museum** of Kraków Jewry including a permanent exhibition of traditional art by Polish Jews (daily 10am–5pm, Mon 10am–2pm; 6zł). The museum provides an excellent English-language introduction to the basic beliefs and rituals of Judaism. Another good place to visit is the refurbished **Synagoga Izaaka** (Isaac Synagogue) at ul Kupa 18, which has an exhibition of photographs and short silent films illustrating the life of Kazimierz Jews before the war and after the formation of the Jewish ghetto (Mon–Fri & Sun 9am–7pm; 6zł).

Eating and drinking

The *cukiernia* dotted around the city centre provide delicious cakes to most Kraków cafés, and Kraków's tourist status has resulted in one of the best selections of **bars**, **cafés** and **restaurants** in Central Europe.

Cafés, milk bars and snacks

Babcia Malina ul Sławkowska 17. Good Polish food in a mountain-hut-style basement milk bar.

Bar Grodzki ul Grodzka 47. Filling Polish standards (including excellent potato pancakes or *placki*).

Café Numero Rynek Główny 6. Deliciously glam café serving excellent coffee (try it with syrup).

Chimera ul Św. Anny 3 off the main square. Atmospheric rooms with a terrace upstairs in summer. Offers cheap, mainly veggie meals.

Kawiarnia u Literatów Kanonicza 7. A courtyard-cum-garden retreat for discerning drinkers.

Tajemnicky Ogród ul Bracka 3–5. Lively café with a popular courtyard terrace just of the Rynek.

Unnamed Café ul Meiselska 20. Relaxed atmosphere and excellent cakes in a trendy Kazimierz café. Guests traditionally should pin up a suggestion for the name of the café.

Restaurants

Arka Noego ul Szeroka 2 ☎012/429 15 28. The best-value Jewish restaurant in Kazimierz, with occasional live music.

Greenway ul Mikołajska 12. Charming little vegetarian self-service restaurant with Polish and Mexican specialities.

Morskie Oko pl Szczepański 8 ☎012/431 24 23. Huge piles of meat in a merry Zakopane-type setting with plenty of wood and waitresses in mountain garb.

Szlacheckie Jadło ul Sławkowski 32 ☎012/422 83 24. Polish fare at reasonable prices in a medieval decor; the lunch menu is 14zł.

Bars

Alchemia ul Estery 5. Darkly atmospheric Kazimierz bar catering to a mixture of Bohemian regulars, curious tourists and permanently sozzled Cracovians.

Black Gallery ul Mikołajska 24. Cellar bar with industrial decor and lively crowd. Lovely garden courtyard.

C.K. Browar ul Podwale 6–7. Excellent beer hall that brews on the premises; order a column of their beer and tap yourself. Also has a good restaurant and disco.

Galaria Cocteau ul Karmelicka 10. A popular gay-friendly bar.

Klub Kulturalny ul Szewska 35. Trance and house music in a popular student cellar bar. Open till 2am.

Pod Jemiola ul Floriańska 20. Cramped but cosy "alternative" bar with cutting-edge dance music on the sound system.

Szuflada ul Wiślna 5. Bar with food and surrealist decor – try the zebra table.

Nightlife

Pod Jaszczurami, Rynek Główny 8, is a student **club** – but if you feel too old, head for *Strefa 22*, at Rynek Główny 22, that has the crowds partying to house at weekends. There are plenty of other **disco** options in the streets surrounding the square – *Music Bar 9*, ul Szewska 9, and *Jazz Rock Café*, ul Sławkowska 12, techno-oriented bars with dance floors. There's **live music** at *Stalowe Magnolia*, ul Św. Jana 15 (though drinks don't come cheap), and **jazz** at *U Muniaka*, ul Floriańska 3 (Thurs–Sat 9.30pm). Best of the dance-music DJs and rock bands appear at *Miasto Krakoff*, at ul Lobzowska 3, north of the centre.

Listings

Consulates UK, ul Św. Anny 9 ☎012/421 70 30, eukconsul@bci.krakow.pl; US, ul Stolarska 9 ☎012/429 66 55, ⊛www.usconsulate.krakow.pl.

Internet access Br@cka, above the Tajemnicky Ogród café at ul Bracka 3–5; Looz, ul Mikołajska 13.

Pharmacies Grodzka 26. Rota posted on window.

Post office Ul Westerplatte 20.

Oświęcim: Auschwitz-Birkenau

In 1940, **OŚWIĘCIM**, a small town 70km west of Kraków, became the site of the Oświęcim-Brzeźinka concentration camp, better known by its German name of **Auschwitz-Birkenau**. Of the many camps built by the Nazis in Poland and other countries during World War II, this was the largest and most horrific: something approaching two million people, 85–90 percent of them Jews, died here. If you want all the specifics on the camp, you can pick up a detailed guidebook or join a guided group, often led by former inmates. Children under 13 are not admitted.

Get to Auschwitz-Birkenau from Kraków using one of the regular trains or buses to Oświęcim station. From there it's a short bus ride to the gates of Auschwitz. Some buses will drop you off at the entrance of Auschwitz. There's an hourly shuttle-bus service to the Birkenau section from the car park at Auschwitz; taxis are also available, otherwise it's a 3km walk.

Most of the Auschwitz camp buildings have been preserved as the **Museum of Martyrdom** (⊛www.auschwitz-museum.oswiecim.pl; daily: summer 8am–7pm; winter 8am–3pm; free). The cinema is a sobering starting point: the film was taken by the Soviet troops who liberated the camp in May 1945 – harrowing images of the survivors and the dead. The bulk of the camp consists of the prison cell blocks, the first section dedicated to "exhibits" found in the camp after liberation. Despite last-minute destruction of many of the storehouses used for the possessions of murdered inmates, there are rooms full of clothes and suitcases, toothbrushes, glasses, shoes and a huge mound of women's hair. Many of the camp barracks are given over to national memorials, moving testimonies to the sufferings of inmates of the different countries. The prison blocks terminate by the gas chambers and the ovens where the bodies were incinerated. The frighteningly large **Birkenau camp** (same hours) is much less visited than Auschwitz, though it was here that the majority of captives lived and died. Killing was the main goal of Birkenau, most of it carried out in the huge gas chambers at the back of the camp, damaged but not destroyed by the fleeing Nazis in 1945. Most of the victims arrived in closed trains – cattle cars mostly – to be driven directly into the gas chambers; railway line, ramp, sidings – they are all still there, just as the Nazis abandoned them.

Zakopane and the Tatras

The **Tatra Mountains** – Tatry in Polish – are the most spectacular and most revered part of the almost unbroken chain of ridges extending the whole length of Poland's southern border. Some 80km long, with peaks rising to 2500m, most of the range rises across the border in Slovakia. However, the Polish section has enough to keep most people happy: high peaks for the dedicated mountaineers, excellent trails for hikers, cable cars for day-trippers, and ski slopes in winter.

The major resort on the fringes of the mountains is **ZAKOPANE**, a town which has succumbed wholeheartedly to tourism. It's easily reached by train (3–4 hr) or bus (2–3 hr) from Kraków, and both stations are a ten-minute walk east of the bustling pedestrian main street, **ul Krupówki**. Uphill, the street merges into ul Zamoyskiego, which runs on out of town towards the entrance to the Tatra National Park (4km away at Kuźnice; see below).

The **tourist information centre**, housed in a wooden chalet west of the stations at ul Kościuszki 17 (8am–6/8pm, Sun 9am–5pm; ⓦwww.polskietatry.pl) can book you into private rooms (❶) or *pensions* (❷) and has maps, guidebooks, details on mountain huts and the latest weather forecast. You can hire an English-speaking mountain guide here for 200–450zł per person. Near the entrance of the park, the Tatra National Park Information Centre at ul Chałubińskiego 44 (daily 9am–3pm; ☏018/206 37 99, ✉kozica@tpn.zakopane.pl) also sells maps and has weather details displayed in the window.

For **accommodation** there's a **hostel** just north of the tourist office at ul Nowotarska 45 (☏018/206 62 03; ❶), offering multi-person dorms or neat modern en-suite doubles. The more central *Dom Turysty PTTK*, just off the main drag at ul Zaruskiego 5 (☏018/206 32 81, domturysty@regle.zakopane.pl; ❷), has similar accommodation. The best **pension** in the centre is *Api-2*, north of the tourist office at Kamieniec 13a (☏018/206 29 31; ❶). *Pod Krokwià* **campsite** (☏018/201 22 56), at the end of ul Żeromskiego on the south side of town, has bungalows (❷) on offer, too.

Restaurants and cafés are concentrated on ul Krupówki. Try *Sabala* (no. 11), offering traditional local dishes, outside tables and indoor folk music. *Bąkowo Zohlina*, near the ski slopes at ul Piłsudskiego 6, is a lively mountain-style restaurant with live music and dancing, serving excellent trout. *Paparazzi*, just off the main street at ul Galicy 8, is the most convivial place to **drink**. Upstairs, *Widmo* offers **internet access** (24hr).

Silesia and Wielkopolska

In Poland it's known as Ślàsk, in the Czech Republic as Sleszko, in Germany as Schlesien: all three countries hold part of the frequently disputed province that's called **Silesia** in English. Since 1945, Poland has held all of it except for a few of the westernmost tracts, a dominance gained as compensation for the Eastern Territories, which were incorporated into the USSR in 1939 as a result of the Nazi–Soviet pact, and never returned. Silesia's main city, Wrocław, is one of Central

Europe's most enticing cosmopolitan centres. North of Silesia, the region known as **Wielkopolska** formed the core of the original Polish nation, and its chief interest is supplied by the vibrant regional capital of **Poznań**.

Wrocław

The special nature of **WROCŁAW** comes from the fact that it contains the soul of two great cities. One of these is the city that has long stood on this spot, Slav by origin but for centuries dominated by Germans and generally known as **Breslau**. The other is **Lwów** (now L'viv), capital of Polish Ukraine, which was annexed by the Soviets in 1939. After the war, its displaced population was encouraged to take over the severely depopulated Breslau, which had been confiscated from Germany. The multinational influences which shaped the city are reflected in much of its architecture: huge Germanic churches, Flemish-style mansions and Baroque palaces.

The City

Wrocław's central area is delineated by the River Odra to the north and by the bow-shaped ul Podwale – the latter following the former city walls, whose moat, now bordered by a shady park, still largely survives. At the centre of town is the vast space of the Rynek with its magnificent fifteenth-century town hall. The famous west face and the south facade are the real show-stoppers, the latter with huge windows, filigree friezes of animals and foliage, and rich statuary. The town hall now serves as the **Historical Museum** (Wed–Sat 11am–5pm, Sun 10am–6pm; 5zł).

In the northwest corner of the Rynek are two curious Baroque houses known as **Jaś i Małgosia**, linked by a gateway giving access to the close of **St Elizabeth**, the most impressive of Wrocław's churches. Since the mid-fifteenth century, its huge ninety-metre tower (Mon–Sat 9am–4pm, Sun 1–4pm; 4zł) has been the city's most prominent landmark.

Southwest of the Rynek lies the maze-like former **Jewish quarter**, whose inhabitants fled or were driven from their tenements during the Third Reich. One of the largest synagogues in Poland, the **Synagoga pod Białym Bocianem** (Sun–Fri 10am–5pm, 4zł), lies hidden in a courtyard at ul Włodkowica 9. Though the facade still needs work, the interior has now been refurbished.

Immediately to the east stands the monumental Royal Palace, housing the **Ethnographic Museum** (Tues–Sun 10am–4pm; 4zł, free Sat), its main draw a large collection of dolls dressed in traditional Silesian costumes. Further east, at the northern end of pl Dominikański, are the buildings of the **Dominican monastery**, centred on the thirteenth-century church of **St Adalbert**, which is embellished with fine brickwork and several lavish Gothic and Baroque chapels. Nearby stands the gargantuan former **Bernardine Monastery**, now the **Museum of Architecture** (Wed 10am–4pm, Thurs–Sat 10am–3.30pm, Sun 10am–5pm; 9zł), a fascinating record of the many historic buildings in the city which were destroyed in the war.

Housed in a specially designed concrete rotunda in the nearby park is Wrocław's iconic and best-loved sight, the **Panorama of the Battle of Racławice** (Tues–Sun 9.30am–4.30pm; shows every 30min; 19zł; includes entrance to the National Museum). This painting, 120m long and 15m high, was commissioned in 1894 to celebrate the centenary of the Russian army's defeat by the people's militia of Tadeusz Kościuszko near the village of Racławice, between Kraków and Kielce.

At the opposite end of the park is the ponderously Prussian neo-Renaissance home of the **National Museum** (Tues–Sun 10am–4pm; 10zł, Thurs free). The highlight of the **medieval stone sculpture** section on the ground floor is the poignant early fourteenth-century *Tomb of Henryk the Righteous*, with its group of weeping mourners.

North of the Rynek, the triangular-shaped university quarter, jam-packed with historic buildings, is bounded by two streets: ul Uniwersytecka to the south and ul

Grodzka, which follows the Odra. The principal building of this district is the 171-metre-long **Collegium Maximum**, whose main assembly hall, or **Aula Leopoldina**, upstairs at pl Uniwersytecki 1 (10am–3.30pm; closed Wed; 4zł), is one of the greatest secular interiors of the Baroque age, fusing architecture, painting, sculpture and ornament into one bravura whole.

From the Market Hall, the Piaskowski Bridge leads to the island of **Wyspa Piasek** and the fourteenth-century hall church of **St Mary of the Sands**, majestically vaulted and featuring a wonderfully kitsch animated children's altar.

Two elegant little bridges connect Wyspa Piasek with **Ostrów Tumski**, the city's ecclesiastical heart. Ul Katedralny leads past several Baroque palaces to the twin-towered **Cathedral of St John the Baptist**. Rebuilt after huge wartime damage, the gloomy interior features some worthwhile Gothic and Baroque chapels. Take the lift up the tower (Mon–Fri 10am–5.30pm, Sat & Sun 2–4pm; 4zł) for good views of the city.

Practicalities

The main **train station**, Wrocław Głowny, faces the broad boulevard of ul Piłsudskiego, about fifteen minutes' walk south of the Rynek; the main **bus station** is at the back of the train station. The **tourist office** at Rynek 14 (Mon–Fri 9am–5pm, Sat 10am–2pm; ☎071/344 31 11) has a wealth of information and provides hotel listings, but doesn't book rooms.

A cluster of rather basic **hotels** can be found near the train station – nearest of all is the *Hotel Piast* at ul Piłsudskiego 98 (☎071/343 00 34; ❶), which offers reductions to ISIC holders. Between the stations and the Old Town, the *Savoy*, pl Kośiuszki 19 (☎071/340 32 19; ❷), offers cheap, acceptable en-suites. Best deal in the old town is the *Bursa Nauczycielska* at ul Kotlarska 42 (☎071/344 37 81; ❶), with simple doubles and triples.

The most convenient **hostel** is 100m from the train station at ul Kołłątaja 20, off ul Piłsudskiego (10am–5pm lockout and 10pm curfew; ☎071/343 88 56; ❶). The hostel occupying half of the *Hotel Tumski*, north of the Old Town at Wyspa Słodowa 10 (☎071/322 60 99, ⊛www.hotel-tumski.com.pl; ❷), offers better standards but has the same lockout and curfew. Information on summer student hostels (late June–Sept; ❶) is available at Almatur, ul Tadeusza Kościuszki 34 (Mon–Fri 10am–5pm; ☎071/343 41 35). There's a **campsite** with bungalows (❶) on the east side of town at al Padarewskiego 35 (☎071/348 46 51) – trams #9, #12, #17 and #32 run nearby.

Wrocław has a good selection of places to eat and drink. Try *Mis*, ul Kuźnicza 48 (Mon–Sat till 5/6pm), a student-packed canteen, for cheap Polish standards, or *Vega*, Rynek-Ratusz 27a, for inexpensive vegetarian food (daily till 5/7pm). *Spiż*, Rynek-Ratusz 2, is a restaurant-cum-pub which brews its own beer. The liveliest student haunt in the university quarter is *Kalogródek* at ul Kuźnicza 29b. *Gumowa Róza*, entered from the Św. Wita alley, is a relaxed basement bar with a Bohemian edge. Those interested in **clubbing** can head for the bars on the Rynek or to *Piec Nutek*, Podwale 37/38, which features regular live gigs.

Poznań

Thanks to its position on the Berlin–Warsaw–Moscow rail line, **POZNAŃ** is many visitors' first taste of Poland. In many ways it's the ideal introduction, as no other city is more closely identified with Polish nationhood. In the ninth century the Polonians founded a castle on an island in the River Warta, and in 968 Mieszko I made this one of the two main centres of his duchy and the seat of its first bishop. The settlement that developed here was given the name **Ostrów Tumski** (Cathedral Island), which it still retains. Nowadays Poznań is a city of great diversity and hosts the country's most important trade fair.

The City

For seven centuries the grandiose **Stary Rynek** has been the hub of life in Poznań. The turreted Town Hall boasts a vivacious eastern facade, its lime-green pilasters framing a frieze of Polish monarchs. Inside lies the **Museum of the History of Poznań** (Mon & Tues 10am–4pm, Wed–Fri noon–6pm, Sat 9am–4pm, Sun 10am–3pm; 5.5zł), worth visiting for the stunning Renaissance **Great Hall** on the first floor, its coffered vault bearing polychrome bas-reliefs with scenes of Samson, King David and Hercules. Many a medieval and Renaissance interior lurks behind the Baroque facades of the **gabled houses** lining the outer sides of the Stary Rynek. The **Museum of Musical Instruments** at no. 45 (Mon–Sat 11am–5pm, Sun 11am–3pm; 5.5zł, free Sat) is a fine example, and has the only collection of its kind in Poland.

Just to the west of the Stary Rynek at the end of ul Zamkowa stands a hill with remnants of the inner circle of the medieval walls. This particular section guarded the **Castle**, which was the seat of the rulers of Wielkopolska. Modified down the centuries, it was almost completely destroyed in 1945, but has been partly restored to house the **Museum of Applied Arts** (Tues, Wed & Fri–Sun 10am–3/4pm; 3.5zł), a collection of crafts from medieval times to the present.

Nearby, at al Marcinkowskiego 9, is **Plac Wolności**, where the excellent **National Museum** houses one of the few important displays of old master paintings in Poland (Tues 10am–6pm, Wed 9am–5pm, Thurs & Fri 10am–4pm, Sat 10am–5pm, Sun 11am–4pm; 10zł). Highlights include Zurbarán's *Madonna of the Rosary* and the *Adoration of the Magi* by Joos van Cleve.

East of the Stary Rynek, the Bolesława Chrobrego bridge crosses to the quiet holy island of **Ostrów Tumski**. The first buildings you see are the late-Gothic **Psalteria** and the brick **St Mary's**, while behind that is the **Cathedral of SS Peter and Paul**. Most of this cathedral, Poland's oldest, was restored to its Gothic shape after wartime devastation, but a lack of documentary evidence for the eastern chapels meant that their successors had to be retained, as were the Baroque spires. Inside, the **crypt** has been excavated, uncovering earlier foundations, as well as parts of the sarcophagi of the early Polish monarchs.

Practicalities

The main **train station**, Poznań Główny, is 2km southwest of the historic quarter; tram #5 runs from the western exit beyond platform 7 to the city centre. The **bus station** is five minutes' walk to the east of the train station, across the bridge. The city **tourist office**, next to the EMPiK store on the corner of Ratajczaka and 27 Grudnia (Mon–Fri 10am–7pm, Sat 10am–5pm; ☎061/9431, ⊛www.city.poznan.pl), can book hotel and hostel rooms, hands out free maps and sells the monthly **listings** guide *Iks*. The Wielkopolska regional tourist office at Stary Rynek 59 (Mon–Fri 9am–5pm, Sat 10am–2pm; ☎061/852 61 56) has information on Poznań and the surrounding province and sells the comprehensive *Poznań In Your Pocket*.

Poznań **hotel** prices can double during trade fairs, which take place throughout the year, July and August excepted. The *Mini-Hotelik* (Al Niepodległości 8, entrance on ul Taylora; t061/863 14 15; ❷) is the cheapest hotel, ideally situated in the centre but near the station. Alternatively, try the *PTTK Dom Turysty* at Rynek 91 (☎061/852 88 93, ⊛www.domturysty-hotel.com.pl; ❷); accommodation ranges from four-person dorms to en-suite doubles. There is a **hostel** 500m southwest of the train station at ul Berwińskiego 2/4 (☎061/866 40 40; ❶). Almatur at Ratajczaka 3 (☎061/855 76 34) can arrange accommodation in student hostels from late June till mid-September. **Private rooms** (❷) are available from the Globtour office in the train station (open 24hr; rooms available until 10pm). The nearest **campsite** is *Malta*, ul Krańcowa 98 (☎061/876 62 03; tram #8 from train station), set by a lake 2km east of the centre.

There are plenty of **eating and drinking** possibilities in the main square. Find cheap Polish food at the *Apetyt* milk bar just off the Rynek on Szkolna, or head further south to *Ali Baba*, ul Św. Marcin 11, for filling piles of cheap middle-eastern food. *Bar Wegeterianski* at ul Wrocławska 21 is a healthy and cheap day-time snack bar (open till 5.30pm, Sat 3pm, closed Sun).

Poznań's large student population ensures a lively **nightlife** scene. On his visit in 2002, Russian president Vladimir Putin had a beer at the Danish-owned *Faxe Pub*, Rynek 62, which is jam-packed on weekends. The bars on ul Nowowiejskiego are great for meeting students. *Pod Minogą* (at no. 8) hosts bands on weekends, while next door, the wonderfully Bohemian *W Starym Kinie* shows free art films. Further west at ul Kościuszki, *Blue Note* is a famed jazz bar hosting regular live gigs and club nights.

Internet access is available at *Klik*, south of the Rynek on Jaskółca (daily 10am–4am, Sat & Sun from noon).

Travel details

Trains

Gdańsk to: Kraków (7 daily; 7–10hr overnight); Poznań (7 daily; 4hr); Toruń (6 daily; 3hr); Warsaw (15 daily; 4hr); Wrocław (4 daily; 6–7hr); Zakopane (2 daily; overnight).

Kraków to: Gdańsk (8 daily; 7hr–10hr overnight); Oświęcim/Auschwitz (16 daily; 1hr 30min); Poznań (7 daily; 6–7hr); Toruń (1 daily; overnight); Warsaw (15 daily; 2hr 30min); Wrocław (11 daily; 4hr–4hr 30min); Zakopane (14 daily; 3–4hr).

Poznań to: Gdańsk (7 daily; 4hr); Kraków (6 daily; 6–7hr); Toruń (4 daily; 2–3hr); Warsaw (17 daily; 3hr); Wrocław (20 daily; 2hr).

Toruń to: Gdańsk (5 daily; 3hr); Kraków (2 daily; overnight); Poznań (3 daily; 2hr); Warsaw (5 daily; 3hr); Wrocław (2 daily; 4hr 30min).

Warsaw to: Gdańsk (15 daily; 4hr); Kraków (14 daily; 2hr 30min); Poznań (17 daily; 3hr); Toruń (5 daily; 3hr); Wrocław (10 daily; 5hr); Zakopane (2 daily; 8hr 30min).

Wrocław to: Gdańsk (4 daily; 6–7hr); Kraków (11 daily; 4hr 30min); Poznań (18 daily; 2hr); Toruń (2 daily; 4hr 30min); Warsaw (9 daily; 5hr).

Zakopane to: Kraków (15 daily; 3–4hr).

Buses

Kraków to: Oświęcim/Auschwitz (19 daily; 1hr 30min); Zakopane (56 daily; 2hr 30min).

Portugal

Portugal highlights

* **A night out in Lisbon**
Great city for clubbing;
have a night in the Bairro
Alto or the club Lux to
find out why. See p.832

* **Óbidos** Picturesque village, its dazzling white-
washed houses
enclosed by medieval
walls. See p.836

* **Queima das Fitas,
Coimbra** University town
that celebrates the end
of the academic year big
time every May. See
p.839

* **Port wine lodges, Porto**
Various lodges offer free
tastings. See p.841

* **The Douro rail route** One
of the most beautiful
lines in Europe, along
the foot of the steep
Douro river valley. See
p.847

* **Alfama, Lisbon**
Traditional village life in
the heart of the capital;
getting lost here is half
the fun. See p.830

Introduction and basics

Portugal is around the size of Scotland with twice the population and has tremendous variety both geographically and in its ways of life and traditions. Along the coast around Lisbon, and on the well-developed Algarve in the south, there are highly sophisticated resorts, while the vibrant capital Lisbon has enough going on to please most city devotees. But in its rural areas this is still a conspicuously underdeveloped country, and there are plenty of opportunities to experience smaller towns and countryside regions that have changed little in the last century or so.

In terms of population, and of customs, differences between the **north and south** are particularly striking. Above a line more or less corresponding with the course of the River Tagus, the people are of predominantly Celtic and Germanic stock. It was here, at Guimarães, that the "Lusitanian" nation was born, in the wake of the Christian reconquest from the North African Moors. South of the Tagus, where the Moorish and Roman civilizations were most established, people tend to be darker-skinned and maintain more of a "Mediterranean" lifestyle. More recent events are woven into the pattern. The 1974 **revolution** came from the south – an area of vast estates, rich landowners and a dependent workforce – while the conservative backlash of the 1980s came from the north, with its powerful religious authorities and individual smallholders wary of change. More profoundly even than the revolution, **emigration** has altered people's attitudes and the appearance of the countryside. After Lisbon, the largest Portuguese community is in Paris, and there are migrant workers spread throughout France and Germany. Returning to Portugal, these emigrants have brought in modern ideas and challenged many traditional rural values.

The greatest of all Portuguese influences, however, is **the sea**. The Portuguese are very conscious of themselves as a seafaring race; mariners like Vasco da Gama led the way in the exploration of Africa and the Americas, and until less than thirty years ago Portugal remained a colonial power. The colonies brought African and South American strands to the country's culture: in the distinctive music of *fado*, sentimental songs heard in Lisbon and Coimbra, for example, or in the Moorish-influenced and Manueline architecture that abounds in places like Belém and Lagos.

Since Portugal is so compact, it's easy to take in something of each of its elements. Scenically, the most interesting parts of the country are in the north: the **Minho**, green, damp, and often startling in its rural customs; and the sensational gorge and valley of the **Douro**, followed along its course by the railway, off which antiquated branch lines edge into remote **Trás-os-Montes**. For contemporary interest, spend some time in both **Lisbon** and **Porto**, the only two cities of real size. And if it's monuments you're after, the centre of the country – above all, **Coimbra** and **Évora** – retains a faded grandeur. The **coast** is virtually continuous beach, and apart from the **Algarve** and a few pockets around Lisbon and Porto, resorts remain low-key and thoroughly Portuguese, with great stretches of deserted sands between

Portugal on the net

ⓦ**www.min-cultura.pt/Agenda/Agenda.html** The Ministry of Culture's website, with details of events in major towns

ⓦ**www.portugalinsite.pt** or ⓦ**www.portugal.org** The official Portuguese tourist office websites, with information on various tourist attractions and practical advice

ⓦ**www.portugalvirtual.pt** Comprehensive directory of everything from hotels to shops, tourist sites and culture

ⓦ**www.nexus-pt.com** Detailed site dedicated to the Algarve

them. Perhaps the loveliest are along the northern **Costa Verde**, around Viana do Castelo, or, for isolation, the wild beaches of **southern Alentejo**.

Information and maps

You'll find a tourist office, or **Turismo**, in almost every town of any size. They can help you find a room, and they often have local maps and leaflets. If you're doing any real exploration, or driving, it's worth investing in a good road **map**. The best are those put out by the Automóvel Clube de Portugal, GeoCenter and Michelin #437.

Money and banks

Portugal is one of the twelve European Union countries which have changed over to the **euro** (€).

Your best bet for cheap exchange is to use a credit or bank card at an **ATM**; commission on travellers' cheques can be high. **Banking hours** are Mon–Fri 8.30am–3pm; in Lisbon and in some of the Algarve resorts they may be open in the evening to change money.

Communications

Post offices (*correios*) are normally open Mon–Fri 9am–6pm & Sat 9am–noon. For **poste restante** services, look for a counter marked *encomendas*. The Portuguese postal service is reasonably efficient: mail takes about three days to Europe and just under a week to the U.S.

International **phone calls** can be made direct from any telephone booth or post office in the country. Cards cost €3, €6 or €9, and are available from post offices and the larger newsagents and tobacconists. The domestic operator number is ☏118; for international assistance and collect calls dial ☏098.

Internet cafés are common in most towns and cities and cost €2.5–5/hr. Most major post offices also have internet booths – just buy a card behind the counter.

Getting around

Distances are small in Portugal and you can get almost everywhere easily and efficiently by either train, bus or ferry. Although **trains** are usually cheaper, and some lines are highly scenic, it's often quicker to go by **bus** – especially on shorter or less obvious routes.

Trains

CP, the Portuguese railway company, operates all trains. About ninety percent are designated *Regional* and stop at most stations en route. *Intercidades* are twice as fast and twice as expensive, and you should reserve a seat if using them. The fastest, most luxurious and priciest of all are the *Rápidos* (known as "*Alfa*"), which speed between Lisbon, Coimbra and Porto – sometimes they have only first-class seats. CP sells its own **rail passes** (valid on any train and in first class), but you'd have to do a lot of travelling to make them worthwhile. Both InterRail and Eurail passes are valid, although supplements equal to the difference from a standard fare must be paid to travel on *Intercidades* and *Rápidos*. A complete timetable of CP services can be bought at ticket offices (€2.50) or accessed via the internet at ⓦ www.cp.pt.

Buses

Buses can often be more flexible than trains and fares are usually competitive. On a number of major routes (particularly Lisbon–Algarve) special express coaches can knock hours off the standard multiple-stop bus journeys. Visit ⓦ www.rede-expressos.pt for timetables or dial ☏707 22 33 44 for 24hr national bus information.

Cycling

Although there are few facilities and little respect from motorists, **cycling** is a popular sport in Portugal. Bikes can be transported on any *Regional* or *Interregional* train (in other words, not the fast ones) as long as there is space – check with the baggage office in advance. The charge is usually around €2, or free if the bike is dismantled.

22

Accommodation

In almost any town you should be able to find **accommodation** in a single room for under €25 and a double for under €50. Even in high season you shouldn't have many problems finding a bed, except in Lisbon and the Algarve.

Pensions and hotels

The main budget stand-bys are **pensions**, or *pensões* (*pensão* in the singular), which are graded from one to three stars. A three-star *pensão* is usually about the same price as a one-star **hotel**.

At the higher end of the scale are **pousadas**, run by the state and similar to the Spanish *paradores*. These charge at least four-star hotel prices, but they are often converted from old monasteries or castles and well worth a visit even if you can't afford to stay.

Hostels

There are forty-one **hostels** (*Pousadas de Juventude*) in Portugal and they tend to stay open all year. The price for a dormitory bed is €8–13 a night, depending on season and location; doubles cost €17–€32. Most have a curfew (usually midnight) and all demand a valid HI card.

Private rooms

Seaside resorts invariably have **rooms** (*quartos* or *dormidas*) **to let in private houses**. These are sometimes advertised, or just hawked by people at the bus and train stations. They're slightly cheaper than pension rooms – especially if you haggle, as is expected in the main resorts. Tourist offices have lists.

Camping

Portugal has around two hundred authorized **campsites**, most of them small, low-key and attractively located, and all of them remarkably inexpensive –rarely will you end up paying more than €5 a person. You can get a fairly complete map list from any Portuguese tourist office, or buy a detailed booklet, the *Roteiro Campista*, from bookshops, big newsstands or from Roteiro Campista, Apartado 3168, 1301-902, Lisbon (Ⓦwww .roteiro-campista.pt). **Unofficial camping** is banned in Portugal and beach areas are especially strict about this.

Food and drink

Portuguese food is excellent, cheap and served in quantity. Virtually all cafés will serve you a basic meal, or at least a snack, for under €8, and for a little more you have the run of most of the country's restaurants.

Food

You'll often come across a whole range of dishes at a **café**, but classic snacks include *tosta mistas* (cheese and ham toasties);*prego* (steak sandwich), usually served with a fried egg; *biftoque* (steak, chips, fried egg); *rissóis de carne* (deep-fried meat patties); *pastéis de bacalhau* (codfish cakes); and *sandes* (sandwiches).

Restaurant servings tend to be huge. Indeed, you can usually have a substantial meal by ordering a *meia dose* (half portion), or *uma dose* between two. Meals are often listed like this on the menu and it's normal practice.

Most restaurants serve an *ementa turística* (set meal) which can be good value, particularly in *pensões* that serve meals, or in the cheaper workers' cafés.

Regional differences aren't as marked as in Spain, but it's always worth taking stock of the *prato do dia* (dish of the day) and, if you're on the coast, going for fish and seafood. Typical Portuguese dishes include *sopa de marisco* (shellfish soup), *caldo verde* (finely shredded green kale leaves in broth) and *bacalhau* (dried cod, cooked in a myriad of different ways). *Caldeirada* is a fish stew with as many as nine kinds of fish, cooked with onions and tomatoes. Also typical is *carne de porco á Alentejana*, in which fried pork is covered with a clam, tomato and onion sauce or stewed with tomato and onions. **Meat** is usually excellent, and nearly all restaurants have pork, beef, lamb, goat and chicken dishes. Regional **cheeses** are well worth sampling, particularly goat and sheep cheese. **Puddings** include *arroz doce* (rice pudding), *salada da fruta* (fresh fruit salad) and *nuvens* (egg custard). Portugal's cakes – *bolos* or *pastéis* – are often at their best in *casas de chá* (tearooms), though you'll also find them in cafés and in *pastelarias* (cake shops). Among the best are custard tarts (*pastéis de nata*), marzipan cakes from the Algarve, and the incredibly sweet egg-based *doces de ovos*.

Drink

Portuguese **wines** (*tinto* for red, *branco* for white) are very inexpensive and of an amazing quality overall – even the standard *vinho da casa* that you get in the humblest of cafés. The fortified **port** (*vinho do Porto*) and **madeira** (*vinho da Madeira*) wines are by far the best known, and you should certainly aim to sample them both. Sparkling **rosé wines** are mostly produced for export; Mateus Rosé is one of the most famous. The light, slightly sparkling **vinhos verdes** – "green wines", in age not colour – are produced in the Minho, and are excellent and refreshing served chilled.

Portuguese **brandy** is available in two varieties, Macieiera and Constantino, and like local gin is ridiculously cheap; if you're asking for gin or any other spirits at a bar always specify you want "gin nacional", "vodka nacional", etc – it'll save you a fortune.

The two most common local **beers** (*cervejas*) are Sagres and Super Bock – both are served on tap and are very drinkable. You can order many other bottled foreign brands in most bars. Order *um fino* or *um imperial* if you want a small glass; *uma caneca* will get you a half-litre.

Opening hours and holidays

Shops are generally **open** Mon–Fri 9am–12.30/1pm & 2/2.30–6/6.30pm, Sat 9am–12.30/1pm. Larger supermarkets tend to stay open until 8pm. Museums, churches and monuments open from around 10am to 6pm; almost all museums and monuments, however, are closed on Mondays, and at Easter, when cultural life seems to cease completely.

The main **public holidays** are: Jan 1; Feb (Carnival); Good Fri; April 25 (Revolution day); May 1; Corpus Christi; June 10 (Camões day); June 13 (St Anthony's Day, Lisbon only); Aug 15; Oct 5 (Republic day); Nov 1 ; Dec 1 (Independence day); Dec 8; Dec 25.

Emergencies

Portugal is a reasonably crime-free country, although Lisbon and the larger tourist areas have recently seen significant increases in petty crime.

Drug trafficking carries heavy sentences although possession of any kind of hard or soft drugs no longer constitutes a prisonable offence. Portuguese **police**, though relatively easy-going, carry guns and are not to be argued with.

For minor health complaints people generally go to a *farmácia* (**pharmacy**), which you'll find in almost any village. They are normally open Mon–Fri 9am–1pm & 3–7pm, Sat 9am–1pm. A sign at each one will show the nearest 24hr pharmacy on duty. Pharmacists are highly trained and can dispense many drugs without a prescription. In the case of **serious illness**, you can get the address of an English-speaking doctor from a consular office or, with luck, from the local police or tourist office.

Emergency numbers

For all emergencies dial ☏112.

Lisbon and around

There are few more immediately likeable capitals than **LISBON**. A lively and varied place, it remains in some ways curiously provincial, rooted as much in the 1920s as the 2000s. Wooden trams clank up outrageous gradients, past mosaic pavements, Art Nouveau cafés and the medieval quarter of **Alfama** which hangs below the city's **São Jorge** castle. Modern Lisbon has kept an easy-going, human pace and scale, while boasting a vibrant, cosmopolitan identity. The city invested heavily in rejuvenation during the 1990s – disued dockland was reclaimed and communication links improved, with several showcase pieces of architecture and engineering such as Santiago Calatrava's impressive Gare de Oriente and his sleek fourteen kilometre-long **Vasco da Gama** bridge which links Lisbon airport to a network of national motorways. The city is still focused firmly on the future and is gearing up to host the European Football Championship in 2004.

The **Great Earthquake** of 1755 (followed by a tidal wave and fire) destroyed most of the city's grandest historical buildings and twenty years of frantic reconstruction led to many impressive new palaces and churches, as well as the street grid pattern spanning the seven hills of Lisbon. Several buildings from Portugal's golden age survived the quake – notably the **Torre de Belém**, the **Castelo de São Jorge** and the **Monastery of Jerónimos** at Belém. Many of the city's more modern sites also demand attention: the **Fundação Calouste Gulbenkian**, a museum and cultural complex, with superb collections of ancient and modern art, and the futuristic **Oceanarium** at the Parque das Nações, the largest of its kind in Europe. Half an hour south of Lisbon dunes stretch along the **Costa da Caparica** and 20km north you'll pass the coastal resorts of **Estoril** and **Cascais** before reaching the lush wooded heights and royal palaces of **Sintra** and the monastery of **Mafra**, one of the most extraordinary buildings in the country.

Arrival and information

From Portela **airport** it's just a twenty-minute bus journey to the centre; the Aerobus (#91; every 20min 7am–9pm; €2.30) leaves from right outside the arrivals hall and runs to Praça dos Restauradores, Rossio, Praça do Comércio and Cais do Sodré; the ticket is then valid for transport on buses and trams for that day. Slightly less convenient but a bit cheaper, local buses #44 and #45 (€0.85) run from the road outside the airport to Rossio and Cais do Sodré (train station for Cascais; ☎800 203 067). **Taxis** into the centre of Lisbon should cost under €10, but it is always best to agree a price with the driver first. **Long-distance trains** use the **Santa Apolónia station**, about fifteen minutes' walk from the waterfront Praça do Comércio, or a short ride on buses #9, #39, #46 or #90 to Rossio. **Local trains** from Sintra emerge at the heart of the city in the **Rossio station**, while **trains from the Algarve and south** terminate at **Barreiro**, on the far bank of the river, from where you catch a ferry (included in price of train ticket) to the **Fluvial** station next to the Praça do Comércio. For **train timetables** visit ⓦwww.rede-expressos.pt or call into the information office on the ground floor of Rossio station (Mon–Sat 9am–7pm) on Avenida João Crisostomo (metro Saldanha). Rossio handles most international and domestic departures, including services to the Algarve and Madrid. The Parque das Nações terminal, **Gare do Oriente** (☎800 201 820), also has some international and domestic departures.

The best place for up-to-date information is the stylish city tourist office, **Lisboa Welcome Centre**, on the corner of Praça do Comércio and Rua do Arsenal (daily 9am–9pm; ☎210 312 700, ⓦwww.alt-turismolisboa.pt). For information on the rest of the country, visit the main Portuguese **tourist office** on the western side of Praça dos Restauradores in the Palácio da Foz (daily 9am–8pm; ☎213 463 314, ⓦwww.portugalinsite.pt); there's also a small tourist office at the airport (daily 6am–midnight; ☎218 450 657).

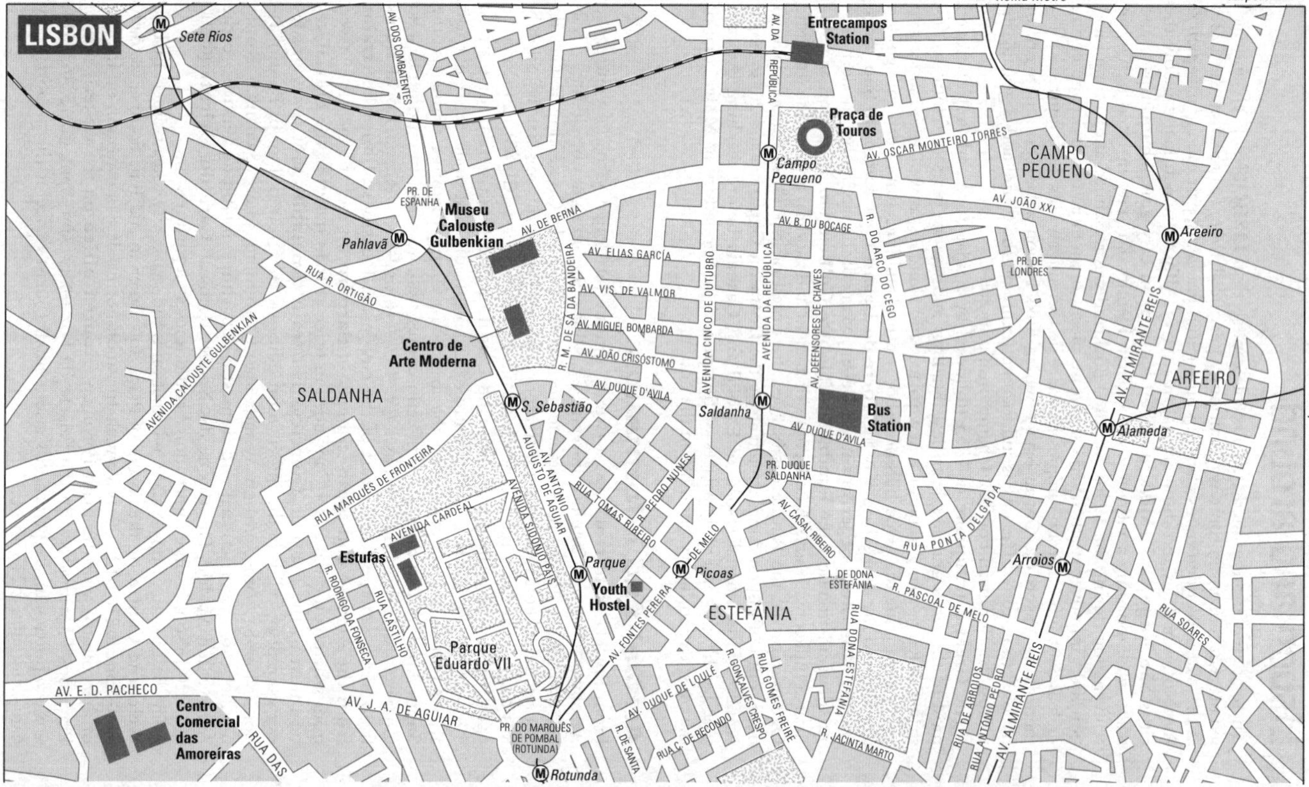
LISBON
Roma Metro
Airport
Expo Site & Gare do Oriente
Sete Ríos
Entrecampos Station
AV. DA REPÚBLICA
AV. DOS COMBATENTES
Praça de Touros
Campo Pequeno
CAMPO PEQUENO
AV. OSCAR MONTEIRO TORRES
AV. JOÃO XXI
Areeiro
PR. DE ESPANHA
Museu Calouste Gulbenkian
Pahlavã
AV. DE BERNA
AV. B. DU BOCAGE
R. DO ARCO DO CEGO
PR. DE LONDRES
RUA R. ORTIGÃO
AV. ELIAS GARCÍA
AV. VIS. DE VALMOR
AV. MIGUEL BOMBARDA
AV. JOÃO CRISÓSTOMO
R. M. DE SÁ DA BANDEIRA
AVENIDA CINCO DE OUTUBRO
AVENIDA DA REPÚBLICA
AV. DEFENSORES DE CHAVES
AV. ALMIRANTE REIS
AREEIRO
AVENIDA CALOUSTE GULBENKIAN
Centro de Arte Moderna
SALDANHA
AV. DUQUE D'AVILA
S. Sebastião
Saldanha
Bus Station
Alameda
PR. DUQUE SALDANHA
AV. ANTÓNIO AUGUSTO DE AGUIAR
AVENIDA SIDÓNIO PAIS
RUA MARQUÊS DE FRONTEIRA
AVENIDA CARDEAL
RUA TOMAS RIBEIRO
R. PEDRO NUNES
AV. CASAL RIBEIRO
RUA PONTA DELGADA
Estufas
Parque
Youth Hostel
Picoas
DE MELO
L. DE DONA ESTEFÂNIA
R. PASCOAL DE MELO
Arroios
R. RODRIGO DA FONSECA
RUA CASTILHO
ESTEFÂNIA
RUA SOARES
Parque Eduardo VII
AV. FONTES PEREIRA
R. GONÇALVES CRESPO
RUA GOMES FREIRE
RUA DONA ESTEFÂNIA
AV. E. D. PACHECO
AV. J. A. DE AGUIAR
PR. DO MARQUÊS DE POMBAL (ROTUNDA)
AV. DUQUE DE LOULÉ
RUA DE ARROIOS
RUA ANTÓNIO PEDRO
Centro Comercial das Amoreíras
RUA DAS
R. DE SANTA
RUA C. DE RECONDO
R. JACINTA MARTO
Rotunda

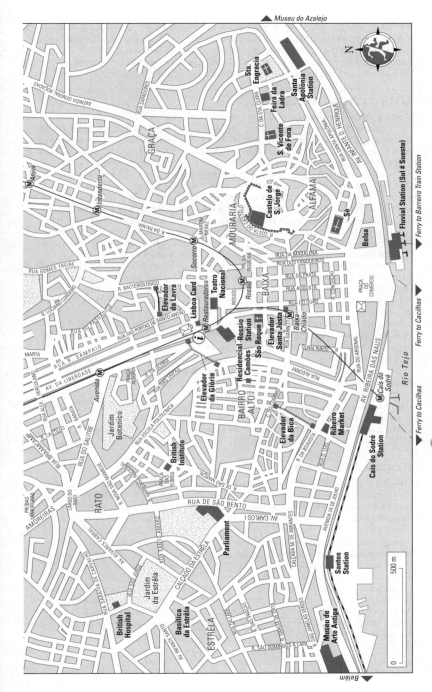

Museu do Azalejo

N

Sta.
Engracia

Feira da
Ladra

Santa
Apolónia
Station

S. Vicente
de Fora

GRAÇA

Anjos

Intendente

ALFAMA

Castelo de
S. Jorge

MOURARIA

Fluvial Station (Sul # Sueste)

Ferry to Barreiro Train Station

Socorro

Sé

Bolsa

RUA GOMES FREIRE

RUA DA MADALENA

RUA DOS FANQUEIROS

R. BACTERIOLOGICO

Elevador
da Lavra

Lisboa Card

Teatro
Nacional

Rossio

BAIXA

RUA DA PRATA

RUA DA PALMA

PR. DA
FIGUEIRA

RUA AUGUSTA

PRAÇA
DO
COMÉRCIO

Restauradores

RUA DO OURO

R. LUCIANO CORDEIRO

RUA DAS PORTAS DE SANTO ANTÃO

Rossio
Station

São Roque

Elevador
Santa Justa

Baixa-
Chiado

AV. DA LIBERDADE

Avenida

Residencial
Camões

Cais do
Sodré

Rio Tejo

MARTA

RUA R. SAMPAIO

HERCULANO

PRAÇA
ALEGRIA

Elevador
da Glória

BAIRRO
ALTO

Elevador
da Bica

Ribeiro
Market

Cais do Sodré
Station

Ferry to Cacilhas

Jardim
Botânico

British
Institute

PRAÇA
DAS
FLORES

RATO

Ferry to Cacilhas

AMOREIRAS

PR. DAS
AMOREIRAS

LARGO DO
RATO

RUA DE SÃO BENTO

AV CARLOS I

AVENIDA 24 DE JULHO

Santos
Station

Parliament

British
Hospital

Jardim
da Estrêla

Basílica
da Estrêla

ESTRÊLA

Museu de
Arte Antiga

500 m

0

R. SÃO DOMINGOS A LAPA

PORTUGAL

22

827

Belém

Museu do Azalejo

It's well worth investing in a good **map** to help you find your way around the narrow streets of the Alfama and Bairro Alto district. The best is the *Falkplan* map which shows all the minor streets not usually shown on other maps; it's sold in the newsagent next to the tourist office in Praça dos Restauradores. Alternatively log on to ⊛www.EUnet.pt/Lisboa and print out a copy of their excellent city maps.

City transport

Getting around Lisbon presents few problems. Most places of interest are within easy walking distance – and transport connections are detailed in the text for those that aren't. The vastly improved **metro** (☎21 798 0600, ⊛www.metrolisboa.pt) now covers most of the city and is by far the fastest way of getting around; tickets cost €0.50 each, €4.50 for a block of ten or €1.40 for a day pass. Also a good bet are **trams**, perhaps the most enjoyable way of getting around, and **buses** (☎21 362 044, ⊛www.carris.pt) – tickets (valid on both buses and trams) can be used for two journeys (€0.85) when purchased in advance from kiosks, or for one journey when bought on board. You can also buy a day **travel pass** (*bilhete turístico*) for just €2.50, which allows unlimited travel on buses, trams and the metro until midnight; alternatively, there are Passe Turístico bus/metro/*elevador* **passes**, valid for four days (€9.25) or seven days (€13.10), available from booths. The bus and tram networks operate from around 6am to midnight and the metro until 1am.

If you want to do some really intensive sightseeing, it's worth investing in the **Lisboa Card**, which gives unlimited travel on all the city's public transport, entry to 26 museums and discounts on a host of tourist-related activities. The cards cost €11 for one day, €18 for two, or €23 for three and are available from any tourist office.

Taxis are reasonably cheap: a short hop shouldn't cost more than €10. All journeys are metered (daytime rate starting at €1.80, at night from €2.10, plus €0.50 for each item of luggage carried). They can be found quite easily by day, especially around the main squares, but at night they're more difficult to get hold of – if you're leaving a bar or club it's usually best to arrange for one by phone; try Rádio Táxis de Lisboa (☎21 811 9000) or Teletáxis (☎21 811 1100).

Ferries are particularly useful in the summer for short trips to various points on the other side of the Tagus river; most are operated by Transtejo (☎21 322 4000, ⊛www.transtejo.pt; €0.55–1.55) and arrive at Belém, Cais do Sodré and Praça do Comércio. There are also 24-hour **water taxis**, operated by Taxitour (☎21 397 2783), which depart from a number of clearly marked points along the river.

Accommodation

Lisbon has scores of small, cheap **pensions**, most of which are found around Rua das Portas de Santo Antão and Rua da Glória. Bairro Alto is the most atmospheric part of the city in which to stay, though rooms can be hard to come by and noisy. At Easter and in midsummer, room availability is stretched to the limit: many single rooms are "converted" to doubles and prices may start as high as €25. Fortunately, during most of the year you should have little difficulty finding a place, and for maybe a third less than the midsummer prices. For more expensive **hotels**, you can save yourself a lot of walking if you use the **24hr reservation service** (☎21 314 1562) at the Praça dos Restauradores tourist office or the airport; there is no commission charge. If you're looking for general backpacking information, free internet and bargain places to stay, try the youth organization **Movijovem**, Avda. Duque de Ávila 137 (☎21 359 6000, ⊛www.sej.pt). Most of the pensions listed below are one- or two-star; **addresses**, written as 53-3°, for example, specify the street number followed by the floor.

Hostels

Pousada de Juventude da Catalazete Estrada Marginal ☎21 443 0638, ⓔcatalazete@movijovem.pt. Overlooking the beach at Oeiras, 15km outside the city. Take any train from Cais do Sodré and follow signs from Oeiras station. It's small, so phone before setting out to be sure of getting a room. Reception is open 6–11pm. Dorms ❷

Pousada de Juventude de Lisboa Rua Andrade Corvo 46 ☎21 353 2696, ⓔlisboa@movijovem.pt. Lisbon's main hostel, with good facilities and no curfew. Book in advance. One block north of the Picoas metro stop, or take buses #1, #21 or #36 from Restauradores or Rossio. Dorms ❷

Casa de Juventude Lisboa Parque das Nações Rua da Moscavide 47–101, Parque das Nações ☎21 892 0890, ⓔliboaparque@movijovem.pt. Modern hostel, a twenty-minute bus/train journey from the centre but right on the banks of the Tagus. No curfew. Take Metro to Oriente. Dorms ❷

Hotels

Residencial Camões Trav. do Poço da Cidade 38-1° ☎21 346 7510. Brilliant location right in the heart of Bairro Alto, though invest in some earplugs for streetside rooms at weekends. Breakfast included in high season, English spoken. ❹

Pensão Coimbra e Madrid Praça da Figueira 3-3°, Baixa ☎21 342 1760. Superb views, though the rooms are noisy. Decent proprietors, shabby though clean furnishings and a TV room, too. ❹

Residencial Florescente Rua das Portas de Santo Antão 99, Baixa ☎21 342 6609. One of the city's best-value establishments, with lots of rooms, some with TV, some without windows, so ask about alternatives. ❻

Pensão Ninho das Águias Costa do Castelo 74, Alfama ☎21 885 4070. Bright, light rooms with a lovely garden terrace overlooking the city. ❺

Pensão Prata Rua da Prata 71-3°, Baixa ☎21 346 8908. Small rooms, some with showers, up three extremely steep flights of stairs in a welcoming, family-run apartment. Book ahead. ❸

Pensão São João de Praça Rua São João de Praça 97-2°, Alfama ☎21 886 2591. Clean, quiet and friendly place in a lovely old town house just below the cathedral. Front rooms have wrought-iron balconies. During high season half-board is compulsory. ❻

Campsites

Parque Municipal de Campismo ☎21 762 3100. Main city campsite, in the Parque Florestal Monsanto, about 6km west of the centre. The entrance is on Estrada da Circunvalação on the park's west side. Take bus #43 from Praça da Figueira.

Camping Obitur-Guincho Lugar da Areia, Guincho ☎21 487 0450, ⓔinfo@orbitur.pt. A well located site some way out of the city in surfer's mecca Guincho. Has a supermarket as well as sports facilities and cabins to rent. From Cais do Sodré catch the train to Cascais, then a bus to Guincho.

The City

The heart of the capital is the lower town – the **Baixa**, housing many of the country's administrative departments, banks and business offices. Europe's first great example of Neoclassical design and urban planning, it remains an imposing quarter of rod-straight streets, cobbled underfoot and either streaming with traffic or turned over to pedestrians and pavement artists. Architecturally, the most interesting places in the Baixa are the squares – the Rossio, Praça da Figueira and Praça do Comércio – and, on the periphery, the lanes leading east to the cathedral and west up towards Bairro Alto. Between the two districts, half-way up the hill, lies an area known as the **Chiado**, which suffered much damage from a fire that swept across the Baixa in 1988 but has been elegantly rebuilt by Portugal's premier architect Alvaro Siza Viera and remains the city's most affluent quarter, focused on the fashionable shops and the beautiful old tearooms of the **Rua Garrett**.

The **Rossio** square is very much a focus for the city; its main concession to grandeur is the **Teatro Nacional**, built along the north side in the 1840s. At the waterfront end of the Baixa lies the city's other main square, the beautiful arcaded **Praça do Comércio**. A couple of blocks east stands the **Sé Cathedral** (daily 8.30am–6pm). Founded in 1150 to commemorate the city's reconquest from the Moors, it occupies the site of the principal mosque of Moorish Lishbuna. Like so many of the country's cathedrals, it is Romanesque and extraordinarily restrained in both size and decoration. You'll need to pay to visit the thirteenth-century cloisters

(€0.50) and the Baroque **sacristy** (€2.50), with its small museum of treasures – including the relics of St Vincent.

From the Sé, Rua Augusto Rosa winds up towards the Castelo, past sparse ruins of a Roman theatre and the **Miradouro de Santa Luzia**, which offers spectacular views over the Tejo. The **Castelo São Jorge** (daily 9am–dusk; free) contains the shell of the Moorish palace that once stood here; now it hosts Olispónia (daily 10am–1pm & 2–6pm; €3), a multimedia show which makes an excellent introduction to the history of the city. The castle itself is an enjoyable place to spend a couple of hours, wandering amid the ramparts and towers and looking down upon the city.

The **Alfama** quarter, tumbling from the walls of the Castelo to the banks of the Tejo, is the oldest part of Lisbon. In Arab times it was the city's grandest district, but with subsequent earthquakes the new Christian nobility moved out, leaving it to the fishing community. Despite some commercialization, the quarter still retains a largely traditional life of its own. The **Feira da Ladra**, Lisbon's rambling **flea market**, fills the Campo de Santa Clara, at the edge of Alfama, every Tuesday and Saturday. While at the flea market, take a look inside **Santa Engrácia** (Tues–Sun 10am–6pm; €2), the loftiest and most tortuously built church in the city – begun in 1682, its vast dome was finally completed in 1966. Through the tiled cloisters of nearby **São Vicente de Fora** you can visit the old monastic refectory, since 1855 the pantheon of the Bragança dynasty (Tues–Sun 10am–5.30pm; €2). Here, in more or less complete (though unexciting) sequence, are the bodies of all Portuguese kings from João IV, who restored the monarchy in 1640, to Manuel II, who lost it and died in exile in England in 1932.

High above and to the west of the Baixa is **Bairro Alto**, the focus of the city's nightlife. The district can be reached by one of two funicular-like trams – the Elevador da Glória from the Praça dos Restauradores or the Elevador da Bica from Rua de São Paulo/Rua da Moeda (both €1 one-way). The other means of access, the great street *elevador* (Elevador Santa Justa), built by Eiffel disciple Raul Mésnier de Ponsard, is currently closed. Hanging almost directly above the exit of Mésnier's funicular are the ruined Gothic arches of the **Convento do Carmo** (Tues–Sun 10am–6pm; €2.50). Once the largest church in the city, this was half-destroyed by the earthquake and is perhaps even more beautiful as a result; its small archeological museum contains treasures from monasteries that were dissolved after the 1834 Liberal revolution.

The Parque Eduardo VII and the Calouste Gulbenkian Museum

North of the Praça dos Restauradores are the city's principal gardens, the **Parque Eduardo VII**, most easily approached by metro Marquês de Pombal. Though there are some pleasant cafés here, the park's big attractions are the **Estufas** (daily 9am–4.30/5.30pm; €1.10), huge and wonderful glasshouses filled with tropical plants, flamingo pools, and endless varieties of palms and cacti.

The **Museu Calouste Gulbenkian** (Tues 2–6pm, Wed–Sun 10am–6pm; €3, free on Sun, combined ticket with Centro de Arte Moderna €5), the great museum of Portugal, is ten minutes' walk north of the Parque Eduardo VII – take bus #31 or #46 from the Restauradores, or the metro to São Sebastião or Praça de Espanha. Established by the Armenian oil magnate Calouste Gulbenkian, the Fundação helps finance various aspects of Portugal's cultural life – including an orchestra, three concert halls and two galleries for temporary exhibitions on the site. This showpiece museum is divided into two distinct parts – the first devoted to Egyptian, Greco-Roman, Islamic and Oriental arts, the second to European, including paintings from all the major schools. There are outstanding portraits by Rubens and Rembrandt, while Fragonard ushers in an excellent showing of work from France, featuring Corot, Manet and Monet. There's also a stunning room full of Art

Nouveau jewellery by René Lalique. Across the gardens, the separate **Centro de Arte Moderna** (same hours; €3, combined ticket with Museu Calouste Gulbenkian €5) has all the big names on the twentieth-century Portuguese scene.

Museu Nacional de Arte Antiga

The one other museum that stands up to Gulbenkian standards is the national art collection, the **Museu Nacional de Arte Antiga** (Tues 2–6pm, Wed–Sun 10am–6pm; €3), situated near the riverfront to the west of the city at Rua das Janelas Verdes 95 (bus #40 or #60 from Praça do Comércio). Its core is formed by fifteenth- and sixteenth-century Portuguese works, the acknowledged masterpiece being Nuno Gonçalves' *St Vincent Altarpiece*, a brilliantly marshalled canvas depicting Lisbon's patron receiving homage from all ranks of its citizens. After Gonçalves and his contemporaries, the most interesting works are by Flemish and German artists (Cranach, Bosch – a fabulous *Temptation of St Anthony* – and Dürer), and miscellaneous gems by Raphael, Zurbarán and Rodin.

Belém and the Monastery of Jerónimos

Even before the Great Earthquake, the **Monastery of Jerónimos** (Mosteiro dos Jerónimos; daily 10am–5/6.30pm; cloisters same hours €3; tram #15 from Praça do Comércio or #14 from Praça da Figuera) at **Belém** was Lisbon's finest monument: since then, it has stood quite without comparison. It was from Belém in 1497 that Vasco da Gama set sail for India, and it was here, too, that he was welcomed home by Dom Manuel. The monastery was funded by a levy on the fruits of his discovery – a five-percent tax on all spices other than pepper, cinnamon and cloves, whose import had become the sole preserve of the Crown. Begun in 1502, this is the most ambitious achievement of Manueline architecture. The main entrance to the church is a complex, shrine-like hierarchy of figures centred around Henry the Navigator. Vaulted throughout and fantastically embellished, the cloister is one of the most original and beautiful pieces of architecture in the country, holding Gothic forms and Renaissance ornamentation in an exuberant balance.

The **Torre de Belém** (Tues–Sun 10am–5/6.30pm; €3), guarding the entrance to the port around 500m from the monastery, is a multi-turreted whimsy built over the last five years of Dom Manuel's reign. The interior is unremarkable, but it's worth visiting for the views from the top. Back towards the monastery are a number of museums, of which the best are the **Museu de Arte Popular** (Tues–Sun 10am–12.30pm & 2–5pm; €1.75, free Sun am), a province-by-province display of Portugal's folk arts, and the **Museu do Design** (daily 11am–8pm; €3) in the Centro Cultural de Belém, featuring design classics from the twentieth century. Opposite is the vast concrete **Monument to the Discoveries** (Tues–Sun 9am–5/7pm; €2), erected in 1960 to commemorate the 500th anniversary of the death of Henry the Navigator; inside, a small exhibition space has changing displays on the city's history.

Eating and drinking

Lisbon has some great **cafés and restaurants** serving large portions of food at sensible prices. **Seafood** is widely available – there's an entire central street, Rua das Portas de Santo Antão, as well as a whole enclave of restaurants across the River Tejo at Cacilhas, that specialize in it. Lisbon also has a rich vein of inexpensive **foreign restaurants** featuring food from the former colonies: Brazil, Mozambique, Angola and Goa. There are plenty of lunchtime restaurants scattered around the Baixa. **At night** head for the Bairro Alto or the slightly more expensive Docas area. For a teatime treat try one of the *pastelarias*, specializing in cakes. Note that many restaurants are **closed on Sundays**, while on Saturday nights you may need to book for the more popular places. Assume moderate **prices** at all the restaurants listed below – no more than €17.50 per person – unless otherwise stated.

Restaurants

Restaurante Andorra Rua das Portas de Santo
Antão 82, Baixa. Not cheap but good grills and well
positioned for people-watching, with outdoor tables.
Bota Alta Trav. da Queimada 37, Bairro Alto. Old
tavern restaurant that pulls in the punters for its
large portions of traditional Portuguese food.
Closed Sat lunch & Sun.
Restaurante Calcuta Rua do Norte 17, Bairro
Alto. Popular Indian restaurant with lots of chicken,
seafood and lamb curries, tandooris, good
vegetarian options. Closed Sun.
O Cantinho do Bem Estar Rua do Norte 46,
Bairro Alto. Inexpensive Alentejan restaurant that's
as friendly and authentic as you can get.
Carvoeiro Rua Vieira Portuense 66–68, Belém.
One of many inexpensive fish restaurants near the
monastery, with outdoor tables. Closed Mon.
Casa Faz Frio Rua Dom Pedro V 96, Bairro Alto. A
beautiful, very traditional restaurant, with tiny
cubicles. Around €10 for a full meal and wine.
Casanova Armazém B, Cais da Pedra à Bica do
Sapato, Santa Apolónia. Fashionable riverside
restaurant serving pizza, pasta and crostini with
great views from its outside terrace. It's
phenomenally popular and you can't book, so turn
up early. Closed all Mon & Tues lunch.
Cervejaria da Trindade Rua Nova da Trindade 20.
Wonderful, vaulted beer-hall restaurant, the oldest
in the city, with a tiny patio garden. Expensive.
Hell´s Kitchen Rua da Atalaia 176. Right at the
top of the Bairro Alto and well worth finding for a
menu of world foods that includes several
vegetarian dishes. Closed Mon.
Mestré André Calçadinha de Santo Estêvão 4–6,
Alfama. A fine neighbourhood tavern, with good

grills (*churrasco*). Outdoor seating in summer.
Closed Sun.
Rei dos Frangos/Bom Jardim Trav. de Santo
Antão 11–18, Baixa. Excellent for spit-roast
chicken – a whole one with fries for about €8.
Adega Santo Antão Rua das Portas de Santo
Antão 42. Good value *adega* with local character.
Bustling bar area and tables inside and out
offering great grilled meat and fish. Closed Mon.
Solmar Rua das Portas de Santo Antão 108, Baixa
☎21 342 3371. Noisy but atmospheric seafood
restaurant/beerhall, with fountain and marine
mosaics.
Teatro Taborda Costelo 75. Fashionable theatre
café/restaurant with fine views from the terrace,
serving fresh vegetarian dishes and Greek salads.
Closed Mon.
Os Tibetanos Rua da Salitre 117, Rato. Fine
vegetarian restaurant run by Buddhists serving
organic food. Closed Sat & Sun.

Cafés

Antiga Confeitaria de Belém Rua de Belém 90,
Belém. Historic tiled café famous for its delicious
custard tarts or *pastéis de nata*.
Café a Brasileira Rua Garrett 120. The most
famous of Rua Garrett's old-style coffee houses.
Open until 2am.
Café Nicola Praça Dom Pedro IV 26. On the west
side of Rossio, this grand old place is a good stop
for breakfast. Closed Sat afternoon and all day Sun.
Café Pastelaria Bernard Rua Garrett 104.
Superb cakes and an outdoor terrace on Chiado's
most fashionable street.
Café Suiça Praça Dom Pedro IV 96. Famous for
cakes and pastries.

Entertainment and nightlife

For night-time drinking, the densest concentration of designer **bars and clubs** is
found in **Bairro Alto** – Lisbon's traditional centre of nightlife. Late-night (though
pricier) action can also be found out in the **Docas** (Docklands) district, just east of
the 25 de Abril bridge (train to Alcântara Mar from Cais do Sodré or tram #15 or
#18). Converted warehouses at the **Doca de Santo Amaro** are host to waterfront
bars and cafés, while a little closer to the city centre the **Doca de Alcântara** has
emerged as the hangout for Lisbon's chic. Clubs don't really get going until around
2am and tend to stay open till 6am. Admission fees are usually about €10 (usually
including one or two drinks), although some Lisbon clubs leave the cover charge to
the doorman's discretion – anything from €5 to €50.

Tourist brochures tend to suggest that Lisbon entertainment begins and ends with
fado, a form of music that developed in Lisbon in the early nineteenty century. It is
a mournful, romantic singing style somewhere between blues and flamenco and
bemoans lost loves and better times (try Bairro Alto or Alfama and expect to pay
over €15). Portuguese **jazz** can be good, **rock** can occasionally surprise, and if you
check out the posters around Restauradores there's a good chance of catching
African music from the former colonies. Entertainment **listings** are available in
the *Agenda Cultural*, a free monthly booklet issued by Lisbon city council, or in the

magazines which come with the Friday editions of the *Independente* or *Diario de Noticias* newspapers.

Bars

Bar Ártis Rua Diário Notícias 95, Bairro Alto. Chill to mellow jazz with a good mix of locals. Closed Mon.

Cena de Copos Rua da Barroca 103–105, Bairro Alto. The place to be if it's after midnight, you're under 25 and you're bursting with energy.

Instituto do Vinho do Porto Rua de São Pedro de Alcântara 45, Bairro Alto. Over 200 types and vintages of port, from €1 a glass upwards. Closed Sun.

Pavilhão Chinês Rua Dom Pedro V 89, Bairro Alto. Overly-decorated bar, completely lined with cabinets of bizarre artefacts. Daily till 2am. Very expensive.

A Tasca Trav. da Quiemada 13–15, Bairro Alto. Cheerful and welcoming tequila bar.

Clubs

Doca de Santo Doca de Santo Amaro, under Ponte 25 de Abril. Large palm-fringed club, one of the first and the most popular in this area.

Kapital Avda. 24 de Julho 68, opposite Santos station. Sweaty outmoded dance venue where you can have a laugh until 6am.

Kasino Rua Cozinha Económica 11, Alcântara. Big house/techno spot. Wed–Sat only.

Kremlin Escadinhas da Praia 5. One of the city's most snobbish nightspots, packed with flash young Lisboetas. Techno still rules. Closed Sun & Mon.

Lux Cais da Pedra a Santa Apolónia, opposite Santa Apolónia station. Recently voted one of the best 35 clubs in the world. Top Portuguese DJs as well as big European names. Closes 6am.

Queens Rua Cintura do Porto de Lisboa, Doca da Alcântâra. A huge place which can hold 2500 people. Tuesday night is Ladies' Night involving a male strip show; visiting DJs on other nights. Wed–Sat only.

Salsa Latina Gare Marítima de Alcântara, Doca de Santo Amaro. A bar/restaurant and club in a fantastic 1940s maritime station, offering salsa Tuesday to Saturday and live music at weekends.

Closed Sun.

Trumps Rua da Imprensa Nacional 104b, Rato, north of Bairro Alto. The biggest gay disco in Lisbon with a reasonably relaxed door policy. Closed Mon.

WIP Elevador da Bica. Halfway down the hill, this bar has a host of different DJs covering mellow sounds from reggae/Afro through soul to drum'n'bass.

Fado and other live music

Adega do Ribatejo Rua do Diário de Notícias 23, Bairro Alto ☏ 21 346 8343. Popular *fado* venue and has a lower-than-usual minimum charge. Singers include a couple of professionals, the manager and even the cooks. Closed Sun.

Atlantic Pavilion Parque das Nações ☏ 218 918 440. Portugal's largest indoor venue, which hosts big-name stars and holds up to 17,000 spectators.

B.leza Largo do Conde Barão 50, Santos. Live African music most nights in this wonderful sixteenth-century building, with space to dance in, tables to relax at, and Cape Verdean food too. Closed Sun.

Chafarica Calçada de São Vicente 81, Alfama. Tiny, long-established Brazilian bar with live music every night. Best after midnight, especially after a few *caipirinhas*.

Hot Clube de Portugal Praça da Alegria 39, off Avda. da Liberdade. Tiny basement jazz club which hosts local and visiting artists. Closed Mon.

Paradise Garage Rua João de Oliveira Miguens 38, Alcântara ☏ 213 955 977. Big on the club scene, this venue also hosts regular gigs. It's on a tiny side road off Rua da Cruz à Alcântara. Thurs–Sat only.

O Senhor Vinho Rua do Meio a Lapa 18, Lapa ☏ 21 397 2681. Famous Lapa club sporting some of the best *fado* singers in Portugal.

A Severa Rua das Gáveas 51–61, Bairro Alto ☏ 21 342 8341. A city institution featuring big *fado* names at big prices. Closed Thurs.

Listings

Banks Main branches in the Baixa. Exchange office at the airport (24hr) and at Santa Apolónia station (daily 8.30am–4pm).

Embassies Australia, Avda. da Liberdade 198–2° ☏ 21 310 1500; Canada, Avda. da Liberdade 196–200 ☏ 21 316 4600; Ireland, Rua da Imprensa à Estrela 1–4° ☏ 213 929 440; UK, Rua de São Marçal 174 ☏ 213 929 440; US, Avda. das Forças Armadas ☏ 21 727 3300.

Hospital British Hospital, Rua Saraiva de Carvalho 46 ☏ 213 955 067.

Internet Ask Me Lisboa, above the Lisbon Welcome Centre in Praça do Comércio; Web C@fe, Ruo do Diário de Notícias 126, Bairro Alto.

Laundry Lava Neve, Rua de Alegría 37, Bairro Alto (closed Sat pm & all Sun).

Post offices Praça dos Restauradores 58.

Around Lisbon

The long beaches of **Caparica** – which the quirks of the Tejo currents have large-ly spared from the pollution of Lisbon – and the architectural attractions of **Sintra** and **Mafra** can each be reached on a day-trip from Lisbon; but to do justice to Sintra you'll need to stay overnight.

Caparica

A short journey east of the capital, **CAPARICA** is a thoroughly Portuguese resort, popular with surfers and crammed with restaurants and beach cafés, yet solitude is easy enough to find, thanks to the mini-railway (*transpraia*) that runs along the 8km of dunes in summer. The most enjoyable way to get there is to take a **ferry** from the Fluvial station by Praça do Comércio, or from Cais do Sodré, to **Cacilhas**, and then pick up the connecting bus. Alternatively, you can take a **bus** direct to Caparica from Praça de Espanha (metro Praça de Espanha). Buses either stop at a bus park by the beach, or at the station five minutes back from the sands. From the latter, walk up to the main road, turn right and keep walking until you reach Praça da Liberdade, the main square, where there's a **tourist office** (Mon–Sat 9am–1pm & 2–5.30pm; summer also Sun same times; ☎212 900 071), market, cinema and banks. The tourist office can direct you to one of several hotels in Caparica, though buses run back to Lisbon/Cacilhas at regular intervals throughout the day. **Campsites**, which range along the first few kilometres of the beach, are on the whole overcrowded and overpriced, but functional enough. There are dozens of good, relaxed, cheap **fish and seafood** places, as well as beach bars, along the main Rua dos Pescadores, which leads from the square to the beach. Try getting off at *transpraia* stop 12 to try the excellent food at the *Cabana do Pescador* restaurant.

Sintra

SINTRA is one of Portugal's most spectacular sights and one of the country's few UNESCO World Heritage sites. Its extraordinary subtropical microclimate allows for an abundance of cool, deciduous woodland which attracted Moorish lords and the kings of Portugal here from Lisbon during the hot summer months. The layout of Sintra – an amalgamation of three villages – can be confusing, but the extraordi-nary **Palácio Nacional** (10am–5.30pm, closed Wed; €3), about twenty minutes' walk from the station, is an obvious landmark. The palace was probably in existence under the Moors, but takes its present form from the rebuilding commissioned by Dom João I and his successor, Dom Manuel, in the fourteenth and fifteenth cen-turies. Its style is a fusion of Gothic and the latter king's Manueline additions. The chapel and its adjoining chamber – its floor worn by the incessant pacing of the half-mad Afonso VI who was confined here for six years by his brother Pedro I – are well worth seeing.

The charms of Sintra, famously penned by Lord Byron, lie as much in its build-ings as in its **walks and paths**; one of the best walks leads past the church of Santa Maria and up to the ruined ramparts of the **Moorish Castle** (daily 10am–5/7pm; €3), from where the views are extraordinary. Beyond the castle, a steep ninety-minute walk from town, is the lower entrance to the immense **Pena Park**, at the top end of which rears the fabulous **Palácio de Pena** (Tues–Sun 10am–5/7pm; €5; gardens only €3), a wild 1840s fantasy of domes, towers and a drawbridge that does not draw. The interior has been preserved exactly as left by the royal family on their flight from Portugal in 1910.

Another must-see site is **Quinta da Regaleira** (tours 1hr 30min; every 30min–1hr; reserve in advance on ☎219 106 650; €10), one of Sintra's most elabo-rate private estates, lying just five minutes' walk west out of town on the Seteais-Monserrate road. The palace and its fantastic gardens were built at the turn of the last century by a theatrical set designer for one of the richest industrialists in Portugal. The highlight is the Initiation Well, inspired by the initiation practices of the Knight Templars and Freemasons. Entering via an Indiana Jones-style revolving stone door, you can walk down a moss-covered spiral stairway to the foot of the well and to a tunnel, which eventually resurfaces at the edge of a lake. Beyond Quinta da Regaleira, the road leads past a series of beautiful private estates to **Monserrate** – about an hour's walk. It's difficult to do justice to the beauty of Monserrate, whose vast **gardens** (daily 9am–5/7pm; €3), filled with endless varieties of exotic trees and subtropical shrubs and plants, extend as far as the eye can see.

Finding **accommodation** at Sintra in summer can be a problem, though if you arrive early in the day you should end up with something. There are a fair number of pensions: best value is probably *Adelaide*, Rua Guilherme Gomes Fernandes 11 (☎219 230 873; ❸), midway between the train station and Sintra village. *Pielas* (☎219 241 691; ❺), on Rua João de Deus 70–72 near the station, offers superb rooms above a café, though is due to move to Avda. Desiderio Cambournac 1–3 in 2003. A little further out, in São Pedro, *Residencial Sintra*, Travessa dos Alvares (☎219 230 738; ❾), is a fantastic place with a rambling garden, swimming pool and giant rooms which can easily accommodate extra beds.

Alternatively, some cheap **private rooms** (❷) can be booked through the extremely helpful **tourist office** (daily 9am–7/8pm; ☎219 231 157), just off the central Praça da República. There's a **hostel** (☎219 241 210; ✉sintra@movi-jovem.pt; dorms ❷, doubles ❺; closed noon–6pm) at Santa Eufemia, in the hills above Sintra, 5km from town – take a local bus to São Pedro from outside the train station and walk from there (2km). The nearest **campsite** is out of town at Praia Grande, served by regular bus. **Restaurants** are generally poor value, relying heavily on the tour parties. Try *Tulhas* behind the turismo (closed Wed) or *Casa da Avo* on nearby Rua Visdonde de Monserrate 46 (closed Thurs).

Mafra

Connected by regular buses from Sintra train station and from outside the Campo Grande metro stop in Lisbon, **MAFRA** is dominated by one building: the vast, pink marble **Palace–Convent** (10am–5pm, closed Tues; €3), built in emulation of Madrid's El Escorial in 1717 by João V, the wealthiest and most extravagant of all Portuguese monarchs. The convent was initially intended for just thirteen Franciscan friars, but as more gold poured in from Brazil, João expanded it into the world's largest basilica, with two royal wings and monastic quarters for 300 monks and 150 novices. The sheer magnitude of the building is what stands out: there are 5200 doorways, 2500 windows, and two bell towers each containing over 50 bells. The highlight is the magnificent Rococo library, rivalling that of Coimbra in both design and grandeur. The basilica is no less imposing, with the multicoloured marble designs of its floor mirrored in the ceiling decoration.

Central Portugal

The **Estremadura** region has played a crucial role in each phase of the nation's history – and the monuments are there to prove it. A comparatively small area, it boasts a quite extraordinary concentration of vivid architecture and engaging towns. **Alcobaça**, **Batalha**, **Óbidos** and **Tomar** – home to the most exciting buildings in Portugal – all lie within ninety minutes' bus ride of one another, as does the pilgrimage centre of **Fátima**. With its fertile rolling hills, Estremadura is second in beauty only to Minho, but the adjoining bull-breeding lands of **Ribatejo** fade into the dull expanses of northwestern Alentejo, and there's no great reason to cross the river unless you're pushing on to Évora or can catch up with one of the region's traditional festivals.

North of Estremadura, life on the fertile plain of the **Beira Litoral** has been conditioned over the centuries by the twin threats of floodwaters from Portugal's highest mountains and silting by the restless Atlantic. The highlight here is **Coimbra**, an ancient university town stacked high on the right bank of the Mondego.

Óbidos

ÓBIDOS is a small town of whitewashed houses draped in bougainvillea and encircled by lofty medieval walls. "The Wedding Town" was the traditional bridal gift of the kings of Portugal to their queens, a custom begun in 1282 by Dom Dinis. The town – a couple of hours from Lisbon by train – can hardly have changed in appearance since then: its cobbled streets and steep staircases wind up to the ramparts, from where you can gaze across a fable-like countryside of windmills and vineyards. The parish church, **Igreja de Santa Maria**, in the central Praça, was chosen for the wedding of the 10-year-old child-king Afonso V and his 8-year-old cousin, Isabel, in 1444. The interior, lined with seventeenth-century blue *azulejos*, contains a retable in a side chapel to the right painted by Josefa de Óbidos, one of the finest Portuguese painters and one of the few women artists afforded any reputation by art historians. One corner of the triangular fortifications is occupied by a massively towered **Castle** built by Dom Dinis and now converted into a *pousada* (☎262 959 105; ❾).

Other **hotels** in Óbidos also tend to be expensive. Your cheapest option is to consult the list of private houses offering **rooms** posted in the **tourist office**, on Rua Direita 51 (daily 9.30am–1pm & 2–7pm; ☎262 959 231); there are comfortable rooms at Rua Direita 40 (☎262 959 188; ❸). If you do feel like splashing out try the *Estalagem Do Convento*, Rua Dr João de Ornelas (☎262 959 214; ❺), housed in an early-nineteenth-century convent, or the *Casa d'Óbidos* (☎258 950 924; ❻), about 1km south of the town walls. Built in 1889 it has beautiful gardens and an air of faded grandeur. One of the better budget places to **eat** is the *Café 1° de Dezembro*, next to the church of São Pedro.

Leiria

With regular bus services to the three big sites of northern Estremadura – Alcobaça, Batalha and Fátima – **LEIRIA** makes a handy centre for excursions. The chief sight in Leiria itself is the **Castle** (daily 9/10am–5.30/6.30pm; €1.50), incorporating an elegant royal palace with a magnificent balcony high above the River Lis. At the heart of the old town, Praça Rodrigues Lobo is surrounded by beautiful buildings and arcades. The **tourist office** (daily: summer 10am–1pm & 3–7pm; winter 2–6pm; ☎244 814 748) and **bus station** are on opposite sides of a park overlooking the river in the modern city centre. The **train station** is about 4km out of town, with a connecting bus service. **For internet** access try *Arquivo Coffee Shop*, Rua Combatentes Grande Guerra, 53 (daily 9.30am–midnight). For **accommodation**, check the **pensions** such as *Pensão Berlinga*, Rua Miguel Bombarda 3D (☎244 823 846; ❸), and restaurants (some offering rooms) around Praça Rodrigues Lobo and on narrow side streets such as Rua Mestre Aviz and Rua Miguel Bombarda. There's also a fancy **hostel** with a good atmosphere at Largo Cândido dos Reis 9 (☎244 831 868; ❷). As for **restaurants**, try the seafood at *Jardim*, by the tourist office (closed Mon), or slightly more expensive Portuguese cuisine at *Montecarlo*, Rua Dr Correia Mateus 32–34.

Alcobaça

From the twelfth century until the middle of the nineteenth, the Cistercian **Abbey of Alcobaça** (9am–5/7pm; €2.50) was one of the greatest in the Christian world. Owning vast tracts of farmland, orchards and vineyards, it held jurisdiction over a dozen towns and three seaports until its ultimate dissolution in 1834. The monastery was originally founded by Dom Afonso Henriques in 1147 in celebration of the liberation of Santarém from the Moors, and is a truly vast complex – its main **Church** (free entry) is the largest in Portugal. The exterior is disappointing, as the Gothic facade has been superseded by unexceptional Baroque additions. Inside, however, all later adornments have been swept away, restoring the narrow soaring aisles to their original vertical simplicity. The only exception to this Gothic purity is the frothy Manueline doorway to the sacristy, hidden behind the high altar.

The abbey's most precious treasures are the fourteenth-century **tombs of Dom Pedro and Dona Inês de Castro**, each occupying one of the transepts and sculpted with phenomenal wealth of detail to show the story of Pedro's love for Inês de Castro, the daughter of a Galician nobleman. Fearing Spanish influence over the Portuguese throne, Pedro's father, Afonso V, forbade their marriage. The ceremony nevertheless took place in secret, whereupon Afonso sanctioned his daughter-in-law's murder. When Pedro succeeded to the throne in 1357 he exhumed the corpse of his lover, forcing the entire royal circle to acknowledge her as queen by kissing her decomposing hand. The tombs – inscribed with the motto "Até o Fim do Mundo" (Until the End of the World) – have been placed foot to foot so that on the Day of Judgement the lovers may rise and immediately feast their eyes on one another.

The most amazing room in the building is the **kitchen**, with its cellars and gargantuan conical chimney, supported by eight trunk-like iron columns. A stream tapped from the River Alcôa still runs straight through the room: it was used not merely for cooking and washing but also to provide a constant supply of fresh fish. The **Sala dos Reis** (Kings' Room), off the beautiful **Cloisters of Silence**, displays statues of virtually every king of Portugal down to Dom José, who died in 1777. The rest of the abbey, including four cloisters, seven dormitories and endless corridors, is closed to the public.

Alcobaça's **tourist office** (daily 10am–1pm & 3–6/7pm; ☎262 582 377) is opposite the abbey on Praça 25 de Abril. **Internet access** is available at *Ciber Café*, Rua Dr Francisco Zagelo (daily 10am–midnight). The best budget place to stay is *Pensão Corações Unidos* (☎262 582 142; ❸), around the corner at Rua Frei António Brandão 39. There's also a **campsite** (☎262 582 265), ten minutes north of the bus station along Avenida Manuel da Silva Carolino. Good-value places to **eat** include the touristy *Frei Bernado*, Rua D Pedro V 17–19, a huge place serving copious meals, and *Celeiro dos Frades*, atmospherically situated under the arches alongside the abbey.

Batalha

The **Mosteiro de Santa Maria da Vitória**, better known as the **Mosteiro de Batalha** (daily 9am–5.30/6.30pm; €2.50), is the finest building in Portugal, classified on the UNESCO's World Heritage list, and an enduring symbol of national pride. It was originally founded to commemorate the Battle of Aljubarrota (1385), which sealed Portugal's independence after decades of Spanish intrigue. It's easily reached on a day-trip from Leiria (5 buses daily).

The honey-coloured abbey was transformed by Manueline additions in the late fifteenth and early sixteenth centuries, but the bulk was completed between 1388 and 1434 in a profusely ornate version of French Gothic. Within this flamboyant framework there are also strong elements of the English Perpendicular style, an influence explained by the **Capela do Fundador** (Founder's Chapel), directly to the right upon entering the church: beneath the octagonal lantern rests the tomb of Dom João I and Philippa of Lancaster, their hands clasped in the ultimate expression of harmonious relations between Portugal and England. Their four younger sons are buried along the south wall of the Capela do Fundador in a row of recessed arches. Second from the right is the **Tomb of Prince Henry the Navigator**, who guided the exploration of Madeira, the Azores and the African coast as far as Sierra. The **Claustro Real** (Royal Cloister) dates from this period of burgeoning self-confidence under Manuel I (1495–1521), its intricate stone grilles being added by Diogo de Boitaca, architect of the cloisters at Belém and the prime genius of Manueline art. Off the east side, the early-fifteenth-century **Sala do Capítulo** (Chapter House) is remarkable for the unsupported span of its ceiling. The Church authorities were convinced that the whole chamber would come crashing down and only employed as labourers criminals already condemned to death.

The **Capelas Imperfeitas** (Unfinished Chapels) form a separate structure tacked on to the east end of the church and accessible only from outside the main complex. Dom Duarte, eldest son of João and Philippa, commissioned them in 1437 as a royal mausoleum but the original design was transformed beyond all recognition by Dom Manuel's architects. It is unique among examples of Christian architecture in its evocation of the great shrines of Islam and Hinduism: perhaps inspired by the tales of Indian monuments that filtered back along the eastern trade routes.

Fátima

FÁTIMA is one of the most important centres of pilgrimage in the Catholic world, a status deriving from the six **Apparitions of the Virgin Mary**. On May 13 1917, three children from the village were tending their parents' flock when, in a flash of lightning, they were confronted with "a lady brighter than the sun" sitting in the branches of a tree. The vision returned on the thirteenth day of the next five months, culminating in the so-called Miracle of the Sun on October 13, when a swirling ball of fire cured lifelong illnesses. To commemorate these extraordinary events a vast white **Basilica** and gigantic esplanade have been built, more than capable of holding the crowds of 100,000 who congregate here for the main **pilgrimages** (May 12 & 13; Oct 12 & 13). In the church the tombs of two of the children, who died in the European flu epidemic of 1919–20, are the subject of constant attention. Hospices and convents have sprung up in the shadow of the basilica, and inevitably the fame of Fátima has resulted in its commercialization.

Pensions and **restaurants** abound, but there's little reason to stay except during the big pilgrimages to witness the midnight processions. Regular **bus services** to Fátima from Tomar make a day-trip easy. **Internet** access is available at *Centro de Copias*, R.S. João de Deus, Edif. Varandas de Fátima 13 (daily 10am–7pm).

Tomar

TOMAR, 34km east of Fátima, is famous for the Convento de Cristo, an artistic *tour de force* which entwines the main military, religious and imperial strands in the history of Portugal. However, it's an attractive town in its own right – especially during the *Festas dos Tabuleiros*, in the first week of July, when the place goes wild – and you should aim to spend a couple of days here if you can.

Built on a simple grid plan, Tomar's old quarters preserve all their traditional charm, with whitewashed cottages lining narrow cobbled streets. On the central Praça da República stands an elegant seventeenth-century town hall, a ring of houses of the same period and the Manueline church of **São João Baptista**, remarkable for its octagonal belfry and elaborate doorway. Nearby, at Rua Joaquim Jacinto 73, you'll find an excellently preserved fourteenth-century **Synagogue**, now the **Museu Luso-Hebraicoa Abraham Zacuto** (daily 10am–7pm; free); in 1496, Dom Manuel ordered the expulsion or conversion of all Portuguese Jews, and the synagogue at Tomar was one of the few to survive.

The **Convento de Cristo** (Tues–Sun: summer 9.15am–12.30pm & 2–6pm; winter 2–5pm; €2.50) is set among pleasant gardens with splendid views, about a quarter of an hour's walk uphill from the centre of town. Founded in 1162 by Gualdim Pais, first Master of the Knights Templar, it was the headquarters of the Order. The heart of the complex remains the **Charola**, the temple from which the knights drew their moral conviction. It's a strange place, more suggestive of the occult than of Christianity; like almost every circular church, it's based on the Church of the Holy Sepulchre in Jerusalem, for whose protection the Knights Templar were originally founded.

The highlight of the convent is the ornamentation of the windows on the main facade of its **Chapter House**, where maritime motifs form a memorial to the sailors who established the Portuguese empire. Later João III (1521–1557) transformed the convent into a thoroughgoing monastic community, adding dormitories, kitchens and no fewer than four cloisters. The adjoining two-tiered **Great Cloisters** comprise one of the purest examples of the Renaissance style in Portugal.

Tomar's **turismo** (daily 10am–6/7pm; ☎249 322 427) is at the top of Avenida Dr Cândido Madureira. There is a pleasant all-year **campsite** (☎249 322 608) in town and a number of reasonable **pensions**, each with a **restaurant**: *Tomarense*, Avda. Torres Pinheiro 13 (☎249 312 948; ❸), near the bus station; *Luz*, Rua Serpa Pinto 144 (☎249 312 317; ❹), with **internet** access; and the very popular *Residencial União*, Rua Serpa Pinto 94 (☎249 323 161; ❹), in the centre of town.

Coimbra

COIMBRA was Portugal's capital from 1143 to 1255 and it ranks behind only the cities of Lisbon and Porto in historic importance. Its university, founded in 1290 and finally established here in 1537 after a series of moves back and forth to Lisbon, was the only one existing in Portugal until the beginning of the last century. For a provincial town it has remarkable riches, and it's an enjoyable place to be, too – lively when the students are in town, sleepy during the holidays. The best time of all to be here is in May, when the students celebrate the end of the academic year in the **Queima das Fitas**, tearing or burning their gowns and faculty ribbons. This is when you're most likely to hear the Coimbra *fado*, distinguished from the Lisbon version by its mournful pace and complex lyrics.

Old Coimbra sits on a hill on the right bank of the River Mondego, with the university crowding its summit. The main buildings of the **Old University**, dating from the sixteenth century, are set around a courtyard dominated by a Baroque clocktower and a statue of João III. The chapel is covered with *azulejos* and intricate decoration, but takes second place to the **Library** (daily 9.30am–12.30pm & 2–5.30/7.30pm; €2.50), a Baroque fantasy presented to the faculty by João V in the early eighteenth century.

Below the university, a good first stop is the **Museu Machado de Castro** (Tues–Sun 9.30am–12.30pm & 2–5.15pm; €3), just down from the unprepossessing Sé Nova (New Cathedral). Named after an eighteenth-century sculptor, the museum is housed in the former archbishop's palace. It's positively stuffed with sculpture, paintings, furniture and ceramics. The **Sé Velha** (Old Cathedral; Mon–Thurs & Sat 10am–5pm, Fri 10am–2pm), halfway down the hill, is one of the most important Romanesque buildings in Portugal. Solid and square on the outside, it's also stolid and simple within, the decoration confined to a few giant conch shells and some unobtrusive *azulejos*.

Restraint and simplicity certainly aren't the chief qualities of the **Igreja de Santa Cruz** (Mon–Sat 9am–noon & 2–5.45pm, Sun 4–6pm; €1 for cloister), at the bottom of the hill past the city gates. Although it was founded before the Old Cathedral, nothing remains that has not been substantially remodelled. In the early sixteenth century, Coimbra was the site of a major sculptural school; the new tombs for Portugal's first kings, Afonso Henriques and Sancho I, and the elaborately carved pulpit, are among its very finest works. The Manueline theme is at its clearest in the airy arches of the Cloister of Silence, its walls decorated with bas-relief scenes from the life of Christ.

Practicalities

Most mainline **trains** stop at Coimbra B, 3km north of the city, from where there are frequent connecting services to Coimbra A, right at the heart of things. The main **bus station** is on Avenida Fernão de Magalhães, about fifteen minutes' walk from the centre – turn right out of the bus station and head down the main road. The **tourist office** (Mon–Fri 9am–5/6pm, Sat & Sun 9/10am–1pm & 2.30–5/5.30pm; ☎239 855 930, ⍟www.turismo-centro.pt) is opposite the bridge in the Largo da Portagem.

Near the station, the sleazy Rua da Sota and its side streets have a few **pensões** that aren't as bad as they look – try the *Pensão Vitória* at Rua da Sota 9 & 19 (☎239 824 049; ➍), or the *Residencial Domus* at Rua Adelino Veiga 62 (☎239 828 584; ➎). Alternatively, there are several options east of the university; beneath the aqueduct, at Rua Castro Matoso 8, *Antunes* (☎239 854 720; ➏) offers good service. The **hostel**, above the park on Rua Henrique Seco 14 (☎239 822 955; ➋), is friendly and immaculately run – it's a twenty-minute walk from Coimbra A, or take bus #7, #☎29 or #46. The **campsite** is currently closed in preparation for the Euro 2004 soccer competition.

There are plenty of inexpensive **places to eat** around the centre. For really basic fare, served up with loads of atmosphere, try the little dives tucked into the tiny alleys between the Largo da Portagem, Rua da Sota and Praça do Comércio. *Adega Paço do Conde* on Rua Paço do Conde is a cavernous, locally renowned *churrasqueira*. Be sure, also, to try one of the traditional **coffee houses** along Rua Ferreira Borges – notably *Café Santa Cruz* – and Rua Visconde da Luz.

Northern Portugal

PORTO, European City of Culture 2001, and the country's second largest city, is an attractive and convenient centre from which to begin an exploration of the region. Magnificently set on a rocky cliff astride the River Douro, it is perhaps most famous for the port-producing suburb of **Vila Nova de Gaia**, the ageing centre for wines supplied by vineyards further inland along the river. The **Douro Valley** is traced by a spectacular **rail route**, with equally impressive branch lines following valleys to the north – along the River Tâmega to Amarante and along the Corgo to Vila Real – the main centre for transport connections into the ancient, isolated region of **Trás-os-Montes** and its famous old capital of **Bragança**. In the northwest, the **Minho**, considered by many to be the most beautiful part of the country, is a lush wilderness of rolling mountain forests and rugged coastlines (the Costa Verde), with some of the most unspoilt beaches in Europe. A quietly conservative region, its towns have a special charm and beauty, amongst them the religious centre of **Braga**, and the self-proclaimed birthplace of the nation, **Guimarães**. **Viana do Castelo** and **Vila do Conde** are enjoyably low-key beach resorts on the Minho coast, both within commuting distance of Porto.

Porto

Capital of the north, **PORTO** is very different from Lisbon – unpretentious, inward-looking, unashamedly commercial. As the local saying goes: "Coimbra sings; Braga prays; Lisbon shows off; and Porto works." The attraction of the city lies largely in the contrast between the prosperous business core of the centre and the timeless charm of its **Ribeira** area, a UNESCO World Heritage site. Here the cobbled warren of steep alleys and passages is alive with bars and restaurants, in a setting that appears unchanged for hundreds of years.

To get your bearings, it's worth climbing the 250 steps of the Baroque **Igreja e Torre dos Clérigos** (Mon–Sat 10am–7pm, Sun 10am–noon; €1), once the tallest building in Portugal. To the south, a statue of Porto's most famous son, Henry the Navigator, provides the centrepiece of a square that bears his name. His birthplace is on one of the streets running down from here towards the river. On the west side of the square is the extravagant facade of the glass-domed former **Stock Exchange** and behind it, the most extraordinary church in Porto, **São Francisco** (daily 9am–5/6pm; €2.50 including museum). It's rather plain from the outside, but inside, once your eyes adjust to the gloom, you are greeted by a fabulously opulent eighteenth-century refurbishment, with gold dripping from every corner. Don't miss the church's small **museum**, set in an eerie underground crypt, and containing an *ossário*, a collection of bones dating from before the time of public cemeteries.

The **Museu Nacional Soares dos Reis** at Rua de Dom Manuel II (Tues 2–6pm, Wed–Sun 10am–12.30pm & 1.30–6pm; €2.50), over to the west behind the city hospital, was the first national museum in Portugal. Its collection includes glass, ceramics and a formidable array of eighteenth- and nineteenth-century paintings, as well as the late-nineteenth-century sculptures of Soares dos Reis – his *O Desterro* (The Exile) is probably the best-known work in Portugal. Follow the road past the museum, or take any bus from the Cordoaria stop except #6 and #18, and you'll come to the **Jardim do Palácio de Cristal**, a peaceful park dominated by a space-age domed pavilion which now serves as a sports centre. In summer the park is home to a vast funfair. On the far side of the park, below the **Museu Romântico** is the **Solar do Vinho do Porto** (Mon–Sat 11am–10.45pm), where you can sample one of hundreds of varieties of **port** on the relaxing river terrace.

Vila Nova de Gaia

Vila Nova de Gaia, essentially a city in its own right, is dominated by the port trade. From the north bank of the river, the names of the various companies (Croft's, Taylor's, Sandeman, Graham's), spelled out in neon letters across the terracotta roofs of the lodges, leave you in no doubt as to what awaits you when you cross. You can walk to Gaia across the **Ponte Dom Luís I**: the most direct route to the wine lodges is across the lower level from the Cais da Ribeira, but if you've a head for heights it's an amazing sensation to walk over the upper deck; otherwise, take bus #32, #57 or #91 from São Bento. Almost all the companies offer free **tasting** and tours of their lodges, although some of the bigger names like Sandeman charge €2.50, redeemable against the price of a bottle. There's little pressure to buy anything – but do try the dry white ports, which are often unobtainable elsewhere.

Practicalities

Most trains from the south will drop you at the distant **Estação de Campanhã**; you should change here for a local train to the central **São Bento** – it takes about five minutes and there should never be more than a twenty-minute wait. The walls of São Bento station are adorned with dramatic *azulejos* (ornamental tiles) that are almost worth the journey themselves. Trains no longer run to the Minho and the north, although they will eventually be linked by Porto's ambitious new metro system, expected to be operational by 2005. As a general rule, **buses** from the south come in around Rua Alexandre Herculano, and those from the north to the new bus station at Rua Dr Alfredo Magalhães 46, about 250m north of the defunct Estação da Trindade. All major European airlines fly to Porto's Francisco Sá Carneiro **international airport** (☎22 941 2534), 10km north from the city centre. The Aerobus (7.45am–7.15pm; every 30min; €2.49, free if you fly with TAP) stops at **Avenida dos Aliados**, a few yards north of the central São Bento station. This is Porto's main commercial centre, which culminates at Praça Dom João I, 43, site of the central **post office** and the main **tourist office** (daily 9am–7pm; ☎22 317 514). **Internet access** is available a few doors down at *PortWeb* (Mon–Sat 9am–2am).

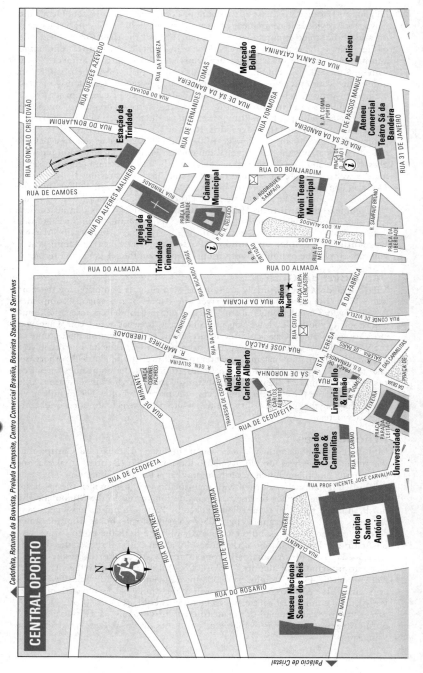

22

842

CENTRAL OPORTO

◄ Cedofeita, Rotunda da Boavista, Prelada Campsite, Centro Comercial Brasília, Boavista Stadium & Serralves

▲ Palácio de Cristal

N

RUA DO ROSARIO

RUA DO BREYNER

RUA DO DO JARDIM

RUA DE CEDOFEITA

RUA DE MIGUEL BOMBARDA

RUA DE CEDOFETA

RUA PROF. VICENTE JOSÉ CARVALHO

Museu Nacional
Soares dos Reis

R. D. MANUEL II

RUA CLEMENTE

MENERES

Hospital
Santo
António

Universidade

Igrejas do
Carmo &
Carmelitas

RUA DO CARMO

Livraria Lello
& Irmão

PRAÇA
PARADA
LEITÃO

PR. GOMES
TEIXEIRA

Auditorio
Nacional
Carlos Alberto

PRAÇA
CARLOS
ALBERTO

PRAÇA
CORONEL
PACHECO

RUA DE
MIRANTE

TRAVESSA DE CEDOFEITA

R. PINHEIRO

R. GEN. SILVEIRA

RUA DE CONCEIÇÃO

R. MARTIRES LIBERDADE

SÁ DE NORONHA

RUA JOSÉ FALCÃO

RUA CEUTA

PRAÇA FILIPA
DE LENCASTRE

Bus Station
North

RUA DA PICARIA

RUA DO ALMADA

RUA DO ALMADA

RUA RICARDO JORGE

Trindade
Cinema

Igreja da
Trindade

PRAÇA
DA
TRINDADE

RUA DE CAMOES

RUA DO ALFERES MALHEIRO

Estação da
Trindade

RUA GONÇALO CRISTOVÃO

RUA DO BONJARDIM

RUA DA TRINDADE

RUA GUEDES AZEVEDO

RUA DA FIRMEZA

RUA DO BOLHÃO

RUA DE SÁ DA BANDEIRA

RUA DE FERNANDES TOMAS

RUA FORMOSA

Mercado
Bolhão

RUA DE SANTA CATARINA

Coliseu

Ateneu
Comercial
Teatro Sá da
Bandeira

R. DE PASSOS MANUEL

RUA 31 DE JANEIRO

RUA DO BONJARDIM

Câmara
Municipal

R. RODRIGUES
SAMPAIO

Rivoli Teatro
Municipal

PRAÇA
DA
LIBERDADE

AV. DOS ALIADOS

R. SAMPAIO BRUNO

PRAÇA DE
D. JOÃO I

R. AT. COMM.
PORTO

RUA DE SÁ DA BANDEIRA

P. G. H. DELGADO

R. E
ORTIGÃO

R. J.
MELO

Câmara
Municipal

R. STA. TERESA

G.G. FERNANDES

GALERIA DE PARIS

RUA CONDE DE VIZELA

R. DA FÁBRICA

R. DAS CARMELITAS

PRAÇA DE

DA SILVA

PRAÇA DE
D. JOÃO I

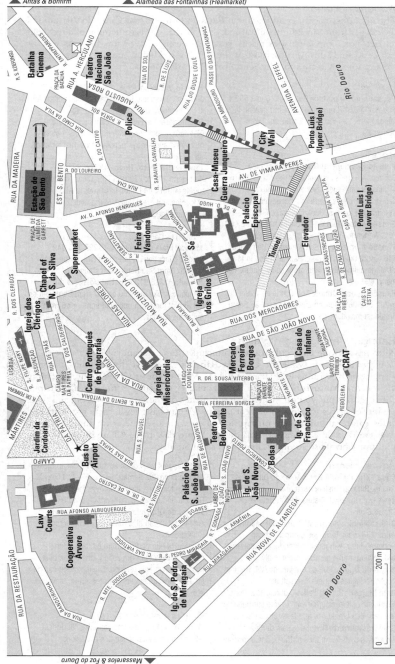

Batalha Cinema

Teatro Nacional São João

Police

RUA A. HERCULANO

R. DOS ANTEPASSEROS

R. S. ILDEFONSO

PRAÇA DA BATALHA

RUA DO SOL

R. DE S. LUIS

RUA DO DUQUE LOULÉ

PASSE D. DAS FONTAINHAS

Rio Douro

AVENIDA G. EIFFEL

RUA DO MIRADOURO

Ponte Luis I (Upper Bridge)

▼ Port Lodges ▼ Vila Nova de Gaia

City Wall

AV. DE VIMARA PERES

Casa-Museu Guerra Junqueiro

Palácio Episcopal

Ponte Luis I (Lower Bridge)

RUA DA MADEIRA

Estação de São Bento

PRAÇA DE ALMEIDA GARRETT

Supermarket

Chapel of N. S. da Silva

Igreja dos Clérigos

R. DOS CLÉRIGOS

LISBOA

R. FILIPE NERY

R. S. ASSUNÇÃO

MARTIRES

CAMPO MARTIRES DA PATRIA

C. DA FERREIRA

Jardim da Cordoaria

Bus to Airport ★

Law Courts

Cooperativa Arvore

RUA DA RESTAURAÇÃO

RUA DA BANDEIRINHA

▲ Massarelos & Foz do Douro

Centro Português de Fotografia

Igreja da Misericórdia

RUA DA VITÓRIA

RUA S. BENTO DA VITÓRIA

RUA DAS TAIPAS

RUA S. MIGUEL

Teatro de Belomonte

Palácio de S. João Novo

Ig. de S. João Novo

Ig. de S. Pedro de Miragaia

RUA DAS VIRTUDES

RUA AFONSO ALBUQUERQUE

R. DR. B. DE CASTRO

FR. ROC. SOARES

R. T. GONZAGA S. JOÃO NOVO

LARGO DE S. JOÃO NOVO

R. S. PEDRO MIRAGAIA

RUA MIRAGAIA

R. MTE. JUDEUS

RUA NOVA DE ALFANDEGA

R. ARMÉNIA

Feira de Vandoma

AV. D. AFONSO HENRIQUES

Sé

Igreja dos Grilos

RUA MOUZINHO DA SILVEIRA

RUA DAS FLORES

RUA DOS MERCADORES

RUA DE SÃO JOÃO NOVO

Mercado Ferreira Borges

Casa do Infante

CRAT

Bolsa

Ig. de S. Francisco

RUA FERREIRA BORGES

R. DR. SOUSA VITERBO

LARGO S. DOMINGOS

RUA INFANTE D. HENRIQUE

PALÁCIO INFANTE D. HENRIQUE

LARGO DO TERREIRO

R. REBOLEIRA

Tunnel

Elevador

RUA DA ALFÂNDEGA

CAIS DA RIBEIRA

PRAÇA DA RIBEIRA

CAIS DA ESTIVA

RUA DE CIMA DO MURO

RUA DAS CANASTREIROS

RUA DA LAPA

Rio Douro

0   200 m

Accommodation

The **cheapest rooms** in town are on Ruas do Loureiro and Cimo do Vila, around the corner from São Bento. Be warned, though, that this is something of a red-light district. For more salubrious places, your best bet is to head for the areas west or east of Avenida dos Aliados; most of the hotels listed below are to the west. There are also some bargain rooms around lively Praça da Batalha.

Hostel

Pousada de Juventude Rua Paulo Gama 552 ☎226 177 257. Large and clean but lacking in atmosphere. Bus #35 from Largo Dos Loios. Dorms ❷

Hotels

Pensão Residencial Duas Nações Praça Guilherme Gomes Fernandes 59 ☎222 081 616, ✉duasnacoes@mail.teleweb.pt. Cheap and dependable, offering en-suite accommodation and free internet access. Book in advance. ❹
Pensão Estoril Rua de Cedofeita 193 ☎222 002 751. Wonderful-value en-suite rooms. ❹
Pensão Monte Sinai Rua Alexandre Herculano 146 ☎222 008 218. The cheapest option in town, although a little dingy and often noisy. Not for the fussy. ❷
Pensão Oporto Chique Rua Conde de Vizela 26 ☎222 080 069. Reasonable and near São Bento. Breakfast included. ❹

Pensão Universal Avda. dos Aliados 38 ☎222 006 758. Clean and in a perfect position, although it can be noisy. Breakfast included. ❺
Residencial Paris Rua da Fábrica 27–29 ☎222 073 140. An old hotel with huge rooms; recently renovated and always popular. Breakfast included. ❺
Residencial Porto Novo Rua Alexandre Herculano 185 ☎222 055 739. Clean, modern rooms with TV and bath, back rooms with balconies and great views of the river. Recommended. ❸

Campsites

Marisol Praia da Madalena ☎227 115 942. Stunning location on the south side of the river; bus #57 from São Bento train station.
Prelada ☎228 312 616. The closest of the campsites; take bus #56 or #87 from Cordoaria or the airport (both run until midnight) or #6 from Avda dos Aliados.

Eating, drinking and nightlife

Porto has a strong **café culture** which includes some elegant rivals to *the fin-de-siècle* places in Lisbon, while the **Cais da Ribeira** waterfront district offers a vibrant scene at night with its lively bars and clubs. Most of the city's big nightclubs are in the outlying **Matosinhos** district. Porto's culinary speciality is *Tripas á Modo* (tripe). Don't let this put you off – there's always plenty of choice on the menu, and there are lots of places where you can eat cheaply. At the basic level, there are **workers' cafés** galore, all with wine on tap, and often with a set menu for the day. Prime areas are Rua do Almada and Rua de São Bento da Vitória. All are busy at midday and invariably close around 7.30pm and all of Sunday.

Restaurants

Casa Filha da Mãe Preta Arcos do Douro 2–3, Cais da Ribeira. Bustling restaurant with excellent views over the river. Dishes cost around €9. Closed Sun.
Churrasqueira de Brasil Campo dos Mártires da Pátria 136, near Torre dos Clerigos. Cheap workers' diner with a lively, friendly atmosphere, and serving ample portions. Open daily.
Ginjal do Oporto Rua do Bonjardim 724. Bargain local specialities in a no-frills setting.
Café Majestic Rua de Santa Catarina 112. Porto's best loved café/restaurant with ornate surroundings and delicious breakfasts and teas. Closed Sun.
Café Restaurant Miradouro Cais da Ribeira, on the arches by the entrance to the bridge. A popular

local hangout with great salads and cheap meals.
Montecarlo Rua Santa Catarina 17-2°. Looks like a 1930s tearoom, has views over the Praça da Batalha and serves good food. Closed Sun.
Adega do Olho Rua Alfonso Martins Alho 6. Traditional cheap dive full of local character. Closed Sun.
Regaleira Rua do Bonjardim 87, around the corner from Praça Dom João I. One of the best places for fish and seafood. English menu can be a little perplexing, but worth persevering. Mains cost €5–12.50.

Cafés and bars

Aniki-Bóbó Rua da Fonte Taurinha 36. Upbeat late-night acid jazz/house bar. Occasional alternative happenings (eg theatre). Till 4am. Closed Sun.

Bar da Praia do Ourigo Esplanada do Castelo. Trendy tapas bar frequented by students, also serves good coffee on the beach.

Quando-Quando Avda. do Brasil 60, Foz do Douro. Popular waterfront hotspot for the in-crowd. Closed Sun & Mon.

Taberna da Ribeira Praça da Ribeira. Prime riverside spot with outdoor tables. Open till 2am.

Clubs

Hard Club Cais de Gaia, Vila Nova de Gaia ☎223 753 819; night bus #91. Porto's main venue for DJs and live music, including a good number of British and Stateside acts.

Industria Avda. Brasil 843. Like its Lisbon namesake attracts a mixed crowd out for a good time. Open Fri–Sun 11pm–6am.

River Café Cançada João do Carmo 31. Pricey entrance fee and and strict dress code but worth it for the chilled, jazzy atmosphere. Open Wed–Sat.

Swing Praçeta Enginheiro Amaro da Costa 766. Fun Seventies-revival disco. Smart dress code. Daily till 2am.

Tomate Rua Manuel Pinto de Azevedo 15. Current hot spot in a warehouse atmosphere with visiting DJs playing drum'n'bass and trance. Closed Sun.

Braga and around

BRAGA, a city with ecclesiastical pretensions, claims to be Portugal's answer to Rome. It was probably founded by the Bracari Celts, hence the name, and was taken by the Romans in 279BC. Later occupied by the Moors, it was reconquered early in the eleventh century and by the end of the century its archbishops were pressing for recognition as "Primate of the Spains", a title they disputed with Toledo over the next six centuries. It is still Portugal's religious capital – the scene of spectacular **Easter celebrations** with torchlight processions.

You won't be able to miss the **Archbishop's Palace**, a great fortress-like building, right at the centre of the old town. Nearby is the **Sé**, which, like the palace, encompasses Gothic, Renaissance and Baroque styles. It was founded in 1070 and its south doorway is a survival from this earliest building; its most striking element, however, is the intricate ornamentation of the roofline, executed by João de Castilho, later the architect of Lisbon's Jerónimos Monastery. A guided tour of the interior (daily 8.30am–1pm & 2–6.30pm; free, museum and Capela dos Reis €1.50) takes you through three Gothic chapels, of which the outstanding specimen is the **Capela dos Reis** (King's Chapel), built to house the tombs of Henry of Burgundy and his wife Teresa, the cathedral's founders and the parents of Afonso Henriques, founder of the kingdom.

The Art Deco **tourist office** (Mon–Fri 9am–7pm, Sat 9am–12.30pm & 2–5.30pm; ☎253 262 550) at the corner of Praça da República has copies of *Cultura Norte*, listing – in Portuguese – most events in the region. Two **hotels** offering excellent value are the *Pensão Francfort*, Avda. Central 1–7 (☎253 262 648; ❹), and the well-located *Grande Residencia Avenida*, Avda. da Liberdade 738 (☎253 262 955; ❹). Braga's well-equipped **hostel** is at Rua Santa Margarida 6 (☎253 616 163; ❹), off Avenida Central; the **campsite** (☎253 273 355) is a two-kilometre walk along the Guimarães road, but is very cheap and right next to the municipal swimming pool. *Churrasqueira Lareira do Conde*, on Praça Conde de Agrolongo, serves reasonably priced, quality **food** in generous quantities, as does the *Restaurante Moçambicana* at Rua Andrade Corvo 8, one of several excellent cheap restaurants grouped around the Arco da Porta Nova. Mahogany-panelled *Café Astória,* Praça da Republica, is by far the best of the old **coffee houses**. **Internet access** is available at *Netstation*, on Rua de Santa Margarida 13, by Largo de Infias.

Bom Jesus

The glorious ornamental stairway of **BOM JESUS**, 3km outside Braga, is one of Portugal's best-known images. Set on a wooded hillside, high above the city, it's a monumental place of pilgrimage created by Braga's archbishop in the early eighteenth century. There is no particular reason for its presence, no miracle or vision, yet it remains an object of devoted pilgrimage, penitents often climbing up on their knees. **Buses** run from near the post office on Avda. da Liberdade in Braga to the foot of the stairway about every thirty minutes at weekends when half the city piles up there to picnic.

If you resist the temptation of the funicular (€1) and climb up the stairway, Bom Jesus's simple allegory unfolds. Each landing has a fountain: the first symbolizes the wounds of Christ, the next five the Senses, and the final three represent the Virtues. At each corner are chapels with mouldering wooden tableaux of the life of Christ, leading to the Crucifixion at the altar of the church. Beyond are wooded gardens, grottoes and miniature boating pools, and several cheap, lively **restaurants**.

Guimarães

Birthplace of Afonso Henriques and first capital of medieval Portucale, **GUIMARÃES** remains a lively and atmospheric university town. The town's chief attraction is the **Castelo** (Tues–Sun 9.30am–12.30pm & 2–5.30pm; free), whose square keep and seven towers are an enduring symbol of the emergent Portuguese nation. Built by the Countess of Mumadona and extended by Henry of Burgundy, it became the stronghold of his son, Afonso Henriques. From here the Reconquest began along with the creation of a kingdom which, within a century of Afonso's death, was to stretch to its present borders. Afonso is said to have been born in the keep, and may have been baptized in the font of the Romanesque chapel of **São Miguel** on the grassy slope below. The third building here, the **Paço dos Duques**, was once the palace of the Dukes of Bragança, but under the Salazar dictatorship was "restored" as an official residence. Looking like a mock-Gothic Victorian folly, it now houses dull collections of portraits, furniture and porcelain.

The **other two museums** in Guimarães are, in contrast, among the best outside Lisbon. The **Museu Alberto Sampaio**, ten minutes' walk south of the castle (Tues–Sun 10am–12.30pm & 2–5.30pm, July & Aug till 7pm; €2, free Sun am), is mostly the treasury of the adjoining Colegiada church and the monastery that used to be here. The highlight is a silver-gilt *Triptych of the Nativity*, said to have been found in the king of Castile's tent after the Portuguese victory at Aljubarrota. Like Batalha, the **Colegiada** itself was built in honour of a vow made by João I before that decisive battle. In front of it stands a Gothic canopy-shrine that marks the spot where Wamba, unwillingly elected king of the Visigoths, drove a pole into the ground swearing that he would not reign until it blossomed. Naturally it sprouted immediately. João, feeling this a useful precedent of divine favour, set out to meet the Castilians from this very point. Equally stunning is the **Museu Arqueológico Martins Sarmento** (Tues–Sun 10am–noon & 2–5pm; €1.50), housed in a former convent and containing displays of finds from the nearby *citânia* of Briteiros, a Celtic hill settlement.

The finest church in town is **São Francisco**, a short distance east of the tourist office, with its huge eighteenth-century *azulejos*, of St Francis preaching to the fishes and its elegant Renaissance cloister and fountain.

Practicalities

Guimarães' **bus station** is fifteen minutes' walk west of town, near the football stadium; the **train station** is to the south. You'll pass one **tourist office** (Mon–Fri 9.30am–12.30pm & 2–6.30pm; ☎253 412 450, ⓦwww.cm-guimaraes.pt) as you walk from here to the centre; the other office is in the centre of the old town in Praça de Santiago (same hours; summer also Sat 10am–1pm & 3–6pm, Sun 10am–1pm; ☎253 518 790). There is very little in the way of cheap **accommodation**: try *Casa dos Pombais*, Avda. de Londres 40 (☎253 412 917; ❺), which has beautiful rooms overlooking attractive gardens, or the less expensive but spartan *Casa dos Retiros*, Rua Francisco Agra 163 (☎253 511 515; ❸). The cheapest option, with good reason, is the dated *Pensão Imperial* (☎253 415 163; ❷). The town's

campsite (☎253 515 912) is 6km away at Penha; take the São Roque bus (daily 6am–8pm; every 30min) from the main *turismo* and get off at "Costa"; or take the cable car from the end of Rua de Dr José Sanpaio (11am–6/7pm; €2.50 return). For **food**, *O Telheiro*, Rua Dom João I 39–41, above *Café Dom João*, serves great dishes in basic but bustling surroundings, and *Oriental* on Largo do Toural has very good regional specialities. *El Rei Dom Alfonso*, Praça de Santiago, is worth the moderate rise in price for its location in the heart of the old town.

The Douro Line

The valleys of **the Douro** and its tributaries are among the most spectacular landscapes in Portugal, and the Douro Valley itself, a narrow, winding gorge for the majority of its long route, is the most beautiful of all. The Douro **rail route**, which joins the river about 60km inland and then sticks to it across the country, is one of those journeys that needs no justification other than the trip itself. There are regular connections along the line as far as Peso da Régua, first capital of the demarcated port-producing region; beyond Régua, there are less frequent connections to Tua and Pocinho, which marks the end of the line.

At Livração, about an hour from Porto, the Tâmega line cuts off for the lovely mountain town of **AMARANTE**. The journey is spectacular, the rickety, single-carriage train struggling through pine woods and vineyards on the climb, with the river visible like a piece of lapis lazuli far below. Amarante is a fine place to stop, with much of its history revolving around the thirteenth-century hermit **Gonçalo**, who is credited with a hand in the founding of just about everything in the town. Although it has a nice **church** and unusual modernist **museum**, the main attraction is the setting, peaceful family atmosphere and relaxing old streets. A good cheap place to stay is *Residencial A Raposeira* on Largo António Cândido 53 (☎255 432 221; ❷), above the restaurant of the same name, which serves huge, if basic, meals.

Shortly after Livração, the main line finally reaches the Douro and heads upstream until, at Mesão Frio, the valley broadens into the little plain commanded by **PESO DA RÉGUA**, the depot through which port wine must pass on its way from Pinhão – the centre of production – to Porto. About 10km south of Peso da Régua is the wealthy town of **LAMEGO**, famed for its Baroque mansions and an imitation of Braga's Bom Jesus steps, leading up to the celebrated shrine of **Nossa Senhora dos Remédios**.

Beyond Peso da Régua begin the terraced slopes where the **port vines** are grown: they look their best in August, with the grapes ripening, and in September when the harvest has begun. The country continues in this vein, craggy and beautiful, with the softer hills of the interior fading dark green into the distance, to Tua (junction for the Corgo line with services to the transport centre of **Vila Real**, the gateway to Tras-os-Montes) and Pocinho, where buses take over for routes east towards Miranda do Douro.

Bragança

Trás-os-Montes – literally meaning "behind the mountains" – is a province untouched by time. Here traditional customs are upheld and old farming methods adhered to. Until the country's admission into the European Union in 1992, this glacial tabletop of granite boulders and rural communities was one of the most isolated pockets of the Continent, but as more and more EU investment pours in, improved transport links are making even the furthest reaches more accessible. On a hillock above **BRAGANÇA**, the small and remote provincial capital, stands a pristine circle of walls, enclosing a medieval village and castle that represent one of Portugal's most atmospheric sights – the extraordinary **Cidadela**. Along with the fine local museum, it is the principal reason for a visit to the town and includes the

Domus Municipalis, a twelfth-century pentagonal Romanesque civic building, the only one of its kind in Europe. Next to it is the church of **Santa Maria**, with its eighteenth-century barrel-vaulted, painted ceiling – a feature common to several churches in Bragança. Towering above these two is the **Castle** (Mon–Wed & Fri–Sun 9am–noon & 2–5pm; €1.50, free Sun am), which the Portuguese royal family rejected as a residence in favour of their vast estate in the Alentejo. At its side a curious pillory rises from the back of a prehistoric granite pig, or *porca*, thought to have been a fertility idol of a prehistoric cult. Celtic-inspired medieval tombstones rub shoulders with a menagerie of *porcas* in the gardens of **Museu do Abade de Baçal**, between the citadel and cathedral in Rua Abílio Beça (Tues–Fri 10am–5pm, Sat & Sun 10am–6pm; €1.25, free on Sun). Inside, a collection of sacred art and the watercolours of Alberto Souza are the highlights.

The helpful **tourist office** (Mon–Fri 9am–12.30pm & 2–5/7pm; ☎273 381 273, ⓦwww.brancanet.pt) is on an extension of Avenida Cidade de Zamora, a couple of hundred metres north of the cathedral. The cheapest **pension** in town is the very basic *Hospedaria Brigantina*, next to the post office on Rua Almirante Reis (☎273 324 321; ❷). For somewhere more comfortable pay a little more for the *Residencial Poças*, Rua Combatentes da G. Guerra 200 (☎273 331 428; ❷). The nearest **campsite** (☎273 351 535; closed Nov–April) is 6km out of town on the França road; a better option is the plush, private site *Cepo Verde* (☎073 999 371; closed Nov–April), 8km down the Vinhais road, with good facilities and a pool. As for **restaurants**, two favourites are *Restaurante Poças*, next to the *Residencial*, serving big, wholesome meals, and *Restaurante D Fernando*, Cidadela 197, inside the walled old town.

Crossing the border

From Bragança the most obvious route into Spain is via Quintanilha (34km), the nearest town to the **San Martin** border post. There are one or two direct buses daily direct to Quintanilha. You can stay above the *Evaristo*, San Martin's only shop, restaurant and **pension**. At 7am there's a bus to Zamora, connected to Madrid by road and rail. In Bragança there's also the possibility of reserving a seat on the Zamora–Valladolid–Madrid **express bus** (Mon, Tues, Thurs & Fri; ⓦwww.alsa.es/internacional).

South of Bragança

South of Bragança, hugging the border with Spain in the east, is the vast and beautiful wilderness of the newly designated **Parque Natural do Douro Internacional**, home to Europe's largest concentration of Egyptian Vultures and a huge number of other birds of prey. The best place to base yourself for a visit is the town of **MOGADOURO**, site of the park's headquarters and connected by daily weekday bus from Bragança (1hr 40min). Accommodation is plentiful: try the *Pensão Russo* (☎279 342 134; ❶), on Rua das Eiras.

Just to the west of the southern reaches of the park lies the **Parque Arqueológico do Vale do Côa**, containing one of the world's largest collections of outdoor Palaeolithic rock art, dating back 22,000 years. The art was only discovered in 1992 and rescued from imminent submersion by a proposed dam scheme thanks to a remarkable "people's campaign", vindicated in 1998 when it was designated a UNESCO World Heritage Site. Visits are by appointment only from the headquarters in **VILA NOVA DE FOZ CÔA** (Tues–Sun 9am–12.30pm & 2–5.30pm, €5 per site; ☎279 768 260), a quiet village bizarrely awarded the status of a city in recognition of the importance of the nearby finds.

Vila Nova can be reached by one of the daily buses from **Pocinho** at the eastern end of the Douro Train Line. Access from the north is more difficult. Three daily buses run south from Mogadouro to Torre de Moncorvo, from where one bus a day makes the journey on to Vila Nova de Foz Côa via Pocinho. If you miss it, taxis will make the journey for around €12. Best bets for **accommodation** are *Residencial Avenida* (☎271 762 112; ❷), Avda. Gago Coutinho 8, and *Residencial Marina* (☎271 762 175; ❷), next door; both offer en-suite bathrooms and TV.

Southern Portugal

The huge, sparsely populated plains of the **Alentejo**, to the southeast of Lisbon, are overwhelmingly agricultural, dominated by vast cork plantations well suited to the low rainfall, sweltering heat and arid soil. This impoverished province is divided into vast estates which provide nearly half of the world's cork but only a sparse living for its rural inhabitants. Visitors to the Alentejo often head for **Évora**, the province's dominant and most historic city. But the Alentejo's **Costa Azul** is a breath of fresh air after the stifling plains of the inland landscape.

With its long, sandy beaches and picturesque rocky coves, the southern coast of the **Algarve** is the most visited and developed region in the country. The coastline has two different characters. **West of Faro**, the lively capital of the Algarve, you'll find the classic postcard images of the province – a series of tiny bays and coves, broken up by weird rocky outcrops and fantastic grottoes, at their most exotic around the resort of **Lagos**. To the **east of Faro** lie the less developed sandy off-shore islets, **the Ilhas** – which front the coastline for some 25 miles – and the lower-key resorts of **Olhão** and **Tavira**. Throughout the Algarve **accommodation** can be a major problem in summer, with hotels block-booked by package companies and pensions filling up early in the day; private rooms or campsites help fill in the gaps. If you fancy something a little less touristy, head inland where you'll find a more Portuguese way of life at **Silves**, the impressive former capital of the Moors.

Évora

ÉVORA is one of the most impressive cities in Portugal, its provincial atmosphere the perfect setting for a range of memorable and often intriguing monuments. The Romans were in occupation for four centuries and the Moors, who settled for just as long, have left their stamp in the tangle of narrow alleys which rise steeply among the whitewashed houses. Most of the monuments, however, date from the fourteenth to the sixteenth centuries, when, with royal encouragement, the city was one of the leading centres of Portuguese art and architecture.

Used as a slaughterhouse until 1870, the **Temple of Diana** in the central square is the best-preserved Roman temple in Portugal, its stark remains consisting of a small platform supporting more than a dozen granite columns with a marble entablature. Directly opposite, the former **Convento dos Lóios**, now converted into a luxurious *pousada*, has been partly attributed to Francisco de Arruda, architect of the Tower of Belém in Lisbon. To the left of the *pousada* lies the church of the convent, dedicated to **São João Evangelista**. This is the private property of the ducal Cadaval family, who still occupy a wing or two of the adjacent ancestral palace. Some rooms of the palace, containing *azulejos*, trick paintings and ossuary, are open to visitors (Tues–Sun 9.30am–12.30pm & 2.30–5pm; €2.50).

The **Cathedral**, or **Sé** (daily 9am–12.30pm & 2–5pm), was begun in 1186, about twenty years after the reconquest of Évora from the Moors, and the Romanesque solidity of its two huge square towers and battlemented roofline contrasts sharply with the pointed Gothic arches of the porch and central window. The interior is more straightforwardly Gothic, although the choir and high altar were remodelled in the eighteenth century. Adjacent, in the archbishop's palace, is the excellent **Museu Municipal** (Tues 2.30–5.30pm, Wed–Sun 9.30am–12.30pm & 2.30–5pm; €2), which houses important collections of fifteenth- and sixteenth-century Flemish and Portuguese paintings assembled from the city's churches and convents.

Perhaps the most memorable sight in Évora is the **Capela dos Ossos** (9am–1pm & 2.30–5.30/6.30pm; €1) in the church of **São Francisco**, close to the bus station. A gruesome reminder of mortality, the walls and pillars of this chilling chamber are entirely covered with the bones of more than 5000 monks; an inscription over the door reads, "Nós ossos que aqui estamos, Pelos vossos esperamos" – We bones here are waiting for your bones.

Practicalities

Both Évora's **bus station** and **train station** are about 1km out of the old town, though there are regular green buses from the former that run to **Praça do Giraldo**, centre of Évora's lively student scene. Here you can find the **tourist office** (daily 9am–12.30pm & 2–5.30/7pm; ☎266 702 671) and a couple of outdoor cafés. All the cheaper **places to stay** are within five minutes' walk, but Évora's tourist appeal pushes prices way over the norm. Best options are *Os Manuéis*, just west of the square at Rua do Raimundo 35 (☎266 702 861; ❺); *Pensão Invicta*, Rua Romão Ramalho 37a, overlooking São Francisco (☎266 702 047; ❹); and *Pensão Giraldo* at Rua dos Mercadores 15 & 27 (☎266 702 833; ❸). Évora's **hostel** (☎266 744 843; ❷) is just off Praça do Giraldo at Rua Miguel Bombarda 40. If you're stuck for a room, the tourist office will sometimes arrange accommodation in **private homes**. The **campsite** (☎266 705 190) is 2km out of town on the Alcáçovas road; bus #5 goes there eight times daily from Praça do Giraldo (except Sun). **Restaurants** abound in the centre: for inexpensive food try *Adego do Neto*, Rua dos Mercadores 46, or the homely *O Portão*, on Rua do Cano 27 alongside the aqueduct. For slightly more you could sample the outstanding Italian food at the enormously popular *Pane & Vino*, Patio do Salema (entrance on Rua Diogo Focardo). *Ofici@n@bar*, at Rua da Moeda 27, is an easy-going **bar** that also offers **internet access** (closed Sat pm & all day Sun).

The Alentejo coast

The coast south of Lisbon features towns and beaches as inviting as those of the Algarve. Admittedly, it's exposed to the winds and waves of the Atlantic, and the waters are colder, but it's fine for summer swimming and far quieter. Access is straightforward, with local bus services and the twice-daily Zambujeira Express from Lisbon, which takes you within easy range of the whole coastline and stops at the beaches of Vila Nova de Milfontes and Zambujeira do Mar.

Five buses a day run from Lisbon to Alcacer do Sal, from where there are reasonable connections south to **SANTIAGO DO CACÉM**, a pleasant little town overlooked by a castle. In turn, there are five buses daily (in summer) from Santiago to **Lagoa de Santo André** and the adjoining **Lagoa de Melides**, with two of the best beaches in the country. The **campsites** at both places are of a high standard and there are masses of signs offering rooms, chalets and houses to let. Beyond the beach-cafés and ice-cream stalls miles and miles of sand stretch all the way to Comporta in the north and Sines in the south. The sea is enticing, with high waves and good surf, but take local advice on water conditions, as the undertow can be fierce. If you want to base yourself at Santiago rather than at the beaches, there's no shortage of good **food and accommodation**. The *Restaurante Covas*, by the bus station at Rua Cidade de Setúbal 10 (☎269 822 675; ❸), is recommended both for its **rooms** and for its outstanding meals. There are plenty of other places around town advertising rooms, and there's another great **restaurant** – *Praceta,* at Largo Zeca Afonso (behind the bus station).

Forty kilometres southwest of Santiago do Cacém lies the popular resort of **PORTO CÔVO**, which, although overdeveloped, has plentiful accommodation, a campsite and beautiful beaches to the south. The larger resort of **VILA NOVA DE MILFONTES** lies a little to the south on the estuary of the River Mira, whose sandy banks gradually expand and merge into the coastline. This is generally the most crowded and popular resort in the Alentejo, with lines of villas and hotels radiating from the centre of the old village. It's still a pretty place, though, with a handsome little castle and an ancient port, reputed to have harboured Hannibal and his Carthaginians during a storm. Finding reasonable **rooms** shouldn't be a problem, and there are a couple of large **campsites** to the north of the village: *Parque de Milfontes* (☎283 996 104) and the more modest *Campiférias* (☎283 996 409). The *Casa Amarela* on Rua D. Luis de Castro e Almeida offers **internet** facilities (open daily).

If you prefer to stay away from the crowds, head for the main inland base, **ODEMIRA**. It's a quiet, unspoiled country town, connected by eight daily buses to Vila Nova de Milfontes. There are several restaurants and **pensions**, including *Residencial Rita*, Largo do Poço Novo (☎283 322 531; ❹), and *Residencial Idálio*, Rua Eng. Arantes Oliveira 28 (☎283 322 156; ❸), just to the left when you come out of the bus station. Of the **restaurants**, try *O Tarro*, near the main road junction.

South of Odemira at **ZAMBUJEIRA DO MAR**, a large cliff provides a dramatic backdrop to the beach, more than compensating for the winds. There are only a few small **pensions**, such as the *Mar-e-Sol* (☎283 961 171; ❸), a few *dormidas* and a couple of bars, as well as a reasonable **campsite** (☎283 961 172), about 1km from the cliffs.

Faro

FARO is the capital of the Algarve and has all the facilities of a modern European town, with an attractive shopping area, some decent restaurants and a "real" Portuguese feel in contrast to many nearby resorts. Excellent **beaches**, too, are within easy reach, and in summer there's quite a nightlife scene, as thousands of travellers pass through on their way to and from the airport, 6km west of the town.

Sacked and burned by the Earl of Essex in 1596, and devastated by the Great Earthquake of 1755, the town has few historic buildings. By far the most curious sight is the Baroque **Igreja do Carmo** (Mon–Fri 10am–1pm & 3–5pm, Sat 10am–1pm) near the central post office on Largo do Carmo. A door to the right of the altar leads to a macabre **Capela dos Ossos** (€1), its walls decorated with bones disinterred from the adjacent cemetery. This aside, the most interesting buildings are all in the old, semi-walled quarter on the south side of the harbour, centred around the majestic Largo da Sé and entered through the eighteenth-century town gate, the **Arco da Vila**. The Largo is flanked by the bishop's palace and the **Sé** itself (Mon–Sat 10am–12.30pm & 1.30–5.30pm, Sun for Mass only; €1), a miscellany of Gothic, Renaissance and Baroque styles, heavily remodelled after the Great Earthquake. More impressive is the nearby **Museu Arqueológico** (Mon & Sat 2/2.30–5.30/6pm, Tues–Fri 9.30/10am–5.30/6pm; €2), installed in a fine sixteenth-century convent. The most striking exhibit is a third-century Roman mosaic of Neptune and the four winds, unearthed near Faro train station.

Practicalities

Taxis from the **airport** to the centre should cost around €8, or take bus #16 (8am–8.30/11pm; every 45min; €1), a twenty-minute journey to town. From June to October there is also a free Aerobus service (hourly 9am–8pm; not Tues) for air-ticket holders. The **bus station** is right in the centre, behind the *Hotel Eva*, across from the old town; you'll find the **train station** a few minutes beyond, up the Avenida da República. There's a **tourist office** at the airport (daily 10am–midnight; ☎289 818 582). The main office is near the harbour at Rua da Misericórdia 8 (Mon–Fri 9.30am–5.30/7pm, Sat & Sun 9.30am–12.30pm & 2–5.30pm/7; ☎289 803 604).

Pensões are concentrated just northeast of the harbour. Among the better places are *Pensão Madalena* (☎289 805 806; ❹) at Rua C. Bivar 109; *Pensão São Félipe*, Rua Infante Don Henrique 55a (☎289 824 182; ❸); and *Residencial Pinto*, Rua 1° de

Maio 27 (℡289 807 417; ❸). *Casa de Hóspedes Adelaide* (℡289 802 383; ❹), near the bus station at Rua Cruz das Mestras 7–9, is the best budget choice – during the summer they also open the roof as a dorm and charge around €5–6.25 per person. The **campsite** (℡289 817 876) is at Praia de Faro, and is always packed in summer – phone ahead; take bus #16 from town. There are **restaurants** to meet most budgets: try the characterful *Adega Dois Irmãos*, on Largo Terreiro do Bispo 13, or for something less expensive, cram in with locals at *Adega Nova*, Rua Francisco Barreto 24, close to the train station. The town's **nightlife** centres around cobbled Rua do Prior; *Millennium III* is one of the best discos. **Internet access** is available at *Papanet*, Rua Dr Justino Cúmano 38 (closed Sat & Sun).

Olhão

OLHÃO, 8km east of Faro, is the largest fishing port on the Algarve and an excellent base for visiting the sandbank islands (*ilhas*). **Train** and **bus** stations are near each other off the Avenida da República northeast of town. The **tourist office**, just off Rua do Comércio (Mon–Fri 9.30am–5.30pm; ℡289 713 936), will provide a town map and advice on rooms. You can get prepaid cards to use the **internet** at the post office on Avenida da República (closed Sat & Sun). For **accommodation**, try the highly rated *Pensão Bela Vista* (℡289 702 538; ❹), right out of the tourist office then first right; or the *Pensão Boémia*, slightly further out of the centre at Rua da Cerca 20, off Rua 18 de Junho (℡289 714 513; ❹). The nearest **campsite** (℡289 700 300) is at Marim, 3km east – buses hourly till 7pm from the main station. There are clusters of **restaurants** and **bars** around Rua do Comércio and on the seafront: *A Bote*, near the market on Avda. 5 de Outubro, is good (closed Mon), or for something cheaper try *Restaurante Bela Vista*, near the tourist office on Rua Dr Teofilio Braga 59 (closed Sun).

Ferries leave for the **Ilhas of Armona** and **Culatra** from the jetty at the far end of Olhão's municipal gardens, five minutes from the market. The service to **ARMONA** (15min; €0.90 each way) drops you off at a long strip of holiday chalets and huts that stretches right across the island on either side of the main path. The only type of **accommodation** available here is in chalets (April–Oct only), and you'll be lucky to get one in summer; phone ahead to book (℡289 714 173). On the ocean side, the beach disappears into the distance and a short walk will take you to totally deserted stretches of sand and dune. Boats to the more distant **Ilha of Culatra** (35–45min; €1–1.20 each way) call first at unattractive Culatra town, then at **FAROL**, a pretty village of holiday homes edged by beautiful beaches on the ocean side.

Tavira

TAVIRA is a clear winner if you are looking for an urban base on the eastern stretch. It's a good-looking little town with superb island beaches within easy reach, and despite ever-increasing visitors it continues to make its living as a tuna-fishing port. **Buses** pull up at the terminal by the river, a two-minute walk from the central square, the Praça da República; the **train station** is 1km from the centre of town, straight up the Rua da Liberdade. From July to mid-September, **boats** to the beach on **Ilha de Tavira** depart from the quayside in Tavira at the town side of the flyover (daily 8am–7.30pm; €1 return). In addition, all-year boats cross from Quatro Águas (every 15min–1hr; €0.75 return), 2km east of town. The beach is backed by dunes and stretches west almost as far as Fuzeta, some 14km away. Despite increasing development – a small chalet settlement, watersports, beach umbrellas and half a dozen bar/restaurants facing the sea – it's an enjoyable spot in which to hang out.

There's a **campsite** (℡281 324 455; closed Nov–March), a minute from the sands, but by far the best place **to stay** in Tavira is the *Residencial Lagoas Bica*, north of the river at Rua Almirante Cândido dos Reis 24 (☎281 322 252; ❹), with the bonus of the budget eatery, *Bica*, below. Alternatives include the smart *Pensão do Castelo* (☎281 320 790; ❹) at Rua da Liberdade 22, the *Residencial Mirante* at Rua da Liberdade 83 (☎281 322 255; ❹, with breakfast) just up the main road (though it can be a bit noisy), and the lovely *Residencial Princesa do Gilão*, across the river on the quayside (☎281 325 171; ❺), whose front rooms have balconies overlooking the river. If these options fail to produce a bed, the **tourist office** just off the main Praça da República (Mon & Fri–Sun 9.30am–1pm & 2–5/6pm, Tues–Thurs 9.30am–7pm; ☎281 322 511) may be able to find you a **private room**. For accesss to the **internet**, head to *Café Bela Fria*, Rua das Polanos 1 (closed Sun), opposite the bus station.

A succession of **bars and restaurants** line the gardens along the bank of the River Gilão, which flows through the centre of town. Probably the best of the restaurants here is the *Imperial*, which serves seafood at fairly reasonable prices. Also good are *Anazu*, Rua Jacques Pessoa 13, a riverfront café, and *Beira Rio*, at Rua Borda da Àgua de Assêca 46–48, a riverside bar/restaurant with tree-shaded tables serving pizza, pasta and salads. The *Arco*, at Rua Almirante Cândido dos Reis 67, is a laid-back, gay-friendly **bar**. Tavira's only **disco**, *UBI* (closed Mon), is reached by following Rua Almirante Cândido dos Reis to the outskirts of town; it's housed in the huge, shiny, metallic warehouse on the right.

Silves

SILVES is the one inland Algarve town that really merits a detour. Capital of the Moorish kings of the al-Gharb (now Algarve), it's still an imposing place and has a lively summer beer festival. The **train station** – an easy approach from Lagos or Faro – lies 2km outside the town; there is a connecting bus, but it's worth walking, allowing the town and its fortress to appear slowly as you emerge from the wooded hills. Under the Moors, Silves was a place of grandeur and industry, described in contemporary accounts as being "of shining brightness". In 1189 an army led by Sancho I put an end to this splendour, killing some 6000 Moors in the process. The impressively complete sandstone walls of the Moorish **fortress** (daily 9am–5.30/8pm; €1.25) retain their towers and elaborate communication system, but the inside is disappointing: apart from the great vaulted water cisterns that still serve the town, there's nothing left of the old citadel. Just below the fortress is Silves' **Cathedral** (daily 8.30am–6.30pm, Sun between masses only), built on the site of the mosque in the thirteenth century. The nearby **Museu Arqueologia** (Mon–Sat 9am–6pm; €1.50) is an engaging museum that romps through the history of Silves from the year dot to the sixteenth century with displays of local archeological finds.

The **tourist office**, in the heart of the town on Rua 25 de Abril 26 (daily 9.30am–1pm & 2–5.30pm; ☎282 442 255), will help you find a **private room**. Recommended are those at Rua Cândido dos Reis 36 (☎282 442 667; ❸), where you share the use of a kitchen and a little outdoor terrace. Another promising option is the *Residencial Sousa* **pension** at Rua Samora Barros 17 (☎282 442 502; ❺).

Lagos

LAGOS is a thriving fishing port and market centre as well as being one of the most popular tourist destinations in the Algarve. Within walking distance of some superb beaches, the town is also an interesting historical centre. It was a favoured residence of Henry the Navigator, who used Lagos as a base for the African trade. Europe's first **slave market** was built here in 1441 in the arches of the **Customs House** which still stands in the Praça da República near the waterfront. On the waterfront and to the rear of the town are the remains of Lagos's once impregnable fortifications, devastated by the Great Earthquake. One rare and beautiful church which did survive for restoration was the **Igreja de Santo António**; decorated around 1715, its gilt and carved interior is wildly obsessive, every inch filled with a private fantasy of cherubic youths struggling with animals and fish. The church forms part of a visit to the **Museu Municipal** next door (Tues–Sun 9.30am–12.30pm & 2–5pm; €1.70), housing an extraordinarily eclectic collection of artefacts including Roman busts and deformed animal foetuses.

To the **east** of Lagos is a splendid sweep of sand – **Meia Praia** – where there's space even at the height of summer. The promontory **south** is fringed by extravagantly eroded cliff faces that shelter a series of tiny **cove beaches**. All are within easy walking distance of the old town. **Praia de Dona Ana** is considered the most picturesque of the beaches, though its crowds make the smaller coves of **Praia do Pinhão**, down a track just opposite the fire station, and **Praia Camilo**, a little further along, just as appealing.

Practicalities

The **train station** is across the river, fifteen minutes' walk from the centre via a swing bridge in the marina; the **bus station** is a bit closer in, a block back from the main Avenida dos Descobrimentos. The **tourist office** is inconveniently located about fifteen minutes from the centre on the first main roundabout on the Portimão road (June to mid-Sept daily 9.30am–12.30pm & 2/3–5.30/7pm; mid-Sept to May Wed–Sat only; ☎282 763 031). They can help find a room for you, but most economical are the **private rooms** (❸) touted at the bus station. Two of the more convenient and pleasant **pensions** are the *Pensão Caravela* at Rua 25 de Abril 16 (☎282 763 361; ❹) and the *Residencial Marazul*, nearby at no. 13 (☎282 769 143; ❺). There's an **hostel** at Rua de Lançarote de Freites 50 (☎282 761 970; ❷), which also has **internet** connection. Lagos's **campsite**, *Campismo da Trindade* (☎282 763 893), is on the way to Praia de Dona Ana but gets very crowded. In season a regular bus service marked "D. Ana/Oporto de Mós" connects it to town; on foot, follow the main road beyond the fort.

Lagos is packed with **restaurants**. Some of the better ones are the fish and shell-fish places by the market, where Rua das Portas de Portugal meets the main avenue, Avenida dos Descobrimentos. On the latter, the popular *Casa do Zé* is open 24 hours a day. For authentic *piri-piri* chicken try the tiny and inexpensive *O Franguinho* at Rua Luís de Azevedo 25 (closed Mon). *Casa Rosa,* on Rua do Ferrador 22, serves substantial €3.5 set meals and is a backpackers' favourite (closed Mon). *Mullens* **bar**, Rua Cândido dos Reis 86, serves meals until 10pm, plays jazz, salsa and soul on the sound system and stays open until 2am. *Hideaway*, Travessa 1° de Maio 9, just off Praça Luís Camões, is a cosily atmospheric bar, also open till 2am. *Eddies*, Rua 25 de Abril 99, is popular with the energetic and also offers **internet** access during the day. For contemporary club sounds, try **Bar Vivante**, on Rua 25 de Abril 105, with its "tropical" roof terrace (till 4am).

Travel details

Trains

Coimbra to: Aveiro (hourly; 45min–1hr); Lisbon (13 daily; 2–3hr); Porto (12 daily; 1hr 20min–2hr).
Faro to: Lagos (7 daily; 1hr 40min); Lisbon (4 daily; 5hr 30min–6hr); Olhão (16 daily; 10min); Silves (7 daily; 1hr–1hr 15min); Tavira (12–17 daily; 35–45min).
Lagos to: Faro (7 daily; 1hr 40min); Lisbon (4 daily; 5hr 15min); Silves (13 daily; 30–50min).

Lisbon to: Braga (2 daily; 4hr 40min); Coimbra (13 daily; 2–3hr); Évora (2 daily via Barreiro and Casa Branca; 3hr); Faro (4 daily; 5hr 30min–6hr); Leiria (5 daily; 2–3hr); Óbidos (change at Cacém; 11 daily; 2hr); Porto (10–13 daily; 3hr 30min–4hr); Sintra (every 15min; 45min); Tavira (4 daily; 6–7hr); Tomar (7 daily; 2hr).
Porto to: Aveiro (every 30min; 1hr 20min); Barcelos (11 daily; 1hr 10min–1hr 40min); Braga (13–16 daily; 1hr–1hr 45min); Coimbra (15–19

daily; 2hr); Lisbon (12 daily; 3–4hr 20min); Madrid (2 daily; 12hr); Peso da Régua (14–15 daily; 2hr 10min–2hr 30min); Viana do Castelo (7 daily; 1hr 36min–2hr); Vigo (Spain; 3 daily; 4hr 30min). **Peso da Régua** to: Porto (14–15 daily; 2hr 10min–2hr 30min); Vila Real (5 daily; 1hr).

Buses

Lisbon to: Alcobaça (3–4 daily; 2hr); Coimbra (16 daily; 2hr 30min); Évora (6–12 daily; 2hr); Faro (5–10 daily; 4hr 20 min); Fátima (7 daily; 1hr 45min–2hr 15min); Leiria (9 daily; 1hr–2hr 10min); Mafra (hourly; 1hr 30 min); Porto (hourly; 3hr); Tomar (2–4 daily; 1hr 45min–2hr); Zambujeira do Mar (1 daily; 4hr 45min).
Braga to: Barcelos (Mon–Fri every 30min, Sat & Sun hourly; 30–50min); Guimarães (every 30min; 30min–1hr); Porto (every 30min; 1hr); Viana do

Castelo (4–10 daily; 1hr 40min).
Coimbra to: Fátima (5 daily; 1hr–1hr 30min); Lisbon (16 daily; 2hr 20min); Leiria (10 daily; 1hr); Porto (8–10 daily; 1hr 30min–2hr 45min); Tomar (2 daily; 2hr).
Faro to: Évora (4 daily; 3hr 30min–4hr); Huelva (for connections to Sevilla; 2 daily; 4hr); Lagos (8 daily, 1hr 45 min); Lisbon (5–10 daily; 4hr 20min); Olhão (every 15min–1hr; 20min); Tavira (7–11 daily; 1hr).
Leiria to: Alcobaça (4 daily; 50min); Batalha (5 daily; 15min); Coimbra (10 daily; 50min); Fátima (9 daily; 25min); Tomar (2 daily; 1hr 10min–2hr).
Porto to: Braga (hourly; 1hr); Bragança (3 daily; 1hr 50min–3hr); Coimbra (8–10 daily; 1hr 30min); Guimarães (12 daily; 2hr); Viana do Castelo (12–14 daily; 2hr); Vila Real (9 daily; 2hr).

Romania

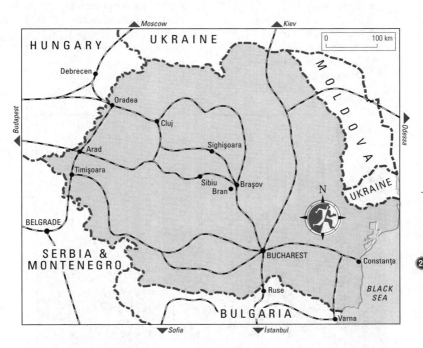

Romania highlights

* **Bucharest** Hectic traffic, Stalinist architecture, pretty residential streets and good dining and nightlife: love it or hate it, Bucharest is unmissable. **See p.863**

* **The Carpathians** Stunning mountain scenery, easily reached from Braşov or Bucharest. **See p.868**

* **Sighişoara** Beautiful, quiet medieval town in the heart of Transylvania. **See p.870**

* **Open air museum, Sibiu** A fascinating overview of Romanian village architecture, including houses, mills and churches. **See p.871**

Introduction and basics

No journey to Eastern Europe would be complete without paying a visit to **Romania**. The country has suffered from a poor public image, but don't be deterred by this – travel in Romania is as rewarding as it is challenging. Outstanding landscapes, a huge diversity of wildlife and bizarre mix of cultures and people await those willing to seek them out. However, it remains one of the hardest countries of the former Eastern bloc to cope with. The regime of Nicolae Ceauşescu left the country on the verge of bankruptcy, and the semi-reformed economy that has since emerged seems to be characterized by hustle and sharp practice.

Romanians trace their ancestry back to the Romans, and a mix of Latin and Balkan traits prevails. The people are generally warm, spontaneous, anarchic, and appreciative of style and life's pleasures. In addition to ethnic Romanians, there are communities from half a dozen other races and cultures: Transylvanian Germans (Saxons) reside around the fortified towns and churches built to guard the mountain passes during the Middle Ages; so do some one and a half million Magyars (Hungarians), many of whom pursue a traditional lifestyle long since vanished in Hungary; and elsewhere there are Jews, Ukrainians, Serbs, Bulgarians, Gypsies, Turks and Tatars.

The capital, **Bucharest**, is perhaps daunting for the first-time visitor – its savage history is only too evident – but parts of this once-beautiful city retain a certain voyeuristic appeal. More attractive by far – and easily accessible on public transport – is **Transylvania**, a region steeped in history and legend, offering some of the most beautiful, but least known, mountain scenery in Europe.

Information and maps

Getting hold of **information** remains a nightmare in Romania. Western-style tourist offices are virtually nonexistent, and the authorities still don't have a clue about what foreign visitors really need. You're best off going to privately run **tourist agencies**, many of which have English-speaking staff. Town and country **maps** (*harta*) are easier to come by. Most bookshops and street vendors selling magazines and books have up-to-date maps, though it remains best to buy them in your home country.

Money and banks

Romania's currency, the **leu** (plural lei), comes in notes of 1000, 2000, 5000, 10,000, 50,000, 100,000 and 500,000 lei, with coins of 500, 1000 and 5000 lei. Many new plastic notes are entering circulation, so when changing money it's best to ask for these. Although hyperinflation has ended, the leu has not been tamed yet, and still devalues slowly against the dollar.

Exchanging money in most towns and cities should not be a problem, and is best done at private exchange bureaux rather than hotels or banks, as they offer competitive rates. Never change money on the streets. The easiest way to get money is from an **ATM**, of which there are plenty in towns and cities. **Travellers' cheques** are seldom accepted, a hassle to change, and

---

Romania on the net

ⓦ **www.turism.ro** Official tourism site
ⓦ **www.ici.ro/romania** General information and news
ⓦ **www.inyourpocket.com** Online guides to Bucharest, Transylvania and the coast
ⓦ **www.geocities.com/Yosemite/2017** Hiking information and links

have high commission rates. **Credit cards are becoming increasingly accepted** at hotels and upmarket shops.

For the Western tourist, **costs** in Romania are pretty low, though prices in Bucharest are higher than elsewhere. Travel is generally cheap – your biggest expense will be accommodation.

Communications

Post offices (*pošta*) in towns are open Mon–Fri 7am–8pm, Sat 8am–noon. **Stamps** (*timbru*) and envelopes (*plic*) can be bought here.

Telephone calls can be made from the orange cardphones or from post offices. **Phonecards** (50,000 or 100,000 lei – you'll need the latter for international calls) are available from post offices and some kiosks. Rates are lower between 11pm and 7am.

Internet access is available in every town and city, and is cheap, though not always fast.

Telephone prefixes

Note that **all telephone prefixes changed in 2002**, with a 2 being added after the 0 (Bucharest's 01 prefix changing to 021); the 9 of three-digit mobile phone prefixes has been changed to 72, 74, 76 or 78. A recorded message should tell you what the new prefix is if you dial the old one.

Getting around

Public transport in Romania is cheap and reliable, though both the trains and roads are poorly maintained. The country is relatively large so allow plenty of time for getting around.

Trains

Travelling by **train** is the best way of covering distances of over 100km on public transport. Of the services available, *InterCity* trains are the most expensive, clean and comfortable; they're followed by *Rapid* and *Acelerat* trains, which stop more often.

Personal trains stop everywhere and are excruciatingly slow, generally grubby and crowded. Most overnight trains have **sleeping carriages** (*vagon de dormit*) and **couchettes** (*cušet*) for a modest surcharge. Smoking is only allowed in the corridors and bear in mind that locals hate having the train windows open, even on hot days, as they "might catch a cold".

Seat reservations are required for all fast trains, and are automatically included with locally purchased tickets. You'll also need one for travelling on **international trains** that do not require a reservation before entering Romania, so make sure to buy one before departure or face fines.

InterRail passes are valid throughout the network, **Eurail** is not; Eurodominos are only worth buying if you plan to cover huge distances by train. The best place to **buy tickets** and book seats is at the local Agenția SNCFR – offices are generally open Mon–Fri 8am–7pm. Tickets can be booked up to ten days in advance through these; at the station you can only book up to one hour in advance.

Buses

Rural **bus** (*autobuz*) services should really only be used if a train does not serve your destination. Most routes offer only a few buses each day and some don't even run to a timetable. A number of new **intercity minibus services** compete with rising train prices and lumbering state-run buses. Usually departing from near the train station, buses depart regularly or when they fill up. Expect to pay half the price of the train ticket, but do not count on a relaxing or particularly safe trip.

Taxis

Most **taxis** are now honest, very cheap and therefore an attractive alternative to crowded public transport. Avoid drivers that approach you in or near the train stations, using instead only taxis that have clearly marked company names, telephone numbers and working meters.

Accommodation

Though it will be your largest expense, **accommodation** in Romania is affordable. Apart from a growing number of four- and five-star hotels offering Western comforts (and prices), **hotel** standards tend to be fairly low. The cheaper hotels will cost £5–8/$7–12 per person per night, for a reasonably clean room and shared shower; breakfast is normally an extra £1.50/$2. An alternative is to take a **private room** (*cazare la persoane particulare*), which may actually be the only option in smaller towns and villages. You'll usually come across people offering accommodation at the train or bus station; if approached ask them "*Cât costă pe noapte?*" ("How much per night?"). Expect to pay around £6/$10 per night.

Though they're still fairly scarce, the number of **official hostels** is growing; see the HI site at ⊛ www.dntcj.ro/yhr for addresses. University towns will have **student accommodation** *(caminul de studenţi)* from late June to August, which should cost around £1.50/$2 per night. **Campsites** are usually very basic. Expect to pay around £2.25/$3 per night for tent space, with little more than a tap and dirty loo.

Food and drink

During the Ceauşescu years **food** became a precious commodity in what had been known as the breadbasket of Eastern Europe. Luckily, the situation is now far better. **Breakfast** (*micul dejun*) is typically a light meal, featuring rolls and butter (*chifle cu unt*) and an *omleta* washed down with a coffee (*cafea*) or tea (*ceai*). As for **snacks** the most common are flaky pastries (*pateuri*) filled with cheese (*cu brânză*) or meat (*cu carne*); and a variety of spicy grilled sausages and meatballs such as *mici* and *chiftele*.

The menus of most Romanian **restaurants** concentrate on grilled meats, or *friptura*. *Cotlet de porc* is the common pork chop, while *muşchi de vacă* is fillet of beef. Dishes usually arrive with a garnish of soggy French fries and a minimalist side salad. At smarter restaurants you can sample traditional **Romanian dishes**, which can be delicious. The best known of these is *sarmale* – pickled cabbage stuffed with rice, meat and herbs, usually served with sour cream. Stews (*tocană*) and other dishes often feature a combination of meat and dairy products. **Vegetarians** in ordinary restaurants could try asking for *caşcaval pane* (hard cheese fried in breadcrumbs); *ghiveci* (mixed fried veg); *ardei umpluţii* (stuffed peppers) or vegetables and salads. When in doubt, stipulate something "*fără carne, vă rog*" (without meat, please).

Establishments called **cofetărie** serve coffee and cakes, and sometimes beer and ice cream. Coffee, whether *cafea naturală* (finely ground and cooked Turkish fashion), *filtru* (filtered), or *nes* (instant coffee), is usually drunk black and sweet; ask for it *cu lapte* or *fără zahăr* if you prefer it with milk or without sugar. **Cakes** and **desserts** are sweet and sticky, as throughout the Balkans. Romanians enjoy pancakes (*clătite*) and pies (*plăcintă*) with various fillings; Turkish-influenced *baclava* and *cataif cu frisca*; and the traditional *dulceaţă*, or glass of jam.

Evening **drinking** takes place in outdoor beer gardens, *cramas* (beer cellars), restaurants (where boozers often outnumber the diners), and in a growing number of Western-style cafés and bars. As an aperitif, or at any other time, people like to drink **ţuică**, a powerful plum brandy taken neat; in rural areas, it is home-made and often twice distilled to yield fearsomely strong *palincă*. Most **beer** (*bere*) is Germanic-style lager. Romania's best **wines** are Grasca and Feteasca Neagră from the vineyards of Cotnari and Dealul Mare, and the sweet dessert wines of Murfatlar. Romania has a huge amount of natural springs, and mineral water (*apă minerală*) is readily available.

Opening hours and holidays

Like so many things in Romania, **opening hours** are unreliable. You'll find most shops open Mon–Fri 9am–6pm, with some supermarkets open until 8pm. Museums and castles are open at similar times (though most are closed on Mon or Tues); **admission charges** are minimal and have therefore not been listed in the *Guide*. **National holidays** are: Jan 1 & 2; Easter Monday; May 1; Dec 1; and Dec 25 & 26.

Emergencies

Petty crime is the only problem you're likely to encounter in Romania. Keep an eye on your belongings at all times, and be aware of pickpockets in crowded buses and trams and when getting on or off trains. Do not believe anyone claiming to be a policeman and asking to see your passport and the contents of your wallet; keep walking, offer to go to a police station or simply scream *poliţia!* (police!).

Make sure you have health insurance before going to Romania. In the event of a **health emergency,** dial the number given below. Bucharest's central emergency hospital is up to Western standards and Medicover, Calea Plevnei 96 (☏021/310 4410), also offers Western-standard care, with English-speaking doctors. **Pharmacies** (*farmacie*) are usually well-stocked. Standard **opening hours** are Mon–Sat 9am–6pm; every town will have at least one place that is open 24hr.

Emergency numbers

For all emergencies dial ☏112.

Bucharest

The reaction of most tourists on arriving in **BUCHAREST** (Bucureşti) is the urgent will to leave as soon as possible, but to do this would be missing the heart of Romania. Bucharest does have its charm and elegance – it's just that it does it in its own way. Added to which, it's a dynamic city, changing quicker than any other in Romania. Old, dusty residential areas with beautiful but crumbling eclectic architecture surround the centre and show what the city was like in a bygone era. Head south and you'll come across unfinished projects from Ceauşescu's reign littering the landscape. Seeing the true scale of what a dictatorship can do is something you won't forget. Love it or hate it, Bucharest is a must-see.

Arrival, information and transport

The modern **Otopeni Airport** is 16km north of the city; ignore the rip-off taxi drivers and head for the #783 bus stop just outside to make the thirty-minute journey to the centre. Buy your two-ride ticket from the aluminium RATB kiosk, stamp it yourself and don't hand it to the driver. Virtually all **trains** terminate at Gara de Nord. The station has done much to improve its dodgy reputation, though it's still wise to keep a sharp eye on your belongings. Use the ATM or the adjacent **currency exchange** to get cash and head straight for the **metro station** to get to the centre (reach Piaţa Universitaţii by changing trains at Piaţa Victoriei). All taxi drivers offering you a ride will overcharge; honest ones can only be found outside the main entrance beyond the Wasteels ticket office – look for the yellow Cristaxi or Cobalcescu cars. Note that Bucharest has a reputation for being rife with danger for inattentive travellers, but the number of **scams** has decreased (still, never pay anything to anyone in advance or without being aware of the exchange rate, and never hand your passport or wallet to anyone claiming to be a policeman).

Incredibly, Bucharest still has no **tourist office**; the Elvis' Villa Hostel information booth at Gara de Nord can give basic directions. The excellent bi-monthly English-language **city guide** *Bucharest In Your Pocket* (Ⓦwww.inyourpocket.com; $2) is essential reading, with maps and witty reviews of accommodation, restaurants, nightlife and sights; it can be bought at Gara de Nord's Wasteels office, the airport kiosk or from hotels and bookstores.

Public transport, although crowded, is efficient and cheap. The most useful lines of the strangely lit metro system are the M1 (an almost circle line) and the more used M2 (north–south). Above ground, you'll find a strange array of trams, buses and trolleybuses. Buy a **ticket** from the kiosks located near the bus stops and validate it in the machine on board. At night, you'll have to depend on **taxis**; thanks to the strict mayor, they tend to be honest and cheap now, charging about $0.2/km; try Meridian (☎9444 or 9888), XXL (☎9791) or Cobalcescu (☎9451), and make sure the driver has the meter running.

Accommodation

Many budget hotels have been renovated in recent years, making them good value for hostel-haters. A good alternative for hotels, especially for those travelling in groups, are **private apartments**, which start at $30 per night and are often better and more spacious than hotel rooms; *Adrian Accommodation* (☎0723/34 7192, Ⓦwww.bucharest-accommodation.ro) and *George* (☎0722/36 75 68, Ⓦwww.for-rent.ro) have good options. Bucharest's *Băneasa* **campsite** (☎021/230 5203) is out towards the airport – take bus #301 from Piaţa Romana and get off at the Casa Alba complex.

Hostels

Elvis' Villa Str Avram Iancu ☎021/315 5273, Ⓦwww.elvisvilla.ro. Australian-run, luxurious,

clean and fun – Elvis is alive, and runs an HI hostel with air-conditioned rooms sleeping 2–8 people. Laundry, breakfast, drinks and internet are all

CENTRAL BUCHAREST

Gara de Nord ◄

Amzei Market

STR. JULLES MICHELET

British Embassy

STRADA PICTOR ARTUR VERONA

STR. GEN. BERTHELOT

Athénée Palace

Romanian Athenaeum

Royal Palace

PIAŢA REVOLUŢIEI

University Library

Theodor Aman's House

STRADA ŞTIRBEI VODĂ

Cişmigiu Gardens

PIAŢA REVOLUŢIEI

PIAŢA WALTER MĂRĂCINEANU

Creţulescu Church

Former Communist Party Headquarters

US Embassy

Enei Church

National Theatre of Bucharest

STR. M. MILLO

University

STR. C. MILLE

STRADA EDGAR QUINET

CAROL I

Cercul Militar

Doamnei Church

PIAŢA UNIVERSITĂŢII

Bucharest History Museum

Colţea Church

B-DUL REGINA ELISABETA

CFR/TAROM

STRADA EFORIE

Police Headquarters

PASAGIUL VILLACROSSE

Russian Church

PIAŢA SF. GHEORGHE

STRADA LIPSCANI

Sf Nicolae-Mihai Vodă Church

STRADA MIHAI VODĂ

New St George's

STR. STAVROPOLEOS

Stavropoleos Church

STRADA LIPSCANI

Choral Temple

National History Museum

Curtea Veche

Pedestrian Bridge

STRADA IULIU MANIU

B-DUL NAŢIUNILE UNITE

SPLAIUL INDEPENDENTEI

St Apostoli Church

Hanul Lur Manuc

Unirea Market

Domniţa Bălaşa Church

Unirea Department Store

Piaţa Unirii

B-DUL UNIRII

Arcade
Pedestrianized Street

0   100 m

included, and there's a kitchen and TV room. Their information kiosk at the station will help you get here, otherwise take any modern trolleybus from Piaţa Universităţii east to the Calea Mosilor stop. ❶

Funky Chicken Guesthouse Str Gen. Berthelot 63 ☏ 021/312 1425. A cheap new hostel, located between the station and the centre and near Cişmigiu park. It has clean communal bathrooms, a TV room, kitchen, laundry service ($1.5) and a chicken. No reservations, but guaranteed accommodation for everyone who turns up. From Gara de Nord, follow B-dul Golescu, cross Str Berzei and enter the street next to the pharmacy. ❶

Villa Helga Str Salcâmilor 2 ☏ 021/610 2214, ⓦ www.rotravel.com/hotels/helga. For years the only hostel in town, Helga remains a popular and friendly HI hostel, and a good place to meet up with other travellers. It has new beds in doubles as well as in mixed and female-only dorms, and free laundry. Take trolleybus #79 or #86 or bus #133 from Gara de Nord and get off two stops after Piaţa Romana; walk further down B-dul Dacia, turning right at the Villa Helga sign. ❶

Villa 11 Str Institutul Medico Militar 11 ☏ 0722/ 495 900, ⓔ vila11bb@hotmail.com. This friendly

and quiet family-run twelve-bed hostel offers standard facilities including free laundry and is near to the Gara de Nord. Phone ahead to book and to be picked up from the station. ❷

Hotels

Bucegi Str Witing 2 ☏ 021/212 71 54, ⓦ www.stalingrad.ro. A cheap and grubby hotel near the station with cramped doubles with shared facilities and larger en suites. ❷

Cerna Str Golescu 29 ☏ 021/311 05 35. Opposite the station; rooms are clean and light; en-suite doubles also include breakfast. ❶

Carpaţi Str Matei Millo 16 ☏ 021/315 0140, ⓦ www.carpatihotel.compace.ro. The best of the cheapies; near Cişmigiu park, quiet and with helpful staff. Rooms with shared showers or toilet and some en suites. ❷

Marna Str Buzeşti 3 ☏ 021/212 7582. Renovated budget hotel near Gara de Nord with en suites and shared showers. ❷

Muntenia Str Academiei 19–21 ☏ 021/313 6010, ⓦ muntenia.kappa.ro. Old fashioned hotel in a central but slightly noisy location. En suites and shared showers. ❷

The City

"A savage hotch-potch" was Ferdinand Lasalle's verdict on Bucharest between the wars, with its boulevards and nightlife, its slums and beggars, its aristocratic mansions and crumbling Orthodox churches. The extremes of wealth and poverty have been mitigated, but otherwise the city has retained many of its old characteristics. Woodlands and a girdle of lakes freshen its northern outskirts, beyond a triumphal arch and a tree-lined avenue extending from Bucharest's main thoroughfare, the Calea Victoriei.

The majority of inner-city sights are within walking distance of **Calea Victoriei**, an avenue of vivid contrasts, scattered with vestiges of *ancien régime* elegance interspersed with apartment blocks, glass and steel facades and cake shops. Fulcrum of the avenue is **Piaţa Revoluţiei**, created during the 1930s on Carol II's orders to ensure a field of fire around the Royal Palace. The palace now contains the excellent **National Art Museum** (Wed–Sun 10/11am–6/7pm; ⓦ art.museum.ro; $3, free first Wed of month) including works by Rembrandt, Monet and Sisley – as well as galleries of modern and ancient Romanian art.

North of the palace, the **Athénée Palace Hotel** (now part of the Hilton chain) has always been a hive of intrigue, but was a veritable "intelligence factory" in the 1950s, with bugged rooms, tapped phones and informer prostitutes. Opposite the palace stands the grand **Romanian Atheneum**, the main concert hall, which can be visited by asking the concierge, and the **University Library**, torched, allegedly by the Securitate, in the confused fighting of the 1989 revolution, but now rebuilt and only recently reopened. Just south of here is the former Communist Party HQ, now the Senate, which dominated TV screens worldwide in 1989. The low balcony is where Nicolae Ceauşescu made his last speech on December 21. Minutes into his speech the booing took over and the dictator's disbelief was broadcast to the nation just before the screens went blank. The next day Ceauşescu and his wife Elena escaped by helicopter from the roof, only to fly to their eventual execution on Christmas Day.

Opposite, the restored eighteenth-century **Creţulescu Church** fronts a tangle of streets wending west towards **Cişmigiu Park**, Bucharest's oldest, containing a boating lake, playgrounds, summer terraces and animated chess players.

Beyond the Creţulescu

Beyond the grand **Cercul Militar** building on the junction with B-dul Regina Elisabeta, the main east–west boulevard, Calea Victoriei continues southwards past the police headquarters. Directly opposite is the **Pasagiul Vilacrosse** arcade, one of the remnants of the Bucharest that used to be known as the "Paris of the East". Near the river, the **National History Museum** at no. 1 (Tues–Sun 10am–6pm) is worth visiting for the cellar vault with superb gold and silverware left by Romania's pre-Christian inhabitants, the Dacians.

Nearby is Bucharest's **historical centre**; a maze of dusty cobblestone streets with decrepit houses and tiny shops, concentrated around the pedestrianized Strada Lipscani. The whole area is slated for a major EU-funded renovation project, urgently necessary to save what's left, but which no doubt will cause the area to lose some of its authenticity.

Just south of Strada Lipscani stands the small **Stavropoleos Church**; built in the 1720s, it has gorgeous, almost arabesque, patterns decorating its facade, and an elegant columned portico. Further south are the modest remains of the **Curtea Veche** (Old Court; daily 10am–4pm), Vlad the Impaler's fifteenth century citadel. Dating from 1559, the adjacent Old Court church is Bucharest's oldest church.

Inside the large white building opposite the church you'll find the lush courtyard of the **Hanul lui Manuc** inn, now home to an over-priced restaurant and wine cellar. The inn's southern wall forms one side of **Piaţa Unirii**, which is where the old Bucharest makes way for the new.

The Centru Civic and Piaţa Universităţii

The infamous **Centru Civic** was Ceauşescu's pet urban project. After an earthquake in 1977 damaged much of the city, Ceauşescu took the opportunity to remodel the entire southern portion of central Bucharest as a monument to Communism. By the early 1980s bulldozers had moved in to clear the way for the Victory of Socialism Boulevard (now **Bulevard Unirii**), taking with them thousands of architecturally significant houses, churches and monuments. The eastern end of the boulevard is now a banking district, while the other end is dominated by the **Palatul Parlamentului** (Parliament Palace), the second-largest administration building in the world. The structure was started in 1984 and still has not been completed, despite the efforts of 100,000 workers, toiling in shifts. The building which has 1100 rooms and a nuclear shelter now housing the Romanian Parliament and a conference centre. **Guided tours** in English (daily 10am–4pm; $3) start at the northern entrace, to the right-hand side of the building.

Returning northwards from Piaţa Unirii along B-dul Brătianu, you'll see the *Hotel Intercontinental* towering above busy **Piaţa Universităţii**. This is where the students pitched their post-revolution City of Peace encampment, which was violently overrun, together with the illusion of true democracy, by the miners that President Iliescu had called in to "restore order" in June 1990. The miners returned to Bucharest in 1991, this time in protest against the government rather than as its storm troopers. When they advanced again in 1999, Bucharest politicians had riot police prevent them from approaching the capital.

Just to the east rises Elena Ceauşescu's **National Theatre**, resembling an Islamicized reworking of the Colosseum. On the corner opposite, **Bucharest University's** its forecourt is thronged with students, snack stands and book vendors. The bulbous domes of the **Students' Church**, originally a Russian church, appear through a gap in the grand buildings lining the southern side of the boulevard.

The northern districts

Stretching north from Piaţa Victoriei, Şoseaua Kiseleff leads into the more pleasant, leafy suburbs. At no. 3, the **Museum of the Romanian Peasant** (Tues–Sun 9am–7pm), www.itcnet.ro/mtr) is a must-see, giving an insight into the country's varied rural traditions, with exhibits on everything from costume to religious icons, and with excellent souvenir and book shops. At the northern end of the Şoseaua is the **Arcul de Triumf**, commemorating Romania's participation on the side of the Allied victors in World War I. Just to the north of the arch is **Herǎstrǎu Park**, the city's largest. Inside the park, just off the northern end of Şoseaua Kiseleff, is the **Village Museum** (daily 9am–5/7pm), boasting wooden houses, churches and windmills from various regions of the country.

Eating

Traditional fresh **snacks**, such as *gogoşi* (Romanian doughnuts) and *covrigi* (pretzels), are sold all over the city. Though the usual fast-food joints are here, it's more fun and often cheaper to eat at a restaurant. Some still have the nasty habit of charging food by the weight – check the real price with the waiter if the menu shows the cost per 100 grams.

Restaurants

Barka Saffron Str Av Sănătescu 1, near Piaţa Domeni on B-dul Mihalache ☎021/224 1004. Trendy, with charming staff and excellent international, Indian and vegetarian food. Worth the trip north of the centre.

La Belle Epoque Str Beller 6, just off Piaţa Dorobanţi ☎021/230 0770. Traditional Belgian dishes are on offer here, served in a traditional Belgian atmosphere. Hoegaarden and Leffe beer on tap.

La Mama Str Văcărescu 3 ☎021/212 4086. Possibly the best place for Romanian food, *La Mama* is good value, very popular, and has great wines – booking ahead is essential. Metro Ştefan cel Mare.

La 'mpinge Tava Piaţa Rosetti 4. A cheap and popular self-service restaurant serving Romanian food and a few vegetarian options till 6pm. Closed Sat & Sun.

Nicoreşti Str Maria Rosetti 40. All the traditional Romanian dishes at rock-bottom prices; accompanied with live music.

Paradis Str Hristo Botev 10. Excellent, inexpensive Lebanese food served just east of Piaţa Universităţii.

Smarts Str Donici 14 ☎211 9035. In a beautifully quiet tree-lined street, this quiet and friendly bar serves up French food alongside the more usual local dishes. Nice bar downstairs.

Drinking and nightlife

Bucharest's nightlife is becoming increasingly good, offering something for pretty much all tastes. The most popular **nightclubs** are the crowded *Club A*, Str Blanari 14, which caters for a studenty crowd; *Studio Martin*, B-dul Iancu de Hunedoara 41, which brings in the ravers with its international guest DJs and gay-friendly atmosphere; and *Twice*, Str Sf. Vineri 4, which has to be Bucharest's biggest club. Weekly **gay and lesbian** nights are held at *Havana*, Str Tunari 67–69, and *Casablanca*, Sala Polivalenta in Tineretului park. The streets around Strada Gabroveni in the historic centre are attracting many new bars and crowds. In summer, the clubs and restaurants around Herăstrău lake are popular – but don't expect good service. For full **listings** of eating and drinking options, get hold of the English-language city guide *Bucharest In Your Pocket*; it's available at the hostels, hotels, book-stores and at ⓦwww.inyourpocket.com. The weekly Romanian-language *Şapte Seri* magazine, found free at bars, has events and cinema listings.

Cafés and bars

Amsterdam Grand Café Str Covaci 22. Heralded as the best new place in Bucharest, this spacious Dutch-run café in the historic centre has a relaxed atmosphere, good service, a reading table, and serves inexpensive food as well as Dutch and Belgian beer.

Jukebox Str Sepcari 22. Opposite Hanul lui Manuc, this cheerful cellar bar comes alive at night with live music and karaoke along with the beer.

Lăptăria lui Enache 4th floor of the National Theatre, Piața Universității. Justifiably one of Bucharest's most popular bars. Cool and with live music in winter, in summer you can watch free films on the rooftop terrace (*La Motor*). Entrance next to the hotel near the Dominuszart sign.

Planter's Str Mendleev 10. Immensely popular bar with a small dancefloor.

Yellow Bar Str E. Quinet 10. Trendy cellar lounge bar with comfortable sofas. Near Piața Universitații.

Listings

Embassies and consulates Australia (Consulate), B-dul Unirii 74 ☎021/320 98 02; Canada, Str N. Iorga 36 ☎021/307 5000; UK, Str J. Michelet 24 ☎021/312 0303; US, Str T. Arghezi 7–9 ☎021/210 4042.

Gay and lesbian Now that Romania has changed the law against "scandalous" single-sex relationships, gay life is starting to flourish. For information, contact Accept, Str Lirei 10 ☎021/252 1637, ☏www.accept-romania.ro.

Internet Brit C@fe, Calea Dorobanților 14; Internet Café, Calea Victoriei 136 and B-dul Carol 1 25.

Hospital Spitalul Clinic de Urgența, Calea Floreasca 8 ☎021/230 0106. Medicover, Calea Plevnei 96 ☎021/310 4410.

Post office Str M. Millo 10.

Transylvania and the Banat

Trains from Bucharest and Hungary follow one of two main rail routes through **Transylvania**. Whether you take the line via Arad, or the longer one via Cluj, you should disembark to see the best of the country. Thanks to Bram Stoker, Transylvania is famed abroad as the homeland of **Dracula**. But although the mountain scenery is dramatic, and despite one Vlad nicknamed "The Impaler", the Dracula image is just one element of Transylvania. Its 99,837sq km takes in caves, alpine meadows, dense forests sheltering bears, and lowland valleys with quaint villages and buffalo cooling off in the rivers.

The population is a mix of Romanians, Magyars, Germans, Gypsies and others, thanks to centuries of migration and colonization. The Trianon Treaty of 1920 placed Transylvania within the Romanian state, but the character of many towns still reflects past patterns of settlement. Most striking are the former seats of Saxon power with their medieval streets, defensive towers and fortified churches. **Sighişoara** is the most picturesque but could be the Saxons' cenotaph: their culture has evaporated here, as it threatens to do in **Braşov**, **Sibiu** and in the old German settlements around. A similarly complex ethnic mix is found in **the Banat**, to the east of Transylvania; the chief town here is **Timişoara**, crucible of the 1989 revolution.

Braşov and around

With an eye for trade and invasion routes, the medieval Saxons sited their largest settlements near Transylvania's mountain passes. **BRAŞOV**, which they called Kronstadt, grew prosperous as a result, and for centuries the Saxons constituted an elite whose economic power long outlasted their feudal privileges. The Communist government brought thousands of Moldavian villagers to Braşov to work in the new factories. As a result, there are two parts to Braşov: the quasi-Gothic bit coiled beneath Mount Tâmpa, which looks great, and the surrounding sprawl of flats, which doesn't.

The park beside B-dul Eroilor meets the eastern end of the pedestrianized Str Republicii, the hub of Braşov's social life. At the top of Str Republicii, sturdy buildings line Piața Sfatului, the main square. The fifteenth-century council house in the centre is now the **History Museum** (Tues–Sun 10am–5pm). The exhibits illustrate the power of the Saxon guilds, whose main hangout was the red **Merchants' Hall** opposite. The Gothic pinnacles of the town's most famous landmark, the **Black Church** (Mon–Sat 10am–3.30pm), stab upwards like a series of daggers. An endearingly monstrous hall-church that took almost a century to complete (1385–1477), it is so called for its soot-blackened walls, the result of being torched by the Austrian army in 1689. Inside, by contrast, the church is startlingly white, with Oriental carpets creating splashes of colour along the walls of the nave. In summer (June–Sept Tues, Thurs & Sat at 6pm), the church's 4000-pipe **organ** is used for concerts.

A length of fortress wall runs along the foot of Mount Tâmpa, behind which a **cable car** whisks tourists up to the summit. Of the original seven bastions the best preserved is that of the weavers, on Str Coşbuc. This complex of wooden galleries and bolt-holes now contains the **Museum of the Bârsa Land Fortifications** (Tues–Sun 10am–4pm). Inside are models and weaponry recalling the bad old days when the region was repeatedly attacked by Tatars, Turks and by Dracula, who impaled hundreds of captives to terrorize the townsfolk. The Saxons widely publicized stories of Dracula's cruelty, unwittingly contributing to Transylvania's dark image and eventually catching Bram Stoker's attention.

Practicalities

Braşov's **train station** is northeast of the old town, 2km from the centre – take bus #4 into town or spend $1 on a taxi. You're likely to be offered **private rooms** (❶) outside the station, but fun-loving backpackers should look in the station hall for the kiosk of the excellent new *Elvis' Hostel*. Located south of the old town at Str Democraţiei 2B (☎0740/844 940, ⓦwww.elvisvilla.com; ❷), it has many free perks, including a free laundry service, and organizes trips to Europe's highest bungee-jump and skiing in winter. The more central *Beke Guesthouse*, Str Cerbului 32 (☎0723/461 888; ❷), is cosy and quiet. Alternatively, there's the British-run *Casa Speranţei*, Str Piatra Mare 101 (☎0268/151 501, ⓔmedipal@deuroconsult.ro; ❷), where a portion of the room-rates goes to help cancer victims. Cheapest of the **hotels** is the basic *Aro Sport*, Str Sfântu Ioan 3 (☎0268/142840; ❶). Campers have the suburban *Dârste* **campsite**, Calea Bucureşti 285 (☎0268/259 080), on the road to Bucharest; it's best reached by taxi.

The old town is dotted with affordable **restaurants** and **cafés**. Good Romanian food is served at *Blue Corner*, Piaţa Enescu 13 (☎0268/478 590), through the archway next to the Orthodox church on Piaţa Sfatului. Next door at #11, the pricier *Bistro De L'Arte* (☎0268/473 994) has bistro dishes and breakfasts. A great **place to drink** is *Festival 39*, Str Mureşenilor 23, which is full of the strangest things – from badly stuffed animals and fake plastic trophies to a barman from Cuba. A few doors up the street, *Saloon* at no. 11–13 has more seating and bar food, while the cosy *Cabana*, Str Hirsher 1, is decked out like a mountain hut. The Romanian-language magazine *Zile şi Nopţi*, free at bars, lists **events**.

Internet **cafés** are a-plenty in Braşov, for instance inside the Orient café, Str Republicii 12.

Bran Castle, Râşnov and Zărneşti

Cosy little **BRAN**, 28km by bus from Braşov, is situated at the foot of the stunning Bucegi mountains. Despite what you may hear, its **Castle** (Tues–Sun 9am–5pm) has only tenuous associations with Dracula – aka Vlad the Impaler – who may have attacked it in 1460. Hyperbole is forgivable, though, as Bran really does look like a vampire count's residence. The castle was built in 1377 by the Saxons of Braşov to safeguard what used to be the main route into Wallachia, and it rises in tiers of towers and ramparts from amongst the woods, against a glorious mountain background. A warren of stairs, nooks and chambers around a small courtyard, the interior is filled with elaborately carved four-poster beds, throne-like chairs and portraits of grim-faced boyars. For a more authentic experience than Bran, jump off the Braşov bus in nearby **RÂŞNOV**, where the hilltop fortress ruins – and the views – are stunning. The nearby town of **ZĂRNEŞTI** is home to the **Carpathian Large Carnivore Project** (ⓔinfo@clcp.ro, ⓦwww.clcp.ro), an ecotourism outfit, which has information on the local wildlife – wolves, bears and lynx populate the nearby Piatra Craiului range – and can **organize guided walks** tracking the animals (advance booking required).

Buses to Bran and Zărneşti leave from bus station #2, 3km west of central Braşov at the end of Str Lungă; take bus #28 from Braşov's central park or bus #10 from the train station. Bran has wholeheartedly succumbed to **tourism**, and there's no shortage of private rooms; Ovi-Tours, Str Bologa 15 (☎0268/420 286), can help book one. For a near-medieval mountain escape, spend a night at *Cabana Montana* (☎0268/238 084; ❶), in the picturesque hamlet of Magură, on the flanks of the Piatra Craiului mountains just south of Zărneşti. Be sure to phone ahead and they'll pick you up from Zărneşti's bus station.

Sighişoara

A forbidding silhouette of battlements and needle spires looms over the citadel of **SIGHIŞOARA**, perched on a hill overlooking the Tărnave Mare valley, and it seems fitting that this was the birthplace of **Vlad Ţepeş** – the man known to posterity as Dracula. Plans to build a **Dracula-land** theme park nearby were aborted after widespread protest, and formed yet another another illustration of Romania's inability to decide what kind of tourism it wishes to promote. Look out for the yearly **Medieval Art Festival** in July, when Sighişoara gets overrun by thousands of beer-guzzling youngsters.

The route from the train station to the centre passes the **Romanian Orthodox Cathedral**, its gleaming white, multifaceted facade a striking contrast to the dark interior. Across the Tărnave Mare river, the **Citadel** dominates the town from a hill whose slopes support a jumble of ancient houses. Steps lead up from the lower town's main square, Piaţa Hermann Oberth, to the main gateway, above which rises the mighty **Clock Tower**. The tower was founded in the fourteenth century when Sighişoara became a free town controlled by craft guilds – each of which had to finance the construction of a bastion and defend it during wartime. Sighişoara grew rich on the proceeds of trade with Moldavia and Wallachia, as attested by the regalia and strongboxes in the tower's **museum** (daily 10am–4/6.30pm). The ticket also gives access to the seventeenth century **torture chamber** and the **Museum of Armaments** next door with its small and poorly presented Dracula Exhibition.

In 1431 or thereabouts, the child later known as **Dracula** was born in a two-storey house near the clock tower at Str Muzeului 6. At the time his father – Vlad Dracul – was commander of the mountain passes into Wallachia, but the younger Vlad's privileged childhood ended eight years later, when he and his brother Radu were sent to Anatolia as hostages to the Turks. There Vlad observed the Turks' use of terror, which he would later turn against them, earning the nickname of "The Impaler". Nowadays, Vlad's **birthplace** is a mediocre tourist restaurant.

The **Klosterkirche** (mid-April to mid-Oct 11am–4pm) has a stark, whitewashed interior and is hung with colourful sixteenth century Anatolian carpets, as in Braşov's Black Church. The other German church, the **Bergkirche** (same times), is approached by an impressive covered wooden stairway which ascends steeply from the far end of Str Şcolii. Massively buttressed, the austere roomy interior church has been extensively renovated over the past six years.

Practicalities

Sighişoara's **train station** is on the northern edge of the town, on Str Libertaţii. The town has finally seen major investments in accommodation. Backpackers are met at the station by employees of the excellent new *Elvis' Villa Hostel*, nearby at Str Libertăţii 10 (☎0265/772 546, ✆www.elvisvilla.com; ❷), which has all the perks of the other Elvis hostels, including free laundry. Less fun, but potentially better, is the German-run *Interetnică Hostel* in the citadel's oldest house at Str Bastionului 4–6 (☎065/722 234, ✉info@ibz.org.ro; ❶); under construction at the time of writing, it is expected to open its doubles and dorms by the end of 2002. There's a charming pension run by the Faur family in the citadel at Str Cojocarilor 1 (☎0744/119 211; ❶). The friendly *Pensiunea Turistică Hera*, just south of the centre at Str Eminescu 62 (☎0265/778 850; ❷), is spacious and cheap. *Hotel Poienţa*, one valley east of the centre at Str D. Cantemir 24 (☎0265/772739; ❷), has a swimming pool. Romantics will like the new excellent-value *Casa cu Cerb* **hotel** at Str Şcolii 1 (☎0265/774 625, ⓦwww.ar-messerschmidt-s.ro; ❸) as the bathtubs fit two and the content of the mini-bar are included in the price.

The **restaurant** in the *Casa cu Cerb* hotel is the best option in the citadel, while in the lower town *Jo*, overlooking the field at Str Goga 12, is the best pizzeria. *Rustic*, Str 1 Decembrie 1918 5, offers fairly good food and becomes a popular **bar** at night. The *Culture Pub* in the basement of the *Interetnică Hostel* has an **internet café** as well as a cellar hosting regular live music.

Sibiu

"I rubbed my eyes in amazement", wrote Walter Starkie of **SIBIU** in 1929. "The town where I found myself did not seem to be in Transylvania . . . the narrow streets and old gabled houses made me think of Nuremberg." Nowadays the illusion is harder to sustain, but Sibiu's older quarters could still serve to illustrate fairy-tales. Called *Hermannstadt* in German, Sibiu was the Saxons' main town, and nowadays seems to have stronger and more lucrative links with Germany than any Transylvanian town, with many people speaking German.

Like Braşov, Sibiu was founded by Germans invited by the Hungarian King Géza II to colonize strategic regions of Transylvania in 1143. Its inhabitants came to dominate trade in Transylvania and Wallachia, forming exclusive guilds under royal charter. Alas for the Saxons, their citadels were no protection against the tide of history, which eroded their influence after the eighteenth century. Within the last decades almost the entire Saxon community has left Romania.

To reach the centre from the main train station, cross the square and follow Str Gen. Magheru until you hit **Piaţa Mare**. Traditionally the hub of public life, it's surrounded by the houses of sixteenth- and seventeenth-century merchants. On its western side stands the **Brukenthal Museum** (Tues–Sun 9am–5pm), one of the finest in Romania with an evocative collection of works by Transylvanian painters. The city's **History Museum** (Tues–Sun 9am–5pm) is housed in the impressive Old City Hall, just to the north.

On the north side of Piaţa Mare, the huge Catholic church stands next to the **Council Tower** (daily 10am–6pm), which offers fine views over Sibiu's rooftops and the Carpathians. To the north, Piaţa Mică is surrounded by arcaded medieval houses. Just beyond, on Piaţa Huet, the **Evangelical Cathedral** (10am–6pm, Sun from 11am) – a massive hall-church raised during the fourteenth and fifteenth centuries – dominates its neighbours. You can climb the tower (Mon–Sat noon–4pm). The crypt, entered from outside, contains impressive tombstones of local mayors, priests and other notables as well as the tomb of Mihnea the Bad, Dracula's son, who was stabbed to death outside here in 1510.

Head down into the rambling **lower town** using one of two staircases behind the cathedral – one overshadowed by arches and the medieval citadel wall. Alternatively use the road from Piaţa Mică, which is spanned by the elegant **Liars' Bridge** – so called because of the legend that no one can stand on it and tell a lie without the structure collapsing – or from the corner of the square via another ancient stairway, pock-marked with medieval windows, doorways and turrets.

Easily outclassing that of Bucharest, Sibiu has an outstanding open-air museum, the **Muzeul Civilizaţiei Populare** on Calea Răşinari, south of the centre; take trolleybus #1. The museum offers a fantastic insight into Romanian rural life, with authentic wooden houses, churches and mills, plus a traditional inn serving local food and drink.

Practicalities

The **train and bus stations** are next to each other on Piaţa 1 Dec 1918, 400m northeast of the main square. Sibiu's **tourist office**, inside the Schiller bookstore on Piaţa Mare (☎0269/211 110, ✉turism@primsb.ro), is not as helpful as it could be, but sells maps and the excellent *Southern Transylvania In Your Pocket* city guide and hands out the *Sibiu Live* **listings magazine**.

The pensions in the lower town offer the best value **accommodation**. Pensiunea Leu, at Str Moş Ion Roata 6 (☎0269/218 392; ❶), and family-run *Podul Minciunilor* at Str Azilului 1 (☎0269/217 259; ❶) both have adequate doubles with shared bathrooms. The *Evangelisches Pfarrhaus* next to the cathedral at Piaţs Huet 1 (☎0269/211 203; ❶) has a **hostel** with simple rooms sleeping two to four. *Gasthof Clara*, Str Râului 24 (☎0269/222 914; ❷), is the best **hotel** in town, with large beds, en-suite bathrooms and breakfasts.

Excellent local **food** is served up at *Mara*, Str Băcescu 21 (☎0269/217 025), and at *La Turn*, on Piaţa Mare next to the Council Tower. *Michelangelo* at Str Turnului 3 serves good pizzas. For something different, head to *Gasthof Clara* (details above), which has Thai food as well as local and German dishes. Sibiu effectively closes down at 9pm. However, the *Art Café*, Str Filarmonicii 2 (till 2.30am), has occasional **jazz concerts** and is full of smoke and arty types. The trendy and popular *Cotton Club*, Str Ion Raţiu 9, is open till 5am, while the *Chill Out Club* at Piaţa Mică 23 holds out till 6am, playing mostly **house music**. Find an **internet café** at the side entrance of the Împăratul Romanilor hotel, Str Bălcescu 4.

Timişoara

TIMIŞOARA, 50km south of the rail junction at Arad and 250km west of Sibiu, evolved around a Magyar fortress, and from the fourteenth century onwards functioned as the capital of the Banat. The Turks conquered the town in 1552, and ruled the surrounding area from here until 1716. The Habsburgs who ejected them proved relatively benign masters, and during the late nineteenth century the municipality rode a wave of progress, becoming one of the first towns in the world to have horse-drawn trams and the first in Europe to install electric street-lighting. Nowadays, Timişoara is one of the most westward-oriented cities of Romania, its good location and multilingual inhabitants attracting many foreign investments.

Timişoara's fame abroad rests on its crucial role in the overthrow of the Ceauşescu regime. A local Hungarian priest, Lászlo Tökes, took a stand on the rights of his community, and when the police came to turf him out of his house on December 16, 1989, his parishioners barred their way. The five-day battle that ensued provided crucial inspiration for the people of Bucharest, so that Timişoara now regards itself as the guardian of the revolution.

Approaching from the train station, you'll enter the centre at Piaţa Victoriei, Romania's most pleasant pedestrian area. Focal point is the huge **Romanian Orthodox Cathedral**; completed in 1946, it blends neo-Byzantine and Moldavian architectural elements and exhibits a collection of icons (ask at the bookstall) in its basement. At the other end, the plush **Opera House** stands near the **castle** once extended by Iancu de Hunedoara, which now houses the stuffy and very missable Museum of the Banat.

Antiquated trams trundle past the Baroque **Town Hall** on the central Piaţa Libertăţii, while two blocks north the marvellous Piaţa Unirii is dominated by the monumental **Roman Catholic and Serbian Orthodox Cathedrals**. Built between 1736 and 1773, the former is a fine example of Viennese Baroque, the latter is roughly contemporaneous and almost as impressive. The huge baroque palace on the southern side of the square houses the **Museum of Fine Arts**, usually displaying work by minor Italian, German and Flemish masters, but currently undergoing extensive renovations.

In 1868, the municipality demolished most of the redundant citadel, leaving two **Bastions** to the east and west of Piaţa Unirii. The part to the east is occupied by an **Ethnographic Museum** (Tues–Sun 10am–5pm). Varied folk costumes, painted glass icons and furnished rooms illustrate the region's ethnic diversity effectively, but in an anodyne fashion – for example, there's no mention of the thousands of Serbs deported in 1951 when the Party turned hostile towards Tito's neighbouring Yugoslavia. The museum has a good souvenir shop.

Practicalities

Timişoara's **train station**, Timişoara Nord, is a fifteen-minute walk east of the centre, along B-dul Republicii. There's no tourist office, but the free **listings magazine** *Timişoara What Where When*, found at some hotels, has a basic map. The **hostel** *Timişoara* is located south of the centre on the third floor of the *Casa Tineretului* youth centre at Str Arieş 19 (☎0256/191 170, ✉fitt@xnet.ro; ❶). Get there by trolleybus #19 from near the castle. On the edge of the city and best reached by taxi, the slightly tacky *Hotel Arizona*, at Str Muzicescu 168 (☎0256/185 557; ❶), is the cheapest **hotel**, with en-suite rooms, and a sauna and swimming pool in summer. The cheapest option in the centre is the *Banatul*, B-dul Republicii 5 (☎0256/190 130; ❷), which has surprisingly good rooms fitted with bathrooms and TV. Just a notch more upscale, the glam *Central* at Str Lenau 6 (☎0256/190 091, ✉central@online.ro; ❷) is the best of the mid-range hotels; the en-suite rooms all have air conditioning. The fairly basic **campsite** on Aleea Pădurea Verde (☎0256/208 925) can be reached by trolleybus #11 from the train station.

For good Romanian **food**, try *Club XXI*, Piaţa Victoriei 2, which offers large, hearty meals, or *Grizzly*, Str Ungureanu 7, which has good vegetarian options. A concentration of **cafés and bars** can be found west of Piaţa Unirii; *Evolution* on Str Lazăr 5 is a laid-back lounge with a cellar club while *Café Corso* on Str Savoya 24 is a popular new drinking den that also serves good breakfasts; both are open round the clock. In the evenings, the canal-side *Jazz Club Pod 16*, behind the Orthodox Cathedral, is great for **live music**. Party animals should head straight for the lively **student area**, just across the Michelangelo bridge, where there are numerous cheap restaurants, terrace cafés as well as **clubs** such as the excellent *The Note*, on Str Fagului 22. Find out what's going on in the weekly *Unde mergi?* and *DeWest* **listings magazines**, found free at most bars. The *Java Coffeehouse*, Str Rodnei 6, is a hip **internet café**.

Travel details

Trains

Bucharest to: Braşov (15 daily; 3hr); Sibiu (3 daily; 6hr); Sighişoara (9 daily; 5hr); Timişoara (9 daily; 8–9hr).

Braşov to: Bucharest (15 daily; 3hr); Sibiu (4 daily; 2hr 30min); Sighişoara (12 daily; 1hr 30min); Timişoara (3 daily; 8hr 30min–9hr 30min).

Sibiu to: Braşov (5 daily; 2hr 30min); Bucharest (4 daily; 6–7hr); Sighişoara (change at Copşa Mică; 4 daily; 2hr); Timişoara (1 daily; 6hr).

Sighişoara to: Braşov (11 daily; 1hr 30min); Bucharest (9 daily; 5hr); Sibiu (change at Copşa Mică; 4 daily; 2hr).

Timişoara to: Bucharest (9 daily; 8–9hr); Braşov (1 daily; 9hr 30min); Sibiu (1 daily; 6hr).

Buses

Braşov to: Bran (7am–6pm every 30min; 45 min).

Russia

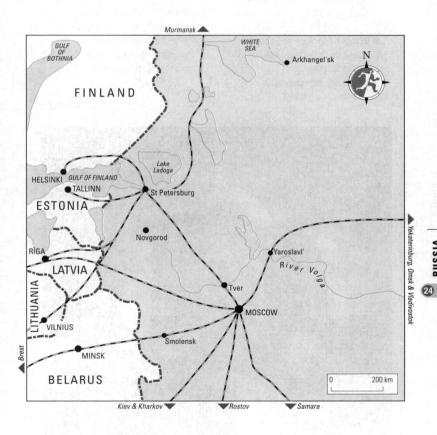

Russia highlights

* **Kremlin, Moscow** A cheat to call this one highlight, of course, as its a whole complex of political, architectural and artistic associations. See p.887

* **VDNKh, Moscow** Stalinist excess, overlaid with Wild Capitalism – all in the very worst possible taste. See p.890

* **Hermitage, St Petersburg** Defines the heart of the city architecturally, intellectually and historically. See p.896

* **Vasilevskiy Island** Walk across Dvortsoviy most with its fabulous views to reach the island's museum. See p.898

Introduction and basics

European **Russia** stretches from the borders of the states of Belarus and Ukraine to the Ural mountains, over 1000km east of Moscow; even without the rest of the Russian Federation, it constitutes by far the largest country in Europe. It was also, for many years, one of the hardest to visit. Today Russia is far more accessible, and although visas are still obligatory and accommodation often has to be booked in advance, independent travel is becoming increasingly popular. Moscow and St Petersburg remain the easiest places to visit, and these are covered below. For the adventurous, travel further afield can be booked through numerous agencies in Russia and abroad, and there are an increasing number of websites offering advice and travel services for the less standard routes.

Moscow and St Petersburg are mutually complementary. **Moscow**, the capital, is chaotic and not a beautiful city by any means. Moscow's central core, however, reflects Russia's long and fascinating history, whether in the relics of the Communist years, the Kremlin with its palaces and churches of the tsars, the wooden buildings still tucked away in back streets, or in the massive building projects of recent years which have radically changed the face of the centre.

By contrast, Russia's second city, **St Petersburg**, is Europe at its most gracious, an attempt by the eighteenth-century tsar Peter the Great to re-create the best of Western European elegance in what was then a far-flung outpost. Its position in the delta of the River Neva is unparalleled, full of watery vistas of huge and faded palaces. St Petersburg has not been revamped anywhere near as much as Moscow, and it preserves a unity and stability lacking in the capital.

You will not be bothered by the so-called Russian mafia in either city, but, as in any other big city, you should beware of petty crime.

Information and maps

Russia has few **tourist offices**. Most travellers use the information desks at hotels and hostels, but the best resources are English-language newspapers, such as the *Moscow Times* (daily) or *St Petersburg Times* (twice weekly), and free quarterly magazines available at leading hotels.

High-quality **maps** in English at very low prices are widely available from kiosks and central department stores. Those produced in the West do not take account of street-name changes or of new metro lines.

RUSSIA | Basics

24

Money and banks

The official **currency** of Russia is the ruble, which is divided into one hundred kopeks: there are 1, 5, 10 and 50 kopek coins, 1, 2 and 5 ruble coins, and notes to the value of 5, 10, 50, 100, 500 and 1000 rubles. Only notes and coins dated 1997 or after are valid.

Despite the end of soaring inflation, **prices** in this chapter are given in US dollars, a fairly stable measure of real costs. In practice though, everything is charged and paid for in rubles; it's illegal to pay in foreign currency. The black market offers nothing but risks: always **change money** in an official bank or currency exchange. Most **banks** are open Mon–Sat 10am–6/8pm, or later.

ATMs are now found in plenty, and using your **credit or debit card** to obtain cash from them is a safe way to get money in Russia. Some, however, have a very low cash limit per transaction, which may make your rubles expensive. **Travellers' cheques** are time-consuming and expensive. Many banks offer Western Union **bank transfer** services.

Be warned that Moscow is an expensive city, and the daily cost of living can be twice that of St Petersburg. In the provinces, on the other hand, life becomes ridiculously cheap.

Communications

Most **post offices** are open Mon–Sat 8am–7pm. All district post offices have **poste restante** (*do vostrébovaniya*) services. Both Moscow and St Petersburg have excellent express-letter post companies, such as Post International and Westpost, which despatch mail via Finland or the US for moderate sums.

Street phones are good for local and international calls. To use them you need a **phonecard** (available from newspaper kiosks and post offices). Moscow's public phones are less numerous and less efficient than those in St Petersburg. Phone booths in airports and major hotels aren't always run by the city phone network, and are much more expensive, but usually take Amex or Visa cards. **Mobile phones** abound in both cities, and GSM users will have no trouble plugging in to the local system. **Email** and internet access is cheap and offered at a number of internet cafés.

Getting around

With an extensive and relatively efficient network of trains and buses, you'll have few problems **getting around** the most populated parts of Russia.

Trains and buses

Buying **tickets** for long-distance and international trains is easy these days and foreigners no longer pay more for tickets than Russians. A dozen trains leave Moscow's Leningrad Station within an hour or so of midnight for the eight-hour journey to St Petersburg, the most historic being the Red Arrow (#2). Many prefer the day train, the Aurora, which takes six hours, or the evening train, at just four hours. All trains are safe and reliable – and cheap.

Most of Moscow's and St Petersburg's outlying sights are easily reached by metro, suburban buses and efficient minibuses from the end of a metro line. Fares are also low, although non-commercial lines are often packed.

Hitching

Many Russians **hitch**, especially after the public transport system closes down, when you'll see people flagging down anything that moves. If the driver finds the destination acceptable, he'll state a price, which may or may not be negotiable; if you're not happy, wait for another car. Russians will usually pay the ruble equivalent of a dollar or so to ride several kilometres; foreigners are likely to be charged more. Don't get into a vehicle which has more than one person in it, and never accept lifts from anyone who approaches you, particularly outside restaurants and nightclubs. Single women should stick to official taxis.

Accommodation and visas

Anyone travelling on a tourist visa to Russia must (technically) have **accommodation** arranged before arrival, but this is increasingly easy to get round. Hostels can usually provide invitations for a stay of any length as long as you spend just one night there. Unless otherwise stated, all hostels and hotels listed here can arrange the necessary visa support for you. Note that it's important to register your visa with your hotel or hostel when you arrive, otherwise you face a fine. Visitors travelling on a business visa (more expensive than a tourist visa) are not obliged to prebook accommodation. You can apply online for visas from ⓦwww.Infinity.ru, ⓦwww.ostwest.com or ⓦwww.visatorussia.com – this last also provides up-to-the-minute info on visa requirements, local embassies, etc.

As **hotels** in Moscow and St Petersburg are expensive, anyone on a tight budget will almost certainly do better by opting for a **hostel** or **private accommodation**. Only St Petersburg has a decent **campsite**, albeit at some distance. Note that cheaper hotels often have "improved" rooms which cost a few dollars more but have better bathroom facilities and newer furniture – it's always worth asking.

Hostels and private accommodation

Hostels are definitely the best-value accommodation in Russia. They are safer and cleaner than most hotels offering similar rates, and can help with many of the problems that face budget travellers. **Reservations** should be made at least three to four weeks in advance. Note that there is no age restriction.

Private accommodation for tourists is catching on, and both Moscow and St Petersburg have agencies providing self-contained **apartments** or **bed and breakfast** in Russian households. The cost varies from $15 to $70 per person per night, depending on the location and whether you opt for B&B or full board.

Hotels

Russian hotels are star-rated from two to five. Two-star **hotels** tend to consist of 1950s low-rises with matchbox-sized rooms; three-star hotels are typically 1960s and 1970s high-rises, equipped with several

restaurants, bars and nightclubs. Recent years have seen the appearance of central "family" hotels, with a tiny number of clean, attractive rooms, though these are not cheap (around $70 a night). Most hotels include **breakfast** in the price, but in cheaper places it's wise to check if there is a restaurant or only a bar.

Whatever class of accommodation you stay in, don't leave **valuables** in your room; put your money in the hotel safe and lock the door before going to sleep.

Food and drink

Moscow and St Petersburg abound in **cafés and restaurants**, offering everything from pizza to Indian, French and Chinese food. Many cater to the new rich or foreign businessmen, but cheap and mid-range establishments are plentiful, serving food with a local flavour. Credit cards are increasingly accepted, though not in the cheaper establishments. Some of the cheaper joints may prove hard to find – sometimes their entrance looks like that of any other building, with no sign outside.

Food

Despite the increasing popularity of **fast food** and foreign cuisine, Russians remain loyal to their culinary heritage, above all to **zakuski** – small dishes consumed before a meal with vodka, as a snack or as a light meal in themselves. Herring is a firm favourite, as are gherkins, assorted cold meats and salads. Pancakes (*bliny*), served with caviar (*ikra*), are to be recommended; red caviar is very cheap and a worthy rival to the black.

Traditionally, Russians take **breakfast** (*zavtrak*) seriously, tucking into calorific pancakes or porridge (*kasha*), with curd cheese (*tvorog*) and sour cream (*smetana*). Hotels usually serve a "Continental" breakfast, probably just fried egg, bread, butter and jam. The main meal of the day in urban Russia is **supper** (*uzhin*). **Restaurants** tend to offer inexpensive business lunch menus, but make much more of the evening meal. **Menus** in smaller establishments are usually written in Russian only, but some have an English version (not always regularly updated).

You can always ask what they recommend ("*shto-by vy porekomendovali?*").

After the *zakuski*, the menu continues with **soup** – typically, cabbage soup (*shchi*), served with a generous dollop of sour cream, much tastier than it sounds, or the gourmet version, *zelyonye shchi* – green (or sorrel) soup; beetroot soup (*borshch*) or *ukha*, fish soup. Russians don't regard even large meaty soups (*kharcho* or *solyanka*) as a main meal.

Main courses are overwhelmingly based on meat (*myaso*), sometimes accompanied by a mushroom, sour cream or cheese sauce. Meat also makes its way into *pelmeny*, a Russian version of ravioli. Georgian restaurants always have interesting **vegetarian** dishes, such as bean stew or stuffed aubergines. Marinated **fish** is a popular starter (try *selyodka pod shuboy*, herring "in a fur coat" of beetroot, carrot, egg and mayonnaise), while fresh fish – usually salmon, sturgeon or pike-perch – appears as a main course in all self-respecting eateries.

Pastries (*pirozhnoe*) are available from cake shops (*konditerskaya*). Savoury pies (*pirozhki*) with cabbage, curd cheese or rice are very popular, but steer clear of the deep-fried ones at all times and never buy from street vendors.

Desserts (*sladkoe*) are not a strong feature of Russian cuisine. Ice cream and sweet pancakes (*blinchiki*) are restaurant perennials (Russian ice cream is outstanding and is eaten even on the street when the temperature drops to minus 20°C). There are many varieties of **cake** (*tort*), but all tend to have an excess of butter-cream.

Drink

Vodka (*vódka*) is still the national drink, though sales have been overtaken by beer recently. Vodka is normally served chilled and drunk neat in one gulp, followed by a mouthful of *zakuska*. Numerous flavoured vodkas come and go, Pertsovka (hot pepper vodka) having a kick that cures all colds in seconds, but true connoisseurs stick to the straight stuff.

Russians drink **beer** (*pívo*) in the morning to alleviate a hangover, or merely as a thirst quencher, and in recent years the country has begun to understand the term "lager lout". The numerous local brands (in bottles and on tap) have an excellent fresh taste, with fewer preservatives than imports.

Wine (*vinó*) comes mostly from the vineyards of Moldavia, Georgia and the Crimea. Georgian dry and semi-sweet wines (such as Stalin's favourite, Khvanchkara) can be excellent, but Moldavian dry wine is more consistently reliable. The Crimea produces mainly fortified wines (*kheres* or sherry and Madeira) from Massandra.

Tea (*chay*) is traditionally brewed and stewed for hours, and topped up with boiling water from a samovar (though cafés have discovered the convenience of teabags). Russians drink tea without milk; if you ask for milk it's likely to be UHT. **Coffee** (*kófe*) is readily available. Sadly, though, the traditional cafés offering excellent Turkish coffee are losing out to increasingly ubiquitous chains of coffee shops. Tea and coffee often have sugar already added unless you specifically ask for them without. **Juices and soft drinks** from the usual market leaders – Pepsi, Coca-Cola and Schweppes – are available, but Russians love the bitter *kvas* and carbonated *Baikal*. Local **mineral waters**, with or without gas, can be recommended.

Opening hours and holidays

Most **shops** open Mon–Sat 10am–7pm or later; few close for lunch. Department stores, bars and restaurants stay open on Sundays.

Opening hours for **museums** are 10am–5/6pm. They are invariably closed one day a week, with one day in the month set aside as a "cleaning day". Ticket offices always close one hour before the museum itself. **Churches** are accessible from 8am until the end of the evening service.

Russia's official **national holidays** have at last settled down, those associated with the former Soviet regime now replaced by traditional religious holidays. The current public holidays are: Jan 1; Jan 6 or 7 (Orthodox Christmas); Feb 23; March 8 (Women's Day); May 1 & 2; May 9 (Victory Day); June 12 (Independence Day); Nov 7; Dec 12 (Constitution Day). Russians also informally celebrate the unofficial Old New Year on 13 or 14 Jan – according to the Julian calendar.

Emergencies

As far as petty crime goes, **pickpocketing** is all that should worry you in Russia. Sensible precautions include making photocopies of your passport and visa, leaving passports and tickets in the hotel safe, and noting down travellers' cheque and credit card numbers. It's unwise to carry large sums of money on you, and you should use a money belt if possible.

The **police** (*militsia*) can be recognized by their blue-grey uniforms and are sometimes armed. If you have anything **stolen** you should report it to the *militsia*. The phrase "*Menya obokrali*" ("I have been robbed") should work. It's unlikely that your belongings will be retrieved, but you'll need a statement detailing what you've lost for your insurance claim.

Visitors to Russia are advised to get **booster-shots** for diphtheria and tetanus. If you are on prescribed medication (particularly insulin), bring enough supplies for your stay, although high-street pharmacies (*aptéka*) offer many familiar medicines over the counter. Foreigners tend to rely for treatment on **private clinics**, which charge excessively high rates, so it's a good idea to take out insurance.

Emergency numbers

Police ☏02; ambulance ☏03; fire ☏01.

Moscow

MOSCOW is all things to all people. For Westerners, the city may look European, but its unruly spirit seems closer to Central Asia. To Muscovites, however, Moscow is both a "Mother City" and a "big village", a tumultuous community which possesses an underlying collective instinct that shows itself in times of trouble. Its beauty and ugliness are inseparable, its sentimentality the obverse of a brutality rooted in centuries of despotism, while private and cultural life in the city are as passionate as business and politics are cynical.

Moscow has been imbued with a sense of its own destiny since the fourteenth century, when the principality of Muscovy took the lead in the struggle against the Mongol-Tatars who had reduced the Kievan state to ruins. Under Ivan the Great and Ivan the Terrible its realm came to encompass everything from the White Sea to the Caspian, while after the fall of Constantinople to the Turks, Moscow assumed Byzantium's suzerainty over the Orthodox world. Despite the changes wrought by Peter the Great – not least the transfer of the capital to St Petersburg – Moscow kept its mystique and bided its time until the Bolsheviks made it the fountainhead of a new creed.Since the fall of Communism, Muscovites have given themselves over largely to the "Wild Capitalism" that intoxicates the city, and major building programmes are changing the face of the city more radically than at any time since the Stalin era.

Arrival and information

Arriving by **train** from London, Berlin or Warsaw, you'll end up at **Belarus Station**, about 1km northwest of the Garden Ring. Services from Budapest terminate at **Kiev Station**, south of the Moskva River. From St Petersburg, Finland or Estonia, you'll arrive at **Leningrad Station**. To get into the centre from any of these stations, it's best to take the **metro**, as **taxi** drivers are notorious for overcharging. Eurolines **buses** from Germany and eastern Europe terminate near the Leningrad Station.

The main **international airport** is Sheremetevo-2, 28km northwest of the city centre. The *Travellers Guest House* (see "Accommodation" below) and most hotels can arrange for you to be met by car. The fee ($40 plus) helps avoid haggling. If you have no booking, the desk in the centre of the arrivals hall should be able to book you a taxi (around $60). More hassle, but much cheaper, is public transport: this involves taking a **bus** or **express bus** (under $1) from outside the arrivals terminal to metro station Rechnoy vokzal, on the outskirts of the city.

The best place for leaflets, maps and general **information** about what's going on in and around Moscow, is the information desk of the *Metropol Hotel*, Teatralniy pr. 1/4 (℗095/927 6000). The *Travellers Guest House* also functions as an excellent information centre. Russian-speakers couldn't do better than to buy the glossy bi-weekly *Afisha* (℠www.afisha.ru), Moscow's equivalent of *Time Out*.

City transport

Although central Moscow is best explored on foot, the city is so big that you're bound to use its famous **metro** system at some point (check out its stunning interiors at ℠www.metro.ru). Trains run daily from 6am to 1am, with services every two to five minutes.You can buy travel cards valid for anything from one to sixty rides, at around 20 cents per ride. Providing you don't leave the metro, you can travel any distance, and change lines as many times as you like for the cost of one ride. Stations are marked with a large neon "M", all signs and maps are in Russian, including "entrance" (*vkhód*), "exit" (*vykhod*) and "passage to another line" (*perekhód*).

Buses, trolleybuses and trams operate from 5.30am until about 11pm. Bus stops are marked with yellow signs and trolleybus stops have blue and white signs suspended, like those for tram stops, from overhead cables. **Tickets** (*talony*) for buses, trolleybuses and trams are available from kiosks or the driver of the vehicle (single tickets and batches of ten for around $1). Some buses and trams have conductors who sell and check tickets. In general, overground transport is inefficient in central Moscow and you're best off sticking with the metro.

Official **taxis** come in all shapes and sizes. Since taxi drivers often don't use their meters, it's best to establish your fare before getting in to avoid any unpleasant surprises, especially as foreigners are likely to be overcharged. **Private cars** will also stop if you stick your hand out and can be considerably cheaper than an official taxi with its meter off. They're generally safe, though women travelling alone at night are advised to avoid them.

Accommodation

Budget travellers will find the accommodation situation in Moscow dispiriting. Most of the city's **hotels** are overpriced, particularly those in the centre. Areas like Oktyabrskaya ploshchad, Leninskiy prospekt and the Sparrow Hills (Vorobyovie gory), south and southwest of the Kremlin, offer a wider range of cheaper accommodation. The best budget options, though, are a **hostel**, or **private accommodation**, which you can arrange in advance through the *Travellers Guest House* (see below) or the St Petersburg-based *HOFA* (☎812/275 19 92, ✆homestay@yahoo .com). Both of these can also arrange onward travel in Russia.

Hostels

7th Floor pr. Vernadskogo 88☎/1 ☎095/956 6038, ✉adm@7floor.ru; Yugo-Zapadnaya metro (30min ride from the centre). Not strictly a hostel, rather a small B&B with efficient and friendly staff. ⑤

Prakash Guest House Profsoyuznaya ul. 83/1; ☎095/334 2598, ✉standkoindo@yahood.com; Belyayevo metro. Indian-run and offering full tourist support. ③

The Travellers Guest House Bolshaya Pereyaslavskaya ul. 50 ☎095/971 40 59, ✆tgh@startravel.ru; ten-minute walk from Prospekt Mira metro. Hidden away on the tenth floor, this American-run hostel is pleasant, clean and fairly central, with a laundry, café and bar. It also provides excellent tourist information and advice. ③

Hotels

Izmailovo Complex – Delta Izmailovskoe shosse 71 ☎095/166 4345, ✆www.izmailovo.ru; Izmailovskiy Park metro. A vast, modern complex near the park, offering rooms of all standards, from dead cheap to "luxury". ⑤

Minsk Hotel Tverskaya ul. 22 ☎095/299 13 49; Mayakovskaya or Pushkinskaya metro. Anonymous 1960s high-rise right in the centre, with a business centre and sauna. ③

Moskva Okhotniy ryad 2 ☎095/960 2060; Okhotniy ryad metro. For location and view nothing beats this Stalin-era hotel. ⑥

Pekin ul. Bolshaya-Sadovaya 5/1 ☎095/209 2442; Mayakovskaya metro. Genuine period charm, plus a Chinese restaurant and a sauna. ⑤

Rossiya Hotel ul. Varvarka 6 ☎095/232 6046; Ploshchad Revolyutsii metro. Gigantic labyrinth, with 3070 rooms, in a great location just off Red Square. ⑤

Tsentralnaya Tverskaya ul. 10 ☎095/229 8957; Tverskaya, Pushkinskaya and Chekhovskaya metros. Extremely central, characterful hotel, but with a shady clientele. No credit cards and no visa support. ③

Yunost Khamovnicheskiy val 34 ☎095/242 4861; Sportivnaya metro. All mod-cons and very nicely located near the Novodevichy Convent. Much better than the centre in summer. ③

The City

Discounting a couple of satellite towns beyond the outer ring road, Moscow covers an area of about 900 square kilometres. Yet, despite its size and the inhuman scale of many of its buildings and avenues, the city's general layout is easily grasped – a series of concentric circles and radial lines emanating from the Kremlin – and the centre is compact enough to explore on foot.

Red Square and the **Kremlin** are the historic nucleus of the city, signifying a great sweep of history that encompasses Ivan the Terrible, Peter the Great, Stalin and Gorbachev. Here you'll find Lenin's Mausoleum and St Basil's Cathedral, the famous GUM department store, and the Kremlin itself, whose splendid cathedrals

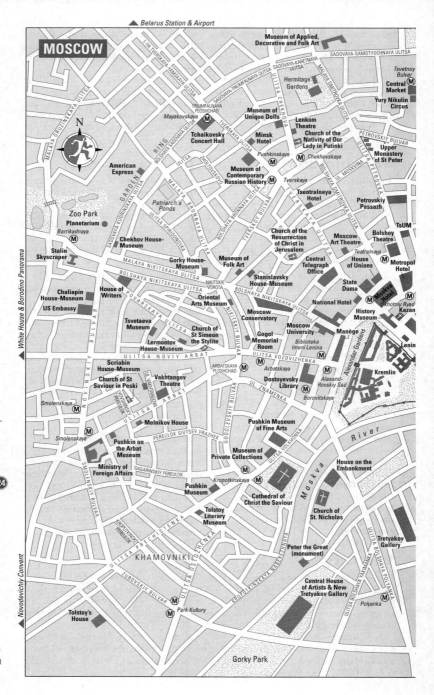

▲ Belarus Station & Airport

Museum of Applied,
Decorative and Folk Art

SADOVAYA-SAMOTYOCHNAYA ULITSA

LYA TVERSKAYA-YAMSKAYA ULITSA

SADOVAYA-KARETNAYA ULITSA

Tsvetnoy
Bulvar

Central
Market Ⓜ

Hermitage
Gardens

ULITSA CHEKHOVA

MALAYA DMITROVKA ULITSA

SADOVAYA-TRIUMFALNAYA ULITSA

Yury Nikulin
Circus

TRIUMFALNAYA
PLOSHCHAD

Mayakovskaya Ⓜ

Museum of
Unique Dolls

Lenkom
Theatre

PETROVSKIY BULVAR

Tchaikovsky
Concert Hall

Minsk
Hotel

Church of the
Nativity of Our
Lady in Putinki

Upper
Monastery
of St Peter

BOLSHAYA SADOVAYA ULITSA

Pushkinskaya Ⓜ

Ⓜ Chekhovskaya

RING

American
Express

BOLSHAYA DMITROVKA ULITSA

Museum of
Contemporary
Russian History Ⓜ

Tverskaya Ⓜ

Tsentralnaya
Hotel

Petrovskiy
Passazh

GARDEN

Patriarch's
Ponds

MALAYA BRONNAYA ULITSA

BOLSHAYA BRONNAYA ULITSA

TVERSKOY BULVAR

BOLSHAYA DMITROVKA ULITSA

TsUM

ULITSA SPIRIDONOVKA

Church of the
Resurrection
of Christ in
Jerusalem

Moscow
Art Theatre

Bolshoy
Theatre

Zoo Park
Planetarium Ⓜ

SADOVAYA-KUDRINSKAYA ULITSA

Barrikadnaya Ⓜ

Chekhov House-
Museum

Gorky House-
Museum

Museum of
Folk Art

Central
Telegraph
Office

House
of Unions Ⓜ

Teatralnaya

Metropol
Hotel

Stalin
Skyscraper Ⓜ

MALAYA NIKITSKAYA ULITSA

Stanislavsky
House-Museum

NIKITSKIE
VOROTA

State
Duma

BOLSHAYA NIKITSKAYA ULITSA

Okhotniy Ryad
Kazan Ⓜ

Moskva
Hotel Ⓜ

BOLSHAYA NIKITSKAYA ULITSA

National Hotel

History
Museum

Chaliapin
House-Museum

House
of Writers

POVARSKAYA ULITSA

Oriental
Arts Museum

Moscow
Conservatory

US Embassy

NIKITSKIY BULVAR

Moscow
University

Manège

Bibiloteka
Imeni Lenina

Lenin

Tsvetaeva
Museum

Church of
St Simeon
the Stylite

Gogol
Memorial
Room

Lermontov
House-Museum

ULITSA NOVIY ARBAT

ULITSA VOZDVIZHENKA

Alexander Gardens

Kremlin

ARBATSKAYA
PLOSHCHAD Ⓜ

Arbatskaya Ⓜ

Scriabin
House-Museum

GOGOLEVSKIY BULVAR

Church of St
Saviour in Peski

Vakhtangov
Theatre

ARBAT

Dostoyevsky
Library

Alexand-
Rovskiy Sad Ⓜ

Smolenskaya Ⓜ

UL ZNAMENKA

Borovitskaya Ⓜ

Melnikov House

PEREULOK SIVTSEV VRAZHEK

Pushkin Museum
of Fine Arts

Smolenskaya Ⓜ

River

Pushkin on
the Arbat
Museum

Museum of
Private Collections

House on the
Embankment

ULITSA VOLKHONKA

Ministry of
Foreign Affairs

GAGARINSKIY PEREULOK

Kropotkinskaya Ⓜ

Moskva

Pushkin
Museum

SMOLENSKIY BULVAR

Tolstoy
Literary
Museum

Cathedral of
Christ the Saviour

Church of
St. Nicholas

ULITSA PRECHISTENKA

ULITSA OSTOZHENKA

KROPOTKINSKIY PEREULOK

Tretyakov
Gallery

KHAMOVNIKI

Peter the Great
(monument)

ZUBOVSKIY BULVAR

KROPOTKINSKAYA NABEREZHNAYA

ULITSA BOLSHAYA POLYANKA

ULITSA BOLSHAYA YAKIMANKA

Central House
of Artists & New
Tretyakov Gallery

Park Kultury Ⓜ

Polyanka

Tolstoy's
House

RUSSIA

24

▲ White House & Borodino Panorama

▲ Novodevichiy Convent

Gorky Park

Ⓜ Komsomolskaya

Kazan Station

SADOVAYA-SUKHAREVSKAYA ULITSA

Sheremetev Hospital

Sukharevskaya Ⓜ

SADOVAYA-SPASSKAYA ULITSA

Krasnye Vorota

Stalin Skyscraper Ⓜ

PROSPEKT AKADEMIKA SAKHAROVA

Krasnye Vorota Ⓜ

TSVETNOY BULVAR

LUKoil

ULITSA SRETENKA

ULITSA MYASNITSKAYA

SADOVAYA-CHERNOGRYAZSKAYA ULITSA

TRUBNAYA PLOSHCHAD

BOULEVARD RING

Convent of the Nativity

Turgenevskaya Ⓜ

Sandunovskiy Baths

Chistye Prudy

Perlov Tea House

ULITSA BOLSHAYA LUBYANKA

ULITSA MYASNITSKAYA

Main Post Office

CHISTOPRUDNIY BULVAR

BOLSHOY KHARITONEVSKIY PEREULOK

FURMANNIY PEREULOK

A. Vasnetsov Flat-Museum

ULITSA POKROVKA

ULITSA ZEMLYANIY VAL

Kuznetskiy Most Ⓜ

Lubyanka

Churches of the Archangel Gabriel & St Theodor Stratilites

Moscow Lights Museum

Detskiy Mir

Lubyanka Ⓜ

ARMYANSKIY PEREULOK

Figurniy dom

SLAVYANSKAYA PLOSHCHAD

Krasnye Vorota

Kurskaya Ⓜ

Kursk Station

Kitay-Gorod Wall

NIKOLSKAYA ULITSA

Politechnical Museum

ULITSA MAROSEYKA

Church of SS Cosmas & Damian

POKROVSKIY BULVAR

Apraksin Mansion

Church of the Presentation in Barashi

PODSOSENSKIY PEREULOK

Kurskaya Ⓜ

Ⓜ *Chkalovskaya*

Moscow History Museum

Cathedral

ULITSA ILINKA

Church of St Vladimir in the Old Garden

Church of the Trinity in Khokhovskiy

KAZARMENNIY PEREULOK

GUM

Monastery of the Sign

Choral Synagogue

ULITSA ZABELINA

Ivanovskiy Convent

Church of the Trinity in Kulishki

Mausoleum

Church of St Barbara

Palace of the Romanov Boyars

ULITSA VARVARKA

Kitay-gorod Ⓜ

PODKOLOKOLNIY PEREULOK

ULITSA ZEMLYANOY VAL

RED SQUARE

English Court

St Basil's Cathedral

Church of the Nativity

Church of Peter & Paul at the Yauza Gate

ZAYAUZE

Kitay-Gorod Wall

Church of the Trinity in Serebryaniki

Rossiya Hotel

ULITSA SOLYANKA

River Yauza

M o s k v a

Balschug Kempinski Hotel

SADOVNICHESKAYA ULITSA

River

SADOVNICHESKAYA NABEREZHNAYA

Kotelnicheskaya Apartments

GONCHARNAYA ULITSA

ULITSA BOLSHAYA ORDYNKA

SADOVNICHESKAYA ULITSA

PYATNITSKAYA ULITSA

Novokuznetskaya Ⓜ

T A G A N K A

Taganka Theatre

Taganskaya Ⓜ

Ⓜ *Marxistskaya*

Furniture Museum

Tretyakovskaya Ⓜ

ZAMOSKVORECHE

Ⓜ

Taganskaya Ⓜ

0   500m

and Armoury museum head the list of attractions. The Kremlin is ringed by two quarters defined by boulevards built over the original ramparts of medieval times, when Moscow's residential areas were divided into the inner **Beliy Gorod** and the humbler outer **Zemlyanoy Gorod**. The cosy **Zamoskvoreche** area to the south is home to the Tretyakov Gallery of Russian art and Gorky Park.

Beyond this core lie some key sites best reached by metro. To the southwest, **Novodevichiy Convent** nestles in the loop of the River Moskva and Moscow State University rises high up on the Sparrow Hills; south is the romantic ex-royal estate of **Kolomenskoe**. In the north sprawls the **VDNKh**, a huge Stalinist exhibition park with amazing statues and pavilions, while in the east lies the **Andrei Rublev Museum of Old Russian Art and Culture**.

Red Square

Every visitor to Moscow is irresistibly drawn to **Red Square**, the historic and spiritual heart of the city, so loaded with associations and drama that it seems to embody all of Russia's triumphs and tragedies. In fact, the name Red Square (Krasnaya ploshchad) has nothing to do with communism, but derives from "krasniy", the old Russian word for "beautiful".

The square came into being towards the end of the fifteenth century and remained an important political and cultural landmark until Peter the Great moved the capital to St Petersburg in 1712. Only when the Bolsheviks moved the capital back to Moscow in 1918 did the square regain its political significance as the centre for huge parades and demonstrations. On the west side the Lenin Mausoleum squats beneath the ramparts of the Kremlin and on the other sprawls **GUM** – what was during Soviet times the State Department Store" – built in 1890–93, and now a hymn to expensive fashion outlets, while **St Basil's Cathedral** erupts in a profusion of onion domes and spires at the far end.

In post-Communist Russia, the **Lenin Mausoleum** (Tues, Wed, Thurs, Sat & Sun 10am–1pm; free) can be seen as either an awkward reminder or a cherished relic of the old days. While leaving Lenin's embalmed corpse *in situ* seems inappropriate (he apparently wished to be buried beside his mother in St Petersburg's Volkov Cemetery), the Mausoleum deserves to be preserved as a stylish piece of architecture. When Boris Yeltsin suggested closing the Mausoleum in 1997, Communist extremists blew up a monument to Nicholas II on the outskirts of Moscow in protest, and although the subject occasionally comes up, emotions are always high and it is allowed to drop after a few weeks of hysteria. Behind the Mausoleum, the **Kremlin wall** – 19m high and 6.5m thick – contains a mass grave of Bolsheviks who perished during the battle for Moscow in 1917 and the ashes of an array of luminaries including writer Maxim Gorky and Yuriy Gagarin, first man in space, and John Reed, the American Communist who witnessed the Revolution. Beyond lie the graves of a select group of Soviet leaders, each with his own bust: a pompous Brezhnev and a benign-looking Stalin.

No description can do justice to **St Basil's Cathedral** (10am–4.30pm, closed Tues; $2), silhouetted against the skyline where Red Square slopes down towards the Moskva River. Commissioned by Ivan the Terrible to celebrate his capture of the Tatar stronghold of Kazan in 1552, its popular title commemorates a "holy fool", St Basil the Blessed, who foretold the fire that swept Moscow in 1547. Stalin hated the building, resenting the fact that it prevented his troops from marching out of Red Square en masse.

At the other end of the square is the **State History Museum** (11am–7pm, closed Tues; $3), with only a tiny proportion of its varied collection of everything from archeological finds to Soviet badges and textiles on display. Beyond, to the north, is the supreme symbol of Moscow's exchange of communism for capitalism: in place of the empty space formerly used for parades and displays of military hardware is the vast underground shopping centre, **Okhotniy ryad**, buried beneath a mass of tasteless landscaping.

The Kremlin

Brooding and glittering in the heart of Moscow, the Kremlin (10am–5pm, closed Thurs) thrills and tantalizes whenever you see its towers against the skyline, or its cathedrals and palaces arrayed above the Moskva River. Its name is synonymous with Russia's government, and in modern times assumed connotations of a Mecca for believers, and the seat of the Antichrist for foes of communism.

The founding of the Kremlin is attributed to Prince Yuriy Dolgorukiy, who erected a wooden fort above the confluence of the Moskva and Neglinna rivers in about 1147. Under Grand Duke Ivan III (1462–1505) this "kremlin" grew to confirm Moscow's stature as the centre of Russia.

One **ticket**, costing $8, admits you to the Kremlin and cathedrals, while separate tickets are required for the Patriarch's Palace and exhibitions ($5). A couple of visits are needed to do it all justice: one to see the cathedrals, and another for touring the Armoury Palace, which can only be entered at set times.

Roughly two-thirds of the Kremlin is off-limits to tourists, the accessible part beginning around the corner from the Great Kremlin Palace. From here the **Patriarch's Palace** heaves into view. This now houses a **Museum of Seventeenth-Century Life and Applied Art**, displaying ecclesiastical regalia, period furniture and domestic utensils. The exhibition concludes in the former **Cathedral of the Twelve Apostles**, which forms part of the same structure. Further along, the **Tsar Cannon**, cast in 1586, is one of the largest cannons ever made and was intended to defend the Saviour Gate, but has never been fired. Close by looms the earthbound **Tsar Bell**, the largest bell in the world, cast in 1655. Beyond the Patriarch's Palace lies **Cathedral Square**, the historic heart of the Kremlin, dominated by the magnificent, white **Ivan the Great Bell Tower**, the tallest structure within the Kremlin's walls. Opposite stands the oldest and most important of the Kremlin churches, the **Cathedral of the Assumption**, which has symbolized Moscow's claim to be the protector of the seat of Russian Orthodoxy ever since the seat of the Church was transferred here from Vladimir in 1326. Rebuilt in 1479 by the Bolognese architect Alberti Fioravanti, its subsequent history reflects its role as Russia's premier church, used throughout tsarist times for coronations and solemn acts of state. Its exterior is remarkably plain, while the interior is spacious, light and echoing, its walls, roof and pillars entirely covered with icons and frescoes. Tucked away next door is the lowly white **Church of the Deposition of the Robe**.

Last of the great churches is the **Cathedral of the Archangel**, built in 1505–08; around the walls and pillars cluster the tombs of Russia's rulers from Grand Duke Ivan I to Tsar Ivan V. Across from here glints the golden-domed **Cathedral of the Annunciation**, the private royal church. Lofty and narrow, it has an interior that seems far more "Russian" than the other Kremlin cathedrals. It also houses some of the finest icons in Russia, with works by Theophanes the Greek and Andrei Rublev.

Situated between the Great Kremlin Palace and the Borovitskiy Gate, the **Armoury Palace** (by ticket purchased in advance; $10) conceals a staggering array of treasures – among them the tsars' coronation robes, carriages, jewellery, dinner services and armour – well worth the trouble and expense involved in seeing them. The palace also houses the **State Diamond Fund** (20min guided tours; tickets around $12), which contains the most valuable gems in Russia.

The Beliy Gorod

The **Beliy Gorod** or "White Town" is the historic name of the residential district that encircled the Kremlin. Multi-domed churches cluster along ulitsa Varvarka, and around Kitay-gorod east of the Kremlin: this was the very heart of the city during the sixteenth century, and even today it has a strongly medieval feel. Its main seventeenth-century thoroughfare, Tverskaya ulitsa, owes its present form to a massive reconstruction programme during the mid-1930s, and yet, despite the scale of some

24

of its gargantuan buildings, the variety of older, often charming sidestreets gives the avenue a distinctive character.

There are countless museums and sights situated in the Beliy Gorod. Those interested in Russia's Communist past and turbulent politics should pay a visit to the **Museum of Contemporary Russian History** (Tues–Sun 10am–5pm; $1), at Tverskaya 21, formerly the Museum of the Revolution. Its bold displays of propaganda posters, photographs and state gifts to Lenin and Stalin are fascinating even if you cannot read the Russian labelling.

South of Tverskaya, Moscow's **Pushkin Museum of Fine Arts**, at Volkhonka ul. 12 (Tues–Sun 10am–7pm; $5), has a rich collection of European painting, from Italian High Renaissance works to Rembrandt and Poussin, and an outstanding display of Impressionists. It also has charming Egyptian portraits, and of course the magnificent gold of the lost city of Troy, removed from Germany at the end of World War II and still the subject of conflict between the two countries.

In 1994, Moscow's Mayor Luzhkov took the populist step of announcing the rebuilding of the **Cathedral of Christ the Redeemer** opposite the museum. The vast original structure, built 1839–83, had been blown up by the Soviet government in 1934 and a swimming pool built on the site. Financed largely by donations and perceived as a symbol of Moscow's (and Russia's) revival, the cathedral is today a monument to one man's overweening pride and ambition. Luzhkov appears smiling broadly in numerous photographs in the museum recording the history of the building, housed in the crypt (daily 10am–6pm; free).

The Zemlyanoy Gorod

In medieval times, the white-walled Beliy Gorod was encircled by a humbler **Zemlyanoy Gorod** or "Earth Town". Separated from the Beliy Gorod by the tree-lined "boulevard ring", this is one of the best-looking parts of Moscow, with neoclassical and Art Nouveau mansions on every corner of the backstreets around the **Patriarch's Ponds**. West of here, the **Arbat** once stood for bohemian Moscow in the way that Carnaby Street represented swinging London, and still has a vibrant streetlife.

Admirers of Bulgakov, Chekhov, Lermontov, Gorky and Pushkin will find their former homes preserved as museums in the pretty, leafy backstreets around the **Patriarch's Ponds**, southwest of Tverskaya. The Patriarch's Ponds are, in fact, one large pond, which forms the heart of a square surrounded by wrought-iron railings and mature trees. At Bolshaya Sadovaya ul. 10, a plaque attests that Mikhail Bulgakov lived here from 1921 to 1924; his satirical fantasy *The Master and Margarita* is indelibly associated with this area in particular. It's usually possible to visit: go into the courtyard and look for entrance 6, on the left; the apartment (no. 50) is at the top of the stairs. Anton Chekhov lived at Sadovaya-Kudrinskaya ul. 6, in what is now the **Chekhov House-Museum** (Tues, Thurs & Sat 11am–5pm, Wed & Fri 2–6pm; $4), while Maxim **Gorky's house-museum** (Mon & Thurs 10am–4.30pm, Tues, Wed & Fri noon–6pm; closed last Thurs of month; $4), on the corner of Povarskaya ulitsa and ulitsa Spiridonovka, is worth seeing purely for its amazing Art Nouveau decor, both inside and out.

Once the **Arbat** was the heart of a bohemian quarter, where writers, actors and scientists hung out. It retains some of these characteristics today, with its array of cafés and antique shops. It tends to get busier beyond the **Peace Wall** – a cute example of propaganda against Reagan's Star Wars. Portrait artists, buskers and photographers offering a range of props from Gorby to Mickey Mouse are a few of the sights on offer.

West of the Zemlyanoy Gorod

West of the Zemlyanoy Gorod, over the river, patriotic ardour finds an outlet at the immense **Borodino Panorama** at Kutuzovskiy pr. 38 (daily 10am/noon–6pm;

$1), housing a painting 115m long and 15m high, with 3000 figures. This monument to the Battle of Borodino, fought against Napoleon in 1812, was completed as late as 1912. It was dismantled soon after the Revolution, then re-established here thirty years later.

South of here, **Moscow State University** occupies the largest of the city's seven 1950s Stalinist-Gothic skyscrapers, dominating the plateau of the **Sparrow Hills** (Vorobyovie gory), overlooking the Moskva River. Besides the university, the attraction is quite simply the panoramic view of Moscow, with Luzhniki stadium and the Novodevichiy Convent in the foreground, the Kremlin in the middle distance, and six more Stalinist skyscrapers ranged across the city.

Novodevichiy Convent

Where the Moskva River begins its loop around the marshy tongue of Luzhniki, southwest of the Zemlyanoy Gorod, a cluster of shining domes above a fortified rampart proclaims the presence of the lovely **Novodevichiy Convent** (daily 8am–7pm for worship). At its heart stands the white Cathedral of the Virgin of Smolensk, with a superb interior. To get there take the metro out to Sportivnaya, taking the ulitsa 10-ti Letiya Oktyabrya exit; a ten-minute walk to the end of the road brings you within sight of the convent's towers and ramparts.

Beyond the convent's south wall lies the venerable **Novodevichiy Cemetery** (daily 10am–6pm), burial place of numerous famous writers, musicians and artists, including Gogol, Chekhov, Stanislavsky, Bulgakov and Shostakovich. Krushchev is also here – he died out of office, and was denied burial in the Kremlin wall.

Zamoskvoreche

South of the Kremlin lies **Zamoskvoreche** (simply "Across the Moskva River"), an area dating back to medieval times and preserving a host of colourful churches and the mansions of civic-minded merchants. One of the most charming parts of the city, with a strongly residential feel, it can be easily traversed on one of the trams which start from Chistye prudy metro.

Founded in 1892 by the financier Pavel Tretyakov, the **Tretyakov Gallery** (Tues–Sun 10am–7.30pm; ⊛www.tretyakov.ru; $5), five minutes' walk from Tretyakovskaya metro, displays an outstanding collection of Russian art before the Revolution. Russian **icons** – which originally came to Russia from Byzantium and were valued for their religious and spiritual content rather than artistic merit – are magnificently displayed on the second floor. The exhibition continues through to the late nineteenth century, with one vast room filled with the nightmare-like, fantastical works of Mikhail Vrubel. Twentieth-century and contemporary art (dominated by Tatlin, Chagall and Malevich) is on show at the **New Tretyakov** opposite the entrance to Gorky Park, at Krymskiy val 10 (Tues–Sun 10am–7.30pm; $4).

Gorky Park is famous abroad from Martin Cruz Smith's classic thriller. Inaugurated in 1928, the Soviet Union's first "Park of Culture and Rest" covers 300 acres and includes funfairs, a large outdoor skating rink and lots of woodland (daily 10am–10pm; $1).

Kolomenskoe

On the steep west bank of the Moskva River, 10km southeast of the Kremlin, **Kolomenskoe** (grounds daily 9am–7pm, free; museum Tues–Sun 10am–6pm, $2) was once a royal summer retreat. Though its legendary wooden palace no longer exists, Kolomenskoe still has one of the finest churches in the whole of Russia, the **Church of the Ascension** (services Sun 8am), and vintage wooden structures such as Peter the Great's cabin, set amid hoary oaks above a great bend in the river. In summer, Muscovites flock here for the fresh air and to sunbathe. Getting here is easy: ride four stops on the metro from Teatralnaya, near the Bolshoy Theatre, to Kolomenskaya, fifteen minutes' walk from the site itself.

Andronikov Monastery complex

The fourteenth-century **Andronikov Monastery** is situated on the steep east bank of the Yauza. Its most famous monk was the great icon painter Andrei Rublev, canonized by the Russian Orthodox Church in 1989 and buried in the grounds. At the centre of the monastery stands Moscow's oldest architectural monument, the **Church of the Saviour** (1420s), with wall paintings by Rublev himself (currently undergoing restoration), which now houses the **Andrei Rublev Museum of Old Russian Art and Culture** at Andronyevskaya pl. 10 (11am–6pm, closed Wed; $3; Ploshchad Ilyicha metro). The most famous icons may be in the Tretyakov, but the atmosphere here is something else – you retire from the noise and bustle of the city and enter a peaceful, serene land. Even the fact that until the 1950s the church housed the archive of the Ministry of State Security could do nothing to destroy its romance.

The VDNKh – the northern suburbs

The Exhibition of Economic Achievements – or **VDNKh** (daily 10am–7pm) – is a permanent trade-fair-cum-shopping-centre which reflects the state of the national economy more faithfully than its founders intended. Its genesis was the All-Union Agricultural Exhibition of 1939, a display of the fruits of socialism and a showpiece of Stalinist monumental art. Scores of pavilions trumpeted the achievements of the Soviet republics and the planned economy. Today, imported cars have ousted Soviet products. Shoppers, lured by "Wild Capitalism" rather than the Five Year Plan, ignore the gilded fountains and the sows that once attested to the fecundity of Soviet livestock. Shorn of ideological pretensions, it has been renamed the **All-Russia Exhibition Centre** (VVTs) – but everyone still calls it VDNKh.

Near the main entrance stands one of the best-ever Soviet monuments, the **Space Obelisk**, a rocket blasting nearly 100m into the sky on a stylized plume of energy clad in shining titanium. It was unveiled in 1964, three years after Gagarin orbited the earth, an unabashed expression of pride in this unique feat. On the other side of the entrance is the famous monument of the Worker and Collective Farm Girl, colossal twin figures intended to embody Soviet industrial progress, though in fact they were handmade.

Eating and drinking

It's no problem finding food and drink in Moscow these days and most places have a member of staff with a rudimentary grasp of English. This list is weighted towards more traditional Russian eateries. **Cafés** serve plentiful and excellent food at much lower prices than full-blown restaurants, and seldom require bookings, making them a boon for budget travellers. In recent years a large number of small rock **clubs** and **bars** have opened up, many open all night. A full list of literally hundreds of worthy places can be found in the *Moscow Times* supplement, *Metropolis*.

Cafés, bars and fast food

Amalteya Stremyanny per. 28/1; Serpukhovksya metro. Choose from a vast range of *meze* in this cheap Turkish café, which has a singer in the evenings.

Clone ul. Bolshaya Dmitrovka 16; Okhotnyy Ryad metro. Minimalist (same could be said of the portions) interior with huge window seats for people-watching on this trendy central street. You pay for style and location, but it's worth it.

Dioscarius Merzlyakovskiy per. 2; Arbatskaya metro. Georgian food and great variety of Georgian wine, right in the centre of town.

Donna Clara Malaya Bronnaya ul. 21/13; Mayakovskaya metro. Small café in the heart of literary Moscow, offering great window seats.

Dzhagannat Express inside Dom Khudozhnika (House of Artists), ul. Kuznetskiy Most; Kuznetskiy Most metro. Rare, centrally located vegetarian café, offering take away, but with no alcohol.

Kofe-In (Caffeine) Bolshaya Dmitrovka ul. 15; Teatralnaya metro. A few main meals, but mainly great coffee and desserts.

Kot Begemot Spiridonyevskiy per. 10A; Mayakovskaya metro. Food nearly as good as the location.

Ogonyok Krasnaya Presnaya ul. 36; 1905-goda metro. Russian food that doesn't limit itself to *pelmeni* and beetroot. No credit cards.

PiR O.G.I. Pyatnitskaya ul. 29I; Novokuznetskaya metro. Great food and beer.

Taras Bulba ul. Petrovka 30/7; Pyatnitskaya ul. 14; Sadovo-Samotechnaya ul. 13; etc. Chain of Ukrainian cafés; their borshch is something else.

U Nikitskikh Vorot Bolshaya Nikitskaya ul. 23/9; Okhotny Ryad metro. Cheap Georgian food, in a comfortable bar (rather plain restaurant).

Yolki-Palki Bolshaya Dmitrovka ul. 23/8; Klimentovskiy per. 14/1; Novyy Arbat ul. 11; etc. If you want to eat Russian/Ukrainian/Mongolian food at rock-bottom prices, join the queue at one of ten or so branches of this popular eatery.

Restaurants

Petrovich Club Myasnitskaya ul. 24 ☎095/923 0082; Chistiye Prudy metro. Russian *nouvelle cuisine* and nostalgia for a Soviet childhood in the 1960s and 1970s. No credit cards.

Praga ul. Arbat 2 ☎095/290 61 71; Arbatskaya metro. Impossible to get into without a bribe during the Soviet period and a ghastly dump in the early years of perestroika, the place lived on its reputation as a pre-Revolutionary palace of *haute cuisine* and high society. Now easily back in the running for quality, it should be visited if only for its place in Moscow's social history.

Raisky Dvor Spiridonovka ul. 25 ☎095/290 13 41; Mayakovskaya metro. Russian and European food, inside an *Animal Farm*-inspired decor.

Nightlife and entertainment

Disco has had its day in Moscow. The city's **nightlife** scene is now given over to scores of small, intimate nightclubs and great **live music** of all genres. Alongside the city's restaurants and clubs, there's a rich **cultural life** in Moscow. Classical music, opera and ballet are strongly represented with a busy schedule of concerts and performances throughout the year, sometimes held in palaces, churches or – in summer – parks and gardens. Puppet and circus shows are also popular and transcend language barriers, while several cinemas, such as the **America Cinema** at the *Radisson-Slavyanskaya Hotel* (☎095/941 87 47; Kievskaya metro; discount for students), show films in their original language. *The Moscow Times* has a reasonable listings section in English, but if you speak a little Russian it's worth buying the more comprehensive listings magazine *Afisha*.

Clubs and live music

Dom Bolshoy Ovchinnikovskiy per. 24/4; Novokuznetskaya metro. For the hip "intellectual" crowd. Thurs–Sun only.

Hungry Duck 9 Pushechnaya ul.; Kuznetskiy Most metro. Renowned for its bad-taste raucous entertainments – entrance fee for men.

Kitayskiy Lyotchik Dzhao Da Lubyanskiy proezd 25; ⊛www.jao-da.ru; Kitay-gorod metro. Coolest place to be seen and hear the best bands on offer. No credit cards. Open 24 hr.

Mesto Vstrechi Maly Gnezdnikovskiy per. 9/8, Building 7; Pushkinskaya metro. The name comes from a cult 1970s TV series and it means "meeting place". Open 24 hr.

Project O.G.I. Potapovskiy per. 8/12; Chistiye prudy metro. Hip club, bar and restaurant with sessions for kids in the mornings. No credit cards.

Propaganda Bolshoy Zlatoustinskiy per. 7; Kitay-gorod metro. Very young, still some of the city's best DJs. No credit cards.

Staraya ploshchad Bolshoy Cherkasskiy per. 8; Kitay-gorod metro. Cellar club for the down-to-earth. No credit cards.

Svalka Profsoyuznaya ul. 27/1; Profsoyuznaya metro. Best for grunge – *Svalka* does, after all,

mean "rubbish dump". Cover charge can be very high, depending on event – and gender.

Opera and ballet

Bolshoy Theatre Teatralnaya pl. 1 ☎095/292 0050; Teatralnaya metro. Fighting hard in its rivalry with Petersburg's Mariinskiy, the competition is great for standards. The ballet and Russian opera are still stupendous. Decent tickets cost $40 or more for foreigners. Performances Tues–Sun at 7pm, matinée on Sun.

Helikon Opera Bolshaya Nikitskaya ul. ☎095/290 0971; Pushkinskaya metro. Small theatre offering intimate, small-scale productions, including works by Handel and Bach.

Circus

New Circus pr. Vernadskovo 7 ☎095/930 28 15; Universitet metro. One of the finest in the world, though still uses animal acts. Performances Wed–Sun.

Yuriy Nikulin Circus Tsvetnoy bul. 13 ☎095/200 06 68; Tsvetnoy bulvar metro. Great atmosphere in this small circus, where clowns are the forte. Performances Thurs–Sun.

Listings

Embassies Australia, Kropotkinskiy per. 13 ⊕095/956 6070; Canada, Starokonyushenniy per. 23 ⊕095/956 6666; Ireland, Grokholskiy per. 5 ⊕095/937 5911; New Zealand, Povarskaya ul. 44 ⊕095/956 3579; UK, Smolenskaya nab. 10 ⊕095/956 72 00; US, Novinskiy bulvar 19/23 ⊕095/728 5000.

Emergencies American Medical Center, Grokholskiy per. 1 ⊕095/933 7700; European Medical Centre, 2-oy Tverskoy-Yamskoy per. 10 ⊕095/787 7000. Both recognized by international insurance companies.

Exchange Official currency exchanges and ATMs all over the centre of Moscow.

Internet cafés Cafemax ul. Pyatnitskaya 25, Novokuznetskaya metro; Image.ru

Novoslobodskaya ul. 16, Mendeleyevskaya metro; Internet Club Kuznetskiy most 12, Kuznetskiy Most metro.

Laundry California Cleaners, Petrovska 27 ⊕095/200 6400.

Left luggage Most train stations have lockers and/or a 24hr left-luggage office, but you would be tempting fate to use them.

Pharmacy Staryy Arbat, Arbatskaya ul. 25; Multifarma, Turistkaya ul. 27; 24hr pharmacy at pr. Mira 71.

Post office Central Telegraph Office, Tverskaya ul. 7; Main Post Office, Myasnitskaya ul. 26/2, 101000. Express postal services via Courier Service, Bolshaya Sadovaya 10 ⊕095/209 1735 (Mayakovskaya metro).

St Petersburg

ST PETERSBURG, Petrograd, Leningrad and St Petersburg again – the city's succession of names mirrors Russia's turbulent history. Founded in 1703 as a "window on the West" by Peter the Great, the city celebrates its **three hundredth anniversary** with great pomp in 2003; details of the city's numerous special events throughout the year can be found on the site ⓦwww.spb300.com. For two centuries the capital of the tsarist empire, synonymous with excess and magnificence, the city was the cradle of the revolutions that overthrew the monarchy and brought the Bolsheviks to power in 1917. As Leningrad it epitomized the Soviet Union's heroic sacrifices in the war, withstanding nine hundred days of Nazi siege. Then, in 1991 – the year the USSR collapsed – the change of name back to St Petersburg proved deeply symbolic of the country's mood.

St Petersburg's sense of its own identity owes much to its origins and to the interweaving of myth and reality throughout its history. Created by the will of an autocrat, the imperial capital embodied both Peter the Great's rejection of Old Russia – represented by "Asiatic" Moscow, the former capital – and of his embrace of Europe. Intensely proud of itself, of its intellectual – and its workers' revolutionary – past, St Petersburg is an easy and relaxing city. It's also one of contrasts: beautiful yet drab. Beggars and nouveaux riches rub shoulders on Nevskiy prospekt, yet after the enormous changes of recent years a sense of stability and relative wellbeing has at last arrived, reaching even beyond the historic centre to the sprawling outer ring of high-rise blocks.

Arrival and information

Trains from Helsinki bring you to the famous Finland Station (the train on which Lenin arrived to start the Revolution in 1917 stands beside platform), while those from Europe usually terminate at the scruffy and disreputable Baltic Station. Trains from Moscow draw into Moscow Station. All are on the metro. St Petersburg's **international airport**, Pulkovo-2 (⊕812/104 3444), is 17km south of the city centre. Take a bus (#13) or minibus from the stop nearest the arrivals building (purchase your flat-fare ticket from the conductor) to Moskovskaya ploshchad, then change onto the metro. It's best to avoid taxis, as drivers often open the bidding at $40 or more. Eurolines **buses** from Germany and the Baltic States can drop you anywhere in the centre of town.

ST PETERSBURG

River Neva

Smolniy Convent
Smolniy Institute

Finland Station
Ploshchad Lenina

Tauride Gardens

Chernyshevskaya

KIROCHNAYA ULITSA

Alexander Nevsky Monastery

LITEYNIY PROSPEKT

Aurora

River Neva

Summer Garden

Church on Spilled Blood

Mikhailovsky Castle

PETROGRAD SIDE

Gorkovskaya

Peter & Paul Fortress

Winter Palace & Hermitage

Mikhailovsky Palace & Russian Museum

Vladimir Church

Mayakovskaya

Moscow Station

LIGOVSKIY PROSPEKT

Ploshchad Vosstaniya

Vladimirskaya
Dostoevskaya

Rostral Columns

Kunstkammer

THE STRELKA

Nevskiy Prospekt

Kazan Cathedral

Nevskiy Prospekt

Gostiny Dvor

Russian Museum

Pushkinskaya

River Fontanka

Sportivnaya

University

Admiralty Garden

Admiralty

St Isaac's Cathedral

Semyonnaya Ploshchad/ Sadovaya

Vitebsk Station

Vasileostrovskaya
Vasilevskiy Ostrov

River Moyka

VOZNESENSKIY PROSPEKT

MOSKOVSKIY PROSPEKT

▼ Baltic Station

Martinskiy Theatre

St Nicholas Cathedral

Canal Griboedov

Smolensk Cemetery

VASILEVSKIY ISLAND

SREDNY PROSPEKT

BOLSHOY PROSPEKT

Sea Terminal

N

0   1 km

RUSSIA | St Petersburg

24

893

The first thing a visitor should do is pick up *St Petersburg: The Official City Guide*, the best of several quarterly English freebies. They also have a website: @ www.city-guide.spb.ru. The Friday edition of *The St Petersburg Times* and the monthly *Pulse* are also free and have good listings and reviews. Major hostels can provide everything from visa support to theatre tickets and general help should something go wrong. The **City Tourist Information Office** at Nevskiy pr. 41 (☎812/311 2843) is still near the bottom of a steep learning curve.

City transport

St Petersburgers walk everywhere, summer or winter. Yet it is a big city, and sooner or later you're going to want to use its cheap and relatively efficient **public transport** system. Unlike Moscow, overground transport is more useful in the centre than the fast **metro** network (6am–midnight). Choose from **trams**, **buses** and **trolleybuses** (tickets from the conductor), or the efficient commercial **minibuses** (tickets from the driver). **Taxis** and **private cars** operate in the same way as in Moscow; see p.883 for further details. One of the best ways to see St Petersburg May to October is by **boat** – either a private motorboat from any bridge on Nevskiy prospekt (from $50/hr), or a large tour boat by the Anichkov Bridge ($5). Remember that May to October all bridges across the Neva are raised between 2am and 5am – a beautiful sight which draws crowds to watch, but can be inconvenient if you are on the wrong side of the river.

Accommodation

As with Moscow, the range of **accommodation** in St Petersburg is rather limited. Centrally located **hotels** are few in number and expensive. Just a little further out, there are some pleasant and inexpensive options, but **hostels** offer the best alternative: they're reasonably central and have decent facilities, and there's no age restriction. Travellers on a tight budget might also consider **bed and breakfast** accommodation with families, which can be arranged with the well-established agencies *HOFA* (☎812/275 1992, @Russianstay@yahoo.com) and NotaBene (@homestays@nb.spb.su); they can also help plan onward travel in Russia and the CIS. OstWest (☎812/ 327 3416, @www.ostwest.com) will book more or less any kind of accommodation, plus tours and onward travel. For a small group of people it might work out cheaper to rent an **apartment** for several days: try BedandBreakfast (☎812/315 1917, @travelspb@hotmail.com) or Pulford Estates (☎812/325 6277, @www.pulford.com). Note that accommodation will be at a premium in 2003 owing to the three hundredth anniversary celebrations, so booking well in advance is strongly recommended.

Hostels

Bolshoy Teatr Kukol ul. Nekrasov 12 ☎812/273 3996; Chernyshevskaya metro. Although technically a hotel, the level is pretty basic, but it has all you need and the location is unbeatable. No visa support. **❶**

Health Hostel pr. Lunacharskogo 41 ☎812/559 9685; Ozerki metro. Not central, but cheap, clean and reliable, and the air's good out here in the suburbs. **❸**

Herzen University Hostel Kazanskaya ul. 6 ☎812/314 7472; Nevskiy Prospekt/Gostiniy Dvor metro. Great location, just behind the Kazan Cathedral off Nevskiy prospekt, with decent facilities, including a solarium and masseur. No visa support. **❹**

Hostel Holiday Mikhaylova ul. 1 ☎812/327 1070, @www.hostel.ru; Ploshchad Lenina metro. Good, large, busy hostel with full range of services, including email and internet access; some rooms overlook the River Neva. **❸**

St Petersburg International Hostel 3-ya Sovetskaya ul. 28 ☎812/329 8018, @www.ryh.ru; Ploshchad Vosstaniya metro. The independent traveller's dream. Book ahead. Can provide invitations even if you are not intending to stay in the hostel. Has attached student travel agency, Sindbad. **❸**

Hotels

Mir ul. Gastello 17 ☎812/108 49 10; Moskovskaya metro. Clean, modest and very efficient, not central but convenient for the metro. No credit cards. **⑤**

Neva Chaykovskovo ul. 17 ☎812/278 0504; Chernyshevskaya metro. Old-fashioned, even quaint, and just a hop away from the Summer Garden. **⑤**

Oktyabrskaya Ligovskiy pr. 10 ☎812/277 63 30, ⊛hotel@spb.cityline.ru; Ploshchad Vosstaniya/Mayakovskaya metro. Nineteenth-century warren – with gloomy service but an indefinable charm – overlooking Moscow Station. Ask for an "upgraded room" – the plumbing is better. **⑥**

Rossiya Chernyshevskogo pl. 11 ☎812/329 3909; Park Pobedy metro. Average everything, a frequent choice for the budget-oriented. **④**

Sovetskaya Lermontovskiy pr. 43/1 ☎812/329 0000, ⊛www.sovetskaya.com; Tekhnologicheskiy Institut metro. Modern hotel offering excellent views of the River Fontanka. **⑦**

Campsites

Olgino Camping Primorskoe shossee 59 ☎812/238 3671; bus or local train to Olgino. The air is fresh, the pine forest healthy, the Gulf of Finland not far away. Perfect for summer. **③**

The City

Everything in St Petersburg is built on a grand scale. The city is split by the **River Neva** and its tributaries, with further sections delineated by the course of the canalized Moyka and Fontanka rivers, all of which conveniently divide St Petersburg into a series of islands, making it fairly easy to get your bearings. St Petersburg's centre lies on the south bank of the Neva, with the curving **River Fontanka** marking its southern boundary. The area within the **Fontanka** is riven by a series of wide avenues which fan out from the most obvious landmark on the south bank of the Neva, the Admiralty. Many of the city's greatest sights and monuments – the Hermitage, the Russian Museum, the Mikhail Castle, the Summer Garden and the St Isaac and Kazan cathedrals – are located on and around **Nevskiy prospekt**, the main avenue.

Across the River Neva is **Vasilevskiy Island**, the largest of the city's islands. In an area known as the **Strelka**, located on the island's eastern tip, are some of St Petersburg's oldest institutions: the Academies of Arts and Sciences, the University and the former Stock Exchange, as well as some fascinating museums.

On the north side of the River Neva, opposite the Winter Palace, is the island known as the Petrograd Side, home to the **Peter and Paul Fortress**, whose construction is seen as marking the foundation of the city itself. As well as its strategic and military purpose, it also housed St Petersburg's first prison and cathedral.

Back on the mainland, east of the River Fontanka, the conventional sights are more dispersed, the two most popular destinations being the **Smolniy**, from where the Bolsheviks orchestrated the October Revolution, and the **Alexander Nevsky Monastery**.

Nevskiy prospekt

Stretching from the Alexander Nevsky Monastery to Palace Square and the Hermitage, **Nevskiy prospekt** has been the backbone and heart of the city for the last three centuries. Built on an epic scale during the reign of Peter the Great, under the direction of the Frenchman Jean-Baptiste Le Blond, it manifests every style of architecture from eighteenth-century Baroque to 1950s Stalinist Classicism, and is home to the city's main sights.

Near the striking Dom Knigi bookshop, former emporium of the Singer sewing-machine company, is **Kazan Cathedral**, built betwen 1801 and 1811 (services daily 9am & 6pm), one of the city's grandest churches, modelled on St Peter's in the Vatican. The cathedral was built to house the venerated icon, Our Lady of Kazan, reputed to have appeared miraculously overnight in Kazan in 1579, and transferred by Peter the Great to St Petersburg, where it resided until its disappearance in 1904. In Soviet times the cathedral housed the Museum of Religion and Atheism.

The Winter Palace

The two-hundred-metre long **Winter Palace** (1762), at the westernmost end of Nevskiy prospekt on the Neva embankment, is the finest example of Russian Baroque in St Petersburg, the largest, most opulent palace within the city. As loaded with history as it is with gilt and stucco, the palace was the official residence of the tsars, not to mention the court and 1500 servants. The main building was finished in 1762 and later new buildings were added to the east: the **Small** and **Large Hermitages** were added by Catherine the Great to enable her to be alone with her friends and her paintings, while the **New Hermitage** (now the Hermitage museum) was launched as Russia's first public art museum in 1852. Beyond stands the **Hermitage Theatre**, Catherine the Great's private theatre, now used for concerts, ballet and conferences.

The Hermitage

The **Hermitage** (Tues–Sun 10.30am–5pm; ⊛www.hermitagemuseum.org; $10) is one of the world's greatest museums. Of awesome size and diversity, it embraces some three million objects, everything from ancient Scythian gold and Kyoto woodcuts to Cubism.

The **Italian art** section has works by Leonardo, Botticelli, Michelangelo, Raphael, Titian, Veronese and Tiepolo; the **Dutch and Flemish art** collection features magnificent selections of paintings by Rembrandt, Rubens and Van Dyck; and there is an impressive collection of seventeenth- and eighteenth-century **French art**. After the state rooms and the Gold Collection, the most universally popular section of the Hermitage is that covering **modern European art** from the nineteenth and twentieth centuries, with a fine spread of Impressionist paintings and works by Matisse and Picasso. Look out, too, for the work of Rodin, Gauguin, Van Gogh, Henri Rousseau, Delacroix, Cézanne, Pissarro, Monet, Degas and Renoir. Paintings by Bonnard and Denis are on display in the museum annexe housed in the majestically curving General Staff Building on the other side of Palace Square.

North of Nevskiy prospekt

Visible from Nevskiy prospekt is the multicoloured, onion-domed **Church on Spilled Blood** (11am–7pm; closed Wed; $8), begun in 1882 to commemorate Tsar Alexander II, who had been assassinated on the site the previous year. Designed in pseudo-traditional Russian style, stuffed full of thousands of metres of mosaics, it is one of St Petersburg's most striking landmarks, quite unlike the city's dominant neoclassical architecture.

East of the church stands the vast **Mikhail Palace**, housing the Russian Museum, its long facade dominating Ploshchad Iskusstv, a neoclassical, harmonious public space lined with museums, theatres and concert halls.

The Russian Museum

The **Russian Museum** contains the finest collection of Russian art in the world. On the **upper floor** are icons and paintings from the fourteenth to nineteenth centuries, including works by Russia's greatest icon painter, the monk Andrei Rublev (c.1340–1430). The **lower floor** demonstrates how Russian art came of age in the late nineteenth century. Highlights are the vast historical canvases of Vasiliy Surikov (1846–1916) and the socially conscious realism of Ilya Repin (1844–1930). A corridor leads from room 48 to the **Benois Wing**, which, as well as housing temporary exhibitions, presents the movements of the early twentieth century, from Symbolism to Analytical Art. Disappointingly, despite the museum's vast holdings, there are only ever a few paintings by the artists of the avant-garde, such as Kazimir Malevich (1878–1935), on display. The Benois Wing also has its own entrance off Griboyedov Canal.

The Mikhail castle and Marsovo Pole

Moving north up Sadovaya ulitsa, you'll come across the idiosyncratic and heavily fortified **Mikhail Castle**, built by Paul I in 1801 shortly after he came to the throne, to protect him from the assassination attempt he feared. However, his precautions were all to no avail: he was murdered in his bedroom there just three weeks after moving in. Now a branch of the Russian Museum (same hours), the castle is due to reopen in 2003 after major work to reconstruct the original defensive moats. The **Mikhail Garden** next door (behind the Russian Museum) is much loved by St Petersburgers for its truly relaxed atmosphere.

Between the River Moyka and the Neva embankment, **Marsovo pole** (Field of Mars), with its Eternal Flame at the centre, is heavy with the scent of lilac in spring. At its northwestern corner stands the **Marble Palace**, designed by Antonio Rinaldi for Catherine the Great's lover, Count Orlov. Another annexe of the Russian Museum (same hours; $4), it displays works by foreign artists living in Russia in the eighteenth and nineteenth centuries and contemporary art.

The Summer Garden and palace

East of Marsovo pole is the **Summer Garden** (daily 8/11am–6/10pm; small admission fee in summer), the city's most treasured public garden, commissioned by Peter the Great in 1704. The Frenchman, Le Blond, was to design a formal garden in the style of Versailles, with numerous marble statues and fountains. However, after the disastrous flood of 1777, which wrecked the garden, Catherine the Great ordered its reconstruction in the less formal, less spectacular English style that survives today. In the northeastern corner, Domenico Trezzini erected a **Summer Palace** (May–Nov 11am–7pm, closed Tues; $3) for Peter the Great in 1710; it's a modest two-storey building of brick and stucco – one of the first such structures in the city.

Southwest of Nevskiy prospekt

The **Admiralty** standing at the western end of Nevskiy prospekt is one of the world's most magnificent expressions of naval triumphalism, extending 407m (1300ft) along the waterfront, from Palace Square (Dvortsovaya ploshchad) to Decembrists' Square (ploshchad Dekabristov). Originally founded by Peter the Great in 1704 as a fortified shipyard, with a primitive wooden tower and spire, the Admiralty gradually became purely administrative in function and a suitable building was erected in the early 1820s. Today, the key feature of the building is still its central tower (72.5m high), culminating in a slender spire.

Largely obscuring the Admiralty, the wooded **Admiralty Garden** leads towards Decembrists' Square. The square is named after a group of reformist officers who, in December 1825, marched three thousand soldiers into the square in an attempt to proclaim a constitutional monarchy. Farce turned to tragedy when Tsar Nicholas I ordered his loyalist troops to attack and crush the rebellion. Today the square is dominated by the **Bronze Horseman**, Falconet's renowned statue of Peter the Great and the city's unofficial symbol. The square is also popular with newlyweds, who traditionally come here to be photographed.

Looming majestically above the square, **St Isaac's Cathedral** (11am–7pm, colonnade till 5pm; closed Wed; $8, colonnade $3) is one of the glories of St Petersburg's skyline. Its gilded dome is the third largest in Europe. The opulent interior is equally impressive, decorated with fourteen kinds of marble. The cathedral's height (101.5m) and rooftop statues are best appreciated by climbing the 262 steps to the outside colonnade.

More intimate in mood is the **St Nicholas Cathedral**, to the south near Theatre Square (Teatralnaya ploshchad). Traditionally the church of naval officers, it is a lovely example of eighteenth-century Russian Baroque – painted ice blue with white Corinthian pilasters, crowned with five gilded onion domes. Its low, vaulted interior is festooned with icons, and during services (6pm) the cathedral resounds with the sonorous Orthodox liturgy, chanted and sung amid clouds of incense.

Vasilevskiy Island

Buffeted by storms from the Gulf of Finland, pear-shaped **Vasilevskiy Island** (Vasilevskiy ostrov) cleaves the River Neva into its Bolshaya and Malaya branches. The island forms a strategic wedge, whose eastern "spit", or **Strelka**, is as much a part of St Petersburg's waterfront as the Winter Palace or Admiralty. Originally, Peter envisaged making the island the centre of his capital, compelling rich landowners and merchants to settle here. By 1726 the island had ten streets and over a thousand inhabitants, but wilderness still predominated and there were no bridges: the hazardous crossing by boat destroyed any hope of the island becoming the centre.

Although you can reach the Strelka by trolleybus (#1, #7 and #10), bus (#7) or numerous expresses (including #47, #T128, #T129) from Nevskiy prospekt, it's better to walk across **Dvortsoviy most** (Palace Bridge), which offers fabulous views of both banks of the Neva (all richly illuminated at night). On the Strelka are the weird **Rostral Columns** and Classical **Stock Exchange** building (now housing the Naval Museum), an ensemble created at the beginning of the nineteenth century by Thomas de Thomon, who also designed the granite embankments and cobbled ramps leading down to the Neva – reminders that the city's port and commercial centre were once located here.

Facing Dvortsoviy most is the **Zoological Museum** (11am–6pm, closed Fri; $1). It was founded in 1832 and has one of the finest collections of its kind in the world, with over one hundred thousand specimens, including a set of stuffed animals that once belonged to Peter the Great and a 44,000-year-old mammoth found in the permafrost of Yakutia in 1903. Even more alluring – or repulsive – is the **Kunstkammer** (11am–6pm, closed Mon; $4), founded by Peter in 1714. Its name (meaning "art chamber" in German) dignified Peter's fascination for curiosities and freaks: he offered rewards for "human monsters" and unknown birds and animals, which were preserved in vinegar or vodka. To attract visitors, each received a glass of vodka or a cup of coffee.

The Peter and Paul Fortress

Across the Neva from the Winter Palace, on a small island, stands the **Peter and Paul Fortress**, built to secure Russia's hold on the Neva delta. Forced labourers toiled from dawn to dusk to construct the fortress in just seven months. The day of its foundation, 27 May 1703, is considered to mark the founding of the city. Its anniversary in 2003 is set to be the high point of the city's celebration of its three hundred years.

The fortress is permanently open – with no admission charge – but its **cathedral** and numerous **museums** (covering the history of the city and Russian life) keep regular visiting hours (11am–6pm, closed Wed) and require tickets (around $5 for all the museums). The midday gun which is fired daily from the roof resounds across the city centre, making windows shake and setting off nearby car alarms.

The Dutch-style **Peter and Paul Cathedral**, completed in 1733, remained the tallest structure (122m) in the city until the 1960s. Sited around the nave are the tombs of the Romanov monarchs from Peter the Great onwards – excluding Peter II, Ivan VI and Nicholas II. Nicholas and his family, whose bones were discovered in a mine shaft in the Urals in 1989, were finally buried in a chapel beside the cathedral in July 1998.

Nestling in a bend of the River Neva, northeast of Nevskiy prospekt, lies the quiet **Smolniy district**, whose sleepy streets lined with nineteenth-century apartment blocks belie the area's turbulent historic past. Lenin ran the Revolution from the Smolniy Institute, and for the 74 years of Communist rule, the word "Smolniy" was synonymous with the Revolution and the Party.

Towering on the eastern horizon, at the heart of the district, is the glorious ice-blue cathedral, the focal point and architectural masterpiece of the former **Smolniy**

Convent, founded in the eighteenth century by the Empress Elizabeth. Rastrelli's grandiose Rococo plans – including a 140-metre-high bell tower, which would have been the tallest structure in the city – were never completed, and the building was only finished in 1835 by Stasov in a more restrained neoclassical fashion. The cathedral's austere white interior (10am–5pm, closed Thurs) is disappointingly severe and is used to host temporary exhibitions and concerts. The **Smolniy Institute**, now the Governor's Headquarters, was built in 1806–08 to house the Institute for Young Noblewomen, but it's best known as the headquarters of the Petrograd Soviet, which was installed here from August 1917 until March 1918, when the city's vulnerability in the Civil War impelled the government to move to Moscow.

Alexander Nevsky Monastery

At the southeastern end of Nevskiy prospekt lies the **Alexander Nevsky Monastery**, founded in 1713 by Peter the Great. From 1797 it became one of only four monasteries in the Russian Empire to be given the title of *lavra*, the highest rank in Orthodox monasticism.

There are two main cemeteries within the monastery. The most famous names reside in the **Tikhvin Cemetery**, also known as Necropolis for Masters of the Arts: here lie Dostoyevsky, Rimsky-Korsakov, Tchaikovsky, Rubinstein and Glinka. Directly opposite is the smaller **Lazarus Cemetery** (Necropolis of the Eighteenth Century), the oldest in the city. **Tickets** are required for entry to both cemeteries (10.30am–4/6pm, closed Thurs; $2), and foreigners are increasingly asked to make a "contribution" before entering the monastery proper. To reach the **monastery** (daily dawn to dusk), continue along the walled path past Trezzini's **Church of the Annunciation** (11am–5pm, closed Mon & Thurs; $2), the original burial place of Peter III, Catherine the Great's deposed husband. Trezzini also drew up an ambitious design for the monastery's **Trinity Cathedral**, but failed to orientate it towards the east, as Orthodox custom required, so the plans were scrapped. The job was left to Ivan Starov, who completed a more modest building in a neoclassical style which now sits awkwardly with the rest of the complex.

Round the back of the cathedral the **Nicholas Cemetery**, an overgrown graveyard where the monastery's scholars and priests, nobles and intellectuals are buried, has become a "fashionable" burial place once more, partly since Galina Starovoitova, reformer and liberal politician, was buried here in 1998.

Eating and drinking

In recent years a growing number of more modestly priced, intimate establishments have opened up in St Petersburg, serving good food and offering a better feel of local life than those aiming to imitate Western stereotypes and prices. The selection offered here are mentioned either for their convenient location or for outstanding food.

Cafés and bars

BBC Sadovaya ul. 12; Gostiniy Dvor metro. Cheap and cheerful café where you're likely to be the only foreigners.

Cynic Goncharnaya ul. 4; Moskovkiy vokzal metro. Grungy student crowds overflow onto the street. Unpredictable, but can be fun.

Green Crest Salad Bar Vladimirskiy pr. 7; Vladimirskaya/Dostoevskaya metro. Salads, salads and more salads – good healthy eating.

Idiot nab. reki Moyki 82; trolleybus #5 or #22, minibus 190 or 169 from Nevskiy prospekt.

Vegetarian bar with books and board games, stuffed with foreigners and social-climbing Russians.

Krokodil Galernaya ul. 181; trolleybus #5 or #22, minibus 190 or 169 from Nevskiy prospekt. Café for the in-crowd, with some performances – anything from jazz to performance art. Original menu, all fresh food. It's particularly good at lunchtime.

Layma nab. kanala Griboedova 16; Gostiniy Dvor/Nevskiy Prospekt metro. Excellent fast food, including steaks and salads, plus beer; great for late, late suppers. Open 24hr.

Minutka Nevskiy pr. 20; Gostiniy Dvor/Nevskiy Prospekt metro. American-style sandwich and salad bar.

Mukha Tsokotukha Solyanoy per. 14; Chernyshevskaya metro. Armenian cuisine, transforms into a mellow jazz club in the evening, with small cover charge.

Russkie bliny ul. Furmanova 13. Ornate, cosy, very popular and cheap lunchtime spot, off Liteyniy prospekt. Traditional Russian pancakes, both savoury and sweet.

Sunduk Art Cafe Furshtatskaya ul. 42; Chernyshevskaya metro. Great food and cocktails, live jazz most evenings (small cover charge), comfortable decor.

Staroe Kafe nab. reki Fontanki 108; Tekhnologicheskiy Institut metro. Tiny, cosy café with traditional Russian food and great pianist.

Vegetarian Bistro Vladimirsky pr. 1; Vladimirskaya/ Dosotevskaya metro. Dead cheap, two steps off Nevskiy prospekt, and darn tasty it all is too.

Restaurants

Demyanova Ukha Kronverkskiy pr. 53 ☏ 812/232 8090; Gorkovskaya metro. Serves fish and nothing else; a little touristy these days. Reservations essential.

Krunk Solyanoy per. 14; Chernyshevskaya metro or a 5min walk from Summer Garden. Armenian food and a friendly atmosphere, opposite the Stieglitz Art School.

Patio Pizza Nevskiy pr. 30 ☏ 812/271 3177; Gostiniy Dvor/Nevskiy Prospekt metro. Best salad bar in town.

Rioni Shpalernaya ul. 24 ☏ 812/273 3261. Excellent Georgian food, tucked away up a side alley. Order lots of different *zakuski*!

Nightlife and entertainment

St Petersburg offers plenty of potential for a wild night out. It has a wide range of **clubs** – from just plain tacky to the spartan underground atmosphere of warehouse clubs. For Russians, the city is associated with several home-grown legendary bands and is the most hip place in the country – a sort of Russian Manchester or Seattle.

St Petersburg also has a wide variety of cultural events, such as **classical concerts**, **ballet** and **opera**. For ballet, it's best to avoid performances in the Hermitage Theatre or at the Mussorgsky Theatre and stick to the Mariinskiy (former Kirov). For details of what's happening, check the listings in the free English-language papers: the Friday edition of *The St Petersburg Times* (excellent club reviews) and *Pulse*. The fullest listings in Russian are to be found in the weekly *Vash Dosug*.

Nightclubs and live music

Decadence Admiralteyskaya nab. 12; Nevskiy Prospekt metro. If you can get past the face control (are you beautiful enough?) you'll love both the jazz/blues and the food.

Front Chernyakhovskovo ul. 31; Ligovskiy prospekt metro. In an underground bunker, with rock and alternative acts.

Griboedov Voronezhskaya ul. 2a; Ligovskiy Prospekt metro. Still the coolest of cool dance clubs, in a former bomb shelter.

Fish Fabrique Pushkinskaya ul. 10 (entrance from Ligovskiy pr. 53); Mayakovskovo metro. Café club at the heart of the city's famous artists' colony.

JFC Jazz Club Shpalernaya ul. 33; Chernyshevskaya metro. The city's most exciting jazz programme. Tucked away in a courtyard.

Jimi Hendrix Liteynyy pr. 33; Chernyshevskaya metro. Some of the bands are really bad, but most aren't – the food's good too. Open 24hr.

Moloko Perekupnoy per. 12; Ploshchad Aleksandra Nevskovo metro. Underground rock club with a reputation for discovering great acts.

Money Honey Saloon Apraksin Dvor 14 (in yard); Gostiniy Dvor/Nevskiy Prospekt metro. Russian rockabilly, cheap beer, always packed; don't forget the leather jacket and quiff.

Tunnel bunker on corner of Lyubanskiy per. And Zverinskaya ul.; Gorkovskaya metro. The home of techno and electronic dance music. Fri & Sat only.

Classical, opera and ballet

Mariinskiy (former Kirov) Theatre Teatralnaya pl. 1 ☏ 812/114 5264. Foreigners will pay $50 upwards for seats in the stalls but seats are available in the gods for $5. Performances at 7pm with Sunday matinées at noon. Note that the company goes on tour July to Sept, and any performances then will likely be by the D-team.

Shostakovich Philharmonia Mikhaylovskaya ul. 2 ☏ 812/311 7333; Nevskiy Prospekt metro. Draws international classical musicians as well as Russia's best. Performances at 7pm.

Listings

Consulates Canada, Malodetskoselsky pr. 32
☏812/325 8448; UK, pl. Proletarskoy diktatury 5
☏812/320 3200; US, Furshtadtskaya ul. 15
☏812/275 1701.

Emergencies International Clinic, Dostoevskovo
ul. 19/21 ☏812/320 3870; Euromed, Suvorovskiy
pr. 60 ☏812/327 0301; American Medical Centre,
Serpukhovskaya ul. 10 ☏812/326 1730. All open
24hr and recognized by international insurance
companies.

Exchange Best ATM machine (24hr) at Sberbank,
Dumskaya ul. 3.

Internet access Quo Vadis, Nevskiy pr. 24 (24hr),
or Westpost at Nevskiy pr. 86.

Laundry Laundromat, 11ya liniya 46
(Vasilievostrovskaya metro).

Pharmacy Petropharm, at Nevskiy pr. 22 (24hr).
Other branches at nos. 50, 66 & 83.

Post office Pochtamskaya ul. 9, just off St Isaac's
Square. Express letter post: Westpost, Nevskiy pr.
86 ☏812/327 3092. Letters can be sent abroad
via Finnish post at the service desk of the *Grand
Hotel Europe*.

Around St Petersburg

There are five imperial summer palaces set in rich parks just outside St Petersburg.
In summer, most visitors opt for **Peterhof**, 29km west of the city, renowned for its
fountains, while in winter **Pavlovsk** and **Tsarskoye Selo** are more striking. Little-
visited **Oranienbaum** is also rewarding. For a view of Old Russia, go to
Novgorod, 190km south; this is the archetypal medieval Russian city. All are easily
accessible by public transport and make perfect day-trips.

Peterhof

First of the great palatial ensembles to be founded outside St Petersburg, **Peterhof**
embodies nearly three hundred years of tsarist self-aggrandisement. It was started
by Peter the Great and completed under the reign of Empress Elizabeth
(1741–1761).

The yellow, white and gold **Great Palace** (10.30am–5pm, closed Mon; $9) is
impressive but cold, far removed from the palace originally designed by Le Blond
(1714–1721), but despite later additions, there's a superb cohesion at work, a tribute
to both the vision of the palace's creators and the skills of the craftsmen who rebuilt
Peterhof from its ashes after World War II.

Peterhof's chief attraction, however, is the **Lower Park** ($6), with its famous
fountains (late-May to late-Sept), among them the Grand Cascade, which drops
down to the sea, and joke fountains which spout water on (supposedly) unsuspect-
ing passers-by.

Finding the Great Palace "unbearable", Empress Aleksandra Fyodorovna pressed
Nicholas I to build a home suited to a cosier, bourgeois lifestyle: the resulting neo-
gothic **Cottage Palace** (May–Oct daily except Fri 10am–5pm; Oct–April Sat &
Sun 10am–5pm; $5) is definitely worth the fifteen-minute walk through the over-
grown Alexandria Park.

In summer the best way to get here is by **hydrofoil** ($5 each way) from outside
the Winter Palace (hourly 9.30am–5pm). Alternatively, take one of the frequent
minibuses from Avtovo metro station (50¢). The best place for **lunch** is at the tiny
Trapeza, just outside the east entrance to the park and palace.

Oranienbaum

A bus or minibus from Peterhof will take you on to **Oranienbaum** (May–Oct
daily except Tues 11am–5pm), stopping by the northeast corner of the park. The
only one of the suburban palaces not destroyed during the German occupation, it is
– most undeservedly – the least visited of them all. Hugely overgrown, in summer
the place vibrates with the drone of dragonflies and bees, rarely disturbed by the
coach parties which throng to all the other summer palaces. Visit the **Chinese
Palace** (same times; $7), Rinaldi's magnificent little Rococo masterpiece, each

RUSSIA | St Petersburg

24

room exquisitely decorated – in one, the walls are stitched with tiny glass beads – and then cut across the park to the **Sliding Hill** (same times; $5), the elegant remains of an eighteenth-century roller-coaster. There's nowhere to eat, so you'll need to bring a picnic.

Tsarskoe Selo

Tsarskoe Selo (also known as Pushkin), 17km southeast of St Petersburg, was Catherine the Great's favourite summer residence. The palace is a dauntingly vast blue and white Baroque structure, set in a richly landscaped park, which is popular with locals all year round. Frequent **minibuses** (50¢) run from Moskovskaya metro station and stop near the palace.

Catherine the Great hated the Baroque **palace** (10am–5pm, closed Tues; $10) and immediately got Scottish architect Charles Cameron to design neoclassical private apartments, the rich Agate Rooms (a bathhouse-cum-summer pavilion) and the supremely elegant Cameron Gallery, stretching high above the park. In 1775, she installed the famous **Amber Room**: stolen by the Germans during the war, the amber panels have fascinated scholars and amateurs, who regularly argue as to whether they were destroyed or still lie buried in some unknown location. Meanwhile, the Amber Room is being re-created for St Petersburg's three-hundredth anniversary.

Pavlovsk

Just beyond Tsarskoe Selo lies the neoclassical **Pavlovsk** (same minibuses as for Tsarskoe Selo). Its **Great Palace** (10am–5pm, closed Fri; $8) is a monument to the taste and habits of Paul I's wife Maria Fyodorovna. Light, airy, and feminine, the palace is renowned for its collection of eighteenth-century furniture and interior fittings. Pavlovsk **park** is perhaps the most beloved of all the parks around the city by St Petersburg's inhabitants, who walk here and feed the squirrels in summer, and ski through the grounds in winter.

Novgorod

Despite its name, **NOVGOROD** ("New Town") is one of Russia's oldest cities, founded, according to popular belief, by Prince Rurik in 862 AD. Excursion **buses** run from beside the portico on Nevskiy prospekt 33 (tickets from kiosk; $4), although the tours are in Russian only. For information on all museums in Novgorod, check out the site ⓦwww.novgorod-museum.ru. Between the twelfth and fifteenth century Novgorod's republican-minded nobles bestowed a fantastic architectural legacy upon the town, including a Kremlin (a fortified inner city), Russia's oldest cathedral and numerous onion-domed stone churches. The impressive, nine-metre-high, red-brick walls of the **Kremlin** date from the fifteenth century, when they formed the inner ring of an entire series of fortifications. As many as eighteen churches and 150 houses were once crammed inside these walls. The Kremlin's main landmark is **St Sophia's Cathedral** (Sofiyskiy sobor), the city's earliest and largest cathedral by far, its five bulbous domes clustered around a slightly raised, golden helmet dome. The cathedral now doubles as a working **church** and **museum** (10am–6pm, closed Tues; there may be an entry charge). Inside, the well-preserved iconostasis is one of the oldest in Russia and includes works from the eleventh to seventeenth centuries.

From the riverbank on the east side of the Kremlin, there's a great view of the **Commercial Side**, site of Novgorod's medieval market. All that remains now is a long section of the old seventeenth-century arcade. Immediately behind the arcade, where the palace of Yaroslav the Wise once stood, is a grassy area still known as **Yaroslav's Court**. Its most important surviving building is the **Cathedral of St Nicholas** (10am–6pm, closed Tues), built in 1113 in a Byzantine style that was a deliberate challenge to St Sophia's.

All that survives of the **Yuryev Monastery**, founded by Prince Vsevolod in 1117, is the majestic **Cathedral of St George**, which was built by a "Master Peter", renowned as the first truly Russian architect, and which is one of the last great churches to be built by the Novgorod princes. Inside, some twelfth-century frescoes survive, but most date from the nineteenth century. The cathedral has been rapidly restored in recent years and the monastery revived – you should dress accordingly (covered head and no trousers for women). In the woods nearby is the Vitoslavitsy **Outdoor Museum of Wooden Architecture** (10am–4/6pm; closed Wed; $4), an inspiring collection of timber constructions, including two churches and several peasant houses, some dating back to the sixteenth century. The best place to **eat** is the excellent little café, the *Detinets*, in the Pokrov Tower of the Kremlin.

Slovakia

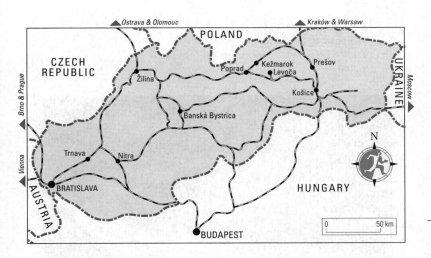

Slovakia highlights

* **High Tatras** These jagged, granite peaks – the most spectacular mountains in Slovakia – rise up dramatically from the Poprad plain. **See p.917**

* **Levoča** Attractive walled medieval town, originally settled by Saxons. **See p.919**

* **Spišský hrad** This sprawling medieval castle is the most stunning hilltop ruin in Slovakia. **See p.920**

Introduction and basics

The republic of **Slovakia** – independent since 1993 – consists of the long, narrow strip of land that stretches from the fertile plains of the Danube basin up to the peaks of the High Tatras – perhaps Europe's most exhilarating mountain range outside of the Alps. The country's numerous mountains have long formed barriers to industrialization and modernization, and parts of the country remain surprisingly rural and unspoilt, some to the point of neglect.

There was only one independent Slovak state before 1993 – when the Slovaks split from the Czechs in 1938, forming an independent state allied to Nazi Germany, a period in the nation's **history** that remains contentious even today. Before 1918, current-day Slovakia was known as Upper Hungary and lay under Magyar rule for roughly a millennium; Bratislava even became the Hungarian capital when the rest of Hungary was occupied by the Turks. In 1918, however, the Slovaks threw their lot in with their Slav neighbours, the Czechs, forming **Czechoslovakia**. This lasted 75 years until the country's "velvet divorce" took place in 1993. Although many Slovaks were ready to go it alone, it has to be said that others had major reservations about this, and none was given the chance to decide in a referendum. Political corruption, nationalism and slow-moving reforms put off overseas investors until a change of government in 1998, since when the country's economic prospects under Prime Minister Dzurinda have brightened and firm steps towards joining the European Union have begun.

For the first-time visitor, perhaps the most striking cultural difference from the Czechs is the Slovak attitude to religion. **Catholicism** is much stronger here than in the Czech Republic, and the churches are often full to overflowing on Sundays. The republic also has a more diverse population, with over half a million ethnic **Hungarians** in the south, as well as thousands of Romanies (Gypsies), who live a fairly miserable existence throughout the country, and several thousand Ruthenians (Rusyns) in the east. **Bratislava**, the capital, is disappointing for those who arrive expecting a Slovak Prague. Taken on its own terms, however, the city is a rewarding, lively place with a compact old town. **Poprad** provides the transport hub for the **High Tatras**, the most spectacular of Slovakia's many mountain ranges, and is also the starting point for exploring the intriguing medieval towns of the **Spiš** region, east Slovakia's architectural high point. Further east still, **Prešov** is the cultural centre of the Ruthenian minority, while **Košice**, Slovakia's vibrant second city, boasts a fine Gothic cathedral, ethnic diversity and a lively independence from much of the rest of Slovakia.

Information and maps

There's some kind of **tourist office** (*informačné centrum*) in just about every town in Slovakia. In summer they're generally open Mon–Fri 9am–6pm, Sat & Sun 9am–2pm; in winter they tend to be shut on Sundays and close an hour earlier on other days. Most tourist offices have English speakers.

Maps are available, often very cheaply, from bookshops and some hotels – ask for

SLOVAKIA | Basics

25

Slovakia on the net

ⓦ **www.slovakspectator.sk** Online version of Bratislava-based English-language weekly, with news, sport, weather and listings

ⓦ **www.tatry.sk** Excellent guide to the High Tatras, with plenty of info, travel and accommodation details; particularly good for walkers, climbers and skiers

ⓦ **www.sacr.sk** Official Slovak Tourist Board website with basic but useful information on the country

a *plán mesta* or *orientačná mapa* (both town plans). Bookshops sell a huge range of Autoatlases, and a specific booklet, *Autokempingy*, produced by the Slovak tourist board, detailing routes, campsites, petrol stations, border crossings and even sites of historic interest. For hiking, the VNÚ's 1:50,000 series details the country's complex network of footpaths.

Money and banks

The local currency is the **Slovak crown** or *Slovenská koruna* (abbreviated to Sk), which is divided into 100 heller or *halér* (abbreviated to h). Notes come in 20Sk, 50Sk, 100Sk, 200Sk, 500Sk, 1000Sk (less frequently 5000Sk) denominations; coins as 1Sk, 2Sk, 5Sk and 10Sk, plus 10h, 20h, 50h. At the time of going to press there were around 70Sk to the pound sterling, 45Sk to the euro and around 50Sk to the US dollar. The Slovak crown is not fully convertible, which theoretically means you can't buy any currency until you arrive in the country.

Travellers' cheques are no longer the cheapest nor the most convenient option for getting local currency, but they do offer safety against loss or theft. **Credit and debit cards** are more convenient, and can be used either in ATMs or over the counter. They are also accepted in most upmarket hotels and restaurants and some shops, though it's a good idea to keep at least some hard currency in **cash** for emergencies. Exchange offices (*zmenáreň*) can be found in all major hotels, travel agencies and department stores.

Communications

Most **post offices** (*pošta*) are open Mon–Fri 8am–5pm – you can also buy stamps (*známky*) from some tobacconists (*tabák*) and street kiosks. Poste restante services are available in major towns, but remember to write *Pošta 1* (the main office), followed by the name of the town.

Cheap local calls can be made from any **phone**, but for international calls it's best to use a card phone, for which you need to buy a telephone card (*telefonná karta*) from a tobacconist or post office. **Internet cafés** have appeared in the larger cities and towns; expect to pay 60–120Sk/hr.

Getting around

With two-thirds of the Slovak **train** network made up of single-track lines, services are predictably slow, but some of the journeys are worth it for the scenery alone. Travelling by **bus** is quicker and covers a more extensive network. In most cities the bus and train stations are neighbours, so you can easily check out both.

Trains

Slovak Railways (*Železnice Slovenskej republiky* or *ŽSR*) run two main types of service: *rýchlik* trains are the faster, stopping only at major towns; the *osobný vlak*, or local train, stops everywhere and averages about 30kmh. **Tickets** (*lístok*) for domestic journeys can be bought at the station (*stanica*) before or on the day of departure. Fares are cheap, but prices are slowly increasing, and supplements are payable on all EC trains, and occasionally for IC and Ex trains. ŽSR run reasonably priced sleepers (*lôžkový vozeň*) and couchettes (*ležadlový vozeň*), to and from a number of places – make sure you book as far in advance as possible and no later than six hours before departure. **EuroDomino** and **InterRail** passes are valid; **Eurail** passes require supplements.

Buses

Buses (*autobus*) are mostly run by the state bus company, *Slovenská automobilová doprava* or *SAD*. The usual practice is to buy your ticket from the driver – often the only option, since the ticket offices are often closed. If you can, it's a good idea to book your ticket in advance if you're travelling at the weekend or early in the morning on one of the main routes.

Accommodation

The **accommodation** situation is much better than it used to be, though it remains the most expensive aspect of travelling in Slovakia. There is no real network of hostels, though a few are now affiliated to Hostelling International and others come under CKM, the student travel agency (@www.ckm.sk). If you're travelling in July or August and want to save yourself hassle, it's always a good idea to arrange accommodation as far in advance as possible.

Hotels and private rooms

Some **hotels** have double pricing, with higher rates for foreigners, but a basic room for £6/$9 per head is not hard to find in any city outside Bratislava, though probably with an extra £1/$1.50 for breakfast. While the old state hotels and spa complexes are slowly being refurbished, their rooms are usually box-like and overpriced; the new hotels and pensions that have opened up, particularly in the more heavily touristed areas, are often a better bet and far better value for money. **Private rooms** are a good option in many towns – keep your eyes peeled for signs saying *Zimmer Frei*. Prices start at around £5/$7.50 per person per night – only slightly below the cheaper hotel rates.

Hostels and campsites

Bratislava has a few private **hostels** which offer varying degrees of discomfort. Elsewhere, the student travel organization, CKM, or local tourist offices can give information on cheap **student accommodation** in the big university towns during July and August. In the High Tatras, in addition to panel-built spa accommodation, you can find a fair number of chalet-style **refuges** (*chata*) scattered about the hillsides. Some are little less than hotels and cost around £10/$15 a bed, less for the simpler, more isolated wooden shelters.

Campsites are plentiful all over Slovakia. Many of the sites feature simple **bungalows** (again, known as *chata*), often available for upwards of £5/$8 a bed. A few sites remain open all year round, but about half don't open until May, at the earliest, and close at the end of September. Even though prices are sometimes inflated for foreigners, costs are reasonable.

Food and drink

Slovak food is no-nonsense, filling fare and pretty similar to Czech cuisine, although traces of Hungarian, Polish and Ukrainian influences can be found in different regions.

Food

The usual mid-morning Slovak snack at the **bufet** (stand-up canteen) is *párek*, perhaps the most ubiquitous **takeaway food** in Central Europe, a hot frankfurter, dipped in mustard or horseradish and served inside a white roll. The Slovak national dish is *bryndzové halušky* – gnocchi with a thick sheep's cheese sauce and crumbled grilled bacon, but Hungarian influences are strong here, too. Goulash is very popular (although a mild stew rather than the authentic spicy soup), as are *langoše* – deep-fried dough smothered in a variety of toppings.

Most menus start with **soup** (*polievka*), one of the country's culinary strong points and served at both midday and evening meals. **Main courses** are overwhelmingly based on pork or beef, but trout and carp are usually featured somewhere on the menu and you may find catfish or pike-perch if you're lucky, and occasionally lamb. Most main courses are served with delicious potatoes (*zemiaky*) – but fresh salads or green vegetables are still a rarity in local restaurants. In addition to *palačinky* (cold pancakes) filled with chocolate, fruit and cream, Slovak **desserts** invariably feature apple or cottage-cheese strudel and ice cream.

In the last few years an increasing number of **restaurants** offering international cuisine have sprouted up, from the omnipresent fast-food joints and pizzerias to Bratislava's many Oriental eateries. **Opening times** have been extended too – though in outlying regions closing time will still be 9 or 10pm, the bigger cities have restaurants open till 11pm or later. Menus and prices are nearly always displayed outside.

Coffee (*káva*) is drunk black – espresso style in the big cities, but sometimes simply hot water poured over ground coffee in the smaller towns and villages (described rather hopefully as "Turkish" or *turecká*). The **cake shop** (*cukráreň*) is an important part of the country's social life, particularly on Sunday mornings when it's often the only place that's open in town. Whatever the season, Slovaks love to have their daily fix of **ice cream** (*zmrzlina*), available at *cukráreň* or dispensed from little window kiosks in the sides of buildings.

Drink

The vineyards in the south of Slovakia produce some pretty good medium-quality white **wines**, which share characteristics with their Hungarian and Austrian neighbours. The home production of brandies is a national pastime, resulting sometimes in almost terminally strong brews. The most famous is *slivovice*, a plum **brandy**, originally from the border hills between the Czech and Slovak Republics, but now available just about everywhere.

After more than seventy years of close association with the Czechs, the Slovaks have also learnt to love draught **beer**, but the *pivnica*, where most heavy drinking goes on, is still less common in Slovakia than in the Czech Republic. Slovaks tend to head instead for restaurants or **wine bars** (*vináreň*), which usually have slightly later opening hours and often double as nightclubs.

Opening hours and holidays

Opening hours for shops in Slovakia are Mon–Fri 9am–6pm, Sat 8am–noon, with some shops and most supermarkets staying open late. Smaller shops close for lunch for an hour or so sometime between noon and 2pm. Most shops are closed on Sunday, but supermarkets and out-of-town hypermarkets are open all day in large towns and cities.

The basic opening hours for **castles** and **monasteries** are Tues–Sun 9am–5pm, though last admission will be at least half an hour before closing. In April and October, opening hours are often restricted to weekends and holidays. From the end of October to the beginning of April, most castles are closed. When visiting a sight, always ask for an *anglický text*, an often unintentionally hilarious English resumé. In Bratislava the main **museums** open Tues–Fri 10am–5pm, Sat & Sun 11am–6pm, though there are exceptions. In winter, many museums close half an hour earlier than the times quoted in this guide. **Entrance tickets** for all sights rarely costs more than £1/$1.50 – hence no prices are quoted in the text.

Public holidays include Jan 1 (Independence Day); Jan 6 (Epiphany); Good Fri; Easter Mon; May 1; May 8; July 5 (SS Cyril and Methodius day); Aug 29 (Slovak National Uprising); Sept 1 (Constitution Day); Sept 15 (Our Lady of Sorrows); Nov 1; and Dec 24, 25 & 26.

Emergencies

There are two types of **police** (*polícia*): the state police, who wear the standard khaki-green uniforms that are a hangover from Communist days, and the local municipal or *mestská polícia*, who wear a variety of natty outfits depending on the fashion-consciousness of the local council. For tourists, theft from cars and hotel rooms is the biggest worry – the best way to protect yourself against such disasters is to take out travel insurance. If you are unlucky enough to have something stolen, report it immediately to the nearest police station in order to get a statement detailing what you've lost for your insurance claim. Everyone is obliged to carry some form of ID and you should carry your **passport** with you at all times, though realistically you're extremely unlikely to get stopped.

Minor ailments can be easily dealt with by the **pharmacist** (*lekáreň*), but language is likely to be a major problem. If it's a repeat prescription you want, take any empty bottles or remaining pills along with you. If the pharmacy can't help, they'll be able to direct you to a **hospital** (*nemocnica*). If you do have to pay for any medication, keep the receipts for claiming on your insurance once you're home.

Emergency numbers

Police ☎ 158; Ambulance/First Aid ☎ 155; Fire ☎ 150.

Bratislava

BRATISLAVA has two distinct sides: the old quarter is an attractive slice of Habsburg Baroque, while the rest of the city has the brash and butchered feel of the average East European metropolis. More buildings have been destroyed here since the war than were bombed out during it, the whole Jewish quarter having been bulldozed to make way for a colossal suspension bridge and highway. Yet, even though the multicultural atmosphere of the prewar days has gone, there is a certain Central European cosmopolitanism here, at the meeting of three nations.

Arrival, information and city transport

Most people flying into Bratislava simply use Vienna's **Schwechat Airport**, 45km away to the west, linked by a bus service (every 2hr) to the main bus station in Bratislava (payment in euros) – be sure to book your seat for the return journey as places sell out fast. Bratislava does have its own **M.R.Štefánik airport** (☎02/4857 3353), 14km northeast of the city centre; bus #61 goes to the main train station, or else you could catch the ČSA bus, which runs a shuttle service to and from the ČSA office on Štúrova 13, timed to coincide with the flight schedule.

A short distance north of the city centre is Bratislava's scruffy main **train station**, Bratislava-hlavná stanica, where most international and long-distance trains pull in. Once you've arrived, go down to the tram terminus below and, having bought your ticket from one of the machines on the platform, hop on tram #1 into town. Some trains, particularly those heading for destinations within west Slovakia, pass through Bratislava's Nové Mesto station, 4km northeast of the centre and linked by tram #6. **Buses** usually arrive at the main bus station, Bratislava autobusová stanica, on Mlynské nivy, fifteen minutes' walk east of the city centre; trolleybus #208 will take you across town to the main train station, while #217 will drop you on Hodžovo námestie. Bratislava's **tourist office**, BIS, is at Klobučnícka 2 (Mon–Fri 8am–4.30/7pm, Sat & Sun 8am–1pm; ☎54 43 37 15, ⑩www.bratislava.sk/bis); it's good for general queries and getting hold of a map and the monthly **listings magazine**, *Kam v Bratislave*; it also books accommodation (50Sk fee). There's an additional, smaller office in the main train station. For news and current affairs, plus a few **listings**, one publication worth getting is the weekly *Slovak Spectator* (⑩www.slovakspectator.sk), available from the tourist office and most downtown news kiosks and hotels.

The best way to see Bratislava is to walk – in fact it's the only way to see the pedestrianized old town, or staré mesto, where most of the sights are concentrated. However, if you're staying outside the city centre or visiting the suburbs, you'll need to make use of the city's inexpensive and comprehensive **transport system**. Buy your ticket (12Sk to the centre) beforehand (from newsagents, kiosks, hotel lobbies or ticket machines), validate it as soon as you get on, and use a fresh ticket each time you change; if you're going to use the system a lot, go to the small booth on the left outside the main entrance of the train station, near the bus departure points, for a one/two-day pass (70Sk/130Sk). **Night buses** congregate at námestie SNP, every quarter to the hour.

Accommodation

Bratislava's proximity to Vienna, and its capital-city status, mean that **hotels** are more expensive than anywhere else in the country. This makes **private rooms** the most popular option for most budget travellers – SATUR, Jesenského 3 (Mon–Fri 9am–6pm, Sat 9am–noon), and BIS, on Klobučnícka (see above), can book centrally located private rooms (①) for a small fee.

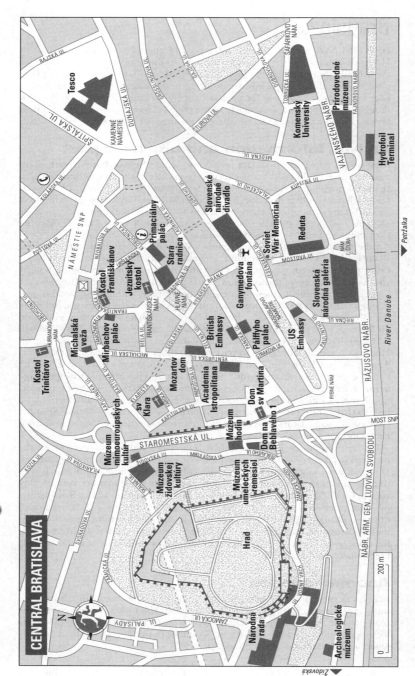

CENTRAL BRATISLAVA

Tesco

Kostol Trinitárov

Michalská veža

sv Klara

Mirbachov palác

Mozartov dom

Academia Istropolitana

Múzeum mimoeurópskych kultúr

Múzeum hodín

Dom sv Martina

Dom na Beblavého 1

Múzeum židovskej kultúry

Múzeum umeleckých remesiel

Hrad

Národná rada

Archeologické múzeum

Kostol Františkánov

Jezuitský kostol

Primaciálny palác

Stará radnica

British Embassy

Pálffyho palác

Ganymedova fontána

US Embassy

Slovenské národné divadlo

Soviet War Memorial

Reduta

Slovenská národná galéria

Komenský University

Prírodovedné múzeum

Hydrofoil Terminal

River Danube

Petržalka

Žilovská

NÁMESTIE SNP

STAROMESTSKÁ UL.

HLAVNÉ NÁM.

FRANTIŠKÁNSKE NÁM.

N

0   200 m

Hostels

Bernolák Bernolákova ☏02/5249 7724. The liveliest hostel in the city, only a short tram ride northeast of the centre. Own bar with regular discos and gigs. July & Aug only. Tram #7 or #11 from Kamenné námestie. ❶

Nešporák Svoradova 13 ☏02/5441 5386. Another bustling, youthful hostel; centrally located just two blocks north of the castle. July & Aug only. ❶

Spirit Vančurova 1 ☏t02/5477 7817, ⓦunivers.host.sk. Welcoming yet bizarre hostel-cum-hotel round the back of the railway station that also houses a school for psychics. ❸

Hotels and pensions

Arcus Moskovská 5 ☏02/5557 2522. Small pension within walking distance of the old town, just east of Americké námestie. Clean, quiet, comfortable and affordable. Take any tram heading up Špitalská from Kamenné námestie. ❹

Baronka Murdorchova 2 ☏02/4488 2089, ⓦwww.baronka.sk. Comfortable, refurbished hotel with swimming pool, fitness centre and restaurant, outside the city centre on tram #3. ❸

Clubhotel Odbojárov 3 ☏02/4425 6369. Drab but clean and with a decent restaurant, this is one of the city's few really inexpensive hotels. Located 3km northeast of the centre, but easily reached by tram #2 from the main train station and #4 or #6 from Kamenné námestie. ❷

Gremium Gorkého 11 ☏02/5413 1025. The only halfway decent, relatively inexpensive option in the old town. Clean, with extremely basic en-suite bathrooms, plus a great café on the ground floor. ❹

Rybársky cech Žižkova 1a ☏02/5441 8332. Pleasant rooms in an old fisherman's lodge by the busy road just below the Hrad, and, given its proximity to the old town, a bargain – although noisy thanks to passing trams. ❸

Campsites

Zlaté Piesky Intercamp ☏02/4445 7373, ⓦwww.intercamp.sk. Two fairly grim campsites, 8km northeast of the city centre, near the swimming lake of the same name. Bungalows on offer all year round; tents May–Sept only. Tram #2 from the main train station or #4 from town. All ❶

The City

Trams from the main train station offload their shoppers and sightseers behind the *Hotel Fórum* in Obchodná – literally Shop Street – which descends into Hurbanovo námestie, a busy junction on the northern edge of the old town (staré mesto). Here you'll find the hefty mass of the **Kostol trinitárov**, one of the city's finest churches, its exuberant trompe l'oeil frescoes creating a magnificent false cupola.

Opposite the church, a footbridge passes under a tower of the city's last remaining double gateway. Below is a small section of what used to be the city moat, now a garden belonging to the Baroque apothecary called *U červeného raka*, on your left between the towers, which now houses a **Pharmaceutical Museum** (Tues–Fri 10am–5pm, Sat & Sun 11am–6pm), displaying everything from seventeenth-century drug grinders to reconstructed period pharmacies. The second and taller of the towers is the **Michalská veža** (daily 10am–5pm), an evocative and impressive entrance to the old town and now a weapons museum.

Michalská and Ventúrska, which run into each other, have both been beautifully restored and are lined with some of Bratislava's finest Baroque palaces. There are usually plenty of students milling about amongst the shoppers, as the main university library is on this thoroughfare. The palaces of the Austro-Hungarian aristocracy continue into Panská, starting with the **Pálffy Palace**, at Panská 19, today an **art gallery** (Tues–Sun 10am–5/6pm), housing a patchy collection of Slovak paintings from the nineteenth and twentieth centuries.

A little northeast of here are the adjoining main squares of the old town – **Hlavné námestie** and **Františkánske námestie** – on the east side of which is the **Old Town Hall** (Tues–Sun 9.30am–4.30pm), a lively hotchpotch of Gothic, Renaissance and nineteenth-century styles containing the Municipal Museum – worth visiting if only for the medieval torture exhibition in the basement dungeons. The Counter-Reformation, which gripped the parts of Hungary not under Turkish occupation, issues forth from the square's **Jesuit Church**, whose best feature is its richly gilded pulpit. Diagonally opposite is the **Mirbach Palace** (Tues–Sun 10am–5pm), arguably the finest of Bratislava's Rococo buildings, preserving much of its original stucco decor. The permanent collection of Rococo and Baroque art and sculpture inside isn't up to much, save for the room of wall-to-wall miniatures set into the wood panelling.

Round the back of the Old Town Hall is the **Primaciálne námestie**, dominated by the neoclassical **Primate's Palace** (Tues–Sun 10am–5pm), whose pediment frieze is topped by a cast-iron cardinal's hat. The palace's main claim to fame is its Hall of Mirrors, where Napoleon and the Austrian emperor signed the Peace of Pressburg (as Bratislava was then called) in 1805. You can now visit this, and several other rooms hung with portraits of the Habsburgs and minor works by seventeenth-century Dutch and Italian masters.

From the Cathedral to the Castle

On the west side of the old town, the most insensitive of Bratislava's postwar developments took place. After the annihilation of the city's Jewish population by the Nazis, the Communist authorities tore down virtually the whole of the Jewish quarter in order to build the brutal showpiece bridge, the SNP Bridge, now known as the Nový most or New Bridge (see below). The traffic which now tears along Staromestská has seriously undermined the foundations of the **Cathedral of St Martin** (Mon–Sat 10–11.45am & 2–4.45pm, Sun 2–4.45pm), the Gothic coronation church of the kings and queens of Hungary for over 250 years, whose ill-proportioned steeple is topped by a tiny gilded Hungarian crown.

As you pass under the approach road for the new bridge, you'll notice the **Clock Museum** at Židovská 1 (9.30am–6pm, closed Tues), with a display of brilliantly kitsch Baroque and Empire clocks. To pay tribute to the large prewar Slovak Jewish population, largely decimated in concentration camps, there is a **Jewish Museum** at Židovská 17 (11am–5pm, closed Sat), with a display of Judaica and a brief history of Slovak Jews.

The **Castle** (daily 9am–8pm), is an unwelcoming giant box built in the fifteenth century by Emperor Sigismund and burnt down by its own drunken soldiers in 1811. It houses the half of the uneven collections of the **Slovak Historical Museum** (Tues–Sun 9am–5pm), which features Slovak trades, handicrafts and folk art, and the **Music Museum** (Tues–Sun 9am–5pm), which contains traditional Slovak instruments. The castle's small collection of old clocks is also worth viewing, and you also get the chance to climb to the top of one of the castle's four corner towers, for an incredible view south across the Danube plain to the Petržalka housing estate, where a third of the city's population lives.

Along the waterfront

Despite the fast dual carriageway of the embankment, it is just about possible to enjoy a stroll along the banks of the (far from blue) **River Danube** – *Dunaj* in Slovak. In addition to a terminal for boats to Budapest and Vienna, there's a summer ferry service across the river, an alternative to crossing by either of the two bridges, the larger of which is the infamous "Bridge of the Slovak National Uprising" or **Nový most** as it's now known. Its one support column leans at an alarming angle, topped by a saucer-like, pricey penthouse café reminiscent of the *Starship Enterprise*.

While you're in the waterfront district, the **Slovak National Gallery** (Tues–Sun 10am–6pm) is worth exploring. There are two entrances: the one on the embankment lets you into the main building, a converted naval barracks, while the one on Stúrovo námestie gives access to the Esterházy Palace wing – inside, both parts connect on the upper floor. The permanent collection in the main building is an exhaustive rundown of Slovak art from Gothic times to the late nineteenth century, while the Esterházy Palace houses thirteenth- to eighteenth-century paintings of dubious merit. You're better off heading straight for the fascinating top-floor display of twentieth-century applied arts, architecture and design.

Further along the quayside, past the rather tatty **Natural History Museum** (Tues–Sun 9am–5pm) and hidden away behind Safárikovo námestie, is Ödön

Lechner's concrete, sky-blue Art Nouveau **Blue Church** at Bezručova 2, a lost monument to this once-Hungarian city, abandoned in the Slovak capital and dedicated to St Elizabeth, the city's one and only famous saint, born in Bratislava in 1207.

Eating and drinking

The choice of places **to eat** in Bratislava has improved over the last few years, as have standards. The most memorable aspect of the whole experience is often the ambience, and exploring the atmospheric streets of the old town by night is all part of the fun. In addition, you can also be fairly sure that, away from the places catering for those on expenses, prices remain uniformly low.

Cafés, bars and pubs

Gremium Gorkého 11. Wonderful, smoky café/gallery in the centre, with a high ceiling and a nice balcony where you can play pool.

Hradná vináreň Mudroňov 1. Stunning wine bar with separate restaurant, serving excellent wine and Slovak specialities with breath-taking views.

Kaffee Mayer Hlavné námestie 4. A resurrected turn-of-the-century café that emulates its Viennese-style ancestor – very popular with the city's older cake-and-coffee fans.

Korzo Hviezdoslavovo námestie 11. Passable shot at a Viennese-style café and a possible breakfast halt, with tables outside overlooking Rybné námestie and the Nový most.

Slovenská pivnica Dunajská 18. A traditional Slovak beer that in the unlikely setting of noisy Kamenné námestie, but its prices are low and the atmosphere is good.

Stará sladovňa Cintorínska 32. The city's malthouse until 1976, *Mamut*, as it's known, is Bratislava's most famous (and largest) pub. Czech Budvar on tap, big band and country & western music Thurs–Sat, and a bingo hall and casino on site as well.

Restaurants

Chez David Zamocká 13 ☎02/5441 3824. Strictly kosher restaurant serving fresh, beautifully prepared Jewish cuisine, but pricey for Bratislava. Closed Sat.

Corleone Hviezdoslavovo námestie 21. The best pizza joint in the city, with a good range of moderately priced, thin-base pizzas.

Mekong Palackého 18. Swish Thai restaurant with, strangely, Italianate decor, and slap-up Thai classics.

Modrá hviezda Beblavého 14. Restaurant en route to the castle serving decent Slovak and Hungarian specialities. Closed Sun.

Rybársky cech Žižkova 1 ☎02/5441 3049. Popular, reliably good but pricey fish restaurant on the ground floor of a former fisherman's house down by the waterfront below the castle (there's a posher, more expensive version upstairs). Reservations recommended.

Vegetarian Laurinská 8. Plain and simple vegetarian lunch spot, with a short list of salads and soya-based main dishes. Closed Sat & Sun.

Nightlife and entertainment

Bratislava's **nightlife** is heavily biased towards high culture, with **opera** and **ballet** at the Slovak National Theatre (@www.snd.sk) and orchestral concerts at the Reduta, as well as the varied programme put on at the modern Istropolis complex on Trnavské myto (tram #2 from the station; tram #4 or #6 from the centre). Bratislava hosts a couple of annual large-scale **festivals**, the most prestigious being the classical music festival in October – without the big names of Prague's, but a lot easier to get tickets for.

The longest-serving **nightspot** is the *Charlie centrum*, Špitálska 4, the entrance is one block east of the *Hotel Kyjev* on Rajská. Inside there's a multiscreen art-house **cinema**, and a late-night bar/disco in the basement. **Clubs** include the *U-Club*. a cheap, loud and slightly weird club located in an old nuclear bunker underneath the castle – access from nábrežie arm. gen. L. Svobodu. *Hystéria*, Odbojárov 9, behind the ice hockey stadium (tram #4 or #6 from Kamenné námestie), is worth the trek for its Tex-Mex food, pool and regular live music.

The mountain regions

The great virtue of Slovakia is its mountains, particularly the **High Tatras**, which, in their short span, reach alpine heights and have a bleak, stunning beauty. By far the republic's most popular destination, they are, in fact, the least typical of Slovakia's mountains, which are predominantly densely forested, round-topped limestone ranges. In the heart of the mountains is **Banská Bystrica**, one of the many towns in the region originally settled by German miners, and still redolent of those times. Generally, though, the towns in the valley bottoms have been fairly solidly industrialized, and are only good as bases for exploring the surrounding countryside. Railways, where they do exist, make for some of the most scenic train journeys in the country.

Banská Bystrica

Lying at the very heart of Slovakia's mountain ranges, the old medieval German mining town of **BANSKÁ BYSTRICA** is a useful introduction to the area and it's also a handsome historic town in its own right – once you've made it through the tangled suburbs of the burgeoning cement- and logging-industries.

Námestie SNP, the old medieval marketplace, is still the centre of life here. The black obelisk of the Soviet war memorial and a revolving fountain, enthusiastically chucking water over a pile of mossy rocks, form the square's centrepiece. One or two of the burgher houses bear closer inspection, particularly the **Venetian House** at no. 16, with its slender first-floor arcaded loggia. The sgraffitoed building opposite is now an art gallery. Just a few doors down is the most imposing building on the square, the honey-coloured Thurzo Palace at no. 4, decorated like a piece of embroidery and sporting cute oval portholes, and now housing the **town museum** (Mon–Fri 9am–noon & 1–5pm, Sun 9am–4pm), with a small selection of folk art and period furniture.

At the top end of the square, beyond the leaning clock tower, there's an interesting ensemble of buildings – all that's left of the old castle. The first building in view is the last remaining **barbican**, curving snugly round a Baroque tower. Next door, the former **town hall** (Tues–Fri 9am–5pm, Sat & Sun 10am–4pm), a boxy little Renaissance structure, is now the town's main art gallery, which puts on temporary exhibitions from its extensive catalogue of modern Slovak art. Behind it is the rouge-red church of **Panna Mária**, which dates back to the thirteenth century; the north side chapel contains the town's greatest art treasure, a carved late-Gothic altarpiece by Master Pavol of Levoča.

A short distance southeast of námestie SNP on Kapitulská, 200m south of the clock tower, is the **SNP Museum** at no. 23 (Tues–Sun 8/9am–4/6pm), looking like an intergalactic mushroom chopped in half and dating from 1969. The museum deals as best it can with the complex issues raised by the Slovak National Uprising (SNP) against the Nazis (and the Slovak puppet regime), which began on August 29, 1944, in Banská Bystrica and which was eventually crushed by the Germans two months later, just a month or so before the town's liberation. Outside on the grass you'll notice an exhibition of tanks, an armoured train and guns from the uprising amid the bushes and the town's last two surviving medieval bastions.

Practicalities

Banská Bystrica's main **bus and train stations** are in the modern part of town, ten minutes' walk east of the centre; if you arrive on a slow train, you can alight at Banská Bystrica mesto train station, just five minutes' walk south of the main square. There's a **tourist office** inside the barbican (Mon–Fri 8am–7pm, Sat 8am–3pm; ☎048/415 5085, ◉www.isternet/sk/pkobb), which can help you arrange **accommodation**. The late-nineteenth-century *Národný dom* (☎048/412 37 37 or 412 50 14; ❸), at Národná 11, is a central option, has a wonderful café, casino and restaurant, but is a little dated in decor and facilities. Two other cheap options are the *Penzión Uhlisko* (☎048/414 56 12; ❸), at Lesná 3, across the river from the stations, and the private rooms offered at *Privát Hodžová*, M. Hodžu 5 (☎048/415 31 19; booking essential; ❶), east of the old town – walk to the end of Dolná, cross the bridge and turn right onto J. Kráľa, then left onto M. Hurbana. There's also a **campsite** on Tajovského 180, 1km west of the main square, just by the turn-off to Tajov. For **food**, try *EVIJO*, at no. 8 on the main square, which dishes out huge pizzas made before your very eyes, or, for hearty Bohemian fare, head for the *Staročeská reštaurácia* on námestie Slobody 9. Try *Lotos* for vaguely Asian delights at no. 3 or enjoy wonderful pub grub at *Reštaurácia U Tigra* at Dolná 36.

The High Tatras

Rising like a giant granite reef above the patchwork Poprad plain, the **High Tatras** are for many people the main reason for venturing this far into Slovakia. Even after all the tourist-board hype, they are still an inspirational sight. A wilderness, however, they are not; all summer, visitors are shoulder to shoulder in the necklace of resorts which sit at the foot of the mountains. But once you're above the tree line, surrounded by bare primeval scree slopes and icy blue tarns, nothing can take away the exhilaration or the breathtaking views.

Poprad

The mainline train station for the Tatras is Poprad-Tatry in **POPRAD**, an unprepossessing town on the plain. With its great swathe of off-white high-rise housing encircling a small old centre, it is best viewed (if at all) as a stop-over on the way to the mountains proper. Poprad's **tourist office**, PIA (May–Sept Mon–Fri 8.30am–5/6pm, Sat & Sun 8.30am–1pm; ☎052/16186, ⓦwww.poprad.sk), at the western end of námestie sv Egídia, can organize private rooms in town and all types of **accommodation** elsewhere in the Tatras. From the high-level platform at Poprad-Tatry, cute red tram-like trains trundle across the fields, linking Poprad with the string of resorts and spas halfway up the Tatras and lying within the **Tatra National Park** or **TANAP**. They range from tasteless new hotels to turreted edifices from the nineteenth century set in civilized spa gardens and pine woods – but it's the mountains to which they give access that make them worth visiting.

Starý Smokovec – and Tatra hikes

The best base for accommodation in the Tatras is the scattered settlement of **STARÝ SMOKOVEC**, whose nucleus is the stretch of lawn between the half-timbered supermarket and the sandy-yellow *Grand Hotel*. The best place to head for help with **accommodation** is T-Ski (daily 9am–5pm; ☎052/442 32 65, ⓦwww.slovakiatravel.sk), up by the cable car (they also rent out skis and bikes), or to book yourself into a **mountain chata** head for Slovakoturist (Mon–Fri 8am–4pm), a couple of minutes' walk east of the main train station in Horný Smokovec (the closest station is Pekná Vyhliadka). The best **campsite** is *Eurocamp FICC*, just south of Tatranská Lomnica (get off at Tatranská Lomnica-Eurocamp FICC station), with bungalows, a restaurant and café, hot showers and many other facilities. Serious climbers and hikers can get information from Horská služba, the **24-hour mountain rescue service** next door to SATUR in Starý Smokovec (☎052/442 28 20, ⓦwww.horska-sluzba.sk).

If the weather's reasonably good, the most straightforward and rewarding climb is to follow the blue-marked path that leads from behind the *Grand Hotel* to the summit of **Slavkovský štít** (2452m), a return journey of nine hours. Alternatively, there's also a narrow-gauge funicular, again starting from behind the *Grand* (every 30min), which climbs 250m to **HREBIENOK** (45min on foot), one of the lesser ski resorts on the edge of the pine forest. The smart wooden *Bilíkova chata* (☎052/442 24 39; ❸) is a five-minute walk from the top of the funicular – even if you don't stay there you should stop for a drink on the balcony. Beyond the *chata*,

25

the path continues through the wood, joining two others, from Tatranská Lesná and Tatranská Lomnica respectively, before passing the gushing waterfalls of the **Studenovodské vodopády**.

Just past the waterfall, a whole variety of trekking possibilities opens up. The right-hand fork takes you up the **Malá Studená dolina** and then zigzags above the tree line to the *Téryho chata*, set in a lunar landscape by the shores of the **Päť Spišských ples**. Following the spectacular trail over the Prieane sedlo to *Zbojnicka chata*, you can return via the **Vejká studená dolina** – an eight-hour round trip from Hrebienok. Another possibility is to take the left-hand fork to the *Zbojnicka chata*, and continue to Zamruznuté pleso, which sits in the shadow of **Východná Vysoká** (2428m); only a thirty-minute hike from the lake, this peak dishes out the best view of **Gerlachovský stít** – the highest peak in the Tatras and a symbol of Slovak nationhood – that a non-climber can get.

East Slovakia

Stretching from the High Tatras east to the Ukrainian border, the landscape of **East Slovakia** is decidedly different from the rest of the country. Ethnically, this is probably the most diverse region in the country, with different groups coexisting even within a single valley. The majority of the country's Romanies live here, mostly on the edge of Slovak villages, in shanty towns of almost medieval squalor. In the ribbon-villages of the north and east, the Rusyn minority struggle to preserve their culture and religion, while along the southern border there are large numbers of Hungarians. After spending time in the rural backwaters, **Košice**, Slovakia's second largest city, can be a welcome though somewhat startling return to city life. Gradually realizing its potential as a diverse and vibrant cosmopolitan centre, it certainly contains enough of interest for at least a day's stopover.

The Spiš region

The land that stretches northeast up the Poprad Valley to the Polish border and east along the River Hornád towards Prešov is known as the **Spiš region**, for centuries a semi-autonomous province within the Hungarian kingdom. After the devastation of the mid-thirteenth-century Tatar invasions, the Hungarian Crown encouraged Saxon families to repopulate the area. The wealthy settlers built some wonderful Gothic churches, and later enriched almost every town and village with the distinctive touch of the Renaissance. Today, with only a few of its ethnic Germans and Hungarians remaining, the Spiš shares the low-living standards of the rest of East Slovakia. But the region's architectural richness offers a glimmer of hope in the growth of tourism – indeed in the high seasons, in towns such as **Levoča**, you can often hardly move for the tour buses.

Kežmarok

Just 14km up the road from Poprad, **KEŽMAROK** is one of the easiest Spiš towns to visit from the High Tatras. It's an odd place, combining the distinctive traits of a Teutonic town with the dozy feel of an oversized Slovak village. Kežmarok is dominated by the giant, gaudy **Lutheran Church** (May–Oct daily 9am–noon & 2–5pm; Nov–April Tues & Fri 9am–noon & 2–4pm), built by Theophil Hansen, the Danish architect responsible for much of late-nineteenth-century Vienna, and funded by the town's merchants. It's a seemingly random fusion of styles – Renaissance campanile, Moorish dome, classical dimensions, all dressed up in grey-green and rouge rendering. Next door is an even more remarkable **wooden Lutheran Church** (times as above), a work of great carpentry and artistry whose ornately decorated interior is capable of seating almost 1500 people.

The old town itself is little more than two long leafy streets that fork off from the important-looking central town hall. The town's Catholic basilica of **sv Kríž** is tucked away in the tangle of dusty back alleys between the two prongs, once surrounded by its own line of fortifications. It is now protected by a Renaissance belfry whose uppermost battlements burst into sgraffito life in the best Spiš tradition. The **Castle** (May–Sept Tues–Sun hourly 9am–4pm; Oct–April Tues–Sat 9–11am & 1–4pm), at the end of the right-hand fork, is impressively fortified and decorated with Renaissance crenellations, but the interior doesn't really justify signing up for the compulsory hour-long guided tour. A better idea is to head for the **town museum**, back along the street at Hradné námestie 55 (Tues–Sat 9am–noon & 1–5pm), which contains, among other things, the personal effects of Countess Hedviga Mária Szirmayova-Badányiova.

The **tourist office** or KIA (Mon–Fri 8.30am–5pm, Sat & Sun 9am–2pm; winter closed Sun; ✪ kezmarok.tripod.com/english), on the main square at Hlavné námestie 46, can book cheap **private rooms**; otherwise the best option is the excellent *Hotel Club,* on ulica MUDr Alexandra (☎052/452 4051, ✉hotelclub @kk.sinet.sk; ❸), an efficiently run, tastefully modernized place right in the old town, with an excellent restaurant on the ground floor. For budget travellers there's the *Hotel Štart* (☎052/452 2916; ❷), which lies in the woods to the north of the castle, a good twenty-minute walk from the train station. The *Castellan Club* tucked into the side of the castle provides a watering-hole late at night.

Levoča

Some 25km east of Poprad, across the broad sweep of Spiš countryside, the ravishingly beautiful walled town of **LEVOČA**, set on a slight incline, makes a wonderfully medieval impression, and is very much a Gothic and Renaissance haven. The Euclidian efficiency with which the old town is laid out means you'll inevitably end up at the main square, **námestie Majstra Pavla**. To the north is the square's least distinguished but most important building, the municipal weigh-house; a law of 1321 obliged every merchant passing through the region to hole up at Levoča for fourteen days, pay various taxes and allow the locals first refusal on their goods.

Of the three freestanding buildings on the main square paid for with these riches, it's the Catholic church of **sv Jakub** (Mon & Sun 1–4.30/6pm, Tues–Sat 8.30/9am–4.30/6pm) that has the most valuable booty. The church can be visited only with a guide, and **tours** (every 30min, hourly in winter) leave from the *kassa* opposite the main entrance. Every nook and cranny is crammed with religious art, the star attraction being the magnificent sixteenth-century wooden **altarpiece** by Master Pavol of Levoča, which, at 18.6m, is reputedly the tallest of its kind in the world. A small **museum** (daily 9am–5pm) dedicated to Master Pavol stands opposite the church on the eastern side of the square. South of the church is the **town hall** (Tues–Sun 9am–5pm), built in a sturdy Renaissance style. On the first floor, there's a museum on the Spiš region, and some fine examples of Spiš handicrafts on the top floor. The last building in the centre of the square is the oddly squat **Lutheran Church**, built in an uncompromisingly neoclassical style.

You can get to Levoča by train from Poprad, but you must change at Spišská Nová Ves – much easier to take a bus from either Poprad, Prešov or Košice. The **train and bus stations** are southeast of the old town. Outside the annual pilgrimage in early July, accommodation shouldn't be hard to find; the helpful **tourist office** (Mon–Fri 9am–4.30pm; May–Sept also Sat & Sun 9.30am–1.30pm; ☎053/451 3763, ✪www.levoca.sk) in the northwest corner of the square can book private rooms. Otherwise, best choice for **accommodation** is the comfortable *Hotel Barbakan* at Košická 15 (☎053/451 4310, ✪www.barbakan; ❸), which includes a buffet breakfast in the price and rents out bikes; alternatively, there's the *Penzión pri Košickej bráne* (☎053/451 2879; ❷) next door; the **campsite** is 3km north of Levoča. Authentic Slovak pub **food** can be had from *U Janusa*, Klástorská 22 (closed Sat & Sun), and from the atmospheric *U troch apoštolov*, above a butcher's, on the east side of the main square. There's a self-service lunchtime-only vegetarian restaurant, *Vegeterián*, at Uholná 3, northwest of the main square, and a *Pizzeria* nearby on Vetrová.

Spišský hrad

The road east from Levoča takes you to the edge of Spiš territory, clearly defined by the Branisko ridge which blocks the way to Prešov. Even if you're not going any further east, you should at least take the bus as far as **SPIŠSKÉ PODHRADIE**, for arguably the most spectacular sight in the whole country – the **Spišský hrad** (daily 9am–5/6pm). This pile of chalk-white ruins, strung out on a bleak green hill, is irresistibly photogenic and finds its way into almost every tourist hand-out in the country. The ruins themselves don't quite live up to expectations, though the view from the top is pretty good. The *Penzíon Podzámok* at Podzámková 28 (☎053/454 1 755; ❷) is a good place **to stay**, with superb views up to the castle.

Prešov

Capital of the Slovak Šariš region and a cultural centre for the Rusyn (Ruthenian) minority, **PREŠOV** has been treated to a wonderful face-lift over the last few years. There's not much of interest beyond its main square, but it's a refreshingly youthful and vibrant town, partly due to its university.

The lozenge-shaped main square, **Hlavná ulica**, is flanked by creamy, pastel-coloured, almost edible eighteenth-century facades. At the square's southern tip is the **Greek-Catholic Cathedral**, a wonderful Rococo affair with a fabulously huge iconostasis. Further along, on the same side of the square, is Prešov's **town hall**, from whose unsuitably small balcony Béla Kun's Hungarian Red Army declared the short-lived Slovak Socialist Republic in 1919. Further north along the square, the **town museum**, situated in the dogtooth-gabled Rákociho dom at no. 86 (Tues–Fri 9am–5pm, Sat 9am–1pm, Sun 1–5pm), offers a thorough retelling of the history of the town and the Šariš region.

Prešov's Catholic and Protestant churches vie with each other at the widest point of the square. The fourteenth-century Catholic church of **sv Mikuláš** has the edge, not least for its modern Moravian stained-glass windows and its sumptuous Baroque altarpiece. Behind sv Mikulás, the much plainer **Lutheran Church**, built in the mid-seventeenth century, bears witness to the strength of religious reformism in the outer reaches of Hungary at a time when the rest of the Habsburgs' lands were suffering the full force of the Counter-Reformation.

Lastly, the town's ornate *fin-de-siècle* **synagogue** in the northwest corner of the old town – access from Svermova – has been turned into a small **Museum of Judaica** (Tues & Wed 11am–4pm, Thurs 3–6pm, Fri 10am–1pm, Sun 1–5pm), with an exhibition on Judaism and the region's Jewish community, 6000 of whom perished in the Holocaust.

The **bus** and **train stations** are situated opposite one another about 1km south of the main square; the best buses and trolleybuses into town are those which stop at Na Hlavnej. There's a **tourist office** (Mon–Fri 10am–6pm, Sat 9am–1pm; ☎051/731 113) near the town hall. The best budget **accommodation** is at the *Sen*, Vajanského 65 (☎051/773 3170; ❶), two blocks east of the main square; otherwise there's the newly done-up *Senator*, at Hlavná 67 (☎051/773 1092; ❶), above the tourist office. A few **restaurants** spill out onto the square in summer, including the *Melódia* at no. 61, which has a satisfyingly long menu that doesn't overlook the needs of vegetarians. For more traditional fare, the *Slovenská reštaurácia* at no. 11 (closed Sun), is pleasant and unpretentious, and the basement *U richtára*, nearby at no. 71, is also appealing.

Košice

Slovak towns rarely amount to much more than their one long main square, and even **KOŠICE**, Slovakia's second largest city, is no exception. Rather like Bratislava,

Košice was, until relatively recently, a modest little town on the edge of the Hungarian plain. Then, in the 1950s, the Communists established a giant steel works on the outskirts of the city. Forty years on, it has a population of over 250,000, a number of worthwhile museums, the best cathedral in the republic, and a lively cosmopolitanism that can be quite reassuring after a week or so in the Slovak back-of-beyond. Just 21km north of the Hungarian border, Košice also acts as a magnet for the Hungarian community – to whom the city is known as *Kassa* – and the terminally under-employed Romanies of the surrounding region, lending it a diversity and vibrancy absent from small-town Slovakia, and only recently viewed as contributing positively to the town.

Almost everything of interest is situated on Košice's long pedestrianized main square, which is called **Hlavná ulica** at its northern and southern extremities, **Hlavné námestie** to the north of the cathedral, and **Námestie slobody** to the south of the cathedral. Lined with handsome Baroque and Neoclassical palaces, it's dominated by the city's unorthodox Gothic **Cathedral of St Elizabeth**, its charcoal-coloured stone now sandblasted back to its original honeyed hue. Begun in 1378, it's an unusual building from the outside, with striped roof tiles and two contorted towers. Inside, imposing Gothic furnishings add an impressive touch to an otherwise plain nave, the main gilded altar depicting scenes from the life of the cathedral's patron saint. On the busy north side of the cathedral is the fourteenth-century **Urbanova veža**, standing on its own set of mini-arcades. The public park and fountains beyond are a favourite spot for hanging out and make an appropriately graceful approach to the city's grand Austro-Hungarian **theatre**.

The peculiar **Vojtech Löffler Museum**, at Alžbetina 20 (Tues–Sat 10am–6pm, Sun 1–5pm), west off the main square, features the work and private collections of Košice's most prominent Communist-sanctioned sculptor. Another unusual attraction is the **Mikluš Prison** (Tues–Sat 9am–5pm, Sun 9am–1pm), east off the square down Univerzitna, whose original dimly lit dungeons and claustrophobic cells graphically transport you into its history as the city prison and torture chamber. At the northern tip of the main square, námestie Maratónu mieru is flanked to the east and west by the bulky nineteenth-century **East Slovak Museum** (Tues–Sat 9am–5pm, Sun 10am–1pm). The western building is worth visiting for its basement collection of fifteenth- to seventeenth-century **gold coins** – 2920 in all – minted at Kremnica, but stashed away by city burghers and discovered by accident in 1935. Hidden round the back of the museum is a wooden Greek-Catholic Church, brought here from the Ukrainian borderlands.

Practicalities

The **train and bus stations** are opposite each other, ten minutes' walk east of the old town. The city **tourist office** is at Hlavná ulica 2 (Mon–Fri 9am–6pm, Sat 9am–1pm; ☎055/16186, ✆www.kosice.sk); another, equally useful information service is located in the Dargov department store at the southern end of the square (same hours). Both can help with finding **accommodation**, including private rooms. Otherwise, try *Atlantik*, Rázusova 1 (☎T055/622 65 01; ❷), a small, simple, central pension that's often fully booked, so it's worth calling well in advance. *Domov mládeže* (☎T055/643 56 88; ❶) is a year-round **hostel** on Medická, west of the centre via bus #17 or #34, or follow Poštovna to Vojenská, which becomes Ondavská, and turn left on Považská. Cheap dorm beds are also available at the *Student Hostel* (☎T055/633 34 37; ❶: July & Aug only) at Podhradová 11. The nearest **campsite** (closed Oct to mid-April) is 5km south of the city centre and also rents out bungalows; take tram #1 or #4, or bus #22 or #52, from the *Slovan* hotel to the flyover, then get off and walk the remaining 500m west along Alejová, the road to Rožňava.

The best **places to eat** are located in the streets to the east of the main square: *Ajvega*, Orlia 10, is a popular vegetarian place with a summer terrace, and serves soya versions of standard Slovak dishes, washed down with fresh juices. The seafood and fish restaurant *Caravella*, just up the street at Orlia 4, does an admirable job considering its distance from the ocean. *Sedliacky dvor*, at Biela 3, is a hymn to Slovak folk culture and cuisine. *Kleopatra Pizza Bar*, south of the cathedral at no. 24, occupies one of the finest settings of all, with outdoor tables overlooking a small park. The city has plenty of options for **drinking**: the *Green Crow Club* in a one-time nuclear shelter at Kasárenské námestie offers jazz along with the booze; *Music Bar Diesel* at Hlavná 92 has frequent live music and a good atmosphere. Košice's **nightlife** revolves around the main square (more a long boulevard).

To find out what's on, get hold of the free **listings booklet** *Kultúrny informátor* from the tourist office. Mainstream culture still predominates, though it's worth knowing that Košice has a **Hungarian theatre**, Thália, on Mojmírova, and also boasts Slovakia's one and only **Romany theatre**, Romathan, Štefánikova 4, which puts on a whole range of events from concerts to plays. You can catch **live jazz** most nights at the city's smoky *Jazz Club*, Kováčska 39, and the occasional **folk gig** takes place at *Klub M*, Moldavská 37.

Travel details

Trains

Bratislava to: Banská Bystrica (1 daily; 3hr 45min); Poprad-Tatry (every 2hr; 4hr 40min); Košice (every 2hr; 6hr).
Poprad-Tatry to: Starý Smokovec (hourly; 35min); Kežmarok (every 2hr; 25min); Košice (every 2hr; 1hr 15min).

Buses

Levoča to: Spišské Podhradie (up to 10 daily; 30min).
Poprad to: Levoča (up to 12 daily; 30–50min); Spišské Podhradie (up to 12 daily; 30–45min); Prešov (up to 10 daily; 2hr).

Slovenia

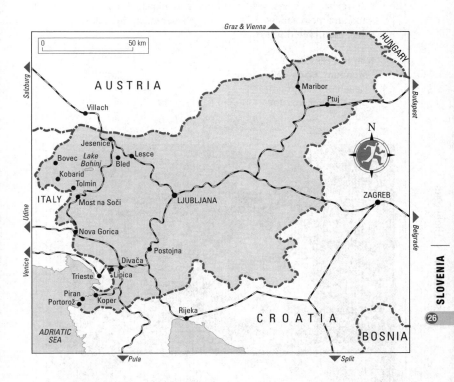

Slovenia highlights

✳ **Old Town, Ljubljana**
Stunning architecture, a
hilltop castle and leafy
riverside cafés. **See p.931**

✳ **Lake Bohinj** Pearl of
Slovenian lakes, less visited and more serene
than Bled. **See p.937**

✳ **Kobarid Historical
Museum, Soča Valley**
Beautiful valley, com-
pelling museum. **See
p.938**

✳ **Kurenti, Ptuj** Slovenia's
most extravagant festi-
val. **See p.939**

✳ **Postojna Caves**
Subterranean wonder-
land, highlight of the
Karst region. **See p.934**

Introduction and basics

The northernmost republic of what was once Yugoslavia, **Slovenia** currently appears the most stable, prosperous and welcoming of all Europe's erstwhile communist countries. It was always the richest and most westernized of the Yugoslav federation, and apart from the Ten-Day War which brought it independence in 1991, it has avoided the strife which has plagued the republics to the south. For centuries, Slovenia was administered by German-speaking overlords and was, until 1918, part of the Austro-Hungarian empire. The Slovenes absorbed the culture of their captors during this period while managing to retain a strong sense of ethnic identity through the Slav-rooted Slovene language, a close relation of Czech, Serbo-Croat and Slovak.

Slovenia's landscape is as varied as it is beautiful: along the Austrian border the **Julian Alps** provide stunning mountain scenery, most accessibly at **Lake Bled** and **Lake Bohinj**; further south, the brittle karst scenery is riddled with spectacular caves like those at **Postojna**. Slovenia's capital, **Ljubljana**, is easily the best of the cities, a vital, youthful place, manageably small and cluttered with Baroque and Habsburg buildings, while the short stretch of Slovenian coast, along the northern edge of the Istrian peninsula, is punctuated by a couple of towns that were among the most attractive resorts of the former Yugoslavia – **Piran** and **Portorož**. Despite its relative isolation in the eastern part of the country, the well preserved town of **Ptuj** is also worth a visit.

Information and maps

There is an excellent network of local authority-run **tourist information centres** in most towns and well-touristed places. As well as providing local information and maps, many centres supply information on other parts of the country, and some also act as an agency for private rooms. A high standard of English is spoken pretty much everywhere.

Freytag & Berndt publishes a good 1:300,000 **map** of Slovenia, while excellent small-scale hiking maps are published by the Slovene Alpine Association (Planinska zveza Slovenije; Dvoržakova ulica 9; ☎01/231-2553, ⓦwww.pzs.si) and are widely available in bookshops in Slovenia.

Money and banks

Slovenia's unit of **currency** is the tolar, divided into 100 stotini. Coins come in denominations of 50 stotini and 1, 2, 5 and 10 tolars; and there are notes of 10, 20, 50, 100, 200, 500, 1000, 5000 and 10,000 tolars. Prices are usually followed by the initials SIT. The exchange rate is currently around 350SIT to £1, and 240SIT to $1.

Banks (*banka*) are generally open Mon–Fri 8.30am–12.30pm & 2–5pm & Sat 8.30am–11/noon. Money can also be changed in tourist offices, post offices, travel agencies and exchange bureaux (*menjalnica*), all of which have more flexible hours. Credit cards are accepted In a large number of hotels and restaurants; they're also useful for getting cash advances from cash dispensers and in the bigger banks.

Prices for accommodation and tours are sometimes given in euros – although payment is usually made in tolars.

Slovenia on the net

ⓦ**www.matkurja.com** Comprehensive site
ⓦ**www.slovenia-tourism.si** Official tourist board
ⓦ**www.ljubljana.si** Sights in the capital
ⓦ**www.bled.si** Useful site on Slovenia's premier attraction

Communications

Most **post offices** (*pošta*) are open Mon–Fri 8am–6pm and Sat 8am–noon. Stamps (*znamke*) can also be bought at newsstands.

Public **phone** boxes use cards (*telekartice*) which come in denominations of 700SIT, 1000SIT, 1700SIT and 3500SIT; you can buy these from post offices, newspaper kiosks and tobacco shops. When making long-distance and international calls it's usually easier to go to the post office, where you're assigned to a cabin and given the bill afterwards.

Internet access is quite poor, even in the capital. Where you do find a terminal, expect to pay around 500SIT/hr.

Getting around

Traversing Slovenia by any kind of public transport is relatively easy and usually very scenic. Generally speaking, trains provide the fastest means of travelling on the main routes linking the capital with Maribor and Koper, or with Austria and Italy. Everywhere else, buses are far more convenient.

Trains and buses

Slovene railways (Slovenske ˇzeleznice) run a smooth and efficient service. **Trains** (*vlaki*) are divided into *potniški* (slow ones which stop at every halt) and *IC* (intercity trains which are faster and slightly more expensive). Some of the latter, colloquially known as *zeleni vlaki* (green trains) and designated on timetables by the initials ICZV, are express services on which prior seat reservations (*rezervacije*) are obligatory. Most timetables have explanations in English, and timetable leaflets (*vozni red*) are sometimes available from counters. *Odhodi* are departures, *prihodi* arrivals. Both Eurail and InterRail passes are valid.

Slovenia's **bus** network consists of an array of small local companies, but their services are well co-ordinated. Towns such as Ljubljana, Maribor and Koper have big bus stations with computerized booking facilities where you can buy your tickets hours (if not days) in advance – recommended if you're travelling between Ljubljana and the coast in high season. Elsewhere, simply pile onto the bus and pay the driver or conductor. You'll be charged extra for cumbersome items of baggage, like a backpack, which must be stored in the hold.

Accommodation

While tourist **accommodation** is universally clean and good quality, it doesn't come much cheaper than in neighbouring Italy or Austria unless you opt for a private room.

Hotels, guest houses and private rooms

Apart from a couple of *fin-de-siècle* establishments in Ljubljana, Slovene **hotels** tend to be high-rise concrete affairs providing modern comforts but little atmosphere. They are classified according to the international five-star system, with three-star places (usually offering rooms with en-suite facilities and TV) making up the bulk of the hotel stock. Cheaper two-star places are occasionally available, but anything lower than this is very rare. Expect to pay £30/$45 upwards for a double at two-star hotels, £40/$60 upwards for a three-star. In recent years there's been an increase in the number of family-run **pensions** in rural Slovenia, especially in the alpine regions, offering the same facilities as hotels (and rated according to the same star system), but usually with a cosier atmosphere and a lower price. Outside alpine resorts, however, pensions tend to be well away from town centres and are therefore hard to find unless you have your own transport.

Private rooms (*zasebne sobe*) are available throughout Slovenia, with bookings administered by tourist information centres in places like Ljubljana, or by travel agents like Slovenijaturist or Kompas elsewhere. Agencies are usually open daily 9am–7/8pm in summer. Private rooms are pretty good value at about £14–20/$21–30 a double, although stays of three nights or under are invariably subject to a thirty-percent surcharge. The more expensive private rooms will have en-suite bathrooms, perhaps even a TV. Self-catering **apartments** (*apartmaji*) are also plentiful in the mountains and on the coast, with per-person rates working out the same as, or sometimes cheaper than, private rooms if there are more than two people travelling together.

Hostels and campsites

Hostels are thin on the ground in Slovenia, although there's a scattering of student hostels (*dijaški dom*) which open their doors to non-students over the summer and at weekends at other times of year. Beds in all hostels are in short supply, and advance booking is advised. Expect to pay about £8–12/$12–18 per person per night.

Campsites are plentiful in the mountains and on the coast and tend to be well-organized affairs with good facilities, restaurants and shops. Two people travelling with a tent can expect to pay £8–10/$12–15; add another £2/$3 for a vehicle. The majority of campsites are open from May to September. Camping rough without permission is punishable by a spot fine.

Serious hikers planning an assault on the peaks of Slovenia's Julian Alps could make use of **mountain huts** (*planinske koče*). The ones on the way up Mount Triglav are little less than hotels; elsewhere they are much more basic. You'll need to book in advance or arrive early. Details can be obtained from the Slovene Alpine Association (see p.925), or from tourist information centres once you arrive.

Food and drink

Slovene cuisine draws on Austrian, Italian and Balkan influences. There's a native Slovene tradition, too, based on age-old peasant recipes, although this is gradually losing out as restaurants and cafés become increasingly international.

Food

Slovenia's supermarkets and *delikatesa* are good places to stock up on **sandwich and picnic ingredients**, like local cheese (*sir*) and salami (*salama*). Buy fresh fruit and vegetables from outdoor markets or roadside stalls, and bread (*kruh*) from a *pekarna* (bakery).

For **breakfast and quick snacks**, *okrepčevalnice* (snack bars) and street kiosks dole out *burek*, a flaky pastry filled with cheese (*sirov burek*) or meat (*burek z mesom*). Sausages come in various forms, most commonly hot dogs, *hrenovke* (Slovene frankfurters), or *kranjska klobasa* (big spicy sausages).

Menus in a Slovene *restavracija* (restaurant) or *gostilna* (inn) are dominated by roast meats (*pečenka*) and schnitzels (*zrezek*), mostly pork (*svinjina*) and veal (*teletina*). The Slovenes are unsqueamish about offal: liver (*jetra*) and grilled or fried brains (*možgani*) are popular standbys in cheaper restaurants. Goulash (*golaž*) is found almost everywhere; *segedin* is goulash with lashings of sauerkraut. Two traditional Slovene dishes are *žlikrofi*, ravioli filled with potato, onion and bacon; and *žganci*, once the staple diet of rural Slovenes, a buckwheat or maize porridge often served with sauerkraut. *Ocvrti sir* (cheese fried in breadcrumbs) is one of the few dishes that will appease vegetarians. On the coast you'll find plenty of fish (*riba*), mussels (*žkoljke*) and squid (*kalamari*). Italian pasta dishes appear on most restaurant menus, and no Slovene high street is without at least one pizzeria.

Typical desserts include several solid Central European favourites: strudel, filled with apple or rhubarb; *žtruklji*, dumplings with fruit filling; *potica*, a doughy roll filled with nuts and honey; and *prekmurska gibanica*, a delicious local cheesecake.

Drink

Daytime drinking takes place in small café/bars, or in a *kavarna*, where a range of cakes, pastries and ice cream is usually on offer. Coffee (*kava*) is usually served black unless specified otherwise – ask for *mleko* (milk) or *smetana* (cream) – and often drunk alongside a glass of mineral water (*mineralna voda*). Tea (*čaj*) is usually served black. Familiar nonalcoholic drinks such as Coca-Cola, Pepsi and Sprite are all fairly ubiquitous.

Evening drinking usually goes on in small European-style bars or the more traditional *pivnica* (beer hall) or *vinarna* (wine cellar). Slovene beer (*pivo*) is of the Pilsner type and is usually excellent (*Lažko Zlatorog* is considered the best), although most breweries also produce *temno pivo* (literally "dark beer"), a Guinness-like stout. The local wine (*vino*) is either *črno* (red) or *belo* (white) and has an international reputation: dry whites like *Lazki rizling* and *Ljutomerčan* are regularly found on Western supermarket shelves. Best of the reds are the light *Cviček* and the dark, dry *Kraški teran*. Favourite aperitifs include *slivovka* (plum brandy), *vilijemovka* (pear brandy), the fiery *sadjevec*, a brandy made from various fruits, and the gin-like juniper-based *brinovec*.

Opening hours and holidays

Most **shops** open Mon–Fri 8am–7pm and Sat 8am–1pm, with an increasing number opening up on Sundays. Some shops outside major centres may take lengthy lunch breaks. Museum times differ from place to place, but they're usually closed on Mondays.

All shops and banks are closed on the following **public holidays**: Jan 1 & 2; Feb 8 (Day of Slovene Culture); Easter Mon; April 27 (Resistance Day); May 1 & 2; June 25 (Day of Slovene Statehood); Aug 15 (Assumption); Oct 31 (Reformation Day); Nov 1; and Dec 25 & 26.

Emergencies

Slovenia's crime rate is low and you're unlikely to have much contact with Slovene **police** (*policija*); if you do, they're generally easy-going and helpful, but unlikely to speak English. As far as health is concerned, citizens of the EU are entitled to free health care. **Pharmacies** (*lekarna*) tend to follow normal shopping hours, and a rota system covers night-time and weekend opening; details are posted in the window of each pharmacy.

Emergency numbers

Police ☏113; ambulance and fire ☏112.

Ljubljana and around

LJUBLJANA curls under its castle-topped hill, an old centre marooned in the shapeless modernity that stretches out across the plain, a vital and self-consciously growing capital. The city's sights are only part of the picture; first and foremost Ljubljana is a place to meet people and to get involved in the nightlife – the buildings just provide the backdrop.

Arrival, information and city transport

Your likely point of arrival (and drop-off point for buses from Brnik airport, 23km north of the city) is the main **train and bus station**, located on Trg Osvobodilne fronte, ten minutes' walk north of the centre. The main **Tourist Information Office (TIC)** is in the old town on Stritarjeva next to the Triple Bridge (daily 8/10am–6/8pm; ☎01/306-1215, ⊛www.ljubljana.si). There's also an information office at the train station (Mon–Fri 8/10am–5.30/9pm; June–Sept also Sat & Sun; ☎01/433-9475). Ljubljana's buses are cheap and frequent. You can pay on the bus – put your money in a box next to the driver (230SIT per journey) – or buy tokens (*žetoni*; 170SIT) in advance, sold at post offices and most newspaper kiosks.

Accommodation

Finding cheap accommodation in Ljubljana is tough. Inexpensive **hotels** are in short supply and the TIC has just a limited stock of central **private rooms** (❸), which can only be booked on the day. Plans are afoot for an official HI hostel; until then your best bet is one of the **student hostels** (July & Aug only; ❷) at the following locations: *Dijaški Dom Tabor*, the most central, at Vidovdanska 7 (☎01/234-8840); *Dijaški Dom Poljane*, at Potočnikova 3 (☎01/300-3137); and *Dijaški Dom I Cankarja*, at Poljanska 26 (☎01/474-8600).

Five kilometres north of the centre is the pleasant Ježica **campsite** (☎01/568-3913), with a few bungalows (❸) – take bus #6 or #8 north along Dunajska cesta.

Hotels

BIT Center Litijska 57 ☎01/548-0055, ⊛www.bit-center.net. Modern, functional rooms in this sports centre 2km east of the centre; 50-percent discount on use of sporting facilities and free use of pool in summer. Buses # 5, #9 and #13. ❸

Lipa Celovška 264 ☎01/519-2125, ✉aa-lipa@siol.net. Comfortable though not ideally located pension: it's 5km northwest of the centre, beside a busy main road. Buses #1, #15, #16. ❸

M Hotel Derčeva 4 ☎01/513-7000, ⊛www.m-hotel.si. An uninspiring but acceptable modern hotel, 2.5km northwest of the city centre off Celovška cesta. ❸

Park Tabor 9 ☎01/433-1306, ✉hotel.park@siol.net. High-rise located amidst a jumble of apartment buildings a few blocks east of the station with shabby, bare rooms, some with en-suite facilities. ❸

Pri Mrak-u Rimska 4 ☎01/421-9600, ⊛www.daj-dam.si. Smallish downtown pension, with comfortable en-suite rooms. 10-percent discount for stays of more than 3 nights. Good restaurant. ❸

Turist Dalmatinova 15 ☎01/234-9130, ⊛www.hotelturist.si. Reasonable downtown hotel with a mix of older, bland rooms and modern, refurbished rooms; all rooms en suite. ❸

The City

Ljubljana's main point of reference is Slovenska cesta, a busy north–south thoroughfare that slices the city down the middle. Most of the sights are within easy walking distance of here, with the Old Town straddling the River Ljubljanica to the south and east and the nineteenth-century quarter to the west, where the principal museums and galleries are to be found.

Museum of Contemporary History

Rožnik Hills

Postojna Caves, Trieste & the Coast

Train Station

TRG OSVOBODILNE FRONTE

Bus Station

CELOVŠKA

TIVOLSKA CESTA

Tivoli Sports Centre

Tivoli Park

DUNAJSKA

PRAŽAKOVA ULICA

KERSNIKOVA

SLOVENSKA CESTA

CIGALETOVA

TRDINOVA ULICA

GOSPOSVETSKA CESTA

National Gallery Extension

Park Adjovščina

ADJOVŠČINA

TAVČARJEVA ULICA

MIKLOŠIČEVA CESTA

KOLODVORSKA

ŽUPANČIČEVA ULICA

Miklošičev Park

DALMATINOVA ULICA

KIDRIČEVA ULICA

Museum of Modern Art

National Gallery

BEETHOVNOVA

PREŠERNOVA

CANKARJEVA CESTA

NAZORJEVA

BRLČNA

Opera House

TOMŠIČEVA ULICA

SLOVENSKA CESTA

ČOPOVA

Franciscan Church

TRUBARJEVA

TRG NARODNIH HEROJEV

PREŠERNOV TRG

PETKOVŠKOVO NABREŽJE

National Museum

River Ljublanica

TRG REPUBLIKE

Triple Bridge

St Nicholas' Cathedral

Market

WOLFOVA

CIRIL METODOV TRG

Cankarjev Dom

Ursuline Church

KONGRESNI TRG

HRIBARJEVO NABREŽJE

CANKARJEVO NABREŽJE

Fountain

MESTNI TRG

Town Hall

ERJAVČEVA CESTA

Slovene Philharmonic

JURČIČEV TRG

GREGORČIČEVA

GOSPOSKA ULICA

NOVI TRG

Castle

BRASKI

RIMSKA CESTA

TRG FRANCOSKE REVOLUCIJE

Municipal Museum

BREG

GALLUSOVO NABREŽJE

STARI TRG

N

AŠKERČEVA CESTA

Križanke

EMONKSA

GORENJI TRG

Roman Town Walls

MIRJE

ROŽNA ULICA

0   100 m

LJUBLJANA

Zagreb

Architecture Museum

The Old Town

From the bus and train stations head south down Miklošičeva for ten minutes and you're on **Prešernov trg**, the hub around which everything in Ljubljana's delightful **Old Town** revolves. Overlooking the bustling square and the River Ljubljanica, the seventeenth-century **Franciscan Church** (daily 7am–1.30pm & 3–8pm) blushes a sandy red: in the tired-feeling interior the old wall paintings look like faded photographs, and even Francesco Robba's Baroque high altar seems a little weary. Robba, an Italian architect and sculptor, was brought in to remodel the city in its eighteenth-century heyday.

Across the elegant Tromostovje, or Triple Bridge, a **fountain**, also by Robba, symbolizes the meeting of the rivers Sava, Krka and Ljubljanica, and the whole stretch down from Prešernov trg west of the river consists of decaying Baroque grandeur. East of the river along Gallusovo Nabrežje most of the houses are ramshackle and medieval, occasionally slicked up as clothes shops and stores.

Opposite Robba's fountain on Mestni trg is the **Town Hall** (Magistrat) – an undistinguished Baroque building around a courtyard. A little east of here **St Nicholas' Cathedral** (daily 6am–noon & 3–6pm) on Ciril-Metodov trg is the most sumptuous and overblown of Ljubljana's Baroque statements. Designed by Andrea Pozzo, this is the best preserved of the city's ecclesiastical buildings. Just to the west of the cathedral buildings, along the riverside, you can't fail to miss the brash, free-for-all **general market** (not Sun).

Opposite the market, Študentovska winds up the thickly wooded hillside to the **Castle**, visible from all over town and currently being restored to its former glory – what's left today dates mainly from a sixteenth-century rebuilding. Within the castle is the **Virtual Museum** (10am–7pm; 700SIT), which presents the development of the city via imaginative interactive displays. Climb the **clock tower** for a superlative view of the Old Town below, the urban sprawl of high-rises beyond and the Kamniške Alps to the north.

Central Ljubljana and beyond

Back on the western side of the river, the broad slash of **Slovenska cesta** forms the commercial heart of Ljubljana. Dominated by nineteenth- and twentieth-century shops and offices, it's a place to do business rather than sightsee. Further south along here, the park-like expanse of Kongresni trg slopes away from the early-eighteenth-century **Ursuline Church** (Uršulinska Cerkev), whose looming Baroque coffee-cake exterior is one of the city's most imposing. Lower down, by the side of the main university building, Vegova Ulica leads south from Kongresni trg towards Trg francoske revolucije, passing on the way the chequered pink, green and grey brickwork of the University Library. This was designed in the late 1930s by **Jože Plečnik** (1872–1957), the architect who more than any other determined the appearance of present-day Ljubljana. The whole atmosphere around the River Ljubljanica, including the riverbanks and several bridges, is the result of rebuilding work by Plečnik. His legacy, in the shape of neoclassical columns, pillars and miniature brick pyramids scattered all over the city, is impossible to avoid.

One such oddity is the **Illyrian Monument** on Trg francoske revolucije, erected in 1930 in belated recognition of Napoleon's short-lived attempt to create a fiefdom of the same name centred on Ljubljana. Virtually next door is the seventeenth-century monastery complex of **Križanke**: originally the seat of a thirteenth-century order of Teutonic Knights, its delightful colonnaded courtyard was restored by Plečnik to form a permanent venue for the Summer Festival (see p.932). Across Gosposka, at no. 15, the seventeenth-century Turjak Palace contains the **Municipal Museum**, currently undergoing a major transformation and due to reopen in 2004.

Beyond Trg francoske revolucije there's little of importance to see, except for a remaining stretch of the town's **Roman Walls** (rearranged by Plečnik) on Mirje, and, a little further on, Plečnik's old house – now an **Architectural Museum**

(Tues & Thurs 10am–2pm; 600SIT) at Karunova 4, where you can wander around Plečnik's ascetic living quarters.

West of Slovenska: museums and Tivoli Park

West of Slovenska, Cankarjeva heads down towards a neatly ordered corner of town that contains the city's most important **museums**. The **National Museum** (Tues–Sun 10am–6pm, Thurs till 8pm; 700SIT; ⓦwww.narmuz-lj.si), at Muzejska 1, contains numerous dim halls of archeological objects, most famous of which is the **Vačka Situla**, a locally found Iron Age cauldron decorated with scenes of ritual feasting. The museum's natural history section is notable only for having the one complete mammoth skeleton found in Europe. The **National Gallery** (Tues–Sun 10am–6pm; 700SIT, free Sat pm; ⓦwww.ng-slo.si) at Cankarjeva 20 is housed in the former Narodni Dom, built in the 1890s to accommodate Slovene cultural institutions in defiance of the Habsburgs. The gallery is rich in local medieval Gothic work, although most visitors gravitate towards the halls devoted to the Slovene Impressionists Rihard Jakopič, Ivan Grohar, Matija Jama and Matej Sternen. There's more Gothic stuff, as well as high-profile temporary exhibitions in a new **extension** to the gallery (same times & prices) one block to the north at Puharjeva 9. Back on the Cankarjeva, the **Museum of Modern Art** at no. 15 (Tues–Sat 10am–6/7pm, Sun 10am–1pm; 500SIT; ⓦwww.mg-lj.si) carries on where the National Gallery left off, showing how the Slovene Impressionists developed more experimental styles in the early years of the twentieth century.

Beyond the art galleries lies **Tivoli Park**, an expanse of lawns and tree-lined walkways backed by dense woodland. Most of Ljubljana's recreational and sporting facilities can be found in the sports centre at the northern end of the park. A villa above the centre contains the most enjoyable of Ljubljana's museums, the **Museum of Modern History** (Tues–Sun 10am–6pm; 500SIT, free first Sun of the month; ⓦwww.muzej-nz.si) with dioramas, video screens and period music combining to produce an evocative journey through twentieth-century Slovene history.

Eating, drinking and nightlife

As befits its sophisticated, cosmopolitan image, Ljubljana is able to boast a tight concentration of **restaurants**, most of which offer excellent value for money. The best choice for **snacks** are the burek kiosks near the stations and the stands scattered throughout town selling hot dogs and the local *gorenjska* sausages. The **market** on Vodnikov trg is the best place to stock up on fresh produce.

On summer evenings the **cafés and bars** of Ljubljana's Old Town spill out onto the streets with the hectic atmosphere of a mass open-air bar. A wander up and down the banks of the River Ljubljanica and along Stari trg and Mestni trg will yield an interesting locale every fifty yards or so. Major gig **venues** are KUD France Preseren at Karunova 14, the Cankarjev Dom Congress Centre on Trg republike, and the open-air stage at Križanke, Trg francoske revolucije. The free English-language *Ljubljana Life* magazine (ⓦwww.ljubljanalife.com), available from the tourist office, has excellent bar and club listings.

For a relatively small city, Ljubljana offers a surprisingly rich diet of **classical culture**. The Cankarjev Dom, Prešernova 10, is the scene of major orchestral and theatrical events, as well as occasional folk and jazz concerts (ticket office Mon–Fri 10am–2pm & 4.30–8pm, Sat 10am–1pm; also 1hr before each performance; ☎01/241-7299). Ljubljana's energetic **symphony orchestra**, the Slovenska Filharmonija, performs at Kongresni trg 9 (☎01/241-0800), while the republic's **opera and ballet** companies are housed in the Slovene National Theatre (Slovensko Narodno Gledališče), Župančičeva 1 (ticket office Mon–Fri 2–5pm, Sat 6–7pm; also 1hr before each performance; ☎01/425-4840, ⓦwww.sngdrama-lj.si). The city's major annual festival, taking place throughout July and August, is the **International Summer Festival**, featuring orchestral concerts at venues such as the Križanke Theatre, Cankarjev Dom and castle (festival box office: ☎061/426-4340, ⊕www.festival-lj.si). The monthly *Where To? Events* pamphlet, available free from the TIC, has complete listings of concerts and events.

Restaurants

As Čopova (entry Knafljev prehod) ☎01/425-8822. Superb fish restaurant between Slovenska and the Triple Bridge. Not cheap, but tell them your budget and they will cook a meal to fit it.

Casa del Papa Celovška 54a. International food in rooms decorated on an Ernest Hemingway theme (there's a Key West room, a Cuba room and so on).

Emonska Klet Plečnikov trg 1. Once the halls of the Ursuline convent, this capacious cellar restaurant serves up pizzas, salads and Slovenian dishes. Nightly live music and a cracking bar turns this into a bit of a party place in the evenings.

Figovec Gosposvetska 1. Charmingly old-fashioned downtown restaurant specializing in pony steaks (sic), horsemeat goulash and traditional Slovene standards.

Lovec Trg mladinskih delovnih brigad 1. One of the more characterful places in which to eat medium-priced Slovene standards, five minutes' west of Trg francoske revolucije. Good range of pizzas too.

Pizzeria Foculus Gregorčičeva 3. Extensive range of affordable pizzas in lively surroundings, including several vegetarian options and a generous salad buffet.

Rio Slovenska 28. Massive beer garden in a cobbled courtyard serving inexpensive grills and stews.

Šestica Slovenska 40. Traditional place on the main street with elegant vine-trellised interior. Slovene, meat-heavy menu. Closed Sun.

Zlata Ribica Cankarjevo Nabrežje 5. With arguably the best outdoor dining area in the city, this modest and inexpensive fish restaurant by the River Ljubljanica ls delightful.

Cafés and bars

Čajna Hiša Stari trg 3. Bijou café serving the best teas in town, excellent sandwiches and cakes and decent breakfasts. Closed Sun.

Café Gaudi Nazorjeva 10. Delightful interior and seductive range of coffees makes this a terrific place for a coffee stop.

Kratochwill Kolodvorska 14. Bar with a Czech beer-hall atmosphere which brews its own ale. Try the *mešano pivo* (a mixture of stout and lager).

Maček Krojaška 5. Stylish café with large outdoor terrace. The place to be seen on Ljubljana's riverfront, and consequently crammed. Happy hour 4–7pm.

Petite Café Trg francoske revolucije 4. Atmospheric place, ideal for a coffee and croissant as well as for an evening drinking session.

Pr'skelet Ključavničarska 5. Devilishly original bar – it's full of skeletons.

Ragamuffin Krojaška 4. In an alleyway just behind *Maček* (see above). Small, reggae-oriented café/bar, good for a daytime chill-out or more boisterous evening drink.

Salon Trubarjeva 23. Trendy hangout with loud hip-hop and techno music.

Clubs and discos

Gajo Jazz Club Beethovnova 8. Refined late-night jazz club with quality offerings by both domestic and foreign acts. See ⊕www.jazzclubgajo.com for programme.

Hound Dog *M Hotel*, Derčeva. Animated basement bar with regular live (rock) music. A fifteen-minute walk northeast of the centre.

K4 Kersnikova 4. Mecca of Ljubljana's alternative scene, offering different styles of music on different nights – including at least one gay night (currently Sun).

Metelkova Metelkova cesta. Old barracks just east of the train station which now functions as an alternative cultural centre. Club nights, gigs and happenings.

Orto Bar Grablovičeva 1. Stylish media haunt east of the train station with decor reminiscent of the interior of a submarine. Frequent live-rock evenings.

Propaganda Grablovičeva 1. Techno and jungle-oriented club with dance floor. Wed–Sat only.

Listings

Embassies and consulates Australia, Trg republike 3 ☎01/425-4252; Canada, Miklošičeva 19 ☎01/430-3570; UK, Trg republike 3 ☎01/200-3910; US, Prešernova 31 ☎01/200-5500.
Exchange At the train station.
Hospital Bohoričeva 4 ☎01/232-3060.
Internet access Čerin, Trubarjeva 52 (closed Sat & Sun); Cyber Café, Slovenska 10 (closed Sun).

Laundry Chemo-express, Wolfova 12 (closed Sat & Sun; ☎01/251-4404).
Left Luggage Train station (24hr).
Pharmacies Lekarna Miklošič, Miklošičeva 24 ☎01/231 4558 (24hr).
Post office/Telephones Slovenska 32.

The rest of the country

Emphatically not to be missed while you're in Ljubljana is a visit to the **Postojna Caves** – easily managed either as a day-trip from the capital or en route south to Slovene Istria, to Croatia or to Italy. A more low-key alternative to the cave stopoff is **Lipica**, where the celebrated white Lipizzaner horses are bred, or **Predjamski Grad**, near Postojna, an atmospherically sombre castle high above a cave entrance in the midst of a dramatic landscape.

Close to the borders with Italy and Croatia, the towns of **Slovene Istria** have long been popular resorts, yet have still managed to retain some charm and identity. Much of this stems from their Italian character, a legacy of four hundred years of Venetian rule. The coast's main draw is **Piran**, which, with its cobbled piazzas, shuttered houses and back alleys laden with laundry, is almost overwhelmingly pretty. By way of contrast, **Portorož** is Slovenia's brashest beach resort.

To the northwest of Ljubljana, and within easy reach of the capital, are the **mountain lakes** of **Bled** and **Bohinj**, Slovenia's number-one tourist attraction. The magnificent **Soča valley**, on the western side of the Slovene alps, is much less touristed, although small towns like **Kobarid** and **Bovec** are excellent bases from which to engage in rafting and walking. East of Ljubljana on the main route to Hungary, **Ptuj** is Slovenia's oldest town and one of its most attractive.

Postojna

POSTOJNA is on the main rail route south, 65km from Ljubljana, but as the walk to the caves from Postojna train station is further than from the bus stop, most people go by one of the regular buses. Once in the town, signs direct you to the **caves** (daily 9/10am–4/6pm; tours every 1–2hr, last tour 1hr before closing; 2400SIT; ⓦ www.postojna-cave.com). Inside, a railway whizzes you through 2km of preliminary systems before the guided tour starts. The vast and fantastic jungles of rock formations are quite breathtaking.

Accommodation in private rooms (②) is arranged by Kompas in the town centre at Titov trg 2a (Mon–Fri 8am–7pm, Sat 9am–1pm; ☎05/726-4281, ⓔinfo@kompas-postojna.si). They can also supply information on the town and the caves. There's a **campsite**, the *Pivka Jama* (☎05/726-5382), 4km beyond the cave entrance and not served by public transport, which also has four-person bungalows for about £12/$18 per person. There are only two **hotels** in town, both of which are very drab: the *Kras*, in the town centre at Tržaška 1 (☎05/726-4071; ④), and *Jama* (☎05/728-2400; ④), by the caves. *Pizzeria Minutka*, at Ljubljankska 14, is a pleasant alternative to the tourist eateries by the caves.

Predjamski Grad

The other site you're steered to near Postojna is **Predjamski Grad** (daily 9/10am–4/7pm; 700SIT), 7km from Postojna and well signposted from the caves. It's walkable if you're in the mood or you can book a taxi through Kompas; otherwise it's only accessible with your own transport or on an organized trip. Pushed up high against a cave entrance in the midst of karst landscape, the sixteenth-century castle is an impressive sight and affords excellent views of the surrounding countryside. Its damp and rather melancholy interior is less rewarding, unimproved by a museum holding a lacklustre collection of odds and ends from this and an earlier castle that stood nearby. There are **guided tours** of the cave below the castle (May–Sept daily 11am, 1pm, 3pm & 5pm; 800SIT).

Lipica

After Postojna, Slovenia's most emblematic tourist draw is probably **LIPICA**. Located 7km west of the drab railway-junction town of Divača near the Italian border, Lipica gave its name to the **Lipizzaner** horses that are associated with the Spanish Riding School of Vienna. There are three hundred horses here, the results of fastidious breeding that can be dated back to 1580, when the Austrian Archduke Charles established the farm in order to add Spanish and Arab blood to the Lipizzaner strain that was first used by the Romans for chariot races. Tours are given round the **stud farm** (daily 9/11am–3/6pm; 1300SIT; ⊛www.lipica.org), and the horses give the elegant displays for which they're famous (April Fri & Sun at 3pm; May–Oct Tues, Fri & Sun at 3pm; 2300SIT). Guided group rides (3500SIT) are also possible. Public **transport** is limited: a few buses run from Divača weekday mornings, but you have little time to look around before catching the last bus back. Alternatives include spending a night here in one of the hotels – the *Klub* or *Maestoso* (both ⊕05/739-1580; ❺) – or joining a weekend excursion run by travel agents in Ljubljana or Portorož. One-day tours combining Postojna and Lipica currently cost around £35/$50 per person.

The coast: Portorož and Piran

Easily reached by bus from the coastal town of Koper, **PORTOROŽ** ("Port of Roses") sprawls at the end of a long, tapering peninsula that projects like a lizard's tail north into the Adriatic. Already known as early as the end of the nineteenth century for its mild climate and the health-inducing properties of its salty mud baths, the resort is now one of the most developed stretches of coast in all Istria, a vibrant strip of hotels and (largely concrete) beaches. Combining Portorož's modernity with the charm of Piran (a short bus ride or forty-minute walk away; see below) is the key to enjoying this brash, consumption-oriented place. The **tourist office** is on the main coastal strip, Obala Maršala Tita, just down from the bus terminal (July & Aug 9am–1.30pm & 3–9pm; rest of year 10am–5pm; ⊕05/674-0231, ⊛www.portoroz.si). **Private rooms** (❷) are available from Maona, just across the road from the tourist office (⊕05/674-0363, ⊛www.maona.si). There are two **campsites**, 500m apart, 2km south of the bus station near the Marina. Obala Maršala Tita is also the place to choose from any number of places to **eat**.

PIRAN, at the very tip of the peninsula 4km from Portorož's bus station, couldn't be more different. Although there are many tourists here too, the town preserves tangible remnants of atmosphere in its sloping web of arched alleys and little Italianate squares. The centre, a couple of hundred metres around the harbour from where the buses stop, is **Tartinijev trg**, named after the eighteenth-century Italian violinist and composer Giuseppe Tartini, who was born in a house on the square and is commemorated by a bronze statue in the centre. With its striking oval-shaped interior, it's one of the loveliest squares on this coast, fringed by a mix of Venetian palaces and an ostentatious Austrian town hall. Across the harbour, the **Maritime Museum** (Tues–Sun 9am–noon & 3/6–6/9pm; 400SIT) houses a collection of fine model ships, along with an interesting display on Piran's salt industry. Follow Ulica IX Korpusa uphill from the square to the barnlike Baroque **Church of Sv Jurij**, crowning a commanding spot on the far side of Piran's peninsula. Five minutes' walk further up, the town's formidable sixteenth-century **walls** stagger across the hill, the remaining towers providing excellent views of the town.

Piran's **tourist office** is on Tartinijev trg (July & Aug daily 9am–1.30pm & 3–9pm; rest of year Mon–Fri 9am–4pm, Sat 10am–2pm; ⊕05/673-0220). **Rooms** can be booked through Maona, between the bus station and the square at Cankarjevo nabrežje 7 (⊕05/673-4520). The **HI hostel**, *Val*, in the old town at Gregorčičeva 38 (⊕05/673-2555, ⊛www.hostel-val.com; ❸), has excellent facilities, as well as a delightful restaurant. The Fiesa **campsite** is 1km away – follow the trail from the church. For **eating**, the main square offers a couple of good possibilities; *Batana*, on Kidričevo Nabrežje, is a stylish pizzeria with pleasant terrace, and *Mario*, up a flight of steps from Tartinijev trg, has good-value fish and meat dishes. Numerous more expensive seafood restaurants line the seafront. *Kavana Galerija*

Tartini, on Tartinijev trg, is the most relaxing place for a daytime or evening **drink**. Liveliest of the **bars** is *Da Noi*, a cellar-like space next to the *Pavel* restaurant on the seafront.

Bled and Bohinj

Fifty kilometres northwest of Ljubljana, towards Austria and at the eastern end of the Julian Alps, are the **mountain lakes** of **Bled** and **Bohinj**, Slovenia's number one tourist attraction. While Bled, surrounded by Olympian mountains and oozing charm, lives up to expectations, it's also chock-full with tourists, which can't help but temper its delights. Bohinj, in contrast, is less visited, more beautiful and much cheaper. If you're interested in serious **hiking**, good maps are essential: your best bets are the 1:50,000 *Triglav National Park*, the 1:25,000 *Mount Triglav* and the 1:25,000 *Bled and environs* – all published by the Slovene alpine association. Pick them up in Ljubljana bookshops or from the tourist offices in Bled and Ribčev Laz.

Buses are the easiest way to reach both Bled and Bohinj (hourly from Ljubljana; 1hr 15min to Bled, 2hr to Bohinj). **Rail** access to the region is either via the main northbound line from Ljubljana, which calls at Bled-Lesce 3km southeast of Bled itself (and linked to Bled by a regular bus), or a branch line which leaves the main Ljubljana–Villach route at Jesenice and crosses the mountains towards Italy and the coast, calling at Bled-Jezero and Bohinjska Bistrica on the way. The trip from Jesenice, chugging steadily through the mountains and karst, is as impressive as you'd imagine. Train buffs should note that a **steam train** is laid on in summer months, at considerable additional expense (9600SIT).

Bled

There's no denying that the lake resort of **BLED** has all the right ingredients for a memorable visit – a placid mirror lake with a romantic island, a fairy-tale castle high on a bluff, leafy lanes and a backdrop of snow-tipped mountains. In summer, the lake, fed by warm-water springs that take the water temperature up to 76°F, forms the setting for a whole host of water sports – major rowing contests are held here throughout summer – and in winter the surface becomes a giant skating rink.

Paths run uphill from the bus station to **Bled Castle** (daily 8am–5/8pm; 700SIT), which has wonderful views and houses a small sixteenth-century chapel and a very ordinary museum tracing the history of Bled.

During the day a constant relay of stretched gondolas leaves from below the *Park Hotel*, the bathing resort below the castle and Mlino, towards the western end of the lake, ferrying tourists back and forth to Bled's picturesque **island** (1800SIT return). With an early start (and by renting your own rowing boat or canoe from the same place as the gondolas) you can beat them to it. Crowning the island, the Baroque-decorated **Church of Sv Marika Božja** is the last in a line of churches on a spot that's long held religious significance: under the present building are remains of early graves and, below the north chapel, a pre-Roman temple. In summer months it's feasible to swim from the western end of the lake to the island; during winter, under the snug muffle of alpine snow, you can walk or skate across.

The main attraction in the outlying hills is the **Vintgar Gorge** (May–Oct daily 8am–7pm; 500SIT), 5km north of town, an impressive defile accessed by a wooden walkway. To get there, head northwest out of Bled on the Vintgar road (just up from the bus station), turning right on the outskirts of town towards the villages of Gmajna and Zasip. Head uphill through Zasip to the hilltop chapel of Sv Katarina before picking up a path through the forest to the gorge entrance. You could alternatively get there by the daily bus (mid-June to Sept) from *Hotel Jelovica*.

The helpful **tourist office**, down behind the *Park Hotel* at Cesta svobode 15 (July & Aug daily 8am–10pm; rest of year Mon–Sat 8am–5/8pm, Sun 10am/noon–5/6pm; ☎04/574-1122, ⊛www.bled.si). **Private rooms** are available through Kompas, in the shopping centre at Ljubljanska 4 (☎04/574-1515, ⊛www.kompas-bled.si).

There's an outstanding **HI hostel** (℡04/574-5250, ✉www.mlino.si; ❸) just above the bus station at Grajska 17, and some reasonable **pensions** – the smallish *Pletna* at Cesta svobode 37 (℡04/574-3702; ❸); the *Mlino*, further along at no. 45 (℡04/574-1404; ❸); and the *Alp*, 2km west of town along the lakeside road at Cankarjeva 20a (℡04/534-1616; ❹). Bled **campsite** (℡04/575-2000) is beautifully located at the western end of the lake amid the pines and with its own stretch of beach; catch a bus towards Bohinj and ask to be set down near the access road.

The best places for **eating** are in the hillside area between Bled's bus station and castle. *Gostilna Pri Planincu*, Grajska 8, offers solid Slovene home cooking; *Pizzeria Portobello* on Rikljeva is probably the best of the Italian places; and the hostel restaurant is pretty decent too.

Lake Bohinj

It's 30km from Bled to Lake Bohinj and buses run hourly through the **Sava Bohinjka Valley** – dense, verdant and often laden with mist and low cloud. In appearance and character **Lake Bohinj** is utterly different from Bled: the lake crooks a narrow finger under the wild mountains, woods slope gently down to the water, and a lazy stillness hangs over all.

RIBČEV LAZ (often referred to as Jezero on bus timetables), at the eastern end of the lake, is where most facilities are based, including the **tourist office** (July & Aug daily 8am–8pm; rest of year Mon–Sat 8am–6pm, Sun 9am–3pm; ℡04/572-3370, ✉www.bohinj.si), which offers rooms (❷) and apartments around Ribčev Laz and in the idyllic village of **STARA FUŽINA**, 1km north. The main attraction in Ribčev Laz is the **Church of Sv Janez** (July & Aug daily 9am–noon & 4–7pm; other times contact the tourist office), a solid-looking structure whose nave and frescoes date back to the fourteenth century. **Walking trails** lead round both sides of the lake, or north onto the eastern shoulders of the Triglav range. One route leads north from Stara Fužina into the Voje valley, passing through the dramatic **Mostrica Canyon**, a popular local beauty spot.

Five kilometres from Ribčev Laz at the western end of the lake is the hamlet of **UKANC** (sometimes referred to as Zlatorog), site of the **Kravji Bal** or "Cow Dance", a mass booze-up which celebrates the return of the cattle from alpine pastures; this usually takes place in the second or third week of September. There are several **private rooms** (❷) and apartments here, which you can book through the tourist office in Ribčev Laz. The **campsite** (℡04/572-3483), just east of the bus stop, occupies an idyllic lakeside position. An easy walk back east takes you to the **cable car** (daily 8am–6pm every 30min; closed Nov; 1600SIT return) at the foot of **Mt Vogel** (1540m). If the Alps look dramatic from the lakeside, from Vogel's summit they're breathtaking.

An hour's walk north from Ukanc are the photogenic **Savica Waterfalls** (mid–April to Oct 8am–6pm; 300SIT). The falls themselves mark the start of one of the most popular hiking routes up Mount Triglav, which zigzags up the mountain wall to the north before bearing northwest into the **Valley of the Seven Lakes** – an area strewn with eerie boulders and hardy firs – before continuing to the summit of Triglav itself. It's not a hike of great technical difficulty, though it's steep in parts and good maps and careful planning are required. The Seven Lakes can be treated as a day-long hiking expedition from Bohinj, but the assault on Triglav itself necessitates at least one night in a mountain hut. The tourist office in Ribčev Laz will supply details and book you a place, although huts on Triglav are only open from late June to late September – the upper stretches of the mountain shouldn't be tackled outside these times.

The Soča valley

On the other, less-touristed side of the mountains from Bohinj, the river Soča cuts through the western spur of the Julian alps, running parallel with Slovenia's border with Italy. During World War I, the Soča marked the front line between the Italian and Austro-Hungarian armies, and three years of bitter warfare on the surrounding peaks rivalled the Western Front in terms of futile offensives and wasted lives. Memorial chapels and abandoned fortifications abound, located incongruously amidst awesome alpine scenery. The valley is also a major centre for activity-based tourism, with the foaming river itself providing the ideal venue for **rafting** and **kayaking** throughout the spring and summer. Main tourist centres are **Kobarid** and **Bovec**, both small towns with a range of **walking** possibilities right on their doorstep. The 1:50,000 *Posočje* **map** covers trails in the region: it's best to pick it up in Ljubljana if you can, as not all local shops have it.

Although both places are served by four daily buses from Ljubljana, transport connections with the rest of Slovenia are patchy. Approaching the Soča valley from the Bled-Bohinj area involves catching one of six daily trains from Bled-Jezero or Bohinjska Bistrica to **Most na Soči**, where five buses daily run onwards up the valley. Getting here from the coast entails catching buses plying the Koper-Sežana-Nova Gorica-Tolmin-Kobarid route (min. 4hr, depending on connections), although you might have to change at each stage of the journey.

Kobarid

It was at the little alpine town of **KOBARID** that German and Austrian troops finally broke through Italian lines in 1917, almost knocking Italy out of the war in the process. Ernest Hemingway, then a volunteer ambulance driver on the Italian side, took part in the chaotic retreat that followed – an experience which resurfaced in his novel *A Farewell to Arms*. A processional way leads up from Kobarid's main square to a monumental, three-tiered **Italian War Memorial** officially opened by Benito Mussolini in 1938, and a fitting place from which to enjoy views of the surrounding alps and ponder Kobarid's violent past. Back in town, the **Kobarid museum** at Gregorčičeva 10 (Mon–Fri 9/10am–5/6pm, Sat & Sun 9am–6/7pm; 700SIT; ⊛www.kobariski-muzej.si) presents a thoughtful and balanced record of the war with a gripping collection of photographs, maps and mementoes. Continue past the museum, head downhill and take the Drežnica road across the river Soča to pick up trails to the **Kozjak waterfall** (50min), less impressive for its height than for the cavern-like space which it has carved out of the surrounding rock. Numerous paths branch off from here into the wooded hills, passing trench systems dug by the Italians during the war.

The staff in the museum can furnish you with **tourist information** (same times; ☎05/389-9200, ⊛www.kobarid.si); they also have a limited number of **private rooms** (❷) in Kobarid and surrounding villages. The chic rooms at the *Hvala* **hotel** on the main square (☎05/389-9300, ⊛www.topli-val-sp.si; ❺) are remarkably good value for the level of comfort on offer. There's also a **campsite**, the *Koren* (☎05/388-5312), about 500m out of town on the way towards the Kozjak waterfall. As for **eating**, there's nowhere cheap in town save for *Pizzeria pri Vitku*, hidden away in a residential district at Pri Malnik 41 (take the road south out of town and follow the signs). The *Topli Val*, attached to the *Hotel Hvala* (see above), is one of the best restaurants in the country and is well worth the expense.

The main **rafting** company in town is Point Extreme (☎041-692-290, ⊛x.point@siol.net), at the northern end of Trg Svobode; they also organize a range of other outdoor activities. Expect to pay around £20/$30 for a rafting trip.

Bovec

Twenty-five kilometres up the valley from Kobarid, the village of **BOVEC** straggles between imperious mountain ridges. A useful base for the Soča Valley, it has more in the way of accommodation than Kobarid because of its status as a winter ski resort. It's also the location of most of the rafting and adventure sport companies, and is the departure point for any number of alpine walks. The quickest route up into the mountains is provided by the **gondola** (July & Aug Sat & Sun; 2400SIT return) at the southern entrance to the village, which ascends to the pasture-cloaked Mt Kanin over to the west. The **tourist office** is in the Bovec Community Centre at Trg golobarskih žrtev 8 (July & Aug daily 9am–8pm; rest of year Mon–Fri 9am–5pm, Sat & Sun 9am–noon; ☎05/384-1919, ⊛www.bovec.si). Private **rooms** (❷) and apartments are available from either *Gotour*, at Trg golobarskih žrtev 50 (☎05/389-6366, ⊛www.gotourbovec.com), or *Avrigo*, at no. 47 (☎05/384-1150). The nearest **campsite** is *Polovnik*, Ledina 8 (☎05/388-6069); follow the road north out of the village and it's signed to the right after 500m. There are plenty of places to eat and drink on and around the main square. *Stari Kovač*, down from the main square on Rupa 3, has a long list of inexpensive pizzas alongside the usual schnitzels. Soča Rafting (☎05/389-6200, ⊛www.arctur.si/soca_rafting), in the Sports Centre, up the road from the tourist office, is the biggest of many companies grouped around the main square offering **rafting** trips (with prices working out much the same as in Kobarid; see above). It also organizes kayaking and canyoning and rents out mountain bikes.

Ptuj

Located 120km northeast of Ljubljana, **PTUJ** is the oldest town in Slovenia and about the most attractive as well, rising up from the Drava Valley in a flutter of red roofs and topped by a friendly looking castle. But the best thing is its streets, with scaled-down mansions standing shoulder to shoulder on scaled-down boulevards, medieval fantasies crumbling next to Baroque extravagances.

Ptuj is on the main rail line from Ljubljana to Budapest (the Venice–Ljubljana–Budapest express passes through here once a day in both directions), and can also be reached by bus from Slovenia's second-largest city **Maribor**, which is on the Ljubljana-Vienna line. On arriving at Maribor, turn left outside the train station and head downhill – the bus station is on the other side of the crossroads.

Ptuj's main street, Prešernova cesta, snakes along the base of the castle-topped hill. At its eastern end is a sixteenth-century bell tower and the **Priory Church of St George** (open am only), a building of twelfth-century origin that holds a statue of its patron nonchalantly killing a rather homely dragon.

From here Prešernova cesta leads to the **Archeological Museum** (mid-April to Dec daily 10am–5pm; 600SIT), housed in what was once a Dominican monastery, gutted in the eighteenth century and now hung with spidery decoration, and worth a look for the carvings and statuary around its likeably dishevelled cloisters.

A path opposite the monastery winds up to the **Castle** (daily 9am–5/6pm; July & Aug Sat & Sun till 8pm; 600SIT). There's been a castle of sorts here for as long as there's been a town, since Ptuj was the only bridging point across the Drava for miles around, holding the defences against the tribes of the north. An agglomeration of styles from the fourteenth to the eighteenth centuries, the castle was home to a succession of noble families. Most prominent were the Herbersteins, Austro–Slovene aristocrats who made their fortune in the Habsburg Empire's wars against the Turks. Their portraits hang on the walls of the castle's **museum**, containing period rooms with original tapestries and wallpaper.

At Shrovetide (late Feb/early March) Ptuj is the venue of one of the oldest and most unusual customs in Slovenia. The *Kurenti* **processions** are a sort of fertility rite and celebration of the dead confused together: participants wear sinister masks of sheepskin and feathers with a coloured beak for a nose and white beads for teeth. So dressed, the *Kurenti* move in hopping procession from house to house, scaring off evil spirits with the din from the cowbells tied to their costumes.

Practicalities

Ptuj's **train station** is 500m northeast of the centre on Osojnikova cesta, the **bus station** 100m nearer town on the same road. From both points, walk down Osojnikova to its junction with ul Heroja Lacka: a right turn here lands you straight in the centre. The **tourist office** in the clocktower outside the church (July & Aug

Mon–Fri 8am–6pm, Sat 8am–4pm, Sun 10am–3pm; rest of the year closed Sun; ☎02/779-6011, ✆www.ptuj.si) has **private rooms** in the town itself and in local farmhouses (❷). The superb new **hostel** is located midway between the stations and the town centre at Osojnikova 9 (☎02/780-5540; ❸). There are two very affordable **hotels**: the central *Mitra*, Prešernova 6 (☎02/774-210; ❹); and the *Poetovio*, near the bus station at Trstenjakova 13 (☎02/779-8201; ❸). The well-regimented Terme Ptuj **campsite**, Pot v Toplice 9 (☎02/782-7821, ✆terme.ptuj@siol.net), lies among fields 2km east of town.

For **eating**, try *Slonček*, Prešernova 19, a decent pizzeria in the centre of town, or *Amadeus*, a little further along at no. 36, serving Slovene standards. *Café Europa*, on Slovenski trg, is the current in-place, while *Café Bo* and *Café Orfei* on Prešernova are both also good places to enjoy an evening **drink**.

Travel details

Trains

Bohinjska Bistrica to: Most na Soai (6 daily; 45min).
Ljubljana to: Divača (hourly; 1hr 30min); Koper (5 daily; 2hr 30min); Maribor (hourly; 2hr 20min–3hr 20min); Postojna (hourly; 1hr); Ptuj (7 daily; 2hr 30min).

Buses

Kobarid to: Bovec (5 daily; 40min); Ljubljana (3 daily; 4hr); Nova Gorica (3 daily; 1hr 15min).
Koper to: Bled (1 daily; 3hr 30min); Piran (every 20min; 40min); Portorož (every 20min; 30min); Trieste (Mon–Sat hourly; 1hr).
Ljubljana to: Bled (hourly; 1hr 15min); Bohinj (hourly; 2hr); Bovec (4 daily; 4hr 45min); Divača (10 daily; 1hr 30min); Kobarid (4 daily; 4hr); Koper (9 daily; 2hr); Maribor (7 daily; 3hr 45min); Piran (6 daily; 2hr 40min); Portorož (6 daily; 2hr 30 min); Postojna (hourly; 1hr).
Maribor to: Ptuj (every 30min; 40min).

Spain

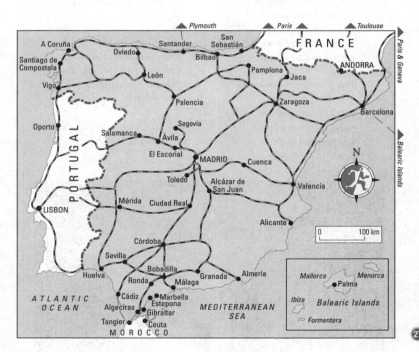

Spain highlights

✱ **Plaza Mayor, Salamanca** The finest square in one of the finest cities in Northern Spain. **See p.979**

✱ **Guggenheim, Bilbao** The billowing curves of Gehry's building are as big an attraction as the art inside. **See p.985**

✱ **The Pyrenees** Get away from it all on a trek through some of the most wonderful and least visited scenery in Spain. **See p.989**

✱ **San Fermín, Pamplona** Make like Hemingway and run with the bulls. **See p.989**

✱ **Parc Güell, Barcelona** A Modernist haven in an architect's city. **See p.1003**

✱ **Ibiza** One of Europe's trendiest resorts, and *the* place to go clubbing. **See p.1010**

Introduction and basics

Spain might appear from the tourist brochures to be no more than a clichéd whirl of bullfights and crowded beaches, castles and Moorish palaces. Travel for any length of time, however, and the sheer variety of this huge country, which in the north can look like Ireland and in the south like Morocco, cannot fail to impress. The separate kingdoms which made up the original Spanish nation remain very much in evidence, in a diversity of language, culture and artistic traditions.

Modern Spain – the country of world-renowned architecture, music festivals, museums and chic city-life – has really only been ten years In the making. Since 1992, when Barcelona hosted the Olympics, Sevilla the World Fair, and Madrid was official Cultural Capital of Europe, Spain hasn't looked back and has seen an ever-more impressed selection of tourists come to explore her every corner. In 2002, the ancient university city of Salamanca became Spain's latest European cultural capital – celebrated, In true Spanish style, with much eating, drinking and fiesta.

In the **cities** there is always something happening – in clubs, on the streets, in fashion, in politics – and even in the most out-of-the-way places there's nightlife, music and entertainment, not to mention the more traditional fiestas. In the **countryside** you can still find villages that have been decaying steadily since Columbus set sail: rural areas are more and more depopulated as the young head for the cities. Yet for the visitor the landscape retains its fascination; even local variations can be so extreme that a journey of just a few hours can take you through scenes of total contrast. Spain is as mountainous a nation as any in Europe and the sierras have always formed formidable barriers to centralization.

It's almost impossible to summarize Spain as a single country. **Catalunya** is vibrant and go-ahead; **Galicia** a verdant rural idyll; the **Basque** country grappling with postindustrial depression and its own identity; **Castile** and the south still, somehow, quintessentially "Spanish". There are definite highlights to Spanish travel: the three great cities of **Barcelona**, **Madrid** and **Sevilla**; the Moorish monuments of **Andalucía** and the Christian ones of **Old Castile**; beach-life in **Ibiza** or on the more deserted sands around **Cádiz** and in the north; and, for some of the best trekking in Europe, the **Pyrenees** and the Asturian **Picos de Europa**.

Information and maps

The **Spanish National Tourist Office** (*Información* or *Oficina de turismo*) has a branch in virtually every major town, giving away a variable array of maps, accommodation lists and leaflets – in the busiest towns

Spain on the net

ⓦ **www.tourspain.es** Comprehensive and highly recommended site with extensive information, in English

ⓦ **www.guiadelocio.com** Major nightlife, art, restaurant and entertainment listings for most Spanish cities, updated weekly. In Spanish

ⓦ **www.alsa.es** Buses throughout southeastern and northwestern Spain, and major cities

ⓦ **www.renfe.es/ingles/hir/index.html** Train timetables and fares, in English

ⓦ **www.mtas.es/injuve/index2/html** Spanish branch of the IYHF with a comprehensive hostel directory

ⓦ **www.hostelspain.com** Hostelworld network of budget hotels and youth hostels throughout the country

SPAIN | Basics

27

they often run out. Offices are often supplemented by provincial or municipal **Turismos**, which vary in quality. Both types are usually open Mon–Fri 9/10am–1pm & 4–7/8pm, Sat 9am–1/2pm.

Among the best **maps** are those published by Editorial Almax (www.almax-editores.com). Good alternatives are the 1:800,000 map produced by RV (Reise- und Verkehrsverlag, Stuttgart) and packaged in Spain by Plaza & Janes, and the less detailed offerings from Michelin, Firestone or Rand McNally. Serious **trekkers** should look for topographical maps issued by the IGN (Instituto Geográfico Nacional) and the SGE (Servicio Geográfico del Ejército), although in the northern mountain areas, Editorial Alpina is more practical.

Money and banks

Spain is one of twelve European Union countries which have changed over to a single currency, the **euro** (€).

Banks and *cajas de ahorro* (equivalent to a building society or savings and loan) have branches in all but the smallest towns. **Hours** are Mon–Fri 8.30am–2pm, also Sat in low season. Outside these times it's usually possible to change cash at larger hotels (generally bad rates, but low commission), with travel agents in the cities and big resorts, and at most El Corte Inglés department stores, which have surprisingly reasonable rates. In tourist areas you'll also find **casas de cambio**, with more convenient hours, but worse exchange rates. ATMs are widespread and accept both credit and debit cards.

For a Western European country, Spain is a relatively cheap place to visit. Public transport is subsidized, museums are generally inexpensive and food and accommodation are normally reasonably priced. If you are eligible, it's always worth asking for student or senior citizen reductions as many tourist sites offer discounts.

Communications

Post offices (*correos*) are open Mon–Fri 8.30am–2pm & Sat 9am–noon, though big branches in large cities have longer afternoon and Sunday hours. Queues can be long, but stamps are also sold at tobacconists (*estancos*). **Poste restante** should be addressed to "Lista de Correos", followed by the name of the town and province. **American Express** in Madrid and Barcelona will hold mail for a month for cardholders.

You can make **international phone calls** from almost any phone box. The various brands of discount long-distance cards for domestic and overseas calls are the cheapest and most convenient way to pay (available from tobacconists, *locutorios* and many Internet cafés). Most phone boxes accept coins as well as cards. The **operator** number is ☏1003 for domestic calls, ☏025 for international information. Note that all regional prefixes are an integral part of **telephone numbers**. For example, in Madrid the two-digit prefix is 91 and it is necessary to dial these digits even when calling from within the city. However, on business cards and other publicity these preliminary digits may not appear, and people don't always include them when giving out a number.

The **internet** is widely available – at internet cafés, some computer shops and many phone centres. Prices vary; in cities hourly rates can be as little as €0.90, rising to around €3 in some smaller towns and €9 if you use the kiosks at bus and train stations.

Getting around

Most of Spain is well covered by both bus and rail networks and for journeys between major towns there's often little to choose between the two in cost or speed. On shorter or minor routes buses tend to be quicker and will normally take you closer to your destination.

Trains

RENFE, the Spanish rail company, operates a horrendously complicated variety of **train** services. It is divided into three sections: *Cercanías* (red) are local commuter trains in and around the major cities; *Regionales* (orange) are equivalent to buses in speed and cost, and run between cities – *regional* *exprés* and *delta* trains can cover longer distances; and *Largo recorrido* express trains (some variation on grey) have a bewildering number of names – in ascending order of speed and luxury, they are known as *Diurno, Intercity (IC), Estrella (*), Talgo, Talgo Pendular, Talgo 200 (T200),* and *Trenhotel.* Anything above Intercity can cost upwards of twice as much as standard second class. There is also a growing number of private super-high-speed trains from Madrid, such as *AVE* to Sevilla, *Alaris* between Madrid and Valencia, and *Euromed* and *Altaria* to Alicante. These are white, look like aeroplanes, and for those who can afford it have cut travelling times drastically.

A good way to avoid the queues is to buy tickets at travel agents which display the RENFE sign – they can also make seat reservations (€3.01), which are obligatory on *largo recorrido* trains; the cost is the same as at the station. Most larger towns also have a RENFE office in the centre. You can also book on ☎902 240 202 (24hr).

InterRail and Eurail passes are valid on all RENFE trains and also on *EuroMed,* but supplements are charged on the fastest trains, as well as a reservation fee (see above).

Buses

Many smaller villages are accessible only by **bus**, almost always leaving from the capital of their province. Service varies in quality, but buses are often faster than trains and are usually as reliable and comfortable, with prices pretty standard at around €6/100km. Many towns still have no main station, and buses may leave from a variety of places. Services are drastically reduced on **Sundays and holidays** – so it's best to avoid travelling to out-of-the-way places on these days.

Accommodation

Simple, reasonably priced rooms are widely available in rural Spain, and in most towns you'll be able to get a double for around €22, €14 a single – though major resorts and big cities will generally charge more. Outside of high season, it's worth bargaining over room prices. For groups, most places have rooms with three or four beds for not a great deal more than the double-room rate.

Hotels

The one thing all travellers need to master is the elaborate variety of types and places of hotel-type accommodation. Cheapest of all, but increasingly rare, are **fondas** (identifiable by a square blue sign with a white F on it), closely followed by **casas de huéspedes** (CH on a similar sign), **pensiones** (P) and, less commonly, **hospedajes**. Distinctions between all of these are rather blurred, but in general you might find food served at both *fondas* and *pensiones* (some of which may offer rooms only on a meals-inclusive basis). *Casas de huéspedes* – literally "guest houses" – were traditionally for longer stays, and to some extent they still are.

Slightly more expensive than all these, but far more common, are **hostales** (marked Hs) and **hostal-residencias** (HsR). These are categorized from one- to three-stars, but prices vary enormously according to location. Most *hostales* offer good functional rooms, usually with private shower, and, for doubles at least, they can be excellent value.

Moving up the scale you finally reach **hoteles** (H), again star-graded by the authorities. One-star hotels cost no more than three-star *hostales* – sometimes they're actually cheaper – but at three stars you pay a lot more, at four or five you're in the luxury class with prices to match. Near the top end of this scale there are also state-run **paradores**: beautiful places, often converted from castles, monasteries and other minor Spanish monuments. **Tourist offices** always have lists of places to stay, but often miss the cheaper deals.

Private rooms and hostels

Outside the above categories, you will sometimes see **camas** (beds) and **habitaciones** (rooms) advertised in private houses or above bars, often with the phrase "*camas y comidas*" (beds and meals) – these can be the cheapest of all options.

Hostels (*Albergues Juveniles*), on the other hand, are rarely very practical, except in northern Spain, where it can be difficult for solo travellers to find any other bed in summer. Few stay open all year, and in towns they are often inconveniently located. They tend to have curfews, are often block-reserved by school groups, and demand production of an HI card (though this is generally available on the spot). At €7–22 per person, you can easily pay more to stay in a hostel than for sharing a cheap double room in a *fonda* or *casa de huéspedes*.

It is sometimes possible to stay at Spanish **monasteries**, which may let empty cells for around €3 per person, but if you want to be sure of a reception it's best to approach the local tourist office first, and phone ahead. Throughout the country there are *agroturismo* and *casa rural* programmes that offer excellent cheap accommodation in rural areas, usually in beautifully preserved and well-maintained private houses. Full lists are available from the relevant tourist offices.

Camping

There are over 350 authorized **campsites** in Spain, mostly on the coast and holiday areas. They work out at about €3 per person plus the same again for a tent. If you plan to camp extensively pick up the free *Mapa de Campings* from the National Tourist Board, the more complete *Guía de Campings* (€6) or see ⊛ www.vayacamping.net.

Camping rough is generally not a good idea, although exact laws vary from province to province. It is unwise to set up a tent anywhere near a tourist beach or campsite, though, as this can result in a hefty fine. Wherever you decide to pitch up, check first with the local *Ayuntamiento* (Town Hall).

Food and drink

There are two ways to eat in Spain: you can go to a *restaurante* or *comedor* (dining room) and have a full meal, or you can have a succession of tapas (small snacks) or *raciones* (larger ones) at one or more bars.

Food

Bars and cafés are best for **breakfast**, which can consist of *churros con chocolate* – long tubular doughnuts with thick drinking chocolate – *tostadas* (toasted bread) with oil

(con aceite) or butter and jam (con mantequilla y mermelada), or more substantial egg dishes such as *tortilla* (omelette). **Coffee and pastries** (*bollería*) are available at the many excellent *pastelerías* and *confiterías*.

Sandwiches (*bocadillos*) make excellent lunches. **Tabernas**, **tascas**, **bodegas**, **cervecerias** and **bars** als serve **tapas** or *pinchos*: mini portions of meat, fish, tortilla or salad for €1.20–2.80 a plate. Their big brothers, **raciones** (€3–9), make a sufficient meal in themselves. Note that sitting at the bar is the cheapest way to eat, a table costs almost twice as much, and a seat outside even more.

Two- or three-course main meals (*cubierto*, *menú del día* or *menú de la casa*) with wine are served at **comedores** or **cafeterías** (€5–8). *Cafeterías* all serve rather bland *platos combinados* such as egg and fries or *calamares* and salad, with bread and a drink included (€3.50–6). **Restaurants** are graded on a scale of one to five forks, with the cheapest full meal plus wine costing €5–10 – but prices escalate rapidly above two forks.

Fish and seafood are fresh and excellent, particularly regional specialities such as Galician fish stews (*zarzuelas*) and Valencian paellas (which also contain meat). Restaurants serving exclusively fish and seafood are called **marisquerías**.

Spain is hard for **vegetarians**, and normal veggie staples such as salads often include tuna or egg, while beans and lentil dishes are cooked with bacon and tortillas come with ham. Most large cities will have a vegetarian restaurant or an all-you-can-eat buffet bar – if not, think omelettes, green salad and bread.

Drink

Wine, either *tinto* (red), *blanco* (white) or *rosado/clarete* (rosé), is cheap and drinkable – the most common variety is Valdepeñas, from New Castile or Rioja. Good regional wines include Penedès and Bach from Catalunya, Ribera del Duero from Castilla, Albariño from Galicia and Mendizabal, a light Rioja rosé.

Vino de Jerez, Andalucian **sherry**, is served chilled and either *fino/jerez seco* (dry), *amontillado* (medium), or *oloroso/jerez dulce* (sweet). **Cerveza**, lager-type beer, is more expensive than wine but also good – local brands, such as Cruzcampo in Sevilla or Alhambra in Granada, are usually the best. **Sangría**, a wine-and-fruit punch, and **sidra**, a dry farmhouse cider most typical in the Basque Country and Asturias, should also be tried.

Spaniards often take a *copa* of **liqueur** with their coffee; the best are *anís* (like Pernod) or *coñac*, excellent local brandy with a distinct vanilla flavour. There are cheaper Spanish equivalents (*nacional*) of most **spirits**, so specify if you are on a tight budget. Measures are large.

Coffee is invariably espresso, unless you specify *cortado* (with a drop of milk), *con leche* (a more generous dollop) or *americano* (weaker black coffee). **Tea** is also drunk black. If you want milk, ask afterwards: ordering *té con leche* might well get you a glass of milk with a teabag floating on top. Herbal teas, such as *tila* (lime blossom), *menta* (mint) and *manzanilla* (camomile), are also available.

Opening hours and holidays

Almost everywhere closes for a **siesta** of at least two hours in the hottest part of the day. There's a lot of variation, and certain **shops** now stay open all day, especially the big department stores, but basic summer hours are Mon–Sat 9.30am–1.30pm & 4.30–8pm. **Museums**, with few exceptions, take a break between 1 and 4pm, and are closed Sunday afternoon and usually all day Monday. The really important **churches**, including most cathedrals, operate similarly; others open only for worship in the early morning and/or the evening.

There are twelve national **holidays** and scores of local ones. The national ones are: Jan 1; Jan 6; Maundy Thurs; Good Fri; Easter Sun; May 1; Aug 15; Oct 12; Nov 1; Dec 6; Dec 8; Dec 25. Certain Comunidades (regions) also observe Easter Mon; May 2 (Madrid only); May 20 (Barcelona only); Corpus Christi (early or mid-June); June 24; and July 25.

Emergencies

The paramilitary **Guardia Civil** (green uniforms and patent-leather hats or green kepis) still police some rural areas, borders and most highways. In Catalunya, some of their responsibilities have devolved to the **Mossos d'Esquadra**, and in the Basque country, to the **Ertzaintza**. In cities, you'll find the **Policía Nacional** (talk to them if you get robbed) and the **Policía Municipal** (for traffic infractions), and there is a **Patrulla Rural** in some outlying areas. A common source of trouble is **petty theft**, which can be particularly bad in some cities and during fiestas; be sure to use common sense and keep an eye (and an arm) on your things at all times.

For minor **health** complaints it's easiest to go to a *farmacia*, which you'll find in almost any town. In more serious cases you can head directly to *Urgencias* at the nearest **hospital**, or get the address of an English-speaking doctor from the nearest relevant consulate, or from a *farmacia*, the local police or tourist office.

Emergency numbers
All emergencies ☏112
Ambulance ☏081

Madrid

MADRID became Spain's capital by grace of its geography; when Philip II moved the seat of government here in 1561, his aim was to create a symbol of Spanish unification and centralization. However, the city has few natural advantages – it is 300km from the sea on a 650-metre-high plateau, freezing in winter, burning in summer – and it was only the determination of successive rulers to promote a strong central capital that ensured its success. Today, Madrid is a predominantly modern city, but the streets at her heart are a pleasant surprise, hiding odd pockets of medieval buildings and atmospheric, narrow alleys. There are admittedly few sights of great architectural interest, but it is home to some of Spain's best art: the monarchs acquired outstanding picture collections which went on to form the basis of the Prado museum. This has long ensured the city a place on any European art-tour, and the more so since the 1990s arrival of the Reina Sofía and Thyssen-Bornemisza galleries, state-of-the-art homes to fabulous arrays of modern Spanish painting (including Picasso's *Guernica*) and European and American masters.

Galleries and sights aside, though, the capital has enough going for it in its own city life and style to ensure a diverting stay. You soon realize that it's the inhabitants – some 5,300 000 Madrileños – that are the capital's key attraction: hanging out in the traditional cafés and *Chocolaterías* or the summer *terrazas*, packing the lanes of the Sunday Rastro flea market, or playing hard and very, very late in a thousand bars, clubs, discos and *tascas*. Whatever Barcelona or San Sebastián might claim, the Madrid scene remains as it is immortalized in the movies of Pedro Almodóvar – vibrant, noisy and lots of fun.

Arrival and information

Barajas airport is 16km out of town and connected with the centre by metro line #8 and bus #89 to Plaza de Colon. Trains from the north and from Portugal arrive at the **Estación de Chamartín**, rather isolated in the north of the city, but connected to the centre – and all major city locations – via metro line #10. The much more central **Estación de Atocha** serves the south, east and west of Spain. Local trains use the **Estaciónde Príncipe Pío**, more widely known as **Estación del Norte**, below the central Plaza de España. **Bus terminals** are scattered throughout the city, but the largest – used by all international services – is the **Estación Sur** (Metro Mendez Alvaró) on c/Mendez Alvaró, south of Atocha station.

Madrid's **tourist offices** aren't great, but they're a good place to start; the main municipal branch is at Plaza Mayor 3 (Mon–Sat 10am–8pm, Sun 10am–3pm; ☏915 881 636); there's also a branch at the airport (daily 8am–8pm; ☏913 058 656). For details of **what's on**, check out the weekly *Guía del Ocio* (available from newsstands; ☼www.guiadelocio.com/madrid), the Friday and Saturday editions of *El País* and *El Mundo* (newspapers) and the free monthly *En Madrid*, available at tourist offices and bars.

City transport

The centre is comfortably walkable, but Madrid also has a good **metro system** that serves most places you're likely to want to get to. It runs from 6am until 1.30am with a flat fare of €0.95, €5 for the metrobus ten-ride ticket, valid for both bus (same flat-fare rate) and metro. The urban **bus network** is more comprehensive than the metro, but also more complicated – trust the transport information stand in the Plaza de Cibeles before the myriad and quickly outdated handouts. Buses run from 6am to 11.30pm, but there are also several nightbus lines in the centre, from Plaza de Cibeles and Puerta del Sol (midnight–3am every 30min, 3–6am hourly). Hop-on hop-off bus companies have stops at all the major sights (€9.62/day, €12.02/two days).

Accommodation

The cheapest accommodation is around the **Estación de Atocha**, though places closest to the station are rather grim, and the area can feel somewhat threatening at night. A better option is to head up c/Atocha towards Sol, to the streets surrounding the buzzing **Plaza Santa Ana**. Prices rise as you reach the Plaza Mayor and Puerta del Sol, but even here there are affordable options. Other promising areas include **Gran Vía**, where the huge old buildings hide a vast array of hotels and *hostales*, and north of here up noisy **c/Fuencarral** towards Chueca and Malsaña.

Hostels

Hostal Barbieri c/Barbieri 15 ☎915 310 258, ✉www.barbierihostel.com. Basic dorm accommodation plus kitchen in youthful, hip Chueca. Rate includes breakfast. **②**

Hostel Los Amigos Campomanes 6, 4th floor ☎915 471 707, ✉www.losamigoshostel.com. Very friendly dorm-only hostel with full kitchen on a quiet street between Sol and the Palacio Real. Metro Opera. Rate includes breakfast. **②**

Hostel Richard Schirmann in the Casa del Campo ☎914 635 699, ✉www.reaj.com. Friendly, comfortable and clean HI place, but way out of the city in a seedy area – taxis are advisable at night. Roughly 1km from Metro El Lago. **①**

Hostel Santa Cruz de Marcenado c/Santa Cruz de Marcenado 28 ☎915 474 532. North of the Plaza de España near the Palacio Liria; reasonably pleasant, modern and quiet HI place. Curfew 1.30am. Books up fast. Metro Argüelles. **①**

Hotels

Hostal Aguilar Carrera San Jerónimo 32 ☎914 293 951. One of several in a building packed with possibilities. **③**

Hostal Alcázar Regis Gran Vía 61 ☎915 479 317. Near the Plaza de España, deservedly popular and often full. **③**

Hostal Alonso c/Espoz y Mina 17 ☎915 315 679.

Very cheap, if a little shabby; family-run, great location. **②**

Hostal Aranzazu c/Doctor Mata 1–3 ☎915 394 846. Centrally located near Atocha and well equipped. **③**

Hostal Armesto c/San Agustin 6 ☎914 299 031. Small, very pleasant *hostal*, well positioned for the Santa Ana area and the art galleries. **③**

Hostal Conchita II c/Campomanes 11 ☎915 475 061. Great location just off Opera, near the Palacio Real and Puerta del Sol. **②**

Hostal Horizonte c/Atocha 28, 2nd floor ☎913 690 996, ✉www.hostalhorizonte.com. Super-friendly hotel with well-maintained and characterful rooms near the Plaza Santa Ana. **②**

Hostal Lisboa c/Ventura de la Vega 17 ☎914 297 481. Good three-star *hostal*, central but not too hectic. **③**

Hostal Carreras c/del Principe 18 ☎915 220 036. Comfortable place in elegant old building off Plaza Santa Ana. **③**

Hostal Riosol c/Mayor 5 ☎915 323 142. Just off Puerta del Sol towards Plaza Mayor. Most rooms en suite. **②**

Hostal Sud-Americana Paseo del Prado 12 ☎914 292 564. Almost opposite the Prado; though standards vary, there are some excellent rooms here. Closed Aug. **②**

The City

Central **Puerta del Sol**, with its bustling crowds and traffic, is as good a place as any to start a tour of Madrid. This is officially the centre of the nation: a stone slab in the pavement outside the main building on the south side marks **Kilometre Zero**, from where six of Spain's National Routes begin, while beneath the streets, three of the city's ten metro lines converge. A statue of a bear pawing a *madroño* bush lies on the north side; this is both the emblem of the city and a favourite meeting place.

Immediately north of Sol, c/de Preciados and c/del Carmen head towards the Gran Vía; both are pedestrianized and constitute the most popular **shopping area** in Madrid. West, c/del Arenal heads directly towards the Opera and Royal Palace, but there's more of interest along **c/Mayor**, one of Madrid's oldest thoroughfares, which runs southwest through the heart of the medieval city, also to end close to the Royal Palace.

CENTRAL MADRID

Conv. de las Comendadoras

Montserrat

Las Maravillas

S. Marcos

Torre de Madrid

Museo Cerralbo

Edificio España

Parque del Oeste

Templo de Debod

Parque de la Montaña

Jardines de Ferraz

Casa de Campo

Parque del Oeste

PLAZA DE ESPAÑA

Pza. de España

Noviciado

S. Antonio de los Alemanes

San Plácido

S. Martín

Palacio de la Prensa

Sto. Domingo

PL. DE SANTO DOMINGO

Cine Callao

Callao

Descalzas Reales

El Carmen

Convento de la Encarnación

Jardines de Sabatini

Jardines del Cabo Noval

Ópera

Teatro Real

PLAZA DE ORIENTE

PLAZA DE ISABEL II

Palacio Real

Armería Real

Campo del Moro

Iglesia de Santiago

San Ginés

PUERTA DEL SOL

Sol

Catedral Ntra. Sra. de la Almudena

San Nicolás

Casa de Cisneros

Los Lujanes

PLAZA MAYOR

Parque Emir Mohamed

Muralla árabe

Las Vistillas

Capitania General

Ayuntamiento

San Miguel

Minist. de Asuntos Exteriores

LA VISTILLAS

PLAZA DE GABRIEL MIRÓ

Capilla del Obispo

San Pedro

San Andrés

San Isidro

Tirso de Molina

Hemeroteca Nacional

La Latina

San Francisco el Grande

Puerta de Toledo

GLORIETA PUERTA DE TOLEDO

La Corrala

SPAIN | Madrid

27

950

0   200 m

▼ Estadio Vicente Calderón

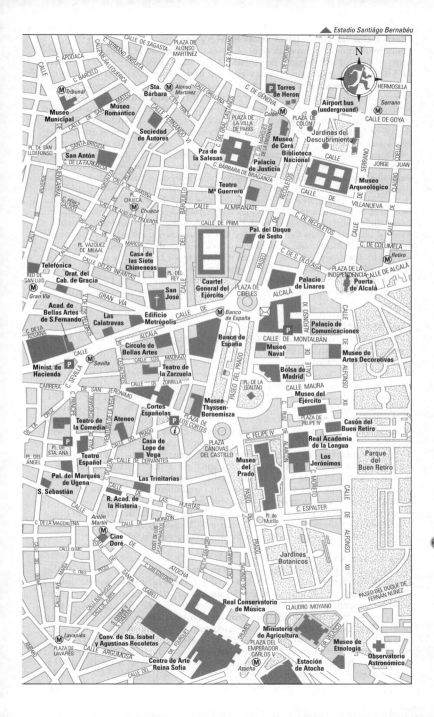

SPAIN | Madrid

Plaza de la Villa and Plaza Mayor

About two-thirds of the way along c/Mayor is the **Plaza de la Villa**, almost a case-book of Spanish architectural development. The oldest survivor here is the **Torre de los Lujanes**, a fifteenth-century building in Mudéjar style; next in age is the **Casa de Cisneros**, built by a nephew of Cardinal Cisneros in sixteenth-century Plateresque style; and to complete the picture is the **Ayuntamiento** (tours Mon at 5pm; free), begun in the seventeenth century, but later remodelled in Baroque mode. Baroque is taken a stage further around the corner in c/San Justo, where the church of **San Miguel** shows the unbridled imagination of its eighteenth-century Italian architects.

Walking straight from the Puerta del Sol to the Plaza de la Villa, it's easy to miss altogether the **Plaza Mayor**, the most important architectural and historical land-mark in Madrid. This almost perfectly preserved, extremely beautiful, seventeenth-century arcaded square, set back from the street, was planned by Philip II and Juan Herrera as the public meeting place of the new capital: *autos-da-fé* (trials of faith) were held by the Inquisition here, kings were crowned, festivals and demonstrations staged, bulls fought and gossip spread. The more important of these events would be watched by royalty from the be-frescoed **Casa Panadería**, named after the bakery that it replaced. Along with its popular but pricey cafés, the plaza still performs several public functions today: in summer, it's an outdoor theatre and music stage; in autumn, a book fair; and just before Christmas it becomes a bazaar for festive decorations and religious regalia. The warren of streets surrounding the Plaza Mayor are well worth exploring, housing as they do a treasure trove of great tapas bars and restaurants.

The Palacio Real

Calle del Arenal ends at the Plaza Isabel II opposite the **Teatro Real** or Opera House, which is separated from the Palacio Real by the newly renovated **Plaza de Oriente**. The chief attraction of the area is the grandiose **Palacio Real**, or Royal Palace (Mon–Fri 9am–5/6pm, Sat & Sun 9am–2/3pm; €6, free Wed to EU citizens). Built after the earlier Muslim Alcázar burned down on Christmas Day 1734, this was the principal royal residence until Alfonso XIII went into exile in 1931. The present royal family inhabits a more modest residence on the western outskirts of the city, using the Palacio Real only on state occasions. The building scores high on statistics: it claims more rooms than any other European palace; a **library** with one of the biggest collections of books, manuscripts, maps and musical scores in the world; an **armoury** with an unrivalled and often bizarre collection of weapons dating back to the fifteenth century; and an original **pharmacy**, a curious mixture of alchemist's den and early laboratory, its walls lined with jars labelled for various remedies. Take your time to contemplate the extraordinary opulence of the place: acres of Flemish and Spanish tapestries, endless Rococo decoration, bejewelled clocks and pompous portraits of the monarchs. In the **Sala del Trono** (Throne Room) there's a magnificent frescoed ceiling by Tiepolo representing the glory of Spain – an extraordinary achievement for an artist by then in his 70s.

The Gran Vía

North from the palace, c/Bailén runs into the Plaza de España, longtime home of the tallest skyscrapers in the city. From here join **Gran Vía**; it was once the capital's major thoroughfare and effectively divides the old city to the south from the newer parts. Permanently crowded with shoppers and sightseers, the street is appropriately named, with splendidly quirky Art Nouveau and Art Deco facades fronting its banks, offices and apartments, and huge hand-painted posters on the cinemas. At its far end, by the magnificent cylindrical **Edificio Metropolis**, it joins with c/Alcalá on the approach to Plaza de la Cibeles. Just across the junction is the majestic old **Círculo de las Bellas Artes**, a contemporary art space with a trendy café/bar (entry €0.80, €1 after 4pm).

On an entirely different plane, the **Monasterio de las Descalzas Reales** (Tues–Sun 10.30/11am–12.45/1.45pm, Tues, Thurs & Fri also 4–5.45pm; €4.81), one of the hidden treasures of the city, lies just south of the Gran Vía on the Plaza de las Descalzas. This convent was founded by Juana de Austria, daughter of Carlos V, sister of Philip II and, at 19, already the widow of Prince Don Juan of Portugal. In her wake came a succession of titled ladies who brought fame and, above all, fortune. It's an amazingly rich and beautiful locale, the tranquillity within its thick walls making an extraordinary contrast to the frenzied commercialism all around. A whistle-stop guided tour takes you through the cloisters and up an overly ornate stairway to a series of chambers packed with art and treasures of every kind.

The Prado

Just across the Paseo del Prado from the Círculo de la Bellas Artes lies Madrid's **Museo del Prado** (Tues–Sat 9am–7pm, Sun 9am–2pm; ⓦmuseoprado.mcu.es; €3, free Sat after 2.30pm & all Sun), which has been one of Europe's key art galleries ever since it was opened to the public in 1819. It houses the finest works accumulated by Spanish royalty as well as standout items from other Iberian sources: over three thousand paintings in all, including the world's finest collections of Goya, Velázquez and Bosch. The most rewarding approach to the museum is perhaps through the Puerta de Goya, on c/Felipe IV; pick up a free leaflet at the entrance to find your way round.

Even in a full day you couldn't hope to do justice to everything in the Prado, and it's much more enjoyable to make short visits with a clear idea of what you want to see. In the first rooms on the ground floor are early Spanish paintings, mostly religious subjects, then in a series of rooms to your left the early **Flemish masters** are displayed. The great triptychs of Hieronymus Bosch – the early *Hay Wain*, the middle-period *Garden of Earthly Delights* and the late *Adoration of the Magi* – are familiar from countless reproductions, and there's much more of his work here, along with that of Pieter Bruegel the Elder, Rogier van der Weyden, Memling, Bouts, Gerard David and Massys. Dürer dominates the small German collection. The museum's collection of over 160 works of later Flemish and Dutch art has been imaginatively rehoused in a new suite of twelve rooms off the main gallery on the first floor. Rubens is extensively represented – by the beautifully restored *Three Graces* among others – as are van Dyck and Jan Brueghel.

The long, central downstairs gallery houses the **early Spanish collection**, and a dazzling array of portraits and religious paintings by El Greco, among them his mystic and hallucinatory *Crucifixion* and *Adoration of the Shepherds*. Beyond this is the beginning of the Prado's **Italian** treasures: the superb Titian portraits of Charles V and Philip II, as well as works by Tintoretto, Bassano, Caravaggio and Veronese. Upstairs are Goya's unmissable Black Paintings – completed in his autumn years and best seen after visiting the rest of his work on the top floor – and, to the left of the Puerta de Goya entrance, a series of panels by Botticelli illustrating a story from the Decameron.

Continuing on the **first floor** you come to the great Spanish painters, where the outstanding presence is **Velázquez** – among the collection are intimate portraits of the family of Felipe IV, most famously his masterpiece *Las Meninas*. Adjacent are important works by Zurbarán and Murillo.

The **top floor** of the building is devoted almost entirely to **Francisco de Goya**, whose many portraits of his patron, Charles IV, are remarkable for their lack of any attempt at flattery, while those of Queen María Luisa, whom he despised, are downright ugly. He was an enormously versatile artist: contrast the voluptuous *Majas* with the horrors depicted in *The Second of May* and *The Third of May*, on-the-spot portrayals of the rebellion against Napoleon and the subsequent reprisals.

The Thyssen-Bornemisza collection

The **Colleción Thyssen-Bornemisza** (Tues–Sun 10am–7pm; temporary collection €3.60, whole collection €6.60; ⊕www.museothyssen.org) occupies the old Palacio de Villahermosa, diagonally opposite the Prado. In 1993, this prestigious site played a large part in Spain's acquisition of what was perhaps the world's greatest private art collection, with important works from every major period and movement. From Duccio and Holbein, through El Greco and Caravaggio, to Schiele and Rothko; from a strong showing of nineteenth-century Americans to some very early and very late Van Goghs, and side-by-side hangings of parallel Cubist studies by Picasso, Braque and Mondrian, the collection is both rich and extensive. There's a **bar and café** in the basement and re-entry is allowed, so long as you get your hand stamped at the exit desk.

Centro de Arte Reina Sofía

The **Centro de Arte Reina Sofía** (Mon & Wed–Sat 10am–11pm, Sun 10am–2.30pm; ⊕museoreinasofia.mcu.es; €3, free Sat after 2.30pm & all Sun), facing Atocha station at the end of Paseo del Prado, keeps different opening hours and days from its neighbours, which is fortunate because this leading exhibition space, and permanent collection of modern Spanish art, is another essential stop on the Madrid art scene. The museum, a massive former convent and hospital, is a kind of Madrid response to the Pompidou centre in Paris. Transparent lifts shuttle visitors up the outside of the building, whose levels feature a cinema, excellent art and design bookshops, a print, music and photographic library, restaurant, bar and café, as well as the exhibition halls (top floor) and the collection of twentieth-century art (second floor).

It is for **Picasso's Guernica** that most visitors come to the Reina Sofía, and rightly so. Superbly displayed along with its preliminary studies, this icon of twentieth-century Spanish art and politics – a response to the fascist bombing of the Basque town of Guernica in the Spanish Civil War – carries a shock that defies all familiarity. Other halls are devoted to **Dalí** and Surrealism, early-twentieth-century Spanish artists including **Miró** and post-World War II figurative art, mapping the beginning of abstraction through to Pop and avant-garde.

The Rastro

The area south of the Plaza Mayor and c/Atocha has traditionally been a tough, working-class district and in many places the old houses survive, huddled together in narrow streets. However, an influx of youthful, fashionable residents has changed the character of **La Latina** and **Lavapiés** over the last decade, making it pleasantly hip. Partly responsible for this change is the **Rastro** (Metro La Latina), which is as much part of Madrid's weekend ritual as a Mass or a *paseo*. This gargantuan, thriving, thieving shambles of a **street market** sprawls south from Metro La Latina to the Ronda de Toledo, and is particularly busy along c/Ribera de Curtidores; crowds flood through between 10am and 3pm on Sundays and holidays. Don't expect to find fabulous bargains; the serious antiques trade has mostly moved off the streets and into the shops. It's definitely worth a visit, though, if only to see the locals out in their thousands and to do as they do – recover in a selection of traditional tapas bars – after the madness has subsided. Keep a tight grip on your bags, pockets, cameras and jewellery. Afterwards head over to the bars and *terrazas* around Puerta de Moros where half of Madrid congregates for an *aperitivo* and to while away the afternoon.

Retiro and other parks

Madrid's many parks provide great places to escape the sightseeing for a few hours. The most central and most popular is the **Parque del Buen Retiro** behind the Prado, a stunning mix of formal gardens and wilder spaces. In its 1.3 sq km you can jog, row a boat, picnic, have your fortune told, and above all promenade – on

Sunday afternoon half of Madrid turns out for the *paseo*. Travelling art exhibitions are frequently housed in the beautiful **Palacio de Velázquez** and the nearby **Palacio de Cristal** (times and prices vary according to exhibition). The nearby **Jardines Botanicos** (daily 10am–sunset; €1.50; Metro Atocha), whose entrance faces the southern end of the Prado, are also delightful.

Eating and drinking

There can be few places in the world that can rival the area around **Puerta del Sol** in either quantity or variety of outlets. And the feasts continue in all directions, especially towards **Plaza Santa Ana** and along **c/de las Huertas** to Atocha, but also south in the neighbourhood haunts of **La Latina** and **Lavapiés**, and north in the gay *barrio* **Chueca** and the alternative **Malsaña**. The streets between Lope de Vega, Plaza Santa Ana and c/Echegary are especially pleasant for bar-hopping.

In summer, all areas of the city have pavement café/bars, where coffees are taken by day and drinks pretty much all night. The prime area is **Paseo Castellana**, where many of the top discos can be found. Smaller scenes are in Plaza de **Chueca**, Paseo **Rosales** del Pintor along the Parque del Oeste, the more relaxed and pleasant **c/Argumosa** in Lavapies/Atocha, **Puerta de Moros** in La Latina and **Las Vistillas**, on the south side of the viaduct on c/Bailén, due south of the royal palace.

Tapas bars

Casa Alberto c/de las Huertas 18. One of the most traditional Huertas bars: very friendly, lots of tables and huge portions. Also a restaurant at the back.

El Anciano Rey de los Vinos c/Bailén. Wine and sherry in the traditional manner straight from the barrel.

Las Bravas c/Espoz y Mina, Huertas. The original premises of this Madrid institution, which now has branches throughout the city; sample their famous *patatas bravas* at the bar under glaring neon lights.

Café Comercial Glorieta de Bilbao. Traditional café and meeting place; linger over coffee, *coñac* or cakes.

Café Gijón Paseo de Recoletos 21, north of Plaza de Cibeles. Traditional nineteenth-century café, tremendously atmospheric. Lunchtime *menú* and pricey summer terrace.

La Mi Venta Plaza de la Marina española. A charming 30-year old establishment specializing in jamón and fish and much frequented by locals.

Mejillonera El Pasaje Pasaje Matheu, off c/Victoria, near Sol. One of many places filling this narrow street with outdoor tables – this one specializes in mussels.

Melo's c/Ave María 44. Excellent-value Galician place serving huge portions. A Lavapiés institution.

Museo del Jamón Carrera San Jerónimo 6, Puerta del Sol end. Extraordinary place where hundreds of hams hang from the ceiling, and you can sample the different (expensive) varieties over a glass or two; also has full meals and the best breakfast deals in town. Numerous other branches.

Viña P Plaza de Santa Ana 3. Friendly bar, decked out in bullfighting mementoes, serving a great range of tapas.

Mainly-for-drinking bars

Cervecería Alemána Plaza Santa Ana. One of Hemingway's favourite haunts and consequently full of Americans; good traditional atmosphere none the less.

Bodega Ángel Sierra Plaza Chueca. Great old bar right on the square, just the place for an apéritif.

Casa Antonio c/de Latoneros near the Plaza Mayor. Specializes in sherries and fine wines.

I Latina Teatro de la Latina, Plaza de la Cebada 2. Hip, modern and friendly bar in the cellar of one of Madrid's theatrical landmarks.

La Nina del Exorcista C/Fernando el Catolico 76. Eclectic new horror-themed bar, where you can feed piranhas or watch horror flicks while you quaff.

Los Gabrieles c/Echegaray 17. One of the most spectacular tiled bars in Madrid, with fabulous nineteenth-century drinking scenes on the glazed ceramic tileworks, including a great version of Velázquez's *Los Borrachos* (The Drunkards). Great service, too.

La Luna Amor de Diós 13, off Huertas. A perennially popular dive.

Star Café c/Marqués de Valdeiglesias 5. Hip, happening gay/mixed bar. Funky grooves in the basement at weekends. Closed Sun.

La Venencia c/Echegaray 7. Marvellous old wooden bar, serving sherry only and the most basic of tapas – cheese and pressed tuna. A must.

Restaurants

Artemisa c/Ventura de la Vega 4. Decent low-priced vegetarian restaurant.

Casa Ciriaco c/Mayor 84. Good, traditional restaurant, not too expensive for the area.

Casa Eduardo Cava San Miguel, next to the market behind Plaza Mayor. Outdoor tables, Galician specialties and very cheap set *menú*.

Champagner'a Gala c/Moratín 22. Excellent value colourful paella restaurant with a lovely conservatory at the back.

Creperie Ma Bretagne c/San Vicente Ferrer. Tiny place with good pancakes.

El Estragón Plaza de la Paja 10. Good vegetarian tapas and an economical *menú del día* in an attractive plaza.

Elqui c/Buenavista 18. One of Madrid's best vegetarian restaurants. Self-service with excellent lunchtime *menú*.

Fernández c/Palma 6. Simple, inexpensive restaurant, always packed with locals and adventurous low-budget travellers.

Casa Mingo Paseo de la Florida, next to chapel of San Antonio de la Florida. Asturian place where you eat roast chicken washed down with cider. Good value and great fun, especially on Sun pm.

La Mordida c/Belén 13 and c/Las Fuentes 3. Mexican food round the clock; good, fresh and filling.

Mushashi c/Conchas 4. Taking advantage of Madrid's role as the second biggest fish market in the world, this basic, friendly restaurant serves very tasty sushi at reasonable prices.

Sabatini c/Bailén 15, opposite Jardines Sabatini. Outdoor tables looking towards the Palacio Real in summer; the food's significantly less expensive than you might expect.

Viuda de Vacas c/Cava Alta 23. Good-value no-frills Castilian restaurant in an area packed with great bars.

Nightlife

The **bars, clubs and discos** of Malsaña, and Huertas around Plaza Santa Ana or a little further south in Lavapiés, could easily occupy your whole stay in Madrid, with the many clubs starting around 1am and staying open until well beyond dawn. The names and styles change constantly but even where a place has closed down a new alternative usually opens up at the same address. To supplement our **listings**, check out the English-language magazine *En Madrid*, or the quarterly *Madrid Concept*.

Music concerts – classical, flamenco, salsa, jazz and rock – are advertised on posters around Sol and are also listed in the *Guia del Ocio* and in the newspaper *El Pais*. In July and especially in August there's not too much happening inside, but the city council sponsors a *Veranos de la Villa* programme of concerts and free cinema in some attractive outside venues. If you find that you've somehow stayed out all night and feel in need of early morning sustenance, a final station on the clubbers' circuit is the *Chocolatería San Gines* (Tues–Sun 10am–7pm) on c/de Coloreros, just off c/Mayor, for a *chocolate con churros*.

Discos, music bars and nightclubs

Discos and **music bars** can be found all over the city. Of the big **nightclubs**, *Pacha*, c/Barcelo 11, is the eternal survivor – it's exceptionally cool during the week, less so at weekends when the out-of-towners take over. Another biggie is *Maxime*, Puerta de Toledo 1 (Metro Puerta de Toledo), hosting both underground and celebrity techno and house DJs. Weekend alternatives are the revolving nights at *Macumba*, above Chamartín station, where the likes of Ministry of Sound hit the decks until 9am; *El Sol* on c/Jardines 3 (Metro Gran Vía), for house, soul and acid jazz, plus live music; *Soul Kitchen* on Traves de San Mateo 1 (Metro Tribunal) and *The Notorious Club* (c/Luchana s/n c/Covarrubias) for R&B, soul and reggae; *Ya'sta* on c/ Valverde 10 for techno, house and drum'n'bass; *Sala Público* (Plaza de los Mostenses 11, s/n Gran Vía 68) for house; *Suga House Club* on Av.Logroño, 323 (Metro Barajas) for dub; and *Café La Palma* (c/La Palma 62) for a little bit of everything. *Shangay Tea Dance* (Gran Vía 37) on Sunday nights from 10pm, is one of the most popular **gay nights** in town.

For diving in and out of clubs, however, as Madrileños like to do, the student area of **Malsaña**, focused on Plaza Dos de Mayo, holds most promise and the music in the clubs is more of a grunge scene. A key street to start off explorations is c/San

Vicente Ferrer, where *Taboo* at no. 23 often has live music, while *La Habana* at Atocha no. 107 has a great mix of salsa and reggae. For more of a chance to talk, try *Café Manuela* on c/San Vicente Ferrer, or any of the pubs in the Plaza Dos de Mayo: *El Arco–Café Mahon* is a good place to start. **Chueca** is more exclusively (but not entirely) **gay** – c/Pelayo is a good point to start, with several gay bars including *New Leather* at no. 42 and *LL* at no. 11. Finally, the up-and-coming **Lavapiés/ Anton Martín** area, south of Sol, is a popular bar and club locale: try *La Ventura* at c/Olmo 31 for some of Madrid's top *electronica* DJs, or the hip *El Mojito* at c/Olmo 6.

Live music

The music scene in Madrid sets the pattern for the rest of the country, and the best rock **bands** either come from here or make their name here. For young local groups try *Taboo* at c/San Vicente Ferrer 22, and *Moby Dick Club*, Avenida de Brasil 5; cool foreign independents often play at Gruta 77, c/Nicolas Morales, s/n c/Cucillo 6. Bigger rock concerts are usually held in one of the football stadiums or at *La Riviera* on Paseo Bajo de la Virgen del Puerto. A good array of **jazz bars** includes the topnotch *Central Café*, Plaza del Ángel 10, near Sol, *Clamores* in c/Albuquerque 14, and *Café Berlin* at c/Jacometrezo 4. Fans of **electronica** might want to check out the quality names at *Nasti*, c/San Vicente Ferrer 23 or the smaller *Siroco*, c/San Dimas 3. **South American** music is on offer at various venues, especially during summer festivals; the best year-round club is the *Café del Mercado* in the Mercado Puerta de Toledo, which puts on live salsa more or less every night. **Flamenco** can also be heard at its best in the summer **festivals**, especially at the *noches de flamenco* in the beautiful courtyard of the old barracks on c/de Conde Duque. Promising year-round venues include *Caracol*, c/Bernardino Obregón 18; *Café de Chinitas*, c/Torija 7; *La Soleá*, Cava Baja 34; *Casa Patas*, Cañizares 10; and at *Suristán*, c/de la Cruz 7 (Wed only), which is the place to head most nights for live performances of all types of **World Music**.

Film and theatre

Cinema-going is a passion in Madrid, reflected in the queues outside the huge-capacity cinemas on Gran Vía. The Spanish routinely dub foreign movies, but a few cinemas specialize in original-language screenings. These include the Alphaville and Renoir theatres at c/Martín de los Heros 14 and 12, near Plaza de España, the tiny California at c/Andrés Mellado 47 (Metro Moncloa) and the Círculo de Bellas Artes, on Marqués de Casa Riera. A bargain (€1.35) programme of classic films is shown at the lovely Art Deco Filmoteca at c/Santa Isabel 3, which has a pleasant bar and, in summer, an outdoor *cine-terraza*.

Classical Spanish **theatre** performances can be seen at the Teatro Español, Plaza Santa Ana, and the Teatro Real, Plaza de Oriente; more modern works are at the Centro Cultural de la Villa, Plaza de Colón, and in the beautiful Círculo de Bellas Artes, Marqués de Casa Riera 2. Cultural events in English are held from time to time at the **British Institute**, c/Almagro 5 (☎913 373 500; Metro Alonso Martínez), which can also be a useful point for contacts.

Listings

Banks and Exchanges Large branches of most major banks on c/Alcalá and Gran Vía. Round the clock currency exchange at the airport; the *Banco Central* is best for American Express travellers' cheques.

Bullfights Madrid's Plaza de Toros – *Las Ventas* – hosts some of the year's most prestigious events, especially during the May/June San Isidro festivities. Tickets for all but the biggest events are available at the box office (☎913 562 200, ⓦwww.las-ventas.com).

Embassies Australia, Plaza Descubridor Diego de Ordás, 3 ☎914 416 025; Canada, Nuñez de Balboa 35 ☎914 233 252; Ireland, Paseo de la Castellana 46 ☎914 364 093; New Zealand, Plaza de la Lealtad 2 ☎915 230 226; UK, c/de Fernando

el Santo 16 ☎917 008 200, ⊕www.ukinspain
.com; US, c/Serrano 75 ☎915 774 000.
Hospitals La Paz del Insalud, Paseo Castellana
261 ☎917 277 000 (Metro Begoñ); Hospital de
Madrid, Plaza Conde del Valle de Suchil 16 ☎914
476 600 (Metro Quevedo or San Bernardo).
Internet access easyEverything, c/Montera 10;
Ciber Natura, Gran Via 16; Vortex Madrid, c/Ave
Maria 20.
Laundry c/Barco 26 (Metro Gran Vía); c/Cervantes

1 (Metro Anton Martin); c/Pelayo 44 (Metro Chueca).
Left luggage At the bus and train stations ad the
airport terminal.
Pharmacies Farmacía Lopez Vicente, c/Gran Vía,
26 ☎915 213 148; Farmacia de la Paloma,
c/Toledo, 46 ☎913 653 458; Farmacía Atocha,
c/Atocha 114 ☎ 915 273 415. For nearest 24hr
pharmacy call ☎098.
Post office Palacio de Comunicaciones in the
Plaza de las Cibeles.

Around Madrid

Surrounding the capital are some of Spain's most fascinating cities, all an easy day-trip from Madrid, or a convenient stopoff on the main routes out. From **Toledo** you can turn south to Andalucía or strike west towards Extremadura. To the north-west the roads lead past **El Escorial**, from where a bus runs to Franco's tomb at **El Valle de los Caídos**, and through the dramatic scenery of the Sierra de Guadarrama, with Madrid's weekend ski resorts, to Segovia. Southwest of here lies the graceful walled city of Salamanca, with Galicia beyond, while to the east there's less of interest, but Alcalá de Henares and Guadalajara can both offer a worthwhile break on the journey into Aragón and Catalunya.

Toledo

Capital of medieval Spain until 1560, **TOLEDO** remains the seat of the Catholic primate and a city redolent of past glories. Set in a desolate landscape, it rests on a rocky mound isolated on three sides by a looping gorge of the Río Tajo (Tagus). Every available inch of this outcrop has been built on: houses, synagogues, churches and mosques are heaped upon one another in a haphazard spiral which the cobbled lanes infiltrate as best they can. The sightseeing hordes are easy enough to avoid; simply slip into the backstreets or stay the night; by 6pm the tour buses have all gone home.

The City

Right at the heart of the city sits the **Cathedral** (Mon–Sat 10.30am–2pm & 4–6.30pm; museum €4.80), a robust Gothic construction which took over 250 years to complete (1227–1493). The exterior is best appreciated from outside the city, from where the hundred-metre spire and the weighty buttressing can be seen to advantage. Inside at the heart of the church, blocking the nave, is the Choir, or **Coro** (closed Sun am), with two tiers of magnificently carved wooden stalls. Directly opposite stands the gargantuan altarpiece of the **Capilla Mayor**, one of the triumphs of Gothic art, overflowing with intricate detail; it contains a synopsis of the entire New Testament, culminating in a Calvary at the summit. Directly behind the main altar is an extraordinary piece of fantasy, the **Transparente**: won-derfully Baroque, with marble cherubs sitting on fluffy marble clouds, it's especially magnificent when the sun reaches through the hole punched in the roof (designd specifically for that purpose). Over twenty chapels are dotted around the walls, all of them of interest. In the **Capilla Mozárabe** Mass is still celebrated daily according to the ancient Visigothic rites; if you want to look inside, get there for Mass (9.30am). You should also see the Capilla de San Juan, housing the riches of the cathedral **Treasury**; the **Sacristía**, with the cathedral's finest paintings, including works by El Greco, Velázquez and Goya; and the **New Museums**, with more work from El Greco, who was born in Crete but settled in Toledo in about 1577.

Toledo is physically dominated by the bluff, imposing **Alcázar** (Tues–Sun 9.30am–2pm; €1.20), to the east of the cathedral in a site that has housed many destroyed fortresses throughout the years. The most recent devastation was wrought in 1936 during a symbolic episode of the Civil War, when some six hundred barricaded Nationalists held out against relentless Republican attack for over two months until finally relieved by one of Franco's armies. Franco's regime completely rebuilt the fortress as a monument to the endurance and glory of its defenders.

An excellent collection of El Grecos can be seen to the north of here in the **Museo de Santa Cruz** (Tues–Sat 10am–6.30pm, Sun 10am–2pm; €1.20, free Sat pm & Sun am), a superlative Renaissance building that also boasts outstanding works by Goya and Ribera, a huge collection of ancient carpets and faded tapestries, sculpture and a small archeological collection. **The Museo de los Concilios y de la Cultura Visigótica** (Tues–Sat 10am–2pm & 4–6.30pm, Sun 10am–2pm; €0.60, free Sat pm & Sun am), in the Mudéjar church of **San Román**, a short way northwest of the cathedral, is also well worth a visit. The building, a delightful combination of Moorish and Christian elements, perhaps even outshines the Visigothic artefacts within.

El Greco's masterpiece, *The Burial of the Count of Orgaz*, is housed in an annexe to the nearby church of **Santo Tomé** (daily 10am–6/7pm; €1.20). From Santo Tomé the c/de San Juan de Dios leads down to the old Jewish quarter and, on c/Reyes Católicos, the synagogue of **El Tránsito**, built along Moorish lines by Samuel Levi in 1366. The only other surviving synagogue, **Santa María la Blanca** (10am–2pm & 3.30–6/7pm; €1.20), is a short way down the same street. Like El Tránsito, which it predates by over a century, it has been both church and synagogue, though it looks more like a mosque.

Continuing down c/Reyes Católicos, you come to the superb church of **San Juan de los Reyes** (daily 10am–2pm & 3.30–6/7pm; €1.20), with its magnificent double-storey cloister. If you leave the city here by the **Puerta de Cambrón** you can follow the Paseo de Recaredo, which runs alongside a stretch of Moorish walls towards the **Hospital de Tavera** (10.30am–1.30pm & 3.30–6pm; €3), a Renaissance palace with beautiful twin patios, which houses a number of fine paintings. Heading back to town, you can pass through the main city gate, the **Nueva Puerta de Bisagra**, marooned by a constant swirl of traffic. The main road bears to the left, but on foot you can climb towards the centre of town by a series of stepped alleyways, past the intriguing Mudéjar church of **Santiago del Arrabal** and the tiny mosque of **Santo Cristo de la Luz**. Built in the tenth century on the foundations of a Visigothic church, this is one of the oldest Moorish monuments surviving in Spain. Only the nave, however, with its nine different cupolas, is the original Arab construction.

Practicalities

Toledo's **train station** is a beautiful but uphill twenty-minute walk to the central Plaza Zocódover (bus #5 or #6). The **bus station** is on Avenida de Castilla la Mancha in the modern, lower part of the city; it's a ten-minute walk from the Plaza, and buses run frequently. From Madrid, buses to Toledo run from Madrid's Estación del Sur, while *cercanía* trains run from both Atocha and Chamartín. The last bus to Madrid leaves Toledo at 10pm (Sun 11.30pm); the last train at 8.56pm. The main **tourist office** (Mon–Sat 9am–6/7pm, Sun 9am–3pm; ☎925 22 08 43), outside the walls opposite the Puerta de Bisagra, has full lists of places to stay; there's also a useful office in the Plaza Ayuntamiento (daily 10.30am–2.30pm & 4.30–7pm, closed Mon pm).

In summer **rooms** can be very hard to find, so it's worth arriving early. Among the more central and inexpensive options, try *Virgen de la Estrella*, Real del Arrabal 18 (☎925 256 318; ❷); *Pension Segovia*, Recoletos 2 (☎925 211 124; ❷); *Pension Castilla*, Recoletos 6 (☎925 256 318, ❷); or *Posada del Estudiante*, hidden behind the cathedral at San Pedro 2 (☎925 210 069; ❷). The **hostel** is about fifteen minutes' walk out of town, in a wing of the Castillo San Servando (☎925 267 700; ●) and affords wonderful views of the city. The nearest **campsite**, *El Circo Romano* (☎925 220 442), is a ten-minute walk from the Puerta de Bisagra along Avda. Carlos III and also enjoys great city views.

Food is relatively expensive and not always very good quality, but it's easy to find. *La Bisagra*, c/Arrabal 14, just uphill from the Puerta Bisagra, and *Arrabal*, opposite, are touristy but reasonably priced. For similar places try the Plaza Magdalena, southwest of Zocódover; one of the best here is *Casa Ludeña* at no. 13, with a cheap set menu. Northeast of Zocódover, c/Santa Fe has several outdoor cafés popular with a young crowd in the evenings. Less obvious places, all with good-value lunchtime menus, include the well-hidden *Posada del Estudiante*, c/de San Pedro 2, behind the cathedral; the pricier *Restaurante Palacios*, c/Alfonso X El Sabio 3; *El Rincón* on c/San Tomé 30; and *La Estrella*, c/Airosas 1, for paella and fish. At night there's not a lot of youthful action unless you're willing to head out to the hip neighbourhood of Rafael (buses #1, #2 & #3), but there are a couple of late **bars**: try *Theo* on Callejón de la Sillería, s/n, for loud drinking. For **live music**, *Picaro* on c/Cadenas 6, has a different genre every night, and *El Último*, Plaza Colegio Infantes 4, hosts regular live blues and jazz. For **discos**, try the music-bars along c/de Gerardo Lobo, the long-established and mainstream *Sithon's* on Callejón de Lucio 1, or the excellent *Venta de Alma*, housed in an old farmhouse across the Puente de San Martín on the Carretera de Piedrabuena.

El Escorial and El Valle de Los Caídos

Northwest of Madrid is the line of mountains formed by the Sierra de Guadarrama and the Sierra de Gredos, snowcapped and forbidding even in summer. Beyond them lies Segovia, but on the near side, in the foothills of the Guadarrama, are **SAN LORENZO DEL ESCORIAL** and the bleak monastery of **El Escorial** (Tues–Sun 10am–5/6pm; €6.91, free on Wed for EU citizens). Enormous and overbearing, its severe grandeur can be impressive, but all too often it's just depressing. Planned by Philip II as a monastery and mausoleum, it was the centre of his web of letters, a place from which he boasted he could "rule the world with two inches of paper".

To avoid the worst of the crowds, come just before lunch, or at least visit the royal apartments – focus of all the bus tours – at that time. If you can afford to avoid coming on Wednesday, even better. A good starting place is the **west gateway**, facing the mountains, and through the traditional main entrance. It leads into the **Patio de los Reyes**, where to the left is a school, to the right the monastery, both of them still in use, and straight ahead the **church**. In here, notice the flat vault of the *coro* above your head as you enter, apparently entirely without support, and the white marble Christ carved by Benvenuto Cellini.

Back outside and around to the left are the **Sacristía** and the **Salas Capitulares** (Chapterhouses), which contain many of the monastery's religious treasures, including paintings by Titian, Velázquez and Ribera. Beside the sacristy a staircase leads down to the **Panteón de los Reyes**, the final resting place of virtually all Spanish monarchs since Charles V. Just above the entrance is the *Pudrería*, where their bodies are laid to rot for twenty years or so before the cleaned skeletons are moved. The younger Royal corpses are laid in the **Panteón de los Infantes**. Nearby are the **Library**, with probably the most valuable collection of books in Spain, and the so-called **New Museums**, where much of the Escorial's art collection – works by Bosch, Gerard David, Dürer, Titian, Zurbarán and many others – is kept in an elegant suite of rooms.

Finally, there's the **Palace** itself, including the spartan quarters inhabited by Philip II. Later, less ascetic monarchs enlarged and richly decorated the palace apartments, but Philip's simple rooms, with the chair that supported his gouty leg and the deathbed from which he could look down into the church where Mass was constantly celebrated, remain the most fascinating. Adding a splash of colour and considerably less morose than the rest of the complex is the **Jardín de los Frailes** (same hours), which offers spectacular views of the surrounding countryside.

North of El Escorial by 9km is **El Valle de los Caídos** (Tues–Sun 10am–6/7pm; €4.81, joint ticket with El Escorial €8.41; free on Wed for EU citizens). This is an equally megalomaniacal yet far more chilling monument than El Escorial: an underground basilica hewn under Franco's orders, allegedly as a monument to the Civil War dead of both sides, though in reality it's a memorial to the *Generalísimo* and his regime. The dictator himself lies buried behind the high altar, while the only other named tomb is that of his guru, the Falange leader José Antonio Primo de Rivera, who was shot dead by Republicans at the beginning of the war. The "other side" is present only in the fact that the complex was built by the Republican army's survivors – political prisoners on quarrying duty. Above the complex is a vast **cross**, reputedly the largest in the world, and visible for miles around.

Practicalities

Trains run daily from Madrid Atocha to El Escorial, though **buses** leaving from Moncloa are faster, slightly cheaper and take you right to the monastery. If you arrive by train, get on the local bus up to the centre of town; it leaves promptly and it's a long uphill walk if you miss it. From El Escorial, the local bus run by Herranz makes the **day-trip** from the bus station to El Valle de los Caídos (departs Tues–Sun 3.15pm, returning 5.30pm). The **tourist office** is near the monastery at c/Grimaldi 2 (Mon–Thurs 11am–6pm, Fri–Sun 10am–7pm; ☎918 905 313).

Though usually visited on a day-trip, El Escorial does offer **accommodation**, which is useful if you're making a trip to El Valle de los Caídos; cheap *hostales* include *Pensión El Retiro*, c/Aulencia 17 (☎918 900 946; ❷) and *Hostal Vasco*, Plaza Santiago (☎918 901 619; ❷). There's also a **campsite** (☎918 902 412) 2km out on the road to Segovia and a **hostel** (☎918 905 924; ❷), usually crowded with school groups, at c/Residencia 14.

Eating is expensive everywhere, but try the bar just inside the gate. Otherwise, there are several inexpensive places along c/Juan de Toledo, off Plaza Virgen de Gracia, and up the hill on c/Pozas.

Segovia

For such a small city, **SEGOVIA** has a remarkable number of outstanding architectural monuments. Most celebrated are the Roman aqueduct, the cathedral and the fairy-tale Alcázar, but the less obvious attractions – the cluster of ancient churches and the many mansions found in the lanes of the old town, all in a warm, honey-coloured stone – are what really make it worth visiting. In winter, at over 1000m, it can be very cold here.

The **Cathedral** (daily 9am–6/7pm) was the last major Gothic building in Spain and it takes that style to its logical extreme, with pinnacles and flying buttresses tacked on at every conceivable point. The interior is, however, surprisingly bare, and spoiled by a great green marble *coro* at its very centre. The treasures are almost all confined to the **museum** which opens off the cloisters (€1.50).

Beside the cathedral, c/de Daoiz leads past a line of souvenir shops to the church of San Andrés and on to a small park in front of the **Alcázar** (daily 10am–6/7pm; €2.25). It's an extraordinary fantasy of a castle which, with its narrow towers and many turrets, looks like something out of Disneyland. And indeed it is a sham – originally built in the fourteenth and fifteenth centuries but almost completely destroyed by fire in 1862 and rebuilt as a hyperbolic parody of the original. Still, it should be visited, if only for the magnificent panoramas from the tower.

The **Aqueduct**, over 800m long and at its highest point towering some 30m above the Plaza de Azoguejo, stands up without a drop of mortar or cement. No one knows exactly when it was built, but it was probably around the end of the first century AD under the emperor Trajan. If you climb the stairs beside the aqueduct, you can get a view looking down over it from a surviving fragment of the city walls – though frankly it's more impressive from a distance.

Segovia is an excellent city for walking, with some fine views and beautiful churches to be enjoyed just outside the boundaries. Perhaps the most interesting of all the ancient churches here is **Vera Cruz** (Tues–Sun 10.30am–1.30pm & 3.30–6/7pm), a remarkable twelve-sided building in the valley facing the Alcázar. It was built by the Knights Templar in the early thirteenth century on the pattern of the church of the Holy Sepulchre in Jerusalem, and once housed part of the True Cross. Inside, the nave is circular, its heart occupied by a strange two-storeyed chamber – again twelve-sided – in which the knights, as part of their initiation, stood vigil over the cross. Climb the tower for a highly photogenic vista of the city. While you're over here you could also visit the prodigiously walled **Convento de los Carmelitas** (daily 10am–1.30pm & 4–7/8pm, closed Mon am), with the gaudy mausoleum of its founder-saint, and the rather damp, ramshackle **Monasterio del Parral** (Mon–Sat 10am–11.30am/12.30pm & 4–6.30pm, Sun 10am–11.30pm).

Practicalities

You can get to Segovia by *cercanía* **train** from Atocha or Chamartín stations or **bus** from the main bus station in Madrid. The **train station** is some distance out of town; take any bus (every 15min) marked Puente Hierro/Estación Renfe to the central Plaza Mayor. The main **tourist office** is at Plaza del Azoguejo 1 (daily 10am–8pm; ☎921 462 906).

For **somewhere to stay**, try one of two *pensiones* – *Cubo* (☎921 460 318; **②**) or *Aragón* (☎921 460 914; **②**) – on different floors of the same building at Plaza Mayor 4; or *Hostal Juan Bravo*, on c/Juan Bravo 12 (☎921 463 413; **②**), which has lots of big comfortable rooms. There are other cheap possibilities in the streets behind the plaza or near the aqueduct. The well-equipped **hostel** (☎921 441 111; **②**) is on Paseo Conde de Sepulveda near the train station and there's a **campsite**, *Camping Acueducto* (closed Oct–March), 2km out on the road to La Granja.

The Calle de la Infanta Isabella, which opens off the Plaza Mayor beside the **local tourist office** (Mon–Fri 9am–2pm & 5–7pm, Sat 10am–2pm & 5–8pm; ☎921 460 334) is packed with noisy **bars** and cheap **places to eat**. *Mesón de Cándido*, on Plaza del Azonguejo next to the aqueduct, is one of the best restaurants, pricey, but well worth it. Other places worth a try include *José María*, c/Cronista Lecea 11; *Narízotas*, Plaza de San Martin; and, for bar food and good, filling dishes, *El Portón Bar & Grill*, c/Romero 10.

Extremadura

The harsh environment of **Extremadura**, west of Madrid, was the cradle of the *conquistadores*, men who opened up a new world for the Spanish Empire. Remote before and forgotten since, Extremadura enjoyed a brief golden age when the heroes returned with their gold to live in a flourish of splendour. **Cáceres** preserves an entire town built with conquistador wealth, the streets crowded with the ornate mansions of returning empire builders. An even more ancient past becomes tangible in the wonders of **Mérida**, the most completely preserved Roman city in Spain.

Cáceres

Old **CÁCERES** was largely built on the proceeds of American exploration, but today it has perhaps been over-restored. Yet it remains a rapidly growing provincial capital, which is also home to the University of Extremadura.

Any visit should begin with Plaza Mayor, opposite the tourist office, in the old town. Almost every building here is magnificent. It features ancient walls pierced by the low **Arco de la Estrella**, the **Torre del Bujaco** – whose foundations date back to Roman times – and in the **Torre del Horno**, one of the best-preserved Moorish mud-brick structures in Spain. Look out too for the family crests adorning many of the mansions. Another highlight, through the Estrella gate, is the **Casa de Toledo-Montezuma** to which a follower of Cortés brought back one of the New World's more exotic prizes – a daughter of the Aztec emperor as his bride.

In the Casa de las Valetas, on Plaza San Mateo, is the **Museo Provincial** (Tues–Sat 9am–2.30pm, Sun 10.15am–2.30pm; free); its highlight is the cistern of the original Moorish Alcázar, with rooms of wonderful horseshoe arches. The **Fine Arts** section in the Casa de los Caballos behind it is part of the same complex, with its mixture of religious and contemporary art, including work by Miró and Picasso.

Cáceres' **train and bus stations** face each other across the Carretera Sevilla, some way out of town; bus #1 runs from here (every 15min) to Plaza de San Juan, a square near the centre, with signs leading on towards the Plaza Mayor and the **tourist office** (Mon–Fri 9.30am–2pm & 4–6.30/7.30pm, Sat & Sun 9.30am–2pm; ☎927 246 347, ⊛www.turismoextremadura.com). The best **places to stay** are all near the Plaza Mayor – try *Pensión Carretero* at no. 23 (☎927 247 482; ❷) or *Pensión Márquez* (☎927 244 960; ❷), just off the plaza at c/Gabriel y Galán 2. Right on Plaza Mayor, *El Pato* and *El Puchero* are options for **dinner**, as is the more expensive *El Figón*, in Plaza San Juan just off c/Pintores. For **bar-hopping**, try c/de Pizarro, just outside the walls on the west side of the old town, or, just north, the Plaza Mayor.

Mérida

Former capital of the Roman province of Lusitania, **MÉRIDA** contains one of the most remarkable concentrations of Roman monuments to be found anywhere: scattered in the midst of the modern city are remains of everything from engineering works to domestic villas. With the aid of a map and a little imagination, it's not hard to reconstruct the Roman city within the not especially attractive modern town. A **combined ticket** (€7.20) gives access to all the sites (all open daily 9.30am–1.45pm & 5–6.15pm).

By far the best site is the **Teatro Romano and Anfiteatro**. It was a present to the city from Agrippa around 15 BC, and today is one of the most beautiful monuments of the Roman world. The stage is in a particularly good state of repair and in July it plays host to a season of classical plays. In its day the adjacent amphitheatre could accommodate up to 15,000 people – almost half Mérida's population today. Also worth seeing is the magnificent **Puente Romano**, the Roman bridge across the islet-strewn Guadiana – sixty arches long, which is defended by an enormous, plain, Moorish **Alcazaba**. Nearby is the sixteenth-century **Plaza de España**, the heart of the modern town. Just across from it is the vast, red-brick bulk of the **Museo Nacional de Arte Romano** (Mon–Sat 10am–2pm & 4/5–6/7pm, Sun 10am–2pm; free), a magnificent museum by the architect Rafael Moneo, which does full justice to its high-class collection, including portrait statues of Augustus, Tiberius and Drusus, and some glorious mosaics. Of the two Roman villas in Mérida, the **Casa Romana Anfiteatro**, which lies immediately below the museum, has perhaps the best mosaics.

Mérida's **tourist office** is at the entrance to the Roman theatre site on Paseo José Saenz de Burnaga (Mon–Fri 9am–2pm & 4/5–6.30/7.15pm, Sat & Sun 9.30am–2pm; ☎924 315 353, ⊛www.turismoextremadura.com). Budget **accommodation** isn't plentiful. Try *Hostal Nueva España*, Avda. Extremadura 6 (☎924 313 356; ❷), or *Hostal Salud*, c/Vespasiano 41 (☎924 31 22 59; ❷). There's an all-year **campsite** (☎924 303 453) not far out of town towards Lisbon, on the Madrid-Lisbon highway, and a more attractive site at Proserpina (☎924 123 055; closed

Oct–March), some 5km north, where you can swim in the reservoir. Mérida is a lively place for its size, and the whole area between the train station and the Plaza de España is full of **bars and restaurants**. Inexpensive food in the town is hard to come by – try *Restaurante Briz*, just off the main plaza at Félix Valverde Lillo 5.

Andalucía

Andalucía is likely to both meet your pre-conceptions of Spain, and defy them. Everywhere there is evidence of this passionate, parched country at its most exuberant: it is the home of flamenco and the bullfight, tradition and fierce pride. But it's also much more than the cliché. In Andalucía the great Moorish monuments vie for your attention. Extraordinary and breathtaking, the evidence of the Moors' sophistication remains visible to this day in **Córdoba**, in **Sevilla** and, particularly, in **Granada's Alhambra**. On **the coast** you could despair. Extending to either side of **Málaga** is the **Costa del Sol**, Europe's most developed resort area, with its beaches hidden behind a remorseless curtain of concrete. But there is life beyond the Costa del Sol, especially the beaches of the Costa de la Luz. Here, **Tarifa** sits on the most southerly tip of Europe, its exposed position drawing swarms of windsurfers. Andalucía is also where Europe stops and Africa begins; in places the mountains of that great continent appear almost close enough to touch, in reality they are just half an hour away by ferry.

Córdoba

CÓRDOBA is a minor provincial capital, prosperous in a modest sort of way. Once, however, it was the largest city of Roman Spain, and for three centuries it formed the heart of the great medieval caliphate of the Moors. For visitors, its main attraction comes down to a single building: **La Mezquita** – the grandest and most beautiful mosque ever constructed by the Moors. This stands right in the centre of the city, surrounded by the labyrinthine Jewish and Moorish quarters, and is a building of extraordinary mystical and aesthetic power. La Mezquita apart, Córdoba is an engaging, atmospheric city, easily explored and with some excellent budget accommodation.

Córdoba's domination of Moorish Spain began thirty years after the conquest, in 756 AD, when the city was placed under **Abd ar-Rahman I**, who established control over all but the north of Spain. It was he who commenced the building of the Great Mosque – in Spanish, La Mezquita – which remains a sublime example of Moorish religious architecture, and one of the key sights of Andalucía. **La Mezquita** (Mon–Sat 10am–7.30pm, Sun am for worship & 2–7.30pm; €6.50) is approached through the **Patio de los Naranjos**, a classic Islamic court which preserves both its orange trees and fountains for ritual purification before prayer. Inside, nearly a thousand twin-layered red and white pillars combine to mesmeric effect, the harmony culminating only at the foot of the beautiful **Mihrab** (prayer niche). Later, Christian, additions – including a vulgar Renaissance Choir – jar but don't manage to destroy the exquisite, hypnotic interior.

North of La Mezquita lies the **Judería**, Córdoba's old Jewish quarter, a fascinating network of lanes that are more atmospheric and less commercialized than Sevilla's. Near the heart of the quarter, at c/Maimonides 18, is a tiny **synagogue** (Tues–Sat 10am–1.30pm & 3.30–5.30pm, Sun 10am–1.30pm; €0.30), one of only three in Spain that survived the Jewish expulsion of 1492 – the other two are in Toledo. East of the Judería, the **Museo Arqueológico** (Tues 3–8pm, Wed–Sat 9am–8pm, Sun 9am–3pm; €1.50) occupies a small Renaissance mansion in which Roman foundations were discovered during conversion: these have been incorporated into an imaginative and enjoyable display.

Practicalities

Close to the **train and bus stations**, the broad Avda. del Gran Capitán leads down to the old quarters and La Mezquita – a 25-minute walk, or short ride on bus #3. The **tourist office** is at the Palacio de Congresos y Exposiciones, c/Torrijos 10, alongside La Mezquita (Mon–Fri 9.30am–7/8pm, Sat 10am–7/8pm, Sun 10am–2pm; ℡957 471 235, ⊛www.ayuncordoba.es).

The best **places to stay** are concentrated in the maze of streets northeast of La Mezquita, many with beautifuly tiled courtyards. Amongst the most atmospheric is *Hostal Deanes*, c/ Deanes 6 (℡957 293 744; ❸). Calle Rey Heredia also has some good places; try the pleasant Hostal *Rey Heredia* at no. 26 (℡957 474 182; ❸). Less savoury, but likely to have room, are the cheap, run-down *fondas* in the ramshackle Plaza de la Corredera: *Fonda Corredera* (℡957 470 581; ❷), at the corner of the Plaza and c/Rodríguez Marin, is clean and friendly. You pay a little more at *Hostal Maestre*, at c/Romero Barros 16 (℡957 475 395; ❸), where you'll get an en-suite room. There's also an HI **hostal** in the Juderia, a few minutes' walk from La Mezquita at Plaza Juda Levi (℡957 290 166; ❷, includes breakfast). It's very modern, and all rooms have a bathroom, but it's antiseptic compared to what's on offer nearby. Córdoba's main **campsite**, *Campamento Municipal El Brillante* (℡957 282 165), is 2km north on the road to Villaviciosa; take bus #10 or #11.

Bars and **restaurants** are on the whole reasonably priced – save for the touristy places around La Mezquita. Loads of alternatives can be found not too far away in the Judería and in the old quarters off to the east, above the Paseo de la Ribera: try *El Extremeño* at Plaza Agrupación de Cofradías, just north of the Mesquita. Alternatively try the *Cafeteria Juda Levi*, opposite the hostel, which does main courses from €6. For **internet** access, head for Ch@t-is, at Claudio Marcelo 15, near the Plaza Tendillas. There's lots of choice for **drinking** and tapas. The local barrelled **wine** is mainly *Montilla* or *Moriles* – both are magnificent, vaguely resembling mellow, dry sherries. For samples, head for *Taberna San Miguel*, a Córdoba institution, affectionately known as *El Pisto*, at Plaza San Miguel 1. **Flamenco** performances take place at *La Bulería*, c/Pedro López 3 (from 10.30pm), but it's poor fare compared to what you can see in Sevilla or Granada.

Sevilla

SEVILLA is the great city of the Spanish south, intensely hot in summer and with an abiding reputation for theatricality and intensity. It has three important monuments – the **Giralda tower**, the **Cathedral** and the **Alcázar** – and an illustrious history, but it's the living self of this city of Carmen, Don Juan and Figaro that remains the great attraction. It is expressed on a phenomenally grand scale at the city's two great festivals – **Semana Santa**, during the week before Easter, and the **April Feria**, which lasts a week at the end of the month. Sevilla is also Spain's second most important centre for **bullfighting**, after Madrid.

Sevilla was the site of the Expo 92 world fair but, despite all the attendant benefits, it remains poor: petty crime is a big problem, especially in the form of bag-snatching. On a more positive note, while the architectural legacy and infrastructure from this Expo are not a patch on Sevilla's 1929 effort, the hi-tech new bridges and few remaining pavilions add an upbeat modern dimension to the city. The soul of Sevilla lies in its historic town centre, however, where minarets jostle for space among cupolas and palms, against a latticework of narrow streets, patios and plazas.

Arrival, information and accommodation

The San Justa **train station** is a fair way out of the centre on Avda. Kansas City, which is also the airport road; bus C1 connects it to the centre and the El Prado de San Sebastián bus station. There is an hourly bus service (6.15am–9.30pm; €2.10) connecting the **airport** to the town. The main **bus station** is at the Plaza de Armas beside the river by the Puente del Cachorro, but buses for destinations within Andalucía (plus Barcelona, Alicante and Valencia) leave from the more central terminal at Plaza de San Sebastián. Bus #C4 connects the two terminals. The **tourist office** is at Avda. de la Constitución 21 (Mon–Fri 9am–7pm, Sat 10am–2pm & 3–7pm, Sun 10am–2pm; ☎954 221 404, ⊛www.turismo.sevilla.org).

The most attractive **area to stay** in town is undoubtedly the maze-like **Barrio Santa Cruz**, near the cathedral, although this is generally reflected in the prices you have to pay. Rooms are almost impossible to find during the big festivals. If you can't find anything in the Barrio, try on its periphery or slightly further out beyond the Plaza Nueva, over towards the river and the Plaza de Armas bus stations. The prices below will double during Easter week and the April fair.

Hostel

Albergue Juvenil Sevilla c/Isaac Peral 2 ☎955 056 500. Refurbished HI hostel some way out in the university district; can get crowded. Take bus #34 from Puerta de Jerez or Plaza Nueva. Breakfast included. **❶**

Hotels

Hostal Arizona Pedro del Torro 14 ☎954 216 042. Near the Plaza de Armas bus station, basic rooms, with and without bath, gets busy so arrive early or phone ahead. **❷**

Hostal Buen Dormir c/Farnesio 8 ☎954 217 492. In the Bario Santa Cruz. Good value, friendly place, with a roof patio, in a street with several possibilities. **❷**

Hostal Bienvenido c/Archeros 14 ☎954 413 655. Near *Buen Dormir* but a little more expensive, small rooms with nice roof terrace. **❸**

Hostal Capitol Zaragoza 66 ☎954 212 441. Just off Plaza Nueva – a range of rooms and prices, so look first. **❸**

Hostal Gala c/Gravina 52 ☎954 214 503. One of several clustered on this street near the Plaza de Armas bus station. Functional, with some en-suite rooms. **❸**

Hostal El Giraldill c/Gravina 23 ☎954 224 275. Has some airy rooms with tiny balconies. Also some with baths. **❸**

Hostal Gravina c/Gravina 46 ☎954 216 414. Basic but cheap and clean. The owner also runs three other places nearby. **❸**

Hostal Monreal c/Rodrigo Caro 8 ☎954 214 166. Great location in the Bario Santa Cruz, plenty of rooms in a newly converted town house. Tiled courtyard café down stairs. **❷**

Hotel Alcantara Ximenez de Enciso 28 ☎954 500 595, ⊛ www.hotelalcantra.net. Great hotel in a great location, an oasis of quiet in the middle of the Barrio de Santa Cruz. Modern, stylish and friendly. **❺**

Campsites

Camping Sevilla ☎954 514 379. By the airport, with its own pool, minibus service connects the site to central Sevilla three times a day.

The City

Sevilla was one of the earliest **Moorish conquests** (in 712 AD) and, as part of the Caliphate of Córdoba, became the second city of al-Andalus. When the caliphate broke up in the early eleventh century it was the most powerful of the independent states to emerge, and under the Almohad dynasty became the capital of the last real Moorish empire in Spain from 1170 until 1212. The Almohads rebuilt the Alcázar, enlarged the principal **mosque** and erected a new and brilliant minaret – the **Giralda** (Mon–Sat 11am–5pm, Sun 2.30–6pm; €6, including entrance to cathedral, free on Sun) – topped with four copper spheres that could be seen from miles round. Today, it still dominates the skyline. You can ascend it for a remarkable view of the city, but most impressive of all is the tower's inner construction: a series of 35 gentle ramps wide enough to allow two mounted guards to pass. The Giralda was so venerated by the Moors that they wanted to destroy it before the Christian conquest of the city. Instead it became the bell tower of the Christian's cathedral in 1402. The **Cathedral** (same hours as Giralda) was completed in just over a century and is the largest Gothic church in the world by cubic capacity. Its centre is dominated by a vast Gothic **retable** composed of 45 carved scenes from the life of Christ. The lifetime's work of a single craftsman, Pierre Dancart, this is the largest altarpiece in the world.

Across the Plaza del Triunfo from the Cathedral lies the **Alcázar** (Tues–Sat 9.30am–7pm, Sun 9.30am–2.30/6pm; €5). Rulers of Sevilla have occupied this site from the time of the Romans. Under the Almohads, the complex was turned into an enormous citadel, forming the heart of the town's fortifications. Parts of the walls survive, but the palace was rebuilt in the Christian period by **Pedro the Cruel** (1350–1369). His works, some of the best surviving examples of **Mudéjar architecture**, form the nucleus of the Alcázar today. Later additions include a wing in which early expeditions to the Americas were planned, and the huge

Renaissance apartments of Charles V. Don't miss the beautiful and rambling **Alcázar gardens**, the confused but enticing product of several eras.

Just ten minutes' walk to the south of the cathedral, the **Plaza de España** and adjoining **María Luisa Park**, laid out in 1929 for an abortive "Fair of the Americas", are an ideal place to spend the middle part of the day. En route you pass by the **Fábrica de Tabacos**, the old tobacco factory that was the setting for Bizet's *Carmen*. Nowadays it's part of the university. Towards the end of the María Luisa Park, the grandest surviving pavilions from the fair (scuppered by the Wall Street Crash) have been adapted as museums. The furthest contains the city's **archeology** collections (Tues 3–8pm, Wed–Sat 9am–8pm, Sun 9am–2pm; €1.50), and opposite is the **Popular Arts Museum** (Tues 3–8pm, Wed–Sat 9am–8pm, Sun 9am–2pm; €1.50), with interesting displays relating to the April *feria*.

A further twenty minutes' walk northwest along the river, the **Río Guadalquivir**, takes you to the twelve-sided **Torre del Oro**, built in 1220 as part of the Alcázar fortifications. The tower later stored the gold brought back to Sevilla from the Americas – hence its name. One block away is the **Hospital de la Caridad** (Mon–Sat 9am–1.30pm & 3.30–6.30pm, Sun 9am–1pm; €3) founded in 1676 by Don Miguel de Manara, the inspiration for Byron's Don Juan, who repented his youthful excesses and set up this hospital for the relief of the dying and destitute. There are some magnificent paintings by Murillo and Valdés Leal inside. There's more art further along at the **Museo de Bellas Artes** on Plaza del Museo (Tues 3–8pm, Wed–Sat 9am–8pm, Sun 9am–2pm; €1.50,), housed in a beautiful former convent. Outstanding are the paintings by Zurbarán of Carthusian monks at supper and El Greco's portrait of his son.

Across the river lies the **Triana** barrio that was once home to the city's gypsy community and is still a lively and atmospheric place. At Triana's northern edge lies **La Cartuja** (Tues–Fri 10am–8pm, Sat 11am–8pm, Sun 10am–3pm; €1.80), a fourteenth-century former Carthusian monastery. Part of the complex is now given over to the **Museo del Arte Contemporáneo** (Tues–Sat 10am–8pm, Sun 10am–3pm; €1.80), which, in addition to work by *Andaluz* artists, frequently stages important exhibitions by international artists.

Eating, drinking and nightlife

Sevilla is a tremendously atmospheric place, and the city is packed with lively bars. Remember, though, that it can also be expensive, particularly in the Barrio Santa Cruz. If you want to **eat** well and cheaply you'll generally have to steer clear of the sights, but there are exceptions: c/Sta María La Blanca has several reasonable restaurants – notably the *Alta Mira* – as does c/Mateus Gago opposite La Giralda – try the *Alcazaba* or the *Café Bar Campanario*, where two large bulls' heads will watch you eat. Other central areas to try are the streets around Plaza Nueva. On c/Albareda in the atmospheric *Cassa la Vidan* you can get a tasty breakfast for a few euros and cheap eats later on. While just off the south of the square on c/Zaragoza, *Café Bar Vina* offers a set menu for just €5. There are similar bargains to be had on c/Jimios nearby. *Habanita* is a pleasant **vegetarian** Cuban restaurant on c/Golfo just off c/Pérez Galdos in the Alfalfa area.

For straight drinking and occasional **tapas** there are **bars** all over town – a high concentration of them with barrelled sherries from nearby Jerez and Sanlúcar (the locals drink the cold, dry *fino*). In the centre of **Santa Cruz** one of the liveliest places is *Las Teresas* in c/Ximénez de Enciso (expensive tapas), but perhaps the best tapas bar in the city, with just about every imaginable snack, is the *Bar Modesto* at c/Cano y Cuento 5, up at the north corner of the quarter by Avda. Menéndez Pelayo. The innocuous-looking *Bodeguita* at c/Arfe 5, south of Plaza Nueva, is also worth searching out and less expensive, while *Bar Giralda* at c/Mateus Gago is also excellent, as is the *Bodega Santa Cuiz* on c/Rodrigo Caro just off Mateus Gago. The Alfalfa area just north of the cathedral is a lively area at night with loud **music** in many of the bars: *Bar Nao* and *Sopa de Ganso* in c/Pérez Galdos are both worth a look. The other main area for nightlife, popular with the substantial foreign student population, is just across the river on c/Betis.

Flamenco – or more accurately *Sevillanas* – music and dance are offered at dozens of places in the city, some of them extremely tacky and expensive. An alternative is the regular, and good, performances at a museum in the heart of the old city: the Casa de la Memoria de Al-Andalus, c/Ximenez de Enciso 28 (☎954 560 670; nightly in the summer at 9pm; €11,), which aims to preserve traditional flamenco. Although worth seeing, you'll still get a very different experience in the bars – an excellent place to try, which often has spontaneous *Sevillanas*, is *La Carbonería* at c/Levías 18, just northeast of the Iglesia de Santa Cruz.

Listings

Banks and exchanges All the main banks and several cambios can be found around the tourist information centre on the Avenida de la Constitución, which runs down the west side of the Cathedral.

Bullfighting The season starts with the April *feria* and continues until September with most corridas being held on Sunday evenings. Tickets can be bought from the Maestranza bullring, Paseo de Colón 12 ☎954 501 382. Prices vary dramatically, but start from as little as €10.

Consulates Australia, Federico Rubio 14 ☎954 220 971; Ireland, Plaza de Santa Cruz 6 ☎954 216 361; UK, Apdo. Correos 143 ☎954 155 018; US, Paseo de las Delicias 7 ☎954 231 885.

Hospital Hospital Universitario, Avda. Dr. Fedriani 3 ☎954 557 400. Also, emergency clinic just behind the Alcázar, at corner of Menendez Pelayo and Avd. de Cádiz.

Internet Odisea, Avenida de la Constitución opposite the tourist office; Seville Internet Centre, c/Almirantazgo.

Laundry c/Castelar 2.

Left luggage At the train station (24hr).

Pharmacy Opposite the Cathedral on Avda. de la Constitución; in the Barrio de Santa Cruz, on the corner of Mateos Gago and Rodrigo Caro.

Police Plaza de la Gavidia ☎954 228 840.

Post office Avda. de la Constitución 32, by the cathedral.

Jerez de la Frontera

JEREZ DE LA FRONTERA is the home and heartland of sherry – and also, less known but equally important, of Spanish brandy. Outside of the the two big **festivals** – the May Horse Fair and the celebration of the vintage towards the end of September – you're unlikely to want to make more than a quick visit (and tasting) between buses; the town itself is hardly distinctive. The **tours of the sherry and brandy bodegas** can be interesting, however. Many were founded by British Catholic refugees who even now form a kind of Anglo-Andalucian aristocracy; but note that most close in August. One exception is also one of the most central: next to the ruins of the Moorish Alcázar on Manuel Maria González is **González Byass** (tours Mon–Sat hourly 11.30am–5.30pm; ☎956 357 016; €7). Most of the other bodegas are on the outskirts of town; pick up a plan from the tourist office.

The **train and bus stations** are close to each other, eight blocks east of the González bodega and the central Plaza de los Reyes Católicos. The **tourist office** is at c/Alameda Christina (Mon–Fri 9.30am–2.30pm & 4.30–6.30pm; ☎956 331 150, ✆www.webjerez.com), by the Claustros de Santa Dominga. For **accommodation**, head for c/Higueras, off c/Medina (left out of the bus station and 3 blocks along), or c/Morenos, off the parallel c/Arcos. There's also a **hostel** at Avda. Carrero Blanco 30 (☎956 143 901; ❷; includes breakfast).

Cádiz

CÁDIZ is among the oldest settlements in Spain, founded about 1100 BC by the Phoenicians, and has been one of the country's principal ports ever since. Its heyday was the eighteenth century, when it enjoyed a virtual monopoly on the Spanish-

American trade in gold and silver. Central Cádiz, built on a peninsula-island, remains much as it must have looked in those days, with its grand open squares, sailors' alleyways and high, turreted houses. It's also the spiritual home of flamenco, and you get a sense of that to this day; the city, crumbling from the effect of sea air on soft limestone, has a tremendous atmosphere – slightly seedy, definitely in decline, but still full of mystique. Cádiz's big party time is its annual carnival, normally held in February and early March; expect frenzied celebrations, masked processions and satirical digs at the local big shots.

With its blind alleys, cafés and backstreets, Cádiz is fascinating to wander around. To understand the city's layout, climb the **Torre Tavira**, Marques del Real Tesoro 10 (daily 10am–6pm; €3), tallest of the 160 lookout towers in the city, with an excellent camera obscura. Some specific sites to check out are the huge **Catedral Nueva** (Tues–Fri 10am–1pm & 4.30–7.30pm, Sat & Sun 10am–1pm; €3) – an unusually successful blend of High Baroque and neoclassical styles, decorated entirely in stone. The oval, eighteenth-century chapel of **Santa Cueva,** c/Rosario (Tues–Fri 10am–1pm & 4.30–7.30pm, Sat & Sun 10am–1pm; €1.50), has eight magnificent arches decorated with frescoes by Goya.

Arriving by **train** you'll have journeyed through field upon field of sunflowers, before finding yourself on the periphery of the old town, close to the Plaza de San Juan de Dios, the busiest of the many squares. This is home to the local **tourist office** (Mon–Fri 9am–2pm & 4–6pm; ☎956 241 001, ⱳwww.cadizayto.es). By **bus** you'll be a few blocks further north, along the water. Note that the ferry route from Cádiz to Tangier doesn't operate any more; to get to Morocco you'll have to go either to Algeciras or Tarifa. Plaza de San Juan de Dios, protruding across the neck of the peninsula from the port, has several **cafés** and cheap **restaurants**. *La Caleta*, whose interior is built like the bow of a ship, is particularly good. There's plenty of budget **accommodation** in the dense network of alleyways around Plaza de San Juan de Dios. The best bets are *Pension Fantoni*, c/Flamenco 5 (☎956 282 704; ❸), and *Pension Colon*, c/Marques de Cadiz 6 (☎956 285 351; ❷), which has a roof terrace. A few doors down *Hostal España*, c/Marquez de Cádiz 9 (☎956 285 500; ❷), is also worth a try. There's a privately owned **hostel** *Quo Qádis* on c/Diego Arias 1 (☎956 221 939; ❶), ten minutes' walk from the train station.

Tarifa

If there is one thing that defines **TARIFA**, it is the wind. It's the most southerly point in Europe and in the summer the prevailing, massively powerful, levant has made it one of the most popular destinations for **windsurfers** anywhere in the world. The area is also harnessing the element in other ways; hundreds of huge wind turbines stud the hills on the outskirts of town, and these ultra-modern versions of Don Quixote's obsession provide enough electricity to power a small town. The elements aside, there's a good feel to the place – with its funky, laid-back atmosphere and maze of narrow streets – which may encourage you to stay a few days. Africa feels very close, too, with its Rif Mountains clearly visible.

The ten-kilometre white, sandy **beaches**, Playa de los Lances and Playa Valdevaqueros, are the places to head for wind- and kite-surfing. In summer they're connected to the town by a shuttle bus. Just to the east of town, nearer and often missed by tourists, are the rocky coves of La Caleta. If you're not an experienced surfer, but feel like having a go after watching the scores of sails skid across the water, remember these winds can reach storm force ten: be sure to join a course such as the one run by *Tarifa Spinout* (☎956 236 352; from €49/2hr). You can also **whale- and dolphin-watch** from Tarifa: book in advance through one of the two, non-profitmaking trips: Whale Watch España, Avenida de la Constitución 6 (☎639 476 544; €36), or Tarifa, Pedro Cortez 4 (☎956 627 008; €36).

Practicalities

Buses drop off at the stop on the main Cádiz-Algeciras road, Batalla del Salado; there is no train station. Head downhill for the ancient archway into the old town. Most of what you need is near here. EU citizens can also make the **ferry crossing to Morocco**; boats sail to Tangier (summer 4 daily; winter 5 weekly; €22.50 one way. The town's **tourist office** is on the fringes of the old town at Paseo de la Alameda (Mon–Sat 10am–2pm & 6–8pm, Sun 10am–2pm; ☎956 680 993).

In the summer finding **somewhere to stay** can be tricky, making it advisable to book in advance. Your best bet is *Hostal Africa*, c/Maria Antonia Toledo 12 (☎956 680 220; ❷), in the old town: great value, atmospheric decoration, and a fantastic view of Africa from its large roof terrace. Also in the old town, near San Mateo church, is the lovely *Pension Correo*, c/Coronel Moscardo 8 (☎956 680 206; ❸). Another useful area is around the bus stop on Batalla del Salado; try *Hostal Facundo*, at no. 47 (☎956 684 298; ❸). Nearby you'll find *Hostal Tarik*, c/San Sebastian 34 (☎956 680 648; ❸), with en-suite rooms and companionable balconies. Round the corner, *Hostal Alborada*, c/San Jose 52 (☎956 681 140; ❸), is pleasant. Another possibility is *Hostal el Asturiano*, Amador de los Rios 8 (☎956 680 619; ❸), by the archway into the old town. **Camping** is a good option, with several sites near the main windsurfing beaches: try *Tarifa*, (☎956 684 778), *Paloma* (☎956 684 203) or *Torre de la Pena* (☎956 684 903).

For **food**, a kiosk on the central Plaza de Oviedo by the church sells bocadillos, falafal and kebabs, while *Café Central* is a cosmopolitan hangout on the same square, and just off it *La Capricciosa*, c/San Francisco 6, does great pizza, and is popular with locals and tourists alike. Another good area is around the Paseo de la Alameda. There are plenty of **bars** – in the old town one of the best is *La Ruina*, c/ Trinidad, which has a roof that comes off in the summer. *Pepes*, c/Calestar 4, is popular, as is the always-crowded *Pasaje*, c/Pedro Cortez, and the *Soul Café*, c/Trinidad. Away from the centre, **clubs** include *Far Out Club*, which plays house, trance and funk, and the seasonal *Jungle Playa* and *La Jaima*; to get there look out for the free night buses.

Algeciras

The main reason to visit **ALGECIRAS**, along the coast from Cádiz, is for the **ferry to Morocco**. The crossings are **to Tangier** (10 daily; 1hr 30min) and **tickets** (€22 one way) are available at scores of travel agents along the waterside and on most approach roads. Wait till Tangier before buying any Moroccan currency.

The number of people passing through guarantees plenty of inexpensive **rooms**. If you have trouble finding space, pick up a plan and check out the list in the **tourist office** on c/Juan de la Cierva (Mon–Fri 9am–2pm; ☎956 572 636), towards the river and rail line from the port. A good bet for cheap **places to eat** is c/Emilio Castelar in the centre.

The Costa del Sol

Perhaps the outstanding feature of the **Costa del Sol** is its ease of access. Hundreds of charter flights arrive here every week, which means that it's often possible to get an absurdly cheap ticket from London. **Málaga airport** is positioned midway between Málaga, the main city on the coast, and Torremolinos, its most grotesque resort. You can get to either town cheaply and easily by taking the train (every 30min) along the coast between Málaga and Fuengirola. Granada, Córdoba and Sevilla are all within easy reach of Málaga; so too are Ronda and the white villages (*pueblos blancos*). In some ways then, this coast's enormous popularity isn't surprising: what is surprising is that the **beaches** are generally grit-grey rather than golden and the sea is none too clean.

Málaga

MÁLAGA is the second city of the south, after Sevilla, and also one of the poorest. Yet though the clusters of high-rises look pretty grim as you approach, it can be a surprisingly attractive place. Around the old fishing villages of El Palo and Pedregalejo, now absorbed into the suburbs, are a series of small beaches and an avenue, or *paseo*, lined with some of the best fish and seafood cafés in the province. Overlooking the town and port are the Moorish citadels of the **Alcazaba** (Tues–Sun 9.30am–6/8pm; €1.80), where the lengthy excavation of a **Roman amphitheatre** continues; and the **Gibralfaro castle** (daily 9am–6/8pm; €1.80), just fifteen minutes' walk from the train or bus stations, and visible from most central points.

Practicalities

Buses #5 and #18 connect the centre to the main **train and bus stations**, which are very close to each other. The main **tourist office** is at Pasaje de Parque 1 (Mon–Fri 9.30am–1.30pm & 4.30–7.30pm, Sat & Sun 9.30am–1.30pm; ☎952 604 410, ✉info@malagaturismo.com), supplemented by two kiosks (one at the bus station and the other on the Puente de Tetuan) and yellow-jacketed information officers who roam the main tourist drags. Arriving at the **airport**, catch the electric train to the main train station, or continue another stop to Málaga Centro: Alameda for the city centre. Málaga has a number of reasonably priced **rooms**, especially in the grids of streets north and south of the Alameda. A couple to try are the *Hostal La Palma*, c/Martínez 7 (☎952 226 772; €17), and the recently refurbished *Hostal Castilla*, c/Córdoba 7 (☎952 218 635; €21). Just across the road but slighty more up-market is the Hotel Lis, c/Córdoba 7 (☎952 227 300; €23). The closest **campsite** (☎952 382 602) is at Torremolinos on Ctra. National; take the Málaga-Torremolinos bus from the main RENFE station in the centre of town.

Scant attractions aside, Málaga is of interest for its cuisine: **fried fish** and sweet **Malaga wine**, enjoyed at a vast choice of tapas bars and restaurants. One of the most atmospheric spit 'n' sawdust style **bodegas** is *Antigua Casa de Guardia*, Alameda Principal 16, reputed to be the oldest bar in town, where you can sample both, with wine served straight from the barrel. You'll find plenty of other bars in the area between Plaza de la Merced and Plaza de los Martires, which is buzzing till late at the weekend. There are many fish restaurants around the Alameda, but for the very best you need to head out to the suburbs of Pedregalejo and El Palo.

Along the coast

It's estimated that 300,000 foreigners live on the **Costa del Sol**, the richest and fastest-growing resort area in the Mediterranean. Approached in the right kind of spirit it's possible to have fun in **TORREMOLINOS**, a resort so over-the-top it's magnificent, and with furious competition keeping prices down. The concrete is a little less in evidence in the suburb of **Carihuela**, some fifteen minutes' walk west of Torremolinos station. For **somewhere to stay**, try *Hostal Flor Blanco*, Paseo Maritimo La Carihuela 4 (☎952 382 071; ❷). A good time costs more in chic **MARBELLA**, where there are bars and nightclubs galore alongside a surprisingly well-preserved old village and some wonderfully conspicuous consumption. At **ESTEPONA** there's a **campsite** and a number of **hostales**, including the *Vista al Mar*, c/Real 154 (☎952 803 247; ❷),

Ronda

Andalucía is dotted with small, brilliantly whitewashed settlements known as the **Pueblos Blancos** or "white villages", most often straggling up hillsides towards a castle or towered church. The most spectacular lie in a roughly triangular area between Málaga, Algeciras and Sevilla, at whose centre is the startling town of

SPAIN | Andalucía

27

972

RONDA, connected by a marvellous rail line to Algeciras. Built on an isolated ridge of the sierra, and ringed by dark, angular mountains, Ronda is split in half by a gaping river gorge that drops sheer for 130m. Still more spectacular, the gorge is spanned by a stupendous eighteenth-century arched **bridge**, while tall white-washed houses lean from its precipitous edges. The town itself is fascinating to wander around and has sacrificed surprisingly little of its character to the flow of day-trippers from the the coast.

Crossing the eighteenth-century **Puente Nuevo** from the Plaza de España takes you from the modern **Mercadillo** quarter to the old Moorish town, the **Ciudad**, centred on the church of **Santa María la Mayor**, originally the mosque. Turning off the main street to the left takes you steeply down to the old bridges – the **Puente Viejo** of 1616 and the Roman single-span **Puente Arabe**. Nearby, on the southeast bank of the river, are the distinctive **Baños Árabes** (Tues 9.30am–1.30pm & 4–6pm, Wed–Sat 9.30am–3.30pm; free). Crossing the old bridge takes you back to the modern town via the **Jardín de la Mina**, which ascends the gorge in a series of stepped terraces with superb views of the river, new bridge and remarkable stairway of the **Casa del Rey Moro** (daily 10am–7pm; €4), an early eighteenth-century mansion built on Moorish foundations whose 365 steps were cut by Christian slaves in the fourteenth century and were intended to guarantee a water supply in times of siege. Behind the church is the **Palacio de Mondragón** (Mon–Fri 10am–6/7pm, Sat & Sun 10am–3pm; €2), probably the palace of the Moorish kings and now home to the **Museo Municipal** – a steep path descends to the river from here. The principal gate of the town, through which the Christian conquerors passed, stands at the entrance to the suburb of San Francisco, beside the ruins of the **Alcázar**, destroyed by the French in 1809. Back in the Mercadillo quarter is the **bullring** (daily 10am–8pm; €4, including museum) – one of the most prestigious in Spain – and the beautiful clifftop *paseo*, facing the open valley and the dramatic mountains of the Serranía de Ronda.

Practicalities

The **tourist office** is opposite the entrance to the bullring at Plaza de Toros (Mon–Fri 9.30am–7.30pm, Sat & Sun 10am–2pm & 5.30–6.30pm; ☏952 187 119, ⓦwww.ronda.net). The regional tourist office is at Plaza de España (Mon–Fri 9am–7pm, Sat & Sun 10am–2pm; ☏952 871 272, ⓦwww.andalucia.org). All the **places to stay** are in the Mercadillo quarter. A good starting point is the area around Plaza del Socorro, c/Almendra (a continuation of c/Lorenzo Borrego), which has several options including the basic but cheap *Hostal Ronda Sol* at no. 11 (☏952 874 497; ❶); a few doors up at no. 7 is *Pension Hostal Biarritz* (☏952 872 910; ❶), which has some rooms with baths. Also worth a try, on nearby c/Sevilla, is *La Purisma* at no. 10 (☏952 871 050; ❷). In the same area you'll find the more upmarket *Hotel Virgen de los Reyes*, c/Lorenzo Borrego 13 (☏952 871 140; ❸), where all rooms are en suite. There are three **campsites**; the best is *El Sur* (☏952 875 939), 1.5km down the Algeciras road.

As for **eating**, most of the bargain options are grouped round the far end of the Plaza del Socorro as you leave it on c/Almendra. *El Brillante* on c/Sevilla is friendly and cheap, as is *Pizzeria Michel Angelo* on c/Lorenzo Borrego. Slightly more expensive – but worth the extra few euros if you have them – is *Taberna de Santo Domingo*, on the road of the same name, just across the Puente Nuevo into the old town. At the weekend, Ronda's **nightlife** kicks off along c/Niño and c/Jerez, and around Plaza de C. Abela.

For the energetic, *Pangea Active Nature*, c/Dolores Ibarruri 4 (☏952 873 496, ⓦwww.pangea-ronda.com), arranges **hiking**, **mountain-biking** and **kayaking** through the spectacular local scenery; a half-day bike-trip costs €27, half-day kayaking €29.

27

Granada

If you see only one town in Spain it should be **GRANADA**. For here, extraordinarily well preserved and in a tremendous natural setting, stands the **Alhambra** – the spectacular and serene climax of Moorish art in Spain. Granada was established as an independent kingdom in 1238 by **Ibn Ahmar**, a prince of the Arab Nasrid tribe which had been driven south from Zaragoza. By a series of shrewd manoeuvres, the Moors of Granada maintained their autonomy for two and a half centuries, but by 1490 only the city itself remained in Muslim hands. **Boabdil**, the last Moorish king, appealed in vain for help from his fellow Muslims in Morocco, Egypt and Turkey, and in the following year Ferdinand and Isabella marched on Granada with an army said to total 150,000 troops. For seven months, through the winter of 1491, they laid siege to the city. On January 2, 1492, Boabdil surrendered: the Christian Reconquest of Spain was complete.

Arrival, information and accommodation

The **train station** is 1km or so out of town on the Avda. de Andaluces, and is connected to the centre by buses #3, #6, #9 and #11. The main **bus station**, on the Carretera de Jaén, is a bit further out; bus #3 runs into town. A bus also (8am–6pm; up to 7 daily; €3) connects the **airport** with the Gran Vía de Colón. Details and timetables of all buses, trains, and much else besides, are posted on the walls of the **tourist office**, which is within the beautiful Corral del Carbon on c/Mariana Pineda off c/Reyes Católicos (Mon–Sat 9am–7pm, Sun 10am–2pm; ☎958 225 990).

The **Gran Vía** is Granada's main street, cutting through the middle of town. It forms a "T" at its end with **c/Reyes Católicos**, which runs east to the **Plaza Nueva** and west to the **Puerta Real**, the city's two main squares. Finding a **place to stay** in this area is easy, except at the very height of the season. Try the streets to either side of the Gran Vía, at the back of the Plaza Nueva, around the Puerta Real and Plaza del Carmen (particularly c/de Navas), the Plaza de la Trinidad, or along the Cuesta de Gomérez, which leads up from the Plaza Nueva towards the Alhambra.

Hostels

Albergue Juvenil Granada Avda. Ramón y Cajal 2 ☎902 510 000. Handy for the train station: turn left onto c/del Halcón, then first left across the railway line. Lots of facilities, including a pool, but very institutional. ❷

Pension Doña Lupe Avda. del Generalife, Alhambra ☎958 221 473. On the road leading up to the cemetery, this is the cheapest option up here. It also has a summertime terrace offering fantastic views. Book ahead if possible. Dorms ❷

Hotels

Hostal Antares Cetti Meriem 10 ☎958 228 313. Good, central location just off the Gran Vía, near the Cathedral. Clean and airy, some rooms en suite. ❷

Hostal Atenas Gran Vía de Colón 38 ☎958 278 750, ✉hatenas@moebius.es. Large, if characterless place. Some rooms en suite. ❸

Pension Los Montes Arteaga 3 ☎958 277 930. Just off the Gran Vía, pleasant rooms, some with baths. ❷

Hostal Olimpia Alvaro de Bazán 6, off Gran Vía de Colón ☎958 278 238. Central, good-value place. ❷

Pension Romero Silleria de Mesones 1 ☎958 266 079. Just off Plaza de la Trinidad. Quite basic, some rooms overlook the square. ❷

Pension Zacatin c/Ermita 11, signed off the Plaza Bib-Rambla ☎958 221 155. Light, atmospheric place, accessed through a tiny alleyway crammed during the day with leather goods. Run by pleasant couple. ❷

Pension Zurita Plaza de la Trinidad 7 ☎958 275 020. Right on the square, airy, family-run place. Some rooms with bath, there's a good café downstairs. ❸

Campsites

Camping Sierra Nevada Avda. de Madrid 107 ☎958 150 062. A surprisingly leafy and relatively central site, within easy walking distance of the train station. Closed Nov–Feb.

The City

There are three distinct groups of buildings on the **Alhambra** hill: the **Palacios Reales** (Royal Palace), the palace gardens of the **Generalife**, and the **Alcazaba**. The latter was all that existed when Ibn Ahmar made Granada his capital, but from its reddish walls the hilltop had already taken its name: *al-Hamra* in Arabic means "the red". Ibn Ahmar rebuilt the Alcazaba and added to it the huge circuit of walls and towers. Within the walls he began a palace, which he supplied with running water by diverting the River Darro; water is an integral part of the Alhambra and this engineering feat was Ibn Ahmar's greatest contribution. The palace was essentially the product of his fourteenth-century successors, particularly Mohammed V. After their conquest of the city, Ferdinand and Isabella lived for a while in the Alhambra. They restored some rooms and converted the mosque but left the palace structure unaltered. As at Córdoba and Sevilla, it was their grandson Charles V who wreaked the most destruction: he demolished a whole wing to build yet another grandiose Renaissance palace. This and the Alhambra itself were simply ignored by his successors, and by the eighteenth century the Royal Palace was in use as a prison. In 1812 it was taken and occupied by Napoleon's forces, who looted and damaged whole sections of the palace, and on their retreat from the city tried (but fortunately failed) to blow up the entire complex.

Alhambra

The standard approach to the **Alhambra** (daily 8.30am–8pm; €7) is along the Cuest de Gomérez, the road that climbs uphill from Plaza Nueva. You need to book in advance or at least arrive early. Buy your ticket from the booth at the entrance, from any Banco BBVA in Spain (including the one in town at Plaza Isabel la Católica); by phone (☎902 224 460; credit cards only; €0.88 booking fee); or online (🌐www.alhambratickets.com). Tickets are timed for the Palacio Nazaries; if you get the choice, opt for later in the day, after most tour groups have left.

Ideally you should start your visit with the earliest, most ruined, part of the fortress – the **Alcazaba**. At the summit of the Alcazaba is the **Torre de la Vela**, named after a huge bell on its turret, from where there's a fine overview of the whole area. The buildings in the **Palacios Nazaries** show a brilliant use of light and space with ornamental stucco decoration, in rhythmic repetitions of supreme beauty. Arabic inscriptions feature prominently: some are poetic eulogies of the buildings and rulers, but most are taken from the Koran.

The Palacios Nazaries is in three parts. The sultans used the **Mexuar**, the first series of rooms, for business and judicial purposes, and this is as far as most people would have penetrated. In the **Serallo**, beyond, they received distinguished guests: here is the royal throne room, known as the **Hall of the Ambassadors**, the largest room of the palace. The last section, the **Harem**, formed their private living quarters and would have been entered by no one but their family or servants. These are the most beautiful rooms of the palace, and include the **Court of the Lions**, which has become the archetypal image of Granada.

You can exit the Palacios Nazaries through the courtyard of the **Charles V's palace**, once the scene of bullfights, which now houses a museum and, although wilfully out of place here, is a distinguished piece of Renaissance design. Still on Alhambra Hill, a short walk from here takes you to the gardens of the **Generalife**. Paradise is described in the Koran as a shaded, leafy garden refreshed by running water where the "fortunate ones" may take their rest under tall canopies. It is an image that perfectly describes the Generalife, the gardens and summer palace of the sultans. Its name means "garden of the architect" and the grounds consist of a luxuriantly imaginative series of patios, enclosed gardens and walkways.

The rest of the city

From just below the entrance to the Generalife the **Cuesta del Rey Chico** winds down towards the River Darro and the old Arab quarter of the Albaicín. Here the

GRANADA

SACROMONTE

Casa del Chapiz

CUESTA DEL CHAPIZ

SAN LUIS

SAN GREGORIO ALTO

ALBAICÍN

Iglesia del Salvador

PL. DE OYTEGAS

MINAS

PANADEROS

Mirador de San Nicolás

S. Juan de los Reyes

PLAZA LARGA

AGUA

CARLOS S. AGUSTÍN

SAN JUAN DE

San Bartolomé

Arco de las Pesas

PL. DE S. NICOLÁS

NICOLÁS

Cvto. de la Concepción

SAN CRISTÓBAL

LARGA

MURCIA

MIRADOR DE ROLANDO

CARNICEROS

NUEVA DE SAN

PILAR SECO

TRILLO

IRIS

AGIBE DE

MULADAR

San Cristóbal

CUESTA DE LA ALHACABA

Palacio de Dar-al-Horra

SANTA ISABEL

Cvto. de Sta. Isabel la Real

Casa de Porras

QUINTA

CARRETERA

DE

Murallas de Albaycín

CUESTA DE LA

Mirador del Carril de la Lona

SAN JOSÉ

San José

CRUZ DE QUIROS

San Gregorio Bético

Hospital Real

PL. DE LA MERCED

ZENETE

AVENIDA

Iglesia de San Ildefonso

AV. CAP MORENO

Arco o Puerta de Elvira

PLAZA DEL TRIUNFO

PL. DE LOS NARANJOS

ELVIRA

CAPUCHINOS

HOSPICIO

Fuente Del Triunfo

GRAN VÍA DE COLÓN

GRAN VÍA DE COLÓN

C. BAZÁN

SAN AGUSTÍN

AVDA. DE LA CONSTITUCIÓN

SAN JUAN

MENDOZA

PL. DE S. AGUSTÍN

Catedral

CÁRCEL

ACERA DEL TRIUNFO

DE DIOS

MANO DE HIERRO

TENDILLAS

JERÓNIMO

Colegio de Niñas Nobles

SANTA

DR. SEVERO OCHOA

BARBARA

ARGUETA

ARRIOLA

Igl. de los Santos Justo y Pastor

SAN

RECTOR

LÓPEZ

Hospital e Iglesia de San Juan de Dios

S. Felipe Neri

Colegio de San Bartolomé y Santiago

Universidad

DUQUESA

CONDE INFANTES

PLAZA DE LA TRINIDAD

Monasterio e Iglesia de San Jerónimo

FÁBRICA VIEJA

MÁLAGA

BUENSUCESO

PLAZA LOBOS

POLÍG UNIVERSITARIO

N

Guadix & Murcia ▲

Jaén, Madrid & Bus Station ▲

Train Station, Airport & Seville ▲

▼ Antequera & Málaga

SPAIN | The Costa del Sol

27

976

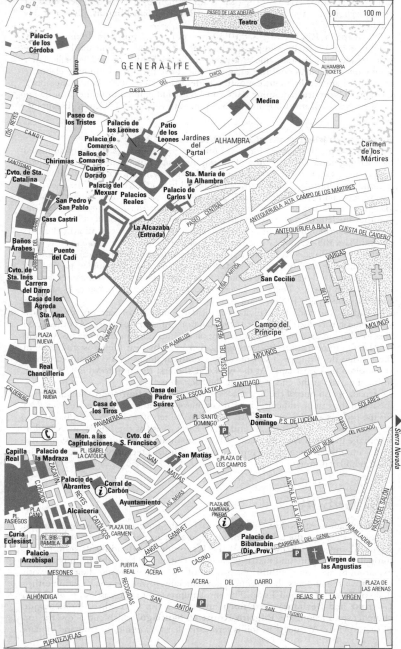

Camino del Sacromonte

PASEO DE LAS ADELFAS
Teatro

0   100 m

Palacio
de los
Córdoba

GENERALIFE

CUESTA DEL REY CHICO

ALHAMBRA TICKETS

Río Darro

Medina

ALHAMBRA

Carmen
de los
Mártires

Paseo de
los Tristes
Palacio de
los Leones
Palacio de
Comares
Baños de
Comares
Chirimías
Cuarto
Dorado
Palacio del
Mexuar

Patio
de los
Leones

Jardines
del
Partal

Cvto. de Sta.
Catalina

San Pedro y
San Pablo
Casa Castril

Sta. María de
la Alhambra
Palacio de Carlos V

Palacios
Reales

CAMPO DE LOS MÁRTIRES

Baños
Árabes
Puente
del Cadí

La Alcazaba
(Entrada)

PASEO CENTRAL

ANTEQUERUELA ALTA

ANTEQUERUELA BAJA   CUESTA DEL CAIDERO

Cvto. de
Sta. Inés
Carrera
del Darro
Casa de los
Agreda
Sta. Ana

PEÑA PARTIDA

San Cecilio

VARGAS

BELÉN

MOLINOS

PLAZA
NUEVA

CUESTA DE GOMÉREZ

LOS ALAMILLOS

Campo del
Príncipe

MOLINOS

Real
Chancillería

CUESTA DEL REALEJO

SANTIAGO

SOLARES

PLAZA
NUEVA

STA. ESCOLÁSTICA

CALDERERÍA

Casa del
Padre Suárez

Casa de
los Tiros
PAVANERAS

PL. SANTO
DOMINGO

Santo
Domingo

P.S. DE LUCENA

DEL PESCADO

Mon. a las
Capitulaciones

PL. ISABEL
LA CATÓLICA

Cvto. de
S. Francisco

CUARTO REAL

Capilla
Real
Palacio de
la Madraza

SAN MATÍAS

San Matías

PLAZA DE
LOS CAMPOS

ANCHA DE LA VIRGEN

PASEO DE SALÓN

Palacio de
Abrantes
Corral de
Carbón

LAS NAVAS

HUMILLADERO

Alcaicería

Ayuntamiento

PLAZA DE
MARIANA
PINEDA

REYES CATÓLICOS

CÓRDOBA

ZACATÍN

PL. A.
CAÑO

PL.
PASIEGOS

PLAZA DEL
CARMEN

Curia
Eclesiást.

PL. BIB.
RAMBLA

ÁNGEL GANIVET

Palacio de
Bibataubín
(Dip. Prov.)

CARRERA DEL GENIL

Virgen de
las Angustias

Palacio
Arzobispal

PUERTA
REAL

CASINO

PLAZA DE
LAS ARENAS

MESONES

ACERA   DEL   DARRO

ALHÓNDIGA

RECOGIDAS

SAN   ANTÓN

ACERA   DEL

REJAS   DE   LA   VIRGEN

SAN   ISIDRO

PUENTEZUELAS

Purchil & Motril

SPAIN | The Costa del Sol

27

Sierra Nevada

977

little-visited **Baños Árabes** (Tues–Sat 10am–2pm; free) at Corredera del Darro 31 are marvellous, and the plaza in front of the church of **San Nicolás** offers probably the best view of the Alhambra in town.

The **Capilla Real** (Mon–Sat 10.30am–1pm & 4–7pm, Sun 10am–noon & 4–8pm; €2.50) is itself an impressive building, late Gothic in style and built in the first decades of Christian rule as a mausoleum for Ferdinand and Isabella. Their tombs are as simple as could be imagined, but above them is a fabulously elaborate monument erected by their grandson Charles V. For all its stark Renaissance bulk, Granada's **Cathedral**, adjoining the Capilla Real and entered from the door beside it (Mon–Sat 10.30am–1.30pm & 4–6.30pm, Sun 4–7pm; €2.50), is a disappointment.

Eating, drinking and nightlife

You don't come to Granada for the cuisine, but the centre has plenty of animated bars serving good, cheap **food** and staying open late. The open-air places on Plaza Nueva are great to while away some time, but pricey if you eat. Better-value dining, and numerous late-night bars, can be found in "Little Morocco", the warren of streets between here and the Gran Vía: good-value choices here include the *Nueva Bodega* at c/Cetti Merién 3, and its neighbour *Cafetería-Restaurante La Riviera*. Another nucleus of reasonable eateries is the area around Plaza del Carmen (near the *Ayuntamiento*) and along c/Navas. There's great people-watching in the bars around Plaza Bib-Rambla, while the tiny *Café Bar Soria* and *Cafetería Guerrero*, both on the nearby Plaza de la Trinidad, are good places to soak up the local atmosphere. Moroccan-style teashops known as **teterías** are increasingly popular, particularly with students, and serve a wide choice of herb teas (*infusiones*), accompanied by traditional Arab pastries. There are several **internet** cafés around c/Santa Escolastica; one of the best value is Net, Plaza de los Gironez 3.

Nightlife is focused on c/Elvira, with its large number of bars; one of the most atmospheric is *Bodegas Castañeda*, at the junction with c/Almireceros. Another good area for drinking is around the university, on c/Gran Capitán and c/Pedro Antonio de Alarcón. In term-time, students also gather in **pubs** near the bus station around the Campo del Príncipe, a square on the southern slopes of the Alhambra, where you'll often find great tapas. At the weekend, the best **disco** in town is *El Camborio* inside the caves at the end of Camino del Sacromonte.

Granada is also one of the best places in Spain to hear **flamenco**, though finding the real thing can be difficult. There are numerous – and mostly lame – *espectaculares* for the tourists around Sacromonto, but you're better off going to the Albaicin district and searching the bars around Plaza Larga, west of the Iglesia del Salvador, where the gypsies play spontaneously. Be aware though that this area has seen a rise in the number of thefts from tourists; take the usual precautions and keep to the more populated streets.

Old Castile

The foundations of modern Spain were laid in the kingdom of **Castile**. A land of frontier fortresses – the *castillos* from which it takes its name – it became the most powerful and centralizing force of the Reconquest, extending its domination through military gains and marriage alliances. The monarchs of this triumphant and expansionist age were enthusiastic patrons of the arts, endowing their cities with superlative monuments above which, quite literally, tower the great Gothic cathedrals of **Salamanca** and **León**. The most impressive of the castles are at **Coca**, **Gormaz** and **Berlanga de Duero**, and there's also a wealth of Romanesque churches spread along the **Pilgrim Route to Santiago**, which cuts across the top of the province. Although its soil is fertile, the harsh extremes of land and climate don't encourage rural settlement, and the vast central plateau is given over almost entirely to grain. The sporadic and depopulated villages are rarely of interest – travel consists of getting quickly from one grand town to the next.

Salamanca

SALAMANCA is probably the most graceful city in Spain, home to what was once one of the most prestigious universities in the world and still boasting an unmistakable atmosphere of erudition. It's a small place and a remarkably pleasant one, given a gorgeous harmony by the golden sandstone from which almost the entire city seems to be constructed. The architectural hoard is huge: two cathedrals, one Gothic, the other Romanesque, vie for attention with Renaissance palaces; the Plaza Mayor is the finest in Spain; and the surviving university buildings are tremendous. And as if that weren't enough, Salamanca's student population ensure their town is always lively at night.

Two great architectural styles were developed, and see their finest expression, in Salamanca. **Churrigueresque**, a particularly florid form of Baroque, takes its name from José Churriguera (1665–1723), the dominant member of a prodigiously creative family. **Plateresque** came earlier, a decorative technique of shallow relief and intricate detail named for its alleged resemblance to the art of the silversmith (*platero*).

The City

A postcard-worthy overview of Salamanca is easy to attain: go to the extreme south of the city and cross its oldest surviving monument, the much-restored **Puente Romano** (Roman Bridge), some 400m long and worth seeing in itself. To explore Salamanca from the inside, though, make for the grand **Plaza Mayor**, its bare central expanse enclosed by a four-storey building decorated with iron balconies and medallion portraits. Nowhere is the Churrigueras' inspired variation of Baroque so refined as here, where the restrained elegance of the designs is heightened by the changing strength and angle of the sun. From the south side, Rua Mayor leads to the vast Baroque church of **La Clerecía**, seat of the Pontifical University (open for visits 1hr before Mass, which takes place Mon–Fri 1.30pm, Sat 7.30pm, Sun 12.30pm), and the celebrated **Casa de las Conchas**, or House of Shells (Mon–Fri 9am–9pm, Sat & Sun 10am–2pm & 4–7pm; free), so called because its facades are decorated with rows of carved scallop shells, symbol of the pilgrimage to Santiago.

From the Casa de las Conchas, c/Libreros leads to the **Patio de las Escuelas** and the Renaissance entrance to the **University** (Mon–Sat 9.30am–1.30pm & 4–7/7.30pm, Sun 10am–1.30pm; €2.40, free Mon am). The ultimate achievement of Plateresque art, this reflects the tremendous reputation of Salamanca in the early sixteenth century, when it was one of Europe's greatest universities – nowadays its prestige is social rather than academic.

As a further declaration of Salamanca's standing, and in a glorious last-minute assertion of Gothic, the **Catedral Nueva** (daily 9am–1pm & 4–6/8pm; free) was begun in 1512. It was built within a few yards of the university and acted as a buttress for the Old Cathedral, which was in danger of collapsing. The main Gothic-Plateresque facade is contemporary with that of the university and equally dazzling in its wealth of ornamental detail. Alberto Churriguera and his brother Joaquín both worked here – the former on the choir stalls, the latter on the dome. Entry to the **Catedral Vieja** (daily 10am–12.30pm & 4–5.30/7.30pm; €3) is through the first chapel on the right. Tiny by comparison and a stylistic hotch-potch of the Romanesque and Gothic, its most striking feature is the huge fifteenth-century retable. In the chapterhouse there's a small **museum** with a fine collection of works by Fernando Gallego, Salamanca's most famous painter.

Another faultless example of Plateresque art, the **Convento de San Esteban** (daily 9am–1pm & 4–6/8pm; €1.20), is a short walk down c/del Tostado from the

Plaza de Anaya at the side of the Catedral Nueva. Its golden facade is divided into three horizontal sections and covered in a veritable tapestry of sculpture, while the east end of the church is occupied by a huge Baroque retable by José Churriguera himself. The monastery's cloisters, through which you enter, are magnificent too, but the most beautiful cloisters in the city stand across the road in the **Convento de las Dueñas** (daily 10.30am–1pm & 4.30–7pm; €1.50). Built on an irregular pentagonal plan in the Renaissance-Plateresque style, its unmissable upper-storey capitals are wildly carved with fantastical writhing demons and realistically pained human skulls. You should also see the **Convento de Las Claras** (Mon–Fri 9.30am–1.40pm & 4–6.40pm, Sat & Sun 9am–2.40pm; €1.20), outwardly plain but with interior features in virtually every important Spanish style.

The latest jewel in Salamanca's crown is no less spectacular. The **Museo Casa Lis** (Tues–Fri 11am–2pm & 4/5–7/9pm, Sat & Sun 11am–8/9pm; €2.10; ⓦwww.museocasalis.org) near the Roman Bridge on c/Gilbratar 14 houses a spectacular collection of Art Nouveau and Art Deco furniture, ornaments and glass; the building itself – with its extravagant use of stained glass and light – is an extra treat.

Practicalities

The **bus and train stations** are on opposite sides of the city, each about fifteen minutes' walk from the centre. The municipal **tourist office** is at the edge of Plaza Mayor 14 (daily 9/10am–2pm & 4.30–6.30pm; ☎923 218 342), and the regional office at Casa de las Conchas (Mon–Sat 9am–2pm & 5–7pm, Sun 10am–2pm & 4–7pm; ☎923 268 571). **Accommodation** is reasonably priced, but can be hard to find in high season – especially at fiesta time in September, and touts tend to be out in force at the RENFE station during the summer. The Plaza Mayor is the best place to look – the small, cobbled streets around house scores of small *fondas* and *hostales*, most of a high standard: *Pensión Estefania*, at c/Jesus 3 (☎923 217 372; ❷), and pensiones *Lisboa* (☎923 214 333; ❶) and *Barez* (☎923 217 495; ❶), on c/Melendez 1 and 19, are particularly good. There's also a friendly **HI hostel** (☎923 269 141; ⓦwww.alberguesalamanca.com; ❷) on c/Escoto 13–15, just off the Plaza Mayor, with six-bed dorms and excellent facilities. There are several **campsites** nearby, the least expensive being *Don Quijote* (☎923 209 052) at Cabrerizos, about 4km out but served by bus #2 from Gran Vía.

The **cafés** in Plaza Mayor are pricey, but worth it for the splendour and atmosphere of the square. Close by in Plaza del Mercado (by the **market**, itself a good source of provisions), there's a row of lively tapas bars, while the university area has loads of good-value bars and restaurants catering to student budgets. Good-value food places include *Cervecería del Comercio*, c/Poco Amarillo 23, and *El Bardo*, c/Compañia 8, selling vegetarian food and alcohol. About the cheapest *menús del día* are at *Restaurante Bar Llamas*, c/Pavel 9, which also has outdoor seating and good sanwiches, and at places along the streets around the market and towards the bus station. Late-night **bars** abound in the Gran Vía area; among the most popular are *El Corrillo*, c/Melendez, for jazz, and *El Callejón*, Gran Vía 68, for folk. The most popular **clubs** include *El Cum Laude*, on c/Prior off Plaza Mayor, which attracts mainly teenagers at weekends; *Potemkin*, off Gran Vía, which is open until sunrise, and *El Puerto de Chus*, on Plaza de San Julián.

León

The stained glass in the cathedral of **LEÓN** and the Romanesque wall paintings in its Royal Pantheon are reason enough for many people to visit the city, but León is also – unusually for this part of the country – as attractive and enjoyable in its modern quarters as it is in those areas that remain from its heyday. The city has a rich history: in 914, as the Reconquest edged its way south from Asturias, this became the Christian capital, and along with its territories it grew so rapidly that by 1035 the county of Castile had matured into a fully fledged kingdom. For the next two centuries León and Castile jointly spearheaded the war against the Moors, but by the thirteenth century Castile's power had eclipsed that of even her mother territory.

León's **Cathedral** (daily 8.30am–1.30pm & 4–7/8pm) dates from the city's final years of greatness. It is said to be a miracle that it's still standing: it has the largest proportion of window to stone of any Gothic cathedral. The kaleidoscopic stained-glass **windows** present one of the most magical and harmonious spectacles in Spain, and the colours used – reds, golds and yellows – could only be Spanish; the bewildering sensation of refracting light was further enhanced by the addition last century of a glass screen, allowing a clear view up to the altar. Outside, the west facade, dominated by a massive rose window, is also magnificent.

The city's other great attraction is the **Real Colegiata de San Isidoro**, the **pantheon** of which houses the bodies of the early kings of León and Castile. Ferdinand I, who united the two kingdoms in 1037, commissioned the complex as a shrine for the bones of St Isidore, which lie in a reliquary on the high altar, and a mausoleum for himself and his successors. The pantheon (Tues–Sat 10am–1.30pm & 4–6.30pm, Sun 10am–1.30pm €2.40), a pair of small crypt-like chambers, is in front of the west facade. One of the earliest Romanesque buildings in Spain (1054–1063), it was decorated towards the end of the twelfth century with some of the most imaginative and impressive paintings of Romanesque art. They are extraordinarily well preserved and their biblical and everyday themes are perfectly adapted to the architecture of the vaults. Eleven kings and twelve queens were laid to rest here, but the chapel was desecrated during the Peninsular War and their tombs command little attention in such a marvellous setting.

Also worth seeing is the opulent **Monasterio de San Marcos**, built in 1168 for the Knights of Santiago and one of several chivalric orders founded in the twelfth century both to protect pilgrims on their way to Santiago de Compostela and to lead the Reconquest. In the sixteenth century the monastery was rebuilt as a pala-tial headquarters for the order, its massive facade lavishly embellished with Plateresque designs. Fittingly, it has been converted into a *parador*, where the guests enjoy the luxury of a magnificent church of their own, the **Iglesia San Marcos**. The church can be visited by non-patrons too; its sacristy houses a small **museum** (Tues–Sat 10am–2pm & 4–7/8pm, Sun 10am–2pm; €1.20, free Sat) of beautiful and priceless exhibits, housed in a room separated from the hotel lobby by a thick pane of glass.

Practicalities

The **train and bus stations** are both just south of the river: the train station at the end of Avenida de Palencia, the bridge across into town, and the bus station on Paseo Ingeniero Saenz de Miera – from here, turn left onto Paseo Ingeniero Miera to reach the bridge. From the roundabout, just across the river at Glorieta Guzmán El Bueno, you can see straight down the Avenida de Ordoño II and across the Plaza de Santo Domingo to the cathedral. Directly opposite the cathedral's west facade stands the friendly **tourist office** (Mon–Fri 9am–2pm & 5–7pm, Sat & Sun 10am–2pm & 5–8pm; ☎987 237 082, ⊛www.jcyl.es/turismo).

There are plenty of **places to stay**, particularly on the main roads leading off the Glorieta, Avda. de Roma and Avda. Ordoño II: try the *Hostal Central,* Avda. Ordoño II 27-3° (☎987 251 806; ❷); other good options are the *Pensión Suarez*, right next to the cathedral on c/Ancha 7-2° (☎987 254 288; ❶), and *Pensión Puerta del Sol* (☎987 211 966; ❷), overlooking the Plaza Mayor. There's a summer-only HI **hos-tel** with a pool at c/de la Corredera 4 (☎987 203 414; ❶); follow Avda. de Independencia from Plaza de Santo Domingo, and another at c/Campos Góticos 3 (☎897 261 174; ❶), about twenty minutes' walk from both the cathedral and the stations, by the *plaza de toros*. The city **campsite** (☎987 680 233) is 5km out on the Valladolid road – unfortunately there's no bus.

For sheer enjoyment, the best time of year to be in León is for the **fiesta** of St Peter in the last week of June. The rest of the year, the liveliest places tend to be the

bars and restaurants in the small square of San Martín, behind Plaza Mayor, and the dark narrow streets which surround it. You'll find good food at the *Restaurante Fornos*, c/Cid 8, or *Mesón Leones Racimo de Oro*, Caño Badillo 2 (closed Tues), and a surprisingly tasty, cheap menu at *Parada de Postas*, in the bus station.

The north coast

Spain's **north coast** veers wildly from the typical conception of the country, with a rocky, indented coastline full of cove beaches and fjord-like *rías*. It's an immensely beautiful region – mountainous, green and thickly forested, and frequent rains often shroud the countryside in a fine mist. The summers are temperately warm and, if you don't mind the occasional shower, are a glorious escape from the unrelenting heat of the south.

In the east, butting against France, is **Euskadi** – the **Basque Country** – which, despite some of the heaviest industrialization on the peninsula, remains remarkably unspoiled: neat and quiet inland, rugged and enclosed along the coast, with easy, efficient transport everywhere. **San Sebastián** is the big seaside attraction, a major resort with superb but crowded beaches, but there are any number of lesser-known, equally attractive coastal villages all the way to **Bilbao** and beyond. Note that the Basque **language**, Euskera, bears almost no relation to Spanish and is widespread here (we've given the alternative Basque names where popularly used) – it's perhaps the most obvious sign of Spain's strongest separatist movement.

To the west lies **Cantabria**, centred on the port of **Santander**, with more good beaches and superb trekking in the mountains of the **Picos de Europa**. The mountains extend into **Asturias**, the one part of Spain never to be conquered by the Moors. It remains today an idiosyncratic principality standing slightly apart from the rest of the nation. Its high, remote valleys are mining country, providing the raw materials for the heavy industry of the three cities: **Gijón, Avilés** and **Oviedo**.

In the far west, **Galicia** looks like Ireland, and there are further parallels in its climate, culture and – despite its fertile appearance – its history of famine and poverty. While right-wing Galicia may not share the radical traditions of the Basque country or of industrial Asturias it does treasure its independence, and Gallego is still spoken by around 85 percent of the population – again, we've given Gallego place names in parentheses. For travellers, the obvious highlight is **Santiago de Compostela**, the greatest goal for pilgrims in medieval Europe.

Once you leave the Basque country, communications in this region are generally slow. If you're not in a great hurry, you may want to make use of the independent **FEVE rail line** (☎914 533 800, ⓦwww.feve.es; rail passes are not valid). The rail line begins at Bilbao and follows the coast, with inland branches to Oviedo and León, all the way to El Ferrol in Galicia. Despite recent major repairs and upgrading, it's still slow, but it's cheap and a terrific journey, skirting beaches, crossing rivers and snaking through a succession of limestone gorges.

San Sebastián

The undisputed queen of the Basque resorts, **SAN SEBASTIÁN** (Donostia), just an hour by road from Bilbao (see below), is a picturesque – though expensive – town with excellent beaches, restaurants and bars. Along with Santander, it has always been the most fashionable place to escape the heat of the southern summers, and in July and August it's packed – though its customers are more likely to be well-to-do-families rather than the glitzy B-list celebrities found in its Riviera counterparts. Set around the deep, still bay of La Concha and enclosed by rolling low hills, Donostia is beautifully situated; the old town sits on the eastern promontory, its back to the wooded slopes of Monte Urgull, while newer development has spread inland along the banks of the River Urumea and around the edge of the bay to the foot of Monte Igùeldo.

The **old quarter** is the centre of interest – cramped and noisy streets where crowds congregate in the evenings to wander among the small bars and shops or sample the shellfish from the traders down by the fishing harbour. Prices tend to reflect the popularity of the area, especially in the waterside restaurants, but it's no hardship to survive on the delicious tapas, which are laid out in all but the fanciest bars – check the prices first, as it's quite easy to run up a sizeable bill: around €1.20 per *pintxo* is the norm. Here too are the town's chief sights: the gaudy Baroque facade of the church of **Santa María**, and the more elegantly restrained sixteenth-century **San Vicente**. The centre of the old part is the Plaza de la Constitución, known locally as "La Consti"; the numbers on the balconies of the buildings around the square refer to the days when it was used as a bullring. Just behind San Vicente, the excellent **Museo de San Telmo** (Tues–Sat 10.30am–1.30pm & 4–8pm, Sun 10.30am–2pm; free) is a fascinating jumble of Basque folklore, funerary relics and assorted artworks. Behind this, **Monte Urgull** is crisscrossed by winding footpaths to the top. From the mammoth figure of Christ on its summit there are great views out to sea and back across the bay to the town, weather permitting. Still better views across the bay can be had from the top of **Monte Igüeldo**; take bus #16 or walk around the bay to its base, from where a funicular (daily 11am–8pm, closed Wed in winter; €1.50 return) will carry you to the summit, the home of a **funfair** (€1.10).

There are three **beaches** in San Sebastián: Playa de la Concha, Playa de Ondaretta and Playa de la Zurriola. **La Concha** is the most central and the most celebrated, a wide crescent of yellow sand stretching round the bay from the town. Despite the almost impenetrable mass of flesh here during most of the summer, this is the best of the beaches. Out in La Concha bay is a small island, **Isla de Santa Clara**, which makes a good spot for picnics; a boat leaves from the Paseo Mollaberria (summer 10am–8.30pm every 30min; €1.20). **Ondaretta**, considered the best beach for swimming and never quite as packed as La Concha, is a continuation of the same strand beyond the rocky outcrop that supports the **Palacio Miramar** (gardens open 9/10am–sunset; free), once a summer home of Spain's royal family. The atmosphere here is rather more staid – it's known as *La Diplomática* for the number of Madrid's "best" families who holiday here. Far less crowded, and popular with surfers, **Playa de Zurriola** and the adjacent **Playa de Gros** were regraded during the 1990s and breakwaters added to shield them from dangerous currents.

Should you tire of sun and antiquity, head for the sparkling new conference and cultural centre, the **Palacio Kursaal** (guided tours Mon–Fri at 1.30pm, Sat & Sun 11.30am, 12.30pm, 1.30pm; €1.80) on Avenida de Zurriola. Designed by the architect Rafael Moneo, and set on the banks of the River Urmuea by Playa de Zurriola, the building consists of two translucent glass cubes not dissimilar to Japanese lanterns – an elegant sight at night.

Practicalities

National **buses** use the terminal at Plaza Pío XII (the ticket office is round the corner on c/Hiribidea), twenty minutes' walk inland along the river, while regional ones go from the Plaza de Guipúzcoa. The main-line **train station** is across the River Urumea on the Paseo de Francia, although local lines to Hendaye and Bilbao have their terminus on c/Easo (rail passes not valid). The **tourist office**, on c/Reina Regente 8 in the old town (winter Mon–Sat 8/9am–2pm & 3.30–7/8pm, Sun 10am–1pm; ☎943 481 166, ✆www.sansebastianturismo.com), is very helpful in finding a place to stay and providing accommodation.

Accommodation, though plentiful, is not cheap and can be very hard to come by in season and at weekends. A good way to ensure a place is to use the central reservations service online: ✆www.paisvasco.com/centralreservas. In the old town, look around La Consti and c/San Jerónimo; in the central district there's better value around the cathedral, especially calles Easo, San Martín and San Bartolomé; or on the other side of the river try behind the Plaza de Cataluña, where you'll also find excellent tapas bars. Places to try in the old part include *Pensión San Jerómino*, c/San Jerómino 25-2° (☎943 420 830; ❸); *Pensión Urgull*, c/Esterlines 10-3° (☎943 430 047; ❷); and *Pensión Anne*, c/Esterlines 15-2° (☎943 421 438, ⓦwww.pension-anne.es.org; ❸). Around the cathedral, try the *Pensión Artea*, c/San Bartolomé 33-1° (☎943 455 100; ❸); *Pensión La Perla*, c/Loyola 10-1° (☎943 428 123; ❸); *Pensión Añorga*, c/Easo 12-1° (☎943 467 945; ❷); or the more expensive *Pensión San Martín*, c/San Martín 10-1° (☎943 428 714; ❸). San Sebastián's **campsite** (☎943 214 502) is excellent, but it's a long way from the centre on the landward side of Monte Igüeldo, reached by bus #16 from the Alameda del Boulevard. The **hostel** (☎943 310 268; ❷), known as *La Sirena*, is located on Paseo de Igüeldo, just a few minutes' walk back from the end of Ondarreta Beach, but away from the centre. There are **internet** cafés at c/San Jerónimo 8 and c/San Lorenzo 6 in the old town.

San Sebastián has some of the best **restaurants** in the country. Luckily for the more impecunious, help is at hand in the good-value, delicious *pintxos* which are set out in all but the fanciest of bars, or try the fixed menus at places near the cathedral such as *Ardandegi*, c/Reyes Católicos 7, the highly recommended *La Barranquesa*, c/Larramendi 21, or, in the old quarter, *Morgan Jatetxea* on c/Narrika Kalea. Alternatively, order some well-priced *raciones* at either *Gaztelu*, c/31 de Agosto 22, or *Beti-Jai*, both on c/Narrika, in the old town. In the evenings you'll find no shortage of action, with **clubs** and **bars** wherever the tourists congregate. The fanciest are along the promenade by the beach, Paseo de la Concha, where you'll pay €12–18 to get in; the cheaper places are mostly in the old town where people normally start the evening off – later everyone heads to the area along c/Reyes Católicos behind the cathedral or c/San Bartolomé. For late nights, head for *Etxekalte* at c/Mari Kalea 11, overlooking the port and beach, where a young clientele groove to choice jazz, urban soul and hip-hop (free entry). A recent addition to Donostia's night scene are growshops, a blend of Amsterdam café, art gallery and bar – Soma *107*, on c/Larramendi 4, is one of the city's best; try also *Kaya*, on Paseo de Colón 46, or *La Mota*, at Aldamar 32.

The Donostian summer is full of **festivals**, many involving Basque sports such as the annual rowing races between the villages along the coast. The *International Jazz Festival* (ⓦwww.jazzaldia.com), at different locations throughout the town in the third week of July, invariably attracts top performers as well as hordes of people on their way home from the fiesta in Pamplona.

Bilbao

Although traditionally an industrial city, **BILBAO** (Bilbo) has given itself a makeover and is now a priority destination on any Spanish tour. And no surprise: a state-of-the-art metro (designed by Lord Norman Foster) links the city's widespread attractions; the breathtaking **Guggenheim Museum** by Frank O. Gehry – along with Jeff Koons' puppy sculpture in flowers – is a major draw; the airport and one of the many dramatic river bridges are Calatrava-designed, and there are various bids to further develop the riverfront with university buildings and public parks connected by footpaths, more bridges and a tramway. Coupled with a vibrant, friendly atmosphere, lots of elegant green spaces and some of the best cafés, restaurants and bars in Euskadi, these all make Bilbao a city that's here to stay.

The **Casco Viejo**, the old quarter on the east bank of the river, is still a main point of interest for the beautiful **Teatro Arriaga**, the elegantly arcaded **Plaza Nueva**, the Gothic **Catedral de Santiago** (Tues–Sat 10am–1.30pm & 4–7pm, Sun 10.30am–1.30pm; free) and the interesting **Basque Museum** on Plaza Miguel de Unamuno, 4 (Tues–Sat 11am–5pm, Sun 11am–2pm; €3, free Thurs).

It is along the Río Nervión that a whole number of exciting new buildings have appeared. A good route through leads from the Casco Viejo down the river past Santiago Calatrava's delightfully modern Campo Volantin footbridge and the more imposing Zubizuri bridge to the billowing curves of the **Guggenheim Museum** (Tues–Sun 10am–8pm; €7), itself more of an attraction than most of the art inside. Two of the best-loved features here are the sculptures outside – one, Louise Bourgeois' *Maman*, is a giant metal spider set between the museum and the river – the other is Jeff Koons' inaugural piece, *Puppy*, a giant dog made from flowers. Inside, the art is divided in two: the permanent collection is housed in more traditional (rectangular) galleries; temporary exhibitions and individual artists' collections are displayed in the huge sculptural spaces nearer the river. Further along the river from the Guggenheim, on the edge of the Parque de Doña Casilda de Hurriza, is the **Museo de Bellas Artes** (Tues–Sat 10am–8pm, Sun 10am–2pm; €4.50, free on Wed), which houses works by Goya and El Greco and some fine temporary exhibitions.

Practicalities

The FEVE and RENFE **train stations** are conveniently located just over the river from the Casco Viejo, while most **buses** arrive some way out of the centre at San Mamés – from here you can catch the metro to the centre. Buses from Barcelona and Madrid arrive on c/Autonomía, a twenty-minute walk via Plaza de Zabálburu from the old town. The **airport**, again designed by Calatrava, is accessible by a bus (daily 6am–10pm; every 30min–1hr; €1) which leaves from just outside the terminal building and runs to Plaza Moyua in the centre. The **tourist office** (Mon–Fri 9am–2pm & 4–7.30pm, Sat 9am–2pm, Sun 10am–2pm; ☎944 795 760, ⊛www .bilbao.net) is just north of the Teatro Arriaga on Paseo del Arenal; there's another branch just outside the Guggenheim (Tues–Fri 11am–2pm & 4–6pm, Sat 11am–2pm & 5–7pm, Sun 11am–2pm) and an information booth at the airport. The best **places to stay** are almost all in the Casco Viejo – especially along and around the streets leading off c/Bidebarrieta, which leads from Plaza Arriaga to the cathedral. Prices have risen substantially since the opening of the Guggenheim, but good possibilities are: the *Hostal Gurea*, c/Bidebarrieta 14 (☎944 163 299; ❷); the superb pensiones *Ladero*, c/Lotería 1 (☎944 150 932; ❷), and *Mendez*, c/Santa Maria 13 (☎944 160 364; ❷), where some rooms have balconies; *Pensión Serantes*, c/Somera 14 (☎944 151 557; ❷); and *Hostal Roquefer*, c/Lotería 2 (☎944 150 755; ❷). In summer and at weekends, booking ahead is advisable. **Internet access** is available at Laser, c/Sendaja 31.

Eating and drinking are also best in the Casco Viejo, although there are few regular restaurants – this is one of those cities where the most enjoyable way to eat is to move from bar to bar, snacking on tapas: Plaza Nueva and the area known as the *siete calles* have numerous options. For breakfast try the excellent *Café Boulevard* on Paseo del Arenal, and for a mid-afternoon coffee you can't beat the Arabic-style *Café Iruña* across the river at c/Jardines de Albia 5. If you do fancy a sit-down meal, try the highly recommended Basque restaurant *Bar Rio-Oja*, c/Perro 4, just west of the cathedral; there are other good restaurants and bars along the same street. Bilbao can be very lively indeed at **night** – and totally wild during the August **fiesta**, *La Semana Grande* (from first Sat after Aug 15), with scores of open-air bars, live music and impromptu dancing in an incredible atmosphere. Head for the streets around c/Licenciado Poza and c/Ledesma.

Santander

Long a favourite summer resort of Madrileños, **SANTANDER** has a French feel – an elegant, reserved resort in a similar vein to San Sebastián. Some people find it a clean, restful base for a short stay; for others it is dull and snobbish. On a brief visit, the balance is tipped in its favour by its excellent (and no longer polluted) beaches, and the sheer style of its setting. The narrow **Bahía de Santander** is dramatic, with the city and port on one side in clear view of open countryside and high mountains on the other; a great first view of Spain if you're arriving on the **ferry** from Plymouth.

Santander was severely damaged by fire in 1941, and what's left of the city divides into two parts: the **town and port**, clumsily reconstructed on the old grid around a mundane cathedral; and the beach suburb of **El Sardinero**, a twenty-minute walk (or bus #1, #3, #4, #7 or #9) from the centre, more if you follow the coast around the wooded headland of **La Magdalena**. There are few real sights to distract you, and it's for the glorious **beaches** that most people come. The first of these, **Playa de la Magdalena**, begins on the near side of the headland. The beautiful yellow strand, sheltered by cliffs and flanked by a summer windsurfing school, is deservedly popular, as is **El Sardinero** itself. If you find both beaches too crowded for your taste, head for the long stretches of dunes across the bay at **Somo** (which has windsurfing boards for rent and a summer campsite) or **Pedreña**; to get to them, jump on a *lancha*, a cheap taxi-ferry (€2.50 return; every 15min) from the central Puerto Chico dock.

Practicalities

The RENFE and FEVE **train and bus stations** are central and side by side, near the waterfront at Plaza Porticada. There are two **tourist offices**: the best is in the Jardines de la Pereda (July–Sept daily 9am–9pm; rest of year Mon–Fri 9.30am–1.30pm & 4–7pm, Sat 9.30am–1.30pm; ☎942 203 000); the other is in front of the casino at El Sardinero (same hours). Good places to look for **rooms** are c/de Rodríguez in front of the station – *San Miguel* at no. 9 (☎942 220 363; ❷) is an option – and Avda. de los Castros, which runs all the way across the northeastern side of town, where you'll find many budget options, such as *La Soledad* at no. 17 (☎942 270 936; ❷). There are some very popular cheapish places by the beach, on the Avda. de los Castros at Sardinero, including the *Botín* at c/Isabel Segundo 1 (☎942 210 094; ❷), and a **campsite** (☎942 391 530) a short walk further down the coast on Cabo Mayor. There's also a summer-only **hostel**, *Albaicín*, at c/Francisco Palazuelos, 21–23 (☎942 217 753; ❷). **Food** options are plentiful along c/San Simón and – for great tapas and a good **drinking** scene – c/Río de la Pila, above Plaza de Velarde, as well as around the main square and station. If you're after seafood, wander down to the fishing port (*puerto pesquero*), to the east of the ferry port and stations; there's no shortage of places along the c/Marqués de la Ensanada, but check prices before ordering – *Casa José* on nearby c/Mocejón is more reasonably priced than most.

Picos de Europa National Park

The **Picos de Europa** offer some of the finest hiking, canoeing and other mountain activity in Spain, and this national park – the country's first – is a delightful, densely forested place to enjoy this breathtaking countryside. The park boasts two glacial lakes, a series of peaks over 2400m high and diverse wildlife ranging from otters and doormice to wolves and bears; it is also a site of historic and religious interest: the Covadonga monastery is situated here.

From Santander, about 80km east, the park is reached by passing through San Vicente de la Barquera, Unquera and Cares; alternative access is from Oviedo in the south, a spectacular drive of 80km along winding, narrow roads. There's a **visitors' centre**, Casa Dago, at Cangas de Onís, a major gateway to the park (daily 9am–2pm & 4–6.30/9pm; Dec & Jan closed Sat & Sun; ☎985 241 412, ✆www.cangasdeonis.com); for more information on hiking, contact the Federación Española de Montañismo (☎914 451 438). **To stay**, head for the **Hospedería del Peregrino**, right in the park at Covadonga (☎985 846 047, ✆www.picosdeuropa.net/peregrino; ❷); or, in Cangas de Onís, try *Hospedaje Torreón* (☎985 848 211, ✆www.iespana.es/pensiontorreon; ❷). There's also a **campsite** at Soto de Cangas,

3.5km west of Cangas de Onís (☎985 940 097), and a private **hostel**, *Albergue La Posada del Monasterio* (☎985 848 553, ⓦwww.posadadelmonasterio.com; ➋), in an old monastery in La Vega-Villanueva, 2km northwest of Cangas de Onís; the management organize canoeing, hiking and other activities in the park.

Santiago de Compostela

SANTIAGO DE COMPOSTELA, built in a warm golden granite, is one of the most beautiful of all Spanish cities. The whole of this medieval place has been declared a national monument and it remains remarkably uniform in its charm, the more so for being almost wholly pedestrianized. The **pilgrimage** to Santiago (see box) captured the imagination of medieval Christian Europe on an unprecedented scale; during the eleventh and twelfth centuries, when the city was at the height of its popularity, it received half a million pilgrims each year. People of all social backgrounds came to visit the supposed shrine of St James the Apostle (Santiago to the Spanish), making this the third-holiest site in Christendom, after Jerusalem and Rome. These days, tourists are as likely to be attracted by art and history as by religion, but the all-round atmosphere of the place must not be dissimilar to that of the pilgrim days. Once host to kings and all manner of society, Santiago is by no means a dead city now – it's the seat of Galicia's regional government, and houses a great contemporary art gallery and a large student population too. It's also a manageable size – fifteen minutes' walk from the centre, you're in open countryside.

The City

All roads to Santiago lead to the **Cathedral** (daily 7.30am–9pm; tourist visits 10am–noon & 1.30–6pm), whose sheer grandeur you first appreciate upon venturing into the vast expanse of the Plaza de Obradoiro. Directly ahead stands a fantastic Baroque pyramid of granite, flanked by immense bell towers and everywhere adorned with statues of St James in his familiar pilgrim guise with staff, broad hat and scallop-shell badge. This **Obradoiro facade** was built in the mid-eighteenth century by an obscure Santiago-born architect, Fernando Casas y Novoa, and no other work of Spanish Baroque can compare with it.

The main body of the cathedral is Romanesque, rebuilt in the eleventh and twelfth centuries after a devastating raid by the Moors. The building's highlight is the **Pórtico de Gloria**, the original west front, which now stands inside the cathedral behind the Obradoiro. This was both the culmination of all Romanesque

---

The Camino de Santiago

The most famous Christian pilgrimage in the world, the **Camino de Santiago** – or Way of St James – traces routes through France and Spain to the world's third most visited pilgrimage site: **Santiago de Compostela**. If you're travelling in this part of the world, you will doubtless see many pilgrims, identified – mainly to each other – by the coquille St Jacques, a large effigy of a scallop shell, that they wear attached to their backpack.

Santiago de Compostela comes from the Latin, Santiago de Campus Stella or "James of the field of stars"; it's named after a peasant who had a vision in a field of stars near where the town now lies; soon after, the Catholic Church miraculously discovered that the disciple James had been buried in that very spot. There are those that scoff at the notion that James was ever in Spain, never mind buried here; some see it as an early church PR exercise to garner some enthusiasm against the Moors. Whether you believe or not, the reality is that millions *do* – if not in the legend, at least in the physical and mental challenge of a pilgrimage on foot.

Should you be interested in walking, cycling, or even cheating and taking the train, check the **website** ⓦwww.caminosantiago.com.

sculpture and a precursor of fingers of one hand pressed into the roots of the *Tree of Jesse* below the saint. So many millions have performed this act of supplication that five deep and shiny holes have been worn into the solid marble. On the other side of the pillar, kneeling at the foot, is the sculptor himself, Maestro Mateo. Pilgrims would touch the statue's head with their foreheads to absorb his wisdom.

The spiritual climax of the pilgrimage was the approach to the **High Altar**. This remains a peculiar experience: you climb steps behind the altar, embrace the Most Sacred Image of Santiago, kiss his bejewelled cape, and are handed, by way of certification, a document in Latin called a *Compostela*. The altar is an exuberant creation of eighteenth-century Churrigueresque, but the statue has stood there for seven centuries and the procedure is quite unchanged. You'll notice an elaborate pulley system in front of the altar. This is for moving the immense incense-burner – *El Botafumeira* – which, operated by eight priests, is swung in a vast ceiling-to-ceiling arc across the transept. It is stunning to watch, but takes place only during certain services such as Friday and Saturday Mass at noon – check with the tourist office.

You can visit the treasury, cloisters, archeological museum and beautiful crypt (Mon–Sat 10am–1.30pm & 4–6.30pm, Sun 10am–1.30pm; €3). The late Gothic **cloisters** in particular are worth seeing: from the plain, mosque-like courtyard you get a wonderful view of the riotous mixture of the exterior, crawling with pagodas, domes, obelisks, battlements, scallop shells and cornucopias.

Further afield, the main interest lies in the multifarious monasteries and convents. The enormous Benedictine **San Martín** stands close to the cathedral, the vast altarpiece in its church depicting its patron riding alongside St James. Nearby is **San Francisco**, reputedly founded by the saint himself during his pilgrimage to Santiago. In the north of the city are Baroque **Santa Clara**, with a unique curving facade, and a little beyond it, **Santo Domingo**. This last is perhaps the most interesting of the buildings, featuring a magnificent seventeenth-century triple stairway, each spiral leading to a different storey of a single tower, and a fascinating museum of Gallego crafts and traditions, the **Museo do Pobo Gallego** (Mon–Sat 10am–1pm & 4–7pm; free). A symbol of Santiago's enduring creativity and charm lies just next door, in the **Centro Galego de Arte Contemporánea** (Tues–Sun 11am–8pm; free), a beautiful gallery designed by Portuguese architect Álvaro Siza and host to a revolving triumvirate of challenging visiting exhibitions: previous artists include Mona Hatoum and Anish Kapoor.

Practicalities

Arriving at the **bus station** you are 1km or so north of the town centre; bus #10 will take you in to the Plaza de Galicia at the southern edge of the old city. The **train station** is a walkable distance south of this plaza along c/del Horreo. The **tourist office** is at Rúa do Vilar 43 (Mon–Fri 10am–2pm & 4–7pm, Sat 11am–2pm & 5–7pm, Sun 11am–2pm; ☏981 584 081, ✇www.santiagoturismo .com), and can provide complete lists of accommodation. There is **internet access** at Cibernova, c/Rúa Nova 50.

You should have no difficulty finding an inexpensive **room** in Santiago, though note that *pensiones* here are often called *hospedajes*. The biggest concentration of places is on the three parallel streets leading down from the cathedral: Rúa Nueva, Rúa do Vilar and c/del Franco. *Hospedaje Santa Cruz*, Rúa do Vilar 42 (☏981 582 362; ❷), has very friendly English-speaking owners; *Rajoy*, Avda. Raxoi, 3-2° (☏981 583 968; ❷), just off Plaza Obradoiro, has rooms overlooking the front of the cathedral; and *Hostal Barbantes II*, c/del Franco 1 (☏981 581 077; ❷), has a lively bar and restaurant. Another very cheap place is *Hospedaje Viño* on Praza de Mazarelos 7 (☏981 585 185; ❷) – the indomitable owner also has dozens of other rooms across town. There's a summer-only **pilgrim refuge** at Avda. Quiroga Palacios (☏981 589 200; €3) and a **hostel** with good facilities 3km out of town at Monte de Gozo (☏981 558 942; ❶) – take the U1 bus from Praza de Galicia. The **campsite**,

Camping As Cancelas (☎981 580 266), 2.5km north of the cathedral, is excellent; take the airport bus or city bus #9.

Thanks, perhaps, to the students, there are plenty of cheap places to eat here, along with excellent bars; it's also the best place in Galicia to hear local Breton-style music, played on *gaitas* (bagpipes). An excellent student eatery is the surprisingly cheap and pleasant *Casa Manolo* at Rúa Traviesa 27; seafood and fish are good at Bodegón de Xulio, Rúa Franco 24, and there are good tapas bars nearby, such as *Tacita de Juan* at Rúa Hórreo 31 and the gorgeous green-tiled and mirrored *Cafetería Paradiso*, rúa do Vilar 29, where you'll even get a few tapas for free. For **drinking** you're spoilt for choice in Santiago; good starting points are the inebriated *El Retablo* at Rúa Nova 13, the alternative *Bar Tolo* on Fonte de San Miguel or the popular *A Reixa* at Tras de Salomé 3.

The Pyrenees

With the singular exception of **Pamplona** at the time of its bull-running fiesta, the area around the Spanish Pyrenees is little visited – most people who come here at all travel straight through. In doing so they miss out on some of the most wonderful scenery in Spain, and some of the country's most attractive trekking. You'll also be struck by the slower pace of life, especially in **Navarra** (in the west, a partly Basque region) and **Aragón** (in the centre) – the Catalan Pyrenees (for which, see Catalunya; p.994) are more developed. There are few cities here – Pamplona itself and **Zaragoza**, with its fine Moorish architecture, are the only large centres – but there are plenty of attractive small towns and, of course, the mountains themselves, with several beautiful **national parks** as a focus for exploration.

Pamplona

PAMPLONA (Iruña) has been the capital of Navarra since the ninth century, and long before that was a powerful fortress town defending the northern approaches to Spain. Even now it has something of the appearance of a garrison city, with its hefty walls and elaborate pentagonal citadel. There's plenty to look at – the elaborately restored **Cathedral** with its magnificent cloister and interesting **Museo Diocesano** (Mon–Fri 10am–1.30pm & 4–7pm, Sat 10am–1.30pm; €3.61), the colossal **city walls** and **citadel**, the display of regional archeology, history and art in the **Museo de Navarra** (Tues–Sat 10am–2pm & 5–7pm, Sun 11am–2pm; €1.80, free Sat pm & all Sun), and much more – but most visitors come here for just one thing: the thrilling week of the **Fiesta of San Fermín**. From midday on July 6 until midnight on July 14 the city gives itself up to riotous nonstop celebration.

The centre of the festivities is the **encierro**, or running of the bulls – in which the animals decisively have the upper hand. Six bulls are released each morning at eight to run from their corral near the Plaza San Domingo to the bullring. In front, around and occasionally under them run the hundreds of locals and tourists who are foolish or drunk enough to test their daring against the horns. It was Hemingway's *The Sun Also Rises* that really put this on the map, and the area in front of the Plaza de Toros has been renamed Plaza Hemingway by a grateful council. To watch the *encierro* it's essential to arrive early – crowds have already formed an hour before it starts. The best **vantage points** are near the starting point or on the wall leading to the bullring. The event divides into two parts: there's the actual running of the bulls; and then after the bulls have been through the streets, bullocks with padded horns are let loose on the crowd in the bullring. If you watch the actual running, you won't be able to get into the bullring, so go on two separate mornings to see both. **Bullfights** take place daily at 6.30pm, with the bulls that ran that morning; tickets are expensive (€12–180 from the Plaza de Toros one day before the show) and are fiendishly difficult to obtain, as most are reserved for members of the bullring. At midnight on July 14 there's a mournful candlelit procession, the **Pobre De Mi**, at which the festivities are officially wound up for another year.

Practicalities

The **train station** is a long way from the old part of town, but bus #9 runs every twenty minutes to the end of Paseo de Sarasate, a few minutes' walk from the central Plaza del Castillo – there is a RENFE ticket office at c/Estella 8. The **bus station** is more central, on c/Conde Oliveto in front of the citadel, while the **tourist office** (summer Mon–Sat 10am–2pm & 4–7pm, Sun 10am–2pm; ☎948 206 540, ⓦwww.cfnavarra.es/turismonavarra) is at c/Esclava on Plaza San Francisco.

You'll find a cluster of cheap **hostales** on noisy c/San Nicolás and its continuation c/San Gregorio, off Plaza del Castillo. Rooms are in short supply during summer, and at fiesta time you've virtually no chance of a place without booking – and most at least double their prices during the fiesta. Good places to try include *La Montanesa*, c/San Gregorio 2 (☎948 224 380; ❷), and *Casa García*, c/San Gregorio 12 (☎948 223 893; ❷). Otherwise, try nearer the cathedral – *Santa Cecilia*, c/Navarrería 17 (☎948 222 230; ❷), is atmospheric and good. There's a **campsite**, *Ezcaba* (☎948 330 315), 7km out of town on the road to France; again it fills several days before the fiesta. Bus #4 runs to the campsite but there are only four daily departures. If you end up **sleeping rough**, remember that there is safety in numbers – head for one of the many parks such as Vuelta del Castillo or Media Luna and bring a sleeping bag, as the nights are cool. To clean off, there are public baths at c/Eslava (Tues–Sat 8.30am–8pm, Sun 8.30am–1pm; ☎948 221 738), where you can have a hot shower/bath. For more information about what to expect, check out: ⓦwww.encierro.com or ⓦwww.sanfermin.net.

The best **bars** are on and around c/San Nicolás, and during San Fermín on c/Jarauta and c/San Lorenzo too, as well as a number of grungy late-night dives on Calderia S. Augustín on the other side of the square. **Food** is expensive in Pamplona and you'll be hard pressed to find a set menu for less than €7 – about the cheapest option is *Catachu*, c/Indatxikia 16, parallel to Paseo de Sarasate. Alternatively, try the streets around c/Mayor, in particular *Bar la Cepa* or *Bar Poliki* on c/San Lorenzo and *Bar la Campana* on c/de la Campana, all of which offer a combination of *bocadillos* and good menus. C/San Nicolás also has several reasonable restaurants including *Dom Luis* and the excellent vegetarian *Sarasate*. *Café Roch* on c/ Comedias is great for tapas or, to get away from the crowds, go to the elegant *Bar Meson Caballo Blanco* on c/Redin up above the ramparts behind the cathedral. The elegant *Café Iruña*, on Plaza del Castillo, is the place to sit over a leisurely coffee.

Zaragoza

ZARAGOZA is the capital of Aragón, and easily its largest and liveliest city, with over half the province's one million people and the majority of its industry. There are some excellent bars and restaurants tucked in among its remarkable monuments, and it's also a handy transport centre, with good connections into the Pyrenees and east towards Barcelona. Try and be here for **Semana Santa** – the week before Easter – for the spectacular street processions.

The most imposing of the city's churches, majestically fronting the Río Ebro, is the **Basilica de Nuestra Señora del Pilar** (daily 5.45am–8.30/9.30pm), one of Zaragoza's two cathedrals. It takes its name from the column which the Virgin is said to have brought from Jerusalem during her lifetime to found the first Marian chapel in Christendom. Topped by a diminutive image of the Virgin, the pillar forms the centrepiece in the Holy Chapel and is the focal point for pilgrims, who line up to kiss an exposed section encased in a silver sheath. The cathedral has a few minor dome frescoes by Goya, and a curious display of two unexploded bombs dropped on the cathedral during the Civil War, but in terms of beauty it can't compare with the nearby Gothic-Mudéjar old cathedral, **La Seo** (Tues–Fri 10am–2pm & 4–6/7pm, Sat & Sun 10am–noon/1pm & 4/5–6/7pm), at the far end of the pigeon-thronged Plaza del Pilar. Just south of the Cathedral, at c/Espoz y Mina 23, lies an attraction of a different order, the wonderful Museo Camón Aznar (Tues–Fri 9am–2.15pm & 6–9pm; Sat 10am–2pm & 6–9pm, Sun 11am–2pm; €0.60) – an absolute must for Goya fans.

The city has recently been bringing to light its **Roman past** in three underground excavations: the Forum and River port (just off the Plaza del Pilar) and the Roman Baths (all Tues–Sat 10am–2pm & 5–8pm, Sun 10am–2pm; €1.80 each, or €3.60 combined ticket from the Forum). You can also see the remains of the amphitheatre in c/Veronica.

The highlight of Zaragoza, however, which you should see even if you plan to do no more than change trains or buses here, is the city's only surviving legacy from Moorish times. From the tenth to the eleventh century this was the centre of an independent dynasty, the Beni Kasim. Their palace, the newly restored **Aljafería** (Mon–Wed & Sat 10am–2pm & 4–6.30/8pm, Fri 4.30–6.30/8pm, Sun 10am–2pm; €1.80), was built in the heyday of their rule in the mid-eleventh century, and thus predates the Alhambra in Granada as well as Sevilla's Alcázar. From the original design the foremost relic is a tiny and beautiful mosque adjacent to the ticket office. Further on is an intricately decorated court, the Patio de Santa Isabella. Crossing from here, the Grand Staircase (added in 1492) leads to a succession of mainly fourteenth-century rooms, remarkable chiefly for their carved ceilings.

Practicalities

Points of arrival in Zaragoza are rather scattered. From *El Portillo* **train station**, walk down the short c/General Mayandia, turn right onto Paseo María Agustín and take bus #22 to Plaza España – or walk it in about twenty minutes. There are various **bus terminals**: most local and national services use the Agreda terminal at Paseo María Agustín 7 (right from the train station). The main **tourist office** is in the Plaza del Pilar (daily 10am–8pm; ☎976 393 537, ⊛www.turismozaragoza.com) with another at the Torreón de la Zuda (same times; ☎976 201 200) – part of the city fortifications overlooking the river.

There are **rooms** – and some cheap restaurants – close to the train station, along c/Madre Sacramento, parallel to Paseo María Agustín. *Fonda Miramar*, c/Capitán Casado 17 (☎976 281 094; ❷), is better than most. However, there's more atmosphere, better accommodation possibilities and most of the city's nightlife crowded into an area known as El Tubo, between c/de Alfonso I and c/Don Jaime I, close to the Plaza del Pilar. There are upwards of a dozen cheap *pensiones* here: try *Pensión Satue*, Espoz y Mina 4 (☎976 390 709; ❶), or *El Borjano* (☎976 394 875; ❷) at c/Estébares 4. Other places to try include the HI **hostel** (☎976 551 387, ⊛raaj@aragob.es; ❷), out of the centre but near the train station on c/Franco y Lopez 4, and the unofficial, hostel, *Ambos Mundos* (☎976 299 704; ❷). located right in the centre at Plaza Pilar 16. You can **camp** at the barren *Camping Casablanca* (☎976 753 870), 2km west of the city on Paseo de Canal – take bus #36 or #42 from the train station or Plaza de España. For **food** in El Tubo, try *Casa Lac* on c/Mártiries, supposedly the oldest restaurant in Spain, which is atmospheric and not too costly, or *La Tasquilla de don Pedro,* c/Cinegio, for tapas. Alternatives include *El Fuelle* on c/Mayor near Plaza de Pilar and, for tapas, *Bar Erzo* on c/Santa Catalina.

Jaca

Heading towards the Pyrenees from Zaragoza, **JACA** is the northernmost town of any size in Aragón and an obvious staging post. It's also a place of considerable interest – an early capital of the kingdom of Aragón that lay astride one of the main medieval pilgrim routes to Santiago. Accordingly, a magnificent **Cathedral** (daily 9am–1.30pm & 4–8pm), the first in Spain to be built in the Romanesque style, dominates the centre of town from its position at the north edge of the old quarter. It remains impressive despite much internal remodelling over the centuries, and there's a powerful added attraction in its **Museo Diocesano** (daily 11am–1.30pm & 4–6.30pm; winter closed Mon; €1.80). The dark cloisters are home to a collection of beautiful twelfth- to fifteenth-century frescoes, gathered from village churches in the area and from higher up in the Pyrenees.

Although barely 800m up, Jaca ranks as a Pyrenean resort, becoming crowded in August; even at other times of the year accommodation prices tend to be pushed up by the ski- and cross-border trade. But Jaca is foremost an army town, with a mass of conscripts attending the local mountain warfare academy. The military connection is nothing new: the **Ciudadela**, a sixteenth-century fort built to the stellar ground plan in vogue at the time, still offers good views of surrounding peaks. You can visit the interior (daily 11am–noon & 5–6pm; €1.80 including guided tour), but it's hardly worth it, as the outside, with slumbering deer in the dry moat, is by far the most interesting part.

Practicalities

Arriving in Jaca by **train**, you'll find yourself 1km or so out of town; move quickly and take the city bus, which connects with most trains. The more central **bus station** is on Avda. Jacetania, 200m northwest of the cathedral. The **tourist office** (Mon–Fri 9am–1.30/2pm & 4.30–7/8pm, Sat 9/10am–1.30pm & 5–7/8pm; summer also Sun 10am–1.30pm; ☎974 360 098, ⊛www.jaca.com) – worth a browse for its noticeboards offering all sorts of sport- and mountaineering-related services – is on Avda. Regimiento Galicia, just downhill from the bus stop and Ciudadela. All of Jaca's budget **accommodation** is on the northeast edge of the old town, with two good, quiet choices being *Hostal París* by the cathedral, Plaza de San Pedro 5 (☎974 361 020, ⊛hostalparisjaca@terra.es; ❷), and a bit closer to the action *Hostal Residencia El Abeto*, c/Bellido 15 (☎974 361 642; ❷). There's also a **hostel** (☎974 360 536, ⊛epiasj@planalfa.es; ❶) on Avda. Perimetral, next to the ice rink at the southern end of town, and two **campsites** – the closer but more basic *Victoria* (☎974 360 323) is 1km west of town on the Pamplona road, the wooded *Peña Oroel* (☎974 360 215) is 3km down the Sabiñanigo road. Good-value **eating** is found in the same part of the old district: carnivores will appreciate *La Fragua*, at c/Gil Berges 4 (closed Wed), while *La Cadiera* on c/Domingo Midal and *La Campanilla*, c/Escuelas Pias 8, both offer cheap but filling set menus.

The Aragonese Pyrenees

If you're not a keen trekker or skier, then the foothill villages of **ANSÓ** and **ECHO** (sometimes spelt with a preceding "h") set in their beautiful namesake valleys are perhaps your best single target in the **Aragonese Pyrenees**: they're noted for their distinctive, imposing architecture, and are accessible by a bus (Mon–Sat 6.30pm) from Jaca, returning early in the morning (Ansó 6am; Echo 6.45am). There are summer-only **tourist offices** in both villages: c/ Sta. Bárbara s/n, Ansó (☎974 370 210), and Plaza Conde Xiquena 1, Echo (☎974 375 329). Echo, to the east, is more visited and inevitably more expensive for **accommodation and food**: try *De La Val*, Cruz Alta 1 (☎974 375 028; ❸), and the *comedor* at the *Fonda Lo Foratón* (☎974 375 247; ❷). There's also a delightful **campsite**, *Valle de Echo* (☎974 375 361). In the westerly valley, less-frequented Ansó offers several reasonable places to stay and eat, including *Hostal Aisa* (☎974 370 009; ❶) on Plaza Domingo Miral.

A worthwhile target for a winter visit to alpine Aragón are the adjacent ski resorts of **ASTÚN-CANDANCHU**, north of Jaca, which are easily reached by bus. Hostales are uniformly pricey; if your budget is limited and/or you're primarily interested in skiing, then either of the two year-round *albergues*, the highly rated *El Aguila* (☎974 373 291; ⊛www.infobide.com/elaguila; ❸), or *Valle de Aragón* (☎974 373 222; ❸), should suit you nicely. Between Jaca and the slopes lies

CANFRANC, the final stop on the rail line up from Zaragoza since the French discontinued the onward section of track in a fit of pique over the success of the Spanish ski resorts. There are trains from Jaca, or use the same buses as for Candanchú. The small village is rather forlorn now, and you wouldn't come especially to see it, but there's a **tourist office** (Tues 9.30am–1pm, Wed–Sat 9am–1.30pm & 3.30–7pm; ☎974 373 141, ⊛www.canfranc.com) and a couple of places to stay and eat – try *Hotel Ara* at c/Fernando el Católico 1 (☎974 373 028; ②), and *Flores* at the other end of the street respectively.

For summertime walking, there's no better destination than the **Parque Nacional de Ordesa**, centred on a vast, trough-like valley flanked by imposingly striated limestone palisades. An *Alosa* bus (Mon–Sat 10.15am; ☎974 355 060) from Jaca serves Sabiñanigo, from where there's a *Hudebus* bus (11am, also 6.30pm in high season; ☎974 213 277) to **Torla**, the best base for the park (see below). Approaching Sabiñanigo by bus or train from Zaragoza, you'll need departures before 8.30am and 7.15am respectively to make the connection. Vehicle **entrance to the park** lies 5km beyond Torla, but trekkers should opt instead for the lovely trail (1hr 30min) on the far side of the river, well marked as part of the Pyrenean GR (long-distance path) system. Further **treks** can be as gentle or as strenuous as you like, the most popular outing being the all-day trip to the **Circo de Soaso** waterfalls. For detailed information on all activities offered in the park, head first for the **Oficina del Parque Nacional**, Ctra. de Ordesa, s/n (☎974 486 472; ⊜pnomp.torla@terra.es) in Torla.

TORLA itself, a formerly sleepy, stone-built village, has, since the 1980s, been overwhelmed in its role as gateway to the park; the older corners though are still visually attractive. Don't hope for a **room** or refuge bed from late July to late August, however, without reserving well in advance – even the two **campsites**, *San Antón* (☎974 486 063, ⊛www.ordesa.net/camping-sananton) and *Valle de Bujaruelo* (☎974 486 348, ⊛www.ordesa.net/camping-valledebujaruelo), 2km and 3km north, can often fill up. The latter also has an albergue with bunks (①). At other times of the year you can usually find space at the central *Hotel Ballarín* (☎974 486 155; ⊜hotelballarin@staragon.com; ③) and *Hostal Alto Aragón* (☎974 486 172; ②), both at Capuvita 11; or try the 43-bunk *Refugio Lucien Briet* (☎974 486 221, ⊜lucienbriet@staragon.com; ①). Both the *Fonda* and the *Bar Brecha*, which manages the *albergue*, serve good-value **meals**.

Several valleys east of Torla and cradled between the two highest summits in the Pyrenees, **BENASQUE** serves as another favourite jump-off point for mountain rambles. There is a daily bus service from Jaca (at 3pm, change at Huesca), and there's a marginally better chance of finding a bed here during high season. The **tourist office** is at c/San Sebastián 5 (☎974 551 289, ⊛www.benasque.com). For **accommodation** try *Pensión Veselia*, c/Mayor 5 (☎974 551 654; ②), the budget standby – they also serve cheap meals; or *Hostal Valero* (☎974 551 061; ⊛www.hoteles-valero.com/spain/hostalvalero; ②), on c/Ctra. Anciles. Decent food is to be had at *Restaurante Pilar*, c/ Ctra. de Francia, and the Basque *Restaurante Ampriu*, c/Las Plazas.

Catalunya

With its own language, culture and, to a degree, government, **Catalunya** (Cataluña in Castilian Spanish, Catalonia in English) has a unique identity. **Barcelona**, the capital, is very much the main event. One of the most vibrant and exciting cities in Europe, it is the kind of place where you end up staying far longer than planned. Inland, the monastery of **Montserrat**, Catalunya's main "sight", is perched on one of the most unusual rock formations in Spain, and the **Catalan Pyrenees**, while more developed than their western neighbours, are easier to access and breathtaking nonetheless. Sadly, large tracts of the coastline are a disaster, with much of the **Costa Brava** in particular a turgid sprawl of concrete. There are parts of the north-ernmost stretch that have managed to retain some attraction but on the whole, if it's beaches you're after you'd do better to keep going south – or take a ferry from Barcelona for the Balearics. Since the use of the Catalan language is so widespread, we've used Catalan spellings, with Castilian equivalents in parentheses.

The Catalan Pyrenees

The **Catalan Pyrenees**, every bit as spectacular as their Aragonese neighbours, have been exploited for far longer. While this has resulted in numerous less-than-aesthetic ski resorts and hydroelectric projects, it also means good public transport and a well-developed tourism infrastructure. In the less frequented corners, such as the westerly **Parc Nacional**, the scenery is the equal of any in Europe, while even the touristy train ride up to **Núria** to the east rarely fails to impress.

The Parc Nacional and around

After Ordesa, the most popular target of trekkers in the Pyrenees is the **Parc Nacional d'Aigüestortes y Estani de Sant Maurici**, covering nearly 200 sq km of forest, lakes and cirques, presided over by 3000m snow-capped peaks. For the less adventurous, there are lower-altitude tracks through fine scenery and visits to several villages around the park.

The main **access town** is **Pobla de Segur**, reached by train from Barcelona. The **best bases**, however, are Boí and Espot, both 60km north of Pobla and, west and east of the park boundaries respectively, with Capdella to the south a less busy alter-native; all are set in their own gorgeous valleys. **BOÍ** is on the main road up to the Viella tunnel, served by daily bus from Pobla via Pont de Suert. In the town itself, the tiny old quarter is dwarfed by modern construction, and tourism facilities are expensive. Exceptions include a few nameless *habitaciones* (❸), in the old quarter, or try *Pensión Pascual* (☎973 696 014; ❷). *Casa Higinio*, 200m up the road to Taüll, is a good place to **eat**. If you draw a blank here, head for the more handsome neigh-bouring village of **TAÜLL**, 3km uphill to the east. It has a couple of decent *pen-siones* – *Sant Climent*, c/Les Feixes 8 (☎973 696 052; ❷), and *La Coma* (☎973 696 147; ❷) – and an attractive **campsite** (☎973 696 174). **Within the park** itself, camping is forbidden and accommodation is limited to four **mountain refuges** (❷). Trails are, not surprisingly, well marked, and you rarely have to walk for more than four hours between huts.

North of the park, the long, narrow **Vall d'Aran**, with the giant Baqueira-Beret ski complex, is now easily the most expensive corner of Catalunya outside of Barcelona, and only worth passing through on your way to or from Aigüestortes. Near the top of the valley, **SALARDÚ** will be your most likely target, the meeting point of two walking routes serving the national park. There are several reasonable places to **stay**, among which the *Pension Montaña*, c/Major (☎973 644 108; ❷), can be singled out, along with the hostel *Era Garona* at Ctra. de Vielha, s/n (☎973 645 271, ⓦwww.aranweb.com/garona; ❷). **VIELLA**, 9km west and much lower,

---

Activities in the park

No activity that may pollute the water is allowed in the **Parc Nacional d'Aigüestortes** – and that includes all watersports. However, there is ample oppor-tunity for hiking, climbing, potholing and paragliding: for more information about the park and activities, contact the visitors' centres at Plaça del Treio 3, in Boí (9am–1pm & 3.30–7pm, closed Sun pm in winter; ☎973 696 189), or Prat del Guarda 4 in Espot (same hours; ☎973 624 036).

is the capital of the region and cross point for the two bus routes from Pobla: one (summer only) via Baqueira-Beret and Salardú, the other (all year) through the namesake tunnel. It's not a particularly memorable town, but if you're forced by the bus schedules to **stay**, try the *Pension Busquets*, c/Major 9 (☎973 640 238; ❷), or the *Pensión Puig*, north of the main drag at c/Camí Reiau 6 (☎973 640 031; ❸).

Núria and beyond

For a beautiful but easy way to see the Pyrenees, look no further than the rack-and-pinion rail line up to the cirque and shrine at **NÚRIA**. After a leisurely start from Ribes de Freser (see below), the tiny two-carriage train lurches up into the mountains, following a river between great crags. Occasionally it stops, the track only inches away from a terrifying drop, a sheer rock face soaring way above you. Once through a final tunnel, the train emerges alongside a small lake (dry in summer), at the other side of which is the one giant building that constitutes Núria. A severe stone structure, it combines church, café, hotel and ski centre all in one; behind it is an official **campsite**. The *Hotel Vall de Núria* (☎972 732 000; ❺, half-board) is expensive in summer, but the price plummets in winter; there are also several dorm-style **refuges** around, though they are often full of groups, in which case you'll have to use the **campsite** (pay at the tourist office; ☎972 732 020) or the **hostel**, *Pic de l'Aliga* (☎972 732 048; ❷), at the end of the cable car. You'll need good equipment, even in summer, since it gets cold at night. As for **food**, you can buy hot snacks or breakfast at the *Bar Finestrelles*; there's a self-service place for lunch or an evening meal; the hotel dining room is another possibility.

Moving on, the privately owned Núria train (🌐www.valldenuria.com) runs year round (except Nov), from Ribes-Enllaç, via the towns of Ribes de Freser and Queralbs, where there are also places to stay. Trains from Barcelona connect with the Cremallera train at Ribes-Enllaç. Mainline trains continue to Puigcerdà, on the French frontier, astride the only surviving rail link over the Pyrenees to France. Four trains a day currently leave for La Tour de Carol, 3km over the border, but if you miss them it's easy enough to walk a slightly shorter distance east to Bourg-Madame, the actual border town. **PUIGCERDÀ** is a lot cheaper than anywhere in France, should schedules compel an **overnight stay**: try the *Hostal La Muntanya*, c/Coronel Molera 1 (☎972 880 202; ❸, including breakfast), or *Pensión Cerdanya*, c/Ramon Losp 7 (☎972 880 010; ❷). **Restaurant** prices are slightly inflated by the cross-border trade, but good bets include *La Cantonada*, c/Major 46 (beyond the bell tower), and *Bar-Restaurant Kennedy*, Pl. Héroes 2.

The Costa Brava

The **Costa Brava** (Rugged Coast), stretching for 145km from the French border to the town of **Blanes**, boasts wooded coves, high cliffs, pretty beaches and deep blue water, and was once the most beautiful part of the Spanish coast. However, greed and development have led to what seems like a determined effort to completely destroy this area's natural beauty forever and the region's an almost total disaster, with a density of concrete tourist developments greater even than the Costa del Sol. The southern part, including the monstrous resort of Lloret de Mar, is the worst: further up the main road runs inland and coastal development is relatively low-key. Attractions here are the ancient Greek site of **Empúries**, and Dalí's birthplace **Figueres**.

Buses in the region are almost all operated by SARFA, with an office in every town. Although they are reasonably efficient in the summer months, it can be frustrating either trying to get to some of the smaller coastal villages or simply attempting to stick to the coast. A car or bike solves all your problems; otherwise it's worth considering using Figueres as a base for lateral trips to the coast.

Palafrugell and Empúries

One of the few places to stop along this stretch of coast is **PALAFRUGELL**, an old town at its liveliest during the morning market. It's not much to get excited about, but it has been overlooked by most tourists and hence remains a pleasant place to be. It's also a convenient and relatively cheap base for the remaining delightful coastline a few kilometres away: pine-covered slopes and some quiet little coves with scintillatingly turquoise waters. *Fonda la Estrella* at c/de les Quatre Cases 13–17 (☎972 300 005; ❷) is the cheapest **accommodation** in Palafrugell; *El Jardinet* on c/Bruguerol 9 serves great tapas, has a reasonable menu and an attractive terrace, and *Cafèteria Pingüins* on Plaça Nova 12 is a popular meeting place. Such is the popularity of the nearby **beaches** that in summer a virtual shuttle bus runs from the **bus station** to Calella and then on to Llafranc. Get off at Calella – a beautiful fishing port with tiny, crowded beaches – since Llafranc is only a twenty-minute walk away from it.

From Palafrugell you're within striking distance of **EMPÚRIES**, one of the most interesting archeological sites in Spain. It started life in 550 BC as Greek *Emporion* (literally "Trading Station") and for three centuries conducted a vigorous trade throughout the Mediterranean. Later a splendid Roman city with an amphitheatre, fine villas and a broad marketplace grew up above the old Greek town. The Romans were replaced in turn by the Visigoths, who built several basilicas and made it the seat of a bishopric. The **site** (daily 10am–6/8pm; €2.40) lies behind a sandy bay about 2km north of L'Escala. The remains of the original Greek colony occupy the lower ground, where remains of temples, the town gate, agora and several streets can easily be made out, along with a mass of house foundations (some with mosaics) and the ruins of the Visigoth basilicas. A small **museum** (€1.80) stands above, and beyond it stretches the vast but only partly excavated Roman town.

There are buses to **L'ESCALA** from Palafrugell and Figueres, from the SARFA company's office just down the road from the combined tourist office/post office at the top of town. L'Escala usually has **rooms** available but it's an expensive and unattractive place – you're still a fair walk from the ruins and the good beaches. You could instead **camp** out on the beaches and in the woods around the archeological site, where there's little development apart from the two-star *Ampurias* (☎972 770 207; ❺, half-board; closed Oct to mid May–Sept) and a few villas. Alternatively there's a **hostel**, *L'Escala*, c/Les Coves 41 (☎972 771 200, ✉alberg_empuries @tujuca.com; ❷), with **camping**, right on the beach by the ruins, though this is often full.

Figueres

The northernmost resorts of the Costa Brava are reached via **FIGUERES**, a provincial Catalan town with a lively Rambla and plenty of cheap food and accommodation. The place would pass almost unnoticed, however, were it not for the most visited museum in Spain after the Prado: the **Museu Dalí** (June–Sept daily 9/10.30am–5.45/7.45pm; Oct–May Tues–Sun 10.30am–5.45pm; €9). Dalí was born in Figueres and on, January, 23, 1989, died there; his embalmed body now lies in a glass case inside the museum. Installed by the artist in a building as surreal as the exhibits, the Museu Dalí is a treat, appealing to everyone's innate love of fantasy, absurdity and participation.

To make your way into the middle of town, simply follow the "Museu Dalí" signs from the **train station**. The **tourist office** (summer Mon–Sat 9am–9pm, Sun 9am–3pm; rest of year Mon–Fri 8.30am–3pm, Sat 10am–1.30pm & 3.30–6.30pm; ☎972 503 155) is in front of the post office building by the Plaça del Sol. For a comfortable **room** try the *Pensión Bartis*, c/Méndez Núñez 2 (☎972 501 473; ❶); the town **campsite**, *Pous* (☎972 675 496), is on the way to the castle. There's a gaggle of cheap tourist restaurants in the narrow streets around the Dalí museum and, although a little more expensive, some nice pavement cafés lining the Rambla.

Barcelona

BARCELONA, the self-confident and progressive capital of Catalunya, is a tremendous place to be. Though it boasts outstanding Gothic and Art Nouveau buildings, and some great museums – most notably those dedicated to Picasso, Miró and Catalan art – its main appeal lies in getting lost in the narrow sidestreets, stopping in at bars and cafés, rising, eating and drinking late and soaking up the atmosphere. A thriving port and the most prosperous commercial centre in Spain, it has a sophisticated and cultural dynamism way ahead of the rest of the country. But Barcelona has also evolved an individual and eclectic cultural identity, most perfectly and eccentrically expressed in the architecture of **Antoni Gaudí**. The planning for the 1992 Olympics led to a new wave of civic pride, culminating in gleaming, renovated monuments and some spectacular modern buildings too. There are, however, darker sides to this prosperity and confidence: there is a great deal of poverty and a considerable drug problem, which means that the **petty crime** rate is very high. It's not unusual for tourists to feel threatened in the seedier areas flanking the Ramblas. It's wise to take a few precautions: leave passports and tickets locked up in your hotel, don't be too conspicuous with expensive cameras and, if attacked, don't offer any resistance. Be especially careful at Estació de Sants and in the old city where gangs of pickpockets and bag-snatchers target tourists.

Arrival and information

The **airport**, 12km southwest of the city, is linked by a train service (daily 6am–10pm every 30min; €2.15) to the main **Estació de Sants**, from where you can take the metro to the city centre (line #3 to Liceu for the Ramblas). Many trains from the airport also run on to **Plaça de Catalunya**, a more direct way of reaching the Barri Gòtic. Alternatively, there's the efficient **Airbus** (5.30/6am–midnight every 15min; €3.30), which departs from outside the terminals on a circular route and runs into the centre via Plaça d'Espanya, Gran Vía and Plaça de Catalunya. A **taxi** to the centre will cost around €20.

Estació de Sants is the city's main **train station**, for national and some international arrivals – many national buses also stop here; metro line #3 takes you directly to the Ramblas. The **Estació de França**, next to the Parc de la Ciutadella, is the terminal for long-distance Spanish and European express and intercity trains. Leaving França you can take the metro (line #4) from nearby Barceloneta, or simply walk (5min) into the Barri Gòtic, up Vía Laietana and into c/Jaume. The main **bus terminal** is the **Estació del Nord** (three blocks north of the Parc de la Ciutadella; Metro Arc de Triomf). If, by chance, you don't arrive here, you'll be dropped at a central point within easy reach of a metro station. Arriving by **ferry** from the Balearics, you'll dock at the Estació Marítima at the bottom of the Ramblas on Moll de Barcelona.

The best **tourist office** is beneath the Plaça de Catalunya (daily 9am–9pm; ☎906 301 282, ⓦwww.barcelonaturisme.com). Other branches can be found at Plaça Sant Jaume (Mon–Fri 9am–8pm, Sat 10am–8pm, Sun 10am–2pm), and at the airport (daily 9am–9pm). The Plaça de Catalunya branch books accommodation.

City transport

The quickest way of getting around is by the modern and efficient **metro** (5/6am–11pm/midnight, 2am at weekends); stations are marked by a red diamond sign. **Bus** routes (6.30am–10pm) are far more complicated, but every bus stop displays a comprehensive route map. For more information on both go to ⓦwww.tmb.net. There's a flat **fare** on both metro and buses (€1). If you're staying a couple of days or more it's better to buy a ticket strip or **targeta** or T-10 (€5.60); available at any metro station ticket office, it covers the metro, buses, and some regional train lines within the city (passes are also available for outlying zones). Similarly, there are daily passes (T-Dia) which offer unlimited travel within the

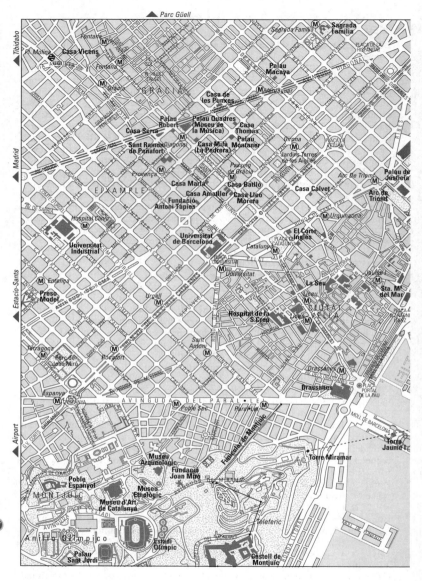

▲ Parc Güell

specified time (from €4.20/one day to €16.50/five days). You can also buy an **aer-obus card** (€12/two days, €14.80/three days, €17.50/four days, €19.50/five days), covering transport to/from the airport, plus all city bus and metro journeys. A limited number of yellow **night buses** (10.30/11.30pm–3.30/4.30am) run from, or pass through, Plaça de Catalunya; they cost a little more than daytime services. The two routes of the **bus turístic** link 27 of Barcelona's major sights, at which

BARCELONA

N

MEDITERRANEAN SEA

Els
Encants

PLAÇA
DE LES GLÒRIES
CATALANES
Glòries

SANT MARTÍ

Llacuna

Marina

Estació
del Nord

Bogatell

VILA OLÍMPICA

PASSEIG DE
LLUIS COMPANYS
Parc
de la
Ciutadella

Museu de
Zoologia
Hivernacle

Museu
Geologia

Mercat
del Born

Parc
Zoològic

Ciutadella

Globo
Turistic

Parlament de
Catalunya

Port
Olímpic

Estació
de
França

RONDA LITORAL

Barceloneta

BARCELONETA

Platja de la Barceloneta

ADMIRALL
AIXADA

Teleferic — ● **Torre Sant Sebastià**

0   500m

you can hop off and on at your leisure (€14/day, €18/two days). Tickets are available at tourist offices or on the bus itself and include a booklet of discount coupons for museums, shops and restaurants.

Black and yellow **taxis** (with a green roof-light lit when available) are inexpensive, plentiful and very useful late at night. There's a minimum charge of €1.10, €1.25 after 10pm, and after that it's around €0.75/km, depending on the time of day.

Accommodation

Accommodation in Barcelona is among the most expensive in Spain and unless you stay in a hostel, you'll be hard pushed to find a room for under €30 for a double. The tourist offices dish out lists of **hotels** and **hostales**, but these are hardly necessary as a walk through the streets of the old town reveals heavy concentrations of places to stay. Most of the **cheapest accommodation** is to be found in the side streets off and around the Ramblas, a convenient and atmospheric area in which to base yourself. The further down towards the port you get, the less salubrious and noisier the surroundings: as a general rule, anything above c/Escudellers tends to be all right. Perhaps the best hunting ground for cheap rooms is between the Ramblas and the Plaça de Sant Jaume, in the area bordered by c/Escudellers and c/de la Boqueria near Plaça Reial. The tourist office at Plaça de Catalunya can help, or you can use Barcelona Online (☎933 437 993, ✆www.barcelona-on-line.es/reserves/index.htm), or the online hostel and hotel reservation service ✆www.hostelbarcelona.com. Be warned that finding a bed in the city can be a nightmare at any time of year. Visitors are strongly advised to book at least the first two nights of accommodation as far ahead as possible.

There are several official and unofficial **hostels** in Barcelona, where accommodation is in multi-bedded dorm rooms, and there are hundreds of **campsites** on the coast in either direction, but none less than 11km from the city; we've detailed the easiest to access below.

Hostels

Alberg Kabul Pl Reial 17 ☎933 185 190, ✆www.kabul-hostel.com. Grotty dorms but a great atmosphere and lots of facilities, overlooking a beautiful square. **2**

Albergue Mare de Déu de Montserrat Passeig Mare de Déu del Coll 41–51 ☎934 838 363. A beautiful HI hostel a little more than half an hour from the city centre. Metro Vallcarca. **2**

Center Ramblès c/Hospital 63 ☎934 838 363. Large, modern hostel just off the Ramblas, with lots of facilites and no curfew. **2**

Gothic Point Hostel c/ Vigatans 5–9 ☎932 687 808, ✆wwww.gothicpoint.com. Lively place with big dorms and good facilities. Very popular with younger travellers and, hence, noisy. Breakfast included. **3**

Ideal Youth Hostel c/Unió 12 ☎933 426 711. Four- to eight-bed dorms in this old building right by the opera house. All have Individual WC, shower and balcony, and there's free internet access for guests. **2**

Youth Hostel Barcelona Mar Carrer San Pau 80 ☎933 248 530. New hostel with laundry and internet access, close to MACBA and the Ramblas. **3**

Hotels

Hostal Centric c/Casanova 13 ☎934 267 573, ✆www.hostalcentric.com. Just renovated, good value rooms In a quiet street that's central to the action nonetheless. **3**

Hostal Gat Raval c/Joaquím Costa 44 ☎934 816 670, ✆www.gataccommodation.com. Sleek minimalist design and helpful, friendly staff in this refreshingly clean, bright and youthful hotel in the hip environs of MACBA. **3**

Hostería Grau c/Ramelleres 22 ☎933 018 135, ✆www.intercom.es/grau. Bright *pensión* with a lovely café/bar in an unbeatable location just off Plaça Catalunya. **3**

Hotel La Terrassa c/Junta del Comerç 11 ☎933 025 174. Clean and atmospheric budget favourite, with plain singles, doubles and triples, some en suite, and a pleasant terrace. **2**

Itaca Hostel c/Ripoll 21 ☎933 019 751, ✆www.Itacahostel.com. Extremely popular and pleasant new hostel In the heart of things, with internet access, café, dining room and book exchange. **2**

Pension Bahia c/Canuda 4 ☎933 026 153, ✆www.pensionbahia.com. Cheap and serviceable but up lots of stairs, in a great location just off the Ramblas and Plaça Catalunya. **3**

The City

Scattered as Barcelona's main sights may be, the greatest area of interest is the **old town** (*la ciutat vella*). These cramped streets above the harbour are easily manageable, and far more enjoyable, on foot. Start, as everyone else does, with the Ramblas.

Around the Ramblas

Only in Barcelona could a street – or, strictly, streets – be a highlight. But the Ramblas are not just any street – here you will find everything from flower markets to fire eaters, performers to pet shops, and in the evening, all of Barcelona out taking a stroll. Heading down from the Plaça de Catalunya, you gradually leave the opulent facades of the banks and department stores for a seedier area towards the port, where the Ramblas cut right through the heart of the notorious red-light district, and side streets are packed with dimly lit clubs, bars and sex shops. However, this harbour end is much less threatening than it once was: the Olympic clean-up and the transformation of the Port Vell area has meant new hip bars and clubs now rub shoulders with sleazy old ones.

On your way down there are plenty of interesting buildings, some of them open for visits: don't miss the glorious **La Boqueria**, the city's main food market (Mon–Sat 8am–8pm), a splendid gallery of sights and smells with several excellent snack bars and a restaurant at the back selling market-fresh dishes. Almost adjacent is the majestic **Liceu**, Barcelona's celebrated opera house now renovated after it went up in smoke in January 1994. More or less opposite is the famous *Café de l'Ópera*, an opulent high-society meeting place – though not as expensive as you might imagine. A few minutes' walk north of here is the stunning **Museu d'Art Contemporani** or MACBA (Mon & Wed–Fri 11am–7.30pm, Sat 10am–8pm, Sun 10am–3pm; €5.11, discount on Wed) with exciting displays by international and national artists.

A little way down from the Liceu, hidden behind an archway just off the Ramblas and easy to miss, lies the elegant nineteenth-century **Plaça Reial**. Decorated with tall palm trees and iron lamps (designed by the young Gaudí), it's the haunt of crusties, Catalan eccentrics, the odd drunk and hundreds of alfresco diners and drinkers. Gaudí's magnificent **Palau Güell** (Mon–Sat 10am–2pm & 4–7.30pm; €3) stands just off the Ramblas, towards the bottom, at c/Nou de la Rambla 3. Much of Gaudí's early career was spent constructing elaborate follies for wealthy patrons, the most important of whom was Don Eusebio Güell, a shipowner and industrialist. In 1885 he commissioned this mansion, where Gaudí's feel for different materials and textures is astounding. Wrought iron supports blend magnificently with granite, marble, ceramics, woodwork and stained and etched glass. Don't miss the roof.

Right at the harbour end of the Ramblas, Columbus stands pointing out to sea from the top of a tall, grandiose column, the **Mirador de Colón** (Mon–Sat 9/10am–1.30pm & 3.30–6.30/8.30pm, Sun 10am–6.30/8.30pm; €1.80). Risk the lift to his head (it fell down in 1976) for a fine view of the city. Opposite, to the west side of the Ramblas, are the Drassanes, medieval shipyards dating from the thirteenth century. The impressive stone-vaulted buildings are home to a fine **Museu Marítim** (daily 10am–7pm, €5.40), whose star exhibit is a sixteenth-century Royal Galley.

The Barri Gòtic

A remarkable concentration of beautiful medieval Gothic buildings just blocks from the Ramblas, the **Barri Gòtic** forms the very heart of the old city. Today's old town dates principally from the fourteenth and fifteenth centuries, when Catalunya reached the height of its commercial prosperity. The quarter is centred on the **Plaça de Sant Jaume**, on one side of which stands the restored town hall, the **Ajuntament**. Across the square rises the **Palau de la Generalitat**, home of the Catalan government; restored during the sixteenth century in Renaissance style, it has a beautiful cloister on the first floor with superb coffered ceilings. Just behind the square **La Seu**, Barcelona's cathedral (daily 10am–1pm & 4/5–6.30pm; free), is one of the great Gothic buildings of Spain. Modern lighting shows off the soaring airiness of the interior superbly. Outside, the magnificent **cloisters** (9am–1pm & 4–7pm) look over a lush tropical garden with soaring palm trees and white geese, and open into, among other things, the small **cathedral museum** (daily 11am–1pm & 4–6.30pm; €0.60).

The cathedral and its associated buildings aside, the most concentrated batch of historic monuments in the Barri Gòtic is the grouping around the nearby **Plaça del Rei**. Barcelona's finest Roman remains were uncovered beneath the **Palau Reial** (the former palace of the counts of Barcelona), which now houses the **Museu d'Història de la Ciutat** (Tues–Sat 9/10am–2pm & 4–8/11.30pm, Sun 10am–2pm; July also Mon 9–11.30pm; €3.60, free first Sat of month). Here, both Roman and Visigothic remains have been preserved where they were found during building work in the 1930s.

For a quick respite from the city centre, nip into the greenery and relative peace of **Parc de la Ciutadella**, which is within easy walking distance of the Barri Gòtic. Its attractions include a lake, Gaudí's monumental fountain and the city zoo (daily 10am–5/7.30pm; €10, €6.50 after 5pm in summer), and you'll also find the meeting place of the Catalan parliament.

Picasso and the Carrer de Montcada

Heading east from the Plaça de Sant Jaume, you'll cross Vía Laietana and reach the Carrer de Montcada, crowded with beautifully restored old buildings. One of these houses the **Museu Picasso** (Tues–Sat 10am–8pm, Sun 10am–3pm; €4.80, free first Sun of month), one of the most important collections of Picasso's work in the world and the only one of any significance in his native country, although it's a rather selective collection and contains none of his best-known work. Continue down the street and you'll come out opposite the great basilica of **Santa María del Mar** (daily 9am–1.30pm & 4.30–8pm; Sun choral Mass at 1pm), built on what was the seashore in the fourteenth century. Its soaring lines were the symbol of Catalan supremacy in Mediterranean commerce and it's still much dearer to the heart of the average local than the cathedral. The stained glass is especially beautiful.

Port Vell and Villa Olympica

The whole **Port Vell** area has been revitalized, notably with the construction of the harbourside *passeig* and the vast new Maremagnum complex reached from near the Monument a Colom via a dramatic wooden walkway. The city planners' desire to refocus attention on the sea has provided an upmarket shopping mall, an excellent aquarium, a cinema, an IMAX theatre and a multitude of cheesy bars and over-priced restaurants all grouped together in the old harbour area. This lies on the fringe of the **Barceloneta district**, home to Barcelona's cleaned-up beaches and seafood restaurants. *Telefèrics* (cable cars) run from here to Montjuïc via Port Vell (10.30am–5.30/7/8pm; €6 one way, €7.20 return). Walk 1km east along the beach and you'll find Port Olímpic with its myriad bars and restaurants. At night the tables are stacked up, dance floors emerge and the area hosts one of the city's most vibrant dance scenes. Dozens of bars pump out a pulsating mix of salsa, house and techno to an uptown clientele.

Antoni Gaudí and the Sagrada Família

Besides modern art, Barcelona offers – above all through the work of **Antoni Gaudí** (1852–1926) – some of the most fantastic and exciting modern architecture to be found anywhere in the world. Without doubt his most famous creation is the incomplete **Temple Expiatori de la Sagrada Família** (daily 9am–6/8pm; €6, lift €1.50; Metro Sagrada Família), a good way northeast of the Plaça de Catalunya. Amid great controversy, work to complete the cathedral has begun, turning the interior into a giant building site, but it's fascinating to watch Gaudí's last-known plans being slowly realized. The size alone is startling, with eight spires rising to over 100m. For Gaudí these were metaphors for the Twelve Apostles; he planned to build four more above the main facade and to add a 180m tower topped with a gallery over the transept, itself to be surrounded by four smaller towers symbolizing the Evangelists. Take the lift, or climb up one of the towers, and you can enjoy a dizzy view down over the whole complex and clamber still further round the walls and into the towers.

Inside the Temple a small **Gaudí museum** traces the career of the architect and the history of the building. The tourist offices also issue a handy leaflet describing all his works, with a map of their locations. Above all, check out the **Parc Güell** (daily 10am–6/9pm; free), his most ambitious project after the Sagrada Família. This almost hallucinatory experience, with giant decorative lizards and a vast Hall of Columns, contains another small **museum** (daily 10am–7.45pm; €3) with some of the furniture Gaudí designed. To get there, take the metro to Lesseps or bus #24 from the Plaça de Catalunya to Travesera de Dalt, from where it's a half-kilometre walk to the main gates on c/d'Olot.

Montjuïc

The hill of **Montjuïc** has yet more varied attractions – five museums, the "Spanish Village", the Olympic arena and a castle with grand views of the city. The most obvious way to approach is to take a bus or metro to the Plaça d'Espanya and walk from there up the imposing Avda. de la Reina María Cristina, past the 1929 International Fair buildings and the rows of fountains. If you'd rather start with the castle, take the **funicular railway** (daily 9am–10pm every 10min; €2 return), which runs from Parallel metro station to the start of the cable car (summer only), which in turn leads to the castle; or take bus #50 along Plaça Universitat and Gran Vía up to Parc Montjuïc.

If you tackle the stiff climb from the Plaça d'Espanya you'll arrive at the **Palau Nacional**, centrepiece of Barcelona's 1929 International Fair and now home to one of Spain's great museums, the **Museu Nacional d'Art de Catalunya** (Tues–Sat 10am–7pm, Sun 10am–2.30pm; €6, free first Thurs of month). Its enormous collection includes the fascinating Gothic section, but it's the Romanesque section that is the more remarkable, perhaps the best collection of its kind in the world: 35 rooms of eleventh- and twelfth-century frescoes, meticulously removed from a series of small Pyrenean churches and beautifully displayed. There is also a substantial collection of Baroque and Renaissance works. The **Museu d'Art Modern** (Mon & Wed–Sat 10am–7pm, Sun 10am–2.30pm; €3, free first Thurs of month) displays a collection that ranges from the eighteenth century to the 1980s, but it is in the process of being shifted to the MNAC; during the move – which is set to be completed during 2003 – some of the collection remains open to visitors.

Barcelona's important **Museu Arqueologia de Catalunya** (Tues–Sat 9.30am–7pm, Sun & hols 10am–2.30pm; €2.40) containing exhibits mostly from the Roman period, but also Carthaginian and Etruscan relics, stands to the east of the Palau Nacional, lower down the hill. Nearby is the **Fundació Joan Miró** (Tues–Sat 10am–7pm, Thurs till 9.30pm, Sun & hols closes 2.30pm; €7.20), the most adventurous of Barcelona's art museums, devoted to one of the greatest Catalan artists. A beautiful white building houses a permanent collection of paintings, graphics, tapestries and sculptures donated by Miró himself and covering the period from 1914 to 1978.

A short walk over to the other side of the Palau Nacional will bring you to the **Poble Espanyol** or "Spanish Village" (Mon 9am–8pm, Tues–Sat 9am–2/4am, Sun 9am–midnight; guided visit €3), consisting of replicas of famous or characteristic buildings from all over Spain, and with a lively club scene at night. Prices, especially for products of the "genuine Spanish workshops" (and in the bars), are exorbitant. Just down the road, the reconstruction of the **Mies van der Rohe Pavilion** for the 1929 Exhibition (daily 10am–8pm; €3.40) is a far greater treat.

From the Poble Espanyol, the main road climbs around the hill to what was the principal **Olympic arena** in 1992, passing some dazzling new buildings – the Picornell swimming pools and the Japanese-designed Palau Sant Jordi. These are overshadowed only by the Olympic Stadium itself, the **Estadi Olimpic** (daily

10am–6/8pm; free), built originally for the 1929 Exhibition and completely refitted to accommodate the 1992 opening and closing ceremonies. The Olympic museum, the **Galeria Olímpica**, on Passeig Olímpic (Tues–Sat 10am–2pm & 4–6/7pm, Sun 10am–2pm; €2.40), is a hands-on affair covering the staging of the Games in the city. Far above this complex of museums and sports arenas, and offering magnificent views across the city, stands the eighteenth-century **Castell de Montjuïc**, built on seventeenth-century ruins.

Eating, drinking and nightlife

There's a huge variety of **food** available in Barcelona and even low-budget travellers can do well for themselves. Be aware that a lot of places close on Sundays and throughout August, and that the *menú del día* is rarely available in the evening. If you want to buy picnic material, head for the covered **market** (Mercat Sant Josep/La Boqueria) off the Ramblas.

There are hundreds of excellent **bars** and **cafés** in the city centre, including the lively tapas places in the Barri Gòtic. Around the Museu Picasso is a particularly good area: the Passeig del Born, the square at the end of c/Montcada behind Santa María del Mar, is crowded with popular bars. Gràcia, north of the centre, is the most studenty area in Barcelona and ideal for low-key drinking, especially on the numerous little squares around the main Plaça del Sol, itself bordered by café terraces. Barcelona's **nightlife** is some of Europe's most exciting. It keeps going all night too, the music bars closing at 3am, the discos at 4/5am, and some clubs open between 5am and 9am at weekends. Among the more expensive, trendier places, *bars modernos* are still in fashion, hi-tech theme palaces concentrated mainly in the Eixample, or in the rich kids' stamping ground bordered by c/Ganduxer, Avda. Diagonal and Vía Augusta, west of Gràcia. Drinks are expensive, the music echoes the often elaborate decorations, and the "in" places change rapidly, with new ones starting up all the time. Laid back and/or alternative places can be found in the small streets around MACBA and south, and the waterfront Port Olimpic area currently seems to be in favour with rich and bored youth, although weekdays out of summer are dead. **Clubbing** can be more expensive still; in the most exclusive places even a beer is going to cost you roughly ten times what it costs in the bar next door.

For **listings** of almost anything you could want in the way of entertainment and culture, buy a copy of the weekly *Guía del Ocio* from any newsstand or check ⓦ www.guiadelociobcn.com. There's a thriving **gay scene** in Barcelona: *Sex Tienda*, at c/Rauric 11 (very near Plaça Reial), supplies free maps of gay Barcelona with a list of bars, clubs and contacts.

Tapas bars

Amaya Rambla Santa Mónica 20–24. Busy, smoke-filled tapas bar on one side, with a mid-range restaurant on the other. Serves Basque specialities, but the tapas are best.
Jai-Ca c/Ginebra 13, Barceloneta. Small, cornerside bar with some of the best tapas in Barceloneta.
Euskal Etxea Placeta Montcada 1–3, Barri Gòtic. A Basque restaurant specializing in mouthwatering tapas. Closed Mon.
El Xampanyet c/de Montcada 22, Barri Gòtic. Terrific blue-tiled champagne bar with fine seafood tapas, *cava* by the glass and local *sidra*. Unmissable. Closed Sun, Mon & all Aug.

Restaurants

Can Ros L'Almirall Aixada 7, Ciutat Vella ☎932 215 049. Unbeatable fish and seafood straight from the harbour. Closed Wed, Sun pm.
Casa de Madrid Ausias Marc 37, Eixample ☎932 656 723. Great neighbourhood find offering a cheap menu and dishes from the Spanish regions. Booking advised.
Comme-Bio & Comme-Bio II Via Layetana, Barrio Gòtic & Gran Vía 603 (corner Rambla de Catalunya), Eixample; Metro Catalunya. Sibling vegetarian restaurants that double as health-food stores.
La Fonda c/Escudellers 10, Drassanes. Hugely popular place with good Mediterranean cuisine and tables on two levels and outdoors. The lunchtime menu is a steal. They don't take bookings, so be prepared to queue.
La Vaca Paca Passeig de Gràcia 21. The mother of all stuff-yourself-silly buffets, for the rock-bottom price of €6.60.
PK2 c/ Mallorca 197, Universitat. Cheap, tasty and

filling Uruguayan food in a friendly, rustic atmosphere, with temporary art exhibitions on the walls. Closed Sun.

Pollos del Llull Ramón Turró 13, Ciutadella & Nápols 272, Sagrada Família. Super-cheap and simple restaurant offering a comprehensive lunchtime menu, but specializing in chicken with trimmings.

Illa de Gràcia c/Sant Doménec 19. Bright vegetarian restaurant serving decent salads, pasta, rice dishes, omelettes and crepes.

Llar del Filador c/ Cortines 13, Barri Gòtic ☎933 192 690. Tucked away in a dark lane in the Ribera, this renovated workshop is the place to enjoy meat, cheese and dessert fondues in a subdued and romantic atmosphere.

Perú Passeig de Bourbó 10, Barceloneta. Barcelona's best seafood. Good value *menú del día*.

Pitarra c/d'Avinyó 56, Barri Gòtic. A Catalan cookery in operation since 1890, lined with paintings and serving good, reasonably priced food. Closed Sun.

Pollo Rico c/Sant Pau 31, Barri Xines. Spit-roasted chicken, fries and a glass of *cava* for under €5 make this one of the area's most popular budget spots. Closed Wed.

Silenus c/Angeles 8, Raval. Just round the corner from the MACBA and with a decidedly hip clientele, this billowing white space of an eatery serves reasonably priced, delicious and health-conscious fare.

Cafés and bars

Café de l'Òpera Ramblas 74. Elegant *fin-de-siècle* café/bar with fine coffee and a range of cakes and snacks.

Café del Sol Plaça del Sol 29, Gràcia. Trendy hangout, just one of several similar places in this square.

El Café Que Pone Muebles Navarro Riera Alta 4–6, Raval. Gorgeously laid-back café/bar with big, comfy sofas and big, strong drinks. Popular with a gay crowd, but open to all.

Casa Almirall c/Joaquím Costa 33, Raval. The oldest functioning bar in Barcelona, this place makes judicious use of wood, comfy sofas and a

very cool neighbourhood.

London Bar c/Nou de la Rambla 34, Barri Xines. Laid-back 1920s bar with live music daily – mainly jazz and blues. Cabaret after midnight Thurs & Sun.

Mojito Bar Port Vell, Maremagnum. Perfect mojitos, daily salsa classes and live music until late on weekends make this the perfect place to finish off an exhausting shopping trip.

Parnasse c/Gignás 21. Laid-back and friendly atmosphere in this hip bar. Listen to jazz, and drink modestly priced single-malt whiskies or the legendary absinthe, *à la française*. Closed Sun & Mon.

Téxtil Café c/Montcada, 12. In the atmospheric medieval courtyard of the textile museum, with braziers in winter, although fairly pricey drinks keep out the art students.

Els Quatre Gats c/Montsió 5, Barri Gòtic. *Modernista*-designed haunt of Picasso and his contemporaries, still an interesting and arty place for a drink and nibble. Closed Sun lunch.

Live music and clubs

Apolo c/Nou de la Rambla 113, Barri Xines. Trip-hop and techno for a gay/straight crowd, old-town location. Metro Parallel.

Club Nitsa Nou de la Rambla 113. Biggish names and burgeoning stars play live, from the worlds of alternative rock, electronica and techno. Metro Parallel.

La Cova de Drac Vallmajor 33. One of the city's hippest locations for both jazz and dance. Metro Muntaner.

KGB c/Alegre de Dalt 55. Multifarious club with good alternative rock and pop acts. Metro Joanic.

The Loft Pamplona 88. The place to go for hard, fast house. Metro Bogatell.

Metro Sepúlveda 185. The original Barcelona gay club has seen everyone from Marc Almond to Jean Paul Gaultier through its doors, and it's still pulling in the crowds. Metro Plaça Universitat.

Moog Arc del Teatre 3, Barri Xines. Techno temple. Regular appearances from top UK and Euro DJs. Best on Wed & Sun. Metro Drassanes.

Razmatazz c/Almogavers 122. Underground rock and punk. Metro Bogatell.

Listings

Banks and exchanges Most banks are located in Plaça de Catalunya and Pg. de Gràcia. Money exchange at the airport; Estacío de Sants; Víajes Marsans, Ramblas 134; Caixa Catalunya in the tourist office at Pl. Catalunya; and at Casas de Cambio throughout the centre.

Consulates Australia, Gran Vía Carles III 98 ☎933 309 496; Canada, c/Elisenda de Pinós 10 ☎932 042 700; Ireland, Gran Vía Carles III 94 ☎934 915 021; New Zealand, Trav. de Gràcia 64 ☎932 090 399; UK, Avda. Diagonal 477 ☎933 666 200; US, Passeig de la Reina Elisenda 23 ☎932 802 227.

27

Hospitals Hospital de la Creu Roja, c/Dos de Maig 301 ☎935 072 700; Policlínica Barcelona, Guillem Tell 4, Gràcia ☎934 161 616; Centro Médico Cruz Blanco, Pelai 40, Ciutat Vella ☎934 121 212.
Internet Cafés easyEverything, Ronda de L'Universitat; Conectate, c/Atagón 283.
Left luggage Lockers at Sants station; Estació Marítima; Estació de França; Estació del Nord; and the airport.

Laundry Martin c/Carme 65.
Police Turisme Attention, Las Ramblas 43 ☎933 019 060.
Pharmacies Farmacia Ivarez, Pº Grácia 26, Eixample ☎933 021 124; Farmacia Clapés Antoja, La Rambla 98, Ciutat Vella ☎933 012 843.
Post office Correus, Plaça Antoni Lòpez at the bottom of Vía Laietana.

Valencia and the east coast

Much of Valencia's coast is a landscape of over-development, a land of villas and vacation homes linked by the southbound highway. But the area still has its attractions: the stretch of coast between Jávea and Altea has escaped the worst excesses, and the cities – vibrant **Valencia**, with its a strong nightlife scene, and relaxed **Alicante** with its holiday atmosphere – are well worth a visit.

Valencia

VALENCIA, one of the largest cities in Spain, may not approach the vitality of Barcelona or the cultural variety of Madrid, but it does have a lively night scene, and its clothes and furniture designers are renowned throughout Spain. As a whole the city is sprawling and confused, marred by thoughtless modernization, but there are some exquisite corners away from the crowds, a few really fine buildings and a couple of excellent museums. The most interesting area for wandering is undoubtedly the maze-like **Barrio del Carmen**, the oldest part of town, roughly between c/de Caballeros and the Río Turia around the Puerta de Serranos. Among Valencia's renowned **fiestas** is Las Fallas de San José (early March) when dozens of giant wooden caricatures are displayed and then ceremoniously burned amidst a riot of fireworks that explode on the final night of the festival.

Arrival, information and accommodation

Valencia's **train station** is reasonably central: head straight out, keeping the unmistakable bullring to your right, along the Avda. Marqués de Sotelo for the main Plaza del Ayuntamiento, beyond which lie the old parts of the city. The **bus station** is further out, at Avda. Menéndez Pidal 13, on the far bank of the dried-up river. From here it's easier to take local bus #8 into the centre; allow twenty minutes if you decide to walk. The **Balearic ferry terminal** is connected to Plaza del Ayuntamiento by bus #19. This square is also home to the main **tourist office** (Mon–Fri 8.30am–2.15pm & 4.15–6.15pm, Sat 9.15am–12.45pm; ☎963 510 417); there's aslo a branch inside the train station (Mon–Fri 9am–6.30pm).

Most of the cheaper **places to stay** are very near the train station, on c/Bailén and c/Pelayo, which run parallel to the tracks off c/Játiva. This area, however, is pretty sleazy; you may feel more comfortable paying a little more for somewhere in the centre, or staying much further out near the beach. Worth trying near the station is the friendly *Hostal-Residencia Lyon*, c/Xátiva 10 (☎963 517 247; ❷). Other options in the streets off central Plaza del Ayuntamiento are the pleasant *Pensión Paris*, c/Salva 12 (☎963 526 766; ❷); the friendly if oddly partitioned *Hostal Universal*, c/Barcas 5 (☎963 515 384; ❷), and the basic *Hostal San Jose*, c/Transits 5 (963 940 152; ❷). Further north, near Plaza del Mercado, is the excellently sited and very good value *Hostal El Rincón*, c/Carda 11 (☎963 916 083; ❶); while out near the beach, the *Hotel La Pepica*, Paseo de Neptuno 2 (☎963 714 111; ❶), offers good-value rooms with bath, and an excellent restaurant. There are two **hostels**:

the more regimented one is halfway to the port on Avda. del Puerto 69 (☎963 617 459; **❶**; midnight curfew); the other, *Hostal Las Arenas*, c/Egenia Viñes 24 (☎963 564 288; **❷**), is a bit decrepit, but is also a real backpackers' hangout, with a great atmosphere, a grassy court yard and a fire most summer nights. It's right by the southern end of Malvarossa beach at the end of bus line #32. The most convenient **campsite** is the *Devesa Gardens* (☎961 611 136), 15km out on the Nazaret-Oliva road by La Albufera; take the hourly bus from Plaza de los Toros.

The City

The distinctive feature of Valencian architecture is its wealth of elaborate Baroque facades – you'll see them on almost every old building in town, but none so extraordinary or rich as the **Palacio del Marqués de Dos Aguas**, a short walk north of the train station. Hipólito Rovira, who designed its amazing alabaster doorway, died insane in 1740, which should come as no surprise to anyone who's seen it. Inside is the **Museo Nacional de Cerámica** (Tues–Sat 10am–2pm & 4–8pm, Sun 10am–2pm; €2.40), with a vast collection of ceramics from all over Spain. Nearby, in the Plaza Patriarca, is the neoclassical former university – with its beautiful cloisters and a series of classical concerts in July – and the beautiful Renaissance **Colegio del Patriarca**, whose small **art museum** (daily 11am–1.30pm; €1.20) includes excellent works by El Greco, Morales and Ribalta.

It's not far from here, up c/de la Paz, to the **Plaza Zaragoza** and Valencia's **Cathedral**. The plaza is dominated by two octagonal towers, the florid spire of the church of Santa Catalina and the **Miguelete**, the unfinished bell-tower of the cathedral. You can make the long climb up to its roof (daily 10.30am–12.30pm & 4.30–6pm; €1.20) for a fantastic view over the city with its many blue-domed churches. The cathedral's most attractive feature is the lantern above the crossing, its windows glazed with sheets of alabaster; there's also a **museum** (daily 10.30am–1pm & 4.30–6pm; €1.20), whose exhibits include a gold and agate cup (the Santo Cáliz) said to be the one used by Christ at the Last Supper – the Holy Grail itself.

Other museums worth visiting include **IVAM**, the modern art museum on c/Guillém de Castro 118 (Tues–Sun 10am–8pm; €2.10), and the **Museo de Bellas Artes** on c/San Pío V (Tues–Sun 10am–8pm; free). A real curiosity is the city's old riverbed. The Río Turia was diverted after serious flooding in 1956, which damaged much of the old city, and is no more than a trickle now – with a huge park being landscaped in the riverbed. On one former bank stands the **Palau de la Música**, a futuristic glass-structure venue for concerts, and the site of the **City of Arts and Sciences**, an ambitious Expo-style group of pavilions including more concert halls, a science museum, and a giant oceanographic theme park, still partly under construction.

Five minutes' walk away from the Cathedral is the enormous **Mercado Central**, a huge iron and glass structure housing one of the biggest markets in Europe, full of amazing local fruit, fish and vegetables; it closes around 2pm every day.

Eating, drinking and nightlife

The quality of **restaurant** food in Valencia can be poor, especially considering that this is the home of paella. However, there are decent mid-range possibilities, including *El Generalife*, behind the cathedral on Plaza de la Virgen, and *Bar Cánovas*, Plaza Cánovas Castillo, one of the city's best tapas bars. For bistros and cheap restaurants the best area is Barrio del Carmen around c/Caballeros. A traditional place to go for *mejillones* (mussels) is the *Bar Pilar* on the corner of c/Moro Zeit, on Plaza del Espart off c/Caballeros. For paella, try Malvarossa's *La Pepica*, Paseo Neptuno 6.

Valencia can seem dead at night, but only because the action is widely dispersed. The best of the city-centre **nightlife** is centred on the Barrio del Carmen (c/Caballeros and c/Quart). *Café Sant Jaume* is a central place to start; there's also good bar-hopping on the adjoining c/Alta. The *Radio City Bar*, c/Santa Teresa 19, has a mainly young ex-pat clientele. Another area to try is near the Gran Vía de Fernando el Católico, along c/Juan Llorens and c/Calixto, where the *Café Carioca*, c/Juan Llorens 52, plays funk and R&B. The university area, around Avda. Blasco Ibáñez, is also popular: the *Rocafull Cafe* at Plaza Xuquer 14 – is an old student favourite. For salsa head for *Café Bachata*, c/Bachata 31, or the bars on Juan Llorens. Many of the **discos** are in the university area – they include the perennially popular *Warthol*, Blasco Ibañez 111. Otherwise, head for the big techno club *The Face*, Camino Montares 141, with its summertime terrace, and *Le Club*, Ctra. Fuente en Corts; both a ten-minute taxi ride from the centre. If this is a stretch, try *La Marxa*, Cocina 5, just off c/Caballeros, which draws a lively, diverse crowd; or the three-floor *Carmen Sui Generis*, c/Caballeros 38. The best **gay bars and discos** are in and around c/Quart; for dancing try *Venial*, c/Quart 34, or *La Goulue*, a few doors down.

For more information about what's on, buy one of the two weekly **listings guides**, *Qué y Dónde* and *Turia* – or pick up the free English-language *24-7 Valencia* from the tourist office.

Listings

Banks and exchanges Main branches of most banks are around the Plaza del Ayuntamiento or along c/Játiva 24. Outside banking hours, try: Caja de Ahorros, c/Játiva 14, to the left as you come out of the train station.

Consulates UK, Plaza Calvo Sotelo 1–2, Alicante ☎965 216 022; US, c/Romagosa 1 ☎963 516 973.

Hospitals Avda. Cid, at the Tres Cruces junction ☎963 862 900.

Internet access Confederation, near the train station at c/Ribera 8.

Left luggage At the train station.

Laundry Plaza del Mercado 12, by the Mercado Central.

Pharmacy Plaza del Mercado 37; at corner of Plaza del Ayuntamiento and c/Periodista Azzati.

Police Gran Vía Ramón y Cajal 40 ☎963 539 539.

Post office Plaza del Ayuntamiento 24.

The Costa Blanca

South of Valencia stretches the **Costa Blanca**, a long strip of country with, between Gandía and Benidorm, some of the best beaches on this coast. Much of it, though, suffers from the worst excesses of package tourism and in the summer it's hard to get a room anywhere – in August virtually impossible. Campers have it somewhat easier – there are hundreds of campsites.

DENIA is a sizeable town even without its summer visitors, and less appealing. You might, though, be tempted to take the **boat to Palma de Mallorca** or **Ibiza** (summer only; daily). A rattling narrow-gauge **rail line** (FGV) runs hourly down the coast from Alicante. Beneath the wooded capes beyond, bypassed by the main road, stretch probably the most beautiful beaches on this coastline, centred on Javea – but you'll need a car to get to any of them, and even if you have a vehicle there's barely a cheap room to be found.

Back on the main road again, **ALTEA** is set on a small hill overlooking this whole stretch of coastline. Restrained tourist development is centred on the seafront, and being so close to Benidorm it does receive some overspill. In character, however, it's a world apart. The old village up the hill is picturesquely attractive with its white houses, blue-domed church and profuse blossoms.

Beyond Altea there's nothing between you and the crowded beaches at **BENIDORM**. If you want hordes of British and Scandinavian sunseekers, scores of "English" pubs, at least seventy discos, and bacon and eggs for breakfast, this is the place to come. The beach – nearly 6km of it, regularly topped up with imported Moroccan sand – is undeniably impressive, backed by a Manhattan skyline. Outside August, you can usually find a room in Benidorm, though it takes a lot of walking. The cheaper places are all near the centre and away from the sea, but out of season many of the giant hotels and apartment buildings slash their prices dramatically.

Check with the **tourist office** (Mon–Sat 10am–2pm & 4–8/9pm; ℡965 851 311, Ⓦwww.gva.es/benid/benidorm) at the bottom of Avda. Martínez Alejos, near the old village.

Alicante

Despite being a package-holiday destination, **ALICANTE** is a living, thoroughly Spanish city. There are good beaches nearby, lively nightlife in season and plenty of cheap places to stay and to eat. Wide esplanades such as the Rambla de Méndez Núñez give the town an elegant air, and around the Plaza de Luceros and along the seafront *paseo* you can relax in style at terrace cafés – paying a bit extra for the palm-tree setting, of course. Links between Alicante and Algeria have always been strong, and boats depart from here for Oran twice a week. If you can, time your visit to coincide with the *Fogueres de Sant Joan*, an elaborate, month-long extravaganza of processions, fire and fireworks which culminates in an orgy of burning on the feast night of St John the Baptist, towards the end of June.

The towering **Castillo de Santa Bárbara** (daily 9am–7pm; €2.40 for the lift) on the bare rock behind the town beach is Alicante's only real "sight" – with a tremendous view from the top. Access it from Playa Postiguet via a tunnel, then a lift shaft – cut straight up through the rock. For the best local **beaches** head for San Juan de Alicante, 6km out, reached either by bus from the Plaza del Mar or the FGV rail line. Still better, take a trip to the **island of Tabarca** to the south; boats leave from Puerto on the Explanada de España, weather permitting (summer only; €13).

Practicalities

The main **train station** is on Avda. Salamanca, but trains on the private FGV line to Benidorm and Denia leave from the small station at the far end of the Playa del Postiguet. The **bus station** for local and international services is in c/Portugal. The **airport**, 12km west, is connected with the centre by a special bus service #C6, which stops at the central Avda. Rambla Mendez Nuñez. Here, at no. 23, you'll find the very helpful **tourist office** (Mon–Sat 10am–7/8pm; ℡965 200 000); there are additional offices at the train and bus stations and the airport.

Except towards the end of June and in August, you should have little problem finding a **room**, with the bulk of the possibilities concentrated at the lower end of the old town, above the Explanada de España – especially on c/San Fernando, c/Jorge Juan and c/Castaño. Options include the friendly *Hostal Ventura*, c/San Fernando 10 (℡965 208 337; ❷) and *Hostal San Fernando*, at no. 34 (℡965 213 656; ❷); note, though that there are several nightclubs nearby. There are cheaper places on c/San Francisco, but many are pretty seedy and not advisable for women travelling alone. On a quieter street is *Hostal Mayor*, c/Mayor 5 (℡965 201 383; ❷), while *Pension Ayuntamiento*, Plaza del Ayuntamiento 3 (℡965 216 223; ❸) leaves you perfectly placed to enjoy some of the events of the Fogueres de Sant Joan. More upmarket, but a bargain out of season, when prices drop a code, is the beautiful *Les Monges*, c/San Agustin 4 (℡965 215 046; ❸). There are several **campsites**, including *El Molino* at Playa de San Juan to the north (connected by FGV train and bus #21) and *La Marina*, south of town in woods on a good beach and connected by Costa Azul buses.

Cheap **restaurants** are clustered around the Ayuntamiento, including a couple of places where you can eat couscous on c/Miguel Soler; there are other cheap eateries on c/Mayor. For tapas, try the atmospheric *Mesón de Labradores* near the cathedral at c/Labradores 19. For **bars** and the best **nightlife**, head into the Barrio Santa Cruz, whose narrow streets lie roughly between the cathedral, Plaza Carmen and Plaza San Cristóbal. An excellent starting point is *Desden*, c/Labradores 22, which plays jazz in the afternoon and house, dance and funk through the night till 4am. Several other **nightclubs** are concentrated on c/San Fernando, while the bars along the Playa de San Juan are a popular summertime haunt. For **internet** access try *Zipposbar*, c/Labradores 1, or *Yazzgo Internet*, Explanada de España 3.

The Balearic islands

The four chief **Balearic islands** – Ibiza, Formentera, Mallorca and Menorca – maintain a character distinct from the mainland and from each other. **Ibiza**, firmly established among Europe's trendiest resorts, has an intense, outrageous street life and a floating summer population that seems to include every club-going Spaniard from Sevilla to Barcelona. It can be fun, if this sounds like your idea of island activity, and above all if you're gay – Ibiza has a particularly good scene. Neighbouring **Formentera** is small and windswept with some gloriously undeveloped beaches. **Mallorca**, the largest of the Balearics, battles with its image, popularly reckoned as little more than sun, booze and beach parties. In reality you'll find all the clichés, most of them crammed into the mega-resorts of the Bay of Palma, but there's certainly much else besides: mountains, lively fishing ports, some beautiful coves and the Balearics' one real city, **Palma**. And last, to the east, there is **Menorca** – more conservative in its development, more modest in its clientele and, after the others, possibly a little dull.

Ferries from mainland Spain (and Marseille) are severely overpriced considering the distances involved; likewise, monopolies keep rates high for inter-island ferries. It can be cheaper to fly. The catch here is that in mid-season flights are often booked out: the solution is to get up before dawn, head for the airport and get yourself on a waiting list for the first flight. As "holiday islands", each with a buoyant international tourist trade, the Balearics charge considerably above mainland prices for **rooms** – which from mid-June to mid-September are in very short supply. It's sensible to try to fix up some kind of reservation in advance.

Ibiza

IBIZA (Eivissa in Catalan) is an island of excess. Beautiful and indented with scores of barely accessible coves, it's nevertheless the islanders and their visitors who make it special. However outrageous you may want to be (and outrageousness is the norm), the locals have seen it all before. For years it was the European hippy escape, but nowadays it is as synonymous with the European club scene as with its 1960s denizens, who keep coming back.

Ibiza Town

In physical as well as atmospheric terms, **IBIZA TOWN** is the most attractive place on the island. Most people stay in rented apartments or small *pensiones* which means fewer hotels to ruin the skyline and no package incursions. Approach by sea and you'll get the full effect of the old town's walls rising like a natural extension of the rocky cliffs that protect the port. Within the walls, the ancient quarter is topped by a sturdy **Cathedral**, whose illuminated clock shines out across the harbour throughout the night.

Practicalities

The capital is a simple enough place to find your way around. From the **ferry terminal**, the old streets of the Sa Peña quarter lead straight ahead towards the walls of the ancient city, which has been declared a UNESCO world heritage site. If you fly in you'll arrive at the **airport** about 6km out; there's a regular bus from here (7.30am–10.30pm), or you can take a taxi (€10). There's an efficient **tourist office** at the airport (May–Oct Mon–Sat 9am–2pm & 4–9pm, Sun 9am–2pm), but the main office is directly opposite the ferry building, on Passeig des Moll (Mon–Fri 9.30am–1.30pm & 5–7.30pm, Sat 10.30am–1.30pm; ☎971 301 900, ⊛www. visitbalears.com). **Internet cafés** in Ibiza Town include Surf@net, c/Riambau 4.

Most of the cheaper **hotels** are a short walk away around Paseo Vara del Rey. A couple of starter possibilities are *Hostal Sol y Brisa*, Avda. Bartolome Vicente Ramón 15 (☎971 310 818; ❸), near the port in the street parallel to Vara de Rey. In the same area, *Hostal Ripoll*, Vicente Cuervo 14 (☎971 314 275 ❸), is good value, busy and clean, while a little further out is *Ebusitana*, Obispo Huix 17 (☎971 300 050; ❷). Near the port and right in the heart of things is *La Marina*, c/Barcelona 7 (☎971 310 172; ❹), where all rooms are en suite. Another notch up is *Hostal Parque*, Plaza del Parque 4 (☎971 301 358; ❹). There are four **campsites** on the island, the nearest to Ibiza Town is the inland *Camping Cala Bassa* (☎971 344 599), 13km away near Sant Josep.

Most of the cheaper places **to eat** are in the Sa Peña quarter. One of the best bets is smoky *C'an Costa* at c/Cruz 19; along the road on the corner, *La Victoria*, c/Rimbau 1, also has cheap main meals. The *Croissant Show*, Mercado Viejo, only closes for a few hours between five and seven in the morning and there are several good options on Plaza del Parque.

The bulk of the **bars** in which to begin your night are in the area around the port, though some can be overpriced even during happy hour. *Dome*, Alfonso XII 5, between the port and the old town, is an old favourite with a mixed crowd; *Mike and Claire's Diner*, Acinguada D-Andenes, has a 24-hour drinks licence, while *The Soap Café*, Manuel Sora 4, is a popular, new-ish arrival, which serves good food day and night. As for **clubs**, some highlights are: the luxurious *Pacha*; *Space*, with its legendary terrace; the wildly extravagant *Privilege* and the cavernous *Amnesia*. None of them really gets going before 1am, and the dancing goes on until dawn. The **Discobus** links them with the centre and runs through the night (€2 single fare). The clubbing season lasts from June to September, with the best time to party being the first and last two weeks. Be prepared to spend a lot of money, with entrance fees upwards of €27 and astronomical bar prices. With this in mind, its best to watch out for the free invites distributed by PR side-shows, which parade through the streets each night. Ibiza has one of the best **gay scenes** in Europe, with the action centred on the sometimes notorious c/Virgin. *Teatro*, at no. 83, remains a popular bar, as does *Capricho* at no. 42. If drag is your thing, try *Samsara Shows*, at no. 44. There's only one dedicated gay club (men only): *Anfora*, c/San Carlos 7, in the old town, but many of the island's big-name clubs hold a gay night once a week. For the free full-moon beach-parties, try asking around in the hippy markets in Es Canar, Las Dalias or Santa Eularía.

Around the island

Nowhere else can compare to the capital, certainly not the second city, San Antonio Abad, which is a highly avoidable package-resort nightmare, though it can be quite pleasant out of season. **SANTA EULALIA**, the only other real town, retains a certain charm in its hilltop church looking down over the sprawling old town and modern seafront, while close by the persistent can find a number of relatively empty beaches. The same holds true for most of the rest of the coast – plenty of golden sands, but a good deal of effort required to reach them. The one major exception is the northern bay of **Portinatx**, connected by a relatively major road and, despite hotel development, with a number of clean, not overly populated beaches. **Inland** there's little to divert you – a few villages and holiday homes.

There's a good **bus service** between Ibiza Town, San Antonio Abad, Santa Eulalia, Portinatx and a few of the larger beaches.

Formentera

If Ibiza's hedonism is not your thing, or if you just need to recover after enjoying it, **FORMENTERA** is the place to go. Just three nautical miles south of its more boisterous neighbour, with a population of just 8000, it is the smallest of the inhabited Balearics and is almost completely barren, the few crops having to be protected, as on Menorca, against the lashing of winter winds. Most of the island is covered in wild rosemary, and crawling with thousands of brilliant green lizards. Its income is derived from tourism (especially German and Italian), visitors taking advantage of

27

some of Spain's longest, whitest and least-crowded beaches. The shortage of fresh water, fortunately, continues to keep away the crowds and for the most part visitors here are seeking escape with little in the way of sophistication. It is, however, becoming more popular, and is certainly not the paradise it once was.

The crossing from Ibiza is short, but strong currents ensure that it's slow (30min–1hr; €18, or €27 by catamaran), and there are usually rival sailings to choose from: check the return times before deciding. Boats dock at the tiny but functional harbour of **LA SAVINA**, where the two waterside streets are lined with places offering cars, mopeds or bicycles for rent, interspersed with the odd bar and café. If you need to get mobile, this is the place to come, but note that authorities would much rather you cycled; and, if you can manage the heat, it's an option worth considering as the island is relatively flat. The island's only **tourist office** is by the harbour (Mon–Fri 10am–2pm & 5–7pm; ☏971 322 057, ⓦwww.illadeformentera).

The capital, **SANT FRANCESC DE FORMENTERA** (usually shortened to Sant Francesc), is 2km away from La Savina. As well as the whitewashed fortified church – now stripped of its defensive cannon – you'll find several restaurants and cafés, at least five banks, ten bars, a hotel, supermarkets, a pharmacist and a doctor. The island's main road continues from Sant Francesc to the easternmost point at La Mola. Along it, or just off it, are almost all of the island's settlements and most of its **beaches**.

The next largest town, **SANT FERRAN** – with a clutch of good bars and cheap places to stay – serves the north coast beach of Es Pujols where the package-tour industry, such as it is, is concentrated. Despite relative crowding, it's a beautiful coast with clear water and pure white sand dunes backed by low pines. Further to the west the **beaches** Illetes and Llevant sit on either side of a thin spur of undeveloped land which has been designated a nature reserve. While on the south coast, Platja de Migjorn, is a five-kilometre stretch of sand broken only by the occasional bar or hotel, and is also an area popular with nude sunbathers.

Practicalities

Most people treat Formentera as a day-trip from Ibiza, and if you want to be one of the few who **stay**, you may have difficulty finding anywhere not given over to agency reservations. One option with a great setting is *Hostal La Sabina,* near the port at Avenida Mediterranea 22–40 (☏971 322 279; ❺; call ahead), which backs onto a tranquil lagoon specked with yachts. Sant Ferran has a number of possibilities: the rooms at *Hostal Pepe,* c/Major 68-76 (☏971 328 033; ❸), are all en suite, and breakfast is included in the rate; *Hostal Illes Pitiuses* (☏971 328 740; ❸) is on the main road through the village; and the pleasant *Pension Bon Sol,* c/Major 84-76 (☏971 328 882; ❷), is one of the cheapest places to stay. **Camping** is illegal.

There are a number of relatively cheap **places to eat**: try c/Major in Sant Ferran, where *Pepe's* is something of a local institution. There are **supermarkets** in Sant Francesc and Sant Ferran. Don't miss the fantastic *Blue Bar*, at the end of a dirt track on Platja de Migjorn, signed off the main Sant Ferran to La Mola road: go for a swim, then experience seriously chilled music and seriously good food in one of the best beach bars in the Balearics (snacks from €3, mains from €7).

Mallorca

MALLORCA has a split identity. A popular place that pulls in an estimated three million tourists a year, there are sections of its coast where high-rise hotels and shopping centres are continuous, wedged beside and upon one another and broken only by a dual carriageway leading to more of the same. But the spread of development, even after 25 years, is surprisingly limited: the high-rises occupy only the Bay of Palma, a forty-kilometre strip flanking the island capital. Beyond, to the north and east, things are very different. Not only are there good cove beaches, but there's a really startling variety and physical beauty to the land itself, which makes the island many people's favourite in the Balearics.

Palma

You may arrive by boat from Menorca at Puerto de Alcúdia in the north of the island, but the odds are you'll find yourself in **PALMA DE MALLORCA**, the capital and the only real "city" in the Balearics. Palma is in some ways like a mainland Spanish city – lively, solid and industrious – though it is immediately set apart by its insular, Mediterranean aura. The port is by far the largest in the Balearics, the evening *paseo* the most ingrained, and, in the evenings at least, you feel the city has only passing relevance to the tourist enclaves around its bay. Arriving by sea, it's beautiful and impressive, with the grand limestone bulk of the cathedral towering above the old town and the remnants of medieval walls.

The **ferry** port is some 3.5km west of the city centre, connected to Palma by bus #1; Palma **airport**, 9km east of the city, is served by bus #25 (every 20min) to the Passeig Mallorca. Finding your way around is fairly straightforward once you're in the centre. Around the Cathedral, containing Gaudí features, is the Portela quarter, "Old" Palma, a cluster of alleyways and lanes that become more spacious and ordered as you move towards the zigzag of avenues built beside or in place of the city walls. Cutting up from the sea, beside the cathedral, is Paseo Borne, garden promenade as well as boulevard, and way up the hill to the northeast lies the Plaza Mayor, target for most of the day-tripping tourists.

Practicalities

There are hundreds of *pensiones* and hotels, and your first move in the summer should be to pick up the official lists of these from the **tourist office** at Plaça de la Reina 2 (daily 9am–8pm; ☎971 712 216, ⊛www.visitbalears.com). The best areas to try for **accommodation** are around the Passeig Mallorca, on c/Apuntadores or c/San Felio running west from Paseo Borne (cheaper), and on c/San Jaime at the top of the Paseo Borne (mid-range). Specific recommendations are probably futile in summer, but some to try are *Hostal Apuntadores*, c/ Apuntadores 8 (☎971 713 491; ❷), the neighbouring *Hostal Ritzi* (☎971 714 610; ❸), and *Hostal Pons*, c/Vi 8, in an old Palma house (☎971 722 658; ❷). There's also a **hostel** at c/Costa Brava 13 in El Arenal (☎971 260 892; ❷), but it's often booked by school groups; take bus #15 from Plaza de España or Plaza de la Reina. There are **no official campsites** on the island. For **internet access** head to Big Byte Palma, c/Apuntadores 6.

Eating in Palma can be cheaper than anywhere in the Balearics. There are plenty of touristy places along the Passeig des Borns, but better fare is available nearby in the Barrio de Llotje between c/Apuntados and the seafront. Here you'll find several lower-priced, low-key restaurants, including *Vecchio Giovani*, c/San Juan 3. Head up the Passeig des Borns for the quirky but fantastic *El Pilon*, on the tiny alley, c/Cifre 4 – bags of local atmosphere and great tapas from €4.50. **Nightlife** here is picking up influences from its neighbours. You might want to start the evening in the Barrio de Llotja, then move on to the waterfront venue: *Pacha*, Avgda. Gabriel Roca 42, which has guest DJs from Ibiza. *Tito's*, Placa Gomila 3, is another hardy perennial of the Palma scene.

Around the island

When you feel you've exhausted the city's possibilities move across to **SÓLLER**, **DEIÁ**, **PUERTO POLLENSA**, **PUERTO DE ALCÚDIA** or one of the small resorts around **PORTO CRISTO** on the southeast coast. **Accommodation** is reasonable at each of these towns, though in July or August it'll be almost impossible to find. Mallorca's **bus service** is good and there are even a couple of **train lines** – one, a beautiful ride up through the mountains from Palma to Sóller, is an attraction in itself. Transport of your own, though, is a strong advantage.

Menorca

Second largest of the Balearics, **MENORCA** is littered with stone reminders of its prehistoric past: rock mounds known as *talayots*, megalithic *taulas* (huge stones topped with another to form a T, around 4m high) and *navetas*, stone slab constructions shaped like an inverted loaf tin. These, and the incessant wind, are the island's most characteristic features. There's not much in the way of excitement, but if you're looking for peace and for some beautiful, relatively isolated **beaches**, head for the sheltered Cala Turqueta on the southwest coast or more windswept Cala Pregonda near Fornells on the north.

The island is boomerang-shaped, stretching from Mahón (*Maó* in Catalan) in the east to the smaller, pretty port of Ciudadela (*Ciutadella*), in the west. The **airport** is 5km out of Mahón and is served only by taxi (€9). **Bus** routes are limited, adhering mostly to the main central road between Mahón and Ciudadela, occasionally branching off to the major coastal towns. You'll need your own vehicle to get to any of the more attractive beaches. There are a few points to remember though: if you're on a moped the winds can be uncomfortably strong, to reach the emptier sands you'll have to negotiate very rough tracks, and petrol stations are few and far between. After 10pm and on Sundays and fiestas, only a few pumps are open; take note of the rota posted outside and keep a full tank.

Accommodation is at a premium, with almost nothing beyond the bigger coastal towns. Once you find something reasonable, stay there. There are two **campsites** both on the south coast: the *S'Atalaia*, Carretera de Cala Galdana (☎971 374 232) and the much bigger *Son Bou*, Carretera de San Jaime (☎971 372 727).

Mahón

If you arrive by ferry from Barcelona or Palma you'll sail into the vast natural harbour of **MAHÓN**, the island capital. It's a quiet, respectable town: the architecture is a strange hybrid of Georgian bay-windowed town houses and tall, gloomy Spanish apartment buildings. Four adjacent squares form a hub close to the docks. The **Plaza España** is reached by a twisting flight of steps from the pier and offers great views right across the port and bay; there's a fish market here in the early mornings, and a recently renovated general market. Immediately behind is the **Plaza Carmen**, with a simple Carmelite church whose cloisters have been adapted to house a small museum. Wander on from here up c/Virgen del Carmen and take any of the streets to the left to reach one of the oldest and most atmospheric parts of town, overlooking the port from on high.

The main **tourist office**, c/ de Sa Rovellada de Dalt 24 (Mon–Fri 9am–1pm & 5–7pm; ☎971 363 790, ⓦwww.visitbalears.com), is near Plaza Explanada, the main square. Mahón is the best bet for **accommodation** on the island, and most options are fairly central. Head for the area around Plaza Reial, where you'll find the American/Scottish-owned *Hostal Orsi* at c/Infanta 19 (☎971 364 751; ❷), *Hostal La Isla* at c/Santa Caterina 4 (☎971 366 492; ❸), and the functional *Hostal Reynes,* c/des Comerc 26 (☎971 364 059; ❸). Mahón has a place in culinary history as the birthplace of mayonnaise (*mahonesa*), and you should have no problem finding somewhere to eat. The majority of **restaurants** are down by the port. For local food try *Ca'n Sintes,* off Plaça Princep at c/Camí de's Castell 203–205, *Café Baixamar,* Moll de Ponent 17, or *Le St Tropez*, Moll de Llevant 107. **Nightlife** is generally focused along the harbour road: try *Tse Tse*, Cuesta del General 15, for drum 'n' bass; *Akelarre*, Moll de Ponent 41–43, is popular with a cosmopolitan crowd.

Travel details

Trains

Madrid to: Algeciras (2 daily; 6hr–10hr 30min); Alicante (10 daily; 3hr 45min); Barcelona (8 daily; 6hr 30min); Bilbao (2–3 daily; 6hr 30min); Cáceres (5 daily; 4hr 30min); Cádiz (2 daily; 5hr); Córdoba (28 daily; 1hr 40min–4hr 45min); Granada (2 daily; 6–8hr); Jaca (1 daily; 7hr); León (7 daily; 4hr); Málaga (6 daily; 4–7hr); Oviedo (2–3 daily; 6hr–7hr 30min); Pamplona (2 daily; 5hr); Salamanca (3 daily; 2hr 40min–3hr 15min); San Sebastián (3 daily; 6hr 30min–8hr); Santander (2–3 daily; 5hr 40min); Santiago (2 daily; 8hr–8hr 30min); Segovia (7–9 daily; 2hr); Sevilla (14 daily; 3hr 30min); Toledo (7–9 daily; 1hr 30min); Valencia (11 daily; 3hr 30min); Zaragoza (13 daily; 3–4hr).

Algeciras to: Córdoba (2 daily; 2hr 50min); Granada (1 daily; 4hr); Ronda (6 daily; 1hr 40min).

Barcelona to: Bilbao (2 daily; 9hr–10hr 20min); Figueres (hourly; 1hr 30min–2hr); Puigcerdà (6 daily; 3hr); Valencia (14 daily; 3–5hr); Zaragoza (15 daily; 3hr 40min–4hr 30min).

Bilbao to: Barcelona (1–2 daily; 9hr–10hr 20min); León (1 daily; 4hr 40min); Madrid (2 daily; 5hr 30min–9hr); San Sebastián (every 30min; 2hr 30min); Santander (4 daily; 2hr).

Córdoba to: Madrid (28 daily; 1hr 40min–4hr 45min); Malaga (10 daily; 2hr 10min); Sevilla (4–6 daily; 1hr–1hr 30min).

Granada to: Madrid (2 daily; 5hr 50min); Ronda (1 daily; 4hr 20min); Valencia (1–2 daily; 8hr 20min).

León to: Barcelona (3–4 daily; 9hr 30min–11hr 40min); Madrid (7 daily; 4hr 15min); Oviedo (5 daily; 2hr); Salamanca (6 daily; 3–5hr); San Sebastián (1 daily; 5hr); Santiago (1 daily; 5hr 40min).

Málaga to: Córdoba (10 daily; 2hr 30min–3hr 30min); Madrid (9 daily; 4–7hr); Ronda (1 daily; 2hr); Sevilla (6 daily; 3hr).

Salamanca to: Madrid (3 daily; 2hr 30min).

San Sebastián to: Bilbao (9 daily; 2hr 30min–3hr); Madrid (3 daily; 8hr 30min–9hr 45min); Pamplona (1–2 daily; 2hr); Salamanca (2 daily; 6hr); Valencia (1 weekly; 10hr); Zaragoza (1–2 daily; 4hr–5hr 10min).

Santiago to: León (1 daily; 6hr); Madrid (2 daily; 7hr 30min–9hr).

Zaragoza to: Barcelona (14–16 daily; 3–6hr); Canfranc (2 daily; 3hr 30min); Jaca (3 daily; 3hr 10min); Madrid (13 daily; 3hr–4hr 30min); Pamplona (5 daily; 1hr 45min–2hr 40min).

Buses

Madrid to: Alicante (5 daily; 5hr 15min); Barcelona (7 daily; 7hr 30min); Bilbao (11 daily; 4hr 45min); Cáceres (8–10 daily; 4hr); Cádiz (6 daily; 7hr); Córdoba (6 daily; 4hr 30min); Granada (9 daily; 6hr); Málaga (7 daily; 7hr); Oviedo (12 daily; 5hr 30min); Pamplona (4 daily; 6hr); Salamanca (21 daily; 3hr); San Sebastián (9 daily; 6hr); Santander (8 daily; 6hr); Santiago (1 daily; 9hr); Sevilla (11 daily; 6hr); Toledo (every 30min; 1hr); Valencia (13 daily; 4hr).

Alicante to: Barcelona (7 daily; 8hr); Granada (5 daily; 5hr); Madrid (9 daily; 8hr); Málaga (5 daily; 8hr); Valencia (hourly; 4hr).

Barcelona to: Alicante (7 daily; 8hr); Madrid (15 daily; 7hr 30min); Seu d'Urgell (4 daily; 5hr); Valencia (14–17 daily; 4hr 15min–5hr); the Vall d'Aran (1 daily; 6hr 30min); Zaragoza (22–25 daily; 3hr 30min–5hr).

Córdoba to: Granada (7 daily; 3hr); Madrid (4 daily; 4hr 30min); Málaga (5 daily; 3hr–3hr 30min); Sevilla (10 daily–2hr 30min).

Figueres to: Barcelona (3–6 daily; 2hr 15min); Cadaqués (3 daily; 1hr); L'Escala (5 daily; 45min); Palafrugell (4 daily; 1hr 30min).

Granada to: Alicante (3 daily; 5hr); Cádiz (2 daily; 6hr); Córdoba (7 daily; 3hr); Madrid (6–9 daily; 6hr); Sevilla (7–9 daily; 4hr 30min); Valencia (3 daily; 7hr).

León to: Madrid (11 daily; 4hr); Oviedo (8 daily; 1hr 30min); Salamanca (2 daily; 2hr); Santander (1 daily; 5hr).

Málaga to: Algeciras (10 daily; 3hr); Córdoba (5 daily; 3hr); Granada (14 daily; 2hr); Ronda (6 daily; 3hr); Sevilla (11 daily; 3hr); Torremolinos (every 30min; 30min).

Oviedo to: León (8 daily; 1hr 30min); Madrid (12 daily; 5hr 30min).

Salamanca to: León (2 daily; 2hr); Madrid (15 daily; 2hr 30min–3hr); Mérida (5 daily; 4hr 30min); Santander (2 daily; 5hr); Sevilla (5 daily; 8hr).

San Sebastián to: Bilbao (1–2 hourly; 1hr 10min); Madrid (8 daily; 6hr 30min); Pamplona (13 daily; 2hr).

Santander to: Bilbao (18 daily; 1hr 30min); Madrid (6 daily; 6hr); Oviedo (4 daily; 3hr 30min); Pamplona (2 daily; 3hr 45min).

Santiago to: Bilbao (3 daily; 11–12hr); Madrid (4 daily; 8–9hr); Porto (2 weekly; 3hr).

Sevilla to: Cádiz (11 daily; 2hr); Córdoba (10 daily; 2hr 30min); Granada (9 daily; 3hr 30min–4hr 30min); Madrid (11 daily; 8hr).

SPAIN | Travel details

1015

Valencia to: Alicante (hourly; 4hr); Barcelona (14–17 daily; 4–5hr); Madrid (13 daily; 4hr); Sevilla (3 daily; 11hr).

Zaragoza to: Barcelona (15 daily; 3hr 30min–5hr); Madrid (15 daily; 3hr 30min); Pamplona (7–8 daily; 2hr–2hr 45min).

Ferries

Barcelona to: Ibiza (4–6 weekly; 9hr 30min); Mahón (3–8 weekly; 9hr); Palma (2–4 daily; 8hr 30min).

Ibiza to: Formentera (6–9 daily; 40min–1hr 30min); Palma (1–3 weekly; 6hr 30min); Valencia (1–6 weekly; 9hr).

Palma to: Ibiza (1–3 weekly; 6hr 30min); Mahón (1 weekly; 6hr 30min).

Valencia to: Ibiza (1–6 weekly; 7hr); Palma (6–13 weekly; 9hr).

Sweden

Sweden highlights

✳ Gamla Stan, Stockholm
One of Europe's most elegant and best pre-served medieval centres. **See p.1018**

✳ Avenyn, Gothenburg This stylish boulevard is the place to sit and sip a coffee and watch the world go by. **See p.1033**

✳ Inlandsbanan Single track rail line that winds its way through virgin forest and past crystal clear streams en route to Lapland. **See p.1039**

✳ Lake Siljan, Dalarna
Sweden's most beautiful lake surrounded by wooden cottages bedecked with summer flowers. **See p.1039**

✳ Jokkmokk, Arctic Circle
This village close to the Arctic Circle makes an excellent base from which to explore the wilds of Swedish Lapland. **See p.1040**

Introduction and basics

Sweden is a large, geographically varied and strangely little-known country whose sense of space is one of its best features. Away from the relatively densely populated south, travelling without seeing a soul is not uncommon. The south and southwest of the country are gently undulating, picturesque holiday lands, long-disputed Danish territory, and fringed with some of Europe's finest beaches. The west coast harbours a host of historic ports – Gothenburg, Helsingborg and Malmö, which is now linked by bridge to Copenhagen – but it is Stockholm, the capital, that is the country's supreme attraction, a bundle of islands housing monumental architecture, fine museums and the country's most active culture and nightlife. The two university towns, Lund and Uppsala, demand a visit too, while, moving northwards, Östersund and Gällivare both make justified demands on your time. This area, central and northern Sweden, is the country of tourist brochures: great swathes of forest, inexhaustible lakes – around 96,000 – and some of the best wilderness hiking in Europe. Two train routes link it with the south. The eastern run, close to the Bothnian coast, passes old wood-built towns and planned new ones such as likeable Sundsvall. In the centre, the trains of the Inlandsbanan strike off through lakelands and mountains, clearing reindeer off the track as they go. The routes meet in Sweden's far north – home of the Sámi, the oldest indigenous Scandinavian people.

Information and maps

Almost all towns in Sweden have a **tourist office**, giving out maps and timetables, and usually able to book private rooms, rent bikes and change money. Some also sell discount cards during the summer which give reductions on local travel, museum entry and other freebies. The best general **map** of Sweden is the Motormännens *Sveriges Atlas*.

Money and banks

Swedish **currency** is the krona (plural kronor), made up of 100 öre. It comes in coins of 50öre, 1kr, 5kr and 10kr; and notes of 20kr, 50kr, 100kr, 500kr, 1000kr and 10,000kr.

Banks are open Mon–Fri 9.30am–3pm, Thurs also 4–5.30pm. Outside normal banking hours you can **change money** in exchange offices at airports and ferry terminals, and in post offices (look for the "Växel" sign), as well as at Forex exchange offices, which usually offer the best rates – expect to pay a minimum 20kr commission or 15kr per travellers' cheque. Bankomat machines give cash advances and accept most credit cards – check with your bank before you go.

Communications

Post offices are open Mon–Fri 9am–6pm, Sat 10am–1pm. You can buy stamps at post offices, supermarkets, newspaper kiosks, tobacconists and hotels.

Sweden on the net

ⓦ **www.cityguide.se** Up-to-date guide to events and entertainment in the main Swedish cities.
ⓦ **www.sunet.se** In-depth regional information
ⓦ **www.sverigeturism.se** – the largest single source of information in English on Sweden, its provinces, nature, culture and society. Not that frequently updated though

For international **telephone** calls you can dial direct from public phones. Card phones have now replaced coin-operated phone boxes; cards (telefonkort) are available from newsagents and kiosks. It is also possible to use credit cards in many payphones, marked with the "CCC" sign. All operators speak English (domestic directory enquiries ☎118 118, international ☎118 119).

Internet cafés are surprisingly thin on the ground, though you should find at least one in the larger towns. An alternative is the local library, where access is free; otherwise expect to pay 40–60kr.

Getting around

Sweden's internal transport system is quick and efficient and runs through all weathers. Services are often reduced in the winter, but it's unlikely you'll ever get stranded. In summer, when everyone is on holiday, trains and buses are packed: on long journeys it's a good idea to make reservations. One booklet worth picking up is the quarterly *SJ Tågtider* **timetable** from any train station, an accurate and comprehensive list of the most useful train services in the country, except for those of the Inlandsbanan up to northern Sweden and the Pågatågen private rail line in the south (InterRail valid on both). The Inlandsbanan is only open from late June to early August.

Trains

Swedish State Railways (*SJ* or *Statens Järnvägar*) have an extensive network, running as far north as Sundsvall and Östersund. Trains of the private company *Tågkompaniet* (rail cards valid) run right into the north of the country above the Arctic Circle and on into Norway. **Tickets** are good value, and you'll rarely have to pay the full rate. **InterRail and Eurail passes** are valid, as is the ScanRail pass (see p.29).

To ensure a seat, you might want to make a **reservation**; on some trains – indicated by an "IC" in the timetable – this costs 30kr; on the high-speed X2000 trains and most national routes reservations are mandatory, though the fee is included in the price. If you are using a travel pass, you must reserve

seats separately before the journey (30kr).

For all train travel north of the line between Sundsvall and Östersund, you have to book tickets through **Tågkompaniet** (☎020/44 41 11). They will also book SJ tickets, but SJ will not book Tågkompaniet.

Buses

Complementing the rail system are **long-distance buses** (*Expressbussar*), operated by Swebus and Svenska Buss. Services tend to be cheaper and slower than the equivalent train ride. In the north, buses are more frequent since they are used to carry mail to isolated regions. Several companies operate daily services, and fares are broadly similar.

Ferries

Unlike Norway and Finland, there are few domestic **ferry** services in Sweden. The various archipelagoes on the southeast coast are served by small ferries, the most comprehensive network being within the Stockholm archipelago, for which you can buy an island-hopping boat pass.

Accommodation

Finding somewhere cheap to sleep is not too much hassle. There's an excellent network of HI hostels and campsites, while in the cities private rooms and bed and breakfast places are a common alternative to hotels.

Hotels and private rooms

Hotels come cheaper than you'd think, especially in Stockholm and the bigger cities during the summer, when many Swedes are out of the country and hotels slash their prices massively. Reduced summer prices are identical to prices charged at weekends during the rest of the year (out of season midweek are therefore the most expensive): on average, for a room with TV and bathroom you can expect to pay from 500kr a double. All hotels include breakfast in the price, which can be a useful bonus. **Package deals** operating in Malmö, Stockholm and Gothenburg, bookable through the tourist office, get you a hotel bed for one night, breakfast and the relevant city discount card from around 370–450kr per person. These schemes are generally valid from mid-June to mid-August and at weekends throughout the year. A further option in the larger towns is a **private room** booked through the tourist office. These usually cost about the same as a bed at a youth hostel, though they're often located some way out of the centre.

Hostels

The country has a huge chain of **hostels** – 280 in all – operated by the Svenska Turistföreningen (STF), Box 25, 101 20, Stockholm (☎08/463 21 00, ⌨www.mer-avsverige.nu). Usually they offer single and double rooms as well as dorms, and virtually all have well-equipped self-catering kitchens and serve a buffet breakfast. Prices are low (120–150kr); non-HI/YHA members pay around an extra 40kr a night. There's also an increasingly large number of non STF-affiliated hostels, mostly run by SVIF (☎0413/55 34 50, ⌨www.svif.se).

Campsites and cabins

Practically every town or village has at least one **campsite**, generally of a high standard. Pitching a tent costs from 90kr for two people sharing in July and August, a little less during the rest of the year, though all costs are considerably higher near the big cities. Most sites are open June to September, some throughout the year, and most are approved and classified by the Swedish Tourist Board; a comprehensive listings book, Camping Sverige, is available at larger sites and most Swedish bookshops. Note that at most sites you'll need a camping card (49kr from your first stop). Many campsites also boast cabins, usually decked out with bunk beds and kitchen equipment but not sheets. These start at 250–350kr for a four-bedded affair.

Food and drink

Eating and drinking is nothing like as expensive as it used to be in Sweden. At its best,

Swedish food is excellent, largely meat-, fish- and potato-based, but varied and generally tasty and filling. Specialities include northern Swedish delicacies – reindeer and elk meat, and wild berries – and herring in many different guises.

Food

Breakfast (frukost) is invariably a help-yourself buffet – served in most hostels for around 50kr, and free in hotels – consisting of juice, cereals, bread, boiled eggs, jams, salami, tea and coffee on even the most limited tables. Something to watch out for is the jug of filmjölk next to the ordinary milk, a thicker, sour milk for pouring on cereals. **Coffee** in Sweden is usually of the filter variety and can be bitter. It's often free after the first cup. **Tea** is weak as a rule but costs around the same – 10–15kr. For **snacks** and lighter meals the choice expands. A Gatukök (street kitchen) or Korvstånd (hot-dog stall) will serve a selection of hot dogs, burgers, chips and the like for around 30kr. **Burger bars** are just about everywhere now and a hefty burger and chips meal will set you back a shade over 50kr. If you can afford a little extra, it's far better to hit the coffee shops (konditori), which always display a range of freshly baked pastries and cakes. They're not particularly cheap (coffee and cake for 20–35kr), but are generally good, also serving smörgåsar, **open sandwiches** piled high with toppings for 30–40kr a time.

Eating in a **restaurant** is fantastic value at lunchtime, when most places offer something called the Dish of the Day (Dagens Rätt) at 60–70kr, often the only affordable way to sample real Swedish cooking. Served between 11am and 2pm, it consists of a main dish with bread and salad, sometimes a drink, and coffee. More expensive but good for a blowout are restaurants and hotels that put out the smörgåsbord at lunchtime for 150–200kr, where you help yourself to unlimited portions of herring, smoked and fresh salmon, hot and cold meats, potatoes, salad, cheese and fruit.

If you don't eat the set lunch, meals in restaurants, especially at **dinner** (middag), can be expensive: 150–200kr for a three-course affair, plus 30–50kr for a beer and at least 120kr for a bottle of house plonk. Pizzerias and Chinese restaurants offer better value. Large pizzas cost 40–60kr, usually with free salad and bread, and the price is generally the same at lunch and dinner. Chinese restaurants nearly always offer a set lunch for around 50kr, though they're pricier in the evening.

Drink

Drinking in Sweden now costs the same as in most European capitals, including London. The cheapest choice is beer. You'll pay 35–50kr for 500ml of lager-type drink – a *storstark*. Unless you specify, it will be *starköl*, the strongest Class III beer, or the slightly weaker *mellanöl*; *folköl* is the Class II and cheaper and weaker brew; cheapest (around half the price) is *lättöl*, a Class I concoction that is virtually nonalcoholic. Classes I and II are available in supermarkets; Class III is only on sale in state-licensed liquor stores (*Systembolaget*), where it's around a third of the price you'll pay in a bar. A glass of **wine** in a bar or restaurant costs around 35–45kr, while you can buy a whole bottle for a little more in a state off-licence. For experimental drinking, **akvavit** is a good bet, served ice-cold in tiny shots and washed down with beer.

You'll find **bars** in all towns and cities and most villages. In Stockholm and the larger cities the move is towards British-style pubs, though wherever you drink, you'll find that things close down at around midnight, a little later in Gothenburg and Stockholm.

Opening hours and holidays

Shops are open Mon–Fri 9am–6pm, Sat 9am–1/4pm. Some larger department stores stay open until 8/10pm, and open Sun noon–4pm. Banks, offices and shops close on the following days and may close early on the preceding day: Jan 1; Jan 6; Good Fri; Easter Sun & Mon; May 1; Ascension (mid-May); Whit Sun & Mon; Midsummer's Eve & Day; Nov 1; Dec 24, 25, 26 & 31.

Emergencies

Sweden has a relatively low **crime** rate, but if you do need to contact the police you'll find them courteous and generally able to speak English. In case of **health problems** you should go direct to a hospital with your passport (there is no GP system), where for a maximum of 240kr you'll receive treatment; if you have to stay in hospital it will cost you an additional 80kr per day. To obtain medicine, take your prescription to a **pharmacist** – *Apotek* – which will be open shop hours, although Stockholm has a 24-hour pharmacy. Larger towns operate a rota system of late opening, with the address of the nearest late-opener posted on the door of each pharmacy.

Emergency numbers

All emergencies ☎112.

Stockholm and around

STOCKHOLM comes lauded as Sweden's most beautiful city, and largely lives up to it – it's delightful, not least as a contrast to the apparently endless lakes and forests of the rest of the country. It's also a remarkably disparate capital, one whose tracts of water and range of monumental buildings give it an ageing, lived-in feel, quite at odds with its status as Sweden's most forward-looking city.

Built on fourteen islands, Stockholm was a natural site for the fortifications, erected by one Birger Jarl in 1255, that grew into the current city. In the sixteenth century, the city fell to King Gustav Vasa, a century later becoming the centre of the Swedish trading empire that covered present-day Scandinavia and beyond. Following the waning of Swedish power it only rose to prominence again in the nineteenth century when industrialization sowed the seeds of the Swedish economic miracle.

Arrival and information

By **train**, you arrive at **Central Station**, a cavernous structure on Vasagatan in Norrmalm. All branches of the Tunnelbana, Stockholm's underground system, meet at T-Centralen, the station directly below Central Station. **Cityterminalen**, adjacent, handles all the **bus** services, both domestic and international, including the airport bus. Viking Line **ferries** arrive at **Tegelvikshamnen** in Södermalm, in the south of the city, a thirty-minute walk from the centre, or connected by bus to Slussen and then by Tunnelbana to T-Centralen. The Silja Line terminal is in the northeastern reaches of the city, a short walk from Gärdet or Ropsten underground stations. **Arlanda airport** is 45km north of Stockholm; buses run every ten minutes to Cityterminalen (6.40am–11.45pm; journey time 40min; 80kr), and high-speed trains leave every fifteen minutes from **Arlanda Norra** and **Södra** stations beneath the airport for the city's Central Station (5am–midnight; journey time 20min; 140kr).

You should be able to pick up a map of the city at most points of arrival, but it's worth making your way to the city **tourist office** (Mon–Fri 9am–6pm, Sat & Sun 9am–3pm; ☎08/789 24 90, ⊛www.stockholmtown.com), on Hamngatan in Norrmalm, on the ground floor of Sverigehuset, which hands out fistfuls of free information and sells decent maps for 20kr. You can also buy the useful **Stockholm Card** here (220kr/day, 380kr/two days, 540kr/three days), which gives unlimited travel on city transport (except on direct buses to the airport or on the connecting night bus to the Nynäshamn ferry terminal), free entry to most museums and free sightseeing boat tours. The office also stocks free copies of *What's On*, which lists forthcoming events.

City transport

The best way to explore Stockholm's initially confusing centre is to **walk** – it takes about 25 minutes to cross central Stockholm on foot – but to reach the more distant sights you'll have to use some form of **transport**. Storstockholms Lokaltrafik (SL) operates a comprehensive system of buses and trains (underground and local) reaching well out of the city centre. Quickest of the transport systems is the **Tunnelbana** (T-bana) underground, based on three main lines. **Buses** can be less direct owing to the nature of Stockholm's islands and central pedestrianization. **Ferries** also link some of the central islands: Djurgården is connected with Nybroplan in Norrmalm (summer only) and Skeppsbron in Gamla Stan (all year). Ferry trips cost 20kr one way, while land transport costs 20kr within one zone, 10kr for each additional zone – so you're normally better off investing in a **pass**. Do not confuse the Stockholm Card (see above) with the more limited **24-hour** and **72-hour cards**, costing 80kr and 150kr respectively, which give unlimited

28

1024

STOCKHOLM

▲ TV Tower

◄ Estline Ferry to Estonia

LADUGÅRDSGÄRDET

Technical Museum

DJURGÅRDEN

Skansen

Djurgårdsbrunnsviken

DJURGÅRDSBRUNNSVÄGEN

ROSENDALSVÄGEN

500m

0

Vasa Museum

Estonia Memorial

Nordic Museum

Gröna Lunds Tivoli

BECKHOLMEN

Viking Line Terminal

Saltsjön

KARLAVÄGEN

LINNÉGATAN

History Museum

Museum of Far Eastern Antiquities

Museum of Modern Art

SKEPPSHOLMEN

KASTELLHOLMEN

KATARINAVÄGEN

Katarina Kyrka

Karlaplan Ⓣ

NARVAVÄGEN

STRANDVÄGEN

STRÖMGATAN

◄ Ropsten

ÖSTERMALM

Music Museum

Summer only

Vasa Museum

All year

Royal Theatre of Drama

NYBROPLAN

National Art Museum

Kungsträdgården

Strömmen

Kungl. Slottet

SKEPPSBRON

Ⓣ *Slussen*

KARL JOH TORG

Östermalmstorg Ⓣ

ÖSTERMALMSTORG

STUREGATAN

BIRGER JARLSG.

NORRMALM

Adolf Fred. Kyrka

Concert House

Hötorget Ⓣ

Kulturhuset

SVEAVÄGEN

Sverigehuset (Tourist Office) ℹ

Kungsträdgården Ⓣ

Opera House

Helgeandsholmen

Riksdagshuset

VASABRON

Riddarhuset

Storkyrkan

GAMLA STAN

Ⓣ *Gamla Stan*

Tyska Kyrkan

SÖDER MÄLARSTRAND

DROTTNINGGATAN

Klara Kyrka

ℹ

T-Centralen Ⓣ

Cityterminalen

Central Station

Stadshuset ℹ

RIDDARHOLMEN

Riddarholms Kyrkan

Mälaren

Ⓣ *Rådhuset*

Hospital

VASAGATAN

KUNGSHOLMSGATAN

FLEMINGGATAN

VÄSTMANNAGATAN

SÖDERMALM

Maria Magdalena Kyrka

Ⓣ *Mariatorget*

SANKT PAULSGATAN

HORNSGATAN

Ⓣ *Zinkensdamm*

N

◄ Smedsudden Beach

travel on public transport within Stockholm county. Alternatively, you can buy a strip of twenty transferable SL **ticket coupons** (*Rabattkuponger*; 110kr); you'll need two coupons for any single journey in the centre. Buy SL tickets and cards from the tourist office and SL offices inside T-Centralen or Central Station. **Taxis** can be hailed in the street, or booked on ☏08/15 00 00. A trip across the city centre costs 100–150kr, more in the evenings and at weekends (women get a 5–10 percent discount at weekends).

Accommodation

There's plenty of **accommodation** in Stockholm, especially for budget travellers, but don't turn up late in summer and expect to get a cheap bed. Booking your first night's accommodation in advance is always a good idea, either through the Sverigehuset tourist centre or by phoning direct. The cheapest choices, on the whole, are found to the north of Cityterminalen, in the streets to the west of Adolf Fredriks Kyrka. There's also **Hotellcentralen**, a booking service on the lower level of Central Station (daily 8/9am–6/8pm; ☏08/789 24 25, ✉hotels@stoinfo.se), which charges a fee of 50kr per room, 20kr for a hostel if you go in person, but is free over the telephone. For **private rooms**, contact Hotelltjänst, Vasagatan 15–17 (☏08/545 291 30), which can fix you up with a double room for around 250kr per person.

Hostels

Af Chapman Skeppsholmen ☏08/463 22 66, ⊕www.stfchapman.com. Official hostel on a ship moored at Skeppsholmen. Without a reservation, the chances of a bed in summer are negligible. ❸
City Backpackers Upplandsgatan 2A, Norra Bantorget ☏08/20 69 20, ⊕www.citybackpackers.se. Curfewless non-STF hostel with four-bed rooms and cheaper eight-bed dorms. ❸
Columbus Hotell & Vandrarhem Tjärhovsgatan 11, Södermalm ☏08/503 112 00, ⊕www.columbus.se. A friendly, non-STF hostel with cheap dorm beds and more expensive doubles ❻, housed in a former brewery. T-bana Medborgarplatsen.
Långholmen Kronohäktet, Långholmen ☏08/668 05 10, ⊕www.langholmen.com. Stockholm's grandest official hostel, in an old prison on Långholmen island, with ordinary doubles in summer as well as hostel beds. T-bana to Hornstull. Turn left and follow the signs. ❻
M/S Rygerfjord Söder Mälarstrand-Kaj 12 ☏08/84 08 30, ⊕www.rygerfjord.se. Homely hostel-ship moored on Södermalm close to Slussen T-bana station. ❸
Zinkensdamm Zinkens väg 20, Södermalm ☏08/616 81 00, ⊕www.zinkensdamm.com. Huge official hostel with kitchen facilities. Nicely situated by the water. T-bana Zinkensdamm. ❸

Hotels and pensions

Anno 1647 Mariagränd 3 ☏08/442 16 80, ⊕www.anno1647.se. Near Slussen, a handy location for the old town. ❾
Gustav Vasa Västmannagatan 61 ☏08/34 38 01, ⊕www.hotel.wineasy.se/gustav.vasa. Early twentieth-century place and not a bad location, in the northern part of Norrmalm. T-bana Odenplan. ❽
Tre små rum Högbergsgatan 81 ☏08/641 23 71, ⊕www.tresmarum.se. T-bana Mariatorget. Seven bright modern non-smoking rooms in the heart of Söder. No en-suites. ❺

Campsites

Ängby ☏08/37 04 20. West of the city on Lake Mälaren and near the beach. T-bana to Ängbyplan, then a 300-metre walk. Book in advance Sept–April.
Bredäng ☏08/97 70 71. Pricey place with a hostel and restaurant on site. Ten kilometres southwest of the centre and also by Lake Mälaren. Take T-bana to Bredäng from where it's a 700-metre walk. Closed Nov–March.
Östermalms Citycamping Fiskartorpsvägen 2 ☏08/10 29 03. Stockholm's most centrally located campsite at the Östermalm sports ground surrounded by woodland. Late June to mid-Aug only.

The City

The **Stadshuset**, Hantverkargatan 1 (guided tours 10am & noon; June–Aug 2pm; rest of year 50kr; T-Centralen), at the water's edge near Central Station, and in particular its gently-tapering 106-metre high red-brick **tower** (May–Sept daily

10am–4.30pm; 15kr), has the best fix on the city's layout. The building itself, a flagship of the National Romantic movement in the 1910s and 1920s, draws heavily on Swedish materials and themes, exemplified in the cavernous Blue Room, where the Nobel prize-givings are held, and the Golden Room, where a précis of Swedish history covers the walls in a gilt mosaic.

Gamla Stan

Three islands – Riddarholmen, Staden and Helgeandsholmen – make up **Gamla Stan** or **Old Stockholm**, a clutter of seventeenth- and eighteenth-century Renaissance buildings, hairline medieval alleys and tall, dark houses whose intricate doorways still bear the arms of the wealthy merchants who once dwelled within. In front of the Swedish parliament building, Riksdagshuset, accessible by a set of steps leading down from Norrbro, the **Medeltidsmuseum** (Tues–Sun 11am–4/6pm; 40kr; T-Gamla Stan) is the best city-related historical collection in Stockholm. Ruins of medieval tunnels and walls were discovered during excavations under the parliament building, and they've been incorporated into a walk-through underground exhibition here.

Over a second set of bridges is the most distinctive monumental building in Stockholm, the **Kungliga Slottet** (Royal Palace; T-Gamla Stan), a beautiful Renaissance successor to the original castle of Stockholm. Finished in 1760, it's a striking achievement, outside sombre, inside a magnificent Baroque and Rococo swirl. The **Apartments** (May to mid-Aug daily 10am–4pm; rest of year Tues–Sun noon–3pm; 70kr) form a relentlessly linear collection of furniture and tapestries; the **Treasury** (same times as apartments; 70kr) has ranks of jewel-studded crowns, the oldest that of Karl X (1650). Also worth catching is **Livrustkammaren**, the Royal Armoury (same times as apartments; 65kr), less to do with weapons than with ceremony – suits of armour, costumes and horse-drawn coaches from the sixteenth century onwards, most notably the stuffed horse and mud-spattered garments of King Gustav II Adolf, who died in the Battle of Lützen in 1632.

Beyond the palace lies Gamla Stan proper, where the streets suddenly narrow and darken. The first major building is the **Storkyrkan** (daily 9am–4/6pm; 10kr, free in winter), consecrated in 1306 and technically Stockholm's cathedral – the monarchs of Sweden are married and crowned here. The Baroque interior is marvellous, with an animated fifteenth-century sculpture of *St George and the Dragon*, the royal pews, more like golden billowing thrones, and a monumental black and silver altarpiece. **Stortorget**, Gamla Stan's main square, is handsomely proportioned and crowded with eighteenth-century buildings. The surrounding narrow streets house a succession of arts and craft shops, restaurants and discreet fast-food outlets, clogged by summer buskers and evening strollers.

Keep right on as far as the handsome Baroque **Riddarhuset** (Mon–Fri 11.30am–12.30pm; 40kr), in whose Great Hall the Swedish aristocracy met during the seventeenth-century Parliament of the Four Estates. Their coats of arms – around 2500 of them – are splattered across the walls. From here it's a matter of seconds across the bridge onto **Riddarholmen** ("Island of the Knights"), and to **Riddarholms Kyrkan** (May–Sept daily 10am–4pm; 30kr), originally a Franciscan monastery and long the burial place of Swedish royalty. You'll find the unfortunate Gustav II Adolf in the green marble sarcophagus.

Skeppsholmen

Off Gamla Stan's eastern reaches, but not connected by bridge from the old town, the island of **Skeppsholmen** is home to the **National Art Museum** (Tues–Sun 11am–5pm, Tues till 8pm; 75kr; T-Kungsträdgården), an impressive collection of applied art – beds slept in by kings, cabinets used by queens, alongside Art Nouveau coffee pots and vases and examples of Swedish furniture design. Upstairs there is a plethora of European sculpture, mesmerizing sixteenth- and seventeenth-century Russian Orthodox icons, and a quality selection of paintings. Unfortunately,

Skeppsholmen's other museum of note, the **Moderna Muséet**, one of the best collections of modern art in Europe, is currently closed and not due to reopen until sometime in 2004.

Norrmalm and Östermalm

Modern Stockholm lies immediately to the north of Gamla Stan. It's split into two distinct sections: the central **Norrmalm** and the classier, residential streets of **Östermalm** to the east – though there's not much apart from a couple of specialist museums to draw you here. On the waterfront, at the foot of Norrbro, is **Gustav Adolfs Torg**, more a traffic island than a square, with the eighteenth-century **Opera House** its proudest and most notable building. It was at a masked ball here in 1792 that King Gustav III was shot; you'll find Gustav's ball costume, as well as the assassin's pistols and mask, displayed in the palace armoury in Gamla Stan. Norrmalm's eastern boundary is marked by **Kungsträdgården**, the most fashionable and central of the city's numerous parks – once royal gardens and now Stockholm's main meeting place, especially in summer when there's almost always something going on.

On the opposite side of Norrmalm in Östermalm is the **Historiska Muséet** (Tues–Sun 11am–5pm; 70kr; T-Karlaplan). Ground-floor highlights include a Stone Age household and a mass of Viking weapons, coins and boats, while upstairs there's a worthy collection of medieval church art and architecture, evocatively housed in massive vaulted rooms, including some rare reassembled bits of stave churches uncovered on the Baltic island of Gotland.

Djurgården

A former royal hunting ground, **Djurgården** is Stockholm's nearest large expanse of park. You could walk to the park from Central Station, but it's quite a hike: you can take the bus instead – #44 from Karlaplan or #47 from Nybroplan – or in summer, the ferry from Nybroplan, or year round from Slussen.

In the northeast of the park you can get excellent views from 155-metre-high **Kaknäs TV tower** (daily 10am–9pm; 25kr), one of Scandinavia's tallest structures. South over Djurgårdsbron are numerous museums. Palatial **Nordiska Muséet** (Tues–Sun 10am–5pm; 60kr) is a good attempt to represent Swedish cultural history in an accessible fashion, with a particularly interesting Sámi section. Close by, the **Vasa Muséet** (daily 10am–5/7pm; 70kr) is an essential stop, displaying the *Vasa* warship which sank in Stockholm harbour after just twenty minutes of its maiden voyage in 1628. Preserved in mud, the ship was raised along with 12,000 objects in 1961. Walkways bring you nose to nose with the cannon hatches and restored decorative relief, exhibition halls display the retrieved bits and pieces, while films and videos explain the social and political life of the period – all with excellent English notes and regular English-language **guided tours**.

Södermalm

It's worth venturing beyond Slussen's traffic interchange for the heights of **Södermalm**'s crags, an area largely neglected by most visitors to the city. The perched buildings are vaguely forbidding, but get beyond the speeding main roads skirting the island and a lively and surprisingly green area unfolds – full of neighbourhood bars and restaurants. To get there by bus, take the #48 from Norrmalm getting off at Bondegatan or the #53 from Tegelbacken to Folkungagatan, or use the T-bana and get off at either Slussen or Medborgarplatsen (on Götgatan). Walking, you reach the island over a double bridge from Gamla Stan, to the south of which is the rewarding **Stadsmuseet** (Tues–Sun 11am–5pm, Thurs till 9pm; 50kr), hidden in a basement courtyard, and housing a set of collections relating to the city's history as a sea port and industrial centre. Nearby, take a look at the **Katarina kyrka**, rebuilt in Renaissance style in the eighteenth century. On this site the victims of the so-called "Stockholm Blood Bath" were buried in 1520, the betrayed nobility of Sweden who had opposed King Christian II's Danish invasion and were burned as heretics outside the city walls.

Eating and drinking

The three main areas for decent **eating**, day or night, are Norrmalm, Gamla Stan and Södermalm. The Hötorgshallen in Hötorget is a cheap and varied indoor market, useful for those planning on **self-catering** and awash with small cafés and ethnic snacks. Outside is an excellent daily fruit and vegetable market too. There's a fairly fine line between cafés, restaurants and bars in Stockholm, many offering music and entertainment in the evening and food during the day. The city boasts an ever-increasing number of stylish **cafés**, perfect for coffee, cake and people-watching, either during the day or in the evening.

Cafés and restaurants

Babs Kök & Bar Birger Jarlsgatan 37. Lively, young and laid-back atmosphere at this quirky restaurant/bar. Interesting eats such as duck terrine with pear and raisin. Mostly meat dishes.

Blå Lotus Katrina Bangata 21. The hangout of the alternative crowd – always has an intellectual buzz.

Café Art Västerlånggatan 60–62, Gamla Stan. A fifteenth-century arty cellar-café with sandwiches, good coffee and cakes.

Chokladdcoppen Stortorget 18, Gamla Stan. Overlooking the grand old square, this is a fabulous café specializing in rich chocolate tart.

Collage Smålandsgatan 2, Norrmalm. Fill up on huge portions from the short meat and fish menu. Try the delicious Africana pork with bananas, peanuts and mandarins.

Cosmic Café Wollmar Yxkullsgatan 5B, Södermalm, opposite Mariatorget T-bana. A tiny, fun, wholefood vegetarian café with very good-value salads, pastas and great fresh fruit milkshakes.

Creperie Fyra Knop Svartensgatan 4. Excellent-value crepes served in this dark, evocative restaurant which is fashionably tatty and plays the likes of Leonard Cohen.

Hannas Café Hornsgatan 156, Södermalm. Small, gay-friendly café serving cheap coffee. Also hosts regular art exhibitions.

Hermitage Stora Nygatan 11. Excellent, vegetarian place with delicious fresh salads and breads.

Lasse i Parken Högalidsgatan 56, Södermalm. Beautiful daytime café in an eighteenth-century house with a pleasant garden. Summer daily 11am–5pm. T-bana Hornstull.

String Café Nytorgsgatan 38, Södermalm. Ultra laid-back retro café full of young studenty types who love the mirror. Lots of big, cheapish coffees with muffins, brownies and the like.

Bars, brasseries and pubs

Fenix Götgatan 40, Södermalm. Trendy and lively American-style bar. Good selection of beers and cheapish food.

Gråmunken Västerlånggatan 18, Gamla Stan. Cosy café with live jazz several nights a week.

Hannas Krog Skånegatan 80. A restaurant with a lively basement bar. *Hannas Deli* opposite is more relaxed and has *Bar K* in the basement.

Mushrooms Nybroplan 6. Always full to bursting with loud, happy beer-drinkers.

O'Learys Götgatan 11, Södermalm. A good bar/restaurant for watching sport on the widescreen TV.

Sloppy's Hamngatan 2. A popular bar and nightclub open until 5am; serves food, too. Sat is *Propaganda*, a gay disco.

Söders Hjärta Bellmansgatan 22, Södermalm. Swanky restaurant with a less intimidating and friendly bar on the mezzanine floor.

Nightlife

There's plenty to keep you occupied at night in Stockholm and the city's tag of being prohibitively expensive is less and less true. As well as the weekend, Wednesday night is an active time, with usually plenty going on and queues at the more popular places. At specifically **live music venues** you'll pay 60–100kr entrance. For up-to-date **what's on information**, check *På Stan*, the Friday supplement of the *Dagens Nyheter* newspaper, or ask at the tourist office.

Live music

Engelen Kornhamnstorg 59, Gamla Stan. Jazz, rock and blues nightly.

Fasching Kungsgatan 63, Norrmalm. Stockholm's premier jazz venue, with local acts and big names.

Kaos Stora Nygatan 21, Gamla Stan. Good live music from 9pm nightly; rock bands on Fri and Sat in the cellar and reasonable late-night food.

Nalen Regeringsgatan 74. The place to go for boogie, R & B, swing and rock & roll bands playing regularly.

Stampen Stora Nygatan 5, Gamla Stan. Long-established and rowdy jazz club.

Discos and clubs

Collage Smålandsgatan 2, Norrmalm. Upstairs from the restaurant is a lively bar and dance floor with a noisy young crowd. Black jack is also played. Open Wed–Sat only.

La Isla Fridhemsplan. Latin platters into the small hours, as well as salsa dancing. Underground in the Fridhemsplan T-bana station complex.

Sture Compagniet Sturegatan 4, Norrmalm. Terrific light show with house and techno sounds blaring on three floors of bars.

Gay Stockholm

Although Stockholm's **gay scene** is still disappointingly small, considering the general tolerance of alternative lifestyles afforded in the city, the action is by no means as limited as it once was. The city's main gay centre is *Tip Top* at Sveavägen 57 (℡08/736 02 12; T-bana Rådmansgatan), which has a bookshop, counselling and meeting facilities, as well as a bar/restaurant. On the floor above are the national offices of Sweden's gay rights group RFSL (⌨www.rfsl.se), which has an excellent free paper, *Kom Ut*. Also pick up the widely available *QX* paper from gay venues.

Bitch Girl Club Kolingsborg, Slussen. Scandinavia's biggest lesbian club. Every other Fri in summer & Sat rest of year.

Häktet Hornsgatan 82; Zinkensdamm T-bana. A friendly neighbourhood bar always packed out. Summer terrace with decent food. Open Wed (mostly women) & Fri.

Regnbågsrummet Sturecompagniet, Stureplan. Currently the hippest spot – hence long queues. Fri & Sat only.

Stargayte Södra Riddarholmshammen 19, next to the Mälardrottningen ship, Gamla Stan. Three bars and two dance floors attracting party animals of all ages. Fri & Sat only.

Patricia Stadsgårdskajen; Slussen T-bana. Drag shows, dancing and comedy on what was the Queen Mother's royal yacht. Also an excellent restaurant on the upper deck. Gay on Sun only.

TipTop (see above). Particularly popular on Fri and Sat.

Listings

Doctor Medical Care Information ℡08/411 71 77.

Embassies Australia, Sergels Torg 12 ℡08/613 29 00; Ireland, Östermalmsgatan 97 ℡08/661 80 05; UK, Skarpögatan 6–8 ℡08/671 30 00; Canada, Tegelbacken 4 ℡08/453 30 00; US, Dag Hammarskjöldsväg 31 ℡08/783 53 00.

Exchange At Arlanda airport; Forex offices at Central Station and Cityterminalen.

Internet access Internet Café, 3rd floor, Pub department store, 63 Drottningatan; Café Access, Kulturhuset, Sergels torg.

Left luggage Lockers on the lower level of the Central Station.

Pharmacy C.W. Scheele, Klarabergsgatan 64 ℡08/454 81 30 (24hr).

Post office Drottninggatan 53.

Millesgården and Drottningholm

Just a short way to the northeast of the city centre, on the mainly residential island of **Lindingö**, the **Millesgården** (May–Sept daily 10am–5pm; Oct–April Tues–Sun noon–4pm; 75kr) is the outdoor sculpture garden of Carl Milles (1875–1955), one of Sweden's greatest sculptors. Arranged on a number of garden terraces carved from the steep cliffs, this is one of the most enticing visual attractions within easy reach of central Stockholm – to get there, take the T-bana to Ropsten and then go on by train one stop to Torvikstorg before walking down Herserudsvägen.

Try also to visit the harmonious royal palace of **Drottningholm** (daily 10am/noon–3.30/4.30pm; guided tours noon, 1pm & 2pm; 60kr), beautifully located on the shores of leafy Lovön island, 11km west of the centre. It's a lovely fifty-minute boat trip there (85kr return); ferries leave every thirty minutes from Stadshusbron to coincide with the opening times. You could also take the T-bana to Brommaplan and then bus #177, #301–323, #336 or #338 – a less thrilling ride,

28

but free with the Stockholm Card. Modelled in a thoroughly French style, Drottningholm is perhaps the greatest achievement of the architects Tessin – father and son – and was begun in 1662 on the orders of King Karl X's widow, Eleonora. Good English notes are available to help you sort out the riot of Rococo decoration.

Uppsala and around

Forty minutes' train ride north of Stockholm, **UPPSALA** is regarded as the historical and religious centre of the country. It's a tranquil daytime alternative to the capital, with a delightful river-cut centre, not to mention an active student-geared nightlife. At the centre of the medieval town, a ten-minute walk from the train station, is the great **Domkyrkan** (daily 8am–6pm; free), Scandinavia's largest cathedral. The echoing interior remains impressive, particularly the French Gothic ambulatory, with its tiny chapels, one of which contains a lively set of restored fourteenth-century wall paintings that tell the legend of St Erik, Sweden's patron saint, while another contains his relics. Poke around and you'll also find the tombs of Reformation rebel monarch Gustav Vasa and his son Johan III, and that of the great botanist Carl Von Linné (self styled as Carolus Linnaeus), who lived in Uppsala.

Opposite the cathedral is the **Gustavianum** (daily 11am–4/5pm; mid-Sept to mid-May closed Mon; 40kr), built in 1625 as part of the university, and much touted for its tidily preserved anatomical theatre. The same building houses a couple of small collections of Egyptian, Classical and Nordic antiquities and the **Uppsala University Museum**, which contains the glorious Augsburg Art Cabinet, an ebony treasure chest presented to Gustav II Adolf. The **Castle** (June–Aug Mon–Fri daily noon–4pm, Sat & Sun 11am/5pm; 60kr) has recently been made open to the public – a 1702 fire that destroyed three-quarters of the city did away with all but one side and two towers of this opulent palace. Now you can wander around the excavations and peruse the waxworks in authentic costumes.

Practicalities

Uppsala's **train** and **bus stations** are adjacent to each other, not far from the **tourist office** (Mon–Fri 10am–6pm, Sat 10am–3pm; July to mid-Aug also Sun noon–4pm; ☎018/27 48 00, ⊛www.res.till.uppland.nu), Fyris Torg 8, which hands out an English guide to the town with a map inside. The beautifully sited official HI **hostel** is 6km south at Sunnerstavägen 24 (☎018/32 42 20; ❸) – take bus #20, #25 or #50 from Stora Torget. For a central **hotel** try *Basic*, Kungsgatan 27 (☎018/480 50 00, ⊛www.basichotel.com; ❹), with bright, clean rooms and weekend reductions. For **camping** as well as two- to four-berth cabins (250–400kr a night), *Sunnersta Camping* (☎018/27 60 84) is at a site 7km out by Lake Mälaren at Graneberg; take bus #20, #22 or #50 from the centre.

It's difficult to beat **lunch** at *Sten Sture & Co.*, a large wooden house immediately below the castle off Nedre Slottsgatan, with a good range of meat-based dishes during the day and live bands in the evening. The best **cafés** are *Ofvandahls*, Sysslomansgatan 5, a student classic, but only fun for smokers, and *Güntherska*, Östra Ågatan 31, another favourite and strictly non-smoking. Also popular is the *Katalin and all that jazz* at Östra Station, behind the train station, which holds sporadic jazz nights. The best café of all, though, is *Wayne's Coffee*, Smedgränd 4, with vast windows looking out onto the street. There's a wide range of excellent **restaurants**, such as *Svenssons krog/bakficka*, Sysslomansgatan 15, the best place for fish dishes and traditional Swedish fare. During the summer, the outdoor café/bar *Lilla Helgonet*, right by the river at Eriks Torg, is a popular spot.

Gamla Uppsala

Five kilometres north of town, three huge **barrows**, atmospheric royal burial mounds dating back to the sixth century, mark the original site of Uppsala,

GAMLA UPPSALA – reached on frequent buses #2, #20, #24 or #54 from Stora Torget. This was a pagan settlement and a place of ancient sacrificial rites: every ninth year a festival demanded the death of nine men, hanged from a nearby tree until their corpses rotted. The pagan temple where this took place is marked by the Christian **Gamla Uppsala Kyrka** (daily 9am–4/6pm), built when the Swedish kings first took baptism in the new faith. Look in for the faded wall paintings and the tomb of Celsius. The worthwhile **Historical Centre** (May–Aug daily 11am–5pm; Sept–April Sun noon–3pm; ✪www.raa.se/gamlauppsala; 50kr) explains the origin of local myths from Roman times and Uppsala's era of greatness until the thirteenth century.

Southern Sweden

Southern Sweden is a nest of coastal provinces, extensive lake and forest regions, gracefully ageing cities and superb beaches. Much of the area, especially the south-west coast, is the target of Swedish holiday-makers, with a wealth of campsites and cycle tracks, yet retaining a sense of space and tranquillity as well as plenty of historical and cultural high points. The grandest coastal city is **Gothenburg**, Sweden's charming second city and well deserving of far more exploration beyond its gargantuan shipyards than the traditional post-ferry exodus allows.

South of here, **Helsingborg**, a stone's throw from Denmark, and **Malmö**, still solidly sixteenth century at its centre, are both worth a day or two each for their charismatic charms, and **Lund**, a medieval cathedral and university town, is a convenient and enjoyable point between the two.

Gothenburg

Although **GOTHENBURG** is Scandinavia's largest port, shipbuilding has long since taken a back seat to ferry arrivals – those from Newcastle alongside the dock-strewn river, and those from Denmark right in the centre of the port and shipyards. Beyond the shipyards, Gothenburg is the prettiest of Sweden's cities, with broad avenues split and ringed by an elegant seventeenth-century, Dutch-designed canal system.

Arrival and information

You're likely to arrive in Gothenburg by **ferry**. DFDS ferries from England dock at Frihamnen, opposite the Opera House. Trams #2 and #5 will trundle you from here to the centre in around ten minutes. Other arrival points are strung out along the docks. Stena Line ferries from Frederikshavn in Denmark dock within twenty minutes' walk of the centre, the Kiel ferries another ten minutes away (3km from the centre in all). Trams #3 and #9 run past both to the centre. **Trains** arrive at Central Station on Drottningtorget. **Buses** from all destinations use Nils Ericsonsplatsen bus terminal. The **airport** is 25km east of the city, linked with the centre by buses running every fifteen minutes from Gate 21 in Nils Ericsonsplatsen (20min; 45kr).

Gothenburg has two **tourist offices**: a kiosk in Nordstan, the shopping centre next to Central Station (Mon–Fri 9.30am–6pm, Sat 10am–4pm, Sun noon–3pm) and a main office on the canal front at Kungsportsplatsen 2 (June–Aug daily 9am–6/8pm; rest of year Mon–Fri 9am–5/6pm; ✪www.goteborg.com). They sell the **Gothenburg Card**, giving unlimited bus and tram travel, free or half-price museum entry and other concessions, including a free boat trip to Elfsborgs fortress and free entry to the Liseberg amusement park, though not the rides there. The card is valid for 24 hours and costs 95kr. Gothenburg is perhaps the most immediately attractive Swedish city around which to **walk**, though you may well use the **public transport** system of trams and buses. Each city journey costs 16kr for

GOTHENBURG

Landvetter Airport ▲

Liseberg

Museum of Ethnography & Scandinavium

Gamla Ulevi Stadium

Lorensburg Theatre

Konstmuseet

Museum of Theatre History

Library

Concert House

Nordstan Shopping Centre ℹ and Forex (Money Exchange)

Forex — (Money Exchange)

Central Station

Train Station

Bus Station (to all destinations)

Palm House

Trädgårdsföreningen

Great Synagogue

Heden Bus Terminal

Forex

Röhsska Museum

VASATAN

Copper Mare (Monument)

Kungsparken

ℹ

Uttiken

Boats to Elfsborg Fortress

LILLE BOMMEN

STORG

Maritima Centrum

Opera House

Kronhusbodarna & Kronhuset

Rådhus.

Stadmuseum

Stora Antikhallarna

Domkyrkan

Saluhall (Market)

HAGA

Feskekörkan ('Fish Church')

Skansparken

Skansen Kronan

LINNE

Stena Line Terminal

Slottskogens Youth Hostel

Stenpiren

Docks

Göta River

N

0   500 m

1032

Frederikshavn ▼

adults, though it's cheaper to buy a ten-trip Rabattkort for 120kr. Tickets can be bought from the driver, but are cheaper from *Tidpunkten* and *Pressbyrån* kiosks around the city. Just get on and punch "2" for city rides and "BYTE" if you are continuing on another bus or tram. **Night time** bus/tram tickets are double the daytime rates. **Taxi** rides (℡031/65 00 00) within the city centre cost around 70kr, and there are 20-percent discounts for women travelling at night, but check with the driver first.

Accommodation

Of the **hostels**, the most central and best appointed is the excellent *Slottsskogen*, Vegagatan 21 (℡031/42 65 20, ✆www.slottsskogenvh.se; ❷), two minutes' walk from Linnégatan – take tram #1 or #2 to Olivedahlsgatan. Another fine option, and well placed for ferries to Denmark, is *Stigbergsliden*, Stigbergsliden 10 (℡031/24 16 20, ✆www.hostel-gothenburg.com; ❷). If you want something a little more peaceful try *Kvibergs*, Kvibergsvägen 5 (℡031/43 50 55, ✆www.vandrarhem.com; ❷), housed in an old barracks building and close to Gothenburg's largest weekend fleamarket – take tram #6 or #7 to Kviberg. If it's vital to stay right in the middle of things, take advantage of the tourist office's special **hotel deal**, called the **Gothenburg package** (from 390kr/person), which gets you a room in a central hotel, with breakfast and a free Gothenburg Card. The package operates every weekend from early June to August, though some hotels extend this limit. If this is beyond your budget, the tourist office can book **private rooms** for around 175kr a head. Alternatively, try the friendly *Lilton*, Föreningsgatan 9 (℡031/82 88 08, ✆www.hotellilton.se; ❸), in a charming old house tucked away close to the Haga area and offering a homely atmosphere. For character and great location, opt for the 1907 sailing ship *Barken Viking*, Gullbergskajen (℡031/63 58 00, ✆barken.viking@liseberg.se; ❹), moored outside the Opera House on the river and very comfortable.

The all-year *Kärralunds* **campsite** (✆www.liseberg.se; 140kr/pitch) is 4km out (tram #5 to Welandergatan) and has four-bed cabins from 600kr and an attached **hostel** (℡031/84 02 00; ❷).

The City

King Gustav II Adolf, looking for western trade, founded Gothenburg in the early seventeenth century as a response to the high tolls charged by the Danes for using the narrow sound between the two countries. As a Calvinist and businessman, Gustav much admired Dutch merchants, inviting them to trade and live in Gothenburg, and it's their influence that shaped the city, parts of which have an oddly Dutch feel. The area defined by the central canal represents what's left of old Gothenburg, centring on **Gustav Adolfs Torg**, a windswept square flanked by the nineteenth-century **Börshuset** (Exchange Building), and the fine **Rådhus**, originally built in 1672. Around the corner, the **Kronhuset**, off Kronhusgatan, built in 1643, is a typical seventeenth-century Dutch construction, and looks like the backdrop to a Vermeer. The cobbled courtyard outside is flanked by the mid-eighteenth-century **Kronhusbodarna** (Mon–Fri 11am–4pm, Sat 11am–2pm), now togged up as period craft shops selling sweets and souvenirs.

The **Stadsmuseum**, Norra Hamngatan 12 (daily 10am–5pm; 40kr), is worth a visit for its rich collection of archeological, cultural and industrial exhibits. Close by, the **Maritima Centrum** (March–Nov daily 10am–4/9pm; 50kr) allows you to clamber aboard a destroyer and submarine moored at the quayside. It is worth coming down here just to look at the shipyards beyond, like a rusting Meccano set put into sharp perspective by the striking **Opera House** (daily noon–6pm; ℡031/10 82 03; tickets from 50kr), a graceful and imaginative ship-like structure.

Crossing the canal from Kungsportsplatsen and running all the way up to Götaplatsen, Kungsportsavenyn is Gothenburg's showiest thoroughfare. Known simply as **Avenyn**, this wide strip was once flanked by private houses fronted by gardens and is now lined with overpriced, posey yet popular pavement restaurants and brasseries. About halfway down, the excellent **Röhsska Museum of Arts and Crafts** at Vasagatan 37–39 (Tues–Sun noon–5pm, Tues till 9pm; 40kr), celebrates Swedish design through the ages, among other things. At the top end, **Götaplatsen** is the modern cultural centre of Gothenburg, home to a concert hall, theatre and **Art Museum** (daily 11am–5/6pm, Wed till 9pm; 40kr), whose enormous collections include a good selection of Impressionist paintings, Pop Art and – most impressively – superb Swedish work in the Furstenburg galleries on the sixth floor. Just a few minutes' walk to the west from Avenyn, the old working-class district of **Haga** is now a picturesque area of gentrified chic with plenty of daytime cafés and boutiques, while **Linnégatan**, a few steps further, is a more charismatic and cosmopolitan version of Avenyn with the most diverse places to eat, drink and stroll. Just five minutes' walk southeast of Götaplatsen, on the edge of the centre, is **Liseberg**, a surprisingly aesthetic amusement park (late April to late Aug daily noon/3–11pm; Sept Sat 1–11pm, Sun noon–8pm; 50kr) with some high-profile rides and acres of gardens, restaurants and fast food. In the opposite direction, great views of the harbour and surrounding area can be had from the excursion boats that run from Lilla Bommen to the **Nya Elfsborg Fortress** (early May to mid-Aug daily 9.30am–3pm; 70kr, including guided tour of fortress), a seventeenth-century island defence guarding the harbour entrance, whose surviving buildings have been turned into a museum and café.

Eating and drinking

There's no shortage of places to **eat** in Gothenburg, and the city's range of ethnic restaurants is particularly good, reflecting its trading past. For **picnic food**, Saluhallen, the indoor market in Kungstorget, is tempting beyond words, and houses the two cheapest snack bars in town. In Linne, *Saluhall Briggen*, Tredje Långgatan, is smaller but brimming with mouthwatering fish, cheeses and cheap cafés. Many of the glitziest places to **eat** flank Avenyn, though with the exception of *Junggrens Café* at no. 37 – a Gothenburg institution – they are generally samey, packed and overpriced; less obvious, and usually cheaper, places can be found in the streets clustered on Haga Nygatan: the cheapest, offering filling lunches, is *Café Kringlan*, Haga Nygatan 13. For friendly, laid-back atmosphere try *Café Engelen* and *Tintin Café*, just a few steps from each other on Engelbrecktsgatan, off Avenyn – both are open round the clock. Another good choice is *Cyrano*, Prinsgatan 7 (℡031/14 31 10), an authentic Provençal bistro. For **vegetarian** and vegan meals, the classic place is *Solrosen*, Kaponjärgatan 4a in Haga district, which turns into a lively drinking venue at night.

There's an excellent choice of places to **drink**, some staying open well into the small hours. Avenyn is the focal point of much of night-time Gothenburg. At the junction of Avenyn and Kristinelundsgatan, *Java Café*, at Vasagatan 23, is a studenty coffee house with a Parisian feel. *Napoleon* at Vasagatan 11 has a lovely, mellow interior and is set in a fabulous old house with exterior wall paintings. *Greta's*, Drottninggatan 35, is a stylish yet casual bar/restaurant, very popular as a **gay** venue and also serving good food. There's live music at the *Auld Dubliner* at Ostra Hamngatan 50b, which claims to have been established in 1870 and serves Guinness and whisky. *Nefertiti*, Hvitfeldtsplatsen 6, is one of the best places to see live jazz and world **music**. The city's large student community means lots of local **live bands**. The best place to hear them is at *Kompaniet*, Kungsgatan, which has a bar on the top floor and dancing downstairs.

Listings

Exchange Forex exchange office inside Central Station and at Avenyn 22.
Pharmacy Apoteket Vasen, Götagatan 10

℡031/80 44 10, in the Nordstan shopping centre, is open till 10pm daily.
Post office Main office in Nordstan.

Helsingborg

At **HELSINGBORG** only a narrow sound separates Sweden from Denmark; indeed, Helsingborg was Danish for most of the Middle Ages, with a castle controlling the southern regions of what is now Sweden. The town's enormously important strategic position meant that it bore the brunt of repeated attacks and rebellions, the Swedes conquering the town on six separate occasions, only to lose it back to the Danes each time. Finally, in 1710, a terrible battle saw off the Danes for the last time, and the battered town lay dormant for almost two hundred years, depopulated and abandoned. Only in the nineteenth century, when the harbour was expanded and the railway constructed, did Helsingborg find new prosperity.

Today, the dramatically redeveloped harbour area has breathed new life into this likeable, relaxed town. Directly south of the the the North Harbour café/bars, the strikingly designed **Henry Dunker Cultural House**, named after the city's foremost industrialist benefactor, is due to open as we go to press, and aims to provide a full vision of the city's history in context. East from Hamntorget and the harbours, the massive, neo-Gothic **Rådhus** marks the bottom of **Stortorget**, the long thin square sloping up to the lower battlements of what's left of Helsingborg's castle, the **kärnan** or keep (daily: April–Sept 9/10am–4/7pm; Oct–March 10am–2pm; 15kr), a fourteenth-century brick tower, the only survivor from the original fortress. The views from the top are worth the entrance fee although you don't miss much from the lower (free) battlements. Off Stortorget, **Norra Storgatan** contains Helsingborg's oldest buildings, attractive seventeenth- and eighteenth-century merchants' houses with quiet courtyards.

Apart from the Sundbussarna passenger ferry to Helsingør, which pulls up across an arm of the docks, all **ferries**, **trains** and **buses** arrive at Knutpunkten, the harbourside **central terminal**. It's just a couple of minutes' walk from here up Stortorget to the **tourist office** at Södra Storgatan 1 (Mon–Fri 9am–6/8pm, Sat 9/10am–2/5pm; June–Aug also Sun 9am–5pm; ☎042/10 43 50, ⊕www.visit.helsingborg.se), which has free city maps and books **private rooms** at 125kr per person. Otherwise, the cheapest of the central **hotels** is *Linnea*, Prästgatan 4 (☎042/21 46 60; ❸), which drops prices in summer and at weekends. The *Villa Thalassa* **hostel** (☎042/21 03 84; ❷; bus #7, or #44 after 7pm) is 4km north along Drottninggatan. For **camping**, try the waterfront site at Kustgatan Råå, 5km southeast; bus #1A or #1B from outside the Rådhus.

You shouldn't have any difficulty finding somewhere to eat. Daytime **cafés** include the classic *Fahlmans* on Stortorget and the charismatic *Ebba's Fik*, Bruksgatan 20, decked out with authentic 1950s memorabilia. There are plenty of harbour-front bars. The cheapest **restaurant** is the unglamorous *Graffitti* on the first floor at Knutpunkten.

There are several good **clubs**, including Sweden's biggest jazz club, *Jazz Klubben*, Nedre Långvinkelsgatan 22 (Wed, Fri & Sat), and the noisy, popular *Tivoli* club, Hamntorget 11, where you can get down to the very latest sounds for a 65kr entrance.

Lund

Just forty minutes south of Helsingborg and fifteen minutes from Malmö, **LUND** is the most obvious target for a trip, a beautiful university town with a picturesque medieval centre and a unique buzz thanks to the student population. This does mean, though, that the life drains out of the place during the summer when the students are on vacation. Its weather-beaten **Domkyrkan** (Mon–Fri 8am–6pm, Sat & Sun 9.30am–5pm), consecrated in 1145, is considered by many to be Scandinavia's finest medieval building. Its plain interior culminates in a delicate, semicircular apse with a gleaming fifteenth-century altarpiece and a mosaic of Christ surrounded by angels – although what draws most attention is a fourteenth-century astronomical clock, revealing an ecclesiastical Punch and Judy show daily at noon and 3pm.

Outside the cathedral, **Kyrkogatan**, lined with staunch, solid, nineteenth-century civic buildings, leads into the main square, **Stortorget**, off which **Kattesund** is home to a glassed-in set of excavated medieval walls. Adjacent is the **Drottens Kyrkoruin** (Tues–Fri & Sun 9am–4pm, Sat 10am–2pm; 10kr), the remains of a medieval church in the basement of another modern building, but the real interest is in the powerful atmosphere of the old streets behind the Domkyrkan. In this web of streets, **Kulturen** (daily 11am/noon–4/5pm; Oct to mid-April closed Tues; 40kr) is a village in itself of indoor and open-air collections of southern Swedish art, silverware, ceramics, musical instruments, etc. Worth a visit at Finngatan 2 is **Skissernas Museum** (Tues–Sat noon–4pm, Sun 1–5pm; exhibitions 30kr) – though renovations may involve temporary closure. Inside the museum is an amazing collection of models, maquettes and sketches of internationally renowned works from Chagall to Matisse, Picasso to Henry Moore. Finish off your meanderings with a visit to the **Botaniska Trädgård** (daily 6am–8pm) just beyond, an extensive botanical garden.

Trains arrive on the western edge of town, an easy walk from the centre. The **tourist office** is opposite the Domkyrkan at Kyrkogatan 11, and is well signposted from the train station (June–Aug Mon–Fri 10am–6pm, Sat & Sun 10am–2pm; rest of year Mon–Fri 10am–5pm; ☎046/ 35 50 40, ✆www.lund.se/english). **Internet access** is available at the city library, St Petri Kyrkogata 6.

Lund makes an appealing alternative stopover to Malmö or Helsingborg by virtue of private rooms which the tourist office can book for 175kr. Its unusual **hostel**, Tåget, Vävaregatan 22 (☎046/14 28 20; ❶), packs you into three-tiered sleeping compartments of six 1940s carriages parked on a branch line behind the train station; turn right and follow the signs. For a good-value central **hotel**, check into *Ahlström*, Skomakaregatan 3 (☎046/211 01 74; ❸; closed June–Aug), or *Hotel Överliggaren*, Bytaregatan 14 (☎046/15 72 30; ❸).

There are plenty of cheap places to **eat**. *Café Ariman*, attached to the Nordic Law Department on Kungsgatan, has been updated, but maintains its shabby, left-wing coffee house appeal with good, cheap, light food; while *Conditori Lundagård* on Kyrkogatan is the classic student café. *Fellini*, opposite the train station, is a popular Italian eatery. *Tegners*, next to the student union, serves really fine food at student prices. Lund's most popular meeting place is the *Stortorget* on Stortorget with a bar, restaurant and club. The best **club** is *Palladium*, Stora Södergatan 13, just south of Stortorget – it has a soul night on Thursdays, minimum age 20.

Malmö

The third largest city in Sweden, **MALMÖ**, won back for Sweden from Denmark by Karl X in the seventeenth century, was a handsome city then and is now, with a cobbled medieval core that has a lived-in, workaday feel worlds apart from the museum-piece quality of most other Swedish town centres. With the opening in 2000 of the **Øresund Link**, a sensational seventeen-kilometre-long road and rail bridge, Malmö really is the Swedish gateway from continental Europe, and after years in the doldrums, it is enjoying an economic revival.

Arrival, information and accommodation

Trains arrive at Central Station, including the local Pågatåg services (to and from Helsingborg and Lund; rail passes valid). The train station also has showers (20kr) and beds (5.30am–11pm; 15kr/hour). The main **bus terminal** is outside Central Station, in Centralplan, though buses from Stockholm, Helsingborg and Gothenburg arrive at Slussplan, east of Central Station, at the end of Norra Vallgatan.

The **tourist office** is inside the station (Mon–Fri 9am–5/8pm, Sat 9/10am–2/5pm; June–Aug also Sun 9am–5pm; ☎040/34 12 00, ✆www.malmo.se/turist). It stocks the handy *Malmö This Month* and sells the **Malmö Card** (150kr/day, 275Kr/two days, 400kr/three days), which gives free museum entry, free travel on city buses, free car parking in public places and discounts on restaurants and certain shops. For **internet** use, head for *Surfer's Paradise*, Amiralsgatan 14, or *Cyber Space*, Engelbrektsgatan 13a.

Malmö is one of the easier places in the south to find good, cheap **accommodation**. The tourist office sells the useful **Malmö Package**, providing a double room in a central **hotel**, breakfast and Malmö Card, for 410kr per person. Of the many hotels within the scheme, one comfortable option is the *Ibis Hotel Malmö City*, Citadellvägen 4 (☎040/23 96 05; ❸), which is far more pleasant than its drab 1950s office-block facade would suggest. There is just one HI **hostel**, the inconveniently placed *STF Vandrarhem*, Backavägen 18 (☎040/822 20; ❸; closed Christmas and New Year), 5km out – take bus #21A from Central Station. A better bet is *Bosse's Gäst och Företagsvåningar*, Södra Förstadsgatan 110B (☎040/32 62 50; ❷), a comfortable **B&B**, twenty minutes' walk south from the station or bus #17 to Södervarn. The nearest **campsite** is *Sibbarps Camping* (☎040/34 26 50) on Strandgatan; bus #82 from Central Station.

The City

Few places in Sweden are more enjoyable – or more conducive to a leisurely stroll – than Malmö, with its canals, parks and largely pedestrianized streets and squares. Most of the medieval centre was taken apart in the early sixteenth century to make way for **Stortorget**, a vast market square. It's as impressive today as it must have been when it first appeared, flanked on one side by the **Rådhus**, built in 1546 and covered with statuary and spiky accoutrements; there are tours of the well-preserved interior (check with the tourist office for times). **Södergatan**, Malmö's main pedestrianized shopping street, runs south from here towards the canal. Behind the Rådhus stands the **St Petri Kyrka** (daily 8/10am–6pm), a fine Gothic church with an impressively decorative pulpit and a four-tiered altarpiece. **Lilla Torget** is everyone's favourite part of the city – indeed, it's been voted the most popular square in Sweden. It's a late-sixteenth-century spin-off from an overcrowded Stortorget, usually full and doing a roaring trade from jewellery stalls and summer buskers. The southern side of the square is formed by a row of mid-nineteenth-century brick and timber warehouses; the shops around here sell books, antiques and gifts, though the best place to drop into is the nearby **Saluhallen**, an excellent indoor market. Further west still lie the **Kungsparken** and the **Malmöhus** (daily 10am/noon–4pm; 40kr), a low fortified castle defended by a wide moat, two circular keeps and grassy ramparts, raised by Danish king Christian III in 1536. For a time a prison (Bothwell, third husband of Mary, Queen of Scots, was the most notable inmate), the castle and its outbuildings now constitute a series of exhibitions including Malmö's main **museum**, though unfortunately with no information in English. The grounds, peppered with small lakes and an old windmill, are good for a stroll.

Eating, drinking and nightlife

The Saluhall on Landbygatan by Lilla Torget stocks a marvellous array of picnic supplies. For **lunch**, a delightful option is the quirky *Café Siesta*, Ostindiefararegatan – turn right at the western end of Landbygatan off Lilla Torget – a fun café serving filling sandwiches and home-made apple cake. *Bageri Café* at Saluhall (Mon–Fri 8am–6pm, Sat 10am–4pm) is excellent for filled baguettes and health foods. *Spot* **restaurant**, Stora Nygatan 33 (Mon–Fri 9am–6pm, Sat 10am–5pm), is a chic Italian and very good for cheese, fish and meat. A charming restaurant is *QD*, Erik Dahlbergsgatan 3 (☎040/12 83 71), an intimate place with an intriguing menu including vegetables in coconut and delicious meat dishes which aren't over-priced. For **drinking**, Lilla Torget swarms with bustling venues through the evening. *Gustav Adolf*, Gustav Adolfs Torg, is popular at weekends. The best place for occasional **live music** is *Matssons Musikpub*, Göran Olsgatan 1, behind the Rådhus. A twenty-minute walk south from the docks is Möllevångens Torget, where *Nyhavn* is one of the more appealing of the bar/pubs that are springing up all across the south city's trendy immigrant quarter. The best **gay club** is the long-established and friendly *Fyran* (Fri & Sat 11pm–3am; 70kr) at Snapperupsgatan 4.

Central and northern Sweden

In many ways, the long wedge of land that comprises **central and northern Sweden** – from the northern shores of Lake Vänern to the Finnish border – is Sweden as seen in the brochures – lakes, holiday cottages, forests and reindeer. On the eastern side, Sweden's coast forms one edge of the **Gulf of Bothnia**. With its jumble of erstwhile fishing towns and squeaky-clean contemporary urban planning, this corridor of land together with its regional town, **Sundsvall**, is worth stopping off in if you're travelling north or have just arrived from Finland by ferry. Though the weather isn't as reliable as further south, you are guaranteed clean beaches, crystal-clear waters and fine hiking. To the west, folklorish **Dalarna** county is the most picturesque region, with sweeping green countryside and inhabitants who maintain a cultural heritage (echoed in contemporary handicrafts and traditions) that goes back to the Middle Ages. This is *the* place to spend midsummer, particularly Midsummer's Night when the whole region erupts in celebration. The **Inlandsbanan**, the great Inland Railway, cuts right through this area from Lake Siljan through the modern lakeside town of **Östersund** to **Gällivare** above the Arctic Circle. An enthralling 1300-kilometre, two-day ride, it ranks with the best European train journeys.

Sundsvall

Known as the "Stone City", **SUNDSVALL** is immediately and obviously different. Once home to a rapidly expanding nineteenth-century sawmill industry, the whole city burned down in 1888 and a new centre built completely of stone emerged within ten years. The result is a living document of early-twentieth-century urban architecture, designed by architects who were engaged in rebuilding Stockholm's residential areas at the same time.

The materials are limestone and brick, the style simple and the size often overwhelming. The **Esplanaden**, a wide central avenue, cuts the grid in two, itself crossed by **Storgatan**, the widest street. The area around **Stortorget** is still the roomy commercial centre that was envisaged. Behind the mock-Baroque exterior of the **Sundsvall Museum** (Mon–Fri 10am–6/7pm, Sat & Sun 11am–4pm; June–Aug 20kr, otherwise free), four late nineteenth-century warehouses have been developed into a cultural complex called Kulturmagasinet devoted to art exhibits and city history. The **Gustav Adolfs Kyrkan** (daily 11am–2/4pm) – a soaring red-brick structure whose interior looks like a large Lego set – marks one end of the new town. To get the best perspective on the city's plan, climb to the heights of **Gaffelbyn** and the **Norra Bergets Hantverksmuseum** (Mon–Fri 9am–4pm; June–Aug also Sat & Sun 11am–4pm; free), an open-air crafts museum down Storgatan and over the main bridge.

From the **train station** the centre is five minutes' walk away, with the **tourist office** in the main Stortorget (Mon–Fri 10am–6pm, Sat 10am–2pm; ☎060/61 04 50, ✆info@sundsvallturism.com). The **bus station** is at the bottom of Esplanaden. The renovated **hostel** (☎060/61 21 19; 4–6pm; ❷) at Norra Berget takes about half an hour to walk to from the centre. The tourist office will help book accommodation for a 20kr fee, but does not book private rooms; otherwise, *Svea Hotel*, Rådhusgatan 11 (☎060/61 16 05; ❷), has the cheapest doubles in town. For **eating**, Storgatan is lined with restaurants, most offering daily lunch menus, while *La Spezia*, Sjögatan 6, has bargain pizzas from 35kr.

Dalarna

Dalarna holds a special, misty-eyed place in the Swedish heart and should certainly be seen, though not to the exclusion of points further north. **Lake Siljan**, at the heart of the province, is the major draw, its gentle surroundings, traditions and local handicrafts weaving a subtle spell. If you've only got time to see part of the lake, **MORA** is as good a place as any, and a starting point for the Inlandsbanan rail route (see below). At the northwestern corner of Lake Siljan, the little town is a showcase for the work of Anders Zorn, the Swedish painter who lived in Mora and whose work is exhibited in the **Zorn Museum**, Vasagatan 36 (Mon–Sat 9am–5pm, Sun 11am/1–5pm; 35kr), along with his small but well-chosen personal collection. Zorn's oils reflect a passion for Dalarna's pastoral lifestyle, but it's his earlier water-colours of southern Europe and North Africa that really stand out. The **tourist office** (Mon–Fri 9/10am–5/7pm, Sat 10am–1/5pm; mid-June to mid-Aug also Sun 10am–5pm; ☎0250/56 76 00, ✉mora@stab.se) is at Mora station, and the HI **hostel** at Fredsgatan 6 (☎0250/381 96, ✉info@maalkullann.se; ❷).

LEKSAND is perhaps the most popular and traditional of the Dalarna villages and certainly worth making the effort to reach at midsummer, when the festivals recall age-old maypole dances, the celebrations culminating in the **church boat races**, an aquatic procession of decorated longboats which the locals once rowed to church every Sunday. The **tourist office** in the train station building (Mon–Fri 9/10am–5/7pm, Sat 10am–1/5pm; mid-June to mid-Aug also Sun 10am–5pm; ☎0247/79 61 30, ✉leksand@stab.se) has lots of information on the area, as does the **hostel** (☎0247/152 50; ❶), 2km south of the centre at Parkgården.

The Inlandsbanan

The **Inlandsbanan** (Inland Railway; ☎020/53 53 53, ⊛www.inlandsbanan.se), linking central Sweden with Gällivare 1300km further north, is the most charismatic of Scandinavian rail routes, the trip everyone wants to make. Long under threat of closure, the line has been privatized and looks like surviving for the moment, but only operates between late June and early August. InterRail pass holders under the age of 26 travel for free while those over 26 pay full fare. With a Scanrail Pass there is a 25 percent discount on individual journeys, but you do get a 25 percent discount off an Inland Railway Card which otherwise costs 950kr and which offers unlimited travel on the line for fourteen days. The full fare, travelling second class from Mora to Östersund, a seven-hour trip, costs from 240kr, plus an optional 50kr seat reservation.

Mora to Östersund

The Inlandsbanan begins in Mora, making its first stop at **ORSA**, fifteen minutes up the line, where the nearby **Grönklitt bear park** (mid-May to mid-Sept daily 10am–3pm; 75kr) provides the best chance to see the bears that roam the countryside. The **hostel** at the park (☎0250/462 00; ❶) has fine facilities.

Several hours north of here, the line's halfway point is marked by **ÖSTERSUND**. It's a welcoming place, and its **Storsjön** – or Great Lake – gives it a holiday atmosphere unusual this far north. The lake is also alleged to be the home of a Loch Ness-style monster. In summer, you can make a tour of the lake on a **steamboat cruise**, stopping off on the small island of Verkön (check with tourist office for times; 95kr). Otherwise, the main thing to do in town is to visit **Jamtli** (late June to mid-Aug daily 11am–5pm; rest of year closed Mon; 90kr), an impressive open-air museum fifteen minutes' walk north from the centre along Rådhusgatan, full of volunteers milling around in traditional country costume encouraging visitors to join in baking, tree-felling and grass-cutting. On the way in, the **museum** (late June to mid-Aug daily 11am–5pm; rest of year closed Mon;

entry covered by the Jamtli ticket) proudly shows off the ninth-century **Överhog-dal tapestries**, whose simple handwoven patterns of horses, dogs and other beasts is quite breathtaking. It's also home to a small collection of monster-catching gear from the nineteenth century. Back in the centre, the town slopes steeply down to the water, and it's tiring work strolling the pedestrianized streets that run around Stortorget. From the **harbour** you can take the bridge over the lake to **Frösön** island, site of the original Viking settlement here.

The **tourist office** is at Rådhusgatan 44 (Mon–Fri 9am–5/9pm; June–Aug also Sat & Sun 9am–3/9pm; ☎063/14 40 01, ⓦwww.turist.ostersund.se) and sells the *Östersundskortet*, valid nine days (June to mid-Aug; 120kr), giving free access to the town's sights, half-price round-trip bus journeys (normally 90kr) and half-price on the steamboat cruise. For a central **hotel**, try either *Hotell Aston*, Köpmansgatan 40 (☎063/ 51 08 51; ❹), or the *Hotell Linden*, close to the train station at Storgatan 64 (☎063/51 73 35; ❹). The STF **hostel** in Östersund (☎063/13 91 00; ❷) is a ten-minute walk from the train station at Södra Gröngatan 32 in the town centre. More atmospheric is the **hostel** at Jamtli (☎063/12 20 60; ❸; take bus #2 to the end of the line) – although slightly more expensive, staying there saves on entrance fees to the museum. **Campers** can stay at either *Östersunds Camping*, 2km down Rådhusgatan (☎063/14 46 15), or on Frösön island at *Fröso Camping* (☎063/14 46 15; June to early Aug only; bus #3 or #4 from the centre). For **food**, try the young and trendy *Brunkullans* restaurant with its outdoor garden at Postgränd 5, or the daily specials at the Australian *Captain Cook,* Hamngatan 9 – cheaper than *Brunkullans*, with live entertainment on Wednesdays, and very popular for **drinking** too.

Storuman, Arvidsjaur and the Arctic Circle

Travelling on the Inlandsbanan, you may well spend the night at **STORUMAN**, five and a half hours north of Östersund and ten hours from Gällivare. The **tourist office** (Mon–Fri 9am–5/8pm; mid-June to mid-Aug also Sat & Sun 11am–5pm; ☎0951/105 00, ⓔentrelappland@swipnet.se) is just to the right of the train station, and will give you details of the excellent mountain hiking to be had around the town. There's a **hostel** in the same building as the tourist office (☎0951/777 00; ❷). **ARVIDSJAUR**, the next major stop on the Inlandsbanan, contains Sweden's oldest surviving Sámi village, dating from the late eighteenth century, a huddle of houses that was once the centre of a great winter market. They were not meant to be permanent homes, but rather a meeting place during festivals, and the last week-end in August is still taken up by a great celebratory shindig. There's a cosy private **hostel** at Västra Skolgatan 9 (☎0960/124 13; ❷), and *Camp Gielas*, beside one of the lakes 1km south of the station, has cabins from 375kr. Three and a half hours north of Arvidsjaur, the Inlandsbanan finally crosses the **Arctic Circle**, signalled by a bout of whistle-blowing as the train pulls up. Painted white rocks curve away over the hilly ground, a crude but popular representation of the Circle.

Jokkmokk

In the midst of remote, densely forested, marshy country, **JOKKMOKK** is a welcome oasis. Once wintertime Sámi quarters, the town is today a renowned handicraft centre, with a Sámi educational college keeping the language and culture alive. The **Ájtte Museum** (Mon–Fri 9/10–4/6pm; Sat & Sun 9am/noon–4/6pm; Oct–April closed Sat; 40kr) on Kyrkegatan is the place to see some of the intricate work. Have a glance, too, at the so-called **Lapp Kyrka**, enclosed by a wide wooden fence, in which corpses were interned during winter, waiting for the thaw when the Sámi could go out and dig graves. The great **winter market** still survives, now nearly 400 years old, held on the first Thursday, Friday and Saturday of each February, when 30,000 people gather in town. It's the best time to be in Jokkmokk, and staying means booking accommodation a good six months in advance. A smaller, less traditional autumn fair at the end of August is an easier though poorer option. The **tourist office** is at Stortorget 4 (mid-June to mid-Aug daily 9am–7pm; during winter market Thurs–Sun 8am–6pm; rest of year Thurs–Sat 8.30am–4pm; ☎0971 121 40, ⓦwww.turism.jokkmokk.se). In summer there should be no problem getting a place at the HI **hostel** at Åsgatan 20 (☎0971/559 77; ❷); just follow the signs from the station. The **campsite** is 3km east on route 97.

Gällivare

GÄLLIVARE, at the junction of the Inlandsbanan and the main line from Stockholm, is one of Europe's most important sources of iron ore, while Europe's largest open-cast copper mine sears the landscape 20km to the south. The tourist office ferries trips to the **iron ore mines** (June to Aug once daily; 200kr) and **copper mine** (June–Aug Mon–Fri 1.30pm; 160kr). Astounding statistics – 300 tonnes of high explosives are used for each blast – pepper the tour, which also takes in **Kåkstan**, a rebuilt shantytown on the site of the original iron ore mine; and you stop long enough to sample local delicacies like reindeer, salmon and lingonberry juice, all for 75kr at the teetotal *Café Endast för Nyktra*. Little remains of the seventeenth-century Sámi village, and the river and surrounding mountains are really the nicest feature of the town itself. You can walk up to **Björnfällan**, a four-kilometre hike on a well-marked path – the views are magnificent. Buses make the journey (200kr return) to the summit 3km north beyond Björnfällan to see the Midnight Sun daily between mid-June and mid-July. Departures are from the train station at 11pm, returning at 1am.

The **tourist office** is at Storgatan 16 (Mon–Fri 9am–4/6pm; June to mid-Aug also Sat & Sun 10am–5pm; ☎0970/166 60, ⓦwww.gellivare.se). Its long summer hours are aimed at late Inlandsbanan arrivals, and the office has a café downstairs and a museum upstairs dealing with Sámi history. The **hostel** (☎0970/143 80; ❶) is at Barnhemsvägen 2, behind the train station, and offers accommodation in small two-person cabins (no bed linen provided), though there are a few three- and four-bed cabins too. There's also a **hotel**, the *Hotell Dundret*, Per Högströmsgatan 1 (☎0970/550 40; ❹), close to the station. The **campsite** (☎0970/100 10) is by the river; for **snacks** or an evening coffee and cakes by the river, make for the *Strandcaféet* near the campsite at Malmbergsvägen 2. Otherwise a good choice is *Restaurang Peking* at Storgatan 21B, which dishes up the usual array of Chinese food.

Travel details

Trains

Gällivare to: Narvik (2 daily; 4hr 40min).
Gothenburg to: Copenhagen (2–3 daily; 4hr 20min); Helsingborg (6–9 daily; 2hr 40min); Kalmar (3–5 daily; 4hr 40min); Lund (6–9 daily; 3hr 30min); Malmö (8–12 daily; 3hr by X2000, 3hr 45min InterCity); Oslo (4 daily; 4hr 40min).
Malmö to: Helsingborg (at least hourly; 50min); Lund (at least hourly; 15min); Ystad (Mon–Fri hourly, Sat & Sun 4–6 daily; 50min).
Stockholm to: Gällivare (2 daily; 16hr); Gävle (hourly; 1hr 20min); Gothenburg (21 daily; 3hr 10min by X2000, 4hr 30min InterCity); Helsingborg (14 daily; 5hr by X2000, 6hr 30min InterCity); Kalmar, change at Alvesta (8 Mon–Sat, 3 Sun;

6hr); Lund (6 daily; 4hr 40min); Malmö (11 daily; 4hr 30 min by X2000; Mora (11 daily; 3hr 30min by X2000); Narvik (2 daily; 20hr); Östersund (6 daily; 6hr); Sundsvall (9 daily; 3hr 30min by X2000); Uppsala (half hourly; 40min).
Sundsvall to: Gävle (8 daily; 2hr 30min); Östersund (5 daily; 2hr 15min).
Uppsala to: Gävle (hourly; 40 min); Mora (11 daily; 2hr 15min by X2000).

Buses

Gothenburg to: Gävle (1–2 daily; 10hr); Kalmar (1 Fri, 1 Sun; 6hr 30min); Malmö (3 Fri, 3 Sun; 4hr 40min); Oslo (3–4 daily; 4hr 50min); Uppsala (1 Fri, 1 Sun; 8hr).

Stockholm to: Gävle (3 Fri, 1 Sat, 4 Sun; 2hr 20min); Gothenburg (2–5 daily; 4hr 30min, or 7hr 20min via Jönköping); Helsingborg (1 daily, 2 Fri & Sun; 8hr); Kalmar (2–5 daily; 6hr 30min); Malmö (1 Fri, 1 Sun; 10hr 20min); Nynäshamn (3 daily; 1hr); Oskarshamn (2–5 daily; 4hr 30min); Oslo (1 Fri, 1 Sun; 9hr); Sundsvall (3 Fri, 1 Sat, 4 Sun; 6hr); Uppsala (3 Fri, 1 Sat, 4 Sun; 1hr).

International ferries

Gothenburg to: Frederikshavn (4–8 daily; 3hr 15min); Newcastle (4 weekly; 24hr); Kiel (1 daily; 14hr).

Helsingborg to: Helsingor (3 hourly; 25min).

Malmö to: Copenhagen (every 30min; 40min).

Stockholm to: Helsinki (Helsingsfors), Finland (2 daily; 15hr); Tallinn (summer 1 daily plus 1 every 2 days; 15hr); Turku (Åbo), Finland (4 daily; 13hr).

Trelleborg to: Rostock (3 daily; 6hr); Travemünde (2 daily; 7–9hr).

Switzerland
and Liechtenstein

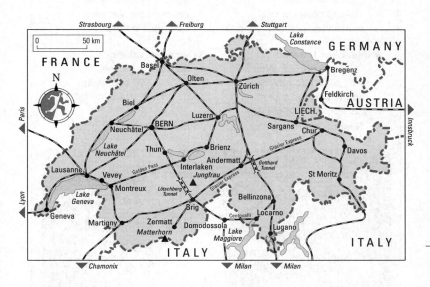

Switzerland highlights

✴ **Lausanne** Geneva's unsung neighbour, with bags of style, sass and lakeside charm. **See p.1053**

✴ **Lake Luzern** Take a cruise on Switzerland's most scenic lake, nestling between high peaks. **See p.1064**

✴ **Interlaken** Base for exploring the high Alps, with access to adventure sports plus the superb Schilthorn cable-car ride. **See p.1067**

✴ **The Matterhorn** The most famous mountain in the world, with guaranteed skiing and snowboarding year-round. **See p.1069**

✴ **World's highest bungee jump** A death-defying 220m off the Verzasca Dam. **See p.1072**

✴ **Centovalli railway** Narrow-gauge line offering a scenic back-country detour on a route to or from Milan. **See p.1072**

Introduction and basics

Switzerland is one of Europe's most visited countries, but one of its least understood. Pass through for a day or two, as most people do, and you'll get the quaint stereotype of Switzerland that the locals deem suitable for public consumption – the Alpine idyll of cheese and chocolate, Heidi and the Matterhorn. Stay longer though and another Switzerland will emerge, the one which the Swiss inhabit, and one which can be an infinitely more rewarding place to explore. Sights are breathtaking, transport links are excellent, costs are no higher than in Britain or Germany, and the locals are unfailingly courteous. Almost everyone speaks some English along with at least one of the official Swiss languages (German, French, Italian, and, in the southeast, Romansh).

Notoriously placid these days, Switzerland nonetheless spent the first 500 years of its existence rent by conflict, and fought a civil war as recently as 1847. The Swiss Confederation (abbreviated to "**CH**") dates back to 1291, when Alpine peasants formed an alliance to defend themselves against the Habsburgs. By the early 1500s, the Confederation had grown into a military superpower feared throughout Europe. It was only with the Reformation that the Swiss began to earn their reputation for neutrality, a reputation which served them well right through to the boom years after World War II. In the 1990s, the country's image was tainted, as exposés uncovered Swiss banks' dubious wartime collusion with the Nazis. Public soul-searching in the aftermath of the scandal is heralding Switzerland's first tentative steps towards ending its dogged isolation and joining the EU and the UN.

As for where to go, Switzerland invented tourism: the country's breathtaking scenery has drawn travellers since the early 1800s. The most visited Alpine area is the central **Bernese Oberland**, which has the highest concentration of picturesque peaks and mountainside villages, although the loftiest Alps are further south, where the small but crowded resort of **Zermatt** provides access to the country's most distinctive mountain, the Toblerone-peaked **Matterhorn**. In the southeastern corner of the country, wild, thickly forested mountain slopes provide the setting for the world-famous resort of **St Moritz**. Of the northern German-speaking cities, Zürich has a wealth of sightseeing and nightlife possibilities and provides easy access to the tiny independent principality of **Liechtenstein** overlooking the Rhine. **Basel** and especially the capital **Bern** are quieter, each with an attractive historic core, while **Luzern** is in an appealing setting close to lakes and mountains. In the French-speaking west, the cities lining the northern shore of Lake Geneva –notably **Geneva** itself, and **Lausanne** –make up the heart of **Suisse-Romande**. South of the Alps, sunny, Italian-speaking **Ticino** can seem a world apart from the rest of the country, particularly the palm-fringed lakeside resorts of **Lugano** and **Locarno**, with their Mediterranean, riviera atmosphere.

Information and maps

Almost all towns have a **tourist office** (*Verkehrsverein or Tourismus; Office du*

Switzerland and Liechtenstein on the net

ⓦ**www.myswitzerland.com** Tourist office portal
ⓦ**www.rail.ch** Train information
ⓦ**www.post.ch** Bus information
ⓦ**www.museums.ch** Information on Swiss museums
ⓦ**www.swissinfo.org** News database
ⓦ**www.tourismus.li** Tourist information about Liechtenstein

Tourisme; *Ente Turistico*), invariably located near the train station and always extremely useful. Most staff speak English and are scrupulously helpful, but **opening hours** in smaller towns allow for a long lunch and can be limited at weekends and in the off-season. All of them have lists of local accommodation and transport information, and provide local and regional **maps**. The Federal Office of Topography (*www.swisstopo.ch*) has excellent 1:50,000 and 1:25,000 walkers' maps.

Money and banks

The **currency** of Switzerland and Liechtenstein is the Swiss franc (Sfr). Each franc is divided into 100 Rappen (Rp), centimes or centisimi (c). There are coins of 5c, 10c, 20c, 50c, Sfr1, Sfr2 and Sfr5, and notes of Sfr10, Sfr20, Sfr50, Sfr100, Sfr200 and Sfr1000. Train stations are the best places for **changing money**; almost all have a commission-free change counter that is open long hours. You can also change money at **banks**, which are usually open Mon–Fri 8.30am–4.30pm (small-town branches often close noon–2pm). Some city and tourist-resort banks also open Sat 9am–4pm, although times vary. Post offices give a similar exchange rate to banks, and **ATMs** are everywhere.

Communications

Post offices tend to open Mon–Fri 7.30am–noon & 1.30–6.30pm, Sat 8–11am,

although watch out for regional variations and restricted hours in smaller branches. Public **phones** are operated by Swisscom; a few still accept coins, but the majority take only phonecards (*taxcards*), available from post offices, newsagents and vending machines in Sfr5, Sfr10 and Sfr20 denominations. Phones that take phonecards also accept credit cards. Many news kiosks and train stations also sell good-value cards from other companies (such as diAx) for calling internationally. The expensive **operator** is on ☎111 (domestic) and ☎1141 (international); directory enquiries is on ☎111. You can use Swisscom phonecards in Liechtenstein.

For **internet access**, there are cybercafés in all towns (Sfr8–20/hr), and you'll also find access at some hostels, main train stations and for free at the airports. You can send a short email from the screens in all phone-booths for Sfr0.90, but you can't pick up any email this way. The same screens let you send an SMS text message to any mobile phone for Sfr0.90.

Getting around

The efficiency of the massively comprehensive Swiss **public transport** system remains one of the wonders of the modern world. Services depart on the dot, and train timetables are well integrated with those of the postbus system, which operates on rural routes not covered by trains. Main stations keep a public copy of the **national timetable**, which covers all rail, bus, boat and cable-car services.

Adventure sports

With its landscape of mountains, glaciers, deep gorges and fast-flowing rivers, Switzerland is ideal territory for **adventure sports**. Dozens of companies, based in all the main resorts, offer thrill-making schemes galore through the summer – choose from **canyoning** (Sfr100/half-day), **river-rafting** (Sfr100/half-day), **bungee-jumping** (Sfr80/100m; Sfr220/180m), **zorbing** (where you're strapped inside a giant plastic sphere and rolled down a mountainside; Sfr50), **house-running** (where you hook a rope round yourself and run full-tilt down the side of a tall building; Sfr70), **flying fox** (where you glide down a vertical cliff on a rope; Sfr75); and, of course, **hang-gliding** (Sfr130), **paragliding** (Sfr170) and **skydiving** from 4000m (Sfr400), which can all be done alone or in tandem with an instructor. Interlaken and Luzern are two popular centres; for full details, check with the local tourist office.

Trains and buses

Travelling through Switzerland by **train** is invariably comfortable, hassle-free and extremely scenic, with many mountain routes an attraction in their own right. The main network, run by SBB CFF FFS (*Schweizerische Bundesbahnen, Chemins de Fer Fédéraux, Ferrovie Federali Svizzere*), covers much of the country, but many routes, especially Alpine lines, are operated by the smaller companies which pioneered them a century or more ago. **Buses** take over where train track runs out. These are generally yellow postbuses (⊛ www.post.ch), which depart from train-station forecourts.

InterRail (also EuroDomino) and **Eurail** passes are vaild on SBB and most smaller lines, but the discounts they bring are patchy on boats, cable cars and mountain railways (specified in the text as IR for InterRail and ER for Eurail). Postbuses are free to holders of all **Swiss passes** (see p.29) – although certain Alpine routes command a Sfr5–10 supplement, along with advance seat reservation) – but not to Eurail and InterRail pass holders.

Boats

All of Switzerland's bigger lakes are crossed by **ferry** services of one sort or another. Most run only during the summer season (June–Sept), and duplicate routes which can be covered more cheaply and quickly by rail. But if you have the time, cruising through the Alpine foothills to Interlaken or between villages on the Lake Geneva shoreline beats the equivalent train journeys hands down.

Accommodation

Accommodation is expensive, but nearly always excellent. Tourist offices can generally book rooms for free in their area, and they normally have a display-board on the street with details of the region's hotels, often with a courtesy phone. In many cases you'll find these boards at train stations. When you check in, you should always ask for a guest card (*Göstekarte, carte des visiteurs, tessera di soggiorno*): these can give substantial discounts on local attractions and transport.

Hotels

Just about every Swiss settlement offers a choice of **hotels**, where accommodation is of a uniformly high standard, and not excessively expensive. The Swiss Hotel Association (⊛ www.swisshotels.ch) has a list of approved establishments, and occasional offers. Double rooms with a shared shower and toilet can cost as little as Sfr85, though a more usual average is Sfr110. Ensuite hotel rooms cost from around Sfr135.

Hostels and campsites

If you're travelling on a budget, a **hostel** (*Jugend-herberge; Auberge de Jeunesse; Albergo/Ostello per la Giovent'*) is likely to be your accommodation of choice; Switzerland has an extensive network, with most places offering very good value. You should definitely book ahead between June and September. **HI hostels** (⊛ www.youthhostel.ch) are of a universally high standard and feature a good proportion of double rooms as well as small dorms. Prices range from Sfr19 to Sfr40; the average is Sfr25 for a dorm bed including breakfast and bedding. Non-HI members pay Sfr5 extra. Note that under-25s are given priority and that there's usually a three-night maximum stay during summer in the towns. Meals, where available, are around Sfr10. A rival group known as **Swiss Backpackers** (⊛ www.backpacker.ch) has lively hostels that are less institutional, often in prime locations in the town and city centres, and are priced to compete; they're specified in the text as "**SB**". Outside the towns and cities, **Naturfreunde hostels**

are a good budget option, located in wilder areas well off any beaten tracks (🌐www .naturfreunde.ch).

The typical Swiss **campsite** is clean and well equipped, although the higher the altitude the more limited the opening times; many close altogether outside the summer season (June–Sept). Prices tend to be around Sfr8 per person plus Sfr8–12 per pitch and per vehicle. Many sites require an international camping carnet. Camping outside official sites is against the law. For those hiking in the mountains there's a network of **Swiss Alpine Club** huts, where dorm beds cost around Sfr30 per night (🌐www .sac-cas.ch).

Food and drink

Food and drink can inflict a fairly massive hole in your budget if you're not careful. Prices are high across the board, although by combining a judicious choice of eateries with forays into picnicking and self-catering you can survive on a tight budget without any compromise on nutrition.

Food

Dairy products find their way into most Swiss dishes. All but a handful of places offer **vegetarian** set menus, but veggies should be aware that most restaurants default onto standard meat-based dishes: fresh salads may come layered with cold meats. Co-operative-run diners, many located in squats in the major cities, offer budget vegetarian and vegan meals as standard.

Burgers, pizza slices, kebabs and falafels are universal **snack** standbys. You'll also find various different kinds of **sausage**; the most popular are pork *Bratwürste*. Cheese **fondue** – a pot of wine-laced molten cheese into which you dip cubes of bread or potato – is the national dish. It's usually priced as a two-person (or more) deal, or as an all-you-can-eat deal (à *discrétion* or à *gogo*). Another speciality is **raclette** – piquant molten cheese is spread on a plate and scooped up with bread or potato. A Swiss-German staple is **Rösti**, grated potatoes

fried to a golden-brown hash and often topped with cheese, chopped ham or a fried egg.

The line between a **café** and a **restaurant** is blurred: both serve meals, although usually at set times (noon–2pm & 6–10pm), with only snacks available in between. To get the best value, make lunch your main meal, and always plump for the dish of the day (*Tagesmenu*, *Tagesteller*, *Tageshit*; *plat/assiette du jour*; *piatto del giorno*) – good, substantial nosh for Sfr15 or less. The same meal in the evening, or choosing à *la carte* anytime, can cost double. **Department stores** have surprisingly good self-service diners attached, where pick-and-choose meals can be just Sfr13. Most also let you pay Sfr6/10 for a small/large plate, with no limit on the quantity of fresh salad or hot daily special you can pile onto it, and some offer a twenty-percent discount to students.

Drink

Cafés are open from breakfast till midnight/1am and often sell alcohol; **bars** and **pubs** tend to open their doors for late-afternoon and evening business only. Daytime places for tea and cakes are dubbed **tearooms**. Table service is ubiquitous, except at the English or Irish pubs gracing most towns.

Beers vary from region to region but are invariably excellent, costing Sfr3–4 for a third of a litre. Even the simplest bars and restaurants have **wine**, most affordably as *Offene Wein*, *vin ouvert*, *vino aperto*, a handful of house reds and whites chalked up on a board (small glass Sfr3–5). Premier Swiss wines are the Valais whites (*Fendant*) and reds (*Dôle*). Also look out for local **spirits/liquors** (*Schnapps*, *eau-de-vie*, *aquavite*), including cherry **Kirsch**, aromatic pear **Williamine**, and Ticinese **grappa**.

Opening hours and holidays

Shop hours are Mon–Fri 9am–noon & 2–6.30pm, Sat 8.30am–noon, although it's becoming common in the cities to ignore the lunch break and stay open on Saturday until

4pm; the flipside is that many places close for Monday morning. Most shops now have one day of late-opening, often Thurs till 9pm; those in the subterranean malls at train stations are open daily, and close later. Most big-city stations also have 24-hour vending machines dispensing loaves of bread, cheese and cartons of milk. **Museums** and attractions are often open on Sundays, but generally closed on Mondays.

Almost everything is closed on the following **public holidays**: Jan 1; Good Fri & Easter Mon; Ascension Day; Whit Mon; Dec 25 & 26. In **Switzerland**, shops and banks tend to close for all or part of Swiss National Day (Aug 1) and on a range of local holidays as well. As well as the above, **Liechtenstein** keeps May 1 as a public holiday, and Aug 15 as the national holiday.

Emergencies

The Swiss are scrupulously law-abiding, rendering even the minimal **police** presence superfluous.

Regarding **health** problems, the E111 is valid in Liechtenstein, but not in Switzerland, so you must have private insurance. Virtually every **hospital** (*Spital*, *hôpital*, *ospedale*) has some kind of 24-hour service, although you will have to pay hefty medical bills upfront and claim expenses back later; make sure you keep full receipts and doctors' reports. Every district has a rota system whereby one local **pharmacy** (*Apotheke*, *pharmacie*, *farmacia*) stays open outside normal shopping hours. Each pharmacy will have a sign in the window telling you where the nearest open one is. Local newspapers also have details.

> **Emergency numbers**
>
> Police ☏117; Fire ☏118; Ambulance ☏144.

Suisse-Romande

French-speaking Switzerland, or **Suisse-Romande**, occupies the western third of the country, comprising the shores of Lake Geneva and the hills and lakes leading north almost to Basel. The ambience here is thoroughly Gallic: historical animosity between Calvinist Geneva and Catholic France has nowadays given way to a yearning on the part of most francophone Swiss to abandon their bumpkin compatriots in the east and embrace the EU.

Geneva, at the southwestern tip of **Lake Geneva** (*Lac Léman* in French) was once a haven for free-thinkers from all over Europe; now it's a city of diplomats and big business. Halfway around the lake, **Lausanne** is full of young people, an energetic, town acclaimed as the skateboarding capital of Europe. Further east, the lakeshore is lined with vineyards and opulent villas – **Montreux** is particularly chic – although you can still taste the unspoilt paradise, evoked by the stunning medieval **Château de Chillon**, which drew Byron and the Romantic poets and which inspired Mary Shelley to write *Frankenstein*. Mont Blanc, Western Europe's highest mountain (4807m), is visible from Geneva city centre, while Montreux and neighbouring **Vevey** have breathtaking views across the water to the French Alps. On a sunny day, the train ride around the vineyard-rich northern shore is memorably scenic, but taking advantage of the lake's excellent **boat** service (IR no discount; ER & SP free; ⑩www.cgn.ch) will help bring home the full grandeur of the setting.

Geneva

The Puritanism of **GENEVA** is inextricably linked with the city's struggle for independence. Long ruled by the dukes of Savoy, who regarded the local bishopric as their private property, sixteenth-century Genevans saw the Reformation in neighbouring Switzerland as a useful aid in their struggle to rid themselves of Savoyard influence. By the time the city's independence was won in 1602, its religious zeal had painted it as the "Protestant Rome". What continues to be known today as the Republic and Canton of Geneva remained outside the Swiss Confederation until 1815 (the Catholic cantons opposed its entry), and acquired a reputation for joylessness which it still struggles to shake off. Today, it's a working city that remains sharply focused on its prominent role in international diplomacy and big business. Time and effort are needed to penetrate the facade of money and power.

Arrival, information and accommodation

The main **train station**, Gare de Cornavin, lies at the head of Rue du Mont-Blanc in the city centre. Expresses from Paris and Lyon arrive in a separate French section (passport control), but local French trains from Annecy/Chamonix terminate at Gare des Eaux-Vives on the east side of town (tram #12 or #16 into the centre). From the **airport**, 5km northwest, trains and bus #10 run regularly into the city. The international **bus station** is on Place Dorcière in the centre. The **tourist office** is in the main post office at 18 Rue du Mont-Blanc (Mon–Sat 9am–6pm; July & Aug also Sun 9am–6pm; ☏0229 097 000, ⑩www.geneve-tourisme.ch), where you can pick up the weekly **listings** magazine *Genève Agenda*, and the excellent *Info-Jeunes* brochure, geared towards budget travellers. There's also an information office on the Pont de la Machine (Mon noon–6pm, Tues–Fri 9am–6pm, Sat 10am–5pm; ☏0223 11 9 970, ⑩www.ville-ge.ch), and a CAR info-bus parked at the Mont-Blanc exit of the train station (mid-June to early Sept daily 9am–11pm; ☏0228 392 081).

Geneva has plenty of budget **accommodation** – ask at the tourist office about cut-price multi-night deals.

▲ Hermance

N

200 m
0

Parc La Grange

Lake Geneva

Jet d'Eau

Boat Launches

QUAI GUSTAVE ADOR

AVENUE W. FAVRE

D'AUBIGNÉ
R. DU CLOS
R. DE LA NAVIGATION
R. DES VOLLANDES
R. DU ROVERAY
TRENTE-ET-UN-DÉCEMBRE
LA MAIRE
AV. PICTET-DE-ROCHEMONT
ROUTE DE FRONTENEX
ROUTE DE CHÊNE

EAUX-VIVES

Gare des Eaux-Vives

AV. DE CHAMONIX
AV. DE LA GRENADE

R. DE VILLE-REUSE
R. DE LA TERRASSIÈRE
R. H. A. LACHENAL
R. DES GLACIS-DE-RIVE

Russian Church
Collections Baur

Grand Casino

Boat Launches

QUAI DU MONT-BLANC

Jardin d'Anglais

BLVD HELVÉTIQUE

Petit-Palais

Musée d'Art et d'Histoire

Cathédrale St-Pierre

Maison Tavel

Hôtel de Ville

Parc des Bastions

Musée Rousseau

Musée Barbier-Müller

Musée Rath

Wall of the Reformation
University Library

Grand Théâtre

PONT DU MONT-BLANC

Île Rousseau

Gare Routière

Gare du Mont-Blanc

LES PÂQUIS

RUE DE LAUSANNE

UN & Musée International de la Croix-Rouge ◀

RUE DU MONT-BLANC

PONT DES BERGUES
PONT DE LA MACHINE
PONT DE L'ÎLE

PLACE BEL-AIR

Gare de Cornavin

BLVD J. FAZY

Rhône

PONT DE LA COULOUVRENIÈRE

Bâtiments des Forces-Motrices

BOULEVARD G. FAVON

BOULEVARD GEORGES-FAVON

Plaine de Plainpalais

AVENUE DU MAIL

MAMCO

RUE DES BAINS

R. DE LA PRAIRIE

Jonction ▼

Carouge ▼

SWITZERLAND | Suisse-Romande

29

1051

Hostels

Auberge de Jeunesse 30 Rue Rothschild ☏0227 326 260, ⍟www.yh-geneva.ch. Big, bustling HI hostel with dorms in the north of the Paquis. Bus #1 to Wilson. ❸

City Hostel Geneva 2 Rue Ferrier ☏0229 011 500, ⍟www.cityhostel.ch. Dorms and doubles; kitchen facilities and internet access. Free lockers. No curfew. ❸

Cité Universitaire 46 Avenue Miremont ☏0228 392 222, ⍟www.unige.ch/cite-uni. Dorms and cut-price rooms. Bus #3 to Champel. ❸

Home St-Pierre 4 Cour St-Pierre ☏0223 103 707, ⍟www.homestpierre.ch. Women only hostel with one dorm for men. Reception closed noon–4pm. ❸

Hotels

De la Cloche 6 Rue de la Cloche ☏0227 329 481, ⍟www.smpage.ch/cloche. Clean, characterful place in a quiet area of the Paquis. Reservations recommended. ❺

Luserna 12 Ave de Luserna ☏0223 454 676, ⍟www.hotel.luserna.ch. Friendly and quiet, family-run place north of the centre. Bus #10 to Servette. ❹

Campsite

Camping d'Hermance 14km northeast, just before the French frontier ☏0227 511 483. Free lake access. Closed Oct–March. Bus #W from the train station

The City

Orientation in the city centres on the Rhône, which flows from the lake west into France. The **Rive Gauche**, on the south bank, takes in a grid of waterfront streets which comprise the main shopping and business districts and the adjacent high ground of the Old Town. Behind the grand hotels lining the northern **Rive Droite** waterfront is the main station and the cosmopolitan (and sometimes sleazy) Les Pâquis district, filled with cheap restaurants. Further north are the offices of the dozens of international organizations headquartered in Geneva, including the UN.

On the Rive Gauche, beyond the ornamental flowerbeds of the **Jardin Anglais**, erupts the roaring 140-metre-high plume of Geneva's trademark **Jet d'Eau**. Nearby is the main thoroughfare of the Old Town, the cobbled, steeply ascending **Grande Rue**. Here, among the secondhand bookshops and galleries, you'll find the atmospheric seventeenth-century **Hôtel de Ville** and the arcaded **armoury**, backed by a lovely terrace with the longest wooden bench in the world (126m). A block away is the huge late-Romanesque **Cathedral** (Mon–Sat 9/10am–5/7pm, Sun 11am–5/7pm), with an incongruous eighteenth-century portal and a plain, soaring interior. The frescoes of the internal Chapelle des Maccabées, with their intricate floral patterns and lute-strumming angels, are modern versions of the faded fifteenth-century originals now in Geneva's main museum. Round the corner is the hub of the Old Town, **Place du Bourg-de-Four**, a picturesque split-level square perched on the hillside and ringed by cafés. Alleys wind down from here to the university park and its austere **Wall of the Reformation** (1909–1917) alongside busy Place Neuve.

A few metres east of the Old Town is the gigantic **Musée d'Art et d'Histoire**, 2 Rue Charles Galland (Tues–Sun 10am–5pm; free; ⍟www.mah.ville-ge.ch). Upstairs are three stunning sculptures – a graceful *Venus and Adonis* by Canova and two powerful pieces by Rodin. The fine-art collection is crowned by Konrad Witz's famous altarpiece, made for the cathedral in 1444, showing Christ and the fishermen transposed onto Lake Geneva. Other highlights are by local artist Félix Vallotton; Cézanne, Renoir and Modigliani; and some striking blue Swiss landscapes by Bern-born Symbolist Ferdinand Hodler. The basement holds the massive archeological collection, including Egyptian mummies and Greek and Roman statuary. Nearby is the astonishing **Collections Baur**, 8 Rue Munier-Romilly (Tues–Sun 2–6pm; Sfr5), the country's premier collection of East Asian art, featuring luminescent yellow Yongzhang ceramics and spectacular porcelain and jade. Make time also for **MAMCO**, a top-quality museum of modern and contemporary art housed in an old factory west of the Old Town at 10 Rue des Vieux-Grenadiers (Tues–Sun noon–6pm; Sfr9; ⍟www.mamco-ge.tripod.com).

About 1km north of the station, opposite the UN complex on Avenue de la Paix, is the thought-provoking **Musée International de la Croix-Rouge** (Mon & Wed–Sun 10am–5pm; Sfr10; ⊛www.micr.ch; bus #8 or #F to Appia), which documents the origins, growth and achievements of the Red Cross without resorting to self-congratulation. Carefully chosen audiovisual material combines with quietly dramatic exhibits – such as the 34 footprints in a tiny cell-space where a delegate found 17 people crammed together – to leave a powerful impression.

Twenty minutes south of the centre by tram #11 lies the late-Baroque suburb of **Carouge**, built by the king of Sardinia in the eighteenth century as a separate town. Its low Italianate houses and leafy lanes are now largely occupied by fashion designers and small galleries, and the area's **reputation** as an outpost of tolerance and hedonism beyond Geneva's jurisdiction lives on in its numerous cafés and music bars. Carouge hosts a colourful **market** (Wed & Sat); the flea market (same days) at Plainpalais, near Geneva's Old Town, is also worth a browse.

Eating and drinking

Central Geneva has plenty of **cafés** and **bars** offering lunchtime *plats du jour*, as well as inexpensive evening **food**.

Restaurants

Al-Amir 12 Rue des Alpes. Excellent Lebanese kebabs and falafel from Sfr7.

Au Petit Chalet 17 Rue de Berne. Unpretentious city-centre place serving Swiss cuisine.

Café Gallay 42 Boulevard St Georges. Friendly neighbourhood café/bar attracting students and theatre people. Inexpensive food. Closed Sun.

Hang-Zhou 19 Rue de la Coulouvreniere. Inexpensive Chinese with a full vegetarian menu. Closed Sun.

Jeck's 14 Rue de Neuchatel. Affordable Thai dishes with lunches from Sfr15.

Le Zofage 6 Rue des Voisins. University cafeteria open to all.

L'Usine Place des Voltaires ☎0223 280 818. Alternative arts venue serving meals from Sfr10.

Manora 4 Rue de Cornavin. High-quality self-service restaurant with plentiful vegetarian selections and meals from Sfr12.

Drinking

Café des Amis 23 Rue Ancienne. The oldest traditional café on Ancienne.

Café Mozart 4 Quai des Forces Motrices. Waterfront wine-bar with live classical music and jazz (Thurs–Sat). Closed Sun & Mon.

Chat Noir 13 Rue Vautier. Bar and cellar venue dedicated to live performance.

La Bretelle 15 Rue des Etuves. Tiny, kitsch tavern with a live accordion and/or drag cabaret (Thurs–Sat).

La Marchand de Sable 4 Rue Vautier. Loud, graffitied little nook with a rough edge.

Le 2e Bureau 9 Rue du Stand. Sleek bar thumping with deep beats.

Listings

Consulates Australia, 2 Chemin des Fins ☎0227 999 100; Canada, 5 Ave de L'Ariana ☎0229 199 200; New Zealand, 2 Chemin des Fins ☎0229 290 350; UK, 37 Rue de Vermont ☎0229 182 400; US, 29 Route de Pré-Bois ☎0228 405 160.

Hospital Hôpital Cantonal, 24 Rue Micheli-du-Crest ☎0223 723 311.

Internet access Café Video ROM, 19 Rue des Alpes; Charly's, 7 Rue de Fribourg (closed Sun).

Laundry Lavseul, 29 Rue de Monthoux.

Post office 18 Rue du Mont-Blanc.

Lausanne

Geneva's neighbour **LAUSANNE** is interesting, attractive, worldly and well aware of how to have a good time – in short, Switzerland's sexiest city. Tiered above the lake on a succession of south-facing terraces, with the Old Town at the top, the train station and commercial districts in the middle, and the one-time fishing village of **Ouchy**, now prime territory for waterfront café-lounging and strolling, at the bottom, it has incredibly steep hills which may do your legs in after a while. If so, copy the locals and catch a bus into the Joret forests above the city, and then blade or **skateboard** your way down to Ouchy: aficionados have been clocked doing 90kph through the streets here. Intrepid Lausannois have even been known to ski down to Ouchy after days of heavy snow. Switzerland's biggest university aids the youthful spirit, and a wealth of international student programmes feeds an unusually diverse, multi-ethnic makeup.

To get to the central **Place St François** from the train station, either walk up the steep Rue du Petit-Chêne, or take the metro to Flon; from the metro platforms, lifts shuttle you up to the level of the giant **Grand Pont**, between Place Bel-Air on the left and St François on the right. Glitzy **Rue de Bourg** entices shoppers uphill from St François; beside it, Rue St François drops down into the valley and up the other side to the cobbled **Place de la Palud**, an ancient, fountained square flanked by the arcades of the Renaissance town hall. From here the medieval **Escaliers du Marché** lead up to the **Cathedral** (daily 8am–7pm), a fine Romanesque-Gothic jumble, its clean lines only peripherally adorned with memorials and fifteenth-century frescoes. Opposite, in the former bishop's palace, is the **Musée Historique** (Tues–Sun 11am–6pm, Thurs till 8pm; Sfr4), which houses a model of old Lausanne – invaluable for grasping the city's confusing topography. Lausanne suffered from many medieval fires, and is the last city in Europe to keep alive the tradition of the nightwatch: every night, on the hour (10pm–2am), a sonorous-voiced civil servant calls out from the cathedral tower "*C'est le guet; il a sonné l'heure*" ("This is the nightwatch; the hour has struck"), assuring the lovers and assorted drunks below that all is well.

West of the cathedral hill is **Place de la Riponne**, an arid expanse of concrete dominated by the splendidly ostentatious Palais de Rumine, housing the university library and various museums. Save your francs for the outstanding **Collection de l'Art Brut**, 11 Ave des Bergières (Tues–Sun 11am–1pm & 2–6pm; Sfr6; Ⓦwww.artbrut.ch), ten minutes' walk northwest of Riponne on Ave Vinet, or bus #2 or #3 to Jomini. This unique gallery is filled with the work of "outsider" artists – ordinary people who discovered their talents late in life, the mentally ill, long-term prisoners, lone obsessives, and so on.

In a park on the Ouchy waterfront sits Lausanne's flagship **Olympic Museum** (daily 9am–6pm, Thurs till 8pm; Oct–April closed Mon; Sfr14; Ⓦwww.museum.olympic.org), a vacuous and expensive place that trumpets the Olympic ideal by means of snippets of archive footage, stirring music and Carl Lewis's and Cathy Freeman's old running shoes. Bypass it for the **Musée de l'Elysée**, an outstanding museum of photography in the same park (Tues–Sun 10am–6pm, Thurs till 9pm; Sfr8; Ⓦwww.elysee.ch).

Practicalities

The **tourist office** has branches in the train station (daily 9am–7pm; ☎0216 137 373, Ⓦwww.lausanne-tourisme.ch), and beside Ouchy metro station (daily: April–Sept 9am–8pm; Oct–March 9am–6pm; same phone and website). A two-day **Lausanne Card** (Sfr15) offers free transport, reduced museum entry, and discounts on meals at *Manora*. **Internet** access can be found opposite the train station at Quanta, 4 Place de la Gare (closed Sun).

Accommodation

Hotel du Raisin 19 Place de la Palud ☎0213 122 756. Atmospheric and characterful place located in the heart of the old town. ❺

Jeunotel 36 Chemin du Bois-de-Vaux ☎0216 260 222, Ⓦwww.jeunotel.ch. HI hostel with internet access, laundry, bar (Tues–Sat) and self-service restaurant (Mon–Fri). No curfew. Bus #2 direction Bourdonnette to Bois de Vaux. ❸

La Croisée 15 Ave Marc-Dufour ☎0213 210 909, Ⓦwww.ferienhotels.ch. Hostel with dorms and doubles, laundry facilities, internet access and kitchen. No curfew. ❸

Lausanne Guesthouse & Backpackers 4 Chemin des Epinettes ☎0216 018 000, Ⓦwww.lausanne-guesthouse.ch. Dorms and doubles overlooking Lake Geneva and the Alps. Kitchen and laundry facilities, internet access and fully equipped for the disabled. No curfew. ❸

Pension Old Inn 11 Ave de la Gare ☎0213 236 221, Ⓔold_inn@bluewin.ch. Rather spartan little pension, but friendly. ❹

Vidy ☎0216 242 031, Ⓦwww.campinglausannevidy.ch. Campsite close to the *Jeunotel*. Closed Oct–April.

Restaurants and cafés

Au Couscous 2 Rue Enning. Arabic, veggie and macrobiotic dishes from Sfr15.

Bleu Lezard 10 Rue Enning. Chic and lively café/bar. Pricey food (veggie options) in the evening.

La Bossette Calm and cosy local café serving speciality beers and excellent food.

Café de l'Évêché 4 Rue Curtat. Atmospheric haunt just below the cathedral. Popular with students and Old timers. Good for morning coffee and authentic fondue.

Café Romand Place St François (under *Pizza Hut*). Heartwarming place for beer, coffee or Swiss belt-busters.

Laxmi 5 Escaliers du Marché. Genuine excellent Indian/veggie food.

Ma Jong 3 Escaliers du Grand-Pont. Sushi and great-value wok-fried meals for Sfr14.

Manora 17 Place St-François. Self-service restaurant with a wide range of excellent cheap food.

Bars, nightlife and festivals

Ouchy's waterfront hosts regular free music events all summer, and people come down here to do a spot of café sunbathing, or blade-cruising (rent blades or skates from beside Ouchy Metro). Lausanne's big party is the **Festival de la Cité** held in early July (ⓦwww.lausanne.ch) featuring music, dance, drama and mime on several open-air stages in the old town. Also check out the prestigious, big-name **Paleo Rock Festival**, in Nyon, in late July (ⓦwww.paleo.ch).

Au Chateau 1 Place du Tunnel. Funky music and flavourful home-brewed beers at this bar.

D! Place Centrale. Happening basement club playing house and jungle. Closed Mon–Wed.

Lecaféthéâtre 10 Rue de Genève. Café/bar with live entertainment most nights.

Le Loft 1 Escaliers Bel-Air. Techno club with a tough reputation.

MAD (Moulin à Danse) 23 Rue de Genève. Cutting-edge dance club with adjoining theatre, art galleries and alternative-style café.

VO Le Jazz Café 11 Place du Tunnel. Café/bar and live venue with regular DJ nights.

Vevey and Montreux

East of Lausanne, trains meander through steep vineyards to **VEVEY**, a small market town looking over to the French Alps across the lake. Vevey's charm centres on the huge lakeside **Grande Place**, a few minutes' walk southeast of the station – known also as **Place du Marché** and packed with market stalls (Tues & Sat) – and the narrow streets which lead off into the old town to the east. Vevey's excellent fine-art museum, **Musée Jenisch** on Rue de la Gare (Tues–Sun 11am/2–5.30pm; Sfr10) has Europe's largest collection of Rembrandt lithographs, as well as graphic works by Dürer, Corot, Le Corbusier and others. East of Place du Marché is a statue of Charlie Chaplin, "The Tramp", who moved to Vevey from the US in the 1950s to escape McCarthyism. To head on to Montreux and Chillon, ditch the train in favour of bus #1, which plies the coast road every 10min. If you have time, walk the floral lakeside path.

MONTREUX, 6km east of Vevey, is a snooty place, full of money and not particularly exciting, but it enjoys spectacular views of the Dents-du-Midi peaks opposite and hosts a colourful Friday market. The whole town is protected from chill northerly winds by a wall of mountains and so basks in its own microclimate, nurturing lakeside palm trees and exotic flowers. The zigzagging streets and hillside terraces of the old quarter above the train station provide marginally more interest than the Grand-Rue below (head 100m left out of the station and cut down the stairs between buildings), although you should make time for the statue of one-time resident **Freddie Mercury** silently serenading the swans on the lakefront beside the vast covered market.

The climax of a journey around Lake Geneva is the stunning thirteenth-century **Château de Chillon** (daily: 9/10am–5/6pm; last entry 1hr before closing; Sfr8.50; ⓦwww.chillon.ch), one of the best-preserved medieval castles in Europe. Whether you opt for the 45-minute shoreline walk east from Montreux, take bus #1 from Vevey or Montreux, a local train, a bike, or, best of all, a lake steamer, your first glimpse of the castle is unforgettable – an elegant, turreted pile jutting out into the water, framed by trees and craggy mountains. At the gate you'll get a follow-the-numbers pamphlet, which starts you off in the dungeons where the dukes of Savoy imprisoned François Bonivard, a Genevan priest, from 1530 to 1536 (he was manacled to the fifth pillar along); Lord Byron, after a sailing trip here with Shelley in 1816, was so affected by the story that he spent the next day in his Ouchy hotel room writing the poem *The Prisoner of Chillon*. Byron's signature, scratched on the dungeon's third pillar, probably isn't genuine, but has been absorbed into the legend nonetheless. As you look out onto the lake, it's sobering to realize how sheer the rock is that Chillon's built on: just below the castle walls yawns 165m of cold water, enough to swallow the Eiffel Tower without a trace. Upstairs you'll find more wonders: gloriously grand knights' halls, secret twisting passages between lavish bedchambers, Gothic windows with dreamy views and a frescoed chapel.

Practicalities

Tourist offices are on Grande Place in Vevey (Mon–Fri 8.30am–noon & 1.30–6pm; July–Sept also Sat & Sun 9am –1pm; ☎0219 222 020, ⊛www.montreux-vevey.com); and beside the ferry landing-stage in Montreux (Mon–Fri 9/9.30am–noon & 1–5.30/6pm, Sat & Sun 10am–2/5pm; ☎0219 628 436). The excellent brochure *On The Trail of Hemingway* pinpoints a welter of sites in the area with famous-name associations. The pristine *Riviera Lodge* SB **hostel**, 5 Grande Place in Vevey (☎0219 238 040, ⊛www.rivieralodge.ch; ❷), is cheaper and easier to get to than the HI hostel at 8 Passage de l'Auberge, beside Territet station just east of Montreux (☎0219 634 934, ⊛www.youthhostel.ch; ❸). The best budget **hotels** are in Vevey: central *Des Négociants*, 27 Rue du Conseil (☎0219 227 011, ⊛www.cyber-hotel.ch; ❺); and rustic *De La Place*, 5 Place du Temple in Corsier (☎0219 211 2 87, ⊛www.swissnew.ch/hoteldelaplace; ❺; bus #11). In Montreux, aim for *Hôtel Elite*, 25 Ave du Casino (☎0219 660 303, ⊛www.montreux.ch; ❹). You can **camp** east of Vevey at lakeside *La Maladaire* (☎0219 443 137).

Vevey has a self-service *Manora* **restaurant** in the St Antoine mall outside the station, and plenty of pavement cafés in the centre. The food at *Hôtel des Négociants* is good. Cyberworld, 4 Rue du Torrent in Vevey, has **internet** access. Montreux has plenty of eateries outside the station on Ave des Alpes, including some with lakeview terraces, as well as the oriental-fantasy *Palais Hoggar*, 14 Quai du Casino, which serves Arabic specialities (meals from Sfr25) and Moroccan mint tea to accompany the lake sunset. The star-studded **Montreux Jazz Festival** (July) features world-famous artists from REM to B.B. King. Tickets (Sfr40–100; ⊛www.montreuxjazz.com) need to be booked well in advance; but if you don't have one, you can still enjoy the street parties and free entertainment all over town. Vevey holds a **Street Artists' Festival** (late Aug), jugglers, acrobats and mime artists performing on the lakeside.

Above Montreux

A scenic narrow-gauge train line climbs through the hills behind Montreux on the flagship **Golden Pass** route, which is well worth incorporating into an eastward journey (ER, IR & SP free; reservations in the special panoramic carriages cost Sfr4–8; ⊛www.goldenpass.ch). The memorable route switchbacks up to a series of tunnels beneath the prominent Dent de Jaman peak before meandering on a single track through lush, quiet and beautiful countryside to the exclusive Alpine resort of **Gstaad**, and then on to **Zweisimmen**, from where connections continue to Spiez, Bern, Interlaken and Luzern.

The northern cities

Northern Switzerland, much of it known as the Schweizer Mittelland – the populated countryside between the Jura to the north and the high Alps to the south – is a region of gentle hills, lakes and some high peaks, though ones by no means as grandiose as the heights further south. There's a wealth of cultural and historical interest in the German-speaking cities of **Zürich**, **Basel**, **Luzern** and the federal capital, **Bern**. Wherever you base yourself, the mountains are never more than a couple of hours away by train.

Zürich

Not so long ago, **ZÜRICH** was famed for being the most icily calm, cleanest city in Europe. Apocryphal stories abound from the 1970s of tourists setting out to find a cigarette butt or a food wrapper discarded on the streets and drawing a blank every time. But there's a lot more to Zürich these days than its obsessive cleanliness. This most beautiful of cities, astride a river and turned towards a crystal-clear lake and distant snowy peaks, has plenty to recommend it. Now you can people-watch on crowded, multi-ethnic streets, drink, dance or hang out at bars and clubs as hip and varied as those in more celebrated European cities, and feel a lived-in urban buzz that contradicts the Swiss stereotype. The steep, cobbled alleys of the Old Town are great to wander around, and with an engaging café culture and a wealth of nightlife, you could easily spend days here.

Arrival, information and accommodation

The giant **train station** is in the city centre on Bahnhofstrasse, served by trains from all over Europe and from the **airport** (every 15min), 11km northeast; the international **bus station** is 50m north on Sihlquai. The **tourist office** on the station concourse (Mon–Sat 8.30am–7/8.30pm, Sun 9am–6.30pm; ☏012 154 000, Ⓦ www.zuerich.com) will book rooms for free, and sells the **Zürich Card** (Sfr15/one day, Sfr30/three days), which entitles you to free rides on all forms of public transport and free entry to museums. They also have the useful **listings** booklets *Zürich News* (Ⓦ www.zuerich.ch), the *Events Guide Zurich* or the *City Guide Zürich* (Ⓦ www.HelloVisitors.com).

You can cover most sights by walking, but the **public transport** system is easy to use. The most important hubs are the city squares of Bahnhofplatz and, on the east side of the river, Central and Bellevue. Buy tickets from machines at every stop: choose between the green button (24hr; Sfr7.20); blue button (1hr; Sfr3.60); or yellow button (short one-way hop; Sfr2.10). All tickets are valid on trams, buses, some boats and local city trains (not to/from the airport).

Hostels

City Backpacker Niederdorfstrasse 5 ☏012 519 015, Ⓦ www.backpacker.ch. SB place, friendly and close to the action. Internet access, kitchen facilities. No curfew. Eight-min walk from the train station. ❸

Zuerich Jugendherberge Mutschellenstrasse 114 ☏014 823 544, Ⓦ www.youthhostel.ch. HI hostel way south of the centre; take tram #7 to Morgental, from where it's a five-minute walk. ❸

Hotels

Martahaus Zähringerstrasse 36 ☏012 514 550, Ⓦ www.martahaus.ch. Clean, secure hotel in the Old Town. Rooms with TV and phone. Breakfast

included. Single-sex dorms also available. ❹

Otter Oberdorfstrasse 7 ☏012 512 207, Ⓦ www.wueste.ch. Comfy, colourful, laid-back and popular with students and artists. Shared facilities. ❺

Rothaus Sihlhallenstrasse 1 ☏012 412 451. On the hip Langstrasse – the clean, spacious rooms are a bargain, if you can overlook the neighbourhood's red-light tendencies. ❹

Splendid Rosengasse 5 ☏012 525 850, Ⓦ www.hotelsplendid.ch. Plain and basic. Hotel door locked 3–5.30am. ❹

Villette Kruggasse 4 ☏012 512 335. Family hotel with homely atmosphere. Near the Bellevue in the heart of the city. ❺

Platzspitz

Schweizerisches
Landesmuseum

MUSEUMSTRASSE

Hauptbahnhof

NEUMÜHLEQUAI

STAMPFENBACH-
PLATZ

STAMPFENBACHSTRASSE

SIHLQUAISTRASSE

CLAUSIUSSTRASSE

WEINBERGSWEG

SONNEGG-STR.

WEINBERGSTRASSE

WALCHEBRÜCKE

NEUMÜHLEQUAI

LEONHARDSTRASSE

AUF DER MAUER

SONNEGG-STR.

BAHNHOFPLATZ

BAHNHOFBRÜCKE

CENTRAL

Polybahn

TANNENSTR.

LÖWENSTRASSE

SCHÜTZENGASSE

BEATEN-
PLATZ

BAHNHOFSTRASSE

BEATENGASSE

BAHNHOFQUAI

Federal Institute of
Technology (ETHZ)

HIRSCHENGRABEN

RAMISTRASSE

LINTHESCHERGASSE

LINTHESCHERGASSE

LISTERSTRASSE

WERDMÜHLESTRASSE

MÜHLESTEG

AM RANK

ZÄHRINGERSTRASSE

SCHIENHUUSS

KÜNSTLERGASSE

KARL-SCHMID-STR.

University

URANIASTRASSE

WERDMÜHLE-
PLATZ

RUDOLF-BRUN BR.

LIMMATQUAI

STRASSE

MÜHLE-

ZÄHRINGER-
PLATZ

SPITALGASSE

Predigerkirche

SEILERGRABEN

SEMPERSTEIG

OETENBACHGASSE

BAHNHOFSTRASSE

RENNWEG

FORTUNAGASSE

SCHIPFE

Limmat

NIEDERDORFSTRASSE

HIRSCHEN-
PLATZ

BRUNNGASSE

FROSCHAUG.

PREDIGERG.

NEUMARKT

FLORHOFGASSE

LINDENHOF

KUTTELGASSE

AUGUSTINERG.

STRELHGASSE

RINDERMARKT

OBMANNAMTSGASSE

ZEHNDERWEG

HEIMSTRASSE

James Joyce
Foundation

Augustinerkirche

WEIN-
PLATZ

WÜHRE

RATHAUSBRÜCKE

MARKTGASSE

SPIEGELGASSE

OBERE ZÄUNE

OBMANNAMTSGASSE

FLORHOFGASSE

Kunsthaus

ST. PETER-
STRASSE

St Peters-
Kirche

IN GASSEN

STORCHENGASSE

Rathaus

MÜNSTERGASSE

Grossmünster

KIRCHGASSE

HIRSCHENGRABEN

HEIM-
PLATZ

BÄRENGASSE

Zunfthaus
zur Meisen

MÜNSTER-
HOF

BLAUFAHNENSTR.-ZÄUNE

TRITTLIGASSE

HIRSCHENGRABEN

PARADE-
PLATZ

POSTSTRASSE

Fraumünster

MÜNSTERBRÜCKE

Wasserkirche

KIRCHGASSE

OBERDORFSTRASSE

RAMISTRASSE

BLEICHERWEG

BAHNHOFSTRASSE

TALSTRASSE

KAPPELERSTRASSE

STADTHAUSQUAI

FRAUMÜNSTERSTRASSE

LIMMATQUAI

BÖRSENSTRASSE

BÖRSE

BELLEVUE-
PLATZ

Stadelhofen
Station

STADELHOFERSTRASSE

SCHANZEN...

QUAIBRÜCKE

SECHSELÄUTEN-
PLATZ

THEATERSTRASSE

STADELHOFER-
PLATZ

KREUZBÜHLSTRASSE

BÜRKLI-
PLATZ

Lake
Zürich

N

UTOQUAI

Opera
House

FALKENSTRASSE

CLARIDENSTRASSE

GENERAL GUISAN QUAI

Tonhalle
Concert Hall

0   100 m

SEEHOFSTR.

Boats

Zürich West

Langstrasse

Campsite

Campsite

Seebucht Seestrasse 559 ☎014 821 612, ⊛www.camping-zurich.ch. Located 2km from the city centre, right on the lake. Closed Oct–April. Take bus #161 or #165 from Bürkliplatz to Stadtgrenze.

The City

From the station, the narrow pedestrian-only streets of the medieval **Niederdorf** district stretch south along the east bank of the River Limmat, tranquil during the day and bustling after dark. The waterfront is lined with fine Baroque *Zunfthäuser* (guildhalls), arcaded lower storeys fronting the quayside, their extravagantly decorated dining-rooms now mostly upmarket restaurants. One block in is **Niederdorfstrasse**, initially tacky, but offering plenty of opportunities to explore atmospheric cobbled side-alleys and secluded courtyards: Spiegelgasse 14 was Lenin's digs in 1917 (pre-Revolution), while a pub at Spiegelgasse 1 once housed the *Cabaret Voltaire*, birthplace of the Dada art movement. Just south is Zürich's trademark **Grossmünster** (Mon–Sat 9/10am–5/6pm), where Huldrych Zwingli, father of Swiss Protestantism, began preaching in 1519. Its exterior is largely fifteenth-century, while its twin towers were topped with distinctive octagonal domes in the seventeenth century, after a fire had all but destroyed them. The interior is austere but for the intensely coloured choir windows by Augusto Giacometti and the Romanesque crypt which contains an oversized fifteenth-century statue of Charlemagne, popularly associated with the foundation of the church in the ninth century. A door, to the right on exiting, gives into the atmospheric **cloister**. Alleys behind the church lead up the hill to Switzerland's best gallery, the **Kunsthaus** (Tues–Sun 10am–5/9pm, Sfr10; ⊛www.kunsthaus.ch). Some fascinating late-Gothic paintings, a roomful of Venetian masters and plenty of Flemish work are fleshed out by Swiss artists, among them Füssli, whose macabre fantasies contrast with the restrained classicism of his compatriot Angelika Kauffmann. The collection of twentieth-century art is stunning: works by Miró, Dalí and De Chirico head a wonderful Surrealist overview; Picasso, Chagall, Klee and Kandinsky all have rooms to themselves; there are two of Monet's most beautiful waterlily canvases, plenty of Warhols, an array of Giacometti's sculpture, and the largest Munch collection outside Scandinavia.

The **west bank** is the site of most business and commercial activity. Leading south from the station, **Bahnhofstrasse** is one of the most prestigious shopping streets in Europe. This is the gateway into the modern city, and is where all of Zürich strolls, to browse at the inexpensive department stores that crowd the first third of the street, or to splash away Sfr25,000 on a Rolex watch or a Vuitton bag at the understated super-chic boutiques further south. Two-thirds of the way down is **Paradeplatz**, a tram-packed little square offering some of the best people-watching in the city, and where most of Switzerland's banks have their HQs: Bahnhofstrasse, if not paved with gold, is at least founded on the stuff, with ingots piled high in well-protected vaults beneath the pavement. The narrow lanes between Bahnhofstrasse and the river lead up to the **Lindenhof** courtyard, site of a Roman fortress and customs post. James Joyce wrote *Ulysses* in Zürich (1915–1919), and the Joyce Foundation, nearby at Augustinergasse 9 (Tues–Sun noon–6pm, Thurs till 8pm; ⊛www.joycefoundation.ch), can point you to his various hangouts, and his grave. Steps away is the **Peterskirche** (Mon–Fri 8am–6pm, Sat 9am–4pm), renowned for the enormous sixteenth-century clock face – the largest in Europe. Immediately south rises the slender-spired Gothic **Fraumünster** (Mon–Sat 9/10am–4/6pm), which began life as a convent in 853; its spectacular stained glass by Marc Chagall is unmissable.

A pleasant diversion from the city, savouring an essence of Switzerland, is the **Lindt and Sprungli Chocolate Factory**, Seestrasse 204, Kilchberg (Wed–Fri 10am–noon & 1–4pm; free; ☎0171 162 233). Factory tours aren't possible, but there's a small exhibition area (German descriptions, but English-language folders available on request). The main draw, however, is the opportunity to ensure that

Lindt's chocolate standards aren't slipping by sampling the free samples offered to visitors. To get there take the S-train to Kilchberg (10min) and walk (a further 10min) in the direction of the fresh-chocolate smell.

Eating and drinking

Zürich offers a wealth of places to **eat cheaply**, with *Manora*, Bahnhofstrasse 75, offering best value. The train station, in addition to the good-value *Nordsee* seafood bar opposite the tourist office, hides *Suan Long* on the lower shopping-level, which does filling stir-fries (Sfr13–15; stand-up only). *Mensa Polyterrasse*, on Künstlergasse at the university, is a student cafeteria open to all. A wander through Niederdorf will turn up dozens of falafel, sausage, noodle and French-fry stalls, plus beer halls serving up daily specials for about Sfr13.

Restaurants

Bodega Espanola, Munstergasse 15. Unmissable, deeply atmospheric tapas bar and paella restaurant.

Hiltl Sihlstrasse 28. Top-quality vegetarian buffet, with budget prices for takeaway.

Pinte Vaudoise Kruggasse 4. Serves what's been voted the best fondue in Zürich.

Schlauch Upstairs at Münstergasse 20. Health food served in a quiet atmosphere.

Schober Napfgasse 4. Don't leave Zürich without sampling the hot chocolate here.

Zähringer Zähringerplatz 11. Co-operative-run café/bar with an alternative-minded clientele.

Bars

Babalu Schmidgasse 6. Chic and back-lit, trendy – and tiny – bar.

James Joyce Pelikanstrasse 8. Comprises an original nineteenth-century bar interior, transported here piece by piece from Dublin. Closed Sat from 7pm & all Sun.

Les Halle Pfingstweldstrasse 6. Highly atmospheric bar featuring a small health-food shop beyond the array of mismatched chairs and tables. Tram #4 or #13 to Escher-wyss Platz.

Odeon Limmatquai 2. Lenin once watched the world go by from the big-windowed bar here.

Oepfelchammer Rindermarkt 12. Legend has it that, if you can swing up and wriggle your way through the gap between beam and ceiling, then your beers are on the house.

Pigalle Marktgasse 14. Popular hangout filled with the elegantly wasted.

Nelson Beatengasse 11. Massive, noisy pub near the train station. Cheap beer, live music, late opening and a somewhat predictable pick-up joint.

Noble Dubliner Talstrasse 82. Cosy, comfy pub with good beer and a talkative atmosphere. Popular with locals and ex-pats.

Rheinfelder Bierhalle Niederorfstrasse 76. Choice of the hearty beer halls.

Wuste Oberdorfstrasse 7. Mellow and comfortable.

Nightlife

Supplementing its lively **music** venues, Zürich's **club** scene has skyrocketed recently, and you'll find dance floors heaving. The hip quarter around Langstrasse, west of the centre, is full of club/bars, and the industrial quarter to the northwest is where the best underground clubs hide themselves; check flyers on Langstrasse or at Zap Records, Zähringerstrasse 47. August sees *the* **Street Parade** (⊛www.street-parade.ch), a hedonistic weekend of techno street-dancing second only to Berlin's Love Parade. **Listings** are in *ZüriTipp* (⊛www.zueritipp.ch) and the Friday supplement of the *Tages Anzeiger* newspaper.

Abart Manessestrasse 170. Good live music from local and foreign bands.

Casa Bar Münstergasse 20. Zürich's longest-running jazz venue with live music nightly.

Dynamo Wasserwerkstrasse 21. Alternative, punkish bands and dance nights.

Labyrinth Pfingstweidstrasse 70. Hard house at this mixed gay/straight venue.

Moods Schiffbaustrasse 6 ⊛www.moods.ch. The city's premier jazz club enticing top acts. Good but expensive restaurant attached. Tram #4 or #13 to Escher-wyss Platz.

Oxa Andreasstrasse 70. Techno and house. Famous for its after-hours parties (Sat & Sun 5–11am).

Rote Fabrik Seestrasse 395 ⊛www.rotefabrik.ch. Former squat venue with live bands and big-name DJs (as well as excellent cheap food).

Listings

Bike rental Workfare, Platform 18 at the train station ☎ 013 053 010/079 431 4838, ⑩ www.vbz.ch/html/mobil/gratis_velos. Free bicycles year round if you provide a deposit (Sfr20), which is refunded on return of the bike, and valid ID.

Consulates UK, Minervastrasse 117 ☎ 013 836 560.

Internet access Stars, in the station; Café Urania, Uraniastrasse 3 (closed Sun); Quanta SA, Limmatquai 94.

Laundry Mühlegasse 11, Niederdorf.

Hospital Permanence Medical Centre, Bahnhofplatz 15 ☎ 0121 544 44.

Pharmacy Bellevue, Theaterstrasse 14 (24hr).

Post office Kasernenstrasse, beside the station.

The Rhine falls

An excellent fine-weather excursion from Zürich is to the **Rhine falls**, Europe's largest waterfalls, which tumble 3km west of the northern Swiss town of **SCHAFFHAUSEN**. They are truly magnificent, not so much for their height (a mere 23m) as for their impressive breadth (150m) and the sheer drama of the place, with spray rising in a cloud of rainbows above the forested banks. The turreted castle **Schloss Laufen** on the south bank completes the spectacle. Be here on August 1, Switzerland's National Day, for a famous fireworks display. Damp steps lead down from the castle souvenir shop to platforms at the water's edge (Sfr1), where the falls roar inches from your nose. In summer, the best views are from daredevil boats, which scurry about in the spray (Sfr5–7).

Trains from Zürich Central run to Winterthur, from where you can make a connection (summer only) for Schaffhausen; get off at the Schloss Laufen am Rheinfall stop.

Basel (Bâle)

With both a gigantic river-port on the Rhine – Switzerland's only outlet to the sea – and the research HQs of several pharmaceutical multinationals, **BASEL** (Bâle) nurtures a reputation as Switzerland's wealthiest city. Its medieval past is endowed with some of the greatest minds of European history, including Erasmus, Zwingli, and later Nietzsche and Hesse, and its long-standing patronage of the arts has resulted in a panoply of first-rate museums and galleries. However, it's almost as if the citizens lost the plot when it came to defining their city for today. You might expect it, situated exactly where Switzerland, Germany and France touch noses, to hum with pan-European energy, but the close proximity of foreign languages and cultures has introverted the city rather than energized it: Basel's a curiously measured place, where equilibrium is everything. Even the city's massive carnival is a rigorously organized set-piece.

The City

Basel's old town lies to the north of the main train station. It revolves around the photogenic main square **Barfüsserplatz**, ringed by higgledy-piggledy medieval buildings, where the city's cultural pre-eminence in the fifteenth and sixteenth centuries is amply demonstrated in the splendid Barfüsserkirche, now home to the **Historisches Museum** (10am–5pm, closed Tues; ⑩ www.historischesmuseum-umbasel.ch); don't miss the sumptuous medieval tapestries, hidden behind protective blinds. Shop-lined Gerbergasse and Freiestrasse run north from the square to Marktplatz, which boasts the elaborate scarlet facade of the **Rathaus**, the central section of which is sixteenth-century. Just beyond Marktplatz is **Schifflände**, site of the main tourist office and from where **boats** depart regularly for trips along the Rhine. Alongside is the **Mittlere Brücke**, which for many centuries was the only bridge across the Rhine between its source and the sea. The working-class quarter across the river, known as Kleinbasel, was traditionally the object of scorn for the cosmopolitan merchants of the city centre: their **Lällekönig** bust still faces down the bridge, sticking out its tongue at the Kleinbaslers.

From Barfüsserplatz, Steinenberg climbs south to a junction; head left to the superb Greek and Etruscan pottery and Egyptian antiquities in the **Antikenmuseum**, St Alban-Graben 5 (Tues–Sun 10am–5pm; Sfr7, free first Sun of month; ⊛www.antikenmuseumbasel.ch). Opposite is the absorbing **Kunstmuseum**, St Alban-Graben 16 (Tues–Sun 10am–5pm; Sfr10, also covers entry to Museum für Gegenwartskunst; free first Sun of month; ⊛www.kunstmuseumbasel.ch). Its dazzling array of twentieth-century art, including paintings by Léger, Chagall, Munch, Braque and the Impressionists, is surpassed by a medieval collection featuring roomfuls of works by the prolific Holbein family. Down to the river, then right, is the **Museum für Gegenwartskunst** (Tues–Sun 11am–5pm; ticket as for Kunstmuseum; ⊛www.mgkbasel.ch), St Alban-Rheinweg 60, with installations by Frank Stella and Joseph Beuys sharing space with video art. A walk away on the north bank, in Solitude Park, is the beautifully designed **Museum Jean Tinguely** (Tues–Sun 11am–7pm; Sfr10; ⊛www.tinguely.ch), dedicated to one of Switzerland's best-loved artists. Tinguely's Monty-Pythonesque mechanical sculptures are endearing, and though most are imbued with an irreverent sense of humour, some, such as the *Mengele-Dance of Death*, are darkly apocalyptic.

Sixteenth-century Rittergasse leads from the Kunstmuseum up to the impressive sandstone **Münster**, overlooking the Rhine (Mon–Sat 10/11am–4/5pm, Sun 1/2–4/5pm). Medieval stone carving above the main portal shows the cathedral's founder, Emperor Heinrich II, holding a model of the church; beside him is a Foolish Virgin. Inside, in the north aisle, is the tomb of the Renaissance humanist Erasmus, who lived in Basel from 1521 until his death in 1536. The large adjoining **cloisters** are memorably atmospheric.

Basel's finest gallery is **Fondation Beyeler** (daily 9am–8pm; Sfr16, Sfr20 at weekends; ⊛www.beyeler.com; tram #6 to Riehen Dorf from Barfüsserplatz), sympathetically designed by Renzo Piano, architect of Paris's Pompidou Centre. A small but exceptionally high-quality collection features some of the best works by Picasso, Giacometti, Rothko, Rodin, Bacon, Miró and others. Sink into a huge white sofa opposite a giant Monet, where piped Debussy (daily at 1pm) fuels dreamy contemplation of the waterlilies.

Practicalities

Basel has two **train stations** straddling three countries. Basel SBB is the main one, most of it in Switzerland, although the section entitled Bâle SNCF is in French territory, receiving trains from Paris and Strasbourg (passport control); trams #8 and #11 shuttle to Barfüsserplatz. Some trains from Germany terminate at Basel Badischer Bahnhof (Basel Bad. for short), in a German enclave on the north side of the river (passport control); tram #6 runs to Barfüsserplatz. At the time of writing the **tourist office** has branches at SBB station (Mon–Fri 8.30am–6/7pm, Sat 8.30am–noon; June–Sept also Sat 1.30–6pm & Sun 10am–2pm), and in the centre at Schifflände 5 (Mon–Fri 8.30am–6pm, Sat 10am–4pm); it is not clear yet where they will move, but their telephone number and website (both offices: ☎061/268 68 68, ⊛www.baseltourismus.ch) will remain the same. Booking a room through them costs Sfr10. Basel thrives on conference business, so accommodation prices drop at weekends. Ask for a **Mobility Card** giving free city transport when you check in. You can also buy a **Basel Card** (Sfr25/one day, Sfr33/two days, Sfr45/three days) here which entitles you free city tours, ferries, and entry to the museums and zoo as well as discounts in some shops, restaurants, entertainment venues, and on transport. **Internet access** can be had at Manor AG Warenhaus, Greifengasse 22 (closed Sun).

Try and be here for Basel's February **Carnival**. The famous masked parades and musical festivities begin at 4am on the first day (in 2003, that's March 10) and last for three full days (⊛www.fasnacht.ch).

Hostels

Baselbackpack Dornacherstrasse 192 ☎0613 330 037, ⊛www.baselbackpack.ch. New hostel, with internet access, bar, community kitchen and homely atmosphere. A seven-min walk from the main station. ❸

Riverside hostel St Alban-Kirchrain 10 ☎0612
720 572, ⓦwww.youthhostel.ch. Quiet, spotless HI
place. Well run. ❸

Hotels

Hecht am Rhein Rheingasse 8 in Kleinbasel
☎0616 912 2 20. Friendly, plain and unfussy. ❺
Stadthof Gerbergasse 84 ☎0162 618 711,
ⓦwww.stadthof.ch. Simple and plain place on the
main shopping drag. No en-suites. ❻

Restaurants

Kunsthalle Steinenberg 7. Arty literati meet at the
gallery with a leafy terrace-café.
Pfalz Münsterberg 11. Fresh juices and a salad
buffet. Closed Sat & Sun.
Parterre Klybeckstrasse 1. Friendly place serving
excellent food. Closed Sun.
Zum Isaak Munsterplatz 16. Tranquil tea-drinkers'
café. Serves snacks and full meals. Closed Mon.
Zum Roten Engel Andreasplatz. Pleasant
vegetarian café with snacks, full meals and fresh
juices.

Bars, clubs and music venues

Atlantis Klosterberg 10 ⓦwww.atlan-tis.ch.
Regular music and dance in the evenings at this
bar/restaurant.
Bird's Eye Kohlenberg 20 ⓦwww.birdseye.ch.
Club hosting live jazz. Popular and lively.
Fischerstube Rheingasse 45. Excellent
atmospheric beer hall with a hearty clientele.
Hirscheneck Lindenberg 23. Co-op owned
graffitied budget café/bar/restaurant. Loud music
and generous portions of simple food.
Kaserne Klybeckstrasse 1. Alternative hang-out
offering veggie choices. Mutates on Tues into
Basel's premier gay/lesbian meeting-point.

Luzern and Lake Luzern

An hour south of Basel and Zürich is beautiful **LUZERN**, offering captivating
mountain views, lake cruises and a picturesque medieval quarter. The giant Mount
Pilatus (see below) rears up behind the town, which is split by the River Reuss,
flowing rapidly out of the northwestern end of the oddly shaped
Vierwaldstättersee ("Lake of the Four Forest Cantons" or plain Lake Luzern). In
the Middle Ages, the communities dotted around the lake guarded the northern
approaches to the Gotthard Pass, the main route between northern and southern
Europe. When Habsburg overlords tried to encroach on their privileges, the communities formed an alliance at the lakeside **Rütli Meadow** (in 1291), which was to
prove the beginning of the Swiss Confederation. Luzern, as the principal market
town for the region, was drawn into the bond shortly after. About this time in
Altdorf, just around the lake, **William Tell** shot the apple from his son's head; the
Tell legend lies at the core of Swiss national identity, and the semi-mystical
Vierwaldstättersee is the spiritual as well as the geographical centre of the country.

Luzern was (and is) the main town of the region, and evidence of its medieval
prosperity is manifest in the frescoed facades of its charming Old Town and the two
surviving covered wooden bridges spanning the river, both formerly part of the
city's fortifications and both boasting unique triangular paintings fixed to their roof-
beams. In 1993, fire almost destroyed the fourteenth-century **Kapellbrücke**, a dog-
leg angled around the squat mid-river **Wasserturm**; it was reconstructed with fac-
similes of the roof-paintings (although a few charred originals remain) – check out
no. 31's William Tell. The **Spreuerbrücke** downstream is also worth a look for its
macabre "Dance of Death" paintings. The north bank is home to a compact cluster
of medieval houses, with Mühlenplatz, Weinmarkt, Hirschenplatz and Kornmarkt
forming an ensemble of cobbled, fountained squares ringed by colourful facades.
Next to the Renaissance town hall on Kornmarkt is the **Picasso Museum** in Am
Rhyn-Haus, Furrengasse 21, containing a small fine-art collection supplemented by
hundreds of intimate photographs of the artist's later years (daily 10/11am–4/6pm;
Sfr6). Northeast of the Old Town is Löwenplatz. To the north of the square is the
moving **Löwendenkmal**, a dying lion hewn out of a cliff-face to commemorate
the seven hundred Swiss mercenaries killed by French revolutionaries in 1792 for
defending Louis XVI.

A big reason to visit Luzern is the **Verkehrshaus**, 2km east of the centre at
Lidostrasse 5 (daily 9/10am–5/6pm; Sfr21; ⓦwww.verkehrshaus.org) – take bus #6

or #8 from the station, or have a pleasant walk along the lakeside. The museum, inadequately translated as the "Transport Museum", is a vast complex that could keep you amused all day. It's packed with loads of hands-on technology including videophones and fully equipped TV and radio studios, various original space capsules, railway locomotives (including a walk-through account of the digging of the Gotthard tunnel, dramatized with slides and soundtrack), aeroplanes, cable cars and more. An incongruous highlight is an excellent museum housing the whimsical and attractive works of the little-known Swiss artist **Hans Erni**. Adjoining the complex is an **IMAX cinema**, with shows throughout the day (Sfr16, or Sfr31 joint admission with museum; ⊛www.imax.ch). The newest attraction is a tethered helium balloon known as the **Hiflyer**, which can lift thirty people up to a height of about 150m (daily 11am–5pm; Sfr20; ⊛www.hiflyer.ch).

Practicalities

Luzern's **train station** is on the south bank, where the lake narrows into the river, across from the Kapellbrücke and beside a stunning Convention Centre designed by French architect Jean Nouvel. The **tourist office** is on platform #3 (Mon–Sat 8.30/9am–6/8.30pm, Sun 8.30/9am–1/8.30pm; ☏0412 271 717, ⊛www.luzern.org). Luzern's **HI hostel** is northwest of town by Lake Rotsee, Sedelstrasse 12 (☏0414 208 800, ⊛www.youthhostel.ch; ❸), take bus #18 to Jugendherberge; there's also the friendly SB *Backpackers* at Alpenquai 42 (☏0413 600 420, ⊛www.backpacker.ch; ❸), take bus #6/7/8 to Weinbergli, then cut left. The central *Tourist Hotel*, St Karliquai 12 (☏0414 102 474, ⊛www.touristhotel.ch; ❹), also has dorms. Of the **hotels**, *Löwengraben*, in the Old Town at Löwengraben 18 (☏0414 171 212, ⊛www.loewengraben.ch; ❺), was Luzern's prison from 1862 to 1998: now you can bed down in the comfortably refurbished cells; it also has dorms (❸), as does the *Lido* **campsite**, Lidostrasse 8 (☏0413 702 146, ⊛www.camping-international.ch). Wherever you check in, ask for a stamped **visitors' card**, which grants plenty of discounts around town (including a three-day bus pass from the tourist office for Sfr8). Luzern is a major centre for **adventure sports**; the main operator is Outventure (☏0416 111 441, ⊛www.outventure.ch), which offers canyoning, bungee-jumping and more. **Internet** access is available at the tourist office.

Eating and **drinking** venues crowd the waterfront and the Old Town squares. *Manora* has a rooftop terrace at Weggisgasse 11; shabby *Bahnhof Buffet* on the top floor of the station charges budget prices for gourmet dishes prepared by *Au Premier* adjacent. *Hofgarten*, Stadthofstrasse 14, has excellent veggie food; relaxed *Parterre*, Mythenstrasse 7, offers internet access. Top **bars** include the buzzing *Jazz Kantine*, Grabenstrasse 8, with DJs and live bands downstairs; *Wärchhof*, Werkhofstrasse 11, is another music venue, this one with women-only nights (Mon); chic *Löwengraben* (see above) and frenetic *Schüür*, Tribschenstrasse 1, have excellent music and cheap weekday lunches. Luzern's infamously raucous six-day **Carnival**, ending on Ash Wednesday, is the biggest and best in Switzerland, a constant round of drinking, dancing and partying.

Lake Luzern

You shouldn't leave Luzern without taking a trip on the **lake**, Switzerland's most beautiful and dramatic by far, the thickly wooded slopes rising sheer from the water, bays and peninsulas giving constantly changing views. The regional tourist office also has full details (no public office; ☏041/227 17 17, ⊛www.centralswitzerland.ch). Of the lakeside towns, **VITZNAU** is the base-station of the oldest rack-railway in the world, serving the majestic **Mount Rigi** (IR no discount, ER discount; ⊛www.rigi.ch); and **KEHRSITEN** has a funicular up to **Bürgenstock**, from where a twenty-minute clifftop walk brings you to Europe's fastest outdoor lift, swishing you in seconds to the Hammetschwand summit. From **ALPNACHSTAD**, the steepest rack-railway in the world climbs to the top of **Mount Pilatus**

(IR half-price; SP/ER 30/35 percent discount; ⊛www.pilatus.com). Taking a leisurely boat ride to the far point of the lake at **FLÜELEN** (3hr) connects with mainline trains running west to Luzern and Basel, north to Zürich and south to Lugano and Milan.

Bern

Of all the Swiss cities, **BERN** is perhaps the most immediately charming. Founded in 1191 by the powerful local Zähringen dynasty, it began life as a fortress town peopled by knights. The growth of the Swiss Confederation in subsequent centuries owed much to the conquests of the warlike Bernese. Crammed onto a steep-sided peninsula in a crook of the fast-flowing River Aare, the city's quiet, cobbled lanes, lined with sandstone arcaded buildings, have changed barely at all in over five hundred years. The hills all around, and the steep banks of the river, are still liberally wooded. It's sometimes hard to remember that this quiet, attractive town of just 130,000 people is the nation's capital.

Bern's old centre – designated a UNESCO World Heritage Site in 1983 for the preservation of its medieval street plan – is best explored from the focal east–west **Spitalgasse**. As it leads away from the train station, Spitalgasse becomes Marktgasse, Kramgasse, and then Gerechtigkeitsgasse, but all the way down is lined with seventeenth- and eighteenth-century houses, fountains and arcaded shops. Some 200m east of the station, the street crosses **Bärenplatz**, scene of much outdoor daytime drinking and a lively Saturday-morning market; to the right of it is the **Bundeshaus** or Federal Parliament Building, a domed neo-Renaissance edifice. Beyond Bärenplatz, Marktgasse continues under the oft-rebuilt **Käfigturm** (prisoners' tower), a thirteenth-century town gate. Further along is an eleventh-century gate which was converted in the sixteenth century into the **Zytglogge** – a distinctively top-heavy clocktower adorned with brightly coloured figures that judder into movement four minutes before each hour. (To the left, in Kornhausplatz, is the most famous of Bern's many ornate fountains, the horrific **Kindlifresserbrunnen**, depicting an ogre devouring a struggling baby.) Münstergasse, one block south, leads to the fifteenth-century Gothic **Münster** (Tues–Sat 10am–4/5pm, Sun 11.30am–2/5pm), noted for the magnificently gilded high-relief *Last Judgement* above the main entrance and the elegant buttressed terrace on its south side. Its 254-stepped **tower** (closes 30min earlier; Sfr3), the tallest in Switzerland, offers terrific views of the city and distant mountains. At the eastern end of the centre, the Nydeggbrücke crosses the river to the **Bärengraben** (daily 8/9am–4/6pm), Bern's famed bear-pits, which have housed generations of morose shaggies since the early sixteenth century. Legend has it that the town's founder Berchtold V of Zähringen named Bern after killing one of the beasts during a hunt; the bear has remained a symbol of the town ever since.

Bern's magical **Kunstmuseum**, near the station at Hodlerstrasse 8–12 (Tues–Sun 10am–5/9pm; Sfr7; ⊛wwwkunstmuseumbern.ch), is especially strong on twentieth-century art, with plenty of works by Matisse, Kandinsky, Braque and Picasso, whole rooms devoted to Paul Klee, who was born in Bern and who returned here from Germany after the rise of Nazism, and a good selection of contemporary art as well. More museums are grouped around **Helvetiaplatz**, south of the river: the **Alpine Museum** houses detailed and interesting displays exploring mountain culture (Mon 2–5pm, Tues–Sun 10am–5pm; Sfr7; ⊛www.alpinesmuseum.ch). You could also spend hours in the fascinating seven-floored **Bernisches Historisches Museum** (Tues–Sun 10am–5pm, Wed till 8pm; Sfr5; ⊛www.bhm,ch); check out the "Dance of Death" sequence in the basement, and their fine late-medieval Flemish tapestries and weaponry.

Practicalities

Bern's main **train station** is at the western end of the old centre; cross Bahnhofplatz and turn left to reach Spitalgasse. The **tourist office** is in the station

(Mon–Sat 9am–6.30/8.30pm, Sun 9/10am–5/8.30pm; ☎0313 281 212, ⓦwww.bernetourism.ch), plus a desk at the Bärengraben (daily 9/10am–4/6pm). The riverside **HI hostel**, Weihergasse 4 (☎0313 116 316, ⓦwww.jugibern.ch; ❸), is below the Bundeshaus; the SB place, *Landhaus*, Altenbergstrasse 4 (☎0313 314 166, ⓦwww.backpacker.ch; ❸), is good value, and *Glocke* is very central at Rathausgasse 75 (☎0313 113 771, ⓦwww.chilisbackpackers.com; ❸); both have dorms and rooms. *Eichholz* **campsite**, Strandweg 49 (☎0319 612 602, ⓦwww.campingeich-holz.ch; closed Oct–April), is a fifteen-minute tram ride (#9) towards Wabern. For **eating**, *Manora*, just off Bahnhofplatz, has filling cheap food, and the popular *Reitschule*, a dilapidated squat-cum-arts centre beside the tracks northeast of the station, offers a Sfr5 meal daily along with its cheap beer and liberal smoking policy. Cosy *Brasserie Lorraine*, Quartiergasse 17, has a top Sunday brunch; *Café Bubenberg Vegi*, upstairs at Bubenbergplatz 8, offers quality veggie menus for Sfr15; *Anker* tavern, Kornhausplatz 16, serves fondue and *Rösti*; and the old Toblerone factory at Länggassstrasse 49a (bus #12), now absorbed by the university, has a lively student café at the back. There's no shortage of good **café/bars**, including plenty ringing Bärenplatz; *Café des Pyrénées*, a jovial hangout on Kornhausplatz for artists, alcoholics and others with loud voices; *Drei Eidgenossen*, Rathausgasse 69; traditional *Klötzlikeller*, Gerechtigkeitsgasse 62; and the colourful *Art'Café*, Gurtengasse 3. The *Reitschule* (see above) and *Dampfzentrale*, Marzilistrasse 47, are the two premier venues for **live music** and dance; *J2K*, Junkerngasse 1, is a DJ-bar in an old-town cellar; *ISC*, Neubrückstrasse 10, is a student gig venue. **Listings** are in *Berner Woche*, the Thursday supplement of *Der Bund* newspaper, free from many cinemas; the free fortnightly *What's On* has information and some listings. Bern hosts a **Carnival** in February, a major jazz festival in May and a huge open-air rock event in July.

Listings

Embassies Canada, Kirchenfeldstrasse 88 ☎0313 573 200; Ireland, Kirchenfeldstrasse 68 ☎031/352 14 42; UK, Thunstrasse 50 ☎0313 597 700; US, Jubiläumsstrasse 93 ☎0313 57 7 011.
Internet access Jäggi Bucher, Loeb department store basement, opposite the station (closed Sun);

the Media Center, Zeughausgasse 14 (closed Sun).
Hospital Inselspital University Hospital, Freiburgstrasse ☎0316 322 111.
Pharmacy Hörning, in the station.
Post office Schanzenstrasse, behind the station.

Alpine Switzerland

South of Bern and Luzern lies the grand Alpine heart of Switzerland, a massively impressive region of classic Swiss scenery – high peaks, sheer valleys and cool lakes – that makes for great hiking and gentle walking, not to mention world-class winter sports. The **Bernese Oberland** is the most accessible and touristed area, but beyond this first great wall of peaks is another even more daunting range in which the **Matterhorn**, marking the Italian border, is star attraction. The wild summits and remote valleys in the southeastern corner of Switzerland shelter the world-famous mountain resort of **St Moritz**.

Note that very little happens in the low seasons (April, May, Oct & Nov); shops and hotels may be shut at these times, cable cars may be closed for renovations, and smaller resorts may be virtually deserted.

The Bernese Oberland

Most spectacular of the Alpine regions, the **Bernese Oberland** is best known for a grand triple-peaked ridge – the Eiger, Mönch and Jungfrau, which crests at 4000m. The excursion that is endlessly touted hereabouts is the rack-railway up to the **Jungfraujoch**, the highest train station in Europe at 3454m. The cable-car ride up to the **Schilthorn** (2970m) gets second billing, and is rejected by most visitors, but is in fact quicker, cheaper, offers a more scenic ride up, and has better mountain-top views. (Local cable-TV broadcasts live pictures from both summits round the clock, to help plan a trip.) Most beautiful of the region's countryside is the **Lauterbrunnen valley**, overlooked by the resort of **Mürren**, which provides an excellent base for winter skiing and summer hiking, as does **Grindelwald**, in its own valley slightly east. **Interlaken** is the main transport hub for the region, but the sheer volume of tourist traffic passing through the town can make it a less-than-restful place to stay. Tourist offices can provide details of the region's numerous **mountain huts** (June–Sept), which exist to offer hikers a bed and simple comforts in the wilds of nature. **Ski passes** are not cheap: a half-day costs Sfr40, a full day Sfr52 in a single sector; or Sfr109 for a two-day universal pass.

Interlaken

INTERLAKEN isn't much more than its long main street, **Höheweg**, with a train station at each end. It has little to amuse the trippers passing through on their way to the mountains, save for the cafés and hotel bars lining this main drag and some great **views** towards the Jungfrau massif, perfectly framed between two hills and best savoured from Höhematte, a central grassy rectangle of parkland. As its name suggests, the town lies on a neck of land between two of Switzerland's most attractive **lakes**, and the best way to arrive is by boat.

Interlaken Ost is the terminus of mainline trains and the departure point for branch lines into the mountains (see below); boats also dock here from Brienz, on the Luzern rail line. Trains from the Bern/Zürich direction pass first through **Interlaken West** (docking point for Thunersee boats), and this station is nearer to the **tourist office**, which sits beneath the town's tallest building at Höheweg 37 (Mon–Fri 8am–noon & 1.30–6pm, Sat 8/9am–noon/5pm; July & Aug also Sun 10am–noon & 4–6pm; ☎0338 265 300, ◉www.interlakentourism.ch). You can access the **internet** at the tourist office and at Yess, Centralestrasse 6.

Beware that **accommodation** fills up very quickly in the summer and winter high seasons; there are hotel lists and courtesy phones at both stations. Interlaken's **HI hostel** is 2km east, at Aareweg 21 in Bönigen (☎0338 224 353, ◉www.youth-hostel.ch; ❸; bus #1); you'd do better joining the backpacker crowd at the excellent SB *Balmer's Herberge*, fifteen minutes south of town at Hauptstrasse 23, Matten (☎0338 221 961, ◉www.balmers.com; ❷). There are quieter hostels in town, pick of which is SB *Backpackers Villa Sonnenhof*, Alpenstrasse 16 (☎0338 267 171, ◉www.villa.ch; ❸), which has internet access. Of the dozens of **hotels**, *Alphorn*, Rugenaustrasse 8 (☎0338 223 051, ◉www.hotel-alphorn.ch; ❺), is a charming, well-run little place. The nearest **campsite** is *Sackgut* behind Ost station (☎0338 224 4 34, ◉www.campinginterlaken.ch; closed Oct–March).

For budget **food**, visit *PizPaz* on Centralstrasse for pasta, pizza and fish dishes (closed Mon); or *El Azteca*, Jungfraustrasse 30, offering Mexican set-meals from Sfr14. *Café Runft* opposite West station is a tearoom, snackerie and **bar** open until 3am; *Positiv Einfach*, Centralstrasse 11, is a small but hip music bar; and *Balmer's* hostel has cheap beer. Interlaken is also a good sport for **adventure sports**: Alpin Raft (☎033/823 41 00, ◉www.alpinraft.ch) is the local leader, with loads of activities daily from skydiving to horse trekking.

Lauterbrunnen

It's hard to overstate just how stunning the **Lauterbrunnen valley** is. An immense U-shaped cleft with bluffs on either side rising 1000m sheer, doused by some 72 waterfalls, it is utterly spectacular. The **Staubbach falls**, the highest in Switzerland at nearly 300m, tumble just beyond the village of **LAUTERBRUNNEN** at the valley entrance. The **tourist office** is opposite Lauterbrunnen's station (Mon–Fri 8am–6pm, Sat 9am–5pm; July & Aug also Sun 10am–3pm; ☎0338 568 568, ◉www.wengen-muerren.ch), with internet access. Down by the tracks is *Valley*

Hostel (☎0338 552 008, ✆www.valleyhostel.ch; ❸); *Matratzenlager Stocki* just over the river has dorms in a converted farmhouse (☎0338 551 754; ❷; closed Nov & Dec). Among cheaper **hotels** are *Horner* at the far end of the village (☎0338 551 673, ✆www.hornerpub.ch; ❺); and *Bahnhof* beside the station (☎0338 551 723, ✆www.bahnhof-hotel.ch; ❸). There are two **campsites**: *Jungfrau* (☎0338 562 010, ✆www.camping-jungfrau.ch) and the quieter *Schützenbach* (☎0338 551 268, ✆www.schutzenbachretreat.ch), both with dorms (❷). From Lauterbrunnen, a bus or a scenic three-kilometre walk along the valley floor takes you to the spectacular **Trümmelbach falls** (daily 9/10am–5/6pm; Sfr10), a series of thunderous waterfalls – the runoff from the high mountain glaciers – which have carved corkscrew channels into the valley walls. The same bus continues 1.5km to **STECHELBERG** at the end of the road, where you'll find a *Naturfreundehaus* (☎033/855 12 02; ❷).

Further up on the train line is **KLEINE SCHEIDEGG**, whose station has comfortable rooms and dorms (☎0338 551 151; ❸). The scenic hike (1hr 30min) from Kleine Scheidegg to **Männlichen**, perched on a ridge, is particularly lovely; from Männlichen a cable car runs down to Wengen on one side, or you can take a gondola in the other direction for an amazing half-hour ride to Grindelwald-Grund (ER & IR no discount; SP 25 percent discount).

Mürren and the Schilthorn

From just before Stechelberg, Schilthornbahn cable cars (see below) leap the valley's west wall to reach the quiet hamlet of **GIMMELWALD**, with the popular self-catering *Mountain Hostel* (☎033/855 17 04, ✆www.gimmelwald-news.ch; ❷), then rise further to **MÜRREN**, another endearing car-free village which has managed to retain its atmosphere of isolation (in the off season at least). Mürren is also accessible from directly opposite Lauterbrunnen station via the BLM Bergbahn – a steep funicular to Grütschalp and a spectacular little cliff-edge **train** from there (IR no discount; ER 25-percent discount; SP free). Whichever way you arrive, it's worth it for the views. From Mürren, the valley floor is 800m straight down, and the panorama of peaks filling the sky is dazzling. The sports centre houses the **tourist office** (Mon–Fri 9am–noon & 1–5/6.30pm, Sat & Sun 1–5/5.30pm; May, June, Oct & Nov closed Sat & Sun; ☎0338 568 686, ✆www.wengen-muerren.ch). For **accommodation**, try *Eiger* (☎0338 553 535, ✆www.muerren.ch/eiger; ❸), which is outside the train station, or *Regina* (☎0338 554 242, ✉regina.muerren@swissonline.ch; ❸), at the other end of the village near the cable-car station. The cable car continues from Mürren on a breathtaking ride (20min) up to the 2970m summit of the **SCHILTHORN**, where you can enjoy exceptional panoramic views and sip cocktails in the revolving *Piz Gloria* summit restaurant, featured in the James Bond film *On Her Majesty's Secret Service*. Schilthornbahn **prices**, compared to the Jungfraujoch ride, are a bargain. From Stechelberg, a round-trip is Sfr89, from Mürren Sfr62.60 (IR no discount; ER 25 percent discount; SP free to Mürren, then 25 percent discount). Make the trip before 9am or after 3.30pm, or any time in May or October, and these drop to Sfr66.80/45.20 (discounts don't apply).

Grindelwald

Valley-floor trains from Interlaken Ost also run to the more popular and visited holiday centre of **GRINDELWALD** in its own broad valley further east, nestling under the craggy trio of the Wetterhorn, Mettenberg and Eiger. Numerous trails around **Pfingstegg** and especially **First** – both at the end of gondola lines from Grindelwald – provide excellent hiking, and the icy caverns of the Oberer Gletscher are 890 stairs, or an hour-and-a-half's walk, away (May–Oct daily 9am–6pm; Sfr5). The **tourist office** (Mon–Fri 8am–6/7pm, Sat 8am–5pm; July & Aug also Sun 9–11am & 3–5pm; ☎0338 541 212, ✆www.grindelwald.ch) is near the station, alongside the region's main **Bergsteigerzentrum**, which offers easy guided ascents, canyon jumps, glacier abseils, and more; call ☎0338 531 200.

Grindelwald is famous **paragliding** country, and Tandem Flights (☎0338 535 553, ⓦ www.paragliding-grindelwald.ch) offers accompanied jumps from Sfr150. A bus from opposite *Hotel Bernerhof*, or a steep fifteen-minute walk, will get you to Terrassenweg, a quiet lane running above the village, where there's an excellent **HI hostel** (☎0338 531 009, ⓦ www.youthhostel.ch; ❸) and a *Naturfreundehaus* (☎0338 531 333; ❸). SB *Mountain Hostel* (☎0338 533 900, ⓦ www.mountainhostel.ch; ❸) is on the valley floor beside Grindelwald-Grund station. (Trains from Grindelwald pass through Grund on their way up to Kleine Scheidegg.) You can **camp** at *Aspen* (☎0338 531 124, ⓦ www.aspen.ch; closed Nov–Feb). **Internet** access is available at the *Parkhotel Schoenegg*, which is just off the main road next to the First Gondola station, and in the Photoshop Schudel in the tourist office building.

The Jungfraujoch

Switzerland's most popular (and expensive) mountain railway trundles through lush countryside south from Interlaken before coiling spectacularly up across mountain pastures, breaking the treeline and tunnelling clean through the Eiger to emerge at the **JUNGFRAUJOCH** (3454m), an icy, windswept col just beneath the Jungfrau summit with the awesome Aletsch glacier, longest in the Alps, for company. The journey up is scenic in parts, but very long (two-and-a-half hours from Interlaken, with most of the final hour climbing in a pitch-dark tunnel), and the top station, inevitably, is a tourist circus of ice sculptures, husky sleigh rides, glacier walks, a short ski run, restaurants and a post office, all invariably overflowing with tour-groups. Nonetheless, on a clear day and with time to spare, it's worth the expense. Panoramic views from the Sphinx Terrace (3571m) to Germany's Black Forest in one direction and across a gleaming wasteland to the Italian Alps in the other are heart-thumping – as is the thin air.

There are two **routes** to the top. Trains head southwest from Interlaken Ost along the valley floor to Lauterbrunnen, from where you pick up the mountain line which climbs through Wengen; trains also head southeast from Interlaken Ost to Grindelwald, where you change for the climb, arriving from the other direction. All trains terminate at Kleine Scheidegg, where you must change for the final pull to Jungfraujoch; the popular practice is to go up one way and down the other. The adult round-trip **fare** from Interlaken is a budget-crunching Sfr162.80 (IR no discount; ER 25 percent discount; SP free to Wengen or Grindelwald then 25 percent discount). The best deal is the discounted **Good Morning ticket**, valid if you travel up on the first train of the day (6.35am from Interlaken), and leave the summit by noon; this costs Sfr125.80 from Interlaken, Sfr108.60 from Lauterbrunnen or Grindelwald, Sfr97 from Wengen, or Sfr62 from Kleine Scheidegg. **Walking** some sections of the journey, up or down, is perfectly feasible in summer, and can save a lot of money. Excellent transport networks and vista-rich footpaths linking all intermediate points mean that with judicious use of a hiking map and train timetable you can see and do a great deal in a day and still get back to Interlaken, or even Bern or Zürich, by bedtime.

Zermatt and the Matterhorn

The shark's-tooth **Matterhorn** (4478m) is the most famous of Switzerland's peaks, and no other natural or human structure in the whole country is so immediately recognizable: in most people's minds, the Matterhorn stands for Switzerland like the Eiffel Tower stands for France. One reason it's so famous is that it stands alone, its impossibly pointy shape sticking up from an otherwise uncrowded horizon above **ZERMATT** village; another is that the quintessential Swiss chocolate, Toblerone, is modelled on it. The only way to reach Zermatt is on the spectacular narrow-gauge BVZ train line (ER no discount, IR half-price for under-26s only, SP free), accessed from mainline junctions at **Brig** and **Visp**. BVZ trains depart on tracks laid in the road outside both stations. The most celebrated way to arrive is on the long east–west St Moritz-to-Zermatt **Glacier Express**, which takes in some of Switzerland's finest scenery in a day-long journey by panoramic train (reserve at any train station; ER & SP free; IR under 26 only half-price; small supplement payable on the Disentis–Brig section; ◉www.glacierexpress.ch). Coming from Zürich, head for Göschenen, where you switch onto the narrow-gauge FO Furka-Oberalp line through Andermatt to Brig (ER & SP free; IR half-price).

Zermatt's main street throngs year-round with an odd mixture of professional climbers, tour-groups, backpackers and fur-clad socialites. Electric minibuses ferry people between the train station at the northern end of the village and the cable-car terminus 1km south. In the village, the **Alpine Museum** (May–Oct daily 10am–noon & 4.30–6.30pm; Nov–April Mon–Fri & Sun 4.30–6.30pm; Sfr5) commemorates the tragic first ascent of the Matterhorn, led by Edward Whymper in 1865: one of his party slipped on the way down, sending four people to their deaths. They, and many more Matterhorn hopefuls, are commemorated in the town's burgeoning cemetery. Opposite the station, GGB Gornergrat-Bahn trains (ER no discount, SP 25 percent discount, IR under 26 only half-price) climb above the village, giving spectacular Matterhorn views (sit on the right) all the way up to the **Gornergrat**, a vantage point with a magnificent Alpine panorama including Switzerland's highest peak, the Dufourspitze (4634m). In summer, GGB trains leave Zermatt once-weekly at dawn to arrive in time for a breathtaking Alpine sunrise. At the south end of Zermatt village a cable car heads up via Furi to the **Schwarzsee** (2583m), the most popular point from which to view the peak and, in summer, the trailhead for a zigzag walk (2hr) to the Berghaus Matterhorn inn (3260m), right below the mountain. All of Zermatt's cable cars and trains bring you to trailheads and spectacular views, and lifts to **Trockener Steg** give access to 21km of ski runs and a snowboard half-pipe that are open all **summer** long (day-pass Sfr60).

Practicalities

There's a hotel list and courtesy phone in the station; otherwise consult the helpful **tourist office** nearby (Mon–Fri 8.30am–noon & 1.30–6pm, Sat 8.30am–noon/6.30pm, Sun 9.30am–noon & 4–6pm; ☎0279 668 100, ◉www.zermatt.ch). The **mountain guides** office (Mon–Fri 9.30am–noon & 4–6.30pm; ☎0279 662 460) organizes tours and climbs. The excellent **HI hostel** is on the east side of the village (☎0279 672 320, ◉www.youthhostel.ch; ❹); nearby is the SB *Matterhorn Hostel* (☎0279 681 919, ◉www.matterhornhostel.com; ❸) and a *Naturfreundehaus* (☎0279 672 788, ✉naturfreunde.zermatt@spectraweb.ch; ❹). *Camping Zermatt* (☎0279 675 414; closed Oct–May) is north of the station. Of the many **hotels**, *Mischabel*, down by the river, is quiet and characterful (☎0279 671 131, ◉www.zermatt.ch/mischabel; ❺), while youthful *Post*, in the centre, is livelier (☎0279 671 932, ◉www.postzermatt.com; ❻) and offers internet access. Plenty of mountain inns and huts bring you closer to the elements, including at Schwarzsee (☎0279 672 263; dorms ❼) and the *Berghaus Matterhorn* (☎0279 672 264, ◉www.zermatt.ch/matterhorn-group/berghaus-matterhorn; dorms ❽; closed Oct–June); rates include half-board. There are plenty of places to **eat** all along Zermatt's main drag: *Hotel Post* has budget pizza/pasta, as does the popular *North Wall* après-ski bar, on the other side of the river. Pleasant *Café du Pont*, just past the church, serves affordable **fondues** and other snacks.

St Moritz

Plopped down amidst the quiet villages of the wild and beautiful **Engadine Valley** that runs for 100km along the south side of the Alps, brassy **ST MORITZ** is the prime winter retreat of the international jet set, who over the years have created a mini-Manhattan of Vuitton and Armani in this stunningly romantic setting of forest, lake and mountains; when the tourist office trumpets St Moritz's "champagne climate", they don't necessarily mean the sparkling sunshine (although there's an amazing 322 days of that a year on average). The town spans two villages, St Moritz-Bad on the lake and St Moritz-Dorf on the hillside 2km above, linked by the main Via dal Bagn. Dorf is the upmarket one, while Bad – site of a Roman spa – is more down-to-earth. The area boasts legendary bob and toboggan courses, including the death-defying 1.2km **Cresta Run** (end Dec to Feb; Sfr450/five rides; no credit cards; booking not possible; ⊛ www.cresta-run.com). You can rent wooden sleds for the famous winter **Preda–Bergün toboggan run** (daily 10am–5pm; Sfr4/hr or Sfr10/day; ⊛ www.berguen.ch), starting from Preda train station and taking a zigzag for 5km down through the scenic Albula valley to Bergün, where trains cart you back to the beginning; the course is floodlit at night (not Mon).

Via Serlas winds up from the **train station** below Dorf to a central square, from where the **tourist office** is 100m east at Via Maistra 12 (Mon–Sat 9am–6pm; Christmas–March also Sun 4–6pm; ☎0818 373 333, ⊛ www.stmoritz.ch). The **HI hostel** *Stille*, Via Surpunt 60 (☎0818 333 9 69, ⊛ www.youthhostel.ch/stmoritz; ❹), is a twenty-minute walk around the lake next to the *Stille* **hotel** (☎0818 336 948, ⊛ www.hotelstille.ch; ❺; closed Nov–May) and near the *Olympiaschanze* **campsite** (☎0818 334 090; closed Oct–May). *Hotel Bellaval* (☎0818 333 245, ⊛ www.bellaval-stmoritz.ch; ❺) is beside Dorf station. Most **restaurants** are ridiculously expensive; affordable ones include *Boccalino* pizzeria, Via dal Bagn 6, but with this kind of scenery all around, you might prefer to picnic. Your best bet for a **drink** is *Bobby's Pub*, Via dal Bagn 52.

Ticino

The Italian-speaking canton of **Ticino** (*Tessin* in German and French) occupies the balmy, lake-laced southern foothills of the Alps. It's radically different from the rest of the country in almost every way: culture, food, architecture, attitude and driving style owe more to Milan than Zürich, and the glamour of the place – its lushly wooded hills, azure lakes and date palms – often seems to blind outsiders with romance. The German Swiss in particular fall head over heels for the Latin paradise on their doorstep: it takes just three hours from the grey streets of suburban Zürich to the fragrant subtropical gardens of Lugano, and you'll find throughout the canton that printed information tends to be in Italian and German, sidelining English. Switzerland has controlled the area since the early 1500s, when it moved to secure the southern approaches of the St Gotthard Pass against the dukes of Milan. It's a cruel irony that the determinedly patriotic Ticinesi now suffer the country's highest unemployment rates, even while the region's service industries thrive, staffed by Italian guest-workers and paid for by thousands of Swiss-German tourists and second-home-owners.

The main attractions are the lakeside resorts of **Locarno** and **Lugano**, where mountain scenery merges with the subtropical flora encouraged by the warm climate. The area is also known for its old churches, many containing medieval frescoes and most featuring huge external murals of St Christopher, patron saint of travellers. Unless you approach from Italy, there's only one train line in – through the 16km **Gotthard Tunnel**.

Locarno

Mainline trains speed south to Lugano and Milan, while a branch line heads west from Bellinzona to Lake Maggiore and its principal Swiss resort, **LOCARNO**, overrun with the rich and wannabe-famous on summer weekends yet still managing to retain its Mediterranean, shades-and-*gelati* cool. The focus of town is **Piazza**

Grande; a busy arcaded square just off the palm-fringed lakefront. Most interest lies in the narrow streets of the characterful Old Town, ranged on gently rising ground behind Piazza Grande. From the west end of the piazza, lanes run up to Via Cittadella and the richly Baroque **Chiesa Nuova**, with a sumptuously stuccoed ceiling. Alleys lead south downhill to the thirteenth-century **Castello Visconteo**, housing an archeological museum (April–Oct Tues–Sun 10am–5pm; Sfr5), especially strong on beautiful Roman glass. Most striking of all, though, is the church of **Madonna del Sasso** (daily 7am–7pm), an impressive ochre vision floating above the town founded in 1480. The walk up (or down) through a wooded ravine and past decaying shrines is glorious; or take the funicular from just west of the station to Ticino's greatest photo-opportunity, looking down on the church and lake. From the top, a cable car runs further up to **Cardada** on the ridge, where there are more walking routes and a chairlift whisking you up to the spectacular views at Cimetta. East of Locarno is **Valle Verzasca**, where deathwish freaks can re-enact the opening scene of the James Bond film *Goldeneye*, by bungeeing a world-record 220m off the **Verzasca Dam** (Sfr255; book on ☏0848 808 007 or ✆www.trekking.ch; closed Nov–March).

Practicalities

Locarno's **train station** is 150m northeast of Piazza Grande. Between the two is the landing stage on the lake; summer boats run to nearby Swiss lakeside resorts such as Ascona, and way south to Italian ones such as Stresa (no discounts). The **tourist office** is in the Casino complex opposite the landing stage (Mon–Fri 9am–6pm; March–Oct also Sat 10am–5pm, Sun 10am–noon & 1–3pm; ☏0917 910 091, ✆www.maggiore.ch). There's **internet** at Cinema Rialto, Via S. Gottardo 1. Both the modern **HI hostel** *Ostello Palagiovani*, Via Varenna 18 (☏0917 561 500, ✆www.youthhostel.ch; ❸; bus #31/#36 to Cinque Vie), and central *Città Vecchia*, Via Torretta 13 (☏0917 514 554, ✆www.cittavecchia.ch; ❸; closed Nov–Feb), have dorms and rooms. The pricey *Delta* **campsite** (☏0917 516 081, ✆www.campingdelta.com) is fifteen minutes south along the lakeshore. There's a self-service *Manor* beside the station and Piazza Grande is full of cafés and pizzerias buzzing from morning until after midnight, although **eating** and **drinking** is more atmospheric in the Old Town alleys. *Cittadella*, at no.18 on the street of the same name, serves affordable pizzas and fish dishes; friendly *Bar del Pozzo* is on Piazza Sant'Antonio; *Cantina Canetti* off Piazza Grande has live accordion on weekend nights; *Simba*, Lungolago 3a, is a popular DJ bar. Music festivals devoted to country, blues, funk and jazz follow hot on each other's heels during June and July, while early August's excellent **Locarno International Film Festival** (✆www.pardo.ch) is stealing a march on Cannes for movie quality and star-appeal; catch nightly offerings on Europe's largest movie screen, set up in Piazza Grande.

The Centovalli railway

Locarno is the eastern terminus of the dramatic **Centovalli railway** (ER, IR & SP free), well worth putting aside half a day for. Clanky little trains run from beneath Locarno's station west into the impressive Centovalli – so named for its "hundred" side-valleys – most of the time sidewinding above ravine-like depths; sit on the left for the best views. After the border at **Camedo** (passport needed), trains roll on through rustic villages amid spectacular scenery before easing down into the Italian town of **DOMODOSSOLA**. Swiss express trains from here run west to Brig (for Zermatt), Geneva and Bern; Italian ones head south to Milan.

Lugano

With its compact cluster of Italianate piazzas and extensive tree-lined promenades, **LUGANO** is the most alluring of Ticino's lake resorts, less touristic than Locarno but with, if anything, double the chic. Centre of town is **Piazza di Riforma**, a huge café-lined square, while Lugano's exceptionally beautiful lake is metres away, as are the characterful steep lanes of the old town. Through the maze northwest of Riforma, Via Cattedrale dog-legs up to **Cattedrale San Lorenzo**, characterized by a fine Renaissance portal, fragments of interior frescoes, and spectacular views from its terrace. Also from Riforma, narrow Via Nassa – rivalling Zürich's Bahnhofstrasse for big-name designer glitz – heads southwest to the medieval church of **Santa Maria degli Angioli**, containing a stunning wall-sized fresco of the Crucifixion. A little further south is the **Museo d'Arte Moderna**, Riva Caccia 5 (Tues–Sun 9am–7pm; Sfr10), with world-class exhibitions; and a little further still is the modestly named district of **Paradiso**, from where a funicular rises to **San Salvatore**, a rugged rock pinnacle offering fine views of the lake and surrounding countryside. East from Riforma along the shore on foot or with bus #1, you'll come to the gates of **Villa Favorita** – which are permanently closed, but the setting is impressive and the villa can only be approached on foot via a long cypress-lined path through lavishly beautiful waterside gardens. The slopes of **Monte Brè** behind are home to most of Lugano's many millionaires, while a funicular rises from the adjacent district of **Cassarate** to the summit, with bracing walks and views. The best of the lake is behind (south of) San Salvatore on the Ceresio peninsula, accessed by boats or postbuses. Here you'll find tiny **Montagnola**, where the writer Hermann Hesse lived for 43 years; his first house, Casa Camuzzi, is now a small **museum** (March–Oct Tues–Sun 10am–12.30pm & 2–6.30pm; Nov–Feb Sat & Sun only; Sfr6; @www.tcp.ch/cultura), with an excellent 45-minute English film on Hesse's life in Ticino. Jewel of the lake, however, is **Morcote** on the gorgeous southern tip of the peninsula. Tranquil stepped lanes lead up to its photogenic church of Santa Maria del Sasso, with striking interior frescoes and a grand vista. Several walks explore the lush woodlands, including a trail back to San Salvatore (2hr 30min).

Practicalities

Lugano's **train station** overlooks the town from the west, linked to the centre by a short funicular or by steps down to Via Cattedrale. The **tourist office** is in Palazzo Civico, between Riforma and the lake (Mon–Fri 9am–5.30/7.30pm; April–Oct also Sat 9am–5.30pm, Sun 10am–4pm; ☎0919 133 232, @www.lugano-tourism.ch). **Boats** around the lake (IR & ER no discount, SP free) depart from opposite the tourist office. One of Switzerland's best-value **HI hostels** (complete with swimming pool) is at Via Cantonale 13, Savosa (☎0919 662 728, @www.youthhostel.ch; ❷; closed Nov–March) – take bus #5 to Crocifisso from the stop 200m left out of the train station; there's another HI place at Figino, southwest of town (☎0919 951 151; ❷; closed Nov–March) – take postbus from Riforma to Casoro. The SB *Montarina*, behind the station at Via Montarina 1 (☎0919 667 272, @www.montarina.ch; ❸), also has dorms. Affordable **hotels** include *Ginevra*, Via Ginevra 7 (☎0919 236 170; ❹). *Molinazzo* (☎0916 051 877, @molinazo@bluewin.ch) is one of several lakeside **campsites** in Agno, a short train-ride west. Lugano is blessed with fine espresso, served at *La Cafferia Cattedrale*, Via Cattedrale 6, and reasonably priced **eateries** on all the central squares: Piazza Cioccaro, the lower terminus of the funicular, is home to a big *Inova* and *Sayonara* where you can find inexpensive pasta and pizzas, while *La Tinèra*, off Via dei Gorini, behind Riforma, has tasty Ticinese chicken stews and *Hotel Pestalozzi* (see above) has a good vegetarian restaurant. Although the many bars and cafés around Riforma are packed with evening **drinkers**, hip Luganesi tuck themselves away elsewhere: in the unlikely warren of the Quartiere Maghetti nearby is *Etnic*, with superb inexpensive Mediterranean-style food, beer, cocktails and a cosy studentish atmosphere. **Internet** access is available at Manor, Piazza Dante 2.

Liechtenstein

Only slightly larger than Manhattan island, **Liechtenstein** is the world's fourth-smallest country. It's a quiet, unassuming place, ruled over by His Serene Highness Prince Hans Adam II, and has made a mint from nursing some Sfr90 billion in its numbered bank accounts, a living that has inevitably laid it open to accusations of dubious practice. Money-laundering aside, the main reason to visit is inevitably the novelty value. You have to feel sorry for little **VADUZ**, labouring under the weight of being capital of a historical oddity: the tiny town bulges with glass-plated banks and squadrons of whistle-stop visitors aimless with anticlimax. Central hub is the post office, where all buses stop, midway between the two parallel main streets, Äulestrasse and pedestrianized Städtle. Facing it is the sleek new **Kunstmuseum** (Tues–Sun 10am–5pm, Thurs till 8pm; Sfr5; ☻ www.kunstmuseum.li), holding the world-famous private **art** collection inherited – and added to – by the prince, which includes exquisite works by Rubens, Rembrandt and others. Perched picturesquely on the forested hillside above the town is the prince's restored sixteenth-century **castle** (no public access). If you have some time to spare, catch bus #10 to Liechtenstein's sole mountain resort of **MALBUN**, a small, blissfully quiet retreat up at 1602m.

Practicalities

Bus #1 shuttles over the Rhine to Vaduz from **Sargans** train station on the Zürich–Chur line (no border controls). Postbuses from Vaduz serve all points in Liechtenstein as well as **Feldkirch** just across the border in Austria (passport needed), from where trains run on to Bregenz, Innsbruck and Vienna. All Swiss transport passes are valid on Liechtenstein buses.

The Vaduz **tourist office**, Städtle 37 (April–Oct Mon–Fri 8am–5.30pm, Sat 9/10am–5pm; May–Sept also Sun 9/10am–5pm; Nov–March Mon–Fri 8am–5.30pm; ☎232 14 43, ☻ www.liechtenstein.li), has good information and will bang a stamp into your passport as a memento (Sfr2). There's an **HI hostel** at Untere Rüttigasse 6, beside Mühleholz bus stop in **SCHAAN**, 2km north of Vaduz (☎232 50 22; ❸; closed Dec–Feb). The best-value **hotel** is the central *Landgasthof Au, Austrasse 2* (☎232 11 17; ❺). At **STEG**, near Malbun, *Sücka* doubles as a working farm and guest house, with dorms (☎263 25 79, ☻suecka1@adon.li; ❸). In the countryside near **TRIESEN**, 5km south of Vaduz, is the Mittagspitz **campsite** (☎392 36 77). For **food** in Vaduz, *Cesare*, Städtle 15 (closed Sat & Sun), offers good Italian food; while gourmet stand-up deli *Eredi Florini*, Herrengasse 9 (closed Sun), has delicious point-and-choose meals. **Internet** access can be found at the Telecom Shop, Austrasse 77 (closed Sun; free).

Travel details

Trains

Basel to: Bern (hourly; 1hr); Geneva (hourly; 2hr 50min); Interlaken Ost (hourly; 2hr 10min); Lausanne (hourly; 2hr 30min); Lugano (hourly; 3hr 50min); Luzern (hourly; 1hr 5min); Zürich (every 30min; 1hr).
Bern to: Basel (hourly; 1hr); Geneva (every 30min; 1hr 45min); Interlaken Ost (hourly; 45min); Lausanne (every 30min; 1hr 10min); Luzern (every 2hr; 1hr 20min); Zürich (every 30min; 1hr 10min).

Geneva to: Basel (hourly; 2hr 50min); Bern (hourly; 1hr 45min); 20min); Lausanne (3 hourly; 35min); Montreux (hourly; 1hr 5min); Vevey (hourly; 1hr); Zürich (every 30min; 3hr).
Grindelwald to: Interlaken Ost (hourly; 20min); Jungfraujoch (every 30min; 1hr 30min – change at Kleine Scheidegg).
Interlaken Ost to: Bern (hourly; 50min); Grindelwald (hourly; 40min); Jungfraujoch (hourly; 2hr 30min – change at Grindelwald or Lauterbrunnen, then Kleine Scheidegg);

Lauterbrunnen (hourly; 20min); Luzern (hourly; 1hr 55min); Zürich (hourly; 2hr 15min).
Kleine Scheidegg to: Grindelwald (every 30min; 35min); Jungfraujoch (every 30min; 50min); Lauterbrunnen (every 30min; 1hr).
Lausanne to: Basel (hourly; 2hr 30min); Bern (every 30min; 1hr 10min); Geneva (3 hourly; 35min); Montreux (every 20min; 25min); Vevey (every 20min; 15min); Zürich (every 30min; 2hr 30min).
Lauterbrunnen to: Interlaken Ost (hourly; 20min); Jungfraujoch (every 20min; 1hr 40min – change at Kleine Scheidegg).
Lugano to: Luzern (hourly; 2hr 50min); Zürich (hourly; 3hr 10min).
Luzern to: Basel (hourly; 1hr 15min); Bern (every 2hr; 1hr 20min); Interlaken Ost (hourly; 1hr 55min); Lugano (hourly; 2hr 50min); Zürich (every 30min; 45min).
Montreux to: Geneva (twice hourly; 1hr 20min); Interlaken (every 2hr; 3hr – change at Zweisimmen & Spiez); Lausanne (every 20min; 25min); Vevey (3 hourly; 10min).
Vevey to: Geneva (twice hourly; 1hr 10min); Lausanne (every 20min; 15min); Montreux (3 hourly; 10min).

Zürich to: Basel (every 30min; 1hr); Bern (every 30min; 1hr 10min); Geneva (every 30min; 3hr); Interlaken Ost (hourly; 2hr 15min); Lausanne (every 30min; 2hr 30min); Lugano (hourly; 3hr 10min); Luzern (hourly; 50min); Sargans (hourly; 1hr 10min).

Buses

Lugano to: St Moritz (twice daily; 4hr).
Sargans to: Vaduz (every 20min; 30min).
Vaduz to: Malbun (hourly; 30min).

Boats

The following times are for May–Sept only; very few boats run outside these months.

Geneva to: Lausanne (3 daily; 3hr 30min); Montreux (3 daily; 5hr); Vevey (3 daily; 4hr 30min).
Lausanne to: Geneva (3 daily; 3hr 30min); Montreux (5 daily; 1hr 30min); Vevey (5 daily; 1hr).
Luzern to: Alpnachstad (6 daily; 1hr 40min); Flüelen (8 daily; 2hr 50min); Kehrsiten (hourly; 35min); Vitznau (hourly; 1hr).

Turkey

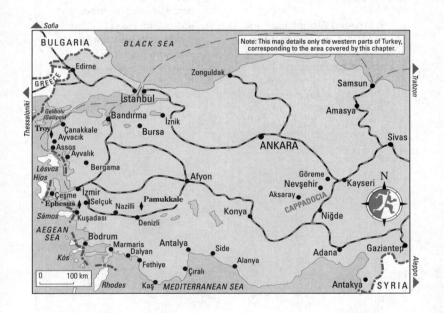

Turkey highlights

✳ **Aya Sofya, İstanbul**
Sixth-century cathedral, built by Justinian. A fascinating glimpse into the city's Byzantium past. **See p.1086**

✳ **Covered Bazaar, Istanbul**
With over 3000 shops, stalls and workshops, and the ubiquitous haggling, this is one of the world's great markets. **See p.1090**

✳ **Ephesus** The best-preserved archeological site in the country. **See p.1107**

✳ **Cappadocia** Lunar landscape shaped by nature and human hands, replete with eerie caves, rock dwellings and underground cities. **See p.1123**

Introduction and basics

Turkey is a country with multiple identities, poised uneasily between East and West. The only NATO member in the Middle East region, the country has recently been accepted as a candidate for membership of the EU. Yet although in many respects Western, Turkey retains its frustrating differences, and its contradictions: mosques coexist with churches, and remnants of the Roman Empire crumble alongside ancient Hittite and Neolithic sites. Politically, modern Turkey was a bold experiment and almost entirely the creation of a single man, **Mustafa Kemal Atatürk**. An explicitly secular republic, though one in which the majority of the inhabitants are at least nominally Muslim, it's a vast country and incorporates large disparities in levels of development. It's an immensely rewarding place to travel, not least because of the people, whose reputation for friendliness and hospitality is richly deserved.

Western Turkey is the most visited and economically developed part of the country. **İstanbul**, straddling the Bosphorus straits and the Marmara coast, is a heady mix of the European and Oriental. It's the country's cultural and commercial centre and also visibly the old imperial capital. Flanking İstanbul on opposite sides of the **Sea of Marmara** are the two earlier Ottoman capitals, **Bursa** and **Edirne**, and the former Byzantine capital of **İznik**, with, just beyond, the World War I battlefields of the **Dardanelles**.

Moving south, on the **Aegean Coast** small country towns such as **Ayvalık** are swathed in olive groves, while the area is littered with ancient sites, including **Assos, Pergamon** and **Ephesus**, which have been a magnet for travellers since the eighteenth century. Beyond the functional but not unattractive city of **İzmir**, the Aegean coast is Turkey at its most developed, with large numbers of visitors drawn to resorts such as **Çeşme**, **Bodrum** and **Marmaris**, beyond which the Mediterranean coast begins. There are remnants of the Lycians at **Xanthos**, and more resorts in **Kaş** and **Fethiye**, along the aptly named "Turquoise Coast".

On the Mediterranean coast, **Antalya** is one of Turkey's fastest-growing cities, a useful starting-point on the stretch towards the Syrian border, featuring extensive sands and archeological sites – most notably at **Perge** and **Aspendos** – until castle-topped **Alanya**, where the tourist numbers begin to diminish. It's worth heading inland from here for the spectacular attractions of **Cappadocia**, with its famous rock churches, subterranean cities and landscape studded with cave dwellings, as well as the Selçuk architecture and dervish associations of **Konya**. Further north, **Ankara**, Turkey's capital, is a planned city whose contrived Western feel gives some indication of the priorities of the modern Turkish Republic.

Information and maps

Most Turkish towns of any size will have a **tourist office** (*Turizm Danışma Bürosu*) generally open Mon–Fri 8.30am–12.30pm & 1.30–5.30pm, with extended evening and weekend hours in big resorts and cities, and during the peak summer season. Staff outside the larger cities and resorts may not

TURKEY | Basics

speak English, but they often have good brochures and maps, and should at least be able to help you with accommodation.

The best available **maps** are produced by Geo Centre/RV ("Turkey West" and "Turkey East"), sold separately as sheets or together in book form at most major resorts. City tourist offices normally stock reasonable **street plans**. *The A–Z Atlas of İstanbul* (pub. Asya) is a worthwhile investment if you're spending time in the city.

Money and banks

Turkish **currency** is the lira, abbreviated as TL. There are coins of 50,000 (written on the coin as "50 bin") and 100,000, and notes of 250,000, 500,000, 1,000,000, 5,000,000 and 10,000,000. Bear in mind that the 10,000,000 note looks very similar to the 1,000,000 one, and it's not unknown for visitors to be fooled into accepting the lower denomination. **Rates** for foreign currency are always better inside Turkey, and because of the TL's constant devaluation you should change money only as you need it. Many pensions and hotels, particularly in the popular destinations, will quote prices in **US dollars** (and increasingly **euros**) as well as TL and you can pay in both.

Banks are open Mon–Fri 8.30am–noon & 1.30–5pm, and some, notably Garanti Bankasi, open at lunchtimes and on Saturdays. Most charge a commission of about US$2.50 for travellers' cheques. Between April and October many coastal resorts between Çanakkale and Alanya have weekend and evening hours at specific *nöbetçi* banks; a list is posted in the window or door of each branch. You can also use the **exchange booths** run by banks in coastal resorts, airports and ferry docks, though some charge a small commission. Easiest option is a private exchange office, which will offer competitive rates and charge no commission. Almost all bank branches have **ATMs** which accept Cirrus and Plus, but it's wise to use them during banking hours in case your card is swallowed; avoid stand-alone ATMs for the same reason. **Post offices** in sizeable towns also sometimes change currency and travellers' cheques, for a one-percent commission.

Communications

Most **post offices** (PTT) are open Mon–Sat 8am–5pm, with main branches staying open till 7/8pm and opening on Sun. Post boxes are clearly labelled with categories of destination – *yurtdışı* means overseas.

Phone calls can be made from Turk Telecom booths and the PTT. Post offices and kiosks sell phonecards (30, 60 and 100 units) and *jetons* (tokens), and have both types of phone, as well as metered phones. A new generation of payphones accepting credit cards has appeared, as have numerous private **phone shops** *(Köntürlü telefon)* offering metered calls at dubious, unofficial rates. Call ☎118 for **directory** enquiries, ☎115 for the international **operator**. There are three GSM **mobile-phone** companies, all of which sell pre-paid SIM cards for around $20. Top-up cards are widely available.

Internet access is excellent, with cybercafés in most towns charging $0.50–1.50/hr depending on location and the mode of access (dial-up or leased-line).

Getting around

Public transport is easy and inexpensive. The train system is limited and slow, but there's a myriad of private buses, as used by most Turks. Short stretches are best covered by *dolmuš* – a shared taxi in towns or a minibus linking rural villages.

Buses and dolmuşes

Long-distance bus is the best way of getting around. There's no national bus company; most routes are covered by several competing firms, which will all have ticket booths at the bus stations (*otogars* or *terminal*) from which they operate, as well as offices in the relevant town centres. There's no such thing as a comprehensive **timetable**. Better companies will have a seasonal schedule of sorts, but even these are subject to change; bigger companies tend to make fewer stops en route, which means their quoted journey time is generally more accurate. **Fares** vary only slightly between companies: as a broad guideline, expect to pay $3/100km. Top companies such as Ulusoy, Pamukkale, Kamil Koç and Varan are worth the bit extra in comfort, service and safety. From October to April, the bigger companies may stop running buses altogether along routes that are popular with summer visitors, in which case you may have to make do with local minibus services; in extreme cases you may not find any transport at all.

For short hops you're most likely to use a **dolmuş**, a car or minibus that follows a set route, picking up and dropping off along the way; sometimes the destination will be posted on a sign at the kerbside, and sometimes within the *dolmuš* itself, though you'll generally have to ask. On busy urban routes it's better to take the *dolmuš* from the start of its run; otherwise, hail it like a taxi to stop it in the street. **Fares** are very low.

Trains

Turkey's **train network**, run by the TCDD, is patchy. The most useful services are the expresses between İstanbul and Ankara, and other long-distance links to main provincial cities such as Edirne, Konya, Eskişehir, Denizli and İzmir. Most routes are slow, tortuous and wonderfully scenic. Sleeper cabins are available on overnight services at very reasonable rates. Reservations for most journeys can be made in İstanbul, İzmir or Ankara, though they're really only necessary at weekends or on national holidays. Basic prices are about as for buses; an ISIC card will get you a twenty-percent discount. **InterRail** is valid, **Eurail** isn't.

Ferries

Nearly all **ferries** are run by *Türkiye Denizcilik İşletmesi* (Turkish Maritime Lines or TDİ), who operate everything from inner-city shuttles and inter-island lines to international routeings. Overnight services are popular, and you should buy tickets well in advance through authorized TDİ agents. **Fares** are reasonable; for example, a third-class double cabin from İstanbul to İzmir costs about $60 per person,. Students aged 28 or under get a thirty-percent discount with an ISIC card.

Accommodation

Finding **accommodation** is generally no problem, except in high season at the busier coastal resorts and in the larger towns. The economic crisis of early 2001 left prices distinctly low by northern European standards, although it remains to be seen how long this will last.

Hotels and pensions

Many **hotels** are graded by the tourism ministry on a scale of one to five stars. Ungraded establishments, which can be either hotels or **pensions** *(pansiyons)*, are licensed by municipalities, and may be as good as equivalent graded ones. A double room in a one-star hotel costs $15–30 in season, with breakfast sometimes included. The most basic ungraded places may offer spartan rooms, with or without toilet, washbasin and/or shower, for as low as $12 per person. A new type of "bijou" hotel/pension, often in historic buildings, offers high levels of comfort, sometimes at surprisingly reasonable prices.

There's also a well-established breed of "**backpacker**" hotels/pensions. In the coastal resorts and other tourist targets, touts acting for these places meet every incoming bus, *dolmuş* and ferry. Rooms tend to be sparse but clean, and cost $10–20 for an en-suite double, $5–10 for a dorm bed. Where places are open during low season (Nov–April), prices tend to drop to half the summer rates; however, most resort-based places close in winter, so it would be wise to call ahead or check with the local tourist office.

Hostels and campsites

Turkey has a small chain of **hostels** under the banner "Turkish YHA", but of these only one is actually HI-affiliated (the *Interyouth* hostel in İstanbul). That said, hostels differ little in price and facilities from the backpacker-oriented hotels and pensions outlined above.

Campsites are common on the coast and in national parks, but rare elsewhere. Charges per person run from $2 for the most basic places to $10 in a well-appointed site at a major resort in season, plus $3–4 per tent. Campsites often rent out tents or provide chalet accommodation for $10–20. Camping rough is not illegal, but hardly anybody does it except when trekking in the mountains. The tourism ministry produces an excellent **map and guide** for recommended campsites, which is generally available from tourist offices.

Food and drink

At its finest, Turkish **food** is one of the world's great cuisines, yet prices are on the whole affordable. Unadventurous travellers are prone to get stuck in a kebab rut, but everyone apart from the most dedicated vegetarians should find enough variety to keep meals interesting.

Food

These days the Turkish **breakfast** (*kahvaltı*) served at hotels and *pansiyons* is usually an open buffet, offering bread or toast along with butter, cheese, jam, honey and olives. There's usually unlimited quantities of tea, but coffee is generally extra. Many workers start the morning with a *börek* or a *poça*, pastries filled with meat, cheese or potato that are sold at a tiny *büfe* (stall/café) or at street carts. Others make do with a simple *simit* (sesame-seed bread ring). The traditional eastern Anatolian breakfast is a bowl of *mercimek çorba* (lentil soup) served with lemon and chilli powder.

Later in the day, vendors hawk *lahmacun*, small "pizzas" with meat-based toppings, and, in coastal cities, *midye tava* (deep-fried mussels). Another option is *pide*, or Turkish pizza – flat bread with various toppings – served at a *pideci* or *pide salonu*. Another snack speciality is *mantı*, meat-filled ravioli drenched in yoghurt and oil.

Restaurants (*lokanta*) serve more substantial hot dishes, which will include a number of vegetable dishes, though they're invariably prepared with lamb- or chicken-based stock. Meat dishes include several variations on the kebab (*kebap*) – such as *İskender kebap* (slices of meat on *pide*, with spicy tomato sauce, yoghurt and salad), *köfte* (meatballs), *šiš* (grilled meat chunks)

and *çöp šiš* (small bits of lamb). Fish and seafood are good, if usually pricey, and sold by weight more often than by item. Budget mainstays include freshly grilled *sardalya* (sardines), *palamut* (bonito), *ıskumru* (mackerel), *kalkan* (turbot) and *kefal* (grey mullet). Most budget restaurants are alcohol-free; some places marked *içkili* (licensed) may be more expensive. A useful exception is a *meyhane* (tavern), which usually serves *mezes* – an extensive array of cold appetizers – as well as grilled kebabs and fish as the focus for a full evening's eating and drinking. **Mezes** come in all shapes and sizes, the most common being *dolma* (peppers or vine leaves stuffed with rice), *patlıcan salata* (aubergine in tomato sauce), and *acılı* (a mixture of tomato paste, onion, chilli and parsley), as well as seafood salads and pickled fish.

Finally, those with a **sweet** tooth will find every imaginable concoction at a *pastane* (sweet-shop): best are the honey-soaked *baklava*, and a variety of milk puddings, most commonly *sütlaç* (rice pudding), which is available in restaurants, too. Other sweets include *ašure* (Noah's pudding), a sort of rosewater jelly laced with pulses, raisins and nuts, and the best-known Turkish sweet, *lokum* or **Turkish Delight** – solidified sugar and pectin, flavoured with rosewater or pistachios, and sprinkled with powdered sugar.

Drink

Tea (*çay*) is the Turkish national drink, served in tiny tulip-shaped glasses, with sugar on the side but no milk. **Turkish coffee** (*kahve*) is served in tiny cups; don't drink the last mouthful (it's the grounds). Instant coffee is thankfully losing ground to fresh filter coffee in trendier cafés. **Fruit juices** (*meyva suyu*) can be excellent but are usually sweetened. Mineral water, either still (*su*) or fizzy (*maden suyu*), is found at the tableside in most restaurants. *Mešrubat* is the generic term for all carbonated **soft drinks**. You'll also come across *ayran*, watered-down yoghurt, which makes a refreshing drink.

Alcoholic drinks (*içkiler*) are available without restriction in resorts and in most other places, though you may have some thirsty moments in smaller interior towns in the east. The main locally brewed brands of **beer** (*bira*) are Efes Pilsen and Tuborg;

In recent years it's become clear that there's a thriving trade in **stolen British passports** in Turkey, and it would appear that British Asians are at particular risk of being robbed; several people have even gone missing, and there's been at least one murder. You should exercise caution, particularly in İstanbul, and particularly if you're travelling alone.

imported beers are available, but at a horrendous mark-up. Turkish **wine** *(šarap)* varies alarmingly in quality; the commonest labels are Kavaklıdere and Doluca, which both offer a variety of vintages. The national aperitif is anis-flavoured **rakı** – stronger than Greek ouzo, it's usually drunk with ice and topped up with water.

Opening hours and holidays

Shops are generally open Mon–Sat 9am–7/8pm, and possibly Sun, depending on the owner.

The two **religious holidays** are the Şeker Bayram (Sugar Holiday), which marks the end of the Muslim fasting month of Ramadan (Dec 6–8, 2002, Nov 26, 2003), and Kurban Bayram (the Feast of the Sacrifice) which falls about six weeks later (Feb 22–25, 2002; March 5–8, 2003). Confusingly, if either falls midweek, the government may choose to extend the holiday period to as much as nine days – announcing it only a couple of weeks beforehand. In main tourist resorts, museums generally stay open but in smaller towns they may close. Many shops and restaurants also close as their owners return to their home towns for the holiday. Four **secular holidays** involve the closure of banks and public offices: Jan 1; May 19 (Atatürk's birthday); Aug 30 (victory over the Greeks in 1922); and Oct 29 (proclamation of the republic).

Emergencies

Despite exaggerated reports of football-related violence, you're unlikely to encounter any **trouble** in Turkey, save for passport-related crime (see box below). Violent street crime is uncommon, theft is rare and the authorities usually treat tourists with courtesy. Keep your wits about you and an eye on your belongings and you shouldn't have any problems. The **police** come in a variety of subdivisions; all wear dark blue uniforms with baseball caps, and have their division – *trafik, narkotik*, etc – clearly marked. Confusingly, the *Belediye Zabitas*, a sort of trading standards police, also wear dark blue, while in rural areas, you'll find the camouflage-clad *Jandarma*, a division of the regular army.

For minor health complaints head for the nearest **pharmacy** *(eczane)*, though you may find it difficult to find exact equivalents to any home prescriptions. Night-duty pharmacists are known as **nöbet(ci)**; the current rota is posted in every pharmacy's front window. For more serious ailments, your consulate or the tourist office may be able to provide you with the address of an English-speaking doctor. Otherwise it's best to go direct to a **hospital** *(klinik)* – either public *(Devlet Hastane* or *SSK Hastanesi)*, or private *(Özel Hastane)*. Private hospitals are far preferable in terms of cleanliness and standards of care, and since all foreigners must pay for medical attention, you might as well get the best available.

TURKEY | Basics

30

İstanbul

Arriving in **İSTANBUL** can come as a shock. Most visitors head for the old city in and around **Sultanahmet**, where back streets teem with traders pushing hand-carts, stevedores carrying burdens twice their size, and omnipresent shoeshine boys. Men still monopolize the public bars and teahouses, while many women cover their heads. Yet this is merely one aspect of modern İstanbul; only a couple of kilo-metres to the north you'll find the former European quarter of **Beyoğlu**, with its trendy bars and cutting-edge dance clubs, while north again are the pavement cafés and restaurants of **Ortaköy** and the swish Bosphorus suburbs of Arnavutköy, Bebek and Etiler. These days the city has a social and cultural diversity to match any of its Western counterparts.

İstanbul is the only city in the world to have played capital to consecutive Christian and Islamic empires, and retains features of both. **Byzantium**, as the city was formerly known, was an important trading centre, but only gained power in the fourth century AD, when Constantine chose it as the new capital of the **Roman Empire**. Later, as **Constantinople**, the city became increasingly dissociat-ed from Rome, adopting the Greek language and Christianity and becoming the capital of an independent empire. In 1203 the city was sacked by the Crusaders. As the Byzantines declined, the **Ottoman Empire** prospered, and in 1453 the city was captured by Mehmet the Conqueror, who shortly after began rebuilding works. In the following century, the victory was reinforced by the great military achievements of Selim the Grim and by the reign of Süleyman the Magnificent. By the nineteenth century, however, the glory days of Ottoman domination were firm-ly over. Defeat in World War I was followed by the **War of Independence**, after which Atatürk created a new capital in Ankara – although İstanbul retained its importance as a centre of trade and commerce. In **recent years**, the population of the city has reached twelve million, a fifth of the country's total, and is still on the rise, adding further to the cacophony and congestion.

The city is divided in two by the **Bosphorus**, which runs between the Black Sea and the Sea of Marmara, dividing Europe from Asia. At right angles to it, the inlet of the **Golden Horn** cuts the European side in two. The old centre of Sultanahmet, occupying the tip of the peninsula south of the Golden Horn, is home to the city's main sightseeing attractions: the cathedral of **Aya Sofya**, **Topkapı Palace** and the **Blue Mosque**, and as such many people find that they spend all their time here. Annoying hustlers mean first impressions can be negative, but tourist police will respond quickly to any problems you may have. Further west, near the **city walls** lies the **Kariye Camii**, which contains the city's finest surviv-ing Byzantine mosaics and frescoes. Across the Golden Horn to the north, the **Galata Tower** offers superb panoramic views over the city.

Arrival and information

İstanbul's **airport** is 24km west of the city. Buses run to Taksim Square northeast of Beyoğlu ($4). Taxis taking the direct route along the seafront road (Sahil Yolu) cost $10–15 – make sure they use the meter. The new airport metro, which is nearing completion, will give a direct link to the centre. There are two main **train stations**: trains from Europe terminate at **Sirkeci**, linked to Sultanahmet by a short tram ride; trains from Asia end at **Haydarpaşa** on the east bank of the Bosphorus, from where you can get a **ferry** to Karaköy and a bus from there to Sultanahmet. From İstanbul's **bus station** at Esenler, around 15km northwest, the better bus companies run courtesy minibuses to various points in the city, although if you're heading for Sultanahmet it might be quicker to take the **metro** (actually an express tramway) to Aksaray and change to the Eminönü-bound tram line which passes through Sultanahmet and Sirkeci. Most buses arrive at the Esenler station, including

European and Asian services, although some also stop at the Harem bus station on the Asian side, from where there are regular *dolmuşes* to Haydarpaşa station.

The most central **tourist office** is in Sultanahmet near the Hippodrome on Divanyolu Caddesi (daily 9am–5pm; ☎0212/518 8754); there are branches at the airport and the two train stations.

City transport

The **public transport system** is improving. Single-journey **metro** tickets ($0.40) are available from a counter (*gişe*) at station entrances. There are two kinds of **buses** serving the same routes, both of which come in a confusing array of colours. The first is a private service, Halk Otobus, for which you pay the conductor on entry ($0.40). More common are the municipality buses (marked IETT), for which you have to buy tickets ($0.40) in advance from bus stations, newspaper kiosks or fast-food booths; some longer routes, usually served by double-deckers, require two advance tickets (look for the sign *iki bilet geçerlidir*). Tickets should be deposited next to the driver on boarding. There are route maps at main bus stops. The European side has two **tram** lines, one running from Eminönü through Sultanahmet to Topkapı and outlying suburbs, the other running along İstiklâl Caddesi from Beyoğlu to Taksim using antique trams; buy tokens (*jetons*; about $0.40) from a booth before you enter the platform. There's also a **municipal train** network, consisting of two lines running along the Marmara shore – west from Sirkeci station on the European side, and east from Haydarpaşa on the Asian. Make sure you check which station your train is leaving from and allow at least an hour to get to the Asian station from the centre. Journeys cost the same as for buses; on the European side you buy a token to let you through the turnstile onto the platform, while on the Asian side you buy a ticket. There are also **dolmuşes**, which have their point of departure and destination displayed somewhere about the windscreen.

Ferries run between Eminönü and Karaköy on the European side, and Üsküdar, Kadiköy and Haydarpaşa in Asia; buy your ticket from the dockside kiosks (about $0.5). The journeys north along the Bosphorus are one of the city's highlights. There are special sightseeing boats throughout the year from Eminönü ($6/2hr journey to Anadolu Kavağı). Ordinary ferries on the same routes are reasonably frequent and much cheaper. Last return boat from Anadolu Kavağı in summer is at 5pm, after which you must resort to a bus or *dolmuş*.

Accommodation

Finding **accommodation** in İstanbul is rarely a problem, but it's best to phone ahead to avoid a lot of trudging; in high season anything up to a week's advance booking is advisable. Some of the city's best small hotels and *pansiyons* are situated in **Sultanahmet**, right at the heart of the city, particularly around Yerebatan Caddesi and the backstreets between the Blue Mosque and the sea. Prices here vary enormously and it's worth shopping around for a good deal; most hotels include breakfast in the price and some offer air-con and cable TV, while some hostels offer inclusive deals and even free internet access. **Taksim** is also a convenient base, and comes into its own at night, when it becomes a centre of cultural and culinary activity; to get there from Sultanahmet, take bus #14, which runs via Karaköy. From Eminönü and Aksaray, any number of buses pass through either Karaköy or Taksim, or both.

Sultanahmet
Alp Guesthouse Adliye Sok 4, Sultanahmet
☎0212/517 9570, ✉alpguesthouse@turk.net.
Friendly place with clean and pleasant, if slightly pricey, rooms. Breakfast on the roof terrace included. ❹

And Yerebatan Cad. Cami Cikmazi 36–40
☎0212/512 0207. Central hotel near Aya Sofya.
Includes breakfast on the roof, with stunning views of the city. ❺

Antique Küçük Ayasoyfa Cad, Oğul Sok 17
☎0212/516 4936, ✆www.hotelantique.com.

Quiet, comfortable hotel – the top rooms have excellent sea views. ❸

Buhara Küçük Ayasoyfa Cad, Yeğen Sok 11 ☎0212/517 3427. Pleasant hotel with outstanding views from its rooftop terrace. ❷

Fehmi Bey Uçler Sok 15 ☎0212/638 9083. Friendly bijou hotel with period furniture, en-suite rooms with TV, air-con and breakfast included. ❺

Hanedan Akbıyık Cad, Adliye Sok 3 ☎0212/516 4869. Uninspiring but clean and central, with good views from the rooftop café. ❷

Interyouth Hostel Caferiye Sok 6/1 ☎0212/513 6150, ✆www.yucelhostel.com. The country's only HI hostel. Large, well-managed, with friendly staff, and ideally located next to Aya Sofya. Has café, terrace, laundry and internet access. Dorms ❶

İstanbul Hostel Kutlugün Sok 35 ☎0212/516 9380, ✆www.istanbul-hostel.com. Friendly hostel, also with internet access. Dorms ❶

Mavi Guesthouse İshak Paşa Cad, Kutlugün Sok 3 ☎0212/516 5878, ✆www.maviguesthouse.com. Backpacker-friendly place just round the corner from the *Alp*. Dorms and terrace space ❶

Merih Alemdar Cad 24 ☎0212/526 9708, ✉merihotel@superonline.com. Accommodating hostel-style hotel just down from Aya Sofya; front rooms can be noisy. Dorms ❶

Orient International Youth Hostel Akbıyık Cad 13 ☎0212/517 9493, ✆www.hostels.com /orienthostel. Long-established hostel with internet access. Dorms ❶

Sıde Hotel and Pansiyon Utangaç Sok 20 ☎0212/517 6590, ✆www.sidehotel.com. Welcoming staff, with clean rooms and excellent sea views from the terrace. ❷

Star Guest House Yeni Akbıyık Cad 10 ☎0212/638 2302. Friendly place with neat rooms. ❶

Taksim and Beyoğlu

Büyük Londra Oteli Meşrutiyet Cad 117, Tepebaşı ☎0212/249 1025. Italian-built hotel more than a century ago and full of character, with spacious, well-furnished rooms. Bargaining has been known to halve the price. ❻

Dünya Meşrutiyet Cad 79, Tepebaşı ☎0212/244 0940. Run-down and seedy, but with clean, bargain en-suite rooms. ❶

Gezi Mete Cad 42 ☎0212/251 7430. Classy and well-run, with Bosphorus views from the restaurant and some of the rooms. ❺

Plaza Aslanyatağa Sok 19–21, Sıraselviler Cad, Taksim ☎0212/274 1313. Quiet backwater with large but basic en-suites and marvellous Bosphorus views. ❸

Campsite

Londra Camping Londra Asfaltı, beyond Ataköy ☎0212/560 4200. Pretty grim location 16km from the centre, on the E5 motorway next to a lorry park. From the airport, take a taxi (10min, \$5); from Taksim Square, take bus #73T.

The City

The old imperial centre of İstanbul stretches from the **Sultanahmet** district – home to the **Aya Sofya**, **Topkapı Palace** and the **Blue Mosque** – northwest to the Süleymaniye mosque complex, the covered bazaar and the remains of the city walls. To the north, across the Galata Bridge, the old Levantine areas of **Galata** and **Pera** are home to one of the city's most famous landmarks, the Galata tower. Close by is the entrance to the **Tünel**, an underground funicular railway running from Karaköy up to the start of İstiklâl Caddesi, home to many of the city's restaurants and much of the nightlife, and on to **Taksim Square**, the heart of modern İstanbul.

Aya Sofya

In the heart of **Sultanahmet**, and readily visible thanks to its massive domed structure, is perhaps the single most compelling sight in the city: the former Byzantine cathedral of **Aya Sofya**. Commissioned in the sixth century by the Emperor Justinian, it was converted to a mosque in 1453, after which the minarets were added. In 1934 it became a **museum** (Tues–Sun 9.15am–4.30pm; \$10). For centuries this was the largest enclosed space in the world, and the interior – filled with shafts of light from the high windows around the dome – is still profoundly impressive.

Scaffolding for a massive **restoration** programme currently obscures part of the dome's interior, but nevertheless helps bring home the scale of the place. Inside there are a few features left over from its time as a mosque – a *mihrab* (niche indicating the direction of Mecca), a *mimber* (pulpit) and the enormous wooden plaques which bear sacred names of God, the prophet Muhammad and the first four caliphs – but the most interesting elements are the Byzantine ones. Between the four great piers that hold up the dome, columns of green marble support the galleries; the smaller columns above are a deep red. The balconies, pediments and capitals are of white marble, many bearing the monograms of Justinian and his wife Theodora. Upstairs in the western gallery a large circle of green Thessalian marble marks the position of the throne of the empress.

There are also remains of abstract and figurative **mosaics**. Two of the most beautiful of all the mosaics can be seen upstairs, where the figures of Christ and Virgin with Child, as depicted on countless posters and postcards, can be found.

The Topkapı Palace

Immediately to the north of Aya Sofya, the **Topkapı Palace** (daily 9am–5pm; $10) is the other unmissable sight in the area. Shortage of funds and ongoing restoration work means parts of the museum and some less important palace rooms are often closed, but this is unlikely to spoil your visit – there's still plenty of interest on view. Built between 1459 and 1465, the palace consists of a collection of buildings arranged around a series of courtyards and was the centre of the Ottoman Empire for nearly four centuries. The first courtyard, as service area of the palace, was always open to the general public and is today home to the ticket office. The second courtyard is the site of the now beautifully restored **Divan**, with the Imperial Council Hall and the couch which gave the institution its name. The **Divan tower**, visible from many vantage points across the city, was rebuilt in 1825 by Mahmut II. Next door is the **Inner Treasury**, a six-domed hall that holds an exhibition of arms and armour. Across the courtyard are the **palace kitchens**, with their magnificent rows of chimneys. The furthest rooms house a fascinating array of utensils, while others display a collection of some fine porcelain and silverware.

Around the corner is the **Harem**, which, consisting of over 400 rooms, is well worth the obligatory guided tour (9.30am–noon & 1–4pm every 30min; $10; buy your ticket at least 15min in advance). The only men that were allowed to enter the harem were eunuchs and the imperial guardsmen, who were only employed at certain hours and even then blinkered. Many rooms have never been opened to the public and are awaiting restoration, but the tour takes in a good part of the complex, including the **Hünkar Sofası** (Imperial Hall) where the sultan entertained his visitors, and the bedchamber of Murat III covered in sixteenth-century İznik tiles and kitted out with a marble fountain and bronze fireplace.

Back in the main body of the palace, in the third courtyard, the **throne room**, mainly dating from the reign of Selim I, was where the sultan awaited the outcome of sessions of the Divan in order to give his assent or otherwise to their proposals. Nearby, the **Pavilion of the Conqueror** houses the Topkapı treasury, filled with excesses such as the Topkapı Dagger, decorated with three enormous emeralds, and the Spoonmaker's Diamond, the fifth largest in the world. Across the courtyard from the treasury, the **Pavilion of the Holy Mantle** houses the holy relics brought home by Selim the Grim after his conquest of Egypt in 1517. Next door, the **Privy Chamber** holds a collection of portraits of sultans. Beyond, the fourth courtyard consists of gardens graced with pavilions such as the **circumcision room** decorated with sixteenth-century İznik tiles and the **Baghdad Pavilion**, decorated with tiles and ivory inlaid ceilings. The sumptuously decorated **Mecidiye Köşkü** commands the best view of any of the Topkapı pavilions.

Just north of Topkapı, **Gülhane Parkı**, once the palace gardens, now houses the **Archeological Museum** (Tues–Sun 9am–5pm; $3). Sadly some of the galleries are unaccountably closed, but it's still worth the admission to see the collection of sarcophagi, sculptures and other remains of past civilizations. The adjacent **Çinili Köşk** is the oldest secular building in İstanbul, now a **Museum of Ceramics** (Tues–Sun 9.30am–5pm; $4), housing a small but superb collection of İznik ware

SEA OF MARMARA

- - - - - Fast Tramway

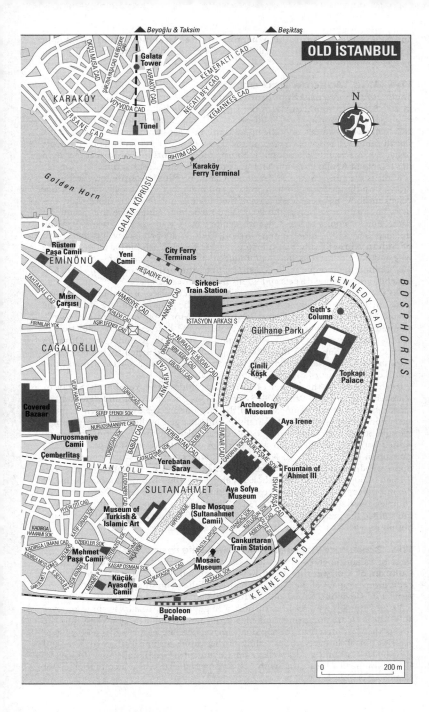

and Seljuk tiles. Nearby, the **Museum of the Ancient Orient** (Wed–Sun 9.30am–5pm; $4) contains a small but dazzling collection of Anatolian, Egyptian and Mesopotamian artefacts.

The Blue Mosque and around

South of Aya Sofya, the **Hippodrome** arena was constructed by Septimus Severus in 200 AD. At its southern end is the **Egyptian Obelisk**, commissioned to commemorate the campaigns of Thutmos III in Egypt during the sixteenth century BC. Originally 60m tall, only the upper third survived shipment from Egypt in the fourth century. The scenes carved on the base record its erection in Constantinople under the direction of Theodosius I. Nearby, the **Serpentine Column** comes from the Temple of Apollo at Delphi and was brought here by Constantine.

With its six minarets, the Sultanahmet Camii, or **Blue Mosque**, on the hippodrome's southeast side, is both impressive and instantly recognizable; inside, its four "elephant foot" pillars obscure parts of the building and dwarf the dome they support. The main attraction is the 20,000-odd blue tiles which give the mosque its name. Fine examples of late-sixteenth-century İznik ware, they include flower and tree panels as well as more abstract designs. Outside the precinct wall is the **Tomb of Sultan Ahmet** (daily 8.30am–5pm), where the sultan is buried along with his wife and three of his sons; like the mosque, it's tiled with seventeenth-century İznik tiles. Behind the mosque is the **Vakıf Carpet Museum** (Tues–Sat 9am–4pm; $2), which houses antique carpets and kilims from all over Turkey.

On the west side of the Hippodrome, the former palace of İbrahim Paşa, completed in 1524 for the grand vizier of Süleyman the Magnificent, is a fitting home for the **Museum of Turkish and Islamic Art** (Mon–Sun 9am–5pm; $2), a well-planned museum containing what is probably the best-exhibited collection of Islamic artefacts in the world, with examples of Selçuk, Mamluk and Ottoman Turkish art. İbrahim Paşa's magnificent audience hall is devoted to a collection of Turkish carpets; on the ground floor, in rooms off the central courtyard, is an exhibition of the folk art of the Yörük tribes of Anatolia.

To the north, on the corner of Yerebatan Caddesi, the **Yerebatan Saray** or "Sunken Palace" (daily 9am–4.30/5.30pm; $4) is one of several underground cisterns which riddle the foundations of the city, but are yet to have been properly excavated. Probably built by Constantine and enlarged by Justinian, the cistern is thought to have supplied water to the Great Palace of the Byzantine emperors. Raised pathways allow you to walk through the cistern's forest of columns, and gaze upon the monumental Medusa heads which support two of them. In the opposite direction from Sultan Ahmet, the **Mosaic Museum** (Tues–Sun 9.15am–4.30pm; $1), on Torun Sokak behind the Blue Mosque, displays some of the magnificent mosaics that once decorated the floors of the Great Palace. This vast complex once stretched from the Hippodrome down to the sea walls, where you can still see the great marble-framed windows of the **Bucoleon**, a pavilion looking out on to what was once the emperors' private harbour.

The Covered Bazaar and the Sülemaniye Camii

West of Sultanahmet, continue along the run-down and busy **Divan Yolu** to the **Column of Constantine (Cemberlitaş)**, erected in 330 AD to mark the city's dedication as capital of the Roman Empire. Off the main street to the right lies the district of **Beyazıt**, centred on the **Kapalı Çarşı**, or Covered Bazaar (Mon–Sat 8.30am–7pm; @www.kapali-carsi.com), a huge web of passageways housing over 4000 shops. It has long since spilled out of the covered area, sprawling into the streets that lead down to the Golden Horn. There are carpet shops everywhere catering for all budgets, shops selling leather goods around Kurkçular Kapı and Perdahçılar Cad, and gold jewellery on Kuyumcular Cad. Don't forget to haggle. When you need a break, the swish *Fes Café* on Halıcılar Cad is a comfortable spot to gloat over your booty.

West of the bazaar, peek into the **Beyazit Camii**, completed in 1506 and the oldest surviving imperial mosque in the city, with a beautiful, sombre courtyard full of richly coloured marble. Beyond the Covered Bazaar, in a pleasant area of shady courtyards behind the university, stands one of the finest of all the Ottoman mosque complexes, the **Süleymaniye Camii**. Outside, the **cemetery** (Wed–Sun 9.30am–4.30/6.30pm) holds the tomb of Süleyman the Magnificent and of Roxelana, his powerful wife. Süleyman's tomb is particularly impressive, with doors inlaid with ebony and ivory, silver and jade. The rest of the complex is made up of the famous **Süleymaniye library**, established by Süleyman in an effort to bring together collections of books scattered throughout the city, and the **Tomb of Mimar Sinan**, a simple tomb except for a magnificent carved turban.

Eminönü and beyond

The area sloping down to the river behind the bazaar is known as **Eminönü**, adjacent to which lies **Sırkecı**, home to the main train station and ferry docks. Close by, on the waterfront, is the last of İstanbul's imperial mosques, **Yeni Camii**. A large, grey edifice, it's also one of the least impressive of the city-centre mosques, partly owing to the heavy layer of soot that covers its walls and windows. Next door, the **Mısır Çarşısı** (Egyptian Bazaar), also known as the Spice Bazaar, sells everything from saffron to aphrodisiacs. A short walk west, the **Rüştem Paşa Camii** is one of the most attractive of İstanbul's smaller mosques, with tiles from the finest period of İznik tile production. On the waterfront, the most prominent landmark is the **Galata Bridge**, a modern two-tier structure that provides access to the opposite bank of the Golden Horn.

West to the city walls

West of Beyazit, İstanbul becomes tattier and more intimate, almost like a collection of villages intersected by major roads. These areas contain some of the city's most compelling sites, including the magnificent Byzantine mosaics and frescoes in the **Kariye Camii** and the great **Land Walls** that barred the peninsula to attackers for 800 years, and there are several other sites worth visiting on the way.

On the far side of the **Aqueduct of Valens** – part of a fourth-century water system that remained in use right up to the end of the nineteenth century – is **Şehzade Camii**, the Mosque of the Sultan's Son, commissioned in 1543. Across Atatürk Bulvarı, the aqueduct continues into **Zeyrek**, an attractively rundown area notable for its steep, cobbled streets and ramshackle wooden houses. At the top of the hill stands **Zeyrek Camii**, the twelfth-century Byzantine monastery church of Christ Pantocrator, which served as a mausoleum for the Comneni dynasty before being converted to a mosque. Beyond Zeyrek, **Fatih** ("the Conqueror") is a fundamentalist area, where you'll notice that more women cover themselves. In the centre of the district, the **Fatih Camii** on İslambol Caddesi was begun in 1463 and rebuilt after an eighteenth-century earthquake.

Twenty minutes' walk north of here, **Yavuz Selim Camii**, on Yavuz Selim Caddesi, holds a commanding position over the surrounding suburbs. It was begun in the reign of Selim the Grim, after whom it is named, and the bleak exterior seems a fitting memorial to a man with such a reputation for cruelty. Once inside, though, it's one of the most attractive of all the imperial mosques. The **Tomb of Selim the Grim** next door (Wed–Sun 9.30am–4.30pm; free) has lost its original interior decoration, but retains two beautiful tiled panels on either side of the door.

About 25 minutes' walk northwest of the Selim mosque is one of the city's most compelling sights, **Kariye Camii** (9.30am–6pm, closed Wed; $5), the former church of St Saviour in Chora, built in the early twelfth century, with some superbly preserved fourteenth-century frescoes and mosaics. It can also be reached by taking the metro to Topkapı (a western district, not the city-centre palace) and walking north beside the city walls as far as the Edirnekapa gate, from where it's signposted.

The walls

Over 6km long, İstanbul's western **Land Walls** are among the most fascinating Byzantine remains in Turkey. Raised by the Emperor Theodosius II, they are the result of a hasty rebuilding to repel Attila the Hun's forces in 447 AD; an ancient edict was brought into effect whereby all citizens, regardless of rank, were required to help, and 16,000 men finished the project in just two months. Most of the outer wall and its 96 towers are still standing, and although long sections have been rebuilt rather tastelessly and closed off, untouched sections can still be examined in detail if you're willing to clamber in the dirt and brick dust. Do pay attention to your personal security here, especially in the evening.

Plenty of **buses** run this way from Eminönü and Sultanahmet, including bus #80 to Yedikule, #84 to Topkapı and #86 to Edirnekapı, and the **tram** line runs west from Aksaray to the Topkapı gate. However, the best way to get here is to take the scenic **train** ride along the coast from Eminönü to **Yediküle**, a district lying at the southern end of the walls in the attractive former Greek quarter of Samatya (apparent from the number of Orthodox churches). It also has a few reasonable restaurants and cafés where you can stop before setting off on your exploration of the walls. The **Ottoman fortress of Yediküle**, off Yediküle Caddesi, encompasses one of the best-preserved sections of wall, including the legendary **Golden Gate**. The fortress is open as a **museum** (9.30am–6.30pm, closed Wed; $1), in which the most interesting exhibit is a section of graffiti left by European inhabitants prior to their brutal demise.

Across the Golden Horn: Karaköy and Beyoğlu

Across the Galata Bridge from the old centre, the separate township district of **Karaköy** (formerly Galata) has its own fascinating history. By the fifth century the area already had city walls, soon after which Tiberius built a fortress here – part of which remains as the Yeraltı Camii on Kemankeş Cad. In 1261 Galata became a Genoese trading colony, and during the early centuries of Ottoman rule it functioned as the capital's "European" quarter, home to non-Muslim Jewish, Greek and Armenian minorities. Overcrowding during the subsequent centuries saw the Europeans gradually spread from Galata into **Beyoğlu** which boasts fashionable music halls, cinemas and restaurants. After the exodus of much of the Greek population from Beyoğlu in the 1960s the area began to lose its cosmopolitan flavour, becoming home to brothels, pick-up joints and sex cinemas, but has since undergone a metamorphosis and now plays host to trendy café/bars, restaurants and clubs coexisting alongside a seedy "red light district".

The **Galata Tower** (daily 9am–6.30pm; $2), built in 1348, is the area's most obvious landmark; its viewing galleries, reached by means of a modern lift, offer the best panoramas of the city. Up towards **İstiklâl Caddesi**, Beyoğlu's main boulevard, an unassuming doorway leads to the courtyard of the **Galata Mevlevihane** (9.30am–4.30pm, closed Tues; $1), a former monastery and ceremonial hall of the Whirling Dervishes, a sect founded in the thirteenth century by Muslim mystic, Mavlana, and now a museum of the Mevlevi order. Exhibits include instruments and dervish costumes, and the building itself has been beautifully restored to late eighteenth-century splendour. Staged dervish ceremonies take place in December and on specific summer evenings (call for information on ☎0212/245 4141). The best way to continue along from the bottom of İstiklâl Caddesi, formerly La Grande Rue de Pera, is to hop on the antique tram which trundles along its 1200-metre length to **Taksim Square**, taking in the sumptuous *fin-de-siècle* architecture. The **Military Museum** (Wed–Sun 9am–5pm; $1), about 1.5km north along Cumhuriyet Caddesi, is worth visiting mainly for the Mehter band, which plays traditional Ottoman music (3–4pm). The wide assortment of Ottoman armour and weaponry should appeal to military buffs.

North along the Bosphorus shore

Beyond Taksim, along the European shore of the Bosphorus, the most obvious place to head for is **Beşiktaş** (best reached from Eminönü by bus #43k, #43r or #51e; or from Taksim by bus #30b or frequent *dolmuşes*), where the huge, sumptuous **Dolmabahçe Palace** (Tues, Wed & Fri–Sun 9am–4pm; guided tours only; $5–8) was built in the mid-nineteenth century to replace Topkapı as the imperial residence of the Ottoman sultans. To the contemporary eye it's not so much magnificent as an ostentatious display of wealth, suggesting that good taste suffered along with the fortunes of the Ottoman Empire. But it retains an Oriental feel in the organization of its rooms, divided into *selâmlık* and harem by the enormous throne room – where the ceremonies were watched by women of the harem through grilles.

Back towards the ferry landing, the **Maritime Museum** (Wed–Sun 9am–noon & 1–5pm; $1) has a collection divided between two buildings, one facing the water housing seagoing craft, and the other, on Cezayir Caddesi, devoted to the maritime history of the Ottoman Empire and the Turkish Republic. A quarter-hour walk north along the coast road is the **Yıldız Parkı** (daily 9am–11pm), a vast wooded area dotted with lakes and gardens, which formed the grounds of Yıldız Palace, to the north. The most important surviving building is **Yıldız Şale** (Tues, Wed & Fri–Sun 9.30am–5pm; $3), built for the first visit of Kaiser Wilhelm II in 1889. **Yıldız Palace** itself (Tues–Sun 9.30am–4.30pm; $3) is entered from Beşiktaş' other main road, Barbaros Bulvarı and consists of a collection of structures in old Ottoman and Art Nouveau styles.

Eating

The historical centre around Sultanahmet is increasingly well-served by decent **restaurants**, although there's also now a concentration of eateries around Taksim and Beyoğlu; the Balık Pazar, behind the Çiçek Pasajı off İstiklâl Caddesi, is a great area for *mezes*, kebabs and fish, while Çiçek Pasajı itself offers similar fare but is now somewhat overpriced and touristy. **Snack** options – which abound in all areas – vary from the dubious fish sandwiches served off boats by fishermen in Kadıköy, Karaköy and Eminönü, to *kokoreç* (skeins of sheep's innards) sold from booths in less salubrious areas.

Afacan İstiklâl Cad 331, Beyoğlu. Very reasonably priced lunch stop with an excellent take on Turkish home cooking and some of the best stews in town. There's a second branch in the building next to İstiklâl Cad's only mosque.

Alem Nevizade Sok, Balık Pazarı, Beyoğlu. Newish place serving *meze*, fish and kebabs, with a huge upstairs dining room. Popular with a younger crowd.

Boncuk Nevizade Sok, Balık Pazarı, Beyoğlu. Old, traditional restaurant, still serving some of the best food on this street despite the ever-growing competition.

Çatı İstiklâl Cad, A. Apaydın Sok 20, Baro Han, floor 7, Beyoğlu ☏ 0212/251 0000. Long-established place, and still popular among İstanbul's intelligentsia. Mixed Turkish and international cuisine plus assorted live music. Good views of the city lights. Closed Sun.

Cennet Divan Yolu Cad 90. Serves only two dishes: *Gözleme* (fried pastries with various fillings) and *Mantı* (Turkish ravioli), consumed from cushions on the floor to a backdrop of traditional decor and live music. Immense fun and reasonably priced.

Darüzziyafe Şifahane Cad 33. Reasonably priced Ottoman cuisine in a Sinan-designed annexe to his masterpiece mosque. Live traditional music most evenings.

Doy Doy Şifa Hamamı Sok 13, off Küçükayasofya Cad at the Hippodrome end. Well known venue offering good, cheap kebabs, *pide* and stews.

Dubb Indian Restaurant İncili Çavuş Sok 10, Sultanahmet. Offers a reasonable but vaguely Turkish take on Indian standards in a small, restored Ottoman house.

Hacı Abdullah Sakızağa Cad 19, Beyoğlu. A legend among locals, offering stunning home cooking at very reasonable prices. Packed at weekends. No alcohol.

İlhamenin Yeri Osmanzade Sok 6, Ortaköy. Last of the real *meyhanes* in this former quiet fishing village turned night-time haunt. Excellent *mezes*, kebabs and fish.

Kör Agop Ördekli Bakkal Cad 7–9, Kumkapı. Third-generation Armenian-owned joint in this block of fish restaurants. One of the oldest in town, still offering great fish dishes, *mezes* and salads.
Nature and Peace Büyükparmakkapı Cad 21, İstikal Cad, Beyoğlu. Vegetarian place three blocks away from Taksim, offering lentil köfte and other veggie favourites.
Nizam Pide Büyükparmakkapı Sok & Kalyoncu Kulluğu Sok, Beyoğlu. Two branches serving excellent *pide*, beans and rice. Cheap and very popular, especially after the bars close.

Şehzade Mehmet Efendi Şehzade Camii, Şehzadebaşı Cad. Wonderfully atmospheric restaurant located in the *medrese* of the Şehzade mosque. Excellent value *pide*, kebabs and stews, and exemplary service.
Türkistan Aşevi Tavukhane Sokağı 36. Behind the Blue Mosque, a conventional Ottoman house specializing in central Asian cuisine with a good set menu. You'll be asked to take off your shoes.
Yeni İskele İskele Sok 17, Yeniköy. Lively Bosphorus fish restaurant with less common specialities such as fishcakes and stuffed squid.

Nightlife

Traditional İstanbul **nightlife** used to centre on restaurants and *gazinos* – clubs where *meze* is served, accompanied by singers and Oriental dancers. These days, Western-style bars and clubs – the latter invariably trendy and expensive – have all but taken over, packed with younger revellers, although traditional music is making something of a comeback, with some laid-back bar/restaurants serving food accompanied by an ever-changing crowd of musicians. Venues tend to be around Taksim and in its nearby suburbs, and along the Bosphorus, particularly the district of Ortaköy, just beyond Beşıktaş.

Bars

Baraka 2nd floor, Ezine Apt, Balo Sok, İstiklâl Cad, Beyoğlu. Noisy hangout with cheap beer and good music.
Cheers Bar Akbıyık Cad 20. Loud music, cheap beer and a backpackerish clientele.
Gizli Bahçe Nevizade Sok 27, İstiklâl Cad, Beyoğlu. Cutting-edge dance music in this bar housed in a dilapidated Ottoman town house. Very young crowd, and deliciously illicit atmosphere.
Hayal Kahvesi Büyükparmakkapı Sok 19, İstiklâl Cad, Beyoğlu. Upmarket café/bar with live jazz and blues.
Line Bar Büyükparmakkapı Sok 14. Hi-tech rock venue with live music every night. Unusually affordable drinks. Closes 2am.
Madrid Bar İpek Sok 20, Beyoğlu. Cheap bar popular with students and impecunious expats alike.
Pano Şaraphanesi Hamalbaşı Cad 26, opposite the British Consulate, Beyoğlu. Greek wine bar 120 years old, reborn as a unique tapas-bar-like drinking den also offering a wide variety of Turkish and international cuisine. Packed at weekends.
Sal Bar Büyükparmakkapı Sok 18a, Beyoğlu. Traditional Turkish music and beer. Try also *Ekin* and *Barabar* on the same street.

Clubs and discos

Babylon Şeybender Sok 3, Asmalımescit, Tünel ⦁www.babylon-ist.com. Purpose-built club and venue with regular stints by foreign bands and DJs alike. Expensive, but occasionally has special offers.
Kemona Taksim. Offers jazz music on the first floor, rock music on the second and pop music on the third.
Milk Akarsu Sok 5, İstiklâl Cad, Beyoğlu. Hi-tech dance venue sometimes calling itself *Magma*. Weekends till 4am.
Mojo İstiklâl Cad, Akarsu Sok 5, Beyoğlu. Trendy basement dive with live bands most nights. Closes 4am.
People Muallin Nacı Cad, Kuruçeşme, Ortaköy. Outdoor dance club overlooking the Bosphorus – popular but pricey. Closed Oct–May.
Roxy Aslanyatağı Sok 113, Siraselviler Cad, Taksim. DJs and regular live bands in a well-known but pricey, yuppy-oriented bar/disco.
Shaft Osmancık Sok 13, Serasker Cad, Kadıköy. Live blues and jazz club on the Asian shore.
Switch Muammer Karaca Çıkmazı, İstiklâl Cad, Taksim. Underground dance club with local and foreign DJs.

Listings

Exchange Best rates from Döviz Burosu offices, throughout the city.
Consulates Australia, Tepecik Yolu 58, Etiler ⦁0212/257 7050; Canada, Buyukdere Cad 107/3

Begun Han, Gayrettepe ⦁0212/272 5174; Ireland, Cumhuriyet Cad 26a, Elmadağ ⦁0212/246 6025; Netherlands, İstiklâl Cad 393, Galatasaray, Beyoğlu ⦁0212/251 5030; UK, Meşrutiyet Cad 34,

Tepebazı, Beyoğlu ☎0212/293 7546; US,
Meşrutiyet Cad 104–108, Tepebaşı, Beyoğlu
☎0212/251 3602.
Hospitals American Hospital, Güzelbahçe Sok 20,
Nişantaşı ☎0212/231 4050; International Hospital,
İstanbul Cad 82, Yeşilköy ☎0212/663 3000.
Internet Internet Café, 2nd floor, Divan Yolu, İncili
Çavuş Sok 31; Blue Internet Café, Yerbatan Cad
54; Yağmur, Şeyh Bender Sok 18, Tünel, Beyoğlu.
Laundry Active, Dr Eminpasa Sok 14, off Divan
Yolu; the Hobby, Caferiya Sok 6/1, Sultanahmet.
Left luggage in both Sirkeci and Haydarpaşa train
stations.

Police The tourist police are at Yerebatan Cad,
Sultanahmet ☎0212/527 4503.
Post office Yeni Posthane Cad, Sirkeci.
Turkish baths The most central, and most
frequented by tourists, are the 400-year-old
Çemberlitaş Hamam on Divan Yolu, and Cağaoğlu
Hamam, Hilali Ahmed Cad 34 (daily: men
7am–10pm; women 8am–8pm; $10–30). Outside
the main tourist areas *hamams* are much cheaper;
the 500-year-old Tophane Hamam on the
Bosphorus at Tophane costs only $3 (daily
7am–10pm).

Around the Sea of Marmara

Despite their proximity to İstanbul, the shores and hinterland of the **Sea of Marmara** are relatively neglected by foreign travellers. The border town of **Edirne**, at the end of the Roman and Byzantine Via Egnatia, later the medieval route to the Ottoman parts of Europe, was once the Ottoman capital. To the east the quaint country town of **İznik** was briefly the Byzantine capital and boasts extensive ruins, while nearby **Bursa** – on many routes towards the Aegean coast – was the first Ottoman capital and aside from many fine buildings has an exquisite city centre. Many visitors also stop off at the extensive World War I battlefields and cemeteries of the **Gelibolu peninsula** (Gallipoli), using either the port of **Gelibolu** as a base, or, more commonly, **Çanakkale** – from where it's also easy to visit the ruins of ancient **Troy**.

Edirne

EDİRNE, a former Ottoman capital, boasts an impressive number of elegant monuments and makes for an easily digestible introduction to Turkey, on the borders with both Greece and Bulgaria. It's a lively city, albeit somewhat seedy thanks to vast numbers of truck drivers and assorted East European traders who pass through.

The main sights of Edirne are best seen on foot; allow a full day as there are myriad lesser monuments and old houses that are well worth a detour. The best starting point is the **Eski Camii** bang in the centre, the oldest mosque in town, begun in 1403. Recently completed restoration work has revealed the splendour of the calligraphy for which the mosque is justly famous. Just across the way, the **Bedesten** was Edirne's first covered market, though the plastic goods it now touts are no match for the building. Nearby, the **Semiz Ali Paşa Çarşısı** is the other main bazaar, begun by Sinan in 1568. A short way north of here is the bizarrely beautiful **Üç Şerefeli Camii**, dating from 1447; its name means "three-balconied", derived from the presence of three galleries for the muezzin on the tallest of the four idiosyncratic minarets. A little way west, the masterly **Selimiye Camii** was designed by Sinan. Its four slender minarets, among the tallest in the world, also have three balconies; the interior is most impressive, its dome planned to surpass that of Aya Sofya in İstanbul. Next door, the **Museum of Turkish and Islamic Arts** (Tues–Sun 9am–1pm & 2.30–6.30pm; $1) houses assorted wooden, ceramic and martial knick-knacks from the province. The main **Archeological Museum** (Tues–Sun 9am–noon & 2.30–6.30pm; $1), just east of the mosque, contains an assortment of Greco-Roman fragments, some Neolithic finds and an ethnographic section that focuses on local crafts. Ten minutes down the slope and up Mimar Sinan Caddesi, the **Muradiye Camii** was built as a sanctuary for Mevlevi dervishes by Murat II in 1435, its interior distinguished by some of the best İznik tiles outside Bursa.

Practicalities

The new **bus station** is around 4km southeast of the centre, from where there are frequent *dolmuşes* and less frequent free city buses to the town centre. The **train station** is 3km southeast of the centre. There are two **tourist offices**, both on Talat Paşa Cad; the main one is about 500m west towards the Gazi Mihal bridge at no. 76a, and an annexe is up near Hürriyet Meydanı by the traffic signals (both daily 8am–5.30pm; ☎0284/213 9208).

Edirne's few budget **hotels** are either grim dosshouses or booked solid by truck drivers. The *Rüştem Paşa Kervanseray*, just off the main Hürriyet Meydanı on İki Kapılı Han Cad (☎0284/225 2195, ✉k.saray@netone.com; ❺), offers overpriced rooms in a restored Ottoman caravanserai; bargaining is recommended. Cheapest place is the seedy but otherwise friendly *Aksaraylı Hotel*, Alipaşa Ortakapı Cad 10 (☎0284/212 6035; ❶), a dilapidated old house where most rooms come with bathroom and TV. It's worth paying the extra for the relative comfort of *Şaban Açikgöz*, Çilingirler Cad 9 (☎0284/213 0313; ❷), which has nicer en-suite rooms with TV; or *Efe*, 13 Maarif Cad (☎0284/213 6166, ✇www.efehotel.com; ❸), which offers the same plus air-conditioning. The only nearby **campsite** is *Fifi Mocamp* (☎0284/226 0101), 8km along the road to İstanbul, which also has en-suite motel rooms (❷).

Restaurants in Edirne mainly cater for pass-through trade and do little to encourage return custom. Look out for the tiny *ciğerci* shops serving the city speciality, deep-fried liver. The lower end of Saraçlar Cad offers some reasonable options: the licensed *Café London* offers a daily special plus Western fast-food and sandwiches, and is also the only place in town to get a decent filter coffee; *Urfa-Gaziantep Kepapcisi* at no. 33 has good-value kebab fare and an upstairs dining room for women; *Balkan Piliç* at no. 14 offers various chicken options; and all along the street you'll find stalls packed with every kind of Turkish pudding and sweet. Good **internet** facilities can be found at *Eska Internet Café*, along from the *Kervanseray* at İlk Kapalıhan Cad 5.

Çanakkale and around

Though celebrated for its setting on the Dardanelles, **ÇANAKKALE** has little to detain you. However, it is a useful base for visiting the **Gelibolu (Gallipoli)** sites and the sparse ruins of **Troy**. Almost everything of interest in Çanakkale is within walking distance of the **ferry docks**, close to the start of the main Demircioğlu Caddesi. In the town, the **Çimenlik Park** (daily 9am–8pm), southwest of the bazaar, houses a replica of the minelayer Nusrat, which stymied the Allied fleet by re-mining zones at night that the French and British had swept clean by day. The **Naval Museum** nearby (daily 9am–noon & 1.30–5pm; $1) features photos and military paraphernalia. Some 2km south of the centre, the **Archeological Museum** (daily 8am–noon & 1–5pm; $1) is accessible by any *dolmuş* along Atatürk Caddesi labelled "Kepez" or "Güzelyalı" and has exhibits from all over the area, including exquisite gold jewellery from nearby tombs.

Practicalities

The **bus station** is out on the coastal highway Atatürk Caddesi, a fifteen-minute walk from the waterfront; if you're arriving on the bus from İstanbul, get off at the ferry rather than going out to the bus station. The **tourist office**, beside the ferry docks (daily 8am–5/8pm; ☎0286/217 1187), is worth a stop if only for their free map of the Gallipoli battlefields.

Except for a crowded couple of weeks during Çanakkale/Troy Festival (the mid-Aug), or on ANZAC Day (April 25), when the town is inundated with Antipodeans, you'll have little trouble finding budget **accommodation**. *Anzac House*, Cumhuriyet Meydanı 61 (☎0286/213 5969, ✇www.anzachouse.com; ❷), has small but neat rooms, dorm beds (❶) and internet access. The clean and airy, newly renovated *Yellow Rose*, Yeni Sok 5 (☎0286/217 3343, ✇www.yellowrose.4mg.com; ❶), in the street behind *Kervanseray*, is a good option with some en-suite rooms, internet access and dorms (**①**). The dilapidated *Kervanseray* round the corner at Fetvahane Sok 13 (☎0286/217 8192; **①**) is a quiet place in an old mansion. More upmarket, the *Anafartalar*, overlooking the ferry landing (☎0286/217 4454; **③**), offers en-suite doubles with TV and fabulous views over the straits; breakfast is included. There are several **campsites** – at Güzelyalı, Dardanos and Kepez – all accessible by minibus.

The expansion of the local university has led to a broadening of Çannakale's **restaurant** and café options. On the quayside south of the ferry jetty, the *Entellektüel* isn't cheap but offers great fish and scenic views. *Dadaşım*, 17 Yalı Cad, offers a good range of kebabs and stews, while the female-run *Köy Ev*, 15 Fetvahane Sok, offers a taste of real Turkish home cooking. Nearby on Cumhuriyet Cad, *Taş Fırın* does a brisk trade in *lahmacun* and *pide*-style fast food. For **drinking**, there is a burgeoning café- and bar-scene on Yalı Cad and Fetvahane Sok, with the latter boasting the current top spot, *Depo*. The *TNT* bar on Saat Kule Meydanı is popular with the Anzac crowd. There are also numerous **internet** cafés in this area.

The Gelibolu peninsula (Gallipoli)

Though endowed with spendid scenery and beaches, the slender **Gelibolu peninsula (Gallipoli)**, which forms the northwest side of the **Dardanelles**, is mainly known for its grim military history. In April 1915 it was the site of a plan, devised by Winston Churchill, to land Allied troops, many of them Australian and New Zealand units, with a view to putting Turkey out of the war. It failed miserably, with massive casualties. Nevertheless, this was the first time Australian and New Zealand soldiers had seen action under their own commanders; the date of the first landings, April 25, is celebrated as **ANZAC Day**. Various companies currently offer **tours** of the Gallipoli battlefields, two of them based in Çanakkale and both offering English-speaking guides: Hassle Free Tours, which is owned by *Anzac House Pension*, and the *Yellow Rose Pension*. Prices are around $20 per person: for a group of four or five, renting a car and doing it yourself would work out cheaper.

The **World War I battlefields** and **Allied cemeteries** scattered along the Gelibolu peninsula are by turns moving and numbing in the sheer multiplicity of graves, memorials and obelisks. It's difficult to imagine the bare desolation of 1915 in the lush landscape of much of the area, but the final 20km have been designated a **national park**. The open-air sites have no admission fees or restricted hours, but since there's little public transport through the area you should take a **tour** unless you have your own vehicle. The first stop on most tours is the **Kabatepe Orientation Centre and Museum** (daily 8am–6pm; $1), 6km along, beyond which are the **Beach**, **Shrapnel Valley** and **Shell Green** cemeteries, followed by **Anzac Cove** and **Arıburnu**, site of the ANZAC landing and ringed by more graves. Beyond Arıburnu, a left fork leads towards the beaches and salt lake at **Cape Suvla**, today renamed Kemikli Burnu; most tourists bear right for Büyük Anafartalar village and **Çonkbayırı Hill**, where there's a massive New Zealand memorial and a Turkish memorial describing Atatürk's words and deeds. Working your way back down towards the visitors' centre, you pass **The Nek**, **Walker's Ridge** and **Quinn's Post**, where the trenches of the opposing forces lay within a few metres of each other: the modern road corresponds to no-man's-land. From here the perilous supply line ran down-valley to the present location of **Beach Cemetery**.

The peninsula's principal town, **GELİBOLU** – an inviting place with a colourful fishing harbour ringed by cafés and restaurants – is, like its neighbour **ECEABAT**, a good alternative to Çanakkale at which to base yourself for visits to the battle sites. The **ferry** jetty in Gelibolu is right at the inner harbour entrance; the new **bus terminal** is on the coast road 1km east of the town centre. In Eceabat, the hourly **ferry** from Carmakale arrices at the jetty in the centre of town, near where **buses** drop you off. There's a good range of excellent-value **accommodation** in both towns. *Hotel Yılmaz*, Liman Cad 6 (☎0286/566 1256; **①**), is the backpacker stopover, but the friendly *Hotel Oya*, Miralay Şeflik Aker Cad 7 (☎0286/566 0392; **①**), is quieter with en-suite rooms. Very cheap accommodation in Eceabat is offered at two hostels: *Ece Hotel Backpackers Guest House* (℡0286/814 1210, ✉berkonz.hotmail.com; ❶), which organize tours and bus tickets; and *TJs*, Cumhuriyer Cad. 5a (℡0286 814 3121, ✉anzacgallipollitours.com; ❶), which also offers tours. There's a municipal **campsite** on the beach to the west of Gelıbolu. Waterfront **restaurants in** Gelibolu include the *İmren*, the *İlhan* and the *Yelkenci*, all of which are licensed and offer several variations on the local speciality, sardines. For **eats** in Eceabat, try the bluefish at *Gul Restaurant* along the seafront. **Internet** access is available at Gina Café Bar in Eceabat, beside the police station, at Cumhuriyat Cad.

Troy

Although not the most spectacular archeological site in Turkey, **TROY** (Truva) is probably the most celebrated, thanks to its key role in Homer's *Iliad*. The ruins of the ancient city, just west of the main road around 20km south of Çanakkale, are on a much smaller scale than other sites, consisting mainly of defensive walls, a small theatre and the remains of a temple. Some visitors may come away disappointed, but it's worth remembering that the settlement dates back to the late Bronze Age, making Troy far older than most other classical cities. Until 1871, when Heinrich Schliemann excavated the site, it had generally been thought to have existed in legend only. Schliemann's work caused a certain amount of damage and he removed many of his discoveries to Germany without permission, but his digging uncovered nine layers of remains, representing developments spanning four millennia. The oldest, Troy I, dates back to about 3600 BC and was followed by four similar settlements. Troy VI is known to have been destroyed by an earthquake in about 1275 BC, while Troy VII shows signs of having been destroyed by fire about 25 years later, around the time historians generally estimate the Trojan War to have taken place. Troy VIII, which thrived from 700 to 300 BC, was a Greek city, while the final layer of development, Troy IX, was built between 300 BC and 300 AD, during the heyday of the Roman Empire.

Çanakkale is the most sensible base for seeing Troy: take one of the frequent *dolmuşes* ($1), which run from Çanakkale's minibus station direct to the site, rather than forking out $10–12 to join an organized tour. The **site** (daily 8am–5/7pm; $4) is signalled by the ticket office opposite the bus drop-off point, from where a road leads to a giant wooden horse. Just beyond is the ruined city itself, a craggy outcrop overlooking the plain, which stretches about 8km to the sea. It's a fantastic view, and despite the sparseness of the remains, as you stand on what's left of the ramparts and look out across the plain, it's not too difficult to imagine a besieging army camped out below. Walking around the site, the **walls** of Troy VI are the most obvious feature, curving around in a crescent from the entrance; there are also more definite and visible remains from Troys VIII and IX, including a council chamber and a small theatre a little way north.

İznik

Tucked away at the eastern end of the lake that bears its name, the sleepy little town of **İZNİK** boasts extensive, well-preserved ruins. Originally the ancient Greek city of Nicaea, when İstanbul fell to the Crusaders in 1204 it became the Byzantine capital. Under the Ottomans, the city became a centre for ceramic production, an art that has recently been revived. You're free to wander the length of the Byzantine city walls that enclose almost everything of interest. In the centre of town sits the **Aya Sofya Museum** (daily 9am–noon & 1–6.30pm; $1), the remains of a Byzantine church originally founded by Justinian. To the northeast lie the **Hacı Özbek Camii** – the earliest-known Ottoman mosque, built in 1333 – and the later **Yeşil Camii**, named for the green tiles decorating its minaret. Across the park sprawls the fourteenth-century **Nilüfer Hatun İmareti**, a religious hostel that nowadays houses İznik's **Archeological Museum** (daily 9.30am–noon &

1–6.30pm; $1), displaying artefacts from nearby Neolithic settlements and some fabulous examples of Ottoman İznik ceramics. In the mid-1990s, the **İznik Foundation** restarted local ceramic production using original materials and techniques; their factory (tours daily 9am–7pm; free; ◍www.iznik.com) is signposted as *İznik Vakfı* on Halı Saha Arkası, beyond the remains of the **Roman amphitheatre**, outside the walls to the southwest.

Buses arrive at İznik's tiny bus station, southeast of the centre, from where everything is within walking distance. The **tourist office** is in the centre of town, opposite the Aya Sofya, at Kılıçaslan Cad 130 (Mon–Fri 8.30am–noon & 1–5.30pm; ☎0224/757 1933). In summer, what **accommodation** there is tends to fill up fast; if you can, reserve in advance. *Kaynarca Pansiyon*, Gündem Sok 1 (☎0224/757 1723; ❶), is backpacker-friendly and provides a useful map; there's satellite TV in every room and an attached **internet** café. For views over the lake, try the *Çamlık Motel* (☎0224/757 1631; ❷), with en-suite doubles, or *Cem Pansiyon* (☎0224/757 1687; ❶), with some en-suites. The fish **restaurants** on the coast road Sahil Yolu are so-so, but try the *Sahil Restaurant*, which can manage grills and has a good range of *meze*. There's a row of cheap restaurants behind Aya Sofya, including the funky old *Konat Barbeku Izgara*, which has good stews and *pide*.

Bursa

Draped along the leafy lower slopes of Uludağ, which towers more than 2000m above, **BURSA** – first capital of the Ottoman Empire and the burial place of several sultans – does more justice to its setting than any other Turkish city besides İstanbul. Gathered here are some of the finest early Ottoman monuments in Turkey, in a tidy and appealing city centre.

Flanked by the busy Atatürk Cad, the compact **Koza Parkı**, with its fountains, benches, crowds and cafés, is the real heart of Bursa. On the far side looms the fourteenth century **Ulu Camii**, whose interior is dominated by a huge *şadırvan* pool for ritual ablutions in the centre, and an intricate walnut *mimber*. Close by is Bursa's covered market, the **Bedesten**, given over to the sale of jewellery and precious metals, and the **Koza Hanı**, flanking the park, still entirely occupied by silk and brocade merchants. Across the river to the east, the **Yeşil Camii** (daily 8am–8.30pm) is easily the most spectacular of Bursa's imperial mosques. The hundreds of green tiles inside give the mosque its name. The nearby hexagonal **Yeşil Türbe** (daily 8am–noon & 1–7pm; free) contains the sarcophagus of Çelebi Mehmet I and assorted offspring. The immediate environs of the mosque are a busy tangle of cafés and souvenir shops. The *medrese*, the largest surviving dependency of the mosque, now houses Bursa's **Museum of Turkish and Islamic Art** (Tues–Sun 8.30am–noon & 1–5pm; $1.50), with İznik ware, Çanakkale ceramics, glass items and a mock-up of an Ottoman circumcision chamber.

West from the centre of town, the **Hisar** ("citadel") district was Bursa's original nucleus. A warren of narrow lanes wind up through dilapidated Ottoman houses, while new walkways clinging to the rock face offer fabulous views. The best-preserved dwellings are a little way west in medieval **Muradiye**, where the **Muradiye Külliyesi** mosque and *medrese* complex was begun in 1424. This is the last imperial foundation in Bursa, although it's most famous for its **tombs**, set in lovingly tended gardens. From Muradiye it's a short walk down to Çekirge Caddesi and the southeast gate of the **Kültür Parkı** (daily 9.30am–12.30pm & 1.30–6.30pm; $0.10) where there's a popular tea garden, a small boating lake and three pricey restaurants. At the far end there's also an **Archeological Museum** (Tues–Sun 8am–noon & 1–5pm; $1), whose exhibits include metal jewellery from all over Anatolia, a collection of Roman glass items, and Byzantine and Roman bronzes. Just beyond the Kültür Parkı, the **Yeni Kaplıca** (daily 9am–11pm; $2) are the nearest of Bursa's baths, a faded reminder of the days when the town was patronized as a spa.

Practicalities

Bursa's new **bus terminal** is 5km north on the main road to İstanbul, from where bus #90a (every 15min) runs to Koza Parkı in a subterranean mall, at one corner of which is Bursa's **tourist office** (Mon–Fri 8.30am–5.30pm; ☏0224/220 1848). Avoid the few grim **hotels** around the old bus station, now the main *dolmuş* garage: better options lie in the centre and the leafy spa suburb of Çekirge, a *dolmuş* ride to the north. In the centre, *Hotel Dikmen*, Maksem Cad 78 (☏0224/224 1840; ❸), is clean and friendly; or there's the female-run *Çeşmeli* at Heykel Gümüşçeken Cad 6 (☏0224/224 1512; ❷), which has great views from the upper rooms, while the brand-new *Hotel Efehan* at no. 34 (☏0224/225 2260, ✆www.efehan.com.tr; ❷) offers extremely comfortable rooms complete with TV. In Çekirge, the *Demirci Otel*, Hammamlar Cad 33 (☏0224/236 5104; ❷), is unpretentious, as is the *Özha Yat Hotel* over the road at no. 31 (☏0224/236 5105; ❶). Both have their own *hamams*.

The rather touristy *Hunkar Kebap* next to the *Yeşil Camii* offers good **kebabs** with views over the valley. In the central Heykel district, *Kebapçı İskender*, Unlu Cad 7 is one of a number of **restaurants** on Unlu Cad offering Bursa's speciality, *İskender kebap*; others include *Adanur Hacibey* and *Yilmaz İşhani Girizi*. Close to the tourist office at Belediye Cad 15, the more elegant *Çiçek Izgara* offers a decent take on many Ottoman dishes. The old fish market on Sakarya Caddesi at the foot of the citadel is dominated by lively fish restaurants, of which *Arap Şükrü*, at no. 6, is reasonably priced. This street also boasts a number of reasonable **bars**, including *Barantico*, *Cevriye* and, tucked down an adjacent side street, *Kuytu*. There are plenty of **internet** cafés: try Ernet, Bozkurt Cad 3/C, or Elite Internet Café just behind the Yeşil Turbe.

The Aegean coast

The **Aegean coast** is, in many ways, Turkey's most enticing destination, home to some of the best of its classical antiquities and the most appealing resorts. The north shore is a quiet, rocky region, well endowed with Hellenistic remains but with few sandy beaches – and so is spared the tourist excesses of the south. Tiny **Assos** with its ancient ruins is one of the gems of the coast. **Ayvalık**, the north's longest-established resort, makes an excellent place to stop for a few days, with good beaches and easy access to **Bergama**, a little inland, with its unmissable ruins. Off the north-west coast, the island of **Bozcaada** has the best beaches of the region. Further south, the city of **İzmir** serves as a base for day-trips to adjacent sights and beaches. The territory to the south is home to the best concentration of classical, Hellenistic and Roman ruins, notably **Ephesus** and the remains inland at **Aphrodisias** and **Hierapolis** – although the latter is more often visited for the pools and rock formations of adjacent **Pamukkale**. The **coast** itself is better down here, too, and although the larger resorts, including **Kuşadası** and **Marmaris**, are beginning to be lost to the developers, **Bodrum** and **Çesme** still have a certain amount of charm.

Bozcaada

South of Troy lies **BOZCAADA,** a small but enticing island just 12km long. **Ferries** run from the mainland at Yukyeri Iskelesi (daily 10am, 2pm, 7pm & 9pm; $0.75). The main settlement, also named Bozcaada, boasts a fifteenth-century **Venetian Castle** (9am–5pm; $0.50). Minibuses run from the town square to the excellent **beaches** on the south of the island, such as Ayazma Plaji for superb swimming in pristine water.

There's no **tourist office** on the island, but the friendly *Café Ada*, at Cinar Cesme 4, the town's main square (☏0286/697 8795), provides helpful advice, hotel reservations and a map. While you're there, sample the tasty chocolate brownies. There are plenty of budget **pensions** to choose from. The friendly *Ergin*, near the castle at Arkasi Sukran Sk. (☎0286 697 84 29; ❷), has four pensions, with good quality rooms, some with a sea view. A family-run pension handy for the beach is *Sekeraga* (☎0532 677 8009, ✉sirmakonat@hotmail.com). Bozcaada's **restaurants** offer Greek and Turkish dishes; for a tasty meal, try *Salkim*, Cinarcarsi Cad 20, or *Lodos*, just along the street. The island is known for its wines and there are three wineries you can visit.

Assos

ASSOS, 70km south of Çanakkale, is a tiny stone village built on a hill around the ruins of the ancient town, founded in the sixth century BC and once home to Aristotle. The old-town ruins (daily 8.30am–5/7pm; $1) are for the most part blissfully quiet; the **Temple of Athena** has had its Doric columns re-erected, and there are breathtaking views from here to the Greek island of Lésvos 10km offshore, while downhill lie the recently unearthed **theatre** and **necropolis**.

The only transport is a minibus from Ayvacik, 25km to the north, which passes through both the upper village of Assos and its twin settlement downhill around the fishing harbour; it runs according to demand, so out of season you may have a long wait. **Pensions** in the upper village are all in restored stone houses and include the delightful *Timur Pansiyon* (☎0286/721 7449, ⒲www.hitit.co.uk/timur; ❶), which offers doubles with shared facilities, and *Dolunay* (☎0286/721 7172; ❷), which has en-suite doubles; both include breakfast. Down on the shore are several beautiful but expensive stone-built **hotels**, which can generally be bargained down in midweek and also offer half-board; also try the unlikely named *Dr No Pansiyon* (☎0286/721 7076; ❶), which has doubles, some en suite, the rest with shared facilities. Further along the shore are several small **campsites** including *Çatır* (☎0286/721 7048), which also has several shacks for rent (❷). Note that on summer weekends, finding a room anywhere may be tricky, and prices will be double or triple those of midweek.

Ayvalık and around

AYVALİK, 2km west of the main coast road, is a small fishing port that also makes a living from olive-oil production and low-key tourism; it makes a good base for beach-lounging, and for visiting the ruins at Bergama, 70km southeast. The town lost its mainly Greek inhabitants during the exchange of populations that followed the Greek–Turkish war of 1920–1922. There's not a great deal to see, though its tangle of central streets, lined with terraces of sumptuous Greek houses and clattering with speeding horsecarts, is worth a wander, and there are some decent beaches in the surrounding area.

The centre is focused on the small square İskele Meydanı, 1.5km south of the main **bus station**. The **tourist office** (Mon–Fri 8am–noon & 1–5/6pm; summer also Sat 9am–noon & 2–6pm; ☎0266/312 2122) is about fifteen minutes' walk south of the centre on the main coast road. There's a wealth of **pensions** in Ayvalık's old houses, the best by far being the beautiful *Taksiyarhis* (☎0266/312 1494, ✉info@taksiyarhis.com; ❷), behind the Taksiyarhis church, signposted inland and uphill from the seafront. The breakfast terrace and some rooms offer delightful views of the town and sea. Alternatives are *Yalı* (☎0266/312 2423; ❷), housed in a lovely old seafront mansion, and, also signposted from the seafront, *Chez Beliz*, Fethiye Mahallesi, Marezal Çakmak Cad 28 (☎0266/312 4897; ❷; closed Oct–April). **Eating** possibilities include *Osmanlı Mutfağı* on Talatpaşa Cad, which offers well-priced superior Turkish dishes; *Kardeşler Pide Salonu*, opposite the PTT on İnönü Cad, with a good choice of kebabs; and *Öz Canlı Balık* on the seafront, specializing in fish and *mezes*. There's a clutch of **drinking** dens between the main street Edremit Caddesi and the parallel İnönü Caddesi, plus *Circus Bar*, on Gümrük Sok. **Internet** access is at Star Internet, 39 Atatürk Cad, five minutes' walk south of the tourist office.

You can take a boat tour of the smaller islands with set intervals for a swim, using one of the many boat companies along the seafront. Tickets can be bought for **ferries** to the Greek island of Lésvos at Jale Tour, Gümrük Cad 24 (June–Sept Mon–Sat; $40 one-way, $50 open return; ☎0266/312 2740), and Yeni İstanbulTur next to the *Aziz Arslan Otel* (June–Sept 3 weekly; same prices; ☎0266/312 6123).

Bergama

Frequently touted as a day-trip from Ayvalık, **BERGAMA** is the site of the Hellenistic – and later Roman – city of Pergamon, ruled for several centuries by a powerful local dynasty. Excavations were completed here in 1886, but unfortunately much of what was found has since been carted off to Germany. However, the acropolis of Eumenes II remains a major attraction, and there are a host of lesser sights and an old quarter of chaotic charm.

The old town lies at the foot of the acropolis, about ten minutes' walk from the bus station. Its foremost attraction is the **Kızıl Avlu** (daily 8.30am–5.30pm; $2), a huge edifice on the river not far from the acropolis, originally built as a temple to the Egyptian god Osiris and converted to a basilica by the early Christians, when it was one of the Seven Churches of Asia Minor addressed by St John in the Book of Revelation. Crumbling but still impressive, it houses a mosque in one of its towers. The area around the basilica is a jumble of ramshackle buildings, carpet and antique shops, mosques and maze-like streets. South along the main street is the **Archeological Museum** (Tues–Sun 8.30am–6pm; $2), which has a large collection of locally unearthed booty, including a statue of Hadrian from the Asclepion (see below), and busts of Zeus and Socrates along with a model of the Zeus altar, complete with the reliefs, that are now in Berlin. Bergama has a particularly good **hamam**, the *Haci Hekim*, Bankalar Cad 32 (from $5).

Pergamon, the ancient city of kings, is set on top of a rocky bluff towering over modern Bergama, with an evocative **Acropolis** (daily 9am–5/7pm; $4). Taking a short cut through the old town still means an uphill walk of around half an hour. By taxi, the ride costs $10 or more; a taxi-tour around all Bergama's sights costs about $15–20. The first main attraction on the acropolis is the huge horseshoe-shaped **Altar of Zeus**, built during the reign of Eumenes II to commemorate his father's victory over the Gauls. Even today its former splendour is apparent. North of the Zeus altar lie the sparse remains of a **Temple of Athena**, above which loom the restored columns of the **Temple of Trajan**, where the deified Roman emperor and his successor Hadrian were revered in the imperial era. From the Temple of Athena a narrow staircase leads down to the theatre, the most spectacular part of the ruined acropolis, capable of seating 10,000 spectators, and a **Temple of Dionysos**, just off-stage to the northwest. Lower down the hill and less well-marked – but just as impressive – are the remains of the **Gymnasium** where the city's children were educated.

Bergama's other significant archeological site is the **Asclepion** (daily 8.30am–6.30pm; $4), a Greco-Roman medical centre which can be reached on foot from the road beginning at the Kurşunlu Camii in the modern town. Much of what can be seen today was built during the first- and second-century heyday of the centre, when its function was similar to that of the nineteenth-century spa. The main features are a **Propylon** or monumental entrance gate, built during the third century AD, and a circular **Temple of Asclepios**, dating from 150 AD and modelled on the Pantheon in Rome. At the western end of the northern colonnade is a **theatre** seating 3500, while at the centre of the open area a **sacred fountain** still gushes mildly radioactive drinking water, near to which an underground passage leads to the two-storey circular **Temple of Telesphorus**.

Practicalities

Bergama's **bus station** is on the main road, about 500m from the town centre, and within fifteen minutes' walk of most accommodation. The **tourist office** (daily

8.30am–5.30pm; ☏0232/633 1862) is further along the same road. Many of the budget **hotels** are located in the old town; *Athena*, Barbaros Mahallı, İmam Çıkmazı 5 (☏0232/633 3420, ✆www.athenapension.8m.com; ❶), has elegant rooms in a nineteenth-century mansion, plus en-suite rooms in a newer annexe; over the bridge, the family-run *Nike Pansiyon* (☏0232/633 3901, ✉fikretnike@yahoo.com; ❶) has clean rooms around a tidy garden with shared bathrooms; *Pergamon Pansiyon* (☏0232/632 3492; ❶) occupies an atmospheric old stone house in the town centre; *Bobligen*, Zafer Mah, Cad 2 (☏0232/633 2153; ❶), is a clean and well-run option on the way to the Asclepion.

If you're on a day-trip from Ayvalık don't feel obliged to eat at the restaurant stop: cheaper and better options abound. The **restaurant** in the *Pergamon Pansiyon*'s courtyard has excellent home cooking; *Sağlam*, Hükümet Meydanı 29, has a good range of traditional Turkish food and a shady courtyard. There's a number of outdoor **drinking** places opposite the museum.

İzmir

Turkey's third city and its second port after İstanbul, **İZMİR** – ancient Smyrna – is home to nearly three million people. Mostly burned down in the Turkish-Greek war of 1922, İzmir has been built pretty much from scratch and is nowadays booming and cosmopolitan. Its hot climate is offset by its location, straddling a (heavily polluted) 50km-long gulf fed by several streams and flanked by mountains on all sides. Despite an illustrious history, much of the city is relentlessly modern.

Orientation can be confusing – many streets are unmarked – but most points of interest lie near each other and walking is the most enjoyable way of exploring. İzmir cannot be said to have a single centre, although **Konak**, the busy park, bus terminal and shopping centre on the waterfront, is where visitors spend most time. It's marked by the ornate **Saat Kulesi** (clock tower), the city's official symbol, and the **Konak Camii**, distinguished by its facade of enamelled tiles. Southwest of here, the **Archeological Museum** (Tues–Sun 9am–noon & 1–5pm; $1) features an excellent collection of finds from all over İzmir province, including some stunning marble statues and sarcophagi. Opposite it is the **Ethnographic Museum** (Tues–Sun 9am–noon & 1–5pm; $0.50).

Immediately east of Konak is İzmir's **bazaar**. The main drag, Anafartalar Caddesi, is lined with clothing, jewellery and shoe shops; Fevzipaşa Bulvarı and the alleys just south are strong on leather garments. Worth seeking out is the handsome vaulted **Kızılara Gazi Kervanseray** on 871 Sok, which has antique and carpet shops and houses a popular café in its midst. East, across Gaziosmanpaşa Bulvarı, the **Agora** (daily 9am–5pm; $1), commercial centre of the classical city, dates back to the early second century BC. Above this is the unmissable **Kadifekale**, an irregularly shaped fortress dating from Byzantine and Ottoman times that gives great views over the city from its pine-shaded tea garden (daily 9am–9pm). The less energetic can take a red-and-white city bus #33 from Konak, but it's worth trying the walk up from the agora, threading through once-elegant narrow streets past dilapidated pre-1922 houses. To the north can be seen the **Kulturpark**, a large park where sanctuary from the sometimes oppressive heat can be sought.

Practicalities

Ferries anchor at the **Alsancak terminal**, 2km north of the centre, where there's also a Turkish Maritime Lines office selling onward boat tickets; a taxi into town costs $2 or you could walk 250m south and pick up bus #2 (blue-and-white) or bus #12 (red-and-white) from Alsancak train station. Intercity **trains** pull in at **Basmane station**, 1km from the seafront at the eastern end of Fevzipaşa Bulvarı. From the **airport**, there's an hourly shuttle train to Alsancak train station, as well as Havaş buses (14 daily) to the main THY office at the central *Efes Hotel*. The **bus station** is way out on the east side of the city, from where buses #50, #51 and #54 run to Basmane and Konak. Buses to and from destinations on the Çeşme peninsula depart from the separate Uçkuyular bus station, accessible by bus #12 and #169 from Konak. There's a **tourist office** in the *Efes Hotel* at Akdeniz Mah. 1344 Sok 2 (daily 8am–7pm; ℡0232/445 7390), and a smaller one just in front of the Kulturpark (same hours).

The main areas for budget **hotels** are Çankaya, Akinci and Altınordu, immediately west and southwest of Basmane train station, around Fevzipaşa Bulvarı and Anafartalar Caddesi. Opposite the Kulturpark, the *Hotel Zeybek* (℡0232 489 6694; ❷) offers a range of rooms. In Akinci, *Hikmet Otel,* 945 Sok 25 (℡0232/484 2672; ❷), has some en-suites; while the rooms at *Nil Otel*, Fevzipaşa Bul 155 (℡0232/483 5228; ❷), are all en suite, though the ones at the front may be noisy. In Çankaya, *Oba*, 1369 Sok 27 (℡0232/483 5474; ❷), is worth trying, as is *Güzel İzmir*, 1368 Sok 8 (℡0232/483 5069; ❷).

İzmir boasts many **restaurant** options. *Ömür*, Anafartalar Cad 794, is cheap and friendly, serving ready-prepared dishes but no alcohol; while *Bolulu Hasan Usta*, 853 Sok 13/B, does the best pudding and ice cream in town – but nothing else. The best eating options by far, hwoever, are in Alsancak on the Birinci Kordon, and on and around the pedestrianized Kıbrıs Şehit Caddesi: try *La Sera*, Birinci Kordon 190a, with kebabs, fish and desserts plus live music evenings; or *Café Reci* on 398 Sok, serving salads, crêpes and ice cream. More upmarket is the pricey *Kemal'ın Yeri*, 1453 Sok 20/A, which is famous for its seafood, while for the budget-conscious the *Kurçiçeği* at 75 Kıbrıs Şehit Caddesi is the place to go. Best-value **bar** is the long-standing *Eko* on the corner of Pilevne Bul and Cumhuriyet Cad, which also serves kebabs and chips. Further along on 1482 Sok *Kahve Bahane* and *Kaos* are brisk, inexpensive student hangouts housed in a row of dilapidated old Greek merchants' houses. Splendid views of the bay are offered by the *Pagos Café*, just in front of the castle at 5250 Sok 3a. There are several **internet** cafés around Alsancak, including Chat Internet Café, 1453 Sok 14a.

Çeşme

A once-attractive town of old Greek houses wrapped around a castle, **ÇEŞME** these days is little more than İzmir on holiday, and a convenient stopover on the way to the Greek island of Híos. The town's two main streets are **İnkilap Caddesi**, the main bazaar thoroughfare, and its continuation Çarşı Caddesi, which saunters south along the waterfront. The **sights** comprise the town's thirteenth-century Genoese **castle** (daily 8.30am–noon & 1–5.30pm; $1), with a museum containing finds from the nearby site of Erythrae, and the *Kervanseray*, a few paces south, dating from the reign of Süleyman the Magnificent but now a somewhat dubious luxury hotel.

Coming by **ferry** from Híos in Greece (Chios in Turkish), you arrive at the small jetty in front of the castle. By **bus** from İzmir you'll probably arrive at the station 1km south, although some services meet the top of İnkilap Cad. **Dolmuşes** to Dalyan leave from the roundabout at the northeast of İnkilap Cad; those to other nearby attractions depart from next to the harbourside **tourist office** (daily 8.30/9am–noon & 1–5/5.30pm; ℡0232/712 6653). There are many options for **accommodation**, with a clutch of pensions on the right-hand side of the castle as it faces the sea. The efficient *Avrupalı* (℡0232/712 7039; ❶) has a picturesque garden and well-appointed rooms including suites with kitchenettes, while *Özge* (℡0232/712 7021; ❶) is immaculately kept and comfortable. A bit further along and away from the harbour past the local *hamam* is the friendly, clean and basic *Aras Apartments* (℡0232/712 7375; ❶), which offers rooms with balconies. Down in the flatlands, the *Alim Pansiyon*, Müftü Sok 3 (℡0232/712 8319; ❶), has simple en-suites, while in the opposite direction, a ten-minute walk beyond the harbour, is the pleasant two-star *Kerman Otel* (℡0232/712 7112, ✉kerman2001@anet.com.tr; ❷), overlooking the beach.

Among Çeşme's better **restaurants** are the *Rıhtım* and *Marina*, both overlooking the fishing harbour; *Körfez*, on the marina, is possibly the most elegant, serving up excellent, if pricey, charcoal-grilled fish. Best-value is the nearby *Kordon Pide* next to the post office. *Rumeli Pastanesi* at İnkilap Cad 44 serves some of the best ice-cream on the Aegean, and specializes in desserts and jams made from the sap of gum trees. *Lezzet Aş Evi* at no. 14 offers good basic *lokanta* fare. **Internet** access is at Emre Internet Café, Kutludal Sok 11.

Kuşadası

KUŞADASI is Turkey's most bloated resort, a brash coastal playground that extends along several kilometres of seafront. In just three decades its population has swelled from 6000 to around 50,000, though far fewer stay year-round. The town is many people's introduction to the country: efficient ferry services link it with the Greek islands of Sámos and Míkonos, plus the resort is an obligatory port of call for Aegean cruise ships, which disgorge vast numbers in summer.

Liman Caddesi runs from the ferry port up to **Atatürk Bulvarı**, the main harbour esplanade, from which pedestrianized **Barbaros Hayrettin Bulvarı** ascends the hill. To the left of here, the **Kale** district, huddled inside the town walls, is the oldest and most appealing part of town, with an eponymous mosque and some fine traditional houses. Kuşadası's most famous **beach**, the **Kadınlar Denizi**, around 3km southwest of town, is a popular strand, usually too crowded for its own good in season. **Güvercin Island**, closer to the centre, is mostly landscaped terraces, dotted with tea gardens and snack bars. For the closest sandy beach, head 500m further south to the small beach, just before **Yılancı Burnu**, or 7km north of town to **Tusan** beach; these are served by all Kuşadası–Selçuk *dolmuşes*, as well as more frequent ones labelled *Şehir İçi*. Much the best beach in the area is **Pamucak**, at the mouth of the Kücük Menderes River 15km north, an exposed a 4km stretch of sand that is as yet little developed; it's served by regular *dolmuşes* from both Kuşadası and Selçuk in season.

Practicalities

Ferries arrive at Liman Cad, right by the **tourist office** (Mon–Fri 8am–5.30pm; summer also Sat & Sun; ☎0256/614 1103), which has exhaustive lists of accommodation. The combined **dolmuş** and long-distance **bus station** is around 2km out, past the end of Kahramanlar Cad on the ring road to Söke, while the *dolmuş* stop is closer to the centre on Adnan Menderes Bulvara.

There are plenty of **places to stay**, though you'll need to exercise caution; the collapse in tourism in 1999 saw many hotels and pensions, especially those in areas favoured by backpackers, open their doors to East European prostitutes and their unsavoury minders. Most of the good pensions, as well as some to be avoided, are just south of the core of the town, uphill from Barbaros Hayrettin Bulvarı. *Sezgin Hotel*, Zafer Sok 15 (☎0256/614 4225, ✉sezgin@ispro.net.tr; ❷), has comfortable en-suite rooms and internet access, while lively and friendly *Sammy's Palace*, Kıbrıs Cad 14 (☎0256/612 2588, ⓦwww.hotelsammyspalace.com; ❷), is firmly on the ANZAC network. *Golden Bed*, Aslanlar Cad, Uğurlu Çıkmazı 4 (☎0256/614 8708; ❷), is similarly friendly and has en-suite rooms. Behind the tourist office at Buyral Sok 4 is *Hotel Liman* (☎0256/614 7770, ✉hasandegirmenci@superonline.com; ❷), which has air-conditioned rooms with sea views and some dorm space on the roof. For **campers**, the *Turyat* out at Tusan beach is well-appointed but expensive; *Önder* and *Yat*, both behind the yacht marina, are marginally cheaper, well-kept and popular.

Eating out is unlikely to be memorable, with few options between the over-priced tourist traps and more basic establishments. *Konyalı*, Saglik Cad 40, is a standard kebab place popular with locals and open round the clock. *Öz Urfa*, in the Kale district on Cephane Sok, has excellent-value *lahmacun* and *pide*; while the *Avlu*, also on Cephane Sok, has a wide range of kebab and steam-tray food and a cosy outdoor courtyard. *Kapı*, Cephane Sok 20, offers reasonable kebabs and *meze* with live traditional *fasil* music. If you want to eat by the water without emptying your entire wallet, try *Ada Restaurant-Plaj-Café*, on Güvercin Adası. The *She* **bar** is on the corner of Bahar and Sakarya Sokaks, with half-a-dozen more along nearby Kışla Sok.

Ferries to Samos are subject to predicted demand; there are no scheduled services in winter and up to three boats a day in high summer. Diana on Kıbrıs Cad (☎0256/614 3859) runs up to two boats daily in summer; the morning Turkish boat is handled by Azim, on Liman Cad Yayla Pasajı (☎0256/614 1553). Fares are $30 single, $35 day return and $55 open return. The Minoan Lines **ferries to Greece and Italy** are handled by Karavan, Kıbrıs Cad 2/1 (☎0256/614 1279).

Selçuk and around

SELÇUK has been catapulted into the limelight of first-division tourism by its proximity to the ruins of **Ephesus**, and a number of other attractions within the city limits and around. The flavour of tourism here, though, is different from that at nearby Kuşadası, its inland location and ecclesiastical connections making it a haven for a disparate mix of backpackers and Bible-bashers from every corner of the globe. Furthermore the beaches in and around Kuşadası are easily accessible from here on a short *dolmuş* ride.

The **hill of Ayasoluk** (daily 8am–6.30pm; $2), the traditional burial place of St John the Evangelist, who died here around 100 AD, boasts the remains of a basilica built by Justinian that was one of the largest Byzantine churches in existence; various colonnades and walls have been re-erected, giving a hint of the building's magnificence. The tomb of the evangelist is marked by a slab at the former site of the altar; beside the nave is the baptistry, where religious tourists pose in the act of dunking as friends' cameras click. The virtually empty **castle**, 200m past the church, is closed. Just behind the tourist office, the **Archeological Museum** (daily 8.30am–noon & 1–5pm; $3) has galleries of finds from Ephesus. Beyond the museum, 600m along the road toward Ephesus, are the scanty remains of the **Artemision** or sanctuary of Artemis, a massive Hellenistic structure that was considered one of the Seven Wonders of the Ancient World, though this is hard to believe today. Within sight of here, the fourteenth-century **İsa Bey Camii** is the most distinguished of various Selçuk monuments.

At the base of the castle hill, a pedestrian precinct leads east to the **train station**. Following the main highway a bit further south brings you to the **bus** and **dolmuş** terminal, opposite which is the **tourist office** (Mon–Fri 8.30am–noon & 1–5pm; summer also Sat & Sun). The majority of pensions and hotels will organize a free lift from the bus station if you call them on arrival, and many will arrange free lifts to Ephesus and some other local sights. *Pension Karahan,* 11 Ataturk Mah. Siegburg Cad. (☎0232 892 2575, ⓔpensionkarahan@hotmail.com; ❷) is a delightfully hospitable and spotless pension run by a local family, only too willing to help you out. Also recommended is *Kiwi Pension,* Ataturk Mah. 1038 Sok. 26 (☎0232 892 4892, ⓔkiwipension@hotmail.com; ❶), run by a friendly expat, with a range of clean rooms and facilities such as a swimming pool on offer. The large *Artemis Guest House "Jimmy's Place"*, 1012 Sok 2 (☎0232/892 1982, ⓦwww.artemisguesthouse.com; ❷), has en-suite doubles, some with nice views, internet access and veggie food. *Otel Ürkmez*, Namık Kemal Cad 20 (☎0232/892 6312, ⓔurkmez35@hotmail.com; ❷), near the *hamam*, has en-suite facilities and a roof terrace. More upmarket is the hospitable and beautifully furnished, female-run *Nilya*, Atatürk Mah 1051 Sok 7 (☎0232/892 9081; ❹), which offers delightful accommodation, combined with splendid views over the Artemision. Selçuk's **campsite**, *Garden*, lies just beyond the IsaBey Camii and is well rated; alternatively, there's the *Blue Moon/Develi*, 9km west at Pamucak Beach, served by Selçuk–Kuşadası *dolmuşes*. The better **restaurants** are in the centre of town. *Kalenin Prensi*, Kale Alti, is a new restaurant, owned by the family of Sagturk, the famous Turkish ballet dancer, offering delightful ancient Roman and Turkish dishes. *Köşk pide* on Zigberg Cad, and *Ephesus* on Namik Kemal Cad, are worth a try, as is the licensed *Old House* restaurant on Deniz Topel Cad. Try Turkish style on cushions and enjoy apple tea in the beautiful garden of *Karamese* café, Tarihi Isabey Camii Onu, opposite the ancient mosque. Internet facilities can be found at the Nutuk Internet Café, Ataturk Mah. 1040 Sok.6. The **hamam** (daily 6.30am–11pm; full treatment approx. $9, plus small tip for masseur), next to the main police station, offers a cheap introduction to good Turkish scrub and massage.

Around Selçuk

Some 8km southwest of Selçuk lies **Meryemana** (daily dawn–dusk; $3), a tiny Greek chapel where some Orthodox theologians believe the Virgin Mary passed her last years, having travelled to the region with St John the Evangelist, who is buried on Ayasoluk hill. Evidence of Mary's residence is somewhat circumstantial but that doesn't stop coach tours to Ephesus making the detour. The chapel's appeal is all spiritual, with regular Catholic masses (summer daily 7.15am, Sun also 10.30am).

ŞIRINCE, to the south and served by hourly minibuses from Selçuk, is a 600-year-old Greek stone village where, against the odds, the wine-making tradition has been continued by Muslim Turks who settled here in the 1920s. Numerous local vintages are on offer in the village's many shops. There are several **accommodation** options, including the beautifully restored village houses which make up *Şirince Evler* (☎0232/898 3209; ➒).

Efes (Ephesus)

With the exception of Pompeii and some hard-to-reach ruins in Libya and Albania, **EPHESUS** is the largest and best-preserved ancient city around the Mediterranean. Not surprisingly, the ruins are busy in summer, although with a little planning and initiative it's possible to tour the site in relative peace. Certainly, it's a place you should not miss. You'll need at least three or four partly shady hours, and a water bottle.

Originally situated close to a temple devoted to the goddess Artemis, Ephesus' location by a fine harbour was the secret of its success in ancient times, eventually making it the wealthy capital of Roman Asia, ornamented with magnificent public buildings by a succession of emperors. During the Byzantine era the city went into decline, owing to the abandoning of Artemis worship, Arab raids, and (worst of all) the final silting up of the harbour, leading the population to siphon off to the nearby hill crowned by the tomb and church of St John, future nucleus of the town of Selçuk.

Approaching from Kuşadası, get the *dolmuş* to drop you at the Tusan Motel junction, 1km from the gate. From Selçuk, it's a 3km walk. In the centre of the **site** (daily 8am–4.30/6.30pm; $6) is the **Arcadian Way**, which was once lined with hundreds of shops and illuminated at night. These days it's generally closed in summer, since grass presents a fire risk. The nearby **theatre** has been partly restored to allow its use for open-air concerts and occasional summer festivals; it's worth the climb to the top for the views over the surrounding countryside. From the theatre, the **Marble Street** heads south, passing the main **agora**, and a **Temple of Serapis** where the city's Egyptian merchants would have worshipped. About halfway along is a footprint, a female head and a heart etched into the rock – an alleged signpost for a **brothel** – at the junction with the Street of the Curetes, the other main street. Inside are some fine floor mosaics denoting the four seasons. On the side of the terraced hill, the superb **Slope Houses** (additional charge $20) were once the preserve of the rich and are still being excavated; you can see some outstanding murals here.

Across the intersection looms the **Library of Celsus**, erected by the consul Gaius Julius Aquila between 110 and 135 AD as a memorial to his father Celsus Polemaeanus, entombed under the west wall. The elegant, two-storey facade was fitted with niches for statues of the four personified intellectual virtues, today filled with copies (the originals are in Vienna). Just uphill from here, a **Byzantine fountain** looks across the Street of the Curetes to the **public latrines**, a favourite with visitors owing to the graphic obviousness of their function. Continuing along the same side of the street, you'll come to the so-called **Temple of Hadrian**, actually donated in 118 AD by a wealthy citizen in honour of Hadrian, Artemis and the city in general. Behind sprawl the **Baths of Scholastica**, so named after a fifth-century Byzantine woman whose headless statue adorns the entrance and who restored the then 400-year-old complex. On the far side of the street from the Hadrian shrine lies a huge pattern **mosaic**, which once fronted a series of shops. Further up Curetes, you pass the **Temple of Domitian**, the lower floor of which houses a mildly interesting **Museum of Inscriptions**, on the way to the large, overgrown **upper agora**, fringed by a colonnade to the north, and a restored *odeion* and *prytaneum* or civic office.

Bodrum

In the eyes of its devotees, **BODRUM** – ancient Halicarnassos – with its whitewashed houses and subtropical gardens, is the most attractive Turkish resort, a quality outfit in comparison to its upstart Aegean rivals. And it is a pleasant town in most senses, despite having no real beach, although development has proceeded apace over the last couple of decades. The centrepiece of Bodrum is the **Castle of St Peter** (daily 8.30am–6pm; $5), built by the Knights of St John over a Selçuk fortress between 1437 and 1522. Inside, there are bits of ancient masonry incorporated into the walls, coats of arms, and a chapel housing a local Bronze Age and Mycenean collection. The various towers house a **Museum of Underwater Archeology**, which includes coin and jewellery rooms, classical and Hellenistic statuary and Byzantine relics retrieved from two wrecks, alongside a diorama explaining salvage techniques. The **Carian princess hall** (daily 10am–noon & 2–4pm; $2 extra) displays the skeleton and sarcophagus of a fourth-century BC Carian noblewoman unearthed in 1989. There is also the **Glass Wreck Hall** (daily 10–11am & 2–4pm; $2 extra) containing the wreck and cargo of an ancient Byzantine ship, which sank at Serce near Marmaris.

Immediately north of the castle lies the **bazaar**, most of which is pedestrianized along the main thoroughfares of Kale Caddesi and Dr Alim Bey Caddesi. From here, stroll up Türkkuyusu Caddesi and turn left to the town's other main sight, the **Mausoleum** (daily 8.30am–6pm; $3). This is the burial place of Mausolus, who ruled Halicarnassos in the fourth century BC, greatly increasing its power and wealth. His tomb, completed by Artemisia II, his sister and wife, was regarded as one of the Seven Wonders of the Ancient World, giving rise to the noun "mausoleum", but the bulk of it is now in London's British Museum. By way of contrast, the ancient amphitheatre, just above the main highway to the north, has been restored and is used during the September festival. Begun by Mausolus, it was modified in the Roman era and originally seated thirteen thousand, though it has a present capacity of about half that.

Dolmuşes from Bodrum's main bus station head to nearby **AKYARLAR**, which offers the combination of the best sandy beach around and some quiet *pansiyons* and restaurants, as well as one of only two campsites on the Bodrum peninsula.

Practicalities

Ferries dock at the jetty west of the castle, quite close to the **tourist office** on İskele Meydanı (Mon–Fri 8.30am–5.30pm; summer also Sat & Sun). The **bus station** is 500m up Cevat Şakir Cad, which divides the town roughly in two. Some of the best **accommodation** is southeast of the bus station in Kumbahçe. *Emiko Pansiyon*, Atatürk Cad, Uslu Sok 11 (☎0252/316 5560, ✉emiko@turk.net; ❷), has a pleasant courtyard and quiet en-suite rooms. *Durak*, Rasthane Sok 8 (☎0252/316

1564; ❶), has clean, tidy en-suites, some with balconies, as does the friendly *Uğur*, just across the road at no. 13 (☎0252/316 2106; ❷). West of the bus station, *Melis*, Türkkuyusu Cad 50 (☎0252/316 0560; ❷), has en-suite rooms and attractive courtyards. The nearby *Dönen* (☎0252/316 4017; ❷) is a quiet family-run operation with a garden and ample parking.

You don't come to Bodrum to ease your budget, and **eating out** is no exception. Best of the budget places are the *Zetaş Ocakbaşı* and the *Kaş Buhara Et Lokantası*, both on Atatürk Cad, which offer good *pide* and meat dishes and are frequented by local artists. *Gemibaşi*, opposite the yacht harbour, on the corner of Firkayten Sok and Neyzen Tevfik, is good for a no-nonsense meat meal. The Karadeniz cake shop on Dr Alim Bey Cad does wonderful fruit and cream cakes. The same street boasts many of the town's fast-changing **bars**, which currently include the *Robin Hood* and the *White House*. There are also a number of good bars along Neyzen Tevfik Cad. For **clubs**, the *Halikarnas* disco at the east end of Cumhuriyet Cad is the most famous on the Aegean, while the *M&M Marine Club* is reputedly the biggest floating disco in the world; it sets sail at 2am when the onshore establishments close. **Internet** access is at Palmiye Internet Café, opposite the Marina.

Tickets for the **ferry to Kos** are best booked through the two main agents, beside each other at the ferry dock: Bodrum Express Lines (☎0252/316 1087) handles hydrofoils ($20 one-way; $30 return), and Bodrum Ferryboat Association (☎0252/316 0882) handles ferries ($12 one-way; $15 day return; $25 open return) as well as domestic services to Datça. You must pay a port tax of $10 on arrival in Greece if you're not returning the same day.

Marmaris and around

MARMARIS rivals Kuşadası as the largest and most developed Aegean resort. Its huge marina and proximity to Dalaman airport mean that tourists pour in more or less nonstop during the warmer months. According to legend, the place was named when Süleyman the Magnificent, not finding the castle here to his liking, was heard to mutter *Mimarı as* ("Hang the architect") – a command which should perhaps still apply to the designers of the seemingly endless high-rises. Ulusal Egemenlik Bulvarı cuts Marmaris in half, and the maze of narrow streets east of it is home to most things of interest, though little is left of the sleepy fishing village that Marmaris was a mere two decades ago. The bazaar is now little more than an area of covered streets, and only the **Kaleiçi** district, the warren of streets at the base of the tiny castle, offers a pleasant wander. The **castle museum** (Tues–Sun 8am–noon & 1–5.30pm; $1) has a worthwhile archeology and ethnography collection.

A new bus station has recently opened about 1.5km south of the town centre, from where you can pick up a *dolmuş* to take you to the town centre. Many of the bus companies also offer a free transfer minibus to their offices in the centre. The **ferry** dock abuts İskele Meydanı, on one side of which stands the very helpf┆ **tourist office** (Mon–Fri 8.30am–noon & 1–5.30/7.30pm; summer also Sa┆ Sun). The development of package tourism has ensured that **hotels** here are exⁱ┆ sive and welcoming *pansiyons* few and far between – but the tourist office is ᵉᵈ in to the needs of backpackers and can help out. The cheapest option the *Interyouth Hostel* at Tepe Mahallesi 42, Sok 45, in the bazaar close to the ᵗürk statue (☎0252/412 3687, ✉interyouth@turk.net; ❶), with around 180 be ᵃ pri- vate rooms as well as dorms, a lively rooftop café, and facilities includⁱ ᵗernet access and a competitively priced travel service. Behind the huge tan┐ᵒᵖᵖⁱⁿg centre is the *Nadir* (☎0252/412 1167; ❷) which has both en-suite p┐ⁿ rooms and hotel rooms complete with air-conditioning. Another good bu┐ᵉⁿˢⁱᵒⁿ is the *Yeşim*, west of the centre towards Uzunyalı beach at Atatürk┐₆₀, Sok 3 (☎0252/412 3001; ❷), a well-maintain┄┄ ┄┄ ᵃ┐ᵒms. More upmarket is the great-value *Marin* ┄┄┄┄ terrace. ┐ʷʷᵤᵣquaz-guide .net; ❷), which has clean e┄

The fabulous *Kırçiçeği* on Kübilay Alpagün Cad behind the bazaar offers excellent traditional Turkish **food** at reasonable prices. In the bazaar area, *Marmaris* and *Liman* are both acceptable and are frequented by the locals. To the west, Uzunyali harbours various pizza joints and a reasonable Turkish restaurant, *Turhan*, at Uzunyali 26. For **drinking**, *Panorama*, up on the castle hill, offers great views, and the nearby Hacı Mustafa Sokaği contains a wealth of other drinking venues, such as *Davy Jones' Locker* and *Casablanca*. Lin Net, 38 Atatürk Cad, opposite the Atatürk statue, has **internet** access.

Ferries to Rhodes ($35 one-way, $50 open return) run daily in high season, weekly in winter. Agents include Yeşil Marmaris, Barbaros Cad 13 (℡0252/412 2290), and Engin Turizm, 3rd floor, G. Mustafa Cad 16 (℡0252/412 6944).

Pamukkale and Hierapolis

The rock formations of **PAMUKKALE** (literally "Cotton Castle"), some 140km northeast of Marmaris, are perhaps the most-visited attraction in this part of Turkey, a series of white terraces saturated with dissolved calcium bicarbonate, bubbling up from the feet of the Çal Dağı Mountains beyond. As the water surges over the edge of the plateau and cools, carbon dioxide is given off and calcium carbonate precipitated as hard chalk or travertine. The spring emerges in what was once the exact middle of the ancient city of **Hierapolis**, the ruins of which would merit a stop even if they weren't coupled with the natural phenomenon. An official rescue campaign has returned the terraces to their pristine whiteness, now enhanced by nighttime illumination.

The **travertine terraces** (daily 24hr; $4) are deservedly the first item on most visitors' agenda, but you should bear in mind the fragility of this natural phenomenon. Nowadays most of the pools are very shallow and closed off, with tourists confined to walking on specially marked routes, though this is, thankfully, having a positive effect, as the travertines slowly return to their former grandeur. Up on the plateau is what is spuriously billed as the **sacred pool** of the ancients, which, with mineral water bubbling up from its bottom at 35°C, is open for bathing (daily 8am–8pm; $4). In reality, though, it's little more than a few big lumps of carved marble submerged in a concrete pool.

The archeological zone of **HIERAPOLIS** lies west of Pamukkale Köyü, via a narrow road winding up past the *Turism Motel*. Its main features include a **temple of Apollo** and the adjacent **Plutonium** – the latter a cavern emitting a toxic mixture of sulphur dioxide and carbon dioxide, capable of killing man and beast alike. There's also a restored **Roman theatre** just east of here, dating from the second century AD, with most of the stage buildings and their elaborate reliefs intact. Arguably the most interesting part of the city, though, is the colonnaded street which once extended for almost 1km from a gate 400m southeast of the sacred pool, terminating in monumental portals a few paces outside the walls – only the most northerly of which, a triple arch flanked by towers and dedicated to the emperor Domitian in 84 AD, still stands. Just south of the arch is the elaborate tomb of Flavius Zeuxis – the first of more than a thousand tombs constituting the necropolis, the largest in Asia Minor, extending for nearly 2km along the road. There's also a **museum** (Tues–Sun 8am–noon & 1–6.30pm; $4), housed in the restored, second-century baths, whose disappointing collection consists of statuary, sarcophagi and masonry fragments.

Practicalities

With over forty pensions, there's no shortage of **accommodation** in the nearby village of **PAMUKKALE KÖYÜ**, and touts at the bus stand can be particularly aggressive. The largest and friendliest is the air-conditioned *Koray* (℡0258/272 2222; ❷), with garden and buffet meals. The *Meltem Guest House*

(☎0258/272 3134; ❷) and *Meltem Motel Backpacker's Inn* (☎0258/272 2413, ✉meltemmotel@superonline.com.tr; ❶) both have en-suite doubles and internet access. Up the hill, the family-owned *Kervanseray* (☎0258/272 2209; ❷) also has a number of decent en-suite doubles and internet access. Most of the handful of **restaurants** are attached to hotels such as the *Mustafa*, which offers vegetarian dishes cooked to order, but you'd probably do best eating at your *pansiyon*.

Aphrodisias

Situated on a high plateau around 100km inland, **APHRODISIAS** is one of the more isolated of Turkey's major archeological sites. It was one of the earliest occupied centres in Anatolia, but remained a shrine for many centuries, and only really grew into a major cultural centre in the second century BC. It was renowned in particular for its school of sculpture, benefiting from nearby quarries of high-grade marble, examples of which adorned every corner of the empire.

A loop path around the site (daily 8am–5.30pm; $4) passes all of the major monuments, beginning with the virtually intact **theatre**, founded in the first century BC but extensively modified by the Romans three centuries later. Further on you pass the **double agora**, two squares ringed by Ionic and Corinthian stoas, and the fine **baths of Hadrian**, well-preserved right down to the floor tiles and the odd mosaic. North of the baths, several columns sprout from a multi-roomed structure commonly known as the **bishop's palace**, east of which is the appealing Roman **odeon**, with nine rows of seats. Perhaps the most impressive feature of the site is, however, the 30,000-seat **stadium**, a little way north, one of the largest and best preserved in Anatolia. The **museum** (daily 8am–5.30pm; $3) consists almost entirely of sculpture recovered from the ruins, including statuary related to the cult of Aphrodite, a joyous satyr carrying the child Dionysus in his arms, and a quasi-satirical portrait of Flavius Palmatus, Byzantine governor of Asia.

The nearest sizeable town is **KARACASU**, 13km west, connected by frequent **dolmuş** to **NAZİLLİ**, 50km northwest. If you're staying in Pamukkale, it's tempting to try and devise a loop to Aphrodisias via Nazilli, and then back to Pamukkale the other way, through Tavas, but you must get to Tavas in time for the last *dolmuş* back to Denizli, and thence to Pamukkale, which is difficult. Whatever happens, try to avoid getting stranded at Aphrodisias or Karacasu. **GEYRE**, 600m from Aphrodisias on the main Karacasu–Tavas highway, has the *Chez Mestan* **campsite/pension** (☎0256/448 8046; ❶).

The Mediterranean coast

The first stretch of Turkey's **Mediterranean Coast**, dominated by the Arkdağ and Bey mountain ranges of the Taurus chain and known as the "**Turquoise Coast**", is perhaps its most popular, famed for its pine-studded shore, minor ruins and beautiful scenery. Most of this is connected by Highway 400, which winds precipitously above the sea from Marmaris to Antalya. In the west of the region, **Dalyan** is renowned for its beach – a breeding ground of loggerhead turtles. West, **Fethiye**, along with the nearby lagoon of **Ölüdeniz**, is a full-blown regional centre, and gives good access to the pick of the region's Lycian ruins, such as **Xanthos**. The region's second major resort, **Kaş**, smaller than Fethiye but no less popular, is a good base for scenery, which becomes increasingly spectacular as you head towards the site of **Olympos**. Further along, past the port and major city of **Antalya**, the landscape is less dramatic but is home to yet more impressive ruins, notably those of the old Pamphylian cities of **Perge** and **Aspendos**. **Sıde**, too, has its share of antiquities, although it's better known as a tourist resort, as is the former pirate refuge of **Alanya**, set on a spectacular headland topped by a stunning Selçuk citadel.

Dalyan

DALYAN, 7km off Highway 400, is one of the calmer resorts along this stretch of coast, and a good base. Life here centres on the Dalyan River, which flows past the village: the one drawback in the summer months is mosquitoes, especially along the riverbank. There are a string of pleasant **pensions**, one of the nicest being *Midas* (☎0252/284 2195; ❷), at the far end of the riverbank, and the newly refurbished *Lindos* (☎0252/284 2005, ✉lindos@superonline.com; ❷), next door, also has a couple of cabin rooms right on the water; other good options are *Aktaş* (☎0252/284 2042; ❷), or its friendly neighbour, *Miletos* (☎0252/284 2532; ❷), both of which include breakfast in the room price. **Restaurants** are fairly undistinguished; the riverfront *Denizatı* and *Caretta* are typical – and pricey. There's better home cooking at *Dostlar Sofrası*, below *Altay Pansiyon*, where you'll come away replete for less than $3.

İstuzu Beach, a twenty-minute ride by boat from Dalyan, is the breeding ground of the loggerhead turtle (May–Oct no admission at night). During the day the beach is open to the public, and is a good place to swim and sunbathe, although you should be careful of disturbing the turtle eggs and nests, which are easily disrupted. You can also visit the nearby ruins of the Greek city of **KAUNOS**; it's a river-boat crossing away ($1), followed by a twenty-minute walk.

Fethiye and around

FETHİYE is well-situated for access to some of the region's ancient sites, many of which date from the time when this area was the independent kingdom of Lycia. The best **beaches**, around the Ölüdeniz Lagoon, are now much too crowded for comfort, but unlike Kaş, which is confined by its sheer rock backdrop, Fethiye is still a real market town and has been able to spread to accommodate increased tourist traffic.

Fethiye occupies the site of the Lycian city of **TELMESSOS**, little of which remains other than the impressive ancient **theatre**, which was only unearthed in 1992, and a number of Lycian rock tombs on the hillside above the bus station. Most notable is the Amyntas Tomb, carved in close imitation of the facade of a temple. You can also visit the remains of the medieval fortress, on the hillside behind the harbour area of town. In the centre of town, off Atatürk Caddesi, the small **museum** (Tues–Sun 10am–6.30pm; $1.50) has some fascinating exhibits from local sites and a good ethnographic section.

One of the most dramatic sights in the area is the ghost village of **KAYA KÖYÜ** (Levissi), 7km out of town, served by *dolmuşes* from behind the PTT. The village was abandoned in 1923, when its Anatolian-Greek population were relocated, along with more than a million others. All you see now is a hillside covered with more than 2000 ruined cottages and an attractive **basilica**, one of three churches to the right of the main path 200m up the hill from the road.

Ölüdeniz is about two hours on foot from Kaya Köyü – through the village, over the hill and down to the lagoon – or a *dolmuşes*-ride from Fethiye. The warm waters of this lagoon make for pleasant swimming, if you don't mind paying the small entrance fee, although the crowds can reach saturation level in high season – in which case the nearby, more prosaic, beaches of Belceğiz and Kidrak are better bets. Ölüdeniz is also the starting point for the **Lycian Way**, Turkey's only marked trekking route, which starts from near the Montana Holiday Village on the Fethiye–Ölüdeniz road and winds along the coast almost as far as Antalya.

Practicalities

Fethiye's **bus station** is about 2km east of the centre; *dolmuşes* to and from Ölüdeniz, Çalış beach and Kaya village use the old station, east of the central market. The **tourist office** is close to the theatre, near the harbour at İskele Meydanı 1 (daily 8/8.30am–5/7pm; ☎0252/612 1975). There are two main concentrations of **hotels** – in the downtown area and in the suburb of Karagözler overlooking the marina to the west (there are direct *dolmuşes* to Karagözler from the bus station). Downtown, the *Ülgen Pansiyon* (☎0252/614 3491; ❶), up the stairs beyond Paspatir Cad, has simple en-suites. Southeast of the centre and handiest for the bus station is *Sinderella*, Merdivenli Geçit 3 (☎0252/614 2288; ❶). In quieter Karagözler, *Savaşci* (☎0252/614 4108; ❷) is a long hike up above the marina but boasts great views, while *Pinara*, Fevzi Çakmak Cad 39 (☎0252/614 2151; ❶), is slightly noisier but friendly. Just behind it and before you reach the *Savaşci* is *Ideal* (☎0252/614 1981; ❶), similarly friendly and popular with backpackers, and with a great terrace. Along from the *Ideal* on Ordu Cad is the *Duygu Pansiyon* (☎0252/614 3563; ❷). All these include breakfast in the room price. For **camping**, one of the best sites is the *Ölüdeniz*, which has its own beach and restaurant; it's just past the entrance to Ölüdeniz Lagoon on the left.

Some of Fethiye's best **food** is at *Paşa Kebap* on Çarşi Cad; *Sedir*, Tütün Sok 3, offers excellent, reasonably priced *pide* and home-cooked stews. Also reasonable is *Birlik Lokanta* opposite the PTT on Atatürk Cad, which offers traditional Turkish cooking and ice cream. Outdoor seafront cafés provide ample **drinking** opportunities, while the hillside above the tourist office offers the garish *Yasmin*, specializing in live Turkish music; the *Music Factory* and *Car Cemetery Bar*, both on Paspartu Sok, vie for being the hottest joint in town. **Internet** access is at Line Bilgisayer, Yalı Sok 5b.

The Lycian sites

East of Fethiye lies the heartland of ancient Lycia, home to a number of archeological sites, all within easy reach of the resort. The closest is the **LETOÖN**, accessible by *dolmuş* from Fethiye to Kumluova, the site lying 4km off the main highway. The Letoön was the official sanctuary of the Lycian Federation, and the extensive **ruins** bear witness to its importance (daily 7am–7.30pm; admission $1.50). The low ruins of three **temples** occupy the centre of the site, the westernmost of which bears a dedication to Leto. The central temple, dating from the fourth century BC, is identified by a dedication to Artemis, while the easternmost temple has a floor mosaic of a lyre, bow and quiver, suggesting a dedication to Artemis and Apollo. Beyond the temple to the southwest is a **nymphaeum** with statue niches, though it's now permanently flooded. There is also a large, well-preserved **theatre** on the right, entered through a vaulted passage.

On the other side of the valley, the remains of the hilltop city of **XANTHOS** are perhaps the most fascinating of the Lycian sites, though the most important relic discovered at the site, the fourth-century Nereid Monument, is now in the British Museum, London. However, there is still enough to see here to reward a lengthy visit. Buses between Fethiye and **Patara** drop you off in Kanak, from where it's a ten-minute walk up to the **ruins** (daily 7am–7.30pm; $2). West of the car park are the acropolis and agora and a Roman theatre, beside which are two Lycian tombs – the so-called **Harpy Tomb**, a cement cast of the original decorated with pairs of bird-woman figures carrying children in their arms, and a Lycian-type **sarcophagus** standing on a pillar tomb. Northeast of the agora looms a structure known popularly as the Xanthian obelisk – in fact the remains of a pillar tomb covered on all four sides by the longest-known Lycian inscription. The nearby Roman theatre is pretty complete.

Kaş and around

KAŞ, southeast of Fethiye, is beautifully situated, nestled in a curving bay against a backdrop of vertical, 500m-high cliffs. However, what was a quaint fishing village as recently as the early 1980s has grown to become a tourist metropolis. There's no beach to speak of, but there's plenty to see in the countryside around, and the town does get lively at night. It's also the site of ancient **Antiphellos**, the ruins of which litter the streets of the modern town, as well as covering the peninsula to the west. Most interesting of these is the **lion tomb**, a towering structure that had two burial chambers, at the top of Uzun Çarşı. Some 500m from the main square, along Hastane Caddesi, a small, almost complete Hellenistic **theatre** looks out to sea; on a nearby hilltop stands a unique rock-cut **Doric tomb**, also almost completely intact.

From the **bus station** it's a five-minute walk downhill to the waterfront. The **tourist office** at Cumhuriyet Meydanı 5 (Mon–Fri 8am–5/7pm; summer also Saat & Sun; ☎0242/836 1238) has lists of **acccommodation**. Cheapest options can be found west of the centre along Hastane Cad *Yalı*, Hastane Cad 11 (☎0242/836 1132; ❷), has en-suite rooms and sea views plus a shared kitchen, as does the next door *Andiflı* (☎0242/836 1042; ❷), which includes breakfast. Further along, the *Gülşen*, Hastane Cad 23 (☎0242/836 1171; ❶), has rooms and a few sea-facing balconies. The *Karakedi Korsan* hotel up the hill to the north at Yeni Camii Sok 7 (☎0242/836 1887; ❷) features a roof terrace overlooking the amphitheatre, plus a pool and internet access. There are two nearby **campsites**: the tidy *Olympos* (☎0242/836 2252) is about 2km from the centre on the Kalkan road, while *Kaş Camping* (☎0242/836 1050) is 1km west of town on Hastane Caddesi, and has its own seaside diving platform, restaurant and bar.

Cheapest **restaurant** is the unlicensed *Mevlana*, Elmalı Cad, offering simple kebab dishes; *Smiley's*, 11 Gursoy Sok, also offers good simple Turkish fare, as does *Oba*, behind the main post office – though at a price. *Chez Evy*, in the backstreets east of the waterfront at Terzi Sok 2, serves up an enticing blend of Turkish and French cuisine. The current crop of **bars** includes the *Red Post*, round the corner from *Chez Evy*, and the *Déjà Vu*, east of the harbour, which has live music. For **internet** access, *Magicomm* and *Net House* are beside the post office.

Demre, Myra and Andriake

A winding 45-minute drive beyond Kaş lies the river delta town of **DEMRE** (officially **KALE**), a rather scruffy citrus- and tomato-growing town afforded more attention by tour parties than it can really deal with. However, it is worth visiting for its **Church of St Nicholas** (daily 9am–7pm; $5) on Müze Caddesi. The saint's sarcophagus, left of the entrance, is not considered the genuine article. The remains of the ancient Lycian city of **MYRA** (daily 9am–7pm; $1), 2km north of the centre, make up one of the most beautiful Lycian sites, consisting mainly of a large theatre and some of the best examples of house-style rock tombs to be seen in Lycia. And the site of the ancient city's port, **Andriake**, now known as Çayağzı, 2km west of Demre, is also worth a visit, itself close to a minimally developed sandy **beach**; however, there are no minibuses, so you'll need to get a taxi. The substantial remains of the so-called **Hadrian's granary** are the most prominent feature of the site, built between 119 and 139 AD by the Emperor Hadrian and consisting of eight rooms. Above the main gate are busts of Hadrian and a woman who is thought to be the Empress Sabina.

It's best to treat Demre as a day-trip from Kaş, as decent **pensions** are few and far between. Best is the family-run *Kent* (☎0242/871 2042; ❶), 2km north of the centre on the road to Myra. The closest **campsite** is the *Ocakbaşi*, at Andriake.

Olympos and Çıralı

Around 50km east of Demre is another Lycian city, **OLYMPOS**, an idyllic site (free access), located on a beautiful sandy bay and the banks of a largely dry river. Close to the beach are some recently excavated tombs with a quay wall, as well as a warehouse; to the east on the same side lie the walls of a Byzantine church; while further back, in the undergrowth, there is a theatre, most of whose seats have gone. On the north side of the river are more striking ruins, namely a well-preserved marble temple entrance. Beyond is a Byzantine bath-house with mosaic floors, and a Byzantine canal which would have carried water to the heart of the city.

A pleasant 1.5km walk away is the village of **ÇIRALI**. About an hour's well-marked stroll above the village's citrus groves flickers the dramatic **Chimaera**, a series of eternal flames issuing from cracks in the bare rock – you can put them out, but they will always re-ignite. The fire has been burning since antiquity, and inspired the Lycians to worship the god Hephaestos (or Vulcan to the Romans) here. The mountain was also associated with a fire-breathing monster, also known as the Chimaera, with a lion's head, a goat's rear and a snake for a tail.

There are one or two **minibuses** a day from Antalya to Çıralı in season; otherwise you'll have to take a taxi ($10) from the main road. To get directly to Olympos, catch any Kaş–Antalya bus to the Olympos minibus stop on the main highway 8km up from the shore; there are hourly minibuses in season. Çıralı now boasts around forty **pensions** ranging from the fairly basic to the frankly luxurious, all hidden in the citrus groves behind the beach – but the area is a national park and nesting turtles mean that camping on the beach, and night access in general, is forbidden. A reasonably priced option is *Blue and White* (☎0242/825 7006, ✉bluewhite@tr.net; ❷), which offers spotless air-conditioned en-suite lodges; *Yavuz* (☎0242/825 7021; ❷) is a moderately priced two-storey motel tucked inside a grove of poplars, all rooms are en suite. *Olympos Lodge* (☎0242/825 7171, ⓦwww.olymposlodge.com; ❾), offering a small taste of heaven with half-board, is located in a paradisal garden overlooking the beach. Back along the beach and ranged along the road behind the ruins are a group of backpacker "tree-house" camps, including *Kadir* (☎0242/892 1250, ⓦwww.olympostreehouse.com; ❶) and *Bayram's* (☎0242/892 1243, ⓦwww.bayrams.com; ❶); these offer a variety of huts and **internet** access, but both can get fairly rowdy. The handful of beach **restaurants**, such as the *Orange*, the *Kadir* and the *Azur*, are simple and uninspiring; you'd do better eating in your hotel. Note, too, that there are no **banks** in Olympos or Çıralı, so make sure you have enough cash before arriving.

Antalya

Turkey's fastest growing city, **ANTALYA** is also the one metropolis besides İstanbul that is also a major destination. Blessed with an ideal climate and a stunning setting, it has seen its annual tourist influx grow to almost match its permanent population, which now stands at just under half-a-million. Despite the grim appearance of its concrete sprawl, it's an agreeable place, although the main area of interest for visitors is confined to the relatively small old quarter; its beaches don't rate much consideration. The city also makes a good base for visiting the nearby ancient sites of Perge and Aspendos.

The intersection of Cumhuriyet Caddesi and Sarampol is the most obvious place to begin a tour of Antalya, dominated by the **Yivli Minare** or "Fluted Minaret", erected in the thirteenth century. Downhill from here is the **old harbour**, recently restored and site of the evening promenade. North is the disappointing bazaar, while south, beyond the Saat Kalesi, lies **Kaleiçi** or the old town, with every house being redone as a carpet shop, café or pension. On the far side, on Atatürk Caddesi, the triple-arched **Hadrian's Gate** recalls a visit by the emperor in 130 AD, while Hesapçı Sokak leads south past the **Kesik Minare** to a number of tea gardens and the **Hıdırlık Kulesi**, of indisputable Roman vintage but ambiguous function – it could have been a lighthouse, bastion or tomb. The one thing you shouldn't miss is the **Archeological Museum** (Tues–Sun 8/9am–5/6.30pm; $5), one of the top five archeological collections in the country; it's on the western edge of town at the far end of Kenan Evren Bulvarı, easily reachable by a tram that departs from the clock tower in Kaleiçi. Highlights include an array of Bronze Age urn burials, second-century statuary, an adjoining sarcophagus wing, a number of mosaics, not to mention an ethnography section with ceramics, household implements, weapons and embroidery and a small but well-thought-out children's section.

Antalya's main **bus station** is 8km north of town, although regular *dolmuşes* run from here to a terminal at the top of Kazım Özalp Cad, still known by its old name of Sarampol, which runs for just under 1km down to the Saat Kulesi on the fringe of the old town. About 5km west of the centre is the **ferry dock**, connected to the centre by *dolmuş*. The **airport** is around 10km northeast; Havaş buses into town depart from the domestic terminal, five minutes' walk from the international terminal, while city-centre-bound *dolmuşes* pass nearby. The main **tourist office**, a fifteen-minute walk west from the clock tower on Cumhuriyet Cad (daily 8am–6/7pm; ☎0242/241 1747), provides free city maps but otherwise only very basic information.

Most travellers **stay** in the atmospheric old town, where almost every other building is a *pansiyon*, although there's also a nucleus of **hotels** between the bus station and the bazaar. *Sabah Pansiyon*, Hesapçı Sok 60/A (☎0242/247 5345; ❶), is clean, well-run and the owner speaks English; book ahead in season. Near the Hadarlak Kulesi, the ageing *Hadrianus*, Zeytin Sok 4/A (☎0242/244 0030; ❷), has a wonderful garden, but the rooms are musty. There are unparalleled rooftop sea views from *Keskin 1*, Hadarlak Sok 35 (☎0242/244 0135; ❶), and the family-run *Senem,* Zeytingeçidi Sok 9 (☎0242/247 1752; ❷). *Keskin 2*, Hadarlak Sok 37 (☎0242/242 3941; ❷), has no views but a nice orange garden in which to breakfast. The *Adler*, Barbaros Mahalle Civelek Sok 16 (☎0242/241 7818; ❶), is one of the cheapest but most characterful of the old town pensions; there are no en-suites. Best of all is the *Antique Pansiyon*, Tuzcular Mah, Paşa Camii Sok 28 (☎0242/242 4615, ✉antique@ixir.com; ❷), housed in an old Ottoman building and boasting internet access as well as an English-speaking owner. *Bambus* **camping** (☎0242/322 5557), 3km south of town on the Lara road, is expensive but has its own rocky cove for swimming.

Many Kaleiçi *pansiyons* have their own **restaurant**. For elegant dining, *Antique Pansiyon's* evening menu is particularly good; otherwise, the licensed *Parlak*, just off Sarampol Cad, mainly serves delicious grilled chicken while the *Sim*, Kaledibi Sok 7, offers reasonably priced home cooking. Cumhuriyet Cad is the location of a number of eating-places with terraces offering excellent views of the harbour that are good for leisurely breakfasts. The covered pedestrian precinct, Eski Sebzeciler İçi Sokak, has a small number of restaurants serving the local speciality *tandır kebap* (mutton roasted in a clay pot). The *Gaziantep* eatery, at the edge of the bazaar through the *pasaj* at İsmet Paşa Cad 3, is excellent. Two other quality choices are *Karadeniz Pideci* on Recep Peker Cad, which offers a good take on standard *pide* fare, and *Ol Gunegliler*, just north of the clock tower, serving southeastern specialities. **Nightlife** is mostly located around the harbour. The popular *Café İskele* has tables grouped around a fountain, while the nearby *Cece* often has live music and *Club 29*, an expensive disco, boasts a terrace with pool and a restaurant. A little inland in the Kale district, *İçi Karatayhan Pansiyon* boasts the reasonably priced and laid back *Gizli Bahçe* bar. Further out, the *Olympos* disco, beside *Falez Hotel* near the archeological museum, is a popular late-night dance venue. There's an **internet** café on Recep Peker Sok near Hadrian's Gate.

The Pamphylian cities

East of Antalya lies an area known in ancient times as **Pamphylia**, a remote region that was home to four great cities – Perge, Sillyon, Aspendos and Sıde.

PERGE, about 15km east of Antalya, can be reached by taking a *dolmuş* to the village of Aksu on the main eastbound road, from where it's a fifteen-minute walk to the site (daily 8/8.30am–5/7pm; $6, stadium free). It was founded around 1000 BC and is an enticing spot, the ruins expansive and impressive. Just beyond the site entrance, the **theatre** was originally constructed by the Greeks, but substantially altered by the Romans in the second century AD; built into the side of a hill, it could accommodate 14,000 people on 42 seating levels. Northeast of here is Perge's massive horseshoe-shaped **stadium**, the largest in Asia Minor and excellently preserved. East of the stadium is the city proper, marked by a cluster of souvenir and soft drinks stands. Just in front of the outer gates is the **tomb of Plancia Magna**, a benefactress of the city, whose name appears later on a number of inscriptions. Inside is a **Byzantine basilica**, beyond which lies the fourth-century AD **agora**; southwest are some **Roman baths**, a couple of whose pools have been exposed. At the northwest corner of the agora is Perge's **Hellenistic Gate**, with its two mighty circular towers, the only building to have survived from the period. Behind, there's a 300m-long colonnaded street, with a water channel running down the middle and shells of shops on either side.

ASPENDOS (daily 7.30/8am–5.30/7.30pm; $7) lies off the main road close to the villages of Serik and Belkis, accessible from Antalya by regular *dolmuş* during summer. The principal feature is the well-preserved **theatre**, built in the second century AD to a Roman design, with an elaborate stage behind which the scenery could be lowered. The stage, auditorium and arcade above are all intact, and what you see today is pretty much what the spectators saw during the theatre's heyday.

About 25km east of Aspendos, **SİDE**, a one-time port and trysting place of Antony and Cleopatra, was perhaps the foremost of the Pamphylian cities. The ruins of the ancient port just about survive; over the last ten years or so, the development of myriad theme-hotel complexes has obliterated areas of real archeological interest. The **beaches** are superb, but if you're more interested in the ruins, try and visit out of season. Fortunately, the buildings and monuments that remain are still impressive. The **city walls** are particularly well preserved, with a number of towers still in place, and the **agora** is today fringed with the stumps of many remaining columns. Opposite the agora is the site of the former **Roman baths**, now restored to house a **museum** (Tues–Sun 9am–noon & 1.30–5pm; $5) with a cross-section of locally unearthed objects – mainly Roman statuary, reliefs and sarcophagi. South of here, a still-intact monumental gateway serves as an entrance to the modern resort and to Side's 15,000-seat **theatre**, the largest in Pamphylia, and supported by arched vaults. At the back of the theatre is a row of ancient toilets, complete with niches for statues facing the cubicles. To the **west** of town, the beach stretches for about 10km, lined by hotels and beach clubs, though the crowds can be heavy during high season. To the **east** the sands are emptier and stretch all the way to Alanya, though there's less in the way of facilities.

Buses from Antalya most often drop off at Manavgat, 10km east of Side; **dolmuşes** from the street behind Manavgat's bus station will take you to Side's new station, around 1km from the central waterfront, close to the monumental gateway. From here you can either walk, take a taxi or a tractor-drawn "tourist train" into the centre. Travelling on from Side, the best bus connections are from Manavgat. Side's **tourist office** (Mon–Fri 8/9am–5/6pm; summer also Sat & Sun; ☎0242/753 1265) is out of town, 300m from the station. **Accommodation** is plentiful, although Side is thronging with package tourists from mid-March onwards and *pansiyon* prices are relatively steep. Most options are in the warren of alleys east of the main street. *Morning Star* (☎0242/753 1134; ❶) is friendly and has en-suite rooms, upper-floor ones with balconies; *Evin* (☎0242/753 1074; ❶) has clean, bright rooms near the agora, beside the friendly *Yıldırım Pansiyon* (☎0242/753 3209; ❶), with a shaded courtyard and pool table; while *Hanimeli Pansiyon* (☎0242/753 1789; ❷) on Turgut Reis Sok offers en-suite doubles. For **camping**, there are a number of sites along the western beach, beginning about 500m from the theatre. There's no shortage of places to **eat and drink**: pricey *Charlies Restaurant* off Liman Cad offers locally caught fish and kebabs and nice views over the harbour; the better-value *Aphrodite* offers a variety of fish dishes including excellent swordfish. The *Apollonik*, just west of the temple of Apollo, is an atmospheric **bar**, while *Pasakoy Bar* on Liman Cad is notable as a masterpiece of kitsch. Further east, *Stones Bar* and *Barracuda* are louder and offer fine views out onto the Mediterranean. Side Internet Café is near the harbour.

Alanya

Now one of the Mediterranean coast's major resorts, **ALANYA** is a booming place that has fortunately managed to hold on to much of its character and is much less crowded than Side, even in midsummer. Most of its old town lies on the great rocky promontory that juts out into the sea, the bulk of which is occupied by the **castle** – an hour's winding climb or a short ride on an hourly bus from the tourist office. At the end of the road is the **İç Kale**, or inner fortress (daily 8am–sunset; $5), built in 1226 and virtually intact, with the shell of a Byzantine **church**, decorated with fading frescoes, in the centre. A platform in a corner of the fortress gives fine views of the western beaches and the mountains, though this originally served as a springboard from which prisoners were thrown to their deaths on the rocks below. On the opposite side of the promontory, the **Kızılkule** is a 35m-high defensive tower that today houses a pedestrian **Ethnographic Museum** (daily 8am–noon & 1.30–5.30pm; $4), and has a roof terrace that overlooks the town's eastern harbour. Back down at sea-level, apart from the hotels and restaurants, modern Alanya has little to offer. On the western side of the promontory, the **Alanya Museum** (daily 9am–noon & 1.30–6.30pm; $1) is filled with local archeological finds and ethnological ephemera, its garden a former Ottoman graveyard. Nearby, the **Damlataş** (daily: 6–10am for asthma sufferers; 10am–sunset for others; $1.50), is a stalactite- and stalagmite-filled cavern with a moist, warm atmosphere said to ease asthma; it's accessible from behind the *Damlataş* restaurant.

Alanya's **beaches**, though not particularly clean, are extensive, stretching 3km west and 8km east. Finer sand and fewer crowds can be found 23km away on the road to Side at **İncekum**, still a beautiful spot despite recent bouts of hotel building.

Practicalities

Alanya's **bus station** is a twenty-minute walk from the centre, but if you come in by local bus from Side or Manavgat you'll probably arrive at the *dolmuş* terminal, five minutes north of the centre. The **tourist office** is at Çarşı Mahallesi, Kalearkası (daily 8.30am–5.30pm; ☏0242/513 1240), opposite the town museum. As in Side, **accommodation** soon fills up and prices can be high, although there's a concentration of *pansiyons* in the grid of streets between the bus station and the seafront. *Oba*, Meteoroloji Sok 8 (☏0242/513 2675; ❷), is a good budget choice, as is *Üstün Pansiyon* on the same street (☏0242/513 2262; ❷). Nearer the centre, behind Damlataş Cad, *Pension Best*, Alaaddinoğlu Sok 23 (☏0242/513 0446; ❶), has immaculately clean rooms and apartments. Two other central alternatives are *Hotel Günaydın*, Kültür Cad 26 (☏0242/513 1943; ❶), and *Pansiyon Alanya*, Nergis Sok 4 (☏0242/513 1897; ❶). **Campers** can head to the Forestry Authority-run *Orman Kamp*, 30km to the west, or *Perle*, 15km to the east. The small streets running between Gazipaşa Cad and Hükümet Cad have lots of cheap *pide* and **kebab** places. *Burak,* Müftüler Cad, Kalgadam Sok 7, and *Buhara* and *Gülistan* on Kuyular Önü Sok offer excellent steam-tray and grilled **food** at reasonable prices. *Kale*, overlooking the harbour, offers good food and views, but at a price. My Donose Chatroom is one of a number of **internet** cafés on İskele Caddesi.

Central Turkey

When the first Turkish nomads arrived in **Anatolia** during the tenth and eleventh centuries, the landscape must have been strongly reminiscent of their Central Asian homeland. The terrain that so pleased the tent-dwelling herdsmen of a thousand years ago, however, has few attractions for modern visitors: monotonous, rolling vistas of stone-strewn grassland, dotted with rocky outcrops, hospitable only to sheep. In winter it can be numbingly cold, while in summer, temperatures can rise to unbearable levels.

It seems appropriate that the heart of original Turkish settlement should be home to the political and social centre of modern Turkey – **Ankara**, a modern European-style capital, symbol of Atatürk's dream of a secular Turkish republic. The south-central part of the country draws more visitors, not least for **Cappadocia** in the far east of the region, where water and wind have created a land of fantastic forms from the soft tufa rock, including forests of cones, table mountains and canyon-like valleys, all further hewn by civilizations that have found the area sympathetic to their needs. Further south still, **Konya** is best known as the birthplace of the mystical **Sufi** sect and is a good place to stop over between Cappadocia and the coast.

Ankara

Modern **ANKARA** is really two cities, a double identity that is due to the break-neck pace at which it has developed since being declared capital of the Turkish Republic in 1923. Until then Ankara – known as Angora – had been a small provincial city, famous chiefly for the production of soft goat's wool. This city still exists, in and around the old citadel that was the site of the original settlement. The other Ankara is the modern metropolis that has grown up around a carefully planned attempt to create a seat of government worthy of a modern, Western-looking state. It's worth visiting just to see how successful this has been, although there's not much else to the place, and the museums and handful of other sights need only detain you for a day or two at most.

Arrival, information and accommodation

Ankara's Esenboğa **airport** is 33km north of town. Havaş buses meet incoming Turkish Airlines flights; a taxi could set you back $30. The imposing new **bus station** lies around 8km to the southeast; some companies run service minibuses to the centre, otherwise take the **Ankaray** rapid transit system ($0.50), which will take you to Kızılay, in the heart of modern Ankara, or catch a *dolmuş* to Ulus, where most of the budget hotels are located, follow the signs to the Ankaray station and ascend to street level. Otherwise you can change from the Ankaray onto the city's other underground system, the **metro**, at Kızılay and take this to Ulus. The main **train station** is at the corner of Talat Paşa Cad and Cumhuriyet Bulvarı, from where frequent buses run to Kızılay and Ulus.

City transport is no problem, with plenty of **buses** running the length of the main Atatürk Bulvarı. Buy bus tickets in advance from kiosks next to the main bus stops (it's a good idea to stock up on tickets, as some areas have no kiosks). Ankara has two linked underground train systems: the metro runs from Kızılay northbound through Ulus, and the Ankaray cuts east to west with an interchange at Kızılay; tickets are interchangable between the two systems. There's a **tourist office** across from the train station at Gazi Mustafa Kemal Bulvarı 121, just outside Maletepe station on the Ankaray (Mon–Fri 9am–5/6.30pm, Sat 9/10am–5pm; summer also Sun ; ☎0312/231 5572).

Most of the cheaper **hotels** are in the streets east of Atatürk Bulvarı between Ulus and Opera Meydanı; there are a few more upmarket places north of Ulus, on and around Çankırı Cad, and clusters of options along Gazi Mustafa Kemal Bulvarı in Maltepe and on Atatürk Bulvarı south of Kızılay, with prices increasing as you move south.

Angora House Kalekapası, Kaleiçi ☎0312/309 8380. Pricey but beautifully renovated house in the old castle. The hosts are attentive and the rooms are sumptuous. **❺**

Buhara Sanayi Cad 13, Ulus ☎0312/310 7999. One of the better choices in Ulus, with en-suites. **❷**

Devran Sanayi Cad. Tavus Sok.8, Ulus

☎0312/311 0485. Small, clean en-suite rooms. **❶**

Ergen Karanfil Sok 48, Kızılay ☎0312/425 7819. Not a budget choice but very comfortable, with TV, air-con and en-suite rooms. **❸**

Güleryüz Sanayi Cad 37, Ulus ☎0312/310 4910. Comfortable, but slightly shabby and distinctly overpriced. All rooms en suite with TV. **❸**

Mithat İtfaiye Meydanı, Tavus Sok 2, Ulus

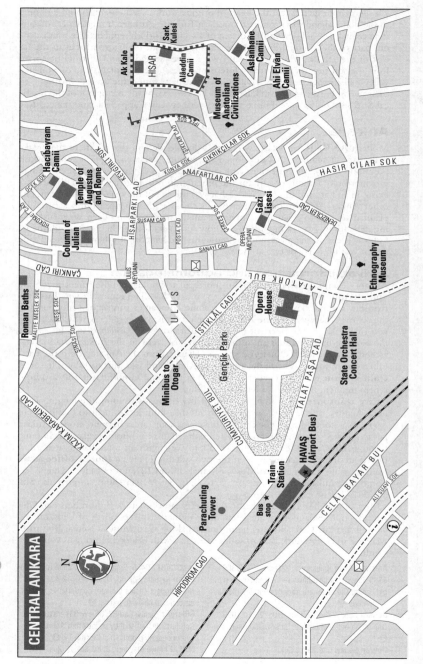

CENTRAL ANKARA

N

Şark Kulesi

Ak Kale

HISAR

Alâeddin Camii

Aslanhane Camii

Ahi Elvan Camii

Museum of Anatolian Civilizations

İPEK SOK

KEÇECİLİ SOK

Hacıbayram Camii

ÇİÇEK SOK

Temple of Augustus and Rome

KONYA SOK

İSTİKLÂT CAD

ÇIKRIKÇILAR SOK

ANAFARTLAR CAD

HASIR CILAR SOK

Column of Julian

HÜKÜME CAD

HİSARPARKI CAD

SUSAM CAD

POSTA CAD

ÇERKEŞ SOK

Gazi Lisesi

DENİZCİLER CAD

ÇANKIRI CAD

SANAYİ CAD

OPERA MEYDANI

Ethnography Museum

Roman Baths

MALİYE MESLEK SOK

NEŞE SOK

SİNASİ SOK

ULUS MEYDANI

ULUS

ATATÜRK BUL

Opera House

Minibus to Otogar

İSTİKLÂL CAD

CUMHURİYET BUL

Gençlik Parkı

State Orchestra Concert Hall

TALAT PAŞA CAD

KAZIM KARABEKİR CAD

HAVAŞ (Airport Bus)

Parachuting Tower

Bus stop

Train Station

CELÂL BAYAR BUL

ALİ SUAVİ SOK

HİPODROM CAD

i

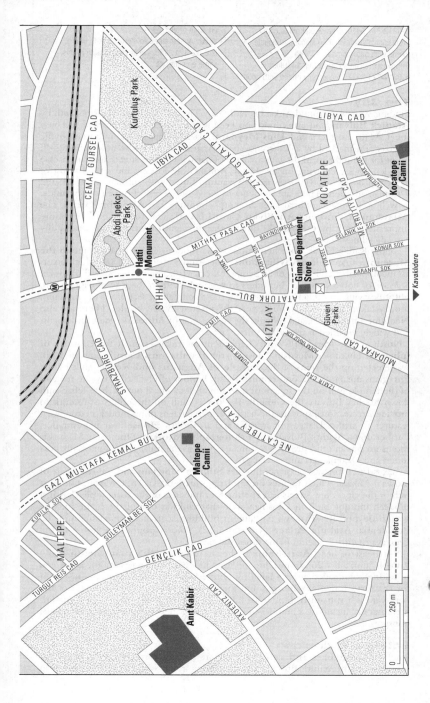

Kavaklıdere ▼

TURKEY

30

1121

— Metro

0   250 m

⌕0312/311 5410, ⌨www.otelmithat.com.tr.
Professionally run, offering single and double
rooms with bathrooms and TV. ❸
Olimpiyat Rüzgarlı Eşdost Sok 14, Ulus
⌕0312/324 3331. Reasonably priced with good

en-suite rooms. ❷
Yavuz Anafartalar Cad, Konya Sok 6, Ulus
⌕0312/324 3255. Clean, presentable rooms,
some en suite. ❶

The City

Finding your way around Ankara is fairly easy. The city is bisected north–south by **Atatürk Bulvarı**, and everything you need is in easy reach of this broad and busy street. At the northern end, **Ulus Meydanı**, a large square and an important traffic intersection marked by a huge equestrian Atatürk statue, is the best jumping-off point for the old part of the city, a village of narrow cobbled streets and ramshackle wooden houses centring on the **Hisar**, Ankara's old fortress and citadel. Most of what can be seen today dates from Byzantine times, with substantial Selçuk and Ottoman additions. There are tremendous views of the rest of the city from inside, as well as an unexceptional twelfth-century mosque, the **Alâeddin Camii**. The **Aslanhane Camii** and **Ali Elvan Camii** bazaar areas to the south are more impressive, built by the Selçuks during the thirteenth century, with beautifully carved ceilings.

Follow Kadife Sokak from here towards the modern city and you come to **the Museum of Anatolian Civilizations** (Tues–Sun 8.30am–5pm; $3), which boasts an incomparable collection of archeological objects housed in a restored Ottoman *bedesten*, or covered market, but offers frustratingly little in the way of explanation. Hittite carving and relief work form the most compelling section of the museum, mostly taken from Carchemish, near the present Syrian border. There are also Neolithic finds from Çatal Höyük, the site of one of Anatolia's oldest settlements and widely regarded as the world's first "city".

North of Ulus Meydanı is what's left of Roman Ankara, namely the **Column of Julian** on Hükümet Meydanı. Close by, the **Hacıbayram Camii**, built in 1400, was erected on the ruins of the **Temple of Augustus and Rome**, built by the Phrygians during the second century BC in honour of Cybele. Today the remains of the temple wall on the square next to the mosque are about all that's left. South down Atatürk Bulvarı, the **Gençlik Parkı** was built on the orders of Atatürk to provide a recreational spot for the hard-working citizens of his model metropolis; it features an artificial lake, funfair, cafés and an **Opera House** near the entrance. Further down Atatürk Bulvarı, the **Ethnography Museum** (Tues–Sun; $1) boasts rooms used as an office by the great man, as well as the usual collection of folk costumes and Ottoman art and artefacts.

Across the main west–east rail line lies **Sıhhıye Meydanı** and the real heart of modern Ankara, which focuses on the large square of Kızılay, the main transport hub of the city. A few streets east rise the four minarets of the **Kocatepe Camii**, a modern mosque built in Ottoman-style that ranks as one of the biggest in the world. Beyond lies Turkey's parliament building, a strip of embassies and the Presidential **Atakule Palace** (Tues–Sun; $2), whose grounds are home to the Çankaya Atatürk Museum (same times and ticket).

Northeast of here, **Anıt Kabir** is the site of **Atatürk's mausoleum** (daily 9am–4/5pm; bus #265 from Ulus and near Tandoğan Ankaray station), at the end of a long colonnaded avenue lined by Hittite lions. It's almost bare inside except for the forty-tonne sarcophagus and the guards. At the southeastern end of the courtyard is a **museum** (Sun 1.30–4.30pm) containing various pieces of Atatürk memorabilia, including a number of Lincoln limousines which served as his official transport.

Eating and drinking

There are some **bars and cafés** in the more affluent parts of town towards the southern end of Atatürk Bulvarı. A good starting point would also be Sakarya Cad in Kızılay where there are a number of decent watering holes in the neighbouring streets. Two worthwhile options are *Café Seven*, Reşit Galip Cad 57/A in Gaziosmanpaşa, a café/bar student hangout with live music in the evening and some snack food; and *London Pub*, 40 Arjantin Cad, Kavaklıdere, popular with richer students and professionals, and packed at the weekends.

Standard *pide* and kebab places can be found on just about every street in Ankara and there's an abundance of good sweet and cake shops, though really good **restaurants** are surprisingly rare. Ulus, particularly along Çankırı Cad, is a good place to look for cheap lunchtime venues, although most night-time eating and drinking takes place in the modern centre around Kızılay where a grid of streets comprising Sakarya, Selanik and Bayindir Soks harbours a range of possibilities, or further south in the well-heeled district of Kavaklıdere.

For **nightlife**, Ankara's citizens are proud of the Opera House at Opera Meydanı, which is great value: admission is usually $5 or under for lively and well-attended performances of works such as *Madame Butterfly* and *La Bohème*. **Discos** can be found at *Graffiti* and *Complex*, both on Farabi Sok, Çankaya.

Altin Şiş Karanfil Sok 17, Kızılay. A reasonably priced kebab place which does good puddings.

Çiçek Lokantası Çankırı Cad 12A, Kavaklidere. One of Ankara's mainstays, serving traditional dishes in regal splendour, albeit at a price.

Gaziantepli Fethi Bey Kebab Sanaycilar Cad 35, Ulus. Good variations on standard southeastern specialities.

Hisar Kule On the left inside the entrance to the Kule ☎0312/309 7898. One of several old-citadel restaurants in restored houses. Wonderful views from the terrace. Book ahead for evenings.

Hünkar kebap Selanik Sok 16, Kızılay. Excellent place to savour *İskender kebap* dishes.

Kebabıstan Karanfil Sok/Yüksel Cad, Kızılay. Plush kebab restaurant, offering all kinds of kebab including excellent mushroom *şiş*.

Körfez Lokantası Bayındır Sok 24. Arguably the best restaurant in town, always packed, and serving good-sized portions of excellent, moderately priced Turkish food.

Samsun & Bafra Selanik Cad 6, Kızılay. Great *pide* and friendly staff at the heart of the Kızılay restaurant quarter.

Listings

Embassies Australia, Nenehatun Cad 83, Gaziosmanpaşa ☎0312/446 1180; Canada, Nenehatun Cad 75, Gaziosmanpaşa ☎0312/459 9200; UK, Şehit Ersan Cad 46/A, Çankaya ☎0312/455 3344; US, Atatürk Bulvarı 110, Kavaklıdere ☎0312/455 5555.

Hamams Karacabey Hamami, Talat Paşa Bulvarı 101 (men 6.30am–11pm; women 8am–7pm; from around $5).

Hospital Hacettepe University Medical faculty, west of Hasırcılar Sok in Sıhhıye ☎0312/311 9393.

Internet Internet Evi, 3rd floor Altın Çarşısı, Ziya Gökalp Cad.

Left luggage At the bus and train stations.

Post office Merkez Postahane, on Atatürk Bulvarı, Kızılay.

Cappadocia

A land created by the complex interaction of natural and human forces over vast spans of time, **Cappadocia**, around 150km southeast of Ankara, is initially a disturbing place, the great expanses of bizarrely eroded volcanic rock giving an impression of barrenness. It's in fact an exceedingly fertile region, and one whose weird formations of soft, dusty rock have been adapted over millennia by many cultures, from Hittites to later Christians hiding away from Arab marauders. There are more than a thousand rock-churches in Cappadocia, dating from the earliest days of Christianity to the thirteenth century, and some caves are still inhabited; and pottery is still made from the clay of the Kızılırmak River. It's a popular area with tourists, and getting more so, but the crowds are largely confined to a few areas.

The **best-known sites** are located within the triangle delineated by the roads connecting Nevşehir, Avanos and Ürgüp. Within this region is the greater part of the valleys of **fairy chimneys**, which are formed when patches of hard lava have settled on top of the soft greyish bedrock (composed of compacted volcanic ash); the areas topped by lava chunks resist erosion, eventually forming 50m-high cones which dot the landscape. Also here are the rock-cut churches of the **Göreme** open-air museum, with their amazing selection of frescoes, and the **Zelve** monastery, a complex of troglodyte dwellings and churches hewn out of the rock. **Nevşehir** itself isn't much of a town, but it's an important travel centre, and while **Ürgüp** makes perhaps a more attractive base from which to tour the surrounding valleys, it isn't as well served by public transport. Outside the triangle to the south are the underground cities of **Derinkuyu** and **Kaymaklı**, fascinating warrens attesting to the ingenuity of the ancient inhabitants.

Nevşehir

Though said to be Turkey's richest town, **NEVŞEHİR**, at the very heart of the region, can hardly be accused of ostentatious wealth. It is the **regional transport hub**: frequent bus services all over Cappadocia run from here, and you'll probably find yourself detouring through when travelling between other apparently neighbouring towns. The **Ottoman castle** at the heart of the old city, southwest of the modern centre, is a good landmark. The new city below is divided by two main streets, **Atatürk Bulvarı**, on which are situated most of the hotels and restaurants, and **Lale Caddesi**, turning into Gülzehir Caddesi to the north, where you'll find the main *dolmuş* station. The remains of the citadel are no big deal in themselves but the views are good. On the side of the hill, the impressive eighteenth-century **Damat İbrahim Paşa Camii** is set in a large precinct surrounded by narrow streets, and has a cool, dark interior enhanced by small decorative details. Opposite, the **Damat İbrahim Paşa Hamamı** (daily 6am–midnight: women only Wed 10am–4pm, men only at other times; $5) is also in good working order and well run. The **Nevşehir Museum**, on Yeni Kayseri Caddesi (Tues–Sun 8.30am–5/6pm; $1), is worth a visit for a collection that includes three terracotta sarcophagi dating from the third to the fourth century AD, finds from the Phrygian and Byzantine periods, and Turkish carpets, kilims and looms.

The **tourist office** is on Atatürk Bulvarı, on the right as you head downhill towards Ürgüp (Mon–Fri 9am–5/5.30pm; summer also Sat & Sun; ☎0384/213 3659). There's also a private information office near the bus station, run by a tour company. **Pensions** in Nevşehir are neither as cheap nor as good as elsewhere in Cappadocia. *Hotel Şems* (☎0384/213 3597; ❷), on Atatürk Bulvarı next to the *Aspava Restaurant*, is comfortable and friendly. A step up, *Orsan*, Atatürk Bulvarı (☎0384/213 2115; ❷), is comfortable and has a swimming pool. Just opposite the *Orsan* on Yeni Kayseri Cad is the friendly and clean *Hotel Seven Brothers* (☎0384/213 4979; ❷). The nicest of the **campsites** in the region, the *Koru Mocamp*, is signposted off to the right as you turn from Nevşehir into Üçhisar. For **food**, the *Aspava Restaurant*, Atatürk Bulvarı 29, serves well-prepared dishes, and the *Sölen*, just before *Hotel Şems* on Atatürk Bulvarı, has a good choice of *mezes* and kebabs. The *Park-Bostan*, in gardens just off Atatürk Bulvarı, is more pricey but licensed. *Uzay Internet* is on Atatürk Bulvarı opposite the *Göreme Hotel*.

Derinkuyu and Kaymaklı

Among the most extraordinary phenomena of the Cappadocia region are the remains of a number of **underground settlements**, some of them large enough to have accommodated up to 30,000 people. The cities are thought to date back to Hittite times, though the complexes were later enlarged by Christian communities who created missionary schools, churches and wine cellars. A total of forty such settlements, from villages to vast cities, have been discovered, but only a few are open to the public. The most thoroughly excavated is in the village of **DERİNKUYU** (daily dawn–dusk; $4), 29km from Nevşehir and accessible by *dolmuş*. The city is well lit and the original ventilation system still functions remarkably well, but some of the passages are small and cramped. The size of this rock-cut warren is difficult to comprehend even on a thorough exploration, since only part of what has been excavated is open, and even this is thought to comprise only a quarter of the original city. The area consists of a total of eight floors and includes stables, wine presses and a dining hall or schoolroom with two long, rock-cut tables; living quarters, churches, armouries and tunnels; and a cruciform church, a meeting hall, a dungeon and a grave.

Some 10km north of Derinkuyu is **KAYMAKLI** (daily 8am–5/6pm; $4). Smaller and less popular than Derinkuyu, only five of its underground levels have been excavated to date. The layout is very similar, networks of streets with small living spaces leading off into underground plazas with various functions, the more obvious of which are stables, smoke-blackened kitchens, storage spaces and wine presses.

Göreme and around

The small town of **GÖREME** is of central importance to Cappadocian tourism, principally because it is the best-known of the few remaining Cappadocian villages whose rock-cut houses and **fairy chimneys** are still inhabited. However, in the last few years these ancient living quarters have slowly been destroyed by development and tourism, which has led to a "Save Göreme" campaign. It is still possible to get away from what is now essentially a holiday village, though, and the tufa landscapes are just a short stroll away. Göreme also makes a good base from which to explore the nearby attractions and sites. When approaching Göreme from elsewhere in Turkey, bear in mind that only two **bus companies** – Göreme and Nevtour – actually travel here direct. Other firms may sell you a ticket to Göreme, but will actually drop you off in Nevşehir, from where you'll have to continue your journey by local bus or *dolmuş* (the last of which leaves Nevşehir at about 6pm).

There are two **churches** in the hills above, the **Durmuş kadir kilisesi**, clearly visible across the vineyard next to a cave-house with rock-cut steps, and the double-domed **Karşıbucak yusuf koç kilisesi**, which houses frescoes in very good condition. About 2km outside the village, the **Göreme open-air museum** (daily 8am–5/6pm; $5) is the best known and most visited of all the monastic settlements in the region, the site of over thirty churches, mainly dating from the ninth to the end of the eleventh century and containing some of the best of all the frescoes in Cappadocia. Most are barely discernible from the outside, apart from a few small holes serving as windows or air shafts. But inside, the churches re-create many of the features of Byzantine buildings, with domes, barrel-vaulted ceilings and cruciform plans supported by mock pillars, capitals and pendentives. The best-preserved church is the **Tokalı kilise**, located away from the others on the opposite side of the road about 50m back towards the village. It's two churches, in fact, both frescoed, an **old church**, dating from the 920s, and a **new church**, whose frescoes represent some of the finest examples of tenth-century Byzantine art. The best known of the churches in the main complex are the three columned churches, the **Elmalı kilise**, the **Karanlık kilise** ($10 extra) whose frescoes have recently been restored, and the **Carıklı kilise** – eleventh-century churches heavily influenced by Byzantine forms and painted with superb skill. Look, too, at the church of **St Barbara**, named after the depiction of the saint on the north wall.

Practicalities

There is no official **tourist office** in Göreme, although numerous private tour operators offer information; bear in mind that they're unlikely to be objective and may be taking commission for recommending accommodation. Cheapest of the **pensions** is probably the *Tuna Caves* (☎0384/271 2681; ❷; closed Nov–March), which has cave rooms/dorms and a pleasant terrace, while the *Blue Moon*, just east of the bus station (☎0384/271 2433; ❷), has immaculate en-suite rooms. Friendly *Paradise* towards the Open-Air Museum (☎0384/271 2248, ✉mbozlak@hotmail.com; ❶) has constant hot water, some cave rooms and a cave bar, while nearby is *Peri*

Pansiyon (☎0384/271 2136, ✉peripansiyon@yahoo.com; ❷), and *L'Elysee Pension* (☎0384/271 2244, ✉elyseegoreme@yahoo.tr; ❷), with clean simple rooms. For luxury try *Göreme House* (☎0384/271 2668; ❷), just up a cobbled road behind the mosque, which has excellent en-suite rooms, central heating and a fantastic terrace. This place can be a real bargain in winter and some rooms even have jacuzzis. There are several **campsites** on the fringes of Göreme. The best are *Panorama*, 1km out on the Üçhisar road, and *Dilek,* on the Ürgüp road near the *Peri Pansiyon*, which is more sheltered and has a nice little restaurant. Both have swimming pools. There's **internet** access at the Neşe Café in the town centre, not far from the Ürgüp road.

Ürgüp

There is also plenty of accommodation in **ÜRGÜP**, a pretty old town with its own cave dwellings 5km east of Göreme. In some ways, this can make a more sophisticated alternative to Göreme as it has managed to accommodate tourism much better and still allows access to the more traditional aspects of Turkish life. Ürgüp's informative **tourist office** (Mon–Fri 8/8.30am–5/7pm; summer also Sat & Sun; ☎0384/341 4059) on the main shopping street, Kayseri Cad, maintains an up-to-date price list of **hotels and pensions**. There are several decent accommodation options on the way in from Nevşehir: *Hotel Hitit* (☎0384 341 4481; ❷) has decent rooms, as well as a lovely rose garden, and is well situated beside a pock-marked cliff; the *Asia Minor* (☎0384/341 4645; ❸), with its courtyard, is one of Ürgüp's most attractive buildings; the *Otel Melis*, out of the centre on the Nevşehir road (☎0384/341 2495, ✉rdvw@hotmail.com; ❸), has a variety of pleasant en-suite rooms ranged around a swimming pool; the *Sun Pansiyon*, behind the *hamam* on İstiklâl Cad (☎0384/341 4493; ❷), has a few cave rooms reputed to be a thousand years old; and the *Yıldız Hotel*, just past the police station on the Kayseri road (☎0384/341 4610; ❷), has basic, spacious en-suites. There are numerous **tour operators** in Ürgüp; try Magic Valley, next to the bus station at Güllüce Cad 7 (☎0384/341 2145). *Kaya Bar* on Cumhuriyet Meydanı doubles as an **internet** café.

Eating in Göreme can prove expensive. *Hotel Ataman* has the best **restaurant**, serving everything from local specialities to French soufflés; the *Ottoman House* is another place to sample traditional cuisine. Among the handful of overpriced restaurants on the main road, *Sultan* serves vegetarian food and pasta while *Sedef* is more lively. Ürgüp's eating options include *Cirahan Restaurant,* Cumhuriyet Meydani, beside the *hamam* which serves traditional Turkish dishes. Also in the central square there is the *Şömine,* Cumhuriyet Meydanı, serving well-prepared specialities. Another excellent and very affordable choice is the *Kervan* courtyard restaurant, serving quality home cooking. *Kardeşler 2* offers an excellent vegetarian casserole (*güveç*). Cheaper options include the *Kardeşler Pide Salonu*, Dumlupınar Cad 13, which serves good *pide*, and the neighbouring *Kent*, with excellent *saç kavurma* (fried beef). The *Prokopi* Bar, Istikal Cad 46, provides an atmospheric place for a drink.

Zelve

The deserted **monastery complex** in the three valleys of **ZELVE** (daily 8am–5.30pm; $4), a few kilometres north of Göreme off the Avanos–Çavuşin road, is accessible by an hourly *dolmuş* from Göreme. The churches here date back to before the ninth century, but then the valley was inhabited by Turkish Muslims, who hacked their dwellings out of the tufa rock face. On the left-hand side of the first valley are the remains of a small Ottoman mosque, the prayer hall and *mihrab* of which are partly hewn from the rock, and a large number of chapels and medieval oratories are scattered through the valleys, many of them decorated with carved crosses. A thorough exploration really requires a torch: some of the rooms are entered by means of precarious steps, others by swinging up through holes in the floors, and, on occasion, massive leaps to a lower floor – good fun if you're reasonably energetic and have a head for heights.

Konya

Roughly midway between Antalya and Nevşehir, **KONYA** is a place of pilgrimage for the Muslim world – the home of Celalledin Rumi or the **Mevlâna** ("Our Master"), the mystic who founded the Mevlevî or **Whirling Dervish** sect, and the centre of **Sufic** mystical practice and teaching. It was also something of a capital during the Selçuk era, many of the buildings from which are still standing, along with examples of their highly distinctive crafts and applied arts, now on display in Konya's museums.

The **Mevlâna Müzesi** (Mon 10am–5pm, Tues–Sun 9am–5pm; $2) is among Turkey's more rewarding sights, housed in the first lodge (*tekke*) of the Mevlevî dervish sect, at the eastern end of Mevlâna Bulvarı, and easily recognizable by its distinctive fluted turquoise dome. The main building of the museum holds the mausoleum containing the tombs of the Mevlâna, his father and other notables – as with mosques, shoes must be left at the door, women must cover their heads, and whether you're male or female, if you're wearing shorts you'll be given a skirt-like affair to cover your legs. It is permitted to take photographs of the mausoleum, but remember to be respectful; it is an extremely holy and venerated site. In the adjoining room, the original *semahane* (ceremonial hall) exhibits include some of the musical instruments of the first dervishes, the original illuminated poetical work of the Mevlâna and silk and woollen carpets, including one 500-year-old silk carpet from Selçuk Persia that is supposedly the finest ever woven. The latticed gallery above was for women spectators, a modification introduced by the followers of the Mevlâna after his death. In the adjoining room, a casket containing hairs from the beard of the Prophet Muhammad is displayed alongside illuminated medieval Korans. A separate building houses an exhibition of dervish memorabilia and some bizarre waxwork figures.

At the opposite end of Mevlâna Caddesi (later Alâeddin Caddesi, once west of Aziziye Caddesi) from the Mevlâna Müzesi, the **Alâeddin Parkı** is a nice place to stroll. This is the site of the original Selçuk acropolis and the source of finds dating back to 7000 BC, most of which are now in the museum in Ankara. At the foot of the hill to the north are the scant remains of a Selçuk palace, although you'd do better to head straight for the imposing **Alâeddin mosque** (daily 9.30am–5.30pm) begun in 1130 and completed in 1221. Recently restored, the interior has distinctly Selçuk features, such as a network of wooden beams. The nearby **Karatay Medrese** on Alâeddin Bulvarı (daily 9am–noon & 1.30–5.30pm; $1.50) is another important Selçuk monument, built in 1251. Inside, the symmetrical design of the dome of stars forms a perfect backdrop for the **Selçuk ceramics** on display, which are covered with striking images of birds, animals and even angels. Behind its fine Selçuk portal the **İnce Minare Medrese**, below the park on Alâeddin Bulvarı, is also now a museum, featuring stone and woodcarving, with exhibits from the palace on the present site of the Alâeddin Parkı, but is currently closed for restoration. The other museum worthy of note is the **Museum of Archeology** (Tues–Sun 8am–noon & 1.30–5.30pm; $1) in the south of the city, containing the only pre-Selçuk remains in the city, including Hittite and Roman artefacts.

Practicalities

Konya's new **bus station** is 10km out of town, from where the Konak *dolmuş* connects with the town centre; the **train station** is around 2km out of the centre at the far end of İstasyon Cad, connected to the centre by regular *dolmuşes*. The **tourist office** is at Mevlâna Cad 21 (Mon–Fri 8am–5.30pm; ☎0332/351 1074). Konya's better **hotels** are on or just north of Mevlâna Cad. The recently renovated *Otel Tur*, Esarizade Sok 13 (☎0332/351 9825; ❷), is quiet, comfortable and friendly; the *Yeni Köşk*, Kadılar Sok 28 (☎0332/352 0671; ❷), has clean rooms with en-suite facilities and is probably the best of the cheaper options; and the *Otel Çeşme* at Akifpaşa Sok 21, off İstanbul Cad (☎0322/351 2426; ❶), has rooms with baths;

outside the annual Mevlâna festival (Dec) rates can usually be bargained down. As for **eating**, the *Şifa Lokantası*, Mevlâna Cad 29, is popular and very reasonably priced and the nearby *Sema* offers reasonable kebab options. The *Tilsum Restaurant*, west of the centre on Meram Cad, serves excellent kebabs but closes early. The *Köşk* next to the Mevlâna museum serves local Konya kebab specialities and has live music. **Express Internet** is at 21 Alâeddin Bulvarı, and Online Internet at İnceminare Sok 81c.

Travel details

Trains

Ankara to: İzmir (2 daily; 14hr).
İstanbul to: Ankara (5 daily; 8hr); Edirne (1 daily; 6hr 30min); Denizli (1 daily; 14hr 30min); İzmir (2 daily; 11hr); Konya (3 daily; 14hr).
İzmir to: Selçuk (6 daily; 2hr).

Buses and dolmuşes

Ankara to: Antalya (12 daily; 10hr); Bodrum (10 daily; 12hr); Bursa (hourly; 7hr); İstanbul (every 30min; 6hr); İzmir (hourly; 9hr); Konya (14 daily; 3hr 30min); Nevşehir (12 daily; 4hr 30min).
Antalya to: Alanya (hourly; 2hr); Antakya (1 daily; 12hr); Denizli (6 daily; 5hr 30min); Fethiye, by inland route (3 daily; 4hr); İzmir (6 daily; 9hr 30min); Kaş (7 daily; 4hr 30min); Konya (6 daily; 6hr 30min); Sıde (3 per hour; 1hr 15min).
Ayvalık to: Bergama (8 daily; 1hr); Bursa (10 daily; 4hr 30min); Çanakkale (hourly; 3hr); İzmir (hourly; 2hr 30min).
Bergama to: Ayvalık (8 daily; 1hr); İzmir (12 daily; 2hr).
Bodrum to: Ankara (several daily; 13hr); Fethiye (6 daily; 4hr 30min); Marmaris (8 daily; 3hr 15min).
Bursa to: Ankara (hourly; 7hr); Çanakkale (hourly; 6hr); İstanbul (hourly; 5hr); İzmir (15 daily; 7hr).
Çanakkale to: Ayvalık (hourly; 3hr); Bursa (16 daily; 6hr); İzmir (hourly; 5hr 30min).
Datça to: Ankara (3 daily; 15hr); Marmaris (13 daily; 2hr 15min).
Denizli to: Antalya (8 daily; 5hr 30min); Bodrum (2–3 daily; 4hr 30min); Konya (several daily; 7hr 30min); Marmaris (6 daily; 4hr).
Edirne to: Çanakkale (2 daily; 4hr 30min); İstanbul (hourly; 3hr).
Fethiye to: Ankara (2 daily; 12hr); Antalya (8 daily; 4hr); Bodrum (6 daily; 5hr); Denizli (5 daily; 4hr); İzmir (every 30min; 7hr); Kaş (15 daily; 2hr 30min); Marmaris (10 daily; 3hr); Patara (10 daily; 1hr 30min).

Kuşadası to: Bodrum (3 daily; 3hr); Pamukkale (12 daily; 3hr 30min).
İstanbul to: Alanya (hourly; 14hr); Ankara (every 30min; 6hr); Antalya (4 daily; 12hr); Ayvalık (4 daily; 9hr); Bodrum (4 daily; 12hr); Bursa (hourly; 5hr); Çanakkale (hourly; 5hr 30min); Datça (1 daily; 17hr); Denizli (hourly; 15hr); Fethiye (hourly; 15hr); İzmir (hourly; 10hr); Göreme (5 daily; 12hr 30min); Kuşadası (3 daily; 11hr); Marmaris (4 daily; 13hr); Nevşehir (3 daily; 12hr); Sıde (1 daily; 13hr); Ürgüp (5 daily; 12hr 30min); Konya (7 daily; 11hr).
İzmir to: Ankara (8 daily; 9hr); Antalya (8 daily; 8hr 30min); Ayvalık (every 30min; 2hr 30min); Bergama (hourly; 2hr); Bodrum (hourly; 4hr); Bursa (6 daily; 7hr); Çanakkale (4 daily; 5hr 30min); Çeşme (every 15–20min; 1hr 30min); Datça (hourly; 7hr); Denizli (hourly; 4hr); Fethiye (12–18 daily; 7hr); Kuşadası (every 30min; 1hr 40min); Marmaris (hourly; 5hr); Selçuk (every 20min; 1hr 20min).
Kaş to: Antalya (6 daily; 5hr); Bodrum (3 daily; 7hr); Fethiye (8 daily; 2hr 30min); Marmaris (4 daily; 4hr 30min); Pamukkale (2 daily; 10hr).
Marmaris to: Ankara (14 daily; 13hr); Bodrum (8 daily; 3hr 15min); Dalaman (hourly; 1hr 30min); Denizli (6 daily; 4hr); Fethiye (10 daily; 3hr).
Nevşehir to: Antalya (1 daily; 11hr); İzmir (1 daily; 12hr); Konya (4 daily; 3hr); Marmaris (1 daily; 14hr).
Selçuk to: Bodrum (hourly; 3hr); İzmir (hourly; 1hr); Kuşadası (every 30min; 40min).

Domestic ferries

Çanakkale to: Eceabat (hourly; 20min).
Datça to: Bodrum (April–Oct 2 daily; 2hr).
Gelibolu to: Lapseki (15 daily; 20min).
İzmir to: İstanbul (1 weekly; 19hr).
Kilitbahir to: Çanakkale (hourly; 10min).

Language

Language

Language

I f you're making a general tour of Europe you can't hope always to speak the language of the country you're travelling in, and in any case in Germany, Scandinavia, and especially the Netherlands and Switzerland, many people, particularly the young, speak reasonable English. That said, it is polite to know at least a few very basic words and phrases wherever you happen to be, which is why we've included the chart on the following pages, and a smattering of French, German or Russian is handy everywhere as a common language if English fails.

Rough Guides phrasebooks are now available for Czech, Dutch, French, German, Greek, Hungarian, Italian, Polish, Portuguese, Russian, Spanish and Turkish, and there's also a European Languages phrasebook. Pocket **dictionaries** can easily be bought for most European languages in the countries where they are spoken, and usually at home too. If you want to get to grips further with any of the languages, Routledge's "Colloquial" series is the best place you could start.

Bulgarian, Croatian and Czech

	Bulgarian	Croatian	Czech
Yes	Da	Da	Ano
No	Ne	Ne	Ne
Please	Molya	Molim	Prosím
Thank you	Blagodarya	Hvala	Děkuju
Hello/Good day	Dobâr den	Bog/Dobar dan	Dobý, den/ahoj
Goodbye	Dovizhdane	Bog/Do vidjenja	Na shledanou
Excuse me	Izvinyavaĭte	Izvinite	Promiňte
Where	Kude	Gdje	Kde
When	Koga	Kada	Kdy
How	Kak	Kako	Jak
Left	Lyavo	Lijevo	Vlevo
Right	Dyasno	Desno	Vpravo
Large	Golyama	Veliko	Velký
Small	Malko	Malo	Malý
Good	Dobro	Dobro	Dobrý
Bad	Plosho	Loše	Spatný
Near	Blizo	Blizu	Blízko
Far	Daleche	Daleko	Daleko
Cheap	Eftino	Jeftino	Levný
Expensive	Skupo	Skupo	Drahý
Open	Otvoreno	Otvoreno	Oteřueno
Closed	Zatvoreno	Zatvoreno	Zavřeno
Today	Dnes	Danas	Dnes
Yesterday	Vechera	Juče	Včera
Tomorrow	Utre	Sutra	Zítra

	Bulgarian	Croatian	Czech
Day	Den	Dan	Den
Week	Sedmitza	Tjedan	Týden
Month	Mesetz	Mjesec	Měsíc
Year	Godina	Godina	Rok
How much is...?	Kolko stroova?	Koliko stoji...?	Kolík stojí...?
What time is it?	Kolko e chasut?	Koliko je sati?	Kolík je hodin?
Where is...?	Kude e...?	Gdje je...?	Kde je...?
I don't understand	Ne razbiram	Ne razumijem	Nerozumím
Do you speak English?	Govorite li Angliski?	Govorite li engleski?	Miuvíte Anglicky?
Please write it down	Molya napishete go	Našiyite ga molim	Prosím, napište to
One	Edin/edna	Jedan	Jeden
Two	Dve	Dva	Dva
Three	Tri	Tri	Tři
Four	Chetiri	Četiri	Čtyři
Five	Pet	Pet	Pět
Six	Shest	Šest	Šest
Seven	Sedem	Sedam	Sedm
Eight	Osem	Osam	Osum
Nine	Devet	Devet	Devět
Ten	Deset	Deset	Deset

Danish, Dutch and Estonian

	Danish	Dutch	Estonian
Yes	Ja	Ja	Jah
No	Nej	Nee	Ei
Please	Vaer så venlig	Alstublieft	Palun
Thank you	Tak	Dank u/Bedankt	Aitäh/tänan
Hello/Good day	Goddag	Hallo	Tere
Goodbye	Farvel	Dag/Tot ziens	Head aega
Excuse me	Undskyld	Pardon	Vabandage
Where	Hvor	Waar	Kus
When	Hvornår	Wanneer	Millal
How	Hvordan	Hoe	Kuidas
Left	Venstre	Links	Vasak
Right	Højre	Rechts	Parem
Large	Stor	Groot	Suur
Small	Lille	Klein	Väike
Good	God	Goed	Hea
Bad	Dårlig	Slecht	Halb
Near	Naer	Dichtbij	Lähedal
Far	Fjern	Ver	Kaugel
Cheap	Billig	Goedkoop	Odav
Expensive	Dyr	Duur	Kallis
Open	Åben	Open	Avatud
Closed	Lukket	Dicht	Suletud

	Danish	Dutch	Estonian
Today	I dag	Vandaag	Täna
Yesterday	I går	Gisteren	Eile
Tomorrow	I morgen	Morgen	Homme
Day	Dag	Dag	Päev
Week	Uge	Week	Nädal
Month	Måned	Maand	Kuu
Year	År	Jaar	Aasta
How much is....?	Hvor meget koster...?	Wat kost...?	Kui palju maksab...?
What time is it?	Hvad er klokken?	Hoe laat is het?	Mis kell praegu on?
Where is...?	Hvor er...?	Waar is...?	Kus on...?
I don't understand	Jeg forstår ikke	Ik begrijp het niet	Ma ei saa aru
Do you speak English?	Taler de Engelsk?	Spreekt u Engels?	Kas te räägite inglise keelt?
Please write it down	Vaer venlig at skrive det	Wilt u het opschrijven, alstublieft	Palun kirjutage see üles
One	En	Een	Uks
Two	To	Twee	Tkaks
Three	Tre	Drie	Kolm
Four	Fire	Vier	Neli
Five	Fem	Vijf	Viis
Six	Seks	Zes	Kuus
Seven	Syv	Zeven	Seitse
Eight	Otte	Acht	Kaheksa
Nine	Ni	Negen	Uheksa
Ten	Ti	Tien	Kümme

Finnish, French and German

	Finnish	French	German
Yes	Kyllä	Oui	Ja
No	Ei	Non	Nein
Please	Olkaa hyvä	S'il vous plaît	Bitte
Thank you	Kiitos	Merci	Danke
Hello/Good day	Hyvää	Bonjour	Güten Tag
Goodbye	Hyvästi	Au revoir/à bientôt	Auf Wiedersehen
Excuse me	Anteeksi	Pardon	Entschuldigen Sie, bitte
Where	Missä	Où	Wo
When	Milloin	Quand	Wann
How	Kuinka	Comment	Wie
Left	Vasen	Gauche	Links
Right	Oikea	Droit	Rechts
Large	Suuri	Grand	Gross
Small	Pieni	Petit	Klein
Good	Hyvä	Bon	Gut
Bad	Paha	Mauvais	Schlecht
Near	Lähellä	Près	Nah
Far	Kaukana	Loin	Weit

	Finnish	French	German
Cheap	Halpa	Bon marché	Billig
Expensive	Kallis	Cher	Teuer
Open	Avoin	Ouvert	Offen
Closed	Suljettu	Fermé	Geschlossen
Today	Tänään	Aujourd'hui	Heute
Yesterday	Eilen	Hier	Gestern
Tomorrow	Huomenna	Demain	Morgen
Day	Päivä	Jour	Tag
Week	Viikko	Semaine	Woche
Month	Kuukausi	Mois	Monat
Year	Vuosi	Année	Jahr
How much is....?	Kuinka paljon on...?	Combien coûte...?	Wieviel kostet...?
What time is it?	Paljonko kello on?	Quelle heure est-il?	Wieviel Uhr ist es?
Where is...?	Missä on...?	Où est...?	Wo ist...?
I don't understand	En ymmärrä	Je ne comprends pas	Ich verstehe nicht
Do you speak English?	Puhutteko Englantia?	Parlez-vous anglais?	Sprechen Sie Englisch?
Please write it down	Olkaa hyvä ja kiarjoittakaa se	Veuillez me l'écrire	Bitte schreiben Sie es
One	Yksi	Un	Eins
Two	Kaksi	Deux	Zwei
Three	Kolme	Trois	Drei
Four	Neljä	Quatre	Vier
Five	Viisi	Cinq	Fünf
Six	Kuusi	Six	Sechs
Seven	Seitsemän	Sept	Sieben
Eight	Kahdeksan	Huit	Acht
Nine	Yhdeksän	Neuf	Neun
Ten	Kymmenen	Dix	Zehn

Greek, Hungarian and Italian

	Greek	Hungarian	Italian
Yes	Néh	Igen	Sì
No	Óhi	Nem	No
Please	Parakaló	Kérem	Per favore
Thank you	Efharistó	Köszönöm	Grazie
Hello/Good day	Yássas/hérete	Jó napot	Ciao/buon giorno
Goodbye	Adío	Viszontlátásra	Ciao/arrivederci
Excuse me	Signómi	Bocsánat	Mi scusi/prego
Where	Pou	Hol	Dove
When	Póte	Mikor	Quando
How	Pos	Hogyan	Come
Left	Aristerá	Balra	Sinistra
Right	Dheksiá	Jobbra	Destra
Large	Megálo	Nagy	Grande
Small	Mikró	Kicsi	Piccolo

L

	Greek	Hungarian	Italian
Good	Kaló	Jó	Buono
Bad	Kakó	Rossz	Cattivo
Near	Kondá	Közel	Vicino
Far	Makriá	Távol	Lontano
Cheap	Fthinós	Olcsó	Buon mercato
Expensive	Akrivós	Drága	Caro
Open	Aniktós	Nyitva	Aperto
Closed	Klistós	Zárva	Chiuso
Today	Símera	Ma	Oggi
Yesterday	Khthés	Tegnap	Ieri
Tomorrow	Ávrio	Holnap	Domani
Day	Méra	Nap	Giorno
Week	Iméra	Hét	Settimana
Month	Evdomáda	Hónap	Mese
Year	Chrónos	Év	Anno
How much is....?	Póso káni...?	Mennyibe kerül...?	Quanto è...?
What time is it?	Ti óra inai...?	Hány óra?	Che ore sono?
Where is...?	Pou íne...?	Hol van?	Dov'è...?
I don't understand	Dhen katalavéno	Nem értem	Non ho capito
Do you speak English?	Ksérite Angliká?	Beszél Angolul?	Parla Inglese?
Please write it down	Parakaló grápiste to	Legyen szíves, írja le	Lo scriva, per favore
One	Éna/mía	Egy	Uno
Two	Dhío	Kettö	Due
Three	Tría	Három	Tre
Four	Tésera	Négy	Quattro
Five	Pénde	Öt	Cinque
Six	Éksi	Hat	Sei
Seven	Eftá	Hét	Sette
Eight	Októ	Nyolc	Otto
Nine	Enyá	Kilenc	Nove
Ten	Dhéka	Tíz	Dieci

Latvian, Lithuanian and Norwegian

	Latvian	Lithuanian	Norwegian
Yes	Jā	Taip	Ja
No	Nē	Ne	Nei
Please	Lüdzu	Prašau	Vaer så god
Thank you	Paldies	Ačiu	Takk
Hello/Good day	Labdien	Labas	God dag
Goodbye	Uz redzēšanos	Viso gero	Adjø
Excuse me	Atvainojiet	Atsiprašau	Unnskyld
Where	Kur	Kur	Hvor
When	Kad	Kada	Når
How	Cik	Kaip	Hvordan
Left	Kreisi	Kairė	Venstre

	Latvian	Lithuanian	Norwegian
Right	Labi	Deyinė	Høyre
Large	Liels	Didelis	Stor
Small	Mazs	Mažas	Liten
Good	Labs	Geras	God
Bad	Slikts	Blogas	Dårlig
Near	Tuvs	Artimas	I naerheten
Far	Tāls	Tolimas	Langt Borte
Cheap	Lēts	Pigus	Billig
Expensive	Dārgs	Brangus	Dyr
Open	Atvērts	Atidarytas	Åpen
Closed	Slēgts	Uždarytas	Lukket
Today	Yodien	Šiandien	I dag
Yesterday	Vakar	Vakar	I går
Tomorrow	Rīt	Rytdiena	I morgen
Day	Diena	Diena	Dag
Week	Nedela	Savaitė	Uke
Month	Menesis	Mėnuo	Måned
Year	Gads	Metai	År
How much is....?	Cik tas maksā...?	Kiek kainuoja ...?	Hvor mye er...?
What time is it?	Cik ir pulkstenis?	Kiek valandų?	Hvor mange er
Where is...?	Kur ir...?	Kur yra...?	klokken?
I don't understand	Es nesaprotu	Nesuprantu	Hvor er...?
Do you speak	Vai jūs runājat	Ar jųs kalbate	Jeg forstår ikke
English?	Angliski?	angliškai?	Snakker de Englesk?
Please write it down	Lūdzu uzrakstiet	Prašau užrašyti	Vennligst skriv det
			ned
One	Viens	Vienas	En
Two	Divi	Du/dvi	To
Three	Trīs	Trys	Tre
Four	Četri	Keturi	Fire
Five	Pieci	Penki	Fem
Six	Seyi	Šeši	Seks
Seven	Septiņi	Septyni	Sju
Eight	Astoņi	Aštuoni	Åtte
Nine	Deviņi	Devyni	Ni
Ten	Desmit	Dešimt	Ti

Polish, Portuguese and Romanian

	Polish	Portuguese	Romanian
Yes	Tak	Sim	Da
No	Nie	Não	Nu
Please	Proszę	Por favor	Vă rog
Thank you	Dzęlkuję	Obrigado	Mulţumesc
Hello/Good day	Dzień dobry	Olá	Salut/buna ziua
Goodbye	Do widzenia	Adeus	La revedere
Excuse me	Przepraszam	Desculpe	Permitemi-mi

	Polish	Portuguese	Romanian
Where	Gdzie	Onde	Unde
When	Kiedy	Quando	Când
How	Jak	Como	Cum
Left	Na lewo	Esquerda	Stânga
Right	Na prawo	Direita	Dreapta
Large	Duży	Grande	Mare
Small	Mały	Pequeno	Mic
Good	Dobry	Bom	Bun/bine
Bad	Zły	Mau	Rău
Near	Bliski	Perto	Apropriat
Far	Daleko	Longe	Departe
Cheap	Tani	Barato	Ieftin
Expensive	Drogi	Caro	Scump
Open	Otwarty	Aberto	Închis
Closed	Zamknięty	Fechado	Deschis
Today	Dziś	Hoje	Azi
Yesterday	Wczoraj	Ontem	Ieri
Tomorrow	Jutro	Amanhã	Mâine
Day	Dzień	Dia	Zi
Week	Tydzień	Semana	Săptămână
Month	Miesiąc	Mês	Lund
Year	Rok	Ano	An
How much is....?	Ile kosztuje...?	Quanto é... ?	Cât costa...?
What time is it?	Która godzina?	Que horas são?	Ce ora este?
Where is...?	Gdzie jest...?	Onde é...?	Unde este...?
I don't understand	Nie rozemiem	Não comprendo	Nu înțeleg
Do you speak English?	Pan(i) mówi po Angielsku?	Fala Inglés?	Vorbiți Englezește?
Please write it down	Proszę to napisać	Escreva-mo, por favor	Vă rog scriemi
One	Jeden	Um	Unu
Two	Dwa	Dois	Doi
Three	Trzy	Três	Trei
Four	Cztery	Quatro	Patru
Five	Pięć	Cinco	Cinci
Six	Sześć	Seis	Şase
Seven	Siedem	Sete	Şapte
Eight	Osiem	Oito	Opt
Nine	Dziewięć	Nove	Noua
Ten	Dziesięć	Dez	Zece

Russian, Slovene and Spanish

	Russian	Slovene	Spanish
Yes	Da	Ja	Sí
No	Net	Ne	No
Please	Pozháluysta	Prosim	Por favor
Thank you	Spasíbo	Hvala	Gracias

	Russian	Slovene	Spanish
Hello/Good day	Zdrávstvuyte	Živjo/dober dan	Hola
Goodbye	Do svidániya	Nasvidenje	Adiós
Excuse me	Izvinite	Oprostite	Con permiso
Where	Gde	Kje	¿Dónde?
When	Kogdá	Kdaj	¿Cuándo?
How	Kak	Kako	¿Cómo?
Left	Nalévo	Levo	Izquierda
Right	Naprávo	Desno	Derecha
Large	Bolshóy	Veliko	Gran
Small	Málenkiy	Majhno	Pequeño
Good	Khoróshiy	Dobro	Buen
Bad	Plokhóy	Slabo	Mal
Near	Bleezkiy	Blizu	Próximo
Far	Da-lyiko	Daleč	Lejos
Cheap	Dyi-shovee	Poceni	Barato
Expensive	Daragoy	Drago	Caro
Open	Otkryto	Odprto	Abierto
Closed	Zakryto	Zaprto	Cerrado
Today	Syivo-dnya	Danes	Hoy
Yesterday	Vcherá	Včeraj	Ayer
Tomorrow	Závtra	Jutri	Mañana
Day	Dyin	Dan	Día
Week	Nyi-dyel-ya	Teden	Semana
Month	Mye-syats	Mesec	Mes
Year	Got	Leto	Año
How much is....?	Skólko stóit?	Koliko stane?	¿Cuánto cuesta...?
What time is it?	Katoree chass?	Koliko je ura?	¿Tiene la hora?
Where is...?	Gde...?	Kje je	¿Dónde está...?
I don't understand	Ya ne ponimáyu	Ne razumem	No entiendo
Do you speak English?	Vy govoríte po-anglíyski?	Govorite angleško?	¿Habla inglés?
Please write it down	Zapishíte éto pozháluysta?	Prosim, če mi napišete	Escríbamelo, por favor
One	Odín	Ena	Un/Una
Two	Dva	Dve	Dos
Three	Tri	Tri	Tres
Four	Chetyre	Ytiri	Cuatro
Five	Pyat	Pet	Cinco
Six	Shest	Yest	Seis
Seven	Sem	Sedem	Siete
Eight	Vósem	Osem	Ocho
Nine	Dévyat	Devet	Nueve
Ten	Désyat	Deset	Diez

Swedish and Turkish

	Swedish	Turkish
Yes	Ja	Evet
No	Nej	Hayır/yok
Please	Var så god	Lütfen
Thank you	Tack	Teşkküler/mersi/sağol
Hello/Good day	Hej	Merhaba
Goodbye	Adjö	Qxyi günler/görüşurüz
Excuse me	Ursäkta mig	Pardon
Where	Var	...nereye
When	När	Ne zaman
How	Hur	Nasfl
Left	Vänster	Sol
Right	Höger	Sağ
Large	Stor	Büyuk
Small	Liten	Kücük
Good	Bra	İyi
Bad	Dalig	Kötü
Near	Nära	Yakın
Far	Avlägsen	Uzak
Cheap	Billig	Ucuz
Expensive	Dyr	Pahalı
Open	Öppen	Açık
Closed	Stängd	Kapalf
Today	I dag	Bugün
Yesterday	I går	Dün
Tomorrow	I morgon	Yarın
Day	Dag	Gün
Week	Vecka	Hafta
Month	Månad	Ay
Year	Är	Sene
How much is....?	Vad kostar det...?	Ne kadar...?
What time is it?	Hur mycket är klockan?	Saatınız var mi?
Where is...?	Var är...?	Nerede...?
I don't understand	Jag förstår int	Anlamadım Qxngilizce
Do you speak English?	Talar ni Engelska?	Biliyormusunuz?
Please write it down	Skulle ni kunna skriva det?	Onu yazarmqxsqxnqxz
One	Ett	Bir
Two	Två	İki
Three	Tre	Uç
Four	Fyra	Dört
Five	Fem	Beş
Six	Sex	Altf
Seven	Sju	Yedi
Eight	Ätta	Sekiz
Nine	Nio	Dokuz
Ten	Tio	On

Index

and small print

Index

Map entries are in colour

A

E

Twenty Years of Rough Guides

In the summer of 1981, Mark Ellingham, Rough Guides' founder, knocked out the first guide on a typewriter, with a group of friends. Mark had been travelling in Greece after university, and couldn't find a guidebook that really answered his needs.There were heavyweight cultural guides on the one hand – good on museums and classical sites but not on beaches and tavernas – and on the other hand student manuals that were so caught up with how to save money that they lost sight of the country's significance beyond its role as a place for a cool vacation. None of the guides began to address Greece as a country, with its natural and human environment, its politics and its contemporary life.

Having no urgent reason to return home, Mark decided to write his own guide. It was a guide to Greece that tried to combine some erudition and insight with a thoroughly practical approach to travellers' needs. Scrupulously researched listings of places to stay, eat and drink were matched by careful attention to detail on everything from Homer to Greek music, from classical sites to national parks and from nude beaches to monasteries. Back in London, Mark and his friends got their Rough Guide accepted by a farsighted commissioning editor at the publisher Routledge and it came out in 1982.

The Rough Guide to Greece was a student scheme that became a publishing phenomenon. The immediate success of the book – shortlisted for the Thomas Cook award – spawned a series that rapidly covered dozens of countries. The Rough Guides found a ready market among backpackers and budget travellers, but soon acquired a much broader readership that included older and less impecunious visitors. Readers relished the guides' wit and inquisitiveness as much as the enthusiastic, critical approach that acknowledges everyone wants value for money – but not at any price.

Rough Guides soon began supplementing the "rougher" information – the hostel and low-budget listings – with the kind of detail that independent-minded travellers on any budget might expect. These days, the guides – distributed worldwide by the Penguin group – include recommendations spanning the range from shoestring to luxury, and cover more than 200 destinations around the globe. Our growing team of authors, many of whom come to Rough Guides initially as outstandingly good letter-writers telling us about their travels, are spread all over the world, particularly in Europe, the USA and Australia. As well as the travel guides, Rough Guides publishes a series of dictionary phrasebooks covering two dozen major languages, an acclaimed series of music guides running the gamut from Classical to World Music, a series of music CDs in association with World Music Network, and a range of reference books on topics as diverse as the Internet, Pregnancy and Unexplained Phenomena. Visit **www.roughguides.com** to see what's cooking.

Rough Guide Credits

Text editor: Judith Bamber
Series editor: Mark Ellingham
Editorial: Martin Dunford, Jonathan Buckley, Kate Berens, Ann-Marie Shaw, Helena Smith, Olivia Swift, Ruth Blackmore, Geoff Howard, Claire Saunders, Gavin Thomas, Alexander Mark Rogers, Polly Thomas, Joe Staines, Richard Lim, Duncan Clark, Peter Buckley, Lucy Ratcliffe, Clifton Wilkinson, Alison Murchie, Matthew Teller, Andrew Dickson, Fran Sandham (UK); Andrew Rosenberg, Stephen Timblin, Yuki Takagaki, Richard Koss, Hunter Slaton, Julie Feiner (US)
Production: Susanne Hillen, Andy Hilliard, Link Hall, Helen Prior, Julia Bovis, Michelle Draycott, Katie Pringle, Zoë Nobes, Rachel Holmes, Andy Turner

Cartography: Melissa Baker, Maxine Repath, Ed Wright, Katie Lloyd-Jones
Cover art direction: Louise Boulton
Picture research: Sharon Martins, Mark Thomas
Online: Kelly Cross, Anja Mutic-Blessing, Jennifer Gold, Audra Epstein, Suzanne Welles, Cree Lawson (US)
Finance: John Fisher, Gary Singh, Edward Downey, Mark Hall, Tim Bill
Marketing & Publicity: Richard Trillo, Niki Smith, David Wearn, Chloë Roberts, Demelza Dallow, Claire Southern (UK); Simon Carloss, David Wechsler, Kathleen Rushforth (US)
Administration: Tania Hummel, Julie Sanderson, Karoline Densley

Publishing Information

This ninth edition published November 2002 by **Rough Guides Ltd**,
80 Strand, London WC2R 0RL.
345 Hudson St, 4th Floor,
New York, NY 10014, USA.
Distributed by the Penguin Group
Penguin Books Ltd,
80 Strand, London WC2R ORL
Penguin Putnam, Inc.
375 Hudson Street, NY 10014, USA
Penguin Books Australia Ltd,
487 Maroondah Highway, PO Box 257,
Ringwood, Victoria 3134, Australia
Penguin Books Canada Ltd,
10 Alcorn Avenue, Toronto, Ontario,
Canada M4V 1E4
Penguin Books (NZ) Ltd,
182–190 Wairau Road, Auckland 10,
New Zealand
Typeset in Bembo and Helvetica to an original design by Henry Iles.

Printed in Italy by LegoPrint S.p.A

1192pp includes index
A catalogue record for this book is available from the British Library
ISBN 1-85828-914-9

The publishers and authors have done their best to ensure the accuracy and currency of all the information in **The Rough Guide to Europe**, however, they can accept no responsibility for any loss, injury or inconvenience sustained by any traveller as a result of information or advice contained in the guide.

Help us update

We've gone to a lot of effort to ensure that the ninth edition of **The Rough Guide to Europe** is accurate and up-to-date. However, things change – places get "discovered", opening hours are notoriously fickle, restaurants and rooms raise prices or lower standards. If you feel we've got it wrong or left something out, we'd like to know, and if you can remember the address, the price, the time, the phone number, so much the better.

We'll credit all contributions, and send a copy of the next edition (or any other Rough Guide if you prefer) for the best letters. Everyone who writes to us and isn't already a subscriber will receive a copy of our full-colour thrice-yearly newsletter. Please mark letters: "**Rough Guide to Europe Update**" and send to: Rough Guides, 80 Strand, London WC2R 0RL, or Rough Guides, 4th Floor, 345 Hudson St, New York, NY 10014. Or send an email to **mail@roughguides.com**.

Have your questions answered and tell others about your trip at **www.roughguides.atinfopop.com**.

Acknowledgements

Thanks are due to Ruth Blackmore and Clifton Wilkinson for helping out with editing; Katie Lloyd-Jones and Ed Wright for the maps; to Ken Bell for proofreading; Andy Turner for typesetting; and Zoë Nobes for picture research. And most of all to all those readers who wrote in with comments and updates on the previous edition.

Photo Credits

Cover Credits

Main front picture Siena, Italy ©Robert Harding
Front (small top image) Pompidou Centre, Paris ©Robert Harding
Front (small bottom image) St Basil's Cathedral, Moscow, Russia ©Michael Jenner
Back top photo Strasbourg, Germany ©Stone
Back lower photo Matterhorn, Switzerland ©Image Bank

Colour introduction

Title page – Bamburgh Castle, Northumbria, Britain ©Edmund Nagele
Main full page – Zaanse Schans, near Amsterdam, Netherlands ©Roy Rainford/Robert Harding
The Matterhorn, Switzerland ©Roy Rainford/Robert Harding
Vai beach, Crete, Greece ©Peter Wilson
Vineyards and farm house near Jonjieux, France ©Michael Busselle/Robert Harding
Running of the bulls, Pamplona, Spain. ©Roberto Arakaki/Robert Harding
Hot-air balloon festival, Château d'Oex, Switzerland ©Neil Egerton/travel Ink

Things not to miss

1. Carnevale, Venice, Italy ©Simon Harris/Robert Harding
2. Puente Nuevo, Ronda, Spain ©2000 Ruth Tomlinson/Robert Harding
3. Edinburgh Festival, Britain ©F. Good/Trip
4. Ljubljana, Slovenia ©C Bowman
5. Oktoberfest, Munich, Germany ©Robert Harding
6. Cappadocia, Turkey ©M Jenkin/TRIP
7. Belgian chocolates ©Nigel Francis/Robert Harding
8. Diocletian's Palace, Split, Croatia ©K. Gillham/Robert Harding
9. Pont St-Bénézet and Petit Palais, Avignon, France ©Charles Bowman
10. Sighişoara, Romania ©Christopher Rennie/Robert Harding
11. Tate Modern, London, Britain ©Nelly Boyd/Robert Harding
12. Brouwers Gracht, Amsterdam, Netherlands ©R. Rainford/Robert Harding
13. The Kremlin, Moscow, Russia ©Dominic Harcourt-Webster/Robert Harding
14. Café Central, Austria, Vienna ©Robert Harding
15. Mykonos Town, Greece ©Ellen Rooney/Robert Harding
16. Nyhavn, Copenhagen, Denmark ©Dean Miculinic/Travel Ink
17. La Sagrada Família, Barcelona, Spain ©Joe Beynon/Axiom
18. Viking carving, Urnes stave church, Norway ©Phil Lee
19. Nevsky Cathedral, Tallinn, Estonia ©Robert Harding
20. Atlas Mountains, Morocco ©M Jelliffe/Trip
21. Courchevel Hotel, Pralong, France ©Adam Woolfitt/Robert Harding
22. The Parthenon, Athens, Greece ©Roy Rainford/Robert Harding
23. April Feria, Sevilla, Spain ©K. Gillham/Robert Harding
24. Reindeers grazing, Lapland, Finland ©Leo F. Postl/Travel Ink
25. Charles Bridge, Prague, Czech Republic ©Greg Evans
26. Main Square, Kraków old town, Poland ©K Gillham/Robert Harding
27. Király Baths, Budapest, Hungary ©A Woolfitt/Robert Harding
28. Pub sign, Cork, Ireland ©Michael Jenner/Robert Harding
29. Aurora Borealis, Lapland, Sweden ©C Gibson/Trip
30. Tatra Mountains, Poland ©K. Gillham/Robert Harding

Black and White Photos

Schönbrunn Palace, Vienna, Austria ©Gavin Hellier/Robert Harding (p.62)
Het Gravensteen, Ghent, Belgium ©B.Bott/Robert Harding (p.94)
Eden Project, Britain ©R.Westlake/Trip (p.126)
Aleksandâr Nevski Cathedral, Sofia, Bulgaria ©Kyle Clapham (p.204)
Dubrovnik, Croatia ©Ken Gillham/Robert Harding (p.226)
Prague Castle ©John Probert (p.250)
Tivoli Gardens, Copenhagen, Denmark ©Robert Harding (p.274)

SMALL PRINT

Nevsky Cathedral, Tallinn, Estonia ©Robert Harding (p.302)

Olavinlinna Castle, Savonlinna, Finland ©Ken Gillham/Robert Harding (p.320)

Chenonceau, Loire Valley, France ©Chris Coe/Axiom (p.340)

Oktoberfest beer tent, Munich, Germany ©Robert Harding (p.414)

Acropolis, Athens, Greece ©Robert Harding (p.486)

Communist Statue Park, Budapest, Hungary ©C Garnham/Trip (p.532)

Slieve League, Ireland ©Gavin Hellier/Robert Harding 9 (p.554)

The Palio, Siena, Italy ©Loirat Ly/Robert Harding/Explorer (p.588)

Freedom momument, Rīga, Latvia ©Robert Harding (p.682)

Trakai Castle, Lithuania ©G R Richardson/Robert Harding (p.696)

Water seller, Djemaa el Fna, Marrakesh, Morocco ©J Sweeney/Trip (p.712)

Rijksmuseum, Amsterdam, Netherlands ©Robert Harding (p.738)

Fjærlandford, Norway ©Chris Coe (p.766)

Main Square, Old Town, Kraków, Poland ©K Gillham/Robert Harding (p.794)

Alfama, Lisbon, Portugal ©Peter Wilson (p.820)

Carpathian Mountains, Romania ©W Jacobs/Trip (p.858)

Cathedral of the Annunciation, The Kremlin, Moscow, Russia ©Dominic Harcourt-Webster/Robert Harding (p.876)

Poprad Slovakia, Tratas Mountains- walker Lichen on Rocks ©N McDiarmid/Trip (p.906)

Mestni Trg Fountain, Ljubljana, Slovenia ©Phil Robinson/Robert Harding (p.924)

Puente Nuevo, Ronda, Spain ©2000 Ruth Tomlinson/Robert Harding (p.942)

Stockholm, Sweden ©Paul van Riel/Robert Harding (p.1018)

Sprungli Chocolate Shop, Zürich, Switzerland ©John Miller/Robert Harding (p.1044)

Sultan Ahmet (Blue Mosque), İstanbul, Turkey ©A. Bedding/Travel Ink (p.1078)

SMALL PRINT

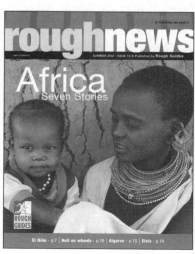

Europe

Algarve
Amsterdam
Andalucia
Austria
Barcelona
Belgium
  & Luxembourg
Berlin
Britain
Brittany
  & Normandy
Bruges & Ghent
Brussels
Budapest
Bulgaria
Copenhagen
Corsica
Costa Brava
Crete
Croatia
Cyprus
Czech & Slovak
  Republics
Devon & Cornwall
Dodecanese
  & East Aegean
Dordogne
  & the Lot
Dublin
Edinburgh
England
Europe
First-Time Europe
Florence
France
French Hotels
  & Restaurants
Germany
Greece
Greek Islands
Holland
Hungary
Ibiza
  & Formentera
Iceland
Ionian Islands
Ireland
Italy
Lake District

Languedoc
  & Roussillon
Lisbon
London
London Mini Guide
London
  Restaurants
Madeira
Madrid
Mallorca
Malta & Gozo
Menorca
Moscow
Norway
Paris
Paris Mini Guide
Poland
Portugal
Prague
Provence & the
  Côte d'Azur
Pyrenees
Romania
Rome
Sardinia
Scandinavia
Scotland
Scottish Highlands
  & Islands
Sicily
Spain
St Petersburg
Sweden
Switzerland
Tenerife & La
  Gomera
Turkey
Tuscany & Umbria
Venice
  & The Veneto
Vienna
Wales

Asia

Bali & Lombok
Bangkok
Beijing
Cambodia
China

First-Time Asia
Goa
Hong Kong
  & Macau
India
Indonesia
Japan
Laos
Malaysia,
  Singapore
  & Brunei
Nepal
Singapore
South India
Southeast Asia
Thailand
Thailand Beaches
  & Islands
Tokyo
Vietnam

Australasia

Australia
Gay & Lesbian
  Australia
Melbourne
New Zealand
Sydney

North America

Alaska
Big Island of
  Hawaii
Boston
California
Canada
Florida
Hawaii
Honolulu
Las Vegas
Los Angeles
Maui
Miami & the
  Florida Keys
Montréal
New England
New Orleans
New York City

New York City
  Mini Guide
New York
  Restaurants
Pacific Northwest
Rocky Mountains
San Francisco
San Francisco
  Restaurants
Seattle
Southwest USA
Toronto
USA
Vancouver
Washington DC
Yosemite

Caribbean & Latin America

Antigua & Barbuda
Argentina
Bahamas
Barbados
Belize
Bolivia
Brazil
Caribbean
Central America
Chile
Costa Rica
Cuba
Dominican
  Republic
Ecuador
Guatemala
Jamaica
Maya World
Mexico
Peru
St Lucia
Trinidad & Tobago

Africa & Middle East

Cape Town
Egypt
Israel & Palestinian
  Territories

Jerusalem
Jordan
Kenya
Morocco
South Africa,
  Lesotho
  & Swaziland
Syria
Tanzania
Tunisia
West Africa
Zanzibar
Zimbabwe

Dictionary Phrasebooks

Czech
Dutch
European
  Languages
French
German
Greek
Hungarian
Italian
Polish
Portuguese
Russian
Spanish
Turkish
Hindi & Urdu
Indonesian
Japanese
Mandarin Chinese
Thai
Vietnamese
Mexican Spanish
Egyptian Arabic
Swahili

Maps

Amsterdam
Dublin
London
Paris
San Francisco
Venice

Rough Guides publishes new books every month

Rough Guides music, reference & CDs

Rough Guide chronicles series

The Rough Guide Chronicle
China
JUSTIN WINTLE

The Rough Guide Chronicle
England
ROBIN EAGLES

The Rough Guide Chronicle
France
IAN LITTLEWOOD

The Rough Guide Chronicle
India
DILIP HIRO

Dip into the past

'Uniquely accessible pocket histories' — History Today

A vital pocket history series for travellers and students alike

Series price £7.99

The ideas expressed in this code were developed by and for independent travellers.

Learn About The Country You're Visiting

Start enjoying your travels before you leave by tapping into as many sources of information as you can.

The Cost Of Your Holiday

Think about where your money goes - be fair and realistic about how cheaply you travel. Try and put money into local peoples' hands; drink local beer or fruit juice rather than imported brands and stay in locally owned accommodation. Haggle with humour and not aggressively. Pay what something is worth to you and remember how wealthy you are compared to local people.

Embrace The Local Culture

Open your mind to new cultures and traditions - it will transform your experience. Think carefully about what's appropriate in terms of your clothes and the way you behave. You'll earn respect and be more readily welcomed by local people. Respect local laws and attitudes towards drugs and alcohol that vary in different countries and communities. Think about the impact you could have on them.

Exploring The World – The Travellers' Code

Being sensitive to these ideas means getting more out of your travels - and giving more back to the people you meet and the places you visit.

Minimise Your Environmental Impact

Think about what happens to your rubbish - take biodegradable products and a water filter bottle. Be sensitive to limited resources like water, fuel and electricity. Help preserve local wildlife and habitats by respecting local rules and regulations, such as sticking to footpaths and not standing on coral.

Don't Rely On Guidebooks

Use your guidebook as a starting point, not the only source of information. Talk to local people, then discover your own adventure!

Be Discreet With Photography

Don't treat people as part of the landscape, they may not want their picture taken. Ask first and respect their wishes.

We work with people the world over to promote tourism that benefits their communities, but we can only carry on our work with the support of people like you. For membership details or to find out how to make your travels work for local people and the environment, visit our website.

www.tourismconcern.org.uk

TourismConcern
Campaigning for Ethical and Fairly Traded Tourism